Presented to:

_____

By

_____

On

_____

Serendipity is
the facility
of making happy
chance discoveries.

Horace Walpole, 1743

Leading a
Small Group
Just Got
Easier!

See page 22

Serendipity
Bible

10th
Anniversary
Edition

NEW INTERNATIONAL VERSION

ZondervanPublishingHouse
Grand Rapids, MI 49530

Serendipity House
Littleton, CO 80120

Dedicated To:

Kevin Lyman Coleman

1968-1995

"I carried you on eagles' wings
and brought you to myself."
                                    Exodus 19:4

CONTENTS

Page

Books of the Bible, Abbreviations Key 9

Contributors. 10

The Story Behind This Bible. 13

Since You Asked

      ❏ About Small Groups 15

      ❏ About the 3-Part Agenda for Group Meetings. 17

      ❏ About the Ready-Made Questionnaires 19

      ❏ About the Ready-Made Courses for Groups. 21

Find Your Kind of Group (60 Ready-Made Courses). 24

    Men's Courses 26

    Women's Courses. 28

    Singles Courses 30

    Marriage Courses 32

    Parenting Courses 34

    Youth Courses 36

    Marketplace Courses 38

    Spiritual Formation Courses 40

    Special Needs Courses. 42

    Recovery Courses 44

Preface to the New International Version 46

Table of Weights and Measures. 1745

Contents of Back Material 1747

BOOKS OF THE BIBLE

OLD TESTAMENT

	Page
Genesis (Ge)	51
Exodus (Ex)	133
Leviticus (Lev)	191
Numbers (Nu)	227
Deuteronomy (Dt)	283
Joshua (Jos)	328
Judges (Jdg)	361
Ruth (Ru)	395
1 Samuel (1Sa)	403
2 Samuel (2Sa)	449
1 Kings (1Ki)	490
2 Kings (2Ki)	533
1 Chronicles (1Ch)	574
2 Chronicles (2Ch)	618
Ezra (Ezr)	661
Nehemiah (Ne)	676
Esther (Est)	696
Job (Job)	707
Psalms (Ps)	756
Proverbs (Pr)	886

	Page
Ecclesiastes (Ecc)	930
Song of Songs (SS)	944
Isaiah (Isa)	958
Jeremiah (Jer)	1056
Lamentations (La)	1144
Ezekiel (Eze)	1156
Daniel (Da)	1220
Hosea (Hos)	1242
Joel (Joel)	1258
Amos (Am)	1265
Obadiah (Ob)	1278
Jonah (Jnh)	1281
Micah (Mic)	1286
Nahum (Na)	1297
Habakkuk (Hab)	1302
Zephaniah (Zep)	1308
Haggai (Hag)	1314
Zechariah (Zec)	1317
Malachi (Mal)	1330

NEW TESTAMENT

	Page
Matthew (Mt)	1337
Mark (Mk)	1390
Luke (Lk)	1427
John (Jn)	1487
Acts (Ac)	1528
Romans (Ro)	1579
1 Corinthians (1Co)	1599
2 Corinthians (2Co)	1617
Galatians (Gal)	1629
Ephesians (Eph)	1636
Philippians (Php)	1643
Colossians (Col)	1649
1 Thessalonians (1Th)	1654
2 Thessalonians (2Th)	1659

	Page
1 Timothy (1Ti)	1663
2 Timothy (2Ti)	1669
Titus (Tit)	1674
Philemon (Phm)	1677
Hebrews (Heb)	1679
James (Jas)	1694
1 Peter (1Pe)	1700
2 Peter (2Pe)	1706
1 John (1Jn)	1710
2 John (2Jn)	1716
3 John (3Jn)	1718
Jude (Jude)	1719
Revelation (Rev)	1722

Abbreviations Key:

	f – verse following	e.g. – for example
	ff – verses following	i.e. – that is
v. – verse	ch – chapter(s)	NT – New Testament
vv. – verses	c. – about, approximately	OT – Old Testament

CONTRIBUTORS

EDITOR-IN-CHIEF

Lyman Coleman.

FIRST EDITION EDITORS

Gary Christopherson, Tucson, AZ; William F. Cutler, Auburn, ME; Dietrich R. Gruen, Madison, WI; Mary H. Naegeli, Moraga, CA; Richard V. Peace, Hamilton, MA; Lance Pierson, London, England; Denny Rydberg, Colorado Springs, CO.

10TH ANNIVERSARY EDITION EDITORS

Brenda Quinn, Andrew Sloan, Stephen Sheely, Cathy Tardif, Alfred Shepard, Kathleen Lintelmann.

MARGIN QUESTIONS

Genesis: Gary Christopherson, Tucson, AZ; Richard C. Meyer, Omaha, NE; **Exodus:** Gary Christopherson, Tucson, AZ; Mary H. Naegeli, Moraga, CA; **Leviticus:** Gary Christopherson, Tucson, AZ; James E. Erwin, Cleveland, TN; **Numbers:** Ken Anderson, Belair, AU; Gary Christopherson, Tucson, AZ; John Mallison, Sydney, AU; **Deuteronomy:** Gary Christopherson, Tucson, AZ; Doug L. Perkins, Bethesda, MD; James M. Singleton, Jr., South Hamilton, MA; Jeanie Thorndike, Pasadena, CA; **Joshua:** David Montzingo, Lemon Grove, CA; Phil Nelson, Oak Brook, IL; **Judges:** Richard C. Meyer, Omaha, NE; **Ruth:** Gary Christopherson, Tucson, AZ; **1,2 Samuel:** Mark Dubis, Newton, MA; Gregoire Benoit, Ashaway, RI; Doug L. Perkins, Bethesda, MD; **1,2 Kings:** Mark Dubis, Newton, MA; Mark Fackler, Wheaton, IL; Steven Saint, San Diego, CA; **1,2 Chronicles:** Mark Fackler, Wheaton, IL; David and Ruth Montzingo, Lemon Grove, CA; **Ezra:** Larry A. Moody, Mansfield, WI; **Nehemiah:** Mark Horton, Bethel, CT; **Esther:** Michael R. Mitchell, Overland Park, KS; **Job:** David G. Horn, South Hamilton, MA; Doug L. Perkins, Bethesda, MD; **Psalms:** Sharon Blackmon, Thousand Oaks, CA; William F. Cutler, Auburn, ME; Peter Pagan, Dallas, TX; Lance Pierson, London, UK; Steven Saint, San Diego, CA; **Proverbs:** Edward C. Grube, Addison, IL; Michael R. Mitchell, Overland Park, KS; **Ecclesiastes:** John T. Anderson, Lancaster, NY; Gregoire Benoit, Ashaway, RI; Chris Powell, Coventry, UK; **Song of Songs:** Dietrich R. Gruen, Madison, WI; John U'Ren, Melbourne, AU; **Isaiah:** David Bolster, Luton, UK; William F. Cutler, Auburn, ME; Gregoire Benoit, Ashaway, RI; **Jeremiah:** Chris Powell, Coventry, UK; Steven Saint, San Diego, CA; Charles E. White, Spring Arbor, MI; **Lamentations:** Gregoire Benoit, Ashaway, RI; Chris Powell, Coventry, UK; Christopher J. Weinhold, Worcester, MA; **Ezekiel:** Rob Frost, Chearn, UK; Steven Saint, San Diego, CA; Charles E. White, Spring Arbor, MI: **Daniel:** James E. Erwin, Cleveland, TN; Larry A. Moody, Marshfield, WI; **Hosea:** Christopher J. Weinhold, Worcester, MA; Graham Young, Durham, UK; **Joel:**

Luther H. Thoreson, Ruthven, IA; **Amos:** Doug Haugen, Auburn, CA; Richard C. Meyer, Omaha, NE; **Obadiah:** Luther H. Thoreson, Ruthven, IA; **Jonah:** Luther H. Thoreson, Ruthven, IA; Graham Young, Durham, UK; **Micah:** Gary Hofmeyer, Sheboygan, WI; Graham Young, Durham, UK; **Nahum:** Gregoire Benoit, Ashaway, RI; Mark Horton, Bethel, CT; Graham Young, Durham, UK; **Habakkuk:** Luther H. Thoreson, Ruthven, IA; Graham Young, Durham, UK; **Zephaniah:** Mark Horton, Bethel, CT; Graham Young, Durham, UK; **Haggai:** Luther H. Thoreson, Ruthven, IA; **Zechariah:** Mark Horton, Bethel, CT; **Malachi:** Mark Horton, Bethel, CT; **Matthew:** Mari R. Anderson, Lancaster, NY; Mary H. Naegeli, Moraga, CA; James M. Singleton, Jr., South Hamilton, MA; **Mark:** Verne Becker, Wheaton, IL; Mary H. Naegeli, Moraga, CA; James M. Singleton, Jr., South Hamilton, MA; **Luke:** Verne Becker, Wheaton, IL; Carol Detoni, Arcadia, CA; **John:** Mari R. Anderson, Lancaster, NY; William F. Cutler, Auburn, ME; **Acts:** William F. Cutler, Auburn, ME; Doug LaBudde, Beverly, MA; **Romans:** Verne Becker, Wheaton, IL; William F. Cutler, Auburn, ME; **1,2 Corinthians:** John T. Anderson, Lancaster, NY; William F. Cutler, Auburn, ME; Mark Horton, Bethel, CT; **Galatians:** John T. Anderson, Lancaster, NY; John Crosby, Glen Ellyn, IL; **Ephesians:** Mari R. Anderson, Lancaster, NY; John and Fay Winson, Beverly, MA; Steve and Betsy Crowe, Wenham, MA; **Philippians:** Mari R. Anderson, Lancaster, NY; John and Fay Winson, Beverly, MA; **Colossians:** Mari R. Anderson, Lancaster, NY; John and Fay Winson, Beverly, MA; **1,2 Thessalonians:** John and Fay Winson, Beverly, MA; **1,2 Timothy:** Mari R. Anderson, Lancaster, NY; Judy Johnson, Madison, WI; **Titus:** Mari R. Anderson, Lancaster, NY; **Philemon:** John and Fay Winson, Beverly, MA; **Hebrews:** James M. Singleton, Madison, WI; **James:** Mari R. Anderson, Lancaster, NY; **1,2 Peter:** Mark Shepard, Easton, MA; **1,2,3 John:** Bill Tucker, Dubuque, IA; **Jude:** Mari R. Anderson, Lancaster, NY; **Revelation:** Dietrich R. Gruen, Madison, WI.

FIRST EDITION ART DESIGN PRODUCTION TEAMS

Sally Graves, Brad Folsom, Julie Bergland and Larry Pfander at Art Forms, Englewood, CO; Billie Herwig, Doug LaBudde, Fay and John Winson at Frontline Marketing, Beverly, MA; Hal Hunt at Autographics, Pomona, CA; Therese Bortolussi, Cathy Clayton, Erika Tiepel and Sheryl Tongue at Graphics Plus, Littleton, CO; the production team at Madison, WI, especially Larry Mykytiuk, Roland Pagano and Bobbette Rose.

10TH ANNIVERSARY EDITION ART DESIGN AND PRODUCTION TEAM

Christopher Werner, Erika Tiepel, Sharon Penington, Maurice Lydick.

Q.

What makes this Bible different from all the others?

A.

It is specifically designed for groups!

THE STORY
BEHIND THIS BIBLE

Twenty years and 20,000 questions ago, we had a dream. A dream of a Bible especially designed for groups. All kinds of groups. Bible study groups. Women's groups. Men's groups. Youth groups. Family groups.

The dream was to provide in one Bible everything it would take to get people together. Get acquainted. Study the Bible. Come to love each other. Care for each other's needs. Celebrate "koinonia" (the Greek word for community).

Faith, Hope and a Shoestring
We came up with the idea of putting a column of questions right next to the Bible text, so that groups could refer immediately to the Bible as they discussed the questions. And we wanted the questions to be on three levels: (1) Questions to help the group get acquainted and get ready for Bible study, (2) Questions to dig into the Scripture, and (3) Questions to apply the Scripture to life.

We appealed to our Serendipity family around the world. Dozens responded. Bible scholars. Teachers. Group process trainers. Pastors. Seminary students. We assigned two writers to every book of the Bible: a right-brain person to ask Serendipity-style "off-the-wall" questions about the text, and a left-brain person to ask the inductive, analytical study kind of questions. Then, we assigned an editor to mesh these two sets together into a "flow" process.

Then followed the field testing with hundreds of groups participating around the country. Every book was tested by five churches, and thousands of questions that didn't pass the test were rewritten.

10th Anniversary Edition
The response to the first edition was overwhelming. Letters poured in from groups around the world. One reviewer put it this way: "Have you ever dreamed of a Bible for small groups where all the questions you wanted to ask about the Bible passage were in the margin? Dream no longer! It's here!"

Now, 10 years later, we have added another feature to this Bible—a curriculum of 60 courses to choose from for 10 major target groups in the church. Just choose a course and follow the outline.

For any group, even those just beginning, there is a ready-made discussion questionnaire at the bottom of the page for 200 favorite Bible stories. All you need to add for the meeting is coffee. Also new to this edition is a three-year lectionary with readings corresponding to the church year.

Here's to the dream. Here's to a great God. Here's to his community wherever two or three are gathered together in his name. Here's to the next "serendipity" in your own life together.

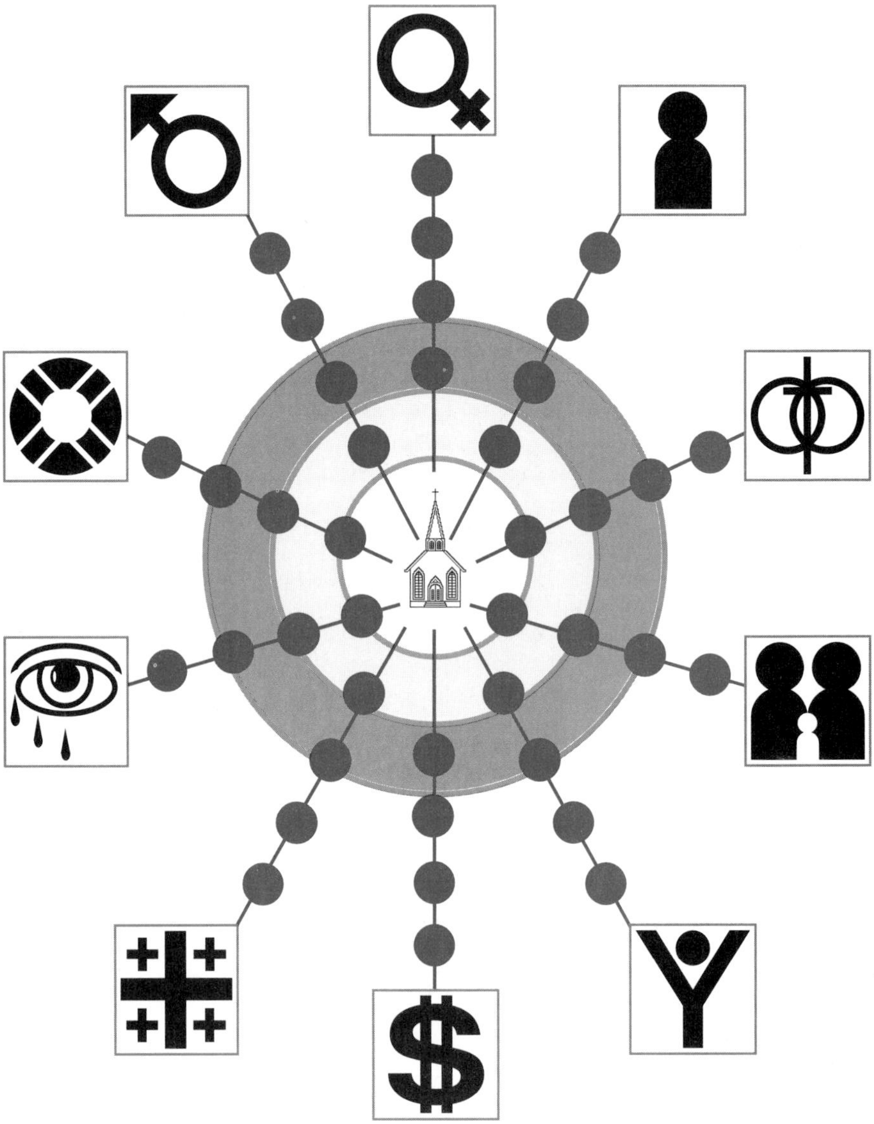

SINCE YOU ASKED

ABOUT SMALL GROUPS

SPECIAL

1. **Why a special study Bible for small groups?** Because small groups need special kinds of discussion questions that help the group to relax and share their own life as well as discuss the Bible.

INTERACTION

2. **What do you call this small group interaction?** Serendipity.

SERENDIPITY

3. **What is "serendipity"?** Originally, it meant "the facility of making happy chance discoveries" (Horace Walpole, 1743). Applied to Bible study, serendipity is what happens when a group of people get together to share their lives around the Scripture and the Holy Spirit does something special.

KOINONIA

4. **What is this "something special"?** Koinonia.

UPPER ROOM

5. **What is "koinonia"?** It is the Greek word for in-depth spiritual community. It is what happened in the Upper Room when a bunch of broken people (the "walking wounded") got together, cared for each other and discovered a whole new power in their lives through the Holy Spirit.

BASEBALL DIAMOND

6. **How do you get to "koinonia" as a group?** Using the illustration of a baseball diamond, "koinonia" is home plate. To get to home plate, the group must go around three bases.

Koinonia

THREE BASES

7. **What are the three bases?** First base is "history giving"—sharing your spiritual story with one another. Second base is "affirmation"—responding in the group to each other's story with words of genuine appreciation and thanks. Third base is "goal setting" or need sharing—identifying where you need to move on in your spiritual life and where you need the support of the group.

GROUP BUILDING

8. **How does this special study Bible fit into this?** *The Serendipity Bible* gives you the tools for building a solid, sturdy, balanced support group.

SHARING

9. **What are the questions for?** To facilitate sharing in groups with questions on three levels—(1) ▽ to start a meeting; (2) ▭ to study together; and (3) ♡ to close.

Sample of Margin Questions

TO START:

How would you arrange for a visiting President to have maximum exposure in your town: What parades? What TV talk shows or radio call-in programs? Where would he eat? Stay the night?

TO STUDY:

1. To what town has Jesus come? Why? **2.** Jesus comes on a donkey and not on a stallion. What does that portray? **3.** What kind of kingdom and king were the people expecting? How do their wishes compare with the reality of Jesus? **4.** How might that discrepancy account for the same crowd jeering and shouting later, "Crucify him!"?

TO CLOSE:

1. What difference does it make to you that Jesus is a gentle King, and not like the one described in 20:25? **2.** How would you have reacted if you had been there to greet Jesus riding into town? Do you jump on political or religious bandwagons today? Why or why not? **3.** Does Jesus' humility work for you? Why or why not?

ABOUT THE 3-PART AGENDA FOR GROUP MEETINGS

COFFEE CUP

10. What are the Coffee Cup questions for? To start off a meeting with a question that levels the playing field—something easy to talk about—and lets the group get to know a little about each other AND to prepare the group for the Bible study to follow.

BOOK

11. What are the Book questions for? To dig into the Scripture to find out what's going on, to figure out the main idea, the plot, the argument, the spiritual principle, etc., and to come up with your own opinion about the interpretation.

HEART

12. What are the Heart questions for? To apply the Scripture to your own life; to take personal inventory and to share with the group what you are going to do as a result.

MODIFYING

13. What if the questions don't fit our situation? Feel free to modify or customize them.

TARGET

14. What kind of group are you aiming at in your questions? This is the hypothetical group we tried to aim at in our questions.

BOB is a space engineer. Bright, but ignorant about the Bible. He comes because his wife makes him. He is very shy.

MARY, Bob's wife, is a graduate of a Bible college. She grew up in a strict religious home and has some bad feelings about the way women were treated in her church.

BILL is an NFL linebacker. He makes $1.5 million a year, but has never read a book in his life.

SALLY and BARB are single parents. One grew up a Baptist, the other an agnostic. They live together in a condo with their teenage children and struggle to pay the bills.

PHIL is a Yuppie. He drives a BMW and has plenty of everything except happiness. He doesn't know where he stands with God, but he's open.

KEVIN arrives at the meeting on a motorcycle in his new "leathers." He is socially outgoing but feels a little insecure around "religious" people.

HONEST

15. Do you really think this kind of group could exist for long? Not really, but it sure did keep us honest in writing questions.

Sample of Questionnaire
With Pictograms to
Target Special Groups

   Genesis 2:4–25   **ADAM AND EVE**

1. If you could have a picture of just one scene in this story, what would it be?
   a. God forming Adam out of the dust
   b. a wide-angle view of the unspoiled Garden of Eden
   c. God bringing the animals to Adam
   d. Adam and Eve seeing each other for the first time.

2. Why didn't God make Adam and Eve at the same time?
   a. to demonstrate that people aren't complete when isolated
   b. to help Adam appreciate his new companion
   c. to establish Adam as the leader in their relationship
   d. to save the best for last

3. What does this story say to you about the nature of men and women?
   a. men and women need each other
   b. men are created with unique authority and responsibility
   c. women are designed to be helpers
   d. men are more task-oriented and women more relational
   e. men and women are more alike than different

4. What did God mean when he described Eve as a "helper"?
   a. she will serve Adam
   b. she will be a great partner
   c. she will be a source of strength
   d. man and woman will work together

5. Why were Adam and Eve naked and not ashamed?
   a. no one told them any different
   b. they were one flesh
   c. they didn't have a knowledge of good and evil
   d. they hadn't sinned yet

6. Describe a time in your life when you were so intensely lonely that you learned the truth of God's statement, "It is not good ... to be alone"?

7. How does this story make you, as a single person, feel?
   a. It reinforces the stigma that I can't be complete without a spouse.
   b. It reassures me that it's normal to need companionship.
   c. It confirms that God is in control of my life and relationships.

   d. It convinces me that God doesn't want me to be lonely.

8. How difficult is it for singles in general to experience companionship apart from marriage? How difficult is it for *you*?

9. What ideas and attitudes do people have about the "submission" of women? How have you, as a woman, felt about this issue? What does this story say to you about God's intent for women?

10. What about your marriage are you most grateful for?
    a. my spouse's help and support
    b. the companionship we share
    c. the sizzle of our romance
    d. the intimacy of knowing each other fully, without shame

11. How could you be more "helpful" to your spouse? How could you deepen your companionship as a couple? Your romance?

Genesis 2:5

without, that special person?

□ 1. Many scholars suggest that verse 4a summarizes the creation account in 1.1–2.3. The creation account in 2:4b–22, is a detailed review of the creation story as it relates to humanity. Why is there a close look at how people fit into the creation account? 2. What do 1:26–28 and 2:7–22 teach about our original nature and character? Our purpose and tasks? Our likeness to the animals? Our likeness to God? 3. Why does God provide this first man with a paradise on earth? Then why (2:9,17; see 3:6) did God place the tree of knowledge of good and evil into this beautiful garden and tell them not to eat from it? 4. What is significant about God creating "woman" last: (a) in the ascending order of creation, she is the "pinnacle"? (b) In being made after man, she is an "after-thought"? (c) "If at first you don't succeed, try, try again"? How do you define "helper"? Does "helper" sound like a lesser person? An equal person? A greater person? 2. A husband and wife become united as one flesh. What does that mean? Are singles incomplete? 6. How would you characterize the rela-

When the LORD G shrub of the field had field had yet sprung earth? and there w came up from the ground— [7]the LORD ground and breathed became a living being

[8]Now the LORD God kinds of trees grow o eye and good for food and the tree of the k

[10]A river watering separated into four h it winds through the there.) [12]The gold of that l the entire land of Cu it runs along the ea Euphrates.

[15]The LORD God to work it and take care "You are free to eat f

[*] Or land; also in verse 6
[#12] Or good; pearls [#13]

  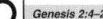 Genesis 2:4–25

1. If you could have a picture of just one scene in this story, what would it be?
   a. God forming Adam out of the dust
   b. a wide-angle view of the unspoiled Garden of Eden
   c. God bringing the animals to Adam
   d. Adam and Eve seeing each other for the first time.

2. Why didn't God make Adam and Eve at the same time?
   a. to demonstrate that people aren't complete when isolated
   b. to help Adam appreciate his new companion
   c. to establish Adam as the leader in their relationship
   d. to save the best for last

3. What does this story say to you about the nature of men and women?
   a. men and women need each other
   b. men are created with unique authority and responsibility
   c. women are designed to be helpers
   d. men are more task-oriented and women more relational
   e. men and women are more alike than different

4. What did God mean when he described Eve as a "helper"?
   a. she will serve Adam
   b. she will be a great partner
   c. she will be a source of strength
   d. man and woman will work together

5. Why were Adam and Eve naked and not ashamed?
   a. no one told them any different
   b. they were one flesh
   c. they didn't have a knowledge of good and evil
   d. they hadn't sinned yet

6. Describe a time in your life when you were so intensely lonely that you learned the truth of God's statement, "It is not good ... to be alone"?

7. How does this story make you, as a single person, feel?
   a. It reinforces the stigma that I can't be complete without a spouse.
   b. It reassures me that it's normal to need companionship.
   c. It confirms that God is in control of my life and relationships.

8. How difficult is it for singles in general to experience companionship apart from marriage? How difficult is it for *you*?

9. What ideas and attitudes do people have about the "submission" of women? How have you, as a woman, felt about this issue? What does this story say to you about God's intent for women?

10. What about your marriage are you most grateful for?
    a. my spouse's help and support
    b. the companionship we share
    c. the sizzle of our romance
    d. the intimacy of knowing each other fully, without shame

11. How could you be more "helpful" to your spouse? How could you deepen your companionship as a couple? Your romance?

ABOUT THE READY-MADE QUESTIONNAIRES

DISCUSSION QUESTIONNAIRES

16. What are the questionnaires at the bottom of some of the pages for? They are especially good for beginning groups and groups that don't know a lot about the Bible.

RIGHT-BRAIN QUESTIONS

17. How are the questionnaires designed? The questionnaire is a series of right-brain questions with multiple-choice options that walk you through a Bible story into your own life—how you relate your story with the story in the Bible.

FAVORITE STORIES

18. How did you go about choosing the stories? We chose 200 of the favorite stories in the Bible (see the list in the back of the Bible).

EASY SHARING

19. Why did you choose stories instead of other Bible passages? It is easier for a small group to relate to a story or parable quickly.

ALL AGES

20. Who are the questionnaires designed for? All ages—from youth to senior citizens.

NO CORRECT ANSWERS

21. In the multiple-choice options, are there any "correct" answers? Not really. Most of the options could be correct, depending on your perspective. This makes for good sharing.

DISCLOSURE SCALE

22. Is there any particular flow in the questions? Yes. The questions are arranged to move across the "Disclosure Scale" from NO RISK at the beginning of the questionnaire to HIGH RISK at the end of the questionnaire.

ESCAPE OPTION

23. Do you mean that these questionnaires could get a group into hot water? It's always possible, but not probable. The multiple-choice options always give an escape option. Otherwise, you can choose to pass.

PICTOGRAMS

24. Why are there pictograms next to some questions? The pictograms indicate questions that are designed for a particular audience, such as Women, Youth, etc. (see course outlines beginning on page 24). You may want to read the question to see if it still relates to your group.

STUDY COURSES

25. How long would you want a group to use the questionnaires? At least six sessions—to get acquainted, share your spiritual story and become a "koinonia" community.

DEEPER

26. What if you want to go deeper? You can always move over to the questions in the margin—especially the BOOK (▢) questions. You can also use CUP (▽) questions as ice-breakers to open your meeting.

Sample of
Six-Session Courses
With Two Tracks

WOMEN'S

		TRACK 1 *Stories / LITE*	TRACK 2 *Teachings / HEAVY*

7. REAL BEAUTY: "LIVING IN A WORLD OF GLITZ"
"It's a constant battle! My hair, my shape and my clothes are never quite right. I know I don't need to measure up to the glamorous stereotype, but where can I find a role model for real beauty?"

1	I DON'T MEASURE UP	Amazing affirmation John 7:53–8:11	[p. 1502]	"How great is the love" 1 John 2:28–3:10	[p. 1712]
2	STRUGGLE TO STAY IN SHAPE	Leah and Rachel Genesis 29:31–30:24	[p. 96]	Training for godliness 1 Timothy 4:1–16	[p. 1666]
3	KEEPING UP MY IMAGE	Queen of Sheba 1 Kings 10:1–13	[p. 508]	Unfading beauty 1 Peter 3:1–7	[p. 1703]
4	FINDING MY OWN STYLE	Stylish love Luke 7:36–50	[p. 1446]	"Be imitators of God" Ephesians 5:1–20	[p. 1640]
5	STAYING FOCUSED	Wealthy women stays focused 2 Kings 4:8–37	[p. 539]	Keeping the goal in sight Ephesians 3:14–21	[p. 1639]
6	ACHIEVING REAL BEAUTY	Mary's song Luke 1:39–56	[p. 1430]	"You surpass them all" Proverbs 31:10–31	[p. 928]

8. CINDERELLA SYNDROME: "WHEN LIFE IS NOT A BALL"
"I never thought my life would be like this. I've had so many disappointments and unfulfilled expectations. I try so hard, but things just don't go the way I've hoped. What am I doing wrong?"

1	WHERE'S THE ROMANCE?	Rachel's romance, Leah's longing Genesis 29:1–30	[p. 95]	Precious in his sight Isaiah 43:1–13	[p. 1018]
2	GROWN UP—AND DOING THIS?	Swallowing pride Jonah 1:1–17	[p. 1282]	Eager to make your calling sure 2 Peter 1:1–11	[p. 1707]
3	WHERE'S MY PICKET FENCE?	The house built on rock Matthew 7:24–29	[p. 1349]	Content in any situation Philippians 4:10–23	[p. 1647]
4	MY PICTURE-PERFECT FAMILY	Rebekah helps trick Isaac Genesis 27:1–40	[p. 95]	A covering of love 1 Peter 4:1–11	[p. 1704]
5	WEREN'T WE BEST FRIENDS?	Hagar's favor turns sour Genesis 16:1–16	[p. 72]	The only faithful One Psalm 146:1–10	[p. 882]

		TRACK 1 *Stories / LITE*	TRACK 2 *Teachings / HEAVY*

7. REAL BEAUTY: "LIVING IN A WORLD OF GLITZ"
"It's a constant battle! My hair, my shape and my clothes are never quite right. I know I don't need to measure up to the glamorous stereotype, but where can I find a role model for real beauty?"

1	I DON'T MEASURE UP	Amazing affirmation John 7:53–8:11	[p. 1502]	"How great is the love" 1 John 2:28–3:10	[p. 1712]
2	STRUGGLE TO STAY IN SHAPE	Leah and Rachel Genesis 29:31–30:24	[p. 96]	Training for godliness 1 Timothy 4:1–16	[p. 1666]
3	KEEPING UP MY IMAGE	Queen of Sheba 1 Kings 10:1–13	[p. 508]	Unfading beauty 1 Peter 3:1–7	[p. 1703]
4	FINDING MY OWN STYLE	Stylish love Luke 7:36–50	[p. 1446]	"Be imitators of God" Ephesians 5:1–20	[p. 1640]
5	STAYING FOCUSED	Wealthy woman stays focused 2 Kings 4:8–37	[p. 539]	Keeping the goal in sight Ephesians 3:14–21	[p. 1639]
6	ACHIEVING REAL BEAUTY	Mary's song Luke 1:39–56	[p. 1430]	"You surpass them all" Proverbs 31:10–31	[p. 928]

ABOUT THE READY-MADE COURSES FOR GROUPS

DECIDING

27. **How do you choose what to study?** Review the courses on pages 24–45 and choose one for your group to study.

DURATION

28. **How long does a study course last?** Six or 12 sessions, depending upon whether you want to study only Track 1—Stories, or Track 2—Teachings, or both.

TWO TRACKS

29. **What is the difference between Track 1 and Track 2?** Track 1 is somewhat easier. All of the studies are taken from stories and have a ready-made questionnaire at the bottom of the text for easy sharing.

TRACK 2

30. **What about Track 2?** Track 2 is somewhat harder. The studies are taken from teachings (mostly from the Epistles) and you will use the questions in the margin.

TARGET GROUPS

31. **How did you arrive at the study courses?** We targeted the 10 affinity groups and tried to deal with the most important issues in each group (see the chart on pages 24–25).

CONTINUING

32. **What do you suggest after completing a course?** Choose another course or move to a book study—such as one of the shorter epistles in the New Testament like Philippians or James.

BOOK STUDY

33. **How do you organize a book study?** The introduction page to each book in the Bible contains a study outline. The outlines include two options for study. Choose the option that fits best with your time schedule. The column for Personal Reading indicates what you can read prior to the meeting. The Group Study Passage indicates the passage your group should focus on, using either the corresponding questionnaire (if applicable) or the margin questions.

DREAM

34. **What is your hope and dream for this Bible?** To provide the tools for groups in the church to study together.

UNIQUENESS

35. **What is the difference between this study Bible and all other study Bibles?** Although this is a valuable tool for personal study, this study Bible was designed primarily to help groups study together. Most other study Bibles are designed only for individual study or teaching.

GROUP vs. PERSONAL BIBLE STUDY

36. **Is there a place for both?** Absolutely. Both are needed. It is important to learn about the Bible and grow in our personal faith. It is also important to belong to a Christian community where we can care for one another. This Bible is designed specifically for this second need.

See!

It's as

Easy as

1, 2, 3!

1. Find Your Kind of Group

2. Pick a Course ... pages 26–45

	WOMEN'S	
	TRACK 1 *Stories / LITE*	**TRACK 2** *Teachings / HEAVY*

7. REAL BEAUTY: "LIVING IN A WORLD OF GLITZ"
"It's a constant battle! My hair, my shape and my clothes are never quite right. I know I don't need to measure up to the glamorous stereotype, but where can I find a role model for real beauty?"

		TRACK 1		TRACK 2	
1	I DON'T MEASURE UP	Amazing affirmation John 7:53–8:11	[p. 1502]	"How great is the love" 1 John 2:28–3:10	[p. 1712]
2	STRUGGLE TO STAY IN SHAPE	Leah and Rachel Genesis 29:31–30:24	[p. 96]	Training for godliness 1 Timothy 4:1–16	[p. 1666]
3	KEEPING UP MY IMAGE	Queen of Sheba 1 Kings 10:1–13	[p. 508]	Unfading beauty 1 Peter 3:1–7	[p. 1703]
4	FINDING MY OWN STYLE	Stylish love Luke 7:36–50	[p. 1446]	"Be imitators of God" Ephesians 5:1–20	[p. 1640]
5	STAYING FOCUSED	Wealthy woman stays focused 2 Kings 4:8–37	[p. 539]	Keeping the goal in sight Ephesians 3:14–21	[p. 1639]
6	ACHIEVING REAL BEAUTY	Mary's song Luke 1:39–56	[p. 1430]	"You surpass them all" Proverbs 31:10–31	[p. 928]

3. Follow a Track

☐ **Track 1** - Bible stories with questionnaires
☐ **Track 2** - Bible teachings with margin questions

See additional course outlines in the back of the Bible.

Find Your Kind of Group

MEN	WOMEN	SINGLES	MARRIAGE	PARENTING
(page 26)	(page 28)	(page 30)	(page 32)	(page 34)
1. MASCULINITY Will the Real Jesus Please Stand Up?	7. REAL BEAUTY Living in a World of Glitz	13. LOVE AND LONELINESS Solitaire on a Saturday Night	19. HONEY, I'M HOME From the Kiss at the Door to the Socks on the Floor	25. PARENTING Not Just a Stroll in the Park
2. ACCOUNT-ABILITY Beyond Football and the Weather	8. CINDERELLA SYNDROME When Life Is Not a Ball	14. PRESSURES Keeping It Together When It's Falling Apart	20. BALANCING ACT Winning at Work Without Losing at Home	26. FAMILY TIME Making Meaningful Memories
3. DISCIPLESHIP Being a Man After God's Own Heart	9. A WOMAN OF EXCELLENCE Being a Godly Woman	15. THE SINGLE JESUS Becoming a Whole in One	21. COMMUNICA-TION AND CON-FLICT Lasting Love	27. PARENTING A STRONG-WILLED CHILD Train Up a Child
4. ATTITUDE ADJUSTMENT Down but Not Out	10. TRANSITIONS Coping With Change	16. DATING DILEMMA In Search of My Better Half	22. INTIMACY The Gift of Sex	28. PARENTING ADOLESCENTS Hair, Hormones and Hassles
5. MEN AT WORK Performance Anxiety	11. ASSERTIVE-NESS Holding Your Own	17. SEXUALITY How Do I Handle My Hormones?	23. SPIRITUALLY SINGLE Solo on Sunday	29. CHALLENG-ING ISSUES FOR PARENTS Special Kids With Special Needs
6. FOR MEN ONLY Issues Men Face	12. FOR WOMEN ONLY Issues Women Face	18. CHOICES Issues Singles Face	24. MISCARRIAGE Why Our Child?	30. PARENTS IN PAIN When Your Child Breaks Your Heart

... and Pick a Course

YOUTH	MARKET-PLACE	SPIRITUAL FORMATION	SPECIAL NEEDS	RECOVERY
(page 36)	(page 38)	(page 40)	(page 42)	(page 44)
31. UP CLOSE Discovering My Real Identity	37. RELATION-SHIPS AT WORK How's Your Serve?	43. SPIRITUAL BASICS Becoming a Christian	49. SELF-ESTEEM Made in the Image of God	55. HEALTHY HABITS Shaping Up
32. BELONGING Finding Friends and Fitting In	38. STRESSED OUT Living in the Fast Lane	44. MATURING IN CHRIST Called to Discipleship	50. FINANCIAL STRESS Making Ends Meet	56. MENDING FENCES Healing Significant Relationships
33. CONFIRMA-TION What Do I Believe?	39. BUSINESS ETHICS A Christian in a Down and Dirty World	45. GIFTS AND CALLING What Is the Will of God for My Life?	51. LIVING WITH PAIN Coping With Life's Hurts	57. DIVORCE RECOVERY Picking Up the Pieces
34. STRESS Surviving Day to Day	40. EMPLOYMENT Over-, Under- and Un-	46. WHOL-I-NESS With Myself, Others and God	52. CAREGIVERS Lifting Others Up Without Getting Down	58. GRIEF AND LOSS Getting Through the Night
35. HASSLES Getting Along With My Parents	41. BORED AND BURNED OUT Assessing Your Career	47. PAIN AND SUFFERING Where Is God When It Hurts?	53. EMPTY NESTERS What Do We Do Now?	59. ABUSE Moving Past the Pain
36. HOT ISSUES I've Got to Talk to Somebody	42. ENTREPRE-NEURS Going Out on a Limb	48. COMING HOME Pilgrims on Their Way Back	54. GROWING OLDER Time to Celebrate Life	60. 12 STEPS The Road to Recovery

See additional course outlines in back of the Bible.

TRACK 1
Stories / LITE

TRACK 2
Teachings / HEAVY

1 MASCULINITY: "WILL THE REAL JESUS PLEASE STAND UP?"

"I get mixed messages about what a man should be—somewhere between macho and milquetoast. I know Jesus is God, but is he also someone I can look to as the ultimate man?"

		Track 1		Track 2	
1	THE DIVINE JESUS	"God with us" Matthew 1:18–25	[p. 1339]	Children of God 1 John 2:28–3:10	[p. 1712]
2	THE HUMAN JESUS	"Isn't this Joseph's son?" Luke 4:14–30	[p. 1438]	Jesus made like his brothers Hebrews 2:1–18	[p. 1681]
3	THE INITIATED JESUS	Baptized and tempted Matthew 3:13–4:11	[p. 1342]	Tempted as we are Hebrews 4:14–5:10	[p. 1683]
4	THE TOUGH JESUS	Temple cleansing time Mark 11:12–19	[p. 1414]	Paul tells it like it is Galatians 1:1–10	[p. 1630]
5	THE TENDER JESUS	"Jesus wept" John 11:1–44	[p. 1509]	"In his steps" 1 Peter 2:13–25	[p. 1702]
6	THE TRIUMPHANT JESUS	Jesus' death Luke 23:44–49	[p. 1484]	"More than conquerors" Romans 8:28–39	[p. 1588]

2 ACCOUNTABILITY: "BEYOND FOOTBALL AND THE WEATHER"

"It's about time men got together and got real. I know what's right and what I need to do. I don't need advice, but I do need a group of guys to listen, keep what I say to themselves, and hold me accountable."

		Track 1		Track 2	
1	OUR NEED FOR OTHERS	Raising the roof for a friend Mark 2:1–12	[p. 1393]	Everybody needs some body 1 Corinthians 12:12–31	[p. 1610]
2	OUR NEED FOR ACCOUNTABILITY	Gehazi caught red-handed 2 Kings 5:1–27	[p. 541]	Paul straightens out Peter Galatians 2:11–21	[p. 1631]
3	OUR NEED FOR SUPPORT	David's mighty men 2 Samuel 23:8–23	[p. 486]	"Spur one another on" Hebrews 10:19–39	[p. 1689]
4	OUR NEED FOR COUNSEL	Rehoboam needs advice 1 Kings 12:1–24	[p. 513]	Going to your brother Matthew 18:15–20	[p. 1366]
5	OUR NEED FOR CORRECTION	Nathan rebukes David 2 Samuel 12:1–14	[p. 464]	Confession and confrontation James 5:7–20	[p. 1698]
6	OUR NEED FOR MENTORING	Moses commissions Joshua Numbers 27:12–23	[p. 271]	"I became your father through the gospel" 1 Corinthians 4:1–21	[p. 1602]

3 DISCIPLESHIP: "BEING A MAN AFTER GOD'S OWN HEART"

"Could anyone tell me what it means to be a man of God? I'm tired of pious Jesus talk and Sunday Christians. If I'm going to go for Christianity, I'm going all the way."

		Track 1		Track 2	
1	FIGHTING SPIRIT	David and Goliath 1 Samuel 17:12–50	[p. 429]	The armor of God Ephesians 6:10–24	[p. 1641]
2	TOTAL COMMITMENT	The rich young man Mark 10:17–31	[p. 1411]	Take up your cross Luke 9:18–27	[p. 1450]
3	OBEDIENCE	Abraham's greatest test Genesis 22:1–19	[p. 82]	Abiding in the vine John 15:1–17	[p. 1516]
4	TEACHABLE SPIRIT	Peter's stretching vision Acts 10:1–23	[p. 1548]	Obey God and your leaders Hebrews 13:1–25	[p. 1692]
5	SPREADING THE WORD	Don't just stand there Acts 1:1–11	[p. 1529]	Christ's ambassadors 2 Corinthians 5:11–6:2	[p. 1621]
6	GOD'S MAN AT HOME	"As for me and my household ... " Joshua 24:1–27	[p. 359]	Love like Christ Ephesians 5:22–6:9	[p. 1641]

COURSES

	TRACK 1 *Stories / LITE*	**TRACK 2** *Teachings / HEAVY*

4 ATTITUDE ADJUSTMENT: "DOWN BUT NOT OUT"

"Pressure is closing in on me. Too many demands. Not enough time. Money. My job. My kids. My marriage. Things are out of control and getting worse. I can't take this rat race anymore."

		Track 1		Track 2	
1	PRESSURES	Three men and a furnace Daniel 3:1–30	[p. 1225]	Pressure beyond our ability to endure 2 Corinthians 1:1–11	[p. 1618]
2	DEMANDS	Moses and his "cry babies" Numbers 11:4–34	[p. 245]	Paul's boasting 2 Corinthians 11:16–33	[p. 1626]
3	CHAOS	Paul and Silas in the slammer Acts 16:16–40	[p. 1559]	Fixing our eyes on the eternal 2 Corinthians 4:1–18	[p. 1620]
4	BLOWING IT	Peter denies Jesus Luke 22:54–62	[p. 1481]	The good news of forgiveness 1 John 1:1–2:14	[p. 1711]
5	FAMILY STRESS	Fracas in the family Luke 15:11–32	[p. 1465]	Good discipline Hebrews 12:1–13	[p. 1691]
6	FOURTH AND GOAL	Peter steps out of the boat Matthew 14:22–33	[p. 1361]	Trials and temptations James 1:1–18	[p. 1695]

5 MEN AT WORK: "PERFORMANCE ANXIETY"

"I constantly feel like my job is on the line. I'm always afraid I'm not measuring up. Even when I'm home I worry about work."

		Track 1		Track 2	
1	WHO IS THE BOSS?	Workers in the vineyard Matthew 20:1–16	[p. 1369]	"Working for the Lord" Colossians 3:1–4:1	[p. 1652]
2	WHAT'S MY RESPONSIBILITY?	Parable of the talents Matthew 25:14–30	[p. 1380]	Work not, eat not 2 Thessalonians 3:1–18	[p. 1661]
3	WHAT'S GOD'S RESPONSIBILITY?	God fights Gideon's battles Judges 7:1–25	[p. 372]	God only knows James 4:13–5:6	[p. 1698]
4	WORKING FOR TYRANTS	Bricks without straw Exodus 5:1–21	[p. 140]	Cruel taskmasters 1 Peter 2:13–25	[p. 1702]
5	WORRY WARTS	Moses under stress Exodus 5:22–6:12	[p. 141]	God knows what you need Matthew 6:19–34	[p. 1347]
6	BEING CONTENT	Abram gives Lot a lot Genesis 13:1–18	[p. 69]	"The secret of being content" Philippians 4:10–23	[p. 1647]

6 FOR MEN ONLY: "ISSUES MEN FACE"

"There are some things I need to talk about, although it won't be easy. I'm sure other guys fight the same battles. We just don't tell each other. I think I'm ready to talk."

		Track 1		Track 2	
1	OPENING UP	A Pharisee and a tax collector Luke 18:9–14	[p. 1471]	You're not alone 1 Corinthians 10:1–13	[p. 1608]
2	FATAL ATTRACTION	David and Bathsheba 2 Samuel 11:1–27	[p. 463]	Lust in the eye—adultery in the heart Matthew 5:21–48	[p. 1345]
3	MY DARK SIDE	Dirty dancing Mark 6:14–29	[p. 1402]	A war within Romans 7:7–25	[p. 1586]
4	MY DOUBTS	I believe; help my unbelief! Mark 9:14–29	[p. 1409]	Real confidence 1 John 5:1–21	[p. 1714]
5	AUTHORITY FIGURES	King Saul blows it 1 Samuel 13:1–15	[p. 421]	"Show proper respect" 1 Peter 2:13–25	[p. 1702]
6	SPIRITUAL RESPONSIBILITY	Eli: A failure at home 1 Samuel 2:12–26	[p. 407]	Family leaders Ephesians 5:22–6:9	[p. 1641]

WOMEN'S

		TRACK 1 *Stories / LITE*		TRACK 2 *Teachings / HEAVY*	

7 REAL BEAUTY: "LIVING IN A WORLD OF GLITZ"

"It's a constant battle! My hair, my shape and my clothes are never quite right. I know I don't need to measure up to the glamorous stereotype, but where can I find a role model for real beauty?"

1	I DON'T MEASURE UP	Amazing affirmation John 7:53–8:11	[p. 1502]	"How great is the love" 1 John 2:28–3:10	[p. 1712]
2	STRUGGLE TO STAY IN SHAPE	Leah and Rachel Genesis 29:31–30:24	[p. 96]	Training for godliness 1 Timothy 4:1–16	[p. 1666]
3	KEEPING UP MY IMAGE	Queen of Sheba 1 Kings 10:1–13	[p. 508]	Unfading beauty 1 Peter 3:1–7	[p. 1703]
4	FINDING MY OWN STYLE	Stylish love Luke 7:36–50	[p. 1446]	"Be imitators of God" Ephesians 5:1–20	[p. 1640]
5	STAYING FOCUSED	Wealthy woman stays focused 2 Kings 4:8–37	[p. 539]	Keeping the goal in sight Ephesians 3:14–21	[p. 1639]
6	ACHIEVING REAL BEAUTY	Mary's song Luke 1:39–56	[p. 1430]	"You surpass them all" Proverbs 31:10–31	[p. 928]

8 CINDERELLA SYNDROME: "WHEN LIFE IS NOT A BALL"

"I never thought my life would be like this. I've had so many disappointments and unfulfilled expectations. I try so hard, but things just don't go the way I've hoped. What am I doing wrong?"

1	WHERE'S THE ROMANCE?	Rachel's romance, Leah's longing Genesis 29:1–30	[p. 95]	Precious in his sight Isaiah 43:1–13	[p. 1018]
2	GROWN UP—AND DOING THIS?	Swallowing pride Jonah 1:1–17	[p. 1282]	Eager to make your calling sure 2 Peter 1:1–11	[p. 1707]
3	WHERE'S MY PICKET FENCE?	The house built on rock Matthew 7:24–29	[p. 1349]	Content in any situation Philippians 4:10–23	[p. 1647]
4	MY PICTURE- PERFECT FAMILY	Rebekah helps trick Isaac Genesis 27:1–40	[p. 91]	A covering of love 1 Peter 4:1–11	[p. 1704]
5	WEREN'T WE BEST FRIENDS?	Hagar's favor turns sour Genesis 16:1–16	[p. 72]	The only faithful One Psalm 146:1–10	[p. 882]
6	NO MORE GOODBYES!	Mary must say another goodbye John 20:1–18	[p. 1524]	"Another Counselor to be with you forever" John 14:15–31	[p. 1515]

9 A WOMAN OF EXCELLENCE: "BEING A GODLY WOMAN"

"What does God want me to be like? How can I apply what the Bible says about women to real life today?"

1	SEEKING GOD'S TRUTH	Queen of Sheba 1 Kings 10:1–13	[p. 508]	"Wisdom is supreme" Proverbs 4:1–27	[p. 891]
2	USING MY GIFTS	Priscilla Acts 18:1–4, 18–28	[p. 1563]	Pleasing God with my gifts Romans 12:1–8	[p. 1593]
3	CARING FOR OTHERS	Shunammite woman 2 Kings 4:8–37	[p. 539]	Sowing generously 2 Corinthians 9:6–15	[p. 1624]
4	BEING BOLD, YET WISE	Esther Esther 4:6–17; 7:1–10	[p. 703]	Deeds done in wisdom James 3:13–18	[p. 1697]
5	TRUSTING GOD IN THE UNKNOWN	Ruth Ruth 1:1–22	[p. 396]	"He guides the humble" Psalm 25:1–22	[p. 775]
6	GIVING GOD THE GLORY	Mary, mother of Jesus Luke 1:39–56	[p. 1430]	"We are God's workmanship" Ephesians 2:1–10	[p. 1638]

COURSES

<table>
<tr><td></td><td></td><td>**TRACK 1**
Stories / LITE</td><td>**TRACK 2**
Teachings / HEAVY</td></tr>
</table>

10 TRANSITIONS: "COPING WITH CHANGE"

"My head is swimming. Last year we moved. I went back to work. My youngest child is starting school. Can somebody throw me a life jacket to survive all the emotions that go along with change?!"

1	MY CHANGING RELATIONSHIPS	Ruth chooses a new family Ruth 1:1–22 [p. 396]	Putting on God's attitude Colossians 3:1–4:1 [p. 1652]
2	MY CHANGING HOME	Abram and Sarai on the move Genesis 11:27–12:9 [p. 68]	Seeking a better home Hebrews 11:1–40 [p. 1689]
3	MY CHANGING CAREER	First disciples called Luke 5:1–11 [p. 1440]	Being worthy of your calling Ephesians 4:1–16 [p. 1639]
4	MY CHANGING CHILDREN	Mary's changing child Luke 2:41–52 [p. 1435]	"As a father deals with his own children" 1 Thessalonians 2:1–16 [p. 1655]
5	MY CHANGING AGE	Sarah receives a promise Genesis 18:1–15 [p. 75]	Groaning for a heavenly home 2 Corinthians 5:1–10 [p. 1621]
6	MY CHANGING SPIRITUAL LIFE	Woman gets "living water" John 4:7–30 [p. 1494]	Love perfected 1 John 4:7–21 [p. 1714]

11 ASSERTIVENESS: "HOLDING YOUR OWN"

"I feel like I'm always giving and always giving in. I want to be a giving person, but I have needs too. How and when do I speak up for myself?"

1	EMPATHY vs. OBSESSION	Jesus mourns with Mary and Martha John 11:1–44 [p. 1509]	The attitude of Christ Philippians 2:1–11 [p. 1645]
2	SERVANTHOOD vs. SETTING LIMITS	Mary chooses not to serve Luke 10:38–42 [p. 1455]	"Neither do we go beyond our limits" 2 Corinthians 10:1–18 [p. 1624]
3	CARING FOR MYSELF	Accepting help from others Exodus 18:1–27 [p. 160]	Give and receive 2 Corinthians 8:1–15 [p. 1623]
4	SPEAKING UP	Esther speaks up for her people Esther 4:6–17; 7:1–10 [p. 703]	Speaking the truth in love Ephesians 4:1–16 [p. 1639]
5	A STRONG WOMAN	Deborah guides Israel Judges 4:1–24 [p. 366]	"Be strong in the Lord" Ephesians 6:10–24 [p. 1641]
6	AT PEACE WITH MYSELF	Jesus at peace in the temple Luke 2:41–52 [p. 1435]	"Peace I leave with you" John 14:15–31 [p. 1515]

12 FOR WOMEN ONLY: "ISSUES WOMEN FACE"

"I wish I could talk to other women about some things I can't escape. Like questions and feelings about career vs. family. About roles at home and church. And issues that require trust to even bring up."

1	TO WORK ... OR NOT TO WORK	Lydia the businesswoman Acts 16:11–15 [p. 1558]	The virtuous woman Proverbs 31:10–31 [p. 928]
2	WHAT ABOUT SUBMISSION?	One flesh Genesis 2:4–25 [p. 54]	As Christ loved Ephesians 5:22–6:9 [p. 1641]
3	MY ROLE AT CHURCH	Priscilla's gift Acts 18:1–4,18–28 [p. 1563]	"Receive her in the Lord" Romans 16:1–27 [p. 1597]
4	CAN I LOVE TOO MUCH?	Learning not to do it all Exodus 18:1–27 [p. 160]	Supplying one another's needs 2 Corinthians 8:1–15 [p. 1623]
5	WHY DIDN'T GOD HELP?	Amnon rapes Tamar 2 Samuel 13:1–22 [p. 467]	Nothing will separate us from God's love Romans 8:28–39 [p. 1588]
6	RECOVERING FROM ABUSE	Jesus heals a bleeding woman Mark 5:24–34 [p. 1400]	"More than all we ask or imagine" Ephesians 3:14–21 [p. 1639]

SINGLES

		TRACK 1 *Stories / LITE*	TRACK 2 *Teachings / HEAVY*

13 LOVE AND LONELINESS: "SOLITAIRE ON A SATURDAY NIGHT"
"I often go for days without a hug or meaningful conversation. Sometimes singleness is like being a social leper. How can I deal with my 'disease'?"

1	I DON'T FIT ANYWHERE	Elijah in the wilderness 1 Kings 19:1–18	[p. 525]	All is loss, compared to knowing Christ Philippians 3:1–11	[p. 1646]
2	MY NEED FOR A LOVING TOUCH	A touching act Luke 7:36–50	[p. 1446]	Love with actions and in truth 1 John 3:11–24	[p. 1713]
3	MY NEED FOR COMMUNICATION	Early connections Acts 2:42–47	[p. 1533]	"Love each other deeply" 1 Peter 4:1–11	[p. 1704]
4	MY NEED FOR COMPANIONSHIP	God provides a companion Genesis 2:4–25	[p. 54]	"The secret of being content" Philippians 4:10–23	[p. 1647]
5	BUSYNESS vs. LONELINESS	Jesus' life of balance Mark 1:29–39	[p. 1392]	Amidst everything—pray! Philippians 4:2–9	[p. 1647]
6	MAKING THE MOST OF MY LIFE	Lydia: A servant open to God Acts 16:11–15	[p. 1558]	"Free from concern" 1 Corinthians 7:25–35	[p. 1605]

14 PRESSURES: "KEEPING IT TOGETHER WHEN IT'S FALLING APART"
"Panic attack ... Dirty laundry. Leaking plumbing. Broken car. Checkbook a disaster. Health problems. I'm a capable person, but how can I survive on my own?!"

1	MAKING MY OWN LIVING	Widow becomes salesperson 2 Kings 4:1–7	[p. 538]	A life worthy of your calling Ephesians 4:1–16	[p. 1639]
2	COPING WITH CRISIS	Joseph holds out under pressure Genesis 39:1–23	[p. 114]	"He will deliver us" 2 Corinthians 1:1–11	[p. 1618]
3	DEALING WITH MY HEALTH	Jesus heals a long sickness John 5:1–15	[p. 1496]	"When I am weak, then I am strong" 2 Corinthians 12:1–10	[p. 1626]
4	MANAGING MY FINANCES	Making the most of what I have Matthew 25:14–30	[p. 1380]	Reap what you sow 2 Corinthians 9:6–15	[p. 1624]
5	DEALING WITH FAMILY ISSUES	God supports Hagar Genesis 21:1–21	[p. 80]	"He himself is our peace" Ephesians 2:11–22	[p. 1638]
6	HANDLING MY EMOTIONS	Paul's vision brings comfort Acts 18:5–17	[p. 1562]	"Set your hearts on things above" Colossians 3:1–4:1	[p. 1652]

15 THE SINGLE JESUS: "BECOMING A WHOLE IN ONE"
"Jesus was single. Is it possible God wants me to remain single for life? How can he call singleness a 'gift'? Couldn't I serve him better with a partner? How can I be 'whole' for him now as a single?"

1	DID JESUS EVER FEEL LONELY?	Alone in the wilderness Matthew 3:13–4:11	[p. 1342]	A gentle and merciful high priest Hebrews 4:14–5:10	[p. 1683]
2	THE *GIFT* OF SINGLENESS?	A high calling Acts 9:1–19	[p. 1545]	Happier as a single 1 Corinthians 7:25–35	[p. 1605]
3	AM I CALLED TO BE SINGLE?	God calls Samuel 1 Samuel 3:1–21	[p. 409]	Each one has his own gift 1 Corinthians 7:36–40	[p. 1606]
4	HOW CAN I BEST SERVE?	The greatest servant Mark 10:35–45	[p. 1412]	The best kind of service 2 Timothy 2:14–26	[p. 1671]
5	HOW SHOULD I PRAY?	Jesus prays for God's will Mark 14:32–42	[p. 1421]	"Present your requests to God" Philippians 4:2–9	[p. 1647]
6	A WHOLE IN ONE	Transfiguration of Jesus Mark 9:2–13	[p. 1408]	"I can do everything ..." Philippians 4:10–23	[p. 1647]

COURSES

		TRACK 1 *Stories / LITE*	TRACK 2 *Teachings / HEAVY*

16 DATING DILEMMA: "IN SEARCH OF MY BETTER HALF"

"The singles bar is a drag ... but the church scene isn't much better. I'm about ready to give up on a real relationship and forget the whole dating game."

		TRACK 1	TRACK 2
1	WHERE SHOULD I LOOK?	Isaac looks for love Genesis 24:1–29,50–66 [p. 84]	No fellowship with darkness 2 Corinthians 6:14–7:1 [p. 1622]
2	STAYING DISCIPLINED	Samson loses control Judges 14:1–20 [p. 383]	Wholly holy living Colossians 3:1–4:1 [p. 1652]
3	FINDING THE RIGHT FIT	Priscilla and Aquila: True partners Acts 18:1–4,18–28 [p. 1563]	"In knowledge and depth of insight" Philippians 1:1–11 [p. 1644]
4	MAKING MYSELF "RIGHT"	Solomon desires God's best 1 Kings 3:1–28 [p. 496]	"An instrument for noble purposes" 2 Timothy 2:14–26 [p. 1671]
5	WHAT ABOUT MY FEARS?	Gideon overcomes his fears Judges 6:1–40 [p. 370]	Relieve the troubles of my heart Psalm 25:1–22 [p. 775]
6	WHEN GOD SAYS "WAIT"	Jacob and Rachel wait Genesis 29:1–30 [p. 95]	"My times are in your hands" Psalm 31:1–24 [p. 779]

17 SEXUALITY: "HOW DO I HANDLE MY HORMONES?"

"The whole world tells me to do it. God gave me these desires. What does he expect me to do with them? Is there anyone out there who struggles with the stuff I struggle with?"

		TRACK 1	TRACK 2
1	ARE MY DESIRES NORMAL?	David is tempted 2 Samuel 11:1–27 [p. 463]	To marry or not 1 Corinthians 7:1–9 [p. 1605]
2	WHAT ARE GOD'S STANDARDS?	Nathan rebukes David 2 Samuel 12:1–14 [p. 464]	"You are not your own" 1 Corinthians 6:12–20 [p. 1604]
3	ISN'T SEX AN ACT OF LOVE?	"Love" gets the best of Samson Judges 16:1–22 [p. 386]	Christ-like commitment Ephesians 5:1–4,22–6:9 [p. 1640]
4	HOW LONG CAN I WAIT?	Jacob puts in his time Genesis 29:1–30 [p. 95]	Controlled by the Spirit Romans 8:1–17 [p. 1587]
5	WHAT IF I'VE MADE MISTAKES?	Jesus forgives a prostitute Luke 7:36–50 [p. 1446]	"That you should be sanctified" 1 Thessalonians 4:1–12 [p. 1656]
6	DEALING WITH MY FRUSTRATIONS	A greater power for Elisha 2 Kings 6:8–23 [p. 543]	"Set your hearts on things above" Colossians 3:1–4:1 [p. 1652]

18 CHOICES: "ISSUES SINGLES FACE"

"What kinds of friends do I look for? How do I keep from being burned again? Should I live in community or alone? Should I go back to school or volunteer overseas? What does God want me to do?"

		TRACK 1	TRACK 2
1	WHOM TO PICK FOR FRIENDS	David's friendship of character 1 Samuel 20:1–42 [p. 435]	An outstanding lineup Romans 16:1–27 [p. 1597]
2	WHEN TO RISK WITH OTHERS	Seventy-seven times Matthew 18:21–35 [p. 1367]	"To this you were called" 1 Peter 3:8–22 [p. 1703]
3	WHERE TO LIVE	Israel's cloud of guidance Numbers 9:15–10:36 [p. 243]	Abraham obeyed and went Hebrews 11:1–19 [p. 1689]
4	HOW TO SPEND MY LIFE	The Good Samaritan Luke 10:25–37 [p. 1454]	"What does the Lord require of you?" Micah 6:1–8 [p. 1293]
5	WHERE TO USE MY TALENTS	David in Saul's service 1 Samuel 16:14–23 [p. 428]	Gifted for God 1 Peter 4:1–11 [p. 1704]
6	WHAT ABOUT THE FUTURE?	Noah waits on God Genesis 8:1–22 [p. 62]	"If it is the Lord's will" James 4:13–5:6 [p. 1698]

MARRIAGE

	TRACK 1 *Stories / LITE*	TRACK 2 *Teachings / HEAVY*

19 HONEY, I'M HOME: "FROM THE KISS AT THE DOOR TO THE SOCKS ON THE FLOOR"
"We don't have a bad relationship, but why isn't marriage more fun? I want to be my spouse's best friend—as well as lover. How can I do a better job of living with the one I married?"

		TRACK 1	TRACK 2
1	IN GOOD TIMES AND BAD	Isaac and Rebekah: First love Genesis 24:1–29,50–66 [p. 84]	Hard times, beautiful times James 1:1–18 [p. 1695]
2	LOVE, HONOR AND CHERISH	Ruth and Boaz: Mutual respect Ruth 2:1–23 [p. 398]	The virtue of submission Ephesians 5:22–6:9 [p. 1641]
3	'TIL DEATH DO US PART	Jacob and Rachel: Worth the wait Genesis 29:1–30 [p. 95]	"What God has joined together" Matthew 19:1–12 [p. 1368]
4	SERVING ONE ANOTHER	Footwashing: Whose job is it? John 13:1–17 [p. 1513]	Putting your "better half" first Philippians 2:1–11 [p. 1645]
5	FRIENDS ...	Adam and Eve: "One flesh" Genesis 2:4–25 [p. 54]	Harmonious matrimony Colossians 3:1–4:1 [p. 1652]
6	AND LOVERS	Viva la difference! Song of Songs 6:13–8:4 [p. 954]	To have and to hold 1 Corinthians 7:1–9 [p. 1605]

20 BALANCING ACT: "WINNING AT WORK WITHOUT LOSING AT HOME"
"We both have so many demands for our time and energy. How can we give our best to our work without it coming at the expense of our family? I don't want to lose what we're supposed to be working for!"

		TRACK 1	TRACK 2
1	TEAMMATES	Adam and Eve: "One flesh" Genesis 2:4–25 [p. 54]	Made to be interdependent 1 Corinthians 11:2–16 [p. 1609]
2	ROOMMATES	Martha in the kitchen Luke 10:38–42 [p. 1455]	"Love is ..." 1 Corinthians 13:1–13 [p. 1611]
3	WORK AND STRESS	Workers in the vineyard Matthew 20:1–16 [p. 1369]	God's rest Hebrews 4:1–13 [p. 1682]
4	STRESS MANAGEMENT	Jesus deals with demands Mark 1:29–39 [p. 1392]	Will the perfect spouse please stand up? Proverbs 31:10–31 [p. 928]
5	SERVING EACH OTHER	Footwashing John 13:1–17 [p. 1513]	Putting your "better half" first Philippians 2:1–11 [p. 1645]
6	FAITHFUL AND FULFILLED	Priscilla and Aquila work together Acts 18:1–4,18–28 [p. 1563]	Serving the Lord Colossians 3:1–4:1 [p. 1652]

21 COMMUNICATION AND CONFLICT: "LASTING LOVE"
"Whether it's how to spend an evening or how to spend our income tax refund—we have a different point of view. How can we relate to each other in a way that pulls us together instead of apart?"

		TRACK 1	TRACK 2
1	POWER OF COMMITMENT	Joseph marries Mary Matthew 1:18–25 [p. 1339]	"Love is ..." 1 Corinthians 13:1–13 [p. 1611]
2	POWER OF WORDS	David and Michal: Cutting words 2 Samuel 6:1–23 [p. 457]	Taming the tongue James 3:1–12 [p. 1697]
3	ACTING ON IMPULSE	Abram, Sarai and Hagar Genesis 16:1–16 [p. 72]	When you don't get your own way James 4:1–12 [p. 1697]
4	DEALING WITH CONFLICT	Abraham and Sarah disagree Genesis 21:1–21 [p. 80]	"In your anger do not sin" Ephesians 4:17–32 [p. 1640]
5	PULLING APART	Adam and Eve play the blame game Genesis 3:1–24 [p. 56]	Putting your "better half" first Philippians 2:1–11 [p. 1645]
6	PULLING TOGETHER	Overcoming differences John 4:7–30 [p. 1494]	Mutual respect Ephesians 5:22–6:9 [p. 1641]

COURSES

<table>
<tr><td></td><td>**TRACK 1**
Stories / LITE</td><td>**TRACK 2**
Teachings / HEAVY</td></tr>
</table>

22 INTIMACY: "THE GIFT OF SEX"

"The world exalts sex as the ultimate high. But we both have different needs. We'd like more romance and sizzle in our love life. How does God want us to enjoy this gift?"

		TRACK 1	TRACK 2
1	GOD'S GIFT	Delighting in love Song of Songs 1:1–14 [p. 945]	"Naked and unashamed" Genesis 2:4–25 [p. 54]
2	SHARING YOURSELF	Wooing words Song of Songs 1:15–2:15 [p. 947]	"Put on love" Colossians 3:1–4:1 [p. 1652]
3	THE RHYTHM OF ROMANCE	Absence makes hearts grow fonder Song of Songs 2:16–3:11 [p. 949]	You're not your own 1 Corinthians 7:1–9 [p. 1605]
4	ONLY YOU	Can't keep my eyes off of you Song of Songs 5:9–6:9 [p. 953]	"Drink water from your own cistern" Proverbs 5:1–23 [p. 892]
5	SENSITIVE SEX	Viva la difference! Song of Songs 6:13–8:4 [p. 954]	"Love is ..." 1 Corinthians 13:1–13 [p. 1611]
6	COMMITTED LOVE	The power of love Song of Songs 8:5–14 [p. 956]	"A profound mystery" Ephesians 5:22–6:9 [p. 1641]

23 SPIRITUALLY SINGLE: "SOLO ON SUNDAYS"

*"Since we've been married, my husband won't come to church with me. I want our children to grow up with Christian teaching, but he doesn't back me up. How can I please God **and** my husband?"*

		TRACK 1	TRACK 2
1	DON'T GIVE UP	A household conversion Acts 16:16–40 [p. 1559]	Don't underestimate your influence 1 Corinthians 7:10–24 [p. 1605]
2	GOD'S LOVE AND OURS	Abraham pleads for Sodom Genesis 18:16–33 [p. 76]	"We love because he first loved us" 1 John 4:7–21 [p. 1714]
3	PUTTING THINGS IN GOD'S HANDS	Abraham's greatest test Genesis 22:1–19 [p. 82]	God's Spirit helps us pray Romans 8:18–27 [p. 1588]
4	WHO'S NUMBER 1?	Take a warning from Solomon 1 Kings 10:23–11:13 [p. 510]	Jesus first Luke 14:25–35 [p. 1462]
5	GOD IS AT WORK	Praying for Peter in prison Acts 12:1–19 [p. 1551]	The power of example 1 Peter 3:1–7 [p. 1703]
6	YOUR SPIRITUAL FAMILY	Mary and John at the cross John 19:16–27 [p. 1522]	"Members of God's household" Ephesians 2:11–22 [p. 1638]

24 MISCARRIAGE: "WHY OUR CHILD?"

"It tears me up to walk past the baby's room. Now I wish we hadn't gotten so excited and made so many plans. I'm dying inside, and I've got to talk to someone who has gone through this."

		TRACK 1	TRACK 2
1	WHEN LIFE FALLS APART	Job's life collapses Job 1:1–22 [p. 708]	Job responds to his pain Job 16:1–17:1 [p. 725]
2	SHATTERED DREAMS	Elisha and a grieving woman 2 Kings 4:8–37 [p. 539]	One day at a time Matthew 6:19–34 [p. 1347]
3	MARITAL STRESS	Jacob and Rachel under stress Genesis 29:31–30:24 [p. 96]	"Love is ..." 1 Corinthians 13:1–13 [p. 1611]
4	RELEASING THE PAIN	Hannah pours out her soul 1 Samuel 1:1–28 [p. 405]	Worn out from weeping Psalm 6:1–10 [p. 760]
5	GOD CARES	Jesus weeps over death John 11:1–44 [p. 1509]	The pain and the hope Romans 8:18–27 [p. 1588]
6	LIFE GOES ON	David pleads, then accepts 2 Samuel 12:15–25 [p. 465]	Nothing will separate us from God's love Romans 8:28–39 [p. 1588]

PARENTING

	TRACK 1 *Stories / LITE*	TRACK 2 *Teachings / HEAVY*

25 PARENTING: "NOT JUST A STROLL IN THE PARK"
"I got into parenting before I was ready. Dr. Spock makes it sound so easy. My mother just laughs. My grand-mother says everything will be okay. But I'm trying to raise my kids without a map. Please help."

1	PREPARATION	Mary and Joseph become parents Luke 2:1–20 [p. 1432]	The pain and the hope Romans 8:18–27 [p. 1588]
2	DEDICATION	Jesus presented in the temple Luke 2:21–40 [p. 1434]	Committed to love 1 Corinthians 13:1–13 [p. 1611]
3	EXPECTATIONS	A mother's high hopes Matthew 20:20–28 [p. 1371]	High standards Colossians 3:1–4:1 [p. 1652]
4	CONFRONTATION	Eli's failure to restrain his sons 1 Samuel 3:1–21 [p. 409]	Godly discipline Hebrews 12:1–13 [p. 1691]
5	CONSECRATION	Abraham's greatest test Genesis 22:1–19 [p. 82]	Godly role models Titus 2:1–15 [p. 1675]
6	CELEBRATION	Homecoming party Luke 15:11–32 [p. 1465]	Passing on the faith Deuteronomy 6:1–25 [p. 292]

26 FAMILY TIME: "MAKING MEANINGFUL MEMORIES"
*"We want to live like a **real** Christian family. Will our kids remember their childhood in a way that feels good to them and honors God?"*

1	PROPER PRIORITIES	God commands a day off Exodus 16:1–35 [p. 157]	Training for godliness 1 Timothy 4:1–16 [p. 1666]
2	TIME TOGETHER	Supper time John 13:1–17 [p. 1513]	"Love is ..." 1 Corinthians 13:1–13 [p. 1611]
3	FAMILY TRADITIONS	Passover: A family ritual Exodus 12:1–30 [p. 150]	"Talk about them ... at home " Deuteronomy 6:1–25 [p. 292]
4	FAMILY VACATIONS	A "vacation" with 5,000 surprises Mark 6:30–44 [p. 1403]	Getting along Ephesians 5:22–6:9 [p. 1641]
5	WORSHIPING TOGETHER	The fellowship of believers Acts 2:42–47 [p. 1533]	The children must hear Deuteronomy 31:1–13 [p. 320]
6	LASTING VALUES	Stones of memorial Joshua 3:14–4:24 [p. 332]	Leaving a legacy 2 Timothy 3:10–4:8 [p. 1672]

27 PARENTING A STRONG-WILLED CHILD: "TRAIN UP A CHILD"
"My daughter always wants to paint outside the lines. She is really a good kid, and I love her a lot, but I don't know what to do. How do you raise a child who was born with a strong will?"

1	WHERE ARE MY INSTRUCTIONS?	Jesus was a strong-willed child Luke 2:41–52 [p. 1435]	When you need wisdom James 1:1–18 [p. 1695]
2	BORN TO BE WILD	The devil made me do it Genesis 3:1–24 [p. 56]	The pain and the hope Romans 8:18–27 [p. 1588]
3	NECESSARY DISCIPLINE	Eli: A parent who failed 1 Samuel 3:1–21 [p. 409]	Discipline is "for our good" Hebrews 12:1–13 [p. 1691]
4	DEALING WITH ANGER	Moses faces backseat back talk Numbers 11:4–34 [p. 245]	"In your anger do not sin" Ephesians 4:17–32 [p. 1640]
5	WHEN THE KIDS DRIVE YOU CRAZY	Little Jacob grabs for power Genesis 25:19–34 [p. 88]	Harmony at home Colossians 3:1–4:1 [p. 1652]
6	HAPPY ENDINGS	Jacob's strength comes through Genesis 32:22–32 [p. 103]	Passing on the faith 2 Timothy 1:1–2:13 [p. 1670]

COURSES

	TRACK 1 *Stories / LITE*	TRACK 2 *Teachings / HEAVY*

28 PARENTING ADOLESCENTS: "HAIR, HORMONES AND HASSLES"

"My teenager is about to drive me crazy. The music. Posters. Clothes. It's outrageous! We can't even talk about it without shouting. How can we make it through adolescence?!"

		TRACK 1		TRACK 2	
1	STRESSFUL TIMES	Fracas in the family Luke 15:11–32	[p. 1465]	Prescriptions for stress Philippians 4:2–9	[p. 1647]
2	CONFUSING TIMES	When Jesus didn't come home Luke 2:41–52	[p. 1435]	Watch your mouth James 1:19–27	[p. 1695]
3	ANGRY TIMES	The golden calf Exodus 32:1–35	[p. 178]	"In your anger do not sin" Ephesians 4:17–32	[p. 1640]
4	DECISIONS, DECISIONS!	Samson's dating fiasco Judges 14:1–20	[p. 383]	Do as I say *and* as I do Titus 2:1–15	[p. 1675]
5	A PARENT'S RESPONSIBILITY	Eli's failure to restrain his sons 1 Samuel 3:1–21	[p. 409]	Discipline: It's for your own good Hebrews 12:1–13	[p. 1691]
6	GETTING ALONG	Joseph: A kid with an "attitude" Genesis 37:1–11	[p. 110]	Harmony at home Colossians 3:1–4:1	[p. 1652]

29 CHALLENGING ISSUES FOR PARENTS: "SPECIAL KIDS WITH SPECIAL NEEDS"

"God gave me a very special child. Now, God needs to give me the wisdom I need to raise this child. I feel somewhat alone and nobody understands."

		TRACK 1		TRACK 2	
1	ADOPTED CHILDREN	Moses: An adopted child Exodus 1:22–2:25	[p. 135]	God's adopted children Ephesians 1:1–14	[p. 1637]
2	CHILDREN OF DIVORCE	Ishmael: Rejected and dejected Genesis 21:1–21	[p. 80]	"Devoted to one another" Romans 12:9–21	[p. 1593]
3	SINGLE-PARENT CHILDREN	Double blessing for a single parent 1 Kings 17:1–24	[p. 521]	"Father" knows best Matthew 6:19–34	[p. 1347]
4	CHILDREN WITH DISABILITIES	Why was he born blind? John 9:1–34	[p. 1505]	"Fearfully and wonderfully made" Psalm 139:1–24	[p. 876]
5	GIFTED CHILDREN	Jesus perplexes his parents Luke 2:41–52	[p. 1435]	Thoughts, attitudes and gifts Romans 12:1–8	[p. 1593]
6	SUBSTITUTE PARENTS	Esther: Raised by a relative Esther 2:1–18	[p. 698]	Pure religion: To look after orphans James 1:19–27	[p. 1695]

30 PARENTS IN PAIN: "WHEN YOUR CHILD BREAKS YOUR HEART"

"Where did we go wrong? I never dreamed our son would make the choices he has. Didn't our values sink in at all? And how do we relate to him now? What should or shouldn't we say to him?"

		TRACK 1		TRACK 2	
1	SHARING YOUR STORY	Prodigal Son: A parable of pain Luke 15:11–32	[p. 1465]	Comfort in the midst of despair 2 Corinthians 1:1–11	[p. 1618]
2	COPING WITH GRIEF	Eli and his wayward sons 1 Samuel 2:12–26	[p. 407]	Painful perspective 1 Peter 4:12–19	[p. 1704]
3	DEALING WITH DISAPPOINTMENT	Bedlam in David's family 2 Samuel 13:23–39	[p. 468]	Sincere love Romans 12:9–21	[p. 1593]
4	KNOWING HOW TO RELATE	David longs for Absalom 2 Samuel 14:1–33	[p. 470]	Slow to speak, slow to anger James 1:19–27	[p. 1695]
5	FEELING THEIR PAIN	Peter disowns Jesus Luke 22:54–62	[p. 1481]	When someone is "caught in sin" Galatians 6:1–18	[p. 1635]
6	BELIEVING IN MIRACLES	Jesus forgives Peter John 21:1–25	[p. 1526]	Waiting with hope Romans 8:18–27	[p. 1588]

YOUTH

TRACK 1 *Stories / LITE*	TRACK 2 *Teachings / HEAVY*

31 UP CLOSE: "DISCOVERING MY REAL IDENTITY"

"I know I'm good at some things and not so good at others. I don't want to be weird, but I do want to be myself. What makes me unique? How can I be all that I was meant to be?"

		TRACK 1	TRACK 2
1	BEING REAL	A Pharisee and a tax collector Luke 18:9–14 [p. 1471]	Children of God 1 John 2:28–3:10 [p. 1712]
2	MY UNIQUENESS	Zacchaeus Luke 19:1–10 [p. 1473]	Finding your place 1 Corinthians 12:1–11 [p. 1610]
3	MY PERSONALITY	Mary and Martha Luke 10:38–42 [p. 1455]	Don't be ashamed of your youth 1 Timothy 4:1–16 [p. 1666]
4	MY ABILITIES	Using your "talents" Matthew 25:14–30 [p. 1380]	You and your gifts Romans 12:1–8 [p. 1593]
5	STRENGTHS AND WEAKNESSES	Gideon's fears and fleeces Judges 6:1–40 [p. 370]	"When I am weak, then I am strong" 2 Corinthians 12:1–10 [p. 1626]
6	GOD'S CALL	Following Jesus Luke 5:1–11 [p. 1440]	New creation 2 Corinthians 5:11–6:2 [p. 1621]

32 BELONGING: "FINDING FRIENDS AND FITTING IN"

"I always feel out of place. It's so hard to fit in. I don't want to come off like I'm either shy or obnoxious. Can I be myself and still have friends?"

		TRACK 1	TRACK 2
1	ACCEPTANCE	Paul's struggle for acceptance Acts 9:20–31 [p. 1546]	Body support 1 Corinthians 12:12–31 [p. 1610]
2	FITTING IN	"The Lord looks at the heart" 1 Samuel 16:1–13 [p. 427]	The Golden Rule Matthew 7:1–29 [p. 1347]
3	BEING MYSELF	David can't use Saul's armor 1 Samuel 17:12–50 [p. 429]	Being who God wants me to be 1 Peter 4:1–11 [p. 1704]
4	FEELING SECURE	David and Jonathan – Part 1 1 Samuel 18:1–30 [p. 432]	"Love never fails" 1 Corinthians 13:1–13 [p. 1611]
5	GETTING CLOSE	David and Jonathan – Part 2 1 Samuel 20:1–42 [p. 435]	The wrong crowd 2 Corinthians 6:14–7:1 [p. 1622]
6	TRUE FRIENDS	Four friends who cared Mark 2:1–12 [p. 1393]	Laying down your life for your friends John 15:1–17 [p. 1516]

33 CONFIRMATION: "WHAT DO I BELIEVE?"

"It's easy to let stuff at church, like the Apostles' Creed, go in one ear and out the other. I think it's time to know what I really believe, and really believe what I already know."

		TRACK 1	TRACK 2
1	GOD THE FATHER ALMIGHTY	Maker of heaven and earth Genesis 1:1–2:3 [p. 53]	The Father's power Ephesians 3:14–21 [p. 1639]
2	JESUS CHRIST	An angel visits Mary Luke 1:26–38 [p. 1429]	The supremacy of Christ Colossians 1:15–23 [p. 1650]
3	HOLY SPIRIT	The Spirit shakes things up Acts 4:1–31 [p. 1535]	Living by the Spirit Galatians 5:16–26 [p. 1634]
4	CHRISTIAN CHURCH	The cost in "being there" Acts 4:32–37 [p. 1537]	Unity in the body of Christ Ephesians 4:1–16 [p. 1639]
5	FORGIVENESS OF SINS	Jesus: My substitute Mark 15:1–15 [p. 1423]	God's gift of grace Ephesians 2:1–10 [p. 1638]
6	RESURRECTION AND LIFE	A new day dawns Matthew 28:1–20 [p. 1388]	Resurrection life 1 Corinthians 15:12–34 [p. 1613]

COURSES

		TRACK 1 *Stories / LITE*		TRACK 2 *Teachings / HEAVY*	

34 STRESS: "SURVIVING DAY TO DAY"
"I have to buy my own clothes. Bum a ride. Make a C average just to stay on the team. Everybody's on my back. And my best friend didn't call tonight. Life stinks."

		TRACK 1		TRACK 2	
1	STRESSED OUT	Facing storms Mark 4:35–41	[p. 1399]	Not to worry Matthew 6:19–34	[p. 1347]
2	DAILY GRIND	Slaving away in Egypt Exodus 5:1–21	[p. 140]	Trials and temptations James 1:1–18	[p. 1695]
3	MAKING THE GRADE	Parable of the talents Matthew 25:14–30	[p. 1380]	Attitudes and gifts Romans 12:1–8	[p. 1593]
4	FEELING ALONE	Jesus in Gethsemane Mark 14:32–42	[p. 1421]	Devoted to one another Romans 12:9–21	[p. 1593]
5	DEALING WITH DISAPPOINTMENT	Jesus betrayed and arrested Matthew 26:47–56	[p. 1384]	Hope doesn't disappoint Romans 5:1–11	[p. 1584]
6	FACING FAILURE	Peter disowns Jesus Luke 22:54–62	[p. 1481]	"More than conquerors" Romans 8:28–39	[p. 1588]

35 HASSLES: "GETTING ALONG WITH MY PARENTS"
"In my parents' eyes, I can't do anything right. I don't look right, act right, study right, spend money right or pick friends right. As long as I'm still at home, will I always be wrong?"

		TRACK 1		TRACK 2	
1	PARENTAL REQUESTS	Jesus and his mom at a wedding John 2:1–11	[p. 1490]	"Love is ..." 1 Corinthians 13:1–13	[p. 1611]
2	PARENTAL EXPECTATIONS	A mother's dream Matthew 20:20–28	[p. 1371]	Harmony at home Colossians 3:1–4:1	[p. 1652]
3	FAMILY TENSION	When Jesus didn't come home Luke 2:41–52	[p. 1435]	Fights and quarrels James 4:1–12	[p. 1697]
4	DEALING WITH FRUSTRATIONS	Jesus and his family Mark 3:20–35	[p. 1396]	"In your anger do not sin" Ephesians 4:17–32	[p. 1640]
5	ARGUING OVER RELATIONSHIPS	Samson and his women Judges 14:1–20	[p. 383]	Who is "the wrong crowd"? 2 Corinthians 6:14–7:1	[p. 1622]
6	MAKING THINGS RIGHT	A son returns home Luke 15:11–32	[p. 1465]	Mending your fences Matthew 5:21–48	[p. 1345]

36 HOT ISSUES: "I'VE GOT TO TALK TO SOMEBODY"
"My friend is pregnant. Another is talking about suicide. What do I do? School is a jungle. People get beat up. Drugs are everywhere. If my parents knew what I have to face every day, they would freak out!"

		TRACK 1		TRACK 2	
1	LIFE IN THE JUNGLE	Jesus is tempted Matthew 3:13–4:11	[p. 1342]	"When you are tempted ..." 1 Corinthians 10:1–13	[p. 1608]
2	LOOSE MORALS	David and Bathsheba 2 Samuel 11:1–27	[p. 463]	Control yourself 1 Thessalonians 4:1–12	[p. 1656]
3	HIDDEN SECRETS	David—You are the man! 2 Samuel 12:1–14	[p. 464]	Confession time James 5:7–20	[p. 1698]
4	DON'T GET USED	Dirty dancing Mark 6:14–29	[p. 1402]	Overcoming evil with good Romans 12:9–21	[p. 1593]
5	JUST SAY NO	Daniel stays "clean" Daniel 1:1–21	[p. 1221]	Controlled by the Spirit Galatians 5:16–26	[p. 1634]
6	TAKE A STAND	Daniel in the lions' den Daniel 6:1–24	[p. 1231]	Take up your cross Luke 9:18–27	[p. 1450]

 # MARKETPLACE

	TRACK 1	TRACK 2
	Stories / LITE	*Teachings / HEAVY*

37 RELATIONSHIPS AT WORK: "HOW'S YOUR SERVE?"
"I don't know which is worse—working under someone or supervising others. I've done both and either way I've been frustrated. How can I get along with the people I work with?"

		TRACK 1	TRACK 2
1	LIFE WITH MY CO-WORKERS	Who is greatest? Mark 10:35–45 [p. 1412]	Life as God's instrument 2 Timothy 2:14–26 [p. 1671]
2	LIFE WITH MY BOSS	David spares Saul 1 Samuel 24:1–22 [p. 440]	Making God attractive Titus 2:1–15 [p. 1675]
3	LIFE AS A SUPERVISOR	Boaz lets Ruth glean Ruth 2:1–23 [p. 398]	Treat them like a brother Philemon 1–25 [p. 1678]
4	LIFE WITH MY COMPETITORS	Elisha deals in strength and grace 2 Kings 6:8–23 [p. 543]	"Live at peace with everyone" Romans 12:9–21 [p. 1593]
5	LETTING GOD BE THE BOSS	Gideon takes orders from God Judges 7:1–25 [p. 372]	Equipped with God's armor Ephesians 6:10–24 [p. 1641]
6	LETTING THE SPIRIT GUIDE ME	Paul follows the Lord's lead Acts 18:5–17 [p. 1562]	Holy Spirit's guidance Romans 8:1–17 [p. 1587]

38 STRESSED OUT: "LIVING IN THE FAST LANE"
"The stress I'm under every day is incredible. Deadlines, projects, personnel—plus home and family. If I don't find a way to release some of this pressure, I'm gonna crack!"

		TRACK 1	TRACK 2
1	STRESS FROM MY WORK	Calm for the storm Mark 4:35–41 [p. 1399]	"Perplexed, but not in despair" 2 Corinthians 4:1–18 [p. 1620]
2	STRESS ON THE JOB	Sexual harassment Genesis 39:1–23 [p. 114]	Harmony 1 Peter 3:8–22 [p. 1703]
3	STRESS IN A SECULAR WORLD	Abraham pleads for Sodom Genesis 18:16–33 [p. 76]	Be still and know Psalm 46:1–10 [p. 795]
4	STRESS FROM A CHANGING WORLD	Tower of Babel Genesis 11:1–9 [p. 66]	Refiner's fire 1 Peter 1:1–12 [p. 1701]
5	BALANCING WORK AND REST	Jesus feeds 5,000 Mark 6:30–44 [p. 1403]	Living holy lives 1 Thessalonians 4:1–12 [p. 1656]
6	KEEPING STRESS UNDER CONTROL	Moses gets a grip Exodus 17:1–16 [p. 159]	Delivered 2 Corinthians 1:1–11 [p. 1618]

39 BUSINESS ETHICS: "A CHRISTIAN IN A DOWN AND DIRTY WORLD"
"It sounds easy on Sunday, but Monday morning the rubber hits the road. Slice the meat a little thinner and say your prayers later. Can you live like a Christian in the business world and try to get ahead?"

		TRACK 1	TRACK 2
1	LIFE OF INTEGRITY	Job loses it all Job 1:1–22 [p. 708]	Pure motives 1 Thessalonians 2:1–16 [p. 1655]
2	LACK OF INTEGRITY	Ananias and Sapphira Acts 5:1–11 [p. 1538]	Living in the light Ephesians 4:17–32 [p. 1640]
3	VALUES OF INTEGRITY	Rich fool faces regret Luke 12:13–21 [p. 1458]	The love of money 1 Timothy 6:3–10 [p. 1667]
4	INTEGRITY AND CONSCIENCE	Parable of the shrewd manager Luke 16:1–15 [p. 1466]	The war within Romans 7:7–25 [p. 1586]
5	INTEGRITY AND AUTHORITY	Paying taxes to Caesar Mark 12:13–17 [p. 1416]	Submission to authorities Romans 13:1–7 [p. 1594]
6	REWARDS OF INTEGRITY	Job receives just reward Job 42:7–17 [p. 754]	"Seek first his kingdom" Matthew 6:19–34 [p. 1347]

COURSES

	TRACK 1 *Stories / LITE*	TRACK 2 *Teachings / HEAVY*

40 EMPLOYMENT: "OVER-, UNDER- AND UN-"

"For years I felt like I was in over my head. Then I didn't even have a job for awhile. And now I'm overqualified and unfulfilled! Will I ever be content?"

		TRACK 1	TRACK 2
1	OVER-QUALIFIED	Jesus takes a job beneath him John 13:1–17 [p. 1513]	Jesus' attitude Philippians 2:1–11 [p. 1645]
2	OVER MY HEAD	Moses asked to do too much Exodus 18:1–27 [p. 160]	"You armed me with strength" Psalm 18:1–50 [p. 768]
3	LAID OFF	Joseph given the boot Genesis 37:12–36 [p. 111]	Endure hardship 2 Timothy 1:1–2:13 [p. 1670]
4	UNEMPLOYED	Moses called in the desert Exodus 3:1–22 [p. 136]	"He may lift you up in due time" 1 Peter 5:1–14 [p. 1705]
5	UNFULFILLED	Bored as a brick maker Exodus 5:1–21 [p. 140]	All I need 2 Peter 1:1–11 [p. 1707]
6	FINDING MY PASSION	Paul's passion revealed Acts 26:1–32 [p. 1574]	The secret Philippians 4:10–23 [p. 1647]

41 BORED AND BURNED OUT: "ASSESSING YOUR CAREER"

"My job is like a broken record. The same thing over and over. By 10 a.m. I'm already tired. By noon, I'm ready to go home. Is it me ... or my work? Maybe I need an attitude adjustment."

1	WHY WORK?	A beachcomber paralytic John 5:1–15 [p. 1496]	A workman not ashamed 2 Timothy 2:14–26 [p. 1671]
2	WHY AM I HERE?	Philip does productive networking Acts 8:26–40 [p. 1544]	"Perplexed, but not in despair" 2 Corinthians 4:1–18 [p. 1620]
3	WHERE AM I HEADING?	Abram's call to move out Genesis 11:27–12:9 [p. 68]	Growing up Ephesians 4:1–16 [p. 1639]
4	HOW CAN GOD USE ME?	Peter's windfall Luke 5:1–11 [p. 1440]	A living sacrifice Romans 12:1–8 [p. 1593]
5	HOW'S MY ATTITUDE?	Trouble in Ocean City Jonah 1:1–17 [p. 1282]	A working attitude 1 Thessalonians 5:12–28 [p. 1657]
6	TO STAY OR TO GO?	Gideon seeks God's guidance Judges 6:1–40 [p. 370]	The main thing Philippians 1:12–30 [p. 1644]

42 ENTREPRENEURS: "GOING OUT ON A LIMB"

"I was excited to start my own business, but now I'm not sure. Rather than working when I want to, I'm working all the time. It's a huge investment. Will my dream become a nightmare?"

1	FOLLOWING MY DREAM	Jacob leaves Laban Genesis 31:1–21 [p. 98]	"The Lord sets prisoners free" Psalm 146:1–10 [p. 882]
2	RISKING MY REPUTATION	Laban pursues Jacob Genesis 31:22–55 [p. 99]	"The Lord who judges" 1 Corinthians 4:1–21 [p. 1602]
3	PAYING THE PRICE	Jacob's financial and emotional toll Genesis 32:1–21 [p. 101]	Sowing and reaping 2 Corinthians 9:6–15 [p. 1624]
4	FORFEITING MY STABILITY	Jacob wrestles with God Genesis 32:22–32 [p. 103]	One day at a time Matthew 6:19–34 [p. 1347]
5	PUTTING IN MY TIME	Jacob's slow going Genesis 33:1–20 [p. 104]	Persevering James 5:7–20 [p. 1698]
6	MEASURING MY SUCCESS	Jacob returns to Bethel Genesis 35:1–15 [p.106]	"Boast in the Lord" 1 Corinthians 1:18–2:5 [p. 1600]

SPIRITUAL

		TRACK 1 *Stories / LITE*		TRACK 2 *Teachings / HEAVY*	

43 SPIRITUAL BASICS: "BECOMING A CHRISTIAN"
"I feel a little stupid and afraid to ask, but I didn't grow up in a church and I never really heard what it means to become a Christian. How do I get to know someone I can't see, touch or hear?"

1	WHO IS CHRIST?	An angel visits Mary Luke 1:26–38	[p. 1429]	Supreme over all Colossians 1:15–23	[p. 1650]
2	HOW DO I RESPOND?	Jesus and Nicodemus John 3:1–21	[p. 1492]	Confess and believe Romans 9:30–10:21	[p. 1590]
3	WHAT ABOUT MY SINS?	Jesus: My substitute Mark 15:1–15	[p. 1423]	God's gift of grace Ephesians 2:1–10	[p. 1638]
4	HOW CAN I BE SURE?	An honest doubter John 20:24–31	[p. 1525]	Confident faith 1 John 5:1–21	[p. 1714]
5	WHAT SHOULD I DO NOW?	Zacchaeus' new life Luke 19:1–10	[p. 1473]	Faith and action Acts 2:42–47	[p. 1533]
6	WHAT DOES IT COST?	Take up your cross Matthew 16:13–28	[p. 1364]	Pressing on toward the goal Philippians 3:12–4:1	[p. 1646]

44 MATURING IN CHRIST: "CALLED TO DISCIPLESHIP"
"Now that I have given my life to Christ, what do I do next? I need to think through my priorities. My relationships. My goals in life. And I need a group of people to help stay the course."

1	UNDER NEW MANAGEMENT	Paul's change of direction Acts 9:1–19	[p. 1545]	Controlled by the Spirit Romans 8:1–17	[p. 1587]
2	ETERNAL VALUES	The rich man and Lazarus Luke 16:19–31	[p. 1467]	Counting the cost Luke 14:25–35	[p. 1462]
3	KINGDOM PRIORITIES	Parable of the great banquet Luke 14:15–24	[p. 1463]	Using your gifts Romans 12:1–8	[p. 1593]
4	QUIET TIME	Jesus: A person of prayer Mark 1:29–39	[p. 1392]	The Lord's Prayer Matthew 6:1–18	[p. 1346]
5	SERVANTHOOD	The Last Supper Luke 22:7–34	[p. 1479]	The attitude of Christ Philippians 2:1–11	[p. 1645]
6	CALLED TO BE WITNESSES	Don't just stand there Acts 1:1–11	[p. 1529]	Called to be change agents 2 Corinthians 5:11–6:2	[p. 1621]

45 GIFTS AND CALLING: "WHAT IS THE WILL OF GOD FOR MY LIFE?"
"I believe I have a gift, but I don't think God wants me to use it the way I've always wanted to. How can I be sure I'm hearing him, and how long must I wait to see what he has for me?"

1	HIGH CALLING	Following Jesus Luke 5:1–11	[p. 1440]	God's instruments 1 Corinthians 12:1–11	[p. 1610]
2	INVESTING YOURSELF	Parable of the talents Matthew 25:14–30	[p. 1380]	Using your gifts Romans 12:1–8	[p. 1593]
3	HEARING GOD	Samuel anoints Saul 1 Samuel 9:1–10:8	[p. 416]	Listening to the Shepherd's voice John 10:1–21	[p. 1507]
4	RUNNING AHEAD	Saul won't wait 1 Samuel 13:1–15	[p. 421]	God only knows James 4:13–5:6	[p. 1698]
5	LAGGING BEHIND	Jonah runs away from God's call Jonah 1:1–17	[p. 1282]	No fear 2 Timothy 1:1–2:13	[p. 1670]
6	WORRYING ABOUT GOD'S WILL	Moses isn't sure Exodus 4:1–17	[p. 138]	Don't worry Matthew 6:19–34	[p. 1347]

FORMATION

		TRACK 1 *Stories / LITE*	**TRACK 2** *Teachings / HEAVY*

46 WHOL-I-NESS: "WITH MYSELF, OTHERS AND GOD"

"Which areas of life do you need to work on to become a whole person? Your physical life? Relational life? Spiritual life? Does anyone else struggle with focusing on all these at the same time?"

1	SPIRITUAL LIFE	Parable of the sower Matthew 13:1–23	[p. 1357]	"Be holy, because I am holy" 1 Peter 1:13–2:3	[p. 1701]
2	PHYSICAL LIFE	Daniel stays "clean" Daniel 1:1–21	[p. 1221]	"Living sacrifices" Romans 12:1–8	[p. 1593]
3	VOCATIONAL LIFE	Parable of the talents Matthew 25:14–30	[p. 1380]	Holy under pressure 2 Corinthians 6:3–13	[p. 1621]
4	EMOTIONAL LIFE	Elijah in the pits 1 Kings 19:1–18	[p. 525]	Peace of mind Philippians 4:2–9	[p. 1647]
5	RELATIONAL LIFE	Miriam and Aaron criticize Moses Numbers 12:1–16	[p. 247]	How's your love life? 1 Corinthians 13:1–13	[p. 1611]
6	VOLITIONAL LIFE	Balaam and his donkey Numbers 22:1–35	[p. 262]	Holy choices 1 Thessalonians 4:1–12	[p. 1656]

47 PAIN AND SUFFERING: "WHERE IS GOD WHEN IT HURTS?"

"My best friend died in a car wreck. My grandfather died of cancer. My sister has MS. My parents got divorced. If God is supposed to be good and loving, how can he allow such terrible things to happen?"

1	HARSH REALITIES	Job loses it all Job 1:1–22	[p. 708]	Paul's thorn in the flesh 2 Corinthians 12:1–10	[p. 1626]
2	WHEN WILL IT END?	Job gets blasted again Job 2:1–10	[p. 710]	The fruit of suffering James 1:1–18	[p. 1695]
3	HARD QUESTIONS	Why was he born blind? John 9:1–34	[p. 1505]	Faith despite circumstances Hebrews 11:1–40	[p. 1689]
4	FINDING GOD	The gentle whisper 1 Kings 19:1–18	[p. 525]	Nothing will separate us from God's love Romans 8:28–39	[p. 1588]
5	COMFORTED BY OTHERS	Four friends who cared Mark 2:1–12	[p. 1393]	Passing on God's comfort 2 Corinthians 1:1–11	[p. 1618]
6	THINGS CAN CHANGE	Job is restored Job 42:7–17	[p. 754]	The pain and the hope Romans 8:18–27	[p. 1588]

48 COMING HOME: "PILGRIMS ON THEIR WAY BACK"

"God, I'm on my way back, but I keep hitting roadblocks. I hear voices from my past reminding me of all the bad things I've done ... and telling me that I will never make it. Please be patient."

1	THE CALL OF LOVE	Parable of the Prodigal Son Luke 15:11–32	[p. 1465]	"We love because he first loved us" 1 John 4:7–21	[p. 1714]
2	HIDE AND SEEK	Adam and Eve: The first prodigals Genesis 3:1–24	[p. 56]	The Good Shepherd John 10:1–21	[p. 1507]
3	STRAYING FROM GOD	Jonah takes a cruise Jonah 1:1–17	[p. 1282]	Struggling with sin Romans 7:7–25	[p. 1586]
4	RETURNING TO GOD	Jonah and Nineveh repent Jonah 2:1–3:10	[p. 1284]	Living by the Spirit Romans 8:1–17	[p. 1587]
5	OBSTACLES IN THE ROAD	Crossing the Red Sea Exodus 14:5–31	[p. 153]	Wrestling with evil Ephesians 6:10–24	[p. 1641]
6	A CLEAN SLATE	Great love, great grace Luke 7:36–50	[p. 1446]	True confessions James 5:7–20	[p. 1698]

SPECIAL

		TRACK 1 *Stories / LITE*	**TRACK 2** *Teachings / HEAVY*

49 SELF-ESTEEM: "MADE IN THE IMAGE OF GOD"

"No matter what others do to show their love for me, I just can't seem to accept it. People say that since God created me I'm special. I want to believe that, but I'm having a hard time feeling it."

1	BY DESIGN	Created in his image Genesis 1:1–2:3	[p. 53]	"Fearfully and wonderfully made" Psalm 139:1–24	[p. 876]
2	ACCEPTED BY GOD	Jesus and Zacchaeus Luke 19:1–10	[p. 1473]	Children of God 1 John 2:28–3:10	[p. 1712]
3	CHOSEN BY GOD	David chosen for his "heart" 1 Samuel 16:1–13	[p. 427]	Chosen and blessed Ephesians 1:1–14	[p. 1637]
4	HEALTHY HUMILITY	A Pharisee and a tax collector Luke 18:9–14	[p. 1471]	Humbled by grace Ephesians 3:1–13	[p. 1638]
5	GIFTED AND ENDOWED	God empowers Moses Exodus 4:1–17	[p. 138]	Me and my gifts Romans 12:1–8	[p. 1593]
6	MAKING A CONTRIBUTION	The widow's offering Mark 12:41–44	[p. 1418]	Important to the body 1 Corinthians 12:12–31	[p. 1610]

50 FINANCIAL STRESS: "MAKING ENDS MEET"

"I've got the mortgage. The loan to pay off. And now these credit card bills. How did I get myself into this? I could ask a relative for a loan, but I would rather die than admit I've blown it. What do I do?"

1	HARD TIMES	Hitting bottom Luke 15:11–32	[p. 1465]	Trials and temptations James 1:1–18	[p. 1695]
2	FACING THE STRESS	Jesus faces pressure Luke 4:14–30	[p. 1438]	Relying on God 2 Corinthians 1:1–11	[p. 1618]
3	TAKING RESPONSIBILITY	Parable of the talents Matthew 25:14–30	[p. 1380]	God is faithful; we should be too 2 Thessalonians 3:1–18	[p. 1661]
4	TOUGH DECISIONS	Parable of the shrewd manager Luke 16:1–15	[p. 1466]	Don't worry Matthew 6:19–34	[p. 1347]
5	MUTUAL AID	Believers share their possessions Acts 4:32–37	[p. 1537]	Giving and receiving 2 Corinthians 9:6–15	[p. 1624]
6	IN GOD WE TRUST	The widow's oil 2 Kings 4:1–7	[p. 538]	In plenty or in want Philippians 4:10–23	[p. 1647]

51 LIVING WITH PAIN: "COPING WITH LIFE'S HURTS"

"I feel like I'm dragging a ball and chain around. How can I deal each day with the pain I'm in, plus the guilt I feel for being such a burden to others?"

1	WHERE IS GOD WHEN I HURT?	The pool paralytic John 5:1–15	[p. 1496]	Groaning for redemption Romans 8:18–27	[p. 1588]
2	PAIN AND BLAME	Why was he born blind? John 9:1–34	[p. 1505]	Patience and forgiveness James 5:7–20	[p. 1698]
3	PAIN AND SHAME	Jesus heals an "unclean" woman Mark 5:24–34	[p. 1400]	"If God is for us, who can be against us?" Romans 8:28–39	[p. 1588]
4	PAIN AND COMFORT	Four friends who cared Mark 2:1–12	[p. 1393]	"The God of all comfort" 2 Corinthians 1:1–11	[p. 1618]
5	PAIN AND PERSPECTIVE	The suffering of Job Job 2:1–10	[p. 710]	The fruit of suffering Romans 5:1–11	[p. 1584]
6	PAIN AND PERSISTENCE	Parable of the persistent widow Luke 18:1–8	[p. 1470]	Paul's thorn in the flesh 2 Corinthians 12:1–10	[p. 1626]

NEEDS

		TRACK 1 *Stories / LITE*	TRACK 2 *Teachings / HEAVY*

52 CAREGIVERS: "LIFTING OTHERS UP WITHOUT GETTING DOWN"

"I want to help any way I can, but their constant demands are so draining. How can I care for others without burning out myself?"

		TRACK 1		TRACK 2	
1	TAKING A BREAK	Manna and the Sabbath Exodus 16:1–35	[p. 157]	Entering God's rest Hebrews 4:1–13	[p. 1682]
2	DEALING WITH DEMANDS	Moses gets weary Exodus 17:1–16	[p. 159]	Paul's boasting 2 Corinthians 11:16–33	[p. 1626]
3	SHARING THE LOAD	Moses decides to delegate Exodus 18:1–27	[p. 160]	Equality in giving 2 Corinthians 8:1–15	[p. 1623]
4	SETTING LIMITS	Mary chooses what's better Luke 10:38–42	[p. 1455]	"Neither do we go beyond our limits" 2 Corinthians 10:1–18	[p. 1624]
5	SURVIVING THE STRESS	Jesus withdraws to pray Mark 1:29–39	[p. 1392]	Peace of mind Philippians 4:2–9	[p. 1647]
6	HEEDING THE CALL	The sheep and the goats Matthew 25:31–46	[p. 1381]	The attitude of Christ Philippians 2:1–11	[p. 1645]

53 EMPTY NESTERS: "WHAT DO WE DO NOW?"

"I guess I wasn't prepared for the kids being gone. It's like part of my identity went with them. I feel like it's half- time and a whole new strategy needs to be made for the second half of life."

		TRACK 1		TRACK 2	
1	TOUGH TIMES	Naomi: A bitter empty nester Ruth 1:1–22	[p. 396]	Trials and temptations James 1:1–18	[p. 1695]
2	NEW PERSPECTIVE	Naomi gets a grandson Ruth 4:1–22	[p. 401]	Nothing will separate us from God's love Romans 8:28–39	[p. 1588]
3	LOOKING AHEAD	Parable of the rich fool Luke 12:13–21	[p. 1458]	God only knows James 4:13–5:6	[p. 1698]
4	HEARING GOD	The call of Abram Genesis 11:27–12:9	[p. 68]	Roll call of the faithful Hebrews 11:1–40	[p. 1689]
5	INVESTING YOURSELF	Moses and the burning bush Exodus 3:1–22	[p. 136]	Using your gifts Romans 12:1–8	[p. 1593]
6	TAKING RISKS	Peter steps out of the boat Matthew 14:22–33	[p. 1361]	Don't worry Matthew 6:19–34	[p. 1347]

54 GROWING OLDER: "TIME TO CELEBRATE LIFE"

"Others may say I'm over the hill, but I want to feel on top of the world? How can I look back with gratitude, and look ahead by passing on to someone else what I've learned?"

		TRACK 1		TRACK 2	
1	FAITH JOURNEY	The call of Abram Genesis 11:27–12:9	[p. 68]	Faithful hall of fame Hebrews 11:1–40	[p. 1689]
2	NEVER TOO OLD	Noah builds a boat Genesis 6:5–7:12	[p. 61]	You and your gifts Romans 12:1–8	[p. 1593]
3	THE POWER OF BLESSING	Simeon and Anna bless Jesus Luke 2:21–40	[p. 1434]	Examples to the younger Titus 2:1–15	[p. 1675]
4	LEAVING A LEGACY	Moses commissions Joshua Numbers 27:12–23	[p. 271]	Passing on the faith 2 Timothy 1:1–2:13	[p. 1670]
5	LOOKING BACK	Remembering God's faithfulness Joshua 23:1–16	[p. 357]	"I have fought the good fight" 2 Timothy 3:10–4:8	[p. 1672]
6	LOOKING AHEAD	Jesus raises Lazarus John 11:1–44	[p. 1509]	"Death has been swallowed up in victory" 1 Corinthians 15:35–58	[p. 1614]

RECOVERY

	TRACK 1 *Stories / LITE*	TRACK 2 *Teachings / HEAVY*

55 HEALTHY HABITS: "SHAPING UP"

"I've tried so many diets and exercise plans. They either don't work or I don't stick with them. I hate what I see in the mirror. But what do I do? I feel like giving up."

		TRACK 1	TRACK 2
1	FRUSTRATIONS	The disciples in Gethsemane Mark 14:32–42 [p. 1421]	I want to, but I can't Romans 7:7–25 [p. 1586]
2	HEALTHY HABITS	Daniel's discipline Daniel 1:1–21 [p. 1221]	Disciplined living Hebrews 12:1–13 [p. 1691]
3	LIVING IN BALANCE	Enough manna for each day Exodus 16:1–35 [p. 157]	Dependent and persistent Luke 11:1–13 [p. 1454]
4	A MATTER OF CONTROL	Israelites crave other food Numbers 11:4–34 [p. 245]	Controlled by the Spirit Romans 8:1–17 [p. 1587]
5	DON'T GIVE UP	Children of Israel turn back Numbers 13:26–14:45 [p. 249]	Pressing on toward the goal Philippians 3:12–4:1 [p. 1646]
6	CONSISTENT AND PERSISTENT	The walls of Jericho Joshua 5:13–6:21 [p. 335]	I can ... through Christ Philippians 4:10–23 [p. 1647]

56 MENDING FENCES: "HEALING SIGNIFICANT RELATIONSHIPS"

"My family and I have hurt each other in the past. We're losing precious time. In my heart I want to make things right—before it's too late. But I'm afraid and need some help."

		TRACK 1	TRACK 2
1	I HAVE A DREAM	Parable of the Prodigal Son Luke 15:11–32 [p. 1465]	True love 1 John 4:7–21 [p. 1714]
2	HEART'S DESIRE	Longing for reconciliation 2 Samuel 14:1–33 [p. 470]	Motivated by love Colossians 3:1–4:1 [p. 1652]
3	CALLED TO RECONCILE	The unmerciful servant Matthew 18:21–35 [p. 1367]	First things first Matthew 5:21–48 [p. 1345]
4	TAKING THE INITIATIVE	Joseph reaches out Genesis 45:1–28 [p. 123]	Sincere love Romans 12:9–21 [p. 1593]
5	ANXIOUS ANTICIPATION	Jacob prepares to meet Esau Genesis 32:1–21 [p. 101]	Overcoming anxiety Philippians 4:2–9 [p. 1647]
6	HOMECOMING	Jacob and Esau reunited Genesis 33:1–20 [p. 104]	"Who shall separate us ...?" Romans 8:28–39 [p. 1588]

57 DIVORCE RECOVERY: "PICKING UP THE PIECES"

"The divorce is final, but I still feel numb. On the outside, things haven't changed that much. But on the inside, it's another matter. I feel lost. Alone with my anger. How can I ever start to heal?"

		TRACK 1	TRACK 2
1	THE DEATH OF A DREAM	Naomi: Empty and bitter Ruth 1:1–22 [p. 396]	Nothing will separate us from God's love Romans 8:28–39 [p. 1578]
2	DEALING WITH ANGER	Cain and Abel Genesis 4:1–26 [p. 58]	"In your anger do not sin" Ephesians 4:17–32 [p. 1640]
3	TAKING THE HIGH ROAD	The unmerciful servant Matthew 18:21–35 [p. 1367]	Loving those who hurt you Luke 6:27–36 [p. 1443]
4	LOST IDENTITY	Jesus heals an "unclean" woman Mark 5:24–34 [p. 1400]	Important parts of the body 1 Corinthians 12:12–31 [p. 1610]
5	GOD CARES	Elijah and a single mother 1 Kings 17:1–24 [p. 521]	"The secret of being content" Philippians 4:10–23 [p. 1647]
6	HOPE FOR HEALING	On the road to Emmaus Luke 24:13–35 [p. 1485]	Hope doesn't disappoint Romans 5:1–11 [p. 1584]

COURSES

		TRACK 1 *Stories / LITE*	**TRACK 2** *Teachings / HEAVY*

58 GRIEF AND LOSS: "GETTING THROUGH THE NIGHT"

"Since he died, I've felt like half of me died, too. Why did he die and leave me so alone? I keep waking up in the night, thinking he's there. What stages do I have to go through to get some relief?"

		Track 1	Track 2
1	DENIAL	Elisha and a woman in denial 2 Kings 4:8–37 [p. 539]	Jesus predicts his death John 12:20–36 [p. 1511]
2	ANGER	Naomi: Empty and bitter Ruth 1:1–22 [p. 396]	"How long, O Lord?" Psalm 13:1–6 [p. 765]
3	BARGAINING	David "bargains" with God 2 Samuel 12:15–25 [p. 465]	Job wants a day in court with God Job 23:1–17 [p. 732]
4	DEPRESSION	Jacob mourns for Joseph Genesis 37:12–36 [p. 111]	Nothing will separate us from God's love Romans 8:28–39 [p. 1588]
5	ACCEPTANCE	The suffering of Job Job 2:1–10 [p. 710]	"The secret of being content" Philippians 4:10–23 [p. 1647]
6	HOPE	Jesus raises Lazarus John 11:1–44 [p. 1509]	The pain and the hope Romans 8:18–27 [p. 1588]

59 ABUSE: "MOVING PAST THE PAIN"

"The hardest thing I ever did was share my darkest secret. Now that I've dared to open up the wound, what can I do to heal the pain? I know I'm not alone, but who can help me through?"

		Track 1	Track 2
1	EXPRESSING EMOTION	Tamar raped by her half brother 2 Samuel 13:1–22 [p. 467]	"In your anger do not sin" Ephesians 4:17–32 [p. 1640]
2	NO MORE SHAME	Jesus heals an "unclean" woman Mark 5:24–34 [p. 1400]	Nothing will separate us from God's love Romans 8:28–39 [p. 1588]
3	MATTERS OF THE HEART	The unmerciful servant Matthew 18:21–35 [p. 1367]	"Overcome evil with good" Romans 12:9–21 [p. 1593]
4	YOU'RE NOT ALONE	God speaks to Elijah 1 Kings 19:1–18 [p. 525]	"If one part suffers, every part suffers" 1 Corinthians 12:12–31 [p. 1610]
5	WALKING IN LOVE	David spares Saul 1 Samuel 24:1–22 [p. 440]	"In his steps" 1 Peter 2:13–25 [p. 1702]
6	HOPE FOR HEALING	On the road to Emmaus Luke 24:13–35 [p. 1485]	The pain and the hope Romans 8:18–27 [p. 1588]

60 12 STEPS: "THE ROAD TO RECOVERY"

"I'm hooked, and this thing is stronger than I am. I know I need a 'Higher Power' and I know that 'Higher Power' is God. How can God help me break the stranglehold of this addiction?"

		Track 1	Track 2
1	GOING BEYOND DENIAL	A Pharisee and a tax collector Luke 18:9–14 [p. 1471]	Admitting we are powerless Romans 7:7–25 [p. 1586]
2	NAMING THE HIGHER POWER	Elijah and the prophets of Baal 1 Kings 18:16–40 [p. 523]	Confess and believe Romans 9:30–10:21 [p. 1590]
3	COMING TO GOD	A possessed man set free Luke 8:26–39 [p. 1449]	Submit to God James 4:1–12 [p. 1697]
4	CONFESSION	Josiah's reform 2 Kings 23:1–25 [p. 569]	"Confess your sins to each other" James 5:7–20 [p. 1698]
5	MAKING AMENDS	Zacchaeus makes things right Luke 19:1–10 [p. 1473]	"Produce fruit in keeping with repentance" Matthew 3:1–17 [p. 1341]
6	AN ADDICTION-FREE LIFESTYLE	Crossing the Red Sea Exodus 14:5–31 [p. 153]	"Be careful that you don't fall!" 1 Corinthians 10:1–13 [p. 1608]

PREFACE

THE NEW INTERNATIONAL VERSION is a completely new translation of the Holy Bible made by over a hundred scholars working directly from the best available Hebrew, Aramaic and Greek texts. It had its beginning in 1965 when, after several years of exploratory study by committees from the Christian Reformed Church and the National Association of Evangelicals, a group of scholars met at Palos Heights, Illinois, and concurred in the need for a new translation of the Bible in contemporary English. This group, though not made up of official church representatives, was transdenominational. Its conclusion was endorsed by a large number of leaders from many denominations who met in Chicago in 1966.

Responsibility for the new version was delegated by the Palos Heights group to a self-governing body of fifteen, the Committee on Bible Translation, composed for the most part of biblical scholars from colleges, universities and seminaries. In 1967 the New York Bible Society (now the International Bible Society) generously undertook the financial sponsorship of the project—a sponsorship that made it possible to enlist the help of many distinguished scholars. The fact that participants from the United States, Great Britain, Canada, Australia and New Zealand worked together gave the project its international scope. That they were from many denominations—including Anglican, Assemblies of God, Baptist, Brethren, Christian Reformed, Church of Christ, Evangelical Free, Lutheran, Mennonite, Methodist, Nazarene, Presbyterian, Wesleyan and other churches—helped to safeguard the translation from sectarian bias.

How it was made helps to give the New International Version its distinctiveness. The translation of each book was assigned to a team of scholars. Next, one of the Intermediate Editorial Committees revised the initial translation, with constant reference to the Hebrew, Aramaic or Greek. Their work then went to one of the General Editorial Committees, which checked it in detail and made another thorough revision. This revision in turn was carefully reviewed by the Committee on Bible Translation, which made further changes and then released the final version for publication. In this way the entire Bible underwent three revisions, during each of which the translation was examined for its faithfulness to the original languages and for its English style.

All this involved many thousands of hours of research and discussion regarding the meaning of the texts and the precise way of putting them into English. It may well be that no other translation has been made by a more thorough process of review and revision from committee to committee than this one.

From the beginning of the project, the Committee on Bible Translation held to certain goals for the New International Version: that it would be an accurate translation and one that would have clarity and literary quality and so prove suitable for public and private reading, teaching, preaching, memorizing and liturgical use. The Committee also sought to preserve some measure of continuity with the long tradition of translating the Scriptures into English.

In working toward these goals, the translators were united in their commitment to the authority and infallibility of the Bible as God's Word in written form. They believe that it contains the divine answer to the deepest needs of humanity, that it sheds unique light on our path in a dark world, and that it sets forth the way to our eternal well-being.

The first concern of the translators has been the accuracy of the translation and its fidelity to the thought of the biblical writers. They have weighed the significance of the lexical and grammatical details of the Hebrew, Aramaic and Greek texts. At the same time, they have striven for more than a word-for-word translation. Because thought patterns and syntax differ from language to language, faithful communication of the meaning of the writers of the Bible demands frequent modifications in sentence structure and constant regard for the contextual meanings of words.

A sensitive feeling for style does not always accompany scholarship. Accordingly, the Committee on Bible Translation submitted the developing version to a number of stylistic consultants. Two of them read every book of both Old and New Testaments twice—once before and once after the last major revision—and made invaluable suggestions. Samples of the translation were tested for clarity and ease of reading by various kinds of people—young and old, highly educated and less well educated, ministers and laymen.

Concern for clear and natural English—that the New International Version should be idiomatic but not idiosyncratic, contemporary but not dated—motivated the translators and consultants. At the same time, they tried to reflect the differing styles of the biblical writers. In view of the international use of English, the translators sought to avoid obvious Americanisms on the one hand and obvious Anglicisms on the other. A British edition reflects the comparatively few differences of significant idiom and of spelling.

As for the traditional pronouns "thou," "thee" and "thine" in reference to the Deity, the translators judged that to use these archaisms (along with the old verb forms such as "doest," "wouldest" and "hadst") would violate accuracy in translation. Neither Hebrew, Aramaic nor Greek uses special pronouns for the persons of the Godhead. A present-day translation is not enhanced by forms that in the time of the King James Version were used in everyday speech, whether referring to God or man.

For the Old Testament the standard Hebrew text, the Masoretic Text as published in the latest edition of *Biblia Hebraica,* was used throughout. The Dead Sea Scrolls contain material bearing on an earlier stage of the Hebrew text. They were consulted, as were the Samaritan Pentateuch and the ancient scribal traditions relating to textual changes. Sometimes a variant Hebrew reading in the margin of the Masoretic Text was followed instead of the text itself. Such instances, being variants within the Masoretic tradition, are not specified by footnotes. In rare cases, words in the consonantal text were divided differently from the way they appear in the Masoretic Text. Footnotes indicate this. The translators also consulted the more important early versions—the Septuagint; Aquila, Symmachus and Theodotion; the Vulgate; the Syriac Peshitta; the Targums; and for the Psalms the *Juxta Hebraica* of Jerome. Readings from these versions were occasionally followed where the Masoretic Text seemed doubtful and where accepted principles of textual criticism showed that one or more of these textual witnesses appeared to provide the correct reading. Such instances are footnoted. Sometimes vowel letters and vowel signs did not, in the judgment of the translators, represent the correct vowels for the original consonantal text. Accordingly some words were read with a different set of vowels. These instances are usually not indicated by footnotes.

The Greek text used in translating the New Testament was an eclectic one. No other piece of ancient literature has such an abundance of manuscript witnesses as does the New Testament. Where existing manuscripts differ, the translators made their choice of readings according to accepted principles of New Testament textual criticism. Footnotes call attention to places where there was uncertainty about what the original text was. The best current printed texts of the Greek New Testament were used.

There is a sense in which the work of translation is never wholly finished. This applies to all great literature and uniquely so to the Bible. In 1973 the New Testament in the New International Version was published. Since then, suggestions for corrections and revisions have been received from various sources. The Committee on Bible Translation carefully considered the suggestions and adopted a number of them. These were incorporated in the first printing of the entire Bible in 1978. Additional revisions were made by the Committee on Bible Translation in 1983 and appear in printings after that date.

As in other ancient documents, the precise meaning of the biblical texts is sometimes uncertain. This is more often the case with the Hebrew and Aramaic texts than with the Greek text. Although archaeological and linguistic discoveries in this century aid in understanding difficult passages, some uncertainties remain. The more significant of these have been called to the reader's attention in the footnotes.

In regard to the divine name *YHWH,* commonly referred to as the *Tetragrammaton,* the translators adopted the device used in most English versions of rendering that name as "Lord" in capital letters to distinguish it from *Adonai,* another Hebrew word rendered "Lord," for which small letters are used. Wherever the two names stand together in the Old Testament as a compound name of God, they are rendered "Sovereign Lord."

Because for most readers today the phrases "the Lord of hosts" and "God of hosts" have little meaning, this version renders them "the Lord Almighty" and "God Almighty." These renderings convey the sense of the Hebrew, namely, "he who is sovereign over all the 'hosts' (powers) in heaven and on earth, especially over the 'hosts' (armies) of Israel." For readers unacquainted with Hebrew this does not make clear the distinction between *Sabaoth* ("hosts" or "Almighty") and *Shaddai* (which can also be translated "Almighty"), but the latter occurs infrequently and is always footnoted. When *Adonai* and *YHWH Sabaoth* occur together, they are rendered "the Lord, the Lord Almighty."

As for other proper nouns, the familiar spellings of the King James Version are generally retained. Names traditionally spelled with "ch," except where it is final, are usually spelled in this translation with "k" or "c," since the biblical languages do not have the sound that "ch" frequently indicates in English—for example, in *chant.* For well-known names such as Zechariah, however, the traditional spelling has been retained. Variation in the spelling of names in the original languages has usually not been indicated. Where a person or place has two or more different names in the Hebrew, Aramaic or Greek texts, the more familiar one has generally been used, with footnotes where needed.

To achieve clarity the translators sometimes supplied words not in the original texts but required by the context. If there was uncertainty about such material, it is enclosed in brackets. Also for the sake of clarity or style, nouns, including some proper nouns, are sometimes substituted for pronouns, and vice versa. And though the Hebrew writers often shifted back and forth between first, second and third personal pronouns without change of antecedent, this translation often makes them uniform, in accordance with English style and without the use of footnotes.

Poetical passages are printed as poetry, that is, with indentation of lines and with separate stanzas. These are generally designed to reflect the structure of Hebrew poetry. This poetry is normally characterized by parallelism in balanced lines. Most of the poetry in the Bible is in the Old Testament, and scholars differ regarding the scansion of Hebrew lines. The translators determined the stanza divisions for the most part by analysis of the subject matter. The stanzas therefore serve as poetic paragraphs.

As an aid to the reader, italicized sectional headings are inserted in most of the books. They are not to be regarded as part of the NIV text, are not for oral reading, and are not intended to dictate the interpretation of the sections they head.

The footnotes in this version are of several kinds, most of which need no explanation. Those giving alternative translations begin with "Or" and generally introduce the alternative with the last word preceding it in the text, except when it is a single-word alternative; in poetry quoted in a footnote a slant mark indicates a line division. Footnotes introduced by "Or" do not have uniform significance. In some cases two possible translations were considered to have about equal validity. In other cases, though the translators were convinced that the translation in the text was correct, they judged that another interpretation was possible and of sufficient importance to be represented in a footnote.

In the New Testament, footnotes that refer to uncertainty regarding the original text are introduced by "Some manuscripts" or similar expressions. In the Old Testament, evidence for the reading chosen is given first and evidence for the alternative is added after a semicolon (for example: Septuagint; Hebrew *father*). In such notes the term "Hebrew" refers to the Masoretic Text.

It should be noted that minerals, flora and fauna, architectural details, articles of clothing and jewelry, musical instruments and other articles cannot always be identified with precision. Also measures of capacity in the biblical period are particularly uncertain (see the table of weights and measures following the text).

Like all translations of the Bible, made as they are by imperfect man, this one undoubtedly falls short of its goals. Yet we are grateful to God for the extent to which he has enabled us to realize these goals and for the strength he has given us and our colleagues to complete our task. We offer this version of the Bible to him in whose name and for whose glory it has been made. We pray that it will lead many into a better understanding of the Holy Scriptures and a fuller knowledge of Jesus Christ the incarnate Word, of whom the Scriptures so faithfully testify.

The Committee on Bible Translation

June 1978
(Revised August 1983)

Names of the translators and editors may be secured from the International Bible Society, translation sponsors of the New International Version, 1820 Jet Stream Drive, Colorado Springs, Colorado 80921-3696 U.S.A

The Old Testament

INTRODUCTION to
GENESIS

Book Study Outline: If you are using Genesis for a study course, here is a 7- or 13-week outline. Use the questions in the margin for your group agenda:

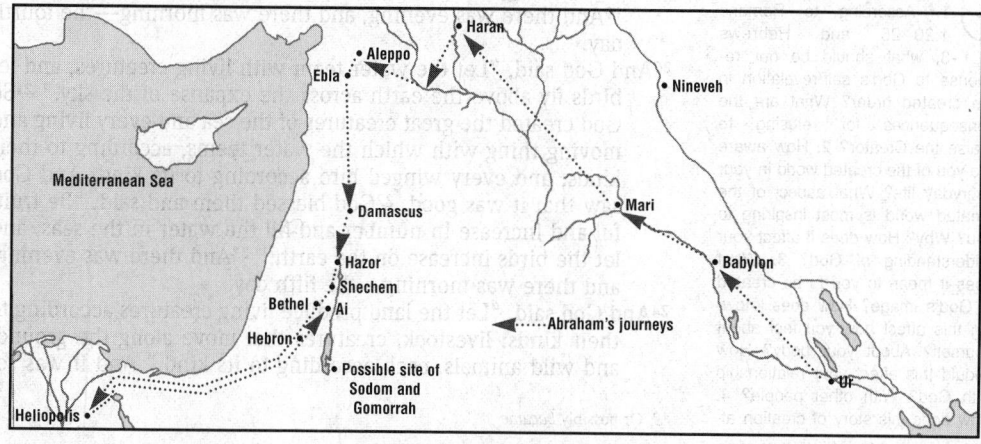

start meeting / 15 min.

read & discuss Bible / 30 min.

close meeting / 15–45 min.

Refer to the Questions and Answers in the front of this Bible for more information.

7-week plan	13-week plan	Personal Reading	Group Study Passage
1	1	1:1–2:3	1:1–2:3/The Creation
	2	3:1–4:26	3:1–24/The Fall
2	3	5:1–10:32	6:5–7:12/The Flood
	4	11:1–26	11:1–9/Tower of Babel
3	5	11:27–14:24	11:27–12:9/Abram's Call
	6	15:1–19:38	18:1–15/The Three Visitors
4	7	20:1–23:20	22:1–19/Abraham Tested
	8	24:1–27:40	27:1–40/Isaac's Blessing
5	9	27:41–31:55	29:1–30/Jacob Marries
	10	32:1–36:43	32:22–32/Jacob Wrestles
6	11	37:1–40:23	37:12–36/Joseph Sold
	12	41:1–44:34	41:1–40/Pharaoh's Dreams
7	13	45:1–50:26	45:1–28/Joseph Reveals Self

Author: Moses is assumed to be the author and editor of most of the first five books of the OT (the Pentateuch).

Date: It is difficult to assign a firm date to the composition of the Pentateuch. Conservative estimates place it in either the fifteenth or thirteenth century B.C., depending on when the Exodus occurred.

Theme: Everything begins with God, who elects a people of his own.

Historical Background: Archaeological findings and extra-biblical evidence have much in common with certain details of the Genesis narrative. Ancient Near Eastern accounts of primeval events bear substantial similarities to those found in Genesis 1–11. The socio-cultural milieu of the patriarchal narratives (Ge 12–50) fits well within the context of the Middle Bronze Age (c. 1950–1550 B.C.) in Palestine.

Characteristics: Organized within a genealogical framework, this "Book of Beginnings" is the origin for many of the major themes discussed in Scripture. Humanity's origin and mission, its fall and predicament, human responsibility and divine sovereignty, God's justice and mercy, his atonement for sin, the transformation of the sinner, the obedience of faith, the covenant of grace—all find their roots in Genesis. But Genesis is perhaps most often read for its vivid account of the pioneers of our faith—Abraham, Isaac and Jacob—through whom God is known and can be trusted.

Genesis

The Beginning

1 In the beginning God created the heavens and the earth. [2]Now the earth was[a] formless and empty, darkness was over the surface of the deep, and the Spirit of God was hovering over the waters.

[3]And God said, "Let there be light," and there was light. [4]God saw that the light was good, and he separated the light from the darkness. [5]God called the light "day," and the darkness he called "night." And there was evening, and there was morning—the first day.

[6]And God said, "Let there be an expanse between the waters to separate water from water." [7]So God made the expanse and separated the water under the expanse from the water above it. And it was so. [8]God called the expanse "sky." And there was evening, and there was morning—the second day.

[9]And God said, "Let the water under the sky be gathered to one place, and let dry ground appear." And it was so. [10]God called the dry ground "land," and the gathered waters he called "seas." And God saw that it was good.

[11]Then God said, "Let the land produce vegetation: seed-bearing plants and trees on the land that bear fruit with seed in it, according to their various kinds." And it was so. [12]The land produced vegetation: plants bearing seed according to their kinds and trees bearing fruit with seed in it according to their kinds. And God saw that it was good. [13]And there was evening, and there was morning—the third day.

[14]And God said, "Let there be lights in the expanse of the sky to separate the day from the night, and let them serve as signs to mark seasons and days and years, [15]and let them be lights in the expanse of the sky to give light on the earth." And it was so. [16]God made two great lights—the greater light to govern the day and the lesser light to govern the night. He also made the stars. [17]God set them in the expanse of the sky to give light on the earth, [18]to govern the day and the night, and to separate light from darkness. And God saw that it was good. [19]And there was evening, and there was morning—the fourth day.

[20]And God said, "Let the water teem with living creatures, and let birds fly above the earth across the expanse of the sky." [21]So God created the great creatures of the sea and every living and moving thing with which the water teems, according to their kinds, and every winged bird according to its kind. And God saw that it was good. [22]God blessed them and said, "Be fruitful and increase in number and fill the water in the seas, and let the birds increase on the earth." [23]And there was evening, and there was morning—the fifth day.

[24]And God said, "Let the land produce living creatures according to their kinds: livestock, creatures that move along the ground, and wild animals, each according to its kind." And it was so.

---

1. What time of day are you most creative? (Are you an early bird or a night owl?) Do you get more done on your "day off" or on "work time"? Do projects wait for a "rainy day" or vacation? 2. If you could create a new animal, what would it be like? What would be its most important feature? Why? What would you call it?

1. Outline Genesis 1:1–2:3 according to the repeated pattern you observe. In this symmetry, what repeated words or phrases do you observe? 2. What does this pattern tell you about the order of creation? Its author? Its purpose? Its climax? Its goodness? Its completeness? 3. Why does God first form the world (on days 1–3) and then fill that world (on days 4–6)? 4. What can you learn about God from his spoken word ("And God said, 'Let ...'") and his sovereign power ("And it was so")? 5. What does John 1:1–3 add to your perception of Genesis 1:1–3 and 1:26? Read Colossians 1:15–20, what is Christ's role in creation? And how does Genesis help you appreciate the nature and work of Christ? 6. For a believer's life and worship, what does it mean that God finishes his work in six days and rests on the seventh (see Ex 20:8–11)? 7. Why do you think the Bible tells us that God created but does not tell us exactly how he created? What does this tell you about the relative importance of the who and how of creation?

1. According to Romans 1:20–25 and Hebrews 11:1–3, what should be our response to God's self-revelation in the created order? What are the consequences for refusing to praise the Creator? 2. How aware are you of the created world in your everyday life? What aspect of the created world is most inspiring to you? Why? How does it affect your understanding of God? 3. What does it mean to you to be created in God's image? How does knowing this affect how you feel about yourself? About your body? How should this affect your relationship with God? With other people? 4. How does this story of creation af-

---

*a*2 Or possibly *became*

²⁵God made the wild animals according to their kinds, the livestock according to their kinds, and all the creatures that move along the ground according to their kinds. And God saw that it was good.

²⁶Then God said, "Let us make man in our image, in our likeness, and let them rule over the fish of the sea and the birds of the air, over the livestock, over all the earth,ᵃ and over all the creatures that move along the ground."

²⁷So God created man in his own image,
in the image of God he created him;
male and female he created them.

²⁸God blessed them and said to them, "Be fruitful and increase in number; fill the earth and subdue it. Rule over the fish of the sea and the birds of the air and over every living creature that moves on the ground."

²⁹Then God said, "I give you every seed-bearing plant on the face of the whole earth and every tree that has fruit with seed in it. They will be yours for food. ³⁰And to all the beasts of the earth and all the birds of the air and all the creatures that move on the ground—everything that has the breath of life in it—I give every green plant for food." And it was so.

³¹God saw all that he had made, and it was very good. And there was evening, and there was morning—the sixth day.

ᵃ26 Hebrew; Syriac *all the wild animals*

fect the way you treat the land, water, plants and animals in God's world? What can you do to help protect the beauty, diversity and fragility of the world God created? **5.** How does Genesis 1 equip you to evaluate popular beliefs of your culture? Using ideas from Genesis 1, how would you counter the gnostic who believes that only the soul matters, as the human body and material things are decadent or non-spiritual? How would you counter the atheist who believes that we are the product of "chance plus time plus energy"? How would you counter the one who reads the daily horoscope, believing that the position of sun, moon and stars ordain our personality and state?

  Genesis 1:1—2:3   **THE BEGINNING**

1. When you read the story of creation, what is your first impression of God?
   a. What a plan!
   b. What an imagination!
   c. What power!
   d. What perfection!

2. What does it mean that man and woman are created "in the image of God"?
   a. They are the most intelligent of God's creatures.
   b. They are God's representatives to care for his creation.
   c. They have creative power.
   d. They can have a relationship with God.

3. Why did God decide to rest on the seventh day?
   a. He was exhausted.
   b. He was satisfied.
   c. Everything was complete.
   d. He was setting a good example for people.

4. How would you compare your spiritual beginnings to the beginning of creation?

   a. It was logical and orderly.
   b. It was the result of my parents' "fruitful" faith.
   c. I experienced a sudden shift from darkness to light.
   d. Visible life didn't appear right away.

5. If you compared your typical week to the creation story, how would you describe it?
   a. formless and empty
   b. very good
   c. full of life
   d. completed

6. When you complete a job or project, what do you usually do?
   a. start another one
   b. rest
   c. play
   d. celebrate
   e. worry

7. Do you wish your response to the last question was different? If so, how? And what can you do to change?

8. How do you feel about the idea that you are made in God's image?
   a. Say what?!
   b. I'm not so sure God would say, "It was very good," about me.
   c. Like the first man and woman, I'm created special!
   d. I don't feel like I've done a very good job of reflecting God's image.
   e. I've felt "rolled over" more than I've felt like I've "ruled over" anything!
   f. other:_____

9. How will you change as a result of this study?
   a. I'll believe there really is a God.
   b. I'll keep an open mind about spiritual things.
   c. I'll be more responsible for taking care of God's creation.
   d. I'll try to let God's plan be worked out in my life.
   e. other:_____

2 Thus the heavens and the earth were completed in all their vast array.

[2]By the seventh day God had finished the work he had been doing; so on the seventh day he rested[a] from all his work. [3]And God blessed the seventh day and made it holy, because on it he rested from all the work of creating that he had done.

Adam and Eve

[4]This is the account of the heavens and the earth when they were created.

When the LORD God made the earth and the heavens— [5]and no shrub of the field had yet appeared on the earth[b] and no plant of the field had yet sprung up, for the LORD God had not sent rain on the earth[b] and there was no man to work the ground, [6]but streams[c] came up from the earth and watered the whole surface of the ground— [7]the LORD God formed the man[d] from the dust of the ground and breathed into his nostrils the breath of life, and the man became a living being.

[8]Now the LORD God had planted a garden in the east, in Eden; and there he put the man he had formed. [9]And the LORD God made all kinds of trees grow out of the ground—trees that were pleasing to the eye and good for food. In the middle of the garden were the tree of life and the tree of the knowledge of good and evil.

[10]A river watering the garden flowed from Eden; from there it

[a]2 Or *ceased*; also in verse 3   [b]5 Or *land*; also in verse 6   [c]6 Or *mist*
[d]7 The Hebrew for *man (adam)* sounds like and may be related to the Hebrew for *ground (adamah)*; it is also the name *Adam* (see Gen. 2:20).

---

1. What is your visual image of the perfect garden? Where would it be? What work would you do there? 2. Who was your first heart-throb? What was life like with, and without, that special person?

1. Many scholars suggest that verse 4a summarizes the creation account in 1:1–2:3. The creation account in 2:4b–25 is a detailed review of the creation story as it relates to humanity. Why are we given a close look at how people fit into the creation account? 2. What do 1:26–29 and 2:7–25 teach about our original nature and character? Our purpose and tasks? Our likeness to the animals? Our likeness to God? 3. Why does God provide this first man with a paradise on earth? Then why did God place the tree of

---

Genesis 2:4–25   ADAM AND EVE

1. If you could have a picture of just one scene in this story, what would it be?
   a. God forming Adam out of the dust
   b. a wide-angle photograph of the unspoiled Garden of Eden
   c. God bringing the animals to Adam
   d. Adam and Eve seeing each other for the first time

2. Why didn't God make Adam and Eve at the same time?
   a. to demonstrate that people aren't complete when isolated
   b. to help Adam appreciate his new companion
   c. to establish Adam as the leader in their relationship
   d. to save the best for last

3. What does this story say to you about the nature of men and women?
   a. Men and women need each other.
   b. Men are created with unique authority and responsibility.
   c. Women are designed to be helpers.
   d. Men are more task-oriented and women more relational.

e. Men and women are more alike than different.

4. What did God mean when he described Eve as a "helper"?
   a. She will serve Adam.
   b. She will be a great partner.
   c. She will be a source of strength.
   d. Adam and Eve will work together.

5. Why were Adam and Eve naked and not ashamed?
   a. No one told them any different.
   b. They were one flesh.
   c. They didn't have a knowledge of good and evil.
   d. They hadn't sinned yet.

6. Describe a time in your life when you were so intensely lonely that you learned the truth of God's statement, "It is not good ... to be alone."

7. How does this story make you, as a single person, feel?
   a. It reinforces the stigma that I can't be complete without a spouse.
   b. It reassures me that it's normal to need companionship.

c. It confirms that God is in control of my life and relationships.
   d. It convinces me that God doesn't want me to be lonely.

8. How difficult is it for singles in general to experience companionship apart from marriage? How difficult is it for *you*?

9. What ideas and attitudes do people have about the "submission" of women? How have you felt about this issue? What does this story say to you about God's intent for women?

10. What about your marriage are you most grateful for?
   a. my spouse's help and support
   b. the companionship we share
   c. the sizzle of our romance
   d. the intimacy of knowing each other fully, without shame

11. How could you be more "helpful" to your spouse? How could you deepen your companionship as a couple? Your romance?

was separated into four headwaters. [11]The name of the first is the Pishon; it winds through the entire land of Havilah, where there is gold. [12](The gold of that land is good; aromatic resin[a] and onyx are also there.) [13]The name of the second river is the Gihon; it winds through the entire land of Cush.[b] [14]The name of the third river is the Tigris; it runs along the east side of Asshur. And the fourth river is the Euphrates.

[15]The LORD God took the man and put him in the Garden of Eden to work it and take care of it. [16]And the LORD God commanded the man, "You are free to eat from any tree in the garden; [17]but you must not eat from the tree of the knowledge of good and evil, for when you eat of it you will surely die."

[18]The LORD God said, "It is not good for the man to be alone. I will make a helper suitable for him."

[19]Now the LORD God had formed out of the ground all the beasts of the field and all the birds of the air. He brought them to the man to see what he would name them; and whatever the man called each living creature, that was its name. [20]So the man gave names to all the livestock, the birds of the air and all the beasts of the field.

But for Adam[c] no suitable helper was found. [21]So the LORD God caused the man to fall into a deep sleep; and while he was sleeping, he took one of the man's ribs[d] and closed up the place with flesh. [22]Then the LORD God made a woman from the rib[e] he had taken out of the man, and he brought her to the man.

[23]The man said,

"This is now bone of my bones
    and flesh of my flesh;
she shall be called 'woman,[f]'
    for she was taken out of man."

[24]For this reason a man will leave his father and mother and be united to his wife, and they will become one flesh.

[25]The man and his wife were both naked, and they felt no shame.

The Fall of Man

3 Now the serpent was more crafty than any of the wild animals the LORD God had made. He said to the woman, "Did God really say, 'You must not eat from any tree in the garden'?"

[2]The woman said to the serpent, "We may eat fruit from the trees in the garden, [3]but God did say, 'You must not eat fruit from the tree that is in the middle of the garden, and you must not touch it, or you will die.'"

[4]"You will not surely die," the serpent said to the woman. [5]"For God knows that when you eat of it your eyes will be opened, and you will be like God, knowing good and evil."

[6]When the woman saw that the fruit of the tree was good for food and pleasing to the eye, and also desirable for gaining wisdom, she took some and ate it. She also gave some to her husband, who was with her, and he ate it. [7]Then the eyes of both of them were opened, and they realized they were naked; so they sewed fig leaves together and made coverings for themselves.

[8]Then the man and his wife heard the sound of the LORD God as he was walking in the garden in the cool of the day, and they hid

knowledge of good and evil into this beautiful garden and tell them not to eat from it (2:9,17; see 3:6)? **4.** What is significant about God creating "woman" last: (a) In the ascending order of creation, she is the "pinnacle"? (b) In being made after man, she is an "afterthought"? (c) "If at first you don't succeed, try, try again"? How do you define "helper"? Does "helper" sound like a lesser person? An equal person? A greater person? **5.** What does it mean: that Adam and Eve were "naked and they felt no shame"? That a husband and wife become one flesh? Are singles incomplete? **6.** How would you characterize the relationship between Adam and this woman? Between God and man? What makes this kind of fellowship possible?

♡ **1.** What can you learn from this passage about your relationships with people of the opposite sex? What do you need to do to apply those principles in your life today? How well does God understand Adam's needs and desires? How well do you feel that God understands your needs and desires? **2.** Have you ever felt alone? How did you make it through that time? What do you need from this group to feel more connected to others? **3.** How are you and your spouse a gift to each other: Spiritually? Emotionally? Physically?

1. What food do you find especially tempting? **2.** When during your growing-up years did you get in big trouble with your parents? **3.** Do you still play hide-and-seek games? With kids? Easter eggs? Scavenger hunt? Why are such games perennial favorites?

1. Who is this serpent: Real creature? Mythical symbol? Or what? (Note: Ancient cults contemporary with Moses' Israelite audience worshiped the serpent-goddess of fertility. Later contemporaries of Jesus identified the serpent as Satan in disguise.) **2.** Which portion of the serpent's statements (vv. 1,4,5) are true and which are false (compare 3:4–5; 3:22; 5:5)? Why do you think the serpent mixes the truth with lies? **3.** Compare Eve's responses (vv. 2,3) with what God actually said and did (2:9,16,17). How does Eve hedge, fixate upon and amplify God's com-

---

[a]12 Or good; pearls   [b]13 Possibly southeast Mesopotamia   [c]20 Or the man
[d]21 Or took part of the man's side   [e]22 Or part   [f]23 The Hebrew for woman
sounds like the Hebrew for man.

mandments? How does that play into Satan's schemes? **4.** How might someone today fall prey to the same tempting question, "Did God really say ...?" **5.** How can something "good"—the beauty, nourishment or wisdom conveyed by the fruit—be "wrong" when it feels so good? What does this imply for our "if-it-feels-good-do-it" generation? **6.** Why do you think Adam eats the fruit? Could he have resisted? What should he have done? Do you think Adam is more, or less, responsible than Eve? Why? **7.** Compare verses 7–13 with the previous chapter. How has the relationship changed between the man and the woman? How has the relationship which they had with God changed? **8.** Why do they engage in the original "cover-up" (2:25; 3:7), "hide-and-seek" (3:8–10) and "who dunnit" games (3:12–13)? **9.** Do you think the punishments detailed in verses 16–24 reflect varying degrees of guilt? Why or why not? Which punishments would have been most difficult for Adam? For Eve? For you? Why? **10.** Why would God allow Adam and Eve to fail when tempted? What does this say about God? About what he wants from us? **11.** From this story, how would you define sin and its consequences? **12.** Where in this story do you find any good news? If Jesus is the ultimate offspring of

from the LORD God among the trees of the garden. ⁹But the LORD God called to the man, "Where are you?"

¹⁰He answered, "I heard you in the garden, and I was afraid because I was naked; so I hid."

¹¹And he said, "Who told you that you were naked? Have you eaten from the tree that I commanded you not to eat from?"

¹²The man said, "The woman you put here with me—she gave me some fruit from the tree, and I ate it."

¹³Then the LORD God said to the woman, "What is this you have done?"

The woman said, "The serpent deceived me, and I ate."

¹⁴So the LORD God said to the serpent, "Because you have done this,

> "Cursed are you above all the livestock
>   and all the wild animals!
> You will crawl on your belly
>   and you will eat dust
>   all the days of your life.
> ¹⁵And I will put enmity
>   between you and the woman,
>   and between your offspringᵃ and hers;
> he will crushᵇ your head,
>   and you will strike his heel."

¹⁶To the woman he said,

> "I will greatly increase your pains in childbearing;
>   with pain you will give birth to children.
> Your desire will be for your husband,
>   and he will rule over you."

¹⁷To Adam he said, "Because you listened to your wife and ate

ᵃ15 Or *seed*   ᵇ15 Or *strike*

     Genesis 3:1–24   **THE FALL**

God made Adam from dust and his "suitable helper" Eve from Adam's rib. Life in the Garden of Eden was a paradise. ... Enter—The serpent!

1. What would you title this story?
   a. Satan's Sneaky Snare
   b. God's Unreasonable Demands
   c. A Declaration of Independence
   d. Playing the Blame Game
   e. Fig Leaves Anonymous
   f. Paradise Lost

2. Why did God command Adam and Eve not to eat from the tree of the knowledge of good and evil?
   a. Ask God—not me!
   b. A little bit of knowledge is a dangerous thing.
   c. They were created to make moral choices.
   d. God knew eating the fruit would cause them to die.

3. Why did Adam and Eve hide from God in the garden?
   a. They were ashamed of their disobedience.
   b. They were now embarrassed about their nakedness.
   c. They were afraid of God's sure judgment.
   d. They didn't deserve to be near God anymore.

4. Why did God deliver his judgment?
   a. because he cannot tolerate sin
   b. as a punishment for disobedience
   c. to limit the corruption of sin
   d. to direct Adam and Eve in the new way of holiness

5. What do you do when you find yourself "naked" (caught in a mistake or sin) before others?
   a. hide
   b. blame someone else

c. say "that's just the way I am" or "nobody's perfect"
d. accept responsibility for myself

6. Who was to blame for the Fall? How do you feel about God's judgment as a result of Adam and Eve's sin?

7. Which character do you most identify with in this story? In what way do you identify? What does this story say to you in your journey with God?

8. What causes you to play the blame game in your marriage? How can you keep this from pulling you apart?

9. How does this story remind you of your "strong-willed child"? How does God's role and response speak to how you can relate to your child?

from the tree about which I commanded you, 'You must not eat of it,'

> "Cursed is the ground because of you;
>> through painful toil you will eat of it
>> all the days of your life.
> [18]It will produce thorns and thistles for you,
>> and you will eat the plants of the field.
> [19]By the sweat of your brow
>> you will eat your food
>> until you return to the ground,
>> since from it you were taken;
>> for dust you are
>> and to dust you will return."

[20]Adam[a] named his wife Eve,[b] because she would become the mother of all the living.

[21]The LORD God made garments of skin for Adam and his wife and clothed them. [22]And the LORD God said, "The man has now become like one of us, knowing good and evil. He must not be allowed to reach out his hand and take also from the tree of life and eat, and live forever." [23]So the LORD God banished him from the Garden of Eden to work the ground from which he had been taken. [24]After he drove the man out, he placed on the east side[c] of the Garden of Eden cherubim and a flaming sword flashing back and forth to guard the way to the tree of life.

Cain and Abel

4 Adam[a] lay with his wife Eve, and she became pregnant and gave birth to Cain.[d] She said, "With the help of the LORD I have brought forth[e] a man." [2]Later she gave birth to his brother Abel.

Now Abel kept flocks, and Cain worked the soil. [3]In the course of time Cain brought some of the fruits of the soil as an offering to the LORD. [4]But Abel brought fat portions from some of the firstborn of his flock. The LORD looked with favor on Abel and his offering, [5]but on Cain and his offering he did not look with favor. So Cain was very angry, and his face was downcast.

[6]Then the LORD said to Cain, "Why are you angry? Why is your face downcast? [7]If you do what is right, will you not be accepted? But if you do not do what is right, sin is crouching at your door; it desires to have you, but you must master it."

[8]Now Cain said to his brother Abel, "Let's go out to the field."[f] And while they were in the field, Cain attacked his brother Abel and killed him.

[9]Then the LORD said to Cain, "Where is your brother Abel?"

"I don't know," he replied. "Am I my brother's keeper?"

[10]The LORD said, "What have you done? Listen! Your brother's blood cries out to me from the ground. [11]Now you are under a curse and driven from the ground, which opened its mouth to receive your brother's blood from your hand. [12]When you work the ground, it will no longer yield its crops for you. You will be a restless wanderer on the earth."

[13]Cain said to the LORD, "My punishment is more than I can bear. [14]Today you are driving me from the land, and I will be

Eve and Adam and is Satan's enemy (v. 15), and if Jesus is the promised tree of life (v. 24; see Revelation 2:7), what does that mean for us sinners?

♡ **1.** Compare Jesus' temptation to this one (see Lk 4:1–13)? How was his similar? How were his responses different? **2.** Can you think of three harder words to say than, "I am sorry"? How easy is it for you to admit you are wrong? **3.** When do you feel most "naked" before God? How does this help you understand Adam and Eve's reactions? **4.** Where in your life is "the serpent" seemingly alive and well?

🍵 **1.** Whom did you envy as a child? Why this person? **2.** As a child, what homemade birthday presents do you recall giving your folks? As a parent, which home-made presents have delighted you? **3.** Did you ever suspect your parents of having "favorites" among your siblings? What was the basis for your suspicion?

📖 **1.** God accepts both animal and grain sacrifices (see Lev 6:14–30). Why then do you think God rejects Cain's sacrifice: (a) Only a blood sacrifice, in place of a human death, could cover sin and guilt (see Lev 4–6)? (b) Cain had a bad attitude or lack of faith (see Heb 11:4; 1Jn 2:9–11)? (c) Cain's offering didn't mean anything to him (see Isa 1:10–20)? (d) Cain's offering did not embody social righteousness (see Am 5:21–24)? **2.** When God tells Cain to "do what is right" (v. 7), what does this tell you about man's source of anger? The strength of anger? God's way of soothing anger? **3.** After the murder of Abel, why do you think God approaches Cain as he does? Why not directly accuse Cain? Why delay punishment? **4.** Why was Cain punished as he was: (a) Wrong sacrifice? (b) Hateful attitude? (c) Murderous act? (d) Failure to master sin? (e) Attempt to cover up sin? **5.** Would honesty with God

[a]20,1 Or *The man*   [b]20 *Eve* probably means *living*.   [c]24 Or *placed in front*
[d]1 *Cain* sounds like the Hebrew for *brought forth* or *acquired.*   [e]1 Or *have acquired*
[f]8 Samaritan Pentateuch, Septuagint, Vulgate and Syriac; Masoretic Text does not have *"Let's go out to the field."*

have reduced his punishment? Why or why not? **6.** Did Cain repent of his sin? How does his confession (vv. 13–14) and the Lord's reply (vv. 15–16) shed light on this? **7.** Why did God protect Cain? In this story of man in exile, where is the cycle of sin, judgment and mercy repeated from chapter 3?

 1. How would you assess the way you handle anger? What might you call yourself: "Vern Volcano"? "Susy Suppression"? "Tina Tightlip"? "Dennis Denial"? Or what? What would you like to do differently with your anger? **2.** Where might God be looking on your life with favor? With disfavor? **3.** Cain is promised frustration at work and restlessness in life (vv. 11–12). How are you experiencing either of these? Lamech remembers God's promise to his forefather, Cain (vv. 23–24). What promises or blessings has God given your ancestors which serve as a comfort to you? **4.** Are you your "brother's keeper"? How so? What kind of "keeping" do you do: Nagging? Parenting? Covenanting? Praying? What brothers (and sisters) do you keep?

hidden from your presence; I will be a restless wanderer on the earth, and whoever finds me will kill me."

¹⁵But the LORD said to him, "Not so*ᵃ*; if anyone kills Cain, he will suffer vengeance seven times over." Then the LORD put a mark on Cain so that no one who found him would kill him. ¹⁶So Cain went out from the LORD's presence and lived in the land of Nod,*ᵇ* east of Eden.

¹⁷Cain lay with his wife, and she became pregnant and gave birth to Enoch. Cain was then building a city, and he named it after his son Enoch. ¹⁸To Enoch was born Irad, and Irad was the father of Mehujael, and Mehujael was the father of Methushael, and Methushael was the father of Lamech.

¹⁹Lamech married two women, one named Adah and the other Zillah. ²⁰Adah gave birth to Jabal; he was the father of those who live in tents and raise livestock. ²¹His brother's name was Jubal; he was the father of all who play the harp and flute. ²²Zillah also had a son, Tubal-Cain, who forged all kinds of tools out of*ᶜ* bronze and iron. Tubal-Cain's sister was Naamah.

²³Lamech said to his wives,

"Adah and Zillah, listen to me;
   wives of Lamech, hear my words.
I have killed*ᵈ* a man for wounding me,
   a young man for injuring me.
²⁴If Cain is avenged seven times,
   then Lamech seventy-seven times."

²⁵Adam lay with his wife again, and she gave birth to a son and named him Seth,*ᵉ* saying, "God has granted me another child in

---

ᵃ15 Septuagint, Vulgate and Syriac; Hebrew *Very well* (see verses 12 and 14).   *ᵇ16 Nod* means *wandering*   *ᶜ22* Or *who instructed all who work in*   *ᵈ23* Or *I will kill*   *ᵉ25 Seth* probably means *granted.*

⊗ *Genesis 4:1–26*   **CAIN AND ABEL**

1. What question does this chapter raise for you?
   a. What kind of worship offering did God require?
   b. Where did Cain get the idea to commit the first murder?
   c. What was the mark that God put on Cain?
   d. Where did the people like Cain's wife come from?

2. Why did Abel's offering please God and Cain's offering didn't?
   a. God liked shepherds more than farmers.
   b. God preferred animal sacrifices.
   c. Abel put more thought and care into his offering.
   d. Only Abel had godly faith and motives.

3. Why did Cain murder Abel?
   a. He took his anger at God out on his brother.
   b. He must have been out to get Abel for awhile.

c. He was jealous.
d. It was the first case of "temporary insanity."

4. Did Cain repent when God confronted him?
   a. Yes—I think he felt genuine remorse.
   b. Sort of—but only because of God's punishment.
   c. No—he just felt sorry for himself again.

5. Why did God protect Cain's life?
   a. pure mercy
   b. so the human race could keep increasing
   c. because two wrongs don't make a right
   d. Being a restless wanderer was enough punishment.

6. What do you learn from the last part of this chapter?
   a. Ungodly character like Cain's tends to get passed on.

b. We should follow Jesus and forgive 77 times instead of wanting to be avenged 77 times like Lamech.
c. God is faithful; he gave Adam and Eve another child.
d. People can change and "call on the name of the Lord."

7. How do you deal with the anger in your life? Do you express it in positive or negative ways? How can your relationship with God make a difference?

8. What does it mean to you to be your "brothers keeper"? Which of your relationships need strengthening or healing?

9. ⊗ How can you relate to Abel? To Cain? What is God saying to you through this study about your recovery from divorce? About your attitude toward your ex-spouse?

place of Abel, since Cain killed him." ²⁶Seth also had a son, and he
named him Enosh.

At that time men began to call on*^a* the name of the LORD.

From Adam to Noah

5 This is the written account of Adam's line.

When God created man, he made him in the likeness of God.
²He created them male and female and blessed them. And when
they were created, he called them "man.*^b*"

³When Adam had lived 130 years, he had a son in his own
likeness, in his own image; and he named him Seth. ⁴After Seth
was born, Adam lived 800 years and had other sons and daughters.
⁵Altogether, Adam lived 930 years, and then he died.

⁶When Seth had lived 105 years, he became the father*^c* of
Enosh. ⁷And after he became the father of Enosh, Seth lived 807
years and had other sons and daughters. ⁸Altogether, Seth lived
912 years, and then he died.

⁹When Enosh had lived 90 years, he became the father of Ke-
nan. ¹⁰And after he became the father of Kenan, Enosh lived 815
years and had other sons and daughters. ¹¹Altogether, Enosh lived
905 years, and then he died.

¹²When Kenan had lived 70 years, he became the father of
Mahalalel. ¹³And after he became the father of Mahalalel, Kenan
lived 840 years and had other sons and daughters. ¹⁴Altogether,
Kenan lived 910 years, and then he died.

¹⁵When Mahalalel had lived 65 years, he became the father of
Jared. ¹⁶And after he became the father of Jared, Mahalalel lived
830 years and had other sons and daughters. ¹⁷Altogether, Mahalalel lived 895 years, and then he died.

¹⁸When Jared had lived 162 years, he became the father of
Enoch. ¹⁹And after he became the father of Enoch, Jared lived 800
years and had other sons and daughters. ²⁰Altogether, Jared lived
962 years, and then he died.

²¹When Enoch had lived 65 years, he became the father of
Methuselah. ²²And after he became the father of Methuselah,
Enoch walked with God 300 years and had other sons and daugh-
ters. ²³Altogether, Enoch lived 365 years. ²⁴Enoch walked with
God; then he was no more, because God took him away.

²⁵When Methuselah had lived 187 years, he became the father
of Lamech. ²⁶And after he became the father of Lamech, Methuselah lived 782 years and had other sons and daughters. ²⁷Altogether,
Methuselah lived 969 years, and then he died.

²⁸When Lamech had lived 182 years, he had a son. ²⁹He named
him Noah*^d* and said, "He will comfort us in the labor and painful
toil of our hands caused by the ground the LORD has cursed."
³⁰After Noah was born, Lamech lived 595 years and had other sons
and daughters. ³¹Altogether, Lamech lived 777 years, and then he
died.

³²After Noah was 500 years old, he became the father of Shem,
Ham and Japheth.

The Flood

6 When men began to increase in number on the earth and
daughters were born to them, ²the sons of God saw that the
daughters of men were beautiful, and they married any of them
they chose. ³Then the LORD said, "My Spirit will not contend

*^a26 Or to proclaim   ^b2 Hebrew adam   ^c6 Father may mean ancestor; also in
verses 7-26.   ^d29 Noah sounds like the Hebrew for comfort.*

---

1. Whom are you most curious about in your family
tree? Why? 2. What do you think
your great-grandchildren will remember about you? Why those
things?

1. As part of the ancient Near
Eastern culture, Genesis
contains a series of genealogies,
as in chapter 5. What purpose do
these selective genealogies serve:
(a) To provide continuity in the narrative (in this case, linking Noah
with Adam)? (b) To provide convenient breaks in the narrative (in this
case, ch. 5 separates Adam's story
from Noah's)? (c) To establish continuity all the way forward to King
David and hence to Jesus Christ
(see Mt 1; Lk 3)? (d) Other? In
short, what's the point of Genesis 5? What do you think about the
incredibly long lifespan Adam and
his descendants enjoyed? 2. What
truth from Genesis is underscored
by the refrain, "And then he died"?
If the line of Cain focuses on sin,
what does the line of Seth focus
on? 3. What is the significance of
Adam having a son "in his own likeness" and "in his image" (see
1:26–27)? What is one exception
to that reign of death (5:24)? What
does it mean for Enoch that "God
took him away"? Why Enoch of all
people (see Heb 11:5f)? Is his experience unique? Or could believers in Christ also enjoy such victory
over death (see 1Co 15:50–51;
1Th 4:13–18)?

Do you have a family historian? A genealogical tree
drawn up to pass down the line?
Why do you suppose genealogies
are less important today than they
were to people in biblical times?
Many of the figures from Biblical
history had meaningful names.
Why were you given your name?
Regarding your spiritual life right
now, what name would describe
you best?

---

1. If you were a zoo keeper,
what animals would you enjoy visiting every day? Which animals would you sooner not see?
2. Suppose the wisest person you
know warns your family tonight of
your town's imminent destruction
(by volcano, forest fire or hurri-

cane), but you have no confirming evidence or experience to draw upon. Which of the following actions typify how members of the family might react: (a) Attend business as usual? (b) Pack a suitcase just in case? (c) Evacuate your kids and pets ASAP? (d) Call around to first see what the neighbors are doing? (e) Perch on your roof, so you can see the end coming? (f) Ridicule the reliability of the source and drive him out of town?

1. Apart from the obscurity of some details in verses 1–5, what do you find most disturbing about the description of human corruption in verse 5? Why? What would most disturb someone who believes human nature is essentially good? 2. Why do you think God feels the way he does about human wickedness (v. 6)? Do you think his decision in verse 7 is justified? Why or why not? Why do you think God went to so much trouble to see that the animals were saved? 3. Compare Genesis 6:6 (where God regrets that he ever made man) with 1 Samuel 15:28–29 (where God "is not like a man that he should change his mind"). How do you reconcile those two apparent contradictions? 4. From verses 8–9, what do you learn about Noah's character? Did Noah become this way because of God's favor? Or did Noah somehow earn God's favor? Why do you think so? 5. Covenants at this time often resembled a contract between a king and his subjects in which sovereign protection is offered in exchange for faithful obedience. How is God's covenant with Noah before the flood (6:13–7:5) like that? 6. Given the unmitigated violence, pervasive corruption and heavy peer pressure surrounding Noah, what might Noah be thinking when God tells him to build the ark? What do you see as the biggest obstacle to his accomplishing that task? How does Noah persevere when the going gets tough? 7. What do you think it must have been like for Noah and his family when they first entered the ark? When they heard the first raindrops? When the ark began to float? When the water began to recede? When the ark came to rest on solid ground? 8. From this story of the great flood (7:6–8:14) and independent accounts of great floods (especially the Babylonian Epic of Gilgamesh), what do you believe about the Flood? Was it

with[a] man forever, for he is mortal[b]; his days will be a hundred and twenty years."

[4]The Nephilim were on the earth in those days—and also afterward—when the sons of God went to the daughters of men and had children by them. They were the heroes of old, men of renown.

[5]The Lord saw how great man's wickedness on the earth had become, and that every inclination of the thoughts of his heart was only evil all the time. [6]The Lord was grieved that he had made man on the earth, and his heart was filled with pain. [7]So the Lord said, "I will wipe mankind, whom I have created, from the face of the earth—men and animals, and creatures that move along the ground, and birds of the air—for I am grieved that I have made them." [8]But Noah found favor in the eyes of the Lord.

[9]This is the account of Noah.

Noah was a righteous man, blameless among the people of his time, and he walked with God. [10]Noah had three sons: Shem, Ham and Japheth.

[11]Now the earth was corrupt in God's sight and was full of violence. [12]God saw how corrupt the earth had become, for all the people on earth had corrupted their ways. [13]So God said to Noah, "I am going to put an end to all people, for the earth is filled with violence because of them. I am surely going to destroy both them and the earth. [14]So make yourself an ark of cypress[c] wood; make rooms in it and coat it with pitch inside and out. [15]This is how you are to build it: The ark is to be 450 feet long, 75 feet wide and 45 feet high.[d] [16]Make a roof for it and finish[e] the ark to within 18 inches[f] of the top. Put a door in the side of the ark and make lower, middle and upper decks. [17]I am going to bring floodwaters on the earth to destroy all life under the heavens, every creature that has the breath of life in it. Everything on earth will perish. [18]But I will establish my covenant with you, and you will enter the ark—you and your sons and your wife and your sons' wives with you. [19]You are to bring into the ark two of all living creatures, male and female, to keep them alive with you. [20]Two of every kind of bird, of every kind of animal and of every kind of creature that moves along the ground will come to you to be kept alive. [21]You are to take every kind of food that is to be eaten and store it away as food for you and for them."

[22]Noah did everything just as God commanded him.

7 The Lord then said to Noah, "Go into the ark, you and your whole family, because I have found you righteous in this generation. [2]Take with you seven[g] of every kind of clean animal, a male and its mate, and two of every kind of unclean animal, a male and its mate, [3]and also seven of every kind of bird, male and female, to keep their various kinds alive throughout the earth. [4]Seven days from now I will send rain on the earth for forty days and forty nights, and I will wipe from the face of the earth every living creature I have made."

[5]And Noah did all that the Lord commanded him.

[6]Noah was six hundred years old when the floodwaters came on the earth. [7]And Noah and his sons and his wife and his sons' wives entered the ark to escape the waters of the flood. [8]Pairs of clean

a3 Or My spirit will not remain in   b3 Or corrupt   c14 The meaning of the Hebrew for this word is uncertain.   d15 Hebrew 300 cubits long, 50 cubits wide and 30 cubits high (about 140 meters long, 23 meters wide and 13.5 meters high) e16 Or Make an opening for light by finishing   f16 Hebrew a cubit (about 0.5 meter) g2 Or seven pairs; also in verse 3

and unclean animals, of birds and of all creatures that move along the ground, [9]male and female, came to Noah and entered the ark, as God had commanded Noah. [10]And after the seven days the floodwaters came on the earth.

[11]In the six hundredth year of Noah's life, on the seventeenth day of the second month—on that day all the springs of the great deep burst forth, and the floodgates of the heavens were opened. [12]And rain fell on the earth forty days and forty nights.

[13]On that very day Noah and his sons, Shem, Ham and Japheth, together with his wife and the wives of his three sons, entered the ark. [14]They had with them every wild animal according to its kind, all livestock according to their kinds, every creature that moves along the ground according to its kind and every bird according to its kind, everything with wings. [15]Pairs of all creatures that have the breath of life in them came to Noah and entered the ark. [16]The animals going in were male and female of every living thing, as God had commanded Noah. Then the LORD shut him in.

[17]For forty days the flood kept coming on the earth, and as the waters increased they lifted the ark high above the earth. [18]The waters rose and increased greatly on the earth, and the ark floated on the surface of the water. [19]They rose greatly on the earth, and all the high mountains under the entire heavens were covered. [20]The waters rose and covered the mountains to a depth of more than twenty feet.[a,b] [21]Every living thing that moved on the earth perished—birds, livestock, wild animals, all the creatures that swarm over the earth, and all mankind. [22]Everything on dry land that had the breath of life in its nostrils died. [23]Every living

[a]20 Hebrew *fifteen cubits* (about 6.9 meters) *and the mountains were covered*   [b]20 Or *rose more than twenty feet,*

world-wide or local? Did it really occur as told in the Genesis account? Was it right to wipe out so many people? **9.** Why do you think God has decided not to destroy the human race again, even though mankind is still evil? Why do you think God made his promise to destroy the human race the way he did (v. 22)? To what future and final solutions does God's mercy point?

♥ **1.** God responded with deep sadness when he saw the evil which was so prevalent in people's lives. Think of times in your own life when you went astray. How does God's sadness about your sin make you feel? Noah was the only one in his generation who was found righteous. Have you ever felt like you were the only one who was trying to be righteous and walk with God? When? Noah is described as a "righteous" and "blameless" man who "walked with God." What would you need to change in your life in order to have a reputation like Noah's? **2.** What is something difficult which God is asking you to do? What one or two obstacles stand in your way? How does God's promise in Noah's situation help in overcoming the obsta-

---

Genesis 6:5–7:12   **THE FLOOD**

1. What does, "The Lord was grieved that he had made man," mean?
   a. God wished he had never made man.
   b. God missed man's affection and worship.
   c. God experienced pain over human rebellion.
   d. God was pouting in heaven.

2. Why do you think God chose Noah?
   a. Noah liked animals.
   b. Noah loved God.
   c. God loved Noah.
   d. Noah was a good man.

3. Why did God want to destroy everyone but Noah's family?
   a. to punish all the other corrupt, violent people
   b. to start the human race over
   c. because Noah was the only one worth keeping

4. If you were Noah, what would you have thought when God told you to build a boat the size of a football stadium in a landlocked area?
   a. A what?!

b. What will the neighbors think?!
c. How long will this take?!
d. How will I finance this project?!
e. I love an adventure!

5. What do you think was the hardest thing Noah faced in building the ark?
   a. designing it and getting all the materials
   b. enduring the community's ridicule
   c. convincing his family this was God's idea
   d. trusting God to come through according to plan
   e. nothing, because God made everything easy

6. What do you find most amazing about this story?
   a. that Noah completed the project
   b. that the animals cooperated
   c. that it rained enough to cause that kind of flood
   d. that a huge boat could survive a violent flood

7. In my life I feel:
   a. discouraged—I feel like I'm alone in trying to obey God.

b. guilty—God is probably grieving over me.
c. grateful—for God's mercy and deliverance.

8. What can you do in light of your response to question 7? What can you do to please God more and grieve God less?

9. How do you feel about the point that Noah was 600 years old at the time of the flood?
   a. That was no big deal back then.
   b. That number must be symbolic rather than literal.
   c. If he lived that long, a project like building the ark wouldn't seem quite as big.
   d. I wish I could live 600 years.
   e. I'm glad I won't live 600 years.

10. As an older person, what activities do you no longer do that you used to enjoy? What activities do you hope to never get too old to do? What would you like to do before you get too old?

cles you are facing? **3.** Take five minutes of silence to listen as you ask God this question, "Where is one place you want me to step out in faith, Lord?" Share with the group what you heard in the silence OR what you felt about this question. Noah worshiped God by building an altar and offering sacrifices to God. How have you expressed your gratitude to God recently when he has brought you through a difficult situation?

thing on the face of the earth was wiped out; men and animals and the creatures that move along the ground and the birds of the air were wiped from the earth. Only Noah was left, and those with him in the ark.

²⁴The waters flooded the earth for a hundred and fifty days.

8 But God remembered Noah and all the wild animals and the livestock that were with him in the ark, and he sent a wind over the earth, and the waters receded. ²Now the springs of the deep and the floodgates of the heavens had been closed, and the rain had stopped falling from the sky. ³The water receded steadily from the earth. At the end of the hundred and fifty days the water had gone down, ⁴and on the seventeenth day of the seventh month the ark came to rest on the mountains of Ararat. ⁵The waters continued to recede until the tenth month, and on the first day of the tenth month the tops of the mountains became visible.

⁶After forty days Noah opened the window he had made in the ark ⁷and sent out a raven, and it kept flying back and forth until the water had dried up from the earth. ⁸Then he sent out a dove to see if the water had receded from the surface of the ground. ⁹But the dove could find no place to set its feet because there was water over all the surface of the earth; so it returned to Noah in the ark. He reached out his hand and took the dove and brought it back to himself in the ark. ¹⁰He waited seven more days and again sent out the dove from the ark. ¹¹When the dove returned to him in the evening, there in its beak was a freshly plucked olive leaf! Then Noah knew that the water had receded from the earth. ¹²He waited seven more days and sent the dove out again, but this time it did not return to him.

¹³By the first day of the first month of Noah's six hundred and first year, the water had dried up from the earth. Noah then removed the covering from the ark and saw that the surface of the

---

 Genesis 8:1–22　　　　　　　　**NOAH WAITS**

1. What do you think Noah and his family did while they waited in the ark over a year for the flood waters to recede?
   a. played a lot of card games
   b. argued about whose turn it was for zoo clean-up duty
   c. kept rejoicing in God's deliverance
   d. became the world's first "small group"

2. On a scale of 1 to 10 (1 being totally laid back and 10 being totally uptight), how impatient would you have been if the dove you sent came back and you had to keep waiting?

3. What kind of waiting is the most frustrating for you?
   a. waiting at red lights or traffic jams
   b. waiting for someone else
   c. waiting for God
   d. being patient with myself

4. How do you think Noah felt when he stepped off the ark onto dry ground?
   a. relieved　　　　d. out of shape
   b. rarin' to go　　　e. thankful
   c. "Now what?"

5. What pleased God about Noah's sacrifice?
   a. the pleasant aroma
   b. Noah's gratitude
   c. the fact that people were worshiping him
   d. the hope it represented that the world would be better than before the flood

6. The good news after the flood is:
   a. God will never again destroy all living creatures.
   b. God still loves people, even though we are sinful.
   c. God is always pleased with sincere worship.
   d. God, like the four seasons, is faithful.

7. The point from this story I need is:
   a. Like the wind sent to recede the waters, I need God's intervention.
   b. Like Noah, I need patience.
   c. Like the dove provided, I need guidance.
   d. Like the rainbow in Genesis 9, I need reassurance that God hasn't forgotten his promises.

8. If you didn't already, share with your group why you answered question 7 the way you did.

9. ▮ How does the story of Noah relate to your situation in life? What message might God want to communicate about your outlook and attitude toward the future?

10. ▮ Of all the choices you face as a single person, which is the most crucial? As this is your last session, how can this group continue to pray for you?

ground was dry. ¹⁴By the twenty-seventh day of the second month the earth was completely dry.

¹⁵Then God said to Noah, ¹⁶"Come out of the ark, you and your wife and your sons and their wives. ¹⁷Bring out every kind of living creature that is with you—the birds, the animals, and all the creatures that move along the ground—so they can multiply on the earth and be fruitful and increase in number upon it."

¹⁸So Noah came out, together with his sons and his wife and his sons' wives. ¹⁹All the animals and all the creatures that move along the ground and all the birds—everything that moves on the earth—came out of the ark, one kind after another.

²⁰Then Noah built an altar to the LORD and, taking some of all the clean animals and clean birds, he sacrificed burnt offerings on it. ²¹The LORD smelled the pleasing aroma and said in his heart: "Never again will I curse the ground because of man, even though*ª* every inclination of his heart is evil from childhood. And never again will I destroy all living creatures, as I have done.

²²"As long as the earth endures,
seedtime and harvest,
cold and heat,
summer and winter,
day and night
will never cease."

God's Covenant With Noah

9 Then God blessed Noah and his sons, saying to them, "Be fruitful and increase in number and fill the earth. ²The fear and dread of you will fall upon all the beasts of the earth and all the birds of the air, upon every creature that moves along the ground, and upon all the fish of the sea; they are given into your hands. ³Everything that lives and moves will be food for you. Just as I gave you the green plants, I now give you everything.

⁴"But you must not eat meat that has its lifeblood still in it. ⁵And for your lifeblood I will surely demand an accounting. I will demand an accounting from every animal. And from each man, too, I will demand an accounting for the life of his fellow man.

⁶"Whoever sheds the blood of man,
by man shall his blood be shed;
for in the image of God
has God made man.

⁷As for you, be fruitful and increase in number; multiply on the earth and increase upon it."

⁸Then God said to Noah and to his sons with him: ⁹"I now establish my covenant with you and with your descendants after you ¹⁰and with every living creature that was with you—the birds, the livestock and all the wild animals, all those that came out of the ark with you—every living creature on earth. ¹¹I establish my covenant with you: Never again will all life be cut off by the waters of a flood; never again will there be a flood to destroy the earth."

¹²And God said, "This is the sign of the covenant I am making between me and you and every living creature with you, a covenant for all generations to come: ¹³I have set my rainbow in the clouds, and it will be the sign of the covenant between me and the earth. ¹⁴Whenever I bring clouds over the earth and the rainbow appears in the clouds, ¹⁵I will remember my covenant between me and you and all living creatures of every kind. Never again will the

ª21 Or man, for

Which best describes your life today: A raging storm, an enclosed ark or a dove with an olive branch? Why?

1. Verses 1–17 stipulate a second covenant which God enters into with Noah and his heirs (see 6:13–7:5). What aspects of this covenant are forever? Which are unconditional? What does this covenant stipulate from the human side (vv. 1–7)? From God's side (vv. 3,5,9–11)? 2. In verses 1–7, why does God repeat for Noah much of what he told Adam? What new instructions does he add about lifeblood and murder? Why? 3. In verses 12–17, what is the sign of this new covenant? What purpose does this sign serve? Does the principle of the reflection of light diminish your belief in God's use of a rainbow to represent his covenant? 4. From elsewhere in the Bible, what do you know about other signs or seals of covenant commitments between God and his people? 5. What does this new covenant teach about the sanctity of life? How might this teaching be especially important to Noah and his sons just now?

1. What does this Flood story add to the overall Genesis themes of judgment and redemption, justice and mercy? 2. What symbolic rainbow have you experienced recently? In what area of your life does this passage bring

you comfort? Where does it challenge you?

――――――――

1. What fruits or vegetables have you grown? 2. What are some favorite recipes for enjoying the "fruit of your labor"?

1. From this story, what is your impression of Noah? Of his sons? How does this compare with the image presented in 6:8–10? 2. What do these contrasting images imply about children respecting parents? About righteousness? (Does "righteous" mean sinless?) 3. What does Noah's prophetic curse mean for his three sons? For the people of Israel descended through Shem? (Note: The Lord is the "God of Shem.") 4. What's the point of including this story in Genesis? 5. Why did Noah curse Canaan for his father's actions? How has your life been affected by the mistakes of your parents? By the successes of your parents?

Why is mocking your father (9:22) so serious, even today (see Eph 6:1–3)? Instead of scoffing, what should you do?

――――――――

1. "The person to whom I am proud to be related is ____." Why? 2. "A nation I have never visited, but would like to, is ____, to see ____, and to do ____." 3. Who was your most famous relative or ancestor?

1. Ancient Near Eastern genealogies were not always to be taken in a strictly literal fashion. How do you feel this one should be taken? (a) The descendants listed indicate direct parent-child relationships? (b) They describe more distant relatives, nations, tribes, cities or clans? (c) Such "relatives" are based on treaty relationships, historical or cultural ties, not at all blood related? 2. Given those possible scenarios, what questions do you have for the compiler of this particular list? 3. Why might it be important for God's people to understand the ties between themselves and the various groups around them? How might a genea-

waters become a flood to destroy all life. [16]Whenever the rainbow appears in the clouds, I will see it and remember the everlasting covenant between God and all living creatures of every kind on the earth."

[17]So God said to Noah, "This is the sign of the covenant I have established between me and all life on the earth."

The Sons of Noah

[18]The sons of Noah who came out of the ark were Shem, Ham and Japheth. (Ham was the father of Canaan.) [19]These were the three sons of Noah, and from them came the people who were scattered over the earth.

[20]Noah, a man of the soil, proceeded[a] to plant a vineyard. [21]When he drank some of its wine, he became drunk and lay uncovered inside his tent. [22]Ham, the father of Canaan, saw his father's nakedness and told his two brothers outside. [23]But Shem and Japheth took a garment and laid it across their shoulders; then they walked in backward and covered their father's nakedness. Their faces were turned the other way so that they would not see their father's nakedness.

[24]When Noah awoke from his wine and found out what his youngest son had done to him, [25]he said,

> "Cursed be Canaan!
> The lowest of slaves
> will he be to his brothers."

[26]He also said,

> "Blessed be the LORD, the God of Shem!
> May Canaan be the slave of Shem.[b]
> [27]May God extend the territory of Japheth[c];
> may Japheth live in the tents of Shem,
> and may Canaan be his[d] slave."

[28]After the flood Noah lived 350 years. [29]Altogether, Noah lived 950 years, and then he died.

The Table of Nations

10 This is the account of Shem, Ham and Japheth, Noah's sons, who themselves had sons after the flood.

The Japhethites

[2]The sons[e] of Japheth:

Gomer, Magog, Madai, Javan, Tubal, Meshech and Tiras.

[3]The sons of Gomer:

Ashkenaz, Riphath and Togarmah.

[4]The sons of Javan:

Elishah, Tarshish, the Kittim and the Rodanim.[f] [5](From these the maritime peoples spread out into their territories by their clans within their nations, each with its own language.)

The Hamites

[6]The sons of Ham:

Cush, Mizraim,[g] Put and Canaan.

――――――――

[a]20 Or soil, was the first   [b]26 Or be his slave   [c]27 Japheth sounds like the Hebrew for extend.   [d]27 Or their   [e]2 Sons may mean descendants or successors or nations; also in verses 3, 4, 6, 7, 20-23, 29 and 31.   [f]4 Some manuscripts of the Masoretic Text and Samaritan Pentateuch (see also Septuagint and 1 Chron. 1:7); most manuscripts of the Masoretic Text Dodanim   [g]6 That is, Egypt; also in verse 13

7The sons of Cush:
  Seba, Havilah, Sabtah, Raamah and Sabteca.
  The sons of Raamah:
  Sheba and Dedan.

8Cush was the father*a* of Nimrod, who grew to be a mighty warrior on the earth. **9**He was a mighty hunter before the LORD; that is why it is said, "Like Nimrod, a mighty hunter before the LORD." **10**The first centers of his kingdom were Babylon, Erech, Akkad and Calneh, in*b* Shinar.*c* **11**From that land he went to Assyria, where he built Nineveh, Rehoboth Ir,*d* Calah **12**and Resen, which is between Nineveh and Calah; that is the great city.

13Mizraim was the father of
  the Ludites, Anamites, Lehabites, Naphtuhites, **14**Pathrusites, Casluhites (from whom the Philistines came) and Caphtorites.
15Canaan was the father of
  Sidon his firstborn,*e* and of the Hittites, **16**Jebusites, Amorites, Girgashites, **17**Hivites, Arkites, Sinites, **18**Arvadites, Zemarites and Hamathites.

Later the Canaanite clans scattered **19**and the borders of Canaan reached from Sidon toward Gerar as far as Gaza, and then toward Sodom, Gomorrah, Admah and Zeboiim, as far as Lasha.
20These are the sons of Ham by their clans and languages, in their territories and nations.

The Semites

21Sons were also born to Shem, whose older brother was*f* Japheth; Shem was the ancestor of all the sons of Eber.

22The sons of Shem:
  Elam, Asshur, Arphaxad, Lud and Aram.
23The sons of Aram:
  Uz, Hul, Gether and Meshech.*g*
24Arphaxad was the father of*h* Shelah,
  and Shelah the father of Eber.
25Two sons were born to Eber:
  One was named Peleg,*i* because in his time the earth was divided; his brother was named Joktan.
26Joktan was the father of
  Almodad, Sheleph, Hazarmaveth, Jerah, **27**Hadoram, Uzal, Diklah, **28**Obal, Abimael, Sheba, **29**Ophir, Havilah and Jobab. All these were sons of Joktan.

30The region where they lived stretched from Mesha toward Sephar, in the eastern hill country.
31These are the sons of Shem by their clans and languages, in their territories and nations.

32These are the clans of Noah's sons, according to their lines of descent, within their nations. From these the nations spread out over the earth after the flood.

---

ogy such as this one help? **4.** Archaeology has taught us much about these ancient places and people groups. Which ones can you find on a Bible map for the post-Flood, pre-Abram period? What do you notice about the spread of these people? About their convergence on the land of Canaan (now called Palestine)? **5.** Archaeologists tell us that in Mesopotamia, these communities each developed their own cultic practices and finally united into political states with their own king, priests and a temple-tower. What caused these nations to eventually scatter, "each with its own language" (v. 5; see 11:1–9)?

♡ **1.** If someone were to write a brief, biblical account of your life, following the pattern of Genesis 10, how would it read? Fill in the blanks: "I was born in _____, to parents who _____. My big accomplishment in life was _____ as typified in my life's motto, _____." **2.** From sharing your accounts in your group, what have you learned you have in common?

---

a8 Father may mean *ancestor* or *predecessor* or *founder*; also in verses 13, 15, 24 and 26.   *b10* Or *Erech and Akkad—all of them in*   *c10* That is, Babylonia
d11 Or *Nineveh with its city squares*   *e15* Or *of the Sidonians, the foremost*
f21 Or *Shem, the older brother of*   *g23* See Septuagint and 1 Chron. 1:17; Hebrew *Mash*   *h24* Hebrew; Septuagint *father of Cainan, and Cainan was the father of*
i25 Peleg means *division*.

What experience do you have with (a) building projects and (b) foreign languages? What most frustrated you about (a) and (b)?

1. Why do they build this tower? Why is such unity wrong?
2. In light of God's early history with mankind, why would the Lord be concerned that "nothing they plan to do will be impossible for them"?
3. What do you learn about God's judgment and mercy?

1. What's the lesson here for empire-building? For church-building? For human ambition? 2. How is unity "in Christ" different from the unity at Babel? 3. Where are you feeling scattered or confused? Why might that be? Have you ever built a "tower" for yourself only to get "scattered" by God? What happened?

 1. Who of your relatives has lived the longest? What do you know or what have you been told about this person? 2. Are you the firstborn of your parents? Or are you among their "other sons and daughters"? What difference did birth order make in how you were raised?

The Tower of Babel

11 Now the whole world had one language and a common speech. [2]As men moved eastward,[a] they found a plain in Shinar[b] and settled there.

[3]They said to each other, "Come, let's make bricks and bake them thoroughly." They used brick instead of stone, and tar for mortar. [4]Then they said, "Come, let us build ourselves a city, with a tower that reaches to the heavens, so that we may make a name for ourselves and not be scattered over the face of the whole earth."

[5]But the LORD came down to see the city and the tower that the men were building. [6]The LORD said, "If as one people speaking the same language they have begun to do this, then nothing they plan to do will be impossible for them. [7]Come, let us go down and confuse their language so they will not understand each other."

[8]So the LORD scattered them from there over all the earth, and they stopped building the city. [9]That is why it was called Babel[c]—because there the LORD confused the language of the whole world. From there the LORD scattered them over the face of the whole earth.

From Shem to Abram

[10]This is the account of Shem.

Two years after the flood, when Shem was 100 years old, he became the father[d] of Arphaxad. [11]And after he became the father of Arphaxad, Shem lived 500 years and had other sons and daughters.

a2 Or *from the east*; or *in the east*   *b2* That is, Babylonia   *c9* That is, Babylon; *Babel* sounds like the Hebrew for *confused*.   *d10 Father* may mean *ancestor*; also in verses 11-25.

$ Genesis 11:1–9   **THE TOWER OF BABEL**

1. When I am with people who speak a different language, I:
   a. feel excluded.
   b. feel frustrated.
   c. think they should learn to speak my language.
   d. think it's a challenge.

2. What advantage did a "common speech" give humankind?
   a. control over circumstances
   b. power to defy God
   c. ability to pool resources
   d. capacity for unrestrained spiritual obedience or rebellion

3. What did the desire to build a tower demonstrate?
   a. pride
   b. no need for God
   c. a desire to meet God
   d. a desire to be God

4. Why was God so concerned about this building project?
   a. because of the pride behind it
   b. because of the threat of human takeover
   c. because their unity would lead to increasing rebellion
   d. because they would discover God's address

5. Why did God confuse their languages and scatter the human race?
   a. to punish their arrogance
   b. to populate the earth
   c. to make the Olympics more interesting
   d. to protect humankind from its own destructive potential

6. Which best describes your faith community?
   a. building towers to heaven
   b. speaking different languages
   c. doing things for God
   d. seeking God's blueprint for life

7. What can you do to help your faith community honor God more?

8. What do you do when God scatters your personal plans?
   a. pound my fist
   b. pick up the pieces and keep going
   c. start another plan
   d. ask for instructions

9. What desire do you have to "build" something? What kind of "name" would this produce? How do you think God feels about your desires and ambitions?

10. **$** How much change has "your world" undergone in the last few years? How have you dealt with the stress that comes from the confusion and scattering of change?

11. **$** How much of the stress you're under do you allow to be put upon you by the vain pressures of the world? What is *God's* definition of success in your life?

12When Arphaxad had lived 35 years, he became the father of Shelah. 13And after he became the father of Shelah, Arphaxad lived 403 years and had other sons and daughters.[a]

14When Shelah had lived 30 years, he became the father of Eber. 15And after he became the father of Eber, Shelah lived 403 years and had other sons and daughters.

16When Eber had lived 34 years, he became the father of Peleg. 17And after he became the father of Peleg, Eber lived 430 years and had other sons and daughters.

18When Peleg had lived 30 years, he became the father of Reu. 19And after he became the father of Reu, Peleg lived 209 years and had other sons and daughters.

20When Reu had lived 32 years, he became the father of Serug. 21And after he became the father of Serug, Reu lived 207 years and had other sons and daughters.

22When Serug had lived 30 years, he became the father of Nahor. 23And after he became the father of Nahor, Serug lived 200 years and had other sons and daughters.

24When Nahor had lived 29 years, he became the father of Terah. 25And after he became the father of Terah, Nahor lived 119 years and had other sons and daughters.

26After Terah had lived 70 years, he became the father of Abram, Nahor and Haran.

27This is the account of Terah.

Terah became the father of Abram, Nahor and Haran. And Haran became the father of Lot. 28While his father Terah was still alive, Haran died in Ur of the Chaldeans, in the land of his birth. 29Abram and Nahor both married. The name of Abram's wife was Sarai, and the name of Nahor's wife was Milcah; she was the daughter of Haran, the father of both Milcah and Iscah. 30Now Sarai was barren; she had no children.

31Terah took his son Abram, his grandson Lot son of Haran, and his daughter-in-law Sarai, the wife of his son Abram, and together they set out from Ur of the Chaldeans to go to Canaan. But when they came to Haran, they settled there.

32Terah lived 205 years, and he died in Haran.

The Call of Abram

12 The LORD had said to Abram, "Leave your country, your people and your father's household and go to the land I will show you.

2"I will make you into a great nation
    and I will bless you;
I will make your name great,
    and you will be a blessing.
3I will bless those who bless you,
    and whoever curses you I will curse;
and all peoples on earth
    will be blessed through you."

4So Abram left, as the LORD had told him; and Lot went with him. Abram was seventy-five years old when he set out from Haran. 5He took his wife Sarai, his nephew Lot, all the possessions they had

a 12,13 Hebrew; Septuagint (see also Luke 3:35, 36 and note at Gen. 10:24) 35 years, he became the father of Cainan. 13And after he became the father of Cainan, Arphaxad lived 430 years and had other sons and daughters, and then he died. When Cainan had lived 130 years, he became the father of Shelah. And after he became the father of Shelah, Cainan lived 330 years and had other sons and daughters

1. What do you learn about Abram, his family and his roots from this passage? Why might Abram migrate with his father and not Nahor? 2. Why might they settle in Haran instead of Canaan, their intended destination: (a) They were tired? (Haran was 600 miles from Ur, and Canaan 400 miles further still.) (b) They were attracted to Haran's moon worship, which reminded them of Ur? (c) They simply lacked the vision and will to "go all the way"? (d) Abram was waiting on God's timing before proceeding further (see Ac 7:2ff)? 3. How does Genesis 11 interlock with the table of nations (ch. 10)? With God's covenant with Noah (ch. 9)? With the genealogy of Adam (ch. 5)? 4. Why would these historical connections be important to Israelites? To you?

1. At this junction between primeval history (ch. 1–11) and patriarchal history (ch. 12–50), a review is in order. What have you learned thus far about: (a) God's original intention for his people and how this paradise was lost? (b) The degeneration of the human race, as well as its generation, since the Fall? (c) The everyday, as well as redemptive, history of God's people? (d) God's covenant with us, which involves judgment, as well as mercy? 2. What new things about God have impacted you in Genesis?

1. Where is "home" for you? When did you first leave there? What for? Who or what did you take with you? And leave behind? 2. What do (or did) you hope to be doing at age 75?

1. What command and promises does God give Abram? With what qualifications? What do you make of their unconditional nature? Their universal scope? Means of fulfillment (v. 7; see 11:30)? 2. Why does God promise Abram a great name (v. 2), when God foiled the name-building efforts of others (see 6:4ff; 11:4ff)? 3. "Actions reveal character": so who is Abram?

1. Describe a time when you made a significant, personal sacrifice in response to God's directive? 2. Of the promises to Abram, which appeal to you and

why? (Would you rather be blessed or be a blessing?) **3.** To what (place, people, priority) might God be calling you? Why not go?

accumulated and the people they had acquired in Haran, and they set out for the land of Canaan, and they arrived there.

[6]Abram traveled through the land as far as the site of the great tree of Moreh at Shechem. At that time the Canaanites were in the land. [7]The LORD appeared to Abram and said, "To your offspring[a] I will give this land." So he built an altar there to the LORD, who had appeared to him.

[8]From there he went on toward the hills east of Bethel and pitched his tent, with Bethel on the west and Ai on the east. There he built an altar to the LORD and called on the name of the LORD. [9]Then Abram set out and continued toward the Negev.

Abram in Egypt

[10]Now there was a famine in the land, and Abram went down to Egypt to live there for a while because the famine was severe. [11]As he was about to enter Egypt, he said to his wife Sarai, "I know what a beautiful woman you are. [12]When the Egyptians see you, they will say, 'This is his wife.' Then they will kill me but will let you live. [13]Say you are my sister, so that I will be treated well for your sake and my life will be spared because of you."

[14]When Abram came to Egypt, the Egyptians saw that she was a very beautiful woman. [15]And when Pharaoh's officials saw her, they praised her to Pharaoh, and she was taken into his palace. [16]He treated Abram well for her sake, and Abram acquired sheep

1. What white lie do you recall telling? **2.** Complete: "When the going gets tough, I _____."

1. When Abram comes to the promised land, only to find a famine there, how might he feel about God's promise? Why? **2.** Sarai was Abram's half-sister (20:12). Does that justify Abram's half-truth? Or does the end (Abram's safety) justify the means (a lie)? What if the end he had in mind was fulfilling God's promise (vv. 2ff)? **3.** Either way, could Abram's sin

[a]7 Or *seed*

   Genesis 11:27–12:9   **THE CALL OF ABRAM**

1. How do you feel when you first move to a new place?

2. Why did Abram settle in Haran at first instead of going on to Canaan?
   a. He was dragging his feet.
   b. He took one step at a time.
   c. Out of respect, he lived where his father wanted to live.
   d. Haran was far enough away.

3. Why did God choose Abram to be the father of his special people?
   a. because Abram was a good man
   b. to demonstrate his power by choosing a childless couple who were up in years
   c. no particular reason
   d. God doesn't need a reason.

4. If you were Abram, what would be most attractive to you about God's promises?
   a. fame and fortune
   b. protection from bullies
   c. opportunity to bring blessing to others
   d. being the founder of a great nation

5. If you were Abram, what would be

hardest to believe about God's promises?

6. Why did Abram travel throughout Canaan after he arrived?
   a. He was looking over his property.
   b. He was claiming it for God.
   c. He was looking for a good place for his family.
   d. He had trouble settling down.

7. Why did Abram build altars in Canaan?
   a. He was relieved.
   b. He was grateful.
   c. He was learning how to worship.
   d. He was reminding God to keep his promises.

8. How have you learned to hear God's call in your life? Who has gone with you on your journey of faith?
   a. a family member(s)
   b. my spouse
   c. Christian friends
   d. I have gone by myself.

9. How does the fact that Abram and Sarai were 75 and 65 years old when they left for Canaan

make you feel? As you grow older, what would you like to accomplish for God? How can you best be a blessing to others?

10. How do you think Sarai felt about all this moving?
    a. "Whatever you want, dear."
    b. "Please make up your mind, Abe."
    c. "Where God sends us, we will go."
    d. "I'm sick of pitching tents!"

11. How many times have you moved as an adult? What other stressful changes have affected your home? How can your faith be an anchor in change?

12. How does your career relate to this story?
    a. I shouldn't have followed in my parents' footsteps.
    b. I wish God would call me somewhere else.
    c. I made a move too, but I regret it.
    d. I'm still searching for my place.

13. What will happen to you if you stay where you are? What hopes and dreams has God given you for your career?

and cattle, male and female donkeys, menservants and maidservants, and camels. [17]But the LORD inflicted serious diseases on Pharaoh and his household because of Abram's wife Sarai. [18]So Pharaoh summoned Abram. "What have you done to me?" he said. "Why didn't you tell me she was your wife? [19]Why did you say, 'She is my sister,' so that I took her to be my wife? Now then, here is your wife. Take her and go!" [20]Then Pharaoh gave orders about Abram to his men, and they sent him on his way, with his wife and everything he had.

Abram and Lot Separate

13 So Abram went up from Egypt to the Negev, with his wife and everything he had, and Lot went with him. [2]Abram had become very wealthy in livestock and in silver and gold.

[3]From the Negev he went from place to place until he came to Bethel, to the place between Bethel and Ai where his tent had been earlier [4]and where he had first built an altar. There Abram called on the name of the LORD.

[5]Now Lot, who was moving about with Abram, also had flocks and herds and tents. [6]But the land could not support them while they stayed together, for their possessions were so great that they were not able to stay together. [7]And quarreling arose between Abram's herdsmen and the herdsmen of Lot. The Canaanites and Perizzites were also living in the land at that time.

[8]So Abram said to Lot, "Let's not have any quarreling between you and me, or between your herdsmen and mine, for we are brothers. [9]Is not the whole land before you? Let's part company. If you go to the left, I'll go to the right; if you go to the right, I'll go to the left."

[10]Lot looked up and saw that the whole plain of the Jordan was well watered, like the garden of the LORD, like the land of Egypt, toward Zoar. (This was before the LORD destroyed Sodom and Gomorrah.) [11]So Lot chose for himself the whole plain of the Jordan and set out toward the east. The two men parted company:

thwart God's plan? How does God extricate Abram from the mess?

1. What sure promise are you questioning? **2.** Have you ever used "the ends justify the means" approach? Explain.

---

1. Who is your favorite aunt or uncle? Your kissin' cousin? Your spoiled nephew? **2.** Where do you like to go for walks?

1. Why do Abram and Lot choose as they do: (a) Rich uncles can afford to be congenial? (b) Nice guys finish last? (c) God will cover for any mistake Abram makes? (d) Good real estate advice is hard to come by? (e) Abram is a righty, Lot a lefty? (f) Abram is more the country pioneer-type, Lot the urban city-type? (g) Lot loves to live a life of sin a lot? **2.** In forsaking rich cities and choosing less fertile land, what does this reveal about Abram (see Heb 11:8–16)? **3.** In reply to Abram's faith, what new promise does God give?

1. If faced with a similar choice, would you have followed the example of Abram, or of Lot? Why? **2.** Would your relationship with God be helped or hurt by a more isolated lifestyle? By a

Genesis 13:1–18   **ABRAM AND LOT SEPARATE**

God called Abram to Canaan, where he promised to make him the founder of a great nation. After a short stay, famine drove Abram, Sarai and their nephew Lot to Egypt. Now they return to the "promised land."

1. What do you think was the main source of conflict between Abram and Lot?
   a. a shortage of good pasture land
   b. competition and jealousy
   c. a codependent relationship
   d. rivalry between their herdsmen

2. How would you have typically handled this kind of problem?

3. What did Abram do by telling Lot to choose?
   a. He took the initiative to solve the problem.
   b. He forced Lot to solve it.

c. He graciously preserved their relationship.
   d. He put his future in God's hands.

4. How do you think Lot felt about Abram's idea?
   a. delighted   c. torn
   b. guilty   d. puzzled

5. How would you have felt if you were in Lot's place?

6. Why did Lot move next to Sodom— "sin city"?
   a. to flirt with temptation
   b. because of the quality of the land
   c. to give his herdsmen something to do Saturday nights
   d. to irritate Uncle Abram

7. What's the "Sodom" in your life? What do you do to keep from getting sucked into sin? How close do you let yourself get?

8. What was the Lord's response to Abram?
   a. "You gave away the family farm, but I'll take care of things."
   b. "Because you gave Lot a lot, I'll give you even more."
   c. "The last shall be first."
   d. "The whole land is as good as yours."

9. What is the difference between being assertive and selfish? Between being a giver and a doormat? How can you apply the lesson of this story to your relationships? How do you need to grow?

10. What does this story teach you about being content? What is God saying about your attitude toward your work? What was the most important thing you gained from this course?

more crowded lifestyle? Why? **3.** What one thing might God be asking you "to lift up your eyes ... look ... see ... go, walk" (vv. 14–17)? **4.** Like Lot, where are you "grabbing for the gusto"? **5.** What promises of God have you taken to heart? What has God promised you that you still have difficulty accepting?

☕ **1.** When was war made most real to you? How did that (book, TV, movie, memorial, protest movement, combat duty) affect you? **2.** How does your family react when one of its members is in trouble? How does this make you feel? **3.** When have you survived a "close call" or brush with death?

📖 **1.** What subtle, but slippery, slope of sin do you see in the lifestyle of Lot? What do you see in this movement from (a) to (e): (a) "moving about with Abram" (13:5), to (b) "quarreling with Abram" (13:8), to (c) "looking toward Zoar" (13:10), to (d) "tenting near Sodom" (13:12), to (e) "living in Sodom" (14:12)? **2.** How does this progressive movement toward Sodom dangerously affect Lot's life (v. 12)? **3.** What is the point of Abram's victory over the four kings (vv. 13–24)? What part do alliances play in his victory and post-victory negotiations? **4.** On what basis does Abram select some allies and reject others? **5.** Abram accepts Melchizedek's blessing and then tithes to him—why? **6.** Given the different way Abram treats the king of Salem and the king of Sodom, what does that tell you about the character and faith of each? How does their contrast sharpen the contrast made between Abram and Lot?

♡ **1.** What alliances do you make? Do you make them readily or reluctantly? Have you ever been burned by a partnership that went bad? Or blessed beyond belief by a serendipitous ally? **2.** Are your influential friends more like the king of Sodom, or the king of Salem? **3.** Which name(s) are akin to how you pledge money or give possessions: "Sensible Sally"? "Extravagant Eddie"? "Rainy Day Ron"? "Giveaway Gert"? "Tight Ted"? Or "Watchful Wanda"? How

---

¹²Abram lived in the land of Canaan, while Lot lived among the cities of the plain and pitched his tents near Sodom. ¹³Now the men of Sodom were wicked and were sinning greatly against the LORD.

¹⁴The LORD said to Abram after Lot had parted from him, "Lift up your eyes from where you are and look north and south, east and west. ¹⁵All the land that you see I will give to you and your offspring[a] forever. ¹⁶I will make your offspring like the dust of the earth, so that if anyone could count the dust, then your offspring could be counted. ¹⁷Go, walk through the length and breadth of the land, for I am giving it to you."

¹⁸So Abram moved his tents and went to live near the great trees of Mamre at Hebron, where he built an altar to the LORD.

Abram Rescues Lot

14 At this time Amraphel king of Shinar,[b] Arioch king of Ellasar, Kedorlaomer king of Elam and Tidal king of Goiim ²went to war against Bera king of Sodom, Birsha king of Gomorrah, Shinab king of Admah, Shemeber king of Zeboiim, and the king of Bela (that is, Zoar). ³All these latter kings joined forces in the Valley of Siddim (the Salt Sea[c]). ⁴For twelve years they had been subject to Kedorlaomer, but in the thirteenth year they rebelled.

⁵In the fourteenth year, Kedorlaomer and the kings allied with him went out and defeated the Rephaites in Ashteroth Karnaim, the Zuzites in Ham, the Emites in Shaveh Kiriathaim ⁶and the Horites in the hill country of Seir, as far as El Paran near the desert. ⁷Then they turned back and went to En Mishpat (that is, Kadesh), and they conquered the whole territory of the Amalekites, as well as the Amorites who were living in Hazazon Tamar.

⁸Then the king of Sodom, the king of Gomorrah, the king of Admah, the king of Zeboiim and the king of Bela (that is, Zoar) marched out and drew up their battle lines in the Valley of Siddim ⁹against Kedorlaomer king of Elam, Tidal king of Goiim, Amraphel king of Shinar and Arioch king of Ellasar—four kings against five. ¹⁰Now the Valley of Siddim was full of tar pits, and when the kings of Sodom and Gomorrah fled, some of the men fell into them and the rest fled to the hills. ¹¹The four kings seized all the goods of Sodom and Gomorrah and all their food; then they went away. ¹²They also carried off Abram's nephew Lot and his possessions, since he was living in Sodom.

¹³One who had escaped came and reported this to Abram the Hebrew. Now Abram was living near the great trees of Mamre the Amorite, a brother[d] of Eshcol and Aner, all of whom were allied with Abram. ¹⁴When Abram heard that his relative had been taken captive, he called out the 318 trained men born in his household and went in pursuit as far as Dan. ¹⁵During the night Abram divided his men to attack them and he routed them, pursuing them as far as Hobah, north of Damascus. ¹⁶He recovered all the goods and brought back his relative Lot and his possessions, together with the women and the other people.

¹⁷After Abram returned from defeating Kedorlaomer and the kings allied with him, the king of Sodom came out to meet him in the Valley of Shaveh (that is, the King's Valley).

¹⁸Then Melchizedek king of Salem[e] brought out bread and wine. He was priest of God Most High, ¹⁹and he blessed Abram, saying,

---

a15 Or *seed*; also in verse 16   *b1* That is, Babylonia; also in verse 9   *c3* That is, the Dead Sea   *d13* Or *a relative*; or *an ally*   *e18* That is, Jerusalem

"Blessed be Abram by God Most High,
  Creator[a] of heaven and earth.
²⁰And blessed be[b] God Most High,
  who delivered your enemies into your hand."

Then Abram gave him a tenth of everything.

²¹The king of Sodom said to Abram, "Give me the people and keep the goods for yourself."

²²But Abram said to the king of Sodom, "I have raised my hand to the Lord, God Most High, Creator of heaven and earth, and have taken an oath ²³that I will accept nothing belonging to you, not even a thread or the thong of a sandal, so that you will never be able to say, 'I made Abram rich.' ²⁴I will accept nothing but what my men have eaten and the share that belongs to the men who went with me—to Aner, Eshcol and Mamre. Let them have their share."

God's Covenant With Abram

15 After this, the word of the Lord came to Abram in a vision:

"Do not be afraid, Abram.
  I am your shield,[c]
  your very great reward.[d]"

²But Abram said, "O Sovereign Lord, what can you give me since I remain childless and the one who will inherit[e] my estate is Eliezer of Damascus?" ³And Abram said, "You have given me no children; so a servant in my household will be my heir."

⁴Then the word of the Lord came to him: "This man will not be your heir, but a son coming from your own body will be your heir." ⁵He took him outside and said, "Look up at the heavens and count the stars—if indeed you can count them." Then he said to him, "So shall your offspring be."

⁶Abram believed the Lord, and he credited it to him as righteousness.

⁷He also said to him, "I am the Lord, who brought you out of Ur of the Chaldeans to give you this land to take possession of it."

⁸But Abram said, "O Sovereign Lord, how can I know that I will gain possession of it?"

⁹So the Lord said to him, "Bring me a heifer, a goat and a ram, each three years old, along with a dove and a young pigeon."

¹⁰Abram brought all these to him, cut them in two and arranged the halves opposite each other; the birds, however, he did not cut in half. ¹¹Then birds of prey came down on the carcasses, but Abram drove them away.

¹²As the sun was setting, Abram fell into a deep sleep, and a thick and dreadful darkness came over him. ¹³Then the Lord said to him, "Know for certain that your descendants will be strangers in a country not their own, and they will be enslaved and mistreated four hundred years. ¹⁴But I will punish the nation they serve as slaves, and afterward they will come out with great possessions. ¹⁵You, however, will go to your fathers in peace and be buried at a good old age. ¹⁶In the fourth generation your descendants will come back here, for the sin of the Amorites has not yet reached its full measure."

¹⁷When the sun had set and darkness had fallen, a smoking firepot with a blazing torch appeared and passed between the

do you feel about "your" name(s)? 4. From what mess would you like to be rescued? 5. Who is blessing you today? Whom might you bless? 6. When have you refused a gift or reward because of your relationship with God?

How do you reassure someone your word is good: (a) "Cross your heart and hope to die"? (b) Give scout's honor? (c) Involve your lawyer? (d) Invoke God's seal? (e) Put up and shut up? Give examples. When was the last time you went stargazing? Describe how you felt.

1. What does Abram fear most (vv. 1–3,8)? What's wrong with wanting reassurance? 2. In adopting a servant heir, is Abram faithless or faithful? What does God think (vv. 4–7,9–21)? 3. If God says it once (12:2–3,7), even twice (13:14–17), why remind Abram again? How has God already been Abram's "shield" and "great reward"? 4. How is "faith" related to "righteousness" (v. 6; see Ro 4:18–22; Gal 3:6–9)? Which comes first? Which comes from God? Which is indispensable to a right relationship with God? 5. In the next scene (vv. 9–21), what do you think the cut animals signify? The blazing torch? The fire passing between the cut pieces? 6. In the dream (vv. 12–16) and after cutting the covenant (vv.18–20), what news is comforting? Discomforting? 7. Why does God initiate such legal contracts with his people? And why a land grant without any obedience required of Abram? Why then the almost 700-year delay in its fulfillment (v. 16; see Heb 11:13–16, 20–22)?

1. Where in your life do you need God to say, "Do not be afraid. I am your shield, your very great reward"? 2. The Lord speaks frequently to Abraham. Does God speak to you? How? 3. Where in your life are you longing for some certainty?

---

a19 Or *Possessor*; also in verse 22   b20 Or *And praise be to*   c1 Or *sovereign*   d1 Or *shield; / your reward will be very great*   e2 The meaning of the Hebrew for this phrase is uncertain.

pieces. [18]On that day the LORD made a covenant with Abram and said, "To your descendants I give this land, from the river[a] of Egypt to the great river, the Euphrates— [19]the land of the Kenites, Kenizzites, Kadmonites, [20]Hittites, Perizzites, Rephaites, [21]Amorites, Canaanites, Girgashites and Jebusites."

Hagar and Ishmael

16 Now Sarai, Abram's wife, had borne him no children. But she had an Egyptian maidservant named Hagar; [2]so she said to Abram, "The LORD has kept me from having children. Go, sleep with my maidservant; perhaps I can build a family through her."

Abram agreed to what Sarai said. [3]So after Abram had been living in Canaan ten years, Sarai his wife took her Egyptian maidservant Hagar and gave her to her husband to be his wife. [4]He slept with Hagar, and she conceived.

When she knew she was pregnant, she began to despise her mistress. [5]Then Sarai said to Abram, "You are responsible for the wrong I am suffering. I put my servant in your arms, and now that she knows she is pregnant, she despises me. May the LORD judge between you and me."

[6]"Your servant is in your hands," Abram said. "Do with her whatever you think best." Then Sarai mistreated Hagar; so she fled from her.

[7]The angel of the LORD found Hagar near a spring in the desert; it was the spring that is beside the road to Shur. [8]And he said, "Hagar, servant of Sarai, where have you come from, and where are you going?"

a 18 Or *Wadi*

1. How long did you (or would you) wait before having kids? Why? **2.** Growing up, who "wore the pants" in your family: Mom? Dad? Kids? Or was decision-making mutual?

1. Of the three main characters in this story—Abram, Sarai and Hagar—which do you like the most? The least? Why? **2.** What might change your opinion of Abram and Sarai: (a) Knowing it was a common cultural practice in their day for childless couples to include as their own any children the man had by his servants? (b) Knowing their attitude and motives are right toward God? (c) Knowing Sarai is now 75 and has always been barren? (d) Knowing it's been 10 years since God promised them a son? **3.** What, if anything, might justify the strategy of surrogate motherhood and "helping out Mother Nature"? **4.** Why does God reject their plan? How does he com-

---

  Genesis 16:1–16   **HAGAR AND ISHMAEL**

Though God had promised Abram a son, Abram and Sarai were now 85 and 75 years old respectively. In this story, they decide to practice a common custom of their time in order to provide the birth of a male heir.

1. What drove Sarai to this course of action?
   a. her guilt and shame
   b. her longing for a family
   c. Abram's longing for a son
   d. social pressure
   e. God—he had the whole thing planned.

2. How do you think Abram felt about Sarai's plan?
   a. "Great idea!"
   b. "What am I getting myself into?!"
   c. "I wonder what God thinks about this."
   d. "I guess God didn't stipulate that Sarai would be my promised son's mother."

3. How do you think Hagar felt about Sarai's plan?
   a. "You've got to be kidding!"

   b. "It's part of the job."
   c. "All right—from servant to wife!"
   d. "What did I do to deserve this?"

4. Why did the plan backfire?
   a. Sarai got jealous.
   b. Hagar got cocky.
   c. Hagar felt used.
   d. Abram didn't have any backbone.
   e. The plan was against God's will.

5. Why did the Lord give Hagar direction, hope and promise?
   a. God felt sorry for her.
   b. God loved her and her son—like he loves everyone.
   c. God felt obligated to take care of the child she was carrying.
   d. God turned a bad idea into his own plan.

6. What in your life have you had to wait a long time for? Are you still waiting? How do you handle the wait?

7. Share a time when you took matters into your own hands. What will prevent you from doing that in the future?

8. Quite possibly Sarai and Hagar had become close friends. When have you lost a close friend? Did your friendship blow up like this one, or did you gradually fade apart?

9. How do you handle conflict with good friends? How hard is it for you to pursue closeness after a friendship has gone sour?

10. How would you describe the communication between Sarai and Abram?
    a. What communication!
    b. Abram always got the last word: "Yes, dear."
    c. They accepted each other's words too quickly, without any discussion.
    d. They both spoke and acted before thinking things through.

11. In what ways does this story remind you of your marriage relationship? How often do you get into impulsive situations that cause conflict? How can you avoid the damage caused by acting on impulse?

"I'm running away from my mistress Sarai," she answered.

⁹Then the angel of the LORD told her, "Go back to your mistress and submit to her." ¹⁰The angel added, "I will so increase your descendants that they will be too numerous to count."

¹¹The angel of the LORD also said to her:

> "You are now with child
> and you will have a son.
> You shall name him Ishmael,ᵃ
> for the LORD has heard of your misery.
> ¹²He will be a wild donkey of a man;
> his hand will be against everyone
> and everyone's hand against him,
> and he will live in hostility
> towardᵇ all his brothers."

¹³She gave this name to the LORD who spoke to her: "You are the God who sees me," for she said, "I have now seenᶜ the One who sees me." ¹⁴That is why the well was called Beer Lahai Roiᵈ; it is still there, between Kadesh and Bered.

¹⁵So Hagar bore Abram a son, and Abram gave the name Ishmael to the son she had borne. ¹⁶Abram was eighty-six years old when Hagar bore him Ishmael.

The Covenant of Circumcision

17 When Abram was ninety-nine years old, the LORD appeared to him and said, "I am God Almightyᵉ; walk before me and be blameless. ²I will confirm my covenant between me and you and will greatly increase your numbers."

³Abram fell facedown, and God said to him, ⁴"As for me, this is my covenant with you: You will be the father of many nations. ⁵No longer will you be called Abramᶠ; your name will be Abraham,ᵍ for I have made you a father of many nations. ⁶I will make you very fruitful; I will make nations of you, and kings will come from you. ⁷I will establish my covenant as an everlasting covenant between me and you and your descendants after you for the generations to come, to be your God and the God of your descendants after you. ⁸The whole land of Canaan, where you are now an alien, I will give as an everlasting possession to you and your descendants after you; and I will be their God."

⁹Then God said to Abraham, "As for you, you must keep my covenant, you and your descendants after you for the generations to come. ¹⁰This is my covenant with you and your descendants after you, the covenant you are to keep: Every male among you shall be circumcised. ¹¹You are to undergo circumcision, and it will be the sign of the covenant between me and you. ¹²For the generations to come every male among you who is eight days old must be circumcised, including those born in your household or bought with money from a foreigner—those who are not your offspring. ¹³Whether born in your household or bought with your money, they must be circumcised. My covenant in your flesh is to be an everlasting covenant. ¹⁴Any uncircumcised male, who has not been circumcised in the flesh, will be cut off from his people; he has broken my covenant."

¹⁵God also said to Abraham, "As for Sarai your wife, you are no longer to call her Sarai; her name will be Sarah. ¹⁶I will bless her

fort Hagar (vv. 7–12)? Why does God insist that she submit to Sarai's authority? **5.** What does Genesis 16 tell you about God? Angels? Human nature? Hagar's heirs (the Arabs)?

1. Where have you been waiting "10 years" for God to fulfill a promise? How do you cope with such delays? **2.** From what are you feeling tempted to run? **3.** Where have you seen God lately? As a result of that encounter, what name would you give to God or to the place where you met him (as in 16:13–14)? If God is "the God who sees," how do you live your life knowing that God is aware of everything about you? (See also Ps 139:1–12.)

1. If you could change your name, what name would you choose? Why? **2.** Who always helps you to laugh? How? **3.** What is the most serious contract you ever signed? How did you confirm it?

1. After 13 years of God's silence, Abram must think Ishmael is the promised heir. How does God show him otherwise? **2.** With his covenant cut with Abram (15:9–21), how does God now confirm it (17:2,4–8)? Why do you think God chose circumcision to ratify his covenant with Abram? What does circumcision demonstrate (15:6; 17:1; see Ro 4:9–12)? **3.** In promising certain privileges, protection and provision to Abram, what does that imply for us, as well? In what way is this promise an "everlasting covenant" (v. 17)? Is it like a coupon good for redemption by anyone, anytime, anywhere? Or is there a catch? **4.** If Abram's only responsibility under the earlier version of the covenant was to "believe" (15:6), what is required this time (17:1,9–14)? **5.** In the ancient world, a name conveyed the essence of a person, and giving a name conveyed rule or ownership. What then do you make of Abram's and Sarai's name change? How might God's view of Abraham differ from Abraham's view of himself? **6.** How does Abraham respond initially (vv. 17–18)? Eventually (vv. 23–27)? How does he know God will keep his word?

ᵃ11 *Ishmael* means *God hears.*   ᵇ12 Or *live to the east / of*   ᶜ13 Or *seen the back of*   ᵈ14 *Beer Lahai Roi* means *well of the Living One who sees me.*   ᵉ1 Hebrew *El-Shaddai*   ᶠ5 *Abram* means *exalted father.*   ᵍ5 *Abraham* means *father of many.*

What example for Christian households does Abraham set here?

♥ 1. If cutting off one's foreskin is no longer required of God's people, what is yet required (see Gal 5:6)? What does faith mean to you? 2. Circumcision then did not confer salvation any more than baptism does today, yet that truth is often missed in both Jewish and Christian circles. Why? 3. Try "strength-bombardment" in your group, in which you affirm the promise you see in each other. How is this exercise similar to what God did with Abraham? 4. Who is your "Ishmael"—the one you want to live under God's blessing?

☕ 1. When did you laugh the hardest last week? 2. What is your favorite brand of humor? What political cartoonist do you like? What comic gets you laughing?

📖 1. Hospitality of strangers was and still is obligatory and virtuous in the Near East. How does Abraham go overboard in showing hospitality to the three visitors (vv. 1–8)? 2. What is the point of the Lord's visit with Abraham? And the Lord's rebuke of Sarah? 3. Why does Sarah laugh? Lie? Disbelieve? How does Sarah's laughter (vv. 12–14) differ from Abraham's (17:17–22), or does it? Why then does God rebuke Sarah but not Abraham for "laughing"?

♥ 1. When in your life is laughter situational? Suppressed? Sadistic? Sarcastic? Sinful? Spiritual? 2. What do you find laughable in this story? Why? 3. Where in your life is God telling you, "It's never too late"? Or where is he saying, "It's okay to laugh"? Or, "No need to rush around"? Or, "Why don't you believe me?" What will you do about that this week?

and will surely give you a son by her. I will bless her so that she will be the mother of nations; kings of peoples will come from her."

[17]Abraham fell facedown; he laughed and said to himself, "Will a son be born to a man a hundred years old? Will Sarah bear a child at the age of ninety?" [18]And Abraham said to God, "If only Ishmael might live under your blessing!"

[19]Then God said, "Yes, but your wife Sarah will bear you a son, and you will call him Isaac.[a] I will establish my covenant with him as an everlasting covenant for his descendants after him. [20]And as for Ishmael, I have heard you: I will surely bless him; I will make him fruitful and will greatly increase his numbers. He will be the father of twelve rulers, and I will make him into a great nation. [21]But my covenant I will establish with Isaac, whom Sarah will bear to you by this time next year." [22]When he had finished speaking with Abraham, God went up from him.

[23]On that very day Abraham took his son Ishmael and all those born in his household or bought with his money, every male in his household, and circumcised them, as God told him. [24]Abraham was ninety-nine years old when he was circumcised, [25]and his son Ishmael was thirteen; [26]Abraham and his son Ishmael were both circumcised on that same day. [27]And every male in Abraham's household, including those born in his household or bought from a foreigner, was circumcised with him.

The Three Visitors

18 The Lord appeared to Abraham near the great trees of Mamre while he was sitting at the entrance to his tent in the heat of the day. [2]Abraham looked up and saw three men standing nearby. When he saw them, he hurried from the entrance of his tent to meet them and bowed low to the ground.

[3]He said, "If I have found favor in your eyes, my lord,[b] do not pass your servant by. [4]Let a little water be brought, and then you may all wash your feet and rest under this tree. [5]Let me get you something to eat, so you can be refreshed and then go on your way—now that you have come to your servant."

"Very well," they answered, "do as you say."

[6]So Abraham hurried into the tent to Sarah. "Quick," he said, "get three seahs[c] of fine flour and knead it and bake some bread."

[7]Then he ran to the herd and selected a choice, tender calf and gave it to a servant, who hurried to prepare it. [8]He then brought some curds and milk and the calf that had been prepared, and set these before them. While they ate, he stood near them under a tree.

[9]"Where is your wife Sarah?" they asked him.

"There, in the tent," he said.

[10]Then the Lord[d] said, "I will surely return to you about this time next year, and Sarah your wife will have a son."

Now Sarah was listening at the entrance to the tent, which was behind him. [11]Abraham and Sarah were already old and well advanced in years, and Sarah was past the age of childbearing. [12]So Sarah laughed to herself as she thought, "After I am worn out and my master[e] is old, will I now have this pleasure?"

[13]Then the Lord said to Abraham, "Why did Sarah laugh and say, 'Will I really have a child, now that I am old?' [14]Is anything too hard for the Lord? I will return to you at the appointed time next year and Sarah will have a son."

---

a 19 Isaac means he laughs.   *b 3 Or O Lord*   *c 6 That is, probably about 20 quarts (about 22 liters)*   *d 10 Hebrew Then he*   *e 12 Or husband*

[15]Sarah was afraid, so she lied and said, "I did not laugh." But he said, "Yes, you did laugh."

Abraham Pleads for Sodom

[16]When the men got up to leave, they looked down toward Sodom, and Abraham walked along with them to see them on their way. [17]Then the LORD said, "Shall I hide from Abraham what I am about to do? [18]Abraham will surely become a great and powerful nation, and all nations on earth will be blessed through him. [19]For I have chosen him, so that he will direct his children and his household after him to keep the way of the LORD by doing what is right and just, so that the LORD will bring about for Abraham what he has promised him."

[20]Then the LORD said, "The outcry against Sodom and Gomorrah is so great and their sin so grievous [21]that I will go down and see if what they have done is as bad as the outcry that has reached me. If not, I will know."

[22]The men turned away and went toward Sodom, but Abraham remained standing before the LORD.[a] [23]Then Abraham approached him and said: "Will you sweep away the righteous with the wicked? [24]What if there are fifty righteous people in the city? Will you really sweep it away and not spare[b] the place for the sake of the fifty righteous people in it? [25]Far be it from you to do such a thing—to kill the righteous with the wicked, treating the righteous and the wicked alike. Far be it from you! Will not the Judge[c] of all the earth do right?"

[26]The LORD said, "If I find fifty righteous people in the city of Sodom, I will spare the whole place for their sake."

[27]Then Abraham spoke up again: "Now that I have been so bold

a22 Masoretic Text; an ancient Hebrew scribal tradition but the LORD remained standing before Abraham   b24 Or forgive; also in verse 26   c25 Or Ruler

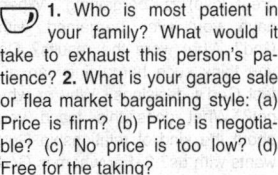

1. Who is most patient in your family? What would it take to exhaust this person's patience? 2. What is your garage sale or flea market bargaining style: (a) Price is firm? (b) Price is negotiable? (c) No price is too low? (d) Free for the taking?

1. What 3-step process in the covenant relationship do you find outlined in verse 19? 2. What "sneak preview" does God show Abraham (vv. 17,20–21)? Why let Abraham in on this? 3. What audacious response does Abraham then make (vv. 22–33)? Why is he daring with God? And so concerned about Sodom and Gomorrah? 4. Do you think Abraham influenced God one way or the other? Why or why not? 5. In Abraham's intercession, what do you admire enough to imitate? In God's successive replies to Abraham, what do you find comforting? Discomforting?

1. How has God shown his patience with you? Do you think that patience will ever run out? How is your answer supported from this passage? What does this say about how we should regard

---

| **Genesis 18:1–15** | **THE THREE VISITORS** |

This story happened soon after the story in Genesis 17—in which the Lord appeared to Abram and again confirmed his covenant with him. God stated that his promise of Abram and Sarai bearing a son was so certain that from that time on they were given new names, Abraham and Sarah.

1. Why did Abraham knock himself out to serve the three visitors?
   a. Eastern culture demanded it.
   b. He knew they were angels.
   c. He was a very hospitable person.
   d. He was looking for something in return.

2. When did Abraham realize the Lord was visiting him?
   a. immediately
   b. when the visitors asked about Sarah by name
   c. when the promise of a son was given
   d. when he was asked why Sarah was laughing to herself

3. If you were Sarah (childless and 89 years old), how would you have felt about what you heard?

4. How would you describe Sarah's laughter?
   a. situational—You had to be there.
   b. suppressed—She was trying to contain herself.
   c. sarcastic—"Yeah, and Abraham will run a marathon!"
   d. sinful—She displayed her lack of faith.
   e. spiritual—She was honest with her feelings.

5. What would it do you good to laugh about right now? What keeps you from doing so?

6. When you were a child, who served as an example of faith to you? What are you doing to pattern your life after that person?

7. What is the purpose of your faith?
   a. to fulfill my dreams
   b. to make me a stronger Christian
   c. to glorify God
   d. to encourage others
   e. to prepare me for eternity
   f. I'm really not sure.

8. Sarah seems to have given up on her desire to have a baby. Where in your life have you given up on your dream? If you're really honest, what seems "too hard for the Lord"?

9. What does this story about Sarah teach you? Where in your life may God be telling you it's never too late? Where might God be saying, "There's still something significant I want to do with your life."

10. What kind of stress does your changing age add to your life? How do you deal with the reality of aging?

our own impatience with others? **2.** One of the five stages in dealing with death and dying (or other great loss) is "bargaining." When have you ever bargained with God? What were the results? Do you think such bargaining can affect God's decisions? Why or why not? What does this teach you about the kind of relationship God wants with us? **3.** For whom is God calling you to intercede as Abraham did? **4.** If you could ask God one question, what would you ask? Why that one?

---

 1. Growing up, who was the disciplinarian in your family? How did that person typically discipline you? **2.** In your punishment, is it easier for you to take it, or to dish it out? Why?

 1. As Abraham did in 18:2–8, how does Lot show hospitality to these angelic visitors in 19:1–8? What might have happened if Lot had not taken them in? In turn, what might have happened

as to speak to the Lord, though I am nothing but dust and ashes, [28]what if the number of the righteous is five less than fifty? Will you destroy the whole city because of five people?"

"If I find forty-five there," he said, "I will not destroy it."

[29]Once again he spoke to him, "What if only forty are found there?"

He said, "For the sake of forty, I will not do it."

[30]Then he said, "May the Lord not be angry, but let me speak. What if only thirty can be found there?"

He answered, "I will not do it if I find thirty there."

[31]Abraham said, "Now that I have been so bold as to speak to the Lord, what if only twenty can be found there?"

He said, "For the sake of twenty, I will not destroy it."

[32]Then he said, "May the Lord not be angry, but let me speak just once more. What if only ten can be found there?"

He answered, "For the sake of ten, I will not destroy it."

[33]When the LORD had finished speaking with Abraham, he left, and Abraham returned home.

Sodom and Gomorrah Destroyed

19 The two angels arrived at Sodom in the evening, and Lot was sitting in the gateway of the city. When he saw them, he got up to meet them and bowed down with his face to the ground. [2]"My lords," he said, "please turn aside to your servant's house. You can wash your feet and spend the night and then go on your way early in the morning."

"No," they answered, "we will spend the night in the square."

[3]But he insisted so strongly that they did go with him and entered his house. He prepared a meal for them, baking bread without yeast, and they ate. [4]Before they had gone to bed, all the men

---

$ 🔷 *Genesis 18:16–33*   **ABRAHAM PLEADS FOR SODOM**

1. What impresses you most about Abraham in this story?
   a. his boldness
   b. his compassion
   c. his influence on God

2. What impresses you most about God in this story?
   a. his confiding in Abraham
   b. his judgment
   c. his mercy

3. What do you think Abraham's motives were? How much of his concern was for his nephew Lot and Lot's family, who lived in Sodom?

4. What did God's openness suggest?
   a. Abraham was getting through to the Lord.
   b. God is just.
   c. Holy people bring benefits to wicked people.
   d. The righteous are important to the Lord.

5. As I discuss my problems with God, I expect he will:

   a. listen patiently.
   b. become angry.
   c. grant my requests.
   d. ignore me.

6. I believe my presence in my community or family has the effect of:
   a. fruitful "salt and light."
   b. a dash of salt in the ocean.
   c. rubbing salt in a wound.

7. What gives me hope for my community and family is:
   a. not much.
   b. the influence of a few righteous people.
   c. God's mercy.
   d. God's all-knowing plan.

8. In order for salvation to come to my community, I am willing to:
   a. pray for it regularly.
   b. share my faith with others.
   c. get involved in the lives of those around me.
   d. contribute to the ministry of my church.

e. engage in community work.

9. In order for salvation to come to all my family, I am willing to:
   a. pray for them regularly.
   b. share my faith with them.
   c. rebuild bridges of trust.
   d. spend less time at church and more time with family.

10. **$** What example does Abraham provide for how to live in a sinful world? In what ways is the environment you live and work in evil? How does that add stress to your life and how do you deal with that stress?

11. **🔷** What does this story say to a spouse who is "spiritually single"? What does it reveal about God's love? About Abraham's love? What applications from this story can you make in your attitude and relationship with your mate?

from every part of the city of Sodom—both young and old—surrounded the house. 5They called to Lot, "Where are the men who came to you tonight? Bring them out to us so that we can have sex with them."

6Lot went outside to meet them and shut the door behind him 7and said, "No, my friends. Don't do this wicked thing. 8Look, I have two daughters who have never slept with a man. Let me bring them out to you, and you can do what you like with them. But don't do anything to these men, for they have come under the protection of my roof."

9"Get out of our way," they replied. And they said, "This fellow came here as an alien, and now he wants to play the judge! We'll treat you worse than them." They kept bringing pressure on Lot and moved forward to break down the door.

10But the men inside reached out and pulled Lot back into the house and shut the door. 11Then they struck the men who were at the door of the house, young and old, with blindness so that they could not find the door.

12The two men said to Lot, "Do you have anyone else here—sons-in-law, sons or daughters, or anyone else in the city who belongs to you? Get them out of here, 13because we are going to destroy this place. The outcry to the LORD against its people is so great that he has sent us to destroy it."

14So Lot went out and spoke to his sons-in-law, who were pledged to marry*a* his daughters. He said, "Hurry and get out of this place, because the LORD is about to destroy the city!" But his sons-in-law thought he was joking.

15With the coming of dawn, the angels urged Lot, saying, "Hurry! Take your wife and your two daughters who are here, or you will be swept away when the city is punished."

16When he hesitated, the men grasped his hand and the hands of his wife and of his two daughters and led them safely out of the city, for the LORD was merciful to them. 17As soon as they had brought them out, one of them said, "Flee for your lives! Don't look back, and don't stop anywhere in the plain! Flee to the mountains or you will be swept away!"

18But Lot said to them, "No, my lords,*b* please! 19Your*c* servant has found favor in your*c* eyes, and you*c* have shown great kindness to me in sparing my life. But I can't flee to the mountains; this disaster will overtake me, and I'll die. 20Look, here is a town near enough to run to, and it is small. Let me flee to it—it is very small, isn't it? Then my life will be spared."

21He said to him, "Very well, I will grant this request too; I will not overthrow the town you speak of. 22But flee there quickly, because I cannot do anything until you reach it." (That is why the town was called Zoar.*d*)

23By the time Lot reached Zoar, the sun had risen over the land. 24Then the LORD rained down burning sulfur on Sodom and Gomorrah—from the LORD out of the heavens. 25Thus he overthrew those cities and the entire plain, including all those living in the cities—and also the vegetation in the land. 26But Lot's wife looked back, and she became a pillar of salt.

27Early the next morning Abraham got up and returned to the place where he had stood before the LORD. 28He looked down toward Sodom and Gomorrah, toward all the land of the plain, and he saw dense smoke rising from the land, like smoke from a furnace.

to Lot had it not been for the intervention of the angelic visitors (vv. 9–11)? **2.** Lot's choice of Sodom is unfortunate, yet he is called a "righteous man" (see 2Pe 2:7). Why is that? (a) Because he was living at odds with this lawless environment (v. 9)? (b) Because he was "sitting in the gateway" (v. 1) as part of Sodom's ruling council? (c) Because he had an "alien" reputation (v. 9)? **3.** How do you explain Lot's decision to offer his own daughters to the mob of men outside his door? Was that a righteous decision? **4.** Why does Lot hesitate to leave this condemned world of Sodom (v. 16)? Is Lot disbelieving? Steeped in sin? Too high up in society? Or compassionately concerned about those who will perish? **5.** From verses 1–11, Ezekiel 16:49ff and Matthew 10:11–16, what reasons warrant the total destruction of Sodom and Gomorrah? What warrants the deliverance of three of its pitiful residents, that is, Lot and his daughters (v. 29)? **6.** In God's dealings with Abraham, Lot and Sodom (18:16–19:29), what do you learn about God's character and purposes? About judgment and mercy for wayward people? **7.** Abraham's plea was redemptive at least for three people (v. 29), whereas Lot's plea was rejected by his sons-in-law (v. 14) and wife (v. 26). Why was Abraham able to exercise more influence than Lot on those people they loved?

1. In reviewing your response to crises during the past year, at what points can you identify with: Abraham, waiting? Lot, hesitant? Angels, rescuing? Sons-in-law, joking? Lot's wife, trapped? **2.** How does your society compare with Sodom? What do you think has prevented total destruction of your society? **3.** When have you "looked back" to the destructive life you were living, even as you were trying to follow the Lord? Sodom and the other cities on the plain had adopted a "corporate immorality." Though we tend to think of morality as a personal matter, have you ever been a part of an organization or group that had noticeably moral or immoral traits? Explain. **4.** What examples does Lot give you to follow, and to avoid, in trying to lead a godly life in a sinful society?

*a*14 Or *were married to*   *b*18 Or *No, Lord*; or *No, my lord*   *c*19 The Hebrew is singular.   *d*22 *Zoar means small.*

1. When have you feared for your safety? 2. As a place to run away, where would you go: Beach? Mountains? A big city? Why?

1. How do you reconcile Lot's description as "a righteous man" with the events of this story? 2. From this story, how would you describe Lot? Lot's daughters? Lot's grandchildren?

1. What bothers you most about this story: The drinking? The deception? The incest? Why? 2. Sexual dysfunction and alcohol abuse have damaged many families. The older daughter gave a justification for this behavior (v. 32.) What justifications have you heard for family problems? Do you accept those justifications? 3. What about Lot's story, or your own, moves you to pray?

1. When have you repeated the same mistake twice? 2. Try a *What's My Line?* game, making three statements about yourself: Two are truthful and one's a well-disguised "line." Have the group guess which was the false line or half-truth. The object is to fool everyone with the best line.

Look for reasons why this story was inserted into the Genesis narrative at this point. 1. Was it for suspense? Will Abraham succeed in jeopardizing God's promise, after all? 2. Was it for irony? Who fears God more — Abraham or Abimelech? After rescuing Lot from his folly, who now needs to be rescued? 3. Was it for anti-climax? After such spiritual exertion for Sodom, isn't it only human for Abraham to relapse? 4. Was it a case of deja vu? When have we seen Abraham commit this same mistake before? 5. Why doesn't God scrap "Plan A" (for Abraham) and go with "Plan B" (a more faithful father)? 6. Instead, how does God remain faithful to his covenant? To Abraham? Sarah? Abimelech? 7. Who is the hero of this story? Why?

1. How can you identify with Abraham in this story: His all-too-human relapse? His repeated

[29]So when God destroyed the cities of the plain, he remembered Abraham, and he brought Lot out of the catastrophe that overthrew the cities where Lot had lived.

Lot and His Daughters

[30]Lot and his two daughters left Zoar and settled in the mountains, for he was afraid to stay in Zoar. He and his two daughters lived in a cave. [31]One day the older daughter said to the younger, "Our father is old, and there is no man around here to lie with us, as is the custom all over the earth. [32]Let's get our father to drink wine and then lie with him and preserve our family line through our father."

[33]That night they got their father to drink wine, and the older daughter went in and lay with him. He was not aware of it when she lay down or when she got up.

[34]The next day the older daughter said to the younger, "Last night I lay with my father. Let's get him to drink wine again tonight, and you go in and lie with him so we can preserve our family line through our father." [35]So they got their father to drink wine that night also, and the younger daughter went and lay with him. Again he was not aware of it when she lay down or when she got up.

[36]So both of Lot's daughters became pregnant by their father. [37]The older daughter had a son, and she named him Moab[a]; he is the father of the Moabites of today. [38]The younger daughter also had a son, and she named him Ben-Ammi[b]; he is the father of the Ammonites of today.

Abraham and Abimelech

20 Now Abraham moved on from there into the region of the Negev and lived between Kadesh and Shur. For a while he stayed in Gerar, [2]and there Abraham said of his wife Sarah, "She is my sister." Then Abimelech king of Gerar sent for Sarah and took her.

[3]But God came to Abimelech in a dream one night and said to him, "You are as good as dead because of the woman you have taken; she is a married woman."

[4]Now Abimelech had not gone near her, so he said, "Lord, will you destroy an innocent nation? [5]Did he not say to me, 'She is my sister,' and didn't she also say, 'He is my brother'? I have done this with a clear conscience and clean hands."

[6]Then God said to him in the dream, "Yes, I know you did this with a clear conscience, and so I have kept you from sinning against me. That is why I did not let you touch her. [7]Now return the man's wife, for he is a prophet, and he will pray for you and you will live. But if you do not return her, you may be sure that you and all yours will die."

[8]Early the next morning Abimelech summoned all his officials, and when he told them all that had happened, they were very much afraid. [9]Then Abimelech called Abraham in and said, "What have you done to us? How have I wronged you that you have brought such great guilt upon me and my kingdom? You have done things to me that should not be done." [10]And Abimelech asked Abraham, "What was your reason for doing this?"

[11]Abraham replied, "I said to myself, 'There is surely no fear of God in this place, and they will kill me because of my wife.' [12]Besides, she really is my sister, the daughter of my father though

---

[a]37 *Moab* sounds like the Hebrew for *from father.*   [b]38 *Ben-Ammi* means *son of my people.*

not of my mother; and she became my wife. ¹³And when God had me wander from my father's household, I said to her, 'This is how you can show your love to me: Everywhere we go, say of me, "He is my brother." ' "

¹⁴Then Abimelech brought sheep and cattle and male and female slaves and gave them to Abraham, and he returned Sarah his wife to him. ¹⁵And Abimelech said, "My land is before you; live wherever you like."

¹⁶To Sarah he said, "I am giving your brother a thousand shekelsᵃ of silver. This is to cover the offense against you before all who are with you; you are completely vindicated."

¹⁷Then Abraham prayed to God, and God healed Abimelech, his wife and his slave girls so they could have children again, ¹⁸for the LORD had closed up every womb in Abimelech's household because of Abraham's wife Sarah.

The Birth of Isaac

21 Now the LORD was gracious to Sarah as he had said, and the LORD did for Sarah what he had promised. ²Sarah became pregnant and bore a son to Abraham in his old age, at the very time God had promised him. ³Abraham gave the name Isaacᵇ to the son Sarah bore him. ⁴When his son Isaac was eight days old, Abraham circumcised him, as God commanded him. ⁵Abraham was a hundred years old when his son Isaac was born to him.

⁶Sarah said, "God has brought me laughter, and everyone who hears about this will laugh with me." ⁷And she added, "Who would have said to Abraham that Sarah would nurse children? Yet I have borne him a son in his old age."

Hagar and Ishmael Sent Away

⁸The child grew and was weaned, and on the day Isaac was weaned Abraham held a great feast. ⁹But Sarah saw that the son whom Hagar the Egyptian had borne to Abraham was mocking, ¹⁰and she said to Abraham, "Get rid of that slave woman and her son, for that slave woman's son will never share in the inheritance with my son Isaac."

¹¹The matter distressed Abraham greatly because it concerned his son. ¹²But God said to him, "Do not be so distressed about the boy and your maidservant. Listen to whatever Sarah tells you, because it is through Isaac that your offspringᶜ will be reckoned. ¹³I will make the son of the maidservant into a nation also, because he is your offspring."

¹⁴Early the next morning Abraham took some food and a skin of water and gave them to Hagar. He set them on her shoulders and then sent her off with the boy. She went on her way and wandered in the desert of Beersheba.

¹⁵When the water in the skin was gone, she put the boy under one of the bushes. ¹⁶Then she went off and sat down nearby, about a bowshot away, for she thought, "I cannot watch the boy die." And as she sat there nearby, sheᵈ began to sob.

¹⁷God heard the boy crying, and the angel of God called to Hagar from heaven and said to her, "What is the matter, Hagar? Do not be afraid; God has heard the boy crying as he lies there. ¹⁸Lift the boy up and take him by the hand, for I will make him into a great nation."

¹⁹Then God opened her eyes and she saw a well of water. So she went and filled the skin with water and gave the boy a drink.

fib? His unwitting test of God's promise? The irony of the rescuer now needing to be rescued? **2.** Who in your life is, or has been, an "Abimelech"—one who bravely sets you straight? Where might God be calling you to be an Abimelech? When have you, made a judgment about someone or a group of people (v. 11) only to be embarrassed later?

What does your name mean? Does it fit you?

1. What does this story reveal about God's faithfulness? Abraham's obedience (see 17:12,19)? Sarah's joyful serendipity? **2.** How might Hagar and Ishmael be feeling just now? **3.** Who gets the last laugh in this serendipitous story?

What personal dream would you like to see fulfilled in your lifetime?

When forced to do what you do not want to do—like saying good-bye or breaking up with someone—what motivates you to do it anyway?

1. From Sarah's perspective, why must Hagar and Ishmael be sent away? Likewise, from God's perspective? **2.** How is Abraham's distress due to past mistakes? Two wives? Two sons? **3.** According to Paul, what truth about God's covenant is illustrated by Sarah and Hagar, Isaac and Ishmael (see Gal 4:21–31; Ro 9:6–9)? **4.** While outside of God's covenant promise, what does Hagar receive instead (vv. 13–21)? Why? What does this reveal about God? **5.** In choosing Isaac and rejecting Ishmael, is God cruel? Arbitrary? Gracious? Sovereign? Merciful?

1. Who, like Sarah or Hagar, is one with whom you don't get along? How are you handling the discord? What can you do to change the situation? **2.** Like Hagar, where do you need God's comforting?

ᵃ16 That is, about 25 pounds (about 11.5 kilograms)   ᵇ3 *Isaac* means *he laughs.*
ᶜ12 Or *seed*   ᵈ16 Hebrew; Septuagint *the child*

²⁰God was with the boy as he grew up. He lived in the desert and became an archer. ²¹While he was living in the Desert of Paran, his mother got a wife for him from Egypt.

The Treaty at Beersheba

²²At that time Abimelech and Phicol the commander of his forces said to Abraham, "God is with you in everything you do. ²³Now swear to me here before God that you will not deal falsely with me or my children or my descendants. Show to me and the country where you are living as an alien the same kindness I have shown to you."

²⁴Abraham said, "I swear it."

²⁵Then Abraham complained to Abimelech about a well of water that Abimelech's servants had seized. ²⁶But Abimelech said, "I don't know who has done this. You did not tell me, and I heard about it only today."

²⁷So Abraham brought sheep and cattle and gave them to Abimelech, and the two men made a treaty. ²⁸Abraham set apart seven ewe lambs from the flock, ²⁹and Abimelech asked Abraham, "What is the meaning of these seven ewe lambs you have set apart by themselves?"

³⁰He replied, "Accept these seven lambs from my hand as a witness that I dug this well."

³¹So that place was called Beersheba,^a because the two men swore an oath there.

³²After the treaty had been made at Beersheba, Abimelech and

^a31 *Beersheba* can mean *well of seven* or *well of the oath.*

1. What frequent complaint do you have with government agencies, corporations or other authorities? 2. Have you ever planted a tree as a memorial? Explain.

1. Why would Abimelech ask Abraham not to deal falsely with him? Is he justified in these concerns (see ch. 20)? 2. What claim is Abraham staking in this story? Why would a semi-nomad like Abraham want to establish legal ownership of property? How does that relate to God's promise (13:14–17)? 3. How is the Abraham-Abimelech treaty confirmed? With what lasting result?

1. What trust relationships are you in now which are patterned after the divine-human covenant? 2. Have you made any agreements or promises that you have not kept? How can you fulfill your end?

Genesis 21:1–21 ISAAC'S BIRTH; HAGAR'S EXPULSION

1. What long-awaited event brought you the most joy?
   a. the birth of a child
   b. a wedding
   c. graduation from school
   d. a new job or promotion
   e. other:_____

2. What blessing can you thank God for right now?

3. How did Sarah seem to feel about giving birth at age 90? How do you think Hagar and Ishmael felt about Isaac's arrival?

4. If you were Hagar, how would you have felt when you heard what Sarah had planned for you?
   a. Where will my son and I find food and shelter?
   b. Who will become our family and friends now?
   c. What will happen to my child?
   d. What have I done to deserve being treated like this?
   e. Should I plead with Abraham to be fair?
   f. I'll be glad to get away from here.

5. God intervened by providing for Hagar and Ishmael's immediate need. What lesson could Hagar learn from this?
   a. When the going gets tough, the tough get going.
   b. The best things in life are free.
   c. There's always a light at the end of the tunnel.
   d. God knows what we need before we ask.
   e. The Lord is faithful to keep his promises.
   f. With God all things are possible.

6. Comparing yourself to Hagar, what are your feelings about God?
   a. I feel bitter toward God because people like Abraham and Sarah have really let me down.
   b. I feel like God has forgotten about me and I'm out in the desert on my own.
   c. I'm hurting right now, but I do believe God hears me.
   d. God gives me what I need when I need it. I'm learning to trust.
   e. God has provided for me, but I'm still concerned about the future.

7. What family relationship causes you the most stress? Why? How do you handle the pressure?

8. As a single person, how can you relate to Hagar? How do you need God's provision or support?

9. How much conflict do you suppose Abraham and Sarah's marriage experienced because of Hagar and Ishmael? What part did God play in resolving that conflict? How does (or could) God and your faith help you deal with conflict in your marriage?

10. As a parent, in what way can you identify with Sarah? With Abraham? With Hagar? What would you like God to say or do for you in your parenting role?

11. What effect has your divorce had on your child(ren)? What can you do to help them not feel like Ishmael—rejected and dejected?

Phicol the commander of his forces returned to the land of the Philistines. ³³Abraham planted a tamarisk tree in Beersheba, and there he called upon the name of the LORD, the Eternal God. ³⁴And Abraham stayed in the land of the Philistines for a long time.

Abraham Tested

22 Some time later God tested Abraham. He said to him, "Abraham!"

"Here I am," he replied.

²Then God said, "Take your son, your only son, Isaac, whom you love, and go to the region of Moriah. Sacrifice him there as a burnt offering on one of the mountains I will tell you about."

³Early the next morning Abraham got up and saddled his donkey. He took with him two of his servants and his son Isaac. When he had cut enough wood for the burnt offering, he set out for the place God had told him about. ⁴On the third day Abraham looked up and saw the place in the distance. ⁵He said to his servants, "Stay here with the donkey while I and the boy go over there. We will worship and then we will come back to you."

⁶Abraham took the wood for the burnt offering and placed it on his son Isaac, and he himself carried the fire and the knife. As the two of them went on together, ⁷Isaac spoke up and said to his father Abraham, "Father?"

"Yes, my son?" Abraham replied.

"The fire and wood are here," Isaac said, "but where is the lamb for the burnt offering?"

⁸Abraham answered, "God himself will provide the lamb for the burnt offering, my son." And the two of them went on together.

⁹When they reached the place God had told him about, Abraham

---

1. At what age do you find children the most adorable? The most exasperating? **2.** What possession would be the hardest for you to give up?

1. In verse 2, what is God emphasizing as he describes Abraham's relationship with Isaac? Why this way of breaking the news? **2.** Knowing God waited 25 years before providing a son for Abraham, how would you expect Abraham to react to God's instructions in verse 2? Why doesn't Abraham object? What do you learn about Abraham based on his prompt, obedient actions (vv. 3–10)? **3.** Do you think Abraham would actually have killed Isaac (vv. 5,8–10)? Why (see Heb 11:17–19)? Why does God wait until the last second to stop Abraham? **4.** For whose benefit does God see how far Abraham will go: His own? Abraham's? Isaac's? Or the readers'? Why do you think so (vv. 11–18)? **5.** Since God already

---

   *Genesis 22:1–19*   **ABRAHAM TESTED**

After years of waiting, Abraham (age 100) and Sarah (age 90) finally had the son God had promised. In this story, God gives Abraham an amazing assignment.

1. Why did Abraham take Isaac to the altar?
   a. He was afraid of God.
   b. He was committed to unquestioning obedience.
   c. He knew it was only a test.
   d. He believed God would raise Isaac from the dead.

2. What did God want from Abraham?
   a. a sacrifice
   b. absolute obedience
   c. to be loved above all else
   d. an example of the sacrificial love that God would demonstrate ultimately at the cross

3. What do you think Isaac felt as he walked with his father?
   a. youthful delight
   b. suspicion
   c. childlike trust
   d. confusion

4. What did Isaac learn from this?
   a. never go with Dad to offer a sacrifice
   b. to be as committed as his father
   c. that God is a jealous God
   d. that Abraham's relationship with God came first

5. What really bothers me about this story is:
   a. how God could put Abraham through such an ordeal.
   b. how God could put Isaac through such an ordeal.
   c. that God would instruct Abraham to kill someone.
   d. that Abraham would actually do what God said.

6. What is the most difficult thing God has ever asked you to do? What is the most difficult thing God is asking you to do right now?

7. What promise does God hold for you if you obey him?
   a. happiness   d. his presence
   b. a godly family   e. eternal life
   c. success

8.  How is Abraham an example of a "man of God"? What area of your life are you holding back from committing totally to the Lord?

9. If I followed Abraham's example in my marriage, I would:
   a. head to the kitchen for a butcher knife!
   b. obey God, no matter what my spouse thinks.
   c. give my spouse more "space."
   d. commit my spouse to God in prayer.

10. If I followed Abraham's example in my life as a parent, I would:
    a. enforce God's standards, even if my child(ren) get angry.
    b. give my child(ren) more "space."
    c. commit my child(ren) to God in prayer.
    d. provide my child(ren) a model of Christian faithfulness.

made his covenant with Abraham, why did he test him and then offer the same covenant again (vv. 15–19)? **6.** What do you see in this news of Nahor's 12 sons? Why is Rebekah's birth noted in this passage (see ch. 24)?

♡ **1.** Some "how-far-will-you-go" tests provide critical turning points in many areas: (a) Graduation from high school or college; (b) Learning to trust our parents, our children, our partner. How have you fared in these two areas, (a) and (b)? **2.** Where do you sense God is testing you now? How are you doing with the test? What are you learning from it? **3.** If the Lord should ask you to give up something or someone special, do you believe he will provide a replacement—beforehand, or afterwards? When have you obeyed and found new reassurance? **4.** Where has God demonstrated his willingness to do as he is asking Abraham to do here? In case of God's sacrificing his own son, how far did he go? Who was there to stop him or provide a substitute? **5.** How is Jesus like Isaac? How is he like the lamb substitute? **6.** How do the examples of Isaac and Jesus apply to your current circumstances and faith? Where do you get the strength to say "Yes" to God when everything else inside of you says "No"?

⎯⎯⎯⎯⎯⎯⎯⎯⎯⎯

☕ What big wheeler-dealer have you been warned about in town? Are you afraid you might not get the better of the deal? Or would you bargain anyway?

📖 **1.** This chapter reflects many Hittite laws and customs, plus one wheeler-dealer who seems generous but also enjoys a hefty price. What is the point of all these details about purchasing a family burial site? **2.** Why might Abraham not want to bury Sarah in one of their tombs? Likewise, why doesn't Abraham bury Sarah where their ancestors live (Mesopotamia), as was the custom in his day? **3.** Why might this property be an important part of God's plan for Abraham (see 25:7–11)? What relationship do you see between this purchased land and the promised land (see 22:15–18)? If this promise had not been made, would landless Abraham have bought this

built an altar there and arranged the wood on it. He bound his son Isaac and laid him on the altar, on top of the wood. ¹⁰Then he reached out his hand and took the knife to slay his son. ¹¹But the angel of the LORD called out to him from heaven, "Abraham! Abraham!"

"Here I am," he replied.

¹²"Do not lay a hand on the boy," he said. "Do not do anything to him. Now I know that you fear God, because you have not withheld from me your son, your only son."

¹³Abraham looked up and there in a thicket he saw a ram[a] caught by its horns. He went over and took the ram and sacrificed it as a burnt offering instead of his son. ¹⁴So Abraham called that place The LORD Will Provide. And to this day it is said, "On the mountain of the LORD it will be provided."

¹⁵The angel of the LORD called to Abraham from heaven a second time ¹⁶and said, "I swear by myself, declares the LORD, that because you have done this and have not withheld your son, your only son, ¹⁷I will surely bless you and make your descendants as numerous as the stars in the sky and as the sand on the seashore. Your descendants will take possession of the cities of their enemies, ¹⁸and through your offspring[b] all nations on earth will be blessed, because you have obeyed me."

¹⁹Then Abraham returned to his servants, and they set off together for Beersheba. And Abraham stayed in Beersheba.

Nahor's Sons

²⁰Some time later Abraham was told, "Milcah is also a mother; she has borne sons to your brother Nahor: ²¹Uz the firstborn, Buz his brother, Kemuel (the father of Aram), ²²Kesed, Hazo, Pildash, Jidlaph and Bethuel." ²³Bethuel became the father of Rebekah. Milcah bore these eight sons to Abraham's brother Nahor. ²⁴His concubine, whose name was Reumah, also had sons: Tebah, Gaham, Tahash and Maacah.

The Death of Sarah

23 Sarah lived to be a hundred and twenty-seven years old. ²She died at Kiriath Arba (that is, Hebron) in the land of Canaan, and Abraham went to mourn for Sarah and to weep over her.

³Then Abraham rose from beside his dead wife and spoke to the Hittites.[c] He said, ⁴"I am an alien and a stranger among you. Sell me some property for a burial site here so I can bury my dead."

⁵The Hittites replied to Abraham, ⁶"Sir, listen to us. You are a mighty prince among us. Bury your dead in the choicest of our tombs. None of us will refuse you his tomb for burying your dead."

⁷Then Abraham rose and bowed down before the people of the land, the Hittites. ⁸He said to them, "If you are willing to let me bury my dead, then listen to me and intercede with Ephron son of Zohar on my behalf ⁹so he will sell me the cave of Machpelah, which belongs to him and is at the end of his field. Ask him to sell it to me for the full price as a burial site among you."

¹⁰Ephron the Hittite was sitting among his people and he replied to Abraham in the hearing of all the Hittites who had come to the gate of his city. ¹¹"No, my lord," he said. "Listen to me; I give[d]

a13 Many manuscripts of the Masoretic Text, Samaritan Pentateuch, Septuagint and Syriac; most manuscripts of the Masoretic Text *a ram behind ⌊him⌋*   b18 Or *seed*
c3 Or *the sons of Heth*; also in verses 5, 7, 10, 16, 18 and 20   d11 Or *sell*

you the field, and I give[a] you the cave that is in it. I give[a] it to you in the presence of my people. Bury your dead."

¹²Again Abraham bowed down before the people of the land ¹³and he said to Ephron in their hearing, "Listen to me, if you will. I will pay the price of the field. Accept it from me so I can bury my dead there."

¹⁴Ephron answered Abraham, ¹⁵"Listen to me, my lord; the land is worth four hundred shekels[b] of silver, but what is that between me and you? Bury your dead."

¹⁶Abraham agreed to Ephron's terms and weighed out for him the price he had named in the hearing of the Hittites: four hundred shekels of silver, according to the weight current among the merchants.

¹⁷So Ephron's field in Machpelah near Mamre—both the field and the cave in it, and all the trees within the borders of the field—was deeded ¹⁸to Abraham as his property in the presence of all the Hittites who had come to the gate of the city. ¹⁹Afterward Abraham buried his wife Sarah in the cave in the field of Machpelah near Mamre (which is at Hebron) in the land of Canaan. ²⁰So the field and the cave in it were deeded to Abraham by the Hittites as a burial site.

Isaac and Rebekah

24 Abraham was now old and well advanced in years, and the LORD had blessed him in every way. ²He said to the chief[c] servant in his household, the one in charge of all that he had, "Put your hand under my thigh. ³I want you to swear by the LORD, the God of heaven and the God of earth, that you will not get a wife for my son from the daughters of the Canaanites, among whom I am living, ⁴but will go to my country and my own relatives and get a wife for my son Isaac."

⁵The servant asked him, "What if the woman is unwilling to come back with me to this land? Shall I then take your son back to the country you came from?"

⁶"Make sure that you do not take my son back there," Abraham said. ⁷"The LORD, the God of heaven, who brought me out of my father's household and my native land and who spoke to me and promised me on oath, saying, 'To your offspring[d] I will give this land'—he will send his angel before you so that you can get a wife for my son from there. ⁸If the woman is unwilling to come back with you, then you will be released from this oath of mine. Only do not take my son back there." ⁹So the servant put his hand under the thigh of his master Abraham and swore an oath to him concerning this matter.

¹⁰Then the servant took ten of his master's camels and left, taking with him all kinds of good things from his master. He set out for Aram Naharaim[e] and made his way to the town of Nahor. ¹¹He had the camels kneel down near the well outside the town; it was toward evening, the time the women go out to draw water.

¹²Then he prayed, "O LORD, God of my master Abraham, give me success today, and show kindness to my master Abraham. ¹³See, I am standing beside this spring, and the daughters of the townspeople are coming out to draw water. ¹⁴May it be that when I say to a girl, 'Please let down your jar that I may have a drink,' and she says, 'Drink, and I'll water your camels too'—let her be the one you have chosen for your servant Isaac. By this I will know that you have shown kindness to my master."

property? Why or why not? **4.** Why is he willing to bury his wife in Canaan but does not allow his son to find a wife there (24:3)? What does this say about Abraham's belief in the promises of land and descendants?

1. How might Sarah have been eulogized at her funeral? **2.** What arrangements have you made for your funeral? If you haven't made any, how come? **3.** What can you learn from Abraham about a husband's love for his wife?

---

1. In high school, what hangout did you frequent in your hometown to meet people of the opposite sex? **2.** What memories do you have of going on a blind date? **3.** If you were to choose a spouse for your son or daughter, what kind would you choose?

1. What problems would be created if Isaac married a Canaanite? How would marrying a relative avoid these problems? How does this demonstrate what is important to Abraham? **2.** What do you make of the role each plays in the fulfillment of Abraham's wish (and God's plan): (a) The chief steward? (b) Rebekah? (c) Laban and Bethuel? **3.** What do you find most compelling about the steward: His earnest piety? Transparent faith? Practical methods? Devotion to his master? Firm resolve? **4.** About Rebekah, what do you like most: Her physical qualities? Servant heart? Willing spirit? Veiled modesty? **5.** About Laban and Bethuel, what attracts you: Their generous hospitality? Spiritual insight? Formal consent? Parental apron strings? Conventional blessing? What is the significance of Isaac bringing Rebekah "into the tent of his mother Sarah"? **6.** How is God's hand evident in this episode, such that all could rightly conclude, "This is from the Lord" (v. 50)? Why does God go to such lengths to provide a wife for Isaac? **7.** Incidental details aside, what do you see as the central issue of this chapter? How does this story make God's point?

---

a11 Or *sell*   b15 That is, about 10 pounds (about 4.5 kilograms)   c2 Or *oldest*
d7 Or *seed*   e10 That is, Northwest Mesopotamia

♡ **1.** Do you suppose that such divine match-making is a precedent we can all rely upon? How applicable do you think the servant's method for finding a wife is for believers today? When, for example, have you prayed a similar prayer asking God for a particular sign? How appropriate is this way of praying? Like the servant, what specific prayer would you like to see answered in the near future? **2.** To what extent is God involved in your mate selection: (a) He has just one person in mind for me? (b) He has a certain "type" in mind for me? (c) He guides me in letting me choose for myself? (d) Anyone is fine with God, as long as he or she is not an unbeliever? (e) He doesn't care who I marry, just the quality of that marriage? **3.** Who consistently goes the extra mile and "waters your camels" for you? This week, how can you be that kind for others, especially your mate? **4.** Likewise, how can you be like the chief steward here and bring honor to your God by being a faithful employee? **5.** If the central issue in this story is an all-knowing, all-powerful, all-loving God working in and through the lives of his covenant people, how does this affect your faith in that God? How is God

¹⁵Before he had finished praying, Rebekah came out with her jar on her shoulder. She was the daughter of Bethuel son of Milcah, who was the wife of Abraham's brother Nahor. ¹⁶The girl was very beautiful, a virgin; no man had ever lain with her. She went down to the spring, filled her jar and came up again.

¹⁷The servant hurried to meet her and said, "Please give me a little water from your jar."

¹⁸"Drink, my lord," she said, and quickly lowered the jar to her hands and gave him a drink.

¹⁹After she had given him a drink, she said, "I'll draw water for your camels too, until they have finished drinking." ²⁰So she quickly emptied her jar into the trough, ran back to the well to draw more water, and drew enough for all his camels. ²¹Without saying a word, the man watched her closely to learn whether or not the LORD had made his journey successful.

²²When the camels had finished drinking, the man took out a gold nose ring weighing a beka[a] and two gold bracelets weighing ten shekels.[b] ²³Then he asked, "Whose daughter are you? Please tell me, is there room in your father's house for us to spend the night?"

²⁴She answered him, "I am the daughter of Bethuel, the son that Milcah bore to Nahor." ²⁵And she added, "We have plenty of straw and fodder, as well as room for you to spend the night."

²⁶Then the man bowed down and worshiped the LORD, ²⁷saying, "Praise be to the LORD, the God of my master Abraham, who has not abandoned his kindness and faithfulness to my master. As for

[a]22 That is, about 1/5 ounce (about 5.5 grams)   [b]22 That is, about 4 ounces (about 110 grams)

Genesis 24:1–29, 50–66   **ISAAC AND REBEKAH**

God had promised that—through his son Isaac—Abraham would become the "father of many nations." Now after Sarah's death, Abraham takes initiative to find Isaac a wife.

1. What title would you give this story?
   a. "Mission Impossible"
   b. "Matchmaker, Matchmaker, Make Me a Match"
   c. "Father Knows Best"
   d. "Love at First Sight"

2. Abraham wanted Isaac to marry one of his own kind because he:
   a. was prejudiced.
   b. liked to be in control.
   c. desired to be the father of an ethnically pure nation.
   d. was determined that Isaac marry a "believer."

3. Why did Abraham object to Isaac going to "the old country" himself?

4. Why did the servant plead to leave as soon as Rebekah's family gave their consent?

a. He was on a roll and didn't want to push his luck.
b. He was afraid Rebekah's family would change their minds.
c. He was afraid Rebekah might refuse to go.
d. He knew Abraham and Isaac were anxiously waiting.

5. What impresses you about the end of the story?
   a. Rebekah's modesty
   b. the dramatic first meeting
   c. the way Isaac and Rebekah both got swept off their feet
   d. the instant success of an arranged marriage

6. What made Abraham's plan successful?
   a. the servant's tenacious faith
   b. some very fortunate timing
   c. God's sovereign control
   d. the gifts that assured Rebekah's family she'd be well off
   e. Rebekah's cooperation
   f. Isaac's acceptance of the plan

7. When have you asked for a sign like the servant did? How valid is it to ask for God's guidance in that way? If you could ask God for one thing, what would it be?

8. ▮ What has been the most frustrating place for you to seek out dating relationships? What does this story say to you about where you should "look"?

9. ▮ How important has dating someone with a similar faith been to you? How have you sensed God's involvement in your dating decisions?

10. ⚭ What was the beginning of your relationship like? How was it like this story?

11. ⚭ What are the best memories of your relationship? What have been some of your hardest times?

me, the LORD has led me on the journey to the house of my master's relatives."

²⁸The girl ran and told her mother's household about these things. ²⁹Now Rebekah had a brother named Laban, and he hurried out to the man at the spring. ³⁰As soon as he had seen the nose ring, and the bracelets on his sister's arms, and had heard Rebekah tell what the man said to her, he went out to the man and found him standing by the camels near the spring. ³¹"Come, you who are blessed by the LORD," he said. "Why are you standing out here? I have prepared the house and a place for the camels."

³²So the man went to the house, and the camels were unloaded. Straw and fodder were brought for the camels, and water for him and his men to wash their feet. ³³Then food was set before him, but he said, "I will not eat until I have told you what I have to say."

"Then tell us," ⌊Laban⌋ said.

³⁴So he said, "I am Abraham's servant. ³⁵The LORD has blessed my master abundantly, and he has become wealthy. He has given him sheep and cattle, silver and gold, menservants and maidservants, and camels and donkeys. ³⁶My master's wife Sarah has borne him a son in herᵃ old age, and he has given him everything he owns. ³⁷And my master made me swear an oath, and said, 'You must not get a wife for my son from the daughters of the Canaanites, in whose land I live, ³⁸but go to my father's family and to my own clan, and get a wife for my son.'

³⁹"Then I asked my master, 'What if the woman will not come back with me?'

⁴⁰"He replied, 'The LORD, before whom I have walked, will send his angel with you and make your journey a success, so that you can get a wife for my son from my own clan and from my father's family. ⁴¹Then, when you go to my clan, you will be released from my oath even if they refuse to give her to you—you will be released from my oath.'

⁴²"When I came to the spring today, I said, 'O LORD, God of my master Abraham, if you will, please grant success to the journey on which I have come. ⁴³See, I am standing beside this spring; if a maiden comes out to draw water and I say to her, "Please let me drink a little water from your jar," ⁴⁴and if she says to me, "Drink, and I'll draw water for your camels too," let her be the one the LORD has chosen for my master's son.'

⁴⁵"Before I finished praying in my heart, Rebekah came out, with her jar on her shoulder. She went down to the spring and drew water, and I said to her, 'Please give me a drink.'

⁴⁶"She quickly lowered her jar from her shoulder and said, 'Drink, and I'll water your camels too.' So I drank, and she watered the camels also.

⁴⁷"I asked her, 'Whose daughter are you?'

"She said, 'The daughter of Bethuel son of Nahor, whom Milcah bore to him.'

"Then I put the ring in her nose and the bracelets on her arms, ⁴⁸and I bowed down and worshiped the LORD. I praised the LORD, the God of my master Abraham, who had led me on the right road to get the granddaughter of my master's brother for his son. ⁴⁹Now if you will show kindness and faithfulness to my master, tell me; and if not, tell me, so I may know which way to turn."

⁵⁰Laban and Bethuel answered, "This is from the LORD; we can say nothing to you one way or the other. ⁵¹Here is Rebekah; take

ᵃ36 Or his

her and go, and let her become the wife of your master's son, as the LORD has directed."

⁵²When Abraham's servant heard what they said, he bowed down to the ground before the LORD. ⁵³Then the servant brought out gold and silver jewelry and articles of clothing and gave them to Rebekah; he also gave costly gifts to her brother and to her mother. ⁵⁴Then he and the men who were with him ate and drank and spent the night there.

When they got up the next morning, he said, "Send me on my way to my master."

⁵⁵But her brother and her mother replied, "Let the girl remain with us ten days or so; then you[a] may go."

⁵⁶But he said to them, "Do not detain me, now that the LORD has granted success to my journey. Send me on my way so I may go to my master."

⁵⁷Then they said, "Let's call the girl and ask her about it." ⁵⁸So they called Rebekah and asked her, "Will you go with this man?"

"I will go," she said.

⁵⁹So they sent their sister Rebekah on her way, along with her nurse and Abraham's servant and his men. ⁶⁰And they blessed Rebekah and said to her,

"Our sister, may you increase
    to thousands upon thousands;
may your offspring possess
    the gates of their enemies."

⁶¹Then Rebekah and her maids got ready and mounted their camels and went back with the man. So the servant took Rebekah and left.

⁶²Now Isaac had come from Beer Lahai Roi, for he was living in the Negev. ⁶³He went out to the field one evening to meditate,[b] and as he looked up, he saw camels approaching. ⁶⁴Rebekah also looked up and saw Isaac. She got down from her camel ⁶⁵and asked the servant, "Who is that man in the field coming to meet us?"

"He is my master," the servant answered. So she took her veil and covered herself.

⁶⁶Then the servant told Isaac all he had done. ⁶⁷Isaac brought her into the tent of his mother Sarah, and he married Rebekah. So she became his wife, and he loved her; and Isaac was comforted after his mother's death.

The Death of Abraham

25 Abraham took[c] another wife, whose name was Keturah. ²She bore him Zimran, Jokshan, Medan, Midian, Ishbak and Shuah. ³Jokshan was the father of Sheba and Dedan; the descendants of Dedan were the Asshurites, the Letushites and the Leummites. ⁴The sons of Midian were Ephah, Epher, Hanoch, Abida and Eldaah. All these were descendants of Keturah.

⁵Abraham left everything he owned to Isaac. ⁶But while he was still living, he gave gifts to the sons of his concubines and sent them away from his son Isaac to the land of the east.

⁷Altogether, Abraham lived a hundred and seventy-five years. ⁸Then Abraham breathed his last and died at a good old age, an old man and full of years; and he was gathered to his people. ⁹His sons Isaac and Ishmael buried him in the cave of Machpelah near Mamre, in the field of Ephron son of Zohar the Hittite, ¹⁰the field Abraham had bought from the Hittites.[d] There Abraham was bur-

---

In your family's "last will and testament", what non-material things would you like to bequeath? To inherit? Why?

1. As the founding father of our faith, Abraham sets an heroic and all-too-human example for us to follow. In Genesis 12–25, what are the most noteworthy character traits which he has left for you to emulate? For you to avoid? 2. Through Abraham's experience of God, what do you learn about the way God treats us when we are obedient? When we are fearful? When we are wayward? 3. How are the themes of sin, judgment and mercy reflected in the faith pilgrimage of Abraham?

---

a55 Or she had taken   b63 The meaning of the Hebrew for this word is uncertain.   c1 Or   d10 Or the sons of Heth

ied with his wife Sarah. ¹¹After Abraham's death, God blessed his son Isaac, who then lived near Beer Lahai Roi.

Ishmael's Sons

¹²This is the account of Abraham's son Ishmael, whom Sarah's maidservant, Hagar the Egyptian, bore to Abraham.

¹³These are the names of the sons of Ishmael, listed in the order of their birth: Nebaioth the firstborn of Ishmael, Kedar, Adbeel, Mibsam, ¹⁴Mishma, Dumah, Massa, ¹⁵Hadad, Tema, Jetur, Naphish and Kedemah. ¹⁶These were the sons of Ishmael, and these are the names of the twelve tribal rulers according to their settlements and camps. ¹⁷Altogether, Ishmael lived a hundred and thirty-seven years. He breathed his last and died, and he was gathered to his people. ¹⁸His descendants settled in the area from Havilah to Shur, near the border of Egypt, as you go toward Asshur. And they lived in hostility toward*ᵃ* all their brothers.

Jacob and Esau

¹⁹This is the account of Abraham's son Isaac.

Abraham became the father of Isaac, ²⁰and Isaac was forty years old when he married Rebekah daughter of Bethuel the Aramean from Paddan Aram*ᵇ* and sister of Laban the Aramean.

²¹Isaac prayed to the LORD on behalf of his wife, because she was barren. The LORD answered his prayer, and his wife Rebekah became pregnant. ²²The babies jostled each other within her, and she said, "Why is this happening to me?" So she went to inquire of the LORD.

²³The LORD said to her,

> "Two nations are in your womb,
>   and two peoples from within you will be
>   separated;
>   one people will be stronger than the other,
>   and the older will serve the younger."

²⁴When the time came for her to give birth, there were twin boys in her womb. ²⁵The first to come out was red, and his whole body was like a hairy garment; so they named him Esau.*ᶜ* ²⁶After this, his brother came out, with his hand grasping Esau's heel; so he was named Jacob.*ᵈ* Isaac was sixty years old when Rebekah gave birth to them.

²⁷The boys grew up, and Esau became a skillful hunter, a man of the open country, while Jacob was a quiet man, staying among the tents. ²⁸Isaac, who had a taste for wild game, loved Esau, but Rebekah loved Jacob.

²⁹Once when Jacob was cooking some stew, Esau came in from the open country, famished. ³⁰He said to Jacob, "Quick, let me have some of that red stew! I'm famished!" (That is why he was also called Edom.*ᵉ*)

³¹Jacob replied, "First sell me your birthright."

³²"Look, I am about to die," Esau said. "What good is the birthright to me?"

³³But Jacob said, "Swear to me first." So he swore an oath to him, selling his birthright to Jacob.

---

1. In comparing your faith journey to Abraham's, what parallels do you see in his call (ch. 12)? His "conversion" (ch. 15)? His covenant (ch. 17)? His concern (ch. 18)? His conniving (ch. 20)? His conflict (ch. 21)? His commitment (ch. 22)? 2. Take time to reassess your group covenant, resolve any internal conflicts and recommit yourselves to sharing your faith stories with others outside the group. Take time to pray toward that end.

---

1. What have you been told about the particulars of your birth? 2. Growing up, were you Mom's favorite or Dad's? How did that feel? 3. Growing up, what was the "worst swap" you ever made with a brother or sister? Why did you do it?

1. From this passage alone, how would you describe Esau? Jacob? Which would you prefer as a son? As a brother? Why? 2. Which of these men does God elect? On what basis? What does this tell you about God (see Ro 9:10–16)? 3. What was the "birthright" which Jacob coveted and Esau despised (vv. 31ff; see v. 5; Heb 12:16ff)?

1. Which of Jacob's traits might fit you: Quiet? Homebound? Mom's boy? A grabber? 2. Which of Esau's traits might fit you: Red-head? Hairy? Hunter? Need instant gratification? Dad's boy? Have you ever gone to your brother or sister for help only to be taken advantage of? Have you ever taken advantage of a family member who came to you in a vulnerable state? Explain. How can you move beyond these incidents to love and forgiveness? 3. In your relationship with your family this week, did you feel more favored, or more overlooked? Why? How did you feel in your relationship with God?

---

a18 Or *lived to the east of*   *b20* That is, Northwest Mesopotamia   *c25 Esau* may mean *hairy*; he was also called *Edom,* which means *red.*   *d26 Jacob* means *he grasps the heel* (figuratively, *he deceives*).   *e30 Edom* means *red.*

34Then Jacob gave Esau some bread and some lentil stew. He ate and drank, and then got up and left.

So Esau despised his birthright.

Isaac and Abimelech

26 Now there was a famine in the land—besides the earlier famine of Abraham's time—and Isaac went to Abimelech king of the Philistines in Gerar. 2The LORD appeared to Isaac and said, "Do not go down to Egypt; live in the land where I tell you to live. 3Stay in this land for a while, and I will be with you and will bless you. For to you and your descendants I will give all these lands and will confirm the oath I swore to your father Abraham. 4I will make your descendants as numerous as the stars in the sky and will give them all these lands, and through your offspring[a] all nations on earth will be blessed, 5because Abraham obeyed me and kept my requirements, my commands, my decrees and my laws." 6So Isaac stayed in Gerar.

7When the men of that place asked him about his wife, he said, "She is my sister," because he was afraid to say, "She is my wife." He thought, "The men of this place might kill me on account of Rebekah, because she is beautiful."

8When Isaac had been there a long time, Abimelech king of the Philistines looked down from a window and saw Isaac caressing his wife Rebekah. 9So Abimelech summoned Isaac and said, "She is really your wife! Why did you say, 'She is my sister'?"

Isaac answered him, "Because I thought I might lose my life on account of her."

a4 Or *seed*

---

1. In what way are you a "chip off the old block"? 2. Who was your childhood enemy? How did you finally agree to "get along"?

1. Compare verses 1–11 with 12:10–20 and 20:1–18. What similarities do you see between Isaac and his father? What differences? (Note: "Abimelech" may be a royal title like "Pharaoh," held by more than one man.) 2. When famine strikes in Isaac's time, what does God say to him (vv. 2–5) and why? What does Gerar have that Egypt does not? Are God's promises to Isaac based on Isaac's obedience? On Abraham's faith? God's initiative? 3. Isaac trusted God by not going to Egypt (v. 6); whereas, under similar circumstances, Abraham had trusted God in going to Egypt (see 12:10). But what does Isaac do here that does show a lack of trust in God, similar to Abraham's? How do you account for this repeated pattern of sin: (a) Sin is inherited? (b) Sinful

---

Genesis 25:19–34   JACOB AND ESAU

1. Choose one of the following to share:
   a. a story about your birth or your child's birth
   b. how your parents chose your name
   c. the meaning of your name
   d. a conflict with a sibling when you were growing up

2. Isaac and Rebekah both learned that God:
   a. knows every detail of your life.
   b. listens to your prayers.
   c. keeps his promises.
   d. gives the desire of your heart.
   e. gives the desire of his heart.

3. What was God saying to Rebekah when he told her about the struggle in her womb?
   a. If you think this is bad, wait until they're born!
   b. It's natural for brothers to fight.
   c. This is more than sibling rivalry.
   d. Rather than with the older, I will continue my covenant with the younger.

4. How would you describe Esau?
   a. all brawn and no brain
   b. a man's man
   c. no spiritual insight
   d. thinks with his stomach

5. How would you describe Jacob?
   a. all brain and no brawn
   b. a sneaky little brother
   c. a man of spiritual insight
   d. a clever opportunist

6. Why did Esau sell his birthright (the oldest son's double share of the inheritance)?
   a. He was hungry.
   b. He was stupid.
   c. He had no respect for the Lord's principles.
   d. He got taken advantage of by Jacob.
   e. It was God's will.

7. What could Isaac and Rebekah have done to avoid this conflict?
   a. always had food in the refrigerator
   b. loved their sons equally
   c. taught Esau the value of his birthright

   d. instilled in their children godly character
   e. nothing—Conflict is unavoidable.
   f. nothing—God had his purposes in it.

8. Do you think what Jacob did was justified? If so, why? How has God blessed you in spite of your faults?

9. Are you taking full advantage of your spiritual "birthright"—the blessings available to God's children? How are you selling God, and yourself, short?

10. In what ways do you imagine Jacob and Esau were strong-willed children? What would have been the challenges and frustrations of parenting them? Which one would have been more difficult for you to deal with?

11. How does your child grab for power? How do you handle power struggles? What do you feel you could do to be a better parent? Is that a legitimate shortcoming, or false guilt?

¹⁰Then Abimelech said, "What is this you have done to us? One of the men might well have slept with your wife, and you would have brought guilt upon us."

¹¹So Abimelech gave orders to all the people: "Anyone who molests this man or his wife shall surely be put to death."

¹²Isaac planted crops in that land and the same year reaped a hundredfold, because the LORD blessed him. ¹³The man became rich, and his wealth continued to grow until he became very wealthy. ¹⁴He had so many flocks and herds and servants that the Philistines envied him. ¹⁵So all the wells that his father's servants had dug in the time of his father Abraham, the Philistines stopped up, filling them with earth.

¹⁶Then Abimelech said to Isaac, "Move away from us; you have become too powerful for us."

¹⁷So Isaac moved away from there and encamped in the Valley of Gerar and settled there. ¹⁸Isaac reopened the wells that had been dug in the time of his father Abraham, which the Philistines had stopped up after Abraham died, and he gave them the same names his father had given them.

¹⁹Isaac's servants dug in the valley and discovered a well of fresh water there. ²⁰But the herdsmen of Gerar quarreled with Isaac's herdsmen and said, "The water is ours!" So he named the well Esek,ᵃ because they disputed with him. ²¹Then they dug another well, but they quarreled over that one also; so he named it Sitnah.ᵇ ²²He moved on from there and dug another well, and no one quarreled over it. He named it Rehoboth,ᶜ saying, "Now the LORD has given us room and we will flourish in the land."

²³From there he went up to Beersheba. ²⁴That night the LORD appeared to him and said, "I am the God of your father Abraham. Do not be afraid, for I am with you; I will bless you and will increase the number of your descendants for the sake of my servant Abraham."

²⁵Isaac built an altar there and called on the name of the LORD. There he pitched his tent, and there his servants dug a well.

²⁶Meanwhile, Abimelech had come to him from Gerar, with Ahuzzath his personal adviser and Phicol the commander of his forces. ²⁷Isaac asked them, "Why have you come to me, since you were hostile to me and sent me away?"

²⁸They answered, "We saw clearly that the LORD was with you; so we said, 'There ought to be a sworn agreement between us'— between us and you. Let us make a treaty with you ²⁹that you will do us no harm, just as we did not molest you but always treated you well and sent you away in peace. And now you are blessed by the LORD."

³⁰Isaac then made a feast for them, and they ate and drank. ³¹Early the next morning the men swore an oath to each other. Then Isaac sent them on their way, and they left him in peace.

³²That day Isaac's servants came and told him about the well they had dug. They said, "We've found water!" ³³He called it Shibah,ᵈ and to this day the name of the town has been Beersheba.ᵉ

³⁴When Esau was forty years old, he married Judith daughter of Beeri the Hittite, and also Basemath daughter of Elon the Hittite. ³⁵They were a source of grief to Isaac and Rebekah.

tendencies are learned? (c) Sinful habits are hard to break? (d) Self-preservation is a prime instinct? (e) Other? 4. Why might it be more dangerous for a woman's "husband" than for her "brother"? Do you think this justifies the use of a lie? Why or why not? 5. Despite his lack of trust and sinful ways, how and why is Isaac blessed by God (vv. 12–33)? 6. From this story, one must conclude that God's blessing is signalled by financial prosperity: True or False? Why? 7. Since we know lying is against God's law (see Ex 20:16), why do you think Abraham and Isaac both prosper, even when they are untruthful? What do these chapters teach you about God's ways? 8. What seems to be the problem between Isaac and Abimelech? What do you learn about each man from the way they settle their dispute and reconcile?

1. Isaac repeats his father's inappropriate behavior. As a "chip off the old block," we do the same. What one "sin" of your parents would you like help in eliminating from your life? What qualities of Abimelech would you like to acquire into your own life? 2. Where in your life would you like the quarreling to stop and the reconciliation to start? What next steps of faith might God want you to take toward that end? 3. What does God's gracious treatment of Isaac and the perpetual nature of his covenant mean to you, as a child of the covenant? As one who repeats mistakes of your fathers? 4. Abraham and Isaac both became very wealthy, even as they were vital participants in God's purposes. Is their wealth more or less important to them than their devotion to God? How do you fit your finances into your participation in God's purposes?

ᵃ20 Esek means dispute.   ᵇ21 Sitnah means opposition.   ᶜ22 Rehoboth means room.   ᵈ33 Shibah can mean oath or seven.   ᵉ33 Beersheba can mean well of the oath or well of seven.

1. Recall that time when you outsmarted your brother or friend. What about that event still brings back an irrepressible smile? 2. When have you played a trick on someone by changing your identity? (a) Getting into a movie under-age? (b) Into a bar under-age? (c) Taking a test for someone playing hooky? (d) Using a "good line" on a date? (e) Trading places at work? (f) Embellishing your resume? (g) Faking your ID? How did you feel then? How do you feel now looking back?

1. In antiquity, both the birth-right and the blessing were of vital importance to a clan. What is Jacob's trickery meant to achieve: (a) He wanted the double portion of his dad's possessions, usually reserved for the first-born? (b) He wanted the leadership of the clan, which went to the one blessed? (c) Other? 2. What do his deceptive actions reveal about his true character? About his trust in or his relationship with God at this point? 3. Could Isaac have taken back the blessing he mistakenly gave Jacob? Why or why not? Why did Isaac's blessing prove so powerful to Jacob, even though it was received under false pretenses? Do you think Jacob's success in this plan demonstrates God's approval? Why or why not? 4. Which member of the family—Isaac, Rebekah, Esau or Jacob—do you think was most wrong here? Why? What should he or she have done instead? How would this have improved things? 5. How do God's prophecy in 25:23 and Esau's actions in 25:29–34 relate to events of chapter 27 (see also Heb 12:16–17)? Why do you think God favors Jacob, a person with such dubious morals? 6. The covenant with Abraham and his descendants owes very little (if anything) to human effort and (almost) everything to God's undeserved grace: True or False? Explain. 7. How do you account for Isaac falling prey to Jacob's obvious trick: (a) Isaac is blind to his own inherited tendency to deceive when threatened? (b) God is just in allowing Isaac to reap what he sows? (c) There's "more than meets the eye" to this story? (d) Even the "oldest trick in the book" will work some of the time? (e) Other?

1. Suppose God's covenant were dependent on cultural custom (favoring the firstborn) or

Jacob Gets Isaac's Blessing

27 When Isaac was old and his eyes were so weak that he could no longer see, he called for Esau his older son and said to him, "My son."

"Here I am," he answered.

²Isaac said, "I am now an old man and don't know the day of my death. ³Now then, get your weapons—your quiver and bow—and go out to the open country to hunt some wild game for me. ⁴Prepare me the kind of tasty food I like and bring it to me to eat, so that I may give you my blessing before I die."

⁵Now Rebekah was listening as Isaac spoke to his son Esau. When Esau left for the open country to hunt game and bring it back, ⁶Rebekah said to her son Jacob, "Look, I overheard your father say to your brother Esau, ⁷'Bring me some game and prepare me some tasty food to eat, so that I may give you my blessing in the presence of the LORD before I die.' ⁸Now, my son, listen carefully and do what I tell you: ⁹Go out to the flock and bring me two choice young goats, so I can prepare some tasty food for your father, just the way he likes it. ¹⁰Then take it to your father to eat, so that he may give you his blessing before he dies."

¹¹Jacob said to Rebekah his mother, "But my brother Esau is a hairy man, and I'm a man with smooth skin. ¹²What if my father touches me? I would appear to be tricking him and would bring down a curse on myself rather than a blessing."

¹³His mother said to him, "My son, let the curse fall on me. Just do what I say; go and get them for me."

¹⁴So he went and got them and brought them to his mother, and she prepared some tasty food, just the way his father liked it. ¹⁵Then Rebekah took the best clothes of Esau her older son, which she had in the house, and put them on her younger son Jacob. ¹⁶She also covered his hands and the smooth part of his neck with the goatskins. ¹⁷Then she handed to her son Jacob the tasty food and the bread she had made.

¹⁸He went to his father and said, "My father."

"Yes, my son," he answered. "Who is it?"

¹⁹Jacob said to his father, "I am Esau your firstborn. I have done as you told me. Please sit up and eat some of my game so that you may give me your blessing."

²⁰Isaac asked his son, "How did you find it so quickly, my son?"

"The LORD your God gave me success," he replied.

²¹Then Isaac said to Jacob, "Come near so I can touch you, my son, to know whether you really are my son Esau or not."

²²Jacob went close to his father Isaac, who touched him and said, "The voice is the voice of Jacob, but the hands are the hands of Esau." ²³He did not recognize him, for his hands were hairy like those of his brother Esau; so he blessed him. ²⁴"Are you really my son Esau?" he asked.

"I am," he replied.

²⁵Then he said, "My son, bring me some of your game to eat, so that I may give you my blessing."

Jacob brought it to him and he ate; and he brought some wine and he drank. ²⁶Then his father Isaac said to him, "Come here, my son, and kiss me."

²⁷So he went to him and kissed him. When Isaac caught the smell of his clothes, he blessed him and said,

> "Ah, the smell of my son
> is like the smell of a field
> that the LORD has blessed.

²⁸May God give you of heaven's dew
and of earth's richness—
an abundance of grain and new wine.
²⁹May nations serve you
and peoples bow down to you.
Be lord over your brothers,
and may the sons of your mother bow down to
you.
May those who curse you be cursed
and those who bless you be blessed."

³⁰After Isaac finished blessing him and Jacob had scarcely left his father's presence, his brother Esau came in from hunting. ³¹He too prepared some tasty food and brought it to his father. Then he said to him, "My father, sit up and eat some of my game, so that you may give me your blessing."

³²His father Isaac asked him, "Who are you?"

"I am your son," he answered, "your firstborn, Esau."

³³Isaac trembled violently and said, "Who was it, then, that hunted game and brought it to me? I ate it just before you came and I blessed him—and indeed he will be blessed!"

³⁴When Esau heard his father's words, he burst out with a loud and bitter cry and said to his father, "Bless me—me too, my father!"

³⁵But he said, "Your brother came deceitfully and took your blessing."

³⁶Esau said, "Isn't he rightly named Jacob^a? He has deceived me these two times: He took my birthright, and now he's taken

^a36 Jacob means he grasps the heel (figuratively, he deceives).

human virtue (no scheming) for its fulfillment. How would that affect Isaac and Jacob? How would that affect you and all other potential heirs of the covenant who have no custom or virtue favoring them? **2.** How could this story be reset in today's world: What would take the place of the birthright? The blessing? What legal consequences would Jacob face for his criminal act? **3.** Whose blessing or approval means the most to you: Dad's? Mom's? Former friend's? Spouse's? Kid's? Boss's? Co-worker's? Pastor's? How might you still be working for their blessing? Whose blessing did you always hunger for but never receive? How did the lack of that blessing affect you? **4.** From what you have learned here about God's justice, sovereignty and unearned grace, why do you think God chose you? **5.** Compared to Jacob, where's your level of trust in God? What can you apply from this story to increase that trust level? What does this story say about the power of the spoken word? How can you be more of a blessing with your words? **6.** Like Esau, where are you experiencing great disappoint-

---

 Genesis 27:1–40   **JACOB GETS ISAAC'S BLESSING**

1. Who is responsible for Jacob getting the blessing?
    a. Isaac—How gullible can you get?!
    b. Rebekah—It was her plan.
    c. Jacob—He pulled it off.
    d. Esau—When he gave up the birthright of the firstborn he was doomed to lose the blessing of the firstborn.

2. The purpose of such a blessing was:
    a. to speak on behalf of God.
    b. to transfer leadership of the clan.
    c. to make the recipient feel good.
    d. to pass on a spiritual inheritance.

3. The hardest thing to understand about this story is:
    a. how Rebekah could so blatantly favor one child over another.
    b. how Jacob could lie to his father and rip off his brother.
    c. why Isaac couldn't revoke Jacob's ill-gotten blessing or at least give Esau a better blessing.
    d. how God could honor Jacob's blessing the way it was achieved.

4. What is the lesson of this story?
    a. Words are very powerful.
    b. It doesn't really matter what you do if God has chosen you.
    c. Character flaws like deception get passed down generations.
    d. We may not understand, but God's ways are just.

5. When God blesses people whom I don't approve of:
    a. I question God's justice.
    b. I pretend not to notice.
    c. I rejoice for them.
    d. I get jealous.

6. What do you do when there is a "Jacob" in your life, scheming to take advantage of you?
    a. try to avoid him (or her)
    b. give him what he wants
    c. fight for what's mine
    d. outsmart him
    e. get him into trouble
    f. calmly confront him

7. When there is competition and conflict in my family, I:

    a. try to prove I am right.
    b. get on the winning side.
    c. try to make peace.
    d. take responsibility for my part.
    e. leave the house.

8. How much of God's covenant with Abraham and his descendants depended on their human merits? Why do you think God chose you?

9. Who can you significantly impact with a "blessing"? How do you plan to do so?

10. Is this story a disappointment or consolation to you about family life? How many of your expectations for family life have been unrealistic? What do you need to do to lower either your expectations or frustrations?

11. In what way is this family like yours? How does Rebekah remind you of yourself? What can you do to improve things?

ment? How can group members help you in this?

1. Which grade school or high school "friend" did you once fear? How did you avoid trouble with this person? **2.** When did your parents help you out of a jam with legal or school authorities?

1. If there was ever any doubt about Jacob's integrity in stealing the blessing from Isaac (see 27:1–40), what do the actions of the people here tell you? Who else is now implicated? **2.** Given Jacob's home-bound nature (see 25:27ff), how was he persuaded to finally leave home? What diplomacy did Rebekah use on Jacob? On Isaac? **3.** Given her apron-string ties to Jacob and the prospect of never seeing him again, how would Rebekah manage to say goodbye? **4.** Upon learning his father's preferences for a suitable mate, what does Esau do (28:8–9)? Why? Do two wrong wives make the third one right? What if she's from Ishmael?

1. In what ways did you once behave like one of Isaac's family? In what family settings do you still behave that way? **2.** What does it mean to you that God chooses you "anyway" (whether you've been good or bad)? **3.** When have you held a long-term grudge? Where might you still be holding one? How has that grudge affected you? Others? **4.** In what sense are (or were) you like Jacob, running from your past, fearing revenge? Pray about that.

my blessing!" Then he asked, "Haven't you reserved any blessing for me?"

[37]Isaac answered Esau, "I have made him lord over you and have made all his relatives his servants, and I have sustained him with grain and new wine. So what can I possibly do for you, my son?"

[38]Esau said to his father, "Do you have only one blessing, my father? Bless me too, my father!" Then Esau wept aloud.

[39]His father Isaac answered him,

"Your dwelling will be
  away from the earth's richness,
  away from the dew of heaven above.
[40]You will live by the sword
  and you will serve your brother.
But when you grow restless,
  you will throw his yoke
  from off your neck."

Jacob Flees to Laban

[41]Esau held a grudge against Jacob because of the blessing his father had given him. He said to himself, "The days of mourning for my father are near; then I will kill my brother Jacob."

[42]When Rebekah was told what her older son Esau had said, she sent for her younger son Jacob and said to him, "Your brother Esau is consoling himself with the thought of killing you. [43]Now then, my son, do what I say: Flee at once to my brother Laban in Haran. [44]Stay with him for a while until your brother's fury subsides. [45]When your brother is no longer angry with you and forgets what you did to him, I'll send word for you to come back from there. Why should I lose both of you in one day?"

[46]Then Rebekah said to Isaac, "I'm disgusted with living because of these Hittite women. If Jacob takes a wife from among the women of this land, from Hittite women like these, my life will not be worth living."

28 So Isaac called for Jacob and blessed[a] him and commanded him: "Do not marry a Canaanite woman. [2]Go at once to Paddan Aram,[b] to the house of your mother's father Bethuel. Take a wife for yourself there, from among the daughters of Laban, your mother's brother. [3]May God Almighty[c] bless you and make you fruitful and increase your numbers until you become a community of peoples. [4]May he give you and your descendants the blessing given to Abraham, so that you may take possession of the land where you now live as an alien, the land God gave to Abraham." [5]Then Isaac sent Jacob on his way, and he went to Paddan Aram, to Laban son of Bethuel the Aramean, the brother of Rebekah, who was the mother of Jacob and Esau.

[6]Now Esau learned that Isaac had blessed Jacob and had sent him to Paddan Aram to take a wife from there, and that when he blessed him he commanded him, "Do not marry a Canaanite woman," [7]and that Jacob had obeyed his father and mother and had gone to Paddan Aram. [8]Esau then realized how displeasing the Canaanite women were to his father Isaac; [9]so he went to Ishmael and married Mahalath, the sister of Nebaioth and daughter of Ishmael son of Abraham, in addition to the wives he already had.

---

[a]1 Or greeted   [b]2 That is, Northwest Mesopotamia; also in verses 5, 6 and 7
[c]3 Hebrew El-Shaddai

Jacob's Dream at Bethel

[10]Jacob left Beersheba and set out for Haran. [11]When he reached a certain place, he stopped for the night because the sun had set. Taking one of the stones there, he put it under his head and lay down to sleep. [12]He had a dream in which he saw a stairway[a] resting on the earth, with its top reaching to heaven, and the angels of God were ascending and descending on it. [13]There above it[b] stood the LORD, and he said: "I am the LORD, the God of your father Abraham and the God of Isaac. I will give you and your descendants the land on which you are lying. [14]Your descendants will be like the dust of the earth, and you will spread out to the west and to the east, to the north and to the south. All peoples on earth will be blessed through you and your offspring. [15]I am with you and will watch over you wherever you go, and I will bring you back to this land. I will not leave you until I have done what I have promised you."

[16]When Jacob awoke from his sleep, he thought, "Surely the LORD is in this place, and I was not aware of it." [17]He was afraid and said, "How awesome is this place! This is none other than the house of God; this is the gate of heaven."

[18]Early the next morning Jacob took the stone he had placed under his head and set it up as a pillar and poured oil on top of it. [19]He called that place Bethel,[c] though the city used to be called Luz.

[20]Then Jacob made a vow, saying, "If God will be with me and will watch over me on this journey I am taking and will give me food to eat and clothes to wear [21]so that I return safely to my father's house, then the LORD[d] will be my God [22]and[e] this stone that I have set up as a pillar will be God's house, and of all that you give me I will give you a tenth."

Jacob Arrives in Paddan Aram

29 Then Jacob continued on his journey and came to the land of the eastern peoples. [2]There he saw a well in the field, with three flocks of sheep lying near it because the flocks were watered from that well. The stone over the mouth of the well was large. [3]When all the flocks were gathered there, the shepherds would roll the stone away from the well's mouth and water the sheep. Then they would return the stone to its place over the mouth of the well.

[4]Jacob asked the shepherds, "My brothers, where are you from?"

"We're from Haran," they replied.

[5]He said to them, "Do you know Laban, Nahor's grandson?"

"Yes, we know him," they answered.

[6]Then Jacob asked them, "Is he well?"

"Yes, he is," they said, "and here comes his daughter Rachel with the sheep."

[7]"Look," he said, "the sun is still high; it is not time for the flocks to be gathered. Water the sheep and take them back to pasture."

[8]"We can't," they replied, "until all the flocks are gathered and the stone has been rolled away from the mouth of the well. Then we will water the sheep."

[9]While he was still talking with them, Rachel came with her father's sheep, for she was a shepherdess. [10]When Jacob saw Rachel daughter of Laban, his mother's brother, and Laban's sheep,

---

In the ebb and flow of your life so far, when have you felt beached, high and dry? When have you felt like "your ship was coming in" with the high tide?

1. What makes Jacob "run"? Being homeless? Landless? Aimless? Sleepless? Friendless? Guiltless? Fearless? 2. What is so remarkable in God's display of grace? Why does God meet Jacob unsolicited and without reproach? 3. What do you think of Jacob's reply upon awakening (vv.16–17)? His actions the next morning (vv. 18–19)? 4. How does Jacob's vow (vv. 20–22) strike you: Mere bargaining chip, unworthy of God? Or growing trust, apropos for Jacob? Or "conversion" event, radical for Jacob? Explain.

1. What childish "deals" with God do you recall making? How did they turn out? As an adult, how do you "deal" with God? Why the difference? 2. Do you think God still speaks through dreams? What are the dangers and benefits of relying on dreams for guidance?

1. What do you recall about that "first kiss"? Was it on a first date or later? How old were you? Or was it just a "kissin' cousin"? 2. What do you know about how your dad first met your mom?

1. Compare Genesis 24:10–32 with this passage. How do you account for the similarities in how Isaac and Jacob met their respective mates: Providence? Coincidence? Like father, like son? 2. How does Jacob discern the woman of God's choosing: From her "drinking habits" (well water, etc.)? Her "drinking companions" (camels, sheep, etc.)? Or what? 3. What likely impressed Rachel about Jacob: His small talk (vv. 4–7)? His new-found energy to roll away the stone all by himself (v. 10)? His ability to express emotion (v. 11)? His family ties (v. 12)? His recent experience with God?

1. What might the power of love energize you to do for someone else? 2. About your "demonstrative" level, do friends tell you to "loosen up," or "calm down"? How can you better demonstrate your love this week? 3.

---

a12 Or *ladder*   b13 Or *There beside him*   c19 *Bethel* means *house of God.*
d20,21 Or *Since God . . . father's house, the* LORD   e21,22 Or *house, and the* LORD *will be my God,* 22*then*

How important are family ties and a common faith to you in your choice of a mate? What else matters to you in this regard?

---

 1. What is a great practical joke you once played on a friend? A great joke played on you? **2.** Who are you often mistaken for? Have you ever played along?

1. Isaac's and Jacob's quest for a wife are similar in many respects, including Laban's common role in both. What was that role? What might Isaac's success and Laban's past service lead Jacob to expect now for his arranged marriage to Rachel? **2.** How are his expectations actually fulfilled here? What does that teach you about how God works? **3.** How could Jacob mistake Leah for Rachel on his

he went over and rolled the stone away from the mouth of the well and watered his uncle's sheep. [11]Then Jacob kissed Rachel and began to weep aloud. [12]He had told Rachel that he was a relative of her father and a son of Rebekah. So she ran and told her father.

[13]As soon as Laban heard the news about Jacob, his sister's son, he hurried to meet him. He embraced him and kissed him and brought him to his home, and there Jacob told him all these things. [14]Then Laban said to him, "You are my own flesh and blood."

Jacob Marries Leah and Rachel

After Jacob had stayed with him for a whole month, [15]Laban said to him, "Just because you are a relative of mine, should you work for me for nothing? Tell me what your wages should be."

[16]Now Laban had two daughters; the name of the older was Leah, and the name of the younger was Rachel. [17]Leah had weak[a] eyes, but Rachel was lovely in form, and beautiful. [18]Jacob was in love with Rachel and said, "I'll work for you seven years in return for your younger daughter Rachel."

[19]Laban said, "It's better that I give her to you than to some other man. Stay here with me." [20]So Jacob served seven years to get Rachel, but they seemed like only a few days to him because of his love for her.

---

[a] 17 Or *delicate*

   Genesis 29:1–30 JACOB MARRIES LEAH AND RACHEL

After deceiving his father to get the blessing intended for his brother Esau, Jacob was running away from Esau's wrath. He was also instructed by his parents to go and marry one of his Uncle Laban's daughters, rather than marry a Canaanite woman.

1. *Men:* If you were Jacob, how would you have felt about your first day in this new place?
   a. God must be with me.
   b. I'm so glad Laban welcomed me.
   c. That Rachel is a real knock-out!
   d. I wonder what Rachel thinks about me.
   e. I wonder if Laban would let me marry Rachel.

2. *Women:* If you were Rachel, how would you have felt about Jacob's entrance on the scene?
   a. How romantic!
   b. God must be with him.
   c. What a gentleman—the way he took care of the sheep for me.
   d. I like a man like Jacob who can show his emotions.
   e. I wonder if he thinks I'm attractive.

3. Why did Laban trick Jacob and give him Leah?

a. It was inappropriate to give the younger daughter first.
b. He wanted another seven years of free labor.
c. He figured both daughters would end up married that way.
d. The deceiver Jacob deserved to be deceived.

4. How could Laban's wedding night scheme work?
   a. That's what I'd like to know!
   b. It must have been really dark.
   c. Leah must have kept her veil on.
   d. Jacob must have gotten drunk.
   e. Leah must have done a good Rachel impersonation.

5. We're told how Jacob and Laban felt (vv. 25–27). How do you think Leah and Rachel felt? How do you think the four of them felt about each other after Laban agreed to let Jacob marry Rachel also?

6. What are you waiting for in your life right now? How are you at waiting? What could you do to be better at it?

7. When have you felt like Leah—unattractive and unloved? When, like Rachel, have you had the rug pulled out from under

your dreams? How does your relationship with God help you cope when the "romance" isn't there?

8. The seven years "seemed like only a few days" to Jacob because of his love for Rachel. Regarding time and my marriage, it seems like:
   a. we have been together forever.
   b. only yesterday we fell in love.
   c. what happened before we met was in another lifetime.
   d. a permanent commitment has been really important.
   e. a lifetime won't be long enough to be together.
   f. we never have enough time.

9. How do you think Jacob and Rachel dealt with waiting seven years (and seven days) to get married? How do you handle times of waiting in your dating life? What helps you keep sexually pure while you wait?

10. What about this course and this group has been helpful in gaining patience and God's perspective for your struggles in sexuality and dating?

21Then Jacob said to Laban, "Give me my wife. My time is completed, and I want to lie with her."

22So Laban brought together all the people of the place and gave a feast. 23But when evening came, he took his daughter Leah and gave her to Jacob, and Jacob lay with her. 24And Laban gave his servant girl Zilpah to his daughter as her maidservant.

25When morning came, there was Leah! So Jacob said to Laban, "What is this you have done to me? I served you for Rachel, didn't I? Why have you deceived me?"

26Laban replied, "It is not our custom here to give the younger daughter in marriage before the older one. 27Finish this daughter's bridal week; then we will give you the younger one also, in return for another seven years of work."

28And Jacob did so. He finished the week with Leah, and then Laban gave him his daughter Rachel to be his wife. 29Laban gave his servant girl Bilhah to his daughter Rachel as her maidservant. 30Jacob lay with Rachel also, and he loved Rachel more than Leah. And he worked for Laban another seven years.

Jacob's Children

31When the LORD saw that Leah was not loved, he opened her womb, but Rachel was barren. 32Leah became pregnant and gave birth to a son. She named him Reuben,a for she said, "It is because the LORD has seen my misery. Surely my husband will love me now."

33She conceived again, and when she gave birth to a son she said, "Because the LORD heard that I am not loved, he gave me this one too." So she named him Simeon.b

34Again she conceived, and when she gave birth to a son she said, "Now at last my husband will become attached to me, because I have borne him three sons." So he was named Levi.c

35She conceived again, and when she gave birth to a son she said, "This time I will praise the LORD." So she named him Judah.d Then she stopped having children.

30 When Rachel saw that she was not bearing Jacob any children, she became jealous of her sister. So she said to Jacob, "Give me children, or I'll die!"

2Jacob became angry with her and said, "Am I in the place of God, who has kept you from having children?"

3Then she said, "Here is Bilhah, my maidservant. Sleep with her so that she can bear children for me and that through her I too can build a family."

4So she gave him her servant Bilhah as a wife. Jacob slept with her, 5and she became pregnant and bore him a son. 6Then Rachel said, "God has vindicated me; he has listened to my plea and given me a son." Because of this she named him Dan.e

7Rachel's servant Bilhah conceived again and bore Jacob a second son. 8Then Rachel said, "I have had a great struggle with my sister, and I have won." So she named him Naphtali.f

9When Leah saw that she had stopped having children, she took her maidservant Zilpah and gave her to Jacob as a wife. 10Leah's servant Zilpah bore Jacob a son. 11Then Leah said, "What good fortune!"g So she named him Gad.h

12Leah's servant Zilpah bore Jacob a second son. 13Then Leah

wedding night? What might have contributed to their mistaken identity? What is the irony in the younger/older role reversal (v. 26)? **4.** Who do you think felt worse: Jacob, Leah or Rachel? Why?

1. "Always a bridesmaid, never a bride"—how does that saying (and Leah's experience) fit you? **2.** For what relationship have you labored, only to find a surprise twist in the end? **3.** When, like Jacob, have you had to suffer such delays in getting what you want? What did God seem to want for you?

1. What size family did you grow up in? Where were you in that birth order? What did you like best and least about being an only child (or the baby, the middle, or the oldest child)? **2.** In your family of origin, what deed (good or bad) got Dad's attention?

1. Knowing that these 12 sons of Jacob become the 12 tribes of Israel, what significance do you see in their birth mothers? Their birth order? Their names? **2.** Regarding their conception, what means seem to be significant: Magic? Superstition? Deception? Manipulation? Surrogate mothers? What was the real source of this blessing (29:31,33; 30:2,6,17,20, 22, 24)? **3.** What seems to be the main problem in this mixed-up, messed-up family? In what sense are Jacob's troubles (vv. 1–4, 15–16) his own fault? **4.** Do you think Jacob enjoys all this attention? Or do you suspect he is worn out from it all? Why do you think so? Why do you think God chose to accomplish so much through such an imperfect family?

1. When in your misery has God showed you the kindness he showed Leah in her misery? **2.** When have you felt like Rachel—unproductive, outnumbered, passed over, or "disgraced"? **3.** Where in your own family can you empathize with Jacob's family: Too many "wives"? Too many kids? Too much competition? Too many conflicts? **4.** Which of these family trials are of your own making? Where is God in all this? **5.** In your own baby-making (if you are so blessed), to what do you attribute

---

a32 Reuben sounds like the Hebrew for he has seen my misery; the name means see, a son. b33 Simeon probably means one who hears. c34 Levi sounds like and may be derived from the Hebrew for attached. d35 Judah sounds like and may be derived from the Hebrew for praise. e6 Dan here means he has vindicated. f8 Naphtali means my struggle. g11 Or "A troop is coming!" h11 Gad can mean good fortune or a troop.

your success? How might modern science and Christian faith be in conflict on this? How might they bear fruit together for you? When have you been used by God despite your mistakes? When have you worked desperately to serve God without seeing any results? What have you learned from these situations?

said, "How happy I am! The women will call me happy." So she named him Asher.[a]

14During wheat harvest, Reuben went out into the fields and found some mandrake plants, which he brought to his mother Leah. Rachel said to Leah, "Please give me some of your son's mandrakes."

15But she said to her, "Wasn't it enough that you took away my husband? Will you take my son's mandrakes too?"

"Very well," Rachel said, "he can sleep with you tonight in return for your son's mandrakes."

16So when Jacob came in from the fields that evening, Leah went out to meet him. "You must sleep with me," she said. "I have hired you with my son's mandrakes." So he slept with her that night.

17God listened to Leah, and she became pregnant and bore Jacob a fifth son. **18**Then Leah said, "God has rewarded me for giving my maidservant to my husband." So she named him Issachar.[b]

19Leah conceived again and bore Jacob a sixth son. **20**Then Leah said, "God has presented me with a precious gift. This time my husband will treat me with honor, because I have borne him six sons." So she named him Zebulun.[c]

21Some time later she gave birth to a daughter and named her Dinah.

22Then God remembered Rachel; he listened to her and opened her womb. **23**She became pregnant and gave birth to a son and said, "God has taken away my disgrace." **24**She named him Joseph,[d] and said, "May the LORD add to me another son."

[a]13 *Asher* means *happy.*   [b]18 *Issachar* sounds like the Hebrew for *reward.*
[c]20 *Zebulun* probably means *honor.*   [d]24 *Joseph* means *may he add.*

  Genesis 29:31–30:24   **JACOB'S CHILDREN**

Jacob traveled to his Uncle Laban's home in hopes of gaining a wife. Jacob fell in love with Laban's younger daughter Rachel and agreed to work for him seven years in exchange for her hand. But at the end of seven years, Laban deceived Jacob and gave him Leah, his other daughter. Laban agreed to let Jacob marry Rachel also, under the condition that Jacob work for him another seven years.

1. What does this sound like?
   a. a soap opera   c. a tug of war
   b. my own family   d. a nightmare

2. If I could say something to Leah, I'd tell her:
   a. You asked for trouble by going along with your father's scheme.
   b. You can't earn a person's love.
   c. God is on your side.
   d. No matter how Jacob feels about you, God still loves you.
   e. No man's worth fighting over.
   f. Your bitterness toward your sister is only hurting you.
   g. Go to Rachel and work things out.

3. If I could say something to Rachel, I'd tell her:
   a. It's not your fault that you can't have children.
   b. Inability to have children doesn't make you any less of a person.
   c. You should be glad your husband loves you.
   d. Having babies is nothing to compete over.
   e. Your jealousy toward your sister is only hurting you.
   f. Go to Leah and work things out.

4. How do you think Jacob felt about all this? What could he have done to reduce the tension and conflict in his household?

5. How could God bless and use such a "dysfunctional" family? What is the biggest problem in your family? How do you contribute to the problem?

6. What effect did Rachel's childlessness have on her and Jacob's marriage?
   a. It brought them closer together.
   b. They both blamed each other.

   c. It drove them to depend on God.
   d. The stress caused them to lash out at each other in anger.

7. How much do you compare yourself with others? How hard is it for you to rejoice with those who have what you want?

8. Would you rather be like Leah—outwardly blessed, but isolated? Or like Rachel—outwardly deprived, but loved? Which one comes closer to describing your life right now?

9. How do Leah and Rachel's struggles remind you of your own? In what areas do you feel compelled to keep up or compete with other women—Physically? Socially? Materially?

10. What effect has your miscarriage had on your marriage? How hard is it to share your feelings with each other? Which of the possibilities in question 6 have been true for you?

Jacob's Flocks Increase

²⁵After Rachel gave birth to Joseph, Jacob said to Laban, "Send me on my way so I can go back to my own homeland. ²⁶Give me my wives and children, for whom I have served you, and I will be on my way. You know how much work I've done for you."

²⁷But Laban said to him, "If I have found favor in your eyes, please stay. I have learned by divination that*a* the LORD has blessed me because of you." ²⁸He added, "Name your wages, and I will pay them."

²⁹Jacob said to him, "You know how I have worked for you and how your livestock has fared under my care. ³⁰The little you had before I came has increased greatly, and the LORD has blessed you wherever I have been. But now, when may I do something for my own household?"

³¹"What shall I give you?" he asked.

"Don't give me anything," Jacob replied. "But if you will do this one thing for me, I will go on tending your flocks and watching over them: ³²Let me go through all your flocks today and remove from them every speckled or spotted sheep, every dark-colored lamb and every spotted or speckled goat. They will be my wages. ³³And my honesty will testify for me in the future, whenever you check on the wages you have paid me. Any goat in my possession that is not speckled or spotted, or any lamb that is not dark-colored, will be considered stolen."

³⁴"Agreed," said Laban. "Let it be as you have said." ³⁵That same day he removed all the male goats that were streaked or spotted, and all the speckled or spotted female goats (all that had white on them) and all the dark-colored lambs, and he placed them in the care of his sons. ³⁶Then he put a three-day journey between himself and Jacob, while Jacob continued to tend the rest of Laban's flocks.

³⁷Jacob, however, took fresh-cut branches from poplar, almond and plane trees and made white stripes on them by peeling the bark and exposing the white inner wood of the branches. ³⁸Then he placed the peeled branches in all the watering troughs, so that they would be directly in front of the flocks when they came to drink. When the flocks were in heat and came to drink, ³⁹they mated in front of the branches. And they bore young that were streaked or speckled or spotted. ⁴⁰Jacob set apart the young of the flock by themselves, but made the rest face the streaked and dark-colored animals that belonged to Laban. Thus he made separate flocks for himself and did not put them with Laban's animals. ⁴¹Whenever the stronger females were in heat, Jacob would place the branches in the troughs in front of the animals so they would mate near the branches, ⁴²but if the animals were weak, he would not place them there. So the weak animals went to Laban and the strong ones to Jacob. ⁴³In this way the man grew exceedingly prosperous and came to own large flocks, and maidservants and menservants, and camels and donkeys.

Jacob Flees From Laban

31 Jacob heard that Laban's sons were saying, "Jacob has taken everything our father owned and has gained all this wealth from what belonged to our father." ²And Jacob noticed that Laban's attitude toward him was not what it had been.

³Then the LORD said to Jacob, "Go back to the land of your fathers and to your relatives, and I will be with you."

a27 Or possibly have become rich and

1. What about sheep do you like: Wool sweaters? Lamb chops? Counting sheep? Stories of "dumb sheep"? Of "black sheep"? 2. Have you raised any pets who had babies? Or do you get them "fixed" so they can't? If your pets ever produced a larger litter than you wanted, how did you decide which babies to keep and which to give away?

There is more to this story than meets the eye. 1. Knowing his scheming son-in-law as he does, what precautions does Laban take (vv. 35–36) after agreeing to the plan (v. 34)? How do you know that Laban likely saw through Jacob's scheme (vv. 31–33)? 2. To the casual observer, what seems to be the cause and effect of Jacob's increase in flocks: The magical power of suggestion (vv. 37–40)? Selective breeding (vv. 40–42)? A fluke in the law of averages? 3. To the eye of faith, what is the secret of Jacob's phenomenal success (see 31:9–12)?

1. Remain silent for five minutes and meditate upon your successes and God's blessings in your life. Ponder the natural or coincidental explanation versus the supernatural or providential explanation for them. Share with the group what you learned or were reminded of during the silence. In what sense are you giving credit where credit is due for the good things that happen to you? 2. We take credit for undeserved blessing, and we pass the buck for deserved blame. What does that say about human nature? 3. Since Jacob is forever the schemer, God must be blessing him despite his flawed character. Why is that? Why does God choose such flawed people to be his special covenant people? What hope does that carry for you?

1. As a kid, did you ever run away from home? How far did you get: Next door? Grandma's? The big city? 2. How do you know when your in-laws start treating you like an "out-law"? What is your first clue?

1. What is a modern equivalent of the livestock in this story? How does that comparison give the story more meaning to you? Compare Jacob's flight from Laban in this passage to his escape from Esau in 27:4–28:5. How has Jacob's character changed, if at all? Is he still driven? Or is he now also called? Why do you think so? **2.** What prompts Jacob to leave without Laban knowing (see 31:31)? What makes him think he could get away unnoticed? **3.** What, if anything, has Jacob learned from his trials? What might he have learned about God? How concerned is he about Laban's well-being? Why? **4.** What changes do you see in Leah's and Rachel's relationship with Jacob (compare ch. 30)? What does the taking of Laban's "household gods" (v. 19) say about Rachel (see 35:2–4)?

1. If you could advise Jacob, what would you tell him to do about his relationship with Laban? **2.** How would that same advice help you better cope with one broken relationship in your own life right now?

⁴So Jacob sent word to Rachel and Leah to come out to the fields where his flocks were. ⁵He said to them, "I see that your father's attitude toward me is not what it was before, but the God of my father has been with me. ⁶You know that I've worked for your father with all my strength, ⁷yet your father has cheated me by changing my wages ten times. However, God has not allowed him to harm me. ⁸If he said, 'The speckled ones will be your wages,' then all the flocks gave birth to speckled young; and if he said, 'The streaked ones will be your wages,' then all the flocks bore streaked young. ⁹So God has taken away your father's livestock and has given them to me.

¹⁰"In breeding season I once had a dream in which I looked up and saw that the male goats mating with the flock were streaked, speckled or spotted. ¹¹The angel of God said to me in the dream, 'Jacob.' I answered, 'Here I am.' ¹²And he said, 'Look up and see that all the male goats mating with the flock are streaked, speckled or spotted, for I have seen all that Laban has been doing to you. ¹³I am the God of Bethel, where you anointed a pillar and where you made a vow to me. Now leave this land at once and go back to your native land.'"

¹⁴Then Rachel and Leah replied, "Do we still have any share in the inheritance of our father's estate? ¹⁵Does he not regard us as foreigners? Not only has he sold us, but he has used up what was paid for us. ¹⁶Surely all the wealth that God took away from our father belongs to us and our children. So do whatever God has told you."

¹⁷Then Jacob put his children and his wives on camels, ¹⁸and drove all his livestock ahead of him, along with all the goods he had accumulated in Paddan Aram,ᵃ to go to his father Isaac in the land of Canaan.

ᵃ18 That is, Northwest Mesopotamia

Genesis 31:1–21   JACOB FLEES FROM LABAN

It has been 20 years since Jacob came to his Uncle Laban. In exchange for marrying Laban's two daughters, Jacob worked for Laban for 14 years. The next six years found Jacob and Laban trying to outsmart each other in the growth of their individual herds of livestock.

1. Why did Jacob leave for Canaan?
   a. He was homesick.
   b. Things were getting really tense with his father-in-law.
   c. God told him to.
   d. He was tired of getting ripped off.
   e. Rachel and Leah were ready to go too.

2. Jacob ran away without telling Laban because he:
   a. hated good-byes.
   b. was in a hurry.
   c. had a habit of operating by deception.
   d. thought Laban would take Rachel and Leah away from him.

   e. was afraid of Laban.

3. Do you think Jacob did the right thing? Why or why not?

4. When I face challenges like Jacob did, I usually:
   a. take off.
   b. fight to the finish.
   c. work out a compromise.
   d. wiggle out of it.
   e. call my parents.

5. If you could change the way you respond to challenges, would you? If so, in what way?

6. What did Rachel's theft of Laban's household gods say about her?
   a. She was a kleptomaniac.
   b. She was an idol-worshipper.
   c. She wanted a keepsake to remember her family.
   d. She did it to spite her father.
   e. She thought they might give her good luck.

   f. She tried to mix her pagan background and her faith in the one true God.

7. When you began your new life in Christ, how hard was it to change your "old ways"? What ongoing struggles do you have between your old life and your new life?

8. **$** How does this story relate to your launching out as an entrepreneur?
   a. I was tired of working for someone else.
   b. I was sick of people taking advantage of me.
   c. I had a problem with a partner.
   d. God gave me a dream.

9. **$** What was your original entrepreneurial dream? How has it unfolded? Do you need to be reminded of your initial vision?

¹⁹When Laban had gone to shear his sheep, Rachel stole her father's household gods. ²⁰Moreover, Jacob deceived Laban the Aramean by not telling him he was running away. ²¹So he fled with all he had, and crossing the River,ᵃ he headed for the hill country of Gilead.

Laban Pursues Jacob

²²On the third day Laban was told that Jacob had fled. ²³Taking his relatives with him, he pursued Jacob for seven days and caught up with him in the hill country of Gilead. ²⁴Then God came to Laban the Aramean in a dream at night and said to him, "Be careful not to say anything to Jacob, either good or bad."

²⁵Jacob had pitched his tent in the hill country of Gilead when Laban overtook him, and Laban and his relatives camped there too. ²⁶Then Laban said to Jacob, "What have you done? You've deceived me, and you've carried off my daughters like captives in war. ²⁷Why did you run off secretly and deceive me? Why didn't you tell me, so I could send you away with joy and singing to the music of tambourines and harps? ²⁸You didn't even let me kiss my grandchildren and my daughters good-by. You have done a foolish thing. ²⁹I have the power to harm you; but last night the God of your father said to me, 'Be careful not to say anything to Jacob, either good or bad.' ³⁰Now you have gone off because you longed to return to your father's house. But why did you steal my gods?"

³¹Jacob answered Laban, "I was afraid, because I thought you would take your daughters away from me by force. ³²But if you find anyone who has your gods, he shall not live. In the presence of our

ᵃ21 That is, the Euphrates

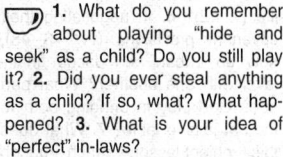

1. What do you remember about playing "hide and seek" as a child? Do you still play it? 2. Did you ever steal anything as a child? If so, what? What happened? 3. What is your idea of "perfect" in-laws?

1. Laban is able to overtake (v. 23) and overpower (v. 29) Jacob. Why doesn't he? How does God intervene (v. 24)? How does this humbling rescue of Jacob from his folly resemble the way God had to rescue two other patriarchs from their misadventures? 2. In verses 25–30, what points does Laban make? Do you think he is justified in his concerns? Why or why not? 3. How does Jacob respond (vv. 36–42)? Do you think he is justified in his concerns? Why or why not? What does this tell you about their relationship? 4. In the interlude (vv. 31–35), what does the reader (and Rachel) know, that Jacob and Laban do not? Is their ignorance

 Genesis 31:22–55   **LABAN PURSUES JACOB**

After years of conflict with Laban, Jacob was called by God to return to his homeland. With the support of his wives Rachel and Leah (Laban's daughters), Jacob fled with his family and possessions.

1. Why did Laban go after Jacob?
   a. to give him his blessing
   b. to do him bodily harm
   c. to force him to work for him again
   d. to take back his daughters
   e. to retrieve his household gods
   f. to see his daughters and grand-children one last time

2. What did God mean when he told Laban "not to say anything to Jacob, either good or bad" (v. 24)?
   a. Don't hurt Jacob.
   b. Don't chew him out.
   c. Listen to his side of the story.
   d. Don't look at the speck in your brother's eye when you've got a plank in your own.

3. What do you think Laban would have done if Jacob had talked to him first rather than running off?

4. Concerning Laban's household gods, Rachel was:
   a. a quick thinker.
   b. fortunate God didn't expose her.
   c. following her father's idolatry.
   d. following her husband's deceit.

5. How do you feel about the end of this story?
   a. They all lived happily ever after, thanks to God's intervention.
   b. Give Laban credit for initiating a truce.
   c. Peace was possible because Jacob moved far from his in-laws.
   d. The sacrifice and special meal proved reconciliation occurred.
   e. Heart to heart reconciliation didn't happen—they just agreed not to bother each other.

6. What is a needed lesson from this story for your life?
   a. Like these people—I need to take initiative to reconcile a relation-ship.
   b. Like Laban—I need to listen when there's conflict.

   c. Like Rachel—I need to quit hiding the skeletons in my closet.
   d. Like Jacob—I need God's help for a situation beyond my control.

7. How do you usually resolve conflict?
   a. I prefer throwing stones to piling them up as a peace memorial.
   b. I try to get the last word before we reach an agreement.
   c. I generally apologize quickly because I think it's my fault.
   d. I ask the other party to sit down and talk things out.
   e. I get knots in my stomach and feel guilty for not doing anything.

8. How much conflict has being an entrepreneur brought to your life? What effect has it had on your family relationships?

9. In what ways have you had to risk your reputation to go into business? What type of accusations have you encountered? How have you sensed "the God of Abraham" with you?

"bliss"? Anger-producing? Or stressful? For whom? **5.** In Jacob's tale of hardships (vv. 38–41), what corrective do you see for the romantic notions of pastor as shepherd? How is Laban's cheating used by God for good in Jacob's life (v. 42)? **6.** In negotiating their covenant provisions (vv. 43–45), how do Laban and Jacob finally level with one another? What part does God play in bringing both to the bargaining table? **7.** What does this object-lesson teach Jacob about fear and faith (compare vv. 31 and 42)? **8.** In verses 45–53, what is meant by the "heap of witness"? By the "watchtower" (*Mizpah*)? By God "judging between us"? By "the name of the Fear of his father Isaac"?

♡ **1.** When God is invoked, as in this chapter, to be witness to the vows and covenants we make, what happens if and when that vow is broken? When have you witnessed such a "self-cursing" vow actually come true? **2.** Deception evidently ran rampant and deep in this patriarchal family. From your own experience and from your review of Genesis to date, do you believe that such sinful patterns are inherited, or are they learned? Would you say that today's abusive sins—child and spouse abuse, drug and alcohol abuse, gambling and theft, lust and adultery—are likewise inherited? Or are they learned by entire families or generations in our society? **3.** How then is one freed from a "family sin" or "inherent sin"? **4.** Judging from your comings and goings last week, which of your pursuits demand and drain the most energy? While on the go, or even on the run, what do you (like Jacob) fear might "catch up with you": (a) False accuser? (b) Ghost from your past? (c) The results of unconfessed sin? (d) Truths you do not want to face? **5.** Where do you see the "hound of heaven" pursuing you? How might you be blind to his loving overtures? Why not ask the group to help you slow down, or do an about-face, long enough to feel the love of God, the Father of Abraham, Isaac, Jacob *and you*?

relatives, see for yourself whether there is anything of yours here with me; and if so, take it." Now Jacob did not know that Rachel had stolen the gods.

[33] So Laban went into Jacob's tent and into Leah's tent and into the tent of the two maidservants, but he found nothing. After he came out of Leah's tent, he entered Rachel's tent. [34] Now Rachel had taken the household gods and put them inside her camel's saddle and was sitting on them. Laban searched through everything in the tent but found nothing.

[35] Rachel said to her father, "Don't be angry, my lord, that I cannot stand up in your presence; I'm having my period." So he searched but could not find the household gods.

[36] Jacob was angry and took Laban to task. "What is my crime?" he asked Laban. "What sin have I committed that you hunt me down? [37] Now that you have searched through all my goods, what have you found that belongs to your household? Put it here in front of your relatives and mine, and let them judge between the two of us.

[38] "I have been with you for twenty years now. Your sheep and goats have not miscarried, nor have I eaten rams from your flocks. [39] I did not bring you animals torn by wild beasts; I bore the loss myself. And you demanded payment from me for whatever was stolen by day or night. [40] This was my situation: The heat consumed me in the daytime and the cold at night, and sleep fled from my eyes. [41] It was like this for the twenty years I was in your household. I worked for you fourteen years for your two daughters and six years for your flocks, and you changed my wages ten times. [42] If the God of my father, the God of Abraham and the Fear of Isaac, had not been with me, you would surely have sent me away empty-handed. But God has seen my hardship and the toil of my hands, and last night he rebuked you."

[43] Laban answered Jacob, "The women are my daughters, the children are my children, and the flocks are my flocks. All you see is mine. Yet what can I do today about these daughters of mine, or about the children they have borne? [44] Come now, let's make a covenant, you and I, and let it serve as a witness between us."

[45] So Jacob took a stone and set it up as a pillar. [46] He said to his relatives, "Gather some stones." So they took stones and piled them in a heap, and they ate there by the heap. [47] Laban called it Jegar Sahadutha,[a] and Jacob called it Galeed.[b]

[48] Laban said, "This heap is a witness between you and me today." That is why it was called Galeed. [49] It was also called Mizpah,[c] because he said, "May the LORD keep watch between you and me when we are away from each other. [50] If you mistreat my daughters or if you take any wives besides my daughters, even though no one is with us, remember that God is a witness between you and me."

[51] Laban also said to Jacob, "Here is this heap, and here is this pillar I have set up between you and me. [52] This heap is a witness, and this pillar is a witness, that I will not go past this heap to your side to harm you and that you will not go past this heap and pillar to my side to harm me. [53] May the God of Abraham and the God of Nahor, the God of their father, judge between us."

So Jacob took an oath in the name of the Fear of his father Isaac. [54] He offered a sacrifice there in the hill country and invited his relatives to a meal. After they had eaten, they spent the night there.

---

[a]47 The Aramaic *Jegar Sahadutha* means *witness heap.*   [b]47 The Hebrew *Galeed* means *witness heap.*   [c]49 *Mizpah* means *watchtower.*

⁵⁵Early the next morning Laban kissed his grandchildren and his daughters and blessed them. Then he left and returned home.

Jacob Prepares to Meet Esau

32 Jacob also went on his way, and the angels of God met him. ²When Jacob saw them, he said, "This is the camp of God!" So he named that place Mahanaim.ᵃ

³Jacob sent messengers ahead of him to his brother Esau in the land of Seir, the country of Edom. ⁴He instructed them: "This is what you are to say to my master Esau: 'Your servant Jacob says, I have been staying with Laban and have remained there till now. ⁵I have cattle and donkeys, sheep and goats, menservants and maidservants. Now I am sending this message to my lord, that I may find favor in your eyes.'"

⁶When the messengers returned to Jacob, they said, "We went to your brother Esau, and now he is coming to meet you, and four hundred men are with him."

⁷In great fear and distress Jacob divided the people who were with him into two groups,ᵇ and the flocks and herds and camels as well. ⁸He thought, "If Esau comes and attacks one group,ᶜ the groupᶜ that is left may escape."

⁹Then Jacob prayed, "O God of my father Abraham, God of my father Isaac, O LORD, who said to me, 'Go back to your country and your relatives, and I will make you prosper,' ¹⁰I am unworthy of all the kindness and faithfulness you have shown your servant. I had only my staff when I crossed this Jordan, but now I have become two groups. ¹¹Save me, I pray, from the hand of my brother Esau,

---

ᵃ2 *Mahanaim* means *two camps.*   ᵇ7 Or *camps*; also in verse 10   ᶜ8 Or *camp*

---

1. What was one meeting you dreaded: Angry boss? Ex-spouse? In-laws? Outlaws? Judge? Hostile sibling? When you went through with it, what happened? 2. When has someone tried to "buy" their way into your good graces? What did they offer you? Did you take it? Did you show mercy anyway?

1. For Jacob, is 20 years away from Esau enough time to heal old wounds? Or does he fear time is on Esau's side, only adding to his desire for revenge? Why do you think so? 2. Are the angels he meets (v. 1) the result of going in faith? Or the reason for faith? 3. Why do you think Esau brings 400 men with him: To intimidate Jacob? Or throw a party for him? What does Jacob think? 4. What do you think of the way Jacob prepares to meet Esau: (a) Jacob is acting out of fear, not faith? (b) Jacob is up to his old tricks again? (c) Jacob is trusting more in Esau's mercy than in God's? Why do you think so? 5. What attitudes

---

  Genesis 32:1–21   **JACOB PREPARES TO MEET ESAU**

Twenty years earlier Jacob had deceitfully stolen the firstborn's blessing their father intended for Jacob's brother Esau. Hearing of Esau's threats to kill him, Jacob fled to the land his family had come from. Now, with his wives, children and possessions, he is about to return home.

1. Why did Jacob send a message ahead to Esau?
a. to get the pain over with
b. to show good faith
c. to get a feel for Esau's attitude toward him
d. to butter him up
e. to reach out before Esau's vengeance was rekindled
f. because angels boosted his confidence that he would be safe

2. Why did Esau come to meet Jacob with 400 men?
a. to break every bone in his body
b. to welcome him with flair
c. to intimidate him
d. to be prepared in case Jacob was tricking him again

3. How do you feel about the way Jacob prepared to meet Esau?
a. He was trying to bribe him.
b. He was using common sense.
c. He was operating out of fear rather than faith.
d. His sincere prayer shows he was totally dependent on God.
e. He was forever trying to manipulate people and events.

4. Is Jacob prepared to admit his wrongdoing and ask Esau to forgive him? Is that imperative for every broken relationship? Why or why not?

5. How do people try to "buy" your favor? Being brutally honest with yourself, how do you try to "buy" the favor of others?

6. What would you like to apply from Jacob's prayer (vv. 9–12) to your own prayer life?
a. What prayer life?!
b. to address God that directly and personally
c. to be absolutely honest
d. to be truly humble

e. to be totally dependent on God
f. to remind God of his promises

7. In your desire to see a significant relationship restored, what positive things from this story can you follow? What negative things does this story caution you to avoid?

8. As you anticipate a meeting with that person, what emotions do you have? Can you and your group commit that to God in prayer?

9. Jacob's new life in Canaan came at the expense of a heavy emotional—and potentially financial—toll. What price, emotionally and financially, have you had to pay as an entrepreneur? Is it worth it? What keeps you going?

10. How would you apply the spirit of Jacob's prayer (vv. 9–12) to your current business life and situation? Conclude your time together with that kind of prayer.

toward God does Jacob display in his naming the place "Mahanaim" (v. 2)? In his escape plans (vv. 7–8)? In his appeasement strategy (vv. 13–21)? Which of these show a true inner change on Jacob's part?

1. For what "showdown" are you preparing? How might your group help you face "your brother" and his "400 men"? 2. What can you learn about prayer from Jacob's prayer in vv. 9–12? When you have wronged someone and want to be forgiven, how do you show you are sincerely sorry? How can Jacob's story help you more effectively ask God or someone else for forgiveness?

1. As a child, did you use your fists, feet, or wits, to get out of trouble? How so? 2. Describe your most mysterious encounter with God.

1. Why do you think Jacob chooses to be alone on the eve of Esau's arrival? 2. What might God be trying to teach Jacob by wrestling with him? Why this method? 3. Who do you think ends up winning? Why? Why is Jacob's hip damaged? 4. In what sense does this story summarize Jacob's life? 5. What does Jacob becoming "Israel" mean?

1. With what are you wrestling: Certain people? God? Evil powers (see Eph 6:12)? 2. Are you winning, losing, or "limping along"? How might your group and God help? Israel means "he struggles with God." What name might God give you?

1. "The best part about fighting is making up"—how might that saying fit your family? 2. What dreaded family reunion turned out better than you expected? Why was it a serendipity for you?

1. How would you judge the success of this meeting? In what sense is Esau like the prodigal's father and Jacob like the

for I am afraid he will come and attack me, and also the mothers with their children. [12]But you have said, 'I will surely make you prosper and will make your descendants like the sand of the sea, which cannot be counted.'"

[13]He spent the night there, and from what he had with him he selected a gift for his brother Esau: [14]two hundred female goats and twenty male goats, two hundred ewes and twenty rams, [15]thirty female camels with their young, forty cows and ten bulls, and twenty female donkeys and ten male donkeys. [16]He put them in the care of his servants, each herd by itself, and said to his servants, "Go ahead of me, and keep some space between the herds."

[17]He instructed the one in the lead: "When my brother Esau meets you and asks, 'To whom do you belong, and where are you going, and who owns all these animals in front of you?' [18]then you are to say, 'They belong to your servant Jacob. They are a gift sent to my lord Esau, and he is coming behind us.'"

[19]He also instructed the second, the third and all the others who followed the herds: "You are to say the same thing to Esau when you meet him. [20]And be sure to say, 'Your servant Jacob is coming behind us.'" For he thought, "I will pacify him with these gifts I am sending on ahead; later, when I see him, perhaps he will receive me." [21]So Jacob's gifts went on ahead of him, but he himself spent the night in the camp.

Jacob Wrestles With God

[22]That night Jacob got up and took his two wives, his two maidservants and his eleven sons and crossed the ford of the Jabbok. [23]After he had sent them across the stream, he sent over all his possessions. [24]So Jacob was left alone, and a man wrestled with him till daybreak. [25]When the man saw that he could not overpower him, he touched the socket of Jacob's hip so that his hip was wrenched as he wrestled with the man. [26]Then the man said, "Let me go, for it is daybreak."

But Jacob replied, "I will not let you go unless you bless me."

[27]The man asked him, "What is your name?"

"Jacob," he answered.

[28]Then the man said, "Your name will no longer be Jacob, but Israel,[a] because you have struggled with God and with men and have overcome."

[29]Jacob said, "Please tell me your name."

But he replied, "Why do you ask my name?" Then he blessed him there.

[30]So Jacob called the place Peniel,[b] saying, "It is because I saw God face to face, and yet my life was spared."

[31]The sun rose above him as he passed Peniel,[c] and he was limping because of his hip. [32]Therefore to this day the Israelites do not eat the tendon attached to the socket of the hip, because the socket of Jacob's hip was touched near the tendon.

Jacob Meets Esau

33 Jacob looked up and there was Esau, coming with his four hundred men; so he divided the children among Leah, Rachel and the two maidservants. [2]He put the maidservants and their children in front, Leah and her children next, and Rachel and Joseph in the rear. [3]He himself went on ahead and bowed down to the ground seven times as he approached his brother.

[4]But Esau ran to meet Jacob and embraced him; he threw his

[a]28 *Israel* means *he struggles with God.*   [b]30 *Peniel* means *face of God.*
[c]31 Hebrew *Penuel,* a variant of *Peniel*

arms around his neck and kissed him. And they wept. ⁵Then Esau looked up and saw the women and children. "Who are these with you?" he asked.

Jacob answered, "They are the children God has graciously given your servant."

⁶Then the maidservants and their children approached and bowed down. ⁷Next, Leah and her children came and bowed down. Last of all came Joseph and Rachel, and they too bowed down.

⁸Esau asked, "What do you mean by all these droves I met?"

"To find favor in your eyes, my lord," he said.

⁹But Esau said, "I already have plenty, my brother. Keep what you have for yourself."

¹⁰"No, please!" said Jacob. "If I have found favor in your eyes, accept this gift from me. For to see your face is like seeing the face of God, now that you have received me favorably. ¹¹Please accept the present that was brought to you, for God has been gracious to me and I have all I need." And because Jacob insisted, Esau accepted it.

¹²Then Esau said, "Let us be on our way; I'll accompany you."

¹³But Jacob said to him, "My lord knows that the children are tender and that I must care for the ewes and cows that are nursing their young. If they are driven hard just one day, all the animals will die. ¹⁴So let my lord go on ahead of his servant, while I move along slowly at the pace of the droves before me and that of the children, until I come to my lord in Seir."

¹⁵Esau said, "Then let me leave some of my men with you."

prodigal (see Lk 15)? **2.** Do you think Esau has forgiven Jacob for his earlier deceptions? Do you think Jacob feels forgiven? Why or why not? (Compare 33:10b with 32:30. What does Jacob see in Esau?) **3.** What do you make of Jacob refusing Esau's offer to travel with him or send along some of his men for protection: (a) Jacob wants no strings attached? (b) "Once burned, twice cautious"? (c) Time does not heal all wounds? (d) Other? **4.** Why do you think Jacob goes to Succoth rather than Seir? What does this tell you about the "reconciliation" between these two men? **5.** How has their relationship changed? Remained the same? Is that good or bad? Why?

1. When is it easier for you to forgive others? When is it harder? When is it easier to feel forgiven? When is it harder? What do your answers reveal about your fears? Your faith? Your Lord? **2.** Tell a happy story of forgiveness received unexpectedly or given unsolicited. **3.** Like Esau, what "gift" from someone are you having difficulty accepting? Why not be gra-

---

   Genesis 32:22–32   **JACOB WRESTLES WITH GOD**

After being gone many years, Jacob is on his way home. He knows Esau, from whom he fled earlier, is coming—along with 400 men—to meet him.

1. Why did Jacob separate himself from his family on the eve of Esau's arrival?
   a. He wanted to be alone.
   b. He figured if Esau came for revenge, at least his family would be spared.
   c. He figured if Esau came for revenge, at least *he* would be spared.
   d. God wanted to get him alone.

2. Which best describes why God chose to wrestle with Jacob?
   a. to show Jacob God's strength
   b. to show Jacob his own strength
   c. to see how much Jacob wanted to be blessed
   d. to correct Jacob's life-long pattern of struggling with people and God

3. Why did God wrench Jacob's hip?
   a. to humble Jacob
   b. as a reminder of God's power
   c. as a reminder of God's favor

d. Pain brings people closer to God.

4. Why did God change Jacob's name (from "He deceives" to "He struggles with God")?
   a. to remind him of this struggle
   b. to mark his personality change
   c. because Jacob finally recognized God as the source of blessing
   d. It was symbolic—the nation of Israel would have a history of struggling with God.

5. How have you discovered your own character?
   a. through struggle
   b. through pain
   c. through God's blessing
   d. through disappointment

6. Right now in my struggles I am (identify all that apply):
   a. wrestling with God.
   b. wrestling with evil.
   c. wrestling with some person(s).
   d. wrestling with a decision.
   e. trying to make it on my own.
   f. gaining the blessing.
   g. losing the battle.
   h. limping along.

7. How can this group pray for you and help you in your struggle(s)?

8. In what ways does being an entrepreneur cost you stability in your life? Who gets the credit if your business succeeds? Who gets the blame if it fails? How much do you struggle to give control of your business to God?

9. How does this story relate to you as a parent?
   a. My child is like Jacob—not letting go until he gets what he wants.
   b. Sometimes I feel like I can't keep up the "fight."
   c. Strong-willed children are tough to deal with but have tremendous potential to be overcomers.
   d. My child may do some "limping," but that's okay.

10. What would be a "happy ending" for you as the parent of a strong-willed child? How can you receive more of God's hope and strength toward that end? How has this Bible study course given you hope and strength?

cious and accept it today? The stories of the patriarchs frequently describe special places these men devote to God. What place holds special meaning in your life?

---

 1. Would you rather be a big brother, or have a big brother? Why? Who served as "big brother" in your life? Was he the kind of big brother that teased and tormented you? Or the kind that defended and rescued you? 2. What or who is the family's pride and joy, the loss of which would be unbearable?

 1. What most disturbs you about this terrible story: The rape of Dinah (v. 2)? The "if they get married what difference does it make" attitude of the Canaanites? The sons' deceit (vv. 13–17)? Or their savage methods of revenge (vv. 25–29)? Why? 2. Why do you

---

"But why do that?" Jacob asked. "Just let me find favor in the eyes of my lord."

[16] So that day Esau started on his way back to Seir. [17] Jacob, however, went to Succoth, where he built a place for himself and made shelters for his livestock. That is why the place is called Succoth.[a]

[18] After Jacob came from Paddan Aram,[b] he arrived safely at the[c] city of Shechem in Canaan and camped within sight of the city. [19] For a hundred pieces of silver,[d] he bought from the sons of Hamor, the father of Shechem, the plot of ground where he pitched his tent. [20] There he set up an altar and called it El Elohe Israel.[e]

Dinah and the Shechemites

34 Now Dinah, the daughter Leah had borne to Jacob, went out to visit the women of the land. [2] When Shechem son of Hamor the Hivite, the ruler of that area, saw her, he took her and violated her. [3] His heart was drawn to Dinah daughter of Jacob, and he loved the girl and spoke tenderly to her. [4] And Shechem said to his father Hamor, "Get me this girl as my wife."

[5] When Jacob heard that his daughter Dinah had been defiled, his sons were in the fields with his livestock; so he kept quiet about it until they came home.

[6] Then Shechem's father Hamor went out to talk with Jacob. [7] Now Jacob's sons had come in from the fields as soon as they

---

[a]17 Succoth means shelters.   [b]18 That is, Northwest Mesopotamia   [c]18 Or arrived at Shalem, a   [d]19 Hebrew hundred kesitahs; a kesitah was a unit of money of unknown weight and value.   [e]20 El Elohe Israel can mean God, the God of Israel or mighty is the God of Israel.

⊗ $ *Genesis 33:1–20*   JACOB MEETS ESAU

Jacob and Esau haven't seen each other since Jacob ran for his life from Esau's spiteful anger 20 years earlier. In preparation for their meeting, Jacob had sent droves of livestock ahead of him as a gift for his twin brother.

1. Jacob bowed down seven times as he approached Esau:
   a. out of total fear.
   b. as a symbol of submission.
   c. because of his guilt.
   d. to beg for mercy.
   e. as a way of apologizing.

2. What happened when Jacob and Esau met?
   a. Esau was overcome with joy to see his brother at last.
   b. Jacob's gifts worked.
   c. Reconciliation occurred.
   d. Jacob got off the hook.
   e. Jacob was forgiven.
   f. Esau was merciful.

3. Why did Jacob insist on giving Esau a present?
   a. to appease his guilt
   b. to buy Esau's future favor

c. to make up for the blessing he had stolen
   d. because God had been so gracious to him
   e. because it was easier than saying "I'm sorry"

4. Why did Jacob tell Esau he would go at his own pace to Seir, but then did not go there?
   a. He got side-tracked.
   b. Things still weren't right between him and Esau.
   c. Always the deceiver, he tricked Esau again.
   d. Though Esau didn't take revenge, Jacob still didn't trust him.
   e. God told him to go elsewhere.

5. Is it harder for you to extend or to accept an apology? Which do you find yourself needing to do more often?

6. ⊗ What's holding you back from making arrangements for reconciling a broken relationship in your life?
   a. Nothing—I'm ready to do it.

b. I'm ready but they're not.
   c. I'm afraid it's too late.
   d. The timing isn't right.
   e. The pain is still too great.
   f. Nothing—I already have!

7. ⊗ As you conclude this course, how would you like the group to remember you in prayer?

8. $ Jacob had to move slowly because of the children and the livestock. How often do you see promising signs in your business, only to encounter delays or setbacks? How often do you feel like your business isn't going anywhere? What difference can your faith make in such times?

9. $ How able are you right now to "slow down" for the sake of your business? Your employees or others involved in your business? Your family? Your friends? Your church? Your relationship with God? Your physical and emotional health?

heard what had happened. They were filled with grief and fury, because Shechem had done a disgraceful thing in*a* Israel by lying with Jacob's daughter—a thing that should not be done.

⁸But Hamor said to them, "My son Shechem has his heart set on your daughter. Please give her to him as his wife. ⁹Intermarry with us; give us your daughters and take our daughters for yourselves. ¹⁰You can settle among us; the land is open to you. Live in it, trade*b* in it, and acquire property in it."

¹¹Then Shechem said to Dinah's father and brothers, "Let me find favor in your eyes, and I will give you whatever you ask. ¹²Make the price for the bride and the gift I am to bring as great as you like, and I'll pay whatever you ask me. Only give me the girl as my wife."

¹³Because their sister Dinah had been defiled, Jacob's sons replied deceitfully as they spoke to Shechem and his father Hamor. ¹⁴They said to them, "We can't do such a thing; we can't give our sister to a man who is not circumcised. That would be a disgrace to us. ¹⁵We will give our consent to you on one condition only: that you become like us by circumcising all your males. ¹⁶Then we will give you our daughters and take your daughters for ourselves. We'll settle among you and become one people with you. ¹⁷But if you will not agree to be circumcised, we'll take our sister*c* and go."

¹⁸Their proposal seemed good to Hamor and his son Shechem. ¹⁹The young man, who was the most honored of all his father's household, lost no time in doing what they said, because he was delighted with Jacob's daughter. ²⁰So Hamor and his son Shechem went to the gate of their city to speak to their fellow townsmen. ²¹"These men are friendly toward us," they said. "Let them live in our land and trade in it; the land has plenty of room for them. We can marry their daughters and they can marry ours. ²²But the men will consent to live with us as one people only on the condition that our males be circumcised, as they themselves are. ²³Won't their livestock, their property and all their other animals become ours? So let us give our consent to them, and they will settle among us."

²⁴All the men who went out of the city gate agreed with Hamor and his son Shechem, and every male in the city was circumcised.

²⁵Three days later, while all of them were still in pain, two of Jacob's sons, Simeon and Levi, Dinah's brothers, took their swords and attacked the unsuspecting city, killing every male. ²⁶They put Hamor and his son Shechem to the sword and took Dinah from Shechem's house and left. ²⁷The sons of Jacob came upon the dead bodies and looted the city where*d* their sister had been defiled. ²⁸They seized their flocks and herds and donkeys and everything else of theirs in the city and out in the fields. ²⁹They carried off all their wealth and all their women and children, taking as plunder everything in the houses.

³⁰Then Jacob said to Simeon and Levi, "You have brought trouble on me by making me a stench to the Canaanites and Perizzites, the people living in this land. We are few in number, and if they join forces against me and attack me, I and my household will be destroyed."

³¹But they replied, "Should he have treated our sister like a prostitute?"

---

think this story is in the Bible? What does this passage teach about rape? About revenge? Family honor? Mixing with foreigners? Marriage? **3.** Instead of returning to Bethel immediately, as commanded by God (see 31:13; 35:1), Jacob lingers at Shechem, which lies along the main road from Peniel to Bethel. How might this put his clan unnecessarily at risk? What reward did Jacob think was worth the risk of "lingering" when God said "Go"? **4.** While Jacob knows enough to never want any of his clan to intermarry with the Canaanites (see 28:1–4), what benefits of association with them does he want? **5.** At the end, what do you think most incensed Jacob: (a) His aborted trade association with the Canaanites? (b) His sons' treachery and massacre? (c) His defiled daughter? (d) His personal safety? Why? (see vv. 5,30; also 49:5–7)? **6.** Where is God in the events of chapter 34? (Note that God's name appears last in 33:20 and first in 35:1 and nowhere in between.) If God appears absent, why is that?

♡ **1.** What does this all-too-human and all-too-modern story of terrorism and counter-terrorism bring to mind for you? What cruelty in your world especially bothers you? **2.** Where do you need to make sure that your anger does not get the best of you? How can this group pray for you? **3.** When are you most likely to seek revenge? How does a desire for revenge affect you and your faith in God? Do you think revenge or retaliation is ever a legitimate response for the Christian? **4.** Is the Bible's concern for cultural and religious purity as important for today's believers as for early Israel? What advice would you give a believer and non-believer who wanted to get married? Why? **5.** In your life, when have you lingered at Shechem (a place to prosper) over Bethel (your designated "house of God")?

---

a7 Or *against* Israel by lying with Jacob's *b10* Or *move about freely*; also in verse 21   *c17* Hebrew daughter   *d27* Or *because*

What place from your past is of spiritual importance to you? What makes this place so meaningful?

📖 **1.** What memories or feelings would Jacob associate with Bethel (see 28:10–22)? Why do you think God now asks him to return there? **2.** How does Jacob's request (v. 2) relate to his clan going up to Bethel? How do they respond to Jacob's request? What then happens (v. 5)? **3.** Why might the "terror of God" have fallen on the towns around Jacob (vv. 4ff; also 34:30)? **4.** Review the promises made to Abraham (12:1–3; 15:17–21; 17:1–8; 22:15–18). How do these compare to the promises God makes to Jacob (vv. 11–12)? What would such continuity mean to Jacob? To God?

♡ **1.** What is your "Bethel"— where God has met you in times of stress? Where do you want God to answer now? **2.** If you were to bury something under the oak at Shechem, what would you bury? **3.** What will you do to thank God for the special places, promises and "fear of God" that he has given to you?

Jacob Returns to Bethel

35 Then God said to Jacob, "Go up to Bethel and settle there, and build an altar there to God, who appeared to you when you were fleeing from your brother Esau."

²So Jacob said to his household and to all who were with him, "Get rid of the foreign gods you have with you, and purify yourselves and change your clothes. ³Then come, let us go up to Bethel, where I will build an altar to God, who answered me in the day of my distress and who has been with me wherever I have gone." ⁴So they gave Jacob all the foreign gods they had and the rings in their ears, and Jacob buried them under the oak at Shechem. ⁵Then they set out, and the terror of God fell upon the towns all around them so that no one pursued them.

⁶Jacob and all the people with him came to Luz (that is, Bethel) in the land of Canaan. ⁷There he built an altar, and he called the place El Bethel,ᵃ because it was there that God revealed himself to him when he was fleeing from his brother.

⁸Now Deborah, Rebekah's nurse, died and was buried under the oak below Bethel. So it was named Allon Bacuth.ᵇ

⁹After Jacob returned from Paddan Aram,ᶜ God appeared to him again and blessed him. ¹⁰God said to him, "Your name is Jacob,ᵈ but you will no longer be called Jacob; your name will be Israel.ᵉ" So he named him Israel.

¹¹And God said to him, "I am God Almightyᶠ; be fruitful and increase in number. A nation and a community of nations will

---

a7 El Bethel means *God of Bethel.*   *b8 Allon Bacuth* means *oak of weeping.*   *c9* That is, Northwest Mesopotamia; also in verse 26   *d10 Jacob* means *he grasps the heel* (figuratively, *he deceives*).   *e10 Israel* means *he struggles with God.*   *f11* Hebrew *El-Shaddai*

$ *Genesis 35:1–15*   **JACOB RETURNS TO BETHEL**

Years before, God had revealed himself to Jacob as he was fleeing his homeland. The Lord promised to bring him back safely, and also transferred to Jacob the covenant promises given to his grandfather Abraham and to his father Isaac. Now God calls him to return to that special place Jacob had named Bethel—the "house of God."

1. What do you think was Jacob's dominant feeling about going back to Bethel?
   a. nostalgia
   b. reverence
   c. gratitude
   d. guilt

2. Why did God call Jacob to return to Bethel?
   a. to get a fresh start
   b. to help him remember his spiritual roots
   c. to convict him of his sins
   d. to renew the covenant with him again
   e. to encourage Jacob to lead his family to worship God alone

3. What do you think was the mood of Jacob's household as they complied with Jacob's request (v. 2)?
   a. anger
   b. sadness
   c. repentance
   d. shame
   e. relief that they saw where Jacob buried their things so they could go back and dig them up!

4. How might God be calling you to go back to Bethel?
   a. by visiting a special place in my spiritual journey
   b. by thanking my parents for what they instilled in me
   c. by worshiping God like I used to
   d. by thanking _____ for the impact they made on my faith

5. Where is your favorite place to meet God now?
   a. church
   b. small group
   c. quiet place at home
   d. special place outdoors
   e. We don't get together much.

6. What do you need to "bury"?
   a. an idol   d. a habit
   b. a grudge   e. an attitude
   c. expectations   f. the past

7. How can this group help you "break ground," and then later not "re-dig"?

8. Jacob erected altars in response to God's blessings. How has God shown his blessings to you lately? How can you express your thanks?

9. **$** The measure of Jacob's success in God's eyes was:
   a. the number of his cattle and sheep.
   b. his trust in God's promises.
   c. the altars he built.
   d. his obedience.
   e. his good deeds.
   f. his influence on his family.

10. **$** How do you measure your success as an entrepreneur? How do you measure your success as a person? How has this course affected your answers?

come from you, and kings will come from your body. [12]The land I gave to Abraham and Isaac I also give to you, and I will give this land to your descendants after you." [13]Then God went up from him at the place where he had talked with him.

[14]Jacob set up a stone pillar at the place where God had talked with him, and he poured out a drink offering on it; he also poured oil on it. [15]Jacob called the place where God had talked with him Bethel.[a]

The Deaths of Rachel and Isaac

[16]Then they moved on from Bethel. While they were still some distance from Ephrath, Rachel began to give birth and had great difficulty. [17]And as she was having great difficulty in childbirth, the midwife said to her, "Don't be afraid, for you have another son." [18]As she breathed her last—for she was dying—she named her son Ben-Oni.[b] But his father named him Benjamin.[c]

[19]So Rachel died and was buried on the way to Ephrath (that is, Bethlehem). [20]Over her tomb Jacob set up a pillar, and to this day that pillar marks Rachel's tomb.

[21]Israel moved on again and pitched his tent beyond Migdal Eder. [22]While Israel was living in that region, Reuben went in and slept with his father's concubine Bilhah, and Israel heard of it.

Jacob had twelve sons:

[23]The sons of Leah:

Reuben the firstborn of Jacob,
Simeon, Levi, Judah, Issachar and Zebulun.

[24]The sons of Rachel:

Joseph and Benjamin.

[25]The sons of Rachel's maidservant Bilhah:

Dan and Naphtali.

[26]The sons of Leah's maidservant Zilpah:

Gad and Asher.

These were the sons of Jacob, who were born to him in Paddan Aram.

[27]Jacob came home to his father Isaac in Mamre, near Kiriath Arba (that is, Hebron), where Abraham and Isaac had stayed. [28]Isaac lived a hundred and eighty years. [29]Then he breathed his last and died and was gathered to his people, old and full of years. And his sons Esau and Jacob buried him.

Esau's Descendants

36 This is the account of Esau (that is, Edom).

[2]Esau took his wives from the women of Canaan: Adah daughter of Elon the Hittite, and Oholibamah daughter of Anah and granddaughter of Zibeon the Hivite— [3]also Basemath daughter of Ishmael and sister of Nebaioth.

[4]Adah bore Eliphaz to Esau, Basemath bore Reuel, [5]and Oholibamah bore Jeush, Jalam and Korah. These were the sons of Esau, who were born to him in Canaan.

[6]Esau took his wives and sons and daughters and all the members of his household, as well as his livestock and all his other animals and all the goods he had acquired in Canaan, and moved to a land some distance from his brother Jacob. [7]Their possessions were too great for them to remain together; the land where they were staying could not support them

a15 *Bethel* means *house of God.*   b18 *Ben-Oni* means *son of my trouble.*
c18 *Benjamin* means *son of my right hand.*

1. How many times have you moved in your lifetime? From where to where? 2. When have you lost a loved one through death?

1. In the context of Genesis, what is the significance of Rachel's death (see 31:32–35)? Of Benjamin's birth (see 30:24)? Of Reuben's shocking sin (see 49:3ff)? Of Isaac's death (see 25:8ff)? 2. What irony do you see in the reunion of Jacob and Esau at their father's death? 3. How does this listing of Jacob's 12 sons by their birth mothers settle legal matters? Or leadership priorities?

1. Are your memories of your parents and grandparents negative, or positive? What is one thing from each for which you are very thankful? What might still need God's healing touch? 2. Consider Isaac's death in v. 29. Describe how you would like to have your own life and death remembered. 3. Compared with Rachel's and Isaac's death, what reunion or transitions would happen with your parents' death?

1. If you had to choose just one, which would you want: Many friends, much money, or numerous descendants? What would you miss most if you lacked any one of those three resources? 2. Recall the last time you were contending for a job promotion, neighborhood turf, committee leadership or marriage proposal. Who was your rival party: Friend, foe, or kinfolk? Suppose you were to find out that one of the parties with whom you were contesting does, in fact, share common roots with you. What difference would that make in your attitudes and your actions?

1. Considering the fact that the Bible does not say much about the descendants of Esau, why do you think so much space is

devoted to his genealogy? Do you think this is meant primarily for the original readers of Genesis, or also for today's reader? Why? **2.** There's actually more to this genealogy than meets the eye of the casual 20th century reader. Where do you see the fulfillment of God's promise (25:23) and Isaac's blessing (27:39–40)? (Note that Amalek [v. 12] will prove to be one of Israel's bitter foes.) **3.** What is significant about the shift in focus from the wives to the livestock in the land of Esau (vv. 1–8)? Likewise, in the shift in focus from the "sons" (vv. 9–14) to the "chiefs" (the head of a clan) of Esau (vv. 15–19)? **4.** What do you see of significance in the "Horite Seir" dynasty: With whom do the Edomites intermarry (match vv. 2 and 24, 12 and 22)? Whom do they then displace altogether (see Dt 2:12,22)? **5.** The dispossessed Esau sees kings and kingdom result from his descendants before Jacob (vv. 31–43). What irony do you see in that (see 17:6; 35:11)? **6.** How does Jacob's "place" in history (37:1) compare with Esau's "place" in history (summarized in 36:43, without any reference to God's covenant provisions)? What bottom line distinction do you see here?

♥ **1.** While Jacob will live almost to the end of Genesis, this chapter marks the end of the narrative concerning Jacob and Esau and the beginning of the one concerning Joseph. Looking back, how have you seen Jacob grow in faith? What turning points were significant that growth? **2.** By the grace of God, "Jacob" became "Israel." What bad traits of a Jacob and good traits of an Israel are reflected in your own growth in character? For example, how is your life, like Jacob's, a struggle with God to see who is in control? **3.** Likewise with Esau, what one lesson from his life could you apply to your own walk with God? For example, Esau's early life was dominated by instant gratification and long-term grudges; later on, he proved to be very magnanimous and God blessed him with "kings." Where on that spectrum would you place your life right now? Looking back on Jacob's deceptive way of getting Esau's blessing and birthright, was Esau's life totally cursed? What does that tell you about God's relationship with Esau? About God's relationship with you?

both because of their livestock. [8]So Esau (that is, Edom) settled in the hill country of Seir.

[9]This is the account of Esau the father of the Edomites in the hill country of Seir.

[10]These are the names of Esau's sons:

Eliphaz, the son of Esau's wife Adah, and Reuel, the son of Esau's wife Basemath.
[11]The sons of Eliphaz:

Teman, Omar, Zepho, Gatam and Kenaz.
[12]Esau's son Eliphaz also had a concubine named Timna, who bore him Amalek. These were grandsons of Esau's wife Adah.
[13]The sons of Reuel:

Nahath, Zerah, Shammah and Mizzah. These were grandsons of Esau's wife Basemath.
[14]The sons of Esau's wife Oholibamah daughter of Anah and granddaughter of Zibeon, whom she bore to Esau:

Jeush, Jalam and Korah.

[15]These were the chiefs among Esau's descendants:
The sons of Eliphaz the firstborn of Esau:

Chiefs Teman, Omar, Zepho, Kenaz, [16]Korah,[a] Gatam and Amalek. These were the chiefs descended from Eliphaz in Edom; they were grandsons of Adah.
[17]The sons of Esau's son Reuel:

Chiefs Nahath, Zerah, Shammah and Mizzah. These were the chiefs descended from Reuel in Edom; they were grandsons of Esau's wife Basemath.
[18]The sons of Esau's wife Oholibamah:

Chiefs Jeush, Jalam and Korah. These were the chiefs descended from Esau's wife Oholibamah daughter of Anah.
[19]These were the sons of Esau (that is, Edom), and these were their chiefs.

[20]These were the sons of Seir the Horite, who were living in the region:

Lotan, Shobal, Zibeon, Anah, [21]Dishon, Ezer and Dishan. These sons of Seir in Edom were Horite chiefs.
[22]The sons of Lotan:

Hori and Homam.[b] Timna was Lotan's sister.
[23]The sons of Shobal:

Alvan, Manahath, Ebal, Shepho and Onam.
[24]The sons of Zibeon:

Aiah and Anah. This is the Anah who discovered the hot springs[c] in the desert while he was grazing the donkeys of his father Zibeon.
[25]The children of Anah:

Dishon and Oholibamah daughter of Anah.
[26]The sons of Dishon[d]:

Hemdan, Eshban, Ithran and Keran.
[27]The sons of Ezer:

Bilhan, Zaavan and Akan.
[28]The sons of Dishan:

Uz and Aran.

[a]16 Masoretic Text; Samaritan Pentateuch (see also Gen. 36:11 and 1 Chron. 1:36) does not have *Korah*.   [b]22 Hebrew *Hemam*, a variant of *Homam* (see 1 Chron. 1:39)
[c]24 Vulgate; Syriac *discovered water*; the meaning of the Hebrew for this word is uncertain.   [d]26 Hebrew *Dishan*, a variant of *Dishon*

²⁹These were the Horite chiefs:

Lotan, Shobal, Zibeon, Anah, ³⁰Dishon, Ezer and Dishan. These were the Horite chiefs, according to their divisions, in the land of Seir.

The Rulers of Edom

³¹These were the kings who reigned in Edom before any Israelite king reigned[a]:

³²Bela son of Beor became king of Edom. His city was named Dinhabah.

³³When Bela died, Jobab son of Zerah from Bozrah succeeded him as king.

³⁴When Jobab died, Husham from the land of the Temanites succeeded him as king.

³⁵When Husham died, Hadad son of Bedad, who defeated Midian in the country of Moab, succeeded him as king. His city was named Avith.

³⁶When Hadad died, Samlah from Masrekah succeeded him as king.

³⁷When Samlah died, Shaul from Rehoboth on the river[b] succeeded him as king.

³⁸When Shaul died, Baal-Hanan son of Acbor succeeded him as king.

³⁹When Baal-Hanan son of Acbor died, Hadad[c] succeeded him as king. His city was named Pau, and his wife's name was Mehetabel daughter of Matred, the daughter of Me-Zahab.

⁴⁰These were the chiefs descended from Esau, by name, according to their clans and regions:

Timna, Alvah, Jetheth, ⁴¹Oholibamah, Elah, Pinon, ⁴²Kenaz, Teman, Mibzar, ⁴³Magdiel and Iram. These were the chiefs of Edom, according to their settlements in the land they occupied.

This was Esau the father of the Edomites.

Joseph's Dreams

37 Jacob lived in the land where his father had stayed, the land of Canaan.

²This is the account of Jacob.

Joseph, a young man of seventeen, was tending the flocks with his brothers, the sons of Bilhah and the sons of Zilpah, his father's wives, and he brought their father a bad report about them.
³Now Israel loved Joseph more than any of his other sons, because he had been born to him in his old age; and he made a richly ornamented[d] robe for him. ⁴When his brothers saw that their father loved him more than any of them, they hated him and could not speak a kind word to him.

⁵Joseph had a dream, and when he told it to his brothers, they hated him all the more. ⁶He said to them, "Listen to this dream I had: ⁷We were binding sheaves of grain out in the field when suddenly my sheaf rose and stood upright, while your sheaves gathered around mine and bowed down to it."

⁸His brothers said to him, "Do you intend to reign over us? Will

1. When, if ever, did you receive a "bad report" in school? What for? By whom? 2. What has been one of your more divisive and memorable experiences with "tattling"?

1. From these verses, how would you describe Joseph to someone who had never met him? Why do you think Joseph behaves the way he does? Would you want him for a brother? Why or why not? 2. If you were Jacob, why play favorites? (Remember how parental favoritism ruined your family ties with brother Esau.) 3. What do these dreams tell us about how the story of Joseph will end? Why might God give these dreams to Joseph at this time? Do such dreams point to human success or God's control? Why?

1. When God wants to give you a special message, how does he do it: Counselors? Circumstances? Group interaction? Script-

---

a31 Or *before an Israelite king reigned over them*   b37 Possibly the Euphrates
c39 Many manuscripts of the Masoretic Text, Samaritan Pentateuch and Syriac (see also 1 Chron. 1:50); most manuscripts of the Masoretic Text *Hadar*   d3 The meaning of the Hebrew for *richly ornamented* is uncertain; also in verses 23 and 32.

ures? How does that way compare to Joseph's dreams? **2.** What is one of your wildest dreams—one "only God" could bring about? **3.** Where are you battling with envy? How would you like to see that change?

---

1. Growing up, how well did you get along with your brothers or sisters? Who was the baby in the family? How was that person treated? **2.** Is your relationship different with them now that you are older? To what do you attribute that: Mellowing with age? Little brother got bigger? Everybody moved away?

1. This family is quite conflicted by all that goes on here. Try to empathize with what each character is feeling: What feelings are aroused by Jacob's sons plot-

you actually rule us?" And they hated him all the more because of his dream and what he had said.

⁹Then he had another dream, and he told it to his brothers. "Listen," he said, "I had another dream, and this time the sun and moon and eleven stars were bowing down to me."

¹⁰When he told his father as well as his brothers, his father rebuked him and said, "What is this dream you had? Will your mother and I and your brothers actually come and bow down to the ground before you?" ¹¹His brothers were jealous of him, but his father kept the matter in mind.

Joseph Sold by His Brothers

¹²Now his brothers had gone to graze their father's flocks near Shechem, ¹³and Israel said to Joseph, "As you know, your brothers are grazing the flocks near Shechem. Come, I am going to send you to them."

"Very well," he replied.

¹⁴So he said to him, "Go and see if all is well with your brothers and with the flocks, and bring word back to me." Then he sent him off from the Valley of Hebron.

When Joseph arrived at Shechem, ¹⁵a man found him wandering around in the fields and asked him, "What are you looking for?"

¹⁶He replied, "I'm looking for my brothers. Can you tell me where they are grazing their flocks?"

 Genesis 37:1–11　　　　　　　　　　**JOSEPH'S DREAMS**

Jacob (given the new name "Israel" by God) had 12 sons. The two youngest were born to him by Rachel, Jacob's favorite wife, who died giving birth to Benjamin. This story, as well as the rest of Genesis, centers around Joseph—Jacob's eleventh son and Rachel's firstborn.

1. If Joseph were my brother, I would:
   a. wring his neck.
   b. ignore his far-out dreams.
   c. mend my ways so he couldn't tattle on me.
   d. conspire with my brothers against him.
   e. compete for my share of Dad's love.
   f. mope with jealousy.

2. If I were Joseph, I would:
   a. do what he did—tell it like it is.
   b. keep my mouth shut.
   c. wear my fancy robe with pride.
   d. ask Dad not to treat me special.
   e. feel like the "black sheep" of the family.

3. If I were Jacob (Israel), I would:
   a. be honest with my feelings like he was.
   b. make a nice robe for all my children or else none of them.
   c. call a family meeting and hash things out.

   d. take Joseph to a counselor.
   e. recognize God's hand in these dreams.

4. What would a family therapist say about this family?
   a. What a case of sibling rivalry!
   b. Joseph is a spoiled brat.
   c. Jacob is an unfit parent.
   d. Joseph has a sleeping disorder.
   e. There's no hope for this family!

5. Why did God give these dreams to Joseph?
   a. He didn't.
   b. because he loved Joseph more than his brothers
   c. because Joseph was Jacob's favorite son
   d. God used them for his purposes later on.

6. When I have dreams of personal success, I:
   a. assume they are from God.
   b. assume they aren't from God.
   c. figure I ate too much before bed.
   d. keep them to myself.
   e. tell everyone who will listen.

7. When are you tempted to be jealous? What needs to happen to change that?

8. What is the number one cause of conflict in your family? What positive things might God be trying to do through it? How could you help your family get along better?

9. How could Jacob correct Joseph without squelching his potential and his dreams? How can you do the same with your child or others close to you?

10. How does this story remind you of your life as a parent? (And what can you do about it?)
    a. I deal with lots of tattling.
    b. I deal with lots of sibling rivalry.
    c. I have a hard time not playing favorites.
    d. My teenager has an "attitude."
    e. My teenager thinks I should "bow down" to what he or she wants.
    f. I "rebuke" my teen a lot.

11. What has been the most helpful thing you have learned about parenting your adolescent during this course? What do you appreciate about this group? Have one member at a time listen silently while others express their affirmation or encouragement to that person.

17"They have moved on from here," the man answered. "I heard them say, 'Let's go to Dothan.'"

So Joseph went after his brothers and found them near Dothan. 18But they saw him in the distance, and before he reached them, they plotted to kill him.

19"Here comes that dreamer!" they said to each other. 20"Come now, let's kill him and throw him into one of these cisterns and say that a ferocious animal devoured him. Then we'll see what comes of his dreams."

21When Reuben heard this, he tried to rescue him from their hands. "Let's not take his life," he said. 22"Don't shed any blood. Throw him into this cistern here in the desert, but don't lay a hand on him." Reuben said this to rescue him from them and take him back to his father.

23So when Joseph came to his brothers, they stripped him of his robe—the richly ornamented robe he was wearing— 24and they took him and threw him into the cistern. Now the cistern was empty; there was no water in it.

25As they sat down to eat their meal, they looked up and saw a caravan of Ishmaelites coming from Gilead. Their camels were loaded with spices, balm and myrrh, and they were on their way to take them down to Egypt.

26Judah said to his brothers, "What will we gain if we kill our brother and cover up his blood? 27Come, let's sell him to the Ishmaelites and not lay our hands on him; after all, he is our brother, our own flesh and blood." His brothers agreed.

28So when the Midianite merchants came by, his brothers pulled

ting revenge on Joseph (vv. 18ff)? By Reuben's rescue attempt and sense of loss (vv. 21f,29ff)? By Judah's successful intervention (vv. 26f)? By the sons' deception of Jacob (vv. 31–33)? By Jacob's lament (vv. 34ff)? By Joseph's actual fate (vv. 28,36)? **2.** With such empathy, how do you account for why they do what they do? **3.** Joseph's story in chapters 37–50 abounds with irony. In chapter 37, how much irony can you find? What future irony do you anticipate in the rest of this story?

1. If you were Joseph just now, would you be despising your dreams from God, or drawing comfort from them? Why? **2.** As this chapter draws to a close, one can see Jacob and Joseph struggling, as we do, with the "if-only's." Complete these sentences: (Jacob) "If only I hadn't sent him to Shechem ..."; (Joseph) "If only I hadn't been so cocky ..." **3.** What is one of your biggest regrets? "If only I hadn't ... then ..." **4.** The cruelty of Joseph's brothers not only hurt Joseph, but also Jacob. When you hurt someone, whether or not

---

  Genesis 37:12–36   **JOSEPH SOLD BY HIS BROTHERS**

Jacob's favorite son Joseph was already despised by his brothers when he shared about his dreams that elevated him above the rest of the family.

1. What was behind the 10 brothers' desire to kill Joseph?
   a. resentment of his dreams
   b. clashing egos
   c. jealousy of their father's favoritism
   d. mob hysteria

2. Reuben tried to rescue Jacob because:
   a. of his love for Joseph.
   b. of his love for their father.
   c. he had no stomach for blood.
   d. as the oldest he felt responsible.

3. Why did the brothers end up selling Joseph instead of killing him?
   a. They had second thoughts.
   b. They got a chance to make money.
   c. They had some conscience.
   d. God protected Joseph.

4. By their scheming and covering up the brothers were:
   a. keeping out of trouble.
   b. insuring their inheritance.

c. following their father's deceit.
d. beginning to fulfill Joseph's dreams.

5. If you were Joseph, how would you be feeling?
   a. bitterly betrayed
   b. shaken and confused
   c. enjoying the adventure
   d. regretting my dreams
   e. holding on to my dreams

6. Concerning God's part in this drama, I think he:
   a. set it up.
   b. seems conspicuously absent.
   c. made the most of a bad situation.
   d. was involved but I'm not sure how.

7. What do you do when you are betrayed by people close to you?
   a. want to get even
   b. vow never to get close again
   c. assume it's part of God's plan
   d. get depressed

8. This story is filled with loss and regrets. What is your deepest regret in life? How much pain is that regret causing you now? Is the pain getting better or worse?

9. 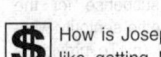 How is Joseph's experience like getting laid off or fired from a job?
   a. the rejection
   b. the loss of dignity and self-respect
   c. being hurt by people you trusted
   d. being at the mercy of others
   e. the uncertainty of the future

10. What dreams has God given you for your future career? What can you do to allow God to unfold his plans for your life?

11. On a scale from 1 to 10, how much is your grief like Jacob's in the following aspects?
    a. I've been mourning for many days.
    b. I refuse to be comforted by others.
    c. I expect to be in mourning still when I die.
    d. I can't stop crying.

12. Regarding the "depression" stage of grief and loss, are you facing it, denying it, in the middle of it, or mostly past it? How can others, especially in this group, help you?

you make it right, do you consider the implications of your actions on people other than the direct recipient of your behavior?

1. When have you been awakened by a friend or family member in need? Likewise, who has been a "3 a.m. friend" for you in your hour of acute need? 2. If you were to exchange IOU's for every act of friendship above and beyond the call of duty, would your IOU ledger for the last year make you a debtor, or a creditor? What does that debt ratio tell you?

1. Why is this digression about Tamar inserted into the Genesis narrative about Joseph: (a) To create suspense for the reader? (b) To settle seniority within Judah's clan? (c) To provide a contrasting backdrop for Joseph's loyalty and chastity, as described in the next chapter? (d) To teach responsibility for one's own family in need? Support your answer(s) from the text. 2. Read Deuteronomy 25:5–10 on brother-in-law marriages. Why would this law be important for widows in ancient Israel, where they had no welfare system? 3. What is the duty of Judah's sons, and even Judah himself, to Tamar? Why is it wrong for Judah to refuse his son's marriage to Tamar? 4. Do you think Tamar acts morally here? Why or why not? In what sense is Tamar "more righteous" than Judah? 5. Of all the Hebrew tribes, why would God choose Judah for the line of King David and Christ Jesus (see Mt 1:3,6, 16), given that tribe's dubious beginning here?

1. What situations, if any, would ever justify wrong acts to achieve something right? How is your answer supported by Genesis 38? 2. What role (match-maker,

Joseph up out of the cistern and sold him for twenty shekels[a] of silver to the Ishmaelites, who took him to Egypt.

²⁹When Reuben returned to the cistern and saw that Joseph was not there, he tore his clothes. ³⁰He went back to his brothers and said, "The boy isn't there! Where can I turn now?"

³¹Then they got Joseph's robe, slaughtered a goat and dipped the robe in the blood. ³²They took the ornamented robe back to their father and said, "We found this. Examine it to see whether it is your son's robe."

³³He recognized it and said, "It is my son's robe! Some ferocious animal has devoured him. Joseph has surely been torn to pieces."

³⁴Then Jacob tore his clothes, put on sackcloth and mourned for his son many days. ³⁵All his sons and daughters came to comfort him, but he refused to be comforted. "No," he said, "in mourning will I go down to the grave[b] to my son." So his father wept for him.

³⁶Meanwhile, the Midianites[c] sold Joseph in Egypt to Potiphar, one of Pharaoh's officials, the captain of the guard.

Judah and Tamar

38 At that time, Judah left his brothers and went down to stay with a man of Adullam named Hirah. ²There Judah met the daughter of a Canaanite man named Shua. He married her and lay with her; ³she became pregnant and gave birth to a son, who was named Er. ⁴She conceived again and gave birth to a son and named him Onan. ⁵She gave birth to still another son and named him Shelah. It was at Kezib that she gave birth to him.

⁶Judah got a wife for Er, his firstborn, and her name was Tamar. ⁷But Er, Judah's firstborn, was wicked in the LORD's sight; so the LORD put him to death.

⁸Then Judah said to Onan, "Lie with your brother's wife and fulfill your duty to her as a brother-in-law to produce offspring for your brother." ⁹But Onan knew that the offspring would not be his; so whenever he lay with his brother's wife, he spilled his semen on the ground to keep from producing offspring for his brother. ¹⁰What he did was wicked in the LORD's sight; so he put him to death also.

¹¹Judah then said to his daughter-in-law Tamar, "Live as a widow in your father's house until my son Shelah grows up." For he thought, "He may die too, just like his brothers." So Tamar went to live in her father's house.

¹²After a long time Judah's wife, the daughter of Shua, died. When Judah had recovered from his grief, he went up to Timnah, to the men who were shearing his sheep, and his friend Hirah the Adullamite went with him.

¹³When Tamar was told, "Your father-in-law is on his way to Timnah to shear his sheep," ¹⁴she took off her widow's clothes, covered herself with a veil to disguise herself, and then sat down at the entrance to Enaim, which is on the road to Timnah. For she saw that, though Shelah had now grown up, she had not been given to him as his wife.

¹⁵When Judah saw her, he thought she was a prostitute, for she had covered her face. ¹⁶Not realizing that she was his daughter-in-law, he went over to her by the roadside and said, "Come now, let me sleep with you."

"And what will you give me to sleep with you?" she asked.

---

[a]28 That is, about 8 ounces (about 0.2 kilogram)   [b]35 Hebrew *Sheol*
[c]36 Samaritan Pentateuch, Septuagint, Vulgate and Syriac (see also verse 28); Masoretic Text *Medanites*

[17]"I'll send you a young goat from my flock," he said.

"Will you give me something as a pledge until you send it?" she asked.

[18]He said, "What pledge should I give you?"

"Your seal and its cord, and the staff in your hand," she answered. So he gave them to her and slept with her, and she became pregnant by him. [19]After she left, she took off her veil and put on her widow's clothes again.

[20]Meanwhile Judah sent the young goat by his friend the Adullamite in order to get his pledge back from the woman, but he did not find her. [21]He asked the men who lived there, "Where is the shrine prostitute who was beside the road at Enaim?"

"There hasn't been any shrine prostitute here," they said.

[22]So he went back to Judah and said, "I didn't find her. Besides, the men who lived there said, 'There hasn't been any shrine prostitute here.'"

[23]Then Judah said, "Let her keep what she has, or we will become a laughingstock. After all, I did send her this young goat, but you didn't find her."

[24]About three months later Judah was told, "Your daughter-in-law Tamar is guilty of prostitution, and as a result she is now pregnant."

Judah said, "Bring her out and have her burned to death!"

[25]As she was being brought out, she sent a message to her father-in-law. "I am pregnant by the man who owns these," she said. And she added, "See if you recognize whose seal and cord and staff these are."

[26]Judah recognized them and said, "She is more righteous than I, since I wouldn't give her to my son Shelah." And he did not sleep with her again.

[27]When the time came for her to give birth, there were twin boys in her womb. [28]As she was giving birth, one of them put out his hand; so the midwife took a scarlet thread and tied it on his wrist and said, "This one came out first." [29]But when he drew back his hand, his brother came out, and she said, "So this is how you have broken out!" And he was named Perez.[a] [30]Then his brother, who had the scarlet thread on his wrist, came out and he was given the name Zerah.[b]

Joseph and Potiphar's Wife

39 Now Joseph had been taken down to Egypt. Potiphar, an Egyptian who was one of Pharaoh's officials, the captain of the guard, bought him from the Ishmaelites who had taken him there.

[2]The LORD was with Joseph and he prospered, and he lived in the house of his Egyptian master. [3]When his master saw that the LORD was with him and that the LORD gave him success in everything he did, [4]Joseph found favor in his eyes and became his attendant. Potiphar put him in charge of his household, and he entrusted to his care everything he owned. [5]From the time he put him in charge of his household and of all that he owned, the LORD blessed the household of the Egyptian because of Joseph. The blessing of the LORD was on everything Potiphar had, both in the house and in the field. [6]So he left in Joseph's care everything he had; with Joseph in charge, he did not concern himself with anything except the food he ate.

Now Joseph was well-built and handsome, [7]and after a while

[a]29 *Perez* means *breaking out.*   [b]30 *Zerah* can mean *scarlet* or *brightness.*

sugar daddy, etc.) do you assume in meeting the very real needs of unmarried people in your family? Do you feel the same sense of duty toward the extended family (in-laws, etc.)? **3.** Where are you finding it hard to live up to your part of the bargain? What does the Judah and Tamar story remind you to do that would be "righteous" concerning the needs of your nuclear and extended family? **4.** Where have you experienced a "double standard"—one for men, another for women—such as was evident for Judah and Tamar? Judah's role in salvation history is crucial, yet, as with his forefathers, perfection was not a requirement in order to be a part of God's purposes. In Judah's case, sexual sin was part of his imperfection. Do you consider any of your sins, sexual or otherwise, as too shameful to allow you to glorify God and fulfill his purposes? What would God say about this? **5.** When has God brought something good out of a bad situation for you? Where would you like to see some good come out of a bad situation today?

1. In what job setting have you enjoyed the most "success"? **2.** What kind of "boss" would you make: Everyone's pal? Law and order tough guy? A hands-on operator? A detached delegator?

1. How do Joseph's prospects look in verse 1? In verse 20? How real do you think his dreams (37:5–11) are to him at these times? **2.** Given his turnabout in fortune, what might Joseph be thinking now? Why do you think God allowed this to happen? What does this say about human perversity? About God's plans for Joseph? For us? **3.** What tactics does Potiphar's wife use to tempt Joseph (vv. 7,10,12)? In each case, how does Joseph resist? Must the circumstances and reasons cited by Joseph in verses 8–9 necessarily lead one to conclude as he did in verse 9c? **4.** What truths about God and Joseph are conveyed by the symmetry of Joseph, the trusted slave (vv. 1–6) and trusted prisoner (vv. 19–23)? **5.** Does Potiphar buy his wife's story "hook, line and sinker"? If so, why doesn't Joseph receive the prescribed death penalty for adulterers?

1. When might you be more tempted to sexual indiscretion and why: (a) When left alone with an attractive member of the opposite sex? (b) When in the company of others who are breaking all the rules? (c) In a foreign culture, where you don't know all the rules and cultural trappings? (d) On your way to the top, when you feel invincible? **2.** "Lord, I can resist anything but temptation." "Tough times never last, tough people do." "The Lord gave him success in whatever he did." How do those sayings fit Joseph? How do they fit you? **3.** How would Romans 8:28–29 fit Joseph just now? And how would it fit you?

his master's wife took notice of Joseph and said, "Come to bed with me!"

[8]But he refused. "With me in charge," he told her, "my master does not concern himself with anything in the house; everything he owns he has entrusted to my care. [9]No one is greater in this house than I am. My master has withheld nothing from me except you, because you are his wife. How then could I do such a wicked thing and sin against God?" [10]And though she spoke to Joseph day after day, he refused to go to bed with her or even be with her.

[11]One day he went into the house to attend to his duties, and none of the household servants was inside. [12]She caught him by his cloak and said, "Come to bed with me!" But he left his cloak in her hand and ran out of the house.

[13]When she saw that he had left his cloak in her hand and had run out of the house, [14]she called her household servants. "Look," she said to them, "this Hebrew has been brought to us to make sport of us! He came in here to sleep with me, but I screamed. [15]When he heard me scream for help, he left his cloak beside me and ran out of the house."

[16]She kept his cloak beside her until his master came home. [17]Then she told him this story: "That Hebrew slave you brought us came to me to make sport of me. [18]But as soon as I screamed for help, he left his cloak beside me and ran out of the house."

[19]When his master heard the story his wife told him, saying, "This is how your slave treated me," he burned with anger. [20]Joseph's master took him and put him in prison, the place where the king's prisoners were confined.

But while Joseph was there in the prison, [21]the LORD was with him; he showed him kindness and granted him favor in the eyes of

---

   Genesis 39:1–23   **JOSEPH AND POTIPHAR'S WIFE**

Due to their jealousy, Joseph's brothers had sold him to a caravan of Ishmaelite merchants passing through Canaan on their way to Egypt.

1. What was the greatest challenge Joseph faced in Egypt?
   a. slavery
   b. injustice
   c. sexual harassment
   d. sexual temptation

2. What was Joseph's most important asset?
   a. good luck   d. his faith
   b. good looks   e. God's favor
   c. his management abilities

3. What tactics did Potiphar's wife use on Joseph?
   a. seduction
   b. persistence
   c. the direct approach
   d. intimidation

4. Which tactic would be hardest for you to resist?

5. Joseph resisted Potiphar's wife by:

   a. not being attracted to her.
   b. not letting himself entertain the thought of having sex with her.
   c. realizing he'd sin against his employer, Potiphar.
   d. realizing he'd sin against God.
   e. doing whatever he had to—even running away.

6. How could Joseph's example help you resist temptation in general, and sexual temptation in particular?

7. Why was it that Joseph didn't seem to protest his "sentence"?
   a. No one would believe him.
   b. It would have made things worse.
   c. He was glad to get away from Potiphar's wife.
   d. He knew God was in control of his life.

8. Right now my life is most like Joseph's when he:
   a. didn't know where he was going.
   b. was blessed with success.
   c. was mistreated by others.
   d. was imprisoned in a bad situation.
   e. made the most of his suffering.

9. To what degree are you subjected to sexual harassment at your job?
   a. not at all
   b. directly
   c. indirectly
   d. by gender discrimination

10. How do you deal with sexual harassment or discrimination? How else does Joseph's experience remind you of the stress you battle at work?

11. Which of the pressures Joseph faced do you face also?
    a. sexual temptation
    b. the pressure to be in a relationship
    c. responsibility of running a household
    d. things seeming to go from bad to worse

12. In what way can you sense that "the Lord is with you," as he was with Joseph, in the midst of pressure? If you could ask God to do one thing to help you cope, what would you request?

the prison warden. ²²So the warden put Joseph in charge of all those held in the prison, and he was made responsible for all that was done there. ²³The warden paid no attention to anything under Joseph's care, because the LORD was with Joseph and gave him success in whatever he did.

The Cupbearer and the Baker

40 Some time later, the cupbearer and the baker of the king of Egypt offended their master, the king of Egypt. ²Pharaoh was angry with his two officials, the chief cupbearer and the chief baker, ³and put them in custody in the house of the captain of the guard, in the same prison where Joseph was confined. ⁴The captain of the guard assigned them to Joseph, and he attended them.

After they had been in custody for some time, ⁵each of the two men—the cupbearer and the baker of the king of Egypt, who were being held in prison—had a dream the same night, and each dream had a meaning of its own.

⁶When Joseph came to them the next morning, he saw that they were dejected. ⁷So he asked Pharaoh's officials who were in custody with him in his master's house, "Why are your faces so sad today?"

⁸"We both had dreams," they answered, "but there is no one to interpret them."

Then Joseph said to them, "Do not interpretations belong to God? Tell me your dreams."

⁹So the chief cupbearer told Joseph his dream. He said to him, "In my dream I saw a vine in front of me, ¹⁰and on the vine were three branches. As soon as it budded, it blossomed, and its clusters ripened into grapes. ¹¹Pharaoh's cup was in my hand, and I took the grapes, squeezed them into Pharaoh's cup and put the cup in his hand."

¹²"This is what it means," Joseph said to him. "The three branches are three days. ¹³Within three days Pharaoh will lift up your head and restore you to your position, and you will put Pharaoh's cup in his hand, just as you used to do when you were his cupbearer. ¹⁴But when all goes well with you, remember me and show me kindness; mention me to Pharaoh and get me out of this prison. ¹⁵For I was forcibly carried off from the land of the Hebrews, and even here I have done nothing to deserve being put in a dungeon."

¹⁶When the chief baker saw that Joseph had given a favorable interpretation, he said to Joseph, "I too had a dream: On my head were three baskets of bread.ᵃ ¹⁷In the top basket were all kinds of baked goods for Pharaoh, but the birds were eating them out of the basket on my head."

¹⁸"This is what it means," Joseph said. "The three baskets are three days. ¹⁹Within three days Pharaoh will lift off your head and hang you on a tree.ᵇ And the birds will eat away your flesh."

²⁰Now the third day was Pharaoh's birthday, and he gave a feast for all his officials. He lifted up the heads of the chief cupbearer and the chief baker in the presence of his officials: ²¹He restored the chief cupbearer to his position, so that he once again put the cup into Pharaoh's hand, ²²but he hangedᶜ the chief baker, just as Joseph had said to them in his interpretation.

²³The chief cupbearer, however, did not remember Joseph; he forgot him.

1. What recurrent dreams do you have? What "believe-it-or-not" dream have you had? 2. Which of your dreams illumine the past? Which reveal the future?

1. Why do you think Joseph winds up in prison with officials of the Egyptian government? 2. How does Joseph show concern for the cupbearer and the baker (vv. 6–8)? Does Joseph's reference to God ring true? Is that a force of pious habit or trained mind? Or is he being opportunistic, intrusive or worse? Why do you think so? 3. As dream interpretations belong to God, and as Joseph invites others to tell him their dreams, what does that tell you about Joseph's abilities (see v. 16)? About his relationship with God? About God's hidden language? About the value of keeping a dream journal? 4. What strikes you most about the two dreams, their interpretation and fulfillment? 5. Why might the chief cupbearer forget Joseph (v. 23)? How might this make Joseph feel? 6. As Joseph—forgotten in prison, foiled in your hope for release, but secure in your role as dream interpreter—how would you now see your own God-given dreams (of 37:5–11)?

1. Where in your life are you feeling imprisoned? Left out of the feast? What is your prayer for release? What fellowship do you want restored? What do you sense is God's answer to those prayers? Has God ever spoken to you through your dreams? How? 2. What is your "dream" for the future? Do you feel that your dreams will be realized or not? 3. How do these dreams and feelings affect your relationship with God? How does that spiritual tie maintain your hope despite circumstances to the contrary?

ᵃ16 Or three wicker baskets   ᵇ19 Or and impale you on a pole   ᶜ22 Or impaled

1. If you could have one, which would you choose: A glimpse of the future or a journey into the past? Why? 2. If you were suddenly summoned to meet the head of state, what would be your first thought? Second thought? What do such thoughts reveal about you? About your view toward government leaders? 3. Which current head of state would you like to meet?

1. How do you account for the significant role dreams play in chapters 37,40,41? What evidence do you see that through dreams God exerts his control of events and that God (not Joseph) is the hero (or villain)? 2. How are these dreams similar? Different? How are they interpreted? Consequently, what action is called for? 3. In Pharaoh's dreams, what do you make of the impending famine? Is it a judgment or punishment from God? Or is it one of life's "natural," however unusual, disasters? Why do you think so? 4. In either event, what kind of response to "what God is about to do" (vv. 25,28) does the dream call for: Repentance in the face of deserved judgment? Or wise precautions in the face of a friendly warning? 5. What does each dream episode teach about Joseph? About his relationship with God? About God's concern for his people? 6. Of the major changes in circumstances faced by Joseph in chapters 37,39–41, which turn of events do you see as deserved? As undeserved? Which are "cruel and unusual punishment"? Which do you consider to be fortunate? Ironic? Coincidental? Providential? 7. When in Joseph's changing circumstances is he gutsy? Shrewd? Opportunistic? Faithless? Cocky? Humble?

1. What do you see as God's role in all this? Why do you think God chooses to work with Joseph (and some of us) in this manner? 2. When was the last time you wondered if God had forgotten about you? How did he show you he hadn't? How might this story help you remember that God is always there? 3. As Joseph resisted the temptation to take pride in his own abilities (v. 16), when have you likewise given God the credit for something he has done in your life recently? For what would you like to give him credit today? 4. As Joseph suggested plans to Phar-

Pharaoh's Dreams

41 When two full years had passed, Pharaoh had a dream: He was standing by the Nile, 2when out of the river there came up seven cows, sleek and fat, and they grazed among the reeds. 3After them, seven other cows, ugly and gaunt, came up out of the Nile and stood beside those on the riverbank. 4And the cows that were ugly and gaunt ate up the seven sleek, fat cows. Then Pharaoh woke up.

5He fell asleep again and had a second dream: Seven heads of grain, healthy and good, were growing on a single stalk. 6After them, seven other heads of grain sprouted—thin and scorched by the east wind. 7The thin heads of grain swallowed up the seven healthy, full heads. Then Pharaoh woke up; it had been a dream.

8In the morning his mind was troubled, so he sent for all the magicians and wise men of Egypt. Pharaoh told them his dreams, but no one could interpret them for him.

9Then the chief cupbearer said to Pharaoh, "Today I am reminded of my shortcomings. 10Pharaoh was once angry with his servants, and he imprisoned me and the chief baker in the house of the captain of the guard. 11Each of us had a dream the same night, and each dream had a meaning of its own. 12Now a young Hebrew was there with us, a servant of the captain of the guard. We told him our dreams, and he interpreted them for us, giving each man the interpretation of his dream. 13And things turned out exactly as he interpreted them to us: I was restored to my position, and the other man was hanged.[a]"

14So Pharaoh sent for Joseph, and he was quickly brought from the dungeon. When he had shaved and changed his clothes, he came before Pharaoh.

15Pharaoh said to Joseph, "I had a dream, and no one can interpret it. But I have heard it said of you that when you hear a dream you can interpret it."

16"I cannot do it," Joseph replied to Pharaoh, "but God will give Pharaoh the answer he desires."

17Then Pharaoh said to Joseph, "In my dream I was standing on the bank of the Nile, 18when out of the river there came up seven cows, fat and sleek, and they grazed among the reeds. 19After them, seven other cows came up—scrawny and very ugly and lean. I had never seen such ugly cows in all the land of Egypt. 20The lean, ugly cows ate up the seven fat cows that came up first. 21But even after they ate them, no one could tell that they had done so; they looked just as ugly as before. Then I woke up.

22"In my dreams I also saw seven heads of grain, full and good, growing on a single stalk. 23After them, seven other heads sprouted—withered and thin and scorched by the east wind. 24The thin heads of grain swallowed up the seven good heads. I told this to the magicians, but none could explain it to me."

25Then Joseph said to Pharaoh, "The dreams of Pharaoh are one and the same. God has revealed to Pharaoh what he is about to do. 26The seven good cows are seven years, and the seven good heads of grain are seven years; it is one and the same dream. 27The seven lean, ugly cows that came up afterward are seven years, and so are the seven worthless heads of grain scorched by the east wind: They are seven years of famine.

28"It is just as I said to Pharaoh: God has shown Pharaoh what he is about to do. 29Seven years of great abundance are coming throughout the land of Egypt, 30but seven years of famine will follow them. Then all the abundance in Egypt will be forgotten, and the famine will ravage the land. ³¹The abundance in the land will not be remembered, because the famine that follows it will be so severe. ³²The reason the dream was given to Pharaoh in two forms is that the matter has been firmly decided by God, and God will do it soon.

³³"And now let Pharaoh look for a discerning and wise man and put him in charge of the land of Egypt. ³⁴Let Pharaoh appoint commissioners over the land to take a fifth of the harvest of Egypt during the seven years of abundance. ³⁵They should collect all the food of these good years that are coming and store up the grain under the authority of Pharaoh, to be kept in the cities for food. ³⁶This food should be held in reserve for the country, to be used during the seven years of famine that will come upon Egypt, so that the country may not be ruined by the famine."

³⁷The plan seemed good to Pharaoh and to all his officials. ³⁸So Pharaoh asked them, "Can we find anyone like this man, one in whom is the spirit of God[a]?"

³⁹Then Pharaoh said to Joseph, "Since God has made all this known to you, there is no one so discerning and wise as you. ⁴⁰You shall be in charge of my palace, and all my people are to submit to your orders. Only with respect to the throne will I be greater than you."

Joseph in Charge of Egypt

⁴¹So Pharaoh said to Joseph, "I hereby put you in charge of the whole land of Egypt." ⁴²Then Pharaoh took his signet ring from his finger and put it on Joseph's finger. He dressed him in robes of fine

[a]38 Or of the gods

---

aoh (vv. 33–36), where would you like to design a specific plan of action in your life today? Joseph has finally gotten a break after suffering from a situation which was not his fault and waiting for things to be made right. How have you suffered for things which weren't your fault or when life was unfair? How did it feel? How did God make things right? Or, if you are still waiting for things to be made right, what can you learn from Joseph's story?

---

1. If you were King or Queen for a day, what would you do? 2. When in your life were you helped to feel "I am somebody special"? 3. What is the story behind the ring(s) on your finger(s)?

Genesis 41:1–40   JOSEPH INTERPRETS PHARAOH'S DREAMS

First, Joseph was sold into slavery by his jealous brothers. He came to be in charge of his master's household in Egypt, until he was falsely accused of assaulting his master's wife—for which he was thrown in prison. While in prison, he accurately interpreted the dreams of two fellow inmates.

1. After being in prison now for a minimum of two years, how do you think Joseph was feeling?
   a. weary
   b. angry
   c. resigned
   d. cautiously optimistic
   e. forever hopeful

2. Why did Joseph shave and change clothes before his appearance with Pharaoh?
   a. to freshen up
   b. to look his best
   c. to look as much like an Egyptian as possible
   d. because he saw this as a job interview

3. Joseph answered Pharaoh the way he did in verse 16:
   a. because he was humble.
   b. to acknowledge God as the source of his ability.
   c. to have an excuse if he was wrong.
   d. as a witness of his faith.
   e. to get on Pharaoh's good side.

4. Why did Pharaoh so readily accept Joseph's interpretation and plan?
   a. They had the "ring of truth."
   b. Joseph had been right before.
   c. God was obviously directing Joseph, and Pharaoh sensed it.
   d. Joseph's confidence was so convincing.
   e. God had the whole thing planned.

5. What quality in Joseph's life stands out the most in this story?
   a. patience—as he sat in prison
   b. intimacy with God—as he interpreted dreams
   c. humility—as he gave God the credit
   d. diplomacy—in relating to people

e. wisdom—as he designed a solution for a problem
   f. cleverness—as he recommended a "discerning and wise man" to be put in charge of the land
   g. faithfulness—as he endured much suffering

6. Which of these qualities do you most need or desire for yourself? Why?

7. How are you at waiting for things to be "right"? How long are you prepared to wait?

8. In what way does life seem unfair to you? How often do you feel like God has forgotten you? How can this story renew your perspective that God indeed is always there?

9. How are you at discerning God's guidance? What issues and questions need to be addressed in your life? In your family? In your vocational calling? In your faith community? How can you contribute to the process of discovering God's will?

1. Has Joseph gone too far in taking on ring, robes, chauffeured chariot, name change, native wife and all? How would becoming more like an Egyptian help Joseph to fulfill his new role? 2. Why do you think the Bible does not criticize Joseph for taking a foreign wife, contrary to his family values? How does Joseph's behavior differ from Esau's wife-taking (see 28:6–9; 36:2)? 3. How is the Joseph of chapter 41 unlike the Joseph of chapter 37? How do you account for his maturity, zeal and wisdom to run the government and travel throughout Egypt? Might the 13 intervening years of humiliation and prison (ch. 39–40) have gifted or energized him?

1. Like Joseph, what past trouble would you like God to help you "forget"? 2. In what ways have you changed from what you were 13 years ago? What did God do during that time to mold your character? 3. Where are you now experiencing a "famine": Physically? Socially? Culturally? Spiritually? What traits of Joseph's will help you survive such famine-like trials?

1. When there's "more month left at the end of the money," what usual grocery items do you do without? What must you buy anyway? 2. What is the tenderest expression of love your father has ever shared with you? 3. What is the longest period of time you have been separated from your family? What was memorable about your reunion?

1. As this chapter unfolds, what vantage point does the reader have that the brothers do not have when Joseph pretends not to know his brothers? When he accuses them of being spies? When he puts them in jail? When he forces Simeon to remain in Egypt as a hostage? Why does Joseph put his brother's money in their sacks of grain? 2. How do the brothers react to this treatment? How does Jacob respond? How

linen and put a gold chain around his neck. 43He had him ride in a chariot as his second-in-command,ᵃ and men shouted before him, "Make wayᵇ!" Thus he put him in charge of the whole land of Egypt.

44Then Pharaoh said to Joseph, "I am Pharaoh, but without your word no one will lift hand or foot in all Egypt." 45Pharaoh gave Joseph the name Zaphenath-Paneah and gave him Asenath daughter of Potiphera, priest of On,ᶜ to be his wife. And Joseph went throughout the land of Egypt.

46Joseph was thirty years old when he entered the service of Pharaoh king of Egypt. And Joseph went out from Pharaoh's presence and traveled throughout Egypt. 47During the seven years of abundance the land produced plentifully. 48Joseph collected all the food produced in those seven years of abundance in Egypt and stored it in the cities. In each city he put the food grown in the fields surrounding it. 49Joseph stored up huge quantities of grain, like the sand of the sea; it was so much that he stopped keeping records because it was beyond measure.

50Before the years of famine came, two sons were born to Joseph by Asenath daughter of Potiphera, priest of On. 51Joseph named his firstborn Manassehᵈ and said, "It is because God has made me forget all my trouble and all my father's household." 52The second son he named Ephraimᵉ and said, "It is because God has made me fruitful in the land of my suffering."

53The seven years of abundance in Egypt came to an end, 54and the seven years of famine began, just as Joseph had said. There was famine in all the other lands, but in the whole land of Egypt there was food. 55When all Egypt began to feel the famine, the people cried to Pharaoh for food. Then Pharaoh told all the Egyptians, "Go to Joseph and do what he tells you."

56When the famine had spread over the whole country, Joseph opened the storehouses and sold grain to the Egyptians, for the famine was severe throughout Egypt. 57And all the countries came to Egypt to buy grain from Joseph, because the famine was severe in all the world.

Joseph's Brothers Go to Egypt

42 When Jacob learned that there was grain in Egypt, he said to his sons, "Why do you just keep looking at each other?" 2He continued, "I have heard that there is grain in Egypt. Go down there and buy some for us, so that we may live and not die."

3Then ten of Joseph's brothers went down to buy grain from Egypt. 4But Jacob did not send Benjamin, Joseph's brother, with the others, because he was afraid that harm might come to him. 5So Israel's sons were among those who went to buy grain, for the famine was in the land of Canaan also.

6Now Joseph was the governor of the land, the one who sold grain to all its people. So when Joseph's brothers arrived, they bowed down to him with their faces to the ground. 7As soon as Joseph saw his brothers, he recognized them, but he pretended to be a stranger and spoke harshly to them. "Where do you come from?" he asked.

"From the land of Canaan," they replied, "to buy food."

ᵃ43 Or in the chariot of his second-in-command; or in his second chariot   ᵇ43 Or Bow down   ᶜ45 That is, Heliopolis; also in verse 50   ᵈ51 Manasseh sounds like and may be derived from the Hebrew for forget.   ᵉ52 Ephraim sounds like the Hebrew for twice fruitful.

⁸Although Joseph recognized his brothers, they did not recognize him. ⁹Then he remembered his dreams about them and said to them, "You are spies! You have come to see where our land is unprotected."

¹⁰"No, my lord," they answered. "Your servants have come to buy food. ¹¹We are all the sons of one man. Your servants are honest men, not spies."

¹²"No!" he said to them. "You have come to see where our land is unprotected."

¹³But they replied, "Your servants were twelve brothers, the sons of one man, who lives in the land of Canaan. The youngest is now with our father, and one is no more."

¹⁴Joseph said to them, "It is just as I told you: You are spies! ¹⁵And this is how you will be tested: As surely as Pharaoh lives, you will not leave this place unless your youngest brother comes here. ¹⁶Send one of your number to get your brother; the rest of you will be kept in prison, so that your words may be tested to see if you are telling the truth. If you are not, then as surely as Pharaoh lives, you are spies!" ¹⁷And he put them all in custody for three days.

¹⁸On the third day, Joseph said to them, "Do this and you will live, for I fear God: ¹⁹If you are honest men, let one of your brothers stay here in prison, while the rest of you go and take grain back for your starving households. ²⁰But you must bring your youngest brother to me, so that your words may be verified and that you may not die." This they proceeded to do.

²¹They said to one another, "Surely we are being punished because of our brother. We saw how distressed he was when he pleaded with us for his life, but we would not listen; that's why this distress has come upon us."

²²Reuben replied, "Didn't I tell you not to sin against the boy? But you wouldn't listen! Now we must give an accounting for his blood." ²³They did not realize that Joseph could understand them, since he was using an interpreter.

²⁴He turned away from them and began to weep, but then turned back and spoke to them again. He had Simeon taken from them and bound before their eyes.

²⁵Joseph gave orders to fill their bags with grain, to put each man's silver back in his sack, and to give them provisions for their journey. After this was done for them, ²⁶they loaded their grain on their donkeys and left.

²⁷At the place where they stopped for the night one of them opened his sack to get feed for his donkey, and he saw his silver in the mouth of his sack. ²⁸"My silver has been returned," he said to his brothers. "Here it is in my sack."

Their hearts sank and they turned to each other trembling and said, "What is this that God has done to us?"

²⁹When they came to their father Jacob in the land of Canaan, they told him all that had happened to them. They said, ³⁰"The man who is lord over the land spoke harshly to us and treated us as though we were spying on the land. ³¹But we said to him, 'We are honest men; we are not spies. ³²We were twelve brothers, sons of one father. One is no more, and the youngest is now with our father in Canaan.'

³³"Then the man who is lord over the land said to us, 'This is how I will know whether you are honest men: Leave one of your brothers here with me, and take food for your starving households and go. ³⁴But bring your youngest brother to me so I will know that

does all this fulfill Joseph's dream (37:7,9) and his eventual plan (see ch. 43ff)? **3.** By forcing the brothers to endure all the things they had forced him to endure, is Joseph primarily seeking revenge? Repentance? Or what? **4.** What is Benjamin's role in the family (vv. 36–38)? Why would Joseph be so interested in how the brothers feel about the "baby in the family" (see 35:24)? **5.** In verses 21–22, what do you think the brothers experience: True penitence? Worldly sorrow? Cursing their misfortune? Why do you think so? Likewise, in verses 27–28? **6.** Why do you think Joseph reacts as he does in verse 24? Why doesn't he reveal himself now? How do you think Joseph feels as he talks to his brothers? If Joseph did not know about Benjamin and thought that he himself was the youngest son, how do you think he felt?

♡ **1.** Define "repentance." Should true repentance be judged on its intention, its emotion, or on its result? Why do you think so? **2.** When someone has deeply wronged you, are you most likely to seek revenge or reconciliation? (Be honest.) What does this tell you about yourself? About your trust in God and his ways? **3.** Like Jacob's sons (vv. 21–22), where are you still paying the price or reaping the effects of a mistake you made? Is God speaking to you in this? **4.** Like Jacob (vv. 36–38), what situation in your life seems "hopeless" at the moment? From this chapter, what will you keep in mind as you face your situation with hope? **5.** What does this story tell you about the phrase, "What goes around comes around," or "You reap what you sow"? What, if anything, can you do now to avoid a later repayment for ways you have mistreated others?

you are not spies but honest men. Then I will give your brother back to you, and you can trade*a* in the land.' "

³⁵As they were emptying their sacks, there in each man's sack was his pouch of silver! When they and their father saw the money pouches, they were frightened. ³⁶Their father Jacob said to them, "You have deprived me of my children. Joseph is no more and Simeon is no more, and now you want to take Benjamin. Everything is against me!"

³⁷Then Reuben said to his father, "You may put both of my sons to death if I do not bring him back to you. Entrust him to my care, and I will bring him back."

³⁸But Jacob said, "My son will not go down there with you; his brother is dead and he is the only one left. If harm comes to him on the journey you are taking, you will bring my gray head down to the grave*b* in sorrow."

The Second Journey to Egypt

43 Now the famine was still severe in the land. ²So when they had eaten all the grain they had brought from Egypt, their father said to them, "Go back and buy us a little more food."

³But Judah said to him, "The man warned us solemnly, 'You will not see my face again unless your brother is with you.' ⁴If you will send our brother along with us, we will go down and buy food for you. ⁵But if you will not send him, we will not go down, because the man said to us, 'You will not see my face again unless your brother is with you.' "

⁶Israel asked, "Why did you bring this trouble on me by telling the man you had another brother?"

⁷They replied, "The man questioned us closely about ourselves and our family. 'Is your father still living?' he asked us. 'Do you have another brother?' We simply answered his questions. How were we to know he would say, 'Bring your brother down here'?"

⁸Then Judah said to Israel his father, "Send the boy along with me and we will go at once, so that we and you and our children may live and not die. ⁹I myself will guarantee his safety; you can hold me personally responsible for him. If I do not bring him back to you and set him here before you, I will bear the blame before you all my life. ¹⁰As it is, if we had not delayed, we could have gone and returned twice."

¹¹Then their father Israel said to them, "If it must be, then do this: Put some of the best products of the land in your bags and take them down to the man as a gift—a little balm and a little honey, some spices and myrrh, some pistachio nuts and almonds. ¹²Take double the amount of silver with you, for you must return the silver that was put back into the mouths of your sacks. Perhaps it was a mistake. ¹³Take your brother also and go back to the man at once. ¹⁴And may God Almighty*c* grant you mercy before the man so that he will let your other brother and Benjamin come back with you. As for me, if I am bereaved, I am bereaved."

¹⁵So the men took the gifts and double the amount of silver, and Benjamin also. They hurried down to Egypt and presented themselves to Joseph. ¹⁶When Joseph saw Benjamin with them, he said to the steward of his house, "Take these men to my house, slaughter an animal and prepare dinner; they are to eat with me at noon."

¹⁷The man did as Joseph told him and took the men to Joseph's house. ¹⁸Now the men were frightened when they were taken to his house. They thought, "We were brought here because of the

1. What one "fancy meal" stands out in your memory? Why that one? **2.** If you had the choice, would you want to be the youngest in the family? The oldest? Why? **3.** When decision-making in your family reaches an impasse, what or who usually breaks the deadlock: (a) Someone gives in or becomes a martyr? (b) Might makes right? (c) The one who cries the loudest wins over the others? (d) Father knows best? (e) The favorite gets favored treatment?

1. In what ways does chapter 43 continue the action in chapter 42? What plot twist is introduced? **2.** If Genesis 43 were part of a movie, what would the camera shoot close up? With what sound effects and mood music? What happens off-camera? Any narration? What's the emotional peak? Do you play this as a mawkish tearjerker? A family sitcom? A scary adventure story? Why? **3.** What do you think of Joseph's performance in this scene: Too cautious? Too risky? Too weepy? Too generous? If you were Joseph's "stage manager," how would you have staged things differently? Why? **4.** Why is Judah successful in prevailing upon Israel (vv. 3–10), whereas Reuben's similar offer of surety was rejected (42:37–38)? **5.** Compare Judah's words in 43:8–9 with 37:26–27. Do you think he has changed much? How so? **6.** How does Jacob compare with Abraham in their willingness to lose beloved sons (see ch. 22)? **7.** Which is the primary focal point of Jacob's decision-making dilemma (vv.1–14): Benjamin? Simeon? The famine? The money? Himself? Why do you think so? **8.** Why do you think Joseph takes his brothers to his own house and has a meal with them

silver that was put back into our sacks the first time. He wants to attack us and overpower us and seize us as slaves and take our donkeys."

¹⁹So they went up to Joseph's steward and spoke to him at the entrance to the house. ²⁰"Please, sir," they said, "we came down here the first time to buy food. ²¹But at the place where we stopped for the night we opened our sacks and each of us found his silver—the exact weight—in the mouth of his sack. So we have brought it back with us. ²²We have also brought additional silver with us to buy food. We don't know who put our silver in our sacks."

²³"It's all right," he said. "Don't be afraid. Your God, the God of your father, has given you treasure in your sacks; I received your silver." Then he brought Simeon out to them.

²⁴The steward took the men into Joseph's house, gave them water to wash their feet and provided fodder for their donkeys. ²⁵They prepared their gifts for Joseph's arrival at noon, because they had heard that they were to eat there.

²⁶When Joseph came home, they presented to him the gifts they had brought into the house, and they bowed down before him to the ground. ²⁷He asked them how they were, and then he said, "How is your aged father you told me about? Is he still living?"

²⁸They replied, "Your servant our father is still alive and well." And they bowed low to pay him honor.

²⁹As he looked about and saw his brother Benjamin, his own mother's son, he asked, "Is this your youngest brother, the one you told me about?" And he said, "God be gracious to you, my son." ³⁰Deeply moved at the sight of his brother, Joseph hurried out and looked for a place to weep. He went into his private room and wept there.

³¹After he had washed his face, he came out and, controlling himself, said, "Serve the food."

³²They served him by himself, the brothers by themselves, and the Egyptians who ate with him by themselves, because Egyptians could not eat with Hebrews, for that is detestable to Egyptians. ³³The men had been seated before him in the order of their ages, from the firstborn to the youngest; and they looked at each other in astonishment. ³⁴When portions were served to them from Joseph's table, Benjamin's portion was five times as much as anyone else's. So they feasted and drank freely with him.

A Silver Cup in a Sack

44 Now Joseph gave these instructions to the steward of his house: "Fill the men's sacks with as much food as they can carry, and put each man's silver in the mouth of his sack. ²Then put my cup, the silver one, in the mouth of the youngest one's sack, along with the silver for his grain." And he did as Joseph said.

³As morning dawned, the men were sent on their way with their donkeys. ⁴They had not gone far from the city when Joseph said to his steward, "Go after those men at once, and when you catch up with them, say to them, 'Why have you repaid good with evil? ⁵Isn't this the cup my master drinks from and also uses for divination? This is a wicked thing you have done.'"

⁶When he caught up with them, he repeated these words to them. ⁷But they said to him, "Why does my lord say such things? Far be it from your servants to do anything like that! ⁸We even brought back to you from the land of Canaan the silver we found inside the mouths of our sacks. So why would we steal silver or

(v. 16)? What do the brothers think will happen there (v. 18)? How will the fear engendered in the brothers help Joseph complete his plan? **9.** Why do you think Joseph chooses not to reveal himself to his brothers, even at the poignant moment of greeting Benjamin (vv. 29ff)? What does Joseph want? What more does Benjamin get (v. 34)? Why does he get more?

♡ **1.** Where is the "cupboard bare" in your life? And where are you feasting "five times as much as anyone else"? **2.** Judah is very practical in this story. When have you put being practical over the best interests of someone? When have you put someone's best interests over practicality? **3.** Who would you like to see? What one person who means a lot to you have you been wanting to see again? Why do you feel that way for that person? Why do you think God gave us the capacity to have such strong feelings for people?

🍵 **1.** What was something valuable you lost or misplaced? Did you ever find it? If not, did you replace it? What did the loss cost you? **2.** What did you once dread telling your father or mother? What happened when you finally did?

📖 **1.** As this story unfolds, what role is played by Joseph? By the steward? Judah? Benjamin? In what sense does Benjamin occupy the same position in the family that Joseph occupied in chapter 37? **2.** In the scheme of things, why does Joseph place the silver cup in Benjamin's sack? Why the suspenseful delay in sending the steward after them? When accused by the steward (vv. 4–6), how do the brothers respond (vv. 7–9)? **3.** Do you suppose Joseph could have foreseen their self-condemning response? What else in this story seems to happen outside Joseph's plan (but within God's control)? **4.** How do the brothers respond when the planted cup is found in Benjamin's sack? How do these feelings compare with their feelings at the end of chapter 43? With what Joseph felt at the end of chapter 37? **5.** How do their actions here compare to the way they acted in chapter 37? What changes have taken place in their lives? **6.** How do Judah's actions here (vv. 18–34) compare with his vow in 43:8–9? How great a sacrifice is he willing to make? For whose sake, primarily: His own? Benjamin's? Jacob's? Why do you think so? What does this tell you about how Judah has matured? **7.** How does Judah's compelling speech bring Joseph to the breaking point (see 45:1ff)? Do you think this climactic ending was the way Joseph envisioned it? Was he desirous of reconciliation, after all? Or was he genuinely stunned by this serendipity? Why?

♡ **1.** What would be your "silver cup"—something material which you highly prize? Would you say that you possess it, or that it possesses you? What might God be saying to you in this? **2.** Where in your family or at work have you seen someone whose "walk matched His talk"? Where in your life has this been observed? Where is it tougher for you to achieve this? Why? **3.** Where, like Joseph, have you given "your brothers" the chance to prove themselves or be reconciled? When has this chance to forgive and forget been offered to you? What did you do with that chance? **4.** With whom do you still hold out hope for a reconciliation? What hope does this story give?

gold from your master's house? [9]If any of your servants is found to have it, he will die; and the rest of us will become my lord's slaves."

[10]"Very well, then," he said, "let it be as you say. Whoever is found to have it will become my slave; the rest of you will be free from blame."

[11]Each of them quickly lowered his sack to the ground and opened it. [12]Then the steward proceeded to search, beginning with the oldest and ending with the youngest. And the cup was found in Benjamin's sack. [13]At this, they tore their clothes. Then they all loaded their donkeys and returned to the city.

[14]Joseph was still in the house when Judah and his brothers came in, and they threw themselves to the ground before him. [15]Joseph said to them, "What is this you have done? Don't you know that a man like me can find things out by divination?"

[16]"What can we say to my lord?" Judah replied. "What can we say? How can we prove our innocence? God has uncovered your servants' guilt. We are now my lord's slaves—we ourselves and the one who was found to have the cup."

[17]But Joseph said, "Far be it from me to do such a thing! Only the man who was found to have the cup will become my slave. The rest of you, go back to your father in peace."

[18]Then Judah went up to him and said: "Please, my lord, let your servant speak a word to my lord. Do not be angry with your servant, though you are equal to Pharaoh himself. [19]My lord asked his servants, 'Do you have a father or a brother?' [20]And we answered, 'We have an aged father, and there is a young son born to him in his old age. His brother is dead, and he is the only one of his mother's sons left, and his father loves him.'

[21]"Then you said to your servants, 'Bring him down to me so I can see him for myself.' [22]And we said to my lord, 'The boy cannot leave his father; if he leaves him, his father will die.' [23]But you told your servants, 'Unless your youngest brother comes down with you, you will not see my face again.' [24]When we went back to your servant my father, we told him what my lord had said.

[25]"Then our father said, 'Go back and buy a little more food.' [26]But we said, 'We cannot go down. Only if our youngest brother is with us will we go. We cannot see the man's face unless our youngest brother is with us.'

[27]"Your servant my father said to us, 'You know that my wife bore me two sons. [28]One of them went away from me, and I said, "He has surely been torn to pieces." And I have not seen him since. [29]If you take this one from me too and harm comes to him, you will bring my gray head down to the grave[a] in misery.'

[30]"So now, if the boy is not with us when I go back to your servant my father and if my father, whose life is closely bound up with the boy's life, [31]sees that the boy isn't there, he will die. Your servants will bring the gray head of our father down to the grave in sorrow. [32]Your servant guaranteed the boy's safety to my father. I said, 'If I do not bring him back to you, I will bear the blame before you, my father, all my life!'

[33]"Now then, please let your servant remain here as my lord's slave in place of the boy, and let the boy return with his brothers. [34]How can I go back to my father if the boy is not with me? No! Do not let me see the misery that would come upon my father."

---

[a]29 Hebrew *Sheol*; also in verse 31

Joseph Makes Himself Known

45 Then Joseph could no longer control himself before all his attendants, and he cried out, "Have everyone leave my presence!" So there was no one with Joseph when he made himself known to his brothers. ²And he wept so loudly that the Egyptians heard him, and Pharaoh's household heard about it.

³Joseph said to his brothers, "I am Joseph! Is my father still living?" But his brothers were not able to answer him, because they were terrified at his presence.

⁴Then Joseph said to his brothers, "Come close to me." When they had done so, he said, "I am your brother Joseph, the one you sold into Egypt! ⁵And now, do not be distressed and do not be angry with yourselves for selling me here, because it was to save lives that God sent me ahead of you. ⁶For two years now there has been famine in the land, and for the next five years there will not be plowing and reaping. ⁷But God sent me ahead of you to preserve for you a remnant on earth and to save your lives by a great deliverance.ª

⁸"So then, it was not you who sent me here, but God. He made me father to Pharaoh, lord of his entire household and ruler of all Egypt. ⁹Now hurry back to my father and say to him, 'This is what your son Joseph says: God has made me lord of all Egypt. Come

ª7 Or *save you as a great band of survivors*

1. Who in your family makes the most noise when crying? Who "never" cries? When was the last time you wept openly? For what? **2.** Who in your family is the one who will forgive anyone anything? For whom does forgiveness come only with difficulty? Which one are you like? How so?

1. If you were visited by a loved one who came back 22 years later "from the dead," as it were, what proof would you need that this person was indeed the one you had given up for dead? What proof does Joseph offer his brothers (vv. 3–13)? His father (vv. 9–11,21–23)? **2.** How does Joseph's bombshell strike the brothers (vv. 3,14)? Pharaoh's palace (vv. 2,16)? Their father (vv. 26–28)? **3.** Has Joseph truly forgiven his brothers? Why do you think so? But are they convinced of their forgiveness? Why or why not (see 50:15ff)? Why do you think Joseph and Benjamin have a special relationship? **4.** Why do you suppose

---

 Genesis 45:1–28   **JOSEPH MAKES HIMSELF KNOWN**

Joseph had gone from slave to prisoner to second in command in Egypt. When Joseph's brothers came to buy grain, Joseph recognized them but they didn't recognize him. He refused to let them buy more food unless they returned with his beloved younger brother Benjamin. Later, when Joseph sent them on their way again, he had his own silver cup planted in Benjamin's sack. When Joseph declared Benjamin's punishment would be to become his slave, the others fell down and begged for mercy.

1. Why did Joseph wait so long to reveal his identity to his brothers?
   a. He wanted revenge.
   b. He enjoyed the irony and suspense.
   c. They needed to feel the pain their sin had caused.
   d. Joseph's dreams required them to bow before him in total submission.

2. Why did Joseph finally spill the beans?
   a. He was in deep pain.
   b. They had learned their lesson.
   c. He was overcome with emotion.
   d. He couldn't wait to embrace them and send them to get his father.

3. If you had been one of Joseph's brothers, how would you have felt when he revealed himself?
   a. shocked
   b. afraid of what he would do to me
   c. ashamed
   d. relieved

4. How could Joseph embrace them after what they'd done to him?
   a. He had forgiven them.
   b. He understood God had a purpose for the whole thing.
   c. Family is more important than a grudge.
   d. Seeing them squirm made it easier for him.
   e. Time heals all wounds.

5. When confronted with the pain I have caused others, I:
   a. am embarrassed.
   b. pretend it didn't happen.
   c. seek their forgiveness.
   d. fear I will be punished.

6. When I have the opportunity to forgive others, I:
   a. avoid the issue.
   b. make sure they know how badly I was hurt.
   c. feel relieved to get it resolved.
   d. enjoy getting back together.

7. How do you feel about Joseph's perspective that God, rather than his brothers, actually put him through the things he experienced? How does that make you feel about your own trials and suffering? How would your attitude and relationship with God be different if you shared Joseph's view?

8. In your situation of living with a broken relationship, how can you relate to this story?
   a. Things have been strained for a long time.
   b. I'd love to experience that kind of a happy ending.
   c. I'd like to see them squirm a little.
   d. They would be shocked if I had Joseph's attitude.
   e. I would be shocked if they had Joseph's attitude.
   f. I can see God's purposes to an extent in what they've done to me.

9. What would it take for you to reach out and take the initiative like Joseph did? How much is your willingness to reach out affected by the response you expect to get?

Joseph sent off his brothers with the final word, "Don't quarrel on the way!"? 5. As Joseph reveals himself for who he really is, how does he also make God known for who He is, has been and will be (vv. 5–11)? 6. How would you typify God's actions in this whole episode: Involved? Laid back? Enjoying the last laugh? Crying the first tear? Giving hugs all around? 7. Based on Joseph's story, how would you define "divine providence"?

1. When in your life have you enjoyed "God's provision"—sovereignly, redemptively, or materially? What would you like to see God provide today? 2. What would bring "tears of joy" if it happened for you sometime soon? Joseph saw God's sovereignty in every aspect of his life. Do you see God's sovereignty in all areas of your life? What areas more than others? 3. What is one thing you have learned from Joseph's story that would be most helpful to share with someone experiencing tough times? Why not share with that person this week?

1. If you had to move to a new country to live, which one would you choose? Why? What would you miss most about your roots? If you had known ahead of time that you would never return once you left, would you still move? 2. How close do you and your relatives now live? Do you consider that "too close" or "too far away"? Why?

1. What frame of mind do you suppose Jacob is in (vv. 1–4)? How can you tell? 2. What concerns Jacob as he leaves his homeland of Canaan? As he prepares to meet long-lost Joseph? As he goes where he has never been before, an alien, likely never to return? How does God speak to

down to me; don't delay. [10]You shall live in the region of Goshen and be near me—you, your children and grandchildren, your flocks and herds, and all you have. [11]I will provide for you there, because five years of famine are still to come. Otherwise you and your household and all who belong to you will become destitute.'

[12]"You can see for yourselves, and so can my brother Benjamin, that it is really I who am speaking to you. [13]Tell my father about all the honor accorded me in Egypt and about everything you have seen. And bring my father down here quickly."

[14]Then he threw his arms around his brother Benjamin and wept, and Benjamin embraced him, weeping. [15]And he kissed all his brothers and wept over them. Afterward his brothers talked with him.

[16]When the news reached Pharaoh's palace that Joseph's brothers had come, Pharaoh and all his officials were pleased. [17]Pharaoh said to Joseph, "Tell your brothers, 'Do this: Load your animals and return to the land of Canaan, [18]and bring your father and your families back to me. I will give you the best of the land of Egypt and you can enjoy the fat of the land.'

[19]"You are also directed to tell them, 'Do this: Take some carts from Egypt for your children and your wives, and get your father and come. [20]Never mind about your belongings, because the best of all Egypt will be yours.'"

[21]So the sons of Israel did this. Joseph gave them carts, as Pharaoh had commanded, and he also gave them provisions for their journey. [22]To each of them he gave new clothing, but to Benjamin he gave three hundred shekels[a] of silver and five sets of clothes. [23]And this is what he sent to his father: ten donkeys loaded with the best things of Egypt, and ten female donkeys loaded with grain and bread and other provisions for his journey. [24]Then he sent his brothers away, and as they were leaving he said to them, "Don't quarrel on the way!"

[25]So they went up out of Egypt and came to their father Jacob in the land of Canaan. [26]They told him, "Joseph is still alive! In fact, he is ruler of all Egypt." Jacob was stunned; he did not believe them. [27]But when they told him everything Joseph had said to them, and when he saw the carts Joseph had sent to carry him back, the spirit of their father Jacob revived. [28]And Israel said, "I'm convinced! My son Joseph is still alive. I will go and see him before I die."

Jacob Goes to Egypt

46 So Israel set out with all that was his, and when he reached Beersheba, he offered sacrifices to the God of his father Isaac.

[2]And God spoke to Israel in a vision at night and said, "Jacob! Jacob!"

"Here I am," he replied.

[3]"I am God, the God of your father," he said. "Do not be afraid to go down to Egypt, for I will make you into a great nation there. [4]I will go down to Egypt with you, and I will surely bring you back again. And Joseph's own hand will close your eyes."

[5]Then Jacob left Beersheba, and Israel's sons took their father Jacob and their children and their wives in the carts that Pharaoh had sent to transport him. [6]They also took with them their livestock and the possessions they had acquired in Canaan, and Jacob and all his offspring went to Egypt. [7]He took with him to Egypt his

a22 That is, about 7 1/2 pounds (about 3.5 kilograms)

sons and grandsons and his daughters and granddaughters—all his offspring.

[8]These are the names of the sons of Israel (Jacob and his descendants) who went to Egypt:

Reuben the firstborn of Jacob.
[9]The sons of Reuben:
Hanoch, Pallu, Hezron and Carmi.
[10]The sons of Simeon:
Jemuel, Jamin, Ohad, Jakin, Zohar and Shaul the son of a Canaanite woman.
[11]The sons of Levi:
Gershon, Kohath and Merari.
[12]The sons of Judah:
Er, Onan, Shelah, Perez and Zerah (but Er and Onan had died in the land of Canaan).
The sons of Perez:
Hezron and Hamul.
[13]The sons of Issachar:
Tola, Puah,[a] Jashub[b] and Shimron.
[14]The sons of Zebulun:
Sered, Elon and Jahleel.
[15]These were the sons Leah bore to Jacob in Paddan Aram,[c] besides his daughter Dinah. These sons and daughters of his were thirty-three in all.

[16]The sons of Gad:
Zephon,[d] Haggi, Shuni, Ezbon, Eri, Arodi and Areli.
[17]The sons of Asher:
Imnah, Ishvah, Ishvi and Beriah.
Their sister was Serah.
The sons of Beriah:
Heber and Malkiel.
[18]These were the children born to Jacob by Zilpah, whom Laban had given to his daughter Leah—sixteen in all.

[19]The sons of Jacob's wife Rachel:
Joseph and Benjamin. [20]In Egypt, Manasseh and Ephraim were born to Joseph by Asenath daughter of Potiphera, priest of On.[e]
[21]The sons of Benjamin:
Bela, Beker, Ashbel, Gera, Naaman, Ehi, Rosh, Muppim, Huppim and Ard.
[22]These were the sons of Rachel who were born to Jacob—fourteen in all.

[23]The son of Dan:
Hushim.
[24]The sons of Naphtali:
Jahziel, Guni, Jezer and Shillem.
[25]These were the sons born to Jacob by Bilhah, whom Laban had given to his daughter Rachel—seven in all.

[26]All those who went to Egypt with Jacob—those who were his direct descendants, not counting his sons' wives—numbered sixty-six persons. [27]With the two sons[f] who had been born to Joseph in

these concerns? **3.** In what respects is Jacob a broken man as a result of the 22 years since the events of chapter 37? Besides having more grandsons, how else has he aged or matured? **4.** How is Jacob's preparation for and actual meeting with Joseph like, and unlike, his other long overdue family reunion—the one with Esau (ch. 32–33)? How does the Joseph story help to account for the differences in Jacob this time around? **5.** How does Joseph pave the way for his family's reception by the Pharaoh (46:31–34)? **6.** In the interview which follows (47:1–10), how do these pilgrim people conduct themselves on alien turf before a mighty temporal power? How does Jacob portray himself?

♡ **1.** If God were calling you, rather than Jacob, what would God be asking you to leave behind? Why this? What would God want you to keep for the journey? How would God calm your fears? Jacob and Joseph's reunion was quite touching. With which person would you like to have a reunion like that? **2.** When God wants you to alter your lifestyle, what does he do? How does he get your attention? What might God be asking you to change about your lifestyle now? **3.** What does the story of Joseph and his family tell you about the importance God places on human relationships? Does your church emphasize the importance of relationships among church members? Jacob had one wish (to see Joseph alive) which he wanted to see fulfilled before he (Jacob) died. What one wish would you like to see come true before you die? What would you be willing to sacrifice toward that end?

---

[a]13 Samaritan Pentateuch and Syriac (see also 1 Chron. 7:1); Masoretic Text *Puvah*
[b]13 Samaritan Pentateuch and some Septuagint manuscripts (see also Num. 26:24 and 1 Chron. 7:1); Masoretic Text *Iob*   [c]15 That is, Northwest Mesopotamia
[d]16 Samaritan Pentateuch and Septuagint (see also Num. 26:15); Masoretic Text *Ziphion*
[e]20 That is, Heliopolis   [f]27 Hebrew; Septuagint *the nine children*

Egypt, the members of Jacob's family, which went to Egypt, were seventy[a] in all.

[28]Now Jacob sent Judah ahead of him to Joseph to get directions to Goshen. When they arrived in the region of Goshen, [29]Joseph had his chariot made ready and went to Goshen to meet his father Israel. As soon as Joseph appeared before him, he threw his arms around his father[b] and wept for a long time.

[30]Israel said to Joseph, "Now I am ready to die, since I have seen for myself that you are still alive."

[31]Then Joseph said to his brothers and to his father's household, "I will go up and speak to Pharaoh and will say to him, 'My brothers and my father's household, who were living in the land of Canaan, have come to me. [32]The men are shepherds; they tend livestock, and they have brought along their flocks and herds and everything they own.' [33]When Pharaoh calls you in and asks, 'What is your occupation?' [34]you should answer, 'Your servants have tended livestock from our boyhood on, just as our fathers did.' Then you will be allowed to settle in the region of Goshen, for all shepherds are detestable to the Egyptians."

47 Joseph went and told Pharaoh, "My father and brothers, with their flocks and herds and everything they own, have come from the land of Canaan and are now in Goshen." [2]He chose five of his brothers and presented them before Pharaoh.

[3]Pharaoh asked the brothers, "What is your occupation?"

"Your servants are shepherds," they replied to Pharaoh, "just as our fathers were." [4]They also said to him, "We have come to live here awhile, because the famine is severe in Canaan and your servants' flocks have no pasture. So now, please let your servants settle in Goshen."

[5]Pharaoh said to Joseph, "Your father and your brothers have come to you, [6]and the land of Egypt is before you; settle your father and your brothers in the best part of the land. Let them live in Goshen. And if you know of any among them with special ability, put them in charge of my own livestock."

[7]Then Joseph brought his father Jacob in and presented him before Pharaoh. After Jacob blessed[c] Pharaoh, [8]Pharaoh asked him, "How old are you?"

[9]And Jacob said to Pharaoh, "The years of my pilgrimage are a hundred and thirty. My years have been few and difficult, and they do not equal the years of the pilgrimage of my fathers." [10]Then Jacob blessed[d] Pharaoh and went out from his presence.

[11]So Joseph settled his father and his brothers in Egypt and gave them property in the best part of the land, the district of Rameses, as Pharaoh directed. [12]Joseph also provided his father and his brothers and all his father's household with food, according to the number of their children.

Joseph and the Famine

[13]There was no food, however, in the whole region because the famine was severe; both Egypt and Canaan wasted away because of the famine. [14]Joseph collected all the money that was to be found in Egypt and Canaan in payment for the grain they were buying, and he brought it to Pharaoh's palace. [15]When the money of the people of Egypt and Canaan was gone, all Egypt came to Joseph and

1. If you needed to pawn something for quick cash, what would be one of the first things you would consider pawning? Why this item? 2. If you could "rent a kid" for a week around your house or place of work, what would you be willing to pay? For what chores?

a27 Hebrew (see also Exodus 1:5 and footnote); Septuagint (see also Acts 7:14) seventy-five   b29 Hebrew *around him*   c7 Or *greeted*   d10 Or *said farewell to*

said, "Give us food. Why should we die before your eyes? Our money is used up."

[16]"Then bring your livestock," said Joseph. "I will sell you food in exchange for your livestock, since your money is gone." [17]So they brought their livestock to Joseph, and he gave them food in exchange for their horses, their sheep and goats, their cattle and donkeys. And he brought them through that year with food in exchange for all their livestock.

[18]When that year was over, they came to him the following year and said, "We cannot hide from our lord the fact that since our money is gone and our livestock belongs to you, there is nothing left for our lord except our bodies and our land. [19]Why should we perish before your eyes—we and our land as well? Buy us and our land in exchange for food, and we with our land will be in bondage to Pharaoh. Give us seed so that we may live and not die, and that the land may not become desolate."

[20]So Joseph bought all the land in Egypt for Pharaoh. The Egyptians, one and all, sold their fields, because the famine was too severe for them. The land became Pharaoh's, [21]and Joseph reduced the people to servitude,[a] from one end of Egypt to the other. [22]However, he did not buy the land of the priests, because they received a regular allotment from Pharaoh and had food enough from the allotment Pharaoh gave them. That is why they did not sell their land.

[23]Joseph said to the people, "Now that I have bought you and your land today for Pharaoh, here is seed for you so you can plant the ground. [24]But when the crop comes in, give a fifth of it to Pharaoh. The other four-fifths you may keep as seed for the fields and as food for yourselves and your households and your children."

[25]"You have saved our lives," they said. "May we find favor in the eyes of our lord; we will be in bondage to Pharaoh."

[26]So Joseph established it as a law concerning land in Egypt—still in force today—that a fifth of the produce belongs to Pharaoh. It was only the land of the priests that did not become Pharaoh's.

[27]Now the Israelites settled in Egypt in the region of Goshen. They acquired property there and were fruitful and increased greatly in number.

[28]Jacob lived in Egypt seventeen years, and the years of his life were a hundred and forty-seven. [29]When the time drew near for Israel to die, he called for his son Joseph and said to him, "If I have found favor in your eyes, put your hand under my thigh and promise that you will show me kindness and faithfulness. Do not bury me in Egypt, [30]but when I rest with my fathers, carry me out of Egypt and bury me where they are buried."

"I will do as you say," he said.

[31]"Swear to me," he said. Then Joseph swore to him, and Israel worshiped as he leaned on the top of his staff.[b]

Manasseh and Ephraim

48 Some time later Joseph was told, "Your father is ill." So he took his two sons Manasseh and Ephraim along with him. [2]When Jacob was told, "Your son Joseph has come to you," Israel rallied his strength and sat up on the bed.

[3]Jacob said to Joseph, "God Almighty[c] appeared to me at Luz in the land of Canaan, and there he blessed me [4]and said to me, 'I am going to make you fruitful and will increase your numbers. I will

1. How severe are the next years of this famine? To what do the people finally resort? What do you think of this "everyone-pays-his-own-way" axiom, typical of the ancient world, but so rare in our welfare state? 2. In theory, all land in Egypt belonged to the Pharaoh anyway, with the notable exception of the land allocated to the priests. How is that theory faithfully put into practice by Joseph's economic policy during these hard times? 3. How does he thus save the people? How does he also enslave them? How does Joseph thus set the stage for what happens in the first chapters of Exodus? 4. While the land aspect of Abraham's covenant loses ground, how is the people side of the covenant gaining?

1. Do you think his actions here are what keep Joseph from being as big a hero in the history of Israel as Abraham and Jacob? Why or why not? 2. Loyalty and kindness were two strong suits of Joseph, but they were played inconsistently "on the job." Of loyalty and kindness, which is your strong suit? In what settings are you more loyal or more kind? In what area does Joseph's story urge you to demonstrate loyalty, or kindness, this week? 3. What about the old "everyone-pays-his-own-way" axiom from Joseph's day would you like to see implemented in your society? On the other hand, what about that law would be unfair if applied to all? 4. Of the three things the people of Egypt relinquished to Pharaoh—money, property and independence—which would be the easiest for you to give up? Which would be hardest? With which are you struggling the most today?

1. Are you a lefty or a righty? What things do you do equally well left-handed and right-handed? 2. What is a favorite memory you have about your grandparents? 3. What "privilege of rank" did you have as a child that your siblings or friends did not seem to have?

1. Consider this departure from the rule: Who was Abraham's first-born son (see ch. 16)?

[a]21 Samaritan Pentateuch and Septuagint (see also Vulgate); Masoretic Text *and he moved the people into the cities*   [b]31 Or *Israel bowed down at the head of his bed*
[c]3 Hebrew *El-Shaddai*

But which son received the blessing (see ch. 25)? Who was Isaac's
first-born son (see ch. 25)? But
which son received the birthright
(see ch. 27)? Who was Jacob's
first-born son (see ch. 29)? But
who received his blessing (27:3)?
Who was Joseph's first-born son
(vv. 14,18)? But who received the
favored blessing (vv. 9–20)? **2.**
What do you make of this unconventional pattern? What does this
teach you about how God chooses
his servants? **3.** What irony do you
see in the crisscross way Jacob
blesses Ephraim and Manasseh?
Instead of faithless scheming and
bitter grudges, what do you see in
how these sons and their parent
accept this reversal?

1. Out of all the events in Jacob's 147 years, why do you
think this one act of blessing Joseph's sons is singled out by the
writer of Hebrews (Heb 11:21) as
an example of outstanding faith? In
adopting Joseph's sons as his own
(v. 5), how did Jacob thus determine the structure and leadership
of his 12 tribes (see 1Ch 5:1ff)? **2.**
If Hebrews 11 were to include you
in its "Hall of Faith," what event in
your life would stand out as evidence of great faith? **3.** In what respects do you identify with Ephraim? With Manasseh? How does
their story and yours illustrate the
point, "But for the grace of God,
there go I"? **4.** As Jacob invokes
God's blessing on Joseph, he recalls how God has been his guiding
shepherd and guardian angel (vv.
15–16). Which of Jacob's pivotal
encounters was he likely reflecting
upon? **5.** As you recall God's dealings with Jacob, which of your own
faith encounters with God come to
mind? Why not thank him today for
the special way the God of Jacob
has been your own Shepherd and
Angel?

make you a community of peoples, and I will give this land as an
everlasting possession to your descendants after you.'

[5]"Now then, your two sons born to you in Egypt before I came to
you here will be reckoned as mine; Ephraim and Manasseh will be
mine, just as Reuben and Simeon are mine. [6]Any children born to
you after them will be yours; in the territory they inherit they will
be reckoned under the names of their brothers. [7]As I was returning
from Paddan,[a] to my sorrow Rachel died in the land of Canaan
while we were still on the way, a little distance from Ephrath. So I
buried her there beside the road to Ephrath" (that is, Bethlehem).

[8]When Israel saw the sons of Joseph, he asked, "Who are
these?"

[9]"They are the sons God has given me here," Joseph said to his
father.

Then Israel said, "Bring them to me so I may bless them."

[10]Now Israel's eyes were failing because of old age, and he could
hardly see. So Joseph brought his sons close to him, and his father
kissed them and embraced them.

[11]Israel said to Joseph, "I never expected to see your face again,
and now God has allowed me to see your children too."

[12]Then Joseph removed them from Israel's knees and bowed
down with his face to the ground. [13]And Joseph took both of them,
Ephraim on his right toward Israel's left hand and Manasseh on his
left toward Israel's right hand, and brought them close to him.
[14]But Israel reached out his right hand and put it on Ephraim's
head, though he was the younger, and crossing his arms, he put his
left hand on Manasseh's head, even though Manasseh was the
firstborn.

[15]Then he blessed Joseph and said,

> "May the God before whom my fathers
>   Abraham and Isaac walked,
> the God who has been my shepherd
>   all my life to this day,
> [16]the Angel who has delivered me from all harm
>   —may he bless these boys.
> May they be called by my name
>   and the names of my fathers Abraham and
>   Isaac,
> and may they increase greatly
>   upon the earth."

[17]When Joseph saw his father placing his right hand on Ephraim's head he was displeased; so he took hold of his father's hand to
move it from Ephraim's head to Manasseh's head. [18]Joseph said to
him, "No, my father, this one is the firstborn; put your right hand
on his head."

[19]But his father refused and said, "I know, my son, I know. He
too will become a people, and he too will become great. Nevertheless, his younger brother will be greater than he, and his descendants will become a group of nations." [20]He blessed them that day
and said,

> "In your[b] name will Israel pronounce this
>   blessing:
> 'May God make you like Ephraim and
>   Manasseh.'"

So he put Ephraim ahead of Manasseh.

---

a7 That is, Northwest Mesopotamia   b20 The Hebrew is singular.

²¹Then Israel said to Joseph, "I am about to die, but God will be with you*ᵃ* and take you*ᵃ* back to the land of your*ᵃ* fathers. ²²And to you, as one who is over your brothers, I give the ridge of land*ᵇ* I took from the Amorites with my sword and my bow."

Jacob Blesses His Sons

49 Then Jacob called for his sons and said: "Gather around so I can tell you what will happen to you in days to come.

²"Assemble and listen, sons of Jacob;
  listen to your father Israel.

³"Reuben, you are my firstborn,
  my might, the first sign of my strength,
  excelling in honor, excelling in power.
⁴Turbulent as the waters, you will no longer excel,
  for you went up onto your father's bed,
  onto my couch and defiled it.

⁵"Simeon and Levi are brothers—
  their swords*ᶜ* are weapons of violence.
⁶Let me not enter their council,
  let me not join their assembly,
for they have killed men in their anger
  and hamstrung oxen as they pleased.
⁷Cursed be their anger, so fierce,
  and their fury, so cruel!
I will scatter them in Jacob
  and disperse them in Israel.

⁸"Judah,*ᵈ* your brothers will praise you;
  your hand will be on the neck of your enemies;
  your father's sons will bow down to you.
⁹You are a lion's cub, O Judah;
  you return from the prey, my son.
Like a lion he crouches and lies down,
  like a lioness—who dares to rouse him?
¹⁰The scepter will not depart from Judah,
  nor the ruler's staff from between his feet,
until he comes to whom it belongs*ᵉ*
  and the obedience of the nations is his.
¹¹He will tether his donkey to a vine,
  his colt to the choicest branch;
he will wash his garments in wine,
  his robes in the blood of grapes.
¹²His eyes will be darker than wine,
  his teeth whiter than milk.*ᶠ*

¹³"Zebulun will live by the seashore
  and become a haven for ships;
  his border will extend toward Sidon.

¹⁴"Issachar is a rawboned*ᵍ* donkey
  lying down between two saddlebags.*ʰ*
¹⁵When he sees how good is his resting place
  and how pleasant is his land,
  he will bend his shoulder to the burden

---

1. What major, non-material blessing have you inherited from your parents or grandparents? 2. What nicknames were you saddled with by your grandfather?

1. As you read through these oracles, list the sons and the most important prediction made about each. What does this list tell you about Jacob? About his sons? About their family life? What surprises you? Angers you? 2. Where do you see moral judgments made here about events told earlier without comment? Where do you see the sons' achievement falling short of their promise? 3. In verse 18, Jacob pauses for prayer. What about the two sons mentioned previously (vv. 14–17) gives Jacob pause for such prayer? 4. What does this last of the great blessings, curses, promises and judgments, contribute to the overall themes or thrust of Genesis?

1. What would the first readers of this account know about the general fulfillment of these prophecies? To what books of the Bible would you turn next for the fulfillment of these prophecies? 2. Which prophecy points to the Messiah who will rule the nations (see vv. 10–12)? Could this be a reference to King David or Christ, the King of kings? 3. With which of the blessings do you most identify today? That is, how are you like turbulent waters, sword fighter, lion's cub, ship's haven, stubborn donkey, biting serpent, king's chef, playful doe, fruitful vine, or ravenous wolf? 4. Add your own name to the list of sons and their blessings: What fun, good and harsh blessings have you received? (No fair identifying only with the fun or good ones.) 5. Which blessings and images do you associate with others in your group? Have a "blessed" time sharing these associations! 6. Which of your better qualities would you like to hand down to your kids? Which of your not-so-flattering qualities do you wish would sooner skip a generation or two? What will you do to help your children acquire and exhibit more of the "good" and less of the "bad" or "ugly" side of you? 7. What not-so-good blessing have you received from someone that affects

---

ᵃ21 The Hebrew is plural.   *ᵇ22* Or *And to you I give one portion more than to your brothers—the portion*   *ᶜ5* The meaning of the Hebrew for this word is uncertain.   *ᵈ8* *Judah* sounds like and may be derived from the Hebrew for *praise.*   *ᵉ10* Or *until Shiloh comes*; or *until he comes to whom tribute belongs*   *ᶠ12* Or *will be dull from wine, / his teeth white from milk*   *ᵍ14* Or *strong*   *ʰ14* Or *campfires*

your life in a not-so-positive way? What great blessing have you received from someone that inspires you to live a courageous, God-glorifying life? **8.** Take turns sharing one way that each group member has blessed your life.

16"Dan[a] will provide justice for his people
    as one of the tribes of Israel.
17Dan will be a serpent by the roadside,
    a viper along the path,
that bites the horse's heels
    so that its rider tumbles backward.

18"I look for your deliverance, O LORD.

19"Gad[b] will be attacked by a band of raiders,
    but he will attack them at their heels.

20"Asher's food will be rich;
    he will provide delicacies fit for a king.

21"Naphtali is a doe set free
    that bears beautiful fawns.[c]

22"Joseph is a fruitful vine,
    a fruitful vine near a spring,
    whose branches climb over a wall.[d]
23With bitterness archers attacked him;
    they shot at him with hostility.
24But his bow remained steady,
    his strong arms stayed[e] limber,
because of the hand of the Mighty One of Jacob,
    because of the Shepherd, the Rock of Israel,
25because of your father's God, who helps you,
    because of the Almighty,[f] who blesses you
with blessings of the heavens above,
    blessings of the deep that lies below,
    blessings of the breast and womb.
26Your father's blessings are greater
    than the blessings of the ancient mountains,
    than[g] the bounty of the age-old hills.
Let all these rest on the head of Joseph,
    on the brow of the prince among[h] his
      brothers.

27"Benjamin is a ravenous wolf;
    in the morning he devours the prey,
    in the evening he divides the plunder."

28All these are the twelve tribes of Israel, and this is what their father said to them when he blessed them, giving each the blessing appropriate to him.

The Death of Jacob

29Then he gave them these instructions: "I am about to be gathered to my people. Bury me with my fathers in the cave in the field of Ephron the Hittite, 30the cave in the field of Machpelah, near Mamre in Canaan, which Abraham bought as a burial place from Ephron the Hittite, along with the field. 31There Abraham and his wife Sarah were buried, there Isaac and his wife Rebekah were buried, and there I buried Leah. 32The field and the cave in it were bought from the Hittites.[i]"

1. How many different places have you lived in your life? Of these, which was your favorite? Which was "home"? **2.** When you die, which would you most like to have perform at your funeral: (a) 76 trombones? (b) An electric guitar? (c) A simple banjo? (d) A full orchestra in tails? What does your choice say about how you hope to live?

1. Why is it so important to Jacob that he be buried in Canaan (see 46:1–4; 47:29–31)? What does this say about Jacob's faith in God's promises? **2.** What

a16 Dan here means he provides justice.   b19 Gad can mean attack and band of raiders.   c21 Or free; / he utters beautiful words   d22 Or Joseph is a wild colt, / a wild colt near a spring, / a wild donkey on a terraced hill   e23,24 Or archers will attack . . . will shoot . . . will remain . . . will stay   f25 Hebrew Shaddai   g26 Or of my progenitors, / as great as   h26 Or the one separated from   i32 Or the sons of Heth

[33]When Jacob had finished giving instructions to his sons, he drew his feet up into the bed, breathed his last and was gathered to his people.

50 Joseph threw himself upon his father and wept over him and kissed him. [2]Then Joseph directed the physicians in his service to embalm his father Israel. So the physicians embalmed him, [3]taking a full forty days, for that was the time required for embalming. And the Egyptians mourned for him seventy days.

[4]When the days of mourning had passed, Joseph said to Pharaoh's court, "If I have found favor in your eyes, speak to Pharaoh for me. Tell him, [5]'My father made me swear an oath and said, "I am about to die; bury me in the tomb I dug for myself in the land of Canaan." Now let me go up and bury my father; then I will return.'"

[6]Pharaoh said, "Go up and bury your father, as he made you swear to do."

[7]So Joseph went up to bury his father. All Pharaoh's officials accompanied him—the dignitaries of his court and all the dignitaries of Egypt— [8]besides all the members of Joseph's household and his brothers and those belonging to his father's household. Only their children and their flocks and herds were left in Goshen. [9]Chariots and horsemen[a] also went up with him. It was a very large company.

[10]When they reached the threshing floor of Atad, near the Jordan, they lamented loudly and bitterly; and there Joseph observed a seven-day period of mourning for his father. [11]When the Canaanites who lived there saw the mourning at the threshing floor of Atad, they said, "The Egyptians are holding a solemn ceremony of mourning." That is why that place near the Jordan is called Abel Mizraim.[b]

[12]So Jacob's sons did as he had commanded them: [13]They carried him to the land of Canaan and buried him in the cave in the field of Machpelah, near Mamre, which Abraham had bought as a burial place from Ephron the Hittite, along with the field. [14]After burying his father, Joseph returned to Egypt, together with his brothers and all the others who had gone with him to bury his father.

Joseph Reassures His Brothers

[15]When Joseph's brothers saw that their father was dead, they said, "What if Joseph holds a grudge against us and pays us back for all the wrongs we did to him?" [16]So they sent word to Joseph, saying, "Your father left these instructions before he died: [17]'This is what you are to say to Joseph: I ask you to forgive your brothers the sins and the wrongs they committed in treating you so badly.' Now please forgive the sins of the servants of the God of your father." When their message came to him, Joseph wept.

[18]His brothers then came and threw themselves down before him. "We are your slaves," they said.

[19]But Joseph said to them, "Don't be afraid. Am I in the place of God? [20]You intended to harm me, but God intended it for good to accomplish what is now being done, the saving of many lives. [21]So then, don't be afraid. I will provide for you and your children." And he reassured them and spoke kindly to them.

The Death of Joseph

[22]Joseph stayed in Egypt, along with all his father's family. He lived a hundred and ten years [23]and saw the third generation of

impact does Jacob's death have on Joseph? On his family? On the Egyptians? On Pharaoh's court? **3.** Why such a large company of mourners? What does that say about fulfilling the people aspect of the covenant? **4.** Why such details concerning the funeral? What does this say about the importance of Jacob? Of Joseph? Of custom?

1. Where would you like to be buried? Will your funeral be bigger or smaller than your wedding or your graduation party? What does that say about how long you expect to live or how many survivors and friends you will have accumulated? **2.** How do you feel about death and dying? Are you afraid of dying? Why or why not? Have you managed to avoid talking about it with your family? Why? Why not talk about it sometime soon?

1. Which memory is harder for you to shake: Rejection or guilt? Why? **2.** Which is harder for you to accept: Mercy or judgment?

1. What do you make of the brothers' fear as described here? Is it justified? Why or why not? **2.** How does Joseph's story reveal the truth of verses 19–21?

1. What low lights and high lights come to mind when you apply verses 19–21 to your life? **2.** When last week were you tempted to replace God in judging others? In judging yourself?

Complete the sentence: "When I die, my family will smile when they remember the time ..."

---

[a]9 Or *charioteers*   [b]11 *Abel Mizraim* means *mourning of the Egyptians.*

How is Joseph's last request tied to God's promises? To the precedent of his father, grandfather and great grandfather? To the anticipation of Exodus?

1. What outstanding characteristic of Joseph's life would you like to make a part of yours? 2. What does this "Book of Beginnings" teach you about your own roots? About the faith of your fathers? About your own faith? About God's promises to you and your children?

Ephraim's children. Also the children of Makir son of Manasseh were placed at birth on Joseph's knees. [a]

24Then Joseph said to his brothers, "I am about to die. But God will surely come to your aid and take you up out of this land to the land he promised on oath to Abraham, Isaac and Jacob." 25And Joseph made the sons of Israel swear an oath and said, "God will surely come to your aid, and then you must carry my bones up from this place."

26So Joseph died at the age of a hundred and ten. And after they embalmed him, he was placed in a coffin in Egypt.

---

a23 That is, were counted as his

INTRODUCTION to
EXODUS

Book Study Outline: If you are using Exodus for a study course, here is a 7- or 13-week outline. Use the questions in the margin for your group agenda:

🍵 start meeting / 15 min.

📖 read & discuss Bible / 30 min.

♡ close meeting / 15–45 min.

Refer to the Questions and Answers in the front of this Bible for more information.

Author: Moses is assumed to be the author and editor of most of the first five books of the OT (the Pentateuch).

7-week plan	13-week plan	Personal Reading	Group Study Passage
1	1	Ge 50:22–Ex. 2:25	1:22–2:25/Moses' Beginnings
	2	3:1–4:31	3:1–22/God Calls Moses
2	3	5:1–6:27	5:22–6:12/God's Promise
	4	6:28–10:29	6:28–7:24/Plagues Begin
3	5	11:1–13:16	12:1–30/The Passover
	6	13:17–15:21	14:5–31/Crossing the Sea
4	7	15:22–16:36	16:1–35/Manna and Quail
	8	17:1–18:27	18:1–27/Jethro Visits Moses
5	9	19:1–24:18	19:10–20:21/Ten Commandments
	10	25:1–33:6	32:1–35/The Golden Calf
6	11	33:7–34:35	33:12–23/Moses Sees God
	12	35:1–39:43	39:32–43/ Tabernacle Inspected
7	13	40:1–38	40:34–38/Glory of the Lord

Date: It is difficult to assign a firm date to the composition of the Pentateuch. Conservative estimates place it in either the fifteenth or thirteenth century B.C., depending on when the Exodus occurred.

Theme: Deliverance from Egypt; giving the Law; building the Tabernacle.

Historical Background: No direct evidence fixes the events of this book within a specifically dated historical context. The Bible does not provide the name of the Pharaoh of the Exodus, and extra-biblical texts and archaeology are silent concerning the Israelites' sojourn in and escape from Egypt. Indirect evidence present throughout the Bible can be used to support a wide range of dates. Certain recent archaeological evidence from Palestine suggests a late thirteenth century date for the appearance of the Israelites in Canaan, by which it would be inferred that Moses and the events of this book may date earlier in this same century, sometime between 1300 and 1250 B.C.

Characteristics: The book of Exodus is dominated by the life and actions of Moses and arranged around two outstanding redemptive acts, the Exodus from Egypt and the establishment of the Covenant at Sinai. In fact, Moses and these events are so fundamental to an understanding of God's plan for the redemption of humanity that it could be argued that much of the Bible is a dialogue which reacts to, explains, implements, elaborates and completes the redemptive plan of God as it is revealed in this book.

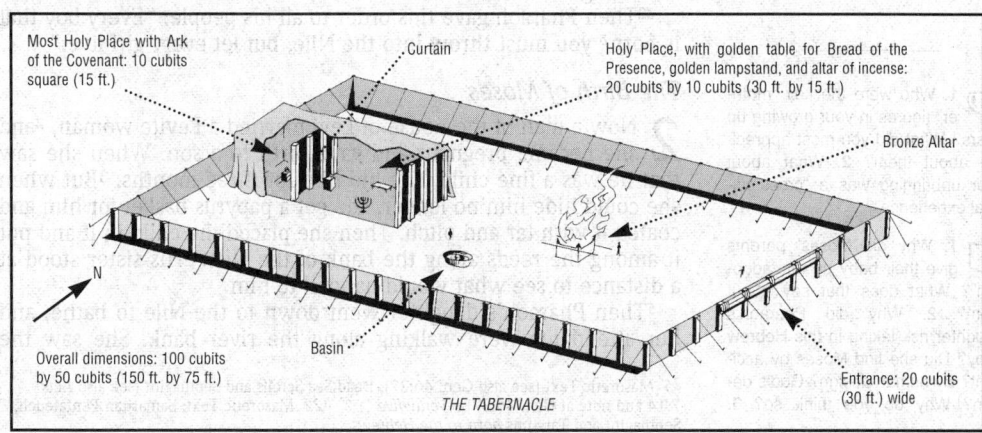

Most Holy Place with Ark of the Covenant: 10 cubits square (15 ft.)

Curtain

Holy Place, with golden table for Bread of the Presence, golden lampstand, and altar of incense: 20 cubits by 10 cubits (30 ft. by 15 ft.)

Bronze Altar

N

Overall dimensions: 100 cubits by 50 cubits (150 ft. by 75 ft.)

Basin

Entrance: 20 cubits (30 ft.) wide

THE TABERNACLE

Exodus

The Israelites Oppressed

1 These are the names of the sons of Israel who went to Egypt with Jacob, each with his family: [2]Reuben, Simeon, Levi and Judah; [3]Issachar, Zebulun and Benjamin; [4]Dan and Naphtali; Gad and Asher. [5]The descendants of Jacob numbered seventy[a] in all; Joseph was already in Egypt.

[6]Now Joseph and all his brothers and all that generation died, [7]but the Israelites were fruitful and multiplied greatly and became exceedingly numerous, so that the land was filled with them.

[8]Then a new king, who did not know about Joseph, came to power in Egypt. [9]"Look," he said to his people, "the Israelites have become much too numerous for us. [10]Come, we must deal shrewdly with them or they will become even more numerous and, if war breaks out, will join our enemies, fight against us and leave the country."

[11]So they put slave masters over them to oppress them with forced labor, and they built Pithom and Rameses as store cities for Pharaoh. [12]But the more they were oppressed, the more they multiplied and spread; so the Egyptians came to dread the Israelites [13]and worked them ruthlessly. [14]They made their lives bitter with hard labor in brick and mortar and with all kinds of work in the fields; in all their hard labor the Egyptians used them ruthlessly.

[15]The king of Egypt said to the Hebrew midwives, whose names were Shiphrah and Puah, [16]"When you help the Hebrew women in childbirth and observe them on the delivery stool, if it is a boy, kill him; but if it is a girl, let her live." [17]The midwives, however, feared God and did not do what the king of Egypt had told them to do; they let the boys live. [18]Then the king of Egypt summoned the midwives and asked them, "Why have you done this? Why have you let the boys live?"

[19]The midwives answered Pharaoh, "Hebrew women are not like Egyptian women; they are vigorous and give birth before the midwives arrive."

[20]So God was kind to the midwives and the people increased and became even more numerous. [21]And because the midwives feared God, he gave them families of their own.

[22]Then Pharaoh gave this order to all his people: "Every boy that is born[b] you must throw into the Nile, but let every girl live."

The Birth of Moses

2 Now a man of the house of Levi married a Levite woman, [2]and she became pregnant and gave birth to a son. When she saw that he was a fine child, she hid him for three months. [3]But when she could hide him no longer, she got a papyrus basket for him and coated it with tar and pitch. Then she placed the child in it and put it among the reeds along the bank of the Nile. [4]His sister stood at a distance to see what would happen to him.

[5]Then Pharaoh's daughter went down to the Nile to bathe, and her attendants were walking along the river bank. She saw the

---

1. How many times have you moved in your lifetime? In your most significant move, who moved with you? Whom did you leave behind? How did you feel about all that moving (or staying put)? 2. In your working career, who has been one very unreasonable boss? How so? How did you respond?

1. How does this story pick up where the other left off (see Ge 45:8–11; 46:8ff)? 2. What did the king "who did not know Joseph" fear about the Hebrews (vv. 8ff)? Why? What does Pharaoh's fear lead him to do? 3. The Israelites were forced into hard labor. Describe a time when you were forced to work hard. How did it feel? What does this say about the power of Pharaoh? Of midwives? Of fearing men vs. fearing God? 4. By disobeying Pharaoh, what are the midwives risking? What does God think of their disobedience?

1. What do you fear? In your life, when is fear "good"? Or "bad"? How do you know when your fear prompts you to do good or do bad? 2. What does the faith of the midwives say about the morality of "civil disobedience"? Discuss this in view of Romans 13. 3. As a Hebrew midwife, what would you have done? Why? When have you acted likewise in disobeying an oppressive regime or boss?

---

1. Who were the key "mother" figures in your growing up years? What did you most appreciate about them? 2. What about your upbringing was a "cross-cultural experience"?

1. Why did Moses' parents give their baby up for "adoption"? What does that say about them? 2. Why did Pharaoh's daughter risk taking in this Hebrew baby? Did she find Moses by accident? By human design? God's design? Why do you think so? 3.

---

[a]5 Masoretic Text (see also Gen. 46:27); Dead Sea Scrolls and Septuagint (see also Acts 7:14 and note at Gen. 46:27) *seventy-five*   [b]22 Masoretic Text; Samaritan Pentateuch, Septuagint and Targums *born to the Hebrews*

basket among the reeds and sent her slave girl to get it. [6]She opened it and saw the baby. He was crying, and she felt sorry for him. "This is one of the Hebrew babies," she said.

[7]Then his sister asked Pharaoh's daughter, "Shall I go and get one of the Hebrew women to nurse the baby for you?"

[8]"Yes, go," she answered. And the girl went and got the baby's mother. [9]Pharaoh's daughter said to her, "Take this baby and nurse him for me, and I will pay you." So the woman took the baby and nursed him. [10]When the child grew older, she took him to Pharaoh's daughter and he became her son. She named him Moses,[a] saying, "I drew him out of the water."

Moses Flees to Midian

[11]One day, after Moses had grown up, he went out to where his own people were and watched them at their hard labor. He saw an Egyptian beating a Hebrew, one of his own people. [12]Glancing this way and that and seeing no one, he killed the Egyptian and hid him in the sand. [13]The next day he went out and saw two Hebrews fighting. He asked the one in the wrong, "Why are you hitting your fellow Hebrew?"

[14]The man said, "Who made you ruler and judge over us? Are you thinking of killing me as you killed the Egyptian?" Then Moses was afraid and thought, "What I did must have become known."

[15]When Pharaoh heard of this, he tried to kill Moses, but Moses fled from Pharaoh and went to live in Midian, where he sat down by a well. [16]Now a priest of Midian had seven daughters, and they came to draw water and fill the troughs to water their father's

[a]10 *Moses* sounds like the Hebrew for *draw out*.

What would Moses gain by growing up "royal"? How might this be good, or bad, for Israel?

1. Pharaoh's daughter felt sorry for the Hebrew baby despite her father's ruling. Have you ever felt love for someone that others oppressed or neglected? 2. What unusual events shaped your place in God's purposes?

Have you ever tried breaking up a fight among siblings or good friends? Why? What happened? Did they turn on you?

1. In scene I (vv. 11–15), how does the royal Moses identify with the "lowly" Hebrews? Why do the Hebrews fail to identify with him? Why does Moses flee? 2. How does scene II (vv. 15–25) relate to scene I? How might the "long period" in desolate Midian (see Ac 7:29–30) influence Moses' role in God's redemptive purposes? 3. What character traits do scenes I and II bring out in Moses? How is Moses being prepared to be the deliverer of God's people?

 Exodus 1:22–2:25   **BEGINNING OF MOSES' LIFE**

About 400 years earlier, Jacob (Israel) and his family moved to Egypt. Since then the Egyptians became so fearful of the rapidly growing population of Israelites that they enslaved them and now even ordered them to drown male newborns in the Nile.

1. What was Moses' mother thinking as she hid her son in the Nile?
   a. I'm sorry I can't keep you.
   b. At least you'll have a chance.
   c. God will take care of you.
   d. Don't worry—I've got a plan.

2. If I had been Pharaoh's daughter, when I saw Moses in the basket I would have:
   a. screamed.
   b. thrown him in the river.
   c. called social services.
   d. sent out a search team for his mother.
   e. taken him home and loved him as my own.

3. Moses killed the Egyptian because:
   a. of his strong sense of justice.
   b. he thought no one was looking.

c. he was a bully.
d. in his heart he was an Israelite.
e. the Egyptian deserved it.

4. What was the most important need God met in this story?
   a. a baby's need for loving care
   b. a mother's need to see her baby survive
   c. an adoptive mother's longing for a son of her own
   d. a people's need for a leader
   e. God's need of a deliverer for his people

5. Why didn't the Israelites appreciate what Moses did for them?

6. When have you been like Moses in trying to "make things right"? How do you know if God is leading you or if you're taking matters into your own hands?

7. I wouldn't be interested in Bible study and growing in my faith if it had not been for:
   a. my parents.
   b. a Sunday School teacher.

c. a pastor.
d. a friend.
e. my spouse.

8. In my faith adventure right now I am:
   a. struggling to keep my head above water.
   b. still cuddled by my parents' faith.
   c. out in the reeds waiting for something to happen.
   d. exposed to options other than Christianity.
   e. launching into the world with a solid Christian identity.

9. 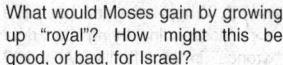 In what ways does this story relate to your child and his or her adoption? How can you explain to your child God's role in his or her adoption story?

10. Has your adopted child expressed an interest in his or her birth family roots? If so, how do you feel about it? If not, how will you feel if it occurs in the future? What other critical issues face you as an adoptive family?

1. When have you been like Moses in trying to right "wrongs" in your family? At work? 2. Have you dropped out, been biding your time, or simply waited on God's plans for you? What for? How did this better prepare you for your future? 3. How do you feel about God using a murderer to further his plans? How has God used a personal flaw or failure of yours for his greater glory?

1. On Monday mornings, what is "business as usual" for you? When you then see, hear or smell something strange going on there, what do you do about it? 2. In taking on new work, do you "bite off more than you can chew"? Do you "chomp at the bit"? Why?

flock. [17]Some shepherds came along and drove them away, but Moses got up and came to their rescue and watered their flock.

[18]When the girls returned to Reuel their father, he asked them, "Why have you returned so early today?"

[19]They answered, "An Egyptian rescued us from the shepherds. He even drew water for us and watered the flock."

[20]"And where is he?" he asked his daughters. "Why did you leave him? Invite him to have something to eat."

[21]Moses agreed to stay with the man, who gave his daughter Zipporah to Moses in marriage. [22]Zipporah gave birth to a son, and Moses named him Gershom,[a] saying, "I have become an alien in a foreign land."

[23]During that long period, the king of Egypt died. The Israelites groaned in their slavery and cried out, and their cry for help because of their slavery went up to God. [24]God heard their groaning and he remembered his covenant with Abraham, with Isaac and with Jacob. [25]So God looked on the Israelites and was concerned about them.

Moses and the Burning Bush

3 Now Moses was tending the flock of Jethro his father-in-law, the priest of Midian, and he led the flock to the far side of the desert and came to Horeb, the mountain of God. [2]There the angel of the LORD appeared to him in flames of fire from within a bush. Moses saw that though the bush was on fire it did not burn up. [3]So

[a]22 *Gershom* sounds like the Hebrew for *an alien there.*

  Exodus 3:1–22   **MOSES AND THE BURNING BUSH**

Though an Israelite by birth, Moses was adopted by Pharaoh's daughter. After killing an Egyptian slave driver who was beating an Israelite slave, Moses fled to Midian—where he married and became a shepherd.

1. Why did God use a burning bush to get Moses' attention?
   a. It would add a lot to movies like "The Ten Commandments."
   b. It signaled the beginning of a new and more intimate relationship with him.
   c. It would help Moses remember his calling later when he really needed to.
   d. The fire emphasized how holy the event was.
   e. God demonstrated his power by the bush not burning up.

2. If you had been Moses, what would you have thought about this event?
   a. I must have eaten too many anchovies.
   b. Why does God want me for this?
   c. I thought I could get away from God out here in the desert.

d. God, don't talk to me about your problems; I've enough of my own.
   e. God, I am your humble servant.

3. Why is Moses reluctant to go back to Egypt and do what God asks? What reassurances does God give him?

4. If I were in Moses' sandals, I would share his:
   a. fear of looking God in the eye.
   b. reverence in taking off my sandals.
   c. sense of inadequacy to do God's work.
   d. concern for what others think.
   e. wondering if God's plan will work.

5. The burning bush (God's attention-getter) in my life has been:
   a. a personal experience with God.
   b. a near disaster.
   c. frustrated plans.
   d. special blessings.
   e. personal crisis.
   f. a meaningful worship experience.
   g. a particular Scripture passage.
   h. a life-changing relationship.

6. What has been God's "call" in your life? What would it take to get your

attention and commitment to accept a new mission in life?

7. What is God's name to you? I AM:
   a. forgiving.   d. tough.
   b. loving.   e. with you.
   c. patient.   f. all you'll ever need.

8. How would you describe your relationship with God right now?
   a. a burning bush
   b. a flickering bush
   c. a few ashes from the past
   d. What bush?!

9. In terms of fulfilling God's calling, Moses was "unemployed" at this time in his life. How have you dealt with being unemployed? How can you relate to Moses being asked to take a "job" with which he wasn't comfortable?

10. At the "empty nest" stage of life, how can you relate to Moses' being called at a mature age to something so different? How could you better invest yourself and your gifts in the "second half of life"?

Moses thought, "I will go over and see this strange sight—why the bush does not burn up."

⁴When the LORD saw that he had gone over to look, God called to him from within the bush, "Moses! Moses!"

And Moses said, "Here I am."

⁵"Do not come any closer," God said. "Take off your sandals, for the place where you are standing is holy ground." ⁶Then he said, "I am the God of your father, the God of Abraham, the God of Isaac and the God of Jacob." At this, Moses hid his face, because he was afraid to look at God.

⁷The LORD said, "I have indeed seen the misery of my people in Egypt. I have heard them crying out because of their slave drivers, and I am concerned about their suffering. ⁸So I have come down to rescue them from the hand of the Egyptians and to bring them up out of that land into a good and spacious land, a land flowing with milk and honey—the home of the Canaanites, Hittites, Amorites, Perizzites, Hivites and Jebusites. ⁹And now the cry of the Israelites has reached me, and I have seen the way the Egyptians are oppressing them. ¹⁰So now, go. I am sending you to Pharaoh to bring my people the Israelites out of Egypt."

¹¹But Moses said to God, "Who am I, that I should go to Pharaoh and bring the Israelites out of Egypt?"

¹²And God said, "I will be with you. And this will be the sign to you that it is I who have sent you: When you have brought the people out of Egypt, you*ᵃ* will worship God on this mountain."

¹³Moses said to God, "Suppose I go to the Israelites and say to them, 'The God of your fathers has sent me to you,' and they ask me, 'What is his name?' Then what shall I tell them?"

¹⁴God said to Moses, "I AM WHO I AM.*ᵇ* This is what you are to say to the Israelites: 'I AM has sent me to you.'"

¹⁵God also said to Moses, "Say to the Israelites, 'The LORD,*ᶜ* the God of your fathers—the God of Abraham, the God of Isaac and the God of Jacob—has sent me to you.' This is my name forever, the name by which I am to be remembered from generation to generation.

¹⁶"Go, assemble the elders of Israel and say to them, 'The LORD, the God of your fathers—the God of Abraham, Isaac and Jacob—appeared to me and said: I have watched over you and have seen what has been done to you in Egypt. ¹⁷And I have promised to bring you up out of your misery in Egypt into the land of the Canaanites, Hittites, Amorites, Perizzites, Hivites and Jebusites—a land flowing with milk and honey.'

¹⁸"The elders of Israel will listen to you. Then you and the elders are to go to the king of Egypt and say to him, 'The LORD, the God of the Hebrews, has met with us. Let us take a three-day journey into the desert to offer sacrifices to the LORD our God.' ¹⁹But I know that the king of Egypt will not let you go unless a mighty hand compels him. ²⁰So I will stretch out my hand and strike the Egyptians with all the wonders that I will perform among them. After that, he will let you go.

²¹"And I will make the Egyptians favorably disposed toward this people, so that when you leave you will not go empty-handed. ²²Every woman is to ask her neighbor and any woman living in her house for articles of silver and gold and for clothing, which you will put on your sons and daughters. And so you will plunder the Egyptians."

1. Why do you think God used the burning bush to get Moses' attention (vv. 1–3)? What if he had simply begun speaking instead? What is the resulting effect on Moses (vv. 5–6)? What relationship with Moses has God initiated here (vv. 1–6)? 2. What does God ask Moses to do for Israel (vv. 7–10)? Why? 3. How does Moses reply (vv.11ff)? Is Moses more uncertain of himself or God? Why? What range of emotion might Moses have had in this encounter with God? 4. What reassurances does God give him? How does "I AM" uniquely designate God? 5. How does Jesus take on that name for himself and with what implication (consider his "I am" statements in John's Gospel)? 6. Who is responsible for carrying out God's plan (vv. 16–22)? What is the part to be played by God? Moses? The elders of Israel? The king of Egypt? The Hebrew women? 7. What motivates God to save his people? Why wait so long? What needs to take place first?

1. Recall an event in your life when you felt like you were "standing on holy ground." What was sacred about that moment? How has that moment served to establish a right relationship between God and you? 2. If God were to identify himself as "I AM _____," how would he fill in the blank for you? 3. Have you ever felt called by God to do a particular task? What task? How did you respond? 4. What would God have to do to get your attention and commitment to take on a new mission in life? How would you likely respond if he called you by name? 5. What would your "land of milk and honey" be like? 6. To get there, what route do you imagine having to take? What "king" stands in your way? What "elders" will you consult? 7. Do you think God will come through for you as he promised to Moses? Why?

ᵃ12 The Hebrew is plural.   *ᵇ14* Or *I WILL BE WHAT I WILL BE*   *ᶜ15* The Hebrew for LORD sounds like and may be derived from the Hebrew for *I AM* in verse 14.

1. As a child, what was one chore you hated? How did you try to avoid doing it? 2. What's the best excuse you've heard lately from a determined procrastinator?

1. What three objections does Moses raise here? What do they sound like to you: False issues? Legitimate ones? True humility? Stubborn resistance? 2. How does God respond to each? What do his signs look like to you: Hocus-pocus? Irrefutable evidence? Miracles which need an interpreter? 3. What do you think of God's persuasive efforts? What's their net effect on Moses? If Moses were a "pushover" instead of a "hard sell," how would this conversation have gone? 4. Why is God so angry (vv. 13–14)? Why do you think God deals with Moses' final objection as he does? Is God taking back part of the job he had assigned Moses? Or assuring him success with "Plan B"? Why does he involve Aaron?

1. When has God reassured you of his presence and power: (a) At the outset of your spiritual life? (b) When you took some specific calling? (c) Making a tough de-

Signs for Moses

4 Moses answered, "What if they do not believe me or listen to me and say, 'The LORD did not appear to you'?"

²Then the LORD said to him, "What is that in your hand?"

"A staff," he replied.

³The LORD said, "Throw it on the ground."

Moses threw it on the ground and it became a snake, and he ran from it. ⁴Then the LORD said to him, "Reach out your hand and take it by the tail." So Moses reached out and took hold of the snake and it turned back into a staff in his hand. ⁵"This," said the LORD, "is so that they may believe that the LORD, the God of their fathers—the God of Abraham, the God of Isaac and the God of Jacob—has appeared to you."

⁶Then the LORD said, "Put your hand inside your cloak." So Moses put his hand into his cloak, and when he took it out, it was leprous,ᵃ like snow.

⁷"Now put it back into your cloak," he said. So Moses put his hand back into his cloak, and when he took it out, it was restored, like the rest of his flesh.

⁸Then the LORD said, "If they do not believe you or pay attention to the first miraculous sign, they may believe the second. ⁹But if they do not believe these two signs or listen to you, take some water from the Nile and pour it on the dry ground. The water you take from the river will become blood on the ground."

¹⁰Moses said to the LORD, "O Lord, I have never been eloquent,

ᵃ6 The Hebrew word was used for various diseases affecting the skin—not necessarily leprosy.

  Exodus 4:1–17   **SIGNS FOR MOSES**

God has just revealed himself to Moses at the burning bush—telling him to return to Egypt to lead the Israelites out of bondage.

1. What was behind Moses' first objection in verse 1? (Actually Moses had objected twice already in ch 3.)
 a. an honest question
 b. a poor excuse
 c. a need for people's approval
 d. lack of trust in God
 e. memories of past rejection

2. What was the point of the miraculous signs?
 a. God was showing off.
 b. God was answering Moses' objection about people not believing him.
 c. God was demonstrating his power to Moses.
 d. God was transferring his power to Moses.

3. If it were you, what effect would the miracles have on you and your reluctance to do what God asked?

4. What was behind Moses' second objection in verse 10?
 a. a speech impediment
 b. an inability to think on his feet
 c. low self-esteem
 d. humility
 e. pride

5. How did God respond to this objection? How would that have made you feel? How has God responded to your limitations or insecurities?

6. What was behind Moses' third objection in verse 13?
 a. laziness   d. fear
 b. rebellion   e. lack of confidence
 c. isolation

7. How did God respond to this objection? Overall, how would you characterize God's dealings with Moses?
 a. loving   c. angry
 b. patient   d. accommodating

8. What excuses do you make to God? How do you think he feels about them?

9. What gifts has God given you? What gifts do you see in the others in your group?

10. What excuses do you use for failing to acknowledge and/or use your gifts? What do you need to stop making these excuses?
 a. a miraculous sign
 b. encouragement from God
 c. an encourager like Aaron
 d. God's wrath

11. How can you relate to Moses' uncertainty about God's will? How much of your uncertainty is honest searching, and how much of it is making excuses? How can you worry less about your future?

12. How has your perception of the way God wants to use your gifts changed during this course? How can your group continue to support you in your quest to know and follow God's will?

neither in the past nor since you have spoken to your servant. I am slow of speech and tongue."

11The LORD said to him, "Who gave man his mouth? Who makes him deaf or mute? Who gives him sight or makes him blind? Is it not I, the LORD? 12Now go; I will help you speak and will teach you what to say."

13But Moses said, "O Lord, please send someone else to do it."

14Then the LORD's anger burned against Moses and he said, "What about your brother, Aaron the Levite? I know he can speak well. He is already on his way to meet you, and his heart will be glad when he sees you. 15You shall speak to him and put words in his mouth; I will help both of you speak and will teach you what to do. 16He will speak to the people for you, and it will be as if he were your mouth and as if you were God to him. 17But take this staff in your hand so you can perform miraculous signs with it."

Moses Returns to Egypt

18Then Moses went back to Jethro his father-in-law and said to him, "Let me go back to my own people in Egypt to see if any of them are still alive."

Jethro said, "Go, and I wish you well."

19Now the LORD had said to Moses in Midian, "Go back to Egypt, for all the men who wanted to kill you are dead." 20So Moses took his wife and sons, put them on a donkey and started back to Egypt. And he took the staff of God in his hand.

21The LORD said to Moses, "When you return to Egypt, see that you perform before Pharaoh all the wonders I have given you the power to do. But I will harden his heart so that he will not let the people go. 22Then say to Pharaoh, 'This is what the LORD says: Israel is my firstborn son, 23and I told you, "Let my son go, so he may worship me." But you refused to let him go; so I will kill your firstborn son.'"

24At a lodging place on the way, the LORD met ⌊Moses⌋a and was about to kill him. 25But Zipporah took a flint knife, cut off her son's foreskin and touched ⌊Moses'⌋ feet with it.b "Surely you are a bridegroom of blood to me," she said. 26So the LORD let him alone. (At that time she said "bridegroom of blood," referring to circumcision.)

27The LORD said to Aaron, "Go into the desert to meet Moses." So he met Moses at the mountain of God and kissed him. 28Then Moses told Aaron everything the LORD had sent him to say, and also about all the miraculous signs he had commanded him to perform.

29Moses and Aaron brought together all the elders of the Israelites, 30and Aaron told them everything the LORD had said to Moses. He also performed the signs before the people, 31and they believed. And when they heard that the LORD was concerned about them and had seen their misery, they bowed down and worshiped.

Bricks Without Straw

5 Afterward Moses and Aaron went to Pharaoh and said, "This is what the LORD, the God of Israel, says: 'Let my people go, so that they may hold a festival to me in the desert.'"

2Pharaoh said, "Who is the LORD, that I should obey him and let Israel go? I do not know the LORD and I will not let Israel go."

3Then they said, "The God of the Hebrews has met with us. Now let us take a three-day journey into the desert to offer sacri-

---

cision? (d) Just last week? Explain. 2. Consider verse 11. How has God exercised his sovereignty over your limitations? 3. What concerns do you still have about doing God's will or following his lead? What do you hear God saying about your excuses? Who has been an "Aaron" in your life?

1. What do you like best about "going home"? What do you do when you get there? 2. What did you start as a youngster, but never finished even as an adult? Would you go back to that unfinished task now?

1. What promptings, promises and provisions does Moses receive to encourage him on his way home (vv. 18–23)? 2. What failure on Moses' part almost ends Moses' opportunity to lead the Israelites? Why is circumcision so important (see Ge 17:9–14)? 3. How does Aaron fulfill his part of the plan (vv. 27–30)? With what response (v. 31)?

1. Where are your spiritual roots? What would it take to set you free to return there? 2. From the example of Moses, what will you apply this week to help ensure that God's future plans for you are not frustrated? 3. Like Zipporah helping Moses, who has helped you fulfill the difficult requirements of your spiritual life?

1. What frustrating experience gets your goat nearly every time? The last time, how did you respond to it? What could have been done to fix it? 2. Do you prefer physical or non-physical jobs? Why? Cite examples of each from your work experience.

---

a24 Or ⌊Moses' son⌋; Hebrew him   b25 Or and drew near ⌊Moses'⌋ feet

1. How do you think the Israelites felt as Moses bid Pharaoh to let them go? Who would be surprised most by Pharaoh's answer (vv. 4–9): Moses? The Israelites? The slave drivers? God? Why do you think so? 2. How would you characterize the response of the people when faced with extra work? Now who is surprised? Why? 3. In this classic power struggle, what is the root problem? Whose problem is it to solve? What do the other players do until it is solved? Why? 4. How is Israel's vision and Moses' leadership now tested? 5. How do you think Moses felt when the foremen, who had been beaten, came to him in frustration?

1. Where do you see your vision being tested by "temporary" setbacks? To what extent are you responding like Israel here? 2. When have you suffered for what was not your fault? Who did you then scapegoat? Why do you think God allows such injustice? 3. When frustrated by a "laugh-or-cry" situation, what reassurance do you draw from Israel's experience that this can be resolved or tolerated? 4. Has your obedience to God ever

fices to the LORD our God, or he may strike us with plagues or with the sword."

4But the king of Egypt said, "Moses and Aaron, why are you taking the people away from their labor? Get back to your work!" 5Then Pharaoh said, "Look, the people of the land are now numerous, and you are stopping them from working."

6That same day Pharaoh gave this order to the slave drivers and foremen in charge of the people: 7"You are no longer to supply the people with straw for making bricks; let them go and gather their own straw. 8But require them to make the same number of bricks as before; don't reduce the quota. They are lazy; that is why they are crying out, 'Let us go and sacrifice to our God.' 9Make the work harder for the men so that they keep working and pay no attention to lies."

10Then the slave drivers and the foremen went out and said to the people, "This is what Pharaoh says: 'I will not give you any more straw. 11Go and get your own straw wherever you can find it, but your work will not be reduced at all.'" 12So the people scattered all over Egypt to gather stubble to use for straw. 13The slave drivers kept pressing them, saying, "Complete the work required of you for each day, just as when you had straw." 14The Israelite foremen appointed by Pharaoh's slave drivers were beaten and were asked, "Why didn't you meet your quota of bricks yesterday or today, as before?"

15Then the Israelite foremen went and appealed to Pharaoh: "Why have you treated your servants this way? 16Your servants are given no straw, yet we are told, 'Make bricks!' Your servants are being beaten, but the fault is with your own people."

17Pharaoh said, "Lazy, that's what you are—lazy! That is why

   Exodus 5:1–21   **BRICKS WITHOUT STRAW**

God has called Moses, with the help of his brother Aaron, to lead the Israelites out of slavery into the promised land.

1. What do you think was Moses' mood as he approached Pharaoh?
   a. excited
   b. fearful
   c. optimistic—because of his faith
   d. pessimistic—because God said Pharaoh wouldn't let them go

2. Why did he ask Israel to be permitted to offer sacrifices in the desert?
   a. He was following God's orders.
   b. The Israelites needed to worship.
   c. Their sacrifices were disgusting to the Egyptians.
   d. It was ridiculous to ask Pharaoh to allow them to leave permanently.

3. Pharaoh refused Moses' request because he:
   a. didn't know the Lord.
   b. couldn't afford to give the Hebrews time off.
   c. had a hard heart.
   d. knew his slaves wouldn't return.

4. How did the Israelites feel about Pharaoh's response?
   a. angry at Pharaoh
   b. angry at Moses
   c. angry at God
   d. wished Moses hadn't interfered
   e. They called out to the Lord.

5. How do you think Moses felt about what the foremen said in verse 21?
   a. like a martyr   f. defensive
   b. like a scapegoat g. hopping mad
   c. like running away
   d. like running to God
   e. frustrated with God

6. Which of the possible answers to the last question best describes how you feel when—like both Moses and the Hebrew slaves—you suffer for something that isn't your fault?

7. What do you think God expects of you when you suffer injustice?
   a. not to get mad
   b. not to get even
   c. not to be a doormat
   d. to bring it to God in prayer

e. simply to turn the other cheek

8. How is this story like the stress in your life?
   a. I've got some Pharaohs telling me what to do.
   b. Every day is the same old grind.
   c. I feel like a slave to the expectations of others.
   d. I don't have time to get it all done.
   e. I get blamed for other peoples' problems and mistakes.

9. In your anxiety about work, how do you identify with Moses and the Hebrew slaves? How do you think God wants you to respond to the "tyrants," injustices and frustrations of your job?

10. When have you felt trapped and unfulfilled in your career? What effect do these situations have on your relationship with God? What can you do when you're unfulfilled in your work?

you keep saying, 'Let us go and sacrifice to the LORD.' [18]Now get to work. You will not be given any straw, yet you must produce your full quota of bricks."

[19]The Israelite foremen realized they were in trouble when they were told, "You are not to reduce the number of bricks required of you for each day." [20]When they left Pharaoh, they found Moses and Aaron waiting to meet them, [21]and they said, "May the LORD look upon you and judge you! You have made us a stench to Pharaoh and his officials and have put a sword in their hand to kill us."

God Promises Deliverance

[22]Moses returned to the LORD and said, "O Lord, why have you brought trouble upon this people? Is this why you sent me? [23]Ever since I went to Pharaoh to speak in your name, he has brought trouble upon this people, and you have not rescued your people at all."

6 Then the LORD said to Moses, "Now you will see what I will do to Pharaoh: Because of my mighty hand he will let them go; because of my mighty hand he will drive them out of his country."

[2]God also said to Moses, "I am the LORD. [3]I appeared to Abraham, to Isaac and to Jacob as God Almighty,[a] but by my name the LORD[b] I did not make myself known to them.[c] [4]I also established my covenant with them to give them the land of Canaan, where they lived as aliens. [5]Moreover, I have heard the groaning of the

a3 Hebrew El-Shaddai   b3 See note at Exodus 3:15.   c3 Or Almighty, and by my name the LORD did I not let myself be known to them?

resulted in frustration or difficulty for others? Describe.

---

1. What is your typical reaction when someone makes a promise to you? Trust? Cynicism? Just wait and see? 2. When have you been burned by being too trusting? When has your trust been rewarded?

1. How do you account for Moses' reaction in 5:22–23? Which seems to hold sway with him: The burning bush (ch. 3)? The Egyptian tyrant (ch. 5)? Or the Israelites? Why? 2. In 6:1–8, how does God reaffirm his trustworthiness? 3. As a Hebrew first hearing this (v. 9), what would be most convincing? Least convincing? Why? 4. How did Moses end up feeling?

 Exodus 5:22–6:12   **GOD PROMISES DELIVERANCE**

Pharaoh's response to Moses' request to let the Israelites worship the Lord in the desert was to oppress the Israelite slaves even more. The Hebrew foremen, who were beaten for not meeting their quota of bricks, in turn had just taken their frustrations out on Moses.

1. What was Moses most concerned about?
a. his own feelings
b. the Israelites' suffering
c. God's reputation
d. Pharaoh's power
e. God's seeming inactivity

2. Moses' biggest personal worry was:
a. that God wouldn't come through.
b. that the Israelites would reject him.
c. that Pharaoh would hurt him.
d. that he'd get tongue-tied and ruin everything.

3. What do you think was Moses' reaction to God's words in 6:1–8?
a. I hope these are more than just nice words.
b. I hope my fellow Israelites will believe this.

c. God said it; I believe it.
d. I have some reservations, but I'll hold on to these promises.

4. As this story ends, what stands out to you the most?
a. Moses' discouragement
b. the Israelites' discouragement
c. Moses' lack of confidence
d. the Israelites' lack of confidence in God
e. God's promises
f. God's persistence

5. When has it been the most difficult for you to believe God's promises?

6. Do you ever get frustrated or impatient with God like Moses did? Like the Israelites, do you have a hard time trusting God when you're discouraged or mistreated?

7. When have God's promises been all that's kept you going? Which of God's promises do you most need to hear right now?
a. I will deliver you from bondage to your enemies.

b. I will be your God.
c. I will forgive your sins.
d. I will take care of you.
e. I will help you find your place.
f. other:_____

8. Whom do you know who needs to be reassured of God's love and care? How will you encourage them?

9. What is your greatest anxiety about your job?
a. getting fired or laid off
b. getting stuck where I am
c. making mistakes
d. failing to meet quotas
e. failing to meet deadlines
f. failing to please my boss
g. other:_____

10. When do you worry the most: At work? Traveling to or from work? At home? At night? How can this Bible passage help you?

♡ 1. For you, which works best: (a) Listening to God first, and being encouraged once again? (b) Get myself encouraged first, so that I can then listen to God? Explain the difference. 2. In your own trust walk with God, which has more impact: (a) Past acts of God? (b) Present circumstances? (c) Future promises? Why? 3. Who do you know who needs an encouraging reminder or promise of God's power and presence? How will you model your message to that person today?

☕ 1. Who was the ringleader of your high school class? What qualified that person for the role? 2. Who in your family tree has been a model for you? How are you like, or unlike, that person?

📖 1. Why do you think the author (or editor) inserted this "commercial break" into the action of the story? What does this say about the meaning of genealogies in Moses' day? How would this help them when it was time to leave Egypt (vv. 26–27)? 2. Which of these names are familiar to you? What would a family tree show of their relationship to one another? Why only a partial listing of Israel's 12 sons? 3. With his royal upbringing (in Pharaoh's court), why now are Moses' ethnic roots highlighted (v. 20)?

♡ 1. Looking back on your family tree, who inspires you to glorify God? How? What patterns of behavior in your family make it difficult for you to believe in God's promises? 2. What would a family tree indicate about your extended family and your responsibility to them or for them? 3. Are you the "same" person today as you were in your parents' eyes? Or have you changed in some essential way since then? How so?

Israelites, whom the Egyptians are enslaving, and I have remembered my covenant.

⁶"Therefore, say to the Israelites: 'I am the LORD, and I will bring you out from under the yoke of the Egyptians. I will free you from being slaves to them, and I will redeem you with an outstretched arm and with mighty acts of judgment. ⁷I will take you as my own people, and I will be your God. Then you will know that I am the LORD your God, who brought you out from under the yoke of the Egyptians. ⁸And I will bring you to the land I swore with uplifted hand to give to Abraham, to Isaac and to Jacob. I will give it to you as a possession. I am the LORD.' "

⁹Moses reported this to the Israelites, but they did not listen to him because of their discouragement and cruel bondage.

¹⁰Then the LORD said to Moses, ¹¹"Go, tell Pharaoh king of Egypt to let the Israelites go out of his country."

¹²But Moses said to the LORD, "If the Israelites will not listen to me, why would Pharaoh listen to me, since I speak with faltering lips*a*?"

Family Record of Moses and Aaron

¹³Now the LORD spoke to Moses and Aaron about the Israelites and Pharaoh king of Egypt, and he commanded them to bring the Israelites out of Egypt.

¹⁴These were the heads of their families*b*:

The sons of Reuben the firstborn son of Israel were Hanoch and Pallu, Hezron and Carmi. These were the clans of Reuben.

¹⁵The sons of Simeon were Jemuel, Jamin, Ohad, Jakin, Zohar and Shaul the son of a Canaanite woman. These were the clans of Simeon.

¹⁶These were the names of the sons of Levi according to their records: Gershon, Kohath and Merari. Levi lived 137 years.

¹⁷The sons of Gershon, by clans, were Libni and Shimei.

¹⁸The sons of Kohath were Amram, Izhar, Hebron and Uzziel. Kohath lived 133 years.

¹⁹The sons of Merari were Mahli and Mushi.

These were the clans of Levi according to their records.

²⁰Amram married his father's sister Jochebed, who bore him Aaron and Moses. Amram lived 137 years.

²¹The sons of Izhar were Korah, Nepheg and Zicri.

²²The sons of Uzziel were Mishael, Elzaphan and Sithri.

²³Aaron married Elisheba, daughter of Amminadab and sister of Nahshon, and she bore him Nadab and Abihu, Eleazar and Ithamar.

²⁴The sons of Korah were Assir, Elkanah and Abiasaph. These were the Korahite clans.

²⁵Eleazar son of Aaron married one of the daughters of Putiel, and she bore him Phinehas.

These were the heads of the Levite families, clan by clan.

²⁶It was this same Aaron and Moses to whom the LORD said, "Bring the Israelites out of Egypt by their divisions." ²⁷They were the ones who spoke to Pharaoh king of Egypt about bringing the Israelites out of Egypt. It was the same Moses and Aaron.

---

*a*12 Hebrew *I am uncircumcised of lips*; also in verse 30   *b*14 The Hebrew for *families* here and in verse 25 refers to units larger than clans.

Aaron to Speak for Moses

28Now when the LORD spoke to Moses in Egypt, 29he said to him, "I am the LORD. Tell Pharaoh king of Egypt everything I tell you." 30But Moses said to the LORD, "Since I speak with faltering lips, why would Pharaoh listen to me?"

7 Then the LORD said to Moses, "See, I have made you like God to Pharaoh, and your brother Aaron will be your prophet. 2You are to say everything I command you, and your brother Aaron is to tell Pharaoh to let the Israelites go out of his country. 3But I will harden Pharaoh's heart, and though I multiply my miraculous signs and wonders in Egypt, 4he will not listen to you. Then I will lay my hand on Egypt and with mighty acts of judgment I will bring out my divisions, my people the Israelites. 5And the Egyptians will know that I am the LORD when I stretch out my hand against Egypt and bring the Israelites out of it."

6Moses and Aaron did just as the LORD commanded them. 7Moses was eighty years old and Aaron eighty-three when they spoke to Pharaoh.

Aaron's Staff Becomes a Snake

8The LORD said to Moses and Aaron, 9"When Pharaoh says to you, 'Perform a miracle,' then say to Aaron, 'Take your staff and throw it down before Pharaoh,' and it will become a snake."

10So Moses and Aaron went to Pharaoh and did just as the LORD commanded. Aaron threw his staff down in front of Pharaoh and his officials, and it became a snake. 11Pharaoh then summoned wise men and sorcerers, and the Egyptian magicians also did the same things by their secret arts: 12Each one threw down his staff and it became a snake. But Aaron's staff swallowed up their staffs.

1. What friend could help you be more diplomatic? With whom do you need good PR? 2. What do you imagine yourself doing at age 80?

1. How are Moses and Aaron "like God to Pharaoh"? How was Moses to overcome his speaking handicap? 2. Do you think God caused Pharaoh to harden his heart or that God's actions resulted in Pharaoh hardening his heart? What is the difference? 3. Why would Pharaoh want a miracle performed (v. 9)? What surprises you about the sorcerers' power? How can they do that? 4. What is the meaning of Aaron's snake swallowing theirs?

1. When has God asked you to do something beyond your natural abilities? Why were you chosen when an "Aaron" could more easily have done your job? 2. When you did "mission impossible," was it due to God's strength, others' input, or your own initiative? 3. Technology does modern miracles. How does that affect our view of God's power today?

Exodus 6:28–7:24   THE PLAGUES BEGIN

Pharaoh was not receptive to Moses' and Aaron's first visit. He not only refused to let the Israelites go worship the Lord, he increased their suffering.

1. When God told Moses he would be "like God to Pharaoh," he meant:
   a. "What you say goes."
   b. "You'll be my representative."
   c. "Pharaoh will submit to you."
   d. "Pharaoh will resist you."

2. Moses would overcome his "faltering lips" by:
   a. a miracle.
   b. trusting God.
   c. Aaron filling in the gap.
   d. accepting his limitations.
   e. positive thinking.
   f. forcing himself to keep going.

3. Why would Pharaoh want Moses and Aaron to perform a miracle (v. 9)?
   a. to test their god
   b. to show them up with his sorcerers
   c. because they were in a power struggle
   d. because supernatural events were so common then

4. How were the Egyptian magicians able to duplicate Moses' and Aaron's miracles?
   a. by illusion
   b. by demonic power
   c. with God's permission
   d. by God's plan

5. Aaron's staff/snake swallowed the others:
   a. because it was hungry.
   b. because it was stronger.
   c. because the others weren't real.
   d. to prove the Lord was greater than the Egyptians' gods.

6. What was the main reason God initiated the plagues?
   a. to make life miserable for the idolatrous Egyptians
   b. to force Pharaoh to free God's people
   c. to demonstrate his power to the Egyptians
   d. to demonstrate his power to the Israelites
   e. to set the stage for the grand finale later at the Passover

7. Why was Pharaoh so stubborn?
   a. He hardened his heart.
   b. God hardened his heart.
   c. His authority was challenged.
   d. He didn't want to lose his slaves.
   e. He wouldn't let anyone tell him what to do—even God.

8. How do you feel when someone tells you what to do? In what situations are you the most stubborn? What would you like to do about it?

9. How does God respond to sin-hardened hearts today? When have you observed God working through "mighty acts of judgment"?

10. When have you felt, like Moses, that God was asking you to do something you couldn't do? What is the most difficult thing God is asking you to do right now?

11. Who has been your "Aaron"—the person you've leaned on to accomplish hard tasks or help you get through tough times? How long has it been since you thanked them?

1. What do you do at the sight of blood? Turn away? Faint? Get a closer look? 2. What is the most obnoxious water you have swam in or fallen into?

1. How important was the Nile River to Egypt? By this plague of blood in that river, what do you think God is trying to tell the Egyptians? The Israelites? 2. What kind of pressures does this plague put on Pharaoh? On his sorcerers? What was his response (vv. 22–23)? 3. How might Moses and Aaron have felt after the plague of blood?

1. Given the eyes of faith, what mighty acts (or gentle touches) of God have you perceived in your life? Have you seen any heaven-sent plagues lately? 2. Who (or what) are the "sorcerers" in your life that imitate God's work today and hinder your trust in the real thing? How do you cope with that?

Describe a time when you found an unwanted creature in your food.

1. What are the key elements in Moses' message to Pharaoh (vv. 1–4)? 2. What elements in the river (polluted for seven days) might have caused the frogs to "come up" onto land and swarm the country? What possible link do you see between the plague of blood and this one? 3. Why does Pharaoh appeal to Moses and Aaron, when sorcery "works"? 4. Why do you think the magicians have been able to match each miracle so far? 5. Given a most timely answer to his "prayer" (vv. 9–15), how does the Pharaoh react? Why?

1. How do you feel about the way God works in this story? Does God "stink up the works" when he wants to get your attention? How so? 2. When have you taken answered prayer for granted? Do you pray more when things are going your way? Or when "in a foxhole"? Why? 3. By now, Aaron or Moses may be feeling used or

¹³Yet Pharaoh's heart became hard and he would not listen to them, just as the LORD had said.

The Plague of Blood

¹⁴Then the LORD said to Moses, "Pharaoh's heart is unyielding; he refuses to let the people go. ¹⁵Go to Pharaoh in the morning as he goes out to the water. Wait on the bank of the Nile to meet him, and take in your hand the staff that was changed into a snake. ¹⁶Then say to him, 'The LORD, the God of the Hebrews, has sent me to say to you: Let my people go, so that they may worship me in the desert. But until now you have not listened. ¹⁷This is what the LORD says: By this you will know that I am the LORD: With the staff that is in my hand I will strike the water of the Nile, and it will be changed into blood. ¹⁸The fish in the Nile will die, and the river will stink; the Egyptians will not be able to drink its water.'"

¹⁹The LORD said to Moses, "Tell Aaron, 'Take your staff and stretch out your hand over the waters of Egypt—over the streams and canals, over the ponds and all the reservoirs'—and they will turn to blood. Blood will be everywhere in Egypt, even in the wooden buckets and stone jars."

²⁰Moses and Aaron did just as the LORD had commanded. He raised his staff in the presence of Pharaoh and his officials and struck the water of the Nile, and all the water was changed into blood. ²¹The fish in the Nile died, and the river smelled so bad that the Egyptians could not drink its water. Blood was everywhere in Egypt.

²²But the Egyptian magicians did the same things by their secret arts, and Pharaoh's heart became hard; he would not listen to Moses and Aaron, just as the LORD had said. ²³Instead, he turned and went into his palace, and did not take even this to heart. ²⁴And all the Egyptians dug along the Nile to get drinking water, because they could not drink the water of the river.

The Plague of Frogs

8 ²⁵Seven days passed after the LORD struck the Nile. ¹Then the LORD said to Moses, "Go to Pharaoh and say to him, 'This is what the LORD says: Let my people go, so that they may worship me. ²If you refuse to let them go, I will plague your whole country with frogs. ³The Nile will teem with frogs. They will come up into your palace and your bedroom and onto your bed, into the houses of your officials and on your people, and into your ovens and kneading troughs. ⁴The frogs will go up on you and your people and all your officials.'"

⁵Then the LORD said to Moses, "Tell Aaron, 'Stretch out your hand with your staff over the streams and canals and ponds, and make frogs come up on the land of Egypt.'"

⁶So Aaron stretched out his hand over the waters of Egypt, and the frogs came up and covered the land. ⁷But the magicians did the same things by their secret arts; they also made frogs come up on the land of Egypt.

⁸Pharaoh summoned Moses and Aaron and said, "Pray to the LORD to take the frogs away from me and my people, and I will let your people go to offer sacrifices to the LORD."

⁹Moses said to Pharaoh, "I leave to you the honor of setting the time for me to pray for you and your officials and your people that you and your houses may be rid of the frogs, except for those that remain in the Nile."

¹⁰"Tomorrow," Pharaoh said.

Moses replied, "It will be as you say, so that you may know there is no one like the LORD our God. 11The frogs will leave you and your houses, your officials and your people; they will remain only in the Nile."

12After Moses and Aaron left Pharaoh, Moses cried out to the LORD about the frogs he had brought on Pharaoh. 13And the LORD did what Moses asked. The frogs died in the houses, in the court-yards and in the fields. 14They were piled into heaps, and the land reeked of them. 15But when Pharaoh saw that there was relief, he hardened his heart and would not listen to Moses and Aaron, just as the LORD had said.

The Plague of Gnats

16Then the LORD said to Moses, "Tell Aaron, 'Stretch out your staff and strike the dust of the ground,' and throughout the land of Egypt the dust will become gnats." 17They did this, and when Aaron stretched out his hand with the staff and struck the dust of the ground, gnats came upon men and animals. All the dust throughout the land of Egypt became gnats. 18But when the magicians tried to produce gnats by their secret arts, they could not. And the gnats were on men and animals.

19The magicians said to Pharaoh, "This is the finger of God." But Pharaoh's heart was hard and he would not listen, just as the LORD had said.

The Plague of Flies

20Then the LORD said to Moses, "Get up early in the morning and confront Pharaoh as he goes to the water and say to him, 'This is what the LORD says: Let my people go, so that they may worship me. 21If you do not let my people go, I will send swarms of flies on you and your officials, on your people and into your houses. The houses of the Egyptians will be full of flies, and even the ground where they are.

22"'But on that day I will deal differently with the land of Go-shen, where my people live; no swarms of flies will be there, so that you will know that I, the LORD, am in this land. 23I will make a distinction*a* between my people and your people. This miracu-lous sign will occur tomorrow.'"

24And the LORD did this. Dense swarms of flies poured into Phar-aoh's palace and into the houses of his officials, and throughout Egypt the land was ruined by the flies.

25Then Pharaoh summoned Moses and Aaron and said, "Go, sacrifice to your God here in the land."

26But Moses said, "That would not be right. The sacrifices we offer the LORD our God would be detestable to the Egyptians. And if we offer sacrifices that are detestable in their eyes, will they not stone us? 27We must take a three-day journey into the desert to offer sacrifices to the LORD our God, as he commands us."

28Pharaoh said, "I will let you go to offer sacrifices to the LORD your God in the desert, but you must not go very far. Now pray for me."

29Moses answered, "As soon as I leave you, I will pray to the LORD, and tomorrow the flies will leave Pharaoh and his officials and his people. Only be sure that Pharaoh does not act deceitfully again by not letting the people go to offer sacrifices to the LORD."

30Then Moses left Pharaoh and prayed to the LORD, 31and the LORD did what Moses asked: The flies left Pharaoh and his officials

a23 Septuagint and Vulgate; Hebrew *will put a deliverance*

manipulated by unrepentant Phar-aoh. When have you felt conned by a non-believer who "took you for a ride"? How do you respond?

1. Why does God now begin doing things the magicians could not? 2. What does "finger of God" imply (see Lk 11:20)? 3. How come "Pharaoh's heart was hard" this time?

When have you hardened your heart in light of God's working?

1. What is your sure-fire way for catching flies? 2. What "fly in the ointment" once spoiled an important event in your family?

1. Why do you think God now distinguishes between the "land of Goshen" (v. 22) and the rest of Egypt (vv. 21,23; also 9:4,6,26; 10:23; 11:7)? What is he trying to tell Pharaoh? The Israel-ites? 2. Who is deceiving who here: Is Moses lying by saying the Exo-dus will be a "three-day" journey? Is Pharaoh consciously lying when he initially lets God's people go and asks Moses for prayer? Is God be-hind any of these "lies," as he is plainly behind the flies? Why or why not? 3. What do you suppose is "detestable" to the Egyptians about Hebrew sacrifices (v. 26; see Ge 43:32)? Is Moses really fearful of them? Or is he just trying to "buy time"? Why?

1. Is God singling out the Is-raelites for special favors be-cause they are choice (the best)? Or because they are chosen (elected)? Why do you think so? 2. In what way does God make simi-lar distinctions today between his followers and others? How does God's favor make you feel? How will you express that to God, right now?

and his people; not a fly remained. [32]But this time also Pharaoh hardened his heart and would not let the people go.

The Plague on Livestock

9 Then the LORD said to Moses, "Go to Pharaoh and say to him, 'This is what the LORD, the God of the Hebrews, says: "Let my people go, so that they may worship me." [2]If you refuse to let them go and continue to hold them back, [3]the hand of the LORD will bring a terrible plague on your livestock in the field—on your horses and donkeys and camels and on your cattle and sheep and goats. [4]But the LORD will make a distinction between the livestock of Israel and that of Egypt, so that no animal belonging to the Israelites will die.' "

[5]The LORD set a time and said, "Tomorrow the LORD will do this in the land." [6]And the next day the LORD did it: All the livestock of the Egyptians died, but not one animal belonging to the Israelites died. [7]Pharaoh sent men to investigate and found that not even one of the animals of the Israelites had died. Yet his heart was unyielding and he would not let the people go.

The Plague of Boils

[8]Then the LORD said to Moses and Aaron, "Take handfuls of soot from a furnace and have Moses toss it into the air in the presence of Pharaoh. [9]It will become fine dust over the whole land of Egypt, and festering boils will break out on men and animals throughout the land."

[10]So they took soot from a furnace and stood before Pharaoh. Moses tossed it into the air, and festering boils broke out on men and animals. [11]The magicians could not stand before Moses because of the boils that were on them and on all the Egyptians. [12]But the LORD hardened Pharaoh's heart and he would not listen to Moses and Aaron, just as the LORD had said to Moses.

The Plague of Hail

[13]Then the LORD said to Moses, "Get up early in the morning, confront Pharaoh and say to him, 'This is what the LORD, the God of the Hebrews, says: Let my people go, so that they may worship me, [14]or this time I will send the full force of my plagues against you and against your officials and your people, so you may know that there is no one like me in all the earth. [15]For by now I could have stretched out my hand and struck you and your people with a plague that would have wiped you off the earth. [16]But I have raised you up[a] for this very purpose, that I might show you my power and that my name might be proclaimed in all the earth. [17]You still set yourself against my people and will not let them go. [18]Therefore, at this time tomorrow I will send the worst hailstorm that has ever fallen on Egypt, from the day it was founded till now. [19]Give an order now to bring your livestock and everything you have in the field to a place of shelter, because the hail will fall on every man and animal that has not been brought in and is still out in the field, and they will die.' "

[20]Those officials of Pharaoh who feared the word of the LORD hurried to bring their slaves and their livestock inside. [21]But those who ignored the word of the LORD left their slaves and livestock in the field.

[22]Then the LORD said to Moses, "Stretch out your hand toward the sky so that hail will fall all over Egypt—on men and animals

---

[a]16 Or have spared you

---

1. Why is Pharaoh so stubborn? 2. What will Egypt lose as their livestock (lifestyle and livelihood) dies? 3. How do you think the Egyptians felt about all this?

1. How could you sustain the loss of your livelihood, food, transportation or status? 2. When has someone else's stubbornness against God caused you pain and frustration?

What part is played by the soot? The boils (see Dt 28:27,35)? The magicians? Pharaoh's heart?

1. Is your heart toward God soft as putty? Firm and cautious? Or rock hard? Why? 2. If God wants all men to know him, why harden Pharaoh's heart?

1. Recount the most severe winter storm you were in. What did you see? Hear? Smell? Feel? Where did you find shelter? 2. What have you seen 2-to 4-year olds do to get their way? Did it work?

1. How has Moses' tough talk gotten tougher (vv. 12–19)? The plagues are hitting Egypt's food sources, yet not without an escape clause (v. 32). Why do you think he is doing this? What does this say about God's ultimate goal? 2. What does the Egyptian response reveal (vv. 20–21)? What does the full force of this plague do? Sparing who? Why? 3. After the hailstorm, what new tactic does Pharaoh use in this battle of the wills? What does Moses see behind this facade? 4. What do the undamaged crops (vv. 31–32) allow Pharaoh to do (vv. 34–35)? How is this second sin worse than the first? In letting Pharaoh have his way, what can you learn about God's mercy? God's judgment?

and on everything growing in the fields of Egypt." ²³When Moses stretched out his staff toward the sky, the LORD sent thunder and hail, and lightning flashed down to the ground. So the LORD rained hail on the land of Egypt; ²⁴hail fell and lightning flashed back and forth. It was the worst storm in all the land of Egypt since it had become a nation. ²⁵Throughout Egypt hail struck everything in the fields—both men and animals; it beat down everything growing in the fields and stripped every tree. ²⁶The only place it did not hail was the land of Goshen, where the Israelites were.

²⁷Then Pharaoh summoned Moses and Aaron. "This time I have sinned," he said to them. "The LORD is in the right, and I and my people are in the wrong. ²⁸Pray to the LORD, for we have had enough thunder and hail. I will let you go; you don't have to stay any longer."

²⁹Moses replied, "When I have gone out of the city, I will spread out my hands in prayer to the LORD. The thunder will stop and there will be no more hail, so you may know that the earth is the LORD's. ³⁰But I know that you and your officials still do not fear the LORD God."

³¹(The flax and barley were destroyed, since the barley had headed and the flax was in bloom. ³²The wheat and spelt, however, were not destroyed, because they ripen later.)

³³Then Moses left Pharaoh and went out of the city. He spread out his hands toward the LORD; the thunder and hail stopped, and the rain no longer poured down on the land. ³⁴When Pharaoh saw that the rain and hail and thunder had stopped, he sinned again: He and his officials hardened their hearts. ³⁵So Pharaoh's heart was hard and he would not let the Israelites go, just as the LORD had said through Moses.

The Plague of Locusts

10 Then the LORD said to Moses, "Go to Pharaoh, for I have hardened his heart and the hearts of his officials so that I may perform these miraculous signs of mine among them ²that you may tell your children and grandchildren how I dealt harshly with the Egyptians and how I performed my signs among them, and that you may know that I am the LORD."

³So Moses and Aaron went to Pharaoh and said to him, "This is what the LORD, the God of the Hebrews, says: 'How long will you refuse to humble yourself before me? Let my people go, so that they may worship me. ⁴If you refuse to let them go, I will bring locusts into your country tomorrow. ⁵They will cover the face of the ground so that it cannot be seen. They will devour what little you have left after the hail, including every tree that is growing in your fields. ⁶They will fill your houses and those of all your officials and all the Egyptians—something neither your fathers nor your forefathers have ever seen from the day they settled in this land till now.' " Then Moses turned and left Pharaoh.

⁷Pharaoh's officials said to him, "How long will this man be a snare to us? Let the people go, so that they may worship the LORD their God. Do you not yet realize that Egypt is ruined?"

⁸Then Moses and Aaron were brought back to Pharaoh. "Go, worship the LORD your God," he said. "But just who will be going?"

⁹Moses answered, "We will go with our young and old, with our sons and daughters, and with our flocks and herds, because we are to celebrate a festival to the LORD."

¹⁰Pharaoh said, "The LORD be with you—if I let you go, along

1. Could God have achieved his goals without the plagues? If so, how? If not, why? What do you see as God's main purpose in causing Egypt to suffer the plagues? Were they primarily for the benefit of Egypt or for Israel (see 6:1–8)? **2.** How has God shown his mighty "right hand" and his merciful "left hand" to you? With what plague-like, attention-getting devices? With what escape clauses? **3.** Does God still send "plagues" on people? Or are most diseases and disasters self-inflicted or due to natural causes? Why do you think so? (How would you categorize the AIDS epidemic?) **4.** Why is it so important to God that you recognize him as the Lord? **5.** Have you ever made a promise to God you did not keep? What happened?

---

1. What was your childhood method of catching grasshoppers? How do you feel about killing them? Eating them? **2.** How were you like a plague to your family growing up: (a) Like a frog, warts and all? (b) A gnat, buzzing in their ears? (c) A fly, flitting from one thing to another? (d) A sick cow, always complaining? (e) Bad case of acne, breaking out with stress? (f) Hail storm, pelting with insults? (g) A grasshopper, gangly and clumsy?

1. Of the many references so far to Pharaoh's hardened heart (see 7:3,13,14,22; 8:15, 19,32; 9:7,12,34–35), what's new about the way the Lord informs Moses this time (vv. 1–2)? When is Pharaoh the sole active agent in hardening his own heart? And when is the Lord actively confirming that choice? How would the hard heart of Pharaoh have helped God to reach his objectives? **2.** Why do you think God removes the plague each time Pharaoh promises to let the Israelites go, even though he changes his mind each time? What further point does that prove? **3.** Where do you think

Pharaoh feels the most pressure: From God? Moses? His officials? The locusts? His guilty conscience? **4.** How does he diffuse that pressure? With what results?

1. Does God often cause people to harden their hearts (see Ro 9:17–18)? For what purpose? **2.** If you were in Pharaoh's place, would you have given in by now? Why or why not? Why is it that some would rather self-destruct than admit they were wrong? How would God view their predicament? **3.** Which would you rather be: Strong and self-sufficient? Or humble and dependent upon God? Why is the choice so difficult? Where does each ultimately lead? Where do you want to end up? **4.** Who was your Moses—the one who forced you to see the need for God in your life? How did you react to this person, back then? And now?

As a child, was darkness: Fearful? Fascinating? Frustrating?

1. What is missing from the onset of this plague (also the third and sixth plagues)? What do you make of that? **2.** What effect would three days of darkness have? How effective is Pharaoh's offer and threat (vv. 24,28)? **3.** If each of the nine plagues can be viewed as the defeat of an Egyptian deity (sun god, etc.), what effect would this have had on Egypt? On Israel? Who stood to gain the most?

1. Against which gods of your culture have you seen God display his power? How does this compare to his use of the plagues? What does this say about God's desire for you? **2.** How do you know when estrangement is irreversible (say, with a spouse)? Can anyone ever be permanently estranged from God? How so?

If your neighbor asked you for your silver and gold, what would your reaction be?

1. How is this plague to be different from the others? **2.** Why do you think Pharaoh disregards Moses' warning here (vv. 9–10)? **3.** This short chapter is a

with your women and children! Clearly you are bent on evil.[a] ¹¹No! Have only the men go; and worship the LORD, since that's what you have been asking for." Then Moses and Aaron were driven out of Pharaoh's presence.

¹²And the LORD said to Moses, "Stretch out your hand over Egypt so that locusts will swarm over the land and devour everything growing in the fields, everything left by the hail."

¹³So Moses stretched out his staff over Egypt, and the LORD made an east wind blow across the land all that day and all that night. By morning the wind had brought the locusts; ¹⁴they invaded all Egypt and settled down in every area of the country in great numbers. Never before had there been such a plague of locusts, nor will there ever be again. ¹⁵They covered all the ground until it was black. They devoured all that was left after the hail—everything growing in the fields and the fruit on the trees. Nothing green remained on tree or plant in all the land of Egypt.

¹⁶Pharaoh quickly summoned Moses and Aaron and said, "I have sinned against the LORD your God and against you. ¹⁷Now forgive my sin once more and pray to the LORD your God to take this deadly plague away from me."

¹⁸Moses then left Pharaoh and prayed to the LORD. ¹⁹And the LORD changed the wind to a very strong west wind, which caught up the locusts and carried them into the Red Sea.[b] Not a locust was left anywhere in Egypt. ²⁰But the LORD hardened Pharaoh's heart, and he would not let the Israelites go.

The Plague of Darkness

²¹Then the LORD said to Moses, "Stretch out your hand toward the sky so that darkness will spread over Egypt—darkness that can be felt." ²²So Moses stretched out his hand toward the sky, and total darkness covered all Egypt for three days. ²³No one could see anyone else or leave his place for three days. Yet all the Israelites had light in the places where they lived.

²⁴Then Pharaoh summoned Moses and said, "Go, worship the LORD. Even your women and children may go with you; only leave your flocks and herds behind."

²⁵But Moses said, "You must allow us to have sacrifices and burnt offerings to present to the LORD our God. ²⁶Our livestock too must go with us; not a hoof is to be left behind. We have to use some of them in worshiping the LORD our God, and until we get there we will not know what we are to use to worship the LORD."

²⁷But the LORD hardened Pharaoh's heart, and he was not willing to let them go. ²⁸Pharaoh said to Moses, "Get out of my sight! Make sure you do not appear before me again! The day you see my face you will die."

²⁹"Just as you say," Moses replied, "I will never appear before you again."

The Plague on the Firstborn

11 Now the LORD had said to Moses, "I will bring one more plague on Pharaoh and on Egypt. After that, he will let you go from here, and when he does, he will drive you out completely. ²Tell the people that men and women alike are to ask their neighbors for articles of silver and gold." ³(The LORD made the Egyptians favorably disposed toward the people, and Moses himself was highly regarded in Egypt by Pharaoh's officials and by the people.)

⁴So Moses said, "This is what the LORD says: 'About midnight I

will go throughout Egypt. 5Every firstborn son in Egypt will die, from the firstborn son of Pharaoh, who sits on the throne, to the firstborn son of the slave girl, who is at her hand mill, and all the firstborn of the cattle as well. 6There will be loud wailing throughout Egypt—worse than there has ever been or ever will be again. 7But among the Israelites not a dog will bark at any man or animal.' Then you will know that the LORD makes a distinction between Egypt and Israel. 8All these officials of yours will come to me, bowing down before me and saying, 'Go, you and all the people who follow you!' After that I will leave." Then Moses, hot with anger, left Pharaoh.

9The LORD had said to Moses, "Pharaoh will refuse to listen to you—so that my wonders may be multiplied in Egypt." 10Moses and Aaron performed all these wonders before Pharaoh, but the LORD hardened Pharaoh's heart, and he would not let the Israelites go out of his country.

The Passover

12 The LORD said to Moses and Aaron in Egypt, 2"This month is to be for you the first month, the first month of your year. 3Tell the whole community of Israel that on the tenth day of this month each man is to take a lamb*a* for his family, one for each household. 4If any household is too small for a whole lamb, they must share one with their nearest neighbor, having taken into account the number of people there are. You are to determine the amount of lamb needed in accordance with what each person will eat. 5The animals you choose must be year-old males without defect, and you may take them from the sheep or the goats. 6Take care of them until the fourteenth day of the month, when all the people of the community of Israel must slaughter them at twilight. 7Then they are to take some of the blood and put it on the sides and tops of the doorframes of the houses where they eat the lambs. 8That same night they are to eat the meat roasted over the fire, along with bitter herbs, and bread made without yeast. 9Do not eat the meat raw or cooked in water, but roast it over the fire—head, legs and inner parts. 10Do not leave any of it till morning; if some is left till morning, you must burn it. 11This is how you are to eat it: with your cloak tucked into your belt, your sandals on your feet and your staff in your hand. Eat it in haste; it is the LORD's Passover.

12"On that same night I will pass through Egypt and strike down every firstborn—both men and animals—and I will bring judgment on all the gods of Egypt. I am the LORD. 13The blood will be a sign for you on the houses where you are; and when I see the blood, I will pass over you. No destructive plague will touch you when I strike Egypt.

14"This is a day you are to commemorate; for the generations to come you shall celebrate it as a festival to the LORD—a lasting ordinance. 15For seven days you are to eat bread made without yeast. On the first day remove the yeast from your houses, for whoever eats anything with yeast in it from the first day through the seventh must be cut off from Israel. 16On the first day hold a sacred assembly, and another one on the seventh day. Do no work at all on these days, except to prepare food for everyone to eat—that is all you may do.

17"Celebrate the Feast of Unleavened Bread, because it was on this very day that I brought your divisions out of Egypt. Celebrate this day as a lasting ordinance for the generations to come. 18In the

study in contrasts: How many can you find?

1. How do you feel when someone rejects your warning? Anything like Moses? Or God? 2. Why do you think people disregard God's warnings today? Have you rejected any warnings recently? 3. How can the memory of these plagues help you heed his warnings and find mercy for doing his will?

1. Where do you fall in the birth order of your family? What great expectations and special privileges fell to the oldest? To the youngest? What was allowed and allotted to you? 2. When it's "just family," what's the biggest spread of the year your parents put on the table?

1. What do you find noteworthy about this Passover observance? For example, when on the calendar is this event commemorated? Why then? How so? With whom? What for? 2. What is the connection between blood and death in this passage? Why is blood a protection against death? 3. What would an Israelites' obedience or disobedience regarding God's instructions about the lamb, the blood and the unleavened bread indicate about their faith in God? 4. God surely could have accomplished the Exodus without the death of all the firstborn of Egypt. So why do you think he chose to do it this way? In what sense was this a "judgment on all the gods of Egypt" (12:12)? In what sense was this a "wonder of God" (11:9)? Or perhaps you find any such killing altogether unforgivable? Why? 5. What influence was the Passover event intended to have on Pharaoh? On the Egyptians? On the Hebrews? On future Israelites? Do you think it succeeded? How so? 6. Regarding the Passover commemoration, for whose benefit does God institute this feast on the same night that he passes over the Egyptians? What does this Jewish feast have in common with its Christian counterpart (Holy Communion)?

a3 The Hebrew word can mean *lamb* or *kid*; also in verse 4.

♡ **1.** What are the gods of your culture? Do you believe that the God of Israel is more powerful than they are? How does he show you his wondrous power? **2.** How does this passage help you see the purpose for Jesus' death and shed blood? How do you remember "the Lamb who was slain" (v. 21; see Rev 5:12)? **3.** What part do ceremonies, such as communion or the Easter family meal, play in helping you remember what God has done for you, back then and now? How do (or will) you keep these memories alive in your children? **4.** Why do you think God determined that it was necessary for Egypt to suffer so much? What does that tell you about the importance of the role of the Israelites in God's purposes? How do you feel about how God sees your role in his purposes?

first month you are to eat bread made without yeast, from the evening of the fourteenth day until the evening of the twenty-first day. ¹⁹For seven days no yeast is to be found in your houses. And whoever eats anything with yeast in it must be cut off from the community of Israel, whether he is an alien or native-born. ²⁰Eat nothing made with yeast. Wherever you live, you must eat unleavened bread."

²¹Then Moses summoned all the elders of Israel and said to them, "Go at once and select the animals for your families and slaughter the Passover lamb. ²²Take a bunch of hyssop, dip it into the blood in the basin and put some of the blood on the top and on both sides of the doorframe. Not one of you shall go out the door of his house until morning. ²³When the LORD goes through the land to strike down the Egyptians, he will see the blood on the top and sides of the doorframe and will pass over that doorway, and he will not permit the destroyer to enter your houses and strike you down.

²⁴"Obey these instructions as a lasting ordinance for you and your descendants. ²⁵When you enter the land that the LORD will give you as he promised, observe this ceremony. ²⁶And when your children ask you, 'What does this ceremony mean to you?' ²⁷then tell them, 'It is the Passover sacrifice to the LORD, who passed over the houses of the Israelites in Egypt and spared our homes when he struck down the Egyptians.'" Then the people bowed down and worshiped. ²⁸The Israelites did just what the LORD commanded Moses and Aaron.

²⁹At midnight the LORD struck down all the firstborn in Egypt, from the firstborn of Pharaoh, who sat on the throne, to the firstborn of the prisoner, who was in the dungeon, and the firstborn of

 Exodus 12:1–30   **THE PASSOVER**

In spite of nine spectacular plagues, Pharaoh had repeatedly refused to let the Israelite slaves hold a worship festival in the desert. Finally, Moses warned that Pharaoh would actually beg the Hebrews to leave after the firstborn of Egypt were killed.

1. What do you think the Israelites thought about these instructions?
   a. This is weird.
   b. This is great.
   c. It's about time.
   d. Let's hope this works.

2. If you were an Israelite, how would you have felt after that fateful night?
   a. awestruck
   b. relieved
   c. worshipful
   d. sorry for the Egyptians

3. How do you think the Egyptians felt?
   a. in shock   c. devastated
   b. angry   d. repentant

4. Through this event God was bringing "judgment on all the gods of Egypt" (v. 12). What are the gods of our culture? How does the Lord

show himself to be more powerful?

5. What was the reason for sprinkling blood on the doorframes?
   a. The blood of a sacrifice was the most important part.
   b. The "destroyer" would know which houses to pass over.
   c. It was an act of faith.
   d. It put into effect the substitution of the animal's life for human life.

6. What was the primary principle behind the requirement that only animals without defect be chosen?
   a. It was the least a person could do.
   b. Defective sacrifices violate God's holiness.
   c. We should give our best to God.
   d. A sacrifice without defect pointed toward Jesus.

7. Why did small households need to share the Passover with others?
   a. to learn to be neighborly
   b. to make the atmosphere festive
   c. so food wouldn't be wasted
   d. so this would be both a community and a family experience

8. How does this story shed light on the purpose and benefits of Christ's death and shed blood? How does the Passover meal remind you of the Lord's Supper?

9. How do rituals, such as communion, help you remember what God has done for you? How can you share those memories and values rather than just keep them to yourself?

10. What has been one of your family's most meaningful traditions?
    a. birthdays and anniversaries
    b. holidays, especially_____
    c. family nights
    d. special meals
    e. family communion services
    f. other:_____

11. How could you get your children more involved in planning and celebrating family traditions? Are there ways you could enhance the spiritual dimension of your traditions?

all the livestock as well. [30]Pharaoh and all his officials and all the Egyptians got up during the night, and there was loud wailing in Egypt, for there was not a house without someone dead.

The Exodus

[31]During the night Pharaoh summoned Moses and Aaron and said, "Up! Leave my people, you and the Israelites! Go, worship the LORD as you have requested. [32]Take your flocks and herds, as you have said, and go. And also bless me."

[33]The Egyptians urged the people to hurry and leave the country. "For otherwise," they said, "we will all die!" [34]So the people took their dough before the yeast was added, and carried it on their shoulders in kneading troughs wrapped in clothing. [35]The Israelites did as Moses instructed and asked the Egyptians for articles of silver and gold and for clothing. [36]The LORD had made the Egyptians favorably disposed toward the people, and they gave them what they asked for; so they plundered the Egyptians.

[37]The Israelites journeyed from Rameses to Succoth. There were about six hundred thousand men on foot, besides women and children. [38]Many other people went up with them, as well as large droves of livestock, both flocks and herds. [39]With the dough they had brought from Egypt, they baked cakes of unleavened bread. The dough was without yeast because they had been driven out of Egypt and did not have time to prepare food for themselves.

[40]Now the length of time the Israelite people lived in Egypt[a] was 430 years. [41]At the end of the 430 years, to the very day, all the LORD's divisions left Egypt. [42]Because the LORD kept vigil that night to bring them out of Egypt, on this night all the Israelites are to keep vigil to honor the LORD for the generations to come.

Passover Restrictions

[43]The LORD said to Moses and Aaron, "These are the regulations for the Passover:

"No foreigner is to eat of it. [44]Any slave you have bought may eat of it after you have circumcised him, [45]but a temporary resident and a hired worker may not eat of it.

[46]"It must be eaten inside one house; take none of the meat outside the house. Do not break any of the bones. [47]The whole community of Israel must celebrate it.

[48]"An alien living among you who wants to celebrate the LORD's Passover must have all the males in his household circumcised; then he may take part like one born in the land. No uncircumcised male may eat of it. [49]The same law applies to the native-born and to the alien living among you."

[50]All the Israelites did just what the LORD had commanded Moses and Aaron. [51]And on that very day the LORD brought the Israelites out of Egypt by their divisions.

Consecration of the Firstborn

13 The LORD said to Moses, [2]"Consecrate to me every firstborn male. The first offspring of every womb among the Israelites belongs to me, whether man or animal."

[3]Then Moses said to the people, "Commemorate this day, the day you came out of Egypt, out of the land of slavery, because the LORD brought you out of it with a mighty hand. Eat nothing containing yeast. [4]Today, in the month of Abib, you are leaving. [5]When the LORD brings you into the land of the Canaanites, Hittites, Amo-

---

[a]40 Masoretic Text; Samaritan Pentateuch and Septuagint *Egypt and Canaan*

What is your favorite fast food restaurant? How often do you eat there?

1. From Pharaoh's response, how does this tenth plague differ in its impact from all the others? 2. Why do you think he asked for a blessing? As they left Egypt in haste, how do you think the Hebrews felt? The Egyptians (vv. 33–36; 3:21–22; 11:2)? 3. In the "430 years", whose patience was most tested—God's or the Hebrews'? Whose word was vindicated? Whose power was broken?

1. What three things have most blessed your life? What part did you play in these divine events? What part did the opposition play? What part did God alone play? 2. What does this tell you about how God works in our lives? 3. What event from your spiritual life do you remember annually?

Did you grow up with many rules about table meals? Which ones have stuck with you?

1. Which rules governing Passover seem exclusive? Inclusive? 2. Without these rules, what would happen? What does this say about the importance of Passover to God? To Israel?

1. As the Exodus is for Israel, what event and ceremony are foundational for Christians? Why? 2. What equivalent to the Jewish Passover rules do you see in the Lord's Supper? 3. What do these Jewish and Christian celebrations mean to you?

At age 13, what set you apart from other kids in school? What groups you belonged to helped define who you were back then?

1. Why is God particularly concerned that the firstborn be consecrated to him (vv. 2,12,15; see 4:22–23; 12:12–13)? How does one "give over" a child to the Lord? 2. What does this say about the position God wanted to occupy

in the lives of the Israelites? **3.** By what sign does God want this remembered? What do the specifics of this observance mean?

♡ **1.** When were you "dedicated" by your parents? "Confirmed" in faith? Baptized? Bar Mitzvahed? **2.** What difference have such childhood observances made in your faith as an adult? If your child or any child were to ask you the meaning of baptism, communion, prayer, worship or ordination (choose one), how would you answer? **3.** By what symbolic meals or other signs do you let God and your family know that he really is number one in your life? **4.** What have you given up or set apart to memorialize what God has done to rescue you?

☕ **1.** When you travel away from home, what one possession do you take along to keep from getting homesick? **2.** What was your most frightening experience in water: Boat capsize? Shark alert? Surf undertow pull you down? Tidal wave wipe out your sand castle? How has that experience affected your feelings about water?

📖 **1.** At the outset of this journey to the sea, what is God's assessment of the Israelite's emotional state? How did he allow for that? With God having defeated all the gods of Egypt (see 12:12), why do you think the Israelites were afraid of one more battle? Would you have been fearful, too? **2.** What significance do Joseph's bones have for the people (13:19; see Ge 50:24–25; Jos 24:32; Heb 11:22)? **3.** With what resources (human, natural and divine) did God lead the people out of Egypt? Which ones were easier to follow than others? **4.** Why did God have the people backtrack from Migdol so soon after their departure (14:2)? What was the strategy behind that? **5.** How does Pharaoh end up showing his true colors (14:5,8)? Why do you think God is concerned that "the Egyptians will

rites, Hivites and Jebusites—the land he swore to your forefathers to give you, a land flowing with milk and honey—you are to observe this ceremony in this month: ⁶For seven days eat bread made without yeast and on the seventh day hold a festival to the LORD. ⁷Eat unleavened bread during those seven days; nothing with yeast in it is to be seen among you, nor shall any yeast be seen anywhere within your borders. ⁸On that day tell your son, 'I do this because of what the LORD did for me when I came out of Egypt.' ⁹This observance will be for you like a sign on your hand and a reminder on your forehead that the law of the LORD is to be on your lips. For the LORD brought you out of Egypt with his mighty hand. ¹⁰You must keep this ordinance at the appointed time year after year.

¹¹"After the LORD brings you into the land of the Canaanites and gives it to you, as he promised on oath to you and your forefathers, ¹²you are to give over to the LORD the first offspring of every womb. All the firstborn males of your livestock belong to the LORD. ¹³Redeem with a lamb every firstborn donkey, but if you do not redeem it, break its neck. Redeem every firstborn among your sons.

¹⁴"In days to come, when your son asks you, 'What does this mean?' say to him, 'With a mighty hand the LORD brought us out of Egypt, out of the land of slavery. ¹⁵When Pharaoh stubbornly refused to let us go, the LORD killed every firstborn in Egypt, both man and animal. This is why I sacrifice to the LORD the first male offspring of every womb and redeem each of my firstborn sons.' ¹⁶And it will be like a sign on your hand and a symbol on your forehead that the LORD brought us out of Egypt with his mighty hand."

Crossing the Sea

¹⁷When Pharaoh let the people go, God did not lead them on the road through the Philistine country, though that was shorter. For God said, "If they face war, they might change their minds and return to Egypt." ¹⁸So God led the people around by the desert road toward the Red Sea.ᵃ The Israelites went up out of Egypt armed for battle.

¹⁹Moses took the bones of Joseph with him because Joseph had made the sons of Israel swear an oath. He had said, "God will surely come to your aid, and then you must carry my bones up with you from this place."ᵇ

²⁰After leaving Succoth they camped at Etham on the edge of the desert. ²¹By day the LORD went ahead of them in a pillar of cloud to guide them on their way and by night in a pillar of fire to give them light, so that they could travel by day or night. ²²Neither the pillar of cloud by day nor the pillar of fire by night left its place in front of the people.

14 Then the LORD said to Moses, ²"Tell the Israelites to turn back and encamp near Pi Hahiroth, between Migdol and the sea. They are to encamp by the sea, directly opposite Baal Zephon. ³Pharaoh will think, 'The Israelites are wandering around the land in confusion, hemmed in by the desert.' ⁴And I will harden Pharaoh's heart, and he will pursue them. But I will gain glory for myself through Pharaoh and all his army, and the Egyptians will know that I am the LORD." So the Israelites did this.

⁵When the king of Egypt was told that the people had fled, Pharaoh and his officials changed their minds about them and said, "What have we done? We have let the Israelites go and have lost their services!" ⁶So he had his chariot made ready and took his

ᵃ18 Hebrew *Yam Suph*; that is, Sea of Reeds   ᵇ19 See Gen. 50:25.

army with him. **7**He took six hundred of the best chariots, along with all the other chariots of Egypt, with officers over all of them. **8**The LORD hardened the heart of Pharaoh king of Egypt, so that he pursued the Israelites, who were marching out boldly. **9**The Egyptians—all Pharaoh's horses and chariots, horsemen[a] and troops—pursued the Israelites and overtook them as they camped by the sea near Pi Hahiroth, opposite Baal Zephon.

10As Pharaoh approached, the Israelites looked up, and there were the Egyptians, marching after them. They were terrified and cried out to the LORD. **11**They said to Moses, "Was it because there were no graves in Egypt that you brought us to the desert to die? What have you done to us by bringing us out of Egypt? **12**Didn't we say to you in Egypt, 'Leave us alone; let us serve the Egyptians'? It would have been better for us to serve the Egyptians than to die in the desert!"

13Moses answered the people, "Do not be afraid. Stand firm and you will see the deliverance the LORD will bring you today. The Egyptians you see today you will never see again. **14**The LORD will fight for you; you need only to be still."

15Then the LORD said to Moses, "Why are you crying out to me? Tell the Israelites to move on. **16**Raise your staff and stretch out your hand over the sea to divide the water so that the Israelites can go through the sea on dry ground. **17**I will harden the hearts of the Egyptians so that they will go in after them. And I will gain glory through Pharaoh and all his army, through his chariots and his horsemen. **18**The Egyptians will know that I am the LORD when I gain glory through Pharaoh, his chariots and his horsemen."

a9 Or *charioteers*; also in verses 17, 18, 23, 26 and 28

know that I am Lord"? Compassion? Justice? Vengeance? Explain. **6.** How equipped were the Egyptians? The Israelites? How did that make the Israelites react (14:6–12)? **7.** Instead of that revolutionary cry, "Give me liberty, or give me death," what is the cry of the Hebrews? Why do you think slavery is preferable to death for them (14:10–12)? **8.** What pressures are piling up for Moses (14:13–16)? How does he handle the stress? Why do you think God spoke to Moses the way he did in verse 15? **9.** As the drama of the sea crossing is played out, who is the director? Script writer? Hero? Supporting cast? Villain? What "special effects" are used? **10.** What is the dramatic punch line? What camera angles and hidden mikes would you have used to record how God gains glory? **11.** How would that glory be reflected in this miracle? In the Egyptians' death? In the Hebrews' salvation? **12.** Retrace the Israelites' movement from fear (14:10–12) to faith (14:29–31). What was instrumental? What do you think it meant to the Israelites that the same sea which "piled up" in their favor also

  Exodus 14:5–31   **CROSSING THE SEA**

As a result of the tenth plague—the death of the Egyptian firstborn on the night of Passover—Pharaoh had finally let the Israelites go.

1. Why did Pharaoh change his mind and go after the Israelites?
   a. He had been in a state of shock.
   b. He realized what he had lost.
   c. God hardened his heart.
   d. His pride was wounded.

2. If I looked up and saw the Egyptian army coming, I would:
   a. cry out to God in fear.
   b. get upset and blame Moses.
   c. wait assuredly for another miracle.
   d. surrender—because slavery is better than death.
   e. fight to the finish—because death is better than slavery.

3. What was going through Moses' head as he raised his staff at the Red Sea?
   a. This better work!
   b. We're number 1!
   c. Praise the Lord!
   d. Ta-dah!

4. As the Israelites walked across on dry ground, they:
   a. took their time.
   b. kept their eyes on the walls of water.
   c. walked with confidence.
   d. sprinted in terror.

5. The Lord chose this way of escape for the Israelites in order to:
   a. teach Pharaoh a lesson.
   b. wipe out the Egyptians at the same time.
   c. gain glory through the event.
   d. teach Israel to trust him.
   e. teach Israel to trust Moses.
   f. form Israel into a bonded people.

6. How have you experienced God through the "Red Sea" of your life?
   a. as rescuer
   b. as guide
   c. as victor over opposition
   d. as freedom-giver

7. How have you grown as a result of your "Red Sea" experience?
   a. I trust God more.
   b. I know myself better.

c. I feel prepared for the next crisis.
d. I take one day at a time.
e. I depend on others more.
f. I feel closer to God's people.

8. What is the most troubling situation in your life? How can this passage in general, and verses 13–14 in particular, help you and encourage you?

9. What are the biggest obstacles you face in your spiritual journey? How often do you feel like "going back to Egypt"? What do you do when you feel that way?

10. What does this story say to you about living an addiction-free lifestyle?
    a. The Lord will fight for me.
    b. I don't have to be enslaved.
    c. I need to trust God when tempted.
    d. I need an influence like Moses.

11. How are you doing in your quest to be addiction-free? What about this course and this group has been the greatest help in your road to recovery?

destroyed the Egyptians? 13. How do you think the Israelites would have described God to someone who had not seen these events firsthand?

1. What is the one "pursuing army" you fear in your life right now? Why this? How is God leading you up to this point: In circles? In the dark? Through fire? Or do you feel abandoned by those you've trusted? 2. In what ways might this passage help you to trust God with your fears? What one battle would you like God to fight for you this week? 3. Based on your own life story, how would you describe God's power to someone else who wasn't there when he rescued you? How does that compare to the power he demonstrates in this passage? With whom will you share your Exodus story this week?

How do you celebrate a long-awaited goal or unexpected victory? This year, which did you celebrate in that fashion: (a) Winning sports team? (b) Business deal? (c) Academic achievement? (d) Family success? (e) Other?

1. What was the cause for breaking into song? Who was the victor? The villain? The results? 2. Now for an inside look: What inner motivations seem to characterize the enemy (vv. 9–10)? What emotions within the victors does this song reflect? 3. What main idea does each stanza of this song reinforce (see 14:4)? What variations on this theme do you see (or hear)? What do you learn about God's character in this song? 4. In celebrating the defeat of one opponent, who do they serve notice to (vv. 13–18)? What will their great God do next? 5. What is noteworthy about Miriam's role in this celebration (vv. 20–21)? Later what does this same Miriam do that contrasts sharply with the spirit of this song (see Nu 12)?

¹⁹Then the angel of God, who had been traveling in front of Israel's army, withdrew and went behind them. The pillar of cloud also moved from in front and stood behind them, ²⁰coming between the armies of Egypt and Israel. Throughout the night the cloud brought darkness to the one side and light to the other side; so neither went near the other all night long.

²¹Then Moses stretched out his hand over the sea, and all that night the LORD drove the sea back with a strong east wind and turned it into dry land. The waters were divided, ²²and the Israelites went through the sea on dry ground, with a wall of water on their right and on their left.

²³The Egyptians pursued them, and all Pharaoh's horses and chariots and horsemen followed them into the sea. ²⁴During the last watch of the night the LORD looked down from the pillar of fire and cloud at the Egyptian army and threw it into confusion. ²⁵He made the wheels of their chariots come off[a] so that they had difficulty driving. And the Egyptians said, "Let's get away from the Israelites! The LORD is fighting for them against Egypt."

²⁶Then the LORD said to Moses, "Stretch out your hand over the sea so that the waters may flow back over the Egyptians and their chariots and horsemen." ²⁷Moses stretched out his hand over the sea, and at daybreak the sea went back to its place. The Egyptians were fleeing toward[b] it, and the LORD swept them into the sea. ²⁸The water flowed back and covered the chariots and horsemen—the entire army of Pharaoh that had followed the Israelites into the sea. Not one of them survived.

²⁹But the Israelites went through the sea on dry ground, with a wall of water on their right and on their left. ³⁰That day the LORD saved Israel from the hands of the Egyptians, and Israel saw the Egyptians lying dead on the shore. ³¹And when the Israelites saw the great power the LORD displayed against the Egyptians, the people feared the LORD and put their trust in him and in Moses his servant.

The Song of Moses and Miriam

15 Then Moses and the Israelites sang this song to the LORD:

"I will sing to the LORD,
    for he is highly exalted.
The horse and its rider
    he has hurled into the sea.
²The LORD is my strength and my song;
    he has become my salvation.
He is my God, and I will praise him,
    my father's God, and I will exalt him.
³The LORD is a warrior;
    the LORD is his name.
⁴Pharaoh's chariots and his army
    he has hurled into the sea.
The best of Pharaoh's officers
    are drowned in the Red Sea.[c]
⁵The deep waters have covered them;
    they sank to the depths like a stone.

⁶"Your right hand, O LORD,
    was majestic in power.
Your right hand, O LORD,

a25 Or He jammed the wheels of their chariots (see Samaritan Pentateuch, Septuagint and Syriac)   b27 Or from   c4 Hebrew Yam Suph; that is, Sea of Reeds; also in verse 22

shattered the enemy.
[7]In the greatness of your majesty
   you threw down those who opposed you.
You unleashed your burning anger;
   it consumed them like stubble.
[8]By the blast of your nostrils
   the waters piled up.
The surging waters stood firm like a wall;
   the deep waters congealed in the heart of the
     sea.

[9]"The enemy boasted,
   'I will pursue, I will overtake them.
I will divide the spoils;
   I will gorge myself on them.
I will draw my sword
   and my hand will destroy them.'
[10]But you blew with your breath,
   and the sea covered them.
They sank like lead
   in the mighty waters.

[11]"Who among the gods is like you, O Lord?
   Who is like you—
     majestic in holiness,
     awesome in glory,
     working wonders?
[12]You stretched out your right hand
   and the earth swallowed them.

[13]"In your unfailing love you will lead
   the people you have redeemed.
In your strength you will guide them
   to your holy dwelling.
[14]The nations will hear and tremble;
   anguish will grip the people of Philistia.
[15]The chiefs of Edom will be terrified,
   the leaders of Moab will be seized with
     trembling,
the people[a] of Canaan will melt away;
[16] terror and dread will fall upon them.
By the power of your arm
   they will be as still as a stone—
until your people pass by, O Lord,
   until the people you bought[b] pass by.
[17]You will bring them in and plant them
   on the mountain of your inheritance—
the place, O Lord, you made for your dwelling,
   the sanctuary, O Lord, your hands established.
[18]The Lord will reign
   for ever and ever."

[19]When Pharaoh's horses, chariots and horsemen[c] went into the sea, the Lord brought the waters of the sea back over them, but the Israelites walked through the sea on dry ground. [20]Then Miriam the prophetess, Aaron's sister, took a tambourine in her hand, and all the women followed her, with tambourines and dancing. [21]Miriam sang to them:

   "Sing to the Lord,

1. Now for an editorial opinion: Do you think this singing is an appropriate response to someone else's death? How do God's apparently violent actions (vv. 3–8) square with his unfailing love (v. 13)? 2. How else could God have achieved his loving purpose for Israel, other than by destroying the Egyptians? 3. By the same token, what would be the most effective means for God to deal with the evil threatening your life: For whom would that be painful? Fearful? Troublesome? Loving? How do you feel about celebrating the tragedy of someone who has wrongly hurt you or aggressively hindered your efforts to do God's will? 4. What miracle has God done for you that you could sing (or crow) about? What song can you think of that best fits a victory God has accomplished in your life? Would you be willing to "personalize" the lyrics for your next meeting? What common victories do the people in your group share? What song, refrain or individual stanza could your group sing to share? 5. What role does your creativity (in music, art, drama, dance) play in relationship to God? How could you use your creativity more often to praise God for the wondrous things he has done in your life? 6. Would you be willing to share the fruit of your creative, devotional expression with your group? Your church?

> for he is highly exalted.
> The horse and its rider
>   he has hurled into the sea."

The Waters of Marah and Elim

22Then Moses led Israel from the Red Sea and they went into the Desert of Shur. For three days they traveled in the desert without finding water. 23When they came to Marah, they could not drink its water because it was bitter. (That is why the place is called Marah.a) 24So the people grumbled against Moses, saying, "What are we to drink?"

25Then Moses cried out to the LORD, and the LORD showed him a piece of wood. He threw it into the water, and the water became sweet.

There the LORD made a decree and a law for them, and there he tested them. 26He said, "If you listen carefully to the voice of the LORD your God and do what is right in his eyes, if you pay attention to his commands and keep all his decrees, I will not bring on you any of the diseases I brought on the Egyptians, for I am the LORD, who heals you."

27Then they came to Elim, where there were twelve springs and seventy palm trees, and they camped there near the water.

Manna and Quail

16 The whole Israelite community set out from Elim and came to the Desert of Sin, which is between Elim and Sinai, on the fifteenth day of the second month after they had come out of Egypt. 2In the desert the whole community grumbled against Moses and Aaron. 3The Israelites said to them, "If only we had died by the LORD's hand in Egypt! There we sat around pots of meat and ate all the food we wanted, but you have brought us out into this desert to starve this entire assembly to death."

4Then the LORD said to Moses, "I will rain down bread from heaven for you. The people are to go out each day and gather enough for that day. In this way I will test them and see whether they will follow my instructions. 5On the sixth day they are to prepare what they bring in, and that is to be twice as much as they gather on the other days."

6So Moses and Aaron said to all the Israelites, "In the evening you will know that it was the LORD who brought you out of Egypt, 7and in the morning you will see the glory of the LORD, because he has heard your grumbling against him. Who are we, that you should grumble against us?" 8Moses also said, "You will know that it was the LORD when he gives you meat to eat in the evening and all the bread you want in the morning, because he has heard your grumbling against him. Who are we? You are not grumbling against us, but against the LORD."

9Then Moses told Aaron, "Say to the entire Israelite community, 'Come before the LORD, for he has heard your grumbling.'"

10While Aaron was speaking to the whole Israelite community, they looked toward the desert, and there was the glory of the LORD appearing in the cloud.

11The LORD said to Moses, 12"I have heard the grumbling of the Israelites. Tell them, 'At twilight you will eat meat, and in the morning you will be filled with bread. Then you will know that I am the LORD your God.'"

13That evening quail came and covered the camp, and in the

a23 *Marah* means *bitter.*

---

1. How can these people turn from prison to praise to protest so quickly? 2. What is the essence of their complaint and God's cure? Why hadn't God led Israel to sweet water in the first place? What was his object lesson? 3. What does that say about human patience? God's provision? His discipline?

1. What's your "sweet and sour" experience of this year? 2. Are you most open to God's leading in feast or famine? Why? 3. God makes a promise in verse 26. What promises has God given to you?

1. What were the "good ol' days" like for you? What made them so "good"? 2. Who cooked Sunday dinner in your childhood home? Who cooks it now? What's the last time you served some new dish and your family asked, "What is it"? (What was it?) 3. If there's one chore you excuse yourself or your family from doing on Sunday, what is it?

1. How adequate do you think Israel's cache of resources (see 12:34–36) was for a prolonged wilderness journey? What do you see as other problems (physical, emotional, spiritual) faced by Israel on their trip? 2. Given the miraculous escape from Egypt, how do you account for the people complaining so soon (about 45 days): Short memory? Long, forced marches? Harsh physical conditions? Finicky eaters? Ill-mannered kids? 3. Does Moses think their complaints about the food were justified? Would you? If they hadn't "grumbled," would God have heard them? Why or why not? What does that tell you about their relationship with God, as it was? As God wanted it to be? Likewise, what do their complaints say about how they treated Moses and Aaron? 4. How do you account for the presence of "manna"? Do you think it was a natural food or something unique and supernatural? 5. What were the promises and requirements associated with God's provision of the manna?

morning there was a layer of dew around the camp. ¹⁴When the dew was gone, thin flakes like frost on the ground appeared on the desert floor. ¹⁵When the Israelites saw it, they said to each other, "What is it?" For they did not know what it was.

Moses said to them, "It is the bread the LORD has given you to eat. ¹⁶This is what the LORD has commanded: 'Each one is to gather as much as he needs. Take an omer*ᵃ* for each person you have in your tent.'"

¹⁷The Israelites did as they were told; some gathered much, some little. ¹⁸And when they measured it by the omer, he who gathered much did not have too much, and he who gathered little did not have too little. Each one gathered as much as he needed.

¹⁹Then Moses said to them, "No one is to keep any of it until morning."

²⁰However, some of them paid no attention to Moses; they kept part of it until morning, but it was full of maggots and began to smell. So Moses was angry with them.

²¹Each morning everyone gathered as much as he needed, and when the sun grew hot, it melted away. ²²On the sixth day, they gathered twice as much—two omers*ᵇ* for each person—and the leaders of the community came and reported this to Moses. ²³He said to them, "This is what the LORD commanded: 'Tomorrow is to be a day of rest, a holy Sabbath to the LORD. So bake what you want to bake and boil what you want to boil. Save whatever is left and keep it until morning.'"

²⁴So they saved it until morning, as Moses commanded, and it

ᵃ16 That is, probably about 2 quarts (about 2 liters); also in verses 18, 32, 33 and 36
ᵇ22 That is, probably about 4 quarts (about 4.5 liters)

Why allow some to gather much and some little (vv. 16–18)? Why provide food that lasts only one day (vv. 19–21)? What was different about the sixth and seventh days (vv. 22–30)? Where does the idea of resting on the seventh day come from? Why is it important to God that the day of rest be remembered? **6.** What does this say about the trust relationship God desires?

♡ **1.** If you were the trip organizer for thousands of men, women and kids, traveling 300 miles of desert, how would you have prepared for their needs: Meals on wheels? AAA bed and board oasis inns? One Great Hour of Sharing? Other? Have you ever grumbled against someone who was actually doing exactly what the Lord wanted them to do? What happened? **2.** How does it feel to know that God wants to provide for all your needs? What if that included manna pancakes and quail casserole every day? **3.** What has been the value of the Sabbath rest in your life lately? What Sabbath activities do you consider truly restful and which are drudgery? How can God help you observe the Sab-

---

Exodus 16:1–35   MANNA FROM THE LORD

God has just delivered the Israelites from bondage in Egypt and miraculously led them through the Red Sea.

1. How could the people, having so recently seen God's awesome power, complain so soon?
   a. They were spoiled rotten.
   b. The desert heat gave them short-term memory loss.
   c. They were finicky eaters.
   d. They hadn't planned ahead.
   e. It was typical of human nature.
   f. Genuine faith doesn't necessarily come from seeing miracles.

2. Why did God send manna and quail?
   a. to quiet their complaints
   b. to meet their needs
   c. to demonstrate his power
   d. to test their obedience

3. Why did God give them only one day's supply of manna at a time?
   a. to establish a routine in the desert
   b. so they'd have to trust God daily
   c. because there was no place to store leftovers
   d. He enjoyed meeting their needs.

4. The reason for the Sabbath was:
   a. God needed rest from providing manna.
   b. the people needed rest from collecting manna.
   c. to learn that nothing important is lost by observing a day of rest.
   d. to learn how to plan ahead.
   e. to worship God regularly.

5. Why was the Sabbath idea so hard for the Israelites?
   a. It was brand new.
   b. They weren't sure God could be trusted.
   c. When you're hungry you don't think straight.
   d. People are greedy.
   e. It's hard to let God meet your needs on *his* terms.

6. The idea of receiving "bread from heaven" daily is:
   a. a little strange.   c. exciting.
   b. something I need.   d. too routine.

7. The kind of spiritual "bread" I am getting right now is:
   a. 100% whole wheat—satisfying and nutritious.

b. cracked wheat—a few good kernels here and there.
c. cheap white bread—bleached out and without substance.
d. moldy.

8. To what extent do you observe the principle of a Sabbath rest? Are you satisfied with that? Do you think God is satisfied?

9. How hard is it for you to set aside "family time"? What have you found to be most helpful to make sure your family gets priority time?

10. What is the most demanding thing about your role as a "caregiver"? How difficult is it for you to take a break from your responsibilities? Do you feel guilty when you take a break? How come?

11. How does God call the Israelites to a life of balance? In your desire to "shape up" physically, what do you think would help you do healthy things like eat sensibly each day?

bath rest? **4.** What applications does Jesus make of this "manna" provision (see Mt 4:4; Lk 11:3; Jn 6 for several key ideas)? What does that suggest for how to resist temptation, pray for others, and trust Christ as the "true bread from heaven"? **5.** Describe a time when you were "stranded in the desert." What one piece of advice would you have given to the Israelites in this passage? If you were in their place, would you take your own advice? Why or why not?

"How do I love thee? Let me count the ways ..." If someone wanted to show how much they loved you, what proof would satisfy you?

1. "Same song, second verse." How does this passage compare with 16:1–4? Do you think their complaints are valid? Why? **2.** Was thirst the only problem? What was the deeper object lesson? How well do you suppose they learned this lesson (see Nu 20:1–13, for a repeated incident at Meribah)?

1. What does this passage teach about the authority of Moses and God? About stress? Obedience? Trust? **2.** Who or what usually gets the brunt of your frustration? How will you "let go and let God" next time you "thirst"?

With raised arms see who can keep them up the longest. Have two people prop up the arms of the group leader: What would happen after 12 hours?

1. What leadership is exerted here by Moses? Joshua? Aaron and Hur? **2.** What do you think is the significance of Moses' raised hands in this story? **3.** Why do you think God might want to blot out the memory of the Amalekites?

did not stink or get maggots in it. ²⁵"Eat it today," Moses said, "because today is a Sabbath to the Lord. You will not find any of it on the ground today. ²⁶Six days you are to gather it, but on the seventh day, the Sabbath, there will not be any."

²⁷Nevertheless, some of the people went out on the seventh day to gather it, but they found none. ²⁸Then the Lord said to Moses, "How long will you[a] refuse to keep my commands and my instructions? ²⁹Bear in mind that the Lord has given you the Sabbath; that is why on the sixth day he gives you bread for two days. Everyone is to stay where he is on the seventh day; no one is to go out." ³⁰So the people rested on the seventh day.

³¹The people of Israel called the bread manna.[b] It was white like coriander seed and tasted like wafers made with honey. ³²Moses said, "This is what the Lord has commanded: 'Take an omer of manna and keep it for the generations to come, so they can see the bread I gave you to eat in the desert when I brought you out of Egypt.'"

³³So Moses said to Aaron, "Take a jar and put an omer of manna in it. Then place it before the Lord to be kept for the generations to come."

³⁴As the Lord commanded Moses, Aaron put the manna in front of the Testimony, that it might be kept. ³⁵The Israelites ate manna forty years, until they came to a land that was settled; they ate manna until they reached the border of Canaan.

³⁶(An omer is one tenth of an ephah.)

Water From the Rock

17 The whole Israelite community set out from the Desert of Sin, traveling from place to place as the Lord commanded. They camped at Rephidim, but there was no water for the people to drink. ²So they quarreled with Moses and said, "Give us water to drink."

Moses replied, "Why do you quarrel with me? Why do you put the Lord to the test?"

³But the people were thirsty for water there, and they grumbled against Moses. They said, "Why did you bring us up out of Egypt to make us and our children and livestock die of thirst?"

⁴Then Moses cried out to the Lord, "What am I to do with these people? They are almost ready to stone me."

⁵The Lord answered Moses, "Walk on ahead of the people. Take with you some of the elders of Israel and take in your hand the staff with which you struck the Nile, and go. ⁶I will stand there before you by the rock at Horeb. Strike the rock, and water will come out of it for the people to drink." So Moses did this in the sight of the elders of Israel. ⁷And he called the place Massah[c] and Meribah[d] because the Israelites quarreled and because they tested the Lord saying, "Is the Lord among us or not?"

The Amalekites Defeated

⁸The Amalekites came and attacked the Israelites at Rephidim. ⁹Moses said to Joshua, "Choose some of our men and go out to fight the Amalekites. Tomorrow I will stand on top of the hill with the staff of God in my hands."

¹⁰So Joshua fought the Amalekites as Moses had ordered, and Moses, Aaron and Hur went to the top of the hill. ¹¹As long as Moses held up his hands, the Israelites were winning, but whenever he lowered his hands, the Amalekites were winning. ¹²When

---

[a]28 The Hebrew is plural.   [b]31 Manna means What is it? (see verse 15).
[c]7 Massah means testing.   [d]7 Meribah means quarreling.

Moses' hands grew tired, they took a stone and put it under him and he sat on it. Aaron and Hur held his hands up—one on one side, one on the other—so that his hands remained steady till sunset. [13]So Joshua overcame the Amalekite army with the sword.

[14]Then the LORD said to Moses, "Write this on a scroll as something to be remembered and make sure that Joshua hears it, because I will completely blot out the memory of Amalek from under heaven."

[15]Moses built an altar and called it The LORD is my Banner. [16]He said, "For hands were lifted up to the throne of the LORD. The[a] LORD will be at war against the Amalekites from generation to generation."

Jethro Visits Moses

18 Now Jethro, the priest of Midian and father-in-law of Moses, heard of everything God had done for Moses and for his people Israel, and how the LORD had brought Israel out of Egypt. [2]After Moses had sent away his wife Zipporah, his father-in-law Jethro received her [3]and her two sons. One son was named Gershom,[b] for Moses said, "I have become an alien in a foreign land"; [4]and the other was named Eliezer,[c] for he said, "My father's God was my helper; he saved me from the sword of Pharaoh."

[5]Jethro, Moses' father-in-law, together with Moses' sons and wife, came to him in the desert, where he was camped near the

---

[a]16 Or *"Because a hand was against the throne of the LORD, the*   [b]3 *Gershom* sounds like the Hebrew for *an alien there.*   [c]4 *Eliezer* means *my God is helper.*

---

1. When have you needed your faith propped up by someone else? **2.** What battle has God won in your life lately? What would you name your altar: "The Lord is my:?"

1. Right now, which is stacked higher: Your IN basket or your OUT basket? How are you coping? **2.** What is your image of the ideal father-in-law? For what advice have you leaned on him before? What advice would you welcome from him now?

1. From what you've read so far, what can you infer was Moses' job description? What were his priorities? How well was he leading and others following? What additional expectations did this raise in their mind? **2.** What kind of

---

   Exodus 17:1–16   **GOD USES MOSES' HANDS**

After bringing the Israelites out of bondage in Egypt, God quieted their complaints and met their need for food by providing "manna" every day.

1. If you were Moses, what would you have said in response to the people?
   a. "Quit your snivelling."
   b. "Go ahead—you can try to do it without me."
   c. "I'm doing my best to address your frustrations and concerns."
   d. "Lord, why me?!"

2. Wandering homeless in the desert, what would you have said to Moses?
   a. "You're doing a great job—keep up the good work."
   b. "This is quite an adventure—thanks for bringing me along!"
   c. "Excuse me—perhaps you haven't noticed, but there's no water out here."
   d. "Don't worry, we're tough—who needs water anyway?"
   e. "Hey, what are you trying to do—kill us?!"

3. God waited to meet the peoples' needs until they complained:
   a. to test them.

b. because he needed time to provide a solution.
   c. to develop character in them.
   d. to establish Moses' leadership.

4. What do you do when you get frustrated?
   a. strike a rock
   b. kick the dog
   c. yell at_____
   d. cry out to the Lord
   e. take a walk
   f. other:_____

5. Why did the Israelites win the battle only when Moses raised his staff?
   a. It was just a coincidence.
   b. There was power in the staff.
   c. It was a motivational tool.
   d. God responded to the appeal for help and empowerment.
   e. God works through his servants' hands.

6. Who has held up your arms during times of crises or great stress? How are you at being an Aaron or Hur and giving support to others?

7. What battle would you like the Lord to fight for you right now? How do

you feel about enlisting the help of others?

8. As these stories illustrate, I can deal with stress by:
   a. realizing even a person like Moses was criticized and stressed out.
   b. realizing it is God's idea to ventilate feelings and frustrations.
   c. putting my hands in God's hands.
   d. accepting help from others instead of always trying to make it on my own.

9. When those you are caring for complain or get on your nerves, what can you do? (How well do you practice your answer?)
   a. Get away from them for awhile.
   b. Talk to them about how I feel.
   c. Look to God for help.
   d. Ask_____ for assistance.
   e. Remind myself of my own shortcomings and limitations.

10. What was most helpful about this small group course? How will you continue to build upon that in your management of stress?

relationship did Moses enjoy with his father-in-law: Relaxed or cautious? Trusting or suspicious? Affirming or critical? Explain. **3.** Role play one of you being Jethro, the others all chiming in with stories that flesh out the meaning of verses 8–9. What does your group report suggest? **4.** What gave Jethro the right to challenge Moses' way of doing things (vv. 13–14)? How do you suppose Moses felt after this critique of his leadership? **5.** What were the key elements of Jethro's plan (vv. 17–23)? What would have appealed to Moses, and to the people, about delegated leadership? What would have been hard for either one to swallow about this idea? **6.** Note the way Jethro delivered his constructive criticism. What makes it possible for Moses to hear and act on it? Indeed, what does Moses do (vv. 24–27; see chs. 19–20)?

 1. How did you react the last time you were corrected or criticized by your boss? Your spouse? Your in-laws? **2.** How open are you to criticism and feedback from others? Whose criticism do you receive the best? How do they get through to you? **3.** What

mountain of God. ⁶Jethro had sent word to him, "I, your father-in-law Jethro, am coming to you with your wife and her two sons."

⁷So Moses went out to meet his father-in-law and bowed down and kissed him. They greeted each other and then went into the tent. ⁸Moses told his father-in-law about everything the LORD had done to Pharaoh and the Egyptians for Israel's sake and about all the hardships they had met along the way and how the LORD had saved them.

⁹Jethro was delighted to hear about all the good things the LORD had done for Israel in rescuing them from the hand of the Egyptians. ¹⁰He said, "Praise be to the LORD, who rescued you from the hand of the Egyptians and of Pharaoh, and who rescued the people from the hand of the Egyptians. ¹¹Now I know that the LORD is greater than all other gods, for he did this to those who had treated Israel arrogantly." ¹²Then Jethro, Moses' father-in-law, brought a burnt offering and other sacrifices to God, and Aaron came with all the elders of Israel to eat bread with Moses' father-in-law in the presence of God.

¹³The next day Moses took his seat to serve as judge for the people, and they stood around him from morning till evening. ¹⁴When his father-in-law saw all that Moses was doing for the people, he said, "What is this you are doing for the people? Why do you alone sit as judge, while all these people stand around you from morning till evening?"

¹⁵Moses answered him, "Because the people come to me to seek God's will. ¹⁶Whenever they have a dispute, it is brought to me, and I decide between the parties and inform them of God's decrees and laws."

¹⁷Moses' father-in-law replied, "What you are doing is not good.

   Exodus 18:1–27   **JETHRO VISITS MOSES**

1. How did Jethro respond to Moses' report about what God had done for Moses and the Israelites?
   a. He wasn't really interested.
   b. He rejoiced with them.
   c. It made him want to hear more.
   d. He worshiped the Lord as a new convert.

2. Why did Moses work so hard?
   a. No one else could do what he did.
   b. He was a workaholic.
   c. He was a perfectionist.
   d. He hated to say no.
   e. He liked to be in control.
   f. He had a need to please others.
   g. He thought he was doing what God wanted.
   h. A creative solution hadn't been suggested.

3. To the extent you work too hard at something, which of the reasons above are true of you?

4. Why did Moses accept Jethro's advice?
   a. because he was intimidated by his father-in-law

   b. because he was very mature and personally secure
   c. because it came from family
   d. because it was great advice
   e. because of the tactful way it was presented
   f. Moses just needed someone else to confirm what he already knew.
   g. Moses realized God was inspiring Jethro's plan.

5. What was the benefit of the plan for Moses? For the people? What did it cost Moses? What were the potential risks?

6. On a scale of 1 (lowest) to 10 (highest), how are you at:
   a. settling other people's disputes?
   b. listening to suggestions?
   c. giving constructive criticism?
   d. accepting criticism?
   e. delegating responsibility?
   f. organizing people and events?
   g. releasing control of situations?

7. In which area listed in the previous question do you most want to

change? What can you learn from this story to help you? What is one thing you can do to grow in that area?

8. In your relationships, do you feel like typically you are on the giving or the receiving end? What does this passage say to you about your own needs? About doing more than you should? About accepting help from others?

9. When have you felt as overwhelmed as Moses must have as he tried to judge all the people's disputes? What—if anything— did you do to relieve the pressure? How does Jethro's advice apply to your current employment situation?

10. In your caregiving, how much have you tried to "share the load" with others? To what degree do you share Jethro's concern that you and those you care for will "wear yourselves out"?

[18]You and these people who come to you will only wear yourselves out. The work is too heavy for you; you cannot handle it alone. [19]Listen now to me and I will give you some advice, and may God be with you. You must be the people's representative before God and bring their disputes to him. [20]Teach them the decrees and laws, and show them the way to live and the duties they are to perform. [21]But select capable men from all the people—men who fear God, trustworthy men who hate dishonest gain—and appoint them as officials over thousands, hundreds, fifties and tens. [22]Have them serve as judges for the people at all times, but have them bring every difficult case to you; the simple cases they can decide themselves. That will make your load lighter, because they will share it with you. [23]If you do this and God so commands, you will be able to stand the strain, and all these people will go home satisfied."

[24]Moses listened to his father-in-law and did everything he said. [25]He chose capable men from all Israel and made them leaders of the people, officials over thousands, hundreds, fifties and tens. [26]They served as judges for the people at all times. The difficult cases they brought to Moses, but the simple ones they decided themselves.

[27]Then Moses sent his father-in-law on his way, and Jethro returned to his own country.

At Mount Sinai

19 In the third month after the Israelites left Egypt—on the very day—they came to the Desert of Sinai. [2]After they set out from Rephidim, they entered the Desert of Sinai, and Israel camped there in the desert in front of the mountain.

[3]Then Moses went up to God, and the LORD called to him from the mountain and said, "This is what you are to say to the house of Jacob and what you are to tell the people of Israel: [4]'You yourselves have seen what I did to Egypt, and how I carried you on eagles' wings and brought you to myself. [5]Now if you obey me fully and keep my covenant, then out of all nations you will be my treasured possession. Although the whole earth is mine, [6]you[a] will be for me a kingdom of priests and a holy nation.' These are the words you are to speak to the Israelites."

[7]So Moses went back and summoned the elders of the people and set before them all the words the LORD had commanded him to speak. [8]The people all responded together, "We will do everything the LORD has said." So Moses brought their answer back to the LORD.

[9]The LORD said to Moses, "I am going to come to you in a dense cloud, so that the people will hear me speaking with you and will always put their trust in you." Then Moses told the LORD what the people had said.

[10]And the LORD said to Moses, "Go to the people and consecrate them today and tomorrow. Have them wash their clothes [11]and be ready by the third day, because on that day the LORD will come down on Mount Sinai in the sight of all the people. [12]Put limits for the people around the mountain and tell them, 'Be careful that you do not go up the mountain or touch the foot of it. Whoever touches the mountain shall surely be put to death. [13]He shall surely be stoned or shot with arrows; not a hand is to be laid on him.

[a]5,6 Or possession, for the whole earth is mine. [6]You

Where were you when you first experienced the reality of God? What happened there? What feelings do you have for this place?

1. From verses 4–6, what does God expect from the people? What does he promise will result? What right does God have to dictate the terms of this covenant? **2.** How does this language compare with God's covenant with Abram (see Ge 12:1–3)? **3.** How do God's people become "a kingdom of priests and a holy nation" (vv. 6,10–15)? **4.** Why do you think so much emphasis is placed on barring people from the mountain (vv. 12–13; 21–24; see Nu 3:28)? On washing their clothes? On abstaining from sex? On special effects (dense cloud, thunder, lightning, trumpet blast, smoke, earth tremors)? What does this tell you about the importance of the events about to take place? **5.** As this covenant is with all the people, why do you think God wants only Moses on the mountain with him (vv. 9,19–20)? What role do the elders and Aaron play in this (vv. 7–8,24)?

1. After all was said and done, who met with God that day: Only Moses? Aaron and the priests, too? The people, as well? Explain how each may have met God. **2.** When did you last truly experience the presence of God?

What impact did that have on you? **3.** Would you even want to meet God face-to-face like Moses did? Who would you trust to send in your place? What questions would you want asked of God? **4.** What feelings do you have toward the person who walks close with God and talks to him: Apathy? Jealousy? Fear? Relief? Curiosity? Deference? **5.** How do Christians "wash" or "abstain" to get ready for church? How else do you draw near to God? **6.** What barriers has Jesus set aside so that we can draw near to God with confidence (see Heb 10:19ff)? What does Peter urge us to do to become "a chosen people, a royal priesthood, a holy nation, belonging to God" (1Pe 2:9)? What will you do about this, today?

Whether man or animal, he shall not be permitted to live.' Only when the ram's horn sounds a long blast may they go up to the mountain."

[14]After Moses had gone down the mountain to the people, he consecrated them, and they washed their clothes. [15]Then he said to the people, "Prepare yourselves for the third day. Abstain from sexual relations."

[16]On the morning of the third day there was thunder and lightning, with a thick cloud over the mountain, and a very loud trumpet blast. Everyone in the camp trembled. [17]Then Moses led the people out of the camp to meet with God, and they stood at the foot of the mountain. [18]Mount Sinai was covered with smoke, because the LORD descended on it in fire. The smoke billowed up from it like smoke from a furnace, the whole mountain[a] trembled violently, [19]and the sound of the trumpet grew louder and louder. Then Moses spoke and the voice of God answered him.[b]

[20]The LORD descended to the top of Mount Sinai and called Moses to the top of the mountain. So Moses went up [21]and the LORD said to him, "Go down and warn the people so they do not force their way through to see the LORD and many of them perish. [22]Even the priests, who approach the LORD, must consecrate themselves, or the LORD will break out against them."

[23]Moses said to the LORD, "The people cannot come up Mount Sinai, because you yourself warned us, 'Put limits around the mountain and set it apart as holy.'"

[24]The LORD replied, "Go down and bring Aaron up with you. But

[a]18 Most Hebrew manuscripts; a few Hebrew manuscripts and Septuagint *all the people*
[b]19 Or *and God answered him with thunder*

Exodus 19:10–20:21   RECEIVING THE TEN COMMANDMENTS

While the Israelites were camped by Mt. Sinai, God powerfully appeared to them. As part of that revelation, the Lord spoke to his people what came to be known as the Ten Commandments.

1. The dense cloud, thunder and lightning, trumpet blasts, smoke and earth tremors were:
   a. a heavenly attention-grabber.
   b. a visible demonstration of God's holiness.
   c. a prelude to the "earth-shaking" event of receiving God's covenant.
   d. God instilling the "fear of the Lord" in his people.

2. Why did God give strict orders not to touch the mountain?
   a. It was holy ground.
   b. He was testing their obedience.
   c. They had to wait until God called them to it to speak to them.

3. How would you have reacted when Moses said it was time to go to the foot of the mountain to meet God?

a. ran to the mountain
b. ran for a video camcorder
c. ran for my life
d. asked Moses to speak instead of God
e. stayed at a distance
f. trembled with fear like everybody else

4. Of all of the Ten Commandments (20:3–17), which does our society most need to hear? Which do you most need to hear?

5. What are some modern idols and false gods? How do you avoid them?

6. How do you think the Lord wants you to remember the Sabbath? How often do you take time off for rest, spiritual rejuvenation and worship?

7. How do you recall Jesus referring to some of the commandments (for instance, in Matthew 5:21–30)? Did his inclusion of anger in murder and his inclusion of lust in adultery change the Ten Commandments or

merely zero in on the heart of them?

8. What does it mean to fear God? How accurately were Moses' words to the Israelites that "the fear of God will be with you to keep you from sinning" (20:20) fulfilled? How can the fear of God keep you from sinning?

9. What is your first memory of experiencing the presence of God? Was it a dramatic, "mountain-top" experience—or more tranquil? What feelings do you have when you remember that time and/or place?

10. When did you last truly experience the Lord's presence? What impact did that have on you?

11. Are you satisfied with the way you are "meeting" with God now? If not, what needs to happen?

12. What could you, your small group, and your church do to "consecrate" or prepare yourselves to meet God?

the priests and the people must not force their way through to come up to the Lord, or he will break out against them."

²⁵So Moses went down to the people and told them.

The Ten Commandments

20 And God spoke all these words:

²"I am the Lord your God, who brought you out of Egypt, out of the land of slavery.

³"You shall have no other gods before*ᵃ* me.

⁴"You shall not make for yourself an idol in the form of anything in heaven above or on the earth beneath or in the waters below. ⁵You shall not bow down to them or worship them; for I, the Lord your God, am a jealous God, punishing the children for the sin of the fathers to the third and fourth generation of those who hate me, ⁶but showing love to a thousand ⌐generations⌐ of those who love me and keep my commandments.

⁷"You shall not misuse the name of the Lord your God, for the Lord will not hold anyone guiltless who misuses his name.

⁸"Remember the Sabbath day by keeping it holy. ⁹Six days you shall labor and do all your work, ¹⁰but the seventh day is a Sabbath to the Lord your God. On it you shall not do any work, neither you, nor your son or daughter, nor your manservant or maidservant, nor your animals, nor the alien within your gates. ¹¹For in six days the Lord made the heavens and the earth, the sea, and all that is in them, but he rested on the seventh day. Therefore the Lord blessed the Sabbath day and made it holy.

¹²"Honor your father and your mother, so that you may live long in the land the Lord your God is giving you.

¹³"You shall not murder.

¹⁴"You shall not commit adultery.

¹⁵"You shall not steal.

¹⁶"You shall not give false testimony against your neighbor.

¹⁷"You shall not covet your neighbor's house. You shall not covet your neighbor's wife, or his manservant or maidservant, his ox or donkey, or anything that belongs to your neighbor."

¹⁸When the people saw the thunder and lightning and heard the trumpet and saw the mountain in smoke, they trembled with fear. They stayed at a distance ¹⁹and said to Moses, "Speak to us yourself and we will listen. But do not have God speak to us or we will die."

²⁰Moses said to the people, "Do not be afraid. God has come to test you, so that the fear of God will be with you to keep you from sinning."

²¹The people remained at a distance, while Moses approached the thick darkness where God was.

Idols and Altars

²²Then the Lord said to Moses, "Tell the Israelites this: 'You have seen for yourselves that I have spoken to you from heaven: ²³Do not make any gods to be alongside me; do not make for yourselves gods of silver or gods of gold.

²⁴"'Make an altar of earth for me and sacrifice on it your burnt offerings and fellowship offerings,ᵇ your sheep and goats and your

---

ᵃ3 Or *besides*   ᵇ24 Traditionally *peace offerings*

Who laid down the law in your home? How did you try to bend the rules?

1. What does it mean that God is jealous? How does that trait define the terms of this covenant? **2.** What passed for an idol, back then (see Dt 4:15ff)? And now? (What about money, things, celebrities, church art?) **3.** How do we misuse the Lord's name in deed and word? **4.** What is the rationale for the Sabbath (vv. 8–11; see 16:21–30; Dt 5:14–15)? **5.** Behavior that honors parents—what does it look like? Who then is blessed? **6.** How does murder vary from killing? What does Jesus add to this (see Mt 5:21–22)? **7.** What happens to a couple when one commits adultery? What does Jesus add to this (see Mt 5:28)? **8.** What passes for stealing? What forms of stealing are worse than others? **9.** Is lying okay if it doesn't injure another, as false witness does? How about little white lies? **10.** What passes for coveting (v. 17) as Jesus defines sins of the heart (see Mt 5:21–30)? **11.** What shift in focus do you see between verses 3–11 and 12–17? What links the two sets of laws? **12.** What link do you see between verses 18–21 and verses 1–17? What does it mean—"Fear not, fear God" (v. 20)?

1. Restate each of these Ten Commandments positively as the "Ten Freedoms." **2.** What "other gods" (objects, goals, people) has the one true God freed you from to serve him only?

---

1. How does verse 23 compare with 20:3–4? What can the one true God do that metal gods can't (see 32:1–10)? **2.** Why only an earthen altar and not one of "dressed" (hewn) stone? (Might this be akin to a graven image?) **3.** What does "nakedness" refer to? What does this say about the place where God is worshiped? What can distract you from meeting God?

___

If you could be the slave of any famous person, who would you choose to be your master?

1. How does God's law about Hebrews serving Hebrews differ from their days serving Pharaoh? 2. What freedoms, rights and needs is God protecting? 3. How will that affect class barriers?

1. Do these laws condone slavery? Why? How do God's instructions about slavery differ from how slaves were treated in pre-Civil War America? 2. How does this passage enable you to cope with "enslaving" situations? 3. How does your treatment of employees and fellow workers fit within God's directives?

___

How were you punished when you were a child? Did the punishments vary according to the seriousness of the offense?

1. What affirmation of life and justice is conveyed by these death penalties (vv. 12–17)? 2. How does God look after victims? Their families? Their property? 3. What hierarchy of values do you see here? How do these laws expand the Ten Commandments? 4. What was the "law of retaliation" meant to achieve (vv. 23–25)? How would this law likely be received by a quick-tempered person? By a person with no convictions? 5. What liability does one have for the actions of one's animal (vv. 28–36)? How is that liability limited?

1. Who decided what was "fair" punishment when you were growing up? How did you respond to this punishment? 2. Has your view of this changed as you've matured? How so? 3. What misunderstanding of these laws was Jesus' teaching on "eye for eye" meant to correct (see Mt 5:38–42)? 4. In these laws, what value does God seem to hold dear:

cattle. Wherever I cause my name to be honored, I will come to you and bless you. [25]If you make an altar of stones for me, do not build it with dressed stones, for you will defile it if you use a tool on it. [26]And do not go up to my altar on steps, lest your nakedness be exposed on it.'

21

"These are the laws you are to set before them:

Hebrew Servants

[2]"If you buy a Hebrew servant, he is to serve you for six years. But in the seventh year, he shall go free, without paying anything. [3]If he comes alone, he is to go free alone; but if he has a wife when he comes, she is to go with him. [4]If his master gives him a wife and she bears him sons or daughters, the woman and her children shall belong to her master, and only the man shall go free.

[5]"But if the servant declares, 'I love my master and my wife and children and do not want to go free,' [6]then his master must take him before the judges.[a] He shall take him to the door or the doorpost and pierce his ear with an awl. Then he will be his servant for life.

[7]"If a man sells his daughter as a servant, she is not to go free as menservants do. [8]If she does not please the master who has selected her for himself,[b] he must let her be redeemed. He has no right to sell her to foreigners, because he has broken faith with her. [9]If he selects her for his son, he must grant her the rights of a daughter. [10]If he marries another woman, he must not deprive the first one of her food, clothing and marital rights. [11]If he does not provide her with these three things, she is to go free, without any payment of money.

Personal Injuries

[12]"Anyone who strikes a man and kills him shall surely be put to death. [13]However, if he does not do it intentionally, but God lets it happen, he is to flee to a place I will designate. [14]But if a man schemes and kills another man deliberately, take him away from my altar and put him to death.

[15]"Anyone who attacks[c] his father or his mother must be put to death.

[16]"Anyone who kidnaps another and either sells him or still has him when he is caught must be put to death.

[17]"Anyone who curses his father or mother must be put to death.

[18]"If men quarrel and one hits the other with a stone or with his fist[d] and he does not die but is confined to bed, [19]the one who struck the blow will not be held responsible if the other gets up and walks around outside with his staff; however, he must pay the injured man for the loss of his time and see that he is completely healed.

[20]"If a man beats his male or female slave with a rod and the slave dies as a direct result, he must be punished, [21]but he is not to be punished if the slave gets up after a day or two, since the slave is his property.

[22]"If men who are fighting hit a pregnant woman and she gives birth prematurely[e] but there is no serious injury, the offender must be fined whatever the woman's husband demands and the court allows. [23]But if there is serious injury, you are to take life for

___

[a]6 Or *before God*   [b]8 Or *master so that he does not choose her*   [c]15 Or *kills*
[d]18 Or *with a tool*   [e]22 Or *she has a miscarriage*

life, [24]eye for eye, tooth for tooth, hand for hand, foot for foot, [25]burn for burn, wound for wound, bruise for bruise.

[26]"If a man hits a manservant or maidservant in the eye and destroys it, he must let the servant go free to compensate for the eye. [27]And if he knocks out the tooth of a manservant or maidservant, he must let the servant go free to compensate for the tooth.

[28]"If a bull gores a man or a woman to death, the bull must be stoned to death, and its meat must not be eaten. But the owner of the bull will not be held responsible. [29]If, however, the bull has had the habit of goring and the owner has been warned but has not kept it penned up and it kills a man or woman, the bull must be stoned and the owner also must be put to death. [30]However, if payment is demanded of him, he may redeem his life by paying whatever is demanded. [31]This law also applies if the bull gores a son or daughter. [32]If the bull gores a male or female slave, the owner must pay thirty shekels[a] of silver to the master of the slave, and the bull must be stoned.

[33]"If a man uncovers a pit or digs one and fails to cover it and an ox or a donkey falls into it, [34]the owner of the pit must pay for the loss; he must pay its owner, and the dead animal will be his.

[35]"If a man's bull injures the bull of another and it dies, they are to sell the live one and divide both the money and the dead animal equally. [36]However, if it was known that the bull had the habit of goring, yet the owner did not keep it penned up, the owner must pay, animal for animal, and the dead animal will be his.

Protection of Property

22 "If a man steals an ox or a sheep and slaughters it or sells it, he must pay back five head of cattle for the ox and four sheep for the sheep.

[2]"If a thief is caught breaking in and is struck so that he dies, the defender is not guilty of bloodshed; [3]but if it happens[b] after sunrise, he is guilty of bloodshed.

"A thief must certainly make restitution, but if he has nothing, he must be sold to pay for his theft.

[4]"If the stolen animal is found alive in his possession—whether ox or donkey or sheep—he must pay back double.

[5]"If a man grazes his livestock in a field or vineyard and lets them stray and they graze in another man's field, he must make restitution from the best of his own field or vineyard.

[6]"If a fire breaks out and spreads into thornbushes so that it burns shocks of grain or standing grain or the whole field, the one who started the fire must make restitution.

[7]"If a man gives his neighbor silver or goods for safekeeping and they are stolen from the neighbor's house, the thief, if he is caught, must pay back double. [8]But if the thief is not found, the owner of the house must appear before the judges[c] to determine whether he has laid his hands on the other man's property. [9]In all cases of illegal possession of an ox, a donkey, a sheep, a garment, or any other lost property about which somebody says, 'This is mine,' both parties are to bring their cases before the judges. The one whom the judges declare[d] guilty must pay back double to his neighbor.

[10]"If a man gives a donkey, an ox, a sheep or any other animal to his neighbor for safekeeping and it dies or is injured or is taken away while no one is looking, [11]the issue between them will be settled by the taking of an oath before the LORD that the neighbor

(a) Limiting revenge? (b) Mandating punishment? (c) Deterring crime? (d) Redressing victims? Keeping his chosen people on track? **5.** Rank order these four values to reflect your hierarchy of justice values. **6.** Would you vote for capital punishment if you are among the jurors finding someone guilty of murder, as defined in verse 14? **7.** What do these laws say to the one who believes "Don't get mad, get even"? **8.** How easy is it for you to live up to the standard set forth here? What would be toughest for you to adhere to? **9.** How would you respond to someone, who opposed the death penalty, saying, "The God of the Old Testament was brutal and merciless"?

1. Have you ever had something stolen from you? What happened? How did you feel about that? **2.** As a child, when did you learn a lesson about stealing?

1. What kinds of property are protected? From an inventory of the protected items, what things are important in this society? What does this teach you about the kind of people the Israelites were? **2.** Why doesn't the principle of "eye for eye" apply in crimes against property? What essential difference does this affirm? **3.** What role do judges play? Why are they needed (see ch. 18)? **4.** What extenuating circumstances limit liability? **5.** How would an oath settle an issue in dispute (v. 11)?

1. If you were to rewrite the list of property protected under God's law, what would you include from your world? What does that tell you about today's society? **2.** How do you feel about stealing? How do you define stealing? What about taking office supplies from work? Calling long distance or cellular on someone else's dime? Fudging on your income tax? What criteria should we use to determine whether or not we are stealing from someone or an organization?

[a]32 That is, about 12 ounces (about 0.3 kilogram) [b]3 Or *if he strikes him* [c]8 Or *before God*; also in verse 9 [d]9 Or *whom God declares*

did not lay hands on the other person's property. The owner is to accept this, and no restitution is required. [12]But if the animal was stolen from the neighbor, he must make restitution to the owner. [13]If it was torn to pieces by a wild animal, he shall bring in the remains as evidence and he will not be required to pay for the torn animal.

[14]"If a man borrows an animal from his neighbor and it is injured or dies while the owner is not present, he must make restitution. [15]But if the owner is with the animal, the borrower will not have to pay. If the animal was hired, the money paid for the hire covers the loss.

Social Responsibility

[16]"If a man seduces a virgin who is not pledged to be married and sleeps with her, he must pay the bride-price, and she shall be his wife. [17]If her father absolutely refuses to give her to him, he must still pay the bride-price for virgins.

[18]"Do not allow a sorceress to live.

[19]"Anyone who has sexual relations with an animal must be put to death.

[20]"Whoever sacrifices to any god other than the LORD must be destroyed.[a]

[21]"Do not mistreat an alien or oppress him, for you were aliens in Egypt.

[22]"Do not take advantage of a widow or an orphan. [23]If you do and they cry out to me, I will certainly hear their cry. [24]My anger will be aroused, and I will kill you with the sword; your wives will become widows and your children fatherless.

[25]"If you lend money to one of my people among you who is needy, do not be like a moneylender; charge him no interest.[b] [26]If you take your neighbor's cloak as a pledge, return it to him by sunset, [27]because his cloak is the only covering he has for his body. What else will he sleep in? When he cries out to me, I will hear, for I am compassionate.

[28]"Do not blaspheme God[c] or curse the ruler of your people.

[29]"Do not hold back offerings from your granaries or your vats.[d]

"You must give me the firstborn of your sons. [30]Do the same with your cattle and your sheep. Let them stay with their mothers for seven days, but give them to me on the eighth day.

[31]"You are to be my holy people. So do not eat the meat of an animal torn by wild beasts; throw it to the dogs.

Laws of Justice and Mercy

23 "Do not spread false reports. Do not help a wicked man by being a malicious witness.

[2]"Do not follow the crowd in doing wrong. When you give testimony in a lawsuit, do not pervert justice by siding with the crowd, [3]and do not show favoritism to a poor man in his lawsuit.

[4]"If you come across your enemy's ox or donkey wandering off, be sure to take it back to him. [5]If you see the donkey of someone who hates you fallen down under its load, do not leave it there; be sure you help him with it.

[6]"Do not deny justice to your poor people in their lawsuits. [7]Have nothing to do with a false charge and do not put an innocent or honest person to death, for I will not acquit the guilty.

What outcast or needy group do you most sympathize with in your community? What effect has your involvement had?

1. How do these laws relate to the Ten Commandments? To the sovereignty of God? To your culture? 2. How are the Israelites to be different ("holy") compared to the pagans around them? 3. Who is singled out for special attention by God? What social responsibility does this place on God's people?

1. As a group, whittle these laws into a few principles for social action. What do you come up with? 2. Choose one: Widow, orphan, alien or a poor person. How could your group take responsibility for the special needs of that person? 3. How could you, your church or community align its social programs more with these priorities for "holy" living? What will you do this week in response to become holy people? 4. Have you ever been or are you currently being mistreated or taken advantage of? How does verse 27b sound to you?

When, perhaps as a child, did you get caught in a lie? How did you learn "honesty is the best policy"?

1. To which of the Ten Commandments do these laws relate? How are justice and mercy related here? 2. How do these laws relate to the "see no evil, hear no evil, speak no evil" mentality? 3. What incentive does God give them for doing this?

How can you show justice and mercy to fellow workers, students, customers, family or strangers because of what God has done for you?

---

[a]20 The Hebrew term refers to the irrevocable giving over of things or persons to the LORD, often by totally destroying them.   [b]25 Or *excessive interest*   [c]28 Or *Do not revile the judges*   [d]29 The meaning of the Hebrew for this phrase is uncertain.

[8]"Do not accept a bribe, for a bribe blinds those who see and twists the words of the righteous.

[9]"Do not oppress an alien; you yourselves know how it feels to be aliens, because you were aliens in Egypt.

Sabbath Laws

[10]"For six years you are to sow your fields and harvest the crops, [11]but during the seventh year let the land lie unplowed and unused. Then the poor among your people may get food from it, and the wild animals may eat what they leave. Do the same with your vineyard and your olive grove.

[12]"Six days do your work, but on the seventh day do not work, so that your ox and your donkey may rest and the slave born in your household, and the alien as well, may be refreshed.

[13]"Be careful to do everything I have said to you. Do not invoke the names of other gods; do not let them be heard on your lips.

The Three Annual Festivals

[14]"Three times a year you are to celebrate a festival to me.

[15]"Celebrate the Feast of Unleavened Bread; for seven days eat bread made without yeast, as I commanded you. Do this at the appointed time in the month of Abib, for in that month you came out of Egypt.

"No one is to appear before me empty-handed.

[16]"Celebrate the Feast of Harvest with the firstfruits of the crops you sow in your field.

"Celebrate the Feast of Ingathering at the end of the year, when you gather in your crops from the field.

[17]"Three times a year all the men are to appear before the Sovereign LORD.

[18]"Do not offer the blood of a sacrifice to me along with anything containing yeast.

"The fat of my festival offerings must not be kept until morning.

[19]"Bring the best of the firstfruits of your soil to the house of the LORD your God.

"Do not cook a young goat in its mother's milk.

God's Angel to Prepare the Way

[20]"See, I am sending an angel ahead of you to guard you along the way and to bring you to the place I have prepared. [21]Pay attention to him and listen to what he says. Do not rebel against him; he will not forgive your rebellion, since my Name is in him. [22]If you listen carefully to what he says and do all that I say, I will be an enemy to your enemies and will oppose those who oppose you. [23]My angel will go ahead of you and bring you into the land of the Amorites, Hittites, Perizzites, Canaanites, Hivites and Jebusites, and I will wipe them out. [24]Do not bow down before their gods or worship them or follow their practices. You must demolish them and break their sacred stones to pieces. [25]Worship the LORD your God, and his blessing will be on your food and water. I will take away sickness from among you, [26]and none will miscarry or be barren in your land. I will give you a full life span.

[27]"I will send my terror ahead of you and throw into confusion every nation you encounter. I will make all your enemies turn their backs and run. [28]I will send the hornet ahead of you to drive the Hivites, Canaanites and Hittites out of your way. [29]But I will not drive them out in a single year, because the land would become desolate and the wild animals too numerous for you. [30]Little by

What is your favorite place to relax? To work?

1. What would happen if you followed these laws? How would this be good for you? Bad for you? 2. How does this help you see the reason for these laws? What will you do today to get the spiritual refreshment God wants for you?

What's your favorite holy day and holiday? Why?

1. What do these three festivals celebrate? 2. Why does God forbid sacrifice with leaven, fat to remain overnight, or boiling a kid in its mother's milk (see 12:15; 34:18,26)?

1. What can you or do you do to celebrate God's provision in your life? 2. Where do you contend with the presence of "yeast" (sin) and "blood sacrifice" (forgiveness) in your life? What would it take to remove the yeast and celebrate? Where does Jesus Christ fit in?

1. What kind of driver are you: (a) "Map-reader"? (b) "Keep-driving-til-you-find-it"? (c) Easily lost? (d) "Lead foot"? (e) Scenic "Sunday driver"? (f) Hand-on-the-horn-road-hog? 2. What about your life is like the way you drive?

1. Why tell Israel that God is sending his angel to prepare their way? 2. How else does God ensure that Israel will reach their goal? What do health and fertility have to do with that (vv. 25,26,30)? 3. What conditions or roadblocks are put on them?

1. Would you rather have God's game plan for you all laid out from the outset, or revealed one step at a time? Why? 2. Where in the world are you headed? Who in that world poses a threat to your faith? 3. Do you tend to focus on

God's warnings or God's promises? Why? Why is God emphatic on driving out the people native to the land?

---

1. How do you rate yourself at keeping promises? (How might other people rate you?) 2. As a young child, how did you picture God?

1. What surprise twists in plot do you see in this drama since 20:21? 2. How does the voice of the people strike you (vv. 3,7): Idealistic? Realistic? Self-defeating? Enthusiastic? Boastful? 3. Do you think either Moses or God expected the people to meet all their covenant duties? Why or why not? 4. Who makes this covenant between the people and God? What did the blood on the altar signify? The blood sprinkled on the people? 5. In what sense do the men "see" God (vv. 9–11,15–18)? What is God like: Sapphire? Consuming fire? Dense fog? Well-camouflaged? 6. Why does God let Moses and the seventy see him but not Moses alone? Why does God make Moses wait six days? 7. How can any person claim to have "seen" God (see Jn 1:18)? What about Jacob (see Ge 32:30)? Even Moses early on (3:6) and later on (33:20–23)?

1. In what sense have you seen God: In Christ? In others? In church? In Bible study? 2. What kinds of promises have you made to God? Have you found it difficult to keep these promises? Why or why not? 3. Is God's covenant with his people, then and now, sustained by their obedience, or by his grace? Why do you think so? How will that affect your promise-making, today?

When are you most generous? (a) Right after payday? (b) To fill a need that you see? (c) To meet a pledge? (d) Every time you are asked? When are you most stingy?

1. Why did God want them to collect these things? Where does God dwell now? What

---

little I will drive them out before you, until you have increased enough to take possession of the land.

31"I will establish your borders from the Red Sea[a] to the Sea of the Philistines,[b] and from the desert to the River.[c] I will hand over to you the people who live in the land and you will drive them out before you. 32Do not make a covenant with them or with their gods. 33Do not let them live in your land, or they will cause you to sin against me, because the worship of their gods will certainly be a snare to you."

The Covenant Confirmed

24 Then he said to Moses, "Come up to the LORD, you and Aaron, Nadab and Abihu, and seventy of the elders of Israel. You are to worship at a distance, 2but Moses alone is to approach the LORD; the others must not come near. And the people may not come up with him."

3When Moses went and told the people all the LORD's words and laws, they responded with one voice, "Everything the LORD has said we will do." 4Moses then wrote down everything the LORD had said.

He got up early the next morning and built an altar at the foot of the mountain and set up twelve stone pillars representing the twelve tribes of Israel. 5Then he sent young Israelite men, and they offered burnt offerings and sacrificed young bulls as fellowship offerings[d] to the LORD. 6Moses took half of the blood and put it in bowls, and the other half he sprinkled on the altar. 7Then he took the Book of the Covenant and read it to the people. They responded, "We will do everything the LORD has said; we will obey."

8Moses then took the blood, sprinkled it on the people and said, "This is the blood of the covenant that the LORD has made with you in accordance with all these words."

9Moses and Aaron, Nadab and Abihu, and the seventy elders of Israel went up 10and saw the God of Israel. Under his feet was something like a pavement made of sapphire,[e] clear as the sky itself. 11But God did not raise his hand against these leaders of the Israelites; they saw God, and they ate and drank.

12The LORD said to Moses, "Come up to me on the mountain and stay here, and I will give you the tablets of stone, with the law and commands I have written for their instruction."

13Then Moses set out with Joshua his aide, and Moses went up on the mountain of God. 14He said to the elders, "Wait here for us until we come back to you. Aaron and Hur are with you, and anyone involved in a dispute can go to them."

15When Moses went up on the mountain, the cloud covered it, 16and the glory of the LORD settled on Mount Sinai. For six days the cloud covered the mountain, and on the seventh day the LORD called to Moses from within the cloud. 17To the Israelites the glory of the LORD looked like a consuming fire on top of the mountain. 18Then Moses entered the cloud as he went on up the mountain. And he stayed on the mountain forty days and forty nights.

Offerings for the Tabernacle

25 The LORD said to Moses, 2"Tell the Israelites to bring me an offering. You are to receive the offering for me from each man whose heart prompts him to give. 3These are the offerings you are to receive from them: gold, silver and bronze; 4blue, purple and scarlet yarn and fine linen; goat hair; 5ram skins dyed red and hides

---

[a]31 Hebrew *Yam Suph*; that is, Sea of Reeds　　　[b]31 That is, the Mediterranean
[c]31 That is, the Euphrates　　　[d]5 Traditionally *peace offerings*　　　[e]10 Or *lapis lazuli*

of sea cows[a]; acacia wood; [6]olive oil for the light; spices for the anointing oil and for the fragrant incense; [7]and onyx stones and other gems to be mounted on the ephod and breastpiece.

[8]"Then have them make a sanctuary for me, and I will dwell among them. [9]Make this tabernacle and all its furnishings exactly like the pattern I will show you.

The Ark

[10]"Have them make a chest of acacia wood—two and a half cubits long, a cubit and a half wide, and a cubit and a half high.[b] [11]Overlay it with pure gold, both inside and out, and make a gold molding around it. [12]Cast four gold rings for it and fasten them to its four feet, with two rings on one side and two rings on the other. [13]Then make poles of acacia wood and overlay them with gold. [14]Insert the poles into the rings on the sides of the chest to carry it. [15]The poles are to remain in the rings of this ark; they are not to be removed. [16]Then put in the ark the Testimony, which I will give you.

[17]"Make an atonement cover[c] of pure gold—two and a half cubits long and a cubit and a half wide.[d] [18]And make two cherubim out of hammered gold at the ends of the cover. [19]Make one cherub on one end and the second cherub on the other; make the cherubim of one piece with the cover, at the two ends. [20]The cherubim are to have their wings spread upward, overshadowing the cover with them. The cherubim are to face each other, looking toward the cover. [21]Place the cover on top of the ark and put in the ark the Testimony, which I will give you. [22]There, above the cover between the two cherubim that are over the ark of the Testimony, I will meet with you and give you all my commands for the Israelites.

The Table

[23]"Make a table of acacia wood—two cubits long, a cubit wide and a cubit and a half high.[e] [24]Overlay it with pure gold and make a gold molding around it. [25]Also make around it a rim a handbreadth[f] wide and put a gold molding on the rim. [26]Make four gold rings for the table and fasten them to the four corners, where the four legs are. [27]The rings are to be close to the rim to hold the poles used in carrying the table. [28]Make the poles of acacia wood, overlay them with gold and carry the table with them. [29]And make its plates and dishes of pure gold, as well as its pitchers and bowls for the pouring out of offerings. [30]Put the bread of the Presence on this table to be before me at all times.

The Lampstand

[31]"Make a lampstand of pure gold and hammer it out, base and shaft; its flowerlike cups, buds and blossoms shall be of one piece with it. [32]Six branches are to extend from the sides of the lampstand—three on one side and three on the other. [33]Three cups shaped like almond flowers with buds and blossoms are to be on one branch, three on the next branch, and the same for all six branches extending from the lampstand. [34]And on the lampstand there are to be four cups shaped like almond flowers with buds and blossoms. [35]One bud shall be under the first pair of branches ex-

---

[a]5 That is, dugongs   [b]10 That is, about 3 3/4 feet (about 1.1 meters) long and 2 1/4 feet (about 0.7 meter) wide and high   [c]17 Traditionally a mercy seat   [d]17 That is, about 3 3/4 feet (about 1.1 meters) long and 2 1/4 feet (about 0.7 meter) wide   [e]23 That is, about 3 feet (about 0.9 meter) long and 1 1/2 feet (about 0.5 meter) wide and 2 1/4 feet (about 0.7 meter) high   [f]25 That is, about 3 inches (about 8 centimeters)

---

changed? 2. What need has God for such riches? Will their offerings secure God's relationship?

What heirlooms or treasures do you have in an old trunk stashed in your attic or basement?

1. As a cubit was about 18 inches, how big was this "treasure chest" (ark)? What in your home would compare in size? 2. What memories should this ark rekindle for the Israelites? What is this "Testimony" (see 31:18)? 3. Why should the ark be portable? How does it signify their relationship with God? 4. Since graven images are prohibited (see 20:4ff), why are the cherubim on the ark's cover?

What might you carry around with you to remind you of God's past actions and continuing presence in your life?

What was your first table grace? What do you say now?

1. What does this table and gold say about God's relationship with his people? 2. What is the "bread of the Presence" (see Lev 24:5–9)? Why is this a perpetual element?

How does this table for the Lord compare to your church's?

What do you enjoy most about your favorite lamp in the house: (a) Home-made? (b) Its value? (c) Location? (d) Light?

1. What features define the lamp described here? Why the number seven? The blossom motif? The pure gold? 2. Why did God tell them to build this lamp? What did its light represent for early Israel? What did this lamp represent for the early Church (see Heb 8:5; Rev 1–3)?

1. Do you think this pattern set forth by Moses is necessary to adequately worship God? 2.

What one way can you brighten your lamp to reflect God's powerful light in your life?

---

1. What is the most awesome church building you can remember being in? Did this building make you feel like worshiping God? Why or why not? 2. What is the most unlikely place you have ever worshiped? What drew your attention to God?

1. Why did the Israelites need a tabernacle? What had they been using in the meantime (see 33:7–11)? 2. Based on the "blue print" here, work as a group to determine the dimensions of the tabernacle. (A cubit equals about 18 inches.) To what can you compare the total size of this structure? 3. What jobs do you see in action here? Who in your group might aspire to be the architect? The structural engineer? Foreman? Weaver? Goldsmith? Interior decorator? Laborer? Embroiderer? 4. Why do you think there is such precision as to the sizes, the colors and the materials of the different parts used in the construction of the tabernacle? What do these materials tell you about the lifestyle of Israelites? About the nature of God? 5. What about the arrangement and purpose of the furnishings draws your attention to God? Why, for example, were the Holy Place and Most Holy Place separated (vv. 33–35)? Why was the ark placed behind the curtain, out of view?

1. When Jesus died, the curtain in the temple tore from top to bottom (see Mk 15:38; Heb 10:19–22). Why was this good news to his followers? What bad news do you see in the fact that God still separates himself from humanity, in that "a veil covers their hearts" (see 2Co 3:14–15)? What does this say about the kind of relationship he wants, that only he can establish? 2. How do you think it affected those Israelite craftsmen to be asked to use their skills for God's purposes? What unusual skills have you used to glorify God? How do you feel when you use your skills to glorify God? 3. If you

tending from the lampstand, a second bud under the second pair, and a third bud under the third pair—six branches in all. 36The buds and branches shall all be of one piece with the lampstand, hammered out of pure gold.

37"Then make its seven lamps and set them up on it so that they light the space in front of it. 38Its wick trimmers and trays are to be of pure gold. 39A talent*a* of pure gold is to be used for the lampstand and all these accessories. 40See that you make them according to the pattern shown you on the mountain.

The Tabernacle

26 "Make the tabernacle with ten curtains of finely twisted linen and blue, purple and scarlet yarn, with cherubim worked into them by a skilled craftsman. 2All the curtains are to be the same size—twenty-eight cubits long and four cubits wide.*b* 3Join five of the curtains together, and do the same with the other five. 4Make loops of blue material along the edge of the end curtain in one set, and do the same with the end curtain in the other set. 5Make fifty loops on one curtain and fifty loops on the end curtain of the other set, with the loops opposite each other. 6Then make fifty gold clasps and use them to fasten the curtains together so that the tabernacle is a unit.

7"Make curtains of goat hair for the tent over the tabernacle—eleven altogether. 8All eleven curtains are to be the same size—thirty cubits long and four cubits wide.*c* 9Join five of the curtains together into one set and the other six into another set. Fold the sixth curtain double at the front of the tent. 10Make fifty loops along the edge of the end curtain in one set and also along the edge of the end curtain in the other set. 11Then make fifty bronze clasps and put them in the loops to fasten the tent together as a unit. 12As for the additional length of the tent curtains, the half curtain that is left over is to hang down at the rear of the tabernacle. 13The tent curtains will be a cubit*d* longer on both sides; what is left will hang over the sides of the tabernacle so as to cover it. 14Make for the tent a covering of ram skins dyed red, and over that a covering of hides of sea cows.*e*

15"Make upright frames of acacia wood for the tabernacle. 16Each frame is to be ten cubits long and a cubit and a half wide,*f* 17with two projections set parallel to each other. Make all the frames of the tabernacle in this way. 18Make twenty frames for the south side of the tabernacle 19and make forty silver bases to go under them—two bases for each frame, one under each projection. 20For the other side, the north side of the tabernacle, make twenty frames 21and forty silver bases—two under each frame. 22Make six frames for the far end, that is, the west end of the tabernacle, 23and make two frames for the corners at the far end. 24At these two corners they must be double from the bottom all the way to the top, and fitted into a single ring; both shall be like that. 25So there will be eight frames and sixteen silver bases—two under each frame.

26"Also make crossbars of acacia wood: five for the frames on one side of the tabernacle, 27five for those on the other side, and five for the frames on the west, at the far end of the tabernacle. 28The center crossbar is to extend from end to end at the middle of

---

a39 That is, about 75 pounds (about 34 kilograms)   *b2* That is, about 42 feet (about 12.5 meters) long and 6 feet (about 1.8 meters) wide   *c8* That is, about 45 feet (about 13.5 meters) long and 6 feet (about 1.8 meters) wide   *d13* That is, about 1 1/2 feet (about 0.5 meter)   *e14* That is, dugongs   *f16* That is, about 15 feet (about 4.5 meters) long and 2 1/4 feet (about 0.7 meter) wide

the frames. ²⁹Overlay the frames with gold and make gold rings to hold the crossbars. Also overlay the crossbars with gold.

³⁰"Set up the tabernacle according to the plan shown you on the mountain.

³¹"Make a curtain of blue, purple and scarlet yarn and finely twisted linen, with cherubim worked into it by a skilled craftsman. ³²Hang it with gold hooks on four posts of acacia wood overlaid with gold and standing on four silver bases. ³³Hang the curtain from the clasps and place the ark of the Testimony behind the curtain. The curtain will separate the Holy Place from the Most Holy Place. ³⁴Put the atonement cover on the ark of the Testimony in the Most Holy Place. ³⁵Place the table outside the curtain on the north side of the tabernacle and put the lampstand opposite it on the south side.

³⁶"For the entrance to the tent make a curtain of blue, purple and scarlet yarn and finely twisted linen—the work of an embroiderer. ³⁷Make gold hooks for this curtain and five posts of acacia wood overlaid with gold. And cast five bronze bases for them.

The Altar of Burnt Offering

27 "Build an altar of acacia wood, three cubits[a] high; it is to be square, five cubits long and five cubits wide.[b] ²Make a horn at each of the four corners, so that the horns and the altar are of one piece, and overlay the altar with bronze. ³Make all its utensils of bronze—its pots to remove the ashes, and its shovels, sprinkling bowls, meat forks and firepans. ⁴Make a grating for it, a bronze network, and make a bronze ring at each of the four corners of the network. ⁵Put it under the ledge of the altar so that it is halfway up the altar. ⁶Make poles of acacia wood for the altar and overlay them with bronze. ⁷The poles are to be inserted into the rings so they will be on two sides of the altar when it is carried. ⁸Make the altar hollow, out of boards. It is to be made just as you were shown on the mountain.

The Courtyard

⁹"Make a courtyard for the tabernacle. The south side shall be a hundred cubits[c] long and is to have curtains of finely twisted linen, ¹⁰with twenty posts and twenty bronze bases and with silver hooks and bands on the posts. ¹¹The north side shall also be a hundred cubits long and is to have curtains, with twenty posts and twenty bronze bases and with silver hooks and bands on the posts.

¹²"The west end of the courtyard shall be fifty cubits[d] wide and have curtains, with ten posts and ten bases. ¹³On the east end, toward the sunrise, the courtyard shall also be fifty cubits wide. ¹⁴Curtains fifteen cubits[e] long are to be on one side of the entrance, with three posts and three bases, ¹⁵and curtains fifteen cubits long are to be on the other side, with three posts and three bases.

¹⁶"For the entrance to the courtyard, provide a curtain twenty cubits[f] long, of blue, purple and scarlet yarn and finely twisted linen—the work of an embroiderer—with four posts and four bases. ¹⁷All the posts around the courtyard are to have silver bands and hooks, and bronze bases. ¹⁸The courtyard shall be a hundred cubits long and fifty cubits wide,[g] with curtains of finely twisted

---

a1 That is, about 4 1/2 feet (about 1.3 meters)   b1 That is, about 7 1/2 feet (about 2.3 meters) long and wide   c9 That is, about 150 feet (about 46 meters); also in verse 11   d12 That is, about 75 feet (about 23 meters); also in verse 13   e14 That is, about 22 1/2 feet (about 6.9 meters); also in verse 15   f16 That is, about 30 feet (about 9 meters)   g18 That is, about 150 feet (about 46 meters) long and 75 feet (about 23 meters) wide

---

could design and build a special place where you could feel close to God, what would it be like? How big would it be? How would you furnish it? What would be the focal point? **4.** How do you "come into God's presence" when you can't go to church or some other special place of worship? What makes this challenging?

---

1. How do we know this was an altar for burnt offerings (see Lev 4:7,10,18)? **2.** What distinguishes this altar from God's throne room (ch. 26)?

1. Why such emphasis on physical setting and details? What does this say about worship, then and now? **2.** What is the "altar" where you give an accounting to your Lord: (a) Your calendar? (b) Checkbook? (c) Small group? (d) Confessional?

---

1. What is inviting about the entry way to your house? **2.** What's the best thing about a candle-lit dinner for two?

1. Why was the tabernacle fenced in? How many entrances were there? **2.** Does the physical layout of the courtyard enhance worship of God? Explain how and why. **3.** For whose sake were the lamps to be kept burning? Why? **4.** Imagine you are walking into the Tabernacle, what does it look like?

1. Compare your small group to this "courtyard" for God. Who does your small group attract? Who do you keep out? What entry point to your church does your small group provide? **2.** How might you re-arrange things so that more people feel drawn to God through your group? **3.** Have you entered through the curtain into God's presence? Or are you tiptoeing to see what's on the other side? Or are you feeling that church is a "closed shop" to you?

Why? **4.** Do you often burn the candle at both ends, night and day? What for?

What do your clothes say about you? What is your favorite piece of clothing?

Why the special garments for Aaron and his sons? Could they have done their job effectively without them?

Do you dress differently for church than on other days? Why? Is that good or bad?

If you were to write a book, whose name(s) would appear on the dedication page?

1. Whose names were to be engraved on the stones (vv. 9–11; see Ge 35:23–26)? What would their names memorialize? **2.** What do these names suggest about the priest's role in relation to the people and God?

Whose faith has been a foundation for yours?

---

1. What kind of decision-maker are you: (a) Procrastinator? (b) Impulsive? (c) Pass the buck? (d) Prone to "buyer's regret"? (e) Cast lots or draw straws? **2.** What is your most impressive suit of clothing? When do you wear it? Why at these times?

1. How exactly do the priests go about making decisions for the people (v. 30; see Pr 16:33)? **2.** What other duties of the priest do you see here, especially in the bearing of the names? **3.** How would this elaborate breastpiece help Aaron's decision-mak-

---

linen five cubits[a] high, and with bronze bases. ¹⁹All the other articles used in the service of the tabernacle, whatever their function, including all the tent pegs for it and those for the courtyard, are to be of bronze.

Oil for the Lampstand

²⁰"Command the Israelites to bring you clear oil of pressed olives for the light so that the lamps may be kept burning. ²¹In the Tent of Meeting, outside the curtain that is in front of the Testimony, Aaron and his sons are to keep the lamps burning before the LORD from evening till morning. This is to be a lasting ordinance among the Israelites for the generations to come.

The Priestly Garments

28 "Have Aaron your brother brought to you from among the Israelites, along with his sons Nadab and Abihu, Eleazar and Ithamar, so they may serve me as priests. ²Make sacred garments for your brother Aaron, to give him dignity and honor. ³Tell all the skilled men to whom I have given wisdom in such matters that they are to make garments for Aaron, for his consecration, so he may serve me as priest. ⁴These are the garments they are to make: a breastpiece, an ephod, a robe, a woven tunic, a turban and a sash. They are to make these sacred garments for your brother Aaron and his sons, so they may serve me as priests. ⁵Have them use gold, and blue, purple and scarlet yarn, and fine linen.

The Ephod

⁶"Make the ephod of gold, and of blue, purple and scarlet yarn, and of finely twisted linen—the work of a skilled craftsman. ⁷It is to have two shoulder pieces attached to two of its corners, so it can be fastened. ⁸Its skillfully woven waistband is to be like it—of one piece with the ephod and made with gold, and with blue, purple and scarlet yarn, and with finely twisted linen.

⁹"Take two onyx stones and engrave on them the names of the sons of Israel ¹⁰in the order of their birth—six names on one stone and the remaining six on the other. ¹¹Engrave the names of the sons of Israel on the two stones the way a gem cutter engraves a seal. Then mount the stones in gold filigree settings ¹²and fasten them on the shoulder pieces of the ephod as memorial stones for the sons of Israel. Aaron is to bear the names on his shoulders as a memorial before the LORD. ¹³Make gold filigree settings ¹⁴and two braided chains of pure gold, like a rope, and attach the chains to the settings.

The Breastpiece

¹⁵"Fashion a breastpiece for making decisions—the work of a skilled craftsman. Make it like the ephod: of gold, and of blue, purple and scarlet yarn, and of finely twisted linen. ¹⁶It is to be square—a span[b] long and a span wide—and folded double. ¹⁷Then mount four rows of precious stones on it. In the first row there shall be a ruby, a topaz and a beryl; ¹⁸in the second row a turquoise, a sapphire[c] and an emerald; ¹⁹in the third row a jacinth, an agate and an amethyst; ²⁰in the fourth row a chrysolite, an onyx and a jasper.[d] Mount them in gold filigree settings. ²¹There are to be twelve stones, one for each of the names of the

---

[a]18 That is, about 7 1/2 feet (about 2.3 meters)   [b]16 That is, about 9 inches (about 22 centimeters)   [c]18 Or *lapis lazuli*   [d]20 The precise identification of some of these precious stones is uncertain.

sons of Israel, each engraved like a seal with the name of one of the twelve tribes.

²²"For the breastpiece make braided chains of pure gold, like a rope. ²³Make two gold rings for it and fasten them to two corners of the breastpiece. ²⁴Fasten the two gold chains to the rings at the corners of the breastpiece, ²⁵and the other ends of the chains to the two settings, attaching them to the shoulder pieces of the ephod at the front. ²⁶Make two gold rings and attach them to the other two corners of the breastpiece on the inside edge next to the ephod. ²⁷Make two more gold rings and attach them to the bottom of the shoulder pieces on the front of the ephod, close to the seam just above the waistband of the ephod. ²⁸The rings of the breastpiece are to be tied to the rings of the ephod with blue cord, connecting it to the waistband, so that the breastpiece will not swing out from the ephod.

²⁹"Whenever Aaron enters the Holy Place, he will bear the names of the sons of Israel over his heart on the breastpiece of decision as a continuing memorial before the LORD. ³⁰Also put the Urim and the Thummim in the breastpiece, so they may be over Aaron's heart whenever he enters the presence of the LORD. Thus Aaron will always bear the means of making decisions for the Israelites over his heart before the LORD.

Other Priestly Garments

³¹"Make the robe of the ephod entirely of blue cloth, ³²with an opening for the head in its center. There shall be a woven edge like a collar^a around this opening, so that it will not tear. ³³Make pomegranates of blue, purple and scarlet yarn around the hem of the robe, with gold bells between them. ³⁴The gold bells and the pomegranates are to alternate around the hem of the robe. ³⁵Aaron must wear it when he ministers. The sound of the bells will be heard when he enters the Holy Place before the LORD and when he comes out, so that he will not die.

³⁶"Make a plate of pure gold and engrave on it as on a seal: HOLY TO THE LORD. ³⁷Fasten a blue cord to it to attach it to the turban; it is to be on the front of the turban. ³⁸It will be on Aaron's forehead, and he will bear the guilt involved in the sacred gifts the Israelites consecrate, whatever their gifts may be. It will be on Aaron's forehead continually so that they will be acceptable to the LORD.

³⁹"Weave the tunic of fine linen and make the turban of fine linen. The sash is to be the work of an embroiderer. ⁴⁰Make tunics, sashes and headbands for Aaron's sons, to give them dignity and honor. ⁴¹After you put these clothes on your brother Aaron and his sons, anoint and ordain them. Consecrate them so they may serve me as priests.

⁴²"Make linen undergarments as a covering for the body, reaching from the waist to the thigh. ⁴³Aaron and his sons must wear them whenever they enter the Tent of Meeting or approach the altar to minister in the Holy Place, so that they will not incur guilt and die.

"This is to be a lasting ordinance for Aaron and his descendants.

Consecration of the Priests

29 "This is what you are to do to consecrate them, so they may serve me as priests: Take a young bull and two rams without defect. ²And from fine wheat flour, without yeast, make bread, and cakes mixed with oil, and wafers spread with oil. ³Put them in

^a32 The meaning of the Hebrew for this word is uncertain.

---

ing? What do you think is the "Urim and Thummim"? **4.** How does this way of making decisions differ from Jethro's idea of decentralized decision-making (see 18:13–23)?

1. How do you determine what is the will of God in a particular situation? Whose names are engraved on your "breastplate of decision-making"? **2.** What kind of decisions are your pastor and church leaders required to make? How do they know God's will for sure? **3.** Are they alone with God in their decision-making? How might you support them in this?

---

1. What colors do you wear most often? What do they make you feel like? **2.** Are any of your clothes home-made? Which one is most special to you? Why?

1. What do clothes and bells have to do with nearing God? **2.** With the tabernacle (furnishings and priestly garments), how are all five senses satisfied in worship? **3.** What do these colorful images, costly materials, lively sounds and pungent smells say about God, the priests and the people? **4.** The gold-plated, "Holy to the Lord," served what purpose: Reminder? Exhortation? Hope? **5.** The linen underwear served what purpose (vv. 42–43)?

How do you think the other Israelites felt about Aaron, who risked his life to take their guilt to God? How do you feel toward Christ for doing the same thing, and more, for you?

---

1. Which of your past spiritual leaders has made the deepest impression at a formative stage in your life? What set that person apart from the rest? **2.** Have you ever attended an ordination service for someone entering the ministry? What was it like? **3.**

What experience have you had with week-long church camps, week-long honeymoons, or any week-long celebration? How would you describe your feelings?

1. What is the basic order of events for an ordination service? Which parts of the service would seem most complex to a first-time participant? 2. From the complex dynamics of this service, define "consecration" and "ordination." From verses 44–46, what does such consecration do for God? For the priest? For the people? 3. In this detailed service of installing priests, God seeks to ensure the sacredness and completeness of any and all sacrifices to him. How does each element of the service, in turn, serve this larger purpose of God? For example, what was the purpose of the washing (v. 4; see Heb 10:22)? Of new garments (vv. 5–6) which are later re-used (vv. 29–30)? 4. What was indispensable about the anointing oil (v. 7; see Isa 61:1)? The laying on of hands (vv. 10,15,19)? The sprinkling of blood (vv. 16,20)? The burnt sin offering (vv. 13–14)? The wave offering (vv. 23–26)? The ram for ordination and eating (vv. 31–34)? 5. Why apply blood to the right ears, the right thumbs and their right big toe (v. 20)? Do you think the consecration process could have taken place without the any of these? Why or why not? 6. Why would God choose sacrifice of animals and sprinkling of blood for the consecration process? What does this say about the importance of a right relationship with God? 7. What facets of the consecration are seven days long and which are offered daily? Is ordination a "once-for-all-time" event or a continual process?

1. Do you think ritual consecration of ministers is as important for the Church today as it was for ancient Israel? Why or why not? Were these rituals mainly for God's benefit, the priest's benefit, or the people's benefit? Why? 2. Is consecration for all believers, or only for "professional" ministers? Why? 3. What do you do that consecrates yourself for the Lord's work—either daily, annually or once-for-all? What part does ritual play in that? Does ritual draw you closer to God, or does it hinder your ability to feel his presence? 4. Who among your church leaders (lay and clergy) would you want to

a basket and present them in it—along with the bull and the two rams. ⁴Then bring Aaron and his sons to the entrance to the Tent of Meeting and wash them with water. ⁵Take the garments and dress Aaron with the tunic, the robe of the ephod, the ephod itself and the breastpiece. Fasten the ephod on him by its skillfully woven waistband. ⁶Put the turban on his head and attach the sacred diadem to the turban. ⁷Take the anointing oil and anoint him by pouring it on his head. ⁸Bring his sons and dress them in tunics ⁹and put headbands on them. Then tie sashes on Aaron and his sons.ᵃ The priesthood is theirs by a lasting ordinance. In this way you shall ordain Aaron and his sons.

¹⁰"Bring the bull to the front of the Tent of Meeting, and Aaron and his sons shall lay their hands on its head. ¹¹Slaughter it in the Lord's presence at the entrance to the Tent of Meeting. ¹²Take some of the bull's blood and put it on the horns of the altar with your finger, and pour out the rest of it at the base of the altar. ¹³Then take all the fat around the inner parts, the covering of the liver, and both kidneys with the fat on them, and burn them on the altar. ¹⁴But burn the bull's flesh and its hide and its offal outside the camp. It is a sin offering.

¹⁵"Take one of the rams, and Aaron and his sons shall lay their hands on its head. ¹⁶Slaughter it and take the blood and sprinkle it against the altar on all sides. ¹⁷Cut the ram into pieces and wash the inner parts and the legs, putting them with the head and the other pieces. ¹⁸Then burn the entire ram on the altar. It is a burnt offering to the Lord, a pleasing aroma, an offering made to the Lord by fire.

¹⁹"Take the other ram, and Aaron and his sons shall lay their hands on its head. ²⁰Slaughter it, take some of its blood and put it on the lobes of the right ears of Aaron and his sons, on the thumbs of their right hands, and on the big toes of their right feet. Then sprinkle blood against the altar on all sides. ²¹And take some of the blood on the altar and some of the anointing oil and sprinkle it on Aaron and his garments and on his sons and their garments. Then he and his sons and their garments will be consecrated.

²²"Take from this ram the fat, the fat tail, the fat around the inner parts, the covering of the liver, both kidneys with the fat on them, and the right thigh. (This is the ram for the ordination.) ²³From the basket of bread made without yeast, which is before the Lord, take a loaf, and a cake made with oil, and a wafer. ²⁴Put all these in the hands of Aaron and his sons and wave them before the Lord as a wave offering. ²⁵Then take them from their hands and burn them on the altar along with the burnt offering for a pleasing aroma to the Lord, an offering made to the Lord by fire. ²⁶After you take the breast of the ram for Aaron's ordination, wave it before the Lord as a wave offering, and it will be your share.

²⁷"Consecrate those parts of the ordination ram that belong to Aaron and his sons: the breast that was waved and the thigh that was presented. ²⁸This is always to be the regular share from the Israelites for Aaron and his sons. It is the contribution the Israelites are to make to the Lord from their fellowship offerings.ᵇ

²⁹"Aaron's sacred garments will belong to his descendants so that they can be anointed and ordained in them. ³⁰The son who succeeds him as priest and comes to the Tent of Meeting to minister in the Holy Place is to wear them seven days.

³¹"Take the ram for the ordination and cook the meat in a sacred place. ³²At the entrance to the Tent of Meeting, Aaron and his sons

ᵃ9 Hebrew; Septuagint *on them*   ᵇ28 Traditionally *peace offerings*

are to eat the meat of the ram and the bread that is in the basket.
[33]They are to eat these offerings by which atonement was made for
their ordination and consecration. But no one else may eat them,
because they are sacred. [34]And if any of the meat of the ordination
ram or any bread is left over till morning, burn it up. It must not be
eaten, because it is sacred.

[35]"Do for Aaron and his sons everything I have commanded you,
taking seven days to ordain them. [36]Sacrifice a bull each day as a
sin offering to make atonement. Purify the altar by making atonement for it, and anoint it to consecrate it. [37]For seven days make
atonement for the altar and consecrate it. Then the altar will be
most holy, and whatever touches it will be holy.

[38]"This is what you are to offer on the altar regularly each day:
two lambs a year old. [39]Offer one in the morning and the other at
twilight. [40]With the first lamb offer a tenth of an ephah[a] of fine
flour mixed with a quarter of a hin[b] of oil from pressed olives, and
a quarter of a hin of wine as a drink offering. [41]Sacrifice the other
lamb at twilight with the same grain offering and its drink offering
as in the morning—a pleasing aroma, an offering made to the LORD
by fire.

[42]"For the generations to come this burnt offering is to be made
regularly at the entrance to the Tent of Meeting before the LORD.
There I will meet you and speak to you; [43]there also I will meet
with the Israelites, and the place will be consecrated by my glory.

[44]"So I will consecrate the Tent of Meeting and the altar and will
consecrate Aaron and his sons to serve me as priests. [45]Then I will
dwell among the Israelites and be their God. [46]They will know that
I am the LORD their God, who brought them out of Egypt so that I
might dwell among them. I am the LORD their God.

The Altar of Incense

30 "Make an altar of acacia wood for burning incense. [2]It is to
be square, a cubit long and a cubit wide, and two cubits
high[c]—its horns of one piece with it. [3]Overlay the top and all the
sides and the horns with pure gold, and make a gold molding
around it. [4]Make two gold rings for the altar below the molding—
two on opposite sides—to hold the poles used to carry it. [5]Make
the poles of acacia wood and overlay them with gold. [6]Put the altar
in front of the curtain that is before the ark of the Testimony—before the atonement cover that is over the Testimony—where I will
meet with you.

[7]"Aaron must burn fragrant incense on the altar every morning
when he tends the lamps. [8]He must burn incense again when he
lights the lamps at twilight so incense will burn regularly before
the LORD for the generations to come. [9]Do not offer on this altar any
other incense or any burnt offering or grain offering, and do not
pour a drink offering on it. [10]Once a year Aaron shall make atonement on its horns. This annual atonement must be made with the
blood of the atoning sin offering for the generations to come. It is
most holy to the LORD."

Atonement Money

[11]Then the LORD said to Moses, [12]"When you take a census of the
Israelites to count them, each one must pay the LORD a ransom for

lay hands on you and set you apart
for some special task? For what
mission would you have (or have
you had) this special dedication or
commissioning? 5. What other elements of the consecration ceremony in this passage might you include in commissioning you to
serve in the church? What elements of this ceremony have you
seen adopted for use in the ordination of others? 6. The process of
consecration and the offering of
sacrifices was a very precise,
bloody, and time-consuming process. Do you think the priests and
the Israelites considered it a worthwhile endeavor? Why? Do your efforts to devote yourself to God ever
seem burdensome? Why or why
not?

1. What images come to
mind when you smell in-
cense: Drug pushers? Lifeless ritual? Religious high? Alien culture?
2. If you could choose a Christian
fragrance, what would it be: (a) Floral (sweet and uplifting)? (b) Cajun
(spicy and eye-watering)? (c) Old
socks (stinky and unapproachable)? (d) Home-cooking (reassuring and appealing)? 3. What smells
can you identify in the room: Who
is wearing perfume or after-shave?
Who can smell the room freshen-
er? The cooking? The outdoors? 4.
Compare all your answers: Whose
nose knows the most? (Congratu-
lations!)

1. What does incense, as
used here, symbolize (see
Ps 141:2; Rev 5:8; 8:3–5)? Where
is it placed? When does it burn?
Who attends it? 2. What meaning
does the incense have when God
is present to meet his own (vv.
6,36)? What meaning does it have
the rest of the time when no people
are present? 3. What were the benefits (spiritual and military) to the
Israelites of census-taking (v. 12;

---

[a]40 That is, probably about 2 quarts (about 2 liters)   [b]40 That is, probably about 1
quart (about 1 liter)   [c]2 That is, about 1 1/2 feet (about 0.5 meter) long and wide
and about 3 feet (about 0.9 meter) high

see Nu 26:2)? **4.** What is a "ransom"? How is it like or unlike a bribe, tax or premium due? Why did the Lord require a ransom? On what basis were rich and poor ransomed? **5.** What could be the symbolism of the priest's regular washing (vv. 17–21)? What effect on their relationship with God was this washing intended to make? What abuses is this practice open to (see Mk 7:1–23)? **6.** After sacrificing the animals and applying blood and water to the priests, what was the purpose of the perfume (vv. 22–33)? Why was it so fragrant and so sacred? **7.** What fear of the Lord is attached to these oils and incense (vv. 32–33,37–38)? Who has a monopoly on these products? Why?

♡ **1.** Do you "smell" like a Christian? How can you tell? What reaction from others would you expect if you did? **2.** How can you become a "fragrant aroma" to God (see 2Co 2:14–16)? What burning releases your heavenly aroma? **3.** How, in your busy life, can you keep the incense of prayer burning, always? **4.** What "ransom payment" has superseded the need for all others (see 1Ti 2:5–6)? In response, or in addition, what do you feel you owe to God? What symbolic ransom payment have you made to God? **5.** How have you been washed clean (see Heb 10:19–22)? What affect does this have on your worship of God?

his life at the time he is counted. Then no plague will come on them when you number them. [13]Each one who crosses over to those already counted is to give a half shekel,[a] according to the sanctuary shekel, which weighs twenty gerahs. This half shekel is an offering to the LORD. [14]All who cross over, those twenty years old or more, are to give an offering to the LORD. [15]The rich are not to give more than a half shekel and the poor are not to give less when you make the offering to the LORD to atone for your lives. [16]Receive the atonement money from the Israelites and use it for the service of the Tent of Meeting. It will be a memorial for the Israelites before the LORD, making atonement for your lives."

Basin for Washing

[17]Then the LORD said to Moses, [18]"Make a bronze basin, with its bronze stand, for washing. Place it between the Tent of Meeting and the altar, and put water in it. [19]Aaron and his sons are to wash their hands and feet with water from it. [20]Whenever they enter the Tent of Meeting, they shall wash with water so that they will not die. Also, when they approach the altar to minister by presenting an offering made to the LORD by fire, [21]they shall wash their hands and feet so that they will not die. This is to be a lasting ordinance for Aaron and his descendants for the generations to come."

Anointing Oil

[22]Then the LORD said to Moses, [23]"Take the following fine spices: 500 shekels[b] of liquid myrrh, half as much (that is, 250 shekels) of fragrant cinnamon, 250 shekels of fragrant cane, [24]500 shekels of cassia—all according to the sanctuary shekel—and a hin[c] of olive oil. [25]Make these into a sacred anointing oil, a fragrant blend, the work of a perfumer. It will be the sacred anointing oil. [26]Then use it to anoint the Tent of Meeting, the ark of the Testimony, [27]the table and all its articles, the lampstand and its accessories, the altar of incense, [28]the altar of burnt offering and all its utensils, and the basin with its stand. [29]You shall consecrate them so they will be most holy, and whatever touches them will be holy.

[30]"Anoint Aaron and his sons and consecrate them so they may serve me as priests. [31]Say to the Israelites, 'This is to be my sacred anointing oil for the generations to come. [32]Do not pour it on men's bodies and do not make any oil with the same formula. It is sacred, and you are to consider it sacred. [33]Whoever makes perfume like it and whoever puts it on anyone other than a priest must be cut off from his people.' "

Incense

[34]Then the LORD said to Moses, "Take fragrant spices—gum resin, onycha and galbanum—and pure frankincense, all in equal amounts, [35]and make a fragrant blend of incense, the work of a perfumer. It is to be salted and pure and sacred. [36]Grind some of it to powder and place it in front of the Testimony in the Tent of Meeting, where I will meet with you. It shall be most holy to you. [37]Do not make any incense with this formula for yourselves; consider it holy to the LORD. [38]Whoever makes any like it to enjoy its fragrance must be cut off from his people."

---

[a]13 That is, about 1/5 ounce (about 6 grams); also in verse 15   [b]23 That is, about 12 1/2 pounds (about 6 kilograms)   [c]24 That is, probably about 4 quarts (about 4 liters)

Bezalel and Oholiab

31 Then the LORD said to Moses, [2]"See, I have chosen Bezalel son of Uri, the son of Hur, of the tribe of Judah, [3]and I have filled him with the Spirit of God, with skill, ability and knowledge in all kinds of crafts— [4]to make artistic designs for work in gold, silver and bronze, [5]to cut and set stones, to work in wood, and to engage in all kinds of craftsmanship. [6]Moreover, I have appointed Oholiab son of Ahisamach, of the tribe of Dan, to help him. Also I have given skill to all the craftsmen to make everything I have commanded you: [7]the Tent of Meeting, the ark of the Testimony with the atonement cover on it, and all the other furnishings of the tent— [8]the table and its articles, the pure gold lampstand and all its accessories, the altar of incense, [9]the altar of burnt offering and all its utensils, the basin with its stand— [10]and also the woven garments, both the sacred garments for Aaron the priest and the garments for his sons when they serve as priests, [11]and the anointing oil and fragrant incense for the Holy Place. They are to make them just as I commanded you."

The Sabbath

[12]Then the LORD said to Moses, [13]"Say to the Israelites, 'You must observe my Sabbaths. This will be a sign between me and you for the generations to come, so you may know that I am the LORD, who makes you holy.[a]

[14]"'Observe the Sabbath, because it is holy to you. Anyone who desecrates it must be put to death; whoever does any work on that day must be cut off from his people. [15]For six days, work is to be done, but the seventh day is a Sabbath of rest, holy to the LORD. Whoever does any work on the Sabbath day must be put to death. [16]The Israelites are to observe the Sabbath, celebrating it for the generations to come as a lasting covenant. [17]It will be a sign between me and the Israelites forever, for in six days the LORD made the heavens and the earth, and on the seventh day he abstained from work and rested.'"

[18]When the LORD finished speaking to Moses on Mount Sinai, he gave him the two tablets of the Testimony, the tablets of stone inscribed by the finger of God.

The Golden Calf

32 When the people saw that Moses was so long in coming down from the mountain, they gathered around Aaron and said, "Come, make us gods[b] who will go before us. As for this fellow Moses who brought us up out of Egypt, we don't know what has happened to him."

[2]Aaron answered them, "Take off the gold earrings that your wives, your sons and your daughters are wearing, and bring them to me." [3]So all the people took off their earrings and brought them to Aaron. [4]He took what they handed him and made it into an idol cast in the shape of a calf, fashioning it with a tool. Then they said, "These are your gods,[c] O Israel, who brought you up out of Egypt."

[5]When Aaron saw this, he built an altar in front of the calf and announced, "Tomorrow there will be a festival to the LORD." [6]So the next day the people rose early and sacrificed burnt offerings and presented fellowship offerings.[d] Afterward they sat down to eat and drink and got up to indulge in revelry.

---

[a]13 Or who sanctifies you; or who sets you apart as holy   [b]1 Or a god; also in verses 23 and 31   [c]4 Or This is your god; also in verse 8   [d]6 Traditionally peace offerings

1. Do you work best with ideas, things, or people? 2. What do you (or your group) think is your most creative talent?

1. What qualified Bezalel for artistic director (vv. 1–5)? Who helps out? 2. What does this say about the way God equips people for leadership? 3. Having just set before the people all the work there is to do, and the workers to do it (vv. 1–11), why does God remind them about the Sabbath (vv. 12–17)? If the project is top priority, why not work overtime? What values are held in tension here? 4. Verse 18 records the end of what God gave to Moses on Mount Sinai. What is the beginning point for these covenant terms? Where does that leave Moses and Israel?

1. What do such hand-picked, skilled craftsmen say about the value of the fine arts in any project worthy of God's dwelling? 2. Describe a skill you have used to serve God—a skill you could not have accomplished without God's intervention in your life. 3. What is the place of the fine arts where you worship? What part in creative worship have you had? 4. How do you view the Sabbath rest: Necessity, or luxury? Guilt-relieving or guilt-inducing? How might the book *When I Relax, I Feel Guilty* depict you? 5. What duties crowd out your Sabbath rest? Which can be shifted next Sunday?

1. Recall when you worried excessively about your parents: Where were they? What kept them? How did you handle their unaccounted for absence? 2. What was the most defiant thing you ever did against your parents' wishes—something you can laugh about now but perhaps wasn't so funny at the time?

1. If this dramatic golden calf incident were made for TV, it might be scripted in five parts: Scene 1 (vv. 1–6); Scene 2 (vv. 7–14); Scene 3 (vv. 15–20); Scene 4 (vv. 21–35); and Scene 5 (33:1–6). What headings would you assign to each of these scenes? 2. Scene 1: (vv. 1–6) How long has Moses been away on the mountain (v. 1; see Ex 24:18)? How do you think the people felt about being in the middle of the desert with no leader? Do you see

an attempted "coup" here? **3.** How do their subsequent actions violate the Ten Commandments they had heard earlier? What does Aaron do for stress management and damage control? What instincts is he drawing upon? Where did the people learn to worship in this manner? Where do you assign the blame for making the calf? **4.** Scene 2: (vv. 7–14) How do God and Moses feel about the golden calf? On what basis is each justified in taking a stand? Why does God back down? What about God does not change (see v. 34; Nu 23:19)? **5.** Scene 3: (vv. 15–20) What do you think was Moses' frame of mind while he was coming down the mountain? What angers him? What might be symbolized in Moses' "tantrum": (a) Punishment to fit the crime? (b) Purging the evil from their midst? (c) Bringing the curse of a broken covenant against them? (d) Venting pent-up frustration from a long road trip? **6.** As an Israelite in the midst of revelry, how would you feel about the forced drinking (v. 20)? **7.** Scene 4: (vv. 21–35) Who points the finger at whom? Why? What was the main concern for Aaron? For Moses?

⁷Then the LORD said to Moses, "Go down, because your people, whom you brought up out of Egypt, have become corrupt. ⁸They have been quick to turn away from what I commanded them and have made themselves an idol cast in the shape of a calf. They have bowed down to it and sacrificed to it and have said, 'These are your gods, O Israel, who brought you up out of Egypt.'

⁹"I have seen these people," the LORD said to Moses, "and they are a stiff-necked people. ¹⁰Now leave me alone so that my anger may burn against them and that I may destroy them. Then I will make you into a great nation."

¹¹But Moses sought the favor of the LORD his God. "O LORD," he said, "why should your anger burn against your people, whom you brought out of Egypt with great power and a mighty hand? ¹²Why should the Egyptians say, 'It was with evil intent that he brought them out, to kill them in the mountains and to wipe them off the face of the earth'? Turn from your fierce anger; relent and do not bring disaster on your people. ¹³Remember your servants Abraham, Isaac and Israel, to whom you swore by your own self: 'I will make your descendants as numerous as the stars in the sky and I will give your descendants all this land I promised them, and it will be their inheritance forever.'" ¹⁴Then the LORD relented and did not bring on his people the disaster he had threatened.

¹⁵Moses turned and went down the mountain with the two tablets of the Testimony in his hands. They were inscribed on both sides, front and back. ¹⁶The tablets were the work of God; the writing was the writing of God, engraved on the tablets.

¹⁷When Joshua heard the noise of the people shouting, he said to Moses, "There is the sound of war in the camp."

 Exodus 32:1–35   **THE GOLDEN CALF**

Forty days earlier, Moses (accompanied by Joshua) had been called up to Mt. Sinai to meet with God. During this time that God engraved the Ten Commandments onto tablets of stone, trouble was brewing in the camp below.

1. After waiting 40 days for Moses, the Israelites were:
   a. impatient.
   b. starting to doubt God.
   c. longing to worship.
   d. ready to party.

2. The Israelites stooped to wanting a graven image because they:
   a. wanted a god they could control.
   b. didn't understand the Ten Commandments they'd heard earlier.
   c. wanted a visible representation of the Lord.
   d. reverted to the pagan practices they grew up with in Egypt.

3. After making the golden calf, why did Aaron announce a festival to God?
   a. He felt guilty about the calf.
   b. He was trying to turn the people back to God.

   c. He thought the Lord would inhabit the calf.
   d. He wanted to appease the people *and* worship God.

4. What did it mean when Moses threw the stone tablets to the ground?
   a. Stop the music!
   b. He was angry.
   c. They had broken the covenant.
   d. They didn't deserve the Law.
   e. His time on the mountain had been for nothing.

5. What was God's reaction to what the people did? How did Moses respond to the Lord?

6. How can God's "changing his mind" encourage you about situations that look hopeless? About the effects of your prayers?

7. The worst thing I ever did contrary to God's will resulted in:
   a. a series of heartaches.
   b. my greatest spiritual growth, eventually.
   c. alienation from those close to me.
   d. my turning away from God.

   e. some deep emotional scars.

8. When you sin and get caught, how do you usually respond? What does it mean to you to be "for the Lord" (v. 26) in the challenges you face in your spiritual life?

9. How does this story remind you of your relationship with your teenager?
   a. Earrings, music and parties cause problems between us too!
   b. Like the Israelites, my teen doesn't have a proper attitude toward God.
   c. Like the Israelites, my adolescent breaks the rules.
   d. Like Aaron, my kid gives excuses.
   e. Like God and Moses, I get angry.
   f. Like Moses, I have to decide whether to bail my child out.
   g. Like Moses, I plead with God on my teen's behalf.

10. How do you react when your teenager makes you angry? In what way would you like to cope differently?

[18]Moses replied:

"It is not the sound of victory,
it is not the sound of defeat;
it is the sound of singing that I hear."

[19]When Moses approached the camp and saw the calf and the dancing, his anger burned and he threw the tablets out of his hands, breaking them to pieces at the foot of the mountain. [20]And he took the calf they had made and burned it in the fire; then he ground it to powder, scattered it on the water and made the Israelites drink it.

[21]He said to Aaron, "What did these people do to you, that you led them into such great sin?"

[22]"Do not be angry, my lord," Aaron answered. "You know how prone these people are to evil. [23]They said to me, 'Make us gods who will go before us. As for this fellow Moses who brought us up out of Egypt, we don't know what has happened to him.' [24]So I told them, 'Whoever has any gold jewelry, take it off.' Then they gave me the gold, and I threw it into the fire, and out came this calf!"

[25]Moses saw that the people were running wild and that Aaron had let them get out of control and so become a laughingstock to their enemies. [26]So he stood at the entrance to the camp and said, "Whoever is for the LORD, come to me." And all the Levites rallied to him.

[27]Then he said to them, "This is what the LORD, the God of Israel, says: 'Each man strap a sword to his side. Go back and forth through the camp from one end to the other, each killing his brother and friend and neighbor.'" [28]The Levites did as Moses commanded, and that day about three thousand of the people died. [29]Then Moses said, "You have been set apart to the LORD today, for you were against your own sons and brothers, and he has blessed you this day."

[30]The next day Moses said to the people, "You have committed a great sin. But now I will go up to the LORD; perhaps I can make atonement for your sin."

[31]So Moses went back to the LORD and said, "Oh, what a great sin these people have committed! They have made themselves gods of gold. [32]But now, please forgive their sin—but if not, then blot me out of the book you have written."

[33]The LORD replied to Moses, "Whoever has sinned against me I will blot out of my book. [34]Now go, lead the people to the place I spoke of, and my angel will go before you. However, when the time comes for me to punish, I will punish them for their sin."

[35]And the LORD struck the people with a plague because of what they did with the calf Aaron had made.

33 Then the LORD said to Moses, "Leave this place, you and the people you brought up out of Egypt, and go up to the land I promised on oath to Abraham, Isaac and Jacob, saying, 'I will give it to your descendants.' [2]I will send an angel before you and drive out the Canaanites, Amorites, Hittites, Perizzites, Hivites and Jebusites. [3]Go up to the land flowing with milk and honey. But I will not go with you, because you are a stiff-necked people and I might destroy you on the way."

[4]When the people heard these distressing words, they began to mourn and no one put on any ornaments. [5]For the LORD had said to Moses, "Tell the Israelites, 'You are a stiff-necked people. If I were to go with you even for a moment, I might destroy you. Now take off your ornaments and I will decide what to do with you.'" [6]So the Israelites stripped off their ornaments at Mount Horeb.

Who kills whom? Why is this a "blessing" in disguise (v. 29)? **8.** What is Moses' role in setting things right again? In what sense is he an army general? A prophet? A priest? A sacrificial lamb? What exemplary qualities are evident in his plea bargaining with God (vv. 30–34)? **9.** What options does God leave open for himself? How is this both merciful and just? What does God's provision of options, an angel, mediator and the plague say about the nature of God? His view of sin? Of the law? **10.** Scene 5: (33:1–6) Why does God say he will not go with the people, but sends an angel instead? In this decision, which is good news? Bad news? How will God resolve this dilemma? **11.** If God does not go with Israel through the wilderness, what are their prospects physically? Emotionally? Spiritually?

♥ **1.** What do you do when you feel God has stopped speaking to you: (a) Keep trying to get his attention? (b) Run wild? (c) Take your "gold" (other resources) and make another god? (d) Blame it on the leadership of your church? (e) Fall back on secular coping methods available outside the church? (f) Wait for God to break the silence? **2.** When someone "lets you off the hook" (forgives a debt, withholds a penalty, gives a second chance), how do you feel about that person? When has that happened recently? Likewise, how does God want you to feel about his forgiveness? **3.** When you sin and get caught, what would you instinctively prefer: (a) Immediate forgiveness? (b) The punishment due? (c) Living with the unforgiven, unpunished sin? (d) A hearing to appeal your case? **4.** How would you have responded to the call in verse 26? What does it mean for you to be "for" the Lord? What risks would that entail where you live? **5.** How do you feel about Aaron's behavior? Do you ever have trouble "fessing up" to your sin? Why?

📖 1. How does this rendezvous serve as a break in the action of chapters 32–33? How is this "word from our Sponsor" vital to the action? 2. Why would Moses seek God's face at a time like this? What were the people expecting?

♡ 1. Where do you meet with God? What does meeting him as a "friend" mean for Moses? For you? 2. Do you consider God a friend? How can you more fully enjoy his friendship?

☕ In heaven, what three questions will you ask God?

📖 1. What three concerns does Moses bring to God? What do these concerns have in common with the people (see 32:1)? 2. What does the presence of God (or the lack of it) mean to him? What ensures Israel's continuing existence? 3. What in Moses' bold appeal do you think persuades God to do an "about-face"? What is Moses shown and told? Why does God set limits? When is Moses' prayer more fully answered (see Lk 9:30–32)?

♡ 1. Describe a time when, while doing something for God, you were absolutely confident that his presence was with you. 2. When have you gone to God in a time of great duress? What was his reply? How does your memory of this make you feel about God's ability to take care of your problems now?

☕ 1. When you were a child, after they had punished you, how did your parents let you know that they still loved you? Were their messages of "tough love" clear, or confusing, to you? How so? 2. When you break something, when do you replace it: (a) Right away, if it belongs to someone else? (b) Only when the rest of the set breaks? (c) Only after I've saved up more money? (d) Only if I'm asked to? (e) Never, even if it was unique?

📖 1. Why was it important to have a new set of stone tab-

The Tent of Meeting

7Now Moses used to take a tent and pitch it outside the camp some distance away, calling it the "tent of meeting." Anyone inquiring of the LORD would go to the tent of meeting outside the camp. 8And whenever Moses went out to the tent, all the people rose and stood at the entrances to their tents, watching Moses until he entered the tent. 9As Moses went into the tent, the pillar of cloud would come down and stay at the entrance, while the LORD spoke with Moses. 10Whenever the people saw the pillar of cloud standing at the entrance to the tent, they all stood and worshiped, each at the entrance to his tent. 11The LORD would speak to Moses face to face, as a man speaks with his friend. Then Moses would return to the camp, but his young aide Joshua son of Nun did not leave the tent.

Moses and the Glory of the LORD

12Moses said to the LORD, "You have been telling me, 'Lead these people,' but you have not let me know whom you will send with me. You have said, 'I know you by name and you have found favor with me.' 13If you are pleased with me, teach me your ways so I may know you and continue to find favor with you. Remember that this nation is your people."

14The LORD replied, "My Presence will go with you, and I will give you rest."

15Then Moses said to him, "If your Presence does not go with us, do not send us up from here. 16How will anyone know that you are pleased with me and with your people unless you go with us? What else will distinguish me and your people from all the other people on the face of the earth?"

17And the LORD said to Moses, "I will do the very thing you have asked, because I am pleased with you and I know you by name."

18Then Moses said, "Now show me your glory."

19And the LORD said, "I will cause all my goodness to pass in front of you, and I will proclaim my name, the LORD, in your presence. I will have mercy on whom I will have mercy, and I will have compassion on whom I will have compassion. 20But," he said, "you cannot see my face, for no one may see me and live."

21Then the LORD said, "There is a place near me where you may stand on a rock. 22When my glory passes by, I will put you in a cleft in the rock and cover you with my hand until I have passed by. 23Then I will remove my hand and you will see my back; but my face must not be seen."

The New Stone Tablets

34 The LORD said to Moses, "Chisel out two stone tablets like the first ones, and I will write on them the words that were on the first tablets, which you broke. 2Be ready in the morning, and then come up on Mount Sinai. Present yourself to me there on top of the mountain. 3No one is to come with you or be seen anywhere on the mountain; not even the flocks and herds may graze in front of the mountain."

4So Moses chiseled out two stone tablets like the first ones and went up Mount Sinai early in the morning, as the LORD had commanded him; and he carried the two stone tablets in his hands. 5Then the LORD came down in the cloud and stood there with him and proclaimed his name, the LORD. 6And he passed in front of Moses, proclaiming, "The LORD, the LORD, the compassionate and gracious God, slow to anger, abounding in love and faithfulness, [7]maintaining love to thousands, and forgiving wickedness, rebellion and sin. Yet he does not leave the guilty unpunished; he punishes the children and their children for the sin of the fathers to the third and fourth generation."

[8]Moses bowed to the ground at once and worshiped. [9]"O Lord, if I have found favor in your eyes," he said, "then let the Lord go with us. Although this is a stiff-necked people, forgive our wickedness and our sin, and take us as your inheritance."

[10]Then the Lord said: "I am making a covenant with you. Before all your people I will do wonders never before done in any nation in all the world. The people you live among will see how awesome is the work that I, the Lord, will do for you. [11]Obey what I command you today. I will drive out before you the Amorites, Canaanites, Hittites, Perizzites, Hivites and Jebusites. [12]Be careful not to make a treaty with those who live in the land where you are going, or they will be a snare among you. [13]Break down their altars, smash their sacred stones and cut down their Asherah poles.[a] [14]Do not worship any other god, for the Lord, whose name is Jealous, is a jealous God.

[15]"Be careful not to make a treaty with those who live in the land; for when they prostitute themselves to their gods and sacrifice to them, they will invite you and you will eat their sacrifices. [16]And when you choose some of their daughters as wives for your sons and those daughters prostitute themselves to their gods, they will lead your sons to do the same.

[17]"Do not make cast idols.

[18]"Celebrate the Feast of Unleavened Bread. For seven days eat bread made without yeast, as I commanded you. Do this at the appointed time in the month of Abib, for in that month you came out of Egypt.

[19]"The first offspring of every womb belongs to me, including all the firstborn males of your livestock, whether from herd or flock. [20]Redeem the firstborn donkey with a lamb, but if you do not redeem it, break its neck. Redeem all your firstborn sons.

"No one is to appear before me empty-handed.

[21]"Six days you shall labor, but on the seventh day you shall rest; even during the plowing season and harvest you must rest.

[22]"Celebrate the Feast of Weeks with the firstfruits of the wheat harvest, and the Feast of Ingathering at the turn of the year.[b] [23]Three times a year all your men are to appear before the Sovereign Lord, the God of Israel. [24]I will drive out nations before you and enlarge your territory, and no one will covet your land when you go up three times each year to appear before the Lord your God.

[25]"Do not offer the blood of a sacrifice to me along with anything containing yeast, and do not let any of the sacrifice from the Passover Feast remain until morning.

[26]"Bring the best of the firstfruits of your soil to the house of the Lord your God.

"Do not cook a young goat in its mother's milk."

[27]Then the Lord said to Moses, "Write down these words, for in accordance with these words I have made a covenant with you and with Israel." [28]Moses was there with the Lord forty days and forty nights without eating bread or drinking water. And he wrote on the tablets the words of the covenant—the Ten Commandments.

lets? In the days before computers and instant copiers, what was involved in replacing the first set (vv. 1–5,27–28)? **2.** How does God's description of himself in verses 6–7 fit the action of chapters 32–34? How is God able to both forgive and punish sin (see Isa 53)? **3.** What are the key lessons God wanted to teach his people about his nature? About worship? Obedience? Covenant relationships? Separation from other peoples and their gods? **4.** Where have you seen these specific covenant terms of verses 15–26 before? **5.** Moses was again gone 40 days. What do you suppose the Israelites did this time around, as they waited for his return?

1. How does God's self-revelation in verses 6–7 compare with your experience of him? What aspects of his character were made real to you in a crisis of faith? Likewise, in the day-to-day routine of last week? **2.** How did you come by the basic rules that you live by? How are those rules consistent with the lessons of this renewed covenant, which God identifies as key for Israel? **3.** From this study, which basic rules from God's list will you add to your own? **4.** What are the other "gods" of the 20th century that we are prone to worship and with whom we "make treaties"? Which of those gods are most alluring to you? What can you do to remove them from your midst? **5.** Moses' encounter with God must have been incredibly awesome. Did Moses return to the people and proclaim the details of his personal experiences with God? Or did Moses proclaim what God wanted the people to do? Do you ever over-emphasize your private experiences with God at the expense of what you need to do in obedience to God? Explain.

[a]13 That is, symbols of the goddess Asherah   [b]22 That is, in the fall

1. Why does Moses' face shine? Why is that a cause for fear? 2. What must Moses have said to bring the people back (v. 31)? 3. For whose sake is Moses' face veiled: His own? The people's? God's? 4. Why is the veil lifted when Moses speaks with God? What does this say about his relationship with God? With the people? (For another account, see 2Co 3:7–18.)

1. How do you "veil" God's glory in your life: Doubt? Timidity? Forgetfulness? Mistrust? Intimidation? Defensiveness? 2. If you were to drop this veil, how would your relationships and witness be different?

---

1. How do you prepare yourself to start, work on and complete a big project? 2. When has this working strategy been effective? When has it backfired?

1. Why is Sabbath observance so central to the commandments of God? What is its relation to the offerings and work details which follow? 2. What kind of materials were needed for this building project? What impresses you about them: (a) Extravagant? (b) Useless to God? (c) Nothing but the best for God? (d) Gifts of love? (e) Eminently useful? (f) Colorfully symbolic? (g) Out of place in the wilderness? 3. Who is expected to give what? When (see 36:3)? How much (see 36:6–7)?

1. Would you say the Sabbath is as much a focus of your life as it was for the Israelites? Why or why not? 2. If your church were to use the same fund-raising method, how would such a fiscal policy be viewed: (a) Responsible? (b) Naive? (c) Unnecessary? (d) Impossible? 3. Why might a church today look askance at this fiscal policy: (a) Economic times have changed? (b) Human nature has changed? (c) Pastoral authority has changed? (d) Other? 4. What do you bring God when you worship him? How is this like the precious items brought by the Israelites? 5. Which are you more willing and able to contribute to a project for the Lord: (a) Your time? (b) Manual labor? (c) Supervisory skills? (d) Money? 6. In your opinion, is giving a private matter, or a corporate duty? How does giving demonstrate something of God's

The Radiant Face of Moses

29When Moses came down from Mount Sinai with the two tablets of the Testimony in his hands, he was not aware that his face was radiant because he had spoken with the LORD. 30When Aaron and all the Israelites saw Moses, his face was radiant, and they were afraid to come near him. 31But Moses called to them; so Aaron and all the leaders of the community came back to him, and he spoke to them. 32Afterward all the Israelites came near him, and he gave them all the commands the LORD had given him on Mount Sinai.

33When Moses finished speaking to them, he put a veil over his face. 34But whenever he entered the LORD's presence to speak with him, he removed the veil until he came out. And when he came out and told the Israelites what he had been commanded, 35they saw that his face was radiant. Then Moses would put the veil back over his face until he went in to speak with the LORD.

Sabbath Regulations

35 Moses assembled the whole Israelite community and said to them, "These are the things the LORD has commanded you to do: 2For six days, work is to be done, but the seventh day shall be your holy day, a Sabbath of rest to the LORD. Whoever does any work on it must be put to death. 3Do not light a fire in any of your dwellings on the Sabbath day."

Materials for the Tabernacle

4Moses said to the whole Israelite community, "This is what the LORD has commanded: 5From what you have, take an offering for the LORD. Everyone who is willing is to bring to the LORD an offering of gold, silver and bronze; 6blue, purple and scarlet yarn and fine linen; goat hair; 7ram skins dyed red and hides of sea cows[a]; acacia wood; 8olive oil for the light; spices for the anointing oil and for the fragrant incense; 9and onyx stones and other gems to be mounted on the ephod and breastpiece.

10"All who are skilled among you are to come and make everything the LORD has commanded: 11the tabernacle with its tent and its covering, clasps, frames, crossbars, posts and bases; 12the ark with its poles and the atonement cover and the curtain that shields it; 13the table with its poles and all its articles and the bread of the Presence; 14the lampstand that is for light with its accessories, lamps and oil for the light; 15the altar of incense with its poles, the anointing oil and the fragrant incense; the curtain for the doorway at the entrance to the tabernacle; 16the altar of burnt offering with its bronze grating, its poles and all its utensils; the bronze basin with its stand; 17the curtains of the courtyard with its posts and bases, and the curtain for the entrance to the courtyard; 18the tent pegs for the tabernacle and for the courtyard, and their ropes; 19the woven garments worn for ministering in the sanctuary—both the sacred garments for Aaron the priest and the garments for his sons when they serve as priests."

20Then the whole Israelite community withdrew from Moses' presence, 21and everyone who was willing and whose heart moved him came and brought an offering to the LORD for the work on the Tent of Meeting, for all its service, and for the sacred garments. 22All who were willing, men and women alike, came and brought gold jewelry of all kinds: brooches, earrings, rings and ornaments. They all presented their gold as a wave offering to the LORD. 23Ev-

---

a7 That is, dugongs; also in verse 23

eryone who had blue, purple or scarlet yarn or fine linen, or goat hair, ram skins dyed red or hides of sea cows brought them. ²⁴Those presenting an offering of silver or bronze brought it as an offering to the LORD, and everyone who had acacia wood for any part of the work brought it. ²⁵Every skilled woman spun with her hands and brought what she had spun—blue, purple or scarlet yarn or fine linen. ²⁶And all the women who were willing and had the skill spun the goat hair. ²⁷The leaders brought onyx stones and other gems to be mounted on the ephod and breastpiece. ²⁸They also brought spices and olive oil for the light and for the anointing oil and for the fragrant incense. ²⁹All the Israelite men and women who were willing brought to the LORD freewill offerings for all the work the LORD through Moses had commanded them to do.

Bezalel and Oholiab

³⁰Then Moses said to the Israelites, "See, the LORD has chosen Bezalel son of Uri, the son of Hur, of the tribe of Judah, ³¹and he has filled him with the Spirit of God, with skill, ability and knowledge in all kinds of crafts— ³²to make artistic designs for work in gold, silver and bronze, ³³to cut and set stones, to work in wood and to engage in all kinds of artistic craftsmanship. ³⁴And he has given both him and Oholiab son of Ahisamach, of the tribe of Dan, the ability to teach others. ³⁵He has filled them with skill to do all kinds of work as craftsmen, designers, embroiderers in blue, purple and scarlet yarn and fine linen, and weavers—all of them master **36** craftsmen and designers. ¹So Bezalel, Oholiab and every skilled person to whom the LORD has given skill and ability to know how to carry out all the work of constructing the sanctuary are to do the work just as the Lord has commanded."

²Then Moses summoned Bezalel and Oholiab and every skilled person to whom the LORD had given ability and who was willing to come and do the work. ³They received from Moses all the offerings the Israelites had brought to carry out the work of constructing the sanctuary. And the people continued to bring freewill offerings morning after morning. ⁴So all the skilled craftsmen who were doing all the work on the sanctuary left their work ⁵and said to Moses, "The people are bringing more than enough for doing the work the LORD commanded to be done."

⁶Then Moses gave an order and they sent this word throughout the camp: "No man or woman is to make anything else as an offering for the sanctuary." And so the people were restrained from bringing more, ⁷because what they already had was more than enough to do all the work.

The Tabernacle

⁸All the skilled men among the workmen made the tabernacle with ten curtains of finely twisted linen and blue, purple and scarlet yarn, with cherubim worked into them by a skilled craftsman. ⁹All the curtains were the same size—twenty-eight cubits long and four cubits wide.ᵃ ¹⁰They joined five of the curtains together and did the same with the other five. ¹¹Then they made loops of blue material along the edge of the end curtain in one set, and the same was done with the end curtain in the other set. ¹²They also made fifty loops on one curtain and fifty loops on the end curtain of the other set, with the loops opposite each other. ¹³Then they made fifty gold clasps and used them to fasten the two sets of curtains together so that the tabernacle was a unit.

ᵃ9 That is, about 42 feet (about 12.5 meters) long and 6 feet (about 1.8 meters) wide

nature? **7.** Why is willingness emphasized so much in this passage? How important is a willing heart to God when it comes to giving (see 2Co 9:7)? Do you give willingly or out of a sense of obligation or compulsion? Explain.

Who is the talented and creative one in your family? What is that person's unique gift?

1. What skills and resources do Bezalel and Oholiab possess? How did they come by their skills: Inherited? God-given? Taught? Caught? **2.** Why might God have equipped them with teaching skills, as well as artistic and practical skills? **3.** Among this mostly repeated material (see 31:2–6), what stands out as surprising? Why has the giving exceeded all expectations?

1. How would your church react if the people gave too much this year: (a) Give the surplus to missions, or to the poor? (b) Give the salaried ministers a big bonus? (c) Save for a rainy day? (d) Dream up a new ministry project? (e) Build a new building? (f) Add more staff? (g) Tell people to stop giving? **2.** What skill do you have that you could teach others? **3.** How does this scene compare with a recent church building project? What lessons apply?

1. What is your earliest memory of church or Sunday School? If you were not raised in a church-going family, what did you substitute for church on the weekend? **2.** Have you ever been someplace and felt that "this is where God must live"? What was it about that place that made you feel this way? **3.** What pets do you have? What is the strangest pet you have ever owned?

1. Briefly compare Exodus 36–39 with the specifications for the tabernacle furnishings and the priestly garments in Exodus

25–31. Given the amount of Bible coverage devoted to the tabernacle and the priestly clothes, how important do you think these things were to the Israelites? To God? 2. The people did everything "as the Lord commanded Moses" (explicit in 39:1,7,21,31, but implied throughout this duplicate section). What does this say about the authority of God? Of Moses? Of Scripture? 3. In the unparalleled verses (38:21–31), what do you learn about what the project cost in terms of raw materials, fiscal resources and manpower? 4. Considering the importance of animals for sacrifice and for the building of the tabernacle, what can you deduce about the role of animals in God's creation? About the relationship between people and animals?

1. Who was the creative genius behind this project? How do the contributions of the other players compare to that Master Builder? 2. The Bible never speaks of persons as "creative"; only God creates. Yet creativity is evident as imagination, artistic ability and resourcefulness in people like Bezalel and Oholiab. Is creativity an essential aspect of people made in God's image? Why? What limits to our creativity and freedom do you see given here in the very laws of God? 3. What does this teach about the purpose of physical representations of our faith to our relationship with God? How can physical items (church buildings, furnishings, art, etc.) help your faith? 4. When you see a room full of religious objects, do they draw your attention toward God, or away from God? What is the difference between these physical aids and religious idols? What can you do to ensure that they remain aids and do not become idols? 5. Relative to what you spend on your own home, how much time and energy do you devote to the place where God dwells with his people, the local tabernacle? How can you make sure that you provide a worthy dwelling place for God? 6. Is the tabernacle concept rather an Old Testament idea? According to the New Testament, where does God "dwell"? Why there? What changed? 7. How do you feel about being able to devote your creative abilities to glorify the Lord and share Christ with others? Encouraged? Ignored? Tolerated? Rejected? Challenged? Explain your answers.

[14]They made curtains of goat hair for the tent over the tabernacle—eleven altogether. [15]All eleven curtains were the same size—thirty cubits long and four cubits wide.[a] [16]They joined five of the curtains into one set and the other six into another set. [17]Then they made fifty loops along the edge of the end curtain in one set and also along the edge of the end curtain in the other set. [18]They made fifty bronze clasps to fasten the tent together as a unit. [19]Then they made for the tent a covering of ram skins dyed red, and over that a covering of hides of sea cows.[b]

[20]They made upright frames of acacia wood for the tabernacle. [21]Each frame was ten cubits long and a cubit and a half wide,[c] [22]with two projections set parallel to each other. They made all the frames of the tabernacle in this way. [23]They made twenty frames for the south side of the tabernacle [24]and made forty silver bases to go under them—two bases for each frame, one under each projection. [25]For the other side, the north side of the tabernacle, they made twenty frames [26]and forty silver bases—two under each frame. [27]They made six frames for the far end, that is, the west end of the tabernacle, [28]and two frames were made for the corners of the tabernacle at the far end. [29]At these two corners the frames were double from the bottom all the way to the top and fitted into a single ring; both were made alike. [30]So there were eight frames and sixteen silver bases—two under each frame.

[31]They also made crossbars of acacia wood: five for the frames on one side of the tabernacle, [32]five for those on the other side, and five for the frames on the west, at the far end of the tabernacle. [33]They made the center crossbar so that it extended from end to end at the middle of the frames. [34]They overlaid the frames with gold and made gold rings to hold the crossbars. They also overlaid the crossbars with gold.

[35]They made the curtain of blue, purple and scarlet yarn and finely twisted linen, with cherubim worked into it by a skilled craftsman. [36]They made four posts of acacia wood for it and overlaid them with gold. They made gold hooks for them and cast their four silver bases. [37]For the entrance to the tent they made a curtain of blue, purple and scarlet yarn and finely twisted linen—the work of an embroiderer; [38]and they made five posts with hooks for them. They overlaid the tops of the posts and their bands with gold and made their five bases of bronze.

The Ark

37 Bezalel made the ark of acacia wood—two and a half cubits long, a cubit and a half wide, and a cubit and a half high.[d] [2]He overlaid it with pure gold, both inside and out, and made a gold molding around it. [3]He cast four gold rings for it and fastened them to its four feet, with two rings on one side and two rings on the other. [4]Then he made poles of acacia wood and overlaid them with gold. [5]And he inserted the poles into the rings on the sides of the ark to carry it.

[6]He made the atonement cover of pure gold—two and a half cubits long and a cubit and a half wide.[e] [7]Then he made two cherubim out of hammered gold at the ends of the cover. [8]He made one cherub on one end and the second cherub on the other; at the two ends he made them of one piece with the cover. [9]The cheru-

a15 That is, about 45 feet (about 13.5 meters) long and 6 feet (about 1.8 meters) wide　b19 That is, dugongs　c21 That is, about 15 feet (about 4.5 meters) long and 2 1/4 feet (about 0.7 meter) wide　d1 That is, about 3 3/4 feet (about 1.1 meters) long and 2 1/4 feet (about 0.7 meter) wide and high　e6 That is, about 3 3/4 feet (about 1.1 meters) long and 2 1/4 feet (about 0.7 meter) wide

bim had their wings spread upward, overshadowing the cover with them. The cherubim faced each other, looking toward the cover.

The Table

[10]They[a] made the table of acacia wood—two cubits long, a cubit wide, and a cubit and a half high.[b] [11]Then they overlaid it with pure gold and made a gold molding around it. [12]They also made around it a rim a handbreadth[c] wide and put a gold molding on the rim. [13]They cast four gold rings for the table and fastened them to the four corners, where the four legs were. [14]The rings were put close to the rim to hold the poles used in carrying the table. [15]The poles for carrying the table were made of acacia wood and were overlaid with gold. [16]And they made from pure gold the articles for the table—its plates and dishes and bowls and its pitchers for the pouring out of drink offerings.

The Lampstand

[17]They made the lampstand of pure gold and hammered it out, base and shaft; its flowerlike cups, buds and blossoms were of one piece with it. [18]Six branches extended from the sides of the lampstand—three on one side and three on the other. [19]Three cups shaped like almond flowers with buds and blossoms were on one branch, three on the next branch and the same for all six branches extending from the lampstand. [20]And on the lampstand were four cups shaped like almond flowers with buds and blossoms. [21]One bud was under the first pair of branches extending from the lampstand, a second bud under the second pair, and a third bud under the third pair—six branches in all. [22]The buds and the branches were all of one piece with the lampstand, hammered out of pure gold.

[23]They made its seven lamps, as well as its wick trimmers and trays, of pure gold. [24]They made the lampstand and all its accessories from one talent[d] of pure gold.

The Altar of Incense

[25]They made the altar of incense out of acacia wood. It was square, a cubit long and a cubit wide, and two cubits high[e]—its horns of one piece with it. [26]They overlaid the top and all the sides and the horns with pure gold, and made a gold molding around it. [27]They made two gold rings below the molding—two on opposite sides—to hold the poles used to carry it. [28]They made the poles of acacia wood and overlaid them with gold.

[29]They also made the sacred anointing oil and the pure, fragrant incense—the work of a perfumer.

The Altar of Burnt Offering

38 They[f] built the altar of burnt offering of acacia wood, three cubits[g] high; it was square, five cubits long and five cubits wide.[h] [2]They made a horn at each of the four corners, so that the horns and the altar were of one piece, and they overlaid the altar with bronze. [3]They made all its utensils of bronze—its pots, shovels, sprinkling bowls, meat forks and firepans. [4]They made a grating for the altar, a bronze network, to be under its

---

[a]10 Or *He*; also in verses 11-29   [b]10 That is, about 3 feet (about 0.9 meter) long, 1 1/2 feet (about 0.5 meter) wide, and 2 1/4 feet (about 0.7 meter) high   [c]12 That is, about 3 inches (about 8 centimeters)   [d]24 That is, about 75 pounds (about 34 kilograms)   [e]25 That is, about 1 1/2 feet (about 0.5 meter) long and wide, and about 3 feet (about 0.9 meter) high   [f]1 Or *He*; also in verses 2-9   [g]1 That is, about 4 1/2 feet (about 1.3 meters)   [h]1 That is, about 7 1/2 feet (about 2.3 meters) long and wide

ledge, halfway up the altar. 5They cast bronze rings to hold the poles for the four corners of the bronze grating. 6They made the poles of acacia wood and overlaid them with bronze. 7They inserted the poles into the rings so they would be on the sides of the altar for carrying it. They made it hollow, out of boards.

Basin for Washing

8They made the bronze basin and its bronze stand from the mirrors of the women who served at the entrance to the Tent of Meeting.

The Courtyard

9Next they made the courtyard. The south side was a hundred cubits*a* long and had curtains of finely twisted linen, 10with twenty posts and twenty bronze bases, and with silver hooks and bands on the posts. 11The north side was also a hundred cubits long and had twenty posts and twenty bronze bases, with silver hooks and bands on the posts.

12The west end was fifty cubits*b* wide and had curtains, with ten posts and ten bases, with silver hooks and bands on the posts. 13The east end, toward the sunrise, was also fifty cubits wide. 14Curtains fifteen cubits*c* long were on one side of the entrance, with three posts and three bases, 15and curtains fifteen cubits long were on the other side of the entrance to the courtyard, with three posts and three bases. 16All the curtains around the courtyard were of finely twisted linen. 17The bases for the posts were bronze. The hooks and bands on the posts were silver, and their tops were overlaid with silver; so all the posts of the courtyard had silver bands.

18The curtain for the entrance to the courtyard was of blue, purple and scarlet yarn and finely twisted linen—the work of an embroiderer. It was twenty cubits*d* long and, like the curtains of the courtyard, five cubits*e* high, 19with four posts and four bronze bases. Their hooks and bands were silver, and their tops were overlaid with silver. 20All the tent pegs of the tabernacle and of the surrounding courtyard were bronze.

The Materials Used

21These are the amounts of the materials used for the tabernacle, the tabernacle of the Testimony, which were recorded at Moses' command by the Levites under the direction of Ithamar son of Aaron, the priest. 22(Bezalel son of Uri, the son of Hur, of the tribe of Judah, made everything the LORD commanded Moses; 23with him was Oholiab son of Ahisamach, of the tribe of Dan—a craftsman and designer, and an embroiderer in blue, purple and scarlet yarn and fine linen.) 24The total amount of the gold from the wave offering used for all the work on the sanctuary was 29 talents and 730 shekels,*f* according to the sanctuary shekel.

25The silver obtained from those of the community who were counted in the census was 100 talents and 1,775 shekels,*g* according to the sanctuary shekel— 26one beka per person, that is, half a shekel,*h* according to the sanctuary shekel, from everyone who had crossed over to those counted, twenty years old or more,

---

a9 That is, about 150 feet (about 46 meters)   *b12* That is, about 75 feet (about 23 meters)   *c14* That is, about 22 1/2 feet (about 6.9 meters)   *d18* That is, about 30 feet (about 9 meters)   *e18* That is, about 7 1/2 feet (about 2.3 meters)   *f24* The weight of the gold was a little over one ton (about 1 metric ton).   *g25* The weight of the silver was a little over 3 3/4 tons (about 3.4 metric tons).   *h26* That is, about 1/5 ounce (about 5.5 grams)

a total of 603,550 men. **27**The 100 talents*a* of silver were used to cast the bases for the sanctuary and for the curtain—100 bases from the 100 talents, one talent for each base. **28**They used the 1,775 shekels*b* to make the hooks for the posts, to overlay the tops of the posts, and to make their bands.

29The bronze from the wave offering was 70 talents and 2,400 shekels.*c* **30**They used it to make the bases for the entrance to the Tent of Meeting, the bronze altar with its bronze grating and all its utensils, **31**the bases for the surrounding courtyard and those for its entrance and all the tent pegs for the tabernacle and those for the surrounding courtyard.

The Priestly Garments

39 From the blue, purple and scarlet yarn they made woven garments for ministering in the sanctuary. They also made sacred garments for Aaron, as the LORD commanded Moses.

The Ephod

2They*d* made the ephod of gold, and of blue, purple and scarlet yarn, and of finely twisted linen. **3**They hammered out thin sheets of gold and cut strands to be worked into the blue, purple and scarlet yarn and fine linen—the work of a skilled craftsman. **4**They made shoulder pieces for the ephod, which were attached to two of its corners, so it could be fastened. **5**Its skillfully woven waistband was like it—of one piece with the ephod and made with gold, and with blue, purple and scarlet yarn, and with finely twisted linen, as the LORD commanded Moses.

6They mounted the onyx stones in gold filigree settings and engraved them like a seal with the names of the sons of Israel. **7**Then they fastened them on the shoulder pieces of the ephod as memorial stones for the sons of Israel, as the LORD commanded Moses.

The Breastpiece

8They fashioned the breastpiece—the work of a skilled crafts-man. They made it like the ephod: of gold, and of blue, purple and scarlet yarn, and of finely twisted linen. **9**It was square—a span*e* long and a span wide—and folded double. **10**Then they mounted four rows of precious stones on it. In the first row there was a ruby, a topaz and a beryl; **11**in the second row a turquoise, a sapphire*f* and an emerald; **12**in the third row a jacinth, an agate and an amethyst; **13**in the fourth row a chrysolite, an onyx and a jasper.*g* They were mounted in gold filigree settings. **14**There were twelve stones, one for each of the names of the sons of Israel, each en-graved like a seal with the name of one of the twelve tribes.

15For the breastpiece they made braided chains of pure gold, like a rope. **16**They made two gold filigree settings and two gold rings, and fastened the rings to two of the corners of the breastpiece. **17**They fastened the two gold chains to the rings at the corners of the breastpiece, **18**and the other ends of the chains to the two settings, attaching them to the shoulder pieces of the ephod at the front. **19**They made two gold rings and attached them to the other two corners of the breastpiece on the inside edge next to the ephod. **20**Then they made two more gold rings and attached them

a27 That is, about 3 3/4 tons (about 3.4 metric tons)   *b28* That is, about 45 pounds (about 20 kilograms)   *c29* The weight of the bronze was about 2 1/2 tons (about 2.4 metric tons).   *d2* Or *He*; also in verses 7, 8 and 22   *e9* That is, about 9 inches (about 22 centimeters)   *f11* Or *lapis lazuli*   *g13* The precise identification of some of these precious stones is uncertain.

to the bottom of the shoulder pieces on the front of the ephod, close to the seam just above the waistband of the ephod. [21]They tied the rings of the breastpiece to the rings of the ephod with blue cord, connecting it to the waistband so that the breastpiece would not swing out from the ephod—as the LORD commanded Moses.

Other Priestly Garments

[22]They made the robe of the ephod entirely of blue cloth—the work of a weaver— [23]with an opening in the center of the robe like the opening of a collar,[a] and a band around this opening, so that it would not tear. [24]They made pomegranates of blue, purple and scarlet yarn and finely twisted linen around the hem of the robe. [25]And they made bells of pure gold and attached them around the hem between the pomegranates. [26]The bells and pomegranates alternated around the hem of the robe to be worn for ministering, as the LORD commanded Moses.

[27]For Aaron and his sons, they made tunics of fine linen—the work of a weaver— [28]and the turban of fine linen, the linen headbands and the undergarments of finely twisted linen. [29]The sash was of finely twisted linen and blue, purple and scarlet yarn—the work of an embroiderer—as the LORD commanded Moses.

[30]They made the plate, the sacred diadem, out of pure gold and engraved on it, like an inscription on a seal: HOLY TO THE LORD. [31]Then they fastened a blue cord to it to attach it to the turban, as the LORD commanded Moses.

Moses Inspects the Tabernacle

[32]So all the work on the tabernacle, the Tent of Meeting, was completed. The Israelites did everything just as the LORD commanded Moses. [33]Then they brought the tabernacle to Moses: the tent and all its furnishings, its clasps, frames, crossbars, posts and bases; [34]the covering of ram skins dyed red, the covering of hides of sea cows[b] and the shielding curtain; [35]the ark of the Testimony with its poles and the atonement cover; [36]the table with all its articles and the bread of the Presence; [37]the pure gold lampstand with its row of lamps and all its accessories, and the oil for the light; [38]the gold altar, the anointing oil, the fragrant incense, and the curtain for the entrance to the tent; [39]the bronze altar with its bronze grating, its poles and all its utensils; the basin with its stand; [40]the curtains of the courtyard with its posts and bases, and the curtain for the entrance to the courtyard; the ropes and tent pegs for the courtyard; all the furnishings for the tabernacle, the Tent of Meeting; [41]and the woven garments worn for ministering in the sanctuary, both the sacred garments for Aaron the priest and the garments for his sons when serving as priests.

[42]The Israelites had done all the work just as the LORD had commanded Moses. [43]Moses inspected the work and saw that they had done it just as the LORD had commanded. So Moses blessed them.

Setting Up the Tabernacle

40 Then the LORD said to Moses: [2]"Set up the tabernacle, the Tent of Meeting, on the first day of the first month. [3]Place the ark of the Testimony in it and shield the ark with the curtain. [4]Bring in the table and set out what belongs on it. Then bring in the lampstand and set up its lamps. [5]Place the gold altar of incense

---

Did your folks ever inspect your room? How thorough were they? Where did you put things you didn't want them to see?

1. What about this passage reminds you of the creation narrative (see Ge 2:1–3)? 2. Why was it necessary for Moses to inspect the work of the people? 3. How do you think they felt when he blessed them (v. 43)? How do you think this made them feel about the work they had just done and the God they served?

1. What have you done for God this past month? If Moses had inspected your work, would he have blessed you? Why or why not? 2. Are you motivated to keep doing your best and receive from God that ultimate blessing, "Well done, good and faithful servant" (Mt 25:21)? Why?

1. What "odd jobs" have you done at the church? 2. What project can you say was completed without the help of anyone else?

1. Who set up this tabernacle and its courtyard? Where were the others all this time? How might they have felt about what

---

a23 The meaning of the Hebrew for this word is uncertain.   b34 That is, dugongs

in front of the ark of the Testimony and put the curtain at the entrance to the tabernacle.

⁶"Place the altar of burnt offering in front of the entrance to the tabernacle, the Tent of Meeting; ⁷place the basin between the Tent of Meeting and the altar and put water in it. ⁸Set up the courtyard around it and put the curtain at the entrance to the courtyard.

⁹"Take the anointing oil and anoint the tabernacle and everything in it; consecrate it and all its furnishings, and it will be holy. ¹⁰Then anoint the altar of burnt offering and all its utensils; consecrate the altar, and it will be most holy. ¹¹Anoint the basin and its stand and consecrate them.

¹²"Bring Aaron and his sons to the entrance to the Tent of Meeting and wash them with water. ¹³Then dress Aaron in the sacred garments, anoint him and consecrate him so he may serve me as priest. ¹⁴Bring his sons and dress them in tunics. ¹⁵Anoint them just as you anointed their father, so they may serve me as priests. Their anointing will be to a priesthood that will continue for all generations to come." ¹⁶Moses did everything just as the LORD commanded him.

¹⁷So the tabernacle was set up on the first day of the first month in the second year. ¹⁸When Moses set up the tabernacle, he put the bases in place, erected the frames, inserted the crossbars and set up the posts. ¹⁹Then he spread the tent over the tabernacle and put the covering over the tent, as the LORD commanded him.

²⁰He took the Testimony and placed it in the ark, attached the poles to the ark and put the atonement cover over it. ²¹Then he brought the ark into the tabernacle and hung the shielding curtain and shielded the ark of the Testimony, as the LORD commanded him.

²²Moses placed the table in the Tent of Meeting on the north side of the tabernacle outside the curtain ²³and set out the bread on it before the LORD, as the LORD commanded him.

²⁴He placed the lampstand in the Tent of Meeting opposite the table on the south side of the tabernacle ²⁵and set up the lamps before the LORD, as the LORD commanded him.

²⁶Moses placed the gold altar in the Tent of Meeting in front of the curtain ²⁷and burned fragrant incense on it, as the LORD commanded him. ²⁸Then he put up the curtain at the entrance to the tabernacle.

²⁹He set the altar of burnt offering near the entrance to the tabernacle, the Tent of Meeting, and offered on it burnt offerings and grain offerings, as the LORD commanded him.

³⁰He placed the basin between the Tent of Meeting and the altar and put water in it for washing, ³¹and Moses and Aaron and his sons used it to wash their hands and feet. ³²They washed whenever they entered the Tent of Meeting or approached the altar, as the LORD commanded Moses.

³³Then Moses set up the courtyard around the tabernacle and altar and put up the curtain at the entrance to the courtyard. And so Moses finished the work.

The Glory of the LORD

³⁴Then the cloud covered the Tent of Meeting, and the glory of the LORD filled the tabernacle. ³⁵Moses could not enter the Tent of Meeting because the cloud had settled upon it, and the glory of the LORD filled the tabernacle.

³⁶In all the travels of the Israelites, whenever the cloud lifted

was going on? 2. Was this solo job an ego trip for Moses? Didn't he trust others at this point? Was he resentful because he was stuck with the job? Or was Moses serving more as a prophet and priest? What highlights from Moses' "career" so far would confirm your view? What does the theme of obedience suggest (vv. 19,21,23, 25,27,29,32)? 3. Why do you think God wanted this tabernacle in the first place? How would focusing their attention help his people to understand him and to communicate with him? 4. What is the danger of localizing God to the tabernacle or its furnishings? How does God seek to avoid this danger? How does this passage illustrate his desire for correct worship?

1. How do you know when it's time to do the job yourself, rather than teach someone else how to do it or delegate the task? When is doing something yourself a sign of arrogance? Of humility? Of obedience? Of personal commitment? 2. What next job will you handle by yourself? Why? 3. How can a finite mind understand an infinite God without the help of "boundaries," as symbolized by a tabernacle? What boundaries do you use in order to understand God better with your finite mind? 4. Many people try to put "God in a box," meaning they try to define what God can and cannot do by the systematic constructs of their mind. How do you ensure that you use these boundaries to understand God and not to limit him?

Recall a summer or a time that you lived "on the road." What were your favorite travel songs? Travel games? Favorite fast food chains? Motel chains? What made you the most sick and tired?

1. The tabernacle was not finished up to this point. Why? Why was it impossible to Moses to finish the tabernacle himself? 2. How important was the physical presence of God to the Israelites when compared to their exodus from Egypt and the giving of the Law? Why? 3. What purpose for the tabernacle do the cloud and the fire confirm? What role did the Lord's cloud and fire play in confirming when it was time to hit the road again?

1. When in your life did you most noticeably feel the physical presence of God? How is the glory of the Lord made real to you at every waking moment? How would you explain this to someone who has not experienced God? With whom will you share this week? 2. During your travels, what most reassures you about God's presence in your life? 3. When do you know it's time to move on with the Lord? What tells you that the Lord has lifted his presence from your work or home or church setting and is relocating himself "on the road again"? How willing are you to set up shop as the Lord directs? 4. What in your group life has been the climax of your Exodus studies? Which of Israel's feasts would be a fitting way to celebrate your life together and your experience of God? Come, let us celebrate!

from above the tabernacle, they would set out; [37]but if the cloud did not lift, they did not set out—until the day it lifted. [38]So the cloud of the LORD was over the tabernacle by day, and fire was in the cloud by night, in the sight of all the house of Israel during all their travels.

INTRODUCTION to
LEVITICUS

Book Study Outline: If you are using Leviticus for a study course, here is a 7- or 13-week outline. Use the questions in the margin for your group agenda:

🍵 start meeting / 15 min.

📖 read & discuss Bible / 30 min.

♡ close meeting / 15–45 min.

Refer to the Questions and Answers in the front of this Bible for more information.

Author: Moses is assumed to be the author and editor of most of the first five books of the OT (the Pentateuch).

7-week plan	13-week plan	Personal Reading	Group Study Passage
1	1	1:1–5:13	1:1–17/Burnt Offerings
	2	5:14–7:38	7:11–21/Fellowship Offerings
2	3	8:1–36	8:1–36/Ordination of Aaron
	4	9:1–10:20	10:1–20/Nadab and Abihu
3	5	11:1–13:59	11:1–47/Clean and Unclean
	6	14:1–15:33	14:1–32/Skin Diseases
4	7	16:1–17:16	16:1–34/Day of Atonement
	8	18:1–20:27	19:1–37/Various Laws
5	9	21:1–22:33	21:1–22:16/Rules for Priests
	10	23:1–24:23	23:1–44/Rules for Feasts
6	11	25:1–55	25:8–55/Year of Jubilee
	12	26:1–46	26:14–46/Punishments
7	13	27:1–34	27:1–34/Redeeming Values

Date: It is difficult to assign a firm date to the composition of the Pentateuch. Conservative estimates place it in either the fifteenth or thirteenth century B.C., depending on when the Exodus occurred.

OLD TESTAMENT SACRIFICES

Burnt Offering:
References: Lev 1; 6:8–13; 8:18–21; 16:24.

Elements: Bull, ram or male bird (dove or young pigeon for the poor); wholly consumed; no defect

Purpose: Voluntary act of worship; atonement for unintentional sin; expression of commitment, devotion and surrender to God.

Grain Offering:
References: Lev 2; 6:14–23

Elements: Grain, fine flour, olive oil, incense, baked bread, salt; no yeast or honey; accompanied burnt

and fellowship offerings (along with drink offering)

Purpose: Voluntary act of worship; recognition of God's goodness and provision; expression of devotion.

Fellowship Offering:
References: Lev 3; 7:11–34

Elements: Any animal without defect from herd or flock; variety of breads

Purpose: Voluntary act of worship; thanksgiving and fellowship (it included a communal meal)

Sin Offering:
References: Lev 4:1–5:13; 6:24–30; 8:14–17; 16:3–22

Elements: 1. Young bull for priest and congregation; 2. Male goat for leader; 3. Female goat or lamb for commoner; 4. Dove or

pigeon for poor; 5. Tenth of an ephah of fine flour for very poor

Purpose: Mandatory atonement for specific unintentional sin; confession, forgiveness of sin; cleansing from defilement

Guilt Offering:
References: Lev 5:14–6:7; 7:1–6

Elements: Ram or lamb

Purpose: Mandatory atonement for unintentional sin requiring restitution; cleansing from defilement; make restitution; pay 20% fine

---

Theme: Reconciliation and sanctification.

Historical Background: The events of this book take place after the Exodus from Egypt and the giving of the Law at Sinai, and concern the formalizing of Israelite religious practice. In Exodus, instructions were given for the building of the tabernacle; here in Leviticus, regulations are given for how to worship there.

Characteristics: After the covenant at Sinai, Israel was the earthly representation of God's kingdom (the theocracy), and, as her King, the Lord established his administration over all of Israel's life. Her religious, communal and personal life were so regulated as to establish her as God's holy people and to instruct her in holiness. To the modern reader, Leviticus may appear hopelessly outdated with its strange, disturbing economic practices, and the blood and gore of animal sacrifice, yet the questions it seeks to answer are as important for us as they were for the Israelites. How do we remain reconciled to God? What is the proper way to worship a holy God? How are we to act toward each other within the context of God's covenant? Leviticus answers these and other questions faced by the Israelites using symbols familiar to them. For us, then, the key to understanding Leviticus is looking beyond these strange symbols to the underlying principles describing God's way of holiness and reconciliation.

Leviticus

The Burnt Offering

1 The LORD called to Moses and spoke to him from the Tent of Meeting. He said, [2]"Speak to the Israelites and say to them: 'When any of you brings an offering to the LORD, bring as your offering an animal from either the herd or the flock.

[3]" 'If the offering is a burnt offering from the herd, he is to offer a male without defect. He must present it at the entrance to the Tent of Meeting so that it[a] will be acceptable to the LORD. [4]He is to lay his hand on the head of the burnt offering, and it will be accepted on his behalf to make atonement for him. [5]He is to slaughter the young bull before the LORD, and then Aaron's sons the priests shall bring the blood and sprinkle it against the altar on all sides at the entrance to the Tent of Meeting. [6]He is to skin the burnt offering and cut it into pieces. [7]The sons of Aaron the priest are to put fire on the altar and arrange wood on the fire. [8]Then Aaron's sons the priests shall arrange the pieces, including the head and the fat, on the burning wood that is on the altar. [9]He is to wash the inner parts and the legs with water, and the priest is to burn all of it on the altar. It is a burnt offering, an offering made by fire, an aroma pleasing to the LORD.

[10]" 'If the offering is a burnt offering from the flock, from either the sheep or the goats, he is to offer a male without defect. [11]He is to slaughter it at the north side of the altar before the LORD, and Aaron's sons the priests shall sprinkle its blood against the altar on all sides. [12]He is to cut it into pieces, and the priest shall arrange them, including the head and the fat, on the burning wood that is on the altar. [13]He is to wash the inner parts and the legs with water, and the priest is to bring all of it and burn it on the altar. It is a burnt offering, an offering made by fire, an aroma pleasing to the LORD.

[14]" 'If the offering to the LORD is a burnt offering of birds, he is to offer a dove or a young pigeon. [15]The priest shall bring it to the altar, wring off the head and burn it on the altar; its blood shall be drained out on the side of the altar. [16]He is to remove the crop with its contents[b] and throw it to the east side of the altar, where the ashes are. [17]He shall tear it open by the wings, not severing it completely, and then the priest shall burn it on the wood that is on the fire on the altar. It is a burnt offering, an offering made by fire, an aroma pleasing to the LORD.

The Grain Offering

2 " 'When someone brings a grain offering to the LORD, his offering is to be of fine flour. He is to pour oil on it, put incense on it [2]and take it to Aaron's sons the priests. The priest shall take a handful of the fine flour and oil, together with all the incense, and burn this as a memorial portion on the altar, an offering made by fire, an aroma pleasing to the LORD. [3]The rest of the grain offering belongs to Aaron and his sons; it is a most holy part of the offerings made to the LORD by fire.

[4]" 'If you bring a grain offering baked in an oven, it is to consist

Sidebar questions

☕ 1. What was the biggest thing your parents ever gave up for you? Why do you think they did it? 2. What is the biggest thing you ever had to give up for someone else? Why did you do it? What did you learn in the process?

📖 1. Beginning with Cain and Abel (see Ge 4 and here in Lev), why do you think God chose "animal sacrifice" to restore broken relationships? Couldn't God forgive sins without sacrifice? Why or why not? 2. Regarding the "burnt offering," what do you think these numerous regulations imply: Why a male, and without defect? Why the laying on of hands? Why sprinkle blood? Why complete burning? Why three categories? 3. How does an "aroma pleasing to the Lord" (vv. 9,13,17) foreshadow Christ and Christian charity (see Eph 5:2; Php 4:18)?

♡ 1. How would you define "sacrifice"? How does your definition differ from others in the group? Does true sacrifice have to *hurt*? 2. How do your sacrifices define your value system? For whom do you make sacrifices? What sacrifices have you, or can you, make for God (see Ro 12:1–2; Heb 13:15)? 3. In your experience, how has God reconciled you to himself? What sacrifice has accomplished that?

☕ 1. Describe the best tasting bread or pastry you've ever eaten. What made it so good? 2. What aromas bring back positive childhood memories?

📖 1. What is significant about grain used as an offering? How is this like, and unlike, the "burnt offering" (see ch. 1)? As a bloodless offering, was it ever sufficient in itself (see Nu 6:14–23)? 2. Regarding the "grain offering," why do you think these regulations were mandatory? What did they imply?

---

a3 Or *he*   b16 Or *crop and the feathers*; the meaning of the Hebrew for this word is uncertain.

of fine flour: cakes made without yeast and mixed with oil, or^a wafers made without yeast and spread with oil. ⁵If your grain offering is prepared on a griddle, it is to be made of fine flour mixed with oil, and without yeast. ⁶Crumble it and pour oil on it; it is a grain offering. ⁷If your grain offering is cooked in a pan, it is to be made of fine flour and oil. ⁸Bring the grain offering made of these things to the LORD; present it to the priest, who shall take it to the altar. ⁹He shall take out the memorial portion from the grain offering and burn it on the altar as an offering made by fire, an aroma pleasing to the LORD. ¹⁰The rest of the grain offering belongs to Aaron and his sons; it is a most holy part of the offerings made to the LORD by fire.

¹¹"'Every grain offering you bring to the LORD must be made without yeast, for you are not to burn any yeast or honey in an offering made to the LORD by fire. ¹²You may bring them to the LORD as an offering of the firstfruits, but they are not to be offered on the altar as a pleasing aroma. ¹³Season all your grain offerings with salt. Do not leave the salt of the covenant of your God out of your grain offerings; add salt to all your offerings.

¹⁴"'If you bring a grain offering of firstfruits to the LORD, offer crushed heads of new grain roasted in the fire. ¹⁵Put oil and incense on it; it is a grain offering. ¹⁶The priest shall burn the memorial portion of the crushed grain and the oil, together with all the incense, as an offering made to the LORD by fire.

The Fellowship Offering

3 "'If someone's offering is a fellowship offering,^b and he offers an animal from the herd, whether male or female, he is to present before the LORD an animal without defect. ²He is to lay his hand on the head of his offering and slaughter it at the entrance to the Tent of Meeting. Then Aaron's sons the priests shall sprinkle the blood against the altar on all sides. ³From the fellowship offering he is to bring a sacrifice made to the LORD by fire: all the fat that covers the inner parts or is connected to them, ⁴both kidneys with the fat on them near the loins, and the covering of the liver, which he will remove with the kidneys. ⁵Then Aaron's sons are to burn it on the altar on top of the burnt offering that is on the burning wood, as an offering made by fire, an aroma pleasing to the LORD.

⁶"'If he offers an animal from the flock as a fellowship offering to the LORD, he is to offer a male or female without defect. ⁷If he offers a lamb, he is to present it before the LORD. ⁸He is to lay his hand on the head of his offering and slaughter it in front of the Tent of Meeting. Then Aaron's sons shall sprinkle its blood against the altar on all sides. ⁹From the fellowship offering he is to bring a sacrifice made to the LORD by fire: its fat, the entire fat tail cut off close to the backbone, all the fat that covers the inner parts or is connected to them, ¹⁰both kidneys with the fat on them near the loins, and the covering of the liver, which he will remove with the kidneys. ¹¹The priest shall burn them on the altar as food, an offering made to the LORD by fire.

¹²"'If his offering is a goat, he is to present it before the LORD. ¹³He is to lay his hand on its head and slaughter it in front of the Tent of Meeting. Then Aaron's sons shall sprinkle its blood against the altar on all sides. ¹⁴From what he offers he is to make this offering to the LORD by fire: all the fat that covers the inner parts or is connected to them, ¹⁵both kidneys with the fat on them near the loins, and the covering of the liver, which he will remove with the

Why grill it? Why without yeast or honey? Why the specified amounts? Why so "fine"? Why salt? Why leave some for Aaron and his sons? **3.** How are these laws part of the reconciliation between God and his people?

1. How would you describe your "offering" to God? How is it like and unlike the grain offering prescribed here? How does your offering help the reconciliation process? **2.** How do you feel about the offering plate at your church? About sermons on stewardship? In what ways are they related to the "grain offering"? **3.** What can you do to ensure a proper attitude toward giving to the church? **4.** If you won a sweepstakes, what would you offer to God?

How do you feel when you are alienated from a close friend? How then do you try to make peace with that person? What do you send or say?

1. Define "fellowship." With this definition, what do you see as the purpose of this offering? How would the various aspects of the offering help to accomplish this? **2.** The Hebrew word for "fellowship" used here can also be translated "peace" or "wholeness." How does this help to explain the function of this offering? **3.** How do the various laws fit the idea of reconciliation between God and his people: The part played by the offerer? The priest? Blood? Fat? Fire? Altar? **4.** Why was eating any of the fat or blood strictly prohibited (v. 17; see 17:11; Dt 12:23–25)?

1. When have you felt most alienated from God? How important is it to you that *all* barriers between yourself and God be removed? Why? **2.** What do you do to rebuild close fellowship with him: Say your prayers? Read his book? Give more money? Give more of yourself? Or what? How does this compare with the "fellowship offering"? **3.** What will you do today to improve relations between you and God?

^a4 Or and   ^b1 Traditionally *peace offering*; also in verses 3, 6 and 9

kidneys. [16]The priest shall burn them on the altar as food, an offering made by fire, a pleasing aroma. All the fat is the LORD's.

[17]"'This is a lasting ordinance for the generations to come, wherever you live: You must not eat any fat or any blood.'"

The Sin Offering

4 The LORD said to Moses, [2]"Say to the Israelites: 'When anyone sins unintentionally and does what is forbidden in any of the LORD's commands—

[3]"'If the anointed priest sins, bringing guilt on the people, he must bring to the LORD a young bull without defect as a sin offering for the sin he has committed. [4]He is to present the bull at the entrance to the Tent of Meeting before the LORD. He is to lay his hand on its head and slaughter it before the LORD. [5]Then the anointed priest shall take some of the bull's blood and carry it into the Tent of Meeting. [6]He is to dip his finger into the blood and sprinkle some of it seven times before the LORD, in front of the curtain of the sanctuary. [7]The priest shall then put some of the blood on the horns of the altar of fragrant incense that is before the LORD in the Tent of Meeting. The rest of the bull's blood he shall pour out at the base of the altar of burnt offering at the entrance to the Tent of Meeting. [8]He shall remove all the fat from the bull of the sin offering—the fat that covers the inner parts or is connected to them, [9]both kidneys with the fat on them near the loins, and the covering of the liver, which he will remove with the kidneys— [10]just as the fat is removed from the ox[a] sacrificed as a fellowship offering.[b] Then the priest shall burn them on the altar of burnt offering. [11]But the hide of the bull and all its flesh, as well as the head and legs, the inner parts and offal— [12]that is, all the rest of the bull—he must take outside the camp to a place ceremonially clean, where the ashes are thrown, and burn it in a wood fire on the ash heap.

[13]"'If the whole Israelite community sins unintentionally and does what is forbidden in any of the LORD's commands, even though the community is unaware of the matter, they are guilty. [14]When they become aware of the sin they committed, the assembly must bring a young bull as a sin offering and present it before the Tent of Meeting. [15]The elders of the community are to lay their hands on the bull's head before the LORD, and the bull shall be slaughtered before the LORD. [16]Then the anointed priest is to take some of the bull's blood into the Tent of Meeting. [17]He shall dip his finger into the blood and sprinkle it before the LORD seven times in front of the curtain. [18]He is to put some of the blood on the horns of the altar that is before the LORD in the Tent of Meeting. The rest of the blood he shall pour out at the base of the altar of burnt offering at the entrance to the Tent of Meeting. [19]He shall remove all the fat from it and burn it on the altar, [20]and do with this bull just as he did with the bull for the sin offering. In this way the priest will make atonement for them, and they will be forgiven. [21]Then he shall take the bull outside the camp and burn it as he burned the first bull. This is the sin offering for the community.

[22]"'When a leader sins unintentionally and does what is forbidden in any of the commands of the LORD his God, he is guilty. [23]When he is made aware of the sin he committed, he must bring as his offering a male goat without defect. [24]He is to lay his hand on

---

1. "It was an accident, I didn't mean to do it"—where have you heard that recently from your children? Your partner? From your excusing conscience? 2. "What they don't know won't hurt them"— Did you ever use this logic to hide some "private" matter from your parents or someone else? What happened when they eventually found out? 3. What childish notion of "sin" do you still have? What do you see as "childish" about it?

1. How would you define "unintentional sin" (v.1)? How is your definition supported by the examples in 5:1–4? If sin that is "unintentional" is still sin by God's definition, what does that say about God's law? 2. Which different individuals and groups are addressed in this passage (4:3,13,22,27; 5:7)? On what basis do these various regulations distinguish the sacrifices required. 3. Why is the "sin offering" of the priest required in each instance (4:3,20,25,29,34) along with their own respective sin offerings? 4. Why must the rest of his bull be taken "outside the camp" (v. 12; also 16:26–28; see Heb 13:11–13, where Christ is crucified outside Jerusalem)? 5. Choose one set of regulations for a particular group: What do you see as the purpose of each? In what sense might they be part of the reconciliation process between people and God? 6. Leviticus repeats the idea that such sacrifices are "an aroma pleasing to God" (1:17; 2:9; 3:5; 4:31). Why do you think it pleases him? What does this say about God's desire for intimate fellowship with us? 7. What other oft-repeated phrases give you clues as to the central concern of this passage? The phrase "will be forgiven (by God)" is repeated nine times. What does that mean?

1. Do you feel responsible for sins that are "unintentional"? What do terms like vehicular homicide, unwitting accomplice, involuntary manslaughter, "pre-meditated" or "malice aforethought" bring to mind? 2. Some say, "Ignorance is bliss." When is that true for you? When is ignorance *not* bliss, but guilt, for you? 3. In your experience, what does unintentional sin do to your relationship with God?

---

[a]10 The Hebrew word can include both male and female.   [b]10 Traditionally *peace offering*; also in verses 26, 31 and 35

the goat's head and slaughter it at the place where the burnt offering is slaughtered before the LORD. It is a sin offering. ²⁵Then the priest shall take some of the blood of the sin offering with his finger and put it on the horns of the altar of burnt offering and pour out the rest of the blood at the base of the altar. ²⁶He shall burn all the fat on the altar as he burned the fat of the fellowship offering. In this way the priest will make atonement for the man's sin, and he will be forgiven.

²⁷" 'If a member of the community sins unintentionally and does what is forbidden in any of the LORD's commands, he is guilty. ²⁸When he is made aware of the sin he committed, he must bring as his offering for the sin he committed a female goat without defect. ²⁹He is to lay his hand on the head of the sin offering and slaughter it at the place of the burnt offering. ³⁰Then the priest is to take some of the blood with his finger and put it on the horns of the altar of burnt offering and pour out the rest of the blood at the base of the altar. ³¹He shall remove all the fat, just as the fat is removed from the fellowship offering, and the priest shall burn it on the altar as an aroma pleasing to the LORD. In this way the priest will make atonement for him, and he will be forgiven.

³²" 'If he brings a lamb as his sin offering, he is to bring a female without defect. ³³He is to lay his hand on its head and slaughter it for a sin offering at the place where the burnt offering is slaughtered. ³⁴Then the priest shall take some of the blood of the sin offering with his finger and put it on the horns of the altar of burnt offering and pour out the rest of the blood at the base of the altar. ³⁵He shall remove all the fat, just as the fat is removed from the lamb of the fellowship offering, and the priest shall burn it on the altar on top of the offerings made to the LORD by fire. In this way the priest will make atonement for him for the sin he has committed, and he will be forgiven.

5 " 'If a person sins because he does not speak up when he hears a public charge to testify regarding something he has seen or learned about, he will be held responsible.

²" 'Or if a person touches anything ceremonially unclean—whether the carcasses of unclean wild animals or of unclean livestock or of unclean creatures that move along the ground—even though he is unaware of it, he has become unclean and is guilty.

³" 'Or if he touches human uncleanness—anything that would make him unclean—even though he is unaware of it, when he learns of it he will be guilty.

⁴" 'Or if a person thoughtlessly takes an oath to do anything, whether good or evil—in any matter one might carelessly swear about—even though he is unaware of it, in any case when he learns of it he will be guilty.

⁵" 'When anyone is guilty in any of these ways, he must confess in what way he has sinned ⁶and, as a penalty for the sin he has committed, he must bring to the LORD a female lamb or goat from the flock as a sin offering; and the priest shall make atonement for him for his sin.

⁷" 'If he cannot afford a lamb, he is to bring two doves or two young pigeons to the LORD as a penalty for his sin—one for a sin offering and the other for a burnt offering. ⁸He is to bring them to the priest, who shall first offer the one for the sin offering. He is to wring its head from its neck, not severing it completely, ⁹and is to sprinkle some of the blood of the sin offering against the side of the altar; the rest of the blood must be drained out at the base of the altar. It is a sin offering. ¹⁰The priest shall then offer the other

Why is that? What is your major concern as you reflect on this? **4.** Without offerings to burn, how is it possible to create "an aroma pleasing to God"? How would you go about doing this (see 2Co 2:14–17)? How might this affect your relationship with God? With others? What will you do about it this week?

as a burnt offering in the prescribed way and make atonement for him for the sin he has committed, and he will be forgiven.

11 " 'If, however, he cannot afford two doves or two young pigeons, he is to bring as an offering for his sin a tenth of an ephah[a] of fine flour for a sin offering. He must not put oil or incense on it, because it is a sin offering. 12He is to bring it to the priest, who shall take a handful of it as a memorial portion and burn it on the altar on top of the offerings made to the LORD by fire. It is a sin offering. 13In this way the priest will make atonement for him for any of these sins he has committed, and he will be forgiven. The rest of the offering will belong to the priest, as in the case of the grain offering.' "

The Guilt Offering

14The LORD said to Moses: 15"When a person commits a violation and sins unintentionally in regard to any of the LORD's holy things, he is to bring to the LORD as a penalty a ram from the flock, one without defect and of the proper value in silver, according to the sanctuary shekel.[b] It is a guilt offering. 16He must make restitution for what he has failed to do in regard to the holy things, add a fifth of the value to that and give it all to the priest, who will make atonement for him with the ram as a guilt offering, and he will be forgiven.

17"If a person sins and does what is forbidden in any of the LORD's commands, even though he does not know it, he is guilty and will be held responsible. 18He is to bring to the priest as a guilt offering a ram from the flock, one without defect and of the proper value. In this way the priest will make atonement for him for the wrong he has committed unintentionally, and he will be forgiven. 19It is a guilt offering; he has been guilty of[c] wrongdoing against the LORD."

6 The LORD said to Moses: 2"If anyone sins and is unfaithful to the LORD by deceiving his neighbor about something entrusted to him or left in his care or stolen, or if he cheats him, 3or if he finds lost property and lies about it, or if he swears falsely, or if he commits any such sin that people may do— 4when he thus sins and becomes guilty, he must return what he has stolen or taken by extortion, or what was entrusted to him, or the lost property he found, 5or whatever it was he swore falsely about. He must make restitution in full, add a fifth of the value to it and give it all to the owner on the day he presents his guilt offering. 6And as a penalty he must bring to the priest, that is, to the LORD, his guilt offering, a ram from the flock, one without defect and of the proper value. 7In this way the priest will make atonement for him before the LORD, and he will be forgiven for any of these things he did that made him guilty."

The Burnt Offering

8The LORD said to Moses: 9"Give Aaron and his sons this command: 'These are the regulations for the burnt offering: The burnt offering is to remain on the altar hearth throughout the night, till morning, and the fire must be kept burning on the altar. 10The priest shall then put on his linen clothes, with linen undergarments next to his body, and shall remove the ashes of the burnt offering that the fire has consumed on the altar and place them beside the altar. 11Then he is to take off these clothes and put on others, and carry the ashes outside the camp to a place that is

---

Have you ever had to buy back something you lost or sold? How did you arrive at a monetary limit for that special something?

1. How is a "guilt offering" different than a "sin offering" (chs. 4–5)? 2. For what kinds of sin is restitution possible and therefore required (5:16; 6:1–5)? Which require a 20 percent fine? 3. What does this teach you about God's view of sin? God's view of the reconciliation process? His desire for his followers?

1. If you were to assign a "money value" to your sins, what would they be worth? How far "in debt" would you be: (a) One week's allowance? (b) One month's wages? (c) Half this country's foreign trade imbalance? (d) More than the national deficit? 2. How will such debts be cancelled: By you? Your creditors? God? When in your experience has God cancelled your debt of guilt? What will it "cost" you to let God cancel your total debt (see Mt 18:21–35)?

1. What memories do you have about one of your "old flames"? Will that love ever die? 2. As a child, what foods were considered "off limits"? Why? 3. When you were growing up, who had to do the dishes most often? For what occasions did you bring out the special plates and silverware?

1. Why do you think God wants the fires for the burnt offerings to burn continuously (vv. 8–13)? What might this say about the perpetual need for, and offer of,

---

a11 That is, probably about 2 quarts (about 2 liters) b15 That is, about 2/5 ounce (about 11.5 grams) c19 Or has made full expiation for his

ceremonially clean. [12]The fire on the altar must be kept burning; it must not go out. Every morning the priest is to add firewood and arrange the burnt offering on the fire and burn the fat of the fellowship offerings[a] on it. [13]The fire must be kept burning on the altar continuously; it must not go out.

The Grain Offering

[14]" 'These are the regulations for the grain offering: Aaron's sons are to bring it before the LORD, in front of the altar. [15]The priest is to take a handful of fine flour and oil, together with all the incense on the grain offering, and burn the memorial portion on the altar as an aroma pleasing to the LORD. [16]Aaron and his sons shall eat the rest of it, but it is to be eaten without yeast in a holy place; they are to eat it in the courtyard of the Tent of Meeting. [17]It must not be baked with yeast; I have given it as their share of the offerings made to me by fire. Like the sin offering and the guilt offering, it is most holy. [18]Any male descendant of Aaron may eat it. It is his regular share of the offerings made to the LORD by fire for the generations to come. Whatever touches them will become holy.[b]' "

[19]The LORD also said to Moses, [20]"This is the offering Aaron and his sons are to bring to the LORD on the day he[c] is anointed: a tenth of an ephah[d] of fine flour as a regular grain offering, half of it in the morning and half in the evening. [21]Prepare it with oil on a griddle; bring it well-mixed and present the grain offering broken[e] in pieces as an aroma pleasing to the LORD. [22]The son who is to succeed him as anointed priest shall prepare it. It is the LORD's regular share and is to be burned completely. [23]Every grain offering of a priest shall be burned completely; it must not be eaten."

The Sin Offering

[24]The LORD said to Moses, [25]"Say to Aaron and his sons: 'These are the regulations for the sin offering: The sin offering is to be slaughtered before the LORD in the place the burnt offering is slaughtered; it is most holy. [26]The priest who offers it shall eat it; it is to be eaten in a holy place, in the courtyard of the Tent of Meeting. [27]Whatever touches any of the flesh will become holy, and if any of the blood is spattered on a garment, you must wash it in a holy place. [28]The clay pot the meat is cooked in must be broken; but if it is cooked in a bronze pot, the pot is to be scoured and rinsed with water. [29]Any male in a priest's family may eat it; it is most holy. [30]But any sin offering whose blood is brought into the Tent of Meeting to make atonement in the Holy Place must not be eaten; it must be burned.

The Guilt Offering

7 " 'These are the regulations for the guilt offering, which is most holy: [2]The guilt offering is to be slaughtered in the place where the burnt offering is slaughtered, and its blood is to be sprinkled against the altar on all sides. [3]All its fat shall be offered: the fat tail and the fat that covers the inner parts, [4]both kidneys with the fat on them near the loins, and the covering of the liver, which is to be removed with the kidneys. [5]The priest shall burn them on the altar as an offering made to the LORD by fire. It is a guilt offering. [6]Any male in a priest's family may eat it, but it must be eaten in a holy place; it is most holy.

reconciliation? 2. Compare verses 14–23 with 2:1–16. Who brings the two grain offerings (2:1; 6:14)? Who could eat whose offering? And where (6:16,22–23)? 3. What further regulations apply to the grain offering of a priest (vv. 19–23)? 4. What do such differences tell you about the function of the grain offering? About its place in the process of rebuilding a proper relationship with God? 5. What is "holy" and "most holy" about the "sin offering" (vv. 24–30)? How does this paragraph epitomize all that's been said so far in Leviticus about our relationship with a holy and righteous God?

1. When have you seen your fire for God almost die out? When has God's eternal love rekindled your flame? When have you felt as if you couldn't be reconciled to God? 2. What do burnt offerings suggest about how to go about keeping a right relationship with God when you are under conviction of sin? 3. What do burnt, grain and sin offerings teach you about the process of reconciliation, then and now? 4. How is your way of restoring a right relationship with God like the one described in chapter 6? 5. How do you explain your way to an unbeliever? With whom will you share this good news today?

1. What meat dishes are your favorite? What makes them so tasty? 2. In what "ceremonial" ways do you show gratitude to your parents: Flowers? Breakfast in bed? Dinner out? Or what?

1. What regulations define the guilt offering? How does this help define the reconciliation process? 2. Why do you think God specifies the sprinkling of blood? And the offering of "all" the fat? 3. What belongs only to priests? Why is that? 4. What is the relation between the blood in this passage and that in Hebrews 9:11–28?

---

[a]12 Traditionally *peace offerings*   [b]18 Or *Whoever touches them must be holy*; similarly in verse 27   [c]20 Or *each*   [d]20 That is, probably about 2 quarts (about 2 liters)   [e]21 The meaning of the Hebrew for this word is uncertain.

How has the believer's relation with God been affected by the blood of Christ's sacrifice? **5.** In what ways do fellowship offerings (vv. 11–21) vary from those for sin (6:24–30) and guilt (7:1–10)? **6.** Why do you think animal sacrifice was appropriate for vows, freewill and thanksgiving offerings, as well as for sin offerings? **7.** What is the distinction between "clean" and "unclean" in verse 19 (also 4:12)? Does this convey ritual purity, physical cleanliness or what? **8.** What does it mean to be "cut off from his people" (vv. 20–21)? Does this convey God's judgment by execution, banishment, or what? What does this say about the importance of one's fellowship with God?

♡ **1.** When you are particularly thankful to God, how do you show it? In what ways is this like the thanksgiving offering depicted in verses 12–15? **2.** For what are you particularly thankful today? How will you express this to God?

☕ **1.** Have you ever had to turn down some particular food served to you? What for? **2.** When something breaks down and needs replacement, do you buy a new one, borrow a used one or fix the old one? Cite an example.

📖 **1.** What links this food law to the laws about animal sacrifice (see chs. 3–4)? **2.** In ancient Israel, all tribes were given land, except "Levites" (the priestly tribe) who were to live off the offerings of others (vv. 35–36; see 10:12–15; Nu 18:8–20; Dt 18:1–5). Being landless and dependent—would that help, or hinder their performance? How so? **3.** What does this teach you about God's desire for his priests? For his people?

7 " 'The same law applies to both the sin offering and the guilt offering: They belong to the priest who makes atonement with them. 8The priest who offers a burnt offering for anyone may keep its hide for himself. 9Every grain offering baked in an oven or cooked in a pan or on a griddle belongs to the priest who offers it, 10and every grain offering, whether mixed with oil or dry, belongs equally to all the sons of Aaron.

The Fellowship Offering

11 " 'These are the regulations for the fellowship offering[a] a person may present to the LORD:

12 " 'If he offers it as an expression of thankfulness, then along with this thank offering he is to offer cakes of bread made without yeast and mixed with oil, wafers made without yeast and spread with oil, and cakes of fine flour well-kneaded and mixed with oil. 13Along with his fellowship offering of thanksgiving he is to present an offering with cakes of bread made with yeast. 14He is to bring one of each kind as an offering, a contribution to the LORD; it belongs to the priest who sprinkles the blood of the fellowship offerings. 15The meat of his fellowship offering of thanksgiving must be eaten on the day it is offered; he must leave none of it till morning.

16 " 'If, however, his offering is the result of a vow or is a freewill offering, the sacrifice shall be eaten on the day he offers it, but anything left over may be eaten on the next day. 17Any meat of the sacrifice left over till the third day must be burned up. 18If any meat of the fellowship offering is eaten on the third day, it will not be accepted. It will not be credited to the one who offered it, for it is impure; the person who eats any of it will be held responsible.

19 " 'Meat that touches anything ceremonially unclean must not be eaten; it must be burned up. As for other meat, anyone ceremonially clean may eat it. 20But if anyone who is unclean eats any meat of the fellowship offering belonging to the LORD, that person must be cut off from his people. 21If anyone touches something unclean—whether human uncleanness or an unclean animal or any unclean, detestable thing—and then eats any of the meat of the fellowship offering belonging to the LORD, that person must be cut off from his people.' "

Eating Fat and Blood Forbidden

22The LORD said to Moses, 23"Say to the Israelites: 'Do not eat any of the fat of cattle, sheep or goats. 24The fat of an animal found dead or torn by wild animals may be used for any other purpose, but you must not eat it. 25Anyone who eats the fat of an animal from which an offering by fire may be[b] made to the LORD must be cut off from his people. 26And wherever you live, you must not eat the blood of any bird or animal. 27If anyone eats blood, that person must be cut off from his people.' "

The Priests' Share

28The LORD said to Moses, 29"Say to the Israelites: 'Anyone who brings a fellowship offering to the LORD is to bring part of it as his sacrifice to the LORD. 30With his own hands he is to bring the offering made to the LORD by fire; he is to bring the fat, together with the breast, and wave the breast before the LORD as a wave offering. 31The priest shall burn the fat on the altar, but the breast belongs to Aaron and his sons. 32You are to give the right thigh of

a11 Traditionally *peace offering*; also in verses 13-37   b25 Or *fire is*

your fellowship offerings to the priest as a contribution. [33]The son of Aaron who offers the blood and the fat of the fellowship offering shall have the right thigh as his share. [34]From the fellowship offerings of the Israelites, I have taken the breast that is waved and the thigh that is presented and have given them to Aaron the priest and his sons as their regular share from the Israelites.'"

[35]This is the portion of the offerings made to the Lord by fire that were allotted to Aaron and his sons on the day they were presented to serve the Lord as priests. [36]On the day they were anointed, the Lord commanded that the Israelites give this to them as their regular share for the generations to come.

[37]These, then, are the regulations for the burnt offering, the grain offering, the sin offering, the guilt offering, the ordination offering and the fellowship offering, [38]which the Lord gave Moses on Mount Sinai on the day he commanded the Israelites to bring their offerings to the Lord, in the Desert of Sinai.

The Ordination of Aaron and His Sons

8 The Lord said to Moses, [2]"Bring Aaron and his sons, their garments, the anointing oil, the bull for the sin offering, the two rams and the basket containing bread made without yeast, [3]and gather the entire assembly at the entrance to the Tent of Meeting." [4]Moses did as the Lord commanded him, and the assembly gathered at the entrance to the Tent of Meeting.

[5]Moses said to the assembly, "This is what the Lord has commanded to be done." [6]Then Moses brought Aaron and his sons forward and washed them with water. [7]He put the tunic on Aaron, tied the sash around him, clothed him with the robe and put the ephod on him. He also tied the ephod to him by its skillfully woven waistband; so it was fastened on him. [8]He placed the breastpiece on him and put the Urim and Thummim in the breastpiece. [9]Then he placed the turban on Aaron's head and set the gold plate, the sacred diadem, on the front of it, as the Lord commanded Moses.

[10]Then Moses took the anointing oil and anointed the tabernacle and everything in it, and so consecrated them. [11]He sprinkled some of the oil on the altar seven times, anointing the altar and all its utensils and the basin with its stand, to consecrate them. [12]He poured some of the anointing oil on Aaron's head and anointed him to consecrate him. [13]Then he brought Aaron's sons forward, put tunics on them, tied sashes around them and put headbands on them, as the Lord commanded Moses.

[14]He then presented the bull for the sin offering, and Aaron and his sons laid their hands on its head. [15]Moses slaughtered the bull and took some of the blood, and with his finger he put it on all the horns of the altar to purify the altar. He poured out the rest of the blood at the base of the altar. So he consecrated it to make atonement for it. [16]Moses also took all the fat around the inner parts, the covering of the liver, and both kidneys and their fat, and burned it on the altar. [17]But the bull with its hide and its flesh and its offal he burned up outside the camp, as the Lord commanded Moses.

[18]He then presented the ram for the burnt offering, and Aaron and his sons laid their hands on its head. [19]Then Moses slaughtered the ram and sprinkled the blood against the altar on all sides. [20]He cut the ram into pieces and burned the head, the pieces and the fat. [21]He washed the inner parts and the legs with water and burned the whole ram on the altar as a burnt offering, a pleasing aroma, an offering made to the Lord by fire, as the Lord commanded Moses.

[22]He then presented the other ram, the ram for the ordination,

1. Some take passages like 7:22–27 as reason to refrain from eating meat or eating only "kosher" meat? What do you think? How else might you show respect for the symbol of life, which is the blood? 2. How is your pastor like and unlike the priests of the OT? 3. How might the living standards for clergy outlined here fit, or not fit, your church? How can you help (not hinder) your pastor by your "offerings"?

1. Which pastor or Sunday School teacher from your growing up years has left the deepest impression on you? What makes that person so memorable? 2. Imagine an ordination service for someone entering the ministry. What images come to mind: Wedding? Graduation? Coronation? Funeral Wake? Other?

1. Imagine yourself "on deck" watching, listening, touching, smelling and tasting what goes on. As an onlooker, what impresses you? As a Levite getting ordained, what impresses you? 2. What lasting impression do you think God intended this proceeding to make on one and all? What was his purpose in setting aside Aaron and his sons in this public and sacred way? 3. How does the elaborate ceremony in this chapter demonstrate the importance of the consecration of the priests to God? 4. More specifically, what is the purpose of their "sacred garments" (vv. 2, 6–10,30; see Ex 28:2; 39:1)? The breastpiece with the "Urim and Thummim" (v. 8; see Ex 28:15,30)? The "anointing oil" (vv. 10–12,30; see Ps 133)? 5. If the "sin offering" (vv. 14ff) was for atonement (see 4:3–12), what was the "burnt offering" for (v. 18)? Why two ram offerings (vv. 18, 22)? Why the "wave offering" (vv. 26–29), as well? And why apply blood to the high priest on his right ear, thumb and toe (v. 23)? 6. Why do you think God saw this ritual cleanliness as important? What do you see as the link between ritual cleanliness and true spiritual cleanliness? Do you think ritual cleanliness was required mainly for God's benefit or for the people's benefit? Why?

and Aaron and his sons laid their hands on its head. ²³Moses slaughtered the ram and took some of its blood and put it on the lobe of Aaron's right ear, on the thumb of his right hand and on the big toe of his right foot. ²⁴Moses also brought Aaron's sons forward and put some of the blood on the lobes of their right ears, on the thumbs of their right hands and on the big toes of their right feet. Then he sprinkled blood against the altar on all sides. ²⁵He took the fat, the fat tail, all the fat around the inner parts, the covering of the liver, both kidneys and their fat and the right thigh. ²⁶Then from the basket of bread made without yeast, which was before the LORD, he took a cake of bread, and one made with oil, and a wafer; he put these on the fat portions and on the right thigh. ²⁷He put all these in the hands of Aaron and his sons and waved them before the LORD as a wave offering. ²⁸Then Moses took them from their hands and burned them on the altar on top of the burnt offering as an ordination offering, a pleasing aroma, an offering made to the LORD by fire. ²⁹He also took the breast—Moses' share of the ordination ram—and waved it before the LORD as a wave offering, as the LORD commanded Moses.

³⁰Then Moses took some of the anointing oil and some of the blood from the altar and sprinkled them on Aaron and his garments and on his sons and their garments. So he consecrated Aaron and his garments and his sons and their garments.

³¹Moses then said to Aaron and his sons, "Cook the meat at the entrance to the Tent of Meeting and eat it there with the bread from the basket of ordination offerings, as I commanded, saying,ᵃ 'Aaron and his sons are to eat it.' ³²Then burn up the rest of the meat and the bread. ³³Do not leave the entrance to the Tent of Meeting for seven days, until the days of your ordination are completed, for your ordination will last seven days. ³⁴What has been done today was commanded by the LORD to make atonement for you. ³⁵You must stay at the entrance to the Tent of Meeting day and night for seven days and do what the LORD requires, so you will not die; for that is what I have been commanded." ³⁶So Aaron and his sons did everything the LORD commanded through Moses.

The Priests Begin Their Ministry

9 On the eighth day Moses summoned Aaron and his sons and the elders of Israel. ²He said to Aaron, "Take a bull calf for your sin offering and a ram for your burnt offering, both without defect, and present them before the LORD. ³Then say to the Israelites: 'Take a male goat for a sin offering, a calf and a lamb—both a year old and without defect—for a burnt offering, ⁴and an oxᵇ and a ram for a fellowship offeringᶜ to sacrifice before the LORD, together with a grain offering mixed with oil. For today the LORD will appear to you.'"

⁵They took the things Moses commanded to the front of the Tent of Meeting, and the entire assembly came near and stood before the LORD. ⁶Then Moses said, "This is what the LORD has command-ed you to do, so that the glory of the LORD may appear to you."

⁷Moses said to Aaron, "Come to the altar and sacrifice your sin offering and your burnt offering and make atonement for yourself and the people; sacrifice the offering that is for the people and make atonement for them, as the LORD has commanded."

⁸So Aaron came to the altar and slaughtered the calf as a sin offering for himself. ⁹His sons brought the blood to him, and he dipped his finger into the blood and put it on the horns of the altar;

ᵃ31 Or *I was commanded;* also in verses 18 and 19. ᵇ4 The Hebrew word can include both male and female; ᶜ4 Traditionally *peace offering;* also in verses 18 and 22

the rest of the blood he poured out at the base of the altar. ¹⁰On the altar he burned the fat, the kidneys and the covering of the liver from the sin offering, as the LORD commanded Moses; ¹¹the flesh and the hide he burned up outside the camp.

¹²Then he slaughtered the burnt offering. His sons handed him the blood, and he sprinkled it against the altar on all sides. ¹³They handed him the burnt offering piece by piece, including the head, and he burned them on the altar. ¹⁴He washed the inner parts and the legs and burned them on top of the burnt offering on the altar.

¹⁵Aaron then brought the offering that was for the people. He took the goat for the people's sin offering and slaughtered it and offered it for a sin offering as he did with the first one.

¹⁶He brought the burnt offering and offered it in the prescribed way. ¹⁷He also brought the grain offering, took a handful of it and burned it on the altar in addition to the morning's burnt offering.

¹⁸He slaughtered the ox and the ram as the fellowship offering for the people. His sons handed him the blood, and he sprinkled it against the altar on all sides. ¹⁹But the fat portions of the ox and the ram—the fat tail, the layer of fat, the kidneys and the covering of the liver— ²⁰these they laid on the breasts, and then Aaron burned the fat on the altar. ²¹Aaron waved the breasts and the right thigh before the LORD as a wave offering, as Moses commanded.

²²Then Aaron lifted his hands toward the people and blessed them. And having sacrificed the sin offering, the burnt offering and the fellowship offering, he stepped down.

²³Moses and Aaron then went into the Tent of Meeting. When they came out, they blessed the people; and the glory of the LORD appeared to all the people. ²⁴Fire came out from the presence of the LORD and consumed the burnt offering and the fat portions on the altar. And when all the people saw it, they shouted for joy and fell facedown.

The Death of Nadab and Abihu

10 Aaron's sons Nadab and Abihu took their censers, put fire in them and added incense; and they offered unauthorized fire before the LORD, contrary to his command. ²So fire came out from the presence of the LORD and consumed them, and they died before the LORD. ³Moses then said to Aaron, "This is what the LORD spoke of when he said:

> "'Among those who approach me
> I will show myself holy;
> in the sight of all the people
> I will be honored.'"

Aaron remained silent.

⁴Moses summoned Mishael and Elzaphan, sons of Aaron's uncle Uzziel, and said to them, "Come here; carry your cousins outside the camp, away from the front of the sanctuary." ⁵So they came and carried them, still in their tunics, outside the camp, as Moses ordered.

⁶Then Moses said to Aaron and his sons Eleazar and Ithamar, "Do not let your hair become unkempt,ᵃ and do not tear your clothes, or you will die and the LORD will be angry with the whole community. But your relatives, all the house of Israel, may mourn for those the LORD has destroyed by fire. ⁷Do not leave the entrance to the Tent of Meeting or you will die, because the LORD's anointing oil is on you." So they did as Moses said.

ᵃ6 Or *Do not uncover your heads*

significance of the fiery "grand finale" (vv. 23–24)? What does this say about Aaron's role in the process of restoring the people to a right relationship with God? **6.** Later Jesus assumes this role. How is Jesus, the High Priest who descended from the tribe of Judah, related to Aaron and his sons, who are descended from the tribe of Levi (see Heb 7:11–28)?

♡ **1.** Do you need someone to stand between you and God in your own process of reconciliation? Why or why not? **2.** Do you think you can be your own "high priest," offering sacrifices and dispensing with formal clergy altogether? Why or why not? **3.** Hebrews 7:11–28 tells us that Jesus is now our High Priest. How does that affect your spiritual pilgrimage? **4.** How would you explain God's process of reconciliation to someone who did not understand it? With whom will you share it?

☕ **1.** As a child, what were you told about keeping up your appearance (hair, clothes, eating habits)? If you looked "unkempt," what would your parents say? How did you respond? **2.** What was your first experience with death: Close friend, aging relative or long-time pet? How old were you then? How did that affect you?

📖 **1.** Why do you think the death of Aaron's sons is included here (after ch. 8–9)? Why were their lives taken (vv. 3,10)? Why do you think repeated mention is made of their death elsewhere (see Ex 6:23; 24:1,9; 28:1; Nu 3:2–4; 26:60–61; 1Ch 6:3; 24:1–2)? **2.** At other turning points in God's redemptive history, those who have trifled with holy things have also died suddenly. What do you know about Achan (Jos 7), Uzzah (2Sa 6:1–7), Ananias and Saphira (Ac 5:1–11)? **3.** What new respect for God does this teach you? By his silence (v. 3), what is Aaron learning about obeying God? Do you think this "object lesson" was too harsh? Why or why not? **4.** In the context of Leviticus, and in the deaths of Nadab and Abihu, what is meant by verse 10? What actions in this chapter could be categorized "holy"? Which are "common"? **5.** It seems Aaron might likewise lose his remaining sons (vv. 16ff). On what basis is Moses "satisfied" with Aaron's intentions?

♡ **1.** What does your church do to help distinguish between the sacred and the secular? Compare your lists. In your opinion, what is "sacrilegious"? What examples support your definition? **2.** Where are you most likely to have problems separating the sacred from the secular? What can you learn from Aaron's sons to help you keep these distinct? **3.** How can your small group keep you accountable and help you avoid becoming sacrilegious?

⊔ **1.** What can you still hear your mother saying about foods that were good, and not good, for you to eat? **2.** What animals head up your "All Ugly Team" by virtue of their features, habits or taste? **3.** What animals head up your "Mr. Clean Team" by virtue of their features, habits or taste? **4.** By whatever definition, which restaurant in your area would you classify as a "clean" establishment? Which one fails to meet your criteria?

📖 **1.** How is this chapter an extension of the principles in the previous one (v. 47)? **2.** Although it is not clear today why certain animals were listed as fit for human consumption and others were not, what reasons might there be back then for such an action by God? How would the reasons you have listed help the people, both physically and spiritually? **3.** Given the situation the people find themselves in, why would cleanliness be

[8]Then the LORD said to Aaron, [9]"You and your sons are not to drink wine or other fermented drink whenever you go into the Tent of Meeting, or you will die. This is a lasting ordinance for the generations to come. [10]You must distinguish between the holy and the common, between the unclean and the clean, [11]and you must teach the Israelites all the decrees the LORD has given them through Moses."

[12]Moses said to Aaron and his remaining sons, Eleazar and Ithamar, "Take the grain offering left over from the offerings made to the LORD by fire and eat it prepared without yeast beside the altar, for it is most holy. [13]Eat it in a holy place, because it is your share and your sons' share of the offerings made to the LORD by fire; for so I have been commanded. [14]But you and your sons and your daughters may eat the breast that was waved and the thigh that was presented. Eat them in a ceremonially clean place; they have been given to you and your children as your share of the Israelites' fellowship offerings.[a] [15]The thigh that was presented and the breast that was waved must be brought with the fat portions of the offerings made by fire, to be waved before the LORD as a wave offering. This will be the regular share for you and your children, as the LORD has commanded."

[16]When Moses inquired about the goat of the sin offering and found that it had been burned up, he was angry with Eleazar and Ithamar, Aaron's remaining sons, and asked, [17]"Why didn't you eat the sin offering in the sanctuary area? It is most holy; it was given to you to take away the guilt of the community by making atonement for them before the LORD. [18]Since its blood was not taken into the Holy Place, you should have eaten the goat in the sanctuary area, as I commanded."

[19]Aaron replied to Moses, "Today they sacrificed their sin offering and their burnt offering before the LORD, but such things as this have happened to me. Would the LORD have been pleased if I had eaten the sin offering today?" [20]When Moses heard this, he was satisfied.

Clean and Unclean Food

11 The LORD said to Moses and Aaron, [2]"Say to the Israelites: 'Of all the animals that live on land, these are the ones you may eat: [3]You may eat any animal that has a split hoof completely divided and that chews the cud.

[4]"'There are some that only chew the cud or only have a split hoof, but you must not eat them. The camel, though it chews the cud, does not have a split hoof; it is ceremonially unclean for you. [5]The coney,[b] though it chews the cud, does not have a split hoof; it is unclean for you. [6]The rabbit, though it chews the cud, does not have a split hoof; it is unclean for you. [7]And the pig, though it has a split hoof completely divided, does not chew the cud; it is unclean for you. [8]You must not eat their meat or touch their carcasses; they are unclean for you.

[9]"'Of all the creatures living in the water of the seas and the streams, you may eat any that have fins and scales. [10]But all creatures in the seas or streams that do not have fins and scales—whether among all the swarming things or among all the other living creatures in the water—you are to detest. [11]And since you are to detest them, you must not eat their meat and you must detest their carcasses. [12]Anything living in the water that does not have fins and scales is to be detestable to you.

[a]14 Traditionally *peace offerings*   [b]5 That is, the hyrax or rock badger

¹³" 'These are the birds you are to detest and not eat because they are detestable: the eagle, the vulture, the black vulture, ¹⁴the red kite, any kind of black kite, ¹⁵any kind of raven, ¹⁶the horned owl, the screech owl, the gull, any kind of hawk, ¹⁷the little owl, the cormorant, the great owl, ¹⁸the white owl, the desert owl, the osprey, ¹⁹the stork, any kind of heron, the hoopoe and the bat.^a

²⁰" 'All flying insects that walk on all fours are to be detestable to you. ²¹There are, however, some winged creatures that walk on all fours that you may eat: those that have jointed legs for hopping on the ground. ²²Of these you may eat any kind of locust, katydid, cricket or grasshopper. ²³But all other winged creatures that have four legs you are to detest.

²⁴" 'You will make yourselves unclean by these; whoever touches their carcasses will be unclean till evening. ²⁵Whoever picks up one of their carcasses must wash his clothes, and he will be unclean till evening.

²⁶" 'Every animal that has a split hoof not completely divided or that does not chew the cud is unclean for you; whoever touches ⌊the carcass of⌋ any of them will be unclean. ²⁷Of all the animals that walk on all fours, those that walk on their paws are unclean for you; whoever touches their carcasses will be unclean till evening. ²⁸Anyone who picks up their carcasses must wash his clothes, and he will be unclean till evening. They are unclean for you.

²⁹" 'Of the animals that move about on the ground, these are unclean for you: the weasel, the rat, any kind of great lizard, ³⁰the gecko, the monitor lizard, the wall lizard, the skink and the chameleon. ³¹Of all those that move along the ground, these are unclean for you. Whoever touches them when they are dead will be unclean till evening. ³²When one of them dies and falls on something, that article, whatever its use, will be unclean, whether it is made of wood, cloth, hide or sackcloth. Put it in water; it will be unclean till evening, and then it will be clean. ³³If one of them falls into a clay pot, everything in it will be unclean, and you must break the pot. ³⁴Any food that could be eaten but has water on it from such a pot is unclean, and any liquid that could be drunk from it is unclean. ³⁵Anything that one of their carcasses falls on becomes unclean; an oven or cooking pot must be broken up. They are unclean, and you are to regard them as unclean. ³⁶A spring, however, or a cistern for collecting water remains clean, but anyone who touches one of these carcasses is unclean. ³⁷If a carcass falls on any seeds that are to be planted, they remain clean. ³⁸But if water has been put on the seed and a carcass falls on it, it is unclean for you.

³⁹" 'If an animal that you are allowed to eat dies, anyone who touches the carcass will be unclean till evening. ⁴⁰Anyone who eats some of the carcass must wash his clothes, and he will be unclean till evening. Anyone who picks up the carcass must wash his clothes, and he will be unclean till evening.

⁴¹" 'Every creature that moves about on the ground is detestable; it is not to be eaten. ⁴²You are not to eat any creature that moves about on the ground, whether it moves on its belly or walks on all fours or on many feet; it is detestable. ⁴³Do not defile yourselves by any of these creatures. Do not make yourselves unclean by means of them or be made unclean by them. ⁴⁴I am the LORD your God; consecrate yourselves and be holy, because I am holy. Do not make yourselves unclean by any creature that moves about on the ground. ⁴⁵I am the LORD who brought you up out of Egypt to be your God; therefore be holy, because I am holy.

so important? How would making cleanliness part of their ritual life help the ancient Israelites? **4.** To this point, Leviticus has been a list of rules for restoring a right relationship with God. How does this chapter develop that theme? What added purpose and incentives to holiness does God give them here (vv. 43–45)?

1. In Daniel 1, we see where strict adherence to such dietary laws help strengthen God's people and establish his purpose. How might God's cause be better served today by following dietary food laws in a self-indulgent culture? **2.** However, in Acts 10:9–23, the regulations concerning clean and unclean animals are apparently lifted. Why do you think this is? In what sense would the removal of these laws help spread the Gospel? **3.** Diets abound in today's society, for all kinds of reasons. What is the latest diet you have heard about? Why are some people always "going on a diet"? When is the last time you went on one? Why did you diet? For any reasons akin to the ones listed in this chapter? **4.** Who has the most to say about the food you eat: (a) TV ads? (b) Your mom? (c) Your spouse? (d) Your physician? (e) Food and Drug Administration? (f) Your sweet tooth? What do they have to say about what is "clean" or "unclean" for you? What do you feel is "clean" or "unclean" for you? **5.** In this chapter, diet and religion seem to be blended. What are the ways you feel food and faith may be appropriately blended? In what ways should the two never mix?

^a19 The precise identification of some of the birds, insects and animals in this chapter is uncertain.

46" 'These are the regulations concerning animals, birds, every living thing that moves in the water and every creature that moves about on the ground. 47You must distinguish between the unclean and the clean, between living creatures that may be eaten and those that may not be eaten.' "

Purification After Childbirth

12 The LORD said to Moses, 2"Say to the Israelites: 'A woman who becomes pregnant and gives birth to a son will be ceremonially unclean for seven days, just as she is unclean during her monthly period. 3On the eighth day the boy is to be circumcised. 4Then the woman must wait thirty-three days to be purified from her bleeding. She must not touch anything sacred or go to the sanctuary until the days of her purification are over. 5If she gives birth to a daughter, for two weeks the woman will be unclean, as during her period. Then she must wait sixty-six days to be purified from her bleeding.

6" 'When the days of her purification for a son or daughter are over, she is to bring to the priest at the entrance to the Tent of Meeting a year-old lamb for a burnt offering and a young pigeon or a dove for a sin offering. 7He shall offer them before the LORD to make atonement for her, and then she will be ceremonially clean from her flow of blood.

" 'These are the regulations for the woman who gives birth to a boy or a girl. 8If she cannot afford a lamb, she is to bring two doves or two young pigeons, one for a burnt offering and the other for a sin offering. In this way the priest will make atonement for her, and she will be clean.' "

Regulations About Infectious Skin Diseases

13 The LORD said to Moses and Aaron, 2"When anyone has a swelling or a rash or a bright spot on his skin that may become an infectious skin disease,a he must be brought to Aaron the priest or to one of his sonsb who is a priest. 3The priest is to examine the sore on his skin, and if the hair in the sore has turned white and the sore appears to be more than skin deep,c it is an infectious skin disease. When the priest examines him, he shall pronounce him ceremonially unclean. 4If the spot on his skin is white but does not appear to be more than skin deep and the hair in it has not turned white, the priest is to put the infected person in isolation for seven days. 5On the seventh day the priest is to examine him, and if he sees that the sore is unchanged and has not spread in the skin, he is to keep him in isolation another seven days. 6On the seventh day the priest is to examine him again, and if the sore has faded and has not spread in the skin, the priest shall pronounce him clean; it is only a rash. The man must wash his clothes, and he will be clean. 7But if the rash does spread in his skin after he has shown himself to the priest to be pronounced clean, he must appear before the priest again. 8The priest is to examine him, and if the rash has spread in the skin, he shall pronounce him unclean; it is an infectious disease.

9"When anyone has an infectious skin disease, he must be brought to the priest. 10The priest is to examine him, and if there is a white swelling in the skin that has turned the hair white and if there is raw flesh in the swelling, 11it is a chronic skin disease

---

a2 Traditionally *leprosy*; the Hebrew word was used for various diseases affecting the skin—not necessarily leprosy; also elsewhere in this chapter.   b2 Or *descendants*
c3 Or *be lower than the rest of the skin*; also elsewhere in this chapter

---

What feelings do you have about babies? Why is that?

Do you think it really takes twice as long to become clean after giving birth to a girl? What do these regulations tell you about the values of this culture? About the relationship of culture and law?

How do these purification regulations make you feel? How does modern culture affect worship and ritual practices at your church? Is this necessarily bad? Why or why not?

1. What disease do you fear most? Why? Is the one you fear considered fatal, contagious, inherited, inevitable, crippling, embarrassing or what? 2. With whom do you find it easier to talk more openly: Your doctor or your pastor? Why do you think this is?

1. Given the situation the Israelites find themselves in, why would it be smart to be concerned about infectious diseases? (Note that the Hebrew word translated "infectious skin diseases" also means "mildew," as in vv. 47–49). How would good physical health promote good spiritual health? 2. Why do you think health laws, such as those in this passage, are part of Israelite religion? Why, for example, must diseased persons be isolated for "seven days" (vv. 4,21,26,31)? Why must infectious people live alone and outside the camp while proclaiming themselves "unclean" (v. 46)? 3. What do preliminary symptoms ("white spots") of these various skin diseases (leprosy, rashes, boils, burns, sores) have to do with religious defilement? 4. How does this compare to the treatment of the sick by Jesus (see Mt 8:1–4)? Why

and the priest shall pronounce him unclean. He is not to put him in isolation, because he is already unclean.

¹²"If the disease breaks out all over his skin and, so far as the priest can see, it covers all the skin of the infected person from head to foot, ¹³the priest is to examine him, and if the disease has covered his whole body, he shall pronounce that person clean. Since it has all turned white, he is clean. ¹⁴But whenever raw flesh appears on him, he will be unclean. ¹⁵When the priest sees the raw flesh, he shall pronounce him unclean. The raw flesh is unclean; he has an infectious disease. ¹⁶Should the raw flesh change and turn white, he must go to the priest. ¹⁷The priest is to examine him, and if the sores have turned white, the priest shall pronounce the infected person clean; then he will be clean.

¹⁸"When someone has a boil on his skin and it heals, ¹⁹and in the place where the boil was, a white swelling or reddish-white spot appears, he must present himself to the priest. ²⁰The priest is to examine it, and if it appears to be more than skin deep and the hair in it has turned white, the priest shall pronounce him unclean. It is an infectious skin disease that has broken out where the boil was. ²¹But if, when the priest examines it, there is no white hair in it and it is not more than skin deep and has faded, then the priest is to put him in isolation for seven days. ²²If it is spreading in the skin, the priest shall pronounce him unclean; it is infectious. ²³But if the spot is unchanged and has not spread, it is only a scar from the boil, and the priest shall pronounce him clean.

²⁴"When someone has a burn on his skin and a reddish-white or white spot appears in the raw flesh of the burn, ²⁵the priest is to examine the spot, and if the hair in it has turned white, and it appears to be more than skin deep, it is an infectious disease that has broken out in the burn. The priest shall pronounce him unclean; it is an infectious skin disease. ²⁶But if the priest examines it and there is no white hair in the spot and if it is not more than skin deep and has faded, then the priest is to put him in isolation for seven days. ²⁷On the seventh day the priest is to examine him, and if it is spreading in the skin, the priest shall pronounce him unclean; it is an infectious skin disease. ²⁸If, however, the spot is unchanged and has not spread in the skin but has faded, it is a swelling from the burn, and the priest shall pronounce him clean; it is only a scar from the burn.

²⁹"If a man or woman has a sore on the head or on the chin, ³⁰the priest is to examine the sore, and if it appears to be more than skin deep and the hair in it is yellow and thin, the priest shall pronounce that person unclean; it is an itch, an infectious disease of the head or chin. ³¹But if, when the priest examines this kind of sore, it does not seem to be more than skin deep and there is no black hair in it, then the priest is to put the infected person in isolation for seven days. ³²On the seventh day the priest is to examine the sore, and if the itch has not spread and there is no yellow hair in it and it does not appear to be more than skin deep, ³³he must be shaved except for the diseased area, and the priest is to keep him in isolation another seven days. ³⁴On the seventh day the priest is to examine the itch, and if it has not spread in the skin and appears to be no more than skin deep, the priest shall pronounce him clean. He must wash his clothes, and he will be clean. ³⁵But if the itch does spread in the skin after he is pronounced clean, ³⁶the priest is to examine him, and if the itch has spread in the skin, the priest does not need to look for yellow hair; the

do you think these differences exist? **5.** Why do you think the burden for health inspection and law enforcement falls to the priests? What does this say about the position of priests in Israel?

♡ **1.** How important is good health to you? Rank yourself on a scale of 1 (sickly slob) to 10 (health nut). How do you think your lifestyle promotes good health? **2.** In what ways does maintaining good health promote your spiritual vitality? **3.** How do you react to sickness in others and/or in yourself? Do you see ill health as a sign of something wrong "spiritually"? What can you do to make sure that you make the proper response to illness? What do you think about testing for infectious diseases? About quarantines? **4.** What role should Christians take in the care of the sick, especially the "unclean" members of our society, such as AIDS victims?

person is unclean. [37]If, however, in his judgment it is unchanged and black hair has grown in it, the itch is healed. He is clean, and the priest shall pronounce him clean.

[38]"When a man or woman has white spots on the skin, [39]the priest is to examine them, and if the spots are dull white, it is a harmless rash that has broken out on the skin; that person is clean.

[40]"When a man has lost his hair and is bald, he is clean. [41]If he has lost his hair from the front of his scalp and has a bald forehead, he is clean. [42]But if he has a reddish-white sore on his bald head or forehead, it is an infectious disease breaking out on his head or forehead. [43]The priest is to examine him, and if the swollen sore on his head or forehead is reddish-white like an infectious skin disease, [44]the man is diseased and is unclean. The priest shall pronounce him unclean because of the sore on his head.

[45]"The person with such an infectious disease must wear torn clothes, let his hair be unkempt,[a] cover the lower part of his face and cry out, 'Unclean! Unclean!' [46]As long as he has the infection he remains unclean. He must live alone; he must live outside the camp.

Regulations About Mildew

[47]"If any clothing is contaminated with mildew—any woolen or linen clothing, [48]any woven or knitted material of linen or wool, any leather or anything made of leather— [49]and if the contamination in the clothing, or leather, or woven or knitted material, or any leather article, is greenish or reddish, it is a spreading mildew and must be shown to the priest. [50]The priest is to examine the mildew and isolate the affected article for seven days. [51]On the seventh day he is to examine it, and if the mildew has spread in the clothing, or the woven or knitted material, or the leather, whatever its use, it is a destructive mildew; the article is unclean. [52]He must burn up the clothing, or the woven or knitted material of wool or linen, or any leather article that has the contamination in it, because the mildew is destructive; the article must be burned up.

[53]"But if, when the priest examines it, the mildew has not spread in the clothing, or the woven or knitted material, or the leather article, [54]he shall order that the contaminated article be washed. Then he is to isolate it for another seven days. [55]After the affected article has been washed, the priest is to examine it, and if the mildew has not changed its appearance, even though it has not spread, it is unclean. Burn it with fire, whether the mildew has affected one side or the other. [56]If, when the priest examines it, the mildew has faded after the article has been washed, he is to tear the contaminated part out of the clothing, or the leather, or the woven or knitted material. [57]But if it reappears in the clothing, or in the woven or knitted material, or in the leather article, it is spreading, and whatever has the mildew must be burned with fire. [58]The clothing, or the woven or knitted material, or any leather article that has been washed and is rid of the mildew, must be washed again, and it will be clean."

[59]These are the regulations concerning contamination by mildew in woolen or linen clothing, woven or knitted material, or any leather article, for pronouncing them clean or unclean.

---

1. Do the clothes you are wearing say anything about you as a person? How does this make you feel? 2. Are you a "pack rat"? If so, why? If not, when do you decide to finally toss out old clothes or those never-used items in the basement, garage or attic?

1. What do these regulations about clothing have in common with the previous regulations about skin diseases? (Note that the Hebrew word for "mildew" is the same one translated "infectious skin diseases.") 2. What do these rules about mildew reveal about the value of clothes in the ancient world? Why might this value make such rules necessary?

1. What objects have a high value for you? How might the value of these articles become dangerous to your physical well-being? To your spiritual well-being? 2. What new insights does this passage give you into Jesus' teaching on "treasures that moth and rust destroy" (see Mt 6:19ff)?

---

a45 Or clothes, uncover his head

Cleansing From Infectious Skin Diseases

14 The LORD said to Moses, ²"These are the regulations for the diseased person at the time of his ceremonial cleansing, when he is brought to the priest: ³The priest is to go outside the camp and examine him. If the person has been healed of his infectious skin disease,ᵃ ⁴the priest shall order that two live clean birds and some cedar wood, scarlet yarn and hyssop be brought for the one to be cleansed. ⁵Then the priest shall order that one of the birds be killed over fresh water in a clay pot. ⁶He is then to take the live bird and dip it, together with the cedar wood, the scarlet yarn and the hyssop, into the blood of the bird that was killed over the fresh water. ⁷Seven times he shall sprinkle the one to be cleansed of the infectious disease and pronounce him clean. Then he is to release the live bird in the open fields.

⁸"The person to be cleansed must wash his clothes, shave off all his hair and bathe with water; then he will be ceremonially clean. After this he may come into the camp, but he must stay outside his tent for seven days. ⁹On the seventh day he must shave off all his hair; he must shave his head, his beard, his eyebrows and the rest of his hair. He must wash his clothes and bathe himself with water, and he will be clean.

¹⁰"On the eighth day he must bring two male lambs and one ewe lamb a year old, each without defect, along with three-tenths of an ephahᵇ of fine flour mixed with oil for a grain offering, and one logᶜ of oil. ¹¹The priest who pronounces him clean shall present both the one to be cleansed and his offerings before the LORD at the entrance to the Tent of Meeting.

¹²"Then the priest is to take one of the male lambs and offer it as a guilt offering, along with the log of oil; he shall wave them before the LORD as a wave offering. ¹³He is to slaughter the lamb in the holy place where the sin offering and the burnt offering are slaughtered. Like the sin offering, the guilt offering belongs to the priest; it is most holy. ¹⁴The priest is to take some of the blood of the guilt offering and put it on the lobe of the right ear of the one to be cleansed, on the thumb of his right hand and on the big toe of his right foot. ¹⁵The priest shall then take some of the log of oil, pour it in the palm of his own left hand, ¹⁶dip his right forefinger into the oil in his palm, and with his finger sprinkle some of it before the LORD seven times. ¹⁷The priest is to put some of the oil remaining in his palm on the lobe of the right ear of the one to be cleansed, on the thumb of his right hand and on the big toe of his right foot, on top of the blood of the guilt offering. ¹⁸The rest of the oil in his palm the priest shall put on the head of the one to be cleansed and make atonement for him before the LORD.

¹⁹"Then the priest is to sacrifice the sin offering and make atonement for the one to be cleansed from his uncleanness. After that, the priest shall slaughter the burnt offering ²⁰and offer it on the altar, together with the grain offering, and make atonement for him, and he will be clean.

²¹"If, however, he is poor and cannot afford these, he must take one male lamb as a guilt offering to be waved to make atonement for him, together with a tenth of an ephahᵈ of fine flour mixed with oil for a grain offering, a log of oil, ²²and two doves or two

1. What makes you feel "clean all over"? Why this? 2. What was your parents' or grandparents' favorite prescription "for whatever ails ya"? What did it look, feel, taste or smell like? Did it work?

1. Review the command in Leviticus 13:45–46. Given such socially ostracizing regulations for infectious skin diseases, how tough do you think it would be for someone healed of a skin disease to then reenter the social life of the Israelite camp? Who do you think would have the tougher adjustment: The person healed, or the people already in the camp? Why? 2. How would the rituals detailed here help both parties overcome their respective difficulties? Of these rituals, which seem to you to have actual "medicinal" value? Which have largely "ceremonial" value? Which may have "relational" value? 3. In this regard, why kill one bird (v. 5) and release the other (v. 7)? Likewise, why the offerings for sin or guilt together with offerings for worship and thanks ("burnt" and "grain" offerings)? Why the repeated use of "seven times" (vv. 7,16,51)? What special provisions were made for the poor (vv. 21–32)? 4. What does all this say about God's concern for the "sick"? The "well"? The "poor"? The "outsiders"? The "insiders"? 5. Who was Jesus more concerned about (see Mt 9:12–13): The "sick" or the "healthy"? Those "sinners" who know they need the Physician, or those "righteous" who deny it?

1. What people does the Christian community ostracize today? Who are the "lepers" of your society? Who are the "outsiders"? The "poor"? 2. Whom does your group tend to screen out? How could your small group help re-incorporate these people into the church? 3. How would you or your group go about beginning this process? With whom will you begin such reconciliation during the next "seven days"? 4. What role should Christians take in the area of public health? In health legislation?

ᵃ3 Traditionally *leprosy*; the Hebrew word was used for various diseases affecting the skin—not necessarily leprosy; also elsewhere in this chapter.   ᵇ10 That is, probably about 6 quarts (about 6.5 liters)   ᶜ10 That is, probably about 2/3 pint (about 0.3 liter); also in verses 12, 15, 21 and 24   ᵈ21 That is, probably about 2 quarts (about 2 liters)

young pigeons, which he can afford, one for a sin offering and the other for a burnt offering.

23"On the eighth day he must bring them for his cleansing to the priest at the entrance to the Tent of Meeting, before the LORD. 24The priest is to take the lamb for the guilt offering, together with the log of oil, and wave them before the LORD as a wave offering. 25He shall slaughter the lamb for the guilt offering and take some of its blood and put it on the lobe of the right ear of the one to be cleansed, on the thumb of his right hand and on the big toe of his right foot. 26The priest is to pour some of the oil into the palm of his own left hand, 27and with his right forefinger sprinkle some of the oil from his palm seven times before the LORD. 28Some of the oil in his palm he is to put on the same places he put the blood of the guilt offering—on the lobe of the right ear of the one to be cleansed, on the thumb of his right hand and on the big toe of his right foot. 29The rest of the oil in his palm the priest shall put on the head of the one to be cleansed, to make atonement for him before the LORD. 30Then he shall sacrifice the doves or the young pigeons, which the person can afford, 31one*a* as a sin offering and the other as a burnt offering, together with the grain offering. In this way the priest will make atonement before the LORD on behalf of the one to be cleansed."

32These are the regulations for anyone who has an infectious skin disease and who cannot afford the regular offerings for his cleansing.

Cleansing From Mildew

33The LORD said to Moses and Aaron, 34"When you enter the land of Canaan, which I am giving you as your possession, and I put a spreading mildew in a house in that land, 35the owner of the house must go and tell the priest, 'I have seen something that looks like mildew in my house.' 36The priest is to order the house to be emptied before he goes in to examine the mildew, so that nothing in the house will be pronounced unclean. After this the priest is to go in and inspect the house. 37He is to examine the mildew on the walls, and if it has greenish or reddish depressions that appear to be deeper than the surface of the wall, 38the priest shall go out the doorway of the house and close it up for seven days. 39On the seventh day the priest shall return to inspect the house. If the mildew has spread on the walls, 40he is to order that the contaminated stones be torn out and thrown into an unclean place outside the town. 41He must have all the inside walls of the house scraped and the material that is scraped off dumped into an unclean place outside the town. 42Then they are to take other stones to replace these and take new clay and plaster the house.

43"If the mildew reappears in the house after the stones have been torn out and the house scraped and plastered, 44the priest is to go and examine it and, if the mildew has spread in the house, it is a destructive mildew; the house is unclean. 45It must be torn down—its stones, timbers and all the plaster—and taken out of the town to an unclean place.

46"Anyone who goes into the house while it is closed up will be unclean till evening. 47Anyone who sleeps or eats in the house must wash his clothes.

48"But if the priest comes to examine it and the mildew has not spread after the house has been plastered, he shall pronounce the house clean, because the mildew is gone. 49To purify the house he

1. How would you describe your housekeeping: Comfortable for humanity? Greenhouse for mildew? "Spotless"? What does your spouse or your mom have to say about your housekeeping? 2. What would you prefer to live in: (a) Luxury condo? (b) Older, restored home? (c) Fixer-upper? 3. What difficulties have you encountered remodeling your home?

1. In addition to health and clothing inspector, what new role is cut out for the priests? Why them? 2. What similarities do you see here between cleansing the house and cleansing the leper (14:1–32)? 3. At this time, Israel still lives in tents and has not yet entered Canaan (v. 34a). Why then give laws regarding houses even before the Israelites own any? 4. Of these rituals, which appear to have actual "cleansing" value? Which appear to be largely "ceremonial"? 5. How do you account for verse 34b: (a) God inflicts a plague on a house due to the sin of its builder? (b) God does not talk of germs or other secondary causes to pre-scientific people who would not understand them? (c) Other? 6. What does chapter 14 say about how God cares to restore his people?

a31 Septuagint and Syriac; Hebrew 31*such as the person can afford, one*

is to take two birds and some cedar wood, scarlet yarn and hyssop. [50]He shall kill one of the birds over fresh water in a clay pot. [51]Then he is to take the cedar wood, the hyssop, the scarlet yarn and the live bird, dip them into the blood of the dead bird and the fresh water, and sprinkle the house seven times. [52]He shall purify the house with the bird's blood, the fresh water, the live bird, the cedar wood, the hyssop and the scarlet yarn. [53]Then he is to release the live bird in the open fields outside the town. In this way he will make atonement for the house, and it will be clean."

[54]These are the regulations for any infectious skin disease, for an itch, [55]for mildew in clothing or in a house, [56]and for a swelling, a rash or a bright spot, [57]to determine when something is clean or unclean.

These are the regulations for infectious skin diseases and mildew.

Discharges Causing Uncleanness

15 The LORD said to Moses and Aaron, [2]"Speak to the Israelites and say to them: 'When any man has a bodily discharge, the discharge is unclean. [3]Whether it continues flowing from his body or is blocked, it will make him unclean. This is how his discharge will bring about uncleanness:

[4]"'Any bed the man with a discharge lies on will be unclean, and anything he sits on will be unclean. [5]Anyone who touches his bed must wash his clothes and bathe with water, and he will be unclean till evening. [6]Whoever sits on anything that the man with a discharge sat on must wash his clothes and bathe with water, and he will be unclean till evening.

[7]"'Whoever touches the man who has a discharge must wash his clothes and bathe with water, and he will be unclean till evening.

[8]"'If the man with the discharge spits on someone who is clean, that person must wash his clothes and bathe with water, and he will be unclean till evening.

[9]"'Everything the man sits on when riding will be unclean, [10]and whoever touches any of the things that were under him will be unclean till evening; whoever picks up those things must wash his clothes and bathe with water, and he will be unclean till evening.

[11]"'Anyone the man with a discharge touches without rinsing his hands with water must wash his clothes and bathe with water, and he will be unclean till evening.

[12]"'A clay pot that the man touches must be broken, and any wooden article is to be rinsed with water.

[13]"'When a man is cleansed from his discharge, he is to count off seven days for his ceremonial cleansing; he must wash his clothes and bathe himself with fresh water, and he will be clean. [14]On the eighth day he must take two doves or two young pigeons and come before the LORD to the entrance to the Tent of Meeting and give them to the priest. [15]The priest is to sacrifice them, the one for a sin offering and the other for a burnt offering. In this way he will make atonement before the LORD for the man because of his discharge.

[16]"'When a man has an emission of semen, he must bathe his whole body with water, and he will be unclean till evening. [17]Any clothing or leather that has semen on it must be washed with water, and it will be unclean till evening. [18]When a man lies with a woman and there is an emission of semen, both must bathe with water, and they will be unclean till evening.

[19]"'When a woman has her regular flow of blood, the impurity

1. How do you feel about receiving advanced warnings: Grateful? Resentful? Suspicious? **2.** When has God told you about some "house" or "illness" to be faced in the future? How would you compare that advance warning to the one given here? **3.** What does all this say about God's total restoration of you (not just your house)?

1. As a child, what was the best part about taking a bath? What was the worst part? **2.** How many baths or showers do you take now: 3/day? 1/week? Only when it rains? How much water do you use: Just a bird-bath? Enough to create a water shortage? What if there was only enough to drink?

1. For what reason are these laws concerning uncleanness given to Israel (v. 31)? Was their uncleanness primarily "physical" and hygienic or "spiritual"? Why do you think so? **2.** Of the various "discharges" listed here, why do you think each would defile God's dwelling place? **3.** Given this extensive list, how much time do you think the average Israelite spent "unclean"? Would this affect his or her relationship with God negatively? Or positively? **4.** Of these various rituals, which do you see that have some real cleansing value? Which ones are largely ceremonial? **5.** What do you see as the function of the sacrifices associated with ceremonial cleansing (vv. 13–15,28–30)? **6.** How do you think these ceremonies would make one feel about: (a) Lengthy discharges (diarrhea, hemorrhaging)? (b) Normal human discharges? (c) Sexual relations? (d) About him or herself as an adolescent coming into puberty? **7.** Now two "Bible trivia" questions: (a) Which rule listed here is the background for David's sin with Bathsheba (2Sa 11:4)? (b) Which rule echoes earlier times when Rachel deceived Laban (Ge 31:35)? **8.** Another not so trivial question: Where would a desert people get all the water for the many prescribed baths?

♡ 1. In what ways might these laws concerning cleanliness relate to hygiene today? In what ways might they relate to worship attendance (compare Heb 9:10)? What do they teach you about God, his relationship to us, and the things which separate us from him? **2.** Many people today find the implications of this passage to be a turnoff. Why would that be? Need that be the case? **3.** When do you feel unworthy to approach God: (a) When my self-esteem is low? (b) When I've had a defeating day at work or home? (c) When I know I've sinned? (d) During a bout of lengthy sickness? (e) When I miss church? Why might someone feel unworthy at those times? **4.** What provisions has God made for you to feel better about yourself? What will you do to remind yourself about these provisions the next time you feel "unclean"? **5.** Jesus often healed people miraculously with very human means, including the instruction to "go and wash" (see Jn 9:7). In this regard, what "baths" has Christ provided for your salvation and wholeness?

☞ 1. Describe the most loved qualities of your best friend. What do you feel like when you have a major disagreement? Why do you feel this way? **2.** When did you last attend a family reunion? What was the best part of it? Why?

📖 1. Based on this chapter, how would you describe the human condition? How do Aaron and his two sons (Nadab and Abihu) typify this basic character flaw (vv. 1–2; see 10:1–3)? **2.** What is God's typical response to that? How does this affect one's fellowship with God? **3.** Why do you think God chose animal sacrifice to reconcile the differences between sinful people and sinless God? Why is it that "without the shedding of blood there is no forgiveness" (Heb 9:22)? **4.** What does the fact that this "Day of Atonement" took place *only* "once a year" (v. 34) tell you about its importance? What does the fact that it must be repeated *every* year ("a lasting ordinance") tell you about human nature? And

of her monthly period will last seven days, and anyone who touches her will be unclean till evening.

²⁰ "'Anything she lies on during her period will be unclean, and anything she sits on will be unclean. ²¹Whoever touches her bed must wash his clothes and bathe with water, and he will be unclean till evening. ²²Whoever touches anything she sits on must wash his clothes and bathe with water, and he will be unclean till evening. ²³Whether it is the bed or anything she was sitting on, when anyone touches it, he will be unclean till evening.

²⁴ "'If a man lies with her and her monthly flow touches him, he will be unclean for seven days; any bed he lies on will be unclean.

²⁵ "'When a woman has a discharge of blood for many days at a time other than her monthly period or has a discharge that continues beyond her period, she will be unclean as long as she has the discharge, just as in the days of her period. ²⁶Any bed she lies on while her discharge continues will be unclean, as is her bed during her monthly period, and anything she sits on will be unclean, as during her period. ²⁷Whoever touches them will be unclean; he must wash his clothes and bathe with water, and he will be unclean till evening.

²⁸ "'When she is cleansed from her discharge, she must count off seven days, and after that she will be ceremonially clean. ²⁹On the eighth day she must take two doves or two young pigeons and bring them to the priest at the entrance to the Tent of Meeting. ³⁰The priest is to sacrifice one for a sin offering and the other for a burnt offering. In this way he will make atonement for her before the LORD for the uncleanness of her discharge.

³¹ "'You must keep the Israelites separate from things that make them unclean, so they will not die in their uncleanness for defiling my dwelling place,ᵃ which is among them.'"

³²These are the regulations for a man with a discharge, for anyone made unclean by an emission of semen, ³³for a woman in her monthly period, for a man or a woman with a discharge, and for a man who lies with a woman who is ceremonially unclean.

The Day of Atonement

16 The LORD spoke to Moses after the death of the two sons of Aaron who died when they approached the LORD. ²The LORD said to Moses: "Tell your brother Aaron not to come whenever he chooses into the Most Holy Place behind the curtain in front of the atonement cover on the ark, or else he will die, because I appear in the cloud over the atonement cover.

³"This is how Aaron is to enter the sanctuary area: with a young bull for a sin offering and a ram for a burnt offering. ⁴He is to put on the sacred linen tunic, with linen undergarments next to his body; he is to tie the linen sash around him and put on the linen turban. These are sacred garments; so he must bathe himself with water before he puts them on. ⁵From the Israelite community he is to take two male goats for a sin offering and a ram for a burnt offering.

⁶"Aaron is to offer the bull for his own sin offering to make atonement for himself and his household. ⁷Then he is to take the two goats and present them before the LORD at the entrance to the Tent of Meeting. ⁸He is to cast lots for the two goats—one lot for the LORD and the other for the scapegoat.ᵇ ⁹Aaron shall bring the goat whose lot falls to the LORD and sacrifice it for a sin offering. ¹⁰But the goat chosen by lot as the scapegoat shall be presented

ᵃ31 Or *my tabernacle*   ᵇ8 That is, the goat of removal; Hebrew *azazel*; also in verses 10 and 26

alive before the LORD to be used for making atonement by sending it into the desert as a scapegoat.

[11] "Aaron shall bring the bull for his own sin offering to make atonement for himself and his household, and he is to slaughter the bull for his own sin offering. [12]He is to take a censer full of burning coals from the altar before the LORD and two handfuls of finely ground fragrant incense and take them behind the curtain. [13]He is to put the incense on the fire before the LORD, and the smoke of the incense will conceal the atonement cover above the Testimony, so that he will not die. [14]He is to take some of the bull's blood and with his finger sprinkle it on the front of the atonement cover; then he shall sprinkle some of it with his finger seven times before the atonement cover.

[15] "He shall then slaughter the goat for the sin offering for the people and take its blood behind the curtain and do with it as he did with the bull's blood: He shall sprinkle it on the atonement cover and in front of it. [16]In this way he will make atonement for the Most Holy Place because of the uncleanness and rebellion of the Israelites, whatever their sins have been. He is to do the same for the Tent of Meeting, which is among them in the midst of their uncleanness. [17]No one is to be in the Tent of Meeting from the time Aaron goes in to make atonement in the Most Holy Place until he comes out, having made atonement for himself, his household and the whole community of Israel.

[18] "Then he shall come out to the altar that is before the LORD and make atonement for it. He shall take some of the bull's blood and some of the goat's blood and put it on all the horns of the altar. [19]He shall sprinkle some of the blood on it with his finger seven times to cleanse it and to consecrate it from the uncleanness of the Israelites.

[20] "When Aaron has finished making atonement for the Most Holy Place, the Tent of Meeting and the altar, he shall bring forward the live goat. [21]He is to lay both hands on the head of the live goat and confess over it all the wickedness and rebellion of the Israelites—all their sins—and put them on the goat's head. He shall send the goat away into the desert in the care of a man appointed for the task. [22]The goat will carry on itself all their sins to a solitary place; and the man shall release it in the desert.

[23] "Then Aaron is to go into the Tent of Meeting and take off the linen garments he put on before he entered the Most Holy Place, and he is to leave them there. [24]He shall bathe himself with water in a holy place and put on his regular garments. Then he shall come out and sacrifice the burnt offering for himself and the burnt offering for the people, to make atonement for himself and for the people. [25]He shall also burn the fat of the sin offering on the altar.

[26] "The man who releases the goat as a scapegoat must wash his clothes and bathe himself with water; afterward he may come into the camp. [27]The bull and the goat for the sin offerings, whose blood was brought into the Most Holy Place to make atonement, must be taken outside the camp; their hides, flesh and offal are to be burned up. [28]The man who burns them must wash his clothes and bathe himself with water; afterward he may come into the camp.

[29] "This is to be a lasting ordinance for you: On the tenth day of the seventh month you must deny yourselves[a] and not do any work—whether native-born or an alien living among you— [30]because on this day atonement will be made for you, to cleanse you.

a29 Or must fast; also in verse 31

what about the lasting effect of this sacrifice (see Heb 9:9–10)? 5. As important as this Day was to Israel for restoring a correct relationship with God, how much more important and lasting is Christ's "once for all" sacrifice (see Heb 9:11– 10:14)? 6. What are the major elements involved in the Day of Atonement? How would each have helped the Israelites to understand: (a) The necessity for having a right relationship with God? (b) The consequences to them if they did not make atonement for sin? 7. What, for example, was the purpose of: (a) The ritual cleanliness? (b) The sacrifice for the priest? (c) Blood sprinkled on certain places? 8. The role of the two goats (vv. 20–22) shows us that no single offering could fully typify the sacrifice of Christ, "the Lamb of God, who takes away the sin of the world" (Jn 1:29). What aspect of his atonement is typified by the goat that is killed? What distinct aspect of Christ is typified by the scapegoat? 9. By establishing this process for ancient Israel to be reconciled with their Lord, what does that tell you about his yearning for a right relationship with us?

1. What is your favorite "scapegoat" to blame when things go wrong? 2. Do you think the basic character of human beings is much different today than in the days of Moses? Why or why not? 3. How about God's character: Is he much different now than back then? Why or why not? How does this affect the continuing need to apply the principles of reconciliation outlined here? 4. How do you handle problems? Do you blame God? Do you consider them the result of a wrong relationship with God? Or are they simply a part of life (or "they come with the territory")? How do you think God would like to help you resolve your problems? 5. If reconciliation is so necessary, why don't Christians follow the rituals outlined in this chapter? How does Hebrews 9–10 help you better understand Leviticus 16? How do these principles help you better understand God's desire for a right relationship with you?

Then, before the LORD, you will be clean from all your sins. ³¹It is a sabbath of rest, and you must deny yourselves; it is a lasting ordinance. ³²The priest who is anointed and ordained to succeed his father as high priest is to make atonement. He is to put on the sacred linen garments ³³and make atonement for the Most Holy Place, for the Tent of Meeting and the altar, and for the priests and all the people of the community.

³⁴"This is to be a lasting ordinance for you: Atonement is to be made once a year for all the sins of the Israelites."

And it was done, as the LORD commanded Moses.

Eating Blood Forbidden

17 The LORD said to Moses, ²"Speak to Aaron and his sons and to all the Israelites and say to them: 'This is what the LORD has commanded: ³Any Israelite who sacrifices an ox,[a] a lamb or a goat in the camp or outside of it ⁴instead of bringing it to the entrance to the Tent of Meeting to present it as an offering to the LORD in front of the tabernacle of the LORD—that man shall be considered guilty of bloodshed; he has shed blood and must be cut off from his people. ⁵This is so the Israelites will bring to the LORD the sacrifices they are now making in the open fields. They must bring them to the priest, that is, to the LORD, at the entrance to the Tent of Meeting and sacrifice them as fellowship offerings.[b] ⁶The priest is to sprinkle the blood against the altar of the LORD at the entrance to the Tent of Meeting and burn the fat as an aroma pleasing to the LORD. ⁷They must no longer offer any of their sacrifices to the goat idols[c] to whom they prostitute themselves. This is to be a lasting ordinance for them and for the generations to come.'

⁸"Say to them: 'Any Israelite or any alien living among them who offers a burnt offering or sacrifice ⁹and does not bring it to the entrance to the Tent of Meeting to sacrifice it to the LORD—that man must be cut off from his people.

¹⁰"'Any Israelite or any alien living among them who eats any blood—I will set my face against that person who eats blood and will cut him off from his people. ¹¹For the life of a creature is in the blood, and I have given it to you to make atonement for yourselves on the altar; it is the blood that makes atonement for one's life. ¹²Therefore I say to the Israelites, "None of you may eat blood, nor may an alien living among you eat blood."

¹³"'Any Israelite or any alien living among you who hunts any animal or bird that may be eaten must drain out the blood and cover it with earth, ¹⁴because the life of every creature is its blood. That is why I have said to the Israelites, "You must not eat the blood of any creature, because the life of every creature is its blood; anyone who eats it must be cut off."

¹⁵"'Anyone, whether native-born or alien, who eats anything found dead or torn by wild animals must wash his clothes and bathe with water, and he will be ceremonially unclean till evening; then he will be clean. ¹⁶But if he does not wash his clothes and bathe himself, he will be held responsible.'"

Unlawful Sexual Relations

18 The LORD said to Moses, ²"Speak to the Israelites and say to them: 'I am the LORD your God. ³You must not do as they do in Egypt, where you used to live, and you must not do as they do in the land of Canaan, where I am bringing you. Do not follow

---

Judging from the number of Christmas letters you send and receive, how many "friends" do you have? Of those, how many are "close" enough to see regularly?

1. What problems might arise if sacrifices were offered in an uncontrolled context (vv. 7,10,13–16)? How would limiting sacrifice to the Tent of Meeting help reduce these problems (vv. 3–6)? 2. What consequences befall those who fail to follow God's command in this regard (vv. 4,9,10,14–16)? 3. A major theme in Leviticus is that blood covers the people's sins and reconciles them to God. Why do you think God chose blood to do that (vv. 10–14)? 4. What does this say about the seriousness of sin? The seriousness of reconciliation?

1. How important to you is taking time to be a friend with God? How much time do you spend maintaining friendship with God: (a) Twice a year at Christmas and Easter? (b) Once a month? (c) Once a week? (d) Daily? 2. What are some things you do now to increase your time with God? 3. Do you always worship alone—by yourself and as you please, even in the "open fields," as it were? Or do you gather with others at the "Tent of Meeting" to worship God as part of the body of Christ? 4. What is the most important thing you have learned from chapter 17 about maintaining fellowship with God? How will you begin to incorporate this into your life today?

1. When do you feel "odd" or different from everyone else? What is special about you that sets you apart from others? 2. Were you raised with more "Dos" or with more "Don'ts" in your sex education? Explain.

ᵃ3 The Hebrew word can include both male and female.   ᵇ5 Traditionally *peace offerings*   ᶜ7 Or *demons*

their practices. ⁴You must obey my laws and be careful to follow my decrees. I am the LORD your God. ⁵Keep my decrees and laws, for the man who obeys them will live by them. I am the LORD.

⁶" 'No one is to approach any close relative to have sexual relations. I am the LORD.

⁷" 'Do not dishonor your father by having sexual relations with your mother. She is your mother; do not have relations with her.

⁸" 'Do not have sexual relations with your father's wife; that would dishonor your father.

⁹" 'Do not have sexual relations with your sister, either your father's daughter or your mother's daughter, whether she was born in the same home or elsewhere.

¹⁰" 'Do not have sexual relations with your son's daughter or your daughter's daughter; that would dishonor you.

¹¹" 'Do not have sexual relations with the daughter of your father's wife, born to your father; she is your sister.

¹²" 'Do not have sexual relations with your father's sister; she is your father's close relative.

¹³" 'Do not have sexual relations with your mother's sister, because she is your mother's close relative.

¹⁴" 'Do not dishonor your father's brother by approaching his wife to have sexual relations; she is your aunt.

¹⁵" 'Do not have sexual relations with your daughter-in-law. She is your son's wife; do not have relations with her.

¹⁶" 'Do not have sexual relations with your brother's wife; that would dishonor your brother.

¹⁷" 'Do not have sexual relations with both a woman and her daughter. Do not have sexual relations with either her son's daughter or her daughter's daughter; they are her close relatives. That is wickedness.

¹⁸" 'Do not take your wife's sister as a rival wife and have sexual relations with her while your wife is living.

¹⁹" 'Do not approach a woman to have sexual relations during the uncleanness of her monthly period.

²⁰" 'Do not have sexual relations with your neighbor's wife and defile yourself with her.

²¹" 'Do not give any of your children to be sacrificedᵃ to Molech, for you must not profane the name of your God. I am the LORD.

²²" 'Do not lie with a man as one lies with a woman; that is detestable.

²³" 'Do not have sexual relations with an animal and defile yourself with it. A woman must not present herself to an animal to have sexual relations with it; that is a perversion.

²⁴" 'Do not defile yourselves in any of these ways, because this is how the nations that I am going to drive out before you became defiled. ²⁵Even the land was defiled; so I punished it for its sin, and the land vomited out its inhabitants. ²⁶But you must keep my decrees and my laws. The native-born and the aliens living among you must not do any of these detestable things, ²⁷for all these things were done by the people who lived in the land before you, and the land became defiled. ²⁸And if you defile the land, it will vomit you out as it vomited out the nations that were before you.

²⁹" 'Everyone who does any of these detestable things—such persons must be cut off from their people. ³⁰Keep my requirements and do not follow any of the detestable customs that were practiced

1. In chapter 18, Israel is called to be different than other nations (vv. 3,21,24–30). What does this tell you about the sexual practices of these other nations? 2. How would participation in the fertility religions of these nations have harmed Israel's relationship with God? 3. Almost all cultures have incest taboos. Judging from the reasons given here (vv. 7–18), why is that? What is most dishonoring or detestable about that? 4. Which of these laws brings to mind the experience of Judah and Tamar (see Ge 38)? Of Amnon and another Tamar (see 2Sa 13)? Of Jacob with Leah and Rachel (see Ge 29)? 5. What other sexual practices does the Lord prohibit here and why (vv. 19,20,22, 23)? 6. What does it mean that those who keep or obey God's laws "will live by them" (v. 5)? Is law-keeping a way of salvation for the lost (see Ro 10:5; Gal 3:12)? Or is law-keeping a way of life for the redeemed (see Ex 19:6; Eze 20:11,13,21)? 7. What else do you learn from this chapter about maintaining a correct relationship with a holy and jealous God, who redeems you and calls you to a different life?

1. How does this list of unlawful sexual practices strike you: Makes sense? Out-of-date? Up-to-date? Arbitrary? Confining? Liberating? Illustrate your answer. 2. What aspects of Western culture could be called modern day "fertility religions"? How can Christians protect themselves against these aspects of our culture? 3. How has your community already been touched by incest, adultery or homosexuality? How has your faith helped you cope with the pain and brokenness of that? What healing can be found by sharing your experiences with trusted members of your group?

ᵃ21 Or *to be passed through ⌞the fire⌟*

1. In your growing up years, who was the disciplinarian in your family? Why that parent? 2. In your household now, who sets most of the rules? Who has to enforce them? Why? Which of your parents are you like in this regard? How so?

1. Chapter 19 contains a list of various laws which expand on the Ten Commandments. What do you think is their purpose? In what sense are laws needed to maintain a relationship with God? 2. Choose five of these laws and explain how each would help the Israelites to maintain their relationship with God. 3. Which law detailed here was quoted by Jesus, Paul and James? In this context, who is one's "brother" and "neighbor" (vv. 14–18)? Which laws show compassion and economic justice for the poor? The handicapped? The alien? 4. Which laws speak of cultic and occult practices? Of parental respect and family values? Of international relations? 5. Of all these laws, which seem to you to have their application limited to the ancient Israelites? Which laws seem to apply universally, to all people, for all time? How do you make that distinction?

1. This chapter provides many rules to live by and train children on. How can two parents from different backgrounds agree on one set of rules for their children to live by? 2. In your own life, how has God delivered you from some sin mentioned in chapter 19? 3. How does this deliverance help you to live better with your God? With your family? Your neighbors? The disadvantaged? 4. Together with your group, pick one of the laws to put into practice? How will you begin? Where? When? Whom will you befriend and reach out to? 5. What is your chief incentive to be "holy"? How might this passage have given rise to the notion of "holier-than-thou"? How can you avoid that tag and still be the holy person God wants you to be?

before you came and do not defile yourselves with them. I am the LORD your God.'"

Various Laws

19 The LORD said to Moses, [2]"Speak to the entire assembly of Israel and say to them: 'Be holy because I, the LORD your God, am holy.

[3]"Each of you must respect his mother and father, and you must observe my Sabbaths. I am the LORD your God.

[4]"Do not turn to idols or make gods of cast metal for yourselves. I am the LORD your God.

[5]"When you sacrifice a fellowship offering[a] to the LORD, sacrifice it in such a way that it will be accepted on your behalf. [6]It shall be eaten on the day you sacrifice it or on the next day; anything left over until the third day must be burned up. [7]If any of it is eaten on the third day, it is impure and will not be accepted. [8]Whoever eats it will be held responsible because he has desecrated what is holy to the LORD; that person must be cut off from his people.

[9]"When you reap the harvest of your land, do not reap to the very edges of your field or gather the gleanings of your harvest. [10]Do not go over your vineyard a second time or pick up the grapes that have fallen. Leave them for the poor and the alien. I am the LORD your God.

[11]"Do not steal.

"'Do not lie.

"'Do not deceive one another.

[12]"Do not swear falsely by my name and so profane the name of your God. I am the LORD.

[13]"Do not defraud your neighbor or rob him.

"'Do not hold back the wages of a hired man overnight.

[14]"Do not curse the deaf or put a stumbling block in front of the blind, but fear your God. I am the LORD.

[15]"Do not pervert justice; do not show partiality to the poor or favoritism to the great, but judge your neighbor fairly.

[16]"Do not go about spreading slander among your people.

"'Do not do anything that endangers your neighbor's life. I am the LORD.

[17]"Do not hate your brother in your heart. Rebuke your neighbor frankly so you will not share in his guilt.

[18]"Do not seek revenge or bear a grudge against one of your people, but love your neighbor as yourself. I am the LORD.

[19]"Keep my decrees.

"'Do not mate different kinds of animals.

"'Do not plant your field with two kinds of seed.

"'Do not wear clothing woven of two kinds of material.

[20]"If a man sleeps with a woman who is a slave girl promised to another man but who has not been ransomed or given her freedom, there must be due punishment. Yet they are not to be put to death, because she had not been freed. [21]The man, however, must bring a ram to the entrance to the Tent of Meeting for a guilt offering to the LORD. [22]With the ram of the guilt offering the priest is to make atonement for him before the LORD for the sin he has committed, and his sin will be forgiven.

[23]"When you enter the land and plant any kind of fruit tree, regard its fruit as forbidden.[b] For three years you are to consider it forbidden[b]; it must not be eaten. [24]In the fourth year all its fruit will be holy, an offering of praise to the LORD. [25]But in the fifth year

[a]5 Traditionally *peace offering*   [b]23 Hebrew *uncircumcised*

you may eat its fruit. In this way your harvest will be increased. I am the LORD your God.

26 "'Do not eat any meat with the blood still in it.

"'Do not practice divination or sorcery.

27 "'Do not cut the hair at the sides of your head or clip off the edges of your beard.

28 "'Do not cut your bodies for the dead or put tattoo marks on yourselves. I am the LORD.

29 "'Do not degrade your daughter by making her a prostitute, or the land will turn to prostitution and be filled with wickedness.

30 "'Observe my Sabbaths and have reverence for my sanctuary. I am the LORD.

31 "'Do not turn to mediums or seek out spiritists, for you will be defiled by them. I am the LORD your God.

32 "'Rise in the presence of the aged, show respect for the elderly and revere your God. I am the LORD.

33 "'When an alien lives with you in your land, do not mistreat him. 34The alien living with you must be treated as one of your native-born. Love him as yourself, for you were aliens in Egypt. I am the LORD your God.

35 "'Do not use dishonest standards when measuring length, weight or quantity. 36Use honest scales and honest weights, an honest ephah*a* and an honest hin.*b* I am the LORD your God, who brought you out of Egypt.

37 "'Keep all my decrees and all my laws and follow them. I am the LORD.'"

Punishments for Sin

20 The LORD said to Moses, 2"Say to the Israelites: 'Any Israelite or any alien living in Israel who gives*c* any of his children to Molech must be put to death. The people of the community are to stone him. 3I will set my face against that man and I will cut him off from his people; for by giving his children to Molech, he has defiled my sanctuary and profaned my holy name. 4If the people of the community close their eyes when that man gives one of his children to Molech and they fail to put him to death, 5I will set my face against that man and his family and will cut off from their people both him and all who follow him in prostituting themselves to Molech.

6 "'I will set my face against the person who turns to mediums and spiritists to prostitute himself by following them, and I will cut him off from his people.

7 "'Consecrate yourselves and be holy, because I am the LORD your God. 8Keep my decrees and follow them. I am the LORD, who makes you holy.*d*

9 "'If anyone curses his father or mother, he must be put to death. He has cursed his father or his mother, and his blood will be on his own head.

10 "'If a man commits adultery with another man's wife—with the wife of his neighbor—both the adulterer and the adulteress must be put to death.

11 "'If a man sleeps with his father's wife, he has dishonored his father. Both the man and the woman must be put to death; their blood will be on their own heads.

12 "'If a man sleeps with his daughter-in-law, both of them must

1. When you were a child, what did your family consider to be the worst thing you could do? 2. What took them the longest to finally forgive? 3. What kinds of punishment were ordinarily handed out in your family? What severe punishment was handed out only in extra-ordinary circumstances?

1. Chapter 20 contains a list of additional laws, as well as punishments for breaking these laws: What do you think is their purpose (vv. 8, 22,26)? Do you see these laws and their punishments serving more as deterrents to wrong behavior? Or as exhortations to right behavior? How might each be effective and necessary to maintain unbroken fellowship with a holy and jealous God? 2. Choose three of these laws and their punishments: How would they help the Israelites to maintain fellowship with God? 3. Which laws detailed here single out religious practices which King Manasseh (see 2Ch 33:6) and King Saul (see 1Sa 28) were guilty of following?

1. Where do you see Satanic, cultic or occult practices today? What does this say about humanity's continuing search for a power or experience "higher" than itself? 2. While most of these laws

---

a36 An ephah was a dry measure.   *b36* A hin was a liquid measure.   *c2* Or
sacrifices; also in verses 3 and 4   *d8* Or *who sanctifies you*; or *who sets you apart as
holy*

seem to have retained their application to all people for all time, most societies have done away with the death penalty as a social deterrent. Why is that? **3.** Do you see the death penalty as "cruel and unusual punishment"? In all cases? For anything but murder or treason? Why or why not? **4.** In what sense has God "made you holy" or set you aside for his purpose? What purpose is that? How tough is it for you to remain "set apart from the world"? **5.** What aspect of the world is tough for you to separate yourself from? Why? How can the message of chapter 20 and the support of your small group help you to remain separated successfully?

---

be put to death. What they have done is a perversion; their blood will be on their own heads.

¹³ "If a man lies with a man as one lies with a woman, both of them have done what is detestable. They must be put to death; their blood will be on their own heads.

¹⁴ "If a man marries both a woman and her mother, it is wicked. Both he and they must be burned in the fire, so that no wickedness will be among you.

¹⁵ "If a man has sexual relations with an animal, he must be put to death, and you must kill the animal.

¹⁶ "If a woman approaches an animal to have sexual relations with it, kill both the woman and the animal. They must be put to death; their blood will be on their own heads.

¹⁷ "If a man marries his sister, the daughter of either his father or his mother, and they have sexual relations, it is a disgrace. They must be cut off before the eyes of their people. He has dishonored his sister and will be held responsible.

¹⁸ "If a man lies with a woman during her monthly period and has sexual relations with her, he has exposed the source of her flow, and she has also uncovered it. Both of them must be cut off from their people.

¹⁹ "Do not have sexual relations with the sister of either your mother or your father, for that would dishonor a close relative; both of you would be held responsible.

²⁰ "If a man sleeps with his aunt, he has dishonored his uncle. They will be held responsible; they will die childless.

²¹ "If a man marries his brother's wife, it is an act of impurity; he has dishonored his brother. They will be childless.

²² "Keep all my decrees and laws and follow them, so that the land where I am bringing you to live may not vomit you out. ²³You must not live according to the customs of the nations I am going to drive out before you. Because they did all these things, I abhorred them. ²⁴But I said to you, "You will possess their land; I will give it to you as an inheritance, a land flowing with milk and honey." I am the LORD your God, who has set you apart from the nations.

²⁵ "You must therefore make a distinction between clean and unclean animals and between unclean and clean birds. Do not defile yourselves by any animal or bird or anything that moves along the ground—those which I have set apart as unclean for you. ²⁶You are to be holy to me*a* because I, the LORD, am holy, and I have set you apart from the nations to be my own.

²⁷ "A man or woman who is a medium or spiritist among you must be put to death. You are to stone them; their blood will be on their own heads.'"

Rules for Priests

21 The LORD said to Moses, "Speak to the priests, the sons of Aaron, and say to them: 'A priest must not make himself ceremonially unclean for any of his people who die, ²except for a close relative, such as his mother or father, his son or daughter, his brother, ³or an unmarried sister who is dependent on him since she has no husband—for her he may make himself unclean. ⁴He must not make himself unclean for people related to him by marriage,*b* and so defile himself.

⁵ "Priests must not shave their heads or shave off the edges of their beards or cut their bodies. ⁶They must be holy to their God and must not profane the name of their God. Because they present

---

1. What are the qualities in a pastor you would seek out for counseling? **2.** What qualities would turn you away? **3.** Which of these qualities in a preacher would impress you more than the others: (a) Honesty? (b) Good speaker? (c) Able to be "human"? (d) Witty sense of humor? (e) Gives short sermons?

1. Based on this passage, how important would you say the sacrificial system was to God? To the Israelite religion? **2.** Why do you think these rules for priests

---

a26 Or *be my holy ones*   *b4* Or *unclean as a leader among his people*

the offerings made to the LORD by fire, the food of their God, they are to be holy.

⁷"'They must not marry women defiled by prostitution or divorced from their husbands, because priests are holy to their God. ⁸Regard them as holy, because they offer up the food of your God. Consider them holy, because I the LORD am holy—I who make you holy.ᵃ

⁹"'If a priest's daughter defiles herself by becoming a prostitute, she disgraces her father; she must be burned in the fire.

¹⁰"'The high priest, the one among his brothers who has had the anointing oil poured on his head and who has been ordained to wear the priestly garments, must not let his hair become unkemptᵇ or tear his clothes. ¹¹He must not enter a place where there is a dead body. He must not make himself unclean, even for his father or mother, ¹²nor leave the sanctuary of his God or desecrate it, because he has been dedicated by the anointing oil of his God. I am the LORD.

¹³"'The woman he marries must be a virgin. ¹⁴He must not marry a widow, a divorced woman, or a woman defiled by prostitution, but only a virgin from his own people, ¹⁵so he will not defile his offspring among his people. I am the LORD, who makes him holy.ᶜ'"

¹⁶The LORD said to Moses, ¹⁷"Say to Aaron: 'For the generations to come none of your descendants who has a defect may come near to offer the food of his God. ¹⁸No man who has any defect may come near: no man who is blind or lame, disfigured or deformed; ¹⁹no man with a crippled foot or hand, ²⁰or who is hunchbacked or dwarfed, or who has any eye defect, or who has festering or running sores or damaged testicles. ²¹No descendant of Aaron the priest who has any defect is to come near to present the offerings made to the LORD by fire. He has a defect; he must not come near to offer the food of his God. ²²He may eat the most holy food of his God, as well as the holy food; ²³yet because of his defect, he must not go near the curtain or approach the altar, and so desecrate my sanctuary. I am the LORD, who makes them holy.ᵈ'"

²⁴So Moses told this to Aaron and his sons and to all the Israelites.

22 The LORD said to Moses, ²"Tell Aaron and his sons to treat with respect the sacred offerings the Israelites consecrate to me, so they will not profane my holy name. I am the LORD.

³"Say to them: 'For the generations to come, if any of your descendants is ceremonially unclean and yet comes near the sacred offerings that the Israelites consecrate to the LORD, that person must be cut off from my presence. I am the LORD.

⁴"'If a descendant of Aaron has an infectious skin diseaseᵉ or a bodily discharge, he may not eat the sacred offerings until he is cleansed. He will also be unclean if he touches something defiled by a corpse or by anyone who has an emission of semen, ⁵or if he touches any crawling thing that makes him unclean, or any person who makes him unclean, whatever the uncleanness may be. ⁶The one who touches any such thing will be unclean till evening. He must not eat any of the sacred offerings unless he has bathed himself with water. ⁷When the sun goes down, he will be clean, and after that he may eat the sacred offerings, for they are his food.

1. Do your have any prejudices or rules for priests? How do they vary from this list? What does this say about a difference in priestly function or in cultural values? (Read Heb 7:26–28. How does this help to account for this difference in function?) 2. What do such passages imply about the attitude necessary for anyone to approach God? How would you depict your own attitude in approaching God: Casual or formal? Confident or subservient? On your tip-toes or on your knees? 3. What kind of behavior do you expect of your religious leaders today? In what areas do you have one set of standards for clergy but another set for non-clergy? What physical qualities do you like in a pastor? 4. How could you bring your approach to God more into line with the intent of this passage? What will you do today to "get in line"?

(Questions column: were given to "all the Israelites" (21:24) and not just given to the priests in their private education? 3. How would you feel about these rules if you were a close relative of this priest? If you were married to one? If you wanted to marry one? If you were handicapped in any way? If you wanted him to conduct or attend your mom's funeral? If you wanted to host him as a dinner guest with leftovers from worship? 4. Why do you think there's such an emphasis on physical perfection, ceremonial cleanliness and abstinence for the priests? 5. How does this relate to God's holiness (21:6,12,15,23; 22:1,9,16)? Likewise, how does this relate to the function of the priests (which is to restore the nation to a right relationship with God)? In this regard, what object lesson do Nadab and Abihu bring to mind (see 10:1–3)? 6. Do you think 21:16–23 indicates that handicapped persons are of less value to God? Why?)

ᵃ8 Or who sanctify you; or who set you apart as holy   ᵇ10 Or not uncover his head   ᶜ15 Or who sanctifies him; or who sets him apart as holy   ᵈ23 Or who sanctifies them; or who sets them apart as holy   ᵉ4 Traditionally leprosy; the Hebrew word was used for various diseases affecting the skin—not necessarily leprosy.

[8]He must not eat anything found dead or torn by wild animals, and so become unclean through it. I am the LORD.

[9]" 'The priests are to keep my requirements so that they do not become guilty and die for treating them with contempt. I am the LORD, who makes them holy.[a]

[10]" 'No one outside a priest's family may eat the sacred offering, nor may the guest of a priest or his hired worker eat it. [11]But if a priest buys a slave with money, or if a slave is born in his household, that slave may eat his food. [12]If a priest's daughter marries anyone other than a priest, she may not eat any of the sacred contributions. [13]But if a priest's daughter becomes a widow or is divorced, yet has no children, and she returns to live in her father's house as in her youth, she may eat of her father's food. No unauthorized person, however, may eat any of it.

[14]" 'If anyone eats a sacred offering by mistake, he must make restitution to the priest for the offering and add a fifth of the value to it. [15]The priests must not desecrate the sacred offerings the Israelites present to the LORD [16]by allowing them to eat the sacred offerings and so bring upon them guilt requiring payment. I am the LORD, who makes them holy.' "

Unacceptable Sacrifices

[17]The LORD said to Moses, [18]"Speak to Aaron and his sons and to all the Israelites and say to them: 'If any of you—either an Israelite or an alien living in Israel—presents a gift for a burnt offering to the LORD, either to fulfill a vow or as a freewill offering, [19]you must present a male without defect from the cattle, sheep or goats in order that it may be accepted on your behalf. [20]Do not bring anything with a defect, because it will not be accepted on your behalf. [21]When anyone brings from the herd or flock a fellowship offering[b] to the LORD to fulfill a special vow or as a freewill offering, it must be without defect or blemish to be acceptable. [22]Do not offer to the LORD the blind, the injured or the maimed, or anything with warts or festering or running sores. Do not place any of these on the altar as an offering made to the LORD by fire. [23]You may, however, present as a freewill offering an ox[c] or a sheep that is deformed or stunted, but it will not be accepted in fulfillment of a vow. [24]You must not offer to the LORD an animal whose testicles are bruised, crushed, torn or cut. You must not do this in your own land, [25]and you must not accept such animals from the hand of a foreigner and offer them as the food of your God. They will not be accepted on your behalf, because they are deformed and have defects.' "

[26]The LORD said to Moses, [27]"When a calf, a lamb or a goat is born, it is to remain with its mother for seven days. From the eighth day on, it will be acceptable as an offering made to the LORD by fire. [28]Do not slaughter a cow or a sheep and its young on the same day.

[29]"When you sacrifice a thank offering to the LORD, sacrifice it in such a way that it will be accepted on your behalf. [30]It must be eaten that same day; leave none of it till morning. I am the LORD.

[31]"Keep my commands and follow them. I am the LORD. [32]Do not profane my holy name. I must be acknowledged as holy by the Israelites. I am the LORD, who makes[d] you holy[e] [33]and who brought you out of Egypt to be your God. I am the LORD."

1. What care do you take in giving gifts at Christmas time: (a) Most anything will do, within a certain price range? (b) Only gifts from a "want list" will do? (c) Used gifts or hand-me-downs are acceptable sometimes? (d) Only new items will do, preferably deluxe editions? (e) Most any gift covering will do? (f) Each gift must be carefully wrapped, with ribbons, bows and cute tags? 2. Describe a time when you took special care in choosing and wrapping a gift.

1. What do you think of God's "want list"? Why do you think God accepts only "perfect" sacrifices or gift offerings? 2. What does this desire for perfection say about the value of the gift? Of the recipient? Of the donor? 3. What do God's values say about his expectations for approaching him?

1. In what area are you giving God less than your "best"? Where are you trying to just get by with offering God "leftovers"? 2. What is keeping you from offering God your best? What will you do today to begin giving him your best?

---

[a]9 Or who sanctifies them; or who sets them apart as holy; also in verse 16   [b]21 Traditionally peace offering   [c]23 The Hebrew word can include both male and female.   [d]32 Or made   [e]32 Or who sanctifies you; or who sets you apart as holy

23
The LORD said to Moses, [2]"Speak to the Israelites and say to them: 'These are my appointed feasts, the appointed feasts of the LORD, which you are to proclaim as sacred assemblies.

The Sabbath

[3]" 'There are six days when you may work, but the seventh day is a Sabbath of rest, a day of sacred assembly. You are not to do any work; wherever you live, it is a Sabbath to the LORD.

The Passover and Unleavened Bread

[4]" 'These are the LORD's appointed feasts, the sacred assemblies you are to proclaim at their appointed times: [5]The LORD's Passover begins at twilight on the fourteenth day of the first month. [6]On the fifteenth day of that month the LORD's Feast of Unleavened Bread begins; for seven days you must eat bread made without yeast. [7]On the first day hold a sacred assembly and do no regular work. [8]For seven days present an offering made to the LORD by fire. And on the seventh day hold a sacred assembly and do no regular work.' "

Firstfruits

[9]The LORD said to Moses, [10]"Speak to the Israelites and say to them: 'When you enter the land I am going to give you and you reap its harvest, bring to the priest a sheaf of the first grain you harvest. [11]He is to wave the sheaf before the LORD so it will be accepted on your behalf; the priest is to wave it on the day after the Sabbath. [12]On the day you wave the sheaf, you must sacrifice as a burnt offering to the LORD a lamb a year old without defect, [13]together with its grain offering of two-tenths of an ephah[a] of fine flour mixed with oil—an offering made to the LORD by fire, a pleasing aroma—and its drink offering of a quarter of a hin[b] of wine. [14]You must not eat any bread, or roasted or new grain, until the very day you bring this offering to your God. This is to be a lasting ordinance for the generations to come, wherever you live.

Feast of Weeks

[15]" 'From the day after the Sabbath, the day you brought the sheaf of the wave offering, count off seven full weeks. [16]Count off fifty days up to the day after the seventh Sabbath, and then present an offering of new grain to the LORD. [17]From wherever you live, bring two loaves made of two-tenths of an ephah of fine flour, baked with yeast, as a wave offering of firstfruits to the LORD. [18]Present with this bread seven male lambs, each a year old and without defect, one young bull and two rams. They will be a burnt offering to the LORD, together with their grain offerings and drink offerings—an offering made by fire, an aroma pleasing to the LORD. [19]Then sacrifice one male goat for a sin offering and two lambs, each a year old, for a fellowship offering.[c] [20]The priest is to wave the two lambs before the LORD as a wave offering, together with the bread of the firstfruits. They are a sacred offering to the LORD for the priest. [21]On that same day you are to proclaim a sacred assembly and do no regular work. This is to be a lasting ordinance for the generations to come, wherever you live.

[22]" 'When you reap the harvest of your land, do not reap to the very edges of your field or gather the gleanings of your harvest. Leave them for the poor and the alien. I am the LORD your God.' "

---

1. What big occasions do you celebrate each year with family? Which one is the biggest? What is your favorite festive meal? 2. Describe the "perfect day off." What would you like to be doing, say, 50 days from now? 3. What is the most fun outing you've had?

1. Why is it most important that Israel remember what God did to bring them out of Egypt (see Ex 12:1–27)? How would this feast help them to remember this and thus maintain a right relationship with God? 2. How does this feast bring to mind the work of Christ, "our Passover lamb" (see 1Co 5:7)? 3. From the various aspects of this "feast of weeks," what do you see as its basic purpose? How would this festival help to maintain a correct relationship with God? 4. What is the New Testament name for this festival (see Ac 2:1)? What insights into Pentecost do you "glean" from this festival as it is described here? Even in its original context, how is this worship related to mission (v. 22)? 5. What call to action do you associate with the sound of trumpets? Why do you think God chose trumpets for the Jewish "New Year's" feast (vv. 23–25)? 6. Why do you think Israel was not allowed to work on feast days (vv. 3,7,21,25,28–32,35–36)? What does this rule say about the relative importance of God and work? How would this rule help the people to focus on the meaning of the different feasts? 7. The consequences for working on the Sabbath and appointed feast days is underscored for the "Day of Atonement" in particular. Why do you suppose that is? How has the "work" of Christ fulfilled the original purpose for this day (see Heb 9:7–15; 10:1–10; 13:11–12)? 8. Why would God want the Israelites to especially remember their time in the wilderness (vv. 33–44)? How would the feast of tabernacles remind them of their wilderness journeys? Of God delivering them? 9. Given the significance of this feast, why do you think Jesus chose to reveal himself on the greatest day of this feast (see Jn 7:37–39)? Might this account for Peter referring to "shelters" in reply to Jesus' transfiguration (see Mk 9:5–6)?

1. How did you include worship in your "perfect day off"? 2. What is God saying by requiring

---

a13 That is, probably about 4 quarts (about 4.5 liters); also in verse 17   b13 That is, probably about 1 quart (about 1 liter)   c19 Traditionally *peace offering*

the "first" of their harvest? Do you think he still expects this of his people? If so, how do you give God "first-fruits" of your labor, income and time? **3.** What additional light is shed by the New Testament on investing disposable income or discretionary time? **4.** Describe the various aspects of your favorite religious festival. What do you see as its purpose? How does your favorite festival help you sustain a correct relationship with God? What does this teach you about the importance of religious festivals to the Christian life? **5.** What redemptive actions has God taken in your life? What has he used to re-enact or remind you of them: Any "tent" meetings? "Wilderness" excursions? "Feast" times? **6.** Which of these memorable events is most important to you? Why? What feelings did this event give you for God? What will you do to regularly remind yourself of this? **7.** If you faithfully observed all these feasts outlined in chapter 23, and maintained your present work responsibilities, how could you afford to "do no regular work" so often? Or would putting God first take care of that? Explain.

When do you do your best work? Are you one who regularly "burns the midnight oil"?

1. Do you think God really needed oil lamps and bread? How would these things function in the Israelite's everyday life? **2.** How

Feast of Trumpets

23The LORD said to Moses, 24"Say to the Israelites: 'On the first day of the seventh month you are to have a day of rest, a sacred assembly commemorated with trumpet blasts. 25Do no regular work, but present an offering made to the LORD by fire.'"

Day of Atonement

26The LORD said to Moses, 27"The tenth day of this seventh month is the Day of Atonement. Hold a sacred assembly and deny yourselves,*a* and present an offering made to the LORD by fire. 28Do no work on that day, because it is the Day of Atonement, when atonement is made for you before the LORD your God. 29Anyone who does not deny himself on that day must be cut off from his people. 30I will destroy from among his people anyone who does any work on that day. 31You shall do no work at all. This is to be a lasting ordinance for the generations to come, wherever you live. 32It is a sabbath of rest for you, and you must deny yourselves. From the evening of the ninth day of the month until the following evening you are to observe your sabbath."

Feast of Tabernacles

33The LORD said to Moses, 34"Say to the Israelites: 'On the fifteenth day of the seventh month the LORD's Feast of Tabernacles begins, and it lasts for seven days. 35The first day is a sacred assembly; do no regular work. 36For seven days present offerings made to the LORD by fire, and on the eighth day hold a sacred assembly and present an offering made to the LORD by fire. It is the closing assembly; do no regular work.

37("'These are the LORD's appointed feasts, which you are to proclaim as sacred assemblies for bringing offerings made to the LORD by fire—the burnt offerings and grain offerings, sacrifices and drink offerings required for each day. 38These offerings are in addition to those for the LORD's Sabbaths and*b* in addition to your gifts and whatever you have vowed and all the freewill offerings you give to the LORD.)

39"'So beginning with the fifteenth day of the seventh month, after you have gathered the crops of the land, celebrate the festival to the LORD for seven days; the first day is a day of rest, and the eighth day also is a day of rest. 40On the first day you are to take choice fruit from the trees, and palm fronds, leafy branches and poplars, and rejoice before the LORD your God for seven days. 41Celebrate this as a festival to the LORD for seven days each year. This is to be a lasting ordinance for the generations to come; celebrate it in the seventh month. 42Live in booths for seven days: All native-born Israelites are to live in booths 43so your descendants will know that I had the Israelites live in booths when I brought them out of Egypt. I am the LORD your God.'"

44So Moses announced to the Israelites the appointed feasts of the LORD.

Oil and Bread Set Before the LORD

24 The LORD said to Moses, 2"Command the Israelites to bring you clear oil of pressed olives for the light so that the lamps may be kept burning continually. 3Outside the curtain of the Testimony in the Tent of Meeting, Aaron is to tend the lamps before the

---

a27 Or *and fast*; also in verses 29 and 32   b38 Or *These feasts are in addition to the LORD's Sabbaths, and these offerings are*

LORD from evening till morning, continually. This is to be a lasting ordinance for the generations to come. [4]The lamps on the pure gold lampstand before the LORD must be tended continually.

[5]"Take fine flour and bake twelve loaves of bread, using two-tenths of an ephah[a] for each loaf. [6]Set them in two rows, six in each row, on the table of pure gold before the LORD. [7]Along each row put some pure incense as a memorial portion to represent the bread and to be an offering made to the LORD by fire. [8]This bread is to be set out before the LORD regularly, Sabbath after Sabbath, on behalf of the Israelites, as a lasting covenant. [9]It belongs to Aaron and his sons, who are to eat it in a holy place, because it is a most holy part of their regular share of the offerings made to the LORD by fire."

A Blasphemer Stoned

[10]Now the son of an Israelite mother and an Egyptian father went out among the Israelites, and a fight broke out in the camp between him and an Israelite. [11]The son of the Israelite woman blasphemed the Name with a curse; so they brought him to Moses. (His mother's name was Shelomith, the daughter of Dibri the Danite.) [12]They put him in custody until the will of the LORD should be made clear to them.

[13]Then the LORD said to Moses: [14]"Take the blasphemer outside the camp. All those who heard him are to lay their hands on his head, and the entire assembly is to stone him. [15]Say to the Israelites: 'If anyone curses his God, he will be held responsible; [16]anyone who blasphemes the name of the LORD must be put to death. The entire assembly must stone him. Whether an alien or native-born, when he blasphemes the Name, he must be put to death.

[17]"'If anyone takes the life of a human being, he must be put to death. [18]Anyone who takes the life of someone's animal must make restitution—life for life. [19]If anyone injures his neighbor, whatever he has done must be done to him: [20]fracture for fracture, eye for eye, tooth for tooth. As he has injured the other, so he is to be injured. [21]Whoever kills an animal must make restitution, but whoever kills a man must be put to death. [22]You are to have the same law for the alien and the native-born. I am the LORD your God.'"

[23]Then Moses spoke to the Israelites, and they took the blasphemer outside the camp and stoned him. The Israelites did as the LORD commanded Moses.

The Sabbath Year

25 The LORD said to Moses on Mount Sinai, [2]"Speak to the Israelites and say to them: 'When you enter the land I am going to give you, the land itself must observe a sabbath to the LORD. [3]For six years sow your fields, and for six years prune your vineyards and gather their crops. [4]But in the seventh year the land is to have a sabbath of rest, a sabbath to the LORD. Do not sow your fields or prune your vineyards. [5]Do not reap what grows of itself or harvest the grapes of your untended vines. The land is to have a year of rest. [6]Whatever the land yields during the sabbath year will be food for you—for yourself, your manservant and maidservant, and the hired worker and temporary resident who live among you, [7]as well as for your livestock and the wild animals in your land. Whatever the land produces may be eaten.

[a]5 That is, probably about 4 quarts (about 4.5 liters)

does this help to explain why they are included in the law?

♡ Do you burn more energy in your diligence for the Lord, or for your own work? What are the important things in your life? How do you give these things to God? What does this say about your relationship with him?

🗩 1. Recall that childhood boast, "My daddy can beat your daddy." In what area was your dad "unbeatable"? 2. If your parents had taken "eye for eye" or "tooth for tooth" every time you fought, what would you look like?

📖 1. Define "blasphemy." Why is this such a serious offense? What lesson do you think the people learned from this event? 2. In what sense do the laws for collecting damages in disputes (vv.17–22) limit vengeance? What does this suggest about "cruel" practices of other nations? How would Israel's limitations help maintain a correct relationship with God? 3. What do these two stories teach you about God's justice and mercy?

♡ 1. When are you tempted to use curses that invoke God's name? 2. How can you let God be your avenger?

🗩 1. If you could take a year off with all expenses paid, what would you like to do? 2. Think about how much you owe your creditors right now. How would you feel if someone paid off all your debts?

📖 1. What would be the direct consequences of this year-long sabbath (vv. 1–7)? What affects might such land management have on Israel's local economy? On their relationship with God? 2. What are the regulations about agricultural land in the 50th year? What would be the immediate consequences of these regulations? The long-range consequences? 3.

Why do you think God made these consequences part of his law (vv. 23–24)? Any other reasons? **4.** Why do you think there is a distinction made between walled cities and villages with regard to the sale and redemption of houses (vv. 29–31)? How might the inherent differences between village and city help to explain this law? **5.** What does it say about the position of the Levites that they are exempted from the regulation concerning sale of property in the city (vv. 32–34)? **6.** What provisions does God stipulate must happen "if one of your countrymen becomes poor" (vv. 25ff, 32ff, 39ff, 47ff)? What is the rationale behind these stipulations? How are these designed to help this person retain his dignity? **7.** Compare the regulations here which concern "slavery" (vv. 39ff, 44ff): Why do you think God distinguishes among Israelites and non-Israelites with regard to slavery? If God opposes slavery for Israelites (v. 39), and if God has just delivered them from slavery in Egypt, then why do you think he allows them to sell themselves for up to 50 years (v. 41)? How would this regulation help them maintain their legal and social standing in the community (vv. 54–55)? **8.** State in your own words the "right of redemption" concerning property and people (vv. 48–53)? What do these laws say about the relationship between God and his people?

♡ **1.** What most excites you about the sabbath year principle? If implemented today, what justice and mercy would be introduced for migrant workers and refugees? Why don't more nations and communities do this, even on a small scale? **2.** What most excites you about the Year of Jubilee? If the Year of Jubilee were to be observed where you live, what would be the consequences of such radical economic reform? **3.** What do you learn from this passage about relations between employer and employee? Lender and borrower? Property owner and tenant? Rich and poor? Countrymen and foreigners? **4.** Optional activity if time permits: Choose one set of the above relationships and plan a small scale activity which puts the Jubilee Year principle in effect. What do you come up with? **5.** On a scale of 1 (low) to 10 (high), rank the priority of importance you place on work? On owning your own place? On earning your own way? On earning the highest rate of in-

The Year of Jubilee

8" 'Count off seven sabbaths of years—seven times seven years—so that the seven sabbaths of years amount to a period of forty-nine years. ⁹Then have the trumpet sounded everywhere on the tenth day of the seventh month; on the Day of Atonement sound the trumpet throughout your land. ¹⁰Consecrate the fiftieth year and proclaim liberty throughout the land to all its inhabitants. It shall be a jubilee for you; each one of you is to return to his family property and each to his own clan. ¹¹The fiftieth year shall be a jubilee for you; do not sow and do not reap what grows of itself or harvest the untended vines. ¹²For it is a jubilee and is to be holy for you; eat only what is taken directly from the fields.

13" 'In this Year of Jubilee everyone is to return to his own property.

14" 'If you sell land to one of your countrymen or buy any from him, do not take advantage of each other. ¹⁵You are to buy from your countryman on the basis of the number of years since the Jubilee. And he is to sell to you on the basis of the number of years left for harvesting crops. ¹⁶When the years are many, you are to increase the price, and when the years are few, you are to decrease the price, because what he is really selling you is the number of crops. ¹⁷Do not take advantage of each other, but fear your God. I am the LORD your God.

18" 'Follow my decrees and be careful to obey my laws, and you will live safely in the land. ¹⁹Then the land will yield its fruit, and you will eat your fill and live there in safety. ²⁰You may ask, "What will we eat in the seventh year if we do not plant or harvest our crops?" ²¹I will send you such a blessing in the sixth year that the land will yield enough for three years. ²²While you plant during the eighth year, you will eat from the old crop and will continue to eat from it until the harvest of the ninth year comes in.

23" 'The land must not be sold permanently, because the land is mine and you are but aliens and my tenants. ²⁴Throughout the country that you hold as a possession, you must provide for the redemption of the land.

25" 'If one of your countrymen becomes poor and sells some of his property, his nearest relative is to come and redeem what his countryman has sold. ²⁶If, however, a man has no one to redeem it for him but he himself prospers and acquires sufficient means to redeem it, ²⁷he is to determine the value for the years since he sold it and refund the balance to the man to whom he sold it; he can then go back to his own property. ²⁸But if he does not acquire the means to repay him, what he sold will remain in the possession of the buyer until the Year of Jubilee. It will be returned in the Jubilee, and he can then go back to his property.

29" 'If a man sells a house in a walled city, he retains the right of redemption a full year after its sale. During that time he may redeem it. ³⁰If it is not redeemed before a full year has passed, the house in the walled city shall belong permanently to the buyer and his descendants. It is not to be returned in the Jubilee. ³¹But houses in villages without walls around them are to be considered as open country. They can be redeemed, and they are to be returned in the Jubilee.

32" 'The Levites always have the right to redeem their houses in the Levitical towns, which they possess. ³³So the property of the Levites is redeemable—that is, a house sold in any town they hold—and is to be returned in the Jubilee, because the houses in the towns of the Levites are their property among the Israelites.

³⁴But the pastureland belonging to their towns must not be sold; it is their permanent possession.

³⁵" 'If one of your countrymen becomes poor and is unable to support himself among you, help him as you would an alien or a temporary resident, so he can continue to live among you. ³⁶Do not take interest of any kind[a] from him, but fear your God, so that your countryman may continue to live among you. ³⁷You must not lend him money at interest or sell him food at a profit. ³⁸I am the LORD your God, who brought you out of Egypt to give you the land of Canaan and to be your God.

³⁹" 'If one of your countrymen becomes poor among you and sells himself to you, do not make him work as a slave. ⁴⁰He is to be treated as a hired worker or a temporary resident among you; he is to work for you until the Year of Jubilee. ⁴¹Then he and his children are to be released, and he will go back to his own clan and to the property of his forefathers. ⁴²Because the Israelites are my servants, whom I brought out of Egypt, they must not be sold as slaves. ⁴³Do not rule over them ruthlessly, but fear your God.

⁴⁴" 'Your male and female slaves are to come from the nations around you; from them you may buy slaves. ⁴⁵You may also buy some of the temporary residents living among you and members of their clans born in your country, and they will become your property. ⁴⁶You can will them to your children as inherited property and can make them slaves for life, but you must not rule over your fellow Israelites ruthlessly.

⁴⁷" 'If an alien or a temporary resident among you becomes rich and one of your countrymen becomes poor and sells himself to the alien living among you or to a member of the alien's clan, ⁴⁸he retains the right of redemption after he has sold himself. One of his relatives may redeem him: ⁴⁹An uncle or a cousin or any blood relative in his clan may redeem him. Or if he prospers, he may redeem himself. ⁵⁰He and his buyer are to count the time from the year he sold himself up to the Year of Jubilee. The price for his release is to be based on the rate paid to a hired man for that number of years. ⁵¹If many years remain, he must pay for his redemption a larger share of the price paid for him. ⁵²If only a few years remain until the Year of Jubilee, he is to compute that and pay for his redemption accordingly. ⁵³He is to be treated as a man hired from year to year; you must see to it that his owner does not rule over him ruthlessly.

⁵⁴" 'Even if he is not redeemed in any of these ways, he and his children are to be released in the Year of Jubilee, ⁵⁵for the Israelites belong to me as servants. They are my servants, whom I brought out of Egypt. I am the LORD your God.

Reward for Obedience

26 " 'Do not make idols or set up an image or a sacred stone for yourselves, and do not place a carved stone in your land to bow down before it. I am the LORD your God.

²" 'Observe my Sabbaths and have reverence for my sanctuary. I am the LORD.

³" 'If you follow my decrees and are careful to obey my commands, ⁴I will send you rain in its season, and the ground will yield its crops and the trees of the field their fruit. ⁵Your threshing will continue until grape harvest and the grape harvest will continue until planting, and you will eat all the food you want and live in safety in your land.

[a] 36 Or *take excessive interest*; similarly in verse 37

terest you can on your money at work for you? **6.** How does the way you ranked yourself help or hinder your relationship with God? What can you do to improve your relationship with God in these areas of your life? **7.** You have been bought with a price, redeemed by God to become his "servant" (v. 55). How do your actions demonstrate your redemption (see Ro 6:15–23)? What will you do to remind yourself of your Christian "servanthood?"

1. What awards have you received (as a student, athlete, employee, manager, volunteer, etc.)? **2.** Why were you given them? Were they worth it?

1. Why does this chapter begin with a list of rewards for obedience? What does this teach you about human nature? And God's nature? **2.** What rewards for obedience listed here most appeal to you? What kind of life would obedience to God's law provide? **3.** How does this blessed life compare with the one promised in Deuteronomy 28:1–14?

1. Are the rewards you receive for your faith in God anything like the rewards promised here? If so, how? If not, why? 2. What do your rewards teach you about "cause and effects" in the abundant life? 3. What possible misuses of this doctrine of the abundant life can you foresee? (Does obedience always "pay"? Does abundance always imply obedience?)

1. How strict were your parents? Did they use the "stick" more than the "carrot"? Or was their "bark" worse than their "bite"? Were the rules and the consequences clearly spelled out? 2. What is the most severe punishment you recall getting from your parents?

1. Of the punishments listed in verses 14–39, which ones seem most severe? Why do you think God found it necessary to include this list in the context with the rewards (26:1–13)? What does it teach you about human nature that one list is substantially longer than the other? How do you feel about that? 2. What hope does God hold out for his people that these punishments will not be necessary? (Note the five conditional "if" clauses in vv. 14–39.) Hence, is there *always* an opportunity for repentance even within God's pronouncements of doom? 3. What new mood is created by making repentance, forgiveness and restoration more explicit (vv. 40–45)? In what sense does God's re-affirmation of the covenant seek the same thing as the list of punishments (vv. 14–39)? 4. How does Paul pick up on this same theme (see Ro 11)? What do these parallel themes teach you about God's nature and his irrevocable covenant? About his desire for a relationship with us? 5. In one paragraph, summarize all of chapter 26 emphasizing how these rewards and punishments would help the people maintain a correct relationship with God?

1. In what two ways are you intentionally like, and unlike, your parents as a disciplinarian? 2. Has human nature changed much since these lists of rewards and punishments were first written? In

6 " 'I will grant peace in the land, and you will lie down and no one will make you afraid. I will remove savage beasts from the land, and the sword will not pass through your country. 7You will pursue your enemies, and they will fall by the sword before you. 8Five of you will chase a hundred, and a hundred of you will chase ten thousand, and your enemies will fall by the sword before you.

9 " 'I will look on you with favor and make you fruitful and increase your numbers, and I will keep my covenant with you. 10You will still be eating last year's harvest when you will have to move it out to make room for the new. 11I will put my dwelling place[a] among you, and I will not abhor you. 12I will walk among you and be your God, and you will be my people. 13I am the LORD your God, who brought you out of Egypt so that you would no longer be slaves to the Egyptians; I broke the bars of your yoke and enabled you to walk with heads held high.

Punishment for Disobedience

14 " 'But if you will not listen to me and carry out all these commands, 15and if you reject my decrees and abhor my laws and fail to carry out all my commands and so violate my covenant, 16then I will do this to you: I will bring upon you sudden terror, wasting diseases and fever that will destroy your sight and drain away your life. You will plant seed in vain, because your enemies will eat it. 17I will set my face against you so that you will be defeated by your enemies; those who hate you will rule over you, and you will flee even when no one is pursuing you.

18 " 'If after all this you will not listen to me, I will punish you for your sins seven times over. 19I will break down your stubborn pride and make the sky above you like iron and the ground beneath you like bronze. 20Your strength will be spent in vain, because your soil will not yield its crops, nor will the trees of the land yield their fruit.

21 " 'If you remain hostile toward me and refuse to listen to me, I will multiply your afflictions seven times over, as your sins deserve. 22I will send wild animals against you, and they will rob you of your children, destroy your cattle and make you so few in number that your roads will be deserted.

23 " 'If in spite of these things you do not accept my correction but continue to be hostile toward me, 24I myself will be hostile toward you and will afflict you for your sins seven times over. 25And I will bring the sword upon you to avenge the breaking of the covenant. When you withdraw into your cities, I will send a plague among you, and you will be given into enemy hands. 26When I cut off your supply of bread, ten women will be able to bake your bread in one oven, and they will dole out the bread by weight. You will eat, but you will not be satisfied.

27 " 'If in spite of this you still do not listen to me but continue to be hostile toward me, 28then in my anger I will be hostile toward you, and I myself will punish you for your sins seven times over. 29You will eat the flesh of your sons and the flesh of your daughters. 30I will destroy your high places, cut down your incense altars and pile your dead bodies on the lifeless forms of your idols, and I will abhor you. 31I will turn your cities into ruins and lay waste your sanctuaries, and I will take no delight in the pleasing aroma of your offerings. 32I will lay waste the land, so that your enemies who live there will be appalled. 33I will scatter you among the nations and will draw out my sword and pursue you. Your land will

a 11 Or my tabernacle

be laid waste, and your cities will lie in ruins. ³⁴Then the land will enjoy its sabbath years all the time that it lies desolate and you are in the country of your enemies; then the land will rest and enjoy its sabbaths. ³⁵All the time that it lies desolate, the land will have the rest it did not have during the sabbaths you lived in it.

³⁶"'As for those of you who are left, I will make their hearts so fearful in the lands of their enemies that the sound of a windblown leaf will put them to flight. They will run as though fleeing from the sword, and they will fall, even though no one is pursuing them. ³⁷They will stumble over one another as though fleeing from the sword, even though no one is pursuing them. So you will not be able to stand before your enemies. ³⁸You will perish among the nations; the land of your enemies will devour you. ³⁹Those of you who are left will waste away in the lands of their enemies because of their sins; also because of their fathers' sins they will waste away.

⁴⁰"'But if they will confess their sins and the sins of their fathers—their treachery against me and their hostility toward me, ⁴¹which made me hostile toward them so that I sent them into the land of their enemies—then when their uncircumcised hearts are humbled and they pay for their sin, ⁴²I will remember my covenant with Jacob and my covenant with Isaac and my covenant with Abraham, and I will remember the land. ⁴³For the land will be deserted by them and will enjoy its sabbaths while it lies desolate without them. They will pay for their sins because they rejected my laws and abhorred my decrees. ⁴⁴Yet in spite of this, when they are in the land of their enemies, I will not reject them or abhor them so as to destroy them completely, breaking my covenant with them. I am the LORD their God. ⁴⁵But for their sake I will remember the covenant with their ancestors whom I brought out of Egypt in the sight of the nations to be their God. I am the LORD.'"

⁴⁶These are the decrees, the laws and the regulations that the LORD established on Mount Sinai between himself and the Israelites through Moses.

Redeeming What Is the LORD's

27 The LORD said to Moses, ²"Speak to the Israelites and say to them: 'If anyone makes a special vow to dedicate persons to the LORD by giving equivalent values, ³set the value of a male between the ages of twenty and sixty at fifty shekels*ᵃ* of silver, according to the sanctuary shekel*ᵇ*; ⁴and if it is a female, set her value at thirty shekels.*ᶜ* ⁵If it is a person between the ages of five and twenty, set the value of a male at twenty shekels*ᵈ* and of a female at ten shekels.*ᵉ* ⁶If it is a person between one month and five years, set the value of a male at five shekels*ᶠ* of silver and that of a female at three shekels*ᵍ* of silver. ⁷If it is a person sixty years old or more, set the value of a male at fifteen shekels*ʰ* and of a female at ten shekels. ⁸If anyone making the vow is too poor to pay the specified amount, he is to present the person to the priest, who will set the value for him according to what the man making the vow can afford.

⁹"'If what he vowed is an animal that is acceptable as an offering to the LORD, such an animal given to the LORD becomes holy. ¹⁰He must not exchange it or substitute a good one for a bad one, or a

what ways is today's church no different than ancient Israel? **3.** What do you think would be included in a similar list of "rewards and punishments" drafted by your pastor with you and your church in mind? What would that list look like if drafted by your small group? (Try it and see.) **4.** What is most difficult for you about sustaining a right relationship with God? How can this chapter help you with this? **5.** How have you experienced the forgiveness and restoration of God, as specified in verses 40–45? What was this experience like? How does that re-affirmation help you to remain reconciled to God? How would you explain this to someone who has not experienced it? With whom will you share it this week?

🍵 **1.** Have you ever been to an auction? Did you get the item you wanted? At the price you wanted? **2.** Have you ever offered or had to buy back a "lost and found" item? What did you lose? What was its posted reward?

📖 **1.** What do you see as the purpose of these laws concerning servants, animals, houses or lands? **2.** Why do you think it was necessary to set a monetary value on people dedicated to the Lord? On other things dedicated to the Lord? What does this tell you about the "give and take" of Israel's relationship with God? **3.** Why do you think the people would want to make these gifts to the Lord beyond their regular tithes? What does this tell you about the people? About their relationship with God? **4.** What stories do you know of Bible characters being "dedicated" or "devoted" to the Lord in the special sense intended here? How does the story of Hannah dedicating

---

ᵃ3 That is, about 1 1/4 pounds (about 0.6 kilogram); also in verse 16   *ᵇ3* That is, about 2/5 ounce (about 11.5 grams); also in verse 25   *ᶜ4* That is, about 12 ounces (about 0.3 kilogram)   *ᵈ5* That is, about 8 ounces (about 0.2 kilogram)   *ᵉ5* That is, about 4 ounces (about 110 grams); also in verse 7   *ᶠ6* That is, about 2 ounces (about 55 grams)   *ᵍ6* That is, about 1 1/4 ounces (about 35 grams)   *ʰ7* That is, about 6 ounces (about 170 grams)

Samuel (1Sa 1:11, 22, 28) illustrate this point? What motivates parents like Hannah to irrevocably give over their children to the Lord?

1. What is something you have recently given to the Lord? Have you ever wanted it back? At what cost? How is this similar to the things dedicated here in this chapter? How is it different? 2. What does this tell you about your value system? Your sense of stewardship vs. ownership? Your hope of "return on investment" in the Lord's work? (Or do you have no thought of return?) 3. Why do you give things to God? When is it easiest for you to dedicate things to the Lord? When is it most difficult for you? What can you and your group do to overcome this difficulty? What will you do today to begin this process? 4. Looking back, what do you see as the overall theme of Leviticus? What other major ideas or points of application will you take with you from your group study? Why not try a study of Hebrews next? More than any other book, Hebrews builds on the rich "typology" (analogous or corresponding truth) of Leviticus, and so points to Christ as the fulfillment of the old covenant. 5. To close out your group study of Leviticus on a redemptive note, try this fun auction game. You have only $1000 to spend on "redeeming" all aspects of your life—the good, the bad and the ugly. Using no more than the $1000 as your spending limit, with $200 as a minimum bid, which qualities of these biblical characters would you "buy" for yourself? $____ for the faith of Abraham; $____ for the patience of Job; $____ for the generosity of Joseph; $____ for the humility of Moses; $____ for the joy of David; $____ for the service of Paul; $____ for the wisdom of Solomon; $____ for the hope of the Prophets. 6. Thank the Lord that his death was limitless and sufficient to buy back all of you, and the whole world besides!

bad one for a good one; if he should substitute one animal for another, both it and the substitute become holy. 11If what he vowed is a ceremonially unclean animal—one that is not acceptable as an offering to the Lord—the animal must be presented to the priest, 12who will judge its quality as good or bad. Whatever value the priest then sets, that is what it will be. 13If the owner wishes to redeem the animal, he must add a fifth to its value.

14"If a man dedicates his house as something holy to the Lord, the priest will judge its quality as good or bad. Whatever value the priest then sets, so it will remain. 15If the man who dedicates his house redeems it, he must add a fifth to its value, and the house will again become his.

16"If a man dedicates to the Lord part of his family land, its value is to be set according to the amount of seed required for it—fifty shekels of silver to a homer[a] of barley seed. 17If he dedicates his field during the Year of Jubilee, the value that has been set remains. 18But if he dedicates his field after the Jubilee, the priest will determine the value according to the number of years that remain until the next Year of Jubilee, and its set value will be reduced. 19If the man who dedicates the field wishes to redeem it, he must add a fifth to its value, and the field will again become his. 20If, however, he does not redeem the field, or if he has sold it to someone else, it can never be redeemed. 21When the field is released in the Jubilee, it will become holy, like a field devoted to the Lord; it will become the property of the priests.[b]

22"If a man dedicates to the Lord a field he has bought, which is not part of his family land, 23the priest will determine its value up to the Year of Jubilee, and the man must pay its value on that day as something holy to the Lord. 24In the Year of Jubilee the field will revert to the person from whom he bought it, the one whose land it was. 25Every value is to be set according to the sanctuary shekel, twenty gerahs to the shekel.

26"'No one, however, may dedicate the firstborn of an animal, since the firstborn already belongs to the Lord; whether an ox[c] or a sheep, it is the Lord's. 27If it is one of the unclean animals, he may buy it back at its set value, adding a fifth of the value to it. If he does not redeem it, it is to be sold at its set value.

28"'But nothing that a man owns and devotes[d] to the Lord—whether man or animal or family land—may be sold or redeemed; everything so devoted is most holy to the Lord.

29"'No person devoted to destruction[e] may be ransomed; he must be put to death.

30"'A tithe of everything from the land, whether grain from the soil or fruit from the trees, belongs to the Lord; it is holy to the Lord. 31If a man redeems any of his tithe, he must add a fifth of the value to it. 32The entire tithe of the herd and flock—every tenth animal that passes under the shepherd's rod—will be holy to the Lord. 33He must not pick out the good from the bad or make any substitution. If he does make a substitution, both the animal and its substitute become holy and cannot be redeemed.'"

34These are the commands the Lord gave Moses on Mount Sinai for the Israelites.

---

a16 That is, probably about 6 bushels (about 220 liters)   b21 Or priest   c26 The Hebrew word can include both male and female.   d28 The Hebrew term refers to the irrevocable giving over of things or persons to the Lord.   e29 The Hebrew term refers to the irrevocable giving over of things or persons to the Lord, often by totally destroying them.

INTRODUCTION to
NUMBERS

Book Study Outline: If you are using Numbers for a study course, here is a 7- or 13-week outline. Use the questions in the margin for your group agenda:

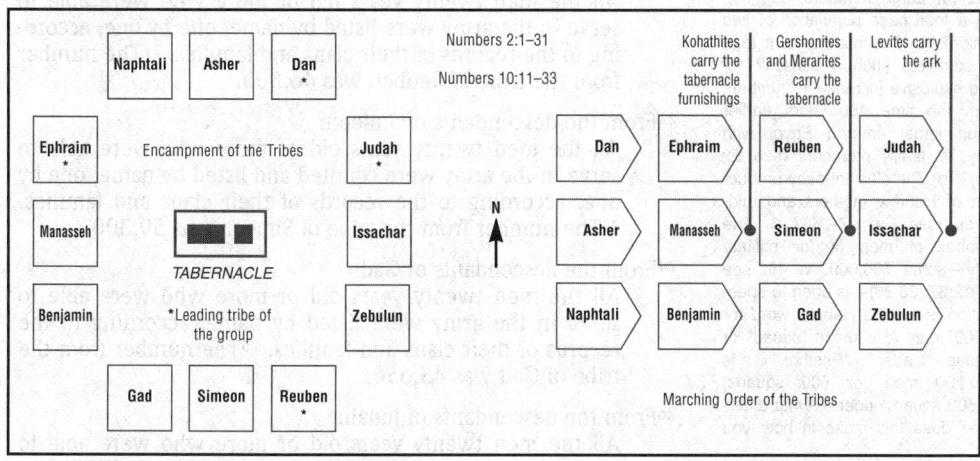 start meeting / 15 min.

read & discuss Bible / 30 min.

close meeting / 15–45 min.

Refer to the Questions and Answers in the front of this Bible for more information.

7-week plan	13-week plan	Personal Reading	Group Study Passage
1	1	1:1–6:21	6:1–21/The Nazirite
	2	6:22–8:26	8:5–26/The Levites
2	3	9:1–10:36	9:15–10:36/Cloud of Guidance
	4	11:1–11:35	11:4–35/Quail From God
3	5	12:1–16	12:1–16/Opposition to Moses
	6	13:16–14:45	13:26–14:45/God's Plan Rejected
4	7	15:1–16:50	16:1–50/Korah's Rebellion
	8	17:1–20:13	20:1–13/Water From the Rock
5	9	20:14–21:35	21:1–9/Bronze Snake
	10	22:1–24:25	22:1–35/Balaam's Donkey
6	11	25:1–26:65	25:1–18/Moab Seduces Israel
	12	27:1–32:42	27:12–23/Joshua Succeeds Moses
7	13	33:1–36:13	33:1–56/Way Stations

Author: Moses is assumed to be the author and editor of most of the first five books of the OT (the Pentateuch).

Date: It is difficult to assign a firm date to the composition of the Pentateuch. Conservative estimates place it in either the fifteenth century or thirteenth century B.C., depending on when the Exodus occurred.

Theme: God's faithfulness despite Israel's rebellion, resulting in 40 years of misery and mercy.

Historical Background: The Book of Numbers relates the story of the 40 years during which Israel journeyed from Mount Sinai to the edge of Canaan. This was a time of great turmoil for Israel in which the people expressed not gratitude for deliverance from Egypt, but rebellion against God. Consequently, they lived out their lives in the desert.

Characteristics: Arranged around the Israelites' wilderness wanderings, the book chronicles God's actions in leading his people toward the land of promise. What makes these actions truly remarkable is that they establish God's faithfulness in spite of the people's rebellious nature. The central human figure in all this is Moses. He combines his many talents with a humble spirit to act as intermediary between his God and his people. The Book of Numbers provides us with a dramatic portrait of Moses, the Israelites, and God as they struggle to turn the disaster of the wilderness wanderings into success.

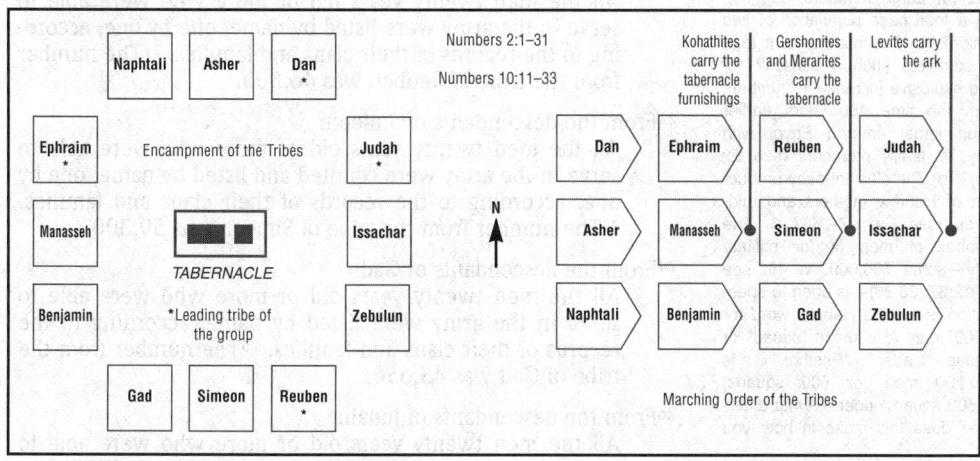

Numbers 2:1–31

Numbers 10:11–33

Encampment of the Tribes

Naphtali	Asher	Dan
Ephraim*		Judah*
Manasseh	TABERNACLE	Issachar
Benjamin	*Leading tribe of the group	Zebulun
Gad	Simeon	Reuben*

Kohathites carry the tabernacle furnishings

Gershonites and Merarites carry the tabernacle

Levites carry the ark

Dan	Ephraim	Reuben	Judah
Asher	Manasseh	Simeon	Issachar
Naphtali	Benjamin	Gad	Zebulun

Marching Order of the Tribes

Numbers

🍵 **1.** How large is the family you grew up in? Your family now? Would you have wanted a larger family anywhere along the way? Why or why not? **2.** What have you been "surveyed" for: Voter opinion? Product testing? Consumer choice? Program evaluation? What do you like or not like about such polls? **3.** Who was your first pastor? What do you remember that was "special" or unique about him or her?

📖 **1.** How does 1:1 serve as the preamble to the whole book of Numbers: Who speaks to whom? (This is stated more than 150 times, 20 different ways in Numbers alone.) Where are they located now? Where are they coming from? What is the turning point or crossroads event for this book? **2.** Compare just the preambles to the five books in the Pentateuch. What do these few verses tell you about where Numbers fits in with the rest? **3.** The "whole Israelite community" is at Mount Sinai preparing for a journey through the wilderness to the land of Canaan. What do you see as the main purpose for taking a census at this point? How might this help to prepare them for the trip? Remind them of God's covenant? **4.** What is significant about who was polled (and who was not)? Why would only men "20 years old or more" be counted? **5.** What is significant to you about the results of the census: (a) Large numbers, suggesting a total base population of two million? (b) The manpower it took to complete such a census? (c) The explosive increase in numbers from the time 400 years earlier when Israel entered Egypt with only 70 family members (see Ex 1:5)? (d) The efficient baby production of Hebrew mothers and midwives (see Ex 1:7–12)? **6.** The number of men fit for military duty—some 600,000 (v. 46; see Ex 12:37; 38:26)—is open to speculation, since the Hebrew word for "1000" may also mean "squad" or "squad leader." Whether it is 600,000 men, or 600 squads, or 600 squad leaders—what difference does this make in how you

The Census

1 The LORD spoke to Moses in the Tent of Meeting in the Desert of Sinai on the first day of the second month of the second year after the Israelites came out of Egypt. He said: ²"Take a census of the whole Israelite community by their clans and families, listing every man by name, one by one. ³You and Aaron are to number by their divisions all the men in Israel twenty years old or more who are able to serve in the army. ⁴One man from each tribe, each the head of his family, is to help you. ⁵These are the names of the men who are to assist you:

> from Reuben, Elizur son of Shedeur;
> ⁶from Simeon, Shelumiel son of Zurishaddai;
> ⁷from Judah, Nahshon son of Amminadab;
> ⁸from Issachar, Nethanel son of Zuar;
> ⁹from Zebulun, Eliab son of Helon;
> ¹⁰from the sons of Joseph:
> from Ephraim, Elishama son of Ammihud;
> from Manasseh, Gamaliel son of Pedahzur;
> ¹¹from Benjamin, Abidan son of Gideoni;
> ¹²from Dan, Ahiezer son of Ammishaddai;
> ¹³from Asher, Pagiel son of Ocran;
> ¹⁴from Gad, Eliasaph son of Deuel;
> ¹⁵from Naphtali, Ahira son of Enan."

¹⁶These were the men appointed from the community, the leaders of their ancestral tribes. They were the heads of the clans of Israel.

¹⁷Moses and Aaron took these men whose names had been given, ¹⁸and they called the whole community together on the first day of the second month. The people indicated their ancestry by their clans and families, and the men twenty years old or more were listed by name, one by one, ¹⁹as the LORD commanded Moses. And so he counted them in the Desert of Sinai:

²⁰From the descendants of Reuben the firstborn son of Israel:
> All the men twenty years old or more who were able to serve in the army were listed by name, one by one, according to the records of their clans and families. ²¹The number from the tribe of Reuben was 46,500.

²²From the descendants of Simeon:
> All the men twenty years old or more who were able to serve in the army were counted and listed by name, one by one, according to the records of their clans and families. ²³The number from the tribe of Simeon was 59,300.

²⁴From the descendants of Gad:
> All the men twenty years old or more who were able to serve in the army were listed by name, according to the records of their clans and families. ²⁵The number from the tribe of Gad was 45,650.

²⁶From the descendants of Judah:
> All the men twenty years old or more who were able to

serve in the army were listed by name, according to the records of their clans and families. ²⁷The number from the tribe of Judah was 74,600.

²⁸From the descendants of Issachar:

All the men twenty years old or more who were able to serve in the army were listed by name, according to the records of their clans and families. ²⁹The number from the tribe of Issachar was 54,400.

³⁰From the descendants of Zebulun:

All the men twenty years old or more who were able to serve in the army were listed by name, according to the records of their clans and families. ³¹The number from the tribe of Zebulun was 57,400.

³²From the sons of Joseph:

From the descendants of Ephraim:

All the men twenty years old or more who were able to serve in the army were listed by name, according to the records of their clans and families. ³³The number from the tribe of Ephraim was 40,500.

³⁴From the descendants of Manasseh:

All the men twenty years old or more who were able to serve in the army were listed by name, according to the records of their clans and families. ³⁵The number from the tribe of Manasseh was 32,200.

³⁶From the descendants of Benjamin:

All the men twenty years old or more who were able to serve in the army were listed by name, according to the records of their clans and families. ³⁷The number from the tribe of Benjamin was 35,400.

³⁸From the descendants of Dan:

All the men twenty years old or more who were able to serve in the army were listed by name, according to the records of their clans and families. ³⁹The number from the tribe of Dan was 62,700.

⁴⁰From the descendants of Asher:

All the men twenty years old or more who were able to serve in the army were listed by name, according to the records of their clans and families. ⁴¹The number from the tribe of Asher was 41,500.

⁴²From the descendants of Naphtali:

All the men twenty years old or more who were able to serve in the army were listed by name, according to the records of their clans and families. ⁴³The number from the tribe of Naphtali was 53,400.

⁴⁴These were the men counted by Moses and Aaron and the twelve leaders of Israel, each one representing his family. ⁴⁵All the Israelites twenty years old or more who were able to serve in Israel's army were counted according to their families. ⁴⁶The total number was 603,550.

⁴⁷The families of the tribe of Levi, however, were not counted along with the others. ⁴⁸The LORD had said to Moses: ⁴⁹"You must not count the tribe of Levi or include them in the census of the other Israelites. ⁵⁰Instead, appoint the Levites to be in charge of the tabernacle of the Testimony—over all its furnishings and everything belonging to it. They are to carry the tabernacle and all its

understand this passage (and other large clan numbers in the exodus and conquest stories)? 7. From verses 47–53, of what importance were the Levites? What is the "Testimony" (vv. 50,53; see Ex 31:18)? What could the Levites do that was prohibited for anyone else (v. 51; see 3:10,38)? 8. Why do you think God wants the census of the Levites (chs. 3–4) separated from that of the people (ch. 1)? How would this affect the way the people viewed the Levites? What's the connection between this and Numbers 8:5–26?

1. What is the most significant crossroads event that separates the "before" and "after" of your life's journey? 2. Israel was in a holding pattern for 13 months following the major crossroads event of all time, the Exodus. How about you: What did you do in the first year following your big event (if there was one)? What aspect of that journey are you embarking on now? 3. How has God especially prepared you for a spiritual journey? In what sense has this preparation made your life's pilgrimage easier? More difficult? 4. How might Israel's numerical growth in the previous 400 years be related to God's promises to Abraham (see Ge 12:2; 15:5; 17:4–6; 22:17)? What does this tell you about God's concern for your growth and success in the Christian life? 5. In what sense is your pastor set apart? How is this demonstrated by his or her role in the community? How then do you feel toward your pastor?

furnishings; they are to take care of it and encamp around it. ⁵¹Whenever the tabernacle is to move, the Levites are to take it down, and whenever the tabernacle is to be set up, the Levites shall do it. Anyone else who goes near it shall be put to death. ⁵²The Israelites are to set up their tents by divisions, each man in his own camp under his own standard. ⁵³The Levites, however, are to set up their tents around the tabernacle of the Testimony so that wrath will not fall on the Israelite community. The Levites are to be responsible for the care of the tabernacle of the Testimony."

⁵⁴The Israelites did all this just as the Lord commanded Moses.

The Arrangement of the Tribal Camps

2 The Lord said to Moses and Aaron: ²"The Israelites are to camp around the Tent of Meeting some distance from it, each man under his standard with the banners of his family."

³On the east, toward the sunrise, the divisions of the camp of Judah are to encamp under their standard. The leader of the people of Judah is Nahshon son of Amminadab. ⁴His division numbers 74,600.

⁵The tribe of Issachar will camp next to them. The leader of the people of Issachar is Nethanel son of Zuar. ⁶His division numbers 54,400.

⁷The tribe of Zebulun will be next. The leader of the people of Zebulun is Eliab son of Helon. ⁸His division numbers 57,400.

⁹All the men assigned to the camp of Judah, according to their divisions, number 186,400. They will set out first.

¹⁰On the south will be the divisions of the camp of Reuben under their standard. The leader of the people of Reuben is Elizur son of Shedeur. ¹¹His division numbers 46,500.

¹²The tribe of Simeon will camp next to them. The leader of the people of Simeon is Shelumiel son of Zurishaddai. ¹³His division numbers 59,300.

¹⁴The tribe of Gad will be next. The leader of the people of Gad is Eliasaph son of Deuel.^a ¹⁵His division numbers 45,650.

¹⁶All the men assigned to the camp of Reuben, according to their divisions, number 151,450. They will set out second.

¹⁷Then the Tent of Meeting and the camp of the Levites will set out in the middle of the camps. They will set out in the same order as they encamp, each in his own place under his standard.

¹⁸On the west will be the divisions of the camp of Ephraim under their standard. The leader of the people of Ephraim is Elishama son of Ammihud. ¹⁹His division numbers 40,500.

²⁰The tribe of Manasseh will be next to them. The leader of the people of Manasseh is Gamaliel son of Pedahzur. ²¹His division numbers 32,200.

²²The tribe of Benjamin will be next. The leader of the people of Benjamin is Abidan son of Gideoni. ²³His division numbers 35,400.

²⁴All the men assigned to the camp of Ephraim, according to their divisions, number 108,100. They will set out third.

²⁵On the north will be the divisions of the camp of Dan,

When was the last time you went camping? How long did this trip last? What did you take with you? What did you end up wishing you had brought along?

1. Why do you think God is so concerned about the arrangements of the Israelite tents? How would deciding on the placement of the tents make the Israelite's trip through the wilderness easier? 2. Draw a baseball diamond, with each base one of four compass points, and with the 12 tribes apportioned at each base camp. Who's on first? Second? Third? Home? Who's on the pitcher's mound? Whose tents are immediately surrounding that mound, keeping the others "some distance from it" (vv. 2,17)? 3. Given their great size, their recent enslavement and later disobedience, what do you find remarkable about their compliance to Moses' command (v. 34; also 1:54)? 4. What does this teach you about God's concern for order and structure among his people? How would this have made the Israelite "mob" feel?

1. Do you think God is concerned about the everyday aspects of your life? How does he show you this concern (or lack of it)? 2. How would you relate Israel's impressive organization to a large rally (mass crusade, political convention or festive celebration) you have witnessed? What does this teach you about human nature and our need for organization from on high?

a14 Many manuscripts of the Masoretic Text, Samaritan Pentateuch and Vulgate (see also Num. 1:14); most manuscripts of the Masoretic Text *Reuel*

under their standard. The leader of the people of Dan is Ahie-zer son of Ammishaddai. [26]His division numbers 62,700.
[27]The tribe of Asher will camp next to them. The leader of the people of Asher is Pagiel son of Ocran. [28]His division numbers 41,500.
[29]The tribe of Naphtali will be next. The leader of the people of Naphtali is Ahira son of Enan. [30]His division numbers 53,400.
[31]All the men assigned to the camp of Dan number 157,600. They will set out last, under their standards.

[32]These are the Israelites, counted according to their families. All those in the camps, by their divisions, number 603,550. [33]The Levites, however, were not counted along with the other Israelites, as the LORD commanded Moses.

[34]So the Israelites did everything the LORD commanded Moses; that is the way they encamped under their standards, and that is the way they set out, each with his clan and family.

The Levites

3 This is the account of the family of Aaron and Moses at the time the LORD talked with Moses on Mount Sinai.
[2]The names of the sons of Aaron were Nadab the firstborn and Abihu, Eleazar and Ithamar. [3]Those were the names of Aaron's sons, the anointed priests, who were ordained to serve as priests. [4]Nadab and Abihu, however, fell dead before the LORD when they made an offering with unauthorized fire before him in the Desert of Sinai. They had no sons; so only Eleazar and Ithamar served as priests during the lifetime of their father Aaron.
[5]The LORD said to Moses, [6]"Bring the tribe of Levi and present them to Aaron the priest to assist him. [7]They are to perform duties for him and for the whole community at the Tent of Meeting by doing the work of the tabernacle. [8]They are to take care of all the furnishings of the Tent of Meeting, fulfilling the obligations of the Israelites by doing the work of the tabernacle. [9]Give the Levites to Aaron and his sons; they are the Israelites who are to be given wholly to him.[a] [10]Appoint Aaron and his sons to serve as priests; anyone else who approaches the sanctuary must be put to death."
[11]The LORD also said to Moses, [12]"I have taken the Levites from among the Israelites in place of the first male offspring of every Israelite woman. The Levites are mine, [13]for all the firstborn are mine. When I struck down all the firstborn in Egypt, I set apart for myself every firstborn in Israel, whether man or animal. They are to be mine. I am the LORD."
[14]The LORD said to Moses in the Desert of Sinai, [15]"Count the Levites by their families and clans. Count every male a month old or more." [16]So Moses counted them, as he was commanded by the word of the LORD.
[17]These were the names of the sons of Levi:
    Gershon, Kohath and Merari.
[18]These were the names of the Gershonite clans:
    Libni and Shimei.
[19]The Kohathite clans:
    Amram, Izhar, Hebron and Uzziel.
[20]The Merarite clans:
    Mahli and Mushi.
These were the Levite clans, according to their families.

[a]9 Most manuscripts of the Masoretic Text; some manuscripts of the Masoretic Text, Samaritan Pentateuch and Septuagint (see also Num. 8:16) *to me*

Who was the "firstborn" in your family? What special rights did they have? What special responsibilities? How did you feel about this?

1. What does the story of Nadab and Abihu illustrate (vv. 4,10,38; see Lev 10:1–3)? When else in God's redemptive history has the Lord made object lessons of those who would trifle with holy vows (see Jos 7; 2Sa 6:7; Ac 5:1–11, for similar judgments)? **2.** In verses 5–10 (also 8:5–26), what distinctions are made between the work of *priests* (sons of Aaron) and *Levites*? **3.** Why do you think God set aside an entire tribe to take care of the tabernacle and the other religious aspects of Israel's life? What does this say about the importance of religious life to God? To the Israelites? **4.** Since Aaron and his sons were a part of the tribe of Levi, do you think the other Levites were jealous of Aaron's family's role as priests? Or more relieved? How is this similar to your attitude toward spiritual leaders? Do you want to jump in and join them or just support them in their big responsibility? **5.** What is God's point in claiming all firstborn (v. 13)? What would this teach the Israelites about God? **6.** In comparison to the other tribes (chs. 1–2), how and why are the Levites counted (vv. 15–39)? Why the different method? **7.** What problems might have arisen if God had asked for the firstborn of every Israelite? How would substituting the Levites solve this problem? Do you think the Israelites would still get God's point? Why? **8.** How do the subtotals (vv. 22,28,34) and total number of Levites (v. 39) compare? How does this 22,000+ figure compare with the total number of firstborn males (v. 43)? **9.** How is Moses to "redeem" (or account for) the remainder of firstborn, not substituted for by the Levites (vv. 45–58)? **10.** What do you find noteworthy about Moses' obedience (vv.16,39,42,49,51)?

♡ **1.** Do you think God still requires our "first" or our "best"? In what sense do you give God your first or best? How do you feel about this? **2.** How much faith in God would it take for you to let him have your children? Do you have this much faith? What will you do this week to make sure that, when called upon, your faith will meet the challenge? **3.** What principle of substitution and redemption does God use today (see Ro 5)? If a redemption price were still required for your life or your children's, what would it be? What price has God paid on your behalf (see Heb 9:15)? **4.** What new appreciation does this chapter give you for the awesome gravity of holy tasks performed by your pastor or priest? As one of God's ministers (lay or clergy), how would you approach God's sanctuary? *Word of caution:* Aren't you among those who would "surely die" if they approached the sanctuary (vv. 10,38; see Heb 4:14–16; 10:19–25)? At what risk do you proceed?

21To Gershon belonged the clans of the Libnites and Shimeites; these were the Gershonite clans. 22The number of all the males a month old or more who were counted was 7,500. 23The Gershonite clans were to camp on the west, behind the tabernacle. 24The leader of the families of the Gershonites was Eliasaph son of Lael. 25At the Tent of Meeting the Gershonites were responsible for the care of the tabernacle and tent, its coverings, the curtain at the entrance to the Tent of Meeting, 26the curtains of the courtyard, the curtain at the entrance to the courtyard surrounding the tabernacle and altar, and the ropes—and everything related to their use.

27To Kohath belonged the clans of the Amramites, Izharites, Hebronites and Uzzielites; these were the Kohathite clans. 28The number of all the males a month old or more was 8,600.ᵃ The Kohathites were responsible for the care of the sanctuary. 29The Kohathite clans were to camp on the south side of the tabernacle. 30The leader of the families of the Kohathite clans was Elizaphan son of Uzziel. 31They were responsible for the care of the ark, the table, the lampstand, the altars, the articles of the sanctuary used in ministering, the curtain, and everything related to their use. 32The chief leader of the Levites was Eleazar son of Aaron, the priest. He was appointed over those who were responsible for the care of the sanctuary.

33To Merari belonged the clans of the Mahlites and the Mushites; these were the Merarite clans. 34The number of all the males a month old or more who were counted was 6,200. 35The leader of the families of the Merarite clans was Zuriel son of Abihail; they were to camp on the north side of the tabernacle. 36The Merarites were appointed to take care of the frames of the tabernacle, its crossbars, posts, bases, all its equipment, and everything related to their use, 37as well as the posts of the surrounding courtyard with their bases, tent pegs and ropes.

38Moses and Aaron and his sons were to camp to the east of the tabernacle, toward the sunrise, in front of the Tent of Meeting. They were responsible for the care of the sanctuary on behalf of the Israelites. Anyone else who approached the sanctuary was to be put to death.

39The total number of Levites counted at the Lord's command by Moses and Aaron according to their clans, including every male a month old or more, was 22,000.

40The Lord said to Moses, "Count all the firstborn Israelite males who are a month old or more and make a list of their names. 41Take the Levites for me in place of all the firstborn of the Israelites, and the livestock of the Levites in place of all the firstborn of the livestock of the Israelites. I am the Lord."

42So Moses counted all the firstborn of the Israelites, as the Lord commanded him. 43The total number of firstborn males a month old or more, listed by name, was 22,273.

44The Lord also said to Moses, 45"Take the Levites in place of all the firstborn of Israel, and the livestock of the Levites in place of their livestock. The Levites are to be mine. I am the Lord. 46To redeem the 273 firstborn Israelites who exceed the number of the Levites, 47collect five shekelsᵇ for each one, according to the

ᵃ28 Hebrew; some Septuagint manuscripts 8,300   ᵇ47 That is, about 2 ounces (about 55 grams) sanctuary shekel, which weighs twenty gerahs. 48Give the money for the redemption of the additional Israelites to Aaron and his sons."

49So Moses collected the redemption money from those who exceeded the number redeemed by the Levites. 50From the first-born of the Israelites he collected silver weighing 1,365 shekels,*a* according to the sanctuary shekel. 51Moses gave the redemption money to Aaron and his sons, as he was commanded by the word of the LORD.

The Kohathites

4 The LORD said to Moses and Aaron: 2"Take a census of the Kohathite branch of the Levites by their clans and families. 3Count all the men from thirty to fifty years of age who come to serve in the work in the Tent of Meeting.

4"This is the work of the Kohathites in the Tent of Meeting: the care of the most holy things. 5When the camp is to move, Aaron and his sons are to go in and take down the shielding curtain and cover the ark of the Testimony with it. 6Then they are to cover this with hides of sea cows,*b* spread a cloth of solid blue over that and put the poles in place.

7"Over the table of the Presence they are to spread a blue cloth and put on it the plates, dishes and bowls, and the jars for drink offerings; the bread that is continually there is to remain on it. 8Over these they are to spread a scarlet cloth, cover that with hides of sea cows and put its poles in place.

9"They are to take a blue cloth and cover the lampstand that is for light, together with its lamps, its wick trimmers and trays, and all its jars for the oil used to supply it. 10Then they are to wrap it and all its accessories in a covering of hides of sea cows and put it on a carrying frame.

11"Over the gold altar they are to spread a blue cloth and cover that with hides of sea cows and put its poles in place.

12"They are to take all the articles used for ministering in the sanctuary, wrap them in a blue cloth, cover that with hides of sea cows and put them on a carrying frame.

13"They are to remove the ashes from the bronze altar and spread a purple cloth over it. 14Then they are to place on it all the utensils used for ministering at the altar, including the firepans, meat forks, shovels and sprinkling bowls. Over it they are to spread a covering of hides of sea cows and put its poles in place.

15"After Aaron and his sons have finished covering the holy furnishings and all the holy articles, and when the camp is ready to move, the Kohathites are to come to do the carrying. But they must not touch the holy things or they will die. The Kohathites are to carry those things that are in the Tent of Meeting.

16"Eleazar son of Aaron, the priest, is to have charge of the oil for the light, the fragrant incense, the regular grain offering and the anointing oil. He is to be in charge of the entire tabernacle and everything in it, including its holy furnishings and articles."

17The LORD said to Moses and Aaron, 18"See that the Kohathite tribal clans are not cut off from the Levites. 19So that they may live and not die when they come near the most holy things, do this for them: Aaron and his sons are to go into the sanctuary and assign to each man his work and what he is to carry. 20But the Kohathites must not go in to look at the holy things, even for a moment, or they will die."

Of all your worldly goods, which one has the mark of a family heirloom that you want to be sure to pass along to a special member of your family?

1. Why is this second census of the Levites taken (v. 3)? As the age for beginning service in the tabernacle was 25 (see 8:24), what do you suppose these Levites did between the ages of 25 and 30? 2. What care or precaution goes into moving the temple furnishings (vv. 4ff)? How could they go about the work of moving the holy things without "touching" (v. 15) or "looking" (v. 20) at them, lest they die? 3. What does this teach about the importance of the holy things? Of those who care for them? And of the one who could draw near to the holy things on everyone's behalf (vv. 16,19)? 4. Why do you think God cares so much that these furnishings be moved in a "proper" way? How would this help Israel to better understand the nature of God and what he expects of them?

1. What ceremonies, or traditions, does your church practice with respect to the "holy things"? Who is in charge of that work? How does this benefit you? 2. What does this passage teach you about maintaining a correct relationship with God? How casual or careful are you with this relationship: (a) God and I are best friends? (b) I can drop in on him any time? (c) I see him on a "reservations only" basis? (d) Mine is a "dinner suits only" with God? (e) Others, who know the right language and etiquette, talk to God for me?

---

a50 That is, about 35 pounds (about 15.5 kilograms)   *b6* That is, dugongs; also in verses 8, 10, 11, 12, 14 and 25

What, if any, religious duties were you assigned: (a) As a youth, or following confirmation of your faith? (b) As an adult, when joining a church on your own?

1. What duties are assigned to the Gershonites (vv. 24–28)? To the Merarites (vv. 31–33)? How do they complement the Kohathites? 2. Given the mobile nature of the Israelites, how important would the work of the Gershonites and Merarites be in the religious life of the Israelites? How would their work enhance the worship of all Israel? What does this say about the nature of worship?

1. Who takes care of the physical aspects of worship in your church (setting up chairs, unlocking doors, cleaning the communion cups, etc.)? 2. How does this aid in your own worship? How will you show your appreciation to one such worship aide today?

How many different churches have you attended over the years? How did you settle on the one you are in now? Was it because someone asked you to get involved?

1. What do you learn about the scope of Israelite worship from the numbers of people involved in physical aspects of the tabernacle? 2. What does this teach you about the importance of worship for the Israelites? Of the work that goes into worship?

1. How many people are involved in making your church services worshipful? How important to the attitude of worship are those that work in the nursery, Sunday school, as greeters or ushers? 2. Which of those roles do you like serving in? How might you show your appreciation to others in that role?

The Gershonites

21The LORD said to Moses, 22"Take a census also of the Gershonites by their families and clans. 23Count all the men from thirty to fifty years of age who come to serve in the work at the Tent of Meeting.

24"This is the service of the Gershonite clans as they work and carry burdens: 25They are to carry the curtains of the tabernacle, the Tent of Meeting, its covering and the outer covering of hides of sea cows, the curtains for the entrance to the Tent of Meeting, 26the curtains of the courtyard surrounding the tabernacle and altar, the curtain for the entrance, the ropes and all the equipment used in its service. The Gershonites are to do all that needs to be done with these things. 27All their service, whether carrying or doing other work, is to be done under the direction of Aaron and his sons. You shall assign to them as their responsibility all they are to carry. 28This is the service of the Gershonite clans at the Tent of Meeting. Their duties are to be under the direction of Ithamar son of Aaron, the priest.

The Merarites

29"Count the Merarites by their clans and families. 30Count all the men from thirty to fifty years of age who come to serve in the work at the Tent of Meeting. 31This is their duty as they perform service at the Tent of Meeting: to carry the frames of the tabernacle, its crossbars, posts and bases, 32as well as the posts of the surrounding courtyard with their bases, tent pegs, ropes, all their equipment and everything related to their use. Assign to each man the specific things he is to carry. 33This is the service of the Merarite clans as they work at the Tent of Meeting under the direction of Ithamar son of Aaron, the priest."

The Numbering of the Levite Clans

34Moses, Aaron and the leaders of the community counted the Kohathites by their clans and families. 35All the men from thirty to fifty years of age who came to serve in the work in the Tent of Meeting, 36counted by clans, were 2,750. 37This was the total of all those in the Kohathite clans who served in the Tent of Meeting. Moses and Aaron counted them according to the LORD's command through Moses.

38The Gershonites were counted by their clans and families. 39All the men from thirty to fifty years of age who came to serve in the work at the Tent of Meeting, 40counted by their clans and families, were 2,630. 41This was the total of those in the Gershonite clans who served at the Tent of Meeting. Moses and Aaron counted them according to the LORD's command.

42The Merarites were counted by their clans and families. 43All the men from thirty to fifty years of age who came to serve in the work at the Tent of Meeting, 44counted by their clans, were 3,200. 45This was the total of those in the Merarite clans. Moses and Aaron counted them according to the LORD's command through Moses.

46So Moses, Aaron and the leaders of Israel counted all the Levites by their clans and families. 47All the men from thirty to fifty years of age who came to do the work of serving and carrying the Tent of Meeting 48numbered 8,580. 49At the LORD's command through Moses, each was assigned his work and told what to carry.

Thus they were counted, as the LORD commanded Moses.

The Purity of the Camp

5 The LORD said to Moses, [2]"Command the Israelites to send away from the camp anyone who has an infectious skin disease[a] or a discharge of any kind, or who is ceremonially unclean because of a dead body. [3]Send away male and female alike; send them outside the camp so they will not defile their camp, where I dwell among them." [4]The Israelites did this; they sent them outside the camp. They did just as the LORD had instructed Moses.

Restitution for Wrongs

[5]The LORD said to Moses, [6]"Say to the Israelites: 'When a man or woman wrongs another in any way[b] and so is unfaithful to the LORD, that person is guilty [7]and must confess the sin he has committed. He must make full restitution for his wrong, add one fifth to it and give it all to the person he has wronged. [8]But if that person has no close relative to whom restitution can be made for the wrong, the restitution belongs to the LORD and must be given to the priest, along with the ram with which atonement is made for him. [9]All the sacred contributions the Israelites bring to a priest will belong to him. [10]Each man's sacred gifts are his own, but what he gives to the priest will belong to the priest.' "

The Test for an Unfaithful Wife

[11]Then the LORD said to Moses, [12]"Speak to the Israelites and say to them: 'If a man's wife goes astray and is unfaithful to him [13]by sleeping with another man, and this is hidden from her husband and her impurity is undetected (since there is no witness against her and she has not been caught in the act), [14]and if feelings of jealousy come over her husband and he suspects his wife and she is impure—or if he is jealous and suspects her even though she is not impure— [15]then he is to take his wife to the priest. He must also take an offering of a tenth of an ephah[c] of barley flour on her behalf. He must not pour oil on it or put incense on it, because it is a grain offering for jealousy, a reminder offering to draw attention to guilt.

[16]" 'The priest shall bring her and have her stand before the LORD. [17]Then he shall take some holy water in a clay jar and put some dust from the tabernacle floor into the water. [18]After the priest has had the woman stand before the LORD, he shall loosen her hair and place in her hands the reminder offering, the grain offering for jealousy, while he himself holds the bitter water that brings a curse. [19]Then the priest shall put the woman under oath and say to her, "If no other man has slept with you and you have not gone astray and become impure while married to your husband, may this bitter water that brings a curse not harm you. [20]But if you have gone astray while married to your husband and you have defiled yourself by sleeping with a man other than your husband"— [21]here the priest is to put the woman under this curse of the oath—"may the LORD cause your people to curse and denounce you when he causes your thigh to waste away and your abdomen to swell.[d] [22]May this water that brings a curse enter your body so that your abdomen swells and your thigh wastes away.[e]"

" 'Then the woman is to say, "Amen. So be it."

[23]" 'The priest is to write these curses on a scroll and then wash

---

[a]2 Traditionally *leprosy*; the Hebrew word was used for various diseases affecting the skin—not necessarily leprosy.   [b]6 Or *woman commits any wrong common to mankind*   [c]15 That is, probably about 2 quarts (about 2 liters)   [d]21 Or *causes you to have a miscarrying womb and barrenness*   [e]22 Or *body and cause you to be barren and have a miscarrying womb*

---

1. What contagious illness have you had? 2. Ever been teased about being a "kleptomaniac" of anything: Clerks' pens? Library books? Copyrighted material? Food? Souvenirs? Kisses? Other?

1. What's the object lesson in verses 1–4? In verses 5–10? 2. How would these two sets of laws help the Israelites on their journey? 3. How would making these laws part of their religion help to make sure they were obeyed?

1. Which of these two object lessons do you think is tougher to administer? Why? 2. Where does the priest come in? Where does forgiveness enter?

1. What is the closest thing to a "lie detector test" you have ever taken or witnessed? How do you feel about the experience? 2. As a child, were you more forgiving or more suspicious? How have you changed since then? What does this tell you about yourself?

1. What would you say is the overall theme of chapter 5? Why is more instruction devoted to the "private" sin of adultery compared to ritual uncleanness and public injustice? 2. Why would it be important to maintain group and family harmony during Israel's journey through the wilderness? How would even the possibility of adultery damage this harmony? 3. What effect would this test have on someone considering adultery? On someone hiding the fact of adultery? Are the effects primarily physical, psychological, social, magical or spiritual? Why do you think so? 4. How could a jealous husband disrupt the harmony of the group? How would this test help to defuse this situation? 5. Do you think this test for adultery is meant primarily for the benefit of the husband, the wife, or both? Why? In the absence of such a test and appeal to the priest, what would be the social consequences?

1. How important is group and family harmony to your own relationship to God? What is most likely to destroy this harmony? What can you do to avoid this problem? 2. When you are jealous

of someone, how is your worship affected? What actions can you take to remove these feelings of jealousy? What will you do to remind yourself to take these actions the next time you become jealous? **3.** What jealousies in your small group are threatening the quality of your worship? How will you deal with these, now?

1. When have you promised your parents, spouse or children, that you would pray for them or remember them in a special way? How successful were you in keeping that promise? How did you feel about that? **2.** What broken promise are you still feeling the pain of? How did you make amends?

1. The Nazirite's vow involved what three prohibitions (vv. 3–6)? Why do you think each of these was prohibited? What would this vow tell other people about the Nazirite? How would such abstinence and austerity draw the Nazirite close to God (vv. 2,8)? **2.** How do these vows compare to the ones that priests had to make (vv. 5–6; see Lev 21:1–5)? **3.** What exceptions were anticipated and why? **4.** Why do you think there is such an elaborate ceremony ending the Nazirite's vow (vv. 13–21)? What would this ceremony tell the people about the Nazirite? About God's relationship with his people? **5.** What do you know about these famous Nazirites: Samuel? Samson? How do they help you to understand the purpose of his vow?

1. Have you ever made a special vow to God: For Lent? New Year's? Marriage? Baby's birth? Explain. **2.** How did you prove your seriousness about this vow? In what ways was this similar to the Nazirite's vow of temperance: Diet? Associations? Appearance? Other? In what ways was it different? **3.** What advantage can you see in making your vows

them off into the bitter water. 24He shall have the woman drink the bitter water that brings a curse, and this water will enter her and cause bitter suffering. 25The priest is to take from her hands the grain offering for jealousy, wave it before the LORD and bring it to the altar. 26The priest is then to take a handful of the grain offering as a memorial offering and burn it on the altar; after that, he is to have the woman drink the water. 27If she has defiled herself and been unfaithful to her husband, then when she is made to drink the water that brings a curse, it will go into her and cause bitter suffering; her abdomen will swell and her thigh waste away,[a] and she will become accursed among her people. 28If, however, the woman has not defiled herself and is free from impurity, she will be cleared of guilt and will be able to have children.

29"'This, then, is the law of jealousy when a woman goes astray and defiles herself while married to her husband, 30or when feelings of jealousy come over a man because he suspects his wife. The priest is to have her stand before the LORD and is to apply this entire law to her. 31The husband will be innocent of any wrongdoing, but the woman will bear the consequences of her sin.'"

The Nazirite

6 The LORD said to Moses, 2"Speak to the Israelites and say to them: 'If a man or woman wants to make a special vow, a vow of separation to the LORD as a Nazirite, 3he must abstain from wine and other fermented drink and must not drink vinegar made from wine or from other fermented drink. He must not drink grape juice or eat grapes or raisins. 4As long as he is a Nazirite, he must not eat anything that comes from the grapevine, not even the seeds or skins.

5"'During the entire period of his vow of separation no razor may be used on his head. He must be holy until the period of his separation to the LORD is over; he must let the hair of his head grow long. 6Throughout the period of his separation to the LORD he must not go near a dead body. 7Even if his own father or mother or brother or sister dies, he must not make himself ceremonially unclean on account of them, because the symbol of his separation to God is on his head. 8Throughout the period of his separation he is consecrated to the LORD.

9"'If someone dies suddenly in his presence, thus defiling the hair he has dedicated, he must shave his head on the day of his cleansing—the seventh day. 10Then on the eighth day he must bring two doves or two young pigeons to the priest at the entrance to the Tent of Meeting. 11The priest is to offer one as a sin offering and the other as a burnt offering to make atonement for him because he sinned by being in the presence of the dead body. That same day he is to consecrate his head. 12He must dedicate himself to the LORD for the period of his separation and must bring a year-old male lamb as a guilt offering. The previous days do not count, because he became defiled during his separation.

13"'Now this is the law for the Nazirite when the period of his separation is over. He is to be brought to the entrance to the Tent of Meeting. 14There he is to present his offerings to the LORD: a year-old male lamb without defect for a burnt offering, a year-old ewe lamb without defect for a sin offering, a ram without defect for a fellowship offering,[b] 15together with their grain offerings and drink offerings, and a basket of bread made without yeast—cakes made of fine flour mixed with oil, and wafers spread with oil.

[a]27 Or suffering; she will have barrenness and a miscarrying womb
[b]14 Traditionally peace offering; also in verses 17 and 18

16" 'The priest is to present them before the LORD and make the sin offering and the burnt offering. 17He is to present the basket of unleavened bread and is to sacrifice the ram as a fellowship offering to the LORD, together with its grain offering and drink offering.

18" 'Then at the entrance to the Tent of Meeting, the Nazirite must shave off the hair that he dedicated. He is to take the hair and put it in the fire that is under the sacrifice of the fellowship offering.

19" 'After the Nazirite has shaved off the hair of his dedication, the priest is to place in his hands a boiled shoulder of the ram, and a cake and a wafer from the basket, both made without yeast. 20The priest shall then wave them before the LORD as a wave offering; they are holy and belong to the priest, together with the breast that was waved and the thigh that was presented. After that, the Nazirite may drink wine.

21" 'This is the law of the Nazirite who vows his offering to the LORD in accordance with his separation, in addition to whatever else he can afford. He must fulfill the vow he has made, according to the law of the Nazirite.' "

The Priestly Blessing

22The LORD said to Moses, 23"Tell Aaron and his sons, 'This is how you are to bless the Israelites. Say to them:

24" ' "The LORD bless you
and keep you;
25the LORD make his face shine upon you
and be gracious to you;
26the LORD turn his face toward you
and give you peace." '

27"So they will put my name on the Israelites, and I will bless them."

Offerings at the Dedication of the Tabernacle

7 When Moses finished setting up the tabernacle, he anointed it and consecrated it and all its furnishings. He also anointed and consecrated the altar and all its utensils. 2Then the leaders of Israel, the heads of families who were the tribal leaders in charge of those who were counted, made offerings. 3They brought as their gifts before the LORD six covered carts and twelve oxen—an ox from each leader and a cart from every two. These they presented before the tabernacle.

4The LORD said to Moses, 5"Accept these from them, that they may be used in the work at the Tent of Meeting. Give them to the Levites as each man's work requires."

6So Moses took the carts and oxen and gave them to the Levites. 7He gave two carts and four oxen to the Gershonites, as their work required, 8and he gave four carts and eight oxen to the Merarites, as their work required. They were all under the direction of Ithamar son of Aaron, the priest. 9But Moses did not give any to the Kohathites, because they were to carry on their shoulders the holy things, for which they were responsible.

10When the altar was anointed, the leaders brought their offerings for its dedication and presented them before the altar. 11For the LORD had said to Moses, "Each day one leader is to bring his offering for the dedication of the altar."

12The one who brought his offering on the first day was Nahshon son of Amminadab of the tribe of Judah.

13His offering was one silver plate weighing a hundred and

---

public, as did the Nazirite? What advantage can you see in keeping your vows private? **4.** How could your group help in a positive way to focus attention on your own vows? Do you have a vow you wish to make public for this purpose?

What farewell blessing is most common to your family? Why do you like it?

1. In what ways has God's power been evident in your life recently? How does that reflect the three-fold blessing here? **2.** What does this priestly blessing say about what God wants for you and your life?

1. What gift from your last birthday do you still remember? What made this such a memorable one? **2.** What is one gift you most enjoyed giving to someone else?

1. In chapter 7, each tribe presents a gift for the dedication of the altar (summed up in 7:84–88). How does this relate to the blessing just received (see 6:24–26)? **2.** How would this act help the people to identify with the tabernacle? Of what importance would this identification be to them in their journey through the wilderness? **3.** Why do you think each tribe gave an identical gift? How would this help to build unity between the tribes? How would it help them to concentrate on the reasons for giving the gift? **4.** What literary and theological climax do you see in this long chapter?

1. What kinds of gifts do you give to God in time, money or talent? What motivates you to give these gifts? How do these gifts make you feel about God? Why?

How does God use these gifts to aid you in your spiritual pilgrimage? **2.** How could "competitive" giving misdirect the reason for giving gifts to God? What can you and your group do to avoid this problem among yourselves?

thirty shekels,[a] and one silver sprinkling bowl weighing seventy shekels,[b] both according to the sanctuary shekel, each filled with fine flour mixed with oil as a grain offering; [14]one gold dish weighing ten shekels,[c] filled with incense; [15]one young bull, one ram and one male lamb a year old, for a burnt offering; [16]one male goat for a sin offering; [17]and two oxen, five rams, five male goats and five male lambs a year old, to be sacrificed as a fellowship offering.[d] This was the offering of Nahshon son of Amminadab.

[18]On the second day Nethanel son of Zuar, the leader of Issachar, brought his offering.

[19]The offering he brought was one silver plate weighing a hundred and thirty shekels, and one silver sprinkling bowl weighing seventy shekels, both according to the sanctuary shekel, each filled with fine flour mixed with oil as a grain offering; [20]one gold dish weighing ten shekels, filled with incense; [21]one young bull, one ram and one male lamb a year old, for a burnt offering; [22]one male goat for a sin offering; [23]and two oxen, five rams, five male goats and five male lambs a year old, to be sacrificed as a fellowship offering. This was the offering of Nethanel son of Zuar.

[24]On the third day, Eliab son of Helon, the leader of the people of Zebulun, brought his offering.

[25]His offering was one silver plate weighing a hundred and thirty shekels, and one silver sprinkling bowl weighing seventy shekels, both according to the sanctuary shekel, each filled with fine flour mixed with oil as a grain offering; [26]one gold dish weighing ten shekels, filled with incense; [27]one young bull, one ram and one male lamb a year old, for a burnt offering; [28]one male goat for a sin offering; [29]and two oxen, five rams, five male goats and five male lambs a year old, to be sacrificed as a fellowship offering. This was the offering of Eliab son of Helon.

[30]On the fourth day Elizur son of Shedeur, the leader of the people of Reuben, brought his offering.

[31]His offering was one silver plate weighing a hundred and thirty shekels, and one silver sprinkling bowl weighing seventy shekels, both according to the sanctuary shekel, each filled with fine flour mixed with oil as a grain offering; [32]one gold dish weighing ten shekels, filled with incense; [33]one young bull, one ram and one male lamb a year old, for a burnt offering; [34]one male goat for a sin offering; [35]and two oxen, five rams, five male goats and five male lambs a year old, to be sacrificed as a fellowship offering. This was the offering of Elizur son of Shedeur.

[36]On the fifth day Shelumiel son of Zurishaddai, the leader of the people of Simeon, brought his offering.

[37]His offering was one silver plate weighing a hundred and thirty shekels, and one silver sprinkling bowl weighing seventy shekels, both according to the sanctuary shekel, each filled with fine flour mixed with oil as a grain offering; [38]one gold dish weighing ten shekels, filled with incense; [39]one young bull, one ram and one male lamb a year old, for a burnt

a13 That is, about 3 1/4 pounds (about 1.5 kilograms); also elsewhere in this chapter
b13 That is, about 1 3/4 pounds (about 0.8 kilogram); also elsewhere in this chapter
c14 That is, about 4 ounces (about 110 grams); also elsewhere in this chapter
d17 Traditionally *peace offering*; also elsewhere in this chapter

offering; ⁴⁰one male goat for a sin offering; ⁴¹and two oxen, five rams, five male goats and five male lambs a year old, to be sacrificed as a fellowship offering. This was the offering of Shelumiel son of Zurishaddai.

⁴²On the sixth day Eliasaph son of Deuel, the leader of the people of Gad, brought his offering.
⁴³His offering was one silver plate weighing a hundred and thirty shekels, and one silver sprinkling bowl weighing seventy shekels, both according to the sanctuary shekel, each filled with fine flour mixed with oil as a grain offering; ⁴⁴one gold dish weighing ten shekels, filled with incense; ⁴⁵one young bull, one ram and one male lamb a year old, for a burnt offering; ⁴⁶one male goat for a sin offering; ⁴⁷and two oxen, five rams, five male goats and five male lambs a year old, to be sacrificed as a fellowship offering. This was the offering of Eliasaph son of Deuel.

⁴⁸On the seventh day Elishama son of Ammihud, the leader of the people of Ephraim, brought his offering.
⁴⁹His offering was one silver plate weighing a hundred and thirty shekels, and one silver sprinkling bowl weighing seventy shekels, both according to the sanctuary shekel, each filled with fine flour mixed with oil as a grain offering; ⁵⁰one gold dish weighing ten shekels, filled with incense; ⁵¹one young bull, one ram and one male lamb a year old, for a burnt offering; ⁵²one male goat for a sin offering; ⁵³and two oxen, five rams, five male goats and five male lambs a year old, to be sacrificed as a fellowship offering. This was the offering of Elishama son of Ammihud.

⁵⁴On the eighth day Gamaliel son of Pedahzur, the leader of the people of Manasseh, brought his offering.
⁵⁵His offering was one silver plate weighing a hundred and thirty shekels, and one silver sprinkling bowl weighing seventy shekels, both according to the sanctuary shekel, each filled with fine flour mixed with oil as a grain offering; ⁵⁶one gold dish weighing ten shekels, filled with incense; ⁵⁷one young bull, one ram and one male lamb a year old, for a burnt offering; ⁵⁸one male goat for a sin offering; ⁵⁹and two oxen, five rams, five male goats and five male lambs a year old, to be sacrificed as a fellowship offering. This was the offering of Gamaliel son of Pedahzur.

⁶⁰On the ninth day Abidan son of Gideoni, the leader of the people of Benjamin, brought his offering.
⁶¹His offering was one silver plate weighing a hundred and thirty shekels, and one silver sprinkling bowl weighing seventy shekels, both according to the sanctuary shekel, each filled with fine flour mixed with oil as a grain offering; ⁶²one gold dish weighing ten shekels, filled with incense; ⁶³one young bull, one ram and one male lamb a year old, for a burnt offering; ⁶⁴one male goat for a sin offering; ⁶⁵and two oxen, five rams, five male goats and five male lambs a year old, to be sacrificed as a fellowship offering. This was the offering of Abidan son of Gideoni.

⁶⁶On the tenth day Ahiezer son of Ammishaddai, the leader of the people of Dan, brought his offering.
⁶⁷His offering was one silver plate weighing a hundred and thirty shekels, and one silver sprinkling bowl weighing seven-

ty shekels, both according to the sanctuary shekel, each filled with fine flour mixed with oil as a grain offering; [68]one gold dish weighing ten shekels, filled with incense; [69]one young bull, one ram and one male lamb a year old, for a burnt offering; [70]one male goat for a sin offering; [71]and two oxen, five rams, five male goats and five male lambs a year old, to be sacrificed as a fellowship offering. This was the offering of Ahiezer son of Ammishaddai.

[72]On the eleventh day Pagiel son of Ocran, the leader of the people of Asher, brought his offering.

[73]His offering was one silver plate weighing a hundred and thirty shekels, and one silver sprinkling bowl weighing seventy shekels, both according to the sanctuary shekel, each filled with fine flour mixed with oil as a grain offering; [74]one gold dish weighing ten shekels, filled with incense; [75]one young bull, one ram and one male lamb a year old, for a burnt offering; [76]one male goat for a sin offering; [77]and two oxen, five rams, five male goats and five male lambs a year old, to be sacrificed as a fellowship offering. This was the offering of Pagiel son of Ocran.

[78]On the twelfth day Ahira son of Enan, the leader of the people of Naphtali, brought his offering.

[79]His offering was one silver plate weighing a hundred and thirty shekels, and one silver sprinkling bowl weighing seventy shekels, both according to the sanctuary shekel, each filled with fine flour mixed with oil as a grain offering; [80]one gold dish weighing ten shekels, filled with incense; [81]one young bull, one ram and one male lamb a year old, for a burnt offering; [82]one male goat for a sin offering; [83]and two oxen, five rams, five male goats and five male lambs a year old, to be sacrificed as a fellowship offering. This was the offering of Ahira son of Enan.

[84]These were the offerings of the Israelite leaders for the dedication of the altar when it was anointed: twelve silver plates, twelve silver sprinkling bowls and twelve gold dishes. [85]Each silver plate weighed a hundred and thirty shekels, and each sprinkling bowl seventy shekels. Altogether, the silver dishes weighed two thousand four hundred shekels,[a] according to the sanctuary shekel. [86]The twelve gold dishes filled with incense weighed ten shekels each, according to the sanctuary shekel. Altogether, the gold dishes weighed a hundred and twenty shekels.[b] [87]The total number of animals for the burnt offering came to twelve young bulls, twelve rams and twelve male lambs a year old, together with their grain offering. Twelve male goats were used for the sin offering. [88]The total number of animals for the sacrifice of the fellowship offering came to twenty-four oxen, sixty rams, sixty male goats and sixty male lambs a year old. These were the offerings for the dedication of the altar after it was anointed.

[89]When Moses entered the Tent of Meeting to speak with the LORD, he heard the voice speaking to him from between the two cherubim above the atonement cover on the ark of the Testimony. And he spoke with him.

---

a85 That is, about 60 pounds (about 28 kilograms)   b86 That is, about 3 pounds (about 1.4 kilograms)

Setting Up the Lamps

8 The LORD said to Moses, 2"Speak to Aaron and say to him, 'When you set up the seven lamps, they are to light the area in front of the lampstand.'"

3Aaron did so; he set up the lamps so that they faced forward on the lampstand, just as the LORD commanded Moses. 4This is how the lampstand was made: It was made of hammered gold—from its base to its blossoms. The lampstand was made exactly like the pattern the LORD had shown Moses.

The Setting Apart of the Levites

5The LORD said to Moses: 6"Take the Levites from among the other Israelites and make them ceremonially clean. 7To purify them, do this: Sprinkle the water of cleansing on them; then have them shave their whole bodies and wash their clothes, and so purify themselves. 8Have them take a young bull with its grain offering of fine flour mixed with oil; then you are to take a second young bull for a sin offering. 9Bring the Levites to the front of the Tent of Meeting and assemble the whole Israelite community. 10You are to bring the Levites before the LORD, and the Israelites are to lay their hands on them. 11Aaron is to present the Levites before the LORD as a wave offering from the Israelites, so that they may be ready to do the work of the LORD.

12"After the Levites lay their hands on the heads of the bulls, use the one for a sin offering to the LORD and the other for a burnt offering, to make atonement for the Levites. 13Have the Levites stand in front of Aaron and his sons and then present them as a wave offering to the LORD. 14In this way you are to set the Levites apart from the other Israelites, and the Levites will be mine.

15"After you have purified the Levites and presented them as a wave offering, they are to come to do their work at the Tent of Meeting. 16They are the Israelites who are to be given wholly to me. I have taken them as my own in place of the firstborn, the first male offspring from every Israelite woman. 17Every firstborn male in Israel, whether man or animal, is mine. When I struck down all the firstborn in Egypt, I set them apart for myself. 18And I have taken the Levites in place of all the firstborn sons in Israel. 19Of all the Israelites, I have given the Levites as gifts to Aaron and his sons to do the work at the Tent of Meeting on behalf of the Israelites and to make atonement for them so that no plague will strike the Israelites when they go near the sanctuary."

20Moses, Aaron and the whole Israelite community did with the Levites just as the LORD commanded Moses. 21The Levites purified themselves and washed their clothes. Then Aaron presented them as a wave offering before the LORD and made atonement for them to purify them. 22After that, the Levites came to do their work at the Tent of Meeting under the supervision of Aaron and his sons. They did with the Levites just as the LORD commanded Moses.

23The LORD said to Moses, 24"This applies to the Levites: Men twenty-five years old or more shall come to take part in the work at the Tent of Meeting, 25but at the age of fifty, they must retire from their regular service and work no longer. 26They may assist their brothers in performing their duties at the Tent of Meeting, but they themselves must not do the work. This, then, is how you are to assign the responsibilities of the Levites."

1. What purpose do the seven lamps serve? What is noteworthy about where they were placed? And how they were made? 2. How are you like a lamp for the Lord?

1. In how many ways are you dependent upon representatives serving in your stead: At church? In government? At parent-teacher councils? Other committees? 2. What representative roles do you have?

1. What does it mean to be "set apart"? How would the ritual in verses 5–14 illustrate this concept? What does this teach you about God's desires for his own? 2. How does this setting apart of the Levites compare with how the Nazirites (ch. 6) were set apart? 3. In comparison to the cleansing of the Levites for ministry, how were Aaron's sons set apart for the priesthood (see Lev 8)? What do you make of the difference in: (a) "Make holy" vs. "cleanse"? (b) "Anointed" vs. "sprinkled"? (c) "New" garments vs. "washed" ones? (d) Blood "applied to" vs. blood "waved over" the principles? 4. How would these distinctions affect how the people perceived Levites different than priests? Would the people more likely see Levites as "one of them" (vv. 10–11,16–19)? Why? 5. How is the Levites' ordination a picture of how Israel is to relate with other nations? How might this help prepare Israel for entering the land of Canaan? 6. What does the age of service (25 years) and age of semi-retirement (50 years) say about the nature of the Levites' duties?

1. What are the dangers of becoming isolated from the real world in which we live? 2. How can we keep the balance between separation and involvement in the world?

How often does your church traditionally serve communion? How often would you like to partake?

1. Who feels excluded from this celebration (vv. 6,14)? Why exclude someone contaminated by a dead body (see Nu 19:11–22)? What must an alien do to participate (see Ex 12:48)? 2. Why would this first celebration of Passover since Egypt (see Ex 12) be so important to the Israelites? What does it say about God that he allows unclean Israelites to celebrate this feast late, after they are ceremonially clean? 3. Why do you think verse 13 is included in this passage? What's wrong with neglecting Passover?

1. When are you and your church likely to be too *firm* about matters of faith and worship? For example, how "open" is your communion service? How might this hinder a real relationship with God? 2. When are you and your church likely to be too *flexible* about such matters? How might that hinder a real relationship with God?

Describe an experience when "your head was in the clouds."

1. How many times and ways does this passage refer to the cloud? 2. What do you think God meant by choosing a cloud? How would this help Moses lead the people? Why were the people so obedient now (in contrast to ch. 11)?

1. How does God guide spiritual leaders today? How does this compare to his guidance here? 2. When God wants you to do something, how does he let you know? How are you sure it is God's guidance? In what ways is this similar to his guidance of the Israelites here?

The Passover

9 The LORD spoke to Moses in the Desert of Sinai in the first month of the second year after they came out of Egypt. He said, 2"Have the Israelites celebrate the Passover at the appointed time. 3Celebrate it at the appointed time, at twilight on the fourteenth day of this month, in accordance with all its rules and regulations."

4So Moses told the Israelites to celebrate the Passover, 5and they did so in the Desert of Sinai at twilight on the fourteenth day of the first month. The Israelites did everything just as the LORD commanded Moses.

6But some of them could not celebrate the Passover on that day because they were ceremonially unclean on account of a dead body. So they came to Moses and Aaron that same day 7and said to Moses, "We have become unclean because of a dead body, but why should we be kept from presenting the LORD's offering with the other Israelites at the appointed time?"

8Moses answered them, "Wait until I find out what the LORD commands concerning you."

9Then the LORD said to Moses, 10"Tell the Israelites: 'When any of you or your descendants are unclean because of a dead body or are away on a journey, they may still celebrate the LORD's Passover. 11They are to celebrate it on the fourteenth day of the second month at twilight. They are to eat the lamb, together with unleavened bread and bitter herbs. 12They must not leave any of it till morning or break any of its bones. When they celebrate the Passover, they must follow all the regulations. 13But if a man who is ceremonially clean and not on a journey fails to celebrate the Passover, that person must be cut off from his people because he did not present the LORD's offering at the appointed time. That man will bear the consequences of his sin.

14" 'An alien living among you who wants to celebrate the LORD's Passover must do so in accordance with its rules and regulations. You must have the same regulations for the alien and the native-born.' "

The Cloud Above the Tabernacle

15On the day the tabernacle, the Tent of the Testimony, was set up, the cloud covered it. From evening till morning the cloud above the tabernacle looked like fire. 16That is how it continued to be; the cloud covered it, and at night it looked like fire. 17Whenever the cloud lifted from above the Tent, the Israelites set out; wherever the cloud settled, the Israelites encamped. 18At the LORD's command the Israelites set out, and at his command they encamped. As long as the cloud stayed over the tabernacle, they remained in camp. 19When the cloud remained over the tabernacle a long time, the Israelites obeyed the LORD's order and did not set out. 20Sometimes the cloud was over the tabernacle only a few days; at the LORD's command they would encamp, and then at his command they would set out. 21Sometimes the cloud stayed only from evening till morning, and when it lifted in the morning, they set out. Whether by day or by night, whenever the cloud lifted, they set out. 22Whether the cloud stayed over the tabernacle for two days or a month or a year, the Israelites would remain in camp and not set out; but when it lifted, they would set out. 23At the LORD's command they encamped, and at the LORD's command they set out. They obeyed the LORD's order, in accordance with his command through Moses.

The Silver Trumpets

10 The LORD said to Moses: [2]"Make two trumpets of hammered silver, and use them for calling the community together and for having the camps set out. [3]When both are sounded, the whole community is to assemble before you at the entrance to the Tent of Meeting. [4]If only one is sounded, the leaders—the heads of the clans of Israel—are to assemble before you. [5]When a trumpet blast is sounded, the tribes camping on the east are to set out. [6]At the sounding of a second blast, the camps on the south are to set out. The blast will be the signal for setting out. [7]To gather the assembly, blow the trumpets, but not with the same signal.

[8]"The sons of Aaron, the priests, are to blow the trumpets. This is to be a lasting ordinance for you and the generations to come. [9]When you go into battle in your own land against an enemy who is oppressing you, sound a blast on the trumpets. Then you will be remembered by the LORD your God and rescued from your enemies. [10]Also at your times of rejoicing—your appointed feasts and New Moon festivals—you are to sound the trumpets over your burnt offerings and fellowship offerings,[a] and they will be a memorial for you before your God. I am the LORD your God."

The Israelites Leave Sinai

[11]On the twentieth day of the second month of the second year, the cloud lifted from above the tabernacle of the Testimony. [12]Then the Israelites set out from the Desert of Sinai and traveled

a 10 Traditionally peace offerings

What does the sound of trumpets make you feel like doing?

1. What are the various functions of the trumpets here? How will this help the Israelites journey through the wilderness? **2.** What does it say about God that he is concerned with such details?

1. What aspects of your own life has God shown special concern over the last 12 months? How does he show his concerns? What does this teach you about him? About you? **2.** When God wants to get your attention and give you marching orders, what "trumpet blast" does he use?

---

1. When was the last time you took a "family holiday"? What was the best part of that experience? The worst? **2.** How well organized are your vacations?

Numbers 9:15–23; 10:11–13, 29–36   THE CLOUD OF GUIDANCE

From the time the Israelites fled Egypt and entered the wilderness, God accompanied them periodically by means of a special cloud. One year later, Israel set up the tabernacle—which housed the ark of the covenant and where the Lord met with the people.

1. Why do you think God used a cloud in his relationship with Israel?
   a. to demonstrate his glory to them
   b. to remind them of his presence
   c. to make sure they didn't make a wrong turn
   d. to teach them to respect their place of worship
   e. to accommodate their desire for a visible representation of God

2. In contrast to other times, why were the people so obedient now?
   a. Following a cloud was easy.
   b. It was fun to follow the cloud.
   c. They were taking a break from being disobedient.
   d. The cloud didn't go anywhere the people didn't want to go.
   e. They were probably still complaining about *something* as they went.

3. Since the cloud was leading Israel, why did Moses plead with his brother-in-law Hobab to be their "eyes"?
   a. The cloud hadn't traveled through the wilderness like Hobab had.
   b. Moses didn't really trust the cloud.
   c. It's always good to get a second opinion.
   d. God also uses people to guide us.
   e. Moses wanted Hobab to share in the blessings of the promised land.

4. Moses' attitude whenever the ark of the covenant set out (10:35) was:
   a. Go get 'em, God!
   b. Wherever you lead us, we will go.
   c. We're number 1!
   d. We can't make it without you.

5. How does this passage compare with how God guides people today?
   a. Following God is an adventure.
   b. God still wants to be in control.
   c. It's clear what God wants us to do.
   d. It's not nearly so clear what God wants us to do.
   e. We have means of guidance they didn't have—the Scriptures and the Holy Spirit within us.

f. God expects us to rely on the common sense he gave us.
g. God is much more interested in our hearts than our daily routine.

6. When God wants you to do something, how does he let you know? How are you sure it is his guidance?

7. What adventure has God called you, your small group, or your church to? Who is the "Hobab" you hope to persuade to join the adventure?

8. How do you respond to this passage?
   a. I wish God would send a cloud to guide me.
   b. Even though I can't physically see it, I know God is leading me.
   c. I need a Hobab to help me find God's direction.
   d. I need a Hobab who has been this way before.

9. What major questions about your future (where to live, for example) are you asking? How can this group help you pray and discern God's guidance?

What does such organization do to
your trip?

1. As the Israelites begin
their journey from Sinai to the
"Promised Land," what impressions
do you get about the journey from
this passage? Who's in charge?
How well do they mobilize the people for this trip? 2. Despite such
preparations, what problems are
they likely to encounter in the wilderness? How would including Hobab on their journey (vv. 29–32)
help solve some of these problems? 3. What image comes to
mind as you hear verses 35–36
(also Ps 68:1) ring out? 4. What do
you see as the chances for the
Lord's army successfully journeying through the wilderness, as that
story unfolds over the next 12
chapters?

1. What adventure has God
prepared and mobilized you
(your small group or church) to do?
How have you prepared? What
problems do you anticipate? 2.
Who is the "Hobab" you hope to
persuade to join you in this adventure of faith? How else has God
helped to fill out your team for this
adventure? 3. What does this
chapter teach you about God?
About his desire for your success?

1. Why do you think God
sends this fire? What does
this teach you about human nature? God? And intercessory
prayer? 2. How have your own acts
or attitudes been affected by a
"Taberah"?

from place to place until the cloud came to rest in the Desert of
Paran. [13]They set out, this first time, at the LORD's command
through Moses.

[14]The divisions of the camp of Judah went first, under their
standard. Nahshon son of Amminadab was in command. [15]Nethan-
el son of Zuar was over the division of the tribe of Issachar, [16]and
Eliab son of Helon was over the division of the tribe of Zebulun.
[17]Then the tabernacle was taken down, and the Gershonites and
Merarites, who carried it, set out.

[18]The divisions of the camp of Reuben went next, under their
standard. Elizur son of Shedeur was in command. [19]Shelumiel son
of Zurishaddai was over the division of the tribe of Simeon, [20]and
Eliasaph son of Deuel was over the division of the tribe of Gad.
[21]Then the Kohathites set out, carrying the holy things. The tabernacle was to be set up before they arrived.

[22]The divisions of the camp of Ephraim went next, under their
standard. Elishama son of Ammihud was in command. [23]Gamaliel
son of Pedahzur was over the division of the tribe of Manasseh,
[24]and Abidan son of Gideoni was over the division of the tribe of
Benjamin.

[25]Finally, as the rear guard for all the units, the divisions of the
camp of Dan set out, under their standard. Ahiezer son of Ammishaddai was in command. [26]Pagiel son of Ocran was over the
division of the tribe of Asher, [27]and Ahira son of Enan was over the
division of the tribe of Naphtali. [28]This was the order of march for
the Israelite divisions as they set out.

[29]Now Moses said to Hobab son of Reuel the Midianite, Moses'
father-in-law, "We are setting out for the place about which the
LORD said, 'I will give it to you.' Come with us and we will treat you
well, for the LORD has promised good things to Israel."

[30]He answered, "No, I will not go; I am going back to my own
land and my own people."

[31]But Moses said, "Please do not leave us. You know where we
should camp in the desert, and you can be our eyes. [32]If you come
with us, we will share with you whatever good things the LORD
gives us."

[33]So they set out from the mountain of the LORD and traveled for
three days. The ark of the covenant of the LORD went before them
during those three days to find them a place to rest. [34]The cloud of
the LORD was over them by day when they set out from the camp.
[35]Whenever the ark set out, Moses said,

> "Rise up, O LORD!
>   May your enemies be scattered;
>   may your foes flee before you."

[36]Whenever it came to rest, he said,

> "Return, O LORD,
>   to the countless thousands of Israel."

Fire From the LORD

11 Now the people complained about their hardships in the
hearing of the LORD, and when he heard them his anger was
aroused. Then fire from the LORD burned among them and consumed some of the outskirts of the camp. [2]When the people cried
out to Moses, he prayed to the LORD and the fire died down. [3]So
that place was called Taberah,[a] because fire from the LORD had
burned among them.

a3 Taberah means burning.

Quail From the LORD

⁴The rabble with them began to crave other food, and again the Israelites started wailing and said, "If only we had meat to eat! ⁵We remember the fish we ate in Egypt at no cost—also the cucumbers, melons, leeks, onions and garlic. ⁶But now we have lost our appetite; we never see anything but this manna!"

⁷The manna was like coriander seed and looked like resin. ⁸The people went around gathering it, and then ground it in a handmill or crushed it in a mortar. They cooked it in a pot or made it into cakes. And it tasted like something made with olive oil. ⁹When the dew settled on the camp at night, the manna also came down.

¹⁰Moses heard the people of every family wailing, each at the entrance to his tent. The LORD became exceedingly angry, and Moses was troubled. ¹¹He asked the LORD, "Why have you brought this trouble on your servant? What have I done to displease you that you put the burden of all these people on me? ¹²Did I conceive all these people? Did I give them birth? Why do you tell me to carry them in my arms, as a nurse carries an infant, to the land you promised on oath to their forefathers? ¹³Where can I get meat for all these people? They keep wailing to me, 'Give us meat to eat!' ¹⁴I cannot carry all these people by myself; the burden is too heavy for me. ¹⁵If this is how you are going to treat me, put me to death right now—if I have found favor in your eyes—and do not let me face my own ruin."

¹⁶The LORD said to Moses: "Bring me seventy of Israel's elders who are known to you as leaders and officials among the people. Have them come to the Tent of Meeting, that they may stand there

1. What is your favorite food? To what lengths will you go to get this food? 2. What food did mother serve "because it was good for you," but you simply refused to eat? 3. What kind of eater are you now: Like a bird (too little)? Like a dog (too eager)? Like a cat (too finicky)?

1. What is the attitude of the Israelites in this chapter (compare Ex 16)? How has their attitude changed since 9:15–23 and 10:11–36? 2. Why do you think their attitude has deteriorated so rapidly? (Do you suppose their food allotment in Egypt was much meatier? More varied?) Does Moses consider their complaints valid? Would you? Why or why not? 3. From this chapter and Exodus 16, how do you account for the presence of this "manna"? Do you think it was a natural food or something unique and supernatural? 4. What has been the net effect on Moses of all the complaints from the rabble-rousers? Why does Moses want to quit (vv. 10–15)? Why does he doubt the Lord's promise of regrettable abundance (vv.

   Numbers 11:4–34   **QUAIL FROM THE LORD**

For over a year God had been caring for the Israelites in the wilderness, including the provision of manna—"bread from heaven" which appeared along with the dew every morning.

1. What was the biggest reason the Israelites were complaining?
   a. They were fed up with manna.
   b. The rabble stirred them up.
   c. Complaining had become a way of life for them.
   d. They missed their favorite foods.
   e. Their past life (as slaves) came to be viewed as the good old days.

2. Why did the Lord get angry?
   a. Meat was too expensive.
   b. He insisted that they would be vegetarians.
   c. The people were ungrateful.
   d. God was freeing them and they wanted to return to slavery.
   e. Spurning his gifts meant spurning their relationship with God.

3. How was Moses affected by the people's complaints?
   a. He got angry with the people.
   b. He got angry with God.

c. He felt sorry for himself.
d. He got depressed.
e. He was near burnout.
f. He desperately wanted to quit.
g. He lost sight of God's power.

4. How did God deal with Moses' complaints? How did God deal with the people's complaints? Why were his responses so different?

5. What happened when the 70 elders met with God at the Tent of Meeting?
   a. They became prophets.
   b. They were empowered by God to become *spiritual* leaders.
   c. Moses got the help he needed.
   d. They got a preview of the outpouring God had planned for future times.

6. What does it say about Moses that he desires God's Spirit on all the people? What do you think God would like the Spirit to do in your life: For your sake? For others' sake?

7. What kinds of complaints or cravings do you have? How do you think God feels about those complaints or

cravings? How do they affect your relationship with the Lord?

8. How do you react when, like Moses, others put lots of demands on you? Which answers in question 3 are typical of you? How would you like to change?

9. What do you identify with most in this story (and what can you do about it)?
   a. craving food I know I shouldn't eat, like:_____
   b. complaining about tasteless food or unpleasant exercise
   c. eating so much that I loathe what I'm eating
   d. feeling God's anger because of my unhealthy habits
   e. being drawn back to the slavery of compulsive habits
   f. feeling depressed and alone

10. Regarding your strong-willed child's worst behavior: What effect does it have on you? How do you deal with your anger? How do you deal with your child's anger?

18–22)? Why does he wish that all God's people could prophesy, as did the 70 elders (vv. 25–29)? **5.** How does God appear to you (unfair, justified, merciful, angry) here: In verse 10? In verses 16–17? In verses 18–20? In verse 23? In verse 33? Why? **6.** How would God's varied response to Israel, and Israel's memorial death camp (v. 34), help them succeed in their journey through the wilderness?

1. When are you, like Israel and Moses, most likely to become discouraged with your allotment or position in life? When discouraged, do you listen more to people's complaints, to God's provision, or to inner doubts? **2.** What kind of complaints or cravings damage your fellowship with God? Your self-confidence? **3.** How do you think God feels when we complain about our lives or crave things he has not provided for us? How does he communicate his will to you in this regard? In what ways is that similar to the events in this chapter: What have you coveted, which in turn God gave you so much of, that you became sick of it? **4.** How is the story of Jesus feeding the multitudes with loaves and fish like and unlike this story of God providing manna and quail? **5.** What does God's handling of this situation teach you about dealing with a demanding child? **6.** How can God's "manna" and "quail," in this story and in your life, help you build a correct relationship with God?

1. Growing up, who did you want to be like? Did this person inspire you or make you feel jealous? **2.** Who in your family is the "speaker of the house"? Who is the best listener?

1. How would you describe Aaron and Miriam in this story (vv. 1–2)? How does this com-

with you. 17I will come down and speak with you there, and I will take of the Spirit that is on you and put the Spirit on them. They will help you carry the burden of the people so that you will not have to carry it alone.

18"Tell the people: 'Consecrate yourselves in preparation for tomorrow, when you will eat meat. The LORD heard you when you wailed, "If only we had meat to eat! We were better off in Egypt!" Now the LORD will give you meat, and you will eat it. 19You will not eat it for just one day, or two days, or five, ten or twenty days, 20but for a whole month—until it comes out of your nostrils and you loathe it—because you have rejected the LORD, who is among you, and have wailed before him, saying, "Why did we ever leave Egypt?" '"

21But Moses said, "Here I am among six hundred thousand men on foot, and you say, 'I will give them meat to eat for a whole month!' 22Would they have enough if flocks and herds were slaughtered for them? Would they have enough if all the fish in the sea were caught for them?"

23The LORD answered Moses, "Is the LORD's arm too short? You will now see whether or not what I say will come true for you."

24So Moses went out and told the people what the LORD had said. He brought together seventy of their elders and had them stand around the Tent. 25Then the LORD came down in the cloud and spoke with him, and he took of the Spirit that was on him and put the Spirit on the seventy elders. When the Spirit rested on them, they prophesied, but they did not do so again.[a]

26However, two men, whose names were Eldad and Medad, had remained in the camp. They were listed among the elders, but did not go out to the Tent. Yet the Spirit also rested on them, and they prophesied in the camp. 27A young man ran and told Moses, "Eldad and Medad are prophesying in the camp."

28Joshua son of Nun, who had been Moses' aide since youth, spoke up and said, "Moses, my lord, stop them!"

29But Moses replied, "Are you jealous for my sake? I wish that all the LORD's people were prophets and that the LORD would put his Spirit on them!" 30Then Moses and the elders of Israel returned to the camp.

31Now a wind went out from the LORD and drove quail in from the sea. It brought them[b] down all around the camp to about three feet[c] above the ground, as far as a day's walk in any direction. 32All that day and night and all the next day the people went out and gathered quail. No one gathered less than ten homers.[d] Then they spread them out all around the camp. 33But while the meat was still between their teeth and before it could be consumed, the anger of the LORD burned against the people, and he struck them with a severe plague. 34Therefore the place was named Kibroth Hattaavah,[e] because there they buried the people who had craved other food.

35From Kibroth Hattaavah the people traveled to Hazeroth and stayed there.

Miriam and Aaron Oppose Moses

12 Miriam and Aaron began to talk against Moses because of his Cushite wife, for he had married a Cushite. 2"Has the LORD spoken only through Moses?" they asked. "Hasn't he also spoken through us?" And the LORD heard this.

---

a25 Or prophesied and continued to do so　　*b31 Or They flew*　　*c31 Hebrew two cubits (about 1 meter)*　　*d32 That is, probably about 60 bushels (about 2.2 kiloliters)*　　*e34 Kibroth Hattaavah means graves of craving.*

3(Now Moses was a very humble man, more humble than anyone else on the face of the earth.)

4At once the LORD said to Moses, Aaron and Miriam, "Come out to the Tent of Meeting, all three of you." So the three of them came out. 5Then the LORD came down in a pillar of cloud; he stood at the entrance to the Tent and summoned Aaron and Miriam. When both of them stepped forward, 6he said, "Listen to my words:

> "When a prophet of the LORD is among you,
>   I reveal myself to him in visions,
>   I speak to him in dreams.
> 7But this is not true of my servant Moses;
>   he is faithful in all my house.
> 8With him I speak face to face,
>   clearly and not in riddles;
>   he sees the form of the LORD.
> Why then were you not afraid
>   to speak against my servant Moses?"

9The anger of the LORD burned against them, and he left them. 10When the cloud lifted from above the Tent, there stood Miriam—leprous,a like snow. Aaron turned toward her and saw that she had leprosy; 11and he said to Moses, "Please, my lord, do not hold against us the sin we have so foolishly committed. 12Do not let

a 10 The Hebrew word was used for various diseases affecting the skin—not necessarily leprosy.

pare with the picture of Moses in verse 3? 2. What is the most awesome part of this story for its principles? And for you? 3. How does the picture of Moses given in verses 6–8 relate to that in verse 3? What distinguishes Moses from all other prophets? 4. Why do you think God prefers Moses and punishes Miriam? What does this say about the kind of person God wants to lead his people? 5. What does it say about Moses that he enjoys this kind of fellowship with God and yet remains humble? 6. What does Aaron's repentance and Moses' plea teach about how God wants us to approach him?

♡ 1. To whom in your circle of friends might verse 3 aptly fit? How does that person exemplify humility? 2. Relative to Moses and the prophets, how does God "speak" with you? How does that help you to be a person God can use? 3. In what ways are you like Miriam and Aaron? What does this do to your relationship with God? With others?

✠ **Numbers 12:1–16**   MIRIAM AND AARON OPPOSE MOSES

This story begins with Moses' brother and sister talking against him for marrying a "Cushite." Whether this refers to his wife of many years or to a recent marriage, she was not an ethnic Jew.

1. What was the problem with Miriam and Aaron and Moses' wife?
   a. They didn't like their sister-in-law.
   b. They felt she was an unbeliever.
   c. They were prejudiced.
   d. It was just a smoke screen for their jealousy of Moses.

2. What must have been the most painful thing about this for Moses?
   a. being attacked by family
   b. being attacked publicly
   c. having his character maligned
   d. continually having "enemies" arise from within his own camp

3. God's response:
   a. was swift and stern.
   b. fit the offense.
   c. could have been more severe.
   d. doesn't really seem fair.
   e. was harder on Miriam because she was the instigator.

4. Do you think Aaron's repentance was sincere? Was he more concerned about his sister or about what might happen to himself?

5. What motivates you to repent?
   a. guilt
   b. God's love
   c. fear of God
   d. fear of consequences
   e. fear of getting caught
   f. fear of the sin becoming addictive
   g. the pain of fellowship with God having been broken

6. What has happened in your life to enable you to identify with the breakdown of relationships in this story? What resolution has taken place? How has your faith in God made a difference?

7. What was the greatest way Moses demonstrated his humility?
   a. He didn't defend himself.
   b. He didn't strike back.
   c. He cried out to God for his sister's healing after how she treated him.
   d. He spoke to God "face to face" and remained humble.

   e. He was the head of a nation without it "going to his head."

8. ✠ What's the most needed lesson and challenge of this story for your relational life?
   a. not to be jealous of others
   b. not to be critical of others
   c. if I have a problem with someone to go to them instead of to others
   d. to accept criticism without being defensive
   e. not to strike back when unjustly accused
   f. to forgive and pray for those who hurt me
   g. to deepen my relationship with God, letting him "talk" to me and defend me

9. ✠ How do the various aspects of life connect in this story—for example, the effect of Miriam and Aaron's relational behavior on their physical and spiritual life; and the consequences of Moses' vocational life for his emotional life? What does this say to you about focusing on all areas of life?

her be like a stillborn infant coming from its mother's womb with its flesh half eaten away."

[13] So Moses cried out to the LORD, "O God, please heal her!"

[14] The LORD replied to Moses, "If her father had spit in her face, would she not have been in disgrace for seven days? Confine her outside the camp for seven days; after that she can be brought back." [15] So Miriam was confined outside the camp for seven days, and the people did not move on till she was brought back.

[16] After that, the people left Hazeroth and encamped in the Desert of Paran.

Exploring Canaan

13 The LORD said to Moses, [2] "Send some men to explore the land of Canaan, which I am giving to the Israelites. From each ancestral tribe send one of its leaders."

[3] So at the LORD's command Moses sent them out from the Desert of Paran. All of them were leaders of the Israelites. [4] These are their names:

from the tribe of Reuben, Shammua son of Zaccur;
[5] from the tribe of Simeon, Shaphat son of Hori;
[6] from the tribe of Judah, Caleb son of Jephunneh;
[7] from the tribe of Issachar, Igal son of Joseph;
[8] from the tribe of Ephraim, Hoshea son of Nun;
[9] from the tribe of Benjamin, Palti son of Raphu;
[10] from the tribe of Zebulun, Gaddiel son of Sodi;
[11] from the tribe of Manasseh (a tribe of Joseph), Gaddi son of Susi;
[12] from the tribe of Dan, Ammiel son of Gemalli;
[13] from the tribe of Asher, Sethur son of Michael;
[14] from the tribe of Naphtali, Nahbi son of Vophsi;
[15] from the tribe of Gad, Geuel son of Maki.

[16] These are the names of the men Moses sent to explore the land. (Moses gave Hoshea son of Nun the name Joshua.)

[17] When Moses sent them to explore Canaan, he said, "Go up through the Negev and on into the hill country. [18] See what the land is like and whether the people who live there are strong or weak, few or many. [19] What kind of land do they live in? Is it good or bad? What kind of towns do they live in? Are they unwalled or fortified? [20] How is the soil? Is it fertile or poor? Are there trees on it or not? Do your best to bring back some of the fruit of the land." (It was the season for the first ripe grapes.)

[21] So they went up and explored the land from the Desert of Zin as far as Rehob, toward Lebo[a] Hamath. [22] They went up through the Negev and came to Hebron, where Ahiman, Sheshai and Talmai, the descendants of Anak, lived. (Hebron had been built seven years before Zoan in Egypt.) [23] When they reached the Valley of Eshcol,[b] they cut off a branch bearing a single cluster of grapes. Two of them carried it on a pole between them, along with some pomegranates and figs. [24] That place was called the Valley of Eshcol because of the cluster of grapes the Israelites cut off there. [25] At the end of forty days they returned from exploring the land.

Report on the Exploration

[26] They came back to Moses and Aaron and the whole Israelite community at Kadesh in the Desert of Paran. There they reported to them and to the whole assembly and showed them the fruit of

---

1. If you could explore, at ground level, the highways and byways of any country, which country would you choose? 2. What kind of artifacts or souvenirs do you pick up from road trips that serve as "show-and-tell" items?

1. Israel is on the brink of realizing their dream of the promised land. How do you think they feel? 2. Why send out spies to explore this land (v. 2; see Dt 1:20–23)? Who stands out among the list? 3. What were the spies looking for (vv. 17–20)? What did they find (vv. 23–25)? After being gone 40 days, what should be the people's reaction to all this? 4. With their extensive preparation and organization (chs. 1–10), effective leadership (ch. 12) and a history of defeating strong opposition (see Ex 14–15), what odds would you give the Israelite army for a successful entry into the land of Canaan?

1. Where are you in your exploration of the abundant life in Christ? Are the "grapes" still as big as ever, even bigger, or going sour? 2. What has God done, recently, to keep you on the growing edge of the Christian adventure? Any command to obey, or promise to claim, from the adventure of the Israelites here? 3. What is the goal of your small group? What "40-day" spying mission might help you realize that?

1. What kind of report do you think the people were expecting? How does that compare to the news they got? 2. With their history of victories (see Ex 7–15), why and

---

[a] 21 Or *toward the entrance to*   [b] 23 *Eshcol* means *cluster*; also in verse 24.

the land. ²⁷They gave Moses this account: "We went into the land to which you sent us, and it does flow with milk and honey! Here is its fruit. ²⁸But the people who live there are powerful, and the cities are fortified and very large. We even saw descendants of Anak there. ²⁹The Amalekites live in the Negev; the Hittites, Jebusites and Amorites live in the hill country; and the Canaanites live near the sea and along the Jordan."

³⁰Then Caleb silenced the people before Moses and said, "We should go up and take possession of the land, for we can certainly do it."

³¹But the men who had gone up with him said, "We can't attack those people; they are stronger than we are." ³²And they spread among the Israelites a bad report about the land they had explored. They said, "The land we explored devours those living in it. All the people we saw there are of great size. ³³We saw the Nephilim there (the descendants of Anak come from the Nephilim). We seemed like grasshoppers in our own eyes, and we looked the same to them."

The People Rebel

14 That night all the people of the community raised their voices and wept aloud. ²All the Israelites grumbled against Moses and Aaron, and the whole assembly said to them, "If only we had died in Egypt! Or in this desert! ³Why is the LORD bringing us to this land only to let us fall by the sword? Our wives and children will be taken as plunder. Wouldn't it be better for us to go

how do you think Israel should be able to overcome the giants?

♡ 1. What "handicap" or difficulties has God helped you to overcome? 2. In doing God's work, do you feel like a "grasshopper"? How so? How will your memory of God's past help affect the way you face this present difficulty?

☕ 1. When you hear the word "rebel," what is your first thought? Your second thought? 2. Were you ever a "rebel"? Against who or what were you rebelling?

 Numbers 13:26–14:10, 26–45   **SPYING ON THE PROMISED LAND**

At the people's bidding, the Lord had Moses send a representative from the 12 tribes of Israel to spy out Canaan. After exploring the length of the land, the spies brought back a mixed report.

1. What didn't the spies agree on?
a. "The land is good."
b. "The people are powerful."
c. "We're stronger than they are."
d. "The cities are well-fortified."
e. "Let's go for it."

2. What made the majority report a "bad report"?
a. It was grossly exaggerated.
b. It came from fear rather than faith.
c. It discouraged the people.
d. Speaking negatively of the land was speaking negatively of God.

3. How did Caleb and Joshua feel?
a. indifferent
b. angry at the other spies
c. grieved by the people's response
d. "holier than thou"
e. blindly optimistic
f. full of faith

4. Why did the Israelites pull back from their goal of reaching Canaan?

a. They were chicken.
b. The devil made them do it.
c. The 10 spies scared them off.
d. They looked at circumstances and forgot about God's past miracles.
e. They had never owned it as a goal.

5. In the end the Israelites:
a. ate their words the next 40 years.
b. repented.
c. were filled with regret but not repentance.
d. changed their minds too late.
e. by heading for Canaan found out two wrongs don't make a right.

6. When I realize I've blown it, I:
a. feel terrible.
b. try to cover things up.
c. try to patch things up.
d. ask for forgiveness.
e. accept the consequences.
f. look for someone to blame.
g. act like nothing happened.

7. What "giants" are you facing? How can your memory of God's help in the past keep you from feeling like a "grasshopper in your own eyes"?

8. Where would you place yourself in this story?
a. heading for the promised land
b. exploring the promised land
c. turning away from the promised land
d. enjoying the promised land
e. trying to believe there is a promised land

9. Rate each statement on a scale from 1 to 10:
a. I feel like a "giant" when I look in the mirror.
b. I feel like a "grasshopper" when I think about my ability to get in shape.
c. I have bitter regrets when I blow it.
d. I am negatively influenced by my environment—other people, social pressures, media messages, etc.
e. I am tempted to give up reaching the physically fit promised land.

10. What is your long-term goal for your physical condition? What's the next step you need to take to get there? How can this group help you not to turn back from pursuing your goal?

1. Within reach of the promised land, the Israelites now pull back from their goal. Why do you think they do this? What are the specific complaints made by the Israelites here? 2. Based on the spies' report (Nu 13:26–33), do you consider their fears valid? Based on the events of Exodus 7–15, are their fears valid? 3. What is significant about God's display of his "glory" (vv. 10–12)? What would that look like? Sound like? Do you think God's anger with the Israelites is justified? Why would he want to start over again with Moses? 4. What do you see as the genius of the minority report submitted by Caleb and Joshua (vv. 6–9)? Likewise, of Moses' argument against God destroying the rebel Israelites (vv. 13–19)? 5. What about God's character is reflected in the oft-quoted verse 18? Note that this verse is based on the Ten Commandments (see Ex 20:5–6; 34:6–7).

1. What "giants" are you afraid of in your school or career path? How can these fears harm your attempts to achieve your goals? 2. What spiritual goals has God given to you? How might your fears keep you from reaching these?

What consequences for "rebel behavior" did you suffer as a teenager? Did it feel like you suffered more, or less, than your siblings or peers? Did you ever get off scot-free? For what?

1. Are you surprised that God relents? Was Moses able to change God's mind, or was "Plan B" what God had in mind all along, if only Moses would pray for it? 2. In what different ways does God punish the people (vv. 20–35)? 3. God promises that Israel will eat its very words (v. 28). How does God's discipline (vv. 29–35) relate to their complaints (14:1–14)? 4. The Lord is said to have been "tested ten times" (v. 22). How many testings can you recall from your reading of Exodus and Numbers? 5. Do you think wrath, or mercy, better fits the spies' crime? What would later become of Caleb (v. 24;

back to Egypt?" 4And they said to each other, "We should choose a leader and go back to Egypt."

5Then Moses and Aaron fell facedown in front of the whole Israelite assembly gathered there. 6Joshua son of Nun and Caleb son of Jephunneh, who were among those who had explored the land, tore their clothes 7and said to the entire Israelite assembly, "The land we passed through and explored is exceedingly good. 8If the LORD is pleased with us, he will lead us into that land, a land flowing with milk and honey, and will give it to us. 9Only do not rebel against the LORD. And do not be afraid of the people of the land, because we will swallow them up. Their protection is gone, but the LORD is with us. Do not be afraid of them."

10But the whole assembly talked about stoning them. Then the glory of the LORD appeared at the Tent of Meeting to all the Israelites. 11The LORD said to Moses, "How long will these people treat me with contempt? How long will they refuse to believe in me, in spite of all the miraculous signs I have performed among them? 12I will strike them down with a plague and destroy them, but I will make you into a nation greater and stronger than they."

13Moses said to the LORD, "Then the Egyptians will hear about it! By your power you brought these people up from among them. 14And they will tell the inhabitants of this land about it. They have already heard that you, O LORD, are with these people and that you, O LORD, have been seen face to face, that your cloud stays over them, and that you go before them in a pillar of cloud by day and a pillar of fire by night. 15If you put these people to death all at one time, the nations who have heard this report about you will say, 16'The LORD was not able to bring these people into the land he promised them on oath; so he slaughtered them in the desert.'

17"Now may the Lord's strength be displayed, just as you have declared: 18'The LORD is slow to anger, abounding in love and forgiving sin and rebellion. Yet he does not leave the guilty unpunished; he punishes the children for the sin of the fathers to the third and fourth generation.' 19In accordance with your great love, forgive the sin of these people, just as you have pardoned them from the time they left Egypt until now."

20The LORD replied, "I have forgiven them, as you asked. 21Nevertheless, as surely as I live and as surely as the glory of the LORD fills the whole earth, 22not one of the men who saw my glory and the miraculous signs I performed in Egypt and in the desert but who disobeyed me and tested me ten times— 23not one of them will ever see the land I promised on oath to their forefathers. No one who has treated me with contempt will ever see it. 24But because my servant Caleb has a different spirit and follows me wholeheartedly, I will bring him into the land he went to, and his descendants will inherit it. 25Since the Amalekites and Canaanites are living in the valleys, turn back tomorrow and set out toward the desert along the route to the Red Sea.a"

26The LORD said to Moses and Aaron: 27"How long will this wicked community grumble against me? I have heard the complaints of these grumbling Israelites. 28So tell them, 'As surely as I live, declares the LORD, I will do to you the very things I heard you say: 29In this desert your bodies will fall—every one of you twenty years old or more who was counted in the census and who has grumbled against me. 30Not one of you will enter the land I swore with uplifted hand to make your home, except Caleb son of Jephunneh and Joshua son of Nun. 31As for your children that you

a25 Hebrew Yam Suph; that is, Sea of Reeds

said would be taken as plunder, I will bring them in to enjoy the land you have rejected. ³²But you—your bodies will fall in this desert. ³³Your children will be shepherds here for forty years, suffering for your unfaithfulness, until the last of your bodies lies in the desert. ³⁴For forty years—one year for each of the forty days you explored the land—you will suffer for your sins and know what it is like to have me against you.' ³⁵I, the LORD, have spoken, and I will surely do these things to this whole wicked community, which has banded together against me. They will meet their end in this desert; here they will die."

³⁶So the men Moses had sent to explore the land, who returned and made the whole community grumble against him by spreading a bad report about it— ³⁷these men responsible for spreading the bad report about the land were struck down and died of a plague before the LORD. ³⁸Of the men who went to explore the land, only Joshua son of Nun and Caleb son of Jephunneh survived.

³⁹When Moses reported this to all the Israelites, they mourned bitterly. ⁴⁰Early the next morning they went up toward the high hill country. "We have sinned," they said. "We will go up to the place the LORD promised."

⁴¹But Moses said, "Why are you disobeying the LORD's command? This will not succeed! ⁴²Do not go up, because the LORD is not with you. You will be defeated by your enemies, ⁴³for the Amalekites and Canaanites will face you there. Because you have turned away from the LORD, he will not be with you and you will fall by the sword."

⁴⁴Nevertheless, in their presumption they went up toward the high hill country, though neither Moses nor the ark of the LORD's covenant moved from the camp. ⁴⁵Then the Amalekites and Canaanites who lived in that hill country came down and attacked them and beat them down all the way to Hormah.

Supplementary Offerings

15 The LORD said to Moses, ²"Speak to the Israelites and say to them: 'After you enter the land I am giving you as a home ³and you present to the LORD offerings made by fire, from the herd or the flock, as an aroma pleasing to the LORD—whether burnt offerings or sacrifices, for special vows or freewill offerings or festival offerings— ⁴then the one who brings his offering shall present to the LORD a grain offering of a tenth of an ephah[a] of fine flour mixed with a quarter of a hin[b] of oil. ⁵With each lamb for the burnt offering or the sacrifice, prepare a quarter of a hin of wine as a drink offering.

⁶"'With a ram prepare a grain offering of two-tenths of an ephah[c] of fine flour mixed with a third of a hin[d] of oil, ⁷and a third of a hin of wine as a drink offering. Offer it as an aroma pleasing to the LORD.

⁸"'When you prepare a young bull as a burnt offering or sacrifice, for a special vow or a fellowship offering[e] to the LORD, ⁹bring with the bull a grain offering of three-tenths of an ephah[f] of fine flour mixed with half a hin[g] of oil. ¹⁰Also bring half a hin of wine as a drink offering. It will be an offering made by fire, an aroma pleasing to the LORD. ¹¹Each bull or ram, each lamb or young goat,

see Jos 14:10–14)? Why do you think God strikes dead the 10 spies, but not the people who listened to them (vv. 36–38)? **6.** What is your impression of the people's actions in verses 39–45: (a) "Better late then never"? (b) "Better dead than red"? (c) "Better quit while you're ahead"? (d) Other? Why do you think God allows Israel to be defeated?

1. Rebel Israel would eat its words for 40 years (vv. 28–35). When have you suffered any such "time out period"? For what offense? How did you cope? How did you change as a result? **2.** How does the composite picture of God in this story compare to your own experience of him? Where would you place yourself in this story? **3.** How has God helped you to reach "insurmountable" goals or helped you overcome "giants" in your path? How can you use such past triumphs to overcome your present fears?

1. What kind of meals do you prepare for yourself: Gourmet? TV dinners only? Finger food? Casseroles from scratch? **2.** What would your "perfect meal" consist of?

1. What amazing juxtaposition do you see between chapters 14 and 15? What does this tell you about the covenant-keeping nature of God? **2.** The requirements for offerings listed in verses 3–12 sound much like a meal recipe. What is noteworthy about the size and need for the grain offerings? **3.** What does it mean that the alien and the native-born are the same before God (vv. 14–16)? Why do you think God affirms their essential equality in this context? **4.** Why do you think God makes these requirements even though he does not need to eat? How might these requirements be influenced by culture?

1. What do these requirements of Israel reveal about the nature of God and what he expects of the Church? **2.** What

a4 That is, probably about 2 quarts (about 2 liters)   b4 That is, probably about 1 quart (about 1 liter); also in verse 5   c6 That is, probably about 4 quarts (about 4.5 liters)   d6 That is, probably about 1 1/4 quarts (about 1.2 liters); also in verse 7   e8 Traditionally *peace offering*   f9 That is, probably about 6 quarts (about 6.5 liters)   g9 That is, probably about 2 quarts (about 2 liters); also in verse 10

things do Christians today offer to God? In what ways are these similar to the offerings of food in this passage? **3.** What do such offerings teach you about God? About what he wants from us?

What difference did it make in how you were punished as a child if you said, "It was an accident," or "I didn't mean to"?

1. What differentiation is made here between intentional (vv. 30–31) and unintentional sin (vv. 22–29)? Why is there little mercy for the "defiant" sinner? What distinctions are made between the communal sin and the individual sin? What does this say about God's view of sin? **2.** Why do you think sacrifice is required for unintentional sin? What does this say about God's nature? Human nature? What does this teach about reconciliation?

Although sacrifice is not required of Christians, how do you deal with each kind of sin? How does this help to mend your relationship with God?

1. How serious is God about his people keeping the Sabbath holy (see Ex 31:12–17)? **2.** How did Jesus get in trouble with this law (see Mk 2:23–28)? **3.** What comes first for you: Personal needs or Sabbath principle? How will you model Jesus' priorities?

is to be prepared in this manner. ¹²Do this for each one, for as many as you prepare.

¹³" 'Everyone who is native-born must do these things in this way when he brings an offering made by fire as an aroma pleasing to the LORD. ¹⁴For the generations to come, whenever an alien or anyone else living among you presents an offering made by fire as an aroma pleasing to the LORD, he must do exactly as you do. ¹⁵The community is to have the same rules for you and for the alien living among you; this is a lasting ordinance for the generations to come. You and the alien shall be the same before the LORD: ¹⁶The same laws and regulations will apply both to you and to the alien living among you.' "

¹⁷The LORD said to Moses, ¹⁸"Speak to the Israelites and say to them: 'When you enter the land to which I am taking you ¹⁹and you eat the food of the land, present a portion as an offering to the LORD. ²⁰Present a cake from the first of your ground meal and present it as an offering from the threshing floor. ²¹Throughout the generations to come you are to give this offering to the LORD from the first of your ground meal.

Offerings for Unintentional Sins

²²" 'Now if you unintentionally fail to keep any of these commands the LORD gave Moses— ²³any of the LORD's commands to you through him, from the day the LORD gave them and continuing through the generations to come— ²⁴and if this is done unintentionally without the community being aware of it, then the whole community is to offer a young bull for a burnt offering as an aroma pleasing to the LORD, along with its prescribed grain offering and drink offering, and a male goat for a sin offering. ²⁵The priest is to make atonement for the whole Israelite community, and they will be forgiven, for it was not intentional and they have brought to the LORD for their wrong an offering made by fire and a sin offering. ²⁶The whole Israelite community and the aliens living among them will be forgiven, because all the people were involved in the unintentional wrong.

²⁷" 'But if just one person sins unintentionally, he must bring a year-old female goat for a sin offering. ²⁸The priest is to make atonement before the LORD for the one who erred by sinning unintentionally, and when atonement has been made for him, he will be forgiven. ²⁹One and the same law applies to everyone who sins unintentionally, whether he is a native-born Israelite or an alien.

³⁰" 'But anyone who sins defiantly, whether native-born or alien, blasphemes the LORD, and that person must be cut off from his people. ³¹Because he has despised the LORD's word and broken his commands, that person must surely be cut off; his guilt remains on him.' "

The Sabbath-Breaker Put to Death

³²While the Israelites were in the desert, a man was found gathering wood on the Sabbath day. ³³Those who found him gathering wood brought him to Moses and Aaron and the whole assembly, ³⁴and they kept him in custody, because it was not clear what should be done to him. ³⁵Then the LORD said to Moses, "The man must die. The whole assembly must stone him outside the camp." ³⁶So the assembly took him outside the camp and stoned him to death, as the LORD commanded Moses.

Tassels on Garments

[37]The LORD said to Moses, [38]"Speak to the Israelites and say to them: 'Throughout the generations to come you are to make tassels on the corners of your garments, with a blue cord on each tassel. [39]You will have these tassels to look at and so you will remember all the commands of the LORD, that you may obey them and not prostitute yourselves by going after the lusts of your own hearts and eyes. [40]Then you will remember to obey all my commands and will be consecrated to your God. [41]I am the LORD your God, who brought you out of Egypt to be your God. I am the LORD your God.'"

Korah, Dathan and Abiram

16 Korah son of Izhar, the son of Kohath, the son of Levi, and certain Reubenites—Dathan and Abiram, sons of Eliab, and On son of Peleth—became insolent[a] [2]and rose up against Moses. With them were 250 Israelite men, well-known community leaders who had been appointed members of the council. [3]They came as a group to oppose Moses and Aaron and said to them, "You have gone too far! The whole community is holy, every one of them, and the LORD is with them. Why then do you set yourselves above the LORD's assembly?"

[4]When Moses heard this, he fell facedown. [5]Then he said to Korah and all his followers: "In the morning the LORD will show who belongs to him and who is holy, and he will have that person come near him. The man he chooses he will cause to come near him. [6]You, Korah, and all your followers are to do this: Take censers [7]and tomorrow put fire and incense in them before the LORD. The man the LORD chooses will be the one who is holy. You Levites have gone too far!"

[8]Moses also said to Korah, "Now listen, you Levites! [9]Isn't it enough for you that the God of Israel has separated you from the rest of the Israelite community and brought you near himself to do the work at the LORD's tabernacle and to stand before the community and minister to them? [10]He has brought you and all your fellow Levites near himself, but now you are trying to get the priesthood too. [11]It is against the LORD that you and all your followers have banded together. Who is Aaron that you should grumble against him?"

[12]Then Moses summoned Dathan and Abiram, the sons of Eliab. But they said, "We will not come! [13]Isn't it enough that you have brought us up out of a land flowing with milk and honey to kill us in the desert? And now you also want to lord it over us? [14]Moreover, you haven't brought us into a land flowing with milk and honey or given us an inheritance of fields and vineyards. Will you gouge out the eyes of[b] these men? No, we will not come!"

[15]Then Moses became very angry and said to the LORD, "Do not accept their offering. I have not taken so much as a donkey from them, nor have I wronged any of them."

[16]Moses said to Korah, "You and all your followers are to appear before the LORD tomorrow—you and they and Aaron. [17]Each man is to take his censer and put incense in it—250 censers in all—and present it before the LORD. You and Aaron are to present your censers also." [18]So each man took his censer, put fire and incense in it, and stood with Moses and Aaron at the entrance to the Tent of Meeting. [19]When Korah had gathered all his followers in opposition to them at the entrance to the Tent of Meeting, the glory of the LORD appeared to the entire assembly. [20]The LORD said to Moses

---

1. How would such tassels fulfill their stated purpose (see Dt 6:4–9)? 2. What "tassels" do you put before you to remember what God wants in your fellowship with him? Which ones work best?

1. How good are you at starting fires: (a) One match does the trick every time? (b) Lighter fluid is a must? (c) Spontaneous combustion follows me wherever I go? 2. What fatal natural disaster have you witnessed? How did that experience change you? 3. What art objects, if any, have you made out of scrap or sheet metal? What did you do with them?

1. What are the specific complaints these people make against Moses and Aaron (vv. 3,13–14)? How do they make their power play sound "spiritual"? Why do you think these complaints are directed only at Moses and Aaron? Who are they ultimately directed at (v. 11)? 2. How does Moses respond to this revolt by Korah and his followers (vv. 5–11,16–17)? How does he plead his case and their case before the Lord (vv. 4, 15, 22)? 3. How were Moses and the rebels thinking the trial by fire would vindicate them (vv. 18–21)? Ironically, what trial by fire does the Lord have in mind (v. 35)? What else does Moses say, and the Lord do, that leaves no room for doubt as to the possible meaning of the divine judgment to come (vv. 28–30)? 4. What further charges are brought against Moses and Aaron (v. 41)? Why hasn't the priests' object lesson from the day before made any difference in the common people? 5. What would have happened if Aaron and Moses had not interceded with God? What happened anyway?

1. How might such revolts against their leaders undermine the Israelites' ability to survive the wilderness wanderings? How does this help to explain the severity of God's punishment? 2. What does this teach you about God's concern for his people's survival? About God's faithfulness concerning those he has chosen as leaders? 3. What struggles for power go on in your church at the local

---

[a]1 Or *Peleth—took men*   [b]14 Or *you make slaves of*; or *you deceive*

level? State or synod level? National and international level? Pick one to talk about in light of this chapter and the next two sets of questions. Do so without gossiping or naming names, but with a genuine concern for God's beloved people. **4.** When are you likely to become dissatisfied with your spiritual leaders? When are you likely to vie for sharing power with them? How does this affect your own relationship with God? **5.** What can you do to react more positively to your leaders, even though you may be unhappy with them? What example does Aaron and Eleazar set for you in this regard? What prayers can your group offer right now for your respective pastors? Out of what "ashes of conflict" might God want you to make something new? **6.** Who in your small group has *never* complained about the conditions of their life? When we complain about these things, what does this say about our level of trust in God? How does this damage fellowship with him? **7.** With what area of your life is *your* trust in God wavering? How might this lack of trust undermine your ability to succeed in this area? What will you do this week to begin trusting God alone? (You might have to resist those who presume to speak for God.)

and Aaron, [21]"Separate yourselves from this assembly so I can put an end to them at once."

[22]But Moses and Aaron fell facedown and cried out, "O God, God of the spirits of all mankind, will you be angry with the entire assembly when only one man sins?"

[23]Then the LORD said to Moses, [24]"Say to the assembly, 'Move away from the tents of Korah, Dathan and Abiram.'"

[25]Moses got up and went to Dathan and Abiram, and the elders of Israel followed him. [26]He warned the assembly, "Move back from the tents of these wicked men! Do not touch anything belonging to them, or you will be swept away because of all their sins." [27]So they moved away from the tents of Korah, Dathan and Abiram. Dathan and Abiram had come out and were standing with their wives, children and little ones at the entrances to their tents.

[28]Then Moses said, "This is how you will know that the LORD has sent me to do all these things and that it was not my idea: [29]If these men die a natural death and experience only what usually happens to men, then the LORD has not sent me. [30]But if the LORD brings about something totally new, and the earth opens its mouth and swallows them, with everything that belongs to them, and they go down alive into the grave,[a] then you will know that these men have treated the LORD with contempt."

[31]As soon as he finished saying all this, the ground under them split apart [32]and the earth opened its mouth and swallowed them, with their households and all Korah's men and all their possessions. [33]They went down alive into the grave, with everything they owned; the earth closed over them, and they perished and were gone from the community. [34]At their cries, all the Israelites around them fled, shouting, "The earth is going to swallow us too!"

[35]And fire came out from the LORD and consumed the 250 men who were offering the incense.

[36]The LORD said to Moses, [37]"Tell Eleazar son of Aaron, the priest, to take the censers out of the smoldering remains and scatter the coals some distance away, for the censers are holy— [38]the censers of the men who sinned at the cost of their lives. Hammer the censers into sheets to overlay the altar, for they were presented before the LORD and have become holy. Let them be a sign to the Israelites."

[39]So Eleazar the priest collected the bronze censers brought by those who had been burned up, and he had them hammered out to overlay the altar, [40]as the LORD directed him through Moses. This was to remind the Israelites that no one except a descendant of Aaron should come to burn incense before the LORD, or he would become like Korah and his followers.

[41]The next day the whole Israelite community grumbled against Moses and Aaron. "You have killed the LORD's people," they said.

[42]But when the assembly gathered in opposition to Moses and Aaron and turned toward the Tent of Meeting, suddenly the cloud covered it and the glory of the LORD appeared. [43]Then Moses and Aaron went to the front of the Tent of Meeting, [44]and the LORD said to Moses, [45]"Get away from this assembly so I can put an end to them at once." And they fell facedown.

[46]Then Moses said to Aaron, "Take your censer and put incense in it, along with fire from the altar, and hurry to the assembly to make atonement for them. Wrath has come out from the LORD; the plague has started." [47]So Aaron did as Moses said, and ran into the midst of the assembly. The plague had already started among

[a]30 Hebrew *Sheol*; also in verse 33

the people, but Aaron offered the incense and made atonement for them. [48]He stood between the living and the dead, and the plague stopped. [49]But 14,700 people died from the plague, in addition to those who had died because of Korah. [50]Then Aaron returned to Moses at the entrance to the Tent of Meeting, for the plague had stopped.

The Budding of Aaron's Staff

17 The LORD said to Moses, [2]"Speak to the Israelites and get twelve staffs from them, one from the leader of each of their ancestral tribes. Write the name of each man on his staff. [3]On the staff of Levi write Aaron's name, for there must be one staff for the head of each ancestral tribe. [4]Place them in the Tent of Meeting in front of the Testimony, where I meet with you. [5]The staff belonging to the man I choose will sprout, and I will rid myself of this constant grumbling against you by the Israelites."

[6]So Moses spoke to the Israelites, and their leaders gave him twelve staffs, one for the leader of each of their ancestral tribes, and Aaron's staff was among them. [7]Moses placed the staffs before the LORD in the Tent of the Testimony.

[8]The next day Moses entered the Tent of the Testimony and saw that Aaron's staff, which represented the house of Levi, had not only sprouted but had budded, blossomed and produced almonds. [9]Then Moses brought out all the staffs from the LORD's presence to all the Israelites. They looked at them, and each man took his own staff.

[10]The LORD said to Moses, "Put back Aaron's staff in front of the Testimony, to be kept as a sign to the rebellious. This will put an end to their grumbling against me, so that they will not die." [11]Moses did just as the LORD commanded him.

[12]The Israelites said to Moses, "We will die! We are lost, we are all lost! [13]Anyone who even comes near the tabernacle of the LORD will die. Are we all going to die?"

Duties of Priests and Levites

18 The LORD said to Aaron, "You, your sons and your father's family are to bear the responsibility for offenses against the sanctuary, and you and your sons alone are to bear the responsibility for offenses against the priesthood. [2]Bring your fellow Levites from your ancestral tribe to join you and assist you when you and your sons minister before the Tent of the Testimony. [3]They are to be responsible to you and are to perform all the duties of the Tent, but they must not go near the furnishings of the sanctuary or the altar, or both they and you will die. [4]They are to join you and be responsible for the care of the Tent of Meeting—all the work at the Tent—and no one else may come near where you are.

[5]"You are to be responsible for the care of the sanctuary and the altar, so that wrath will not fall on the Israelites again. [6]I myself have selected your fellow Levites from among the Israelites as a gift to you, dedicated to the LORD to do the work at the Tent of Meeting. [7]But only you and your sons may serve as priests in connection with everything at the altar and inside the curtain. I am giving you the service of the priesthood as a gift. Anyone else who comes near the sanctuary must be put to death."

Offerings for Priests and Levites

[8]Then the LORD said to Aaron, "I myself have put you in charge of the offerings presented to me; all the holy offerings the Israelites give me I give to you and your sons as your portion and regular

1. Does anything in your life "sprout, bud, blossom and produce fruit"—all on schedule? What would be your reaction if something did? 2. When have you come out on the "short end of the stick" in some dispute?

1. How is this chapter related to the previous one? Why might questions about Aaron's leadership persist? How does God address such concerns this time? 2. Why do you think God asked for 12 staffs, rather than just Aaron's? How would this symbolic act help mitigate danger for Israel? What new fears arise?

1. Why is it that some people seem to be dogged by persistent critics? Is this happening to anyone you know at work, school or church (no names)? 2. How can you be more sensitive and supportive to them?

1. In light of the problems highlighted in Numbers 16–17, why do you think God has "gifted" priestly duties solely to Aaron's clan? How would such consolidation help mediate these problems? 2. What might Aaron be thinking as such weighty spiritual matters are again placed in the hands of his family and tribe?

1. What kind of person would sacrifice personal well-being for the national interest? 2. Do you think God is still concerned with the spiritual well-being of his followers? How does he help you to maintain your spiritual wellness? How is this similar to measures taken here?

1. What were your first acts of economic independence from your parents? When did you start buying those things that they

used to pay for? **2.** When did you first assume economic responsibility for someone else: (a) As a parent with kids? (b) As a child of an aging parent? (c) As a donor to church or other faith mission?

1. In what sense do the duties of the priests and Levites (18:1–7) provide for the spiritual health of the Israelites? How would they fare without such leaders? **2.** How might material concerns damage the ability of the priests and Levites to adequately complete their job? Would the laws set forth in this passage remove these difficulties, or create new ones? Why do you think so? **3.** Why do you think God allows priests and Levites to eat the sacrifices made to him, even the "first" and "finest" of them (vv. 12–13)? What does this teach about the meaning of temple workers in God's eyes? **4.** In turn, what are the Levites to give back to the Lord and why (vv. 26–32)? **5.** To what might the everlasting "covenant of salt" refer (v. 19; see 2Ch 13:5; Lev 2:13)? How might salty offerings and salty meals serve to remind one of God's permanent covenant? **6.** How is the priests inheritance different than the others (v. 20,24)?

1. Your pastor works, like salty priests and Levites, to preserve the spiritual health of your church. How might material concerns prevent him or her from doing an adequate job? How does (or could) such money matters hinder any of us? **2.** What does your church do to avoid this problem: Free manse? Food baskets? Expense allowance? Enough salary and pension to avoid working an extra job? **3.** Israel's ministers received the "first" or "finest" from their people, and the early Church believed in "equal pay for equal work" of the minister (see 1Co 9:3–10). What is the salary scale like for your pastors: (a) Tops? (b) Better than most? (c) Better than average? (d) On a par with everyone else? (e) Below par? Why is that? **4.** How has your pastor helped you with a specific spiritual problem? What is something tangible you could do this week to show your gratitude?

share. ⁹You are to have the part of the most holy offerings that is kept from the fire. From all the gifts they bring me as most holy offerings, whether grain or sin or guilt offerings, that part belongs to you and your sons. ¹⁰Eat it as something most holy; every male shall eat it. You must regard it as holy.

¹¹"This also is yours: whatever is set aside from the gifts of all the wave offerings of the Israelites. I give this to you and your sons and daughters as your regular share. Everyone in your household who is ceremonially clean may eat it.

¹²"I give you all the finest olive oil and all the finest new wine and grain they give the Lord as the firstfruits of their harvest. ¹³All the land's firstfruits that they bring to the Lord will be yours. Everyone in your household who is ceremonially clean may eat it.

¹⁴"Everything in Israel that is devoted[a] to the Lord is yours. ¹⁵The first offspring of every womb, both man and animal, that is offered to the Lord is yours. But you must redeem every firstborn son and every firstborn male of unclean animals. ¹⁶When they are a month old, you must redeem them at the redemption price set at five shekels[b] of silver, according to the sanctuary shekel, which weighs twenty gerahs.

¹⁷"But you must not redeem the firstborn of an ox, a sheep or a goat; they are holy. Sprinkle their blood on the altar and burn their fat as an offering made by fire, an aroma pleasing to the Lord. ¹⁸Their meat is to be yours, just as the breast of the wave offering and the right thigh are yours. ¹⁹Whatever is set aside from the holy offerings the Israelites present to the Lord I give to you and your sons and daughters as your regular share. It is an everlasting covenant of salt before the Lord for both you and your offspring."

²⁰The Lord said to Aaron, "You will have no inheritance in their land, nor will you have any share among them; I am your share and your inheritance among the Israelites.

²¹"I give to the Levites all the tithes in Israel as their inheritance in return for the work they do while serving at the Tent of Meeting. ²²From now on the Israelites must not go near the Tent of Meeting, or they will bear the consequences of their sin and will die. ²³It is the Levites who are to do the work at the Tent of Meeting and bear the responsibility for offenses against it. This is a lasting ordinance for the generations to come. They will receive no inheritance among the Israelites. ²⁴Instead, I give to the Levites as their inheritance the tithes that the Israelites present as an offering to the Lord. That is why I said concerning them: 'They will have no inheritance among the Israelites.'"

²⁵The Lord said to Moses, ²⁶"Speak to the Levites and say to them: 'When you receive from the Israelites the tithe I give you as your inheritance, you must present a tenth of that tithe as the Lord's offering. ²⁷Your offering will be reckoned to you as grain from the threshing floor or juice from the winepress. ²⁸In this way you also will present an offering to the Lord from all the tithes you receive from the Israelites. From these tithes you must give the Lord's portion to Aaron the priest. ²⁹You must present as the Lord's portion the best and holiest part of everything given to you.'

³⁰"Say to the Levites: 'When you present the best part, it will be reckoned to you as the product of the threshing floor or the winepress. ³¹You and your households may eat the rest of it anywhere, for it is your wages for your work at the Tent of Meeting. ³²By presenting the best part of it you will not be guilty in this matter;

---

a14 The Hebrew term refers to the irrevocable giving over of things or persons to the Lord.   b16 That is, about 2 ounces (about 55 grams)

then you will not defile the holy offerings of the Israelites, and you will not die.' "

The Water of Cleansing

19 The LORD said to Moses and Aaron: ²"This is a requirement of the law that the LORD has commanded: Tell the Israelites to bring you a red heifer without defect or blemish and that has never been under a yoke. ³Give it to Eleazar the priest; it is to be taken outside the camp and slaughtered in his presence. ⁴Then Eleazar the priest is to take some of its blood on his finger and sprinkle it seven times toward the front of the Tent of Meeting. ⁵While he watches, the heifer is to be burned—its hide, flesh, blood and offal. ⁶The priest is to take some cedar wood, hyssop and scarlet wool and throw them onto the burning heifer. ⁷After that, the priest must wash his clothes and bathe himself with water. He may then come into the camp, but he will be ceremonially unclean till evening. ⁸The man who burns it must also wash his clothes and bathe with water, and he too will be unclean till evening.

⁹"A man who is clean shall gather up the ashes of the heifer and put them in a ceremonially clean place outside the camp. They shall be kept by the Israelite community for use in the water of cleansing; it is for purification from sin. ¹⁰The man who gathers up the ashes of the heifer must also wash his clothes, and he too will be unclean till evening. This will be a lasting ordinance both for the Israelites and for the aliens living among them.

¹¹"Whoever touches the dead body of anyone will be unclean for seven days. ¹²He must purify himself with the water on the third day and on the seventh day; then he will be clean. But if he does not purify himself on the third and seventh days, he will not be clean. ¹³Whoever touches the dead body of anyone and fails to purify himself defiles the LORD's tabernacle. That person must be cut off from Israel. Because the water of cleansing has not been sprinkled on him, he is unclean; his uncleanness remains on him.

¹⁴"This is the law that applies when a person dies in a tent: Anyone who enters the tent and anyone who is in it will be unclean for seven days, ¹⁵and every open container without a lid fastened on it will be unclean.

¹⁶"Anyone out in the open who touches someone who has been killed with a sword or someone who has died a natural death, or anyone who touches a human bone or a grave, will be unclean for seven days.

¹⁷"For the unclean person, put some ashes from the burned purification offering into a jar and pour fresh water over them. ¹⁸Then a man who is ceremonially clean is to take some hyssop, dip it in the water and sprinkle the tent and all the furnishings and the people who were there. He must also sprinkle anyone who has touched a human bone or a grave or someone who has been killed or someone who has died a natural death. ¹⁹The man who is clean is to sprinkle the unclean person on the third and seventh days, and on the seventh day he is to purify him. The person being cleansed must wash his clothes and bathe with water, and that evening he will be clean. ²⁰But if a person who is unclean does not purify himself, he must be cut off from the community, because he has defiled the sanctuary of the LORD. The water of cleansing has not been sprinkled on him, and he is unclean. ²¹This is a lasting ordinance for them.

"The man who sprinkles the water of cleansing must also wash his clothes, and anyone who touches the water of cleansing will be unclean till evening. ²²Anything that an unclean person touches

---

1. How did you react to the first death among your significant friends or family? What did you learn about yourself from that? 2. What experience have you had with putting a favorite pet "to sleep" and burying it?

1. Given the open living conditions of life in the desert, why would special regulations to limit contact with dead bodies be necessary for ancient Israel? 2. Without professionals to take care of the dead, how likely is it that an Israelite will eventually come into contact with an "unclean" corpse? How would such regulations likely make the Israelites feel about coming into contact, or even proximity, with dead bodies? (How would you feel?) 3. Of these cleansing regulations, which ones appear to be for hygienic reasons? Which are largely social or ceremonial? Which seem to offer spiritual value? 4. How do these values help to explain the variety of cleansing regulations outlined here? 5. The regulation involving the "red heifer" is unprecedented in the Old Testament (contrast Lev 1:3–9, for the usual pattern of burnt offerings). What makes this animal killing unique (vv. 2–10)?

1. Is it possible to live in today's world and never come into contact with sin? How do you feel when you are confronted with sin? What sorts of things do you do to avoid being "contaminated" by the "uncleanness" around you? 2. When you sin, how do you feel about yourself? About your damaged relationship with God? What do you do to restore this relationship? How is that similar to the "water of cleansing" in this chapter? 3. How does the cleansing power of Christ's blood relate to the point of this chapter (see Heb 9:13–14)?

When you're in a difficult situation that feels like a repeat, only different, what do you do?

1. Read Exodus 17:1–7, which recounts a nearly identical scene 40 years earlier. Compare what God told Moses to do then with what he tells him to do here. How do the two outcomes compare? **2.** How do you explain Moses' failure here following his earlier success: (a) If striking the rock worked once, it should work twice? (b) Moses didn't believe words alone would suffice? (c) After 40 years, his pent-up anger spilled out, as well as the water? (d) Moses "choked" in the clutch? (e) One glitch is enough to get in trouble with God?

1. What is something you are very successful at? How might this success cause you to trust in yourself instead of in God? **2.** What about Moses' hard lesson, or your own "Meribah," reminds you that you need God in your "40th year," as well as your first?

When road repair or an accident makes you late for an appointment, how do you feel?

1. Why would the king of Edom be suspicious of letting "brother" Israel pass through his territory? What difference do their promises of good behavior make? **2.** Given the king's concerns, what do you think of his rebuff? With Israel's God on their side and the promised land so close, what do you think of the Israelites' "timid" response (see Dt 2:4–6)? **3.** What do you learn about God's timing in this story?

1. What are some long-term spiritual promises God has made to you? Which of these are you still waiting for? How patient are you in waiting? **2.** From this story, and your own story of God's detours, what do you learn about God's promises? About patience? How can your small group help you in this?

becomes unclean, and anyone who touches it becomes unclean till evening."

Water From the Rock

20 In the first month the whole Israelite community arrived at the Desert of Zin, and they stayed at Kadesh. There Miriam died and was buried.

²Now there was no water for the community, and the people gathered in opposition to Moses and Aaron. ³They quarreled with Moses and said, "If only we had died when our brothers fell dead before the LORD! ⁴Why did you bring the LORD's community into this desert, that we and our livestock should die here? ⁵Why did you bring us up out of Egypt to this terrible place? It has no grain or figs, grapevines or pomegranates. And there is no water to drink!"

⁶Moses and Aaron went from the assembly to the entrance to the Tent of Meeting and fell facedown, and the glory of the LORD appeared to them. ⁷The LORD said to Moses, ⁸"Take the staff, and you and your brother Aaron gather the assembly together. Speak to that rock before their eyes and it will pour out its water. You will bring water out of the rock for the community so they and their livestock can drink."

⁹So Moses took the staff from the LORD's presence, just as he commanded him. ¹⁰He and Aaron gathered the assembly together in front of the rock and Moses said to them, "Listen, you rebels, must we bring you water out of this rock?" ¹¹Then Moses raised his arm and struck the rock twice with his staff. Water gushed out, and the community and their livestock drank.

¹²But the LORD said to Moses and Aaron, "Because you did not trust in me enough to honor me as holy in the sight of the Israelites, you will not bring this community into the land I give them."

¹³These were the waters of Meribah,ᵃ where the Israelites quarreled with the LORD and where he showed himself holy among them.

Edom Denies Israel Passage

¹⁴Moses sent messengers from Kadesh to the king of Edom, saying:

"This is what your brother Israel says: You know about all the hardships that have come upon us. ¹⁵Our forefathers went down into Egypt, and we lived there many years. The Egyptians mistreated us and our fathers, ¹⁶but when we cried out to the LORD, he heard our cry and sent an angel and brought us out of Egypt.

"Now we are here at Kadesh, a town on the edge of your territory. ¹⁷Please let us pass through your country. We will not go through any field or vineyard, or drink water from any well. We will travel along the king's highway and not turn to the right or to the left until we have passed through your territory."

¹⁸But Edom answered:

"You may not pass through here; if you try, we will march out and attack you with the sword."

¹⁹The Israelites replied:

"We will go along the main road, and if we or our livestock

ᵃ13 Meribah means quarreling.

drink any of your water, we will pay for it. We only want to pass through on foot—nothing else."

20Again they answered:

"You may not pass through."

Then Edom came out against them with a large and powerful army. 21Since Edom refused to let them go through their territory, Israel turned away from them.

The Death of Aaron

22The whole Israelite community set out from Kadesh and came to Mount Hor. 23At Mount Hor, near the border of Edom, the LORD said to Moses and Aaron, 24"Aaron will be gathered to his people. He will not enter the land I give the Israelites, because both of you rebelled against my command at the waters of Meribah. 25Get Aaron and his son Eleazar and take them up Mount Hor. 26Remove Aaron's garments and put them on his son Eleazar, for Aaron will be gathered to his people; he will die there."

27Moses did as the LORD commanded: They went up Mount Hor in the sight of the whole community. 28Moses removed Aaron's garments and put them on his son Eleazar. And Aaron died there on top of the mountain. Then Moses and Eleazar came down from the mountain, 29and when the whole community learned that Aaron had died, the entire house of Israel mourned for him thirty days.

Arad Destroyed

21 When the Canaanite king of Arad, who lived in the Negev, heard that Israel was coming along the road to Atharim, he attacked the Israelites and captured some of them. 2Then Israel made this vow to the LORD: "If you will deliver these people into our hands, we will totally destroy[a] their cities." 3The LORD listened to Israel's plea and gave the Canaanites over to them. They completely destroyed them and their towns; so the place was named Hormah.[b]

The Bronze Snake

4They traveled from Mount Hor along the route to the Red Sea,[c] to go around Edom. But the people grew impatient on the way; 5they spoke against God and against Moses, and said, "Why have you brought us up out of Egypt to die in the desert? There is no bread! There is no water! And we detest this miserable food!"

6Then the LORD sent venomous snakes among them; they bit the people and many Israelites died. 7The people came to Moses and said, "We sinned when we spoke against the LORD and against you. Pray that the LORD will take the snakes away from us." So Moses prayed for the people.

8The LORD said to Moses, "Make a snake and put it up on a pole; anyone who is bitten can look at it and live." 9So Moses made a bronze snake and put it up on a pole. Then when anyone was bitten by a snake and looked at the bronze snake, he lived.

The Journey to Moab

10The Israelites moved on and camped at Oboth. 11Then they set out from Oboth and camped in Iye Abarim, in the desert that faces Moab toward the sunrise. 12From there they moved on and camped

a2 The Hebrew term refers to the irrevocable giving over of things or persons to the LORD, often by totally destroying them; also in verse 3.　b3 *Hormah* means *destruction.*
c4 Hebrew *Yam Suph*; that is, Sea of Reeds

---

1. What problem might Aaron's death cause for Israel? Why do you think God keeps him from entering the land? Why is he singled out with Moses (v. 24; see 20:7–8)? 2. How would Eleazar's presence lessen the impact of Aaron's death?

1. What turning point does chapter 20 signal in Israel's desert wanderings? 2. What tearful "passing of the old guard" have you witnessed at work, home, school or church? What new thing emerged from that transition?

---

1. After avoiding Edom, why does Israel destroy Arad? How do you feel about such destruction? What does this say about God's relationship with the Israelites? 2. Having destroyed Arad, why do the people complain (again) about the bread? Why and how does God judge them for this? 3. Why and how does he provide relief from the snakes? 4. What does this say about repentance and mercy?

1. What does God do when you need discipline? When you need relief? How does this compare to God's actions in this passage? 2. What use of this incident does Jesus make (see Jn 3:14–15; 6:32–40)? How have you availed yourself of the lifted up Healer and the Bread of life?

When you vacation, do you like going from place to place? Or do you prefer the same bed for a week at a time? What do you tend to bring back as mementos: Post cards? T-shirts? Suntan? Rocks? Other?

1. Why would it be important that the Israelites remember this trip? How would the songs in this passage help them do that? 2. What recurring themes do you see here?

1. Which event in your spiritual pilgrimage during this past year was most significant? 2. Why is it important that you remember this event? What will you do to ensure you do?

1. Would you ever engage in wrestling or fisticuffs to settle a dispute? When was the last time? Did the fight resolve anything or teach you any lessons? (What?) 2. If not the fighting type, how do you channel your aggression? What non-combative way have you found for settling your differences?

1. How do the events here compare to those in Numbers 20:14–21? How do you account for such different outcomes this time around? What reason does Moses have for being less afraid? 2. What does the defeat of Og and Sihon do for Israel (vv. 27–31; see Ps 135:11; 136:19–20)? 3. What do "war songs" say about God's desire for his people? For their enemies?

1. When confronted by opponents, are you more likely to "fight" or "flee"? Why? What does that say about you? 2. Is it always right to fight? To retreat? How can you know which is the right response to a particular situation? 3. How can Israel's encounter with Edom and Sihon help you to sort out a proper response?

in the Zered Valley. [13]They set out from there and camped alongside the Arnon, which is in the desert extending into Amorite territory. The Arnon is the border of Moab, between Moab and the Amorites. [14]That is why the Book of the Wars of the LORD says:

> ". . . Waheb in Suphah[a] and the ravines,
>   the Arnon [15]and[b] the slopes of the ravines
> that lead to the site of Ar
>   and lie along the border of Moab."

[16]From there they continued on to Beer, the well where the LORD said to Moses, "Gather the people together and I will give them water."

[17]Then Israel sang this song:

> "Spring up, O well!
>   Sing about it,
> [18]about the well that the princes dug,
>   that the nobles of the people sank—
> the nobles with scepters and staffs."

Then they went from the desert to Mattanah, [19]from Mattanah to Nahaliel, from Nahaliel to Bamoth, [20]and from Bamoth to the valley in Moab where the top of Pisgah overlooks the wasteland.

Defeat of Sihon and Og

[21]Israel sent messengers to say to Sihon king of the Amorites:

[22]"Let us pass through your country. We will not turn aside into any field or vineyard, or drink water from any well. We will travel along the king's highway until we have passed through your territory."

[23]But Sihon would not let Israel pass through his territory. He mustered his entire army and marched out into the desert against Israel. When he reached Jahaz, he fought with Israel. [24]Israel, however, put him to the sword and took over his land from the Arnon to the Jabbok, but only as far as the Ammonites, because their border was fortified. [25]Israel captured all the cities of the Amorites and occupied them, including Heshbon and all its surrounding settlements. [26]Heshbon was the city of Sihon king of the Amorites, who had fought against the former king of Moab and had taken from him all his land as far as the Arnon.

[27]That is why the poets say:

> "Come to Heshbon and let it be rebuilt;
>   let Sihon's city be restored.
>
> [28]"Fire went out from Heshbon,
>   a blaze from the city of Sihon.
> It consumed Ar of Moab,
>   the citizens of Arnon's heights.
> [29]Woe to you, O Moab!
>   You are destroyed, O people of Chemosh!
> He has given up his sons as fugitives
>   and his daughters as captives
> to Sihon king of the Amorites.
>
> [30]"But we have overthrown them;
>   Heshbon is destroyed all the way to Dibon.

a 14 The meaning of the Hebrew for this phrase is uncertain.   b 14,15 Or "I have been given from Suphah and the ravines / of the Arnon [15]to

We have demolished them as far as Nophah,
which extends to Medeba."

31So Israel settled in the land of the Amorites.

32After Moses had sent spies to Jazer, the Israelites captured its surrounding settlements and drove out the Amorites who were there. 33Then they turned and went up along the road toward Bashan, and Og king of Bashan and his whole army marched out to meet them in battle at Edrei.

34The LORD said to Moses, "Do not be afraid of him, for I have handed him over to you, with his whole army and his land. Do to him what you did to Sihon king of the Amorites, who reigned in Heshbon."

35So they struck him down, together with his sons and his whole army, leaving them no survivors. And they took possession of his land.

Balak Summons Balaam

22 Then the Israelites traveled to the plains of Moab and camped along the Jordan across from Jericho.[a]

2Now Balak son of Zippor saw all that Israel had done to the Amorites, 3and Moab was terrified because there were so many people. Indeed, Moab was filled with dread because of the Israelites.

4The Moabites said to the elders of Midian, "This horde is going to lick up everything around us, as an ox licks up the grass of the field."

So Balak son of Zippor, who was king of Moab at that time, 5sent messengers to summon Balaam son of Beor, who was at Pethor, near the River,[b] in his native land. Balak said:

"A people has come out of Egypt; they cover the face of the land and have settled next to me. 6Now come and put a curse on these people, because they are too powerful for me. Perhaps then I will be able to defeat them and drive them out of the country. For I know that those you bless are blessed, and those you curse are cursed."

7The elders of Moab and Midian left, taking with them the fee for divination. When they came to Balaam, they told him what Balak had said.

8"Spend the night here," Balaam said to them, "and I will bring you back the answer the LORD gives me." So the Moabite princes stayed with him.

9God came to Balaam and asked, "Who are these men with you?"

10Balaam said to God, "Balak son of Zippor, king of Moab, sent me this message: 11'A people that has come out of Egypt covers the face of the land. Now come and put a curse on them for me. Perhaps then I will be able to fight them and drive them away.'"

12But God said to Balaam, "Do not go with them. You must not put a curse on those people, because they are blessed."

13The next morning Balaam got up and said to Balak's princes, "Go back to your own country, for the LORD has refused to let me go with you."

14So the Moabite princes returned to Balak and said, "Balaam refused to come with us."

1. What kind of mail do you open first? Last? 2. When you come home to phone messages, are you eager to listen to them? Or do you feel annoyed? What is the funniest greeting you've heard when reaching someone else's answering machine?

1. Given the events of the previous chapter, but with no sign that Israel is intent on attacking him, why is Balak worried about Israel? How is his reaction to Israel's "threat" like and unlike that of Sihon and Og? 2. What role does divine help play in this ancient culture's problem-solving? What does this say about their belief in the supernatural? 3. Balak sends all the way to the Euphrates River basin for Balaam, twice (vv. 5,15). What does that tell you about Balak's fear? About his difficulty in getting hold of Balaam? About Balaam's popular acclaim in this culture? 4. What does Balak want Balaam to do, ultimately? What does this reveal about his view of the relationship between man and God? How does his view differ from Balaam's? 5. Why does Balaam deny the messengers the first time (vv. 12–13)? Why, if he had a sure word from God then, does Balaam still inquire of God again (vv. 18–19)? Why does God permit Balaam to go the second time but not at first? 6. Does Balaam strike you as a "captive agent," loyal only to Yahweh? Or an "independent agent," brokering for any god (see 24:1) and the highest bidder? Explain.

1. What is your initial reaction to conflict: Like Balak? Like Balaam? Or what? 2. Judging from your prayer life, are you doing God's bidding? Or is he doing

---

a1 Hebrew *Jordan of Jericho*; possibly an ancient name for the Jordan River   b5 That is, the Euphrates

yours? What does that say about your relationship with God? **3.** What steps will you take to ensure that you maintain a proper, deferential relationship with God?

If you were to typecast your personality with that of an animal stereotype, which animal would fit you and why?

1. What does Balak want Balaam to do? In what sense would this be opposing God? What does Balaam want his donkey to do? In what sense was he opposing God? **2.** Why do you think God is angry with Balaam for leaving (v. 22), since just prior, he had told him to go and later repeats that

[15]Then Balak sent other princes, more numerous and more distinguished than the first. [16]They came to Balaam and said:

"This is what Balak son of Zippor says: Do not let anything keep you from coming to me, [17]because I will reward you handsomely and do whatever you say. Come and put a curse on these people for me."

[18]But Balaam answered them, "Even if Balak gave me his palace filled with silver and gold, I could not do anything great or small to go beyond the command of the LORD my God. [19]Now stay here tonight as the others did, and I will find out what else the LORD will tell me."

[20]That night God came to Balaam and said, "Since these men have come to summon you, go with them, but do only what I tell you."

Balaam's Donkey

[21]Balaam got up in the morning, saddled his donkey and went with the princes of Moab. [22]But God was very angry when he went, and the angel of the LORD stood in the road to oppose him. Balaam was riding on his donkey, and his two servants were with him. [23]When the donkey saw the angel of the LORD standing in the road with a drawn sword in his hand, she turned off the road into a field. Balaam beat her to get her back on the road.

[24]Then the angel of the LORD stood in a narrow path between two vineyards, with walls on both sides. [25]When the donkey saw the angel of the LORD, she pressed close to the wall, crushing Balaam's foot against it. So he beat her again.

✚✚ **Numbers 22:1–35**   **BALAK, BALAAM AND HIS DONKEY**
✚✚

Settled in the plains of Moab, the children of Israel were preparing to invade the promised land. Although the Israelites had passed by Moab peacefully, Balak, the king of Moab, devised a scheme—along with the neighboring Midianites—against Israel.

1. What was Balak trying to do?
   a. relieve his fears
   b. drive away the Israelites
   c. rent a renowned sorcerer
   d. manipulate the gods

2. How would you describe Balaam?
   a. a true prophet
   b. a false prophet
   c. a wishy-washy prophet
   d. a for-profit prophet

3. Since the Lord told Balaam to go with the messengers, why was God angry with him?
   a. Earlier Balaam had asked God if he could go and God said no.
   b. Balaam was motivated by greed to prophesy.
   c. God knew Balaam was thinking of disobeying him cursing Israel.

4. What is the most comical thing about this story?
   a. that the professional seer could not see what his donkey could see
   b. that Balaam got mad at his donkey while she was saving his life
   c. that the donkey could talk
   d. that Balaam got into a conversation with his donkey

5. Where do you identify with Balaam the most?
   a. ignoring God and going ahead
   b. kidding myself about my motives
   c. experiencing adversity as a way God gets my attention
   d. beating the one voice that could really help me
   e. recognizing the holiness of God the hard way
   f. being willing to turn back when God says so

6. When the direction of my life is undergoing a "mid-course correction," I respond by:
   a. getting mad at God.
   b. getting defensive.
   c. lashing out at others.

d. beating up on myself.
e. asking for forgiveness.
f. following the new path without hesitation.

7. Who or what can you trust to help you follow the right path?
   a. my upbringing
   b. my feelings
   c. my mind
   d. my faith
   e. my conscience
   f. my small group
   g. an angel
   h. my family
   i. my pastor
   j. I'm not sure.

8. Judging from your prayer life, are you doing God's bidding? Or is God constantly being asked to do yours?

9. ✚✚ How do you know if you are ✚✚ in God's will? How can you keep your own will in line with God's will?

10. ✚✚ How have these studies ✚✚ about "whol-i-ness" been a mid-course correction in your: (a) view of making choices; (b) priorities for personal growth; and (c) plan for a life of wholeness?

²⁶Then the angel of the LORD moved on ahead and stood in a narrow place where there was no room to turn, either to the right or to the left. ²⁷When the donkey saw the angel of the LORD, she lay down under Balaam, and he was angry and beat her with his staff. ²⁸Then the LORD opened the donkey's mouth, and she said to Balaam, "What have I done to you to make you beat me these three times?"

²⁹Balaam answered the donkey, "You have made a fool of me! If I had a sword in my hand, I would kill you right now."

³⁰The donkey said to Balaam, "Am I not your own donkey, which you have always ridden, to this day? Have I been in the habit of doing this to you?"

"No," he said.

³¹Then the LORD opened Balaam's eyes, and he saw the angel of the LORD standing in the road with his sword drawn. So he bowed low and fell facedown.

³²The angel of the LORD asked him, "Why have you beaten your donkey these three times? I have come here to oppose you because your path is a reckless one before me.ᵃ ³³The donkey saw me and turned away from me these three times. If she had not turned away, I would certainly have killed you by now, but I would have spared her."

³⁴Balaam said to the angel of the LORD, "I have sinned. I did not realize you were standing in the road to oppose me. Now if you are displeased, I will go back."

³⁵The angel of the LORD said to Balaam, "Go with the men, but speak only what I tell you." So Balaam went with the princes of Balak.

³⁶When Balak heard that Balaam was coming, he went out to meet him at the Moabite town on the Arnon border, at the edge of his territory. ³⁷Balak said to Balaam, "Did I not send you an urgent summons? Why didn't you come to me? Am I really not able to reward you?"

³⁸"Well, I have come to you now," Balaam replied. "But can I say just anything? I must speak only what God puts in my mouth."

³⁹Then Balaam went with Balak to Kiriath Huzoth. ⁴⁰Balak sacrificed cattle and sheep, and gave some to Balaam and the princes who were with him. ⁴¹The next morning Balak took Balaam up to Bamoth Baal, and from there he saw part of the people.

Balaam's First Oracle

23 Balaam said, "Build me seven altars here, and prepare seven bulls and seven rams for me." ²Balak did as Balaam said, and the two of them offered a bull and a ram on each altar.

³Then Balaam said to Balak, "Stay here beside your offering while I go aside. Perhaps the LORD will come to meet with me. Whatever he reveals to me I will tell you." Then he went off to a barren height.

⁴God met with him, and Balaam said, "I have prepared seven altars, and on each altar I have offered a bull and a ram."

⁵The LORD put a message in Balaam's mouth and said, "Go back to Balak and give him this message."

⁶So he went back to him and found him standing beside his offering, with all the princes of Moab. ⁷Then Balaam uttered his oracle:

> "Balak brought me from Aram,
>   the king of Moab from the eastern mountains.

ᵃ32 The meaning of the Hebrew for this clause is uncertain.

---

command (vv. 20,35)? **3.** How might this be explained by the interaction and insights of Balaam and his donkey? What do you think God is trying to teach the opportunistic and spiritually blind Balaam through his loyal and spiritually alert donkey? Does God succeed in this (vv. 37–38; see 23:12,20, 26)? **4.** Which was the greater miracle: God opening Balaam's eyes (v. 31), or his donkey's mouth (v. 28)? Why do you think so?

1. Are you like Balaam or his donkey? How so? When have you suddenly and stubbornly found yourself opposing God, much to your surprise? How did he point out your error? How many run-ins with God's angel or roadblocks did it take before he opened your eyes? **2.** Do you think it is possible to always know God's will every step of the way? Why or why not? **3.** What are some ways we can attune ourselves to God's will for us? Which of these will you begin incorporating into your life, now?

Who is the one person you'd like to affirm? What gift would you give him or her?

1. In this first oracle, what is Balak's desire? Balaam's desire? God's desire? **2.** Hence, how would each see the function of the seven altars and sacrifices? **3.** How do these disparate views help to explain what's going on in this oracle? (Nowhere else does the term "oracle" describe the speech of God's true prophets.) **4.** Why can't Balaam bring himself to curse Israel? What truth secures Israel's blessing forever?

1. When you want to know God's will for your life, what do you do? How is that similar to Balaam's altars and sacrifices in this passage? How successful is this method for determining God's desires? **2.** When are your desires most likely to conflict with God's desires? Have you ever tried to convince God that your way is better? What was the result of that attempt? **3.** In this story, are you more like *Balak* (cursing others, opposing God) or *Balaam* (blessing others, obeying God)? What can you do to ensure that, like Balaam, you mold your desires to fit God's?

☕ "If at first you don't succeed, try, try again," the saying goes. What major test have you flunked, only to pass it on a subsequent try, perhaps even an umpteenth try: (a) Driver's test? (b) College exam? (c) Lovers' quarrel? (d) Work requirement?

📖 **1.** Why is Balak back again giving it the "old college try"? What does he know about Balaam or God that leads him to believe either one can be bought? What is God's answer to this presumption of Balak's (vv. 18–20)? **2.** What do you see as the central message or key verse of this oracle? How does the blessing of this second oracle compare in scope to the first one? What is Balak's response to this greater blessing? **3.** How does its message fit into the larger story of Balak and Balaam (chs. 22–24)?

♥ **1.** When are God's decrees hardest for you to accept? How is God not like a parent or a spouse or a politician who can and do change their minds? **2.** How do your reactions at these times help you to understand Balak in this story? If you could give Balak one piece of advice, what would it be? What will you do to ensure you follow your own advice? **3.** In verse 25, Balak admits that this whole exercise is backfiring on him. When have you felt like Balak in this regard? **4.** How can you avoid situations like that? How might the story of Balak and Balaam help you do just that, "the next time"?

'Come,' he said, 'curse Jacob for me;
come, denounce Israel.'
[8]How can I curse
those whom God has not cursed?
How can I denounce
those whom the LORD has not denounced?
[9]From the rocky peaks I see them,
from the heights I view them.
I see a people who live apart
and do not consider themselves one of the nations.
[10]Who can count the dust of Jacob
or number the fourth part of Israel?
Let me die the death of the righteous,
and may my end be like theirs!"

[11]Balak said to Balaam, "What have you done to me? I brought you to curse my enemies, but you have done nothing but bless them!"

[12]He answered, "Must I not speak what the LORD puts in my mouth?"

Balaam's Second Oracle

[13]Then Balak said to him, "Come with me to another place where you can see them; you will see only a part but not all of them. And from there, curse them for me." [14]So he took him to the field of Zophim on the top of Pisgah, and there he built seven altars and offered a bull and a ram on each altar.

[15]Balaam said to Balak, "Stay here beside your offering while I meet with him over there."

[16]The LORD met with Balaam and put a message in his mouth and said, "Go back to Balak and give him this message."

[17]So he went to him and found him standing beside his offering, with the princes of Moab. Balak asked him, "What did the LORD say?"

[18]Then he uttered his oracle:

"Arise, Balak, and listen;
hear me, son of Zippor.
[19]God is not a man, that he should lie,
nor a son of man, that he should change his mind.
Does he speak and then not act?
Does he promise and not fulfill?
[20]I have received a command to bless;
he has blessed, and I cannot change it.

[21]"No misfortune is seen in Jacob,
no misery observed in Israel.[a]
The LORD their God is with them;
the shout of the King is among them.
[22]God brought them out of Egypt;
they have the strength of a wild ox.
[23]There is no sorcery against Jacob,
no divination against Israel.
It will now be said of Jacob
and of Israel, 'See what God has done!'
[24]The people rise like a lioness;
they rouse themselves like a lion

[a]21 Or *He has not looked on Jacob's offenses / or on the wrongs found in Israel.*

that does not rest till he devours his prey
  and drinks the blood of his victims."

²⁵Then Balak said to Balaam, "Neither curse them at all nor bless them at all!"

²⁶Balaam answered, "Did I not tell you I must do whatever the LORD says?"

Balaam's Third Oracle

²⁷Then Balak said to Balaam, "Come, let me take you to another place. Perhaps it will please God to let you curse them for me from there." ²⁸And Balak took Balaam to the top of Peor, overlooking the wasteland.

²⁹Balaam said, "Build me seven altars here, and prepare seven bulls and seven rams for me." ³⁰Balak did as Balaam had said, and offered a bull and a ram on each altar.

24 Now when Balaam saw that it pleased the LORD to bless Israel, he did not resort to sorcery as at other times, but turned his face toward the desert. ²When Balaam looked out and saw Israel encamped tribe by tribe, the Spirit of God came upon him ³and he uttered his oracle:

"The oracle of Balaam son of Beor,
  the oracle of one whose eye sees clearly,
⁴the oracle of one who hears the words of God,
  who sees a vision from the Almighty,ᵃ
  who falls prostrate, and whose eyes are opened:

⁵"How beautiful are your tents, O Jacob,
  your dwelling places, O Israel!

⁶"Like valleys they spread out,
  like gardens beside a river,
like aloes planted by the LORD,
  like cedars beside the waters.
⁷Water will flow from their buckets;
  their seed will have abundant water.

"Their king will be greater than Agag;
  their kingdom will be exalted.

⁸"God brought them out of Egypt;
  they have the strength of a wild ox.
They devour hostile nations
  and break their bones in pieces;
  with their arrows they pierce them.
⁹Like a lion they crouch and lie down,
  like a lioness—who dares to rouse them?

"May those who bless you be blessed
  and those who curse you be cursed!"

¹⁰Then Balak's anger burned against Balaam. He struck his hands together and said to him, "I summoned you to curse my enemies, but you have blessed them these three times. ¹¹Now leave at once and go home! I said I would reward you handsomely, but the LORD has kept you from being rewarded."

¹²Balaam answered Balak, "Did I not tell the messengers you sent me, ¹³'Even if Balak gave me his palace filled with silver and gold, I could not do anything of my own accord, good or bad, to go beyond the command of the LORD—and I must say only what the

ᵃ4 Hebrew *Shaddai*; also in verse 16

What is the one mistake you have repeated at least three times? Why do you think this is?

1. Why do you think Balak asks Balaam a third time to curse the Israelites? After this third oracle, has Balak changed? Based on these three oracles, how would you describe Balak's view of God? 2. How might Balaam's abandonment of sorcery (v. 1) have helped him realize that God wants to bless Israel? How might Balaam's sorcery be related to Balak's desire to influence God? 3. Do you think Balaam has changed since the first oracle? How so (vv. 2–4)? 4. What does verse 2 imply: (a) Prophet's anointing? (b) Personal Pentecost? (c) Inspired message? (d) Other? 5. Compare the first two oracles with this one as to what they say about the Israelites. What do you notice that is the same? Different? 6. What does Balak's angry outburst against Balaam (vv. 10–11) say about their inner motives? What legacy of guilt does Balaam carry forward from this (see 2Pe 2:15–16; Jude 11; Rev 2:14)? Might this explain his yearning to be covered by Israel's blessing (v. 9; 23:10)? 7. What do you see as God's purpose in giving these oracles to someone as greedy or as pagan as Balaam? Who do you think such oracles are aimed primarily for: Balak? Balaam? Israel?

1. Do you think that God wishes for you all the goodness that he decrees for the Israelites in these oracles? In what ways has he blessed you this last year? How does this make you feel? 2. Do you always believe that God wants only good for you? When is it most difficult for you to believe this? If you could believe this at all times, how would it change your prayer life? Your view of God? 3. What lesson do you learn from this passage about abandoning your former ways and accepting God's will? 4. How will you reply to those who get angry with you, because you are no longer acting or believing like you used to? Anything like Balaam (vv. 12–14)?

LORD says'? [14]Now I am going back to my people, but come, let me warn you of what this people will do to your people in days to come."

Balaam's Fourth Oracle

[15]Then he uttered his oracle:

"The oracle of Balaam son of Beor,
    the oracle of one whose eye sees clearly,
[16]the oracle of one who hears the words of God,
    who has knowledge from the Most High,
who sees a vision from the Almighty,
    who falls prostrate, and whose eyes are opened:

[17]"I see him, but not now;
    I behold him, but not near.
A star will come out of Jacob;
    a scepter will rise out of Israel.
He will crush the foreheads of Moab,
    the skulls[a] of[b] all the sons of Sheth.[c]
[18]Edom will be conquered;
    Seir, his enemy, will be conquered,
    but Israel will grow strong.
[19]A ruler will come out of Jacob
    and destroy the survivors of the city."

Balaam's Final Oracles

[20]Then Balaam saw Amalek and uttered his oracle:

"Amalek was first among the nations,
    but he will come to ruin at last."

[21]Then he saw the Kenites and uttered his oracle:

"Your dwelling place is secure,
    your nest is set in a rock;
[22]yet you Kenites will be destroyed
    when Asshur takes you captive."

[23]Then he uttered his oracle:

"Ah, who can live when God does this?[d]
[24]   Ships will come from the shores of Kittim;
they will subdue Asshur and Eber,
    but they too will come to ruin."

[25]Then Balaam got up and returned home and Balak went his own way.

Moab Seduces Israel

25 While Israel was staying in Shittim, the men began to indulge in sexual immorality with Moabite women, [2]who invited them to the sacrifices to their gods. The people ate and bowed down before these gods. [3]So Israel joined in worshiping the Baal of Peor. And the LORD's anger burned against them.

[4]The LORD said to Moses, "Take all the leaders of these people, kill them and expose them in broad daylight before the LORD, so that the LORD's fierce anger may turn away from Israel."

[5]So Moses said to Israel's judges, "Each of you must put to death

---

1. What do you like best about the end of a fireworks display or the end of an opera? 2. Which are you more inclined to do: (a) Speak first and ask questions later? (b) Look first and speak about whatever you see? (c) Look first to see if anyone is listening? Explain.

1. How are these oracles like and unlike Balaam's previous ones? How do they continue the "theme song" of the "Balaam and Balak Show"? 2. In these oracles, who is the "star" on the horizon (v. 17; compare Rev 22:16)? Who is the "scepter" of Israel? The "ruler" of Jacob? What initial and ultimate fulfillments of these prophecies do you see? 3. How do these four oracles relate to each other? What unifying theme do you see? 4. What do the theme song and future prophecies add to the story of Balak and Balaam (chs. 22–24)? 5. What does this passage teach you about God? About deliverance?

1. What "enemies" (people or things which keep you from doing God's work) do you face in your everyday life? How are these enemies similar to those facing ancient Israel? In the face of such enemies, what hope can you draw from this passage? 2. In the past year, how has God removed obstacles keeping you from serving him? What part did you play in their removal?

How old were you when you realized what pornography was? How did you react to it then? And now?

1. In the fertility religions of Canaanite culture, sexual intercourse was part of worship. Why might missionaries from these groups be popular with Israelites? What danger does such immorality and Baal worship pose to God's covenant with Israel (vv. 1–4, 11–13)? 2. Since God says, "You shall not murder" (Ex 20:13), why do you think he rewards Phin-

---

[a]17 Samaritan Pentateuch (see also Jer. 48:45); the meaning of the word in the Masoretic Text is uncertain.   [b]17 Or possibly *Moab, / batter*   [c]17 Or *all the noisy boasters*   [d]23 Masoretic Text; with a different word division of the Hebrew *A people will gather from the north.*

those of your men who have joined in worshiping the Baal of Peor."

⁶Then an Israelite man brought to his family a Midianite woman right before the eyes of Moses and the whole assembly of Israel while they were weeping at the entrance to the Tent of Meeting. ⁷When Phinehas son of Eleazar, the son of Aaron, the priest, saw this, he left the assembly, took a spear in his hand ⁸and followed the Israelite into the tent. He drove the spear through both of them—through the Israelite and into the woman's body. Then the plague against the Israelites was stopped; ⁹but those who died in the plague numbered 24,000.

¹⁰The LORD said to Moses, ¹¹"Phinehas son of Eleazar, the son of Aaron, the priest, has turned my anger away from the Israelites; for he was as zealous as I am for my honor among them, so that in my zeal I did not put an end to them. ¹²Therefore tell him I am making my covenant of peace with him. ¹³He and his descendants will have a covenant of a lasting priesthood, because he was zealous for the honor of his God and made atonement for the Israelites."

¹⁴The name of the Israelite who was killed with the Midianite woman was Zimri son of Salu, the leader of a Simeonite family. ¹⁵And the name of the Midianite woman who was put to death was Cozbi daughter of Zur, a tribal chief of a Midianite family.

¹⁶The LORD said to Moses, ¹⁷"Treat the Midianites as enemies and kill them, ¹⁸because they treated you as enemies when they deceived you in the affair of Peor and their sister Cozbi, the daughter of a Midianite leader, the woman who was killed when the plague came as a result of Peor."

The Second Census

26 After the plague the LORD said to Moses and Eleazar son of Aaron, the priest, ²"Take a census of the whole Israelite community by families—all those twenty years old or more who are able to serve in the army of Israel." ³So on the plains of Moab by the Jordan across from Jericho,ᵃ Moses and Eleazar the priest spoke with them and said, ⁴"Take a census of the men twenty years old or more, as the LORD commanded Moses."

These were the Israelites who came out of Egypt:

⁵The descendants of Reuben, the firstborn son of Israel, were:
   through Hanoch, the Hanochite clan;
   through Pallu, the Palluite clan;
   ⁶through Hezron, the Hezronite clan;
   through Carmi, the Carmite clan.
⁷These were the clans of Reuben; those numbered were 43,730.
⁸The son of Pallu was Eliab, ⁹and the sons of Eliab were Nemuel, Dathan and Abiram. The same Dathan and Abiram were the community officials who rebelled against Moses and Aaron and were among Korah's followers when they rebelled against the LORD. ¹⁰The earth opened its mouth and swallowed them along with Korah, whose followers died when the fire devoured the 250 men. And they served as a warning sign. ¹¹The line of Korah, however, did not die out.

¹²The descendants of Simeon by their clans were:
   through Nemuel, the Nemuelite clan;
   through Jamin, the Jaminite clan;
   through Jakin, the Jakinite clan;

ᵃ3 Hebrew *Jordan of Jericho*; possibly an ancient name for the Jordan River; also in verse 63

---

ehas for his actions? What makes his actions different from murder? **3.** Define "zealous." How is this zeal overt in the actions of Phinehas killing the two culprits? Likewise, in the actions of God sending the plague? Why such a graphic picture of the sex and killing involved? **4.** Why are Midianites seen as "enemies" (vv. 17–18; see 22:4,7)? **5.** What does this teach you about honoring God's name? Keeping his covenant? Deterring sin? Treating enemies?

♡ **1.** What are some modern cultural practices that could erode the purity of the Christian faith? Which of these do you consider the most dangerous? **2.** Would the actions of Phinehas be a fitting response to this danger today? Why or why not? What does it mean to be zealous for the Lord in today's culture?

☕ **1.** Would you characterize your family as large or small? What advantages and disadvantages does this size give your family? **2.** How many children and grandchildren have been added to your clan in the last 38 years? How many do you anticipate in the next 38 years?

📖 **1.** It's been 38 years since the census taken in chapter 1. In what ways would a census taken just prior to their entry into the promised land help the Israelites? **2.** What is the main problem this census is meant to eliminate (vv. 52–56)? How would it achieve this? Do you think this way of attacking this possible problem is a just way? Why or why not? **3.** For what other reason is this census important (vv. 63–65)? Why distinguish these Israelites from those counted in the earlier census (see Nu 1 and 14:20–24)? **4.** What is noteworthy about the survivors listed here: Who has lost numbers in the intervening 38 years and why? Who has gained the most ground and why? How do the bottom line totals compare between the two censuses (v. 51; see 1:46)? What names are listed here to remind readers of their infamy (vv. 9,19,33)? **5.** In addition to the distinctive numbers and names of the survivors, what does this census say about their historical roots? Why would people entering the promised land want to know they had common historical roots but a completely separate identity from those in the earlier census?

♡ **1.** For what meaningful groups are you counted among their membership rolls? **2.** What is one advantage and disadvantage of being part of each meaningful grouping? How have these pluses and minuses affected your faith in God? **3.** Can you imagine being a follower of Jesus if you had been born into another family or cultural group? In what ways is your privileged position similar to that of the Israelites in this census? **4.** What can you do to make sure that the positive parts of your past are accentuated in your trust relationship with God: Would tracing your family and spiritual roots help? Would redeeming your spiritual inheritance help? Other? **5.** Of all the things you could do, what *will* you do today to ensure that this is the case?

[13]through Zerah, the Zerahite clan;
    through Shaul, the Shaulite clan.
[14]These were the clans of Simeon; there were 22,200 men.

[15]The descendants of Gad by their clans were:
    through Zephon, the Zephonite clan;
    through Haggi, the Haggite clan;
    through Shuni, the Shunite clan;
[16]through Ozni, the Oznite clan;
    through Eri, the Erite clan;
[17]through Arodi,[a] the Arodite clan;
    through Areli, the Arelite clan.
[18]These were the clans of Gad; those numbered were 40,500.

[19]Er and Onan were sons of Judah, but they died in Canaan.
[20]The descendants of Judah by their clans were:
    through Shelah, the Shelanite clan;
    through Perez, the Perezite clan;
    through Zerah, the Zerahite clan.
[21]The descendants of Perez were:
    through Hezron, the Hezronite clan;
    through Hamul, the Hamulite clan.
[22]These were the clans of Judah; those numbered were 76,500.

[23]The descendants of Issachar by their clans were:
    through Tola, the Tolaite clan;
    through Puah, the Puite[b] clan;
[24]through Jashub, the Jashubite clan;
    through Shimron, the Shimronite clan.
[25]These were the clans of Issachar; those numbered were 64,300.

[26]The descendants of Zebulun by their clans were:
    through Sered, the Seredite clan;
    through Elon, the Elonite clan;
    through Jahleel, the Jahleelite clan.
[27]These were the clans of Zebulun; those numbered were 60,500.

[28]The descendants of Joseph by their clans through Manasseh and Ephraim were:

[29]The descendants of Manasseh:
    through Makir, the Makirite clan (Makir was the father of Gilead);
    through Gilead, the Gileadite clan.
[30]These were the descendants of Gilead:
    through Iezer, the Iezerite clan;
    through Helek, the Helekite clan;
[31]through Asriel, the Asrielite clan;
    through Shechem, the Shechemite clan;
[32]through Shemida, the Shemidaite clan;
    through Hepher, the Hepherite clan.
[33](Zelophehad son of Hepher had no sons; he had only daughters, whose names were Mahlah, Noah, Hoglah, Milcah and Tirzah.)
[34]These were the clans of Manasseh; those numbered were 52,700.

[35]These were the descendants of Ephraim by their clans:
    through Shuthelah, the Shuthelahite clan;

---

[a]17 Samaritan Pentateuch and Syriac (see also Gen. 46:16); Masoretic Text *Arod*
[b]23 Samaritan Pentateuch, Septuagint, Vulgate and Syriac (see also 1 Chron. 7:1); Masoretic Text *through Puvah, the Punite*

through Beker, the Bekerite clan;
through Tahan, the Tahanite clan.
36These were the descendants of Shuthelah:
through Eran, the Eranite clan.
37These were the clans of Ephraim; those numbered were 32,500.

These were the descendants of Joseph by their clans.

38The descendants of Benjamin by their clans were:
through Bela, the Belaite clan;
through Ashbel, the Ashbelite clan;
through Ahiram, the Ahiramite clan;
39through Shupham,ª the Shuphamite clan;
through Hupham, the Huphamite clan.
40The descendants of Bela through Ard and Naaman were:
through Ard,ᵇ the Ardite clan;
through Naaman, the Naamite clan.
41These were the clans of Benjamin; those numbered were 45,600.

42These were the descendants of Dan by their clans:
through Shuham, the Shuhamite clan.
These were the clans of Dan: 43All of them were Shuhamite clans;
and those numbered were 64,400.

44The descendants of Asher by their clans were:
through Imnah, the Imnite clan;
through Ishvi, the Ishvite clan;
through Beriah, the Beriite clan;
45and through the descendants of Beriah:
through Heber, the Heberite clan;
through Malkiel, the Malkielite clan.
46(Asher had a daughter named Serah.)
47These were the clans of Asher; those numbered were 53,400.

48The descendants of Naphtali by their clans were:
through Jahzeel, the Jahzeelite clan;
through Guni, the Gunite clan;
49through Jezer, the Jezerite clan;
through Shillem, the Shillemite clan.
50These were the clans of Naphtali; those numbered were 45,400.

51The total number of the men of Israel was 601,730.

52The LORD said to Moses, 53"The land is to be allotted to them as
an inheritance based on the number of names. 54To a larger group
give a larger inheritance, and to a smaller group a smaller one; each
is to receive its inheritance according to the number of those
listed. 55Be sure that the land is distributed by lot. What each group
inherits will be according to the names for its ancestral tribe.
56Each inheritance is to be distributed by lot among the larger and
smaller groups."

57These were the Levites who were counted by their clans:
through Gershon, the Gershonite clan;
through Kohath, the Kohathite clan;
through Merari, the Merarite clan.
58These also were Levite clans:
the Libnite clan,

ª39 A few manuscripts of the Masoretic Text, Samaritan Pentateuch, Vulgate and Syriac
(see also Septuagint); most manuscripts of the Masoretic Text *Shephupham*
ᵇ40 Samaritan Pentateuch and Vulgate (see also Septuagint); Masoretic Text does not have
through Ard.

the Hebronite clan,
the Mahlite clan,
the Mushite clan,
the Korahite clan.
(Kohath was the forefather of Amram; 59the name of Amram's wife was Jochebed, a descendant of Levi, who was born to the Levites*a* in Egypt. To Amram she bore Aaron, Moses and their sister Miriam. 60Aaron was the father of Nadab and Abihu, Eleazar and Ithamar. 61But Nadab and Abihu died when they made an offering before the LORD with unauthorized fire.)

62All the male Levites a month old or more numbered 23,000. They were not counted along with the other Israelites because they received no inheritance among them.

63These are the ones counted by Moses and Eleazar the priest when they counted the Israelites on the plains of Moab by the Jordan across from Jericho. 64Not one of them was among those counted by Moses and Aaron the priest when they counted the Israelites in the Desert of Sinai. 65For the LORD had told those Israelites they would surely die in the desert, and not one of them was left except Caleb son of Jephunneh and Joshua son of Nun.

Zelophehad's Daughters

27 The daughters of Zelophehad son of Hepher, the son of Gilead, the son of Makir, the son of Manasseh, belonged to the clans of Manasseh son of Joseph. The names of the daughters were Mahlah, Noah, Hoglah, Milcah and Tirzah. They approached 2the entrance to the Tent of Meeting and stood before Moses, Eleazar the priest, the leaders and the whole assembly, and said, 3"Our father died in the desert. He was not among Korah's followers, who banded together against the LORD, but he died for his own sin and left no sons. 4Why should our father's name disappear from his clan because he had no son? Give us property among our father's relatives."

5So Moses brought their case before the LORD 6and the LORD said to him, 7"What Zelophehad's daughters are saying is right. You must certainly give them property as an inheritance among their father's relatives and turn their father's inheritance over to them.

8"Say to the Israelites, 'If a man dies and leaves no son, turn his inheritance over to his daughter. 9If he has no daughter, give his inheritance to his brothers. 10If he has no brothers, give his inheritance to his father's brothers. 11If his father had no brothers, give his inheritance to the nearest relative in his clan, that he may possess it. This is to be a legal requirement for the Israelites, as the LORD commanded Moses.'"

Joshua to Succeed Moses

12Then the LORD said to Moses, "Go up this mountain in the Abarim range and see the land I have given the Israelites. 13After you have seen it, you too will be gathered to your people, as your brother Aaron was, 14for when the community rebelled at the waters in the Desert of Zin, both of you disobeyed my command to honor me as holy before their eyes." (These were the waters of Meribah Kadesh, in the Desert of Zin.)

15Moses said to the LORD, 16"May the LORD, the God of the spirits of all mankind, appoint a man over this community 17to go out and come in before them, one who will lead them out and bring them

---

What unresolved situation are you facing, for which you'd like "special case consideration"?

1. What do you admire about these gutsy daughters (vv. 1–4)? **2.** Why were the Israelites concerned that a man's name not "disappear from his clan" (v. 4; see Dt 25:5–10)? **3.** Sometimes innocent family members do suffer for the sin of their father (see Da 6:24). On what basis do these daughters win their case? **4.** How does this case law (vv. 8–11) affect property accumulation? Social relations? Economic justice for all? **5.** Given the importance of Moses, what problems would his death bring to Israel? **6.** If a merciful exception to God's law could be found for Zelophehad's daughters, why not for Moses (vv. 12–14)? How does Moses respond to God's hard line? **7.** What hardships would Moses' successor likely face? How would anointing a successor before Moses dies help to avoid those problems? **8.** What is this ceremony (vv. 18–21) designed to do for Joshua? For the people he leads?

1. Why is equality among believers important? In what areas is equality most important to you? **2.** What does equality imply today: Uniformity? Fairness? "Special case" treatment under the law? **3.** What will you do to bring more equality to your work or home situation? **4.** Who was your "Moses"? What problems arose when "Josh-

---

a59 Or Jochebed, a daughter of Levi, who was born to Levi

in, so the LORD's people will not be like sheep without a shepherd." [18]So the LORD said to Moses, "Take Joshua son of Nun, a man in whom is the spirit,[a] and lay your hand on him. [19]Have him stand before Eleazar the priest and the entire assembly and commission him in their presence. [20]Give him some of your authority so the whole Israelite community will obey him. [21]He is to stand before Eleazar the priest, who will obtain decisions for him by inquiring of the Urim before the LORD. At his command he and the entire community of the Israelites will go out, and at his command they will come in."

[22]Moses did as the LORD commanded him. He took Joshua and had him stand before Eleazar the priest and the whole assembly. [23]Then he laid his hands on him and commissioned him, as the LORD instructed through Moses.

Daily Offerings

28 The LORD said to Moses, [2]"Give this command to the Israelites and say to them: 'See that you present to me at the appointed time the food for my offerings made by fire, as an aroma pleasing to me.' [3]Say to them: 'This is the offering made by fire that you are to present to the LORD: two lambs a year old without defect, as a regular burnt offering each day. [4]Prepare one lamb in the morning and the other at twilight, [5]together with a grain offering of a tenth of an ephah[b] of fine flour mixed with a quarter of a hin[c] of oil from pressed olives. [6]This is the regular burnt offering insti-

[a]18 Or *Spirit*   [b]5 That is, probably about 2 quarts (about 2 liters); also in verses 13, 21 and 29   [c]5 That is, probably about 1 quart (about 1 liter); also in verses 7 and 14

1. Is your church a high expectation, high commitment church? Or is yours a voluntary association with a lowest common denominator as criteria for membership? 2. How is that reflected in your church-wide programs: What does your church do on a daily basis? On a weekly basis? Monthly? Annually? 3. Which of these church functions are indispensible to you?

1. What feelings do you think these daily offerings are meant to evoke in the Israelites (vv.

  Numbers 27:12–23   **JOSHUA TO SUCCEED MOSES**

After 40 years in the wilderness, the Israelites are stationed just across the Jordan River—ready to enter the promised land. The Lord repeats his pronouncement that Moses will not be allowed to enter the land because of an earlier act of disobedience.

1. If you were Moses, how do you think you would have reacted to God's words in verses 12–14?
   a. "Nobody's perfect—can't I have another chance?"
   b. "I really don't want to die!"
   c. "At least I get to see the land."
   d. "After all I've done for you, this is what I get?!"
   e. "The Lord gives and takes away; blessed be the name of the Lord."

2. What does Moses' response (vv. 16–17) say about him?
   a. He wasn't a whiner.
   b. He was ready to die.
   c. His focus was on others' needs.
   d. He was willing to step aside and let someone else take over.
   e. He let God dictate the future.

3. Which of the statements in the last question is most true of you? Which one do you most need to work on?

4. What would Moses' successor most need in order to be successful?
   a. big feet to fill Moses' sandals
   b. wisdom and experience
   c. youthful enthusiasm
   d. a shepherd's heart
   e. military genius
   f. the people's respect
   g. God's Spirit
   h. Moses' blessing

5. What would commissioning Joshua before Moses died do for Joshua? For the people? For Moses?

6. When have you lost someone who has been a spiritual leader or shepherd in your life? How did you handle that experience and the transition to a new leader or shepherd?

7. What does this story say to you about getting older?
   a. Life and death are in God's hands.
   b. Power to influence the next generation is in my hands.

c. There's something special about touching another person.
d. Older believers aren't "over the hill," they're on the mountain waiting to enter the promised land.
e. I want to do all I can for my "community" before I'm gone.

8. How are you preparing for the day you will be "gathered to your people"? What legacy do you hope to leave behind?

9. Joshua had been Moses' trusted aide for many years. Who is your "Moses"—the man you look to as a mentor? Who is your "Joshua"—the man you are helping to be all God wants him to be?

10. What was the highlight of this course for you? How well did your group meet the objectives you set for being a men's accountability group? What are your plans for continuing to meet and/or to hold each other accountable?

1–8)? How does their everyday regularity help to maintain fellowship with God? What work would all this create for the priests to oversee? **2.** Of what importance do you think monthly offerings were to Israel? To God? Who do you think they were primarily aimed at? **3.** What event does the Passover commemorate (vv. 16–25; see Ex 12:17, 24–28)? Why do you think God wants Israel to celebrate this event after they have entered the land? **4.** What do you make of the 7's (and 14) in this Passover celebration? How will this symbolism complete their faith? **5.** What link does Passover have with the Feast of Unleavened Bread (see Lev 23:4–8)? **6.** For agricultural people, why would the early harvest be crucial? Why do you think God requires this "sacred assembly" after this harvest (v. 26)? **7.** What does it say about God that he gets the "first" of their fruit?

♡ **1.** What serves as a daily reminder of what God has done for you? In what sense are your daily reminders similar to what the Israelites offer daily? **2.** What do these actions do for you? For God? **3.** What special things do you do on Sunday to remind you of what God has done for you? How do these things help to strengthen your relationship with God? **4.** What special, once-a-month religious celebrations do you appreciate most? Why? What benefits do you get from these celebrations? What benefits does God receive? **5.** What does the Passover meal bring to mind for Christians (see 1Co 5:7, where Christ is "our Passover lamb")? What can you do to commemorate Easter in terms of the Exodus? **6.** What "aromatic" things do you do simply to please God for sustaining you? Are you giving him your "firsts" or your "lasts"? Cite an example of each.

tuted at Mount Sinai as a pleasing aroma, an offering made to the LORD by fire. [7]The accompanying drink offering is to be a quarter of a hin of fermented drink with each lamb. Pour out the drink offering to the LORD at the sanctuary. [8]Prepare the second lamb at twilight, along with the same kind of grain offering and drink offering that you prepare in the morning. This is an offering made by fire, an aroma pleasing to the LORD.

Sabbath Offerings

[9]" 'On the Sabbath day, make an offering of two lambs a year old without defect, together with its drink offering and a grain offering of two-tenths of an ephah[a] of fine flour mixed with oil. [10]This is the burnt offering for every Sabbath, in addition to the regular burnt offering and its drink offering.

Monthly Offerings

[11]" 'On the first of every month, present to the LORD a burnt offering of two young bulls, one ram and seven male lambs a year old, all without defect. [12]With each bull there is to be a grain offering of three-tenths of an ephah[b] of fine flour mixed with oil; with the ram, a grain offering of two-tenths of an ephah of fine flour mixed with oil; [13]and with each lamb, a grain offering of a tenth of an ephah of fine flour mixed with oil. This is for a burnt offering, a pleasing aroma, an offering made to the LORD by fire. [14]With each bull there is to be a drink offering of half a hin[c] of wine; with the ram, a third of a hin[d]; and with each lamb, a quarter of a hin. This is the monthly burnt offering to be made at each new moon during the year. [15]Besides the regular burnt offering with its drink offering, one male goat is to be presented to the LORD as a sin offering.

The Passover

[16]" 'On the fourteenth day of the first month the LORD's Passover is to be held. [17]On the fifteenth day of this month there is to be a festival; for seven days eat bread made without yeast. [18]On the first day hold a sacred assembly and do no regular work. [19]Present to the LORD an offering made by fire, a burnt offering of two young bulls, one ram and seven male lambs a year old, all without defect. [20]With each bull prepare a grain offering of three-tenths of an ephah of fine flour mixed with oil; with the ram, two-tenths; [21]and with each of the seven lambs, one-tenth. [22]Include one male goat as a sin offering to make atonement for you. [23]Prepare these in addition to the regular morning burnt offering. [24]In this way prepare the food for the offering made by fire every day for seven days as an aroma pleasing to the LORD; it is to be prepared in addition to the regular burnt offering and its drink offering. [25]On the seventh day hold a sacred assembly and do no regular work.

Feast of Weeks

[26]" 'On the day of firstfruits, when you present to the LORD an offering of new grain during the Feast of Weeks, hold a sacred assembly and do no regular work. [27]Present a burnt offering of two young bulls, one ram and seven male lambs a year old as an aroma pleasing to the LORD. [28]With each bull there is to be a grain offering of three-tenths of an ephah of fine flour mixed with oil; with the

[a]9 That is, probably about 4 quarts (about 4.5 liters); also in verses 12, 20 and 28
[b]12 That is, probably about 6 quarts (about 6.5 liters); also in verses 20 and 28
[c]14 That is, probably about 2 quarts (about 2 liters)   [d]14 That is, probably about 1 1/4 quarts (about 1.2 liters)

ram, two-tenths; [29]and with each of the seven lambs, one-tenth. [30]Include one male goat to make atonement for you. [31]Prepare these together with their drink offerings, in addition to the regular burnt offering and its grain offering. Be sure the animals are without defect.

Feast of Trumpets

29 " 'On the first day of the seventh month hold a sacred assembly and do no regular work. It is a day for you to sound the trumpets. [2]As an aroma pleasing to the LORD, prepare a burnt offering of one young bull, one ram and seven male lambs a year old, all without defect. [3]With the bull prepare a grain offering of three-tenths of an ephah[a] of fine flour mixed with oil; with the ram, two-tenths[b]; [4]and with each of the seven lambs, one-tenth.[c] [5]Include one male goat as a sin offering to make atonement for you. [6]These are in addition to the monthly and daily burnt offerings with their grain offerings and drink offerings as specified. They are offerings made to the LORD by fire—a pleasing aroma.

Day of Atonement

[7]" 'On the tenth day of this seventh month hold a sacred assembly. You must deny yourselves[d] and do no work. [8]Present as an aroma pleasing to the LORD a burnt offering of one young bull, one ram and seven male lambs a year old, all without defect. [9]With the bull prepare a grain offering of three-tenths of an ephah of fine flour mixed with oil; with the ram, two-tenths; [10]and with each of the seven lambs, one-tenth. [11]Include one male goat as a sin offering, in addition to the sin offering for atonement and the regular burnt offering with its grain offering, and their drink offerings.

Feast of Tabernacles

[12]" 'On the fifteenth day of the seventh month, hold a sacred assembly and do no regular work. Celebrate a festival to the LORD for seven days. [13]Present an offering made by fire as an aroma pleasing to the LORD, a burnt offering of thirteen young bulls, two rams and fourteen male lambs a year old, all without defect. [14]With each of the thirteen bulls prepare a grain offering of three-tenths of an ephah of fine flour mixed with oil; with each of the two rams, two-tenths; [15]and with each of the fourteen lambs, one-tenth. [16]Include one male goat as a sin offering, in addition to the regular burnt offering with its grain offering and drink offering.

[17]" 'On the second day prepare twelve young bulls, two rams and fourteen male lambs a year old, all without defect. [18]With the bulls, rams and lambs, prepare their grain offerings and drink offerings according to the number specified. [19]Include one male goat as a sin offering, in addition to the regular burnt offering with its grain offering, and their drink offerings.

[20]" 'On the third day prepare eleven bulls, two rams and fourteen male lambs a year old, all without defect. [21]With the bulls, rams and lambs, prepare their grain offerings and drink offerings according to the number specified. [22]Include one male goat as a sin offering, in addition to the regular burnt offering with its grain offering and drink offering.

[23]" 'On the fourth day prepare ten bulls, two rams and fourteen male lambs a year old, all without defect. [24]With the bulls, rams and lambs, prepare their grain offerings and drink offerings accord-

---

What is your favorite way of spending New Year's Eve? New Year's Day?

1. If these trumpets are blown for God, what praise or action would that spark? Why would trumpets herald the Jewish "New Year's Day" feast? **2.** What purpose does this Day of Atonement serve (see Lev 16:29–34; 23:26–32)? **3.** How has Christ's "work" fulfilled the purpose of this feast day when all others were to "do no work" (see Heb 9:7–15; 10:10; 13:11–12)?

1. What do you use to praise God that serves a similar function to the trumpets here? Why not praise God in this way, now? **2.** Define "atonement." What meaning does this word have in your life? How does at-one-ment affect your relation with God and fellow believers?

---

1. Do you think you could live for a week in a tent? What would you like best about that? What would you like least? Why? **2.** Among your group, see if you can recall all 12 sets of gifts given on "The Twelve Days of Christmas."

1. Where do you suppose this festival gets its name (see Lev 23:33,42–43)? What memories and feelings would be associated with living in "booths"? What would God want Israel to always remember about their wanderings in the wilderness? **2.** What is noteworthy about the ingredients for each sacrifice? About the order of the sacrifices listed here? About the other aspects of this celebration (see Lev 23:39ff)? **3.** What do you think the daily sacrifices would add to the Israelites' celebration of this feast? To their memory of the wilderness wanderings? To the strengthening of their fellowship with God?

1. Given the significance of this feast to Israel, why do you think Jesus chose to reveal himself on the greatest day of this feast (see Jn 7:37–39)? How might

---

[a]3 That is, probably about 6 quarts (about 6.5 liters); also in verses 9 and 14   [b]3 That is, probably about 4 quarts (about 4.5 liters); also in verses 9 and 14   [c]4 That is, probably about 2 quarts (about 2 liters); also in verses 10 and 15   [d]7 Or *must fast*

that account for Peter's reference to "shelters" in his response to Jesus' transfiguration (see Mk 9:5–6)? **2.** When you look back on your life, has God met more often with you during "wilderness" excursions, or at "feast" times? Why do you think that is? **3.** What do you view as *the* wilderness period for you? Why? What was most difficult about this for you? What good came out of this experience? At the time, how did it affect your relationship with others? With God? **4.** As you recall this desert experience, what painful and joyful feelings linger? What do these lasting memories make you want to do, now? Why? How can you use this to strengthen your faith in God? Your service to others?

Did you keep your New Year's resolution of last year? Do you even recall what it was?

1. What complications does the father-daughter relationship pose for the woman wanting to make a vow or being held responsible for it (vv. 3–5)? **2.** What complications does the husband-wife relationship present (vv. 6–8,10–15)? **3.** Who alone is free to be her own agent and why? **4.** Do you think these rules are meant primarily to relieve women, and their fathers and husbands, in case they can't keep their vows? Or to bind them to these oaths? Why? **5.** What does this teach you about the position of women in Israelite culture? How do you feel about that? **6.** Why does God place so much importance on vows? What does this say about God and his promises? About human nature and our promises?

ing to the number specified. 25Include one male goat as a sin offering, in addition to the regular burnt offering with its grain offering and drink offering.

26"'On the fifth day prepare nine bulls, two rams and fourteen male lambs a year old, all without defect. 27With the bulls, rams and lambs, prepare their grain offerings and drink offerings according to the number specified. 28Include one male goat as a sin offering, in addition to the regular burnt offering with its grain offering and drink offering.

29"'On the sixth day prepare eight bulls, two rams and fourteen male lambs a year old, all without defect. 30With the bulls, rams and lambs, prepare their grain offerings and drink offerings according to the number specified. 31Include one male goat as a sin offering, in addition to the regular burnt offering with its grain offering and drink offering.

32"'On the seventh day prepare seven bulls, two rams and fourteen male lambs a year old, all without defect. 33With the bulls, rams and lambs, prepare their grain offerings and drink offerings according to the number specified. 34Include one male goat as a sin offering, in addition to the regular burnt offering with its grain offering and drink offering.

35"'On the eighth day hold an assembly and do no regular work. 36Present an offering made by fire as an aroma pleasing to the LORD, a burnt offering of one bull, one ram and seven male lambs a year old, all without defect. 37With the bull, the ram and the lambs, prepare their grain offerings and drink offerings according to the number specified. 38Include one male goat as a sin offering, in addition to the regular burnt offering with its grain offering and drink offering.

39"'In addition to what you vow and your freewill offerings, prepare these for the LORD at your appointed feasts: your burnt offerings, grain offerings, drink offerings and fellowship offerings.ᵃ'"

40Moses told the Israelites all that the LORD commanded him.

Vows

30 Moses said to the heads of the tribes of Israel: "This is what the LORD commands: 2When a man makes a vow to the LORD or takes an oath to obligate himself by a pledge, he must not break his word but must do everything he said.

3"When a young woman still living in her father's house makes a vow to the LORD or obligates herself by a pledge 4and her father hears about her vow or pledge but says nothing to her, then all her vows and every pledge by which she obligated herself will stand. 5But if her father forbids her when he hears about it, none of her vows or the pledges by which she obligated herself will stand; the LORD will release her because her father has forbidden her.

6"If she marries after she makes a vow or after her lips utter a rash promise by which she obligates herself 7and her husband hears about it but says nothing to her, then her vows or the pledges by which she obligated herself will stand. 8But if her husband forbids her when he hears about it, he nullifies the vow that obligates her or the rash promise by which she obligates herself, and the LORD will release her.

9"Any vow or obligation taken by a widow or divorced woman will be binding on her.

10"If a woman living with her husband makes a vow or obligates

---

ᵃ39 Traditionally *peace offerings*

herself by a pledge under oath ¹¹and her husband hears about it but says nothing to her and does not forbid her, then all her vows or the pledges by which she obligated herself will stand. ¹²But if her husband nullifies them when he hears about them, then none of the vows or pledges that came from her lips will stand. Her husband has nullified them, and the LORD will release her. ¹³Her husband may confirm or nullify any vow she makes or any sworn pledge to deny herself. ¹⁴But if her husband says nothing to her about it from day to day, then he confirms all her vows or the pledges binding on her. He confirms them by saying nothing to her when he hears about them. ¹⁵If, however, he nullifies them some time after he hears about them, then he is responsible for her guilt."

¹⁶These are the regulations the LORD gave Moses concerning relationships between a man and his wife, and between a father and his young daughter still living in his house.

Vengeance on the Midianites

31 The LORD said to Moses, ²"Take vengeance on the Midianites for the Israelites. After that, you will be gathered to your people."

³So Moses said to the people, "Arm some of your men to go to war against the Midianites and to carry out the LORD's vengeance on them. ⁴Send into battle a thousand men from each of the tribes of Israel." ⁵So twelve thousand men armed for battle, a thousand from each tribe, were supplied from the clans of Israel. ⁶Moses sent them into battle, a thousand from each tribe, along with Phinehas son of Eleazar, the priest, who took with him articles from the sanctuary and the trumpets for signaling.

⁷They fought against Midian, as the LORD commanded Moses, and killed every man. ⁸Among their victims were Evi, Rekem, Zur, Hur and Reba—the five kings of Midian. They also killed Balaam son of Beor with the sword. ⁹The Israelites captured the Midianite women and children and took all the Midianite herds, flocks and goods as plunder. ¹⁰They burned all the towns where the Midianites had settled, as well as all their camps. ¹¹They took all the plunder and spoils, including the people and animals, ¹²and brought the captives, spoils and plunder to Moses and Eleazar the priest and the Israelite assembly at their camp on the plains of Moab, by the Jordan across from Jericho.ᵃ

¹³Moses, Eleazar the priest and all the leaders of the community went to meet them outside the camp. ¹⁴Moses was angry with the officers of the army—the commanders of thousands and commanders of hundreds—who returned from the battle.

¹⁵"Have you allowed all the women to live?" he asked them. ¹⁶"They were the ones who followed Balaam's advice and were the means of turning the Israelites away from the LORD in what happened at Peor, so that a plague struck the LORD's people. ¹⁷Now kill all the boys. And kill every woman who has slept with a man, ¹⁸but save for yourselves every girl who has never slept with a man.

¹⁹"All of you who have killed anyone or touched anyone who was killed must stay outside the camp seven days. On the third and seventh days you must purify yourselves and your captives. ²⁰Purify every garment as well as everything made of leather, goat hair or wood."

²¹Then Eleazar the priest said to the soldiers who had gone into battle, "This is the requirement of the law that the LORD gave

---

ᵃ12 Hebrew *Jordan of Jericho*; possibly an ancient name for the Jordan River

1. How would a breach of promise discredit today's banking industry? International relations? Employees? Your spouse and kids? What does this tell you about what holds modern society together? 2. What is the most rash promise you can recall making? What promise have you made lately "with your fingers crossed"? Did you keep either one?

1. What did your mom used to say when you came in from playing outside in wet conditions? Did you ever get in trouble for breaking her rule? How so? 2. As a teen, who was the one who might have influenced you for "evil"? How did you resist his or her advances?

1. What happened at Peor (v. 16; see ch. 25)? What must have been "Balaam's advice"? Does this prove Balaam never was a true prophet? Or only that he backslid since chapters 22–24? Why do you think so? 2. How might the very existence of Midian jeopardize God's plans for Israel? 3. How do you feel about their near annihilation? Why were the virgins spared by Moses, but not the rest (vv. 15–18; see 25:1–4, 16–18)? Do you think the danger they posed to Israel merited their destruction? What clues tell you this is a "holy war"? 4. What do you see as the main reason for the army's purification rites (vv. 19–24): Sanitation? Holy war requirement? Ceremonial purity? 5. Do you think this ceremony would have helped the people view any more seriously their actions? Themselves? Their relationship with God? Why do you think so?

1. What enemies, or threats to God's covenant, do Christians face today? How might their existence jeopardize God's plans for his people? How serious do you feel this threat is? 2. In what situations would you declare "the moral equivalent of war" on this perceived threat? Anything like what Israel did to Midian? How so? 3. For what abuses of this "holy war" principle

are believers (Christians, Moslems, Jews and others) guilty?

☕ **1.** In fighting for what you want, do you get more enjoyment out of *pursuing* your opponent, or *possessing* the victor's spoils? **2.** What does that say about your approach to goal-setting and the attainment of those goals? How do you feel once you attain the goal?

📖 **1.** What need does God have of this booty (vv. 28–30)? What lessons might he be trying to teach Israel by asking for one-fifth of 1 percent of the spoils? How might giving God a share enhance their fellowship with him? **2.** Why do you think God's share was given to Eleazar and the Levites? What does this say about their role in Israel's military success? **3.** Why is the booty shared equally among those who fought on front lines and those who stayed home? What does this say about comparable worth? **4.** Compare the giving of gifts in verses 25–47 with the giving of gifts in verses 48–54. What are the differences? What does it say about these officers that their gifts were unsolicited? How is this similar to the "freewill" offerings in 29:39?

♡ **1.** Which do you think brings greater joy to the Lord and the giver: Giving by assessed quotas, or by voluntary donations? Why are both needed to run the church? **2.** Of what military significance are today's religious leaders and those on the home front? How does that compare with the value ascribed to the Israelites? **3.** How do you share your triumphs in life with God? What "spoils" do you give him? What do you withhold? **4.** "Life is God's gift to you. What you do with that life is your gift to God." Does that fit you? How so?

Moses: 22Gold, silver, bronze, iron, tin, lead 23and anything else that can withstand fire must be put through the fire, and then it will be clean. But it must also be purified with the water of cleansing. And whatever cannot withstand fire must be put through that water. 24On the seventh day wash your clothes and you will be clean. Then you may come into the camp."

Dividing the Spoils

25The LORD said to Moses, 26"You and Eleazar the priest and the family heads of the community are to count all the people and animals that were captured. 27Divide the spoils between the soldiers who took part in the battle and the rest of the community. 28From the soldiers who fought in the battle, set apart as tribute for the LORD one out of every five hundred, whether persons, cattle, donkeys, sheep or goats. 29Take this tribute from their half share and give it to Eleazar the priest as the LORD's part. 30From the Israelites' half, select one out of every fifty, whether persons, cattle, donkeys, sheep, goats or other animals. Give them to the Levites, who are responsible for the care of the LORD's tabernacle." 31So Moses and Eleazar the priest did as the LORD commanded Moses.

32The plunder remaining from the spoils that the soldiers took was 675,000 sheep, 3372,000 cattle, 3461,000 donkeys 35and 32,000 women who had never slept with a man.

36The half share of those who fought in the battle was:

337,500 sheep, 37of which the tribute for the LORD was 675; 3836,000 cattle, of which the tribute for the LORD was 72; 3930,500 donkeys, of which the tribute for the LORD was 61; 4016,000 people, of which the tribute for the LORD was 32.

41Moses gave the tribute to Eleazar the priest as the LORD's part, as the LORD commanded Moses.

42The half belonging to the Israelites, which Moses set apart from that of the fighting men— 43the community's half—was 337,500 sheep, 4436,000 cattle, 4530,500 donkeys 46and 16,000 people. 47From the Israelites' half, Moses selected one out of every fifty persons and animals, as the LORD commanded him, and gave them to the Levites, who were responsible for the care of the LORD's tabernacle.

48Then the officers who were over the units of the army—the commanders of thousands and commanders of hundreds—went to Moses 49and said to him, "Your servants have counted the soldiers under our command, and not one is missing. 50So we have brought as an offering to the LORD the gold articles each of us acquired— armlets, bracelets, signet rings, earrings and necklaces—to make atonement for ourselves before the LORD."

51Moses and Eleazar the priest accepted from them the gold—all the crafted articles. 52All the gold from the commanders of thousands and commanders of hundreds that Moses and Eleazar presented as a gift to the LORD weighed 16,750 shekels.[a] 53Each soldier had taken plunder for himself. 54Moses and Eleazar the priest accepted the gold from the commanders of thousands and commanders of hundreds and brought it into the Tent of Meeting as a memorial for the Israelites before the LORD.

---

a52 That is, about 420 pounds (about 190 kilograms)

The Transjordan Tribes

32 The Reubenites and Gadites, who had very large herds and flocks, saw that the lands of Jazer and Gilead were suitable for livestock. ²So they came to Moses and Eleazar the priest and to the leaders of the community, and said, ³"Ataroth, Dibon, Jazer, Nimrah, Heshbon, Elealeh, Sebam, Nebo and Beon— ⁴the land the Lord subdued before the people of Israel—are suitable for livestock, and your servants have livestock. ⁵If we have found favor in your eyes," they said, "let this land be given to your servants as our possession. Do not make us cross the Jordan."

⁶Moses said to the Gadites and Reubenites, "Shall your countrymen go to war while you sit here? ⁷Why do you discourage the Israelites from going over into the land the Lord has given them? ⁸This is what your fathers did when I sent them from Kadesh Barnea to look over the land. ⁹After they went up to the Valley of Eshcol and viewed the land, they discouraged the Israelites from entering the land the Lord had given them. ¹⁰The Lord's anger was aroused that day and he swore this oath: ¹¹'Because they have not followed me wholeheartedly, not one of the men twenty years old or more who came up out of Egypt will see the land I promised on oath to Abraham, Isaac and Jacob— ¹²not one except Caleb son of Jephunneh the Kenizzite and Joshua son of Nun, for they followed the Lord wholeheartedly.' ¹³The Lord's anger burned against Israel and he made them wander in the desert forty years, until the whole generation of those who had done evil in his sight was gone.

¹⁴"And here you are, a brood of sinners, standing in the place of your fathers and making the Lord even more angry with Israel. ¹⁵If you turn away from following him, he will again leave all this people in the desert, and you will be the cause of their destruction."

¹⁶Then they came up to him and said, "We would like to build pens here for our livestock and cities for our women and children. ¹⁷But we are ready to arm ourselves and go ahead of the Israelites until we have brought them to their place. Meanwhile our women and children will live in fortified cities, for protection from the inhabitants of the land. ¹⁸We will not return to our homes until every Israelite has received his inheritance. ¹⁹We will not receive any inheritance with them on the other side of the Jordan, because our inheritance has come to us on the east side of the Jordan."

²⁰Then Moses said to them, "If you will do this—if you will arm yourselves before the Lord for battle, ²¹and if all of you will go armed over the Jordan before the Lord until he has driven his enemies out before him— ²²then when the land is subdued before the Lord, you may return and be free from your obligation to the Lord and to Israel. And this land will be your possession before the Lord.

²³"But if you fail to do this, you will be sinning against the Lord; and you may be sure that your sin will find you out. ²⁴Build cities for your women and children, and pens for your flocks, but do what you have promised."

²⁵The Gadites and Reubenites said to Moses, "We your servants will do as our lord commands. ²⁶Our children and wives, our flocks and herds will remain here in the cities of Gilead. ²⁷But your servants, every man armed for battle, will cross over to fight before the Lord, just as our lord says."

²⁸Then Moses gave orders about them to Eleazar the priest and Joshua son of Nun and to the family heads of the Israelite tribes. ²⁹He said to them, "If the Gadites and Reubenites, every man armed for battle, cross over the Jordan with you before the Lord,

1. Which of you or your siblings was the first to move away from home? How did the rest of the family feel about this? How did you feel? 2. Which family member lives farthest from you? How does this affect your kinship? What do you do on a regular basis that keeps you in touch? What special event has brought you all together as never before or since?

1. Locate the lands of Gilead and Jazer on a Bible map. Although there would not be a great physical distance between the tribes, what obstacles do you imagine they would confront crossing the deep Jordan Valley? How would this affect communication between tribes on either side of this great divide? 2. With less communication, how is this likely to affect kinship between tribes? What external dangers does this pose for Israel? Which of these dangers does Moses address in his speech (vv. 6–15)? 3. Do you think Moses is justified in his concerns (for personal honesty, wholehearted commitment, mutiny in the ranks, mustering enough troops, sharing in the promise)? Why or why not? 4. What affect do you think the compromise offer made by the Reubenites and Gadites (vv. 16–19) would have on the relationship between all the tribes? 5. Do you think this offer appeases Moses? Why or why not? When it is not their land, cities, wives, children or herds they are fighting for, how will Moses know whether the tribes east of the Jordan will be effective fighters for their fellow tribes (vv. 20–24)? 6. What repeated assurances do the Gadites and Reubenites give? How does Moses bind them to their word? 7. How green does the grass prove to be on this "other side" (vv. 33–42)?

1. Today, what natural and spiritual barriers to unity exist between isolated *believers*? What dangers are there for lone-wolf Christians? What would you do to break this isolation and bring people together? 2. In what ways are *churches* isolated from one another? What dangers are there in such prolonged isolation? 3. What would you do to bridge the divide and build trust? How willing are you to go to bat for someone else when it's not your turf at stake? How is your proposal like the one made in verses 16–19? 4. Are you, your small group or your church isolated

and going it alone? How so? What problems is this causing you? What will you do this week to begin breaking this isolation?

then when the land is subdued before you, give them the land of Gilead as their possession. 30But if they do not cross over with you armed, they must accept their possession with you in Canaan."

31The Gadites and Reubenites answered, "Your servants will do what the LORD has said. 32We will cross over before the LORD into Canaan armed, but the property we inherit will be on this side of the Jordan."

33Then Moses gave to the Gadites, the Reubenites and the half-tribe of Manasseh son of Joseph the kingdom of Sihon king of the Amorites and the kingdom of Og king of Bashan—the whole land with its cities and the territory around them.

34The Gadites built up Dibon, Ataroth, Aroer, 35Atroth Shophan, Jazer, Jogbehah, 36Beth Nimrah and Beth Haran as fortified cities, and built pens for their flocks. 37And the Reubenites rebuilt Heshbon, Elealeh and Kiriathaim, 38as well as Nebo and Baal Meon (these names were changed) and Sibmah. They gave names to the cities they rebuilt.

39The descendants of Makir son of Manasseh went to Gilead, captured it and drove out the Amorites who were there. 40So Moses gave Gilead to the Makirites, the descendants of Manasseh, and they settled there. 41Jair, a descendant of Manasseh, captured their settlements and called them Havvoth Jair.a 42And Nobah captured Kenath and its surrounding settlements and called it Nobah after himself.

Stages in Israel's Journey

33 Here are the stages in the journey of the Israelites when they came out of Egypt by divisions under the leadership of Moses and Aaron. 2At the LORD's command Moses recorded the stages in their journey. This is their journey by stages:

3The Israelites set out from Rameses on the fifteenth day of the first month, the day after the Passover. They marched out boldly in full view of all the Egyptians, 4who were burying all their firstborn, whom the LORD had struck down among them; for the LORD had brought judgment on their gods.

5The Israelites left Rameses and camped at Succoth.

6They left Succoth and camped at Etham, on the edge of the desert.

7They left Etham, turned back to Pi Hahiroth, to the east of Baal Zephon, and camped near Migdol.

8They left Pi Hahirothb and passed through the sea into the desert, and when they had traveled for three days in the Desert of Etham, they camped at Marah.

9They left Marah and went to Elim, where there were twelve springs and seventy palm trees, and they camped there.

10They left Elim and camped by the Red Sea.c

11They left the Red Sea and camped in the Desert of Sin.

12They left the Desert of Sin and camped at Dophkah.

13They left Dophkah and camped at Alush.

14They left Alush and camped at Rephidim, where there was no water for the people to drink.

15They left Rephidim and camped in the Desert of Sinai.

16They left the Desert of Sinai and camped at Kibroth Hatta-avah.

1. What trip in your life took you the farthest from home in terms of miles travelled or time away? 2. What unforgettable event on this trip was captured for all time in your notebook or photo album? 3. In your travels around the country, how many states or provinces have you been to? Who in your group has been to the most?

1. What have we here: (a) Moses' diary? (b) Missionary slide show? (c) Archeologist's hidden treasure map? (d) Tourist's guide to the "Top 40" hot spots to visit next time you are in the Sinai Peninsula? (e) Other? Why do you think so? 2. Of the men now preparing to enter the promised land, how many had experienced firsthand the Exodus from Egypt (see 32:11–13)? How might this affect their view of the task ahead of them? And their trust in God's power? 3. Of these stages in Israel's journey, which ones do you recognize from your previous reading? How many are obscure to you? What happened at the sites you recognize? Can you see the parched Israelites with that hang-dog look, perpetually searching for water (vv. 8,9,14,36,48)? 4. What impression does this listing give you of the twists and turns in their journey? How might a list like this help those who had not actually experienced the early parts of the journey? How might it affect their

a41 Or *them the settlements of Jair*   b8 Many manuscripts of the Masoretic Text, Samaritan Pentateuch and Vulgate; most manuscripts of the Masoretic Text *left from before Hahiroth*   c10 Hebrew *Yam Suph*; that is, Sea of Reeds; also in verse 11

17They left Kibroth Hattaavah and camped at Hazeroth.
18They left Hazeroth and camped at Rithmah.
19They left Rithmah and camped at Rimmon Perez.
20They left Rimmon Perez and camped at Libnah.
21They left Libnah and camped at Rissah.
22They left Rissah and camped at Kehelathah.
23They left Kehelathah and camped at Mount Shepher.
24They left Mount Shepher and camped at Haradah.
25They left Haradah and camped at Makheloth.
26They left Makheloth and camped at Tahath.
27They left Tahath and camped at Terah.
28They left Terah and camped at Mithcah.
29They left Mithcah and camped at Hashmonah.
30They left Hashmonah and camped at Moseroth.
31They left Moseroth and camped at Bene Jaakan.
32They left Bene Jaakan and camped at Hor Haggidgad.
33They left Hor Haggidgad and camped at Jotbathah.
34They left Jotbathah and camped at Abronah.
35They left Abronah and camped at Ezion Geber.
36They left Ezion Geber and camped at Kadesh, in the Desert of Zin.
37They left Kadesh and camped at Mount Hor, on the border of Edom. 38At the LORD's command Aaron the priest went up Mount Hor, where he died on the first day of the fifth month of the fortieth year after the Israelites came out of Egypt. 39Aaron was a hundred and twenty-three years old when he died on Mount Hor.
40The Canaanite king of Arad, who lived in the Negev of Canaan, heard that the Israelites were coming.
41They left Mount Hor and camped at Zalmonah.
42They left Zalmonah and camped at Punon.
43They left Punon and camped at Oboth.
44They left Oboth and camped at Iye Abarim, on the border of Moab.
45They left Iyim*a* and camped at Dibon Gad.
46They left Dibon Gad and camped at Almon Diblathaim.
47They left Almon Diblathaim and camped in the mountains of Abarim, near Nebo.
48They left the mountains of Abarim and camped on the plains of Moab by the Jordan across from Jericho.*b* 49There on the plains of Moab they camped along the Jordan from Beth Jeshimoth to Abel Shittim.

50On the plains of Moab by the Jordan across from Jericho the LORD said to Moses, 51"Speak to the Israelites and say to them: 'When you cross the Jordan into Canaan, 52drive out all the inhabitants of the land before you. Destroy all their carved images and their cast idols, and demolish all their high places. 53Take possession of the land and settle in it, for I have given you the land to possess. 54Distribute the land by lot, according to your clans. To a larger group give a larger inheritance, and to a smaller group a smaller one. Whatever falls to them by lot will be theirs. Distribute it according to your ancestral tribes.

55" 'But if you do not drive out the inhabitants of the land, those you allow to remain will become barbs in your eyes and thorns in your sides. They will give you trouble in the land where you will live. 56And then I will do to you what I plan to do to them.' "

a45 That is, Iye Abarim   *b48* Hebrew *Jordan of Jericho;* possibly an ancient name for the Jordan River; also in verse 50

belief in the reality of God's power? 5. Why do you think God is so concerned about the people whom the Israelites will displace (vv. 50–56)? How would driving them out of the land solve this problem? What does this teach you about God's concern for the people and land of his covenant?

♥ 1. What parallels do you see in the Exodus and Wilderness experience of the Israelites as compared with the pilgrimage of many who come to faith in Christ today? 2. Of what importance is ancient Israel's story to your own faith? How does their documented journey enhance your faith in the power of God? 3. What would you add to this list from your own journey with God? When has God "parted the waters" for you? When has he helped you to find "water from a rock"? When has he helped a "grasshopper" like you face "giants in the land"? When has he led you out of your desert wanderings to the brink of some Jordan River? 4. It would build up the faith of your small group and your descendants for them to hear the stages of your journey. Why not recount your faith story for their benefit this week? With whom will you begin?

1. As a child, what were your territorial boundaries? How far could you go before you were "off limits" or "out of bounds"? How large did this "home turf" seem to you? 2. How have your boundaries changed over the years? How far does your present "home turf" extend before you start feeling like a "stranger in a strange land"?

1. What sort of transporting, organizing and authority problems would face the Israelites as they took possession of the land? What tribal feuds might break out as a result? How might these problems affect their relationship with God? What affect would this have on their chances for success over the Canaanites? 2. What three steps are taken here to lessen these problems (vv. 1–12, 13–15, and 16–29)? What specific problems are each of these steps aimed at? 3. How would a strategy of defined boundaries, parceled out by lot, and implemented by chosen leaders, help to alleviate these problems and improve their chances for success?

1. What administrative problems face your church as you seek to enter the next growth stage God wills? In what sense are your problems like the problems faced by Israel as they entered the land? 2. How do these problems affect fellowship and factions within the church? Likewise, the mission of the church? 3. Which of these problems do you think is the most serious? Why? What could your small group do to help alleviate this problem: (a) Define parameters? (b) Assign responsibility? (c) Use available leadership? (d) Train new leaders? 4. What will you do this week to begin working on this problem?

Boundaries of Canaan

34 The LORD said to Moses, [2]"Command the Israelites and say to them: 'When you enter Canaan, the land that will be allotted to you as an inheritance will have these boundaries:

[3]" 'Your southern side will include some of the Desert of Zin along the border of Edom. On the east, your southern boundary will start from the end of the Salt Sea,[a] [4]cross south of Scorpion[b] Pass, continue on to Zin and go south of Kadesh Barnea. Then it will go to Hazar Addar and over to Azmon, [5]where it will turn, join the Wadi of Egypt and end at the Sea.[c]

[6]" 'Your western boundary will be the coast of the Great Sea. This will be your boundary on the west.

[7]" 'For your northern boundary, run a line from the Great Sea to Mount Hor [8]and from Mount Hor to Lebo[d] Hamath. Then the boundary will go to Zedad, [9]continue to Ziphron and end at Hazar Enan. This will be your boundary on the north.

[10]" 'For your eastern boundary, run a line from Hazar Enan to Shepham. [11]The boundary will go down from Shepham to Riblah on the east side of Ain and continue along the slopes east of the Sea of Kinnereth.[e] [12]Then the boundary will go down along the Jordan and end at the Salt Sea.

" 'This will be your land, with its boundaries on every side.' "

[13]Moses commanded the Israelites: "Assign this land by lot as an inheritance. The LORD has ordered that it be given to the nine and a half tribes, [14]because the families of the tribe of Reuben, the tribe of Gad and the half-tribe of Manasseh have received their inheritance. [15]These two and a half tribes have received their inheritance on the east side of the Jordan of Jericho,[f] toward the sunrise."

[16]The LORD said to Moses, [17]"These are the names of the men who are to assign the land for you as an inheritance: Eleazar the priest and Joshua son of Nun. [18]And appoint one leader from each tribe to help assign the land. [19]These are their names:

Caleb son of Jephunneh,
    from the tribe of Judah;
[20]Shemuel son of Ammihud,
    from the tribe of Simeon;
[21]Elidad son of Kislon,
    from the tribe of Benjamin;
[22]Bukki son of Jogli,
    the leader from the tribe of Dan;
[23]Hanniel son of Ephod,
    the leader from the tribe of Manasseh son of Joseph;
[24]Kemuel son of Shiphtan,
    the leader from the tribe of Ephraim son of Joseph;
[25]Elizaphan son of Parnach,
    the leader from the tribe of Zebulun;
[26]Paltiel son of Azzan,
    the leader from the tribe of Issachar;
[27]Ahihud son of Shelomi,
    the leader from the tribe of Asher;
[28]Pedahel son of Ammihud,
    the leader from the tribe of Naphtali."

[29]These are the men the LORD commanded to assign the inheritance to the Israelites in the land of Canaan.

---

a3 That is, the Dead Sea; also in verse 12   b4 Hebrew *Akrabbim*   c5 That is, the Mediterranean; also in verses 6 and 7   d8 Or *to the entrance to*   e11 That is, Galilee   f15 *Jordan of Jericho* was possibly an ancient name for the Jordan River.

Towns for the Levites

35 On the plains of Moab by the Jordan across from Jericho,[a] the LORD said to Moses, [2]"Command the Israelites to give the Levites towns to live in from the inheritance the Israelites will possess. And give them pasturelands around the towns. [3]Then they will have towns to live in and pasturelands for their cattle, flocks and all their other livestock.

[4]"The pasturelands around the towns that you give the Levites will extend out fifteen hundred feet[b] from the town wall. [5]Outside the town, measure three thousand feet[c] on the east side, three thousand on the south side, three thousand on the west and three thousand on the north, with the town in the center. They will have this area as pastureland for the towns.

Cities of Refuge

[6]"Six of the towns you give the Levites will be cities of refuge, to which a person who has killed someone may flee. In addition, give them forty-two other towns. [7]In all you must give the Levites forty-eight towns, together with their pasturelands. [8]The towns you give the Levites from the land the Israelites possess are to be given in proportion to the inheritance of each tribe: Take many towns from a tribe that has many, but few from one that has few."

[9]Then the LORD said to Moses: [10]"Speak to the Israelites and say to them: 'When you cross the Jordan into Canaan, [11]select some towns to be your cities of refuge, to which a person who has killed someone accidentally may flee. [12]They will be places of refuge from the avenger, so that a person accused of murder may not die before he stands trial before the assembly. [13]These six towns you give will be your cities of refuge. [14]Give three on this side of the Jordan and three in Canaan as cities of refuge. [15]These six towns will be a place of refuge for Israelites, aliens and any other people living among them, so that anyone who has killed another accidentally can flee there.

[16]"'If a man strikes someone with an iron object so that he dies, he is a murderer; the murderer shall be put to death. [17]Or if anyone has a stone in his hand that could kill, and he strikes someone so that he dies, he is a murderer; the murderer shall be put to death. [18]Or if anyone has a wooden object in his hand that could kill, and he hits someone so that he dies, he is a murderer; the murderer shall be put to death. [19]The avenger of blood shall put the murderer to death; when he meets him, he shall put him to death. [20]If anyone with malice aforethought shoves another or throws something at him intentionally so that he dies [21]or if in hostility he hits him with his fist so that he dies, that person shall be put to death; he is a murderer. The avenger of blood shall put the murderer to death when he meets him.

[22]"'But if without hostility someone suddenly shoves another or throws something at him unintentionally [23]or, without seeing him, drops a stone on him that could kill him, and he dies, then since he was not his enemy and he did not intend to harm him, [24]the assembly must judge between him and the avenger of blood according to these regulations. [25]The assembly must protect the one accused of murder from the avenger of blood and send him back to the city of refuge to which he fled. He must stay there until the death of the high priest, who was anointed with the holy oil.

[26]"'But if the accused ever goes outside the limits of the city of

---

[a1] Hebrew *Jordan of Jericho*; possibly an ancient name for the Jordan River
[b4] Hebrew *a thousand cubits* (about 450 meters)   [c5] Hebrew *two thousand cubits* (about 900 meters)

1. As a child, did you ever run away from home? Where did you go? Why there? 2. What experience have you had with an overseas embassy? With political asylum? Refugees? 3. Where you work and live, where do people go to get away from the boss or the parent with an "axe to grind"?

1. With duties that kept them on the go, how would the landless Levites manage to live in dispersed towns (vv. 1–5; see Jos 21, for how this was actually done)? 2. Secure as their own tribal unit, but scattered among the people, how would this affect their job performance? 3. What is Israel's legal definition of murder (vv. 16–21)? How does this compare with their definition of accidental death (vv. 22–24)? Why would it be important to establish these definitions before entering the land? 4. Who was the "avenger of blood" (see Lev 24:17; also Ru 3:9, where this word is translated "kinsman-redeemer")? How would you explain to someone unfamiliar with the Bible what is the duty of the injured party's nearest kin? 5. Under certain circumstances, might it be legal for the avenger to kill the accused, even in the case of accidental death, without incurring any guilt himself (v. 27)? What does this tell you about the strength of kinship ties in this society? 6. Given these legal definitions and the practice of blood vengeance in ancient Israel, how necessary were the cities of refuge? How would you describe their function: (a) Safety for criminals awaiting trial? (b) Time for relationships to heal? (c) Interruption of the vicious life-for-life principle? (d) Other? 7. Re-read this passage and plot the actions which would occur in the case of an accidental death and in the case of murder. In this sequence, do such laws allow *justice* to be served? Or do they delay, even deny, justice in favor of *mercy*? Why do you think so?

1. In what ways are your Christian duties like those of the Levites? Do you think these duties are best done in isolation? Or out in the "real world"? Is that true for all believers? Why? 2. If commissioned to create a feature film based on the cities of refuge passage, what would you entitle the film? Who would you cast in the various parts? Which character would be the hero in your film: (a) The accused? (b) The mayor of the

city of refuge? (c) The blood avenger? (d) The victim or martyr? What does your casting reveal about your understanding of this passage? **3.** Have you ever been accidentally hurt by a friend? How serious was this? How did this situation make you feel? How did it affect your friendship? **4.** When you have conflicts with other Christians, how do you resolve them, short of killing them? How might a "city of refuge" help you to subdue your desire for revenge?

Is there an heirloom in your family that gets passed down from generation to generation? Who gets it and why?

1. If this were a letter, then 36:5–9 would be the "P.S." to 27:1–11. When the question of Zelophehad's daughters is first raised, what is the main concern of this clan? What new concern is raised here to address the loophole left in the chapter 27 regulations? **2.** What does this appendix tell you about the overriding importance of tribal and clan unity for the Israelites? How will this emphasis help them as they settle the land and settle their differences?

1. What distinguishes a "connectional" (Presbyterian-type) church from an "independent" (Baptist-type) fellowship? How do each of these values affect a church's mission? What's the fine line between these two? **2.** What are some signs that a church has moved from unity to isolation? If this is your situation, how would Moses' case law apply, so as to encourage your church to remain connected and not isolated? **3.** Before you go your separate ways, celebrate the group unity that God has given you in your sharing or reliving the desert wanderings with Moses and the mob of Israelites.

refuge to which he has fled ²⁷and the avenger of blood finds him outside the city, the avenger of blood may kill the accused without being guilty of murder. ²⁸The accused must stay in his city of refuge until the death of the high priest; only after the death of the high priest may he return to his own property.

²⁹"'These are to be legal requirements for you throughout the generations to come, wherever you live.

³⁰"'Anyone who kills a person is to be put to death as a murderer only on the testimony of witnesses. But no one is to be put to death on the testimony of only one witness.

³¹"'Do not accept a ransom for the life of a murderer, who deserves to die. He must surely be put to death.

³²"'Do not accept a ransom for anyone who has fled to a city of refuge and so allow him to go back and live on his own land before the death of the high priest.

³³"'Do not pollute the land where you are. Bloodshed pollutes the land, and atonement cannot be made for the land on which blood has been shed, except by the blood of the one who shed it. ³⁴Do not defile the land where you live and where I dwell, for I, the LORD, dwell among the Israelites.'"

Inheritance of Zelophehad's Daughters

36 The family heads of the clan of Gilead son of Makir, the son of Manasseh, who were from the clans of the descendants of Joseph, came and spoke before Moses and the leaders, the heads of the Israelite families. ²They said, "When the LORD commanded my lord to give the land as an inheritance to the Israelites by lot, he ordered you to give the inheritance of our brother Zelophehad to his daughters. ³Now suppose they marry men from other Israelite tribes; then their inheritance will be taken from our ancestral inheritance and added to that of the tribe they marry into. And so part of the inheritance allotted to us will be taken away. ⁴When the Year of Jubilee for the Israelites comes, their inheritance will be added to that of the tribe into which they marry, and their property will be taken from the tribal inheritance of our forefathers."

⁵Then at the LORD's command Moses gave this order to the Israelites: "What the tribe of the descendants of Joseph is saying is right. ⁶This is what the LORD commands for Zelophehad's daughters: They may marry anyone they please as long as they marry within the tribal clan of their father. ⁷No inheritance in Israel is to pass from tribe to tribe, for every Israelite shall keep the tribal land inherited from his forefathers. ⁸Every daughter who inherits land in any Israelite tribe must marry someone in her father's tribal clan, so that every Israelite will possess the inheritance of his fathers. ⁹No inheritance may pass from tribe to tribe, for each Israelite tribe is to keep the land it inherits."

¹⁰So Zelophehad's daughters did as the LORD commanded Moses. ¹¹Zelophehad's daughters—Mahlah, Tirzah, Hoglah, Milcah and Noah—married their cousins on their father's side. ¹²They married within the clans of the descendants of Manasseh son of Joseph, and their inheritance remained in their father's clan and tribe.

¹³These are the commands and regulations the LORD gave through Moses to the Israelites on the plains of Moab by the Jordan across from Jericho.ᵃ

---

a 13 Hebrew *Jordan of Jericho;* possibly an ancient name for the Jordan River

INTRODUCTION to
DEUTERONOMY

Book Study Outline: If you are using Deuteronomy for a study course, here is a 7- or 13-week outline. Use the questions in the margin for your group agenda:

🥤 start meeting / 15 min.

📖 read & discuss Bible / 30 min.

♡ close meeting / 15–45 min.

Refer to the Questions and Answers in the front of this Bible for more information.

7-week plan	13-week plan	Personal Reading	Group Study Passage
1	1	1:1–2:37	1:19–46/Review of Rebellion
	2	3:1–4:43	4:1–14/Obedience Commanded
2	3	4:44–5:33	5:1–33/Ten Commandments
	4	6:1–25	6:1–25/Great Commandment
3	5	7:1–9:29	8:1–20/Do Not Forget the Lord
	6	10:1–11:32	11:1–32/Love and Obey God
4	7	12:1–17:7	13:1–18/Following Other Gods
	8	17:8–21:21	19:1–19/Cities of Refuge
5	9	21:22–26:19	23:1–25:19/Various Laws
	10	27:1–28:68	28:15–68/Various Curses
6	11	29:1–30:20	30:11–20/Life or Death
	12	31:1–32:43	31:30–32:43/Song of Moses
7	13	32:44–34:12	34:1–12/Death of Moses

Author: Moses is assumed to be the author and editor of most of the first five books of the OT (the Pentateuch).

Date: It is difficult to assign a firm date to the composition of the Pentateuch. Conservative estimates place it in either the fifteenth or thirteenth century B.C., depending on when the Exodus occurred.

Theme: God's covenant and Moses' personal plea with Israel.

Historical Background: The events of this book take place on the plains of Moab as the Israelites are poised to enter the promised land. Moses oversees the important task of transferring his leadership to Joshua. He gives his final instructions to the people. The book ends with his death.

Characteristics: Arranged around three sermons given by Moses (1:1–4:43; 4:44–26:19; 29:1–32:47), Deuteronomy introduces the reader to the great theological themes of Judaism. Hence, we read of a God who acts in history for the redemption of his elect; we confront the Israelite concepts of sin, punishment and reward; and we are introduced to the essential creed of Judaism, "Hear, O Israel: the Lord our God, the Lord is one" (6:4). Behind these themes, and binding them together, is the covenant between God and Israel. It is this covenant which provides the driving force of the message of Deuteronomy, leaving no doubt as to the responsibilities, rewards and punishments inherent in the covenant. Deuteronomy's spiritual emphasis and its call to total commitment to the Lord in worship and obedience inspired references to its message throughout the rest of Scripture.

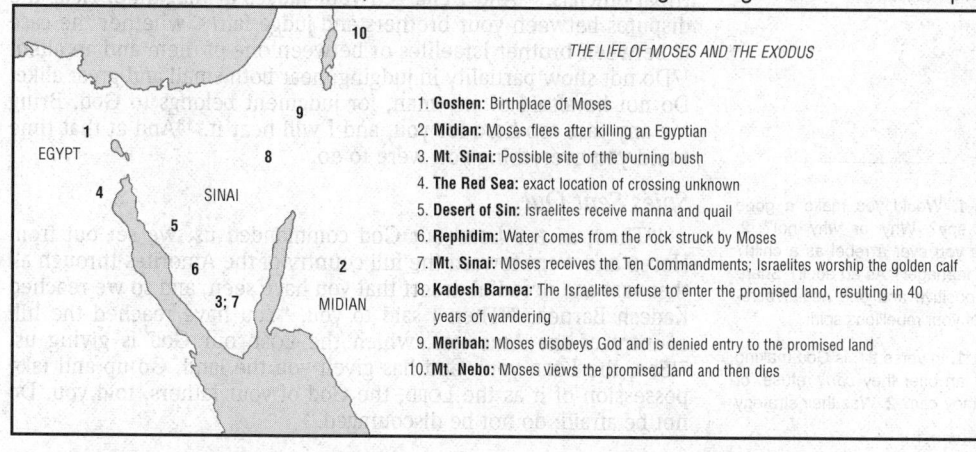

THE LIFE OF MOSES AND THE EXODUS

1. **Goshen:** Birthplace of Moses
2. **Midian:** Moses flees after killing an Egyptian
3. **Mt. Sinai:** Possible site of the burning bush
4. **The Red Sea:** exact location of crossing unknown
5. **Desert of Sin:** Israelites receive manna and quail
6. **Rephidim:** Water comes from the rock struck by Moses
7. **Mt. Sinai:** Moses receives the Ten Commandments; Israelites worship the golden calf
8. **Kadesh Barnea:** The Israelites refuse to enter the promised land, resulting in 40 years of wandering
9. **Meribah:** Moses disobeys God and is denied entry to the promised land
10. **Mt. Nebo:** Moses views the promised land and then dies

Deuteronomy

The Command to Leave Horeb

☕ 1. Where on earth is your idea of the "promised land"? 2. Do you daydream more about the past or the future? Share a recent daydream. 3. On trips, do you like being in the driver's seat (taking directions) or the back seat (giving them)? What recent "misadventure" proves your point?

📖 1. Where are they encamped? What "time" is it? Why is that significant (see Nu 14:33–34; 21:21–26)? 2. Where are they to go? To do what? Why? 3. Consult a map of this period. How could the God of Israel expect desert nomads to take possession of all that? 4. Why is Moses eager to share leadership (vv. 9–18)? 5. What's the wisdom of his proposal? 6. Who qualified to be a judge? Whose justice did they represent? 7. In what sense is Moses' job now both lighter and heavier? How will this help the Israelites as they enter the promised land?

♥ 1. Who has been like a Moses to you, reminding you of God's faithfulness (past and future)? 2. Is it time for you to move on in your spiritual journey? Where to? With whom? What for? What is your next step? What has prepared you so far for this? 3. What "shared ministry" model do you see here that might apply to your church's small group ministry? 4. For what counsel might your peers look to you? In turn, where do you find justice?

☕ 1. Would you make a good spy? Why or why not? 2. Were you ever a rebel as a child? As a teenager? As an adult? Share one positive and one negative result of your rebellious spirit.

📖 1. In verse 21, is God making an offer they *can't* refuse, or one they *can*? 2. Was their strategy

1 These are the words Moses spoke to all Israel in the desert east of the Jordan—that is, in the Arabah—opposite Suph, between Paran and Tophel, Laban, Hazeroth and Dizahab. ²(It takes eleven days to go from Horeb to Kadesh Barnea by the Mount Seir road.)

³In the fortieth year, on the first day of the eleventh month, Moses proclaimed to the Israelites all that the LORD had commanded him concerning them. ⁴This was after he had defeated Sihon king of the Amorites, who reigned in Heshbon, and at Edrei had defeated Og king of Bashan, who reigned in Ashtaroth.

⁵East of the Jordan in the territory of Moab, Moses began to expound this law, saying:

⁶The LORD our God said to us at Horeb, "You have stayed long enough at this mountain. ⁷Break camp and advance into the hill country of the Amorites; go to all the neighboring peoples in the Arabah, in the mountains, in the western foothills, in the Negev and along the coast, to the land of the Canaanites and to Lebanon, as far as the great river, the Euphrates. ⁸See, I have given you this land. Go in and take possession of the land that the LORD swore he would give to your fathers—to Abraham, Isaac and Jacob—and to their descendants after them."

The Appointment of Leaders

⁹At that time I said to you, "You are too heavy a burden for me to carry alone. ¹⁰The LORD your God has increased your numbers so that today you are as many as the stars in the sky. ¹¹May the LORD, the God of your fathers, increase you a thousand times and bless you as he has promised! ¹²But how can I bear your problems and your burdens and your disputes all by myself? ¹³Choose some wise, understanding and respected men from each of your tribes, and I will set them over you."

¹⁴You answered me, "What you propose to do is good."

¹⁵So I took the leading men of your tribes, wise and respected men, and appointed them to have authority over you—as commanders of thousands, of hundreds, of fifties and of tens and as tribal officials. ¹⁶And I charged your judges at that time: Hear the disputes between your brothers and judge fairly, whether the case is between brother Israelites or between one of them and an alien. ¹⁷Do not show partiality in judging; hear both small and great alike. Do not be afraid of any man, for judgment belongs to God. Bring me any case too hard for you, and I will hear it. ¹⁸And at that time I told you everything you were to do.

Spies Sent Out

¹⁹Then, as the LORD our God commanded us, we set out from Horeb and went toward the hill country of the Amorites through all that vast and dreadful desert that you have seen, and so we reached Kadesh Barnea. ²⁰Then I said to you, "You have reached the hill country of the Amorites, which the LORD our God is giving us. ²¹See, the LORD your God has given you the land. Go up and take possession of it as the LORD, the God of your fathers, told you. Do not be afraid; do not be discouraged."

²²Then all of you came to me and said, "Let us send men ahead to spy out the land for us and bring back a report about the route we are to take and the towns we will come to."

²³The idea seemed good to me; so I selected twelve of you, one man from each tribe. ²⁴They left and went up into the hill country, and came to the Valley of Eshcol and explored it. ²⁵Taking with them some of the fruit of the land, they brought it down to us and reported, "It is a good land that the LORD our God is giving us."

Rebellion Against the LORD

²⁶But you were unwilling to go up; you rebelled against the command of the LORD your God. ²⁷You grumbled in your tents and said, "The LORD hates us; so he brought us out of Egypt to deliver us into the hands of the Amorites to destroy us. ²⁸Where can we go? Our brothers have made us lose heart. They say, 'The people are stronger and taller than we are; the cities are large, with walls up to the sky. We even saw the Anakites there.'"

²⁹Then I said to you, "Do not be terrified; do not be afraid of them. ³⁰The LORD your God, who is going before you, will fight for you, as he did for you in Egypt, before your very eyes, ³¹and in the desert. There you saw how the LORD your God carried you, as a father carries his son, all the way you went until you reached this place."

³²In spite of this, you did not trust in the LORD your God, ³³who went ahead of you on your journey, in fire by night and in a cloud by day, to search out places for you to camp and to show you the way you should go.

³⁴When the LORD heard what you said, he was angry and solemnly swore: ³⁵"Not a man of this evil generation shall see the good land I swore to give your forefathers, ³⁶except Caleb son of Jephunneh. He will see it, and I will give him and his descendants the land he set his feet on, because he followed the LORD wholeheartedly."

³⁷Because of you the LORD became angry with me also and said, "You shall not enter it, either. ³⁸But your assistant, Joshua son of Nun, will enter it. Encourage him, because he will lead Israel to inherit it. ³⁹And the little ones that you said would be taken captive, your children who do not yet know good from bad—they will enter the land. I will give it to them and they will take possession of it. ⁴⁰But as for you, turn around and set out toward the desert along the route to the Red Sea.ᵃ"

⁴¹Then you replied, "We have sinned against the LORD. We will go up and fight, as the LORD our God commanded us." So every one of you put on his weapons, thinking it easy to go up into the hill country.

⁴²But the LORD said to me, "Tell them, 'Do not go up and fight, because I will not be with you. You will be defeated by your enemies.'"

⁴³So I told you, but you would not listen. You rebelled against the LORD's command and in your arrogance you marched up into the hill country. ⁴⁴The Amorites who lived in those hills came out against you; they chased you like a swarm of bees and beat you down from Seir all the way to Hormah. ⁴⁵You came back and wept before the LORD, but he paid no attention to your weeping and turned a deaf ear to you. ⁴⁶And so you stayed in Kadesh many days—all the time you spent there.

ᵃ40 Hebrew *Yam Suph*; that is, Sea of Reeds

---

in verse 22 borne out of fear or faith? Head or heart? Wisdom or folly? **3.** Can you fill in the details of the spy mission (see Nu 13–14)? **4.** Why didn't Israel take the land (vv. 26–28)? Are their fears valid? Why or why not? **5.** How did the Lord address the real issue (vv. 29–33)? How does he build his case? With what images? Toward what end? **6.** Why is the Lord so angry, even with Moses? Why does he make an exception of Caleb and Joshua (vv. 36,38)? **7.** What punishment is meted out to everyone else (vv. 35–40)? What about that seems fair? Unfair? Merciful? Harsh? **8.** What response does this punishment elicit: (a) Repentance? (b) True grit? (c) Bravado? (d) Presumptuous faith? (e) Stubbornness? (f) Controlling behavior? Explain. **9.** Why does God respond as he does (v. 42)? **10.** What must Israel still learn about God before they re-enter the land? How would remembering this history lesson from Moses help them to learn this?

1. Spying might be a delaying tactic. How do you try to confirm God's will rather than do it? Are your eyes of faith bigger than your stomach of fear? How so? **2.** God carried Israel as a father carries a son (v. 31). What do you recall about your father "carrying you"? Did that help or hinder your learning to trust God's love? How so? **3.** What "frightening" thing have you attempted for God? Did fear get the best of you? Or did he calm your fears? How? **4.** What "miraculous" thing has he done for you? What impact has that had on your faith? On your family's faith?

1. What's the longest you have ever lived out of a suitcase? What did you like and dislike? 2. How did you feel as a child or teenager about entering a new school for the first time?

1. Trace on a map the Israelites' route in this passage. What territories and peoples do they see? 2. What are God's commands and reminders here? 3. Using Genesis 19:30–38 and 28:1–8 as background, what run-ins have the Israelites had with each of these people groups? How do you think the Israelites feel about God's command to leave these people alone? What does this say about God? 4. As the Israelites prepare to enter the land which God has given them, what fears might they have about the people who live there? How might the events of this passage, and the demonstration of God 's care for the Moabites, Ammonites and Edomites, help the Israelites face their fears?

1. What has been a desert experience in your life and how did you sense God's provisional plan for you? 2. How do you feel about non-believers who are successful? Do you think any of their success is attributable to God? Why or why not? 3. In what sense is God concerned about the welfare of non-believers today? What examples can you give? How are these similar to this passage? 4. What challenge are you facing in your life today? What provision do you need from God? What have you learned here about God's character that can help calm and strengthen you for that challenge?

Wanderings in the Desert

2 Then we turned back and set out toward the desert along the route to the Red Sea,[a] as the LORD had directed me. For a long time we made our way around the hill country of Seir.

2Then the LORD said to me, 3"You have made your way around this hill country long enough; now turn north. 4Give the people these orders: 'You are about to pass through the territory of your brothers the descendants of Esau, who live in Seir. They will be afraid of you, but be very careful. 5Do not provoke them to war, for I will not give you any of their land, not even enough to put your foot on. I have given Esau the hill country of Seir as his own. 6You are to pay them in silver for the food you eat and the water you drink.'"

7The LORD your God has blessed you in all the work of your hands. He has watched over your journey through this vast desert. These forty years the LORD your God has been with you, and you have not lacked anything.

8So we went on past our brothers the descendants of Esau, who live in Seir. We turned from the Arabah road, which comes up from Elath and Ezion Geber, and traveled along the desert road of Moab.

9Then the LORD said to me, "Do not harass the Moabites or provoke them to war, for I will not give you any part of their land. I have given Ar to the descendants of Lot as a possession."

10(The Emites used to live there—a people strong and numerous, and as tall as the Anakites. 11Like the Anakites, they too were considered Rephaites, but the Moabites called them Emites. 12Horites used to live in Seir, but the descendants of Esau drove them out. They destroyed the Horites from before them and settled in their place, just as Israel did in the land the LORD gave them as their possession.)

13And the LORD said, "Now get up and cross the Zered Valley." So we crossed the valley.

14Thirty-eight years passed from the time we left Kadesh Barnea until we crossed the Zered Valley. By then, that entire generation of fighting men had perished from the camp, as the LORD had sworn to them. 15The LORD's hand was against them until he had completely eliminated them from the camp.

16Now when the last of these fighting men among the people had died, 17the LORD said to me, 18"Today you are to pass by the region of Moab at Ar. 19When you come to the Ammonites, do not harass them or provoke them to war, for I will not give you possession of any land belonging to the Ammonites. I have given it as a possession to the descendants of Lot."

20(That too was considered a land of the Rephaites, who used to live there; but the Ammonites called them Zamzummites. 21They were a people strong and numerous, and as tall as the Anakites. The LORD destroyed them from before the Ammonites, who drove them out and settled in their place. 22The LORD had done the same for the descendants of Esau, who lived in Seir, when he destroyed the Horites from before them. They drove them out and have lived in their place to this day. 23And as for the Avvites who lived in villages as far as Gaza, the Caphtorites coming out from Caphtor[b] destroyed them and settled in their place.)

---

a 1 Hebrew *Yam Suph*; that is, Sea of Reeds   b 23 That is, Crete

Defeat of Sihon King of Heshbon

24"Set out now and cross the Arnon Gorge. See, I have given into your hand Sihon the Amorite, king of Heshbon, and his country. Begin to take possession of it and engage him in battle. 25This very day I will begin to put the terror and fear of you on all the nations under heaven. They will hear reports of you and will tremble and be in anguish because of you."

26From the desert of Kedemoth I sent messengers to Sihon king of Heshbon offering peace and saying, 27"Let us pass through your country. We will stay on the main road; we will not turn aside to the right or to the left. 28Sell us food to eat and water to drink for their price in silver. Only let us pass through on foot— 29as the descendants of Esau, who live in Seir, and the Moabites, who live in Ar, did for us—until we cross the Jordan into the land the LORD our God is giving us." 30But Sihon king of Heshbon refused to let us pass through. For the LORD your God had made his spirit stubborn and his heart obstinate in order to give him into your hands, as he has now done.

31The LORD said to me, "See, I have begun to deliver Sihon and his country over to you. Now begin to conquer and possess his land."

32When Sihon and all his army came out to meet us in battle at Jahaz, 33the LORD our God delivered him over to us and we struck him down, together with his sons and his whole army. 34At that time we took all his towns and completely destroyed^a them— men, women and children. We left no survivors. 35But the livestock and the plunder from the towns we had captured we carried off for ourselves. 36From Aroer on the rim of the Arnon Gorge, and from the town in the gorge, even as far as Gilead, not one town was too strong for us. The LORD our God gave us all of them. 37But in accordance with the command of the LORD our God, you did not encroach on any of the land of the Ammonites, neither the land along the course of the Jabbok nor that around the towns in the hills.

Defeat of Og King of Bashan

3 Next we turned and went up along the road toward Bashan, and Og king of Bashan with his whole army marched out to meet us in battle at Edrei. 2The LORD said to me, "Do not be afraid of him, for I have handed him over to you with his whole army and his land. Do to him what you did to Sihon king of the Amorites, who reigned in Heshbon."

3So the LORD our God also gave into our hands Og king of Bashan and all his army. We struck them down, leaving no survivors. 4At that time we took all his cities. There was not one of the sixty cities that we did not take from them—the whole region of Argob, Og's kingdom in Bashan. 5All these cities were fortified with high walls and with gates and bars, and there were also a great many unwalled villages. 6We completely destroyed^a them, as we had done with Sihon king of Heshbon, destroying^a every city—men, women and children. 7But all the livestock and the plunder from their cities we carried off for ourselves.

8So at that time we took from these two kings of the Amorites the territory east of the Jordan, from the Arnon Gorge as far as Mount Hermon. 9(Hermon is called Sirion by the Sidonians; the

---

When have you dug in your heels and refused to budge? Why? What resulted?

1. How different are the instructions concerning Heshbon in verse 24 from those in verses 5,9 and 19? Why the difference? What were the Israelites to do? What was God going to do? 2. What part does God play in Sihon's refusal to allow the Israelites to pass through his territory? What does this reveal about God? 3. How do you think the Israelites felt as they prepared to confront Sihon? How complete was the destruction of Heshbon? Why? 4. What does this story reveal about how God works to prepare his people to carry out his plan?

1. What part of your life seems directionless? How do you go about seeking God's will in that area? 2. If God solves life's problems in different ways, what advice would you give to someone approaching God with a problem? Why is it sometimes difficult for us to discern God's guidance?

1. What is the worst place you've ever slept? 2. What kind of sleeper are you: (a) Toss and turn? (b) Snore up a storm? (c) Sleep like a log?

1. Compare the defeat of Bashan with that of Heshbon (2:24–35). 2. How does the conquest of Bashan begin to fulfill God's promise in 2:25? What makes the defeat of King Og a powerful victory? 3. On a map, locate the territory conquered here and in 2:24–27. What do these conquests reveal about how God works to prepare people for the promised land?

1. Where do you see God at work right now in your life? What might the "promised land" look like? 2. What about your relationship with God continues to amaze you?

---

^a34,6 The Hebrew term refers to the irrevocable giving over of things or persons to the LORD, often by totally destroying them.

Amorites call it Senir.) [10]We took all the towns on the plateau, and all Gilead, and all Bashan as far as Salecah and Edrei, towns of Og's kingdom in Bashan. [11](Only Og king of Bashan was left of the remnant of the Rephaites. His bed[a] was made of iron and was more than thirteen feet long and six feet wide.[b] It is still in Rabbah of the Ammonites.)

Division of the Land

[12]Of the land that we took over at that time, I gave the Reubenites and the Gadites the territory north of Aroer by the Arnon Gorge, including half the hill country of Gilead, together with its towns. [13]The rest of Gilead and also all of Bashan, the kingdom of Og, I gave to the half tribe of Manasseh. (The whole region of Argob in Bashan used to be known as a land of the Rephaites. [14]Jair, a descendant of Manasseh, took the whole region of Argob as far as the border of the Geshurites and the Maacathites; it was named after him, so that to this day Bashan is called Havvoth Jair.[c]) [15]And I gave Gilead to Makir. [16]But to the Reubenites and the Gadites I gave the territory extending from Gilead down to the Arnon Gorge (the middle of the gorge being the border) and out to the Jabbok River, which is the border of the Ammonites. [17]Its western border was the Jordan in the Arabah, from Kinnereth to the Sea of the Arabah (the Salt Sea[d]), below the slopes of Pisgah.

[18]I commanded you at that time: "The LORD your God has given you this land to take possession of it. But all your able-bodied men, armed for battle, must cross over ahead of your brother Israelites. [19]However, your wives, your children and your livestock (I know you have much livestock) may stay in the towns I have given you, [20]until the LORD gives rest to your brothers as he has to you, and they too have taken over the land that the LORD your God is giving them, across the Jordan. After that, each of you may go back to the possession I have given you."

Moses Forbidden to Cross the Jordan

[21]At that time I commanded Joshua: "You have seen with your own eyes all that the LORD your God has done to these two kings. The LORD will do the same to all the kingdoms over there where you are going. [22]Do not be afraid of them; the LORD your God himself will fight for you."

[23]At that time I pleaded with the LORD: [24]"O Sovereign LORD, you have begun to show to your servant your greatness and your strong hand. For what god is there in heaven or on earth who can do the deeds and mighty works you do? [25]Let me go over and see the good land beyond the Jordan—that fine hill country and Lebanon."

[26]But because of you the LORD was angry with me and would not listen to me. "That is enough," the LORD said. "Do not speak to me anymore about this matter. [27]Go up to the top of Pisgah and look west and north and south and east. Look at the land with your own eyes, since you are not going to cross this Jordan. [28]But commission Joshua, and encourage and strengthen him, for he will lead this people across and will cause them to inherit the land that you will see." [29]So we stayed in the valley near Beth Peor.

---

1. When growing up, did you share your bedroom or have it to yourself? What was this like? 2. What did your parents used to say about sharing? How have their sayings influenced your sharing?

1. Why do the Reubenites, Gadites and the half-tribe of Manasseh want to live apart from the other tribes (see Nu 32:1–5)? 2. What would allow them to settle east of the Jordan (see Nu 32:6–27)? Why? 3. How would all parties involved benefit from these instructions? 4. The Jordan Valley was a geographical barrier to their communication. What inter-tribal problems might this create? Why do you think God allows them to remain in separate camps? 5. What is Joshua told and why (vv. 21–22)? 6. What does Moses' prayer (vv. 24–25) reveal about his relationship with God? 7. How do you think Moses felt looking at the promised land? Commissioning Joshua?

1. How is your group or extended family interwoven and interdependent? What communication problems have you had to bridge? 2. When has someone shared the battles of life with you? How did their presence make a difference in the outcome? 3. When have you, like Moses, been prevented from experiencing a much-anticipated event? How did you feel? What did you do? 4. At what stage are you in your Christian journey: (a) On the outside looking in? (b) Waiting to cross over? (c) Newly arrived on the other side? (d) Taking possession of God's gift? (e) Other? 5. What are you doing to prepare yourself to move on from that stage? Who in your Christian community might God be encouraging you to assist along the way?

---

a11 Or sarcophagus   b11 Hebrew nine cubits long and four cubits wide (about 4 meters long and 1.8 meters wide)   c14 Or called the settlements of Jair
d17 That is, the Dead Sea

Obedience Commanded

4 Hear now, O Israel, the decrees and laws I am about to teach you. Follow them so that you may live and may go in and take possession of the land that the LORD, the God of your fathers, is giving you. ²Do not add to what I command you and do not subtract from it, but keep the commands of the LORD your God that I give you.

³You saw with your own eyes what the LORD did at Baal Peor. The LORD your God destroyed from among you everyone who followed the Baal of Peor, ⁴but all of you who held fast to the LORD your God are still alive today.

⁵See, I have taught you decrees and laws as the LORD my God commanded me, so that you may follow them in the land you are entering to take possession of it. ⁶Observe them carefully, for this will show your wisdom and understanding to the nations, who will hear about all these decrees and say, "Surely this great nation is a wise and understanding people." ⁷What other nation is so great as to have their gods near them the way the LORD our God is near us whenever we pray to him? ⁸And what other nation is so great as to have such righteous decrees and laws as this body of laws I am setting before you today?

⁹Only be careful, and watch yourselves closely so that you do not forget the things your eyes have seen or let them slip from your heart as long as you live. Teach them to your children and to their children after them. ¹⁰Remember the day you stood before the LORD your God at Horeb, when he said to me, "Assemble the people before me to hear my words so that they may learn to revere me as long as they live in the land and may teach them to their children." ¹¹You came near and stood at the foot of the mountain while it blazed with fire to the very heavens, with black clouds and deep darkness. ¹²Then the LORD spoke to you out of the fire. You heard the sound of words but saw no form; there was only a voice. ¹³He declared to you his covenant, the Ten Commandments, which he commanded you to follow and then wrote them on two stone tablets. ¹⁴And the LORD directed me at that time to teach you the decrees and laws you are to follow in the land that you are crossing the Jordan to possess.

Idolatry Forbidden

¹⁵You saw no form of any kind the day the LORD spoke to you at Horeb out of the fire. Therefore watch yourselves very carefully, ¹⁶so that you do not become corrupt and make for yourselves an idol, an image of any shape, whether formed like a man or a woman, ¹⁷or like any animal on earth or any bird that flies in the air, ¹⁸or like any creature that moves along the ground or any fish in the waters below. ¹⁹And when you look up to the sky and see the sun, the moon and the stars—all the heavenly array—do not be enticed into bowing down to them and worshiping things the LORD your God has apportioned to all the nations under heaven. ²⁰But as for you, the LORD took you and brought you out of the iron-smelting furnace, out of Egypt, to be the people of his inheritance, as you now are.

²¹The LORD was angry with me because of you, and he solemnly swore that I would not cross the Jordan and enter the good land the LORD your God is giving you as your inheritance. ²²I will die in this land; I will not cross the Jordan; but you are about to cross over and take possession of that good land. ²³Be careful not to forget the covenant of the LORD your God that he made with you; do not make for yourselves an idol in the form of anything the LORD your God

1. If you were founding a new country, what would you include first in your constitution? How would this help to make your country a better place to live? 2. If you were President for a day, what would you sign into law?

1. What two reasons does God give for the necessity of his law to the new nation (vv. 3–8)? What do these reasons reveal about God's expectations for his people? 2. "Do not forget the things your eyes have seen" (v. 9). What is the relationship between this directive and obedience to the law? What does this connection between God's actions and his law tell you about how he works?

1. Would a non-believer's commentary on your life resemble what the nations would say about Israel (vv. 6–8)? Why or why not? How does this make you feel? 2. When is it hardest for you to give God's Word its due place in your life? What needs to happen this week to make sure God's Word receives the proper emphasis in your life? 3. Can you recall a specific time when God's Word brought clarity and guidance to your life? What happened? How did Scripture fill your ache for God then?

1. What do you like to collect? How did you get started? What is a favorite piece in your collection? 2. What God-given gifts do you admire in others?

1. Ancient peoples often used animal figurines to represent their gods or characteristics of their gods. In what ways is this an attempt to control or limit these gods? 2. Why would this be of such concern to God? What is the importance of God acting without form at Horeb (Mt. Sinai)? In what ways are the Israelites the image of the unseen God (v. 20)? 3. In what way is Moses' inability to cross the Jordan a redemptive suffering for Israel (vv. 21–24)? How could the death of Moses strengthen their covenant relationship with God? 4. What is the "if … then" logic of verses 25–31? What does this reveal about God's desires for his

people? What is the only way to find God?

1. In what ways do we attempt to limit or control God? How is this like the function of idols in the ancient world? 2. When you are most likely to try to limit or control God, do you think the "if … then" statements of verses 25–31 apply to you? If so, how? If not, why? 3. What does it mean for your daily life to seek God with all your heart and soul?

———————

Who was a special childhood friend? What did you enjoy doing together?

1. If God is known by his actions, what did the Israelites know about God? 2. Why does God choose Israel (vv. 35,37)? In what ways do his actions fit his motive? Do you think God provided enough evidence to demonstrate his great love? 3. What response and result is expected (vv. 39–40)?

1. What events in your life do you see as God's choosing of you? If God is known by his actions, what have you come to know about God? What further evidence (of his love or your election) are you looking for? 2. What do you believe God wants from you? Why would he choose you? What can you do to embrace God's choice of you?

———————

What room was your family gathering-place? What memories of security does it bring to mind?

1. What was the purpose of the cities of refuge? How were they regulated (see Nu 35:6–34)? Where were these cities located (see a map)? How did their locale help fulfill their function? 2. What is the point of emphasizing the conquests in verses 44–49? Why would this be an important backdrop to the giving of the law?

has forbidden. 24For the LORD your God is a consuming fire, a jealous God.

25After you have had children and grandchildren and have lived in the land a long time—if you then become corrupt and make any kind of idol, doing evil in the eyes of the LORD your God and provoking him to anger, 26I call heaven and earth as witnesses against you this day that you will quickly perish from the land that you are crossing the Jordan to possess. You will not live there long but will certainly be destroyed. 27The LORD will scatter you among the peoples, and only a few of you will survive among the nations to which the LORD will drive you. 28There you will worship manmade gods of wood and stone, which cannot see or hear or eat or smell. 29But if from there you seek the LORD your God, you will find him if you look for him with all your heart and with all your soul. 30When you are in distress and all these things have happened to you, then in later days you will return to the LORD your God and obey him. 31For the LORD your God is a merciful God; he will not abandon or destroy you or forget the covenant with your forefathers, which he confirmed to them by oath.

The LORD Is God

32Ask now about the former days, long before your time, from the day God created man on the earth; ask from one end of the heavens to the other. Has anything so great as this ever happened, or has anything like it ever been heard of? 33Has any other people heard the voice of God[a] speaking out of fire, as you have, and lived? 34Has any god ever tried to take for himself one nation out of another nation, by testings, by miraculous signs and wonders, by war, by a mighty hand and an outstretched arm, or by great and awesome deeds, like all the things the LORD your God did for you in Egypt before your very eyes?

35You were shown these things so that you might know that the LORD is God; besides him there is no other. 36From heaven he made you hear his voice to discipline you. On earth he showed you his great fire, and you heard his words from out of the fire. 37Because he loved your forefathers and chose their descendants after them, he brought you out of Egypt by his Presence and his great strength, 38to drive out before you nations greater and stronger than you and to bring you into their land to give it to you for your inheritance, as it is today.

39Acknowledge and take to heart this day that the LORD is God in heaven above and on the earth below. There is no other. 40Keep his decrees and commands, which I am giving you today, so that it may go well with you and your children after you and that you may live long in the land the LORD your God gives you for all time.

Cities of Refuge

41Then Moses set aside three cities east of the Jordan, 42to which anyone who had killed a person could flee if he had unintentionally killed his neighbor without malice aforethought. He could flee into one of these cities and save his life. 43The cities were these: Bezer in the desert plateau, for the Reubenites; Ramoth in Gilead, for the Gadites; and Golan in Bashan, for the Manassites.

Introduction to the Law

44This is the law Moses set before the Israelites. 45These are the stipulations, decrees and laws Moses gave them when they came

a33 Or of a god

out of Egypt [46]and were in the valley near Beth Peor east of the Jordan, in the land of Sihon king of the Amorites, who reigned in Heshbon and was defeated by Moses and the Israelites as they came out of Egypt. [47]They took possession of his land and the land of Og king of Bashan, the two Amorite kings east of the Jordan. [48]This land extended from Aroer on the rim of the Arnon Gorge to Mount Siyon[a] (that is, Hermon), [49]and included all the Arabah east of the Jordan, as far as the Sea of the Arabah,[b] below the slopes of Pisgah.

The Ten Commandments

5 Moses summoned all Israel and said:
Hear, O Israel, the decrees and laws I declare in your hearing today. Learn them and be sure to follow them. [2]The LORD our God made a covenant with us at Horeb. [3]It was not with our fathers that the LORD made this covenant, but with us, with all of us who are alive here today. [4]The LORD spoke to you face to face out of the fire on the mountain. [5](At that time I stood between the LORD and you to declare to you the word of the LORD, because you were afraid of the fire and did not go up the mountain.) And he said:

[6]"I am the LORD your God, who brought you out of Egypt, out of the land of slavery.

[7]"You shall have no other gods before[c] me.

[8]"You shall not make for yourself an idol in the form of anything in heaven above or on the earth beneath or in the waters below. [9]You shall not bow down to them or worship them; for I, the LORD your God, am a jealous God, punishing the children for the sin of the fathers to the third and fourth generation of those who hate me, [10]but showing love to a thousand ⌊generations⌋ of those who love me and keep my commandments.

[11]"You shall not misuse the name of the LORD your God, for the LORD will not hold anyone guiltless who misuses his name.

[12]"Observe the Sabbath day by keeping it holy, as the LORD your God has commanded you. [13]Six days you shall labor and do all your work, [14]but the seventh day is a Sabbath to the LORD your God. On it you shall not do any work, neither you, nor your son or daughter, nor your manservant or maidservant, nor your ox, your donkey or any of your animals, nor the alien within your gates, so that your manservant and maidservant may rest, as you do. [15]Remember that you were slaves in Egypt and that the LORD your God brought you out of there with a mighty hand and an outstretched arm. Therefore the LORD your God has commanded you to observe the Sabbath day.

[16]"Honor your father and your mother, as the LORD your God has commanded you, so that you may live long and that it may go well with you in the land the LORD your God is giving you.

[17]"You shall not murder.

[18]"You shall not commit adultery.

[19]"You shall not steal.

[20]"You shall not give false testimony against your neighbor.

[21]"You shall not covet your neighbor's wife. You shall not set your desire on your neighbor's house or land, his man-

[a]48 Hebrew; Syriac (see also Deut. 3:9) *Sirion*   [b]49 That is, the Dead Sea
[c]7 Or *besides*

What people, places or practices have been helpful to you in understanding God's Word?

---

1. What were the three most important rules in your home when you were growing up? What do these reveal about your family? **2.** What are the three most important rules in your present home? What do they reveal about you?

1. This chapter is the first in a long discussion of decrees and laws (chs. 5–26). Why begin this extended sermon with the Ten Commandments? In what sense are these 10 laws the prologue or parent of the other laws? **2.** The first four commandments (vv. 7–15) concern our relationship with God. What do each of these say about the kind of relationship God wants with us? What does this teach you about his nature? **3.** The final six commandments (vv. 16–21) concern human relationships. What do each of these say about the kind of relationships God desires for us and for his creation? **4.** What might you infer about human nature in Moses' day from these 10 laws? Is this an acknowledgment of sinful humanity, or are these laws an attempt to change humanity? Explain. **5.** Were the Israelites in this passage present at Mt. Sinai when the law was first given? How will this covenant help them to establish a new nation? **6.** How was the law given (vv. 4–5,22–31)? What does this scene convey about the importance of these laws to God? About the well-being of the Israelites? About the function of the law itself? **7.** What do verses 32–33 say in summary fashion about the function of these laws?

1. As a child, why did you obey rules? Is this different from why you obey rules today? Why or why not? **2.** What effect have these ancient laws had on the shaping of law today? What does this tell you about these laws? **3.** Do you think human nature has changed since these laws were first given to Moses? Why or why not? **4.** Although most of these are written in the negative, they also imply a positive behavior and a divine freedom. For example, "You shall not steal" implies, "Respect personal belongings ... All things ultimately belong to and are given by God, which frees you from worry." Re-state in your own words the positive behaviors and divine freedoms contained in each commandment. **5.** In what ways might your relationship with God and with others be changed if you lived by the positive and freeing intent of the Ten Commandments? **6.** Which do you think is the most difficult of the 10 to follow? Why? What promises and resources (v. 33) do you have to help you follow this?

servant or maidservant, his ox or donkey, or anything that belongs to your neighbor."

²²These are the commandments the LORD proclaimed in a loud voice to your whole assembly there on the mountain from out of the fire, the cloud and the deep darkness; and he added nothing more. Then he wrote them on two stone tablets and gave them to me.

²³When you heard the voice out of the darkness, while the mountain was ablaze with fire, all the leading men of your tribes and your elders came to me. ²⁴And you said, "The LORD our God has shown us his glory and his majesty, and we have heard his voice from the fire. Today we have seen that a man can live even if God speaks with him. ²⁵But now, why should we die? This great fire will consume us, and we will die if we hear the voice of the LORD our God any longer. ²⁶For what mortal man has ever heard the voice of the living God speaking out of fire, as we have, and survived? ²⁷Go near and listen to all that the LORD our God says. Then tell us whatever the LORD our God tells you. We will listen and obey."

²⁸The LORD heard you when you spoke to me and the LORD said to me, "I have heard what this people said to you. Everything they said was good. ²⁹Oh, that their hearts would be inclined to fear me and keep all my commands always, so that it might go well with them and their children forever!

³⁰"Go, tell them to return to their tents. ³¹But you stay here with me so that I may give you all the commands, decrees and laws you are to teach them to follow in the land I am giving them to possess."

³²So be careful to do what the LORD your God has commanded you; do not turn aside to the right or to the left. ³³Walk in all the way that the LORD your God has commanded you, so that you may live and prosper and prolong your days in the land that you will possess.

Love the LORD Your God

6 These are the commands, decrees and laws the LORD your God directed me to teach you to observe in the land that you are crossing the Jordan to possess, ²so that you, your children and their children after them may fear the LORD your God as long as you live by keeping all his decrees and commands that I give you, and so that you may enjoy long life. ³Hear, O Israel, and be careful to obey so that it may go well with you and that you may increase greatly in a land flowing with milk and honey, just as the LORD, the God of your fathers, promised you.

⁴Hear, O Israel: The LORD our God, the LORD is one.^a ⁵Love the LORD your God with all your heart and with all your soul and with all your strength. ⁶These commandments that I give you today are to be upon your hearts. ⁷Impress them on your children. Talk about them when you sit at home and when you walk along the road, when you lie down and when you get up. ⁸Tie them as symbols on your hands and bind them on your foreheads. ⁹Write them on the doorframes of your houses and on your gates.

¹⁰When the LORD your God brings you into the land he swore to your fathers, to Abraham, Isaac and Jacob, to give you—a land with large, flourishing cities you did not build, ¹¹houses filled with all kinds of good things you did not provide, wells you did not dig, and

1. Share a fond childhood memory of your parents or a significant adult. What makes this special for you? **2.** As a child, what was one lesson you were taught by an adult for which you are most grateful today?

1. Who and what are the commandments and decrees intended for? Why do you think Moses keeps emphasizing these points? **2.** In the context of her surrounding nations, what is meant by "The Lord our God, the Lord is one" (v. 4)? How is verse 5 related to the first four commandments (5:7–15)? **3.** Why such a strong emphasis on teaching these laws and decrees to children (vv. 6–9, 20–25)? How would you characterize this method of teaching? Why might this method be best suited to the task? How do these practices support the assertion of verse 5? **4.** Why is Moses apprehensive (vv. 10–16)? How would the instructions in verses 1–9 help alleviate Moses' fears? **5.** What is the essence of

^a4 Or *The LORD our God is one LORD*; or *The LORD is our God, the LORD is one*; or *The LORD is our God, the LORD alone*

vineyards and olive groves you did not plant—then when you eat and are satisfied, ¹²be careful that you do not forget the LORD, who brought you out of Egypt, out of the land of slavery.

¹³Fear the LORD your God, serve him only and take your oaths in his name. ¹⁴Do not follow other gods, the gods of the peoples around you; ¹⁵for the LORD your God, who is among you, is a jealous God and his anger will burn against you, and he will destroy you from the face of the land. ¹⁶Do not test the LORD your God as you did at Massah. ¹⁷Be sure to keep the commands of the LORD your God and the stipulations and decrees he has given you. ¹⁸Do what is right and good in the LORD's sight, so that it may go well with you and you may go in and take over the good land that the LORD promised on oath to your forefathers, ¹⁹thrusting out all your enemies before you, as the LORD said.

²⁰In the future, when your son asks you, "What is the meaning of the stipulations, decrees and laws the LORD our God has commanded you?" ²¹tell him: "We were slaves of Pharaoh in Egypt, but the LORD brought us out of Egypt with a mighty hand. ²²Before our eyes the LORD sent miraculous signs and wonders—great and terrible—upon Egypt and Pharaoh and his whole household. ²³But he brought us out from there to bring us in and give us the land that he promised on oath to our forefathers. ²⁴The LORD commanded us to obey all these decrees and to fear the LORD our God, so that we might always prosper and be kept alive, as is the case today. ²⁵And if we are careful to obey all this law before the LORD our God, as he has commanded us, that will be our righteousness."

Driving Out the Nations

7 When the LORD your God brings you into the land you are entering to possess and drives out before you many nations— the Hittites, Girgashites, Amorites, Canaanites, Perizzites, Hivites and Jebusites, seven nations larger and stronger than you— ²and when the LORD your God has delivered them over to you and you have defeated them, then you must destroy them totally.ᵃ Make no treaty with them, and show them no mercy. ³Do not intermarry with them. Do not give your daughters to their sons or take their daughters for your sons, ⁴for they will turn your sons away from following me to serve other gods, and the LORD's anger will burn against you and will quickly destroy you. ⁵This is what you are to do to them: Break down their altars, smash their sacred stones, cut down their Asherah polesᵇ and burn their idols in the fire. ⁶For you are a people holy to the LORD your God. The LORD your God has chosen you out of all the peoples on the face of the earth to be his people, his treasured possession.

⁷The LORD did not set his affection on you and choose you because you were more numerous than other peoples, for you were the fewest of all peoples. ⁸But it was because the LORD loved you and kept the oath he swore to your forefathers that he brought you out with a mighty hand and redeemed you from the land of slavery, from the power of Pharaoh king of Egypt. ⁹Know therefore that the LORD your God is God; he is the faithful God, keeping his covenant of love to a thousand generations of those who love him and keep his commands. ¹⁰But

those who hate him he will repay to their face by destruction;

---

the story recounted in verses 20–25? What meaning does this story give to the commands and decrees?

1. How do you demonstrate your love for God? How does this fulfill verse 5? What will you do today to demonstrate this love? 2. Do you have more trouble recalling God's role in your life during times of failure, or in success? How is this a reflection of Moses' fears in verses 10–16? What can you do to combat this tendency? 3. In what ways is God responsible for the successes you enjoy in life? How do you know this? 4. How important is it to you that the children in your life grow up to celebrate God's love and appreciate his role in their life? How can you build traditions that teach them about God's love?

1. What people groups or "ites" (Wisconsinites, etc.) are represented in your family tree or surrounding you in your community? 2. What demolition work have you witnessed, even participated in?

1. List the commands which God gives to the Israelites concerning the people they will encounter when they enter the land (vv. 1–5). Which of these commands make you uncomfortable? Can this be reconciled with the picture of God as merciful (4:31)? Why or why not? Why the harshness? Why should Israel strictly follow this? 2. List the rewards for obedience (vv. 12–16). How does this list compare to verses 1–5? What do you see as the function of these rewards, as compared to the commands? What do both reveal about the nature of God? 3. According to verses 7–11, why did God choose the Israelites? Why do you think God reminds them of this? What are the mutual obligations of God and Israel? What does this reveal about both parties to this covenant? 4. What kind of life do you think the Israelites had in the wilderness, as compared to the more urban population of Canaan? How might this affect the Israelites' will to conquer the nations of Ca-

---

ᵃ2 The Hebrew term refers to the irrevocable giving over of things or persons to the LORD, often by totally destroying them; also in verse 26.   ᵇ5 That is, symbols of the goddess Asherah; here and elsewhere in Deuteronomy

naan? **5.** If the Israelites view these nations as strong, how will this affect their opinion of the gods of these nations? What kinds of problems might this create for the Israelites as they attempt to establish themselves in Canaan? **6.** How does Moses anticipate that? How do verses 17–26 relate to their very real fears?

1. In what sense has God "chosen" you? Why do you think he has done this? How is this similar to his choice of the Israelites? What obligations does this imply for God? For you? **2.** In comparing yourself with your non-believer friends, in what areas do they seem stronger than you? What are the symbols of this strength? In what ways are these symbols similar to the silver and gold idols of the Canaanites? **3.** How do you show that your God is stronger than the "gods" of non-believers? What actions can you take today to strengthen your belief?

he will not be slow to repay to their face those who hate him.

[11]Therefore, take care to follow the commands, decrees and laws I give you today.

[12]If you pay attention to these laws and are careful to follow them, then the LORD your God will keep his covenant of love with you, as he swore to your forefathers. [13]He will love you and bless you and increase your numbers. He will bless the fruit of your womb, the crops of your land—your grain, new wine and oil—the calves of your herds and the lambs of your flocks in the land that he swore to your forefathers to give you. [14]You will be blessed more than any other people; none of your men or women will be childless, nor any of your livestock without young. [15]The LORD will keep you free from every disease. He will not inflict on you the horrible diseases you knew in Egypt, but he will inflict them on all who hate you. [16]You must destroy all the peoples the LORD your God gives over to you. Do not look on them with pity and do not serve their gods, for that will be a snare to you.

[17]You may say to yourselves, "These nations are stronger than we are. How can we drive them out?" [18]But do not be afraid of them; remember well what the LORD your God did to Pharaoh and to all Egypt. [19]You saw with your own eyes the great trials, the miraculous signs and wonders, the mighty hand and outstretched arm, with which the LORD your God brought you out. The LORD your God will do the same to all the peoples you now fear. [20]Moreover, the LORD your God will send the hornet among them until even the survivors who hide from you have perished. [21]Do not be terrified by them, for the LORD your God, who is among you, is a great and awesome God. [22]The LORD your God will drive out those nations before you, little by little. You will not be allowed to eliminate them all at once, or the wild animals will multiply around you. [23]But the LORD your God will deliver them over to you, throwing them into great confusion until they are destroyed. [24]He will give their kings into your hand, and you will wipe out their names from under heaven. No one will be able to stand up against you; you will destroy them. [25]The images of their gods you are to burn in the fire. Do not covet the silver and gold on them, and do not take it for yourselves, or you will be ensnared by it, for it is detestable to the LORD your God. [26]Do not bring a detestable thing into your house or you, like it, will be set apart for destruction. Utterly abhor and detest it, for it is set apart for destruction.

Do Not Forget the LORD

8 Be careful to follow every command I am giving you today, so that you may live and increase and may enter and possess the land that the LORD promised on oath to your forefathers. [2]Remember how the LORD your God led you all the way in the desert these forty years, to humble you and to test you in order to know what was in your heart, whether or not you would keep his commands. [3]He humbled you, causing you to hunger and then feeding you with manna, which neither you nor your fathers had known, to teach you that man does not live on bread alone but on every word that comes from the mouth of the LORD. [4]Your clothes did not wear out and your feet did not swell during these forty years. [5]Know then in your heart that as a man disciplines his son, so the LORD your God disciplines you.

[6]Observe the commands of the LORD your God, walking in his ways and revering him. [7]For the LORD your God is bringing you into

1. What memory aids do you use to keep from forgetting things? What do you tend to forget, despite all efforts to remind you? **2.** What memory of your father disciplining you do you recall from your growing up years?

1. In this context (vv. 1–4,15–16), what does it mean to be disciplined by God "as a man disciplines his son" (v. 5)? What is the intended effect of God's actions in the wilderness? Why do you think the Israelites needed to experience this discipline before entering the promised land? **2.** What distinguishes this

a good land—a land with streams and pools of water, with springs flowing in the valleys and hills; 8a land with wheat and barley, vines and fig trees, pomegranates, olive oil and honey; 9a land where bread will not be scarce and you will lack nothing; a land where the rocks are iron and you can dig copper out of the hills.

10When you have eaten and are satisfied, praise the LORD your God for the good land he has given you. 11Be careful that you do not forget the LORD your God, failing to observe his commands, his laws and his decrees that I am giving you this day. 12Otherwise, when you eat and are satisfied, when you build fine houses and settle down, 13and when your herds and flocks grow large and your silver and gold increase and all you have is multiplied, 14then your heart will become proud and you will forget the LORD your God, who brought you out of Egypt, out of the land of slavery. 15He led you through the vast and dreadful desert, that thirsty and waterless land, with its venomous snakes and scorpions. He brought you water out of hard rock. 16He gave you manna to eat in the desert, something your fathers had never known, to humble and to test you so that in the end it might go well with you. 17You may say to yourself, "My power and the strength of my hands have produced this wealth for me." 18But remember the LORD your God, for it is he who gives you the ability to produce wealth, and so confirms his covenant, which he swore to your forefathers, as it is today.

19If you ever forget the LORD your God and follow other gods and worship and bow down to them, I testify against you today that you will surely be destroyed. 20Like the nations the LORD destroyed before you, so you will be destroyed for not obeying the LORD your God.

Not Because of Israel's Righteousness

9 Hear, O Israel. You are now about to cross the Jordan to go in and dispossess nations greater and stronger than you, with large cities that have walls up to the sky. 2The people are strong and tall—Anakites! You know about them and have heard it said: "Who can stand up against the Anakites?" 3But be assured today that the LORD your God is the one who goes across ahead of you like a devouring fire. He will destroy them; he will subdue them before you. And you will drive them out and annihilate them quickly, as the LORD has promised you.

4After the LORD your God has driven them out before you, do not say to yourself, "The LORD has brought me here to take possession of this land because of my righteousness." No, it is on account of the wickedness of these nations that the LORD is going to drive them out before you. 5It is not because of your righteousness or your integrity that you are going in to take possession of their land; but on account of the wickedness of these nations, the LORD your God will drive them out before you, to accomplish what he swore to your fathers, to Abraham, Isaac and Jacob. 6Understand, then, that it is not because of your righteousness that the LORD your God is giving you this good land to possess, for you are a stiff-necked people.

The Golden Calf

7Remember this and never forget how you provoked the LORD your God to anger in the desert. From the day you left Egypt until you arrived here, you have been rebellious against the LORD. 8At Horeb you aroused the LORD's wrath so that he was angry enough

promised land (vv. 6–9)? What must the Israelites guard against (vv. 10–20)? What aspects of "spiritual gluttony" do you see here? 3. What relationship choices are set before the Israelites as they enter the promised land? What kind of relationship does God want with his followers and why?

1. When, if ever, have you experienced "God's wilderness" in your life? In what respect was it like a "desert"? In what sense was it disciplinary? What role did God play in this? In what ways is life different because of that? 2. How are producing wealth and accumulating wealth different? What does this chapter teach you about your capacity to produce wealth? Is it harder for you to maintain a proper relationship with God in prosperity or in hardship? Why? 3. How might the warning of verses 19–20 apply to you in your world?

When in your life have you been the underdog and beaten all odds to claim victory?

1. What are the enemies like who live in this land? How are they to be conquered? What role is Israel to play? What role is God to play? 2. Why does God select the Israelites? What does this reveal about God?

1. In what ways do you feel like underdog Israel? How has God used you, despite the odds, to further his kingdom? How does this make you feel? 2. When are you most likely to forget that your victory is from God? What will you do this week to "remember" him?

1. What memorable incident from your childhood will simply not go away? What are you meant to learn from it? 2. Apart from God, who has forgiven you

the most? What do you think makes this person so forgiving?

1. How long is Moses on the mountain with God? What kinds of stress might this situation create for the Israelites? 2. In what sense is the golden calf a response to this stress (see Ex 32:1–4)? Why is making the calf so wrong? What do you think they should have done? 3. To whom does God speak in verse 14? Do you think this verse is a direct prohibition of, or an invitation to, intercession by Moses? 4. What is meant by Moses' breaking the two tablets? What is he feeling? 5. How and why does Moses intercede for Israel (vv. 18–21)? Consequently, Israel is spared but are they any better off, or do they learn their lesson? Why or why not? 6. In verses 25–29, how does Moses demonstrate his understanding of the heart and plans of God? 7. How do you think this story would make the Israelites feel, especially in the context of 9:1–6? Why is this story important for the people as they prepare to enter Canaan?

1. What situations are most stressful for you? How do you respond to stress? What affect does it have on your relationship with others? With God? Are any of your stress management techniques similar to the Israelites? 2. In your own life, what has been your "golden calf"? How did this affect your relationship with God? How have you seen God's forgiving nature at work in your life? How have you shown him your thanks?

to destroy you. ⁹When I went up on the mountain to receive the tablets of stone, the tablets of the covenant that the LORD had made with you, I stayed on the mountain forty days and forty nights; I ate no bread and drank no water. ¹⁰The LORD gave me two stone tablets inscribed by the finger of God. On them were all the commandments the LORD proclaimed to you on the mountain out of the fire, on the day of the assembly.

¹¹At the end of the forty days and forty nights, the LORD gave me the two stone tablets, the tablets of the covenant. ¹²Then the LORD told me, "Go down from here at once, because your people whom you brought out of Egypt have become corrupt. They have turned away quickly from what I commanded them and have made a cast idol for themselves."

¹³And the LORD said to me, "I have seen this people, and they are a stiff-necked people indeed! ¹⁴Let me alone, so that I may destroy them and blot out their name from under heaven. And I will make you into a nation stronger and more numerous than they."

¹⁵So I turned and went down from the mountain while it was ablaze with fire. And the two tablets of the covenant were in my hands.ᵃ ¹⁶When I looked, I saw that you had sinned against the LORD your God; you had made for yourselves an idol cast in the shape of a calf. You had turned aside quickly from the way that the LORD had commanded you. ¹⁷So I took the two tablets and threw them out of my hands, breaking them to pieces before your eyes.

¹⁸Then once again I fell prostrate before the LORD for forty days and forty nights; I ate no bread and drank no water, because of all the sin you had committed, doing what was evil in the LORD's sight and so provoking him to anger. ¹⁹I feared the anger and wrath of the LORD, for he was angry enough with you to destroy you. But again the LORD listened to me. ²⁰And the LORD was angry enough with Aaron to destroy him, but at that time I prayed for Aaron too. ²¹Also I took that sinful thing of yours, the calf you had made, and burned it in the fire. Then I crushed it and ground it to powder as fine as dust and threw the dust into a stream that flowed down the mountain.

²²You also made the LORD angry at Taberah, at Massah and at Kibroth Hattaavah.

²³And when the LORD sent you out from Kadesh Barnea, he said, "Go up and take possession of the land I have given you." But you rebelled against the command of the LORD your God. You did not trust him or obey him. ²⁴You have been rebellious against the LORD ever since I have known you.

²⁵I lay prostrate before the LORD those forty days and forty nights because the LORD had said he would destroy you. ²⁶I prayed to the LORD and said, "O Sovereign LORD, do not destroy your people, your own inheritance that you redeemed by your great power and brought out of Egypt with a mighty hand. ²⁷Remember your servants Abraham, Isaac and Jacob. Overlook the stubbornness of this people, their wickedness and their sin. ²⁸Otherwise, the country from which you brought us will say, 'Because the LORD was not able to take them into the land he had promised them, and because he hated them, he brought them out to put them to death in the desert.' ²⁹But they are your people, your inheritance that you brought out by your great power and your outstretched arm."

ᵃ15 Or And I had the two tablets of the covenant with me, one in each hand

Tablets Like the First Ones

10 At that time the LORD said to me, "Chisel out two stone tablets like the first ones and come up to me on the mountain. Also make a wooden chest.[a] ²I will write on the tablets the words that were on the first tablets, which you broke. Then you are to put them in the chest."

³So I made the ark out of acacia wood and chiseled out two stone tablets like the first ones, and I went up on the mountain with the two tablets in my hands. ⁴The LORD wrote on these tablets what he had written before, the Ten Commandments he had proclaimed to you on the mountain, out of the fire, on the day of the assembly. And the LORD gave them to me. ⁵Then I came back down the mountain and put the tablets in the ark I had made, as the LORD commanded me, and they are there now.

⁶(The Israelites traveled from the wells of the Jaakanites to Moserah. There Aaron died and was buried, and Eleazar his son succeeded him as priest. ⁷From there they traveled to Gudgodah and on to Jotbathah, a land with streams of water. ⁸At that time the LORD set apart the tribe of Levi to carry the ark of the covenant of the LORD, to stand before the LORD to minister and to pronounce blessings in his name, as they still do today. ⁹That is why the Levites have no share or inheritance among their brothers; the LORD is their inheritance, as the LORD your God told them.)

¹⁰Now I had stayed on the mountain forty days and nights, as I did the first time, and the LORD listened to me at this time also. It was not his will to destroy you. ¹¹"Go," the LORD said to me, "and lead the people on their way, so that they may enter and possess the land that I swore to their fathers to give them."

Fear the LORD

¹²And now, O Israel, what does the LORD your God ask of you but to fear the LORD your God, to walk in all his ways, to love him, to serve the LORD your God with all your heart and with all your soul, ¹³and to observe the LORD's commands and decrees that I am giving you today for your own good?

¹⁴To the LORD your God belong the heavens, even the highest heavens, the earth and everything in it. ¹⁵Yet the LORD set his affection on your forefathers and loved them, and he chose you, their descendants, above all the nations, as it is today. ¹⁶Circumcise your hearts, therefore, and do not be stiff-necked any longer. ¹⁷For the LORD your God is God of gods and Lord of lords, the great God, mighty and awesome, who shows no partiality and accepts no bribes. ¹⁸He defends the cause of the fatherless and the widow, and loves the alien, giving him food and clothing. ¹⁹And you are to love those who are aliens, for you yourselves were aliens in Egypt. ²⁰Fear the LORD your God and serve him. Hold fast to him and take your oaths in his name. ²¹He is your praise; he is your God, who performed for you those great and awesome wonders you saw with your own eyes. ²²Your forefathers who went down into Egypt were seventy in all, and now the LORD your God has made you as numerous as the stars in the sky.

Love and Obey the LORD

11 Love the LORD your God and keep his requirements, his decrees, his laws and his commands always. ²Remember today that your children were not the ones who saw and experienced the discipline of the LORD your God: his majesty, his mighty

[a] 1 That is, an ark

---

1. What have you broken that got you in trouble with the powers that be: Window? Car? Family heirloom? Curfew? Training rules? Other? **2.** Were you given a second chance?

1. Many formal agreements in the ancient Near East were carved in stone. What does it signify about the nature of Israel's laws, and about its relationship with God, that their laws were written in stone? Why might this be important as they enter the promised land? **2.** Why does God instruct Moses to prepare two new tablets of stone? What does this tell you about God's nature? **3.** What is unique about the Levites (vv. 8–10)? In what way is the Lord their inheritance? In what ways will the Levites benefit all of Israel as the people enter Canaan?

What are the bases of the Christian life? How are these similar to the tablets of stone? How do these things help you?

When have you been an alien? How were you treated? How did you feel? Is the memory of it still vivid? Why?

1. What five responses does God want from his people (vv. 12–13)? How would you define each? What kind of relationship with God would these produce? **2.** How is God described in verses 14–22? How are the Israelites described? In what way do these explain the quality of relationship God seeks with Israel? How do these descriptions relate to verses 12–13?

1. Does the description in verses 14–22 still hold true for God? For his followers? How so? **2.** How will you "fear the Lord" (vv. 12–13) this week?

---

1. In your family, what material possessions have been treasured and passed on? Are you the keeper of any of these? **2.** What family traditions have you also received to be kept?

1. How are the Israelites asked to love God (vv. 1–9)? What is the link between *remembering, loving and obeying*? 2. What would the names of Dathan and Abiram bring to mind for the Israelites (see Nu 16:1–34)? How can this memory help them as they enter Canaan? 3. How is the promised land different from Egypt (vv. 10–12)? How is this new land to be a living reminder (vv. 13–15)? 4. Why might the Israelites be tempted to worship other gods in this new land? What will be the consequences for disobedience and obedience (vv. 16–17,22–25)? 5. To avoid such temptation, what will they have to remember always (vv. 1–7,22–25) and practice daily (vv. 18–21)? 6. Sum up the past memories and living reminders God has given to Israel (vv. 1–32). What is their purpose?

1. When in your life has God acted "miraculously"? What did you learn? Does this memory affect your present obedience? How so? 2. Put your name in verses 7–8. What is God's personal message to you? What risks are involved? Do these risks draw you to God? Why? What commands might God give you as you enter your promised land? 3. When have you experienced the blessings of following God's commands? What (reasons, resources, rewards) helped you to obey? Was your obedience willing or reluctant? How so? 4. What "curses" have you or your nation experienced as the result of disobedience? What is the lesson in that for you? 5. How would you explain to a new Christian the goodness that comes from obeying God?

hand, his outstretched arm; [3]the signs he performed and the things he did in the heart of Egypt, both to Pharaoh king of Egypt and to his whole country; [4]what he did to the Egyptian army, to its horses and chariots, how he overwhelmed them with the waters of the Red Sea[a] as they were pursuing you, and how the LORD brought lasting ruin on them. [5]It was not your children who saw what he did for you in the desert until you arrived at this place, [6]and what he did to Dathan and Abiram, sons of Eliab the Reubenite, when the earth opened its mouth right in the middle of all Israel and swallowed them up with their households, their tents and every living thing that belonged to them. [7]But it was your own eyes that saw all these great things the LORD has done.

[8]Observe therefore all the commands I am giving you today, so that you may have the strength to go in and take over the land that you are crossing the Jordan to possess, [9]and so that you may live long in the land that the LORD swore to your forefathers to give to them and their descendants, a land flowing with milk and honey. [10]The land you are entering to take over is not like the land of Egypt, from which you have come, where you planted your seed and irrigated it by foot as in a vegetable garden. [11]But the land you are crossing the Jordan to take possession of is a land of mountains and valleys that drinks rain from heaven. [12]It is a land the LORD your God cares for; the eyes of the LORD your God are continually on it from the beginning of the year to its end.

[13]So if you faithfully obey the commands I am giving you today—to love the LORD your God and to serve him with all your heart and with all your soul— [14]then I will send rain on your land in its season, both autumn and spring rains, so that you may gather in your grain, new wine and oil. [15]I will provide grass in the fields for your cattle, and you will eat and be satisfied.

[16]Be careful, or you will be enticed to turn away and worship other gods and bow down to them. [17]Then the LORD's anger will burn against you, and he will shut the heavens so that it will not rain and the ground will yield no produce, and you will soon perish from the good land the LORD is giving you. [18]Fix these words of mine in your hearts and minds; tie them as symbols on your hands and bind them on your foreheads. [19]Teach them to your children, talking about them when you sit at home and when you walk along the road, when you lie down and when you get up. [20]Write them on the doorframes of your houses and on your gates, [21]so that your days and the days of your children may be many in the land that the LORD swore to give your forefathers, as many as the days that the heavens are above the earth.

[22]If you carefully observe all these commands I am giving you to follow—to love the LORD your God, to walk in all his ways and to hold fast to him— [23]then the LORD will drive out all these nations before you, and you will dispossess nations larger and stronger than you. [24]Every place where you set your foot will be yours: Your territory will extend from the desert to Lebanon, and from the Euphrates River to the western sea.[b] [25]No man will be able to stand against you. The LORD your God, as he promised you, will put the terror and fear of you on the whole land, wherever you go.

[26]See, I am setting before you today a blessing and a curse— [27]the blessing if you obey the commands of the LORD your God that I am giving you today; [28]the curse if you disobey the commands of the LORD your God and turn from the way that I command you today by following other gods, which you have not known. [29]When

a4 Hebrew *Yam Suph*; that is, Sea of Reeds   b24 That is, the Mediterranean

the LORD your God has brought you into the land you are entering to possess, you are to proclaim on Mount Gerizim the blessings, and on Mount Ebal the curses. [30]As you know, these mountains are across the Jordan, west of the road,[a] toward the setting sun, near the great trees of Moreh, in the territory of those Canaanites living in the Arabah in the vicinity of Gilgal. [31]You are about to cross the Jordan to enter and take possession of the land the LORD your God is giving you. When you have taken it over and are living there, [32]be sure that you obey all the decrees and laws I am setting before you today.

The One Place of Worship

12 These are the decrees and laws you must be careful to follow in the land that the LORD, the God of your fathers, has given you to possess—as long as you live in the land. [2]Destroy completely all the places on the high mountains and on the hills and under every spreading tree where the nations you are dispossessing worship their gods. [3]Break down their altars, smash their sacred stones and burn their Asherah poles in the fire; cut down the idols of their gods and wipe out their names from those places.

[4]You must not worship the LORD your God in their way. [5]But you are to seek the place the LORD your God will choose from among all your tribes to put his Name there for his dwelling. To that place you must go; [6]there bring your burnt offerings and sacrifices, your tithes and special gifts, what you have vowed to give and your freewill offerings, and the firstborn of your herds and flocks. [7]There, in the presence of the LORD your God, you and your families shall eat and shall rejoice in everything you have put your hand to, because the LORD your God has blessed you.

[8]You are not to do as we do here today, everyone as he sees fit, [9]since you have not yet reached the resting place and the inheritance the LORD your God is giving you. [10]But you will cross the Jordan and settle in the land the LORD your God is giving you as an inheritance, and he will give you rest from all your enemies around you so that you will live in safety. [11]Then to the place the LORD your God will choose as a dwelling for his Name—there you are to bring everything I command you: your burnt offerings and sacrifices, your tithes and special gifts, and all the choice possessions you have vowed to the LORD. [12]And there rejoice before the LORD your God, you, your sons and daughters, your menservants and maidservants, and the Levites from your towns, who have no allotment or inheritance of their own. [13]Be careful not to sacrifice your burnt offerings anywhere you please. [14]Offer them only at the place the LORD will choose in one of your tribes, and there observe everything I command you.

[15]Nevertheless, you may slaughter your animals in any of your towns and eat as much of the meat as you want, as if it were gazelle or deer, according to the blessing the LORD your God gives you. Both the ceremonially unclean and the clean may eat it. [16]But you must not eat the blood; pour it out on the ground like water. [17]You must not eat in your own towns the tithe of your grain and new wine and oil, or the firstborn of your herds and flocks, or whatever you have vowed to give, or your freewill offerings or special gifts. [18]Instead, you are to eat them in the presence of the LORD your God at the place the LORD your God will choose—you, your sons and daughters, your menservants and maidservants, and the Levites from your towns—and you are to rejoice before the

[a]30 Or *Jordan, westward*

1. What has been a memorable worship experience in your life? Why? 2. What alternative "worship" centers are popular with people where you live: Sports arena? Cadillac showroom? Civic Center? Museum? Shopping mall? Campus union? Marketplace? Lake cabin? Lawn and garden? 3. What is the object of worship in each?

1. Chapter 12 begins a long section of supplementary requirements to follow the demand for absolute allegiance (4:44–11:32). Why do you think Moses begins with the commands about places of worship? 2. How complete was the destruction to be (vv. 2–3,29–30)? Why? 3. What do you learn about the practices of pagan worship (vv. 2–3,31)? 4. Why might the Israelites be tempted to try other ways of worship? (How might their change from nomadic to city life contribute to their curiosity?) 5. "*Who* we worship is always more important than *how* or *where* we worship"—Is that trendy statement true or false, according to Moses? Why? (Why would it be wrong to worship God as the Canaanites worshiped their gods? Why is the one not-yet-specified place of worship also important? What do you think was God's purpose in repeating these commands?) 6. Why did the Lord forbid Israel to drink the blood of their animals? What were they to learn from this? 7. In what other ways was Israel to be "*in* Canaan" but not "*of* Canaan"? (That is, how will "promised-land" worship be different from "nomadic" worship [v. 8]? What attitudes does God desire to be a part of worship [vv. 7, 12–13,18–19,28]? How is this different from pagan worship?)

1. Do some worship commands apply only to Israel and not to Christians? Which ones? Why? 2. What "pagan shrines and gods" are in today's

culture? Are these a source of temptation to you? Why? **3.** In what ways are you to be "*in the world*," but not "*of the world*" in your worship of God? **4.** How *holy* are holidays today? How can worship of God be enhanced on these days? **5.** What is the difference between worshiping at church on Sunday or on the tennis court (etc.)? **6.** What does this chapter teach you about corporate worship that might apply to your church as a whole? How can your small group rejoice in the Lord? **7.** What kinds of offerings do you bring to God? How are these offerings like and unlike the ones in this chapter? **8.** How much relative emphasis do you think belongs on each aspect of worship—the who, how, where, when, what and why of worship?

LORD your God in everything you put your hand to. ¹⁹Be careful not to neglect the Levites as long as you live in your land.

²⁰When the LORD your God has enlarged your territory as he promised you, and you crave meat and say, "I would like some meat," then you may eat as much of it as you want. ²¹If the place where the LORD your God chooses to put his Name is too far away from you, you may slaughter animals from the herds and flocks the LORD has given you, as I have commanded you, and in your own towns you may eat as much of them as you want. ²²Eat them as you would gazelle or deer. Both the ceremonially unclean and the clean may eat. ²³But be sure you do not eat the blood, because the blood is the life, and you must not eat the life with the meat. ²⁴You must not eat the blood; pour it out on the ground like water. ²⁵Do not eat it, so that it may go well with you and your children after you, because you will be doing what is right in the eyes of the LORD.

²⁶But take your consecrated things and whatever you have vowed to give, and go to the place the LORD will choose. ²⁷Present your burnt offerings on the altar of the LORD your God, both the meat and the blood. The blood of your sacrifices must be poured beside the altar of the LORD your God, but you may eat the meat. ²⁸Be careful to obey all these regulations I am giving you, so that it may always go well with you and your children after you, because you will be doing what is good and right in the eyes of the LORD your God.

²⁹The LORD your God will cut off before you the nations you are about to invade and dispossess. But when you have driven them out and settled in their land, ³⁰and after they have been destroyed before you, be careful not to be ensnared by inquiring about their gods, saying, "How do these nations serve their gods? We will do the same." ³¹You must not worship the LORD your God in their way, because in worshiping their gods, they do all kinds of detestable things the LORD hates. They even burn their sons and daughters in the fire as sacrifices to their gods.

³²See that you do all I command you; do not add to it or take away from it.

Worshiping Other Gods

13 If a prophet, or one who foretells by dreams, appears among you and announces to you a miraculous sign or wonder, ²and if the sign or wonder of which he has spoken takes place, and he says, "Let us follow other gods" (gods you have not known) "and let us worship them," ³you must not listen to the words of that prophet or dreamer. The LORD your God is testing you to find out whether you love him with all your heart and with all your soul. ⁴It is the LORD your God you must follow, and him you must revere. Keep his commands and obey him; serve him and hold fast to him. ⁵That prophet or dreamer must be put to death, because he preached rebellion against the LORD your God, who brought you out of Egypt and redeemed you from the land of slavery; he has tried to turn you from the way the LORD your God commanded you to follow. You must purge the evil from among you.

⁶If your very own brother, or your son or daughter, or the wife you love, or your closest friend secretly entices you, saying, "Let us go and worship other gods" (gods that neither you nor your fathers have known, ⁷gods of the peoples around you, whether near or far, from one end of the land to the other), ⁸do not yield to him or listen to him. Show him no pity. Do not spare him or shield him. ⁹You must certainly put him to death. Your hand must be the first in putting him to death, and then the hands of all the people.

---

1. What fad in clothing, recreation or hair did you once follow that now brings a smile to your face? **2.** What dated religious fad did you once follow?

1. Of what three sources of danger were the Israelites to be wary (vv. 1–3,6–8,12–14)? **2.** Why might Israel be tempted to follow a prophet who worshiped other gods? How was Israel to know if a prophet was from God (vv. 2–4)? What were the consequences for a false prophet? **3.** How could family and friends be a source of temptation (vv. 6–7)? How was a person to respond and why? **4.** What threat does a town to be conquered pose? What were the Israelites to do (vv. 12–14)? What were the consequences for the town and for Israel (vv. 15–18)? **5.** What are the limits of God's tolerance? What are the blessings of faithfulness?

¹⁰Stone him to death, because he tried to turn you away from the LORD your God, who brought you out of Egypt, out of the land of slavery. ¹¹Then all Israel will hear and be afraid, and no one among you will do such an evil thing again.

¹²If you hear it said about one of the towns the LORD your God is giving you to live in ¹³that wicked men have arisen among you and have led the people of their town astray, saying, "Let us go and worship other gods" (gods you have not known), ¹⁴then you must inquire, probe and investigate it thoroughly. And if it is true and it has been proved that this detestable thing has been done among you, ¹⁵you must certainly put to the sword all who live in that town. Destroy it completely,ᵃ both its people and its livestock. ¹⁶Gather all the plunder of the town into the middle of the public square and completely burn the town and all its plunder as a whole burnt offering to the LORD your God. It is to remain a ruin forever, never to be rebuilt. ¹⁷None of those condemned thingsᵃ shall be found in your hands, so that the LORD will turn from his fierce anger; he will show you mercy, have compassion on you, and increase your numbers, as he promised on oath to your forefathers, ¹⁸because you obey the LORD your God, keeping all his commands that I am giving you today and doing what is right in his eyes.

Clean and Unclean Food

14 You are the children of the LORD your God. Do not cut yourselves or shave the front of your heads for the dead, ²for you are a people holy to the LORD your God. Out of all the peoples on the face of the earth, the LORD has chosen you to be his treasured possession.

³Do not eat any detestable thing. ⁴These are the animals you may eat: the ox, the sheep, the goat, ⁵the deer, the gazelle, the roe deer, the wild goat, the ibex, the antelope and the mountain sheep.ᵇ ⁶You may eat any animal that has a split hoof divided in two and that chews the cud. ⁷However, of those that chew the cud or that have a split hoof completely divided you may not eat the camel, the rabbit or the coney.ᶜ Although they chew the cud, they do not have a split hoof; they are ceremonially unclean for you. ⁸The pig is also unclean; although it has a split hoof, it does not chew the cud. You are not to eat their meat or touch their carcasses.

⁹Of all the creatures living in the water, you may eat any that has fins and scales. ¹⁰But anything that does not have fins and scales you may not eat; for you it is unclean.

¹¹You may eat any clean bird. ¹²But these you may not eat: the eagle, the vulture, the black vulture, ¹³the red kite, the black kite, any kind of falcon, ¹⁴any kind of raven, ¹⁵the horned owl, the screech owl, the gull, any kind of hawk, ¹⁶the little owl, the great owl, the white owl, ¹⁷the desert owl, the osprey, the cormorant, ¹⁸the stork, any kind of heron, the hoopoe and the bat.

¹⁹All flying insects that swarm are unclean to you; do not eat them. ²⁰But any winged creature that is clean you may eat.

²¹Do not eat anything you find already dead. You may give it to an alien living in any of your towns, and he may eat it, or you may sell it to a foreigner. But you are a people holy to the LORD your God.

Do not cook a young goat in its mother's milk.

1. How does falsehood among religious teachers, family members, or a whole community apply today? Is one a source of danger for you? How so? What can you do about that? 2. How can you know if a person or teaching is from God? How do you seek discernment? 3. What do you think should be "limits of toleration" for a committed Christian? Should these limits be extended, or relaxed, in relation to those outside the Christian faith? Why? 4. In what way is historic Christianity an intolerant faith? How does this shape your life today?

What foods don't you like? What do you like best? What would get you to eat something you don't like, or to stop eating something you do like?

1. Why would the mourning customs of verse 1 be prohibited. (see 1Ki 18:28)? 2. What is the overall purpose of these dietary commands (v. 2)? What do the phrases "holy to the Lord" and "unclean" imply? 3. How would these laws help Israel to become a distinctive and holy people?

1. In what ways are Christians called to be separate and holy? In what area of your life would you like to grow in holiness? How so? How can your small group assist you? 2. Are there any ungodly customs you have adopted which interfere with your holiness? What will you do about them? When? 3. What are the pros, and cons, for you as a Christian in being holy and separate?

ᵃ15,17 The Hebrew term refers to the irrevocable giving over of things or persons to the LORD, often by totally destroying them.   ᵇ5 The precise identification of some of the birds and animals in this chapter is uncertain.   ᶜ7 That is, the hyrax or rock badger

Who is (or was) the generous giver in your family? How so?

1. What were the Israelites to do (vv. 22–23)? How would this help them to "revere the Lord"? **2.** How was the Israelite personally involved in giving (vv. 24–26)? What was to accompany this giving? Why? **3.** What happened at the end of three years and why?

1. Why do you think God commands us to give? What do you feel about the giving that is commanded? How have you been blessed through giving? **2.** How do you decide who to give to and how much to give? How can verses 27–29 help you? **3.** When there is not enough money to meet your monthly budget of needs, do you give more, the same or less of your money to God? Why?

———

Apart from your parents, which persons are you most "indebted" to for getting where you are and becoming who you are?

1. By this principle of cancelling debts, what attitude, behavior and theology is Moses trying to teach Israel? How is each of these three related? **2.** Why should Israel be so generous (v. 4)? What promises are given for a generous heart (vv. 5–6,10,18)? **3.** Is verse 11 an excuse or an appeal? For what?

1. What attitudes and behaviors can and will you adopt from verses 1–11? **2.** What promises in Scripture and role models in your community do you have for becoming more generous? What can you adopt from their example? **3.** What causes a "tight fist"? In what ways would you like to become more "open-handed"? How will you begin this week?

———

What was your first "real job" and how long did it last?

1. What rights did Jewish slaves have? What responsibilities did owners have? **2.** In what way do these instructions help Israel prevent slavery (vv. 13–14)? **3.** Why do you think God

Tithes

22Be sure to set aside a tenth of all that your fields produce each year. 23Eat the tithe of your grain, new wine and oil, and the firstborn of your herds and flocks in the presence of the LORD your God at the place he will choose as a dwelling for his Name, so that you may learn to revere the LORD your God always. 24But if that place is too distant and you have been blessed by the LORD your God and cannot carry your tithe (because the place where the LORD will choose to put his Name is so far away), 25then exchange your tithe for silver, and take the silver with you and go to the place the LORD your God will choose. 26Use the silver to buy whatever you like: cattle, sheep, wine or other fermented drink, or anything you wish. Then you and your household shall eat there in the presence of the LORD your God and rejoice. 27And do not neglect the Levites living in your towns, for they have no allotment or inheritance of their own.

28At the end of every three years, bring all the tithes of that year's produce and store it in your towns, 29so that the Levites (who have no allotment or inheritance of their own) and the aliens, the fatherless and the widows who live in your towns may come and eat and be satisfied, and so that the LORD your God may bless you in all the work of your hands.

The Year for Canceling Debts

15 At the end of every seven years you must cancel debts. 2This is how it is to be done: Every creditor shall cancel the loan he has made to his fellow Israelite. He shall not require payment from his fellow Israelite or brother, because the LORD's time for canceling debts has been proclaimed. 3You may require payment from a foreigner, but you must cancel any debt your brother owes you. 4However, there should be no poor among you, for in the land the LORD your God is giving you to possess as your inheritance, he will richly bless you, 5if only you fully obey the LORD your God and are careful to follow all these commands I am giving you today. 6For the LORD your God will bless you as he has promised, and you will lend to many nations but will borrow from none. You will rule over many nations but none will rule over you.

7If there is a poor man among your brothers in any of the towns of the land that the LORD your God is giving you, do not be hardhearted or tightfisted toward your poor brother. 8Rather be openhanded and freely lend him whatever he needs. 9Be careful not to harbor this wicked thought: "The seventh year, the year for canceling debts, is near," so that you do not show ill will toward your needy brother and give him nothing. He may then appeal to the LORD against you, and you will be found guilty of sin. 10Give generously to him and do so without a grudging heart; then because of this the LORD your God will bless you in all your work and in everything you put your hand to. 11There will always be poor people in the land. Therefore I command you to be openhanded toward your brothers and toward the poor and needy in your land.

Freeing Servants

12If a fellow Hebrew, a man or a woman, sells himself to you and serves you six years, in the seventh year you must let him go free. 13And when you release him, do not send him away empty-handed. 14Supply him liberally from your flock, your threshing floor and your winepress. Give to him as the LORD your God has blessed you. 15Remember that you were slaves in Egypt and the LORD your God redeemed you. That is why I give you this command today.

[16]But if your servant says to you, "I do not want to leave you," because he loves you and your family and is well off with you, [17]then take an awl and push it through his ear lobe into the door, and he will become your servant for life. Do the same for your maidservant.

[18]Do not consider it a hardship to set your servant free, because his service to you these six years has been worth twice as much as that of a hired hand. And the LORD your God will bless you in everything you do.

The Firstborn Animals

[19]Set apart for the LORD your God every firstborn male of your herds and flocks. Do not put the firstborn of your oxen to work, and do not shear the firstborn of your sheep. [20]Each year you and your family are to eat them in the presence of the LORD your God at the place he will choose. [21]If an animal has a defect, is lame or blind, or has any serious flaw, you must not sacrifice it to the LORD your God. [22]You are to eat it in your own towns. Both the ceremonially unclean and the clean may eat it, as if it were gazelle or deer. [23]But you must not eat the blood; pour it out on the ground like water.

Passover

16 Observe the month of Abib and celebrate the Passover of the LORD your God, because in the month of Abib he brought you out of Egypt by night. [2]Sacrifice as the Passover to the LORD your God an animal from your flock or herd at the place the LORD will choose as a dwelling for his Name. [3]Do not eat it with bread made with yeast, but for seven days eat unleavened bread, the bread of affliction, because you left Egypt in haste—so that all the days of your life you may remember the time of your departure from Egypt. [4]Let no yeast be found in your possession in all your land for seven days. Do not let any of the meat you sacrifice on the evening of the first day remain until morning.

[5]You must not sacrifice the Passover in any town the LORD your God gives you [6]except in the place he will choose as a dwelling for his Name. There you must sacrifice the Passover in the evening, when the sun goes down, on the anniversary[a] of your departure from Egypt. [7]Roast it and eat it at the place the LORD your God will choose. Then in the morning return to your tents. [8]For six days eat unleavened bread and on the seventh day hold an assembly to the LORD your God and do no work.

Feast of Weeks

[9]Count off seven weeks from the time you begin to put the sickle to the standing grain. [10]Then celebrate the Feast of Weeks to the LORD your God by giving a freewill offering in proportion to the blessings the LORD your God has given you. [11]And rejoice before the LORD your God at the place he will choose as a dwelling for his Name—you, your sons and daughters, your menservants and maidservants, the Levites in your towns, and the aliens, the fatherless and the widows living among you. [12]Remember that you were slaves in Egypt, and follow carefully these decrees.

Feast of Tabernacles

[13]Celebrate the Feast of Tabernacles for seven days after you have gathered the produce of your threshing floor and your wine-

[a]6 Or *down, at the time of day*

---

reminds the Israelites that they had once been slaves? **4.** What is the new relationship in verses 16–17? How is this different from the previous relationship? **5.** How is 15:19–23 linked with 12:1–19? What do both passages affirm about God? About Israel's giving?

1. In what ways have we as Christians been freed from slavery? How is this to influence our care for others? **2.** What implications do these verses have for employees? Employers? **3.** What do these verses tell you about God's priorities in relationships and property?

---

1. What is your favorite celebration or holiday? Why? **2.** What favorite dessert or snack, if made for your family tonight, would be "gone by morning"? **3.** Name one from your church or from your community who is making a go of it, despite being a foreigner, an orphan or a widow?

1. What was the purpose of the Passover celebration (v. 3)? **2.** What were the Israelites to remember about God? Do you think such remembrances would become "old hat"? Why? **3.** Where and when was the Passover to be celebrated (v. 6)? Why is that significant? (How is God relevant to darkness?) **4.** What did the Feast of Weeks celebrate (vv. 9–12) that was different than the Feast of Tabernacles (vv. 13–17)? **5.** In what ways were both a memory party for all kinds of people? Why were children included at this party? Why do you think God wanted different social classes, age-groups, and ethnic-groups to celebrate together? **6.** How were these feasts tied to the economy? How similar in scope was it to an American Thanksgiving? **7.** What was to be the emotional tone of these feasts? Why? **8.** What is the link between this worship of God and the administration of law (vv. 18–20)? What warning is given in verse 19? What goal is set before the Israelites in verse 20? **9.** What did these feasts and judges teach Israel about God?

1. Why is it important to have special holidays or holy days to remember God's intervention? 2. What Christian holidays have helped you to remember who God is? How so? 3. What upcoming Christian holiday do you want to celebrate more meaningfully than before? What will you do differently this time? 4. What principles of celebration should Christians adapt from the feasts in this chapter? 5. What have you learned about God from these three feasts? 6. What part does justice play in your worship of God?

1. What in creation reflects God's image for you? Why? 2. When have you used the "court of appeal" available to you at work, school, church, state or home? With what results?

1. Why the prohibitions of cult objects (16:21–22; see 7:5; Ex 34:13) and flawed animals (17:1; compare Mal 1:8)? 2. What is attractive about the sun, moon, and stars? What is dangerous about worshiping these? 3. Why would false worship lead to potential death? What safeguards against false accusations are given here? 4. What is the role of these law courts? How are their rulings to be treated? 5. Why do you think the penalty for contempt was death? What contempt-of-court exists in your system today? 6. What do you know about the time, anticipated by Moses, when Israel would ask for a king (17:14; see 1Sa 8:4–9)? Why should the king be an Israelite? What should he refrain from accumulating and why? Who do you know that violated this? 7. Instead, how is the king to live each day? What will be his inspiration?

1. What role does this text suggest believers should play in each other's life when one "breaks covenant" with God? 2. In what ways do we bear false witness against each other? 3. What guidelines for justice from these verses are still at work today in civic and church governing bodies? 4. How should Christians respond to another's contempt for the law? 5.

press. ¹⁴Be joyful at your Feast—you, your sons and daughters, your menservants and maidservants, and the Levites, the aliens, the fatherless and the widows who live in your towns. ¹⁵For seven days celebrate the Feast to the LORD your God at the place the LORD will choose. For the LORD your God will bless you in all your harvest and in all the work of your hands, and your joy will be complete.

¹⁶Three times a year all your men must appear before the LORD your God at the place he will choose: at the Feast of Unleavened Bread, the Feast of Weeks and the Feast of Tabernacles. No man should appear before the LORD empty-handed: ¹⁷Each of you must bring a gift in proportion to the way the LORD your God has blessed you.

Judges

¹⁸Appoint judges and officials for each of your tribes in every town the LORD your God is giving you, and they shall judge the people fairly. ¹⁹Do not pervert justice or show partiality. Do not accept a bribe, for a bribe blinds the eyes of the wise and twists the words of the righteous. ²⁰Follow justice and justice alone, so that you may live and possess the land the LORD your God is giving you.

Worshiping Other Gods

²¹Do not set up any wooden Asherah pole[a] beside the altar you build to the LORD your God, ²²and do not erect a sacred stone, for these the LORD your God hates.

17 Do not sacrifice to the LORD your God an ox or a sheep that has any defect or flaw in it, for that would be detestable to him.

²If a man or woman living among you in one of the towns the LORD gives you is found doing evil in the eyes of the LORD your God in violation of his covenant, ³and contrary to my command has worshiped other gods, bowing down to them or to the sun or the moon or the stars of the sky, ⁴and this has been brought to your attention, then you must investigate it thoroughly. If it is true and it has been proved that this detestable thing has been done in Israel, ⁵take the man or woman who has done this evil deed to your city gate and stone that person to death. ⁶On the testimony of two or three witnesses a man shall be put to death, but no one shall be put to death on the testimony of only one witness. ⁷The hands of the witnesses must be the first in putting him to death, and then the hands of all the people. You must purge the evil from among you.

Law Courts

⁸If cases come before your courts that are too difficult for you to judge—whether bloodshed, lawsuits or assaults—take them to the place the LORD your God will choose. ⁹Go to the priests, who are Levites, and to the judge who is in office at that time. Inquire of them and they will give you the verdict. ¹⁰You must act according to the decisions they give you at the place the LORD will choose. Be careful to do everything they direct you to do. ¹¹Act according to the law they teach you and the decisions they give you. Do not turn aside from what they tell you, to the right or to the left. ¹²The man who shows contempt for the judge or for the priest who stands ministering there to the LORD your God must be put to death. You must purge the evil from Israel. ¹³All the people will hear and be afraid, and will not be contemptuous again.

a21 Or Do not plant any tree dedicated to Asherah

The King

14When you enter the land the LORD your God is giving you and have taken possession of it and settled in it, and you say, "Let us set a king over us like all the nations around us," 15be sure to appoint over you the king the LORD your God chooses. He must be from among your own brothers. Do not place a foreigner over you, one who is not a brother Israelite. 16The king, moreover, must not acquire great numbers of horses for himself or make the people return to Egypt to get more of them, for the LORD has told you, "You are not to go back that way again." 17He must not take many wives, or his heart will be led astray. He must not accumulate large amounts of silver and gold.

18When he takes the throne of his kingdom, he is to write for himself on a scroll a copy of this law, taken from that of the priests, who are Levites. 19It is to be with him, and he is to read it all the days of his life so that he may learn to revere the LORD his God and follow carefully all the words of this law and these decrees 20and not consider himself better than his brothers and turn from the law to the right or to the left. Then he and his descendants will reign a long time over his kingdom in Israel.

Offerings for Priests and Levites

18 The priests, who are Levites—indeed the whole tribe of Levi—are to have no allotment or inheritance with Israel. They shall live on the offerings made to the LORD by fire, for that is their inheritance. 2They shall have no inheritance among their brothers; the LORD is their inheritance, as he promised them.

3This is the share due the priests from the people who sacrifice a bull or a sheep: the shoulder, the jowls and the inner parts. 4You are to give them the firstfruits of your grain, new wine and oil, and the first wool from the shearing of your sheep, 5for the LORD your God has chosen them and their descendants out of all your tribes to stand and minister in the LORD's name always.

6If a Levite moves from one of your towns anywhere in Israel where he is living, and comes in all earnestness to the place the LORD will choose, 7he may minister in the name of the LORD his God like all his fellow Levites who serve there in the presence of the LORD. 8He is to share equally in their benefits, even though he has received money from the sale of family possessions.

Detestable Practices

9When you enter the land the LORD your God is giving you, do not learn to imitate the detestable ways of the nations there. 10Let no one be found among you who sacrifices his son or daughter in*a* the fire, who practices divination or sorcery, interprets omens, engages in witchcraft, 11or casts spells, or who is a medium or spiritist or who consults the dead. 12Anyone who does these things is detestable to the LORD, and because of these detestable practices the LORD your God will drive out those nations before you. 13You must be blameless before the LORD your God.

The Prophet

14The nations you will dispossess listen to those who practice sorcery or divination. But as for you, the LORD your God has not permitted you to do so. 15The LORD your God will raise up for you a prophet like me from among your own brothers. You must listen to him. 16For this is what you asked of the LORD your God at Horeb

a10 Or *who makes his son or daughter pass through*

What still tempts people in places of leadership? How can power often corrupt? How would application of this passage help prevent corruption? What part will you play in its application this week?

1. Who in the clergy has played an important role in your life? How so? 2. Has anyone ever tried to interest you in ouija boards or astrology? What might intrigue you about such practices?

1. What was the Levites' inheritance? Is their freedom from property and dependence on others a good thing? Why or why not? 2. How would you characterize the offerings they live on: (a) Leftovers? (b) Luxuries? (c) Just dues? 3. How were all God's people involved with the priests' sustenance? What was the goal behind the "detestable" practices of other nations?

1. Today, should clergy put laity first, or vice versa? Why? How so? 2. What has God given you as an "inheritance"? Are you to share this? How so? 3. Who, caught up in spiritism, may you pray for tonight? How else may you be of help? 4. Why does God want you "blameless" (v. 13)?

Would it frighten or delight you to be a prophet? Why?

1. What provision does God make for Israel (vv. 14–15)? Why? 2. What was the duty of the prophet, as compared with a priest? 3. What kinds of prophets were the Israelites to avoid (vv.

10–11,22)? How do you account for miraculous signs performed by false prophets? **4.** What was the responsibility of the true prophet? Of the people?

♡ **1.** Today, who might qualify as a prophet in the biblical tradition? How can you recognize such? What from these verses applies today? **2.** Who in your group or church might have the gift of prophecy? How can you tell? How can you help one another be good stewards of this gift?

☕ **1.** Where do you feel most safe and sheltered from harm or stress? Why there? **2.** Have you ever been seriously misjudged or gossiped about? How so?

📖 **1.** What geographical guidelines were given for these cities of refuge (vv. 2–3)? **2.** How were these cities an inheritance for everyone? **3.** Why distinguish between intentional and unintentional murder? (Isn't murder still murder?) **4.** How do these cities honor God and human life? **5.** What promise and penalty is associated with the use and abuse of these cities (vv. 8–9)? Why? **6.** Why should judges interrogate witnesses so thoroughly (vv. 16–20)? **7.** Is this passage more concerned with innocence or guilt? Why do you think that is? **8.** To whom should "no pity" be shown? How might the cities of refuge apply here?

♡ **1.** What does this passage affirm about human life and divine justice and mercy that applies today? (E.g.: What laws today are similar to the ancient cities of refuge)? **2.** What impact does bearing false witness have on your life with God, self and others? **3.** What can your group cultivate to help eradicate gossip and false accusations among God's people?

on the day of the assembly when you said, "Let us not hear the voice of the LORD our God nor see this great fire anymore, or we will die."

[17]The LORD said to me: "What they say is good. [18]I will raise up for them a prophet like you from among their brothers; I will put my words in his mouth, and he will tell them everything I command him. [19]If anyone does not listen to my words that the prophet speaks in my name, I myself will call him to account. [20]But a prophet who presumes to speak in my name anything I have not commanded him to say, or a prophet who speaks in the name of other gods, must be put to death."

[21]You may say to yourselves, "How can we know when a message has not been spoken by the LORD?" [22]If what a prophet proclaims in the name of the LORD does not take place or come true, that is a message the LORD has not spoken. That prophet has spoken presumptuously. Do not be afraid of him.

Cities of Refuge

19 When the LORD your God has destroyed the nations whose land he is giving you, and when you have driven them out and settled in their towns and houses, [2]then set aside for yourselves three cities centrally located in the land the LORD your God is giving you to possess. [3]Build roads to them and divide into three parts the land the LORD your God is giving you as an inheritance, so that anyone who kills a man may flee there.

[4]This is the rule concerning the man who kills another and flees there to save his life—one who kills his neighbor unintentionally, without malice aforethought. [5]For instance, a man may go into the forest with his neighbor to cut wood, and as he swings his ax to fell a tree, the head may fly off and hit his neighbor and kill him. That man may flee to one of these cities and save his life. [6]Otherwise, the avenger of blood might pursue him in a rage, overtake him if the distance is too great, and kill him even though he is not deserving of death, since he did it to his neighbor without malice aforethought. [7]This is why I command you to set aside for yourselves three cities.

[8]If the LORD your God enlarges your territory, as he promised on oath to your forefathers, and gives you the whole land he promised them, [9]because you carefully follow all these laws I command you today—to love the LORD your God and to walk always in his ways—then you are to set aside three more cities. [10]Do this so that innocent blood will not be shed in your land, which the LORD your God is giving you as your inheritance, and so that you will not be guilty of bloodshed.

[11]But if a man hates his neighbor and lies in wait for him, assaults and kills him, and then flees to one of these cities, [12]the elders of his town shall send for him, bring him back from the city, and hand him over to the avenger of blood to die. [13]Show him no pity. You must purge from Israel the guilt of shedding innocent blood, so that it may go well with you.

[14]Do not move your neighbor's boundary stone set up by your predecessors in the inheritance you receive in the land the LORD your God is giving you to possess.

Witnesses

[15]One witness is not enough to convict a man accused of any crime or offense he may have committed. A matter must be established by the testimony of two or three witnesses.

[16]If a malicious witness takes the stand to accuse a man of a

crime, [17]the two men involved in the dispute must stand in the presence of the LORD before the priests and the judges who are in office at the time. [18]The judges must make a thorough investigation, and if the witness proves to be a liar, giving false testimony against his brother, [19]then do to him as he intended to do to his brother. You must purge the evil from among you. [20]The rest of the people will hear of this and be afraid, and never again will such an evil thing be done among you. [21]Show no pity: life for life, eye for eye, tooth for tooth, hand for hand, foot for foot.

Going to War

20 When you go to war against your enemies and see horses and chariots and an army greater than yours, do not be afraid of them, because the LORD your God, who brought you up out of Egypt, will be with you. [2]When you are about to go into battle, the priest shall come forward and address the army. [3]He shall say: "Hear, O Israel, today you are going into battle against your enemies. Do not be fainthearted or afraid; do not be terrified or give way to panic before them. [4]For the LORD your God is the one who goes with you to fight for you against your enemies to give you victory."

[5]The officers shall say to the army: "Has anyone built a new house and not dedicated it? Let him go home, or he may die in battle and someone else may dedicate it. [6]Has anyone planted a vineyard and not begun to enjoy it? Let him go home, or he may die in battle and someone else enjoy it. [7]Has anyone become pledged to a woman and not married her? Let him go home, or he may die in battle and someone else marry her." [8]Then the officers shall add, "Is any man afraid or fainthearted? Let him go home so that his brothers will not become disheartened too." [9]When the officers have finished speaking to the army, they shall appoint commanders over it.

[10]When you march up to attack a city, make its people an offer of peace. [11]If they accept and open their gates, all the people in it shall be subject to forced labor and shall work for you. [12]If they refuse to make peace and they engage you in battle, lay siege to that city. [13]When the LORD your God delivers it into your hand, put to the sword all the men in it. [14]As for the women, the children, the livestock and everything else in the city, you may take these as plunder for yourselves. And you may use the plunder the LORD your God gives you from your enemies. [15]This is how you are to treat all the cities that are at a distance from you and do not belong to the nations nearby.

[16]However, in the cities of the nations the LORD your God is giving you as an inheritance, do not leave alive anything that breathes. [17]Completely destroy[a] them—the Hittites, Amorites, Canaanites, Perizzites, Hivites and Jebusites—as the LORD your God has commanded you. [18]Otherwise, they will teach you to follow all the detestable things they do in worshiping their gods, and you will sin against the LORD your God.

[19]When you lay siege to a city for a long time, fighting against it to capture it, do not destroy its trees by putting an ax to them, because you can eat their fruit. Do not cut them down. Are the trees of the field people, that you should besiege them?[b] [20]However, you may cut down trees that you know are not fruit trees and use them to build siege works until the city at war with you falls.

1. What has been a recent "victory" in your life? How was the "war" won? 2. Share a major unfinished duty you'd like to carry to completion this year.

1. When going to war, what were the Israelites to trust? What memory was to strengthen them? Why does the Lord enter into their world of war? 2. When most armies *build up*, why did Israel *scale down*? 3. How was Israel to approach its enemies (vv. 10–15)? Why? How was this different from conquered people in the Promised Land (vv. 16–18)? Why does property (vv. 19–20) seem to receive preferential treatment over these people? 4. Some theologians term this killing in the Promised Land part of the intrusion ethic—that is, exceptions made for this "intrusion" only. Do you think such an "ethic" is consistent with God's character? Why?

1. Does verse 4 apply to military wars today? When might it be correct to say God takes sides? 2. Are the exemptions of verses 5–8 more important than going to war? Why? How might they apply today? 3. How does verse 4 apply to situations outside a military setting? How does it apply now to you? 4. Which is more effective "in battle" for God: a small, single-minded, dedicated body of believers, or a large, half-hearted, discontented body? Why? 5. What competes for your allegiance in busy stretches of your life? How do you follow through with God?

---

a17 The Hebrew term refers to the irrevocable giving over of things or persons to the LORD, often by totally destroying them. b19 Or *down to use in the siege, for the fruit trees are for the benefit of man.*

Who has been your favorite fictitious detective? Why? How often is homicide involved? When and how is the typical mystery solved?

1. Why the instructions in verses 3–9 (see Dt 19:6)? 2. What were the elders and priests acknowledging in verse 7? How is God described in the very next verse? 3. What did the death of the heifer signify? Why the prayer? For what might you have expected them to pray?

1. Does your government have any homicide laws like this? What is your responsibility when a person is killed by an unknown murderer? 2. Have you ever received an anonymous hate note? Been harmed by someone you didn't know? What did you learn about justice? Mercy? Peace? How do you hope to react next time?

1. For what would you shave your head? 2. Share an instance of rebelliousness in your childhood and how just or merciful your parents were in response to it. How did you feel?

1. What were the rights of a prisoner of war? Of the conqueror? 2. What attitude on the part of God toward women lies behind the instructions in verses 10–14? Why? 3. What were the rights of the firstborn (vv. 15–17)? What was to be the father's attitude? How does this reflect God's justice and love? 4. Why the severe penalty of rebellious children in verses 18–21? What commandment lies behind this regulation (see 5:16)?

1. What specific passion for God's justice do you glean from this passage? Do you know of anyone suffering from injustice? How may you help him or her this week? 2. Have you ever felt "disinherited" by family, friends or employers? How can your small group help you handle this?

What important thing have you once lost and then found? What was it like to *discover* your loss? To *recover* your loss?

Atonement for an Unsolved Murder

21 If a man is found slain, lying in a field in the land the LORD your God is giving you to possess, and it is not known who killed him, [2]your elders and judges shall go out and measure the distance from the body to the neighboring towns. [3]Then the elders of the town nearest the body shall take a heifer that has never been worked and has never worn a yoke [4]and lead her down to a valley that has not been plowed or planted and where there is a flowing stream. There in the valley they are to break the heifer's neck. [5]The priests, the sons of Levi, shall step forward, for the LORD your God has chosen them to minister and to pronounce blessings in the name of the LORD and to decide all cases of dispute and assault. [6]Then all the elders of the town nearest the body shall wash their hands over the heifer whose neck was broken in the valley, [7]and they shall declare: "Our hands did not shed this blood, nor did our eyes see it done. [8]Accept this atonement for your people Israel, whom you have redeemed, O LORD, and do not hold your people guilty of the blood of an innocent man." And the bloodshed will be atoned for. [9]So you will purge from yourselves the guilt of shedding innocent blood, since you have done what is right in the eyes of the LORD.

Marrying a Captive Woman

[10]When you go to war against your enemies and the LORD your God delivers them into your hands and you take captives, [11]if you notice among the captives a beautiful woman and are attracted to her, you may take her as your wife. [12]Bring her into your home and have her shave her head, trim her nails [13]and put aside the clothes she was wearing when captured. After she has lived in your house and mourned her father and mother for a full month, then you may go to her and be her husband and she shall be your wife. [14]If you are not pleased with her, let her go wherever she wishes. You must not sell her or treat her as a slave, since you have dishonored her.

The Right of the Firstborn

[15]If a man has two wives, and he loves one but not the other, and both bear him sons but the firstborn is the son of the wife he does not love, [16]when he wills his property to his sons, he must not give the rights of the firstborn to the son of the wife he loves in preference to his actual firstborn, the son of the wife he does not love. [17]He must acknowledge the son of his unloved wife as the firstborn by giving him a double share of all he has. That son is the first sign of his father's strength. The right of the firstborn belongs to him.

A Rebellious Son

[18]If a man has a stubborn and rebellious son who does not obey his father and mother and will not listen to them when they discipline him, [19]his father and mother shall take hold of him and bring him to the elders at the gate of his town. [20]They shall say to the elders, "This son of ours is stubborn and rebellious. He will not obey us. He is a profligate and a drunkard." [21]Then all the men of his town shall stone him to death. You must purge the evil from among you. All Israel will hear of it and be afraid.

Various Laws

[22]If a man guilty of a capital offense is put to death and his body is hung on a tree, [23]you must not leave his body on the tree overnight. Be sure to bury him that same day, because anyone who

is hung on a tree is under God's curse. You must not desecrate the land the LORD your God is giving you as an inheritance.

22 If you see your brother's ox or sheep straying, do not ignore it but be sure to take it back to him. ²If the brother does not live near you or if you do not know who he is, take it home with you and keep it until he comes looking for it. Then give it back to him. ³Do the same if you find your brother's donkey or his cloak or anything he loses. Do not ignore it.

⁴If you see your brother's donkey or his ox fallen on the road, do not ignore it. Help him get it to its feet.

⁵A woman must not wear men's clothing, nor a man wear women's clothing, for the LORD your God detests anyone who does this.

⁶If you come across a bird's nest beside the road, either in a tree or on the ground, and the mother is sitting on the young or on the eggs, do not take the mother with the young. ⁷You may take the young, but be sure to let the mother go, so that it may go well with you and you may have a long life.

⁸When you build a new house, make a parapet around your roof so that you may not bring the guilt of bloodshed on your house if someone falls from the roof.

⁹Do not plant two kinds of seed in your vineyard; if you do, not only the crops you plant but also the fruit of the vineyard will be defiled.ᵃ

¹⁰Do not plow with an ox and a donkey yoked together.

¹¹Do not wear clothes of wool and linen woven together.

¹²Make tassels on the four corners of the cloak you wear.

Marriage Violations

¹³If a man takes a wife and, after lying with her, dislikes her ¹⁴and slanders her and gives her a bad name, saying, "I married this woman, but when I approached her, I did not find proof of her virginity," ¹⁵then the girl's father and mother shall bring proof that she was a virgin to the town elders at the gate. ¹⁶The girl's father will say to the elders, "I gave my daughter in marriage to this man, but he dislikes her. ¹⁷Now he has slandered her and said, 'I did not find your daughter to be a virgin.' But here is the proof of my daughter's virginity." Then her parents shall display the cloth before the elders of the town, ¹⁸and the elders shall take the man and punish him. ¹⁹They shall fine him a hundred shekels of silverᵇ and give them to the girl's father, because this man has given an Israelite virgin a bad name. She shall continue to be his wife; he must not divorce her as long as he lives.

²⁰If, however, the charge is true and no proof of the girl's virginity can be found, ²¹she shall be brought to the door of her father's house and there the men of her town shall stone her to death. She has done a disgraceful thing in Israel by being promiscuous while still in her father's house. You must purge the evil from among you.

²²If a man is found sleeping with another man's wife, both the man who slept with her and the woman must die. You must purge the evil from Israel.

²³If a man happens to meet in a town a virgin pledged to be married and he sleeps with her, ²⁴you shall take both of them to the gate of that town and stone them to death—the girl because she was in a town and did not scream for help, and the man because he violated another man's wife. You must purge the evil from among you.

ᵃ9 Or *be forfeited to the sanctuary*   ᵇ19 That is, about 2 1/2 pounds (about 1 kilogram)

How much time elapsed in between?

1. What do you think was the original purpose of declaring God's curse on criminals hung on a tree (21:22–23)? How does this apply to Jesus' death on a cross (see Gal 3:13)? 2. What attitude and commandment lies behind the instructions in 22:1–4 (see 5:21)? 3. What was the benefit of distinguishing between a mother and her young (22:6–7)? Of building a parapet (22:8)? Of not commingling seed, beasts of burden or certain clothing (22:9–10)?

1. Have you ever been cared for in the way that 22:1–4 encourages? What happened? 2. What rationale can you find for including in the Bible the seemingly trivial laws listed here?

What if dating relationships and marriages came with "money back guarantees," would you take advantage of them? How rich might you then be?

1. Who or what was at risk in these marriage violations (22:13–21)? What injustices were these instructions meant to prevent? 2. What was to be Israel's attitude toward the unmarried virgin? Toward divorce? Toward pre-marital intercourse? 3. What practices were prohibited in verses 22–30? Why? Who was protected? Which of these did Reuben once violate with dire consequences (see Ge 35:22; 49:3–4)? 4. What was God teaching Israel by these regulations?

1. Why do you think the penalty for improper sexual and social behavior was so harsh? 2. What frightens you most about the changing sexual standards in your community? Have God's restrictions on sexual behavior changed? If so, how? If not, why? Has God's punishment changed? Why or why not? 3. How has the world influenced your views on sexual behavior? What is the connection between your sexual behavior and your relationship with God? 4. What laws does your society have that reflect the rules in this pas-

sage? Who do such rules seek to protect and why?

---

²⁵But if out in the country a man happens to meet a girl pledged to be married and rapes her, only the man who has done this shall die. ²⁶Do nothing to the girl; she has committed no sin deserving death. This case is like that of someone who attacks and murders his neighbor, ²⁷for the man found the girl out in the country, and though the betrothed girl screamed, there was no one to rescue her.

²⁸If a man happens to meet a virgin who is not pledged to be married and rapes her and they are discovered, ²⁹he shall pay the girl's father fifty shekels of silver.ᵃ He must marry the girl, for he has violated her. He can never divorce her as long as he lives.

³⁰A man is not to marry his father's wife; he must not dishonor his father's bed.

Exclusion From the Assembly

23 No one who has been emasculated by crushing or cutting may enter the assembly of the LORD.

²No one born of a forbidden marriageᵇ nor any of his descendants may enter the assembly of the LORD, even down to the tenth generation.

³No Ammonite or Moabite or any of his descendants may enter the assembly of the LORD, even down to the tenth generation. ⁴For they did not come to meet you with bread and water on your way when you came out of Egypt, and they hired Balaam son of Beor from Pethor in Aram Naharaimᶜ to pronounce a curse on you. ⁵However, the LORD your God would not listen to Balaam but turned the curse into a blessing for you, because the LORD your God loves you. ⁶Do not seek a treaty of friendship with them as long as you live.

⁷Do not abhor an Edomite, for he is your brother. Do not abhor an Egyptian, because you lived as an alien in his country. ⁸The third generation of children born to them may enter the assembly of the LORD.

Uncleanness in the Camp

⁹When you are encamped against your enemies, keep away from everything impure. ¹⁰If one of your men is unclean because of a nocturnal emission, he is to go outside the camp and stay there. ¹¹But as evening approaches he is to wash himself, and at sunset he may return to the camp.

¹²Designate a place outside the camp where you can go to relieve yourself. ¹³As part of your equipment have something to dig with, and when you relieve yourself, dig a hole and cover up your excrement. ¹⁴For the LORD your God moves about in your camp to protect you and to deliver your enemies to you. Your camp must be holy, so that he will not see among you anything indecent and turn away from you.

Miscellaneous Laws

¹⁵If a slave has taken refuge with you, do not hand him over to his master. ¹⁶Let him live among you wherever he likes and in whatever town he chooses. Do not oppress him.

¹⁷No Israelite man or woman is to become a shrine prostitute. ¹⁸You must not bring the earnings of a female prostitute or of a male prostituteᵈ into the house of the LORD your God to pay any vow, because the LORD your God detests them both.

¹⁹Do not charge your brother interest, whether on money or

ᵃ29 That is, about 1 1/4 pounds (about 0.6 kilogram)　　ᵇ2 Or *one of illegitimate birth*
ᶜ4 That is, Northwest Mesopotamia　　ᵈ18 Hebrew *of a dog*

food or anything else that may earn interest. [20]You may charge a foreigner interest, but not a brother Israelite, so that the LORD your God may bless you in everything you put your hand to in the land you are entering to possess.

[21]If you make a vow to the LORD your God, do not be slow to pay it, for the LORD your God will certainly demand it of you and you will be guilty of sin. [22]But if you refrain from making a vow, you will not be guilty. [23]Whatever your lips utter you must be sure to do, because you made your vow freely to the LORD your God with your own mouth.

[24]If you enter your neighbor's vineyard, you may eat all the grapes you want, but do not put any in your basket. [25]If you enter your neighbor's grainfield, you may pick kernels with your hands, but you must not put a sickle to his standing grain.

24 If a man marries a woman who becomes displeasing to him because he finds something indecent about her, and he writes her a certificate of divorce, gives it to her and sends her from his house, [2]and if after she leaves his house she becomes the wife of another man, [3]and her second husband dislikes her and writes her a certificate of divorce, gives it to her and sends her from his house, or if he dies, [4]then her first husband, who divorced her, is not allowed to marry her again after she has been defiled. That would be detestable in the eyes of the LORD. Do not bring sin upon the land the LORD your God is giving you as an inheritance.

[5]If a man has recently married, he must not be sent to war or have any other duty laid on him. For one year he is to be free to stay at home and bring happiness to the wife he has married.

[6]Do not take a pair of millstones—not even the upper one—as security for a debt, because that would be taking a man's livelihood as security.

[7]If a man is caught kidnapping one of his brother Israelites and treats him as a slave or sells him, the kidnapper must die. You must purge the evil from among you.

[8]In cases of leprous[a] diseases be very careful to do exactly as the priests, who are Levites, instruct you. You must follow carefully what I have commanded them. [9]Remember what the LORD your God did to Miriam along the way after you came out of Egypt.

[10]When you make a loan of any kind to your neighbor, do not go into his house to get what he is offering as a pledge. [11]Stay outside and let the man to whom you are making the loan bring the pledge out to you. [12]If the man is poor, do not go to sleep with his pledge in your possession. [13]Return his cloak to him by sunset so that he may sleep in it. Then he will thank you, and it will be regarded as a righteous act in the sight of the LORD your God.

[14]Do not take advantage of a hired man who is poor and needy, whether he is a brother Israelite or an alien living in one of your towns. [15]Pay him his wages each day before sunset, because he is poor and is counting on it. Otherwise he may cry to the LORD against you, and you will be guilty of sin.

[16]Fathers shall not be put to death for their children, nor children put to death for their fathers; each is to die for his own sin.

[17]Do not deprive the alien or the fatherless of justice, or take the cloak of the widow as a pledge. [18]Remember that you were slaves in Egypt and the LORD your God redeemed you from there. That is why I command you to do this.

[19]When you are harvesting in your field and you overlook a sheaf, do not go back to get it. Leave it for the alien, the fatherless

---

What great example of human generosity have you experienced? How did you react?

1. What was the function of the certificate of divorce? Who did it protect and why (see Dt 22:22)? How did Jesus qualify this law (see Mt 5:31–32; 19:3–9) 2. What prerogatives does a newly-wed enjoy (v. 5)? Why? 3. What is a security or pledge (vv. 6,10)? How is accepting a pledge different from charging interest? What pledges were accepted? Forbidden (vv. 6,10–13,17)? Why? 4. What are the Israelites to "remember" from Miriam's story (vv. 8–9; see Nu 12:9–15) and from their days in slavery (vv. 18,22)? 5. Who stood to gain from the fair labor law in verses 14–15? How so? 6. Why the need for affirming individual accountability (v. 16; see Eze 18:4)? What misunderstanding of Exodus 20:5 and 34:7 necessitated this? 7. What do verses 19–22 add to the law of gleaning (see Lev 19:9–10; Ru 2). What attitude does this foster?

1. What behavior and attitude is God asking for here from employers? From workers? 2. How can an employer exploit a worker today? What can a worker do? 3. Have you ever felt enslaved? When? How has this influenced your attitude toward others in a similar predicament? 4. Who are the "poor" in your region? What do you have that the poor could "glean"? Where and when would you want to begin in caring for them? Optional: Have your group consult a Christian expert on poverty.

---

a8 The Hebrew word was used for various diseases affecting the skin—not necessarily leprosy.

and the widow, so that the LORD your God may bless you in all the work of your hands. ²⁰When you beat the olives from your trees, do not go over the branches a second time. Leave what remains for the alien, the fatherless and the widow. ²¹When you harvest the grapes in your vineyard, do not go over the vines again. Leave what remains for the alien, the fatherless and the widow. ²²Remember that you were slaves in Egypt. That is why I command you to do this.

25 When men have a dispute, they are to take it to court and the judges will decide the case, acquitting the innocent and condemning the guilty. ²If the guilty man deserves to be beaten, the judge shall make him lie down and have him flogged in his presence with the number of lashes his crime deserves, ³but he must not give him more than forty lashes. If he is flogged more than that, your brother will be degraded in your eyes.

⁴Do not muzzle an ox while it is treading out the grain.

⁵If brothers are living together and one of them dies without a son, his widow must not marry outside the family. Her husband's brother shall take her and marry her and fulfill the duty of a brother-in-law to her. ⁶The first son she bears shall carry on the name of the dead brother so that his name will not be blotted out from Israel.

⁷However, if a man does not want to marry his brother's wife, she shall go to the elders at the town gate and say, "My husband's brother refuses to carry on his brother's name in Israel. He will not fulfill the duty of a brother-in-law to me." ⁸Then the elders of his town shall summon him and talk to him. If he persists in saying, "I do not want to marry her," ⁹his brother's widow shall go up to him in the presence of the elders, take off one of his sandals, spit in his face and say, "This is what is done to the man who will not build up his brother's family line." ¹⁰That man's line shall be known in Israel as The Family of the Unsandaled.

¹¹If two men are fighting and the wife of one of them comes to rescue her husband from his assailant, and she reaches out and seizes him by his private parts, ¹²you shall cut off her hand. Show her no pity.

¹³Do not have two differing weights in your bag—one heavy, one light. ¹⁴Do not have two differing measures in your house—one large, one small. ¹⁵You must have accurate and honest weights and measures, so that you may live long in the land the LORD your God is giving you. ¹⁶For the LORD your God detests anyone who does these things, anyone who deals dishonestly.

¹⁷Remember what the Amalekites did to you along the way when you came out of Egypt. ¹⁸When you were weary and worn out, they met you on your journey and cut off all who were lagging behind; they had no fear of God. ¹⁹When the LORD your God gives you rest from all the enemies around you in the land he is giving you to possess as an inheritance, you shall blot out the memory of Amalek from under heaven. Do not forget!

Firstfruits and Tithes

26 When you have entered the land the LORD your God is giving you as an inheritance and have taken possession of it and settled in it, ²take some of the firstfruits of all that you produce from the soil of the land the LORD your God is giving you and put them in a basket. Then go to the place the LORD your God will choose as a dwelling for his Name ³and say to the priest in office at the time, "I declare today to the LORD your God that I have come to the land the LORD swore to our forefathers to give us." ⁴The priest

---

Do you hold grudges or take revenge? What makes you most angry?

1. Whose welfare is being protected in verses 1–3? Why? 2. What rights and punishment does a lawbreaker have? Why are they spelled out here? 3. What does "muzzle and ox" mean here? What does it mean to Christian ministers (see 1Co 9:9–10)? Why? 4. In verses 5–10, what are the concerns of the wife? What did the birth of a son signify? What did it guarantee the mother? 5. Why should a brother-in-law want to fulfill this duty? (What would happen to their land otherwise?) Why might he not want to marry her? What has the sandal got to do with this (For answers, see also Ge 38:8–10; Ru 4:1–12.) 6. What social problem does God detest and why (vv. 13–16)? 7. What about the Amalekites would Israel never forget (vv. 17–18; see Ex 17:8–16; compare 1Sa 30)?

1. What application of these ancient laws do you see in today's legal system regarding the guilty and innocent? Regarding crime and its punishment? Fair wages? Property rights? Inheritance law? Truth in advertising? Fighting fair and hitting below the belt? 2. How do you think a family should care for a widowed member? Why? 3. Where do your Christian values and marketplace values clash? What can you do to reconcile the two? What support do you need?

What's a favorite thing you do after you cash your paycheck?

1. What are the Israelites asked to do with their firstfruits (vv. 1–11)? 2. What was the purpose of the tithe (vv. 5–10)? How might it be hard for a farmer? 3. What were the Israelites con-

shall take the basket from your hands and set it down in front of the altar of the LORD your God. [5]Then you shall declare before the LORD your God: "My father was a wandering Aramean, and he went down into Egypt with a few people and lived there and became a great nation, powerful and numerous. [6]But the Egyptians mistreated us and made us suffer, putting us to hard labor. [7]Then we cried out to the LORD, the God of our fathers, and the LORD heard our voice and saw our misery, toil and oppression. [8]So the LORD brought us out of Egypt with a mighty hand and an outstretched arm, with great terror and with miraculous signs and wonders. [9]He brought us to this place and gave us this land, a land flowing with milk and honey; [10]and now I bring the firstfruits of the soil that you, O LORD, have given me." Place the basket before the LORD your God and bow down before him. [11]And you and the Levites and the aliens among you shall rejoice in all the good things the LORD your God has given to you and your household.

[12]When you have finished setting aside a tenth of all your produce in the third year, the year of the tithe, you shall give it to the Levite, the alien, the fatherless and the widow, so that they may eat in your towns and be satisfied. [13]Then say to the LORD your God: "I have removed from my house the sacred portion and have given it to the Levite, the alien, the fatherless and the widow, according to all you commanded. I have not turned aside from your commands nor have I forgotten any of them. [14]I have not eaten any of the sacred portion while I was in mourning, nor have I removed any of it while I was unclean, nor have I offered any of it to the dead. I have obeyed the LORD my God; I have done everything you commanded me. [15]Look down from heaven, your holy dwelling place, and bless your people Israel and the land you have given us as you promised on oath to our forefathers, a land flowing with milk and honey."

Follow the LORD's Commands

[16]The LORD your God commands you this day to follow these decrees and laws; carefully observe them with all your heart and with all your soul. [17]You have declared this day that the LORD is your God and that you will walk in his ways, that you will keep his decrees, commands and laws, and that you will obey him. [18]And the LORD has declared this day that you are his people, his treasured possession as he promised, and that you are to keep all his commands. [19]He has declared that he will set you in praise, fame and honor high above all the nations he has made and that you will be a people holy to the LORD your God, as he promised.

The Altar on Mount Ebal

27 Moses and the elders of Israel commanded the people: "Keep all these commands that I give you today. [2]When you have crossed the Jordan into the land the LORD your God is giving you, set up some large stones and coat them with plaster. [3]Write on them all the words of this law when you have crossed over to enter the land the LORD your God is giving you, a land flowing with milk and honey, just as the LORD, the God of your fathers, promised you. [4]And when you have crossed the Jordan, set up these stones on Mount Ebal, as I command you today, and coat them with plaster. [5]Build there an altar to the LORD your God, an altar of stones. Do not use any iron tool upon them. [6]Build the altar of the

fessing? Why? How should confessing climax? **4.** How are verses 12–15 related to worship? Why are these actions so important (see Dt 10:18–19)? What was the temptation (v. 14)? The blessing (v. 15)? **5.** What attitudes do these practices foster toward God? Others? Income? **6.** What is the significance of "heart and soul" (v. 16) when it comes to command-keeping? **7.** In the mutual declarations (vv. 17–19), which come first: God's or the people's? Why is one based on the other?

1. How do you decide how much to give, to whom and why? From this passage, what are God's priorities? **2.** What confession would you make to accompany your giving? **3.** It has been estimated that 99 percent of the money Christians spend is on themselves. How would this passage address that issue? **4.** What do you like about your present giving patterns? What does your giving pattern say about God's character and commands? **5.** What would you like to change about your giving pattern to more closely "walk in his ways" (v. 17)? What first step can you take this week? How might the group help?

1. What did the large stones represent? What function would they serve? **2.** When were these things to be set up (see Jos 8:33–35)? **3.** What attitude is intended?

1. How does building an altar serve as a living reminder? What serves as a living reminder for you to obey God? To what would you build an altar? **2.** Do we have living reminders in church today? What attitudes and principles might still apply? Why?

LORD your God with fieldstones and offer burnt offerings on it to the LORD your God. [7]Sacrifice fellowship offerings[a] there, eating them and rejoicing in the presence of the LORD your God. [8]And you shall write very clearly all the words of this law on these stones you have set up."

Curses From Mount Ebal

[9]Then Moses and the priests, who are Levites, said to all Israel, "Be silent, O Israel, and listen! You have now become the people of the LORD your God. [10]Obey the LORD your God and follow his commands and decrees that I give you today."

[11]On the same day Moses commanded the people:

[12]When you have crossed the Jordan, these tribes shall stand on Mount Gerizim to bless the people: Simeon, Levi, Judah, Issachar, Joseph and Benjamin. [13]And these tribes shall stand on Mount Ebal to pronounce curses: Reuben, Gad, Asher, Zebulun, Dan and Naphtali.

[14]The Levites shall recite to all the people of Israel in a loud voice:

[15]"Cursed is the man who carves an image or casts an idol—a thing detestable to the LORD, the work of the craftsman's hands—and sets it up in secret."

Then all the people shall say, "Amen!"

[16]"Cursed is the man who dishonors his father or his mother."

Then all the people shall say, "Amen!"

[17]"Cursed is the man who moves his neighbor's boundary stone."

Then all the people shall say, "Amen!"

[18]"Cursed is the man who leads the blind astray on the road."

Then all the people shall say, "Amen!"

[19]"Cursed is the man who withholds justice from the alien, the fatherless or the widow."

Then all the people shall say, "Amen!"

[20]"Cursed is the man who sleeps with his father's wife, for he dishonors his father's bed."

Then all the people shall say, "Amen!"

[21]"Cursed is the man who has sexual relations with any animal."

Then all the people shall say, "Amen!"

[22]"Cursed is the man who sleeps with his sister, the daughter of his father or the daughter of his mother."

Then all the people shall say, "Amen!"

[23]"Cursed is the man who sleeps with his mother-in-law."

Then all the people shall say, "Amen!"

[24]"Cursed is the man who kills his neighbor secretly."

Then all the people shall say, "Amen!"

[25]"Cursed is the man who accepts a bribe to kill an innocent person."

Then all the people shall say, "Amen!"

[26]"Cursed is the man who does not uphold the words of this law by carrying them out."

Then all the people shall say, "Amen!"

---

1. What advertisement gets your attention? Why? 2. What injustice in the news this month particularly galled you? Why were you so irritated? 3. Share a time in your life when you wanted to start out "clean" again.

1. Why, where, when, how was this ceremony to be conducted? Why not stay in the valley? 2. Who were the participants? Who said the "curses"? Who responded? What did the "Amen!" represent? 3. What does it mean to be "cursed"? Which curses refer to which of the Ten Commandments (see ch. 5)? 4. Why do the curses come before the blessings? What corresponding blessings do these tribes receive from Moses later in chapter 33?

1. What kinds of oaths does your employer, coach, spouse, or parent implicitly make you take? Anything like this ceremony? 2. To what divine sanctions do you tend to say, "Amen"? Why? Were there any items on this list for which your "Amen" was weakly offered, if at all? 3. Has Jesus ended the "curses" when he hung on a tree (see 21:23; see Gal 3:13)? Or are these curses still somehow woven into the moral fabric of all relationships? What is the good news in this which you will share with someone else this week? 4. If verses 15–25 are sins of *commission*, verse 26 is a sin of *omission*. Why might you pay special heed here?

---

a 7 Traditionally *peace offerings*

Blessings for Obedience

28 If you fully obey the LORD your God and carefully follow all his commands I give you today, the LORD your God will set you high above all the nations on earth. ²All these blessings will come upon you and accompany you if you obey the LORD your God:

³You will be blessed in the city and blessed in the country.
⁴The fruit of your womb will be blessed, and the crops of your land and the young of your livestock—the calves of your herds and the lambs of your flocks.
⁵Your basket and your kneading trough will be blessed.
⁶You will be blessed when you come in and blessed when you go out.

⁷The LORD will grant that the enemies who rise up against you will be defeated before you. They will come at you from one direction but flee from you in seven.
⁸The LORD will send a blessing on your barns and on everything you put your hand to. The LORD your God will bless you in the land he is giving you.
⁹The LORD will establish you as his holy people, as he promised you on oath, if you keep the commands of the LORD your God and walk in his ways. ¹⁰Then all the peoples on earth will see that you are called by the name of the LORD, and they will fear you. ¹¹The LORD will grant you abundant prosperity—in the fruit of your womb, the young of your livestock and the crops of your ground—in the land he swore to your forefathers to give you.
¹²The LORD will open the heavens, the storehouse of his bounty, to send rain on your land in season and to bless all the work of your hands. You will lend to many nations but will borrow from none. ¹³The LORD will make you the head, not the tail. If you pay attention to the commands of the LORD your God that I give you this day and carefully follow them, you will always be at the top, never at the bottom. ¹⁴Do not turn aside from any of the commands I give you today, to the right or to the left, following other gods and serving them.

Curses for Disobedience

¹⁵However, if you do not obey the LORD your God and do not carefully follow all his commands and decrees I am giving you today, all these curses will come upon you and overtake you:

¹⁶You will be cursed in the city and cursed in the country.
¹⁷Your basket and your kneading trough will be cursed.
¹⁸The fruit of your womb will be cursed, and the crops of your land, and the calves of your herds and the lambs of your flocks.
¹⁹You will be cursed when you come in and cursed when you go out.

²⁰The LORD will send on you curses, confusion and rebuke in everything you put your hand to, until you are destroyed and come to sudden ruin because of the evil you have done in forsaking him.ᵃ ²¹The LORD will plague you with diseases until he has destroyed you from the land you are entering to possess. ²²The LORD will strike you with wasting disease, with fever and inflammation, with scorching heat and drought, with blight and mildew, which will plague you until you perish. ²³The sky over your head will be bronze, the ground beneath you iron. ²⁴The LORD will turn the rain

ᵃ20 Hebrew *me*

What do you feel "blessed" with in your life today? How would you like to be blessed?

1. What is the foundation for the blessings: God's work or our obedience? What is the point behind the oft-repeated "if-clause" (vv. 1–2,9,13,14)? 2. What six ways will Israel be blessed (vv. 3–6)? 3. What will God do to bring about these (vv. 7–8,11,12)? 4. How will God be glorified (vv. 9–10)? 5. What status does God promise Israel (vv. 9,13)? What does it mean to be holy? How is holiness inseparable from the promise?

1. Which of these tangible blessings have you seen in your life? Does this sound like the "health-and-wealth" gospel of some modern preaching? What are the similarities? Differences? 2. How would you put verses 3–6 in modern terms? How would it apply to Third World believers? 3. How is God glorified when he blesses you? What is your responsibility with the blessings and their conditions? How do you know if you are fulfilling the terms of the covenant? (By whether or not you are being blessed?) 4. How is obedience itself a blessing?

1. Were you more rebellious as a child, as a teenager, as an adult or as a senior citizen? Share one example to make your point. 2. When was the last time your well-laid plans ended up in total disarray, even backfiring on you? 3. How do you react when everything and everyone seems to be against you? (a) Run and hide? (b) Lash out? (c) Talk to God? (d) Don't talk to God? (e) Wish life would end? (f) Wish tomorrow would come, so things might change?

1. What is the condition for the curses (v. 15)? 2. Paraphrase the six curses listed here (vv. 16–19) in modern terms. What areas of life are covered? 3. How would you categorize the different penalties in verses 20–35? What is their scope? How do they correlate to specific blessings (vv. 1–14)? 4. Where do the penalties of verses 36–46 take place? How did Moses

know Israel would decide to have kings (v. 36) or would go into captivity (v. 41)? How do they correlate to specific blessings (vv. 1–14)? **5.** Who is the agent of judgment in verses 47–57? Why would God use a "secular" means to discipline his people? What will be the net effect of the enemy laying siege to Israel's cities? **6.** What meaning does this chapter give to the "glorious and awesome name" (v. 58) of the Lord God? How could such a great God be so merciless? What does it mean that "the Lord" is injected so often into their lives, especially in verses 58–68? **7.** How may "an anxious mind" and "eyes weary with longing" (v. 65) bring the people back to trust in the Lord? How would "constant suspense … never sure of your life" (v. 66) serve a similar purpose?

♡ **1.** Which curses would seem most terrible to a single person? To a married person? Why? **2.** How do these curses fit with your understanding of God? What if God were just a God of blessing? **3.** Are Christians still under these curses, or has Jesus taken care of that? If so, how? If not, why? **4.** If not in the form of these curses, how do you experience God's correction today in your life? **5.** What do these verses teach you about the exceptional ways God treats his people? **6.** God's sheer power, as shown in this chapter, makes reverence for him the logical outcome. But anything that is pounded into human heads can and will be resisted by those who say, "I've heard it all before." Is that your reaction—boredom? Or are you genuinely awed by this powerful, wrathful God? Where in your life this week does reverence for God need to prevail?

of your country into dust and powder; it will come down from the skies until you are destroyed.

²⁵The Lord will cause you to be defeated before your enemies. You will come at them from one direction but flee from them in seven, and you will become a thing of horror to all the kingdoms on earth. ²⁶Your carcasses will be food for all the birds of the air and the beasts of the earth, and there will be no one to frighten them away. ²⁷The Lord will afflict you with the boils of Egypt and with tumors, festering sores and the itch, from which you cannot be cured. ²⁸The Lord will afflict you with madness, blindness and confusion of mind. ²⁹At midday you will grope about like a blind man in the dark. You will be unsuccessful in everything you do; day after day you will be oppressed and robbed, with no one to rescue you.

³⁰You will be pledged to be married to a woman, but another will take her and ravish her. You will build a house, but you will not live in it. You will plant a vineyard, but you will not even begin to enjoy its fruit. ³¹Your ox will be slaughtered before your eyes, but you will eat none of it. Your donkey will be forcibly taken from you and will not be returned. Your sheep will be given to your enemies, and no one will rescue them. ³²Your sons and daughters will be given to another nation, and you will wear out your eyes watching for them day after day, powerless to lift a hand. ³³A people that you do not know will eat what your land and labor produce, and you will have nothing but cruel oppression all your days. ³⁴The sights you see will drive you mad. ³⁵The Lord will afflict your knees and legs with painful boils that cannot be cured, spreading from the soles of your feet to the top of your head.

³⁶The Lord will drive you and the king you set over you to a nation unknown to you or your fathers. There you will worship other gods, gods of wood and stone. ³⁷You will become a thing of horror and an object of scorn and ridicule to all the nations where the Lord will drive you.

³⁸You will sow much seed in the field but you will harvest little, because locusts will devour it. ³⁹You will plant vineyards and cultivate them but you will not drink the wine or gather the grapes, because worms will eat them. ⁴⁰You will have olive trees throughout your country but you will not use the oil, because the olives will drop off. ⁴¹You will have sons and daughters but you will not keep them, because they will go into captivity. ⁴²Swarms of locusts will take over all your trees and the crops of your land.

⁴³The alien who lives among you will rise above you higher and higher, but you will sink lower and lower. ⁴⁴He will lend to you, but you will not lend to him. He will be the head, but you will be the tail.

⁴⁵All these curses will come upon you. They will pursue you and overtake you until you are destroyed, because you did not obey the Lord your God and observe the commands and decrees he gave you. ⁴⁶They will be a sign and a wonder to you and your descendants forever. ⁴⁷Because you did not serve the Lord your God joyfully and gladly in the time of prosperity, ⁴⁸therefore in hunger and thirst, in nakedness and dire poverty, you will serve the enemies the Lord sends against you. He will put an iron yoke on your neck until he has destroyed you.

⁴⁹The Lord will bring a nation against you from far away, from the ends of the earth, like an eagle swooping down, a nation whose language you will not understand, ⁵⁰a fierce-looking nation without respect for the old or pity for the young. ⁵¹They will devour the young of your livestock and the crops of your land until you are

destroyed. They will leave you no grain, new wine or oil, nor any calves of your herds or lambs of your flocks until you are ruined. 52They will lay siege to all the cities throughout your land until the high fortified walls in which you trust fall down. They will besiege all the cities throughout the land the LORD your God is giving you.

53Because of the suffering that your enemy will inflict on you during the siege, you will eat the fruit of the womb, the flesh of the sons and daughters the LORD your God has given you. 54Even the most gentle and sensitive man among you will have no compassion on his own brother or the wife he loves or his surviving children, 55and he will not give to one of them any of the flesh of his children that he is eating. It will be all he has left because of the suffering your enemy will inflict on you during the siege of all your cities. 56The most gentle and sensitive woman among you—so sensitive and gentle that she would not venture to touch the ground with the sole of her foot—will begrudge the husband she loves and her own son or daughter 57the afterbirth from her womb and the children she bears. For she intends to eat them secretly during the siege and in the distress that your enemy will inflict on you in your cities.

58If you do not carefully follow all the words of this law, which are written in this book, and do not revere this glorious and awesome name—the LORD your God— 59the LORD will send fearful plagues on you and your descendants, harsh and prolonged disasters, and severe and lingering illnesses. 60He will bring upon you all the diseases of Egypt that you dreaded, and they will cling to you. 61The LORD will also bring on you every kind of sickness and disaster not recorded in this Book of the Law, until you are destroyed. 62You who were as numerous as the stars in the sky will be left but few in number, because you did not obey the LORD your God. 63Just as it pleased the LORD to make you prosper and increase in number, so it will please him to ruin and destroy you. You will be uprooted from the land you are entering to possess.

64Then the LORD will scatter you among all nations, from one end of the earth to the other. There you will worship other gods—gods of wood and stone, which neither you nor your fathers have known. 65Among those nations you will find no repose, no resting place for the sole of your foot. There the LORD will give you an anxious mind, eyes weary with longing, and a despairing heart. 66You will live in constant suspense, filled with dread both night and day, never sure of your life. 67In the morning you will say, "If only it were evening!" and in the evening, "If only it were morning!"—because of the terror that will fill your hearts and the sights that your eyes will see. 68The LORD will send you back in ships to Egypt on a journey I said you should never make again. There you will offer yourselves for sale to your enemies as male and female slaves, but no one will buy you.

Renewal of the Covenant

29 These are the terms of the covenant the LORD commanded Moses to make with the Israelites in Moab, in addition to the covenant he had made with them at Horeb.

2Moses summoned all the Israelites and said to them:

Your eyes have seen all that the LORD did in Egypt to Pharaoh, to all his officials and to all his land. 3With your own eyes you saw those great trials, those miraculous signs and great wonders. 4But to this day the LORD has not given you a mind that understands or eyes that see or ears that hear. 5During the forty years that I led you through the desert, your clothes did not wear out, nor did the

What social event would you like to "crash"? Why?

1. Of what does Moses remind the Israelites in verses 2–8? What does each story demonstrate? 2. What people attended this covenant ceremony (v. 11)? Who else was it intended for? Upon whom did the covenant depend (v. 12)? Why? What does this show about the covenant? 3. Why was the covenant necessary?

What has Israel not yet understood (v. 4)? Why? **4.** Why the plea of verses 16–18? What is the allure of pagan idolatry? How could God's redemption be so easily forgotten or taken for granted? **5.** What about their attitude is like a "bitter poison" (v. 18)? Why? What happens to the idolater? To the community? **6.** In verses 19–24, who is being warned? Who is held responsible? What will later generations conclude and why? **7.** What memory does Moses recall (see Ge 19: 24–25)? Why? What questions will the surrounding people ask later (v. 24)? **8.** How are verses 25–29 the answer to that question? Does God always reveal the "why" behind his actions? When he does reveal certain "secret things," what should be our response (v. 29)?

1. What memories help keep you faithful to God? How are they like Israel's memories? **2.** Are Christian's susceptible to the "bitter poison" of verses 18–20? Why? **3.** What is your personal responsibility toward idolatry? Your church's responsibility? **4.** What modern idols are popular right now with the youth of your culture? With the adults? **5.** How do we subtly become like whatever we worship—good or bad? How can idols drive a wedge between us and God and make us drift away from the covenant community? **6.** Mark Twain once said, "It's not the hard-to-understand things in Scripture that make me tremble. Rather, it's those things I *do* understand." How does verse 29 reiterate this? What revealed truth, understandable to you, will you apply this week?

sandals on your feet. 6You ate no bread and drank no wine or other fermented drink. I did this so that you might know that I am the LORD your God.

7When you reached this place, Sihon king of Heshbon and Og king of Bashan came out to fight against us, but we defeated them. 8We took their land and gave it as an inheritance to the Reubenites, the Gadites and the half-tribe of Manasseh.

9Carefully follow the terms of this covenant, so that you may prosper in everything you do. 10All of you are standing today in the presence of the LORD your God—your leaders and chief men, your elders and officials, and all the other men of Israel, 11together with your children and your wives, and the aliens living in your camps who chop your wood and carry your water. 12You are standing here in order to enter into a covenant with the LORD your God, a covenant the LORD is making with you this day and sealing with an oath, 13to confirm you this day as his people, that he may be your God as he promised you and as he swore to your fathers, Abraham, Isaac and Jacob. 14I am making this covenant, with its oath, not only with you 15who are standing here with us today in the presence of the LORD our God but also with those who are not here today.

16You yourselves know how we lived in Egypt and how we passed through the countries on the way here. 17You saw among them their detestable images and idols of wood and stone, of silver and gold. 18Make sure there is no man or woman, clan or tribe among you today whose heart turns away from the LORD our God to go and worship the gods of those nations; make sure there is no root among you that produces such bitter poison.

19When such a person hears the words of this oath, he invokes a blessing on himself and therefore thinks, "I will be safe, even though I persist in going my own way." This will bring disaster on the watered land as well as the dry.ᵃ 20The LORD will never be willing to forgive him; his wrath and zeal will burn against that man. All the curses written in this book will fall upon him, and the LORD will blot out his name from under heaven. 21The LORD will single him out from all the tribes of Israel for disaster, according to all the curses of the covenant written in this Book of the Law.

22Your children who follow you in later generations and foreigners who come from distant lands will see the calamities that have fallen on the land and the diseases with which the LORD has afflicted it. 23The whole land will be a burning waste of salt and sulfur—nothing planted, nothing sprouting, no vegetation growing on it. It will be like the destruction of Sodom and Gomorrah, Admah and Zeboiim, which the LORD overthrew in fierce anger. 24All the nations will ask: "Why has the LORD done this to this land? Why this fierce, burning anger?"

25And the answer will be: "It is because this people abandoned the covenant of the LORD, the God of their fathers, the covenant he made with them when he brought them out of Egypt. 26They went off and worshiped other gods and bowed down to them, gods they did not know, gods he had not given them. 27Therefore the LORD's anger burned against this land, so that he brought on it all the curses written in this book. 28In furious anger and in great wrath the LORD uprooted them from their land and thrust them into another land, as it is now."

29The secret things belong to the LORD our God, but the things

ᵃ19 Or *way, in order to add drunkenness to thirst.*"

revealed belong to us and to our children forever, that we may follow all the words of this law.

Prosperity After Turning to the LORD

30 When all these blessings and curses I have set before you come upon you and you take them to heart wherever the LORD your God disperses you among the nations, ²and when you and your children return to the LORD your God and obey him with all your heart and with all your soul according to everything I command you today, ³then the LORD your God will restore your fortunes[a] and have compassion on you and gather you again from all the nations where he scattered you. ⁴Even if you have been banished to the most distant land under the heavens, from there the LORD your God will gather you and bring you back. ⁵He will bring you to the land that belonged to your fathers, and you will take possession of it. He will make you more prosperous and numerous than your fathers. ⁶The LORD your God will circumcise your hearts and the hearts of your descendants, so that you may love him with all your heart and with all your soul, and live. ⁷The LORD your God will put all these curses on your enemies who hate and persecute you. ⁸You will again obey the LORD and follow all his commands I am giving you today. ⁹Then the LORD your God will make you most prosperous in all the work of your hands and in the fruit of your womb, the young of your livestock and the crops of your land. The LORD will again delight in you and make you prosperous, just as he delighted in your fathers, ¹⁰if you obey the LORD your God and keep his commands and decrees that are written in this Book of the Law and turn to the LORD your God with all your heart and with all your soul.

The Offer of Life or Death

¹¹Now what I am commanding you today is not too difficult for you or beyond your reach. ¹²It is not up in heaven, so that you have to ask, "Who will ascend into heaven to get it and proclaim it to us so we may obey it?" ¹³Nor is it beyond the sea, so that you have to ask, "Who will cross the sea to get it and proclaim it to us so we may obey it?" ¹⁴No, the word is very near you; it is in your mouth and in your heart so you may obey it.

¹⁵See, I set before you today life and prosperity, death and destruction. ¹⁶For I command you today to love the LORD your God, to walk in his ways, and to keep his commands, decrees and laws; then you will live and increase, and the LORD your God will bless you in the land you are entering to possess. ¹⁷But if your heart turns away and you are not obedient, and if you are drawn away to bow down to other gods and worship them, ¹⁸I declare to you this day that you will certainly be destroyed. You will not live long in the land you are crossing the Jordan to enter and possess.

¹⁹This day I call heaven and earth as witnesses against you that I have set before you life and death, blessings and curses. Now choose life, so that you and your children may live ²⁰and that you may love the LORD your God, listen to his voice, and hold fast to him. For the LORD is your life, and he will give you many years in the land he swore to give to your fathers, Abraham, Isaac and Jacob.

a3 *Or will bring you back from captivity*

If you couldn't live in your native land, what country *would* you choose and why?

1. How does Israel come full circle in verses 1–3? 2. What does it mean to "return to the Lord" (vv. 2,4,6,8,10)? 3. What promises from God make this repentance possible (vv. 3,5,7,9)? 4. How does verse 6 fit with 29:4? What about a "circumcised heart" enables one to see with understanding?

1. Has God ever restored you? How so? 2. What does it mean for you to "return to the Lord"? How often do you "return"? Why? 3. How has God changed your heart? 4. Is there any area of your life where you need "heart surgery"? What can you do? 5. What in these verses encourages you? Why?

1. What unspoken objection are verses 11–14 answering? 2. Where can Israel find God's word? 3. What choices does Moses set before Israel? How will Israel show the choice they've made? Who witnesses Israel's choice? 4. What clincher does verse 20 provide for anyone still having to choose?

1. Today, how do life-or-death options present themselves? 2. What modern objections have you heard, or used, which sound like the ones in verses 11–13? 3. From this passage, would you be able to recognize genuine faith when you saw it? How so? By what tell-tale clues? By what action verbs? 4. How can you live out the verbs of verse 20? Would this be difficult? Why? How does God help you?

☕ In whose footsteps would you like to follow? Why? Where do you suspect they would lead you?

📖 1. What events are about to take place? 2. Who will cross the Jordan before Israel? What does this mean in context? 3. Why the tendency toward fear and discouragement? Would you be afraid or dejected in a situation like this? 4. Where will Israel get the strength and courage to go on without Moses? How will Joshua follow in his steps? 5. What three arrangements were made regarding the Law? How does this relate to Joshua's succession of Moses? 6. For whom, when and why was the Law read in public?

♡ 1. For what today do you need strength and courage in your life? Where will you find it? 2. Who has been your mentor? What have you learned? Enough to succeed him or her? Explain. 3. How have you set about reading and listening to God's Word? Is this satisfying to you? Why or why not? Any adjustments pending? 4. How does, or did, your family incorporate the call to worship (vv. 12–13) into your lives together?

☕ 1. What brought out your rebellious side as a teenager? What incident recently brought out the rebellion in you? 2. Who are your favorite songwriters? What music seems the most rebellious to you: Rap? Heavy Metal? Beatles? Punk? Hip Hop? Rock 'n Roll? Other? Explain.

📖 1. What themes from Moses' discourse with God and with Israel are continued here in these verses? 2. What typically happens at the Tent of Meeting (see Ex 29:42; 33:7–11)? What might Joshua expect to happen this time? What does he see and hear instead (vv. 14–18)? 3. Why does God tell both Joshua and Moses to write down this song (v. 19; see ch. 32)? Where else in Moses' family are song-writing gifts evident (see Ex 15:1,21)? How difficult do you think it would be to teach a song? (Or learn one?) Why was it to be taught that very day (v. 22)? 4. What witnesses will be mar-

Joshua to Succeed Moses

31 Then Moses went out and spoke these words to all Israel: 2"I am now a hundred and twenty years old and I am no longer able to lead you. The LORD has said to me, 'You shall not cross the Jordan.' 3The LORD your God himself will cross over ahead of you. He will destroy these nations before you, and you will take possession of their land. Joshua also will cross over ahead of you, as the LORD said. 4And the LORD will do to them what he did to Sihon and Og, the kings of the Amorites, whom he destroyed along with their land. 5The LORD will deliver them to you, and you must do to them all that I have commanded you. 6Be strong and courageous. Do not be afraid or terrified because of them, for the LORD your God goes with you; he will never leave you nor forsake you."

7Then Moses summoned Joshua and said to him in the presence of all Israel, "Be strong and courageous, for you must go with this people into the land that the LORD swore to their forefathers to give them, and you must divide it among them as their inheritance. 8The LORD himself goes before you and will be with you; he will never leave you nor forsake you. Do not be afraid; do not be discouraged."

The Reading of the Law

9So Moses wrote down this law and gave it to the priests, the sons of Levi, who carried the ark of the covenant of the LORD, and to all the elders of Israel. 10Then Moses commanded them: "At the end of every seven years, in the year for canceling debts, during the Feast of Tabernacles, 11when all Israel comes to appear before the LORD your God at the place he will choose, you shall read this law before them in their hearing. 12Assemble the people—men, women and children, and the aliens living in your towns—so they can listen and learn to fear the LORD your God and follow carefully all the words of this law. 13Their children, who do not know this law, must hear it and learn to fear the LORD your God as long as you live in the land you are crossing the Jordan to possess."

Israel's Rebellion Predicted

14The LORD said to Moses, "Now the day of your death is near. Call Joshua and present yourselves at the Tent of Meeting, where I will commission him." So Moses and Joshua came and presented themselves at the Tent of Meeting.

15Then the LORD appeared at the Tent in a pillar of cloud, and the cloud stood over the entrance to the Tent. 16And the LORD said to Moses: "You are going to rest with your fathers, and these people will soon prostitute themselves to the foreign gods of the land they are entering. They will forsake me and break the covenant I made with them. 17On that day I will become angry with them and forsake them; I will hide my face from them, and they will be destroyed. Many disasters and difficulties will come upon them, and on that day they will ask, 'Have not these disasters come upon us because our God is not with us?' 18And I will certainly hide my face on that day because of all their wickedness in turning to other gods.

19"Now write down for yourselves this song and teach it to the Israelites and have them sing it, so that it may be a witness for me against them. 20When I have brought them into the land flowing with milk and honey, the land I promised on oath to their forefathers, and when they eat their fill and thrive, they will turn to other gods and worship them, rejecting me and breaking my covenant. 21And when many disasters and difficulties come upon them, this song will testify against them, because it will not be forgotten by their descendants. I know what they are disposed to do, even before I bring them into the land I promised them on oath." 22So Moses wrote down this song that day and taught it to the Israelites.

23The LORD gave this command to Joshua son of Nun: "Be strong and courageous, for you will bring the Israelites into the land I promised them on oath, and I myself will be with you."

24After Moses finished writing in a book the words of this law from beginning to end, 25he gave this command to the Levites who carried the ark of the covenant of the LORD: 26"Take this Book of the Law and place it beside the ark of the covenant of the LORD your God. There it will remain as a witness against you. 27For I know how rebellious and stiff-necked you are. If you have been rebellious against the LORD while I am still alive and with you, how much more will you rebel after I die! 28Assemble before me all the elders of your tribes and all your officials, so that I can speak these words in their hearing and call heaven and earth to testify against them. 29For I know that after my death you are sure to become utterly corrupt and to turn from the way I have commanded you. In days to come, disaster will fall upon you because you will do evil in the sight of the LORD and provoke him to anger by what your hands have made."

The Song of Moses

30And Moses recited the words of this song from beginning to end in the hearing of the whole assembly of Israel:

32

Listen, O heavens, and I will speak;
    hear, O earth, the words of my mouth.
2Let my teaching fall like rain
    and my words descend like dew,
like showers on new grass,
    like abundant rain on tender plants.

3I will proclaim the name of the LORD.
    Oh, praise the greatness of our God!
4He is the Rock, his works are perfect,
    and all his ways are just.
A faithful God who does no wrong,
    upright and just is he.

5They have acted corruptly toward him;
    to their shame they are no longer his children,
    but a warped and crooked generation.[a]
6Is this the way you repay the LORD,
    O foolish and unwise people?
Is he not your Father, your Creator,[b]
    who made you and formed you?

7Remember the days of old;
    consider the generations long past.
Ask your father and he will tell you,
    your elders, and they will explain to you.
8When the Most High gave the nations their
        inheritance,
    when he divided all mankind,
he set up boundaries for the peoples

---

a5 Or *Corrupt are they and not his children, / a generation warped and twisted to their shame*   b6 Or *Father, who bought you*

---

shalled against Israel (vv. 21,26,28) and why? **5.** Why is Israel's future disobedience described? How is this different from self-fulfilling prophecy?

♡ **1.** Are you encouraged or discouraged by God's knowledge of your future failings? Why? **2.** What aspects of God are revealed in nature? Would you sense that apart from Scripture, such as this chapter? **3.** How do songs and small groups serve similar purposes in your situation? How will this help you in the week ahead?

☕ What kind of music do you like? What local radio station or music group typifies your taste?

📖 Read the song out loud and imagine yourself as an Israelite listening to the song. **1.** Is theological truth being conveyed here in logical, propositional form (stating facts)? Or in feeling tones and painted pictures (stating impressions)? What difference does that make in how you interpret this song? **2.** As you interpret this song, what does it say about God? What poetic images express this theology? **3.** What is the song's purpose (v. 3)? The song's narrative viewpoint? **4.** What might it mean that God is called "the Rock" (vv. 4,15, 18,30–31)? By contrast, how is Israel behaving (vv. 5–6)? **5.** What kind of parent is God (vv. 10–14,18)? By contrast, what kind of child was Israel (vv. 15–18)? Why would they worship a golden calf who is not alive? **6.** Does God's choice of and care for Israel obligate Israel in any way? Does this precedent obligate God in any way to again act redemptively—or is once enough? **7.** What is the extent of their rebellion? What is God's response and action (vv. 19–22)? **8.** What instant recall and vivid memories for Israel are associated with verses 23–25? What are God's intentions (vv. 26–27)? What keeps God from destroying Israel? What does this tell Israel about God? **9.** What does God think about Israel (vv. 28–29)? About Israel's enemies (vv. 30–33,35,40–43)? **10.** What is Israel to conclude about God and itself (vv. 36–39)? **11.** If this song were set to music with solo parts and a common refrain, what verse(s) would you designate as the repeated refrain? What would be the message of your imagined song lyrics? What was Israel to do with the lyrics (vv. 45–46)?

♡ **1.** In what sense is this song your song? Do Christians sing anything similar to the truths of this song? If so, what? **2.** What does it mean that God is your "rock"? How can you live this truth? **3.** Is it harder to follow God in times of prosperity, or in times of adversity? Why? **4.** The Israelites made God jealous by "their worthless idols" (v. 21). How do you make God jealous? **5.** Do verses 28–29 apply to your nation? How so? What can you and your people do to grow in discernment and wisdom? How can you begin this week? **6.** Who or what are you tempted to rely on rather than God? Why? What prompts you to trust and obey God? **7.** What is the lesson of this song for you?

according to the number of the sons of Israel.[a]
9For the LORD's portion is his people,
   Jacob his allotted inheritance.

10In a desert land he found him,
   in a barren and howling waste.
He shielded him and cared for him;
   he guarded him as the apple of his eye,
11like an eagle that stirs up its nest
   and hovers over its young,
that spreads its wings to catch them
   and carries them on its pinions.
12The LORD alone led him;
   no foreign god was with him.

13He made him ride on the heights of the land
   and fed him with the fruit of the fields.
He nourished him with honey from the rock,
   and with oil from the flinty crag,
14with curds and milk from herd and flock
   and with fattened lambs and goats,
with choice rams of Bashan
   and the finest kernels of wheat.
You drank the foaming blood of the grape.

15Jeshurun[b] grew fat and kicked;
   filled with food, he became heavy and sleek.
He abandoned the God who made him
   and rejected the Rock his Savior.
16They made him jealous with their foreign gods
   and angered him with their detestable idols.
17They sacrificed to demons, which are not God—
   gods they had not known,
   gods that recently appeared,
   gods your fathers did not fear.
18You deserted the Rock, who fathered you;
   you forgot the God who gave you birth.

19The LORD saw this and rejected them
   because he was angered by his sons and
      daughters.
20"I will hide my face from them," he said,
   "and see what their end will be;
for they are a perverse generation,
   children who are unfaithful.
21They made me jealous by what is no god
   and angered me with their worthless idols.
I will make them envious by those who are not a
      people;
   I will make them angry by a nation that has no
      understanding.
22For a fire has been kindled by my wrath,
   one that burns to the realm of death[c] below.
It will devour the earth and its harvests
   and set afire the foundations of the mountains.

23"I will heap calamities upon them
   and spend my arrows against them.
24I will send wasting famine against them,

---

a8 Masoretic Text; Dead Sea Scrolls (see also Septuagint) *sons of God*   b15 *Jeshurun*
means *the upright one*, that is, Israel.   c22 Hebrew *to Sheol*

consuming pestilence and deadly plague;
I will send against them the fangs of wild beasts,
    the venom of vipers that glide in the dust.
²⁵In the street the sword will make them childless;
    in their homes terror will reign.
Young men and young women will perish,
    infants and gray-haired men.
²⁶I said I would scatter them
    and blot out their memory from mankind,
²⁷but I dreaded the taunt of the enemy,
    lest the adversary misunderstand
and say, 'Our hand has triumphed;
    the LORD has not done all this.'"

²⁸They are a nation without sense,
    there is no discernment in them.
²⁹If only they were wise and would understand this
    and discern what their end will be!
³⁰How could one man chase a thousand,
    or two put ten thousand to flight,
unless their Rock had sold them,
    unless the LORD had given them up?
³¹For their rock is not like our Rock,
    as even our enemies concede.
³²Their vine comes from the vine of Sodom
    and from the fields of Gomorrah.
Their grapes are filled with poison,
    and their clusters with bitterness.
³³Their wine is the venom of serpents,
    the deadly poison of cobras.

³⁴"Have I not kept this in reserve
    and sealed it in my vaults?
³⁵It is mine to avenge; I will repay.
    In due time their foot will slip;
their day of disaster is near
    and their doom rushes upon them."

³⁶The LORD will judge his people
    and have compassion on his servants
when he sees their strength is gone
    and no one is left, slave or free.
³⁷He will say: "Now where are their gods,
    the rock they took refuge in,
³⁸the gods who ate the fat of their sacrifices
    and drank the wine of their drink offerings?
Let them rise up to help you!
    Let them give you shelter!

³⁹"See now that I myself am He!
    There is no god besides me.
I put to death and I bring to life,
    I have wounded and I will heal,
    and no one can deliver out of my hand.
⁴⁰I lift my hand to heaven and declare:
    As surely as I live forever,
⁴¹when I sharpen my flashing sword
    and my hand grasps it in judgment,
I will take vengeance on my adversaries
    and repay those who hate me.
⁴²I will make my arrows drunk with blood,

while my sword devours flesh:
the blood of the slain and the captives,
the heads of the enemy leaders."

⁴³Rejoice, O nations, with his people,^{a,b}
for he will avenge the blood of his servants;
he will take vengeance on his enemies
and make atonement for his land and people.

⁴⁴Moses came with Joshua^c son of Nun and spoke all the words of this song in the hearing of the people. ⁴⁵When Moses finished reciting all these words to all Israel, ⁴⁶he said to them, "Take to heart all the words I have solemnly declared to you this day, so that you may command your children to obey carefully all the words of this law. ⁴⁷They are not just idle words for you—they are your life. By them you will live long in the land you are crossing the Jordan to possess."

Moses to Die on Mount Nebo

⁴⁸On that same day the LORD told Moses, ⁴⁹"Go up into the Abarim Range to Mount Nebo in Moab, across from Jericho, and view Canaan, the land I am giving the Israelites as their own possession. ⁵⁰There on the mountain that you have climbed you will die and be gathered to your people, just as your brother Aaron died on Mount Hor and was gathered to his people. ⁵¹This is because both of you broke faith with me in the presence of the Israelites at the waters of Meribah Kadesh in the Desert of Zin and because you did not uphold my holiness among the Israelites. ⁵²Therefore, you will see the land only from a distance; you will not enter the land I am giving to the people of Israel."

Moses Blesses the Tribes

33 This is the blessing that Moses the man of God pronounced on the Israelites before his death. ²He said:

"The LORD came from Sinai
and dawned over them from Seir;
he shone forth from Mount Paran.
He came with^d myriads of holy ones
from the south, from his mountain slopes.^e
³Surely it is you who love the people;
all the holy ones are in your hand.
At your feet they all bow down,
and from you receive instruction,
⁴the law that Moses gave us,
the possession of the assembly of Jacob.
⁵He was king over Jeshurun^f
when the leaders of the people assembled,
along with the tribes of Israel.

⁶"Let Reuben live and not die,
nor^g his men be few."

⁷And this he said about Judah:

"Hear, O LORD, the cry of Judah;
bring him to his people.

Whose death in your family was (will be) the toughest on you?

1. How does this scene compare with an earlier version of it in 3:23–28? What does Moses do here and why? 2. What does it mean "be gathered to your people" (v. 50; see Ge 25:8)? 3. Why couldn't Moses enter Canaan (see Nu 20:11–13; 27:14)? 4. What was Moses able to see and why?

1. Do the words of Moses seem like "idle words" or "your life" (v. 47)? How so? 2. Does it seem that God was harsh to Moses? Why? Have you ever felt similarly denied your life goal? 3. What is our hope as we approach death?

What was your prized possession as you were growing up? Why that one?

1. What is a blessing that one person confers on another? How does that compare to God blessing us? Who is being blessed here and by whom? 2. What picture is being painted in verses 1–5? Who is present? Who are the "holy ones"? How do the people respond? What do they receive? 3. How do Moses' blessings (vv. 6–25) compare, tribe for tribe, with Jacob's blessings of his tribes (see Ge 49)? 4. Why is Reuben's life to be cut short (v. 6; see Ge 49:3–4)? How does Judah fare this time around? 5. How does the blessing for Levi fit his role? What are "thummim" and "urim" (v. 8; see Ex 28:30; Nu 27:21)? 6. What is the tone of the blessing for Benjamin this time? Why the change from before? 7. Who are the two tribes of Joseph? What blessings do they receive? Why are they so privileged? 8. How does Moses confirm the blessing conferred by Jacob on Zebulun? What does he add to it? How does Jacob's blessing of Gad fit his personality (as typified by Jacob)? 9. Who is likened to a "lion's

---

^a43 Or *Make his people rejoice, O nations*   ^b43 Masoretic Text; Dead Sea Scrolls (see also Septuagint) *people, / and let all the angels worship him /*   ^c44 Hebrew *Hoshea,* a variant of *Joshua*   ^d2 Or *from*   ^e2 The meaning of the Hebrew for this phrase is uncertain.   ^f5 *Jeshurun* means *the upright one,* that is, Israel; also in verse 26.   ^g6 Or *but let*

With his own hands he defends his cause.
   Oh, be his help against his foes!"

8About Levi he said:

"Your Thummim and Urim belong
   to the man you favored.
You tested him at Massah;
   you contended with him at the waters of
      Meribah.
9He said of his father and mother,
   'I have no regard for them.'
He did not recognize his brothers
   or acknowledge his own children,
but he watched over your word
   and guarded your covenant.
10He teaches your precepts to Jacob
   and your law to Israel.
He offers incense before you
   and whole burnt offerings on your altar.
11Bless all his skills, O LORD,
   and be pleased with the work of his hands.
Smite the loins of those who rise up against him;
   strike his foes till they rise no more."

12About Benjamin he said:

"Let the beloved of the LORD rest secure in him,
   for he shields him all day long,
   and the one the LORD loves rests between his
      shoulders."

13About Joseph he said:

"May the LORD bless his land
   with the precious dew from heaven above
   and with the deep waters that lie below;
14with the best the sun brings forth
   and the finest the moon can yield;
15with the choicest gifts of the ancient mountains
   and the fruitfulness of the everlasting hills;
16with the best gifts of the earth and its fullness
   and the favor of him who dwelt in the burning
      bush.
Let all these rest on the head of Joseph,
   on the brow of the prince among*a* his
      brothers.
17In majesty he is like a firstborn bull;
   his horns are the horns of a wild ox.
With them he will gore the nations,
   even those at the ends of the earth.
Such are the ten thousands of Ephraim;
   such are the thousands of Manasseh."

18About Zebulun he said:

"Rejoice, Zebulun, in your going out,
   and you, Issachar, in your tents.
19They will summon peoples to the mountain
   and there offer sacrifices of righteousness;

cub" by Moses? By Jacob? How do you account for the double use of that metaphor? 10. How is Naphtali twice blessed (v. 23; see Ge 49:21)? 11. In what sense is Asher "most blessed of sons" (vv. 24–25)? 12. Whose arms are "everlasting" (v. 27)? How would this uplift Jeshurun (Israel)? What does God's character mean for Israel in verses 28–29? 13. How does this poem of blessing reinforce the song of chapter 32?

1. What picture of God do you get from these verses? Does that make you want to trust God more, or less? How so? 2. By what names do you call on God? What names from here, implicit in God's blessings, would seem quite strange on your lips? What does that tell you about God and how he is variously known by his people? 3. What is your response to these blessings? Why? What questions does this chapter prompt, especially when compared to Jacob's blessings in Genesis 49? 4. In what sense are we "blessed" as Christians: Generally, with blessings Christ makes available to all? Or specifically, with blessings that come to us "with our name on them"? Why do you think so? Can you give an example of a named blessing? 5. Who would you like to bless? With what? Why?

a 16 Or of the one separated from

they will feast on the abundance of the seas,
on the treasures hidden in the sand."

²⁰About Gad he said:

"Blessed is he who enlarges Gad's domain!
Gad lives there like a lion,
tearing at arm or head.
²¹He chose the best land for himself;
the leader's portion was kept for him.
When the heads of the people assembled,
he carried out the LORD's righteous will,
and his judgments concerning Israel."

²²About Dan he said:

"Dan is a lion's cub,
springing out of Bashan."

²³About Naphtali he said:

"Naphtali is abounding with the favor of the LORD
and is full of his blessing;
he will inherit southward to the lake."

²⁴About Asher he said:

"Most blessed of sons is Asher;
let him be favored by his brothers,
and let him bathe his feet in oil.
²⁵The bolts of your gates will be iron and bronze,
and your strength will equal your days.

²⁶"There is no one like the God of Jeshurun,
who rides on the heavens to help you
and on the clouds in his majesty.
²⁷The eternal God is your refuge,
and underneath are the everlasting arms.
He will drive out your enemy before you,
saying, 'Destroy him!'
²⁸So Israel will live in safety alone;
Jacob's spring is secure
in a land of grain and new wine,
where the heavens drop dew.
²⁹Blessed are you, O Israel!
Who is like you,
a people saved by the LORD?
He is your shield and helper
and your glorious sword.
Your enemies will cower before you,
and you will trample down their high places.ᵃ"

The Death of Moses

34 Then Moses climbed Mount Nebo from the plains of Moab to the top of Pisgah, across from Jericho. There the LORD showed him the whole land—from Gilead to Dan, ²all of Naphtali, the territory of Ephraim and Manasseh, all the land of Judah as far as the western sea,ᵇ ³the Negev and the whole region from the Valley of Jericho, the City of Palms, as far as Zoar. ⁴Then the LORD said to him, "This is the land I promised on oath to Abraham, Isaac and Jacob when I said, 'I will give it to your descendants.' I have let you see it with your eyes, but you will not cross over into it."

What is the last sight you would like to see before you die?

1. How does this final scene compare to its "dress rehearsals" or foreshadowing (see 3:23–28; 4:21–22; 31:1–8; 32:48–52)? What similarities do you see? What differences? **2.** What did it mean, emotionally and spiritually, for Moses to see the promised land? **3.** Who do you suppose buried Moses if he was all

ᵃ29 Or *will tread upon their bodies*   ᵇ2 That is, the Mediterranean

⁵And Moses the servant of the LORD died there in Moab, as the LORD had said. ⁶He buried him*a* in Moab, in the valley opposite Beth Peor, but to this day no one knows where his grave is. ⁷Moses was a hundred and twenty years old when he died, yet his eyes were not weak nor his strength gone. ⁸The Israelites grieved for Moses in the plains of Moab thirty days, until the time of weeping and mourning was over.

⁹Now Joshua son of Nun was filled with the spirit*b* of wisdom because Moses had laid his hands on him. So the Israelites listened to him and did what the LORD had commanded Moses.

¹⁰Since then, no prophet has risen in Israel like Moses, whom the LORD knew face to face, ¹¹who did all those miraculous signs and wonders the LORD sent him to do in Egypt—to Pharaoh and to all his officials and to his whole land. ¹²For no one has ever shown the mighty power or performed the awesome deeds that Moses did in the sight of all Israel.

alone when he died? Who do you suppose wrote this epitaph for Moses (vv. 7,10–12)? **4.** How did Israel respond to the death of Moses, as compared to the death of Jacob (see Ge 50:3)? **5.** What happened to Joshua after this (v. 9; see Jos 1)? Why did the Israelites heed Joshua?

♡ **1.** What about Moses' relationship with God and his people made him unique? What about that relationship was, or could be, common to other believers? **2.** What does it mean to know God "face to face"? Do you know God, at least partially, this way? How did this happen? **3.** Can you do the same kind of things Moses did? Why? **4.** How can you receive the "spirit of wisdom" like Joshua did? What is your source of "mighty power"? **5.** What would you like to do for God? How can your small group band together with you?

a6 Or *He was buried*   *b9* Or *Spirit*

INTRODUCTION to
JOSHUA

Book Study Outline: If you are using Joshua for a study course, here is a 7- or 13-week outline. Use the questions in the margin for your group agenda:

🗣 start meeting / 15 min.

📖 read & discuss Bible / 30 min.

💗 close meeting / 15–45 min.

Refer to the Questions and Answers in the front of this Bible for more information.

7-week plan	13-week plan	Personal Reading	Group Study Passage
1	1	1:1–18	1:1–18/Call of Joshua
	2	2:1–24	2:1–24/Rahab and Spies
2	3	3:1–5:12	3:14–4:24/Crossing Jordan
	4	5:13–6:27	5:13–6:21/Fall of Jericho
3	5	7:1–8:35	7:1–26/Battle of Ai
	6	9:1–27	9:1–27/Gibeonite Deception
4	7	10:1–13:33	10:1–43/Sun Stands Still
	8	14:1–15:63	14:1–15/Caleb's Land
5	9	16:1–19:51	16:1–17:18/Land Allotted
	10	20:1–21:45	20:1–9/Cities of Refuge
6	11	22:1–34	22:1–34/Altar of Offense
	12	23:1–16	23:1–16/Joshua's Farewell
7	13	24:1–33	24:1–27/Covenant Renewal

Author: The author is not identified. The book is named for its main character, Joshua, successor to Moses.

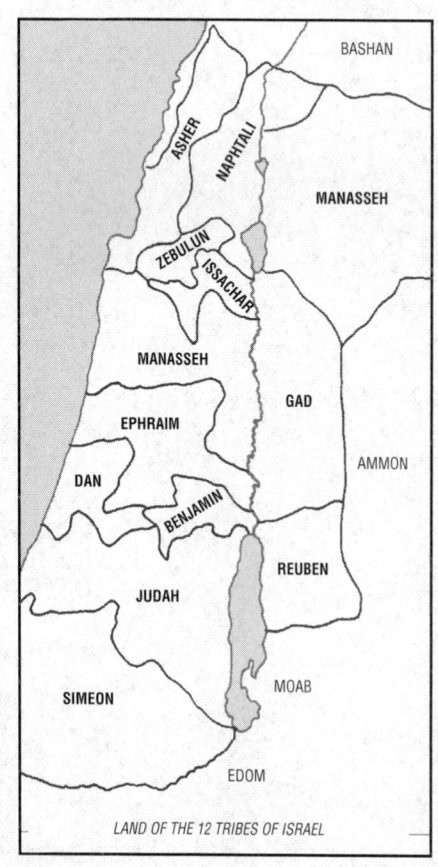

LAND OF THE 12 TRIBES OF ISRAEL

Date: Suggested dates for Joshua range from c. 1405 to 1250 B.C.

Theme: Obedience brings long-awaited victory in the promised land.

Historical Background: Having led the children of Israel to the entrance of the promised land, Moses is forbidden to guide them in. His servant and aide, Joshua, is chosen by God to take the people in, lead them to victory over their enemies, and divide the land among them. Joshua's training has included accompanying Moses partially up Mt. Sinai, being the captain of the army under Moses' direction, and being sent as a spy into Canaan. He was one of only two spies who believed Israel could possess the land by God's enablement.

Characteristics: This book has inspired many hymns and spirituals because of the "good news" character of Joshua's successful leadership of Israel and because of God's active involvement in history. We see this most obviously in the "book of war" (ch. 1–11), which chronicles a series of battles, with victory going to the strong and courageous (a theme repeated at least eight times in God's call to Joshua). When the Israelites do what God calls them to do, they defeat the enemy. When they disobey, they are unable to win. The less action-packed "book of distribution" (ch. 12–24) mostly details allocation of the conquered land, which is depicted in the adjacent map of the tribes' territories.

Joshua

The LORD Commands Joshua

1 After the death of Moses the servant of the LORD, the LORD said to Joshua son of Nun, Moses' aide: ²"Moses my servant is dead. Now then, you and all these people, get ready to cross the Jordan River into the land I am about to give to them—to the Israelites. ³I will give you every place where you set your foot, as I promised Moses. ⁴Your territory will extend from the desert to Lebanon, and from the great river, the Euphrates—all the Hittite country—to the Great Sea*ᵃ* on the west. ⁵No one will be able to stand up against you all the days of your life. As I was with Moses, so I will be with you; I will never leave you nor forsake you.

⁶"Be strong and courageous, because you will lead these people to inherit the land I swore to their forefathers to give them. ⁷Be strong and very courageous. Be careful to obey all the law my servant Moses gave you; do not turn from it to the right or to the left, that you may be successful wherever you go. ⁸Do not let this Book of the Law depart from your mouth; meditate on it day and night, so that you may be careful to do everything written in it. Then you will be prosperous and successful. ⁹Have I not commanded you? Be strong and courageous. Do not be terrified; do not be discouraged, for the LORD your God will be with you wherever you go."

¹⁰So Joshua ordered the officers of the people: ¹¹"Go through the camp and tell the people, 'Get your supplies ready. Three days from now you will cross the Jordan here to go in and take possession of the land the LORD your God is giving you for your own.'"

¹²But to the Reubenites, the Gadites and the half-tribe of Manasseh, Joshua said, ¹³"Remember the command that Moses the servant of the LORD gave you: 'The LORD your God is giving you rest and has granted you this land.' ¹⁴Your wives, your children and your livestock may stay in the land that Moses gave you east of the Jordan, but all your fighting men, fully armed, must cross over ahead of your brothers. You are to help your brothers ¹⁵until the LORD gives them rest, as he has done for you, and until they too have taken possession of the land that the LORD your God is giving them. After that, you may go back and occupy your own land, which Moses the servant of the LORD gave you east of the Jordan toward the sunrise."

¹⁶Then they answered Joshua, "Whatever you have commanded us we will do, and wherever you send us we will go. ¹⁷Just as we fully obeyed Moses, so we will obey you. Only may the LORD your God be with you as he was with Moses. ¹⁸Whoever rebels against your word and does not obey your words, whatever you may command them, will be put to death. Only be strong and courageous!"

Rahab and the Spies

2 Then Joshua son of Nun secretly sent two spies from Shittim. "Go, look over the land," he said, "especially Jericho." So they went and entered the house of a prostitute*ᵇ* named Rahab and stayed there.

ᵃ4 That is, the Mediterranean   *ᵇ1* Or possibly *an innkeeper*

---

1. What employer-employee, teacher-pupil or coach-player relationship has most influenced you? In what ways? **2.** What instructions did your mom usually repeat at least three times as you went off on your own?

1. What has just happened "off-stage" as this scene opens? What does this mean for Joshua? **2.** What promises are given to him (vv. 3–5,9)? Which ones ask Joshua to look back and remember what God has done in the past? Which ones ask him to look ahead and believe God for future blessing? **3.** Which commands accompany the promises? Which would seem most terrifying to one who had to fill Moses' shoes? What is necessary for success and prosperity? What do you think God means here by "success"? **4.** Hence, what does Joshua tell his officers (vv. 10–11)? What exceptions to that general command does he give to the tribes who already possess their land (vv. 12–15)? **5.** In turn, what do they promise? **6.** From their reassuring reply and from the Lord's promises, what do you infer Joshua must be feeling?

1. Which command given to Joshua (vv. 5–9) would be the toughest for you to obey? **2.** Which of his promises would be most helpful to you, if you were left "on your own"? Why? **3.** What challenge lies before you now? How will you "succeed" at it? What do you fear might hinder you? Who can you rally to help you?

---

1. If you went incognito, or "underground" as a spy, what kind of identity would you want? **2.** When you were in senior high, what was one of the most daring things you tried?

1. Why do you suppose Rahab felt safe harboring two spies? What if she had been caught by her own people, or turned against by spies she had no prior reason to trust? 2. Other than safety and an escape plan, what does she provide the spies? Why do those in Jericho feel that way about the Israelites (vv. 9–11)? 3. What was Rahab's request of the spies? In this request, is she being: (a) Self-serving? (b) Other-centered? (c) God-honoring? Why do you think so? 4. What further conditions to her request do the spies and Rahab agree upon (vv. 17–21)? What does their conversation reveal about Israel's intentions? About the binding nature of promises? About Rahab's saving faith? 5. What is the key element in the spies' report (vv. 9,24)? Upon first hearing that report, how would you respond? 6. Given her disreputable occupation and her obvious lie, what in this story builds Rahab's reputation as a woman of faith (see Heb 11:31; Jas 2:25)? How do you react to Rahab's joining the Israelites after the fall of Jericho (Jos 6:22–25) and appar-

²The king of Jericho was told, "Look! Some of the Israelites have come here tonight to spy out the land." ³So the king of Jericho sent this message to Rahab: "Bring out the men who came to you and entered your house, because they have come to spy out the whole land."

⁴But the woman had taken the two men and hidden them. She said, "Yes, the men came to me, but I did not know where they had come from. ⁵At dusk, when it was time to close the city gate, the men left. I don't know which way they went. Go after them quickly. You may catch up with them." ⁶(But she had taken them up to the roof and hidden them under the stalks of flax she had laid out on the roof.) ⁷So the men set out in pursuit of the spies on the road that leads to the fords of the Jordan, and as soon as the pursuers had gone out, the gate was shut.

⁸Before the spies lay down for the night, she went up on the roof ⁹and said to them, "I know that the LORD has given this land to you and that a great fear of you has fallen on us, so that all who live in this country are melting in fear because of you. ¹⁰We have heard how the LORD dried up the water of the Red Sea ᵃ for you when you came out of Egypt, and what you did to Sihon and Og, the two kings of the Amorites east of the Jordan, whom you completely destroyed. ᵇ ¹¹When we heard of it, our hearts melted and everyone's courage failed because of you, for the LORD your God is God in heaven above and on the earth below. ¹²Now then, please swear to me by the LORD that you will show kindness to my family, because I have shown kindness to you. Give me a sure sign ¹³that

ᵃ10 Hebrew *Yam Suph*; that is, Sea of Reeds　　ᵇ10 The Hebrew term refers to the irrevocable giving over of things or persons to the LORD, often by totally destroying them.

Joshua 2:1–24　　　　　　　RAHAB AND THE SPIES

The Israelites are across the Jordan River from Jericho, poised to invade the promised land.

1. Why did the two spies stay at a prostitute's house?
a. for the same reason others would
b. because she operated an inn
c. Being in the city wall, it was the first place they came to.
d. A prostitute was the least likely to be suspected.
e. God led them to her.

2. How do you think Rahab related to God at this point?
a. She was not a believer.
b. She was a closet believer.
c. She feared God but didn't really know him.
d. She was experiencing a "foxhole conversion."

3. Why did Rahab risk her own safety to provide safety for the spies?
a. She was a daredevil.
b. She was a traitor.
c. She had great foresight.
d. She knew they would owe her one.

e. She had faith in their God.

4. The most important intelligence information the spies gained was:
a. a first-hand look at Jericho's walls.
b. discovering the best hiding places in the hills outside Jericho.
c. that the Canaanites had heard of the Israelites' past victories.
d. that the Canaanites were "melting in fear."
e. Rahab's conviction that "the Lord has given this land to you."

5. What do you make of the New Testament's affirmation of "Rahab the prostitute" (Heb 11:31, Jas 2:25), and—as a result of her inclusion in the nation of Israel (Jos 6:22–25)— her apparently becoming a member of Jesus' line of ancestry (Mt 1:5)?
a. She must have changed her lifestyle after she met the spies.
b. God's grace is more inclusive than ours.
c. Prostitution wasn't scorned that much in Old Testament times.
d. God uses "sinners" who are open and available to him.

6. I am most likely to fear God because:
a. of the fear of punishment.
b. of the promise of blessing.
c. there's no one else to believe in.
d. others have believed first.
e. God is so awesome.

7. The "sure sign" for me that God has spared my life is:
a. the promises of Scripture.
b. the word of my parents.
c. the blood of Christ shed for my sins.
d. a life-changing experience.
e. the fact that I want to please him.

8. The "scarlet cord" I've been counting on to hold my weight is:
a. my faith in Jesus Christ.
b. living the best life I can.
c. going to church regularly.
d. God's mercy despite my faults.

9. Rahab's actions would later spare her family as well as herself. What can you do to spare your family from the effects of sin and evil?

you will spare the lives of my father and mother, my brothers and sisters, and all who belong to them, and that you will save us from death."

[14]"Our lives for your lives!" the men assured her. "If you don't tell what we are doing, we will treat you kindly and faithfully when the LORD gives us the land."

[15]So she let them down by a rope through the window, for the house she lived in was part of the city wall. [16]Now she had said to them, "Go to the hills so the pursuers will not find you. Hide yourselves there three days until they return, and then go on your way."

[17]The men said to her, "This oath you made us swear will not be binding on us [18]unless, when we enter the land, you have tied this scarlet cord in the window through which you let us down, and unless you have brought your father and mother, your brothers and all your family into your house. [19]If anyone goes outside your house into the street, his blood will be on his own head; we will not be responsible. As for anyone who is in the house with you, his blood will be on our head if a hand is laid on him. [20]But if you tell what we are doing, we will be released from the oath you made us swear."

[21]"Agreed," she replied. "Let it be as you say." So she sent them away and they departed. And she tied the scarlet cord in the window.

[22]When they left, they went into the hills and stayed there three days, until the pursuers had searched all along the road and returned without finding them. [23]Then the two men started back. They went down out of the hills, forded the river and came to Joshua son of Nun and told him everything that had happened to them. [24]They said to Joshua, "The LORD has surely given the whole land into our hands; all the people are melting in fear because of us."

Crossing the Jordan

3 Early in the morning Joshua and all the Israelites set out from Shittim and went to the Jordan, where they camped before crossing over. [2]After three days the officers went throughout the camp, [3]giving orders to the people: "When you see the ark of the covenant of the LORD your God, and the priests, who are Levites, carrying it, you are to move out from your positions and follow it. [4]Then you will know which way to go, since you have never been this way before. But keep a distance of about a thousand yards[a] between you and the ark; do not go near it."

[5]Joshua told the people, "Consecrate yourselves, for tomorrow the LORD will do amazing things among you."

[6]Joshua said to the priests, "Take up the ark of the covenant and pass on ahead of the people." So they took it up and went ahead of them.

[7]And the LORD said to Joshua, "Today I will begin to exalt you in the eyes of all Israel, so they may know that I am with you as I was with Moses. [8]Tell the priests who carry the ark of the covenant: 'When you reach the edge of the Jordan's waters, go and stand in the river.'"

[9]Joshua said to the Israelites, "Come here and listen to the words of the LORD your God. [10]This is how you will know that the living God is among you and that he will certainly drive out before you the Canaanites, Hittites, Hivites, Perizzites, Girgashites, Amo-

ently becoming an ancestor of Jesus Christ?

♡ **1.** Rahab's actions spare her family. What can you do to help insure the salvation of your family? What "scarlet thread" (or life-line) will you hold out, and hold onto, for life? **2.** When told of how God has worked through those "on the other side," how do you respond: With fear? Jealousy? Vicarious joy? Inspired faith? **3.** What great things has God done "on your side" that might offer hope to others? What groups of people live "on the other side," whom you need to reach out in Christian love to include in your circle?

☕ **1.** When canoeing, camping or fishing, what's your most memorable mishap? **2.** When have you found yourself saying, "Water, water, everywhere": (a) TransAtlantic cruise? (b) Flooded basement? (c) Freezer thawed? (d) Wet season? (e) Other?

📖 **1.** While waiting to cross the Jordan, what do you suppose the people were doing? Feeling? Praying? Anticipating? **2.** What does the ark signify (vv. 3–5,11; see Ex 25:12–22; Nu 4:5; 10:35–36; Dt 10:8; 31:26)? **3.** Why must they wait to see the ark and then keep their distance from it: (a) To keep separate from a holy God? (b) To better see how wonderfully God will lead them? (c) To receive guidance on the way to go? (d) All of the above? Why do you think so? **4.** What does Joshua's call to "consecrate yourselves" imply: Prayers? Cleansing? Give the victory to God, not man? Or what? **5.** Why did God inaugurate Joshua's career with a miracle similar to the one that he gave Moses (vv. 7–8)?

---

[a]4 Hebrew *about two thousand cubits* (about 900 meters)

6. In verses 9–13, what is the relation between word and miracle? **7.** Why did God have the people cross the Jordan at the flood stage (vv. 14–17)?

1. When "you have never been this way before," what do you most need: A guide? A miracle? A signpost? A small group? Where in your life do you need these right now? **2.** In what way can you personally consecrate yourself for the "amazing things" in your life God wants to do?

1. What was one significant place in your formative years? What might you someday tell your child about it? **2.** Which of your folks' childhood memories have you heard over and over again?

rites and Jebusites. ¹¹See, the ark of the covenant of the Lord of all the earth will go into the Jordan ahead of you. ¹²Now then, choose twelve men from the tribes of Israel, one from each tribe. ¹³And as soon as the priests who carry the ark of the LORD—the Lord of all the earth—set foot in the Jordan, its waters flowing downstream will be cut off and stand up in a heap."

¹⁴So when the people broke camp to cross the Jordan, the priests carrying the ark of the covenant went ahead of them. ¹⁵Now the Jordan is at flood stage all during harvest. Yet as soon as the priests who carried the ark reached the Jordan and their feet touched the water's edge, ¹⁶the water from upstream stopped flowing. It piled up in a heap a great distance away, at a town called Adam in the vicinity of Zarethan, while the water flowing down to the Sea of the Arabah (the Salt Sea ᵃ) was completely cut off. So the people crossed over opposite Jericho. ¹⁷The priests who carried the ark of the covenant of the LORD stood firm on dry ground in the middle of the Jordan, while all Israel passed by until the whole nation had completed the crossing on dry ground.

4 When the whole nation had finished crossing the Jordan, the LORD said to Joshua, ²"Choose twelve men from among the people, one from each tribe, ³and tell them to take up twelve stones from the middle of the Jordan from right where the priests stood and to carry them over with you and put them down at the place where you stay tonight."

⁴So Joshua called together the twelve men he had appointed from the Israelites, one from each tribe, ⁵and said to them, "Go

ᵃ16 That is, the Dead Sea

Joshua 3:14–4:24   **CROSSING THE JORDAN**

Forty years after the Israelites left Egypt, the day to enter the promised land finally came. There was only one problem: They had to cross the Jordan River—during flood season no less.

1. What do you suppose the people were thinking as they watched the priests and the ark head for the river?
   a. "I hope these guys can swim."
   b. "I hope the ark can float."
   c. "I guess we're next."
   d. "Lord, have mercy."

2. If the Israelites could have just one picture of this day for their memory album, what would they choose?
   a. the waters receding when the priests entered the river
   b. the waters piled up in a heap upstream
   c. the nation crossing over while the priests stood in the middle
   d. the waters returning to flood stage when the priests came out of the river
   e. the nation gathered around Joshua as he set up the stones in Gilgal

3. What impact do you think this story had on the people? On the priests? On Joshua? What was the reason for God "exalting" Joshua (4:14)?

4. Why did Joshua have the people set up a monument of 12 stones?
   a. as a tribute to Joshua
   b. to remember what they had accomplished
   c. to remember what the Lord had done for them
   d. to commemorate their entrance into the promised land
   e. to remind the 12 tribes that "we're in this together"
   f. to provide a conversation piece for their descendants

5. What are the greatest "stones of memorial" in your life?
   a. my conversion to Christ
   b. an occasion of healing
   c. miraculous provision of resources
   d. spiritual mountain top experience
   e. an incident of God's guidance
   f. other:_____

6. In the future the Israelites would

face battles, discouragement and spiritual backsliding. What struggles or challenges do you face? How can looking again at your stones of memorial help you face them?

7. For what two purposes did God perform this miracle (4:24)? What evidence do others have that "the Lord is powerful" in your life? How have God's actions in the past caused you to "always fear the Lord"?

8. How much of your spiritual journey have you shared with your children? Does anything hold you back from showing them your stones of memorial?

9. How can you formally (e.g. family devotions) and informally (throughout your daily routine) communicate to your children the lasting values of who God is and what he has done?

10. As a result of this course, how are you feeling about your "family time"? In what way will it have more lasting value?

over before the ark of the LORD your God into the middle of the Jordan. Each of you is to take up a stone on his shoulder, according to the number of the tribes of the Israelites, ⁶to serve as a sign among you. In the future, when your children ask you, 'What do these stones mean?' ⁷tell them that the flow of the Jordan was cut off before the ark of the covenant of the LORD. When it crossed the Jordan, the waters of the Jordan were cut off. These stones are to be a memorial to the people of Israel forever."

⁸So the Israelites did as Joshua commanded them. They took twelve stones from the middle of the Jordan, according to the number of the tribes of the Israelites, as the LORD had told Joshua; and they carried them over with them to their camp, where they put them down. ⁹Joshua set up the twelve stones that had been*a* in the middle of the Jordan at the spot where the priests who carried the ark of the covenant had stood. And they are there to this day.

¹⁰Now the priests who carried the ark remained standing in the middle of the Jordan until everything the LORD had commanded Joshua was done by the people, just as Moses had directed Joshua. The people hurried over, ¹¹and as soon as all of them had crossed, the ark of the LORD and the priests came to the other side while the people watched. ¹²The men of Reuben, Gad and the half-tribe of Manasseh crossed over, armed, in front of the Israelites, as Moses had directed them. ¹³About forty thousand armed for battle crossed over before the LORD to the plains of Jericho for war.

¹⁴That day the LORD exalted Joshua in the sight of all Israel; and they revered him all the days of his life, just as they had revered Moses.

¹⁵Then the LORD said to Joshua, ¹⁶"Command the priests carrying the ark of the Testimony to come up out of the Jordan."

¹⁷So Joshua commanded the priests, "Come up out of the Jordan."

¹⁸And the priests came up out of the river carrying the ark of the covenant of the LORD. No sooner had they set their feet on the dry ground than the waters of the Jordan returned to their place and ran at flood stage as before.

¹⁹On the tenth day of the first month the people went up from the Jordan and camped at Gilgal on the eastern border of Jericho. ²⁰And Joshua set up at Gilgal the twelve stones they had taken out of the Jordan. ²¹He said to the Israelites, "In the future when your descendants ask their fathers, 'What do these stones mean?' ²²tell them, 'Israel crossed the Jordan on dry ground.' ²³For the LORD your God dried up the Jordan before you until you had crossed over. The LORD your God did to the Jordan just what he had done to the Red Sea*b* when he dried it up before us until we had crossed over. ²⁴He did this so that all the peoples of the earth might know that the hand of the LORD is powerful and so that you might always fear the LORD your God."

Circumcision at Gilgal

5 Now when all the Amorite kings west of the Jordan and all the Canaanite kings along the coast heard how the LORD had dried up the Jordan before the Israelites until we had crossed over, their hearts melted and they no longer had the courage to face the Israelites.

²At that time the LORD said to Joshua, "Make flint knives and

1. What difficulties are posed for the modern mind by this miraculous river-crossing? (Note: The town of Adam, where the river was "cut off" [3:16], was located 16 miles up river from Jericho, and has experienced a dry river bed on two other occasions, AD 1266 and 1927, due to landslides.) 2. Why did Joshua have the people set up a monument (vv. 6–7,21–22)? Why 12 stones (v. 5; 3:12)? Why from the river? Why two monuments, one in (or by) the river where the priests had stood (v. 9), one taken to Gilgal (vv. 3,19–20)? 3. How does this drama spotlight the role of the ark (vv. 7,9,10,16,18)? Of the priests (vv. 10–11)? Of Joshua (v. 14; see 1:5; 3:7)? But who steals center stage? 4. For what five audiences is this dramatic miracle intended (4:6,7,11,13,24; 5:1)? What prior miracle does this one recall (v. 23)? Who survives as an eye-witness to both (see 5:4,6)? For what two reasons is the new miracle staged?

1. Israel crossed the Jordan "on dry ground," but armed for war, signifying God delivers, but battles will follow. Are you battle-ready or battle-weary these days? 2. What one life-changing encounter with God will you be sure to tell your kids? 3. What "memorial" or other testimonial evidence would your co-workers, neighbors or family come across which might prompt them to ask what God is doing in your life? 4. From your group (or any other), what Jordan-like experience might well be "memorialized"?

What "rite of passage" marked your coming of age into adulthood: Your first cigarette? Voting? Driving? Marriage? Graduation?

1. What is the impact of the miraculous river-crossing on the neighboring kings (v. 1)? 2. Why did God have the children of

---

a 9 Or *Joshua also set up twelve stones*   *b 23* Hebrew *Yam Suph*; that is, Sea of Reeds

Israel wander 40 years in the wilderness (v. 6; see Nu 14:34)? Why circumcise them "again" (vv. 2,5,7)? Why had they not been circumcised before? **3.** Why did all the men of military age die? Who survived (v. 7; see Nu 14:38)? **4.** What does the "reproach of Egypt" imply? What "rolled it away" from Israel? **5.** What is significant about "celebrating the Passover" (v. 10; see Ex 12:42)? "No manna"? "Eating the produce" (v. 12; see Ex 16:35)? How did this force Israel to grow up?

♡ **1.** How has disobeying God's law kept you from enjoying the bounty of his promises? **2.** God rolled away the reproach of Israel's skeptical neighbors with a "seeing-is-believing" miracle. How has God dealt with your own skepticism or that of others watching you? **3.** How has God "stopped the manna" in your life? What has he substituted for it? How has that weaning process helped you be more responsible?

───────────

1. Who was the most intimidating person you ever met: Your prospective father-in-law? The captain of the other team? Your new boss? Your new secretary? **2.** When playing a pickup game or team sport, were you among the first or the last half picked? Why? Who did you most want on your side? Why?

1. Who stands in the way of Joshua (5:13–15)? What does this divine commander want? Why? What is the effect on Joshua? **2.** What is meant by "neither" (5:14): The Lord is neutral? The Lord is holy? The Lord's side is what counts? Or what? **3.** What is meant by "take off your sandals" (5:15)? How is this like Moses' encounter with the "burning bush" (Ex 3:5)? **4.** Is the messenger in 5:13–15 the same as "the Lord" in 6:2? Why do you think so (see Ge 16:7–11 with 16:13)? **5.** How does the battle plan (6:2–5) follow from this divine encounter? How might that determine *how well* Joshua follows the battle plan? And even *whose* battle this really is? **6.** As this battle plan is carried out, what seems strategic to you militarily? Psychologically? Religiously? Why? **7.** What purpose is served by the number seven? By the trumpets' constant blowing? By the people's silence? By their perse-

circumcise the Israelites again." ³So Joshua made flint knives and circumcised the Israelites at Gibeath Haaraloth.ᵃ

⁴Now this is why he did so: All those who came out of Egypt— all the men of military age—died in the desert on the way after leaving Egypt. ⁵All the people that came out had been circumcised, but all the people born in the desert during the journey from Egypt had not. ⁶The Israelites had moved about in the desert forty years until all the men who were of military age when they left Egypt had died, since they had not obeyed the LORD. For the LORD had sworn to them that they would not see the land that he had solemnly promised their fathers to give us, a land flowing with milk and honey. ⁷So he raised up their sons in their place, and these were the ones Joshua circumcised. They were still uncircumcised because they had not been circumcised on the way. ⁸And after the whole nation had been circumcised, they remained where they were in camp until they were healed.

⁹Then the LORD said to Joshua, "Today I have rolled away the reproach of Egypt from you." So the place has been called Gilgalᵇ to this day.

¹⁰On the evening of the fourteenth day of the month, while camped at Gilgal on the plains of Jericho, the Israelites celebrated the Passover. ¹¹The day after the Passover, that very day, they ate some of the produce of the land: unleavened bread and roasted grain. ¹²The manna stopped the day afterᶜ they ate this food from the land; there was no longer any manna for the Israelites, but that year they ate of the produce of Canaan.

The Fall of Jericho

¹³Now when Joshua was near Jericho, he looked up and saw a man standing in front of him with a drawn sword in his hand. Joshua went up to him and asked, "Are you for us or for our enemies?"

¹⁴"Neither," he replied, "but as commander of the army of the LORD I have now come." Then Joshua fell facedown to the ground in reverence, and asked him, "What message does my Lordᵈ have for his servant?"

¹⁵The commander of the LORD's army replied, "Take off your sandals, for the place where you are standing is holy." And Joshua did so.

6 Now Jericho was tightly shut up because of the Israelites. No one went out and no one came in.

²Then the LORD said to Joshua, "See, I have delivered Jericho into your hands, along with its king and its fighting men. ³March around the city once with all the armed men. Do this for six days. ⁴Have seven priests carry trumpets of rams' horns in front of the ark. On the seventh day, march around the city seven times, with the priests blowing the trumpets. ⁵When you hear them sound a long blast on the trumpets, have all the people give a loud shout; then the wall of the city will collapse and the people will go up, every man straight in."

⁶So Joshua son of Nun called the priests and said to them, "Take up the ark of the covenant of the LORD and have seven priests carry trumpets in front of it." ⁷And he ordered the people, "Advance! March around the city, with the armed guard going ahead of the ark of the LORD."

⁸When Joshua had spoken to the people, the seven priests carrying the seven trumpets before the LORD went forward, blowing

ᵃ3 *Gibeath Haaraloth* means *hill of foreskins.*   ᵇ9 *Gilgal* sounds like the Hebrew for *roll.*   ᶜ12 Or *the day*   ᵈ14 Or *lord*

their trumpets, and the ark of the LORD's covenant followed them. 9The armed guard marched ahead of the priests who blew the trumpets, and the rear guard followed the ark. All this time the trumpets were sounding. 10But Joshua had commanded the people, "Do not give a war cry, do not raise your voices, do not say a word until the day I tell you to shout. Then shout!" 11So he had the ark of the LORD carried around the city, circling it once. Then the people returned to camp and spent the night there.

12Joshua got up early the next morning and the priests took up the ark of the LORD. 13The seven priests carrying the seven trumpets went forward, marching before the ark of the LORD and blowing the trumpets. The armed men went ahead of them and the rear guard followed the ark of the LORD, while the trumpets kept sounding. 14So on the second day they marched around the city once and returned to the camp. They did this for six days.

15On the seventh day, they got up at daybreak and marched around the city seven times in the same manner, except that on that day they circled the city seven times. 16The seventh time around, when the priests sounded the trumpet blast, Joshua commanded the people, "Shout! For the LORD has given you the city! 17The city and all that is in it are to be devoted*a* to the LORD. Only Rahab the prostitute*b* and all who are with her in her house shall be spared, because she hid the spies we sent. 18But keep away from the devoted things, so that you will not bring about your own destruction by taking any of them. Otherwise you will make the

a17 The Hebrew term refers to the irrevocable giving over of things or persons to the LORD, often by totally destroying them; also in verses 18 and 21.   b17 Or possibly innkeeper; also in verses 22 and 25

verance? By the ark's position (see 3:4, where the ark is distant from the people)? **8.** How is it that with some divine miracles the people share in them by their obedience, whereas with other miracles they do not? **9.** In verses 17–21, what is meant by "devoted things" and their prohibition? Why is such total destruction of Jericho warranted? **10.** Why spare only Rahab's family (vv. 17,22–25)? Why place them "outside the camp of Israel" (see Eph 3:6)? **11.** What happens to any who rebuild Jericho (v. 26; see 1Ki 16:34)?

 1. When did you discover what it meant to be on God's side and take direction from him, rather than having him serve you on your side? **2.** What crazy battle plan is the Lord calling you to carry out? How will you persevere in that? Who else is on the Lord's side with you in this? Your group? **3.** What walled-in area of your life are you still protecting or hiding behind? How secure do you feel behind that wall? How might God give you victory over those walls if you will follow his ways? **4.** How has your life been spared, even re-

---

 Joshua 5:13–6:21   THE FALL OF JERICHO

The Israelites have just crossed the Jordan River and entered the promised land. Before them stands the fortified city of Jericho.

1. What does the "commander of the army of the Lord" come for?
   a. to give Joshua the battle plan
   b. to call Joshua to reverence
   c. to commission him for holy war
   d. to examine Joshua's feet
   e. to get Joshua pumped up

2. How do you think the Israelites felt about Joshua's battle plan?
   a. "This is weird."
   b. "What will keep them from taking shots at us from inside the city?"
   c. "I hope I don't get dizzy!"
   d. "If God wants us to do it, let's do it."
   e. "I could use the exercise."

3. How do you think the residents of Jericho felt about the plan?
   a. "These people are crazy!"
   b. "These trumpets are driving *me* crazy!"
   c. "I wonder if their god told them to do this."

   d. "These people are persistent."
   e. "I have a bad feeling about this."

4. What was the purpose of the trumpet blast and the people's shout?
   a. The noise would collapse the wall.
   b. It was God's cue.
   c. It was psychological warfare.
   d. It was a test of Israel's obedience.
   e. It was an expression of the people's faith.

5. Why did God call for the total destruction of Jericho?
   a. because of their wickedness and idolatry
   b. to keep the Israelites from becoming like them
   c. to make a statement to the other Canaanites
   d. because the promised land was exclusively for the Israelites now
   e. That's what I'd like to know.

6. When did you realize what it means to be on the Lord's side and take your marching orders from him? How can you tell when you start to stray into enemy lines?

7. What area of your life are you still protecting or hiding behind? How could God give you victory over those walls if you would follow his ways?

8. What crazy battle plan is the Lord calling you to? How will you persevere in the fray? Who can you enlist to join you?

9. 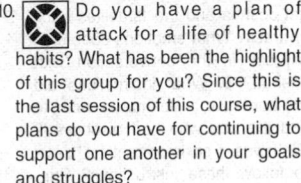 How does this story relate to your struggle to "shape up"?
   a. I need that kind of persistence.
   b. I need that kind of daily exercise.
   c. I've gone around and around with diet plans at least seven times!
   d. I need to find the right battle plan and stick to it.
   e. I know what I need to do, but I can't win this battle on my own.

10. 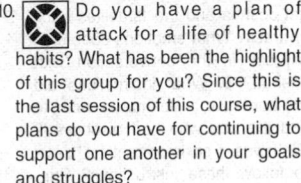 Do you have a plan of attack for a life of healthy habits? What has been the highlight of this group for you? Since this is the last session of this course, what plans do you have for continuing to support one another in your goals and struggles?

deemed, thanks in part to someone else's faithful response to you and their Lord?

camp of Israel liable to destruction and bring trouble on it. ¹⁹All the silver and gold and the articles of bronze and iron are sacred to the LORD and must go into his treasury."

²⁰When the trumpets sounded, the people shouted, and at the sound of the trumpet, when the people gave a loud shout, the wall collapsed; so every man charged straight in, and they took the city. ²¹They devoted the city to the LORD and destroyed with the sword every living thing in it—men and women, young and old, cattle, sheep and donkeys.

²²Joshua said to the two men who had spied out the land, "Go into the prostitute's house and bring her out and all who belong to her, in accordance with your oath to her." ²³So the young men who had done the spying went in and brought out Rahab, her father and mother and brothers and all who belonged to her. They brought out her entire family and put them in a place outside the camp of Israel.

²⁴Then they burned the whole city and everything in it, but they put the silver and gold and the articles of bronze and iron into the treasury of the LORD's house. ²⁵But Joshua spared Rahab the prostitute, with her family and all who belonged to her, because she hid the men Joshua had sent as spies to Jericho—and she lives among the Israelites to this day.

²⁶At that time Joshua pronounced this solemn oath: "Cursed before the LORD is the man who undertakes to rebuild this city, Jericho:

> "At the cost of his firstborn son
>   will he lay its foundations;
> at the cost of his youngest
>   will he set up its gates."

²⁷So the LORD was with Joshua, and his fame spread throughout the land.

Achan's Sin

7 But the Israelites acted unfaithfully in regard to the devoted things[a]; Achan son of Carmi, the son of Zimri,[b] the son of Zerah, of the tribe of Judah, took some of them. So the LORD's anger burned against Israel.

²Now Joshua sent men from Jericho to Ai, which is near Beth Aven to the east of Bethel, and told them, "Go up and spy out the region." So the men went up and spied out Ai.

³When they returned to Joshua, they said, "Not all the people will have to go up against Ai. Send two or three thousand men to take it and do not weary all the people, for only a few men are there." ⁴So about three thousand men went up; but they were routed by the men of Ai, ⁵who killed about thirty-six of them. They chased the Israelites from the city gate as far as the stone quarries[c] and struck them down on the slopes. At this the hearts of the people melted and became like water.

⁶Then Joshua tore his clothes and fell facedown to the ground before the ark of the LORD, remaining there till evening. The elders of Israel did the same, and sprinkled dust on their heads. ⁷And Joshua said, "Ah, Sovereign LORD, why did you ever bring this people across the Jordan to deliver us into the hands of the Amorites to destroy us? If only we had been content to stay on the other

1. When you were 10 years old, where was your favorite hiding place? 2. Can you recall a time when someone did something wrong, but you were punished for it instead? How did you feel? 3. What toy did you always want as a child, but never got?

1. Why was God angry with all the Israelites (see 6:18–19, for God's instructions on the capture of Jericho)? 2. When Israel attacked Ai, what apparently did they expect would happen? What instead was the actual outcome? 3. How would you describe Joshua's reaction to the stunning defeat at Ai: Cowardly? Angry? Whining? Surprised? Or what? What elements of each do you see in your group's reaction (had you been there)? 4. How did the Lord get Joshua and the Israelites back on track? What emotions does God express in the conversation with Joshua? 5. What instructions did the Lord give to Joshua in order to find the one who had disobeyed? Why was it so important for Israel to follow these instructions? Sup-

---

a 1 The Hebrew term refers to the irrevocable giving over of things or persons to the LORD, often by totally destroying them; also in verses 11, 12, 13 and 15.   b 1 See Septuagint and 1 Chron. 2:6; Hebrew *Zabdi*; also in verses 17 and 18.   c 5 Or *as far as Shebarim*

side of the Jordan! ⁸O Lord, what can I say, now that Israel has been routed by its enemies? ⁹The Canaanites and the other people of the country will hear about this and they will surround us and wipe out our name from the earth. What then will you do for your own great name?"

¹⁰The LORD said to Joshua, "Stand up! What are you doing down on your face? ¹¹Israel has sinned; they have violated my covenant, which I commanded them to keep. They have taken some of the devoted things; they have stolen, they have lied, they have put them with their own possessions. ¹²That is why the Israelites cannot stand against their enemies; they turn their backs and run because they have been made liable to destruction. I will not be with you anymore unless you destroy whatever among you is devoted to destruction.

¹³"Go, consecrate the people. Tell them, 'Consecrate yourselves in preparation for tomorrow; for this is what the LORD, the God of Israel, says: That which is devoted is among you, O Israel. You cannot stand against your enemies until you remove it.

¹⁴"'In the morning, present yourselves tribe by tribe. The tribe that the LORD takes shall come forward clan by clan; the clan that the LORD takes shall come forward family by family; and the family that the LORD takes shall come forward man by man. ¹⁵He who is caught with the devoted things shall be destroyed by fire, along with all that belongs to him. He has violated the covenant of the LORD and has done a disgraceful thing in Israel!'"

¹⁶Early the next morning Joshua had Israel come forward by tribes, and Judah was taken. ¹⁷The clans of Judah came forward, and he took the Zerahites. He had the clan of the Zerahites come forward by families, and Zimri was taken. ¹⁸Joshua had his family come forward man by man, and Achan son of Carmi, the son of Zimri, the son of Zerah, of the tribe of Judah, was taken.

¹⁹Then Joshua said to Achan, "My son, give glory to the LORD,ᵃ the God of Israel, and give him the praise.ᵇ Tell me what you have done; do not hide it from me."

²⁰Achan replied, "It is true! I have sinned against the LORD, the God of Israel. This is what I have done: ²¹When I saw in the plunder a beautiful robe from Babylonia,ᶜ two hundred shekelsᵈ of silver and a wedge of gold weighing fifty shekels,ᵉ I coveted them and took them. They are hidden in the ground inside my tent, with the silver underneath."

²²So Joshua sent messengers, and they ran to the tent, and there it was, hidden in his tent, with the silver underneath. ²³They took the things from the tent, brought them to Joshua and all the Israelites and spread them out before the LORD.

²⁴Then Joshua, together with all Israel, took Achan son of Zerah, the silver, the robe, the gold wedge, his sons and daughters, his cattle, donkeys and sheep, his tent and all that he had, to the Valley of Achor. ²⁵Joshua said, "Why have you brought this trouble on us? The LORD will bring trouble on you today."

Then all Israel stoned him, and after they had stoned the rest, they burned them. ²⁶Over Achan they heaped up a large pile of rocks, which remains to this day. Then the LORD turned from his fierce anger. Therefore that place has been called the Valley of Achorᶠ ever since.

pose they hadn't? 6. What exactly was Achan's sin? Why do you think he did it even though he knew God's orders? Describe his state of mind as he watched the tribes, clans, and families file past Joshua. 7. Who all suffered because of Achan's sin? Why do you think the punishment was so severe?

♡ 1. What kinds of things can happen in our lives when we sin and try to hide it? As with the Israelites, has the Lord ever had to "get tough" with you to get you back on track? When? 2. If you had been Joshua, would you have been tempted to let Achan go with a slap on the wrist? Send him packing? Punch him out? Or what? What does this say about your style of disciplining those you feel responsible for at home or work? 3. If you had been Achan's wife or children, how would you have felt? How about the parents of one of the 36 killed in the attack on Ai? 4. Do you think it was fair for God to punish all Israel because just one person sinned? Why or why not?

ᵃ19 A solemn charge to tell the truth   ᵇ19 Or and confess to him   ᶜ21 Hebrew Shinar   ᵈ21 That is, about 5 pounds (about 2.3 kilograms)   ᵉ21 That is, about 1 1/4 pounds (about 0.6 kilogram)   ᶠ26 Achor means trouble.

1. When have you come up a winner the second time around: (a) Entrance exams? (b) Remarriage? (c) Trying to give birth to a new _____? What made the difference the second time? 2. What is one "come-from-behind victory" in your life you still remember fondly?

1. In chapter 7, the first attack on Ai ended in defeat. What does the Lord say to Joshua now to encourage him in a second attack? How is this attack to differ from the first one? 2. Briefly describe the plan of attack that Joshua draws up in verses 3–8. How does this plan make use of the defeat suffered in the first attack? 3. If you had been an Israelite soldier, how would you have felt as Joshua explained his new master plan to you: Wildly enthusiastic? Okay, but …? Forget it? What does Joshua do to encourage any less-than-enthusiastic soldiers before the battle? 4. What do you think was the attitude of Ai's king and soldiers when the battle began? How did this attitude lead them to defeat? 5. What was the final outcome of Israel's attack on Ai? How important was Joshua's leadership? In your opinion, how much of the outcome was due to the Lord's direction and how much was due to human planning and effort? (a) 100 percent the Lord; (b) Mostly the Lord; (c) 50–50; (d) Mostly human planning and effort.

1. Is there some area of your life now in which you hear the Lord saying to you, "Do not be afraid; do not be discouraged"? 2. Have you ever had an occasion when your own self-confidence led you into danger? What great thing might you attempt now in your life if *God* assured you of success? 3. Some say, "The only failure is the failure to learn." Others say, "The only thing you can learn from losing is how to lose." Which would *Joshua* say in this regard? What would *you* say? 4. If you had been an Israelite soldier, how would you have felt about killing the women of Ai? Would the experience of Achan in chapter 7 have made it any easier?

Ai Destroyed

8 Then the Lord said to Joshua, "Do not be afraid; do not be discouraged. Take the whole army with you, and go up and attack Ai. For I have delivered into your hands the king of Ai, his people, his city and his land. ²You shall do to Ai and its king as you did to Jericho and its king, except that you may carry off their plunder and livestock for yourselves. Set an ambush behind the city."

³So Joshua and the whole army moved out to attack Ai. He chose thirty thousand of his best fighting men and sent them out at night ⁴with these orders: "Listen carefully. You are to set an ambush behind the city. Don't go very far from it. All of you be on the alert. ⁵I and all those with me will advance on the city, and when the men come out against us, as they did before, we will flee from them. ⁶They will pursue us until we have lured them away from the city, for they will say, 'They are running away from us as they did before.' So when we flee from them, ⁷you are to rise up from ambush and take the city. The Lord your God will give it into your hand. ⁸When you have taken the city, set it on fire. Do what the Lord has commanded. See to it; you have my orders."

⁹Then Joshua sent them off, and they went to the place of ambush and lay in wait between Bethel and Ai, to the west of Ai—but Joshua spent that night with the people.

¹⁰Early the next morning Joshua mustered his men, and he and the leaders of Israel marched before them to Ai. ¹¹The entire force that was with him marched up and approached the city and arrived in front of it. They set up camp north of Ai, with the valley between them and the city. ¹²Joshua had taken about five thousand men and set them in ambush between Bethel and Ai, to the west of the city. ¹³They had the soldiers take up their positions—all those in the camp to the north of the city and the ambush to the west of it. That night Joshua went into the valley.

¹⁴When the king of Ai saw this, he and all the men of the city hurried out early in the morning to meet Israel in battle at a certain place overlooking the Arabah. But he did not know that an ambush had been set against him behind the city. ¹⁵Joshua and all Israel let themselves be driven back before them, and they fled toward the desert. ¹⁶All the men of Ai were called to pursue them, and they pursued Joshua and were lured away from the city. ¹⁷Not a man remained in Ai or Bethel who did not go after Israel. They left the city open and went in pursuit of Israel.

¹⁸Then the Lord said to Joshua, "Hold out toward Ai the javelin that is in your hand, for into your hand I will deliver the city." So Joshua held out his javelin toward Ai. ¹⁹As soon as he did this, the men in the ambush rose quickly from their position and rushed forward. They entered the city and captured it and quickly set it on fire.

²⁰The men of Ai looked back and saw the smoke of the city rising against the sky, but they had no chance to escape in any direction, for the Israelites who had been fleeing toward the desert had turned back against their pursuers. ²¹For when Joshua and all Israel saw that the ambush had taken the city and that smoke was going up from the city, they turned around and attacked the men of Ai. ²²The men of the ambush also came out of the city against them, so that they were caught in the middle, with Israelites on both sides. Israel cut them down, leaving them neither survivors nor fugitives. ²³But they took the king of Ai alive and brought him to Joshua.

²⁴When Israel had finished killing all the men of Ai in the fields

and in the desert where they had chased them, and when every one of them had been put to the sword, all the Israelites returned to Ai and killed those who were in it. ²⁵Twelve thousand men and women fell that day—all the people of Ai. ²⁶For Joshua did not draw back the hand that held out his javelin until he had destroyed*ᵃ* all who lived in Ai. ²⁷But Israel did carry off for themselves the livestock and plunder of this city, as the LORD had instructed Joshua.

²⁸So Joshua burned Ai and made it a permanent heap of ruins, a desolate place to this day. ²⁹He hung the king of Ai on a tree and left him there until evening. At sunset, Joshua ordered them to take his body from the tree and throw it down at the entrance of the city gate. And they raised a large pile of rocks over it, which remains to this day.

The Covenant Renewed at Mount Ebal

³⁰Then Joshua built on Mount Ebal an altar to the LORD, the God of Israel, ³¹as Moses the servant of the LORD had commanded the Israelites. He built it according to what is written in the Book of the Law of Moses—an altar of uncut stones, on which no iron tool had been used. On it they offered to the LORD burnt offerings and sacrificed fellowship offerings.*ᵇ* ³²There, in the presence of the Israelites, Joshua copied on stones the law of Moses, which he had written. ³³All Israel, aliens and citizens alike, with their elders, officials and judges, were standing on both sides of the ark of the covenant of the LORD, facing those who carried it—the priests, who were Levites. Half of the people stood in front of Mount Gerizim and half of them in front of Mount Ebal, as Moses the servant of the LORD had formerly commanded when he gave instructions to bless the people of Israel.

³⁴Afterward, Joshua read all the words of the law—the blessings and the curses—just as it is written in the Book of the Law. ³⁵There was not a word of all that Moses had commanded that Joshua did not read to the whole assembly of Israel, including the women and children, and the aliens who lived among them.

The Gibeonite Deception

9 Now when all the kings west of the Jordan heard about these things—those in the hill country, in the western foothills, and along the entire coast of the Great Sea*ᶜ* as far as Lebanon (the kings of the Hittites, Amorites, Canaanites, Perizzites, Hivites and Jebusites)— ²they came together to make war against Joshua and Israel.

³However, when the people of Gibeon heard what Joshua had done to Jericho and Ai, ⁴they resorted to a ruse: They went as a delegation whose donkeys were loaded*ᵈ* with worn-out sacks and old wineskins, cracked and mended. ⁵The men put worn and patched sandals on their feet and wore old clothes. All the bread of their food supply was dry and moldy. ⁶Then they went to Joshua in the camp at Gilgal and said to him and the men of Israel, "We have come from a distant country; make a treaty with us."

⁷The men of Israel said to the Hivites, "But perhaps you live near us. How then can we make a treaty with you?"

⁸"We are your servants," they said to Joshua.

When was the last time your "whole family" gathered together? Where? What for?

1. What was the first thing Joshua did after the great victory at Ai? What does this tell you about the kind of man he was? 2. Why assemble all Israel at this place and in this fashion (see Dt 11:29; 27:1–14)? 3. Why do you think the children and aliens were included in this covenant renewal ceremony?

What might it mean for you to "build an altar" to the Lord? What would you offer?

---

1. What was your favorite costume as a child? Why that one? 2. Have you ever bought something that later turned out to be a lemon? How did you feel?

1. How did the kings west of the Jordan react to Israel's conquest of Jericho and Ai? What about the people of Gibeon? How would you have reacted if you had been a king in that area? 2. What was the ruse used by the people of Gibeon to trick Joshua and the Israelites? Why do you suppose it worked? In this regard, what is the significance of the Israelites sampling, but not inquiring? 3. What did the Israelites do when they discovered they had been tricked by the Gibeonites (vv. 16–18)? How did that affect those responsible for the unpopular treaty? 4. How did Joshua finally deal with the Gibeonites (vv. 22–23)? What was their response to Joshua's curse? 5. Locate Gibeon on a map of Joshua's

---

ᵃ26 The Hebrew term refers to the irrevocable giving over of things or persons to the LORD, often by totally destroying them.   *ᵇ31* Traditionally *peace offerings*
ᶜ1 That is, the Mediterranean   *ᵈ4* Most Hebrew manuscripts; some Hebrew manuscripts, Vulgate and Syriac (see also Septuagint) *They prepared provisions and loaded their donkeys*

time. Why was its capture so strategic for Israel?

1. The men of Israel "did not inquire of the Lord" (v. 14), as they should have. Have you ever made an important decision in your life without inquiring of the Lord? What was the result? 2. Have you ever made a promise which later turned out to be difficult or unpopular to keep? What happened? 3. As a fearful and accursed Gibeonite, would you have fought for your freedom or submitted to perpetual slavery? Why? What does that say about your fighting style in general? Do you readily accept, or usually resist, authority imposed on you? Does it depend on who is doing the imposing? How so? 4. Strategy was important for Joshua. What does that say about the use of strategy in planning your life? In doing God's work?

But Joshua asked, "Who are you and where do you come from?" 9They answered: "Your servants have come from a very distant country because of the fame of the LORD your God. For we have heard reports of him: all that he did in Egypt, 10and all that he did to the two kings of the Amorites east of the Jordan—Sihon king of Heshbon, and Og king of Bashan, who reigned in Ashtaroth. 11And our elders and all those living in our country said to us, 'Take provisions for your journey; go and meet them and say to them, "We are your servants; make a treaty with us." ' 12This bread of ours was warm when we packed it at home on the day we left to come to you. But now see how dry and moldy it is. 13And these wineskins that we filled were new, but see how cracked they are. And our clothes and sandals are worn out by the very long journey."

14The men of Israel sampled their provisions but did not inquire of the LORD. 15Then Joshua made a treaty of peace with them to let them live, and the leaders of the assembly ratified it by oath.

16Three days after they made the treaty with the Gibeonites, the Israelites heard that they were neighbors, living near them. 17So the Israelites set out and on the third day came to their cities: Gibeon, Kephirah, Beeroth and Kiriath Jearim. 18But the Israelites did not attack them, because the leaders of the assembly had sworn an oath to them by the LORD, the God of Israel.

The whole assembly grumbled against the leaders, 19but all the leaders answered, "We have given them our oath by the LORD, the God of Israel, and we cannot touch them now. 20This is what we will do to them: We will let them live, so that wrath will not fall on us for breaking the oath we swore to them." 21They continued, "Let them live, but let them be woodcutters and water carriers for the entire community." So the leaders' promise to them was kept.

22Then Joshua summoned the Gibeonites and said, "Why did you deceive us by saying, 'We live a long way from you,' while actually you live near us? 23You are now under a curse: You will never cease to serve as woodcutters and water carriers for the house of my God."

24They answered Joshua, "Your servants were clearly told how the LORD your God had commanded his servant Moses to give you the whole land and to wipe out all its inhabitants from before you. So we feared for our lives because of you, and that is why we did this. 25We are now in your hands. Do to us whatever seems good and right to you."

26So Joshua saved them from the Israelites, and they did not kill them. 27That day he made the Gibeonites woodcutters and water carriers for the community and for the altar of the LORD at the place the LORD would choose. And that is what they are to this day.

The Sun Stands Still

1. As a teenager, did you ever do something risky to defend a friend? What was it? 2. If you could save one day of your life in a bottle to live over and over, what day would it be? 3. If you had a 30-hour day at your disposal tomorrow, how would you spend it?

1. Imagine you are a reporter for the Jerusalem Journal of Joshua's day. Write the headline and opening sentence (the lead) for a story about Joshua's defeat of the Amorites. 2. Who are these

10 Now Adoni-Zedek king of Jerusalem heard that Joshua had taken Ai and totally destroyed[a] it, doing to Ai and its king as he had done to Jericho and its king, and that the people of Gibeon had made a treaty of peace with Israel and were living near them. 2He and his people were very much alarmed at this, because Gibeon was an important city, like one of the royal cities; it was larger than Ai, and all its men were good fighters. 3So Adoni-Zedek king of Jerusalem appealed to Hoham king of Hebron, Piram king of Jarmuth, Japhia king of Lachish and Debir king of Eglon. 4"Come

a 1 The Hebrew term refers to the irrevocable giving over of things or persons to the LORD, often by totally destroying them; also in verses 28, 35, 37, 39 and 40.

up and help me attack Gibeon," he said, "because it has made peace with Joshua and the Israelites."

⁵Then the five kings of the Amorites—the kings of Jerusalem, Hebron, Jarmuth, Lachish and Eglon—joined forces. They moved up with all their troops and took up positions against Gibeon and attacked it.

⁶The Gibeonites then sent word to Joshua in the camp at Gilgal: "Do not abandon your servants. Come up to us quickly and save us! Help us, because all the Amorite kings from the hill country have joined forces against us."

⁷So Joshua marched up from Gilgal with his entire army, including all the best fighting men. ⁸The LORD said to Joshua, "Do not be afraid of them; I have given them into your hand. Not one of them will be able to withstand you."

⁹After an all-night march from Gilgal, Joshua took them by surprise. ¹⁰The LORD threw them into confusion before Israel, who defeated them in a great victory at Gibeon. Israel pursued them along the road going up to Beth Horon and cut them down all the way to Azekah and Makkedah. ¹¹As they fled before Israel on the road down from Beth Horon to Azekah, the LORD hurled large hailstones down on them from the sky, and more of them died from the hailstones than were killed by the swords of the Israelites.

¹²On the day the LORD gave the Amorites over to Israel, Joshua said to the LORD in the presence of Israel:

"O sun, stand still over Gibeon,
     O moon, over the Valley of Aijalon."
  ¹³So the sun stood still,
     and the moon stopped,
        till the nation avenged itself on[a] its enemies,

as it is written in the Book of Jashar.

The sun stopped in the middle of the sky and delayed going down about a full day. ¹⁴There has never been a day like it before or since, a day when the LORD listened to a man. Surely the LORD was fighting for Israel!

¹⁵Then Joshua returned with all Israel to the camp at Gilgal.

Five Amorite Kings Killed

¹⁶Now the five kings had fled and hidden in the cave at Makkedah. ¹⁷When Joshua was told that the five kings had been found hiding in the cave at Makkedah, ¹⁸he said, "Roll large rocks up to the mouth of the cave, and post some men there to guard it. ¹⁹But don't stop! Pursue your enemies, attack them from the rear and don't let them reach their cities, for the LORD your God has given them into your hand."

²⁰So Joshua and the Israelites destroyed them completely—almost to a man—but the few who were left reached their fortified cities. ²¹The whole army then returned safely to Joshua in the camp at Makkedah, and no one uttered a word against the Israelites.

²²Joshua said, "Open the mouth of the cave and bring those five kings out to me." ²³So they brought the five kings out of the cave—the kings of Jerusalem, Hebron, Jarmuth, Lachish and Eglon. ²⁴When they had brought these kings to Joshua, he summoned all the men of Israel and said to the army commanders who had come with him, "Come here and put your feet on the necks of these

people that attack Gibeon? Why do they do so? 3. How do Joshua and the Israelites get involved? If you were Joshua, would you have helped the Gibeonites after their trickery in chapter 9? 4. How does the Lord encourage Joshua in his attack? Where have you heard similar words in the book of Joshua? 5. Where else does the Lord help the Israelites in the battle? Can you think of possible explanations for the miracle in verse 13? 6. Who was actually responsible for Israel's victory? Why is this important in the story?

1. Who in your group do you feel you could call on for help in a tough spot? 2. What are you doing now that you wish God would give you more time to accomplish? If more time is not available but more workers would get the job done, is there a way your small group can help?

1. Ever explore a cave? What do you remember most about your experience? 2. What was the #1 priority in your life this month?

1. What happened to the five Amorite kings? Why do you think they were hiding rather than fighting with their troops (see 10:11)? 2. Who escapes? Why do the "fortified cities" provide what the caves can not? 3. What was the meaning of Joshua's instructions in verse 24? What might be the comparable action today? 4. How did Joshua encourage his troops in word and deed (vv. 25–28)? 5. How might succeeding generations of Israelites have felt when they saw the cave at Makkedah: Disgust? Pride? Curiosity? Or what? Why?

a 13 Or *nation triumphed over*

1. In your life do you feel more like: (a) I've got the enemy trapped but not destroyed? (b) The enemy has me trapped? (c) Battles abound, but I'm not alone? (d) I'm overwhelmed by the battles I still have to face? (e) The enemy doesn't dare utter one word against me? 2. In each instance, who (or what) is your enemy?

When you were a child, what activity gave you the feeling of being part of a team? Where do you experience that feeling now?

1. What major cities did the Israelites attack? What was the outcome of each attack? 2. Do you notice a pattern in how each victory is reported? What is this pattern? 3. What is meant by the repeated phrase, "Then Joshua and all Israel with him …" (vv. 29,31,34,36,38)? 4. According to verses 40–42, how much of the promised land had been conquered up to this point? How long do you think this took: A few days? A month? A year? A long time? Why?

1. Where in your life is it evident that the Lord is fighting for you? Do you have anyone alongside you in that battle? Who? How long is it taking to win your particular battle? 2. Why do you think God commanded the Israelites to destroy the cities *totally*? Might God command something similar today? If so, what "zero tolerance" program comes to mind?

1. What big person or thing scared you as a child? How did you overcome that fear, or did you? 2. Complete this sentence: "In

kings." So they came forward and placed their feet on their necks.

²⁵Joshua said to them, "Do not be afraid; do not be discouraged. Be strong and courageous. This is what the LORD will do to all the enemies you are going to fight." ²⁶Then Joshua struck and killed the kings and hung them on five trees, and they were left hanging on the trees until evening.

²⁷At sunset Joshua gave the order and they took them down from the trees and threw them into the cave where they had been hiding. At the mouth of the cave they placed large rocks, which are there to this day.

²⁸That day Joshua took Makkedah. He put the city and its king to the sword and totally destroyed everyone in it. He left no survivors. And he did to the king of Makkedah as he had done to the king of Jericho.

Southern Cities Conquered

²⁹Then Joshua and all Israel with him moved on from Makkedah to Libnah and attacked it. ³⁰The LORD also gave that city and its king into Israel's hand. The city and everyone in it Joshua put to the sword. He left no survivors there. And he did to its king as he had done to the king of Jericho.

³¹Then Joshua and all Israel with him moved on from Libnah to Lachish; he took up positions against it and attacked it. ³²The LORD handed Lachish over to Israel, and Joshua took it on the second day. The city and everyone in it he put to the sword, just as he had done to Libnah. ³³Meanwhile, Horam king of Gezer had come up to help Lachish, but Joshua defeated him and his army—until no survivors were left.

³⁴Then Joshua and all Israel with him moved on from Lachish to Eglon; they took up positions against it and attacked it. ³⁵They captured it that same day and put it to the sword and totally destroyed everyone in it, just as they had done to Lachish.

³⁶Then Joshua and all Israel with him went up from Eglon to Hebron and attacked it. ³⁷They took the city and put it to the sword, together with its king, its villages and everyone in it. They left no survivors. Just as at Eglon, they totally destroyed it and everyone in it.

³⁸Then Joshua and all Israel with him turned around and attacked Debir. ³⁹They took the city, its king and its villages, and put them to the sword. Everyone in it they totally destroyed. They left no survivors. They did to Debir and its king as they had done to Libnah and its king and to Hebron.

⁴⁰So Joshua subdued the whole region, including the hill country, the Negev, the western foothills and the mountain slopes, together with all their kings. He left no survivors. He totally destroyed all who breathed, just as the LORD, the God of Israel, had commanded. ⁴¹Joshua subdued them from Kadesh Barnea to Gaza and from the whole region of Goshen to Gibeon. ⁴²All these kings and their lands Joshua conquered in one campaign, because the LORD, the God of Israel, fought for Israel.

⁴³Then Joshua returned with all Israel to the camp at Gilgal.

Northern Kings Defeated

11 When Jabin king of Hazor heard of this, he sent word to Jobab king of Madon, to the kings of Shimron and Acshaph, ²and to the northern kings who were in the mountains, in the

Arabah south of Kinnereth, in the western foothills and in Naphoth Dor[a] on the west; [3]to the Canaanites in the east and west; to the Amorites, Hittites, Perizzites and Jebusites in the hill country; and to the Hivites below Hermon in the region of Mizpah. [4]They came out with all their troops and a large number of horses and chariots—a huge army, as numerous as the sand on the seashore. [5]All these kings joined forces and made camp together at the Waters of Merom, to fight against Israel.

[6]The LORD said to Joshua, "Do not be afraid of them, because by this time tomorrow I will hand all of them over to Israel, slain. You are to hamstring their horses and burn their chariots."

[7]So Joshua and his whole army came against them suddenly at the Waters of Merom and attacked them, [8]and the LORD gave them into the hand of Israel. They defeated them and pursued them all the way to Greater Sidon, to Misrephoth Maim, and to the Valley of Mizpah on the east, until no survivors were left. [9]Joshua did to them as the LORD had directed: He hamstrung their horses and burned their chariots.

[10]At that time Joshua turned back and captured Hazor and put its king to the sword. (Hazor had been the head of all these kingdoms.) [11]Everyone in it they put to the sword. They totally destroyed[b] them, not sparing anything that breathed, and he burned up Hazor itself.

[12]Joshua took all these royal cities and their kings and put them to the sword. He totally destroyed them, as Moses the servant of the LORD had commanded. [13]Yet Israel did not burn any of the cities built on their mounds—except Hazor, which Joshua burned. [14]The Israelites carried off for themselves all the plunder and livestock of these cities, but all the people they put to the sword until they completely destroyed them, not sparing anyone that breathed. [15]As the LORD commanded his servant Moses, so Moses commanded Joshua, and Joshua did it; he left nothing undone of all that the LORD commanded Moses.

[16]So Joshua took this entire land: the hill country, all the Negev, the whole region of Goshen, the western foothills, the Arabah and the mountains of Israel with their foothills, [17]from Mount Halak, which rises toward Seir, to Baal Gad in the Valley of Lebanon below Mount Hermon. He captured all their kings and struck them down, putting them to death. [18]Joshua waged war against all these kings for a long time. [19]Except for the Hivites living in Gibeon, not one city made a treaty of peace with the Israelites, who took them all in battle. [20]For it was the LORD himself who hardened their hearts to wage war against Israel, so that he might destroy them totally, exterminating them without mercy, as the LORD had commanded Moses.

[21]At that time Joshua went and destroyed the Anakites from the hill country: from Hebron, Debir and Anab, from all the hill country of Judah, and from all the hill country of Israel. Joshua totally destroyed them and their towns. [22]No Anakites were left in Israelite territory; only in Gaza, Gath and Ashdod did any survive. [23]So Joshua took the entire land, just as the LORD had directed Moses, and he gave it as an inheritance to Israel according to their tribal divisions.

Then the land had rest from war.

---

school I learned that the secret of success is _____." What does your composite essay say about success?

1. How did the northern kings respond when they heard about the Israelite victories in the south (vv. 1–5)? Why might Joshua have been afraid of this army even after his many victories? 2. How does the Lord speak to that fear (v. 6)? Why the instructions about destroying even the horses and chariots (see Ps 33:16–17)? 3. What was the result of Joshua's sudden attack? Why do you think Hazor got special attention (vv. 10,13)? 4. What reason does the author give for the total destruction of these cities (vv. 12–15)? Why is the command to Moses mentioned? 5. Verses 16–20 describe the conquest of the north. What geography lesson do you see here? 6. Why did his campaign take a long time? What was left after it was finished? 7. According to this chapter, why were Joshua and the Israelites successful in their conquest of the promised land, in spite of overwhelming odds against them?

1. At what points can you identify with Joshua: (a) When all his enemies are coming to attack him? (b) When he is winning but the war is lasting a long time? (c) When the land finally had rest from war? 2. Do you always expect success when you are obedient to God? Why or why not?

---

a2 Or *in the heights of Dor*   b11 The Hebrew term refers to the irrevocable giving over of things or persons to the LORD, often by totally destroying them; also in verses 12, 20 and 21.

1. Which grandparent had the most influence on your life? How so? 2. What one accomplishment in your teen years do you take the most pride in? Why? 3. Do you consider yourself more like an "Easterner" or a "Westerner" in your roots and outlook on life? In what way?

1. Verses 1–6 describe the kings defeated by Israel under Moses' leadership. Where were these kings located? Why did Israel end up fighting them (see Nu 21:21–35 and Dt 2:24–37)? What happened to their land? 2. Verses 7–24 list the kings defeated under Joshua's leadership on the west side of the Jordan. Which of these kings do you remember from your study of chapters 1–11? What one battle stands out in your mind? Why? 3. Why do you think so many cities are listed in this chapter? What was the importance of such a list to the people of Israel in later generations?

1. Has God helped you to conquer any of the following in your life: Bad temper? Shyness? Certain phobia? Smoking? Serious illness? Bad marriage? Weight problem? Poor self image? 2. The list could go on. Why not share one of these victories with your group? 3. What one or two people have led the way for your own spiritual growth in the past year?

List of Defeated Kings

12 These are the kings of the land whom the Israelites had defeated and whose territory they took over east of the Jordan, from the Arnon Gorge to Mount Hermon, including all the eastern side of the Arabah:

²Sihon king of the Amorites,
who reigned in Heshbon. He ruled from Aroer on the rim of the Arnon Gorge—from the middle of the gorge—to the Jabbok River, which is the border of the Ammonites. This included half of Gilead. ³He also ruled over the eastern Arabah from the Sea of Kinneretha to the Sea of the Arabah (the Salt Seab), to Beth Jeshimoth, and then southward below the slopes of Pisgah.

⁴And the territory of Og king of Bashan,
one of the last of the Rephaites, who reigned in Ashtaroth and Edrei. ⁵He ruled over Mount Hermon, Salecah, all of Bashan to the border of the people of Geshur and Maacah, and half of Gilead to the border of Sihon king of Heshbon.

⁶Moses, the servant of the LORD, and the Israelites conquered them. And Moses the servant of the LORD gave their land to the Reubenites, the Gadites and the half-tribe of Manasseh to be their possession.

⁷These are the kings of the land that Joshua and the Israelites conquered on the west side of the Jordan, from Baal Gad in the Valley of Lebanon to Mount Halak, which rises toward Seir (their lands Joshua gave as an inheritance to the tribes of Israel according to their tribal divisions— ⁸the hill country, the western foothills, the Arabah, the mountain slopes, the desert and the Negev—the lands of the Hittites, Amorites, Canaanites, Perizzites, Hivites and Jebusites):

⁹the king of Jericho	one
the king of Ai (near Bethel)	one
¹⁰the king of Jerusalem	one
the king of Hebron	one
¹¹the king of Jarmuth	one
the king of Lachish	one
¹²the king of Eglon	one
the king of Gezer	one
¹³the king of Debir	one
the king of Geder	one
¹⁴the king of Hormah	one
the king of Arad	one
¹⁵the king of Libnah	one
the king of Adullam	one
¹⁶the king of Makkedah	one
the king of Bethel	one
¹⁷the king of Tappuah	one
the king of Hepher	one
¹⁸the king of Aphek	one
the king of Lasharon	one
¹⁹the king of Madon	one
the king of Hazor	one
²⁰the king of Shimron Meron	one
the king of Acshaph	one
²¹the king of Taanach	one

a3 That is, Galilee   b3 That is, the Dead Sea

the king of Megiddo	one
22the king of Kedesh	one
the king of Jokneam in Carmel	one
23the king of Dor (in Naphoth Dor[a])	one
the king of Goyim in Gilgal	one
24the king of Tirzah	one

thirty-one kings in all.

Land Still to Be Taken

13 When Joshua was old and well advanced in years, the LORD said to him, "You are very old, and there are still very large areas of land to be taken over.

2"This is the land that remains: all the regions of the Philistines and Geshurites: 3from the Shihor River on the east of Egypt to the territory of Ekron on the north, all of it counted as Canaanite (the territory of the five Philistine rulers in Gaza, Ashdod, Ashkelon, Gath and Ekron—that of the Avvites); 4from the south, all the land of the Canaanites, from Arah of the Sidonians as far as Aphek, the region of the Amorites, 5the area of the Gebalites[b]; and all Lebanon to the east, from Baal Gad below Mount Hermon to Lebo[c] Hamath.

6"As for all the inhabitants of the mountain regions from Lebanon to Misrephoth Maim, that is, all the Sidonians, I myself will drive them out before the Israelites. Be sure to allocate this land to Israel for an inheritance, as I have instructed you, 7and divide it as an inheritance among the nine tribes and half of the tribe of Manasseh."

Division of the Land East of the Jordan

8The other half of Manasseh,[d] the Reubenites and the Gadites had received the inheritance that Moses had given them east of the Jordan, as he, the servant of the LORD, had assigned it to them.

9It extended from Aroer on the rim of the Arnon Gorge, and from the town in the middle of the gorge, and included the whole plateau of Medeba as far as Dibon, 10and all the towns of Sihon king of the Amorites, who ruled in Heshbon, out to the border of the Ammonites. 11It also included Gilead, the territory of the people of Geshur and Maacah, all of Mount Hermon and all Bashan as far as Salecah— 12that is, the whole kingdom of Og in Bashan, who had reigned in Ashtaroth and Edrei and had survived as one of the last of the Rephaites. Moses had defeated them and taken over their land. 13But the Israelites did not drive out the people of Geshur and Maacah, so they continue to live among the Israelites to this day.

14But to the tribe of Levi he gave no inheritance, since the offerings made by fire to the LORD, the God of Israel, are their inheritance, as he promised them.

15This is what Moses had given to the tribe of Reuben, clan by clan:

16The territory from Aroer on the rim of the Arnon Gorge, and from the town in the middle of the gorge, and the whole plateau past Medeba 17to Heshbon and all its towns on the plateau, including Dibon, Bamoth Baal, Beth Baal Meon, 18Jahaz, Kedemoth, Mephaath, 19Kiriathaim, Sibmah, Zereth Sha-

a23 Or in the heights of Dor   b5 That is, the area of Byblos   c5 Or to the entrance to   d8 Hebrew With it (that is, with the other half of Manasseh)

As a child, were you made to finish all the food on your plate? What happened if you didn't? Do you do so now?

1. As Joshua approaches retirement, what does the Lord tell him? How do you think Joshua felt about that? 2. What areas remained to be taken (vv. 2–7)? As far as you know, were they ever conquered by the Israelites?

1. What could you once do, but not anymore, due to "advancing years"? 2. What "unfinished business" is left in your game plan for you to do?

1. What territory do you associate with your grandparents? Is that where they lived the longest? Or where they are buried? Or did you grow up there? 2. What inheritance do you wish you had received from your parents or grandparents?

1. Where generally is the inheritance that half-Manasseh, Reuben and Gad received? How was their inheritance different from the other tribes of Israel? 2. Do you see any potential problems in the inheritance of the two and a half tribes east of the Jordan? What might they be? 3. What is noteworthy about the slaying of Balaam (v. 22)? Why did he deserve that (see Nu 25; 31:8)? 4. Why did the Levites receive no land for an inheritance (vv. 14,33; see Nu 18:20–24)? Would they have felt slighted or doubly blessed by this assignment?

1. What have you received that you feel is a specific inheritance from the Lord? What have you done with it? 2. If you had been a Gadite or Reubenite, what would have been the first thing you would have done in your new land: (a) Build a house to live in? (b) Cook a big feast? (c) Check out the

neighbors? (d) Look for water? (e) Gather for worship and praise? Why?

---

har on the hill in the valley, [20]Beth Peor, the slopes of Pisgah, and Beth Jeshimoth [21]—all the towns on the plateau and the entire realm of Sihon king of the Amorites, who ruled at Heshbon. Moses had defeated him and the Midianite chiefs, Evi, Rekem, Zur, Hur and Reba—princes allied with Sihon—who lived in that country. [22]In addition to those slain in battle, the Israelites had put to the sword Balaam son of Beor, who practiced divination. [23]The boundary of the Reubenites was the bank of the Jordan. These towns and their villages were the inheritance of the Reubenites, clan by clan.

[24]This is what Moses had given to the tribe of Gad, clan by clan:

[25]The territory of Jazer, all the towns of Gilead and half the Ammonite country as far as Aroer, near Rabbah; [26]and from Heshbon to Ramath Mizpah and Betonim, and from Mahanaim to the territory of Debir; [27]and in the valley, Beth Haram, Beth Nimrah, Succoth and Zaphon with the rest of the realm of Sihon king of Heshbon (the east side of the Jordan, the territory up to the end of the Sea of Kinnereth[a]). [28]These towns and their villages were the inheritance of the Gadites, clan by clan.

[29]This is what Moses had given to the half-tribe of Manasseh, that is, to half the family of the descendants of Manasseh, clan by clan:

[30]The territory extending from Mahanaim and including all of Bashan, the entire realm of Og king of Bashan—all the settlements of Jair in Bashan, sixty towns, [31]half of Gilead, and Ashtaroth and Edrei (the royal cities of Og in Bashan). This was for the descendants of Makir son of Manasseh—for half of the sons of Makir, clan by clan.

[32]This is the inheritance Moses had given when he was in the plains of Moab across the Jordan east of Jericho. [33]But to the tribe of Levi, Moses had given no inheritance; the LORD, the God of Israel, is their inheritance, as he promised them.

Division of the Land West of the Jordan

14 Now these are the areas the Israelites received as an inheritance in the land of Canaan, which Eleazar the priest, Joshua son of Nun and the heads of the tribal clans of Israel allotted to them. [2]Their inheritances were assigned by lot to the nine-and-a-half tribes, as the LORD had commanded through Moses. [3]Moses had granted the two-and-a-half tribes their inheritance east of the Jordan but had not granted the Levites an inheritance among the rest, [4]for the sons of Joseph had become two tribes—Manasseh and Ephraim. The Levites received no share of the land but only towns to live in, with pasturelands for their flocks and herds. [5]So the Israelites divided the land, just as the LORD had commanded Moses.

Hebron Given to Caleb

[6]Now the men of Judah approached Joshua at Gilgal, and Caleb son of Jephunneh the Kenizzite said to him, "You know what the LORD said to Moses the man of God at Kadesh Barnea about you and me. [7]I was forty years old when Moses the servant of the LORD sent me from Kadesh Barnea to explore the land. And I brought him back a report according to my convictions, [8]but my brothers who went up with me made the hearts of the people melt with fear. I,

Who made the big decisions in your childhood home? How much input did you have?

1. How did the nine and a half tribes west of the Jordan receive their land? 2. Why treat the two and a half tribes and the Levites differently?

What is your "lot in life"? Did you choose it, or did someone else choose it for you?

Where would you like to spend your retirement? Doing what?

1. Who was Caleb? What was his chief "claim to fame"? 2. "Actions reveal character." If so, what do Caleb's actions say about the kind of man he was in the prime of life (vv. 6–9)? How was he different from the others

[a]27 That is, Galilee

however, followed the LORD my God wholeheartedly. 9So on that day Moses swore to me, 'The land on which your feet have walked will be your inheritance and that of your children forever, because you have followed the LORD my God wholeheartedly.'[a]

10"Now then, just as the LORD promised, he has kept me alive for forty-five years since the time he said this to Moses, while Israel moved about in the desert. So here I am today, eighty-five years old! 11I am still as strong today as the day Moses sent me out; I'm just as vigorous to go out to battle now as I was then. 12Now give me this hill country that the LORD promised me that day. You yourself heard then that the Anakites were there and their cities were large and fortified, but, the LORD helping me, I will drive them out just as he said."

13Then Joshua blessed Caleb son of Jephunneh and gave him Hebron as his inheritance. 14So Hebron has belonged to Caleb son of Jephunneh the Kenizzite ever since, because he followed the LORD, the God of Israel, wholeheartedly. 15(Hebron used to be called Kiriath Arba after Arba, who was the greatest man among the Anakites.)

Then the land had rest from war.

Allotment for Judah

15 The allotment for the tribe of Judah, clan by clan, extended down to the territory of Edom, to the Desert of Zin in the extreme south.

2Their southern boundary started from the bay at the southern end of the Salt Sea,[b] 3crossed south of Scorpion[c] Pass, continued on to Zin and went over to the south of Kadesh Barnea. Then it ran past Hezron up to Addar and curved around to Karka. 4It then passed along to Azmon and joined the Wadi of Egypt, ending at the sea. This is their[d] southern boundary.

5The eastern boundary is the Salt Sea as far as the mouth of the Jordan.

The northern boundary started from the bay of the sea at the mouth of the Jordan, 6went up to Beth Hoglah and continued north of Beth Arabah to the Stone of Bohan son of Reuben. 7The boundary then went up to Debir from the Valley of Achor and turned north to Gilgal, which faces the Pass of Adummim south of the gorge. It continued along to the waters of En Shemesh and came out at En Rogel. 8Then it ran up the Valley of Ben Hinnom along the southern slope of the Jebusite city (that is, Jerusalem). From there it climbed to the top of the hill west of the Hinnom Valley at the northern end of the Valley of Rephaim. 9From the hilltop the boundary headed toward the spring of the waters of Nephtoah, came out at the towns of Mount Ephron and went down toward Baalah (that is, Kiriath Jearim). 10Then it curved westward from Baalah to Mount Seir, ran along the northern slope of Mount Jearim (that is, Kesalon), continued down to Beth Shemesh and crossed to Timnah. 11It went to the northern slope of Ekron, turned toward Shikkeron, passed along to Mount Baalah and reached Jabneel. The boundary ended at the sea.

12The western boundary is the coastline of the Great Sea.[e] These are the boundaries around the people of Judah by their clans.

Moses sent up with him to explore the land? 3. Has Caleb changed much since then (vv. 10–12)? Why or why not? 4. What was the area that Caleb wanted for himself? What does his request show you about his confidence in God? Your own faith in God?

1. Caleb was still going strong at age 85. Do you think you will be? Why? 2. What quality of Caleb's life do you want for yourself and your family? 3. What would it mean practically for you to serve God *wholeheartedly* this year?

1. What kind of fence would you want around your dream house: (a) White picket? (b) Red brick? (c) Split rail? (d) Barbed wire? (e) None? 2. How did your parents first meet? 3. Where did you call "home" when you were 5 years old?

Consult a Bible map for this period to help answer these questions. 1. The first allotment of land west of the Jordan was to Judah. What were the major boundaries of Judah's land? Where was it in relation to the rest of the promised land? 2. What do we learn about Caleb from verses 13–19? What does he do with the portion of land allotted to him? How was he able to get the best out of others? 3. What do you think about Caleb's method for choosing his daughter's husband? 4. How do you think Othniel felt about being the son-in-law of such a hero? What did Othniel later go on to become (see Jdg 3:7–11)? 5. In verses 20–62, what four administrative areas was Judah divided into? Why do you think so much detail is given about Judah's allotment? (Read Ge 49:8–12 for a possible explanation.) 6. What is significant about Judah not being able to dislodge the Jebusites (v. 63; see Jdg 1:8,21, where the Benjamites failed likewise)? Who was finally able to conquer Jerusalem and unite the kingdom at this royal city (see 2Sa 5:6–12)? Why might this knowledge be important for us today?

---

[a]9 Deut. 1:36   [b]2 That is, the Dead Sea; also in verse 5   [c]3 Hebrew *Akrabbim*
[d]4 Hebrew *your*   [e]12 That is, the Mediterranean; also in verse 47

[13]In accordance with the LORD's command to him, Joshua gave to Caleb son of Jephunneh a portion in Judah—Kiriath Arba, that is, Hebron. (Arba was the forefather of Anak.) [14]From Hebron Caleb drove out the three Anakites—Sheshai, Ahiman and Talmai—descendants of Anak. [15]From there he marched against the people living in Debir (formerly called Kiriath Sepher). [16]And Caleb said, "I will give my daughter Acsah in marriage to the man who attacks and captures Kiriath Sepher." [17]Othniel son of Kenaz, Caleb's brother, took it; so Caleb gave his daughter Acsah to him in marriage.

[18]One day when she came to Othniel, she urged him[a] to ask her father for a field. When she got off her donkey, Caleb asked her, "What can I do for you?"

[19]She replied, "Do me a special favor. Since you have given me land in the Negev, give me also springs of water." So Caleb gave her the upper and lower springs.

[20]This is the inheritance of the tribe of Judah, clan by clan:

[21]The southernmost towns of the tribe of Judah in the Negev toward the boundary of Edom were:

Kabzeel, Eder, Jagur, [22]Kinah, Dimonah, Adadah, [23]Kedesh, Hazor, Ithnan, [24]Ziph, Telem, Bealoth, [25]Hazor Hadattah, Kerioth Hezron (that is, Hazor), [26]Amam, Shema, Moladah, [27]Hazar Gaddah, Heshmon, Beth Pelet, [28]Hazar Shual, Beersheba, Biziothiah, [29]Baalah, Iim, Ezem, [30]Eltolad, Kesil, Hormah, [31]Ziklag, Madmannah, Sansannah, [32]Lebaoth, Shilhim, Ain and Rimmon—a total of twenty-nine towns and their villages.

[33]In the western foothills:

Eshtaol, Zorah, Ashnah, [34]Zanoah, En Gannim, Tappuah, Enam, [35]Jarmuth, Adullam, Socoh, Azekah, [36]Shaaraim, Adithaim and Gederah (or Gederothaim)[b]—fourteen towns and their villages.

[37]Zenan, Hadashah, Migdal Gad, [38]Dilean, Mizpah, Joktheel, [39]Lachish, Bozkath, Eglon, [40]Cabbon, Lahmas, Kitlish, [41]Gederoth, Beth Dagon, Naamah and Makkedah—sixteen towns and their villages.

[42]Libnah, Ether, Ashan, [43]Iphtah, Ashnah, Nezib, [44]Keilah, Aczib and Mareshah—nine towns and their villages.

[45]Ekron, with its surrounding settlements and villages; [46]west of Ekron, all that were in the vicinity of Ashdod, together with their villages; [47]Ashdod, its surrounding settlements and villages; and Gaza, its settlements and villages, as far as the Wadi of Egypt and the coastline of the Great Sea.

[48]In the hill country:

Shamir, Jattir, Socoh, [49]Dannah, Kiriath Sannah (that is, Debir), [50]Anab, Eshtemoh, Anim, [51]Goshen, Holon and Giloh—eleven towns and their villages.

[52]Arab, Dumah, Eshan, [53]Janim, Beth Tappuah, Aphekah, [54]Humtah, Kiriath Arba (that is, Hebron) and Zior—nine towns and their villages.

[55]Maon, Carmel, Ziph, Juttah, [56]Jezreel, Jokdeam, Zanoah, [57]Kain, Gibeah and Timnah—ten towns and their villages.

[58]Halhul, Beth Zur, Gedor, [59]Maarath, Beth Anoth and Eltekon—six towns and their villages.

[60]Kiriath Baal (that is, Kiriath Jearim) and Rabbah—two towns and their villages.

a 18 Hebrew and some Septuagint manuscripts; other Septuagint manuscripts (see also note at Judges 1:14) Othniel, he urged her   b 36 Or Gederah and Gederothaim

[61]In the desert:

Beth Arabah, Middin, Secacah, [62]Nibshan, the City of Salt and En Gedi—six towns and their villages.

[63]Judah could not dislodge the Jebusites, who were living in Jerusalem; to this day the Jebusites live there with the people of Judah.

Allotment for Ephraim and Manasseh

16 The allotment for Joseph began at the Jordan of Jericho,[a] east of the waters of Jericho, and went up from there through the desert into the hill country of Bethel. [2]It went on from Bethel (that is, Luz),[b] crossed over to the territory of the Arkites in Ataroth, [3]descended westward to the territory of the Japhletites as far as the region of Lower Beth Horon and on to Gezer, ending at the sea. [4]So Manasseh and Ephraim, the descendants of Joseph, received their inheritance.

[5]This was the territory of Ephraim, clan by clan:

The boundary of their inheritance went from Ataroth Addar in the east to Upper Beth Horon [6]and continued to the sea. From Micmethath on the north it curved eastward to Taanath Shiloh, passing by it to Janoah on the east. [7]Then it went down from Janoah to Ataroth and Naarah, touched Jericho and came out at the Jordan. [8]From Tappuah the border went west to the Kanah Ravine and ended at the sea. This was the inheritance of the tribe of the Ephraimites, clan by clan. [9]It also included all the towns and their villages that were set aside for the Ephraimites within the inheritance of the Manassites.

[10]They did not dislodge the Canaanites living in Gezer; to this day the Canaanites live among the people of Ephraim but are required to do forced labor.

17 This was the allotment for the tribe of Manasseh as Joseph's firstborn, that is, for Makir, Manasseh's firstborn. Makir was the ancestor of the Gileadites, who had received Gilead and Bashan because the Makirites were great soldiers. [2]So this allotment was for the rest of the people of Manasseh—the clans of Abiezer, Helek, Asriel, Shechem, Hepher and Shemida. These are the other male descendants of Manasseh son of Joseph by their clans.

[3]Now Zelophehad son of Hepher, the son of Gilead, the son of Makir, the son of Manasseh, had no sons but only daughters, whose names were Mahlah, Noah, Hoglah, Milcah and Tirzah. [4]They went to Eleazar the priest, Joshua son of Nun, and the leaders and said, "The LORD commanded Moses to give us an inheritance among our brothers." So Joshua gave them an inheritance along with the brothers of their father, according to the LORD's command. [5]Manasseh's share consisted of ten tracts of land besides Gilead and Bashan east of the Jordan, [6]because the daughters of the tribe of Manasseh received an inheritance among the sons. The land of Gilead belonged to the rest of the descendants of Manasseh.

[7]The territory of Manasseh extended from Asher to Micmethath east of Shechem. The boundary ran southward from there to include the people living at En Tappuah. [8](Manasseh had the land of Tappuah, but Tappuah itself, on the boundary of Manasseh, belonged to the Ephraimites.) [9]Then the boundary continued south to the Kanah Ravine. There were towns

1. In what country is your family's "ancestral home"? Have you ever visited there? 2. How do you react when you don't get your fair share of something: Suffer in silence? Pout? Have a fit? Demand your rights? Other? 3. What teacher or coach really challenged you? How so?

Consult a Bible map for this period to help answer these questions. 1. Where in the promised land was the allotment assigned to the descendants of Joseph (the tribes of Ephraim and Manasseh): The north? The center? The south? How would you compare the size of Joseph's area to Judah's? 2. How was their allotment a fulfillment of both God's promise to Jacob and Jacob's blessing of them (see Ge 28:10–19; 48:19–20)? 3. What sour note was recorded in Ephraim's and Manasseh's inheritance? What would you have wanted to do about either situation if you were their tribal leader? 4. What was so unusual about the request made by the daughters of Zelophehad (17:3–6; see Nu 27:1–11; 36)? Why did Joshua grant their request? 5. Why, in the end, were the people of Joseph unhappy with their share of the land (17:14–16)? What was Joshua's bottom line solution? Why wouldn't they buy it? 6. What problems, both external and internal, will the people of Joseph have to overcome if they are to possess all the land Joshua has given them? With which of those problems can you identify?

1. How do you feel when you see a promise of God coming true in your life? Describe an instance where this has happened. 2. What do Zelophehad's daughters encourage you to do: (a) Be assertive? (b) Know my rights? (c) Go straight to the ones in charge? (d) Join with others if I want something? 3. Is there some place where you need to stand up for your rights? How will you do this in a helpful way? 4. Are you satisfied with the size of your Bible study group or church fellowship? Or is it: (a) Not big enough? (b) Not friendly

---

a 1 Jordan of Jericho was possibly an ancient name for the Jordan River.
b 2 Septuagint; Hebrew Bethel to Luz

enough? (c) Not enough outreach into the community? (d) Not enough resources or iron chariots? (e) Not enough _____? **5.** If you are dissatisfied or deficient in any way, what is God calling you to do about it?

What do you do when stuck behind a slow driver: (a) Try to pass even if it's dangerous? (b) Tailgate? (c) Lay on the horn? (d) Relax and enjoy the scenery?

1. Why was Joshua impatient with seven of the tribes when they all gathered at Shiloh? What action did he take to deal with the problem? **2.** What instructions did Joshua give to the surveyors he sent out? Why do you think these surveyors were appointed from each tribe? Would you have volunteered to be one of them? **3.** What was the actual method of dividing up the land? Does this way seem fair? Godly? Pot luck?

What in your life have you begun but never finished? What will it take to get you going?

belonging to Ephraim lying among the towns of Manasseh, but the boundary of Manasseh was the northern side of the ravine and ended at the sea. [10]On the south the land belonged to Ephraim, on the north to Manasseh. The territory of Manasseh reached the sea and bordered Asher on the north and Issachar on the east.

[11]Within Issachar and Asher, Manasseh also had Beth Shan, Ibleam and the people of Dor, Endor, Taanach and Megiddo, together with their surrounding settlements (the third in the list is Naphoth[a]).

[12]Yet the Manassites were not able to occupy these towns, for the Canaanites were determined to live in that region. [13]However, when the Israelites grew stronger, they subjected the Canaanites to forced labor but did not drive them out completely.

[14]The people of Joseph said to Joshua, "Why have you given us only one allotment and one portion for an inheritance? We are a numerous people and the LORD has blessed us abundantly."

[15]"If you are so numerous," Joshua answered, "and if the hill country of Ephraim is too small for you, go up into the forest and clear land for yourselves there in the land of the Perizzites and Rephaites."

[16]The people of Joseph replied, "The hill country is not enough for us, and all the Canaanites who live in the plain have iron chariots, both those in Beth Shan and its settlements and those in the Valley of Jezreel."

[17]But Joshua said to the house of Joseph—to Ephraim and Manasseh—"You are numerous and very powerful. You will have not only one allotment [18]but the forested hill country as well. Clear it, and its farthest limits will be yours; though the Canaanites have iron chariots and though they are strong, you can drive them out."

Division of the Rest of the Land

18 The whole assembly of the Israelites gathered at Shiloh and set up the Tent of Meeting there. The country was brought under their control, [2]but there were still seven Israelite tribes who had not yet received their inheritance.

[3]So Joshua said to the Israelites: "How long will you wait before you begin to take possession of the land that the LORD, the God of your fathers, has given you? [4]Appoint three men from each tribe. I will send them out to make a survey of the land and to write a description of it, according to the inheritance of each. Then they will return to me. [5]You are to divide the land into seven parts. Judah is to remain in its territory on the south and the house of Joseph in its territory on the north. [6]After you have written descriptions of the seven parts of the land, bring them here to me and I will cast lots for you in the presence of the LORD our God. [7]The Levites, however, do not get a portion among you, because the priestly service of the LORD is their inheritance. And Gad, Reuben and the half-tribe of Manasseh have already received their inheritance on the east side of the Jordan. Moses the servant of the LORD gave it to them."

[8]As the men started on their way to map out the land, Joshua instructed them, "Go and make a survey of the land and write a description of it. Then return to me, and I will cast lots for you here at Shiloh in the presence of the LORD." [9]So the men left and went through the land. They wrote its description on a scroll, town by town, in seven parts, and returned to Joshua in the camp at

_a 11_ That is, Naphoth Dor

Shiloh. [10]Joshua then cast lots for them in Shiloh in the presence of the LORD, and there he distributed the land to the Israelites according to their tribal divisions.

Allotment for Benjamin

[11]The lot came up for the tribe of Benjamin, clan by clan. Their allotted territory lay between the tribes of Judah and Joseph:

[12]On the north side their boundary began at the Jordan, passed the northern slope of Jericho and headed west into the hill country, coming out at the desert of Beth Aven. [13]From there it crossed to the south slope of Luz (that is, Bethel) and went down to Ataroth Addar on the hill south of Lower Beth Horon.

[14]From the hill facing Beth Horon on the south the boundary turned south along the western side and came out at Kiriath Baal (that is, Kiriath Jearim), a town of the people of Judah. This was the western side.

[15]The southern side began at the outskirts of Kiriath Jearim on the west, and the boundary came out at the spring of the waters of Nephtoah. [16]The boundary went down to the foot of the hill facing the Valley of Ben Hinnom, north of the Valley of Rephaim. It continued down the Hinnom Valley along the southern slope of the Jebusite city and so to En Rogel. [17]It then curved north, went to En Shemesh, continued to Geliloth, which faces the Pass of Adummim, and ran down to the Stone of Bohan son of Reuben. [18]It continued to the northern slope of Beth Arabah[a] and on down into the Arabah. [19]It then went to the northern slope of Beth Hoglah and came out at the northern bay of the Salt Sea,[b] at the mouth of the Jordan in the south. This was the southern boundary.

[20]The Jordan formed the boundary on the eastern side.

These were the boundaries that marked out the inheritance of the clans of Benjamin on all sides.

[21]The tribe of Benjamin, clan by clan, had the following cities:

Jericho, Beth Hoglah, Emek Keziz, [22]Beth Arabah, Zemaraim, Bethel, [23]Avvim, Parah, Ophrah, [24]Kephar Ammoni, Ophni and Geba—twelve towns and their villages.

[25]Gibeon, Ramah, Beeroth, [26]Mizpah, Kephirah, Mozah, [27]Rekem, Irpeel, Taralah, [28]Zelah, Haeleph, the Jebusite city (that is, Jerusalem), Gibeah and Kiriath—fourteen towns and their villages.

This was the inheritance of Benjamin for its clans.

Allotment for Simeon

19 The second lot came out for the tribe of Simeon, clan by clan. Their inheritance lay within the territory of Judah. [2]It included:

Beersheba (or Sheba),[c] Moladah, [3]Hazar Shual, Balah, Ezem, [4]Eltolad, Bethul, Hormah, [5]Ziklag, Beth Marcaboth, Hazar Susah, [6]Beth Lebaoth and Sharuhen—thirteen towns and their villages;

[7]Ain, Rimmon, Ether and Ashan—four towns and their villages— [8]and all the villages around these towns as far as Baalath Beer (Ramah in the Negev).

This was the inheritance of the tribe of the Simeonites, clan by clan. [9]The inheritance of the Simeonites was taken from the share

---

Which was your best and worst subject in school: (a) History? (b) Geography? (c) Arithmetic? (d) Gym? (e) Lunch?

1. Benjamin was the first to receive its allotment of land under Joshua's lottery system. Why was its territory important? What towns in its territory played an important role in Israel's history? 2. From the description given, would you say Benjamin's territory was larger or smaller than the other tribes around it? Now consult a map to see for yourself. 3. Who were some of the famous Biblical people that came from Benjamin? (See 1Sa 9:1; Est 2:5 and Ro 11:1 for three examples.)

Is "bigger" better, so far as you are concerned? As far as God is concerned? Give a few examples.

What is your birth order among your siblings? Were there any benefits or drawbacks to this position?

1. Where was Simeon's inheritance in relationship to the other tribes? How was this inheritance a fulfillment of Jacob's blessing (see Ge 49:5–7)? 2. Is there anything in the description of the other tribal allotments that strikes you as interesting? What are you curious about, that the text omits? 3. Which of these other allotments do you see as a fulfillment of Jacob's blessing (see Ge 49)? 4. What did the tribes have to do

---

[a]18 Septuagint; Hebrew *slope facing the Arabah*   [b]19 That is, the Dead Sea
[c]2 Or *Beersheba, Sheba*; 1 Chron. 4:28 does not have *Sheba.*

(v. 47) to fully realize the blessing that was theirs by survey work, chance allotment and divine prophecy? **5.** What inheritance did Joshua receive as a reward for his leadership? What is significant about Joshua getting what he asked for?

1. What principles for decision-making do you see between the lines of the chapter that uses chance allotment, survey work, divine prophecy, circumstances and personal desires? **2.** Which of these factors do you weigh more than others in the decisions facing you? **3.** Where are you experiencing difficulty taking possession of your rightful inheritance from Christ? What is holding you back from claiming the victory that is yours in Christ?

of Judah, because Judah's portion was more than they needed. So the Simeonites received their inheritance within the territory of Judah.

Allotment for Zebulun

[10]The third lot came up for Zebulun, clan by clan:

The boundary of their inheritance went as far as Sarid. [11]Going west it ran to Maralah, touched Dabbesheth, and extended to the ravine near Jokneam. [12]It turned east from Sarid toward the sunrise to the territory of Kisloth Tabor and went on to Daberath and up to Japhia. [13]Then it continued eastward to Gath Hepher and Eth Kazin; it came out at Rimmon and turned toward Neah. [14]There the boundary went around on the north to Hannathon and ended at the Valley of Iphtah El. [15]Included were Kattath, Nahalal, Shimron, Idalah and Bethlehem. There were twelve towns and their villages. [16]These towns and their villages were the inheritance of Zebulun, clan by clan.

Allotment for Issachar

[17]The fourth lot came out for Issachar, clan by clan. [18]Their territory included:

Jezreel, Kesulloth, Shunem, [19]Hapharaim, Shion, Anaharath, [20]Rabbith, Kishion, Ebez, [21]Remeth, En Gannim, En Haddah and Beth Pazzez. [22]The boundary touched Tabor, Shahazumah and Beth Shemesh, and ended at the Jordan. There were sixteen towns and their villages.

[23]These towns and their villages were the inheritance of the tribe of Issachar, clan by clan.

Allotment for Asher

[24]The fifth lot came out for the tribe of Asher, clan by clan. [25]Their territory included:

Helkath, Hali, Beten, Acshaph, [26]Allammelech, Amad and Mishal. On the west the boundary touched Carmel and Shihor Libnath. [27]It then turned east toward Beth Dagon, touched Zebulun and the Valley of Iphtah El, and went north to Beth Emek and Neiel, passing Cabul on the left. [28]It went to Abdon,[a] Rehob, Hammon and Kanah, as far as Greater Sidon. [29]The boundary then turned back toward Ramah and went to the fortified city of Tyre, turned toward Hosah and came out at the sea in the region of Aczib, [30]Ummah, Aphek and Rehob. There were twenty-two towns and their villages.

[31]These towns and their villages were the inheritance of the tribe of Asher, clan by clan.

Allotment for Naphtali

[32]The sixth lot came out for Naphtali, clan by clan:

[33]Their boundary went from Heleph and the large tree in Zaanannim, passing Adami Nekeb and Jabneel to Lakkum and ending at the Jordan. [34]The boundary ran west through Aznoth Tabor and came out at Hukkok. It touched Zebulun on the south, Asher on the west and the Jordan[b] on the east. [35]The fortified cities were Ziddim, Zer, Hammath, Rakkath, Kinnereth, [36]Adamah, Ramah, Hazor, [37]Kedesh, Edrei, En Hazor, [38]Iron, Migdal El, Horem, Beth Anath and Beth Shemesh. There were nineteen towns and their villages.

---

[a]28 Some Hebrew manuscripts (see also Joshua 21:30); most Hebrew manuscripts *Ebron*
[b]34 Septuagint; Hebrew *west, and Judah, the Jordan,*

³⁹These towns and their villages were the inheritance of the tribe of Naphtali, clan by clan.

Allotment for Dan

⁴⁰The seventh lot came out for the tribe of Dan, clan by clan. ⁴¹The territory of their inheritance included:

Zorah, Eshtaol, Ir Shemesh, ⁴²Shaalabbin, Aijalon, Ithlah, ⁴³Elon, Timnah, Ekron, ⁴⁴Eltekeh, Gibbethon, Baalath, ⁴⁵Jehud, Bene Berak, Gath Rimmon, ⁴⁶Me Jarkon and Rakkon, with the area facing Joppa.

⁴⁷(But the Danites had difficulty taking possession of their territory, so they went up and attacked Leshem, took it, put it to the sword and occupied it. They settled in Leshem and named it Dan after their forefather.)

⁴⁸These towns and their villages were the inheritance of the tribe of Dan, clan by clan.

Allotment for Joshua

⁴⁹When they had finished dividing the land into its allotted portions, the Israelites gave Joshua son of Nun an inheritance among them, ⁵⁰as the LORD had commanded. They gave him the town he asked for—Timnath Serah[a] in the hill country of Ephraim. And he built up the town and settled there.

⁵¹These are the territories that Eleazar the priest, Joshua son of Nun and the heads of the tribal clans of Israel assigned by lot at Shiloh in the presence of the LORD at the entrance to the Tent of Meeting. And so they finished dividing the land.

Cities of Refuge

20 Then the LORD said to Joshua: ²"Tell the Israelites to designate the cities of refuge, as I instructed you through Moses, ³so that anyone who kills a person accidentally and unintentionally may flee there and find protection from the avenger of blood.

⁴"When he flees to one of these cities, he is to stand in the entrance of the city gate and state his case before the elders of that city. Then they are to admit him into their city and give him a place to live with them. ⁵If the avenger of blood pursues him, they must not surrender the one accused, because he killed his neighbor unintentionally and without malice aforethought. ⁶He is to stay in that city until he has stood trial before the assembly and until the death of the high priest who is serving at that time. Then he may go back to his own home in the town from which he fled."

⁷So they set apart Kedesh in Galilee in the hill country of Naphtali, Shechem in the hill country of Ephraim, and Kiriath Arba (that is, Hebron) in the hill country of Judah. ⁸On the east side of the Jordan of Jericho[b] they designated Bezer in the desert on the plateau in the tribe of Reuben, Ramoth in Gilead in the tribe of Gad, and Golan in Bashan in the tribe of Manasseh. ⁹Any of the Israelites or any alien living among them who killed someone accidentally could flee to these designated cities and not be killed by the avenger of blood prior to standing trial before the assembly.

Towns for the Levites

21 Now the family heads of the Levites approached Eleazar the priest, Joshua son of Nun, and the heads of the other tribal families of Israel ²at Shiloh in Canaan and said to them, "The LORD commanded through Moses that you give us towns to live in, with

1. Do you feel safe on the streets of your city? Why or why not? **2.** What safety issues concern you most about growing up or raising kids where you live now?

1. What was a city of refuge? Why were they set up (see Ex. 21:13 and Nu 35:6–15)? **2.** How did a person find safety in a city of refuge? **3.** What modern principles of justice do you see in this? **4.** Where were the cities of refuge located? Is their placement significant? Could someone "fall through the cracks"? How so?

1. Where do you go or to whom do you turn when you feel in danger? **2.** In what ways could a church today be like a city of refuge?

1. What once-promised, long-awaited birthday gift or Christmas gift did you receive as a child? **2.** Which of the following is the hardest for you to share with others and why: (a) Your car? (b) Your food? (c) Your free time? (d) Your feelings? (e) Your dreams?

a50 Also known as *Timnath Heres* (see Judges 2:9) b8 *Jordan of Jericho* was possibly an ancient name for the Jordan River.

1. Why did the family heads of the Levites approach Eleazar and Joshua at Shiloh? What basis did they have for their claim (see Nu 35:1–8)? 2. Who were the Levites? How were they divided up? What was unique about the Kohathites (see Nu 3 for background information)? 3. Do you think the other tribes had any objections to cities from their territory being given to the Levites? Why or why not? What about Caleb and the city of Hebron in verse 12? How would you have reacted? 4. How many cities of refuge listed in chapter 20 were given to the Levites? Why do you think this was the case? 5. In verses 43–45, what did the Lord give to Israel? What aspects of God's nature shine through these gifts to Israel?

1. What part of your life is God calling you to share with someone else right now? How about your group? 2. Write down some of the things the Lord has given to you this past year. Why not thank God for these good gifts? 3. Can you honestly say from your experience, "Not one of the Lord's promises to me has failed"? If not, would you feel comfortable sharing that disappointment with the group? Likely you are not alone. Together you can discern the Lord's goodness in spite of apparent failure.

pasturelands for our livestock." ³So, as the LORD had commanded, the Israelites gave the Levites the following towns and pasturelands out of their own inheritance:

⁴The first lot came out for the Kohathites, clan by clan. The Levites who were descendants of Aaron the priest were allotted thirteen towns from the tribes of Judah, Simeon and Benjamin. ⁵The rest of Kohath's descendants were allotted ten towns from the clans of the tribes of Ephraim, Dan and half of Manasseh.

⁶The descendants of Gershon were allotted thirteen towns from the clans of the tribes of Issachar, Asher, Naphtali and the half-tribe of Manasseh in Bashan.

⁷The descendants of Merari, clan by clan, received twelve towns from the tribes of Reuben, Gad and Zebulun.

⁸So the Israelites allotted to the Levites these towns and their pasturelands, as the LORD had commanded through Moses.

⁹From the tribes of Judah and Simeon they allotted the following towns by name ¹⁰(these towns were assigned to the descendants of Aaron who were from the Kohathite clans of the Levites, because the first lot fell to them):

¹¹They gave them Kiriath Arba (that is, Hebron), with its surrounding pastureland, in the hill country of Judah. (Arba was the forefather of Anak.) ¹²But the fields and villages around the city they had given to Caleb son of Jephunneh as his possession.

¹³So to the descendants of Aaron the priest they gave Hebron (a city of refuge for one accused of murder), Libnah, ¹⁴Jattir, Eshtemoa, ¹⁵Holon, Debir, ¹⁶Ain, Juttah and Beth Shemesh, together with their pasturelands—nine towns from these two tribes.

¹⁷And from the tribe of Benjamin they gave them Gibeon, Geba, ¹⁸Anathoth and Almon, together with their pasturelands—four towns.

¹⁹All the towns for the priests, the descendants of Aaron, were thirteen, together with their pasturelands.

²⁰The rest of the Kohathite clans of the Levites were allotted towns from the tribe of Ephraim:

²¹In the hill country of Ephraim they were given Shechem (a city of refuge for one accused of murder) and Gezer, ²²Kibzaim and Beth Horon, together with their pasturelands—four towns.

²³Also from the tribe of Dan they received Eltekeh, Gibbethon, ²⁴Aijalon and Gath Rimmon, together with their pasturelands—four towns.

²⁵From half the tribe of Manasseh they received Taanach and Gath Rimmon, together with their pasturelands—two towns.

²⁶All these ten towns and their pasturelands were given to the rest of the Kohathite clans.

²⁷The Levite clans of the Gershonites were given:
from the half-tribe of Manasseh,
Golan in Bashan (a city of refuge for one accused of murder) and Be Eshtarah, together with their pasturelands—two towns;
²⁸from the tribe of Issachar,
Kishion, Daberath, ²⁹Jarmuth and En Gannim, together with their pasturelands—four towns;
³⁰from the tribe of Asher,

Mishal, Abdon, ³¹Helkath and Rehob, together with their pasturelands—four towns;
³²from the tribe of Naphtali,
Kedesh in Galilee (a city of refuge for one accused of murder), Hammoth Dor and Kartan, together with their pasturelands—three towns.
³³All the towns of the Gershonite clans were thirteen, together with their pasturelands.

³⁴The Merarite clans (the rest of the Levites) were given:
from the tribe of Zebulun,
Jokneam, Kartah, ³⁵Dimnah and Nahalal, together with their pasturelands—four towns;
³⁶from the tribe of Reuben,
Bezer, Jahaz, ³⁷Kedemoth and Mephaath, together with their pasturelands—four towns;
³⁸from the tribe of Gad,
Ramoth in Gilead (a city of refuge for one accused of murder), Mahanaim, ³⁹Heshbon and Jazer, together with their pasturelands—four towns in all.
⁴⁰All the towns allotted to the Merarite clans, who were the rest of the Levites, were twelve.
⁴¹The towns of the Levites in the territory held by the Israelites were forty-eight in all, together with their pasturelands. ⁴²Each of these towns had pasturelands surrounding it; this was true for all these towns.

⁴³So the LORD gave Israel all the land he had sworn to give their forefathers, and they took possession of it and settled there. ⁴⁴The LORD gave them rest on every side, just as he had sworn to their forefathers. Not one of their enemies withstood them; the LORD handed all their enemies over to them. ⁴⁵Not one of all the LORD's good promises to the house of Israel failed; every one was fulfilled.

Eastern Tribes Return Home

22 Then Joshua summoned the Reubenites, the Gadites and the half-tribe of Manasseh ²and said to them, "You have done all that Moses the servant of the LORD commanded, and you have obeyed me in everything I commanded. ³For a long time now—to this very day—you have not deserted your brothers but have carried out the mission the LORD your God gave you. ⁴Now that the LORD your God has given your brothers rest as he promised, return to your homes in the land that Moses the servant of the LORD gave you on the other side of the Jordan. ⁵But be very careful to keep the commandment and the law that Moses the servant of the LORD gave you: to love the LORD your God, to walk in all his ways, to obey his commands, to hold fast to him and to serve him with all your heart and all your soul."

⁶Then Joshua blessed them and sent them away, and they went to their homes. ⁷(To the half-tribe of Manasseh Moses had given land in Bashan, and to the other half of the tribe Joshua gave land on the west side of the Jordan with their brothers.) When Joshua sent them home, he blessed them, ⁸saying, "Return to your homes with your great wealth—with large herds of livestock, with silver, gold, bronze and iron, and a great quantity of clothing—and divide with your brothers the plunder from your enemies."

⁹So the Reubenites, the Gadites and the half-tribe of Manasseh left the Israelites at Shiloh in Canaan to return to Gilead, their own land, which they had acquired in accordance with the command of the LORD through Moses.

1. What nice thing said about you in recent weeks still rings in your ears? Did you try discounting or disbelieving the statement? Or did you want it repeated? Within others' hearing?) 2. Who was your best friend as a teenager? Do you still stay in touch? 3. How do you typically respond when angered by a friend? Do you: (a) Blast away? (b) Freeze out? (c) Do a slow burn? (d) Pray about it?

1. What did Joshua say to the Reubenites, Gadites and half-tribe of Manasseh that would have made their ears burn? What challenge did he give them? Why are both affirmation and exhortation important for God's people? 2. In what way were the two and one half tribes different from the rest of Israel? 3. What seemingly innocent action did the Reubenites, Gadites, and half-tribe of Manasseh do on their way home (v. 10)? How did the rest of the tribes react to this action? Do you think they overreacted? 4. What was the "sin of Peor" (v. 17; see Nu 25)? In light of

that incident, why do you think Phinehas was chosen to lead the delegation in verses 13–14? Does he seem like a wise choice to you? Why or why not? **5.** What was it about this new altar that got the rest of Israel so upset? What assumptions did they make about this altar? What terrible results did they fear? **6.** How was this current incident like the "sin of Achan" (v. 20; see Jos 7)? How was it different? **7.** When finally given a chance to explain themselves (vv. 21–29), what reasons did the Reubenites, Gadites and half-tribe of Manasseh give for building this altar? How was it to be a positive, not a negative, influence? **8.** How did Phinehas, the leaders of the community, and the rest of Israel each respond to this explanation? What might have happened to Israel had they not taken the time to find out the facts? **9.** Why do you think this story was important for later generations of Israelites? For Christians today?

1. Is there someone near and dear from whom you will soon be parted? What kind of things do you need to say to that person by way of encouragement or challenge? **2.** What lesson do you need to learn from this story: (a) Don't build new altars until you check them out with others? (b) Find out the facts before you judge anyone? (c) Believe the best not the worst about people? (d) Speak directly to people you have a disagreement with? **3.** If someone were to say to you, "You have no share in the Lord," how would you react? What principles of conflict resolution, gleaned from this story, would you use to defend yourself? **4.** What in your group life is like a "Witness between us that the Lord is God"?

[10]When they came to Geliloth near the Jordan in the land of Canaan, the Reubenites, the Gadites and the half-tribe of Manasseh built an imposing altar there by the Jordan. [11]And when the Israelites heard that they had built the altar on the border of Canaan at Geliloth near the Jordan on the Israelite side, [12]the whole assembly of Israel gathered at Shiloh to go to war against them.

[13]So the Israelites sent Phinehas son of Eleazar, the priest, to the land of Gilead—to Reuben, Gad and the half-tribe of Manasseh. [14]With him they sent ten of the chief men, one for each of the tribes of Israel, each the head of a family division among the Israelite clans.

[15]When they went to Gilead—to Reuben, Gad and the half-tribe of Manasseh—they said to them: [16]"The whole assembly of the LORD says: 'How could you break faith with the God of Israel like this? How could you turn away from the LORD and build yourselves an altar in rebellion against him now? [17]Was not the sin of Peor enough for us? Up to this very day we have not cleansed ourselves from that sin, even though a plague fell on the community of the LORD! [18]And are you now turning away from the LORD?

" 'If you rebel against the LORD today, tomorrow he will be angry with the whole community of Israel. [19]If the land you possess is defiled, come over to the LORD's land, where the LORD's tabernacle stands, and share the land with us. But do not rebel against the LORD or against us by building an altar for yourselves, other than the altar of the LORD our God. [20]When Achan son of Zerah acted unfaithfully regarding the devoted things,[a] did not wrath come upon the whole community of Israel? He was not the only one who died for his sin.' "

[21]Then Reuben, Gad and the half-tribe of Manasseh replied to the heads of the clans of Israel: [22]"The Mighty One, God, the LORD! The Mighty One, God, the LORD! He knows! And let Israel know! If this has been in rebellion or disobedience to the LORD, do not spare us this day. [23]If we have built our own altar to turn away from the LORD and to offer burnt offerings and grain offerings, or to sacrifice fellowship offerings[b] on it, may the LORD himself call us to account.

[24]"No! We did it for fear that some day your descendants might say to ours, 'What do you have to do with the LORD, the God of Israel? [25]The LORD has made the Jordan a boundary between us and you—you Reubenites and Gadites! You have no share in the LORD.' So your descendants might cause ours to stop fearing the LORD.

[26]"That is why we said, 'Let us get ready and build an altar—but not for burnt offerings or sacrifices.' [27]On the contrary, it is to be a witness between us and you and the generations that follow, that we will worship the LORD at his sanctuary with our burnt offerings, sacrifices and fellowship offerings. Then in the future your descendants will not be able to say to ours, 'You have no share in the LORD.'

[28]"And we said, 'If they ever say this to us, or to our descendants, we will answer: Look at the replica of the LORD's altar, which our fathers built, not for burnt offerings and sacrifices, but as a witness between us and you.'

[29]"Far be it from us to rebel against the LORD and turn away from him today by building an altar for burnt offerings, grain offerings and sacrifices, other than the altar of the LORD our God that stands before his tabernacle."

[a]20 The Hebrew term refers to the irrevocable giving over of things or persons to the LORD, often by totally destroying them.   [b]23 Traditionally *peace offerings*; also in verse 27

³⁰When Phinehas the priest and the leaders of the community—the heads of the clans of the Israelites—heard what Reuben, Gad and Manasseh had to say, they were pleased. ³¹And Phinehas son of Eleazar, the priest, said to Reuben, Gad and Manasseh, "Today we know that the LORD is with us, because you have not acted unfaithfully toward the LORD in this matter. Now you have rescued the Israelites from the LORD's hand."

³²Then Phinehas son of Eleazar, the priest, and the leaders returned to Canaan from their meeting with the Reubenites and Gadites in Gilead and reported to the Israelites. ³³They were glad to hear the report and praised God. And they talked no more about going to war against them to devastate the country where the Reubenites and the Gadites lived.

³⁴And the Reubenites and the Gadites gave the altar this name: A Witness Between Us that the LORD is God.

Joshua's Farewell to the Leaders

23 After a long time had passed and the LORD had given Israel rest from all their enemies around them, Joshua, by then old and well advanced in years, ²summoned all Israel—their elders, leaders, judges and officials—and said to them: "I am old and well advanced in years. ³You yourselves have seen everything the LORD your God has done to all these nations for your sake; it was the LORD your God who fought for you. ⁴Remember how I have allotted as an inheritance for your tribes all the land of the nations that remain—the nations I conquered—between the Jordan and the Great Seaᵃ in the west. ⁵The LORD your God himself will drive them out of your way. He will push them out before you, and you

a4 That is, the Mediterranean

1. When you were a child, who was the oldest person you knew? What do you recall about him or her? **2.** As a teen, which of the following were you most likely to turn to for advice and why: (a) Parent or grandparent? (b) Teacher? (c) Minister, priest, or rabbi? (d) Close friend your own age? (e) A good book? (f) The Good Book?

1. Whom does Joshua specifically summon to him when he is old? What does he remind them about in verses 3–5? Why is this reminder important? **2.**

 Joshua 23:1–16   **JOSHUA'S FAREWELL ADDRESS**

In his 110 years, Joshua experienced: slavery in Egypt; the plagues; the Exodus; serving as Moses' aide and one of the 12 spies during the 40 years in the wilderness; becoming Moses' successor and leading the Israelites through the miraculous crossing of the Jordan River; and commanding the army of Israel in their conquest of the promised land. As his life draws to an end, Joshua gives a farewell address to Israel—her leaders in particular.

1. How do you think Joshua felt as he looked back on his life?
   a. tired   e. grateful
   b. proud   f. at peace
   c. disillusioned   g. no regrets
   d. filled with praise h. some regrets

2. Which of the answers to the previous question are true of you? Or would you add another?

3. If you were Joshua, what about the past would you celebrate the most?

a. the rest (peace) God provided
b. the many years of his life
c. the richness of those years
d. the miracles he had seen
e. his sense of accomplishment
f. the respect he received
g. God's faithfulness

4. Looking back over your life, what has been the result when you obeyed God? When you disobeyed God?

5. How did Joshua feel about his people's future?
   a. hopeful
   b. worried
   c. optimistic—because of his faith
   d. pessimistic—because of their past failures

6. Which of the answers to the previous question describe how you feel about "the next generation"? Or would you add another?

7. What did Joshua most want to com-

municate to the next generation?
a. Don't forget what God has done for you.
b. Don't forget what God and I have done for you.
c. Don't get proud.
d. Keep your courage.
e. Keep your faith.
f. Follow God's Word.
g. Be careful whose company you keep.
h. Don't throw away what you have.
i. Who—or what—will you worship?

8. 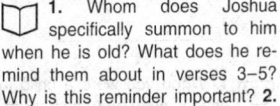 Now that you are growing older, what would you like to say to the next generation, in general? To your own loved ones, in particular? How can you try to communicate that message?

9. What are the best memories of your life? Close your time together by thanking God for those memories and for his faithfulness.

What advice does Joshua give in verses 6–8? Practically speaking, what does it mean for the leaders "to obey all that is written in the Book of the Law of Moses"? **3.** In verses 9–11, what has been the wonderful result of loving and obeying the Lord? **4.** In verses 12–13, how will Israel show it has turned away from the Lord? What are the terrible results of such disobedience? **5.** How would Joshua's words in verses 14–16 have helped the leaders understand God better? Do they help or hinder you? Why?

1. What one piece of advice do you typically give (or receive) on farewell occasions, such as graduation days, going-away parties and the like? **2.** Looking back over your life, what has been the result when you obeyed God? When you disobeyed?

1. When you were a child in school were you ever summoned to the principal's office? For what? **2.** If you could live in any other period of history, when would you choose? Why then? **3.** When presented with a challenge in your life, are you more prone to look before you leap or leap before you look? Give an example.

1. Who were the people gathered at Shechem? Why do you think Joshua gathered them there (see Ge 12:6–7; 3:18–20)? **2.** As Joshua recounts the history of Israel (vv. 2–13), how was God involved in the life of Abraham? In the escape from Egypt? In the battles against people east of the Jordan? In the conquest of the promised land? Where would Israel be without God's help? **3.** Based on all the Lord has done, what does Joshua ask the people to do (vv. 14–15)? What does he plan to do himself? **4.** How do the people respond to Joshua's challenge? Why does Joshua sound dubious about this response (vv. 19–24)? What would you have said and done in his sandals? **5.** How can the people show they are serious about serving the Lord? How would you

will take possession of their land, as the Lord your God promised you.

⁶"Be very strong; be careful to obey all that is written in the Book of the Law of Moses, without turning aside to the right or to the left. ⁷Do not associate with these nations that remain among you; do not invoke the names of their gods or swear by them. You must not serve them or bow down to them. ⁸But you are to hold fast to the Lord your God, as you have until now.

⁹"The Lord has driven out before you great and powerful nations; to this day no one has been able to withstand you. ¹⁰One of you routs a thousand, because the Lord your God fights for you, just as he promised. ¹¹So be very careful to love the Lord your God.

¹²"But if you turn away and ally yourselves with the survivors of these nations that remain among you and if you intermarry with them and associate with them, ¹³then you may be sure that the Lord your God will no longer drive out these nations before you. Instead, they will become snares and traps for you, whips on your backs and thorns in your eyes, until you perish from this good land, which the Lord your God has given you.

¹⁴"Now I am about to go the way of all the earth. You know with all your heart and soul that not one of all the good promises the Lord your God gave you has failed. Every promise has been fulfilled; not one has failed. ¹⁵But just as every good promise of the Lord your God has come true, so the Lord will bring on you all the evil he has threatened, until he has destroyed you from this good land he has given you. ¹⁶If you violate the covenant of the Lord your God, which he commanded you, and go and serve other gods and bow down to them, the Lord's anger will burn against you, and you will quickly perish from the good land he has given you."

The Covenant Renewed at Shechem

24 Then Joshua assembled all the tribes of Israel at Shechem. He summoned the elders, leaders, judges and officials of Israel, and they presented themselves before God.

²Joshua said to all the people, "This is what the Lord, the God of Israel, says: 'Long ago your forefathers, including Terah the father of Abraham and Nahor, lived beyond the River[a] and worshiped other gods. ³But I took your father Abraham from the land beyond the River and led him throughout Canaan and gave him many descendants. I gave him Isaac, ⁴and to Isaac I gave Jacob and Esau. I assigned the hill country of Seir to Esau, but Jacob and his sons went down to Egypt.

⁵" 'Then I sent Moses and Aaron, and I afflicted the Egyptians by what I did there, and I brought you out. ⁶When I brought your fathers out of Egypt, you came to the sea, and the Egyptians pursued them with chariots and horsemen[b] as far as the Red Sea.[c] ⁷But they cried to the Lord for help, and he put darkness between you and the Egyptians; he brought the sea over them and covered them. You saw with your own eyes what I did to the Egyptians. Then you lived in the desert for a long time.

⁸" 'I brought you to the land of the Amorites who lived east of the Jordan. They fought against you, but I gave them into your hands. I destroyed them from before you, and you took possession of their land. ⁹When Balak son of Zippor, the king of Moab, prepared to fight against Israel, he sent for Balaam son of Beor to put a curse on you. ¹⁰But I would not listen to Balaam, so he blessed you again and again, and I delivered you out of his hand.

---

a2 That is, the Euphrates; also in verses 3, 14 and 15   b6 Or charioteers
c6 Hebrew Yam Suph; that is, Sea of Reeds

¹¹"'Then you crossed the Jordan and came to Jericho. The citizens of Jericho fought against you, as did also the Amorites, Perizzites, Canaanites, Hittites, Girgashites, Hivites and Jebusites, but I gave them into your hands. ¹²I sent the hornet ahead of you, which drove them out before you—also the two Amorite kings. You did not do it with your own sword and bow. ¹³So I gave you a land on which you did not toil and cities you did not build; and you live in them and eat from vineyards and olive groves that you did not plant.'

¹⁴"Now fear the LORD and serve him with all faithfulness. Throw away the gods your forefathers worshiped beyond the River and in Egypt, and serve the LORD. ¹⁵But if serving the LORD seems undesirable to you, then choose for yourselves this day whom you will serve, whether the gods your forefathers served beyond the River, or the gods of the Amorites, in whose land you are living. But as for me and my household, we will serve the LORD."

¹⁶Then the people answered, "Far be it from us to forsake the LORD to serve other gods! ¹⁷It was the LORD our God himself who brought us and our fathers up out of Egypt, from that land of slavery, and performed those great signs before our eyes. He protected us on our entire journey and among all the nations through which we traveled. ¹⁸And the LORD drove out before us all the nations, including the Amorites, who lived in the land. We too will serve the LORD, because he is our God."

¹⁹Joshua said to the people, "You are not able to serve the LORD. He is a holy God; he is a jealous God. He will not forgive your rebellion and your sins. ²⁰If you forsake the LORD and serve foreign

show you mean business with the Lord? **6.** What did Joshua do to remind the people of their commitment to the Lord?

1. Looking back over your life so far, can you see any special time in it when God made a difference? How? **2.** Are there other gods that you have been tempted to serve? What are they? How are you able to resist that temptation? **3.** What symbols of commitment does your church use to help people count the cost of following the Lord Jesus? **4.** Frankly speaking, are you really serious about serving the Lord? If so, how do you show it? By what symbols of commitment is that evident to others?

 Joshua 24:1–27   **JOSHUA RENEWS THE COVENANT**

In the closing days of Joshua's life, the last action he would take as Israel's leader was to call the people to renew their covenant with the Lord.

1. What does God mean by verse 13?
   a. You'll always feel out of place here.
   b. I've given you a head start.
   c. All that you have is a gift from me.
   d. You owe me one.

2. After all they've been through, why are the Israelites given a choice now about whom to serve?
   a. Joshua has doubts about their commitment.
   b. Faith is always a choice.
   c. You can't serve God and something else.
   d. Joshua was soliciting support for his leadership.

3. What was behind the people's saying, "We too will serve the Lord"?
   a. unblemished faith and commitment
   b. fear of what God might do otherwise
   c. a little too much self-confidence
   d. a sense of obligation

4. If Joshua comes on a little strong in verses 19–20, it's because:
   a. he was old, so he didn't have to be tactful.
   b. he knew Israel's track record.
   c. once you commit, there's no turning back.
   d. there's a limit to God's patience.
   e. in and of yourself, you're *not* able to serve the Lord.

5. What makes you think the Israelites are going to stay committed?
   a. They had fair warning.
   b. They made a commitment at a solemn public occasion.
   c. They agreed to throw away their old gods.
   d. They had a stone to remind them of their promise.
   e. They were God's people.
   f. Actually, there are no guarantees.

6. What other "gods" besides the Lord are you tempted to serve?
   a. certain people   f. money
   b. an ideal/cause   g. power
   c. security   h. other:_____
   d. leisure
   e. physical gratification

7. How are you able to resist that temptation? What would be the end result of continuing to serve that "god"?

8. What does Joshua's statement, "as for me and my household, we will serve Lord," say to you about your role in the spiritual life of your family? How do you feel about that role and about your influence in the spiritual health of your family?

9. Are you really serious about serving the Lord? If so, conclude this session and this course with the following exercise patterned after the covenant renewal in this passage:
   a. Share one thing God has done for you, your family or your group (vv. 2–13).
   b. Name one concrete spiritual commitment you want to make (vv. 14–18).
   c. Write down on paper the "god" you wish to forsake (vv. 23–24).
   d. Crumple your paper and throw it into a wastebasket (or fire).
   e. Celebrate with a prayer or song.

gods, he will turn and bring disaster on you and make an end of you, after he has been good to you."

21But the people said to Joshua, "No! We will serve the LORD." 22Then Joshua said, "You are witnesses against yourselves that you have chosen to serve the LORD."

"Yes, we are witnesses," they replied.

23"Now then," said Joshua, "throw away the foreign gods that are among you and yield your hearts to the LORD, the God of Israel."

24And the people said to Joshua, "We will serve the LORD our God and obey him."

25On that day Joshua made a covenant for the people, and there at Shechem he drew up for them decrees and laws. 26And Joshua recorded these things in the Book of the Law of God. Then he took a large stone and set it up there under the oak near the holy place of the LORD.

27"See!" he said to all the people. "This stone will be a witness against us. It has heard all the words the LORD has said to us. It will be a witness against you if you are untrue to your God."

Buried in the Promised Land

28Then Joshua sent the people away, each to his own inheritance.

29After these things, Joshua son of Nun, the servant of the LORD, died at the age of a hundred and ten. 30And they buried him in the land of his inheritance, at Timnath Seraha in the hill country of Ephraim, north of Mount Gaash.

31Israel served the LORD throughout the lifetime of Joshua and of the elders who outlived him and who had experienced everything the LORD had done for Israel.

32And Joseph's bones, which the Israelites had brought up from Egypt, were buried at Shechem in the tract of land that Jacob bought for a hundred pieces of silverb from the sons of Hamor, the father of Shechem. This became the inheritance of Joseph's descendants.

33And Eleazar son of Aaron died and was buried at Gibeah, which had been allotted to his son Phinehas in the hill country of Ephraim.

---

1. What age do you think you'll be when you die? Why that age? 2. In your social circles, when is it appropriate to ask or divulge the age of an older female? An older male? 3. Are you keeping your age a secret from the group? Why or why not?

1. What distinguishes the last days, death and burial of Joshua? 2. What brief "obituary" is included here? What more would you add to that from the book of Joshua? 3. Why do you think Joseph's bones were brought from Egypt and buried at Shechem (see Ge 50:24–25)? 4. What era comes to an end with the death of Joshua? With the death of Eleazer?

1. Where would you like to be buried? Why? 2. What one thing do you want people to remember about you when you die? 3. As your group study comes to an end, give each person a proper "send off": What "inheritance" from your group study will each of you come away with?

---

a30 Also known as *Timnath Heres* (see Judges 2:9)   b32 Hebrew *hundred kesitahs*; a kesitah was a unit of money of unknown weight and value.

INTRODUCTION to
JUDGES

Book Study Outline: If you are using Judges for a study course, here is a 7- or 13-week outline. Use the questions in the margin for your group agenda:

☕ start meeting / 15 min.

📖 read & discuss Bible / 30 min.

♡ close meeting / 15–45 min.

Refer to the Questions and Answers in the front of this Bible for more information.

Author: The author of Judges is not identified. Some view Samuel as the author, but this is uncertain.

7-week plan	13-week plan	Personal Reading	Group Study Passage
1	1	1:1–36	1:1–36/Israel Conquers Canaan
	2	2:1–3:6	2:6–3:6/Cycle of Apostasy
2	3	3:7–31	3:12–30/Ehud
	4	4:1–5:31	4:1–24/Deborah Leads Israel
3	5	6:1–40	6:1–40/Gideon and the Fleece
	6	7:1–8:35	7:1–25/Gideon Defeats Midian
4	7	9:1–57	9:1–57/Abimelech
	8	10:1–12:7	11:1–40/Jephthah
5	9	12:8–13:25	13:1–25/Samson's Birth
	10	14:1–16:22	16:1–22/Samson and Delilah
6	11	16:23–31	16:23–31/Samson's Death
	12	17:1–18:31	17:1–13/Micah's Idols
7	13	19:1–21:25	19:1–30/Levite's Concubine

Date: The exact date of authorship is unknown, but Judges may have been written during the early period of the reign of David (c. 1000–980 B.C.). The action recorded here spans the period between the conquest and the monarchy of Israel.

Theme: God is merciful and long-suffering despite the sin of his people.

Historical Background: Two to three hundred years lapse between the conquest of Canaan (after Joshua's death) and the rise of Saul (c. 1050 B.C.). During this time Israel was a loose confederation of tribes spread throughout the promised land. This area was heavily influenced by Canaanite culture and religion. Hence, Israel is repeatedly drawn away from worshiping the Lord in their desire to have a king like their neighbors (17:6; 18:1; 19:1; 21:25).

Characteristics: Once in Canaan, all the Israelites needed to do was obey God; instead, they followed the sinful example of the Canaanites. Their disobedience resulted in a cycle observed throughout the book (see 2:11–19): (1) There is apostasy or rebellion by God's people; (2) God raises up foreign oppressors to chasten his people; (3) A cry of distress goes up from the Israelites; (4) God raises up a "deliverer" or "judge" who takes up arms to defend the homeland and rescue the repentant people. The Book of Judges shows that even in dark, chaotic times, God is in control.

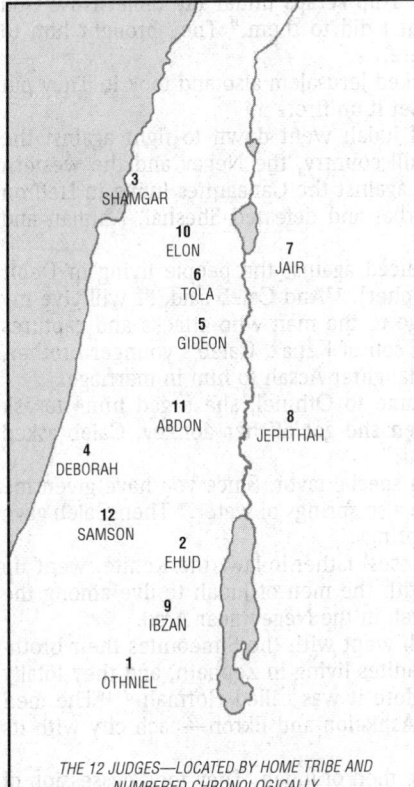

3 SHAMGAR
10 ELON
6 TOLA
7 JAIR
5 GIDEON
11 ABDON
8 JEPHTHAH
4 DEBORAH
12 SAMSON
2 EHUD
9 IBZAN
1 OTHNIEL

THE 12 JUDGES—LOCATED BY HOME TRIBE AND NUMBERED CHRONOLOGICALLY

Judges

☕ 1. Are you more of a "stub-your-toe," "mash-your-fin-ger," or "all-thumbs-and-no-fin-gers" type? Explain. 2. If you had your pick, where would you rather live: In the mountains? Desert? Plains? Or at the beach? Why? 3. From which of these places does your family originate? Which place serves as the family vacation spot or retreat house? Which has been "home" to you for any significant period of time?

📖 1. The author places these events as "after the death of Joshua" (v. 1). What do you recall about Joshua? What were the days of Joshua like? How does the era of the judges figure to be different? 2. How do you suppose the Israel-ites "asked the Lord" and were giv-en such a definitive answer (vv. 1–2; see Ex 28:30)? (In compari-son, how do you discern God's will with certainty?) 3. Why is Judah given the front-line role in this con-quest (v. 2; see 20:18; Ge 49:8–12)? 4. What special favor does Caleb do and why (vv. 12–15; see 1Sa 18:25 on bride-price)? 5. What was the reason for driving the Canaanites from the land (see Ge 15:13–21; Dt 7:1–6)? 6. Within the redemptive purpose and progressive revelation of God and his Prince of Peace, how do you account for the mutilation of POWs (vv. 6–7; see 16:21)? The annihilation of whole cities (v. 17; see Dt 20:16–18)? The enslave-ment of their neighbors (vv. 28ff; see 1Ki 9:15; 2Sa 12:31)? 7. How do you account for their sparing one man and his family (vv. 23–26; see Jos 6:25)? 8. How do you ac-count for Israel's failure to drive out all the Canaanites (vv. 19,27–36; also 2:1–3; 2:20–3:4)?

❤ 1. Does this chapter turn on your competitive drive to win? Or does it turn your stomach in revulsion? Why? 2. Like Adoni-Bezek, when have you experi-enced the "reap-what-you-sow" principle? Were you reaping or sowing? Was it positive or negative fruit you reaped (or sowed)? 3. Where in your life are you feeling under attack or driven out? Where are you holding your ground?

Israel Fights the Remaining Canaanites

1 After the death of Joshua, the Israelites asked the LORD, "Who will be the first to go up and fight for us against the Canaan-ites?"

²The LORD answered, "Judah is to go; I have given the land into their hands."

³Then the men of Judah said to the Simeonites their brothers, "Come up with us into the territory allotted to us, to fight against the Canaanites. We in turn will go with you into yours." So the Simeonites went with them.

⁴When Judah attacked, the LORD gave the Canaanites and Periz-zites into their hands and they struck down ten thousand men at Bezek. ⁵It was there that they found Adoni-Bezek and fought against him, putting to rout the Canaanites and Perizzites. ⁶Adoni-Bezek fled, but they chased him and caught him, and cut off his thumbs and big toes.

⁷Then Adoni-Bezek said, "Seventy kings with their thumbs and big toes cut off have picked up scraps under my table. Now God has paid me back for what I did to them." They brought him to Jerusalem, and he died there.

⁸The men of Judah attacked Jerusalem also and took it. They put the city to the sword and set it on fire.

⁹After that, the men of Judah went down to fight against the Canaanites living in the hill country, the Negev and the western foothills. ¹⁰They advanced against the Canaanites living in Hebron (formerly called Kiriath Arba) and defeated Sheshai, Ahiman and Talmai.

¹¹From there they advanced against the people living in Debir (formerly called Kiriath Sepher). ¹²And Caleb said, "I will give my daughter Acsah in marriage to the man who attacks and captures Kiriath Sepher." ¹³Othniel son of Kenaz, Caleb's younger brother, took it; so Caleb gave his daughter Acsah to him in marriage.

¹⁴One day when she came to Othniel, she urged him[a] to ask her father for a field. When she got off her donkey, Caleb asked her, "What can I do for you?"

¹⁵She replied, "Do me a special favor. Since you have given me land in the Negev, give me also springs of water." Then Caleb gave her the upper and lower springs.

¹⁶The descendants of Moses' father-in-law, the Kenite, went up from the City of Palms[b] with the men of Judah to live among the people of the Desert of Judah in the Negev near Arad.

¹⁷Then the men of Judah went with the Simeonites their broth-ers and attacked the Canaanites living in Zephath, and they totally destroyed[c] the city. Therefore it was called Hormah.[d] ¹⁸The men of Judah also took[e] Gaza, Ashkelon and Ekron—each city with its territory.

¹⁹The LORD was with the men of Judah. They took possession of the hill country, but they were unable to drive the people from the

---

a14 Hebrew; Septuagint and Vulgate *Othniel, he urged her*   b16 That is, Jericho
c17 The Hebrew term refers to the irrevocable giving over of things or persons to the
LORD, often by totally destroying them.   d17 *Hormah* means *destruction.*
e18 Hebrew; Septuagint *Judah did not take*

plains, because they had iron chariots. [20]As Moses had promised, Hebron was given to Caleb, who drove from it the three sons of Anak. [21]The Benjamites, however, failed to dislodge the Jebusites, who were living in Jerusalem; to this day the Jebusites live there with the Benjamites.

[22]Now the house of Joseph attacked Bethel, and the LORD was with them. [23]When they sent men to spy out Bethel (formerly called Luz), [24]the spies saw a man coming out of the city and they said to him, "Show us how to get into the city and we will see that you are treated well." [25]So he showed them, and they put the city to the sword but spared the man and his whole family. [26]He then went to the land of the Hittites, where he built a city and called it Luz, which is its name to this day.

[27]But Manasseh did not drive out the people of Beth Shan or Taanach or Dor or Ibleam or Megiddo and their surrounding settlements, for the Canaanites were determined to live in that land. [28]When Israel became strong, they pressed the Canaanites into forced labor but never drove them out completely. [29]Nor did Ephraim drive out the Canaanites living in Gezer, but the Canaanites continued to live there among them. [30]Neither did Zebulun drive out the Canaanites living in Kitron or Nahalol, who remained among them; but they did subject them to forced labor. [31]Nor did Asher drive out those living in Acco or Sidon or Ahlab or Aczib or Helbah or Aphek or Rehob, [32]and because of this the people of Asher lived among the Canaanite inhabitants of the land. [33]Neither did Naphtali drive out those living in Beth Shemesh or Beth Anath; but the Naphtalites too lived among the Canaanite inhabitants of the land, and those living in Beth Shemesh and Beth Anath became forced laborers for them. [34]The Amorites confined the Danites to the hill country, not allowing them to come down into the plain. [35]And the Amorites were determined also to hold out in Mount Heres, Aijalon and Shaalbim, but when the power of the house of Joseph increased, they too were pressed into forced labor. [36]The boundary of the Amorites was from Scorpion[a] Pass to Sela and beyond.

The Angel of the LORD at Bokim

2 The angel of the LORD went up from Gilgal to Bokim and said, "I brought you up out of Egypt and led you into the land that I swore to give to your forefathers. I said, 'I will never break my covenant with you, [2]and you shall not make a covenant with the people of this land, but you shall break down their altars.' Yet you have disobeyed me. Why have you done this? [3]Now therefore I tell you that I will not drive them out before you; they will be ⌞thorns⌟ in your sides and their gods will be a snare to you."

[4]When the angel of the LORD had spoken these things to all the Israelites, the people wept aloud, [5]and they called that place Bokim.[b] There they offered sacrifices to the LORD.

Disobedience and Defeat

[6]After Joshua had dismissed the Israelites, they went to take possession of the land, each to his own inheritance. [7]The people served the LORD throughout the lifetime of Joshua and of the elders who outlived him and who had seen all the great things the LORD had done for Israel.

[8]Joshua son of Nun, the servant of the LORD, died at the age of a hundred and ten. [9]And they buried him in the land of his inheri-

Where are you compromising the Lord's commands and growing lax? 4. What resources are you drawing upon to "hold your ground" or "seize what is rightfully the Lord's"? How can your small group help you in this regard? 5. Who recently has been a "Caleb," doing a special favor for you? To whom might God be calling you to be a "Caleb"?

Who or what is a "thorn in your side"? For what purpose?

1. Why has Israel disobeyed God? How does God get their attention on this? How do they respond? 2. How do you see God's treatment of Israel: Too harsh? Too soft? Just right?

1. When did you last fail to carry out the boss' (or parents') order? What happened? 2. What experience has come the closest to testing your survival skills or your creative ingenuity? What was the net result of passing the test (if you did)?

---

a36 Hebrew Akrabbim   b5 Bokim means weepers.

1. What do you suppose was the national mood in the days following the death of Joshua? What was their behavior like in the years to follow? 2. In many ways this passage serves as a prologue and "report form" to the rest of Judges, giving the reader an overview of what's to follow. Hence, what repeated themes and cycles of behavior can we expect to be reported on in successive chapters? Compare 2:11 with 3:7; 3:12; 4:1; 6:1; 10:6. What do you see? What other expressions sound like formulas the author will use later on? 3. What does this passage reveal about the justice and mercy of God? 4. Why do you suppose the people did not listen to their assigned leaders (the judges)? 5. What test does God put to Israel? Involving whom? For what purposes (2:20–3:4)?

1. How would *your* life story fit into the Judges' "report form" (of opening word, cycle of apostasy, oppression, distress, deliverance, apt conclusion)? 2. In what one way are you *unlike* your parents? How are you *like* them? How do you feel about the difference and the similarity? 3. Where have you been unable to learn from the past, and thus you find yourself (and your children?) repeating the same mistake? Where have your mistakes accumulated, so that you now feel great distress or hopelessly stuck in some rut? 4. Who or what in times past has come to rescue you from your distress? How might your group be a "lifesaver" in the months to come? 5. When has the Lord ever tested you like he did the Israelites? How are you stronger today, thanks to that testing experience?

1. What does the "Othniel Report" entail? 2. What is so evil about "Baals" and "Asherahs" (see 2Ki 23:4–7)? 3. What role does God's Spirit play here?

When have you burned with rage? Yearned for peace? How was the Lord involved? (Or was he?)

tance, at Timnath Heres[a] in the hill country of Ephraim, north of Mount Gaash.

[10]After that whole generation had been gathered to their fathers, another generation grew up, who knew neither the LORD nor what he had done for Israel. [11]Then the Israelites did evil in the eyes of the LORD and served the Baals. [12]They forsook the LORD, the God of their fathers, who had brought them out of Egypt. They followed and worshiped various gods of the peoples around them. They provoked the LORD to anger [13]because they forsook him and served Baal and the Ashtoreths. [14]In his anger against Israel the LORD handed them over to raiders who plundered them. He sold them to their enemies all around, whom they were no longer able to resist. [15]Whenever Israel went out to fight, the hand of the LORD was against them to defeat them, just as he had sworn to them. They were in great distress.

[16]Then the LORD raised up judges,[b] who saved them out of the hands of these raiders. [17]Yet they would not listen to their judges but prostituted themselves to other gods and worshiped them. Unlike their fathers, they quickly turned from the way in which their fathers had walked, the way of obedience to the LORD's commands. [18]Whenever the LORD raised up a judge for them, he was with the judge and saved them out of the hands of their enemies as long as the judge lived; for the LORD had compassion on them as they groaned under those who oppressed and afflicted them. [19]But when the judge died, the people returned to ways even more corrupt than those of their fathers, following other gods and serving and worshiping them. They refused to give up their evil practices and stubborn ways.

[20]Therefore the LORD was very angry with Israel and said, "Because this nation has violated the covenant that I laid down for their forefathers and has not listened to me, [21]I will no longer drive out before them any of the nations Joshua left when he died. [22]I will use them to test Israel and see whether they will keep the way of the LORD and walk in it as their forefathers did." [23]The LORD had allowed those nations to remain; he did not drive them out at once by giving them into the hands of Joshua.

3 These are the nations the LORD left to test all those Israelites who had not experienced any of the wars in Canaan [2](he did this only to teach warfare to the descendants of the Israelites who had not had previous battle experience): [3]the five rulers of the Philistines, all the Canaanites, the Sidonians, and the Hivites living in the Lebanon mountains from Mount Baal Hermon to Lebo[c] Hamath. [4]They were left to test the Israelites to see whether they would obey the LORD's commands, which he had given their forefathers through Moses.

[5]The Israelites lived among the Canaanites, Hittites, Amorites, Perizzites, Hivites and Jebusites. [6]They took their daughters in marriage and gave their own daughters to their sons, and served their gods.

Othniel

[7]The Israelites did evil in the eyes of the LORD; they forgot the LORD their God and served the Baals and the Asherahs. [8]The anger of the LORD burned against Israel so that he sold them into the hands of Cushan-Rishathaim king of Aram Naharaim,[d] to whom the Israelites were subject for eight years. [9]But when they cried out

[a]9 Also known as *Timnath Serah* (see Joshua 19:50 and 24:30)   [b]16 Or *leaders*; similarly in verses 17-19   [c]3 Or *to the entrance to*   [d]8 That is, Northwest Mesopotamia

to the LORD, he raised up for them a deliverer, Othniel son of Kenaz, Caleb's younger brother, who saved them. [10]The Spirit of the LORD came upon him, so that he became Israel's judge[a] and went to war. The LORD gave Cushan-Rishathaim king of Aram into the hands of Othniel, who overpowered him. [11]So the land had peace for forty years, until Othniel son of Kenaz died.

Ehud

[12]Once again the Israelites did evil in the eyes of the LORD, and because they did this evil the LORD gave Eglon king of Moab power over Israel. [13]Getting the Ammonites and Amalekites to join him, Eglon came and attacked Israel, and they took possession of the City of Palms.[b] [14]The Israelites were subject to Eglon king of Moab for eighteen years.

[15]Again the Israelites cried out to the LORD, and he gave them a deliverer—Ehud, a left-handed man, the son of Gera the Benjamite. The Israelites sent him with tribute to Eglon king of Moab. [16]Now Ehud had made a double-edged sword about a foot and a half[c] long, which he strapped to his right thigh under his clothing. [17]He presented the tribute to Eglon king of Moab, who was a very fat man. [18]After Ehud had presented the tribute, he sent on their way the men who had carried it. [19]At the idols[d] near Gilgal he himself turned back and said, "I have a secret message for you, O king."

The king said, "Quiet!" And all his attendants left him.

[20]Ehud then approached him while he was sitting alone in the upper room of his summer palace[e] and said, "I have a message from God for you." As the king rose from his seat, [21]Ehud reached with his left hand, drew the sword from his right thigh and plunged it into the king's belly. [22]Even the handle sank in after the blade, which came out his back. Ehud did not pull the sword out, and the fat closed in over it. [23]Then Ehud went out to the porch[f]; he shut the doors of the upper room behind him and locked them.

[24]After he had gone, the servants came and found the doors of the upper room locked. They said, "He must be relieving himself in the inner room of the house." [25]They waited to the point of embarrassment, but when he did not open the doors of the room, they took a key and unlocked them. There they saw their lord fallen to the floor, dead.

[26]While they waited, Ehud got away. He passed by the idols and escaped to Seirah. [27]When he arrived there, he blew a trumpet in the hill country of Ephraim, and the Israelites went down with him from the hills, with him leading them.

[28]"Follow me," he ordered, "for the LORD has given Moab, your enemy, into your hands." So they followed him down and, taking possession of the fords of the Jordan that led to Moab, they allowed no one to cross over. [29]At that time they struck down about ten thousand Moabites, all vigorous and strong; not a man escaped. [30]That day Moab was made subject to Israel, and the land had peace for eighty years.

Shamgar

[31]After Ehud came Shamgar son of Anath, who struck down six hundred Philistines with an oxgoad. He too saved Israel.

---

1. When punching out your kid brother, what part of his anatomy would you hit? Why there? 2. What would you hope to do if you were able to use right and left hands equally well?

1. This is the first of five major accounts of national deliverers, all of which are meant to sicken the reader as well as celebrate Israel's deliverance. Which details of this story make you sick? Which make you celebrate? 2. How do you account for the murder of Eglon from the details given here? From the major theme of Judges in 21:25? 3. What, if anything, might be the significance of Ehud's being left-handed (vv. 15,21)? 4. What do you think of Ehud's plan and behavior: (a) Ehud would bring honor to the FBI? (b) Ehud could star in a James Bond movie? (c) Ehud would not be allowed to date any daughter of mine? (d) I would cross to the other side of the street if I ever saw him coming my way? 5. What do you think of Eglon's behavior? And that of Eglon's servants? 6. How does Ehud then deliver Israel from their oppressors (vv. 28–30)? 7. Shamgar is the first of six minor judges: What do you learn about him here? (Note: "Anath," Baal's sister, was a goddess of war.)

1. When have you sent God an "SOS" call for help? How did he answer? Where in your life would you like to experience God answering one of your cries today? 2. If you were to "blow a trumpet" in gratitude for something God has done for you recently, what would it be? 3. If your country's war-torn economy were to enjoy "eighty years of peace" from now on, what would you do to celebrate?

---

a10 Or leader   b13 That is, Jericho   c16 Hebrew a cubit (about 0.5 meter)
d19 Or the stone quarries; also in verse 26   e20 The meaning of the Hebrew for this phrase is uncertain.   f23 The meaning of the Hebrew for this word is uncertain.

1. Apart from your mom or your wife (if married), who is the greatest woman you have ever met? In what areas was she special or a leader? **2.** What "spike-in-the-ground" experience has proved to be a turning point in your life, helping you to make a stand?

1. What familiar cycle is repeated here (vv. 1–3)? **2.** How do you think Barak felt about being called to action by Deborah? Why did he insist on having her go along (vv. 6–8)? Where else (in government, on TV, in your family) have you seen a male-female couple relate like this? **3.** What do you make of Deborah's prophecies (vv. 7,9,14)? How did she know in advance that the Lord would fight Sisera from heaven and flood the Kishon River (5:20–21), thus canceling the advantage of his chariots? How could she know about Jael killing Sisera? (Or did she?) **4.** How do you think Heber responded to his wife's murdering a family friend? What do you think of her use of a tent peg and hammer? **5.** How does this story highlight the role of women over men? What do you think the Israelites felt

Deborah

4 After Ehud died, the Israelites once again did evil in the eyes of the LORD. ²So the LORD sold them into the hands of Jabin, a king of Canaan, who reigned in Hazor. The commander of his army was Sisera, who lived in Harosheth Haggoyim. ³Because he had nine hundred iron chariots and had cruelly oppressed the Israelites for twenty years, they cried to the LORD for help.

⁴Deborah, a prophetess, the wife of Lappidoth, was leading*a* Israel at that time. ⁵She held court under the Palm of Deborah between Ramah and Bethel in the hill country of Ephraim, and the Israelites came to her to have their disputes decided. ⁶She sent for Barak son of Abinoam from Kedesh in Naphtali and said to him, "The LORD, the God of Israel, commands you: 'Go, take with you ten thousand men of Naphtali and Zebulun and lead the way to Mount Tabor. ⁷I will lure Sisera, the commander of Jabin's army, with his chariots and his troops to the Kishon River and give him into your hands.'"

⁸Barak said to her, "If you go with me, I will go; but if you don't go with me, I won't go."

⁹"Very well," Deborah said, "I will go with you. But because of the way you are going about this,*b* the honor will not be yours, for the LORD will hand Sisera over to a woman." So Deborah went with Barak to Kedesh, ¹⁰where he summoned Zebulun and Naphtali. Ten thousand men followed him, and Deborah also went with him.

¹¹Now Heber the Kenite had left the other Kenites, the descen-

a4 Traditionally *judging*   *b9* Or *But on the expedition you are undertaking*

Judges 4:1–24   DEBORAH LEADS ISRAEL

During the period of the "judges" (or "leaders"), God provided deliverance for the Israelites through a chain of human instruments. On this occasion God's instrument was quite unusual for that time and place—a woman.

1. God's response to the Israelites' wickedness was to:
   a. punish them.
   b. send an enemy to harass them.
   c. abandon them.
   d. show them their weakness.

2. What made Deborah a leader in a man's world?
   a. her ability to predict the future
   b. her courage
   c. her military mind
   d. her strong faith
   e. the obvious gifts God gave her
   f. None of the men had her backbone.

3. What was Barak's problem (v. 8)?
   a. He was chicken.
   b. He wasn't sure of the route.
   c. He wasn't convinced that this was the right thing to do.

   d. He wanted a spokesperson for God with him.
   e. He wanted to lean on Deborah.

4. How do you think the Israelite men felt about the honor of victory going to two women? How do you think the Israelite women felt?

5. In this period, Israel went through cycles of turning away from God, suffering from oppression, crying out to the Lord, and being delivered by God through a human agent. When do you most often drift away from the Lord?
   a. when I get too comfortable
   b. when other things demand my attention
   c. when I get tired of being "good"
   d. when I ignore my "quiet time"
   e. when the pressure gets too great
   f. I can't explain it—it just happens.

6. How does God usually seem to "discipline" you?
   a. failure   d. family crises
   b. illness   e. things falling apart
   c. guilt   f. other:_____

7. What is the most effective way for you to "cry out to God"?
   a. "Help!"
   b. talking to a Christian friend
   c. confessing my sin
   d. pouring out my soul in a journal

8. In what way have you experienced God's deliverance?
   a. healing   e. peace
   b. people's help   f. inner strength
   c. provision of resources
   d. spiritual growth through a crisis

9. What quality of Deborah's would you most like to have (and what would you attempt if you had it)?
   a. foresight   d. faith
   b. confidence   e. leadership ability
   c. boldness   f. inner strength

10. How was Deborah able to be an "assertive servant"? What woman today do you look to as a similar example of that kind of strength? What can you do to be more like her and/or Deborah?

dants of Hobab, Moses' brother-in-law,[a] and pitched his tent by the great tree in Zaanannim near Kedesh.

¹²When they told Sisera that Barak son of Abinoam had gone up to Mount Tabor, ¹³Sisera gathered together his nine hundred iron chariots and all the men with him, from Harosheth Haggoyim to the Kishon River.

¹⁴Then Deborah said to Barak, "Go! This is the day the LORD has given Sisera into your hands. Has not the LORD gone ahead of you?" So Barak went down Mount Tabor, followed by ten thousand men. ¹⁵At Barak's advance, the LORD routed Sisera and all his chariots and army by the sword, and Sisera abandoned his chariot and fled on foot. ¹⁶But Barak pursued the chariots and army as far as Harosheth Haggoyim. All the troops of Sisera fell by the sword; not a man was left.

¹⁷Sisera, however, fled on foot to the tent of Jael, the wife of Heber the Kenite, because there were friendly relations between Jabin king of Hazor and the clan of Heber the Kenite.

¹⁸Jael went out to meet Sisera and said to him, "Come, my lord, come right in. Don't be afraid." So he entered her tent, and she put a covering over him.

¹⁹"I'm thirsty," he said. "Please give me some water." She opened a skin of milk, gave him a drink, and covered him up.

²⁰"Stand in the doorway of the tent," he told her. "If someone comes by and asks you, 'Is anyone here?' say 'No.'"

²¹But Jael, Heber's wife, picked up a tent peg and a hammer and went quietly to him while he lay fast asleep, exhausted. She drove the peg through his temple into the ground, and he died.

²²Barak came by in pursuit of Sisera, and Jael went out to meet him. "Come," she said, "I will show you the man you're looking for." So he went in with her, and there lay Sisera with the tent peg through his temple—dead.

²³On that day God subdued Jabin, the Canaanite king, before the Israelites. ²⁴And the hand of the Israelites grew stronger and stronger against Jabin, the Canaanite king, until they destroyed him.

The Song of Deborah

5 On that day Deborah and Barak son of Abinoam sang this song:

²"When the princes in Israel take the lead,
when the people willingly offer themselves—
praise the LORD!

³"Hear this, you kings! Listen, you rulers!
I will sing to[b] the LORD, I will sing;
I will make music to[c] the LORD, the God of
Israel.

⁴"O LORD, when you went out from Seir,
when you marched from the land of Edom,
the earth shook, the heavens poured,
the clouds poured down water.
⁵The mountains quaked before the LORD, the One
of Sinai,
before the LORD, the God of Israel.

⁶"In the days of Shamgar son of Anath,
in the days of Jael, the roads were abandoned;
travelers took to winding paths.

about having a woman judging and delivering them?

♡ 1. Share a time in your life when you may have had a keen sense of God's timing (as does Deborah). How does such foresight differ from the gift of prophecy? 2. Where in your life do you wish you possessed Deborah's certainty and confidence? If God were to tell you something specific about the future, what one thing would you like him to tell you? 3. When have you been under the leadership of a woman who called you forth to undertake new paths of ministry? Did you follow her lead? Or hold back? Why?

🍵 1. When you celebrate a victory, what are you known to do: Cry? Laugh? Shout? Lapse into poetry? Break out in song? Spoil yourself? Treat your friends? 2. When was the last time you recall singing someone's praises without using a hymnbook? Has anyone ever sung your praises? What for? 3. What was one of your favorite popular songs as a teen? How about today?

📖 1. What is the purpose and occasion for this psalm of praise (vv. 1–9)? Who is it for (v. 3)? Who is it by (v. 7; see footnote)? 2. What other songs in Scripture does this one bring to mind? As songwriters, what similarities do Deborah and Barak have with Moses and Miriam (see Ex 15:1–21)? With Mary and Zechariah (See Lk 1:46–55, 68–79)? 3. In this song, what feelings come through about God? What feelings about the nobles and the wealthy (vv. 10–11)? About their fellow

---

a 11 Or *father-in-law*   *b 3* Or *of*   *c 3* Or */ with song I will praise*

warriors (vv. 13–18)? Those who failed to engage in the holy wars of the Lord (v. 23)? The clever but godless Jael (vv. 24–27)? Sisera's mother (vv. 28–30)? **4.** What is your favorite lyric or major theme in this song? Which statements by Deborah seem shocking or in bad taste? **5.** What additional light does this song shed on the events of chapter 4? For example, what was Israel like before God's deliverance (vv. 6–11)? And what natural forces did God use in defeating Sisera (vv. 20–21)? **6.** Of the tribes which participated in the battle (vv. 13–18), which received highest marks? Which the lowest? What might have motivated some to join in and others to abstain? How do you suppose this affected future relations between the 12 tribes of Israel? **7.** On balance, do you like Deborah and Jael? Or do you cringe at the lawlessness of these times Israel had no king?

1. Deborah was a *prophet*, a *leader*, a *songwriter*. If you (or your parents) had to describe yourself in three words, which three would you choose? What is the story behind those words? **2.** Some tribes pitched in to help Deborah, while others did not. In your life, are you experiencing people pitching in to help? How so? Where are you feeling somewhat abandoned? **3.** Other than for God, for whom would you likely compose a song of praise? **4.** What aspect of Deborah's song would best fit your group's song? Try composing one. Is it singable?

⁷Village life*a* in Israel ceased,
　　ceased until I,*b* Deborah, arose,
　　arose a mother in Israel.
⁸When they chose new gods,
　　war came to the city gates,
　　and not a shield or spear was seen
　　among forty thousand in Israel.
⁹My heart is with Israel's princes,
　　with the willing volunteers among the people.
　　Praise the LORD!

¹⁰"You who ride on white donkeys,
　　sitting on your saddle blankets,
　　and you who walk along the road,
　consider ¹¹the voice of the singers*c* at the
　　watering places.
　They recite the righteous acts of the LORD,
　　the righteous acts of his warriors*d* in Israel.

"Then the people of the LORD
　　went down to the city gates.
¹²'Wake up, wake up, Deborah!
　　Wake up, wake up, break out in song!
Arise, O Barak!
　　Take captive your captives, O son of Abinoam.'

¹³"Then the men who were left
　　came down to the nobles;
　the people of the LORD
　　came to me with the mighty.
¹⁴Some came from Ephraim, whose roots were in
　　Amalek;
　　Benjamin was with the people who followed
　　you.
From Makir captains came down,
　　from Zebulun those who bear a commander's
　　staff.
¹⁵The princes of Issachar were with Deborah;
　　yes, Issachar was with Barak,
　　rushing after him into the valley.
In the districts of Reuben
　　there was much searching of heart.
¹⁶Why did you stay among the campfires*e*
　　to hear the whistling for the flocks?
In the districts of Reuben
　　there was much searching of heart.
¹⁷Gilead stayed beyond the Jordan.
　　And Dan, why did he linger by the ships?
Asher remained on the coast
　　and stayed in his coves.
¹⁸The people of Zebulun risked their very lives;
　　so did Naphtali on the heights of the field.

¹⁹"Kings came, they fought;
　　the kings of Canaan fought
　at Taanach by the waters of Megiddo,
　　but they carried off no silver, no plunder.
²⁰From the heavens the stars fought,
　　from their courses they fought against Sisera.

a7 Or *Warriors*　*b7* Or *you*　*c11* Or *archers*; the meaning of the Hebrew for this word is uncertain.　*d11* Or *villagers*　*e16* Or *saddlebags*

²¹The river Kishon swept them away,
  the age-old river, the river Kishon.
  March on, my soul; be strong!
²²Then thundered the horses' hoofs—
  galloping, galloping go his mighty steeds.
²³'Curse Meroz,' said the angel of the LORD.
  'Curse its people bitterly,
because they did not come to help the LORD,
  to help the LORD against the mighty.'

²⁴"Most blessed of women be Jael,
  the wife of Heber the Kenite,
  most blessed of tent-dwelling women.
²⁵He asked for water, and she gave him milk;
  in a bowl fit for nobles she brought him curdled
    milk.
²⁶Her hand reached for the tent peg,
  her right hand for the workman's hammer.
She struck Sisera, she crushed his head,
  she shattered and pierced his temple.
²⁷At her feet he sank,
  he fell; there he lay.
At her feet he sank, he fell;
  where he sank, there he fell—dead.

²⁸"Through the window peered Sisera's mother;
  behind the lattice she cried out,
'Why is his chariot so long in coming?
  Why is the clatter of his chariots delayed?'
²⁹The wisest of her ladies answer her;
  indeed, she keeps saying to herself,
³⁰'Are they not finding and dividing the spoils:
  a girl or two for each man,
  colorful garments as plunder for Sisera,
  colorful garments embroidered,
  highly embroidered garments for my neck—
all this as plunder?'

³¹"So may all your enemies perish, O LORD!
  But may they who love you be like the sun
  when it rises in its strength."

Then the land had peace forty years.

Gideon

6 Again the Israelites did evil in the eyes of the LORD, and for seven years he gave them into the hands of the Midianites. ²Because the power of Midian was so oppressive, the Israelites prepared shelters for themselves in mountain clefts, caves and strongholds. ³Whenever the Israelites planted their crops, the Midianites, Amalekites and other eastern peoples invaded the country. ⁴They camped on the land and ruined the crops all the way to Gaza and did not spare a living thing for Israel, neither sheep nor cattle nor donkeys. ⁵They came up with their livestock and their tents like swarms of locusts. It was impossible to count the men and their camels; they invaded the land to ravage it. ⁶Midian so impoverished the Israelites that they cried out to the LORD for help.

⁷When the Israelites cried to the LORD because of Midian, ⁸he sent them a prophet, who said, "This is what the LORD, the God of Israel, says: I brought you up out of Egypt, out of the land of

1. If some bully were to come to where you live and ruin three resources you use in making a living, what three would they be? 2. Where do you go to get away from it all? Who sometimes meets you there? 3. How would you recognize an "angel" if you saw one face to face? What would be your first clue?

1. In the seven years prior to Gideon coming to save the day, what is the situation in Israel? Sound familiar? Why? 2. This time how are the people responding? Are they *regretful*, or *repentant*? What is the difference between the two? 3. How well do you suppose

the prophet's message went over with Israel (vv. 7–10)? **4.** What is the significance of the angel's word and Gideon's protest concerning the Lord's presence (vv. 11–14)? **5.** Why does Gideon object to being chosen (v. 15): Lack of faith in himself? Or in God? Or in his teammates? **6.** How does the angel of God reassure him? At what point does Gideon recognize the angel for who he is? Why not until then? Why the thought of death? **7.** What is the significance of the altar that Gideon built (vv. 24–32)? How do you account for Gideon's newfound courage and name-change? Where does he still lack courage (vv. 27,30)? What does that tell you about Gideon: Is he a "wimp" or a "family man"? Why do you think so? **8.** What role does the Holy Spirit play in this story (vv. 34ff)? **9.** How do you account for Gideon's need for more signs of God's presence (vv. 36–40)? Why do you suppose God condescended to oblige Gideon's "erratic faith" the first time? The second time? **10.** What lesson is God teaching him (and us) here? Would God have been equally just and merciful in simply reminding Gideon of what

slavery. ⁹I snatched you from the power of Egypt and from the hand of all your oppressors. I drove them from before you and gave you their land. ¹⁰I said to you, 'I am the LORD your God; do not worship the gods of the Amorites, in whose land you live.' But you have not listened to me."

¹¹The angel of the LORD came and sat down under the oak in Ophrah that belonged to Joash the Abiezrite, where his son Gideon was threshing wheat in a winepress to keep it from the Midianites. ¹²When the angel of the LORD appeared to Gideon, he said, "The LORD is with you, mighty warrior."

¹³"But sir," Gideon replied, "if the LORD is with us, why has all this happened to us? Where are all his wonders that our fathers told us about when they said, 'Did not the LORD bring us up out of Egypt?' But now the LORD has abandoned us and put us into the hand of Midian."

¹⁴The LORD turned to him and said, "Go in the strength you have and save Israel out of Midian's hand. Am I not sending you?"

¹⁵"But Lord,ᵃ" Gideon asked, "how can I save Israel? My clan is the weakest in Manasseh, and I am the least in my family."

¹⁶The LORD answered, "I will be with you, and you will strike down all the Midianites together."

¹⁷Gideon replied, "If now I have found favor in your eyes, give me a sign that it is really you talking to me. ¹⁸Please do not go away until I come back and bring my offering and set it before you."

And the LORD said, "I will wait until you return."

¹⁹Gideon went in, prepared a young goat, and from an ephahᵇ of flour he made bread without yeast. Putting the meat in a basket

ᵃ15 Or sir   ᵇ19 That is, probably about 3/5 bushel (about 22 liters)

    Judges 6:1–40   GIDEON'S FEAR, FAITH AND FLEECE

1. How would you describe Gideon?
   a. "mighty warrior"   d. cautious
   b. full of faith   e. diplomatic
   c. full of fear   f. wavering

2. The main reason Gideon balked at God's instruction was because he:
   a. lacked faith in God.
   b. lacked faith in himself.
   c. lacked faith in his countrymen.
   d. was too afraid.
   e. didn't realize whom he was talking to.

3. Who did Gideon fear the most?
   a. the Midianites   c. the Lord
   b. the townspeople d. his family

4. Gideon exhibited the greatest faith when he:
   a. kept working despite oppression of the Midianites.
   b. brought an offering to the angel.
   c. tore down the altar to Baal.
   d. built an altar to the Lord and sacrificed his father's bull on it.
   e. trumpeted the call to arms.
   f. asked for miraculous signs.

5. The Lord was patient with Gideon's requests for signs and "fleeces" because he:
   a. understood Gideon's weakness.
   b. appreciated the risks Gideon took.
   c. saw Gideon's potential.
   d. accepted Gideon's fears.
   e. accepted Gideon's faith.

6. On my spiritual journey, I am:
   a. trying to remain inconspicuous.
   b. noticing an "angel" in my life.
   c. looking for assurance that God is with me.
   d. beginning to "tear down idols."
   e. empowered by God's Spirit.
   f. asking the Lord for confirmation of his will.

7. What is your greatest fear? If you stop and listen, are you able to hear God say—as he did to Gideon—"I will be with you"?

8. Have you ever used a "fleece" to seek direction from God? How do you feel about asking the Lord for signs? In what area of your life do you most need God's direction now?

9. What is the hardest thing about doing God's will?
   a. figuring out what it is
   b. choosing the many options God gives me
   c. taking risks
   d. explaining my actions to others
   e. doing it once I know what it is

10. Which stand out the most to you—Gideon's strengths or his weaknesses? Which stand out the most about yourself? What is your greatest strength? Your greatest weakness?

11. What are your greatest fears or concerns regarding your dating life? How are you encouraged or challenged by this story?

12. What decisions about your career have you made as a result of this course? How are you addressing the major factors in the decisions yet to be made? How can your group continue to support each other in the future?

and its broth in a pot, he brought them out and offered them to him under the oak.

²⁰The angel of God said to him, "Take the meat and the unleavened bread, place them on this rock, and pour out the broth." And Gideon did so. ²¹With the tip of the staff that was in his hand, the angel of the LORD touched the meat and the unleavened bread. Fire flared from the rock, consuming the meat and the bread. And the angel of the LORD disappeared. ²²When Gideon realized that it was the angel of the LORD, he exclaimed, "Ah, Sovereign LORD! I have seen the angel of the LORD face to face!"

²³But the LORD said to him, "Peace! Do not be afraid. You are not going to die."

²⁴So Gideon built an altar to the LORD there and called it The LORD is Peace. To this day it stands in Ophrah of the Abiezrites.

²⁵That same night the LORD said to him, "Take the second bull from your father's herd, the one seven years old.^a Tear down your father's altar to Baal and cut down the Asherah pole^b beside it. ²⁶Then build a proper kind of^c altar to the LORD your God on the top of this height. Using the wood of the Asherah pole that you cut down, offer the second^d bull as a burnt offering."

²⁷So Gideon took ten of his servants and did as the LORD told him. But because he was afraid of his family and the men of the town, he did it at night rather than in the daytime.

²⁸In the morning when the men of the town got up, there was Baal's altar, demolished, with the Asherah pole beside it cut down and the second bull sacrificed on the newly built altar!

²⁹They asked each other, "Who did this?"

When they carefully investigated, they were told, "Gideon son of Joash did it."

³⁰The men of the town demanded of Joash, "Bring out your son. He must die, because he has broken down Baal's altar and cut down the Asherah pole beside it."

³¹But Joash replied to the hostile crowd around him, "Are you going to plead Baal's cause? Are you trying to save him? Whoever fights for him shall be put to death by morning! If Baal really is a god, he can defend himself when someone breaks down his altar." ³²So that day they called Gideon "Jerub-Baal,^e" saying, "Let Baal contend with him," because he broke down Baal's altar.

³³Now all the Midianites, Amalekites and other eastern peoples joined forces and crossed over the Jordan and camped in the Valley of Jezreel. ³⁴Then the Spirit of the LORD came upon Gideon, and he blew a trumpet, summoning the Abiezrites to follow him. ³⁵He sent messengers throughout Manasseh, calling them to arms, and also into Asher, Zebulun and Naphtali, so that they too went up to meet them.

³⁶Gideon said to God, "If you will save Israel by my hand as you have promised— ³⁷look, I will place a wool fleece on the threshing floor. If there is dew only on the fleece and all the ground is dry, then I will know that you will save Israel by my hand, as you said." ³⁸And that is what happened. Gideon rose early the next day; he squeezed the fleece and wrung out the dew—a bowlful of water.

³⁹Then Gideon said to God, "Do not be angry with me. Let me make just one more request. Allow me one more test with the fleece. This time make the fleece dry and the ground covered with

he had already told and shown him? Why do you think so?

1. One time Gideon is so sure of God (vv. 22,24,27a); the next moment he is so *unsure* (vv. 13,15,17,27b,36,39). How are you like Gideon in this regard? 2. When have you resorted to using "Gideon's fleece"? What happened? Were you tempted to do it over again? Why? 3. In the past five years, what have been two "sure" signs of God's presence with you? What are two present signs? 4. Where are you uncertain, afraid or overly cautious of God's call to you right now? 5. Gideon built an altar and tore one down overnight. What would you like to "tear down" in your life, if you could? And what would you like to "build up" to the glory of God? How can your small group help you get started in this "overnight" project?

---

^a25 Or *Take a full-grown, mature bull from your father's herd*   ^b25 That is, a symbol of the goddess Asherah; here and elsewhere in Judges   ^c26 Or *build with layers of stone an*   ^d26 Or *full-grown*; also in verse 28   ^e32 *Jerub-Baal* means *let Baal contend*.

dew." ⁴⁰That night God did so. Only the fleece was dry; all the ground was covered with dew.

Gideon Defeats the Midianites

7 Early in the morning, Jerub-Baal (that is, Gideon) and all his men camped at the spring of Harod. The camp of Midian was north of them in the valley near the hill of Moreh. ²The LORD said to Gideon, "You have too many men for me to deliver Midian into their hands. In order that Israel may not boast against me that her own strength has saved her, ³announce now to the people, 'Anyone who trembles with fear may turn back and leave Mount Gilead.'" So twenty-two thousand men left, while ten thousand remained.

⁴But the LORD said to Gideon, "There are still too many men. Take them down to the water, and I will sift them for you there. If I say, 'This one shall go with you,' he shall go; but if I say, 'This one shall not go with you,' he shall not go."

⁵So Gideon took the men down to the water. There the LORD told him, "Separate those who lap the water with their tongues like a dog from those who kneel down to drink." ⁶Three hundred men lapped with their hands to their mouths. All the rest got down on their knees to drink.

⁷The LORD said to Gideon, "With the three hundred men that lapped I will save you and give the Midianites into your hands. Let all the other men go, each to his own place." ⁸So Gideon sent the rest of the Israelites to their tents but kept the three hundred, who took over the provisions and trumpets of the others.

Now the camp of Midian lay below him in the valley. ⁹During

1. What dream still sticks in your mind? What's so bothersome or motivational about that dream? **2.** What camping experience (recent or childhood) tested your ingenuity or your survival skills?

1. Why did God want to reduce the size of Gideon's army? Why send the others home (vv. 3,7; see Dt 20:8)? Might they be useful later, if not now (vv. 23f; see 8:1)? **2.** What do you think of God's "winnowing" process? Which makes more sense to you—the reduction having to do with fear, or the one having to do with lapping water? What does lapping water have to do with anything? **3.** As Gideon, how would you feel when God says, "You have too many men. Send some home." What was God trying to teach Gideon: Risk-taking? Trust? Budget-cutting? **4.** Why did Gideon take his servant Purah down to the enemies' camp (vv. 9–12)? Was this a spying mission to gather secret military intelli-

---

  Judges 7:1–25   **GIDEON DEFEATS THE MIDIANITES**

Rather reluctantly, Gideon has accepted God's call to lead Israel against her oppressors—the Midianites.

1. What was going through Gideon's mind when God was telling him he had too many men?
   a. "You've got to be kidding!"
   b. "This is going to be great!"
   c. "I'll bow out myself, then."
   d. "What's he trying to prove?"
   e. "As you please."

2. What was going through God's mind?
   a. God was only looking for a few good men.
   b. God wanted to get the credit.
   c. God wanted to show that bigger isn't always better.
   d. God didn't want the Israelites to get big heads.
   e. God was teaching Gideon to take risks.
   f. God was teaching Gideon simply to trust him.

3. What was the qualification for joining this army?
   a. faith
   b. a team spirit
   c. drinking etiquette
   d. trumpeting ability
   e. strength
   f. courage

4. Where did Gideon get his battle plan?
   a. old war movies
   b. God
   c. his brilliant military mind
   d. being inspired by his visit to the enemy camp

5. The Israelites won because:
   a. they were a cracker-jack strike force.
   b. they caught the enemy sleeping.
   c. the Midianites were overcome with fear.
   d. God was on their side.
   e. they followed Gideon's orders.
   f. they followed God's orders.

6. Where are you feeling outnumbered or in need of immediate intervention?

7. How do you feel about letting God fight that battle for you?
   a. Anything is better than what I've been doing.
   b. I really want to do that.
   c. I still think I can handle it myself.
   d. Okay, but how do I turn the situation over to him?

8. Why is it important that God get the credit for winning your battles?
   a. because he fights them
   b. because he needs the applause
   c. because I need to praise him
   d. because he deserves the credit

9. How does this story relate to you and your work?
   a. I never have enough help.
   b. Sometimes I'm afraid to attack job problems.
   c. I have found that when I am weak, God is strong.
   d. If I'm faithful to God, my battles are really his.

10. How do you think working relationships in Gideon's army were affected by letting God be in command? How could you better let God be the "boss" in your job and in your working relationships?

that night the LORD said to Gideon, "Get up, go down against the camp, because I am going to give it into your hands. ¹⁰If you are afraid to attack, go down to the camp with your servant Purah ¹¹and listen to what they are saying. Afterward, you will be encouraged to attack the camp." So he and Purah his servant went down to the outposts of the camp. ¹²The Midianites, the Amalekites and all the other eastern peoples had settled in the valley, thick as locusts. Their camels could no more be counted than the sand on the seashore.

¹³Gideon arrived just as a man was telling a friend his dream. "I had a dream," he was saying. "A round loaf of barley bread came tumbling into the Midianite camp. It struck the tent with such force that the tent overturned and collapsed."

¹⁴His friend responded, "This can be nothing other than the sword of Gideon son of Joash, the Israelite. God has given the Midianites and the whole camp into his hands."

¹⁵When Gideon heard the dream and its interpretation, he worshiped God. He returned to the camp of Israel and called out, "Get up! The LORD has given the Midianite camp into your hands." ¹⁶Dividing the three hundred men into three companies, he placed trumpets and empty jars in the hands of all of them, with torches inside.

¹⁷"Watch me," he told them. "Follow my lead. When I get to the edge of the camp, do exactly as I do. ¹⁸When I and all who are with me blow our trumpets, then from all around the camp blow yours and shout, 'For the LORD and for Gideon.'"

¹⁹Gideon and the hundred men with him reached the edge of the camp at the beginning of the middle watch, just after they had changed the guard. They blew their trumpets and broke the jars that were in their hands. ²⁰The three companies blew the trumpets and smashed the jars. Grasping the torches in their left hands and holding in their right hands the trumpets they were to blow, they shouted, "A sword for the LORD and for Gideon!" ²¹While each man held his position around the camp, all the Midianites ran, crying out as they fled.

²²When the three hundred trumpets sounded, the LORD caused the men throughout the camp to turn on each other with their swords. The army fled to Beth Shittah toward Zererah as far as the border of Abel Meholah near Tabbath. ²³Israelites from Naphtali, Asher and all Manasseh were called out, and they pursued the Midianites. ²⁴Gideon sent messengers throughout the hill country of Ephraim, saying, "Come down against the Midianites and seize the waters of the Jordan ahead of them as far as Beth Barah."

So all the men of Ephraim were called out and they took the waters of the Jordan as far as Beth Barah. ²⁵They also captured two of the Midianite leaders, Oreb and Zeeb. They killed Oreb at the rock of Oreb, and Zeeb at the winepress of Zeeb. They pursued the Midianites and brought the heads of Oreb and Zeeb to Gideon, who was by the Jordan.

Zebah and Zalmunna

8 Now the Ephraimites asked Gideon, "Why have you treated us like this? Why didn't you call us when you went to fight Midian?" And they criticized him sharply.

²But he answered them, "What have I accomplished compared to you? Aren't the gleanings of Ephraim's grapes better than the full grape harvest of Abiezer? ³God gave Oreb and Zeeb, the Midianite leaders, into your hands. What was I able to do compared to you?" At this, their resentment against him subsided.

gence? Or was this mission mostly for morale building? Why do you think so? **5.** How did Gideon's mood change after hearing the dream and its interpretation (vv. 13ff)? What does this incident tell us about God? About his ways of using non-Israeli, even "secular" means of communicating his will? Along with the fleece, what does this incident tell you about Gideon? **6.** Besides God, what did Gideon's battle plan have going for it? What elements of the plan led to its success? What would the horn-blowing contribute?

♡ **1.** In what way is Gideon's winnowing experience similar to Paul's experience of God's grace made perfect in human weakness (see 2Co 12:7–10)? **2.** How do the object lessons of chapters 6 and 7 compare with the prevailing message from today's success-oriented, "bigger-is-better" culture? **3.** In your life, when has God used one of your weaknesses or failures to help someone else? Which weakness of yours does this story prompt you to see differently today? **4.** In the battle you are facing today, which of Gideon's battle armaments do you need most: (a) Horn to blow? (b) Jar to shatter? (c) Torch to shine? or (d) Voice to shout? **5.** Where are you feeling outnumbered or needing immediate intervention from God? **6.** Where else in the Bible do you recall God speaking to someone in a dream? Does God still speak to us in dreams, or is this a thing of the past? Explain.

▽ **1.** What food are you craving right now? **2.** What activity this past month simply exhausted you? **3.** In the A to Z roll call your teachers used for checking attendance and assigning seats, who do you recall was first? Or last? Where were you? How did that make you feel?

1. What do you think of the Ephraimites' behavior (v. 1; see 7:3,7,23–24): Justified? Petty? Was Gideon's response to them appropriate? Diplomatic? Cowardly? Or what (contrast Jephthah and Ephraim, 12:1–6)? 2. After the Ephraimites, Gideon runs into more detours in hot pursuit of Zebah and Zalmunna. Why do you think Succoth and Peniel refuse him food? In your opinion did Gideon overreact to them? Or was he justified? 3. What do you think such detours and criticisms were doing to the "insides" of Gideon? What kept him from turning back and forgetting about Zalmunna and Zebah: God? Pride? Compulsiveness? 4. When Zebah and Zalmunna tell Gideon, "Come, do it yourself," were they afraid? Cocky? Humiliated? 5. What is an "ephod" (v. 27; see Ex 28:6–14, for its holy use; Jdg 18:14–17, for its pagan use)? 6. How could Gideon resist the Israelites' invitation to rule in the place of God (v. 22), yet worship an ephod in God's stead (v. 27)? Was he greedy? Shortsighted? Losing his zeal for the Lord? 7. How does Gideon's flaw relate to the lawlessness of those times Israel had no king (see 21:25)? 8. Years later, how do you suppose Gideon's young son Jether will remember what happened here? How will he remember his dad?

1. On a scale of 1–10, what marks would you give yourself in handling criticism? What marks would others give you? What would you like to do differently about this, if anything? 2. Gideon hotly pursued Zebah and Zalmunna. How about you? If someone were to write a story of your past month, what pursuit or pursuits would be recorded? How do you feel about those pursuits? What obstacles are in your way? What "bread" do you need to succeed? 3. What do you want to pursue this year, even next month? Where are you likely to face some detours or setbacks in your life's pursuit? How can the small group help you with this? 4. What tends to become an "ephod" in your life: Family? Car? Work? Prized possession? A hobby? How will you submit that to God?

[4] Gideon and his three hundred men, exhausted yet keeping up the pursuit, came to the Jordan and crossed it. [5] He said to the men of Succoth, "Give my troops some bread; they are worn out, and I am still pursuing Zebah and Zalmunna, the kings of Midian."

[6] But the officials of Succoth said, "Do you already have the hands of Zebah and Zalmunna in your possession? Why should we give bread to your troops?"

[7] Then Gideon replied, "Just for that, when the LORD has given Zebah and Zalmunna into my hand, I will tear your flesh with desert thorns and briers."

[8] From there he went up to Peniel[a] and made the same request of them, but they answered as the men of Succoth had. [9] So he said to the men of Peniel, "When I return in triumph, I will tear down this tower."

[10] Now Zebah and Zalmunna were in Karkor with a force of about fifteen thousand men, all that were left of the armies of the eastern peoples; a hundred and twenty thousand swordsmen had fallen. [11] Gideon went up by the route of the nomads east of Nobah and Jogbehah and fell upon the unsuspecting army. [12] Zebah and Zalmunna, the two kings of Midian, fled, but he pursued them and captured them, routing their entire army.

[13] Gideon son of Joash then returned from the battle by the Pass of Heres. [14] He caught a young man of Succoth and questioned him, and the young man wrote down for him the names of the seventy-seven officials of Succoth, the elders of the town. [15] Then Gideon came and said to the men of Succoth, "Here are Zebah and Zalmunna, about whom you taunted me by saying, 'Do you already have the hands of Zebah and Zalmunna in your possession? Why should we give bread to your exhausted men?'" [16] He took the elders of the town and taught the men of Succoth a lesson by punishing them with desert thorns and briers. [17] He also pulled down the tower of Peniel and killed the men of the town.

[18] Then he asked Zebah and Zalmunna, "What kind of men did you kill at Tabor?"

"Men like you," they answered, "each one with the bearing of a prince."

[19] Gideon replied, "Those were my brothers, the sons of my own mother. As surely as the LORD lives, if you had spared their lives, I would not kill you." [20] Turning to Jether, his oldest son, he said, "Kill them!" But Jether did not draw his sword, because he was only a boy and was afraid.

[21] Zebah and Zalmunna said, "Come, do it yourself. 'As is the man, so is his strength.'" So Gideon stepped forward and killed them, and took the ornaments off their camels' necks.

Gideon's Ephod

[22] The Israelites said to Gideon, "Rule over us—you, your son and your grandson—because you have saved us out of the hand of Midian."

[23] But Gideon told them, "I will not rule over you, nor will my son rule over you. The LORD will rule over you." [24] And he said, "I do have one request, that each of you give me an earring from your share of the plunder." (It was the custom of the Ishmaelites to wear gold earrings.)

[25] They answered, "We'll be glad to give them." So they spread out a garment, and each man threw a ring from his plunder onto it. [26] The weight of the gold rings he asked for came to seventeen

a8 Hebrew *Penuel*, a variant of *Peniel*; also in verses 9 and 17

hundred shekels,[a] not counting the ornaments, the pendants and the purple garments worn by the kings of Midian or the chains that were on their camels' necks. [27]Gideon made the gold into an ephod, which he placed in Ophrah, his town. All Israel prostituted themselves by worshiping it there, and it became a snare to Gideon and his family.

Gideon's Death

[28]Thus Midian was subdued before the Israelites and did not raise its head again. During Gideon's lifetime, the land enjoyed peace forty years.

[29]Jerub-Baal son of Joash went back home to live. [30]He had seventy sons of his own, for he had many wives. [31]His concubine, who lived in Shechem, also bore him a son, whom he named Abimelech. [32]Gideon son of Joash died at a good old age and was buried in the tomb of his father Joash in Ophrah of the Abiezrites.

[33]No sooner had Gideon died than the Israelites again prostituted themselves to the Baals. They set up Baal-Berith as their god and [34]did not remember the LORD their God, who had rescued them from the hands of all their enemies on every side. [35]They also failed to show kindness to the family of Jerub-Baal (that is, Gideon) for all the good things he had done for them.

Abimelech

9 Abimelech son of Jerub-Baal went to his mother's brothers in Shechem and said to them and to all his mother's clan, [2]"Ask all the citizens of Shechem, 'Which is better for you: to have all seventy of Jerub-Baal's sons rule over you, or just one man?' Remember, I am your flesh and blood."

[3]When the brothers repeated all this to the citizens of Shechem, they were inclined to follow Abimelech, for they said, "He is our brother." [4]They gave him seventy shekels[b] of silver from the temple of Baal-Berith, and Abimelech used it to hire reckless adventurers, who became his followers. [5]He went to his father's home in Ophrah and on one stone murdered his seventy brothers, the sons of Jerub-Baal. But Jotham, the youngest son of Jerub-Baal, escaped by hiding. [6]Then all the citizens of Shechem and Beth Millo gathered beside the great tree at the pillar in Shechem to crown Abimelech king.

[7]When Jotham was told about this, he climbed up on the top of Mount Gerizim and shouted to them, "Listen to me, citizens of Shechem, so that God may listen to you. [8]One day the trees went out to anoint a king for themselves. They said to the olive tree, 'Be our king.'

[9]"But the olive tree answered, 'Should I give up my oil, by which both gods and men are honored, to hold sway over the trees?'

[10]"Next, the trees said to the fig tree, 'Come and be our king.'

[11]"But the fig tree replied, 'Should I give up my fruit, so good and sweet, to hold sway over the trees?'

[12]"Then the trees said to the vine, 'Come and be our king.'

[13]"But the vine answered, 'Should I give up my wine, which cheers both gods and men, to hold sway over the trees?'

[14]"Finally all the trees said to the thornbush, 'Come and be our king.'

[15]"The thornbush said to the trees, 'If you really want to anoint me king over you, come and take refuge in my shade; but if not,

---

1. Once "weakest in Manasseh" and "least in my family" (6:15), how have things changed for Gideon? As a result of doing what good things (see ch. 6—8)? 2. What are "the Baals" (v. 33; see 2:11—13)? What then is the moral of this Gideon story?

1. Gideon's people soon forgot God. What can you and your group do to help ensure that does not happen to you? 2. To whom is God calling you to express kindness this week? How will you?

---

1. What period of your life was characterized with "reckless adventure"? Describe one incident from that period of your life. What is something reckless you might want to do at your current stage in life? 2. If you had to liken yourself and your past week to a tree, would you be: (a) Oak tree, "solid and sturdy"? (b) Almond tree, "a little nutty"? (c) Palm tree, "warm and comfortable in a tropical climate"? (d) Evergreen, "staying green in the midst of winter's blast"? (e) Date tree, "thankful for, or in need of, human companionship"? 3. What was "an offer you couldn't refuse" which turned out to be not so great after all?

1. Who was Abimelech's mother (see 8:31; 9:18; Ge 16:2)? What is the difference between a wife and a concubine? How might such an upbringing affect Abimelech? 2. The name Abimelech literally means "My Father is king." What additional insight might this give us about him? 3. What images does Jotham evoke in his parable of the trees? Which tree corresponds to Abimelech and his evil deed? What is the main point of that parable? How did that go over with the folk of Shechem? 4. What admirable qualities do you see in Jotham? How would you characterize his tone of voice as he speaks to the people of Shechem: Compassionate? Angry? Sarcastic? Fearful? 5. How can evil proceed *from* God (v. 23; see 1Sa

---

[a]26 That is, about 43 pounds (about 19.5 kilograms)   [b]4 That is, about 1 3/4 pounds (about 0.8 kilogram)

16:14; 18:10, where Saul is also visited by an "evil spirit from God")? **6.** Would you say Gaal's bold statements · about Abimelech were premeditated? Or were they the result of having too much to drink? Why do you think so? **7.** What do you think motivated Zebul to tell Abimelech about Gaal: Loyalty? Civic duty? Self-interest? Or what? **8.** One would think that after getting rid of his chief critic (v. 41), Abimelech would have gone back home. Why didn't he (vv. 42ff)? What further vengeance does he take out on the tower of Shechem? Why? Why then would he go to the city of Thebez and try to wipe it out, too? **9.** What does all this hot pursuit and indiscriminate violence tell you about Abimelech's mental state at this time? **10.** How much pleasure does the author of Judges (and you) take in seeing Abimelech meet his demise? What would be the big deal in being killed by a woman? Why is taking your own life (or being assisted in doing so) a preferable fate (see 1Sa 31:4; 2Sa 11:21)? **11.** In contrast to Gideon, how is Abimelech the antithesis of what God appointed the judges to be? What did the two stand for? What did they each oppose? What was the resulting effect on the people?

♡ **1.** Where in your life is God calling you to be a "Jotham" and to stand up to an "Abimelech"? What might frighten you about that assignment? **2.** Sooner or later, God repays wickedness. What does that inspire in you: Awe? Comfort? Guilt? Fear? Of what wicked thing would you like to rid yourself? **3.** In your life, when has God brought an unexpected deliverance, as he did with the people of Thebez? From what "enemy" would you like to be delivered now? How can your small group help?

then let fire come out of the thornbush and consume the cedars of Lebanon!'

[16]"Now if you have acted honorably and in good faith when you made Abimelech king, and if you have been fair to Jerub-Baal and his family, and if you have treated him as he deserves— [17]and to think that my father fought for you, risked his life to rescue you from the hand of Midian [18](but today you have revolted against my father's family, murdered his seventy sons on a single stone, and made Abimelech, the son of his slave girl, king over the citizens of Shechem because he is your brother)— [19]if then you have acted honorably and in good faith toward Jerub-Baal and his family today, may Abimelech be your joy, and may you be his, too! [20]But if you have not, let fire come out from Abimelech and consume you, citizens of Shechem and Beth Millo, and let fire come out from you, citizens of Shechem and Beth Millo, and consume Abimelech!"

[21]Then Jotham fled, escaping to Beer, and he lived there because he was afraid of his brother Abimelech.

[22]After Abimelech had governed Israel three years, [23]God sent an evil spirit between Abimelech and the citizens of Shechem, who acted treacherously against Abimelech. [24]God did this in order that the crime against Jerub-Baal's seventy sons, the shedding of their blood, might be avenged on their brother Abimelech and on the citizens of Shechem, who had helped him murder his brothers. [25]In opposition to him these citizens of Shechem set men on the hilltops to ambush and rob everyone who passed by, and this was reported to Abimelech.

[26]Now Gaal son of Ebed moved with his brothers into Shechem, and its citizens put their confidence in him. [27]After they had gone out into the fields and gathered the grapes and trodden them, they held a festival in the temple of their god. While they were eating and drinking, they cursed Abimelech. [28]Then Gaal son of Ebed said, "Who is Abimelech, and who is Shechem, that we should be subject to him? Isn't he Jerub-Baal's son, and isn't Zebul his deputy? Serve the men of Hamor, Shechem's father! Why should we serve Abimelech? [29]If only this people were under my command! Then I would get rid of him. I would say to Abimelech, 'Call out your whole army!' " [a]

[30]When Zebul the governor of the city heard what Gaal son of Ebed said, he was very angry. [31]Under cover he sent messengers to Abimelech, saying, "Gaal son of Ebed and his brothers have come to Shechem and are stirring up the city against you. [32]Now then, during the night you and your men should come and lie in wait in the fields. [33]In the morning at sunrise, advance against the city. When Gaal and his men come out against you, do whatever your hand finds to do."

[34]So Abimelech and all his troops set out by night and took up concealed positions near Shechem in four companies. [35]Now Gaal son of Ebed had gone out and was standing at the entrance to the city gate just as Abimelech and his soldiers came out from their hiding place.

[36]When Gaal saw them, he said to Zebul, "Look, people are coming down from the tops of the mountains!"

Zebul replied, "You mistake the shadows of the mountains for men."

[37]But Gaal spoke up again: "Look, people are coming down from

---

a29 Septuagint; Hebrew *him.*" Then he said to Abimelech, "Call out your whole army!"

[13]The king of the Ammonites answered Jephthah's messengers, "When Israel came up out of Egypt, they took away my land from the Arnon to the Jabbok, all the way to the Jordan. Now give it back peaceably."

[14]Jephthah sent back messengers to the Ammonite king, [15]saying:

"This is what Jephthah says: Israel did not take the land of Moab or the land of the Ammonites. [16]But when they came up out of Egypt, Israel went through the desert to the Red Sea[a] and on to Kadesh. [17]Then Israel sent messengers to the king of Edom, saying, 'Give us permission to go through your country,' but the king of Edom would not listen. They sent also to the king of Moab, and he refused. So Israel stayed at Kadesh.

[18]"Next they traveled through the desert, skirted the lands of Edom and Moab, passed along the eastern side of the country of Moab, and camped on the other side of the Arnon. They did not enter the territory of Moab, for the Arnon was its border.

[19]"Then Israel sent messengers to Sihon king of the Amorites, who ruled in Heshbon, and said to him, 'Let us pass through your country to our own place.' [20]Sihon, however, did not trust Israel[b] to pass through his territory. He mustered all his men and encamped at Jahaz and fought with Israel.

[21]"Then the LORD, the God of Israel, gave Sihon and all his men into Israel's hands, and they defeated them. Israel took over all the land of the Amorites who lived in that country, [22]capturing all of it from the Arnon to the Jabbok and from the desert to the Jordan.

[23]"Now since the LORD, the God of Israel, has driven the Amorites out before his people Israel, what right have you to take it over? [24]Will you not take what your god Chemosh gives you? Likewise, whatever the LORD our God has given us, we will possess. [25]Are you better than Balak son of Zippor, king of Moab? Did he ever quarrel with Israel or fight with them? [26]For three hundred years Israel occupied Heshbon, Aroer, the surrounding settlements and all the towns along the Arnon. Why didn't you retake them during that time? [27]I have not wronged you, but you are doing me wrong by waging war against me. Let the LORD, the Judge,[c] decide the dispute this day between the Israelites and the Ammonites."

[28]The king of Ammon, however, paid no attention to the message Jephthah sent him.

[29]Then the Spirit of the LORD came upon Jephthah. He crossed Gilead and Manasseh, passed through Mizpah of Gilead, and from there he advanced against the Ammonites. [30]And Jephthah made a vow to the LORD: "If you give the Ammonites into my hands, [31]whatever comes out of the door of my house to meet me when I return in triumph from the Ammonites will be the LORD's, and I will sacrifice it as a burnt offering."

[32]Then Jephthah went over to fight the Ammonites, and the LORD gave them into his hands. [33]He devastated twenty towns from Aroer to the vicinity of Minnith, as far as Abel Keramim. Thus Israel subdued Ammon.

[34]When Jephthah returned to his home in Mizpah, who should come out to meet him but his daughter, dancing to the sound of

5. What new dynamics turn the story from talk to action (vv. 29–33)? What do you think is the decisive factor in Israel's victory over the Ammonites: (a) God's Spirit upon Jephthah? (b) Jephthah's vow to the Lord? (c) Jephthah's military strategy? 6. What is the purpose of this story about Jephthah and his daughter? What is so crucial about keeping one's vow to the Lord? What is so detestable about human sacrifice? 7. What do you suppose was the exact nature of Jephthah's vow (vv. 30–31,39)? Surely the Lord would let him off the hook as he did Abraham (see Ge 22:1–19; compare Nu 30; Dt 23:21–23; Ecc 5:4–5)? 8. In God's plan, is human sacrifice ever acceptable? Which do you think takes precedence, Jephthah's vow or God's rejection of human sacrifice? How do Jephthah's actions reflect the theme of this book (see 21:25)? 9. How has your opinion of Jephthah changed by the end of chapter 11? Did he do the right thing regarding his daughter? Or did he act hastily and needlessly? Why do you think so?

1. Jephthah's story can be summed up in four words— *rejection, vindication, victory* and *heartache.* Which of these words touch upon stages in your life right now? When have you won a hard-fought battle, only to lose a heartfelt love? 2. What did God see in Jephthah that others found hard to see? What does God see in *you* that others might miss on first meeting you? If you have trouble answering, ask your small group members what God sees in you! 3. When have you attempted to argue your case *pro se* (by yourself, without legal counsel)? What arguments did you put in your defense, petition, or complaint? What happened? 4. What is the status of vows in your society? What are some unpopular vows you have made and kept? Which has caused you more heartache—the ones you've kept, or the ones you've broken? Confidentially, share your heartache with your group. 5. If keeping a vow meant you would have to sin, would you keep it? Why or why not? How can this passage help you to keep your vows in perspective?

---

[a]16 Hebrew *Yam Suph*; that is, Sea of Reeds   [b]20 Or *however, would not make an agreement for Israel*   [c]27 Or *Ruler*

tambourines! She was an only child. Except for her he had neither son nor daughter. ³⁵When he saw her, he tore his clothes and cried, "Oh! My daughter! You have made me miserable and wretched, because I have made a vow to the LORD that I cannot break."

³⁶"My father," she replied, "you have given your word to the LORD. Do to me just as you promised, now that the LORD has avenged you of your enemies, the Ammonites. ³⁷But grant me this one request," she said. "Give me two months to roam the hills and weep with my friends, because I will never marry."

³⁸"You may go," he said. And he let her go for two months. She and the girls went into the hills and wept because she would never marry. ³⁹After the two months, she returned to her father and he did to her as he had vowed. And she was a virgin.

From this comes the Israelite custom ⁴⁰that each year the young women of Israel go out for four days to commemorate the daughter of Jephthah the Gileadite.

Jephthah and Ephraim

12 The men of Ephraim called out their forces, crossed over to Zaphon and said to Jephthah, "Why did you go to fight the Ammonites without calling us to go with you? We're going to burn down your house over your head."

²Jephthah answered, "I and my people were engaged in a great struggle with the Ammonites, and although I called, you didn't save me out of their hands. ³When I saw that you wouldn't help, I took my life in my hands and crossed over to fight the Ammonites, and the LORD gave me the victory over them. Now why have you come up today to fight me?"

⁴Jephthah then called together the men of Gilead and fought against Ephraim. The Gileadites struck them down because the Ephraimites had said, "You Gileadites are renegades from Ephraim and Manasseh." ⁵The Gileadites captured the fords of the Jordan leading to Ephraim, and whenever a survivor of Ephraim said, "Let me cross over," the men of Gilead asked him, "Are you an Ephraimite?" If he replied, "No," ⁶they said, "All right, say 'Shibboleth.'" If he said, "Sibboleth," because he could not pronounce the word correctly, they seized him and killed him at the fords of the Jordan. Forty-two thousand Ephraimites were killed at that time.

⁷Jephthah led*ᵃ* Israel six years. Then Jephthah the Gileadite died, and was buried in a town in Gilead.

Ibzan, Elon and Abdon

⁸After him, Ibzan of Bethlehem led Israel. ⁹He had thirty sons and thirty daughters. He gave his daughters away in marriage to those outside his clan, and for his sons he brought in thirty young women as wives from outside his clan. Ibzan led Israel seven years. ¹⁰Then Ibzan died, and was buried in Bethlehem.

¹¹After him, Elon the Zebulunite led Israel ten years. ¹²Then Elon died, and was buried in Aijalon in the land of Zebulun.

¹³After him, Abdon son of Hillel, from Pirathon, led Israel. ¹⁴He had forty sons and thirty grandsons, who rode on seventy donkeys. He led Israel eight years. ¹⁵Then Abdon son of Hillel died, and was buried at Pirathon in Ephraim, in the hill country of the Amalekites.

ᵃ7 Traditionally *judged*; also in verses 8-14

☕ Judging from the speech accent of group members, how many states or countries are represented in your group?

📖 1. Compare 12:1–3 with 8:1–3. What seems to be Ephraim's point? Why are they prone to avoid the battle and criticize the victor? How do Jephthah and Gideon differ in their responses? 2. Apparently, the Ephraimites used a dialect which did not use "sh." How would you assess Jephthah's "Shibboleth" test? Did he get carried away in response to what they said to him (v. 4)? Or did Ephraim have it coming? Explain. 3. What is the object lesson here?

♡ 1. Who is a thorn in your side? How do you suppose Christ wants you to deal with this person? 2. By what "accent" can others tell you are a believer?

📖 1. Of the three men, who stands out? Why? 2. What is to be praised or questioned here?

♡ If you could choose three things about which you would like to be remembered, what would they be? How would those distinguish you from your brothers or sisters?

The Birth of Samson

13 Again the Israelites did evil in the eyes of the LORD, so the LORD delivered them into the hands of the Philistines for forty years.

²A certain man of Zorah, named Manoah, from the clan of the Danites, had a wife who was sterile and remained childless. ³The angel of the LORD appeared to her and said, "You are sterile and childless, but you are going to conceive and have a son. ⁴Now see to it that you drink no wine or other fermented drink and that you do not eat anything unclean, ⁵because you will conceive and give birth to a son. No razor may be used on his head, because the boy is to be a Nazirite, set apart to God from birth, and he will begin the deliverance of Israel from the hands of the Philistines."

⁶Then the woman went to her husband and told him, "A man of God came to me. He looked like an angel of God, very awesome. I didn't ask him where he came from, and he didn't tell me his name. ⁷But he said to me, 'You will conceive and give birth to a son. Now then, drink no wine or other fermented drink and do not eat anything unclean, because the boy will be a Nazirite of God from birth until the day of his death.'"

⁸Then Manoah prayed to the LORD: "O Lord, I beg you, let the man of God you sent to us come again to teach us how to bring up the boy who is to be born."

⁹God heard Manoah, and the angel of God came again to the woman while she was out in the field; but her husband Manoah was not with her. ¹⁰The woman hurried to tell her husband, "He's here! The man who appeared to me the other day!"

¹¹Manoah got up and followed his wife. When he came to the man, he said, "Are you the one who talked to my wife?"

"I am," he said.

Fill in the (blanks): "I was born on (date) in (place) to (mother) and (father). My favorite childhood game to play was _____. One thing that sets me apart from other people is _____."

1. Here's the seventh cycle of apostasy. Same song, seventh verse, only the names have been changed. The enemy is now the Philistines. What do you know about their power? Their most famous agent (Goliath)? **2.** Here the people do not cry out for help. Why is that? What substitutes for that typical part of the cycle? **3.** What parallels do you see between Samson's birth and that of Isaac, Samuel, John the Baptist and Jesus? What do you make of that? **4.** How would you assess the spirituality of Samson's parents: Fanatic fundamentalist? Committed Calvinist? Lukewarm Lutheran? Methodical Methodist? Angelic Amish? Other? **5.** How do you assess the quality of this husband-wife, mother-father team? Who seems more devout? More level-headed? More insightful? Explain. **6.** What three vows does the Nazirite make in Nu 6:1–21? (Samson will break all three.) **7.** What is the purpose of this separation and abstinence? Is it to be temporary or life-long? **8.**

Judges 13:1–25   **SAMSON'S BIRTH**

1. Where were you in your family birth order? How did your parents feel knowing you were on the way?

2. Why did the Israelites do evil in God's sight?
   a. It was becoming a habit.
   b. They lacked leadership.
   c. Success made them complacent.
   d. There were so many gods for them to choose from.

3. Why did God give this childless couple a special child?
   a. to deliver Israel from the Philistines
   b. because he felt sorry for them
   c. because he loved them
   d. because of their faith
   e. because he thought they would be good parents

4. If you received the message in verses 3–5, how would you respond?
   a. "Thank you, thank you, thank you, thank you!"
   b. "Would you put that in writing?"

c. "I'm not worthy of this."
d. "How long must I follow this diet?"
e. "This is too good to be true."

5. When it comes to parenting, how would you describe Manoah and his wife?
   a. clueless
   b. teachable
   c. prepared
   d. disciplined
   e. God-fearing

6. How would you describe yourself as a parent or potential parent?

7. If you were Samson, how would you feel about being a life-long Nazirite?
   a. "What a drag!"
   b. "What an honor!"
   c. "What a responsibility!"
   d. "I wish I could have had a choice."
   e. "I wish I could get a hair cut."

8. What was the purpose of Samson being a Nazirite?

a. to keep him from having fun
b. to set him apart from others
c. to set him apart for God
d. to keep his focus on his mission
e. to keep him focused on the Lord

9. How do you attempt to separate yourself from the world and set yourself apart to God?

10. What ministry or task has God set you apart to fulfill? How is the Spirit of the Lord stirring you to action?

11. If you could have one thing from this story, what would it be?
   a. a child
   b. a child committed to the Lord
   c. God's instruction on "how to bring up" my children
   d. deliverance from an enemy
   e. a visit from an angel
   f. an intimate encounter with God
   g. a special mission in life
   h. for the Holy Spirit to be more active in my life

What does this chapter teach you about the nature and ministry of angels?

1. From what you know about those who are "set apart" from birth to serve the Lord, what are its benefits? Its potential drawbacks? 2. How do you go about "separating yourself" to be with God but apart from the world (see Jn 17:13–19)? What aspects of that vow would you keep or alter for you (or your children) in order to best serve the Lord? 3. In what way do you feel separated from others through no choice of your own? How is this separation affecting you and your ministry? 4. Who was the calming, level-headed force in your family when you were a child? And now? Who was the spiritually devout influence then? Now? 5. How can you open yourself to the ministry of angels: (a) Entertain more visitors? (b) Obey what I already have been given to do by God? (c) Believe by faith what is "beyond understanding"?

1. Growing up what friend of yours were your parents not too thrilled about? Did you persist in seeing him or her? 2. What was your first or most romantic moment?

1. It was lust at first sight and Samson turned the arrangements over to his parents. Why would they object to Samson's wishes: Timing? Racism? Generation gap? Lord's prohibition (see 3:5–6; Ex 34:11–16; Dt 7:1–4)? 2. What do you think of Samson taking matters (lion, woman, honey) into his own hands? What were his positive qualities? His negative ones? 3. In touching a dead body (vv. 8–9) and in throwing a drinking party (v. 10), what two Nazirite vows is Samson breaking (see Nu 6:1–8)? From this picture so far, how do you assess Samson as a Nazirite (on a scale of 1–10)? How does Samson's cavalier attitude toward holy vows fit in with these times that Israel had no king (21:25)? 4. What does verse 4 tell

¹²So Manoah asked him, "When your words are fulfilled, what is to be the rule for the boy's life and work?"

¹³The angel of the LORD answered, "Your wife must do all that I have told her. ¹⁴She must not eat anything that comes from the grapevine, nor drink any wine or other fermented drink nor eat anything unclean. She must do everything I have commanded her."

¹⁵Manoah said to the angel of the LORD, "We would like you to stay until we prepare a young goat for you."

¹⁶The angel of the LORD replied, "Even though you detain me, I will not eat any of your food. But if you prepare a burnt offering, offer it to the LORD." (Manoah did not realize that it was the angel of the LORD.)

¹⁷Then Manoah inquired of the angel of the LORD, "What is your name, so that we may honor you when your word comes true?"

¹⁸He replied, "Why do you ask my name? It is beyond understanding.ᵃ" ¹⁹Then Manoah took a young goat, together with the grain offering, and sacrificed it on a rock to the LORD. And the LORD did an amazing thing while Manoah and his wife watched: ²⁰As the flame blazed up from the altar toward heaven, the angel of the LORD ascended in the flame. Seeing this, Manoah and his wife fell with their faces to the ground. ²¹When the angel of the LORD did not show himself again to Manoah and his wife, Manoah realized that it was the angel of the LORD.

²²"We are doomed to die!" he said to his wife. "We have seen God!"

²³But his wife answered, "If the LORD had meant to kill us, he would not have accepted a burnt offering and grain offering from our hands, nor shown us all these things or now told us this."

²⁴The woman gave birth to a boy and named him Samson. He grew and the LORD blessed him, ²⁵and the Spirit of the LORD began to stir him while he was in Mahaneh Dan, between Zorah and Eshtaol.

Samson's Marriage

14 Samson went down to Timnah and saw there a young Philistine woman. ²When he returned, he said to his father and mother, "I have seen a Philistine woman in Timnah; now get her for me as my wife."

³His father and mother replied, "Isn't there an acceptable woman among your relatives or among all our people? Must you go to the uncircumcised Philistines to get a wife?"

But Samson said to his father, "Get her for me. She's the right one for me." ⁴(His parents did not know that this was from the LORD, who was seeking an occasion to confront the Philistines; for at that time they were ruling over Israel.) ⁵Samson went down to Timnah together with his father and mother. As they approached the vineyards of Timnah, suddenly a young lion came roaring toward him. ⁶The Spirit of the LORD came upon him in power so that he tore the lion apart with his bare hands as he might have torn a young goat. But he told neither his father nor his mother what he had done. ⁷Then he went down and talked with the woman, and he liked her.

⁸Some time later, when he went back to marry her, he turned aside to look at the lion's carcass. In it was a swarm of bees and some honey, ⁹which he scooped out with his hands and ate as he went along. When he rejoined his parents, he gave them some, and

ᵃ18 Or *is wonderful*

they too ate it. But he did not tell them that he had taken the honey from the lion's carcass.

[10]Now his father went down to see the woman. And Samson made a feast there, as was customary for bridegrooms. [11]When he appeared, he was given thirty companions.

[12]"Let me tell you a riddle," Samson said to them. "If you can give me the answer within the seven days of the feast, I will give you thirty linen garments and thirty sets of clothes. [13]If you can't tell me the answer, you must give me thirty linen garments and thirty sets of clothes."

"Tell us your riddle," they said. "Let's hear it."

[14]He replied,

> "Out of the eater, something to eat;
> out of the strong, something sweet."

For three days they could not give the answer.

[15]On the fourth[a] day, they said to Samson's wife, "Coax your husband into explaining the riddle for us, or we will burn you and your father's household to death. Did you invite us here to rob us?"

[16]Then Samson's wife threw herself on him, sobbing, "You hate me! You don't really love me. You've given my people a riddle, but you haven't told me the answer."

"I haven't even explained it to my father or mother," he replied, "so why should I explain it to you?" [17]She cried the whole seven days of the feast. So on the seventh day he finally told her, because

[a]15 Some Septuagint manuscripts and Syriac; Hebrew *seventh*

you about the providence or sovereignty of God? Does this mean intermarriage with a Canaanite was "right" for Samson (or anyone else)? Why or why not? **5.** What do you think of the party Samson threw? And his party game, the riddle? **6.** Was Samson justified in killing 30 men of Ashkelon (a Philistine city) to make good on his bet? Why? How do you account for his being enabled by God to do this (v. 19)? **7.** As the chapter ends, do you get the sense that Samson is "A Man of God"? "A Man For All Seasons"? Or "A Man Out of Control"? Why?

1. In your life, where would you like to experience more self-control? Choose one area in which you can have your small group keep you accountable. **2.** What once seemed "right for you," but in hindsight proved to be more wrong than right? What would you do over, if you could? What good has God brought out of that occasion, after all? What comfort has he brought you in that? **3.** As this chapter ends, can you hear Samson's folks saying, "I told you so"? What would your parents have

---

 Judges 14:1–20   **SAMSON'S MARRIAGE**

Before Samson was born, the Lord told his parents he would be "set apart" and used by God in delivering Israel from the Philistines' oppression.

1. What drew Samson to this woman?
   a. love at first sight   c. her charm
   b. lust at first sight   d. his rebellion

2. Why did Samson's parents object to his choice for a wife?
   a. They wanted to make the choice.
   b. Philistines were their enemies.
   c. They were prejudiced.
   d. She wasn't a believer.
   e. God told the Israelites not to marry Philistines.

3. If you were Samson's parents, what would you have done about his plans?
   a. put my foot down
   b. tried to reason with him
   c. let him make his own decisions
   d. asked God for direction

4. If you were Samson's parents, what would you have done at the end of the story?
   a. said "I told you so"

   b. given him space
   c. given him a hug
   d. given him a piece of my mind
   e. tried to help him learn from this

5. Samson's wife tried to get him to explain the riddle because she:
   a. loved riddles.
   b. didn't want secrets between them.
   c. was blackmailed.
   d. was a nag.
   e. was scared.
   f. was a manipulator.

6. What does "this was from the Lord" (v. 4) mean?
   a. God had the whole thing planned.
   b. God had everything under control.
   c. God wanted Samson to marry this woman.
   d. God allowed him to marry her so he could punish the Philistines.
   e. God used Samson's sinful choices for his purposes.

7. How often do you, like Samson, take matters into your own hands? How can you tell if you're "in the flesh" or empowered by God's Spirit?

8. What has been the greatest temptation to lose your discipline in your dating life?
   a. being attracted to unbelievers
   b. going too much by appearances
   c. ignoring my parents' (or others') advice
   d. deceiving myself into thinking that this is "the right one for me"
   e. falling for manipulators
   f. letting physical desire control my decisions

9. How is this story like your parents (and what can you do about it)?
   a. They want to run my life.
   b. They don't like my friends.
   c. We never have these problems.
   d. I may not like it, but my parents do what they think is best for me.

10. In what way is your relationship with your teen like, and unlike, this story? How do you deal with your child when he or she makes decisions you don't approve of—particularly in the area of relationships?

said? What do you hear Samson saying in his defense? What similar after-the-fact rationalizations do you use? What do you hear his wife saying, once her duplicity is exposed? **4.** When have you used the tactic, "If you really loved me, you would _____?"

🍵 **1.** Do you find yourself putting out fires, or starting them? **2.** What or who tends to tie you up in knots?

📖 **1.** Who's fault is the snafu between Samson and his wife (vv. 1–2; see ch. 14)? **2.** Samson says, "This time I have a right to get even" (v. 3). Is this true or false? What does that imply about his previous action? Is revenge ever a "right"? Explain. **3.** What strikes you about Samson torching Philistine fields: Ingenious tactic? Sweet revenge? Horror over the animal cruelty? Typical of what Israelites do when there's no king on the throne? How so? **4.** If Samson's wife were interviewed on your evening news after the fields burnt, what would she say? **5.** At this juncture, who seems to be the enemy for the Israelites: Samson? The Philistines? Both? **6.** Why is Samson so calm when corralled by 3000 of his own countrymen (vv. 11–13)? What's his "secret"? **7.** How would the Israelites have reacted to Samson breaking free and killing 1000 Philistines: With glee? Fear? Anger? Guilt? Why do you think so? **8.** How might these incidents be related to Samson leading (or judging) his people for 20 more years (v. 20)? **9.** What does Samson's prayer, God's response and Samson's long term in office tell you about their relationship (vv. 18–20)?

❤️ **1.** When have you burned with righteous indignation? What is your fuse like: Long? Short? Like a foxtail? **2.** When have you been in on a vicious cycle of revenge? How did it feel? Where

she continued to press him. She in turn explained the riddle to her people.

¹⁸Before sunset on the seventh day the men of the town said to him,

> "What is sweeter than honey?
> What is stronger than a lion?"

Samson said to them,

> "If you had not plowed with my heifer,
> you would not have solved my riddle."

¹⁹Then the Spirit of the LORD came upon him in power. He went down to Ashkelon, struck down thirty of their men, stripped them of their belongings and gave their clothes to those who had explained the riddle. Burning with anger, he went up to his father's house. ²⁰And Samson's wife was given to the friend who had attended him at his wedding.

Samson's Vengeance on the Philistines

15 Later on, at the time of wheat harvest, Samson took a young goat and went to visit his wife. He said, "I'm going to my wife's room." But her father would not let him go in.

²"I was so sure you thoroughly hated her," he said, "that I gave her to your friend. Isn't her younger sister more attractive? Take her instead."

³Samson said to them, "This time I have a right to get even with the Philistines; I will really harm them." ⁴So he went out and caught three hundred foxes and tied them tail to tail in pairs. He then fastened a torch to every pair of tails, ⁵lit the torches and let the foxes loose in the standing grain of the Philistines. He burned up the shocks and standing grain, together with the vineyards and olive groves.

⁶When the Philistines asked, "Who did this?" they were told, "Samson, the Timnite's son-in-law, because his wife was given to his friend."

So the Philistines went up and burned her and her father to death. ⁷Samson said to them, "Since you've acted like this, I won't stop until I get my revenge on you." ⁸He attacked them viciously and slaughtered many of them. Then he went down and stayed in a cave in the rock of Etam.

⁹The Philistines went up and camped in Judah, spreading out near Lehi. ¹⁰The men of Judah asked, "Why have you come to fight us?"

"We have come to take Samson prisoner," they answered, "to do to him as he did to us."

¹¹Then three thousand men from Judah went down to the cave in the rock of Etam and said to Samson, "Don't you realize that the Philistines are rulers over us? What have you done to us?"

He answered, "I merely did to them what they did to me."

¹²They said to him, "We've come to tie you up and hand you over to the Philistines."

Samson said, "Swear to me that you won't kill me yourselves."

¹³"Agreed," they answered. "We will only tie you up and hand you over to them. We will not kill you." So they bound him with two new ropes and led him up from the rock. ¹⁴As he approached Lehi, the Philistines came toward him shouting. The Spirit of the LORD came upon him in power. The ropes on his arms became like charred flax, and the bindings dropped from his hands. ¹⁵Finding a

fresh jawbone of a donkey, he grabbed it and struck down a thousand men.

[16]Then Samson said,

> "With a donkey's jawbone
> I have made donkeys of them.[a]
> With a donkey's jawbone
> I have killed a thousand men."

[17]When he finished speaking, he threw away the jawbone; and the place was called Ramath Lehi.[b]

[18]Because he was very thirsty, he cried out to the LORD, "You have given your servant this great victory. Must I now die of thirst and fall into the hands of the uncircumcised?" [19]Then God opened up the hollow place in Lehi, and water came out of it. When Samson drank, his strength returned and he revived. So the spring was called En Hakkore,[c] and it is still there in Lehi.

[20]Samson led[d] Israel for twenty years in the days of the Philistines.

Samson and Delilah

16 One day Samson went to Gaza, where he saw a prostitute. He went in to spend the night with her. [2]The people of Gaza were told, "Samson is here!" So they surrounded the place and lay in wait for him all night at the city gate. They made no move during the night, saying, "At dawn we'll kill him."

[3]But Samson lay there only until the middle of the night. Then he got up and took hold of the doors of the city gate, together with the two posts, and tore them loose, bar and all. He lifted them to his shoulders and carried them to the top of the hill that faces Hebron.

[4]Some time later, he fell in love with a woman in the Valley of Sorek whose name was Delilah. [5]The rulers of the Philistines went to her and said, "See if you can lure him into showing you the secret of his great strength and how we can overpower him so we may tie him up and subdue him. Each one of us will give you eleven hundred shekels[e] of silver."

[6]So Delilah said to Samson, "Tell me the secret of your great strength and how you can be tied up and subdued."

[7]Samson answered her, "If anyone ties me with seven fresh thongs[f] that have not been dried, I'll become as weak as any other man."

[8]Then the rulers of the Philistines brought her seven fresh thongs that had not been dried, and she tied him with them. [9]With men hidden in the room, she called to him, "Samson, the Philistines are upon you!" But he snapped the thongs as easily as a piece of string snaps when it comes close to a flame. So the secret of his strength was not discovered.

[10]Then Delilah said to Samson, "You have made a fool of me; you lied to me. Come now, tell me how you can be tied."

[11]He said, "If anyone ties me securely with new ropes that have never been used, I'll become as weak as any other man."

[12]So Delilah took new ropes and tied him with them. Then, with men hidden in the room, she called to him, "Samson, the Philistines are upon you!" But he snapped the ropes off his arms as if they were threads.

1. What hair styles have you adopted over the years? When was your hair the shortest? Longest? Kinkiest? 2. Share an April Fool's joke in which you were completely taken in or caught off guard.

1. Gaza was a Philistine city, so why would Samson venture anywhere near such a place: Death wish? Tempting fate? Cockiness? Carelessness? 2. This time (in Gaza), Samson only steals the city gates instead of waging war on the Philistines. What's the meaning of this more symbolic, less violent, response? 3. What did Delilah and Samson have going for them as a couple? What was working against them? 4. What are some possible reasons why Samson did not answer Delilah truthfully until well after her fourth query? Why did he finally give in? 5. Do you think he knew what would then happen (v. 20)? How could Samson be taken in by a woman like this and thus forsake the third of his three vows? Do you see this as tragic? Comic? Ironic? How is this incident typical of the evil chaotic times when Israel had no king (see 21:25)? 6. What likely was going through Samson's mind when he first became aware? When he became blind? When his hair began to grow back?

1. Everyone has their price. How rich was Delilah after this deal (v. 5; see 17:2,10, where ten silver shekels is a priest's annual wages)? How do you imagine Delilah felt about betraying her lover and Israel's deliverer: Sad? Guilty? Numb? Suicidal? In this re-

3. In the ancient Near East, "cities of refuge" were set up to avert endless cycles of revenge (see Jos 20). Samson's wife and her father could have used one. What similar refuge could you use to escape the cycle of revenge "the next time"? 4. Where could you use the Spirit of the Lord to empower you? 5. Where could you use God's thirst-quenching water to revive you?

---

[a]16 Or *made a heap or two*; the Hebrew for *donkey* sounds like the Hebrew for *heap.*
[b]17 *Ramath Lehi* means *jawbone hill.*   [c]19 *En Hakkore* means *caller's spring.*
[d]20 Traditionally *judged*   [e]5 That is, about 28 pounds (about 13 kilograms)
[f]7 Or *bowstrings*; also in verses 8 and 9

gard, how did Judas feel after betraying Jesus (see Mt 27:1–5)? How would you feel in a similar situation? What's your price? Draw from any personal experience you have. **2.** Every strength has its flip side. While Samson had obvious physical strength, what strength was he lacking? What strength are you lacking? Where do you feel like Samson—bound and hoping your hair is growing back? **3.** What positively affects your spiritual strength? What is draining it? How can your small group add and not subtract from that strength? **4.** Where is God calling you to persist, even harass, until you get what you want? Ask yourself: Is that what God wants for me? **5.** What has been nagging at you lately and wearing you down?

[13]Delilah then said to Samson, "Until now, you have been making a fool of me and lying to me. Tell me how you can be tied."

He replied, "If you weave the seven braids of my head into the fabric ⌐on the loom⌐ and tighten it with the pin, I'll become as weak as any other man." So while he was sleeping, Delilah took the seven braids of his head, wove them into the fabric [14]and[a] tightened it with the pin.

Again she called to him, "Samson, the Philistines are upon you!" He awoke from his sleep and pulled up the pin and the loom, with the fabric.

[15]Then she said to him, "How can you say, 'I love you,' when you won't confide in me? This is the third time you have made a fool of me and haven't told me the secret of your great strength." [16]With such nagging she prodded him day after day until he was tired to death.

[17]So he told her everything. "No razor has ever been used on my head," he said, "because I have been a Nazirite set apart to God since birth. If my head were shaved, my strength would leave me, and I would become as weak as any other man."

[18]When Delilah saw that he had told her everything, she sent word to the rulers of the Philistines, "Come back once more; he has told me everything." So the rulers of the Philistines returned with the silver in their hands. [19]Having put him to sleep on her lap, she called a man to shave off the seven braids of his hair, and so began to subdue him.[b] And his strength left him.

[a] 13,14 Some Septuagint manuscripts; Hebrew *"⌐I can⌐ if you weave the seven braids of my head into the fabric ⌐on the loom⌐."* [14]*So she* [b] 19 Hebrew; some Septuagint manuscripts *and he began to weaken*

 Judges 16:1–22 **SAMSON AND DELILAH**

Samson—who had led his people against the Philistines—had incited Israel's enemy by his heroic exploits.

1. What would you title this passage?
   a. Sleeping With the Enemy
   b. Fatal Attraction
   c. Money, Sex and Power
   d. Macho Man Meets His Match

2. What was Samson's downfall?
   a. his sexual appetites
   b. his attraction to Philistine women
   c. his inability to keep his secret
   d. his overconfidence
   e. Delilah's betrayal
   f. his betrayal of God's calling

3. How could Delilah do what she did?
   a. She only pretended to love him.
   b. She was a patriotic Philistine.
   c. She was cold and ruthless.
   d. She took it as a personal challenge.
   e. Everyone has their price.
   f. She didn't realize the Philistines would be so cruel to Samson.

4. What could Samson expect to gain by sharing his secret?

   a. a trusting relationship
   b. relief from the stress of keeping it
   c. Delilah's acceptance
   d. peace and quiet

5. Why did shaving his head cost Samson his power?
   a. His strength was in his hair.
   b. His secret was out.
   c. His vow to God was broken.
   d. The symbol of his being set apart to God was scorned.

6. What was the worst thing that happened to Samson?
   a. He lost his hair.
   b. He lost his honor.
   c. He lost his lover.
   d. He lost his Lord.
   e. He lost his eyes.

7. When have you used the tactic, "If you really loved me, you would _____"?
   a. with my boyfriend/girlfriend
   b. with my spouse
   c. with my parents
   d. with my children
   e. with God

8. What is the secret of your spiritual strength?
   a. daily aerobics
   b. regular prayer
   c. Bible reading
   d. awareness of my weaknesses
   e. a Christian upbringing

9. I feel weakest against temptation when it is:
   a. subtle.
   b. persistent.
   c. particularly attractive.
   d. perfectly reasonable.
   e. something new.
   f. the same old thing.

10. Did Samson operate out of love or lust? What about Delilah? What was missing in this "love" relationship? What makes sex an act of true love?

11. How could Samson better have handled his hormones? Ask yourself the same question; and close with silent prayer—asking God for help, strength, forgiveness, guidance, etc.

20Then she called, "Samson, the Philistines are upon you!"

He awoke from his sleep and thought, "I'll go out as before and shake myself free." But he did not know that the L ORD had left him. **21**Then the Philistines seized him, gouged out his eyes and took him down to Gaza. Binding him with bronze shackles, they set him to grinding in the prison. **22**But the hair on his head began to grow again after it had been shaved.

The Death of Samson

23Now the rulers of the Philistines assembled to offer a great sacrifice to Dagon their god and to celebrate, saying, "Our god has delivered Samson, our enemy, into our hands."

24When the people saw him, they praised their god, saying,

> "Our god has delivered our enemy
>   into our hands,
> the one who laid waste our land
>   and multiplied our slain."

25While they were in high spirits, they shouted, "Bring out Samson to entertain us." So they called Samson out of the prison, and he performed for them.

When they stood him among the pillars, **26**Samson said to the servant who held his hand, "Put me where I can feel the pillars that support the temple, so that I may lean against them." **27**Now the temple was crowded with men and women; all the rulers of the Philistines were there, and on the roof were about three thousand men and women watching Samson perform. **28**Then Samson prayed to the L ORD, "O Sovereign L ORD, remember me. O God, please strengthen me just once more, and let me with one blow get revenge on the Philistines for my two eyes." **29**Then Samson

1. This past week, when and why were you in "high spirits"? 2. What "entertains" you the most?

1. Why didn't the Philistines kill Samson? Why play with him? 2. What does the crowd's mood remind you of? Any modern parallels? 3. What is the object lesson in Samson's prayer life? In his moral life? In his death (v. 30)? 4. Why would God use such a man as this?

1. If a Christian's witness includes "dying well," what witness did Samson have? How do you suppose he was eulogized? How can you prepare yourself to "die well"? 2. What's the relation between "living well" and "dying well," as typified by Samson? Like Samson, where do you feel like you are merely "performing," and not really "living"? 3. What would

---

Judges 16:23–31   **SAMSON'S DEATH**

Samson—the champion of Israel—had been captured by the Philistines, blinded, shackled and relegated to the lowly task of grinding grain.

1. Who was responsible for Samson's demise?
   a. Dagon
   b. Delilah
   c. Samson
   d. the man who shaved Samson's hair off
   e. the Lord

2. Why didn't the Philistines kill Samson?
   a. It gave them a slave to grind grain.
   b. Humiliating him was more fun.
   c. They didn't believe in capital punishment.
   d. They wanted to relish his defeat.
   e. The Lord had other plans.

3. Why did God answer Samson's prayer?
   a. because Samson's hair had begun to grow again

b. because Samson had repented
c. to save face
d. to kill a multitude of Philistines
e. to give Samson revenge
f. to fulfill Samson's destiny
g. to put Samson out of his misery

4. From what you know of Samson, how would you describe him?
   a. strong
   b. weak
   c. driven by his calling
   d. driven by his hormones
   e. filled with the Spirit
   f. filled with himself
   g. a riddle

5. What would you say to the boy who says, "I want to grow up to be like Samson"?

6. The most tragic thing about Samson's life was that he:
   a. lost his eyesight.
   b. lost sight of being set apart to God.
   c. never realized his potential.
   d. woke up and discovered to his shock "that the Lord had left him."

e. died in his prime.
f. surely broke his parents' hearts.

7. What was the most redeeming thing about Samson's life?
   a. He went down swinging.
   b. God used him in spite of his faults.
   c. The New Testament includes him as a hero of faith (Heb 11:32).
   d. Through him God brought justice.
   e. He was dependent on God's Spirit to perform mighty exploits.

8. What has been, or is, the most tragic thing about your life? What has been, or is, the most redeeming?

9. What is your greatest strength that God can use? How can that strength become a weakness? How can you keep it from being your downfall?

10. Where do you feel weak? How do you sense God using you in spite of this? What could energize you? How could this group help strengthen you?

you say to your son who says, "I want to grow up to be like Samson"? **4.** Like Samson, if you could pray for but *one* thing to happen, what would that be? Pray as a group.

---

1. Why did Micah confess what he had done? Was he principled or pragmatic? **2.** What do you think of his mom's response? **3.** What does her use of the 200 shekels say about spiritual values in Micah's home (see Ex 20:1–5)? **4.** What was the spiritual climate of the times (v. 6; see 21:25)? What modern parallels does this bring to mind? **5.** What's wrong with the bargain which Micah struck with the young Levite (see Dt 12:4,14)? How does the 10 shekels compare with the 1100 shekels he stole? What does this tell us about the character of Micah? Of the young Levite? Who's lazy? Greedy? Naive? Desperate? **6.** What bottom line assumption is Micah operating under? Is that true or false?

1. Is this a story of "honesty pays"? "Spare the rod, spoil the child"? "I've got the priest in my pocket"? Or what? **2.** If you were to create God in your own image, what qualities would you include? And exclude? In what way might you be doing this very thing now?

1. Where would you like to retire? Why there? **2.** What prized possession did you used to fight over with "big brother" or "big sister" and hated giving up? How did you feel being short-changed or left empty-handed? **3.** "An offer you couldn't refuse" in your career field would be an offer to _____?

1. Why had the Danites not yet come into their inheritance (v. 1; see 1:34 and Jos 19:40–48)? **2.** How is it "they recognized the voice" of the priest (v. 3)? Had the warriors of Dan known him before? Was he on their *most-wanted list*? Or what? **3.** Instead of roughing him up or restor-

---

reached toward the two central pillars on which the temple stood. Bracing himself against them, his right hand on the one and his left hand on the other, ³⁰Samson said, "Let me die with the Philistines!" Then he pushed with all his might, and down came the temple on the rulers and all the people in it. Thus he killed many more when he died than while he lived.

³¹Then his brothers and his father's whole family went down to get him. They brought him back and buried him between Zorah and Eshtaol in the tomb of Manoah his father. He had led*ᵃ* Israel twenty years.

Micah's Idols

17 Now a man named Micah from the hill country of Ephraim ²said to his mother, "The eleven hundred shekels*ᵇ* of silver that were taken from you and about which I heard you utter a curse—I have that silver with me; I took it."

Then his mother said, "The LORD bless you, my son!"

³When he returned the eleven hundred shekels of silver to his mother, she said, "I solemnly consecrate my silver to the LORD for my son to make a carved image and a cast idol. I will give it back to you."

⁴So he returned the silver to his mother, and she took two hundred shekels*ᶜ* of silver and gave them to a silversmith, who made them into the image and the idol. And they were put in Micah's house.

⁵Now this man Micah had a shrine, and he made an ephod and some idols and installed one of his sons as his priest. ⁶In those days Israel had no king; everyone did as he saw fit.

⁷A young Levite from Bethlehem in Judah, who had been living within the clan of Judah, ⁸left that town in search of some other place to stay. On his way*ᵈ* he came to Micah's house in the hill country of Ephraim.

⁹Micah asked him, "Where are you from?"

"I'm a Levite from Bethlehem in Judah," he said, "and I'm looking for a place to stay."

¹⁰Then Micah said to him, "Live with me and be my father and priest, and I'll give you ten shekels*ᵉ* of silver a year, your clothes and your food." ¹¹So the Levite agreed to live with him, and the young man was to him like one of his sons. ¹²Then Micah installed the Levite, and the young man became his priest and lived in his house. ¹³And Micah said, "Now I know that the LORD will be good to me, since this Levite has become my priest."

Danites Settle in Laish

18 In those days Israel had no king.
And in those days the tribe of the Danites was seeking a place of their own where they might settle, because they had not yet come into an inheritance among the tribes of Israel. ²So the Danites sent five warriors from Zorah and Eshtaol to spy out the land and explore it. These men represented all their clans. They told them, "Go, explore the land."

The men entered the hill country of Ephraim and came to the house of Micah, where they spent the night. ³When they were near Micah's house, they recognized the voice of the young Levite; so they turned in there and asked him, "Who brought you here? What are you doing in this place? Why are you here?"

ᵃ31 Traditionally *judged*   *ᵇ2* That is, about 28 pounds (about 13 kilograms)
ᶜ4 That is, about 5 pounds (about 2.3 kilograms)   *ᵈ8* Or *To carry on his profession*
ᵉ10 That is, about 4 ounces (about 110 grams)

[4]He told them what Micah had done for him, and said, "He has hired me and I am his priest."

[5]Then they said to him, "Please inquire of God to learn whether our journey will be successful."

[6]The priest answered them, "Go in peace. Your journey has the LORD's approval."

[7]So the five men left and came to Laish, where they saw that the people were living in safety, like the Sidonians, unsuspecting and secure. And since their land lacked nothing, they were prosperous.[a] Also, they lived a long way from the Sidonians and had no relationship with anyone else.[b]

[8]When they returned to Zorah and Eshtaol, their brothers asked them, "How did you find things?"

[9]They answered, "Come on, let's attack them! We have seen that the land is very good. Aren't you going to do something? Don't hesitate to go there and take it over. [10]When you get there, you will find an unsuspecting people and a spacious land that God has put into your hands, a land that lacks nothing whatever."

[11]Then six hundred men from the clan of the Danites, armed for battle, set out from Zorah and Eshtaol. [12]On their way they set up camp near Kiriath Jearim in Judah. This is why the place west of Kiriath Jearim is called Mahaneh Dan[c] to this day. [13]From there they went on to the hill country of Ephraim and came to Micah's house.

[14]Then the five men who had spied out the land of Laish said to their brothers, "Do you know that one of these houses has an ephod, other household gods, a carved image and a cast idol? Now you know what to do." [15]So they turned in there and went to the house of the young Levite at Micah's place and greeted him. [16]The six hundred Danites, armed for battle, stood at the entrance to the gate. [17]The five men who had spied out the land went inside and took the carved image, the ephod, the other household gods and the cast idol while the priest and the six hundred armed men stood at the entrance to the gate.

[18]When these men went into Micah's house and took the carved image, the ephod, the other household gods and the cast idol, the priest said to them, "What are you doing?"

[19]They answered him, "Be quiet! Don't say a word. Come with us, and be our father and priest. Isn't it better that you serve a tribe and clan in Israel as priest rather than just one man's household?" [20]Then the priest was glad. He took the ephod, the other household gods and the carved image and went along with the people. [21]Putting their little children, their livestock and their possessions in front of them, they turned away and left.

[22]When they had gone some distance from Micah's house, the men who lived near Micah were called together and overtook the Danites. [23]As they shouted after them, the Danites turned and said to Micah, "What's the matter with you that you called out your men to fight?"

[24]He replied, "You took the gods I made, and my priest, and went away. What else do I have? How can you ask, 'What's the matter with you?'"

[25]The Danites answered, "Don't argue with us, or some hot-tempered men will attack you, and you and your family will lose your lives." [26]So the Danites went their way, and Micah, seeing that they were too strong for him, turned around and went back home.

[27]Then they took what Micah had made, and his priest, and

ing him to his proper place, what immediate and future use do they have for the Levite and his idols (vv. 5–6,14ff)? Why this priest? Would you buy a used car from this guy (or trust his word that God is with them)? **4.** Why would Danites want his religious paraphernalia? What does this tell you about the spiritual maturity of the Danites? How does this relate to the theme of Judges in 21:25? **5.** Why does the priest go along with them: (a) Vanity? (b) Greed? (c) Career advancement? (d) Arm-twisting? (e) Have idols, will travel? (f) Other? **6.** What about Micah's loss is ironic? Tragic? Comic? **7.** What "cover-up" by later scribes do you detect in verse 30? What difference does it make whether this young Levite is a descendant of Moses or Manasseh? **8.** Rank order the following from bad to worse: The Danites? The priest? Micah? What does that ranking reveal about your scale of values? Why would you rank some higher on the "scum chart" than others? **9.** What future of the tribe of Dan would you forecast based on the presence and persistence of such idolatry? **10.** What is the purpose of this chapter? How is it related to chapter 17? What is the object lesson here? If it were cut out of the book, what would we miss?

♡ **1.** When it comes to job-hunting and career changes, in what sense are you like this young Levite: (a) Selling your services short? (b) Eager for advancement? (c) Other? Explain. **2.** What do like about your current job? What is difficult for you on the job? When a new job offer comes your way, what things will you take into consideration? How can your group members pray for you in this area? **3.** List some of your prized possessions. Which, if any, might you be holding too tightly? Which may be hindering your relationship with God? **4.** Chapters 17–18 demonstrate what happened "in those days [when] Israel had no king." What does that imply for you *these days*? What difference has the presence or absence of a (divine) King made in your life?

---

[a]7 The meaning of the Hebrew for this clause is uncertain.   [b]7 Hebrew; some Septuagint manuscripts *with the Arameans*   [c]12 Mahaneh Dan means *Dan's camp.*

went on to Laish, against a peaceful and unsuspecting people. They attacked them with the sword and burned down their city. [28]There was no one to rescue them because they lived a long way from Sidon and had no relationship with anyone else. The city was in a valley near Beth Rehob.

The Danites rebuilt the city and settled there. [29]They named it Dan after their forefather Dan, who was born to Israel—though the city used to be called Laish. [30]There the Danites set up for themselves the idols, and Jonathan son of Gershom, the son of Moses,[a] and his sons were priests for the tribe of Dan until the time of the captivity of the land. [31]They continued to use the idols Micah had made, all the time the house of God was in Shiloh.

A Levite and His Concubine

19 In those days Israel had no king.
Now a Levite who lived in a remote area in the hill country of Ephraim took a concubine from Bethlehem in Judah. [2]But she was unfaithful to him. She left him and went back to her father's house in Bethlehem, Judah. After she had been there four months, [3]her husband went to her to persuade her to return. He had with him his servant and two donkeys. She took him into her father's house, and when her father saw him, he gladly welcomed him. [4]His father-in-law, the girl's father, prevailed upon him to stay; so he remained with him three days, eating and drinking, and sleeping there.

[5]On the fourth day they got up early and he prepared to leave, but the girl's father said to his son-in-law, "Refresh yourself with something to eat; then you can go." [6]So the two of them sat down to eat and drink together. Afterward the girl's father said, "Please stay tonight and enjoy yourself." [7]And when the man got up to go, his father-in-law persuaded him, so he stayed there that night. [8]On the morning of the fifth day, when he rose to go, the girl's father said, "Refresh yourself. Wait till afternoon!" So the two of them ate together.

[9]Then when the man, with his concubine and his servant, got up to leave, his father-in-law, the girl's father, said, "Now look, it's almost evening. Spend the night here; the day is nearly over. Stay and enjoy yourself. Early tomorrow morning you can get up and be on your way home." [10]But, unwilling to stay another night, the man left and went toward Jebus (that is, Jerusalem), with his two saddled donkeys and his concubine.

[11]When they were near Jebus and the day was almost gone, the servant said to his master, "Come, let's stop at this city of the Jebusites and spend the night."

[12]His master replied, "No. We won't go into an alien city, whose people are not Israelites. We will go on to Gibeah." [13]He added, "Come, let's try to reach Gibeah or Ramah and spend the night in one of those places." [14]So they went on, and the sun set as they neared Gibeah in Benjamin. [15]There they stopped to spend the night. They went and sat in the city square, but no one took them into his home for the night.

[16]That evening an old man from the hill country of Ephraim, who was living in Gibeah (the men of the place were Benjamites), came in from his work in the fields. [17]When he looked and saw the traveler in the city square, the old man asked, "Where are you going? Where did you come from?"

[18]He answered, "We are on our way from Bethlehem in Judah to

---

1. When you travel as a family, do you rough it, go first class, or stay with friends? 2. Among your travels, what ranks as the "Baddest" accommodation you have had? 3. Who is your favorite relative to visit? Why? 4. Have you ever "left home without it"? What would it be, in your case?

1. What is a concubine (see Ge 4:19; 16:2 for examples)? How is a concubine different than a wife? 2. What caused the concubine to return to her father? Why then would the Levite want her back? How long before the Levite decided to go and get her? Why the delay on his part: Disinterest? Dismay? Disinformation? Disgust? Distance? Disloyal? Distress? District Attorney's counsel? 3. What are some possible reasons as to why the father kept asking the Levite to stay longer (vv. 4–10)? 4. It is the Near Eastern custom to be hospitable to strangers. How hospitable were the people of Gibeah? How does that compare with the people of your community? 5. This is Sodom and Gomorrah revisited! Compare and contrast what happens here to Genesis 19. What do you make of the frightening parallels? 6. Why would the old man offer two women, even his own virgin daughter, rather than the Levite whom he had only met that night? Why would he offer to send out anyone at all? 7. Assess the passive and reactive behavior of the Levite in this account. What do you like about him? What do you dislike? 8. What could have motivated the Levite to send a piece of the concubine's body to each tribe of Israel (19:29f; 20:1; see 1Sa 11:7)? 9. Would a king on the throne of Israel have prevented, or at least punished, this kind of evil?

1. This chapter has been called the "Sewer of Scripture." Agree or disagree? What

---

[a]30 An ancient Hebrew scribal tradition, some Septuagint manuscripts and Vulgate; Masoretic Text *Manasseh*

a remote area in the hill country of Ephraim where I live. I have been to Bethlehem in Judah and now I am going to the house of the LORD. No one has taken me into his house. ¹⁹We have both straw and fodder for our donkeys and bread and wine for ourselves your servants—me, your maidservant, and the young man with us. We don't need anything."

²⁰"You are welcome at my house," the old man said. "Let me supply whatever you need. Only don't spend the night in the square." ²¹So he took him into his house and fed his donkeys. After they had washed their feet, they had something to eat and drink.

²²While they were enjoying themselves, some of the wicked men of the city surrounded the house. Pounding on the door, they shouted to the old man who owned the house, "Bring out the man who came to your house so we can have sex with him."

²³The owner of the house went outside and said to them, "No, my friends, don't be so vile. Since this man is my guest, don't do this disgraceful thing. ²⁴Look, here is my virgin daughter, and his concubine. I will bring them out to you now, and you can use them and do to them whatever you wish. But to this man, don't do such a disgraceful thing."

²⁵But the men would not listen to him. So the man took his concubine and sent her outside to them, and they raped her and abused her throughout the night, and at dawn they let her go. ²⁶At daybreak the woman went back to the house where her master was staying, fell down at the door and lay there until daylight.

²⁷When her master got up in the morning and opened the door of the house and stepped out to continue on his way, there lay his concubine, fallen in the doorway of the house, with her hands on the threshold. ²⁸He said to her, "Get up; let's go." But there was no answer. Then the man put her on his donkey and set out for home.

²⁹When he reached home, he took a knife and cut up his concubine, limb by limb, into twelve parts and sent them into all the areas of Israel. ³⁰Everyone who saw it said, "Such a thing has never been seen or done, not since the day the Israelites came up out of Egypt. Think about it! Consider it! Tell us what to do!"

Israelites Fight the Benjamites

20 Then all the Israelites from Dan to Beersheba and from the land of Gilead came out as one man and assembled before the LORD in Mizpah. ²The leaders of all the people of the tribes of Israel took their places in the assembly of the people of God, four hundred thousand soldiers armed with swords. ³(The Benjamites heard that the Israelites had gone up to Mizpah.) Then the Israelites said, "Tell us how this awful thing happened."

⁴So the Levite, the husband of the murdered woman, said, "I and my concubine came to Gibeah in Benjamin to spend the night. ⁵During the night the men of Gibeah came after me and surrounded the house, intending to kill me. They raped my concubine, and she died. ⁶I took my concubine, cut her into pieces and sent one piece to each region of Israel's inheritance, because they committed this lewd and disgraceful act in Israel. ⁷Now, all you Israelites, speak up and give your verdict."

⁸All the people rose as one man, saying, "None of us will go home. No, not one of us will return to his house. ⁹But now this is what we'll do to Gibeah: We'll go up against it as the lot directs. ¹⁰We'll take ten men out of every hundred from all the tribes of Israel, and a hundred from a thousand, and a thousand from ten thousand, to get provisions for the army. Then, when the army

would have cleaned it up? For example, what has Hosea done with this same motif of redeeming a faithless woman (typifying God's faithful love for Israel)? **2.** Judging from last year's social calendar, how would you rate in terms of showing hospitality? Are you a "Welcoming Waldo"? "Tolerant Tess"? "Reluctant Rhoda"? Or "Resentful Ralph"? Give one example. What next step do you and your group want to take in this regard? **3.** What evil or inhumane situation in the world especially galls you? What might God be calling you to do about that? **4.** What can you do about the homeless, the sexual perverts, or the violent crimes in the city near where you live? Write a graphic letter about this. Send it to the appropriate people. What visual aids or other dramatic effects will you enclose?

---

1. Are you more motivated to act by a clarion "call to arms," or by a "war protest" movement? What does that say about you? **2.** What large, unified gathering is most memorable to you: Some rock concert? Sporting event? Parade? Memorial service? Or what? **3.** Who are you: A person who would rather "switch than fight," or "fight than switch"? Give an example.

1. What does it mean that Israel "came out," "rose" and "united" *as one man* (vv. 1,8,11; see 1Sa 11:7–8)? What's the point of such phrases? Who was missing from "all Israel" (see 21:8–9)? **2.** What initially motivated Israel to fight the Benjamites: Revenge? Justice? Adventure? Combat pay? Or what? **3.** How did they select the Israelites to join this battle against their fellow brothers? How do you suppose those selected felt: (a)

"Let me at 'em!"? (b) "How come I always get the short straw"? **4.** Why didn't the Benjamites simply turn over the guilty and thus avoid a bloodbath? What does the Benjamite response tell us about them? **5.** When did the Israelites involve God in this process—before, or after, they had decided to attack Benjamin? Whose side is God on? How do you think this civil war affected God? **6.** What point is God trying to make in allowing the Israelites to fail in their first two attacks? How do the Israelites respond to their initial failures? Are they learning their lesson, or storing up more vengeance? How can you tell? **7.** From the two accounts of this battle, how many Benjamites died in battle? How many were left with which to start over again? **8.** Do you think that in the heat of the battle the Israelites went too far, far enough, or not far enough, in this brother vs. brother war? Why do you think so? What did Israel think (see 21:2–3)? **9.** Read Genesis 49:27, where Jacob blesses the tribe of Benjamin, along with his other sons. In what sense has that blessing now come true?

♡ **1.** What intra-family, in-house or inter-church battles have you have fought recently? What are you still battling today? **2.** Where in your life does God seem to be less than willing to answer a prayer in the way you want it answered? When God says, "Wait" or "Maybe" or "No," how do you handle that? What change on your part is called for? **3.** When in the past five years have you experienced the power of unity, of being "one" with a group of people? Would you say such unity characterizes your small group? Your church? What does your unity enable you to do?

arrives at Gibeah[a] in Benjamin, it can give them what they deserve for all this vileness done in Israel." ¹¹So all the men of Israel got together and united as one man against the city.

¹²The tribes of Israel sent men throughout the tribe of Benjamin, saying, "What about this awful crime that was committed among you? ¹³Now surrender those wicked men of Gibeah so that we may put them to death and purge the evil from Israel."

But the Benjamites would not listen to their fellow Israelites. ¹⁴From their towns they came together at Gibeah to fight against the Israelites. ¹⁵At once the Benjamites mobilized twenty-six thousand swordsmen from their towns, in addition to seven hundred chosen men from those living in Gibeah. ¹⁶Among all these soldiers there were seven hundred chosen men who were left-handed, each of whom could sling a stone at a hair and not miss.

¹⁷Israel, apart from Benjamin, mustered four hundred thousand swordsmen, all of them fighting men.

¹⁸The Israelites went up to Bethel[b] and inquired of God. They said, "Who of us shall go first to fight against the Benjamites?"

The LORD replied, "Judah shall go first."

¹⁹The next morning the Israelites got up and pitched camp near Gibeah. ²⁰The men of Israel went out to fight the Benjamites and took up battle positions against them at Gibeah. ²¹The Benjamites came out of Gibeah and cut down twenty-two thousand Israelites on the battlefield that day. ²²But the men of Israel encouraged one another and again took up their positions where they had stationed themselves the first day. ²³The Israelites went up and wept before the LORD until evening, and they inquired of the LORD. They said, "Shall we go up again to battle against the Benjamites, our brothers?"

The LORD answered, "Go up against them."

²⁴Then the Israelites drew near to Benjamin the second day. ²⁵This time, when the Benjamites came out from Gibeah to oppose them, they cut down another eighteen thousand Israelites, all of them armed with swords.

²⁶Then the Israelites, all the people, went up to Bethel, and there they sat weeping before the LORD. They fasted that day until evening and presented burnt offerings and fellowship offerings[c] to the LORD. ²⁷And the Israelites inquired of the LORD. (In those days the ark of the covenant of God was there, ²⁸with Phinehas son of Eleazar, the son of Aaron, ministering before it.) They asked, "Shall we go up again to battle with Benjamin our brother, or not?"

The LORD responded, "Go, for tomorrow I will give them into your hands."

²⁹Then Israel set an ambush around Gibeah. ³⁰They went up against the Benjamites on the third day and took up positions against Gibeah as they had done before. ³¹The Benjamites came out to meet them and were drawn away from the city. They began to inflict casualties on the Israelites as before, so that about thirty men fell in the open field and on the roads—the one leading to Bethel and the other to Gibeah.

³²While the Benjamites were saying, "We are defeating them as before," the Israelites were saying, "Let's retreat and draw them away from the city to the roads."

³³All the men of Israel moved from their places and took up positions at Baal Tamar, and the Israelite ambush charged out of its

a10 One Hebrew manuscript; most Hebrew manuscripts *Geba*, a variant of *Gibeah*
b18 Or *to the house of God*; also in verse 26   c26 Traditionally *peace offerings*

place on the west[a] of Gibeah.[b] ³⁴Then ten thousand of Israel's finest men made a frontal attack on Gibeah. The fighting was so heavy that the Benjamites did not realize how near disaster was. ³⁵The LORD defeated Benjamin before Israel, and on that day the Israelites struck down 25,100 Benjamites, all armed with swords. ³⁶Then the Benjamites saw that they were beaten.

Now the men of Israel had given way before Benjamin, because they relied on the ambush they had set near Gibeah. ³⁷The men who had been in ambush made a sudden dash into Gibeah, spread out and put the whole city to the sword. ³⁸The men of Israel had arranged with the ambush that they should send up a great cloud of smoke from the city, ³⁹and then the men of Israel would turn in the battle.

The Benjamites had begun to inflict casualties on the men of Israel (about thirty), and they said, "We are defeating them as in the first battle." ⁴⁰But when the column of smoke began to rise from the city, the Benjamites turned and saw the smoke of the whole city going up into the sky. ⁴¹Then the men of Israel turned on them, and the men of Benjamin were terrified, because they realized that disaster had come upon them. ⁴²So they fled before the Israelites in the direction of the desert, but they could not escape the battle. And the men of Israel who came out of the towns cut them down there. ⁴³They surrounded the Benjamites, chased them and easily[c] overran them in the vicinity of Gibeah on the east. ⁴⁴Eighteen thousand Benjamites fell, all of them valiant fighters. ⁴⁵As they turned and fled toward the desert to the rock of Rimmon, the Israelites cut down five thousand men along the roads. They kept pressing after the Benjamites as far as Gidom and struck down two thousand more.

⁴⁶On that day twenty-five thousand Benjamite swordsmen fell, all of them valiant fighters. ⁴⁷But six hundred men turned and fled into the desert to the rock of Rimmon, where they stayed four months. ⁴⁸The men of Israel went back to Benjamin and put all the towns to the sword, including the animals and everything else they found. All the towns they came across they set on fire.

Wives for the Benjamites

21 The men of Israel had taken an oath at Mizpah: "Not one of us will give his daughter in marriage to a Benjamite."

²The people went to Bethel,[d] where they sat before God until evening, raising their voices and weeping bitterly. ³"O LORD, the God of Israel," they cried, "why has this happened to Israel? Why should one tribe be missing from Israel today?"

⁴Early the next day the people built an altar and presented burnt offerings and fellowship offerings.[e]

⁵Then the Israelites asked, "Who from all the tribes of Israel has failed to assemble before the LORD?" For they had taken a solemn oath that anyone who failed to assemble before the LORD at Mizpah should certainly be put to death.

⁶Now the Israelites grieved for their brothers, the Benjamites. "Today one tribe is cut off from Israel," they said. ⁷"How can we provide wives for those who are left, since we have taken an oath by the LORD not to give them any of our daughters in marriage?" ⁸Then they asked, "Which one of the tribes of Israel failed to assemble before the LORD at Mizpah?" They discovered that no one

---

a33 Some Septuagint manuscripts and Vulgate; the meaning of the Hebrew for this word is uncertain.   *b33* Hebrew *Geba,* a variant of *Gibeah*   *c43* The meaning of the Hebrew for this word is uncertain.   *d2* Or *to the house of God*   *e4* Traditionally *peace offerings*

What experience have you had with "match-making"? In your social circles, is it always "boy-ask-girl," or can women also ask men for dates? Are there enough to go around? Or is the deck stacked? Which way? How come?

1. What has triggered second thoughts for Israel? Why are they warring one moment, vowing another and weeping the next? 2. What does this tell you about the fickleness of human nature? The foolishness of war? The seriousness of vows? And the bonds of the covenant? 3. Is Israel to be commended or criticized for *making* this vow? What about for *keeping* this vow, once it is made? 4. In all this, where is God: Keeping their feet to the fire? Letting them off the hook? Hearing their complaints? 5. How do they try to *circumvent* the "spirit" of this vow, albeit not the "letter" of their oath? How success-

ful are they in this match-making? Who do they alienate? Why? **6.** What will result from this seizure at Shiloh (see 1Sa 9:20–24)? What does that tell you about God's providence or sovereignty? **7.** In what way is verse 25 an apt bottom line to this chapter? To this entire book?

♡ **1.** With 20–20 hindsight, how do you view some of the reckless things you've said and done in the past? Do you "shoot-first-ask-questions-later"? Or do you have "foot-in-mouth" disease? What did Israel have? **2.** Israel felt like one of its own members had been "cut off" (see Rev 7:4–8, where Benjamin is still missing). Where are you feeling "cut off" these days from your past roots? From your future inheritance? From your current family? **3.** Where do you go to ask God, "Why is this happening to me"? How can your small group be a forum for the situations you grieve over? How would you like God to intervene? **4.** What correctives would you give your child who says, "I want to grow up to be like Deborah"? ... or "Gideon"? ... or "Jephthah"? ... or "Samson"? **5.** What bottom-line slogan sums up your understanding of the book of Judges? What light has this sobering account of Israel's darker history brought to bear on you and your small group? Where do you feel *judged* by the object lessons? Where do you feel *encouraged* by the Judge who delivers his people every time?

from Jabesh Gilead had come to the camp for the assembly. [9]For when they counted the people, they found that none of the people of Jabesh Gilead were there.

[10]So the assembly sent twelve thousand fighting men with instructions to go to Jabesh Gilead and put to the sword those living there, including the women and children. [11]"This is what you are to do," they said. "Kill every male and every woman who is not a virgin." [12]They found among the people living in Jabesh Gilead four hundred young women who had never slept with a man, and they took them to the camp at Shiloh in Canaan.

[13]Then the whole assembly sent an offer of peace to the Benjamites at the rock of Rimmon. [14]So the Benjamites returned at that time and were given the women of Jabesh Gilead who had been spared. But there were not enough for all of them.

[15]The people grieved for Benjamin, because the LORD had made a gap in the tribes of Israel. [16]And the elders of the assembly said, "With the women of Benjamin destroyed, how shall we provide wives for the men who are left? [17]The Benjamite survivors must have heirs," they said, "so that a tribe of Israel will not be wiped out. [18]We can't give them our daughters as wives, since we Israelites have taken this oath: 'Cursed be anyone who gives a wife to a Benjamite.' [19]But look, there is the annual festival of the LORD in Shiloh, to the north of Bethel, and east of the road that goes from Bethel to Shechem, and to the south of Lebonah."

[20]So they instructed the Benjamites, saying, "Go and hide in the vineyards [21]and watch. When the girls of Shiloh come out to join in the dancing, then rush from the vineyards and each of you seize a wife from the girls of Shiloh and go to the land of Benjamin. [22]When their fathers or brothers complain to us, we will say to them, 'Do us a kindness by helping them, because we did not get wives for them during the war, and you are innocent, since you did not give your daughters to them.'"

[23]So that is what the Benjamites did. While the girls were dancing, each man caught one and carried her off to be his wife. Then they returned to their inheritance and rebuilt the towns and settled in them.

[24]At that time the Israelites left that place and went home to their tribes and clans, each to his own inheritance.

[25]In those days Israel had no king; everyone did as he saw fit.

INTRODUCTION to
RUTH

Book Study Outline: If you are using Ruth as a study course, here is a 4-week outline. Use the questions in the margin for your group agenda:

4-week plan	Personal Reading	Group Study Passage
1	1:1–22	1:1–22/Naomi and Ruth
2	2:1–23	2:1–23/Ruth Meets Boaz
3	3:1–18	3:1–18/At the Threshing Floor
4	4:1–22	4:1–22/Boaz Marries Ruth

🍵 start meeting / 15 min.

📖 read & discuss Bible / 30 min.

♡ close meeting / 15–45 min.

Refer to the Questions and Answers in the front of this Bible for more information.

Author: The author of Ruth is unknown.

Date: The date of composition is difficult to fix, though it was probably written during the period of the Israelite monarchy (c. 1000–722 B.C.). An early date is likely, as suggested by the fact that the genealogy in 4:17–22 ends with David.

Theme: Divine providence and human loyalty in the life of one family. The legal procedure of kinsman-redeemer also serves to illustrate the larger biblical theme of redemption.

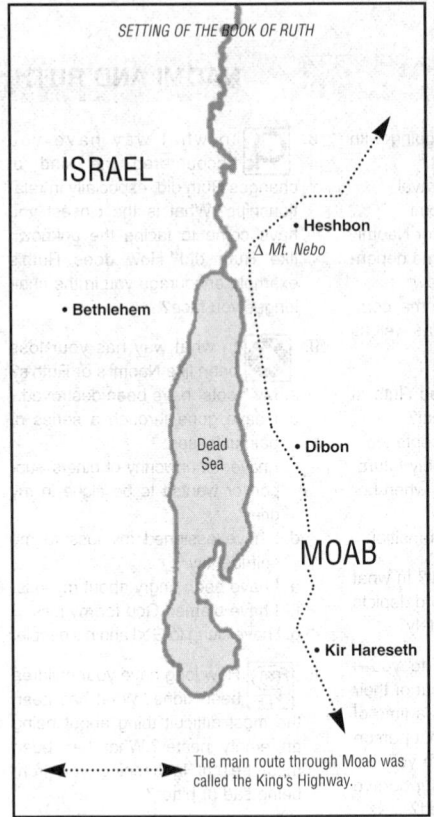

SETTING OF THE BOOK OF RUTH

ISRAEL

• Heshbon
Δ Mt. Nebo

• Bethlehem

Dead Sea

• Dibon

MOAB

• Kir Hareseth

⬅┄┄┄┄┄ The main route through Moab was called the King's Highway.

Historical Background: The action of the book of Ruth is set in the tumultuous period of the judges (c. 1100 B.C.). It may be that the book's original intention was to provide a politically important genealogy for David (4:17–22). The story goes to great lengths to legitimize his Moabite connections. This was important since Moabite women were considered immoral by many in Israel (see Ge 19:30–38; Nu 25:1–3). Modern readers of Ruth, unfamiliar with the background of the "kinsman-redeemer" motif, will also want to read about the plight of bereft widows and disenfranchised poor people, and how the next of kin was obliged to extend the family name (see Dt 25:5–10) and redeem their lost property (see Lev 25:23–28).

Characteristics: This book does not drive home its points, but subtly weaves them into the form of a story. In style, with its condensed action and plot twists, the book of Ruth is like a modern short story. The author has taken the changing fortunes of a single family and created a work of art. The book is interesting for its contrast to the Book of Judges. Though set during the time of the judges, the story of Ruth does not present the dramatic acts of God; in fact, God is not often mentioned in the book. Nonetheless, implied throughout is the quiet and tangible presence of God superintending the action of the story. Above all, this is a book about a loving and righteous woman. The author takes an outsider of questionable background, Ruth, and shows her to be a person about whom God is vitally concerned.

Ruth

Naomi and Ruth

☕ **1.** What was the economic climate like for the family in which you were raised? **2.** When have you felt quite alone in the world, or most cared for? Explain.

📖 **1.** What is the climate of the times for Naomi? What personal disasters befall her (vv. 1–5)? **2.** Without husband or sons, what crises is Naomi facing (vv. 11–13)? In a male-dominated, pre-welfare age, how important would male relatives be for widows? **3.** What ethnic enmity complicates prospects for her daughters-in-law? Why this hatred of the Moabites (see Ge 19:30–38; Nu 25:1–3; Dt 23:2–4)? **4.** Given the social problems facing these widows, why do you think Naomi tells Ruth and Orpah to return to their families? Orpah returns to her family while Ruth remains with Naomi, both out of loyalty. Which action was most

1 In the days when the judges ruled,[a] there was a famine in the land, and a man from Bethlehem in Judah, together with his wife and two sons, went to live for a while in the country of Moab. ²The man's name was Elimelech, his wife's name Naomi, and the names of his two sons were Mahlon and Kilion. They were Ephrathites from Bethlehem, Judah. And they went to Moab and lived there.

³Now Elimelech, Naomi's husband, died, and she was left with her two sons. ⁴They married Moabite women, one named Orpah and the other Ruth. After they had lived there about ten years, ⁵both Mahlon and Kilion also died, and Naomi was left without her two sons and her husband.

⁶When she heard in Moab that the LORD had come to the aid of his people by providing food for them, Naomi and her daughters-in-law prepared to return home from there. ⁷With her two daughters-in-law she left the place where she had been living and set out on the road that would take them back to the land of Judah.

⁸Then Naomi said to her two daughters-in-law, "Go back, each

---

a 1 Traditionally judged

   Ruth 1:1–22   **NAOMI AND RUTH**

1. When famine struck Israel, Naomi, Elimelech and their sons decided to emigrate to Moab. Over the next 10 years all three men died. How would you evaluate this family's decisions?
   a. They should have stayed at home.
   b. You do what you have to do.
   c. God judged them for the sons marrying women who weren't Israelites.
   d. Bad things happen to everyone, so don't second guess yourself.

2. Did Naomi make the right decision to return to Israel?
   a. Yes—go back to your roots.
   b. No—there is no going back.
   c. Be careful—things have changed.

3. Why did Naomi tell her daughters-in-law to return to their homes?
   a. She was concerned about their welfare.
   b. She was immersed in self-pity.
   c. She was tired of them and wanted to gently get rid of them.
   d. She was testing them to see if they really wanted to go with her.
   e. She couldn't bring herself to ask them to leave their people.

4. Why did Ruth insist on going with Naomi?
   a. because she loved to travel
   b. because she loved Naomi
   c. because she felt sorry for Naomi
   d. because she had become dependent on her mother-in-law
   e. because she had become committed to Naomi's God as well as to Naomi

5. What do you think awaited Ruth at the end of the road to Israel?
   a. warm welcome and acceptance
   b. cold shoulder and a lonely future
   c. fears similar to Naomi's when her family moved to Moab
   d. a difficult, but hopeful, transition

6. In what way is your life full? In what way is it empty? Which word depicts your life now more accurately?

7. Who has been a "Ruth" to you—someone who has gone out of their way to be there for you in a time of need? What impact has that person had on you? For whom are you like Ruth—a faithful and supportive friend—in *their* time of need?

8. ☒ In what way have you encountered the kind of changes Ruth did, especially in relationships? What is the closest you have come to facing the unknown like Ruth did? How does Ruth's example encourage you in the challenges you face?

9. ☒ In what way has your loss been like Naomi's or Ruth's?
   a. My "roots" have been destroyed.
   b. I have gone through a series of painful losses.
   c. I have felt unworthy of others' support or wanted to be alone in my grief.
   d. I have assigned my loss to my self-identity.
   e. I have been angry about my loss.
   f. I have blamed God for my loss.
   g. I have clung to God and his people.

10. 👁 How long have your children been gone? What has been the most difficult thing about being an empty nester? What has been most helpful in keeping you from being sad or bitter?

of you, to your mother's home. May the LORD show kindness to you, as you have shown to your dead and to me. ⁹May the LORD grant that each of you will find rest in the home of another husband."

Then she kissed them and they wept aloud ¹⁰and said to her, "We will go back with you to your people."

¹¹But Naomi said, "Return home, my daughters. Why would you come with me? Am I going to have any more sons, who could become your husbands? ¹²Return home, my daughters; I am too old to have another husband. Even if I thought there was still hope for me—even if I had a husband tonight and then gave birth to sons— ¹³would you wait until they grew up? Would you remain unmarried for them? No, my daughters. It is more bitter for me than for you, because the LORD's hand has gone out against me!"

¹⁴At this they wept again. Then Orpah kissed her mother-in-law good-by, but Ruth clung to her.

¹⁵"Look," said Naomi, "your sister-in-law is going back to her people and her gods. Go back with her."

¹⁶But Ruth replied, "Don't urge me to leave you or to turn back from you. Where you go I will go, and where you stay I will stay. Your people will be my people and your God my God. ¹⁷Where you die I will die, and there I will be buried. May the LORD deal with me, be it ever so severely, if anything but death separates you and me." ¹⁸When Naomi realized that Ruth was determined to go with her, she stopped urging her.

¹⁹So the two women went on until they came to Bethlehem. When they arrived in Bethlehem, the whole town was stirred because of them, and the women exclaimed, "Can this be Naomi?"

²⁰"Don't call me Naomi,ᵃ" she told them. "Call me Mara,ᵇ because the Almightyᶜ has made my life very bitter. ²¹I went away full, but the LORD has brought me back empty. Why call me Naomi? The LORD has afflictedᵈ me; the Almighty has brought misfortune upon me."

²²So Naomi returned from Moab accompanied by Ruth the Moabitess, her daughter-in-law, arriving in Bethlehem as the barley harvest was beginning.

Ruth Meets Boaz

2 Now Naomi had a relative on her husband's side, from the clan of Elimelech, a man of standing, whose name was Boaz.

²And Ruth the Moabitess said to Naomi, "Let me go to the fields and pick up the leftover grain behind anyone in whose eyes I find favor."

Naomi said to her, "Go ahead, my daughter." ³So she went out and began to glean in the fields behind the harvesters. As it turned out, she found herself working in a field belonging to Boaz, who was from the clan of Elimelech.

⁴Just then Boaz arrived from Bethlehem and greeted the harvesters, "The LORD be with you!"

"The LORD bless you!" they called back.

⁵Boaz asked the foreman of his harvesters, "Whose young woman is that?"

⁶The foreman replied, "She is the Moabitess who came back from Moab with Naomi. ⁷She said, 'Please let me glean and gather among the sheaves behind the harvesters.' She went into the field and has worked steadily from morning till now, except for a short rest in the shelter."

surprising? Most expected? Why? **5.** Both Ruth (vv. 16–17) and Naomi (vv. 20–21) confess God's sovereign control of events, each in her own way. What truth does each convey of God? Of themselves? Of their success in coping with stress? Which confession do you think would most startle the original readers? Why?

♡ **1.** Like Ruth, have you ever had to crossover to another ethnic or cultural group? Were you able to assimilate or did you remain a stranger? **2.** What kinds of groups do you feel like a stranger among? (On what basis: Social class? Race? Creed? Politics? Past hurts?) **3.** Like Ruth, have you embraced God's people as your own, forever? (For instance, have you settled into a church?) **4.** What has been stressful for you this year? Did you cope like Naomi, Orpah or Ruth? How so? **5.** Who in your life is like Ruth, loyal to you in your emptiness? How can you be like Ruth to someone else in their desolation?

☕ **1.** Have you ever worked on a farm? What was it like? **2.** Have you ever been a part of a harvest? What was it like?

📖 **1.** What signs of hope do you see as this chapter opens (vv. 1–3; also 1:22)? As it is harvest time, how long until Naomi and Ruth can grow their own food? In the meantime, how will they meet their most pressing need? **2.** What initiatives do Naomi, Ruth, Boaz and his men take to meet this need? What does that say about the character of the mother-daughter bond? The owner-harvester rapport? The Hebrew-Moabite fear? The man-woman chemistry? **3.** What hope is awakened at the close of this chapter (vv. 20–22)? What law about "gleanings" is Boaz heeding (see Lev 19:9–10)? What role does a "kinsman-redeemer" play in providing an heir for a brother who had died (see Dt 25:5–10)?

ᵃ20 Naomi means pleasant; also in verse 21.   ᵇ20 Mara means bitter.
ᶜ20 Hebrew Shaddai; also in verse 21   ᵈ21 Or has testified against

In redeeming a relative sold into slavery (see Lev 25:47–49)? Or land sold outside the family (4:3–4; see Lev 25:25–28)? Or avenging a relative's murder (see Nu 35:19ff, where "avenger" means "kinsman-redeemer")? Which of these regulations directly affect the situation Ruth and Naomi find themselves in? **4.** Do you think Naomi dares to hope in any of these provisions (v. 20)? Or is she still feeling like "Mara" (1:20–21)? How has this change been brought about? What does this reveal about the power of God's love? About Naomi, Ruth and Boaz? **5.** Given the sad state of Israel-Moab relations (see Ge 19:30–38; Nu 25:1–3), what surprising turn of events would the original readers see in this chapter? How does Ruth's loyalty to Naomi (vv. 11–12,23), and Boaz's loyalty to Ruth, defy historical prejudices of the original readers? How does their loyalty reflect God's?

1. What mechanisms does your country have for coping with the hungry and the homeless? What is your view of beggars? Of welfare programs? **2.** If you suddenly had no means of supporting yourself, do you think your reaction

[8]So Boaz said to Ruth, "My daughter, listen to me. Don't go and glean in another field and don't go away from here. Stay here with my servant girls. [9]Watch the field where the men are harvesting, and follow along after the girls. I have told the men not to touch you. And whenever you are thirsty, go and get a drink from the water jars the men have filled."

[10]At this, she bowed down with her face to the ground. She exclaimed, "Why have I found such favor in your eyes that you notice me—a foreigner?"

[11]Boaz replied, "I've been told all about what you have done for your mother-in-law since the death of your husband—how you left your father and mother and your homeland and came to live with a people you did not know before. [12]May the LORD repay you for what you have done. May you be richly rewarded by the LORD, the God of Israel, under whose wings you have come to take refuge."

[13]"May I continue to find favor in your eyes, my lord," she said. "You have given me comfort and have spoken kindly to your servant—though I do not have the standing of one of your servant girls."

[14]At mealtime Boaz said to her, "Come over here. Have some bread and dip it in the wine vinegar."

When she sat down with the harvesters, he offered her some roasted grain. She ate all she wanted and had some left over. [15]As she got up to glean, Boaz gave orders to his men, "Even if she gathers among the sheaves, don't embarrass her. [16]Rather, pull out some stalks for her from the bundles and leave them for her to pick up, and don't rebuke her."

[17]So Ruth gleaned in the field until evening. Then she threshed

  Ruth 2:1–23   **RUTH MEETS BOAZ**

Years earlier, Naomi, her husband and their two sons left Israel because of famine. While in Moab, all three men died. Now Naomi has just returned to Israel with her faithful Moabitess daughter-in-law Ruth.

1. What are your first impressions of this story?
a. Sounds like a Harlequin Romance.
b. What a knight in shining armor!
c. I'm glad I wasn't a widow then.
d. A "real man" would have rescued Ruth from the fields altogether.
e. Respect for each other was the basis for a later love relationship.

2. What do you most admire about Boaz in this story?
a. his rapport with his workers
b. his respect for a foreign woman
c. his initiative to protect Ruth from sexual harassment
d. his generosity with his grain

3. What do you most admire about Ruth in this story?
a. her courage and willingness to take risks

b. her loyalty to those she loved
c. her positive attitude about menial work
d. the way she took refuge "under God's wings" (v. 12)
e. the way she respected others and really appreciated what others did for her

4. How would you rate yourself on a scale from 1 to 10 regarding the answers to the previous question?

5. If you are married, what were the most important things your spouse left because of his/her love for you?
a. strong ties to family
b. the area where he/she grew up
c. professional opportunities
d. an old girlfriend/boyfriend
e. the freedoms of single life

6. How does your spouse show the kind of honor that Boaz and Ruth showed each other?
a. by protecting me
b. by affirming me
c. by listening to me
d. by supporting me in my work

e. by discussing important decisions
f. by speaking highly of me to others
g. by speaking to me kindly

7. Which of the answers in the previous question do you need to do more often to "love, honor and cherish" your mate?

8. If you have worked (or are working) as a supervisor, how have you felt about that role? What can you learn from Boaz in the area of management skills?

9. When it comes to positive working relationships, what lesson do you most need to learn?
a. to "bless" my coworkers (v. 4)
b. not to make my coworkers look bad or embarrass them (v. 15)
c. to show gratitude for help I receive
d. to make sure no one I work with is harassed
e. to be generous with those who work for me
f. to respect those I work for

the barley she had gathered, and it amounted to about an ephah.ᵃ
¹⁸She carried it back to town, and her mother-in-law saw how much she had gathered. Ruth also brought out and gave her what she had left over after she had eaten enough.

¹⁹Her mother-in-law asked her, "Where did you glean today? Where did you work? Blessed be the man who took notice of you!"

Then Ruth told her mother-in-law about the one at whose place she had been working. "The name of the man I worked with today is Boaz," she said.

²⁰"The LORD bless him!" Naomi said to her daughter-in-law. "He has not stopped showing his kindness to the living and the dead." She added, "That man is our close relative; he is one of our kinsman-redeemers."

²¹Then Ruth the Moabitess said, "He even said to me, 'Stay with my workers until they finish harvesting all my grain.'"

²²Naomi said to Ruth her daughter-in-law, "It will be good for you, my daughter, to go with his girls, because in someone else's field you might be harmed."

²³So Ruth stayed close to the servant girls of Boaz to glean until the barley and wheat harvests were finished. And she lived with her mother-in-law.

Ruth and Boaz at the Threshing Floor

3 One day Naomi her mother-in-law said to her, "My daughter, should I not try to find a homeᵇ for you, where you will be well provided for? ²Is not Boaz, with whose servant girls you have been, a kinsman of ours? Tonight he will be winnowing barley on the threshing floor. ³Wash and perfume yourself, and put on your best clothes. Then go down to the threshing floor, but don't let him know you are there until he has finished eating and drinking. ⁴When he lies down, note the place where he is lying. Then go and uncover his feet and lie down. He will tell you what to do."

⁵"I will do whatever you say," Ruth answered. ⁶So she went down to the threshing floor and did everything her mother-in-law told her to do.

⁷When Boaz had finished eating and drinking and was in good spirits, he went over to lie down at the far end of the grain pile. Ruth approached quietly, uncovered his feet and lay down. ⁸In the middle of the night something startled the man, and he turned and discovered a woman lying at his feet.

⁹"Who are you?" he asked.

"I am your servant Ruth," she said. "Spread the corner of your garment over me, since you are a kinsman-redeemer."

¹⁰"The LORD bless you, my daughter," he replied. "This kindness is greater than that which you showed earlier: You have not run after the younger men, whether rich or poor. ¹¹And now, my daughter, don't be afraid. I will do for you all you ask. All my fellow townsmen know that you are a woman of noble character. ¹²Although it is true that I am near of kin, there is a kinsman-redeemer nearer than I. ¹³Stay here for the night, and in the morning if he wants to redeem, good; let him redeem. But if he is not willing, as surely as the LORD lives I will do it. Lie here until morning."

¹⁴So she lay at his feet until morning, but got up before anyone could be recognized; and he said, "Don't let it be known that a woman came to the threshing floor."

¹⁵He also said, "Bring me the shawl you are wearing and hold it

would be like *Orpah* (and do what was expected of you)? Like *Ruth* (simple, humbling action)? Or like *Naomi* (with some bitterness creeping in)? Why? **3.** When have you shared Naomi's experience of God using a Ruth to show his kindness to you (as in vv. 11,12)? How did this unmerited act of kindness change you? **4.** Whom do you know who needs to be reminded that God still loves them? What will you do today to demonstrate such love?

1. Did your parents ever encourage you to date, even marry someone? How did you feel about that? **2.** How did (or would) you "pop the question" (or receive it)?

1. What instructions does Naomi give to Ruth (vv. 1–4)? What is their goal? In their male-dominated world, how do you account for such boldness? **2.** What factors could lead readers to believe a sexual indiscretion took place: (a) Boaz's "hung over" condition? (b) The secluded "bed"? (c) Naomi's instructions? (d) Uncovering Boaz? (e) Moabite history (Nu 25:1)? (f) Today's culture? (g) Human nature? **3.** What factors assure you that no sexual encounter took place: (a) Uncovering Boaz's feet was not a sexually forward move, but a way to ensure he'd awake on a cold night? (b) "Spreading the corner of one's garment" signified a request for marriage and an offer to protect (as in Eze 16:8)? (c) Ruth's indisputable moral integrity (v. 11)? (d) The proper deference of Boaz to others in accord with the law of the kinsman-redeemer (v. 13)? **4.** If found together, who'd likely get blamed: Naomi, Ruth or Boaz (vv. 5–6,14)? Why does Boaz not take advantage of her? Why bless her and consider her proposal (vv. 10–13)?

1. If this love story were remade for TV, what liberty with the script might the director take to appeal to viewers? How

---

ᵃ17 That is, probably about 3/5 bushel (about 22 liters)   ᵇ1 Hebrew *find rest* (see Ruth 1:9) might that obscure the main point? For whom is this story most appealing, "as is"? **2.** In your circle of friends, what "dos" and "don'ts" of sexual morality prevail? Which "rules" are the first to be bent or broken? **3.** How would Ruth and Boaz fit into your social circle? How does their example help you say "No"?

_____

1. Do you like going barefoot? When? Where? **2.** When have you sealed a promise in an unusual way (like being "blood-brothers")?

1. From Leviticus 25:23–43 and Deuteronomy 25:5–10, what are God's views on property, poverty and posterity? Given her tenuous position, how would these laws protect Naomi? **2.** What cost is involved for the kinsman-redeemer who follows each of these laws? If a woman marries the kinsman, how much of her property goes to him? How much to her son? How might this account for the nameless redeemer's reluctance to marry Ruth (v. 6)? **3.** What does it say about Boaz that he is

out." When she did so, he poured into it six measures of barley and put it on her. Then he*a* went back to town.

¹⁶When Ruth came to her mother-in-law, Naomi asked, "How did it go, my daughter?"

Then she told her everything Boaz had done for her ¹⁷and added, "He gave me these six measures of barley, saying, 'Don't go back to your mother-in-law empty-handed.'"

¹⁸Then Naomi said, "Wait, my daughter, until you find out what happens. For the man will not rest until the matter is settled today."

Boaz Marries Ruth

4 Meanwhile Boaz went up to the town gate and sat there. When the kinsman-redeemer he had mentioned came along, Boaz said, "Come over here, my friend, and sit down." So he went over and sat down.

²Boaz took ten of the elders of the town and said, "Sit here," and they did so. ³Then he said to the kinsman-redeemer, "Naomi, who has come back from Moab, is selling the piece of land that belonged to our brother Elimelech. ⁴I thought I should bring the matter to your attention and suggest that you buy it in the presence of these seated here and in the presence of the elders of my people. If you will redeem it, do so. But if you*b* will not, tell me, so I will know. For no one has the right to do it except you, and I am next in line."

"I will redeem it," he said.

a15 Most Hebrew manuscripts; many Hebrew manuscripts, Vulgate and Syriac *she*
b4 Many Hebrew manuscripts, Septuagint, Vulgate and Syriac; most Hebrew manuscripts *he*

Ruth 3:1–18   **RUTH AND BOAZ AT THE THRESHING FLOOR**

In Jewish society in Ruth's time, it was understood that when a man died his nearest blood relative would marry the widow to continue the family's name. This person was called a "kinsman-redeemer." Naomi devises a plan to set in motion this process between Ruth and Boaz—who was a relative of Naomi's deceased husband and son.

1. What was Naomi after?
   a. getting rid of Ruth
   b. providing for Ruth's welfare
   c. providing for her own welfare
   d. providing for the continuation of her family line

2. When Ruth went to the threshing floor, what was she after?
   a. a good time
   b. a husband
   c. Naomi's approval
   d. Boaz's acceptance

3. If you were Ruth's best friend, what would you have said to her?
   a. "Get a life!"
   b. "You continually amaze me."

c. "You've done enough for Naomi—do something for yourself."
d. "Good things come to those who do what is right."
e. "There are plenty of younger, more attractive men around."
f. other:_____

4. Ruth's actions and words (v. 9) were apparently a request for marriage. How would you have felt if you were Boaz?
   a. flattered   d. embarrassed
   b. fortunate   e. obligated
   c. excited

5. How was Naomi's "emptiness" starting to turn around?
   a. Ruth didn't return to her "empty-handed" (v. 17).
   b. Her plan was working.
   c. She was getting closer to having a son-in-law and potential family heir.

6. If you had been Ruth, which of these circumstances would have been most difficult for you?

a. experiencing my spouse's death
b. leaving my home and moving to a foreign land
c. living with my mother-in-law
d. taking the initiative at the threshing floor like she did
e. getting romantically involved with someone much older than myself

7. If you could choose three qualities found in Ruth, what would you choose?
   a. devotion   f. respect
   b. integrity   g. faithfulness
   c. love   h. humility
   d. perseverance   i. kindness
   e. service   j. other:_____

8. What would you most like to have?
   a. a "kinsman" to provide for me (v. 1)
   b. someone to share life with (v. 2)
   c. a little kindness (v. 10)
   d. the Lord's blessing (v. 10)
   e. a noble character (v. 11)

9. How have you been "well provided for" by other people? By God? How can you express your thanks?

⁵Then Boaz said, "On the day you buy the land from Naomi and from Ruth the Moabitess, you acquireᵃ the dead man's widow, in order to maintain the name of the dead with his property."

⁶At this, the kinsman-redeemer said, "Then I cannot redeem it because I might endanger my own estate. You redeem it yourself. I cannot do it."

⁷(Now in earlier times in Israel, for the redemption and transfer of property to become final, one party took off his sandal and gave it to the other. This was the method of legalizing transactions in Israel.)

⁸So the kinsman-redeemer said to Boaz, "Buy it yourself." And he removed his sandal.

⁹Then Boaz announced to the elders and all the people, "Today you are witnesses that I have bought from Naomi all the property of Elimelech, Kilion and Mahlon. ¹⁰I have also acquired Ruth the Moabitess, Mahlon's widow, as my wife, in order to maintain the name of the dead with his property, so that his name will not disappear from among his family or from the town records. Today you are witnesses!"

¹¹Then the elders and all those at the gate said, "We are witnesses. May the LORD make the woman who is coming into your home like Rachel and Leah, who together built up the house of Israel. May you have standing in Ephrathah and be famous in Bethlehem. ¹²Through the offspring the LORD gives you by this young woman, may your family be like that of Perez, whom Tamar bore to Judah."

ᵃ5 Hebrew; Vulgate and Syriac *Naomi, you acquire Ruth the Moabitess,*

willing to take on all the expenses and duties, when he will get nothing tangible in return? What ancestor of Boaz was born from the same practice of this kinsman-redeemer law (vv. 12,18–21; see Ge 38)? How might that have influenced his choice of wife?

♡ **1.** How large a social problem are "your poor, your hungry and your homeless"? How could the biblical principle of gleaning (salvaging or recycling) be applied to your situation? **2.** When have you faced great physical need? How did God provide for you? How is your story like Naomi's and Ruth's story of how God cares?

Ruth 4:1–22   BOAZ MARRIES RUTH

After providentially gleaning in Boaz's grain fields, Ruth approached him regarding the law of the kinsman-redeemer. Boaz, a relative of Ruth's late husband, now calls for an official meeting in an effort to redeem the deceased man's land and—in his place—to provide his family an heir.

1. How does this story strike you?
   a. cold and mechanical
   b. warm and inspiring
   c. complicated
   d. chauvinistic

2. What do you think Boaz's motives were?
   a. love
   b. sexual desire
   c. real estate expansion
   d. obligation
   e. honor and integrity
   f. a desire for an extra sandal

3. Why didn't the closer relative want to redeem the piece of land?
   a. He couldn't afford it.
   b. He wasn't willing to get married—especially to someone he didn't know.
   c. He might have to share his own estate with a son born to Ruth.

4. What risks was Boaz taking?
   a. over-extending himself financially
   b. endangering his own estate
   c. adjusting to a marriage with someone from a different culture

5. What was so special about Obed?
   a. He kept a family name from being lost.
   b. He would become King David's grandfather.
   c. He would become an ancestor of Jesus Christ (Lk 3:32).
   d. He brought life and joy to Naomi.
   e. He was a testimony of the Lord's faithful provision.

6. In the end the whole community welcomes Ruth. What brought her from outsider to acceptance?
   a. luck
   b. having a cuddly baby
   c. God's providence
   d. Boaz's good standing
   e. Ruth's character
   f. Ruth's acceptance of them
   g. Naomi's clever maneuvering

7. What can you and your group do to help neglected, unloved "Moabites" feel welcomed and cared for by your community?

8. How do you see God's providence at work in this story? Where have you seen God providentially at work in your life? Where do you need to trust his providence right now?

9. How is Jesus Christ your ultimate "kinsman-redeemer"?

10. 👁 How did Naomi's "empty nest" become full again? What do you think happened to her attitude about life? About herself? About God? What do you want to remember about your attitude after your nest became empty?

11. 👁 What would give you a new or better perspective about being an empty nester?
   a. a grandchild
   b. not feeling so sorry for myself
   c. a new outlet for my energies
   d. a supportive community
   e. deciding to give the Lord praise

1. Of which ancestors are you very proud? Of whom were you embarrassed? 2. What would you like to be famous for?

1. How is the birth of Obed announced? How is Ruth's selfless devotion celebrated? What is the point of this unusual birth announcement? 2. Why do you think the story of Ruth concludes with a genealogy of David? Why two such genealogies (vv. 17 and 18–22)? 3. In ancient Near East, genealogies often served in context to connect two people. For instance, the genealogy in verses 18–22 connects David with Perez, the son of Judah and Tamar, who are also mentioned in verse 12. For David and his descendants, who faced numerous challenges to their right to rule, how would this "famous" connection help to legitimize their claims to royalty (see Ge 49:8–12)? 4. How would Moabite history (see Ge 19:30–38; Nu 25:1–3; Dt 24:2–4) likely affect the Israelites' view of Moabites? And hence, their view of Israelites, such as David, who are linked to Moabites? (vv. 13–17; see 1Sa 22:3–4)? 5. Define "providence." In this story, what evidence do you see for divine providence superseding: (a) Human ingenuity? (b) Cultural prejudice? (c) Marriage and property laws of that day?

1. Where have you seen the God of Ruth and Boaz act providentially and redemptively on your behalf? Where have you seen the God of Israel *and Moab* concern himself equally for any and all people who put their trust in him? 2. Who is the "untouchable Moabite" in your life—the one whom you keep at arm's length? How will you bridge the gap between you? 3. There are two books in the Bible bearing the title of women's names. Both experienced successful cross-cultural marriages. Is there a lesson to be told with respect to this activity? If so, what?

The Genealogy of David

13So Boaz took Ruth and she became his wife. Then he went to her, and the LORD enabled her to conceive, and she gave birth to a son. 14The women said to Naomi: "Praise be to the LORD, who this day has not left you without a kinsman-redeemer. May he become famous throughout Israel! 15He will renew your life and sustain you in your old age. For your daughter-in-law, who loves you and who is better to you than seven sons, has given him birth."

16Then Naomi took the child, laid him in her lap and cared for him. 17The women living there said, "Naomi has a son." And they named him Obed. He was the father of Jesse, the father of David.

18This, then, is the family line of Perez:

Perez was the father of Hezron,
19Hezron the father of Ram,
Ram the father of Amminadab,
20Amminadab the father of Nahshon,
Nahshon the father of Salmon,*a*
21Salmon the father of Boaz,
Boaz the father of Obed,
22Obed the father of Jesse,
and Jesse the father of David.

---

a20 A few Hebrew manuscripts, some Septuagint manuscripts and Vulgate (see also verse 21 and Septuagint of 1 Chron. 2:11); most Hebrew manuscripts *Salma*

INTRODUCTION to
1 SAMUEL

Book Study Outline: If you are using 1 Samuel for a study course, here is a 7- or 13-week outline. Use the questions in the margin for your group agenda:

start meeting / 15 min.

read & discuss Bible / 30 min.

close meeting / 15–45 min.

Refer to the Questions and Answers in the front of this Bible for more information.

7-week plan	13-week plan	Personal Reading	Group Study Passage
1	1	1:1–28	1:1–28/Birth of Samuel
	2	2:1–36	2:12–26/Eli's Wicked Sons
2	3	3:1–7:1	3:1–21/God Calls Samuel
	4	7:2–8:22	8:1–22/Israel Requests King
3	5	9:1–12:25	9:1–10:8/Saul Anointed
	6	13:1–14:52	13:1–15/Samuel Rebukes Saul
4	7	15:1–16:13	16:1–13/David Anointed
	8	16:14–23	16:14–23/David Serves Saul
5	9	17:1–58	17:12–50/David and Goliath
	10	18:1–19:24	18:1–30/Saul's Jealousy
6	11	20:1–23:29	20:1–42/David and Jonathan
	12	24:1–27:12	24:1–22/David Spares Saul
7	13	28:1–31:13	28:1–25/Saul and a Witch

Author: The author of 1 Samuel is not known with certainty. Perhaps a compiler drew from materials written by others such as Samuel, Gad and Nathan (see 1Ch 29:29) in order to produce the final rendition. Note that 1 and 2 Samuel were originally composed as one unit.

Date: Uncertain, though it is possible that this two-volume book was written around the time of Solomon's death (c. 930 B.C.).

Theme: The king-maker (Samuel) and the first king (Saul).

Historical Background: The first book of Samuel narrates a major transition in the life of Israel—the shift from government under judges to a monarchy. Samuel, the last judge, anoints Saul as Israel's first king (c. 1050 B.C.). He later anoints David as the king who will take Saul's place.

Characteristics: This historical book highlights the lives of three central figures: Samuel, Saul and David. Sad elements abound: Eli's sons rebel; faithless Israel rejects her great King; Saul self-destructs in his vicious pursuit of David, reaching his lowest point when he consults a witch. But bright notes also punctuate this sordid story: Samuel stands firm and godly as the prophet of God who is ever faithful to his Lord; David (with soul mate Jonathan) appears youthful, courageous, popular and abounding in faith in the mighty God of Israel. In the context of almost constant warfare, trust in God is either conspicuously present or conspicuously absent. God is seen as the rejected King, the Revealer of the unknown, the Judge of the rebellious, as well as the Deliverer of his people.

DAVID'S FAMILY TREE

RUTH
Boaz .... Jesse .... David

KEY:
RUTH—Female
Jesse—Male
TAMAR—Female Child

Nine other sons of David are listed (without their mother's names) in 1Ch 3:6–8.

DAVID'S WIVES:

MICHAL

AHINOAM .... Amnon

ABIGAIL .... Kileab

MAACAH .... Absalom
.... *TAMAR*

HAGGITH .... Adonijah

ABITAL .... Shephatiah

EGLAH .... Ithream

BATHSHEBA .... Solomon
(plus three other sons)

David's Children:

1 Samuel

The Birth of Samuel

☕ **1.** What has brought you the most joy the past few years? The most grief? What brought relief from your grief? **2.** What does your name mean? Why was that name chosen? How are you like your namesake or like its meaning?

📖 **1.** How does the list of Elkanah's ancestry (v. 1) underscore Hannah's plight? Why is a son so dear to her? **2.** What responses does her not having children evoke in Hannah? In Elkanah? In Peninnah? In Eli? **3.** How does this passage illustrate the evils of polygamy? **4.** What does Hannah intend for her son by her vow (v. 11; see Nu 6:1–8, Jdg 13:7)? What is the irony in Eli's accusation? **5.** Why does Hannah's sadness disappear so quickly (v. 18)?

♡ **1.** What "unchangeable" situation have you grieved over as Hannah does? Was it really unchangeable? **2.** When has God led you into a time of disappointment before granting your heart's desire? Are you in the midst of a time of disappointment now? What encouragement can you find in this passage? In your own experiences of God's faithfulness? **3.** When has the Lord "remembered" you in a time of great need? Has there been a time of need when you suddenly "remembered" the Lord? What helps at such times: recorded prayers? Re-reading your prayers? Reading the Bible? **4.** What prayer will you record to help recall how he has been with you?

1 There was a certain man from Ramathaim, a Zuphite^a from the hill country of Ephraim, whose name was Elkanah son of Jeroham, the son of Elihu, the son of Tohu, the son of Zuph, an Ephraimite. ²He had two wives; one was called Hannah and the other Peninnah. Peninnah had children, but Hannah had none.

³Year after year this man went up from his town to worship and sacrifice to the LORD Almighty at Shiloh, where Hophni and Phinehas, the two sons of Eli, were priests of the LORD. ⁴Whenever the day came for Elkanah to sacrifice, he would give portions of the meat to his wife Peninnah and to all her sons and daughters. ⁵But to Hannah he gave a double portion because he loved her, and the LORD had closed her womb. ⁶And because the LORD had closed her womb, her rival kept provoking her in order to irritate her. ⁷This went on year after year. Whenever Hannah went up to the house of the LORD, her rival provoked her till she wept and would not eat. ⁸Elkanah her husband would say to her, "Hannah, why are you weeping? Why don't you eat? Why are you downhearted? Don't I mean more to you than ten sons?"

⁹Once when they had finished eating and drinking in Shiloh, Hannah stood up. Now Eli the priest was sitting on a chair by the doorpost of the LORD's temple.^b ¹⁰In bitterness of soul Hannah wept much and prayed to the LORD. ¹¹And she made a vow, saying, "O LORD Almighty, if you will only look upon your servant's misery and remember me, and not forget your servant but give her a son, then I will give him to the LORD for all the days of his life, and no razor will ever be used on his head."

¹²As she kept on praying to the LORD, Eli observed her mouth. ¹³Hannah was praying in her heart, and her lips were moving but her voice was not heard. Eli thought she was drunk ¹⁴and said to her, "How long will you keep on getting drunk? Get rid of your wine."

¹⁵"Not so, my lord," Hannah replied, "I am a woman who is deeply troubled. I have not been drinking wine or beer; I was pouring out my soul to the LORD. ¹⁶Do not take your servant for a wicked woman; I have been praying here out of my great anguish and grief."

¹⁷Eli answered, "Go in peace, and may the God of Israel grant you what you have asked of him."

¹⁸She said, "May your servant find favor in your eyes." Then she went her way and ate something, and her face was no longer downcast.

¹⁹Early the next morning they arose and worshiped before the LORD and then went back to their home at Ramah. Elkanah lay with Hannah his wife, and the LORD remembered her. ²⁰So in the course

of time Hannah conceived and gave birth to a son. She named him Samuel,[a] saying, "Because I asked the LORD for him."

Hannah Dedicates Samuel

²¹When the man Elkanah went up with all his family to offer the annual sacrifice to the LORD and to fulfill his vow, ²²Hannah did not go. She said to her husband, "After the boy is weaned, I will take him and present him before the LORD, and he will live there always."

²³"Do what seems best to you," Elkanah her husband told her. "Stay here until you have weaned him; only may the LORD make good his[b] word." So the woman stayed at home and nursed her son until she had weaned him.

²⁴After he was weaned, she took the boy with her, young as he was, along with a three-year-old bull,[c] an ephah[d] of flour and a skin of wine, and brought him to the house of the LORD at Shiloh. ²⁵When they had slaughtered the bull, they brought the boy to Eli, ²⁶and she said to him, "As surely as you live, my lord, I am the woman who stood here beside you praying to the LORD. ²⁷I prayed for this child, and the LORD has granted me what I asked of him. ²⁸So now I give him to the LORD. For his whole life he will be given over to the LORD." And he worshiped the LORD there.

What do you recall about the first time you left home for any significant time?

1. Why do you suppose Hannah neglected the annual sacrifice? **2.** How do you think Hannah felt giving Samuel to someone else to raise? What does Elkanah mean by "may the Lord make good his (or your) word" (v. 23)? **3.** What does the conversation between Elkanah and Hannah show of the nature of their marriage?

1. Have you or your parents made a vow? **2.** If you were "dedicated" early on, how has that affected your life? **3.** What things or people in your life are most indispensable to you? Can you "give them back to God" as Hannah did?

---

a20 Samuel sounds like the Hebrew for *heard of God.*   *b23* Masoretic Text; Dead Sea Scrolls, Septuagint and Syriac *your*   *c24* Dead Sea Scrolls, Septuagint and Syriac; Masoretic Text *with three bulls*   *d24* That is, probably about 3/5 bushel (about 22 liters)

---

 1 Samuel 1:1–28   **THE BIRTH AND DEDICATION OF SAMUEL**

1. What was the worst thing Hannah had to cope with?
   a. her barrenness
   b. an irritating rival
   c. depression
   d. an unsympathetic priest

2. Why did she want a baby so badly?
   a. to prove her worth as a woman
   b. to please her husband
   c. to get back at her rival
   d. because she loved children
   e. because she was lonely
   f. because of social pressure

3. What was the most encouraging thing Hannah had going for her?
   a. a loving husband   c. free time
   b. financial security   d. her faith

4. Why was Hannah's grief especially intense at the annual sacrifices?
   a. Festive occasions highlighted her inward despair.
   b. Focusing on God made her question his goodness.
   c. Seeing all the children tore her up.
   d. Elkanah's favoring her at the feast made Peninnah rub it in more.

5. What caused Hannah to be "no longer downcast" (v. 18)?
   a. She accepted her situation.
   b. She knew she'd get pregnant.
   c. She felt God's peace.

6. How did Hannah feel as she took Samuel to the house of the Lord?
   a. apprehensive   d. regretful
   b. determined   e. overjoyed
   c. grateful   f. torn

7. What in your life gives you a sense of self-worth?
   a. my family   d. people in my life
   b. my job   e. spiritual security
   c. my education   f. other:_____

8. How do you respond when God seems to say no to what you want?
   a. get depressed
   b. get mad at God
   c. keep on praying
   d. rephrase my request
   e. forget it
   f. accept it

9. I felt like Hannah one time when:
   a. I was a single adult.
   b. I was childless.
   c. We had a miscarriage.
   d. I was teased.
   e. I was misunderstood.

10. What encouragement can you find in this story for what you shared or for other disappointments in your life?

11. What should you dedicate to God?
    a. children   e. possessions
    b. childlessness   f. job
    c. spouse   g. talents
    d. home   h. future

12. How does this story reflect your experience of miscarriage?
    a. I know all about bitterness of soul.
    b. Seeing parents with their children tears me up.
    c. I can't seem to stop crying.
    d. I can't seem to comfort my mate.
    e. Other people—even if unintentionally—make me feel worse.
    f. I have poured out my soul to God.
    g. I need to pour out my soul to God.

Hannah's Prayer

2 Then Hannah prayed and said:

"My heart rejoices in the LORD;
    in the LORD my horn[a] is lifted high.
My mouth boasts over my enemies,
    for I delight in your deliverance.

2"There is no one holy[b] like the LORD;
    there is no one besides you;
    there is no Rock like our God.

3"Do not keep talking so proudly
    or let your mouth speak such arrogance,
for the LORD is a God who knows,
    and by him deeds are weighed.

4"The bows of the warriors are broken,
    but those who stumbled are armed with
      strength.
5Those who were full hire themselves out for food,
    but those who were hungry hunger no more.
She who was barren has borne seven children,
    but she who has had many sons pines away.

6"The LORD brings death and makes alive;
    he brings down to the grave[c] and raises up.
7The LORD sends poverty and wealth;
    he humbles and he exalts.
8He raises the poor from the dust
    and lifts the needy from the ash heap;
he seats them with princes
    and has them inherit a throne of honor.

"For the foundations of the earth are the LORD's;
    upon them he has set the world.
9He will guard the feet of his saints,
    but the wicked will be silenced in darkness.

"It is not by strength that one prevails;
10   those who oppose the LORD will be shattered.
He will thunder against them from heaven;
    the LORD will judge the ends of the earth.

"He will give strength to his king
    and exalt the horn of his anointed."

11Then Elkanah went home to Ramah, but the boy ministered before the LORD under Eli the priest.

Eli's Wicked Sons

12Eli's sons were wicked men; they had no regard for the LORD. 13Now it was the practice of the priests with the people that whenever anyone offered a sacrifice and while the meat was being boiled, the servant of the priest would come with a three-pronged fork in his hand. 14He would plunge it into the pan or kettle or caldron or pot, and the priest would take for himself whatever the fork brought up. This is how they treated all the Israelites who came to Shiloh. 15But even before the fat was burned, the servant of the priest would come and say to the man who was sacrificing,

a1 *Horn* here symbolizes strength; also in verse 10.   b2 Or *no Holy One*
c6 Hebrew *Sheol*

"Give the priest some meat to roast; he won't accept boiled meat from you, but only raw."

¹⁶If the man said to him, "Let the fat be burned up first, and then take whatever you want," the servant would then answer, "No, hand it over now; if you don't, I'll take it by force."

¹⁷This sin of the young men was very great in the LORD's sight, for they*a* were treating the LORD's offering with contempt.

¹⁸But Samuel was ministering before the LORD—a boy wearing a linen ephod. ¹⁹Each year his mother made him a little robe and took it to him when she went up with her husband to offer the annual sacrifice. ²⁰Eli would bless Elkanah and his wife, saying, "May the LORD give you children by this woman to take the place of the one she prayed for and gave to the LORD." Then they would go home. ²¹And the LORD was gracious to Hannah; she conceived and gave birth to three sons and two daughters. Meanwhile, the boy Samuel grew up in the presence of the LORD.

²²Now Eli, who was very old, heard about everything his sons were doing to all Israel and how they slept with the women who served at the entrance to the Tent of Meeting. ²³So he said to them, "Why do you do such things? I hear from all the people about these wicked deeds of yours. ²⁴No, my sons; it is not a good report that I hear spreading among the LORD's people. ²⁵If a man sins against another man, God*b* may mediate for him; but if a man sins against the LORD, who will intercede for him?" His sons, however, did not listen to their father's rebuke, for it was the LORD's will to put them to death.

a17 Or *men*   *b25* Or *the judges*

make clothes for Samuel? How does their relationship compare with that between Eli and his sons? How do these relationships affect the children (vv. 12,18,26)? **4.** Why does Eli distinguish between the sins mentioned in verse 25? How does the Lord support his warning?

♡ **1.** Is your example to children like that of Hannah or that of Eli? How so? How can you prepare your children (or those who look up to you) for a life "ministering before the Lord"? Are you prepared for the costly obedience of Hannah? What would that mean in your situation? **2.** How important is it to discipline children today? What does it mean to be a "Hannah" parent? An "Eli" parent?

---

  1 Samuel 2:12–26   **ELI'S WICKED SONS**

Eli, in his later years, was Israel's high priest. In this story we see the stark contrast between Eli's sons, Hophni and Phinehas, who were also priests, and Samuel—who had been dedicated as a child to the Lord's service by his parents Hannah and Elkanah.

1. What were Eli's sons doing wrong?
   a. nothing any red-blooded male wouldn't do given the chance
   b. taking what belonged to God for themselves
   c. serving out of duty rather than love
   d. disregarding God's requirements for worship
   e. using their position for sexual exploitation
   f. dishonoring their holy calling

2. In contrast, why did Samuel enjoy God's favor?
   a. He was still young and innocent.
   b. He had better parenting.
   c. He *chose* to honor the Lord.
   d. He had a special calling and relationship with the Lord.

3. Eli's response to his sons (vv. 23–25) was:
   a. right on.
   b. too little too late.
   c. the best he could do.
   d. a mere scolding when they should have been removed from the priesthood.

4. How come Eli's sons didn't listen to their father's rebuke?
   a. They were too busy having fun.
   b. Their hearts were hardened.
   c. God had other plans for them.
   d. They couldn't help themselves.
   e. They had become so wicked their judgment was already determined.

5. According to the next passage, Eli honored his sons more than the Lord (v. 29). Do you honor anyone or anything more than the Lord? If so, what will you do about it?

6. How can you prepare your children, or others who look up to you, for a life that honors rather than dishonors the Lord?

7. How do you think Eli coped with the grief his sons caused him? How do you cope with the pain your son or daughter has brought into your life?

8. 1 Samuel 3:13 indicates that both Eli *and* his sons failed. Have there been ways you have contributed to your child's waywardness? If so, have you asked God to forgive you? In light of God's grace, do you continue to punish yourself undeservedly?

9. Though Eli was a religious and political leader for 40 years, he was remembered as a failure at home. What will keep that from happening to you? How capable do you feel of assuming spiritual responsibility in your family?

10. What have you appreciated the most about this course and group? Are there any issues you need to talk about that weren't covered? If so, how could you address them?

²⁶And the boy Samuel continued to grow in stature and in favor with the LORD and with men.

Prophecy Against the House of Eli

²⁷Now a man of God came to Eli and said to him, "This is what the LORD says: 'Did I not clearly reveal myself to your father's house when they were in Egypt under Pharaoh? ²⁸I chose your father out of all the tribes of Israel to be my priest, to go up to my altar, to burn incense, and to wear an ephod in my presence. I also gave your father's house all the offerings made with fire by the Israelites. ²⁹Why do you^a scorn my sacrifice and offering that I prescribed for my dwelling? Why do you honor your sons more than me by fattening yourselves on the choice parts of every offering made by my people Israel?'

³⁰"Therefore the LORD, the God of Israel, declares: 'I promised that your house and your father's house would minister before me forever.' But now the LORD declares: 'Far be it from me! Those who honor me I will honor, but those who despise me will be disdained. ³¹The time is coming when I will cut short your strength and the strength of your father's house, so that there will not be an old man in your family line ³²and you will see distress in my dwelling. Although good will be done to Israel, in your family line there will never be an old man. ³³Every one of you that I do not cut off from my altar will be spared only to blind your eyes with tears and to grieve your heart, and all your descendants will die in the prime of life.

³⁴"'And what happens to your two sons, Hophni and Phinehas, will be a sign to you—they will both die on the same day. ³⁵I will raise up for myself a faithful priest, who will do according to what is in my heart and mind. I will firmly establish his house, and he will minister before my anointed one always. ³⁶Then everyone left in your family line will come and bow down before him for a piece of silver and a crust of bread and plead, "Appoint me to some priestly office so I can have food to eat." '"

The LORD Calls Samuel

3 The boy Samuel ministered before the LORD under Eli. In those days the word of the LORD was rare; there were not many visions.

²One night Eli, whose eyes were becoming so weak that he could barely see, was lying down in his usual place. ³The lamp of God had not yet gone out, and Samuel was lying down in the temple^b of the LORD, where the ark of God was. ⁴Then the LORD called Samuel.

Samuel answered, "Here I am." ⁵And he ran to Eli and said, "Here I am; you called me."

But Eli said, "I did not call; go back and lie down." So he went and lay down.

⁶Again the LORD called, "Samuel!" And Samuel got up and went to Eli and said, "Here I am; you called me."

"My son," Eli said, "I did not call; go back and lie down."

⁷Now Samuel did not yet know the LORD: The word of the LORD had not yet been revealed to him.

⁸The LORD called Samuel a third time, and Samuel got up and went to Eli and said, "Here I am; you called me."

Then Eli realized that the LORD was calling the boy. ⁹So Eli told Samuel, "Go and lie down, and if he calls you, say, 'Speak, LORD, for

---

If you could know the date when you will die, would you want to know? Why?

1. What does God expect of his priests? 2. Why does God extend to Eli the responsibility for the sins of his sons (see 3:13)? Why to his son's heirs (see Ex 20:5)? 3. What does it mean to have one's house "firmly established" (v. 35)?

1. What does God expect of us who are priests one to another (see 1Pe 2:5)? What can we expect if we are faithful? Unfaithful? 2. Is your house becoming firmly established? How so? 3. What inheritance are you passing on to your descendants? What is hindering your "ministering before the Lord"? How can the group help you to be more faithful?

1. As a child, did you ever run into your parents' room after a nightmare? What was the dream? 2. Did you ever have trouble (then or now) getting to sleep? What did (or do) you do to help you sleep?

1. What do you make of Eli's physical disability (v. 2; see 2:33)? What might this and the "lamp of the Lord" (v. 3) symbolize? 2. Why is the Lord angry with Eli? How has Eli failed to repent (v. 13)? 3. If you were Eli, how would you have reacted to the Lord's words? If you were Samuel, how would you have felt repeating them to Eli? 4. What does it mean that Samuel "let none of his words fall to the ground" (v. 19)? How does that compare with Eli?

1. Do you tend to be too strict or too permissive/lenient as a parent or in other positions of responsibility? 2. Has the Lord recently convicted you of some sin or

---

^a29 The Hebrew is plural.   ^b3 That is, tabernacle

your servant is listening.'" So Samuel went and lay down in his place.

[10]The LORD came and stood there, calling as at the other times, "Samuel! Samuel!"

Then Samuel said, "Speak, for your servant is listening."

[11]And the LORD said to Samuel: "See, I am about to do something in Israel that will make the ears of everyone who hears of it tingle. [12]At that time I will carry out against Eli everything I spoke against his family—from beginning to end. [13]For I told him that I would judge his family forever because of the sin he knew about; his sons made themselves contemptible,[a] and he failed to restrain them. [14]Therefore, I swore to the house of Eli, 'The guilt of Eli's house will never be atoned for by sacrifice or offering.'"

[15]Samuel lay down until morning and then opened the doors of the house of the LORD. He was afraid to tell Eli the vision, [16]but Eli called him and said, "Samuel, my son."

Samuel answered, "Here I am."

[17]"What was it he said to you?" Eli asked. "Do not hide it from me. May God deal with you, be it ever so severely, if you hide from me anything he told you." [18]So Samuel told him everything, hiding nothing from him. Then Eli said, "He is the LORD; let him do what is good in his eyes."

[19]The LORD was with Samuel as he grew up, and he let none of his words fall to the ground. [20]And all Israel from Dan to Beersheba recognized that Samuel was attested as a prophet of the LORD. [21]The

---

[a]13 Masoretic Text; an ancient Hebrew scribal tradition and Septuagint *sons blasphemed God*

---

     1 Samuel 3:1–21   **THE LORD CALLS SAMUEL**

Young Samuel had been brought by his parents to grow up and serve in the house of the Lord with Eli, the high priest. In this story he experiences his first revelation from God. That message confirms what a prophet had previously told Eli about God's judgment on his family for the corruption Eli's sons had brought the priesthood.

1. Why did the Lord speak to Samuel and not to Eli?
   a. Eli had a hearing problem.
   b. It's hard to hear the truth about yourself.
   c. It was time for Samuel to answer directly to God.
   d. Samuel's ministry as a prophet was about to begin.

2. Why was God angry at Eli?
   a. His sons were wicked.
   b. He didn't do anything about their wickedness.
   c. His attempts to correct them failed.
   d. He had ignored God's warning.

3. If you had been Samuel, how would you have felt about bearing the bad news?

a. afraid of Eli
b. afraid to hurt Eli's feelings
c. afraid to conceal God's message
d. glad to see justice done

4. If you had been Eli, how would you react to the news about your family?
   a. with grief
   b. with resignation
   c. with denial
   d. attempt to change God's mind
   e. with animosity toward Samuel

5. The best way for me to "listen" as God's servant is to:
   a. pay attention in church and small group settings.
   b. start my day with prayer and Bible study.
   c. take a break during the day to "tune in" to God.
   d. take stock of my day at bedtime.
   e. spend time with God out of doors.
   f. learn from God's people.

6. How close are you to an attitude of, "Speak, Lord, for your servant is listening"? How do you, or would you, react if the Lord's message was something you'd rather not hear—

such as a word of correction? Would it make any difference if the message came from another person?

7. How important is it to discipline children? How do you imagine Eli had done in that area when his sons were growing up?

8. In the area of disciplining my child(ren), I have a tendency to:
   a. fail to restrain them.
   b. fail to restrain myself.
   c. be too strict with rules.
   d. be too permissive with rules.
   e. be too harsh when rules are broken.
   f. be too soft when rules are broken.
   g. avoid confrontation.
   h. ride them too much.
   i. be inconsistent.

9. What have you sensed God to be saying about your status as a single person? How open are you to the possibility that God has called you to a life of singleness?

failure? How did you react? **3.** Do you pray with an attitude of: (a) "Speak Lord, your servant listens" or (b) "Listen Lord, for your servant speaks"? How can you learn to listen more and speak less? **4.** How do you treat the word of God? What commands have you "let fall to the ground"?

What superstitions were popular when your grandparents were young? What superstitions do people believe in today?

1. Why do the Israelites bring the ark to the battle front? What's wrong with this thinking? 2. Why did the Lord allow Israel to lose the first battle (v. 2)? Why the second (v. 10)? Why did Israel lose so many men the second time (vv. 2,10)? 3. What do the Philistines know about the Lord (vv. 7–9)? How does this view of him compare with that of the Hebrews?

1. When have you trusted in symbols or rituals instead of the reality to which they point? 2. Role play how each of the following characters would interact with God: (a) Philistine soldier; (b) Hebrew soldier; (c) Eli's sons. Which of these characters had a view of God which is closest to your own?

1. How has war been made most real to you: By TV? Family stories? Do you have any "war stories" of your own? 2. Have you had to be the bearer of "bad news"? How did you break the news?

1. What words from God are fulfilled "that same day" (v. 12; see 2:32–34)? 2. What seems to be Eli's first concern here? What new insight does that give into his character? 3. Why do Eli and the townspeople react so strongly to the news of the ark? Do you suppose they had any premonition of the news to come? How so? 4. At the close of this story, what "good news" helps to offset some of this "bad news"?

1. What low points and high points have marked your spiritual pilgrimage? Where are you just now on the "bad-news-to-good-news" spectrum? 2. When was the last time that you felt de-

LORD continued to appear at Shiloh, and there he revealed himself to Samuel through his word.

4 And Samuel's word came to all Israel.

The Philistines Capture the Ark

Now the Israelites went out to fight against the Philistines. The Israelites camped at Ebenezer, and the Philistines at Aphek. ²The Philistines deployed their forces to meet Israel, and as the battle spread, Israel was defeated by the Philistines, who killed about four thousand of them on the battlefield. ³When the soldiers returned to camp, the elders of Israel asked, "Why did the LORD bring defeat upon us today before the Philistines? Let us bring the ark of the LORD's covenant from Shiloh, so that itᵃ may go with us and save us from the hand of our enemies."

⁴So the people sent men to Shiloh, and they brought back the ark of the covenant of the LORD Almighty, who is enthroned between the cherubim. And Eli's two sons, Hophni and Phinehas, were there with the ark of the covenant of God.

⁵When the ark of the LORD's covenant came into the camp, all Israel raised such a great shout that the ground shook. ⁶Hearing the uproar, the Philistines asked, "What's all this shouting in the Hebrew camp?"

When they learned that the ark of the LORD had come into the camp, ⁷the Philistines were afraid. "A god has come into the camp," they said. "We're in trouble! Nothing like this has happened before. ⁸Woe to us! Who will deliver us from the hand of these mighty gods? They are the gods who struck the Egyptians with all kinds of plagues in the desert. ⁹Be strong, Philistines! Be men, or you will be subject to the Hebrews, as they have been to you. Be men, and fight!"

¹⁰So the Philistines fought, and the Israelites were defeated and every man fled to his tent. The slaughter was very great; Israel lost thirty thousand foot soldiers. ¹¹The ark of God was captured, and Eli's two sons, Hophni and Phinehas, died.

Death of Eli

¹²That same day a Benjamite ran from the battle line and went to Shiloh, his clothes torn and dust on his head. ¹³When he arrived, there was Eli sitting on his chair by the side of the road, watching, because his heart feared for the ark of God. When the man entered the town and told what had happened, the whole town sent up a cry.

¹⁴Eli heard the outcry and asked, "What is the meaning of this uproar?"

The man hurried over to Eli, ¹⁵who was ninety-eight years old and whose eyes were set so that he could not see. ¹⁶He told Eli, "I have just come from the battle line; I fled from it this very day."

Eli asked, "What happened, my son?"

¹⁷The man who brought the news replied, "Israel fled before the Philistines, and the army has suffered heavy losses. Also your two sons, Hophni and Phinehas, are dead, and the ark of God has been captured."

¹⁸When he mentioned the ark of God, Eli fell backward off his chair by the side of the gate. His neck was broken and he died, for he was an old man and heavy. He had ledᵇ Israel forty years.

¹⁹His daughter-in-law, the wife of Phinehas, was pregnant and near the time of delivery. When she heard the news that the ark of

ᵃ3 Or *he*   ᵇ18 Traditionally *judged*

God had been captured and that her father-in-law and her husband were dead, she went into labor and gave birth, but was overcome by her labor pains. 20As she was dying, the women attending her said, "Don't despair; you have given birth to a son." But she did not respond or pay any attention.

21She named the boy Ichabod,a saying, "The glory has departed from Israel"—because of the capture of the ark of God and the deaths of her father-in-law and her husband. 22She said, "The glory has departed from Israel, for the ark of God has been captured."

The Ark in Ashdod and Ekron

5 After the Philistines had captured the ark of God, they took it from Ebenezer to Ashdod. 2Then they carried the ark into Dagon's temple and set it beside Dagon. 3When the people of Ashdod rose early the next day, there was Dagon, fallen on his face on the ground before the ark of the LORD! They took Dagon and put him back in his place. 4But the following morning when they rose, there was Dagon, fallen on his face on the ground before the ark of the LORD! His head and hands had been broken off and were lying on the threshold; only his body remained. 5That is why to this day neither the priests of Dagon nor any others who enter Dagon's temple at Ashdod step on the threshold.

6The LORD's hand was heavy upon the people of Ashdod and its vicinity; he brought devastation upon them and afflicted them with tumors.b 7When the men of Ashdod saw what was happening, they said, "The ark of the god of Israel must not stay here with us, because his hand is heavy upon us and upon Dagon our god." 8So they called together all the rulers of the Philistines and asked them, "What shall we do with the ark of the god of Israel?"

They answered, "Have the ark of the god of Israel moved to Gath." So they moved the ark of the God of Israel.

9But after they had moved it, the LORD's hand was against that city, throwing it into a great panic. He afflicted the people of the city, both young and old, with an outbreak of tumors.c 10So they sent the ark of God to Ekron.

As the ark of God was entering Ekron, the people of Ekron cried out, "They have brought the ark of the god of Israel around to us to kill us and our people." 11So they called together all the rulers of the Philistines and said, "Send the ark of the god of Israel away; let it go back to its own place, or itd will kill us and our people." For death had filled the city with panic; God's hand was very heavy upon it. 12Those who did not die were afflicted with tumors, and the outcry of the city went up to heaven.

The Ark Returned to Israel

6 When the ark of the LORD had been in Philistine territory seven months, 2the Philistines called for the priests and the diviners and said, "What shall we do with the ark of the LORD? Tell us how we should send it back to its place."

3They answered, "If you return the ark of the god of Israel, do not send it away empty, but by all means send a guilt offering to him. Then you will be healed, and you will know why his hand has not been lifted from you."

4The Philistines asked, "What guilt offering should we send to him?"

serted by God? What was the cause? The solution? **3.** Is God currently in your camp? In the Philistines' camp? Somewhere on the road between?

---

1. For what sickness were you bed-ridden? Hospitalized? Contagious? Quarantined? **2.** What gets passed around your family begging for an owner: Hot potato? Unwanted heirloom? White elephant?

1. Dagon was the pagan deity of corn. Why do the Philistines place the ark in Dagon's temple after defeating the Israelites? **2.** Why does Dagon keep falling over? Why does he lose his head and hands? **3.** Why do the Philistines play "hot potato" with the ark and keep passing it around? Why don't they send it back to Israel? **4.** Why is God so "heavy handed" with the Philistines? Who is at fault for the suffering and deaths of the Philistines: The Philistines? The Jews? God?

1. What commandments or "holy things" of God do you treat lightly? How might that be affecting the non-Christians around you? **2.** Is God disciplining you right now? How are you responding: Passing the buck? Replacing idols? Submitting to his hand? **3.** What "enemy" or "false god" in your life would you like to have God topple? How will you take steps this week to cooperate?

---

1. Did you see the popular movie, "Raiders of the Lost Ark"? What do you remember about the scene where the "bad guys" looked into the ark? How did this scene affect you? **2.** When have you lost something precious, only to find it again months later? How did you respond? **3.** Describe a model or sculpture which you built as a child and still take pride in displaying.

1. Why do the religious experts of the Philistines suggest a guilt offering? Why does this offering consist of imitation rats and

---

a21 *Ichabod* means *no glory.*   b6 Hebrew; Septuagint and Vulgate *tumors. And rats appeared in their land, and death and destruction were throughout the city.*   c9 Or *with tumors in the groin* (see Septuagint)   d11 Or *he*

tumors made from gold? Why five of each (vv. 4,17–18)? **2.** What lesson is drawn from the plagues which God sent upon Egypt (v. 6)? **3.** Why do you think they take care to build a new cart and use yet unyoked cows to transport the ark (v. 7)? **4.** How were the Philistines to be assured that the God of Israel had intentionally brought the plague upon them and not by chance (v. 9)? Why take the calves away from their mom, unless to deter the cows from making straight for Beth Shemesh? (Note their "lowing all the way," v. 12.) **5.** If you had been one of the Philistine onlookers (v. 16), what would you have seen and heard and told to your friends back in Ekron? What would you have wished to have happened to the Levites that didn't? **6.** Why weren't the Levites afflicted by the dangerous ark (v. 15), whereas some laymen were (v. 19)? What is the object lesson here (vv. 20–21)? **7.** Why do you suppose the ark was sent to Kiriath Jearim, and not to Shiloh, where it was before its capture (see Jer 7:12–14)?

♡ **1.** When in the last year have you felt like God was angry with you? At such times, do you feel like nothing—not even good behavior or guilt offerings—will please him? What finally turns the tide of his anger? **2.** When do you test God? What do you do to rationalize God's judgment on you for trifling with that which is holy? **3.** When have you treated God and sacred things with too much familiarity? How do you maintain proper respect for his holiness? **4.** Do you use "signs" to determine if God is for or against a plan of yours? Which signs? How do you know if these are from God or not?

They replied, "Five gold tumors and five gold rats, according to the number of the Philistine rulers, because the same plague has struck both you and your rulers. ⁵Make models of the tumors and of the rats that are destroying the country, and pay honor to Israel's god. Perhaps he will lift his hand from you and your gods and your land. ⁶Why do you harden your hearts as the Egyptians and Pharaoh did? When heᵃ treated them harshly, did they not send the Israelites out so they could go on their way?

⁷"Now then, get a new cart ready, with two cows that have calved and have never been yoked. Hitch the cows to the cart, but take their calves away and pen them up. ⁸Take the ark of the LORD and put it on the cart, and in a chest beside it put the gold objects you are sending back to him as a guilt offering. Send it on its way, ⁹but keep watching it. If it goes up to its own territory, toward Beth Shemesh, then the LORD has brought this great disaster on us. But if it does not, then we will know that it was not his hand that struck us and that it happened to us by chance."

¹⁰So they did this. They took two such cows and hitched them to the cart and penned up their calves. ¹¹They placed the ark of the LORD on the cart and along with it the chest containing the gold rats and the models of the tumors. ¹²Then the cows went straight up toward Beth Shemesh, keeping on the road and lowing all the way; they did not turn to the right or to the left. The rulers of the Philistines followed them as far as the border of Beth Shemesh.

¹³Now the people of Beth Shemesh were harvesting their wheat in the valley, and when they looked up and saw the ark, they rejoiced at the sight. ¹⁴The cart came to the field of Joshua of Beth Shemesh, and there it stopped beside a large rock. The people chopped up the wood of the cart and sacrificed the cows as a burnt offering to the LORD. ¹⁵The Levites took down the ark of the LORD, together with the chest containing the gold objects, and placed them on the large rock. On that day the people of Beth Shemesh offered burnt offerings and made sacrifices to the LORD. ¹⁶The five rulers of the Philistines saw all this and then returned that same day to Ekron.

¹⁷These are the gold tumors the Philistines sent as a guilt offering to the LORD—one each for Ashdod, Gaza, Ashkelon, Gath and Ekron. ¹⁸And the number of the gold rats was according to the number of Philistine towns belonging to the five rulers—the fortified towns with their country villages. The large rock, on whichᵇ they set the ark of the LORD, is a witness to this day in the field of Joshua of Beth Shemesh.

¹⁹But God struck down some of the men of Beth Shemesh, putting seventyᶜ of them to death because they had looked into the ark of the LORD. The people mourned because of the heavy blow the LORD had dealt them, ²⁰and the men of Beth Shemesh asked, "Who can stand in the presence of the LORD, this holy God? To whom will the ark go up from here?"

²¹Then they sent messengers to the people of Kiriath Jearim, saying, "The Philistines have returned the ark of the LORD. Come

7 down and take it up to your place." ¹So the men of Kiriath Jearim came and took up the ark of the LORD. They took it to Abinadab's house on the hill and consecrated Eleazar his son to guard the ark of the LORD.

ᵃ6 That is, God   ᵇ18 A few Hebrew manuscripts (see also Septuagint); most Hebrew manuscripts *villages as far as Greater Abel, where*   ᶜ19 A few Hebrew manuscripts; most Hebrew manuscripts and Septuagint *50,070*

Samuel Subdues the Philistines at Mizpah

²It was a long time, twenty years in all, that the ark remained at Kiriath Jearim, and all the people of Israel mourned and sought after the LORD. ³And Samuel said to the whole house of Israel, "If you are returning to the LORD with all your hearts, then rid yourselves of the foreign gods and the Ashtoreths and commit yourselves to the LORD and serve him only, and he will deliver you out of the hand of the Philistines." ⁴So the Israelites put away their Baals and Ashtoreths, and served the LORD only.

⁵Then Samuel said, "Assemble all Israel at Mizpah and I will intercede with the LORD for you." ⁶When they had assembled at Mizpah, they drew water and poured it out before the LORD. On that day they fasted and there they confessed, "We have sinned against the LORD." And Samuel was leaderᵃ of Israel at Mizpah.

⁷When the Philistines heard that Israel had assembled at Mizpah, the rulers of the Philistines came up to attack them. And when the Israelites heard of it, they were afraid because of the Philistines. ⁸They said to Samuel, "Do not stop crying out to the LORD our God for us, that he may rescue us from the hand of the Philistines." ⁹Then Samuel took a suckling lamb and offered it up as a whole burnt offering to the LORD. He cried out to the LORD on Israel's behalf, and the LORD answered him.

¹⁰While Samuel was sacrificing the burnt offering, the Philistines drew near to engage Israel in battle. But that day the LORD thundered with loud thunder against the Philistines and threw them into such a panic that they were routed before the Israelites. ¹¹The men of Israel rushed out of Mizpah and pursued the Philistines, slaughtering them along the way to a point below Beth Car.

¹²Then Samuel took a stone and set it up between Mizpah and Shen. He named it Ebenezer,ᵇ saying, "Thus far has the LORD helped us." ¹³So the Philistines were subdued and did not invade Israelite territory again.

Throughout Samuel's lifetime, the hand of the LORD was against the Philistines. ¹⁴The towns from Ekron to Gath that the Philistines had captured from Israel were restored to her, and Israel delivered the neighboring territory from the power of the Philistines. And there was peace between Israel and the Amorites.

¹⁵Samuel continued as judge over Israel all the days of his life. ¹⁶From year to year he went on a circuit from Bethel to Gilgal to Mizpah, judging Israel in all those places. ¹⁷But he always went back to Ramah, where his home was, and there he also judged Israel. And he built an altar there to the LORD.

Israel Asks for a King

8 When Samuel grew old, he appointed his sons as judges for Israel. ²The name of his firstborn was Joel and the name of his second was Abijah, and they served at Beersheba. ³But his sons did not walk in his ways. They turned aside after dishonest gain and accepted bribes and perverted justice.

⁴So all the elders of Israel gathered together and came to Samuel at Ramah. ⁵They said to him, "You are old, and your sons do not walk in your ways; now appoint a king to leadᶜ us, such as all the other nations have."

⁶But when they said, "Give us a king to lead us," this displeased Samuel; so he prayed to the LORD. ⁷And the LORD told him: "Listen

ᵃ6 Traditionally judge   ᵇ12 Ebenezer means stone of help.   ᶜ5 Traditionally judge; also in verses 6 and 20

reason? **3.** Is rejecting Samuel the same as rejecting God (v. 7)? Why? What pattern does this represent (v. 8)? **4.** If you had heard the warning of verses 11–18, would you have acted as the Israelites did? Why? What's wrong with their willful intent to have a king? What were kings of "other nations" like then (e.g., Pharaoh)? **5.** How can they forget so soon how God has led them into battle (v. 20)? Why does the Lord seem to "give in"?

1. When are you inclined to want or do something just to be "like everyone else"? How do you prevent sin from blinding you in your choices? **2.** How would you distinguish an offense for the sake of Christ and being "just plain offensive"? **3.** When was the last time you bulldozed over God's will, only to find the walls crash in around you? **4.** How can you ask God for something in the confidence he will say "no" if it is bad for you? Do you really want him to?

to all that the people are saying to you; it is not you they have rejected, but they have rejected me as their king. ⁸As they have done from the day I brought them up out of Egypt until this day, forsaking me and serving other gods, so they are doing to you. ⁹Now listen to them; but warn them solemnly and let them know what the king who will reign over them will do."

¹⁰Samuel told all the words of the Lord to the people who were asking him for a king. ¹¹He said, "This is what the king who will reign over you will do: He will take your sons and make them serve with his chariots and horses, and they will run in front of his chariots. ¹²Some he will assign to be commanders of thousands and commanders of fifties, and others to plow his ground and reap his harvest, and still others to make weapons of war and equipment for his chariots. ¹³He will take your daughters to be perfumers and cooks and bakers. ¹⁴He will take the best of your fields and vineyards and olive groves and give them to his attendants. ¹⁵He will take a tenth of your grain and of your vintage and give it to his officials and attendants. ¹⁶Your menservants and maidservants and the best of your cattleᵃ and donkeys he will take for his own use. ¹⁷He will take a tenth of your flocks, and you yourselves will become his slaves. ¹⁸When that day comes, you will cry out for relief from the king you have chosen, and the Lord will not answer you in that day."

¹⁹But the people refused to listen to Samuel. "No!" they said. "We want a king over us. ²⁰Then we will be like all the other nations, with a king to lead us and to go out before us and fight our battles."

²¹When Samuel heard all that the people said, he repeated it

ᵃ16 Septuagint; Hebrew *young men*

1 Samuel 8:1–22   ISRAEL ASKS FOR A KING

For the years since God led the Israelites out of Egypt and into the promised land, Israel had been without a king. Rather, the nation had been led by "judges"—individuals called by God not only to judicial functions, but also to rally the people in times of spiritual and military crises. Now things are about to change.

1. How do you explain the way Samuel's sons turned out?
   a. They rejected Samuel's teaching.
   b. They were typical "preacher's kids."
   c. They got into the wrong crowd.
   d. Samuel was a good prophet but a bad father.
   e. There's no guarantee children will turn out like their parents.

2. Why did the Israelites want a king?
   a. because it was better than having a bad judge
   b. to give the nation more stability
   c. to keep up with the Joneses
   d. for the sake of national security

3. What was God's response to their request?
   a. I don't want any rivals.
   b. You are rejecting me as your king.
   c. I give up on these bellyachers.
   d. Since you've stopped depending on me for help, don't expect any.
   e. People have to learn by their mistakes.
   f. You'll be sorry!

4. Why were the Israelites willing to ignore God's warning?
   a. They didn't believe the bad things would really happen.
   b. They liked living dangerously.
   c. They just wanted to be like their neighbors.
   d. Now is more important than later.

5. Why did God give in to their wishes? Do you think God has ever given you what you wanted even though it wasn't the best thing for you? Why?

6. Have you ever gone through a time of rebellion?

   a. never
   b. never, but I wish I had
   c. once, and I learned my lesson
   d. often, and I wonder if God has given up on me

7. Sometimes I act as though the "king" who rules my life is:
   a. my work.   e. my parents.
   b. my schedule.   f. my fears.
   c. worry about what others think.
   d. my drive for _____.

8. In what way are you most concerned to be like everyone else? How do you keep that desire from enslaving you?

9. What persuades you to submit to God's way for your life?
   a. knowing what God's way is
   b. being assured it will meet my need
   c. being reassured God loves me
   d. knowing it is the right way
   e. having others go that way with me
   f. realizing the alternatives don't measure up

before the LORD. ²²The LORD answered, "Listen to them and give them a king."

Then Samuel said to the men of Israel, "Everyone go back to his town."

Samuel Anoints Saul

9 There was a Benjamite, a man of standing, whose name was Kish son of Abiel, the son of Zeror, the son of Becorath, the son of Aphiah of Benjamin. ²He had a son named Saul, an impressive young man without equal among the Israelites—a head taller than any of the others.

³Now the donkeys belonging to Saul's father Kish were lost, and Kish said to his son Saul, "Take one of the servants with you and go and look for the donkeys." ⁴So he passed through the hill country of Ephraim and through the area around Shalisha, but they did not find them. They went on into the district of Shaalim, but the donkeys were not there. Then he passed through the territory of Benjamin, but they did not find them.

⁵When they reached the district of Zuph, Saul said to the servant who was with him, "Come, let's go back, or my father will stop thinking about the donkeys and start worrying about us."

⁶But the servant replied, "Look, in this town there is a man of God; he is highly respected, and everything he says comes true. Let's go there now. Perhaps he will tell us what way to take."

⁷Saul said to his servant, "If we go, what can we give the man? The food in our sacks is gone. We have no gift to take to the man of God. What do we have?"

⁸The servant answered him again. "Look," he said, "I have a quarter of a shekelᵃ of silver. I will give it to the man of God so that he will tell us what way to take." ⁹(Formerly in Israel, if a man went to inquire of God, he would say, "Come, let us go to the seer," because the prophet of today used to be called a seer.)

¹⁰"Good," Saul said to his servant. "Come, let's go." So they set out for the town where the man of God was.

¹¹As they were going up the hill to the town, they met some girls coming out to draw water, and they asked them, "Is the seer here?"

¹²"He is," they answered. "He's ahead of you. Hurry now; he has just come to our town today, for the people have a sacrifice at the high place. ¹³As soon as you enter the town, you will find him before he goes up to the high place to eat. The people will not begin eating until he comes, because he must bless the sacrifice; afterward, those who are invited will eat. Go up now; you should find him about this time."

¹⁴They went up to the town, and as they were entering it, there was Samuel, coming toward them on his way up to the high place.

¹⁵Now the day before Saul came, the LORD had revealed this to Samuel: ¹⁶"About this time tomorrow I will send you a man from the land of Benjamin. Anoint him leader over my people Israel; he will deliver my people from the hand of the Philistines. I have looked upon my people, for their cry has reached me."

¹⁷When Samuel caught sight of Saul, the LORD said to him, "This is the man I spoke to you about; he will govern my people."

¹⁸Saul approached Samuel in the gateway and asked, "Would you please tell me where the seer's house is?"

ᵃ8 That is, about 1/10 ounce (about 3 grams)

1. How do you feel about your height? Is height a factor in your selection of a mate? In your vote for a political candidate? 2. Who sat where at your family table when you were 12 years old? 3. Were you ever the honored guest at a fancy meal? What for?

1. Outline the chain of "chance" events which the Lord uses to put Saul where he wants him. 2. What physical advantage does Saul have over his peers? How might that impress others with his "electability"? 3. What distinguishes a "man of God" (9:6)? What was the prophetic office like back then? What does Saul's ignorance of Samuel indicate? 4. What is God's purpose for the king-to-be (9:16)? What does this teach us about his mercy? 5. What do you think Samuel saw in Saul's heart (9:19)? In Saul's fortunes and future (9:20)? 6. How does Saul react to such prophetic insight (9:21): With true modesty? Still in ignorance? Fear? Why? 7. In what ways does Samuel honor Saul at the meal (9:22–24)? Do you think Saul knows what Samuel's intentions are? Why or why not? 8. What is the significance of Samuel's private anointing of Saul (10:1)? Why a *private* ceremony when there would be a *public* coronation later on (10:17–25)? 9. What three signs would be given to Saul (10:2–6)? What would these signs confirm (10:7)? If you had been in Saul's sandals at this point, how would you consider this prophecy, given the events of the past 24 hours?

1. If some seer were reading all that was in your heart and telling you where your lost items were, would you have reacted as Saul did? Why or why not? 2. What insight does Samuel give you into Jesus' prophetic ability to know what was in the heart of man (see Jn 2:25)? 3. Likewise, what insight does Saul's search for the lost donkeys give you regarding Jesus' compassion in seeking to save the lost (sheep, coin, son, see Luke 15)? 4. When has God mercifully used your disobedient choices to bring about good in your life

(such as what God mercifully intends to do in spite of Israel's rebellious desire for a king)? **5.** When has God used "chance" events, good or bad, to bring you to the point where he could bless you? **6.** Is God leading you into any new responsibilities? Are past roles changing? How is God confirming that to you? **7.** Any signs that you are to be like Saul—"changed into a different person"? What attitude is especially important for you to maintain in the transition period?

¹⁹"I am the seer," Samuel replied. "Go up ahead of me to the high place, for today you are to eat with me, and in the morning I will let you go and will tell you all that is in your heart. ²⁰As for the donkeys you lost three days ago, do not worry about them; they have been found. And to whom is all the desire of Israel turned, if not to you and all your father's family?"

²¹Saul answered, "But am I not a Benjamite, from the smallest tribe of Israel, and is not my clan the least of all the clans of the tribe of Benjamin? Why do you say such a thing to me?"

²²Then Samuel brought Saul and his servant into the hall and seated them at the head of those who were invited—about thirty in number. ²³Samuel said to the cook, "Bring the piece of meat I gave you, the one I told you to lay aside."

²⁴So the cook took up the leg with what was on it and set it in front of Saul. Samuel said, "Here is what has been kept for you. Eat, because it was set aside for you for this occasion, from the time I said, 'I have invited guests.'" And Saul dined with Samuel that day.

²⁵After they came down from the high place to the town, Samuel talked with Saul on the roof of his house. ²⁶They rose about daybreak and Samuel called to Saul on the roof, "Get ready, and I will send you on your way." When Saul got ready, he and Samuel went outside together. ²⁷As they were going down to the edge of the town, Samuel said to Saul, "Tell the servant to go on ahead of us"—and the servant did so—"but you stay here awhile, so that I may give you a message from God."

---

 1 Samuel 9:1–10:8   **SAMUEL ANOINTS SAUL**

Following the people's complaints and appeals, the Lord has just told the prophet Samuel that he will grant Israel's request for a king.

1. What would you call God's decision to give Israel a king?
   a. preordained
   b. spontaneous
   c. merciful
   d. consequence of Israel's rebellion

2. When God looked for a king, what did he look for?
   a. physical stature
   b. social standing
   c. popular appeal
   d. spiritual perception
   e. family pedigree
   f. openness to the Holy Spirit

3. Since Samuel knew God really did not want Israel to have a king, how do you think Samuel felt in this story?
   a. confused   d. sad
   b. angry   e. relieved
   c. detached   f. jealous

4. If you were Saul, how would you

have felt about being anointed?
   a. confused   d. overwhelmed
   b. proud   e. energized
   c. humble   f. afraid

5. Why did Samuel anoint Saul privately (instead of publicly as later on)?
   a. to get Saul used to the idea
   b. to demonstrate the king's need for the prophet
   c. to encourage Saul to depend on the Spirit before he became a celebrity
   d. to emphasize that God—not the people—chose Saul

6. From what you know of Saul, how much (or for how long) do you think he was actually "changed into a different person" (10:6)? How come?

7. How have you seen God mercifully use your wrong or disobedient choices to bring about good in your life (as he did with Israel's desire for a king)?

8. When has God used what seemed like chance circumstances to bring you to a place where he could bless you or make you a blessing? Does

the Lord seem to be leading you to anything new now?

9. What does this story say to you about hearing God's call in your life?
   a. We may seem to be on a "wild donkey chase," but God is at work (9:3–4).
   b. Status and position don't matter when it comes to God's call (9:21).
   c. God often calls us through others (10:1).
   d. When God calls, the Spirit empowers (10:6).
   e. Letting God change us is more important than what we do (10:6).
   f. Don't back down if you know what God's will is for you (10:7).
   g. If God says wait, that means wait (10:8).

10. Which of the previous points are most relevant to you in your desire to know how God wants to use your life? What input have you received from others about your gifts and calling?

10 Then Samuel took a flask of oil and poured it on Saul's head and kissed him, saying, "Has not the LORD anointed you leader over his inheritance?[a] 2When you leave me today, you will meet two men near Rachel's tomb, at Zelzah on the border of Benjamin. They will say to you, 'The donkeys you set out to look for have been found. And now your father has stopped thinking about them and is worried about you. He is asking, "What shall I do about my son?" '

3"Then you will go on from there until you reach the great tree of Tabor. Three men going up to God at Bethel will meet you there. One will be carrying three young goats, another three loaves of bread, and another a skin of wine. 4They will greet you and offer you two loaves of bread, which you will accept from them.

5"After that you will go to Gibeah of God, where there is a Philistine outpost. As you approach the town, you will meet a procession of prophets coming down from the high place with lyres, tambourines, flutes and harps being played before them, and they will be prophesying. 6The Spirit of the LORD will come upon you in power, and you will prophesy with them; and you will be changed into a different person. 7Once these signs are fulfilled, do whatever your hand finds to do, for God is with you.

8"Go down ahead of me to Gilgal. I will surely come down to you to sacrifice burnt offerings and fellowship offerings,[b] but you must wait seven days until I come to you and tell you what you are to do."

Saul Made King

9As Saul turned to leave Samuel, God changed Saul's heart, and all these signs were fulfilled that day. 10When they arrived at Gibeah, a procession of prophets met him; the Spirit of God came upon him in power, and he joined in their prophesying. 11When all those who had formerly known him saw him prophesying with the prophets, they asked each other, "What is this that has happened to the son of Kish? Is Saul also among the prophets?"

12A man who lived there answered, "And who is their father?" So it became a saying: "Is Saul also among the prophets?" 13After Saul stopped prophesying, he went to the high place.

14Now Saul's uncle asked him and his servant, "Where have you been?"

"Looking for the donkeys," he said. "But when we saw they were not to be found, we went to Samuel."

15Saul's uncle said, "Tell me what Samuel said to you."

16Saul replied, "He assured us that the donkeys had been found." But he did not tell his uncle what Samuel had said about the kingship.

17Samuel summoned the people of Israel to the LORD at Mizpah 18and said to them, "This is what the LORD, the God of Israel, says: 'I brought Israel up out of Egypt, and I delivered you from the power of Egypt and all the kingdoms that oppressed you.' 19But you have now rejected your God, who saves you out of all your calamities and distresses. And you have said, 'No, set a king over us.' So now present yourselves before the LORD by your tribes and clans."

20When Samuel brought all the tribes of Israel near, the tribe of Benjamin was chosen. 21Then he brought forward the tribe of Benjamin, clan by clan, and Matri's clan was chosen. Finally Saul

---

Recall when some employer or talent scout first discovered you had a special ability. How did they affirm that in you? How did you respond?

1. What meaning did events at Gibeah have for Saul? For those who knew him? Why such surprise and cynicism? 2. What do you think is meant by the proverb, "Is Saul also among the prophets" (v. 11)? Was that meant to put down or build up? 3. Why does Saul explain the newfound donkeys but not the kingship (v. 16)? Why does he hide (vv. 21–22)? 4. In publicly anointing Saul, how does Samuel implicitly judge Israel and reward their protest (vv. 17–19; see 8:19–20)? 5. Why the elimination process (vv. 20–21), when Samuel already knew Saul was God's elect: To preserve suspense? To embarrass Saul? To appear judicious? To play "God"? 6. In what sense was there "no one like Saul"? Do you think Samuel has any clue that Saul will turn bad? 7. How do the Israelites respond to their new king (vv. 24–27)? Why this mixed reaction? How does Saul take it? Would your feelings have been more like the "valiant men" or the "troublemakers"?

---

a1 Hebrew; Septuagint and Vulgate over his people Israel? You will reign over the LORD's people and save them from the power of their enemies round about. And this will be a sign to you that the LORD has anointed you leader over his inheritance:
b8 Traditionally peace offerings

1. Describe a time when people were surprised at how God was working in your life. Were you equally surprised by God's grace? **2.** What major "calamity" in your past has God delivered you from? How has the memory of that event shaped your relationship with God now? **3.** In what area of your life right now do you feel the need for some "valiant men" to accompany you? How about your small group?

When have you been physically threatened? How did you feel? What happened?

1. Why does Nahash make such harsh terms of surrender? **2.** Why then does Nahash give the people of Jabesh a chance to fortify their troops? **3.** Had you been there at Gibeah to hear their report, how would you have responded? **4.** How are the troops rallied "as one man": By Saul's threat? By family ties? By the Spirit's power? Or what? **5.** How do the Jabeshites mislead the Ammonites (v. 10, "surrender" more literally means "go out")? **6.** How extensive was the defeat of the Ammonites (v. 11)? What did the victory mean for citizens of Jabesh? For the other Israelites, even "troublemakers" (vv. 12–13)?

1. In what situation have you felt God truly energizing you? What did you do that, without God, you could not have done? **2.** When has God vindicated you in the eyes of troublemakers or skeptics (no names)? **3.** What challenge are you facing now in which you need God to embolden and empower you? **4.** Where does your group or church need to act "as one man" to achieve victory?

1. Why do the people want a purge? Why does Saul stop them? **2.** Why does Samuel "reaffirm" the kingship (v. 14)?

son of Kish was chosen. But when they looked for him, he was not to be found. ²²So they inquired further of the LORD, "Has the man come here yet?"

And the LORD said, "Yes, he has hidden himself among the baggage."

²³They ran and brought him out, and as he stood among the people he was a head taller than any of the others. ²⁴Samuel said to all the people, "Do you see the man the LORD has chosen? There is no one like him among all the people."

Then the people shouted, "Long live the king!"

²⁵Samuel explained to the people the regulations of the kingship. He wrote them down on a scroll and deposited it before the LORD. Then Samuel dismissed the people, each to his own home.

²⁶Saul also went to his home in Gibeah, accompanied by valiant men whose hearts God had touched. ²⁷But some troublemakers said, "How can this fellow save us?" They despised him and brought him no gifts. But Saul kept silent.

Saul Rescues the City of Jabesh

11 Nahash the Ammonite went up and besieged Jabesh Gilead. And all the men of Jabesh said to him, "Make a treaty with us, and we will be subject to you."

²But Nahash the Ammonite replied, "I will make a treaty with you only on the condition that I gouge out the right eye of every one of you and so bring disgrace on all Israel."

³The elders of Jabesh said to him, "Give us seven days so we can send messengers throughout Israel; if no one comes to rescue us, we will surrender to you."

⁴When the messengers came to Gibeah of Saul and reported these terms to the people, they all wept aloud. ⁵Just then Saul was returning from the fields, behind his oxen, and he asked, "What is wrong with the people? Why are they weeping?" Then they repeated to him what the men of Jabesh had said.

⁶When Saul heard their words, the Spirit of God came upon him in power, and he burned with anger. ⁷He took a pair of oxen, cut them into pieces, and sent the pieces by messengers throughout Israel, proclaiming, "This is what will be done to the oxen of anyone who does not follow Saul and Samuel." Then the terror of the LORD fell on the people, and they turned out as one man. ⁸When Saul mustered them at Bezek, the men of Israel numbered three hundred thousand and the men of Judah thirty thousand.

⁹They told the messengers who had come, "Say to the men of Jabesh Gilead, 'By the time the sun is hot tomorrow, you will be delivered.'" When the messengers went and reported this to the men of Jabesh, they were elated. ¹⁰They said to the Ammonites, "Tomorrow we will surrender to you, and you can do to us whatever seems good to you."

¹¹The next day Saul separated his men into three divisions; during the last watch of the night they broke into the camp of the Ammonites and slaughtered them until the heat of the day. Those who survived were scattered, so that no two of them were left together.

Saul Confirmed as King

¹²The people then said to Samuel, "Who was it that asked, 'Shall Saul reign over us?' Bring these men to us and we will put them to death."

¹³But Saul said, "No one shall be put to death today, for this day the LORD has rescued Israel."

¹⁴Then Samuel said to the people, "Come, let us go to Gilgal and there reaffirm the kingship." ¹⁵So all the people went to Gilgal and confirmed Saul as king in the presence of the LORD. There they sacrificed fellowship offerings*a* before the LORD, and Saul and all the Israelites held a great celebration.

Samuel's Farewell Speech

12 Samuel said to all Israel, "I have listened to everything you said to me and have set a king over you. ²Now you have a king as your leader. As for me, I am old and gray, and my sons are here with you. I have been your leader from my youth until this day. ³Here I stand. Testify against me in the presence of the LORD and his anointed. Whose ox have I taken? Whose donkey have I taken? Whom have I cheated? Whom have I oppressed? From whose hand have I accepted a bribe to make me shut my eyes? If I have done any of these, I will make it right."

⁴"You have not cheated or oppressed us," they replied. "You have not taken anything from anyone's hand."

⁵Samuel said to them, "The LORD is witness against you, and also his anointed is witness this day, that you have not found anything in my hand."

"He is witness," they said.

⁶Then Samuel said to the people, "It is the LORD who appointed Moses and Aaron and brought your forefathers up out of Egypt. ⁷Now then, stand here, because I am going to confront you with evidence before the LORD as to all the righteous acts performed by the LORD for you and your fathers.

⁸"After Jacob entered Egypt, they cried to the LORD for help, and the LORD sent Moses and Aaron, who brought your forefathers out of Egypt and settled them in this place.

⁹"But they forgot the LORD their God; so he sold them into the hand of Sisera, the commander of the army of Hazor, and into the hands of the Philistines and the king of Moab, who fought against them. ¹⁰They cried out to the LORD and said, 'We have sinned; we have forsaken the LORD and served the Baals and the Ashtoreths. But now deliver us from the hands of our enemies, and we will serve you.' ¹¹Then the LORD sent Jerub-Baal,*b* Barak,*c* Jephthah and Samuel,*d* and he delivered you from the hands of your enemies on every side, so that you lived securely.

¹²"But when you saw that Nahash king of the Ammonites was moving against you, you said to me, 'No, we want a king to rule over us'—even though the LORD your God was your king. ¹³Now here is the king you have chosen, the one you asked for; see, the LORD has set a king over you. ¹⁴If you fear the LORD and serve and obey him and do not rebel against his commands, and if both you and the king who reigns over you follow the LORD your God—good! ¹⁵But if you do not obey the LORD, and if you rebel against his commands, his hand will be against you, as it was against your fathers.

¹⁶"Now then, stand still and see this great thing the LORD is about to do before your eyes! ¹⁷Is it not wheat harvest now? I will call upon the LORD to send thunder and rain. And you will realize what an evil thing you did in the eyes of the LORD when you asked for a king."

¹⁸Then Samuel called upon the LORD, and that same day the LORD

In victory are you magnanimous? How are you in defeat? When are you more likely to give God the glory? Take pride?

---

1. Have you ever been slandered or falsely accused? Were you later vindicated? How so? 2. What was your attitude toward history courses in school?

1. What do verses 1–5 reveal about Samuel's character, faith, and tactics? Why does he want the Israelites to agree that he is innocent of wrongdoing? 2. What is the purpose of Samuel's history lesson (vv. 6–15)? From verses 8–11, how would you describe God's military record? What response has that winning streak engendered in Israel? 3. What further reason does Samuel cite for Israel's evil desire for a king (v. 12)? How did their desire for a king repeat the cycle of their unfaithfulness? 4. How much faith do you suppose Samuel has in Israel's ability to do the "good" (vv. 14–15)? How much confidence does Israel have? 5. What does Samuel hope to achieve by praying for thunder and rain (in the dry season)? What, in fact, happens? What prior experience with the Lord's thunder may have encouraged their fear (at Mizpah, 7:10; at Sinai, see Ex 19:16)? 6. How does Samuel seek to soothe their fears (vv. 20–23)? When is "failure to pray" a sin against the Lord? 7. What incentives, positive and negative, does he offer for loyal covenant living (vv. 24–25)? 8. Under this new administration of the covenant, whose "neck is in the noose" if the government fails: Prophet, priest or king? And whose office remains the teacher or mediator of that covenant? Why is this?

1. On the strength of his campaign speech, record in office and party platform, would you re-elect Samuel? Or urge him to retire? Why? 2. On a scale of 1 to 10, are you more guilt-free ("1") or guilt-ridden ("10")? Why do you think so? 3. How do you respond when you really blow it before God? What is a biblical response? 4. What "great things" has God done for you the past year? How is that conveyed in your faithfulness to God since then? 5. In what areas of your life has God continually proven faithful, yet you remain

---

a 15 Traditionally *peace offerings*   *b 11* Also called *Gideon*   *c 11* Some Septuagint manuscripts and Syriac; Hebrew *Bedan*   *d 11* Hebrew; some Septuagint manuscripts and Syriac *Samson*

reluctant to trust him in those very areas? **6.** Are you more motivated by *positive* incentives, or *negative* ones? Why?

☕ **1.** If drafted into military service tomorrow, would you go whole-heartedly, reluctantly or not at all? Why? **2.** If you have a date to meet someone, how late can he be before you give up on him?

📖 **1.** Combating the Philistine threat was to be Saul's life work. How does he plan to do it here with his 3000 men divided (v. 2)? Why does he call up the reserves (v. 4) he had just sent home? **2.** What are Israel's odds of victory? Are the odds improved by hiding? **3.** Why did they wait at Gilgal for Samuel (see 10:8)? How would you have reacted as a soldier of Saul: Stayed with him? Hidden? Gone to Gad? Explain why. **4.** How do Saul's reasons for deciding to sacrifice sound to you? How do they sound to Samuel (vv. 13–14)? **5.** What command does Saul violate (see 10:8)? What does this tell you about Samuel's authority and role (9:13)? **6.** What happens as a result of Saul's disobedience? How is David foreshadowed here?

♡ **1.** When you sin, which are you more likely to blame and why: (a) Circumstances? (b) Bad timing? (c) Parents? (d) Others? **2.** When has God been "late" in keeping a promise to you? Did you rush ahead and take things into your own hands? What happened? How did, or can, you make restitution? **3.** How hard is it for you to admit when you are wrong? **4.** What aspects of your faith and personality only come out under crisis circumstances?

---

sent thunder and rain. So all the people stood in awe of the LORD and of Samuel.

[19]The people all said to Samuel, "Pray to the LORD your God for your servants so that we will not die, for we have added to all our other sins the evil of asking for a king."

[20]"Do not be afraid," Samuel replied. "You have done all this evil; yet do not turn away from the LORD, but serve the LORD with all your heart. [21]Do not turn away after useless idols. They can do you no good, nor can they rescue you, because they are useless. [22]For the sake of his great name the LORD will not reject his people, because the LORD was pleased to make you his own. [23]As for me, far be it from me that I should sin against the LORD by failing to pray for you. And I will teach you the way that is good and right. [24]But be sure to fear the LORD and serve him faithfully with all your heart; consider what great things he has done for you. [25]Yet if you persist in doing evil, both you and your king will be swept away."

Samuel Rebukes Saul

13 Saul was ⌞thirty⌟[a] years old when he became king, and he reigned over Israel ⌞forty-⌟[b] two years.

[2]Saul[c] chose three thousand men from Israel; two thousand were with him at Micmash and in the hill country of Bethel, and a thousand were with Jonathan at Gibeah in Benjamin. The rest of the men he sent back to their homes.

[3]Jonathan attacked the Philistine outpost at Geba, and the Philistines heard about it. Then Saul had the trumpet blown throughout the land and said, "Let the Hebrews hear!" [4]So all Israel heard the news: "Saul has attacked the Philistine outpost, and now Israel has become a stench to the Philistines." And the people were summoned to join Saul at Gilgal.

[5]The Philistines assembled to fight Israel, with three thousand[d] chariots, six thousand charioteers, and soldiers as numerous as the sand on the seashore. They went up and camped at Micmash, east of Beth Aven. [6]When the men of Israel saw that their situation was critical and that their army was hard pressed, they hid in caves and thickets, among the rocks, and in pits and cisterns. [7]Some Hebrews even crossed the Jordan to the land of Gad and Gilead.

Saul remained at Gilgal, and all the troops with him were quaking with fear. [8]He waited seven days, the time set by Samuel; but Samuel did not come to Gilgal, and Saul's men began to scatter. [9]So he said, "Bring me the burnt offering and the fellowship offerings.[e]" And Saul offered up the burnt offering. [10]Just as he finished making the offering, Samuel arrived, and Saul went out to greet him.

[11]"What have you done?" asked Samuel.

Saul replied, "When I saw that the men were scattering, and that you did not come at the set time, and that the Philistines were assembling at Micmash, [12]I thought, 'Now the Philistines will come down against me at Gilgal, and I have not sought the LORD's favor.' So I felt compelled to offer the burnt offering."

[13]"You acted foolishly," Samuel said. "You have not kept the command the LORD your God gave you; if you had, he would have established your kingdom over Israel for all time. [14]But now your kingdom will not endure; the LORD has sought out a man after his

---

[a]1 A few late manuscripts of the Septuagint; Hebrew does not have *thirty*.   [b]1 See the round number in Acts 13:21; Hebrew does not have *forty-*.   [c]1,2 Or *and when he had reigned over Israel two years,* [2]*he*   [d]5 Some Septuagint manuscripts and Syriac; Hebrew *thirty thousand*   [e]9 Traditionally *peace offerings*

own heart and appointed him leader of his people, because you have not kept the LORD's command."

[15]Then Samuel left Gilgal[a] and went up to Gibeah in Benjamin, and Saul counted the men who were with him. They numbered about six hundred.

Israel Without Weapons

[16]Saul and his son Jonathan and the men with them were staying in Gibeah[b] in Benjamin, while the Philistines camped at Micmash. [17]Raiding parties went out from the Philistine camp in three detachments. One turned toward Ophrah in the vicinity of Shual, [18]another toward Beth Horon, and the third toward the borderland overlooking the Valley of Zeboim facing the desert.

[19]Not a blacksmith could be found in the whole land of Israel, because the Philistines had said, "Otherwise the Hebrews will make swords or spears!" [20]So all Israel went down to the Philistines to have their plowshares, mattocks, axes and sickles[c] sharpened. [21]The price was two thirds of a shekel[d] for sharpening plowshares and mattocks, and a third of a shekel[e] for sharpening forks and axes and for repointing goads.

[22]So on the day of the battle not a soldier with Saul and Jonathan had a sword or spear in his hand; only Saul and his son Jonathan had them.

[a]15 Hebrew; Septuagint *Gilgal and went his way; the rest of the people went after Saul to meet the army, and they went out of Gilgal*   [b]16 Two Hebrew manuscripts; most Hebrew manuscripts *Geba*, a variant of *Gibeah*   [c]20 Septuagint; Hebrew *plowshares*   [d]21 Hebrew *pim*; that is, about 1/4 ounce (about 8 grams)   [e]21 That is, about 1/8 ounce (about 4 grams)

When you play a game with sporting equipment inferior to your opponent's, how do you feel?

1. How extensive is the Philistines' influence over Israel? **2.** How did their weaponry compare (v. 22)?

1. In what specific ways have you seen God exalted through your weaknesses and "unsharpened swords"? **2.** Which of your inferior tools will you entrust to God for sharpening and for his use today, so that *his* power may be seen?

---

1 Samuel 13:1–15   SAMUEL REBUKES SAUL

Through the prophet Samuel, Saul has just been installed as Israel's first king. After leading the people to victory over the Ammonites, Saul (and his son Jonathan) now faces another enemy—the Philistines.

1. What do you do if someone you are meeting is late?
   a. go on without them
   b. wait a little while
   c. wait a long time
   d. blow a fuse
   e. stay cool

2. Saul's biggest mistake was presuming to:
   a. send most of the troops back home (v. 2).
   b. attack the Philistines (vv. 3–4).
   c. rally a bunch of cowards (vv. 6–7).
   d. offer a sacrifice (v. 9).
   e. disregard the Lord's command through his prophet (vv. 8,13).

3. Who was to blame for Saul getting in trouble?
   a. the Philistines—for oppressing God's people
   b. the Israelites—for deserting Saul

   c. Saul himself—for going ahead
   d. Samuel—for cutting it so close
   e. God—for putting Saul under such pressure

4. Saul's punishment (vv. 13–14):
   a. seems unreasonably severe.
   b. was deserved.
   c. affected his descendants more than Saul himself.
   d. opened the way for a better king (David).

5. What does this story tell you about Samuel and Saul's relationship?
   a. The Lord directed Saul through Samuel.
   b. Samuel was testing Saul.
   c. Saul resisted Samuel's authority.
   d. Samuel was trying to make Saul look bad.

6. What do you do if something in your life seems late in arriving and you feel under a lot of pressure? How often do you take matters into your own hands the way Saul did? Are you in those circumstances now?

7. When you sin, which of the following

are you most likely to blame?
   a. circumstances   e. my past
   b. bad timing   f. my genes
   c. someone else   g. myself
   d. my sin nature   h. God

8. How do you feel about Saul falling so fast from success to failure? In what way are you afraid of failure?

9. How have you related to authority figures: Your father? Mother? School and government authorities? Bosses and employers? Spiritual leaders? God? Do you need to make peace with your past? If so, how?

10. Is relating to persons in authority something you struggle with now? If so, in what way?

11. How have you been tempted to run ahead of God's will for your life in the past? How about now? Specifically, are you anxious to exercise a gift in a way that God hasn't given you a green light to do?

1. Have you ever run an obstacle course or climbed a cliff? Describe the experience. 2. When have you experienced the proverbial truth, "Pride goeth before a fall"?

1. How do you see Jonathan's raid on the Philistine outpost: (a) Outstanding courage? (b) 10-to-1 long shot? (c) Foolhardy presumption? (d) Expectant faith? (e) One-upmanship over Saul? 2. What attitude does the Philistine taunt reveal (vv. 11–12)? What sign from God does that reveal? What's the link between the two? 3. What obstacles did Jonathan and his armor-bearer have to overcome to be victorious? What role did faith play in that? 4. Why do you think Jonathan felt so confident of God's blessing?

1. What "cliffs" do you think God would have you climb for him? How does your response to life's obstacles compare with Jonathan's? 2. What would it take for your Christian walk to be characterized by "expectancy"?

Do you ever experience "panic attacks"? When? What are you panicking about these days? How do you find relief?

1. Why do you think Saul asks for the "ephod" (preferable to "ark"; see footnote)? 2. What is meant by Saul's command to the priest (v. 19; see Ex 28:30)? What does this action reveal about Saul? 3. Who is credited with the Philistine-busting? How is that particularly evident?

On a scale of 1 (trusting God) to 10 (trusting self), how would an impartial observer rate your current trust level? What story lies behind the rating?

Jonathan Attacks the Philistines

23Now a detachment of Philistines had gone out to the pass at Micmash.

14 1One day Jonathan son of Saul said to the young man bearing his armor, "Come, let's go over to the Philistine outpost on the other side." But he did not tell his father.

2Saul was staying on the outskirts of Gibeah under a pomegranate tree in Migron. With him were about six hundred men, 3among whom was Ahijah, who was wearing an ephod. He was a son of Ichabod's brother Ahitub son of Phinehas, the son of Eli, the LORD's priest in Shiloh. No one was aware that Jonathan had left.

4On each side of the pass that Jonathan intended to cross to reach the Philistine outpost was a cliff; one was called Bozez, and the other Seneh. 5One cliff stood to the north toward Micmash, the other to the south toward Geba.

6Jonathan said to his young armor-bearer, "Come, let's go over to the outpost of those uncircumcised fellows. Perhaps the LORD will act in our behalf. Nothing can hinder the LORD from saving, whether by many or by few."

7"Do all that you have in mind," his armor-bearer said. "Go ahead; I am with you heart and soul."

8Jonathan said, "Come, then; we will cross over toward the men and let them see us. 9If they say to us, 'Wait there until we come to you,' we will stay where we are and not go up to them. 10But if they say, 'Come up to us,' we will climb up, because that will be our sign that the LORD has given them into our hands."

11So both of them showed themselves to the Philistine outpost. "Look!" said the Philistines. "The Hebrews are crawling out of the holes they were hiding in." 12The men of the outpost shouted to Jonathan and his armor-bearer, "Come up to us and we'll teach you a lesson."

So Jonathan said to his armor-bearer, "Climb up after me; the LORD has given them into the hand of Israel."

13Jonathan climbed up, using his hands and feet, with his armor-bearer right behind him. The Philistines fell before Jonathan, and his armor-bearer followed and killed behind him. 14In that first attack Jonathan and his armor-bearer killed some twenty men in an area of about half an acre.a

Israel Routs the Philistines

15Then panic struck the whole army—those in the camp and field, and those in the outposts and raiding parties—and the ground shook. It was a panic sent by God.b

16Saul's lookouts at Gibeah in Benjamin saw the army melting away in all directions. 17Then Saul said to the men who were with him, "Muster the forces and see who has left us." When they did, it was Jonathan and his armor-bearer who were not there.

18Saul said to Ahijah, "Bring the ark of God." (At that time it was with the Israelites.)c 19While Saul was talking to the priest, the tumult in the Philistine camp increased more and more. So Saul said to the priest, "Withdraw your hand."

20Then Saul and all his men assembled and went to the battle. They found the Philistines in total confusion, striking each other with their swords. 21Those Hebrews who had previously been with the Philistines and had gone up with them to their camp went over to the Israelites who were with Saul and Jonathan. 22When all the Israelites who had hidden in the hill country of Ephraim heard that

a14 Hebrew half a yoke; a "yoke" was the land plowed by a yoke of oxen in one day.
b15 Or a terrible panic   c18 Hebrew; Septuagint "Bring the ephod." (At that time he wore the ephod before the Israelites.)

the Philistines were on the run, they joined the battle in hot pursuit. ²³So the LORD rescued Israel that day, and the battle moved on beyond Beth Aven.

Jonathan Eats Honey

²⁴Now the men of Israel were in distress that day, because Saul had bound the people under an oath, saying, "Cursed be any man who eats food before evening comes, before I have avenged myself on my enemies!" So none of the troops tasted food.

²⁵The entire army[a] entered the woods, and there was honey on the ground. ²⁶When they went into the woods, they saw the honey oozing out, yet no one put his hand to his mouth, because they feared the oath. ²⁷But Jonathan had not heard that his father had bound the people with the oath, so he reached out the end of the staff that was in his hand and dipped it into the honeycomb. He raised his hand to his mouth, and his eyes brightened.[b] ²⁸Then one of the soldiers told him, "Your father bound the army under a strict oath, saying, 'Cursed be any man who eats food today!' That is why the men are faint."

²⁹Jonathan said, "My father has made trouble for the country. See how my eyes brightened[c] when I tasted a little of this honey. ³⁰How much better it would have been if the men had eaten today some of the plunder they took from their enemies. Would not the slaughter of the Philistines have been even greater?"

³¹That day, after the Israelites had struck down the Philistines from Micmash to Aijalon, they were exhausted. ³²They pounced on the plunder and, taking sheep, cattle and calves, they butchered them on the ground and ate them, together with the blood. ³³Then someone said to Saul, "Look, the men are sinning against the LORD by eating meat that has blood in it."

"You have broken faith," he said. "Roll a large stone over here at once." ³⁴Then he said, "Go out among the men and tell them, 'Each of you bring me your cattle and sheep, and slaughter them here and eat them. Do not sin against the LORD by eating meat with blood still in it.'"

So everyone brought his ox that night and slaughtered it there. ³⁵Then Saul built an altar to the LORD; it was the first time he had done this.

³⁶Saul said, "Let us go down after the Philistines by night and plunder them till dawn, and let us not leave one of them alive."

"Do whatever seems best to you," they replied.

But the priest said, "Let us inquire of God here."

³⁷So Saul asked God, "Shall I go down after the Philistines? Will you give them into Israel's hand?" But God did not answer him that day.

³⁸Saul therefore said, "Come here, all you who are leaders of the army, and let us find out what sin has been committed today. ³⁹As surely as the LORD who rescues Israel lives, even if it lies with my son Jonathan, he must die." But not one of the men said a word.

⁴⁰Saul then said to all the Israelites, "You stand over there; I and Jonathan my son will stand over here."

"Do what seems best to you," the men replied.

⁴¹Then Saul prayed to the LORD, the God of Israel, "Give me the right answer."[d] And Jonathan and Saul were taken by lot, and the

---

1. What is the longest span of time you have gone without food? For what purpose? How did you feel? How did you break the fast? 2. Have you ever done something that everyone knew was forbidden except you? Was "ignorance" your excuse? Were you punished or not?

1. Why does Saul bind his troops with this oath? What does this reveal about Saul: Is he a stubborn fool? Or is he exercising trust in God? 2. What is Jonathan's opinion of his father's oath? Do you sympathize more with Saul's or Jonathan's reasoning? 3. Why is eating meat with blood a sin against God (v. 33; see Lev 17:10–12)? How does Saul respond? 4. What does it say about Saul that before now he had never built an altar (v. 35)? 5. Why do you suppose God refuses to answer Saul (v. 37)? Why does God single out Jonathan (v. 42)? What could God be trying to tell Saul via "casting lots"? (Note: Lots were cast by the Urim and Thummim, the priestly oracle found over the heart in the breastpiece of the ephod or priestly robe, see Ex 28:30.) 6. Why does Saul make the vow of verse 39? What does his response show in verse 44? 7. Where does the loyalty of Saul's troops lie: With Saul? Jonathan? God? Selves? 8. Overall, is Saul a strong leader of Israel? A weak one? Or both? Explain.

1. What position(s) of authority do you presently find yourself in (family, job, church, etc.)? How do you guard yourself from being "a heavy" in exercising that authority? How can you be more Christ-like in the role? 2. In what ways are you, like Saul, impulsive and uncertain in your words? Likewise, are you able to back up what you say? Or are you easily out-voted by others? 3. When you are wrong, what does it take for you to publicly admit it? 4. What do you rely upon as a means for making tough decisions? What is your version of "casting lots"?

---

a25 Or *Now all the people of the land*   b27 Or *his strength was renewed*
c29 Or *my strength was renewed*   d41 Hebrew; Septuagint *"Why have you not answered your servant today? If the fault is in me or my son Jonathan, respond with Urim, but if the men of Israel are at fault, respond with Thummim."*

men were cleared. ⁴²Saul said, "Cast the lot between me and Jonathan my son." And Jonathan was taken.

⁴³Then Saul said to Jonathan, "Tell me what you have done."

So Jonathan told him, "I merely tasted a little honey with the end of my staff. And now must I die?"

⁴⁴Saul said, "May God deal with me, be it ever so severely, if you do not die, Jonathan."

⁴⁵But the men said to Saul, "Should Jonathan die—he who has brought about this great deliverance in Israel? Never! As surely as the LORD lives, not a hair of his head will fall to the ground, for he did this today with God's help." So the men rescued Jonathan, and he was not put to death.

⁴⁶Then Saul stopped pursuing the Philistines, and they withdrew to their own land.

⁴⁷After Saul had assumed rule over Israel, he fought against their enemies on every side: Moab, the Ammonites, Edom, the kings[a] of Zobah, and the Philistines. Wherever he turned, he inflicted punishment on them.[b] ⁴⁸He fought valiantly and defeated the Amalekites, delivering Israel from the hands of those who had plundered them.

Saul's Family

⁴⁹Saul's sons were Jonathan, Ishvi and Malki-Shua. The name of his older daughter was Merab, and that of the younger was Michal. ⁵⁰His wife's name was Ahinoam daughter of Ahimaaz. The name of the commander of Saul's army was Abner son of Ner, and Ner was Saul's uncle. ⁵¹Saul's father Kish and Abner's father Ner were sons of Abiel.

⁵²All the days of Saul there was bitter war with the Philistines, and whenever Saul saw a mighty or brave man, he took him into his service.

The LORD Rejects Saul as King

15 Samuel said to Saul, "I am the one the LORD sent to anoint you king over his people Israel; so listen now to the message from the LORD. ²This is what the LORD Almighty says: 'I will punish the Amalekites for what they did to Israel when they waylaid them as they came up from Egypt. ³Now go, attack the Amalekites and totally destroy[c] everything that belongs to them. Do not spare them; put to death men and women, children and infants, cattle and sheep, camels and donkeys.' "

⁴So Saul summoned the men and mustered them at Telaim—two hundred thousand foot soldiers and ten thousand men from Judah. ⁵Saul went to the city of Amalek and set an ambush in the ravine. ⁶Then he said to the Kenites, "Go away, leave the Amalekites so that I do not destroy you along with them; for you showed kindness to all the Israelites when they came up out of Egypt." So the Kenites moved away from the Amalekites.

⁷Then Saul attacked the Amalekites all the way from Havilah to Shur, to the east of Egypt. ⁸He took Agag king of the Amalekites alive, and all his people he totally destroyed with the sword. ⁹But Saul and the army spared Agag and the best of the sheep and cattle, the fat calves[d] and lambs—everything that was good. These they

[Margin study notes]

❤ 1. What does this outline of Saul's reign tell you about his life-long priorities? 2. What would a 4-verse summary of your family look like? Whom would you list? 3. How would you summarize your life's work in one sentence?

☕ 1. Who were the people you looked up to as a child—those you relished being seen with? What did these "heroes" do to be liked and win your favor? Did they lose your favor and prove to have "feet of clay"? 2. In whose eyes are you a hero? What are you likely to boast about with them? When have you invited them to "tag along"?

📖 1. In verse 3, what exactly does the Lord command Saul to do? What have the Amalekites done to deserve such punishment (v. 2; see Dt 25:17–19)? Why do you think that God commanded even innocent children and animals to be killed? 2. Why are the Kenites spared (v. 6)? 3. What distinguishes the things Israel destroyed from the things they kept (v. 9)? 4. Compare the progression in Saul's responses to Samuel's indictment: How does Saul respond to Samuel's arrival (v. 13)? To Samuel's first rebuke (vv. 14–15)? To the second rebuke (vv. 17–21)? To the third rebuke (vv. 22–25)? 5. Why

---

a47 Masoretic Text; Dead Sea Scrolls and Septuagint *king*   b47 Hebrew; Septuagint *he was victorious*   c3 The Hebrew term refers to the irrevocable giving over of things or persons to the LORD, often by totally destroying them; also in verses 8, 9, 15, 18, 20 and 21.   d9 Or *the grown bulls*; the meaning of the Hebrew for this phrase is uncertain.

were unwilling to destroy completely, but everything that was despised and weak they totally destroyed.

[10]Then the word of the LORD came to Samuel: [11]"I am grieved that I have made Saul king, because he has turned away from me and has not carried out my instructions." Samuel was troubled, and he cried out to the LORD all that night.

[12]Early in the morning Samuel got up and went to meet Saul, but he was told, "Saul has gone to Carmel. There he has set up a monument in his own honor and has turned and gone on down to Gilgal."

[13]When Samuel reached him, Saul said, "The LORD bless you! I have carried out the LORD's instructions."

[14]But Samuel said, "What then is this bleating of sheep in my ears? What is this lowing of cattle that I hear?"

[15]Saul answered, "The soldiers brought them from the Amalekites; they spared the best of the sheep and cattle to sacrifice to the LORD your God, but we totally destroyed the rest."

[16]"Stop!" Samuel said to Saul. "Let me tell you what the LORD said to me last night."

"Tell me," Saul replied.

[17]Samuel said, "Although you were once small in your own eyes, did you not become the head of the tribes of Israel? The LORD anointed you king over Israel. [18]And he sent you on a mission, saying, 'Go and completely destroy those wicked people, the Amalekites; make war on them until you have wiped them out.' [19]Why did you not obey the LORD? Why did you pounce on the plunder and do evil in the eyes of the LORD?"

[20]"But I did obey the LORD," Saul said. "I went on the mission the LORD assigned me. I completely destroyed the Amalekites and brought back Agag their king. [21]The soldiers took sheep and cattle from the plunder, the best of what was devoted to God, in order to sacrifice them to the LORD your God at Gilgal."

[22]But Samuel replied:

"Does the LORD delight in burnt offerings and
        sacrifices
    as much as in obeying the voice of the LORD?
    To obey is better than sacrifice,
        and to heed is better than the fat of rams.
[23]For rebellion is like the sin of divination,
        and arrogance like the evil of idolatry.
    Because you have rejected the word of the LORD,
        he has rejected you as king."

[24]Then Saul said to Samuel, "I have sinned. I violated the LORD's command and your instructions. I was afraid of the people and so I gave in to them. [25]Now I beg you, forgive my sin and come back with me, so that I may worship the LORD."

[26]But Samuel said to him, "I will not go back with you. You have rejected the word of the LORD, and the LORD has rejected you as king over Israel!"

[27]As Samuel turned to leave, Saul caught hold of the hem of his robe, and it tore. [28]Samuel said to him, "The LORD has torn the kingdom of Israel from you today and has given it to one of your neighbors—to one better than you. [29]He who is the Glory of Israel does not lie or change his mind; for he is not a man, that he should change his mind."

[30]Saul replied, "I have sinned. But please honor me before the elders of my people and before Israel; come back with me, so that

does Saul change his tune after the third rebuke? What do you think prompted Saul to disobey God in the first place? 6. Why do you think Saul wants Samuel to go back with him (vv. 25,30)? 7. How do Agag's thoughts compare with Samuel's (vv. 32–33)? How do Saul's compare with Samuel's (vv. 13–14)? With God? 8. Why does Samuel refuse to visit Saul thereafter? Why do you suppose Samuel continues to mourn for Saul nonetheless (v. 35; see 16:1)?

1. If you were only concerned with seeking God's glory and not your own, how would your life be different (at home, work, school)? 2. When were you caught hiding sinful motivations behind a spiritual front? Are you doing so now? Where? 3. When were your "feet of clay" first exposed to adoring eyes who looked up to you as a hero? How did their idealized image of you (perhaps built up by you) eventually lose its luster? 4. Who plays "Samuel" in your life today—instructing you in the ways of God, rebuking you when you fall short, crying out with God's compassion for you? 5. For whom can you be a gentle "Samuel" (without naming names or gossiping)? 6. When does God's grief move you to grieve? How can your mind begin to reflect more and more on God's mind?

I may worship the LORD your God." ³¹So Samuel went back with Saul, and Saul worshiped the LORD.

³²Then Samuel said, "Bring me Agag king of the Amalekites."

Agag came to him confidently,ᵃ thinking, "Surely the bitterness of death is past."

³³But Samuel said,

> "As your sword has made women childless,
>   so will your mother be childless among
>   women."

And Samuel put Agag to death before the LORD at Gilgal.

³⁴Then Samuel left for Ramah, but Saul went up to his home in Gibeah of Saul. ³⁵Until the day Samuel died, he did not go to see Saul again, though Samuel mourned for him. And the LORD was grieved that he had made Saul king over Israel.

Samuel Anoints David

16 The LORD said to Samuel, "How long will you mourn for Saul, since I have rejected him as king over Israel? Fill your horn with oil and be on your way; I am sending you to Jesse of Bethlehem. I have chosen one of his sons to be king."

²But Samuel said, "How can I go? Saul will hear about it and kill me."

The LORD said, "Take a heifer with you and say, 'I have come to sacrifice to the LORD.' ³Invite Jesse to the sacrifice, and I will show you what to do. You are to anoint for me the one I indicate."

⁴Samuel did what the LORD said. When he arrived at Bethlehem, the elders of the town trembled when they met him. They asked, "Do you come in peace?"

⁵Samuel replied, "Yes, in peace; I have come to sacrifice to the LORD. Consecrate yourselves and come to the sacrifice with me." Then he consecrated Jesse and his sons and invited them to the sacrifice.

⁶When they arrived, Samuel saw Eliab and thought, "Surely the LORD's anointed stands here before the LORD."

⁷But the LORD said to Samuel, "Do not consider his appearance or his height, for I have rejected him. The LORD does not look at the things man looks at. Man looks at the outward appearance, but the LORD looks at the heart."

⁸Then Jesse called Abinadab and had him pass in front of Samuel. But Samuel said, "The LORD has not chosen this one either." ⁹Jesse then had Shammah pass by, but Samuel said, "Nor has the LORD chosen this one." ¹⁰Jesse had seven of his sons pass before Samuel, but Samuel said to him, "The LORD has not chosen these." ¹¹So he asked Jesse, "Are these all the sons you have?"

"There is still the youngest," Jesse answered, "but he is tending the sheep."

Samuel said, "Send for him; we will not sit downᵇ until he arrives."

¹²So he sent and had him brought in. He was ruddy, with a fine appearance and handsome features.

Then the LORD said, "Rise and anoint him; he is the one."

¹³So Samuel took the horn of oil and anointed him in the presence of his brothers, and from that day on the Spirit of the LORD came upon David in power. Samuel then went to Ramah.

---

1. What have you bought based on first impressions, only to find out later that the product or person (no names) was not as advertised? **2.** In a job interview, are you swayed by appearance? Why? For your own interviews, how do you "primp"?

1. What is Samuel mourning? Why does God rebuke him? **2.** Why does Samuel hesitate to go to Bethlehem? What do Samuel's fears say about Saul's character? **3.** How does God calm that fear? Is God commanding Samuel to tell a "white lie"? Why or why not? **4.** Why do the elders tremble at the sight of Samuel? What does that say about the Saul-Samuel rift? **5.** Beyond normal worship, what does Samuel's sacrifice signify (v. 5; see 11:14–15)? **6.** Why did Samuel initially think Eliab was the Lord's anointed? What is the irony here (see 10:23–24)? **7.** As one of David's brothers, how would you have felt, being passed over in favor of David? When else has God ignored tradition in choosing one with a heart for God to fulfill his covenant?

1. When have you been ashamed to be seen with a fellow Christian because of appearances (no names)? What difference would it make if you saw him as God does? **2.** What is God calling you to do despite others' protests?

ᵃ32 Or *him trembling, yet around*   ᵇ11 Some Septuagint manuscripts; Hebrew *not gather*

David in Saul's Service

¹⁴Now the Spirit of the LORD had departed from Saul, and an evil[a] spirit from the LORD tormented him.

¹⁵Saul's attendants said to him, "See, an evil spirit from God is tormenting you. ¹⁶Let our lord command his servants here to search for someone who can play the harp. He will play when the evil spirit from God comes upon you, and you will feel better."

¹⁷So Saul said to his attendants, "Find someone who plays well and bring him to me."

¹⁸One of the servants answered, "I have seen a son of Jesse of Bethlehem who knows how to play the harp. He is a brave man and a warrior. He speaks well and is a fine-looking man. And the LORD is with him."

¹⁹Then Saul sent messengers to Jesse and said, "Send me your son David, who is with the sheep." ²⁰So Jesse took a donkey loaded with bread, a skin of wine and a young goat and sent them with his son David to Saul.

²¹David came to Saul and entered his service. Saul liked him very much, and David became one of his armor-bearers. ²²Then Saul sent word to Jesse, saying, "Allow David to remain in my service, for I am pleased with him."

²³Whenever the spirit from God came upon Saul, David would take his harp and play. Then relief would come to Saul; he would feel better, and the evil spirit would leave him.

a 14 Or *injurious*; also in verses 15, 16 and 23

1. What musical instruments do you play or wish you did? 2. When you are depressed, how do you spell relief?

1. How is the Holy Spirit at work in David's life and Saul's (vv. 13–14)? 2. How could the evil spirit tormenting Saul be *from God* (vv. 14,23), when God is holy and loving? Why do you think God sends the spirit? 3. Why is music advised for Saul's troubled soul? How does music make a person feel better? As one of Saul's aides, what would you have recommended? 4. What about David commends him to Saul (v. 18)? What secures David's service?

1. When have you sinned and tried to find relief for your resulting problems in remedies other than repentance? 2. When have people said of you: "The Lord is with him/her"?

---

  1 Samuel 16:1–13   **SAMUEL ANOINTS DAVID**

God had led the prophet Samuel to anoint Saul as Israel's king. Samuel has just told Saul that, because of his disobedience, the kingdom has been torn from him and given to another.

1. Samuel was reluctant to visit Jesse:
   a. because he was afraid of what Saul might do to him.
   b. because he was afraid of what Saul might do to the new king.
   c. because Saul wanted his own son to be the next king.

2. When Samuel said, "I have come to sacrifice to the Lord" (v. 5), he was:
   a. partially right.
   b. being sneaky.
   c. repeating what God told him.
   d. keeping Saul from suspicion.

3. How do you think David's brothers felt as they watched their youngest brother get chosen?
   a. proud   d. relieved
   b. jealous   e. hurt
   c. shocked   f. angry

4. What was God communicating by passing over all Jesse's sons before picking David?

a. God's way of looking at people is different than ours.
b. Shepherds make the best leaders.
c. The most important things about a person are invisible.
d. Whatever is in a person's heart makes the person.

5. Why did Samuel anoint David in the presence of his brothers?
   a. to rub it in
   b. to make God's choice clear
   c. to keep it a secret ceremony
   d. to provide witnesses for future verification
   e. so the Spirit could empower David

6. On what basis do you tend to judge people?
   a. talents   g. lifestyle
   b. appearance   h. education
   c. character   i. faith
   d. intelligence   j. possessions
   e. potential
   f. accomplishments

7. How do you want to be judged by others? Since the Lord judges by the heart, what is really important when it comes to "fitting in"?

8. I can relate to this story because I have felt:
   a. punished for my sins—like Saul.
   b. passed over by God—like David's brothers.
   c. left out by other people—like David.
   d. chosen by God—like David.
   e. the Holy Spirit's power—like David.

9. How does the fact that, "Man looks at the outward appearance, but the Lord looks at the heart" encourage your self-esteem? What can you do to make your heart more pleasing and attractive to God?

10. In your small group, imagine that the person on your right has been anointed to lead God's people. What inner qualities of the heart do you recognize that qualify that person for service?
    a. humility   f. kindness
    b. honesty   g. patience
    c. spiritual gifts   h. courage
    d. unselfishness   i. love
    e. trust in God   j. other:_____

1. How would you feel playing football, alone, against the New York Giants? Which direction would you run? 2. How do you feel when someone casts doubt on your ability to do something? 3. Do others have *more* confidence in you than you do yourself? Or do they have *less*? Why? 4. When have you met up with "lions and tigers and bears—oh my"?

1. What does Goliath's armor and weaponry reveal about him (vv. 4–7)? 2. As an Israelite, how would you view Goliath's proposal (vv. 8–10): (a) With respect? (b) Ridicule? (c) Dismay and terror? (d) Faith and courage? Who would you "volunteer" from your small group to accept his proposal? Why? 3. What motivated David to fight Goliath (vv. 25–27)? What's at stake for the victor? For Israel? 4. How would you describe the sibling rivalry between David and Eliab (vv. 28–30)? What might be the root cause of that jealousy (see 16:6–13)? 5. How did David seek to persuade Saul to let him fight Goliath (vv. 32–37)? Would David's reasoning have persuaded you? 6. Compare the "kingly" be-

David and Goliath

17 Now the Philistines gathered their forces for war and assembled at Socoh in Judah. They pitched camp at Ephes Dammim, between Socoh and Azekah. ²Saul and the Israelites assembled and camped in the Valley of Elah and drew up their battle line to meet the Philistines. ³The Philistines occupied one hill and the Israelites another, with the valley between them.

⁴A champion named Goliath, who was from Gath, came out of the Philistine camp. He was over nine feet[a] tall. ⁵He had a bronze helmet on his head and wore a coat of scale armor of bronze weighing five thousand shekels[b]; ⁶on his legs he wore bronze greaves, and a bronze javelin was slung on his back. ⁷His spear shaft was like a weaver's rod, and its iron point weighed six hundred shekels.[c] His shield bearer went ahead of him.

⁸Goliath stood and shouted to the ranks of Israel, "Why do you come out and line up for battle? Am I not a Philistine, and are you not the servants of Saul? Choose a man and have him come down to me. ⁹If he is able to fight and kill me, we will become your subjects; but if I overcome him and kill him, you will become our subjects and serve us." ¹⁰Then the Philistine said, "This day I defy the ranks of Israel! Give me a man and let us fight each other." ¹¹On hearing the Philistine's words, Saul and all the Israelites were dismayed and terrified.

¹²Now David was the son of an Ephrathite named Jesse, who was from Bethlehem in Judah. Jesse had eight sons, and in Saul's

---

a4 Hebrew *was six cubits and a span* (about 3 meters)   b5 That is, about 125 pounds (about 57 kilograms)   c7 That is, about 15 pounds (about 7 kilograms)

---

 1 Samuel 16:14–23   **DAVID IN SAUL'S SERVICE**

Just before this, the prophet Samuel informed Saul that, due to his disobedience, God was replacing him with "one better than you"; then he secretly anointed David as Israel's next king.

1. How would you describe Saul's relationship with the Lord?
a. washed-up
b. tormented
c. dependent on others
d. on again, off again
e. at odds
f. peaceful

2. What does it mean that "an evil spirit from God came upon Saul"?
a. God directed an evil spirit to afflict Saul.
b. It was assumed that God sent an evil spirit to afflict Saul.
c. God allowed an evil spirit to afflict Saul.
d. Saul was losing his mind.
e. Saul was filled with self-pity and depression.
f. God was working things out so David would get a high profile.

3. If you were Saul's attendant, what would you have suggested he do?
a. snap out of it
b. find a musician
c. find a therapist
d. take some time off
e. resign his office
f. repent

4. What do you find most ironic about this story?
a. A holy God uses an evil spirit.
b. A warrior plays the harp.
c. The king invites his replacement to join the royal court.
d. God's Spirit through David (see 16:13) brings comfort from an evil spirit.
e. Saul is pleased with the person he fears.

5. Which three descriptions of David do you most want to describe you? In which one do you most desire change?
a. brave
b. being a "warrior"
c. skilled in communicating
d. physically attractive

e. empowered by God's Spirit
f. highly talented
g. well-rounded
h. pleasing to others

6. How would you describe your relationship with the Lord right now? Do any of the options in question 1 fit?

7. What would you like to do or to be that would lead people to say (as with David), "The Lord is with you"?

8. What "torments" your life the most right now? What can you do to get relief? What can others, perhaps this group, do to help?

9. What do you feel are your primary talents? How or where would you like to use them? How can you use them in God's service?

10. Later David would go from pleasing to enraging Saul. How are your talents viewed by others? How important is it to you that others appreciate and affirm your talents?

time he was old and well advanced in years. [13]Jesse's three oldest sons had followed Saul to the war: The firstborn was Eliab; the second, Abinadab; and the third, Shammah. [14]David was the youngest. The three oldest followed Saul, [15]but David went back and forth from Saul to tend his father's sheep at Bethlehem.

[16]For forty days the Philistine came forward every morning and evening and took his stand.

[17]Now Jesse said to his son David, "Take this ephah[a] of roasted grain and these ten loaves of bread for your brothers and hurry to their camp. [18]Take along these ten cheeses to the commander of their unit.[b] See how your brothers are and bring back some assurance[c] from them. [19]They are with Saul and all the men of Israel in the Valley of Elah, fighting against the Philistines."

[20]Early in the morning David left the flock with a shepherd, loaded up and set out, as Jesse had directed. He reached the camp as the army was going out to its battle positions, shouting the war cry. [21]Israel and the Philistines were drawing up their lines facing each other. [22]David left his things with the keeper of supplies, ran to the battle lines and greeted his brothers. [23]As he was talking with them, Goliath, the Philistine champion from Gath, stepped out from his lines and shouted his usual defiance, and David heard it. [24]When the Israelites saw the man, they all ran from him in great fear.

[25]Now the Israelites had been saying, "Do you see how this man keeps coming out? He comes out to defy Israel. The king will give

---

havior and attitudes of David and Saul. What do you see? **7.** If you were at ringside for this fight, and placing bets with fellow Israelites and opposing Philistines, what odds would you have given David? Where would you place your money: Where Goliath's mouth was? Or where David's faith was? **8.** Where does David find the confidence to face Goliath? What larger missionary purpose is served by this single fight? How does David's attitude compare with Saul's (v. 11)? **9.** What is the end result of David's boldness for Goliath (vv. 48–51a)? For the men of Israel and Judah (vv. 47,52)? For the Philistines (vv. 47,51b–54)? For David himself (17:55–18:2)? Indeed, for the "whole world" (v. 46)? **10.** Why do you think Saul seems not to know David, despite 16:14–23?

♡ **1.** What giants are drawn up against you in battle? How are they taunting you? Is your attitude toward them more like Saul's or David's? How does that attitude need to change? **2.** What larger missionary purpose might be accomplished for God if you would turn that battle over to the Lord? **3.**

---

[a]17 That is, probably about 3/5 bushel (about 22 liters)   [b]18 Hebrew *thousand*
[c]18 Or *some token;* or *some pledge of spoils*

 **1 Samuel 17:12–50**   **DAVID AND GOLIATH**

The armies of Israel had drawn up a battle line with the Philistines. Day after day Goliath—the 9-foot Philistine champion—came forward to defy the Israelites and challenge them to send a representative to fight him.

1. Why were the Israelites helpless against Goliath?
   a. They were chicken.
   b. They didn't have a plan.
   c. They were intimidated by his size.
   d. They had forgotten about God's promise to fight their battles.

2. What was going on between David and his older brother?
   a. It was a case of sibling rivalry.
   b. David was embarrassing Eliab.
   c. Eliab was jealous of David.
   d. Eliab misread David's motives.

3. Why did David volunteer to take on Goliath?
   a. to get the reward
   b. to marry the king's daughter
   c. to get a tax break
   d. to teach the Philistines a lesson
   e. to prove himself
   f. to vindicate God

4. Why did David refuse to wear Saul's armor?
   a. He didn't want to hide his good looks.
   b. Ill-fitting armor is worse than no armor.
   c. He wanted to be himself.
   d. He wanted to rely on God.

5. David's confidence came from:
   a. killing lions and bears.
   b. his sling-shot abilities.
   c. God's past deliverance.
   d. his conviction that the Lord would fight for his people.

6. The way I usually fight "Goliath" is:
   a. with sticks and stones.
   b. with stinging words from a sharp tongue.
   c. by turning the other cheek.
   d. with calm confrontation.
   e. with the silent treatment.
   f. by calling on the name of God.
   g. by hiding in a foxhole.

7. What is the hardest part of the battle with the giant you are facing now?
   a. trusting the Lord
   b. courage to advance

c. using God's weapons
d. battle fatigue
e. feeling alone
f. facing too many battles at once

8. What is the most reassuring lesson about this story?
   a. Believers always win.
   b. God will fight my battles.
   c. God will train me for battle.
   d. The greatest enemy is never too big for God.

9.  How much of a fighting spirit have you had in your spiritual life? How can you have a fighting spirit and, at the same time, let God fight your battles?

10. When is it hardest for you to be yourself (and what do you do in those situations)?
   a. when someone says, "You don't belong here" (v. 28)
   b. when someone doubts my abilities (v. 33)
   c. when I don't feel comfortable with what's going on (vv. 38–39)
   d. when someone threatens me or puts me down (vv. 41–44)

What's holding you back from taking the bull by the horns (or the Goliath by a slingshot)? What do you fear might happen if you turned and faced the enemy who taunts you and defies God? What's the "worst case scenario"? Having imagined that, now re-write the end result with God on your side. **4.** What Goliaths are there in society, defying God and Christians? How can you, small and unarmed, work to bring them down? What can you as a group do together?

great wealth to the man who kills him. He will also give him his daughter in marriage and will exempt his father's family from taxes in Israel."

26David asked the men standing near him, "What will be done for the man who kills this Philistine and removes this disgrace from Israel? Who is this uncircumcised Philistine that he should defy the armies of the living God?"

27They repeated to him what they had been saying and told him, "This is what will be done for the man who kills him."

28When Eliab, David's oldest brother, heard him speaking with the men, he burned with anger at him and asked, "Why have you come down here? And with whom did you leave those few sheep in the desert? I know how conceited you are and how wicked your heart is; you came down only to watch the battle."

29"Now what have I done?" said David. "Can't I even speak?" 30He then turned away to someone else and brought up the same matter, and the men answered him as before. 31What David said was overheard and reported to Saul, and Saul sent for him.

32David said to Saul, "Let no one lose heart on account of this Philistine; your servant will go and fight him."

33Saul replied, "You are not able to go out against this Philistine and fight him; you are only a boy, and he has been a fighting man from his youth."

34But David said to Saul, "Your servant has been keeping his father's sheep. When a lion or a bear came and carried off a sheep from the flock, 35I went after it, struck it and rescued the sheep from its mouth. When it turned on me, I seized it by its hair, struck it and killed it. 36Your servant has killed both the lion and the bear; this uncircumcised Philistine will be like one of them, because he has defied the armies of the living God. 37The LORD who delivered me from the paw of the lion and the paw of the bear will deliver me from the hand of this Philistine."

Saul said to David, "Go, and the LORD be with you."

38Then Saul dressed David in his own tunic. He put a coat of armor on him and a bronze helmet on his head. 39David fastened on his sword over the tunic and tried walking around, because he was not used to them.

"I cannot go in these," he said to Saul, "because I am not used to them." So he took them off. 40Then he took his staff in his hand, chose five smooth stones from the stream, put them in the pouch of his shepherd's bag and, with his sling in his hand, approached the Philistine.

41Meanwhile, the Philistine, with his shield bearer in front of him, kept coming closer to David. 42He looked David over and saw that he was only a boy, ruddy and handsome, and he despised him. 43He said to David, "Am I a dog, that you come at me with sticks?" And the Philistine cursed David by his gods. 44"Come here," he said, "and I'll give your flesh to the birds of the air and the beasts of the field!"

45David said to the Philistine, "You come against me with sword and spear and javelin, but I come against you in the name of the LORD Almighty, the God of the armies of Israel, whom you have defied. 46This day the LORD will hand you over to me, and I'll strike you down and cut off your head. Today I will give the carcasses of the Philistine army to the birds of the air and the beasts of the earth, and the whole world will know that there is a God in Israel. 47All those gathered here will know that it is not by sword or spear that the LORD saves; for the battle is the LORD's, and he will give all of you into our hands."

⁴⁸As the Philistine moved closer to attack him, David ran quickly toward the battle line to meet him. ⁴⁹Reaching into his bag and taking out a stone, he slung it and struck the Philistine on the forehead. The stone sank into his forehead, and he fell facedown on the ground.

⁵⁰So David triumphed over the Philistine with a sling and a stone; without a sword in his hand he struck down the Philistine and killed him.

⁵¹David ran and stood over him. He took hold of the Philistine's sword and drew it from the scabbard. After he killed him, he cut off his head with the sword.

When the Philistines saw that their hero was dead, they turned and ran. ⁵²Then the men of Israel and Judah surged forward with a shout and pursued the Philistines to the entrance of Gath*ᵃ* and to the gates of Ekron. Their dead were strewn along the Shaaraim road to Gath and Ekron. ⁵³When the Israelites returned from chasing the Philistines, they plundered their camp. ⁵⁴David took the Philistine's head and brought it to Jerusalem, and he put the Philistine's weapons in his own tent.

⁵⁵As Saul watched David going out to meet the Philistine, he said to Abner, commander of the army, "Abner, whose son is that young man?"

Abner replied, "As surely as you live, O king, I don't know."

⁵⁶The king said, "Find out whose son this young man is."

⁵⁷As soon as David returned from killing the Philistine, Abner took him and brought him before Saul, with David still holding the Philistine's head.

⁵⁸"Whose son are you, young man?" Saul asked him.

David said, "I am the son of your servant Jesse of Bethlehem."

Saul's Jealousy of David

18 After David had finished talking with Saul, Jonathan became one in spirit with David, and he loved him as himself. ²From that day Saul kept David with him and did not let him return to his father's house. ³And Jonathan made a covenant with David because he loved him as himself. ⁴Jonathan took off the robe he was wearing and gave it to David, along with his tunic, and even his sword, his bow and his belt.

⁵Whatever Saul sent him to do, David did it so successfully*ᵇ* that Saul gave him a high rank in the army. This pleased all the people, and Saul's officers as well.

⁶When the men were returning home after David had killed the Philistine, the women came out from all the towns of Israel to meet King Saul with singing and dancing, with joyful songs and with tambourines and lutes. ⁷As they danced, they sang:

"Saul has slain his thousands,
    and David his tens of thousands."

⁸Saul was very angry; this refrain galled him. "They have credited David with tens of thousands," he thought, "but me with only thousands. What more can he get but the kingdom?" ⁹And from that time on Saul kept a jealous eye on David.

¹⁰The next day an evil*ᶜ* spirit from God came forcefully upon Saul. He was prophesying in his house, while David was playing the harp, as he usually did. Saul had a spear in his hand ¹¹and he hurled it, saying to himself, "I'll pin David to the wall." But David eluded him twice.

---

1. What astronaut, sports figure, military hero, or miracle worker has become a "household word" to you, almost overnight? 2. When have you been most jealous of another's success: (a) As a jilted lover? (b) As a defeated office-seeker? (c) As a parent beat by your child at your best game? (d) As a displaced employee? (e) Other? 3. Have you ever hit it off with the boss's daughter or son? What happened?

1. Why do you suppose David and Jonathan hit it off so well? (See 14:6 and 17:47.) 2. What especially galls Saul about the refrain in verse 7? 3. Why do the people and Saul see David so differently? 4. Why does Saul offer David his oldest daughter in marriage (v. 17; see 17:25)? Why does she marry another instead? 5. Why does Saul again offer one of his daughters to David? Why does David continue to refuse to become the king's son-in-law? Do you think David suspected Saul's motives? Why or why not? 6. How does Saul react when his offer is accepted (vv. 28–29)? What does this say about Saul's relationship with God?

ᵃ52 Some Septuagint manuscripts; Hebrew *a valley*   *ᵇ5* Or *wisely*   *ᶜ10* Or *injurious*

1. How do you respond to someone out to get you personally or professionally? When has your jealousy been aroused by someone dismissing your achievements in relation to a rival? 2. What do such interpersonal relationships reveal about your relationship with God? 3. In what area of your life are you vulnerable to "comparitivitis"? 4. How can this Saul-David story help cure you of always comparing yourself to others? How can the group help you to more readily rejoice in the accomplishments of others?

¹²Saul was afraid of David, because the LORD was with David but had left Saul. ¹³So he sent David away from him and gave him command over a thousand men, and David led the troops in their campaigns. ¹⁴In everything he did he had great success,ᵃ because the LORD was with him. ¹⁵When Saul saw how successfulᵇ he was, he was afraid of him. ¹⁶But all Israel and Judah loved David, because he led them in their campaigns.

¹⁷Saul said to David, "Here is my older daughter Merab. I will give her to you in marriage; only serve me bravely and fight the battles of the LORD." For Saul said to himself, "I will not raise a hand against him. Let the Philistines do that!"

¹⁸But David said to Saul, "Who am I, and what is my family or my father's clan in Israel, that I should become the king's son-in-law?" ¹⁹Soᶜ when the time came for Merab, Saul's daughter, to be given to David, she was given in marriage to Adriel of Meholah.

²⁰Now Saul's daughter Michal was in love with David, and when they told Saul about it, he was pleased. ²¹"I will give her to him," he thought, "so that she may be a snare to him and so that the hand of the Philistines may be against him." So Saul said to David, "Now you have a second opportunity to become my son-in-law."

²²Then Saul ordered his attendants: "Speak to David privately and say, 'Look, the king is pleased with you, and his attendants all like you; now become his son-in-law.'"

²³They repeated these words to David. But David said, "Do you think it is a small matter to become the king's son-in-law? I'm only a poor man and little known."

²⁴When Saul's servants told him what David had said, ²⁵Saul

ᵃ14 Or *he was very wise*   ᵇ15 Or *wise*   ᶜ19 Or *However,*

---

1 Samuel 18:1–30   **SAUL'S JEALOUSY OF DAVID**

Young David has recently experienced two events which would drastically change his life: First he was anointed by the prophet Samuel—without King Saul's knowledge—to be Israel's next king; then he courageously defeated Goliath in a dramatic duel.

1. What aspect of this passage leaves the greatest impression on you?
   a. the friendship   d. the jealousy
   b. the romance   e. the violence
   c. the political intrigue

2. What does it mean that Saul's son Jonathan "became one in spirit" with David?
   a. He lost his own identity.
   b. Something clicked between them.
   c. They agreed on many issues.
   d. They cared for each other in a way that was beyond words.

3. Why did Jonathan give David gifts?
   a. He wanted David to like him.
   b. He was rich and could afford it.
   c. He was expressing his love.
   d. He was giving David his blessing to be Israel's next king.

e. He was pledging his friendship.

4. Why was Saul so eager to have David marry one of his daughters?
   a. because he knew David would make a good husband
   b. to fulfill his promise to whoever would slay Goliath
   c. to lure David to attack the Philistines and get killed himself
   d. so the next king would at least be his son-in-law

5. What was Saul's worst problem?
   a. his irrational jealousy
   b. an evil spirit
   c. his dependence on David for his sanity and for national security
   d. the Lord leaving him

6. When you are jealous of someone, what is most likely the cause?
   a. their looks
   b. their abilities
   c. their popularity
   d. their possessions
   e. their having taken my place
   f. their social skills—always doing and saying the right thing

7. How much do you play the "comparison game"? What can you do to reduce how much you compare yourself to others?

8. Jonathan gave David his weapons. The thing I need to surrender to have close friendships is my tendency to:
   a. hide my feelings.
   b. act like I don't need anyone.
   c. be jealous.
   d. put myself down.
   e. not let others get close to me.
   f. get caught up with things instead of people.

9. When you're around people you don't know, how do you usually act?
   a. relaxed   d. confident
   b. nervous   e. quiet
   c. clumsy   f. life of the party

10. When you're in those situations, how are you really feeling inside? How can you feel secure with others the way Jonathan and David did with each other?

replied, "Say to David, 'The king wants no other price for the bride than a hundred Philistine foreskins, to take revenge on his enemies.'" Saul's plan was to have David fall by the hands of the Philistines.

²⁶When the attendants told David these things, he was pleased to become the king's son-in-law. So before the allotted time elapsed, ²⁷David and his men went out and killed two hundred Philistines. He brought their foreskins and presented the full number to the king so that he might become the king's son-in-law. Then Saul gave him his daughter Michal in marriage.

²⁸When Saul realized that the LORD was with David and that his daughter Michal loved David, ²⁹Saul became still more afraid of him, and he remained his enemy the rest of his days.

³⁰The Philistine commanders continued to go out to battle, and as often as they did, David met with more success[a] than the rest of Saul's officers, and his name became well known.

Saul Tries to Kill David

19 Saul told his son Jonathan and all the attendants to kill David. But Jonathan was very fond of David ²and warned him, "My father Saul is looking for a chance to kill you. Be on your guard tomorrow morning; go into hiding and stay there. ³I will go out and stand with my father in the field where you are. I'll speak to him about you and will tell you what I find out."

⁴Jonathan spoke well of David to Saul his father and said to him, "Let not the king do wrong to his servant David; he has not wronged you, and what he has done has benefited you greatly. ⁵He took his life in his hands when he killed the Philistine. The LORD won a great victory for all Israel, and you saw it and were glad. Why then would you do wrong to an innocent man like David by killing him for no reason?"

⁶Saul listened to Jonathan and took this oath: "As surely as the LORD lives, David will not be put to death."

⁷So Jonathan called David and told him the whole conversation. He brought him to Saul, and David was with Saul as before.

⁸Once more war broke out, and David went out and fought the Philistines. He struck them with such force that they fled before him.

⁹But an evil[b] spirit from the LORD came upon Saul as he was sitting in his house with his spear in his hand. While David was playing the harp, ¹⁰Saul tried to pin him to the wall with his spear, but David eluded him as Saul drove the spear into the wall. That night David made good his escape.

¹¹Saul sent men to David's house to watch it and to kill him in the morning. But Michal, David's wife, warned him, "If you don't run for your life tonight, tomorrow you'll be killed." ¹²So Michal let David down through a window, and he fled and escaped. ¹³Then Michal took an idol[c] and laid it on the bed, covering it with a garment and putting some goats' hair at the head.

¹⁴When Saul sent the men to capture David, Michal said, "He is ill."

¹⁵Then Saul sent the men back to see David and told them, "Bring him up to me in his bed so that I may kill him." ¹⁶But when the men entered, there was the idol in the bed, and at the head was some goats' hair.

¹⁷Saul said to Michal, "Why did you deceive me like this and send my enemy away so that he escaped?"

[a]30 Or David acted more wisely verse 16   [b]9 Or injurious   [c]13 Hebrew teraphim; also in

1. If you knew the boss was out to get you fired or worse, how would you behave? Could you trust the boss' daughter? The boss' son? Why or why not? 2. When have you taken a stand for a friend at some risk to your own welfare? What happened? 3. When you were young, did you ever sneak out of the house at night? What happened?

1. Why is Saul so eager to kill David? 2. Why do you think Jonathan seems to be more loyal to David than to his own father? Is this right or wrong? 3. Would you trust Saul's vow at this point (vv. 6–7)? Why does David seem to? 4. Why does God send the evil spirit to Saul again? What is God trying to do? Why does David play the harp again, after all he and Saul have been through? 5. What new insights do verses 11–17 give you into Michal's friendship with David? With Saul? With God? 6. The "prophesying" here was probably singing and praising the Lord. Why does prophesying seem to keep Saul's men from capturing David (vv. 20–24)? Why would God use this means to protect David? Why is it ironic that Saul ends up prophesying, too? How might this, too, have been God's mercy toward Saul?

1. How has your loyalty to friends been tested recently? Were you giving the test to others, or taking it yourself? Did you (or they) pass the loyalty test? How so? 2. Is there any situation in your life right now in which you feel like "the enemy is closing in"? Have you devised a plan of escape? Have you had to make good on it yet? 3. Like Saul, have you any less-than-holy plans which God

continues to frustrate despite your persistence? What would it take for you to submit to God's stronger and wiser will? How can you use praise and worship to help you?

1. When you were in high school and needed a long talk with a best friend, where did you go? 2. When growing up, did you have any secret ways of communicating with your friends? Do you still use coded messages? What for?

1. How do you think Jonathan felt upon hearing David's anguish-filled complaint against Saul (vv. 1–3)? Who does he prefer to trust at this point? Why? 2. Which do you think angers Saul more and why: David's absence from the table, or his own son's collusion with David? By what "higher principle" does Saul justify his anger (vv. 30–31)? 3. What does it take for Jonathan to finally catch on to his father's true intent with regard to David? Why is Jonathan so slow to catch on: Does he want to believe the best about his dad at all costs? Or is Saul that good at masking his motives? Why do you think so? 4. Knowing Saul tried to kill him, too, why does Jonathan go back home instead of going into hiding with David? How do you think Jonathan feels to be "caught in the middle"? 5. Do you think Jonathan did the right thing to remain loyal to David? Has he betrayed his father? If so, how? If not, why not?

1. Do you think your parents are (or were) totally honest with you all the time? Why? When have you presumed to know their innermost thoughts, only to be proven wrong in a big way? How did you handle that piercing hurt?

Michal told him, "He said to me, 'Let me get away. Why should I kill you?'"

18When David had fled and made his escape, he went to Samuel at Ramah and told him all that Saul had done to him. Then he and Samuel went to Naioth and stayed there. 19Word came to Saul: "David is in Naioth at Ramah"; 20so he sent men to capture him. But when they saw a group of prophets prophesying, with Samuel standing there as their leader, the Spirit of God came upon Saul's men and they also prophesied. 21Saul was told about it, and he sent more men, and they prophesied too. Saul sent men a third time, and they also prophesied. 22Finally, he himself left for Ramah and went to the great cistern at Secu. And he asked, "Where are Samuel and David?"

"Over in Naioth at Ramah," they said.

23So Saul went to Naioth at Ramah. But the Spirit of God came even upon him, and he walked along prophesying until he came to Naioth. 24He stripped off his robes and also prophesied in Samuel's presence. He lay that way all that day and night. This is why people say, "Is Saul also among the prophets?"

David and Jonathan

20 Then David fled from Naioth at Ramah and went to Jonathan and asked, "What have I done? What is my crime? How have I wronged your father, that he is trying to take my life?"

2"Never!" Jonathan replied. "You are not going to die! Look, my father doesn't do anything, great or small, without confiding in me. Why would he hide this from me? It's not so!"

3But David took an oath and said, "Your father knows very well that I have found favor in your eyes, and he has said to himself, 'Jonathan must not know this or he will be grieved.' Yet as surely as the LORD lives and as you live, there is only a step between me and death."

4Jonathan said to David, "Whatever you want me to do, I'll do for you."

5So David said, "Look, tomorrow is the New Moon festival, and I am supposed to dine with the king; but let me go and hide in the field until the evening of the day after tomorrow. 6If your father misses me at all, tell him, 'David earnestly asked my permission to hurry to Bethlehem, his hometown, because an annual sacrifice is being made there for his whole clan.' 7If he says, 'Very well,' then your servant is safe. But if he loses his temper, you can be sure that he is determined to harm me. 8As for you, show kindness to your servant, for you have brought him into a covenant with you before the LORD. If I am guilty, then kill me yourself! Why hand me over to your father?"

9"Never!" Jonathan said. "If I had the least inkling that my father was determined to harm you, wouldn't I tell you?"

10David asked, "Who will tell me if your father answers you harshly?"

11"Come," Jonathan said, "let's go out into the field." So they went there together.

12Then Jonathan said to David: "By the LORD, the God of Israel, I will surely sound out my father by this time the day after tomorrow! If he is favorably disposed toward you, will I not send you word and let you know? 13But if my father is inclined to harm you, may the LORD deal with me, be it ever so severely, if I do not let you know and send you away safely. May the LORD be with you as he has been with my father. 14But show me unfailing kindness like that of the LORD as long as I live, so that I may not be killed, [15]and do not ever cut off your kindness from my family—not even when the LORD has cut off every one of David's enemies from the face of the earth."

[16]So Jonathan made a covenant with the house of David, saying, "May the LORD call David's enemies to account." [17]And Jonathan had David reaffirm his oath out of love for him, because he loved him as he loved himself.

[18]Then Jonathan said to David: "Tomorrow is the New Moon festival. You will be missed, because your seat will be empty. [19]The day after tomorrow, toward evening, go to the place where you hid when this trouble began, and wait by the stone Ezel. [20]I will shoot three arrows to the side of it, as though I were shooting at a target. [21]Then I will send a boy and say, 'Go, find the arrows.' If I say to him, 'Look, the arrows are on this side of you; bring them here,' then come, because, as surely as the LORD lives, you are safe; there is no danger. [22]But if I say to the boy, 'Look, the arrows are beyond you,' then you must go, because the LORD has sent you away. [23]And about the matter you and I discussed—remember, the LORD is witness between you and me forever."

[24]So David hid in the field, and when the New Moon festival came, the king sat down to eat. [25]He sat in his customary place by the wall, opposite Jonathan,[a] and Abner sat next to Saul, but David's place was empty. [26]Saul said nothing that day, for he thought, "Something must have happened to David to make him ceremonially unclean—surely he is unclean." [27]But the next day, the second day of the month, David's place was empty again. Then

[a]25 Septuagint; Hebrew *wall. Jonathan arose*

2. What does this chapter indicate about the quality of a "Jonathan-David type" friendship? When have you experienced such a covenant bond with a member of the same sex? **3.** Whose circumstances and emotions do you most readily identify with: *Saul*, trying to preserve your own self-interests? *David*, trying to escape and torn by conflict of interests? Or *Jonathan*, losing a loved one? **4.** When is it right to go against authority in obeying God? When is it wrong? What elements in civil or familial disobedience are never right?

---

   1 Samuel 20:1–42   **DAVID AND JONATHAN**

After escaping from King Saul's attempts to kill him, David now goes to his special friend Jonathan.

1. Thinking about this story of David and Jonathan, what comes to mind?
   a. This is beautiful.
   b. This is corny.
   c. This sounds like a Hollywood plot.
   d. I wish I had a friendship like that.

2. If you found out your father was threatening to kill your best friend, how would you feel?
   a. There must be something wrong with my dad.
   b. There must be something wrong with my friend.
   c. There's something wrong with me.
   d. I'd feel terribly torn.

3. When you realized your father was doing this to save the throne for you, how would you have felt?
   a. the same way
   b. unworthy
   c. appreciative
   d. disgusted

4. How do you think Saul was feeling?
   a. insecure
   b. betrayed by his son
   c. unappreciated by his son
   d. deceived by David
   e. blinded by jealousy

5. If you knew the king was trying to kill you, would you trust the location of your hiding place to his son?
   a. Yes—if you can't trust your best friend you've really got a problem.
   b. No—you really can't depend on anyone but yourself.
   c. Only if I had a promise like Jonathan made.

6. What do you think was the secret to David and Jonathan's friendship?
   a. common interests
   b. loyalty
   c. warm affection
   d. trust
   e. the problems they went through together

7. What is the closest you have come to a friendship like theirs?

8. When it comes to making friends, I usually (choose one in each pair):
   a. make friends *quickly* or *slowly?*
   b. change friends *constantly* or *never?*
   c. break off friendships *easily* or *painfully?*
   d. pick the *right* or the *wrong* kind of friends?

9. What has been your basis for choosing friends? Has that led to friendships of character like David and Jonathan's?

10. How do you feel about having a close and trusted friend?
   a. I need a friend like that.
   b. I have friends like that now, and would like more.
   c. I like the idea, but I can't imagine myself with such a friendship.
   d. I'm not sure I want to make the commitment it would take.
   e. I haven't recovered yet from a close friendship that had an unhappy ending.

Saul said to his son Jonathan, "Why hasn't the son of Jesse come to the meal, either yesterday or today?"

²⁸Jonathan answered, "David earnestly asked me for permission to go to Bethlehem. ²⁹He said, 'Let me go, because our family is observing a sacrifice in the town and my brother has ordered me to be there. If I have found favor in your eyes, let me get away to see my brothers.' That is why he has not come to the king's table."

³⁰Saul's anger flared up at Jonathan and he said to him, "You son of a perverse and rebellious woman! Don't I know that you have sided with the son of Jesse to your own shame and to the shame of the mother who bore you? ³¹As long as the son of Jesse lives on this earth, neither you nor your kingdom will be established. Now send and bring him to me, for he must die!"

³²"Why should he be put to death? What has he done?" Jonathan asked his father. ³³But Saul hurled his spear at him to kill him. Then Jonathan knew that his father intended to kill David.

³⁴Jonathan got up from the table in fierce anger; on that second day of the month he did not eat, because he was grieved at his father's shameful treatment of David.

³⁵In the morning Jonathan went out to the field for his meeting with David. He had a small boy with him, ³⁶and he said to the boy, "Run and find the arrows I shoot." As the boy ran, he shot an arrow beyond him. ³⁷When the boy came to the place where Jonathan's arrow had fallen, Jonathan called out after him, "Isn't the arrow beyond you?" ³⁸Then he shouted, "Hurry! Go quickly! Don't stop!" The boy picked up the arrow and returned to his master. ³⁹(The boy knew nothing of all this; only Jonathan and David knew.) ⁴⁰Then Jonathan gave his weapons to the boy and said, "Go, carry them back to town."

⁴¹After the boy had gone, David got up from the south side ⌊of the stone⌋ and bowed down before Jonathan three times, with his face to the ground. Then they kissed each other and wept together—but David wept the most.

⁴²Jonathan said to David, "Go in peace, for we have sworn friendship with each other in the name of the LORD, saying, 'The LORD is witness between you and me, and between your descendants and my descendants forever.'" Then David left, and Jonathan went back to the town.

David at Nob

21 David went to Nob, to Ahimelech the priest. Ahimelech trembled when he met him, and asked, "Why are you alone? Why is no one with you?"

²David answered Ahimelech the priest, "The king charged me with a certain matter and said to me, 'No one is to know anything about your mission and your instructions.' As for my men, I have told them to meet me at a certain place. ³Now then, what do you have on hand? Give me five loaves of bread, or whatever you can find."

⁴But the priest answered David, "I don't have any ordinary bread on hand; however, there is some consecrated bread here—provided the men have kept themselves from women."

⁵David replied, "Indeed women have been kept from us, as usual whenever*a* I set out. The men's things*b* are holy even on missions that are not holy. How much more so today!" ⁶So the priest gave him the consecrated bread, since there was no bread there except the bread of the Presence that had been removed from

What "secret mission" did you once embark on? What for?

1. What does Ahimelech fear (v. 1)? Why? How does David seek to calm his fears? 2. Why does David lie to Ahimelech? Is he justified or guilty? 3. For what reasons has David come to Ahimelech (vv. 3,8; also 22:10)? 4. What's the possible sin involved in consuming the consecrated bread (vv. 4–6; see Lev 24:9)? Why does Ahimelech give it to David? 5. What has God's holiness got to do with sexual abstinence? With this mission (vv. 4–5)? 6. What is so special about David carrying Goliath's sword?

---

a5 Or from us in the past few days since   b5 Or bodies

before the LORD and replaced by hot bread on the day it was taken away.

⁷Now one of Saul's servants was there that day, detained before the LORD; he was Doeg the Edomite, Saul's head shepherd.

⁸David asked Ahimelech, "Don't you have a spear or a sword here? I haven't brought my sword or any other weapon, because the king's business was urgent."

⁹The priest replied, "The sword of Goliath the Philistine, whom you killed in the Valley of Elah, is here; it is wrapped in a cloth behind the ephod. If you want it, take it; there is no sword here but that one."

David said, "There is none like it; give it to me."

David at Gath

¹⁰That day David fled from Saul and went to Achish king of Gath. ¹¹But the servants of Achish said to him, "Isn't this David, the king of the land? Isn't he the one they sing about in their dances:

"'Saul has slain his thousands,
and David his tens of thousands'?"

¹²David took these words to heart and was very much afraid of Achish king of Gath. ¹³So he pretended to be insane in their presence; and while he was in their hands he acted like a madman, making marks on the doors of the gate and letting saliva run down his beard.

¹⁴Achish said to his servants, "Look at the man! He is insane! Why bring him to me? ¹⁵Am I so short of madmen that you have to bring this fellow here to carry on like this in front of me? Must this man come into my house?"

David at Adullam and Mizpah

22 David left Gath and escaped to the cave of Adullam. When his brothers and his father's household heard about it, they went down to him there. ²All those who were in distress or in debt or discontented gathered around him, and he became their leader. About four hundred men were with him.

³From there David went to Mizpah in Moab and said to the king of Moab, "Would you let my father and mother come and stay with you until I learn what God will do for me?" ⁴So he left them with the king of Moab, and they stayed with him as long as David was in the stronghold.

⁵But the prophet Gad said to David, "Do not stay in the stronghold. Go into the land of Judah." So David left and went to the forest of Hereth.

Saul Kills the Priests of Nob

⁶Now Saul heard that David and his men had been discovered. And Saul, spear in hand, was seated under the tamarisk tree on the hill at Gibeah, with all his officials standing around him. ⁷Saul said to them, "Listen, men of Benjamin! Will the son of Jesse give all of you fields and vineyards? Will he make all of you commanders of thousands and commanders of hundreds? ⁸Is that why you have all conspired against me? No one tells me when my son makes a covenant with the son of Jesse. None of you is concerned about me or tells me that my son has incited my servant to lie in wait for me, as he does today."

⁹But Doeg the Edomite, who was standing with Saul's officials, said, "I saw the son of Jesse come to Ahimelech son of Ahitub at

1. Jesus supports David for eating the show bread (see Mt 12:1–4). Why? When is it right to disregard sacred rituals (see Lk 6:6–9)? 2. Does this principle apply to David's lie? To sexual holiness? 3. What "sacred bread" has the Lord fed you with this past week? With what "sword" has he armed you?

What disguises have you worn on stage? At a recent costume party? In real life?

1. Gath is a Philistine stronghold. Why then does David go there? 2. Why does David feel it necessary to act like a madman? What sort of "marks" does he make? Where?

1. When has "playing dumb" worked for you? 2. How do you honestly face fear?

Have you ever visited a cave? Where? What was it like?

1. Why do men join David's band of fugitives? Are they likely to be reliable? 2. Why does David entrust his family to a Moabite king (see Ru 1:1–5; 4:17)?

In what area of your life are you waiting to learn what God will do for you?

What would you find toughest to do and why: (a) Testify against someone if you knew your witness would bring his death? (b) Testify for someone if you knew it may bring your own death? (c) Carry out the death sentence?

1. What is Saul's mental and emotional state? 2. What motivates Doeg the Edomite to testify against Ahimelech? What defense does Ahimelech offer? 3. If David had told Ahimelech the truth (see 21:2–4), do you think Saul

might have not killed him? Is David in fact guilty for these deaths (v. 22)? Explain. **4.** Why do the guards dare refuse the king's edict to kill Ahimelech and his whole family? **5.** What does Saul's twice-issued command reveal about the man he has become? **6.** What kind of person does Doeg the Edomite prove to be? He also proves to be a tool in God's hand: What prophecy does the killing of the priests fulfill (see 2:30–33)? **7.** How does David pray for Doeg (see Ps 52)?

1. When, if ever, have you been consumed with a desire for revenge? If looks or thoughts could kill, how many of your friends would be dead by now: 9? 99? What friends? Are you still bearing any hateful grudges? Any stepping-over-others to get ahead? **2.** What "little sin" have you committed, only to be shocked at its far-reaching consequences? How can you help each other to "count the cost" of each temptation? **3.** The opening question in this session was hypothetical for you, but not for the main characters in this section. With whom do you most readily identify? Which of their weaknesses do you also detect in your own life? **4.** How will you bring these admitted weaknesses under the lordship of Christ?

What is your favorite means of deciding what God's will for your life is?

1. By what means does David inquire of God? **2.** Why do David's men hesitate to go to Keilah (vv. 3,7)? Why is David resolved to proceed?

When faced with a similar call to arms, or to serve, do you respond more like David's men, or like David? Why?

---

1. If you could ask God one "Yes/No" question regarding the future, what would it be? **2.** What one person outside your family especially encouraged you when you were growing up? Why

Nob. [10]Ahimelech inquired of the LORD for him; he also gave him provisions and the sword of Goliath the Philistine."

[11]Then the king sent for the priest Ahimelech son of Ahitub and his father's whole family, who were the priests at Nob, and they all came to the king. [12]Saul said, "Listen now, son of Ahitub."

"Yes, my lord," he answered.

[13]Saul said to him, "Why have you conspired against me, you and the son of Jesse, giving him bread and a sword and inquiring of God for him, so that he has rebelled against me and lies in wait for me, as he does today?"

[14]Ahimelech answered the king, "Who of all your servants is as loyal as David, the king's son-in-law, captain of your bodyguard and highly respected in your household? [15]Was that day the first time I inquired of God for him? Of course not! Let not the king accuse your servant or any of his father's family, for your servant knows nothing at all about this whole affair."

[16]But the king said, "You will surely die, Ahimelech, you and your father's whole family."

[17]Then the king ordered the guards at his side: "Turn and kill the priests of the LORD, because they too have sided with David. They knew he was fleeing, yet they did not tell me."

But the king's officials were not willing to raise a hand to strike the priests of the LORD.

[18]The king then ordered Doeg, "You turn and strike down the priests." So Doeg the Edomite turned and struck them down. That day he killed eighty-five men who wore the linen ephod. [19]He also put to the sword Nob, the town of the priests, with its men and women, its children and infants, and its cattle, donkeys and sheep.

[20]But Abiathar, a son of Ahimelech son of Ahitub, escaped and fled to join David. [21]He told David that Saul had killed the priests of the LORD. [22]Then David said to Abiathar: "That day, when Doeg the Edomite was there, I knew he would be sure to tell Saul. I am responsible for the death of your father's whole family. [23]Stay with me; don't be afraid; the man who is seeking your life is seeking mine also. You will be safe with me."

David Saves Keilah

23 When David was told, "Look, the Philistines are fighting against Keilah and are looting the threshing floors," [2]he inquired of the LORD, saying, "Shall I go and attack these Philistines?"

The LORD answered him, "Go, attack the Philistines and save Keilah."

[3]But David's men said to him, "Here in Judah we are afraid. How much more, then, if we go to Keilah against the Philistine forces!"

[4]Once again David inquired of the LORD, and the LORD answered him, "Go down to Keilah, for I am going to give the Philistines into your hand." [5]So David and his men went to Keilah, fought the Philistines and carried off their livestock. He inflicted heavy losses on the Philistines and saved the people of Keilah. [6](Now Abiathar son of Ahimelech had brought the ephod down with him when he fled to David at Keilah.)

Saul Pursues David

[7]Saul was told that David had gone to Keilah, and he said, "God has handed him over to me, for David has imprisoned himself by entering a town with gates and bars." [8]And Saul called up all his forces for battle, to go down to Keilah to besiege David and his men.

[9]When David learned that Saul was plotting against him, he said to Abiathar the priest, "Bring the ephod." [10]David said, "O LORD, God of Israel, your servant has heard definitely that Saul plans to come to Keilah and destroy the town on account of me. [11]Will the citizens of Keilah surrender me to him? Will Saul come down, as your servant has heard? O LORD, God of Israel, tell your servant."

And the LORD said, "He will."

[12]Again David asked, "Will the citizens of Keilah surrender me and my men to Saul?"

And the LORD said, "They will."

[13]So David and his men, about six hundred in number, left Keilah and kept moving from place to place. When Saul was told that David had escaped from Keilah, he did not go there.

[14]David stayed in the desert strongholds and in the hills of the Desert of Ziph. Day after day Saul searched for him, but God did not give David into his hands.

[15]While David was at Horesh in the Desert of Ziph, he learned that Saul had come out to take his life. [16]And Saul's son Jonathan went to David at Horesh and helped him find strength in God. [17]"Don't be afraid," he said. "My father Saul will not lay a hand on you. You will be king over Israel, and I will be second to you. Even my father Saul knows this." [18]The two of them made a covenant before the LORD. Then Jonathan went home, but David remained at Horesh.

[19]The Ziphites went up to Saul at Gibeah and said, "Is not David hiding among us in the strongholds at Horesh, on the hill of Hakilah, south of Jeshimon? [20]Now, O king, come down whenever it pleases you to do so, and we will be responsible for handing him over to the king."

[21]Saul replied, "The LORD bless you for your concern for me. [22]Go and make further preparation. Find out where David usually goes and who has seen him there. They tell me he is very crafty. [23]Find out about all the hiding places he uses and come back to me with definite information.[a] Then I will go with you; if he is in the area, I will track him down among all the clans of Judah."

[24]So they set out and went to Ziph ahead of Saul. Now David and his men were in the Desert of Maon, in the Arabah south of Jeshimon. [25]Saul and his men began the search, and when David was told about it, he went down to the rock and stayed in the Desert of Maon. When Saul heard this, he went into the Desert of Maon in pursuit of David.

[26]Saul was going along one side of the mountain, and David and his men were on the other side, hurrying to get away from Saul. As Saul and his forces were closing in on David and his men to capture them, [27]a messenger came to Saul, saying, "Come quickly! The Philistines are raiding the land." [28]Then Saul broke off his pursuit of David and went to meet the Philistines. That is why they call this place Sela Hammahlekoth.[b] [29]And David went up from there and lived in the strongholds of En Gedi.

David Spares Saul's Life

24 After Saul returned from pursuing the Philistines, he was told, "David is in the Desert of En Gedi." [2]So Saul took three thousand chosen men from all Israel and set out to look for David and his men near the Crags of the Wild Goats.

[3]He came to the sheep pens along the way; a cave was there, and Saul went in to relieve himself. David and his men were far back in

did he or she take that interest in your life?

1. Why is Saul pleased to hear that David is in Keilah (vv. 7–8)? 2. What are these citizens of Keilah like (compare vv. 12,5)? 3. What do you learn about God from his responses to David (vv. 9–12)? From his control of circumstances (v. 14,26–27)? 4. What are David's motives in leaving Keilah: Purely selfish (v.12)? Concern for others (v. 10; 22:22)? Or what? 5. What motivates the Ziphites to come to Saul (vv. 19–20; compare vv. 10–11)? What irony do you see in verse 21? 6. Is this a casual "cat-mouse" game, or something far more deadly (vv. 22–29)?

1. What distinguishes those who are "driven" as is Saul? Take a good look at the "Saul" within you. In which areas of your life are you prone to explosive anger, to paralyzing self-pity, to compulsive behavior? 2. Who has helped you "find strength in the Lord"? How so? 3. Pick one tough situation facing you right now: How is God in control of that? If you are "on the run" in any way, how does God fit into your flight pattern? Who can encourage you now? 4. Pick another tough situation in which you are more prone to act like the Ziphites and "sell out" or give up: How will you resist that temptation?

When your parents, teachers, or bosses turn their backs on you what do you do? When have you used that occasion to slack off? To show yourself 100 percent faithful?

1. What brings Saul to En Gedi? To this particular cave? 2. Why does David cut off

part of Saul's robe? Why does he feel guilty about that? **3.** Why does David not kill Saul? What pressures did he have which might have "excused" killing him? **4.** Why does David "prostrate" himself before Saul (v. 8)? **5.** Why does David liken himself to a dead dog and a flea (v. 14)? **6.** If you were writing this scene as fiction, how would you have Saul respond to David's rebuke? Do you think Saul's repentance here is sincere? Does David think so? **7.** What irony do you see in verses 21–22? How are their roles reversed?

♡ **1.** When have you let your friends talk you into taking revenge against someone? How did you feel afterwards? **2.** What is your attitude toward authority figures? Which of the following do you see as "God's anointed" and as people's anointed: Parents? Spouse? Clergy? Employer? Police? Corrupt politicians? Explain. **3.** Is there an authority figure in your life whom you have a difficult time submitting to? How would David act in your position? **4.** Are you as content as David seems to be to simply let God effect his will, his

the cave. ⁴The men said, "This is the day the LORD spoke of when he said*ᵃ* to you, 'I will give your enemy into your hands for you to deal with as you wish.'" Then David crept up unnoticed and cut off a corner of Saul's robe.

⁵Afterward, David was conscience-stricken for having cut off a corner of his robe. ⁶He said to his men, "The LORD forbid that I should do such a thing to my master, the LORD's anointed, or lift my hand against him; for he is the anointed of the LORD." ⁷With these words David rebuked his men and did not allow them to attack Saul. And Saul left the cave and went his way.

⁸Then David went out of the cave and called out to Saul, "My lord the king!" When Saul looked behind him, David bowed down and prostrated himself with his face to the ground. ⁹He said to Saul, "Why do you listen when men say, 'David is bent on harming you'? ¹⁰This day you have seen with your own eyes how the LORD delivered you into my hands in the cave. Some urged me to kill you, but I spared you; I said, 'I will not lift my hand against my master, because he is the LORD's anointed.' ¹¹See, my father, look at this piece of your robe in my hand! I cut off the corner of your robe but did not kill you. Now understand and recognize that I am not guilty of wrongdoing or rebellion. I have not wronged you, but you are hunting me down to take my life. ¹²May the LORD judge between you and me. And may the LORD avenge the wrongs you have done to me, but my hand will not touch you. ¹³As the old saying goes, 'From evildoers come evil deeds,' so my hand will not touch you.

ᵃ4 Or "Today the LORD is saying

---

  1 Samuel 24:1–22   **DAVID SPARES SAUL'S LIFE**

Saul has been pursuing David in an attempt to kill him to keep David (who has been chosen by God) from replacing Saul as Israel's king.

1. What brought Saul to this cave?
a. coincidence
b. Saul's fears and jealousy
c. God's leading
d. Saul had to go.

2. David cut off a piece of Saul's robe:
a. to be cute.
b. to serve as a warning.
c. to save as a trophy.
d. because he missed.
e. because he was going to kill Saul and changed his mind.

3. I think David:
a. missed a good chance.
b. let his heart rule his head.
c. showed amazing restraint.
d. made his point with Saul.
e. had an overactive conscience.
f. honored the Lord.

4. How do you react when someone is out to get you?

5. How do you explain Saul's future ongoing quest to destroy David (as in 1Sa 26) in light of his actions here? When have you tried to change but went back to your old ways?

6. Think of the person you have the hardest time getting along with. What would happen if you treated this "Saul" the way David did?
a. nothing
b. "Saul" would faint in amazement.
c. "Saul" would cry.
d. It would transform the relationship.
e. I would change more than "Saul."

7. How do you deal with conflict (and how would you like to change)?
a. avoid it
b. approach it cautiously
c. thrive on it
d. with anger
e. with careful words
f. with actions rather than words

8. Like David, are you content to let God bring to pass his will—in his time and way? Or do you usually try to "help God out" somehow?

9. In what way does this story remind you of your relationship with your boss?
a. Very little—thank God!
b. My boss seems out to get me.
c. I find myself wanting to hide from my boss.
d. I feel guilty for how I've felt and acted toward my boss.
e. I'd have a hard time not striking out at my boss if I had an opportunity.
f. I need to see persons in authority as part of God's plan for my life.

10. How does this story relate to your experience of abuse?
a. I have struggled to forgive my abuser.
b. I have struggled with not seeking revenge.
c. I've confined myself to protective caves and strongholds for a long time.
d. I don't think my abuser, like Saul, will ever change.
e. I am trying to let the Lord "avenge the wrongs done to me."
f. I am starting to realize what God *has* delivered me from.

[14]"Against whom has the king of Israel come out? Whom are you pursuing? A dead dog? A flea? [15]May the LORD be our judge and decide between us. May he consider my cause and uphold it; may he vindicate me by delivering me from your hand."

[16]When David finished saying this, Saul asked, "Is that your voice, David my son?" And he wept aloud. [17]"You are more righteous than I," he said. "You have treated me well, but I have treated you badly. [18]You have just now told me of the good you did to me; the LORD delivered me into your hands, but you did not kill me. [19]When a man finds his enemy, does he let him get away unharmed? May the LORD reward you well for the way you treated me today. [20]I know that you will surely be king and that the kingdom of Israel will be established in your hands. [21]Now swear to me by the LORD that you will not cut off my descendants or wipe out my name from my father's family."

[22]So David gave his oath to Saul. Then Saul returned home, but David and his men went up to the stronghold.

David, Nabal and Abigail

25 Now Samuel died, and all Israel assembled and mourned for him; and they buried him at his home in Ramah.

Then David moved down into the Desert of Maon.[a] [2]A certain man in Maon, who had property there at Carmel, was very wealthy. He had a thousand goats and three thousand sheep, which he was shearing in Carmel. [3]His name was Nabal and his wife's name was Abigail. She was an intelligent and beautiful woman, but her husband, a Calebite, was surly and mean in his dealings.

[4]While David was in the desert, he heard that Nabal was shearing sheep. [5]So he sent ten young men and said to them, "Go up to Nabal at Carmel and greet him in my name. [6]Say to him: 'Long life to you! Good health to you and your household! And good health to all that is yours!

[7]"'Now I hear that it is sheep-shearing time. When your shepherds were with us, we did not mistreat them, and the whole time they were at Carmel nothing of theirs was missing. [8]Ask your own servants and they will tell you. Therefore be favorable toward my young men, since we come at a festive time. Please give your servants and your son David whatever you can find for them.'"

[9]When David's men arrived, they gave Nabal this message in David's name. Then they waited.

[10]Nabal answered David's servants, "Who is this David? Who is this son of Jesse? Many servants are breaking away from their masters these days. [11]Why should I take my bread and water, and the meat I have slaughtered for my shearers, and give it to men coming from who knows where?"

[12]David's men turned around and went back. When they arrived, they reported every word. [13]David said to his men, "Put on your swords!" So they put on their swords, and David put on his. About four hundred men went up with David, while two hundred stayed with the supplies.

[14]One of the servants told Nabal's wife Abigail: "David sent messengers from the desert to give our master his greetings, but he hurled insults at them. [15]Yet these men were very good to us. They did not mistreat us, and the whole time we were out in the fields near them nothing was missing. [16]Night and day they were a wall around us all the time we were herding our sheep near them. [17]Now think it over and see what you can do, because disaster is

---

way, in his time? Or are you likely to "help God out" in some way? Give a recent example. **5.** How can you tell if someone is sincere in wanting to "turn over a new leaf"? **6.** By your own standards, how would *you* do on that sincerity test?

1. When you were growing up, which holiday did you celebrate with "enough food to feed a whole army"? What was your favorite holiday meal? **2.** When you get angry, which are you most like: (a) Match on gasoline? (b) Slow-burning fuse? (c) Smoldering underground fire? **3.** (If married) How did you meet your mate?

1. What do Nabal and Saul have in common? How might this story be a "parable" of Saul's relation to David? **2.** Why does David respond so violently? What breach of diplomacy and oriental cultural values is he reacting to? **3.** Why does David seek to kill Nabal? Why did he react so differently with Saul (24:4)? **4.** In Nabal's refusal, what do you detect: Sarcasm? Disdain for authority? Self-preservation? Genuine ignorance? A cover-up (see vv. 28–30)? **5.** What were David's motives in guarding Nabal's possessions? Does he have a right to be repaid? To exact vengeance when not repaid? **6.** Does Abigail do the right thing in interceding for her husband? What might have happened if she hadn't? What might have happened if she'd "told her husband" (v. 19)? **7.** What happens to Nabal in the next scene (vv. 36–38)? Why? How does David see Nabal's death: (a) God always gets his man? (b) He who laughs last, laughs best? (c) Finder's keepers, loser's weepers? (d) Patience is rewarded? (e) Couldn't happen to a nicer guy? **8.** How does David "remember" Abigail (vv. 31b,39b)?

1. If you were recently widowed, like Abigail, how would you respond to a sudden proposal

---

[a] 1 Some Septuagint manuscripts; Hebrew *Paran*

like David's: (a) "No," pretending to grieve a dead husband you could not stand to live with? (b) "Yes," jumping at this new lease on life? (c) "It all depends on _____"? 2. How faithful are you in leaving revenge to God? When did you most recently give someone "what was coming to him"? When did you most recently return good for evil? 3. How do you react when you don't get what is "rightfully" yours? What can you learn from David's choices and their consequences? 4. If you were in Abigail's sandals, what would you have done? 5. When those in authority over you make bad decisions, should you: Take matters into your own hands? Pray? Try to dissuade the person from error? What about those under your authority? 6. Who is your "Abigail"—one who has kept you from sin by appealing to your conscience? Do you seek this ministry from fellow believers? How so? How often?

hanging over our master and his whole household. He is such a wicked man that no one can talk to him."

¹⁸Abigail lost no time. She took two hundred loaves of bread, two skins of wine, five dressed sheep, five seahs*ᵃ* of roasted grain, a hundred cakes of raisins and two hundred cakes of pressed figs, and loaded them on donkeys. ¹⁹Then she told her servants, "Go on ahead; I'll follow you." But she did not tell her husband Nabal.

²⁰As she came riding her donkey into a mountain ravine, there were David and his men descending toward her, and she met them. ²¹David had just said, "It's been useless—all my watching over this fellow's property in the desert so that nothing of his was missing. He has paid me back evil for good. ²²May God deal with David,*ᵇ* be it ever so severely, if by morning I leave alive one male of all who belong to him!"

²³When Abigail saw David, she quickly got off her donkey and bowed down before David with her face to the ground. ²⁴She fell at his feet and said: "My lord, let the blame be on me alone. Please let your servant speak to you; hear what your servant has to say. ²⁵May my lord pay no attention to that wicked man Nabal. He is just like his name—his name is Fool, and folly goes with him. But as for me, your servant, I did not see the men my master sent.

²⁶"Now since the LORD has kept you, my master, from bloodshed and from avenging yourself with your own hands, as surely as the LORD lives and as you live, may your enemies and all who intend to harm my master be like Nabal. ²⁷And let this gift, which your servant has brought to my master, be given to the men who follow you. ²⁸Please forgive your servant's offense, for the LORD will certainly make a lasting dynasty for my master, because he fights the LORD's battles. Let no wrongdoing be found in you as long as you live. ²⁹Even though someone is pursuing you to take your life, the life of my master will be bound securely in the bundle of the living by the LORD your God. But the lives of your enemies he will hurl away as from the pocket of a sling. ³⁰When the LORD has done for my master every good thing he promised concerning him and has appointed him leader over Israel, ³¹my master will not have on his conscience the staggering burden of needless bloodshed or of having avenged himself. And when the LORD has brought my master success, remember your servant."

³²David said to Abigail, "Praise be to the LORD, the God of Israel, who has sent you today to meet me. ³³May you be blessed for your good judgment and for keeping me from bloodshed this day and from avenging myself with my own hands. ³⁴Otherwise, as surely as the LORD, the God of Israel, lives, who has kept me from harming you, if you had not come quickly to meet me, not one male belonging to Nabal would have been left alive by daybreak."

³⁵Then David accepted from her hand what she had brought him and said, "Go home in peace. I have heard your words and granted your request."

³⁶When Abigail went to Nabal, he was in the house holding a banquet like that of a king. He was in high spirits and very drunk. So she told him nothing until daybreak. ³⁷Then in the morning, when Nabal was sober, his wife told him all these things, and his heart failed him and he became like a stone. ³⁸About ten days later, the LORD struck Nabal and he died.

³⁹When David heard that Nabal was dead, he said, "Praise be to the LORD, who has upheld my cause against Nabal for treating me

a 18 That is, probably about a bushel (about 37 liters)   *b 22* Some Septuagint manuscripts; Hebrew *with David's enemies*

with contempt. He has kept his servant from doing wrong and has brought Nabal's wrongdoing down on his own head."

Then David sent word to Abigail, asking her to become his wife. [40]His servants went to Carmel and said to Abigail, "David has sent us to you to take you to become his wife."

[41]She bowed down with her face to the ground and said, "Here is your maidservant, ready to serve you and wash the feet of my master's servants." [42]Abigail quickly got on a donkey and, attended by her five maids, went with David's messengers and became his wife. [43]David had also married Ahinoam of Jezreel, and they both were his wives. [44]But Saul had given his daughter Michal, David's wife, to Paltiel[a] son of Laish, who was from Gallim.

David Again Spares Saul's Life

26 The Ziphites went to Saul at Gibeah and said, "Is not David hiding on the hill of Hakilah, which faces Jeshimon?"

[2]So Saul went down to the Desert of Ziph, with his three thousand chosen men of Israel, to search there for David. [3]Saul made his camp beside the road on the hill of Hakilah facing Jeshimon, but David stayed in the desert. When he saw that Saul had followed him there, [4]he sent out scouts and learned that Saul had definitely arrived.[b]

[5]Then David set out and went to the place where Saul had camped. He saw where Saul and Abner son of Ner, the commander of the army, had lain down. Saul was lying inside the camp, with the army encamped around him.

[6]David then asked Ahimelech the Hittite and Abishai son of Zeruiah, Joab's brother, "Who will go down into the camp with me to Saul?"

"I'll go with you," said Abishai.

[7]So David and Abishai went to the army by night, and there was Saul, lying asleep inside the camp with his spear stuck in the ground near his head. Abner and the soldiers were lying around him.

[8]Abishai said to David, "Today God has delivered your enemy into your hands. Now let me pin him to the ground with one thrust of my spear; I won't strike him twice."

[9]But David said to Abishai, "Don't destroy him! Who can lay a hand on the Lord's anointed and be guiltless? [10]As surely as the Lord lives," he said, "the Lord himself will strike him; either his time will come and he will die, or he will go into battle and perish. [11]But the Lord forbid that I should lay a hand on the Lord's anointed. Now get the spear and water jug that are near his head, and let's go."

[12]So David took the spear and water jug near Saul's head, and they left. No one saw or knew about it, nor did anyone wake up. They were all sleeping, because the Lord had put them into a deep sleep.

[13]Then David crossed over to the other side and stood on top of the hill some distance away; there was a wide space between them. [14]He called out to the army and to Abner son of Ner, "Aren't you going to answer me, Abner?"

Abner replied, "Who are you who calls to the king?"

[15]David said, "You're a man, aren't you? And who is like you in Israel? Why didn't you guard your lord the king? Someone came to destroy your lord the king. [16]What you have done is not good. As surely as the Lord lives, you and your men deserve to die, because

1. What would it take to rouse you from deep sleep? What is the most embarrassing or damaging thing you have managed to sleep through? 2. Growing up, when were you most homesick? When do you tend to feel homesick now?

1. Compare this passage and David's encounter with Saul in the cave (ch. 24). What are the similarities and differences? How has God humbled Saul? Exalted David? 2. Given this setting, how would you have responded to David's invitation (v. 6): As Ahimelech, or Abishai? Why? 3. Why does David refute Abishai's advice? 4. What evidence do we have that the Lord is with David? Why has the Lord twice delivered Saul into David's hands this way? Would the Lord really have been angry if David had killed Saul? 5. Why is there "no one like Abner in Israel" (v. 15)? If you had been Abner, how would you respond to David's taunts? 6. When David and Saul confer this time (compare with 24:9–22), what is David most concerned to protect: (a) His innocence? (b) His inheritance? (c) His faithfulness to God? (d) To the Lord's anointed? (e) His own life? (f) A place in Israel to properly worship the Lord? Why do you think so? 7. How does David show he is wiser and less trusting of Saul this time around?

1. In what area of your life do you need to be comforted with this reminder, "The Lord rewards righteousness and faithfulness"? Where is your faithfulness being tested? What reward are you anticipating? 2. Failing to see God act on your behalf, are you tempted to take matters into your own hands? In what area? 3. Describe one of your "desert experiences" from the past. Are you in one now?

a44 Hebrew Palti, a variant of Paltiel   b4 Or had come to Nacon

What do you hope to learn from this one?

you did not guard your master, the LORD's anointed. Look around you. Where are the king's spear and water jug that were near his head?"

[17]Saul recognized David's voice and said, "Is that your voice, David my son?"

David replied, "Yes it is, my lord the king." [18]And he added, "Why is my lord pursuing his servant? What have I done, and what wrong am I guilty of? [19]Now let my lord the king listen to his servant's words. If the LORD has incited you against me, then may he accept an offering. If, however, men have done it, may they be cursed before the LORD! They have now driven me from my share in the LORD's inheritance and have said, 'Go, serve other gods.' [20]Now do not let my blood fall to the ground far from the presence of the LORD. The king of Israel has come out to look for a flea—as one hunts a partridge in the mountains."

[21]Then Saul said, "I have sinned. Come back, David my son. Because you considered my life precious today, I will not try to harm you again. Surely I have acted like a fool and have erred greatly."

[22]"Here is the king's spear," David answered. "Let one of your young men come over and get it. [23]The LORD rewards every man for his righteousness and faithfulness. The LORD delivered you into my hands today, but I would not lay a hand on the LORD's anointed. [24]As surely as I valued your life today, so may the LORD value my life and deliver me from all trouble."

[25]Then Saul said to David, "May you be blessed, my son David; you will do great things and surely triumph."

So David went on his way, and Saul returned home.

David Among the Philistines

27 But David thought to himself, "One of these days I will be destroyed by the hand of Saul. The best thing I can do is to escape to the land of the Philistines. Then Saul will give up searching for me anywhere in Israel, and I will slip out of his hand."

[2]So David and the six hundred men with him left and went over to Achish son of Maoch king of Gath. [3]David and his men settled in Gath with Achish. Each man had his family with him, and David had his two wives: Ahinoam of Jezreel and Abigail of Carmel, the widow of Nabal. [4]When Saul was told that David had fled to Gath, he no longer searched for him.

[5]Then David said to Achish, "If I have found favor in your eyes, let a place be assigned to me in one of the country towns, that I may live there. Why should your servant live in the royal city with you?"

[6]So on that day Achish gave him Ziklag, and it has belonged to the kings of Judah ever since. [7]David lived in Philistine territory a year and four months.

[8]Now David and his men went up and raided the Geshurites, the Girzites and the Amalekites. (From ancient times these peoples had lived in the land extending to Shur and Egypt.) [9]Whenever David attacked an area, he did not leave a man or woman alive, but took sheep and cattle, donkeys and camels, and clothes. Then he returned to Achish.

[10]When Achish asked, "Where did you go raiding today?" David would say, "Against the Negev of Judah" or "Against the Negev of Jerahmeel" or "Against the Negev of the Kenites." [11]He did not leave a man or woman alive to be brought to Gath, for he thought, "They might inform on us and say, 'This is what David did.'" And such was his practice as long as he lived in Philistine territory.

1. In your experience with sibling rivalry, were you more often the aggressor, the victim, or the tattler? 2. How did you keep someone from telling Mom or Dad: Arm-twisting? Bribery? Some other threat?

1. Given King Achish's last encounter with David (21:10–15), how do you think Achish felt about David's arrival and settlement in Gath? 2. Why does David desire to move to the country? 3. What was David's motive for totally annihilating those whom he raided? Was David justified in raiding the outlying towns (see 15:2–3; Jos 13:1–2)?

1. David escapes Saul only to land in Achish's lap. When has an escape plan of yours turned into a similar "out-of-the-frying-pan-into-the-fire" escapade? What good, if any, came of that fiery situation? 2. What are you getting away with right now that you fear someone might blow the whistle on? 3. What long-standing commandment or covenant with the Lord remains unfulfilled in your life? How will you begin this week to obey in this area?

¹²Achish trusted David and said to himself, "He has become so odious to his people, the Israelites, that he will be my servant forever."

Saul and the Witch of Endor

28 In those days the Philistines gathered their forces to fight against Israel. Achish said to David, "You must understand that you and your men will accompany me in the army."

²David said, "Then you will see for yourself what your servant can do."

Achish replied, "Very well, I will make you my bodyguard for life."

³Now Samuel was dead, and all Israel had mourned for him and buried him in his own town of Ramah. Saul had expelled the mediums and spiritists from the land.

⁴The Philistines assembled and came and set up camp at Shunem, while Saul gathered all the Israelites and set up camp at Gilboa. ⁵When Saul saw the Philistine army, he was afraid; terror filled his heart. ⁶He inquired of the LORD, but the LORD did not answer him by dreams or Urim or prophets. ⁷Saul then said to his attendants, "Find me a woman who is a medium, so I may go and inquire of her."

"There is one in Endor," they said.

⁸So Saul disguised himself, putting on other clothes, and at night he and two men went to the woman. "Consult a spirit for me," he said, "and bring up for me the one I name."

⁹But the woman said to him, "Surely you know what Saul has done. He has cut off the mediums and spiritists from the land. Why have you set a trap for my life to bring about my death?"

¹⁰Saul swore to her by the LORD, "As surely as the LORD lives, you will not be punished for this."

¹¹Then the woman asked, "Whom shall I bring up for you?"

"Bring up Samuel," he said.

¹²When the woman saw Samuel, she cried out at the top of her voice and said to Saul, "Why have you deceived me? You are Saul!"

¹³The king said to her, "Don't be afraid. What do you see?"

The woman said, "I see a spirit[a] coming up out of the ground."

¹⁴"What does he look like?" he asked.

"An old man wearing a robe is coming up," she said.

Then Saul knew it was Samuel, and he bowed down and prostrated himself with his face to the ground.

¹⁵Samuel said to Saul, "Why have you disturbed me by bringing me up?"

"I am in great distress," Saul said. "The Philistines are fighting against me, and God has turned away from me. He no longer answers me, either by prophets or by dreams. So I have called on you to tell me what to do."

¹⁶Samuel said, "Why do you consult me, now that the LORD has turned away from you and become your enemy? ¹⁷The LORD has done what he predicted through me. The LORD has torn the kingdom out of your hands and given it to one of your neighbors—to David. ¹⁸Because you did not obey the LORD or carry out his fierce wrath against the Amalekites, the LORD has done this to you today. ¹⁹The LORD will hand over both Israel and you to the Philistines, and tomorrow you and your sons will be with me. The LORD will also hand over the army of Israel to the Philistines."

²⁰Immediately Saul fell full length on the ground, filled with fear

a 13 Or *see spirits;* or *see gods*

---

1. If you had the power to go back in time and visit any military leader of the world, which hero would you consult and why? **2.** You have just learned you have 24 hours to live: Which of your current "do today" items do you forsake? What do you do instead?

1. What unspoken thoughts do you suppose David had during his talk with Achish (vv. 1–2)? **2.** How does God communicate his will at this time in Israel's history (v. 6)? Instead, how does Saul seek to know God's will? **3.** Why did Saul expel spiritists and mediums from Israel (see Lev 19:31; 20:6; Dt 18:10–13)? Why then does he consult one anyway? And why covertly? **4.** Why does the woman fear she might die (see Lev 20:27)? Considering Saul's assurance (v. 10), who fears the living God more—the Israelite king or the pagan witch? **5.** Why is she terrified when she sees Samuel? What do you think she *really* sees: Samuel risen from the dead? A spirit impersonating Samuel? Or what? What does this say for the validity of such occult practices? **6.** Why has God stopped responding to Saul when he calls? How has Saul responded to God's calls in the past? In view of his past performances, do you think Saul's prostrated humility (v. 14) is sincere? **7.** How do you suppose the fattened calf tasted to one who now knew he was about to die?

1. Saul was very prone to say one thing (e.g., expel the mediums and spiritists) and do quite another (consult them). In what areas of your life are you like that? Where do your actions speak louder than your words? **2.** What "great distress" in your life has you seeking God's will in earnest? Where are you looking for answers? Whom are you consulting? **3.** Do you temporarily "repent" during hard times, only to "harden your heart" when things get better? **4.** Do you ever read your horoscope? Is that acceptable in God's sight? What other occult things do you play with? Ouija boards? Crystals? Tarot cards? "Visualization"? Other "New Age" trends? How do such things compare with Dt 18:10–13? **5.** In light of your present relationship with God, what are your feelings about death and dying? Do you know with certainty where you are going to spend eternity? What is the basis for your certainty?

because of Samuel's words. His strength was gone, for he had eaten nothing all that day and night.

21When the woman came to Saul and saw that he was greatly shaken, she said, "Look, your maidservant has obeyed you. I took my life in my hands and did what you told me to do. 22Now please listen to your servant and let me give you some food so you may eat and have the strength to go on your way."

23He refused and said, "I will not eat."

But his men joined the woman in urging him, and he listened to them. He got up from the ground and sat on the couch.

24The woman had a fattened calf at the house, which she butchered at once. She took some flour, kneaded it and baked bread without yeast. 25Then she set it before Saul and his men, and they ate. That same night they got up and left.

Achish Sends David Back to Ziklag

29 The Philistines gathered all their forces at Aphek, and Israel camped by the spring in Jezreel. 2As the Philistine rulers marched with their units of hundreds and thousands, David and his men were marching at the rear with Achish. 3The commanders of the Philistines asked, "What about these Hebrews?"

Achish replied, "Is this not David, who was an officer of Saul king of Israel? He has already been with me for over a year, and from the day he left Saul until now, I have found no fault in him."

4But the Philistine commanders were angry with him and said, "Send the man back, that he may return to the place you assigned him. He must not go with us into battle, or he will turn against us during the fighting. How better could he regain his master's favor than by taking the heads of our own men? 5Isn't this the David they sang about in their dances:

> " 'Saul has slain his thousands,
>   and David his tens of thousands'?"

6So Achish called David and said to him, "As surely as the LORD lives, you have been reliable, and I would be pleased to have you serve with me in the army. From the day you came to me until now, I have found no fault in you, but the rulers don't approve of you. 7Turn back and go in peace; do nothing to displease the Philistine rulers."

8"But what have I done?" asked David. "What have you found against your servant from the day I came to you until now? Why can't I go and fight against the enemies of my lord the king?"

9Achish answered, "I know that you have been as pleasing in my eyes as an angel of God; nevertheless, the Philistine commanders have said, 'He must not go up with us into battle.' 10Now get up early, along with your master's servants who have come with you, and leave in the morning as soon as it is light."

11So David and his men got up early in the morning to go back to the land of the Philistines, and the Philistines went up to Jezreel.

David Destroys the Amalekites

30 David and his men reached Ziklag on the third day. Now the Amalekites had raided the Negev and Ziklag. They had attacked Ziklag and burned it, 2and had taken captive the women and all who were in it, both young and old. They killed none of them, but carried them off as they went on their way.

3When David and his men came to Ziklag, they found it destroyed by fire and their wives and sons and daughters taken captive. 4So David and his men wept aloud until they had no strength

1. How successful are you at card games or board games that require some "bluffing" to win? Can others read you "like an open book" or not? 2. How successful would you be as a secret agent?

1. What reservations do the Philistine leaders have about David fighting on their side? What is the view of Achish? Why such conflicting opinions? 2. Do you think David would have fought against Israel? Or was he bluffing?

1. In your life right now, where are you "between a rock and a hard place"—caught in the middle whether you do, or don't do, a particular course of action? 2. In such dilemmas, how does your Christian faith affect how you decide?

1. Has your house or a friend's house ever been destroyed by fire? How did that affect you or your friend: (a) You counted your losses and your blessings? (b) You pitched in and helped out? (c) You provided shelter? (d) Other? 2. What has been your biggest loss from theft? From a hit-and-run ac-

left to weep. 5David's two wives had been captured—Ahinoam of Jezreel and Abigail, the widow of Nabal of Carmel. 6David was greatly distressed because the men were talking of stoning him; each one was bitter in spirit because of his sons and daughters. But David found strength in the LORD his God.

7Then David said to Abiathar the priest, the son of Ahimelech, "Bring me the ephod." Abiathar brought it to him, 8and David inquired of the LORD, "Shall I pursue this raiding party? Will I overtake them?"

"Pursue them," he answered. "You will certainly overtake them and succeed in the rescue."

9David and the six hundred men with him came to the Besor Ravine, where some stayed behind, 10for two hundred men were too exhausted to cross the ravine. But David and four hundred men continued the pursuit.

11They found an Egyptian in a field and brought him to David. They gave him water to drink and food to eat— 12part of a cake of pressed figs and two cakes of raisins. He ate and was revived, for he had not eaten any food or drunk any water for three days and three nights.

13David asked him, "To whom do you belong, and where do you come from?"

He said, "I am an Egyptian, the slave of an Amalekite. My master abandoned me when I became ill three days ago. 14We raided the Negev of the Kerethites and the territory belonging to Judah and the Negev of Caleb. And we burned Ziklag."

15David asked him, "Can you lead me down to this raiding party?"

He answered, "Swear to me before God that you will not kill me or hand me over to my master, and I will take you down to them."

16He led David down, and there they were, scattered over the countryside, eating, drinking and reveling because of the great amount of plunder they had taken from the land of the Philistines and from Judah. 17David fought them from dusk until the evening of the next day, and none of them got away, except four hundred young men who rode off on camels and fled. 18David recovered everything the Amalekites had taken, including his two wives. 19Nothing was missing: young or old, boy or girl, plunder or anything else they had taken. David brought everything back. 20He took all the flocks and herds, and his men drove them ahead of the other livestock, saying, "This is David's plunder."

21Then David came to the two hundred men who had been too exhausted to follow him and who were left behind at the Besor Ravine. They came out to meet David and the people with him. As David and his men approached, he greeted them. 22But all the evil men and troublemakers among David's followers said, "Because they did not go out with us, we will not share with them the plunder we recovered. However, each man may take his wife and children and go."

23David replied, "No, my brothers, you must not do that with what the LORD has given us. He has protected us and handed over to us the forces that came against us. 24Who will listen to what you say? The share of the man who stayed with the supplies is to be the same as that of him who went down to the battle. All will share alike." 25David made this a statute and ordinance for Israel from that day to this.

26When David arrived in Ziklag, he sent some of the plunder to the elders of Judah, who were his friends, saying, "Here is a present for you from the plunder of the LORD's enemies."

cident? What did you do to replace it?

1. How does the Lord once again look after David's interests when his enemies attack him (v. 2; see 27:9)? 2. How do you think David "found strength in the Lord" (v. 6b)? 3. How does the ephod relate to David's inquiry and God's will (vv. 7–8; see 23:9–12)? 4. If you had been the Egyptian, what would you be feeling as your master raided and torched Ziklag? As your master then abandoned you without food and water in the desert? As David and his men then discover you? Feed you? Interrogate you? Follow your lead in pursuit of the Amalekites? 5. While David is destroying the Amalekites, Saul is dying in battle. How does David at this point replace Saul as God's anointed (see 15:2–3)? 6. What dissension in David's ranks now threatens to make this victory bittersweet? How does David deal with that? 7. How does the attitude of David's men toward authority compare with that of David? What might be the key differences (v. 6)? 8. What is David's attitude toward the things he has earned? Toward his "employees"? Toward his friends and benefactors?

1. Divide your group into "thirds" for a role play: one-third the troublemakers among the victors returning with spoils, one-third the ones left behind the front lines to recover health, one-third advisors to David on how to manage this internal conflict. Using chapter 30, any similar experiences of your own, plus your own vivid imaginations as your script, re-enact this drama in conflict management. Which role-plays seem to fit your real life? 2. When harm comes to your family or prize possessions, how do you initially respond: With bitterness and fixing blame, as typified by David's men? Or by finding strength in the Lord, as David does? 3. Where do you need that divine strength now? 4. What commodity (time, money, possessions) are you least likely to be generous with? Why? 5. With whom would you like to be especially generous this week, as a reflection of God's kindness and provision?

27He sent it to those who were in Bethel, Ramoth Negev and Jattir; 28to those in Aroer, Siphmoth, Eshtemoa 29and Racal; to those in the towns of the Jerahmeelites and the Kenites; 30to those in Hormah, Bor Ashan, Athach 31and Hebron; and to those in all the other places where David and his men had roamed.

Saul Takes His Life

31 Now the Philistines fought against Israel; the Israelites fled before them, and many fell slain on Mount Gilboa. 2The Philistines pressed hard after Saul and his sons, and they killed his sons Jonathan, Abinadab and Malki-Shua. 3The fighting grew fierce around Saul, and when the archers overtook him, they wounded him critically.

4Saul said to his armor-bearer, "Draw your sword and run me through, or these uncircumcised fellows will come and run me through and abuse me."

But his armor-bearer was terrified and would not do it; so Saul took his own sword and fell on it. 5When the armor-bearer saw that Saul was dead, he too fell on his sword and died with him. 6So Saul and his three sons and his armor-bearer and all his men died together that same day.

7When the Israelites along the valley and those across the Jordan saw that the Israelite army had fled and that Saul and his sons had died, they abandoned their towns and fled. And the Philistines came and occupied them.

8The next day, when the Philistines came to strip the dead, they found Saul and his three sons fallen on Mount Gilboa. 9They cut off his head and stripped off his armor, and they sent messengers throughout the land of the Philistines to proclaim the news in the temple of their idols and among their people. 10They put his armor in the temple of the Ashtoreths and fastened his body to the wall of Beth Shan.

11When the people of Jabesh Gilead heard of what the Philistines had done to Saul, 12all their valiant men journeyed through the night to Beth Shan. They took down the bodies of Saul and his sons from the wall of Beth Shan and went to Jabesh, where they burned them. 13Then they took their bones and buried them under a tamarisk tree at Jabesh, and they fasted seven days.

How do you think your own death might happen: (a) "Rust out" in old age? (b) "Burn out" in your prime? (c) "Drop out" in a sudden, accidental death? Why do you think so?

1. Why does Saul ask his armor-bearer to kill him? Would this have been akin to a "mercy killing"? Why does he refuse Saul's request (v. 4; see 2Sa 1:14)? 2. Why then does each in turn take his own life? 3. How do you think God views suicide (see Dt 5:17; Pr 3:5–6)? 4. Why do the Philistines cut off Saul's head and put his armor in their temple (see 5:2; 17:51; 21:9)? 5. Why do the people of Jabesh Gilead retrieve the bodies of Saul and his sons (see ch. 11)? 6. Where do you think Saul is spending eternity?

1. As part of the Christian's witness, the Puritans stressed the importance of "dying well." How can you get ready to "die well"? 2. What will you take to heart from this first book of Samuel? Any quotable quotes? Life applications? Group covenants? Pray about these.

INTRODUCTION to
2 SAMUEL

Book Study Outline: If you are using 2 Samuel for a study course, here is a 7- or 13-week outline. Use the questions in the margin for your group agenda:

☕ start meeting / 15 min.

📖 read & discuss Bible / 30 min.

❤ close meeting / 15–45 min.

Refer to the Questions and Answers in the front of this Bible for more information.

7-week plan	13-week plan	Personal Reading	Group Study Passage
1	1	1:1–3:5	2:8–3:5/Civil War Divides
	2	3:6–6:23	6:1–23/David and the Ark
2	3	7:1–9:13	7:1–17/God Promises David
	4	10:1–11:27	11:1–27/David and Bathsheba
3	5	12:1–14	12:1–14/David Rebuked
	6	12:15–31	12:15–25/David Grieves
4	7	13:1–22	13:1–22/Amnon Rapes Tamar
	8	13:23–39	13:23–39/Absalom Kills Amnon
5	9	14:1–15:37	14:1–38/Absalom Returns
	10	16:1–19:8a	18:19–19:8a/David Distressed
6	11	19:8b–21:22	21:1–14/Saul's Sons Destroyed
	12	22:1–23:7	22:1–51/God Delivers David
7	13	23:8–24:25	23:8–23/David's Mighty Men

Author: The author is not known with certainty. Perhaps a compiler drew from materials written by others such as Samuel, Gad and Nathan (see 1 Ch 29:29) in order to produce the final rendition. Note that 1 and 2 Samuel were originally composed as one unit.

Date: Uncertain, though it is possible that this two-volume book was written around the time of Solomon's death (c. 930 B.C.).

Theme: The life and times of King David.

Historical Background: David had been on the run from Saul. Now that Saul has died, David is able to take his rightful place on the throne over all of Israel, but only after he emerges triumphant from a political power struggle. Surrounding nations, especially the Philistines, still pose the threat of war; however, Israel is militarily strong under David's victorious reign.

Characteristics: Second Samuel continues the historical narrative of 1 Samuel, where David's youth and troublesome exile were the focus. Now in "volume two" David reigns as Saul's successor and he must heal and unify the war-torn country. Chapters 1–10 narrate the prosperous early reign of David. He is anointed king over Judah and then over all Israel. He also sustains victory after victory on the battlefield. David's adultery with Bathsheba (ch. 11–12), however, marks a turning point in the book. In the chapters which follow, the "sword never departs from David's house" (12:10). Throughout the book, God forms the backdrop as the One who establishes David upon the throne of Israel and gives him victory over his enemies.

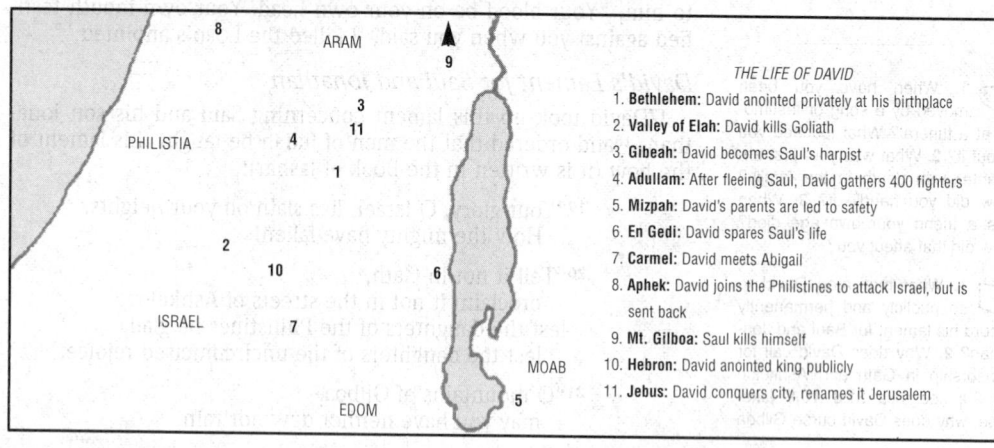

THE LIFE OF DAVID

1. **Bethlehem:** David anointed privately at his birthplace
2. **Valley of Elah:** David kills Goliath
3. **Gibeah:** David becomes Saul's harpist
4. **Adullam:** After fleeing Saul, David gathers 400 fighters
5. **Mizpah:** David's parents are led to safety
6. **En Gedi:** David spares Saul's life
7. **Carmel:** David meets Abigail
8. **Aphek:** David joins the Philistines to attack Israel, but is sent back
9. **Mt. Gilboa:** Saul kills himself
10. **Hebron:** David anointed king publicly
11. **Jebus:** David conquers city, renames it Jerusalem

2 Samuel

David Hears of Saul's Death

1. Where were you upon hearing news of a famous person's (JFK, Martin Luther King, Kurt Cobain, Yitzhak Rabin, etc.) death? How did news of his or her death hit you? 2. Who has lived the longest in your family? Who has died most suddenly? Any for whom tough decisions had to be made about the use of life support systems to prolong life or delay death?

1. How does the Amalekite's account of Saul's death (vv. 6–10) vary from the biblical author's (see 1Sa 31)? Why would the Amalekite lie? 2. What does he bring to David? What would he hope to win by ingratiating himself to David? 3. Which of David's responses (vv. 11–15) surprise you? Why? Does he believe the Amalekite's report or not? Why? 4. How do David and the Amalekite vary in their views of "mercy-killing" (vv. 9–10,14–16)? And of the "Lord's anointed"?

1. When have you fibbed to win someone's favor? How might you be tempted to do so again? 2. Where does your attitude toward your enemies need to change? How so? 3. Where might you be grieving the death of a relationship? How is yours "good grief"?

1 After the death of Saul, David returned from defeating the Amalekites and stayed in Ziklag two days. ²On the third day a man arrived from Saul's camp, with his clothes torn and with dust on his head. When he came to David, he fell to the ground to pay him honor.

³"Where have you come from?" David asked him.

He answered, "I have escaped from the Israelite camp."

⁴"What happened?" David asked. "Tell me."

He said, "The men fled from the battle. Many of them fell and died. And Saul and his son Jonathan are dead."

⁵Then David said to the young man who brought him the report, "How do you know that Saul and his son Jonathan are dead?"

⁶"I happened to be on Mount Gilboa," the young man said, "and there was Saul, leaning on his spear, with the chariots and riders almost upon him. ⁷When he turned around and saw me, he called out to me, and I said, 'What can I do?'

⁸"He asked me, 'Who are you?'

"'An Amalekite,' I answered.

⁹"Then he said to me, 'Stand over me and kill me! I am in the throes of death, but I'm still alive.'

¹⁰"So I stood over him and killed him, because I knew that after he had fallen he could not survive. And I took the crown that was on his head and the band on his arm and have brought them here to my lord."

¹¹Then David and all the men with him took hold of their clothes and tore them. ¹²They mourned and wept and fasted till evening for Saul and his son Jonathan, and for the army of the LORD and the house of Israel, because they had fallen by the sword.

¹³David said to the young man who brought him the report, "Where are you from?"

"I am the son of an alien, an Amalekite," he answered.

¹⁴David asked him, "Why were you not afraid to lift your hand to destroy the LORD's anointed?"

¹⁵Then David called one of his men and said, "Go, strike him down!" So he struck him down, and he died. ¹⁶For David had said to him, "Your blood be on your own head. Your own mouth testified against you when you said, 'I killed the LORD's anointed.'"

David's Lament for Saul and Jonathan

1. When have you been moved by a song or testimony at a funeral? What touched you about it? 2. What was your first encounter with death in the family? How did you handle it? 3. When has a friend your own age died? How did that affect you?

1. What motivated David to so publicly and permanently record his lament for Saul and Jonathan? 2. Why does David call for censorship in Gath and Ashkelon (v. 20; see 1Sa 31:8–10)? Likewise, why does David curse Gilboa

¹⁷David took up this lament concerning Saul and his son Jonathan, ¹⁸and ordered that the men of Judah be taught this lament of the bow (it is written in the Book of Jashar):

¹⁹"Your glory, O Israel, lies slain on your heights.
        How the mighty have fallen!

²⁰"Tell it not in Gath,
        proclaim it not in the streets of Ashkelon,
    lest the daughters of the Philistines be glad,
        lest the daughters of the uncircumcised rejoice.

²¹"O mountains of Gilboa,
        may you have neither dew nor rain,

nor fields that yield offerings ⌊of grain⌋.
  For there the shield of the mighty was defiled,
    the shield of Saul—no longer rubbed with oil.
²²From the blood of the slain,
    from the flesh of the mighty,
  the bow of Jonathan did not turn back,
    the sword of Saul did not return unsatisfied.

²³"Saul and Jonathan—
  in life they were loved and gracious,
    and in death they were not parted.
  They were swifter than eagles,
    they were stronger than lions.

²⁴"O daughters of Israel,
    weep for Saul,
  who clothed you in scarlet and finery,
    who adorned your garments with ornaments of
      gold.

²⁵"How the mighty have fallen in battle!
    Jonathan lies slain on your heights.
²⁶I grieve for you, Jonathan my brother;
    you were very dear to me.
  Your love for me was wonderful,
    more wonderful than that of women.

²⁷"How the mighty have fallen!
    The weapons of war have perished!"

David Anointed King Over Judah

2 In the course of time, David inquired of the LORD. "Shall I go up
to one of the towns of Judah?" he asked.
  The LORD said, "Go up."
  David asked, "Where shall I go?"
  "To Hebron," the LORD answered.
²So David went up there with his two wives, Ahinoam of Jezreel
and Abigail, the widow of Nabal of Carmel. ³David also took the
men who were with him, each with his family, and they settled in
Hebron and its towns. ⁴Then the men of Judah came to Hebron and
there they anointed David king over the house of Judah.
  When David was told that it was the men of Jabesh Gilead who
had buried Saul, ⁵he sent messengers to the men of Jabesh Gilead
to say to them, "The LORD bless you for showing this kindness to
Saul your master by burying him. ⁶May the LORD now show you
kindness and faithfulness, and I too will show you the same favor
because you have done this. ⁷Now then, be strong and brave, for
Saul your master is dead, and the house of Judah has anointed me
king over them."

War Between the Houses of David and Saul

⁸Meanwhile, Abner son of Ner, the commander of Saul's army,
had taken Ish-Bosheth son of Saul and brought him over to Mahanaim. ⁹He made him king over Gilead, Ashuriᵃ and Jezreel, and
also over Ephraim, Benjamin and all Israel.
¹⁰Ish-Bosheth son of Saul was forty years old when he became
king over Israel, and he reigned two years. The house of Judah,

ᵃ9 Or Asher

(v. 21)? **3.** What kind of warriors
were Saul and Jonathan (vv.
22–23)? **4.** What does verse 26 reveal about the David-Jonathan
friendship: (a) This imagery puts
down marriage? (b) Indicates their
sexual preference? (c) David marveling at how one man could be so
unselfishly committed to him? (d)
David idolizing Jonathan, making
him larger in death than he ever
was in life? **5.** From this lament,
what can you tell about how David
treats his enemies? His friends?

♡ **1.** What worst enemy and
best friend can you begin
treating the way David treats Saul
and Jonathan? What is holding you
back? How could you overcome
the hurdles involved and do this
while they are still living? **2.** If you
have experienced a death close to
home recently, how might you
creatively remember him or her?
What do you wish you had said before their death?

How often has your family
moved? Which move was the
hardest?

1. How might David feel as
he returns "home" from exile? What would be hardest for him
in this move? **2.** Why Hebron in Judah of all places to relocate (see
1Sa 30:26–31; Jos 15:13–15)? **3.**
Had you been from Judah, would
you have voted for David as king?
Why? And if you had been from Jabesh Gilead (not in Judah)?

♡ About what future "moves"
are you inquiring of the Lord?
So far what is he telling you to do?

1. How do you feel about
these kinds of sports: (a)
Tag-team wrestling? (b) Boxing?
(c) Cock fights? (d) Jousting? **2.**
How do you respond in sports competition when your opponent is
weaker? When your opponent is
stronger? **3.** What sporting event
brings out the competition in you or

causes you to want to win at any cost?

1. What do you know about Abner from earlier chapters (see 1Sa 17:55–57; 20:25; 26:5,13–16)? What gave him the right of choosing Saul's son as king? **2.** Why was representative combat proposed by Abner and accepted by Joab (see 1Sa 17:8b–9)? **3.** Why are Benjamites conspicuous in Ish-Bosheth's army (2:15,25; see 1Sa 9:1–2)? **4.** Why was the result of this "super-duel" so memorable (2:15–17)? **5.** Why was Asahel so determined to chase Abner? Why did Abner try to discourage Asahel with words first? Then why the spear? **6.** Why the call for an end to all fighting (2:26,30–31)? **7.** How does this gory passage illustrate the general direction of war (3:1–2)? **8.** What about David's family life do you learn from 3:2–5?

1. In what ways are you like *Abner*. When do you manipulate others to your own advantage? When do you make war instead of peace? How do you decide "enough's enough" in your fights? When do you teach "your brother" (the competitor) a "lesson he'll never forget"? **2.** In what ways are you like *Asahel*. What qualities do you possess above your peers, those which could get you in trouble? When do you pursue "enemies" which are best left to someone else? When are your "eyes bigger than your stomach"? Where do you need large doses of wisdom to balance your zeal, lest you come to a premature demise? **3.** In what ways are you like the house of *David*. Are you growing "stronger and stronger"? Are you "missing in action"? Or are you feeling competition in the family (like a third party wife)? To what do you attribute that? Where do you need a ceasefire?

however, followed David. [11]The length of time David was king in Hebron over the house of Judah was seven years and six months.

[12]Abner son of Ner, together with the men of Ish-Bosheth son of Saul, left Mahanaim and went to Gibeon. [13]Joab son of Zeruiah and David's men went out and met them at the pool of Gibeon. One group sat down on one side of the pool and one group on the other side.

[14]Then Abner said to Joab, "Let's have some of the young men get up and fight hand to hand in front of us."

"All right, let them do it," Joab said.

[15]So they stood up and were counted off—twelve men for Benjamin and Ish-Bosheth son of Saul, and twelve for David. [16]Then each man grabbed his opponent by the head and thrust his dagger into his opponent's side, and they fell down together. So that place in Gibeon was called Helkath Hazzurim.[a]

[17]The battle that day was very fierce, and Abner and the men of Israel were defeated by David's men.

[18]The three sons of Zeruiah were there: Joab, Abishai and Asahel. Now Asahel was as fleet-footed as a wild gazelle. [19]He chased Abner, turning neither to the right nor to the left as he pursued him. [20]Abner looked behind him and asked, "Is that you, Asahel?"

"It is," he answered.

[21]Then Abner said to him, "Turn aside to the right or to the left; take on one of the young men and strip him of his weapons." But Asahel would not stop chasing him.

[22]Again Abner warned Asahel, "Stop chasing me! Why should I strike you down? How could I look your brother Joab in the face?"

[23]But Asahel refused to give up the pursuit; so Abner thrust the butt of his spear into Asahel's stomach, and the spear came out through his back. He fell there and died on the spot. And every man stopped when he came to the place where Asahel had fallen and died.

[24]But Joab and Abishai pursued Abner, and as the sun was setting, they came to the hill of Ammah, near Giah on the way to the wasteland of Gibeon. [25]Then the men of Benjamin rallied behind Abner. They formed themselves into a group and took their stand on top of a hill.

[26]Abner called out to Joab, "Must the sword devour forever? Don't you realize that this will end in bitterness? How long before you order your men to stop pursuing their brothers?"

[27]Joab answered, "As surely as God lives, if you had not spoken, the men would have continued the pursuit of their brothers until morning.[b]

[28]So Joab blew the trumpet, and all the men came to a halt; they no longer pursued Israel, nor did they fight anymore.

[29]All that night Abner and his men marched through the Arabah. They crossed the Jordan, continued through the whole Bithron[c] and came to Mahanaim.

[30]Then Joab returned from pursuing Abner and assembled all his men. Besides Asahel, nineteen of David's men were found missing. [31]But David's men had killed three hundred and sixty Benjamites

---

[a] 16 *Helkath Hazzurim* means *field of daggers* or *field of hostilities.*   [b] 27 Or *spoken this morning, the men would not have taken up the pursuit of their brothers*; or *spoken, the men would have given up the pursuit of their brothers by morning*   [c] 29 Or *morning*; or *ravine*; the meaning of the Hebrew for this word is uncertain.

who were with Abner. [32]They took Asahel and buried him in his father's tomb at Bethlehem. Then Joab and his men marched all night and arrived at Hebron by daybreak.

3 The war between the house of Saul and the house of David lasted a long time. David grew stronger and stronger, while the house of Saul grew weaker and weaker.

[2]Sons were born to David in Hebron:

His firstborn was Amnon the son of Ahinoam of Jezreel;

[3]his second, Kileab the son of Abigail the widow of Nabal of Carmel;

the third, Absalom the son of Maacah daughter of Talmai king of Geshur;

[4]the fourth, Adonijah the son of Haggith;

the fifth, Shephatiah the son of Abital;

[5]and the sixth, Ithream the son of David's wife Eglah.

These were born to David in Hebron.

Abner Goes Over to David

[6]During the war between the house of Saul and the house of David, Abner had been strengthening his own position in the house of Saul. [7]Now Saul had had a concubine named Rizpah daughter of Aiah. And Ish-Bosheth said to Abner, "Why did you sleep with my father's concubine?"

[8]Abner was very angry because of what Ish-Bosheth said and he answered, "Am I a dog's head—on Judah's side? This very day I am loyal to the house of your father Saul and to his family and friends. I haven't handed you over to David. Yet now you accuse me of an offense involving this woman! [9]May God deal with Abner, be it ever so severely, if I do not do for David what the LORD promised him on oath [10]and transfer the kingdom from the house of Saul and establish David's throne over Israel and Judah from Dan to Beersheba." [11]Ish-Bosheth did not dare to say another word to Abner, because he was afraid of him.

[12]Then Abner sent messengers on his behalf to say to David, "Whose land is it? Make an agreement with me, and I will help you bring all Israel over to you."

[13]"Good," said David. "I will make an agreement with you. But I demand one thing of you: Do not come into my presence unless you bring Michal daughter of Saul when you come to see me." [14]Then David sent messengers to Ish-Bosheth son of Saul, demanding, "Give me my wife Michal, whom I betrothed to myself for the price of a hundred Philistine foreskins."

[15]So Ish-Bosheth gave orders and had her taken away from her husband Paltiel son of Laish. [16]Her husband, however, went with her, weeping behind her all the way to Bahurim. Then Abner said to him, "Go back home!" So he went back.

[17]Abner conferred with the elders of Israel and said, "For some time you have wanted to make David your king. [18]Now do it! For the LORD promised David, 'By my servant David I will rescue my people Israel from the hand of the Philistines and from the hand of all their enemies.'"

[19]Abner also spoke to the Benjamites in person. Then he went to Hebron to tell David everything that Israel and the whole house of Benjamin wanted to do. [20]When Abner, who had twenty men with him, came to David at Hebron, David prepared a feast for him and his men. [21]Then Abner said to David, "Let me go at once and assemble all Israel for my lord the king, so that they may make a

1. When (at home, work or church) have you felt like a "figurehead," with someone else holding the real reigns of power? **2.** Have you ever been forcibly separated from one in whom you were romantically interested? What happened?

1. Why would Ish-Bosheth be upset if Abner slept with one of Saul's concubines (vv. 6–7; see 12:8; 16:20–22; 1Ki 1:1–4; 2:22)? From the way Abner responds to the accusation, do you think he was guilty? **2.** If Abner has known all along that God promised to make David king (vv. 9,18), why has he opposed him up until now? **3.** Why would Ish-Bosheth assist Abner to leave him and accommodate David (vv. 11,15)? How do you think Paltiel felt about losing Michal? **4.** How extensive is Abner's control over Israel (vv. 17–21)? Why does he want to surrender and come over to David's side?

1. Where in your life do you feel the need to "strengthen your own position," as did Abner? **2.** David experienced the pain of broken promises from Saul, yet trusted in God's promised kingdom. How trusting are you of others' promises? Of God's promises? **3.** To whom were you most loyal today: (a) "To thine own self be true"? (b) To God's chosen King? (c) To some false king of your own making?

compact with you, and that you may rule over all that your heart desires." So David sent Abner away, and he went in peace.

Joab Murders Abner

22Just then David's men and Joab returned from a raid and brought with them a great deal of plunder. But Abner was no longer with David in Hebron, because David had sent him away, and he had gone in peace. 23When Joab and all the soldiers with him arrived, he was told that Abner son of Ner had come to the king and that the king had sent him away and that he had gone in peace.

24So Joab went to the king and said, "What have you done? Look, Abner came to you. Why did you let him go? Now he is gone! 25You know Abner son of Ner; he came to deceive you and observe your movements and find out everything you are doing."

26Joab then left David and sent messengers after Abner, and they brought him back from the well of Sirah. But David did not know it. 27Now when Abner returned to Hebron, Joab took him aside into the gateway, as though to speak with him privately. And there, to avenge the blood of his brother Asahel, Joab stabbed him in the stomach, and he died.

28Later, when David heard about this, he said, "I and my kingdom are forever innocent before the LORD concerning the blood of Abner son of Ner. 29May his blood fall upon the head of Joab and upon all his father's house! May Joab's house never be without someone who has a running sore or leprosy[a] or who leans on a crutch or who falls by the sword or who lacks food."

30(Joab and his brother Abishai murdered Abner because he had killed their brother Asahel in the battle at Gibeon.)

31Then David said to Joab and all the people with him, "Tear your clothes and put on sackcloth and walk in mourning in front of Abner." King David himself walked behind the bier. 32They buried Abner in Hebron, and the king wept aloud at Abner's tomb. All the people wept also.

33The king sang this lament for Abner:

> "Should Abner have died as the lawless die?
> 34 Your hands were not bound,
>   your feet were not fettered.
> You fell as one falls before wicked men."

And all the people wept over him again.

35Then they all came and urged David to eat something while it was still day; but David took an oath, saying, "May God deal with me, be it ever so severely, if I taste bread or anything else before the sun sets!"

36All the people took note and were pleased; indeed, everything the king did pleased them. 37So on that day all the people and all Israel knew that the king had no part in the murder of Abner son of Ner.

38Then the king said to his men, "Do you not realize that a prince and a great man has fallen in Israel this day? 39And today, though I am the anointed king, I am weak, and these sons of Zeruiah are too strong for me. May the LORD repay the evildoer according to his evil deeds!"

---

a29 The Hebrew word was used for various diseases affecting the skin—not necessarily leprosy.

Ish-Bosheth Murdered

4 When Ish-Bosheth son of Saul heard that Abner had died in Hebron, he lost courage, and all Israel became alarmed. ²Now Saul's son had two men who were leaders of raiding bands. One was named Baanah and the other Recab; they were sons of Rimmon the Beerothite from the tribe of Benjamin—Beeroth is considered part of Benjamin, ³because the people of Beeroth fled to Gittaim and have lived there as aliens to this day.

⁴(Jonathan son of Saul had a son who was lame in both feet. He was five years old when the news about Saul and Jonathan came from Jezreel. His nurse picked him up and fled, but as she hurried to leave, he fell and became crippled. His name was Mephibosheth.)

⁵Now Recab and Baanah, the sons of Rimmon the Beerothite, set out for the house of Ish-Bosheth, and they arrived there in the heat of the day while he was taking his noonday rest. ⁶They went into the inner part of the house as if to get some wheat, and they stabbed him in the stomach. Then Recab and his brother Baanah slipped away.

⁷They had gone into the house while he was lying on the bed in his bedroom. After they stabbed and killed him, they cut off his head. Taking it with them, they traveled all night by way of the Arabah. ⁸They brought the head of Ish-Bosheth to David at Hebron and said to the king, "Here is the head of Ish-Bosheth son of Saul, your enemy, who tried to take your life. This day the LORD has avenged my lord the king against Saul and his offspring."

⁹David answered Recab and his brother Baanah, the sons of Rimmon the Beerothite, "As surely as the LORD lives, who has delivered me out of all trouble, ¹⁰when a man told me, 'Saul is dead,' and thought he was bringing good news, I seized him and put him to death in Ziklag. That was the reward I gave him for his news! ¹¹How much more—when wicked men have killed an innocent man in his own house and on his own bed—should I not now demand his blood from your hand and rid the earth of you!"

¹²So David gave an order to his men, and they killed them. They cut off their hands and feet and hung the bodies by the pool in Hebron. But they took the head of Ish-Bosheth and buried it in Abner's tomb at Hebron.

David Becomes King Over Israel

5 All the tribes of Israel came to David at Hebron and said, "We are your own flesh and blood. ²In the past, while Saul was king over us, you were the one who led Israel on their military campaigns. And the LORD said to you, 'You will shepherd my people Israel, and you will become their ruler.'"

³When all the elders of Israel had come to King David at Hebron, the king made a compact with them at Hebron before the LORD, and they anointed David king over Israel.

⁴David was thirty years old when he became king, and he reigned forty years. ⁵In Hebron he reigned over Judah seven years and six months, and in Jerusalem he reigned over all Israel and Judah thirty-three years.

David Conquers Jerusalem

⁶The king and his men marched to Jerusalem to attack the Jebusites, who lived there. The Jebusites said to David, "You will not get in here; even the blind and the lame can ward you off." They thought, "David cannot get in here." ⁷Nevertheless, David captured the fortress of Zion, the City of David.

---

1. What serious injury as a child did you incur? How did it happen? Any lasting repercussions? **2.** Are you easily startled in your sleep? Or would you sleep right through while a noisy burglar made off with everything in your house?

1. Why would Abner's death cause Ish-Bosheth to lose courage (v. 1)? **2.** What is significant about Baanah and Recab being Benjamites (vv. 2–3; see 1Sa 9:1–2)? What motivation to kill Ish-Bosheth does this reveal? **3.** What is the meaning of Jonathan's lame son (v. 4) in relation to David's kingship? **4.** Why do Recab and Baanah cut off Ish-Bosheth's head after killing him? What serious miscalculation do they make in so doing? How are Recab and Baanah like, and unlike, the Amalekite (vv. 5–8; see 1:1–16)? **5.** How does David's treatment of remains compare with that of Recab and Baanah (v. 12)? What does that say about David?

1. "Those who live by the sword, must die by the sword"—how has the sword of revenge backfired on you? Where has mercy prevailed instead of such "justice" and revenge? **2.** David was tempted to profit from someone's demise, but refused. How do you repel such thoughts?

What relatives are you proud to claim? What about the others?

1. Why did Israel's elders believe in David? What is significant about age 30? About the number 40? **2.** What has David's life been like since he was first anointed by Samuel?

Which promises of God are you still patiently waiting to see fulfilled in your lifetime?

"They said it couldn't be done, but you did it!"—when has that been said of you?

1. Who were the Jebusites as portrayed in Judges (Jdg 1:21 and 19:10–12)? How close was that era to this? Do they show similar characteristics? What? How does David react? **2.** Why is David so successful in conquering the city? For whose sake (v. 12)? **3.** What "new" chapter in his family life do you see here (vv. 13–16)?

♡ **1.** If you had absolute assurance that "the Lord was with you," how would your coming week be affected? What fears would dissipate? What new mission would you take on? What old habits would you break? **2.** How has God blessed you to be a blessing to others?

☕ In what order have you placed these priorities and why: (a) Establish family? (b) Establish home? (c) Establish God as the focal point? (d) Establish career?

📖 **1.** What priority does David take on next? What political platform and profile in courage are you getting of the king's "First 100 Days" in office? **2.** What significance for a revived Israel do you see in David's action, prayers, speech, removal of pagan idols, and obedience to God?

♡ **1.** How do you react when "your best shot" requires a second effort: Try the same thing? Try something new? End-run? Punt on fourth down? **2.** What factors help you tune in better to God's game plan?

☕ **1.** Recall when a "party-pooper" (parents? spouse? friend? little brother?) once killed the festive spirit of your celebration. How did you feel at the time? **2.** What would it take to get you "dancing in the streets": A wedding? Nuclear arms reduction treaty? Peace in the Middle East? A lower crime rate? A World Series or Super Bowl win for the home team? School let out early for the year? A healthy baby born?

📖 **1.** How and why is the ark being moved now? Why a "new cart" (see 1Sa 6:1–8)? How had God prescribed that the ark be

[8]On that day, David said, "Anyone who conquers the Jebusites will have to use the water shaft[a] to reach those 'lame and blind' who are David's enemies.[b]" That is why they say, "The 'blind and lame' will not enter the palace."

[9]David then took up residence in the fortress and called it the City of David. He built up the area around it, from the supporting terraces[c] inward. [10]And he became more and more powerful, because the LORD God Almighty was with him. [11]Now Hiram king of Tyre sent messengers to David, along with cedar logs and carpenters and stonemasons, and they built a palace for David. [12]And David knew that the LORD had established him as king over Israel and had exalted his kingdom for the sake of his people Israel.

[13]After he left Hebron, David took more concubines and wives in Jerusalem, and more sons and daughters were born to him. [14]These are the names of the children born to him there: Shammua, Shobab, Nathan, Solomon, [15]Ibhar, Elishua, Nepheg, Japhia, [16]Elishama, Eliada and Eliphelet.

David Defeats the Philistines

[17]When the Philistines heard that David had been anointed king over Israel, they went up in full force to search for him, but David heard about it and went down to the stronghold. [18]Now the Philistines had come and spread out in the Valley of Rephaim; [19]so David inquired of the LORD, "Shall I go and attack the Philistines? Will you hand them over to me?"

The LORD answered him, "Go, for I will surely hand the Philistines over to you."

[20]So David went to Baal Perazim, and there he defeated them. He said, "As waters break out, the LORD has broken out against my enemies before me." So that place was called Baal Perazim.[d] [21]The Philistines abandoned their idols there, and David and his men carried them off.

[22]Once more the Philistines came up and spread out in the Valley of Rephaim; [23]so David inquired of the LORD, and he answered, "Do not go straight up, but circle around behind them and attack them in front of the balsam trees. [24]As soon as you hear the sound of marching in the tops of the balsam trees, move quickly, because that will mean the LORD has gone out in front of you to strike the Philistine army." [25]So David did as the LORD commanded him, and he struck down the Philistines all the way from Gibeon[e] to Gezer.

The Ark Brought to Jerusalem

6 David again brought together out of Israel chosen men, thirty thousand in all. [2]He and all his men set out from Baalah of Judah[f] to bring up from there the ark of God, which is called by the Name,[g] the name of the LORD Almighty, who is enthroned between the cherubim that are on the ark. [3]They set the ark of God on a new cart and brought it from the house of Abinadab, which was on the hill. Uzzah and Ahio, sons of Abinadab, were guiding the new cart [4]with the ark of God on it,[h] and Ahio was walking in front of it. [5]David and the whole house of Israel were celebrating

---

[a]8 Or use scaling hooks　　[b]8 Or are hated by David　　[c]9 Or the Millo　　[d]20 Baal Perazim means the lord who breaks out.　　[e]25 Septuagint (see also 1 Chron. 14:16); Hebrew Geba　　[f]2 That is, Kiriath Jearim; Hebrew Baale Judah, a variant of Baalah of Judah　　[g]2 Hebrew; Septuagint and Vulgate do not have the Name.　　[h]3,4 Dead Sea Scrolls and some Septuagint manuscripts; Masoretic Text cart [4]and they brought it with the ark of God from the house of Abinadab, which was on the hill

with all their might before the LORD, with songs[a] and with harps, lyres, tambourines, sistrums and cymbals.

[6]When they came to the threshing floor of Nacon, Uzzah reached out and took hold of the ark of God, because the oxen stumbled. [7]The LORD's anger burned against Uzzah because of his irreverent act; therefore God struck him down and he died there beside the ark of God.

[8]Then David was angry because the LORD's wrath had broken out against Uzzah, and to this day that place is called Perez Uzzah.[b]

[9]David was afraid of the LORD that day and said, "How can the ark of the LORD ever come to me?" [10]He was not willing to take the ark of the LORD to be with him in the City of David. Instead, he took it aside to the house of Obed-Edom the Gittite. [11]The ark of the LORD remained in the house of Obed-Edom the Gittite for three months, and the LORD blessed him and his entire household.

[12]Now King David was told, "The LORD has blessed the household of Obed-Edom and everything he has, because of the ark of God." So David went down and brought up the ark of God from the house of Obed-Edom to the City of David with rejoicing. [13]When those who were carrying the ark of the LORD had taken six steps, he sacrificed a bull and a fattened calf. [14]David, wearing a linen ephod, danced before the LORD with all his might, [15]while he and the entire house of Israel brought up the ark of the LORD with shouts and the sound of trumpets.

[16]As the ark of the LORD was entering the City of David, Michal daughter of Saul watched from a window. And when she saw King

[a]5 See Dead Sea Scrolls, Septuagint and 1 Chronicles 13:8; Masoretic Text *celebrating before the LORD with all kinds of instruments made of pine.*   [b]8 *Perez Uzzah* means *outbreak against Uzzah.*

moved (see Ex 25:14)? And by whom (see 1Ch 15:11–15; Nu 4:15)? **2.** How is Uzzah's act "irreverent" (vv. 6–7; see 1Sa 6:19)? What does such burning anger reveal about God's holiness? About Jesus, our High Priest? **3.** Upon being given this deadly ark, how do you think Obed-Edom felt? Where else, in your opinion, could David have placed it? **4.** Three months later, how cautious was David in moving the ark? How did he show reverence to God? **5.** Is David's rejoicing *genuine* or *symbolic* as an example to his people? **6.** Why is Michal's bitterness, barrenness and relation to Saul significant here? What does David's reply to her tell of his character?

♡ **1.** What would a worship service led by David be like in your church? How would he be received? What would he have to wear? Why? **2.** In your private worship life, do you treat God with more "reverential awe" or with more "familiarity"? What aspects of David's "serendipity" would be appropriate for a person in your position? Why? Which would be appropriate for your small group? Why? **3.** What objects of worship or

 2 Samuel 6:1–23   **DAVID BRINGS THE ARK TO JERUSALEM**

David has just been anointed king of Israel, brought Jerusalem into Israel's control, and made it the nation's capital. God had told the Israelites that his presence would dwell above the ark, a wooden chest covered with gold. Now David decides to bring the ark, which had been in relative obscurity for at least 20 years, to Jerusalem.

1. What are your first impressions of this passage?
   a. God sure is holy.
   b. God sure is strict.
   c. David would fit right in at my church.
   d. David definitely would not fit in at my church.

2. Why did David want to bring the ark to Jerusalem?
   a. to show off
   b. to honor the Lord as the true King
   c. for political reasons
   d. to restore Israel's worship
   e. to seek God's favor and blessing

3. If you were Obed-Edom, how would you have felt about housing the ark?

   a. petrified
   b. honored
   c. picked on
   d. sorry to see it go

4. David came to realize (1Ch 15) God's stipulations had been ignored: The ark should have been carried on poles (not on a cart), and only priests could touch it. When have you done good things, such as spiritual activities, for the wrong reasons?

5. What was different about the second time the ark was moved?

6. What can you do to keep from taking God's holiness for granted? Do you need to relate to God with more reverence or with more familiarity?

7. What was going on with Michal (one of David's wives)?
   a. She had no appreciation for the spiritual significance of the event.
   b. She felt this was no way for a king to carry on.
   c. She should have been a participant instead of a spectator.

   d. She was a jealous wife.
   e. Her modesty was violated.

8. What happened between David and Michal?
   a. David's plan to "bless his household" was met with Michal's scorn.
   b. David wouldn't hear her concerns.
   c. Sharp words killed their marriage.
   d. The Lord punished her with barrenness.
   e. David made sure she was barren!

9. ⊕ What percentage of the blame for this conflict would you attribute to Michal's words? To David's words? When you have conflict in your marriage, how important is it to assign blame? How willing are you to accept your share of responsibility?

10. ⊕ Which is more powerful: the negative effects of cutting words or the positive effects of caring words? Conclude this study by meeting with your spouse and sharing something positive you appreciate about the other.

means of grace do you "uphold" as sacred? How, then, do you "uphold" them? When have you slipped, like Uzzah, and acted irreverently in this regard? How does Christ the Mediator intercede for you when you fall?

---

1. Describe the house you lived in as a 10-year-old. How did it compare to your neighbors'? 2. What opportunity have you had that your parents never did? What do you want your kids to have that you never did?

1. How prophetic is Nathan's initial counsel (v. 3)? Why does that change? 2. What is God's attitude regarding David's house of cedar (vv. 5–7)? 3. What is meant by God reminding David of his indebtedness? While that might motivate David to build a house for God, how does such dependency actually preclude David from doing God this "favor"? 4. Why does God go on to say "No" to David's "household" (temple) but "Yes" to his "house" (dynasty)? 5. What about God's promises in verses 9b–16 would surprise David? Why? What would most reassure him? Why? What might irk him? Why? 6. In what way today is David's house and kingdom "established forever" (v. 16; see Isa 9:6–7; Lk 1:32–33)?

1. Do you tend to favor God by working for him? Or savor God by worshipping him? Why is that? 2. How many long-lasting promises keep you going at work? Home? What limited contracts get you worried about the future? 3. (For those in mid-life crisis): What life's dream, career goals, or family plans are you beginning to see will not be accomplished by you? Who, then, will see those plans to com-

David leaping and dancing before the Lord, she despised him in her heart.

17They brought the ark of the Lord and set it in its place inside the tent that David had pitched for it, and David sacrificed burnt offerings and fellowship offerings[a] before the Lord. 18After he had finished sacrificing the burnt offerings and fellowship offerings, he blessed the people in the name of the Lord Almighty. 19Then he gave a loaf of bread, a cake of dates and a cake of raisins to each person in the whole crowd of Israelites, both men and women. And all the people went to their homes.

20When David returned home to bless his household, Michal daughter of Saul came out to meet him and said, "How the king of Israel has distinguished himself today, disrobing in the sight of the slave girls of his servants as any vulgar fellow would!"

21David said to Michal, "It was before the Lord, who chose me rather than your father or anyone from his house when he appointed me ruler over the Lord's people Israel—I will celebrate before the Lord. 22I will become even more undignified than this, and I will be humiliated in my own eyes. But by these slave girls you spoke of, I will be held in honor."

23And Michal daughter of Saul had no children to the day of her death.

God's Promise to David

7 After the king was settled in his palace and the Lord had given him rest from all his enemies around him, 2he said to Nathan the prophet, "Here I am, living in a palace of cedar, while the ark of God remains in a tent."

3Nathan replied to the king, "Whatever you have in mind, go ahead and do it, for the Lord is with you."

4That night the word of the Lord came to Nathan, saying:

5"Go and tell my servant David, 'This is what the Lord says: Are you the one to build me a house to dwell in? 6I have not dwelt in a house from the day I brought the Israelites up out of Egypt to this day. I have been moving from place to place with a tent as my dwelling. 7Wherever I have moved with all the Israelites, did I ever say to any of their rulers whom I commanded to shepherd my people Israel, "Why have you not built me a house of cedar?" '

8"Now then, tell my servant David, 'This is what the Lord Almighty says: I took you from the pasture and from following the flock to be ruler over my people Israel. 9I have been with you wherever you have gone, and I have cut off all your enemies from before you. Now I will make your name great, like the names of the greatest men of the earth. 10And I will provide a place for my people Israel and will plant them so that they can have a home of their own and no longer be disturbed. Wicked people will not oppress them anymore, as they did at the beginning 11and have done ever since the time I appointed leaders[b] over my people Israel. I will also give you rest from all your enemies.

"'The Lord declares to you that the Lord himself will establish a house for you: 12When your days are over and you rest with your fathers, I will raise up your offspring to succeed you, who will come from your own body, and I will establish his kingdom. 13He is the one who will build a house for my Name, and I will establish the throne of his kingdom forever.

---

a17 Traditionally peace offerings; also in verse 18   b11 Traditionally judges

¹⁴I will be his father, and he will be my son. When he does wrong, I will punish him with the rod of men, with floggings inflicted by men. ¹⁵But my love will never be taken away from him, as I took it away from Saul, whom I removed from before you. ¹⁶Your house and your kingdom will endure forever before me^a; your throne will be established forever.'"

¹⁷Nathan reported to David all the words of this entire revelation.

David's Prayer

¹⁸Then King David went in and sat before the LORD, and he said:

"Who am I, O Sovereign LORD, and what is my family, that you have brought me this far? ¹⁹And as if this were not enough in your sight, O Sovereign LORD, you have also spoken about the future of the house of your servant. Is this your usual way of dealing with man, O Sovereign LORD?

²⁰"What more can David say to you? For you know your servant, O Sovereign LORD. ²¹For the sake of your word and according to your will, you have done this great thing and made it known to your servant.

²²"How great you are, O Sovereign LORD! There is no one like you, and there is no God but you, as we have heard with our own ears. ²³And who is like your people Israel—the one nation on earth that God went out to redeem as a people for himself, and to make a name for himself, and to perform great and awesome wonders by driving out nations and their gods from before your people, whom you redeemed from Egypt?^b ²⁴You have established your people Israel as your very own forever, and you, O LORD, have become their God.

²⁵"And now, LORD God, keep forever the promise you have made concerning your servant and his house. Do as you promised, ²⁶so that your name will be great forever. Then men will say, 'The LORD Almighty is God over Israel!' And the house of your servant David will be established before you.

²⁷"O LORD Almighty, God of Israel, you have revealed this to your servant, saying, 'I will build a house for you.' So your servant has found courage to offer you this prayer. ²⁸O Sovereign LORD, you are God! Your words are trustworthy, and you have promised these good things to your servant. ²⁹Now be pleased to bless the house of your servant, that it may continue forever in your sight; for you, O Sovereign LORD, have spoken, and with your blessing the house of your servant will be blessed forever."

David's Victories

8 In the course of time, David defeated the Philistines and subdued them, and he took Metheg Ammah from the control of the Philistines.

²David also defeated the Moabites. He made them lie down on the ground and measured them off with a length of cord. Every two lengths of them were put to death, and the third length was allowed to live. So the Moabites became subject to David and brought tribute.

³Moreover, David fought Hadadezer son of Rehob, king of Zobah, when he went to restore his control along the Euphrates

^a16 Some Hebrew manuscripts and Septuagint; most Hebrew manuscripts *you*
^b23 See Septuagint and 1 Chron. 17:21; Hebrew *wonders for your land and before your people, whom you redeemed from Egypt, from the nations and their gods.*

---

pletion? How can you pray now toward that end?

---

1. Describe a time when were you "twice blessed" (as when it's "less filling" and "tastes great"). How do you react to a compliment: With characteristic modesty, or lapping it up? 2. What promise from a parent did you once receive and then continually "beg" for, until delivered?

1. To which of God's promises in this chapter is David answering in verse 18? In verse 19? 2. How is God's sovereignty underscored in the way David addresses him in this prayer? In the actions David ascribes to God? 3. How would you describe Israel's relationship to God here? 4. Why does David want so badly to see God's promise "kept forever" (vv. 25–26)? 5. How does God's action and character give David courage to pray like this? 6. Why does David ask God to do what God has already promised to do?

1. How do you respond to the promises of a trustworthy God? How, primarily, have you addressed God: With introductions? Requests? Confession? Thanksgiving? What does this say about your rapport with him? 2. What would you like to adopt from David's example in this regard? What "good things" do you desire, which conform to God's will?

---

1. If one-third of your group was to be picked for some nasty job, and the other two-thirds were to be spared, how would you go about choosing? 2. What "winning streak" of yours reflects "the good ol' days"? What was so good about them?

1. Why the decimation and subjection of so many people? "The Lord gave David victory wherever he went"—does that say it all? Or does that only beg more questions for you? 2. Why would David hamstring the horses (v. 4)? Why should this act be noted by

the writer (see Dt 17:16)? **3.** Since David is now king, was he entitled to keep the precious-metal gifts from the subdued kings (vv. 9–10)? What is the meaning of David's dedicating them? How was Hebrew dedication done (see Nu 7:10)? **4.** Is God implicated, exonerated, exhilarated or exacerbated by the events in this story? Why do you think so? **5.** Does David's regime (vv. 15–18) look like a true theocracy to you, albeit a human one? How so? How not? (See 1Ki 2:3?)

♥ **1.** Over what "enemies" has God given you victory? Where have you yet to experience his victory? **2.** What God-given possessions, abilities or resources would you like to "dedicate" anew to God, as does David in this story?

🖒 **1.** When have you been favored by a substantial donor, unable to pay back the gift in kind? How did you express thanks? **2.** Describe some of your grandparents' property. What, if any of it, has been passed along? How does it feel to be an "heir"?

📖 **1.** What does David's kindness to Saul's lineage underscore about covenants? (See 1Sa 20:14–15,42?) **2.** Why didn't the writer make Zeba nameless here? Why all the details? How might have Zeba known Mephibosheth was living at Makir's house (vv. 4–5,10b)? According to 17:27 and 29 what kind of region was Lo Debar? What might Mephibosheth have felt as he is escorted back to Jerusalem? To the throne room? To the dining table? **3.** In this regard, what do you make of Mephibosheth's handicap? And his likening himself to a "dead dog"? (What

River. ⁴David captured a thousand of his chariots, seven thousand charioteers[a] and twenty thousand foot soldiers. He hamstrung all but a hundred of the chariot horses.

⁵When the Arameans of Damascus came to help Hadadezer king of Zobah, David struck down twenty-two thousand of them. ⁶He put garrisons in the Aramean kingdom of Damascus, and the Arameans became subject to him and brought tribute. The LORD gave David victory wherever he went.

⁷David took the gold shields that belonged to the officers of Hadadezer and brought them to Jerusalem. ⁸From Tebah[b] and Berothai, towns that belonged to Hadadezer, King David took a great quantity of bronze.

⁹When Tou[c] king of Hamath heard that David had defeated the entire army of Hadadezer, ¹⁰he sent his son Joram[d] to King David to greet him and congratulate him on his victory in battle over Hadadezer, who had been at war with Tou. Joram brought with him articles of silver and gold and bronze.

¹¹King David dedicated these articles to the LORD, as he had done with the silver and gold from all the nations he had subdued: ¹²Edom[e] and Moab, the Ammonites and the Philistines, and Amalek. He also dedicated the plunder taken from Hadadezer son of Rehob, king of Zobah.

¹³And David became famous after he returned from striking down eighteen thousand Edomites[f] in the Valley of Salt.

¹⁴He put garrisons throughout Edom, and all the Edomites became subject to David. The LORD gave David victory wherever he went.

David's Officials

¹⁵David reigned over all Israel, doing what was just and right for all his people. ¹⁶Joab son of Zeruiah was over the army; Jehoshaphat son of Ahilud was recorder; ¹⁷Zadok son of Ahitub and Ahimelech son of Abiathar were priests; Seraiah was secretary; ¹⁸Benaiah son of Jehoiada was over the Kerethites and Pelethites; and David's sons were royal advisers.[g]

David and Mephibosheth

9 David asked, "Is there anyone still left of the house of Saul to whom I can show kindness for Jonathan's sake?"

²Now there was a servant of Saul's household named Ziba. They called him to appear before David, and the king said to him, "Are you Ziba?"

"Your servant," he replied.

³The king asked, "Is there no one still left of the house of Saul to whom I can show God's kindness?"

Ziba answered the king, "There is still a son of Jonathan; he is crippled in both feet."

⁴"Where is he?" the king asked.

Ziba answered, "He is at the house of Makir son of Ammiel in Lo Debar."

⁵So King David had him brought from Lo Debar, from the house of Makir son of Ammiel.

---

a4 Septuagint (see also Dead Sea Scrolls and 1 Chron. 18:4); Masoretic Text *captured seventeen hundred of his charioteers*   b8 See some Septuagint manuscripts (see also 1 Chron. 18:8); Hebrew *Betah*.   c9 Hebrew *Toi*, a variant of *Tou*; also in verse 10   d10 A variant of *Hadoram*   e12 Some Hebrew manuscripts, Septuagint and Syriac (see also 1 Chron. 18:11); most Hebrew manuscripts *Aram*   f13 A few Hebrew manuscripts, Septuagint and Syriac (see also 1 Chron. 18:12); most Hebrew manuscripts *Aram* (that is, Arameans)   g18 Or *were priests*

⁶When Mephibosheth son of Jonathan, the son of Saul, came to David, he bowed down to pay him honor.

David said, "Mephibosheth!"

"Your servant," he replied.

⁷"Don't be afraid," David said to him, "for I will surely show you kindness for the sake of your father Jonathan. I will restore to you all the land that belonged to your grandfather Saul, and you will always eat at my table."

⁸Mephibosheth bowed down and said, "What is your servant, that you should notice a dead dog like me?"

⁹Then the king summoned Ziba, Saul's servant, and said to him, "I have given your master's grandson everything that belonged to Saul and his family. ¹⁰You and your sons and your servants are to farm the land for him and bring in the crops, so that your master's grandson may be provided for. And Mephibosheth, grandson of your master, will always eat at my table." (Now Ziba had fifteen sons and twenty servants.)

¹¹Then Ziba said to the king, "Your servant will do whatever my lord the king commands his servant to do." So Mephibosheth ate at David's*ᵃ* table like one of the king's sons.

¹²Mephibosheth had a young son named Mica, and all the members of Ziba's household were servants of Mephibosheth. ¹³And Mephibosheth lived in Jerusalem, because he always ate at the king's table, and he was crippled in both feet.

David Defeats the Ammonites

10 In the course of time, the king of the Ammonites died, and his son Hanun succeeded him as king. ²David thought, "I will show kindness to Hanun son of Nahash, just as his father showed kindness to me." So David sent a delegation to express his sympathy to Hanun concerning his father.

When David's men came to the land of the Ammonites, ³the Ammonite nobles said to Hanun their lord, "Do you think David is honoring your father by sending men to you to express sympathy? Hasn't David sent them to you to explore the city and spy it out and overthrow it?" ⁴So Hanun seized David's men, shaved off half of each man's beard, cut off their garments in the middle at the buttocks, and sent them away.

⁵When David was told about this, he sent messengers to meet the men, for they were greatly humiliated. The king said, "Stay at Jericho till your beards have grown, and then come back."

⁶When the Ammonites realized that they had become a stench in David's nostrils, they hired twenty thousand Aramean foot soldiers from Beth Rehob and Zobah, as well as the king of Maacah with a thousand men, and also twelve thousand men from Tob. ⁷On hearing this, David sent Joab out with the entire army of fighting men. ⁸The Ammonites came out and drew up in battle formation at the entrance to their city gate, while the Arameans of Zobah and Rehob and the men of Tob and Maacah were by themselves in the open country.

⁹Joab saw that there were battle lines in front of him and behind him; so he selected some of the best troops in Israel and deployed them against the Arameans. ¹⁰He put the rest of the men under the command of Abishai his brother and deployed them against the Ammonites. ¹¹Joab said, "If the Arameans are too strong for me, then you are to come to my rescue; but if the Ammonites are too strong for you, then I will come to rescue you. ¹²Be strong and let

ᵃ*11* Septuagint; Hebrew *my*

---

might be an equivalent self-abasing comment today?)

♡ **1.** In what ways are you like Mephibosheth as you "stand" before God's throne? As you break bread at the Lord's Table? As you are an heir to your heavenly Father's spiritual kingdom? **2.** When have you shown or received God's kindness as a "friend of a friend," as epitomized in this story? To whom can you be that kind of friend this week?

☕ **1.** When traveling in a foreign country through airport security, have you ever been strip-searched or held in suspicion? What for? How did that make you feel? **2.** How do you feel about beards: (a) They look attractive? (b) Feel scratchy? (c) Cover up acne? (d) Save on razor blades? (e) Proof of manliness? (f) Offset baldness? (g) Could cost one a certain job? (h) Could catch a certain girl? (i) Couldn't grow one if I tried?

📖 **1.** Who are the Ammonites (see Ge 19:38; Dt 2:19)? What do we know about Nahash (1Sa 11:1–11)? Why might David be struck by an act of kindness from him? How surprised was David by the suspicion, shaving, and stripping? **2.** Who starts the war? Why? **3.** How does Joab manage the war on two fronts (vv. 9–11)? What does he think about the goodness of God (v. 12)? How consistent is this with David's view? **4.** How does Hadadezer, an earlier foe, think he can outmaneuver David in verses 15–17? Why is his defeat miraculous (vv. 18–19)? How is God's goodness reconciled with all this gore?

♡ **1.** In what area of your life are you feeling the need for "reinforcements"? How might your small group reinforce you? **2.** Do you feel as though you are being attacked from both sides right now? Who or what is on your left? Your right? What good do you think the Lord might bring out of that conflict? **3.** Are you foolishly regrouping, like the Arameans, to fight a lost cause anywhere? What *piece* of the problem are you clinging to, thus forfeiting God's *peace*? How might you "win the war" by "losing the battle"?

1. What's your favorite springtime activity? Where you live, how soon do people begin sun-bathing? **2.** Nearly everyone has a mental image of "the girl next door," or "the big man on campus." Describe the one that still sticks in your mind. What first drew your attention to her or him? **3.** Where did you spend your last getaway weekend with a loved one? Where would you like to go next time?

1. What significance do you see in the timing of David's sin (vv. 1–2)? In the timing of Bathsheba's "purification," meaning she was now ceremonially clean from menstruation (v. 4; see Lev 15:19,28)? **2.** What progression of thought do you think David entertained (vv. 2–5) upon the sight of her? Upon desiring her? Sending for her? Seducing her? Sleeping with her? Could Bathsheba have prevented this seduction? Why or why not? **3.** Where does this passage record David's first fear of the adultery? Why might he fear (see Lev 20:10, Dt 22:22)? How could his attempted cover-up possibly nullify the sin? **4.** What superior character qualities does Uriah exhibit in refusing David's overture (vv. 11,13; see Dt 23:9–10)? What does this reveal about David? Uriah? Joab? **5.** As Joab's messenger, what would you think of the message sent to David (vv. 18–24)? And David's response (v. 25)? **6.** What must Bathsheba be feeling as her identity changes quickly from Uriah's wife, to David's lover, to Uriah's widow, to David's

us fight bravely for our people and the cities of our God. The LORD will do what is good in his sight."

[13]Then Joab and the troops with him advanced to fight the Arameans, and they fled before him. [14]When the Ammonites saw that the Arameans were fleeing, they fled before Abishai and went inside the city. So Joab returned from fighting the Ammonites and came to Jerusalem.

[15]After the Arameans saw that they had been routed by Israel, they regrouped. [16]Hadadezer had Arameans brought from beyond the River[a]; they went to Helam, with Shobach the commander of Hadadezer's army leading them.

[17]When David was told of this, he gathered all Israel, crossed the Jordan and went to Helam. The Arameans formed their battle lines to meet David and fought against him. [18]But they fled before Israel, and David killed seven hundred of their charioteers and forty thousand of their foot soldiers.[b] He also struck down Shobach the commander of their army, and he died there. [19]When all the kings who were vassals of Hadadezer saw that they had been defeated by Israel, they made peace with the Israelites and became subject to them.

So the Arameans were afraid to help the Ammonites anymore.

David and Bathsheba

11 In the spring, at the time when kings go off to war, David sent Joab out with the king's men and the whole Israelite army. They destroyed the Ammonites and besieged Rabbah. But David remained in Jerusalem.

[2]One evening David got up from his bed and walked around on the roof of the palace. From the roof he saw a woman bathing. The woman was very beautiful, [3]and David sent someone to find out about her. The man said, "Isn't this Bathsheba, the daughter of Eliam and the wife of Uriah the Hittite?" [4]Then David sent messengers to get her. She came to him, and he slept with her. (She had purified herself from her uncleanness.) Then[c] she went back home. [5]The woman conceived and sent word to David, saying, "I am pregnant."

[6]So David sent this word to Joab: "Send me Uriah the Hittite." And Joab sent him to David. [7]When Uriah came to him, David asked him how Joab was, how the soldiers were and how the war was going. [8]Then David said to Uriah, "Go down to your house and wash your feet." So Uriah left the palace, and a gift from the king was sent after him. [9]But Uriah slept at the entrance to the palace with all his master's servants and did not go down to his house.

[10]When David was told, "Uriah did not go home," he asked him, "Haven't you just come from a distance? Why didn't you go home?"

[11]Uriah said to David, "The ark and Israel and Judah are staying in tents, and my master Joab and my lord's men are camped in the open fields. How could I go to my house to eat and drink and lie with my wife? As surely as you live, I will not do such a thing!"

[12]Then David said to him, "Stay here one more day, and tomorrow I will send you back." So Uriah remained in Jerusalem that day and the next. [13]At David's invitation, he ate and drank with him, and David made him drunk. But in the evening Uriah went out to sleep on his mat among his master's servants; he did not go home.

[14]In the morning David wrote a letter to Joab and sent it with

---

a 16 That is, the Euphrates 19:18); Hebrew *horsemen* *b 18* Some Septuagint manuscripts (see also 1 Chron. *uncleanness,* *c 4* Or *with her. When she purified herself from her*

Uriah. [15]In it he wrote, "Put Uriah in the front line where the fighting is fiercest. Then withdraw from him so he will be struck down and die."

[16]So while Joab had the city under siege, he put Uriah at a place where he knew the strongest defenders were. [17]When the men of the city came out and fought against Joab, some of the men in David's army fell; moreover, Uriah the Hittite died.

[18]Joab sent David a full account of the battle. [19]He instructed the messenger: "When you have finished giving the king this account of the battle, [20]the king's anger may flare up, and he may ask you, 'Why did you get so close to the city to fight? Didn't you know they would shoot arrows from the wall? [21]Who killed Abimelech son of Jerub-Besheth[a]? Didn't a woman throw an upper millstone on him from the wall, so that he died in Thebez? Why did you get so close to the wall?' If he asks you this, then say to him, 'Also, your servant Uriah the Hittite is dead.'"

[22]The messenger set out, and when he arrived he told David everything Joab had sent him to say. [23]The messenger said to David, "The men overpowered us and came out against us in the open, but we drove them back to the entrance to the city gate. [24]Then the archers shot arrows at your servants from the wall, and some of the king's men died. Moreover, your servant Uriah the Hittite is dead."

[25]David told the messenger, "Say this to Joab: 'Don't let this upset you; the sword devours one as well as another. Press the attack against the city and destroy it.' Say this to encourage Joab."

[a]21 Also known as *Jerub-Baal* (that is, Gideon)

bride? **7.** In what ways does one sin lead to another in this story, until David has broken the 6th, 7th, 9th and 10th Commandments?

1. "Lord, I can resist anything but temptation"—how does that confession fit you? Have you recently faced temptation and resisted it? Would you like to tell about it? **2.** Pretend your friend faces a "shot-gun wedding." What options would you suggest? **3.** Once virginity or fidelity are lost (physically), how can one be a virgin or faithful again (spiritually)? Where do you need "purification" and forgiveness today? Go wash as God directs you.

---

      2 Samuel 11:1–27   **DAVID AND BATHSHEBA**

Everything has been going King David's way. He has acquired the admiration of all Israel, numerous wives and children, stunning military victories and expansion, and God's promise of a perpetual reign for him and his descendants.

1. How do you feel about King David after reading this story?
   a. Hey, everyone makes mistakes.
   b. He was a typical corrupt politician.
   c. They should have thrown him out of office.
   d. You have to balance his successes against his failures.
   e. He was still God's anointed.

2. What really happened to David, "the man after God's own heart"?
   a. He got hit with spring fever.
   b. He didn't need God anymore.
   c. His hormones overtook him.
   d. His achievements made him think he deserved whatever he wanted.
   e. His morality gradually eroded.
   f. He was relaxing at home when he should have been with his men.

3. What do you think Bathsheba's involvement was in the relationship?
   a. She purposely seduced David by bathing where he could see her.
   b. David seduced her.
   c. She didn't have a choice.
   d. She was a willing participant.

4. How does the fact that, according to the Law of Moses, adultery was punishable by death affect the way you feel about this story?
   a. It should have been a deterrent.
   b. When you really want something, you don't think straight.
   c. No wonder David was so desperate to cover things up.
   d. Sin is blind to its consequences.

5. How does this story end?
   a. "happily ever after".
   b. "the calm before the storm"
   c. "all's well that ends well"
   d. "the beginning of the end"

6. How do you deal with temptation?
   a. give in to it
   b. fight it off
   c. ask for God's help
   d. talk to someone about it
   e. just say "no"
   f. do something to get my mind off it
   g. beat myself up with guilt

7. In general, how do you feel about your spiritual life? How have you successfully resisted temptation recently?

8. Since God created David with sexual urges, when did his thoughts or actions become sin? Why did God create us with drives we're not always allowed to satisfy?

9. What would you have done if you were on David's roof? When are you most vulnerable to sexual temptation? What have you found to be the most helpful strategy of resistance?

10. How does this story remind you of your world?
    a. lots of visual stimulation
    b. the pressure to be sexually active
    c. so many kids getting pregnant
    d. worry about who you can trust
    e. the pressure to party
    f. wondering if what I do "displeases the Lord"

26When Uriah's wife heard that her husband was dead, she mourned for him. 27After the time of mourning was over, David had her brought to his house, and she became his wife and bore him a son. But the thing David had done displeased the LORD.

Nathan Rebukes David

12 The LORD sent Nathan to David. When he came to him, he said, "There were two men in a certain town, one rich and the other poor. 2The rich man had a very large number of sheep and cattle, 3but the poor man had nothing except one little ewe lamb he had bought. He raised it, and it grew up with him and his children. It shared his food, drank from his cup and even slept in his arms. It was like a daughter to him.

4"Now a traveler came to the rich man, but the rich man refrained from taking one of his own sheep or cattle to prepare a meal for the traveler who had come to him. Instead, he took the ewe lamb that belonged to the poor man and prepared it for the one who had come to him."

5David burned with anger against the man and said to Nathan, "As surely as the LORD lives, the man who did this deserves to die! 6He must pay for that lamb four times over, because he did such a thing and had no pity."

7Then Nathan said to David, "You are the man! This is what the LORD, the God of Israel, says: 'I anointed you king over Israel, and I delivered you from the hand of Saul. 8I gave your master's house to you, and your master's wives into your arms. I gave you the

---

1. What special meal do you spread out "just for company"? What special meal do you request when you need comfort and cheer? Is "pigging out" one of your weaknesses? **2.** What one weakness of yours do you more readily see in others than in yourself?

1. Why does Nathan speak to David with a parable? How does the parable relate to the events of the previous chapter? **2.** Why does the absence of justice and mercy in Nathan's account so enrage David (vv. 5–6)? How could David have cultivated contentment and thus avoided coveting? What is Nathan's perspective on gratitude (vv. 7–9)? **3.** What three sons will meet violent deaths in fulfillment of prophecy (v. 10; see 13:28–29; 18:14–15; 1Ki 2:25)? Who will "lie with David's wives in broad daylight" (vv. 11–12; see

---

2 Samuel 12:1–14   **NATHAN REBUKES DAVID**

The previous chapter records David's great sin: his adultery with Bathsheba, his attempts to cover up the fact he got her pregnant—ending with his ordering her husband's murder, and then taking Bathsheba as his wife.

1. Why did Nathan start with a story?
   a. to get David's attention
   b. to dramatize his point
   c. to disarm David's defenses
   d. so David would incriminate himself
   e. because prophets often do that

2. David's anger reflects his:
   a. sensitivity to injustice.
   b. awareness of the consequences of sin.
   c. unawareness that this was a parable about himself.
   d. underlying guilt and defensiveness.

3. What right did Nathan have to say, "You are the man!"?
   a. He was a recognized prophet.
   b. He spoke the truth.
   c. He loved David.
   d. God had sent him.

4. What was the Lord's message through Nathan?

a. "You blew it."
b. "I am angry."
c. "Why didn't you come to me?"
d. "Please say you're sorry."
e. "It's too late for apologies."

5. How did David respond to Nathan's words? Was his confession sincere? If so, why didn't he do it sooner?

6. How do you respond when someone corrects or criticizes you?
   a. I want to cry.
   b. I accept it without comment.
   c. I accept it as God's word to me.
   d. I get defensive.
   e. I avoid that person.
   f. I assume I deserved it.

7. Which is the easiest and which is the hardest?
   a. to see sin in myself
   b. to see sin in others
   c. to admit my fault to others
   d. to confront others in love
   e. to receive an apology
   f. to love those who expose my sin

8. If others see something wrong in my life, they:
   a. should let me know.
   b. better be right.

c. should keep it to themselves.
d. need to be subtle.
e. should reassure me of their love.
f. should show me by example.
g. should also praise me when I do something right.

9. How do you feel about God's response to David's confession? Are God's standards for sexual purity: Clear or unclear? Fair or unfair? Outdated or relevant? For our good or needless?

10. How would you feel if a friend confronted you like Nathan did? How would you feel about giving someone (maybe this group) permission to correct you when you sin?

11. Do you have anyone you can talk to about the most personal things in your life? If not what can you do to find somebody? Close this meeting by silently asking yourself, "Is there anything in my life I need to confess to God or talk to someone about?"

house of Israel and Judah. And if all this had been too little, I would have given you even more. ⁹Why did you despise the word of the LORD by doing what is evil in his eyes? You struck down Uriah the Hittite with the sword and took his wife to be your own. You killed him with the sword of the Ammonites. ¹⁰Now, therefore, the sword will never depart from your house, because you despised me and took the wife of Uriah the Hittite to be your own.'

¹¹"This is what the LORD says: 'Out of your own household I am going to bring calamity upon you. Before your very eyes I will take your wives and give them to one who is close to you, and he will lie with your wives in broad daylight. ¹²You did it in secret, but I will do this thing in broad daylight before all Israel.' "

¹³Then David said to Nathan, "I have sinned against the LORD."

Nathan replied, "The LORD has taken away your sin. You are not going to die. ¹⁴But because by doing this you have made the enemies of the LORD show utter contempt,ᵃ the son born to you will die."

¹⁵After Nathan had gone home, the LORD struck the child that Uriah's wife had borne to David, and he became ill. ¹⁶David pleaded with God for the child. He fasted and went into his house and spent the nights lying on the ground. ¹⁷The elders of his household stood beside him to get him up from the ground, but he refused, and he would not eat any food with them.

¹⁸On the seventh day the child died. David's servants were afraid to tell him that the child was dead, for they thought, "While

ᵃ14 Masoretic Text; an ancient Hebrew scribal tradition *this you have shown utter contempt for the LORD*

16:21–22)? **4.** How does David's response to Nathan's rebuke (v. 13; see Ps 51) compare with Saul's response in similar situations (see 1Sa 13:11–12; 15:13–26)? **5.** What is God trying to teach David (and us) by the death of David's son (vv. 13b–23)? What other redemptive purpose is ultimately accomplished by this severe mercy (vv. 24–25)? **6.** Why does Joab call for David to join him in battle (vv. 26–31)? What point does this story serve, inserted here in this context?

1. In what ways has a lack of gratitude led you to sin, as it did David? In being reminded of all that God has done for you, how might you be kept from deliberate sin? **2.** We reap not only what we sow, but also what others have sown. How are you suffering because of what your parents or previous generation did wrong? How might your children be suffering likewise? What hope do you have that the sins of one generation will not be passed to another? **3.** Who is one "Nathan" in your life? How did you respond when confronted

---

   2 Samuel 12:15–25   **DAVID GRIEVES**

King David committed adultery with Bathsheba while her husband was off fighting the king's battles. When she became pregnant, David attempted to cover up his sin—even having her husband killed in battle. David married Bathsheba, who bore him a son. God sent Nathan to confront David about his sin and he immediately repented. David would be spared the decreed death penalty for his sins. But Nathan stated, "the son born to you will die."

1. What is your reaction to this story?
   a. I didn't know the Bible contained soap operas!
   b. I'm glad the Bible doesn't sugar-coat life.
   c. God doesn't seem very loving.
   d. It stirs up feelings I've had myself.

2. How would you describe God's response to David's repentance?
   a. cruel   d. to be expected
   b. merciful   e. not strict enough
   c. justified f. other:_____

3. Who do you relate to in this story?
   a. David—I've suffered some painful consequences for my actions.

b. Nathan—I've had to confront someone about serious issues.
   c. David's servants—I've been confused by another's grief.
   d. The child—Life hasn't seemed fair to me.

4. Why did David fast, weep and spend his nights lying on the ground?
   a. He was consumed with guilt.
   b. He was begging God for the child's life to be spared.
   c. He was tormented by "if only" thoughts.
   d. He was promising not to fail God again, hoping his son would live.

5. David stopped mourning when his son died because he:
   a. accepted the child's death.
   b. was exhausted after seven days of intense grieving.
   c. realized he deserved what he got.
   d. admitted "bargaining" didn't work.

6. What is God trying to teach David (and us) by the death of David's son? What does the birth of Solomon say about David's relationship with God now?

7. What lesson about grief sticks out to you from this story?
   a. Bargaining is a normal part of grief, but don't expect it to work.
   b. Even if bargaining isn't so good to do, prayer and confession is.
   c. Intense grief is awful, but at least it helps you move on with life.
   d. It's possible to worship God even in the midst of terrible loss.

8. How have you engaged in bargaining in regard to your loss? What, if anything, do you need to do to pass through that stage of grief?

9. Are you getting closer to accepting the loss you have experienced through miscarriage? How has this course affected that process?

10. As David comforted Bathsheba, how have you appreciated the comfort of your spouse and this group? What would help you and your marriage receive God's comfort?

with your sin: Like Saul or like David? How so? **4.** How do you imagine the script for this story would have been written if David had confessed his adultery to Uriah and God, and had not engaged in any cover-up operation, much less murder?

the child was still living, we spoke to David but he would not listen to us. How can we tell him the child is dead? He may do something desperate."

¹⁹David noticed that his servants were whispering among themselves and he realized the child was dead. "Is the child dead?" he asked.

"Yes," they replied, "he is dead."

²⁰Then David got up from the ground. After he had washed, put on lotions and changed his clothes, he went into the house of the LORD and worshiped. Then he went to his own house, and at his request they served him food, and he ate.

²¹His servants asked him, "Why are you acting this way? While the child was alive, you fasted and wept, but now that the child is dead, you get up and eat!"

²²He answered, "While the child was still alive, I fasted and wept. I thought, 'Who knows? The LORD may be gracious to me and let the child live.' ²³But now that he is dead, why should I fast? Can I bring him back again? I will go to him, but he will not return to me."

²⁴Then David comforted his wife Bathsheba, and he went to her and lay with her. She gave birth to a son, and they named him Solomon. The LORD loved him; ²⁵and because the LORD loved him, he sent word through Nathan the prophet to name him Jedidiah.ᵃ

²⁶Meanwhile Joab fought against Rabbah of the Ammonites and captured the royal citadel. ²⁷Joab then sent messengers to David, saying, "I have fought against Rabbah and taken its water supply. ²⁸Now muster the rest of the troops and besiege the city and capture it. Otherwise I will take the city, and it will be named after me."

²⁹So David mustered the entire army and went to Rabbah, and attacked and captured it. ³⁰He took the crown from the head of their kingᵇ—its weight was a talentᶜ of gold, and it was set with precious stones—and it was placed on David's head. He took a great quantity of plunder from the city ³¹and brought out the people who were there, consigning them to labor with saws and with iron picks and axes, and he made them work at brickmaking.ᵈ He did this to all the Ammonite towns. Then David and his entire army returned to Jerusalem.

Amnon and Tamar

13 In the course of time, Amnon son of David fell in love with Tamar, the beautiful sister of Absalom son of David. ²Amnon became frustrated to the point of illness on account of his sister Tamar, for she was a virgin, and it seemed impossible for him to do anything to her.

³Now Amnon had a friend named Jonadab son of Shimeah, David's brother. Jonadab was a very shrewd man. ⁴He asked Amnon, "Why do you, the king's son, look so haggard morning after morning? Won't you tell me?"

Amnon said to him, "I'm in love with Tamar, my brother Absalom's sister."

⁵"Go to bed and pretend to be ill," Jonadab said. "When your father comes to see you, say to him, 'I would like my sister Tamar to come and give me something to eat. Let her prepare the food in my sight so I may watch her and then eat it from her hand.'"

⁶So Amnon lay down and pretended to be ill. When the king

1. Whom did you consult regarding your "love life" while in high school? What was some of their worst advice? Their best advice? **2.** From what you know of "blended families" (with stepchildren), what complicated love-hate relationships could occur? How are blood ties thicker than anything else that binds the family?

1. How do you account for Amnon's "lovesickness" regarding Tamar (vv. 1–4)? At first blush, does this strike you as innocent "puppy" love? "Perverse" love? Or what? **2.** What advice does Jonadab offer to woo Tamar (v. 5)? How does David unknowingly collaborate in the charade (vv. 6–7)? Had David been visiting Amnon irregularly (v. 5)? Why did Amnon seek to deceive his dad? How was Tamar's statement about Da-

---

ᵃ25 *Jedidiah* means *loved by the LORD.*   ᵇ30 Or *of Milcom* (that is, Molech)
ᶜ30 That is, about 75 pounds (about 34 kilograms)   ᵈ31 The meaning of the Hebrew for this clause is uncertain.

came to see him, Amnon said to him, "I would like my sister Tamar to come and make some special bread in my sight, so I may eat from her hand."

[7]David sent word to Tamar at the palace: "Go to the house of your brother Amnon and prepare some food for him." [8]So Tamar went to the house of her brother Amnon, who was lying down. She took some dough, kneaded it, made the bread in his sight and baked it. [9]Then she took the pan and served him the bread, but he refused to eat.

"Send everyone out of here," Amnon said. So everyone left him. [10]Then Amnon said to Tamar, "Bring the food here into my bedroom so I may eat from your hand." And Tamar took the bread she had prepared and brought it to her brother Amnon in his bedroom. [11]But when she took it to him to eat, he grabbed her and said, "Come to bed with me, my sister."

[12]"Don't, my brother!" she said to him. "Don't force me. Such a thing should not be done in Israel! Don't do this wicked thing. [13]What about me? Where could I get rid of my disgrace? And what about you? You would be like one of the wicked fools in Israel. Please speak to the king; he will not keep me from being married to you." [14]But he refused to listen to her, and since he was stronger than she, he raped her.

[15]Then Amnon hated her with intense hatred. In fact, he hated her more than he had loved her. Amnon said to her, "Get up and get out!"

[16]"No!" she said to him. "Sending me away would be a greater wrong than what you have already done to me."

vid (v. 13) a rebuke to this? **3.** Why does Amnon end up hating Tamar (v. 15)? Why does Tamar refuse to be banished? What "greater wrong" has she just experienced (see Dt 22:28–29)? **4.** How does Absalom react to Tamar's rape now (v. 20) and later (v. 28)? **5.** How does David respond (v. 21)? Why doesn't he do what any self-respecting king and father would do in this test situation? How might David's credibility have been compromised (see also ch. 11–12)?

♡ **1.** In what ways have you been impacted by sexual sins in the past (your past or another's)? How have you managed to control the damage? To forgive the sinner? To be forgiven? **2.** Who have you ended up "hating" that you started "loving"? Why the sudden and total reversal in the relationship? How can you be more reconciled with your past and with this person? **3.** As a parent, or a potential parent, how do you evaluate your present example for the future generation: one that promotes "loose living," or one that de-

---

  2 Samuel 13:1–22   **AMNON RAPES TAMAR**

As a result of King David's sins, the Lord said through the prophet Nathan that David would reap great calamity from his own household. The trouble begins here with David's son and daughter, Amnon and Tamar.

1. What would you call Amnon's feelings toward his half sister at the beginning of this story?
   a. puppy love   d. obsession
   b. lust   e. innocent
   c. infatuation   f. unnatural

2. What was Jonadab's advice?
   a. Enjoy breakfast in bed.
   b. Deceive your father.
   c. Deceive your half sister.
   d. Force yourself on Tamar.
   e. A prince should get whatever he wants.

3. Why did Amnon force himself on Tamar?
   a. He was a jerk.
   b. He was taking a dare.
   c. He liked challenges.
   d. Moses' Law prohibited having sex with or marrying his sister.

4. What did Tamar appeal to in

attempting to resist Amnon?
   a. his sense of morality
   b. his sense of honor
   c. common sense
   d. his self-interest as heir to the throne
   e. her certain disgrace

5. How do you explain Amnon's reversal from "love" to "hate"?
   a. He was sick.
   b. He only loved himself.
   c. He never understood real love.
   d. He got what he wanted.
   e. He hated Tamar because he hated himself.
   f. His experience didn't live up to his fantasies.
   g. One sin leads to another.

6. Why didn't David do something about what happened?
   a. He was too angry.
   b. He didn't know what to do.
   c. He figured "boys will be boys."
   d. He was a weak disciplinarian.
   e. He would feel like a hypocrite because of his own moral failures.

7. The worst thing that happened to Tamar was that she was:

a. raped.
b. violated by someone she loved.
c. kicked out by her abuser.
d. unprotected by her father.
e. relegated to a life of celibacy.
f. left with the shame of being "spoiled goods."

8. Though you won't find the word "God" in this story, do you think God abandoned Tamar? How do you hold on to your faith in light of the terrible things that happen to innocent people?

9. What's the closest you have come to the kind of despairing experience Tamar suffered? How fully is that situation resolved in your life?

10. How does this story remind you of your own experience of abuse? What do you feel was probably the worst thing about what happened to you?

11. Tamar grieved intensely after she was abused. Do you feel you have adequately expressed your emotions?

ters it? How do you identify with "David the dad" in the passage?

But he refused to listen to her. ¹⁷He called his personal servant and said, "Get this woman out of here and bolt the door after her." ¹⁸So his servant put her out and bolted the door after her. She was wearing a richly ornamented*ᵃ* robe, for this was the kind of garment the virgin daughters of the king wore. ¹⁹Tamar put ashes on her head and tore the ornamented*ᵇ* robe she was wearing. She put her hand on her head and went away, weeping aloud as she went.

²⁰Her brother Absalom said to her, "Has that Amnon, your brother, been with you? Be quiet now, my sister; he is your brother. Don't take this thing to heart." And Tamar lived in her brother Absalom's house, a desolate woman.

²¹When King David heard all this, he was furious. ²²Absalom never said a word to Amnon, either good or bad; he hated Amnon because he had disgraced his sister Tamar.

1. When, if ever, have you "run away"? Where did you go? For how long? What were you escaping? *2.* How do your grandparents spoil you: What might they have asked them for that you wouldn't dare ask your mom or dad for?

Absalom Kills Amnon

²³Two years later, when Absalom's sheepshearers were at Baal Hazor near the border of Ephraim, he invited all the king's sons to come there. ²⁴Absalom went to the king and said, "Your servant has had shearers come. Will the king and his officials please join me?"

1. Why does Absalom ask David, his officials and all his sons to join him (vv. 23–25)? Why was sheep shearing a big event (see 1Sa 25:7–8)? *2.* If you were

²⁵"No, my son," the king replied. "All of us should not go; we would only be a burden to you." Although Absalom urged him, he still refused to go, but gave him his blessing.

ᵃ18 The meaning of the Hebrew for this phrase is uncertain.   *ᵇ19* The meaning of the Hebrew for this word is uncertain.

2 Samuel 13:23–39   ABSALOM KILLS AMNON

The Lord pronounced that King David would experience tragedy within his family because of his sins of adultery and murder. That prophecy began to be fulfilled when David's oldest son Amnon raped David's daughter Tamar (Amnon's half sister). The king, though furious, did nothing about Amnon's offense. However, David's second oldest son Absalom (Tamar's full brother) hated Amnon for what he did, and now acts on his wrath.

1. Why did Absalsom invite David and all his sons and officials to join him?
   a. to help shear the sheep
   b. to party, as was common at sheep-shearing time
   c. to ambush Amnon

2. What did David think when Absalom insisted Amnon come?
   a. He thought nothing of it.
   b. Absalom must want Amnon, as crown prince, to take David's place.
   c. He wondered why Absalom was so insistent.
   d. Knowing his sons' relationship

was strained, he was suspicious.

3. What was the main reason Absalom killed Amnon?
   a. to avenge his sister's rape
   b. to unleash his hatred for Amnon
   c. to be next in line for the throne
   d. to fulfill prophecy

4. Why did Absalom flee the country and live with Talmai (who, as 2Sa 3:3 indicates, was his maternal grandfather)?

5. What was the worst thing David went through?
   a. hearing that Amnon killed all his other sons
   b. waiting to hear what report was true
   c. wondering if this would have happened if he had been there
   d. grieving Amnon's death
   e. grieving Absalom's absence
   f. losing his two oldest sons
   g. feeling responsible for these tragedies

6. What long-term grudges have taken their toll on your relationships with

family or friends? What can you do about them and their effects?

7. From what hurts would you like to run away? Where could you go?

8. Like David, what is your spirit longing for? If you could ask God for one thing, what would it be?

9. How can you, as a "parent in pain," identify with this story?
   a. My child's broken relationships have broken my heart also.
   b. My child's mistakes have caused me deep grief.
   c. I've been tormented by "if only" thoughts concerning my child.
   d. I am alienated from my child.
   e. I have "wept very bitterly" over my child and our relationship.
   f. I have felt responsible for much of my child's pain.

10. What's the most disappointing thing about your wayward child and your relationship with him or her? How are you dealing with that disappointment?

²⁶Then Absalom said, "If not, please let my brother Amnon come with us."

The king asked him, "Why should he go with you?" ²⁷But Absalom urged him, so he sent with him Amnon and the rest of the king's sons.

²⁸Absalom ordered his men, "Listen! When Amnon is in high spirits from drinking wine and I say to you, 'Strike Amnon down,' then kill him. Don't be afraid. Have not I given you this order? Be strong and brave." ²⁹So Absalom's men did to Amnon what Absalom had ordered. Then all the king's sons got up, mounted their mules and fled.

³⁰While they were on their way, the report came to David: "Absalom has struck down all the king's sons; not one of them is left." ³¹The king stood up, tore his clothes and lay down on the ground; and all his servants stood by with their clothes torn.

³²But Jonadab son of Shimeah, David's brother, said, "My lord should not think that they killed all the princes; only Amnon is dead. This has been Absalom's expressed intention ever since the day Amnon raped his sister Tamar. ³³My lord the king should not be concerned about the report that all the king's sons are dead. Only Amnon is dead."

³⁴Meanwhile, Absalom had fled.

Now the man standing watch looked up and saw many people on the road west of him, coming down the side of the hill. The watchman went and told the king, "I see men in the direction of Horonaim, on the side of the hill."[a]

³⁵Jonadab said to the king, "See, the king's sons are here; it has happened just as your servant said."

³⁶As he finished speaking, the king's sons came in, wailing loudly. The king, too, and all his servants wept very bitterly.

³⁷Absalom fled and went to Talmai son of Ammihud, the king of Geshur. But King David mourned for his son every day.

³⁸After Absalom fled and went to Geshur, he stayed there three years. ³⁹And the spirit of the king[b] longed to go to Absalom, for he was consoled concerning Amnon's death.

Absalom Returns to Jerusalem

14 Joab son of Zeruiah knew that the king's heart longed for Absalom. ²So Joab sent someone to Tekoa and had a wise woman brought from there. He said to her, "Pretend you are in mourning. Dress in mourning clothes, and don't use any cosmetic lotions. Act like a woman who has spent many days grieving for the dead. ³Then go to the king and speak these words to him." And Joab put the words in her mouth.

⁴When the woman from Tekoa went[c] to the king, she fell with her face to the ground to pay him honor, and she said, "Help me, O king!"

⁵The king asked her, "What is troubling you?"

She said, "I am indeed a widow; my husband is dead. ⁶I your servant had two sons. They got into a fight with each other in the field, and no one was there to separate them. One struck the other and killed him. ⁷Now the whole clan has risen up against your servant; they say, 'Hand over the one who struck his brother down, so that we may put him to death for the life of his brother whom he killed; then we will get rid of the heir as well.' They

Amnon or David, would you suspect Absalom's party invitation (vv. 26–27)? Why or why not? **3.** Why is revenge still on Absalom's mind? What is significant about the timing ("two years later" and "when Amnon is in high spirits")? What do you think of his tactics? How parallel are these to the tactics of Amnon and Jonadab two years earlier? **4.** Over whom was David mourning after the first (v. 30), second (v. 32–33), and third (v. 35) reports? Does his grieving end here? How possible might it be for David to have penned a psalm here? **5.** Where does Absalom go (v. 37; see 3:3)? What might he get from his grandfather that he dare not ask his father for? With Amnon dead, what might Absalom think as a refugee and heir apparent to David?

♡ **1.** What long-term grudges have taken their toll on your family? With whom are you not now on good speaking terms? How can you "bury the hatchet," instead of using it? **2.** From what hurts do you feel like "running away"? Where would you go?

⌒ **1.** When you want to mask your true identity and show up somewhere "incognito," what do you do: (a) Wear a wig, costume or make-up? (b) Carry a fake ID? (c) Spin a few tales about your past? (d) Create a double to stand in for you? When have you done this before? With what success? **2.** What is the longest your hair has ever been? For what reason were you growing it long? **3.** What is the longest you have been alienated from your parents or children? How did you (or they) finally break the silence: Call? Write? Show up for the holidays?

📖 **1.** Is Joab acting here in the best interests of Absalom, David or himself? Why do you think so? **2.** What acting role does he ask this "wise woman" to assume (vv. 2–3)? How well does she play the part (vv. 4–8)? **3.** What aspects of the woman's clever story appeal

---

[a]34 Septuagint; Hebrew does not have this sentence.   [b]39 Dead Sea Scrolls and some Septuagint manuscripts; Masoretic Text *But ⸤the spirit of⸥ David the king*   [c]4 Many Hebrew manuscripts, Septuagint, Vulgate and Syriac; most Hebrew manuscripts *spoke*

to David: (a) The law which seeks to perpetuate a family name through descendants (see Dt 25:5–6)? (b) The law which permits blood revenge (see Nu 35:19–21)? (c) The clans' motives were more selfish than just? (d) Murder "without malice aforethought" is not punishable by death (see Dt 19:4–6)? **4.** How does the woman's story relate to David and Absalom? **5.** In verses 13–17, what aspects of God's truth does she accurately portray? Which biblical teaching does she distort to effect Absalom's safe return? Once David exposes the true source of her story as being Joab (vv. 18–20), why does he still agree to bring back Absalom? **6.** Why then does David refuse to see Absalom upon his return to Jerusalem (vv. 23–24)? **7.** What TV or movie star would you cast in the role of this handsome dude Absalom (vv. 25–26)? **8.** What's significant about Absalom naming his daughter Tamar (v. 27; see 13:1)? **9.** What kind of person would treat Joab the way Absalom does in verses 28–32? What kind of king would react as David does in

would put out the only burning coal I have left, leaving my husband neither name nor descendant on the face of the earth."

⁸The king said to the woman, "Go home, and I will issue an order in your behalf."

⁹But the woman from Tekoa said to him, "My lord the king, let the blame rest on me and on my father's family, and let the king and his throne be without guilt."

¹⁰The king replied, "If anyone says anything to you, bring him to me, and he will not bother you again."

¹¹She said, "Then let the king invoke the LORD his God to prevent the avenger of blood from adding to the destruction, so that my son will not be destroyed."

"As surely as the LORD lives," he said, "not one hair of your son's head will fall to the ground."

¹²Then the woman said, "Let your servant speak a word to my lord the king."

"Speak," he replied.

¹³The woman said, "Why then have you devised a thing like this against the people of God? When the king says this, does he not convict himself, for the king has not brought back his banished son? ¹⁴Like water spilled on the ground, which cannot be recovered, so we must die. But God does not take away life; instead, he devises ways so that a banished person may not remain estranged from him.

¹⁵"And now I have come to say this to my lord the king because the people have made me afraid. Your servant thought, 'I will speak to the king; perhaps he will do what his servant asks. ¹⁶Perhaps the king will agree to deliver his servant from the hand of the

---

  2 Samuel 14:1–33   ABSALOM RETURNS TO JERUSALEM

King David's son Absalom has murdered David's son Amnon in retaliation for Amnon raping Absalom's sister. Absalom fled the country to Geshur, where he has been for three years.

1. Why did Joab devise this scheme?
   a. He enjoyed playwriting.
   b. He knew what David wanted.
   c. He knew how David responded to stories.
   d. He was concerned for Absalom.
   e. He was concerned that Absalom's absence would cause a struggle to determine the next king.

2. Why hadn't David done anything about Absalom's banishment?
   a. He wasn't sure what to do.
   b. He liked others to take initiative.
   c. He was torn between love and anger.
   d. His acts of adultery and murder had cost him credibility to exert discipline.
   e. Absalom deserved to die for murdering his brother.

3. How does the woman's fabricated story relate to David and Absalom?

How do you feel about Joab's scheme, and about David's decision to bring back Absalom?

4. Why did David refuse to see Absalom when he came back?
   a. He was still too angry.
   b. He was still too hurt.
   c. He couldn't look him in the eye.
   d. He wasn't able to forgive him.
   e. Absalom had not sought forgiveness.

5. What kind of person is Absalom?
   a. charming   d. meek
   b. proud   e. fiery
   c. demanding   f. impatient

6. How do you feel about the way the story ends?
   a. David is forgiving as he should be.
   b. David ignored justice.
   c. Absalom had to come begging.
   d. Absalom never did repent.
   e. True reconciliation occurred.
   f. Only appearances changed.

7. How do you typically respond when you are alienated from another person? Or from God?

8. In your desire to see a significant relationship restored, do you identify more with David or Absalom? Specifically, how does this story relate to your situation?
   a. I have very mixed feelings.
   b. My heart longs for reconciliation, but I'm not sure how to go about it.
   c. Thinking of facing the other person gives me cold sweats.
   d. I'm struggling to be patient.
   e. We're both waiting for the other.
   f. We need a "Joab" to help us.
   g. I want *real* reconciliation, not just surface reconciliation.

9. How much do you identify with David's feelings about relating to a child who has hurt you? Do you understand the longing? The mixed feelings? The hesitancy? The need for a mediator?

10. What is your present relationship with your child like? Now that you know something of each others' stories, how can the members of the group help you with your questions about relating to your child?

man who is trying to cut off both me and my son from the inheritance God gave us.'

¹⁷"And now your servant says, 'May the word of my lord the king bring me rest, for my lord the king is like an angel of God in discerning good and evil. May the LORD your God be with you.'"

¹⁸Then the king said to the woman, "Do not keep from me the answer to what I am going to ask you."

"Let my lord the king speak," the woman said.

¹⁹The king asked, "Isn't the hand of Joab with you in all this?"

The woman answered, "As surely as you live, my lord the king, no one can turn to the right or to the left from anything my lord the king says. Yes, it was your servant Joab who instructed me to do this and who put all these words into the mouth of your servant. ²⁰Your servant Joab did this to change the present situation. My lord has wisdom like that of an angel of God—he knows everything that happens in the land."

²¹The king said to Joab, "Very well, I will do it. Go, bring back the young man Absalom."

²²Joab fell with his face to the ground to pay him honor, and he blessed the king. Joab said, "Today your servant knows that he has found favor in your eyes, my lord the king, because the king has granted his servant's request."

²³Then Joab went to Geshur and brought Absalom back to Jerusalem. ²⁴But the king said, "He must go to his own house; he must not see my face." So Absalom went to his own house and did not see the face of the king.

²⁵In all Israel there was not a man so highly praised for his handsome appearance as Absalom. From the top of his head to the sole of his foot there was no blemish in him. ²⁶Whenever he cut the hair of his head—he used to cut his hair from time to time when it became too heavy for him—he would weigh it, and its weight was two hundred shekels* by the royal standard.

²⁷Three sons and a daughter were born to Absalom. The daughter's name was Tamar, and she became a beautiful woman.

²⁸Absalom lived two years in Jerusalem without seeing the king's face. ²⁹Then Absalom sent for Joab in order to send him to the king, but Joab refused to come to him. So he sent a second time, but he refused to come. ³⁰Then he said to his servants, "Look, Joab's field is next to mine, and he has barley there. Go and set it on fire." So Absalom's servants set the field on fire.

³¹Then Joab did go to Absalom's house and he said to him, "Why have your servants set my field on fire?"

³²Absalom said to Joab, "Look, I sent word to you and said, 'Come here so I can send you to the king to ask, "Why have I come from Geshur? It would be better for me if I were still there!"' Now then, I want to see the king's face, and if I am guilty of anything, let him put me to death."

³³So Joab went to the king and told him this. Then the king summoned Absalom, and he came in and bowed down with his face to the ground before the king. And the king kissed Absalom.

Absalom's Conspiracy

15 In the course of time, Absalom provided himself with a chariot and horses and with fifty men to run ahead of him. ²He would get up early and stand by the side of the road leading to the city gate. Whenever anyone came with a complaint to be placed before the king for a decision, Absalom would call out to

ᵃ26 That is, about 5 pounds (about 2.3 kilograms)

verse 33? What do you find wrong or right with David forgiving Absalom so easily?

1. How do you usually respond when you are alienated from another person? Or from God? What corrective measures right now does this story suggest you take for restoration? 2. How does physical appearance affect your acceptance of others? Or your acceptance of yourself? How might that acceptance level change if you found your self-confidence exclusively in God? 3. How desperate are you these days to get authorities to look favorably upon whatever plight you may be in: (a) Desperate enough to stretch God's truth to your own defense? (b) To pull heart-strings with a sob story? (c) To burn someone's fields or bridges behind you? (d) To solicit group prayer? (Why not pray about it now?)

1. It helps to know people in "high places." Who do you know who can pull strings for you? 2. What "conspiracy theories" or "takeover plots" fascinate you (and why) in 20th-century history: Communists? Religious Right? Political Left? Wall Street brokers? White

supremacists? CIA subversives? Muslims? One-world government?

1. What do "chariots, horses and 50 men" signal of Absalom's ambitions (v. 1; see 1Sa 8:11)? 2. As a victim of injustice, what would you make of Absalom's two decrees (vv. 3,4)? His greeting (v. 5)? 3. Why do you think Absalom waits "four years" (v. 7) to carry out his conspiracy plot? When else has he shown patience in devising evil plans (see 13:23ff)? 4. How can David be so gullible (vv. 7–9)? 5. What steps does David unknowingly take to consolidate Absalom's power (vv. 10–12)?

1. When do you feel frustrated in getting an audience with *your* King? Why? 2. What campaigns of disinformation today seek to discredit God's reign or encourage believers to stray from the faith? How might your group counteract that?

1. When have you set out in your car, just to get away from it all, without knowing where you're going? 2. When you want to go to a specific getaway place, where do you go? With whom? 3. When you have changed jobs or churches or residences, has anyone chosen to move with you? Why?

1. As an official of David's, what is your reaction to the news of Absalom's revolt (vv. 13–18)? How would your response have compared with Ittai's (vv. 19–22)? 2. Why are David's "caretakers" noted (v. 16; see 12:11; 16:21)? 3. Why do the Levites follow David with the ark (v. 24)? What does that do for David's sense of well-being? Whose rule does David confess (v. 26)? 4. How would you describe the roles of Zadok and Abiathar in the struggle between David and Absalom (vv. 27–29, 35–36)? How would you describe David's ascent up the Mount of Olives? Why is he weeping, while other prophets suffer loss without doing so (see Eze 24:16–17)? 5. What answers do you see for his prayer (v. 31; see 16:23; 17:14)? How is Hushai, David's friend, part of the prayer's answer?

him, "What town are you from?" He would answer, "Your servant is from one of the tribes of Israel." ³Then Absalom would say to him, "Look, your claims are valid and proper, but there is no representative of the king to hear you." ⁴And Absalom would add, "If only I were appointed judge in the land! Then everyone who has a complaint or case could come to me and I would see that he gets justice."

⁵Also, whenever anyone approached him to bow down before him, Absalom would reach out his hand, take hold of him and kiss him. ⁶Absalom behaved in this way toward all the Israelites who came to the king asking for justice, and so he stole the hearts of the men of Israel.

⁷At the end of four*a* years, Absalom said to the king, "Let me go to Hebron and fulfill a vow I made to the LORD. ⁸While your servant was living at Geshur in Aram, I made this vow: 'If the LORD takes me back to Jerusalem, I will worship the LORD in Hebron.*b*'"

⁹The king said to him, "Go in peace." So he went to Hebron.

¹⁰Then Absalom sent secret messengers throughout the tribes of Israel to say, "As soon as you hear the sound of the trumpets, then say, 'Absalom is king in Hebron.'" ¹¹Two hundred men from Jerusalem had accompanied Absalom. They had been invited as guests and went quite innocently, knowing nothing about the matter. ¹²While Absalom was offering sacrifices, he also sent for Ahithophel the Gilonite, David's counselor, to come from Giloh, his hometown. And so the conspiracy gained strength, and Absalom's following kept on increasing.

David Flees

¹³A messenger came and told David, "The hearts of the men of Israel are with Absalom."

¹⁴Then David said to all his officials who were with him in Jerusalem, "Come! We must flee, or none of us will escape from Absalom. We must leave immediately, or he will move quickly to overtake us and bring ruin upon us and put the city to the sword."

¹⁵The king's officials answered him, "Your servants are ready to do whatever our lord the king chooses."

¹⁶The king set out, with his entire household following him; but he left ten concubines to take care of the palace. ¹⁷So the king set out, with all the people following him, and they halted at a place some distance away. ¹⁸All his men marched past him, along with all the Kerethites and Pelethites; and all the six hundred Gittites who had accompanied him from Gath marched before the king.

¹⁹The king said to Ittai the Gittite, "Why should you come along with us? Go back and stay with King Absalom. You are a foreigner, an exile from your homeland. ²⁰You came only yesterday. And today shall I make you wander about with us, when I do not know where I am going? Go back, and take your countrymen. May kindness and faithfulness be with you."

²¹But Ittai replied to the king, "As surely as the LORD lives, and as my lord the king lives, wherever my lord the king may be, whether it means life or death, there will your servant be."

²²David said to Ittai, "Go ahead, march on." So Ittai the Gittite marched on with all his men and the families that were with him.

²³The whole countryside wept aloud as all the people passed by. The king also crossed the Kidron Valley, and all the people moved on toward the desert.

²⁴Zadok was there, too, and all the Levites who were with him

---

*a*7 Some Septuagint manuscripts, Syriac and Josephus; Hebrew *forty*   *b*8 Some Septuagint manuscripts; Hebrew does not have *in Hebron*.

were carrying the ark of the covenant of God. They set down the ark of God, and Abiathar offered sacrifices[a] until all the people had finished leaving the city.

25Then the king said to Zadok, "Take the ark of God back into the city. If I find favor in the LORD's eyes, he will bring me back and let me see it and his dwelling place again. 26But if he says, 'I am not pleased with you,' then I am ready; let him do to me whatever seems good to him."

27The king also said to Zadok the priest, "Aren't you a seer? Go back to the city in peace, with your son Ahimaaz and Jonathan son of Abiathar. You and Abiathar take your two sons with you. 28I will wait at the fords in the desert until word comes from you to inform me." 29So Zadok and Abiathar took the ark of God back to Jerusalem and stayed there.

30But David continued up the Mount of Olives, weeping as he went; his head was covered and he was barefoot. All the people with him covered their heads too and were weeping as they went up. 31Now David had been told, "Ahithophel is among the conspirators with Absalom." So David prayed, "O LORD, turn Ahithophel's counsel into foolishness."

32When David arrived at the summit, where people used to worship God, Hushai the Arkite was there to meet him, his robe torn and dust on his head. 33David said to him, "If you go with me, you will be a burden to me. 34But if you return to the city and say to Absalom, 'I will be your servant, O king; I was your father's servant in the past, but now I will be your servant,' then you can help me by frustrating Ahithophel's advice. 35Won't the priests Zadok and Abiathar be there with you? Tell them anything you hear in the king's palace. 36Their two sons, Ahimaaz son of Zadok and Jonathan son of Abiathar, are there with them. Send them to me with anything you hear."

37So David's friend Hushai arrived at Jerusalem as Absalom was entering the city.

David and Ziba

16 When David had gone a short distance beyond the summit, there was Ziba, the steward of Mephibosheth, waiting to meet him. He had a string of donkeys saddled and loaded with two hundred loaves of bread, a hundred cakes of raisins, a hundred cakes of figs and a skin of wine.

2The king asked Ziba, "Why have you brought these?"

Ziba answered, "The donkeys are for the king's household to ride on, the bread and fruit are for the men to eat, and the wine is to refresh those who become exhausted in the desert."

3The king then asked, "Where is your master's grandson?"

Ziba said to him, "He is staying in Jerusalem, because he thinks, 'Today the house of Israel will give me back my grandfather's kingdom.'"

4Then the king said to Ziba, "All that belonged to Mephibosheth is now yours."

"I humbly bow," Ziba said. "May I find favor in your eyes, my lord the king."

Shimei Curses David

5As King David approached Bahurim, a man from the same clan as Saul's family came out from there. His name was Shimei son of Gera, and he cursed as he came out. 6He pelted David and all the

1. Have you made Ittai's promise ("wherever, whatever") to your Master? Or have you qualified your allegiance somewhat? How so? Why not make a commitment without reservations to follow your King this week? 2. David says, "Let God do to me whatever seems good to him." If you could bring yourself to say that, what are you afraid might happen? 3. Where do you need to put "legs to your prayers," as David does in sending Hushai to confound Ahithophel's counsel?

1. When you are catching a meal on the run, what does your "order to go" usually consist of? 2. If you could have 100 portions of any food you like, free, what would you choose?

1. What is Ziba's motive in coming to David, bearing such gifts? 2. Is he trustworthy (v. 3; see 19:24–30)? Why does David think so (see 9:1–11)?

In contrast to the loyalty of Ittai to his master, we have the example of Ziba. Where might you be tempted likewise to betray your loyalties? How will you resist that temptation?

1. When have you been "cussed out." How did that feel? 2. "Sticks and stones may break my bones, but names will never hurt me"—when have you resorted to that childhood refrain?

[a]24 Or Abiathar went up

(In self-defense? In self-pity? In self-deception? In self-affirmation?)

1. What significance do you see in Shimei's family ties (v. 5)? Why else is Shimei so mad (vv. 7–8)? Is his anger justified? What does Abishai think? What does David think (vv. 10–12)? 2. Why does David attribute Shimei's cursing to God? What does this tell you about David's character? About his view of God's character?

1. When have you, like David, been under the Lord's discipline? What for? Could you take "the heat," however it was dished out? How did you respond? 2. When the heat on you is *not* "from the Lord," how do you respond?

---

1. When torn between the counsel of two parties, how do you decide which advice to follow: (a) Flip a coin? (b) Trial and error? (c) Go with the more objective, disinterested party? (d) Go with gut instincts? (e) Ask more questions? (f) Punt. 2. Whose counsel do you seek when it comes to decisions about which school, job or mate to choose? Why? 3. What do you think of professional advice-givers such as Ann Landers, Dr. Ruth, Larry King? Do you read, watch or listen to them regularly? What question would you likely to submit to them?

1. What makes Hushai's words seem credible to Absalom (16:16–19)? 2. What does "lying with the king's concubines … in the sight of all Israel" symbolize (16:21–22; see 12:8–12)? 3. What advice does Ahithophel offer (17:1–3)? With what advice does Hushai counter (17:7–13)? What do you see as the major difference between the two? 4. Why doesn't Absalom go with the one predicting a bloodless, easy victory? What about his counsel was "foolish" (17:14; see 15:31)? 5. What word does Hushai send to David (17:15–16,21)? Why (see 15:36)? Does loyalty to David justify deceiving Absalom or confounding Ahithophel? Why or why not? 6. How does Ahithophel's suicide strike you and why: (a) Odd? (b) Predict-

king's officials with stones, though all the troops and the special guard were on David's right and left. ⁷As he cursed, Shimei said, "Get out, get out, you man of blood, you scoundrel! ⁸The LORD has repaid you for all the blood you shed in the household of Saul, in whose place you have reigned. The LORD has handed the kingdom over to your son Absalom. You have come to ruin because you are a man of blood!"

⁹Then Abishai son of Zeruiah said to the king, "Why should this dead dog curse my lord the king? Let me go over and cut off his head."

¹⁰But the king said, "What do you and I have in common, you sons of Zeruiah? If he is cursing because the LORD said to him, 'Curse David,' who can ask, 'Why do you do this?'"

¹¹David then said to Abishai and all his officials, "My son, who is of my own flesh, is trying to take my life. How much more, then, this Benjamite! Leave him alone; let him curse, for the LORD has told him to. ¹²It may be that the LORD will see my distress and repay me with good for the cursing I am receiving today."

¹³So David and his men continued along the road while Shimei was going along the hillside opposite him, cursing as he went and throwing stones at him and showering him with dirt. ¹⁴The king and all the people with him arrived at their destination exhausted. And there he refreshed himself.

The Advice of Hushai and Ahithophel

¹⁵Meanwhile, Absalom and all the men of Israel came to Jerusalem, and Ahithophel was with him. ¹⁶Then Hushai the Arkite, David's friend, went to Absalom and said to him, "Long live the king! Long live the king!"

¹⁷Absalom asked Hushai, "Is this the love you show your friend? Why didn't you go with your friend?"

¹⁸Hushai said to Absalom, "No, the one chosen by the LORD, by these people, and by all the men of Israel—his I will be, and I will remain with him. ¹⁹Furthermore, whom should I serve? Should I not serve the son? Just as I served your father, so I will serve you."

²⁰Absalom said to Ahithophel, "Give us your advice. What should we do?"

²¹Ahithophel answered, "Lie with your father's concubines whom he left to take care of the palace. Then all Israel will hear that you have made yourself a stench in your father's nostrils, and the hands of everyone with you will be strengthened." ²²So they pitched a tent for Absalom on the roof, and he lay with his father's concubines in the sight of all Israel.

²³Now in those days the advice Ahithophel gave was like that of one who inquires of God. That was how both David and Absalom regarded all of Ahithophel's advice.

17 Ahithophel said to Absalom, "I would*ᵃ* choose twelve thousand men and set out tonight in pursuit of David. ²I would*ᵇ* attack him while he is weary and weak. I would*ᵇ* strike him with terror, and then all the people with him will flee. I would*ᵇ* strike down only the king ³and bring all the people back to you. The death of the man you seek will mean the return of all; all the people will be unharmed." ⁴This plan seemed good to Absalom and to all the elders of Israel.

⁵But Absalom said, "Summon also Hushai the Arkite, so we can hear what he has to say." ⁶When Hushai came to him, Absalom

---

a1 Or *Let me*   *b2* Or *will*

said, "Ahithophel has given this advice. Should we do what he says? If not, give us your opinion."

[7]Hushai replied to Absalom, "The advice Ahithophel has given is not good this time. [8]You know your father and his men; they are fighters, and as fierce as a wild bear robbed of her cubs. Besides, your father is an experienced fighter; he will not spend the night with the troops. [9]Even now, he is hidden in a cave or some other place. If he should attack your troops first,[a] whoever hears about it will say, 'There has been a slaughter among the troops who follow Absalom.' [10]Then even the bravest soldier, whose heart is like the heart of a lion, will melt with fear, for all Israel knows that your father is a fighter and that those with him are brave.

[11]"So I advise you: Let all Israel, from Dan to Beersheba—as numerous as the sand on the seashore—be gathered to you, with you yourself leading them into battle. [12]Then we will attack him wherever he may be found, and we will fall on him as dew settles on the ground. Neither he nor any of his men will be left alive. [13]If he withdraws into a city, then all Israel will bring ropes to that city, and we will drag it down to the valley until not even a piece of it can be found."

[14]Absalom and all the men of Israel said, "The advice of Hushai the Arkite is better than that of Ahithophel." For the LORD had determined to frustrate the good advice of Ahithophel in order to bring disaster on Absalom.

[15]Hushai told Zadok and Abiathar, the priests, "Ahithophel has advised Absalom and the elders of Israel to do such and such, but I have advised them to do so and so. [16]Now send a message immediately and tell David, 'Do not spend the night at the fords in the desert; cross over without fail, or the king and all the people with him will be swallowed up.'"

[17]Jonathan and Ahimaaz were staying at En Rogel. A servant girl was to go and inform them, and they were to go and tell King David, for they could not risk being seen entering the city. [18]But a young man saw them and told Absalom. So the two of them left quickly and went to the house of a man in Bahurim. He had a well in his courtyard, and they climbed down into it. [19]His wife took a covering and spread it out over the opening of the well and scattered grain over it. No one knew anything about it.

[20]When Absalom's men came to the woman at the house, they asked, "Where are Ahimaaz and Jonathan?"

The woman answered them, "They crossed over the brook."[b] The men searched but found no one, so they returned to Jerusalem.

[21]After the men had gone, the two climbed out of the well and went to inform King David. They said to him, "Set out and cross the river at once; Ahithophel has advised such and such against you." [22]So David and all the people with him set out and crossed the Jordan. By daybreak, no one was left who had not crossed the Jordan.

[23]When Ahithophel saw that his advice had not been followed, he saddled his donkey and set out for his house in his hometown. He put his house in order and then hanged himself. So he died and was buried in his father's tomb.

[24]David went to Mahanaim, and Absalom crossed the Jordan with all the men of Israel. [25]Absalom had appointed Amasa over the army in place of Joab. Amasa was the son of a man named

able? (c) Just desserts? (d) Tragic? (e) Comic? (f) Better him than David? (g) An answer to David's prayer? 7. Meanwhile, how has delaying Absalom's attack benefitted David?

1. What risks is the Lord asking you to take for him: What "enemy lines" are you willing to cross, as Hushai did? What "spy messages" will you communicate for your Master in disregard for your own comfort and safety, as Zadok and Abiathar did? What "hiding place" ministry will you conduct to protect innocent people, as did the man and his wife in Bahurim? 2. On the other hand, perhaps you are like Ahithophel. Where are you looking for an "easy victory" in a tough situation? How strong is your desire for the approval of others? Where have you failed to live up to unrealistic "God-like" expectations placed on you (by yourself or others)? What gets you feeling depressed, even "suicidal" at times? (What do you do with those feelings?) 3. How can your small group help you overcome such tendencies of Ahithophel? And take more risks?

a9 Or When some of the men fall at the first attack   b20 Or "They passed by the sheep pen toward the water."

Jether,[a] an Israelite[b] who had married Abigail,[c] the daughter of Nahash and sister of Zeruiah the mother of Joab. [26]The Israelites and Absalom camped in the land of Gilead.

[27]When David came to Mahanaim, Shobi son of Nahash from Rabbah of the Ammonites, and Makir son of Ammiel from Lo Debar, and Barzillai the Gileadite from Rogelim [28]brought bedding and bowls and articles of pottery. They also brought wheat and barley, flour and roasted grain, beans and lentils,[d] [29]honey and curds, sheep, and cheese from cows' milk for David and his people to eat. For they said, "The people have become hungry and tired and thirsty in the desert."

Absalom's Death

18 David mustered the men who were with him and appointed over them commanders of thousands and commanders of hundreds. [2]David sent the troops out—a third under the command of Joab, a third under Joab's brother Abishai son of Zeruiah, and a third under Ittai the Gittite. The king told the troops, "I myself will surely march out with you."

[3]But the men said, "You must not go out; if we are forced to flee, they won't care about us. Even if half of us die, they won't care; but you are worth ten thousand of us.[e] It would be better now for you to give us support from the city."

[4]The king answered, "I will do whatever seems best to you."

So the king stood beside the gate while all the men marched out in units of hundreds and of thousands. [5]The king commanded Joab, Abishai and Ittai, "Be gentle with the young man Absalom for my sake." And all the troops heard the king giving orders concerning Absalom to each of the commanders.

[6]The army marched into the field to fight Israel, and the battle took place in the forest of Ephraim. [7]There the army of Israel was defeated by David's men, and the casualties that day were great— twenty thousand men. [8]The battle spread out over the whole countryside, and the forest claimed more lives that day than the sword.

[9]Now Absalom happened to meet David's men. He was riding his mule, and as the mule went under the thick branches of a large oak, Absalom's head got caught in the tree. He was left hanging in midair, while the mule he was riding kept on going.

[10]When one of the men saw this, he told Joab, "I just saw Absalom hanging in an oak tree."

[11]Joab said to the man who had told him this, "What! You saw him? Why didn't you strike him to the ground right there? Then I would have had to give you ten shekels[f] of silver and a warrior's belt."

[12]But the man replied, "Even if a thousand shekels[g] were weighed out into my hands, I would not lift my hand against the king's son. In our hearing the king commanded you and Abishai and Ittai, 'Protect the young man Absalom for my sake.'[h] [13]And if I had put my life in jeopardy[i]—and nothing is hidden from the king—you would have kept your distance from me."

[14]Joab said, "I'm not going to wait like this for you." So he took three javelins in his hand and plunged them into Absalom's heart

---

Sidebar column

1. Ever play chess? In that game, what role do the pawns often play? Where on the board does the king usually stay? Why is that? What naked moves make the king more vulnerable to attack? **2.** While in the woods horseback riding, hiking, jogging or biking, what is the worst accident that has befallen you?

1. How has David benefitted from the delay of Absalom's attack (vv. 1–2)? With all the betrayal and spying going on, what makes David think he can trust these three generals in particular— Joab, Abishai and Ittai? **2.** Why do they want David to stay behind and let others do the fighting (v. 3)? **3.** In wanting to spare young Absalom, what does this again say about David (v. 5)? **4.** What is significant about the location of the ensuing battle in terms of tactics? Results? Absalom's fate? **5.** What irony do you see in Absalom getting hung up in the end (see 14:25–26)? **6.** How does the man who spotted Absalom respond to Joab's rebuke (vv. 11–13)? Would you have reacted any differently? How so? **7.** What does Joab's treatment of Absalom reveal about him (vv. 11,14–15, 17)? What impact does Absalom's death have on the rest of his men? Later, what still lingers in their memory of Absalom (v. 18)?

1. Why do you believe our King is worth "ten thousand of us"? What other measure of his worth might you use? Why? As pawns sacrifice for their king in chess, and as David's men did for him, what will you do to tangibly demonstrate your belief in the unsurpassed worth of Christ the King? **2.** Recently, what have you tried hiding from God? What brought the hidden truth to light? **3.** When have you had done unto you what you've been dishing out to others? How could you reverse that

---

a25 Hebrew *Ithra*, a variant of *Jether*   b25 Hebrew and some Septuagint manuscripts; other Septuagint manuscripts (see also 1 Chron. 2:17) *Ishmaelite* or *Jezreelite*
c25 Hebrew *Abigal*, a variant of *Abigail*   d28 Most Septuagint manuscripts and Syriac; Hebrew *lentils, and roasted grain*   e3 Two Hebrew manuscripts, some Septuagint manuscripts and Vulgate; most Hebrew manuscripts *care; for now there are ten thousand like us*   f11 That is, about 4 ounces (about 115 grams)   g12 That is, about 25 pounds (about 11 kilograms)   h12 A few Hebrew manuscripts, Septuagint, Vulgate and Syriac; most Hebrew manuscripts may be translated *Absalom, whoever you may be.*
i13 Or *Otherwise, if I had acted treacherously toward him*

while Absalom was still alive in the oak tree. ¹⁵And ten of Joab's armor-bearers surrounded Absalom, struck him and killed him.

¹⁶Then Joab sounded the trumpet, and the troops stopped pursuing Israel, for Joab halted them. ¹⁷They took Absalom, threw him into a big pit in the forest and piled up a large heap of rocks over him. Meanwhile, all the Israelites fled to their homes.

¹⁸During his lifetime Absalom had taken a pillar and erected it in the King's Valley as a monument to himself, for he thought, "I have no son to carry on the memory of my name." He named the pillar after himself, and it is called Absalom's Monument to this day.

David Mourns

¹⁹Now Ahimaaz son of Zadok said, "Let me run and take the news to the king that the LORD has delivered him from the hand of his enemies."

²⁰"You are not the one to take the news today," Joab told him. "You may take the news another time, but you must not do so today, because the king's son is dead."

²¹Then Joab said to a Cushite, "Go, tell the king what you have seen." The Cushite bowed down before Joab and ran off.

²²Ahimaaz son of Zadok again said to Joab, "Come what may, please let me run behind the Cushite."

But Joab replied, "My son, why do you want to go? You don't have any news that will bring you a reward."

²³He said, "Come what may, I want to run."

So Joab said, "Run!" Then Ahimaaz ran by way of the plain*ᵃ* and outran the Cushite.

²⁴While David was sitting between the inner and outer gates, the watchman went up to the roof of the gateway by the wall. As he looked out, he saw a man running alone. ²⁵The watchman called out to the king and reported it.

The king said, "If he is alone, he must have good news." And the man came closer and closer.

²⁶Then the watchman saw another man running, and he called down to the gatekeeper, "Look, another man running alone!"

The king said, "He must be bringing good news, too."

²⁷The watchman said, "It seems to me that the first one runs like Ahimaaz son of Zadok."

"He's a good man," the king said. "He comes with good news."

²⁸Then Ahimaaz called out to the king, "All is well!" He bowed down before the king with his face to the ground and said, "Praise be to the LORD your God! He has delivered up the men who lifted their hands against my lord the king."

²⁹The king asked, "Is the young man Absalom safe?"

Ahimaaz answered, "I saw great confusion just as Joab was about to send the king's servant and me, your servant, but I don't know what it was."

³⁰The king said, "Stand aside and wait here." So he stepped aside and stood there.

³¹Then the Cushite arrived and said, "My lord the king, hear the good news! The LORD has delivered you today from all who rose up against you."

³²The king asked the Cushite, "Is the young man Absalom safe?"

The Cushite replied, "May the enemies of my lord the king and all who rise up to harm you be like that young man."

³³The king was shaken. He went up to the room over the gateway and wept. As he went, he said: "O my son Absalom! My son,

---

ᵃ23 That is, the plain of the Jordan

cycle, so that "what goes around" is good, not evil?

1. If you could be the very first person to do something, what would that something be? 2. What does it feel like to be the bearer of good news? Describe the "fight" to be the first one to share a recent good news event (news of your engagement, pregnancy, job promotion, academic achievement, scientific breakthrough, etc.). 3. When have you nervously paced the living room of your house or the waiting room of a hospital, awaiting some word about a family member's welfare? What was that like? 4. Describe a victory celebration which someone dampened with a "wet blanket." How were you kept from rejoicing?

1. Why does Ahimaaz persist in his request (18:19–23)? 2. What does the choice of messenger depend upon: (a) Favoritism? (b) Running ability? (c) Eagerness? (d) The content of the particular message? (e) Ability to be discreet? 3. Trace David's thinking: On what is he likely focusing before sighting the messengers? After sighting them? After hearing the first? The second? After receiving Joab's rebuke? 4. Why is David so preoccupied with Absalom's safety with so little concern for his own? Knowing this, what do Joab (18:20) and Ahimaaz (18:28–29) seek to do? Instead of cushioning the blow, what does the Cushite do and why? 5. Is Joab justified in his rebuke of David (19:5–7)? Why or why not?

1. What would you have said to David, or to your army, if you were faced with the morale problem described by Joab? 2. From what "enemies" has God recently delivered you? If delivered from your current enemy, what would you do without any more excuses or scapegoats? If that enemy is no longer a threat, with what new set of problems must you now contend? 3. With what have you been preoccupied lately? If the

my son Absalom! If only I had died instead of you—O Absalom, my son, my son!"

19 Joab was told, "The king is weeping and mourning for Absalom." ²And for the whole army the victory that day was turned into mourning, because on that day the troops heard it said, "The king is grieving for his son." ³The men stole into the city that day as men steal in who are ashamed when they flee from battle. ⁴The king covered his face and cried aloud, "O my son Absalom! O Absalom, my son, my son!"

⁵Then Joab went into the house to the king and said, "Today you have humiliated all your men, who have just saved your life and the lives of your sons and daughters and the lives of your wives and concubines. ⁶You love those who hate you and hate those who love you. You have made it clear today that the commanders and their men mean nothing to you. I see that you would be pleased if Absalom were alive today and all of us were dead. ⁷Now go out and encourage your men. I swear by the LORD that if you don't go out, not a man will be left with you by nightfall. This will be worse for you than all the calamities that have come upon you from your youth till now."

⁸So the king got up and took his seat in the gateway. When the men were told, "The king is sitting in the gateway," they all came before him.

David Returns to Jerusalem

Meanwhile, the Israelites had fled to their homes. ⁹Throughout the tribes of Israel, the people were all arguing with each other, saying, "The king delivered us from the hand of our enemies; he is the one who rescued us from the hand of the Philistines. But now he has fled the country because of Absalom; ¹⁰and Absalom, whom we anointed to rule over us, has died in battle. So why do you say nothing about bringing the king back?"

¹¹King David sent this message to Zadok and Abiathar, the priests: "Ask the elders of Judah, 'Why should you be the last to bring the king back to his palace, since what is being said throughout Israel has reached the king at his quarters? ¹²You are my brothers, my own flesh and blood. So why should you be the last to bring back the king?' ¹³And say to Amasa, 'Are you not my own flesh and blood? May God deal with me, be it ever so severely, if from now on you are not the commander of my army in place of Joab.'"

¹⁴He won over the hearts of all the men of Judah as though they were one man. They sent word to the king, "Return, you and all your men." ¹⁵Then the king returned and went as far as the Jordan.

Now the men of Judah had come to Gilgal to go out and meet the king and bring him across the Jordan. ¹⁶Shimei son of Gera, the Benjamite from Bahurim, hurried down with the men of Judah to meet King David. ¹⁷With him were a thousand Benjamites, along with Ziba, the steward of Saul's household, and his fifteen sons and twenty servants. They rushed to the Jordan, where the king was. ¹⁸They crossed at the ford to take the king's household over and to do whatever he wished.

When Shimei son of Gera crossed the Jordan, he fell prostrate before the king ¹⁹and said to him, "May my lord not hold me guilty. Do not remember how your servant did wrong on the day my lord the king left Jerusalem. May the king put it out of his mind. ²⁰For I your servant know that I have sinned, but today I have come here as the first of the whole house of Joseph to come down and meet my lord the king."

---

worst-case scenario comes to pass, what will happen? Then what will you do? What role does your Christian faith and your small group play in this regard?

☕ 1. When do you feel most motivated to ask for someone else's forgiveness? To grant someone forgiveness? Share an instance. 2. When you and a rival sibling fought over how to share your things, what did you ask Mom or Dad to do? Of all the solutions they proposed, which ones worked best? Why? 3. Over the past year, have you given more favors, or received more favors? At year's end, when it's time to balance out "favors receivable" and "favors payable," will you likely be a creditor or a debtor? Why? 4. In politics and sports, whom do you tend to support: (a) Whoever is ahead at the outset? (b) Whoever is behind near the end? (c) Whoever's victory favors you the most? (d) Whoever wins—he/she was your choice all along?

📖 1. If you had previously backed Absalom, why would you now reconfirm David as king (vv. 8b–10)? What about David's appeal (vv. 11–13) would secure your vote of confidence? 2. Why do you think Shimei behaves as he does (vv. 16–20; see 16:5–14)? 3. How and why does David's response vary from Abishai's (vv. 21–23; see 16:9–12)? 4. How does Mephibosheth's side of the story vary from Ziba's (vv. 24–30; see 16:3)? Who do you find more credible—Mephibosheth or Ziba? Why? Who do you think David believes? (Or does it even matter to him?) 5.

21Then Abishai son of Zeruiah said, "Shouldn't Shimei be put to death for this? He cursed the LORD's anointed."

22David replied, "What do you and I have in common, you sons of Zeruiah? This day you have become my adversaries! Should anyone be put to death in Israel today? Do I not know that today I am king over Israel?" 23So the king said to Shimei, "You shall not die." And the king promised him on oath.

24Mephibosheth, Saul's grandson, also went down to meet the king. He had not taken care of his feet or trimmed his mustache or washed his clothes from the day the king left until the day he returned safely. 25When he came from Jerusalem to meet the king, the king asked him, "Why didn't you go with me, Mephibosheth?"

26He said, "My lord the king, since I your servant am lame, I said, 'I will have my donkey saddled and will ride on it, so I can go with the king.' But Ziba my servant betrayed me. 27And he has slandered your servant to my lord the king. My lord the king is like an angel of God; so do whatever pleases you. 28All my grandfather's descendants deserved nothing but death from my lord the king, but you gave your servant a place among those who eat at your table. So what right do I have to make any more appeals to the king?"

29The king said to him, "Why say more? I order you and Ziba to divide the fields."

30Mephibosheth said to the king, "Let him take everything, now that my lord the king has arrived home safely."

31Barzillai the Gileadite also came down from Rogelim to cross the Jordan with the king and to send him on his way from there. 32Now Barzillai was a very old man, eighty years of age. He had provided for the king during his stay in Mahanaim, for he was a very wealthy man. 33The king said to Barzillai, "Cross over with me and stay with me in Jerusalem, and I will provide for you."

34But Barzillai answered the king, "How many more years will I live, that I should go up to Jerusalem with the king? 35I am now eighty years old. Can I tell the difference between what is good and what is not? Can your servant taste what he eats and drinks? Can I still hear the voices of men and women singers? Why should your servant be an added burden to my lord the king? 36Your servant will cross over the Jordan with the king for a short distance, but why should the king reward me in this way? 37Let your servant return, that I may die in my own town near the tomb of my father and mother. But here is your servant Kimham. Let him cross over with my lord the king. Do for him whatever pleases you."

38The king said, "Kimham shall cross over with me, and I will do for him whatever pleases you. And anything you desire from me I will do for you."

39So all the people crossed the Jordan, and then the king crossed over. The king kissed Barzillai and gave him his blessing, and Barzillai returned to his home.

40When the king crossed over to Gilgal, Kimham crossed with him. All the troops of Judah and half the troops of Israel had taken the king over.

41Soon all the men of Israel were coming to the king and saying to him, "Why did our brothers, the men of Judah, steal the king away and bring him and his household across the Jordan, together with all his men?"

42All the men of Judah answered the men of Israel, "We did this because the king is closely related to us. Why are you angry about it? Have we eaten any of the king's provisions? Have we taken anything for ourselves?"

43Then the men of Israel answered the men of Judah, "We have

Why does David seek to reward Barzillai (vv. 24–30)? Why is that offer refused (vv. 34–37)? What face-saving alternative is then proposed and accepted? As Kimham, being singled out for such favor, how would you feel toward your two benefactors? 6. Why are the men of Israel so upset (vv. 41ff)? What's at stake here besides hurt pride?

1. Is the Lord's return of David to power based, at least in part, on David's favoring and forgiving others? Or is David now able to grant general amnesty only because God has first forgiven him? Why do you think so? 2. If King Jesus were to grant amnesty to you for something as particular as what King David offered Shimei, Mephiboseth, Barzillai or Kimham, what would that amnesty cover in your case? Would you accept the King's generous offer? Or would you respectfully "pass" or defer to another? Why? 3. This week, where will you be as forgiving as David? As penitent as Shimei? As generous as Barzillai? As sincere and grateful as Mephibosheth? How can you begin doing this within your small group?

ten shares in the king; and besides, we have a greater claim on David than you have. So why do you treat us with contempt? Were we not the first to speak of bringing back our king?"

But the men of Judah responded even more harshly than the men of Israel.

Sheba Rebels Against David

20 Now a troublemaker named Sheba son of Bicri, a Benjamite, happened to be there. He sounded the trumpet and shouted,

"We have no share in David,
    no part in Jesse's son!
Every man to his tent, O Israel!"

[2]So all the men of Israel deserted David to follow Sheba son of Bicri. But the men of Judah stayed by their king all the way from the Jordan to Jerusalem.

[3]When David returned to his palace in Jerusalem, he took the ten concubines he had left to take care of the palace and put them in a house under guard. He provided for them, but did not lie with them. They were kept in confinement till the day of their death, living as widows.

[4]Then the king said to Amasa, "Summon the men of Judah to come to me within three days, and be here yourself." [5]But when Amasa went to summon Judah, he took longer than the time the king had set for him.

[6]David said to Abishai, "Now Sheba son of Bicri will do us more harm than Absalom did. Take your master's men and pursue him, or he will find fortified cities and escape from us." [7]So Joab's men and the Kerethites and Pelethites and all the mighty warriors went out under the command of Abishai. They marched out from Jerusalem to pursue Sheba son of Bicri.

[8]While they were at the great rock in Gibeon, Amasa came to meet them. Joab was wearing his military tunic, and strapped over it at his waist was a belt with a dagger in its sheath. As he stepped forward, it dropped out of its sheath.

[9]Joab said to Amasa, "How are you, my brother?" Then Joab took Amasa by the beard with his right hand to kiss him. [10]Amasa was not on his guard against the dagger in Joab's hand, and Joab plunged it into his belly, and his intestines spilled out on the ground. Without being stabbed again, Amasa died. Then Joab and his brother Abishai pursued Sheba son of Bicri.

[11]One of Joab's men stood beside Amasa and said, "Whoever favors Joab, and whoever is for David, let him follow Joab!" [12]Amasa lay wallowing in his blood in the middle of the road, and the man saw that all the troops came to a halt there. When he realized that everyone who came up to Amasa stopped, he dragged him from the road into a field and threw a garment over him. [13]After Amasa had been removed from the road, all the men went on with Joab to pursue Sheba son of Bicri.

[14]Sheba passed through all the tribes of Israel to Abel Beth Maacah[a] and through the entire region of the Berites, who gathered together and followed him. [15]All the troops with Joab came and besieged Sheba in Abel Beth Maacah. They built a siege ramp up to the city, and it stood against the outer fortifications. While they were battering the wall to bring it down, [16]a wise woman called

---

1. What are the political leanings of your family? Which way do you lean? **2.** What pressing deadline are you facing right now? What will happen if you don't get it done in the next three days? **3.** When have you lost a job to someone else? Or when have you been passed over for a promotion you felt you deserved? How did you feel about that?

1. In what ways do events of the previous chapter (especially 19:41–43) fuel Sheba's revolt (vv. 1–2)? **2.** Why does David treat his concubines as he does (v. 3; see 16:21–22)? **3.** To squash Sheba's revolt, why does David bypass Joab twice, first favoring Amasa and then Abishai (vv. 4–6)? What particularly galls Joab about Amasa's appointment (see 17:25; 19:13)? **4.** Could it be that Joab catching Amasa by his beard is the origin of that refrain, "I've got you by the hair on your chinny-chin-chin"? **5.** What impact do the blood and guts of Amasa have on Joab's men? What impact do such lurid details have on you? **6.** Is Sheba's revolt a popular uprising (vv. 14ff)? Popular with whom? Betrayed by whom? Beheaded by whom? **7.** Why would "all the people" (v. 22), among whom were Sheba's own followers, behead him? **8.** How does this story illustrate the wisdom of this woman? Who does she remind you of? Why? **9.** How would you evaluate David's cabinet of royal officials? Who has served David most faithfully? Who would you impeach for breaking your "code of ethics"? Who is no longer serving at the post they were first given (see 8:15–18)?

1. When have you been especially tempted to desert your King? For what reason? What kept you from going AWOL? **2.** When your status or authority is diminished by someone else, how does that make you feel? When resentment builds up, how do you keep that in check? Where might resentment be getting the better of you now? **3.** How can your Christian faith and your small group make a difference during such trying times?

---

[a]14 Or Abel, even Beth Maacah; also in verse 15

from the city, "Listen! Listen! Tell Joab to come here so I can speak to him." ¹⁷He went toward her, and she asked, "Are you Joab?"

"I am," he answered.

She said, "Listen to what your servant has to say."

"I'm listening," he said.

¹⁸She continued, "Long ago they used to say, 'Get your answer at Abel,' and that settled it. ¹⁹We are the peaceful and faithful in Israel. You are trying to destroy a city that is a mother in Israel. Why do you want to swallow up the LORD's inheritance?"

²⁰"Far be it from me!" Joab replied, "Far be it from me to swallow up or destroy! ²¹That is not the case. A man named Sheba son of Bicri, from the hill country of Ephraim, has lifted up his hand against the king, against David. Hand over this one man, and I'll withdraw from the city."

The woman said to Joab, "His head will be thrown to you from the wall."

²²Then the woman went to all the people with her wise advice, and they cut off the head of Sheba son of Bicri and threw it to Joab. So he sounded the trumpet, and his men dispersed from the city, each returning to his home. And Joab went back to the king in Jerusalem.

²³Joab was over Israel's entire army; Benaiah son of Jehoiada was over the Kerethites and Pelethites; ²⁴Adoniram^a was in charge of forced labor; Jehoshaphat son of Ahilud was recorder; ²⁵Sheva was secretary; Zadok and Abiathar were priests; ²⁶and Ira the Jairite was David's priest.

The Gibeonites Avenged

21 During the reign of David, there was a famine for three successive years; so David sought the face of the LORD. The LORD said, "It is on account of Saul and his blood-stained house; it is because he put the Gibeonites to death."

²The king summoned the Gibeonites and spoke to them. (Now the Gibeonites were not a part of Israel but were survivors of the Amorites; the Israelites had sworn to ⌊spare⌋ them, but Saul in his zeal for Israel and Judah had tried to annihilate them.) ³David asked the Gibeonites, "What shall I do for you? How shall I make amends so that you will bless the LORD's inheritance?"

⁴The Gibeonites answered him, "We have no right to demand silver or gold from Saul or his family, nor do we have the right to put anyone in Israel to death."

"What do you want me to do for you?" David asked.

⁵They answered the king, "As for the man who destroyed us and plotted against us so that we have been decimated and have no place anywhere in Israel, ⁶let seven of his male descendants be given to us to be killed and exposed before the LORD at Gibeah of Saul—the LORD's chosen one."

So the king said, "I will give them to you."

⁷The king spared Mephibosheth son of Jonathan, the son of Saul, because of the oath before the LORD between David and Jonathan son of Saul. ⁸But the king took Armoni and Mephibosheth, the two sons of Aiah's daughter Rizpah, whom she had borne to Saul, together with the five sons of Saul's daughter Merab,^b whom she had borne to Adriel son of Barzillai the Meholathite. ⁹He handed them over to the Gibeonites, who killed and exposed them on a hill before the LORD. All seven of them fell together; they were put

1. When your prayers go unanswered, what do you assume? What do you do? 2. The last time you pulled an "all-nighter," what kept you up: Illness? Homework? Grief? A baby?

The events of chapters 21–24 are not chronological, yet they tie together the whole book. 1. What caused the famine (vv. 1–2; see Jos 9:20)? Why did Israel make a treaty with the Gibeonites ("Hivites") in the first place (see Jos 9)? 2. Saul decimates the Gibeonites "in his zeal," but David spares them due to an oath "before the Lord." What does this say about the basic differences between the two men? About the seriousness of oaths? About God's judgment? 3. Why does David spare the son of Jonathan but not Saul's other relatives (vv. 7ff; see 4:4; 9:1–13; 1Sa 20:14–17)? What contrast between the two does this again highlight? 4. What is significant about both oaths and executions being made "before the Lord" (vv. 6,7,9)? 5. What link do you see in verses 1 and 9? 6. Rizpah pulls several "all-nighters" (vv.10ff). What does she hope to achieve in the short-run? Long-run? 7. Why would it please God to see Saul's descendants executed (v. 14)?

^a24 Some Septuagint manuscripts (see also 1 Kings 4:6 and 5:14); Hebrew *Adoram*
^b8 Two Hebrew manuscripts, some Septuagint manuscripts and Syriac (see also 1 Samuel 18:19); most Hebrew and Septuagint manuscripts *Michal*

1. Is it appropriate to see God's judgment in famines and other natural disasters today? Why or why not? 2. How would this story apply today to situations where treaty rights are violated, e.g., the treaty rights of Native Americans? 3. About what do you need to seek the face of the Lord, as did David?

to death during the first days of the harvest, just as the barley harvest was beginning.

[10]Rizpah daughter of Aiah took sackcloth and spread it out for herself on a rock. From the beginning of the harvest till the rain poured down from the heavens on the bodies, she did not let the birds of the air touch them by day or the wild animals by night. [11]When David was told what Aiah's daughter Rizpah, Saul's concubine, had done, [12]he went and took the bones of Saul and his son Jonathan from the citizens of Jabesh Gilead. (They had taken them secretly from the public square at Beth Shan, where the Philistines had hung them after they struck Saul down on Gilboa.) [13]David brought the bones of Saul and his son Jonathan from there, and the bones of those who had been killed and exposed were gathered up.

[14]They buried the bones of Saul and his son Jonathan in the tomb of Saul's father Kish, at Zela in Benjamin, and did everything the king commanded. After that, God answered prayer in behalf of the land.

Wars Against the Philistines

[15]Once again there was a battle between the Philistines and Israel. David went down with his men to fight against the Philistines, and he became exhausted. [16]And Ishbi-Benob, one of the descendants of Rapha, whose bronze spearhead weighed three hundred shekels[a] and who was armed with a new ⌊sword⌋, said he would kill David. [17]But Abishai son of Zeruiah came to David's rescue; he struck the Philistine down and killed him. Then David's men swore to him, saying, "Never again will you go out with us to battle, so that the lamp of Israel will not be extinguished."

[18]In the course of time, there was another battle with the Philistines, at Gob. At that time Sibbecai the Hushathite killed Saph, one of the descendants of Rapha.

[19]In another battle with the Philistines at Gob, Elhanan son of Jaare-Oregim[b] the Bethlehemite killed Goliath[c] the Gittite, who had a spear with a shaft like a weaver's rod.

[20]In still another battle, which took place at Gath, there was a huge man with six fingers on each hand and six toes on each foot—twenty-four in all. He also was descended from Rapha. [21]When he taunted Israel, Jonathan son of Shimeah, David's brother, killed him.

[22]These four were descendants of Rapha in Gath, and they fell at the hands of David and his men.

1. What do your feet and hands reveal about the kind of person you are? 2. Share a story which demonstrates how you were "Hero for a Day."

1. Precise identification and dating of these four Philistine episodes is uncertain, but this is not germane to their main point. What main point does each episode serve? 2. How do the heroics of David's men relate to 21:17? To 21:22? To 22:1? 3. We know David killed Goliath (1Sa 17); what explanations can you offer for the apparent contradiction in verse 19?

1. What battles have you recently fought for your King? What battles do you anticipate in the coming week? 2. Who do you regard as your "spiritual heroes," those who have kept their light burning for the Lord and have shared that light with you? How did they conquer sinful habits?

David's Song of Praise

22 David sang to the Lord the words of this song when the Lord delivered him from the hand of all his enemies and from the hand of Saul. [2]He said:

1. Which of the following typifies your way of making music: (a) Composing a song? (b) Singing in the shower? (c) Singing in the church choir? (d) Making a joyful noise? (e) Playing the "Top 40" on the radio? 2. Try picturing God as you did when you were a child: What did you draw for God's face? His body? What were in his hands and feet? What did you color him? What words came out of his mouth? 3. Today, what images do you link with God? What colors? What emotions? What sounds? 4. What one dramatic rescue attempt can you recall hearing about or

> "The Lord is my rock, my fortress and my
>   deliverer;
> [3]   my God is my rock, in whom I take refuge,
>   my shield and the horn[d] of my salvation.
> He is my stronghold, my refuge and my savior—
>   from violent men you save me.
> [4]I call to the Lord, who is worthy of praise,
>   and I am saved from my enemies.
>
> [5]"The waves of death swirled about me;

---

[a]16 That is, about 7 1/2 pounds (about 3.5 kilograms)   [b]19 Or son of Jair the weaver
[c]19 Hebrew and Septuagint; 1 Chron. 20:5 son of Jair killed Lahmi the brother of Goliath
[d]3 Horn here symbolizes strength.

the torrents of destruction overwhelmed me.
⁶The cords of the grave^a coiled around me;
    the snares of death confronted me.
⁷In my distress I called to the LORD;
    I called out to my God.
From his temple he heard my voice;
    my cry came to his ears.

⁸"The earth trembled and quaked,
    the foundations of the heavens^b shook;
    they trembled because he was angry.
⁹Smoke rose from his nostrils;
    consuming fire came from his mouth,
    burning coals blazed out of it.
¹⁰He parted the heavens and came down;
    dark clouds were under his feet.
¹¹He mounted the cherubim and flew;
    he soared^c on the wings of the wind.
¹²He made darkness his canopy around him—
    the dark^d rain clouds of the sky.
¹³Out of the brightness of his presence
    bolts of lightning blazed forth.
¹⁴The LORD thundered from heaven;
    the voice of the Most High resounded.
¹⁵He shot arrows and scattered ⌊the enemies⌋,
    bolts of lightning and routed them.
¹⁶The valleys of the sea were exposed
    and the foundations of the earth laid bare
at the rebuke of the LORD,
    at the blast of breath from his nostrils.

¹⁷"He reached down from on high and took hold of
    me;
    he drew me out of deep waters.
¹⁸He rescued me from my powerful enemy,
    from my foes, who were too strong for me.
¹⁹They confronted me in the day of my disaster,
    but the LORD was my support.
²⁰He brought me out into a spacious place;
    he rescued me because he delighted in me.

²¹"The LORD has dealt with me according to my
    righteousness;
according to the cleanness of my hands he has
    rewarded me.
²²For I have kept the ways of the LORD;
    I have not done evil by turning from my God.
²³All his laws are before me;
    I have not turned away from his decrees.
²⁴I have been blameless before him
    and have kept myself from sin.
²⁵The LORD has rewarded me according to my
    righteousness,
according to my cleanness^e in his sight.

²⁶"To the faithful you show yourself faithful,
    to the blameless you show yourself blameless,

seeing? What's the most memorable rescue effort in which you've been involved?

📖 **1.** If you had to express the emotions of David's song in music, what types of music would you pick and why? What refrains would you dramatize? What solo parts stand out? Where would you signal the musical crescendo? **2.** Would you say this song (also Ps 18) sums up accurately David's life to date and his relationship with God? What about this song reflects his triumph over foreign enemies (8:1–14) and Saul (1Sa 18–31)? Do you suppose this song was written before, or after, his adultery with Bathsheba (ch.11–12)? Why? **3.** David spent much time hiding from Saul in rocks and caves. What insight does this give you into the meaning of God as "my rock," "my fortress" and "my stronghold" (vv. 2–3)? **4.** Nowhere in 1 or 2 Samuel did the cosmic events of verses 5–20 actually happen to David. Why then does he use such figurative language to describe how God saved him? To what other redemptive experiences in Israel's collective history is he alluding? **5.** In likening God's rescue of David to what God did for the nation Israel at the Red Sea or Mt. Sinai, what does that say about God's redemptive love for individuals? What else does vivid imagery say about God's justice? **6.** Here (vv. 21–25) David speaks as though he were sinless, yet elsewhere he is very aware of his failure (see Ps 32; 51). How do you account for this? How could David make such claims about himself? **7.** In verses 21–30, what is going on: Is David indirectly boasting? Or is he only praising God? Why do you think so? How did David's lifestyle influence God's dealings with him: Is he engaging in legalistic exercises to gain God's favor? Or is he basing his appeal on God's sure promise and peculiar delight in him? Why do you think so? **8.** In verses 31–37 and 47–51, what qualities of God do you see through the eyes of David? What effect does God have on him? **9.** In referring to his qualities as a warrior and king (vv. 38–46), what new insights do you gain into David? To what extent was David victorious over his enemies?

❤ **1.** This psalm was used with reference to Jesus (v. 50; see Ro 15:9). What new meaning does that give you here into Da-

---

^a6 Hebrew *Sheol*   ^b8 Hebrew; Vulgate and Syriac (see also Psalm 18:7) *mountains*   ^c11 Many Hebrew manuscripts (see also Psalm 18:10); most Hebrew manuscripts *appeared*   ^d12 Septuagint and Vulgate (see also Psalm 18:11); Hebrew *massed*   ^e25 Hebrew; Septuagint and Vulgate (see also Psalm 18:24) *to the cleanness of my hands*

vid's claim to be sinless? What new insights might these verses give you into the victorious rule of a future Messiah, the Son of David? **2.** Most religions of the world teach their followers to honor, fear or appease their god. What does it mean to you that we can come to our God as David does in verse 2? **3.** When do you feel like God would shake heaven and earth to save you? Or don't you think God would even lift a finger to save you? Why? Knowing you are worth that much effort to him, and that he delights in you, what does that do for your motivation and ability to praise God among the nations who do not know him? **4.** If you had written this song with references to the redemptive experiences of your small group or your church, what would you be singing about? From your personal experience, what would you call God: "My _____"? Recently, when have you been overwhelmed by love for God? In writing a song of your own, praising God, how might that help you become more aware of his love for you this week? **5.** How might God help you prevail over enemies "too strong for you"? Over what "walls" would you like God to help you go? **6.** Habakkuk 3:19 quotes verse 34 (re: "hind's feet in high places") to build up hope in the face of a national crisis. What verse or lyric from David's song would you claim to describe how you want to see God work in your life? Why that verse?

²⁷to the pure you show yourself pure,
    but to the crooked you show yourself shrewd.
²⁸You save the humble,
    but your eyes are on the haughty to bring them low.
²⁹You are my lamp, O LORD;
    the LORD turns my darkness into light.
³⁰With your help I can advance against a troop^a;
    with my God I can scale a wall.

³¹"As for God, his way is perfect;
    the word of the LORD is flawless.
He is a shield
    for all who take refuge in him.
³²For who is God besides the LORD?
    And who is the Rock except our God?
³³It is God who arms me with strength^b
    and makes my way perfect.
³⁴He makes my feet like the feet of a deer;
    he enables me to stand on the heights.
³⁵He trains my hands for battle;
    my arms can bend a bow of bronze.
³⁶You give me your shield of victory;
    you stoop down to make me great.
³⁷You broaden the path beneath me,
    so that my ankles do not turn.

³⁸"I pursued my enemies and crushed them;
    I did not turn back till they were destroyed.
³⁹I crushed them completely, and they could not rise;
    they fell beneath my feet.
⁴⁰You armed me with strength for battle;
    you made my adversaries bow at my feet.
⁴¹You made my enemies turn their backs in flight,
    and I destroyed my foes.
⁴²They cried for help, but there was no one to save them—
    to the LORD, but he did not answer.
⁴³I beat them as fine as the dust of the earth;
    I pounded and trampled them like mud in the streets.

⁴⁴"You have delivered me from the attacks of my people;
    you have preserved me as the head of nations.
People I did not know are subject to me,
⁴⁵   and foreigners come cringing to me;
    as soon as they hear me, they obey me.
⁴⁶They all lose heart;
    they come trembling^c from their strongholds.

⁴⁷"The LORD lives! Praise be to my Rock!
    Exalted be God, the Rock, my Savior!
⁴⁸He is the God who avenges me,
    who puts the nations under me,
⁴⁹   who sets me free from my enemies.

^a30 Or *can run through a barricade*   ^b33 Dead Sea Scrolls, some Septuagint manuscripts, Vulgate and Syriac (see also Psalm 18:32); Masoretic Text *who is my strong refuge*   ^c46 Some Septuagint manuscripts and Vulgate (see also Psalm 18:45); Masoretic Text *they arm themselves.*

> You exalted me above my foes;
>> from violent men you rescued me.
> ⁵⁰Therefore I will praise you, O LORD, among the
>> nations;
> I will sing praises to your name.
> ⁵¹He gives his king great victories;
>> he shows unfailing kindness to his anointed,
>> to David and his descendants forever."

The Last Words of David

23 These are the last words of David:

> "The oracle of David son of Jesse,
>> the oracle of the man exalted by the Most High,
> the man anointed by the God of Jacob,
>> Israel's singer of songs^a:
>
> ²"The Spirit of the LORD spoke through me;
>> his word was on my tongue.
> ³The God of Israel spoke,
>> the Rock of Israel said to me:
> 'When one rules over men in righteousness,
>> when he rules in the fear of God,
> ⁴he is like the light of morning at sunrise
>> on a cloudless morning,
> like the brightness after rain
>> that brings the grass from the earth.'
>
> ⁵"Is not my house right with God?
>> Has he not made with me an everlasting
>>> covenant,
>> arranged and secured in every part?
> Will he not bring to fruition my salvation
>> and grant me my every desire?
> ⁶But evil men are all to be cast aside like thorns,
>> which are not gathered with the hand.
> ⁷Whoever touches thorns
>> uses a tool of iron or the shaft of a spear;
>> they are burned up where they lie."

David's Mighty Men

⁸These are the names of David's mighty men:

Josheb-Basshebeth,^b a Tahkemonite,^c was chief of the Three; he raised his spear against eight hundred men, whom he killed^d in one encounter.

⁹Next to him was Eleazar son of Dodai the Ahohite. As one of the three mighty men, he was with David when they taunted the Philistines gathered ⌊at Pas Dammim⌋^e for battle. Then the men of Israel retreated, ¹⁰but he stood his ground and struck down the Philistines till his hand grew tired and froze to the sword. The LORD brought about a great victory that day. The troops returned to Eleazar, but only to strip the dead.

¹¹Next to him was Shammah son of Agee the Hararite. When the Philistines banded together at a place where there was a field full of lentils, Israel's troops fled from them. ¹²But Shammah took his

As a teen, who was your "singer of songs," or favorite music group? Now what music do you like?

1. Which of his idealized terms (vv. 1–4) apply to David? Which of these images are more fully realized in David's greater son, Jesus, the ideal theocratic ruler yet to come? 2. In these last words, how does David underscore the divine inspiration of *all* his recorded words (vv. 2–3)? 3. How does David know all is right with his house (v. 5; see 7:12–16)? How do evil men compare with him (vv. 6–7)?

1. Regarding divine inspiration, *how* does God's Word come to be in human words? By mechanical dictation? Power of suggestion? Or what? 2. Can God speak through you this week? How is that like or unlike divine inspiration? With whom would you like to share God's Word?

1. What do you consider one of your greatest accomplishments? Why? What obstacles did you have to overcome? 2. Which "mighty man" character was your most favorite and why: Superman? Batman? Lone Ranger? Mighty Mouse? Popeye? Robin Hood? Roy Rogers? James Bond? 3. In the "Greatest Military Heroes of All Time" category (excluding Bible characters), who would you place in your "Top Three"? Pooling the group's nominees for a secret ballot, who would you vote for as "Chief" of your "Mighty Men"?

1. What kind of person do you imagine the typical "mighty man of David" was? Do David's nominees seem "cartoonish" to you? Would they make your all-time list? Why or why not? 2.

a1 Or *Israel's beloved singer*   *b8* Hebrew; some Septuagint manuscripts suggest *Ish-Bosheth,* that is, *Esh-Baal* (see also 1 Chron. 11:11 *Jashobeam*).   *c8* Probably a variant of *Hacmonite* (see 1 Chron. 11:11)   *d8* Some Septuagint manuscripts (see also 1 Chron. 11:11); Hebrew and other Septuagint manuscripts *Three; it was Adino the Eznite who killed eight hundred men*   *e9* See 1 Chron. 11:13; Hebrew *gathered there.*

Which mighty men do you think were David's top "Three" (vv. 8ff,13ff,17,18–19,22–23)? **3.** What do Eleazar and Shammah have in common (vv. 9–12)? Who should get the credit for their victories? **4.** When in David's lifetime do you think the event of verses 13–17 occurred (see 1Sa 22:1–2 or 2Sa 5:17)? How do you think David felt when his three mighty men offered him the water? How would David's soldier's have felt when he then poured it on the ground? **5.** For what was Abishai famous (vv. 18–19)? Why do you think he was *commander* of "the Three," but *not* among them? **6.** For what was Benaiah famous (vv. 20–23)? How was he honored? **7.** What names do you recognize among "the Thirty" (vv. 24–39)? What biblical events do their names bring to mind for you? How many names are listed there? How do you account for the apparent discrepancy? Likewise, what names add up to "thirty-seven" (v. 39)?

 1. Take a sample cross section of 100 "average" Christian soldiers in the Lord's army. Would you place yourself in the top 30? Why or why not? What

stand in the middle of the field. He defended it and struck the Philistines down, and the LORD brought about a great victory.

[13]During harvest time, three of the thirty chief men came down to David at the cave of Adullam, while a band of Philistines was encamped in the Valley of Rephaim. [14]At that time David was in the stronghold, and the Philistine garrison was at Bethlehem. [15]David longed for water and said, "Oh, that someone would get me a drink of water from the well near the gate of Bethlehem!" [16]So the three mighty men broke through the Philistine lines, drew water from the well near the gate of Bethlehem and carried it back to David. But he refused to drink it; instead, he poured it out before the LORD. [17]"Far be it from me, O LORD, to do this!" he said. "Is it not the blood of men who went at the risk of their lives?" And David would not drink it.

Such were the exploits of the three mighty men.

[18]Abishai the brother of Joab son of Zeruiah was chief of the Three.[a] He raised his spear against three hundred men, whom he killed, and so he became as famous as the Three. [19]Was he not held in greater honor than the Three? He became their commander, even though he was not included among them.

[20]Benaiah son of Jehoiada was a valiant fighter from Kabzeel, who performed great exploits. He struck down two of Moab's best men. He also went down into a pit on a snowy day and killed a lion. [21]And he struck down a huge Egyptian. Although the Egyptian had a spear in his hand, Benaiah went against him with a club. He snatched the spear from the Egyptian's hand and killed him with

[a]18 Most Hebrew manuscripts (see also 1 Chron. 11:20); two Hebrew manuscripts and Syriac *Thirty*

---

2 Samuel 23:8–23   DAVID'S MIGHTY MEN

Recorded here are some exploits of King David's most valiant warriors.

1. What would you call this listing?
   a. Israel's Ancient All Stars
   b. David's Daring Dudes
   c. God's Gladiators
   d. Thirty Thugs
   e. Sanctified Super Heroes

2. How do you envision these men?
   a. tough and toothless
   b. sly as a fox
   c. ferocious as a lion
   d. faithful friends

3. What would a guy like Eleazar or Benaiah probably be today?
   a. a middle linebacker
   b. a professional wrestler
   c. a biker
   d. a Green Beret
   e. a Secret Service agent
   f. a street minister
   g. a prayer warrior

4. What made David's mighty men so mighty?
   a. team spirit
   b. brute strength
   c. good leadership
   d. superior strategy
   e. individual heroics
   f. willpower and determination
   g. God's favor

5. What made David long for water from the well near Bethlehem?
   a. It would make him feel pampered.
   b. They had run out of fresh water.
   c. They had to ration their water in the stronghold.
   d. David grew up with that water.

6. How do you think David felt when the three men brought him the water?
   a. overwhelmed with gratitude
   b. tempted to drink it
   c. honored by their support
   d. unworthy of such devotion

7. How do you think the three felt?
   a. foolish for their efforts
   b. unappreciated by their leader
   c. esteemed by David
   d. blessed by David turning their physical sacrifice into a spiritual sacrifice

8. Who have been the "spiritual giants" who have fought at your side?

9. Where God has currently placed you, what would it mean for you to "stand your ground"? What opposition or obstacles would you like to strike down with God's help?

10. Do you feel like you are fighting any battles all by yourself? In what way could your small group provide reinforcements?

11. How much do you feel a need in your life for support from other men?
    a. I really feel that need.
    b. I want to move in that direction, but I feel a little uptight about it.
    c. Strong men stand on their own.
    d. Giving and receiving other men's support is easier said than done.

12. Focusing on the members of your group one at a time, share the strengths you see in that person which make him valuable in the Lord's army.

his own spear. 22Such were the exploits of Benaiah son of Jehoiada; he too was as famous as the three mighty men. 23He was held in greater honor than any of the Thirty, but he was not included among the Three. And David put him in charge of his bodyguard.

24Among the Thirty were:
Asahel the brother of Joab,
Elhanan son of Dodo from Bethlehem,
25Shammah the Harodite,
Elika the Harodite,
26Helez the Paltite,
Ira son of Ikkesh from Tekoa,
27Abiezer from Anathoth,
Mebunnai[a] the Hushathite,
28Zalmon the Ahohite,
Maharai the Netophathite,
29Heled[b] son of Baanah the Netophathite,
Ithai son of Ribai from Gibeah in Benjamin,
30Benaiah the Pirathonite,
Hiddai[c] from the ravines of Gaash,
31Abi-Albon the Arbathite,
Azmaveth the Barhumite,
32Eliahba the Shaalbonite,
the sons of Jashen,
Jonathan 33son of[d] Shammah the Hararite,
Ahiam son of Sharar[e] the Hararite,
34Eliphelet son of Ahasbai the Maacathite,
Eliam son of Ahithophel the Gilonite,
35Hezro the Carmelite,
Paarai the Arbite,
36Igal son of Nathan from Zobah,
the son of Hagri,[f]
37Zelek the Ammonite,
Naharai the Beerothite, the armor-bearer of Joab son of Zeruiah,
38Ira the Ithrite,
Gareb the Ithrite,
39and Uriah the Hittite.
There were thirty-seven in all.

David Counts the Fighting Men

24 Again the anger of the LORD burned against Israel, and he incited David against them, saying, "Go and take a census of Israel and Judah."

2So the king said to Joab and the army commanders[g] with him, "Go throughout the tribes of Israel from Dan to Beersheba and enroll the fighting men, so that I may know how many there are."

3But Joab replied to the king, "May the LORD your God multiply the troops a hundred times over, and may the eyes of my lord the king see it. But why does my lord the king want to do such a thing?"

4The king's word, however, overruled Joab and the army com-

a27 Hebrew; some Septuagint manuscripts (see also 1 Chron. 11:29) *Sibbecai*
b29 Some Hebrew manuscripts and Vulgate (see also 1 Chron. 11:30); most Hebrew manuscripts *Heleb*   c30 Hebrew; some Septuagint manuscripts (see also 1 Chron. 11:32) *Hurai*   d33 Some Septuagint manuscripts (see also 1 Chron. 11:34); Hebrew does not have *son of*.   e33 Hebrew; some Septuagint manuscripts (see also 1 Chron. 11:35) *Sacar*   f36 Some Septuagint manuscripts (see also 1 Chron. 11:38); Hebrew *Haggadi*   g2 Septuagint (see also verse 4 and 1 Chron. 21:2); Hebrew *Joab the army commander*

strengths would you need to develop to be among your King's mighty warriors? **2.** Where God has placed you now, what would it mean for you to "stand your ground"? What major obstacles or opposition would you be able to strike down with God's help? In the near future, in what battle would you like to see God give you the victory? **3.** Do you feel like you are fighting any battles all by yourself? In what way might your small group provide reinforcements?

1. When you were first learning math, what did you use: (a) Computers? (b) Calculators? (c) Adding machines? (d) Slide rules? (e) Abacus? (e) Fingers? **2.** Did your parents ever make you "choose your consequences"? What difficult choices do you remember making?

This story presents us with many theological and ethical problems as we seek insights into David's dilemma. **1.** What prompted David's request to take a census (vv. 1–2): (a) God's anger? (b) Satan's ruse (see 1Ch 21:1)? (c) David's pride? (d) David's insecurity? (e) Some external threat? **2.** What does your answer say about who lies behind evil acts (see Jas 1:13–15)? How could a "man after

God's own heart" be duped by Satan? **3.** As for the census itself (vv 5–9), what's involved in terms of time, money and manpower? **4.** Why is David so conscience-stricken (v. 10)? Is taking a census always wrong, sinful or a foolish waste of human resources (see Nu 1:2–3; 26:2–4)? Didn't the Lord ultimately direct him to do so (v. 1)? **5.** If the Lord did ask David to take the census, then why the subsequent punishment (vv. 11–17)? Why three options? And why punish the people for something *David* ordered? **6.** Is God working at cross-purposes when he grieves over the punishment inflicted on Israel by his own angel (v. 16)?

1. In what ways are you proud of your accomplishments, acquisitions or responsibilities? Behind the proud image you show the world, are you also insecure? Where are you tempted to lean upon the strength of your superior assets rather than in weakness depend on God? **2.** Though you may have prayed for *strength* in order to achieve great things for God, where has God made you *weak*, that you might learn to humbly obey him?

manders; so they left the presence of the king to enroll the fighting men of Israel.

[5]After crossing the Jordan, they camped near Aroer, south of the town in the gorge, and then went through Gad and on to Jazer. [6]They went to Gilead and the region of Tahtim Hodshi, and on to Dan Jaan and around toward Sidon. [7]Then they went toward the fortress of Tyre and all the towns of the Hivites and Canaanites. Finally, they went on to Beersheba in the Negev of Judah.

[8]After they had gone through the entire land, they came back to Jerusalem at the end of nine months and twenty days.

[9]Joab reported the number of the fighting men to the king: In Israel there were eight hundred thousand able-bodied men who could handle a sword, and in Judah five hundred thousand.

[10]David was conscience-stricken after he had counted the fighting men, and he said to the LORD, "I have sinned greatly in what I have done. Now, O LORD, I beg you, take away the guilt of your servant. I have done a very foolish thing."

[11]Before David got up the next morning, the word of the LORD had come to Gad the prophet, David's seer: [12]"Go and tell David, 'This is what the LORD says: I am giving you three options. Choose one of them for me to carry out against you.'"

[13]So Gad went to David and said to him, "Shall there come upon you three[a] years of famine in your land? Or three months of fleeing from your enemies while they pursue you? Or three days of plague in your land? Now then, think it over and decide how I should answer the one who sent me."

[14]David said to Gad, "I am in deep distress. Let us fall into the hands of the LORD, for his mercy is great; but do not let me fall into the hands of men."

[15]So the LORD sent a plague on Israel from that morning until the end of the time designated, and seventy thousand of the people from Dan to Beersheba died. [16]When the angel stretched out his hand to destroy Jerusalem, the LORD was grieved because of the calamity and said to the angel who was afflicting the people, "Enough! Withdraw your hand." The angel of the LORD was then at the threshing floor of Araunah the Jebusite.

[17]When David saw the angel who was striking down the people, he said to the LORD, "I am the one who has sinned and done wrong. These are but sheep. What have they done? Let your hand fall upon me and my family."

David Builds an Altar

[18]On that day Gad went to David and said to him, "Go up and build an altar to the LORD on the threshing floor of Araunah the Jebusite." [19]So David went up, as the LORD had commanded through Gad. [20]When Araunah looked and saw the king and his men coming toward him, he went out and bowed down before the king with his face to the ground.

[21]Araunah said, "Why has my lord the king come to his servant?"

"To buy your threshing floor," David answered, "so I can build an altar to the LORD, that the plague on the people may be stopped."

[22]Araunah said to David, "Let my lord the king take whatever pleases him and offer it up. Here are oxen for the burnt offering, and here are threshing sledges and ox yokes for the wood. [23]O king, Araunah gives all this to the king." Araunah also said to him, "May the LORD your God accept you."

1. Who is the most generous person in your family? Has this person ever given you something for free for which you've insisted on paying? **2.** Were you raised in a strict "each-pays-his-own-way" family? Or in a "we-are-all-in-this-together" family, one where dependency on a certain bread-winner or benefactor was okay as part of a team effort? What part did you play in that?

1. When and where and why is David commanded to build an altar (v. 18)? What is significant about that place (see v. 16)? What is significant about God's command following David's prayer (v. 17)? **2.** You are Araunah: The plague has reached your threshing

---

[a]13 Septuagint (see also 1 Chron. 21:12); Hebrew *seven*

²⁴But the king replied to Araunah, "No, I insist on paying you for it. I will not sacrifice to the LORD my God burnt offerings that cost me nothing."

So David bought the threshing floor and the oxen and paid fifty shekelsᵃ of silver for them. ²⁵David built an altar to the LORD there and sacrificed burnt offerings and fellowship offerings.ᵇ Then the LORD answered prayer in behalf of the land, and the plague on Israel was stopped.

floor, and David wants to buy it to build an altar there. What are you feeling about all this attention? Would you have responded as Araunah does (vv. 22–23)? **3.** David might have expropriated the man's property, or paid a mere pittance for it, as he was king (see 1Sa 8:14). But what does David do instead and why (v. 24)? **4.** What results do the sacrifices bring (v. 25)? What does this say about the relationship between sin and suffering? Between sin and sacrifice? What bearing does this have on your understanding of Jesus' death for our sin and suffering?

♡ **1.** Are you willing to say to your King, "Take whatever pleases you"? What do you fear he might take that you want to keep? **2.** The Lord God accepted David and his sacrifice. How about you? Has the Lord your God accepted you? How do you know for sure? **3.** As a final offering of worship and fellowship as a group, try praising the Lord for all of his attributes which he brings to mind as you pray. Take turns giving thanks for what God has taught you through the study of 2 Samuel.

ᵃ24 That is, about 1 1/4 pounds (about 0.6 kilogram)   ᵇ25 Traditionally *peace offerings*

INTRODUCTION to
1 KINGS

Book Study Outline: If you are using 1 Kings for a study course, here is a 7- or 13-week outline. Use the questions in the margin for your group agenda:

🍵 start meeting / 15 min.

📖 read & discuss Bible / 30 min.

♡ close meeting / 15–45 min.

Refer to the Questions and Answers in the front of this Bible for more information.

7-week plan	13-week plan	Personal Reading	Group Study Passage
1	1	1:1–2:12	1:28–53/Solomon Made King
	2	2:13–3:28	3:1–28/Solomon Gets Wisdom
2	3	4:1–6:38	6:1–38/Temple Built
	4	7:1–8:66	8:22–66/Temple Dedicated
3	5	9:1–10:13	10:1–13/Queen of Sheba
	6	10:14–11:13	10:23–11:13/Solomon's Wives
4	7	11:14–12:24	12:1–24/House Divided
	8	12:25–14:31	14:1–20/Jeroboam Doomed
5	9	15:1–17:24	17:1–24/Widow at Zarephath
	10	16:29–18:46	18:16–40/Elijah vs. Baal
6	11	19:1–20:43	19:1–18/God's Whisper
	12	21:1–29	21:1–29/Ahab vs. Naboth
7	13	22:1–53	22:1–28/Micaiah vs. Ahab

Author: The author of 1 and 2 Kings is not known, but the three literary sources that are named suggest multiple authors and editors: "the Annals of Solomon" (1Ki 11:41); "the Annals of the Kings of Israel" (1Ki 14:19; 2Ki 15:31); and "the Annals of the Kings of Judah" (1Ki 14:29; 2Ki 24:5).

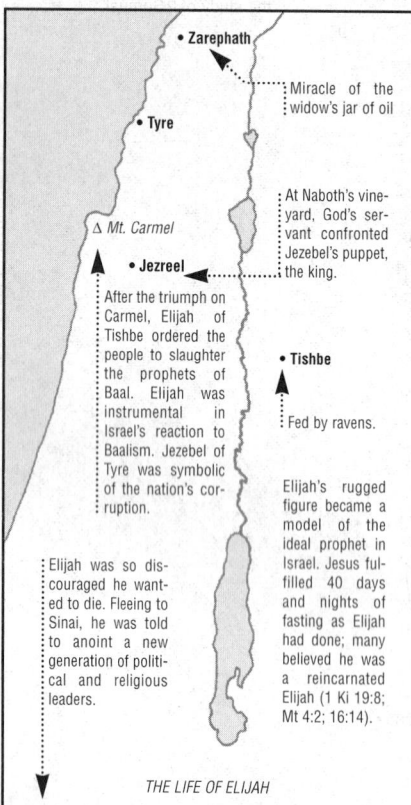

THE LIFE OF ELIJAH

- Zarephath

Miracle of the widow's jar of oil

- Tyre

At Naboth's vineyard, God's servant confronted Jezebel's puppet, the king.

△ Mt. Carmel

- Jezreel

After the triumph on Carmel, Elijah of Tishbe ordered the people to slaughter the prophets of Baal. Elijah was instrumental in Israel's reaction to Baalism. Jezebel of Tyre was symbolic of the nation's corruption.

- Tishbe

Fed by ravens.

Elijah's rugged figure became a model of the ideal prophet in Israel. Jesus fulfilled 40 days and nights of fasting as Elijah had done; many believed he was a reincarnated Elijah (1 Ki 19:8; Mt 4:2; 16:14).

Elijah was so discouraged he wanted to die. Fleeing to Sinai, he was told to anoint a new generation of political and religious leaders.

Date: The account of Jehoiachin's release from prison in 2 Kings 25:27–30 means that the final form of Kings was written after 561 B.C. Nonetheless, the source materials could have been written at the time of the events they describe. These events span almost 400 years.

Theme: Israel's Golden Age—its coronation and corrosion.

Historical Background: Solomon reaps the reward of David's military success. He inherits peace and security and so launches Israel's "Golden Age." Following Solomon's death, the division of the country into the two separate nations of Israel and Judah brings an end to this era of strength. Both nations then enter a period of decline.

Characteristics: The atmosphere in the early chapters of 1 Kings is one of grandeur as Solomon's wealth, wisdom and fame is set forth. But Solomon's end is most pitiful, as he turns to foreign wives and their false gods. Jeroboam follows suit, as do other kings of northern Israel and southern Judah. All told, 19 kings in the North and 20 rulers in the South are alternately profiled in 1 Kings. Tracking the rise and fall of both kingdoms can be confusing, but it helps to remember that none of Israel's kings were faithful to God during this time, while only half of Judah's rulers showed any faithfulness.

1 Kings

Adonijah Sets Himself Up as King

1 When King David was old and well advanced in years, he could not keep warm even when they put covers over him. ²So his servants said to him, "Let us look for a young virgin to attend the king and take care of him. She can lie beside him so that our lord the king may keep warm."

³Then they searched throughout Israel for a beautiful girl and found Abishag, a Shunammite, and brought her to the king. ⁴The girl was very beautiful; she took care of the king and waited on him, but the king had no intimate relations with her.

⁵Now Adonijah, whose mother was Haggith, put himself forward and said, "I will be king." So he got chariots and horses*a* ready, with fifty men to run ahead of him. ⁶(His father had never interfered with him by asking, "Why do you behave as you do?" He was also very handsome and was born next after Absalom.)

⁷Adonijah conferred with Joab son of Zeruiah and with Abiathar the priest, and they gave him their support. ⁸But Zadok the priest, Benaiah son of Jehoiada, Nathan the prophet, Shimei and Rei*b* and David's special guard did not join Adonijah.

⁹Adonijah then sacrificed sheep, cattle and fattened calves at the Stone of Zoheleth near En Rogel. He invited all his brothers, the king's sons, and all the men of Judah who were royal officials, ¹⁰but he did not invite Nathan the prophet or Benaiah or the special guard or his brother Solomon.

¹¹Then Nathan asked Bathsheba, Solomon's mother, "Have you not heard that Adonijah, the son of Haggith, has become king without our lord David's knowing it? ¹²Now then, let me advise you how you can save your own life and the life of your son Solomon. ¹³Go in to King David and say to him, 'My lord the king, did you not swear to me your servant: "Surely Solomon your son shall be king after me, and he will sit on my throne"? Why then has Adonijah become king?' ¹⁴While you are still there talking to the king, I will come in and confirm what you have said."

¹⁵So Bathsheba went to see the aged king in his room, where Abishag the Shunammite was attending him. ¹⁶Bathsheba bowed low and knelt before the king.

"What is it you want?" the king asked.

¹⁷She said to him, "My lord, you yourself swore to me your servant by the LORD your God: 'Solomon your son shall be king after me, and he will sit on my throne.' ¹⁸But now Adonijah has become king, and you, my lord the king, do not know about it. ¹⁹He has sacrificed great numbers of cattle, fattened calves, and sheep, and has invited all the king's sons, Abiathar the priest and Joab the commander of the army, but he has not invited Solomon your servant. ²⁰My lord the king, the eyes of all Israel are on you, to learn from you who will sit on the throne of my lord the king after him. ²¹Otherwise, as soon as my lord the king is laid to rest with his fathers, I and my son Solomon will be treated as criminals."

²²While she was still speaking with the king, Nathan the prophet arrived. ²³And they told the king, "Nathan the prophet is here." So

a5 Or charioteers   b8 Or and his friends

---

1. When you sleep, do you like it cool and breezy or warm and toasty? How does your roommate like it? Does that ever create a problem? 2. Were your parents strict or lenient with regard to your activities, whereabouts or friends? How so? 3. Were you ever shocked or surprised to find yourself not invited to some wedding or social occasion? Did you attend anyway?

1. What is David's condition (vv. 1–4)? To what is an aging king vulnerable? 2. Who arranges for Abishag to wait on David? Why not let one of his wives perform the bed-warming project? 3. Is the monarchy in Israel hereditary (see 2Sa 5:1–4)? Why hasn't David publicly named his successor? 4. What are the pros and cons of making Adonijah king (vv. 5–10)? Is he a champion schemer or an anxious heir apparent? 5. Why does Nathan oppose Adonijah and his plan (vv. 11–14)? Why does Nathan approach Bathsheba? What's the risk of getting involved? 6. What are Nathan and Bathsheba concerned about? What might happen to them if Adonijah comes to power? What will happen to Zadok and Benaiah? 7. How is Nathan's plan supposed to sway the king (vv. 15–21)? How does Nathan's speech compare with Bathsheba's (vv. 17–27)? How would you feel if you were David?

1. In what ways do you feel more vulnerable now than five years ago? What bothers you most about aging: (a) Declining health? (b) Loss of youth? (c) Loss of friends and relations? (d) The inevitability of death? (e) Slow narrowing of options and possibilities? Other? 2. How competitive are you? Would you run over people in order to win? Walk over them? Ask them to kindly step aside? What ambition have you yet to fulfill? 3. On a scale of 1 ("Do it my way") to 10 ("Tell me what to do, please"), rate your need to control. Do you try to control things directly, or do you sway people indirectly? 4. Do you have a family member you don't get along with? What happened? Is reconciliation possible?

Desirable? **5.** In what way do you need to "set your eyes upon your King" for direction at this point in your life?

☕ **1.** What promise did your parents make when you were a child that you can still remember today? Were they big on keeping promises or more forgetful? How long could you live on a "promise alone" before you demanded its fulfillment? **2.** Have you ever felt cheated out of something that was rightfully yours? What do you do when you feel your rights are being violated?

📖 **1.** What is Bathsheba's mood as she comes before David (vv. 28–31)? On hearing David's promise? Knowing David will soon die, and being ambitious for her son, why does Bathsheba want David to live forever? **2.** What ceremonies are involved in the coronation of Solomon (vv. 33–35, 38–40)? What significance do they have? What did Jesus mean by these very same symbols (see Mt 21:1–5)? **3.** Who are Benaiah, the Kerethites and the Pelethites (vv. 36–38; see 2Sa 20:7,23)? What role do they play here? Whose job does Benaiah want? **4.** What is significant about the timing of Solomon's inauguration (v. 41)? How do the various people (townspeople, Jonathan, David's officials, David, Adonijah's guests) respond to news of this event (vv. 40–49)? **5.** Was Solomon the eldest son of David (see 1Ch 3:1–5)? Why is David skipping over Adonijah? **6.** Why does Adonijah go to the altar (v. 50; see Ex 21:12–14)? Is Solomon's response (vv. 52–53) fair or too soft? Should Adonijah be suspicious? Why?

❤️ **1.** Is the Lord "with" you in ways you can feel and know? Do you need more of that kind of "witness"? Why or why not? **2.** When you see a schemer at work, do you step in and get involved? Or keep quiet and mind your own business? Why? **3.** Are there any distant rumbles (worrisome rumors,

---

he went before the king and bowed with his face to the ground.

²⁴Nathan said, "Have you, my lord the king, declared that Adonijah shall be king after you, and that he will sit on your throne? ²⁵Today he has gone down and sacrificed great numbers of cattle, fattened calves, and sheep. He has invited all the king's sons, the commanders of the army and Abiathar the priest. Right now they are eating and drinking with him and saying, 'Long live King Adonijah!' ²⁶But me your servant, and Zadok the priest, and Benaiah son of Jehoiada, and your servant Solomon he did not invite. ²⁷Is this something my lord the king has done without letting his servants know who should sit on the throne of my lord the king after him?"

David Makes Solomon King

²⁸Then King David said, "Call in Bathsheba." So she came into the king's presence and stood before him.

²⁹The king then took an oath: "As surely as the Lord lives, who has delivered me out of every trouble, ³⁰I will surely carry out today what I swore to you by the Lord, the God of Israel: Solomon your son shall be king after me, and he will sit on my throne in my place."

³¹Then Bathsheba bowed low with her face to the ground and, kneeling before the king, said, "May my lord King David live forever!"

³²King David said, "Call in Zadok the priest, Nathan the prophet and Benaiah son of Jehoiada." When they came before the king, ³³he said to them: "Take your lord's servants with you and set Solomon my son on my own mule and take him down to Gihon. ³⁴There have Zadok the priest and Nathan the prophet anoint him king over Israel. Blow the trumpet and shout, 'Long live King Solomon!' ³⁵Then you are to go up with him, and he is to come and sit on my throne and reign in my place. I have appointed him ruler over Israel and Judah."

³⁶Benaiah son of Jehoiada answered the king, "Amen! May the Lord, the God of my lord the king, so declare it. ³⁷As the Lord was with my lord the king, so may he be with Solomon to make his throne even greater than the throne of my lord King David!"

³⁸So Zadok the priest, Nathan the prophet, Benaiah son of Jehoiada, the Kerethites and the Pelethites went down and put Solomon on King David's mule and escorted him to Gihon. ³⁹Zadok the priest took the horn of oil from the sacred tent and anointed Solomon. Then they sounded the trumpet and all the people shouted, "Long live King Solomon!" ⁴⁰And all the people went up after him, playing flutes and rejoicing greatly, so that the ground shook with the sound.

⁴¹Adonijah and all the guests who were with him heard it as they were finishing their feast. On hearing the sound of the trumpet, Joab asked, "What's the meaning of all the noise in the city?"

⁴²Even as he was speaking, Jonathan son of Abiathar the priest arrived. Adonijah said, "Come in. A worthy man like you must be bringing good news."

⁴³"Not at all!" Jonathan answered. "Our lord King David has made Solomon king. ⁴⁴The king has sent with him Zadok the priest, Nathan the prophet, Benaiah son of Jehoiada, the Kerethites and the Pelethites, and they have put him on the king's mule, ⁴⁵and Zadok the priest and Nathan the prophet have anointed him king at Gihon. From there they have gone up cheering, and the city resounds with it. That's the noise you hear. ⁴⁶Moreover, Solomon has taken his seat on the royal throne. ⁴⁷Also, the royal officials

have come to congratulate our lord King David, saying, 'May your God make Solomon's name more famous than yours and his throne greater than yours!' And the king bowed in worship on his bed [48]and said, 'Praise be to the LORD, the God of Israel, who has allowed my eyes to see a successor on my throne today.'"

[49]At this, all Adonijah's guests rose in alarm and dispersed. [50]But Adonijah, in fear of Solomon, went and took hold of the horns of the altar. [51]Then Solomon was told, "Adonijah is afraid of King Solomon and is clinging to the horns of the altar. He says, 'Let King Solomon swear to me today that he will not put his servant to death with the sword.'"

[52]Solomon replied, "If he shows himself to be a worthy man, not a hair of his head will fall to the ground; but if evil is found in him, he will die." [53]Then King Solomon sent men, and they brought him down from the altar. And Adonijah came and bowed down to King Solomon, and Solomon said, "Go to your home."

David's Charge to Solomon

2 When the time drew near for David to die, he gave a charge to Solomon his son.

[2]"I am about to go the way of all the earth," he said. "So be strong, show yourself a man, [3]and observe what the LORD your God requires: Walk in his ways, and keep his decrees and commands, his laws and requirements, as written in the Law of Moses, so that you may prosper in all you do and wherever you go, [4]and that the LORD may keep his promise to me: 'If your descendants watch how they live, and if they walk faithfully before me with all their heart and soul, you will never fail to have a man on the throne of Israel.'

[5]"Now you yourself know what Joab son of Zeruiah did to me— what he did to the two commanders of Israel's armies, Abner son of Ner and Amasa son of Jether. He killed them, shedding their blood in peacetime as if in battle, and with that blood stained the belt around his waist and the sandals on his feet. [6]Deal with him according to your wisdom, but do not let his gray head go down to the grave[a] in peace.

[7]"But show kindness to the sons of Barzillai of Gilead and let them be among those who eat at your table. They stood by me when I fled from your brother Absalom.

[8]"And remember, you have with you Shimei son of Gera, the Benjamite from Bahurim, who called down bitter curses on me the day I went to Mahanaim. When he came down to meet me at the Jordan, I swore to him by the LORD: 'I will not put you to death by the sword.' [9]But now, do not consider him innocent. You are a man of wisdom; you will know what to do to him. Bring his gray head down to the grave in blood."

[10]Then David rested with his fathers and was buried in the City of David. [11]He had reigned forty years over Israel—seven years in Hebron and thirty-three in Jerusalem. [12]So Solomon sat on the throne of his father David, and his rule was firmly established.

Solomon's Throne Established

[13]Now Adonijah, the son of Haggith, went to Bathsheba, Solomon's mother. Bathsheba asked him, "Do you come peacefully?"

He answered, "Yes, peacefully." [14]Then he added, "I have something to say to you."

"You may say it," she replied.

[15]"As you know," he said, "the kingdom was mine. All Israel

[a]6 Hebrew *Sheol*; also in verse 9

---

political maneuvering) which are causing you concern? Can the group help? **4.** In your family, are you the eldest child, the youngest or in any other way "favored" by your parents? How did your parents' fairness (or lack of it) affect you?

In what areas, or for what things, do people seek out your advice? What parental advice do you still remember receiving (or giving)?

1. What kind of king does David want Solomon to be (vv. 2–4)? What does this say about David? **2.** When was David given the promise referred to in verse 4 (see 2Sa 7:12–13,16)? Why does he want it fulfilled? **3.** What kind of advice does David give in verses 5–9? What divisions always plagued him (see 2Sa 2:4,10–17; 5:3–5; 15:13–14)? **4.** Why did Joab kill Abner (see 2Sa 2:22–24) and Amasa (see 2Sa 17:24–26; 19:10–13)? Is David really against vengeance? **5.** Why did Shimei curse David (vv. 8–9; see 2Sa 16:5–8)? How will David set aside his oath?

1. Do you find it hard to "forgive and forget"? Do you hold grudges? How does the desire for vengeance, even if justified, affect your life? **2.** What factions do you find at your church? Are political games played? Does unity mean conformity?

---

1. Was there a member of the opposite sex you once wanted to attract? What silly, abnormal or crazy thing did you do? Was he or she impressed? **2.** Were you ever a petty thief? Small-time crook? Minor league bandit? Friend of bandits? Ever taken in police custody? Ever give police a hard time? **3.** What status symbol are you most tempted to pursue? Why is it appealing?

📖 **1.** Why does Adonijah want Abishag (vv. 13–17; see 1:3–4)? Is he a sore loser? Secretly in love? What did sleeping with a king's wife or concubine symbolize (see 2Sa 12:7–8; 16:21–22)? **2.** Why does he make his request through Bathsheba? What does Solomon see behind his brother's request? **3.** Why does Solomon punish Abiathar and Joab immediately after Adonijah's request? Why does Abiathar deserve to die (v. 26)? Why does Solomon spare him? **4.** Why does Joab flee in verse 28? Why doesn't Benaiah kill Joab immediately (v. 30; see Ex 21:14)? **5.** What justification does Solomon offer for Joab's execution (vv. 31–33)? Is Solomon acting righteously, or is he simply eliminating the opposition to his government? **6.** How does Solomon fill the newly created vacancies in his administration (v. 35)? Does this surprise you? **7.** Why does Shimei respond to Solomon so warmly (vv. 36–38)? Why does Solomon sentence him to house arrest? Why do you think Shimei personally pursues the slaves: (a) He had no one else to do it? (b) He had forgotten the ban? (c) He's testing the new king's mettle? (d) He thinks he's immune from further punishment? **8.** How does Solomon justify Shimei's execution? Compared to when this chapter started, is Solomon's kingdom now more secure? Less naive? More gutsy?

♡ **1.** Solomon acts with traditional wisdom in the affairs of state: "Do unto others before they do unto you." Do you like this unflattering but popular motto? Is it unreasonable to protect yourself? What should the Christian motto be? **2.** In your requests of God, can you ever ask too much of him? What guidelines can keep your ambitions in check? **3.** Many modern governments still use the tactics of assassination, cruel and inhumane punishment and sentencing without trial. This does not support the notion that modern society has improved in the past few centuries. In what sense can it be said mankind is making progress in human rights? In what sense are we no further advanced than the ancient Israelites? **4.** In what instances are you too soft on "enemies"? Too evasive on important decisions?

looked to me as their king. But things changed, and the kingdom has gone to my brother; for it has come to him from the LORD. ¹⁶Now I have one request to make of you. Do not refuse me."

"You may make it," she said.

¹⁷So he continued, "Please ask King Solomon—he will not refuse you—to give me Abishag the Shunammite as my wife."

¹⁸"Very well," Bathsheba replied, "I will speak to the king for you."

¹⁹When Bathsheba went to King Solomon to speak to him for Adonijah, the king stood up to meet her, bowed down to her and sat down on his throne. He had a throne brought for the king's mother, and she sat down at his right hand.

²⁰"I have one small request to make of you," she said. "Do not refuse me."

The king replied, "Make it, my mother; I will not refuse you."

²¹So she said, "Let Abishag the Shunammite be given in marriage to your brother Adonijah."

²²King Solomon answered his mother, "Why do you request Abishag the Shunammite for Adonijah? You might as well request the kingdom for him—after all, he is my older brother—yes, for him and for Abiathar the priest and Joab son of Zeruiah!"

²³Then King Solomon swore by the LORD: "May God deal with me, be it ever so severely, if Adonijah does not pay with his life for this request! ²⁴And now, as surely as the LORD lives—he who has established me securely on the throne of my father David and has founded a dynasty for me as he promised—Adonijah shall be put to death today!" ²⁵So King Solomon gave orders to Benaiah son of Jehoiada, and he struck down Adonijah and he died.

²⁶To Abiathar the priest the king said, "Go back to your fields in Anathoth. You deserve to die, but I will not put you to death now, because you carried the ark of the Sovereign LORD before my father David and shared all my father's hardships." ²⁷So Solomon removed Abiathar from the priesthood of the LORD, fulfilling the word the LORD had spoken at Shiloh about the house of Eli.

²⁸When the news reached Joab, who had conspired with Adonijah though not with Absalom, he fled to the tent of the LORD and took hold of the horns of the altar. ²⁹King Solomon was told that Joab had fled to the tent of the LORD and was beside the altar. Then Solomon ordered Benaiah son of Jehoiada, "Go, strike him down!"

³⁰So Benaiah entered the tent of the LORD and said to Joab, "The king says, 'Come out!'"

But he answered, "No, I will die here."

Benaiah reported to the king, "This is how Joab answered me."

³¹Then the king commanded Benaiah, "Do as he says. Strike him down and bury him, and so clear me and my father's house of the guilt of the innocent blood that Joab shed. ³²The LORD will repay him for the blood he shed, because without the knowledge of my father David he attacked two men and killed them with the sword. Both of them—Abner son of Ner, commander of Israel's army, and Amasa son of Jether, commander of Judah's army—were better men and more upright than he. ³³May the guilt of their blood rest on the head of Joab and his descendants forever. But on David and his descendants, his house and his throne, may there be the LORD's peace forever."

³⁴So Benaiah son of Jehoiada went up and struck down Joab and killed him, and he was buried on his own land*a* in the desert.

a 34 Or buried in his tomb

³⁵The king put Benaiah son of Jehoiada over the army in Joab's position and replaced Abiathar with Zadok the priest.

³⁶Then the king sent for Shimei and said to him, "Build yourself a house in Jerusalem and live there, but do not go anywhere else. ³⁷The day you leave and cross the Kidron Valley, you can be sure you will die; your blood will be on your own head."

³⁸Shimei answered the king, "What you say is good. Your servant will do as my lord the king has said." And Shimei stayed in Jerusalem for a long time.

³⁹But three years later, two of Shimei's slaves ran off to Achish son of Maacah, king of Gath, and Shimei was told, "Your slaves are in Gath." ⁴⁰At this, he saddled his donkey and went to Achish at Gath in search of his slaves. So Shimei went away and brought the slaves back from Gath.

⁴¹When Solomon was told that Shimei had gone from Jerusalem to Gath and had returned, ⁴²the king summoned Shimei and said to him, "Did I not make you swear by the LORD and warn you, 'On the day you leave to go anywhere else, you can be sure you will die'? At that time you said to me, 'What you say is good. I will obey.' ⁴³Why then did you not keep your oath to the LORD and obey the command I gave you?"

⁴⁴The king also said to Shimei, "You know in your heart all the wrong you did to my father David. Now the LORD will repay you for your wrongdoing. ⁴⁵But King Solomon will be blessed, and David's throne will remain secure before the LORD forever."

⁴⁶Then the king gave the order to Benaiah son of Jehoiada, and he went out and struck Shimei down and killed him.

The kingdom was now firmly established in Solomon's hands.

Solomon Asks for Wisdom

3 Solomon made an alliance with Pharaoh king of Egypt and married his daughter. He brought her to the City of David until he finished building his palace and the temple of the LORD, and the wall around Jerusalem. ²The people, however, were still sacrificing at the high places, because a temple had not yet been built for the Name of the LORD. ³Solomon showed his love for the LORD by walking according to the statutes of his father David, except that he offered sacrifices and burned incense on the high places.

⁴The king went to Gibeon to offer sacrifices, for that was the most important high place, and Solomon offered a thousand burnt offerings on that altar. ⁵At Gibeon the LORD appeared to Solomon during the night in a dream, and God said, "Ask for whatever you want me to give you."

⁶Solomon answered, "You have shown great kindness to your servant, my father David, because he was faithful to you and righteous and upright in heart. You have continued this great kindness to him and have given him a son to sit on his throne this very day.

⁷"Now, O LORD my God, you have made your servant king in place of my father David. But I am only a little child and do not know how to carry out my duties. ⁸Your servant is here among the people you have chosen, a great people, too numerous to count or number. ⁹So give your servant a discerning heart to govern your people and to distinguish between right and wrong. For who is able to govern this great people of yours?"

¹⁰The Lord was pleased that Solomon had asked for this. ¹¹So God said to him, "Since you have asked for this and not for long life or wealth for yourself, nor have asked for the death of your enemies but for discernment in administering justice, ¹²I will do what you have asked. I will give you a wise and discerning heart, so that

Too hopeful of pleasing everyone and offending no one?

1. Do you remember dreams? Nightmares? Daydreams? Describe one. 2. Which of these gifts would you give your best friend—fame, wealth, or long life? Which would you like most?

1. Why does Solomon marry a Gentile (v. 1)? Should the politics of Israel differ from that of other nations (see Dt 7:3–4)? How so? 2. Why were the "high places" built (v. 2; see 1Sa 9:12–14)? Since there is no temple, why is there a problem with Solomon's sacrifices at high places (v. 3)? 3. Why does God use dreams to communicate (vv. 5–15; see Ge 20:3; Nu 12:6–8)? Why not be more direct? 4. What is Solomon's agenda as king? Whose interests does he have at heart and why? 5. With what kind of prayers does God seem pleased (vv. 11–12)? 6. What else does God promise Solomon (vv. 13–14)? Why? What saying of Jesus echoes this (see Mt 6:33)? 7. Why does Solomon worship and throw a party (v. 15)?

1. Have you ever sensed God's will in a dream? How does God's word come to you? Do you need a special "appearance" from God sometimes to help you

cope? **2.** Whose interests are close to your heart? Do your own needs weigh heavy? Or are you so concerned about everyone else that you don't take care of yourself? Does anyone have your interests at heart? Who does?

---

1. In what area are you considered "wise"? **2.** Who's your favorite detective? Ever try any detective work yourself?

1. Why should the new king worry about a dispute among prostitutes? What does Solomon know about mothers and babies? **2.** What kind of court system does Israel have (see 2Sa 12:1–6; 14:4ff)? How would this case have been settled in a modern court? What different ideas does your group hold about the power of government (vv. 24–25)? **3.** For what quality is Solomon testing the women (v. 26)? Why not test them for honesty? **4.** Would this story have filled you with awe (v. 28)? Why do you think Israel was so impressed?

there will never have been anyone like you, nor will there ever be. [13]Moreover, I will give you what you have not asked for—both riches and honor—so that in your lifetime you will have no equal among kings. [14]And if you walk in my ways and obey my statutes and commands as David your father did, I will give you a long life." [15]Then Solomon awoke—and he realized it had been a dream.

He returned to Jerusalem, stood before the ark of the Lord's covenant and sacrificed burnt offerings and fellowship offerings.[a] Then he gave a feast for all his court.

A Wise Ruling

[16]Now two prostitutes came to the king and stood before him. [17]One of them said, "My lord, this woman and I live in the same house. I had a baby while she was there with me. [18]The third day after my child was born, this woman also had a baby. We were alone; there was no one in the house but the two of us.

[19]"During the night this woman's son died because she lay on him. [20]So she got up in the middle of the night and took my son from my side while I your servant was asleep. She put him by her breast and put her dead son by my breast. [21]The next morning, I got up to nurse my son—and he was dead! But when I looked at him closely in the morning light, I saw that it wasn't the son I had borne."

[22]The other woman said, "No! The living one is my son; the dead one is yours."

But the first one insisted, "No! The dead one is yours; the living one is mine." And so they argued before the king.

[a]15 Traditionally *peace offerings*

---

1 Kings 3:1–28   SOLOMON'S WISDOM

Solomon, probably only 20 years old, has just succeeded his father David as Israel's king.

1. What were Solomon's motives in the beginning phase of his reign?
   a. political   d. compromising
   b. romantic   e. righteous
   c. God-fearing   f. wise

2. Why did the Lord tell Solomon to, "Ask for whatever you want"?
   a. to reward him
   b. to test him
   c. to honor his father David
   d. to teach him to depend on God
   e. because God loves to give

3. Why did Solomon ask for wisdom?
   a. to walk in his father's footsteps
   b. to avoid his father's mistakes
   c. because of his young age and his inexperience
   d. because he was humble
   e. because he felt insecure as a king

4. By giving Solomon more than he asked for, God was saying:
   a. "I'm pleased with you."

b. "You can be trusted with riches."
c. "I love to bless you."
d. "Seek first my kingdom and all these things will be given to you."

5. In the dispute between the two women, what did the mother of the living baby want? What did the mother of the dead baby want?

6. Why did Solomon call for a sword?
   a. He was impatient.
   b. He was barbaric.
   c. He was forcing the issue.
   d. He had a plan.

7. What was Solomon's priority in this decision?
   a. the mother's feelings
   b. the child's welfare
   c. ending the conflict
   d. doing the right thing

8. How would you describe the way you make tough decisions?
   a. hesitant   e. logical
   b. quick   f. emotional
   c. deliberate   g. firm
   d. impulsive   h. wishy-washy

9. How have you gained wisdom in your life?
   a. through experience
   b. through studying the Bible
   c. from other people
   d. by asking God for it
   e. I'm not sure.

10. What do you hope to receive as a side benefit of living according to God's wisdom?
   a. prosperity   e. fulfillment
   b. a long life   f. peace of mind
   c. happiness   g. success
   d. confidence   h. companionship

11. What present situation do you need God's wisdom to deal with?

12. What does Solomon's example say to you about your dating life and desires? How much of your focus is on finding the "right person" and how much is on making yourself "right"?

13. What might God want to do in you to make you a better partner for someone in the future?

²³The king said, "This one says, 'My son is alive and your son is dead,' while that one says, 'No! Your son is dead and mine is alive.' "

²⁴Then the king said, "Bring me a sword." So they brought a sword for the king. ²⁵He then gave an order: "Cut the living child in two and give half to one and half to the other."

²⁶The woman whose son was alive was filled with compassion for her son and said to the king, "Please, my lord, give her the living baby! Don't kill him!"

But the other said, "Neither I nor you shall have him. Cut him in two!"

²⁷Then the king gave his ruling: "Give the living baby to the first woman. Do not kill him; she is his mother."

²⁸When all Israel heard the verdict the king had given, they held the king in awe, because they saw that he had wisdom from God to administer justice.

Solomon's Officials and Governors

4 So King Solomon ruled over all Israel. ²And these were his chief officials:

Azariah son of Zadok—the priest;
³Elihoreph and Ahijah, sons of Shisha—secretaries;
Jehoshaphat son of Ahilud—recorder;
⁴Benaiah son of Jehoiada—commander in chief;
Zadok and Abiathar—priests;
⁵Azariah son of Nathan—in charge of the district officers;
Zabud son of Nathan—a priest and personal adviser to the king;
⁶Ahishar—in charge of the palace;
Adoniram son of Abda—in charge of forced labor.

⁷Solomon also had twelve district governors over all Israel, who supplied provisions for the king and the royal household. Each one had to provide supplies for one month in the year. ⁸These are their names:

Ben-Hur—in the hill country of Ephraim;
⁹Ben-Deker—in Makaz, Shaalbim, Beth Shemesh and Elon Bethhanan;
¹⁰Ben-Hesed—in Arubboth (Socoh and all the land of Hepher were his);
¹¹Ben-Abinadab—in Naphoth Dor^a (he was married to Taphath daughter of Solomon);
¹²Baana son of Ahilud—in Taanach and Megiddo, and in all of Beth Shan next to Zarethan below Jezreel, from Beth Shan to Abel Meholah across to Jokmeam;
¹³Ben-Geber—in Ramoth Gilead (the settlements of Jair son of Manasseh in Gilead were his, as well as the district of Argob in Bashan and its sixty large walled cities with bronze gate bars);
¹⁴Ahinadab son of Iddo—in Mahanaim;
¹⁵Ahimaaz—in Naphtali (he had married Basemath daughter of Solomon);
¹⁶Baana son of Hushai—in Asher and in Aloth;
¹⁷Jehoshaphat son of Paruah—in Issachar;
¹⁸Shimei son of Ela—in Benjamin;
¹⁹Geber son of Uri—in Gilead (the country of Sihon king of the

^a11 Or in the heights of Dor

1. Do you pursue wisdom? How? How many hours did you seek wisdom this week? 2. What has been your toughest decision this year? What prevailed: Your feelings? Others' advice? Circumstances? 3. Are you considered compassionate? What brings it out? What closes your heart toward others?

1. What one month do you feel free to take your annual vacation? What month is freer than most for volunteer church work? For getting caught up on household chores? 2. Would you ever take up the careers of your parents? Why or why not?

1. Which names here do you recognize? Who seem to be carry-overs from David's administration (vv. 2–6; see 1:32–33; 2Sa 8:16)? 2. Who carry on the professions of their parents, and who seem determined to do otherwise (vv. 2,5)? 3. For what major project will the king use "forced labor" (v. 6; see 5:13–14)? 4. What do verses 7–19 (together with a Bible map) reveal about the extent of Solomon's kingdom? How do you think the district governors will "supply provisions" for the royal court each month? 5. What extra pressure might Ben-Abinadab and Ahimaaz face under Solomon's rule?

1. Of the following, which job pressures affect you positively, and which affect you negatively: Parents' expectation? Monthly routine? Urgent deadlines? Job specs? Getting ahead? 2. When jobs are passed out (at church, on the job, in the home) are you the "can-do" type, the "talk-it-over" type, or what? Give an example. 3. What title would you give your "job" in God's kingdom? How did you find your line of work?

1. How often do you shop for groceries? How many bags a trip? 2. What will history cite as your area of expertise?

1. What is Solomon's Israel like economically? Militarily? Spiritually? 2. What does this passage reveal about taxes? What non-Israelites are taxed (v. 21)? 3. What is the difference between "stall-fed" and "pasture-fed" cattle? Which is more expensive? 4. Is the author exaggerating things to demonstrate a point? To you, what points seem stretched? 5. What are Solomon's areas of expertise? How do you suppose he came by his special wisdom: Private study? International discourse? Practice? Instant answer to prayer?

1. Is Solomon indulgent? Should affluent people consume so much while others go hungry? What sacrifices can you make to help those less fortunate? How so? 2. Is taxation an absolute right of those in power? What do you make of this country's tax system? 3. If Solomon were a member of your group, what would you ask him? 4. In what areas would you like more wisdom? How can you get it?

1. What kinds of things did you trade as a child: Marbles? Dolls? Baseball cards? Mystery books? 2. Have you ever worked away from home? Traveled on the job? Was it fun or tiresome?

1. Why does Hiram send a delegation to Solomon (v. 1)? 2. How do you see Solomon's reply (vv. 3–6): Veiled threat? Peaceful olive branch? Shrewd business deal? Explain. 3. Is Solomon critical of David's violent foreign policy? Is he afraid Hiram might consider him a softy compared to his father? Explain. 4. Why does Solomon want a temple so much? Does God want one (see 2Sa 7:5–7)? 5. Why does Hiram send business envoys instead of an invading army? Why does he ask Solomon for food (vv. 9–11)? Who will be relieved of the burden of

Amorites and the country of Og king of Bashan). He was the only governor over the district.

Solomon's Daily Provisions

20The people of Judah and Israel were as numerous as the sand on the seashore; they ate, they drank and they were happy. 21And Solomon ruled over all the kingdoms from the River[a] to the land of the Philistines, as far as the border of Egypt. These countries brought tribute and were Solomon's subjects all his life.

22Solomon's daily provisions were thirty cors[b] of fine flour and sixty cors[c] of meal, 23ten head of stall-fed cattle, twenty of pasture-fed cattle and a hundred sheep and goats, as well as deer, gazelles, roebucks and choice fowl. 24For he ruled over all the kingdoms west of the River, from Tiphsah to Gaza, and had peace on all sides. 25During Solomon's lifetime Judah and Israel, from Dan to Beersheba, lived in safety, each man under his own vine and fig tree.

26Solomon had four[d] thousand stalls for chariot horses, and twelve thousand horses.[e]

27The district officers, each in his month, supplied provisions for King Solomon and all who came to the king's table. They saw to it that nothing was lacking. 28They also brought to the proper place their quotas of barley and straw for the chariot horses and the other horses.

Solomon's Wisdom

29God gave Solomon wisdom and very great insight, and a breadth of understanding as measureless as the sand on the seashore. 30Solomon's wisdom was greater than the wisdom of all the men of the East, and greater than all the wisdom of Egypt. 31He was wiser than any other man, including Ethan the Ezrahite—wiser than Heman, Calcol and Darda, the sons of Mahol. And his fame spread to all the surrounding nations. 32He spoke three thousand proverbs and his songs numbered a thousand and five. 33He described plant life, from the cedar of Lebanon to the hyssop that grows out of walls. He also taught about animals and birds, reptiles and fish. 34Men of all nations came to listen to Solomon's wisdom, sent by all the kings of the world, who had heard of his wisdom.

Preparations for Building the Temple

5 When Hiram king of Tyre heard that Solomon had been anointed king to succeed his father David, he sent his envoys to Solomon, because he had always been on friendly terms with David. 2Solomon sent back this message to Hiram:

3"You know that because of the wars waged against my father David from all sides, he could not build a temple for the Name of the LORD his God until the LORD put his enemies under his feet. 4But now the LORD my God has given me rest on every side, and there is no adversary or disaster. 5I intend, therefore, to build a temple for the Name of the LORD my God, as the LORD told my father David, when he said, 'Your son whom I will put on the throne in your place will build the temple for my Name.'

6"So give orders that cedars of Lebanon be cut for me. My men will work with yours, and I will pay you for your men

---

a21 That is, the Euphrates; also in verse 24   b22 That is, probably about 185 bushels (about 6.6 kiloliters)   c22 That is, probably about 375 bushels (about 13.2 kiloliters)   d26 Some Septuagint manuscripts (see also 2 Chron. 9:25); Hebrew forty   e26 Or charioteers

whatever wages you set. You know that we have no one so skilled in felling timber as the Sidonians."

[7]When Hiram heard Solomon's message, he was greatly pleased and said, "Praise be to the LORD today, for he has given David a wise son to rule over this great nation."

[8]So Hiram sent word to Solomon:

"I have received the message you sent me and will do all you want in providing the cedar and pine logs. [9]My men will haul them down from Lebanon to the sea, and I will float them in rafts by sea to the place you specify. There I will separate them and you can take them away. And you are to grant my wish by providing food for my royal household."

[10]In this way Hiram kept Solomon supplied with all the cedar and pine logs he wanted, [11]and Solomon gave Hiram twenty thousand cors[a] of wheat as food for his household, in addition to twenty thousand baths[b,c] of pressed olive oil. Solomon continued to do this for Hiram year after year. [12]The LORD gave Solomon wisdom, just as he had promised him. There were peaceful relations between Hiram and Solomon, and the two of them made a treaty.

[13]King Solomon conscripted laborers from all Israel—thirty thousand men. [14]He sent them off to Lebanon in shifts of ten thousand a month, so that they spent one month in Lebanon and two months at home. Adoniram was in charge of the forced labor. [15]Solomon had seventy thousand carriers and eighty thousand stonecutters in the hills, [16]as well as thirty-three hundred[d] foremen who supervised the project and directed the workmen. [17]At the king's command they removed from the quarry large blocks of quality stone to provide a foundation of dressed stone for the temple. [18]The craftsmen of Solomon and Hiram and the men of Gebal[e] cut and prepared the timber and stone for the building of the temple.

Solomon Builds the Temple

6 In the four hundred and eightieth[f] year after the Israelites had come out of Egypt, in the fourth year of Solomon's reign over Israel, in the month of Ziv, the second month, he began to build the temple of the LORD.

[2]The temple that King Solomon built for the LORD was sixty cubits long, twenty wide and thirty high.[g] [3]The portico at the front of the main hall of the temple extended the width of the temple, that is twenty cubits,[h] and projected ten cubits[i] from the front of the temple. [4]He made narrow clerestory windows in the temple. [5]Against the walls of the main hall and inner sanctuary he built a structure around the building, in which there were side rooms. [6]The lowest floor was five cubits[j] wide, the middle floor six cubits[k] and the third floor seven.[l] He made offset ledges around the outside of the temple so that nothing would be inserted into the temple walls.

[7]In building the temple, only blocks dressed at the quarry were

---

a11 That is, probably about 125,000 bushels (about 4,400 kiloliters)   b11 Septuagint (see also 2 Chron. 2:10); Hebrew twenty cors   c11 That is, about 115,000 gallons (about 440 kiloliters)   d16 Hebrew; some Septuagint manuscripts (see also 2 Chron. 2:2, 18) thirty-six hundred   e18 That is, Byblos   f1 Hebrew; Septuagint four hundred and fortieth   g2 That is, about 90 feet (about 27 meters) long and 30 feet (about 9 meters) wide and 45 feet (about 13.5 meters) high   h3 That is, about 30 feet (about 9 meters)   i3 That is, about 15 feet (about 4.5 meters)   j6 That is, about 7 1/2 feet (about 2.3 meters); also in verses 10 and 24   k6 That is, about 9 feet (about 2.7 meters)   l6 That is, about 10 1/2 feet (about 3.1 meters)

---

providing for Hiram's household? Who will carry the burden of both Solomon and Hiram (v. 13)? How did Hiram, a pagan king, get so wise? **6.** Who are the losers in Solomon's projects? How does conscription differ from slavery? Who will work the fields to support this work force? Do you think this project justifies the hardships induced? Why or why not?

1. What would you like to construct for God? How must you prepare for this endeavor? Whose assistance do you need to enlist? **2.** What "enemies" has the Lord recently "put under your feet"? What new opportunities has this opened for you? **3.** Have you ever had to force others to do things they didn't like, in order to get an important job done? What feelings did the project evoke? What prayers? **4.** Do you find the government's financial demands a burden? What else might you do with your money?

1. What do you look for in a church building? Are you a stained glass fan? Pipe organ nut? Beamed ceiling or wood pew aficionado? Steeple junkie? Why is any of this relevant? **2.** If someone from several centuries back examined your bedroom for information about contemporary life, what would they assume? What would reveal the inner you? If you knew they were coming, what would you leave out to explain your values and beliefs? **3.** What would you like to be doing seven years from now? What do you hope and pray you won't be doing?

1. Why is the building of the temple dated in reference to the Exodus (v. 1)? **2.** Are any buildings in your town comparable in size to Solomon's temple? Why is the temple smaller than most churches? **3.** Is there an artist, draftsman or architect in the group who can sketch the temple as described here? Everyone try and compare sketches. Then see the sketch found in the Introduction to 1 Chronicles. **4.** Why such a large portico? Such small windows? Why the side rooms? Why the inner sanctuary (vv. 16,19)? **5.** Why is no iron tool heard at the construction site (v. 7)? **6.** Regarding the promise in verse 12, how, when and why is this promise fulfilled? Is God requiring a temple in return for a blessing? **7.** In what ways does Solomon demonstrate the importance he attaches to the temple? Why is so much value given to this building? **8.** What art adorns the temple (vv. 23–29)? What are cherubim (see Ge 3:24)? Why does Jewish art avoid any human depictions (see Dt 5:8)? **9.** Does the temple say anything about the character of God? What? What do you think it should say?

♡ **1.** Are church buildings as important today as the temple was in Solomon's time? Why or why not? **2.** What percentage of your church's resources go to building facilities? If you can obtain a budget statement from your church, calculate the percentage of money going to the mortgage and upkeep of the building and property. What percentage goes to the poor or missions? **3.** Is the promise God gave the Israelites (vv. 12–13) relevant today? Has your church fulfilled the terms of the promise? **4.** What kind of "temple" is God building (see Eph 2:19–22)? How is the progress in the corner of the project assigned to you? To your small group? To your church? **5.** Is the project "noise-free" or full of static? Explain. How will the laborers be supported? What sacrifices will be needed? **6.** What do you think of religious art? Is it okay to depict Jesus in paintings? Stained glass? Statues? What would this chapter say to that, if anything?

used, and no hammer, chisel or any other iron tool was heard at the temple site while it was being built.

⁸The entrance to the lowest*ᵃ* floor was on the south side of the temple; a stairway led up to the middle level and from there to the third. ⁹So he built the temple and completed it, roofing it with beams and cedar planks. ¹⁰And he built the side rooms all along the temple. The height of each was five cubits, and they were attached to the temple by beams of cedar.

¹¹The word of the LORD came to Solomon: ¹²"As for this temple you are building, if you follow my decrees, carry out my regulations and keep all my commands and obey them, I will fulfill through you the promise I gave to David your father. ¹³And I will live among the Israelites and will not abandon my people Israel."

¹⁴So Solomon built the temple and completed it. ¹⁵He lined its interior walls with cedar boards, paneling them from the floor of the temple to the ceiling, and covered the floor of the temple with planks of pine. ¹⁶He partitioned off twenty cubits*ᵇ* at the rear of the temple with cedar boards from floor to ceiling to form within the temple an inner sanctuary, the Most Holy Place. ¹⁷The main hall in front of this room was forty cubits*ᶜ* long. ¹⁸The inside of the temple was cedar, carved with gourds and open flowers. Everything was cedar; no stone was to be seen.

¹⁹He prepared the inner sanctuary within the temple to set the ark of the covenant of the LORD there. ²⁰The inner sanctuary was twenty cubits long, twenty wide and twenty high.*ᵈ* He overlaid the inside with pure gold, and he also overlaid the altar of cedar. ²¹Solomon covered the inside of the temple with pure gold, and he extended gold chains across the front of the inner sanctuary, which was overlaid with gold. ²²So he overlaid the whole interior with gold. He also overlaid with gold the altar that belonged to the inner sanctuary.

²³In the inner sanctuary he made a pair of cherubim of olive wood, each ten cubits*ᵉ* high. ²⁴One wing of the first cherub was five cubits long, and the other wing five cubits—ten cubits from wing tip to wing tip. ²⁵The second cherub also measured ten cubits, for the two cherubim were identical in size and shape. ²⁶The height of each cherub was ten cubits. ²⁷He placed the cherubim inside the innermost room of the temple, with their wings spread out. The wing of one cherub touched one wall, while the wing of the other touched the other wall, and their wings touched each other in the middle of the room. ²⁸He overlaid the cherubim with gold.

²⁹On the walls all around the temple, in both the inner and outer rooms, he carved cherubim, palm trees and open flowers. ³⁰He also covered the floors of both the inner and outer rooms of the temple with gold.

³¹For the entrance of the inner sanctuary he made doors of olive wood with five-sided jambs. ³²And on the two olive wood doors he carved cherubim, palm trees and open flowers, and overlaid the cherubim and palm trees with beaten gold. ³³In the same way he made four-sided jambs of olive wood for the entrance to the main hall. ³⁴He also made two pine doors, each having two leaves that turned in sockets. ³⁵He carved cherubim, palm trees and open flowers on them and overlaid them with gold hammered evenly over the carvings.

ᵃ8 Septuagint; Hebrew *middle*   *ᵇ16* That is, about 30 feet (about 9 meters)
ᶜ17 That is, about 60 feet (about 18 meters)   *ᵈ20* That is, about 30 feet (about 9 meters) long, wide and high   *ᵉ23* That is, about 15 feet (about 4.5 meters)

36And he built the inner courtyard of three courses of dressed stone and one course of trimmed cedar beams.

37The foundation of the temple of the LORD was laid in the fourth year, in the month of Ziv. **38**In the eleventh year in the month of Bul, the eighth month, the temple was finished in all its details according to its specifications. He had spent seven years building it.

Solomon Builds His Palace

7 It took Solomon thirteen years, however, to complete the construction of his palace. **2**He built the Palace of the Forest of Lebanon a hundred cubits long, fifty wide and thirty high,*a* with four rows of cedar columns supporting trimmed cedar beams. **3**It was roofed with cedar above the beams that rested on the columns—forty-five beams, fifteen to a row. **4**Its windows were placed high in sets of three, facing each other. **5**All the doorways had rectangular frames; they were in the front part in sets of three, facing each other.*b*

6He made a colonnade fifty cubits long and thirty wide.*c* In front of it was a portico, and in front of that were pillars and an overhanging roof.

7He built the throne hall, the Hall of Justice, where he was to judge, and he covered it with cedar from floor to ceiling.*d* **8**And the palace in which he was to live, set farther back, was similar in design. Solomon also made a palace like this hall for Pharaoh's daughter, whom he had married.

9All these structures, from the outside to the great courtyard and from foundation to eaves, were made of blocks of high-grade stone cut to size and trimmed with a saw on their inner and outer faces. **10**The foundations were laid with large stones of good quality, some measuring ten cubits*e* and some eight.*f* **11**Above were high-grade stones, cut to size, and cedar beams. **12**The great courtyard was surrounded by a wall of three courses of dressed stone and one course of trimmed cedar beams, as was the inner courtyard of the temple of the LORD with its portico.

The Temple's Furnishings

13King Solomon sent to Tyre and brought Huram,*g* **14**whose mother was a widow from the tribe of Naphtali and whose father was a man of Tyre and a craftsman in bronze. Huram was highly skilled and experienced in all kinds of bronze work. He came to King Solomon and did all the work assigned to him.

15He cast two bronze pillars, each eighteen cubits high and twelve cubits around,*h* by line. **16**He also made two capitals of cast bronze to set on the tops of the pillars; each capital was five cubits*i* high. **17**A network of interwoven chains festooned the capitals on top of the pillars, seven for each capital. **18**He made pomegranates in two rows*j* encircling each network to decorate the capitals on top of the pillars.*k* He did the same for each capital. **19**The capitals on top of the pillars in the portico were in

---

a2 That is, about 150 feet (about 46 meters) long, 75 feet (about 23 meters) wide and 45 feet (about 13.5 meters) high   *b5* The meaning of the Hebrew for this verse is uncertain.   *c6* That is, about 75 feet (about 23 meters) long and 45 feet (about 13.5 meters) wide   *d7* Vulgate and Syriac; Hebrew *floor*   *e10* That is, about 15 feet (about 4.5 meters)   *f10* That is, about 12 feet (about 3.6 meters)   *g13* Hebrew *Hiram*, a variant of *Huram*; also in verses 40 and 45   *h15* That is, about 27 feet (about 8.1 meters) high and 18 feet (about 5.4 meters) around   *i16* That is, about 7 1/2 feet (about 2.3 meters); also in verse 23   *j18* Two Hebrew manuscripts and Septuagint; most Hebrew manuscripts *made the pillars, and there were two rows*   *k18* Many Hebrew manuscripts and Syriac; most Hebrew manuscripts *pomegranates*

1. Where did you live when you were 10 years old? What was memorable about it? **2.** What weird features or bizarre objects adorn your home now?

1. Which took longer to build—the temple or Solomon's palace (v. 1; see 6:38)? Why does Solomon need so much room? **2.** From its construction, what seems to be the function of this "Palace of the Forest of Lebanon" (vv. 2–6)? **3.** Why does the author describe so carefully buildings that were long since destroyed?

1. Are you involved in a project taking "years" to finish? Does faith make a difference? **2.** Do you resent people in power "living like kings"? Why? Is it important that governments project wealth and power to other nations? **3.** What does Jesus say about such power displays (see Mt 20:25–28)?

1. Have you ever been so dirty you thought you would never get clean, no matter how often you washed? When that dirty, what would you like to do: Hug someone? Jump in a lake? Walk into your bank and conduct some stuffy business? Avoid people contact? **2.** What piece of furniture do you remember breaking as a child? Did you try to repair it before your parents found out? What happened? **3.** Did you ever borrow something and never return it (as when the owner moves, the company goes out of business, or the library forgot)? Do you ever think about returning it still?

1. Why is Huram an ideal worker for this project? What would he bring from the Israelite side of his family (v. 14)? From the pagan side? **2.** Since they do not seem to hold anything up, what do you think is the purpose of the pillars? Why name them (v. 21)? As a group, try drawing a picture of the pillars (as well as the other items in this passage as you go along). **3.** What is the function of the bronze "Sea" (vv. 23–26; see Ex 30: 17–21)? **4.** Is it a good idea to furnish the Temple with bronze bulls, in light of the problems of idolatrous calves (v. 25; see Ex 32; 1Ki 12:28–30)? **5.** What was the purpose of the 10 movable stands (vv. 27–39; see 2Ch 4:6)? Why did God require so much washing? What did water represent in an arid land? **6.** How was the golden altar used (v. 48; see Ex 30:6–10)? The golden table (see Ex 25:23–30)? The lampstands (see Ex 27:20–21)? **7.** What silver and gold "things" had David dedicated (v. 51; see 2Sa 8:9–12)? What administrative problems does Solomon solve by placing these things in the temple treasury? Is it right to put pagan items in the Lord's temple? **8.** Did Solomon slip up in failing to weigh the bronze articles (v. 47)? Why or why not?

♡ **1.** Has God given you any "heavy" assignments lately? At what are you "highly skilled," so that you could do "all the work assigned"? What would you like to be skilled at? **2.** Solomon wanted one place of worship for the entire people of Israel, whereas we often see "a church on every corner." Does this suggest we have lost his vision? Explain. **3.** What would you like to "dedicate" to the Lord and why? **4.** If you could tackle any task for the Lord, what would you like to do and why? **5.** What inscription or message do visitors to your church see when they enter? Does the message offer hope? Judgment? Mercy? Other? **6.** Is your place of worship plainer than this one? What do "plain" churches suggest to you: People are not as skilled? They are unwilling to give? Not eager to build as in Solomon's day? Does God care that much about art? Isn't creativity dangerous? **7.** Do you feel a need to be "cleansed" in any way? How will you go about this? **8.** Do you have all your wealth in one location (or all your eggs in one basket)? How so? Do you worry at all about being attacked and wiped out in one fell swoop? Why or why not?

the shape of lilies, four cubits^a high. ²⁰On the capitals of both pillars, above the bowl-shaped part next to the network, were the two hundred pomegranates in rows all around. ²¹He erected the pillars at the portico of the temple. The pillar to the south he named Jakin^b and the one to the north Boaz.^c ²²The capitals on top were in the shape of lilies. And so the work on the pillars was completed.

²³He made the Sea of cast metal, circular in shape, measuring ten cubits^d from rim to rim and five cubits high. It took a line of thirty cubits^e to measure around it. ²⁴Below the rim, gourds encircled it—ten to a cubit. The gourds were cast in two rows in one piece with the Sea.

²⁵The Sea stood on twelve bulls, three facing north, three facing west, three facing south and three facing east. The Sea rested on top of them, and their hindquarters were toward the center. ²⁶It was a handbreadth^f in thickness, and its rim was like the rim of a cup, like a lily blossom. It held two thousand baths.^g

²⁷He also made ten movable stands of bronze; each was four cubits long, four wide and three high.^h ²⁸This is how the stands were made: They had side panels attached to uprights. ²⁹On the panels between the uprights were lions, bulls and cherubim—and on the uprights as well. Above and below the lions and bulls were wreaths of hammered work. ³⁰Each stand had four bronze wheels with bronze axles, and each had a basin resting on four supports, cast with wreaths on each side. ³¹On the inside of the stand there was an opening that had a circular frame one cubitⁱ deep. This opening was round, and with its basework it measured a cubit and a half.^j Around its opening there was engraving. The panels of the stands were square, not round. ³²The four wheels were under the panels, and the axles of the wheels were attached to the stand. The diameter of each wheel was a cubit and a half. ³³The wheels were made like chariot wheels; the axles, rims, spokes and hubs were all of cast metal.

³⁴Each stand had four handles, one on each corner, projecting from the stand. ³⁵At the top of the stand there was a circular band half a cubit^k deep. The supports and panels were attached to the top of the stand. ³⁶He engraved cherubim, lions and palm trees on the surfaces of the supports and on the panels, in every available space, with wreaths all around. ³⁷This is the way he made the ten stands. They were all cast in the same molds and were identical in size and shape.

³⁸He then made ten bronze basins, each holding forty baths^l and measuring four cubits across, one basin to go on each of the ten stands. ³⁹He placed five of the stands on the south side of the temple and five on the north. He placed the Sea on the south side, at the southeast corner of the temple. ⁴⁰He also made the basins and shovels and sprinkling bowls.

So Huram finished all the work he had undertaken for King Solomon in the temple of the LORD:

⁴¹the two pillars;
the two bowl-shaped capitals on top of the pillars;

^a19 That is, about 6 feet (about 1.8 meters); also in verse 38   ^b21 *Jakin* probably means *he establishes.*   ^c21 *Boaz* probably means *in him is strength.*   ^d23 That is, about 15 feet (about 4.5 meters)   ^e23 That is, about 45 feet (about 13.5 meters)   ^f26 That is, about 3 inches (about 8 centimeters)   ^g26 That is, probably about 11,500 gallons (about 44 kiloliters); the Septuagint does not have this sentence.   ^h27 That is, about 6 feet (about 1.8 meters) long and wide and about 4 1/2 feet (about 1.3 meters) high   ⁱ31 That is, about 1 1/2 feet (about 0.5 meter)   ^j31 That is, about 2 1/4 feet (about 0.7 meter); also in verse 32   ^k35 That is, about 3/4 foot (about 0.2 meter)   ^l38 That is, about 230 gallons (about 880 liters)

the two sets of network decorating the two bowl-shaped capitals on top of the pillars;
42the four hundred pomegranates for the two sets of network (two rows of pomegranates for each network, decorating the bowl-shaped capitals on top of the pillars);
43the ten stands with their ten basins;
44the Sea and the twelve bulls under it;
45the pots, shovels and sprinkling bowls.

All these objects that Huram made for King Solomon for the temple of the LORD were of burnished bronze. 46The king had them cast in clay molds in the plain of the Jordan between Succoth and Zarethan. 47Solomon left all these things unweighed, because there were so many; the weight of the bronze was not determined.

48Solomon also made all the furnishings that were in the LORD's temple:

the golden altar;
the golden table on which was the bread of the Presence;
49the lampstands of pure gold (five on the right and five on the left, in front of the inner sanctuary);
the gold floral work and lamps and tongs;
50the pure gold basins, wick trimmers, sprinkling bowls, dishes and censers;
and the gold sockets for the doors of the innermost room, the Most Holy Place, and also for the doors of the main hall of the temple.

51When all the work King Solomon had done for the temple of the LORD was finished, he brought in the things his father David had dedicated—the silver and gold and the furnishings—and he placed them in the treasuries of the LORD's temple.

The Ark Brought to the Temple

8 Then King Solomon summoned into his presence at Jerusalem the elders of Israel, all the heads of the tribes and the chiefs of the Israelite families, to bring up the ark of the LORD's covenant from Zion, the City of David. 2All the men of Israel came together to King Solomon at the time of the festival in the month of Ethanim, the seventh month.

3When all the elders of Israel had arrived, the priests took up the ark, 4and they brought up the ark of the LORD and the Tent of Meeting and all the sacred furnishings in it. The priests and Levites carried them up, 5and King Solomon and the entire assembly of Israel that had gathered about him were before the ark, sacrificing so many sheep and cattle that they could not be recorded or counted.

6The priests then brought the ark of the LORD's covenant to its place in the inner sanctuary of the temple, the Most Holy Place, and put it beneath the wings of the cherubim. 7The cherubim spread their wings over the place of the ark and overshadowed the ark and its carrying poles. 8These poles were so long that their ends could be seen from the Holy Place in front of the inner sanctuary, but not from outside the Holy Place; and they are still there today. 9There was nothing in the ark except the two stone tablets that Moses had placed in it at Horeb, where the LORD made a covenant with the Israelites after they came out of Egypt.

10When the priests withdrew from the Holy Place, the cloud filled the temple of the LORD. 11And the priests could not perform their service because of the cloud, for the glory of the LORD filled his temple.

1. Complete this sentence: "I come from a long line of _____s." How long a line? Will the line continue? 2. Do you have any heirlooms? How did they come into your hands? Where do you keep them or what do you do with them?

1. From where to where does Solomon move the ark (v. 1)? Why build the temple on Mount Moriah instead of Mount Zion (see 2Ch 3:1; 1Ch 21:25–28)? 2. What has Solomon learned from David's mistakes in moving the ark (vv. 3–5)? What was the purpose of Solomon's sacrifices? 3. Why is the ark placed within the inner sanctuary (vv. 6–9)? Why is the length of the carrying poles noted? Any message here about the character of God? 4. Why does this passage speak of the tablets within the ark? What do pagan temples usually have in the Most Holy Place? 5. Why does God appear as a "dark cloud" (vv. 10–11; see Ex 19:16)? 6. Does Solomon say that God lives in the temple (vv. 15–20)? How does he speak about God's presence there?

1. What is your "ark"—something you must have in your life to feel close to God? Are you close now? If not, what move is needed? 2. When have you felt spiritually "at home"? Are you at home now, or still journeying toward "Zion"? 3. When have you been especially aware of God's holiness, glory or faithfulness? 4. Have you seen God's promises fulfilled in your life recently? 5. Are you shy of speech-making? Is there something the people around you need to hear? Do they seem open to hearing it? What word would you like to give the group?

1. In an average week, what's the toughest "natural disaster" which afflicts you: Grubs in a garden? Bumper crop of weeds? Rainwater in the basement? A month of no rain for your plants and grass? Other? 2. What out-of-the-ordinary "disaster" have you had to contend with this year? 3. What's your number one way to rest and relax? When's the last time you did it?

1. Which of God's promises has Solomon seen fulfilled already (vv. 23–24)? What promises does he hope to see fulfilled in the future (vv. 25–26)? 2. Why does Solomon pray as he does in verses 27–30? What false impression might some get about the temple? About God's locale or sphere of influence? Why then would people pray toward the temple? 3. What form of judgment is this "swearing an oath before the altar" (vv. 31–32; see Nu 5:19–28)? 4. What do the three "disasters" in verses 33–40 have in common? What features of the prayer remain the same, whatever the disaster or its source? What does the sameness say about the trouble people face? About the God who afflicts and answers prayer? 5. How can Israel reverse the curses of disobedience (see Dt 28:15–24)? What does this passage say about repentance and salvation? 6. What do the three pe-

¹²Then Solomon said, "The LORD has said that he would dwell in a dark cloud; ¹³I have indeed built a magnificent temple for you, a place for you to dwell forever."

¹⁴While the whole assembly of Israel was standing there, the king turned around and blessed them. ¹⁵Then he said:

"Praise be to the LORD, the God of Israel, who with his own hand has fulfilled what he promised with his own mouth to my father David. For he said, ¹⁶'Since the day I brought my people Israel out of Egypt, I have not chosen a city in any tribe of Israel to have a temple built for my Name to be there, but I have chosen David to rule my people Israel.'

¹⁷"My father David had it in his heart to build a temple for the Name of the LORD, the God of Israel. ¹⁸But the LORD said to my father David, 'Because it was in your heart to build a temple for my Name, you did well to have this in your heart. ¹⁹Nevertheless, you are not the one to build the temple, but your son, who is your own flesh and blood—he is the one who will build the temple for my Name.'

²⁰"The LORD has kept the promise he made: I have succeeded David my father and now I sit on the throne of Israel, just as the LORD promised, and I have built the temple for the Name of the LORD, the God of Israel. ²¹I have provided a place there for the ark, in which is the covenant of the LORD that he made with our fathers when he brought them out of Egypt."

Solomon's Prayer of Dedication

²²Then Solomon stood before the altar of the LORD in front of the whole assembly of Israel, spread out his hands toward heaven ²³and said:

"O LORD, God of Israel, there is no God like you in heaven above or on earth below—you who keep your covenant of love with your servants who continue wholeheartedly in your way. ²⁴You have kept your promise to your servant David my father; with your mouth you have promised and with your hand you have fulfilled it—as it is today.

²⁵"Now LORD, God of Israel, keep for your servant David my father the promises you made to him when you said, 'You shall never fail to have a man to sit before me on the throne of Israel, if only your sons are careful in all they do to walk before me as you have done.' ²⁶And now, O God of Israel, let your word that you promised your servant David my father come true.

²⁷"But will God really dwell on earth? The heavens, even the highest heaven, cannot contain you. How much less this temple I have built! ²⁸Yet give attention to your servant's prayer and his plea for mercy, O LORD my God. Hear the cry and the prayer that your servant is praying in your presence this day. ²⁹May your eyes be open toward this temple night and day, this place of which you said, 'My Name shall be there,' so that you will hear the prayer your servant prays toward this place. ³⁰Hear the supplication of your servant and of your people Israel when they pray toward this place. Hear from heaven, your dwelling place, and when you hear, forgive.

³¹"When a man wrongs his neighbor and is required to take an oath and he comes and swears the oath before your altar in this temple, ³²then hear from heaven and act. Judge between your servants, condemning the guilty and bringing down on

his own head what he has done. Declare the innocent not guilty, and so establish his innocence.

[33]"When your people Israel have been defeated by an enemy because they have sinned against you, and when they turn back to you and confess your name, praying and making supplication to you in this temple, [34]then hear from heaven and forgive the sin of your people Israel and bring them back to the land you gave to their fathers.

[35]"When the heavens are shut up and there is no rain because your people have sinned against you, and when they pray toward this place and confess your name and turn from their sin because you have afflicted them, [36]then hear from heaven and forgive the sin of your servants, your people Israel. Teach them the right way to live, and send rain on the land you gave your people for an inheritance.

[37]"When famine or plague comes to the land, or blight or mildew, locusts or grasshoppers, or when an enemy besieges them in any of their cities, whatever disaster or disease may come, [38]and when a prayer or plea is made by any of your people Israel—each one aware of the afflictions of his own heart, and spreading out his hands toward this temple— [39]then hear from heaven, your dwelling place. Forgive and act; deal with each man according to all he does, since you know his heart (for you alone know the hearts of all men), [40]so that they will fear you all the time they live in the land you gave our fathers.

[41]"As for the foreigner who does not belong to your people Israel but has come from a distant land because of your name— [42]for men will hear of your great name and your mighty hand and your outstretched arm—when he comes and prays toward this temple, [43]then hear from heaven, your dwelling place, and do whatever the foreigner asks of you, so that all the peoples of the earth may know your name and fear you, as do your own people Israel, and may know that this house I have built bears your Name.

[44]"When your people go to war against their enemies, wherever you send them, and when they pray to the LORD toward the city you have chosen and the temple I have built for your Name, [45]then hear from heaven their prayer and their plea, and uphold their cause.

[46]"When they sin against you—for there is no one who does not sin—and you become angry with them and give them over to the enemy, who takes them captive to his own land, far away or near; [47]and if they have a change of heart in the land where they are held captive, and repent and plead with you in the land of their conquerors and say, 'We have sinned, we have done wrong, we have acted wickedly'; [48]and if they turn back to you with all their heart and soul in the land of their enemies who took them captive, and pray to you toward the land you gave their fathers, toward the city you have chosen and the temple I have built for your Name; [49]then from heaven, your dwelling place, hear their prayer and their plea, and uphold their cause. [50]And forgive your people, who have sinned against you; forgive all the offenses they have committed against you, and cause their conquerors to show them mercy; [51]for they are your people and your inheritance, whom you brought out of Egypt, out of that iron-smelting furnace.

[52]"May your eyes be open to your servant's plea and to the

titions in verses 41–51 have in common? Does this section strike you as: (a) Premonition of the exile to come? (b) Reflection on the Egyptian captivity? (c) Petitions added to Solomon's speech by later editors? **7.** On what basis does Solomon hope for an answer to these prayers (vv. 52–53)? **8.** What does Solomon's body language say about his concept of God? Of prayer? Why does Solomon change posture halfway through this section? What does the change signal? **9.** Why are spoken words so important to Solomon and his people (v. 59; see 4:32,34)? Would private faith, unexpressed and silent, be as powerful? **10.** What blessings does he confer on his people (vv. 55–61)? What does that say about Solomon's understanding of the relationship between God and his people? **11.** Based on Solomon's prayer and blessing, at what points are the people vulnerable or weak? What is the solution to failure of faith?

1. On a scale of 1 ("Jesus is my buddy") to 10 ("God is so holy, who can approach him?"), how would you rate your reverence toward God? In which direction do you want to grow—more casual or more formal? More spontaneous or more serious? **2.** What posture do you normally assume when you pray? Have you ever experimented with other postures? What do you find helpful? Not helpful? **3.** Do you consider afflictions to be punishment for sin—always, sometimes or never? In what cases? What prayers do you want to direct toward God's heavenly temple? Do you first need to confess some sin? **4.** Have you appropriated the promise of "rest" given to God's people (v. 56)? Any preparation needed on your part? What energy for service does that give you? **5.** If you were to fashion a group prayer, what parts of Solomon's would be dropped, substituted, retained, assigned to others? Why are long pastoral or solo prayers not so popular today?

plea of your people Israel, and may you listen to them whenever they cry out to you. ⁵³For you singled them out from all the nations of the world to be your own inheritance, just as you declared through your servant Moses when you, O Sovereign LORD, brought our fathers out of Egypt."

⁵⁴When Solomon had finished all these prayers and supplications to the LORD, he rose from before the altar of the LORD, where he had been kneeling with his hands spread out toward heaven. ⁵⁵He stood and blessed the whole assembly of Israel in a loud voice, saying:

⁵⁶"Praise be to the LORD, who has given rest to his people Israel just as he promised. Not one word has failed of all the good promises he gave through his servant Moses. ⁵⁷May the LORD our God be with us as he was with our fathers; may he never leave us nor forsake us. ⁵⁸May he turn our hearts to him, to walk in all his ways and to keep the commands, decrees and regulations he gave our fathers. ⁵⁹And may these words of mine, which I have prayed before the LORD, be near to the LORD our God day and night, that he may uphold the cause of his servant and the cause of his people Israel according to each day's need, ⁶⁰so that all the peoples of the earth may know that the LORD is God and that there is no other. ⁶¹But your hearts must be fully committed to the LORD our God, to live by his decrees and obey his commands, as at this time."

The Dedication of the Temple

⁶²Then the king and all Israel with him offered sacrifices before the LORD. ⁶³Solomon offered a sacrifice of fellowship offerings*a* to the LORD: twenty-two thousand cattle and a hundred and twenty thousand sheep and goats. So the king and all the Israelites dedicated the temple of the LORD.

⁶⁴On that same day the king consecrated the middle part of the courtyard in front of the temple of the LORD, and there he offered burnt offerings, grain offerings and the fat of the fellowship offerings, because the bronze altar before the LORD was too small to hold the burnt offerings, the grain offerings and the fat of the fellowship offerings.

⁶⁵So Solomon observed the festival at that time, and all Israel with him—a vast assembly, people from Lebo*b* Hamath to the Wadi of Egypt. They celebrated it before the LORD our God for seven days and seven days more, fourteen days in all. ⁶⁶On the following day he sent the people away. They blessed the king and then went home, joyful and glad in heart for all the good things the LORD had done for his servant David and his people Israel.

The LORD Appears to Solomon

9 When Solomon had finished building the temple of the LORD and the royal palace, and had achieved all he had desired to do, ²the LORD appeared to him a second time, as he had appeared to him at Gibeon. ³The LORD said to him:

"I have heard the prayer and plea you have made before me; I have consecrated this temple, which you have built, by putting my Name there forever. My eyes and my heart will always be there.

⁴"As for you, if you walk before me in integrity of heart and

What events (historic and social) have you publicly celebrated this year?

1. Why sacrifice so many animals (vv. 62–63)? 2. Why can't Israel eat fat or blood (v. 64; see Lev 3:16–17)? 3. How do the bronze and gold altars differ (v. 64; also see Ex 30:6–7)? 4. What feast is celebrated at this time of year (see 8:2; Lev 23:34,41–43)? What irony do you see in this timing?

1. What "good things" has God done for you lately? 2. What "sacrifices" does God require today and why?

What place have you once visited or lived that captured your eyes or heart? Why there?

1. What happened at Gibeon (v. 2; see 1Ki 3:5–15)? 2. In what way did God consecrate the temple (v. 3)? Is God more present in the temple than anywhere else? How so? 3. Compare God's words to Solomon with Solomon's words to Israel (v. 4; see 8:61) and David's words to Solomon (see 1Ki 2:2–4). What do you see? Why is

uprightness, as David your father did, and do all I command and observe my decrees and laws, [5]I will establish your royal throne over Israel forever, as I promised David your father when I said, 'You shall never fail to have a man on the throne of Israel.'

[6]"But if you[a] or your sons turn away from me and do not observe the commands and decrees I have given you[a] and go off to serve other gods and worship them, [7]then I will cut off Israel from the land I have given them and will reject this temple I have consecrated for my Name. Israel will then become a byword and an object of ridicule among all peoples. [8]And though this temple is now imposing, all who pass by will be appalled and will scoff and say, 'Why has the LORD done such a thing to this land and to this temple?' [9]People will answer, 'Because they have forsaken the LORD their God, who brought their fathers out of Egypt, and have embraced other gods, worshiping and serving them—that is why the LORD brought all this disaster on them.'"

Solomon's Other Activities

[10]At the end of twenty years, during which Solomon built these two buildings—the temple of the LORD and the royal palace— [11]King Solomon gave twenty towns in Galilee to Hiram king of Tyre, because Hiram had supplied him with all the cedar and pine and gold he wanted. [12]But when Hiram went from Tyre to see the towns that Solomon had given him, he was not pleased with them. [13]"What kind of towns are these you have given me, my brother?" he asked. And he called them the Land of Cabul,[b] a name they have to this day. [14]Now Hiram had sent to the king 120 talents[c] of gold.

[15]Here is the account of the forced labor King Solomon conscripted to build the LORD's temple, his own palace, the supporting terraces,[d] the wall of Jerusalem, and Hazor, Megiddo and Gezer. [16](Pharaoh king of Egypt had attacked and captured Gezer. He had set it on fire. He killed its Canaanite inhabitants and then gave it as a wedding gift to his daughter, Solomon's wife. [17]And Solomon rebuilt Gezer.) He built up Lower Beth Horon, [18]Baalath, and Tadmor[e] in the desert, within his land, [19]as well as all his store cities and the towns for his chariots and for his horses[f]—whatever he desired to build in Jerusalem, in Lebanon and throughout all the territory he ruled.

[20]All the people left from the Amorites, Hittites, Perizzites, Hivites and Jebusites (these peoples were not Israelites), [21]that is, their descendants remaining in the land, whom the Israelites could not exterminate[g]—these Solomon conscripted for his slave labor force, as it is to this day. [22]But Solomon did not make slaves of any of the Israelites; they were his fighting men, his government officials, his officers, his captains, and the commanders of his chariots and charioteers. [23]They were also the chief officials in charge of Solomon's projects—550 officials supervising the men who did the work.

[24]After Pharaoh's daughter had come up from the City of David to the palace Solomon had built for her, he constructed the supporting terraces.

that significant? 4. What happens if Solomon or his heirs are disloyal (vv. 6–9)? Who will scoff?

1. Is Solomon saying, "If we obey we will prosper, if we sin we will suffer"? Is God's love that conditional? 2. Is rejection by God a fear you struggle with? What's to be done about that? 3. What modern gods compete for your allegiance? How does God stake his claim to be "the one and only" in your life?

1. If you could own an entire town, from what section of the country would you choose it? What size town? What essential attractions? 2. (If married) What modifications in your living situation did you undertake when you began living as two? Do two really live more cheaply than one? (If single) What economic factors would affect your decision to wed?

1. How has Hiram helped Solomon with his building projects (vv. 11–14,27–28; see 5:8–9)? What was in it for Hiram? Why does Hiram feel cheated by Solomon? 2. How did Solomon manage to build all that he did (vv. 15,20)? How does the forced labor policy strike you: As fair? Shrewd? Racist? 3. How does Gezer rate as a wedding gift (v. 16)? 4. In what way does Solomon accommodate this Pharaoh's daughter and wife-to-be? 5. Why does Solomon sacrifice three times a year (v. 25; see Ex 23:14–17)?

1. What actions of these ancient regimes would be considered criminal today? What cultural factors and religious beliefs made Solomon's situation different from yours? 2. How do you handle people who are not happy with a gift? With their salary? Their marriage? Their career? Are you able to keep such disappointed people as friends, as Solomon apparently did with Hiram? 3. What ethnic group tends to do the menial tasks in your town? Is this fair? What can you do about it?

---

[a]6 The Hebrew is plural.		[b]13 Cabul sounds like the Hebrew for good-for-nothing.
[c]14 That is, about 4 1/2 tons (about 4 metric tons)		[d]15 Or the Millo; also in verse 24
[e]18 The Hebrew may also be read Tamar.		[f]19 Or charioteers		[g]21 The Hebrew term refers to the irrevocable giving over of things or persons to the LORD, often by totally destroying them.

²⁵Three times a year Solomon sacrificed burnt offerings and fellowship offerings[a] on the altar he had built for the LORD, burning incense before the LORD along with them, and so fulfilled the temple obligations.

²⁶King Solomon also built ships at Ezion Geber, which is near Elath in Edom, on the shore of the Red Sea.[b] ²⁷And Hiram sent his men—sailors who knew the sea—to serve in the fleet with Solomon's men. ²⁸They sailed to Ophir and brought back 420 talents[c] of gold, which they delivered to King Solomon.

The Queen of Sheba Visits Solomon

10 When the queen of Sheba heard about the fame of Solomon and his relation to the name of the LORD, she came to test him with hard questions. ²Arriving at Jerusalem with a very great caravan—with camels carrying spices, large quantities of gold, and precious stones—she came to Solomon and talked with him about all that she had on her mind. ³Solomon answered all her questions; nothing was too hard for the king to explain to her. ⁴When the queen of Sheba saw all the wisdom of Solomon and the palace he had built, ⁵the food on his table, the seating of his officials, the attending servants in their robes, his cupbearers, and the burnt offerings he made at[d] the temple of the LORD, she was overwhelmed.

⁶She said to the king, "The report I heard in my own country about your achievements and your wisdom is true. ⁷But I did not

---

a25 Traditionally *peace offerings*   *b26* Hebrew *Yam Suph*; that is, Sea of Reeds   *c28* That is, about 16 tons (about 14.5 metric tons)   *d5* Or *the ascent by which he went up to*

Sidebar (left column)

What *first* attracted you to your current (or a prospective) mate: Good looks? Good mind? Good listener? Good body? Pretty face? Obvious wealth? What was the *second* thing you noticed?

1. What questions do you suppose the queen of Sheba asks (vv. 2–3)? **2.** What firstly and secondly impresses the queen? How is it she "sees" wisdom (v. 7)? **3.** How does the queen compliment Solomon? **4.** What is the surprise twist and the main point of this whole episode: (a) A *woman* of this era comes to test Solomon? (b) She pays homage to the god of Solomon's territory, Israel?(c) She expresses faith in the God of Israel? (d) She offers extravagant gifts

---

1 Kings 10:1–13   THE QUEEN OF SHEBA VISITS SOLOMON

King Solomon's reputation has become known far and wide. One of those who visited him was the queen of Sheba, who may have come to negotiate a trade agreement as well.

1. What motivated this dignitary to travel 1,200 miles to visit Solomon?
   a. his achievements
   b. his wisdom
   c. his faith
   d. her curiosity
   e. her skepticism
   f. her national interests

2. What impresses you the most about Solomon?
   a. his achievements
   b. his wisdom
   c. his faith
   d. his generosity
   e. his political and economic savvy

3. What impresses me the most about the queen of Sheba was that she:
   a. had the intelligence to test Solomon with hard questions.
   b. saw the connection between Solomon's wisdom and his God.
   c. knew how to flatter Solomon.
   d. didn't seem overly concerned about her image.

4. What were her words in verse 9?
   a. sincere
   b. manipulative
   c. full of understanding
   d. a recognition of the Lord as Solomon's and Israel's God
   e. a confession of the Lord as *her* God, as well

5. What did the queen of Sheba take home with her?
   a. seeds of truth
   b. a new faith
   c. a business deal
   d. wonderful gifts
   e. more than she brought

6. Who is someone whose godly wisdom has drawn you to the Lord? What might you do to express your appreciation to them?

7. If someone could give you "all you desired and asked for," which three of the following would you choose?
   a. great wealth
   b. great health
   c. physical attractiveness
   d. a successful career
   e. a happy family
   f. a life without stress
   g. a close walk with God
   h. a clear sense of purpose
   i. close friends
   j. other:_____

8. What do your choices in the last question indicate about the next steps you need to take in your life?

9. What keeps you from pursuing God's inner beauty in your life?
   a. family demands
   b. television
   c. time with others
   d. lack of discipline
   e. too much time spent on my outward image

10. What are you doing to discover who you really are? What are you doing to discover who God really is?

believe these things until I came and saw with my own eyes. Indeed, not even half was told me; in wisdom and wealth you have far exceeded the report I heard. [8]How happy your men must be! How happy your officials, who continually stand before you and hear your wisdom! [9]Praise be to the LORD your God, who has delighted in you and placed you on the throne of Israel. Because of the LORD's eternal love for Israel, he has made you king, to maintain justice and righteousness."

[10]And she gave the king 120 talents[a] of gold, large quantities of spices, and precious stones. Never again were so many spices brought in as those the queen of Sheba gave to King Solomon.

[11](Hiram's ships brought gold from Ophir; and from there they brought great cargoes of almugwood[b] and precious stones. [12]The king used the almugwood to make supports for the temple of the LORD and for the royal palace, and to make harps and lyres for the musicians. So much almugwood has never been imported or seen since that day.)

[13]King Solomon gave the queen of Sheba all she desired and asked for, besides what he had given her out of his royal bounty. Then she left and returned with her retinue to her own country.

Solomon's Splendor

[14]The weight of the gold that Solomon received yearly was 666 talents,[c] [15]not including the revenues from merchants and traders and from all the Arabian kings and the governors of the land.

[16]King Solomon made two hundred large shields of hammered gold; six hundred bekas[d] of gold went into each shield. [17]He also made three hundred small shields of hammered gold, with three minas[e] of gold in each shield. The king put them in the Palace of the Forest of Lebanon.

[18]Then the king made a great throne inlaid with ivory and overlaid with fine gold. [19]The throne had six steps, and its back had a rounded top. On both sides of the seat were armrests, with a lion standing beside each of them. [20]Twelve lions stood on the six steps, one at either end of each step. Nothing like it had ever been made for any other kingdom. [21]All King Solomon's goblets were gold, and all the household articles in the Palace of the Forest of Lebanon were pure gold. Nothing was made of silver, because silver was considered of little value in Solomon's days. [22]The king had a fleet of trading ships[f] at sea along with the ships of Hiram. Once every three years it returned, carrying gold, silver and ivory, and apes and baboons.

[23]King Solomon was greater in riches and wisdom than all the other kings of the earth. [24]The whole world sought audience with Solomon to hear the wisdom God had put in his heart. [25]Year after year, everyone who came brought a gift—articles of silver and gold, robes, weapons and spices, and horses and mules.

[26]Solomon accumulated chariots and horses; he had fourteen hundred chariots and twelve thousand horses,[g] which he kept in the chariot cities and also with him in Jerusalem. [27]The king made silver as common in Jerusalem as stones, and cedar as plentiful as sycamore-fig trees in the foothills. [28]Solomon's horses were imported from Egypt[h] and from Kue[i]—the royal merchants purchased them from Kue. [29]They imported a chariot from Egypt for six hun-

for his advice? (e) Solomon gives her a "blank check" (v. 13)?

1. What does this story stir up in you: Envy? Suspicion? Unworthiness? Embarrassed by praise or riches? Why? 2. Who truly admires you or seeks out your opinion? How is love for God evident in your talk? 3. What one question would you ask the wisest person in the world? 4. What will you do this week to thank someone you admire?

Know anyone with money to burn? What would you do with all that money?

1. How does this passage strike you: (a) Accurate history? (b) Political boasting? (c) Storybook account? (d) Gold mine? Explain. 2. How does Solomon make his "revenues" (vv. 14–15)? 3. What is significant about his lions, apes and horses? 4. How is God true to his promises to Solomon (vv. 23–24; see 3:12–13)? Is wisdom a money-maker (v. 25)? Or does having money give the appearance of wisdom? 5. How does Solomon profit from the "arms race" (vv. 28–29)? How does he rate with the Mosaic code (see Dt 17:16–17)?

1. Are gold, silver or ivory signs of God's favor today? What seems to have taken their place and why? 2. It is said, "One man's wealth is built on another man's poverty." Does that seem true in Solomon's case? In your case? Who pays for your comfort in terms of low wages, broken treaties, unfair business deals? 3. Is it right for Christians to accumulate large amounts of "silver and gold"? Why?

a 10 That is, about 4 1/2 tons (about 4 metric tons)   b 11 Probably a variant of algumwood; also in verse 12   c 14 That is, about 25 tons (about 23 metric tons)   d 16 That is, about 7 1/2 pounds (about 3.5 kilograms)   e 17 That is, about 3 3/4 pounds (about 1.7 kilograms)   f 22 Hebrew of ships of Tarshish   g 26 Or charioteers   h 28 Or possibly Muzur, a region in Cilicia; also in verse 29   i 28 Probably Cilicia

dred shekels*a* of silver, and a horse for a hundred and fifty.*b* They also exported them to all the kings of the Hittites and of the Arameans.

Solomon's Wives

11 King Solomon, however, loved many foreign women besides Pharaoh's daughter—Moabites, Ammonites, Edomites, Sidonians and Hittites. ²They were from nations about which the LORD had told the Israelites, "You must not intermarry with them, because they will surely turn your hearts after their gods." Nevertheless, Solomon held fast to them in love. ³He had seven hundred wives of royal birth and three hundred concubines, and his wives led him astray. ⁴As Solomon grew old, his wives turned his heart after other gods, and his heart was not fully devoted to the LORD his God, as the heart of David his father had been. ⁵He followed Ashtoreth the goddess of the Sidonians, and Molech*c* the detestable god of the Ammonites. ⁶So Solomon did evil in the eyes of the LORD; he did not follow the LORD completely, as David his father had done.

⁷On a hill east of Jerusalem, Solomon built a high place for Chemosh the detestable god of Moab, and for Molech the detestable god of the Ammonites. ⁸He did the same for all his foreign wives, who burned incense and offered sacrifices to their gods.

⁹The LORD became angry with Solomon because his heart had turned away from the LORD, the God of Israel, who had appeared to him twice. ¹⁰Although he had forbidden Solomon to follow other

a29 That is, about 15 pounds (about 7 kilograms)   b29 That is, about 3 3/4 pounds (about 1.7 kilograms)   c5 Hebrew Milcom; also in verse 33

Sidebar (left column)

All other things being equal, how many wives or husbands could you afford to keep?

1. What was Solomon's weakness (vv. 1–5)? Why didn't his great wisdom save him? **2.** Why is intermarriage forbidden in Jewish law (Dt 7:1–4)? What purpose do royal weddings serve (see 3:1)? Why have concubines? **3.** What happened in the worship of Molech (vv. 7–8; see Lev 20:5; 2Ki 23:10)? **4.** Why is God so harsh, knowing these shrines are only for the wives (v. 8)? **5.** Why does God soften the judgment on Solomon (vv. 12–13; see 2Sa 7:11–16)?

1. What weakness hurts your relationship with God? With others? With health and long life? **2.** What gods divide your attention today? What's wrong with 90 percent devotion to God and 10 percent to modern idols? What is easier to do: get your attention or divide it? Isn't some devotion better than none? **3.** Is it wrong to date a non-

---

1 Kings 10:23–11:13   SOLOMON'S SPLENDOR, SOLOMON'S WIVES

Outwardly, Solomon brought Israel to unparalleled prominence and glory.

1. Solomon's problem was that he:
   a. was rich.
   b. was famous.
   c. was indiscriminate about women.
   d. turned to other gods.

2. What did God have against the Israelites marrying foreigners?
   a. They diverted Israel's attention.
   b. They seduced Israel into idolatry.
   c. They tainted God's pure race.
   d. God didn't love them as much.

3. It appears to me that Solomon:
   a. ignored wisdom in his love life.
   b. knew what he was doing.
   c. didn't know the consequences.
   d. gradually fell away from God.
   e. was fortunate he was David's son.

4. How did Solomon turn away from God as he got older?
   a. Fame and fortune filled his needs.
   b. He tired of resisting temptation.
   c. He let others influence him.
   d. He forgot his heritage.
   e. He wavered in his commitment.

5. In Solomon's case, what would "devoting his heart to the Lord" mean?
   a. celibacy
   b. a busy day in divorce court
   c. giving away his wealth
   d. living by the wisdom he knew
   e. destroying the foreign gods
   f. getting off the fence

6. Devoting myself to God has been:
   a. an event.
   b. a process.
   c. a struggle.
   d. a confusing obligation.
   e. a daily commitment.
   f. something I've been putting off.

7. I notice myself drifting away from the Lord when I:
   a. focus on material things.
   b. get too busy.
   c. don't go to church or small group.
   d. am under stress.
   e. give in to my bad habits.
   f. let others negatively influence me.

8. What difference has it made (or would it make) to be fully devoted to

God: In your social life? In your family life? In your job? In your church?

9. What keeps you from going off the deep end (spiritually, morally, etc.)?
   a. my church
   b. Christian friends
   c. a sense of humor
   d. physical activity
   e. my devotional life
   f. God's grip on me
   g. other:_____

10. As one who is "spiritually single," how does this story make you feel?
   a. condemned for my situation
   b. worried about my future
   c. motivated to learn from Solomon's downfall
   d. convicted about my spiritual life
   e. relieved that it's not too late

11. How does Solomon's example serve as a warning to you about the influence your spouse can have on your spiritual life? How are you able to honor your mate *and* keep God first in your life?

gods, Solomon did not keep the LORD's command. [11]So the LORD said to Solomon, "Since this is your attitude and you have not kept my covenant and my decrees, which I commanded you, I will most certainly tear the kingdom away from you and give it to one of your subordinates. [12]Nevertheless, for the sake of David your father, I will not do it during your lifetime. I will tear it out of the hand of your son. [13]Yet I will not tear the whole kingdom from him, but will give him one tribe for the sake of David my servant and for the sake of Jerusalem, which I have chosen."

Solomon's Adversaries

[14]Then the LORD raised up against Solomon an adversary, Hadad the Edomite, from the royal line of Edom. [15]Earlier when David was fighting with Edom, Joab the commander of the army, who had gone up to bury the dead, had struck down all the men in Edom. [16]Joab and all the Israelites stayed there for six months, until they had destroyed all the men in Edom. [17]But Hadad, still only a boy, fled to Egypt with some Edomite officials who had served his father. [18]They set out from Midian and went to Paran. Then taking men from Paran with them, they went to Egypt, to Pharaoh king of Egypt, who gave Hadad a house and land and provided him with food.

[19]Pharaoh was so pleased with Hadad that he gave him a sister of his own wife, Queen Tahpenes, in marriage. [20]The sister of Tahpenes bore him a son named Genubath, whom Tahpenes brought up in the royal palace. There Genubath lived with Pharaoh's own children.

[21]While he was in Egypt, Hadad heard that David rested with his fathers and that Joab the commander of the army was also dead. Then Hadad said to Pharaoh, "Let me go, that I may return to my own country."

[22]"What have you lacked here that you want to go back to your own country?" Pharaoh asked.

"Nothing," Hadad replied, "but do let me go!"

[23]And God raised up against Solomon another adversary, Rezon son of Eliada, who had fled from his master, Hadadezer king of Zobah. [24]He gathered men around him and became the leader of a band of rebels when David destroyed the forces[a] ⌊of Zobah⌋; the rebels went to Damascus, where they settled and took control. [25]Rezon was Israel's adversary as long as Solomon lived, adding to the trouble caused by Hadad. So Rezon ruled in Aram and was hostile toward Israel.

Jeroboam Rebels Against Solomon

[26]Also, Jeroboam son of Nebat rebelled against the king. He was one of Solomon's officials, an Ephraimite from Zeredah, and his mother was a widow named Zeruah.

[27]Here is the account of how he rebelled against the king: Solomon had built the supporting terraces[b] and had filled in the gap in the wall of the city of David his father. [28]Now Jeroboam was a man of standing, and when Solomon saw how well the young man did his work, he put him in charge of the whole labor force of the house of Joseph.

[29]About that time Jeroboam was going out of Jerusalem, and Ahijah the prophet of Shiloh met him on the way, wearing a new cloak. The two of them were alone out in the country, [30]and Ahijah took hold of the new cloak he was wearing and tore it into twelve

[a]24 Hebrew *destroyed them*   [b]27 Or *the Millo*

Christian? To marry one? What's your advice to "mixed faith" couples? **4.** Why don't we practice polygamy anymore? If it's so bad, why was it practiced in the Old Testament era, even under the Law?

---

1. Did any school-age "adversaries" ever gang up on you and cause you to flee? Do you have any vivid memories of being "on the run" from them? **2.** Have you ever been set up with "someone's sister"?

1. What does it mean that God "raised up" adversaries against Solomon? Didn't they have their own reasons to oppose him? **2.** Why does Hadad give up Egypt's comforts for guerrilla life (vv. 15–22)? Is he a coward waiting for David and Joab to die? Why does Pharaoh try to dissuade him? **3.** From where comes Solomon's second enemy (vv. 23–25; see 2Sa 8:3–6)? **4.** How is God fulfilling his promise to David by giving Solomon these enemies?

1. Are you: (a) Seeking revenge for past wrongs? or (b) Finding yourself the object of others' grudges? How should people respond to unjust treatment? **2.** Who are your adversaries? What word might God be trying to get to you through them?

---

1. Who stole your "first love"? In turn, were you ever the "heart-breaker," forsaking an old friend for a new one? **2.** How have you not lived up to, or rebelled against, your parents' expectations or standards of excellence?

1. What commends Jeroboam for the position he's given (vv. 26–28)? **2.** Do you think Jeroboam opposed Solomon before meeting Ahijah (v. 29)? What grievances might he have had? **3.** How do Ahijah's actions embody God's plans (vv. 30–31)? Hasn't the "cloak" been divided for some time (see 2Sa 5:5; 19:43)? What tribe will Solomon keep (v. 32; see Jos 19:1–9)? What tribes are left (see Jos 21)? **4.** Is God dividing Israel during its golden age, or has Solomon simply failed to unite it? Who does this passage blame for the schism: Jeroboam? Solomon? God? **5.** If you were Solomon, which adversary would cause you the greatest concern: Hadad (see vv. 14–22), Rezon (see vv. 23–25) or Jeroboam? Why? **6.** Why does Solomon try to kill Jeroboam (v. 40)? What must have transpired? How loyal an ally is pharaoh? **7.** What written source no longer exists as far as we know (v. 41)? Why write this account if other ones already exist?

1. Has God torn anything out of your hands lately? Any guess as to God's purpose? What have you learned through this? **2.** The promise of reward is a common motivation for obeying God, but is it a sufficient incentive for you? How so? What promises of reward would you want to keep in mind through the coming week?

---

1. As a kid, were you the type who: (a) Took your ball and went home? (b) Grabbed the ball and forced the game to continue? (c) Punctured the ball to settle everyone's problem? Explain. **2.** What parental advice did you once reject in favor of your peers—advice that you later wished you'd taken? **3.** What hard manual labor have you done? What was your reward?

1. Are all the tribes of Israel sold on Rehoboam (vv. 1–4)? How do they view Solomon's "golden age"? **2.** Rehoboam receives conflicting advice from the elders and his peers. What rationale lies behind each advisory opinion? **3.** How does Rehoboam respond to each? Why does Rehoboam favor the young men's advice (vv. 10–14)? **4.** What is meant by attributing this to the Lord (v. 15; see 11:9–13)? Is the author condoning either Rehoboam's harshness or the people's rebellion? **5.**

pieces. [31]Then he said to Jeroboam, "Take ten pieces for yourself, for this is what the LORD, the God of Israel, says: 'See, I am going to tear the kingdom out of Solomon's hand and give you ten tribes. [32]But for the sake of my servant David and the city of Jerusalem, which I have chosen out of all the tribes of Israel, he will have one tribe. [33]I will do this because they have[a] forsaken me and worshiped Ashtoreth the goddess of the Sidonians, Chemosh the god of the Moabites, and Molech the god of the Ammonites, and have not walked in my ways, nor done what is right in my eyes, nor kept my statutes and laws as David, Solomon's father, did.

[34]" 'But I will not take the whole kingdom out of Solomon's hand; I have made him ruler all the days of his life for the sake of David my servant, whom I chose and who observed my commands and statutes. [35]I will take the kingdom from his son's hands and give you ten tribes. [36]I will give one tribe to his son so that David my servant may always have a lamp before me in Jerusalem, the city where I chose to put my Name. [37]However, as for you, I will take you, and you will rule over all that your heart desires; you will be king over Israel. [38]If you do whatever I command you and walk in my ways and do what is right in my eyes by keeping my statutes and commands, as David my servant did, I will be with you. I will build you a dynasty as enduring as the one I built for David and will give Israel to you. [39]I will humble David's descendants because of this, but not forever.' "

[40]Solomon tried to kill Jeroboam, but Jeroboam fled to Egypt, to Shishak the king, and stayed there until Solomon's death.

Solomon's Death

[41]As for the other events of Solomon's reign—all he did and the wisdom he displayed—are they not written in the book of the annals of Solomon? [42]Solomon reigned in Jerusalem over all Israel forty years. [43]Then he rested with his fathers and was buried in the city of David his father. And Rehoboam his son succeeded him as king.

Israel Rebels Against Rehoboam

12 Rehoboam went to Shechem, for all the Israelites had gone there to make him king. [2]When Jeroboam son of Nebat heard this (he was still in Egypt, where he had fled from King Solomon), he returned from[b] Egypt. [3]So they sent for Jeroboam, and he and the whole assembly of Israel went to Rehoboam and said to him: [4]"Your father put a heavy yoke on us, but now lighten the harsh labor and the heavy yoke he put on us, and we will serve you."

[5]Rehoboam answered, "Go away for three days and then come back to me." So the people went away.

[6]Then King Rehoboam consulted the elders who had served his father Solomon during his lifetime. "How would you advise me to answer these people?" he asked.

[7]They replied, "If today you will be a servant to these people and serve them and give them a favorable answer, they will always be your servants."

[8]But Rehoboam rejected the advice the elders gave him and consulted the young men who had grown up with him and were serving him. [9]He asked them, "What is your advice? How should we answer these people who say to me, 'Lighten the yoke your father put on us'?"

---

[a]33 Hebrew; Septuagint, Vulgate and Syriac *because he has*   [b]2 Or *he remained in*

[10]The young men who had grown up with him replied, "Tell these people who have said to you, 'Your father put a heavy yoke on us, but make our yoke lighter'—tell them, 'My little finger is thicker than my father's waist. [11]My father laid on you a heavy yoke; I will make it even heavier. My father scourged you with whips; I will scourge you with scorpions.'"

[12]Three days later Jeroboam and all the people returned to Rehoboam, as the king had said, "Come back to me in three days." [13]The king answered the people harshly. Rejecting the advice given him by the elders, [14]he followed the advice of the young men and said, "My father made your yoke heavy; I will make it even heavier. My father scourged you with whips; I will scourge you with scorpions." [15]So the king did not listen to the people, for this turn of events was from the LORD, to fulfill the word the LORD had spoken to Jeroboam son of Nebat through Ahijah the Shilonite.

[16]When all Israel saw that the king refused to listen to them, they answered the king:

"What share do we have in David,
    what part in Jesse's son?
To your tents, O Israel!
    Look after your own house, O David!"

So the Israelites went home. [17]But as for the Israelites who were living in the towns of Judah, Rehoboam still ruled over them.

[18]King Rehoboam sent out Adoniram,[a] who was in charge of forced labor, but all Israel stoned him to death. King Rehoboam, however, managed to get into his chariot and escape to Jerusalem.

[a] 18 Some Septuagint manuscripts and Syriac (see also 1 Kings 4:6 and 5:14); Hebrew *Adoram*

How do the Israelites express their rebellion here? What short-term and long-term effect does this have? What does Rehoboam learn from Adoniram's chilling reception? **6.** Why does Judah remain faithful to Rehoboam (vv. 20–21; see also Mt 1:2–7)? **7.** What role and risks does Shemaiah take: (a) Brave diplomat who forestalls a bloody civil war? (b) Wise prophet who convinces the king to swallow his pride and go home? (c) Shrewd spy working for Jeroboam? **8.** Why did his word carry the day? What is the mood of the people of Judah: Resentment? Resignation? Relief?

1. What justification is there for violence, assassination or civil war? Does justice sometimes require that some people die? **2.** Who really listens to your side of the story: Parents? A friend? Boss? Pastor? Who seems to always ignore your feelings and needs? **3.** Do you take advice well? Do you go it alone? What piece of your own advice do you never seem to follow? How can the group help? **4.** How well do you listen? (Are you usually thinking about what you'll say next? Appearing knowledgeable or trendy?) Pair off in your

---

1 Kings 12:1–24   THE KINGDOM IS DIVIDED

Before Solomon died God told him that, due to his spiritual disobedience, he would lose most of the kingdom. However, for the sake of his father David, this would happen to his son. A prophet also promised Jeroboam he would later rule the northern tribes. The southern tribe of Judah naturally accepted David and his descendants since they were from that tribe. Now Rehoboam has succeeded his father Solomon as king, and travels to Shechem in hopes of receiving the continued support of the northern tribes.

1. What did the northern tribes want?
    a. an end to forced labor and military service
    b. lower taxes
    c. a new nation
    d. a new king
    e. a fair king
    f. a reason to rebel

2. What was the philosophy behind the advice of the "elders"?
    a. Politicians should make promises.
    b. Politicians should be servants.

c. Creative solutions are win-win.
d. It takes strength to compromise.

3. What was the philosophy behind the advice of Rehoboam's friends?
    a. Show them who's in charge.
    b. Tread softly and carry a big stick.
    c. Play hardball.
    d. Compromise is for sissies.

4. Why did Rehoboam choose the young men's counsel?
    a. He bowed to peer pressure.
    b. He wanted to look strong.
    c. He thought it was the best way to keep the kingdom together.
    d. It was God's will.

5. Who was responsible for Israel breaking apart?
    a. Rehoboam
    b. Jeroboam
    c. Solomon
    d. Rehoboam's young advisers
    e. the northern tribes
    f. the southern tribe (Judah)
    g. God
    h. no one really—conflict is inevitable

6. How does the story end?
    a. They all live happily ever after.
    b. Rehoboam and Judah wimp out.
    c. Rehoboam and Judah swallow their pride.
    d. A prophet prevents a civil war.
    e. Cooler heads prevail.

7. Do you have a peacemaker like Shemaiah in your family? Your workplace? Your church or small group?

8. When have you rejected good advice (that you later wished you had taken) in favor of your peers?

9. Do you consider yourself a good listener? How well do you take advice? Would you rather go it alone?

10. How important is it for Christians to seek counsel from others? How closely does your practice match your principles?

11. Where do you usually go for counsel? How do you discern good from bad advice? What do you do if you don't like what you hear?

¹⁹So Israel has been in rebellion against the house of David to this day.

²⁰When all the Israelites heard that Jeroboam had returned, they sent and called him to the assembly and made him king over all Israel. Only the tribe of Judah remained loyal to the house of David.

²¹When Rehoboam arrived in Jerusalem, he mustered the whole house of Judah and the tribe of Benjamin—a hundred and eighty thousand fighting men—to make war against the house of Israel and to regain the kingdom for Rehoboam son of Solomon.

²²But this word of God came to Shemaiah the man of God: ²³"Say to Rehoboam son of Solomon king of Judah, to the whole house of Judah and Benjamin, and to the rest of the people, ²⁴'This is what the LORD says: Do not go up to fight against your brothers, the Israelites. Go home, every one of you, for this is my doing.'" So they obeyed the word of the LORD and went home again, as the LORD had ordered.

Golden Calves at Bethel and Dan

²⁵Then Jeroboam fortified Shechem in the hill country of Ephraim and lived there. From there he went out and built up Peniel.^a

²⁶Jeroboam thought to himself, "The kingdom will now likely revert to the house of David. ²⁷If these people go up to offer sacrifices at the temple of the LORD in Jerusalem, they will again give their allegiance to their lord, Rehoboam king of Judah. They will kill me and return to King Rehoboam."

²⁸After seeking advice, the king made two golden calves. He said to the people, "It is too much for you to go up to Jerusalem. Here are your gods, O Israel, who brought you up out of Egypt." ²⁹One he set up in Bethel, and the other in Dan. ³⁰And this thing became a sin; the people went even as far as Dan to worship the one there.

³¹Jeroboam built shrines on high places and appointed priests from all sorts of people, even though they were not Levites. ³²He instituted a festival on the fifteenth day of the eighth month, like the festival held in Judah, and offered sacrifices on the altar. This he did in Bethel, sacrificing to the calves he had made. And at Bethel he also installed priests at the high places he had made. ³³On the fifteenth day of the eighth month, a month of his own choosing, he offered sacrifices on the altar he had built at Bethel. So he instituted the festival for the Israelites and went up to the altar to make offerings.

The Man of God From Judah

13 By the word of the LORD a man of God came from Judah to Bethel, as Jeroboam was standing by the altar to make an offering. ²He cried out against the altar by the word of the LORD: "O altar, altar! This is what the LORD says: 'A son named Josiah will be born to the house of David. On you he will sacrifice the priests of the high places who now make offerings here, and human bones will be burned on you.'" ³That same day the man of God gave a sign: "This is the sign the LORD has declared: The altar will be split apart and the ashes on it will be poured out."

⁴When King Jeroboam heard what the man of God cried out against the altar at Bethel, he stretched out his hand from the altar and said, "Seize him!" But the hand he stretched out toward the man shriveled up, so that he could not pull it back. ⁵Also, the altar

---

group and try listening to someone without attempting to approve, disapprove, analyze, fix, heal, convert or condemn him or her. Does it help them open up? Will they talk to you again?

☕ 1. How far do you travel to church? Why not worship closer to home? 2. Do you sit in the same place every Sunday at church or when the group meets? When did you last break out of the mold?

📖 1. What two threats does Jeroboam feel from Judah (vv. 25–27)? How does he address each? 2. Who does Jeroboam echo (vv. 28–30; see Ex 32:4)? Do the golden calves *replace* or *represent* God? Why two? (Check a map.) 3. How else does Jeroboam's do-it-yourself religion compete with the religious system of Judah (vv. 31–33)? By what authority are the changes made?

♡ 1. Who are your spiritual authorities? Is the church a democracy? 2. How do you tell true from false religion?

☕ 1. Have you ever been threatened by a wild animal? Grizzly bear? Wolf? Lion? Bison? House mice? 2. On vacations, where do you tend to eat: Familiar fast food chains? Exotic native restaurants? Hotels? Truck stops? When do you cultivate your culinary curiosity? 3. What tall tale or legendary story about you got really blown out of proportion? Who contributed to the fantastic distortions?

📖 1. Who is the "man of God"? Couldn't he have delivered his message at Bethel in a more diplomatic way? How so? 2. Does his prediction generate any con-

---

^a25 Hebrew *Penuel,* a variant of *Peniel*

was split apart and its ashes poured out according to the sign given by the man of God by the word of the LORD.

[6]Then the king said to the man of God, "Intercede with the LORD your God and pray for me that my hand may be restored." So the man of God interceded with the LORD, and the king's hand was restored and became as it was before.

[7]The king said to the man of God, "Come home with me and have something to eat, and I will give you a gift."

[8]But the man of God answered the king, "Even if you were to give me half your possessions, I would not go with you, nor would I eat bread or drink water here. [9]For I was commanded by the word of the LORD: 'You must not eat bread or drink water or return by the way you came.'" [10]So he took another road and did not return by the way he had come to Bethel.

[11]Now there was a certain old prophet living in Bethel, whose sons came and told him all that the man of God had done there that day. They also told their father what he had said to the king. [12]Their father asked them, "Which way did he go?" And his sons showed him which road the man of God from Judah had taken. [13]So he said to his sons, "Saddle the donkey for me." And when they had saddled the donkey for him, he mounted it [14]and rode after the man of God. He found him sitting under an oak tree and asked, "Are you the man of God who came from Judah?"

"I am," he replied.

[15]So the prophet said to him, "Come home with me and eat."

[16]The man of God said, "I cannot turn back and go with you, nor can I eat bread or drink water with you in this place. [17]I have been told by the word of the LORD: 'You must not eat bread or drink water there or return by the way you came.'"

[18]The old prophet answered, "I too am a prophet, as you are. And an angel said to me by the word of the LORD: 'Bring him back with you to your house so that he may eat bread and drink water.'" (But he was lying to him.) [19]So the man of God returned with him and ate and drank in his house.

[20]While they were sitting at the table, the word of the LORD came to the old prophet who had brought him back. [21]He cried out to the man of God who had come from Judah, "This is what the LORD says: 'You have defied the word of the LORD and have not kept the command the LORD your God gave you. [22]You came back and ate bread and drank water in the place where he told you not to eat or drink. Therefore your body will not be buried in the tomb of your fathers.'"

[23]When the man of God had finished eating and drinking, the prophet who had brought him back saddled his donkey for him. [24]As he went on his way, a lion met him on the road and killed him, and his body was thrown down on the road, with both the donkey and the lion standing beside it. [25]Some people who passed by saw the body thrown down there, with the lion standing beside the body, and they went and reported it in the city where the old prophet lived.

[26]When the prophet who had brought him back from his journey heard of it, he said, "It is the man of God who defied the word of the LORD. The LORD has given him over to the lion, which has mauled him and killed him, as the word of the LORD had warned him."

[27]The prophet said to his sons, "Saddle the donkey for me," and they did so. [28]Then he went out and found the body thrown down on the road, with the donkey and the lion standing beside it. The lion had neither eaten the body nor mauled the donkey. [29]So the

cern for Jeroboam (vv. 4–5)? What "gives teeth" to the prediction? Why do you think the king invites the man of God to his home? Would you have gone? **3.** Why does the prophet refuse (vv. 8–10)? What might be God's rationale behind these restrictions? **4.** What motivates the old prophet to go after the man of God (vv. 11–19)? Why does the old prophet lie? Whose fault is it that the man of God gets fooled into dinner? How do you suppose the man of God feels when he hears the words in verses 21–22: Trapped? Deserted? Tricked? Hopeless? Repentant? Scared? **5.** Imagine you are playing the game known as, "What's wrong with this picture?" What would you answer about the scene in verses 23–25? What's the message about the man of God's death? **6.** How is the old prophet affected by the death: (a) Worried he will be next? (b) Sorry about lying to the man? (c) Glad to have had a word of prophecy after so long? (d) Other? **7.** Does Jeroboam get the message? Is the message clear enough? Where does Jeroboam go wrong? Is he worried? Scared? **8.** Has anyone in this chapter done right? Does God's work get accomplished? Does this chapter strike you as some kind of Hebrew fairy tale? Why or why not?

♡ **1.** Are you being tempted in any way right now to step off the straight and narrow path? Where might you want to deviate? Is someone else urging you to do so? What rationalizations have arisen in your mind for doing what you know deep down is not right? **2.** How can you tell the difference between a genuine "prophecy" and a lie? **3.** Are any mistakes too severe for God to forgive? What kind? Where does God's love stop and sure judgment begin? **4.** Can "anyone who wants to be" qualify as a preacher or teacher? Who qualifies as spiritual authority? **5.** Where do you plan to be buried? Does it make any difference? What would you like inscribed on your tombstone?

prophet picked up the body of the man of God, laid it on the donkey, and brought it back to his own city to mourn for him and bury him. ³⁰Then he laid the body in his own tomb, and they mourned over him and said, "Oh, my brother!"

³¹After burying him, he said to his sons, "When I die, bury me in the grave where the man of God is buried; lay my bones beside his bones. ³²For the message he declared by the word of the LORD against the altar in Bethel and against all the shrines on the high places in the towns of Samaria will certainly come true."

³³Even after this, Jeroboam did not change his evil ways, but once more appointed priests for the high places from all sorts of people. Anyone who wanted to become a priest he consecrated for the high places. ³⁴This was the sin of the house of Jeroboam that led to its downfall and to its destruction from the face of the earth.

Ahijah's Prophecy Against Jeroboam

14 At that time Abijah son of Jeroboam became ill, ²and Jeroboam said to his wife, "Go, disguise yourself, so you won't be recognized as the wife of Jeroboam. Then go to Shiloh. Ahijah the prophet is there—the one who told me I would be king over this people. ³Take ten loaves of bread with you, some cakes and a jar of honey, and go to him. He will tell you what will happen to the boy." ⁴So Jeroboam's wife did what he said and went to Ahijah's house in Shiloh.

Now Ahijah could not see; his sight was gone because of his age. ⁵But the LORD had told Ahijah, "Jeroboam's wife is coming to ask you about her son, for he is ill, and you are to give her such and such an answer. When she arrives, she will pretend to be someone else."

⁶So when Ahijah heard the sound of her footsteps at the door, he said, "Come in, wife of Jeroboam. Why this pretense? I have been sent to you with bad news. ⁷Go, tell Jeroboam that this is what the LORD, the God of Israel, says: 'I raised you up from among the people and made you a leader over my people Israel. ⁸I tore the kingdom away from the house of David and gave it to you, but you have not been like my servant David, who kept my commands and followed me with all his heart, doing only what was right in my eyes. ⁹You have done more evil than all who lived before you. You have made for yourself other gods, idols made of metal; you have provoked me to anger and thrust me behind your back.

¹⁰"'Because of this, I am going to bring disaster on the house of Jeroboam. I will cut off from Jeroboam every last male in Israel—slave or free. I will burn up the house of Jeroboam as one burns dung, until it is all gone. ¹¹Dogs will eat those belonging to Jeroboam who die in the city, and the birds of the air will feed on those who die in the country. The LORD has spoken!'

¹²"As for you, go back home. When you set foot in your city, the boy will die. ¹³All Israel will mourn for him and bury him. He is the only one belonging to Jeroboam who will be buried, because he is the only one in the house of Jeroboam in whom the LORD, the God of Israel, has found anything good.

¹⁴"The LORD will raise up for himself a king over Israel who will cut off the family of Jeroboam. This is the day! What? Yes, even now.ᵃ ¹⁵And the LORD will strike Israel, so that it will be like a reed swaying in the water. He will uproot Israel from this good land that he gave to their forefathers and scatter them beyond the River,ᵇ because they provoked the LORD to anger by making Ashe-

---

ᵃ14 The meaning of the Hebrew for this sentence is uncertain.   ᵇ15 That is, the Euphrates

rah poles.*a* 16And he will give Israel up because of the sins Jeroboam has committed and has caused Israel to commit."

17Then Jeroboam's wife got up and left and went to Tirzah. As soon as she stepped over the threshold of the house, the boy died. 18They buried him, and all Israel mourned for him, as the LORD had said through his servant the prophet Ahijah.

19The other events of Jeroboam's reign, his wars and how he ruled, are written in the book of the annals of the kings of Israel. 20He reigned for twenty-two years and then rested with his fathers. And Nadab his son succeeded him as king.

Rehoboam King of Judah

21Rehoboam son of Solomon was king in Judah. He was forty-one years old when he became king, and he reigned seventeen years in Jerusalem, the city the LORD had chosen out of all the tribes of Israel in which to put his Name. His mother's name was Naamah; she was an Ammonite.

22Judah did evil in the eyes of the LORD. By the sins they committed they stirred up his jealous anger more than their fathers had done. 23They also set up for themselves high places, sacred stones and Asherah poles on every high hill and under every spreading tree. 24There were even male shrine prostitutes in the land; the people engaged in all the detestable practices of the nations the LORD had driven out before the Israelites.

25In the fifth year of King Rehoboam, Shishak king of Egypt attacked Jerusalem. 26He carried off the treasures of the temple of the LORD and the treasures of the royal palace. He took everything, including all the gold shields Solomon had made. 27So King Rehoboam made bronze shields to replace them and assigned these to the commanders of the guard on duty at the entrance to the royal palace. 28Whenever the king went to the LORD's temple, the guards bore the shields, and afterward they returned them to the guardroom.

29As for the other events of Rehoboam's reign, and all he did, are they not written in the book of the annals of the kings of Judah? 30There was continual warfare between Rehoboam and Jeroboam. 31And Rehoboam rested with his fathers and was buried with them in the City of David. His mother's name was Naamah; she was an Ammonite. And Abijah*b* his son succeeded him as king.

Abijah King of Judah

15 In the eighteenth year of the reign of Jeroboam son of Nebat, Abijah*c* became king of Judah, 2and he reigned in Jerusalem three years. His mother's name was Maacah daughter of Abishalom.*d*

3He committed all the sins his father had done before him; his heart was not fully devoted to the LORD his God, as the heart of David his forefather had been. 4Nevertheless, for David's sake the LORD his God gave him a lamp in Jerusalem by raising up a son to succeed him and by making Jerusalem strong. 5For David had done what was right in the eyes of the LORD and had not failed to keep any of the LORD's commands all the days of his life—except in the case of Uriah the Hittite.

6There was war between Rehoboam*e* and Jeroboam throughout

---

something you'd prefer to leave to your family? Why?

Have you ever been given a warning for a traffic violation, instead of a ticket? How did you respond to the warning?

1. Why does the text mention Rehoboam's ancestral lineage twice (vv. 21,31; see 11:1–2)? 2. Has Solomon's sin born fruit in the life of his son and in Israel (vv. 22–24)? 3. What is the purpose of the Egyptian attack (vv. 25–28)? How would Solomon have felt seeing his precious treasures stolen? How would the forced laborers and craftsmen have felt? 4. Who does the writer imply is to blame for the pillage: Shishak? Rehoboam? The people of Israel? God? What had God warned (see Dt 28:15,25, 29)?

1. What are the modern Asherah poles? What pagan rites today, overt or subtle, lead people away from the true God? 2. How does God warn his people today about sinful practices to be avoided? Have you been warned lately?

1. In what two ways are you like, and unlike, your dad? 2. What chapter from your life would you like to re-write if you could?

1. For what is Abijah's reign remembered? 2. Since Abijah is sinful, why is he given the throne? Why does God continue his line "for David's sake" (v. 4)? 3. What struggle does Abijah inherit?

1. Why will one child follow the parents' ways, another will reject them? Did you follow or reject your parents' beliefs? 2. Does God bless people for the merit of their ancestors?

---

a15 That is, symbols of the goddess Asherah; here and elsewhere in 1 Kings
b31 Some Hebrew manuscripts and Septuagint (see also 2 Chron. 12:16); most Hebrew manuscripts *Abijam*   *c1* Some Hebrew manuscripts and Septuagint (see also 2 Chron. 12:16); most Hebrew manuscripts *Abijam*; also in verses 7 and 8   *d2* A variant of *Absalom*; also in verse 10   *e6* Most Hebrew manuscripts; some Hebrew manuscripts and Syriac *Abijam* (that is, Abijah)

⌐Abijah's⌐ lifetime. 7As for the other events of Abijah's reign, and all he did, are they not written in the book of the annals of the kings of Judah? There was war between Abijah and Jeroboam. 8And Abijah rested with his fathers and was buried in the City of David. And Asa his son succeeded him as king.

Asa King of Judah

9In the twentieth year of Jeroboam king of Israel, Asa became king of Judah, 10and he reigned in Jerusalem forty-one years. His grandmother's name was Maacah daughter of Abishalom.

11Asa did what was right in the eyes of the LORD, as his father David had done. 12He expelled the male shrine prostitutes from the land and got rid of all the idols his fathers had made. 13He even deposed his grandmother Maacah from her position as queen mother, because she had made a repulsive Asherah pole. Asa cut the pole down and burned it in the Kidron Valley. 14Although he did not remove the high places, Asa's heart was fully committed to the LORD all his life. 15He brought into the temple of the LORD the silver and gold and the articles that he and his father had dedicated.

16There was war between Asa and Baasha king of Israel throughout their reigns. 17Baasha king of Israel went up against Judah and fortified Ramah to prevent anyone from leaving or entering the territory of Asa king of Judah.

18Asa then took all the silver and gold that was left in the treasuries of the LORD's temple and of his own palace. He entrusted it to his officials and sent them to Ben-Hadad son of Tabrimmon, the son of Hezion, the king of Aram, who was ruling in Damascus. 19"Let there be a treaty between me and you," he said, "as there was between my father and your father. See, I am sending you a gift of silver and gold. Now break your treaty with Baasha king of Israel so he will withdraw from me."

20Ben-Hadad agreed with King Asa and sent the commanders of his forces against the towns of Israel. He conquered Ijon, Dan, Abel Beth Maacah and all Kinnereth in addition to Naphtali. 21When Baasha heard this, he stopped building Ramah and withdrew to Tirzah. 22Then King Asa issued an order to all Judah—no one was exempt—and they carried away from Ramah the stones and timber Baasha had been using there. With them King Asa built up Geba in Benjamin, and also Mizpah.

23As for all the other events of Asa's reign, all his achievements, all he did and the cities he built, are they not written in the book of the annals of the kings of Judah? In his old age, however, his feet became diseased. 24Then Asa rested with his fathers and was buried with them in the city of his father David. And Jehoshaphat his son succeeded him as king.

Nadab King of Israel

25Nadab son of Jeroboam became king of Israel in the second year of Asa king of Judah, and he reigned over Israel two years. 26He did evil in the eyes of the LORD, walking in the ways of his father and in his sin, which he had caused Israel to commit.

27Baasha son of Ahijah of the house of Issachar plotted against him, and he struck him down at Gibbethon, a Philistine town, while Nadab and all Israel were besieging it. 28Baasha killed Nadab in the third year of Asa king of Judah and succeeded him as king.

29As soon as he began to reign, he killed Jeroboam's whole family. He did not leave Jeroboam anyone that breathed, but destroyed them all, according to the word of the LORD given through

---

1. Have you ever foraged through garbage dumpsters or roadside trash for treasures or food? With whom? What was the loot? 2. How often do you go "garage saling"? What items do you look for? Ever been told you need to hold a garage sale? What's the message there?

1. Why do you think Asa's mother is not mentioned (v. 10)? What could have motivated Asa to break the chain of evil forged by his father and grandfather? 2. What is the function of "male shrine prostitutes" (v. 12; see Dt 23:17–18; Hos 4:14)? 3. What resistance does Asa face in his reforms and why (v. 13)? 4. What is Asa's strategy for national defense (vv. 16–20)? What is the alliance based upon? What short-term benefit might it provide? What is the long-range problem in Asa's military plan?

1. Has your obedience to God ever alienated family or others around you? Was it really your faith or just your "holier-than-thou" attitude? What happened? 2. Is the security of your country in "silver and gold"? Stones and timber? Undercover dealings? Where does real security lie? 3. Do you fear becoming an invalid when you get old? Where will you live when you can no longer get around? How can you best prepare for possible disabling illness?

What silly thing always punches your anger button? How do you show it?

1. What was the sin of Nadab's father (see 12:26–33)? 2. Baasha was likely a military leader. How does his military coup fit in with God's plan (vv. 27–28; see 14:10–16)? 3. Why should the king's children die, too?

his servant Ahijah the Shilonite— ³⁰because of the sins Jeroboam had committed and had caused Israel to commit, and because he provoked the LORD, the God of Israel, to anger.
³¹As for the other events of Nadab's reign, and all he did, are they not written in the book of the annals of the kings of Israel? ³²There was war between Asa and Baasha king of Israel throughout their reigns.

Baasha King of Israel

³³In the third year of Asa king of Judah, Baasha son of Ahijah became king of all Israel in Tirzah, and he reigned twenty-four years. ³⁴He did evil in the eyes of the LORD, walking in the ways of Jeroboam and in his sin, which he had caused Israel to commit.

16 Then the word of the LORD came to Jehu son of Hanani against Baasha: ²"I lifted you up from the dust and made you leader of my people Israel, but you walked in the ways of Jeroboam and caused my people Israel to sin and to provoke me to anger by their sins. ³So I am about to consume Baasha and his house, and I will make your house like that of Jeroboam son of Nebat. ⁴Dogs will eat those belonging to Baasha who die in the city, and the birds of the air will feed on those who die in the country."
⁵As for the other events of Baasha's reign, what he did and his achievements, are they not written in the book of the annals of the kings of Israel? ⁶Baasha rested with his fathers and was buried in Tirzah. And Elah his son succeeded him as king.
⁷Moreover, the word of the LORD came through the prophet Jehu son of Hanani to Baasha and his house, because of all the evil he had done in the eyes of the LORD, provoking him to anger by the things he did, and becoming like the house of Jeroboam—and also because he destroyed it.

Elah King of Israel

⁸In the twenty-sixth year of Asa king of Judah, Elah son of Baasha became king of Israel, and he reigned in Tirzah two years.
⁹Zimri, one of his officials, who had command of half his chariots, plotted against him. Elah was in Tirzah at the time, getting drunk in the home of Arza, the man in charge of the palace at Tirzah. ¹⁰Zimri came in, struck him down and killed him in the twenty-seventh year of Asa king of Judah. Then he succeeded him as king.
¹¹As soon as he began to reign and was seated on the throne, he killed off Baasha's whole family. He did not spare a single male, whether relative or friend. ¹²So Zimri destroyed the whole family of Baasha, in accordance with the word of the LORD spoken against Baasha through the prophet Jehu— ¹³because of all the sins Baasha and his son Elah had committed and had caused Israel to commit, so that they provoked the LORD, the God of Israel, to anger by their worthless idols.
¹⁴As for the other events of Elah's reign, and all he did, are they not written in the book of the annals of the kings of Israel?

Zimri King of Israel

¹⁵In the twenty-seventh year of Asa king of Judah, Zimri reigned in Tirzah seven days. The army was encamped near Gibbethon, a Philistine town. ¹⁶When the Israelites in the camp heard that Zimri had plotted against the king and murdered him, they proclaimed Omri, the commander of the army, king over Israel that very day there in the camp. ¹⁷Then Omri and all the Israelites with him

---

1. Why are so many countries today ruled by military leaders? What must generals believe for civilian rule to prevail? **2.** How does God deal with sinners today? Are fair warnings still given? How so?

For what culinary "feat" (delight or disaster) will you be remembered?

---

1. Are you surprised Baasha lasts 24 years in power (see 15:27–30)? Was he an improvement over the king he replaced? Why or why not? **2.** Is it fair to punish Baasha, and punish in like manner, for destroying the house of Jeroboam (vv. 2–4; see 14:10–16; 15:29)? Why or why not?

---

1. In what ways has God "lifted you up from the dust"? What responsibilities came with the new life? **2.** Ever felt like Jehu, the bearer of bad news? How can good news shine through bad news? **3.** Ever been "caught between a rock and a hard place"? When?

---

1. What might Zimri have against Elah? Is power hazardous to your health? **2.** How is Zimri's rise to power like Baasha's? Is Zimri part of Jehu's prophecy (see 16:3)? Why doesn't Elah suspect Zimri (v. 9)? **3.** Why does Zimri execute the friends, as well as the family, of Baasha (v. 11)?

---

1. Have you ever been betrayed by a friend, or are you a good judge of character? How so? **2.** Can you succeed by being nice in a "dog-eat-dog" world? Do you have to be violent to be safe? Explain.

With what badge of notoriety would you like your name to be associated 3000 years in the future?

---

1. What positions do Zimri and Omri hold in the army (vv. 15–16; see 16:9)? What does

Zimri do during his week as king (see 16:11)? **2.** Does Zimri overestimate his popularity with the military, or does he launch a coup knowing the military won't back him? What does his response to Omri's siege tell you (vv. 17–18)? **3.** Is the writer fair with Zimri or sounding like a broken record (v. 19)? **4.** What opposition does Omri face (v. 21)? How long is the power struggle (vv. 15,23)? In what kind of shape is Tirzah? **5.** What would Omri look for in relocating the capital from Tirzah, building and naming a new one?

♡ **1.** Is popularity important to you? Why or why not? Were you ever shocked to find you weren't as well-liked as you thought? **2.** Are you facing formidable opposition in any area of your life right now? **3.** What do you think of the Christians who tried to kill Hitler? How should Christians handle power struggles?

📖 **1.** What is Ahab's biggest sin (see Dt 7:1–4)? **2.** Why not rebuild Jericho (v. 34; see Jos 6:17–19,26)? **3.** What does Hiel do to his sons?

♡ **1.** Is your competitive edge high, low or medium? How do you channel it? **2.** Would Jesus ask us to annihilate unbelievers today (see Mt 5:44–45)? Why the change?

☕ Describe a time in your life when you had to "skimp" on food. What was your most creative meal?

📖 **1.** Why is a drought on the way (v. 1; see 16:33)? Why is the message open-ended? Dare Ahab try to kill Elijah? **2.** To what authority do the ravens link Elijah (v. 6; see Ex 16:12)? What does his "marking time" in Kerith symbolize? **3.** How did Elijah know it was time to move on (vv. 4,7,8)? Where does God send him and why? **4.** If

withdrew from Gibbethon and laid siege to Tirzah. ¹⁸When Zimri saw that the city was taken, he went into the citadel of the royal palace and set the palace on fire around him. So he died, ¹⁹because of the sins he had committed, doing evil in the eyes of the LORD and walking in the ways of Jeroboam and in the sin he had committed and had caused Israel to commit.

²⁰As for the other events of Zimri's reign, and the rebellion he carried out, are they not written in the book of the annals of the kings of Israel?

Omri King of Israel

²¹Then the people of Israel were split into two factions; half supported Tibni son of Ginath for king, and the other half supported Omri. ²²But Omri's followers proved stronger than those of Tibni son of Ginath. So Tibni died and Omri became king.

²³In the thirty-first year of Asa king of Judah, Omri became king of Israel, and he reigned twelve years, six of them in Tirzah. ²⁴He bought the hill of Samaria from Shemer for two talents*a* of silver and built a city on the hill, calling it Samaria, after Shemer, the name of the former owner of the hill.

²⁵But Omri did evil in the eyes of the LORD and sinned more than all those before him. ²⁶He walked in all the ways of Jeroboam son of Nebat and in his sin, which he had caused Israel to commit, so that they provoked the LORD, the God of Israel, to anger by their worthless idols.

²⁷As for the other events of Omri's reign, what he did and the things he achieved, are they not written in the book of the annals of the kings of Israel? ²⁸Omri rested with his fathers and was buried in Samaria. And Ahab his son succeeded him as king.

Ahab Becomes King of Israel

²⁹In the thirty-eighth year of Asa king of Judah, Ahab son of Omri became king of Israel, and he reigned in Samaria over Israel twenty-two years. ³⁰Ahab son of Omri did more evil in the eyes of the LORD than any of those before him. ³¹He not only considered it trivial to commit the sins of Jeroboam son of Nebat, but he also married Jezebel daughter of Ethbaal king of the Sidonians, and began to serve Baal and worship him. ³²He set up an altar for Baal in the temple of Baal that he built in Samaria. ³³Ahab also made an Asherah pole and did more to provoke the LORD, the God of Israel, to anger than did all the kings of Israel before him.

³⁴In Ahab's time, Hiel of Bethel rebuilt Jericho. He laid its foundations at the cost of his firstborn son Abiram, and he set up its gates at the cost of his youngest son Segub, in accordance with the word of the LORD spoken by Joshua son of Nun.

Elijah Fed by Ravens

17 Now Elijah the Tishbite, from Tishbe*b* in Gilead, said to Ahab, "As the LORD, the God of Israel, lives, whom I serve, there will be neither dew nor rain in the next few years except at my word."

²Then the word of the LORD came to Elijah: ³"Leave here, turn eastward and hide in the Kerith Ravine, east of the Jordan. ⁴You will drink from the brook, and I have ordered the ravens to feed you there."

⁵So he did what the LORD had told him. He went to the Kerith Ravine, east of the Jordan, and stayed there. ⁶The ravens brought

a24 That is, about 150 pounds (about 70 kilograms)   *b1* Or *Tishbite, of the settlers* him bread and meat in the morning and bread and meat in the evening, and he drank from the brook.

The Widow at Zarephath

[7]Some time later the brook dried up because there had been no rain in the land. [8]Then the word of the LORD came to him: [9]"Go at once to Zarephath of Sidon and stay there. I have commanded a widow in that place to supply you with food." [10]So he went to Zarephath. When he came to the town gate, a widow was there gathering sticks. He called to her and asked, "Would you bring me a little water in a jar so I may have a drink?" [11]As she was going to get it, he called, "And bring me, please, a piece of bread."

[12]"As surely as the LORD your God lives," she replied, "I don't have any bread—only a handful of flour in a jar and a little oil in a jug. I am gathering a few sticks to take home and make a meal for myself and my son, that we may eat it—and die."

[13]Elijah said to her, "Don't be afraid. Go home and do as you have said. But first make a small cake of bread for me from what you have and bring it to me, and then make something for yourself and your son. [14]For this is what the LORD, the God of Israel, says: 'The jar of flour will not be used up and the jug of oil will not run dry until the day the LORD gives rain on the land.'"

[15]She went away and did as Elijah had told her. So there was food every day for Elijah and for the woman and her family. [16]For the jar of flour was not used up and the jug of oil did not run dry, in keeping with the word of the LORD spoken by Elijah.

[17]Some time later the son of the woman who owned the house became ill. He grew worse and worse, and finally stopped breath-

you were the widow, how would you have responded to Elijah's words in verses 13–14? Was the woman a believer in the true God, or just in no position to argue? Why does Elijah tell her to provide for him first? Why does the woman comply? **5.** What does the widow assume when her son dies (v. 18; see Job 36:8–9)? Why does Elijah work so hard on the son (vv. 19–21): (a) He rejects the belief that God afflicts people when they sin? (b) He accepts this belief, but feels the widow is not guilty? (c) He wants to be proven a man of God, whose word can be trusted? (d) He wants to see for himself if God answers prayer? **6.** What impact does her son's recovery have on the widow (v. 24)? What other responses can you imagine? Will she lose faith again, at the next crisis?

♡ **1.** How difficult is it for you to stand against the mainstream? Is your Christian commitment a "Kerith Ravine experience" for you? How so? **2.** What "jars and jugs" are running dry for you? Will the Lord do something miraculous for you? Why or why not? **3.** When has a decision to trust God meant burning your bridges behind you?

---

   1 Kings 17:1–24   **ELIJAH AND THE WIDOW AT ZAREPHATH**

As Israel is led by Ahab, the most evil king they have ever had, the prophet Elijah appears on the scene. God tells Elijah to go first to the Kerith Ravine, and then to Zarephath—in the heart of the land from which the idolatrous worship of Baal had come into Israel.

1. Why did Elijah announce the coming of a drought to King Ahab?
   a. to make himself look good
   b. to demonstrate God's power
   c. to warn Ahab and Israel
   d. to punish Ahab and Israel

2. Why did God send Elijah out of the country to a Gentile in Zarephath?
   a. to keep him safe from Ahab
   b. to be provided for by a widow
   c. to provide for a widow
   d. to show Israel's rejection of God

3. If you were the widow, what would you have thought about Elijah's words in verses 13–14?
   a. Preachers want your last dime.
   b. What a deal!
   c. Sounds like a con job.
   d. What have I got to lose?

4. Why did God perform a miracle with the flour and oil?
   a. because of the woman's faith
   b. to keep his word
   c. to keep the mother and son alive
   d. to take care of Elijah

5. What do you think the widow was feeling when her son quit breathing?
   a. anger at Elijah
   b. anger at God
   c. guilt
   d. hopelessness

6. What do you think Elijah was feeling when the boy quit breathing?
   a. anger at himself
   b. anger at God
   c. guilt
   d. hopelessness
   e. faith

7. How was the widow changed after God gave her son back to her?

8. What "jars and jugs" are running dry for you? Does that situation or any other represent a seemingly impossible request you have for the Lord?

9. How did God show love to this woman? How has God shown his love for you in your recovery from divorce?

10. Have you felt let down in any way by God? If so, what would the Lord need to do to show you he cares?

11. The widow and her son were down to their last meal when God intervened in their lives. When have you and your child(ren) felt like you reached the end of your rope?

12. What keeps you from believing your child(ren) will turn out all right?
   a. My faith is weak.
   b. I don't have an Elijah at my house.
   c. I lack confidence in my child(ren).
   d. I'm not sure I can make it as a single parent.
   e. I haven't seen any miracles yet.
   f. The spark of life in my child(ren) is almost out.
   g. I can't let my child(ren) go.

4. Do you have any "impossible" requests to bring before the Lord? **5.** Do you believe God punishes you when you sin? Prospers you when you're good? How fair has God been lately?

1. Ever been flustered at seeing a movie star? A sports figure? An old friend? **2.** If you could pick anyone on earth for a pen pal, who would it be?

1. What is Obadiah's dilemma? Why does he so boldly hide 100 prophets and freely talk about it? Who are these prophets, anyway (vv. 3,13; see 1Sa 10:5)? **2.** Why then doesn't Obadiah also testify about Elijah to Ahab? What is Elijah's reputation (v. 12; see 2Ki 2:15–16)? What is Ahab likely to do? **3.** How do you reconcile the conflicting natures of Ahab: (a) Lover of animals (v. 5)? (b) Trusting of Obadiah (vv. 3,6)? (c) Willing to kill Obadiah over Elijah's whereabouts? **4.** Can Obadiah refuse to help after Elijah's assurance in verse 15?

1. Do you tend to take risks or play it safe? What risks are hardest for you to take? When was the last time you really took a chance? **2.** Are you considered reliable? Punctual? Trustworthy? Why or why not? What would you like your reputation to be? **3.** In what situation do you need to move courageously, putting your confidence in the Lord? What past actions of God would encourage you to trust him?

1. Did you ever get burned playing with fire? How so? **2.** Ever want to get back to your "roots"? What or who encouraged you in that direction?

ing. [18]She said to Elijah, "What do you have against me, man of God? Did you come to remind me of my sin and kill my son?"

[19]"Give me your son," Elijah replied. He took him from her arms, carried him to the upper room where he was staying, and laid him on his bed. [20]Then he cried out to the LORD, "O LORD my God, have you brought tragedy also upon this widow I am staying with, by causing her son to die?" [21]Then he stretched himself out on the boy three times and cried to the LORD, "O LORD my God, let this boy's life return to him!"

[22]The LORD heard Elijah's cry, and the boy's life returned to him, and he lived. [23]Elijah picked up the child and carried him down from the room into the house. He gave him to his mother and said, "Look, your son is alive!"

[24]Then the woman said to Elijah, "Now I know that you are a man of God and that the word of the LORD from your mouth is the truth."

Elijah and Obadiah

18 After a long time, in the third year, the word of the LORD came to Elijah: "Go and present yourself to Ahab, and I will send rain on the land." [2]So Elijah went to present himself to Ahab.

Now the famine was severe in Samaria, [3]and Ahab had summoned Obadiah, who was in charge of his palace. (Obadiah was a devout believer in the LORD. [4]While Jezebel was killing off the LORD's prophets, Obadiah had taken a hundred prophets and hidden them in two caves, fifty in each, and had supplied them with food and water.) [5]Ahab had said to Obadiah, "Go through the land to all the springs and valleys. Maybe we can find some grass to keep the horses and mules alive so we will not have to kill any of our animals." [6]So they divided the land they were to cover, Ahab going in one direction and Obadiah in another.

[7]As Obadiah was walking along, Elijah met him. Obadiah recognized him, bowed down to the ground, and said, "Is it really you, my lord Elijah?"

[8]"Yes," he replied. "Go tell your master, 'Elijah is here.' "

[9]"What have I done wrong," asked Obadiah, "that you are handing your servant over to Ahab to be put to death? [10]As surely as the LORD your God lives, there is not a nation or kingdom where my master has not sent someone to look for you. And whenever a nation or kingdom claimed you were not there, he made them swear they could not find you. [11]But now you tell me to go to my master and say, 'Elijah is here.' [12]I don't know where the Spirit of the LORD may carry you when I leave you. If I go and tell Ahab and he doesn't find you, he will kill me. Yet I your servant have worshiped the LORD since my youth. [13]Haven't you heard, my lord, what I did while Jezebel was killing the prophets of the LORD? I hid a hundred of the LORD's prophets in two caves, fifty in each, and supplied them with food and water. [14]And now you tell me to go to my master and say, 'Elijah is here.' He will kill me!"

[15]Elijah said, "As the LORD Almighty lives, whom I serve, I will surely present myself to Ahab today."

Elijah on Mount Carmel

[16]So Obadiah went to meet Ahab and told him, and Ahab went to meet Elijah. [17]When he saw Elijah, he said to him, "Is that you, you troubler of Israel?"

[18]"I have not made trouble for Israel," Elijah replied. "But you and your father's family have. You have abandoned the LORD's commands and have followed the Baals. [19]Now summon the people

from all over Israel to meet me on Mount Carmel. And bring the four hundred and fifty prophets of Baal and the four hundred prophets of Asherah, who eat at Jezebel's table."

²⁰So Ahab sent word throughout all Israel and assembled the prophets on Mount Carmel. ²¹Elijah went before the people and said, "How long will you waver between two opinions? If the LORD is God, follow him; but if Baal is God, follow him."

But the people said nothing.

²²Then Elijah said to them, "I am the only one of the LORD's prophets left, but Baal has four hundred and fifty prophets. ²³Get two bulls for us. Let them choose one for themselves, and let them cut it into pieces and put it on the wood but not set fire to it. I will prepare the other bull and put it on the wood but not set fire to it. ²⁴Then you call on the name of your god, and I will call on the name of the LORD. The god who answers by fire—he is God."

Then all the people said, "What you say is good."

²⁵Elijah said to the prophets of Baal, "Choose one of the bulls and prepare it first, since there are so many of you. Call on the name of your god, but do not light the fire." ²⁶So they took the bull given them and prepared it.

Then they called on the name of Baal from morning till noon. "O Baal, answer us!" they shouted. But there was no response; no one answered. And they danced around the altar they had made.

²⁷At noon Elijah began to taunt them. "Shout louder!" he said. "Surely he is a god! Perhaps he is deep in thought, or busy, or traveling. Maybe he is sleeping and must be awakened." ²⁸So they shouted louder and slashed themselves with swords and spears, as was their custom, until their blood flowed. ²⁹Midday passed, and they continued their frantic prophesying until the time for the

1. Why does Ahab think Elijah is the "troubler of Israel"? Why does Elijah reverse the charges? **2.** How many people do you think assemble on Mount Carmel (v. 19)? Are the prophets of Baal native Israelites (see 16:31–32)? **3.** Why don't the people say anything in response to Elijah (v. 21)? What attitudes could account for their silence? **4.** What reason does Elijah give for the prophets of Baal going first (vv. 22–26)? **5.** Is this a battle of doctrine? Logic? Power? What's the relationship between power and doctrine? **6.** Is Elijah being overly dramatic by the three water dowsings, the trench and all (vv. 30–35)? Where did they find so much water, given the three-year drought? **7.** Is it over-reacting to have all the priests of Baal slaughtered (v. 40)? Why or why not? **8.** Are the people fickle, following whoever performs the most magnificent miracle? Or are they sincere, eager to return to worshiping the true God? Why do you think so? **9.** Why does Elijah tell Ahab to "eat and drink" and his servant to keep looking (41–44)? What must they be thinking? Why does Elijah as-

---

 1 Kings 18:16–40   **ELIJAH AND THE PROPHETS OF BAAL**

After announcing to wicked King Ahab the beginning of a severe drought, the prophet Elijah left Israel. Now, about three years later, Elijah returns.

1. What was Elijah's main reason for challenging the other prophets?
   a. to show them up
   b. to destroy them
   c. to prove the Lord's superiority
   d. to call Israel back to the Lord

2. Why was Ahab willing to risk a confrontation at Mount Carmel?
   a. He respected Elijah.
   b. He thought that his prophets would win.
   c. He wanted the people to decide.
   d. He would look bad if he refused.
   e. Everyone loves a good contest.

3. Why did the people say nothing when Elijah challenged them (v. 21)?
   a. They were confused.
   b. They were afraid.
   c. They were angry.
   d. They were ashamed.
   e. They thought it was okay to worship both the Lord *and* Baal.

4. The thing that impresses me the most about Elijah in this duel is his:
   a. guts.
   b. faith.
   c. taunting.
   d. theatrical flair.
   e. prayer.
   f. fury.

5. When God sent down fire, he was:
   a. making himself perfectly clear.
   b. venting his anger.
   c. purifying the people.
   d. endorsing Elijah's ministry.

6. When the people shouted, "The Lord—he is God!" they were:
   a. scared to death.
   b. convinced.
   c. humbled.
   d. responding out of emotion.
   e. truly converted.

7. What convinces you that God is more powerful than anything else?
   a. thunder and lightning
   b. seeing how God has changed me
   c. the reality of miracles
   d. the truth of his Word
   e. the sincerity of Christian people
   f. the inadequacy of competing "gods"

8. What would you like God to bring to your life?
   a. an answer to prayer
   b. proof of his existence
   c. his presence
   d. his help for my "wavering"

9. Is your allegiance to God leading you to any "showdowns"? What kind of strength do you need?

10. Why do you suppose the concept of a "Higher Power" is so central to recovery from addiction? What is the biggest obstacle to your submitting to God as your "Higher Power"?

11. What is your greatest need for your "Higher Power"?
    a. someone to love me and help me love myself
    b. someone to empower me to overcome my problems
    c. someone who forgives me and helps me forgive myself
    d. someone with such awesome power that he commands my respect

sume the fetal position on Carmel? What must he be feeling? **10.** How does Elijah outrun the chariot (v. 46; see 18:12)?

♡ **1.** Are you "wavering between two opinions" right now with regard to obeying God's will? Which one will you follow and why? **2.** Is your devotion to God leading you into any "showdowns"? What kind of "betting odds" are you facing? **3.** Are skeptics today more convinced by logical arguments, emotional appeals or miraculous power? Which of these three convinced you of the truth of Christianity? **4.** Does God show power today? Or is Christian witness more one of subtle good deeds and words fitly spoken? **5.** Does God give you extra strength to do his will? What kind of strength do you need right now? Can your small group help? **6.** Have you ever wanted to follow Elijah's example and boldly ask for a public miracle in Jesus' name? Who will look stupid if God doesn't produce? Does doubt create a risk that God won't come through? Or is God out of the flashy miracle business? Have you ever gone ahead and then been left in the lurch by God?

☕ Have you ever had a "midlife crisis" or seen a family member go through it: Once? Never? Several times? Explain what it was like.

📖 **1.** Had Jezebel been on Carmel, would she be invoking her gods in this way (vv. 1–2)? Why? **2.** Why is Elijah suddenly afraid (v. 3)? Is he despondent, ⋯ ⁎ in a post-adrenaline ⋯ hy go to Judah? The ⋯ doesn't God take Eli-

evening sacrifice. But there was no response, no one answered, no one paid attention.

³⁰Then Elijah said to all the people, "Come here to me." They came to him, and he repaired the altar of the LORD, which was in ruins. ³¹Elijah took twelve stones, one for each of the tribes descended from Jacob, to whom the word of the LORD had come, saying, "Your name shall be Israel." ³²With the stones he built an altar in the name of the LORD, and he dug a trench around it large enough to hold two seahs*ᵃ* of seed. ³³He arranged the wood, cut the bull into pieces and laid it on the wood. Then he said to them, "Fill four large jars with water and pour it on the offering and on the wood."

³⁴"Do it again," he said, and they did it again.

"Do it a third time," he ordered, and they did it the third time. ³⁵The water ran down around the altar and even filled the trench.

³⁶At the time of sacrifice, the prophet Elijah stepped forward and prayed: "O LORD, God of Abraham, Isaac and Israel, let it be known today that you are God in Israel and that I am your servant and have done all these things at your command. ³⁷Answer me, O LORD, answer me, so these people will know that you, O LORD, are God, and that you are turning their hearts back again."

³⁸Then the fire of the LORD fell and burned up the sacrifice, the wood, the stones and the soil, and also licked up the water in the trench.

³⁹When all the people saw this, they fell prostrate and cried, "The LORD—he is God! The LORD—he is God!"

⁴⁰Then Elijah commanded them, "Seize the prophets of Baal. Don't let anyone get away!" They seized them, and Elijah had them brought down to the Kishon Valley and slaughtered there.

⁴¹And Elijah said to Ahab, "Go, eat and drink, for there is the sound of a heavy rain." ⁴²So Ahab went off to eat and drink, but Elijah climbed to the top of Carmel, bent down to the ground and put his face between his knees.

⁴³"Go and look toward the sea," he told his servant. And he went up and looked.

"There is nothing there," he said.

Seven times Elijah said, "Go back."

⁴⁴The seventh time the servant reported, "A cloud as small as a man's hand is rising from the sea."

So Elijah said, "Go and tell Ahab, 'Hitch up your chariot and go down before the rain stops you.'"

⁴⁵Meanwhile, the sky grew black with clouds, the wind rose, a heavy rain came on and Ahab rode off to Jezreel. ⁴⁶The power of the LORD came upon Elijah and, tucking his cloak into his belt, he ran ahead of Ahab all the way to Jezreel.

Elijah Flees to Horeb

19 Now Ahab told Jezebel everything Elijah had done and how he had killed all the prophets with the sword. ²So Jezebel sent a messenger to Elijah to say, "May the gods deal with me, be it ever so severely, if by this time tomorrow I do not make your life like that of one of them."

³Elijah was afraid*ᵇ* and ran for his life. When he came to Beersheba in Judah, he left his servant there, ⁴while he himself went a day's journey into the desert. He came to a broom tree, sat down under it and prayed that he might die. "I have had enough, LORD,"

ᵃ32 That is, probably about 13 quarts (about 15 liters)   *ᵇ3* Or *Elijah saw*

he said. "Take my life; I am no better than my ancestors." ⁵Then he lay down under the tree and fell asleep.

All at once an angel touched him and said, "Get up and eat." ⁶He looked around, and there by his head was a cake of bread baked over hot coals, and a jar of water. He ate and drank and then lay down again.

⁷The angel of the Lord came back a second time and touched him and said, "Get up and eat, for the journey is too much for you." ⁸So he got up and ate and drank. Strengthened by that food, he traveled forty days and forty nights until he reached Horeb, the mountain of God. ⁹There he went into a cave and spent the night.

The Lord Appears to Elijah

And the word of the Lord came to him: "What are you doing here, Elijah?"

¹⁰He replied, "I have been very zealous for the Lord God Almighty. The Israelites have rejected your covenant, broken down your altars, and put your prophets to death with the sword. I am the only one left, and now they are trying to kill me too."

¹¹The Lord said, "Go out and stand on the mountain in the presence of the Lord, for the Lord is about to pass by."

Then a great and powerful wind tore the mountains apart and shattered the rocks before the Lord, but the Lord was not in the wind. After the wind there was an earthquake, but the Lord was not in the earthquake. ¹²After the earthquake came a fire, but the Lord was not in the fire. And after the fire came a gentle whisper. ¹³When Elijah heard it, he pulled his cloak over his face and went out and stood at the mouth of the cave.

Then a voice said to him, "What are you doing here, Elijah?"

jah's life (v. 4)? **4.** Is the food here an unmediated miracle, or has some "widow of Zarephath" been watching (v. 6; see 17:9–11)? **5.** What is significant about the 40 days and nights? About Mount Horeb? For what does he hope (see Ex 3:1–2; Dt 4:10–14)? **6.** With what tone does he answer God in verse 10? Whom is Elijah blaming for all the trouble? **7.** What's the point of God's three "false starts" (vv. 11–12; see 9:9,16–19)? How does Elijah's close encounter differ from Moses'? What is God's message when he finally does speak? **8.** Compare verses 13–14 and 9–10 in context: What does Elijah's unchanged answer imply? **9.** In verses 15–18, what is the bad news? The good news? What do the two ancient signs of homage symbolize? **10.** What's the point of the cloak-throw (v. 19)? Of slaughtering oxen and burning the plow (v. 21)?

♡ **1.** Has your life taken a discouraging turn lately? Does God seem to care at all in your struggle? How can you be helped? **2.** Has God ever asked you "What are you doing here"? What was your answer? **3.** What might tempt

---

   1 Kings 19:1–18   **ELIJAH & GOD'S GENTLE WHISPER**

King Ahab, influenced by his foreign wife Jezebel, had led Israel into idolatry. Just before this scene, the power of God came upon Elijah in amazing ways: (1) In a contest with the prophets of Baal, Elijah demonstrated the Lord's superiority over Baal—resulting in the execution of the false prophets according to the Law of Moses; (2) then after a long drought God sent rain in response to Elijah's prayer; and (3) then the Lord empowered Elijah to outrun Ahab's chariot.

1. Why did Elijah run away?
   a. He needed some "R and R."
   b. Jezebel was furious about what he did to her prophets.
   c. He wasn't ready for another fight.
   d. Ahab's troops outnumbered his.

2. Why did Elijah pray to die?
   a. He was afraid.
   b. He was depressed.
   c. He was totally drained.
   d. He was full of self-pity.
   e. He was having a faith crisis.
   f. He felt all alone and unsupported.

3. What did Elijah need the most?
   a. physical replenishment
   b. some peace and quiet
   c. a spiritual retreat
   d. an attitude adjustment
   e. some answers about life
   f. fellowship with other believers
   g. a fresh vision of God

4. What was God saying through the wind, earthquake, fire and whisper?
   a. "I'm in control."
   b. "Stop whining and listen to me."
   c. "Don't expect me to be so dramatic all the time."
   d. "You're not alone."

5. What was God saying to Elijah in verses 15–18?
   a. "Your ministry is far from over."
   b. "Trust me."
   c. "Stop moping and get moving."
   d. "You're not alone."

6. After a great victory, I usually:
   a. bask in it.
   b. rest.
   c. anticipate a letdown.
   d. move on to the next challenge.

7. Which, if any, of the answers in question 2 sound like you? Which of the choices in question 3 do you need the most?

8. How is God trying to communicate to you right now? What's the message of the "gentle whisper"?

9. How can you relate to Elijah's wilderness experience of feeling lonely and excluded? Socially, what is your greatest challenge as a single person?

10. In your healing from the pain of your past, how do you sense God whispering to you, "You're not alone"—in terms of God's presence? In terms of the support of those God has "reserved" for you?

11. When you feel drained by the pressures or injustices of life, what do you do? Is there any action you can take to find God? Or do you have to wait for God to call you out of your "cave"?

you to give up in your service of God? What might prompt you to abandon your chosen profession? Have you "burned the plow" in some other way? **4.** Has God ever appeared in some spectacular way to you? In some "small" way? How so? **5.** Have you admired someone else's spiritual experiences but found they do not happen to you? Do you feel like a failure? Inadequate? Mad at God? **6.** In the midst of all your hard work, are you developing the leadership who will eventually replace you? How so?

1. When have you taken a stand against violence and why? **2.** Do you haggle and barter prices or just ask the price and pay up?

1. Why did Ben-Hadad's father attack Israel 50 years earlier (see 1Ki 15:18–21)? Why does Ben-Hadad II besiege Samaria (v. 1)? **2.** Does Ahab take Ben-Hadad's terms seriously (vv. 2–4)? What terms shock Ahab (vv. 6–7)? Why? **3.** Why do the elders and people counsel resistance? **4.** What's the point of Ahab's proverb (v. 11)? Describe the reaction at Ben-Hadad's camp.

1. What "enemy" haunts you time after time? Will you ever be rid of it (him or her) once and for all? How so? **2.** What could you never give up to someone who asks of you? Would you die for this? **3.** Do you get defensive easily? When do you take off your armor? What is your prized defense mechanism?

---

[14]He replied, "I have been very zealous for the LORD God Almighty. The Israelites have rejected your covenant, broken down your altars, and put your prophets to death with the sword. I am the only one left, and now they are trying to kill me too."

[15]The LORD said to him, "Go back the way you came, and go to the Desert of Damascus. When you get there, anoint Hazael king over Aram. [16]Also, anoint Jehu son of Nimshi king over Israel, and anoint Elisha son of Shaphat from Abel Meholah to succeed you as prophet. [17]Jehu will put to death any who escape the sword of Hazael, and Elisha will put to death any who escape the sword of Jehu. [18]Yet I reserve seven thousand in Israel—all whose knees have not bowed down to Baal and all whose mouths have not kissed him."

The Call of Elisha

[19]So Elijah went from there and found Elisha son of Shaphat. He was plowing with twelve yoke of oxen, and he himself was driving the twelfth pair. Elijah went up to him and threw his cloak around him. [20]Elisha then left his oxen and ran after Elijah. "Let me kiss my father and mother good-by," he said, "and then I will come with you."

"Go back," Elijah replied. "What have I done to you?"

[21]So Elisha left him and went back. He took his yoke of oxen and slaughtered them. He burned the plowing equipment to cook the meat and gave it to the people, and they ate. Then he set out to follow Elijah and became his attendant.

Ben-Hadad Attacks Samaria

20 Now Ben-Hadad king of Aram mustered his entire army. Accompanied by thirty-two kings with their horses and chariots, he went up and besieged Samaria and attacked it. [2]He sent messengers into the city to Ahab king of Israel, saying, "This is what Ben-Hadad says: [3]'Your silver and gold are mine, and the best of your wives and children are mine.'"

[4]The king of Israel answered, "Just as you say, my lord the king. I and all I have are yours."

[5]The messengers came again and said, "This is what Ben-Hadad says: 'I sent to demand your silver and gold, your wives and your children. [6]But about this time tomorrow I am going to send my officials to search your palace and the houses of your officials. They will seize everything you value and carry it away.'"

[7]The king of Israel summoned all the elders of the land and said to them, "See how this man is looking for trouble! When he sent for my wives and my children, my silver and my gold, I did not refuse him."

[8]The elders and the people all answered, "Don't listen to him or agree to his demands."

[9]So he replied to Ben-Hadad's messengers, "Tell my lord the king, 'Your servant will do all you demanded the first time, but this demand I cannot meet.'" They left and took the answer back to Ben-Hadad.

[10]Then Ben-Hadad sent another message to Ahab: "May the gods deal with me, be it ever so severely, if enough dust remains in Samaria to give each of my men a handful."

[11]The king of Israel answered, "Tell him: 'One who puts on his armor should not boast like one who takes it off.'"

[12]Ben-Hadad heard this message while he and the kings were

drinking in their tents,[a] and he ordered his men: "Prepare to attack." So they prepared to attack the city.

Ahab Defeats Ben-Hadad

[13]Meanwhile a prophet came to Ahab king of Israel and announced, "This is what the LORD says: 'Do you see this vast army? I will give it into your hand today, and then you will know that I am the LORD.'"

[14]"But who will do this?" asked Ahab.

The prophet replied, "This is what the LORD says: 'The young officers of the provincial commanders will do it.'"

"And who will start the battle?" he asked.

The prophet answered, "You will."

[15]So Ahab summoned the young officers of the provincial commanders, 232 men. Then he assembled the rest of the Israelites, 7,000 in all. [16]They set out at noon while Ben-Hadad and the 32 kings allied with him were in their tents getting drunk. [17]The young officers of the provincial commanders went out first.

Now Ben-Hadad had dispatched scouts, who reported, "Men are advancing from Samaria."

[18]He said, "If they have come out for peace, take them alive; if they have come out for war, take them alive."

[19]The young officers of the provincial commanders marched out of the city with the army behind them [20]and each one struck down his opponent. At that, the Arameans fled, with the Israelites in pursuit. But Ben-Hadad king of Aram escaped on horseback with some of his horsemen. [21]The king of Israel advanced and overpowered the horses and chariots and inflicted heavy losses on the Arameans.

[22]Afterward, the prophet came to the king of Israel and said, "Strengthen your position and see what must be done, because next spring the king of Aram will attack you again."

[23]Meanwhile, the officials of the king of Aram advised him, "Their gods are gods of the hills. That is why they were too strong for us. But if we fight them on the plains, surely we will be stronger than they. [24]Do this: Remove all the kings from their commands and replace them with other officers. [25]You must also raise an army like the one you lost—horse for horse and chariot for chariot—so we can fight Israel on the plains. Then surely we will be stronger than they." He agreed with them and acted accordingly.

[26]The next spring Ben-Hadad mustered the Arameans and went up to Aphek to fight against Israel. [27]When the Israelites were also mustered and given provisions, they marched out to meet them. The Israelites camped opposite them like two small flocks of goats, while the Arameans covered the countryside.

[28]The man of God came up and told the king of Israel, "This is what the LORD says: 'Because the Arameans think the LORD is a god of the hills and not a god of the valleys, I will deliver this vast army into your hands, and you will know that I am the LORD.'"

[29]For seven days they camped opposite each other, and on the seventh day the battle was joined. The Israelites inflicted a hundred thousand casualties on the Aramean foot soldiers in one day. [30]The rest of them escaped to the city of Aphek, where the wall collapsed on twenty-seven thousand of them. And Ben-Hadad fled to the city and hid in an inner room.

[31]His officials said to him, "Look, we have heard that the kings of

[a]12 Or *in Succoth*; also in verse 16

1. Did you ever move in search of a better-paying job or to pursue a romantic interest? Did the strategy work? 2. What change of heart has come over you in recent years, a change which forced you to eat your earlier words or change your opinion?

1. How vast is "vast" (v. 13; see 20:1)? How could Ahab help but see it? 2. Why do kings want to hear from God about wars but not about righteousness (vv. 14–15)? What makes Ahab nervous about the prophet's advice? 3. If you were a young commander, what would you suspect Ahab was up to? Would you volunteer? 4. What's the sense in Ben-Hadad's instructions (v. 18)? What would have been a better plan? What does this battle tell you about the Aramean army? 5. The second time around, why does Ben-Hadad go to fight Israel at Aphek rather than Samaria (vv. 23–26)? What are the odds in the second battle (v. 27)? 6. What do you suppose happens for six days at the camp at Aphek? What would you be doing during that time? 7. Why does God favor Ahab in this (v. 28)? How accurate was Ben-Hadad's theology? 8. What message do the sackcloth and ropes convey (vv. 31–32)? Why does Ahab let Ben-Hadad live (vv. 33–34)? Is this: (a) A great military idea? (b) A genius-level political idea? (c) A dumb mistake?

1. Are you facing any situation now where the odds are heavily stacked against you? Where does the "opposing army" look strongest to you? Does your faith shape your approach to the problem? How? 2. Why do people limit God to "the hills" today, unable to see him as sovereign? Do you have a stunted view of God? How did you get it? What's to be done? 3. If a drunken bully like Ben-Hadad is given a break, what hope does that give you? What Ben-Hadad character do you know whom you could give a break to, even if, or especially if he doesn't deserve one? 4. If you've recently won a victory, should you be getting ready for round two, as did King Ahab? What battles do you anticipate having to win more than once? 5. Have you ever felt close to God but in a heap of trouble? Ever felt far from

God and things were going great? What's the relationship between feeling close to God and having favorable circumstances?

1. For what reason were you last found standing by a road? 2. Where do you go to sulk?

1. Why does this prophet want to be wounded (vv. 38–40)? What word from the Lord is he acting out? Does that make it okay to fake a wound or tell a tall tale? 2. Why such punishment for the well-meaning soul in verse 36? What story does this echo (see 1Ki 13:20–24)? 3. Likewise, is Ahab's verdict just (v. 40)? Is Ahab like the man whom the prophet portrays (v. 41)? 4. What must Ahab think of these prophets and their God?

1. Would you wound a friend if he or she asked? Why? 2. This king sulks under self-condemnation. When are you moody? How do you deal with it? What role does God play in your moods?

1. What's the weirdest, oldest, ugliest garment you own? When do you wear it? Who nags you about it? 2. Has anyone ever thrown a surprise party for you? What lies did they have to tell to get you there unawares?

1. Why does Ahab want the vineyard (vv. 1–3)? As king, why doesn't he just confiscate it (see Dt 17:18–20)? Why does Naboth refuse his king this request (see Lev 25:23–28; Nu 36:7)? Would you have refused the king? 2. What does Ahab's reaction reveal about him (v. 4)? What other examples of pouting have you seen in Ahab? What tends to cheer him up? 3. What does Jezebel's solu-

the house of Israel are merciful. Let us go to the king of Israel with sackcloth around our waists and ropes around our heads. Perhaps he will spare your life."

32Wearing sackcloth around their waists and ropes around their heads, they went to the king of Israel and said, "Your servant Ben-Hadad says: 'Please let me live.'"

The king answered, "Is he still alive? He is my brother."

33The men took this as a good sign and were quick to pick up his word. "Yes, your brother Ben-Hadad!" they said.

"Go and get him," the king said. When Ben-Hadad came out, Ahab had him come up into his chariot.

34"I will return the cities my father took from your father," Ben-Hadad offered. "You may set up your own market areas in Damascus, as my father did in Samaria."

⌊Ahab said,⌋ "On the basis of a treaty I will set you free." So he made a treaty with him, and let him go.

A Prophet Condemns Ahab

35By the word of the Lord one of the sons of the prophets said to his companion, "Strike me with your weapon," but the man refused.

36So the prophet said, "Because you have not obeyed the Lord, as soon as you leave me a lion will kill you." And after the man went away, a lion found him and killed him.

37The prophet found another man and said, "Strike me, please." So the man struck him and wounded him. 38Then the prophet went and stood by the road waiting for the king. He disguised himself with his headband down over his eyes. 39As the king passed by, the prophet called out to him, "Your servant went into the thick of the battle, and someone came to me with a captive and said, 'Guard this man. If he is missing, it will be your life for his life, or you must pay a talent[a] of silver.' 40While your servant was busy here and there, the man disappeared."

"That is your sentence," the king of Israel said. "You have pronounced it yourself."

41Then the prophet quickly removed the headband from his eyes, and the king of Israel recognized him as one of the prophets. 42He said to the king, "This is what the Lord says: 'You have set free a man I had determined should die.[b] Therefore it is your life for his life, your people for his people.'" 43Sullen and angry, the king of Israel went to his palace in Samaria.

Naboth's Vineyard

21 Some time later there was an incident involving a vineyard belonging to Naboth the Jezreelite. The vineyard was in Jezreel, close to the palace of Ahab king of Samaria. 2Ahab said to Naboth, "Let me have your vineyard to use for a vegetable garden, since it is close to my palace. In exchange I will give you a better vineyard or, if you prefer, I will pay you whatever it is worth."

3But Naboth replied, "The Lord forbid that I should give you the inheritance of my fathers."

4So Ahab went home, sullen and angry because Naboth the Jezreelite had said, "I will not give you the inheritance of my fathers." He lay on his bed sulking and refused to eat.

5His wife Jezebel came in and asked him, "Why are you so sullen? Why won't you eat?"

a39 That is, about 75 pounds (about 34 kilograms) b42 The Hebrew term refers to the irrevocable giving over of things or persons to the Lord, often by totally destroying them.

⁶He answered her, "Because I said to Naboth the Jezreelite, 'Sell me your vineyard; or if you prefer, I will give you another vineyard in its place.' But he said, 'I will not give you my vineyard.' "

⁷Jezebel his wife said, "Is this how you act as king over Israel? Get up and eat! Cheer up. I'll get you the vineyard of Naboth the Jezreelite."

⁸So she wrote letters in Ahab's name, placed his seal on them, and sent them to the elders and nobles who lived in Naboth's city with him. ⁹In those letters she wrote:

"Proclaim a day of fasting and seat Naboth in a prominent place among the people. ¹⁰But seat two scoundrels opposite him and have them testify that he has cursed both God and the king. Then take him out and stone him to death."

¹¹So the elders and nobles who lived in Naboth's city did as Jezebel directed in the letters she had written to them. ¹²They proclaimed a fast and seated Naboth in a prominent place among the people. ¹³Then two scoundrels came and sat opposite him and brought charges against Naboth before the people, saying, "Naboth has cursed both God and the king." So they took him outside the city and stoned him to death. ¹⁴Then they sent word to Jezebel: "Naboth has been stoned and is dead."

¹⁵As soon as Jezebel heard that Naboth had been stoned to death, she said to Ahab, "Get up and take possession of the vineyard of Naboth the Jezreelite that he refused to sell you. He is no longer alive, but dead." ¹⁶When Ahab heard that Naboth was dead, he got up and went down to take possession of Naboth's vineyard.

¹⁷Then the word of the LORD came to Elijah the Tishbite: ¹⁸"Go down to meet Ahab king of Israel, who rules in Samaria. He is now in Naboth's vineyard, where he has gone to take possession of it. ¹⁹Say to him, 'This is what the LORD says: Have you not murdered a man and seized his property?' Then say to him, 'This is what the LORD says: In the place where dogs licked up Naboth's blood, dogs will lick up your blood—yes, yours!' "

²⁰Ahab said to Elijah, "So you have found me, my enemy!"

"I have found you," he answered, "because you have sold yourself to do evil in the eyes of the LORD. ²¹'I am going to bring disaster on you. I will consume your descendants and cut off from Ahab every last male in Israel—slave or free. ²²I will make your house like that of Jeroboam son of Nebat and that of Baasha son of Ahijah, because you have provoked me to anger and have caused Israel to sin.'

²³"And also concerning Jezebel the LORD says: 'Dogs will devour Jezebel by the wall ofª Jezreel.'

²⁴"Dogs will eat those belonging to Ahab who die in the city, and the birds of the air will feed on those who die in the country."

²⁵(There was never a man like Ahab, who sold himself to do evil in the eyes of the LORD, urged on by Jezebel his wife. ²⁶He behaved in the vilest manner by going after idols, like the Amorites the LORD drove out before Israel.)

²⁷When Ahab heard these words, he tore his clothes, put on sackcloth and fasted. He lay in sackcloth and went around meekly.

²⁸Then the word of the LORD came to Elijah the Tishbite: ²⁹"Have you noticed how Ahab has humbled himself before me? Because he has humbled himself, I will not bring this disaster in his day, but I will bring it on his house in the days of his son."

tion reveal about her and her relationship with Ahab (vv. 8–10)? Is she an effective king's wife? A woman to be respected? Feared? Married? **4.** What kind of governors are the elders? How seriously do they view capital punishment (vv. 11–13)? Is it fair to try a capital crime on the testimony of two witnesses (see Lev 24:13–16)? Without cross-examination? No lawyers? **5.** Was Naboth naive? Should he have suspected? Are we dealing with a man of small brain or just great stubbornness? **6.** What does Jezebel's scheme reveal about courts and justice? If the courts are so corrupt, isn't Naboth foolish to think he could keep the vineyard? **7.** How can Ahab simply take a dead man's land? What might he be thinking? **8.** Who cuts short Ahab's sense of conquest again (vv. 17–22)? What is the point of comparing Ahab's fate to that of Jeroboam (see 14:10; 15:28–30) or Baasha (16:3–4, 11–13)? **9.** What is the surprise ending to this episode (v. 27)? What impression are you building of Ahab's mental state: (a) Manic-depressive? (b) Paranoid schizophrenic? (c) A chameleon? (d) Genuinely torn between loyalties? (e) Easily pushed around? **10.** How is Ahab's fate like, and unlike, David's (vv. 28–29; see 2Sa 12:1–14)?

♡ **1.** In what subtle ways, does your life resemble either Ahab or Jezebel: Do you love things? Use people? Throw your weight around? Defame someone's character? Exploit or oppress others (even subtly)? Cite an example from your past. How can you avoid this in the future? **2.** How does God forgive vile sinners today? Does God postpone judgment one generation? **3.** Do you trust the judicial system in this country? Have you ever felt abused as was Naboth? How did you respond?

ª23 Most Hebrew manuscripts; a few Hebrew manuscripts, Vulgate and Syriac (see also 2 Kings 9:26) *the plot of ground at*

1. Have you ever been slapped on the cheek? (In jest? In real anger?) Did you slap back, turn the other cheek or make up? 2. Do you have a friend who is nothing but bad news? Why do you overlook all the negativity?

1. What peace treaty has Ahab struck with Aram (vv. 1–2; see 20:34; compare 1Ki 15:20)? Where is Ramoth Gilead? What has apparently *not* happened? 2. Has Ahab recovered from his meekness (v. 4; see 21:27–29)? Or did Elijah's prophecy make him feel invincible? 3. How "buddy-buddy" are Ahab and Jehoshaphat now (v. 4; see 2Ki 8:16,18)? What does Jehoshaphat's request reveal about him (vv. 5,7)? 4. If Jezebel killed the prophets of God and Elijah killed the prophets of Baal, who are these 400 men (vv. 6–7)? Is prophecy a fairly cushy, in-demand profession? How do the prophets answer Ahab and Jehoshaphat? What does Jehoshaphat make of this bunch? 5. What is the basis for Ahab's assessment of a prophet (v. 8; compare 18:17; 20:42; 21:20)? Is Ahab trying different prophets until he finds one who agrees with him? Why? 6. What kind of advice does the messenger give Micaiah (v. 13)? Why does Micaiah respond as he does in verse 15 (compare v. 12): Is Micaiah lying? Teasing Ahab? What does Ahab think (v. 16)? How does he interpret Micaiah's prophecy? Why? 7. How does Micaiah explain the majority opinion (vv. 19–23)? Is this explanation: (a) The "word of the Lord"? (b) More teasing? (c) A story to confuse Ahab further? 8. Why does Zedekiah slap Micaiah and ask a sarcastic question (v. 24)? How is he put in his place by Micaiah? 9. What is the test of Micaiah's message (vv. 25–28; see Dt 18:21–22)? Why take Micaiah hostage: (a) That will win God's blessing? (b) A hungry Micaiah might pray for his welfare? (c) Bad news prophets must be kept out of sight?

1. Who or what makes a lie okay? Conversely, do you always have to tell everybody anything they ask? Can you protect yourself by letting people be misled? What examples come to mind from this story and elsewhere? 2. Are you so stubborn that your closest friends must scheme to get you to hear their advice? Why are you

Micaiah Prophesies Against Ahab

22 For three years there was no war between Aram and Israel. 2But in the third year Jehoshaphat king of Judah went down to see the king of Israel. 3The king of Israel had said to his officials, "Don't you know that Ramoth Gilead belongs to us and yet we are doing nothing to retake it from the king of Aram?"

4So he asked Jehoshaphat, "Will you go with me to fight against Ramoth Gilead?"

Jehoshaphat replied to the king of Israel, "I am as you are, my people as your people, my horses as your horses." 5But Jehoshaphat also said to the king of Israel, "First seek the counsel of the LORD."

6So the king of Israel brought together the prophets—about four hundred men—and asked them, "Shall I go to war against Ramoth Gilead, or shall I refrain?"

"Go," they answered, "for the Lord will give it into the king's hand."

7But Jehoshaphat asked, "Is there not a prophet of the LORD here whom we can inquire of?"

8The king of Israel answered Jehoshaphat, "There is still one man through whom we can inquire of the LORD, but I hate him because he never prophesies anything good about me, but always bad. He is Micaiah son of Imlah."

"The king should not say that," Jehoshaphat replied.

9So the king of Israel called one of his officials and said, "Bring Micaiah son of Imlah at once."

10Dressed in their royal robes, the king of Israel and Jehoshaphat king of Judah were sitting on their thrones at the threshing floor by the entrance of the gate of Samaria, with all the prophets prophesying before them. 11Now Zedekiah son of Kenaanah had made iron horns and he declared, "This is what the LORD says: 'With these you will gore the Arameans until they are destroyed.'"

12All the other prophets were prophesying the same thing. "Attack Ramoth Gilead and be victorious," they said, "for the LORD will give it into the king's hand."

13The messenger who had gone to summon Micaiah said to him, "Look, as one man the other prophets are predicting success for the king. Let your word agree with theirs, and speak favorably."

14But Micaiah said, "As surely as the LORD lives, I can tell him only what the LORD tells me."

15When he arrived, the king asked him, "Micaiah, shall we go to war against Ramoth Gilead, or shall I refrain?"

"Attack and be victorious," he answered, "for the LORD will give it into the king's hand."

16The king said to him, "How many times must I make you swear to tell me nothing but the truth in the name of the LORD?"

17Then Micaiah answered, "I saw all Israel scattered on the hills like sheep without a shepherd, and the LORD said, 'These people have no master. Let each one go home in peace.'"

18The king of Israel said to Jehoshaphat, "Didn't I tell you that he never prophesies anything good about me, but only bad?"

19Micaiah continued, "Therefore hear the word of the LORD: I saw the LORD sitting on his throne with all the host of heaven standing around him on his right and on his left. 20And the LORD said, 'Who will entice Ahab into attacking Ramoth Gilead and going to his death there?'

"One suggested this, and another that. 21Finally, a spirit came forward, stood before the LORD and said, 'I will entice him.'

22"'By what means?' the LORD asked.

"'I will go out and be a lying spirit in the mouths of all his prophets,' he said.

"'You will succeed in enticing him,' said the LORD. 'Go and do it.'

23"So now the LORD has put a lying spirit in the mouths of all these prophets of yours. The LORD has decreed disaster for you."

24Then Zedekiah son of Kenaanah went up and slapped Micaiah in the face. "Which way did the spirit from[a] the LORD go when he went from me to speak to you?" he asked.

25Micaiah replied, "You will find out on the day you go to hide in an inner room."

26The king of Israel then ordered, "Take Micaiah and send him back to Amon the ruler of the city and to Joash the king's son 27and say, 'This is what the king says: Put this fellow in prison and give him nothing but bread and water until I return safely.'"

28Micaiah declared, "If you ever return safely, the LORD has not spoken through me." Then he added, "Mark my words, all you people!"

Ahab Killed at Ramoth Gilead

29So the king of Israel and Jehoshaphat king of Judah went up to Ramoth Gilead. 30The king of Israel said to Jehoshaphat, "I will enter the battle in disguise, but you wear your royal robes." So the king of Israel disguised himself and went into battle.

31Now the king of Aram had ordered his thirty-two chariot commanders, "Do not fight with anyone, small or great, except the king of Israel." 32When the chariot commanders saw Jehoshaphat, they thought, "Surely this is the king of Israel." So they turned to attack him, but when Jehoshaphat cried out, 33the chariot commanders saw that he was not the king of Israel and stopped pursuing him.

34But someone drew his bow at random and hit the king of Israel between the sections of his armor. The king told his chariot driver, "Wheel around and get me out of the fighting. I've been wounded." 35All day long the battle raged, and the king was propped up in his chariot facing the Arameans. The blood from his wound ran onto the floor of the chariot, and that evening he died. 36As the sun was setting, a cry spread through the army: "Every man to his town; everyone to his land!"

37So the king died and was brought to Samaria, and they buried him there. 38They washed the chariot at a pool in Samaria (where the prostitutes bathed),[b] and the dogs licked up his blood, as the word of the LORD had declared.

39As for the other events of Ahab's reign, including all he did, the palace he built and inlaid with ivory, and the cities he fortified, are they not written in the book of the annals of the kings of Israel? 40Ahab rested with his fathers. And Ahaziah his son succeeded him as king.

Jehoshaphat King of Judah

41Jehoshaphat son of Asa became king of Judah in the fourth year of Ahab king of Israel. 42Jehoshaphat was thirty-five years old when he became king, and he reigned in Jerusalem twenty-five years. His mother's name was Azubah daughter of Shilhi. 43In everything he walked in the ways of his father Asa and did not stray from them; he did what was right in the eyes of the LORD. The high places, however, were not removed, and the people continued to offer

always the last to know? 3. What price have you paid for telling the truth? Was it worth the cost? 4. What major decisions of yours warrant outside counsel? Why do you follow some advice and ignore other views? How do you choose among conflicting opinions? Who is your final arbiter?

1. Have you said hello to a person you'd mistaken for someone else? How did he or she react? What characteristic misled you? 2. Have you been mistaken for someone else? Who?

1. Why does Ahab disguise himself (vv. 29–30)? Why would Jehoshaphat go along? 2. Why does the king of Aram give the command of verse 31? Was the peace treaty a farce? 3. How would the soldiers recognize Ahab (vv. 32–33)? What do you think Jehoshaphat "cried out"? 4. What is the significance of a *random* arrow killing Ahab (v. 34)? 5. How does the end of this story fulfill the prophecy of Micaiah (see 22:20, 28)? Of Elijah (see 21:19–21, 29)? Thus proving what?

Do you believe that God sovereignly controls all of life's circumstances? Is there human choice? Randomness? Explain.

1. In what two ways are you like, and unlike, your father? Your mother? 2. If a biographer were writing the events of your life, what source documents and eyewitnesses would be invaluable?

1. What are Jehoshaphat's big accomplishments? What could he have done better? 2. Why does he succeed in eliminating

a24 Or Spirit of   b38 Or Samaria and cleaned the weapons

male prostitutes, but not pagan pillars and altars? **3.** Why do his ships wreck (v. 48; see 2Ch 20:35–37)? Was it wrong to make peace with Israel? **4.** What is Ahaziah's problem (v. 52)? Who is to blame for this repeated sin?

♡ **1.** The candid and sordid stories of these kings leave much room for pondering "what if" questions. What do you think would have been different if these kings had done right in the sight of the Lord, or if they had listened to the Lord's prophet? Review the book and pick one such errant and evil king and try rewriting a different scenario based on these "what ifs." **2.** Is it possible to know that your life is "right in the eyes of the Lord"? Does it matter if you know or not? How would a one-paragraph biography of you read differently if you were doing "evil in the eyes of the Lord"? **3.** Why do some kids follow their parents while others totally reject them? How does it look like your children will go (if you have any)? How can your group help children turn out right?

sacrifices and burn incense there. ⁴⁴Jehoshaphat was also at peace with the king of Israel.

⁴⁵As for the other events of Jehoshaphat's reign, the things he achieved and his military exploits, are they not written in the book of the annals of the kings of Judah? ⁴⁶He rid the land of the rest of the male shrine prostitutes who remained there even after the reign of his father Asa. ⁴⁷There was then no king in Edom; a deputy ruled.

⁴⁸Now Jehoshaphat built a fleet of trading ships[a] to go to Ophir for gold, but they never set sail—they were wrecked at Ezion Geber. ⁴⁹At that time Ahaziah son of Ahab said to Jehoshaphat, "Let my men sail with your men," but Jehoshaphat refused.

⁵⁰Then Jehoshaphat rested with his fathers and was buried with them in the city of David his father. And Jehoram his son succeeded him.

Ahaziah King of Israel

⁵¹Ahaziah son of Ahab became king of Israel in Samaria in the seventeenth year of Jehoshaphat king of Judah, and he reigned over Israel two years. ⁵²He did evil in the eyes of the LORD, because he walked in the ways of his father and mother and in the ways of Jeroboam son of Nebat, who caused Israel to sin. ⁵³He served and worshiped Baal and provoked the LORD, the God of Israel, to anger, just as his father had done.

a48 Hebrew *of ships of Tarshish*

INTRODUCTION to
2 KINGS

Book Study Outline: If you are using 2 Kings for a study course, here is a 7- or 13-week outline. Use the questions in the margin for your group agenda:

☕ start meeting / 15 min.

📖 read & discuss Bible / 30 min.

♡ close meeting / 15–45 min.

Refer to the Questions and Answers in the front of this Bible for more information.

7-week plan	13-week plan	Personal Reading	Group Study Passage
1	1	1:1–2:25	2:1–18/Elisha Succeeds Elijah
	2	3:1–4:7	4:1–7/The Widow's Oil
2	3	4:8–4:44	4:8–37/Elisha Resurrects Boy
	4	5:1–5:27	5:1–27/Naaman Healed
3	5	6:1–23	6:8–23/Elisha Traps Arameans
	6	6:24–8:15	7:3–20/Aramean Siege Lifted
4	7	8:16–10:17	10:1–17/Ahab Curse Fulfilled
	8	10:18–14:29	13:10–25/Jehoash With Elisha
5	9	15:1–16:20	16:1–20/Ahaz Does Evil
	10	17:1–18:16	17:7–23/Israel Suffers Exile
6	11	18:17–20:21	18:17–37/Sennacherib Warns
	12	21:1–23:35	23:1–25/Covenant Renewed
7	13	23:36–25:30	25:1–26/Jerusalem Sacked

Author: The author of 1 and 2 Kings is not known, but the three literary sources that are named suggest multiple authors and editors: "the Annals of Solomon" (1Ki 11:41); "the Annals of the Kings of Israel" (1Ki 14:19; 2Ki 15:31); and "the Annals of the Kings of Judah" (1Ki 14:29; 2Ki 24:5).

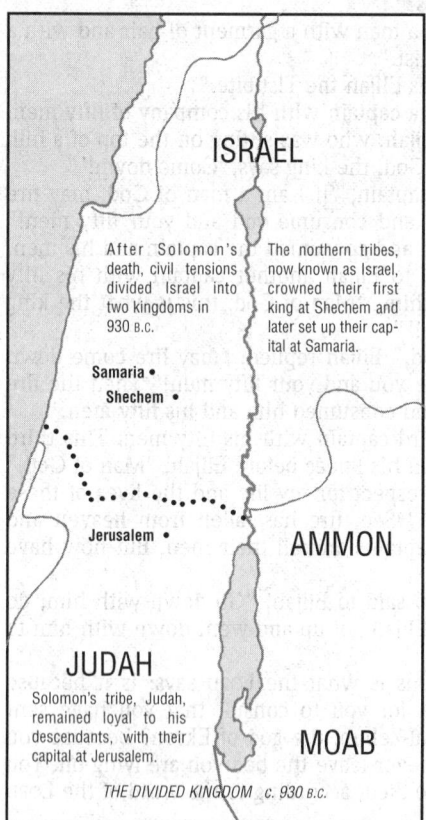

After Solomon's death, civil tensions divided Israel into two kingdoms in 930 B.C.

The northern tribes, now known as Israel, crowned their first king at Shechem and later set up their capital at Samaria.

Samaria •
Shechem •

Jerusalem •

ISRAEL

AMMON

JUDAH
Solomon's tribe, Judah, remained loyal to his descendants, with their capital at Jerusalem.

MOAB

THE DIVIDED KINGDOM c. 930 B.C.

Date: The account of Jehoiachin's release from prison in 2 Kings 25:27–30 means that the final form of Kings was written after 561 B.C. Nonetheless, the source materials could have been written at the time of the events they describe. These events span almost 400 years.

Theme: Israel's and Judah's spiral to destruction.

Historical Background: The divided kingdoms of Israel and Judah continue their political and moral decline. They are oppressed by their enemies, particularly Aram (Syria). The narrative witnesses to the rise of Assyrian power which crushes Israel's capital, Samaria, in 722 B.C. (2Ki 17). The Babylonians succeeded the Assyrians as the dominant power in the region. It was at their hands, in 586 B.C., that Judah's capital, Jerusalem, suffered a fate similar to that of Samaria (2Ki 25).

Characteristics: Second Kings completes the historical narrative begun in 1 Kings. It chronicles the succession of kings in both the northern kingdom of Israel and the southern kingdom of Judah. The verdict upon most of these kings is sadly repetitive: They "did evil in the eyes of the Lord." Elisha succeeds the great prophet, Elijah, and is "doubly blessed" with God's Spirit.

2 Kings

The LORD's Judgment on Ahaziah

1 After Ahab's death, Moab rebelled against Israel. ²Now Ahaziah had fallen through the lattice of his upper room in Samaria and injured himself. So he sent messengers, saying to them, "Go and consult Baal-Zebub, the god of Ekron, to see if I will recover from this injury."

³But the angel of the LORD said to Elijah the Tishbite, "Go up and meet the messengers of the king of Samaria and ask them, 'Is it because there is no God in Israel that you are going off to consult Baal-Zebub, the god of Ekron?' ⁴Therefore this is what the LORD says: 'You will not leave the bed you are lying on. You will certainly die!'" So Elijah went.

⁵When the messengers returned to the king, he asked them, "Why have you come back?"

⁶"A man came to meet us," they replied. "And he said to us, 'Go back to the king who sent you and tell him, "This is what the LORD says: Is it because there is no God in Israel that you are sending men to consult Baal-Zebub, the god of Ekron? Therefore you will not leave the bed you are lying on. You will certainly die!"'"

⁷The king asked them, "What kind of man was it who came to meet you and told you this?"

⁸They replied, "He was a man with a garment of hair and with a leather belt around his waist."

The king said, "That was Elijah the Tishbite."

⁹Then he sent to Elijah a captain with his company of fifty men. The captain went up to Elijah, who was sitting on the top of a hill, and said to him, "Man of God, the king says, 'Come down!'"

¹⁰Elijah answered the captain, "If I am a man of God, may fire come down from heaven and consume you and your fifty men!" Then fire fell from heaven and consumed the captain and his men.

¹¹At this the king sent to Elijah another captain with his fifty men. The captain said to him, "Man of God, this is what the king says, 'Come down at once!'"

¹²"If I am a man of God," Elijah replied, "may fire come down from heaven and consume you and your fifty men!" Then the fire of God fell from heaven and consumed him and his fifty men.

¹³So the king sent a third captain with his fifty men. This third captain went up and fell on his knees before Elijah. "Man of God," he begged, "please have respect for my life and the lives of these fifty men, your servants! ¹⁴See, fire has fallen from heaven and consumed the first two captains and all their men. But now have respect for my life!"

¹⁵The angel of the LORD said to Elijah, "Go down with him; do not be afraid of him." So Elijah got up and went down with him to the king.

¹⁶He told the king, "This is what the LORD says: Is it because there is no God in Israel for you to consult that you have sent messengers to consult Baal-Zebub, the god of Ekron? Because you have done this, you will never leave the bed you are lying on. You will certainly die!" ¹⁷So he died, according to the word of the LORD that Elijah had spoken.

☕ **1.** If someone questioned whether you were a Christian, how would you react and why? **2.** Where is your place to be alone to pray, think and write letters?

📖 **1.** How far out of his way did this king have to go to consult the god of Ekron (see map)? Who is Baal-Zebub (see Lk 11:14–15)? Why does Ahaziah consult this god? **2.** Why do the messengers turn back (vv. 5–8)? Why would a king's squadron obey the word of a single unknown man over the king's order? What tone of voice do you expect from Ahaziah on hearing the man's description? **3.** What could Elijah be doing on a hilltop (vv. 9–12)? Why does he take offense at their question? Are these people slow learners or what? **4.** Why does the third captain succeed (vv. 13–15)? Does this story strike you as: (a) Accurate history of God's methods of persuasion? (b) Folklore revealing how little the ancients respected life? (c) A parable on respecting God's prophets? Other? **5.** How does Elijah's message in person vary from the ones delivered by go-betweens? With what effect? **6.** What would you say God is like if this chapter were your starting point?

❤️ **1.** In the midst of all the demands on your time, do you take time out to think, pray or meditate, as did Elijah on the hilltop? Is it enough time for you to meet God? What would you do with seven uninterrupted minutes each day alone with God? Would you run out of things to talk about? **2.** With which character do you identify: (a) The bed-ridden Ahaziah, fumbling for answers? (b) The first two captains, staunch but sorry loyalists? (c) The third captain, a practical man? (d) Elijah, afraid yet aware of God's true power? **3.** How has God proven himself powerful through a recent victory in your life?

Because Ahaziah had no son, Joram*a* succeeded him as king in the second year of Jehoram son of Jehoshaphat king of Judah. ¹⁸As for all the other events of Ahaziah's reign, and what he did, are they not written in the book of the annals of the kings of Israel?

Elijah Taken Up to Heaven

2 When the LORD was about to take Elijah up to heaven in a whirlwind, Elijah and Elisha were on their way from Gilgal. ²Elijah said to Elisha, "Stay here; the LORD has sent me to Bethel."

But Elisha said, "As surely as the LORD lives and as you live, I will not leave you." So they went down to Bethel.

³The company of the prophets at Bethel came out to Elisha and asked, "Do you know that the LORD is going to take your master from you today?"

"Yes, I know," Elisha replied, "but do not speak of it."

⁴Then Elijah said to him, "Stay here, Elisha; the LORD has sent me to Jericho."

And he replied, "As surely as the LORD lives and as you live, I will not leave you." So they went to Jericho.

⁵The company of the prophets at Jericho went up to Elisha and asked him, "Do you know that the LORD is going to take your master from you today?"

"Yes, I know," he replied, "but do not speak of it."

⁶Then Elijah said to him, "Stay here; the LORD has sent me to the Jordan."

And he replied, "As surely as the LORD lives and as you live, I will not leave you." So the two of them walked on.

⁷Fifty men of the company of the prophets went and stood at a distance, facing the place where Elijah and Elisha had stopped at the Jordan. ⁸Elijah took his cloak, rolled it up and struck the water with it. The water divided to the right and to the left, and the two of them crossed over on dry ground.

⁹When they had crossed, Elijah said to Elisha, "Tell me, what can I do for you before I am taken from you?"

"Let me inherit a double portion of your spirit," Elisha replied.

¹⁰"You have asked a difficult thing," Elijah said, "yet if you see me when I am taken from you, it will be yours—otherwise not."

¹¹As they were walking along and talking together, suddenly a chariot of fire and horses of fire appeared and separated the two of them, and Elijah went up to heaven in a whirlwind. ¹²Elisha saw this and cried out, "My father! My father! The chariots and horsemen of Israel!" And Elisha saw him no more. Then he took hold of his own clothes and tore them apart.

¹³He picked up the cloak that had fallen from Elijah and went back and stood on the bank of the Jordan. ¹⁴Then he took the cloak that had fallen from him and struck the water with it. "Where now is the LORD, the God of Elijah?" he asked. When he struck the water, it divided to the right and to the left, and he crossed over.

¹⁵The company of the prophets from Jericho, who were watching, said, "The spirit of Elijah is resting on Elisha." And they went to meet him and bowed to the ground before him. ¹⁶"Look," they said, "we your servants have fifty able men. Let them go and look for your master. Perhaps the Spirit of the LORD has picked him up and set him down on some mountain or in some valley."

"No," Elisha replied, "do not send them."

¹⁷But they persisted until he was too ashamed to refuse. So he said, "Send them." And they sent fifty men, who searched for three

---

1. What's your longest hike? Was it under duress ? Why? 2. Were you a "hand-me-down" kid? Whose clothes did you get? Whose "outgrown" things would you appreciate these days?

1. Why does Elijah continue to ask Elisha to stay behind (vv. 1–6)? Why does he keep refusing? What does it tell about each man and their relationship? 2. How do the "companies of prophets" know about Elijah's upcoming departure (vv. 3,5)? Do they seem to have a better rapport with Elisha than Elijah? Why does Elisha ask them to keep it "hush-hush"? 3. What does everyone suspect about Elisha (v. 7; see 1Ki 19:19)? 4. Why use a cloak instead of a bridge or boat (vv. 8,14)? To what authority does this action tie him (see Ex 14:21–22; Jos 3:7,13)? 5. What does Elisha mean by "a double portion of your spirit" (v. 9; see Dt 21:17)? Is this a presumptuous request? Why does Elijah say it's a "difficult thing" (v. 10; see Nu 11:17,25)? 6. What do you suppose happened next to Elijah and why? What do the eyewitnesses think happened (vv. 15–18) Why does he get special treatment (compare Enoch, see Ge 5:24)? 7. What does Elisha mean in verse 12? How does he feel? Has he passed Elijah's test (v. 10) or been granted the request (v. 9)? How does he "double check"? 8. Why doesn't Elisha fill the prophets in on the true meaning of these events?

1. Many biblical heroes—Elijah, John the Baptist, Paul, Jesus himself—raised no family. What are the advantages of being single or celibate? Disadvantages? Did you ever consider it an option for you? 2. Have you ever had the mantle of leadership passed onto you? What was it like? Could you truly be yourself? 3. In what company (outside immediate family and friends) would you like to spend a day walking and talking? What would you hope to learn? 4. Would a miracle-working cloak be helpful to you? Why or why not? Is there a modern version of Elijah's cloak? 5. In what manner would you like to die? Is a believer's death like Elijah's? How so?

---

a 17 Hebrew *Jehoram*, a variant of *Joram*

days but did not find him. [18]When they returned to Elisha, who was staying in Jericho, he said to them, "Didn't I tell you not to go?"

Healing of the Water

[19]The men of the city said to Elisha, "Look, our lord, this town is well situated, as you can see, but the water is bad and the land is unproductive."

[20]"Bring me a new bowl," he said, "and put salt in it." So they brought it to him.

[21]Then he went out to the spring and threw the salt into it, saying, "This is what the LORD says: 'I have healed this water. Never again will it cause death or make the land unproductive.'" [22]And the water has remained wholesome to this day, according to the word Elisha had spoken.

Elisha Is Jeered

[23]From there Elisha went up to Bethel. As he was walking along the road, some youths came out of the town and jeered at him. "Go on up, you baldhead!" they said. "Go on up, you baldhead!" [24]He turned around, looked at them and called down a curse on them in the name of the LORD. Then two bears came out of the woods and mauled forty-two of the youths. [25]And he went on to Mount Carmel and from there returned to Samaria.

Moab Revolts

3 Joram[a] son of Ahab became king of Israel in Samaria in the eighteenth year of Jehoshaphat king of Judah, and he reigned twelve years. [2]He did evil in the eyes of the LORD, but not as his father and mother had done. He got rid of the sacred stone of Baal that his father had made. [3]Nevertheless he clung to the sins of Jeroboam son of Nebat, which he had caused Israel to commit; he did not turn away from them.

[4]Now Mesha king of Moab raised sheep, and he had to supply the king of Israel with a hundred thousand lambs and with the wool of a hundred thousand rams. [5]But after Ahab died, the king of Moab rebelled against the king of Israel. [6]So at that time King Joram set out from Samaria and mobilized all Israel. [7]He also sent this message to Jehoshaphat king of Judah: "The king of Moab has rebelled against me. Will you go with me to fight against Moab?"

"I will go with you," he replied. "I am as you are, my people as your people, my horses as your horses."

[8]"By what route shall we attack?" he asked.

"Through the Desert of Edom," he answered.

[9]So the king of Israel set out with the king of Judah and the king of Edom. After a roundabout march of seven days, the army had no more water for themselves or for the animals with them.

[10]"What!" exclaimed the king of Israel. "Has the LORD called us three kings together only to hand us over to Moab?"

[11]But Jehoshaphat asked, "Is there no prophet of the LORD here, that we may inquire of the LORD through him?"

An officer of the king of Israel answered, "Elisha son of Shaphat is here. He used to pour water on the hands of Elijah.[b]"

[12]Jehoshaphat said, "The word of the LORD is with him." So the king of Israel and Jehoshaphat and the king of Edom went down to him.

[13]Elisha said to the king of Israel, "What do we have to do with

---

1. How do you like your water: Tap? Bottled? Babbling? Imported? (Have any on hand?) 2. Who in your family is bald? Do you fear baldness? Why?

1. What might have contaminated the town's water source (v. 21)? 2. What might the new bowl and the salt symbolize (see Nu 18:19)? 3. Is there more behind the youths' harrassment than just Elisha's baldness? Is Elisha being over-bearing? What parable of judgment is enacted here and for what reason?

1. Is any part of your life a rancid spring? What could unleash your potential? 2. Do you ridicule people to their faces, or just behind their backs? What can you do about back-biting?

---

1. Have you ever taken a short-cut home only to get caught in delays or even lost? What happened? 2. What's your favorite thirst-quencher? 3. Ever ask help from a stranger? What happened? Did the episode renew or destroy your faith in human nature?

1. How was Joram like his parents (vv. 1–3)? What reforms did he institute? Why not go all the way and really clean house? 2. Prior to Ahab's death, what was the relationship between Moab and Israel (vv. 4–7)? What are Joram's options in the face of Moab's rebellion? What does his choice of action tell about him? 3. Why does Jehoshaphat appear so eager to help? Has he not learned his lesson about alliances with the North (see 1Ki 22:29–34)? Why not? 4. What big problem does their war strategy encounter (v. 9)? In their risky route to Moab, was this avoidable? How so? Why is it only at this point of desperation that they turn to a prophet of the Lord (v. 11)? 5. How does Elisha respond to Joram and to Jehoshaphat (vv. 13–14)? Why? 6. Why does Elisha want music (v. 15; see 1Sa 10:5–6)? 7. How do you think Elisha's advice will set with the soldiers awaiting relief from thirst (vv. 16–18)? What faith must the troopers and commanders show in order to see God act on their behalf? 8. What purposes does the water fulfill (vv.

---

a1 Hebrew *Jehoram*, a variant of *Joram*; also in verse 6   b11 That is, he was Elijah's personal servant.

each other? Go to the prophets of your father and the prophets of your mother."

"No," the king of Israel answered, "because it was the LORD who called us three kings together to hand us over to Moab."

¹⁴Elisha said, "As surely as the LORD Almighty lives, whom I serve, if I did not have respect for the presence of Jehoshaphat king of Judah, I would not look at you or even notice you. ¹⁵But now bring me a harpist."

While the harpist was playing, the hand of the LORD came upon Elisha ¹⁶and he said, "This is what the LORD says: Make this valley full of ditches. ¹⁷For this is what the LORD says: You will see neither wind nor rain, yet this valley will be filled with water, and you, your cattle and your other animals will drink. ¹⁸This is an easy thing in the eyes of the LORD; he will also hand Moab over to you. ¹⁹You will overthrow every fortified city and every major town. You will cut down every good tree, stop up all the springs, and ruin every good field with stones."

²⁰The next morning, about the time for offering the sacrifice, there it was—water flowing from the direction of Edom! And the land was filled with water.

²¹Now all the Moabites had heard that the kings had come to fight against them; so every man, young and old, who could bear arms was called up and stationed on the border. ²²When they got up early in the morning, the sun was shining on the water. To the Moabites across the way, the water looked red—like blood. ²³"That's blood!" they said. "Those kings must have fought and slaughtered each other. Now to the plunder, Moab!"

²⁴But when the Moabites came to the camp of Israel, the Israelites rose up and fought them until they fled. And the Israelites invaded the land and slaughtered the Moabites. ²⁵They destroyed the towns, and each man threw a stone on every good field until it was covered. They stopped up all the springs and cut down every good tree. Only Kir Hareseth was left with its stones in place, but men armed with slings surrounded it and attacked it as well.

²⁶When the king of Moab saw that the battle had gone against him, he took with him seven hundred swordsmen to break through to the king of Edom, but they failed. ²⁷Then he took his firstborn son, who was to succeed him as king, and offered him as a sacrifice on the city wall. The fury against Israel was great; they withdrew and returned to their own land.

The Widow's Oil

4 The wife of a man from the company of the prophets cried out to Elisha, "Your servant my husband is dead, and you know that he revered the LORD. But now his creditor is coming to take my two boys as his slaves."

²Elisha replied to her, "How can I help you? Tell me, what do you have in your house?"

"Your servant has nothing there at all," she said, "except a little oil."

³Elisha said, "Go around and ask all your neighbors for empty jars. Don't ask for just a few. ⁴Then go inside and shut the door behind you and your sons. Pour oil into all the jars, and as each is filled, put it to one side."

⁵She left him and afterward shut the door behind her and her sons. They brought the jars to her and she kept pouring. ⁶When all the jars were full, she said to her son, "Bring me another one."

But he replied, "There is not a jar left." Then the oil stopped flowing.

22–23)? Of what shaky alliance does the king of Moab hope to take advantage? What happens? **9.** Why does the king of Moab kill his son (v. 27; see Jdg 11:30–31)? What's the cost to him? To the country? Who comes to the rescue—his god or his people?

♥ **1.** Which is worst: (a) Extracting taxes from your neighbor under military threat? (b) Making everyone take sides in a war? (c) Seeking God's favor in a battle? (d) Defoliating the land as you fight? (e) Killing your firstborn son? Who did something right in this chapter? **2.** Does music help you worship or pray? Why? **3.** Does God still come to the aid of his people in dramatic ways? Have you experienced or witnessed it? How so? **4.** In what ways do we "sacrifice" our firstborn today: Early years in day care centers? Less-than-excellent public schools? TV for a baby sitter? Material comforts over spiritual growth? Not protecting their ecological inheritance?

☕ What's more trouble: Having credit cards or not having them? Should you cut yours up?

📖 **1.** How is this story like Elijah with the widow at Zarephath (see 1Ki 17:7–16)? What do widows represent? **2.** Why does the widow obey? What are her alternatives? **3.** Is this a miracle or is there another explanation?

♥ **1.** Does your money help or hinder your trust in God? How so? **2.** How can your family share more with the poor? Write a family budget to see what expenses can be cut or debts eliminated.

⁷She went and told the man of God, and he said, "Go, sell the oil and pay your debts. You and your sons can live on what is left."

The Shunammite's Son Restored to Life

⁸One day Elisha went to Shunem. And a well-to-do woman was there, who urged him to stay for a meal. So whenever he came by, he stopped there to eat. ⁹She said to her husband, "I know that this man who often comes our way is a holy man of God. ¹⁰Let's make a small room on the roof and put in it a bed and a table, a chair and a lamp for him. Then he can stay there whenever he comes to us."

¹¹One day when Elisha came, he went up to his room and lay down there. ¹²He said to his servant Gehazi, "Call the Shunammite." So he called her, and she stood before him. ¹³Elisha said to him, "Tell her, 'You have gone to all this trouble for us. Now what can be done for you? Can we speak on your behalf to the king or the commander of the army?'"

She replied, "I have a home among my own people."

¹⁴"What can be done for her?" Elisha asked.

Gehazi said, "Well, she has no son and her husband is old."

¹⁵Then Elisha said, "Call her." So he called her, and she stood in the doorway. ¹⁶"About this time next year," Elisha said, "you will hold a son in your arms."

"No, my lord," she objected. "Don't mislead your servant, O man of God!"

¹⁷But the woman became pregnant, and the next year about that same time she gave birth to a son, just as Elisha had told her.

¹⁸The child grew, and one day he went out to his father, who was with the reapers. ¹⁹"My head! My head!" he said to his father. His father told a servant, "Carry him to his mother." ²⁰After the

---

Are you the open-heart, open-home type, always ready to entertain? What's neat about such people? What's aggravating about them?

1. What seems strange about this story? (Do rich people often help the prophets?) Why are women particularly sympathetic (see Lk 8:3)? **2.** What does the woman of Shunem suspect after hosting Elisha several times (vv. 9–10)? Does her husband seem to notice? **3.** Why doesn't Elisha speak to the woman directly (vv. 12–15)? Do they need a translator? What is this "home" she refers to? What does that say about her character? **4.** How does Elisha conclude the woman wanted a son? Is the woman lacking faith, being cautiously optimistic or is she realistically hopeful (v. 16)? **5.** What happens to dash those hopes? Was this son's birth and death a set up for greater things to come? Or did his death catch everyone off guard? **6.** What is significant about where she lays the

---

2 Kings 4:1–7   ELISHA AND THE WIDOW'S OIL

Elisha had recently succeeded Elijah as Israel's leading prophet. This story involves the widow of a man who was part of the "company of the prophets," a group zealously committed to God.

1. Why did this woman turn to Elisha?
   a. She trusted him.
   b. She didn't know where else to go.
   c. Elisha was known for his miracles.
   d. She felt like Elisha owed her husband a favor.

2. How come Elisha asked her what she had in her house?
   a. He was nosy.
   b. He needed something to work the miracle with.
   c. He was testing her to see if she was really in need.
   d. God uses whatever you have.

3. What would you think if your neighbor asked for your empty jars?
   a. She must be into recycling.
   b. She must be really desperate.
   c. I wouldn't give them to her unless she told me why she wanted them.
   d. I would be glad to help her out.

4. Why did the oil stop flowing?
   a. because they ran out of jars
   b. because their needs were met
   c. to keep them from getting greedy
   d. to keep them dependent on God
   e. to keep them from making a mess

5. What are you feeling low on?
   a. oil
   b. cash
   c. joy
   d. patience
   e. time
   f. energy
   g. peace
   h. work
   i. income
   j. friends
   k. faith
   l. other:_____

6. God used the widow's own limited resources. Which resource of yours will God likely use to provide for you?
   a. my family
   b. friends I have overlooked
   c. my church or small group
   d. inner strength I didn't know I had
   e. Scripture
   f. my prayer time

7. Does your money help you trust the Lord *more* or *less*? Why?

8. How would you describe your spiritual life right now?
   a. bone dry
   b. running low
   c. making it one day at a time
   d. being replenished
   e. full and overflowing

9. 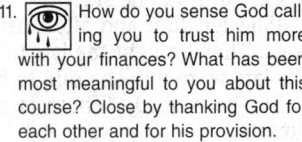 What has been most difficult in surviving as a single? How can this story encourage you in struggling to make it on your own?

10. What do you have in common with this woman?
    a. I feel alone in making ends meet.
    b. Creditors are pursuing me.
    c. I feel like a "slave" to my debts.
    d. My cupboards are almost bare.
    e. Maybe I should ask for some help.
    f. Maybe I should be sharing with those who have less than I do.

11. How do you sense God calling you to trust him more with your finances? What has been most meaningful to you about this course? Close by thanking God for each other and for his provision.

servant had lifted him up and carried him to his mother, the boy sat on her lap until noon, and then he died. ²¹She went up and laid him on the bed of the man of God, then shut the door and went out.

²²She called her husband and said, "Please send me one of the servants and a donkey so I can go to the man of God quickly and return."

²³"Why go to him today?" he asked. "It's not the New Moon or the Sabbath."

"It's all right," she said.

²⁴She saddled the donkey and said to her servant, "Lead on; don't slow down for me unless I tell you." ²⁵So she set out and came to the man of God at Mount Carmel.

When he saw her in the distance, the man of God said to his servant Gehazi, "Look! There's the Shunammite! ²⁶Run to meet her and ask her, 'Are you all right? Is your husband all right? Is your child all right?'"

"Everything is all right," she said.

²⁷When she reached the man of God at the mountain, she took hold of his feet. Gehazi came over to push her away, but the man of God said, "Leave her alone! She is in bitter distress, but the LORD has hidden it from me and has not told me why."

²⁸"Did I ask you for a son, my lord?" she said. "Didn't I tell you, 'Don't raise my hopes'?"

²⁹Elisha said to Gehazi, "Tuck your cloak into your belt, take my staff in your hand and run. If you meet anyone, do not greet him, and if anyone greets you, do not answer. Lay my staff on the boy's face."

dead son (v. 21)? About her secrecy and urgency (vv. 22–23)? About her encounter at Carmel (vv. 26–30)? **7.** Why does the Lord "hide" her problem from Elisha? Why does Elisha delegate the healing mission (vv. 29–31)? How would Gehazi feel? Why doesn't Elisha's staff work magic as his cloak once did? Should he reduce Gehazi's pay for his inability to do the work of a prophet? **8.** Do you suppose Elisha knew for sure that God would raise the boy to life? Otherwise, would he have prayed or worked any differently? **9.** How is this account similar to Elijah and the son of the widow at Zarephath (see 1Ki 17:17–24)?

♡ **1.** Are miraculous faith stories like this a thing of the past? Why or why not? Have you ever witnessed a raising from the dead, or even a miraculous healing? Or is this story simply a parable for God's inner healing? **2.** Many people pray fervently for a terminally ill loved one, yet death comes anyway. What happened to those prayers? As death comes inevitably, isn't all healing temporary? **3.** Are you wrestling with a

---

   2 Kings 4:8–37   **ELISHA AND A GRIEVING WOMAN**

---

1. Why did this woman want to provide accommodations for Elisha?
   a. She was thinking of opening Shunem's first bed and breakfast.
   b. She loved to entertain.
   c. She had the gift of hospitality.
   d. Her heart went out to this traveling minister.
   e. She thought her life would be blessed by blessing a "holy man."

2. After years of hoping, how would you have reacted when Elisha said, "Next year you will hold a son"?
   a. "Sure, Pops!"
   b. "This is too good to be true."
   c. "Don't get my hopes up."
   d. "I'll believe it when I see it."
   e. "I knew God would do it."

3. How do you explain the woman's covering up that her son had died?
   a. She and her husband didn't have good communication.
   b. She was in shock.
   c. She didn't want to say the words.
   d. Laying the boy in the "man of God's" room showed she wasn't willing to accept his death as final.

4. Why did the woman say, "Everything is all right"?
   a. She had accepted her son's death.
   b. She was in denial.
   c. She had faith for a miracle.
   d. She was determined to share her distress with no one but Elisha.

5. How would you describe Elisha's remedies for the dead boy?
   a. bizarre   d. Spirit-led
   b. dramatic   e. successful
   c. courageous   f. hard to believe

6. When was the last time you went out of your way to provide for someone like this woman did? How did you feel about what you did? What reward do you expect for serving others?

7. When you have a problem, to whom can you "tell it like it is" rather than pretend "everything is all right"?

8. ⬛ What was this woman's focus?
   a. herself
   b. others
   c. what she had
   d. what she didn't have

9. ⬛ How would you answer question 8 for *yourself?* How do you balance focusing on your own needs with caring for others?

10. How does your experience of loss relate to this story?
    a. I had a loved one die in my arms.
    b. I couldn't face my loss.
    c. I "froze out" people close to me.
    d. I've hidden my pain from others.
    e. I've resented God for giving me someone only to take them away.

11. ⬛ Do you feel you have passed through the "denial" stage of grief? What about your loss are you still struggling to face?

12. ⬀ How does this story remind you of your experience of miscarriage?
    a. the years of waiting for a child
    b. the shattered dreams and hopes
    c. the difficulty of talking about it with others, even my spouse
    d. the fear of hoping for a child again
    e. pretending "everything is all right"

tragedy "that shouldn't have happened," yet did? What promises have you claimed? What hope? **4.** Have you ever had a friendship with a member of the opposite sex that people didn't quite understand? That you didn't even understand? Is it necessary to label or define relationships? When is it wise to do so?

---

1. What do you like best in a stew? What ruins a stew for you? **2.** Ever run out of food at a picnic, birthday or reception? What happened?

1. What might the famine and the wild gourd symbolize (see Dt 28:18,23–24)? **2.** How would flour neutralize the soup (v. 41)? What is the meaning of this part of the meal? Likewise, this curse of the covenant? **3.** Why hesitate to share (v. 43)? From where comes all the bread? What is the meaning of this part of the meal? How does that compare with Jesus' purpose in feeding the multitudes (see Lk 9:12–17)?

1. Why do people react instantly to physical threat, yet seem indifferent to spiritual threat? **2.** What would you be least willing to share with others? Why?

When's the last time you picked up the entire tab at a restaurant or ball game (other than for your family)? Do you usually pay, let someone else, or do you mostly go "dutch" (and split the bill)?

1. Since Israel and Aram are officially at peace, why is a little captive girl the instigator of this story (vv. 2–3)? What does she tell you about the survival of true faith in Israel? **2.** Why would the pagan king of Aram agree to have his top soldier travel to the heart of Israel for an unlikely cure

---

³⁰But the child's mother said, "As surely as the LORD lives and as you live, I will not leave you." So he got up and followed her. ³¹Gehazi went on ahead and laid the staff on the boy's face, but there was no sound or response. So Gehazi went back to meet Elisha and told him, "The boy has not awakened."

³²When Elisha reached the house, there was the boy lying dead on his couch. ³³He went in, shut the door on the two of them and prayed to the LORD. ³⁴Then he got on the bed and lay upon the boy, mouth to mouth, eyes to eyes, hands to hands. As he stretched himself out upon him, the boy's body grew warm. ³⁵Elisha turned away and walked back and forth in the room and then got on the bed and stretched out upon him once more. The boy sneezed seven times and opened his eyes.

³⁶Elisha summoned Gehazi and said, "Call the Shunammite." And he did. When she came, he said, "Take your son." ³⁷She came in, fell at his feet and bowed to the ground. Then she took her son and went out.

Death in the Pot

³⁸Elisha returned to Gilgal and there was a famine in that region. While the company of the prophets was meeting with him, he said to his servant, "Put on the large pot and cook some stew for these men."

³⁹One of them went out into the fields to gather herbs and found a wild vine. He gathered some of its gourds and filled the fold of his cloak. When he returned, he cut them up into the pot of stew, though no one knew what they were. ⁴⁰The stew was poured out for the men, but as they began to eat it, they cried out, "O man of God, there is death in the pot!" And they could not eat it.

⁴¹Elisha said, "Get some flour." He put it into the pot and said, "Serve it to the people to eat." And there was nothing harmful in the pot.

Feeding of a Hundred

⁴²A man came from Baal Shalishah, bringing the man of God twenty loaves of barley bread baked from the first ripe grain, along with some heads of new grain. "Give it to the people to eat," Elisha said.

⁴³"How can I set this before a hundred men?" his servant asked.

But Elisha answered, "Give it to the people to eat. For this is what the LORD says: 'They will eat and have some left over.'" ⁴⁴Then he set it before them, and they ate and had some left over, according to the word of the LORD.

Naaman Healed of Leprosy

5 Now Naaman was commander of the army of the king of Aram. He was a great man in the sight of his master and highly regarded, because through him the LORD had given victory to Aram. He was a valiant soldier, but he had leprosy.ᵃ

²Now bands from Aram had gone out and had taken captive a young girl from Israel, and she served Naaman's wife. ³She said to her mistress, "If only my master would see the prophet who is in Samaria! He would cure him of his leprosy."

⁴Naaman went to his master and told him what the girl from Israel had said. ⁵"By all means, go," the king of Aram replied. "I will send a letter to the king of Israel." So Naaman left, taking with

---

ᵃ 1 The Hebrew word was used for various diseases affecting the skin—not necessarily leprosy; also in verses 3, 6, 7, 11 and 27.

him ten talents[a] of silver, six thousand shekels[b] of gold and ten sets of clothing. ⁶The letter that he took to the king of Israel read: "With this letter I am sending my servant Naaman to you so that you may cure him of his leprosy."

⁷As soon as the king of Israel read the letter, he tore his robes and said, "Am I God? Can I kill and bring back to life? Why does this fellow send someone to me to be cured of his leprosy? See how he is trying to pick a quarrel with me!"

⁸When Elisha the man of God heard that the king of Israel had torn his robes, he sent him this message: "Why have you torn your robes? Have the man come to me and he will know that there is a prophet in Israel." ⁹So Naaman went with his horses and chariots and stopped at the door of Elisha's house. ¹⁰Elisha sent a messenger to say to him, "Go, wash yourself seven times in the Jordan, and your flesh will be restored and you will be cleansed."

¹¹But Naaman went away angry and said, "I thought that he would surely come out to me and stand and call on the name of the LORD his God, wave his hand over the spot and cure me of my leprosy. ¹²Are not Abana and Pharpar, the rivers of Damascus, better than any of the waters of Israel? Couldn't I wash in them and be cleansed?" So he turned and went off in a rage.

¹³Naaman's servants went to him and said, "My father, if the prophet had told you to do some great thing, would you not have done it? How much more, then, when he tells you, 'Wash and be cleansed'!" ¹⁴So he went down and dipped himself in the Jordan seven times, as the man of God had told him, and his flesh was restored and became clean like that of a young boy.

a5 That is, about 750 pounds (about 340 kilograms)   b5 That is, about 150 pounds (about 70 kilograms)

(vv. 4–6)? 3. Why does Naaman take so much money with him? Why does he take a letter to Joram, king of Israel? 4. On the surface, who shows greater faith—the pagan king of Aram in sending Naaman, or the king of Israel in receiving him (v. 7)? 5. Do you see Elisha chiding the king in verse 8 (compare 3:13–14)? 6. What is significant about the contrast between Naaman's grand arrival and Elisha's quiet, even cool, reception (vv. 9–10)? 7. Why does Naaman become angry (vv. 11–12)? (a) So that his soldiers won't think he's naive? (b) Because Elisha's reception was so cool? (c) Because the healing will require his cooperation? (d) He wanted a big spectacle? Explain. 8. Why are Naaman's servants persuasive in urging him to lighten up and get into the Jordan (v. 13)? (When has their logic been used on you?) What happens to Naaman that he didn't expect and couldn't foresee? 9. Why doesn't Elisha accept any gift of gratitude? Why does Naaman want the dirt (vv. 17–18)? Does Elisha tolerate this outward show of idolatry? (Is idolatry a matter of the outside or inside?) 10. What is Gehazi's root problem (vv. 20–26)? How

2 Kings 5:1–27   NAAMAN HEALED OF LEPROSY

When this story takes place, the people of Aram and Israel were officially at peace, though border skirmishes were not uncommon.

1. Why did the Israelite slave girl urge Naaman to go to the prophet Elisha?
   a. She was a "know-it-all."
   b. She loved her master.
   c. She was amazingly unselfish.
   d. If her idea worked, this could be her ticket home.

2. How would you describe Naaman before he was healed?
   a. respectable   d. superstitious
   b. courageous   e. vain
   c. proud   f. easily offended

3. What do you make of Elisha's attitude toward Naaman?
   a. Naaman's arrival with horses and chariots turned him off.
   b. He was too busy to see Naaman.
   c. He made it clear the Lord would be the healer.
   d. He made it clear Naaman's healing would require faith on his part.

e. Since Elisha didn't do the healing, he wouldn't take any reward from Naaman.

4. How would you describe Naaman after he was healed?
   a. clean   d. grateful
   b. converted   e. humbled
   c. superstitious   f. generous

5. What did Gehazi think?
   a. "Elisha was a fool."
   b. "Naaman got off too easy."
   c. "It's a shame to let Naaman go home with everything he brought."
   d. "If Elisha doesn't want anything, I might as well get something."
   e. "Elisha deserves to be paid."
   f. "I deserve to be paid."

6. What caused Gehazi's leprosy?
   a. greed
   b. lying
   c. getting caught
   d. guilt
   e. It was contagious.

7. What did it take to convince you, like

Naaman, that there is no God in the world except the Lord?

8. Naaman resisted Elisha's message. Are you resisting anything God would like you to do? If so, why?

9. Are there ways you try to "buy" God's blessings or favor, such as by giving your money or your time?

10. How do you feel about a fellow "brother in Christ" holding you accountable the way Elisha did Gehazi?
   a. That would be great!
   b. Yeah, great ... just so he can't see me all the time like Elisha could!
   c. I don't want someone looking over my shoulder.
   d. I can hold myself accountable.
   e. It's scary, but it's also what I need.
   f. That's what this group is all about.

11. If you haven't already let it be known, is there anything you want this group to hold you accountable for?

is it manifested? 11. What's the symbolism in Gehazi being stricken with leprosy? How is it that Naaman, the pagan warlord, enters the "Faith Hall of Fame" while Gehazi, companion of saints, hits the street with a perpetual case of leprosy (see Lk 4:27)? What's the message for all of us?

1. How has greed and its cover-up afflicted the older generation of today? The young professionals? Big business? National government? Even you? 2. What promise of God from this story seems to be too "easy" to be true? Have you virtually ignored, "virtuously" added to, or freely received this promise? 3. When did you come to the settled conviction that there is no God but the God of Israel (v. 15)? What did it take to convince you? 4. Since there is only one God, aren't all religions just different ways to God? Or is the *inside* heart of the person really different, and not just the *outside* form of religion? How do you know? How can you at least give someone the benefit of the doubt, as did Elisha? 5. What is wrong with stretching the truth for a good cause? Does a good cause sometimes justify rotten means? Slightly rotten means? Over-ripe means? 6. Is total honesty always the best policy? Explain.

What have you borrowed that you still haven't returned?

1. Why all the worry over a lost ax head? Why does Elisha care about the place where it fell into the water? 2. What message does this story convey?

1. Does God deal only in the big issues? Do you pray for parking places or good weather? 2. Why doesn't God answer starving Christians who pray for bread?

15Then Naaman and all his attendants went back to the man of God. He stood before him and said, "Now I know that there is no God in all the world except in Israel. Please accept now a gift from your servant."

16The prophet answered, "As surely as the LORD lives, whom I serve, I will not accept a thing." And even though Naaman urged him, he refused.

17"If you will not," said Naaman, "please let me, your servant, be given as much earth as a pair of mules can carry, for your servant will never again make burnt offerings and sacrifices to any other god but the LORD. 18But may the LORD forgive your servant for this one thing: When my master enters the temple of Rimmon to bow down and he is leaning on my arm and I bow there also— when I bow down in the temple of Rimmon, may the LORD forgive your servant for this."

19"Go in peace," Elisha said.

After Naaman had traveled some distance, 20Gehazi, the servant of Elisha the man of God, said to himself, "My master was too easy on Naaman, this Aramean, by not accepting from him what he brought. As surely as the LORD lives, I will run after him and get something from him."

21So Gehazi hurried after Naaman. When Naaman saw him running toward him, he got down from the chariot to meet him. "Is everything all right?" he asked.

22"Everything is all right," Gehazi answered. "My master sent me to say, 'Two young men from the company of the prophets have just come to me from the hill country of Ephraim. Please give them a talent[a] of silver and two sets of clothing.'"

23"By all means, take two talents," said Naaman. He urged Gehazi to accept them, and then tied up the two talents of silver in two bags, with two sets of clothing. He gave them to two of his servants, and they carried them ahead of Gehazi. 24When Gehazi came to the hill, he took the things from the servants and put them away in the house. He sent the men away and they left. 25Then he went in and stood before his master Elisha.

"Where have you been, Gehazi?" Elisha asked.

"Your servant didn't go anywhere," Gehazi answered.

26But Elisha said to him, "Was not my spirit with you when the man got down from his chariot to meet you? Is this the time to take money, or to accept clothes, olive groves, vineyards, flocks, herds, or menservants and maidservants? 27Naaman's leprosy will cling to you and to your descendants forever." Then Gehazi went from Elisha's presence and he was leprous, as white as snow.

An Axhead Floats

6 The company of the prophets said to Elisha, "Look, the place where we meet with you is too small for us. 2Let us go to the Jordan, where each of us can get a pole; and let us build a place there for us to live."

And he said, "Go."

3Then one of them said, "Won't you please come with your servants?"

"I will," Elisha replied. 4And he went with them.

They went to the Jordan and began to cut down trees. 5As one of them was cutting down a tree, the iron axhead fell into the water. "Oh, my lord," he cried out, "it was borrowed!"

6The man of God asked, "Where did it fall?" When he showed

---

a22 That is, about 75 pounds (about 34 kilograms)

him the place, Elisha cut a stick and threw it there, and made the iron float. [7]"Lift it out," he said. Then the man reached out his hand and took it.

Elisha Traps Blinded Arameans

[8]Now the king of Aram was at war with Israel. After conferring with his officers, he said, "I will set up my camp in such and such a place."

[9]The man of God sent word to the king of Israel: "Beware of passing that place, because the Arameans are going down there." [10]So the king of Israel checked on the place indicated by the man of God. Time and again Elisha warned the king, so that he was on his guard in such places.

[11]This enraged the king of Aram. He summoned his officers and demanded of them, "Will you not tell me which of us is on the side of the king of Israel?"

[12]"None of us, my lord the king," said one of his officers, "but Elisha, the prophet who is in Israel, tells the king of Israel the very words you speak in your bedroom."

[13]"Go, find out where he is," the king ordered, "so I can send men and capture him." The report came back: "He is in Dothan." [14]Then he sent horses and chariots and a strong force there. They went by night and surrounded the city.

[15]When the servant of the man of God got up and went out early the next morning, an army with horses and chariots had surrounded the city. "Oh, my lord, what shall we do?" the servant asked.

[16]"Don't be afraid," the prophet answered. "Those who are with us are more than those who are with them."

[17]And Elisha prayed, "O LORD, open his eyes so he may see."

---

1. What might qualify or disqualify you from being a spy?
2. Did you ever receive directions that were totally wrong? Did you find your way, after all?

1. Why is the king of Israel so well prepared for war (vv. 8–10)? Why does this enrage Ben-Hadad, the King of Aram? Why does he suspect it's the work of a double agent (v.11)? Why should he believe their claim that Elisha was the culprit? 2. What is Ben-Hadad's solution (vv. 13–14)? Why does he think he can sneak up on Elisha? Does he (v. 15)? 3. What two miracles does Elisha perform, and for whose benefit (vv. 17–18)? What do you make of this "vision" and "blindness": (a) Total blackout? (b) Fuzzy vision? (c) A mass hallucination? (d) Believing is seeing? 4. Was Elisha's deception in verse 19 okay? Why should the soldiers believe him? 5. Why doesn't Joram kill the POWs (vv. 21–23)? What will releasing them achieve (see 1Ki 20:31)? Is

---

  2 Kings 6:8–23   **ELISHA AND THE CHARIOTS OF FIRE**

1. What about this story do you find the most amazing?
   a. the way the prophet Elisha knew the Arameans' every move
   b. the presence of the heavenly hosts around Elisha
   c. that Elisha and his servant were able to see the heavenly host
   d. that the Arameans were blinded
   e. that Elisha was able to lead the enemy into Samaria—Israel's capital
   f. that the Israelites had a feast for their enemies and then sent them home

2. What made the king of Aram the most upset?
   a. He couldn't defeat Israel.
   b. He suspected a snitch in his army.
   c. He discovered his bedroom had been bugged.

3. Why did the king of Aram go after Elisha?
   a. to dispose of him
   b. to keep him from snitching
   c. to get Elisha on his side

4. How would you feel when Elisha said, "Those who are with us are more than those who are with them"?
   a. Elisha is dreaming.
   b. Our troops must be on the way.
   c. Elisha knows something I don't.
   d. I wish I had Elisha's faith.

5. What would you call Elisha's leading the Arameans to Samaria?
   a. brilliant   d. mean
   b. sneaky   e. inspired
   c. funny   f. incredible

6. Why weren't the Arameans killed?
   a. They were captured by the Lord, not through a human battle.
   b. Israel "turned the other cheek."
   c. Better to "kill them with kindness."
   d. It caused the Arameans to stop raiding Israel's territory.

7. What makes it easier to be kind to your adversaries?
   a. when I have the upper hand
   b. since, as a believer, I always have the upper hand
   c. when I realize the spiritual dimension of the conflict

   d. when I take time to pray for them
   e. when I think about my blessings

8. In what situation do you need some heavenly "horses and chariots of fire" to help you? If they were at your command, how would you deploy them?

9. Who are your competitors in your work? How do you feel about them? What does this story say to you about your attitude and how to relate to them?

10. What does this story communicate about dealing with your frustrations?
    a. God is with me even when I'm not aware of it.
    b. God has ample protective power.
    c. When I'm feeling weak or tempted, I need to remember to pray.
    d. I need to see things as God does.

11. What have you appreciated about this course and this group? How well were your expectations met? How can the group continue to support you in prayer?

Elisha becoming non-violent (see 2:23–25)?

♡ 1. Is it easy to be generous to adversaries when you have the upper hand? Does being one of God's people mean always having the upper hand? Explain. 2. Is a little deception okay, when it achieves a worthwhile goal? 3. What military strategy is Elisha modeling which applies to the evangelism efforts of you and your church? 4. Is love always stronger than violence? Why do we resort to violence more readily than love?

_____

☕ 1. When have you felt under siege or under the gun? Who was putting the gun to your head? (Was it of your own doing or someone else?) 2. What was your hungriest moment? What finally ended it?

📖 1. Is the attack here made by the same Ben-Hadad who made peace with Ahab in 857 B.C. (see 1Ki 20:33–34), or by the Ben-Hadad who fought Jehoahaz in 806 or 796 B.C. (see 13:3)? 2. What is implied in the king invoking the Lord's name in verses 26–27? How severe is the famine (vv. 28–29)? 3. Why does the king tear his robes upon hearing the woman's story (vv. 30–31)? What does the underlying sackcloth reveal (see 1Ki 20:31)? 4. Why is he angry at Elisha? How can Elisha sit around watching the people suffer? What has probably been his advice to the king regarding the siege (v. 33)? 5. What surprise comes to the elders? To the king? To the messenger?

♡ 1. Faced with the choices of the women in this story, what is the right thing to do? Should the king have enforced the verbal contract? 2. When is "helping" a person not helping? Do some people simply have to live through their troubles in order to learn from them? Have you withheld help recently for this reason? 3. Might God be using a hard situation now to bring about a change of heart on your part? How so?

Then the Lord opened the servant's eyes, and he looked and saw the hills full of horses and chariots of fire all around Elisha. [18] As the enemy came down toward him, Elisha prayed to the Lord, "Strike these people with blindness." So he struck them with blindness, as Elisha had asked.

[19] Elisha told them, "This is not the road and this is not the city. Follow me, and I will lead you to the man you are looking for." And he led them to Samaria.

[20] After they entered the city, Elisha said, "Lord, open the eyes of these men so they can see." Then the Lord opened their eyes and they looked, and there they were, inside Samaria.

[21] When the king of Israel saw them, he asked Elisha, "Shall I kill them, my father? Shall I kill them?"

[22] "Do not kill them," he answered. "Would you kill men you have captured with your own sword or bow? Set food and water before them so that they may eat and drink and then go back to their master." [23] So he prepared a great feast for them, and after they had finished eating and drinking, he sent them away, and they returned to their master. So the bands from Aram stopped raiding Israel's territory.

Famine in Besieged Samaria

[24] Some time later, Ben-Hadad king of Aram mobilized his entire army and marched up and laid siege to Samaria. [25] There was a great famine in the city; the siege lasted so long that a donkey's head sold for eighty shekels[a] of silver, and a quarter of a cab[b] of seed pods[c] for five shekels.[d]

[26] As the king of Israel was passing by on the wall, a woman cried to him, "Help me, my lord the king!"

[27] The king replied, "If the Lord does not help you, where can I get help for you? From the threshing floor? From the winepress?" [28] Then he asked her, "What's the matter?"

She answered, "This woman said to me, 'Give up your son so we may eat him today, and tomorrow we'll eat my son.' [29] So we cooked my son and ate him. The next day I said to her, 'Give up your son so we may eat him,' but she had hidden him."

[30] When the king heard the woman's words, he tore his robes. As he went along the wall, the people looked, and there, underneath, he had sackcloth on his body. [31] He said, "May God deal with me, be it ever so severely, if the head of Elisha son of Shaphat remains on his shoulders today!"

[32] Now Elisha was sitting in his house, and the elders were sitting with him. The king sent a messenger ahead, but before he arrived, Elisha said to the elders, "Don't you see how this murderer is sending someone to cut off my head? Look, when the messenger comes, shut the door and hold it shut against him. Is not the sound of his master's footsteps behind him?"

[33] While he was still talking to them, the messenger came down to him. And ⌊the king⌋ said, "This disaster is from the Lord. Why should I wait for the Lord any longer?"

7 Elisha said, "Hear the word of the Lord. This is what the Lord says: About this time tomorrow, a seah[e] of flour will sell for a shekel[f] and two seahs[g] of barley for a shekel at the gate of Samaria."

---

[a]25 That is, about 2 pounds (about 1 kilogram)   [b]25 That is, probably about 1/2 pint (about 0.3 liter)   [c]25 Or of dove's dung   [d]25 That is, about 2 ounces (about 55 grams)   [e]1 That is, probably about 7 quarts (about 7.3 liters); also in verses 16 and 18   [f]1 That is, about 2/5 ounce (about 11 grams); also in verses 16 and 18   [g]1 That is, probably about 13 quarts (about 15 liters); also in verses 16 and 18

[2]The officer on whose arm the king was leaning said to the man of God, "Look, even if the LORD should open the floodgates of the heavens, could this happen?"

"You will see it with your own eyes," answered Elisha, "but you will not eat any of it!"

The Siege Lifted

[3]Now there were four men with leprosy[a] at the entrance of the city gate. They said to each other, "Why stay here until we die? [4]If we say, 'We'll go into the city'—the famine is there, and we will die. And if we stay here, we will die. So let's go over to the camp of the Arameans and surrender. If they spare us, we live; if they kill us, then we die."

[5]At dusk they got up and went to the camp of the Arameans. When they reached the edge of the camp, not a man was there, [6]for the Lord had caused the Arameans to hear the sound of chariots and horses and a great army, so that they said to one another, "Look, the king of Israel has hired the Hittite and Egyptian kings to attack us!" [7]So they got up and fled in the dusk and abandoned their tents and their horses and donkeys. They left the camp as it was and ran for their lives.

[8]The men who had leprosy reached the edge of the camp and entered one of the tents. They ate and drank, and carried away silver, gold and clothes, and went off and hid them. They returned and entered another tent and took some things from it and hid them also.

[9]Then they said to each other, "We're not doing right. This is a day of good news and we are keeping it to ourselves. If we wait until daylight, punishment will overtake us. Let's go at once and report this to the royal palace."

[10]So they went and called out to the city gatekeepers and told them, "We went into the Aramean camp and not a man was there—not a sound of anyone—only tethered horses and donkeys, and the tents left just as they were." [11]The gatekeepers shouted the news, and it was reported within the palace.

[12]The king got up in the night and said to his officers, "I will tell you what the Arameans have done to us. They know we are starving; so they have left the camp to hide in the countryside, thinking, 'They will surely come out, and then we will take them alive and get into the city.'"

[13]One of his officers answered, "Have some men take five of the horses that are left in the city. Their plight will be like that of all the Israelites left here—yes, they will only be like all these Israelites who are doomed. So let us send them to find out what happened."

[14]So they selected two chariots with their horses, and the king sent them after the Aramean army. He commanded the drivers, "Go and find out what has happened." [15]They followed them as far as the Jordan, and they found the whole road strewn with the clothing and equipment the Arameans had thrown away in their headlong flight. So the messengers returned and reported to the king. [16]Then the people went out and plundered the camp of the Arameans. So a seah of flour sold for a shekel, and two seahs of barley sold for a shekel, as the LORD had said.

[17]Now the king had put the officer on whose arm he leaned in charge of the gate, and the people trampled him in the gateway, and he died, just as the man of God had foretold when the king

---

[a]3 The Hebrew word is used for various diseases affecting the skin—not necessarily leprosy; also in verse 8.

1. Are you more of a risk taker than your friends? What one risky thing might you consider: Skydiving? Bungee jumping? A marriage proposal? Volunteering for a mission? Other? 2. Have you ever made a significant discovery that you initially kept under your hat: A wallet full of cash? Tickets to a game? Long-lost _____?

1. Do you buy the logic of the four lepers (vv. 3–4)? Have they missed anything? 2. Did the Arameans have logic on their side when they rushed to the rear (vv. 6–7)? What alternatives did they miss? 3. In what sense was it right for the lepers to eat and drink items not belonging to them (v. 8): (a) "Finders keepers"? (b) "All's fair in love and war"? (c) Only hiding some of their loot was wrong? 4. How does the king sort out the meaning of the good news (v. 12)? Is he being logical, playing it safe, acting in fear, or in faith? What alternatives does he miss? What risk is he willing to take? Should the officer with the plan (v. 13) be promoted to general or demoted? 5. What's the point of the trampled gate officer (vv. 17–20): Never question a prophet's words? Don't let a dumb king lean on you? Never try to control a mob of hungry citizens?

1. Have you ever seen God reverse, unexpectedly, the circumstances in your life? How so? If not, would you like to see God do so? In what arena of your life? 2. Are some behaviors (like plunder and killing) fair "in love and war" that would normally be wrong? Are morals justified by circumstances? 3. Do you prefer complete answers to everything? Or are you content with some issues open-ended? What issues does this chapter leave open-ended for you? 4. This story emphasizes the trustworthiness of God's prophetic word. Where are you with regard to God's word: (a) Still leaning on my reason and trusting only that which I can figure out? (b) Leaning in the direction of God's authority, but not risking too much? (c) Placing my full weight on it, letting it control my actions?

came down to his house. [18]It happened as the man of God had said to the king: "About this time tomorrow, a seah of flour will sell for a shekel and two seahs of barley for a shekel at the gate of Samaria."

[19]The officer had said to the man of God, "Look, even if the LORD should open the floodgates of the heavens, could this happen?" The man of God had replied, "You will see it with your own eyes, but you will not eat any of it!" [20]And that is exactly what happened to him, for the people trampled him in the gateway, and he died.

The Shunammite's Land Restored

8 Now Elisha had said to the woman whose son he had restored to life, "Go away with your family and stay for a while wherever you can, because the LORD has decreed a famine in the land that will last seven years." [2]The woman proceeded to do as the man of God said. She and her family went away and stayed in the land of the Philistines seven years.

[3]At the end of the seven years she came back from the land of the Philistines and went to the king to beg for her house and land. [4]The king was talking to Gehazi, the servant of the man of God, and had said, "Tell me about all the great things Elisha has done." [5]Just as Gehazi was telling the king how Elisha had restored the dead to life, the woman whose son Elisha had brought back to life came to beg the king for her house and land.

Gehazi said, "This is the woman, my lord the king, and this is her son whom Elisha restored to life." [6]The king asked the woman about it, and she told him.

Then he assigned an official to her case and said to him, "Give back everything that belonged to her, including all the income from her land from the day she left the country until now."

Hazael Murders Ben-Hadad

[7]Elisha went to Damascus, and Ben-Hadad king of Aram was ill. When the king was told, "The man of God has come all the way up here," [8]he said to Hazael, "Take a gift with you and go to meet the man of God. Consult the LORD through him; ask him, 'Will I recover from this illness?'"

[9]Hazael went to meet Elisha, taking with him as a gift forty camel-loads of all the finest wares of Damascus. He went in and stood before him, and said, "Your son Ben-Hadad king of Aram has sent me to ask, 'Will I recover from this illness?'"

[10]Elisha answered, "Go and say to him, 'You will certainly recover'; but[a] the LORD has revealed to me that he will in fact die." [11]He stared at him with a fixed gaze until Hazael felt ashamed. Then the man of God began to weep.

[12]"Why is my lord weeping?" asked Hazael.

"Because I know the harm you will do to the Israelites," he answered. "You will set fire to their fortified places, kill their young men with the sword, dash their little children to the ground, and rip open their pregnant women."

[13]Hazael said, "How could your servant, a mere dog, accomplish such a feat?"

"The LORD has shown me that you will become king of Aram," answered Elisha.

[14]Then Hazael left Elisha and returned to his master. When Ben-Hadad asked, "What did Elisha say to you?" Hazael replied, "He told me that you would certainly recover." [15]But the next day

---

a10 The Hebrew may also be read *Go and say, 'You will certainly not recover,' for.*

What great coincidence occurred for you this week?

1. Where did this story leave off (see 4:37)? Why has God sent famine to Israel (see Lev 26:18–20)? Where is the woman's husband (vv. 1–3)? 2. Why does the king speak to Gehazi? Why is Gehazi so eager to speak? 3. What might have happened to the land while the woman was gone? Why does the king treat her well?

1. Do you believe in good luck? Chance? Coincidence? How would that be evident to a casual observer? 2. When blessings overflow, do you feel closer to God, or more independent of him?

1. Were you caught staring at anyone this week: Odd couple? Pretty girl? Good-looking guy? If caught, how did you feel? 2. What dog might you be compared with: Show dog? Mutt? Pit bull? Warm puppy? Trick poodle?

1. Why would a pagan seek the prophet's counsel or be given an audience (vv. 7–8; see 1Ki 19:15)? 2. How do Elisha and Hazael keep the truth from Ben-Hadad (vv. 10,14)? 3. Why the stare (vv. 11–12)? Will Elisha's words avert the disaster, help bring it on, or rationalize it after the fact? 4. Why does Hazael compare himself to a "mere dog" (v. 13)? 5. How does this story relate to the adage: "What he doesn't know won't hurt him"?

1. When might it be okay to tell a lie: (a) To a bandit? (b) To a jilted lover? (c) To a person intent on killing your family? (d) To a cancer patient or AIDS partner not yet ready to hear the truth? 2. What can you tell by a person's eyes? How good are you at "reading" people?

he took a thick cloth, soaked it in water and spread it over the king's face, so that he died. Then Hazael succeeded him as king.

Jehoram King of Judah

[16]In the fifth year of Joram son of Ahab king of Israel, when Jehoshaphat was king of Judah, Jehoram son of Jehoshaphat began his reign as king of Judah. [17]He was thirty-two years old when he became king, and he reigned in Jerusalem eight years. [18]He walked in the ways of the kings of Israel, as the house of Ahab had done, for he married a daughter of Ahab. He did evil in the eyes of the LORD. [19]Nevertheless, for the sake of his servant David, the LORD was not willing to destroy Judah. He had promised to maintain a lamp for David and his descendants forever.

[20]In the time of Jehoram, Edom rebelled against Judah and set up its own king. [21]So Jehoram[a] went to Zair with all his chariots. The Edomites surrounded him and his chariot commanders, but he rose up and broke through by night; his army, however, fled back home. [22]To this day Edom has been in rebellion against Judah. Libnah revolted at the same time.

[23]As for the other events of Jehoram's reign, and all he did, are they not written in the book of the annals of the kings of Judah? [24]Jehoram rested with his fathers and was buried with them in the City of David. And Ahaziah his son succeeded him as king.

Ahaziah King of Judah

[25]In the twelfth year of Joram son of Ahab king of Israel, Ahaziah son of Jehoram king of Judah began to reign. [26]Ahaziah was twenty-two years old when he became king, and he reigned in Jerusalem one year. His mother's name was Athaliah, a granddaughter of Omri king of Israel. [27]He walked in the ways of the house of Ahab and did evil in the eyes of the LORD, as the house of Ahab had done, for he was related by marriage to Ahab's family.

[28]Ahaziah went with Joram son of Ahab to war against Hazael king of Aram at Ramoth Gilead. The Arameans wounded Joram; [29]so King Joram returned to Jezreel to recover from the wounds the Arameans had inflicted on him at Ramoth[b] in his battle with Hazael king of Aram.

Then Ahaziah son of Jehoram king of Judah went down to Jezreel to see Joram son of Ahab, because he had been wounded.

Jehu Anointed King of Israel

9 The prophet Elisha summoned a man from the company of the prophets and said to him, "Tuck your cloak into your belt, take this flask of oil with you and go to Ramoth Gilead. [2]When you get there, look for Jehu son of Jehoshaphat, the son of Nimshi. Go to him, get him away from his companions and take him into an inner room. [3]Then take the flask and pour the oil on his head and declare, 'This is what the LORD says: I anoint you king over Israel.' Then open the door and run; don't delay!"

[4]So the young man, the prophet, went to Ramoth Gilead. [5]When he arrived, he found the army officers sitting together. "I have a message for you, commander," he said.

"For which of us?" asked Jehu.

"For you, commander," he replied.

[6]Jehu got up and went into the house. Then the prophet poured the oil on Jehu's head and declared, "This is what the LORD, the God of Israel, says: 'I anoint you king over the LORD's people Israel.

---

[a]21 Hebrew *Joram,* a variant of *Jehoram*; also in verses 23 and 24   [b]29 Hebrew *Ramah,* a variant of *Ramoth*

Who would you nominate as "Person of the Decade"— one who has most influenced your life?

1. What does Jehoram have going for, and against, him (vv. 16–18; see 1Ki 22:41–44)? How could he stand up to the evil Ahab? **2.** What, if any, conditions does God's promise to David have (v. 19; see 1Ki 11:36–38)? **3.** Who defeated Edom (vv. 20–22; see 1Ki 22:45–47)? Shouldn't they have their own king? What's the political fallout of Edom's revolution? **4.** What does Ahaziah have going for him? Against him (vv. 25–27)? **5.** How does the story of the sons resemble the story of the fathers (vv. 28–29; see 1Ki 22:3–4, 29–34)? Is it the same story, applied to both generations? In what way?

1. Jehoram and Ahaziah could have used better role models. What friends of yours are positive models for your children? For you? **2.** How are you a controlling person? You like to control: (a) The outcome? (b) The means to get there? (c) Your reaction whatever the outcome? (d) Others' reaction to the outcome? Why might it be hard to release control and let others be themselves? **3.** Have the "sins of your fathers" been visited unto you? How so? (Are your relationships with the opposite sex like that of your parents? Do you treat your kids as you were treated?)

1. Have you ever received a *singing* valentine or birthday greeting in front of a group of people? How did you respond? **2.** Has one of your friends ever received a great honor? How did you feel? Jealous? Joyous? Both?

1. Was Elisha supposed to name the new king (vv.1–3; see 1Ki 19:15–17)? Why send the younger prophet? Why must he anoint and run? **2.** Who will Jehu avenge (v. 7; see 1Ki 18:4,13; 19:10; 21:13)? **3.** How will the house of Ahab be like the houses of Jeroboam and Baasha (see 1Ki 15:29–30; 16:11–13)? **4.** Why is Jehu so coy and the military men so fawning about his anointing? **5.** What do verses 11–13 tell you about the mixed feelings people have toward the prophets?

♥ 1. Are you eager for big assignments from God? What holds you back? What propels you on? 2. Have you had to downplay your faith to fit in with your peers? Is this sometimes necessary, or always a compromise? 3. Does the group recognize your gifts in any way? How can the group better call out and honor the gifts of its members?

☕ 1. Can your spouse or roommate tell what kind of day you've had just by the way you walk in the house? How so? 2. Have you ever tried to keep good news secret? How long?

📖 1. If Jehu has just been anointed king (9:1–13), why does he need to conspire against Joram (v. 14)? Is Jehu reluctant to accept kingship? Does he want a peoples' mandate, a bloodless coup or what? 2. Why the secrecy about the news (v. 15b)? Who might profit from communicating with Joram? 3. How can the lookout tell whose troops approach and what their intent is (vv. 17–20)? What happens to the two messengers from Jezreel and why? Do they know what Jehu's up to? 4. Aren't Joram and Ahaziah a bit brash to explore Jehu's motives in person (v. 21)? Isn't Joram supposed to be licking his wounds? 5. Was peace between Joram and Jehu at all possible, or even desirable? Why? 6. How does Jehu justify killing his commander and king (vv. 25–26; see 1Ki 21:18–24)? How far in political savvy has the nation's leadership come since David refused on principle to kill Saul? 7. Why is Ahaziah also a target (v. 27)? Is Jehu truly a "madman" (v. 20), going too far? Or is he fulfilling God's will? Or both? 8. Why such a dishonorable end for Joram? Should the son pay for the sins of the father? Why?

♥ 1. Is treason sometimes okay? Under what circumstances? With what support? What are the risks? Does the driving force of revolution help leaders perform more benevolently or vicious-

⁷You are to destroy the house of Ahab your master, and I will avenge the blood of my servants the prophets and the blood of all the LORD's servants shed by Jezebel. ⁸The whole house of Ahab will perish. I will cut off from Ahab every last male in Israel—slave or free. ⁹I will make the house of Ahab like the house of Jeroboam son of Nebat and like the house of Baasha son of Ahijah. ¹⁰As for Jezebel, dogs will devour her on the plot of ground at Jezreel, and no one will bury her.'" Then he opened the door and ran.

¹¹When Jehu went out to his fellow officers, one of them asked him, "Is everything all right? Why did this madman come to you?"

"You know the man and the sort of things he says," Jehu replied.

¹²"That's not true!" they said. "Tell us."

Jehu said, "Here is what he told me: 'This is what the LORD says: I anoint you king over Israel.'"

¹³They hurried and took their cloaks and spread them under him on the bare steps. Then they blew the trumpet and shouted, "Jehu is king!"

Jehu Kills Joram and Ahaziah

¹⁴So Jehu son of Jehoshaphat, the son of Nimshi, conspired against Joram. (Now Joram and all Israel had been defending Ramoth Gilead against Hazael king of Aram, ¹⁵but King Joram*ᵃ* had returned to Jezreel to recover from the wounds the Arameans had inflicted on him in the battle with Hazael king of Aram.) Jehu said, "If this is the way you feel, don't let anyone slip out of the city to go and tell the news in Jezreel." ¹⁶Then he got into his chariot and rode to Jezreel, because Joram was resting there and Ahaziah king of Judah had gone down to see him.

¹⁷When the lookout standing on the tower in Jezreel saw Jehu's troops approaching, he called out, "I see some troops coming."

"Get a horseman," Joram ordered. "Send him to meet them and ask, 'Do you come in peace?'"

¹⁸The horseman rode off to meet Jehu and said, "This is what the king says: 'Do you come in peace?'"

"What do you have to do with peace?" Jehu replied. "Fall in behind me."

The lookout reported, "The messenger has reached them, but he isn't coming back."

¹⁹So the king sent out a second horseman. When he came to them he said, "This is what the king says: 'Do you come in peace?'"

Jehu replied, "What do you have to do with peace? Fall in behind me."

²⁰The lookout reported, "He has reached them, but he isn't coming back either. The driving is like that of Jehu son of Nimshi—he drives like a madman."

²¹"Hitch up my chariot," Joram ordered. And when it was hitched up, Joram king of Israel and Ahaziah king of Judah rode out, each in his own chariot, to meet Jehu. They met him at the plot of ground that had belonged to Naboth the Jezreelite. ²²When Joram saw Jehu he asked, "Have you come in peace, Jehu?"

"How can there be peace," Jehu replied, "as long as all the idolatry and witchcraft of your mother Jezebel abound?"

²³Joram turned about and fled, calling out to Ahaziah, "Treachery, Ahaziah!"

²⁴Then Jehu drew his bow and shot Joram between the shoulders. The arrow pierced his heart and he slumped down in his

ᵃ15 Hebrew *Jehoram,* a variant of *Joram;* also in verses 17 and 21-24

chariot. 25Jehu said to Bidkar, his chariot officer, "Pick him up and throw him on the field that belonged to Naboth the Jezreelite. Remember how you and I were riding together in chariots behind Ahab his father when the LORD made this prophecy about him: 26'Yesterday I saw the blood of Naboth and the blood of his sons, declares the LORD, and I will surely make you pay for it on this plot of ground, declares the LORD.'ᵃ Now then, pick him up and throw him on that plot, in accordance with the word of the LORD."

27When Ahaziah king of Judah saw what had happened, he fled up the road to Beth Haggan.ᵇ Jehu chased him, shouting, "Kill him too!" They wounded him in his chariot on the way up to Gur near Ibleam, but he escaped to Megiddo and died there. 28His servants took him by chariot to Jerusalem and buried him with his fathers in his tomb in the City of David. 29(In the eleventh year of Joram son of Ahab, Ahaziah had become king of Judah.)

Jezebel Killed

30Then Jehu went to Jezreel. When Jezebel heard about it, she painted her eyes, arranged her hair and looked out of a window. 31As Jehu entered the gate, she asked, "Have you come in peace, Zimri, you murderer of your master?"ᶜ

32He looked up at the window and called out, "Who is on my side? Who?" Two or three eunuchs looked down at him. 33"Throw her down!" Jehu said. So they threw her down, and some of her blood spattered the wall and the horses as they trampled her underfoot.

34Jehu went in and ate and drank. "Take care of that cursed woman," he said, "and bury her, for she was a king's daughter." 35But when they went out to bury her, they found nothing except her skull, her feet and her hands. 36They went back and told Jehu, who said, "This is the word of the LORD that he spoke through his servant Elijah the Tishbite: On the plot of ground at Jezreel dogs will devour Jezebel's flesh.ᵈ 37Jezebel's body will be like refuse on the ground in the plot at Jezreel, so that no one will be able to say, 'This is Jezebel.'"

Ahab's Family Killed

10 Now there were in Samaria seventy sons of the house of Ahab. So Jehu wrote letters and sent them to Samaria: to the officials of Jezreel,ᵉ to the elders and to the guardians of Ahab's children. He said, 2"As soon as this letter reaches you, since your master's sons are with you and you have chariots and horses, a fortified city and weapons, 3choose the best and most worthy of your master's sons and set him on his father's throne. Then fight for your master's house."

4But they were terrified and said, "If two kings could not resist him, how can we?"

5So the palace administrator, the city governor, the elders and the guardians sent this message to Jehu: "We are your servants and we will do anything you say. We will not appoint anyone as king; you do whatever you think best."

6Then Jehu wrote them a second letter, saying, "If you are on my side and will obey me, take the heads of your master's sons and come to me in Jezreel by this time tomorrow."

Now the royal princes, seventy of them, were with the leading men of the city, who were rearing them. 7When the letter arrived,

ly? **2.** The people rallied around Jehu before knowing what kind of king he would be. Have you ever done that with a boss, whom you later regretted choosing? **3.** What's the root cause of the troubles you face? **4.** Is there a role for righteous madmen today, like the prophet and Jehu? Can you exhibit wild abandon for the Lord? How so? Do you?

———

1. Were you forbidden to wear makeup, or do another "grown-up" activity, until a certain age?

1. Does Jezebel know what's coming (vv. 30–31)? **2.** Why does she call Jehu "Zimri" (see 1Ki 16:9–18)? How does she want Jehu to feel? **3.** How does her death confirm Elijah's prophecy (vv. 33–37; see 1Ki 21:23)?

How do you face confrontation: (a) Guns blazing? (b) Peace at any price? (c) Change the subject? (d) Armed with words to twist emotions? Which ways are healthy?

———

1. Have you ever been at a cattle roundup? Did you feel sorry for the animals getting branded, dehorned, castrated, slaughtered? Why? **2.** Who among your friends is the "hyper" type? When is "hyperness" helpful? When does it need a bucket of cold water?

1. To consolidate power, what must Jehu do? What choices are available to him? What choices does Jehu give the elders of Samaria (vv. 1–3)? **2.** Why don't the Samarian leaders negotiate a compromise or take advantage of the city's unique fortifications? How has their fear blinded them to their options and to the ways of Jehu? **3.** What two meanings could Jehu's second letter to Samaria have (v. 6)? How do the Samaritans interpret it? **4.** How could foster parents act so brutally toward their children apparently without a single dissenter (v. 7)? Is this what Jehu had in mind (v. 9)? Why does he

ᵃ26 See 1 Kings 21:19.　　ᵇ27 Or *fled by way of the garden house*　　ᶜ31 Or *"Did Zimri have peace, who murdered his master?"*　　ᵈ36 See 1 Kings 21:23.
ᵉ1 Hebrew; some Septuagint manuscripts and Vulgate *of the city*

pile the heads at the gate? **5.** Is Jehu's rampage what Elijah had in mind (vv. 10–11; see 1Ki 21:21)? Could less bloodshed still have achieved his goals? **6.** Why are the 42 visitors killed (vv. 12–14)? Why is Jehonadab spared and favored (v. 15)? **7.** How does Jehu describe his purge (v.16)? How do you think others might describe it?

♡ **1.** What would you have done if you were raising Joram's children? **2.** What does "zeal for the Lord" (v. 16) mean today? How is it expressed? How can zeal get a person in trouble? How can zeal cloud good judgment? How can "good judgment" squelch zeal? **3.** Is anyone completely "right" when they use violence? What side do you think God takes in current wars?

☕ Allow yourself to brag by completing this sentence comparing you with your father: "My father did _____ a little; I will do that same thing much more" (often, bigger or better). How do you account for the difference?

📖 **1.** Can anyone really be sure of what Jehu is up to (vv. 18–19)? How would the followers of Yahweh feel when Jehu declares his passion for Baal? How would the "Baalophiles" feel? **2.** What logic compels the Baal priests to attend the burnt offering (vv. 20–22)? How does Jehu add luster to his deception as the priests gather? How old a custom is getting dressed up for worship (see Ge 35:2–3)? **3.** Why should the priests be suspicious at Jehu's request that they look out for intruders (v. 23)? What about Jehu would make the 80 posted guards especially vicious that day (v. 24)? **4.** What about Jehu's deception and the guards' demolition work seems excessive (vv. 25–27)? **5.**

these men took the princes and slaughtered all seventy of them. They put their heads in baskets and sent them to Jehu in Jezreel. **8**When the messenger arrived, he told Jehu, "They have brought the heads of the princes."

Then Jehu ordered, "Put them in two piles at the entrance of the city gate until morning."

9The next morning Jehu went out. He stood before all the people and said, "You are innocent. It was I who conspired against my master and killed him, but who killed all these? **10**Know then, that not a word the Lord has spoken against the house of Ahab will fail. The Lord has done what he promised through his servant Elijah." **11**So Jehu killed everyone in Jezreel who remained of the house of Ahab, as well as all his chief men, his close friends and his priests, leaving him no survivor.

12Jehu then set out and went toward Samaria. At Beth Eked of the Shepherds, **13**he met some relatives of Ahaziah king of Judah and asked, "Who are you?"

They said, "We are relatives of Ahaziah, and we have come down to greet the families of the king and of the queen mother."

14"Take them alive!" he ordered. So they took them alive and slaughtered them by the well of Beth Eked—forty-two men. He left no survivor.

15After he left there, he came upon Jehonadab son of Recab, who was on his way to meet him. Jehu greeted him and said, "Are you in accord with me, as I am with you?"

"I am," Jehonadab answered.

"If so," said Jehu, "give me your hand." So he did, and Jehu helped him up into the chariot. **16**Jehu said, "Come with me and see my zeal for the Lord." Then he had him ride along in his chariot.

17When Jehu came to Samaria, he killed all who were left there of Ahab's family; he destroyed them, according to the word of the Lord spoken to Elijah.

Ministers of Baal Killed

18Then Jehu brought all the people together and said to them, "Ahab served Baal a little; Jehu will serve him much. **19**Now summon all the prophets of Baal, all his ministers and all his priests. See that no one is missing, because I am going to hold a great sacrifice for Baal. Anyone who fails to come will no longer live." But Jehu was acting deceptively in order to destroy the ministers of Baal.

20Jehu said, "Call an assembly in honor of Baal." So they proclaimed it. **21**Then he sent word throughout Israel, and all the ministers of Baal came; not one stayed away. They crowded into the temple of Baal until it was full from one end to the other. **22**And Jehu said to the keeper of the wardrobe, "Bring robes for all the ministers of Baal." So he brought out robes for them.

23Then Jehu and Jehonadab son of Recab went into the temple of Baal. Jehu said to the ministers of Baal, "Look around and see that no servants of the Lord are here with you—only ministers of Baal." **24**So they went in to make sacrifices and burnt offerings. Now Jehu had posted eighty men outside with this warning: "If one of you lets any of the men I am placing in your hands escape, it will be your life for his life."

25As soon as Jehu had finished making the burnt offering, he ordered the guards and officers: "Go in and kill them; let no one escape." So they cut them down with the sword. The guards and officers threw the bodies out and then entered the inner shrine of the temple of Baal. 26They brought the sacred stone out of the temple of Baal and burned it. 27They demolished the sacred stone of Baal and tore down the temple of Baal, and people have used it for a latrine to this day.

28So Jehu destroyed Baal worship in Israel. 29However, he did not turn away from the sins of Jeroboam son of Nebat, which he had caused Israel to commit—the worship of the golden calves at Bethel and Dan.

30The LORD said to Jehu, "Because you have done well in accomplishing what is right in my eyes and have done to the house of Ahab all I had in mind to do, your descendants will sit on the throne of Israel to the fourth generation." 31Yet Jehu was not careful to keep the law of the LORD, the God of Israel, with all his heart. He did not turn away from the sins of Jeroboam, which he had caused Israel to commit.

32In those days the LORD began to reduce the size of Israel. Hazael overpowered the Israelites throughout their territory 33east of the Jordan in all the land of Gilead (the region of Gad, Reuben and Manasseh), from Aroer by the Arnon Gorge through Gilead to Bashan.

34As for the other events of Jehu's reign, all he did, and all his achievements, are they not written in the book of the annals of the kings of Israel?

35Jehu rested with his fathers and was buried in Samaria. And Jehoahaz his son succeeded him as king. 36The time that Jehu reigned over Israel in Samaria was twenty-eight years.

Athaliah and Joash

11 When Athaliah the mother of Ahaziah saw that her son was dead, she proceeded to destroy the whole royal family. 2But Jehosheba, the daughter of King Jehorama and sister of Ahaziah, took Joash son of Ahaziah and stole him away from among the royal princes, who were about to be murdered. She put him and his nurse in a bedroom to hide him from Athaliah; so he was not killed. 3He remained hidden with his nurse at the temple of the LORD for six years while Athaliah ruled the land.

4In the seventh year Jehoiada sent for the commanders of units of a hundred, the Carites and the guards and had them brought to him at the temple of the LORD. He made a covenant with them and put them under oath at the temple of the LORD. Then he showed them the king's son. 5He commanded them, saying, "This is what you are to do: You who are in the three companies that are going on duty on the Sabbath—a third of you guarding the royal palace, 6a third at the Sur Gate, and a third at the gate behind the guard, who take turns guarding the temple— 7and you who are in the other two companies that normally go off Sabbath duty are all to guard the temple for the king. 8Station yourselves around the king, each man with his weapon in his hand. Anyone who approaches your ranksb must be put to death. Stay close to the king wherever he goes."

9The commanders of units of a hundred did just as Jehoiada the priest ordered. Each one took his men—those who were going on duty on the Sabbath and those who were going off duty—and came to Jehoiada the priest. 10Then he gave the commanders the spears and shields that had belonged to King David and that were in the temple of the LORD. 11The guards, each with his weapon in his

In verses 28–31, what about this is commendable to God? Is criticized by God? Why didn't Jehu go all the way in this arena as well? Of what excessive zeal, private sins and compromised conscience is he guilty (see 1Ki 12:28–30; Hos 1:4)? **6.** Do you buy Jehu's "zeal for the Lord" (10:16)? What is he really zealous for?

1. Is covert action okay? Should honest alternatives take priority over complex plots and deceptive means? **2.** Do true worshippers seem less forceful today than in Jehu's time? What's the modern equivalent of Jehu's purge in the church?

1. What age were you when your peers or parents gave you your first significant vote of confidence? For example, when were you first given household chores? An allowance? The car? An elected office? **2.** What difference does age make in your vote for national candidates?

1. Why is Athaliah so vicious (v. 1)? What will the death of Ahaziah's heirs accomplish? If successful, could this purge wipe out God's redemptive plan? **2.** Why does Jehosheba subvert Athaliah's plan (vv. 2–3; see 2Ch 22:11)? What faction does she represent? What is their plan? **3.** What risks does Jehoiada take in this conspiracy (vv. 4–11)? What precautions? Why should the soldiers cooperate? **4.** Is this a popular coup? How do they show their support (vv. 12,18,20)? **5.** What choices confront Athaliah as she learns of the coronation? Why are the soldiers so ready to follow the words of a priest to kill the reigning monarch (vv. 15–16)? Why doesn't anyone listen to Athaliah? Why not a judge and jury process before the execution? **6.** What is a "covenant"? What different roles do each of the four covenants play in this conspiracy (vv. 4,12,17)? What obligations does Jehoiada lay on the people?

---

a2 Hebrew *Joram*, a variant of *Jehoram*   b8 Or *approaches the precincts*

Can their lives be the same after this day?

1. Who is as vicious today as Athaliah? What makes them so? Who is as courageous today as Jehosheba and Jehoiada? What builds such courage? **2.** What covenants of responsibility and privilege have you been given: As a child? Teenager? Adult? What covenants have you in turn entered into with others? **3.** What turning points (protective custodians, godly influences, popular mandates) have made your life radically different than if it were not for these agents of God? **4.** Was Mattan just in the wrong place at the wrong time (v. 18)? Would he be allowed to live in the modern era? Why? Is our "religious pluralism" defined as "anything that makes people feel good"? What does that exclude? **5.** Do you have a covenant with God and other people? Or do you prefer private faith? What's the good and bad of each?

1. Who was a personal guide or mentor during your teen years? Are you still in touch with this person? **2.** Have you ever challenged authority when it ran amok? How so? Did you win?

1. What's the connection between Joash and Jehoiada (vv. 2–5; see 11:4,12,15,18)? When does Joash decide it's time to assert his independence? **2.** Is Joash's project worthwhile? Why doesn't Jehoiada cooperate (vv. 6–7)? Who foots the bill for the repairs? How long does it take Joash to notice the work slowdown? **3.** Who wins in the confrontation between Joash and Jehoiada? Any damage to the relationship? Compare the report here with that in 2 Chronicles 24:4–7. What major differences do you see? **4.** Was Joash naive not to require an accounting of the money (v. 15)? Is such trust found anywhere today? **5.** What are Joash's apparent weaknesses (vv. 17–18; see 2Ch 24:17–25, for a glaring weak-

hand, stationed themselves around the king—near the altar and the temple, from the south side to the north side of the temple.

¹²Jehoiada brought out the king's son and put the crown on him; he presented him with a copy of the covenant and proclaimed him king. They anointed him, and the people clapped their hands and shouted, "Long live the king!"

¹³When Athaliah heard the noise made by the guards and the people, she went to the people at the temple of the LORD. ¹⁴She looked and there was the king, standing by the pillar, as the custom was. The officers and the trumpeters were beside the king, and all the people of the land were rejoicing and blowing trumpets. Then Athaliah tore her robes and called out, "Treason! Treason!"

¹⁵Jehoiada the priest ordered the commanders of units of a hundred, who were in charge of the troops: "Bring her out between the ranks[a] and put to the sword anyone who follows her." For the priest had said, "She must not be put to death in the temple of the LORD." ¹⁶So they seized her as she reached the place where the horses enter the palace grounds, and there she was put to death.

¹⁷Jehoiada then made a covenant between the LORD and the king and people that they would be the LORD's people. He also made a covenant between the king and the people. ¹⁸All the people of the land went to the temple of Baal and tore it down. They smashed the altars and idols to pieces and killed Mattan the priest of Baal in front of the altars.

Then Jehoiada the priest posted guards at the temple of the LORD. ¹⁹He took with him the commanders of hundreds, the Carites, the guards and all the people of the land, and together they brought the king down from the temple of the LORD and went into the palace, entering by way of the gate of the guards. The king then took his place on the royal throne, ²⁰and all the people of the land rejoiced. And the city was quiet, because Athaliah had been slain with the sword at the palace.

²¹Joash[b] was seven years old when he began to reign.

Joash Repairs the Temple

12 In the seventh year of Jehu, Joash[c] became king, and he reigned in Jerusalem forty years. His mother's name was Zibiah; she was from Beersheba. ²Joash did what was right in the eyes of the LORD all the years Jehoiada the priest instructed him. ³The high places, however, were not removed; the people continued to offer sacrifices and burn incense there.

⁴Joash said to the priests, "Collect all the money that is brought as sacred offerings to the temple of the LORD—the money collected in the census, the money received from personal vows and the money brought voluntarily to the temple. ⁵Let every priest receive the money from one of the treasurers, and let it be used to repair whatever damage is found in the temple."

⁶But by the twenty-third year of King Joash the priests still had not repaired the temple. ⁷Therefore King Joash summoned Jehoiada the priest and the other priests and asked them, "Why aren't you repairing the damage done to the temple? Take no more money from your treasurers, but hand it over for repairing the temple." ⁸The priests agreed that they would not collect any more money from the people and that they would not repair the temple themselves.

⁹Jehoiada the priest took a chest and bored a hole in its lid. He

---

a 15 Or *out from the precincts*   b 21 Hebrew *Jehoash*, a variant of *Joash*
c 1 Hebrew *Jehoash*, a variant of *Joash*; also in verses 2, 4, 6, 7 and 18

placed it beside the altar, on the right side as one enters the temple of the LORD. The priests who guarded the entrance put into the chest all the money that was brought to the temple of the LORD. ¹⁰Whenever they saw that there was a large amount of money in the chest, the royal secretary and the high priest came, counted the money that had been brought into the temple of the LORD and put it into bags. ¹¹When the amount had been determined, they gave the money to the men appointed to supervise the work on the temple. With it they paid those who worked on the temple of the LORD—the carpenters and builders, ¹²the masons and stonecutters. They purchased timber and dressed stone for the repair of the temple of the LORD, and met all the other expenses of restoring the temple.

¹³The money brought into the temple was not spent for making silver basins, wick trimmers, sprinkling bowls, trumpets or any other articles of gold or silver for the temple of the LORD; ¹⁴it was paid to the workmen, who used it to repair the temple. ¹⁵They did not require an accounting from those to whom they gave the money to pay the workers, because they acted with complete honesty. ¹⁶The money from the guilt offerings and sin offerings was not brought into the temple of the LORD; it belonged to the priests.

¹⁷About this time Hazael king of Aram went up and attacked Gath and captured it. Then he turned to attack Jerusalem. ¹⁸But Joash king of Judah took all the sacred objects dedicated by his fathers—Jehoshaphat, Jehoram and Ahaziah, the kings of Judah—and the gifts he himself had dedicated and all the gold found in the treasuries of the temple of the LORD and of the royal palace, and he sent them to Hazael king of Aram, who then withdrew from Jerusalem.

¹⁹As for the other events of the reign of Joash, and all he did, are they not written in the book of the annals of the kings of Judah? ²⁰His officials conspired against him and assassinated him at Beth Millo, on the road down to Silla. ²¹The officials who murdered him were Jozabad son of Shimeath and Jehozabad son of Shomer. He died and was buried with his fathers in the City of David. And Amaziah his son succeeded him as king.

Jehoahaz King of Israel

13 In the twenty-third year of Joash son of Ahaziah king of Judah, Jehoahaz son of Jehu became king of Israel in Samaria, and he reigned seventeen years. ²He did evil in the eyes of the LORD by following the sins of Jeroboam son of Nebat, which he had caused Israel to commit, and he did not turn away from them. ³So the LORD's anger burned against Israel, and for a long time he kept them under the power of Hazael king of Aram and Ben-Hadad his son.

⁴Then Jehoahaz sought the LORD's favor, and the LORD listened to him, for he saw how severely the king of Aram was oppressing Israel. ⁵The LORD provided a deliverer for Israel, and they escaped from the power of Aram. So the Israelites lived in their own homes as they had before. ⁶But they did not turn away from the sins of the house of Jeroboam, which he had caused Israel to commit; they continued in them. Also, the Asherah pole*ᵃ* remained standing in Samaria.

⁷Nothing had been left of the army of Jehoahaz except fifty horsemen, ten chariots and ten thousand foot soldiers, for the king

ness)? Why would a king so eager to rebuild the temple give so much away to a foreign tyrant? Why would a king who owes his very life and throne to Jehoiada murder that priest's son? What does Joash lose besides the treasures? **6.** Why don't the officials who kill Joash assume power (vv. 20–21; see 2Ch 24:26)?

1. How could a person whose life centered around the temple end on such a downbeat? For what apparent reasons do you see leaders (in church and state) not remaining true to their initial calling? **2.** Are you a role model for someone younger than you? How do you feel about living up to their expectations? What are the pitfalls of being a mentor? **3.** Are you trying to establish your independence, as did Joash, the boy king, in relation to Jehoiada? What role does God play in the process of "becoming your own person"? **4.** Are you as trusting with your money as Joash was with his? When you delegate work without supervising, what happens? If you don't *inspect*, what can you *expect*?

Ever been a loyal fan of a losing team? What's the cost in frustration? What's the fun of it?

1. How does Jehoahaz strike you: Resourceful? Compromiser? Sincere? Victim? Half-hearted? Under-achiever? Why? **2.** Is God a "softy," blessing the people while they commit the very sins Jehu shed blood to punish (vv. 4–6)? **3.** With their depleted resources, how prepared for war is Israel (v. 7; compare 1Ki 20:29)?

1. Is it easier to seek God when you are prospering or struggling? **2.** Have things gone well for you in times of sin? Poorly in times of prayer?

ᵃ6 That is, a symbol of the goddess Asherah; here and elsewhere in 2 Kings

of Aram had destroyed the rest and made them like the dust at threshing time.

[8]As for the other events of the reign of Jehoahaz, all he did and his achievements, are they not written in the book of the annals of the kings of Israel? [9]Jehoahaz rested with his fathers and was buried in Samaria. And Jehoash[a] his son succeeded him as king.

Jehoash King of Israel

[10]In the thirty-seventh year of Joash king of Judah, Jehoash son of Jehoahaz became king of Israel in Samaria, and he reigned sixteen years. [11]He did evil in the eyes of the LORD and did not turn away from any of the sins of Jeroboam son of Nebat, which he had caused Israel to commit; he continued in them.

[12]As for the other events of the reign of Jehoash, all he did and his achievements, including his war against Amaziah king of Judah, are they not written in the book of the annals of the kings of Israel? [13]Jehoash rested with his fathers, and Jeroboam succeeded him on the throne. Jehoash was buried in Samaria with the kings of Israel.

[14]Now Elisha was suffering from the illness from which he died. Jehoash king of Israel went down to see him and wept over him. "My father! My father!" he cried. "The chariots and horsemen of Israel!"

[15]Elisha said, "Get a bow and some arrows," and he did so. [16]"Take the bow in your hands," he said to the king of Israel. When he had taken it, Elisha put his hands on the king's hands.

[17]"Open the east window," he said, and he opened it. "Shoot!" Elisha said, and he shot. "The LORD's arrow of victory, the arrow of victory over Aram!" Elisha declared. "You will completely destroy the Arameans at Aphek."

[18]Then he said, "Take the arrows," and the king took them. Elisha told him, "Strike the ground." He struck it three times and stopped. [19]The man of God was angry with him and said, "You should have struck the ground five or six times; then you would have defeated Aram and completely destroyed it. But now you will defeat it only three times."

[20]Elisha died and was buried.

Now Moabite raiders used to enter the country every spring. [21]Once while some Israelites were burying a man, suddenly they saw a band of raiders; so they threw the man's body into Elisha's tomb. When the body touched Elisha's bones, the man came to life and stood up on his feet.

[22]Hazael king of Aram oppressed Israel throughout the reign of Jehoahaz. [23]But the LORD was gracious to them and had compassion and showed concern for them because of his covenant with Abraham, Isaac and Jacob. To this day he has been unwilling to destroy them or banish them from his presence.

[24]Hazael king of Aram died, and Ben-Hadad his son succeeded him as king. [25]Then Jehoash son of Jehoahaz recaptured from Ben-Hadad son of Hazael the towns he had taken in battle from his father Jehoahaz. Three times Jehoash defeated him, and so he recovered the Israelite towns.

Amaziah King of Judah

14 In the second year of Jehoash[b] son of Jehoahaz king of Israel, Amaziah son of Joash king of Judah began to reign. [2]He was twenty-five years old when he became king, and he reigned in Jerusalem twenty-nine years. His mother's name was

---

☕ **1.** As a child, did you enjoy playing "Simon Says"? How well were you able to do what Simon says? **2.** Now who is always telling you what to do (fixing your grammar, redressing you)? How well do you do what she (or he) says?

📖 **1.** This passage of Scripture weaves together 3–4 stories. Can you find the connective word and "seam" verses tying one story to the other? **2.** Does it sound like Jehoash listened to Elisha and the prophets (vv. 10–11)? How must he be feeling as Elisha dies (v. 14)? What do you associate with this final exclamation (see 2:12)? **3.** Why does the nation's leading prophet even give an evil king two minutes of time, much less a word of encouragement (vv. 15–17)? What happens when people touch hands, as Elisha does to Jehoash? **4.** Why all the precise directives (east window ... shoot ... take the arrows ... strike the ground ... five or six times)? Is he playing an ancient version of "Simon Says"? How can Elisha assure Jehoash of complete victory (v. 17) and then only a partial victory (vv. 19,25)? **5.** What effect do you suppose Elisha's death, prophecy and bones bring to one and all?

♡ **1.** How can Elisha's bones have such power? Have you heard stories of miraculous relics of the Christian era? Share one. **2.** How is your image of God challenged by these stories of miraculous power, fulfilled prophecy, wrath and mercy?

☕ Do you tend to bite off more than you can chew, always testing your limits? Or do you regularly say no and withdraw from challenges that you know are beyond you? Illustrate.

---

a9 Hebrew *Joash*, a variant of *Jehoash*; also in verses 12-14 and 25   b1 Hebrew *Joash*, a variant of *Jehoash*; also in verses 13, 23 and 27

Jehoaddin; she was from Jerusalem. ³He did what was right in the eyes of the LORD, but not as his father David had done. In everything he followed the example of his father Joash. ⁴The high places, however, were not removed; the people continued to offer sacrifices and burn incense there.

⁵After the kingdom was firmly in his grasp, he executed the officials who had murdered his father the king. ⁶Yet he did not put the sons of the assassins to death, in accordance with what is written in the Book of the Law of Moses where the LORD commanded: "Fathers shall not be put to death for their children, nor children put to death for their fathers; each is to die for his own sins."ᵃ

⁷He was the one who defeated ten thousand Edomites in the Valley of Salt and captured Sela in battle, calling it Joktheel, the name it has to this day.

⁸Then Amaziah sent messengers to Jehoash son of Jehoahaz, the son of Jehu, king of Israel, with the challenge: "Come, meet me face to face."

⁹But Jehoash king of Israel replied to Amaziah king of Judah: "A thistle in Lebanon sent a message to a cedar in Lebanon, 'Give your daughter to my son in marriage.' Then a wild beast in Lebanon came along and trampled the thistle underfoot. ¹⁰You have indeed defeated Edom and now you are arrogant. Glory in your victory, but stay at home! Why ask for trouble and cause your own downfall and that of Judah also?"

¹¹Amaziah, however, would not listen, so Jehoash king of Israel attacked. He and Amaziah king of Judah faced each other at Beth Shemesh in Judah. ¹²Judah was routed by Israel, and every man fled to his home. ¹³Jehoash king of Israel captured Amaziah king of Judah, the son of Joash, the son of Ahaziah, at Beth Shemesh. Then Jehoash went to Jerusalem and broke down the wall of Jerusalem from the Ephraim Gate to the Corner Gate—a section about six hundred feet long.ᵇ ¹⁴He took all the gold and silver and all the articles found in the temple of the LORD and in the treasuries of the royal palace. He also took hostages and returned to Samaria.

¹⁵As for the other events of the reign of Jehoash, what he did and his achievements, including his war against Amaziah king of Judah, are they not written in the book of the annals of the kings of Israel? ¹⁶Jehoash rested with his fathers and was buried in Samaria with the kings of Israel. And Jeroboam his son succeeded him as king.

¹⁷Amaziah son of Joash king of Judah lived for fifteen years after the death of Jehoash son of Jehoahaz king of Israel. ¹⁸As for the other events of Amaziah's reign, are they not written in the book of the annals of the kings of Judah?

¹⁹They conspired against him in Jerusalem, and he fled to Lachish, but they sent men after him to Lachish and killed him there. ²⁰He was brought back by horse and was buried in Jerusalem with his fathers, in the City of David.

²¹Then all the people of Judah took Azariah,ᶜ who was sixteen years old, and made him king in place of his father Amaziah. ²²He was the one who rebuilt Elath and restored it to Judah after Amaziah rested with his fathers.

Jeroboam II King of Israel

²³In the fifteenth year of Amaziah son of Joash king of Judah, Jeroboam son of Jehoash king of Israel became king in Samaria, and

1. What tells you that Amaziah might bring a breath of fresh air to Judah (vv. 1–5)? Is he a practical politician? One who is power-hungry? Or one who means well? How would David have done differently? 2. Why should Amaziah respect the Law on inheritance of punishment if his predecessors did not (vv. 5–6)? What's to be gained by respect for the Law? 3. What is Amaziah's character flaw which Jehoash exposes with a riddle or fable (vv. 7–11)? 4. What does that stubborn pride cost Amaziah and his nation? Had he taken lessons from David, how might the flaw have worked out differently? 5. How does Jehoash try to keep the upstart king of the south from causing any more trouble (vv. 11–14)? Is it a merciless drubbing, or charitable under the circumstances? 6. From the evidence, does it appear that Amaziah's assassination was a plot hatched by a few operatives, or supported by a large part of the people (vv. 19–20)? 7. What formidable challenges face the teenage king Azariah (v. 21)?

1. Amaziah aimed too high and ended up six feet under. As for you, is it better to aim high and miss, or aim low and hit? How do you feel about failure? How is success or failure measured? Should "success and failure" be done away with altogether? 2. In some respects, Amaziah had it coming to him. Is it generally okay to beat up on bullies? Why or why not? 3. What traits of God evident in this section comfort you? Alarm you? 4. What is pride? How much of a problem is it for you? What's to be done about this?

When is the last time you felt truly helpless? Who did you call?

ᵃ6 Deut. 24:16   ᵇ13 Hebrew *four hundred cubits* (about 180 meters)   ᶜ21 Also called *Uzziah*

1. What kind of news splash do you suppose the local prophet made when he came by whale and water to Nineveh (see Jnh 1:1)? What does Jonah know about being helpless and being saved? 2. Find on a map Hamath and the Sea of Arabah. Is the author getting a little overheated about Jeroboam's conquests (v. 28)? 3. Is a strong military Israel's real solution (v. 26)?

1. Who are the "helpless" in your world? What role could your church or group play in helping them? 2. If God shows kindness through sinful people (v. 27), how can God show kindness through you?

What was your biggest concern at 16?

1. By what other name is Azariah known (see 2Ch 26)? Why does he have leprosy (v. 5)? Is God always to blame for illness? 2. What happened the year Azariah died (see Isa 6:1)?

1. Do you know anyone with disability? Mental illness? Is God to blame? 2. Do you have problems that never go away? How do you cope?

1. How do you get your news? Do you feel up-to-date or out-of-touch? 2. What could you learn in a month: A language? To swim? Job skills?

1. What surprise comes into Zechariah's life (v. 8)? What are his choices? 2. Is Shallum guilty of murder or fulfilling prophecy (vv. 11–12)? 3. What social conditions breed conspiracies? When is being in power dangerous? When is it relatively safe? 4. Does Shallum get his justice?

1. Is Zechariah's career any admonition to stay abreast of current events? To pay attention to God's word? 2. What hard choices confront you? From whom do you seek advice? 3. Do you always reap what you sow? When were you last on the receiving end of justice? When did you get off easy?

he reigned forty-one years. [24]He did evil in the eyes of the LORD and did not turn away from any of the sins of Jeroboam son of Nebat, which he had caused Israel to commit. [25]He was the one who restored the boundaries of Israel from Lebo[a] Hamath to the Sea of the Arabah,[b] in accordance with the word of the LORD, the God of Israel, spoken through his servant Jonah son of Amittai, the prophet from Gath Hepher.

[26]The LORD had seen how bitterly everyone in Israel, whether slave or free, was suffering; there was no one to help them. [27]And since the LORD had not said he would blot out the name of Israel from under heaven, he saved them by the hand of Jeroboam son of Jehoash.

[28]As for the other events of Jeroboam's reign, all he did, and his military achievements, including how he recovered for Israel both Damascus and Hamath, which had belonged to Yaudi,[c] are they not written in the book of the annals of the kings of Israel? [29]Jeroboam rested with his fathers, the kings of Israel. And Zechariah his son succeeded him as king.

Azariah King of Judah

15 In the twenty-seventh year of Jeroboam king of Israel, Azariah son of Amaziah king of Judah began to reign. [2]He was sixteen years old when he became king, and he reigned in Jerusalem fifty-two years. His mother's name was Jecoliah; she was from Jerusalem. [3]He did what was right in the eyes of the LORD, just as his father Amaziah had done. [4]The high places, however, were not removed; the people continued to offer sacrifices and burn incense there.

[5]The LORD afflicted the king with leprosy[d] until the day he died, and he lived in a separate house.[e] Jotham the king's son had charge of the palace and governed the people of the land.

[6]As for the other events of Azariah's reign, and all he did, are they not written in the book of the annals of the kings of Judah? [7]Azariah rested with his fathers and was buried near them in the City of David. And Jotham his son succeeded him as king.

Zechariah King of Israel

[8]In the thirty-eighth year of Azariah king of Judah, Zechariah son of Jeroboam became king of Israel in Samaria, and he reigned six months. [9]He did evil in the eyes of the LORD, as his fathers had done. He did not turn away from the sins of Jeroboam son of Nebat, which he had caused Israel to commit.

[10]Shallum son of Jabesh conspired against Zechariah. He attacked him in front of the people,[f] assassinated him and succeeded him as king. [11]The other events of Zechariah's reign are written in the book of the annals of the kings of Israel. [12]So the word of the LORD spoken to Jehu was fulfilled: "Your descendants will sit on the throne of Israel to the fourth generation."[g]

Shallum King of Israel

[13]Shallum son of Jabesh became king in the thirty-ninth year of Uzziah king of Judah, and he reigned in Samaria one month. [14]Then Menahem son of Gadi went from Tirzah up to Samaria. He attacked Shallum son of Jabesh in Samaria, assassinated him and succeeded him as king.

---

a25 Or *from the entrance to*   *b25* That is, the Dead Sea   *c28* Or *Judah*
d5 The Hebrew word was used for various diseases affecting the skin—not necessarily leprosy.   *e5* Or *in a house where he was relieved of responsibility*   *f10* Hebrew; some Septuagint manuscripts *in Ibleam*   *g12* 2 Kings 10:30

[15]The other events of Shallum's reign, and the conspiracy he led, are written in the book of the annals of the kings of Israel.

[16]At that time Menahem, starting out from Tirzah, attacked Tiphsah and everyone in the city and its vicinity, because they refused to open their gates. He sacked Tiphsah and ripped open all the pregnant women.

Menahem King of Israel

[17]In the thirty-ninth year of Azariah king of Judah, Menahem son of Gadi became king of Israel, and he reigned in Samaria ten years. [18]He did evil in the eyes of the LORD. During his entire reign he did not turn away from the sins of Jeroboam son of Nebat, which he had caused Israel to commit.

[19]Then Pul[a] king of Assyria invaded the land, and Menahem gave him a thousand talents[b] of silver to gain his support and strengthen his own hold on the kingdom. [20]Menahem exacted this money from Israel. Every wealthy man had to contribute fifty shekels[c] of silver to be given to the king of Assyria. So the king of Assyria withdrew and stayed in the land no longer.

[21]As for the other events of Menahem's reign, and all he did, are they not written in the book of the annals of the kings of Israel? [22]Menahem rested with his fathers. And Pekahiah his son succeeded him as king.

Pekahiah King of Israel

[23]In the fiftieth year of Azariah king of Judah, Pekahiah son of Menahem became king of Israel in Samaria, and he reigned two years. [24]Pekahiah did evil in the eyes of the LORD. He did not turn away from the sins of Jeroboam son of Nebat, which he had caused Israel to commit. [25]One of his chief officers, Pekah son of Remaliah, conspired against him. Taking fifty men of Gilead with him, he assassinated Pekahiah, along with Argob and Arieh, in the citadel of the royal palace at Samaria. So Pekah killed Pekahiah and succeeded him as king.

[26]The other events of Pekahiah's reign, and all he did, are written in the book of the annals of the kings of Israel.

Pekah King of Israel

[27]In the fifty-second year of Azariah king of Judah, Pekah son of Remaliah became king of Israel in Samaria, and he reigned twenty years. [28]He did evil in the eyes of the LORD. He did not turn away from the sins of Jeroboam son of Nebat, which he had caused Israel to commit.

[29]In the time of Pekah king of Israel, Tiglath-Pileser king of Assyria came and took Ijon, Abel Beth Maacah, Janoah, Kedesh and Hazor. He took Gilead and Galilee, including all the land of Naphtali, and deported the people to Assyria. [30]Then Hoshea son of Elah conspired against Pekah son of Remaliah. He attacked and assassinated him, and then succeeded him as king in the twentieth year of Jotham son of Uzziah.

[31]As for the other events of Pekah's reign, and all he did, are they not written in the book of the annals of the kings of Israel?

Jotham King of Judah

[32]In the second year of Pekah son of Remaliah king of Israel, Jotham son of Uzziah king of Judah began to reign. [33]He was twenty-five years old when he became king, and he reigned in Jerusa-

What work around the house or on the job could you use 50 good men to do? Is the work mindless? Costly? Legal? Fun?

1. What is the purpose of military conquest (vv. 19–20)? 2. Why should a desperado like Menahem stoop to such humiliating tactics to get rid of an enemy? 3. Who ends up footing the bill: The government? The wealthy? The little guy? 4. What hints do you see that despite Menahem, the country is enjoying prosperity? 5. Is Pekahiah done in because people are upset with his sinning (vv. 23–25)? 6. What does the quick turnaround in kings say about life in Israel?

1. Is evil tolerable as long as the economy looks bright? Is it better to be poor and Christ-like or comfortable and compromised? What gets your attention most—the bank balance or the word of God? 2. Does God give you some wealth to help fend off evil? What is the purpose of your prosperity?

When you're feeling real low, who can send you even lower: Spouse? Kids? School principal? Boss?

1. What happened the last time Assyria attacked (see 15:19)? 2. With the national treasury empty, the army shoeless and the temples bare, what resource is left to extract (v. 29)? 3. What does Hoshea decide with Assyria advancing on Aram and Philistia (v. 30)? 4. Meanwhile in Judah, what does Jotham have going for him (vv. 32–34)? 5. Who most likely destroyed the Upper Gate (see 14:13)? 6. If Jotham is good and concerned about God's temple, why does God send enemies (v. 37)? Is this author too quick to attribute every military maneuver to God?

---

[a]19 Also called *Tiglath-Pileser*   [b]19 That is, about 37 tons (about 34 metric tons)
[c]20 That is, about 1 1/4 pounds (about 0.6 kilogram)

lem sixteen years. His mother's name was Jerusha daughter of Zadok. [34]He did what was right in the eyes of the LORD, just as his father Uzziah had done. [35]The high places, however, were not removed; the people continued to offer sacrifices and burn incense there. Jotham rebuilt the Upper Gate of the temple of the LORD.

[36]As for the other events of Jotham's reign, and what he did, are they not written in the book of the annals of the kings of Judah? [37](In those days the LORD began to send Rezin king of Aram and Pekah son of Remaliah against Judah.) [38]Jotham rested with his fathers and was buried with them in the City of David, the city of his father. And Ahaz his son succeeded him as king.

Ahaz King of Judah

16 In the seventeenth year of Pekah son of Remaliah, Ahaz son of Jotham king of Judah began to reign. [2]Ahaz was twenty years old when he became king, and he reigned in Jerusalem sixteen years. Unlike David his father, he did not do what was right in the eyes of the LORD his God. [3]He walked in the ways of the kings of Israel and even sacrificed his son in[a] the fire, following the detestable ways of the nations the LORD had driven out before the Israelites. [4]He offered sacrifices and burned incense at the high places, on the hilltops and under every spreading tree.

[5]Then Rezin king of Aram and Pekah son of Remaliah king of Israel marched up to fight against Jerusalem and besieged Ahaz, but they could not overpower him. [6]At that time, Rezin king of Aram recovered Elath for Aram by driving out the men of Judah. Edomites then moved into Elath and have lived there to this day.

[7]Ahaz sent messengers to say to Tiglath-Pileser king of Assyria, "I am your servant and vassal. Come up and save me out of the hand of the king of Aram and of the king of Israel, who are attacking me." [8]And Ahaz took the silver and gold found in the temple of the LORD and in the treasuries of the royal palace and sent it as a gift to the king of Assyria. [9]The king of Assyria complied by attacking Damascus and capturing it. He deported its inhabitants to Kir and put Rezin to death.

[10]Then King Ahaz went to Damascus to meet Tiglath-Pileser king of Assyria. He saw an altar in Damascus and sent to Uriah the priest a sketch of the altar, with detailed plans for its construction. [11]So Uriah the priest built an altar in accordance with all the plans that King Ahaz had sent from Damascus and finished it before King Ahaz returned. [12]When the king came back from Damascus and saw the altar, he approached it and presented offerings[b] on it. [13]He offered up his burnt offering and grain offering, poured out his drink offering, and sprinkled the blood of his fellowship offerings[c] on the altar. [14]The bronze altar that stood before the LORD he brought from the front of the temple—from between the new altar and the temple of the LORD—and put it on the north side of the new altar.

[15]King Ahaz then gave these orders to Uriah the priest: "On the large new altar, offer the morning burnt offering and the evening grain offering, the king's burnt offering and his grain offering, and the burnt offering of all the people of the land, and their grain offering and their drink offering. Sprinkle on the altar all the blood of the burnt offerings and sacrifices. But I will use the bronze altar for seeking guidance." [16]And Uriah the priest did just as King Ahaz had ordered.

[17]King Ahaz took away the side panels and removed the basins

---

1. Have you ever met a refugee? Who is responsible for aiding refugees? **2.** How does the writer's view of God's involvement in human events affect your attitude toward developments on the world scene?

---

1. How photographic is your memory: Once seen, always filed? Overexposed? Out of focus? Needs developing? **2.** When did you purposely copy someone else's dress? Hairstyle? Homework? Recipe? Did they get any credit?

1. What new standards for sinning does Ahaz set (vv. 3–4; see Lev 18:21; Dt 12:2; compare Ex 13:1–2,11–13)? **2.** Why does Israel join Aram in attacking Judah (vv. 5–6; see Isa 7:5–6)? What does Rezin do when he can't take Jerusalem? **3.** What is Ahaz's strategy for repelling Aram and Israel (vv. 7–9)? What has Isaiah warned him about (see Isa 8:6–8, an event which took place in 732 B.C.)? **4.** Why do you think Ahaz meets with Tiglath-Pileser after he defeats Aram (v. 10)? Why does Ahaz want to copy the temple in Damascus (vv. 11–12)? Who is Ahaz's accomplice in all his schemes? **5.** Who consecrates the new altar? Is he qualified? What will it be used for? What's wrong with that (see Dt 18:10)? **6.** What "deference to the king of Assyria" is going on here (vv. 15–18)? What symbols of his royal power is this vassal king handing over to the Assyrian?

1. How do you determine acceptable modes of worship? Are some modes unusual but not a great problem? Are some dead wrong? **2.** Are you in any alliances that pang your conscience from time to time? How should you handle these? **3.** No one held King Ahaz or Uriah the priest accountable for doing things against the Law of God. How do you respectfully call those in spiritual authority to account when they err? How can it be done gracefully? **4.** Where do you go for guidance? How does guidance come? What guidance do you need at this moment?

---

a3 Or even made his son pass through　　b12 Or and went up　　c13 Traditionally peace offerings

from the movable stands. He removed the Sea from the bronze bulls that supported it and set it on a stone base. [18]He took away the Sabbath canopy[a] that had been built at the temple and removed the royal entryway outside the temple of the LORD, in deference to the king of Assyria.

[19]As for the other events of the reign of Ahaz, and what he did, are they not written in the book of the annals of the kings of Judah? [20]Ahaz rested with his fathers and was buried with them in the City of David. And Hezekiah his son succeeded him as king.

Hoshea Last King of Israel

17 In the twelfth year of Ahaz king of Judah, Hoshea son of Elah became king of Israel in Samaria, and he reigned nine years. [2]He did evil in the eyes of the LORD, but not like the kings of Israel who preceded him.

[3]Shalmaneser king of Assyria came up to attack Hoshea, who had been Shalmaneser's vassal and had paid him tribute. [4]But the king of Assyria discovered that Hoshea was a traitor, for he had sent envoys to So[b] king of Egypt, and he no longer paid tribute to the king of Assyria, as he had done year by year. Therefore Shalmaneser seized him and put him in prison. [5]The king of Assyria invaded the entire land, marched against Samaria and laid siege to it for three years. [6]In the ninth year of Hoshea, the king of Assyria captured Samaria and deported the Israelites to Assyria. He settled them in Halah, in Gozan on the Habor River and in the towns of the Medes.

Israel Exiled Because of Sin

[7]All this took place because the Israelites had sinned against the LORD their God, who had brought them up out of Egypt from under the power of Pharaoh king of Egypt. They worshiped other gods [8]and followed the practices of the nations the LORD had driven out before them, as well as the practices that the kings of Israel had introduced. [9]The Israelites secretly did things against the LORD their God that were not right. From watchtower to fortified city they built themselves high places in all their towns. [10]They set up sacred stones and Asherah poles on every high hill and under every spreading tree. [11]At every high place they burned incense, as the nations whom the LORD had driven out before them had done. They did wicked things that provoked the LORD to anger. [12]They worshiped idols, though the LORD had said, "You shall not do this."[c] [13]The LORD warned Israel and Judah through all his prophets and seers: "Turn from your evil ways. Observe my commands and decrees, in accordance with the entire Law that I commanded your fathers to obey and that I delivered to you through my servants the prophets."

[14]But they would not listen and were as stiff-necked as their fathers, who did not trust in the LORD their God. [15]They rejected his decrees and the covenant he had made with their fathers and the warnings he had given them. They followed worthless idols and themselves became worthless. They imitated the nations around them although the LORD had ordered them, "Do not do as they do," and they did the things the LORD had forbidden them to do.

[16]They forsook all the commands of the LORD their God and made for themselves two idols cast in the shape of calves, and an Asherah pole. They bowed down to all the starry hosts, and they wor-

1. What childhood secret have you kept from your parents to this day? **2.** What warning do you habitually ignore which puts you at greater risk: Speed limit? Seat belt signs? Warning labels on cigarette packs?

1. How did Hoshea come to reign (v. 1; see 15:29–30)? What relationship did this create between Israel and Assyria, which Hoshea is betraying (vv. 2–3; compare 16:17–18)? **2.** What clues can you find in verses 3–6 that: (a) Hoshea had traitors in his cabinet? (b) Samaria was one magnificently fortified city? (c) Hoshea was a strong and determined leader? **3.** What's the strategy behind resettling captured people? Isn't it all a lot of work and hardship for everyone? So why does the Assyrian king do it? **4.** This Assyrian exile of the northern kingdom took place in 722 B.C. What is the author's explanation of it (v. 7; compare 1Ki 14:15)? What are the immediate reasons? Long-range political and military reasons? **5.** In what sense can all idolatry be called "secret" (v. 9)? Which of Israel's secrets were apparently done in the open? In ignorance? In defiance? In imitation of neighbor nations? What sin is so heinous for the author, he attributes it to every evil king in his history (vv. 16,21–22; see 1Ki 12:26–30)? **6.** Why is rivalry to the temple so bad? Are the author's southern biases showing through (v. 18)? Or is Judah getting its share of bad press here, as well? **7.** Who tried to turn the rudder of spirituality from retreat to truth (v. 23)? What was the gist of their message? The dominant reply?

1. Is it fair to describe any nation's history as if God was in the business of punishing them for sin? Is this how we see God and history today? Why or why not? **2.** What has God done for you, recently and not-so-recently, that evokes your heart-felt gratitude? If a gratitude meter could be plugged into your heart, what would it read?

---

[a]18 Or the dais of his throne (see Septuagint)   [b]4 Or to Sais, to the; So is possibly an abbreviation for Osorkon.   [c]12 Exodus 20:4, 5

3. Is any part of your life more like the practices of your neighbors than like the commands of God? How so? 4. Any "gods" in your life that would provoke the true God to jealousy? Who functions as the "prophet" in your life? What have you done with his or her spiritual warnings?

---

1. Did you ever get burned trying to date more than one person at a time? What happened? 2. Is teaching slow learners your cup of tea? What are the rewards? The trials?

1. How would a resettlement program build Assyria's empire (v. 24)? What problems do the settlers face (vv. 25–28)? 2. Does the Assyrian king see the truth about God, or is he simply trying to maintain order in one of his remote outposts? What does he believe about local gods? If such deities do not exist, why do people feel they can be appeased? 3. What is the significance of the qualifier, "but they also..." and "even while ..." (vv. 32–33,41): (a) The settlers truly convert to paganism? (b) This is a harmless example of cultural adaptation for the sake of blending in? (c) They are secret believers in Yahweh? (d) They are compromised and condemned by their syncretism? (e) They are doing whatever it takes to escape the lions (v. 26)? 4. Note the repeated phrase, "to this day" (vv. 34,41). Why is this story being told (and retold) here?

1. If you had been the priest selected to return (v. 27), what would be your conditions? The supplies you would insist on? Vacation schedule? Prayer support? 2. How exclusive is your devotion to the one true God? What competes for your heart's loyalty to him? 3. Can people who have never heard of God or Jesus be judged or condemned?

shiped Baal. [17]They sacrificed their sons and daughters in[a] the fire. They practiced divination and sorcery and sold themselves to do evil in the eyes of the LORD, provoking him to anger.

[18]So the LORD was very angry with Israel and removed them from his presence. Only the tribe of Judah was left, [19]and even Judah did not keep the commands of the LORD their God. They followed the practices Israel had introduced. [20]Therefore the LORD rejected all the people of Israel; he afflicted them and gave them into the hands of plunderers, until he thrust them from his presence.

[21]When he tore Israel away from the house of David, they made Jeroboam son of Nebat their king. Jeroboam enticed Israel away from following the LORD and caused them to commit a great sin. [22]The Israelites persisted in all the sins of Jeroboam and did not turn away from them [23]until the LORD removed them from his presence, as he had warned through all his servants the prophets. So the people of Israel were taken from their homeland into exile in Assyria, and they are still there.

Samaria Resettled

[24]The king of Assyria brought people from Babylon, Cuthah, Avva, Hamath and Sepharvaim and settled them in the towns of Samaria to replace the Israelites. They took over Samaria and lived in its towns. [25]When they first lived there, they did not worship the LORD; so he sent lions among them and they killed some of the people. [26]It was reported to the king of Assyria: "The people you deported and resettled in the towns of Samaria do not know what the god of that country requires. He has sent lions among them, which are killing them off, because the people do not know what he requires."

[27]Then the king of Assyria gave this order: "Have one of the priests you took captive from Samaria go back to live there and teach the people what the god of the land requires." [28]So one of the priests who had been exiled from Samaria came to live in Bethel and taught them how to worship the LORD.

[29]Nevertheless, each national group made its own gods in the several towns where they settled, and set them up in the shrines the people of Samaria had made at the high places. [30]The men from Babylon made Succoth Benoth, the men from Cuthah made Nergal, and the men from Hamath made Ashima; [31]the Avvites made Nibhaz and Tartak, and the Sepharvites burned their children in the fire as sacrifices to Adrammelech and Anammelech, the gods of Sepharvaim. [32]They worshiped the LORD, but they also appointed all sorts of their own people to officiate for them as priests in the shrines at the high places. [33]They worshiped the LORD, but they also served their own gods in accordance with the customs of the nations from which they had been brought.

[34]To this day they persist in their former practices. They neither worship the LORD nor adhere to the decrees and ordinances, the laws and commands that the LORD gave the descendants of Jacob, whom he named Israel. [35]When the LORD made a covenant with the Israelites, he commanded them: "Do not worship any other gods or bow down to them, serve them or sacrifice to them. [36]But the LORD, who brought you up out of Egypt with mighty power and outstretched arm, is the one you must worship. To him you shall bow down and to him offer sacrifices. [37]You must always be careful to keep the decrees and ordinances, the laws and commands he wrote for you. Do not worship other gods. [38]Do not forget the

a17 Or *They made their sons and daughters pass through*

covenant I have made with you, and do not worship other gods. ³⁹Rather, worship the LORD your God; it is he who will deliver you from the hand of all your enemies."

⁴⁰They would not listen, however, but persisted in their former practices. ⁴¹Even while these people were worshiping the LORD, they were serving their idols. To this day their children and grand-children continue to do as their fathers did.

Hezekiah King of Judah

18 In the third year of Hoshea son of Elah king of Israel, Hezekiah son of Ahaz king of Judah began to reign. ²He was twenty-five years old when he became king, and he reigned in Jerusalem twenty-nine years. His mother's name was Abijah^a daughter of Zechariah. ³He did what was right in the eyes of the LORD, just as his father David had done. ⁴He removed the high places, smashed the sacred stones and cut down the Asherah poles. He broke into pieces the bronze snake Moses had made, for up to that time the Israelites had been burning incense to it. (It was called^b Nehushtan.^c)

⁵Hezekiah trusted in the LORD, the God of Israel. There was no one like him among all the kings of Judah, either before him or after him. ⁶He held fast to the LORD and did not cease to follow him; he kept the commands the LORD had given Moses. ⁷And the LORD was with him; he was successful in whatever he undertook. He rebelled against the king of Assyria and did not serve him. ⁸From watchtower to fortified city, he defeated the Philistines, as far as Gaza and its territory.

⁹In King Hezekiah's fourth year, which was the seventh year of Hoshea son of Elah king of Israel, Shalmaneser king of Assyria marched against Samaria and laid siege to it. ¹⁰At the end of three years the Assyrians took it. So Samaria was captured in Hezekiah's sixth year, which was the ninth year of Hoshea king of Israel. ¹¹The king of Assyria deported Israel to Assyria and settled them in Halah, in Gozan on the Habor River and in towns of the Medes. ¹²This happened because they had not obeyed the LORD their God, but had violated his covenant—all that Moses the servant of the LORD commanded. They neither listened to the commands nor carried them out.

¹³In the fourteenth year of King Hezekiah's reign, Sennacherib king of Assyria attacked all the fortified cities of Judah and captured them. ¹⁴So Hezekiah king of Judah sent this message to the king of Assyria at Lachish: "I have done wrong. Withdraw from me, and I will pay whatever you demand of me." The king of Assyria exacted from Hezekiah king of Judah three hundred talents^d of silver and thirty talents^e of gold. ¹⁵So Hezekiah gave him all the silver that was found in the temple of the LORD and in the treasuries of the royal palace.

¹⁶At this time Hezekiah king of Judah stripped off the gold with which he had covered the doors and doorposts of the temple of the LORD, and gave it to the king of Assyria.

Sennacherib Threatens Jerusalem

¹⁷The king of Assyria sent his supreme commander, his chief officer and his field commander with a large army, from Lachish to King Hezekiah at Jerusalem. They came up to Jerusalem and stopped at the aqueduct of the Upper Pool, on the road to the

What characteristic sets you off from other people: A rare achievement? Strange behavior? A birthmark? What?

1. What does Hezekiah have going for him (vv. 1–4)? What behaviors show love for God? 2. What is the significance of the bronze snake (v. 4; see Nu 21:8–9; compare Jn 3:14–15)? Why would this antique become a fetish? 3. Why does the author seem to rank Hezekiah greater than David, Solomon or Josiah (vv. 5–8; compare 23:25)? How does Hezekiah succeed where others failed (see 16:7–8 and 2Ch 28:16–18)? 4. Is some of this praise exaggerated in view of verses 13–16? What "wrong" has Hezekiah done that other kings did (compare 18:9–12 with 17:3–7)?

1. If God can raise up for Judah a reformer king like Hezekiah, what does that imply for the future of God's spiritual kingdom? Do you live each day expecting great things from God? 2. God spared Judah from falling to the siege by Assyria in 701 B.C., but it cost Hezekiah more than his silver and gold. Will God aid you when you're in trouble from overreaching? At what cost? 3. Have you ever paid a price for overreaching? Are you recovered? On to greater heights? Do you pray as if God will rescue you at any cost—on your terms or his?

If you won 2000 horses on a quiz show, what would you do with them?

1. This passage is repeated verbatim in Isaiah 36. What advice has Isaiah given Hezekiah on the Assyrian invasion (see Isa 31:1–3)? 2. Isn't paying the tribute

---

^a2 Hebrew *Abi*, a variant of *Abijah*   ^b4 Or *He called it*   ^c4 *Nehushtan* sounds like the Hebrew for *bronze* and *snake* and *unclean thing*.   ^d14 That is, about 11 tons (about 10 metric tons)   ^e14 That is, about 1 ton (about 1 metric ton)

enough (see 18:14–16)? What two plans does Sennacherib figure Judah might pursue (vv. 19–22)? **3.** What do the Assyrians make of the Egypt option? The Yahweh option? What Assyrian option do they propose (vv. 23–25)? Which of the three would you put your money on and why? **4.** Why do Hezekiah's men want the Assyrians to speak in Aramaic (vv. 26–27)? What reason do the Assyrians give for continuing in Hebrew? What is he implying will happen? **5.** If you were a Hebrew standing on the wall, what would you see going on below you? What would you overhear that was not meant for you? How would you feel, knowing Eliakim wants to hide the conversation from you? **6.** If the way to a man's heart is through his stomach, what heart appeal do you smell in verses 31–32? Would tastier food sway them? Why or why not? **7.** How do the Assyrians view the God of Judah (vv. 22,32–35)? The deities in general? Assyrian power compared to deity-power? **8.** Despite this attack on Hezekiah and their God, are the people still loyal to him? How so? **9.** Why do the three palace messengers tear their clothes? Why aren't they dressed for success? Won't their tattered appearance bias their message? How so?

♡ **1.** If your pastor's or president's character were being smeared by outside accusers, would you and your fellow parishioners jump on the band wagon, remain silent, or voice your objections? Why? **2.** Have any friendships been threatened because you took the side of the accuser rather than your friend? **3.** When events look bleak, will friends stand with you? Will God really deliver? How do you go about the process of faithful discovery? **4.** What's the equivalent of torn clothing today? What do you use to get a similar message through?

Washerman's Field. [18]They called for the king; and Eliakim son of Hilkiah the palace administrator, Shebna the secretary, and Joah son of Asaph the recorder went out to them.

[19]The field commander said to them, "Tell Hezekiah:

" 'This is what the great king, the king of Assyria, says: On what are you basing this confidence of yours? [20]You say you have strategy and military strength—but you speak only empty words. On whom are you depending, that you rebel against me? [21]Look now, you are depending on Egypt, that splintered reed of a staff, which pierces a man's hand and wounds him if he leans on it! Such is Pharaoh king of Egypt to all who depend on him. [22]And if you say to me, "We are depending on the LORD our God"—isn't he the one whose high places and altars Hezekiah removed, saying to Judah and Jerusalem, "You must worship before this altar in Jerusalem"?

[23]" 'Come now, make a bargain with my master, the king of Assyria: I will give you two thousand horses—if you can put riders on them! [24]How can you repulse one officer of the least of my master's officials, even though you are depending on Egypt for chariots and horsemen[a]? [25]Furthermore, have I come to attack and destroy this place without word from the LORD? The LORD himself told me to march against this country and destroy it.' "

[26]Then Eliakim son of Hilkiah, and Shebna and Joah said to the field commander, "Please speak to your servants in Aramaic, since we understand it. Don't speak to us in Hebrew in the hearing of the people on the wall."

[27]But the commander replied, "Was it only to your master and you that my master sent me to say these things, and not to the men sitting on the wall—who, like you, will have to eat their own filth and drink their own urine?"

[28]Then the commander stood and called out in Hebrew: "Hear the word of the great king, the king of Assyria! [29]This is what the king says: Do not let Hezekiah deceive you. He cannot deliver you from my hand. [30]Do not let Hezekiah persuade you to trust in the LORD when he says, 'The LORD will surely deliver us; this city will not be given into the hand of the king of Assyria.'

[31]"Do not listen to Hezekiah. This is what the king of Assyria says: Make peace with me and come out to me. Then every one of you will eat from his own vine and fig tree and drink water from his own cistern, [32]until I come and take you to a land like your own, a land of grain and new wine, a land of bread and vineyards, a land of olive trees and honey. Choose life and not death!

"Do not listen to Hezekiah, for he is misleading you when he says, 'The LORD will deliver us.' [33]Has the god of any nation ever delivered his land from the hand of the king of Assyria? [34]Where are the gods of Hamath and Arpad? Where are the gods of Sepharvaim, Hena and Ivvah? Have they rescued Samaria from my hand? [35]Who of all the gods of these countries has been able to save his land from me? How then can the LORD deliver Jerusalem from my hand?"

[36]But the people remained silent and said nothing in reply, because the king had commanded, "Do not answer him."

[37]Then Eliakim son of Hilkiah the palace administrator, Shebna the secretary and Joah son of Asaph the recorder went to Hezekiah,

a24 Or *charioteers*

with their clothes torn, and told him what the field commander had said.

Jerusalem's Deliverance Foretold

19 When King Hezekiah heard this, he tore his clothes and put on sackcloth and went into the temple of the LORD. ²He sent Eliakim the palace administrator, Shebna the secretary and the leading priests, all wearing sackcloth, to the prophet Isaiah son of Amoz. ³They told him, "This is what Hezekiah says: This day is a day of distress and rebuke and disgrace, as when children come to the point of birth and there is no strength to deliver them. ⁴It may be that the LORD your God will hear all the words of the field commander, whom his master, the king of Assyria, has sent to ridicule the living God, and that he will rebuke him for the words the LORD your God has heard. Therefore pray for the remnant that still survives."

⁵When King Hezekiah's officials came to Isaiah, ⁶Isaiah said to them, "Tell your master, 'This is what the LORD says: Do not be afraid of what you have heard—those words with which the underlings of the king of Assyria have blasphemed me. ⁷Listen! I am going to put such a spirit in him that when he hears a certain report, he will return to his own country, and there I will have him cut down with the sword.'"

⁸When the field commander heard that the king of Assyria had left Lachish, he withdrew and found the king fighting against Libnah.

⁹Now Sennacherib received a report that Tirhakah, the Cushite[a] king ⌐of Egypt⌐, was marching out to fight against him. So he again sent messengers to Hezekiah with this word: ¹⁰"Say to Hezekiah king of Judah: Do not let the god you depend on deceive you when he says, 'Jerusalem will not be handed over to the king of Assyria.' ¹¹Surely you have heard what the kings of Assyria have done to all the countries, destroying them completely. And will you be delivered? ¹²Did the gods of the nations that were destroyed by my forefathers deliver them: the gods of Gozan, Haran, Rezeph and the people of Eden who were in Tel Assar? ¹³Where is the king of Hamath, the king of Arpad, the king of the city of Sepharvaim, or of Hena or Ivvah?"

Hezekiah's Prayer

¹⁴Hezekiah received the letter from the messengers and read it. Then he went up to the temple of the LORD and spread it out before the LORD. ¹⁵And Hezekiah prayed to the LORD: "O LORD, God of Israel, enthroned between the cherubim, you alone are God over all the kingdoms of the earth. You have made heaven and earth. ¹⁶Give ear, O LORD, and hear; open your eyes, O LORD, and see; listen to the words Sennacherib has sent to insult the living God.

¹⁷"It is true, O LORD, that the Assyrian kings have laid waste these nations and their lands. ¹⁸They have thrown their gods into the fire and destroyed them, for they were not gods but only wood and stone, fashioned by men's hands. ¹⁹Now, O LORD our God, deliver us from his hand, so that all kingdoms on earth may know that you alone, O LORD, are God."

Isaiah Prophesies Sennacherib's Fall

²⁰Then Isaiah son of Amoz sent a message to Hezekiah: "This is what the LORD, the God of Israel, says: I have heard your prayer

a 9 That is, from the upper Nile region

---

1. Are you a "worry-wart"—one who thinks, "Why pray, when you can worry"? What do you tend to worry about most? 2. When you don't get the answer you want, or you get no answer, do you pray, stew, get on the phone, write a second follow-up RSVP, or what?

1. What is Hezekiah worried about (vv. 1–4)? What does he do to win over worry? Why should a king so faithful also be one of Judah's great worry-warts? 2. How is this dismal situation going to turn out (vv. 6–7)? Thanks to whom? 3. What must Sennacherib suspect when he hears about Tirhakah (v. 9; see 18:21)? Is the Yahweh option still a possibility in his mind (v. 10)? 4. What theological sense does Sennacherib's final threat make (vv. 11–13)? What suggests he still has some good theology to learn? 5. What does Hezekiah do with the threatening letter from Sennacherib (v. 14; see 2Ch 32:17) and why? What hope has Isaiah's earlier message give him (vv. 6,15–16)? 6. Why does Hezekiah pray in the order he does? 7. Where do Hezekiah and Sennacherib agree (vv. 18–19)? Disagree? What is Hezekiah's outreach program?

1. Why do faithful Christians worry? 2. When matters are out of your hands, how do you feel? What do you do (or not do)? 3. In the days of the kings, it seems that war helped determine which people were following the correct religion. Is that any longer true, if it ever was? Why? Why did people on both sides of World War II pray for victory? Should today's soldiers in conflicts pray for victory? Will God take sides?

1. Have you ever felt led around on a short leash like a trained animal: Were you smitten with love? Hen-pecked? Hooked by your boss' deadline? Got an

early hook in some "Gong Show"? Dragged against your will to some wedding, bachelor party or other social function? **2.** Have you ever thought you were really "hot stuff" only to find yourself melting under the spotlight? When?

1. Why doesn't God answer Hezekiah right then and there in the temple (v. 20)? **2.** How is all the arrogance of Assyrian military prowess mocked by God (v. 21)? Who does Sennacherib credit for Assyria's conquests (vv. 23–24)? Who does God credit? **3.** Does God like Sennacherib or just use him? Manipulate him? Why does God want Assyria to destroy so many people? **4.** Like which animal will Sennacherib be made to behave (v. 28)? How will it feel to be lead on a tight leash back to Jerusalem? **5.** What three promises does Isaiah give to Hezekiah (vv. 29–34)? What do you make of the promise of the three years' harvest (v. 29): (a) It will be impossible to farm for two years, but there will be food? (b) Sennacherib will besiege Jerusalem for two years before retreating? (c) Lean years will be followed by prosperity? (d) Other? What would you make of this "sign" if you knew the Assyrians would leave Judah immediately? **6.** Who does the "remnant" mentioned here seem to be (vv. 30–31; see 1Ki 19:18; Isa 4:2–3)? Who will be thought of as the "remnant" after the exile to Babylon (see Eze 12:15–16)? What meaning will the early Christians attach to this remnant idea (see Ro 11:5; Rev 14:1)? **7.** Are these promises connected to one another? Conditional on anything? **8.** Do the events of verses 35–37 fulfill the prophecy? Why does God wait until every other Judean city has fallen to bring the plague? **9.** What curse befalls Sennacherib, just as he hopes to secure the blessing of his own pagan idols (v. 37)?

1. What promising prospect do you feel the next three years hold for you personally? For your family? For your church? Where do such intuitions come from? **2.** Do angels still intervene in human affairs, or are they a thing of the past? When have you sensed the presence of an angel of God intervening when no other explanation suffices? **3.** Do you get arrogant? When? Why? What do you do about it? **4.** Like athletic training or permanent weight loss, the first months of any extended

concerning Sennacherib king of Assyria. [21]This is the word that the LORD has spoken against him:

> " 'The Virgin Daughter of Zion
>   despises you and mocks you.
> The Daughter of Jerusalem
>   tosses her head as you flee.
> [22]Who is it you have insulted and blasphemed?
>   Against whom have you raised your voice
> and lifted your eyes in pride?
>   Against the Holy One of Israel!
> [23]By your messengers
>   you have heaped insults on the Lord.
> And you have said,
>   "With my many chariots
> I have ascended the heights of the mountains,
>   the utmost heights of Lebanon.
> I have cut down its tallest cedars,
>   the choicest of its pines.
> I have reached its remotest parts,
>   the finest of its forests.
> [24]I have dug wells in foreign lands
>   and drunk the water there.
> With the soles of my feet
>   I have dried up all the streams of Egypt."
>
> [25]" 'Have you not heard?
>   Long ago I ordained it.
> In days of old I planned it;
>   now I have brought it to pass,
> that you have turned fortified cities
>   into piles of stone.
> [26]Their people, drained of power,
>   are dismayed and put to shame.
> They are like plants in the field,
>   like tender green shoots,
> like grass sprouting on the roof,
>   scorched before it grows up.
>
> [27]" 'But I know where you stay
>   and when you come and go
>   and how you rage against me.
> [28]Because you rage against me
>   and your insolence has reached my ears,
> I will put my hook in your nose
>   and my bit in your mouth,
> and I will make you return
>   by the way you came.'
>
> [29]"This will be the sign for you, O Hezekiah:
>
> "This year you will eat what grows by itself,
>   and the second year what springs from that.
> But in the third year sow and reap,
>   plant vineyards and eat their fruit.
> [30]Once more a remnant of the house of Judah
>   will take root below and bear fruit above.
> [31]For out of Jerusalem will come a remnant,
>   and out of Mount Zion a band of survivors.

The zeal of the LORD Almighty will accomplish this.

³²"Therefore this is what the LORD says concerning the king of Assyria:

> "He will not enter this city
>   or shoot an arrow here.
> He will not come before it with shield
>   or build a siege ramp against it.
> ³³By the way that he came he will return;
>   he will not enter this city,
>   declares the LORD.
> ³⁴I will defend this city and save it,
>   for my sake and for the sake of David my
>   servant."

³⁵That night the angel of the LORD went out and put to death a hundred and eighty-five thousand men in the Assyrian camp. When the people got up the next morning—there were all the dead bodies! ³⁶So Sennacherib king of Assyria broke camp and withdrew. He returned to Nineveh and stayed there.

³⁷One day, while he was worshiping in the temple of his god Nisroch, his sons Adrammelech and Sharezer cut him down with the sword, and they escaped to the land of Ararat. And Esarhaddon his son succeeded him as king.

Hezekiah's Illness

20 In those days Hezekiah became ill and was at the point of death. The prophet Isaiah son of Amoz went to him and said, "This is what the LORD says: Put your house in order, because you are going to die; you will not recover."

²Hezekiah turned his face to the wall and prayed to the LORD, ³"Remember, O LORD, how I have walked before you faithfully and with wholehearted devotion and have done what is good in your eyes." And Hezekiah wept bitterly.

⁴Before Isaiah had left the middle court, the word of the LORD came to him: ⁵"Go back and tell Hezekiah, the leader of my people, 'This is what the LORD, the God of your father David, says: I have heard your prayer and seen your tears; I will heal you. On the third day from now you will go up to the temple of the LORD. ⁶I will add fifteen years to your life. And I will deliver you and this city from the hand of the king of Assyria. I will defend this city for my sake and for the sake of my servant David.'"

⁷Then Isaiah said, "Prepare a poultice of figs." They did so and applied it to the boil, and he recovered.

⁸Hezekiah had asked Isaiah, "What will be the sign that the LORD will heal me and that I will go up to the temple of the LORD on the third day from now?"

⁹Isaiah answered, "This is the LORD's sign to you that the LORD will do what he has promised: Shall the shadow go forward ten steps, or shall it go back ten steps?"

¹⁰"It is a simple matter for the shadow to go forward ten steps," said Hezekiah. "Rather, have it go back ten steps."

¹¹Then the prophet Isaiah called upon the LORD, and the LORD made the shadow go back the ten steps it had gone down on the stairway of Ahaz.

Envoys From Babylon

¹²At that time Merodach-Baladan son of Baladan king of Babylon sent Hezekiah letters and a gift, because he had heard of Hezekiah's illness. ¹³Hezekiah received the messengers and showed them all that was in his storehouses—the silver, the gold, the spices and

spiritual growth program are the toughest. Rarely do we see results overnight, as in this story. What do you imagine those early months would be like for you? When would you know you were making progress?

What would you like to accomplish in the next 15 years of your life?

1. Why is the good king such a crybaby over the inevitable (vv. 1–3)? **2.** Does God heed Hezekiah's argument, or does he have other reasons for healing him (vv. 4–6)? **3.** Hezekiah died in 686 B.C. The Assyrians invaded in 701 B.C. If Hezekiah was 25 when he took office in 715 B.C. (v. 18:2), then how old is he at this time? What would a man his age likely want to do in the next 15 years? **4.** Do figs have healing qualities, or is the poultice a symbol? Of what? **5.** How do you account for the miracle of the shadow going back 10 steps?

1. What makes prayer more effective: Perseverance? Emotion? Irrefutable logic? High moral arguments? **2.** Can prayer change God's mind? Is God weak if he does change his mind? What does it mean to say that God never changes? **3.** Is it weak to ask God to give miraculous signs? Should the word be enough to ease all doubts?

What room in your house are guests first shown? Which room do guests never see? What is special about each?

1. Why does Hezekiah show the envoys everything (vv. 12–13): Naive hospitality? Protocol? Showing off? 2. What is Isaiah's mood as he probes him: Accusing? Nonchalant? Alarmed? Is Hezekiah as open with Isaiah as he appears to be with the envoys? 3. What do you find remarkable about Isaiah's oracle concerning the Babylonian exile (vv. 16–18)? 4. In verse 19, is Hezekiah selfish? Relieved? Grateful? Callous? Explain.

1. Should nations be hospitable and open or go big on "national security"? Where does true security lie? 2. If God revealed that you would not die for 15 years, would you live more confidently? Daringly? Selfishly?

1. Have you ever destroyed something out of frustration or anger? Did it feel good? What's your number one steam release? 2. Have you ever cried while reading a book? Was the book touching? Disappointing? Overpriced?

1. After what events did Hezekiah sire his son Manasseh (v. 1; see 20:5–6)? Who would have been king if Hezekiah had died from the boil? Viewing Manasseh's career in retrospect, should God have let Hezekiah die? 2. What new customs does Manasseh add to Judah's catalog of sins (vv. 3–5)? Where do you suppose he took his courses in idolatry? 3. Why does the author repeat the old promises in the middle of this story (v. 8)? 4. Is Manasseh a single-handed bandit? Who shares the blame? 5. Who stands in opposition to the king (v. 10)? What happened to them (v. 16)? 6. What is a plumb line (v. 13)? What message does this warning convey? Is God changing his mind here, cancelling previous promises (v. 14)? 7. Is it true that Israel has done nothing good since they left Egypt (v. 15)? Why does this account of Manasseh overlook the story of his conversion (see 2Ch 33:10–17)? 8. Why was Amon's regime so short-lived (v. 23), especially when compared to Manasseh's 55 years? If Amon did as much evil as his father

the fine oil—his armory and everything found among his treasures. There was nothing in his palace or in all his kingdom that Hezekiah did not show them.

[14]Then Isaiah the prophet went to King Hezekiah and asked, "What did those men say, and where did they come from?"

"From a distant land," Hezekiah replied. "They came from Babylon."

[15]The prophet asked, "What did they see in your palace?"

"They saw everything in my palace," Hezekiah said. "There is nothing among my treasures that I did not show them."

[16]Then Isaiah said to Hezekiah, "Hear the word of the LORD: [17]The time will surely come when everything in your palace, and all that your fathers have stored up until this day, will be carried off to Babylon. Nothing will be left, says the LORD. [18]And some of your descendants, your own flesh and blood, that will be born to you, will be taken away, and they will become eunuchs in the palace of the king of Babylon."

[19]"The word of the LORD you have spoken is good," Hezekiah replied. For he thought, "Will there not be peace and security in my lifetime?"

[20]As for the other events of Hezekiah's reign, all his achievements and how he made the pool and the tunnel by which he brought water into the city, are they not written in the book of the annals of the kings of Judah? [21]Hezekiah rested with his fathers. And Manasseh his son succeeded him as king.

Manasseh King of Judah

21 Manasseh was twelve years old when he became king, and he reigned in Jerusalem fifty-five years. His mother's name was Hephzibah. [2]He did evil in the eyes of the LORD, following the detestable practices of the nations the LORD had driven out before the Israelites. [3]He rebuilt the high places his father Hezekiah had destroyed; he also erected altars to Baal and made an Asherah pole, as Ahab king of Israel had done. He bowed down to all the starry hosts and worshiped them. [4]He built altars in the temple of the LORD, of which the LORD had said, "In Jerusalem I will put my Name." [5]In both courts of the temple of the LORD, he built altars to all the starry hosts. [6]He sacrificed his own son in[a] the fire, practiced sorcery and divination, and consulted mediums and spiritists. He did much evil in the eyes of the LORD, provoking him to anger.

[7]He took the carved Asherah pole he had made and put it in the temple, of which the LORD had said to David and to his son Solomon, "In this temple and in Jerusalem, which I have chosen out of all the tribes of Israel, I will put my Name forever. [8]I will not again make the feet of the Israelites wander from the land I gave their forefathers, if only they will be careful to do everything I commanded them and will keep the whole Law that my servant Moses gave them." [9]But the people did not listen. Manasseh led them astray, so that they did more evil than the nations the LORD had destroyed before the Israelites.

[10]The LORD said through his servants the prophets: [11]"Manasseh king of Judah has committed these detestable sins. He has done more evil than the Amorites who preceded him and has led Judah into sin with his idols. [12]Therefore this is what the LORD, the God of Israel, says: I am going to bring such disaster on Jerusalem and Judah that the ears of everyone who hears of it will tingle. [13]I will stretch out over Jerusalem the measuring line used against Samaria

a 6 Or He made his own son pass through

and the plumb line used against the house of Ahab. I will wipe out Jerusalem as one wipes a dish, wiping it and turning it upside down. ¹⁴I will forsake the remnant of my inheritance and hand them over to their enemies. They will be looted and plundered by all their foes, ¹⁵because they have done evil in my eyes and have provoked me to anger from the day their forefathers came out of Egypt until this day."

¹⁶Moreover, Manasseh also shed so much innocent blood that he filled Jerusalem from end to end—besides the sin that he had caused Judah to commit, so that they did evil in the eyes of the LORD.

¹⁷As for the other events of Manasseh's reign, and all he did, including the sin he committed, are they not written in the book of the annals of the kings of Judah? ¹⁸Manasseh rested with his fathers and was buried in his palace garden, the garden of Uzza. And Amon his son succeeded him as king.

Amon King of Judah

¹⁹Amon was twenty-two years old when he became king, and he reigned in Jerusalem two years. His mother's name was Meshullemeth daughter of Haruz; she was from Jotbah. ²⁰He did evil in the eyes of the LORD, as his father Manasseh had done. ²¹He walked in all the ways of his father; he worshiped the idols his father had worshiped, and bowed down to them. ²²He forsook the LORD, the God of his fathers, and did not walk in the way of the LORD.

²³Amon's officials conspired against him and assassinated the king in his palace. ²⁴Then the people of the land killed all who had plotted against King Amon, and they made Josiah his son king in his place.

²⁵As for the other events of Amon's reign, and what he did, are they not written in the book of the annals of the kings of Judah? ²⁶He was buried in his grave in the garden of Uzza. And Josiah his son succeeded him as king.

The Book of the Law Found

22 Josiah was eight years old when he became king, and he reigned in Jerusalem thirty-one years. His mother's name was Jedidah daughter of Adaiah; she was from Bozkath. ²He did what was right in the eyes of the LORD and walked in all the ways of his father David, not turning aside to the right or to the left.

³In the eighteenth year of his reign, King Josiah sent the secretary, Shaphan son of Azaliah, the son of Meshullam, to the temple of the LORD. He said: ⁴"Go up to Hilkiah the high priest and have him get ready the money that has been brought into the temple of the LORD, which the doorkeepers have collected from the people. ⁵Have them entrust it to the men appointed to supervise the work on the temple. And have these men pay the workers who repair the temple of the LORD— ⁶the carpenters, the builders and the masons. Also have them purchase timber and dressed stone to repair the temple. ⁷But they need not account for the money entrusted to them, because they are acting faithfully."

⁸Hilkiah the high priest said to Shaphan the secretary, "I have found the Book of the Law in the temple of the LORD." He gave it to Shaphan, who read it. ⁹Then Shaphan the secretary went to the king and reported to him: "Your officials have paid out the money that was in the temple of the LORD and have entrusted it to the workers and supervisors at the temple." ¹⁰Then Shaphan the secretary informed the king, "Hilkiah the priest has given me a book." And Shaphan read from it in the presence of the king.

(v. 20), why do the people kill those who killed him (v. 24)? How else have the people shown their support for the house of David (11:10–14,18–20; 14:21)?

♥ **1.** What are "good people" to do during evil times? What's the key to surviving the reign of bad kings? **2.** What does this story tell you about the ultimate seat of power? The ultimate disposition of good and evil? What hints here at God's patience and mercy? Which attribute of God—power or mercy—has been most impressed on you recently? **3.** Do you believe in "power to the people," as demonstrated here? What are the benefits and dangers of people power? How can it run amok? **4.** Should God's people ever use violence to achieve justice, as did the run-amok crowd? When?

🍵 **1.** Which three people would you appoint to your personal "advisory board"? What qualifies them? **2.** Ever uncover a library book you'd long forgotten to return? Was the book's fine greater than its purchase price?

📖 **1.** What does Josiah have going for him as he begins his reign (vv. 1–3)? What top priority does he share with another boy king (vv. 4–7; see 12:1–16)? **2.** Why are these kings always hiring tradesmen to refurbish the temple? **3.** What serendipity happens to this good king (v. 8)? This book is probably Deuteronomy—in whole or in part. Do you suppose it was really lost or simply hidden? How could Josiah "do what is right in the eyes of the Lord" (v. 2) his whole life without knowing of this book? **4.** Who makes up the king's advisory board for this Bible study project (vv. 11–14)? Without consulting learned advisors, what does Josiah evidently know about the book? **5.** What does Huldah, as the senior biblical consultant, contribute to this project (vv. 15–20)? What really makes God angry? How does she turn grim news into good news? What then is the state of true worship in Judah? Should Josiah sew up his robes after her report?

♡ 1. What book, apart from the Bible, has most profoundly changed you? How so? How does that book's effect compare with the Bible's effect on your life? 2. How many times have you vowed to rediscover the Scriptures every morning? Will you keep trying or give up? 3. What leadership roles do women play in your church? In the group? Who is your "Huldah"? 4. Has the ultimate bad news of God's judgment been postponed for you? Under what conditions? What does that give you time to do? 5. How well do you know church history? Who are the "Josiahs" that have rediscovered biblical truth in recent centuries? Which Josiah is your denomination indebted to?

☕ 1. Are you a "clean freak" or a "slob"? If your best friend were to hire spring cleaners to help you organize your place, where would they start? What will you never throw out despite all begging? 2. Are sawdust-trail revival meetings part of your family history, past or present? Any memories of powerful speakers? Closing hymns? Heat? 3. What holiday have you *stopped* celebrating and why? Your birthday? Valentine's Day?

📖 1. What does it mean to "renew the covenant" (vv. 1–3)? What must Judah do? What will God do? How extensive is the revival here? 2. What shape is the temple in (vv. 4–7)? Are these repairs the kind that money and manpower alone could fix (see 22:4–7)? What more is necessary? 3. Why were the priests burning incense at the high places (v. 5; see 1Ki 3:2)? Why does Josiah destroy these independent shrines (see Dt 12:2–7)? What do shrine prostitutes do that's so vile (v. 7; see Ex 34:15–16; Dt 23:17–18)? 4. What

11When the king heard the words of the Book of the Law, he tore his robes. 12He gave these orders to Hilkiah the priest, Ahikam son of Shaphan, Acbor son of Micaiah, Shaphan the secretary and Asaiah the king's attendant: 13"Go and inquire of the LORD for me and for the people and for all Judah about what is written in this book that has been found. Great is the LORD's anger that burns against us because our fathers have not obeyed the words of this book; they have not acted in accordance with all that is written there concerning us."

14Hilkiah the priest, Ahikam, Acbor, Shaphan and Asaiah went to speak to the prophetess Huldah, who was the wife of Shallum son of Tikvah, the son of Harhas, keeper of the wardrobe. She lived in Jerusalem, in the Second District.

15She said to them, "This is what the LORD, the God of Israel, says: Tell the man who sent you to me, 16'This is what the LORD says: I am going to bring disaster on this place and its people, according to everything written in the book the king of Judah has read. 17Because they have forsaken me and burned incense to other gods and provoked me to anger by all the idols their hands have made,[a] my anger will burn against this place and will not be quenched.' 18Tell the king of Judah, who sent you to inquire of the LORD, 'This is what the LORD, the God of Israel, says concerning the words you heard: 19Because your heart was responsive and you humbled yourself before the LORD when you heard what I have spoken against this place and its people, that they would become accursed and laid waste, and because you tore your robes and wept in my presence, I have heard you, declares the LORD. 20Therefore I will gather you to your fathers, and you will be buried in peace. Your eyes will not see all the disaster I am going to bring on this place.'"

So they took her answer back to the king.

Josiah Renews the Covenant

23 Then the king called together all the elders of Judah and Jerusalem. 2He went up to the temple of the LORD with the men of Judah, the people of Jerusalem, the priests and the prophets—all the people from the least to the greatest. He read in their hearing all the words of the Book of the Covenant, which had been found in the temple of the LORD. 3The king stood by the pillar and renewed the covenant in the presence of the LORD—to follow the LORD and keep his commands, regulations and decrees with all his heart and all his soul, thus confirming the words of the covenant written in this book. Then all the people pledged themselves to the covenant.

4The king ordered Hilkiah the high priest, the priests next in rank and the doorkeepers to remove from the temple of the LORD all the articles made for Baal and Asherah and all the starry hosts. He burned them outside Jerusalem in the fields of the Kidron Valley and took the ashes to Bethel. 5He did away with the pagan priests appointed by the kings of Judah to burn incense on the high places of the towns of Judah and on those around Jerusalem—those who burned incense to Baal, to the sun and moon, to the constellations and to all the starry hosts. 6He took the Asherah pole from the temple of the LORD to the Kidron Valley outside Jerusalem and burned it there. He ground it to powder and scattered the dust over the graves of the common people. 7He also tore down the quarters

a 17 Or by everything they have done

of the male shrine prostitutes, which were in the temple of the LORD and where women did weaving for Asherah.

[8]Josiah brought all the priests from the towns of Judah and desecrated the high places, from Geba to Beersheba, where the priests had burned incense. He broke down the shrines[a] at the gates—at the entrance to the Gate of Joshua, the city governor, which is on the left of the city gate. [9]Although the priests of the high places did not serve at the altar of the LORD in Jerusalem, they ate unleavened bread with their fellow priests.

[10]He desecrated Topheth, which was in the Valley of Ben Hinnom, so no one could use it to sacrifice his son or daughter in[b] the fire to Molech. [11]He removed from the entrance to the temple of the LORD the horses that the kings of Judah had dedicated to the sun. They were in the court near the room of an official named Nathan-Melech. Josiah then burned the chariots dedicated to the sun.

[12]He pulled down the altars the kings of Judah had erected on the roof near the upper room of Ahaz, and the altars Manasseh had built in the two courts of the temple of the LORD. He removed them from there, smashed them to pieces and threw the rubble into the Kidron Valley. [13]The king also desecrated the high places that were east of Jerusalem on the south of the Hill of Corruption—the ones Solomon king of Israel had built for Ashtoreth the vile goddess of the Sidonians, for Chemosh the vile god of Moab, and for Molech[c] the detestable god of the people of Ammon. [14]Josiah smashed the

[a]8 Or high places   [b]10 Or to make his son or daughter pass through
[c]13 Hebrew Milcom

kings have been responsible for putting up and tearing down these ever-present Asherah poles (vv. 4–7,15; see 1Ki 12:28–33; 2Ki 18:4; 21:7; 2Ch 33:11–15,22)? **5.** What could be the point in scattering Asherah dust over graves (vv. 4,6,14,16; see Nu 19:16)? Who is the man of God who foretold these things and whose bones were left undisturbed (vv. 16–18; see 1Ki 13:1–2, 31–32)? **6.** With regional shrines closed down, where do the priests look for work (vv. 8–9)? **7.** What message does burning tainted military hardware send to the people (v. 11)? Why are altars on rooftops (v. 12; see Jer 19:13)? Which altars are responsible for that (see 16:1–4,10–16; 21:1–3,19–22)? Why had even King Solomon built detestable high places (v. 13; see 1Ki 11:3–8)? **8.** Where does the revival move from Judah (vv. 15,19–20)? Who's living there now (see 17:27–34)? What does this indicate about the current state of Assyrian power? **9.** How long does the author say it has been since the people celebrated Passover (vv. 21–22; compare 2Ch 30:1–5)? **10.** On a scale of 1 to 10, how wholehearted is this

---

 2 Kings 23:1–25   **JOSIAH RENEWS THE COVENANT**

During Josiah's reign in Judah (the southern kingdom of Israel), the Book of the Covenant, containing some or all of the first five books of the Bible, was found in the temple. Josiah was terribly grieved when he realized how its commands and warnings had been disobeyed and neglected.

1. Why did Josiah read the entire Book of the Covenant?
   a. The people had never heard it.
   b. The people had forgotten it.
   c. The people didn't understand it.
   d. The people were breaking it.

2. When Josiah and the people renewed the covenant, what were they committing themselves to do?
   a. obey rules and regulations
   b. follow the Lord
   c. live in relationship
   d. keep reading

3. How had the Israelites compromised their religious practice?
   a. in superficial ways
   b. in the choice of priests
   c. in the temple

   d. in their homes
   e. by bowing to every god there was

4. Why were the people willing to give up their idolatry?
   a. It was just minor housekeeping.
   b. They feared the wrath of God.
   c. They had made a pledge.
   d. Josiah's convictions inspired them.
   e. They did whatever the king said.

5. Why did Josiah destroy everything having to do with other gods?
   a. to remove all temptation
   b. to teach the people a lesson
   c. to fully obey the covenant
   d. because compromise would have been self-destructive

6. What would getting your life in line with God's expectations require?
   a. a little fine tuning
   b. a regular tune-up
   c. major repairs
   d. a complete overhaul

7. Why do you want to obey God?
   a. It's the right thing to do.
   b. I don't want to hurt others.

   c. I love God.
   d. I fear God's punishment.

8. What is one "idol" that would be hard for you to give up?
   a. a relationship
   b. my job
   c. certain possessions
   d. a habit
   e. other:_____

9. 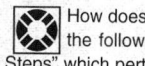 How does this story relate to the following four of the "12 Steps" which pertain to confession?
   a. Made a searching and fearless moral inventory of ourselves.
   b. Admitted to God, to ourselves, and to another human being the exact nature of our wrongs.
   c. Were entirely ready to have God remove these defects of character.
   d. Humbly asked him to remove our shortcomings.

10. 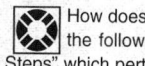 On your road to recovery, how are you doing in practicing these four steps? Is there anything you want to confess to the group right now?

revival? Who else had tried this before (18:4)? What had happened
that Josiah's reform became necessary (21:3–7)? **11.** Why is Josiah so relentless (vv. 25–27)? Does
he get what he hoped for? Is all the
trouble to no avail? Why doesn't all
his good outweigh Manasseh's
evil? (Is God in the weights and
measurements business, anyway?
Is the author grasping for an explanation for Judah's military downfall?) **12.** Why does Josiah face-off
with Pharaoh Neco (v. 29)? Which
side are the Egyptians on (see
7:5–6; 18:19–21)? In what position
will an Egypt-Assyria alliance put
Judah and Samaria?

♡ **1.** What extremes have you
gone to in your efforts to live
a pure faith: Attend Bible study
nightly? Pitch your rock music?
Boycott a business? Would you do
such actions again? **2.** Do you
know any public architecture that
would come down quickly in a real
revival? How would your church
fare in the remodeling? **3.** Do you
feel it's time to renew your commitment to God? How can you and
your group renew your covenant
with each other and with God? **4.**
Once your faith is in order, what will
you do in concert with others to
spread revival? Or is revival dependent all and only on God? **5.** If
psychics, astrologers and channel-
ers are doing the same things as
"mediums and spiritists" were in Josiah's day, should these people be
wiped out today?

sacred stones and cut down the Asherah poles and covered the
sites with human bones.

¹⁵Even the altar at Bethel, the high place made by Jeroboam son
of Nebat, who had caused Israel to sin—even that altar and high
place he demolished. He burned the high place and ground it to
powder, and burned the Asherah pole also. ¹⁶Then Josiah looked
around, and when he saw the tombs that were there on the hillside, he had the bones removed from them and burned on the altar
to defile it, in accordance with the word of the LORD proclaimed by
the man of God who foretold these things.

¹⁷The king asked, "What is that tombstone I see?"

The men of the city said, "It marks the tomb of the man of God
who came from Judah and pronounced against the altar of Bethel
the very things you have done to it."

¹⁸"Leave it alone," he said. "Don't let anyone disturb his bones."
So they spared his bones and those of the prophet who had come
from Samaria.

¹⁹Just as he had done at Bethel, Josiah removed and defiled all
the shrines at the high places that the kings of Israel had built in
the towns of Samaria that had provoked the LORD to anger. ²⁰Josiah
slaughtered all the priests of those high places on the altars and
burned human bones on them. Then he went back to Jerusalem.

²¹The king gave this order to all the people: "Celebrate the
Passover to the LORD your God, as it is written in this Book of the
Covenant." ²²Not since the days of the judges who led Israel, nor
throughout the days of the kings of Israel and the kings of Judah,
had any such Passover been observed. ²³But in the eighteenth year
of King Josiah, this Passover was celebrated to the LORD in Jerusalem.

²⁴Furthermore, Josiah got rid of the mediums and spiritists, the
household gods, the idols and all the other detestable things seen
in Judah and Jerusalem. This he did to fulfill the requirements of
the law written in the book that Hilkiah the priest had discovered
in the temple of the LORD. ²⁵Neither before nor after Josiah was
there a king like him who turned to the LORD as he did—with all
his heart and with all his soul and with all his strength, in accordance with all the Law of Moses.

²⁶Nevertheless, the LORD did not turn away from the heat of his
fierce anger, which burned against Judah because of all that Manasseh had done to provoke him to anger. ²⁷So the LORD said, "I will
remove Judah also from my presence as I removed Israel, and I will
reject Jerusalem, the city I chose, and this temple, about which I
said, 'There shall my Name be.'ᵃ"

²⁸As for the other events of Josiah's reign, and all he did, are
they not written in the book of the annals of the kings of Judah?

²⁹While Josiah was king, Pharaoh Neco king of Egypt went up
to the Euphrates River to help the king of Assyria. King Josiah
marched out to meet him in battle, but Neco faced him and killed
him at Megiddo. ³⁰Josiah's servants brought his body in a chariot
from Megiddo to Jerusalem and buried him in his own tomb. And
the people of the land took Jehoahaz son of Josiah and anointed
him and made him king in place of his father.

Jehoahaz King of Judah

³¹Jehoahaz was twenty-three years old when he became king,
and he reigned in Jerusalem three months. His mother's name was
Hamutal daughter of Jeremiah; she was from Libnah. ³²He did evil

☕ Which are you: (a) I make
quick decisions? (b) I mull
over every decision I make? (c) I
can't decide if I'm indecisive?

ᵃ27 1 Kings 8:29

in the eyes of the Lord, just as his fathers had done. ³³Pharaoh Neco put him in chains at Riblah in the land of Hamath* so that he might not reign in Jerusalem, and he imposed on Judah a levy of a hundred talents* of silver and a talent* of gold. ³⁴Pharaoh Neco made Eliakim son of Josiah king in place of his father Josiah and changed Eliakim's name to Jehoiakim. But he took Jehoahaz and carried him off to Egypt, and there he died. ³⁵Jehoiakim paid Pharaoh Neco the silver and gold he demanded. In order to do so, he taxed the land and exacted the silver and gold from the people of the land according to their assessments.

Jehoiakim King of Judah

³⁶Jehoiakim was twenty-five years old when he became king, and he reigned in Jerusalem eleven years. His mother's name was Zebidah daughter of Pedaiah; she was from Rumah. ³⁷And he did evil in the eyes of the Lord, just as his fathers had done.

24 During Jehoiakim's reign, Nebuchadnezzar king of Babylon invaded the land, and Jehoiakim became his vassal for three years. But then he changed his mind and rebelled against Nebuchadnezzar. ²The Lord sent Babylonian,* Aramean, Moabite and Ammonite raiders against him. He sent them to destroy Judah, in accordance with the word of the Lord proclaimed by his servants the prophets. ³Surely these things happened to Judah according to the Lord's command, in order to remove them from his presence because of the sins of Manasseh and all he had done, ⁴including the shedding of innocent blood. For he had filled Jerusalem with innocent blood, and the Lord was not willing to forgive.

⁵As for the other events of Jehoiakim's reign, and all he did, are they not written in the book of the annals of the kings of Judah? ⁶Jehoiakim rested with his fathers. And Jehoiachin his son succeeded him as king.

⁷The king of Egypt did not march out from his own country again, because the king of Babylon had taken all his territory, from the Wadi of Egypt to the Euphrates River.

Jehoiachin King of Judah

⁸Jehoiachin was eighteen years old when he became king, and he reigned in Jerusalem three months. His mother's name was Nehushta daughter of Elnathan; she was from Jerusalem. ⁹He did evil in the eyes of the Lord, just as his father had done.

¹⁰At that time the officers of Nebuchadnezzar king of Babylon advanced on Jerusalem and laid siege to it, ¹¹and Nebuchadnezzar himself came up to the city while his officers were besieging it. ¹²Jehoiachin king of Judah, his mother, his attendants, his nobles and his officials all surrendered to him.

In the eighth year of the reign of the king of Babylon, he took Jehoiachin prisoner. ¹³As the Lord had declared, Nebuchadnezzar removed all the treasures from the temple of the Lord and from the royal palace, and took away all the gold articles that Solomon king of Israel had made for the temple of the Lord. ¹⁴He carried into exile all Jerusalem: all the officers and fighting men, and all the craftsmen and artisans—a total of ten thousand. Only the poorest people of the land were left.

¹⁵Nebuchadnezzar took Jehoiachin captive to Babylon. He also took from Jerusalem to Babylon the king's mother, his wives, his officials and the leading men of the land. ¹⁶The king of Babylon also

---

*33 Hebrew; Septuagint (see also 2 Chron. 36:3) *Neco at Riblah in Hamath removed him* *33 That is, about 3 3/4 tons (about 3.4 metric tons) *33 That is, about 75 pounds (about 34 kilograms) *2 Or *Chaldean*

1. Josiah dies trying to stop an Egypt-Assyria alliance (v. 29). What choices face Jehoahaz (vv. 31–33)? 2. What do you make of the taxation without representation in verse 33,35? What seems ironic and redundant about this (see 15:19–20; 18:14)? 3. What was Neco trying to accomplish by changing Eliakim's name? By taxing his people? 4. Nebuchadnezzar invades Judah in 605 B.C. (24:1a). Who was warning Jehoiakim about this impending disaster all along, but to no avail (see Jer 36:1–3,22–25)? 5. Jehoiakim changes his strategy for national security a second time (24:1b), and again to no avail (vv. 2–4). What picture of Jehoiakim does this whole sad story impress on you?

1. Jehoiakim goes from one problem to the next. Are you like that? When did you last vow: "I'll never do that again!" Was it a bad business venture? Rejected by the opposite sex? Trying to help someone who didn't want it? 2. What lessons do you learn from repeated mistakes, indecision and stubbornness.

Were you ever banished from the presence of your parents or peers? Where were you sent—your room, the principal's office, a relative's house?

1. How does Jehoiachin continue his father's policies towards God and Babylon (vv. 8–11)? 2. Why not resist the invaders as did Hezekiah (see ch. 19): (a) Judah is weary of war? (b) The prophet is not encouraging (see Jer 22:28–30)? (c) Another miracle would be needed (see 19:35)? (d) Jehoiachin knows the odds? 3. Who does the conquest affect (vv. 12–14)? Who's not affected? Why does Babylon deport the upper class? 4. Why the name change from Mattaniah ("Gift of Yahweh") to Zedekiah ("Righteousness of Yahweh") (vv. 16–17)?

1. When hope for survival dims, how do you cope? What role does faith play in that? 2. Is forgiveness ever beyond reach? Explain. Is the "snowball effect"

sometimes impossible to stop, as in the last days before the fall of Jerusalem? **3.** Why do the poor care the least who holds power? Why do you care about who's in or out of government?

---

1. Are you active in any sports or other competition? Do you win more than lose? Would you keep playing if you always lost? **2.** Do you know anyone who lives in a war zone? Occupied territory? The inner city? Why don't they move?

1. What conflicting counsel must Zedekiah sort through in his decision to resist Babylon (v. 1; see Jer 27:1–15; Eze 17:12–15)? **2.** How long does the siege last (vv. 1–2)? What gave Zedekiah hope that God would save him (see Jer 37:3,5)? Was this realistic? **3.** What does Jeremiah advise when the famine strikes (v. 3; see Jer 38:17–23)? What do Zedekiah's responses reveal about him? **4.** What about Zedekiah's escape plan was lacking (vv. 4–7)? Why are his sons singled out for execution? What is ironic and tragic about Zedekiah's last visual image? **5.** Why does Nebuzaradan parcel out land to the "poorest people" (v. 12)? (To whom will they be grateful—Babylon or the house of David?) **6.** What do you know about Gedaliah's family and political leanings (see 22:1–17; Jer 26:24; 41:10)? What qualities would Nebuchadnezzar be looking for in a governor (vv. 22–24)? Does he get his money's worth when Gedaliah meets with the resistance leaders? **7.** What does Ishmael hope to accomplish by assassinating Gedaliah, the proponent of non-violence (vv. 22–26)? Does he have the support of the other Judean army leaders (see Jer 41:11–14)? What does his flight to Egypt say about his popular support?

deported to Babylon the entire force of seven thousand fighting men, strong and fit for war, and a thousand craftsmen and artisans. ¹⁷He made Mattaniah, Jehoiachin's uncle, king in his place and changed his name to Zedekiah.

Zedekiah King of Judah

¹⁸Zedekiah was twenty-one years old when he became king, and he reigned in Jerusalem eleven years. His mother's name was Hamutal daughter of Jeremiah; she was from Libnah. ¹⁹He did evil in the eyes of the LORD, just as Jehoiakim had done. ²⁰It was because of the LORD's anger that all this happened to Jerusalem and Judah, and in the end he thrust them from his presence.

The Fall of Jerusalem

Now Zedekiah rebelled against the king of Babylon.

25 So in the ninth year of Zedekiah's reign, on the tenth day of the tenth month, Nebuchadnezzar king of Babylon marched against Jerusalem with his whole army. He encamped outside the city and built siege works all around it. ²The city was kept under siege until the eleventh year of King Zedekiah. ³By the ninth day of the ⌊fourth⌋^a month the famine in the city had become so severe that there was no food for the people to eat. ⁴Then the city wall was broken through, and the whole army fled at night through the gate between the two walls near the king's garden, though the Babylonians^b were surrounding the city. They fled toward the Arabah,^c ⁵but the Babylonian^d army pursued the king and overtook him in the plains of Jericho. All his soldiers were separated from him and scattered, ⁶and he was captured. He was taken to the king of Babylon at Riblah, where sentence was pronounced on him. ⁷They killed the sons of Zedekiah before his eyes. Then they put out his eyes, bound him with bronze shackles and took him to Babylon.

⁸On the seventh day of the fifth month, in the nineteenth year of Nebuchadnezzar king of Babylon, Nebuzaradan commander of the imperial guard, an official of the king of Babylon, came to Jerusalem. ⁹He set fire to the temple of the LORD, the royal palace and all the houses of Jerusalem. Every important building he burned down. ¹⁰The whole Babylonian army, under the commander of the imperial guard, broke down the walls around Jerusalem. ¹¹Nebuzaradan the commander of the guard carried into exile the people who remained in the city, along with the rest of the populace and those who had gone over to the king of Babylon. ¹²But the commander left behind some of the poorest people of the land to work the vineyards and fields.

¹³The Babylonians broke up the bronze pillars, the movable stands and the bronze Sea that were at the temple of the LORD and they carried the bronze to Babylon. ¹⁴They also took away the pots, shovels, wick trimmers, dishes and all the bronze articles used in the temple service. ¹⁵The commander of the imperial guard took away the censers and sprinkling bowls—all that were made of pure gold or silver.

¹⁶The bronze from the two pillars, the Sea and the movable stands, which Solomon had made for the temple of the LORD, was more than could be weighed. ¹⁷Each pillar was twenty-seven feet^e high. The bronze capital on top of one pillar was four and a half feet^f high and was decorated with a network and pomegranates of

---

^a3 See Jer. 52:6.   ^b4 Or *Chaldeans*; also in verses 13, 25 and 26   ^c4 Or *the Jordan Valley*   ^d5 Or *Chaldean*; also in verses 10 and 24   ^e17 Hebrew *eighteen cubits* (about 8.1 meters)   ^f17 Hebrew *three cubits* (about 1.3 meters)

bronze all around. The other pillar, with its network, was similar. [18]The commander of the guard took as prisoners Seraiah the chief priest, Zephaniah the priest next in rank and the three door-keepers. [19]Of those still in the city, he took the officer in charge of the fighting men and five royal advisers. He also took the secretary who was chief officer in charge of conscripting the people of the land and sixty of his men who were found in the city. [20]Nebuzaradan the commander took them all and brought them to the king of Babylon at Riblah. [21]There at Riblah, in the land of Hamath, the king had them executed.

So Judah went into captivity, away from her land.

[22]Nebuchadnezzar king of Babylon appointed Gedaliah son of Ahikam, the son of Shaphan, to be over the people he had left behind in Judah. [23]When all the army officers and their men heard that the king of Babylon had appointed Gedaliah as governor, they came to Gedaliah at Mizpah—Ishmael son of Nethaniah, Johanan son of Kareah, Seraiah son of Tanhumeth the Netophathite, Jaazaniah the son of the Maacathite, and their men. [24]Gedaliah took an oath to reassure them and their men. "Do not be afraid of the Babylonian officials," he said. "Settle down in the land and serve the king of Babylon, and it will go well with you."

[25]In the seventh month, however, Ishmael son of Nethaniah, the son of Elishama, who was of royal blood, came with ten men and assassinated Gedaliah and also the men of Judah and the Babylonians who were with him at Mizpah. [26]At this, all the people from the least to the greatest, together with the army officers, fled to Egypt for fear of the Babylonians.

Jehoiachin Released

[27]In the thirty-seventh year of the exile of Jehoiachin king of Judah, in the year Evil-Merodach[a] became king of Babylon, he released Jehoiachin from prison on the twenty-seventh day of the twelfth month. [28]He spoke kindly to him and gave him a seat of honor higher than those of the other kings who were with him in Babylon. [29]So Jehoiachin put aside his prison clothes and for the rest of his life ate regularly at the king's table. [30]Day by day the king gave Jehoiachin a regular allowance as long as he lived.

1. This conflict story poses a dilemma: Is surrender ever honorable? Is resistance always noble? In what way do you need to surrender? To keep fighting? How do you know when to do what? 2. Is God still angry today? Over the same things? Does God judge nations and bring disaster on them? Why or why not? 3. Have you ever witnessed a violent death? How is it different than the endless "deaths" on TV or in movies? Has violence in the media desensitized us to the horror of murder? 4. Has God ever pulled everything out from under you? Without your last crutch or means of support, what happened when you fell? Do you dread falling again? Are you less afraid now?

Did you get an allowance as a youngster? Did this require work? What allowances do you get today?

1. What does Jehoiachin's release say about Evil-Merodach? About Jehoiachin? 2. Jehoiachin went into exile two years before the rest of Judah, but was given amnesty halfway through the 70-year period of exile (see Jer 25:8–11). Why do you suppose that was? 3. After all the judgment in Kings, what's the meaning of this conclusion?

1. Do you need to be released? How long has your exile been? Are there any signs that relief is on the way? 2. Can you live "one day at a time"? Does the past drag you down, or the future worry you? If expectations and obligations set your agenda, what do you have to give up to truly experience the present moment? How can the group help? 3. Does the violent history of Israel's First Commonwealth confuse you? Disturb you? Instruct you? What view of God does the author hold? With what do you agree? Disagree?

INTRODUCTION to
1 CHRONICLES

Book Study Outline: If you are using 1 Chronicles for a study course, here is a 7- or 13-week outline. Use the questions in the margin for your group agenda:

🍵 start meeting / 15 min.

📖 read & discuss Bible / 30 min.

♡ close meeting / 15–45 min.

Refer to the Questions and Answers in the front of this Bible for more information.

7-week plan	13-week plan	Personal Reading	Group Study Passage
1	1	1:1–5:26	5:11–26/God in History
	2	6:1–9:1	6:31–49/God Inspires Worship
2	3	9:2–34	9:2–34/The Returned Exiles
	4	9:35–10:14	10:1–14/The Death of Saul
3	5	11:1–12:40	11:1–9/David Crowned As King
	6	13:1–14:17	13:1–14/The Ark Returns
4	7	15:1–16:43	16:7–43/David's Gratitude
	8	17:1–18:17	17:1–15/God Promises David
5	9	19:1–22:1	21:1–22:1/Counting Off
	10	22:2–24:31	22:2–19/Preparing for Worship
6	11	25:1–26:32	25:1–31/Temple Singers
	12	27:1–34	27:25–34/The King's Officials
7	13	28:1–29:30	29:21–30/Solomon Enthroned

Author: Jewish tradition suggests Ezra as author, with no firm evidence.

Date: Probably written toward the end of the fifth century B.C. or a little later. The actions narrated in the book are centered primarily in the reign of David (c. 1011–971 B.C.).

Theme: A family record to remind exiled and returning Israelites of God's chosen king and their place in the restored Jerusalem.

Historical Background: The reign of David was the golden age of Jewish history. The country was united and military victories allowed David to enlarge his territory. He introduced new administrative organization which brought stability and prosperity. He brought the Ark of the Covenant to Jerusalem and restructured the tabernacle worship.

Characteristics: Chapters 1–9 trace Israel's family record back to Adam. God is very much behind the scenes selecting a people for himself. Chapters 10–29 record the history of David's reign from the viewpoint of the chronicler's priestly interests. His concern is not the ups and downs of one man, but the lasting achievements of David—the monarchy and the temple. David is seen as God's chosen king around whom the welfare of the nation revolves. The chronicler omits much of the personal and family detail recorded in 2 Samuel. Instead, he records the nature of David's reorganization of worship in Jerusalem, detailing his appointments of not only priests but singers, musicians and gatekeepers.

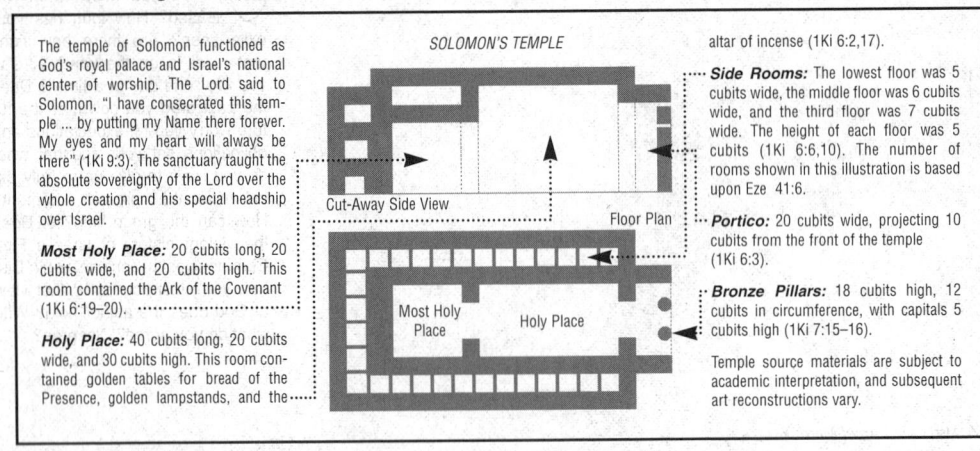

The temple of Solomon functioned as God's royal palace and Israel's national center of worship. The Lord said to Solomon, "I have consecrated this temple ... by putting my Name there forever. My eyes and my heart will always be there" (1Ki 9:3). The sanctuary taught the absolute sovereignty of the Lord over the whole creation and his special headship over Israel.

Most Holy Place: 20 cubits long, 20 cubits wide, and 20 cubits high. This room contained the Ark of the Covenant (1Ki 6:19–20).

Holy Place: 40 cubits long, 20 cubits wide, and 30 cubits high. This room contained golden tables for bread of the Presence, golden lampstands, and the

SOLOMON'S TEMPLE

Cut-Away Side View

Floor Plan

Most Holy Place

Holy Place

altar of incense (1Ki 6:2,17).

Side Rooms: The lowest floor was 5 cubits wide, the middle floor was 6 cubits wide, and the third floor was 7 cubits wide. The height of each floor was 5 cubits (1Ki 6:6,10). The number of rooms shown in this illustration is based upon Eze 41:6.

Portico: 20 cubits wide, projecting 10 cubits from the front of the temple (1Ki 6:3).

Bronze Pillars: 18 cubits high, 12 cubits in circumference, with capitals 5 cubits high (1Ki 7:15–16).

Temple source materials are subject to academic interpretation, and subsequent art reconstructions vary.

1 Chronicles

Historical Records From Adam to Abraham

To Noah's Sons

1 Adam, Seth, Enosh, ²Kenan, Mahalalel, Jared, ³Enoch, Methuselah, Lamech, Noah.

⁴The sons of Noah:ᵃ
  Shem, Ham and Japheth.

The Japhethites

⁵The sonsᵇ of Japheth:
  Gomer, Magog, Madai, Javan, Tubal, Meshech and Tiras.
⁶The sons of Gomer:
  Ashkenaz, Riphathᶜ and Togarmah.
⁷The sons of Javan:
  Elishah, Tarshish, the Kittim and the Rodanim.

The Hamites

⁸The sons of Ham:
  Cush, Mizraim,ᵈ Put and Canaan.
⁹The sons of Cush:
  Seba, Havilah, Sabta, Raamah and Sabteca.
  The sons of Raamah:
  Sheba and Dedan.
¹⁰Cush was the fatherᵉ of
  Nimrod, who grew to be a mighty warrior on earth.
¹¹Mizraim was the father of
  the Ludites, Anamites, Lehabites, Naphtuhites, ¹²Pathrusites, Casluhites (from whom the Philistines came) and Caphtorites.
¹³Canaan was the father of
  Sidon his firstborn,ᶠ and of the Hittites, ¹⁴Jebusites, Amorites, Girgashites, ¹⁵Hivites, Arkites, Sinites, ¹⁶Arvadites, Zemarites and Hamathites.

The Semites

¹⁷The sons of Shem:
  Elam, Asshur, Arphaxad, Lud and Aram.
  The sons of Aramᵍ:
  Uz, Hul, Gether and Meshech.
¹⁸Arphaxad was the father of Shelah,
  and Shelah the father of Eber.
¹⁹Two sons were born to Eber:
  One was named Peleg,ʰ because in his time the earth was divided; his brother was named Joktan.
²⁰Joktan was the father of

ᵃ4 Septuagint; Hebrew does not have *The sons of Noah:*   ᵇ5 *Sons* may mean *descendants* or *successors* or *nations*; also in verses 6-10, 17 and 20.   ᶜ6 Many Hebrew manuscripts and Vulgate (see also Septuagint and Gen. 10:3); most Hebrew manuscripts *Diphath*   ᵈ8 That is, Egypt; also in verse 11   ᵉ10 *Father* may mean *ancestor* or *predecessor* or *founder*; also in verses 11, 13, 18 and 20.   ᶠ13 Or *of the Sidonians, the foremost*   ᵍ17 One Hebrew manuscript and some Septuagint manuscripts (see also Gen. 10:23); most Hebrew manuscripts do not have this line.   ʰ19 *Peleg* means *division*.

---

1. What kind of lists do you depend on (grocery, telephone, Christmas, "to do," etc.) to keep your life organized and efficient? 2. What changes would be forced on you if one of your most used lists were lost forever?

1. Genealogies often introduce stories, but in Chronicles, genealogies seem to *be* the story. What do you think is the purpose behind these lists? (a) To trace one's family tree and the property won? (b) To value the struggles of bygone days? (c) To see God guiding his chosen through thick and thin, heroism and villainy? (d) To show children God's loving kindness to all generations? 2. The purpose of the chronicler may be gleaned from the selective way lists are edited. Already in verse 1, some "glaring omissions" are evident. Which ones can you find? 3. The chronicler highlights past events by arranging "linear genealogies" (a list devoted to a single line from ancestor to descendant) and "segmented genealogies" (a list tracing several lines of descent from a common ancestor). Where do you see the two kinds of lists here? 4. Why so few names with any description? What major events are brought to mind by merely listing names associated with the events? 5. Who is Nimrod (v. 10; see Ge 10:8–12)? Why might Nimrod be closely connected with a bunch of "ites" (tribal groups)? 6. What strange events are linked with Peleg's era (vv. 19–20; see Ge 10:21–11:9)? 7. What troubles and triumphs of history are embraced here? What kind of God (yet unnamed) is implicit in this narrative?

1. Which of those listed were "household names" to you? 2. Likely some important names listed here are virtual unknowns. For example, Seth: Like a substitute player, he takes the field in a world burned by murder and greed (see Ge 4:25). Yet through him, God establishes a chosen nation! For all who live fairly humble, nondescript lives, why should we think our life still counts for something?

Almodad, Sheleph, Hazarmaveth, Jerah, [21]Hadoram, Uzal, Diklah, [22]Obal,[a] Abimael, Sheba, [23]Ophir, Havilah and Jobab. All these were sons of Joktan.

[24]Shem, Arphaxad,[b] Shelah,
[25]Eber, Peleg, Reu,
[26]Serug, Nahor, Terah
[27]and Abram (that is, Abraham).

The Family of Abraham

[28]The sons of Abraham:
Isaac and Ishmael.

Descendants of Hagar

[29]These were their descendants:
Nebaioth the firstborn of Ishmael, Kedar, Adbeel, Mibsam, [30]Mishma, Dumah, Massa, Hadad, Tema, [31]Jetur, Naphish and Kedemah. These were the sons of Ishmael.

Descendants of Keturah

[32]The sons born to Keturah, Abraham's concubine:
Zimran, Jokshan, Medan, Midian, Ishbak and Shuah.
The sons of Jokshan:
Sheba and Dedan.
[33]The sons of Midian:
Ephah, Epher, Hanoch, Abida and Eldaah.
All these were descendants of Keturah.

Descendants of Sarah

[34]Abraham was the father of Isaac.
The sons of Isaac:
Esau and Israel.

Esau's Sons

[35]The sons of Esau:
Eliphaz, Reuel, Jeush, Jalam and Korah.
[36]The sons of Eliphaz:
Teman, Omar, Zepho,[c] Gatam and Kenaz;
by Timna: Amalek.[d]
[37]The sons of Reuel:
Nahath, Zerah, Shammah and Mizzah.

The People of Seir in Edom

[38]The sons of Seir:
Lotan, Shobal, Zibeon, Anah, Dishon, Ezer and Dishan.
[39]The sons of Lotan:
Hori and Homam. Timna was Lotan's sister.
[40]The sons of Shobal:
Alvan,[e] Manahath, Ebal, Shepho and Onam.
The sons of Zibeon:
Aiah and Anah.
[41]The son of Anah:
Dishon.
The sons of Dishon:

---

1. If you were compiling a family tree, how would you decide who gets included and who doesn't? Would you include pirates and other "low-lifes"? Or would you skip them to highlight some high moral purpose? 2. What family embarrassments would give you pause if you were to share that "tree" with your group?

1. Why does the chronicler always call Jacob by his "other" name (v. 34)? 2. This section includes some "firsts" for women in the book of Chronicles. Let's see if you genealogy sleuths can find: (a) The first mention of a woman? (b) Of a daughter? (c) Of a grandmother? 3. What political leader (town or movement) takes on the name of a woman? Why are their names omitted? 4. What developments in the institution of marriage does chapter 1 recount? What happened to Hagar (v. 29; see Ge 21)? Likewise, Sarah (v. 34; see Ge 23)? And Keturah (vv. 32–33; see Ge 25:1–4)? 5. Like a good baseball manager, the chronicler has a strategy in the way he makes out his line-up card of names. From his list of Abraham's sons (vv. 28–34), who seem to be regarded as the most important players? Why are they so vital? 6. In verses 35–54 (also Ge 36:10–14,20–43), why is such unusual detail devoted to people and places having little role in Israel's development? 7. Will the real "Timna" please stand up (vv. 36,39,51 and footnote to v. 36)? Is "she" a wife of Eliphaz? Or is "he" his son? And what kind of mom was she if her son's tribe, the Amalekites, becomes Israel's chief enemy (see 1Sa 15)? 8. What's significant about the kings mentioned here (vv. 43ff)? 9. What does Esau's lineage tell us about God's care for his people?

1. Of all the groups (teams, associations, families) you belong to, which two most define who you are? Which one helps you decide which downtown service agency to help with Thanksgiving meals? Which will help you decide what neighborhood to live in? Or

a22 Some Hebrew manuscripts and Syriac (see also Gen. 10:28); most Hebrew manuscripts Ebal b24 Hebrew; some Septuagint manuscripts Arphaxad, Cainan (see also note at Gen. 11:10) c36 Many Hebrew manuscripts, some Septuagint manuscripts and Syriac (see also Gen. 36:11); most Hebrew manuscripts Zephi d36 Some Septuagint manuscripts (see also Gen. 36:12); Hebrew Gatam, Kenaz, Timna and Amalek e40 Many Hebrew manuscripts and some Septuagint manuscripts (see also Gen. 36:23); most Hebrew manuscripts Alian

Hemdan,[a] Eshban, Ithran and Keran.
[42]The sons of Ezer:

Bilhan, Zaavan and Akan.[b]

The sons of Dishan[c]:

Uz and Aran.

The Rulers of Edom

[43]These were the kings who reigned in Edom before any Israelite king reigned[d]:

Bela son of Beor, whose city was named Dinhabah.

[44]When Bela died, Jobab son of Zerah from Bozrah succeeded him as king.

[45]When Jobab died, Husham from the land of the Temanites succeeded him as king.

[46]When Husham died, Hadad son of Bedad, who defeated Midian in the country of Moab, succeeded him as king. His city was named Avith.

[47]When Hadad died, Samlah from Masrekah succeeded him as king.

[48]When Samlah died, Shaul from Rehoboth on the river[e] succeeded him as king.

[49]When Shaul died, Baal-Hanan son of Acbor succeeded him as king.

[50]When Baal-Hanan died, Hadad succeeded him as king. His city was named Pau,[f] and his wife's name was Mehetabel daughter of Matred, the daughter of Me-Zahab. [51]Hadad also died.

The chiefs of Edom were:

Timna, Alvah, Jetheth, [52]Oholibamah, Elah, Pinon, [53]Kenaz, Teman, Mibzar, [54]Magdiel and Iram. These were the chiefs of Edom.

Israel's Sons

2 These were the sons of Israel:
Reuben, Simeon, Levi, Judah, Issachar, Zebulun, [2]Dan, Joseph, Benjamin, Naphtali, Gad and Asher.

Judah

To Hezron's Sons

[3]The sons of Judah:

Er, Onan and Shelah. These three were born to him by a Canaanite woman, the daughter of Shua. Er, Judah's firstborn, was wicked in the LORD's sight; so the LORD put him to death. [4]Tamar, Judah's daughter-in-law, bore him Perez and Zerah. Judah had five sons in all.

[5]The sons of Perez:

Hezron and Hamul.

[6]The sons of Zerah:

Zimri, Ethan, Heman, Calcol and Darda[g]—five in all.

[7]The son of Carmi:

a41 Many Hebrew manuscripts and some Septuagint manuscripts (see also Gen. 36:26); most Hebrew manuscripts *Hamran*   b42 Many Hebrew and Septuagint manuscripts (see also Gen. 36:27); most Hebrew manuscripts *Zaavan, Jaakan*   c42 Hebrew *Dishon*, a variant of *Dishan*   d43 Or *before an Israelite king reigned over them*   e48 Possibly the Euphrates   f50 Many Hebrew manuscripts, some Septuagint manuscripts, Vulgate and Syriac (see also Gen. 36:39); most Hebrew manuscripts *Pai*   g6 Many Hebrew manuscripts, some Septuagint manuscripts and Syriac (see also 1 Kings 4:31); most Hebrew manuscripts *Dara*

how much income to declare on your income tax forms? Which groups influence your choice of clothes, hairstyle, leisure pursuits? **2.** How might the strange listing of the Edomites make you think twice about which people you view as offensive, unattractive, outside your circles? **3.** Do you think marriage was taken more seriously in Abraham's day than today? Why or why not? Today we have ways of dissolving marriages which insure that the parties of a previous marriage are cared for. By today's standard of equal rights, would Abraham's effort to provide for Hagar have passed muster? If the exiled Hagar and her brood had moved next door to you, would you or your church be ready to assist her? Why or why not?

What about a politician's or clan's "Rise and Fall" most intrigues you? What do you imagine it must be like to be famous and powerful one moment in history, only to be disgraced and banished the next?

1. Much of the Old Testament "Hall of Fame" is contained here. In a quick, first read-through, which names are familiar to you? What stories of God's deliverance and human weakness do these footnotes to history bring to mind? **2.** Now take a closer look at verses 1–9: Of the 12 sons listed in verse 1, why is just one (Judah) explored further? **3.** What harm comes to the house of Judah with his first two sons, Er and Onan (v. 3; see Ge 38:7–10)? They are the first people since the Flood whose death is a direct result of their disobedience to God. What qualities of God would "Er and Onan" recall? **4.** Tamar prostitutes herself (see Ge 38), but is here the first woman in the royal line to be named by the chronicler. What do you recall about the convoluted moral drama she faced? What qualities of God would "Tamar" instantly recall for God's redeemed people? **5.** Achar (v. 7; alias "Achan," see Jos 7) also lives a troubled life; so much so, that his name change is recorded for all time by the chronicler: Why? What purpose was served by reminding people of their troubled past? **6.** In the midst of these examples of shame, "Azariah" reminds us "God has helped." What message is Ethan leaving his heirs with this name for his son (which occurs 24 times in the Old Testament)? **7.** Where do you see the first direct mention of "the Lord" and any explicit qualities attributed to him? What does this tell you about the on-going relationship God has had with all the sons of Judah thus far? Likewise, what could the sons of Hezron be expected to know about their God and the purpose of their lives? **8.** In verses 10–17, we see David's forefathers and family listed. At their family reunions, what tales were likely told and retold about each? Take Eliab, for example (see 1Sa 16:6–7). What famous saying was first told to the expectant Eliab, and what might Eliab have learned about discipleship from his disappointment? Or Asahel (see 2Sa 2:18ff): What mix of qualities did he possess above his peers which, for lack of wisdom, led to his premature death? And which members of David's own family take up arms against him, teaching David (and us) valuable lessons in faith and trust (see 3:2; 2Sa 17:25)? **9.** Of the names listed in verses 18ff, some are linked with stories of faith, such as Bezalel (v. 20; see Ex 31:1–11). He was a peer with Caleb (the one who spied out the land with Joshua and is the great-grandson of the Caleb listed here). Other names are linked with stories of sex (Hezron), money and power (Jair, Geshur, Aram). What does this tell you about how and why God gives good gifts to his people? **10.** God's gift of children is implicit in this chapter. How are the "failures" of Seled (v. 30), Jether (v. 32) and Sheshan (v. 34) each duly noted? Where does Sheshan eventually succeed, whereas the others did not?

♡ **1.** Either Ashhur was born into a single-parent family (v. 24 of the NIV translation), or he's the product of incest (as suggested by the RSV translation of

Achar,ᵃ who brought trouble on Israel by violating the ban on taking devoted things.ᵇ

⁸The son of Ethan:

Azariah.

⁹The sons born to Hezron were:

Jerahmeel, Ram and Caleb.ᶜ

From Ram Son of Hezron

¹⁰Ram was the father of

Amminadab, and Amminadab the father of Nahshon, the leader of the people of Judah. ¹¹Nahshon was the father of Salmon,ᵈ Salmon the father of Boaz, ¹²Boaz the father of Obed and Obed the father of Jesse.

¹³Jesse was the father of

Eliab his firstborn; the second son was Abinadab, the third Shimea, ¹⁴the fourth Nethanel, the fifth Raddai, ¹⁵the sixth Ozem and the seventh David. ¹⁶Their sisters were Zeruiah and Abigail. Zeruiah's three sons were Abishai, Joab and Asahel. ¹⁷Abigail was the mother of Amasa, whose father was Jether the Ishmaelite.

Caleb Son of Hezron

¹⁸Caleb son of Hezron had children by his wife Azubah (and by Jerioth). These were her sons: Jesher, Shobab and Ardon. ¹⁹When Azubah died, Caleb married Ephrath, who bore him Hur. ²⁰Hur was the father of Uri, and Uri the father of Bezalel.

²¹Later, Hezron lay with the daughter of Makir the father of Gilead (he had married her when he was sixty years old), and she bore him Segub. ²²Segub was the father of Jair, who controlled twenty-three towns in Gilead. ²³(But Geshur and Aram captured Havvoth Jair,ᵉ as well as Kenath with its surrounding settlements—sixty towns.) All these were descendants of Makir the father of Gilead.

²⁴After Hezron died in Caleb Ephrathah, Abijah the wife of Hezron bore him Ashhur the fatherᶠ of Tekoa.

Jerahmeel Son of Hezron

²⁵The sons of Jerahmeel the firstborn of Hezron:

Ram his firstborn, Bunah, Oren, Ozem andᵍ Ahijah. ²⁶Jerahmeel had another wife, whose name was Atarah; she was the mother of Onam.

²⁷The sons of Ram the firstborn of Jerahmeel:

Maaz, Jamin and Eker.

²⁸The sons of Onam:

Shammai and Jada.

The sons of Shammai:

Nadab and Abishur.

²⁹Abishur's wife was named Abihail, who bore him Ahban and Molid.

³⁰The sons of Nadab:

Seled and Appaim. Seled died without children.

³¹The son of Appaim:

ᵃ7 *Achar* means *trouble*; *Achar* is called *Achan* in Joshua.   ᵇ7 The Hebrew term refers to the irrevocable giving over of things or persons to the Lord, often by totally destroying them.   ᶜ9 Hebrew *Kelubai*, a variant of *Caleb*   ᵈ11 Septuagint (see also Ruth 4:21); Hebrew *Salma*   ᵉ23 Or *captured the settlements of Jair*   ᶠ24 *Father* may mean *civic leader* or *military leader*; also in verses 42, 45, 49-52 and possibly elsewhere.   ᵍ25 Or *Oren and Ozem, by*

Ishi, who was the father of Sheshan.
Sheshan was the father of Ahlai.
32The sons of Jada, Shammai's brother:
Jether and Jonathan. Jether died without children.
33The sons of Jonathan:
Peleth and Zaza.
These were the descendants of Jerahmeel.
34Sheshan had no sons—only daughters.

He had an Egyptian servant named Jarha. 35Sheshan gave his daughter in marriage to his servant Jarha, and she bore him Attai.

36Attai was the father of Nathan,
Nathan the father of Zabad,
37Zabad the father of Ephlal,
Ephlal the father of Obed,
38Obed the father of Jehu,
Jehu the father of Azariah,
39Azariah the father of Helez,
Helez the father of Eleasah,
40Eleasah the father of Sismai,
Sismai the father of Shallum,
41Shallum the father of Jekamiah,
and Jekamiah the father of Elishama.

The Clans of Caleb

42The sons of Caleb the brother of Jerahmeel:
Mesha his firstborn, who was the father of Ziph, and his son Mareshah,a who was the father of Hebron.
43The sons of Hebron:
Korah, Tappuah, Rekem and Shema. 44Shema was the father of Raham, and Raham the father of Jorkeam. Rekem was the father of Shammai. 45The son of Shammai was Maon, and Maon was the father of Beth Zur.
46Caleb's concubine Ephah was the mother of Haran, Moza and Gazez. Haran was the father of Gazez.
47The sons of Jahdai:
Regem, Jotham, Geshan, Pelet, Ephah and Shaaph.
48Caleb's concubine Maacah was the mother of Sheber and Tirhanah. 49She also gave birth to Shaaph the father of Madmannah and to Sheva the father of Macbenah and Gibea. Caleb's daughter was Acsah. 50These were the descendants of Caleb.

The sons of Hur the firstborn of Ephrathah:
Shobal the father of Kiriath Jearim, 51Salma the father of Bethlehem, and Hareph the father of Beth Gader.
52The descendants of Shobal the father of Kiriath Jearim were:
Haroeh, half the Manahathites, 53and the clans of Kiriath Jearim: the Ithrites, Puthites, Shumathites and Mishraites. From these descended the Zorathites and Eshtaolites.
54The descendants of Salma:
Bethlehem, the Netophathites, Atroth Beth Joab, half the Manahathites, the Zorites, 55and the clans of scribesb who lived at Jabez: the Tirathites, Shimeathites and Sucathites. These are the Kenites who came from Hammath, the father of the house of Recab.c

v. 24). Either way, what would Ashhur's lot in life have been like? How many "Ashhurs" have you known—children of one parent or of mixed-up parentage? What resources today help such children grow to maturity? How can churches or Bible study groups help? **2.** Of what profit to the "Ashhurs" of this world would be a chronicle of their family history? **3.** How has your family overcome disadvantage or hardship in giving birth to their children? In giving birth to their dreams of making a "name" for themselves? **4.** How have the gifts and talents been distributed among your clan? How have they been used? Or abused? **5.** Who in your family is like Bezalel—filled with the Spirit of God *and* with skill, ability and knowledge in all kinds of crafts? How do you respond to those who "have it all"? **6.** In the composite picture of your group, do you have more "Ashhurs" or "Bezalels"? Any with the shenanigans of "Sheshan"?

a42 The meaning of the Hebrew for this phrase is uncertain.   b55 Or *of the Sopherites*   c55 Or *father of Beth Recab*

If tragedy is the bookmark of history, separating chapters into lessons learned and unlearned, then what tragic-type "bookmarks" have shaped your life? Any casualties of war? Any tragic family feuds? Any natural disaster striking close to home?

This chapter divides neatly into three parts, but those who lived in the divisions likely did not think life was too neat at all. **1.** From verses 1–9 (also 2Sa 3:2–5; 5:13–16), what can you tell about David's family life? What must relations among the 19 named siblings and the 7+ sets of half-brothers have been like? **2.** Why do you think the lists vary in name and number between Samuel's account and the chronicler's? **3.** From the story of David's sin with Bathsheba, Solomon seems to be the first child of that union (see 2Sa 12:24–25). In Chronicles, what is Solomon's apparent place? **4.** Why are children of concubines named in other royal family lines (1:32; 2:46), but not in David's (3:9; 14:3–6)? And why list Tamar alone of all his daughters (see 14:3–6)? **5.** David was a "parent in pain," with open disdain, rebellion and sibling rivalry rampant among his sons. How is that evident in the stories of Amnon (see 2Sa 13), Absalom (see 2Sa 16:15ff; 18:31–33) and Adonijah (see 1Ki 1)? **6.** In verses 10–14, we are introduced to the kings of Judah, any of whom could provide interesting tangents to pursue in 1 and 2 Kings. From the heavy-handed reign of Rehoboam, "Israel has been in rebellion against the house of David to this day" (1Ki 12:19). Forced labor, foreign invaders, idol worship, assimilation of their neighbors' worldly values, foreign alliances—all such "evil in the sight of the LORD" spelled doom for Israel. What parallels in modern history seem to replay this Rehoboam to Zedekiah's reign of folly, tyranny and evil? **7.** Now we come back to Jehoiachin (v. 17): What has happened to him, to Jerusalem and to the royal line thereafter?

1. As did many of the Israelites after Solomon died, what legacy of family troubles did you inherit? What have you in turn passed along to others? **2.** When facing conflicts such as these sons of David and kings of Judah must have faced, what kind of bird are you: (a) *Hawk*, flying above it all

The Sons of David

3 These were the sons of David born to him in Hebron:
The firstborn was Amnon the son of Ahinoam of Jezreel;
the second, Daniel the son of Abigail of Carmel;
²the third, Absalom the son of Maacah daughter of Talmai king of Geshur;
the fourth, Adonijah the son of Haggith;
³the fifth, Shephatiah the son of Abital;
and the sixth, Ithream, by his wife Eglah.
⁴These six were born to David in Hebron, where he reigned seven years and six months.

David reigned in Jerusalem thirty-three years, ⁵and these were the children born to him there:
Shammua,ᵃ Shobab, Nathan and Solomon. These four were by Bathshebaᵇ daughter of Ammiel. ⁶There were also Ibhar, Elishua,ᶜ Eliphelet, ⁷Nogah, Nepheg, Japhia, ⁸Elishama, Eliada and Eliphelet—nine in all. ⁹All these were the sons of David, besides his sons by his concubines. And Tamar was their sister.

The Kings of Judah

¹⁰Solomon's son was Rehoboam,
Abijah his son,
Asa his son,
Jehoshaphat his son,
¹¹Jehoramᵈ his son,
Ahaziah his son,
Joash his son,
¹²Amaziah his son,
Azariah his son,
Jotham his son,
¹³Ahaz his son,
Hezekiah his son,
Manasseh his son,
¹⁴Amon his son,
Josiah his son.
¹⁵The sons of Josiah:
Johanan the firstborn,
Jehoiakim the second son,
Zedekiah the third,
Shallum the fourth.
¹⁶The successors of Jehoiakim:
Jehoiachinᵉ his son,
and Zedekiah.

The Royal Line After the Exile

¹⁷The descendants of Jehoiachin the captive:
Shealtiel his son, ¹⁸Malkiram, Pedaiah, Shenazzar, Jekamiah, Hoshama and Nedabiah.
¹⁹The sons of Pedaiah:
Zerubbabel and Shimei.
The sons of Zerubbabel:
Meshullam and Hananiah.
Shelomith was their sister.

ᵃ5 Hebrew *Shimea*, a variant of *Shammua* ᵇ5 One Hebrew manuscript and Vulgate (see also Septuagint and 2 Samuel 11:3); most Hebrew manuscripts *Bathshua* ᶜ6 Two Hebrew manuscripts (see also 2 Samuel 5:15 and 1 Chron. 14:5); most Hebrew manuscripts *Elishama* ᵈ11 Hebrew *Joram*, a variant of *Jehoram* ᵉ16 Hebrew *Jeconiah*, a variant of *Jehoiachin*; also in verse 17

20There were also five others:
    Hashubah, Ohel, Berekiah, Hasadiah and Jushab-Hesed.
21The descendants of Hananiah:
    Pelatiah and Jeshaiah, and the sons of Rephaiah, of Arnan,
    of Obadiah and of Shecaniah.
22The descendants of Shecaniah:
    Shemaiah and his sons:
    Hattush, Igal, Bariah, Neariah and Shaphat—six in all.
23The sons of Neariah:
    Elioenai, Hizkiah and Azrikam—three in all.
24The sons of Elioenai:
    Hodaviah, Eliashib, Pelaiah, Akkub, Johanan, Delaiah and
    Anani—seven in all.

Other Clans of Judah

4 The descendants of Judah:
    Perez, Hezron, Carmi, Hur and Shobal.
2Reaiah son of Shobal was the father of Jahath, and Jahath the
father of Ahumai and Lahad. These were the clans of the
Zorathites.
3These were the sons*a* of Etam:
    Jezreel, Ishma and Idbash. Their sister was named Hazze-
lelponi. 4Penuel was the father of Gedor, and Ezer the
father of Hushah.
These were the descendants of Hur, the firstborn of Ephrathah and father*b* of Bethlehem.
5Ashhur the father of Tekoa had two wives, Helah and Naarah.
6Naarah bore him Ahuzzam, Hepher, Temeni and Haahashtari.
    These were the descendants of Naarah.
7The sons of Helah:
    Zereth, Zohar, Ethnan, 8and Koz, who was the father of
Anub and Hazzobebah and of the clans of Aharhel son of
Harum.

9Jabez was more honorable than his brothers. His mother had
named him Jabez,*c* saying, "I gave birth to him in pain." 10Jabez
cried out to the God of Israel, "Oh, that you would bless me and
enlarge my territory! Let your hand be with me, and keep me from
harm so that I will be free from pain." And God granted his request.

11Kelub, Shuhah's brother, was the father of Mehir, who was
    the father of Eshton. 12Eshton was the father of Beth Ra-
pha, Paseah and Tehinnah the father of Ir Nahash.*d* These
were the men of Recah.

13The sons of Kenaz:
    Othniel and Seraiah.
    The sons of Othniel:
    Hathath and Meonothai.*e* 14Meonothai was the father of
Ophrah.
    Seraiah was the father of Joab,
    the father of Ge Harashim.*f* It was called this because its
people were craftsmen.
15The sons of Caleb son of Jephunneh:
    Iru, Elah and Naam.

---

a3 Some Septuagint manuscripts (see also Vulgate); Hebrew *father*   *b4* *Father* may
mean *civic leader* or *military leader*; also in verses 12, 14, 17, 18 and possibly elsewhere.
c9 *Jabez* sounds like the Hebrew for *pain*.   *d12* Or *of the city of Nahash*
e13 Some Septuagint manuscripts and Vulgate; Hebrew does not have *and Meonothai*.
f14 *Ge Harashim* means *valley of craftsmen*.

and ready to pounce on mistakes?
(b) *Dove,* waging peace instead of
war? (c) *Ostrich,* with your head in
the sand, waiting for the conflict to
blow over? (d) *Turkey,* easily ruf-
fled, always squawking? **3.** What
troubles have you tried tackling this
year: Any of your own making? Any
you've inherited? What help have
you had? What disappointments?
What will you do differently from
here on?

---

1. What period or people of
history do you enjoy reading
about? Of those now in power,
whose family history, royal lineage
or cultural roots would you like to
explore further? Why? **2.** Who in
your group can trace their roots
back the furthest?

1. Verses 1–8 is a curious
replay of an earlier Chronicles listing: Can you "geneatectives" find it? (Note: This coined
term depicts astute Bible students
who can find treasure in trivia and
master God's purpose for these
kingdom genealogies.) **2.** In verses
9–10, geneatectives will find the
first direct quotation, the first
prayer, and the first specific description of God's activity in Chronicles. What do you learn about
God's intentions for human life
from the strange occurrence of
these "firsts"? **3.** How is Jabez's life
different due to his prayer? How
might Jabez's prayer be related to
his mother's pain? What lessons
about prayer does Jabez's life exemplify? **4.** What most unusual
marriage wins a mention here?
What kinds of problems do you
imagine Miriam, Shammai and Ishbah might have had with other kids
at school? What special problems
does Mered likely face by choosing
to marry royalty? **5.** What professional groups are singled out for
special mention here? What does
their mention suggest about the
way extended families learned and
practiced certain crafts?

1. How have family relations
and social institutions
changed since grandparents, parents and children all lived and
worked together? Did your mom or
dad want you to follow in their footsteps family-wise, career-wise or
otherwise? How so? **2.** Mixed marriages violated instructions given to
the people entering the Promised

Land, yet evidence here suggests that all kinds of family units make up the chosen kingdom people. What "odd" families do you admit to your chosen circle of friends (group or church)? **3.** What expectations do you have of your children and their careers? If you joined together to maximize your resources, focus expenses, and train successive generations to do likewise, what might you specialize in? What might you achieve with time?

---

1. That loaf of bread: How many hands contributed to its getting to the grocery store? **2.** Your last hotel stay: How many workers were involved in making it so pleasant? **3.** Why doesn't the little guy ever hear, "What a great sandwich" or "What a good night's sleep"?

1. The little clan of Simeon was absorbed by the bigger tribe of Judah some 400 years after the Exodus. Yet by this genealogy, the chronicler keeps their memory alive. What impresses you from this record of "lost Simeon"? **2.** From other lists of Simeon's sons (see Ge 46; Ex 6; Nu 26), you geneatectives face these conundrums: Will the real third son of Simeon please stand up? How long before the Simeon clan intermarries with native women? Why do Shaul's sons seem so familiar (see 1:29–30)? **3.** What benefits came to the tribe of Judah by their taking in the loyal Simeonites?

How would you feel if all your heritage was lost in a bigger crowd, as was Simeon's? What would you do to recover your lost identity?

The son of Elah:
  Kenaz.
[16]The sons of Jehallelel:
  Ziph, Ziphah, Tiria and Asarel.
[17]The sons of Ezrah:
  Jether, Mered, Epher and Jalon. One of Mered's wives gave birth to Miriam, Shammai and Ishbah the father of Eshtemoa. [18](His Judean wife gave birth to Jered the father of Gedor, Heber the father of Soco, and Jekuthiel the father of Zanoah.) These were the children of Pharaoh's daughter Bithiah, whom Mered had married.
[19]The sons of Hodiah's wife, the sister of Naham:
  the father of Keilah the Garmite, and Eshtemoa the Maacathite.
[20]The sons of Shimon:
  Amnon, Rinnah, Ben-Hanan and Tilon.
The descendants of Ishi:
  Zoheth and Ben-Zoheth.
[21]The sons of Shelah son of Judah:
  Er the father of Lecah, Laadah the father of Mareshah and the clans of the linen workers at Beth Ashbea, [22]Jokim, the men of Cozeba, and Joash and Saraph, who ruled in Moab and Jashubi Lehem. (These records are from ancient times.) [23]They were the potters who lived at Netaim and Gederah; they stayed there and worked for the king.

Simeon

[24]The descendants of Simeon:
  Nemuel, Jamin, Jarib, Zerah and Shaul;
  [25]Shallum was Shaul's son, Mibsam his son and Mishma his son.
[26]The descendants of Mishma:
  Hammuel his son, Zaccur his son and Shimei his son.
[27]Shimei had sixteen sons and six daughters, but his brothers did not have many children; so their entire clan did not become as numerous as the people of Judah. [28]They lived in Beersheba, Moladah, Hazar Shual, [29]Bilhah, Ezem, Tolad, [30]Bethuel, Hormah, Ziklag, [31]Beth Marcaboth, Hazar Susim, Beth Biri and Shaaraim. These were their towns until the reign of David. [32]Their surrounding villages were Etam, Ain, Rimmon, Token and Ashan—five towns— [33]and all the villages around these towns as far as Baalath.[a] These were their settlements. And they kept a genealogical record.

[34]Meshobab, Jamlech, Joshah son of Amaziah, [35]Joel, Jehu son of Joshibiah, the son of Seraiah, the son of Asiel, [36]also Elioenai, Jaakobah, Jeshohaiah, Asaiah, Adiel, Jesimiel, Benaiah, [37]and Ziza son of Shiphi, the son of Allon, the son of Jedaiah, the son of Shimri, the son of Shemaiah.

[38]The men listed above by name were leaders of their clans. Their families increased greatly, [39]and they went to the outskirts of Gedor to the east of the valley in search of pasture for their flocks. [40]They found rich, good pasture, and the land was spacious, peaceful and quiet. Some Hamites had lived there formerly. [41]The men whose names were listed came in the days of Hezekiah king of Judah. They attacked the Hamites in their dwellings and

---

a33 Some Septuagint manuscripts (see also Joshua 19:8); Hebrew *Baal*

also the Meunites who were there and completely destroyed[a] them, as is evident to this day. Then they settled in their place, because there was pasture for their flocks. 42And five hundred of these Simeonites, led by Pelatiah, Neariah, Rephaiah and Uzziel, the sons of Ishi, invaded the hill country of Seir. 43They killed the remaining Amalekites who had escaped, and they have lived there to this day.

Reuben

5 The sons of Reuben the firstborn of Israel (he was the first-born, but when he defiled his father's marriage bed, his rights as firstborn were given to the sons of Joseph son of Israel; so he could not be listed in the genealogical record in accordance with his birthright, 2and though Judah was the strongest of his brothers and a ruler came from him, the rights of the firstborn belonged to Joseph)— 3the sons of Reuben the firstborn of Israel:

Hanoch, Pallu, Hezron and Carmi.

4The descendants of Joel:

Shemaiah his son, Gog his son,

Shimei his son, 5Micah his son,

Reaiah his son, Baal his son,

6and Beerah his son, whom Tiglath-Pileser[b] king of Assyria took into exile. Beerah was a leader of the Reubenites.

7Their relatives by clans, listed according to their genealogical records:

Jeiel the chief, Zechariah, 8and Bela son of Azaz, the son of Shema, the son of Joel. They settled in the area from Aroer to Nebo and Baal Meon. 9To the east they occupied the land up to the edge of the desert that extends to the Euphrates River, because their livestock had increased in Gilead.

10During Saul's reign they waged war against the Hagrites, who were defeated at their hands; they occupied the dwellings of the Hagrites throughout the entire region east of Gilead.

Gad

11The Gadites lived next to them in Bashan, as far as Salecah:

12Joel was the chief, Shapham the second, then Janai and Shaphat, in Bashan.

13Their relatives, by families, were:

Michael, Meshullam, Sheba, Jorai, Jacan, Zia and Eber— seven in all.

14These were the sons of Abihail son of Huri, the son of Jaroah, the son of Gilead, the son of Michael, the son of Jeshishai, the son of Jahdo, the son of Buz.

15Ahi son of Abdiel, the son of Guni, was head of their family.

16The Gadites lived in Gilead, in Bashan and its outlying villages, and on all the pasturelands of Sharon as far as they extended.

17All these were entered in the genealogical records during the reigns of Jotham king of Judah and Jeroboam king of Israel.

18The Reubenites, the Gadites and the half-tribe of Manasseh had 44,760 men ready for military service—able-bodied men who

Do you keep photos of distant relatives you've never met? Why?

Chapter 5 records the "trans-Jordan tribes"—those who settled east of the Jordan, while Joshua led the Hebrews west into Canaan. 1. What privilege did big brother Reuben forfeit? What does this say about God's justice and mercy? 2. Imagine Beerah, cut off from the bulk of Israel by a water barrier, defeated by a pagan king and taken captive: How does he explain his share in the covenant to his children? 3. What special skill do the Reubenites possess (vv. 9f)? Reuben shows that "As you sow, so shall you reap." How does son Hanoch suffer, also?

1. How has your spiritual inheritance been affected, for good and for bad, by your actions? By your parents' decisions? 2. Your family may also have felt cut off by natural boundaries: How so?

1. If you could choose your neighbor, would you prefer: (a) Sheriff's deputy? (b) Retirees? (c) Car mechanic? (d) Or whom? 2. Describe your most friendly neighbor ever.

1. What kind of neighbors were Gadites to Reubenites (vv. 18–19)? 2. Given their valiant bravery and accumulated wealth, how did their history as a tribe end (v. 22)? 3. Even in defeat, how might the Gadites have found faith and hope during their exile? 4. How is God portrayed here?

1. Are periods of prosperity or lack of it a part of your family's life cycle? How so? How would you feel about working hard only to have someone take (or tax) it all away? 2. From what self-imposed or personal "exiles" have you had to recover? How did you recover?

a41 The Hebrew term refers to the irrevocable giving over of things or persons to the Lord, often by totally destroying them.   b6 Hebrew Tilgath-Pilneser, a variant of Tiglath-Pileser; also in verse 26

could handle shield and sword, who could use a bow, and who were trained for battle. [19]They waged war against the Hagrites, Jetur, Naphish and Nodab. [20]They were helped in fighting them, and God handed the Hagrites and all their allies over to them, because they cried out to him during the battle. He answered their prayers, because they trusted in him. [21]They seized the livestock of the Hagrites—fifty thousand camels, two hundred fifty thousand sheep and two thousand donkeys. They also took one hundred thousand people captive, [22]and many others fell slain, because the battle was God's. And they occupied the land until the exile.

The Half-Tribe of Manasseh

[23]The people of the half-tribe of Manasseh were numerous; they settled in the land from Bashan to Baal Hermon, that is, to Senir (Mount Hermon).

[24]These were the heads of their families: Epher, Ishi, Eliel, Azriel, Jeremiah, Hodaviah and Jahdiel. They were brave warriors, famous men, and heads of their families. [25]But they were unfaithful to the God of their fathers and prostituted themselves to the gods of the peoples of the land, whom God had destroyed before them. [26]So the God of Israel stirred up the spirit of Pul king of Assyria (that is, Tiglath-Pileser king of Assyria), who took the Reubenites, the Gadites and the half-tribe of Manasseh into exile. He took them to Halah, Habor, Hara and the river of Gozan, where they are to this day.

Levi

6 The sons of Levi:
  Gershon, Kohath and Merari.
  [2]The sons of Kohath:
  Amram, Izhar, Hebron and Uzziel.
  [3]The children of Amram:
  Aaron, Moses and Miriam.
  The sons of Aaron:
  Nadab, Abihu, Eleazar and Ithamar.
  [4]Eleazar was the father of Phinehas,
  Phinehas the father of Abishua,
  [5]Abishua the father of Bukki,
  Bukki the father of Uzzi,
  [6]Uzzi the father of Zerahiah,
  Zerahiah the father of Meraioth,
  [7]Meraioth the father of Amariah,
  Amariah the father of Ahitub,
  [8]Ahitub the father of Zadok,
  Zadok the father of Ahimaaz,
  [9]Ahimaaz the father of Azariah,
  Azariah the father of Johanan,
  [10]Johanan the father of Azariah (it was he who served as priest in the temple Solomon built in Jerusalem),
  [11]Azariah the father of Amariah,
  Amariah the father of Ahitub,
  [12]Ahitub the father of Zadok,
  Zadok the father of Shallum,
  [13]Shallum the father of Hilkiah,
  Hilkiah the father of Azariah,
  [14]Azariah the father of Seraiah,
  and Seraiah the father of Jehozadak.
[15]Jehozadak was deported when the LORD sent Judah and Jerusalem into exile by the hand of Nebuchadnezzar.

If deputies and doctors are the preferred neighbors, what kind of neighbors must you try extra hard to like?

1. Of the qualities which typify the half-tribe of Manasseh, which do you admire? Despise? Why? 2. How is the Manasseh clan like, and unlike, the Gad clan?

How do the virtues and vices of Manasseh compare to those of your own neighbors?

---

1. Who is your favorite pastor of all time? 2. Who is your favorite minister from your childhood days, if you had one? Why that one? 3. Have you ever aspired to be a minister or priest? Why or why not?

1. What two neat halves does this section divide into? Why does the chronicler seem to begin again in verse 16? 2. What names in this list are familiar to you? Why? 3. The Levites are given as much prominence as what other tribe? Why is that (see Nu 3:5–10)? 4. What trouble did the first chief priest, Aaron, have with his two oldest sons (see Lev 10:1–3)? What attitude does Aaron show after their demise? 5. If Aaron is the first high priest, what is the chronicler's intention in this genealogy? 6. Two of the priests listed here are briefly described (vv. 10,15): Which had the tougher job? 7. Geneatectives may search the following texts (Ne 11:11; 2Ki 22; 25:18,21; 1Chr 29:22; Ezr 3:2) for clues to these four riddles: (a) Which high priest would be remembered as a martyr? (b) Which high priest led a reformation in the worship of God by discovering a long-lost book? (c) Which served Israel the longest following the greatest time-gap in their formal worship? (d) Which served Israel's most famous king? 8. While the terrible

¹⁶The sons of Levi:

Gershon,ᵃ Kohath and Merari.

¹⁷These are the names of the sons of Gershon:

Libni and Shimei.

¹⁸The sons of Kohath:

Amram, Izhar, Hebron and Uzziel.

¹⁹The sons of Merari:

Mahli and Mushi.

These are the clans of the Levites listed according to their fathers:

²⁰Of Gershon:

Libni his son, Jehath his son,

Zimmah his son, ²¹Joah his son,

Iddo his son, Zerah his son

and Jeatherai his son.

²²The descendants of Kohath:

Amminadab his son, Korah his son,

Assir his son, ²³Elkanah his son,

Ebiasaph his son, Assir his son,

²⁴Tahath his son, Uriel his son,

Uzziah his son and Shaul his son.

²⁵The descendants of Elkanah:

Amasai, Ahimoth,

²⁶Elkanah his son,ᵇ Zophai his son,

Nahath his son, ²⁷Eliab his son,

Jeroham his son, Elkanah his son

and Samuel his son.ᶜ

²⁸The sons of Samuel:

Joelᵈ the firstborn

and Abijah the second son.

²⁹The descendants of Merari:

Mahli, Libni his son,

Shimei his son, Uzzah his son,

³⁰Shimea his son, Haggiah his son

and Asaiah his son.

The Temple Musicians

³¹These are the men David put in charge of the music in the house of the Lᴏʀᴅ after the ark came to rest there. ³²They ministered with music before the tabernacle, the Tent of Meeting, until Solomon built the temple of the Lᴏʀᴅ in Jerusalem. They performed their duties according to the regulations laid down for them.

³³Here are the men who served, together with their sons:

From the Kohathites:

Heman, the musician,

the son of Joel, the son of Samuel,

³⁴the son of Elkanah, the son of Jeroham,

the son of Eliel, the son of Toah,

³⁵the son of Zuph, the son of Elkanah,

the son of Mahath, the son of Amasai,

³⁶the son of Elkanah, the son of Joel,

the son of Azariah, the son of Zephaniah,

³⁷the son of Tahath, the son of Assir,

the son of Ebiasaph, the son of Korah,

ᵃ16 Hebrew *Gershom*, a variant of *Gershon*; also in verses 17, 20, 43, 62 and 71
ᵇ26 Some Hebrew manuscripts, Septuagint and Syriac; most Hebrew manuscripts *Ahimoth*
²⁶*and Elkanah. The sons of Elkanah:* ᶜ27 Some Septuagint manuscripts (see also
1 Samuel 1:19,20 and 1 Chron. 6:33,34); Hebrew does not have *and Samuel his son.*
ᵈ28 Some Septuagint manuscripts and Syriac (see also 1 Samuel 8:2 and 1 Chron. 6:33);
Hebrew does not have *Joel.*

Nebuchadnezzar may have seemed invincible to Israel, he is a bit player in a larger drama according to the chronicler. Who writes the script for that drama? **9.** In verses 16ff, what new information is provided? What info is given two or more versions within this section? **10.** For geneatectives only: What well-known person, listed here as a Levite, is linked to a different tribe in the introduction to the Bible book which bears his name?

♡ Levi's descendants had the responsibility of instilling the family values learned from a long genealogy such as this one. This was to prepare them for their priestly duties in the years and centuries ahead. What attitudes, strengths and experiences come to mind by the mere mentioning of your distant relatives, especially your namesake?

☕ **1.** What kind of music gets the most air-time in your home? What instruments make most of that music? **2.** What differences in musical taste are apparent in your family? What accounts for those differences: Generational gap? Influence of rock culture? God-given abilities and preferences? Church-dictated no-no's?

📖 **1.** What does David do here (v. 31)? Up to now, what has he been chiefly concerned about (see 3:1–9)? **2.** Knowing their new king cared much about music and could make music himself (see 1Sa 16:14–23), how might that affect "Mr. and Mrs. Benjamite"? **3.** Would these Levite musicians play their B-flats and C-sharps, leaving the Hebrew equivalent of "heavy metal" to other groups, playing outside the temple? Why do you think so (v. 32)? **4.** Compare this list of Kohathites (vv. 33–38) with the previous ones (6:1ff, 16ff). What differences do you observe? Why trace Heman's contribution to the musicians' guild? **5.** Likewise, what is the meaning of Asaph's contribution among the Gershonites (vv. 38–43)? What do you know about the career of this leading vocalist/instrumentalist of Israel's golden age (see 16:4–7,37; 25:5–6; 2Ch 5:12; 29:30; 35:15; Ne 12:45–47)? What works of this composer do you know (see Ps 50,73–83)? **6.** The third group is the Merarites, featuring Ethan. How many generations of training did Ethan have behind him (vv. 44–47)? **7.** What separates the priestly line of Aaron from the rest of the Levites (vv. 48–49)? To whom does the chronicler trace all "rules and regs" of worship? **8.** Verses 50–53 repeat verses 4–8: What is the author's purpose in linking this list here with verse 49? **9.** Verses 54–81 list what resources? Why is the author so careful to list property outside the city limits? What kind of resources might be attached to such a list of "tax-exempt" real estate today? How might this list have been used to solve legal disputes? **10.** What cities are described in any way? See Numbers 35:5–34 for details about the special status of those cities: Who needed them? What problems did they solve? Why would the Levites be ideal caretakers for such sanctuaries? **11.** The Levites received all their property from allotments given to (or won by) other tribes. In some cases, this meant armed tribes must conquer and bequeath that area for the Levites. What special bonds, and resentments, could this cause?

♥ **1.** If your country's leader was intent on directing all the nation's professional music groups, what skills and ideas would you expect in the candidate of your political party? Would you like to live in a nation where most all music was performed by clergy and church workers? Or not? Why? **2.** Given the generations of training in music built into Heman, Asaph and Ethan, what kind of pressure from the laity are they laboring under? When have you faced similar pressure to perform and live up to your family name? **3.** The priests led Israel in making atonement in their daily worship and ritual. By comparison, how fine-tuned is your sense of God's awesomeness, and your frailty? **4.** The Levite's resources were widely known (once the

³⁸the son of Izhar, the son of Kohath,
  the son of Levi, the son of Israel;
³⁹and Heman's associate Asaph, who served at his right hand:
  Asaph son of Berekiah, the son of Shimea,
⁴⁰the son of Michael, the son of Baaseiah,[a]
  the son of Malkijah, ⁴¹the son of Ethni,
  the son of Zerah, the son of Adaiah,
⁴²the son of Ethan, the son of Zimmah,
  the son of Shimei, ⁴³the son of Jahath,
  the son of Gershon, the son of Levi;
⁴⁴and from their associates, the Merarites, at his left hand:
  Ethan son of Kishi, the son of Abdi,
  the son of Malluch, ⁴⁵the son of Hashabiah,
  the son of Amaziah, the son of Hilkiah,
⁴⁶the son of Amzi, the son of Bani,
  the son of Shemer, ⁴⁷the son of Mahli,
  the son of Mushi, the son of Merari,
  the son of Levi.

⁴⁸Their fellow Levites were assigned to all the other duties of the tabernacle, the house of God. ⁴⁹But Aaron and his descendants were the ones who presented offerings on the altar of burnt offering and on the altar of incense in connection with all that was done in the Most Holy Place, making atonement for Israel, in accordance with all that Moses the servant of God had commanded.

⁵⁰These were the descendants of Aaron:
  Eleazar his son, Phinehas his son,
  Abishua his son, ⁵¹Bukki his son,
  Uzzi his son, Zerahiah his son,
⁵²Meraioth his son, Amariah his son,
  Ahitub his son, ⁵³Zadok his son
  and Ahimaaz his son.

⁵⁴These were the locations of their settlements allotted as their territory (they were assigned to the descendants of Aaron who were from the Kohathite clan, because the first lot was for them): ⁵⁵They were given Hebron in Judah with its surrounding pasturelands. ⁵⁶But the fields and villages around the city were given to Caleb son of Jephunneh. ⁵⁷So the descendants of Aaron were given Hebron (a city of refuge), and Libnah,[b] Jattir, Eshtemoa, ⁵⁸Hilen, Debir, ⁵⁹Ashan, Juttah[c] and Beth Shemesh, together with their pasturelands. ⁶⁰And from the tribe of Benjamin they were given Gibeon,[d] Geba, Alemeth and Anathoth, together with their pasturelands.

These towns, which were distributed among the Kohathite clans, were thirteen in all.

⁶¹The rest of Kohath's descendants were allotted ten towns from the clans of half the tribe of Manasseh.

⁶²The descendants of Gershon, clan by clan, were allotted thirteen towns from the tribes of Issachar, Asher and Naphtali, and from the part of the tribe of Manasseh that is in Bashan.

⁶³The descendants of Merari, clan by clan, were allotted twelve towns from the tribes of Reuben, Gad and Zebulun.

⁶⁴So the Israelites gave the Levites these towns and their pas-

---

^a40 Most Hebrew manuscripts; some Hebrew manuscripts, one Septuagint manuscript and Syriac *Maaseiah*   ^b57 See Joshua 21:13; Hebrew *given the cities of refuge: Hebron, Libnah.*   ^c59 Syriac (see also Septuagint and Joshua 21:16); Hebrew does not have *Juttah.*   ^d60 See Joshua 21:17; Hebrew does not have *Gibeon.*

turelands. 65From the tribes of Judah, Simeon and Benjamin they allotted the previously named towns.

66Some of the Kohathite clans were given as their territory towns from the tribe of Ephraim.

67In the hill country of Ephraim they were given Shechem (a city of refuge), and Gezer,a 68Jokmeam, Beth Horon, 69Aijalon and Gath Rimmon, together with their pasturelands.

70And from half the tribe of Manasseh the Israelites gave Aner and Bileam, together with their pasturelands, to the rest of the Kohathite clans.

71The Gershonites received the following:
From the clan of the half-tribe of Manasseh
    they received Golan in Bashan and also Ashtaroth, together with their pasturelands;
72from the tribe of Issachar
    they received Kedesh, Daberath, 73Ramoth and Anem, together with their pasturelands;
74from the tribe of Asher
    they received Mashal, Abdon, 75Hukok and Rehob, together with their pasturelands;
76and from the tribe of Naphtali
    they received Kedesh in Galilee, Hammon and Kiriathaim, together with their pasturelands.

77The Merarites (the rest of the Levites) received the following:
From the tribe of Zebulun
    they received Jokneam, Kartah,b Rimmono and Tabor, together with their pasturelands;
78from the tribe of Reuben across the Jordan east of Jericho
    they received Bezer in the desert, Jahzah, 79Kedemoth and Mephaath, together with their pasturelands;
80and from the tribe of Gad
    they received Ramoth in Gilead, Mahanaim, 81Heshbon and Jazer, together with their pasturelands.

Issachar

7 The sons of Issachar:
  Tola, Puah, Jashub and Shimron—four in all.
2The sons of Tola:
  Uzzi, Rephaiah, Jeriel, Jahmai, Ibsam and Samuel—heads of their families. During the reign of David, the descendants of Tola listed as fighting men in their genealogy numbered 22,600.
3The son of Uzzi:
  Izrahiah.
  The sons of Izrahiah:
  Michael, Obadiah, Joel and Isshiah. All five of them were chiefs. 4According to their family genealogy, they had 36,000 men ready for battle, for they had many wives and children.
5The relatives who were fighting men belonging to all the clans of Issachar, as listed in their genealogy, were 87,000 in all.

Benjamin

6Three sons of Benjamin:
  Bela, Beker and Jediael.

---

a67 See Joshua 21:21; Hebrew given the cities of refuge: Shechem, Gezer.   b77 See Septuagint and Joshua 21:34; Hebrew does not have Jokneam, Kartah.

---

chronicler published them). For what resources have you been given stewardship duties? Would you mind making them public to your church or even your small group? Why? **5.** If the church is to continue the Levites' role in providing sanctuary, what role would your church be prepared to take regarding criminal refugees? Child abuse refugees? Political refugees? **6.** The armed tribes of Israel were to give a portion of their property to the Levites (and possibly also do battle for them), causing some indebtedness and resentment. We see this today in similar laity and clergy tensions. Which of today's abuses need attention where you live and worship? Why would you share your personal gains with your "Levite" minister?

---

1. In your family tree, are there any branches that had only daughters? Who in your small group comes from a line that produces mostly females? **2.** What names (maiden name, spouse's pet name, childhood nicknames) do you go by in various circles? Would a later generation be able to recognize the one person behind all the names? Why or why not?

1. Comparing the *names* and *numbers* listed here, how many generations do you think are skipped over? What function does this census seem to have served at one time (vv. 2,4,5,7,9,11)? **2.** Comparing these numbers to earlier surveys (see Ge 46:13; Nu 26:25), is Issachar a "growth clan" or a "declining tribe"? **3.** Compare this list of Benjamin's three sons with other lists (see 8:1–2; Ge 46:21; Nu 26:38–39). How do you account for the differences? What does Bela's repeated mention say about the significance of firstborn sons? **4.** Compare the same lists for the sons of that firstborn Bela. Why are no two names the same? What purpose is served by such variable lists? Or do verses 6–12 more suitably fit the clans of Zebulun and Dan (as 7:6–12 does not match with what is known of Benjamin's lineage)? **5.** How might Manasseh qualify for "My Most Unforgettable Character" in *Readers' Digest* (or at least in Joseph's clan, see Ge 41:51)? **6.** Manasseh's clan seems dominated by women: What does that suggest? A wife and sister with the same name (vv. 15–16) implies what? To dismiss one son who "had only daughters" not worth naming (see Nu 26:33) implies what? **7.** Of what famous grandparents can Ephraim's clan brag (see Ge 41:51,52; 46:20)? And of what favorite son, ten generations (400 years) removed from Joseph (vv. 25–27)? **8.** How has Ephraim's clan felt the misfortune of two "cattle thieves" and "frontier justice" (vv. 21b–24)? **9.** From Joshua 16–17, what do you know about the settlements listed in verses 28–29? In limiting Joseph's heirs to this area, what is the chronicler's point? **10.** If Ephraim's clan is noted for its grief and its favorite son Joshua, what are "Asher" (see Ge 30:9–13) and his clan noted for (v. 40)? **11.** Of all the genealogies in chapter 7, which ones are "linear" (tracing a single line of descent) and which are "segmented" (tracing several lines)? What does this say about the chronicler's purpose?

♡ **1.** With this chapter reading like a military roster or draft lottery, the protection function surely dominates the chronicler's concerns. How willing are you to be counted among the protectors of your people? Who in your town could use "fighting men" to escort them? How can you help others feel safe where you live? **2.** How have you learned, like Makir and other descendants of "unforgettable" Manasseh, to forget the troubles of the past (no sons, no eligible women) and make the best of the hand you are dealt? **3.** What grief-stricken families does Ephraim's clan bring to mind for you? What are you all doing to help families recover a sense of hope after suffering loss and grief? **4.** How would this chapter help ancient Israel (and you) answer the age-old question, "Is God still interested in us?"

7The sons of Bela:

Ezbon, Uzzi, Uzziel, Jerimoth and Iri, heads of families—five in all. Their genealogical record listed 22,034 fighting men.

8The sons of Beker:

Zemirah, Joash, Eliezer, Elioenai, Omri, Jeremoth, Abijah, Anathoth and Alemeth. All these were the sons of Beker. **9**Their genealogical record listed the heads of families and 20,200 fighting men.

10The son of Jediael:

Bilhan.

The sons of Bilhan:

Jeush, Benjamin, Ehud, Kenaanah, Zethan, Tarshish and Ahishahar. **11**All these sons of Jediael were heads of families. There were 17,200 fighting men ready to go out to war.

12The Shuppites and Huppites were the descendants of Ir, and the Hushites the descendants of Aher.

Naphtali

13The sons of Naphtali:

Jahziel, Guni, Jezer and Shillem*a*—the descendants of Bilhah.

Manasseh

14The descendants of Manasseh:

Asriel was his descendant through his Aramean concubine. She gave birth to Makir the father of Gilead. **15**Makir took a wife from among the Huppites and Shuppites. His sister's name was Maacah.

Another descendant was named Zelophehad, who had only daughters.

16Makir's wife Maacah gave birth to a son and named him Peresh. His brother was named Sheresh, and his sons were Ulam and Rakem.

17The son of Ulam:

Bedan.

These were the sons of Gilead son of Makir, the son of Manasseh. **18**His sister Hammoleketh gave birth to Ishhod, Abiezer and Mahlah.

19The sons of Shemida were:

Ahian, Shechem, Likhi and Aniam.

Ephraim

20The descendants of Ephraim:

Shuthelah, Bered his son,
Tahath his son, Eleadah his son,
Tahath his son, **21**Zabad his son
and Shuthelah his son.

Ezer and Elead were killed by the native-born men of Gath, when they went down to seize their livestock. **22**Their father Ephraim mourned for them many days, and his relatives came to comfort him. **23**Then he lay with his wife again, and she became pregnant and gave birth to a son. He named him Beriah,*b* because there had been misfortune in his family.

---

a13 Some Hebrew and Septuagint manuscripts (see also Gen. 46:24 and Num. 26:49); most Hebrew manuscripts *Shallum*   *b23* *Beriah* sounds like the Hebrew for *misfortune.*

²⁴His daughter was Sheerah, who built Lower and Upper Beth Horon as well as Uzzen Sheerah.
²⁵Rephah was his son, Resheph his son,ᵃ
Telah his son, Tahan his son,
²⁶Ladan his son, Ammihud his son,
Elishama his son, ²⁷Nun his son
and Joshua his son.

²⁸Their lands and settlements included Bethel and its surrounding villages, Naaran to the east, Gezer and its villages to the west, and Shechem and its villages all the way to Ayyah and its villages. ²⁹Along the borders of Manasseh were Beth Shan, Taanach, Megiddo and Dor, together with their villages. The descendants of Joseph son of Israel lived in these towns.

Asher

³⁰The sons of Asher:
Imnah, Ishvah, Ishvi and Beriah. Their sister was Serah.
³¹The sons of Beriah:
Heber and Malkiel, who was the father of Birzaith.
³²Heber was the father of Japhlet, Shomer and Hotham and of their sister Shua.
³³The sons of Japhlet:
Pasach, Bimhal and Ashvath.
These were Japhlet's sons.
³⁴The sons of Shomer:
Ahi, Rohgah,ᵇ Hubbah and Aram.
³⁵The sons of his brother Helem:
Zophah, Imna, Shelesh and Amal.
³⁶The sons of Zophah:
Suah, Harnepher, Shual, Beri, Imrah, ³⁷Bezer, Hod, Shamma, Shilshah, Ithranᶜ and Beera.
³⁸The sons of Jether:
Jephunneh, Pispah and Ara.
³⁹The sons of Ulla:
Arah, Hanniel and Rizia.
⁴⁰All these were descendants of Asher—heads of families, choice men, brave warriors and outstanding leaders. The number of men ready for battle, as listed in their genealogy, was 26,000.

The Genealogy of Saul the Benjamite

8 Benjamin was the father of Bela his firstborn,
Ashbel the second son, Aharah the third,
²Nohah the fourth and Rapha the fifth.
³The sons of Bela were:
Addar, Gera, Abihud,ᵈ ⁴Abishua, Naaman, Ahoah, ⁵Gera, Shephuphan and Huram.
⁶These were the descendants of Ehud, who were heads of families of those living in Geba and were deported to Manahath:
⁷Naaman, Ahijah, and Gera, who deported them and who was the father of Uzza and Ahihud.
⁸Sons were born to Shaharaim in Moab after he had divorced his wives Hushim and Baara. ⁹By his wife Hodesh he had Jobab, Zibia, Mesha, Malcam, ¹⁰Jeuz, Sakia and Mirmah. These were his sons, heads of families. ¹¹By Hushim he had Abitub and Elpaal.

ᵃ25 Some Septuagint manuscripts; Hebrew does not have *his son*. ᵇ34 Or *of his brother Shomer: Rohgah* ᶜ37 Possibly a variant of *Jether* ᵈ3 Or *Gera the father of Ehud*

1. When have you been jealous of a younger sibling who got more press than you did for similar accomplishments? 2. What did your parents almost name you but didn't? Why not? Likewise, with your children, any leftover or runner-up names?

1. Only Judah and Levi get more press coverage of their descendants by the chronicler. What does the inclusion of this extensive genealogy of Benjamin imply about the purpose of the chronicler? Who from this tribe is he interested in? Why extend his line from the Patriarchs all the way to the Exile? 2. What likely embarrassing social arrangements and family blessings do you see in verses 8–11? From the scant hints offered here, why do you think Shaharaim divorced not one wife,

but two? Could he have acted within his rights? How so? **3.** What relationship do Ner and Kish share here (vv. 31,33)? How does that compare with the record in 1 Samuel 9:1 and 1 Samuel 14:51? Why the variance? **4.** Loyal Israelites despised the pagan god Baal. How then do you account for Baal-names given to Saul's sons and grandsons (vv. 33–34), names which were later changed (see 2Sa 2:8; 4:4)? **5.** What is the "weakest link" in the chain of Saul's descendants? What does this say about God's enduring love for the Benjamite tribe?

♡ **1.** Who do you know who has changed his or her given name? What purpose does a pseudonym serve? Under what conditions would you change yours? **2.** The fortunes of families often change rapidly, being just one generation away from extinction. In the line of King Saul, this is true career-wise, biologically, spiritually. How is that true of your family? Who will inherit the family business? Any male heirs to pass along the family name? Any spiritual heirs to spread God's name? **3.** What's in a name, yours or your children's? How can one overdo the meaning of a name and saddle a kid for life?

1. How many times during the week does the "platoon system" (i.e. working in shifts) help you get things done: Carpooling kids? Relieving shift workers? Assembly line duties? Co-parenting? Babysitting? After-school care? Church work? Health, education and welfare services? Other? **2.** What has happened to you and yours when you try to go it alone

¹²The sons of Elpaal:

Eber, Misham, Shemed (who built Ono and Lod with its surrounding villages), ¹³and Beriah and Shema, who were heads of families of those living in Aijalon and who drove out the inhabitants of Gath.

¹⁴Ahio, Shashak, Jeremoth, ¹⁵Zebadiah, Arad, Eder, ¹⁶Michael, Ishpah and Joha were the sons of Beriah.

¹⁷Zebadiah, Meshullam, Hizki, Heber, ¹⁸Ishmerai, Izliah and Jobab were the sons of Elpaal.

¹⁹Jakim, Zicri, Zabdi, ²⁰Elienai, Zillethai, Eliel, ²¹Adaiah, Beraiah and Shimrath were the sons of Shimei.

²²Ishpan, Eber, Eliel, ²³Abdon, Zicri, Hanan, ²⁴Hananiah, Elam, Anthothijah, ²⁵Iphdeiah and Penuel were the sons of Shashak.

²⁶Shamsherai, Shehariah, Athaliah, ²⁷Jaareshiah, Elijah and Zicri were the sons of Jeroham.

²⁸All these were heads of families, chiefs as listed in their genealogy, and they lived in Jerusalem.

²⁹Jeiel*ᵃ* the father*ᵇ* of Gibeon lived in Gibeon.

His wife's name was Maacah, ³⁰and his firstborn son was Abdon, followed by Zur, Kish, Baal, Ner,*ᶜ* Nadab, ³¹Gedor, Ahio, Zeker ³²and Mikloth, who was the father of Shimeah. They too lived near their relatives in Jerusalem.

³³Ner was the father of Kish, Kish the father of Saul, and Saul the father of Jonathan, Malki-Shua, Abinadab and Esh-Baal.*ᵈ*

³⁴The son of Jonathan:

Merib-Baal,*ᵉ* who was the father of Micah.

³⁵The sons of Micah:

Pithon, Melech, Tarea and Ahaz.

³⁶Ahaz was the father of Jehoaddah, Jehoaddah was the father of Alemeth, Azmaveth and Zimri, and Zimri was the father of Moza. ³⁷Moza was the father of Binea; Raphah was his son, Eleasah his son and Azel his son.

³⁸Azel had six sons, and these were their names:

Azrikam, Bokeru, Ishmael, Sheariah, Obadiah and Hanan. All these were the sons of Azel.

³⁹The sons of his brother Eshek:

Ulam his firstborn, Jeush the second son and Eliphelet the third. ⁴⁰The sons of Ulam were brave warriors who could handle the bow. They had many sons and grandsons—150 in all.

All these were the descendants of Benjamin.

9 All Israel was listed in the genealogies recorded in the book of the kings of Israel.

The People in Jerusalem

The people of Judah were taken captive to Babylon because of their unfaithfulness. ²Now the first to resettle on their own property in their own towns were some Israelites, priests, Levites and temple servants.

³Those from Judah, from Benjamin, and from Ephraim and Manasseh who lived in Jerusalem were:

ᵃ29 Some Septuagint manuscripts (see also 1 Chron. 9:35); Hebrew does not have *Jeiel*.
ᵇ29 Father may mean *civic leader* or *military leader.*   *ᶜ30* Some Septuagint manuscripts (see also 1 Chron. 9:36); Hebrew does not have *Ner*.   *ᵈ33* Also known as *Ish-Bosheth*   *ᵉ34* Also known as *Mephibosheth*

4Uthai son of Ammihud, the son of Omri, the son of Imri, the son of Bani, a descendant of Perez son of Judah.

5Of the Shilonites:

Asaiah the firstborn and his sons.

6Of the Zerahites:

Jeuel.

The people from Judah numbered 690.

7Of the Benjamites:

Sallu son of Meshullam, the son of Hodaviah, the son of Hassenuah;

8Ibneiah son of Jeroham; Elah son of Uzzi, the son of Micri; and Meshullam son of Shephatiah, the son of Reuel, the son of Ibnijah.

9The people from Benjamin, as listed in their genealogy, numbered 956. All these men were heads of their families.

10Of the priests:

Jedaiah; Jehoiarib; Jakin;

11Azariah son of Hilkiah, the son of Meshullam, the son of Zadok, the son of Meraioth, the son of Ahitub, the official in charge of the house of God;

12Adaiah son of Jeroham, the son of Pashhur, the son of Malkijah; and Maasai son of Adiel, the son of Jahzerah, the son of Meshullam, the son of Meshillemith, the son of Immer.

13The priests, who were heads of families, numbered 1,760. They were able men, responsible for ministering in the house of God.

14Of the Levites:

Shemaiah son of Hasshub, the son of Azrikam, the son of Hashabiah, a Merarite; 15Bakbakkar, Heresh, Galal and Mattaniah son of Mica, the son of Zicri, the son of Asaph; 16Obadiah son of Shemaiah, the son of Galal, the son of Jeduthun; and Berekiah son of Asa, the son of Elkanah, who lived in the villages of the Netophathites.

17The gatekeepers:

Shallum, Akkub, Talmon, Ahiman and their brothers, Shallum their chief 18being stationed at the King's Gate on the east, up to the present time. These were the gatekeepers belonging to the camp of the Levites. 19Shallum son of Kore, the son of Ebiasaph, the son of Korah, and his fellow gatekeepers from his family (the Korahites) were responsible for guarding the thresholds of the Tent*a* just as their fathers had been responsible for guarding the entrance to the dwelling of the LORD. 20In earlier times Phinehas son of Eleazar was in charge of the gatekeepers, and the LORD was with him. 21Zechariah son of Meshelemiah was the gatekeeper at the entrance to the Tent of Meeting.

22Altogether, those chosen to be gatekeepers at the thresholds numbered 212. They were registered by genealogy in their villages. The gatekeepers had been assigned to their positions of trust by David and Samuel the seer. 23They and their descendants were in charge of guarding the gates of the house of the LORD—the house called the Tent. 24The gatekeepers were on the four sides: east, west, north and south. 25Their brothers in their villages had to come from time to time and share their duties for seven-day periods. 26But the four principal gatekeepers, who were Levites, were entrusted with the responsibility for the rooms and treasuries in

a 19 That is, the temple; also in verses 21 and 23

and not be bothered with platooning?

📖 1. What is the time gap between verses 1 and 2? After years in captivity, and suffering great personal and material loss, what problems must the Israelites deal with in recovering their grand heritage? For example, how did they settle the issue of who owned what property? And what resources could they rely upon to begin again? 2. Why do you think "some Israelites [laity], priests, Levites and temple servants" (v. 2) were the first to resettle the land? What services would they add to nation-building that valiant warriors or clever architects could not? 3. Where else do the returnees come from (v. 3)? How does this migration from north and south flesh out the meaning of "all Israel" (v. 1; see 11:1–4)? 4. What do priests listed in 9:10–13 have in common with those listed in 6:12–13? What is the meaning of such close ties with the past for contemporary returnees? 5. Why mention here all the gatekeepers and their duties? What other clues do you see here that indicate the restored community of Israel was primarily a religious community? 6. Which of the job assignments seem menial? Which require special skill, the right connections or the trust of VIPs? Which were performed "day and night"? Which required weekly shift rotations? Who had the graveyard shift? What advantages did this platoon system likely hold for Israel? 7. Carrying forward "something old and something new" helps many couples forge a new identity and begin again in married life. How was this true for the returning Israelites who had to forge a new identity out of resources from the past?

♡ 1. Why did the Israelites take such precautions about guarding the "Tent of God"? Today, what sacred buildings are guarded heavily? 2. In what sense have you inherited charge of the key to the house of God? Who are you letting in ... or keeping out? 3. What special offerings and activities does your church reserve for weekly observance? 4. Who carries responsibilities for rules, rituals, receipts and recipes in your place of worship? 5. Why is movement from town to town, such as the weekly Israelite platoon system afforded, important to the life and health of

Christians today? How does your fellowship encourage delegation of its leadership roles and full participation by its members? What re-entry points do you have for people disoriented by great personal and material loss?

What's the "oldest line in the book" when you are trying to get to know someone "new"?

1. Where have you seen these names before? Why dredge up Saul's family line one more time? Why is it repeated in this context? **2.** To you geneatectives, what six variances do you find in the two lists? How do you account for that?

What well-known persons in our day need help in rewriting the public view of them? As with Israel and Saul, how do we overcome the "people we love to hate" syndrome?

---

1. Where were you when JFK or Martin Luther King was shot? How did the news of their deaths hit you? **2.** Which way do you think you might die: "Rust out" (old age)? "Burn out" (in your prime)? Or "drop out" (in some accident)?

1. Put yourself in this story, amid slain comrades, fiercely defending your king: How do you feel when the enemy catches up with Saul and his sons? How do you react to his death? Why do you abandon your homestead just because your king has died? Why do you risk taking Saul's head and armor to a place of honor? **2.** As Saul, why do you ask your armorbearer to kill you? As Saul's armor-

---

the house of God. [27]They would spend the night stationed around the house of God, because they had to guard it; and they had charge of the key for opening it each morning.

[28]Some of them were in charge of the articles used in the temple service; they counted them when they were brought in and when they were taken out. [29]Others were assigned to take care of the furnishings and all the other articles of the sanctuary, as well as the flour and wine, and the oil, incense and spices. [30]But some of the priests took care of mixing the spices. [31]A Levite named Mattithiah, the firstborn son of Shallum the Korahite, was entrusted with the responsibility for baking the offering bread. [32]Some of their Kohathite brothers were in charge of preparing for every Sabbath the bread set out on the table.

[33]Those who were musicians, heads of Levite families, stayed in the rooms of the temple and were exempt from other duties because they were responsible for the work day and night.

[34]All these were heads of Levite families, chiefs as listed in their genealogy, and they lived in Jerusalem.

The Genealogy of Saul

[35]Jeiel the father[a] of Gibeon lived in Gibeon.

His wife's name was Maacah, [36]and his firstborn son was Abdon, followed by Zur, Kish, Baal, Ner, Nadab, [37]Gedor, Ahio, Zechariah and Mikloth. [38]Mikloth was the father of Shimeam. They too lived near their relatives in Jerusalem.

[39]Ner was the father of Kish, Kish the father of Saul, and Saul the father of Jonathan, Malki-Shua, Abinadab and Esh-Baal.[b]

[40]The son of Jonathan:

Merib-Baal,[c] who was the father of Micah.

[41]The sons of Micah:

Pithon, Melech, Tahrea and Ahaz.[d]

[42]Ahaz was the father of Jadah, Jadah[e] was the father of Alemeth, Azmaveth and Zimri, and Zimri was the father of Moza. [43]Moza was the father of Binea; Rephaiah was his son, Eleasah his son and Azel his son.

[44]Azel had six sons, and these were their names:

Azrikam, Bokeru, Ishmael, Sheariah, Obadiah and Hanan. These were the sons of Azel.

Saul Takes His Life

10 Now the Philistines fought against Israel; the Israelites fled before them, and many fell slain on Mount Gilboa. [2]The Philistines pressed hard after Saul and his sons, and they killed his sons Jonathan, Abinadab and Malki-Shua. [3]The fighting grew fierce around Saul, and when the archers overtook him, they wounded him.

[4]Saul said to his armor-bearer, "Draw your sword and run me through, or these uncircumcised fellows will come and abuse me."

But his armor-bearer was terrified and would not do it; so Saul took his own sword and fell on it. [5]When the armor-bearer saw that Saul was dead, he too fell on his sword and died. [6]So Saul and his three sons died, and all his house died together.

[7]When all the Israelites in the valley saw that the army had fled

---

[a]35 *Father* may mean *civic leader* or *military leader.*   [b]39 Also known as *Ish-Bosheth*   [c]40 Also known as *Mephibosheth*   [d]41 Vulgate and Syriac (see also Septuagint and 1 Chron. 8:35); Hebrew does not have *and Ahaz.*   [e]42 Some Hebrew manuscripts and Septuagint (see also 1 Chron. 8:36); most Hebrew manuscripts *Jarah, Jarah*

and that Saul and his sons had died, they abandoned their towns and fled. And the Philistines came and occupied them.

⁸The next day, when the Philistines came to strip the dead, they found Saul and his sons fallen on Mount Gilboa. ⁹They stripped him and took his head and his armor, and sent messengers throughout the land of the Philistines to proclaim the news among their idols and their people. ¹⁰They put his armor in the temple of their gods and hung up his head in the temple of Dagon.

¹¹When all the inhabitants of Jabesh Gilead heard of everything the Philistines had done to Saul, ¹²all their valiant men went and took the bodies of Saul and his sons and brought them to Jabesh. Then they buried their bones under the great tree in Jabesh, and they fasted seven days.

¹³Saul died because he was unfaithful to the LORD; he did not keep the word of the LORD and even consulted a medium for guidance, ¹⁴and did not inquire of the LORD. So the LORD put him to death and turned the kingdom over to David son of Jesse.

David Becomes King Over Israel

11 All Israel came together to David at Hebron and said, "We are your own flesh and blood. ²In the past, even while Saul was king, you were the one who led Israel on their military campaigns. And the LORD your God said to you, 'You will shepherd my people Israel, and you will become their ruler.'"

³When all the elders of Israel had come to King David at Hebron, he made a compact with them at Hebron before the LORD, and they anointed David king over Israel, as the LORD had promised through Samuel.

David Conquers Jerusalem

⁴David and all the Israelites marched to Jerusalem (that is, Jebus). The Jebusites who lived there ⁵said to David, "You will not get in here." Nevertheless, David captured the fortress of Zion, the City of David.

⁶David had said, "Whoever leads the attack on the Jebusites will become commander-in-chief." Joab son of Zeruiah went up first, and so he received the command.

⁷David then took up residence in the fortress, and so it was called the City of David. ⁸He built up the city around it, from the supporting terraces* to the surrounding wall, while Joab restored the rest of the city. ⁹And David became more and more powerful, because the LORD Almighty was with him.

David's Mighty Men

¹⁰These were the chiefs of David's mighty men—they, together with all Israel, gave his kingship strong support to extend it over the whole land, as the LORD had promised— ¹¹this is the list of David's mighty men:

Jashobeam,ᵇ a Hacmonite, was chief of the officersᶜ; he raised his spear against three hundred men, whom he killed in one encounter.

¹²Next to him was Eleazar son of Dodai the Ahohite, one of the three mighty men. ¹³He was with David at Pas Dammim when the Philistines gathered there for battle. At a place where there was a field full of barley, the troops fled from the Philistines. ¹⁴But they took their stand in the middle of the field. They defended it and

---

bearer, why do you refuse to take Saul's life (see 2Sa 1:14), but take your own? **3.** Why does the chronicler say "all his house died together" (v. 6), when one son survives to succeed Saul (see 2Sa 2:8–9)? **4.** What view of Saul's history and God's will does the chronicler offer?

♡ **1.** The Puritans stressed "dying well" as a Christian witness. How can you be prepared to die well? **2.** What is the relation between living well and dying well as typified by Saul? Why is Saul's story sad?

🍵 **1.** Ever since you have been of voting age, how many times have you backed the eventual winning President? What big losers will you admit voting for? **2.** What up-hill battle have you won in recent years? How did that make you feel?

📖 **1.** What unanimous ballot does the chronicler cast for David (see 2Sa 5:4–5, where a split kingdom was indicated)? **2.** What does David do that others said couldn't be done? What managerial and motivational techniques does David use to reach his impossible goal?

♡ Do you think God's will has anything to do with national elections or national prosperity, as was so obvious in David's day?

🍵 **1.** What do you consider one of your greatest accomplishments? Why? What obstacles did you have to overcome to do it? **2.** Which "mighty man" character was your favorite and why: The Bionic Man? Superman? Batman? Lone Ranger? Mighty Mouse? Popeye? Robin Hood? Roy Rogers?

📖 **1.** What in this chapter suggests that David knew he could not fulfill *by himself* God's will for the nation? What kind of person do you imagine the typical "mighty man of David" was? Do they seem cartoonish to you? Or do they remind you of David himself? **2.**

---

a8 Or *the Millo*   *b11* Possibly a variant of *Jashob-Baal*   *c11* Or *Thirty*; some Septuagint manuscripts *Three* (see also 2 Samuel 23:8)

Which mighty men do you think were "the Three" at the top of his list (vv. 12,15,18–19,21,24–25; see 2Sa 23:9b–11a, where a third one is named)? **3.** When in David's lifetime do you think the event of verses 15–19 occurred (see 1Sa 22:1 or 2Sa 5:17)? Why would a great military hero like David be hiding out in a cave? How do you think David felt when his three mighty men offered him the water? How would his men have felt when he then poured it on the ground? **4.** What do Abishai and Jashobeam have in common (vv. 11,20–21)? Why do you think Abishai was "doubly honored," commander of "the Three," but not among them (see 1Sa 26:6ff)? Who should get the greater honor for their victories? **5.** For what was Benaiah famous (vv. 22–25)? How are his exploits like David's? How was he honored? **6.** What names do you recognize among "the Thirty" (vv. 26–47)? What biblical events do their names bring to mind for you (e.g., Uriah the Hittite)? **7.** How many names are listed here (compare 2Sa 23:24–39)? What does the longer list here suggest about the fluidity of David's "thirty" best warriors? (Note, too, who else had "thirty with him.") Why would new officers be needed from time to time? **8.** What does such a loyal following of "chiefs" suggest about the common support David's kingship enjoyed from "all Israel" (v. 10)? What does all this tell you about God's support for David?

♡ **1.** Take a sample cross section of 100 average Christian soldiers in the Lord's army. Would you place yourself in the top 30? Why or why not? What strengths would you need to develop to be among your King's mighty warriors? **2.** When is bravery most obvious? How do you practice day-to-day for the rare crisis moment when such bravery is required? What enemies and obstacles would you bravely hope to strike down with God's help? In the near future, in what battle of yours would you like God to give you the victory? **3.** Do you feel like you are fighting any battles all by yourself? In years past, who have been the *spiritual giants* who have fought with you at your side? In what way might your small group provide reinforcements today? **4.** Every nation memorializes their "mighty" men and women. Where do you find such lists today? **5.** In the

struck the Philistines down, and the LORD brought about a great victory.

[15] Three of the thirty chiefs came down to David to the rock at the cave of Adullam, while a band of Philistines was encamped in the Valley of Rephaim. [16] At that time David was in the stronghold, and the Philistine garrison was at Bethlehem. [17] David longed for water and said, "Oh, that someone would get me a drink of water from the well near the gate of Bethlehem!" [18] So the Three broke through the Philistine lines, drew water from the well near the gate of Bethlehem and carried it back to David. But he refused to drink it; instead, he poured it out before the LORD. [19] "God forbid that I should do this!" he said. "Should I drink the blood of these men who went at the risk of their lives?" Because they risked their lives to bring it back, David would not drink it.

Such were the exploits of the three mighty men.

[20] Abishai the brother of Joab was chief of the Three. He raised his spear against three hundred men, whom he killed, and so he became as famous as the Three. [21] He was doubly honored above the Three and became their commander, even though he was not included among them.

[22] Benaiah son of Jehoiada was a valiant fighter from Kabzeel, who performed great exploits. He struck down two of Moab's best men. He also went down into a pit on a snowy day and killed a lion. [23] And he struck down an Egyptian who was seven and a half feet[a] tall. Although the Egyptian had a spear like a weaver's rod in his hand, Benaiah went against him with a club. He snatched the spear from the Egyptian's hand and killed him with his own spear. [24] Such were the exploits of Benaiah son of Jehoiada; he too was as famous as the three mighty men. [25] He was held in greater honor than any of the Thirty, but he was not included among the Three. And David put him in charge of his bodyguard.

[26] The mighty men were:

Asahel the brother of Joab,
Elhanan son of Dodo from Bethlehem,
[27] Shammoth the Harorite,
Helez the Pelonite,
[28] Ira son of Ikkesh from Tekoa,
Abiezer from Anathoth,
[29] Sibbecai the Hushathite,
Ilai the Ahohite,
[30] Maharai the Netophathite,
Heled son of Baanah the Netophathite,
[31] Ithai son of Ribai from Gibeah in Benjamin,
Benaiah the Pirathonite,
[32] Hurai from the ravines of Gaash,
Abiel the Arbathite,
[33] Azmaveth the Baharumite,
Eliahba the Shaalbonite,
[34] the sons of Hashem the Gizonite,
Jonathan son of Shagee the Hararite,
[35] Ahiam son of Sacar the Hararite,
Eliphal son of Ur,
[36] Hepher the Mekerathite,
Ahijah the Pelonite,
[37] Hezro the Carmelite,
Naarai son of Ezbai,
[38] Joel the brother of Nathan,

---

a23 Hebrew *five cubits* (about 2.3 meters)

Mibhar son of Hagri,
³⁹Zelek the Ammonite,
Naharai the Berothite, the armor-bearer of Joab son of Zeruiah,
⁴⁰Ira the Ithrite,
Gareb the Ithrite,
⁴¹Uriah the Hittite,
Zabad son of Ahlai,
⁴²Adina son of Shiza the Reubenite, who was chief of the Reubenites, and the thirty with him,
⁴³Hanan son of Maacah,
Joshaphat the Mithnite,
⁴⁴Uzzia the Ashterathite,
Shama and Jeiel the sons of Hotham the Aroerite,
⁴⁵Jediael son of Shimri,
his brother Joha the Tizite,
⁴⁶Eliel the Mahavite,
Jeribai and Joshaviah the sons of Elnaam,
Ithmah the Moabite,
⁴⁷Eliel, Obed and Jaasiel the Mezobaite.

Warriors Join David

12 These were the men who came to David at Ziklag, while he was banished from the presence of Saul son of Kish (they were among the warriors who helped him in battle; ²they were armed with bows and were able to shoot arrows or to sling stones right-handed or left-handed; they were kinsmen of Saul from the tribe of Benjamin):

³Ahiezer their chief and Joash the sons of Shemaah the Gibeathite; Jeziel and Pelet the sons of Azmaveth; Beracah, Jehu the Anathothite, ⁴and Ishmaiah the Gibeonite, a mighty man among the Thirty, who was a leader of the Thirty; Jeremiah, Jahaziel, Johanan, Jozabad the Gederathite, ⁵Eluzai, Jerimoth, Bealiah, Shemariah and Shephatiah the Haruphite; ⁶Elkanah, Isshiah, Azarel, Joezer and Jashobeam the Korahites; ⁷and Joelah and Zebadiah the sons of Jeroham from Gedor.

⁸Some Gadites defected to David at his stronghold in the desert. They were brave warriors, ready for battle and able to handle the shield and spear. Their faces were the faces of lions, and they were as swift as gazelles in the mountains.
⁹Ezer was the chief,
Obadiah the second in command, Eliab the third,
¹⁰Mishmannah the fourth, Jeremiah the fifth,
¹¹Attai the sixth, Eliel the seventh,
¹²Johanan the eighth, Elzabad the ninth,
¹³Jeremiah the tenth and Macbannai the eleventh.
¹⁴These Gadites were army commanders; the least was a match for a hundred, and the greatest for a thousand. ¹⁵It was they who crossed the Jordan in the first month when it was overflowing all its banks, and they put to flight everyone living in the valleys, to the east and to the west.

¹⁶Other Benjamites and some men from Judah also came to David in his stronghold. ¹⁷David went out to meet them and said to them, "If you have come to me in peace, to help me, I am ready to have you unite with me. But if you have come to betray me to my enemies when my hands are free from violence, may the God of our fathers see it and judge you."

"Greatest Military Heroes of All Time" category (excluding Bible characters), who would you place in your "Top Three"? Pooling the group's nominees for a secret ballot, who would you vote for as "Chief" of your "Mighty Men"?

1. Who are your favorite outlaws: Jesse James? Bonnie and Clyde? Robin Hood? **2.** For you, what makes some renegades into villains and others into folk heroes: (a) Folk heroes rob from the rich; villains from the poor? (b) Folk heroes defect to the West; villains to the East? (c) Folk heroes kill in self-defense; villains simply kill?

1. What tells you this is a "flashback," pre-dating the events of chapter 11? **2.** What is notable about Saul's own kinsmen (v. 2) coming over to David's side (before "all Israel" did so)? **3.** Where else do the defectors come from? Are they "political dissidents," "proven winners" or "cast offs"? What is their claim to fame? What do you suppose made the Gadite commanders so effective for David? **4.** Why is David cautious about some renegades who join his side (vv. 16–17)? How are his suspicions laid to rest? **5.** Was invoking God's witness (vv. 17–18) enough to cement ties between these two men? Or were careful contractual negotiations between David and Amasai also necessary? Note that Amasai's (Amasa's) treason years later gives David "20/20 hindsight" to confirm his suspicions here (2 Sa 17:25). **6.** What leads David to marvel at God's guidance during this time in exile (v. 22)?

1. What special commandos today might rival the men who joined David in exile? **2.** For what reasons might someone be suspicious of you and withhold their trust? How do you win over those who are suspicious of you? **3.** Like these defectors from Saul pledging themselves to David, to whom have you felt inspired to pledge your service (with heart and will open to God)? What normally prevents such commitment? **4.** Adnah, Jozabad and the others had to surrender loyalty to Saul in order to side with David. How do you decide which way to go when divided loyalties force a choice?

---

1. What event in your life has swelled in importance over the years? Does it now seem as if *everyone* was there? **2.** What events in your social calendar require special catering vs. paper plates for all the guests invited? **3.** Have you ever seen a ticker tape parade? What was it like?

1. What do you think is the chronicler's point in recounting the numbers and nature of those joining David at Hebron, including the two priests named? **2.** What do you make of such *large* numbers (340,800 total men): (a) This is exaggeration, just as "the army of God" (v. 22) must be? (b) This is what "all Israel" (v. 38) means? (c) Only "officers, the commanders of thousands [340] and of hundreds [8]" attended (13:1), not the total figures each represented?

1. While huge numbers eating and drinking at David's three-day coronation may seem problematic, what does such imagery say about the *joy* that attended this banquet? **2.** When have you given *joy* three days of your time? What was the occasion? Why is it we often feel guilty about such time-consuming pleasure? **3.** As a Christian anticipating the final banquet crowning your coming King (see Lk 13:28–30; 14:16–24), what will you do with the limitless opportunity for enjoying your King?

[18]Then the Spirit came upon Amasai, chief of the Thirty, and he said:

> "We are yours, O David!
> We are with you, O son of Jesse!
> Success, success to you,
> and success to those who help you,
> for your God will help you."

So David received them and made them leaders of his raiding bands.

[19]Some of the men of Manasseh defected to David when he went with the Philistines to fight against Saul. (He and his men did not help the Philistines because, after consultation, their rulers sent him away. They said, "It will cost us our heads if he deserts to his master Saul.") [20]When David went to Ziklag, these were the men of Manasseh who defected to him: Adnah, Jozabad, Jediael, Michael, Jozabad, Elihu and Zillethai, leaders of units of a thousand in Manasseh. [21]They helped David against raiding bands, for all of them were brave warriors, and they were commanders in his army. [22]Day after day men came to help David, until he had a great army, like the army of God.[a]

Others Join David at Hebron

[23]These are the numbers of the men armed for battle who came to David at Hebron to turn Saul's kingdom over to him, as the LORD had said:

[24]men of Judah, carrying shield and spear—6,800 armed for battle;

[25]men of Simeon, warriors ready for battle—7,100;

[26]men of Levi—4,600, [27]including Jehoiada, leader of the family of Aaron, with 3,700 men, [28]and Zadok, a brave young warrior, with 22 officers from his family;

[29]men of Benjamin, Saul's kinsmen—3,000, most of whom had remained loyal to Saul's house until then;

[30]men of Ephraim, brave warriors, famous in their own clans—20,800;

[31]men of half the tribe of Manasseh, designated by name to come and make David king—18,000;

[32]men of Issachar, who understood the times and knew what Israel should do—200 chiefs, with all their relatives under their command;

[33]men of Zebulun, experienced soldiers prepared for battle with every type of weapon, to help David with undivided loyalty—50,000;

[34]men of Naphtali—1,000 officers, together with 37,000 men carrying shields and spears;

[35]men of Dan, ready for battle—28,600;

[36]men of Asher, experienced soldiers prepared for battle—40,000;

[37]and from east of the Jordan, men of Reuben, Gad and the half-tribe of Manasseh, armed with every type of weapon—120,000.

[38]All these were fighting men who volunteered to serve in the ranks. They came to Hebron fully determined to make David king over all Israel. All the rest of the Israelites were also of one mind to make David king. [39]The men spent three days there with David, eating and drinking, for their families had supplied provisions for

---

[a]22 Or *a great and mighty army*

them. [40]Also, their neighbors from as far away as Issachar, Zebulun and Naphtali came bringing food on donkeys, camels, mules and oxen. There were plentiful supplies of flour, fig cakes, raisin cakes, wine, oil, cattle and sheep, for there was joy in Israel.

Bringing Back the Ark

13 David conferred with each of his officers, the commanders of thousands and commanders of hundreds. [2]He then said to the whole assembly of Israel, "If it seems good to you and if it is the will of the LORD our God, let us send word far and wide to the rest of our brothers throughout the territories of Israel, and also to the priests and Levites who are with them in their towns and pasturelands, to come and join us. [3]Let us bring the ark of our God back to us, for we did not inquire of[a] it[b] during the reign of Saul." [4]The whole assembly agreed to do this, because it seemed right to all the people.

[5]So David assembled all the Israelites, from the Shihor River in Egypt to Lebo[c] Hamath, to bring the ark of God from Kiriath Jearim. [6]David and all the Israelites with him went to Baalah of Judah (Kiriath Jearim) to bring up from there the ark of God the LORD, who is enthroned between the cherubim—the ark that is called by the Name.

[7]They moved the ark of God from Abinadab's house on a new cart, with Uzzah and Ahio guiding it. [8]David and all the Israelites were celebrating with all their might before God, with songs and with harps, lyres, tambourines, cymbals and trumpets.

[9]When they came to the threshing floor of Kidon, Uzzah reached out his hand to steady the ark, because the oxen stumbled. [10]The LORD's anger burned against Uzzah, and he struck him down because he had put his hand on the ark. So he died there before God.

[11]Then David was angry because the LORD's wrath had broken out against Uzzah, and to this day that place is called Perez Uzzah.[d]

[12]David was afraid of God that day and asked, "How can I ever bring the ark of God to me?" [13]He did not take the ark to be with him in the City of David. Instead, he took it aside to the house of Obed-Edom the Gittite. [14]The ark of God remained with the family of Obed-Edom in his house for three months, and the LORD blessed his household and everything he had.

David's House and Family

14 Now Hiram king of Tyre sent messengers to David, along with cedar logs, stonemasons and carpenters to build a palace for him. [2]And David knew that the LORD had established him as king over Israel and that his kingdom had been highly exalted for the sake of his people Israel.

[3]In Jerusalem David took more wives and became the father of more sons and daughters. [4]These are the names of the children born to him there: Shammua, Shobab, Nathan, Solomon, [5]Ibhar, Elishua, Elpelet, [6]Nogah, Nepheg, Japhia, [7]Elishama, Beeliada[e] and Eliphelet.

David Defeats the Philistines

[8]When the Philistines heard that David had been anointed king over all Israel, they went up in full force to search for him, but David heard about it and went out to meet them. [9]Now the Philistines had come and raided the Valley of Rephaim; [10]so David in-

---

Recall when a party-pooper (parents? spouse? little brother?) once killed the mood of your party: What did you do then?

1. Who made the decision to bring back the ark? Where has it been (see 1Sa 7:1–2)? Why such high priority on bringing it back? 2. How did they move it (v. 7)? Why a "new cart" (see 1Sa 6:7ff)? What's wrong with that? How's the ark supposed to be moved (see Ex 25:14)? And by whom (see 15:2,13–15; Nu 4:15)? 3. How is Uzzah's act "the last straw"? Who then intervenes (vv. 10–12)? 4. What does such anger show about God's holiness? About David's character and sense of responsibility?

1. If you had been given this deadly ark, as was Obed-Edom (vv. 13–14), how would you feel? What steps would you take to avoid God's curse and ensure his blessing? 2. Do you treat God with more reverential awe or more familiarity? Why? 3. Like Uzzah, when have you slipped and acted irreverently? When you fall, who intercedes?

---

1. In what order have you established these priorities: (a) Have kids? (b) Get married? (c) Build a new home? (d) Establish God as the focal point? (e) Prove yourself in your career? 2. How would you order these, ideally? 3. Any step-children in your extended family? How do blended families work out in your experience?

1. What two events and two blessings recorded here are symbolic of David's truly becoming king of Israel? What political and redemptive purpose do they serve? 2. How does this list of the king's kids compare with 1 Chronicles 3:5–8 and 2 Samuel 5:14–15? 3. What priority does David take on next? What political platform do you notice in the king's First 100 Days in office? 4. What strategic

---

a3 Or *we neglected*   b3 Or *him*   c5 Or *to the entrance to*   d11 *Perez Uzzah* means *outbreak against Uzzah.*   e7 A variant of *Eliada*

steps did David take to ensure success against the Philistines? What significance for a revived Israel do you see in his action, prayers, speech, removal of pagan idols, obedience to God and fame among the nations?

♡ **1.** When David was recognized by Hiram, this helped to secure David's sense that God had indeed called him. In this regard, whose recognition is important to you? **2.** David's first victory was insufficient. How do you react when your best shot requires a second effort? Try the same thing? Try something new? **3.** For what things do you "inquire of God"? How do you get your answer?

☕ **1.** "If at first you don't succeed, try, try again"—how does that little pep talk fit a situation you're facing just now? **2.** What would it take to get you "dancing in the streets": Nuclear arms reduction treaty? Peace in the Middle East? A World Series or Super Bowl win for the home team? School let out early for the year? "It's a Boy!" The recipe actually worked!? She said, "I do"?

📖 **1.** What suggests that David has learned a valuable lesson about not playing loose with the rules for worship given by God through Moses? What blame-shifting by the chronicler do you also detect? **2.** What suggests that David is now the leader of all the people, not just a few, and no longer a mere challenger to the incumbent line of Saul? **3.** What three clans of Levi are represented at this religious processional? What all is involved in David's ordering them to "consecrate yourselves" (vv. 12–15; see Ex 29:1–37)? **4.** How does David organize them for worship (vv. 16–28)? List all the musical instruments used here in worship. How will these various sounds revive their awe and love for God? **5.** What experience does Obed-Edom (vv. 18,21,24; see 13:13–14) bring to this? How does he likely feel about getting the ark out of his house after three months? **6.** In what sense does God "help" the Levites carry the ark this time around (v. 26), whereas before (see ch. 13) he had opposed them? **7.** As the ark is being moved to Jerusalem, what is the response of the people (15:25,28; 16:1)? Of David (15:25, 27;

quired of God: "Shall I go and attack the Philistines? Will you hand them over to me?"

The LORD answered him, "Go, I will hand them over to you."

[11]So David and his men went up to Baal Perazim, and there he defeated them. He said, "As waters break out, God has broken out against my enemies by my hand." So that place was called Baal Perazim.[a] [12]The Philistines had abandoned their gods there, and David gave orders to burn them in the fire.

[13]Once more the Philistines raided the valley; [14]so David inquired of God again, and God answered him, "Do not go straight up, but circle around them and attack them in front of the balsam trees. [15]As soon as you hear the sound of marching in the tops of the balsam trees, move out to battle, because that will mean God has gone out in front of you to strike the Philistine army." [16]So David did as God commanded him, and they struck down the Philistine army, all the way from Gibeon to Gezer.

[17]So David's fame spread throughout every land, and the LORD made all the nations fear him.

The Ark Brought to Jerusalem

15 After David had constructed buildings for himself in the City of David, he prepared a place for the ark of God and pitched a tent for it. [2]Then David said, "No one but the Levites may carry the ark of God, because the LORD chose them to carry the ark of the LORD and to minister before him forever."

[3]David assembled all Israel in Jerusalem to bring up the ark of the LORD to the place he had prepared for it. [4]He called together the descendants of Aaron and the Levites:

[5]From the descendants of Kohath,
    Uriel the leader and 120 relatives;
[6]from the descendants of Merari,
    Asaiah the leader and 220 relatives;
[7]from the descendants of Gershon,[b]
    Joel the leader and 130 relatives;
[8]from the descendants of Elizaphan,
    Shemaiah the leader and 200 relatives;
[9]from the descendants of Hebron,
    Eliel the leader and 80 relatives;
[10]from the descendants of Uzziel,
    Amminadab the leader and 112 relatives.

[11]Then David summoned Zadok and Abiathar the priests, and Uriel, Asaiah, Joel, Shemaiah, Eliel and Amminadab the Levites. [12]He said to them, "You are the heads of the Levitical families; you and your fellow Levites are to consecrate yourselves and bring up the ark of the LORD, the God of Israel, to the place I have prepared for it. [13]It was because you, the Levites, did not bring it up the first time that the LORD our God broke out in anger against us. We did not inquire of him about how to do it in the prescribed way." [14]So the priests and Levites consecrated themselves in order to bring up the ark of the LORD, the God of Israel. [15]And the Levites carried the ark of God with the poles on their shoulders, as Moses had commanded in accordance with the word of the LORD.

[16]David told the leaders of the Levites to appoint their brothers as singers to sing joyful songs, accompanied by musical instruments: lyres, harps and cymbals.

[17]So the Levites appointed Heman son of Joel; from his brothers, Asaph son of Berekiah; and from their brothers the Merarites,

---

[a]11 *Baal Perazim* means *the lord who breaks out.*   [b]7 Hebrew *Gershom,* a variant of *Gershon*

Ethan son of Kushaiah; [18]and with them their brothers next in rank: Zechariah,[a] Jaaziel, Shemiramoth, Jehiel, Unni, Eliab, Benaiah, Maaseiah, Mattithiah, Eliphelehu, Mikneiah, Obed-Edom and Jeiel,[b] the gatekeepers.

[19]The musicians Heman, Asaph and Ethan were to sound the bronze cymbals; [20]Zechariah, Aziel, Shemiramoth, Jehiel, Unni, Eliab, Maaseiah and Benaiah were to play the lyres according to *alamoth,*[c] [21]and Mattithiah, Eliphelehu, Mikneiah, Obed-Edom, Jeiel and Azaziah were to play the harps, directing according to *sheminith.*[c] [22]Kenaniah the head Levite was in charge of the singing; that was his responsibility because he was skillful at it.

[23]Berekiah and Elkanah were to be doorkeepers for the ark. [24]Shebaniah, Joshaphat, Nethanel, Amasai, Zechariah, Benaiah and Eliezer the priests were to blow trumpets before the ark of God. Obed-Edom and Jehiah were also to be doorkeepers for the ark.

[25]So David and the elders of Israel and the commanders of units of a thousand went to bring up the ark of the covenant of the LORD from the house of Obed-Edom, with rejoicing. [26]Because God had helped the Levites who were carrying the ark of the covenant of the LORD, seven bulls and seven rams were sacrificed. [27]Now David was clothed in a robe of fine linen, as were all the Levites who were carrying the ark, and as were the singers, and Kenaniah, who was in charge of the singing of the choirs. David also wore a linen ephod. [28]So all Israel brought up the ark of the covenant of the LORD with shouts, with the sounding of rams' horns and trumpets, and of cymbals, and the playing of lyres and harps.

[29]As the ark of the covenant of the LORD was entering the City of David, Michal daughter of Saul watched from a window. And when she saw King David dancing and celebrating, she despised him in her heart.

16 They brought the ark of God and set it inside the tent that David had pitched for it, and they presented burnt offerings and fellowship offerings[d] before God. [2]After David had finished sacrificing the burnt offerings and fellowship offerings, he blessed the people in the name of the LORD. [3]Then he gave a loaf of bread, a cake of dates and a cake of raisins to each Israelite man and woman.

[4]He appointed some of the Levites to minister before the ark of the LORD, to make petition, to give thanks, and to praise the LORD, the God of Israel: [5]Asaph was the chief, Zechariah second, then Jeiel, Shemiramoth, Jehiel, Mattithiah, Eliab, Benaiah, Obed-Edom and Jeiel. They were to play the lyres and harps, Asaph was to sound the cymbals, [6]and Benaiah and Jahaziel the priests were to blow the trumpets regularly before the ark of the covenant of God.

David's Psalm of Thanks

[7]That day David first committed to Asaph and his associates this psalm of thanks to the LORD:

> [8]Give thanks to the LORD, call on his name;
> make known among the nations what he has done.
> [9]Sing to him, sing praise to him;
> tell of all his wonderful acts.
> [10]Glory in his holy name;

---

a18 Three Hebrew manuscripts and most Septuagint manuscripts (see also verse 20 and 1 Chron. 16:5); most Hebrew manuscripts *Zechariah son and* or *Zechariah, Ben and*   *b18* Hebrew; Septuagint (see also verse 21) *Jeiel and Azaziah*   *c20,21* Probably a musical term   *d1* Traditionally *peace offerings*; also in verse 2

16:2–3)? Of the Levites (5:26,28; 16:1,4–6) **8.** By contrast, how does Michal respond? Why is she so upset with David (v. 29; see 2Sa 6:20)? **9.** If "clothes make the man," and if David "dresses for success," what do you make of his attire in verse 27 (see 1Sa 2:18; 22:18)? How is David by his costume thus redefining the role of the king? **10.** In 16:1–3, what is David doing that further identifies him as a priest-king, a type of the Priest-King to come?

1. What would a worship service led by David be like in your church? What sights and sounds would surprise you? How would he be received? What would he have to wear? Why? **2.** How does your attire Sunday morning relate to your duties and approach in worship? What attire is forbidden where you worship? What else are you saying by the way you do and don't dress? **3.** Which of the following would characterize your small group or your personal worship life: (a) Reverential awe? (b) Childlike joy? (c) Special clothing? (d) Conversational prayer? (e) David's serendipity-like dancing? How do you decide what form of worship is appropos for what occasions?

---

1. What about your past week, your dream life or your future vacation plans would you characterize as *awesome*? **2.** What era of your country's history or of world history would you like to visit in a time machine? Why? **3.** Are you the type to relive and reflect on the past? Or do you forget about the past, living only for now? Why?

1. How is David's kingdom further strengthened by giving thanks to the Lord with this psalm? How would this psalm bring the 12 tribes closer together as one people? **2.** In the song's first stanza (vv. 8–13), What does the psalmist urge us to do and why? What memories for Israel are evoked by reference to God's "wonders," "miracles" or "judgments"? **3.** In the second stanza (vv. 14–18), who first understands God's mission in the world? What is the mission? The covenant? What news about God do you suppose Jacob heard through the family grapevine from Isaac, and Isaac from Abraham? **4.** In the third stanza (vv. 19–22), who are the VIPs esteemed by God? How were they protected? What were these relatively few nomads called? That special term is usually reserved for what high office? **5.** In the majestic fourth stanza (vv. 23–33), what actions are we instructed to take (list the verbs)? Who or what is called upon to participate and why? Why "all the earth"? Why "day after day"? **6.** If all these actions are to achieve their purpose, what will have to happen and when? **7.** In the fifth stanza (vv. 34–36), what common human needs are addressed? How will the Lord meet them, as no one else can? **8.** What familiar names appear after the benediction to this psalm? What roles are they given and why? Why does David wait until the end to resume his role as father and husband? **9.** When all is said and done, sung and ascribed, at the close of this chapter, do you think the worship of God by these people fulfills David's prescription (v. 8)? How so?

♡ **1.** The occasion for this psalm was the return of the ark and the establishment of David's reign. For what occasions might Israel and the Church have used this psalm? How might you use it today? **2.** Of the songs often heard or sung by your family and friends, how many are less than 10 years old? Any that are a century old? Any 200 years old? Does your church sing any songs like this one, songs of ancient worship to God (truly oldies but goodies)? **3.** What qualities of Israel's God mentioned in this psalm of praise, are most comforting to you? What about this God do you find most disturbing? Which divine attribute applies to a current worry or problem of yours? **4.** How is the worship in this psalm multi-racial or multilingual? What multi-tunes do you hear? What multitudes are singing? **5.** If your church were to model its worship service after this

let the hearts of those who seek the LORD
    rejoice.
[11]Look to the LORD and his strength;
    seek his face always.
[12]Remember the wonders he has done,
    his miracles, and the judgments he pronounced,
[13]O descendants of Israel his servant,
    O sons of Jacob, his chosen ones.

[14]He is the LORD our God;
    his judgments are in all the earth.
[15]He remembers[a] his covenant forever,
    the word he commanded, for a thousand generations,
[16]the covenant he made with Abraham,
    the oath he swore to Isaac.
[17]He confirmed it to Jacob as a decree,
    to Israel as an everlasting covenant:
[18]"To you I will give the land of Canaan
    as the portion you will inherit."

[19]When they were but few in number,
    few indeed, and strangers in it,
[20]they[b] wandered from nation to nation,
    from one kingdom to another.
[21]He allowed no man to oppress them;
    for their sake he rebuked kings:
[22]"Do not touch my anointed ones;
    do my prophets no harm."

[23]Sing to the LORD, all the earth;
    proclaim his salvation day after day.
[24]Declare his glory among the nations,
    his marvelous deeds among all peoples.
[25]For great is the LORD and most worthy of praise;
    he is to be feared above all gods.
[26]For all the gods of the nations are idols,
    but the LORD made the heavens.
[27]Splendor and majesty are before him;
    strength and joy in his dwelling place.
[28]Ascribe to the LORD, O families of nations,
    ascribe to the LORD glory and strength,
[29] ascribe to the LORD the glory due his name.
  Bring an offering and come before him;
    worship the LORD in the splendor of his[c] holiness.
[30]Tremble before him, all the earth!
    The world is firmly established; it cannot be moved.
[31]Let the heavens rejoice, let the earth be glad;
    let them say among the nations, "The LORD reigns!"
[32]Let the sea resound, and all that is in it;
    let the fields be jubilant, and everything in them!
[33]Then the trees of the forest will sing,

---

[a]15 Some Septuagint manuscripts (see also Psalm 105:8); Hebrew *Remember*
[b]18-20 One Hebrew manuscript, Septuagint and Vulgate (see also Psalm 105:12); most Hebrew manuscripts inherit, / [19]though you are but few in number, / few indeed, and strangers in it." / [20]They   [c]29 Or LORD with the splendor of

they will sing for joy before the LORD,
for he comes to judge the earth.

34Give thanks to the LORD, for he is good;
his love endures forever.
35Cry out, "Save us, O God our Savior;
gather us and deliver us from the nations,
that we may give thanks to your holy name,
that we may glory in your praise."
36Praise be to the LORD, the God of Israel,
from everlasting to everlasting.

Then all the people said "Amen" and "Praise the LORD."

37David left Asaph and his associates before the ark of the covenant of the LORD to minister there regularly, according to each day's requirements. 38He also left Obed-Edom and his sixty-eight associates to minister with them. Obed-Edom son of Jeduthun, and also Hosah, were gatekeepers.

39David left Zadok the priest and his fellow priests before the tabernacle of the LORD at the high place in Gibeon 40to present burnt offerings to the LORD on the altar of burnt offering regularly, morning and evening, in accordance with everything written in the Law of the LORD, which he had given Israel. 41With them were Heman and Jeduthun and the rest of those chosen and designated by name to give thanks to the LORD, "for his love endures forever." 42Heman and Jeduthun were responsible for the sounding of the trumpets and cymbals and for the playing of the other instruments for sacred song. The sons of Jeduthun were stationed at the gate.

43Then all the people left, each for his own home, and David returned home to bless his family.

God's Promise to David

17 After David was settled in his palace, he said to Nathan the prophet, "Here I am, living in a palace of cedar, while the ark of the covenant of the LORD is under a tent."

2Nathan replied to David, "Whatever you have in mind, do it, for God is with you."

3That night the word of God came to Nathan, saying:

4"Go and tell my servant David, 'This is what the LORD says: You are not the one to build me a house to dwell in. 5I have not dwelt in a house from the day I brought Israel up out of Egypt to this day. I have moved from one tent site to another, from one dwelling place to another. 6Wherever I have moved with all the Israelites, did I ever say to any of their leaders*a* whom I commanded to shepherd my people, "Why have you not built me a house of cedar?" '

7"Now then, tell my servant David, 'This is what the LORD Almighty says: I took you from the pasture and from following the flock, to be ruler over my people Israel. 8I have been with you wherever you have gone, and I have cut off all your enemies from before you. Now I will make your name like the names of the greatest men of the earth. 9And I will provide a place for my people Israel and will plant them so that they can have a home of their own and no longer be disturbed. Wicked people will not oppress them anymore, as they did at the beginning 10and have done ever since the time I appointed

a 6 Traditionally judges; also in verse 10

---

multi-pattern, what skills would you have to import? What skills could you grow internally? What would require a spiritual transplant from a donor church? Which donor church would you go to for ideas?

Compare the house you grew up in with yours now. What do you like most about each house?

1. What about David's house bothers him? How is Nathan's reply like a blank check? How does his open-ended counsel (v. 2) change? 2. What is God's attitude toward his own house of cedar (vv. 6)? Why is David reminded of his debt to God (vv. 7–8a)? 3. What kind of "house" does God promise David (v. 10)? What kind will God get (v. 12)? Should this news surprise or irk David? 4. In what sense is God's kingdom "established forever" (v. 14; see Isa 9:6–7; Lk 1:32–33)?

1. When have you felt like doing God a favor? 2. Which do you find motivates you more in your *work*: (a) Guaranteed contracts? (b) Performance incentives? Give an example. 3. Which do you find motivates you more in your *worship*: (a) God's promises, which are not dependent on your performance? (b) God's conditional clauses, where obedience is expected to fully realize the terms of

the covenant? Explain. **4.** David would not realize his dream (a house for the Lord). What life dream or goal are you beginning to see that you will not accomplish yourself? Will a successor of yours be responsible for this?

---

1. When overwhelmed with generosity or a prestigious honor, what do you do? When have you been "twice blessed"? **2.** Is "reverence" necessary in work or worship? Do you like reverent folk?

1. What motivates David to pray? To which of God's promises in this chapter is David answering in verse 16? In verse 17? **2.** How is God's sovereignty underscored in the way David addresses him in this prayer? **3.** Likewise, how is Israel's uniqueness underscored here? **4.** Why does David want so badly to see God's promise "kept forever" (vv. 23–24)? What gives him the courage to pray like this?

1. How do you respond to the promises of a trustworthy God? How do you most often address God? Do you more often ask, or thank, God for things? What does that say about your rapport with him? **2.** Rank 1 to 5 these five activities: corporate worship; table grace; pre-game prayer; solitary prayer; small group prayer. What makes certain prayer situations more satisfying than others? **3.** What does David's prayer inspire you and your small group to pray for?

---

1. What winning streak of yours recalls the good ol' days? What made them so good? **2.** What do you do for the sheer joy of it, regardless of its cost?

1. How do you explain his winning streak? "The Lord gave David victory wherever he went." Does that say it all? Or does that only beg more questions for you? **2.** What does David do with captured soldiers, horses, equip-

leaders over my people Israel. I will also subdue all your enemies.

"'I declare to you that the LORD will build a house for you: ¹¹When your days are over and you go to be with your fathers, I will raise up your offspring to succeed you, one of your own sons, and I will establish his kingdom. ¹²He is the one who will build a house for me, and I will establish his throne forever. ¹³I will be his father, and he will be my son. I will never take my love away from him, as I took it away from your predecessor. ¹⁴I will set him over my house and my kingdom forever; his throne will be established forever.'"

¹⁵Nathan reported to David all the words of this entire revelation.

David's Prayer

¹⁶Then King David went in and sat before the LORD, and he said:

"Who am I, O LORD God, and what is my family, that you have brought me this far? ¹⁷And as if this were not enough in your sight, O God, you have spoken about the future of the house of your servant. You have looked on me as though I were the most exalted of men, O LORD God.

¹⁸"What more can David say to you for honoring your servant? For you know your servant, ¹⁹O LORD. For the sake of your servant and according to your will, you have done this great thing and made known all these great promises.

²⁰"There is no one like you, O LORD, and there is no God but you, as we have heard with our own ears. ²¹And who is like your people Israel—the one nation on earth whose God went out to redeem a people for himself, and to make a name for yourself, and to perform great and awesome wonders by driving out nations from before your people, whom you redeemed from Egypt? ²²You made your people Israel your very own forever, and you, O LORD, have become their God.

²³"And now, LORD, let the promise you have made concerning your servant and his house be established forever. Do as you promised, ²⁴so that it will be established and that your name will be great forever. Then men will say, 'The LORD Almighty, the God over Israel, is Israel's God!' And the house of your servant David will be established before you.

²⁵"You, my God, have revealed to your servant that you will build a house for him. So your servant has found courage to pray to you. ²⁶O LORD, you are God! You have promised these good things to your servant. ²⁷Now you have been pleased to bless the house of your servant, that it may continue forever in your sight; for you, O LORD, have blessed it, and it will be blessed forever."

David's Victories

18 In the course of time, David defeated the Philistines and subdued them, and he took Gath and its surrounding villages from the control of the Philistines.

²David also defeated the Moabites, and they became subject to him and brought tribute.

³Moreover, David fought Hadadezer king of Zobah, as far as Hamath, when he went to establish his control along the Euphrates River. ⁴David captured a thousand of his chariots, seven thousand charioteers and twenty thousand foot soldiers. He hamstrung all but a hundred of the chariot horses.

⁵When the Arameans of Damascus came to help Hadadezer king of Zobah, David struck down twenty-two thousand of them. ⁶He put garrisons in the Aramean kingdom of Damascus, and the Arameans became subject to him and brought tribute. The LORD gave David victory everywhere he went.

⁷David took the gold shields carried by the officers of Hadadezer and brought them to Jerusalem. ⁸From Tebah*a* and Cun, towns that belonged to Hadadezer, David took a great quantity of bronze, which Solomon used to make the bronze Sea, the pillars and various bronze articles.

⁹When Tou king of Hamath heard that David had defeated the entire army of Hadadezer king of Zobah, ¹⁰he sent his son Hadoram to King David to greet him and congratulate him on his victory in battle over Hadadezer, who had been at war with Tou. Hadoram brought all kinds of articles of gold and silver and bronze.

¹¹King David dedicated these articles to the LORD, as he had done with the silver and gold he had taken from all these nations: Edom and Moab, the Ammonites and the Philistines, and Amalek.

¹²Abishai son of Zeruiah struck down eighteen thousand Edomites in the Valley of Salt. ¹³He put garrisons in Edom, and all the Edomites became subject to David. The LORD gave David victory everywhere he went.

David's Officials

¹⁴David reigned over all Israel, doing what was just and right for all his people. ¹⁵Joab son of Zeruiah was over the army; Jehoshaphat son of Ahilud was recorder; ¹⁶Zadok son of Ahitub and Ahimelech*b* son of Abiathar were priests; Shavsha was secretary; ¹⁷Benaiah son of Jehoiada was over the Kerethites and Pelethites; and David's sons were chief officials at the king's side.

The Battle Against the Ammonites

19 In the course of time, Nahash king of the Ammonites died, and his son succeeded him as king. ²David thought, "I will show kindness to Hanun son of Nahash, because his father showed kindness to me." So David sent a delegation to express his sympathy to Hanun concerning his father.

When David's men came to Hanun in the land of the Ammonites to express sympathy to him, ³the Ammonite nobles said to Hanun, "Do you think David is honoring your father by sending men to you to express sympathy? Haven't his men come to you to explore and spy out the country and overthrow it?" ⁴So Hanun seized David's men, shaved them, cut off their garments in the middle at the buttocks, and sent them away.

⁵When someone came and told David about the men, he sent messengers to meet them, for they were greatly humiliated. The king said, "Stay at Jericho till your beards have grown, and then come back."

⁶When the Ammonites realized that they had become a stench in David's nostrils, Hanun and the Ammonites sent a thousand talents*c* of silver to hire chariots and charioteers from Aram Naharaim,*d* Aram Maacah and Zobah. ⁷They hired thirty-two thousand chariots and charioteers, as well as the king of Maacah with his troops, who came and camped near Medeba, while the Ammonites were mustered from their towns and moved out for battle.

⁸On hearing this, David sent Joab out with the entire army of

ment and articles? Why kill off good horses (see Dt 17:16), but dedicate the articles? What does this say about David? **3.** What gruesome story connected to these campaigns does Samuel tell, but is omitted here (see 2Sa 8:2)?

1. Has your nation's army ever adopted the belief that God was on its side? What are the benefits, and the dangers, of such "God-and-country" dogma? If God is credited for David's wins, what about for his losses, and the decimation of others? Is God to blame win, lose or draw? **2.** Over what enemy has God given you victory? Where have you yet to experience his victory? **3.** What possessions, abilities or resources would you like to dedicate anew to God, as does David in this story?

1. Does this regime look like a true (albeit human) theocracy to you? What would a true theocracy look like (see 1Ki 2:3–4)? **2.** What would a dishonest regime look like (see 1Sa 8:3; 12:3)?

1. What's your favorite risk game? Can you put vast fortunes of play money on the line? Are you the "double or nothing" type? **2.** How do you feel about beards: (a) They look attractive? (b) Feel scratchy? (c) Cover up acne? (d) Save on razor blades? (e) Proof of manliness? (f) Offset baldness? (g) The boss won't like it? (h) Flower child at 40? (i) Could catch a certain girl? (j) Couldn't grow one if I tried?

1. Who are the Ammonites (see Ge 19:38; Dt 2:19)? Why are they a particular threat to Israel (see Jdg 11:4–32)? Why does David send messengers to their new king (vv. 1–2a)? What suspicions does that raise? **2.** What was Hanun trying to prove by stripping and shaving David's emissaries? What was the stench all about (v. 5–6)? **3.** Who starts the war? Was it accidental? On purpose? Or "accidentally on purpose"? **4.** How does Joab manage the war on two fronts (vv. 10–13)? Who wins the war? **5.** How does Hadadezer think he can outmaneuver David (vv. 16–18)? When does he finally raise the

a8 Hebrew *Tibhath,* a variant of *Tebah*   *b16* Some Hebrew manuscripts, Vulgate and Syriac (see also 2 Samuel 8:17); most Hebrew manuscripts *Abimelech*   *c6* That is, about 37 tons (about 34 metric tons)   *d6* That is, Northwest Mesopotamia

white flag? **6.** What variations do you find between this account and the parallel one in 2 Samuel 10? What do you make of them? Which numbers make David look like he took the greater risk and won a greater victory?

1. In what area of your life are you feeling the need for reinforcements? How might your small group come to your rescue? **2.** How confident are you in taking risks? In escalating risky confrontations (as David did), even when you're in the right? What's the difference between "stepping out in faith" and risk-taking? **3.** How can children learn loyalty and trust, so that their parents' friends can become their genuine friends as well?

Apart from your parents, spouse or God, to whom do you owe the biggest debt of gratitude for your position in life?

1. Who is the hero in the capture of Rabbah? Who actually gets the credit? **2.** What measure of mercy do you see here? **3.** What does the chronicler omit from his version of this battle (see 2Sa 11:1–12:31)? Why? **4.** What is the main point of these undated wars (vv. 4–8)? **5.** What trouble does David encounter here which the chronicler passes over (see 2Sa 21:15–17)? Why such embellishment?

1. Do you feel you are getting proper credit for the jobs you do well? What reward are you working for? **2.** What giants have you fought for your King? What giants are you preparing for? Training others for? How might the group help you?

fighting men. ⁹The Ammonites came out and drew up in battle formation at the entrance to their city, while the kings who had come were by themselves in the open country.

¹⁰Joab saw that there were battle lines in front of him and behind him; so he selected some of the best troops in Israel and deployed them against the Arameans. ¹¹He put the rest of the men under the command of Abishai his brother, and they were deployed against the Ammonites. ¹²Joab said, "If the Arameans are too strong for me, then you are to rescue me; but if the Ammonites are too strong for you, then I will rescue you. ¹³Be strong and let us fight bravely for our people and the cities of our God. The LORD will do what is good in his sight."

¹⁴Then Joab and the troops with him advanced to fight the Arameans, and they fled before him. ¹⁵When the Ammonites saw that the Arameans were fleeing, they too fled before his brother Abishai and went inside the city. So Joab went back to Jerusalem.

¹⁶After the Arameans saw that they had been routed by Israel, they sent messengers and had Arameans brought from beyond the River,ᵃ with Shophach the commander of Hadadezer's army leading them.

¹⁷When David was told of this, he gathered all Israel and crossed the Jordan; he advanced against them and formed his battle lines opposite them. David formed his lines to meet the Arameans in battle, and they fought against him. ¹⁸But they fled before Israel, and David killed seven thousand of their charioteers and forty thousand of their foot soldiers. He also killed Shophach the commander of their army.

¹⁹When the vassals of Hadadezer saw that they had been defeated by Israel, they made peace with David and became subject to him.

So the Arameans were not willing to help the Ammonites anymore.

The Capture of Rabbah

20 In the spring, at the time when kings go off to war, Joab led out the armed forces. He laid waste the land of the Ammonites and went to Rabbah and besieged it, but David remained in Jerusalem. Joab attacked Rabbah and left it in ruins. ²David took the crown from the head of their kingᵇ—its weight was found to be a talentᶜ of gold, and it was set with precious stones—and it was placed on David's head. He took a great quantity of plunder from the city ³and brought out the people who were there, consigning them to labor with saws and with iron picks and axes. David did this to all the Ammonite towns. Then David and his entire army returned to Jerusalem.

War With the Philistines

⁴In the course of time, war broke out with the Philistines, at Gezer. At that time Sibbecai the Hushathite killed Sippai, one of the descendants of the Rephaites, and the Philistines were subjugated.

⁵In another battle with the Philistines, Elhanan son of Jair killed Lahmi the brother of Goliath the Gittite, who had a spear with a shaft like a weaver's rod.

⁶In still another battle, which took place at Gath, there was a huge man with six fingers on each hand and six toes on each foot—twenty-four in all. He also was descended from Rapha.

ᵃ16 That is, the Euphrates   ᵇ2 Or of Milcom, that is, Molech   ᶜ2 That is, about 75 pounds (about 34 kilograms)

[7]When he taunted Israel, Jonathan son of Shimea, David's brother, killed him.

[8]These were descendants of Rapha in Gath, and they fell at the hands of David and his men.

David Numbers the Fighting Men

21 Satan rose up against Israel and incited David to take a census of Israel. [2]So David said to Joab and the commanders of the troops, "Go and count the Israelites from Beersheba to Dan. Then report back to me so that I may know how many there are."

[3]But Joab replied, "May the LORD multiply his troops a hundred times over. My lord the king, are they not all my lord's subjects? Why does my lord want to do this? Why should he bring guilt on Israel?"

[4]The king's word, however, overruled Joab; so Joab left and went throughout Israel and then came back to Jerusalem. [5]Joab reported the number of the fighting men to David: In all Israel there were one million one hundred thousand men who could handle a sword, including four hundred and seventy thousand in Judah.

[6]But Joab did not include Levi and Benjamin in the numbering, because the king's command was repulsive to him. [7]This command was also evil in the sight of God; so he punished Israel.

[8]Then David said to God, "I have sinned greatly by doing this. Now, I beg you, take away the guilt of your servant. I have done a very foolish thing."

[9]The LORD said to Gad, David's seer, [10]"Go and tell David, 'This is what the LORD says: I am giving you three options. Choose one of them for me to carry out against you.'"

[11]So Gad went to David and said to him, "This is what the LORD says: 'Take your choice: [12]three years of famine, three months of being swept away[a] before your enemies, with their swords overtaking you, or three days of the sword of the LORD—days of plague in the land, with the angel of the LORD ravaging every part of Israel.' Now then, decide how I should answer the one who sent me."

[13]David said to Gad, "I am in deep distress. Let me fall into the hands of the LORD, for his mercy is very great; but do not let me fall into the hands of men."

[14]So the LORD sent a plague on Israel, and seventy thousand men of Israel fell dead. [15]And God sent an angel to destroy Jerusalem. But as the angel was doing so, the LORD saw it and was grieved because of the calamity and said to the angel who was destroying the people, "Enough! Withdraw your hand." The angel of the LORD was then standing at the threshing floor of Araunah[b] the Jebusite.

[16]David looked up and saw the angel of the LORD standing between heaven and earth, with a drawn sword in his hand extended over Jerusalem. Then David and the elders, clothed in sackcloth, fell facedown.

[17]David said to God, "Was it not I who ordered the fighting men to be counted? I am the one who has sinned and done wrong. These are but sheep. What have they done? O LORD my God, let your hand fall upon me and my family, but do not let this plague remain on your people."

[18]Then the angel of the LORD ordered Gad to tell David to go up and build an altar to the LORD on the threshing floor of Araunah the Jebusite. [19]So David went up in obedience to the word that Gad had spoken in the name of the LORD.

a 12 Hebrew; Septuagint and Vulgate (see also 2 Samuel 24:13) *of fleeing*
b 15 Hebrew *Ornan,* a variant of *Araunah;* also in verses 18-28

1. How well can you keep a secret: (a) Your smile gives you away? (b) Sleepless until someone knows? (c) Future career as a double agent? **2.** If you could travel back in history as the invisible person, what private conversations would you sit in on?

1. What prompts David to take a census: (a) God's anger (see 2Sa 24:1)? (b) Satan's ruse? (c) David's pride or insecurity? (d) Some external threat? (e) To keep his men busy between wars? (f) To win power over Joab? (g) Rationale for the temple property (vv. 28ff)? **2.** What does your answer say about who lies behind evil acts (v. 15; see Job 1:12; Jas 1:13–15)? How could a "man after God's own heart" be duped by Satan? **3.** How does Joab remain true to his own conscience while taking David's census? Was his secret (v. 6) a lie? Was it justified by circumstances? **4.** In the actual census-taking, what time, money and manpower are involved (vv. 4–6; see 2Sa 24:8)? **5.** How does David discover his error (see 2Sa 24:10)? How do we know that David confessed his error to his advisors, that he was not trying for a cover-up? **6.** Is God working at cross-purposes when he grieves over what he inflicted on Israel? Why does he punish Israel for what *David* ordered? **7.** After the plague is over, David builds an altar (21:18–22:1). Where? Why there? What does David's prayer have to do with that? **8.** The plague reaches Araunah's threshing floor, and David wants to buy it to build an altar there. Why? For what price (see 1Sa 8:14)? What results? **9.** Why should God's messages go through Gad? **10.** What important conversations does the chronicler know about, but does not detail? **11.** From this story, what do you learn about angels? About God? About David's relationship with God? About the people who suffered, or lost loved ones? **12.** What happens here if, instead of repentant, David gets stubborn, resentful or bitter? Write your own ending to reflect that.

1. How are you like David—proud but insecure in "numbers"? When are you tempted to lean upon your superior assets, rather than in weakness depend on God? When have you, like David, pulled rank instead of listening to your "Joab"? **2.** Taking a cue from Israel's emphasis on body language (falling face down, etc.), how could you non-verbally express your fear, penitence or needs? **3.** Are you ready to say to your King, "Take whatever pleases you"? What freebies would you willingly give up? What costly items do you fear he might take that you want to keep? **4.** What does this story say about the link between sin and suffering? Between sin and sacrifice? Between humility and service? Between wrath and mercy? What bearing does this have on your confidence that God brings good out of the trials we endure? How is that true for you?

1. When have you ever been taken off a job that you very much wanted to complete yourself? How did you feel at the time? **2.** As an employer, when have you had to replace someone who, for one reason or another, was not the right person for the job? How did you feel, having to break the bad news? How did you feel installing a person of your own choosing?

1. What task has David yielded? Was he too defiled by war to build the temple himself (vv. 7–10; see 17:10; 1Ki 5:3)? **2.** What feelings can you read between the lines? Is David able to let go (of his dream and of his son)? Is he looking forward to retirement or an empty nest? **3.** What resources (material and spiritual) does David provide his son? Would that make it easier, or tougher, on Solomon? What burdens does Solomon inherit because of all David's preparations? **4.** How does David greet his son? How does he bid him farewell? What verbal assurances seem most significant in motivating a son to fulfill the assigned task? What virtues does he insist that Solomon cultivate? How will the

20While Araunah was threshing wheat, he turned and saw the angel; his four sons who were with him hid themselves. **21**Then David approached, and when Araunah looked and saw him, he left the threshing floor and bowed down before David with his face to the ground.

22David said to him, "Let me have the site of your threshing floor so I can build an altar to the LORD, that the plague on the people may be stopped. Sell it to me at the full price."

23Araunah said to David, "Take it! Let my lord the king do whatever pleases him. Look, I will give the oxen for the burnt offerings, the threshing sledges for the wood, and the wheat for the grain offering. I will give all this."

24But King David replied to Araunah, "No, I insist on paying the full price. I will not take for the LORD what is yours, or sacrifice a burnt offering that costs me nothing."

25So David paid Araunah six hundred shekels[a] of gold for the site. **26**David built an altar to the LORD there and sacrificed burnt offerings and fellowship offerings.[b] He called on the LORD, and the LORD answered him with fire from heaven on the altar of burnt offering.

27Then the LORD spoke to the angel, and he put his sword back into its sheath. **28**At that time, when David saw that the LORD had answered him on the threshing floor of Araunah the Jebusite, he offered sacrifices there. **29**The tabernacle of the LORD, which Moses had made in the desert, and the altar of burnt offering were at that time on the high place at Gibeon. **30**But David could not go before it to inquire of God, because he was afraid of the sword of the angel of the LORD.

22 Then David said, "The house of the LORD God is to be here, and also the altar of burnt offering for Israel."

Preparations for the Temple

2So David gave orders to assemble the aliens living in Israel, and from among them he appointed stonecutters to prepare dressed stone for building the house of God. **3**He provided a large amount of iron to make nails for the doors of the gateways and for the fittings, and more bronze than could be weighed. **4**He also provided more cedar logs than could be counted, for the Sidonians and Tyrians had brought large numbers of them to David.

5David said, "My son Solomon is young and inexperienced, and the house to be built for the LORD should be of great magnificence and fame and splendor in the sight of all the nations. Therefore I will make preparations for it." So David made extensive preparations before his death.

6Then he called for his son Solomon and charged him to build a house for the LORD, the God of Israel. **7**David said to Solomon: "My son, I had it in my heart to build a house for the Name of the LORD my God. **8**But this word of the LORD came to me: 'You have shed much blood and have fought many wars. You are not to build a house for my Name, because you have shed much blood on the earth in my sight. **9**But you will have a son who will be a man of peace and rest, and I will give him rest from all his enemies on every side. His name will be Solomon,[c] and I will grant Israel peace and quiet during his reign. **10**He is the one who will build a house for my Name. He will be my son, and I will be his father. And I will establish the throne of his kingdom over Israel forever.'

11"Now, my son, the LORD be with you, and may you have suc-

---

a25 That is, about 15 pounds (about 7 kilograms)   b26 Traditionally *peace offerings*   c9 *Solomon* sounds like and may be derived from the Hebrew for *peace.*

cess and build the house of the LORD your God, as he said you would. ¹²May the LORD give you discretion and understanding when he puts you in command over Israel, so that you may keep the law of the LORD your God. ¹³Then you will have success if you are careful to observe the decrees and laws that the LORD gave Moses for Israel. Be strong and courageous. Do not be afraid or discouraged.

¹⁴"I have taken great pains to provide for the temple of the LORD a hundred thousand talents[a] of gold, a million talents[b] of silver, quantities of bronze and iron too great to be weighed, and wood and stone. And you may add to them. ¹⁵You have many workmen: stonecutters, masons and carpenters, as well as men skilled in every kind of work ¹⁶in gold and silver, bronze and iron—craftsmen beyond number. Now begin the work, and the LORD be with you."

¹⁷Then David ordered all the leaders of Israel to help his son Solomon. ¹⁸He said to them, "Is not the LORD your God with you? And has he not granted you rest on every side? For he has handed the inhabitants of the land over to me, and the land is subject to the LORD and to his people. ¹⁹Now devote your heart and soul to seeking the LORD your God. Begin to build the sanctuary of the LORD God, so that you may bring the ark of the covenant of the LORD and the sacred articles belonging to God into the temple that will be built for the Name of the LORD."

The Levites

23 When David was old and full of years, he made his son Solomon king over Israel.

²He also gathered together all the leaders of Israel, as well as the priests and Levites. ³The Levites thirty years old or more were counted, and the total number of men was thirty-eight thousand. ⁴David said, "Of these, twenty-four thousand are to supervise the work of the temple of the LORD and six thousand are to be officials and judges. ⁵Four thousand are to be gatekeepers and four thousand are to praise the LORD with the musical instruments I have provided for that purpose."

⁶David divided the Levites into groups corresponding to the sons of Levi: Gershon, Kohath and Merari.

Gershonites

⁷Belonging to the Gershonites:
   Ladan and Shimei.
   ⁸The sons of Ladan:
   Jehiel the first, Zetham and Joel—three in all.
   ⁹The sons of Shimei:
   Shelomoth, Haziel and Haran—three in all.
   These were the heads of the families of Ladan.
   ¹⁰And the sons of Shimei:
   Jahath, Ziza,[c] Jeush and Beriah.
   These were the sons of Shimei—four in all.
   ¹¹Jahath was the first and Ziza the second, but Jeush and Beriah did not have many sons; so they were counted as one family with one assignment.

Lord help in that? **5.** Are David and Solomon cast from the same mold?

♡ **1.** When have you "passed on the torch" to a subordinate at work? To an heir in the family? **2.** What preparations have you made for passing on your life's work or family values? Would you "arrange" a child's life, as David did for Solomon? **3.** What kind of a head start in life did you get, materially, from your parents? **4.** Imagine greeting your friends, children or colleagues with "The Lord be with you." What would they take that to mean?

☕ Who in your group has the most siblings? The most kids? Most grandkids? Share photos, if you wish.

📖 **1.** How is David handling old age? What troubles does David face among senior management (see 1Ki 1–2)? Why does the chronicler omit such bloody details? **2.** When were priests eligible for service (v. 3; compare 24,27; Nu 4:1–3; 8:24)? **3.** What other provisions for worship does David give? **4.** Ponder verses 7–11. How does this list compare with the one in chapter 6? Is Shimei the son of Libni and/or Gershon and/or Merari? And how many sons does Shimei seem to have (vv. 9–10)? Why reduce the assignment for two of his sons? As Beriah's heir, would you be pleased or resentful?

♡ **1.** How hard is it to turn over power? For David? For you? **2.** David delegated extensively at this stage in his career. What are the modern equivalents for the offices appointed here? Could your town use four times as many pastors as police?

---

a14 That is, about 3,750 tons (about 3,450 metric tons)   b14 That is, about 37,500 tons (about 34,500 metric tons)   c10 One Hebrew manuscript, Septuagint and Vulgate (see also verse 11); most Hebrew manuscripts *Zina*

Who is the most famous person you ever got to shake hands with, get an autograph from or actually visit with? What shirt-tail relative of some reknown do you claim?

1. Levi's tree has three branches. Which one is more famous and why? 2. Is Aaron given busy work, or a creative outlet (v. 13)? What skills would he need to perform that role with excellence?

1. What church fights or political debates would you be spared today, if leaders were appointed "for life," as were the Hebrew priests? 2. What lifelong duties or irrevocable callings have come your way? 3. Where might the Kohath clan have struggled, in trying to maintain the fame resulting from Moses and Aaron? Can you empathize anywhere?

1. "When I relax, I feel guilty"—does that describe you? How so? 2. Who among your friends is an expert at having fun?

1. Of the Merarites, David and the Levites, how did each succeed in their own way? Who seems most successful? 2. What possible misunderstandings might the Hebrews have attached to the "rest" granted to them (v. 25)? How would you re-phrase David's intent here? 3. Why the apparent changes in the age of eligibility for priests (vv. 24,27; see 23:3; Nu 4:1–3; 8:23–24)? 4. What here hints that the Hebrews enjoyed fun and fellowship in their work?

1. For you, is Sunday restful, workful, or worshipful? 2. The Levites had two teams, and membership was a matter of birth, not performance. If you were the chief Levite, what pep talk of yours would get the most out of your team? 3. At age 20, where were you in relation to an organized church: (a) Taking a four-year vacation? (b) Attending when it was convenient? (c) Getting actively involved?

Kohathites

¹²The sons of Kohath:
Amram, Izhar, Hebron and Uzziel—four in all.
¹³The sons of Amram:
Aaron and Moses.
Aaron was set apart, he and his descendants forever, to consecrate the most holy things, to offer sacrifices before the LORD, to minister before him and to pronounce blessings in his name forever. ¹⁴The sons of Moses the man of God were counted as part of the tribe of Levi.
¹⁵The sons of Moses:
Gershom and Eliezer.
¹⁶The descendants of Gershom:
Shubael was the first.
¹⁷The descendants of Eliezer:
Rehabiah was the first.
Eliezer had no other sons, but the sons of Rehabiah were very numerous.
¹⁸The sons of Izhar:
Shelomith was the first.
¹⁹The sons of Hebron:
Jeriah the first, Amariah the second, Jahaziel the third and Jekameam the fourth.
²⁰The sons of Uzziel:
Micah the first and Isshiah the second.

Merarites

²¹The sons of Merari:
Mahli and Mushi.
The sons of Mahli:
Eleazar and Kish.
²²Eleazar died without having sons: he had only daughters. Their cousins, the sons of Kish, married them.
²³The sons of Mushi:
Mahli, Eder and Jerimoth—three in all.

²⁴These were the descendants of Levi by their families—the heads of families as they were registered under their names and counted individually, that is, the workers twenty years old or more who served in the temple of the LORD. ²⁵For David had said, "Since the LORD, the God of Israel, has granted rest to his people and has come to dwell in Jerusalem forever, ²⁶the Levites no longer need to carry the tabernacle or any of the articles used in its service." ²⁷According to the last instructions of David, the Levites were counted from those twenty years old or more.

²⁸The duty of the Levites was to help Aaron's descendants in the service of the temple of the LORD: to be in charge of the courtyards, the side rooms, the purification of all sacred things and the performance of other duties at the house of God. ²⁹They were in charge of the bread set out on the table, the flour for the grain offerings, the unleavened wafers, the baking and the mixing, and all measurements of quantity and size. ³⁰They were also to stand every morning to thank and praise the LORD. They were to do the same in the evening ³¹and whenever burnt offerings were presented to the LORD on Sabbaths and at New Moon festivals and at appointed feasts. They were to serve before the LORD regularly in the proper number and in the way prescribed for them.

³²And so the Levites carried out their responsibilities for the

Tent of Meeting, for the Holy Place and, under their brothers the descendants of Aaron, for the service of the temple of the LORD.

The Divisions of Priests

24 These were the divisions of the sons of Aaron:
The sons of Aaron were Nadab, Abihu, Eleazar and Ithamar. ²But Nadab and Abihu died before their father did, and they had no sons; so Eleazar and Ithamar served as the priests. ³With the help of Zadok a descendant of Eleazar and Ahimelech a descendant of Ithamar, David separated them into divisions for their appointed order of ministering. ⁴A larger number of leaders were found among Eleazar's descendants than among Ithamar's, and they were divided accordingly: sixteen heads of families from Eleazar's descendants and eight heads of families from Ithamar's descendants. ⁵They divided them impartially by drawing lots, for there were officials of the sanctuary and officials of God among the descendants of both Eleazar and Ithamar.

⁶The scribe Shemaiah son of Nethanel, a Levite, recorded their names in the presence of the king and of the officials: Zadok the priest, Ahimelech son of Abiathar and the heads of families of the priests and of the Levites—one family being taken from Eleazar and then one from Ithamar.

⁷The first lot fell to Jehoiarib,
  the second to Jedaiah,
⁸the third to Harim,
  the fourth to Seorim,
⁹the fifth to Malkijah,
  the sixth to Mijamin,
¹⁰the seventh to Hakkoz,
  the eighth to Abijah,
¹¹the ninth to Jeshua,
  the tenth to Shecaniah,
¹²the eleventh to Eliashib,
  the twelfth to Jakim,
¹³the thirteenth to Huppah,
  the fourteenth to Jeshebeab,
¹⁴the fifteenth to Bilgah,
  the sixteenth to Immer,
¹⁵the seventeenth to Hezir,
  the eighteenth to Happizzez,
¹⁶the nineteenth to Pethahiah,
  the twentieth to Jehezkel,
¹⁷the twenty-first to Jakin,
  the twenty-second to Gamul,
¹⁸the twenty-third to Delaiah
  and the twenty-fourth to Maaziah.

¹⁹This was their appointed order of ministering when they entered the temple of the LORD, according to the regulations prescribed for them by their forefather Aaron, as the LORD, the God of Israel, had commanded him.

The Rest of the Levites

²⁰As for the rest of the descendants of Levi:
  from the sons of Amram: Shubael;
    from the sons of Shubael: Jehdeiah.
²¹As for Rehabiah, from his sons:
    Isshiah was the first.
²²From the Izharites: Shelomoth;

1. In your family, how do members decide what joint activity or common cause to engage in: By political or church ties? By geographic locale? By generations? By marriage? 2. Who got you the job you are in now? Did you apply for it? Earn it? Or were you "volunteered"? How so?

1. In the family line of Aaron, what divisions are evident? On the basis of what moral, inherited, and impartial grounds? 2. What is the story behind the two sons who are excluded on moral grounds (v. 2; see Lev 10:1–3)? 3. Who is given the lion's share of the ministerial appointments (vv. 3–4)? On what grounds? 4. By what means are the further divisions made, so as to balance out the natural advantage enjoyed by the more fruitful Eleazar? 5. What might be the purpose of 24 evenly divided shifts? What rotation of duty would that allow them to do? 6. What petty jealousies or party politics might this strategy avert? What might someone chosen first, second, last or second to last feel? 7. What authorities (scribe, temporal and ultimate) stood behind this appointment process? How might that authority assure its rightness, control rumors and squelch any rebellion against these priestly divisions?

1. Who in your life is like the quiet competent scribe, Shemaiah, a "Gal Friday" or "press secretary"? Who do you serve in that manner? 2. Whether you were elected, appointed, or inherited your present job what difference does that make in your job security? In your incentive to excel on the job? What difference does it make knowing God was in that selection process?

What venture or business partnership would you and a sibling consider doing together? How would your brother or sister complement you in this venture?

from the sons of Shelomoth: Jahath.

²³The sons of Hebron: Jeriah the first,[a] Amariah the second, Jahaziel the third and Jekameam the fourth.

²⁴The son of Uzziel: Micah;
from the sons of Micah: Shamir.
²⁵The brother of Micah: Isshiah;
from the sons of Isshiah: Zechariah.
²⁶The sons of Merari: Mahli and Mushi.
The son of Jaaziah: Beno.
²⁷The sons of Merari:
from Jaaziah: Beno, Shoham, Zaccur and Ibri.
²⁸From Mahli: Eleazar, who had no sons.
²⁹From Kish: the son of Kish:
Jerahmeel.
³⁰And the sons of Mushi: Mahli, Eder and Jerimoth.

These were the Levites, according to their families. ³¹They also cast lots, just as their brothers the descendants of Aaron did, in the presence of King David and of Zadok, Ahimelech, and the heads of families of the priests and of the Levites. The families of the oldest brother were treated the same as those of the youngest.

The Singers

25 David, together with the commanders of the army, set apart some of the sons of Asaph, Heman and Jeduthun for the ministry of prophesying, accompanied by harps, lyres and cymbals. Here is the list of the men who performed this service:

²From the sons of Asaph:
Zaccur, Joseph, Nethaniah and Asarelah. The sons of Asaph were under the supervision of Asaph, who prophesied under the king's supervision.
³As for Jeduthun, from his sons:
Gedaliah, Zeri, Jeshaiah, Shimei,[b] Hashabiah and Mattithiah, six in all, under the supervision of their father Jeduthun, who prophesied, using the harp in thanking and praising the LORD.
⁴As for Heman, from his sons:
Bukkiah, Mattaniah, Uzziel, Shubael and Jerimoth; Hananiah, Hanani, Eliathah, Giddalti and Romamti-Ezer; Joshbekashah, Mallothi, Hothir and Mahazioth. ⁵All these were sons of Heman the king's seer. They were given him through the promises of God to exalt him.[c] God gave Heman fourteen sons and three daughters.

⁶All these men were under the supervision of their fathers for the music of the temple of the LORD, with cymbals, lyres and harps, for the ministry at the house of God. Asaph, Jeduthun and Heman were under the supervision of the king. ⁷Along with their relatives—all of them trained and skilled in music for the LORD—they numbered 288. ⁸Young and old alike, teacher as well as student, cast lots for their duties.

⁹The first lot, which was for Asaph, fell to
Joseph,
his sons and relatives,[d]   12[e]
the second to Gedaliah,

a23 Two Hebrew manuscripts and some Septuagint manuscripts (see also 1 Chron. 23:19); most Hebrew manuscripts *The sons of Jeriah:*   b3 One Hebrew manuscript and some Septuagint manuscripts (see also verse 17); most Hebrew manuscripts do not have *Shimei.*   c5 Hebrew *exalt the horn*   d9 See Septuagint; Hebrew does not have *his sons and relatives.*   e9 See the total in verse 7; Hebrew does not have *twelve.*

he and his relatives and sons,   12
10the third to Zaccur,
    his sons and relatives,   12
11the fourth to Izri,[a]
    his sons and relatives,   12
12the fifth to Nethaniah,
    his sons and relatives,   12
13the sixth to Bukkiah,
    his sons and relatives,   12
14the seventh to Jesarelah,[b]
    his sons and relatives,   12
15the eighth to Jeshaiah,
    his sons and relatives,   12
16the ninth to Mattaniah,
    his sons and relatives,   12
17the tenth to Shimei,
    his sons and relatives,   12
18the eleventh to Azarel,[c]
    his sons and relatives,   12
19the twelfth to Hashabiah,
    his sons and relatives,   12
20the thirteenth to Shubael,
    his sons and relatives,   12
21the fourteenth to Mattithiah,
    his sons and relatives,   12
22the fifteenth to Jerimoth,
    his sons and relatives,   12
23the sixteenth to Hananiah,
    his sons and relatives,   12
24the seventeenth to Joshbekashah,
    his sons and relatives,   12
25the eighteenth to Hanani,
    his sons and relatives,   12
26the nineteenth to Mallothi,
    his sons and relatives,   12
27the twentieth to Eliathah,
    his sons and relatives,   12
28the twenty-first to Hothir,
    his sons and relatives,   12
29the twenty-second to Giddalti,
    his sons and relatives,   12
30the twenty-third to Mahazioth,
    his sons and relatives,   12
31the twenty-fourth to Romamti-Ezer,
    his sons and relatives,   12

The Gatekeepers

26 The divisions of the gatekeepers:

From the Korahites: Meshelemiah son of Kore, one of the
    sons of Asaph.
2Meshelemiah had sons:
    Zechariah the firstborn,
    Jediael the second,
    Zebadiah the third,
    Jathniel the fourth,
    3Elam the fifth,

of worship? **2.** The prophecy of musicians in ancient Israel was key to certain military decisions. How does that compare to the relative importance attached to the music program of your school or church? What role do your musicians play in discerning or conveying God's will for the church? **3.** What advantages and disadvantages do you suppose a Minister of Music in David's era would have over today's music ministry? What would your church do with David's 288 trained singers? **4.** Are you able to let go with voice and heart in joyful singing? Or do you feel bashful, untrained, unmelodic? What would it take for you to move from the bashful stage to the kind of leadership shown by Gedaliah, Izri and Joshbekashah? Optional: Try a group sing-along to see what joyful noises and gifted resources you can share. **5.** Assume you are leading a group study on the Bible's view of the family and this is your first meeting. What points could you draw from this chapter? How would you apply them to families in your church? To your own family?

1. Where you live, do you lock up at night? During the day? Your car, too? Is your property fenced in? Is that locked, too? What does that say about your need for, or lack of, security? **2.** What experience have you had giving or receiving "guard duty": Pool life guard? Kid's babysitter? Night watchman? VIP's body guard? National Guard? Palace gatekeeper? Bailiff? Parole officer? Airport security?

a11 A variant of *Zeri*   b14 A variant of *Asarelah*   c18 A variant of *Uzziel*

1. What is this third most important function in Hebrew temple worship? (What were the other two?) What specifically did a gatekeeper do (v. 12; see 9:22–29)? 2. How many gatekeepers in all were there (vv. 6–11; compare 23:5)? Why the vast difference in numbers? 3. Genealogies are loaded with name changes. What variation in Meshelemiah's name occurs in this very section? Likewise, in Ebiasaph's name (see 6:23, 9:19)? 4. What do you remember about Obed-Edom (see 13:13–14)? Though not officially a Levite, how might his being "faithful in little" qualify him for adoption into this honored levitical duty of full-time temple service? 5. How do you picture these guards: Lone Ranger types? All brawn, no brain? Ice in their veins? Stuffy country club types? Heartless tin woodsmen? Or what? 6. How did they avoid petty jealousies, like who got duty at the south gate (the one most often used by the king)?

1. Of the guard duties listed in the "coffee cup" questions, which ones incorporate some aspect of Israel's temple gatekeepers? 2. What security measures do your pastor, church officers, treasurer and janitor take which are akin to the function of these gatekeepers? Whose responsibility is it to guard church property? To guard polity and constitutional concerns? To guard confidences? To guard the Gospel itself? 3. What does your church look for in hiring someone to fill one of these "gatekeeper" duties?

1. Where do you hide extra cash: Shoe box? Refrigerator? 2. Are you ever tempted to go on a shopping spree, using that college fund you've been saving? How do you protect long-range savings from short-term whims?

1. What special service do the Levites offer here? What are these "treasuries" (vv. 20,26–28)? What do the other officials do (vv. 29ff)? 2. How do these "last of the Levites" sustain their enthusiasm at a duller task, while

Jehohanan the sixth
and Eliehoenai the seventh.
⁴Obed-Edom also had sons:
Shemaiah the firstborn,
Jehozabad the second,
Joah the third,
Sacar the fourth,
Nethanel the fifth,
⁵Ammiel the sixth,
Issachar the seventh
and Peullethai the eighth.
(For God had blessed Obed-Edom.)

⁶His son Shemaiah also had sons, who were leaders in their father's family because they were very capable men. ⁷The sons of Shemaiah: Othni, Rephael, Obed and Elzabad; his relatives Elihu and Semakiah were also able men. ⁸All these were descendants of Obed-Edom; they and their sons and their relatives were capable men with the strength to do the work—descendants of Obed-Edom, 62 in all.

⁹Meshelemiah had sons and relatives, who were able men— 18 in all.

¹⁰Hosah the Merarite had sons: Shimri the first (although he was not the firstborn, his father had appointed him the first), ¹¹Hilkiah the second, Tabaliah the third and Zechariah the fourth. The sons and relatives of Hosah were 13 in all.

¹²These divisions of the gatekeepers, through their chief men, had duties for ministering in the temple of the LORD, just as their relatives had. ¹³Lots were cast for each gate, according to their families, young and old alike.

¹⁴The lot for the East Gate fell to Shelemiah.ᵃ Then lots were cast for his son Zechariah, a wise counselor, and the lot for the North Gate fell to him. ¹⁵The lot for the South Gate fell to Obed-Edom, and the lot for the storehouse fell to his sons. ¹⁶The lots for the West Gate and the Shalleketh Gate on the upper road fell to Shuppim and Hosah.

Guard was alongside of guard: ¹⁷There were six Levites a day on the east, four a day on the north, four a day on the south and two at a time at the storehouse. ¹⁸As for the court to the west, there were four at the road and two at the court itself.

¹⁹These were the divisions of the gatekeepers who were descendants of Korah and Merari.

The Treasurers and Other Officials

²⁰Their fellow Levites wereᵇ in charge of the treasuries of the house of God and the treasuries for the dedicated things.

²¹The descendants of Ladan, who were Gershonites through Ladan and who were heads of families belonging to Ladan the Gershonite, were Jehieli, ²²the sons of Jehieli, Zetham and his brother Joel. They were in charge of the treasuries of the temple of the LORD.

²³From the Amramites, the Izharites, the Hebronites and the Uzzielites:

²⁴Shubael, a descendant of Gershom son of Moses, was the officer in charge of the treasuries. ²⁵His relatives through

ᵃ14 A variant of Meshelemiah   ᵇ20 Septuagint; Hebrew As for the Levites, Ahijah was

Eliezer: Rehabiah his son, Jeshaiah his son, Joram his son, Zicri his son and Shelomith his son. ²⁶Shelomith and his relatives were in charge of all the treasuries for the things dedicated by King David, by the heads of families who were the commanders of thousands and commanders of hundreds, and by the other army commanders. ²⁷Some of the plunder taken in battle they dedicated for the repair of the temple of the LORD. ²⁸And everything dedicated by Samuel the seer and by Saul son of Kish, Abner son of Ner and Joab son of Zeruiah, and all the other dedicated things were in the care of Shelomith and his relatives.

²⁹From the Izharites: Kenaniah and his sons were assigned duties away from the temple, as officials and judges over Israel.

³⁰From the Hebronites: Hashabiah and his relatives—seventeen hundred able men—were responsible in Israel west of the Jordan for all the work of the LORD and for the king's service. ³¹As for the Hebronites, Jeriah was their chief according to the genealogical records of their families. In the fortieth year of David's reign a search was made in the records, and capable men among the Hebronites were found at Jazer in Gilead. ³²Jeriah had twenty-seven hundred relatives, who were able men and heads of families, and King David put them in charge of the Reubenites, the Gadites and the half-tribe of Manasseh for every matter pertaining to God and for the affairs of the king.

Army Divisions

27 This is the list of the Israelites—heads of families, commanders of thousands and commanders of hundreds, and their officers, who served the king in all that concerned the army divisions that were on duty month by month throughout the year. Each division consisted of 24,000 men.

²In charge of the first division, for the first month, was Jashobeam son of Zabdiel. There were 24,000 men in his division. ³He was a descendant of Perez and chief of all the army officers for the first month. ⁴In charge of the division for the second month was Dodai the Ahohite; Mikloth was the leader of his division. There were 24,000 men in his division. ⁵The third army commander, for the third month, was Benaiah son of Jehoiada the priest. He was chief and there were 24,000 men in his division. ⁶This was the Benaiah who was a mighty man among the Thirty and was over the Thirty. His son Ammizabad was in charge of his division. ⁷The fourth, for the fourth month, was Asahel the brother of Joab; his son Zebadiah was his successor. There were 24,000 men in his division. ⁸The fifth, for the fifth month, was the commander Shamhuth the Izrahite. There were 24,000 men in his division. ⁹The sixth, for the sixth month, was Ira the son of Ikkesh the Tekoite. There were 24,000 men in his division. ¹⁰The seventh, for the seventh month, was Helez the Pelonite, an Ephraimite. There were 24,000 men in his division. ¹¹The eighth, for the eighth month, was Sibbecai the Hushathite, a Zerahite. There were 24,000 men in his division. ¹²The ninth, for the ninth month, was Abiezer the Anathothite, a Benjamite. There were 24,000 men in his division.

others do more colorful pageantry? **3.** What job pressures do you think faced Shubael when he got to work each day? What character qualities and job skills would be required for excellence in his field **4.** How many officials and judges are required to administer justice outside Jerusalem (vv. 29–32; see 23:4)? If these people had lost their genealogical records (v. 31), how would they know who does what?

1. Does David's method of hiding his stash give you any hints about what to do with your own jar of coins and bills? **2.** What view of the future *promotes* long-term financial planning in the church? What viewpoint *retards* such interest? What ideas about the future seem to lie behind David's planning?

Of all you do each week, what would you gladly stop doing for a whole month? What would be impossible to stop for a month?

1. What monthly duties are parceled out here? What advantage might this rotation of commanders have for David? For the privates and corporals? **2.** Review time for geneatectives (see ch. 11): Who among the army commanders is already known for bravery? For foolhardy pursuit of personal enemies? For killing 300 enemy with a spear in one battle? Who appears by lineage to be a clergy-under-arms? Who also is listed among the roll call of David's "mighty men"? **3.** In delegating authority, is David trusting only hometown buddies and relatives? Or is he rewarding loyalty and experience? **4.** Just how large is this standing army? (Note: The Hebrew word for "1000" may mean "squad" or "squad leader." A squad was likely about 10 men.) **5.** The stress here seems to be on *symmetry* (to complement one another) rather than on *size*. How would this help ensure healthy Levitical divisions?

In listing the physically powerful jobs last (ch. 27) and the artistic and liturgical jobs first (ch. 24–26), what does that suggest to young Hebrews who need heroes and role models? How satisfied are you with today's role models for children?

Who in your group can name your local, state and national representatives? What office holders are hardest to remember?

1. Which names on this list do you recognize from before? What "double duty" are some of them now doing? 2. What two tribes, normally included in the roll call of "all Israel," are absent here? How many are present? 3. What can you infer from verses 23–24 about the kind of work these officers tried to do? 4. What new insight into David's wrong-headed census is provided here?

1. Some jobs are better left undone, like David's ill-advised census. What projects have you unwisely started and wisely aborted? 2. Do you keep a "book of annals"? Does your church?

1. Fill in these blanks: "I am ___ in charge of ___. I want to be in charge of ___, but only for one day." 2. Are you a "take charge" person? Or more laid back? Would you ever take charge of your small group? Or family property?

1. Write one job description for the property overseers (vv. 25–31); a second one for the royal cabinet (vv. 32–34). Include "key objectives" and "skills required." How do the two compare? 2. Why would this "man after God's own heart" need a professional friend or personal pastor? (See 1Ki 2, for the sorry end to this group.)

1. These good people began their careers entrusted with royal resources. Where did you begin your career? Where has it led you? 2. What is your basic job description? Anything like these men? Who is your "friend," counselor or protector?

13The tenth, for the tenth month, was Maharai the Netophathite, a Zerahite. There were 24,000 men in his division. 14The eleventh, for the eleventh month, was Benaiah the Pirathonite, an Ephraimite. There were 24,000 men in his division. 15The twelfth, for the twelfth month, was Heldai the Netophathite, from the family of Othniel. There were 24,000 men in his division.

Officers of the Tribes

16The officers over the tribes of Israel:

over the Reubenites: Eliezer son of Zicri;
over the Simeonites: Shephatiah son of Maacah;
17over Levi: Hashabiah son of Kemuel;
over Aaron: Zadok;
18over Judah: Elihu, a brother of David;
over Issachar: Omri son of Michael;
19over Zebulun: Ishmaiah son of Obadiah;
over Naphtali: Jerimoth son of Azriel;
20over the Ephraimites: Hoshea son of Azaziah;
over half the tribe of Manasseh: Joel son of Pedaiah;
21over the half-tribe of Manasseh in Gilead: Iddo son of Zechariah;
over Benjamin: Jaasiel son of Abner;
22over Dan: Azarel son of Jeroham.
These were the officers over the tribes of Israel.

23David did not take the number of the men twenty years old or less, because the LORD had promised to make Israel as numerous as the stars in the sky. 24Joab son of Zeruiah began to count the men but did not finish. Wrath came on Israel on account of this numbering, and the number was not entered in the book[a] of the annals of King David.

The King's Overseers

25Azmaveth son of Adiel was in charge of the royal storehouses.
Jonathan son of Uzziah was in charge of the storehouses in the outlying districts, in the towns, the villages and the watchtowers. 26Ezri son of Kelub was in charge of the field workers who farmed the land.
27Shimei the Ramathite was in charge of the vineyards.
Zabdi the Shiphmite was in charge of the produce of the vineyards for the wine vats.
28Baal-Hanan the Gederite was in charge of the olive and sycamore-fig trees in the western foothills.
Joash was in charge of the supplies of olive oil.
29Shitrai the Sharonite was in charge of the herds grazing in Sharon.
Shaphat son of Adlai was in charge of the herds in the valleys.
30Obil the Ishmaelite was in charge of the camels.
Jehdeiah the Meronothite was in charge of the donkeys.
31Jaziz the Hagrite was in charge of the flocks.
All these were the officials in charge of King David's property.

32Jonathan, David's uncle, was a counselor, a man of insight and a scribe. Jehiel son of Hacmoni took care of the king's sons.
33Ahithophel was the king's counselor.

a24 Septuagint; Hebrew *number*

Hushai the Arkite was the king's friend. [34]Ahithophel was succeeded by Jehoiada son of Benaiah and by Abiathar.

Joab was the commander of the royal army.

David's Plans for the Temple

28 David summoned all the officials of Israel to assemble at Jerusalem: the officers over the tribes, the commanders of the divisions in the service of the king, the commanders of thousands and commanders of hundreds, and the officials in charge of all the property and livestock belonging to the king and his sons, together with the palace officials, the mighty men and all the brave warriors.

[2]King David rose to his feet and said: "Listen to me, my brothers and my people. I had it in my heart to build a house as a place of rest for the ark of the covenant of the LORD, for the footstool of our God, and I made plans to build it. [3]But God said to me, 'You are not to build a house for my Name, because you are a warrior and have shed blood.'

[4]"Yet the LORD, the God of Israel, chose me from my whole family to be king over Israel forever. He chose Judah as leader, and from the house of Judah he chose my family, and from my father's sons he was pleased to make me king over all Israel. [5]Of all my sons—and the LORD has given me many—he has chosen my son Solomon to sit on the throne of the kingdom of the LORD over Israel. [6]He said to me: 'Solomon your son is the one who will build my house and my courts, for I have chosen him to be my son, and I will be his father. [7]I will establish his kingdom forever if he is unswerving in carrying out my commands and laws, as is being done at this time.'

[8]"So now I charge you in the sight of all Israel and of the assembly of the LORD, and in the hearing of our God: Be careful to follow all the commands of the LORD your God, that you may possess this good land and pass it on as an inheritance to your descendants forever.

[9]"And you, my son Solomon, acknowledge the God of your father, and serve him with wholehearted devotion and with a willing mind, for the LORD searches every heart and understands every motive behind the thoughts. If you seek him, he will be found by you; but if you forsake him, he will reject you forever. [10]Consider now, for the LORD has chosen you to build a temple as a sanctuary. Be strong and do the work."

[11]Then David gave his son Solomon the plans for the portico of the temple, its buildings, its storerooms, its upper parts, its inner rooms and the place of atonement. [12]He gave him the plans of all that the Spirit had put in his mind for the courts of the temple of the LORD and all the surrounding rooms, for the treasuries of the temple of God and for the treasuries for the dedicated things. [13]He gave him instructions for the divisions of the priests and Levites, and for all the work of serving in the temple of the LORD, as well as for all the articles to be used in its service. [14]He designated the weight of gold for all the gold articles to be used in various kinds of service, and the weight of silver for all the silver articles to be used in various kinds of service: [15]the weight of gold for the gold lampstands and their lamps, with the weight for each lampstand and its lamps; and the weight of silver for each silver lampstand and its lamps, according to the use of each lampstand; [16]the weight of gold for each table for consecrated bread; the weight of silver for the silver tables; [17]the weight of pure gold for the forks, sprinkling bowls and pitchers; the weight of gold for each gold dish; the

1. Which PK's (President's Kids) are unforgettable for you? How many former First Family sons or daughters do you know anything about? 2. In what ways are you known by reference to your dad: Same looks? Same career? Same Lord? Same virtues and vice?

1. From clues in just this chapter, what kind of king was David? What kind of father was he? How are the two roles related? 2. How is this account of David and Solomon like and unlike the one in chapter 22? Which one is private? Public? 3. How does this combined account compare to the transition between Moses and Joshua: Who failed to attain their goals? Why? Who succeeds in bringing the people to "rest"? Who has a direct pipeline to God for detailed plans (of tabernacles and temple)? What verbal assurances are given in parallel manner? 4. Enlightening, as well, is the comparison between the version here and the one in 1 Kings 1–2. They present contrasting portraits of David's transition to retirement and Solomon's succession to power. Which one is peaceful and smooth? Uncertain and rocky? Where do you see cynical realism? Or cautious optimism? Bittersweet sorrow? Bloodless coup attempt and bloody rebel purge? 5. What picture of God is drawn here? To whom does the temple belong? And the people? And the kingdom? What difference might that make to Solomon? To Mr. and Mrs. Fig-Farmer? To the remnant of Israel, who were the first readers of the chronicler's book?

1. What parenting model and ministry motivation do you see in this chapter? What can you do to become a "David" to some "Solomon" whom God has chosen to receive blessing through you? 2. How might you apply God's powerful promise (v. 20) to your life's work? Without the assets and assistants Solomon had, what help can you count on to make the promises real? How about your small group? 3. God blesses whom he will, apart from human merit or happenstance of birth (vv. 4–7). His blessing is unfailing and all-sufficient (vv. 20–21). Can that same blessing be forfeited (vv. 8–10)? If not, why? If so, how?

weight of silver for each silver dish; [18]and the weight of the refined gold for the altar of incense. He also gave him the plan for the chariot, that is, the cherubim of gold that spread their wings and shelter the ark of the covenant of the LORD.

[19]"All this," David said, "I have in writing from the hand of the LORD upon me, and he gave me understanding in all the details of the plan."

[20]David also said to Solomon his son, "Be strong and courageous, and do the work. Do not be afraid or discouraged, for the LORD God, my God, is with you. He will not fail you or forsake you until all the work for the service of the temple of the LORD is finished. [21]The divisions of the priests and Levites are ready for all the work on the temple of God, and every willing man skilled in any craft will help you in all the work. The officials and all the people will obey your every command."

Gifts for Building the Temple

29 Then King David said to the whole assembly: "My son Solomon, the one whom God has chosen, is young and inexperienced. The task is great, because this palatial structure is not for man but for the LORD God. [2]With all my resources I have provided for the temple of my God—gold for the gold work, silver for the silver, bronze for the bronze, iron for the iron and wood for the wood, as well as onyx for the settings, turquoise,[a] stones of various colors, and all kinds of fine stone and marble—all of these in large quantities. [3]Besides, in my devotion to the temple of my God I now give my personal treasures of gold and silver for the temple of my God, over and above everything I have provided for this holy temple: [4]three thousand talents[b] of gold (gold of Ophir) and seven thousand talents[c] of refined silver, for the overlaying of the walls of the buildings, [5]for the gold work and the silver work, and for all the work to be done by the craftsmen. Now, who is willing to consecrate himself today to the LORD?"

[6]Then the leaders of families, the officers of the tribes of Israel, the commanders of thousands and commanders of hundreds, and the officials in charge of the king's work gave willingly. [7]They gave toward the work on the temple of God five thousand talents[d] and ten thousand darics[e] of gold, ten thousand talents[f] of silver, eighteen thousand talents[g] of bronze and a hundred thousand talents[h] of iron. [8]Any who had precious stones gave them to the treasury of the temple of the LORD in the custody of Jehiel the Gershonite. [9]The people rejoiced at the willing response of their leaders, for they had given freely and wholeheartedly to the LORD. David the king also rejoiced greatly.

David's Prayer

[10]David praised the LORD in the presence of the whole assembly, saying,

"Praise be to you, O LORD,
    God of our father Israel,
    from everlasting to everlasting.
[11]Yours, O LORD, is the greatness and the power
    and the glory and the majesty and the splendor,

How do you gauge *loyalty* to a grocery store? To a TV network? To a national football or soccer team? To your small group? Are you "loyal"?

1. How does David's use of money become a model of loyalty? To what three things is David most loyal? **2.** To what top priorities are the people loyal (vv. 6–9)? Do their hearts follow their money? Or vice-versa? Why? **3.** As Solomon is still "young and inexperienced," where is David placing his faith (and gifts): In missions? Bricks and mortar? People? Worship? Education? Or?

1. How does David's fundraising strategy rate against all the financial appeals you receive? **2.** If outside auditors were to look over your checkbook, what would they conclude about your top loyalties? How would you like to change that?

---

1. What models of generosity were you raised with: (a) "Neither a borrower, nor a lender be"? (b) "Give unto others as they give unto you"? (c) "You can't outgive God"? (d) Other? **2.** Who gave to you last week? How did you express your gratitude: Returned the favor? Thank-you note? IOU? Took it for granted? Other?

1. As David nears retirement, what three things are upper-

---

[a]2 The meaning of the Hebrew for this word is uncertain.   [b]4 That is, about 110 tons (about 100 metric tons)   [c]4 That is, about 260 tons (about 240 metric tons)   [d]7 That is, about 190 tons (about 170 metric tons)   [e]7 That is, about 185 pounds (about 84 kilograms)   [f]7 That is, about 375 tons (about 345 metric tons)   [g]7 That is, about 675 tons (about 610 metric tons)   [h]7 That is, about 3,750 tons (about 3,450 metric tons)

for everything in heaven and earth is yours.
Yours, O Lord, is the kingdom;
    you are exalted as head over all.
[12]Wealth and honor come from you;
    you are the ruler of all things.
In your hands are strength and power
    to exalt and give strength to all.
[13]Now, our God, we give you thanks,
    and praise your glorious name.

[14]"But who am I, and who are my people, that we should be able to give as generously as this? Everything comes from you, and we have given you only what comes from your hand. [15]We are aliens and strangers in your sight, as were all our forefathers. Our days on earth are like a shadow, without hope. [16]O Lord our God, as for all this abundance that we have provided for building you a temple for your Holy Name, it comes from your hand, and all of it belongs to you. [17]I know, my God, that you test the heart and are pleased with integrity. All these things have I given willingly and with honest intent. And now I have seen with joy how willingly your people who are here have given to you. [18]O Lord, God of our fathers Abraham, Isaac and Israel, keep this desire in the hearts of your people forever, and keep their hearts loyal to you. [19]And give my son Solomon the wholehearted devotion to keep your commands, requirements and decrees and to do everything to build the palatial structure for which I have provided."

[20]Then David said to the whole assembly, "Praise the Lord your God." So they all praised the Lord, the God of their fathers; they bowed low and fell prostrate before the Lord and the king.

Solomon Acknowledged as King

[21]The next day they made sacrifices to the Lord and presented burnt offerings to him: a thousand bulls, a thousand rams and a thousand male lambs, together with their drink offerings, and other sacrifices in abundance for all Israel. [22]They ate and drank with great joy in the presence of the Lord that day.

Then they acknowledged Solomon son of David as king a second time, anointing him before the Lord to be ruler and Zadok to be priest. [23]So Solomon sat on the throne of the Lord as king in place of his father David. He prospered and all Israel obeyed him. [24]All the officers and mighty men, as well as all of King David's sons, pledged their submission to King Solomon.

[25]The Lord highly exalted Solomon in the sight of all Israel and bestowed on him royal splendor such as no king over Israel ever had before.

The Death of David

[26]David son of Jesse was king over all Israel. [27]He ruled over Israel forty years—seven in Hebron and thirty-three in Jerusalem. [28]He died at a good old age, having enjoyed long life, wealth and honor. His son Solomon succeeded him as king.

[29]As for the events of King David's reign, from beginning to end, they are written in the records of Samuel the seer, the records of Nathan the prophet and the records of Gad the seer, [30]together with the details of his reign and power, and the circumstances that surrounded him and Israel and the kingdoms of all the other lands.

most on his mind? What fears may lurk behind those priorities? 2. What is David's view of how a nation prospers? Of who leads a nation? What seems to be his formula for "life, liberty and the pursuit of happiness"? 3. How does David view God: Privately, as his own Savior? Corporately, as Israel's Deliverer and Provider? Cosmically, as Lord of the universe? Or what? 4. By what gesture, rare today, do the people respond to David's prayer?

1. What aspects of this prayer are useful to Christians today? What parts seem outdated? (What about bowing low? Falling prostrate? Praising God aloud?) Paraphrase this prayer in the language and concerns of your small group. 2. How closely does David's prayer follow the script you might use in a retirement speech? How would you say it differently when your "days on earth are like a shadow"? Like David, are you "without hope"? Where do you place your hope?

Who are your favorite kind of party people? Your favorite party food?

1. These final two sections wrap things up neatly. But this final chapter, as others do, says volumes by what is omitted. As it is here, what signs of joy and sadness do you see? Submission and aspiration? Pride and humility? Blessing and bounty? 2. What signs of party unity and total support does the chronicler portray here? Why has he neglected Adonijah's rebellion, which led aides and sons of the king to openly rebel (see 1Ki 1:9,19,25)? Is that why the chronicler refers to "a second time" (v. 22b)? If so, when was the "first time"?

1. How could Israel's economy afford these nation-wide bashes, involving thousands of animals and oil sacrifices, plus bounteous food and drink for everyone? What objections might such extravagant offerings provoke today? 2. In comparison, how did you celebrate the inauguration or coronation of your most recent president or king? How about for a new boss or priest or spouse? 3. What future unity between the royal and priestly offices is anticipated here (v. 22b; see Zec 4:14; 6:13; Ps 110; Heb 7)?

INTRODUCTION to
2 CHRONICLES

Book Study Outline: If you are using 2 Chronicles for a study course, here is a 7- or 13-week outline. Use the questions in the margin for your group agenda:

 start meeting / 15 min.

read & discuss Bible / 30 min.

close meeting / 15–45 min.

Refer to the Questions and Answers in the front of this Bible for more information.

7-week plan	13-week plan	Personal Reading	Group Study Passage
1	1	1–2	1:1–17/Solomon's Wisdom
	2	3–7	7:1–10/Dedicating the Temple
2	3	8–9	9:13–28/Solomon's Splendor
	4	10–12	10:1–11:4/The Great Divide
3	5	13–16	15:1–19/Asa's Reform
	6	17:1–21:3	20:1–30/Jehoshaphat's Reform
4	7	21:4–22:9	21:4–20/Jehoram's Evil Ways
	8	22:10–24:27	24:1–4,17–27/Fickle Joash
5	9	25–26	26:1–23/Uzziah's Reform
	10	27–28	28:1–27Ahaz's "Unjust War"
6	11	29–32	30:1–31:1/Hezekiah's Reform
	12	33:1–36:1	34:14–33/Josiah's Reform
7	13	36:2–23	36:15–23/Jerusalem's Fall

Author: Jewish tradition suggests Ezra as author, with no firm evidence.

Date: Probably written toward the end of the fifth century B.C. or a little later. The events narrated span 970–538 B.C.

Theme: Kingship and worship in Judah from Solomon to the Exile.

Historical Background: After the glory days of Israel under Solomon, warfare and unrest divide the nation, the people forsake temple worship for idols, and they lose their national identity when Jerusalem is totally destroyed in 586 B.C. Along the way, the southern kingdom of Judah is led into slow decline by evil kings and, alternately, into periods of spiritual reformation and restored national pride by Asa, Jehoshaphat, Uzziah, Hezekiah and Josiah. Judah's slow decline (and the chronicler's account) ends with the Exile, but a "postscript" gives us a brief glimpse of future restoration.

Characteristics: The major interests of 1 Chronicles—the Davidic dynasty and the Temple worship—are continued in 2 Chronicles. Compared to the colorful stories in the books of Samuel and Kings, the chronicler has written a blander account. The stains of David's or Solomon's past are not given attention. Instead, the great wealth, worldwide acclaim, political stability, and magnificent temple get full-page treatment (ch. 1–9). Each king is evaluated on the basis of his response to God, especially as to worship of God and obedience to the law. Those who introduce reforms are given top billing and the nature of their reforms is described in some detail.

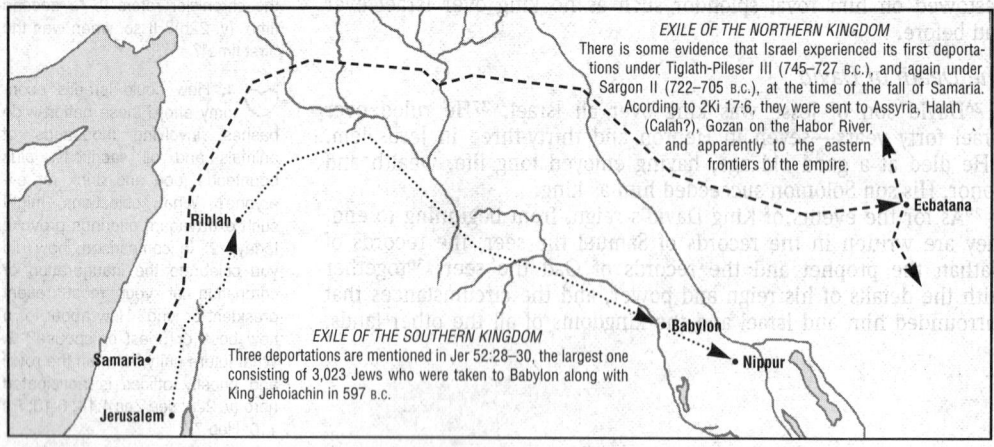

EXILE OF THE NORTHERN KINGDOM
There is some evidence that Israel experienced its first deportations under Tiglath-Pileser III (745–727 B.C.), and again under Sargon II (722–705 B.C.), at the time of the fall of Samaria. According to 2Ki 17:6, they were sent to Assyria, Halah (Calah?), Gozan on the Habor River, and apparently to the eastern frontiers of the empire.

Ecbatana

Riblah

Babylon

Nippur

EXILE OF THE SOUTHERN KINGDOM
Three deportations are mentioned in Jer 52:28–30, the largest one consisting of 3,023 Jews who were taken to Babylon along with King Jehoiachin in 597 B.C.

Samaria

Jerusalem

2 Chronicles

Solomon Asks for Wisdom

1 Solomon son of David established himself firmly over his kingdom, for the LORD his God was with him and made him exceedingly great.

²Then Solomon spoke to all Israel—to the commanders of thousands and commanders of hundreds, to the judges and to all the leaders in Israel, the heads of families— ³and Solomon and the whole assembly went to the high place at Gibeon, for God's Tent of Meeting was there, which Moses the LORD's servant had made in the desert. ⁴Now David had brought up the ark of God from Kiriath Jearim to the place he had prepared for it, because he had pitched a tent for it in Jerusalem. ⁵But the bronze altar that Bezalel son of Uri, the son of Hur, had made was in Gibeon in front of the tabernacle of the LORD; so Solomon and the assembly inquired of him there. ⁶Solomon went up to the bronze altar before the LORD in the Tent of Meeting and offered a thousand burnt offerings on it.

⁷That night God appeared to Solomon and said to him, "Ask for whatever you want me to give you."

⁸Solomon answered God, "You have shown great kindness to David my father and have made me king in his place. ⁹Now, LORD God, let your promise to my father David be confirmed, for you have made me king over a people who are as numerous as the dust of the earth. ¹⁰Give me wisdom and knowledge, that I may lead this people, for who is able to govern this great people of yours?"

¹¹God said to Solomon, "Since this is your heart's desire and you have not asked for wealth, riches or honor, nor for the death of your enemies, and since you have not asked for a long life but for wisdom and knowledge to govern my people over whom I have made you king, ¹²therefore wisdom and knowledge will be given you. And I will also give you wealth, riches and honor, such as no king who was before you ever had and none after you will have."

¹³Then Solomon went to Jerusalem from the high place at Gibeon, from before the Tent of Meeting. And he reigned over Israel.

¹⁴Solomon accumulated chariots and horses; he had fourteen hundred chariots and twelve thousand horses,ᵃ which he kept in the chariot cities and also with him in Jerusalem. ¹⁵The king made silver and gold as common in Jerusalem as stones, and cedar as plentiful as sycamore-fig trees in the foothills. ¹⁶Solomon's horses were imported from Egyptᵇ and from Kueᶜ—the royal merchants purchased them from Kue. ¹⁷They imported a chariot from Egypt for six hundred shekelsᵈ of silver, and a horse for a hundred and fifty.ᵉ They also exported them to all the kings of the Hittites and of the Arameans.

Preparations for Building the Temple

2 Solomon gave orders to build a temple for the Name of the LORD and a royal palace for himself. ²He conscripted seventy thousand men as carriers and eighty thousand as stonecutters in the hills and thirty-six hundred as foremen over them.

ᵃ14 Or charioteers   ᵇ16 Or possibly Muzur, a region in Cilicia; also in verse 17
ᶜ16 Probably Cilicia   ᵈ17 That is, about 15 pounds (about 7 kilograms)
ᵉ17 That is, about 3 3/4 pounds (about 1.7 kilograms)

☕ 1. What living "great person" would you want to spend one day with? Why? 2. If you could have only one of the following, which would you choose: (a) Live to be 100? (b) Write a great novel? (c) Own your own mansion? (d) Raise a happy, well-adjusted family? (e) Travel to every continent? 3. What "things" do you enjoy so much that having 12,000 of them would be heaven on earth?

📖 1. Now that Solomon is established (v. 1), what are his first official acts as king? Where does he do them? Who else is involved? What do each of these actions tell you about Solomon's leadership? 2. What was Solomon's answer to God's surprising question in verse 7? What else might Solomon have asked for? If you had been Solomon, how would you have answered God's question? 3. What other things does God promise to give Solomon? Why do you think God goes beyond the original offer? How do you see God's promises to Solomon fulfilled in verses 14–17? 4. Based solely on this chapter, how would you evaluate Solomon's character? His relationship with God? So far, do you think he deserves to be called "exceedingly great" (v. 1)?

♡ 1. Close your eyes and imagine that God appears to you tonight. What question is he asking you? How do you want to respond? 2. Looking back over your life, do you feel on the whole that you have received more than you asked for or less than you expected from God? How does this chapter speak to your situation? 3. What gifts could you ask God to give to the leaders of your country?

☕ 1. Which of the following have you built yourself or helped to build: (a) Bird house? (b) Tree house? (c) Doll house? (d) Your own house? (e) God's house? 2. What two skills would you make sure to include on your resume? 3. If you could conscript 153,600 people to work for you, what would you have them do?

1. What two major building projects did Solomon set out to accomplish during the early years of his reign? Whom did he use to accomplish them? 2. What kind of help did Solomon request from Hiram king of Tyre? Why did he need this help? What did he offer Hiram in return? Does this sound like a fair trade to you? 3. How does Solomon describe the temple he wants built to Hiram? What is it to be used for? Why do you think its construction was so important to Solomon? 4. What is the tone of Hiram's reply to Solomon in verses 11–16? Comparing his letter with Solomon's message to him, would you conclude: (a) Solomon was Hiram's vassal? (b) Hiram was Solomon's vassal? (c) They were equals, but Hiram was afraid of Solomon? (d) They were friendly allies? 5. Who becomes the chief craftsman for the temple's construction? How would his resume have read in the following areas: Background? Skills? Experience? (Compare with his resume in 1Ki 7:13–14.) 6. How did Solomon procure the necessary labor to build the temple? Do you think this was wise or fair? Why?

1. Considering the whole chapter, what grade (A, B, C, D, F) would you give Solomon in the following areas: Administration? Foreign diplomacy? Civil rights? Religion? 2. If you had unlimited resources, what would you build in the next year for the name of the Lord? For yourself? Whom would you ask to help you? 3. Is it ever permissible to use people to accomplish worthwhile goals as Solomon did? Has this ever happened to you?

³Solomon sent this message to Hiram[a] king of Tyre:

"Send me cedar logs as you did for my father David when you sent him cedar to build a palace to live in. ⁴Now I am about to build a temple for the Name of the Lord my God and to dedicate it to him for burning fragrant incense before him, for setting out the consecrated bread regularly, and for making burnt offerings every morning and evening and on Sabbaths and New Moons and at the appointed feasts of the Lord our God. This is a lasting ordinance for Israel.

⁵"The temple I am going to build will be great, because our God is greater than all other gods. ⁶But who is able to build a temple for him, since the heavens, even the highest heavens, cannot contain him? Who then am I to build a temple for him, except as a place to burn sacrifices before him?

⁷"Send me, therefore, a man skilled to work in gold and silver, bronze and iron, and in purple, crimson and blue yarn, and experienced in the art of engraving, to work in Judah and Jerusalem with my skilled craftsmen, whom my father David provided.

⁸"Send me also cedar, pine and algum[b] logs from Lebanon, for I know that your men are skilled in cutting timber there. My men will work with yours ⁹to provide me with plenty of lumber, because the temple I build must be large and magnificent. ¹⁰I will give your servants, the woodsmen who cut the timber, twenty thousand cors[c] of ground wheat, twenty thousand cors of barley, twenty thousand baths[d] of wine and twenty thousand baths of olive oil."

¹¹Hiram king of Tyre replied by letter to Solomon:

"Because the Lord loves his people, he has made you their king."

¹²And Hiram added:

"Praise be to the Lord, the God of Israel, who made heaven and earth! He has given King David a wise son, endowed with intelligence and discernment, who will build a temple for the Lord and a palace for himself.

¹³"I am sending you Huram-Abi, a man of great skill, ¹⁴whose mother was from Dan and whose father was from Tyre. He is trained to work in gold and silver, bronze and iron, stone and wood, and with purple and blue and crimson yarn and fine linen. He is experienced in all kinds of engraving and can execute any design given to him. He will work with your craftsmen and with those of my lord, David your father.

¹⁵"Now let my lord send his servants the wheat and barley and the olive oil and wine he promised, ¹⁶and we will cut all the logs from Lebanon that you need and will float them in rafts by sea down to Joppa. You can then take them up to Jerusalem."

¹⁷Solomon took a census of all the aliens who were in Israel, after the census his father David had taken; and they were found to be 153,600. ¹⁸He assigned 70,000 of them to be carriers and 80,000 to be stonecutters in the hills, with 3,600 foremen over them to keep the people working.

---

a3 Hebrew *Huram,* a variant of *Hiram*; also in verses 11 and 12　　*b8* Probably a variant of *almug*; possibly juniper　　*c10* That is, probably about 125,000 bushels (about 4,400 kiloliters)　　*d10* That is, probably about 115,000 gallons (about 440 kiloliters)

Solomon Builds the Temple

3 Then Solomon began to build the temple of the LORD in Jerusalem on Mount Moriah, where the LORD had appeared to his father David. It was on the threshing floor of Araunah[a] the Jebusite, the place provided by David. [2]He began building on the second day of the second month in the fourth year of his reign.

[3]The foundation Solomon laid for building the temple of God was sixty cubits long and twenty cubits wide[b] (using the cubit of the old standard). [4]The portico at the front of the temple was twenty cubits[c] long across the width of the building and twenty cubits[d] high.

He overlaid the inside with pure gold. [5]He paneled the main hall with pine and covered it with fine gold and decorated it with palm tree and chain designs. [6]He adorned the temple with precious stones. And the gold he used was gold of Parvaim. [7]He overlaid the ceiling beams, doorframes, walls and doors of the temple with gold, and he carved cherubim on the walls.

[8]He built the Most Holy Place, its length corresponding to the width of the temple—twenty cubits long and twenty cubits wide. He overlaid the inside with six hundred talents[e] of fine gold. [9]The gold nails weighed fifty shekels.[f] He also overlaid the upper parts with gold.

[10]In the Most Holy Place he made a pair of sculptured cherubim and overlaid them with gold. [11]The total wingspan of the cherubim was twenty cubits. One wing of the first cherub was five cubits[g] long and touched the temple wall, while its other wing, also five cubits long, touched the wing of the other cherub. [12]Similarly one wing of the second cherub was five cubits long and touched the other temple wall, and its other wing, also five cubits long, touched the wing of the first cherub. [13]The wings of these cherubim extended twenty cubits. They stood on their feet, facing the main hall.[h]

[14]He made the curtain of blue, purple and crimson yarn and fine linen, with cherubim worked into it.

[15]In the front of the temple he made two pillars, which ⌊together⌋ were thirty-five cubits[i] long, each with a capital on top measuring five cubits. [16]He made interwoven chains[j] and put them on top of the pillars. He also made a hundred pomegranates and attached them to the chains. [17]He erected the pillars in the front of the temple, one to the south and one to the north. The one to the south he named Jakin[k] and the one to the north Boaz.[l]

The Temple's Furnishings

4 He made a bronze altar twenty cubits long, twenty cubits wide and ten cubits high.[m] [2]He made the Sea of cast metal, circular in shape, measuring ten cubits from rim to rim and five cubits[n] high. It took a line of thirty cubits[o] to measure around it. [3]Below the rim, figures of bulls encircled it—ten to a cubit.[p] The bulls were cast in two rows in one piece with the Sea.

---

[a]1 Hebrew *Ornan,* a variant of *Araunah*   [b]3 That is, about 90 feet (about 27 meters) long and 30 feet (about 9 meters) wide   [c]4 That is, about 30 feet (about 9 meters); also in verses 8, 11 and 13   [d]4 Some Septuagint and Syriac manuscripts; Hebrew *and a hundred and twenty*   [e]8 That is, about 23 tons (about 21 metric tons)   [f]9 That is, about 1 1/4 pounds (about 0.6 kilogram)   [g]11 That is, about 7 1/2 feet (about 2.3 meters); also in verse 15   [h]13 Or *facing inward*   [i]15 That is, about 52 feet (about 16 meters)   [j]16 Or possibly *made chains in the inner sanctuary*; the meaning of the Hebrew for this phrase is uncertain.   [k]17 *Jakin* probably means *he establishes.*   [l]17 *Boaz* probably means *in him is strength.*   [m]1 That is, about 30 feet (about 9 meters) long and wide, and about 15 feet (about 4.5 meters) high   [n]2 That is, about 7 1/2 feet (about 2.3 meters)   [o]2 That is, about 45 feet (about 13.5 meters)   [p]3 That is, about 1 1/2 feet (about 0.5 meter)

---

1. Do you have a favorite place to "meet with God"? Where is it? 2. How did you decorate the walls of your bedroom when you were 12? 3. Which room would be the largest in your dream house? The kitchen? The bedroom? The library? The gym? The garage?

1. What was significant about locating the temple in Jerusalem? On Mount Moriah (see Ge 22)? On the threshing floor of Araunah (see 1Ch 21)? 2. What were the three main parts of the temple? (It may be helpful to draw a picture.) How large was each part? Can you think of a room you use comparable in size to each of these parts? (Note: One cubit equals approximately 1 1/2 feet.) 3. How was the main hall of the temple decorated? The Most Holy Place? Why was there so much attention given to the cherubim? 4. What special decorations would you have seen as you approached the temple? What message would they convey?

1. If you had been one of Solomon's advisors, would you have counseled him to spend so much on the temple construction? Or advised a more modest temple so that other things could be done? 2. What, if anything, does this chapter say to you about construction of church buildings today? About their decorations?

1. What piece of furniture do you most remember from your childhood home? 2. Have you ever made anything with your own hands that you were really proud of? If so, what?

1. In verses 1–11, what objects did Solomon have made to furnish the temple? How were each of these items used in worship? Which of them would you have wanted to examine closely? Why? 2. The Sea of cast metal is also described in 1 Kings 7:23–26. What are the differences between that description and the one in this chapter? How might you account for these differences? 3. In verses 12–18, how did Huram, the crafts-

man sent by the king of Tyre, use his skills to decorate the temple? Does it sound as if his work was greatly appreciated by later generations? **4.** How would the furnishings listed in verses 19–22 have helped the Israelites worship God? (Are any of these things important to you for your own worship now? Why?) **5.** In addition to worship, for what other functions does Solomon use the temple?

♡ **1.** How important are beautiful things for your own worship of God? Does a beautifully decorated church or chapel tend to help or hinder your worship? **2.** What skill do you possess that you could use to help others worship God? Where might you use it? **3.** Which of the temple objects mentioned in this chapter play an important role in the New Testament? **4.** Huram was remembered by later generations for his craftsmanship. What have you done in your life that you hope will be appreciated by later generations?

4The Sea stood on twelve bulls, three facing north, three facing west, three facing south and three facing east. The Sea rested on top of them, and their hindquarters were toward the center. **5**It was a handbreadth[a] in thickness, and its rim was like the rim of a cup, like a lily blossom. It held three thousand baths.[b]

6He then made ten basins for washing and placed five on the south side and five on the north. In them the things to be used for the burnt offerings were rinsed, but the Sea was to be used by the priests for washing.

7He made ten gold lampstands according to the specifications for them and placed them in the temple, five on the south side and five on the north.

8He made ten tables and placed them in the temple, five on the south side and five on the north. He also made a hundred gold sprinkling bowls.

9He made the courtyard of the priests, and the large court and the doors for the court, and overlaid the doors with bronze. **10**He placed the Sea on the south side, at the southeast corner.

11He also made the pots and shovels and sprinkling bowls.

So Huram finished the work he had undertaken for King Solomon in the temple of God:

12the two pillars;
  the two bowl-shaped capitals on top of the pillars;
  the two sets of network decorating the two bowl-shaped capitals on top of the pillars;
13the four hundred pomegranates for the two sets of network (two rows of pomegranates for each network, decorating the bowl-shaped capitals on top of the pillars);
14the stands with their basins;
15the Sea and the twelve bulls under it;
16the pots, shovels, meat forks and all related articles.

All the objects that Huram-Abi made for King Solomon for the temple of the LORD were of polished bronze. **17**The king had them cast in clay molds in the plain of the Jordan between Succoth and Zarethan.[c] **18**All these things that Solomon made amounted to so much that the weight of the bronze was not determined.

19Solomon also made all the furnishings that were in God's temple:

  the golden altar;
  the tables on which was the bread of the Presence;
20the lampstands of pure gold with their lamps, to burn in front of the inner sanctuary as prescribed;
21the gold floral work and lamps and tongs (they were solid gold);
22the pure gold wick trimmers, sprinkling bowls, dishes and censers; and the gold doors of the temple: the inner doors to the Most Holy Place and the doors of the main hall.

5 When all the work Solomon had done for the temple of the LORD was finished, he brought in the things his father David had dedicated—the silver and gold and all the furnishings—and he placed them in the treasuries of God's temple.

The Ark Brought to the Temple

2Then Solomon summoned to Jerusalem the elders of Israel, all the heads of the tribes and the chiefs of the Israelite families, to

☕ **1.** When was the last time your whole family got together? What was the occasion? **2.** What was the best thing about a parade when you were a child: (a) The bands? (b) The clowns? (c)

[a]5 That is, about 3 inches (about 8 centimeters) [b]5 That is, about 17,500 gallons (about 66 kiloliters) [c]17 Hebrew *Zeredatha*, a variant of *Zarethan*

bring up the ark of the LORD's covenant from Zion, the City of David. ³And all the men of Israel came together to the king at the time of the festival in the seventh month.

⁴When all the elders of Israel had arrived, the Levites took up the ark, ⁵and they brought up the ark and the Tent of Meeting and all the sacred furnishings in it. The priests, who were Levites, carried them up; ⁶and King Solomon and the entire assembly of Israel that had gathered about him were before the ark, sacrificing so many sheep and cattle that they could not be recorded or counted.

⁷The priests then brought the ark of the LORD's covenant to its place in the inner sanctuary of the temple, the Most Holy Place, and put it beneath the wings of the cherubim. ⁸The cherubim spread their wings over the place of the ark and covered the ark and its carrying poles. ⁹These poles were so long that their ends, extending from the ark, could be seen from in front of the inner sanctuary, but not from outside the Holy Place; and they are still there today. ¹⁰There was nothing in the ark except the two tablets that Moses had placed in it at Horeb, where the LORD made a covenant with the Israelites after they came out of Egypt.

¹¹The priests then withdrew from the Holy Place. All the priests who were there had consecrated themselves, regardless of their divisions. ¹²All the Levites who were musicians—Asaph, Heman, Jeduthun and their sons and relatives—stood on the east side of the altar, dressed in fine linen and playing cymbals, harps and lyres. They were accompanied by 120 priests sounding trumpets. ¹³The trumpeters and singers joined in unison, as with one voice, to give praise and thanks to the LORD. Accompanied by trumpets, cymbals and other instruments, they raised their voices in praise to the LORD and sang:

> "He is good;
>   his love endures forever."

Then the temple of the LORD was filled with a cloud, ¹⁴and the priests could not perform their service because of the cloud, for the glory of the LORD filled the temple of God.

6 Then Solomon said, "The LORD has said that he would dwell in a dark cloud; ²I have built a magnificent temple for you, a place for you to dwell forever."

³While the whole assembly of Israel was standing there, the king turned around and blessed them. ⁴Then he said:

"Praise be to the LORD, the God of Israel, who with his hands has fulfilled what he promised with his mouth to my father David. For he said, ⁵'Since the day I brought my people out of Egypt, I have not chosen a city in any tribe of Israel to have a temple built for my Name to be there, nor have I chosen anyone to be the leader over my people Israel. ⁶But now I have chosen Jerusalem for my Name to be there, and I have chosen David to rule my people Israel.'

⁷"My father David had it in his heart to build a temple for the Name of the LORD, the God of Israel. ⁸But the LORD said to my father David, 'Because it was in your heart to build a temple for my Name, you did well to have this in your heart. ⁹Nevertheless, you are not the one to build the temple, but your son, who is your own flesh and blood—he is the one who will build the temple for my Name.'

¹⁰"The LORD has kept the promise he made. I have succeeded David my father and now I sit on the throne of Israel, just as the LORD promised, and I have built the temple for the

The horses? What's the best part now? **3.** What musical instrument do you play or wish you could play?

1. Whom did Solomon summon to Jerusalem? For what purpose? On what previous occasion were these same people brought together? In moving the ark to the temple, what was the Levites' role? The king's role? The priests' role? (Which of these roles would you have liked to play?) **2.** Where did the ark of the Lord finally end up? Why such a fancy place for it? What attitudes toward God might this place have inspired in the people? In you? **3.** Who provided the music for this great celebration? What instruments were involved? What mark did two of these musicians leave on their peoples' worship (see Ps 39; 50; 62; 73–83; esp. 77)? **4.** What happened in the temple that seems to have resulted from the musical praise to the Lord? What previous experiences in Israel's history does this remind you of (see Ex 19:9 and 40:34)? **5.** How did the priests react when the glory of the Lord filled the temple? How about Solomon? (Which reaction—Solomon's or the priests'—is more characteristic of you in such a situation? Why?) **6.** In Solomon's speech to the people (6:4–11), what do you learn about God? About Solomon's father, King David? About Solomon himself? What main point do you think Solomon tried to make in this speech?

1. Had you received an invitation from Solomon to attend the celebration described in this chapter, why would you have gone: (a) To get a few days off work? (b) To be part of an important event? (c) To hear superb music? (d) To hobnob with the king and important people? (e) To see what was on the inside? **2.** What kind of music is the greatest help for you in your praise and worship with God? Is this preference shared by other people in your group? Family? Church? **3.** If together we are God's temple, as 1 Corinthians 3:16 says, how can we make sure that we are filled with the glory of the Lord when we meet? Or can we?

Name of the LORD, the God of Israel. [11]There I have placed the ark, in which is the covenant of the LORD that he made with the people of Israel."

Solomon's Prayer of Dedication

[12]Then Solomon stood before the altar of the LORD in front of the whole assembly of Israel and spread out his hands. [13]Now he had made a bronze platform, five cubits[a] long, five cubits wide and three cubits[b] high, and had placed it in the center of the outer court. He stood on the platform and then knelt down before the whole assembly of Israel and spread out his hands toward heaven. [14]He said:

"O LORD, God of Israel, there is no God like you in heaven or on earth—you who keep your covenant of love with your servants who continue wholeheartedly in your way. [15]You have kept your promise to your servant David my father; with your mouth you have promised and with your hand you have fulfilled it—as it is today.

[16]"Now LORD, God of Israel, keep for your servant David my father the promises you made to him when you said, 'You shall never fail to have a man to sit before me on the throne of Israel, if only your sons are careful in all they do to walk before me according to my law, as you have done.' [17]And now, O LORD, God of Israel, let your word that you promised your servant David come true.

[18]"But will God really dwell on earth with men? The heavens, even the highest heavens, cannot contain you. How much less this temple I have built! [19]Yet give attention to your servant's prayer and his plea for mercy, O LORD my God. Hear the cry and the prayer that your servant is praying in your presence. [20]May your eyes be open toward this temple day and night, this place of which you said you would put your Name there. May you hear the prayer your servant prays toward this place. [21]Hear the supplications of your servant and of your people Israel when they pray toward this place. Hear from heaven, your dwelling place; and when you hear, forgive.

[22]"When a man wrongs his neighbor and is required to take an oath and he comes and swears the oath before your altar in this temple, [23]then hear from heaven and act. Judge between your servants, repaying the guilty by bringing down on his own head what he has done. Declare the innocent not guilty and so establish his innocence.

[24]"When your people Israel have been defeated by an enemy because they have sinned against you and when they turn back and confess your name, praying and making supplication before you in this temple, [25]then hear from heaven and forgive the sin of your people Israel and bring them back to the land you gave to them and their fathers.

[26]"When the heavens are shut up and there is no rain because your people have sinned against you, and when they pray toward this place and confess your name and turn from their sin because you have afflicted them, [27]then hear from heaven and forgive the sin of your servants, your people Israel. Teach them the right way to live, and send rain on the land you gave your people for an inheritance.

---

1. On which of the following occasions did you pray as a child: (a) Before meals? (b) During church? (c) When in big trouble? (d) Before bed? (e) Never? 2. Where do you feel the closest to heaven? Why? 3. To whom were you most likely to go for help as a teenager: (a) Your parents? (b) Minister, priest, or rabbi? (c) Teacher? (d) Close friend?

1. Where does Solomon position himself to lead his dedication prayer? What body positions does he use? (Which of these do you use in prayer?) 2. Solomon begins his prayer in verses 14–15 by praising God for what? Why is praise so often a good way to begin a prayer? 3. About what promise does Solomon remind God in verses 16–17? What is this promise (found in 2Sa 7:12–17) usually called? What are its conditions? Why does Solomon have to remind God, or is this reminder really for others? 4. How many different ways does Solomon appeal to God to hear his prayer in verses 18–21? Why all the repetition? Where does he think God is (see vv. 21,23,25,27,30, 33,35 and 39)? 5. In verses 22–39, Solomon envisions seven different occasions which call for prayer in or toward the temple (each is introduced by the word *when*). Why do you think the occasion in verses 22–23 is mentioned first? What does this say about the priority of "justice for all" in a society? 6. What are the next three occasions for prayer mentioned by Solomon in verses 24–31? Why has each of these difficulties come about? What specifically must the people do if they want God to answer their prayer? Must they actually be in the temple to pray in each of these situations? 7. In verses 32–33, Solomon prays for foreigners. What would draw a foreigner to the temple? Why does Solomon ask the Lord to answer these "foreign prayers"? Does it seem to you that Solomon expects both of these to happen? How were people supposed to pray to God as captives in a land far away when they couldn't reach the temple? 8. On what note does Solomon conclude his prayer in verses 40–42? Why would these words have been used later by pilgrims

---

a13 That is, about 7 1/2 feet (about 2.3 meters)   b13 That is, about 4 1/2 feet (about 1.3 meters)

28"When famine or plague comes to the land, or blight or mildew, locusts or grasshoppers, or when enemies besiege them in any of their cities, whatever disaster or disease may come, **29**and when a prayer or plea is made by any of your people Israel—each one aware of his afflictions and pains, and spreading out his hands toward this temple— **30**then hear from heaven, your dwelling place. Forgive, and deal with each man according to all he does, since you know his heart (for you alone know the hearts of men), **31**so that they will fear you and walk in your ways all the time they live in the land you gave our fathers.

32"As for the foreigner who does not belong to your people Israel but has come from a distant land because of your great name and your mighty hand and your outstretched arm—when he comes and prays toward this temple, **33**then hear from heaven, your dwelling place, and do whatever the foreigner asks of you, so that all the peoples of the earth may know your name and fear you, as do your own people Israel, and may know that this house I have built bears your Name.

34"When your people go to war against their enemies, wherever you send them, and when they pray to you toward this city you have chosen and the temple I have built for your Name, **35**then hear from heaven their prayer and their plea, and uphold their cause.

36"When they sin against you—for there is no one who does not sin—and you become angry with them and give them over to the enemy, who takes them captive to a land far away or near; **37**and if they have a change of heart in the land where they are held captive, and repent and plead with you in the land of their captivity and say, 'We have sinned, we have done wrong and acted wickedly'; **38**and if they turn back to you with all their heart and soul in the land of their captivity where they were taken, and pray toward the land you gave their fathers, toward the city you have chosen and toward the temple I have built for your Name; **39**then from heaven, your dwelling place, hear their prayer and their pleas, and uphold their cause. And forgive your people, who have sinned against you.

40"Now, my God, may your eyes be open and your ears attentive to the prayers offered in this place.

> **41**"Now arise, O Lᴏʀᴅ God, and come to your
>   resting place,
> you and the ark of your might.
> May your priests, O Lᴏʀᴅ God, be clothed
>   with salvation,
> may your saints rejoice in your goodness.
> **42**O Lᴏʀᴅ God, do not reject your anointed one.
> Remember the great love promised to
>   David your servant."

The Dedication of the Temple

7 When Solomon finished praying, fire came down from heaven and consumed the burnt offering and the sacrifices, and the glory of the Lᴏʀᴅ filled the temple. **2**The priests could not enter the temple of the Lᴏʀᴅ because the glory of the Lᴏʀᴅ filled it. **3**When all the Israelites saw the fire coming down and the glory of the Lᴏʀᴅ above the temple, they knelt on the pavement with their faces to the ground, and they worshiped and gave thanks to the Lᴏʀᴅ, saying,

coming up to Jerusalem to pray at the temple (see Ps 132:8–11)?

1. Where do you think God is when you pray? What do you feel is the best place and posture for personal prayer? For public prayer? Why? **2.** Which of the following is the most important characteristic about God when you pray? (a) God's nearness? (b) God's faithfulness? (c) God's forgiveness? (d) God's tenderness? **3.** Which specific situation mentioned by Solomon do you feel the need to pray for as a group? **4.** Is Solomon's prayer a model for national days of prayer? Why or why not? **5.** What is the first thing for which you would praise God in prayer today?

1. What was the best party you ever attended? How long did it last? How long did you last? **2.** Which "big event" would you want to attend the most and why: (a) The Super Bowl? (b) A presidential inauguration? (c) The Cannes Film Festival? (d) Easter at the Vatican?

1. How did the Lord respond to Solomon's prayer of dedication? What impact did this have on the priests? On all the Israelites? 2. In what loving ways did Solomon, the priests and Levites each worship God? 3. Get out your pocket calculators: If the priests kept the middle courtyard busy around the clock for 14 days, how many sacrifices per hour would they have had to make? Does this sound excessive to you? A waste? Or what? 4. What thoughts and feelings did the people take home with them from this great festival? What would have impressed you the most if you had been there?

1. What makes a celebration enjoyable for you? Is there any time soon your group could have a "Solomon-like" party? 2. What do you offer to God to express your gratitude and thanksgiving?

1. What is the most memorable or emotional dream you have had? What did it mean to you? 2. Which did your parents or guardians use to motivate you as a child: Carrot or stick?

1. This is the second time the Lord appears to Solomon in a dream. (Compare with the first time in 2Ch 1:7ff.) Does this second time smack more of "the carrot" or "the stick"? Explain. 2. What situation and people did verse 14 originally address? How would this verse still apply? 3. In verses 17–22, what are God's promises to Solomon and the kings to follow? What are the warnings to those who don't walk as David did? Do these warnings seem too harsh to you? Why? 4. How would the Lord's promise in verse 18 have affected Israelites in times of national crisis?

1. What might God say if he appeared to your nation's leader tonight as he did to Solomon? 2. Do any of your nation's problems happen because people "serve other gods and worship them" (v. 19)? What should be done about that?

"He is good;
    his love endures forever."

⁴Then the king and all the people offered sacrifices before the LORD. ⁵And King Solomon offered a sacrifice of twenty-two thousand head of cattle and a hundred and twenty thousand sheep and goats. So the king and all the people dedicated the temple of God. ⁶The priests took their positions, as did the Levites with the LORD's musical instruments, which King David had made for praising the LORD and which were used when he gave thanks, saying, "His love endures forever." Opposite the Levites, the priests blew their trumpets, and all the Israelites were standing.

⁷Solomon consecrated the middle part of the courtyard in front of the temple of the LORD, and there he offered burnt offerings and the fat of the fellowship offerings,ᵃ because the bronze altar he had made could not hold the burnt offerings, the grain offerings and the fat portions.

⁸So Solomon observed the festival at that time for seven days, and all Israel with him—a vast assembly, people from Leboᵇ Hamath to the Wadi of Egypt. ⁹On the eighth day they held an assembly, for they had celebrated the dedication of the altar for seven days and the festival for seven days more. ¹⁰On the twenty-third day of the seventh month he sent the people to their homes, joyful and glad in heart for the good things the LORD had done for David and Solomon and for his people Israel.

The LORD Appears to Solomon

¹¹When Solomon had finished the temple of the LORD and the royal palace, and had succeeded in carrying out all he had in mind to do in the temple of the LORD and in his own palace, ¹²the LORD appeared to him at night and said:

"I have heard your prayer and have chosen this place for myself as a temple for sacrifices.

¹³"When I shut up the heavens so that there is no rain, or command locusts to devour the land or send a plague among my people, ¹⁴if my people, who are called by my name, will humble themselves and pray and seek my face and turn from their wicked ways, then will I hear from heaven and will forgive their sin and will heal their land. ¹⁵Now my eyes will be open and my ears attentive to the prayers offered in this place. ¹⁶I have chosen and consecrated this temple so that my Name may be there forever. My eyes and my heart will always be there.

¹⁷"As for you, if you walk before me as David your father did, and do all I command, and observe my decrees and laws, ¹⁸I will establish your royal throne, as I covenanted with David your father when I said, 'You shall never fail to have a man to rule over Israel.'

¹⁹"But if youᶜ turn away and forsake the decrees and commands I have given youᶜ and go off to serve other gods and worship them, ²⁰then I will uproot Israel from my land, which I have given them, and will reject this temple I have consecrated for my Name. I will make it a byword and an object of ridicule among all peoples. ²¹And though this temple is now so imposing, all who pass by will be appalled and say, 'Why has the LORD done such a thing to this land and to this temple?' ²²People will answer, 'Because they have forsaken the

---

ᵃ7 Traditionally *peace offerings*   ᵇ8 Or *from the entrance to*   ᶜ19 The Hebrew is plural.

LORD, the God of their fathers, who brought them out of Egypt, and have embraced other gods, worshiping and serving them—that is why he brought all this disaster on them.' "

Solomon's Other Activities

8 At the end of twenty years, during which Solomon built the temple of the LORD and his own palace, ²Solomon rebuilt the villages that Hiram*a* had given him, and settled Israelites in them. ³Solomon then went to Hamath Zobah and captured it. ⁴He also built up Tadmor in the desert and all the store cities he had built in Hamath. ⁵He rebuilt Upper Beth Horon and Lower Beth Horon as fortified cities, with walls and with gates and bars, ⁶as well as Baalath and all his store cities, and all the cities for his chariots and for his horses*b*—whatever he desired to build in Jerusalem, in Lebanon and throughout all the territory he ruled.

⁷All the people left from the Hittites, Amorites, Perizzites, Hivites and Jebusites (these peoples were not Israelites), ⁸that is, their descendants remaining in the land, whom the Israelites had not destroyed—these Solomon conscripted for his slave labor force, as it is to this day. ⁹But Solomon did not make slaves of the Israelites for his work; they were his fighting men, commanders of his captains, and commanders of his chariots and charioteers. ¹⁰They were also King Solomon's chief officials—two hundred and fifty officials supervising the men.

¹¹Solomon brought Pharaoh's daughter up from the City of David to the palace he had built for her, for he said, "My wife must not live in the palace of David king of Israel, because the places the ark of the LORD has entered are holy."

¹²On the altar of the LORD that he had built in front of the portico, Solomon sacrificed burnt offerings to the LORD, ¹³according to the daily requirement for offerings commanded by Moses for Sabbaths, New Moons and the three annual feasts—the Feast of Unleavened Bread, the Feast of Weeks and the Feast of Tabernacles. ¹⁴In keeping with the ordinance of his father David, he appointed the divisions of the priests for their duties, and the Levites to lead the praise and to assist the priests according to each day's requirement. He also appointed the gatekeepers by divisions for the various gates, because this was what David the man of God had ordered. ¹⁵They did not deviate from the king's commands to the priests or to the Levites in any matter, including that of the treasuries.

¹⁶All Solomon's work was carried out, from the day the foundation of the temple of the LORD was laid until its completion. So the temple of the LORD was finished.

¹⁷Then Solomon went to Ezion Geber and Elath on the coast of Edom. ¹⁸And Hiram sent him ships commanded by his own officers, men who knew the sea. These, with Solomon's men, sailed to Ophir and brought back four hundred and fifty talents*c* of gold, which they delivered to King Solomon.

The Queen of Sheba Visits Solomon

9 When the queen of Sheba heard of Solomon's fame, she came to Jerusalem to test him with hard questions. Arriving with a very great caravan—with camels carrying spices, large quantities of gold, and precious stones—she came to Solomon and talked with him about all she had on her mind. ²Solomon answered all her questions; nothing was too hard for him to explain to her. ³When

---

1. Which of the following occupations are closest to your dream? (a) Astronaut? (b) Movie star? (c) Professional athlete? (d) President? (e) Research scientist? 2. What major project would you like to accomplish in the next five years?

1. After skimming through this chapter, how many different major projects did Solomon accomplish in his career as king? What talents did he demonstrate in these projects? What do you think Solomon did best? 2. Where did Solomon get the labor to do all the building described in verses 1–6? Who were the winners in this arrangement? What precedent did this set? 3. Does Solomon's treatment of his wife in verse 11 seem right to you? What dangers are lurking behind this situation (see 1Ki 11:1–13)? 4. How is Solomon's concern for worship demonstrated in verses 12–16? Whose lead is he following? Does this make him a legalist? A traditionalist? 5. What do verses 17–18 indicate about Solomon's skills in the sphere of international commerce?

1. What do you find admirable in Solomon's accomplishments as king? What would you rather he hadn't done? Why? 2. How is your own worship of God like Solomon's? Does his example suggest any changes you need to make?

1. Whom did you most admire as a teenager? Why? 2. If you could spend a day with one of the following, whom would you prefer and why: (a) Caesar Augustus? (b) Joan of Arc? (c) Queen Elizabeth I? (d) Napoleon?

1. The Queen of Sheba and her retinue probably traveled over 1,000 miles to Jerusalem.

---

a2 Hebrew *Huram*, a variant of *Hiram*; also in verse 18   *b6* Or *charioteers*
c18 That is, about 17 tons (about 16 metric tons)

What reasons can you discover in verses 1–12 for such a spectacular visit? **2.** What kinds of things about Solomon and his capital impressed the Queen? What about Solomon impresses you the most? **3.** How did the Queen show her admiration for Solomon? Do you feel her words of praise in verses 5–8 had some political motivation? Personal attraction? **4.** What precious gifts did the Queen give to Solomon? What did he give to her in return? How did this exchange enhance his greatness?

♡ **1.** Solomon answered all the Queen's questions. What one question would you want Solomon to answer for you? **2.** Who is the one person you turn to when you need wise advice? How has that person demonstrated his or her wisdom to you in the past?

☕ **1.** If you were suddenly given $1,000,000, what is the first thing you would go out and buy? **2.** What one possession were you the most proud of as a teenager? Do you still have it?

📖 **1.** Solomon's wealth is legendary. According to verses 13–28, what were the sources of this wealth? **2.** How did Solomon display his fabulous wealth for people to see? Did any of these projects have a practical value to them, or were they all merely decorative? **3.** Try to sketch a picture of the great throne described in verses 17–19. Do any of the parts seem to have symbolic meanings? What thoughts might visitors have had as they approached this throne? **4.** Why was Solomon considered a world leader of his time? On what was his leadership based? How do you think this "world status" benefited Israel as a people? Hurt them? **5.** The chronicler sees Solomon's reign as an unqualified success. Do you? Why or why not?

♡ **1.** Do you wish you were a wealthy person (if not already)? In what ways would you use your wealth and possessions to bring honor and glory to God?

the queen of Sheba saw the wisdom of Solomon, as well as the palace he had built, ⁴the food on his table, the seating of his officials, the attending servants in their robes, the cupbearers in their robes and the burnt offerings he made at ᵃ the temple of the LORD, she was overwhelmed.

⁵She said to the king, "The report I heard in my own country about your achievements and your wisdom is true. ⁶But I did not believe what they said until I came and saw with my own eyes. Indeed, not even half the greatness of your wisdom was told me; you have far exceeded the report I heard. ⁷How happy your men must be! How happy your officials, who continually stand before you and hear your wisdom! ⁸Praise be to the LORD your God, who has delighted in you and placed you on his throne as king to rule for the LORD your God. Because of the love of your God for Israel and his desire to uphold them forever, he has made you king over them, to maintain justice and righteousness."

⁹Then she gave the king 120 talents ᵇ of gold, large quantities of spices, and precious stones. There had never been such spices as those the queen of Sheba gave to King Solomon.

¹⁰(The men of Hiram and the men of Solomon brought gold from Ophir; they also brought algumwood ᶜ and precious stones. ¹¹The king used the algumwood to make steps for the temple of the LORD and for the royal palace, and to make harps and lyres for the musicians. Nothing like them had ever been seen in Judah.)

¹²King Solomon gave the queen of Sheba all she desired and asked for; he gave her more than she had brought to him. Then she left and returned with her retinue to her own country.

Solomon's Splendor

¹³The weight of the gold that Solomon received yearly was 666 talents, ᵈ ¹⁴not including the revenues brought in by merchants and traders. Also all the kings of Arabia and the governors of the land brought gold and silver to Solomon.

¹⁵King Solomon made two hundred large shields of hammered gold; six hundred bekas ᵉ of hammered gold went into each shield. ¹⁶He also made three hundred small shields of hammered gold, with three hundred bekas ᶠ of gold in each shield. The king put them in the Palace of the Forest of Lebanon.

¹⁷Then the king made a great throne inlaid with ivory and overlaid with pure gold. ¹⁸The throne had six steps, and a footstool of gold was attached to it. On both sides of the seat were armrests, with a lion standing beside each of them. ¹⁹Twelve lions stood on the six steps, one at either end of each step. Nothing like it had ever been made for any other kingdom. ²⁰All King Solomon's goblets were gold, and all the household articles in the Palace of the Forest of Lebanon were pure gold. Nothing was made of silver, because silver was considered of little value in Solomon's day. ²¹The king had a fleet of trading ships ᵍ manned by Hiram's ʰ men. Once every three years it returned, carrying gold, silver and ivory, and apes and baboons.

²²King Solomon was greater in riches and wisdom than all the other kings of the earth. ²³All the kings of the earth sought audience with Solomon to hear the wisdom God had put in his heart. ²⁴Year after year, everyone who came brought a gift—articles of

silver and gold, and robes, weapons and spices, and horses and mules.

²⁵Solomon had four thousand stalls for horses and chariots, and twelve thousand horses,ᵃ which he kept in the chariot cities and also with him in Jerusalem. ²⁶He ruled over all the kings from the Riverᵇ to the land of the Philistines, as far as the border of Egypt. ²⁷The king made silver as common in Jerusalem as stones, and cedar as plentiful as sycamore-fig trees in the foothills. ²⁸Solomon's horses were imported from Egyptᶜ and from all other countries.

Solomon's Death

²⁹As for the other events of Solomon's reign, from beginning to end, are they not written in the records of Nathan the prophet, in the prophecy of Ahijah the Shilonite and in the visions of Iddo the seer concerning Jeroboam son of Nebat? ³⁰Solomon reigned in Jerusalem over all Israel forty years. ³¹Then he rested with his fathers and was buried in the city of David his father. And Rehoboam his son succeeded him as king.

Israel Rebels Against Rehoboam

10 Rehoboam went to Shechem, for all the Israelites had gone there to make him king. ²When Jeroboam son of Nebat heard this (he was in Egypt, where he had fled from King Solomon), he returned from Egypt. ³So they sent for Jeroboam, and he and all Israel went to Rehoboam and said to him: ⁴"Your father put a heavy yoke on us, but now lighten the harsh labor and the heavy yoke he put on us, and we will serve you."

⁵Rehoboam answered, "Come back to me in three days." So the people went away.

⁶Then King Rehoboam consulted the elders who had served his father Solomon during his lifetime. "How would you advise me to answer these people?" he asked.

⁷They replied, "If you will be kind to these people and please them and give them a favorable answer, they will always be your servants."

⁸But Rehoboam rejected the advice the elders gave him and consulted the young men who had grown up with him and were serving him. ⁹He asked them, "What is your advice? How should we answer these people who say to me, 'Lighten the yoke your father put on us'?"

¹⁰The young men who had grown up with him replied, "Tell the people who have said to you, 'Your father put a heavy yoke on us, but make our yoke lighter'—tell them, 'My little finger is thicker than my father's waist. ¹¹My father laid on you a heavy yoke; I will make it even heavier. My father scourged you with whips; I will scourge you with scorpions.'"

¹²Three days later Jeroboam and all the people returned to Rehoboam, as the king had said, "Come back to me in three days." ¹³The king answered them harshly. Rejecting the advice of the elders, ¹⁴he followed the advice of the young men and said, "My father made your yoke heavy; I will make it even heavier. My father scourged you with whips; I will scourge you with scorpions." ¹⁵So the king did not listen to the people, for this turn of events was from God, to fulfill the word the LORD had spoken to Jeroboam son of Nebat through Ahijah the Shilonite.

¹⁶When all Israel saw that the king refused to listen to them, they answered the king:

What spiritual dangers might you encounter? **2.** What three accomplishments do you want mentioned in your obituary? Is there anything you hope gets left out?

1. When faced with a big bully in the school yard, you were trained to: (a) Keep a safe distance? (b) Report him to a teacher? (c) Turn the other cheek? (d) Punch and run? **2.** What one person would you love to give advice to if he or she would listen?

1. Heavily taxed and forced into labor for Solomon's lavish building program, the people of Israel rebelled. Who plays major roles in this succession drama? Is the exiled hero to be blamed for fostering a rebellion (see 1Ki 11:26–40)? **2.** As the sides begin to line up, who has the power? Rehoboam has what going for him? What kind of power does Jeroboam wield? **3.** After Jeroboam and the Israelites visit Rehoboam, Rehoboam consults the elders for advice. What is their advice and why is it rejected? Could Rehoboam read motives into their soft touch? Did Rehoboam have models of successful soft touch kings? **4.** Rehoboam's pals counsel for the stiff punch. Why? Could greed be a motive since they already controlled the school yard? What models of this leadership style did Rehoboam have? **5.** What symbols does Rehoboam choose to show the people the kind of administration he intended to conduct? **6.** Like workers dissatisfied with contract talks, the northern tribes turn thumbs down to Rehoboam's deal. Paraphrase their response (v. 16) in modern terms. **7.** What is God's role in the nation's breakup? Is that surprising to you? Why or why not?

ᵃ25 Or *charioteers*   ᵇ26 That is, the Euphrates   ᶜ28 Or possibly *Muzur,* a region in Cilicia

1. What lessons about youth or wisdom is the chronicler telling through these players? Is it ever wise to give leadership to the young? (Rehoboam was 41 in this chapter.) **2.** Are splits in churches or nations ever right? What conditions might justify a split? What about splits in families? **3.** Have you ever played the part of a "Christian bully"? Is the stiff punch ever necessary, or is the soft touch always the best policy? What Christian standards do you use in solving conflicts?

If you had a backyard bomb shelter what three books would you put in it?

1. What is Rehoboam's strategy for protecting the few against the many? **2.** Why do the Levites come south? How do these refugees strengthen public courage against Jeroboam's northern forces? **3.** Are Rehoboam and the Levites acting out of paranoia or conviction? Fear of man or fear of God? **4.** Geneatectives: Was Maacah a "daughter of Absalom" (v. 21), or more likely, a granddaughter (see 2Sa 14:27)? **5.** What other strategies does Rehoboam employ to coalesce his power (vv. 22–23)?

What would you do if you were forced to leave your job, your property or your family because of your faith?

"What share do we have in David,
  what part in Jesse's son?
To your tents, O Israel!
  Look after your own house, O David!"

So all the Israelites went home. [17]But as for the Israelites who were living in the towns of Judah, Rehoboam still ruled over them.

[18]King Rehoboam sent out Adoniram,[a] who was in charge of forced labor, but the Israelites stoned him to death. King Rehoboam, however, managed to get into his chariot and escape to Jerusalem. [19]So Israel has been in rebellion against the house of David to this day.

11 When Rehoboam arrived in Jerusalem, he mustered the house of Judah and Benjamin—a hundred and eighty thousand fighting men—to make war against Israel and to regain the kingdom for Rehoboam.

[2]But this word of the LORD came to Shemaiah the man of God: [3]"Say to Rehoboam son of Solomon king of Judah and to all the Israelites in Judah and Benjamin, [4]'This is what the LORD says: Do not go up to fight against your brothers. Go home, every one of you, for this is my doing.'" So they obeyed the words of the LORD and turned back from marching against Jeroboam.

Rehoboam Fortifies Judah

[5]Rehoboam lived in Jerusalem and built up towns for defense in Judah: [6]Bethlehem, Etam, Tekoa, [7]Beth Zur, Soco, Adullam, [8]Gath, Mareshah, Ziph, [9]Adoraim, Lachish, Azekah, [10]Zorah, Aijalon and Hebron. These were fortified cities in Judah and Benjamin. [11]He strengthened their defenses and put commanders in them, with supplies of food, olive oil and wine. [12]He put shields and spears in all the cities, and made them very strong. So Judah and Benjamin were his.

[13]The priests and Levites from all their districts throughout Israel sided with him. [14]The Levites even abandoned their pasturelands and property, and came to Judah and Jerusalem because Jeroboam and his sons had rejected them as priests of the LORD. [15]And he appointed his own priests for the high places and for the goat and calf idols he had made. [16]Those from every tribe of Israel who set their hearts on seeking the LORD, the God of Israel, followed the Levites to Jerusalem to offer sacrifices to the LORD, the God of their fathers. [17]They strengthened the kingdom of Judah and supported Rehoboam son of Solomon three years, walking in the ways of David and Solomon during this time.

Rehoboam's Family

[18]Rehoboam married Mahalath, who was the daughter of David's son Jerimoth and of Abihail, the daughter of Jesse's son Eliab. [19]She bore him sons: Jeush, Shemariah and Zaham. [20]Then he married Maacah daughter of Absalom, who bore him Abijah, Attai, Ziza and Shelomith. [21]Rehoboam loved Maacah daughter of Absalom more than any of his other wives and concubines. In all, he had eighteen wives and sixty concubines, twenty-eight sons and sixty daughters.

[22]Rehoboam appointed Abijah son of Maacah to be the chief prince among his brothers, in order to make him king. [23]He acted wisely, dispersing some of his sons throughout the districts of Judah and Benjamin, and to all the fortified cities. He gave them abundant provisions and took many wives for them.

a18 Hebrew *Hadoram*, a variant of *Adoniram*

Shishak Attacks Jerusalem

12 After Rehoboam's position as king was established and he had become strong, he and all Israel[a] with him abandoned the law of the LORD. ²Because they had been unfaithful to the LORD, Shishak king of Egypt attacked Jerusalem in the fifth year of King Rehoboam. ³With twelve hundred chariots and sixty thousand horsemen and the innumerable troops of Libyans, Sukkites and Cushites[b] that came with him from Egypt, ⁴he captured the fortified cities of Judah and came as far as Jerusalem.

⁵Then the prophet Shemaiah came to Rehoboam and to the leaders of Judah who had assembled in Jerusalem for fear of Shishak, and he said to them, "This is what the LORD says, 'You have abandoned me; therefore, I now abandon you to Shishak.'"

⁶The leaders of Israel and the king humbled themselves and said, "The LORD is just."

⁷When the LORD saw that they humbled themselves, this word of the LORD came to Shemaiah: "Since they have humbled themselves, I will not destroy them but will soon give them deliverance. My wrath will not be poured out on Jerusalem through Shishak. ⁸They will, however, become subject to him, so that they may learn the difference between serving me and serving the kings of other lands."

⁹When Shishak king of Egypt attacked Jerusalem, he carried off the treasures of the temple of the LORD and the treasures of the royal palace. He took everything, including the gold shields Solomon had made. ¹⁰So King Rehoboam made bronze shields to replace them and assigned these to the commanders of the guard on duty at the entrance to the royal palace. ¹¹Whenever the king went to the LORD's temple, the guards went with him, bearing the shields, and afterward they returned them to the guardroom.

¹²Because Rehoboam humbled himself, the LORD's anger turned from him, and he was not totally destroyed. Indeed, there was some good in Judah.

¹³King Rehoboam established himself firmly in Jerusalem and continued as king. He was forty-one years old when he became king, and he reigned seventeen years in Jerusalem, the city the LORD had chosen out of all the tribes of Israel in which to put his Name. His mother's name was Naamah; she was an Ammonite. ¹⁴He did evil because he had not set his heart on seeking the LORD.

¹⁵As for the events of Rehoboam's reign, from beginning to end, are they not written in the records of Shemaiah the prophet and of Iddo the seer that deal with genealogies? There was continual warfare between Rehoboam and Jeroboam. ¹⁶Rehoboam rested with his fathers and was buried in the City of David. And Abijah his son succeeded him as king.

Abijah King of Judah

13 In the eighteenth year of the reign of Jeroboam, Abijah became king of Judah, ²and he reigned in Jerusalem three years. His mother's name was Maacah,[c] a daughter[d] of Uriel of Gibeah.

There was war between Abijah and Jeroboam. ³Abijah went into battle with a force of four hundred thousand able fighting men, and Jeroboam drew up a battle line against him with eight hundred thousand able troops.

⁴Abijah stood on Mount Zemaraim, in the hill country of Ephra-

1. Ever get stopped for speeding? Ever talk your way out of a ticket? 2. Likewise, ever get out of punishment you deserved from the hands of your parents? How did you manage that?

1. How does this chapter build on the previous ones? Why does Rehoboam abandon the law of the Lord at this time (v. 1)? Why does that so anger the Lord (see 1Ki 14:22–24)? 2. What prompts Shishak to attack and Shemaiah to warn Jerusalem? With what effect? If not for this prophecy, do you think Rehoboam would have humbled himself anyway, or fought off the attackers? 3. What do you think of Rehoboam's punishment and deliverance: Too soft for a holy God? Too bitter a pill to swallow for a proud king? Just right for God's wrath and mercy? 4. If chapter 12 shows the rewards for obedience to God (prosperity, power, public acclaim, productive family), what covenant principle does chapter 13 illustrate (see also 7:14)? 5. To make this lesson stick, and bring some good out of Judah (v. 12), what part was played by the guards (vv. 9–11)? By Shemaiah and Iddo (v. 15)? By outside forces? By his family?

1. If this chapter was your point for rediscovering God, what would you learn about his character and purpose? 2. What examples does Rehoboam leave you to follow? To avoid? 3. When are you tempted to compromise with God's law: When you feel strongest or most vulnerable? Why is that? 4. Do you have a friend like Shemaiah who keeps you in line by interpreting the meaning of things that are happening to you?

1. If you were chained to the wall in the cellar of a foreign jail, who of the following characters would you like to see leading the rescue team: (a) Indiana Jones? (b) James Bond? (c) Sheriff Matt Dillon? (d) Dr. Who? Why? 2. In what jams have you found yourself this past week?

1. What kind of leader is Abijah: Cautious? Timid? Foolhardy? Righteous? Compare t' picture of Abijah in I Kings 15:' with this chapter: How are the

---

a1 That is, Judah, as frequently in 2 Chronicles   *b3* That is, people from the upper Nile region   *c2* Most Septuagint manuscripts and Syriac (see also 2 Chron. 11:20 and 1 Kings 15:2); Hebrew *Micaiah*   *d2* Or *granddaughter*

ferent? **2.** How many fighting men does Abijah have? What about Jeroboam? What has led to the two armies facing off? **3.** Though Jeroboam has twice the fighting force, Abijah appears confident. Why? What could the strange term "covenant of salt" mean to Abijah (see Lev 2:13; Nu 18:19)? **4.** What clues should show intelligent Israelites the error of Jeroboam's rebellion? **5.** How does Abijah mock Israel's new gods or "not gods" (v. 9)? **6.** While Abijah is speaking, what is Jeroboam's strategy? What turns the battle from a surprise attack into a victorious routing of the Israelites? **7.** Besides the battle what does Jeroboam lose? What does Abijah gain? How is Abijah's leadership rewarded?

♡ **1.** Many Bible stories tell how God routed enemies when his people were outnumbered. What do these stories tell you about God's strategy vs. human strategy? About risk taking? How are you at taking risks? **2.** What gods or "not gods" (v. 9) compete for people's adoration today? Why do these "not gods" have any appeal? What "not gods" tend to compete for your adoration?

im, and said, "Jeroboam and all Israel, listen to me! [5]Don't you know that the LORD, the God of Israel, has given the kingship of Israel to David and his descendants forever by a covenant of salt? [6]Yet Jeroboam son of Nebat, an official of Solomon son of David, rebelled against his master. [7]Some worthless scoundrels gathered around him and opposed Rehoboam son of Solomon when he was young and indecisive and not strong enough to resist them.

[8]"And now you plan to resist the kingdom of the LORD, which is in the hands of David's descendants. You are indeed a vast army and have with you the golden calves that Jeroboam made to be your gods. [9]But didn't you drive out the priests of the LORD, the sons of Aaron, and the Levites, and make priests of your own as the peoples of other lands do? Whoever comes to consecrate himself with a young bull and seven rams may become a priest of what are not gods.

[10]"As for us, the LORD is our God, and we have not forsaken him. The priests who serve the LORD are sons of Aaron, and the Levites assist them. [11]Every morning and evening they present burnt offerings and fragrant incense to the LORD. They set out the bread on the ceremonially clean table and light the lamps on the gold lampstand every evening. We are observing the requirements of the LORD our God. But you have forsaken him. [12]God is with us; he is our leader. His priests with their trumpets will sound the battle cry against you. Men of Israel, do not fight against the LORD, the God of your fathers, for you will not succeed."

[13]Now Jeroboam had sent troops around to the rear, so that while he was in front of Judah the ambush was behind them. [14]Judah turned and saw that they were being attacked at both front and rear. Then they cried out to the LORD. The priests blew their trumpets [15]and the men of Judah raised the battle cry. At the sound of their battle cry, God routed Jeroboam and all Israel before Abijah and Judah. [16]The Israelites fled before Judah, and God delivered them into their hands. [17]Abijah and his men inflicted heavy losses on them, so that there were five hundred thousand casualties among Israel's able men. [18]The men of Israel were subdued on that occasion, and the men of Judah were victorious because they relied on the LORD, the God of their fathers.

[19]Abijah pursued Jeroboam and took from him the towns of Bethel, Jeshanah and Ephron, with their surrounding villages. [20]Jeroboam did not regain power during the time of Abijah. And the LORD struck him down and he died.

[21]But Abijah grew in strength. He married fourteen wives and had twenty-two sons and sixteen daughters.

[22]The other events of Abijah's reign, what he did and what he said, are written in the annotations of the prophet Iddo.

14 And Abijah rested with his fathers and was buried in the City of David. Asa his son succeeded him as king, and in his days the country was at peace for ten years.

Asa King of Judah

[2]Asa did what was good and right in the eyes of the LORD his God. [3]He removed the foreign altars and the high places, smashed the sacred stones and cut down the Asherah poles.[a] [4]He commanded Judah to seek the LORD, the God of their fathers, and to obey his laws and commands. [5]He removed the high places and incense altars in every town in Judah, and the kingdom was at peace under him. [6]He built up the fortified cities of Judah, since

1. What's most fun for you to tear down, take apart or clean up: (a) A campsite? (b) Garden weeds? (c) Car engine? (d) Bicycle? (e) Old apple tree? (f) ⌐e on frying pans? (g) Clothes ⌐hat feels good about it? ⌐e tearing down or taking than setting up and

-8-
dif-

a3 That is, symbols of the goddess Asherah; here and elsewhere in 2 Chronicles

the land was at peace. No one was at war with him during those years, for the LORD gave him rest.

[7] "Let us build up these towns," he said to Judah, "and put walls around them, with towers, gates and bars. The land is still ours, because we have sought the LORD our God; we sought him and he has given us rest on every side." So they built and prospered.

[8] Asa had an army of three hundred thousand men from Judah, equipped with large shields and with spears, and two hundred and eighty thousand from Benjamin, armed with small shields and with bows. All these were brave fighting men.

[9] Zerah the Cushite marched out against them with a vast army[a] and three hundred chariots, and came as far as Mareshah. [10] Asa went out to meet him, and they took up battle positions in the Valley of Zephathah near Mareshah.

[11] Then Asa called to the LORD his God and said, "LORD, there is no one like you to help the powerless against the mighty. Help us, O LORD our God, for we rely on you, and in your name we have come against this vast army. O LORD, you are our God; do not let man prevail against you."

[12] The LORD struck down the Cushites before Asa and Judah. The Cushites fled, [13] and Asa and his army pursued them as far as Gerar. Such a great number of Cushites fell that they could not recover; they were crushed before the LORD and his forces. The men of Judah carried off a large amount of plunder. [14] They destroyed all the villages around Gerar, for the terror of the LORD had fallen upon them. They plundered all these villages, since there was much booty there. [15] They also attacked the camps of the herdsmen and carried off droves of sheep and goats and camels. Then they returned to Jerusalem.

Asa's Reform

15 The Spirit of God came upon Azariah son of Oded. [2] He went out to meet Asa and said to him, "Listen to me, Asa and all Judah and Benjamin. The LORD is with you when you are with him. If you seek him, he will be found by you, but if you forsake him, he will forsake you. [3] For a long time Israel was without the true God, without a priest to teach and without the law. [4] But in their distress they turned to the LORD, the God of Israel, and sought him, and he was found by them. [5] In those days it was not safe to travel about, for all the inhabitants of the lands were in great turmoil. [6] One nation was being crushed by another and one city by another, because God was troubling them with every kind of distress. [7] But as for you, be strong and do not give up, for your work will be rewarded."

[8] When Asa heard these words and the prophecy of Azariah son of[b] Oded the prophet, he took courage. He removed the detestable idols from the whole land of Judah and Benjamin and from the towns he had captured in the hills of Ephraim. He repaired the altar of the LORD that was in front of the portico of the LORD's temple.

[9] Then he assembled all Judah and Benjamin and the people from Ephraim, Manasseh and Simeon who had settled among them, for large numbers had come over to him from Israel when they saw that the LORD his God was with him.

[10] They assembled at Jerusalem in the third month of the fifteenth year of Asa's reign. [11] At that time they sacrificed to the LORD

1. What are Asa's accomplishments (see 1Ki 15:12–15)? Which accomplishments required tough moral fiber? What was Asa's reward? 2. How many fighting men were in Asa's army? What were their weapons? How many fighting men in Zerah's army? Chariots? 3. What is Asa's strategy? Does it work? What happens to the "vast army" of the Cushites? Their villages and camps? 4. The kings of Judah and Israel had lots of influence over the peoples ideas about God. How did Asa witness to his faith in God?

1. If you were to go on a rampage against modern "Asherah poles," what are your top two or three targets? 2. Asa relied on the Lord to fight this battle. What battle are you fighting now? How can you rely on the Lord to fight it?

1. About sermons, what would you say: (a) "I usually remember it"? (b) "I'm glad it's only once a week"? (c) "They don't have much place in my life"? (d) "They're too long!"? 2. What advice would you offer on how to reach people through a sermon?

1. Azariah delivers a dynamite sermon and gets results! What are the main points? What is the impact for Asa? The people? 2. Do you think the command in verse 13 was fair? Why or why not (see Ex 22:20 and Dt 13:6–9)? 3. What political changes took place in the life of the nation as a result of "finding" the Lord? 4. What was Asa's and the nations reward for their actions?

1. Has a sermon ever changed your life or behavior? Tell your group about one that did. 2. How is Asa's response to the sermon a model for people today? In what ways can you "take courage" after a sermon? 3. What would it mean for God to be "found" by your nation? By your church? By you? 4. Do you feel God is in hiding? If so, where is he?

---

[a] 9 Hebrew *with an army of a thousand thousands* or *with an army of thousands upon thousands*   [b] 8 Vulgate and Syriac (see also Septuagint and verse 1); Hebrew does not have *Azariah son of*.

seven hundred head of cattle and seven thousand sheep and goats from the plunder they had brought back. [12]They entered into a covenant to seek the LORD, the God of their fathers, with all their heart and soul. [13]All who would not seek the LORD, the God of Israel, were to be put to death, whether small or great, man or woman. [14]They took an oath to the LORD with loud acclamation, with shouting and with trumpets and horns. [15]All Judah rejoiced about the oath because they had sworn it wholeheartedly. They sought God eagerly, and he was found by them. So the LORD gave them rest on every side.

[16]King Asa also deposed his grandmother Maacah from her position as queen mother, because she had made a repulsive Asherah pole. Asa cut the pole down, broke it up and burned it in the Kidron Valley. [17]Although he did not remove the high places from Israel, Asa's heart was fully committed ˌto the LORDˌ all his life. [18]He brought into the temple of God the silver and gold and the articles that he and his father had dedicated.

[19]There was no more war until the thirty-fifth year of Asa's reign.

Asa's Last Years

16 In the thirty-sixth year of Asa's reign Baasha king of Israel went up against Judah and fortified Ramah to prevent anyone from leaving or entering the territory of Asa king of Judah.

[2]Asa then took the silver and gold out of the treasuries of the LORD's temple and of his own palace and sent it to Ben-Hadad king of Aram, who was ruling in Damascus. [3]"Let there be a treaty between me and you," he said, "as there was between my father and your father. See, I am sending you silver and gold. Now break your treaty with Baasha king of Israel so he will withdraw from me."

[4]Ben-Hadad agreed with King Asa and sent the commanders of his forces against the towns of Israel. They conquered Ijon, Dan, Abel Maim[a] and all the store cities of Naphtali. [5]When Baasha heard this, he stopped building Ramah and abandoned his work. [6]Then King Asa brought all the men of Judah, and they carried away from Ramah the stones and timber Baasha had been using. With them he built up Geba and Mizpah.

[7]At that time Hanani the seer came to Asa king of Judah and said to him: "Because you relied on the king of Aram and not on the LORD your God, the army of the king of Aram has escaped from your hand. [8]Were not the Cushites[b] and Libyans a mighty army with great numbers of chariots and horsemen[c]? Yet when you relied on the LORD, he delivered them into your hand. [9]For the eyes of the LORD range throughout the earth to strengthen those whose hearts are fully committed to him. You have done a foolish thing, and from now on you will be at war."

[10]Asa was angry with the seer because of this; he was so enraged that he put him in prison. At the same time Asa brutally oppressed some of the people.

[11]The events of Asa's reign, from beginning to end, are written in the book of the kings of Judah and Israel. [12]In the thirty-ninth year of his reign Asa was afflicted with a disease in his feet. Though his disease was severe, even in his illness he did not seek help from the LORD, but only from the physicians. [13]Then in the forty-first year of his reign Asa died and rested with his fathers. [14]They buried him in the tomb that he had cut out for himself in the City

---

1. In your youth, who made you angry: Brothers or sisters? Schoolteachers? Bullies? Others? 2. What run-ins today enrage you?

1. What was Baasha, king of Israel, doing to Judah? How did Asa outsmart him and protect his own territory? 2. Was God pleased with Asa's strategy? Why or why not? 3. Hanani the seer delivered the bad news to Asa. What was his message? 4. What was Asa's response? How is Asa's response here different from his response to Azariah (see 2Ch 15:8)? Is there anything in Hanani's message which could have helped Asa to take courage? 5. Asa's anger kept him from seeking help from the Lord in another difficulty. What was it? The consequence?

1. Recall a time when your response to a reprimand was anger. Was there something in it to take courage from instead? 2. Why does God want you to rely on him? Share a time when you relied on the Lord.

---

a4 Also known as Abel Beth Maacah   b8 That is, people from the upper Nile region
c8 Or charioteers

of David. They laid him on a bier covered with spices and various blended perfumes, and they made a huge fire in his honor.

Jehoshaphat King of Judah

17 Jehoshaphat his son succeeded him as king and strengthened himself against Israel. [2]He stationed troops in all the fortified cities of Judah and put garrisons in Judah and in the towns of Ephraim that his father Asa had captured.

[3]The LORD was with Jehoshaphat because in his early years he walked in the ways his father David had followed. He did not consult the Baals [4]but sought the God of his father and followed his commands rather than the practices of Israel. [5]The LORD established the kingdom under his control; and all Judah brought gifts to Jehoshaphat, so that he had great wealth and honor. [6]His heart was devoted to the ways of the LORD; furthermore, he removed the high places and the Asherah poles from Judah.

[7]In the third year of his reign he sent his officials Ben-Hail, Obadiah, Zechariah, Nethanel and Micaiah to teach in the towns of Judah. [8]With them were certain Levites—Shemaiah, Nethaniah, Zebadiah, Asahel, Shemiramoth, Jehonathan, Adonijah, Tobijah and Tob-Adonijah—and the priests Elishama and Jehoram. [9]They taught throughout Judah, taking with them the Book of the Law of the LORD; they went around to all the towns of Judah and taught the people.

[10]The fear of the LORD fell on all the kingdoms of the lands surrounding Judah, so that they did not make war with Jehoshaphat. [11]Some Philistines brought Jehoshaphat gifts and silver as tribute, and the Arabs brought him flocks: seven thousand seven hundred rams and seven thousand seven hundred goats.

[12]Jehoshaphat became more and more powerful; he built forts and store cities in Judah [13]and had large supplies in the towns of Judah. He also kept experienced fighting men in Jerusalem. [14]Their enrollment by families was as follows:

> From Judah, commanders of units of 1,000:
> Adnah the commander, with 300,000 fighting men;
> [15]next, Jehohanan the commander, with 280,000;
> [16]next, Amasiah son of Zicri, who volunteered himself for the service of the LORD, with 200,000.
> [17]From Benjamin:
> Eliada, a valiant soldier, with 200,000 men armed with bows and shields;
> [18]next, Jehozabad, with 180,000 men armed for battle.

[19]These were the men who served the king, besides those he stationed in the fortified cities throughout Judah.

Micaiah Prophesies Against Ahab

18 Now Jehoshaphat had great wealth and honor, and he allied himself with Ahab by marriage. [2]Some years later he went down to visit Ahab in Samaria. Ahab slaughtered many sheep and cattle for him and the people with him and urged him to attack Ramoth Gilead. [3]Ahab king of Israel asked Jehoshaphat king of Judah, "Will you go with me against Ramoth Gilead?"

Jehoshaphat replied, "I am as you are, and my people as your people; we will join you in the war." [4]But Jehoshaphat also said to the king of Israel, "First seek the counsel of the LORD."

[5]So the king of Israel brought together the prophets—four hundred men—and asked them, "Shall we go to war against Ramoth Gilead, or shall I refrain?"

---

1. If you could go back to school to learn anything what subject would you choose? Why? 2. What do you read nearly every day: Newspaper? Funnies? A novel? Billboards? TV guide? A devotional book? The Bible? 3. If "you are what you read," what are you?

1. What made King Jehoshaphat spiritually successful (vv. 1–6)? 2. What unusual social and spiritual enrichment program does Jehoshaphat begin? What is the curriculum of this traveling school? What impact could it have for worship of God? National strength? 3. Where does Jehoshaphat get new economic resources for himself and the nation? How does he use them? 4. How many fighting men did Jehoshaphat amass "for the service of the Lord"? 5. How does Jehoshaphat's closeness to God translate into tangible benefits for himself and Judah?

1. Jehoshaphat had wealth, respect, peace and prosperity. Is it true today that people who are close to God are successful and prosperous, while people who worship false gods pay tribute to the first group? How does the chronicler's lesson apply in your world? 2. If you were to create an itinerant teaching team for churches, what subjects would you have them focus on? What would you like such a team to do for your church? For your group?

---

1. How could the things in your wallet right now help people you don't know to trust you? 2. Did you ever tell a big lie as a child? Were you caught? What happened?

1. What bond tied Jehoshaphat to Ahab, king of Israel? 2. What was Ahab's request of his ally? Jehoshaphat's response? 3. Why do the prophets of Israel make such poor advisors? What is their advice? 4. Who was the prophet of the Lord? How does

Ahab feel about him? Why? **5.** The messenger (v. 12) prompts Micaiah with what Ahab wants to hear. However, what is the "word of the Lord" to Ahab? **6.** How does Micaiah explain the deceit of the other prophets? Is verse 22 part of God's strategy to lure Ahab into his own destruction? **7.** What is Micaiah's reward for speaking the truth?

1. How difficult is it to tell the truth no matter what? To family? At work? To members of this group? To God? **2.** In what situations might lying be wise and/or necessary, if any?

"Go," they answered, "for God will give it into the king's hand."

⁶But Jehoshaphat asked, "Is there not a prophet of the LORD here whom we can inquire of?"

⁷The king of Israel answered Jehoshaphat, "There is still one man through whom we can inquire of the LORD, but I hate him because he never prophesies anything good about me, but always bad. He is Micaiah son of Imlah."

"The king should not say that," Jehoshaphat replied.

⁸So the king of Israel called one of his officials and said, "Bring Micaiah son of Imlah at once."

⁹Dressed in their royal robes, the king of Israel and Jehoshaphat king of Judah were sitting on their thrones at the threshing floor by the entrance to the gate of Samaria, with all the prophets prophesying before them. ¹⁰Now Zedekiah son of Kenaanah had made iron horns, and he declared, "This is what the LORD says: 'With these you will gore the Arameans until they are destroyed.'"

¹¹All the other prophets were prophesying the same thing. "Attack Ramoth Gilead and be victorious," they said, "for the LORD will give it into the king's hand."

¹²The messenger who had gone to summon Micaiah said to him, "Look, as one man the other prophets are predicting success for the king. Let your word agree with theirs, and speak favorably."

¹³But Micaiah said, "As surely as the LORD lives, I can tell him only what my God says."

¹⁴When he arrived, the king asked him, "Micaiah, shall we go to war against Ramoth Gilead, or shall I refrain?"

"Attack and be victorious," he answered, "for they will be given into your hand."

¹⁵The king said to him, "How many times must I make you swear to tell me nothing but the truth in the name of the LORD?"

¹⁶Then Micaiah answered, "I saw all Israel scattered on the hills like sheep without a shepherd, and the LORD said, 'These people have no master. Let each one go home in peace.'"

¹⁷The king of Israel said to Jehoshaphat, "Didn't I tell you that he never prophesies anything good about me, but only bad?"

¹⁸Micaiah continued, "Therefore hear the word of the LORD: I saw the LORD sitting on his throne with all the host of heaven standing on his right and on his left. ¹⁹And the LORD said, 'Who will entice Ahab king of Israel into attacking Ramoth Gilead and going to his death there?'

"One suggested this, and another that. ²⁰Finally, a spirit came forward, stood before the LORD and said, 'I will entice him.'

"'By what means?' the LORD asked.

²¹"'I will go and be a lying spirit in the mouths of all his prophets,' he said.

"'You will succeed in enticing him,' said the LORD. 'Go and do it.'

²²"So now the LORD has put a lying spirit in the mouths of these prophets of yours. The LORD has decreed disaster for you."

²³Then Zedekiah son of Kenaanah went up and slapped Micaiah in the face. "Which way did the spirit from*ᵃ* the LORD go when he went from me to speak to you?" he asked.

²⁴Micaiah replied, "You will find out on the day you go to hide in an inner room."

²⁵The king of Israel then ordered, "Take Micaiah and send him back to Amon the ruler of the city and to Joash the king's son,

ᵃ*23 Or Spirit of*

26and say, 'This is what the king says: Put this fellow in prison and give him nothing but bread and water until I return safely.' "

27Micaiah declared, "If you ever return safely, the LORD has not spoken through me." Then he added, "Mark my words, all you people!"

Ahab Killed at Ramoth Gilead

28So the king of Israel and Jehoshaphat king of Judah went up to Ramoth Gilead. 29The king of Israel said to Jehoshaphat, "I will enter the battle in disguise, but you wear your royal robes." So the king of Israel disguised himself and went into battle.

30Now the king of Aram had ordered his chariot commanders, "Do not fight with anyone, small or great, except the king of Israel." 31When the chariot commanders saw Jehoshaphat, they thought, "This is the king of Israel." So they turned to attack him, but Jehoshaphat cried out, and the LORD helped him. God drew them away from him, 32for when the chariot commanders saw that he was not the king of Israel, they stopped pursuing him.

33But someone drew his bow at random and hit the king of Israel between the sections of his armor. The king told the chariot driver, "Wheel around and get me out of the fighting. I've been wounded." 34All day long the battle raged, and the king of Israel propped himself up in his chariot facing the Arameans until evening. Then at sunset he died.

19 When Jehoshaphat king of Judah returned safely to his palace in Jerusalem, 2Jehu the seer, the son of Hanani, went out to meet him and said to the king, "Should you help the wicked and love*a* those who hate the LORD? Because of this, the wrath of the LORD is upon you. 3There is, however, some good in you, for you have rid the land of the Asherah poles and have set your heart on seeking God."

Jehoshaphat Appoints Judges

4Jehoshaphat lived in Jerusalem, and he went out again among the people from Beersheba to the hill country of Ephraim and turned them back to the LORD, the God of their fathers. 5He appointed judges in the land, in each of the fortified cities of Judah. 6He told them, "Consider carefully what you do, because you are not judging for man but for the LORD, who is with you whenever you give a verdict. 7Now let the fear of the LORD be upon you. Judge carefully, for with the LORD our God there is no injustice or partiality or bribery."

8In Jerusalem also, Jehoshaphat appointed some of the Levites, priests and heads of Israelite families to administer the law of the LORD and to settle disputes. And they lived in Jerusalem. 9He gave them these orders: "You must serve faithfully and wholeheartedly in the fear of the LORD. 10In every case that comes before you from your fellow countrymen who live in the cities—whether bloodshed or other concerns of the law, commands, decrees or ordinances—you are to warn them not to sin against the LORD; otherwise his wrath will come on you and your brothers. Do this, and you will not sin.

11"Amariah the chief priest will be over you in any matter concerning the LORD, and Zebadiah son of Ishmael, the leader of the tribe of Judah, will be over you in any matter concerning the king, and the Levites will serve as officials before you. Act with courage, and may the LORD be with those who do well."

a2 Or *and make alliances with*

You are invited to a masquerade party and told to dress up as your fantasy. What do you come dressed as: Shirley Temple? Mother Teresa? Dorothy of Oz? Caveman? Other?

1. What is Ahab's strategy for saving his own neck in this battle? How about the military strategy of the king of Aram? 2. Why would Jehoshaphat volunteer to become a target in this battle? How did the Lord help Jehoshaphat? 3. What became of Ahab? Was that part of God's plan? 4. Who rebuked Jehoshaphat? What lessons were learned from this battle? About alliances? About God?

Do you generally feel embarrassed to "cry out" for help? Ever have a narrow escape and learned about God from it? What happened?

Which would you prefer to judge and why: (a) Sports event? (b) County fair pie contest? (c) Jazz band competition? (d) Court? (e) Beauty pageant? (f) Other?

1. In chapter 17, Jehoshaphat began a teaching mission and in this chapter he begins judicial reform throughout Judah. What is to be the guiding principle for the judges? What does he warn them against? 2. Who did Jehoshaphat appoint to the Jerusalem court? What serves as the "constitution"? 3. What further instructions does Jehoshaphat give the judges? What is their final appeal for lawful behavior? 4. What quality must judges possess above all others?

1. What would you say is your guiding principle in decision-making everyday? 2. How can knowing God is with you whenever you make a decision affect your decisions?

1. What song title best expresses who you are: (a)
"Somewhere Over the Rainbow"?
(b) "Raindrops Keep Falling on My
Head"? (c) "I Can't Get No Satisfaction"? (d) "I'm So Lonesome I
Could Cry"? (e) "Fools Rush In"? 2.
When you are asked to give a public speech, what is your reaction:
(a) "Not on your life"? (b) "Depends
on the crowd"? (c) "I love an
adrenalin rush"? (d) "Line up the
loudspeakers"?

1. Why does Jehoshaphat
"proclaim a fast" for all of Judah? What has he learned from his
close call in chapters 18 and 19? 2.
In Jehoshaphat's public prayer,
why does he tell God things that
God already knows? Is he coaxing
God's cooperation? Whom does
Jehoshaphat blame for the invasion? How does Jehoshaphat evaluate Judah's chances? 3. Where is
Judah's ultimate focus? What picture do you get from the terse description of verse 13? 4. How does
God get his message to Jehoshaphat and Judah? How does the
messenger's ancestry lend credibility to his words? 5. What are the
key phrases in Jahaziel's message? How was the message received? 6. What reassurances did
Jehoshaphat give on the morning
of the battle? Why does he say
"have faith in his prophets"? Isn't
right faith exclusively in God? 7.
What happened to the invaders? 8.
What role does music play in the
battle? In victory? 9. Instead of disaster and loss, what does this battle hold for Judah? What feelings
are expressed by Jehosophat and
the people? How do they celebrate?

1. Compare the "serendipity"
(happy discovery) in this
chapter with experiences of your
own. Can you share a "battle" God
has won for you? 2. In the midst of
a problem, where is your focus?
On the problem? On the Lord? On
yourself? What are some good
ways to fix your eyes on the Lord?
What kind of music and/or body
language might help? 3. How does
the defeat of Moab and Ammon
warn you about: Alliances with unbelievers? The common idea that
the bigger guys always win?

Jehoshaphat Defeats Moab and Ammon

20 After this, the Moabites and Ammonites with some of the
Meunites[a] came to make war on Jehoshaphat.
²Some men came and told Jehoshaphat, "A vast army is coming
against you from Edom,[b] from the other side of the Sea.[c] It is
already in Hazazon Tamar" (that is, En Gedi). ³Alarmed, Jehoshaphat resolved to inquire of the LORD, and he proclaimed a fast for all
Judah. ⁴The people of Judah came together to seek help from the
LORD; indeed, they came from every town in Judah to seek him.
⁵Then Jehoshaphat stood up in the assembly of Judah and Jerusalem at the temple of the LORD in the front of the new courtyard
⁶and said:

"O LORD, God of our fathers, are you not the God who is in
heaven? You rule over all the kingdoms of the nations. Power
and might are in your hand, and no one can withstand you.
⁷O our God, did you not drive out the inhabitants of this land
before your people Israel and give it forever to the descendants of Abraham your friend? ⁸They have lived in it and have
built in it a sanctuary for your Name, saying, ⁹'If calamity
comes upon us, whether the sword of judgment, or plague or
famine, we will stand in your presence before this temple that
bears your Name and will cry out to you in our distress, and
you will hear us and save us.'
¹⁰"But now here are men from Ammon, Moab and Mount
Seir, whose territory you would not allow Israel to invade
when they came from Egypt; so they turned away from them
and did not destroy them. ¹¹See how they are repaying us by
coming to drive us out of the possession you gave us as an
inheritance. ¹²O our God, will you not judge them? For we
have no power to face this vast army that is attacking us. We
do not know what to do, but our eyes are upon you."

¹³All the men of Judah, with their wives and children and little
ones, stood there before the LORD.
¹⁴Then the Spirit of the LORD came upon Jahaziel son of Zechariah, the son of Benaiah, the son of Jeiel, the son of Mattaniah, a
Levite and descendant of Asaph, as he stood in the assembly.
¹⁵He said: "Listen, King Jehoshaphat and all who live in Judah
and Jerusalem! This is what the LORD says to you: 'Do not be afraid
or discouraged because of this vast army. For the battle is not
yours, but God's. ¹⁶Tomorrow march down against them. They will
be climbing up by the Pass of Ziz, and you will find them at the end
of the gorge in the Desert of Jeruel. ¹⁷You will not have to fight this
battle. Take up your positions; stand firm and see the deliverance
the LORD will give you, O Judah and Jerusalem. Do not be afraid; do
not be discouraged. Go out to face them tomorrow, and the LORD
will be with you.'"
¹⁸Jehoshaphat bowed with his face to the ground, and all the
people of Judah and Jerusalem fell down in worship before the
LORD. ¹⁹Then some Levites from the Kohathites and Korahites stood
up and praised the LORD, the God of Israel, with very loud voice.
²⁰Early in the morning they left for the Desert of Tekoa. As they
set out, Jehoshaphat stood and said, "Listen to me, Judah and
people of Jerusalem! Have faith in the LORD your God and you will
be upheld; have faith in his prophets and you will be successful."
²¹After consulting the people, Jehoshaphat appointed men to sing

---

a1 Some Septuagint manuscripts; Hebrew *Ammonites*   b2 One Hebrew manuscript;
most Hebrew manuscripts, Septuagint and Vulgate *Aram*   c2 That is, the Dead Sea

to the LORD and to praise him for the splendor of his[a] holiness as they went out at the head of the army, saying:

> "Give thanks to the LORD,
>   for his love endures forever."

[22]As they began to sing and praise, the LORD set ambushes against the men of Ammon and Moab and Mount Seir who were invading Judah, and they were defeated. [23]The men of Ammon and Moab rose up against the men from Mount Seir to destroy and annihilate them. After they finished slaughtering the men from Seir, they helped to destroy one another.

[24]When the men of Judah came to the place that overlooks the desert and looked toward the vast army, they saw only dead bodies lying on the ground; no one had escaped. [25]So Jehoshaphat and his men went to carry off their plunder, and they found among them a great amount of equipment and clothing[b] and also articles of value—more than they could take away. There was so much plunder that it took three days to collect it. [26]On the fourth day they assembled in the Valley of Beracah, where they praised the LORD. This is why it is called the Valley of Beracah[c] to this day.

[27]Then, led by Jehoshaphat, all the men of Judah and Jerusalem returned joyfully to Jerusalem, for the LORD had given them cause to rejoice over their enemies. [28]They entered Jerusalem and went to the temple of the LORD with harps and lutes and trumpets.

[29]The fear of God came upon all the kingdoms of the countries when they heard how the LORD had fought against the enemies of Israel. [30]And the kingdom of Jehoshaphat was at peace, for his God had given him rest on every side.

The End of Jehoshaphat's Reign

[31]So Jehoshaphat reigned over Judah. He was thirty-five years old when he became king of Judah, and he reigned in Jerusalem twenty-five years. His mother's name was Azubah daughter of Shilhi. [32]He walked in the ways of his father Asa and did not stray from them; he did what was right in the eyes of the LORD. [33]The high places, however, were not removed, and the people still had not set their hearts on the God of their fathers.

[34]The other events of Jehoshaphat's reign, from beginning to end, are written in the annals of Jehu son of Hanani, which are recorded in the book of the kings of Israel.

[35]Later, Jehoshaphat king of Judah made an alliance with Ahaziah king of Israel, who was guilty of wickedness. [36]He agreed with him to construct a fleet of trading ships.[d] After these were built at Ezion Geber, [37]Eliezer son of Dodavahu of Mareshah prophesied against Jehoshaphat, saying, "Because you have made an alliance with Ahaziah, the LORD will destroy what you have made." The ships were wrecked and were not able to set sail to trade.[e]

21 Then Jehoshaphat rested with his fathers and was buried with them in the City of David. And Jehoram his son succeeded him as king. [2]Jehoram's brothers, the sons of Jehoshaphat, were Azariah, Jehiel, Zechariah, Azariahu, Michael and Shephatiah. All these were sons of Jehoshaphat king of Israel.[f] [3]Their father had given them many gifts of silver and gold and articles of value, as well as fortified cities in Judah, but he had given the kingdom to Jehoram because he was his firstborn son.

What is your dream vessel: Sailboat? Motorboat? Cruise ship? Canoe? Loveboat? Windjammer? Catamaran? Where would you go in your dream boat? What are you afraid might wreck your dream boat?

1. Following a story in which the whole nation is united in praise to God (vv. 13,27), does verse 33 seem unusual to you? Why or why not? 2. Where does this dismal spirituality lead (vv. 35–37)? 3. What evidence from this section shows that Jehosophat was blessed by God? 4. What legacy does Jehoshaphat try to leave the nation? His family?

If tonight you were to die, what legacy would you leave behind? What goals unfinished or not begun?

---

[a]21 Or him with the splendor of   [b]25 Some Hebrew manuscripts and Vulgate; most Hebrew manuscripts *corpses*   [c]26 Beracah means *praise.*   [d]36 Hebrew *of ships that could go to Tarshish*   [e]37 Hebrew *sail for Tarshish*   [f]2 That is, Judah, as frequently in 2 Chronicles

1. What famous bad guy is the most interesting to you and why: Jesse James? Butch Cassidy? Dracula? Darth Vader? Other? 2. If you could get a personal letter in return, who would you like to send a letter to: The President? The Pope? A deceased loved one? What would the essence of your letter be?

1. What sort of person was King Jehoram? His wife? What blame must Jehoshaphat carry for the trouble of Jehoram's reign? 2. Why doesn't God wipe out the whole of Jehoram's family? 3. Why did Libnah revolt? Do all political moves in 2 Chronicles have spiritual causes? 4. What help does Elijah provide Jehoram? Is it too late for Jehoram to put his life in order? What could he do? 5. What consolation does God's vengeance allow Jehoram? 6. How does Jehoram's story end with the king in disgrace and dishonor?

1. In terms of forgiveness and getting right with God, how late is too late? 2. Have you ever received a letter as authoritative as Elijah's to Jehoram? A letter as ominous? What would your first response have been?

What is the most important personality trait your parents passed on to you?

1. Why did Ahaziah, Jehoram's youngest son succeed his father as king of Judah? How old was he when he became king? 2. What was the nature of Ahaziah's brief reign? What role did his mother Athaliah play in that reign? Why do you think she was such a

Jehoram King of Judah

⁴When Jehoram established himself firmly over his father's kingdom, he put all his brothers to the sword along with some of the princes of Israel. ⁵Jehoram was thirty-two years old when he became king, and he reigned in Jerusalem eight years. ⁶He walked in the ways of the kings of Israel, as the house of Ahab had done, for he married a daughter of Ahab. He did evil in the eyes of the LORD. ⁷Nevertheless, because of the covenant the LORD had made with David, the LORD was not willing to destroy the house of David. He had promised to maintain a lamp for him and his descendants forever.

⁸In the time of Jehoram, Edom rebelled against Judah and set up its own king. ⁹So Jehoram went there with his officers and all his chariots. The Edomites surrounded him and his chariot commanders, but he rose up and broke through by night. ¹⁰To this day Edom has been in rebellion against Judah.

Libnah revolted at the same time, because Jehoram had forsaken the LORD, the God of his fathers. ¹¹He had also built high places on the hills of Judah and had caused the people of Jerusalem to prostitute themselves and had led Judah astray.

¹²Jehoram received a letter from Elijah the prophet, which said:

"This is what the LORD, the God of your father David, says: 'You have not walked in the ways of your father Jehoshaphat or of Asa king of Judah. ¹³But you have walked in the ways of the kings of Israel, and you have led Judah and the people of Jerusalem to prostitute themselves, just as the house of Ahab did. You have also murdered your own brothers, members of your father's house, men who were better than you. ¹⁴So now the LORD is about to strike your people, your sons, your wives and everything that is yours, with a heavy blow. ¹⁵You yourself will be very ill with a lingering disease of the bowels, until the disease causes your bowels to come out.'"

¹⁶The LORD aroused against Jehoram the hostility of the Philistines and of the Arabs who lived near the Cushites. ¹⁷They attacked Judah, invaded it and carried off all the goods found in the king's palace, together with his sons and wives. Not a son was left to him except Ahaziah,ᵃ the youngest.

¹⁸After all this, the LORD afflicted Jehoram with an incurable disease of the bowels. ¹⁹In the course of time, at the end of the second year, his bowels came out because of the disease, and he died in great pain. His people made no fire in his honor, as they had for his fathers.

²⁰Jehoram was thirty-two years old when he became king, and he reigned in Jerusalem eight years. He passed away, to no one's regret, and was buried in the City of David, but not in the tombs of the kings.

Ahaziah King of Judah

22 The people of Jerusalem made Ahaziah, Jehoram's youngest son, king in his place, since the raiders, who came with the Arabs into the camp, had killed all the older sons. So Ahaziah son of Jehoram king of Judah began to reign.

²Ahaziah was twenty-twoᵇ years old when he became king, and he reigned in Jerusalem one year. His mother's name was Athaliah, a granddaughter of Omri.

ᵃ17 Hebrew *Jehoahaz*, a variant of *Ahaziah* ᵇ2 Some Septuagint manuscripts and Syriac (see also 2 Kings 8:26); Hebrew *forty-two*

³He too walked in the ways of the house of Ahab, for his mother encouraged him in doing wrong. ⁴He did evil in the eyes of the LORD, as the house of Ahab had done, for after his father's death they became his advisers, to his undoing. ⁵He also followed their counsel when he went with Joram*a* son of Ahab king of Israel to war against Hazael king of Aram at Ramoth Gilead. The Arameans wounded Joram; ⁶so he returned to Jezreel to recover from the wounds they had inflicted on him at Ramoth*b* in his battle with Hazael king of Aram.

Then Ahaziah*c* son of Jehoram king of Judah went down to Jezreel to see Joram son of Ahab because he had been wounded.

⁷Through Ahaziah's visit to Joram, God brought about Ahaziah's downfall. When Ahaziah arrived, he went out with Joram to meet Jehu son of Nimshi, whom the LORD had anointed to destroy the house of Ahab. ⁸While Jehu was executing judgment on the house of Ahab, he found the princes of Judah and the sons of Ahaziah's relatives, who had been attending Ahaziah, and he killed them. ⁹He then went in search of Ahaziah, and his men captured him while he was hiding in Samaria. He was brought to Jehu and put to death. They buried him, for they said, "He was a son of Jehoshaphat, who sought the LORD with all his heart." So there was no one in the house of Ahaziah powerful enough to retain the kingdom.

Athaliah and Joash

¹⁰When Athaliah the mother of Ahaziah saw that her son was dead, she proceeded to destroy the whole royal family of the house of Judah. ¹¹But Jehosheba,*d* the daughter of King Jehoram, took Joash son of Ahaziah and stole him away from among the royal princes who were about to be murdered and put him and his nurse in a bedroom. Because Jehosheba,*d* the daughter of King Jehoram and wife of the priest Jehoiada, was Ahaziah's sister, she hid the child from Athaliah so she could not kill him. ¹²He remained hidden with them at the temple of God for six years while Athaliah ruled the land.

23 In the seventh year Jehoiada showed his strength. He made a covenant with the commanders of units of a hundred: Azariah son of Jeroham, Ishmael son of Jehohanan, Azariah son of Obed, Maaseiah son of Adaiah, and Elishaphat son of Zicri. ²They went throughout Judah and gathered the Levites and the heads of Israelite families from all the towns. When they came to Jerusalem, ³the whole assembly made a covenant with the king at the temple of God.

Jehoiada said to them, "The king's son shall reign, as the LORD promised concerning the descendants of David. ⁴Now this is what you are to do: A third of you priests and Levites who are going on duty on the Sabbath are to keep watch at the doors, ⁵a third of you at the royal palace and a third at the Foundation Gate, and all the other men are to be in the courtyards of the temple of the LORD. ⁶No one is to enter the temple of the LORD except the priests and Levites on duty; they may enter because they are consecrated, but all the other men are to guard what the LORD has assigned to them.*e* ⁷The Levites are to station themselves around the king, each man with his weapons in his hand. Anyone who enters the temple must be put to death. Stay close to the king wherever he goes."

dominant force over her son? (Remember: Athaliah was the daughter of Ahab and Jezebel, see 21:6.) **3.** What "unholy alliance" did Ahaziah enter into? Upon whose advice? With what predictable outcome? **4.** Humanly speaking, who brought about Ahaziah's end in verses 7–9? How? Who was really responsible for his downfall? **5.** What was Ahaziah's brief obituary? Why hadn't his grandfather's faith been passed on to him?

Have you had to struggle with any negative impact from your mother upon your own life? Upon your religious faith? Upon your career?

_____

1. Where was your "secret hiding place" when you were 10 years old? Did anyone ever discover it? **2.** What would it take to get you to join a revolution? Would you be: (a) forever loyal to the government? (b) a revolutionary (fighting for independence)? (c) a fence-sitter? Why?

1. What was Athaliah's plan for herself after the death of her son? What does this tell you about her character? If she had been successful in her scheme, what would have happened to God's covenant with King David? **2.** How was Athaliah's scheme thwarted according to 22:11–23:3? Who were the principal actors in this drama? What might have motivated each of them? **3.** What was Jehoiada's plan for anointing Joash as the king of Judah? Why did he rely so much on the priests and Levites for help? Would you have wanted to participate in this coup? **4.** In verses 12–13, how did Athaliah get wind of the coup against her? What was her reaction? Does it sound to you as if she was popular? Tolerated? Hated? **5.** How did Athaliah meet her fate? Where? What immediate impact did her death have in verses 16–17? Do these results justify her killing? **6.** With Athaliah dead and King Joash only a boy, who really made the decisions in Jerusalem? What kinds of things did he do to insure proper rule and worship? Which of his qualities do you admire?

---

a5 Hebrew *Jehoram*, a variant of *Joram*; also in verses 6 and 7   *b6* Hebrew *Ramah*, a variant of *Ramoth*   *c6* Some Hebrew manuscripts, Septuagint, Vulgate and Syriac (see also 2 Kings 8:29); most Hebrew manuscripts *Azariah*   *d11* Hebrew *Jehoshabeath*, a variant of *Jehosheba*   *e6* Or *to observe the LORD's command ⌐not to enter⌐*

1. Should we ever involve ourselves in violent revolutions? If yes, when? If no, why not? 2. What is the balance between "trusting the Lord" and "taking matters in your own hands" as a Christian? How does this story help you decide? 3. Where do you think God needs to raise up a modern Jehoiada to show his strength?

8The Levites and all the men of Judah did just as Jehoiada the priest ordered. Each one took his men—those who were going on duty on the Sabbath and those who were going off duty—for Jehoiada the priest had not released any of the divisions. 9Then he gave the commanders of units of a hundred the spears and the large and small shields that had belonged to King David and that were in the temple of God. 10He stationed all the men, each with his weapon in his hand, around the king—near the altar and the temple, from the south side to the north side of the temple.

11Jehoiada and his sons brought out the king's son and put the crown on him; they presented him with a copy of the covenant and proclaimed him king. They anointed him and shouted, "Long live the king!"

12When Athaliah heard the noise of the people running and cheering the king, she went to them at the temple of the LORD. 13She looked, and there was the king, standing by his pillar at the entrance. The officers and the trumpeters were beside the king, and all the people of the land were rejoicing and blowing trumpets, and singers with musical instruments were leading the praises. Then Athaliah tore her robes and shouted, "Treason! Treason!"

14Jehoiada the priest sent out the commanders of units of a hundred, who were in charge of the troops, and said to them: "Bring her out between the ranks[a] and put to the sword anyone who follows her." For the priest had said, "Do not put her to death at the temple of the LORD." 15So they seized her as she reached the entrance of the Horse Gate on the palace grounds, and there they put her to death.

16Jehoiada then made a covenant that he and the people and the king[b] would be the LORD's people. 17All the people went to the temple of Baal and tore it down. They smashed the altars and idols and killed Mattan the priest of Baal in front of the altars.

18Then Jehoiada placed the oversight of the temple of the LORD in the hands of the priests, who were Levites, to whom David had made assignments in the temple, to present the burnt offerings of the LORD as written in the Law of Moses, with rejoicing and singing, as David had ordered. 19He also stationed doorkeepers at the gates of the LORD's temple so that no one who was in any way unclean might enter.

20He took with him the commanders of hundreds, the nobles, the rulers of the people and all the people of the land and brought the king down from the temple of the LORD. They went into the palace through the Upper Gate and seated the king on the royal throne, 21and all the people of the land rejoiced. And the city was quiet, because Athaliah had been slain with the sword.

Joash Repairs the Temple

24 Joash was seven years old when he became king, and he reigned in Jerusalem forty years. His mother's name was Zibiah; she was from Beersheba. 2Joash did what was right in the eyes of the LORD all the years of Jehoiada the priest. 3Jehoiada chose two wives for him, and he had sons and daughters.

4Some time later Joash decided to restore the temple of the LORD. 5He called together the priests and Levites and said to them, "Go to the towns of Judah and collect the money due annually from all Israel, to repair the temple of your God. Do it now." But the Levites did not act at once.

6Therefore the king summoned Jehoiada the chief priest and said

1. Which of these organizations do you give to regularly and which not at all: (a) Your church? (b) Your alma mater school? (c) A world mission? (d) A conservation organization? Why? 2. From whom did you learn your most useful skills (for example: sewing, reading, speaking, gardening, driving, cooking)?

1. Joash's reign as king is divided into two parts: the good part (vv. 1–16) and the bad part (vv. 17–32). Why the difference between the two? 2. What was Joash's major accomplishment as

a 14 Or out from the precincts   b 16 Or covenant between ⌊the LORD⌋ and the people and the king that they (see 2 Kings 11:17)

to him, "Why haven't you required the Levites to bring in from Judah and Jerusalem the tax imposed by Moses the servant of the LORD and by the assembly of Israel for the Tent of the Testimony?"

⁷Now the sons of that wicked woman Athaliah had broken into the temple of God and had used even its sacred objects for the Baals.

⁸At the king's command, a chest was made and placed outside, at the gate of the temple of the LORD. ⁹A proclamation was then issued in Judah and Jerusalem that they should bring to the LORD the tax that Moses the servant of God had required of Israel in the desert. ¹⁰All the officials and all the people brought their contributions gladly, dropping them into the chest until it was full. ¹¹Whenever the chest was brought in by the Levites to the king's officials and they saw that there was a large amount of money, the royal secretary and the officer of the chief priest would come and empty the chest and carry it back to its place. They did this regularly and collected a great amount of money. ¹²The king and Jehoiada gave it to the men who carried out the work required for the temple of the LORD. They hired masons and carpenters to restore the LORD's temple, and also workers in iron and bronze to repair the temple.

¹³The men in charge of the work were diligent, and the repairs progressed under them. They rebuilt the temple of God according to its original design and reinforced it. ¹⁴When they had finished, they brought the rest of the money to the king and Jehoiada, and with it were made articles for the LORD's temple: articles for the service and for the burnt offerings, and also dishes and other objects of gold and silver. As long as Jehoiada lived, burnt offerings were presented continually in the temple of the LORD.

¹⁵Now Jehoiada was old and full of years, and he died at the age of a hundred and thirty. ¹⁶He was buried with the kings in the City of David, because of the good he had done in Israel for God and his temple.

The Wickedness of Joash

¹⁷After the death of Jehoiada, the officials of Judah came and paid homage to the king, and he listened to them. ¹⁸They abandoned the temple of the LORD, the God of their fathers, and worshiped Asherah poles and idols. Because of their guilt, God's anger came upon Judah and Jerusalem. ¹⁹Although the LORD sent prophets to the people to bring them back to him, and though they testified against them, they would not listen.

²⁰Then the Spirit of God came upon Zechariah son of Jehoiada the priest. He stood before the people and said, "This is what God says: 'Why do you disobey the LORD's commands? You will not prosper. Because you have forsaken the LORD, he has forsaken you.'"

²¹But they plotted against him, and by order of the king they stoned him to death in the courtyard of the LORD's temple. ²²King Joash did not remember the kindness Zechariah's father Jehoiada had shown him but killed his son, who said as he lay dying, "May the LORD see this and call you to account."

²³At the turn of the year,ᵃ the army of Aram marched against Joash; it invaded Judah and Jerusalem and killed all the leaders of the people. They sent all the plunder to their king in Damascus. ²⁴Although the Aramean army had come with only a few men, the LORD delivered into their hands a much larger army. Because Judah had forsaken the LORD, the God of their fathers, judgment was

king according to verses 4–14? Whom did he enlist to help him in this venture? Why do you think they were hesitant to help him at first? How did Jehoiada help? **3.** How did Joash plan to finance his repairs? Whose legal precedent did he appeal to (see Ex 30:12–16)? What was the response of the people to his plan? **4.** How did Joash use the money he raised at the temple? The excess? Who benefitted from the extensive repair work? **5.** What was Jehoiada's epitaph? In your opinion, did he deserve to be buried with the kings?

♡ **1.** Who is the single most influential religious figure in your life? How has he or she helped you remain faithful to God the way Jehoiada did for Joash? **2.** What would excite you about giving money to a church? What turns you off?

☕ When did you first feel you were "on your own" as an adult? What age were you: 16? 18? 21?

📖 **1.** In verses 17–32, we read about the second part of Joash's reign as king. How did it differ from the first part, when Jehoiada the priest was alive? What does this difference say about the depth of Joash's faith in God? **2.** Following in his father Jehoiada's footsteps, how did Zechariah try to call the people back to obedient faith? What happened to him because of this (compare Mt 5:11–12)? **3.** If the repair of the temple was Joash's major accomplishment, what was the major disaster of his reign? Why did it happen? How could it have been avoided? **4.** How does Joash's death summarize his reign? Why do you think he is left out of the list of Jesus' ancestors in Matthew 1:8?

♡ **1.** In the end, Joash's religious reforms were only skin deep. What should he have done to bring about a deep, long lasting

---

ᵃ23 Probably in the spring

revival in the people of Judah? **2.** What can you do to bring about renewal in your own community? What persecution (and blessing) might you get in return?

☕ If you had $1000 to spend on anything you wanted, what would you buy?

📖 **1.** What is the chronicler's assessment of Amaziah's spirituality in verse 2? **2.** What respect does Amaziah show to the Law in avenging his father's death? **3.** How did Amaziah plan to add to his troops? At what cost? **4.** What message did the "man of God" bring to Amaziah? **5.** Amaziah dismissed these extra troops, but what troubles him about doing so? What simple statement dismisses his worries? (Would it dismiss your worries about losing money?) What was the consequence of hiring these mercenaries in the first place? **6.** What clues from this story hint that life was rough and tumble in ninth century B.C.? (Are values such as mercy and compassion on the upswing today?) **7.** What made God angry with Amaziah (v. 15)? **8.** In Amaziah's response to the prophet, what evidence is there that his military success had gone to his head? **9.** How does Amaziah challenge Jehoash, king of Israel? Do you think Jehoash is trying to avoid bloodshed or coaxing Amaziah into a fury by his response? Could a proud king have just stayed at home after a reply like Jehoash sent? **10.** The two kings met at Beth-Shemesh. Who won? What booty did he take? What happened to Amaziah?

♡ **1.** Why is wholeheartedness so important to God? Isn't a little faith better than no faith at all? **2.** How has your pride gotten you into Amaziah-like trouble in the last year?

executed on Joash. ²⁵When the Arameans withdrew, they left Joash severely wounded. His officials conspired against him for murdering the son of Jehoiada the priest, and they killed him in his bed. So he died and was buried in the City of David, but not in the tombs of the kings.

²⁶Those who conspired against him were Zabad,ᵃ son of Shimeath an Ammonite woman, and Jehozabad, son of Shimrithᵇ a Moabite woman. ²⁷The account of his sons, the many prophecies about him, and the record of the restoration of the temple of God are written in the annotations on the book of the kings. And Amaziah his son succeeded him as king.

Amaziah King of Judah

25 Amaziah was twenty-five years old when he became king, and he reigned in Jerusalem twenty-nine years. His mother's name was Jehoaddinᶜ; she was from Jerusalem. ²He did what was right in the eyes of the LORD, but not wholeheartedly. ³After the kingdom was firmly in his control, he executed the officials who had murdered his father the king. ⁴Yet he did not put their sons to death, but acted in accordance with what is written in the Law, in the Book of Moses, where the LORD commanded: "Fathers shall not be put to death for their children, nor children put to death for their fathers; each is to die for his own sins."ᵈ

⁵Amaziah called the people of Judah together and assigned them according to their families to commanders of thousands and commanders of hundreds for all Judah and Benjamin. He then mustered those twenty years old or more and found that there were three hundred thousand men ready for military service, able to handle the spear and shield. ⁶He also hired a hundred thousand fighting men from Israel for a hundred talentsᵉ of silver.

⁷But a man of God came to him and said, "O king, these troops from Israel must not march with you, for the LORD is not with Israel—not with any of the people of Ephraim. ⁸Even if you go and fight courageously in battle, God will overthrow you before the enemy, for God has the power to help or to overthrow."

⁹Amaziah asked the man of God, "But what about the hundred talents I paid for these Israelite troops?"

The man of God replied, "The LORD can give you much more than that."

¹⁰So Amaziah dismissed the troops who had come to him from Ephraim and sent them home. They were furious with Judah and left for home in a great rage.

¹¹Amaziah then marshaled his strength and led his army to the Valley of Salt, where he killed ten thousand men of Seir. ¹²The army of Judah also captured ten thousand men alive, took them to the top of a cliff and threw them down so that all were dashed to pieces.

¹³Meanwhile the troops that Amaziah had sent back and had not allowed to take part in the war raided Judean towns from Samaria to Beth Horon. They killed three thousand people and carried off great quantities of plunder.

¹⁴When Amaziah returned from slaughtering the Edomites, he brought back the gods of the people of Seir. He set them up as his own gods, bowed down to them and burned sacrifices to them. ¹⁵The anger of the LORD burned against Amaziah, and he sent a

---

ᵃ26 A variant of *Jozabad*   ᵇ26 A variant of *Shomer*   ᶜ1 Hebrew *Jehoaddan,* a variant of *Jehoaddin*   ᵈ4 Deut. 24:16   ᵉ6 That is, about 3 3/4 tons (about 3.4 metric tons); also in verse 9

prophet to him, who said, "Why do you consult this people's gods, which could not save their own people from your hand?"

¹⁶While he was still speaking, the king said to him, "Have we appointed you an adviser to the king? Stop! Why be struck down?"

So the prophet stopped but said, "I know that God has determined to destroy you, because you have done this and have not listened to my counsel."

¹⁷After Amaziah king of Judah consulted his advisers, he sent this challenge to Jehoash[a] son of Jehoahaz, the son of Jehu, king of Israel: "Come, meet me face to face."

¹⁸But Jehoash king of Israel replied to Amaziah king of Judah: "A thistle in Lebanon sent a message to a cedar in Lebanon, 'Give your daughter to my son in marriage.' Then a wild beast in Lebanon came along and trampled the thistle underfoot. ¹⁹You say to yourself that you have defeated Edom, and now you are arrogant and proud. But stay at home! Why ask for trouble and cause your own downfall and that of Judah also?"

²⁰Amaziah, however, would not listen, for God so worked that he might hand them over to ˻Jehoash˼, because they sought the gods of Edom. ²¹So Jehoash king of Israel attacked. He and Amaziah king of Judah faced each other at Beth Shemesh in Judah. ²²Judah was routed by Israel, and every man fled to his home. ²³Jehoash king of Israel captured Amaziah king of Judah, the son of Joash, the son of Ahaziah,[b] at Beth Shemesh. Then Jehoash brought him to Jerusalem and broke down the wall of Jerusalem from the Ephraim Gate to the Corner Gate—a section about six hundred feet[c] long. ²⁴He took all the gold and silver and all the articles found in the temple of God that had been in the care of Obed-Edom, together with the palace treasures and the hostages, and returned to Samaria.

²⁵Amaziah son of Joash king of Judah lived for fifteen years after the death of Jehoash son of Jehoahaz king of Israel. ²⁶As for the other events of Amaziah's reign, from beginning to end, are they not written in the book of the kings of Judah and Israel? ²⁷From the time that Amaziah turned away from following the LORD, they conspired against him in Jerusalem and he fled to Lachish, but they sent men after him to Lachish and killed him there. ²⁸He was brought back by horse and was buried with his fathers in the City of Judah.

Uzziah King of Judah

26 Then all the people of Judah took Uzziah,[d] who was sixteen years old, and made him king in place of his father Amaziah. ²He was the one who rebuilt Elath and restored it to Judah after Amaziah rested with his fathers.

³Uzziah was sixteen years old when he became king, and he reigned in Jerusalem fifty-two years. His mother's name was Jecoliah; she was from Jerusalem. ⁴He did what was right in the eyes of the LORD, just as his father Amaziah had done. ⁵He sought God during the days of Zechariah, who instructed him in the fear[e] of God. As long as he sought the LORD, God gave him success.

⁶He went to war against the Philistines and broke down the walls of Gath, Jabneh and Ashdod. He then rebuilt towns near Ashdod and elsewhere among the Philistines. ⁷God helped him against the Philistines and against the Arabs who lived in Gur Baal

---

a17 Hebrew Joash, a variant of Jehoash; also in verses 18, 21, 23 and 25
b23 Hebrew Jehoahaz, a variant of Ahaziah   c23 Hebrew four hundred cubits (about 180 meters)   d1 Also called Azariah   e5 Many Hebrew manuscripts, Septuagint and Syriac; other Hebrew manuscripts vision

---

1. What do you feel passionately about: The soil? The water? The stage? The mountains? The local sports team? Other? 2. Are any two people in your group passionate about the same thing? What?

1. What strengths and weaknesses do you see in Uzziah, the teenage king? Points of weakness? Why does the chronicler rate him so highly (v. 4), when he spends his latter years under divine punishment? 2. Who contributes to Uzziah's success and why? 3. What are Uzziah's accomplishments (vv. 6–15)? Which one stands out to you as the headliner for this king's resume? 4. What happens to Uzziah midway through life? Any parallels with other lead-

ers of Judah? Why do Judean kings seem to falter at the halfway mark? 5. Was Uzziah's mistake an innocent blunder? Why or why not? 6. What is Uzziah's punishment? Does God allow too little time for repentance? Is it fair? 7. Uzziah not only became leprous but also had to leave the palace and was excluded from the temple. Even in death he was not restored to his former place of honor (v. 23). What lessons were the people of Judah to learn from this tragedy? Where can you see God's mercy at work, as well?

♡ 1. Is success oftentimes a danger to our relationship with God? What does Uzziah's story say to you about this? 2. What consequence have you suffered from a foolish action that you later repented of? Where could you see God's mercy at work in the situation?

and against the Meunites. 8The Ammonites brought tribute to Uzziah, and his fame spread as far as the border of Egypt, because he had become very powerful.

9Uzziah built towers in Jerusalem at the Corner Gate, at the Valley Gate and at the angle of the wall, and he fortified them. 10He also built towers in the desert and dug many cisterns, because he had much livestock in the foothills and in the plain. He had people working his fields and vineyards in the hills and in the fertile lands, for he loved the soil.

11Uzziah had a well-trained army, ready to go out by divisions according to their numbers as mustered by Jeiel the secretary and Maaseiah the officer under the direction of Hananiah, one of the royal officials. 12The total number of family leaders over the fighting men was 2,600. 13Under their command was an army of 307,500 men trained for war, a powerful force to support the king against his enemies. 14Uzziah provided shields, spears, helmets, coats of armor, bows and slingstones for the entire army. 15In Jerusalem he made machines designed by skillful men for use on the towers and on the corner defenses to shoot arrows and hurl large stones. His fame spread far and wide, for he was greatly helped until he became powerful.

16But after Uzziah became powerful, his pride led to his downfall. He was unfaithful to the LORD his God, and entered the temple of the LORD to burn incense on the altar of incense. 17Azariah the priest with eighty other courageous priests of the LORD followed him in. 18They confronted him and said, "It is not right for you, Uzziah, to burn incense to the LORD. That is for the priests, the descendants of Aaron, who have been consecrated to burn incense. Leave the sanctuary, for you have been unfaithful; and you will not be honored by the LORD God."

19Uzziah, who had a censer in his hand ready to burn incense, became angry. While he was raging at the priests in their presence before the incense altar in the LORD's temple, leprosya broke out on his forehead. 20When Azariah the chief priest and all the other priests looked at him, they saw that he had leprosy on his forehead, so they hurried him out. Indeed, he himself was eager to leave, because the LORD had afflicted him.

21King Uzziah had leprosy until the day he died. He lived in a separate houseb—leprous, and excluded from the temple of the LORD. Jotham his son had charge of the palace and governed the people of the land.

22The other events of Uzziah's reign, from beginning to end, are recorded by the prophet Isaiah son of Amoz. 23Uzziah rested with his fathers and was buried near them in a field for burial that belonged to the kings, for people said, "He had leprosy." And Jotham his son succeeded him as king.

Jotham King of Judah

27 Jotham was twenty-five years old when he became king, and he reigned in Jerusalem sixteen years. His mother's name was Jerusha daughter of Zadok. 2He did what was right in the eyes of the LORD, just as his father Uzziah had done, but unlike him he did not enter the temple of the LORD. The people, however, continued their corrupt practices. 3Jotham rebuilt the Upper Gate of the temple of the LORD and did extensive work on the wall at the

---

☕ If you could build your dream house, what style would it be? Where would you build it?

📖 1. Finally, a king who stays true to the Lord. Why are there so few verses allotted to him? What strengths and weaknesses do you see in Jotham? What lasting impact did he have? 2. What accounts for Jotham's success beyond his steadiness and diligence?

a19 The Hebrew word was used for various diseases affecting the skin—not necessarily leprosy; also in verses 20, 21 and 23.   b21 Or in a house where he was relieved of responsibilities

hill of Ophel. [4]He built towns in the Judean hills and forts and towers in the wooded areas.

[5]Jotham made war on the king of the Ammonites and conquered them. That year the Ammonites paid him a hundred talents[a] of silver, ten thousand cors[b] of wheat and ten thousand cors of barley. The Ammonites brought him the same amount also in the second and third years.

[6]Jotham grew powerful because he walked steadfastly before the LORD his God.

[7]The other events in Jotham's reign, including all his wars and the other things he did, are written in the book of the kings of Israel and Judah. [8]He was twenty-five years old when he became king, and he reigned in Jerusalem sixteen years. [9]Jotham rested with his fathers and was buried in the City of David. And Ahaz his son succeeded him as king.

Ahaz King of Judah

28 Ahaz was twenty years old when he became king, and he reigned in Jerusalem sixteen years. Unlike David his father, he did not do what was right in the eyes of the LORD. [2]He walked in the ways of the kings of Israel and also made cast idols for worshiping the Baals. [3]He burned sacrifices in the Valley of Ben Hinnom and sacrificed his sons in the fire, following the detestable ways of the nations the LORD had driven out before the Israelites. [4]He offered sacrifices and burned incense at the high places, on the hilltops and under every spreading tree.

[5]Therefore the LORD his God handed him over to the king of Aram. The Arameans defeated him and took many of his people as prisoners and brought them to Damascus.

He was also given into the hands of the king of Israel, who inflicted heavy casualties on him. [6]In one day Pekah son of Remaliah killed a hundred and twenty thousand soldiers in Judah—because Judah had forsaken the LORD, the God of their fathers. [7]Zicri, an Ephraimite warrior, killed Maaseiah the king's son, Azrikam the officer in charge of the palace, and Elkanah, second to the king. [8]The Israelites took captive from their kinsmen two hundred thousand wives, sons and daughters. They also took a great deal of plunder, which they carried back to Samaria.

[9]But a prophet of the LORD named Oded was there, and he went out to meet the army when it returned to Samaria. He said to them, "Because the LORD, the God of your fathers, was angry with Judah, he gave them into your hand. But you have slaughtered them in a rage that reaches to heaven. [10]And now you intend to make the men and women of Judah and Jerusalem your slaves. But aren't you also guilty of sins against the LORD your God? [11]Now listen to me! Send back your fellow countrymen you have taken as prisoners, for the LORD's fierce anger rests on you."

[12]Then some of the leaders in Ephraim—Azariah son of Jehohanan, Berekiah son of Meshillemoth, Jehizkiah son of Shallum, and Amasa son of Hadlai—confronted those who were arriving from the war. [13]"You must not bring those prisoners here," they said, "or we will be guilty before the LORD. Do you intend to add to our sin and guilt? For our guilt is already great, and his fierce anger rests on Israel."

[14]So the soldiers gave up the prisoners and plunder in the presence of the officials and all the assembly. [15]The men designated by name took the prisoners, and from the plunder they clothed all

Are you more of the super-achiever or "slow-and-steady-wins-the-race" type? What advantages do you see in each? What are the drawbacks?

1. What gifts do you love to receive anytime: Clothes? Perfume? Sports equipment? Jewelry? C.D.'s? Candy? Other? When you were age 7, what was your favorite game: Capture the flag? Freeze tag? Other?

1. What is the chronicler's assessment of Ahaz? What detestable practices did he institute? 2. What punishment was most severe (vv. 5–8)? 3. The Israelites went too far in carrying out retribution. Who rebuked them and what was the message? Israel's response? How does God show mercy to Judah here? 4. Ahaz doesn't learn the lesson and God sends punishment number two. What nations carry out God's vengeance? 5. Ahaz asks Tiglath-Pileser (a powerful adversary in the seventh century B.C.) to be his ally. How did Ahaz try to win Tiglath-Pileser's cooperation? Did it work? 6. Who does Ahaz turn to in his "time of trouble"? Where does he use twisted logic in this episode? 7. After verse 24 it looks like worship of the true God is outlawed in Judah. What could faithful Judeans do to continue the true worship? 8. Ahaz continued to anger the Lord to the end of his life. What hint is there in verse 27 that someone with sense still lived in Judah?

1. When have times of trouble driven you *toward* the Lord? Which have driven you *away* from the Lord? What made the difference? 2. In your memory how has twisted logic been used to rationalize cruelty and terror, close to home or far away? How can you tell twisted logic from the truth? 3. You're a missionary sent to Jerusalem around the time of verses 24–25. What is your message? 4. What support for the "just war"

[a]5 That is, about 3 3/4 tons (about 3.4 metric tons)   [b]5 That is, probably about 62,000 bushels (about 2,200 kiloliters)

theory do you find here? Do you believe there are "just" and "unjust" wars? Or are all wars unjust? Explain.

who were naked. They provided them with clothes and sandals, food and drink, and healing balm. All those who were weak they put on donkeys. So they took them back to their fellow countrymen at Jericho, the City of Palms, and returned to Samaria.

¹⁶At that time King Ahaz sent to the king[a] of Assyria for help. ¹⁷The Edomites had again come and attacked Judah and carried away prisoners, ¹⁸while the Philistines had raided towns in the foothills and in the Negev of Judah. They captured and occupied Beth Shemesh, Aijalon and Gederoth, as well as Soco, Timnah and Gimzo, with their surrounding villages. ¹⁹The LORD had humbled Judah because of Ahaz king of Israel,[b] for he had promoted wickedness in Judah and had been most unfaithful to the LORD. ²⁰Tiglath-Pileser[c] king of Assyria came to him, but he gave him trouble instead of help. ²¹Ahaz took some of the things from the temple of the LORD and from the royal palace and from the princes and presented them to the king of Assyria, but that did not help him.

²²In his time of trouble King Ahaz became even more unfaithful to the LORD. ²³He offered sacrifices to the gods of Damascus, who had defeated him; for he thought, "Since the gods of the kings of Aram have helped them, I will sacrifice to them so they will help me." But they were his downfall and the downfall of all Israel.

²⁴Ahaz gathered together the furnishings from the temple of God and took them away.[d] He shut the doors of the LORD's temple and set up altars at every street corner in Jerusalem. ²⁵In every town in Judah he built high places to burn sacrifices to other gods and provoked the LORD, the God of his fathers, to anger.

²⁶The other events of his reign and all his ways, from beginning to end, are written in the book of the kings of Judah and Israel. ²⁷Ahaz rested with his fathers and was buried in the city of Jerusalem, but he was not placed in the tombs of the kings of Israel. And Hezekiah his son succeeded him as king.

Hezekiah Purifies the Temple

29 Hezekiah was twenty-five years old when he became king, and he reigned in Jerusalem twenty-nine years. His mother's name was Abijah daughter of Zechariah. ²He did what was right in the eyes of the LORD, just as his father David had done.

³In the first month of the first year of his reign, he opened the doors of the temple of the LORD and repaired them. ⁴He brought in the priests and the Levites, assembled them in the square on the east side ⁵and said: "Listen to me, Levites! Consecrate yourselves now and consecrate the temple of the LORD, the God of your fathers. Remove all defilement from the sanctuary. ⁶Our fathers were unfaithful; they did evil in the eyes of the LORD our God and forsook him. They turned their faces away from the LORD's dwelling place and turned their backs on him. ⁷They also shut the doors of the portico and put out the lamps. They did not burn incense or present any burnt offerings at the sanctuary to the God of Israel. ⁸Therefore, the anger of the LORD has fallen on Judah and Jerusalem; he has made them an object of dread and horror and scorn, as you can see with your own eyes. ⁹This is why our fathers have fallen by the sword and why our sons and daughters and our wives are in captivity. ¹⁰Now I intend to make a covenant with the LORD, the God of Israel, so that his fierce anger will turn away from us. ¹¹My sons, do not be negligent now, for the LORD has chosen you to

☕ 1. What is your favorite speed sport: Car racing? Downhill skiing? Sailing? Horse racing? Ice Hockey? Other? 2. Which of the following most needs to be cleaned out right now: Your garage? Your clothes closet? Your refrigerator? Your purse or billfold? 3. Your first official act as president or prime minister of your country would be . . .?

📖 1. How is King Hezekiah introduced to the reader in verses 1 and 2? Given his father's reign, why is this introduction significant? 2. What actions did Hezekiah take in the very first month of his reign? Why did he take these seemingly hasty actions? What does this say about Hezekiah's priorities as king? 3. How did the Levites and priests respond to Hezekiah's orders? Why do you think they were so eager to follow the king's directions? 4. After the temple had been purified, it needed to be rededicated to the Lord. What role did each of the following play in that rededication: The city officials? The priests? The Levites?

a16 One Hebrew manuscript, Septuagint and Vulgate (see also 2 Kings 16:7); most Hebrew manuscripts *kings*   b19 That is, Judah, as frequently in 2 Chronicles   c20 Hebrew *Tilgath-Pilneser*, a variant of *Tiglath-Pileser*   d24 Or *and cut them up*

stand before him and serve him, to minister before him and to burn incense."

¹²Then these Levites set to work:

from the Kohathites,
Mahath son of Amasai and Joel son of Azariah;
from the Merarites,
Kish son of Abdi and Azariah son of Jehallelel;
from the Gershonites,
Joah son of Zimmah and Eden son of Joah;
¹³from the descendants of Elizaphan,
Shimri and Jeiel;
from the descendants of Asaph,
Zechariah and Mattaniah;
¹⁴from the descendants of Heman,
Jehiel and Shimei;
from the descendants of Jeduthun,
Shemaiah and Uzziel.

¹⁵When they had assembled their brothers and consecrated themselves, they went in to purify the temple of the LORD, as the king had ordered, following the word of the LORD. ¹⁶The priests went into the sanctuary of the LORD to purify it. They brought out to the courtyard of the LORD's temple everything unclean that they found in the temple of the LORD. The Levites took it and carried it out to the Kidron Valley. ¹⁷They began the consecration on the first day of the first month, and by the eighth day of the month they reached the portico of the LORD. For eight more days they consecrated the temple of the LORD itself, finishing on the sixteenth day of the first month.

¹⁸Then they went in to King Hezekiah and reported: "We have purified the entire temple of the LORD, the altar of burnt offering with all its utensils, and the table for setting out the consecrated bread, with all its articles. ¹⁹We have prepared and consecrated all the articles that King Ahaz removed in his unfaithfulness while he was king. They are now in front of the LORD's altar."

²⁰Early the next morning King Hezekiah gathered the city officials together and went up to the temple of the LORD. ²¹They brought seven bulls, seven rams, seven male lambs and seven male goats as a sin offering for the kingdom, for the sanctuary and for Judah. The king commanded the priests, the descendants of Aaron, to offer these on the altar of the LORD. ²²So they slaughtered the bulls, and the priests took the blood and sprinkled it on the altar; next they slaughtered the rams and sprinkled their blood on the altar; then they slaughtered the lambs and sprinkled their blood on the altar. ²³The goats for the sin offering were brought before the king and the assembly, and they laid their hands on them. ²⁴The priests then slaughtered the goats and presented their blood on the altar for a sin offering to atone for all Israel, because the king had ordered the burnt offering and the sin offering for all Israel.

²⁵He stationed the Levites in the temple of the LORD with cymbals, harps and lyres in the way prescribed by David and Gad the king's seer and Nathan the prophet; this was commanded by the LORD through his prophets. ²⁶So the Levites stood ready with David's instruments, and the priests with their trumpets.

²⁷Hezekiah gave the order to sacrifice the burnt offering on the altar. As the offering began, singing to the LORD began also, accompanied by trumpets and the instruments of David king of Israel. ²⁸The whole assembly bowed in worship, while the singers sang and the trumpeters played. All this continued until the sacrifice of the burnt offering was completed.

The whole assembly? The king? In which of these roles would you have felt most comfortable? **5.** What is the "order of worship" in verses 27–31 for the rededication ceremony? Why is each part important for worship? **6.** What was the response of the people to the reopening of the temple? What problem did this cause? The remedy? Who is being indirectly criticized for lack of leadership here? **7.** In the final analysis, who was really responsible for reopening the temple? Why is this important for us?

♡ **1.** What do you learn from this chapter about Hezekiah's character? His leadership? Is there anything you see in him that you would like in your own life? **2.** Hezekiah seems to link "right worship" with God's blessing. Do you agree? What evidence would you give from your own life, pro or con? **3.** What is God leading you to rededicate to him? How might these elements of the rededication service outlined here be reflected in what you do? Why not do so right now?

²⁹When the offerings were finished, the king and everyone present with him knelt down and worshiped. ³⁰King Hezekiah and his officials ordered the Levites to praise the LORD with the words of David and of Asaph the seer. So they sang praises with gladness and bowed their heads and worshiped.

³¹Then Hezekiah said, "You have now dedicated yourselves to the LORD. Come and bring sacrifices and thank offerings to the temple of the LORD." So the assembly brought sacrifices and thank offerings, and all whose hearts were willing brought burnt offerings.

³²The number of burnt offerings the assembly brought was seventy bulls, a hundred rams and two hundred male lambs—all of them for burnt offerings to the LORD. ³³The animals consecrated as sacrifices amounted to six hundred bulls and three thousand sheep and goats. ³⁴The priests, however, were too few to skin all the burnt offerings; so their kinsmen the Levites helped them until the task was finished and until other priests had been consecrated, for the Levites had been more conscientious in consecrating themselves than the priests had been. ³⁵There were burnt offerings in abundance, together with the fat of the fellowship offeringsᵃ and the drink offerings that accompanied the burnt offerings.

So the service of the temple of the LORD was reestablished. ³⁶Hezekiah and all the people rejoiced at what God had brought about for his people, because it was done so quickly.

Hezekiah Celebrates the Passover

30 Hezekiah sent word to all Israel and Judah and also wrote letters to Ephraim and Manasseh, inviting them to come to the temple of the LORD in Jerusalem and celebrate the Passover to the LORD, the God of Israel. ²The king and his officials and the whole assembly in Jerusalem decided to celebrate the Passover in the second month. ³They had not been able to celebrate it at the regular time because not enough priests had consecrated themselves and the people had not assembled in Jerusalem. ⁴The plan seemed right both to the king and to the whole assembly. ⁵They decided to send a proclamation throughout Israel, from Beersheba to Dan, calling the people to come to Jerusalem and celebrate the Passover to the LORD, the God of Israel. It had not been celebrated in large numbers according to what was written.

⁶At the king's command, couriers went throughout Israel and Judah with letters from the king and from his officials, which read:

"People of Israel, return to the LORD, the God of Abraham, Isaac and Israel, that he may return to you who are left, who have escaped from the hand of the kings of Assyria. ⁷Do not be like your fathers and brothers, who were unfaithful to the LORD, the God of their fathers, so that he made them an object of horror, as you see. ⁸Do not be stiff-necked, as your fathers were; submit to the LORD. Come to the sanctuary, which he has consecrated forever. Serve the LORD your God, so that his fierce anger will turn away from you. ⁹If you return to the LORD, then your brothers and your children will be shown compassion by their captors and will come back to this land, for the LORD your God is gracious and compassionate. He will not turn his face from you if you return to him."

¹⁰The couriers went from town to town in Ephraim and Manasseh, as far as Zebulun, but the people scorned and ridiculed them.

ᵃ35 Traditionally *peace offerings*

1. When it comes to large get-togethers, which do you tend to avoid: (a) Reunions? (b) Block parties? (c) Patriotic celebrations? (d) Church socials? Why? 2. What was the most important letter you ever received? 3. If you had no limits, where would you spend two weeks on holiday?

1. The second major act of King Hezekiah is to reinstitute the Passover (see Ex 12:1–28). Whom did he invite to come and celebrate the Passover? How? 2. In Hezekiah's invitation to Passover (vv. 6–9), what did he ask the people to do? What were his reasons, positive and negative? Does he seem unduly harsh? 3. What were the various responses to Hezekiah's proclamation? Why the differences? Pride? Politics? Or what? 4. How did "the very large crowd of people assembled in Jerusalem" prepare for the feast? What effect did this have on the priests and Levites? What was wrong with those religious leaders? 5. Where were the rules "bent" in order for many to celebrate the Passover? Why was Hezekiah so confident that this deviation from the Law was okay with God? Do you see a similar line of thought in Psalm 51:10–19? 6. What's the overall tone of this revived Passover celebration? How did Hezekiah keep the festival going for the first week? For the second week?

¹¹Nevertheless, some men of Asher, Manasseh and Zebulun humbled themselves and went to Jerusalem. ¹²Also in Judah the hand of God was on the people to give them unity of mind to carry out what the king and his officials had ordered, following the word of the LORD.

¹³A very large crowd of people assembled in Jerusalem to celebrate the Feast of Unleavened Bread in the second month. ¹⁴They removed the altars in Jerusalem and cleared away the incense altars and threw them into the Kidron Valley.

¹⁵They slaughtered the Passover lamb on the fourteenth day of the second month. The priests and the Levites were ashamed and consecrated themselves and brought burnt offerings to the temple of the LORD. ¹⁶Then they took up their regular positions as prescribed in the Law of Moses the man of God. The priests sprinkled the blood handed to them by the Levites. ¹⁷Since many in the crowd had not consecrated themselves, the Levites had to kill the Passover lambs for all those who were not ceremonially clean and could not consecrate ⌊their lambs⌋ to the LORD. ¹⁸Although most of the many people who came from Ephraim, Manasseh, Issachar and Zebulun had not purified themselves, yet they ate the Passover, contrary to what was written. But Hezekiah prayed for them, saying, "May the LORD, who is good, pardon everyone ¹⁹who sets his heart on seeking God—the LORD, the God of his fathers—even if he is not clean according to the rules of the sanctuary." ²⁰And the LORD heard Hezekiah and healed the people.

²¹The Israelites who were present in Jerusalem celebrated the Feast of Unleavened Bread for seven days with great rejoicing, while the Levites and priests sang to the LORD every day, accompanied by the LORD's instruments of praise.[a]

²²Hezekiah spoke encouragingly to all the Levites, who showed good understanding of the service of the LORD. For the seven days they ate their assigned portion and offered fellowship offerings[b] and praised the LORD, the God of their fathers.

²³The whole assembly then agreed to celebrate the festival seven more days; so for another seven days they celebrated joyfully. ²⁴Hezekiah king of Judah provided a thousand bulls and seven thousand sheep and goats for the assembly, and the officials provided them with a thousand bulls and ten thousand sheep and goats. A great number of priests consecrated themselves. ²⁵The entire assembly of Judah rejoiced, along with the priests and Levites and all who had assembled from Israel, including the aliens who had come from Israel and those who lived in Judah. ²⁶There was great joy in Jerusalem, for since the days of Solomon son of David king of Israel there had been nothing like this in Jerusalem. ²⁷The priests and the Levites stood to bless the people, and God heard them, for their prayer reached heaven, his holy dwelling place.

31 When all this had ended, the Israelites who were there went out to the towns of Judah, smashed the sacred stones and cut down the Asherah poles. They destroyed the high places and the altars throughout Judah and Benjamin and in Ephraim and Manasseh. After they had destroyed all of them, the Israelites returned to their own towns and to their own property.

Contributions for Worship

²Hezekiah assigned the priests and Levites to divisions—each of them according to their duties as priests or Levites—to offer burnt offerings and fellowship offerings,[b] to minister, to give thanks and

Who does Hezekiah remind you of in the history of Israel? 7. What were some of the remarkable results of this Passover celebration in Jerusalem? In Judah? In Israel? Were these responses just emotional froth, or motivated by a new desire to obey the Lord?

1. If you had been an Israelite in Hezekiah's time, what would have moved you to travel to Jerusalem for the Passover? What would have impressed you the most about it? 2. Is it okay to "bend" some of the rules to include people in your church or group? Which ones? 3. What ritual meal in the New Testament takes the place of Passover for us? How could this chapter help us to better celebrate that meal? 4. In what ways are modern missionaries like Hezekiah's couriers? How are the responses to their message like Jesus' parable in Mark 4:1–9?

1. What person or service comes to mind when you hear the word "generous"? 2. What food item do you serve generous heaps of to company?

a21 Or priests praised the LORD every day with resounding instruments belonging to the LORD   b22,2 Traditionally peace offerings

1. What specific things did King Hezekiah do in verses 2–4 to continue the revival of worship? Why was each of these actions important? 2. How did the people respond to Hezekiah's order in verse 5? Why so generous? What lesson did Azariah the chief priest learn from all this? 3. How did Hezekiah plan to handle the "heaps" of things given to the Lord? What responsibilities did he delegate? Why is good delegation so important to successful leadership? 4. Who was provided for under Hezekiah's distribution plan? Why was this so important (see Nu 18)? 5. What most impresses you about Hezekiah from these verses? What was the secret of his success?

1. What kinds of organizations or people do you regularly support with time, talent or treasure (money)? Why these? 2. Are some things better caught than taught? How does this chapter illustrate this to you? 3. Does obedience to the Lord insure prosperity for an individual? A church? A nation? Explain.

to sing praises at the gates of the LORD's dwelling. ³The king contributed from his own possessions for the morning and evening burnt offerings and for the burnt offerings on the Sabbaths, New Moons and appointed feasts as written in the Law of the LORD. ⁴He ordered the people living in Jerusalem to give the portion due the priests and Levites so they could devote themselves to the Law of the LORD. ⁵As soon as the order went out, the Israelites generously gave the firstfruits of their grain, new wine, oil and honey and all that the fields produced. They brought a great amount, a tithe of everything. ⁶The men of Israel and Judah who lived in the towns of Judah also brought a tithe of their herds and flocks and a tithe of the holy things dedicated to the LORD their God, and they piled them in heaps. ⁷They began doing this in the third month and finished in the seventh month. ⁸When Hezekiah and his officials came and saw the heaps, they praised the LORD and blessed his people Israel.

⁹Hezekiah asked the priests and Levites about the heaps; ¹⁰and Azariah the chief priest, from the family of Zadok, answered, "Since the people began to bring their contributions to the temple of the LORD, we have had enough to eat and plenty to spare, because the LORD has blessed his people, and this great amount is left over."

¹¹Hezekiah gave orders to prepare storerooms in the temple of the LORD, and this was done. ¹²Then they faithfully brought in the contributions, tithes and dedicated gifts. Conaniah, a Levite, was in charge of these things, and his brother Shimei was next in rank. ¹³Jehiel, Azaziah, Nahath, Asahel, Jerimoth, Jozabad, Eliel, Ismakiah, Mahath and Benaiah were supervisors under Conaniah and Shimei his brother, by appointment of King Hezekiah and Azariah the official in charge of the temple of God.

¹⁴Kore son of Imnah the Levite, keeper of the East Gate, was in charge of the freewill offerings given to God, distributing the contributions made to the LORD and also the consecrated gifts. ¹⁵Eden, Miniamin, Jeshua, Shemaiah, Amariah and Shecaniah assisted him faithfully in the towns of the priests, distributing to their fellow priests according to their divisions, old and young alike.

¹⁶In addition, they distributed to the males three years old or more whose names were in the genealogical records—all who would enter the temple of the LORD to perform the daily duties of their various tasks, according to their responsibilities and their divisions. ¹⁷And they distributed to the priests enrolled by their families in the genealogical records and likewise to the Levites twenty years old or more, according to their responsibilities and their divisions. ¹⁸They included all the little ones, the wives, and the sons and daughters of the whole community listed in these genealogical records. For they were faithful in consecrating themselves.

¹⁹As for the priests, the descendants of Aaron, who lived on the farm lands around their towns or in any other towns, men were designated by name to distribute portions to every male among them and to all who were recorded in the genealogies of the Levites.

²⁰This is what Hezekiah did throughout Judah, doing what was good and right and faithful before the LORD his God. ²¹In everything that he undertook in the service of God's temple and in obedience to the law and the commands, he sought his God and worked wholeheartedly. And so he prospered.

Sennacherib Threatens Jerusalem

32 After all that Hezekiah had so faithfully done, Sennacherib king of Assyria came and invaded Judah. He laid siege to the fortified cities, thinking to conquer them for himself. [2]When Hezekiah saw that Sennacherib had come and that he intended to make war on Jerusalem, [3]he consulted with his officials and military staff about blocking off the water from the springs outside the city, and they helped him. [4]A large force of men assembled, and they blocked all the springs and the stream that flowed through the land. "Why should the kings[a] of Assyria come and find plenty of water?" they said. [5]Then he worked hard repairing all the broken sections of the wall and building towers on it. He built another wall outside that one and reinforced the supporting terraces[b] of the City of David. He also made large numbers of weapons and shields.

[6]He appointed military officers over the people and assembled them before him in the square at the city gate and encouraged them with these words: [7]"Be strong and courageous. Do not be afraid or discouraged because of the king of Assyria and the vast army with him, for there is a greater power with us than with him. [8]With him is only the arm of flesh, but with us is the LORD our God to help us and to fight our battles." And the people gained confidence from what Hezekiah the king of Judah said.

[9]Later, when Sennacherib king of Assyria and all his forces were laying siege to Lachish, he sent his officers to Jerusalem with this message for Hezekiah king of Judah and for all the people of Judah who were there:

[10]"This is what Sennacherib king of Assyria says: On what are you basing your confidence, that you remain in Jerusalem under siege? [11]When Hezekiah says, 'The LORD our God will save us from the hand of the king of Assyria,' he is misleading you, to let you die of hunger and thirst. [12]Did not Hezekiah himself remove this god's high places and altars, saying to Judah and Jerusalem, 'You must worship before one altar and burn sacrifices on it'?

[13]"Do you not know what I and my fathers have done to all the peoples of the other lands? Were the gods of those nations ever able to deliver their land from my hand? [14]Who of all the gods of these nations that my fathers destroyed has been able to save his people from me? How then can your god deliver you from my hand? [15]Now do not let Hezekiah deceive you and mislead you like this. Do not believe him, for no god of any nation or kingdom has been able to deliver his people from my hand or the hand of my fathers. How much less will your god deliver you from my hand!"

[16]Sennacherib's officers spoke further against the LORD God and against his servant Hezekiah. [17]The king also wrote letters insulting the LORD, the God of Israel, and saying this against him: "Just as the gods of the peoples of the other lands did not rescue their people from my hand, so the god of Hezekiah will not rescue his people from my hand." [18]Then they called out in Hebrew to the people of Jerusalem who were on the wall, to terrify them and make them afraid in order to capture the city. [19]They spoke about the God of Jerusalem as they did about the gods of the other peoples of the world—the work of men's hands.

[20]King Hezekiah and the prophet Isaiah son of Amoz cried out in prayer to heaven about this. [21]And the LORD sent an angel, who

---

1. What is your favorite body of water: (a) Your pool? (b) Secret fishing hole? (c) Stretch of white water rapids? (d) Secluded seashore or lake? **2.** What kept you out of mischief when you were 5 years old?

1. After all his successes, what was the major political crisis Hezekiah faced in his reign? How did he prepare to deal with this crisis (vv. 2–8)? What strikes you about these preparations? **2.** What tactics did Sennacherib use to undermine the morale of Hezekiah and Jerusalem? What did he say about Hezekiah? Himself? The Lord? Does it sound like this psychological warfare was partially successful (compare these verses with Isa 37)? **3.** How was Sennacherib's invasion actually defeated? Did Hezekiah play any role in this defeat? Did he get credit for it?

1. Facing any Sennacheribs in your life right now? How are you preparing to defend yourself? **2.** Has God ever miraculously rescued you from a terrible situation or person? How did it happen?

---

a 4 Hebrew; Septuagint and Syriac *king*   *b* 5 Or *the Millo*

annihilated all the fighting men and the leaders and officers in the camp of the Assyrian king. So he withdrew to his own land in disgrace. And when he went into the temple of his god, some of his sons cut him down with the sword.

²²So the LORD saved Hezekiah and the people of Jerusalem from the hand of Sennacherib king of Assyria and from the hand of all others. He took care of them*a* on every side. ²³Many brought offerings to Jerusalem for the LORD and valuable gifts for Hezekiah king of Judah. From then on he was highly regarded by all the nations.

Hezekiah's Pride, Success and Death

²⁴In those days Hezekiah became ill and was at the point of death. He prayed to the LORD, who answered him and gave him a miraculous sign. ²⁵But Hezekiah's heart was proud and he did not respond to the kindness shown him; therefore the LORD's wrath was on him and on Judah and Jerusalem. ²⁶Then Hezekiah repented of the pride of his heart, as did the people of Jerusalem; therefore the LORD's wrath did not come upon them during the days of Hezekiah.

²⁷Hezekiah had very great riches and honor, and he made treasuries for his silver and gold and for his precious stones, spices, shields and all kinds of valuables. ²⁸He also made buildings to store the harvest of grain, new wine and oil; and he made stalls for various kinds of cattle, and pens for the flocks. ²⁹He built villages and acquired great numbers of flocks and herds, for God had given him very great riches.

³⁰It was Hezekiah who blocked the upper outlet of the Gihon spring and channeled the water down to the west side of the City of David. He succeeded in everything he undertook. ³¹But when envoys were sent by the rulers of Babylon to ask him about the miraculous sign that had occurred in the land, God left him to test him and to know everything that was in his heart.

³²The other events of Hezekiah's reign and his acts of devotion are written in the vision of the prophet Isaiah son of Amoz in the book of the kings of Judah and Israel. ³³Hezekiah rested with his fathers and was buried on the hill where the tombs of David's descendants are. All Judah and the people of Jerusalem honored him when he died. And Manasseh his son succeeded him as king.

Manasseh King of Judah

33 Manasseh was twelve years old when he became king, and he reigned in Jerusalem fifty-five years. ²He did evil in the eyes of the LORD, following the detestable practices of the nations the LORD had driven out before the Israelites. ³He rebuilt the high places his father Hezekiah had demolished; he also erected altars to the Baals and made Asherah poles. He bowed down to all the starry hosts and worshiped them. ⁴He built altars in the temple of the LORD, of which the LORD had said, "My Name will remain in Jerusalem forever." ⁵In both courts of the temple of the LORD, he built altars to all the starry hosts. ⁶He sacrificed his sons in*b* the fire in the Valley of Ben Hinnom, practiced sorcery, divination and witchcraft, and consulted mediums and spiritists. He did much evil in the eyes of the LORD, provoking him to anger.

⁷He took the carved image he had made and put it in God's temple, of which God had said to David and to his son Solomon, "In this temple and in Jerusalem, which I have chosen out of all the

---

1. What was the most traumatic childhood illness you suffered? How did it impact your life? 2. Where do you want to be buried when you die? Why?

1. After all of Hezekiah's accomplishments, what personal crisis did he face? What character flaw did this crisis expose? What lessons do you see in this incident described in verses 24–26? 2. How else was Hezekiah's reign noteworthy according to verses 27–30? Which of his accomplishments is most impressive to you? 3. Where does the chronicler rank Hezekiah among the kings of Judah? Where would you? Why?

1. Hezekiah is criticized for his pride. Is pride always bad? What can make it so objectionable to God? 2. How do you measure greatness in life? How does God measure it?

1. If you had a monument dedicated to your memory, what kind of monument would you prefer: Building? Park? Street? Library? Airport? 2. What did you want to be when you were a child? 3. What did you want to be as a young adult?

1. At the beginning of his reign what sort of king was Manasseh? Why did he make the Lord angry? How "low" do the people go under Manasseh's reign according to the chronicler? 2. What finally turned Manasseh around? How great is God's forgiveness? 3. How does Manasseh show that he really was changed? What proved that the people were not totally changed? 4. How does this history of Manasseh compare to the story in 2 Kings 21:1–18? Why the differ-

---

a22 Hebrew; Septuagint and Vulgate *He gave them rest*   *b6* Or *He made his sons pass through*

tribes of Israel, I will put my Name forever. [8]I will not again make the feet of the Israelites leave the land I assigned to your forefathers, if only they will be careful to do everything I commanded them concerning all the laws, decrees and ordinances given through Moses." [9]But Manasseh led Judah and the people of Jerusalem astray, so that they did more evil than the nations the LORD had destroyed before the Israelites.

[10]The LORD spoke to Manasseh and his people, but they paid no attention. [11]So the LORD brought against them the army commanders of the king of Assyria, who took Manasseh prisoner, put a hook in his nose, bound him with bronze shackles and took him to Babylon. [12]In his distress he sought the favor of the LORD his God and humbled himself greatly before the God of his fathers. [13]And when he prayed to him, the LORD was moved by his entreaty and listened to his plea; so he brought him back to Jerusalem and to his kingdom. Then Manasseh knew that the LORD is God.

[14]Afterward he rebuilt the outer wall of the City of David, west of the Gihon spring in the valley, as far as the entrance of the Fish Gate and encircling the hill of Ophel; he also made it much higher. He stationed military commanders in all the fortified cities in Judah.

[15]He got rid of the foreign gods and removed the image from the temple of the LORD, as well as all the altars he had built on the temple hill and in Jerusalem; and he threw them out of the city. [16]Then he restored the altar of the LORD and sacrificed fellowship offerings[a] and thank offerings on it, and told Judah to serve the LORD, the God of Israel. [17]The people, however, continued to sacrifice at the high places, but only to the LORD their God.

[18]The other events of Manasseh's reign, including his prayer to his God and the words the seers spoke to him in the name of the LORD, the God of Israel, are written in the annals of the kings of Israel.[b] [19]His prayer and how God was moved by his entreaty, as well as all his sins and unfaithfulness, and the sites where he built high places and set up Asherah poles and idols before he humbled himself—all are written in the records of the seers.[c] [20]Manasseh rested with his fathers and was buried in his palace. And Amon his son succeeded him as king.

Amon King of Judah

[21]Amon was twenty-two years old when he became king, and he reigned in Jerusalem two years. [22]He did evil in the eyes of the LORD, as his father Manasseh had done. Amon worshiped and offered sacrifices to all the idols Manasseh had made. [23]But unlike his father Manasseh, he did not humble himself before the LORD; Amon increased his guilt.

[24]Amon's officials conspired against him and assassinated him in his palace. [25]Then the people of the land killed all who had plotted against King Amon, and they made Josiah his son king in his place.

Josiah's Reforms

34 Josiah was eight years old when he became king, and he reigned in Jerusalem thirty-one years. [2]He did what was right in the eyes of the LORD and walked in the ways of his father David, not turning aside to the right or to the left.

[3]In the eighth year of his reign, while he was still young, he began to seek the God of his father David. In his twelfth year he began to purge Judah and Jerusalem of high places, Asherah poles,

---

a16 Traditionally *peace offerings*   *b18* That is, Judah, as frequently in 2 Chronicles
c19 One Hebrew manuscript and Septuagint; most Hebrew manuscripts *of Hozai*

---

ence in the moral verdict on Manasseh? **5.** How was Manasseh's character similar to Hezekiah's? **6.** Amon learned some lessons and rejected others from the life of his father. Which ones? What's the big difference between father and son? **7.** Who assassinated Amon? Is this assassination justifiable? Was it God's idea? What happened to the assassins?

1. Would you have shown Manasseh such mercy? Is there anything God won't forgive if you are truly repentant? **2.** When did God first become real in your life? In what concrete ways did your life begin to change? **3.** Reflect on a time you were in distress and called on the Lord. How did he come to your rescue?

How did you celebrate your 16th birthday? What song was popular at the time?

1. How old was Josiah when he began to seek the Lord? When he began his reforms? **2.** What were the reforms Josiah accomplished? What suggests that there was resistance, use of force and even violence in Josiah's clean-up program? Why did Josiah risk extending his program so far north of Jerusalem (v. 6)? **3.** Why do you think the repair of the temple was not attended to first? What point might Josiah be trying to press? **4.** How was the repair of the temple paid for? What was the extent of repair? Who administered the funds and supervised the workers? From verses 12b and 13a, what might have helped the men do their work more joyfully?

1. What clean-up programs have been top priority with you: Physical? Spiritual? Psychological? Environmental? What people and other resources helped a lot? **2.** What do you think of teenagers in positions of authority? How could you help them seek the Lord?

You are rummaging through an attic and happen upon a big chest covered with dust. Inside what would you prefer to find: (a) Old letters? (b) Old newspaper clippings? (c) Old scrapbook? (d) Old books? (e) Old maps? (f) Antique clothes? (g) Antique jewelry? (h) Old coins? What makes your choice so interesting to you?

1. When does the Book of the Law cease to be a casual find and begin to be the center of great excitement? **2.** What is Josiah's strange and intense reaction to the book? **3.** What role does Huldah play? What is her message? **4.** What is the special message for Josiah? What again signals the most important character trait for a successful king? **5.** How does Josiah take Huldah's message? **6.** What do you make of the people's commitment to the Lord? Where else have you seen something like that?

carved idols and cast images. ⁴Under his direction the altars of the Baals were torn down; he cut to pieces the incense altars that were above them, and smashed the Asherah poles, the idols and the images. These he broke to pieces and scattered over the graves of those who had sacrificed to them. ⁵He burned the bones of the priests on their altars, and so he purged Judah and Jerusalem. ⁶In the towns of Manasseh, Ephraim and Simeon, as far as Naphtali, and in the ruins around them, ⁷he tore down the altars and the Asherah poles and crushed the idols to powder and cut to pieces all the incense altars throughout Israel. Then he went back to Jerusalem.

⁸In the eighteenth year of Josiah's reign, to purify the land and the temple, he sent Shaphan son of Azaliah and Maaseiah the ruler of the city, with Joah son of Joahaz, the recorder, to repair the temple of the Lord his God.

⁹They went to Hilkiah the high priest and gave him the money that had been brought into the temple of God, which the Levites who were the doorkeepers had collected from the people of Manasseh, Ephraim and the entire remnant of Israel and from all the people of Judah and Benjamin and the inhabitants of Jerusalem. ¹⁰Then they entrusted it to the men appointed to supervise the work on the Lord's temple. These men paid the workers who repaired and restored the temple. ¹¹They also gave money to the carpenters and builders to purchase dressed stone, and timber for joists and beams for the buildings that the kings of Judah had allowed to fall into ruin.

¹²The men did the work faithfully. Over them to direct them were Jahath and Obadiah, Levites descended from Merari, and Zechariah and Meshullam, descended from Kohath. The Levites— all who were skilled in playing musical instruments— ¹³had charge of the laborers and supervised all the workers from job to job. Some of the Levites were secretaries, scribes and doorkeepers.

The Book of the Law Found

¹⁴While they were bringing out the money that had been taken into the temple of the Lord, Hilkiah the priest found the Book of the Law of the Lord that had been given through Moses. ¹⁵Hilkiah said to Shaphan the secretary, "I have found the Book of the Law in the temple of the Lord." He gave it to Shaphan.

¹⁶Then Shaphan took the book to the king and reported to him: "Your officials are doing everything that has been committed to them. ¹⁷They have paid out the money that was in the temple of the Lord and have entrusted it to the supervisors and workers." ¹⁸Then Shaphan the secretary informed the king, "Hilkiah the priest has given me a book." And Shaphan read from it in the presence of the king.

¹⁹When the king heard the words of the Law, he tore his robes. ²⁰He gave these orders to Hilkiah, Ahikam son of Shaphan, Abdon son of Micah,ᵃ Shaphan the secretary and Asaiah the king's attendant: ²¹"Go and inquire of the Lord for me and for the remnant in Israel and Judah about what is written in this book that has been found. Great is the Lord's anger that is poured out on us because our fathers have not kept the word of the Lord; they have not acted in accordance with all that is written in this book."

²²Hilkiah and those the king had sent with himᵇ went to speak to the prophetess Huldah, who was the wife of Shallum son of

---

ᵃ20 Also called *Acbor son of Micaiah*   ᵇ22 One Hebrew manuscript, Vulgate and Syriac; most Hebrew manuscripts do not have *had sent with him.*

Tokhath,^a the son of Hasrah,^b keeper of the wardrobe. She lived in Jerusalem, in the Second District.

²³She said to them, "This is what the LORD, the God of Israel, says: Tell the man who sent you to me, ²⁴'This is what the LORD says: I am going to bring disaster on this place and its people—all the curses written in the book that has been read in the presence of the king of Judah. ²⁵Because they have forsaken me and burned incense to other gods and provoked me to anger by all that their hands have made,^c my anger will be poured out on this place and will not be quenched.' ²⁶Tell the king of Judah, who sent you to inquire of the LORD, 'This is what the LORD, the God of Israel, says concerning the words you heard: ²⁷Because your heart was responsive and you humbled yourself before God when you heard what he spoke against this place and its people, and because you humbled yourself before me and tore your robes and wept in my presence, I have heard you, declares the LORD. ²⁸Now I will gather you to your fathers, and you will be buried in peace. Your eyes will not see all the disaster I am going to bring on this place and on those who live here.'"

So they took her answer back to the king.

²⁹Then the king called together all the elders of Judah and Jerusalem. ³⁰He went up to the temple of the LORD with the men of Judah, the people of Jerusalem, the priests and the Levites—all the people from the least to the greatest. He read in their hearing all the words of the Book of the Covenant, which had been found in the temple of the LORD. ³¹The king stood by his pillar and renewed the covenant in the presence of the LORD—to follow the LORD and keep his commands, regulations and decrees with all his heart and all his soul, and to obey the words of the covenant written in this book.

³²Then he had everyone in Jerusalem and Benjamin pledge themselves to it; the people of Jerusalem did this in accordance with the covenant of God, the God of their fathers.

³³Josiah removed all the detestable idols from all the territory belonging to the Israelites, and he had all who were present in Israel serve the LORD their God. As long as he lived, they did not fail to follow the LORD, the God of their fathers.

Josiah Celebrates the Passover

35 Josiah celebrated the Passover to the LORD in Jerusalem, and the Passover lamb was slaughtered on the fourteenth day of the first month. ²He appointed the priests to their duties and encouraged them in the service of the LORD's temple. ³He said to the Levites, who instructed all Israel and who had been consecrated to the LORD: "Put the sacred ark in the temple that Solomon son of David king of Israel built. It is not to be carried about on your shoulders. Now serve the LORD your God and his people Israel. ⁴Prepare yourselves by families in your divisions, according to the directions written by David king of Israel and by his son Solomon.

⁵"Stand in the holy place with a group of Levites for each subdivision of the families of your fellow countrymen, the lay people. ⁶Slaughter the Passover lambs, consecrate yourselves and prepare ⌊the lambs⌋ for your fellow countrymen, doing what the LORD commanded through Moses."

⁷Josiah provided for all the lay people who were there a total of thirty thousand sheep and goats for the Passover offerings, and also three thousand cattle—all from the king's own possessions.

1. What comes easier to you: (a) Obeying rigorously the laws of God? or, (b) Enjoying and taking pleasure in God? Which type of response to God would you like to experience more? 2. How important are the words of the good Book in your daily life? How often do you read it? Do you often make concrete decisions or change behavior based simply on what you read? 3. Who serves the role of Huldah for you? Why is this helpful? How could this service make more of an impact on you?

1. Your parents want to give a large banquet in your honor. You decide the menu. What will you have? 2. What yearly ritual are you certain to observe in some special way: Super Bowl? Fourth of July? Thanksgiving? County Fair? Other?

1. One gets the impression after reading this section that tons of preparation went into the Passover celebration. What is Passover and the Feast of Unleavened Bread (see Ex 12)? 2. What were Josiah's specific instructions for preparing for Passover? 3. Who provided the sheep, goats and cattle for the offerings and the main dish? 4. What was the priests' role? 5. Such a Passover! How good was it (v. 18)?

---

^a22 Also called *Tikvah*   ^b22 Also called *Harhas*   ^c25 Or *by everything they have done*

1. Are rituals as important in your life as they were to the ancient Israelites? How attached are rituals to your faith and spiritual growth? What's the good and bad of rituals? 2. Priests were central in the Passover. Who is a priest to you?

8His officials also contributed voluntarily to the people and the priests and Levites. Hilkiah, Zechariah and Jehiel, the administrators of God's temple, gave the priests twenty-six hundred Passover offerings and three hundred cattle. 9Also Conaniah along with Shemaiah and Nethanel, his brothers, and Hashabiah, Jeiel and Jozabad, the leaders of the Levites, provided five thousand Passover offerings and five hundred head of cattle for the Levites.

10The service was arranged and the priests stood in their places with the Levites in their divisions as the king had ordered. 11The Passover lambs were slaughtered, and the priests sprinkled the blood handed to them, while the Levites skinned the animals. 12They set aside the burnt offerings to give them to the subdivisions of the families of the people to offer to the LORD, as is written in the Book of Moses. They did the same with the cattle. 13They roasted the Passover animals over the fire as prescribed, and boiled the holy offerings in pots, caldrons and pans and served them quickly to all the people. 14After this, they made preparations for themselves and for the priests, because the priests, the descendants of Aaron, were sacrificing the burnt offerings and the fat portions until nightfall. So the Levites made preparations for themselves and for the Aaronic priests.

15The musicians, the descendants of Asaph, were in the places prescribed by David, Asaph, Heman and Jeduthun the king's seer. The gatekeepers at each gate did not need to leave their posts, because their fellow Levites made the preparations for them.

16So at that time the entire service of the LORD was carried out for the celebration of the Passover and the offering of burnt offerings on the altar of the LORD, as King Josiah had ordered. 17The Israelites who were present celebrated the Passover at that time and observed the Feast of Unleavened Bread for seven days. 18The Passover had not been observed like this in Israel since the days of the prophet Samuel; and none of the kings of Israel had ever celebrated such a Passover as did Josiah, with the priests, the Levites and all Judah and Israel who were there with the people of Jerusalem. 19This Passover was celebrated in the eighteenth year of Josiah's reign.

The Death of Josiah

20After all this, when Josiah had set the temple in order, Neco king of Egypt went up to fight at Carchemish on the Euphrates, and Josiah marched out to meet him in battle. 21But Neco sent messengers to him, saying, "What quarrel is there between you and me, O king of Judah? It is not you I am attacking at this time, but the house with which I am at war. God has told me to hurry; so stop opposing God, who is with me, or he will destroy you."

22Josiah, however, would not turn away from him, but disguised himself to engage him in battle. He would not listen to what Neco had said at God's command but went to fight him on the plain of Megiddo.

23Archers shot King Josiah, and he told his officers, "Take me away; I am badly wounded." 24So they took him out of his chariot, put him in the other chariot he had and brought him to Jerusalem, where he died. He was buried in the tombs of his fathers, and all Judah and Jerusalem mourned for him.

25Jeremiah composed laments for Josiah, and to this day all the men and women singers commemorate Josiah in the laments. These became a tradition in Israel and are written in the Laments.

26The other events of Josiah's reign and his acts of devotion, according to what is written in the Law of the LORD— 27all the

What leader's death had the greatest impact on your life?

1. If pious kings succeed in battle, and evil kings do not, why does Josiah get himself shot? 2. For what previous leaders have the Israelites mourned so greatly? Why all the fuss?

Your death can come unexpectedly, just as Josiah's did. Are you prepared to die?

events, from beginning to end, are written in the book of the kings

36
of Israel and Judah. ¹And the people of the land took Jehoahaz son of Josiah and made him king in Jerusalem in place of his father.

Jehoahaz King of Judah

²Jehoahaz*a* was twenty-three years old when he became king, and he reigned in Jerusalem three months. ³The king of Egypt dethroned him in Jerusalem and imposed on Judah a levy of a hundred talents*b* of silver and a talent*c* of gold. ⁴The king of Egypt made Eliakim, a brother of Jehoahaz, king over Judah and Jerusalem and changed Eliakim's name to Jehoiakim. But Neco took Eliakim's brother Jehoahaz and carried him off to Egypt.

Jehoiakim King of Judah

⁵Jehoiakim was twenty-five years old when he became king, and he reigned in Jerusalem eleven years. He did evil in the eyes of the LORD his God. ⁶Nebuchadnezzar king of Babylon attacked him and bound him with bronze shackles to take him to Babylon. ⁷Nebuchadnezzar also took to Babylon articles from the temple of the LORD and put them in his temple*d* there.

⁸The other events of Jehoiakim's reign, the detestable things he did and all that was found against him, are written in the book of the kings of Israel and Judah. And Jehoiachin his son succeeded him as king.

Jehoiachin King of Judah

⁹Jehoiachin was eighteen*e* years old when he became king, and he reigned in Jerusalem three months and ten days. He did evil in the eyes of the LORD. ¹⁰In the spring, King Nebuchadnezzar sent for him and brought him to Babylon, together with articles of value from the temple of the LORD, and he made Jehoiachin's uncle,*f* Zedekiah, king over Judah and Jerusalem.

Zedekiah King of Judah

¹¹Zedekiah was twenty-one years old when he became king, and he reigned in Jerusalem eleven years. ¹²He did evil in the eyes of the LORD his God and did not humble himself before Jeremiah the prophet, who spoke the word of the LORD. ¹³He also rebelled against King Nebuchadnezzar, who had made him take an oath in God's name. He became stiff-necked and hardened his heart and would not turn to the LORD, the God of Israel. ¹⁴Furthermore, all the leaders of the priests and the people became more and more unfaithful, following all the detestable practices of the nations and defiling the temple of the LORD, which he had consecrated in Jerusalem.

The Fall of Jerusalem

¹⁵The LORD, the God of their fathers, sent word to them through his messengers again and again, because he had pity on his people and on his dwelling place. ¹⁶But they mocked God's messengers, despised his words and scoffed at his prophets until the wrath of the LORD was aroused against his people and there was no remedy. ¹⁷He brought up against them the king of the Babylonians,*g* who

If you knew the world would end in six months, how would you spend your time?

1. How much time elapsed from the start of Jehoahaz' reign until the fall of Jerusalem? How many kings in this period? Name each king and in one sentence tell something about him. **2.** What prophets were around at this time? **3.** What kings carried out God's punishment for Judah? What was the ultimate punishment? **4.** Who were the remnant? What happened to them? How long did the captivity last? **5.** How do the people get back to Jerusalem? **6.** What's the irony of Cyrus' being appointed to build the temple for God? What's the lesson in it? **7.** What is the chronicler's final message? What significance did Cyrus' decree play in the exiles return under Ezra (see Ezr 1:1–5; 2Ch 36:23)?

1. The faithfulness of the Lord lasts through generations. Does this chapter depress you or give you hope for the future of Israel? For your own life? For your small group? How so? **2.** In the cycle of good and bad kings and their effect on people, two major compulsions are evident in 2 Chronicles: (a) The compulsion of tyrannized people to assert their freedom; and (b) the compulsion of free people to self-destruct. How is this cycle and these two compulsions evident in your world? **3.** In your own life cycle and struggles with freedom, which do you feel more compelled to do right now?

a2 Hebrew *Joahaz,* a variant of *Jehoahaz;* also in verse 4   *b3* That is, about 3 3/4 tons (about 3.4 metric tons)   *c3* That is, about 75 pounds (about 34 kilograms)   *d7* Or *palace*   *e9* One Hebrew manuscript, some Septuagint manuscripts and Syriac (see also 2 Kings 24:8); most Hebrew manuscripts *eight*   *f10* Hebrew *brother,* that is, relative (see 2 Kings 24:17)   *g17* Or *Chaldeans*

killed their young men with the sword in the sanctuary, and spared neither young man nor young woman, old man or aged. God handed all of them over to Nebuchadnezzar. [18]He carried to Babylon all the articles from the temple of God, both large and small, and the treasures of the LORD's temple and the treasures of the king and his officials. [19]They set fire to God's temple and broke down the wall of Jerusalem; they burned all the palaces and destroyed everything of value there.

[20]He carried into exile to Babylon the remnant, who escaped from the sword, and they became servants to him and his sons until the kingdom of Persia came to power. [21]The land enjoyed its sabbath rests; all the time of its desolation it rested, until the seventy years were completed in fulfillment of the word of the LORD spoken by Jeremiah.

[22]In the first year of Cyrus king of Persia, in order to fulfill the word of the LORD spoken by Jeremiah, the LORD moved the heart of Cyrus king of Persia to make a proclamation throughout his realm and to put it in writing:

[23]"This is what Cyrus king of Persia says:

" 'The LORD, the God of heaven, has given me all the kingdoms of the earth and he has appointed me to build a temple for him at Jerusalem in Judah. Anyone of his people among you—may the LORD his God be with him, and let him go up.' "

INTRODUCTION to
EZRA

Book Study Outline: If you are using Ezra for a study course, here is a 4- or 7-week outline. Use the questions in the margin for your group agenda:

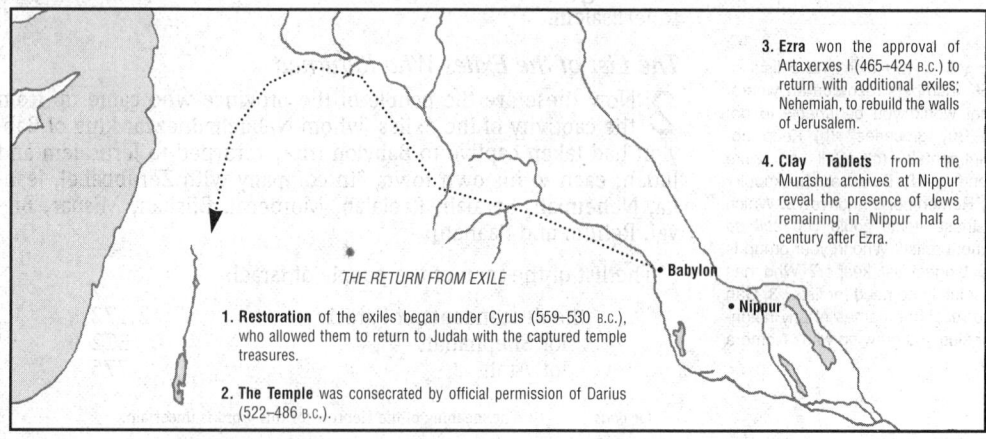

☕ start meeting / 15 min.

📖 read & discuss Bible / 30 min.

♡ close meeting / 15–45 min.

4-week plan	7-week plan	Personal Reading	Group Study Passage
1	1	1:1–2:70	1:1–11/Returning Exiles
	2	3:1–13	3:1–6/Rebuilding the Altar
2	3	4:1–24	4:6–24/Rebuilding Delayed
	4	5:1–6:22	6:1–12/Darius' Decree
3	5	7:1–8:36	7:11–28/Artaxerxes' Letter
	6	9:1–15	9:1–15/Sin of Intermarriage
4	7	10:1–44	10:1–17/Confession of Sin

Refer to the Questions and Answers in the front of this Bible for more information.

Author: The book is named for the principal character, Ezra, but it does not state its author. Whoever it was may have also helped to compile the book of Nehemiah and perhaps 1 and 2 Chronicles.

Date: With an unstated author, precise dating is difficult to determine. The events narrated cover the years c. 538–458 B.C.

Theme: Beginning again, by building the second temple.

Historical Background: Originally this work was one book along with Nehemiah. In the Latin Bible, Ezra and Nehemiah are entitled 1 and 2 Esdras. This book chronicles the restoration of Israel after 70 years of captivity in Babylon. This is accomplished through the help of three Persian kings (Cyrus, Darius and Artaxerxes I). Cyrus was an enlightened king who reversed the oppressive policies of his Assyrian and Babylonian predecessors and encouraged the return of the exiles and the rebirth of their religion. The traditional view is that Ezra arrived in Jerusalem in the seventh year of the reign of Artaxerxes I (458 B.C.) and Nehemiah in the twentieth year of the reign (445 B.C.).

Characteristics: This book weaves together various lists, the first-person and third-person memoirs of Ezra and official documents. These include: (1) the decree of Cyrus (1:2–4); (2) the accusation against the Jews (4:11–16); (3) the response of Artaxerxes (4:17–22); (4) the letter of Tattenai to Darius (5:7–17); (5) a memo (6:2b–5); (6) Darius' reply to Tattenai (6:6–12); and (7) a letter from Artaxerxes I to Ezra (7:12–26). God is shown using Persian kings and Jewish leaders both to bless and to discipline his people. Ezra is often seen as the "father of Judaism" because he promotes a way of life renewed by and centered on unswerving allegiance to the Torah. Ezra's policies saved Judaism from oblivion in this crucial period of transition.

Ezra

Cyrus Helps the Exiles to Return

1 In the first year of Cyrus king of Persia, in order to fulfill the word of the LORD spoken by Jeremiah, the LORD moved the heart of Cyrus king of Persia to make a proclamation throughout his realm and to put it in writing:

2"This is what Cyrus king of Persia says:

" 'The LORD, the God of heaven, has given me all the kingdoms of the earth and he has appointed me to build a temple for him at Jerusalem in Judah. 3Anyone of his people among you—may his God be with him, and let him go up to Jerusalem in Judah and build the temple of the LORD, the God of Israel, the God who is in Jerusalem. 4And the people of any place where survivors may now be living are to provide him with silver and gold, with goods and livestock, and with freewill offerings for the temple of God in Jerusalem.' "

5Then the family heads of Judah and Benjamin, and the priests and Levites—everyone whose heart God had moved—prepared to go up and build the house of the LORD in Jerusalem. 6All their neighbors assisted them with articles of silver and gold, with goods and livestock, and with valuable gifts, in addition to all the freewill offerings. 7Moreover, King Cyrus brought out the articles belonging to the temple of the LORD, which Nebuchadnezzar had carried away from Jerusalem and had placed in the temple of his god.[a] 8Cyrus king of Persia had them brought by Mithredath the treasurer, who counted them out to Sheshbazzar the prince of Judah.

9This was the inventory:

gold dishes	30
silver dishes	1,000
silver pans[b]	29
10gold bowls	30
matching silver bowls	410
other articles	1,000

11In all, there were 5,400 articles of gold and of silver. Sheshbazzar brought all these along when the exiles came up from Babylon to Jerusalem.

The List of the Exiles Who Returned

2 Now these are the people of the province who came up from the captivity of the exiles, whom Nebuchadnezzar king of Babylon had taken captive to Babylon (they returned to Jerusalem and Judah, each to his own town, 2in company with Zerubbabel, Jeshua, Nehemiah, Seraiah, Reelaiah, Mordecai, Bilshan, Mispar, Bigvai, Rehum and Baanah):

The list of the men of the people of Israel:

3the descendants of Parosh	2,172
4of Shephatiah	372
5of Arah	775

Sidebar questions (left column):

1. What historical events have most scattered or restored your family: War? Civil Rights Act? Amnesty? Economic opportunity? Emigration? Persecution? Baby Boom? 2. Where do you fit in this?

1. How does Cyrus' decree strike you: (a) Deja vu (see 2Ch 36:22–23)? (b) Unusual? (c) Note-worthy? (d) Legally binding? (e) Predictable (see Jer 25:11–12; 29:10)? 2. In what sense is Jeremiah's prophecy fulfilled by Cyrus? By the "people of any place" (v. 4)? By their neighbors? By God? Who moves whom to do what? 3. Compare this decree (1:2–4) with its "memo" version (6:3–5). What do you make of the variation? 4. What do you make of the missing or uncounted articles in verses 7–11a (see 2Ki 25:13–15)?

1. Which factors from Cyrus' story have also shaped who you are: (a) Building projects? (b) Mercy toward others? (c) Service offerings? (d) Family ties? 2. God moves hearts of kings and families alike to do his will. How has God "moved your heart" (vv. 1,5)? 3. If you must wait, as Israel did, for God to restore your place in his service, are you content to do so? Or pushing for change? How so?

1. If you didn't have lists or numbers recorded anywhere, what would you be unable to do: (a) Buy groceries? (b) Keep appointments? (c) Call or write friends? (d) Balance checkbook? (e) Remember birthdays? 2. Which of these items could you still do without a list? Who in your group is the biggest list keeper? Who has absolutely no need for lists? 3. Can you recall the names of any neighbor kids you grew up with? Name a few.

---

a7 Or gods   b9 The meaning of the Hebrew for this word is uncertain.

6of Pahath-Moab (through the line of
   Jeshua and Joab)   2,812
7of Elam   1,254
8of Zattu   945
9of Zaccai   760
10of Bani   642
11of Bebai   623
12of Azgad   1,222
13of Adonikam   666
14of Bigvai   2,056
15of Adin   454
16of Ater (through Hezekiah)   98
17of Bezai   323
18of Jorah   112
19of Hashum   223
20of Gibbar   95

21the men of Bethlehem   123
22of Netophah   56
23of Anathoth   128
24of Azmaveth   42
25of Kiriath Jearim,a Kephirah and
   Beeroth   743
26of Ramah and Geba   621
27of Micmash   122
28of Bethel and Ai   223
29of Nebo   52
30of Magbish   156
31of the other Elam   1,254
32of Harim   320
33of Lod, Hadid and Ono   725
34of Jericho   345
35of Senaah   3,630

36The priests:

   the descendants of Jedaiah (through
      the family of Jeshua)   973
37of Immer   1,052
38of Pashhur   1,247
39of Harim   1,017

40The Levites:

   the descendants of Jeshua and Kadmiel
      (through the line of Hodaviah)   74

41The singers:

   the descendants of Asaph   128

42The gatekeepers of the temple:

   the descendants of
      Shallum, Ater, Talmon,
      Akkub, Hatita and Shobai   139

43The temple servants:

   the descendants of
      Ziha, Hasupha, Tabbaoth,
44Keros, Siaha, Padon,
45Lebanah, Hagabah, Akkub,

a25 See Septuagint (see also Neh. 7:29); Hebrew Kiriath Arim.

1. What is the connection between this chapter and the previous one? What transfer of leadership occurs? 2. Nehemiah 7 parallels this chapter, with some important variation in names and numbers. How does verse 2 compare with Nehemiah 7:7? Why might Nehemiah want to include 12 tribes of Israel, but Ezra only 11? 3. Three had Babylonian names (Zerubbabel, Bilshan and Mordecai) and one a Persian name (Bigvai). What does that tell you about the religious and ethnic integration among these Babylonian Jews? 4. What forms the seven organizational divisions for Ezra (vv. 3–58)? When grouping people by their points of departure (vv. 21–35), why do you think Ezra omits any reference to towns in the Negev? (Note: The Negev was a large area south of Judah, which was occupied by the Edomites after Nebuchadnezzar conquered Judah in 597 B.C.) 5. Ezra 2 and Nehemiah 7 agree on the priestly family names, their order and the numbers assigned to each (vv. 36–39). What does that say about their relative importance? 6. What is the ratio between the total number of priests (vv. 36–39) and the total membership for the restored community (v. 64)? Does that ratio sound top-heavy to you? What long-term needs of the community would be served by that many priests? 7. What other professional groups or classes of people are returning from exile? What do their small numbers say about their relative importance? 8. Moses, Joshua and David gave captives to the Levites for service at the Lord's altar (see Nu 31:29–30; Jos 9:22–27). Yet Ezra and Nehemiah talk of temple slaves differently, tracing their heirs by name (vv. 43–54). What change is indicated by their inclusion in this list of returnees? 9. What happened to returnees who could not properly document their family ties (vv. 61–63)? What situation parallels this today? What does that tell you about the importance of keeping family records? What's the "Urim and Thummim" (see Ex 28:30)? Why would they be necessary? 10. What priorities are evident in the inventory of extras (vv. 64–67)? In their designated gifts (vv. 68–69)? Why is it often easier to raise money for a building (as in v. 68) than a church program? 11. In what towns do they all settle after 70 years of exile (v. 70)? How do you explain that:

Good collective memory? Fine-tuned homing instincts? Divine guidance?

1. What is the most ethnically diverse group, of which you are an active part? How does that group help you celebrate differences? 2. What family records do you keep: (a) Diary? (b) Old letters? (c) Photo album? (d) Memorabilia? Why do you keep them? What would an inventory of them indicate about the kind of person you are, or the kind of family you come from? 3. When have you experienced a time of spiritual restoration: After lapsing in your faith? After moving away from organized religion? After a time out to explore other things? After an interaction by someone else? 4. This chapter underscores the importance of spiritual ancestors to Israel. Do you know who are your spiritual ancestors? What has been passed on to you, spiritually, from your ancestors? What one quality are you now developing as one of God's people that you want to pass along to any children and grandchildren? How do you intend to do this? What ideas does this chapter give you in that regard?

⁴⁶Hagab, Shalmai, Hanan,
⁴⁷Giddel, Gahar, Reaiah,
⁴⁸Rezin, Nekoda, Gazzam,
⁴⁹Uzza, Paseah, Besai,
⁵⁰Asnah, Meunim, Nephussim,
⁵¹Bakbuk, Hakupha, Harhur,
⁵²Bazluth, Mehida, Harsha,
⁵³Barkos, Sisera, Temah,
⁵⁴Neziah and Hatipha

⁵⁵The descendants of the servants of Solomon:

the descendants of
   Sotai, Hassophereth, Peruda,
⁵⁶Jaala, Darkon, Giddel,
⁵⁷Shephatiah, Hattil,
   Pokereth-Hazzebaim and Ami

⁵⁸The temple servants and the descendants
   of the servants of Solomon   392

⁵⁹The following came up from the towns of Tel Melah, Tel Harsha, Kerub, Addon and Immer, but they could not show that their families were descended from Israel:

⁶⁰The descendants of
   Delaiah, Tobiah and Nekoda   652

⁶¹And from among the priests:

   The descendants of
   Hobaiah, Hakkoz and Barzillai (a man who
   had married a daughter of Barzillai the
   Gileadite and was called by that name).

⁶²These searched for their family records, but they could not find them and so were excluded from the priesthood as unclean. ⁶³The governor ordered them not to eat any of the most sacred food until there was a priest ministering with the Urim and Thummim.

⁶⁴The whole company numbered 42,360, ⁶⁵besides their 7,337 menservants and maidservants; and they also had 200 men and women singers. ⁶⁶They had 736 horses, 245 mules, ⁶⁷435 camels and 6,720 donkeys.

⁶⁸When they arrived at the house of the LORD in Jerusalem, some of the heads of the families gave freewill offerings toward the rebuilding of the house of God on its site. ⁶⁹According to their ability they gave to the treasury for this work 61,000 drachmas^a of gold, 5,000 minas^b of silver and 100 priestly garments.

⁷⁰The priests, the Levites, the singers, the gatekeepers and the temple servants settled in their own towns, along with some of the other people, and the rest of the Israelites settled in their towns.

Rebuilding the Altar

3 When the seventh month came and the Israelites had settled in their towns, the people assembled as one man in Jerusalem. ²Then Jeshua son of Jozadak and his fellow priests and Zerubbabel son of Shealtiel and his associates began to build the altar of the God of Israel to sacrifice burnt offerings on it, in accordance with what is written in the Law of Moses the man of God. ³Despite their

What's first on your to-do list of building projects?

1. Why are they assembling "as one man" (v. 1; see Lev 23:23–36)? 2. What is first on Jeshua's list? 3. What is the value (symbolic and actual) of building the altar on "its foundation" and in accord with the Law (vv. 2–4)? 4. Why have the people sacrificed be-

^{a}69 That is, about 1,100 pounds (about 500 kilograms) ^{b}69 That is, about 3 tons (about 2.9 metric tons)

fear of the peoples around them, they built the altar on its foundation and sacrificed burnt offerings on it to the LORD, both the morning and evening sacrifices. [4]Then in accordance with what is written, they celebrated the Feast of Tabernacles with the required number of burnt offerings prescribed for each day. [5]After that, they presented the regular burnt offerings, the New Moon sacrifices and the sacrifices for all the appointed sacred feasts of the LORD, as well as those brought as freewill offerings to the LORD. [6]On the first day of the seventh month they began to offer burnt offerings to the LORD, though the foundation of the LORD's temple had not yet been laid.

Rebuilding the Temple

[7]Then they gave money to the masons and carpenters, and gave food and drink and oil to the people of Sidon and Tyre, so that they would bring cedar logs by sea from Lebanon to Joppa, as authorized by Cyrus king of Persia.

[8]In the second month of the second year after their arrival at the house of God in Jerusalem, Zerubbabel son of Shealtiel, Jeshua son of Jozadak and the rest of their brothers (the priests and the Levites and all who had returned from the captivity to Jerusalem) began the work, appointing Levites twenty years of age and older to supervise the building of the house of the LORD. [9]Jeshua and his sons and brothers and Kadmiel and his sons (descendants of Hodaviah[a]) and the sons of Henadad and their sons and brothers—all Levites—joined together in supervising those working on the house of God.

[10]When the builders laid the foundation of the temple of the LORD, the priests in their vestments and with trumpets, and the Levites (the sons of Asaph) with cymbals, took their places to praise the LORD, as prescribed by David king of Israel. [11]With praise and thanksgiving they sang to the LORD:

"He is good;
    his love to Israel endures forever."

And all the people gave a great shout of praise to the LORD, because the foundation of the house of the LORD was laid. [12]But many of the older priests and Levites and family heads, who had seen the former temple, wept aloud when they saw the foundation of this temple being laid, while many others shouted for joy. [13]No one could distinguish the sound of the shouts of joy from the sound of weeping, because the people made so much noise. And the sound was heard far away.

Opposition to the Rebuilding

4 When the enemies of Judah and Benjamin heard that the exiles were building a temple for the LORD, the God of Israel, [2]they came to Zerubbabel and to the heads of the families and said, "Let us help you build because, like you, we seek your God and have been sacrificing to him since the time of Esarhaddon king of Assyria, who brought us here."

[3]But Zerubbabel, Jeshua and the rest of the heads of the families of Israel answered, "You have no part with us in building a temple to our God. We alone will build it for the LORD, the God of Israel, as King Cyrus, the king of Persia, commanded us."

[4]Then the peoples around them set out to discourage the people of Judah and make them afraid to go on building.[b] [5]They hired

---

fore laying the temple foundations (vv. 3–6)?

1. How does your zeal compare to theirs? Does worship come first for you? Why? 2. On what basis are you building your altar to God? What do you sacrifice?

---

1. Have you ever laughed so hard you cried? Or cried at first but ended up laughing? When? 2. What for you were the good ol' days? Why?

1. What did it take to lay the foundation for this new temple (vv. 7–9)? 2. Read 1 Kings 5:1–6:1 to see what went into building Solomon's temple the first time. What parallels do you find? Why does Ezra pointedly accent such parallels (see 3:2)? What does this say about second chances? 3. Why would some who knew the former temple cry while others shout aloud for joy?

1. Ezra had the temple rebuilt on Solomon's original foundations. What is the lesson for you in this? 2. What cornerstone ceremony has helped you celebrate new beginnings (e.g., in your marriage; in your work; your retirement; your life with God)? 3. Ezra waited for the second year post-exile before doing what he wanted. How patient are you (with self, God, others) when waiting for a new beginning?

How do you deal with ridicule: (a) Revenge? (b) Form a protective alliance? (c) Give in?

1. What psychological tool is used here against Israel? With what effect? 2. Why did Zerubbabel and the others respond as they did (v. 3; 3:2)? 3. Cyrus reigned 29 years (559–530 B.C.). What must have been the impact of such protracted opposition (v. 5)?

1. What clues tell you who has a part in God's work, and who is opposed to him? Are such clues presumption or faith? 2. When has someone tried to wear

---

a 9 Hebrew *Yehudah,* probably a variant of *Hodaviah*   *b 4* Or *and troubled them as they built*

you out or scare you away from completing a certain task? Did you continue or quit? Why?

"The pen is mightier than the sword"—when has that proved true for you? Do you fight better with words or with your fists? In fighting with words, do you tend to pout? Tease? Provoke? Ridicule? Do you get your best zingers by thinking quickly on your feet, or by composing your words on paper?

1. Xerxes reigned from 486–465 B.C. and Artaxerxes I from 465–424 B.C. How does the opposition under their reigns compare to the opposition under King Cyrus (see 4:1–6)? How do you account for the perseverance and intensifying of this conflict over such a span of years? 2. Ashurbanipal squelched a major revolt in Babylonia (652–648 B.C.), destroyed the town of Susa (v. 9) in the process, and deported the rebels (v. 10). What irony do you see in what Rehum (and the other descendants of those rebels) are doing two centuries later? 3. What was their letter designed to do (vv. 11–16)? How is that related to what transpired one century earlier (under the reign of King Cyrus)? 4. What is the three-pronged appeal of Rehum's letter? What is this plaintiff more concerned about: City building code violations? Political issues? Advancing his own cause? Revenging himself and his people on Israel? Other? 5. What effect did this letter have on Artaxerxes? On Rehum and associates? On the Jews? And later, on Nehemiah (see Ne 1:3ff, where it is believed he hears news of this episode)? 6. What does Ezra conclude? What happens in the second year of King Darius' rule (v. 24; Hag 1:1–5; Zec 1:1–17)?

1. Rehum's complaints against Israel remind us that our past sometimes lives on to haunt us. Where do you see that proving true today in national or international affairs? In TV evangelists? In churches and denominations? In your personal and family life? 2. When one party says they alone are the true worshippers of God, and all others are a mixed breed, what might be expected in return? How else do you account for the opposition mounted against ancient Israel? 3. On the other

counselors to work against them and frustrate their plans during the entire reign of Cyrus king of Persia and down to the reign of Darius king of Persia.

Later Opposition Under Xerxes and Artaxerxes

[6]At the beginning of the reign of Xerxes,[a] they lodged an accusation against the people of Judah and Jerusalem.

[7]And in the days of Artaxerxes king of Persia, Bishlam, Mithredath, Tabeel and the rest of his associates wrote a letter to Artaxerxes. The letter was written in Aramaic script and in the Aramaic language.[b,c]

[8]Rehum the commanding officer and Shimshai the secretary wrote a letter against Jerusalem to Artaxerxes the king as follows:

[9]Rehum the commanding officer and Shimshai the secretary, together with the rest of their associates—the judges and officials over the men from Tripolis, Persia,[d] Erech and Babylon, the Elamites of Susa, [10]and the other people whom the great and honorable Ashurbanipal[e] deported and settled in the city of Samaria and elsewhere in Trans-Euphrates.

[11](This is a copy of the letter they sent him.)

To King Artaxerxes,

From your servants, the men of Trans-Euphrates:

[12]The king should know that the Jews who came up to us from you have gone to Jerusalem and are rebuilding that rebellious and wicked city. They are restoring the walls and repairing the foundations.

[13]Furthermore, the king should know that if this city is built and its walls are restored, no more taxes, tribute or duty will be paid, and the royal revenues will suffer. [14]Now since we are under obligation to the palace and it is not proper for us to see the king dishonored, we are sending this message to inform the king, [15]so that a search may be made in the archives of your predecessors. In these records you will find that this city is a rebellious city, troublesome to kings and provinces, a place of rebellion from ancient times. That is why this city was destroyed. [16]We inform the king that if this city is built and its walls are restored, you will be left with nothing in Trans-Euphrates.

[17]The king sent this reply:

To Rehum the commanding officer, Shimshai the secretary and the rest of their associates living in Samaria and elsewhere in Trans-Euphrates:

Greetings.

[18]The letter you sent us has been read and translated in my presence. [19]I issued an order and a search was made, and it was found that this city has a long history of revolt against kings and has been a place of rebellion and sedition. [20]Jerusalem has had powerful kings ruling over the whole of Trans-Euphrates, and taxes, tribute and duty were paid to them. [21]Now issue an order to these men to stop work, so that this city will

---

[a]6 Hebrew *Ahasuerus*, a variant of Xerxes' Persian name   [b]7 Or *written in Aramaic and translated*   [c]7 The text of Ezra 4:8—6:18 is in Aramaic.   [d]9 Or *officials, magistrates and governors over the men from*   [e]10 Aramaic *Osnappar*, a variant of Ashurbanipal

not be rebuilt until I so order. 22Be careful not to neglect this matter. Why let this threat grow, to the detriment of the royal interests?

23As soon as the copy of the letter of King Artaxerxes was read to Rehum and Shimshai the secretary and their associates, they went immediately to the Jews in Jerusalem and compelled them by force to stop.

24Thus the work on the house of God in Jerusalem came to a standstill until the second year of the reign of Darius king of Persia.

Tattenai's Letter to Darius

5 Now Haggai the prophet and Zechariah the prophet, a descendant of Iddo, prophesied to the Jews in Judah and Jerusalem in the name of the God of Israel, who was over them. 2Then Zerubbabel son of Shealtiel and Jeshua son of Jozadak set to work to rebuild the house of God in Jerusalem. And the prophets of God were with them, helping them.

3At that time Tattenai, governor of Trans-Euphrates, and Shethar-Bozenai and their associates went to them and asked, "Who authorized you to rebuild this temple and restore this structure?" 4They also asked, "What are the names of the men constructing this building?" a 5But the eye of their God was watching over the elders of the Jews, and they were not stopped until a report could go to Darius and his written reply be received.

6This is a copy of the letter that Tattenai, governor of Trans-Euphrates, and Shethar-Bozenai and their associates, the officials of Trans-Euphrates, sent to King Darius. 7The report they sent him read as follows:

To King Darius:

Cordial greetings.

8The king should know that we went to the district of Judah, to the temple of the great God. The people are building it with large stones and placing the timbers in the walls. The work is being carried on with diligence and is making rapid progress under their direction.

9We questioned the elders and asked them, "Who authorized you to rebuild this temple and restore this structure?" 10We also asked them their names, so that we could write down the names of their leaders for your information.

11This is the answer they gave us:

"We are the servants of the God of heaven and earth, and we are rebuilding the temple that was built many years ago, one that a great king of Israel built and finished. 12But because our fathers angered the God of heaven, he handed them over to Nebuchadnezzar the Chaldean, king of Babylon, who destroyed this temple and deported the people to Babylon.

13"However, in the first year of Cyrus king of Babylon, King Cyrus issued a decree to rebuild this house of God. 14He even removed from the temple b of Babylon the gold and silver articles of the house of God, which Nebuchadnezzar had taken from the temple in Jerusalem and brought to the temple b in Babylon.

"Then King Cyrus gave them to a man named Sheshbazzar,

hand, why was Israel right to insist on religious exclusivity and spiritual purity? Today, when might it be valid to assert one's expression of the faith as the only way? Over against whom? Other denominations? Cults? State religion? Government interference?

Are you a "pack-rat," selective saver or toss-it-all person? How far back do you keep letters? Christmas cards? Bills? Taxes?

1. In what way do the events of verses 1–2 represent a new start (see 4:24; Hag 1:1; Zec 1:1)? 2. Why does the author retrace the rebuilding effort to Shealtiel (v. 2; see 1Ch 3:17–19)? 3. "At that time" (v. 3) can be dated to the period from August 29 to December 18, 520 B.C., one year after the Babylonians failed in their revolt against Persia (November, 521 B.C.). How does that help account for what's going on in verses 3–5? 4. What about this episode is seen as a blessing from God? Why? 5. How is God's hand of blessing evident in Tattenai's letter to Darius (vv. 6–17)? What human instruments has God evidently been using to bless and discipline his people? 6. What is the status of this re-building project to date? Who is to be credited (or blamed) for the "rapid progress"(v. 8)? How about for the "unfinished task" (v. 16)?

1. In 536 B.C. Sheshbazzar presided over laying the temple foundation (vv. 14–16), and in 520 B.C. Zerubbabel presided over laying a second foundation (see Hag 1:14–15)? How do you account for that 16-year delay (see Zec 4:6–10): (a) Israel suffers from strong opposition? (b) From lack of legal authority? (c) From lack of spiritual power? (d) From internal lethargy? (e) Good things, done right, take time? Explain. (Note: Some believe Sheshbazzar [v. 14] was the Babylonian name for Zerubbabel, meaning the two were the same person.) 2. In your life, what has taken many years to get right? How do you account for the delay? 3. In the work God has given you to do, when is his hand of blessing obvious to you: (a) In warding off opponents, as in 5:5? (b) In "making rapid progress," as

---

a4 See Septuagint; Aramaic 4We told them the names of the men constructing this building.   b14 Or palace

in 5:8? (c) Often in construction delays? (d) Only in the project's completion, as in 6:15–17?

1. What might be the oldest document in your family archives: Your birth certificate? High school yearbook? Grandpa's diary? Last year's TV guide? Why have you kept it this long? 2. What court order, parents' ruling or umpire's decision recently went your way in some contested case? How did you feel about that?

1. Compare this Aramaic memo of Cyrus' decree with the Hebrew version in 1:2–4. What additional details do you see here? Why would they have been added? 2. How does Darius' decree (vv. 6–12) expand on that earlier memo? What is his "punch line"? Why might this rub Tattenai the wrong way?

1. When have you invoked God's authority as your own? Where do you draw the line and dare someone to cross over or defy your authority? What defiance (by your kids, partners or subordinates) would trip your trigger and bring them into conflict with you? 2. What sacrifices and prayers are you offering on behalf of those in authority over you (v. 10; see 1Ti 2:1f)? 3. Persian kings made a policy of restoring the religious institutions of native peoples (6:1–12). If this policy were practiced where you live, what native religions might flourish? 4. What restoration projects are you, like Darius, supporting with your money, as well as your mouth?

whom he had appointed governor, [15]and he told him, 'Take these articles and go and deposit them in the temple in Jerusalem. And rebuild the house of God on its site.' [16]So this Sheshbazzar came and laid the foundations of the house of God in Jerusalem. From that day to the present it has been under construction but is not yet finished."

[17]Now if it pleases the king, let a search be made in the royal archives of Babylon to see if King Cyrus did in fact issue a decree to rebuild this house of God in Jerusalem. Then let the king send us his decision in this matter.

The Decree of Darius

6 King Darius then issued an order, and they searched in the archives stored in the treasury at Babylon. [2]A scroll was found in the citadel of Ecbatana in the province of Media, and this was written on it:

Memorandum:

[3]In the first year of King Cyrus, the king issued a decree concerning the temple of God in Jerusalem:

Let the temple be rebuilt as a place to present sacrifices, and let its foundations be laid. It is to be ninety feet[a] high and ninety feet wide, [4]with three courses of large stones and one of timbers. The costs are to be paid by the royal treasury. [5]Also, the gold and silver articles of the house of God, which Nebuchadnezzar took from the temple in Jerusalem and brought to Babylon, are to be returned to their places in the temple in Jerusalem; they are to be deposited in the house of God.

[6]Now then, Tattenai, governor of Trans-Euphrates, and Shethar-Bozenai and you, their fellow officials of that province, stay away from there. [7]Do not interfere with the work on this temple of God. Let the governor of the Jews and the Jewish elders rebuild this house of God on its site.

[8]Moreover, I hereby decree what you are to do for these elders of the Jews in the construction of this house of God:

The expenses of these men are to be fully paid out of the royal treasury, from the revenues of Trans-Euphrates, so that the work will not stop. [9]Whatever is needed—young bulls, rams, male lambs for burnt offerings to the God of heaven, and wheat, salt, wine and oil, as requested by the priests in Jerusalem—must be given them daily without fail, [10]so that they may offer sacrifices pleasing to the God of heaven and pray for the well-being of the king and his sons.

[11]Furthermore, I decree that if anyone changes this edict, a beam is to be pulled from his house and he is to be lifted up and impaled on it. And for this crime his house is to be made a pile of rubble. [12]May God, who has caused his Name to dwell there, overthrow any king or people who lifts a hand to change this decree or to destroy this temple in Jerusalem.

I Darius have decreed it. Let it be carried out with diligence.

a3 Aramaic *sixty cubits* (about 27 meters)

Completion and Dedication of the Temple

[13]Then, because of the decree King Darius had sent, Tattenai, governor of Trans-Euphrates, and Shethar-Bozenai and their associates carried it out with diligence. [14]So the elders of the Jews continued to build and prosper under the preaching of Haggai the prophet and Zechariah, a descendant of Iddo. They finished building the temple according to the command of the God of Israel and the decrees of Cyrus, Darius and Artaxerxes, kings of Persia. [15]The temple was completed on the third day of the month Adar, in the sixth year of the reign of King Darius.

[16]Then the people of Israel—the priests, the Levites and the rest of the exiles—celebrated the dedication of the house of God with joy. [17]For the dedication of this house of God they offered a hundred bulls, two hundred rams, four hundred male lambs and, as a sin offering for all Israel, twelve male goats, one for each of the tribes of Israel. [18]And they installed the priests in their divisions and the Levites in their groups for the service of God at Jerusalem, according to what is written in the Book of Moses.

The Passover

[19]On the fourteenth day of the first month, the exiles celebrated the Passover. [20]The priests and Levites had purified themselves and were all ceremonially clean. The Levites slaughtered the Passover lamb for all the exiles, for their brothers the priests and for themselves. [21]So the Israelites who had returned from the exile ate it, together with all who had separated themselves from the unclean practices of their Gentile neighbors in order to seek the LORD, the God of Israel. [22]For seven days they celebrated with joy the Feast of Unleavened Bread, because the LORD had filled them with joy by changing the attitude of the king of Assyria, so that he assisted them in the work on the house of God, the God of Israel.

Ezra Comes to Jerusalem

7 After these things, during the reign of Artaxerxes king of Persia, Ezra son of Seraiah, the son of Azariah, the son of Hilkiah, [2]the son of Shallum, the son of Zadok, the son of Ahitub, [3]the son of Amariah, the son of Azariah, the son of Meraioth, [4]the son of Zerahiah, the son of Uzzi, the son of Bukki, [5]the son of Abishua, the son of Phinehas, the son of Eleazar, the son of Aaron the chief priest— [6]this Ezra came up from Babylon. He was a teacher well versed in the Law of Moses, which the LORD, the God of Israel, had given. The king had granted him everything he asked, for the hand of the LORD his God was on him. [7]Some of the Israelites, including priests, Levites, singers, gatekeepers and temple servants, also came up to Jerusalem in the seventh year of King Artaxerxes.

[8]Ezra arrived in Jerusalem in the fifth month of the seventh year of the king. [9]He had begun his journey from Babylon on the first day of the first month, and he arrived in Jerusalem on the first day of the fifth month, for the gracious hand of his God was on him. [10]For Ezra had devoted himself to the study and observance of the Law of the LORD, and to teaching its decrees and laws in Israel.

King Artaxerxes' Letter to Ezra

[11]This is a copy of the letter King Artaxerxes had given to Ezra the priest and teacher, a man learned in matters concerning the commands and decrees of the LORD for Israel:

What project was years in the making for you? How did you celebrate? With whom?

1. Who oversees the work on the temple (vv. 13–18)? Who else is involved? How so? Whose authority seems to prevail? Who gets credit without being on the scene? **2.** How does this temple dedication service compare with the previous one (vv. 16–18; see 2Ch 7:1–10)? How do you account for this rather poor showing: (a) Second time around is no big deal? (b) A small temple deserves a token sacrifice? (c) Israel is impoverished by this prolonged building project? **3.** Priests, Levites, the exiles, and converts all celebrate Passover (vv. 19–22). What must each do to participate (see Ex 12:43–50; Nu 9:1–14)?

1. What half-done project does God want you to carry out with diligence: Spring cleaning? This week's to-do list? Last month's do-today-or-else list? Your New Year's resolution from the year___? **2.** Why not get on with it? **3.** How does an outsider get to celebrate the sacraments in your church tradition?

Who in your group is doing what their parents or grandparents did for a living?

1. "After these things" means 60 years later, from 516–458 B.C. (ch. 6–7). What else does 7:1–10 say as to the Who? What? How? When? Where? and Why? about Ezra? **2.** Why was it important to link him to Hilkiah (see 2Ki 22:4)? To Zadok (see 2Sa 8:17)? To the Law of Moses?

1. Ezra was "well-versed" in the Law (vv. 6,10; see Ne 8). What subject matter are you well-versed in? By comparison, how well-versed are you in the Bible? **2.** Who instilled in you a love for the Word?

---

1. What on earth has been for you like a "ticket to heaven": Some letter of recommendation? Some critical acclaim? **2.**

What doors of opportunity did this key open up for you?

1. What doors of opportunity does this letter of endorsement open up for Ezra and his fellow Jews? 2. Besides the royal letter, what other goodies does Ezra have in hand? How does this bounty compare with what was prescribed by Darius (vv. 15–22; see 6:8–9)? 3. What prompts King Artaxerxes to be so generous (vv. 23b,28; compare 6:10)? 4. How long has it taken so far for Jewish refugees to return to their homeland (compare 7:8f with 1:1–4)? Hence, what job promotion and higher authority is Ezra given (vv. 25–26)?

1. How is the "hand of the Lord" (v. 9) evident in your life? What leadership role does that encourage you to take? 2. How does the experience of God's hand differ among your group members? 3. Artaxerxes' letter to Ezra and his commission of Nehemiah (Ne 1:1,11) have been regarded as the first of Daniel's 69 "sevens" (Da 9:24–27). Whichever starting point one uses, Daniel sees the restoration of Israel under Artaxerxes as prefiguring the first coming of Christ. What meaning for Jews and Christians do you ascribe to the historic restoration of Israel, *then* (in 538–430 B.C.) and *now*? 4. Why is it important for some people to have their religious leader's pedigree or ordination related to a great high priest (as in Ezra's lineage, vv. 1–5), or even the High Priest (see Heb 7–8)? 5. What aspect of praise, gratitude and healthy self-esteem does your small group enjoy as a result of your devotion to God's Word? What group doxology would reflect this (as in vv. 27–28)?

^{12a}Artaxerxes, king of kings,

To Ezra the priest, a teacher of the Law of the God of heaven:

Greetings.

^{13}Now I decree that any of the Israelites in my kingdom, including priests and Levites, who wish to go to Jerusalem with you, may go. ^{14}You are sent by the king and his seven advisers to inquire about Judah and Jerusalem with regard to the Law of your God, which is in your hand. ^{15}Moreover, you are to take with you the silver and gold that the king and his advisers have freely given to the God of Israel, whose dwelling is in Jerusalem, ^{16}together with all the silver and gold you may obtain from the province of Babylon, as well as the freewill offerings of the people and priests for the temple of their God in Jerusalem. ^{17}With this money be sure to buy bulls, rams and male lambs, together with their grain offerings and drink offerings, and sacrifice them on the altar of the temple of your God in Jerusalem.

^{18}You and your brother Jews may then do whatever seems best with the rest of the silver and gold, in accordance with the will of your God. ^{19}Deliver to the God of Jerusalem all the articles entrusted to you for worship in the temple of your God. ^{20}And anything else needed for the temple of your God that you may have occasion to supply, you may provide from the royal treasury.

^{21}Now I, King Artaxerxes, order all the treasurers of Trans-Euphrates to provide with diligence whatever Ezra the priest, a teacher of the Law of the God of heaven, may ask of you— ^{22}up to a hundred talents^b of silver, a hundred cors^c of wheat, a hundred baths^d of wine, a hundred baths^d of olive oil, and salt without limit. ^{23}Whatever the God of heaven has prescribed, let it be done with diligence for the temple of the God of heaven. Why should there be wrath against the realm of the king and of his sons? ^{24}You are also to know that you have no authority to impose taxes, tribute or duty on any of the priests, Levites, singers, gatekeepers, temple servants or other workers at this house of God.

^{25}And you, Ezra, in accordance with the wisdom of your God, which you possess, appoint magistrates and judges to administer justice to all the people of Trans-Euphrates—all who know the laws of your God. And you are to teach any who do not know them. ^{26}Whoever does not obey the law of your God and the law of the king must surely be punished by death, banishment, confiscation of property, or imprisonment.

^{27}Praise be to the LORD, the God of our fathers, who has put it into the king's heart to bring honor to the house of the LORD in Jerusalem in this way ^{28}and who has extended his good favor to me before the king and his advisers and all the king's powerful officials. Because the hand of the LORD my God was on me, I took courage and gathered leading men from Israel to go up with me.

^{a}12 The text of Ezra 7:12-26 is in Aramaic. ^{b}22 That is, about 3 3/4 tons (about 3.4 metric tons) ^{c}22 That is, probably about 600 bushels (about 22 kiloliters) ^{d}22 That is, probably about 600 gallons (about 2.2 kiloliters)

List of the Family Heads Returning With Ezra

8 These are the family heads and those registered with them who came up with me from Babylon during the reign of King Artaxerxes:

²of the descendants of Phinehas, Gershom;
of the descendants of Ithamar, Daniel;
of the descendants of David, Hattush ³of the descendants of Shecaniah;

of the descendants of Parosh, Zechariah, and with him were registered 150 men;
⁴of the descendants of Pahath-Moab, Eliehoenai son of Zerahiah, and with him 200 men;
⁵of the descendants of Zattu,ᵃ Shecaniah son of Jahaziel, and with him 300 men;
⁶of the descendants of Adin, Ebed son of Jonathan, and with him 50 men;
⁷of the descendants of Elam, Jeshaiah son of Athaliah, and with him 70 men;
⁸of the descendants of Shephatiah, Zebadiah son of Michael, and with him 80 men;
⁹of the descendants of Joab, Obadiah son of Jehiel, and with him 218 men;
¹⁰of the descendants of Bani,ᵇ Shelomith son of Josiphiah, and with him 160 men;
¹¹of the descendants of Bebai, Zechariah son of Bebai, and with him 28 men;
¹²of the descendants of Azgad, Johanan son of Hakkatan, and with him 110 men;
¹³of the descendants of Adonikam, the last ones, whose names were Eliphelet, Jeuel and Shemaiah, and with them 60 men;
¹⁴of the descendants of Bigvai, Uthai and Zaccur, and with them 70 men.

The Return to Jerusalem

¹⁵I assembled them at the canal that flows toward Ahava, and we camped there three days. When I checked among the people and the priests, I found no Levites there. ¹⁶So I summoned Eliezer, Ariel, Shemaiah, Elnathan, Jarib, Elnathan, Nathan, Zechariah and Meshullam, who were leaders, and Joiarib and Elnathan, who were men of learning, ¹⁷and I sent them to Iddo, the leader in Casiphia. I told them what to say to Iddo and his kinsmen, the temple servants in Casiphia, so that they might bring attendants to us for the house of our God. ¹⁸Because the gracious hand of our God was on us, they brought us Sherebiah, a capable man, from the descendants of Mahli son of Levi, the son of Israel, and Sherebiah's sons and brothers, 18 men; ¹⁹and Hashabiah, together with Jeshaiah from the descendants of Merari, and his brothers and nephews, 20 men. ²⁰They also brought 220 of the temple servants—a body that David and the officials had established to assist the Levites. All were registered by name.

²¹There, by the Ahava Canal, I proclaimed a fast, so that we might humble ourselves before our God and ask him for a safe journey for us and our children, with all our possessions. ²²I was ashamed to ask the king for soldiers and horsemen to protect us

ᵃ5 Some Septuagint manuscripts (also 1 Esdras 8:32); Hebrew does not have Zattu.
ᵇ10 Some Septuagint manuscripts (also 1 Esdras 8:36); Hebrew does not have Bani.

1. How far back in your family tree can you trace native-born sons and daughters before you come to one who was born overseas? What do you know about that first pilgrim? **2.** What long trip have you made away from home? How far away did you go? How long did you stay away? At what point did you get homesick?

1. What shift in the story-teller's viewpoint do you see in 7:27 and continued through chapter 9? What do you make of this first reference to "me"? **2.** Why was this particular genealogical record important for Ezra? **3.** Compare this list with the one in 2:1–70? Which one is shortened in form? Which numbers don't add up the same? What do you make of similarities and differences in names and numbers? **4.** How does Ezra handle the lack of response by the Levites to his planned pilgrimage (vv. 15–20)? Is he end-running divine authority? Or pursuing an additional channel for God's blessing? Why do you think so? (What do the numbers in 2:40 tell you?) **5.** How does Ezra show spiritual dependence, political expediency and common sense in his trek from Ahava to Jerusalem (vv. 21–32)? What do you make of Ezra praying and fasting instead of (not in addition to) the customary escort (see Ne 2:9)? **6.** At face value, it seems Persian kings gave Ezra some 32 tons of silver and gold to underwrite the temple project. What principles of financial accountability do you see in the way Ezra handled this vast amount of money (vv. 24–30)?

1. Is God's hand more directly involved in the lives of those who strip themselves of all visible means of support and protection? Or are God's fingerprints just more obvious or necessary at such times of naked trust? Why do you think so? **2.** The trek from Ahava to Jerusalem around the Euphrates River is about 900 miles. After an 11-day interlude, their journey took 110 days to complete (vv. 21,31; compare 7:9). Nine miles/day was a good pace for a large mass migration back then. When has your journey with the Lord seemed no faster than nine miles/day? What does this say about your need for patience, especially in bringing others along with you in your vision (as did Ezra)? **3.** Ezra fasted before approaching God for direction, as did Jesus and his disciples (see Mt 4:2; 6:16–18). How might fasting help you to know God's answer for an important decision you are facing? **4.** Ezra entrusts 24 men with millions of dollars and holds them accountable for every last talent. For what talents will you be held accountable? How do you see people today being held accountable for their money: Through taxes? Church review boards? Media pressure? For what and by whom is your small group held accountable? **5.** How and when have you sensed God protecting you from enemies? What enemies (internal and external) might you still need God's protection from? **6.** What articles do you so revere that they are consecrated to the Lord? What might the Lord now be asking you to consecrate to him?

---

1. What is your image of confession: (a) Confessional box? (b) "Dear Abby" column? (c) Trusted friends? (d) Good for the soul? (e) Bad public relations? **2.** When have you seen public confession work out for good?

1. How extensive is this problem of intermarriage? What five parties are guilty (vv. 1–2; see 10:18–43, for values)? How long is Ezra on the scene before being brought in for damage control (compare 10:9 and 7:9)? **2.** Ezra wanted to establish a holy nation with pure marriages. What are the pros and cons of this (see Dt 7:1–5; Mal 2:10–16; 2Co 6:14; Ge 41:45; Nu 12:1)? **3.** In Ezra's response what is the emotional tone? The gist of his logic? Why is he so heart-broken? **4.** What five themes do you see in this classic prayer

from enemies on the road, because we had told the king, "The gracious hand of our God is on everyone who looks to him, but his great anger is against all who forsake him." ²³So we fasted and petitioned our God about this, and he answered our prayer.

²⁴Then I set apart twelve of the leading priests, together with Sherebiah, Hashabiah and ten of their brothers, ²⁵and I weighed out to them the offering of silver and gold and the articles that the king, his advisers, his officials and all Israel present there had donated for the house of our God. ²⁶I weighed out to them 650 talents[a] of silver, silver articles weighing 100 talents,[b] 100 talents[b] of gold, ²⁷20 bowls of gold valued at 1,000 darics,[c] and two fine articles of polished bronze, as precious as gold.

²⁸I said to them, "You as well as these articles are consecrated to the LORD. The silver and gold are a freewill offering to the LORD, the God of your fathers. ²⁹Guard them carefully until you weigh them out in the chambers of the house of the LORD in Jerusalem before the leading priests and the Levites and the family heads of Israel." ³⁰Then the priests and Levites received the silver and gold and sacred articles that had been weighed out to be taken to the house of our God in Jerusalem.

³¹On the twelfth day of the first month we set out from the Ahava Canal to go to Jerusalem. The hand of our God was on us, and he protected us from enemies and bandits along the way. ³²So we arrived in Jerusalem, where we rested three days.

³³On the fourth day, in the house of our God, we weighed out the silver and gold and the sacred articles into the hands of Meremoth son of Uriah, the priest. Eleazar son of Phinehas was with him, and so were the Levites Jozabad son of Jeshua and Noadiah son of Binnui. ³⁴Everything was accounted for by number and weight, and the entire weight was recorded at that time.

³⁵Then the exiles who had returned from captivity sacrificed burnt offerings to the God of Israel: twelve bulls for all Israel, ninety-six rams, seventy-seven male lambs and, as a sin offering, twelve male goats. All this was a burnt offering to the LORD. ³⁶They also delivered the king's orders to the royal satraps and to the governors of Trans-Euphrates, who then gave assistance to the people and to the house of God.

Ezra's Prayer About Intermarriage

9 After these things had been done, the leaders came to me and said, "The people of Israel, including the priests and the Levites, have not kept themselves separate from the neighboring peoples with their detestable practices, like those of the Canaanites, Hittites, Perizzites, Jebusites, Ammonites, Moabites, Egyptians and Amorites. ²They have taken some of their daughters as wives for themselves and their sons, and have mingled the holy race with the peoples around them. And the leaders and officials have led the way in this unfaithfulness."

³When I heard this, I tore my tunic and cloak, pulled hair from my head and beard and sat down appalled. ⁴Then everyone who trembled at the words of the God of Israel gathered around me because of this unfaithfulness of the exiles. And I sat there appalled until the evening sacrifice.

⁵Then, at the evening sacrifice, I rose from my self-abasement, with my tunic and cloak torn, and fell on my knees with my hands spread out to the LORD my God ⁶and prayed:

---

a26 That is, about 25 tons (about 22 metric tons)   *b26* That is, about 3 3/4 tons (about 3.4 metric tons)   *c27* That is, about 19 pounds (about 8.5 kilograms)

"O my God, I am too ashamed and disgraced to lift up my face to you, my God, because our sins are higher than our heads and our guilt has reached to the heavens. ⁷From the days of our forefathers until now, our guilt has been great. Because of our sins, we and our kings and our priests have been subjected to the sword and captivity, to pillage and humiliation at the hand of foreign kings, as it is today.

⁸"But now, for a brief moment, the LORD our God has been gracious in leaving us a remnant and giving us a firm place in his sanctuary, and so our God gives light to our eyes and a little relief in our bondage. ⁹Though we are slaves, our God has not deserted us in our bondage. He has shown us kindness in the sight of the kings of Persia: He has granted us new life to rebuild the house of our God and repair its ruins, and he has given us a wall of protection in Judah and Jerusalem.

¹⁰"But now, O our God, what can we say after this? For we have disregarded the commands ¹¹you gave through your servants the prophets when you said: 'The land you are entering to possess is a land polluted by the corruption of its peoples. By their detestable practices they have filled it with their impurity from one end to the other. ¹²Therefore, do not give your daughters in marriage to their sons or take their daughters for your sons. Do not seek a treaty of friendship with them at any time, that you may be strong and eat the good things of the land and leave it to your children as an everlasting inheritance.'

¹³"What has happened to us is a result of our evil deeds and our great guilt, and yet, our God, you have punished us less than our sins have deserved and have given us a remnant like this. ¹⁴Shall we again break your commands and intermarry with the peoples who commit such detestable practices? Would you not be angry enough with us to destroy us, leaving us no remnant or survivor? ¹⁵O LORD, God of Israel, you are righteous! We are left this day as a remnant. Here we are before you in our guilt, though because of it not one of us can stand in your presence."

The People's Confession of Sin

10 While Ezra was praying and confessing, weeping and throwing himself down before the house of God, a large crowd of Israelites—men, women and children—gathered around him. They too wept bitterly. ²Then Shecaniah son of Jehiel, one of the descendants of Elam, said to Ezra, "We have been unfaithful to our God by marrying foreign women from the peoples around us. But in spite of this, there is still hope for Israel. ³Now let us make a covenant before our God to send away all these women and their children, in accordance with the counsel of my lord and of those who fear the commands of our God. Let it be done according to the Law. ⁴Rise up; this matter is in your hands. We will support you, so take courage and do it."

⁵So Ezra rose up and put the leading priests and Levites and all Israel under oath to do what had been suggested. And they took the oath. ⁶Then Ezra withdrew from before the house of God and went to the room of Jehohanan son of Eliashib. While he was there, he ate no food and drank no water, because he continued to mourn over the unfaithfulness of the exiles.

⁷A proclamation was then issued throughout Judah and Jerusalem for all the exiles to assemble in Jerusalem. ⁸Anyone who failed to appear within three days would forfeit all his property, in accor-

(vv. 6f,8f,10ff,13f,15)? **5.** What does this prayer tell you about which is greater—guilt or grace? Slavish habits or new life? God's anger or mercy? **6.** What hope for the remnant do you see (v. 14)?

1. What effect do you suppose this public and published prayer had on the first audience? On later readers? On God? On you? Explain. **2.** Some 25 years later, Nehemiah dealt with the same problem of intermarriage with foreigners, but pulled out more hair than Ezra (see Ne 13:23–29). If confronted with a similarly offensive sin, would you respond more like Nehemiah or Ezra ("beating them" versus "abasing self")? How else do you express your grief over sin? **3.** What problem do you have with people marrying outside the Christian faith? How common is that among your friends? With what results? **4.** What else could compromise a struggling community of faith as much as mixed marriages in ancient Israel? **5.** Do you pray more personal "I-prayers," or more priestly "we-prayers"? Why? **6.** How has God given you new life (v. 9) along your journey: Short-lived? Long-lasting? Or what?

1. What important oaths or covenants have you made: Marriage? Public office? Military service? Ordination? **2.** What held you accountable to your vow: Spouse? Media? Public trust? Conscience? Consequences? **3.** Which vow do you consider most serious? Most silly?

1. What is the effect of Ezra's prayer on the people? What is Shecaniah's message and its effect? **2.** How does Ezra become convinced and, in turn, convince others that this is the will of God? Is he pulling rank, twisting arms, exercising wisdom, or what (vv. 5–8; see 7:25–28)? **3.** What compromise is proposed and why (vv. 12–14)? With what opposition and why (v. 15)? Which view carries the day and why? **4.** Why do you suppose it took so long to process all the cases: (a) Judicial red tape? (b)

Bitter foreign wives? (c) Fearful Israelite men?

♡ **1.** What is the connection
here between repentance
and hope? Between prayer and action? Between unilateral covenant
and mutual agreement? Point of
decision and process of implementation? **2.** Why do many people find
it valuable to make a decision and
act quickly? Why do others procrastinate and compromise? Which
do you like to do and why? **3.** Does
your small group decide things on
their own, independent of higher
authority or church-wide consensus? If so, how do you arrive at
those decisions? **4.** Does your
small group *represent* change to
the larger church, or *resist* change
as suggested by the larger church?
How so? Over what issues do you
covenant for change?

☕ **1.** In whose file are you likely
to find a black mark next to
your name: (a) First grade teacher's? (b) High school's? (c) Pastor
or counselor's? (d) IRS or collection agency? (e) FBI or criminal division? (f) Medical records? (g)
Court records? **2.** Of these files,
which contents would you like to
erase for all time?

📖 **1.** Which of these names
have you seen listed else-
where in Ezra? **2.** What is significant about only one singer and
three gatekeepers marrying pagan
wives (v. 24)? Likewise, why do
you suppose no temple servants or
descendants of Solomon's servants are guilty of this? **3.** Why do
you think children were insufficient
reason for halting the divorce pro-
ceedings (v. 44)? **4.** Why such fu-
ror over relatively few transgressors (27 clergy and 84 laity)?

♡ **1.** What does the total of 111
guilty men, their ex-spouses
and broken homes do for you?
How would you feel seeing your
name listed here? Does such senti-
ment tend to overshadow the principles involved? **2.** This list of guilty
men attests to a momentary purge
and purification of Israel. Some 12

dance with the decision of the officials and elders, and would
himself be expelled from the assembly of the exiles.

⁹Within the three days, all the men of Judah and Benjamin had
gathered in Jerusalem. And on the twentieth day of the ninth
month, all the people were sitting in the square before the house of
God, greatly distressed by the occasion and because of the rain.
¹⁰Then Ezra the priest stood up and said to them, "You have been
unfaithful; you have married foreign women, adding to Israel's
guilt. ¹¹Now make confession to the LORD, the God of your fathers,
and do his will. Separate yourselves from the peoples around you
and from your foreign wives."

¹²The whole assembly responded with a loud voice: "You are
right! We must do as you say. ¹³But there are many people here
and it is the rainy season; so we cannot stand outside. Besides, this
matter cannot be taken care of in a day or two, because we have
sinned greatly in this thing. ¹⁴Let our officials act for the whole
assembly. Then let everyone in our towns who has married a
foreign woman come at a set time, along with the elders and judges
of each town, until the fierce anger of our God in this matter is
turned away from us." ¹⁵Only Jonathan son of Asahel and Jahzeiah
son of Tikvah, supported by Meshullam and Shabbethai the Levite,
opposed this.

¹⁶So the exiles did as was proposed. Ezra the priest selected men
who were family heads, one from each family division, and all of
them designated by name. On the first day of the tenth month they
sat down to investigate the cases, ¹⁷and by the first day of the first
month they finished dealing with all the men who had married
foreign women.

Those Guilty of Intermarriage

¹⁸Among the descendants of the priests, the following had married foreign women:

From the descendants of Jeshua son of Jozadak, and his brothers: Maaseiah, Eliezer, Jarib and Gedaliah. ¹⁹(They all gave
their hands in pledge to put away their wives, and for their
guilt they each presented a ram from the flock as a guilt
offering.)

²⁰From the descendants of Immer:
Hanani and Zebadiah.
²¹From the descendants of Harim:
Maaseiah, Elijah, Shemaiah, Jehiel and Uzziah.
²²From the descendants of Pashhur:
Elioenai, Maaseiah, Ishmael, Nethanel, Jozabad and Elasah.

²³Among the Levites:

Jozabad, Shimei, Kelaiah (that is, Kelita), Pethahiah, Judah
and Eliezer.
²⁴From the singers:
Eliashib.
From the gatekeepers:
Shallum, Telem and Uri.

²⁵And among the other Israelites:

From the descendants of Parosh:
Ramiah, Izziah, Malkijah, Mijamin, Eleazar, Malkijah and
Benaiah.
²⁶From the descendants of Elam:
Mattaniah, Zechariah, Jehiel, Abdi, Jeremoth and Elijah.

27From the descendants of Zattu:

Elioenai, Eliashib, Mattaniah, Jeremoth, Zabad and Aziza.

28From the descendants of Bebai:

Jehohanan, Hananiah, Zabbai and Athlai.

29From the descendants of Bani:

Meshullam, Malluch, Adaiah, Jashub, Sheal and Jeremoth.

30From the descendants of Pahath-Moab:

Adna, Kelal, Benaiah, Maaseiah, Mattaniah, Bezalel, Binnui and Manasseh.

31From the descendants of Harim:

Eliezer, Ishijah, Malkijah, Shemaiah, Shimeon, **32**Benjamin, Malluch and Shemariah.

33From the descendants of Hashum:

Mattenai, Mattattah, Zabad, Eliphelet, Jeremai, Manasseh and Shimei.

34From the descendants of Bani:

Maadai, Amram, Uel, **35**Benaiah, Bedeiah, Keluhi, **36**Vaniah, Meremoth, Eliashib, **37**Mattaniah, Mattenai and Jaasu.

38From the descendants of Binnui:[a]

Shimei, **39**Shelemiah, Nathan, Adaiah, **40**Macnadebai, Shashai, Sharai, **41**Azarel, Shelemiah, Shemariah, **42**Shallum, Amariah and Joseph.

43From the descendants of Nebo:

Jeiel, Mattithiah, Zabad, Zebina, Jaddai, Joel and Benaiah.

44All these had married foreign women, and some of them had children by these wives.[b]

and 25 years later (see Ne 10:30 and 13:23–29), Nehemiah must confront that same sin of mixed marriages. What does that say about human nature? About the tenacity of sin? About the effect of legal sanctions? About the need for continuing to renew divine-human covenants? **3.** Where then would you place your hope for a purified Church today (see Mt 13:24–30)? **4.** In your study of Ezra, what have you learned about your own human nature? About God's nature? About his desires for you? His discipline of you? **5.** What kind of pilgrim would you have made back in Ezra's day? How is that shown in your faith now?

---

[a]37,38 See Septuagint (also 1 Esdras 9:34); Hebrew *Jaasu* 38*and Bani and Binnui,*
[b]44 Or *and they sent them away with their children*

INTRODUCTION to
NEHEMIAH

Book Study Outline: If you are using Nehemiah for a study course, here is a 7- or 13-week outline. Use the questions in the margin for your group agenda:

☕ start meeting / 15 min.

📖 read & discuss Bible / 30 min.

♡ close meeting / 15–45 min.

Refer to the Questions and Answers in the front of this Bible for more information.

7-week plan	13-week plan	Personal Reading	Group Study Passage
1	1	1:1–11	Nehemiah's Passion
	2	2:1–20	Artaxerxes's Permission
2	3	3:1–32	Builders of the Wall
	4	4:1–23	Opposition to the Rebuilding
3	5	5:1–19	Nehemiah Helps the Poor
	6	6:1–7:3	Rebuilding Opposed, Completed
4	7	7:4–73a	List of Exiles Who Returned
	8	7:73b–8:18	Ezra Reads the Law
5	9	9:1–37	Israelites Confess Their Sins
	10	9:38–10:39	Agreement of the People
6	11	11:1–36	New Residents of Jerusalem
	12	12:1–47	Leaders and Wall Dedicated
7	13	13:1–31	Nehemiah's Final Reform

Author: The book is named for the principal character, Nehemiah, but it does not state its author. Whoever it was may have also helped to compile the book of Ezra and perhaps 1 and 2 Chronicles.

Date: With an unstated author, precise dating is difficult to determine. The events narrated cover the years c. 445–432 B.C.

CHRONOLOGY OF EZRA AND NEHEMIAH

YEAR	EVENT	REFERENCE
539 B.C.	Capture of Babylon	Da 5:30
538–7	Cyrus' 1st Year	Ezr 1:1–4
537 (?)	Return under Sheshbazzar	Ezr 1:11
536	Work on temple begun	Ezr 3:8
536–30	Opposition during Cyrus' reign	Ezr 4:1–5
530–20	Work on temple ceased	Ezr 4:24
520	Work on temple renewed under Darius	Ezr 5:2; Hag 1:14
516	Temple completed	Ezr 6:15
458	Ezra departs from Babylon	Ezr 7:6-9
	Ezra arrives in Jerusalem	Ezr 7:8-9
	People assemble	Ezr 10:9
	Committee begins investigation	Ezr 10:16
457	Committee ends investigation	Ezr 10:17
445–4	20th year of Artaxerxes I	Ne 1:1
445	Nehemiah approaches king	Ne 2:1
	Nehemiah arrives in Jerusalem	Ne 2:11
	Completion of wall	Ne 6:15
	Public Assembly	Ne 7:73–8:1
	Feast of Tabernacles	Ne 8:14
	Fast	Ne 9:1
	32nd year of Artaxerxes Nehemiah's recall and return	Ne 5:14; 13:6

Theme: Restoration of the second temple and revival of the people, providing a legacy of God-given leadership principles.

Historical Background: Originally this work was one book along with Ezra. In the Latin Bible, Ezra and Nehemiah are entitled 1 and 2 Esdras. This book complements Ezra in reporting the restoration of Israel after 70 years of captivity in Babylon. Nehemiah's distress over the broken-down walls of Jerusalem (1:3) is probably caused by the episode in Ezra 4:7–23. Ezra's return had revived spiritual and nationalistic fervor in God's people so that they worked to rebuild the walls of Jerusalem (ch. 8–9). But the completion of that task apparently fell to governor Nehemiah, a man dedicated to God.

Characteristics: This book weaves together various lists with first-person and third-person memoirs of Nehemiah, who is the lead actor in this drama. Some of the most moving prayers outside the Psalms are found here (1:5–11; 9:5b–37). With plot twists akin to a modern short story, Nehemiah describes the rebuilding of the Jerusalem walls. The physical condition of the walls (ch. 1–7) parallels the spiritual condition of the people. As the walls are restored, the people are rehabilitated (ch. 8–13).

Nehemiah

Nehemiah's Prayer

1 The words of Nehemiah son of Hacaliah:

In the month of Kislev in the twentieth year, while I was in the citadel of Susa, ²Hanani, one of my brothers, came from Judah with some other men, and I questioned them about the Jewish remnant that survived the exile, and also about Jerusalem.

³They said to me, "Those who survived the exile and are back in the province are in great trouble and disgrace. The wall of Jerusalem is broken down, and its gates have been burned with fire."

⁴When I heard these things, I sat down and wept. For some days I mourned and fasted and prayed before the God of heaven. ⁵Then I said:

"O LORD, God of heaven, the great and awesome God, who keeps his covenant of love with those who love him and obey his commands, ⁶let your ear be attentive and your eyes open to hear the prayer your servant is praying before you day and night for your servants, the people of Israel. I confess the sins we Israelites, including myself and my father's house, have committed against you. ⁷We have acted very wickedly toward you. We have not obeyed the commands, decrees and laws you gave your servant Moses.

⁸"Remember the instruction you gave your servant Moses, saying, 'If you are unfaithful, I will scatter you among the nations, ⁹but if you return to me and obey my commands, then even if your exiled people are at the farthest horizon, I will gather them from there and bring them to the place I have chosen as a dwelling for my Name.'

¹⁰"They are your servants and your people, whom you redeemed by your great strength and your mighty hand. ¹¹O Lord, let your ear be attentive to the prayer of this your servant and to the prayer of your servants who delight in revering your name. Give your servant success today by granting him favor in the presence of this man."

I was cupbearer to the king.

Artaxerxes Sends Nehemiah to Jerusalem

2 In the month of Nisan in the twentieth year of King Artaxerxes, when wine was brought for him, I took the wine and gave it to the king. I had not been sad in his presence before; ²so the king asked me, "Why does your face look so sad when you are not ill? This can be nothing but sadness of heart."

I was very much afraid, ³but I said to the king, "May the king live forever! Why should my face not look sad when the city where my fathers are buried lies in ruins, and its gates have been destroyed by fire?"

⁴The king said to me, "What is it you want?"

Then I prayed to the God of heaven, ⁵and I answered the king, "If it pleases the king and if your servant has found favor in his sight, let him send me to the city in Judah where my fathers are buried so that I can rebuild it."

1. Where is "home" for you? How long have you been away from your roots? 2. What unfinished, even unstarted, projects at home most disturb you?

1. Why is Nehemiah so concerned about Jerusalem? What does he learn about its condition from Hanani and others (vv. 2–4)? How might the events of 2Kings 25:9–21 and Ezra 4:7–24 relate to his present concern? 2. How does Nehemiah respond to this news (v. 4)? What does that say about his relationship with God? 3. How vital a force do you think prayer was for him: Daily routine? Crisis times only? Intimate? Energizing? 4. What do you see of God's nature through Nehemiah's prayer? What does Nehemiah see in himself, the more he focuses on God? What does he recall as he persists in prayer (vv. 8–10)? 5. What then is the basis for his final appeal (v. 11)?

1. How grieved are you about the physical and spiritual state of God's people? Enough to pray? Fast? Act? 2. When news of exiled people, brokenness and famine hits you, do you react anything like Nehemiah? 3. Do you tend to despair over what is? Accept what is? Or pray for what *should be*?

1. Who first broke your heart? How long did it take for your heart to heal? Where did you find comfort? 2. What would you do with a leave of absence from work?

1. In these intervening three months, what do you think Nehemiah has been doing? What does King Artaxerxes notice and why? Why has it taken so long for Nehemiah to express his grief? 2. What does he request the king to do? What three questions does the king have? 3. In Nehemiah's ready response, what do you see that demonstrates his practical wis-

dom? His dependence on God? On human resources? His respect for his superior? **4.** What obstacle to his success looms on the horizon? Why?

♡ **1.** Can others read what you are thinking or feeling, almost like an open book? Or is your heart under lock and key? Why is that? **2.** How can you make your needs known to your King? Do this as a group.

———————

☕ Have you ever witnessed a hurricane, earthquake, house fire, car accident or war? What was it like to walk through the wreckage?

📖 **1.** What do you think Nehemiah did his first three days in Jerusalem? Why was that important? **2.** Why do you think Nehemiah said nothing to those who would be doing the work until he had inspected the walls himself? Why inspect the walls at *night*? **3.** What three points does Nehemiah make publicly to rally the troops to rebuild? Which one do you find most convincing? **4.** What charge do Nehemiah's opponents bring against him? How does he respond?

♡ **1.** When is it hardest for you to act: (a) When your project lies in ruins? (b) When your workers are few? (c) When others mock you? (d) When you must "buck City Hall" to get a permit? **2.** How do you know if God is with you in some enterprise?

———————

☕ **1.** Among the following, which do you prefer and why: (a) Individual or team sports? (b) Solo music performances or group concerts? (c) Living on your own or in some cooperative living arrangement? (d) Self-employment or a closely knit work force? **2.** What are the names of those who lived next to you at your previous place of residence? In the neighborhood where you grew up? **3.** Try another experiment: Give full names for everyone in your group. What do

⁶Then the king, with the queen sitting beside him, asked me, "How long will your journey take, and when will you get back?" It pleased the king to send me; so I set a time.

⁷I also said to him, "If it pleases the king, may I have letters to the governors of Trans-Euphrates, so that they will provide me safe-conduct until I arrive in Judah? ⁸And may I have a letter to Asaph, keeper of the king's forest, so he will give me timber to make beams for the gates of the citadel by the temple and for the city wall and for the residence I will occupy?" And because the gracious hand of my God was upon me, the king granted my requests. ⁹So I went to the governors of Trans-Euphrates and gave them the king's letters. The king had also sent army officers and cavalry with me.

¹⁰When Sanballat the Horonite and Tobiah the Ammonite official heard about this, they were very much disturbed that someone had come to promote the welfare of the Israelites.

Nehemiah Inspects Jerusalem's Walls

¹¹I went to Jerusalem, and after staying there three days ¹²I set out during the night with a few men. I had not told anyone what my God had put in my heart to do for Jerusalem. There were no mounts with me except the one I was riding on.

¹³By night I went out through the Valley Gate toward the Jackal*ᵃ* Well and the Dung Gate, examining the walls of Jerusalem, which had been broken down, and its gates, which had been destroyed by fire. ¹⁴Then I moved on toward the Fountain Gate and the King's Pool, but there was not enough room for my mount to get through; ¹⁵so I went up the valley by night, examining the wall. Finally, I turned back and reentered through the Valley Gate. ¹⁶The officials did not know where I had gone or what I was doing, because as yet I had said nothing to the Jews or the priests or nobles or officials or any others who would be doing the work.

¹⁷Then I said to them, "You see the trouble we are in: Jerusalem lies in ruins, and its gates have been burned with fire. Come, let us rebuild the wall of Jerusalem, and we will no longer be in disgrace." ¹⁸I also told them about the gracious hand of my God upon me and what the king had said to me.

They replied, "Let us start rebuilding." So they began this good work.

¹⁹But when Sanballat the Horonite, Tobiah the Ammonite official and Geshem the Arab heard about it, they mocked and ridiculed us. "What is this you are doing?" they asked. "Are you rebelling against the king?"

²⁰I answered them by saying, "The God of heaven will give us success. We his servants will start rebuilding, but as for you, you have no share in Jerusalem or any claim or historic right to it."

Builders of the Wall

3 Eliashib the high priest and his fellow priests went to work and rebuilt the Sheep Gate. They dedicated it and set its doors in place, building as far as the Tower of the Hundred, which they dedicated, and as far as the Tower of Hananel. ²The men of Jericho built the adjoining section, and Zaccur son of Imri built next to them.

³The Fish Gate was rebuilt by the sons of Hassenaah. They laid its beams and put its doors and bolts and bars in place. ⁴Meremoth son of Uriah, the son of Hakkoz, repaired the next section. Next to

ᵃ13 Or *Serpent* or *Fig*

him Meshullam son of Berekiah, the son of Meshezabel, made repairs, and next to him Zadok son of Baana also made repairs. [5]The next section was repaired by the men of Tekoa, but their nobles would not put their shoulders to the work under their supervisors.[a]

[6]The Jeshanah[b] Gate was repaired by Joiada son of Paseah and Meshullam son of Besodeiah. They laid its beams and put its doors and bolts and bars in place. [7]Next to them, repairs were made by men from Gibeon and Mizpah—Melatiah of Gibeon and Jadon of Meronoth—places under the authority of the governor of Trans-Euphrates. [8]Uzziel son of Harhaiah, one of the goldsmiths, repaired the next section; and Hananiah, one of the perfume-makers, made repairs next to that. They restored[c] Jerusalem as far as the Broad Wall. [9]Rephaiah son of Hur, ruler of a half-district of Jerusalem, repaired the next section. [10]Adjoining this, Jedaiah son of Harumaph made repairs opposite his house, and Hattush son of Hashabneiah made repairs next to him. [11]Malkijah son of Harim and Hasshub son of Pahath-Moab repaired another section and the Tower of the Ovens. [12]Shallum son of Hallohesh, ruler of a half-district of Jerusalem, repaired the next section with the help of his daughters.

[13]The Valley Gate was repaired by Hanun and the residents of Zanoah. They rebuilt it and put its doors and bolts and bars in place. They also repaired five hundred yards[d] of the wall as far as the Dung Gate.

[14]The Dung Gate was repaired by Malkijah son of Recab, ruler of the district of Beth Hakkerem. He rebuilt it and put its doors and bolts and bars in place.

[15]The Fountain Gate was repaired by Shallun son of Col-Hozeh, ruler of the district of Mizpah. He rebuilt it, roofing it over and putting its doors and bolts and bars in place. He also repaired the wall of the Pool of Siloam,[e] by the King's Garden, as far as the steps going down from the City of David. [16]Beyond him, Nehemiah son of Azbuk, ruler of a half-district of Beth Zur, made repairs up to a point opposite the tombs[f] of David, as far as the artificial pool and the House of the Heroes.

[17]Next to him, the repairs were made by the Levites under Rehum son of Bani. Beside him, Hashabiah, ruler of half the district of Keilah, carried out repairs for his district. [18]Next to him, the repairs were made by their countrymen under Binnui[g] son of Henadad, ruler of the other half-district of Keilah. [19]Next to him, Ezer son of Jeshua, ruler of Mizpah, repaired another section, from a point facing the ascent to the armory as far as the angle. [20]Next to him, Baruch son of Zabbai zealously repaired another section, from the angle to the entrance of the house of Eliashib the high priest. [21]Next to him, Meremoth son of Uriah, the son of Hakkoz, repaired another section, from the entrance of Eliashib's house to the end of it.

[22]The repairs next to him were made by the priests from the surrounding region. [23]Beyond them, Benjamin and Hasshub made repairs in front of their house; and next to them, Azariah son of Maaseiah, the son of Ananiah, made repairs beside his house.

these two experiments tell you about your ability to recall names?

1. What was the people's response to Nehemiah's challenge? 2. How many professional groups or classes of the Jewish community participated in Nehemiah's winning team? What, if any, distinctions between clergy and laity do you see? 3. Pick one of the 10 gates and, as a group, give "30-second progress reports" on each section. Decide among yourselves: Who had the most interesting report to share? Why do you think so? 4. What's interesting about Eliashib and his fellow priests (vv. 1,20)? About Shallum's group (v. 12)? Why do you think the "nobles" of Tekoa refused to work? What did that mean for the men of Tekoa (vv. 5,27)? 5. What do you learn from the fact that Nehemiah knew who worked "next to" whom? What does this tell you about the organization and cooperation involved in this nation-wide effort? How much of the wall was repaired during this time (v. 13)? 6. Nehemiah's name is conspicuous by its absence from this chapter. What do you suppose Nehemiah was doing while all the others were "doing the work"?

1. What attitudes and actions from Nehemiah's team of wall-builders fit Christians who want to build the church? Which ones should Christians avoid? 2. Which one do you think is primary to all the others? Which one could you demonstrate at home? At school? At church? 3. Do you know anyone like the nobles from Tekoa who want the benefits of a project without having to work for it (no names)? From Nehemiah, what do you learn about how to deal with them? 4. Who in your small group can you get "next to" for the sake of teaming up to tackle some project bigger than the two of you? Might the group help you tackle some project at church which remains undone for lack of volunteers?

---

[a]5 Or *their Lord* or *the governor*   [b]6 Or *Old*   [c]8 Or *They left out part of*
[d]13 Hebrew *a thousand cubits* (about 450 meters)   [e]15 Hebrew *Shelah,* a variant of
Shiloah, that is, Siloam   [f]16 Hebrew; Septuagint, some Vulgate manuscripts and
Syriac *tomb*   [g]18 Two Hebrew manuscripts and Syriac (see also Septuagint and verse
24); most Hebrew manuscripts *Bavvai*

24Next to him, Binnui son of Henadad repaired another section, from Azariah's house to the angle and the corner, 25and Palal son of Uzai worked opposite the angle and the tower projecting from the upper palace near the court of the guard. Next to him, Pedaiah son of Parosh 26and the temple servants living on the hill of Ophel made repairs up to a point opposite the Water Gate toward the east and the projecting tower. 27Next to them, the men of Tekoa repaired another section, from the great projecting tower to the wall of Ophel.

28Above the Horse Gate, the priests made repairs, each in front of his own house. 29Next to them, Zadok son of Immer made repairs opposite his house. Next to him, Shemaiah son of Shecaniah, the guard at the East Gate, made repairs. 30Next to him, Hananiah son of Shelemiah, and Hanun, the sixth son of Zalaph, repaired another section. Next to them, Meshullam son of Berekiah made repairs opposite his living quarters. 31Next to him, Malkijah, one of the goldsmiths, made repairs as far as the house of the temple servants and the merchants, opposite the Inspection Gate, and as far as the room above the corner; 32and between the room above the corner and the Sheep Gate the goldsmiths and merchants made repairs.

Opposition to the Rebuilding

4 When Sanballat heard that we were rebuilding the wall, he became angry and was greatly incensed. He ridiculed the Jews, 2and in the presence of his associates and the army of Samaria, he said, "What are those feeble Jews doing? Will they restore their wall? Will they offer sacrifices? Will they finish in a day? Can they bring the stones back to life from those heaps of rubble—burned as they are?"

3Tobiah the Ammonite, who was at his side, said, "What they are building—if even a fox climbed up on it, he would break down their wall of stones!"

4Hear us, O our God, for we are despised. Turn their insults back on their own heads. Give them over as plunder in a land of captivity. 5Do not cover up their guilt or blot out their sins from your sight, for they have thrown insults in the face of[a] the builders.

6So we rebuilt the wall till all of it reached half its height, for the people worked with all their heart.

7But when Sanballat, Tobiah, the Arabs, the Ammonites and the men of Ashdod heard that the repairs to Jerusalem's walls had gone ahead and that the gaps were being closed, they were very angry. 8They all plotted together to come and fight against Jerusalem and stir up trouble against it. 9But we prayed to our God and posted a guard day and night to meet this threat.

10Meanwhile, the people in Judah said, "The strength of the laborers is giving out, and there is so much rubble that we cannot rebuild the wall."

11Also our enemies said, "Before they know it or see us, we will be right there among them and will kill them and put an end to the work."

12Then the Jews who lived near them came and told us ten times over, "Wherever you turn, they will attack us."

13Therefore I stationed some of the people behind the lowest points of the wall at the exposed places, posting them by families,

a5 Or have provoked you to anger before

"Stick and stones may break my bones, but names will never hurt me"—How did that childhood taunt affect you? What teasing and name-calling actually did get to you?

1. Why do you think Sanballat was so opposed to Nehemiah's efforts? What weapons does he use against Nehemiah and his team? How effective were their taunts in slowing down the building project? 2. To whom does Nehemiah turn in the face of opposition (v. 4)? What does he say that surprises you? What effect does his prayer have on his own people? 3. What is the next threat brought against Nehemiah's team (vv. 7–8)? How do the Jews meet this threat? 4. The next threat is primarily internal, from within their own ranks—what is it? How does Nehemiah encourage his people to persist? What does he want them to remember (v. 14)? 5. What happens when the Jews return to work? How was the plot of their enemies foiled? 6. How does Nehemiah show his "nitty-gritty" level of involvement in this building effort? How does he show his dependence upon God? Upon strategy use of human resources? Upon his own diligence?

1. When have you or your church ever attempted something so big it was beyond human control, but within God's provision? Describe your big dream or vision. 2. Which gives you more difficulty:

with their swords, spears and bows. [14]After I looked things over, I stood up and said to the nobles, the officials and the rest of the people, "Don't be afraid of them. Remember the Lord, who is great and awesome, and fight for your brothers, your sons and your daughters, your wives and your homes."

[15]When our enemies heard that we were aware of their plot and that God had frustrated it, we all returned to the wall, each to his own work.

[16]From that day on, half of my men did the work, while the other half were equipped with spears, shields, bows and armor. The officers posted themselves behind all the people of Judah [17]who were building the wall. Those who carried materials did their work with one hand and held a weapon in the other, [18]and each of the builders wore his sword at his side as he worked. But the man who sounded the trumpet stayed with me.

[19]Then I said to the nobles, the officials and the rest of the people, "The work is extensive and spread out, and we are widely separated from each other along the wall. [20]Wherever you hear the sound of the trumpet, join us there. Our God will fight for us!"

[21]So we continued the work with half the men holding spears, from the first light of dawn till the stars came out. [22]At that time I also said to the people, "Have every man and his helper stay inside Jerusalem at night, so they can serve us as guards by night and workmen by day." [23]Neither I nor my brothers nor my men nor the guards with me took off our clothes; each had his weapon, even when he went for water.[a]

Nehemiah Helps the Poor

5 Now the men and their wives raised a great outcry against their Jewish brothers. [2]Some were saying, "We and our sons and daughters are numerous; in order for us to eat and stay alive, we must get grain."

[3]Others were saying, "We are mortgaging our fields, our vineyards and our homes to get grain during the famine."

[4]Still others were saying, "We have had to borrow money to pay the king's tax on our fields and vineyards. [5]Although we are of the same flesh and blood as our countrymen and though our sons are as good as theirs, yet we have to subject our sons and daughters to slavery. Some of our daughters have already been enslaved, but we are powerless, because our fields and our vineyards belong to others."

[6]When I heard their outcry and these charges, I was very angry. [7]I pondered them in my mind and then accused the nobles and officials. I told them, "You are exacting usury from your own countrymen!" So I called together a large meeting to deal with them [8]and said: "As far as possible, we have bought back our Jewish brothers who were sold to the Gentiles. Now you are selling your brothers, only for them to be sold back to us!" They kept quiet, because they could find nothing to say.

[9]So I continued, "What you are doing is not right. Shouldn't you walk in the fear of our God to avoid the reproach of our Gentile enemies? [10]I and my brothers and my men are also lending the people money and grain. But let the exacting of usury stop! [11]Give back to them immediately their fields, vineyards, olive groves and houses, and also the usury you are charging them—the hundredth part of the money, grain, new wine and oil."

[a]23 The meaning of the Hebrew for this clause is uncertain.

External criticism or internal fears? Why? 3. Do you usually do things one at a time (or "one-handed")? Or do you like to juggle two or more things ("weapon and water" in hand)? Which of the juggling acts Nehemiah's men were doing would you find toughest to do (see vv. 17,23)? 4. Which do you tend to do "with all your heart": Work? Worry? Worship? Warfare? Why? 5. What is one area of your life where there seems to be "so much rubble"? In what ways are you cooperating with others and trusting God to build something out of that rubble?

1. In your growing up years, what kind of fighter were you (with siblings and others): Scrapper? Underdog? Topdog? Pit bull terrier? 2. How trusting are you of others: (a) In *God* we trust, all others pay cash? (b) *Family*, but only when they need bail money? (c) *Strangers*, never, not even with double collateral? (d) Some *friends*, but only with a legal contract written in blood? (e) *Anyone* with a reason or money enough to back it up? 3. When there's more month left at the end of the money, what do you decide to do without?

1. What is the "great outcry" all about? What needs are going unmet? What do you suppose brought on the economic crisis? What three groups are most affected? How does this affect their common desire to finish the project? 2. How does Nehemiah respond to his brothers' cries for economic justice? Why does he get so angry at the nobles and officials (vv. 7ff; see Lev 25:39–42; Eze 22:12–13)? 3. How does Nehemiah seek to make sure the nobles and officials make their ways right (vv. 9–12)? In what ways does he act wisely? Generously? 4. What changes in the governor's office does Nehemiah enact for the sake of his people (vv. 14–19)? What

does he hope to gain in return for his personal sacrifice? How do you suppose he made ends meet?

1. In your church this past year, what financial crisis, party politics or other morale problems may have hindered your service to God and others? In what ways do you react like, or unlike, Nehemiah? **2.** In money matters, do you deal with a Christian differently than with a non-Christian? Why is that? **3.** Nehemiah shows us that loving God and others may require personal sacrifice. What privileges and rights are you ready to give up so that God's work may prosper? When have your beliefs really cost you something?

---

1. What horror movie, murder mystery or drama-in-real-life has really frightened you? What was so frightening about it? What does that say about you? **2.** What was once rumored to be true about you, but wasn't?

1. As the rebuilding project is almost over, what final threats does Nehemiah face from Sanballat, Tobiah and cohorts? **2.** What does the proposed meeting (v. 2) claim to be? Why does Nehemiah suspect otherwise? Even if it were sincere or well-intentioned, how does Nehemiah not let the "good" get in the way of the "better"? **3.** What impact was the "unsealed letter" intended to have on the public at large? On the ruling Persian king? How scared do you think Nehemiah was, really? Why? How does he face those who would slander him? **4.** What was the prophecy of Shemaiah intended to do? How do you think Nehemiah discerned he was a false prophet? (Note: Only priests could enter the sanctuary, Nu 18:7.)

1. How complete is your defense against those who would sidetrack you? What weak spots in the wall of your heart need shoring up? **2.** In going about doing good, when have you been tempt-

[12]"We will give it back," they said. "And we will not demand anything more from them. We will do as you say."

Then I summoned the priests and made the nobles and officials take an oath to do what they had promised. [13]I also shook out the folds of my robe and said, "In this way may God shake out of his house and possessions every man who does not keep this promise. So may such a man be shaken out and emptied!"

At this the whole assembly said, "Amen," and praised the LORD. And the people did as they had promised.

[14]Moreover, from the twentieth year of King Artaxerxes, when I was appointed to be their governor in the land of Judah, until his thirty-second year—twelve years—neither I nor my brothers ate the food allotted to the governor. [15]But the earlier governors—those preceding me—placed a heavy burden on the people and took forty shekels[a] of silver from them in addition to food and wine. Their assistants also lorded it over the people. But out of reverence for God I did not act like that. [16]Instead, I devoted myself to the work on this wall. All my men were assembled there for the work; we[b] did not acquire any land.

[17]Furthermore, a hundred and fifty Jews and officials ate at my table, as well as those who came to us from the surrounding nations. [18]Each day one ox, six choice sheep and some poultry were prepared for me, and every ten days an abundant supply of wine of all kinds. In spite of all this, I never demanded the food allotted to the governor, because the demands were heavy on these people.

[19]Remember me with favor, O my God, for all I have done for these people.

Further Opposition to the Rebuilding

6 When word came to Sanballat, Tobiah, Geshem the Arab and the rest of our enemies that I had rebuilt the wall and not a gap was left in it—though up to that time I had not set the doors in the gates— [2]Sanballat and Geshem sent me this message: "Come, let us meet together in one of the villages[c] on the plain of Ono."

But they were scheming to harm me; [3]so I sent messengers to them with this reply: "I am carrying on a great project and cannot go down. Why should the work stop while I leave it and go down to you?" [4]Four times they sent me the same message, and each time I gave them the same answer.

[5]Then, the fifth time, Sanballat sent his aide to me with the same message, and in his hand was an unsealed letter [6]in which was written:

"It is reported among the nations—and Geshem[d] says it is true—that you and the Jews are plotting to revolt, and therefore you are building the wall. Moreover, according to these reports you are about to become their king [7]and have even appointed prophets to make this proclamation about you in Jerusalem: 'There is a king in Judah!' Now this report will get back to the king; so come, let us confer together."

[8]I sent him this reply: "Nothing like what you are saying is happening; you are just making it up out of your head."

[9]They were all trying to frighten us, thinking, "Their hands will get too weak for the work, and it will not be completed."

But I prayed, "Now strengthen my hands."

[10]One day I went to the house of Shemaiah son of Delaiah, the

a15 That is, about 1 pound (about 0.5 kilogram)   b16 Most Hebrew manuscripts; some Hebrew manuscripts, Septuagint, Vulgate and Syriac I   c2 Or in Kephirim   d6 Hebrew Gashmu, a variant of Geshem son of Mehetabel, who was shut in at his home. He said, "Let us meet in the house of God, inside the temple, and let us close the temple doors, because men are coming to kill you—by night they are coming to kill you."

[11]But I said, "Should a man like me run away? Or should one like me go into the temple to save his life? I will not go!" [12]I realized that God had not sent him, but that he had prophesied against me because Tobiah and Sanballat had hired him. [13]He had been hired to intimidate me so that I would commit a sin by doing this, and then they would give me a bad name to discredit me.

[14]Remember Tobiah and Sanballat, O my God, because of what they have done; remember also the prophetess Noadiah and the rest of the prophets who have been trying to intimidate me.

The Completion of the Wall

[15]So the wall was completed on the twenty-fifth of Elul, in fifty-two days. [16]When all our enemies heard about this, all the surrounding nations were afraid and lost their self-confidence, because they realized that this work had been done with the help of our God.

[17]Also, in those days the nobles of Judah were sending many letters to Tobiah, and replies from Tobiah kept coming to them. [18]For many in Judah were under oath to him, since he was son-in-law to Shecaniah son of Arah, and his son Jehohanan had married the daughter of Meshullam son of Berekiah. [19]Moreover, they kept reporting to me his good deeds and then telling him what I said. And Tobiah sent letters to intimidate me.

7 After the wall had been rebuilt and I had set the doors in place, the gatekeepers and the singers and the Levites were appointed. [2]I put in charge of Jerusalem my brother Hanani, along with[a] Hananiah the commander of the citadel, because he was a man of integrity and feared God more than most men do. [3]I said to them, "The gates of Jerusalem are not to be opened until the sun is hot. While the gatekeepers are still on duty, have them shut the doors and bar them. Also appoint residents of Jerusalem as guards, some at their posts and some near their own houses."

The List of the Exiles Who Returned

[4]Now the city was large and spacious, but there were few people in it, and the houses had not yet been rebuilt. [5]So my God put it into my heart to assemble the nobles, the officials and the common people for registration by families. I found the genealogical record of those who had been the first to return. This is what I found written there:

[6]These are the people of the province who came up from the captivity of the exiles whom Nebuchadnezzar king of Babylon had taken captive (they returned to Jerusalem and Judah, each to his own town, [7]in company with Zerubbabel, Jeshua, Nehemiah, Azariah, Raamiah, Nahamani, Mordecai, Bilshan, Mispereth, Bigvai, Nehum and Baanah):

The list of the men of Israel:

[8]the descendants of Parosh	2,172
[9]of Shephatiah	372
[10]of Arah	652

[a]2 Or Hanani, that is,

What is the most satisfying project you have completed? What was so special about finishing?

1. What lay in ruins for 140 years has been rebuilt in 52 days? How was this possible? 2. Although most enemies have given up, how does Tobiah extend his subversive tactics (on family ties, see 3:4; 6:18)? 3. What commends Hanani (Hananiah) for his responsible position? 4. What steps does Nehemiah take to secure the city of Jerusalem? What is significant about the timing and placement of his resources?

What importance do you place on setting goals and achieving them? Are you accountable?

ed to settle for second best? 3. How does a Christian distinguish between what is God's will and the words of a false prophet or misguided person? 4. From Nehemiah's example, how will you handle slander?

1. Who were you named after? Where did they come from? Who else shares your family name? 2. What do you know about your genealogy? How far back can you go before you start forgetting names? 3. What would you like to discover about your family tree?

1. How and why does Nehemiah go about re-populating Jerusalem? Why was a genealogical record important for this purpose? What does this tell you about the importance of Jerusalem to God and his people? 2. This genealogical record is nearly the same as in Ezra 2. In comparing the two lists, what do you observe about the functions of genealogies? (Note: Some variance in names and numbers between the two lists may be due to copying errors or, more likely, to the different functions of the genealogies.) 3.

What does the list of localities tell you? What tribes and towns are these people returning from? Likewise, what professional groups or classes of people are returning from exile? **4.** In what towns do they then settle (v. 73; see 11:1–20)? What does this tell you about their collective memory and homing instincts? **5.** What happened to refugees who could not properly document their family ties (vv. 61–65)? What does that say about the importance of keeping family records? **6.** What other kinds of people, livestock and valuables were declared and counted as they enter (vv. 66–72)?

♡ **1.** Do you keep a diary, save old letters or file away memorabilia of your family and relatives? What would an inventory of them reveal about the kind of person you are, or the kind of family you come from? **2.** Who are the meaningful people in your spiritual journey? What has been passed on to you, spiritually, from your forebears? **3.** What one quality are you now developing as one of God's people that you would like to pass on to your children and their children? How do you intend to do this?

[11]of Pahath-Moab (through the line of Jeshua and Joab)	2,818
[12]of Elam	1,254
[13]of Zattu	845
[14]of Zaccai	760
[15]of Binnui	648
[16]of Bebai	628
[17]of Azgad	2,322
[18]of Adonikam	667
[19]of Bigvai	2,067
[20]of Adin	655
[21]of Ater (through Hezekiah)	98
[22]of Hashum	328
[23]of Bezai	324
[24]of Hariph	112
[25]of Gibeon	95
[26]the men of Bethlehem and Netophah	188
[27]of Anathoth	128
[28]of Beth Azmaveth	42
[29]of Kiriath Jearim, Kephirah and Beeroth	743
[30]of Ramah and Geba	621
[31]of Micmash	122
[32]of Bethel and Ai	123
[33]of the other Nebo	52
[34]of the other Elam	1,254
[35]of Harim	320
[36]of Jericho	345
[37]of Lod, Hadid and Ono	721
[38]of Senaah	3,930

[39]The priests:

the descendants of Jedaiah (through the family of Jeshua)	973
[40]of Immer	1,052
[41]of Pashhur	1,247
[42]of Harim	1,017

[43]The Levites:

the descendants of Jeshua (through Kadmiel through the line of Hodaviah)	74

[44]The singers:

the descendants of Asaph	148

[45]The gatekeepers:

the descendants of Shallum, Ater, Talmon, Akkub, Hatita and Shobai	138

[46]The temple servants:

the descendants of
Ziha, Hasupha, Tabbaoth,
[47]Keros, Sia, Padon,
[48]Lebana, Hagaba, Shalmai,
[49]Hanan, Giddel, Gahar,
[50]Reaiah, Rezin, Nekoda,
[51]Gazzam, Uzza, Paseah,
[52]Besai, Meunim, Nephussim,

^{53}Bakbuk, Hakupha, Harhur,
^{54}Bazluth, Mehida, Harsha,
^{55}Barkos, Sisera, Temah,
^{56}Neziah and Hatipha

^{57}The descendants of the servants of Solomon:

the descendants of
Sotai, Sophereth, Perida,
^{58}Jaala, Darkon, Giddel,
^{59}Shephatiah, Hattil,
Pokereth-Hazzebaim and Amon

^{60}The temple servants and the descendants
of the servants of Solomon   392

^{61}The following came up from the towns of Tel Melah, Tel Harsha, Kerub, Addon and Immer, but they could not show that their families were descended from Israel:

^{62}the descendants of
Delaiah, Tobiah and Nekoda   642

^{63}And from among the priests:

the descendants of
Hobaiah, Hakkoz and Barzillai (a man who
had married a daughter of Barzillai the
Gileadite and was called by that name).

^{64}These searched for their family records, but they could not find them and so were excluded from the priesthood as unclean. ^{65}The governor, therefore, ordered them not to eat any of the most sacred food until there should be a priest ministering with the Urim and Thummim.

^{66}The whole company numbered 42,360, ^{67}besides their 7,337 menservants and maidservants; and they also had 245 men and women singers. ^{68}There were 736 horses, 245 mules,^{a} ^{69}435 camels and 6,720 donkeys.

^{70}Some of the heads of the families contributed to the work. The governor gave to the treasury 1,000 drachmas^b of gold, 50 bowls and 530 garments for priests. ^{71}Some of the heads of the families gave to the treasury for the work 20,000 drachmas^c of gold and 2,200 minas^d of silver. ^{72}The total given by the rest of the people was 20,000 drachmas of gold, 2,000 minas^e of silver and 67 garments for priests.

^{73}The priests, the Levites, the gatekeepers, the singers and the temple servants, along with certain of the people and the rest of the Israelites, settled in their own towns.

Ezra Reads the Law

When the seventh month came and the Israelites had settled in their towns, ^{1}all the people assembled as one man in the square before the Water Gate. They told Ezra the scribe to bring out the Book of the Law of Moses, which the LORD had commanded for Israel.

^{2}So on the first day of the seventh month Ezra the priest brought the Law before the assembly, which was made up of men and

Have you ever attended a high school reunion? What one thing most surprised you? How had your classmates changed? What would a picture of you then and now indicate about how you had changed?

1. What was the occasion for assembling the people on the "first day of the seventh month"

$^a68$ Some Hebrew manuscripts (see also Ezra 2:66); most Hebrew manuscripts do not have this verse. $^b70$ That is, about 19 pounds (about 8.5 kilograms) $^c71$ That is, about 375 pounds (about 170 kilograms); also in verse 72 $^d71$ That is, about 1 1/3 tons (about 1.2 metric tons) $^e72$ That is, about 1 1/4 tons (about 1.1 metric tons)

(v. 2; see Lev 23:24; Nu 29:1–6)? And why the public square instead of the temple for this activity? **2.** Ezra first came to Jerusalem in 458 B.C. for the purpose of teaching the Law (see Ezr 7:6–10). Why do you suppose it has taken 13 years from that time until this general assembly (in 445 B.C.) for him to fully and publicly proclaim its truth? **3.** How do the people first respond to the Book of the Law of Moses (vv. 3,5,6,9)? How do you account for this response? **4.** What is the make-up of this large, historic Bible study group? Who is helping them to understand the Scriptures "clearly"? Why can't the lay people understand the Bible on their own? **5.** What happens when they truly understand (vv. 9–12; see Dt 16:14)? Who is in the second, follow-up study (v. 13)? What do they discover and do (vv. 14–17; see Lev 23:34–43)? **6.** What is the link between the Exodus from Egypt and their return from exile? How did this add to their festive spirit?

♡ **1.** How important was the reading of God's Word in your own spiritual renewal? Which had the greater impact on you: Private Bible study or public preaching? Why? **2.** When you "saw the light," did you weep and mourn? Celebrate with joy? Did you then give to the poor or reach out to others on the margins of society? How else did you spread the word? **3.** What acts of God do you celebrate with regularity and joy as one of his pilgrim people? **4.** What three activities from this chapter would be foundational to the renewal of your church? How could your small group help in one such activity?

women and all who were able to understand. ³He read it aloud from daybreak till noon as he faced the square before the Water Gate in the presence of the men, women and others who could understand. And all the people listened attentively to the Book of the Law.

⁴Ezra the scribe stood on a high wooden platform built for the occasion. Beside him on his right stood Mattithiah, Shema, Anaiah, Uriah, Hilkiah and Maaseiah; and on his left were Pedaiah, Mishael, Malkijah, Hashum, Hashbaddanah, Zechariah and Meshullam.

⁵Ezra opened the book. All the people could see him because he was standing above them; and as he opened it, the people all stood up. ⁶Ezra praised the Lord, the great God; and all the people lifted their hands and responded, "Amen! Amen!" Then they bowed down and worshiped the Lord with their faces to the ground.

⁷The Levites—Jeshua, Bani, Sherebiah, Jamin, Akkub, Shabbethai, Hodiah, Maaseiah, Kelita, Azariah, Jozabad, Hanan and Pelaiah—instructed the people in the Law while the people were standing there. ⁸They read from the Book of the Law of God, making it clear[a] and giving the meaning so that the people could understand what was being read.

⁹Then Nehemiah the governor, Ezra the priest and scribe, and the Levites who were instructing the people said to them all, "This day is sacred to the Lord your God. Do not mourn or weep." For all the people had been weeping as they listened to the words of the Law.

¹⁰Nehemiah said, "Go and enjoy choice food and sweet drinks, and send some to those who have nothing prepared. This day is sacred to our Lord. Do not grieve, for the joy of the Lord is your strength."

¹¹The Levites calmed all the people, saying, "Be still, for this is a sacred day. Do not grieve."

¹²Then all the people went away to eat and drink, to send portions of food and to celebrate with great joy, because they now understood the words that had been made known to them.

¹³On the second day of the month, the heads of all the families, along with the priests and the Levites, gathered around Ezra the scribe to give attention to the words of the Law. ¹⁴They found written in the Law, which the Lord had commanded through Moses, that the Israelites were to live in booths during the feast of the seventh month ¹⁵and that they should proclaim this word and spread it throughout their towns and in Jerusalem: "Go out into the hill country and bring back branches from olive and wild olive trees, and from myrtles, palms and shade trees, to make booths"— as it is written.[b]

¹⁶So the people went out and brought back branches and built themselves booths on their own roofs, in their courtyards, in the courts of the house of God and in the square by the Water Gate and the one by the Gate of Ephraim. ¹⁷The whole company that had returned from exile built booths and lived in them. From the days of Joshua son of Nun until that day, the Israelites had not celebrated it like this. And their joy was very great.

¹⁸Day after day, from the first day to the last, Ezra read from the Book of the Law of God. They celebrated the feast for seven days, and on the eighth day, in accordance with the regulation, there was an assembly.

---

a 8 Or *God, translating it*   *b* 15 See Lev. 23:37-40.

The Israelites Confess Their Sins

9 On the twenty-fourth day of the same month, the Israelites gathered together, fasting and wearing sackcloth and having dust on their heads. ²Those of Israelite descent had separated themselves from all foreigners. They stood in their places and confessed their sins and the wickedness of their fathers. ³They stood where they were and read from the Book of the Law of the LORD their God for a quarter of the day, and spent another quarter in confession and in worshiping the LORD their God. ⁴Standing on the stairs were the Levites—Jeshua, Bani, Kadmiel, Shebaniah, Bunni, Sherebiah, Bani and Kenani—who called with loud voices to the LORD their God. ⁵And the Levites—Jeshua, Kadmiel, Bani, Hashabneiah, Sherebiah, Hodiah, Shebaniah and Pethahiah—said: "Stand up and praise the LORD your God, who is from everlasting to everlasting.ᵃ"

"Blessed be your glorious name, and may it be exalted above all blessing and praise. ⁶You alone are the LORD. You made the heavens, even the highest heavens, and all their starry host, the earth and all that is on it, the seas and all that is in them. You give life to everything, and the multitudes of heaven worship you.

⁷"You are the LORD God, who chose Abram and brought him out of Ur of the Chaldeans and named him Abraham. ⁸You found his heart faithful to you, and you made a covenant with him to give to his descendants the land of the Canaanites, Hittites, Amorites, Perizzites, Jebusites and Girgashites. You have kept your promise because you are righteous.

⁹"You saw the suffering of our forefathers in Egypt; you heard their cry at the Red Sea.ᵇ ¹⁰You sent miraculous signs and wonders against Pharaoh, against all his officials and all the people of his land, for you knew how arrogantly the Egyptians treated them. You made a name for yourself, which remains to this day. ¹¹You divided the sea before them, so that they passed through it on dry ground, but you hurled their pursuers into the depths, like a stone into mighty waters. ¹²By day you led them with a pillar of cloud, and by night with a pillar of fire to give them light on the way they were to take.

¹³"You came down on Mount Sinai; you spoke to them from heaven. You gave them regulations and laws that are just and right, and decrees and commands that are good. ¹⁴You made known to them your holy Sabbath and gave them commands, decrees and laws through your servant Moses. ¹⁵In their hunger you gave them bread from heaven and in their thirst you brought them water from the rock; you told them to go in and take possession of the land you had sworn with uplifted hand to give them.

¹⁶"But they, our forefathers, became arrogant and stiff-necked, and did not obey your commands. ¹⁷They refused to listen and failed to remember the miracles you performed among them. They became stiff-necked and in their rebellion appointed a leader in order to return to their slavery. But you are a forgiving God, gracious and compassionate, slow to anger and abounding in love. Therefore you did not desert them, ¹⁸even when they cast for themselves an image of a calf and said, 'This is your god, who brought you up out of Egypt,' or when they committed awful blasphemies.

1. In your growing up years, what did "confession" mean to you? What was required? How often? Who was involved? Why? 2. Do you write down any of your prayers? Why?

1. What is the occasion for this time of corporate confession? How do the Israelites prepare for this? Why do they "separate themselves from all foreigners"? 2. What's the relationship between the three parts of their worship: (a) instruction from the Word, (b) confession of sin, and (c) praise of God? 3. In the prayer recorded here, God's grace and power are reviewed throughout redemptive history. Where do you see God at work in creation? In Abraham? In Egypt? In the Exodus? In the desert? At Mount Sinai? In their possessing of Canaan? In the era of the Judges? Of the prophets? 4. Where is God at work in their present situation? What Psalm(s) does this whole prayer bring to mind for you? 5. In thus seeing God anew in this prayer, how do the people then respond? (Note particularly the verbs.) 6. How do the people think God treated them? What did they say was the source of their problems?

1. The last time you did something "really dumb," requiring confession to your parents or your peers, what was involved? What made it so "dumb"? What brought it out in the open? How was your "confession" received? 2. How does a Christian today show sincerity in one's confession and repentance of sin? In that activity, what part would you assign to God's Word? To other believers? To public or published prayer? To private or silent prayer? How much time would you devote to each part? 3. If you were to write a prayer patterned after verses 5–37, what bench marks or signposts of God's grace would you include? What is the "great distress" from which you want God to deliver you? 4. If such a prayer were written collectively by your small group, what would be included? (Try it and see.)

ᵃ5 Or *God for ever and ever*   ᵇ9 Hebrew *Yam Suph*; that is, Sea of Reeds

[19]"Because of your great compassion you did not abandon them in the desert. By day the pillar of cloud did not cease to guide them on their path, nor the pillar of fire by night to shine on the way they were to take. [20]You gave your good Spirit to instruct them. You did not withhold your manna from their mouths, and you gave them water for their thirst. [21]For forty years you sustained them in the desert; they lacked nothing, their clothes did not wear out nor did their feet become swollen.

[22]"You gave them kingdoms and nations, allotting to them even the remotest frontiers. They took over the country of Sihon[a] king of Heshbon and the country of Og king of Bashan. [23]You made their sons as numerous as the stars in the sky, and you brought them into the land that you told their fathers to enter and possess. [24]Their sons went in and took possession of the land. You subdued before them the Canaanites, who lived in the land; you handed the Canaanites over to them, along with their kings and the peoples of the land, to deal with them as they pleased. [25]They captured fortified cities and fertile land; they took possession of houses filled with all kinds of good things, wells already dug, vineyards, olive groves and fruit trees in abundance. They ate to the full and were well-nourished; they reveled in your great goodness.

[26]"But they were disobedient and rebelled against you; they put your law behind their backs. They killed your prophets, who had admonished them in order to turn them back to you; they committed awful blasphemies. [27]So you handed them over to their enemies, who oppressed them. But when they were oppressed they cried out to you. From heaven you heard them, and in your great compassion you gave them deliverers, who rescued them from the hand of their enemies.

[28]"But as soon as they were at rest, they again did what was evil in your sight. Then you abandoned them to the hand of their enemies so that they ruled over them. And when they cried out to you again, you heard from heaven, and in your compassion you delivered them time after time.

[29]"You warned them to return to your law, but they became arrogant and disobeyed your commands. They sinned against your ordinances, by which a man will live if he obeys them. Stubbornly they turned their backs on you, became stiff-necked and refused to listen. [30]For many years you were patient with them. By your Spirit you admonished them through your prophets. Yet they paid no attention, so you handed them over to the neighboring peoples. [31]But in your great mercy you did not put an end to them or abandon them, for you are a gracious and merciful God.

[32]"Now therefore, O our God, the great, mighty and awesome God, who keeps his covenant of love, do not let all this hardship seem trifling in your eyes—the hardship that has come upon us, upon our kings and leaders, upon our priests and prophets, upon our fathers and all your people, from the days of the kings of Assyria until today. [33]In all that has happened to us, you have been just; you have acted faithfully, while we did wrong. [34]Our kings, our leaders, our priests and our fathers did not follow your law; they did not pay attention to your commands or the warnings you gave them. [35]Even while they were in their kingdom, enjoying your great good-

---

a22 One Hebrew manuscript and Septuagint; most Hebrew manuscripts *Sihon, that is, the country of the*

ness to them in the spacious and fertile land you gave them, they did not serve you or turn from their evil ways. [36]"But see, we are slaves today, slaves in the land you gave our forefathers so they could eat its fruit and the other good things it produces. [37]Because of our sins, its abundant harvest goes to the kings you have placed over us. They rule over our bodies and our cattle as they please. We are in great distress.

The Agreement of the People

[38]"In view of all this, we are making a binding agreement, putting it in writing, and our leaders, our Levites and our priests are affixing their seals to it."

10
Those who sealed it were:

Nehemiah the governor, the son of Hacaliah.

Zedekiah, [2]Seraiah, Azariah, Jeremiah,
[3]Pashhur, Amariah, Malkijah,
[4]Hattush, Shebaniah, Malluch,
[5]Harim, Meremoth, Obadiah,
[6]Daniel, Ginnethon, Baruch,
[7]Meshullam, Abijah, Mijamin,
[8]Maaziah, Bilgai and Shemaiah.
These were the priests.

[9]The Levites:

Jeshua son of Azaniah, Binnui of the sons of Henadad, Kadmiel,
[10]and their associates: Shebaniah,
Hodiah, Kelita, Pelaiah, Hanan,
[11]Mica, Rehob, Hashabiah,
[12]Zaccur, Sherebiah, Shebaniah,
[13]Hodiah, Bani and Beninu.

[14]The leaders of the people:

Parosh, Pahath-Moab, Elam, Zattu, Bani,
[15]Bunni, Azgad, Bebai,
[16]Adonijah, Bigvai, Adin,
[17]Ater, Hezekiah, Azzur,
[18]Hodiah, Hashum, Bezai,
[19]Hariph, Anathoth, Nebai,
[20]Magpiash, Meshullam, Hezir,
[21]Meshezabel, Zadok, Jaddua,
[22]Pelatiah, Hanan, Anaiah,
[23]Hoshea, Hananiah, Hasshub,
[24]Hallohesh, Pilha, Shobek,
[25]Rehum, Hashabnah, Maaseiah,
[26]Ahiah, Hanan, Anan,
[27]Malluch, Harim and Baanah.

[28]"The rest of the people—priests, Levites, gatekeepers, singers, temple servants and all who separated themselves from the neighboring peoples for the sake of the Law of God, together with their wives and all their sons and daughters who are able to understand— [29]all these now join their brothers the nobles, and bind themselves with a curse and an oath to follow the Law of God given through Moses the servant of God and to obey carefully all the commands, regulations and decrees of the LORD our Lord.

1. Recall a significant agreement you put your name to in writing: Was it enlisting for the military? Purchasing a home? Co-signing for a loan? Applying for a driver's license? Settling your marital property? Affiliating with your professional association? 2. In each instance, what did it matter whether the agreement was in writing or not? 3. What is one thing you are waiting on now to be "signed, sealed and delivered"?

1. From verses 1–29, what of significance do you see in the listing of specific names? Where else have you seen most of these names? 2. Do you suppose the original agreement contained all the names of those summarized in verse 28? Why or why not? 3. What subjects are covered by the provisions of this covenant? What rationale can you see for the prohibition in verse 30 (see Ex 34:16)? For the prohibition and duties in verses 31–33 (see Ex 20:8–11; 30:11–16)? For the duties in verses 35–36 (see Dt 26:1–11)? Is Nehemiah prescribing tighter restrictions, or more lenient ones, on his fellow Jews than required by the Law? Why might that be? 4. In verses 37–39, how did the Jews demonstrate they were good stewards? What had neglecting the house of God taught them in the past (see 13:11; Hag 1:4–11)?

1. For the Christian, is there any similar covenant that reflects the values or principles of this chapter? (What about your church's practice of baptism, or new member classes, or your own small group covenant?) What part does putting it in writing play? How might this regulate lifestyle? How could this become legalistic? 2. Is personal stewardship a reliable index of commitment to God and his work? Why or why not? What else might serve that purpose for you? 3. In your church, what seems most neglected and in need of repair: (a) God's house? (b) His Word? (c) His people? (d) His leaders? (e) The Christian lifestyle? (f) Other? Why do you think so? 4.

What will you do next week as a direct result of renewing your covenant vows today?

30"We promise not to give our daughters in marriage to the peoples around us or take their daughters for our sons.

31"When the neighboring peoples bring merchandise or grain to sell on the Sabbath, we will not buy from them on the Sabbath or on any holy day. Every seventh year we will forgo working the land and will cancel all debts.

32"We assume the responsibility for carrying out the commands to give a third of a shekel[a] each year for the service of the house of our God: **33**for the bread set out on the table; for the regular grain offerings and burnt offerings; for the offerings on the Sabbaths, New Moon festivals and appointed feasts; for the holy offerings; for sin offerings to make atonement for Israel; and for all the duties of the house of our God.

34"We—the priests, the Levites and the people—have cast lots to determine when each of our families is to bring to the house of our God at set times each year a contribution of wood to burn on the altar of the LORD our God, as it is written in the Law.

35"We also assume responsibility for bringing to the house of the LORD each year the firstfruits of our crops and of every fruit tree.

36"As it is also written in the Law, we will bring the firstborn of our sons and of our cattle, of our herds and of our flocks to the house of our God, to the priests ministering there.

37"Moreover, we will bring to the storerooms of the house of our God, to the priests, the first of our ground meal, of our ⌐grain⌐ offerings, of the fruit of all our trees and of our new wine and oil. And we will bring a tithe of our crops to the Levites, for it is the Levites who collect the tithes in all the towns where we work. **38**A priest descended from Aaron is to accompany the Levites when they receive the tithes, and the Levites are to bring a tenth of the tithes up to the house of our God, to the storerooms of the treasury. **39**The people of Israel, including the Levites, are to bring their contributions of grain, new wine and oil to the storerooms where the articles for the sanctuary are kept and where the ministering priests, the gatekeepers and the singers stay.

"We will not neglect the house of our God."

The New Residents of Jerusalem

11 Now the leaders of the people settled in Jerusalem, and the rest of the people cast lots to bring one out of every ten to live in Jerusalem, the holy city, while the remaining nine were to stay in their own towns. **2**The people commended all the men who volunteered to live in Jerusalem.

3These are the provincial leaders who settled in Jerusalem (now some Israelites, priests, Levites, temple servants and descendants of Solomon's servants lived in the towns of Judah, each on his own property in the various towns, **4**while other people from both Judah and Benjamin lived in Jerusalem):

From the descendants of Judah:

Athaiah son of Uzziah, the son of Zechariah, the son of Amariah, the son of Shephatiah, the son of Mahalalel, a descendant of Perez; **5**and Maaseiah son of Baruch, the son of Col-Hozeh, the son of Hazaiah, the son of Adaiah, the son of Joiarib, the

1. When you were eligible to serve in your country's army, did you enlist? Were you drafted? Or exempted? Or a conscientious objector? Why? 2. What was the last church, school or community involvement for which you were "volunteered"? Would you do it again? Why or why not? 3. Can you recall any job you've held which paid a bonus for "hazardous duty" or "combat time"? What was it? 4. Do you prefer rural, suburban or city life to raise a family? Why?

1. Why do you think the people were so reluctant to settle in Jerusalem? Why did Nehemiah and the other leaders deem it necessary to re-populate the "holy city"? With what two recruitment policies? 2. What does the list of

a32 That is, about 1/8 ounce (about 4 grams)

son of Zechariah, a descendant of Shelah. ⁶The descendants of Perez who lived in Jerusalem totaled 468 able men.

⁷From the descendants of Benjamin:

Sallu son of Meshullam, the son of Joed, the son of Pedaiah, the son of Kolaiah, the son of Maaseiah, the son of Ithiel, the son of Jeshaiah, ⁸and his followers, Gabbai and Sallai—928 men. ⁹Joel son of Zicri was their chief officer, and Judah son of Hassenuah was over the Second District of the city.

¹⁰From the priests:

Jedaiah; the son of Joiarib; Jakin; ¹¹Seraiah son of Hilkiah, the son of Meshullam, the son of Zadok, the son of Meraioth, the son of Ahitub, supervisor in the house of God, ¹²and their associates, who carried on work for the temple—822 men; Adaiah son of Jeroham, the son of Pelaliah, the son of Amzi, the son of Zechariah, the son of Pashhur, the son of Malkijah, ¹³and his associates, who were heads of families—242 men; Amashsai son of Azarel, the son of Ahzai, the son of Meshillemoth, the son of Immer, ¹⁴and his[a] associates, who were able men—128. Their chief officer was Zabdiel son of Haggedolim.

¹⁵From the Levites:

Shemaiah son of Hasshub, the son of Azrikam, the son of Hashabiah, the son of Bunni; ¹⁶Shabbethai and Jozabad, two of the heads of the Levites, who had charge of the outside work of the house of God; ¹⁷Mattaniah son of Mica, the son of Zabdi, the son of Asaph, the director who led in thanksgiving and prayer; Bakbukiah, second among his associates; and Abda son of Shammua, the son of Galal, the son of Jeduthun. ¹⁸The Levites in the holy city totaled 284.

¹⁹The gatekeepers:

Akkub, Talmon and their associates, who kept watch at the gates—172 men.

²⁰The rest of the Israelites, with the priests and Levites, were in all the towns of Judah, each on his ancestral property.
²¹The temple servants lived on the hill of Ophel, and Ziha and Gishpa were in charge of them.
²²The chief officer of the Levites in Jerusalem was Uzzi son of Bani, the son of Hashabiah, the son of Mattaniah, the son of Mica. Uzzi was one of Asaph's descendants, who were the singers responsible for the service of the house of God. ²³The singers were under the king's orders, which regulated their daily activity.
²⁴Pethahiah son of Meshezabel, one of the descendants of Zerah son of Judah, was the king's agent in all affairs relating to the people.
²⁵As for the villages with their fields, some of the people of Judah lived in Kiriath Arba and its surrounding settlements, in Dibon and its settlements, in Jekabzeel and its villages, ²⁶in Jeshua, in Moladah, in Beth Pelet, ²⁷in Hazar Shual, in Beersheba and its settlements, ²⁸in Ziklag, in Meconah and its settlements, ²⁹in En Rimmon, in Zorah, in Jarmuth, ³⁰Zanoah, Adullam and their villages, in Lachish and its fields, and in Azekah and its settlements. So they were living all the way from Beersheba to the Valley of Hinnom.
³¹The descendants of the Benjamites from Geba lived in Mic-

residents (vv. 3–24) say about the administrative abilities of Nehemiah? Percentage-wise, what relative success did he have in transferring rural folk to the urban center Jerusalem (see 7:66)? Why so few Levites (284) compared with the total number of priests (1192)? Could it be that life in exile was more appealing than the menial tasks of temple service? **3.** What labor divisions and family ties are evident from descriptive notes with each set of residents? Any "young urban professionals" ("Yuppies")? **4.** Why was it crucial that most folk live in villages and settlements outside Jerusalem?

♡ **1.** Is the downtown "center" of worship where you live attractive or unattractive? Why is that? **2.** Would you be willing to relocate to the inner city, maybe forsaking your chosen field or ancestral home, to be of greater use to God and his kingdom? Why or why not? **3.** What is your church doing to promote ministry to those who live and work in the heart of your urban ghettos? What would be the impact if one-tenth of your church families were set aside for this mission? What could your small group do to set an example here?

---

a 14 Most Septuagint manuscripts; Hebrew *their*

mash, Aija, Bethel and its settlements, 32in Anathoth, Nob and Ananiah, 33in Hazor, Ramah and Gittaim, 34in Hadid, Zeboim and Neballat, 35in Lod and Ono, and in the Valley of the Craftsmen.

36Some of the divisions of the Levites of Judah settled in Benjamin.

Priests and Levites

12 These were the priests and Levites who returned with Zerubbabel son of Shealtiel and with Jeshua:

Seraiah, Jeremiah, Ezra,
2Amariah, Malluch, Hattush,
3Shecaniah, Rehum, Meremoth,
4Iddo, Ginnethon,*a* Abijah,
5Mijamin,*b* Moadiah, Bilgah,
6Shemaiah, Joiarib, Jedaiah,
7Sallu, Amok, Hilkiah and Jedaiah.

These were the leaders of the priests and their associates in the days of Jeshua.

8The Levites were Jeshua, Binnui, Kadmiel, Sherebiah, Judah, and also Mattaniah, who, together with his associates, was in charge of the songs of thanksgiving. 9Bakbukiah and Unni, their associates, stood opposite them in the services.

10Jeshua was the father of Joiakim, Joiakim the father of Eliashib, Eliashib the father of Joiada, 11Joiada the father of Jonathan, and Jonathan the father of Jaddua.

12In the days of Joiakim, these were the heads of the priestly families:

of Seraiah's family, Meraiah;
of Jeremiah's, Hananiah;
13of Ezra's, Meshullam;
of Amariah's, Jehohanan;
14of Malluch's, Jonathan;
of Shecaniah's,*c* Joseph;
15of Harim's, Adna;
of Meremoth's,*d* Helkai;
16of Iddo's, Zechariah;
of Ginnethon's, Meshullam;
17of Abijah's, Zicri;
of Miniamin's and of Moadiah's, Piltai;
18of Bilgah's, Shammua;
of Shemaiah's, Jehonathan;
19of Joiarib's, Mattenai;
of Jedaiah's, Uzzi;
20of Sallu's, Kallai;
of Amok's, Eber;
21of Hilkiah's, Hashabiah;
of Jedaiah's, Nethanel.

22The family heads of the Levites in the days of Eliashib, Joiada, Johanan and Jaddua, as well as those of the priests, were recorded in the reign of Darius the Persian. 23The family heads among the descendants of Levi up to the time of Johanan son of Eliashib were recorded in the book of the annals. 24And the leaders of the Levites were Hashabiah, Sherebiah, Jeshua son of Kadmiel, and their associates, who stood opposite them to give praise and thanksgiving,

---

1. Have more "saints," or more "sinners," come over for dinner the last year? What does that say about the company you keep? Judging from the company you keep, what's your reputation? 2. Name four clergy types in your community whom you respect. Why those four?

1. In verses 1–7, Nehemiah lists the divisions of priests and Levites returning from Babylonian exile in 538 B.C. What purpose does this dated list serve? 2. In verses 12–21, Nehemiah updates the list to include those priests who are contemporaries of his and peers to Joiakim (v. 26). What do these two lists have in common? What does that say about God's faithfulness and human loyalty across two generations? 3. What effect would the reading of this list have on the Jews about to dedicate the walls of Jerusalem?

1. If you had or have children—how would you like to be remembered by succeeding generations? What one thing are you doing regularly to help assure this happens? 2. Are you a "traditionalist" (loyal to the ways of your parents and their parents)? Or are you a "pioneer" (charting a new course for future generations to follow)? Give one example.

---

a4 Many Hebrew manuscripts and Vulgate (see also Neh. 12:16); most Hebrew manuscripts *Ginnethoi*   *b5* A variant of *Miniamin*   *c14* Very many Hebrew manuscripts, some Septuagint manuscripts and Syriac (see also Neh. 12:3); most Hebrew manuscripts *Shebaniah's*   *d15* Some Septuagint manuscripts (see also Neh. 12:3); Hebrew *Meraioth's*

one section responding to the other, as prescribed by David the man of God.

²⁵Mattaniah, Bakbukiah, Obadiah, Meshullam, Talmon and Akkub were gatekeepers who guarded the storerooms at the gates. ²⁶They served in the days of Joiakim son of Jeshua, the son of Jozadak, and in the days of Nehemiah the governor and of Ezra the priest and scribe.

Dedication of the Wall of Jerusalem

²⁷At the dedication of the wall of Jerusalem, the Levites were sought out from where they lived and were brought to Jerusalem to celebrate joyfully the dedication with songs of thanksgiving and with the music of cymbals, harps and lyres. ²⁸The singers also were brought together from the region around Jerusalem—from the villages of the Netophathites, ²⁹from Beth Gilgal, and from the area of Geba and Azmaveth, for the singers had built villages for themselves around Jerusalem. ³⁰When the priests and Levites had purified themselves ceremonially, they purified the people, the gates and the wall.

³¹I had the leaders of Judah go up on top*ᵃ* of the wall. I also assigned two large choirs to give thanks. One was to proceed on top*ᵇ* of the wall to the right, toward the Dung Gate. ³²Hoshaiah and half the leaders of Judah followed them, ³³along with Azariah, Ezra, Meshullam, ³⁴Judah, Benjamin, Shemaiah, Jeremiah, ³⁵as well as some priests with trumpets, and also Zechariah son of Jonathan, the son of Shemaiah, the son of Mattaniah, the son of Micaiah, the son of Zaccur, the son of Asaph, ³⁶and his associates—Shemaiah, Azarel, Milalai, Gilalai, Maai, Nethanel, Judah and Hanani—with musical instruments ⌊prescribed by⌋ David the man of God. Ezra the scribe led the procession. ³⁷At the Fountain Gate they continued directly up the steps of the City of David on the ascent to the wall and passed above the house of David to the Water Gate on the east.

³⁸The second choir proceeded in the opposite direction. I followed them on top*ᶜ* of the wall, together with half the people—past the Tower of the Ovens to the Broad Wall, ³⁹over the Gate of Ephraim, the Jeshanah*ᵈ* Gate, the Fish Gate, the Tower of Hananel and the Tower of the Hundred, as far as the Sheep Gate. At the Gate of the Guard they stopped.

⁴⁰The two choirs that gave thanks then took their places in the house of God; so did I, together with half the officials, ⁴¹as well as the priests—Eliakim, Maaseiah, Miniamin, Micaiah, Elioenai, Zechariah and Hananiah with their trumpets— ⁴²and also Maaseiah, Shemaiah, Eleazar, Uzzi, Jehohanan, Malkijah, Elam and Ezer. The choirs sang under the direction of Jezrahiah. ⁴³And on that day they offered great sacrifices, rejoicing because God had given them great joy. The women and children also rejoiced. The sound of rejoicing in Jerusalem could be heard far away.

⁴⁴At that time men were appointed to be in charge of the storerooms for the contributions, firstfruits and tithes. From the fields around the towns they were to bring into the storerooms the portions required by the Law for the priests and the Levites, for Judah was pleased with the ministering priests and Levites. ⁴⁵They performed the service of their God and the service of purification, as did also the singers and gatekeepers, according to the commands of David and his son Solomon. ⁴⁶For long ago, in the days of David and Asaph, there had been directors for the singers and for the

1. What's your idea of a "musical extravaganza": (a) 76-trombone parade? (b) 100-piece orchestra? (c) Half-time at the Super Bowl? (d) Boom-box concert? (e) Other? 2. What do you associate with "Thanksgiving" celebrations: (a) Pilgrims? (b) Grandma's? (c) Football? (d) Turkey? (e) Count your blessings? (f) Other?

1. How did the people celebrate the dedication of the wall of Jerusalem? What specific actions did the priests, Levites and singers take? 2. What was the purpose of the processions? Which groups were included? Who led each group? In which direction did they go? If you were there, what would you see? Hear? Feel? If your local media were covering this event for the evening news, what picture stories and interviews would they be sure to get? 3. What happens off-camera in the "house of God" (vv. 40–43)? What mood typifies the dedication ceremony? What modern music pieces would you have assigned to capture that mood? 4. What steps of appreciation do the people take to ensure that those who serve at the temple—priests, Levites, singers, gatekeepers—are cared for (vv. 44–47)?

1. Review Nehemiah's lonely walk around Jerusalem (ch. 2). How does that compare with the grand procession here? What "before" and "after" story could you write from Nehemiah's diary? Have you seen or experienced anything like that in your life? 2. How would you go about thanking God for shoring up the spiritual resources of your life? 3. How are you, like Ezra and Nehemiah, finding, developing and using your gifts to build God's kingdom? Where would your gifts have placed you in their winning team? 4. What steps as an individual and as a community of faith are you taking to care for those who are serving the Lord as "priests, Levites, singers or gatekeepers"?

songs of praise and thanksgiving to God. 47So in the days of Zerub-babel and of Nehemiah, all Israel contributed the daily portions for the singers and gatekeepers. They also set aside the portion for the other Levites, and the Levites set aside the portion for the descendants of Aaron.

Nehemiah's Final Reforms

13 On that day the Book of Moses was read aloud in the hearing of the people and there it was found written that no Ammonite or Moabite should ever be admitted into the assembly of God, 2because they had not met the Israelites with food and water but had hired Balaam to call a curse down on them. (Our God, however, turned the curse into a blessing.) 3When the people heard this law, they excluded from Israel all who were of foreign descent.

4Before this, Eliashib the priest had been put in charge of the storerooms of the house of our God. He was closely associated with Tobiah, 5and he had provided him with a large room formerly used to store the grain offerings and incense and temple articles, and also the tithes of grain, new wine and oil prescribed for the Levites, singers and gatekeepers, as well as the contributions for the priests.

6But while all this was going on, I was not in Jerusalem, for in the thirty-second year of Artaxerxes king of Babylon I had returned to the king. Some time later I asked his permission 7and came back to Jerusalem. Here I learned about the evil thing Eliashib had done in providing Tobiah a room in the courts of the house of God. 8I was greatly displeased and threw all Tobiah's household goods out of the room. 9I gave orders to purify the rooms, and then I put back into them the equipment of the house of God, with the grain offerings and the incense.

10I also learned that the portions assigned to the Levites had not been given to them, and that all the Levites and singers responsible for the service had gone back to their own fields. 11So I rebuked the officials and asked them, "Why is the house of God neglected?" Then I called them together and stationed them at their posts.

12All Judah brought the tithes of grain, new wine and oil into the storerooms. 13I put Shelemiah the priest, Zadok the scribe, and a Levite named Pedaiah in charge of the storerooms and made Hanan son of Zaccur, the son of Mattaniah, their assistant, because these men were considered trustworthy. They were made responsible for distributing the supplies to their brothers.

14Remember me for this, O my God, and do not blot out what I have so faithfully done for the house of my God and its services.

15In those days I saw men in Judah treading winepresses on the Sabbath and bringing in grain and loading it on donkeys, together with wine, grapes, figs and all other kinds of loads. And they were bringing all this into Jerusalem on the Sabbath. Therefore I warned them against selling food on that day. 16Men from Tyre who lived in Jerusalem were bringing in fish and all kinds of merchandise and selling them in Jerusalem on the Sabbath to the people of Judah. 17I rebuked the nobles of Judah and said to them, "What is this wicked thing you are doing—desecrating the Sabbath day? 18Didn't your forefathers do the same things, so that our God brought all this calamity upon us and upon this city? Now you are stirring up more wrath against Israel by desecrating the Sabbath."

19When evening shadows fell on the gates of Jerusalem before the Sabbath, I ordered the doors to be shut and not opened until

1. When told by Mom or Dad, "Pick up your room, or else" what did the "or else" imply? Did your parents ever follow through on their implied threat? How? 2. Who has recently told you, "Clean house": Your boss, parent, room-mate or pastor? What would it mean for you to "clean house" at work, at home, at church, in your heart? 3. What makes "Sunday" different than other days of the week for you?

1. What happened soon after Nehemiah was no longer governing Jerusalem? What five reforms did Nehemiah make upon his return from Babylon, for which he wanted God to "remember" him? 2. What rule had been set up to exclude what Eliashib did? Why do you suppose Eliashib did this "evil thing": (a) "While the cat is away, the mice will play"? (b) What the boss doesn't know won't hurt him? (c) Tobiah is a friend of the family? (d) People are more valued than property? (e) Tobiah wanted "rent money" to pad the temple treasury? 3. Why did Nehemiah act against Tobiah the way he did (vv. 8–9): (a) To settle an old grudge? (b) Temple needed house-cleaning anyway? (c) God's temple servants and services were being neglected? (d) Trust had been broken? 4. What made it necessary for Nehemiah to rectify "neglect of God's house" (vv. 9–13)? 5. What made Sabbath reform necessary? How does common use of sacred things profane God's name, and thus stir up his wrath? 6. Some 25 years before, Ezra dealt with the same problem of intermarriage with foreigners, but quite differently than Nehemiah here (see Ezra 9). How are they different and why? 7. What made marrying foreign women so wicked? What example of this does Nehemiah make of Solomon and Joiada's son?

1. Which of the reforms addressed by Nehemiah needs attention in your society? Which has contributed more to your people drifting away from God: (a) Not regarding the needs, authority or integrity of clergy? (b) Not keeping the Sabbath holy? (c) Not marrying within the faith? 2. How would you

the Sabbath was over. I stationed some of my own men at the gates so that no load could be brought in on the Sabbath day. 20Once or twice the merchants and sellers of all kinds of goods spent the night outside Jerusalem. 21But I warned them and said, "Why do you spend the night by the wall? If you do this again, I will lay hands on you." From that time on they no longer came on the Sabbath. 22Then I commanded the Levites to purify themselves and go and guard the gates in order to keep the Sabbath day holy.

Remember me for this also, O my God, and show mercy to me according to your great love.

23Moreover, in those days I saw men of Judah who had married women from Ashdod, Ammon and Moab. 24Half of their children spoke the language of Ashdod or the language of one of the other peoples, and did not know how to speak the language of Judah. 25I rebuked them and called curses down on them. I beat some of the men and pulled out their hair. I made them take an oath in God's name and said: "You are not to give your daughters in marriage to their sons, nor are you to take their daughters in marriage for your sons or for yourselves. 26Was it not because of marriages like these that Solomon king of Israel sinned? Among the many nations there was no king like him. He was loved by his God, and God made him king over all Israel, but even he was led into sin by foreign women. 27Must we hear now that you too are doing all this terrible wickedness and are being unfaithful to our God by marrying foreign women?"

28One of the sons of Joiada son of Eliashib the high priest was son-in-law to Sanballat the Horonite. And I drove him away from me.

29Remember them, O my God, because they defiled the priestly office and the covenant of the priesthood and of the Levites.

30So I purified the priests and the Levites of everything foreign, and assigned them duties, each to his own task. 31I also made provision for contributions of wood at designated times, and for the firstfruits.

Remember me with favor, O my God.

start "cleaning house" and restoring clergy credibility and Christian marriages? Whose hair would you pull out: Your own (as did Ezra)? Or "theirs" (as did Nehemiah)? 3. How are you like Eliashib, or like the mice who play while the cat is away? What is one way you take advantage of your privileged position or neglect the needy among the community of faith? 4. What is the most important thing you learned from Nehemiah? What life-changing application are you making? 5. What life application would you like God to favorably "remember"? How can the group help you remember to follow through?

INTRODUCTION to
ESTHER

Book Study Outline: If you are using Esther for a study course, here is a 5- or 10-week outline. Use the questions in the margin for your group agenda:

📖 start meeting / 15 min.

📖 read & discuss Bible / 30 min.

♡ close meeting / 15–45 min.

Refer to the Questions and Answers in the front of this Bible for more information.

5-week plan	10-week plan	Personal Reading	Group Study Passage
1	1	1:1–22	1:1–22/Queen Vashti Deposed
	2	2:1–23	2:1–18/Esther Made Queen
2	3	3:1–15	3:1–15/Haman's Evil Plot
	4	4:1–17	4:1–17/Mordecai's Appeal
3	5	5:1–14	5:1–8/Esther's Request
	6	6:1–14	6:1–14/Mordecai Honored
4	7	7:1–10	7:1–10/Haman Hanged
	8	8:1–17	8:1–17/The King's Edict
5	9	9:1–17	9:1–17/The Jews Triumph
	10	9:18–10:3	9:18–32/Purim Celebrated

Author: Unknown. The author was most likely a Jewish nationalist who was a resident of a Persian city. Some suggest that Mordecai is the author.

Date: No earlier than Xerxes (who reigned c.486–465 B.C.), and probably no later than 331 B.C., when the Persian empire fell to Greece.

OLD TESTAMENT FEASTS AND OTHER SACRED DAYS

Sabbath
Ex 20:8–11; 31:12–17; Lev 23:3; Dt 5:12–15
TIME: 7TH DAY

Sabbath Year
Ex 23:10–11; Lev 25:1–7
TIME: 7TH YEAR

Year of Jubilee
Lev 25:8–55; 27:17–24; Nu 36:4
TIME: 50TH YEAR

Passover
Ex 12:1–14; Lev 23:5; Nu 9:1–14; 28:16; Dt 16:1–3a,4b–7
TIME: 1ST MONTH; (ABIB) 14

Unleavened Bread
Ex 12:15–20; 13:3–10; 23:15; 34:18; Lev 23:6–8; Nu 28:17–25;
Dt 16:3b,4a,8
TIME: 1ST MONTH (ABIB) 15–21

Firstfruits
Lev 23:9–14
TIME: 1ST MONTH (ABIB) 16

Weeks (Pentecost) (Harvest)
Ex 23:16a; 34:22a; Lev 23:15–21; Nu 28:26–31; Dt 16:9–12
TIME: 3RD MONTH (SIVAN) 6

Trumpets (later Rosh Hashanah-New Year's Day)
Lev 23:23–25; Nu 29:1–6
TIME: 7TH MONTH (TISHRI) 1

Day of Atonement (Yom Kippur)
Lev 16; 23:26–32; Nu 29:7–11
TIME: 7TH MONTH (TISHRI) 10

Tabernacles (Booths) (Ingathering)
Ex 23:16b; 34:22b; Lev 23:33–36a,39–43; Nu 29:12–34;
Dt 16:13–15; Zec 14:16–19
TIME: 7TH MONTH (TISHRI) 15–21

Sacred Assembly
Lev 23:36b; Nu 29:35–38
TIME: 7TH MONTH (TISHRI) 22

Purim
Est 9:18–32
TIME: 12TH MONTH (ADAR) 14,15

Theme: The providence of God in the free decisions of people, especially in delivering the Jews under Xerxes; also a profile in human courage.

Historical Background: More than a generation had passed since Cyrus defeated the Babylonians and allowed the Jews to return to Israel. Still, many Jews remained spread throughout the known world, making their home among their captors. The book of Esther features some of these expatriates. It is noteworthy that Artaxerxes, the son of Xerxes, was king during Nehemiah's time. He may have been influenced by Queen Esther in his handling of the Jews (see Ne 2:6).

Characteristics: The Book of Esther recounts how the Feast of Purim came to be celebrated—a feast still observed today by Jews in memory of Jehovah's sovereign, providential care of his people. The story revolves around 10 banquets (1:3–4; 1:5–8; 1:9; 2:18; 3:15; 5:1–8; 7:1–10; 8:17; 9:17; 9:18–32). The banquets culminate in the double celebration of the Feast of Purim. Interestingly, the Book of Esther does not directly name Yahweh. This conspicuous lack of any reference to God focuses attention on what he is doing constantly, behind the scenes, to effect deliverance for the Jews. Esther is a literary masterpiece which reads like a modern suspense novel, complete with plot twists, coincidence, irony, intrigue, revenge and plenty of feasting.

Esther

Queen Vashti Deposed

1 This is what happened during the time of Xerxes,[a] the Xerxes who ruled over 127 provinces stretching from India to Cush[b]: [2]At that time King Xerxes reigned from his royal throne in the citadel of Susa, [3]and in the third year of his reign he gave a banquet for all his nobles and officials. The military leaders of Persia and Media, the princes, and the nobles of the provinces were present.

[4]For a full 180 days he displayed the vast wealth of his kingdom and the splendor and glory of his majesty. [5]When these days were over, the king gave a banquet, lasting seven days, in the enclosed garden of the king's palace, for all the people from the least to the greatest, who were in the citadel of Susa. [6]The garden had hangings of white and blue linen, fastened with cords of white linen and purple material to silver rings on marble pillars. There were couches of gold and silver on a mosaic pavement of porphyry, marble, mother-of-pearl and other costly stones. [7]Wine was served in goblets of gold, each one different from the other, and the royal wine was abundant, in keeping with the king's liberality. [8]By the king's command each guest was allowed to drink in his own way, for the king instructed all the wine stewards to serve each man what he wished.

[9]Queen Vashti also gave a banquet for the women in the royal palace of King Xerxes.

[10]On the seventh day, when King Xerxes was in high spirits from wine, he commanded the seven eunuchs who served him—Mehuman, Biztha, Harbona, Bigtha, Abagtha, Zethar and Carcas—[11]to bring before him Queen Vashti, wearing her royal crown, in order to display her beauty to the people and nobles, for she was lovely to look at. [12]But when the attendants delivered the king's command, Queen Vashti refused to come. Then the king became furious and burned with anger.

[13]Since it was customary for the king to consult experts in matters of law and justice, he spoke with the wise men who understood the times [14]and were closest to the king—Carshena, Shethar, Admatha, Tarshish, Meres, Marsena and Memucan, the seven nobles of Persia and Media who had special access to the king and were highest in the kingdom.

[15]"According to law, what must be done to Queen Vashti?" he asked. "She has not obeyed the command of King Xerxes that the eunuchs have taken to her."

[16]Then Memucan replied in the presence of the king and the nobles, "Queen Vashti has done wrong, not only against the king but also against all the nobles and the peoples of all the provinces of King Xerxes. [17]For the queen's conduct will become known to all the women, and so they will despise their husbands and say, 'King Xerxes commanded Queen Vashti to be brought before him, but she would not come.' [18]This very day the Persian and Median women of the nobility who have heard about the queen's conduct will respond to all the king's nobles in the same way. There will be no end of disrespect and discord.

[a]1 Hebrew *Ahasuerus*, a variant of Xerxes' Persian name; here and throughout Esther
[b]1 That is, the upper Nile region

1. Have you thrown a big banquet or an open-house party? What were you celebrating? 2. What is the biggest bash you have attended in the last few years, and who was invited? 3. Whose pictures do you keep in your wallet? Share a few.

1. What might be the occasion for this opulent banquet thrown by King Xerxes (vv. 3–8)? What would warrant a six-month "open-house"? Who is invited? 2. What do you make of all the architectural, fashion, and wine detail given here? What does that tell you about the king's wealth? Popularity? Ego? 3. Why do you think his wife, Queen Vashti, throws a separate party (v. 9)? Why does he send for her (v. 11)? When she refuses, how does the king react? 4. Who advises the king what to do and why? (Note what shape he's in, and that those who "understood the times" were astrologers.) What is their advice? 5. What is at stake here: (a) The king's honor? (b) Male supremacy? (c) Potential anarchy? (d) Obeying authority? 6. What would cause a government to establish a law that could not be repealed (v. 19; 8:8): (a) They were trapping a king in a moment of weakness (v. 10; 2:1)? (b) Keeping women in their place? (c) Trying to preserve "family values"? Explain.

1. With which of the characters do you most identify? Why? Where in your life are you working on: (a) Obeying authority? (b) Mutual respect? (c) Sharing (not showing) your wealth? (d) Being the host with the most? 2. For what grand occasion would you and yours co-host a gala affair: Your 40th birthday? Silver anniversary? Opening a new business? Graduation? 3. What important decision is pending for you? What input from the group would you like for this? 4. In decisions affecting other people, who is your "Memucan"? Who else would you feel free to call in the middle of the night? 5. The nobles feared anarchy would result if women were as "independent" as Vashti. At home, how do you work out disagreements?

¹⁹"Therefore, if it pleases the king, let him issue a royal decree and let it be written in the laws of Persia and Media, which cannot be repealed, that Vashti is never again to enter the presence of King Xerxes. Also let the king give her royal position to someone else who is better than she. ²⁰Then when the king's edict is proclaimed throughout all his vast realm, all the women will respect their husbands, from the least to the greatest."

²¹The king and his nobles were pleased with this advice, so the king did as Memucan proposed. ²²He sent dispatches to all parts of the kingdom, to each province in its own script and to each people in its own language, proclaiming in each people's tongue that every man should be ruler over his own household.

Esther Made Queen

2 Later when the anger of King Xerxes had subsided, he remembered Vashti and what she had done and what he had decreed about her. ²Then the king's personal attendants proposed, "Let a search be made for beautiful young virgins for the king. ³Let the king appoint commissioners in every province of his realm to bring all these beautiful girls into the harem at the citadel of Susa. Let them be placed under the care of Hegai, the king's eunuch, who is in charge of the women; and let beauty treatments be given to them. ⁴Then let the girl who pleases the king be queen instead of Vashti." This advice appealed to the king, and he followed it.

⁵Now there was in the citadel of Susa a Jew of the tribe of Benjamin, named Mordecai son of Jair, the son of Shimei, the son of Kish, ⁶who had been carried into exile from Jerusalem by Nebuchadnezzar king of Babylon, among those taken captive with Jehoi-

1. If invited for a private audience with the prime minister or president, would you go? What might she or he want to talk to you about? What questions would you pose? How would you dress and prepare yourself? 2. What contest have you ever won? Who was your competition?

1. Verse 1 is a hinge verse, spanning four years (see v. 16 and 1:3). In that time, what has happened to the king's anger? His memory? His decree? To Vashti? 2. As this king's search unfolds, how does it compare to the Joseph story (Ge 37–41)? 3. How

Esther 2:1–18　　　　　　　　　**ESTHER MADE QUEEN**

This story takes place in Susa, one of the capital cities of the Persian Empire. King Xerxes has deposed Queen Vashti for refusing a request he had made of her. Introduced in this chapter are Mordecai and Esther—Jews whose ancestors had been taken into exile from Israel years ago.

1. What would you call this search for a new queen?
   a. a beauty pageant
   b. stupid
   c. exciting
   d. chauvinistic
   e. important

2. What would the Persian people call the search for a new queen?
   a. a beauty pageant
   b. stupid
   c. exciting
   d. chauvinistic
   e. important

3. How would you have felt if you were Esther (who had no choice in the matter) about being selected for the king's harem?

   a. flattered　　d. angry
   b. frightened　　e. proud
   c. embarrassed　f. used

4. Why did Mordecai forbid Esther to reveal that she was a Jew?
   a. He was ashamed of the fact.
   b. He was afraid Esther would be disqualified from being queen.
   c. He was afraid Esther would be persecuted.
   d. He liked to run Esther's life.
   e. Something told him it wasn't the right time.

5. Why did Esther abide by Mordecai's request?

6. How would you describe Esther?
   a. charming　　d. respectful
   b. compliant　　e. victimized
   c. humble　　　f. blessed

7. In your relationship with God, how do you feel right now?
   a. chosen　　　e. pleasing
   b. rejected　　　f. compliant
   c. overlooked　g. "feasting"
   d. "cosmetic"　h. joyful

8. How does your child(ren) respond when you forbid him or her to do something?
   a. with happy compliance
   b. with angry compliance
   c. with much argument
   d. with outright defiance

9. As a parent, how can you relate to this story?
   a. I face the challenges of being a "substitute parent."
   b. My child has had a rough life.
   c. My child gets pampered.
   d. My child knows how to get "anything she (or he) wants."
   e. In spite of the circumstances, my child is turning out pretty well.
   f. other: _____

10. What have you appreciated about this group? What need do you feel for ongoing support? Esther was affirmed by others. One person at a time, listen silently while others in the group take turns affirming or blessing you.

achin[a] king of Judah. [7]Mordecai had a cousin named Hadassah, whom he had brought up because she had neither father nor mother. This girl, who was also known as Esther, was lovely in form and features, and Mordecai had taken her as his own daughter when her father and mother died.

[8]When the king's order and edict had been proclaimed, many girls were brought to the citadel of Susa and put under the care of Hegai. Esther also was taken to the king's palace and entrusted to Hegai, who had charge of the harem. [9]The girl pleased him and won his favor. Immediately he provided her with her beauty treatments and special food. He assigned to her seven maids selected from the king's palace and moved her and her maids into the best place in the harem.

[10]Esther had not revealed her nationality and family background, because Mordecai had forbidden her to do so. [11]Every day he walked back and forth near the courtyard of the harem to find out how Esther was and what was happening to her.

[12]Before a girl's turn came to go in to King Xerxes, she had to complete twelve months of beauty treatments prescribed for the women, six months with oil of myrrh and six with perfumes and cosmetics. [13]And this is how she would go to the king: Anything she wanted was given her to take with her from the harem to the king's palace. [14]In the evening she would go there and in the morning return to another part of the harem to the care of Shaashgaz, the king's eunuch who was in charge of the concubines. She would not return to the king unless he was pleased with her and summoned her by name.

[15]When the turn came for Esther (the girl Mordecai had adopted, the daughter of his uncle Abihail) to go to the king, she asked for nothing other than what Hegai, the king's eunuch who was in charge of the harem, suggested. And Esther won the favor of everyone who saw her. [16]She was taken to King Xerxes in the royal residence in the tenth month, the month of Tebeth, in the seventh year of his reign.

[17]Now the king was attracted to Esther more than to any of the other women, and she won his favor and approval more than any of the other virgins. So he set a royal crown on her head and made her queen instead of Vashti. [18]And the king gave a great banquet, Esther's banquet, for all his nobles and officials. He proclaimed a holiday throughout the provinces and distributed gifts with royal liberality.

Mordecai Uncovers a Conspiracy

[19]When the virgins were assembled a second time, Mordecai was sitting at the king's gate. [20]But Esther had kept secret her family background and nationality just as Mordecai had told her to do, for she continued to follow Mordecai's instructions as she had done when he was bringing her up.

[21]During the time Mordecai was sitting at the king's gate, Bigthana[b] and Teresh, two of the king's officers who guarded the doorway, became angry and conspired to assassinate King Xerxes. [22]But Mordecai found out about the plot and told Queen Esther, who in turn reported it to the king, giving credit to Mordecai. [23]And when the report was investigated and found to be true, the two officials were hanged on a gallows.[c] All this was recorded in the book of the annals in the presence of the king.

do Mordecai and Esther fit in to that model? Who are Mordecai's ancestors (1Sa 9:1)? How do Mordecai and Esther relate to each other? How do they fit the man-woman household rule in 1:22? **4.** What might have happened if Esther had not obeyed Mordecai? How did she manage to keep her ethnic background secret from the king? **5.** Of what significance is the year-long preparation period? What in your culture roughly corresponds to it? **6.** Nothing is said here about the morality of Xerxes seizing or sampling the women as he does. Why is that?

1. Where would you fit yourself into this story: A queen fit for a king? A runner-up? A personal attendant? A fretful, fatherly Mordecai? **2.** If you were one of these characters, what would be your best line? **3.** How important is physical attractiveness to you in courting or keeping your mate? **4.** How would you feel if God, as King, took four years to fill a "vacancy" or solve some other problem in your life? How important (to you and God) is time and timing? **5.** If you were chosen queen (or king), what would be the greatest strength or asset you'd bring to your country? Where are you using that gift now?

How good are you at keeping secrets?

Subplots abound: Secrecy, concubines, obedience, assassins! Which one most concerns Xerxes? Mordecai? Esther?

1. Do you see coincidence or providence at work behind these scenes? How so? **2.** In your life, what do you see more of: Fate? Chance? Design? Destiny? Explain.

---

[a]6 Hebrew *Jeconiah*, a variant of *Jehoiachin*   [b]21 Hebrew *Bigthan*, a variant of *Bigthana*   [c]23 Or *were hung* (or *impaled*) *on poles*; similarly elsewhere in Esther

Haman's Plot to Destroy the Jews

3 After these events, King Xerxes honored Haman son of Hammedatha, the Agagite, elevating him and giving him a seat of honor higher than that of all the other nobles. 2All the royal officials at the king's gate knelt down and paid honor to Haman, for the king had commanded this concerning him. But Mordecai would not kneel down or pay him honor.

3Then the royal officials at the king's gate asked Mordecai, "Why do you disobey the king's command?" 4Day after day they spoke to him but he refused to comply. Therefore they told Haman about it to see whether Mordecai's behavior would be tolerated, for he had told them he was a Jew.

5When Haman saw that Mordecai would not kneel down or pay him honor, he was enraged. 6Yet having learned who Mordecai's people were, he scorned the idea of killing only Mordecai. Instead Haman looked for a way to destroy all Mordecai's people, the Jews, throughout the whole kingdom of Xerxes.

7In the twelfth year of King Xerxes, in the first month, the month of Nisan, they cast the *pur* (that is, the lot) in the presence of Haman to select a day and month. And the lot fell on[a] the twelfth month, the month of Adar.

8Then Haman said to King Xerxes, "There is a certain people dispersed and scattered among the peoples in all the provinces of your kingdom whose customs are different from those of all other people and who do not obey the king's laws; it is not in the king's best interest to tolerate them. 9If it pleases the king, let a decree be issued to destroy them, and I will put ten thousand talents[b] of silver into the royal treasury for the men who carry out this business."

10So the king took his signet ring from his finger and gave it to Haman son of Hammedatha, the Agagite, the enemy of the Jews. 11"Keep the money," the king said to Haman, "and do with the people as you please."

12Then on the thirteenth day of the first month the royal secretaries were summoned. They wrote out in the script of each province and in the language of each people all Haman's orders to the king's satraps, the governors of the various provinces and the nobles of the various peoples. These were written in the name of King Xerxes himself and sealed with his own ring. 13Dispatches were sent by couriers to all the king's provinces with the order to destroy, kill and annihilate all the Jews—young and old, women and little children—on a single day, the thirteenth day of the twelfth month, the month of Adar, and to plunder their goods. 14A copy of the text of the edict was to be issued as law in every province and made known to the people of every nationality so they would be ready for that day.

15Spurred on by the king's command, the couriers went out, and the edict was issued in the citadel of Susa. The king and Haman sat down to drink, but the city of Susa was bewildered.

Mordecai Persuades Esther to Help

4 When Mordecai learned of all that had been done, he tore his clothes, put on sackcloth and ashes, and went out into the city, wailing loudly and bitterly. 2But he went only as far as the king's gate, because no one clothed in sackcloth was allowed to enter it. 3In every province to which the edict and order of the king came,

a7 Septuagint; Hebrew does not have *And the lot fell on.* b9 That is, about 375 tons (about 345 metric tons)

there was great mourning among the Jews, with fasting, weeping and wailing. Many lay in sackcloth and ashes.

⁴When Esther's maids and eunuchs came and told her about Mordecai, she was in great distress. She sent clothes for him to put on instead of his sackcloth, but he would not accept them. ⁵Then Esther summoned Hathach, one of the king's eunuchs assigned to attend her, and ordered him to find out what was troubling Mordecai and why.

⁶So Hathach went out to Mordecai in the open square of the city in front of the king's gate. ⁷Mordecai told him everything that had happened to him, including the exact amount of money Haman had promised to pay into the royal treasury for the destruction of the Jews. ⁸He also gave him a copy of the text of the edict for their annihilation, which had been published in Susa, to show to Esther and explain it to her, and he told him to urge her to go into the king's presence to beg for mercy and plead with him for her people.

⁹Hathach went back and reported to Esther what Mordecai had said. ¹⁰Then she instructed him to say to Mordecai, ¹¹"All the king's officials and the people of the royal provinces know that for any man or woman who approaches the king in the inner court without being summoned the king has but one law: that he be put to death. The only exception to this is for the king to extend the gold scepter to him and spare his life. But thirty days have passed since I was called to go to the king."

¹²When Esther's words were reported to Mordecai, ¹³he sent back this answer: "Do not think that because you are in the king's house you alone of all the Jews will escape. ¹⁴For if you remain silent at this time, relief and deliverance for the Jews will arise from another place, but you and your father's family will perish. And who knows but that you have come to royal position for such a time as this?"

¹⁵Then Esther sent this reply to Mordecai: ¹⁶"Go, gather together all the Jews who are in Susa, and fast for me. Do not eat or drink for three days, night or day. I and my maids will fast as you do. When this is done, I will go to the king, even though it is against the law. And if I perish, I perish."

¹⁷So Mordecai went away and carried out all of Esther's instructions.

Esther's Request to the King

5 On the third day Esther put on her royal robes and stood in the inner court of the palace, in front of the king's hall. The king was sitting on his royal throne in the hall, facing the entrance. ²When he saw Queen Esther standing in the court, he was pleased with her and held out to her the gold scepter that was in his hand. So Esther approached and touched the tip of the scepter.

³Then the king asked, "What is it, Queen Esther? What is your request? Even up to half the kingdom, it will be given you."

⁴"If it pleases the king," replied Esther, "let the king, together with Haman, come today to a banquet I have prepared for him."

⁵"Bring Haman at once," the king said, "so that we may do what Esther asks."

So the king and Haman went to the banquet Esther had prepared. ⁶As they were drinking wine, the king again asked Esther, "Now what is your petition? It will be given you. And what is your request? Even up to half the kingdom, it will be granted."

⁷Esther replied, "My petition and my request is this: ⁸If the king regards me with favor and if it pleases the king to grant my petition

scoop"? For your "gossip column"? Would you name your sources? Why or why not? **2.** Mordecai's crying and penitence were culturally accepted (vv. 1,3). As for Esther, what options are open to her as queen? As a Jew? At what cost? **3.** Which option does Esther finally settle on (vv. 15–16)? What hope does she have for success? What else is she feeling? **4.** What does fasting involve? Where is God in this? **5.** Why do you think Mordecai would break his silence about who Esther is? If she remains silent, what hope is there?

1. "If you're not part of the problem or its solution, let's not waste time talking"—How does this quote apply here? How do you feel when *you* are the innocent or helpless third party? **2.** Do you think Esther was either innocent or helpless? What did Mordecai think? **3.** Can you imagine a crisis in which you would go "against the law," as Esther does, to find a solution? **4.** Have you ever fasted? How long? What for? What was the result? How do you show your readiness to do God's will?

1. Did it help to "dress for success" in your last job interview? How so? **2.** When you want someone to do a special favor for you, how do you convince them?

1. "On the third day"—of what? Why is that detail relevant to the plot? **2.** What might be the purpose of Esther's delaying tactics: Fear? Intriguing the king? Buying time? Waiting for him to up his offer? Building suspense for the reader? Or what? **3.** What is the king's response so far to her requests? What does this imply?

1. If any request could be granted, as was done for Esther, for what would you ask? Why that? **2.** What assurances do you have that when you ask God for something, it will be granted?

---

1. As the tension mounts, so do tempers. Why is Haman in "high spirits"? What's the toasting all about? 2. What infuriates Haman most about Mordecai? What irony do you see here (see 3:2–6)? What does this say about Haman? About human nature?

Comparing yourself to Haman, how do you react when someone touches your "hot button"? Are you like a firecracker with a short fuse or a long fuse? Or are you a "dud"—lots of smoke, but no fire?

What brings on sleep the quickest for you: (a) Hard day's work? (b) Hard day's fun? (c) Big meal? (d) Bible reading? (e) Soft music? (f) Watching TV? What delays sleep for you?

1. Ironies abound! What noise might be keeping the king awake (see 5:14)? What does he do when he can't sleep? 2. What other ironies or coincidences do you see in the hidden identity? In the robe? In the friends' counsel? 3. Where do you see the hand of God in all this: In circumstances? Hearts? Humor?

1. What do Haman's pride and racial hatred bring him? What is the object lesson here for church leaders? For yourself? 2. What do Mordecai's meekness and loyalty bring him? What spiritual law do you see at work here? When not recognized for a "good deed," how do you feel? What recognition or rewards matter most to you? 3. In your life, where do you see the "fickle finger of fate" or the "holy hand of God"? How do you know the difference?

and fulfill my request, let the king and Haman come tomorrow to the banquet I will prepare for them. Then I will answer the king's question."

Haman's Rage Against Mordecai

9Haman went out that day happy and in high spirits. But when he saw Mordecai at the king's gate and observed that he neither rose nor showed fear in his presence, he was filled with rage against Mordecai. 10Nevertheless, Haman restrained himself and went home.

Calling together his friends and Zeresh, his wife, 11Haman boasted to them about his vast wealth, his many sons, and all the ways the king had honored him and how he had elevated him above the other nobles and officials. 12"And that's not all," Haman added. "I'm the only person Queen Esther invited to accompany the king to the banquet she gave. And she has invited me along with the king tomorrow. 13But all this gives me no satisfaction as long as I see that Jew Mordecai sitting at the king's gate."

14His wife Zeresh and all his friends said to him, "Have a gallows built, seventy-five feet[a] high, and ask the king in the morning to have Mordecai hanged on it. Then go with the king to the dinner and be happy." This suggestion delighted Haman, and he had the gallows built.

Mordecai Honored

6 That night the king could not sleep; so he ordered the book of the chronicles, the record of his reign, to be brought in and read to him. 2It was found recorded there that Mordecai had exposed Bigthana and Teresh, two of the king's officers who guarded the doorway, who had conspired to assassinate King Xerxes.

3"What honor and recognition has Mordecai received for this?" the king asked.

"Nothing has been done for him," his attendants answered.

4The king said, "Who is in the court?" Now Haman had just entered the outer court of the palace to speak to the king about hanging Mordecai on the gallows he had erected for him.

5His attendants answered, "Haman is standing in the court."

"Bring him in," the king ordered.

6When Haman entered, the king asked him, "What should be done for the man the king delights to honor?"

Now Haman thought to himself, "Who is there that the king would rather honor than me?" 7So he answered the king, "For the man the king delights to honor, 8have them bring a royal robe the king has worn and a horse the king has ridden, one with a royal crest placed on its head. 9Then let the robe and horse be entrusted to one of the king's most noble princes. Let them robe the man the king delights to honor, and lead him on the horse through the city streets, proclaiming before him, 'This is what is done for the man the king delights to honor!' "

10"Go at once," the king commanded Haman. "Get the robe and the horse and do just as you have suggested for Mordecai the Jew, who sits at the king's gate. Do not neglect anything you have recommended."

11So Haman got the robe and the horse. He robed Mordecai, and led him on horseback through the city streets, proclaiming before him, "This is what is done for the man the king delights to honor!"

a14 Hebrew *fifty cubits* (about 23 meters)

¹²Afterward Mordecai returned to the king's gate. But Haman rushed home, with his head covered in grief, ¹³and told Zeresh his wife and all his friends everything that had happened to him.

His advisers and his wife Zeresh said to him, "Since Mordecai, before whom your downfall has started, is of Jewish origin, you cannot stand against him—you will surely come to ruin!" ¹⁴While they were still talking with him, the king's eunuchs arrived and hurried Haman away to the banquet Esther had prepared.

Haman Hanged

7 So the king and Haman went to dine with Queen Esther, ²and as they were drinking wine on that second day, the king again asked, "Queen Esther, what is your petition? It will be given you. What is your request? Even up to half the kingdom, it will be granted."

³Then Queen Esther answered, "If I have found favor with you, O king, and if it pleases your majesty, grant me my life—this is my petition. And spare my people—this is my request. ⁴For I and my people have been sold for destruction and slaughter and annihilation. If we had merely been sold as male and female slaves, I would have kept quiet, because no such distress would justify disturbing the king.ᵃ"

⁵King Xerxes asked Queen Esther, "Who is he? Where is the man who has dared to do such a thing?"

⁶Esther said, "The adversary and enemy is this vile Haman."

Then Haman was terrified before the king and queen. ⁷The king

ᵃ4 Or *quiet, but the compensation our adversary offers cannot be compared with the loss the king would suffer*

"Make your words sweet, you may have to eat them some day"—When have you seen the truth of that proverb in your life?

1. "The king asked again" (v. 2) implies a previous inquiry. When? Why? What has led up to this dramatic banquet? **2.** What does it reveal about Esther's character: (a) Self-preservation? (b) Selfless loyalty? (c) Royal respect? (d) Sweet revenge? **3.** What about Haman is "vile"? Foolish? Pitiful? Pitiless? **4.** What role does Harbona play (v. 9; see 1:10)? **5.** While this chapter ends with Haman's death, what issues remain unresolved?

1. If you were Esther, would you have handled the situation any differently? How so? **2.** When have you stepped out in

---

 Esther 4:6–17; 7:1–10   **ESTHER ACTS FOR HER PEOPLE**

Beautiful young Esther has been chosen to be the new queen of Persia. Haman, an official who despised Jews in general and Mordecai (Esther's cousin and adopted father) in particular, has just persuaded King Xerxes to order the annihilation of all the Jews in the empire. Though Mordecai earlier instructed Esther not to reveal she was a Jew, when he learns of Haman's plot he challenges her to act on behalf of their people.

1. How did Esther respond to Mordecai's first message?
   a. with fear   d. with honesty
   b. with faith   e. with caution
   c. with open eyes

2. How did Mordecai respond back?
   a. "You are our only hope."
   b. "Buck up!"
   c. "Look at the opportunity you have."
   d. "If you don't risk your life now, you'll lose it later."
   e. "If God doesn't use you, he'll use someone else."
   f. "The ball's in your court."

3. What was Esther feeling as she made the decision to go to the king?
   a. fear   d. hope
   b. faith   e. resignation
   c. humility   f. inadequacy

4. The king *did* receive Esther when she voluntarily approached him (5:1–3). What did Esther's eventual appeal in chapter 7 say about her?
   a. She was interested in herself.
   b. She was most interested in her people.
   c. She was out for revenge.
   d. Her strategy was ingenious.
   e. She knew how to get what she wanted.

5. What's the moral of this story?
   a. Everything will come out all right in the end.
   b. One person *can* make a difference.
   c. No guts—no glory.
   d. What goes around comes around.
   e. Whatever will be will be.
   f. Prayer changes things.

6. When have you stepped out in faith like Esther did? What was at stake? How did things turn out?

7. How do you respond to a crisis?
   a. with fear   d. with prayer
   b. with faith   e. with action
   c. with worry   f. with inaction

8. How do you prepare to do God's will when it isn't easy? Have you ever fasted? Why? With what result?

9. How did Esther most clearly demonstrate wisdom?
   a. the way she respected Mordecai
   b. the way she followed her adopted father's instructions
   c. the way she called for a fast
   d. the way she approached the king

10. What situations or circumstances make it most difficult for you to be assertive? What would make it easier for you to "speak up"?

11. In what area of your life do you desire more wisdom? Where would you like more boldness?

faith, as she did? What was at stake? **3.** What enemy threatens you and your goals or your church and its goals: Prejudice? Apathy? Politics? People like Harbona? **4.** What lesson does Haman's life teach you?

What is the toughest part of seeking a raise: (a) The asking? (b) The amount? (c) Waiting for an answer? When have you had to do that? What answer did you get? How will you approach the boss next time?

1. "It's all over but the shouting"—How might that gleeful commentary from the sports world fit this chapter? What is almost over? What's the shouting all about? **2.** Before the victors dispatch Haman's estate (vv. 1–2; see 5:11), what must be dispatched first? Why the anguish for Esther, who is now quite secure in the king's favor (vv. 1–6)? What is the problem with getting the king to reverse the death sentence on the Jews (v. 8)? **3.** What does the new edict do for the Jews? For others? What seems like "deja vu" or "same song, second verse" about this edict (see 1:19; 3:1–4:3; 6:10)? What is particularly symmetrical about its timing (v. 12; see 3:7,13)? **4.** Verse 17 starts a new theme song. What is it? What is the principle for evangelism here?

1. The Jews had nine months to prepare their defense (vv. 9–12). What could you accomplish in the next nine months that would put your life in better order? What part of that re-ordering will you do this month? **2.** If you were in a position to destroy your enemy without fear of the consequences to you, would you take advantage of the situation? Why or why not? **3.** If the rules of the game are switched on you at halftime, how do you react: (a) Cry foul? (b) Suit up for battle anyway? (c) If you can't fight 'em, join 'em? When have you faced such a dilemma? **4.** Would the way you react to the good things in your

---

got up in a rage, left his wine and went out into the palace garden. But Haman, realizing that the king had already decided his fate, stayed behind to beg Queen Esther for his life.

8Just as the king returned from the palace garden to the banquet hall, Haman was falling on the couch where Esther was reclining.

The king exclaimed, "Will he even molest the queen while she is with me in the house?"

As soon as the word left the king's mouth, they covered Haman's face. 9Then Harbona, one of the eunuchs attending the king, said, "A gallows seventy-five feet[a] high stands by Haman's house. He had it made for Mordecai, who spoke up to help the king."

The king said, "Hang him on it!" 10So they hanged Haman on the gallows he had prepared for Mordecai. Then the king's fury subsided.

The King's Edict in Behalf of the Jews

8 That same day King Xerxes gave Queen Esther the estate of Haman, the enemy of the Jews. And Mordecai came into the presence of the king, for Esther had told how he was related to her. 2The king took off his signet ring, which he had reclaimed from Haman, and presented it to Mordecai. And Esther appointed him over Haman's estate.

3Esther again pleaded with the king, falling at his feet and weeping. She begged him to put an end to the evil plan of Haman the Agagite, which he had devised against the Jews. 4Then the king extended the gold scepter to Esther and she arose and stood before him.

5"If it pleases the king," she said, "and if he regards me with favor and thinks it the right thing to do, and if he is pleased with me, let an order be written overruling the dispatches that Haman son of Hammedatha, the Agagite, devised and wrote to destroy the Jews in all the king's provinces. 6For how can I bear to see disaster fall on my people? How can I bear to see the destruction of my family?"

7King Xerxes replied to Queen Esther and to Mordecai the Jew, "Because Haman attacked the Jews, I have given his estate to Esther, and they have hanged him on the gallows. 8Now write another decree in the king's name in behalf of the Jews as seems best to you, and seal it with the king's signet ring—for no document written in the king's name and sealed with his ring can be revoked."

9At once the royal secretaries were summoned—on the twenty-third day of the third month, the month of Sivan. They wrote out all Mordecai's orders to the Jews, and to the satraps, governors and nobles of the 127 provinces stretching from India to Cush.[b] These orders were written in the script of each province and the language of each people and also to the Jews in their own script and language. 10Mordecai wrote in the name of King Xerxes, sealed the dispatches with the king's signet ring, and sent them by mounted couriers, who rode fast horses especially bred for the king.

11The king's edict granted the Jews in every city the right to assemble and protect themselves; to destroy, kill and annihilate any armed force of any nationality or province that might attack them and their women and children; and to plunder the property of their enemies. 12The day appointed for the Jews to do this in all the provinces of King Xerxes was the thirteenth day of the twelfth

---

a 9 Hebrew *fifty cubits* (about 23 meters)   *b 9* That is, the upper Nile region

month, the month of Adar. [13]A copy of the text of the edict was to be issued as law in every province and made known to the people of every nationality so that the Jews would be ready on that day to avenge themselves on their enemies.

[14]The couriers, riding the royal horses, raced out, spurred on by the king's command. And the edict was also issued in the citadel of Susa.

[15]Mordecai left the king's presence wearing royal garments of blue and white, a large crown of gold and a purple robe of fine linen. And the city of Susa held a joyous celebration. [16]For the Jews it was a time of happiness and joy, gladness and honor. [17]In every province and in every city, wherever the edict of the king went, there was joy and gladness among the Jews, with feasting and celebrating. And many people of other nationalities became Jews because fear of the Jews had seized them.

Triumph of the Jews

9 On the thirteenth day of the twelfth month, the month of Adar, the edict commanded by the king was to be carried out. On this day the enemies of the Jews had hoped to overpower them, but now the tables were turned and the Jews got the upper hand over those who hated them. [2]The Jews assembled in their cities in all the provinces of King Xerxes to attack those seeking their destruction. No one could stand against them, because the people of all the other nationalities were afraid of them. [3]And all the nobles of the provinces, the satraps, the governors and the king's administrators helped the Jews, because fear of Mordecai had seized them. [4]Mordecai was prominent in the palace; his reputation spread throughout the provinces, and he became more and more powerful.

[5]The Jews struck down all their enemies with the sword, killing and destroying them, and they did what they pleased to those who hated them. [6]In the citadel of Susa, the Jews killed and destroyed five hundred men. [7]They also killed Parshandatha, Dalphon, Aspatha, [8]Poratha, Adalia, Aridatha, [9]Parmashta, Arisai, Aridai and Vaizatha, [10]the ten sons of Haman son of Hammedatha, the enemy of the Jews. But they did not lay their hands on the plunder.

[11]The number of those slain in the citadel of Susa was reported to the king that same day. [12]The king said to Queen Esther, "The Jews have killed and destroyed five hundred men and the ten sons of Haman in the citadel of Susa. What have they done in the rest of the king's provinces? Now what is your petition? It will be given you. What is your request? It will also be granted."

[13]"If it pleases the king," Esther answered, "give the Jews in Susa permission to carry out this day's edict tomorrow also, and let Haman's ten sons be hanged on gallows."

[14]So the king commanded that this be done. An edict was issued in Susa, and they hanged the ten sons of Haman. [15]The Jews in Susa came together on the fourteenth day of the month of Adar, and they put to death in Susa three hundred men, but they did not lay their hands on the plunder.

[16]Meanwhile, the remainder of the Jews who were in the king's provinces also assembled to protect themselves and get relief from their enemies. They killed seventy-five thousand of them but did not lay their hands on the plunder. [17]This happened on the thirteenth day of the month of Adar, and on the fourteenth they rested and made it a day of feasting and joy.

life give honor to God and convert anyone to the Christian faith? Why or why not?

1. What have you won (a job, a game, a mate, an appeal) that you were not expected to win? Did you crow about it? Make others eat humble pie? Or what? 2. How often do you cheer for the "underdog"? The "topdog"? When on top, do you ever "pour it on"? Why or why not?

1. To what do you compare the distinct *tone* of this chapter: (a) Nostalgic newsreel of WW II? (b) Teaser for an upcoming horror show? (c) Notes on the jacket of a war novel? (d) Other? 2. How and why were the Jews able to triumph? Who "turned the tables"? When the Jews got the upper hand, how did they handle it: Cruelly? Mercifully? As expected in war? 3. In what sense is this defeat of the Amalekites the very antithesis of what happened in 1 Samuel 15? Why do the Jews seem intent this time to "take no prisoners" and "take no plunder" (vv. 10,15,16)? 4. What does this chapter reveal about the character of Esther? Of God?

1. When might "winning the battle" mean "losing the war"? When might "going easy" on the defeated enemy only invite their revenge later? How do you know the difference? 2. When have you had the tables turned on you? How did that feel? What did you learn from that? 3. How do you square this story of annihilating and humiliating one's enemy with what Jesus stood for: namely, to "love your enemy"? Would it make a difference to you if it were "kill or be killed"? When, if ever, have you faced such a dilemma?

1. What national day of celebration do you enjoy the most? What makes it so special? **2.** Birthdays aside, which event in your life is an annual personal day of celebration? Why?

1. *Purim* is a most revered Jewish festival, celebrated to this day. Why is that? How was it first established? Where did it get its name? **2.** Why is *Purim* celebrated for two days (v. 27)? What customs make *Purim* different from the other feast days of the Jews (see chart in Introduction)? **3.** In recounting the story (vv. 23–28), why do you suppose the narrator chose to start with Haman's plot, instead of "at the beginning," with Esther's rise to prominence in a foreign monarchy (reminiscent of Joseph)?

1. What event in your life has turned sorrow into joy? How have you commemorated that event? How have you shared it with others so that they could join you? **2.** *Purim* is "a day for giving … to one another and … the poor." What prompts you to give to others, especially the poor: Times of tragedy? Only at Christmas? More often than that? How regularly? **3.** What traditions or national customs do you observe regularly as a family? Who joins you from outside the family? Have these traditions gained new meaning, or lost all meaning, over the years? How so? **4.** What "relief from your enemies" have you received lately? What relief are you still seeking? How can your group be a "relief agency" for you and others?

1. What is the central theological point of this book? **2.** Why would a book so obviously Jewish be devoid of any reference to the Lord? **3.** Is the God-story of Esther and Mordecai better suited to its purpose if they are seen as obedient servants of God, or as unknowingly used by a sovereign God?

Purim Celebrated

[18]The Jews in Susa, however, had assembled on the thirteenth and fourteenth, and then on the fifteenth they rested and made it a day of feasting and joy.

[19]That is why rural Jews—those living in villages—observe the fourteenth of the month of Adar as a day of joy and feasting, a day for giving presents to each other.

[20]Mordecai recorded these events, and he sent letters to all the Jews throughout the provinces of King Xerxes, near and far, [21]to have them celebrate annually the fourteenth and fifteenth days of the month of Adar [22]as the time when the Jews got relief from their enemies, and as the month when their sorrow was turned into joy and their mourning into a day of celebration. He wrote them to observe the days as days of feasting and joy and giving presents of food to one another and gifts to the poor.

[23]So the Jews agreed to continue the celebration they had begun, doing what Mordecai had written to them. [24]For Haman son of Hammedatha, the Agagite, the enemy of all the Jews, had plotted against the Jews to destroy them and had cast the *pur* (that is, the lot) for their ruin and destruction. [25]But when the plot came to the king's attention,[a] he issued written orders that the evil scheme Haman had devised against the Jews should come back onto his own head, and that he and his sons should be hanged on the gallows. [26](Therefore these days were called Purim, from the word *pur.*) Because of everything written in this letter and because of what they had seen and what had happened to them, [27]the Jews took it upon themselves to establish the custom that they and their descendants and all who join them should without fail observe these two days every year, in the way prescribed and at the time appointed. [28]These days should be remembered and observed in every generation by every family, and in every province and in every city. And these days of Purim should never cease to be celebrated by the Jews, nor should the memory of them die out among their descendants.

[29]So Queen Esther, daughter of Abihail, along with Mordecai the Jew, wrote with full authority to confirm this second letter concerning Purim. [30]And Mordecai sent letters to all the Jews in the 127 provinces of the kingdom of Xerxes—words of goodwill and assurance— [31]to establish these days of Purim at their designated times, as Mordecai the Jew and Queen Esther had decreed for them, and as they had established for themselves and their descendants in regard to their times of fasting and lamentation. [32]Esther's decree confirmed these regulations about Purim, and it was written down in the records.

The Greatness of Mordecai

10 King Xerxes imposed tribute throughout the empire, to its distant shores. [2]And all his acts of power and might, together with a full account of the greatness of Mordecai to which the king had raised him, are they not written in the book of the annals of the kings of Media and Persia? [3]Mordecai the Jew was second in rank to King Xerxes, preeminent among the Jews, and held in high esteem by his many fellow Jews, because he worked for the good of his people and spoke up for the welfare of all the Jews.

a25 Or *when Esther came before the king*

INTRODUCTION to

JOB

Book Study Outline: If you are using Job for a study course, here is a 7- or 13-week outline. Use the questions in the margin for your group agenda:

🫖 start meeting / 15 min.

📖 read & discuss Bible / 30 min.

♡ close meeting / 15–45 min.

Refer to the Questions and Answers in the front of this Bible for more information.

Author: Not Job himself, but an Israelite who is otherwise unknown.

7-week plan	13-week plan	Personal Reading	Group Study Passage
1	1	1	1:1–22/Job's First Test
	2	2	2:1–10/Job's Second Test
2	3	3–5	3:1–26/Job's Misery
	4	6–8	8:1–22/Job Must Have Sinned
3	5	9–11	11:1–20/Job Is Self-Deceived
	6	12–15	13:1–28/Job Is Misunderstood
4	7	16–18	16:1–22/Job Finds No Relief
	8	19–22	21:1–34/Job Ponders the Wicked
5	9	23–25	25:1–6/Job: A Mere Worm?
	10	26–31	31:1–40/"I Am Innocent!"
6	11	32–37	32:1–33/Job Must Be Guilty
	12	38–41	40:1–24/God Reveals His Glory
7	13	42	42:7–17/Job Is Restored

Date: The events described may have taken place in the patriarchal age, but the book was probably not written in its present form until much later, possibly 600–400 B.C.

Theme: The justice of God in the light of human suffering.

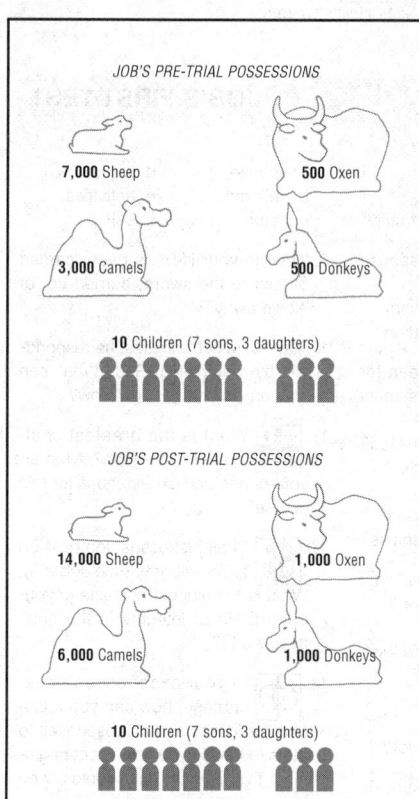

JOB'S PRE-TRIAL POSSESSIONS

7,000 Sheep

500 Oxen

3,000 Camels

500 Donkeys

10 Children (7 sons, 3 daughters)

JOB'S POST-TRIAL POSSESSIONS

14,000 Sheep

1,000 Oxen

6,000 Camels

1,000 Donkeys

10 Children (7 sons, 3 daughters)

Historical Background: Since there is little significant detail given, the precise situation cannot be established with certainty.

Characteristics: The opening verses set the stage for this well-crafted drama. Job is a wealthy, leading citizen, reputed to be very wise. When he loses herds, house and family and is struck down with a painful illness, we see an example in one life of the forms of suffering which afflict so many in our world. As a clue to Job's apparent alienation from God, the reader is shown that Satan, as accuser, is actively driving a wedge between God and his beloved. If Job proves to be righteous only because "it pays," then Satan wins his bet with God. Job's friends do not have the benefit of this insight, but their theology (and Job's) is quite biblical: (1) God is almighty; (2) God is just; (3) No human is entirely innocent in God's eyes. Therefore, say his friends, Job's suffering must be retribution for some sin—a logical answer, but not at all consoling to Job in his despair. Finally, all are silenced, as God breaks in, but he gives no "solution" except to point to his greatness, glory and power. For the most profound insight, we turn to the Cross where God takes on himself human suffering and thus defeats it forever—a solution only hinted at in the book of Job.

Job

Prologue

1 In the land of Uz there lived a man whose name was Job. This man was blameless and upright; he feared God and shunned evil. ²He had seven sons and three daughters, ³and he owned seven thousand sheep, three thousand camels, five hundred yoke of oxen and five hundred donkeys, and had a large number of servants. He was the greatest man among all the people of the East.

⁴His sons used to take turns holding feasts in their homes, and they would invite their three sisters to eat and drink with them. ⁵When a period of feasting had run its course, Job would send and have them purified. Early in the morning he would sacrifice a burnt offering for each of them, thinking, "Perhaps my children have sinned and cursed God in their hearts." This was Job's regular custom.

Job's First Test

⁶One day the angels[a] came to present themselves before the LORD, and Satan[b] also came with them. ⁷The LORD said to Satan, "Where have you come from?"

[a]6 Hebrew *the sons of God*   [b]6 *Satan* means *accuser.*

What makes you "healthy"? "Wealthy"? And "wise"?

1. What does it mean that Job is "blameless and upright" (vv. 1,8)? That he: (a) fears God? (b) shuns evil? (c) is sinless (see 6:24; 7:21)? (d) is fulfilled (as the number 3 and 7 suggest)? (e) is pure as the whitest snow? **2.** Job regularly sacrifices to God, while his children feast (vv. 4–5). What does that suggest?

---

1. "When it rains, it pours"— to what scenario in your life might that saying refer? **2.** "The devil made me do it"—when have you used or heard that excuse recently?

 Job 1:1–22   **JOB'S FIRST TEST**

---

1. What impresses you about Job?
   a. his wealth
   b. his faith
   c. his religious observance
   d. his restraint
   e. his acceptance of loss

2. Had you been Job, how would you have reacted after all these losses?
   a. If any more messengers come, I'm not home!
   b. I must have done something to make God really mad.
   c. There is no God!
   d. If all can be lost so quickly I can't be attached to anything or anyone.
   e. The Lord gave and has taken away; may his name be praised.

3. How did Satan choose Job?
   a. Job posed the greatest challenge.
   b. Job would least expect trouble.
   c. God put Satan up to it.
   d. Job had the most to lose.
   e. God had the most to lose.

4. How did Job view his possessions?
   a. the fruit of his labor
   b. the result of an upright life
   c. gifts from God
   d. of little real value
   e. meaningless compared to family

5. How do you react to Job's response to his misfortune?
   a. disbelief   c. skepticism
   b. curiosity   d. admiration

6. What exactly did this test mean for Job? (And which question is most pressing for you?)
   a. Do I love anything more than God?
   b. Am I strong in spiritual battle?
   c. Is God my friend or foe?
   d. Do I blame God for my losses?
   e. Do I love God just for the benefits?

7. If you lost everything in a day, what would be your biggest question?
   a. Why me?
   b. How could I have prevented this?
   c. What can I learn from this?
   d. Where is God?
   e. How can I recover?
   f. What will my insurance cover?

8. Sometimes I wonder if I really do love God more than my:

   a. spouse.   d. work.
   b. children.   e. activities.
   c. home.   f. self.

9. What in your life has been "carried off, put to the sword, burned up, or blown away"?

10. After all of Job's losses, he responded by worshiping God. What can you praise God for right now?

11. What is the greatest challenge to your faith? What are your hopes and expectations for this course?

12. In all his losses Job held on to his integrity (see Job 2:9). What is the biggest obstacle to your living a life of integrity in the business world?

13. In your experience of miscarriage, how can you relate to Job's losses and his responses to them? How do you feel about beginning this course for couples who have suffered a miscarriage?

Satan answered the LORD, "From roaming through the earth and going back and forth in it."

[8]Then the LORD said to Satan, "Have you considered my servant Job? There is no one on earth like him; he is blameless and upright, a man who fears God and shuns evil."

[9]"Does Job fear God for nothing?" Satan replied. [10]"Have you not put a hedge around him and his household and everything he has? You have blessed the work of his hands, so that his flocks and herds are spread throughout the land. [11]But stretch out your hand and strike everything he has, and he will surely curse you to your face."

[12]The LORD said to Satan, "Very well, then, everything he has is in your hands, but on the man himself do not lay a finger."

Then Satan went out from the presence of the LORD.

[13]One day when Job's sons and daughters were feasting and drinking wine at the oldest brother's house, [14]a messenger came to Job and said, "The oxen were plowing and the donkeys were grazing nearby, [15]and the Sabeans attacked and carried them off. They put the servants to the sword, and I am the only one who has escaped to tell you!"

[16]While he was still speaking, another messenger came and said, "The fire of God fell from the sky and burned up the sheep and the servants, and I am the only one who has escaped to tell you!"

[17]While he was still speaking, another messenger came and said, "The Chaldeans formed three raiding parties and swept down on your camels and carried them off. They put the servants to the sword, and I am the only one who has escaped to tell you!"

[18]While he was still speaking, yet another messenger came and said, "Your sons and daughters were feasting and drinking wine at the oldest brother's house, [19]when suddenly a mighty wind swept in from the desert and struck the four corners of the house. It collapsed on them and they are dead, and I am the only one who has escaped to tell you!"

[20]At this, Job got up and tore his robe and shaved his head. Then he fell to the ground in worship [21]and said:

> "Naked I came from my mother's womb,
>   and naked I will depart.[a]
> The LORD gave and the LORD has taken away;
>   may the name of the LORD be praised."

[22]In all this, Job did not sin by charging God with wrongdoing.

Job's Second Test

2 On another day the angels[b] came to present themselves before the LORD, and Satan also came with them to present himself before him. [2]And the LORD said to Satan, "Where have you come from?"

Satan answered the LORD, "From roaming through the earth and going back and forth in it."

[3]Then the LORD said to Satan, "Have you considered my servant Job? There is no one on earth like him; he is blameless and upright, a man who fears God and shuns evil. And he still maintains his integrity, though you incited me against him to ruin him without any reason."

---

1. What's so unusual about the opening set for this drama? How does that set the stage for the rest of the book? 2. How are the major characters in this drama depicted: God? Satan? Job? Messengers? 3. What action takes place "off stage"? What do the four disasters have in common? 4. What does it mean that the Lord, not Satan, initiates the testing of Job? What limits does God place on Satan? 5. What does Satan want to prove? What does it mean to put a "hedge" around Job? Whose integrity is really at stake here: Job's? Satan's? God's? 6. How does Job score on this first test (vv. 20–22)? How is his faith evident?

1. What in Job's response strikes you as most extraordinary? How would you have responded to similar circumstances? 2. What about the nature of the test do you take exception to? What standards of "fairness" or "human rights" apply to this? 3. If no evil can happen to man apart from God's tacit permission, what problems does that raise for you? (For similar "test cases," compare 1Ch 21:1 with 2Sa 24:1; see 1Sa 16:14; 2Sa 24:16; 1Co 5:5; 2Co 12:7)? How is Job's temptation like and unlike Jesus' temptation?

1. Who is your favorite TV courtroom attorney? Your favorite TV judge? What do you like about them? 2. What experience have you had in court as a witness, defendant or plaintiff?

1. In this heavenly courtroom scene, how would you characterize the defendant? His wife? The prosecuting attorney? The judge? The three witnesses? 2. How does this judge respond to the tactics of the accuser and the rights of the defendant the first time around (v. 3)? And the second time

---

[a]21 Or *will return there*   [b]1 Hebrew *the sons of God*

(vv. 4–6)? Is Satan still on a leash, or given more free reign? **3.** What part does Job's wife play in this courtroom scene? If Job did curse God, what would that prove about Job? About God? About Satan? **4.** Instead, how does Job respond? How do his three friends respond? What do you find commendable in their responses?

♡ **1.** In tests 1 and 2, is Job on trial, or is God in the dock? Why? **2.** Recall the last time you "sat among the ashes." What questions were you asking God then? Who else listened to you? What answers did you get? **3.** When bad things happen to good people, whom do you blame? **4.** When are you most comfortable with silence? Why? When is silence more preferable, even more powerful, than words?

⁴"Skin for skin!" Satan replied. "A man will give all he has for his own life. ⁵But stretch out your hand and strike his flesh and bones, and he will surely curse you to your face."

⁶The LORD said to Satan, "Very well, then, he is in your hands; but you must spare his life."

⁷So Satan went out from the presence of the LORD and afflicted Job with painful sores from the soles of his feet to the top of his head. ⁸Then Job took a piece of broken pottery and scraped himself with it as he sat among the ashes.

⁹His wife said to him, "Are you still holding on to your integrity? Curse God and die!"

¹⁰He replied, "You are talking like a foolish*a* woman. Shall we accept good from God, and not trouble?"

In all this, Job did not sin in what he said.

Job's Three Friends

¹¹When Job's three friends, Eliphaz the Temanite, Bildad the Shuhite and Zophar the Naamathite, heard about all the troubles that had come upon him, they set out from their homes and met together by agreement to go and sympathize with him and comfort him. ¹²When they saw him from a distance, they could hardly recognize him; they began to weep aloud, and they tore their robes and sprinkled dust on their heads. ¹³Then they sat on the ground with him for seven days and seven nights. No one said a word to him, because they saw how great his suffering was.

a10 The Hebrew word rendered *foolish* denotes moral deficiency.

      Job 2:1–10   **JOB'S SECOND TEST**

God has already allowed Satan to attack everything Job had except Job himself. As a result, Job lost his possessions and all 10 of his children.

1. Why did God allow Satan to afflict Job again?
   a. to prove Satan was wrong
   b. to punish Job
   c. to test Job
   d. to strengthen Job
   e. God couldn't prevent it.
   f. It's a mystery.

2. This story shows that Satan:
   a. knows what's happening on earth.
   b. knows what's going on in heaven.
   c. accuses believers.
   d. has little power.
   e. has great power.
   f. is limited by God.

3. What was Job's wife saying?
   a. what Satan wanted Job to hear
   b. "Look where your integrity has gotten you."
   c. "Be honest with your feelings."
   d. "Curse God so you can die."
   e. "It's too late for integrity."

4. After this, some friends came to "comfort" Job. What would you have said or done to help Job?

5. How could Job make such strong statements of faith (Job 1:21, 2:10) after such tragedies?
   a. What happened to him hadn't really sunk in yet.
   b. His faith in God was all he had left.
   c. He thought if he were faithful, God would give everything back.
   d. It was ingrained in him from a life-time of faith-training.
   e. It shows this is fiction—no real person would respond that way!

6. What happened the last time your faith was seriously tested?
   a. I flunked.
   b. I quit before I finished.
   c. I passed after remedial work.
   d. I did about average.
   e. I passed with flying colors.

7. What do you need to do to be ready for the next test?
   a. study more
   b. work on my priorities

   c. take out some insurance
   d. know that God is with me

8. What trouble or suffering are you going through right now? What are you thinking as you "sit among the ashes"? If you could appear before God's heavenly council, what question would you ask?

9. Do you think Job had actually come to the place of accepting his losses (see Job 1:20–21 and 2:10)? What, if anything, keeps you from accepting *your* loss?

10. In light of the suffering you've experienced or observed in others, do you find yourself feeling more like Job or his wife? How can you keep trusting God even when the end isn't in sight?

11. How do you think Job was able to maintain such a positive perspective about living with pain? What is one step you can take to move in that direction?

Job Speaks

3 After this, Job opened his mouth and cursed the day of his birth. ²He said:

³"May the day of my birth perish,
   and the night it was said, 'A boy is born!'
⁴That day—may it turn to darkness;
   may God above not care about it;
   may no light shine upon it.
⁵May darkness and deep shadow^a claim it once
      more;
   may a cloud settle over it;
   may blackness overwhelm its light.
⁶That night—may thick darkness seize it;
   may it not be included among the days of the
      year
   nor be entered in any of the months.
⁷May that night be barren;
   may no shout of joy be heard in it.
⁸May those who curse days^b curse that day,
   those who are ready to rouse Leviathan.
⁹May its morning stars become dark;
   may it wait for daylight in vain
   and not see the first rays of dawn,
¹⁰for it did not shut the doors of the womb on me
   to hide trouble from my eyes.

¹¹"Why did I not perish at birth,
   and die as I came from the womb?
¹²Why were there knees to receive me
   and breasts that I might be nursed?
¹³For now I would be lying down in peace;
   I would be asleep and at rest
¹⁴with kings and counselors of the earth,
   who built for themselves places now lying in
      ruins,
¹⁵with rulers who had gold,
   who filled their houses with silver.
¹⁶Or why was I not hidden in the ground like a
      stillborn child,
   like an infant who never saw the light of day?
¹⁷There the wicked cease from turmoil,
   and there the weary are at rest.
¹⁸Captives also enjoy their ease;
   they no longer hear the slave driver's shout.
¹⁹The small and the great are there,
   and the slave is freed from his master.

²⁰"Why is light given to those in misery,
   and life to the bitter of soul,
²¹to those who long for death that does not come,
   who search for it more than for hidden
      treasure,
²²who are filled with gladness
   and rejoice when they reach the grave?
²³Why is life given to a man
   whose way is hidden,
   whom God has hedged in?
²⁴For sighing comes to me instead of food;

---

1. Imagine if your closest family member or friend had never been born—how would your life be different? 2. What day qualifies as worst day of your life? Explain briefly.

1. Note the change in the text from prose to poetry. What does this change mean? Should poetry be interpreted just like prose, or are the rules different? 2. After *what* (v. 1) does Job speak? What is the relation between their prolonged silence and his eventual speech? 3. Is Job speaking logically? Theologically? Emotionally? How can you tell? 4. How close does Job come to cursing God (vv. 1–10)? Why does Job curse the day of his birth, rather than God? Is cursing God's creation equivalent to cursing God? Or is there a difference? If so, what? 5. In verses 11–26, instead of cursing, what is Job doing? Who is he questioning? What does he prefer to the status quo? 6. By cursing and questioning his own existence, how does this implicate God? What statement of Job's comes closest to challenging God's power? God's wisdom? God's goodness? 7. In light of chapter 1, what irony do you see in verse 23? Who was "hedging" before? Who is hedging now? 8. What does this chapter tell you about Job's health—emotionally, physically and spiritually? What does it tell you, if anything, about his sense of loss? Does that surprise you? How so?

1. When, if ever, have you felt like life was not worth living? What were you feeling? What were the circumstances? What did you end up doing about that? Where was God for you when it hurt the most? 2. How do *you* respond to rhetorical questions, such as Job asks (vv. 11–12,16, 20–23)? Why does he use them? When would you use them? Who do you expect to answer? 3. What three friends of yours are better listeners than most? What might you want to share with them now?

---

^a5 Or *and the shadow of death*   ^b8 Or *the sea*

my groans pour out like water.
²⁵What I feared has come upon me;
    what I dreaded has happened to me.
²⁶I have no peace, no quietness;
    I have no rest, but only turmoil."

Eliphaz

4 Then Eliphaz the Temanite replied:

²"If someone ventures a word with you, will you
    be impatient?
    But who can keep from speaking?
³Think how you have instructed many,
    how you have strengthened feeble hands.
⁴Your words have supported those who stumbled;
    you have strengthened faltering knees.
⁵But now trouble comes to you, and you are
    discouraged;
    it strikes you, and you are dismayed.
⁶Should not your piety be your confidence
    and your blameless ways your hope?

⁷"Consider now: Who, being innocent, has ever
    perished?
    Where were the upright ever destroyed?
⁸As I have observed, those who plow evil
    and those who sow trouble reap it.
⁹At the breath of God they are destroyed;
    at the blast of his anger they perish.
¹⁰The lions may roar and growl,
    yet the teeth of the great lions are broken.
¹¹The lion perishes for lack of prey,
    and the cubs of the lioness are scattered.

¹²"A word was secretly brought to me,
    my ears caught a whisper of it.
¹³Amid disquieting dreams in the night,
    when deep sleep falls on men,
¹⁴fear and trembling seized me
    and made all my bones shake.
¹⁵A spirit glided past my face,
    and the hair on my body stood on end.
¹⁶It stopped,
    but I could not tell what it was.
    A form stood before my eyes,
    and I heard a hushed voice:
¹⁷'Can a mortal be more righteous than God?
    Can a man be more pure than his Maker?
¹⁸If God places no trust in his servants,
    if he charges his angels with error,
¹⁹how much more those who live in houses of clay,
    whose foundations are in the dust,
    who are crushed more readily than a moth!
²⁰Between dawn and dusk they are broken to
    pieces;
    unnoticed, they perish forever.
²¹Are not the cords of their tent pulled up,
    so that they die without wisdom?'ᵃ

What is the very first thought that comes to mind when you hear: (a) "God told me that …"? (b) "If you only had more faith …"? Fill in the blanks from your own experience of dealing with such statements. What impact did they have on you?

1. After seven days of mourning, Eliphaz speaks up. How do his first words strike you: Sympathetic? Instructive? Well-meaning? Pastoral? Dogmatic? Or what? 2. What neat theological formula does Eliphaz urge upon Job as the proper basis for his hope (4:6–11)? How does that view of the "blameless" and the "evildoers" compare with the prevailing theology of that day (see Ps 1)? Is Eliphaz's theology correct? How so? 3. What is Eliphaz's source for his authoritative viewpoint (4:12–16)? How does he describe his spiritual experience? Does that hair-raising, mystical experience sound reliable to you? 4. What does Eliphaz say God told him (4:17–21)? What is the point of the angels-mortals comparison? 5. Who would serve as a mediator to help plead Job's case (5:1; see 9:33; 16:19–20)? Who are these "holy ones" (see 1:6; 2:1)? Why does Job need a mediator (5:2–7)? 6. What is the gist of Eliphaz's advice in 5:8–16? What is his concept of God? His view of God working in history? What, if anything, is wrong with Eliphaz's views? 7. What does Eliphaz imply is the reason for suffering (vv. 17–26)? How would these words likely be received by Job, a "blameless and upright man," a man who has lost his security and children? 8. What is Job supposed to do with Eliphaz's advice (5:27)? What part of Eliphaz's advice is field-tested as true and applicable to Job?

1. What makes you feel most understood by your close friends? What do they say? Not say? What do they do? Not do? 2. Have you ever been totally misunderstood by your closest friend? How did you feel about that? 3. How did your closest friend react the last time you faced personal difficulty? How was he or she most

ᵃ21 Some interpreters end the quotation after verse 17.

5   "Call if you will, but who will answer you?
              To which of the holy ones will you turn?
²Resentment kills a fool,
              and envy slays the simple.
³I myself have seen a fool taking root,
              but suddenly his house was cursed.
⁴His children are far from safety,
              crushed in court without a defender.
⁵The hungry consume his harvest,
              taking it even from among thorns,
              and the thirsty pant after his wealth.
⁶For hardship does not spring from the soil,
              nor does trouble sprout from the ground.
⁷Yet man is born to trouble
              as surely as sparks fly upward.

⁸"But if it were I, I would appeal to God;
              I would lay my cause before him.
⁹He performs wonders that cannot be fathomed,
              miracles that cannot be counted.
¹⁰He bestows rain on the earth;
              he sends water upon the countryside.
¹¹The lowly he sets on high,
              and those who mourn are lifted to safety.
¹²He thwarts the plans of the crafty,
              so that their hands achieve no success.
¹³He catches the wise in their craftiness,
              and the schemes of the wily are swept away.
¹⁴Darkness comes upon them in the daytime;
              at noon they grope as in the night.
¹⁵He saves the needy from the sword in their
                   mouth;
              he saves them from the clutches of the
                   powerful.
¹⁶So the poor have hope,
              and injustice shuts its mouth.

¹⁷"Blessed is the man whom God corrects;
              so do not despise the discipline of the
                   Almighty.ᵃ
¹⁸For he wounds, but he also binds up;
              he injures, but his hands also heal.
¹⁹From six calamities he will rescue you;
              in seven no harm will befall you.
²⁰In famine he will ransom you from death,
              and in battle from the stroke of the sword.
²¹You will be protected from the lash of the tongue,
              and need not fear when destruction comes.
²²You will laugh at destruction and famine,
              and need not fear the beasts of the earth.
²³For you will have a covenant with the stones of
                   the field,
              and the wild animals will be at peace with you.
²⁴You will know that your tent is secure;
              you will take stock of your property and find
                   nothing missing.
²⁵You will know that your children will be many,

helpful? Unhelpful? **4.** What about
when the tables were turned and
your friend was facing difficulty:
What kind of friend did you prove to
be? **5.** Can "correct" theology (all
the right words) ever be "bad" theology in practice? When? What
real or hypothetical situations come
to mind? What part of Eliphaz's advice is true and applicable to you?
In what way?

ᵃ17 Hebrew *Shaddai*; here and throughout Job

and your descendants like the grass of the
earth.
26You will come to the grave in full vigor,
like sheaves gathered in season.

27"We have examined this, and it is true.
So hear it and apply it to yourself."

Job

6

Then Job replied:

2"If only my anguish could be weighed
and all my misery be placed on the scales!
3It would surely outweigh the sand of the seas—
no wonder my words have been impetuous.
4The arrows of the Almighty are in me,
my spirit drinks in their poison;
God's terrors are marshaled against me.
5Does a wild donkey bray when it has grass,
or an ox bellow when it has fodder?
6Is tasteless food eaten without salt,
or is there flavor in the white of an egg*a*?
7I refuse to touch it;
such food makes me ill.

8"Oh, that I might have my request,
that God would grant what I hope for,
9that God would be willing to crush me,
to let loose his hand and cut me off!
10Then I would still have this consolation—
my joy in unrelenting pain—
that I had not denied the words of the Holy
One.

11"What strength do I have, that I should still hope?
What prospects, that I should be patient?
12Do I have the strength of stone?
Is my flesh bronze?
13Do I have any power to help myself,
now that success has been driven from me?

14"A despairing man should have the devotion of
his friends,
even though he forsakes the fear of the
Almighty.
15But my brothers are as undependable as
intermittent streams,
as the streams that overflow
16when darkened by thawing ice
and swollen with melting snow,
17but that cease to flow in the dry season,
and in the heat vanish from their channels.
18Caravans turn aside from their routes;
they go up into the wasteland and perish.
19The caravans of Tema look for water,
the traveling merchants of Sheba look in hope.
20They are distressed, because they had been
confident;
they arrive there, only to be disappointed.

1. In what areas of life are you a noted "heavyweight": (a) Heavy thinker? (b) Heavy player? (c) Heavy worker? (d) Theological heavyweight? (e) Heavy sleeper? (f) Heavy talker? (g) Other? 2. In what areas of life are you considered a "lightweight"?

1. In 6:2–6 and 7:1–6, does Job describe his anguish more in physical terms? Emotional tones? Spiritual ideas? Or what? 2. What images or word pictures carry more of the weight of Job's anguish than any of the others? 3. Who does Job view as the source of his suffering? According to chapters 1–2, is he right? 4. How does Job regard the food for thought offered by Eliphaz (vv. 5–6)? 5. What is Job's request in verses 8–10? Is he thinking of suicide? Is he a masochist? Or what? What does his "consolation" prize (v. 10) say about his priorities? 6. Is Job being too hard on his friends (vv. 14–30)? What does he expect of his "brothers" (compare Gal 6:1–2)? How have they proven to be of no help? What false accusations does he want them to take back? 7. What does Job's "integrity" consist of (v. 29; see 2:9–10)? Why does he think his integrity is at stake here?

1. Have you ever experienced anything like Job's misery, as described in 7:3–4, for months? Several nights? Even one night? What were the circumstances and your response to them? 2. When have you felt like your personal integrity was at stake? What did you do to defend yourself from false accusations? 3. If "silence is golden," what is friendly advice worth to you? When is it priceless? When is it worthless? What does your assessment depend on? 4. What consolation have you experienced from the hand of God?

a6 The meaning of the Hebrew for this phrase is uncertain.

²¹Now you too have proved to be of no help;
    you see something dreadful and are afraid.
²²Have I ever said, 'Give something on my behalf,
    pay a ransom for me from your wealth,
²³deliver me from the hand of the enemy,
    ransom me from the clutches of the ruthless'?

²⁴"Teach me, and I will be quiet;
    show me where I have been wrong.
²⁵How painful are honest words!
    But what do your arguments prove?
²⁶Do you mean to correct what I say,
    and treat the words of a despairing man as
      wind?
²⁷You would even cast lots for the fatherless
    and barter away your friend.

²⁸"But now be so kind as to look at me.
    Would I lie to your face?
²⁹Relent, do not be unjust;
    reconsider, for my integrity is at stake.ᵃ
³⁰Is there any wickedness on my lips?
    Can my mouth not discern malice?

7   "Does not man have hard service on earth?
    Are not his days like those of a hired man?
²Like a slave longing for the evening shadows,
    or a hired man waiting eagerly for his wages,
³so I have been allotted months of futility,
    and nights of misery have been assigned to me.
⁴When I lie down I think, 'How long before I get
      up?'
    The night drags on, and I toss till dawn.
⁵My body is clothed with worms and scabs,
    my skin is broken and festering.

⁶"My days are swifter than a weaver's shuttle,
    and they come to an end without hope.
⁷Remember, O God, that my life is but a breath;
    my eyes will never see happiness again.
⁸The eye that now sees me will see me no longer;
    you will look for me, but I will be no more.
⁹As a cloud vanishes and is gone,
    so he who goes down to the graveᵇ does not
      return.
¹⁰He will never come to his house again;
    his place will know him no more.

¹¹"Therefore I will not keep silent;
    I will speak out in the anguish of my spirit,
    I will complain in the bitterness of my soul.
¹²Am I the sea, or the monster of the deep,
    that you put me under guard?
¹³When I think my bed will comfort me
    and my couch will ease my complaint,
¹⁴even then you frighten me with dreams
    and terrify me with visions,
¹⁵so that I prefer strangling and death,
    rather than this body of mine.

ᵃ29 Or *my righteousness still stands*   ᵇ9 Hebrew *Sheol*

If your under-your-breath conversations were monitored for a day, what would that likely reveal about you: (a) Lots of self-talk, berating myself? (b) Many pep-talks, encouraging myself? (c) Unmentionable cursing? (d) Talk-back sessions? (e) Prayers too deep for words? (f) Last laughs? (g) Imaginary friends?

1. To whom is Job speaking now? Why pray now? **2.** In praying, is Job trying to get God to pay more attention to him? Or is Job trying to get rid of God, who now terrifies him? **3.** Is Job's complaint frivolous, or well founded (vv. 11–16)? **4.** Why does Job doubt his self-worth (vv. 15–17)? Why does he think God created him (vv. 18–21)? **5.** What does it mean to be examined by God, according to Job? According to the psalmist (see Ps 8:4–8; 139)? How are their situations different?

1. Consider a close friend: Would you rather know this person, or be known by this person? What is the difference? 2. Likewise, what does it mean for you to both know God and be known by him? Compared to human friendships, how well do you and God know each other? Does that make you feel comfort or discomfort?

1. Who among your family knows the most: (a) The one who has lived the longest? (b) The one with the most formal education? (c) The one who graduated from the "school of hard knocks"? 2. What invaluable lesson have you learned from your grandparents?

1. How does the tone of Bildad's argument compare to the older Eliphaz? What kind of friend does he appear to be? 2. What is Bildad's view of justice? What "If …, then …" formula does he use on Job? 3. In the eyes of Bildad, what is Job: (a) An evil hypocrite (pretending to be something he is not)? (b) Self-deceived? (c) All talk, no show? (d) "Pure, upright, blameless"? How can you tell (see vv. 2,6,13,20)? 4. At what point is Bildad's prophecy more accurate than he thinks (vv. 6,20; see 42:10–17)? 5. What source does Bildad draw upon for his authoritative view (vv. 8–10)? Does this seem any more reliable to you than Eliphaz's source (see 4:12–16)? How so? 6. What age-old wisdom of former generations does Bildad offer (vv. 11–19)? How does that extended proverb apply to Job's situation (vv. 20–22)?

1. What proverbial wisdom has been effectively passed down in your family by those who have graduated from life's "school of hard knocks"? How would that wisdom apply to Job's situation? To your current situation? 2. What view would Bildad likely have of you and your situation, as compared to Job's? How would you respond to a friend like Bildad?

[16]I despise my life; I would not live forever.
Let me alone; my days have no meaning.

[17]"What is man that you make so much of him,
that you give him so much attention,
[18]that you examine him every morning
and test him every moment?
[19]Will you never look away from me,
or let me alone even for an instant?
[20]If I have sinned, what have I done to you,
O watcher of men?
Why have you made me your target?
Have I become a burden to you?[a]
[21]Why do you not pardon my offenses
and forgive my sins?
For I will soon lie down in the dust;
you will search for me, but I will be no more."

Bildad

8 Then Bildad the Shuhite replied:

[2]"How long will you say such things?
Your words are a blustering wind.
[3]Does God pervert justice?
Does the Almighty pervert what is right?
[4]When your children sinned against him,
he gave them over to the penalty of their sin.
[5]But if you will look to God
and plead with the Almighty,
[6]if you are pure and upright,
even now he will rouse himself on your behalf
and restore you to your rightful place.
[7]Your beginnings will seem humble,
so prosperous will your future be.

[8]"Ask the former generations
and find out what their fathers learned,
[9]for we were born only yesterday and know
nothing,
and our days on earth are but a shadow.
[10]Will they not instruct you and tell you?
Will they not bring forth words from their
understanding?
[11]Can papyrus grow tall where there is no marsh?
Can reeds thrive without water?
[12]While still growing and uncut,
they wither more quickly than grass.
[13]Such is the destiny of all who forget God;
so perishes the hope of the godless.
[14]What he trusts in is fragile[b];
what he relies on is a spider's web.
[15]He leans on his web, but it gives way;
he clings to it, but it does not hold.
[16]He is like a well-watered plant in the sunshine,
spreading its shoots over the garden;
[17]it entwines its roots around a pile of rocks
and looks for a place among the stones.

[a]20 A few manuscripts of the Masoretic Text, an ancient Hebrew scribal tradition and Septuagint; most manuscripts of the Masoretic Text *I have become a burden to myself.*
[b]14 The meaning of the Hebrew for this word is uncertain.

¹⁸But when it is torn from its spot,
  that place disowns it and says, 'I never saw
    you.'
¹⁹Surely its life withers away,
  and*ᵃ* from the soil other plants grow.

²⁰"Surely God does not reject a blameless man
  or strengthen the hands of evildoers.
²¹He will yet fill your mouth with laughter
  and your lips with shouts of joy.
²²Your enemies will be clothed in shame,
  and the tents of the wicked will be no more."

Job

9 Then Job replied:

²"Indeed, I know that this is true.
  But how can a mortal be righteous before God?
³Though one wished to dispute with him,
  he could not answer him one time out of a
    thousand.
⁴His wisdom is profound, his power is vast.
  Who has resisted him and come out unscathed?
⁵He moves mountains without their knowing it
  and overturns them in his anger.
⁶He shakes the earth from its place
  and makes its pillars tremble.
⁷He speaks to the sun and it does not shine;
  he seals off the light of the stars.
⁸He alone stretches out the heavens
  and treads on the waves of the sea.
⁹He is the Maker of the Bear and Orion,
  the Pleiades and the constellations of the south.
¹⁰He performs wonders that cannot be fathomed,
  miracles that cannot be counted.
¹¹When he passes me, I cannot see him;
  when he goes by, I cannot perceive him.
¹²If he snatches away, who can stop him?
  Who can say to him, 'What are you doing?'
¹³God does not restrain his anger;
  even the cohorts of Rahab cowered at his feet.

¹⁴"How then can I dispute with him?
  How can I find words to argue with him?
¹⁵Though I were innocent, I could not answer him;
  I could only plead with my Judge for mercy.
¹⁶Even if I summoned him and he responded,
  I do not believe he would give me a hearing.
¹⁷He would crush me with a storm
  and multiply my wounds for no reason.
¹⁸He would not let me regain my breath
  but would overwhelm me with misery.
¹⁹If it is a matter of strength, he is mighty!
  And if it is a matter of justice, who will
    summon him*ᵇ*?
²⁰Even if I were innocent, my mouth would
  condemn me;

ᵃ19 Or Surely all the joy it has / is that   *ᵇ19 See Septuagint; Hebrew me.*

1. When have you felt small and most overwhelmed by an awesome natural wonder: (a) On top of a mountain or canyon? (b) Flying? (c) Inside a mammoth cave? (d) Sailing the ocean? (e) Gazing at stars? **2.** By contrast, when do you feel big? **3.** Which did you feel last week—small or big? How come?

1. Why does Job ask the same question as Eliphaz (v. 2; see 4:17): (a) Mockery? (b) Flattery? (c) Pursuit of truth? (d) Self-defense? **2.** In what respects does Job agree with his friends on the character of God? On his own character? Where does he go beyond what the others believe? Where is he more modest (vv. 10–11; see 4:15–16)? **3.** If God is undeniably, infinitely *great* (vv. 5–10), does Job believe God's greatness is controlled at all by *goodness* or *justice*? Why or why not? **4.** What would Job like to say to God if granted a day in court with him (vv. 3,14–24)? Who would be on trial? In the witness stand? Who would be the blind-folded judge? The prosecuting attorney? **5.** In Job's case, what would be the reasonable verdict? The morally indifferent verdict? **6.** In what tone of voice can you hear Job setting forth his case: Angry? Bitter? Sarcastic? Humble? Begging? **7.** How does Job think sin and suffering are related? How is that different from his friends? According to Jesus, who gets the greater share of justice or mercy (see Mt 5:45)?

1. How do *you* see sin and suffering related: (a) I suffer the consequences for my sins? (b) I suffer for the sins of others? (c) I suffer without regard to sin? (d) I sin without suffering any immediate consequences? (e) I sin without suffering, period? Give an example to support your case. **2.** Which statement would Job agree with?

Why? **3.** When you do feel guilt, how do you know it is God convicting you, not Satan or self? How do you know the difference between true and false guilt? **4.** What's your answer to the question raised in 9:2 (and 4:17)?

───────────

1. In your no-holds-barred family arguments, who tends to be the position-taker? The conflict-avoider? The negotiator? The scapegoat? Who generally wins and why? **2.** In the "moment's joy" were you given last week?

1. In 9:25–31, Job shifts focus—to what? What feelings can you discern? What flights of fancy? What unsound reasoning? **2.** In 9:32–35, Job resumes the theme of 9:14–21. How so? What puzzling problem comes into sharp focus in 9:32–33? **3.** Is Job eager to make intellectual sense of the problem of suffering? Or is he more eager to attain or preserve a right relationship with God, which makes suffering acceptable, if not intelligible? Is he looking for forgiveness from some divine mediator (see Heb 9:15), or is he desiring someone to attest his innocence? **4.** In the "complaint" of 10:1–7, what is Job appealing to God for? On what basis (10:8–12)? In this is he defiant and arrogant, or puzzled and hurt? **5.** If God's intentions in creating life were good, why would Job go on to conclude that very same life is not worth living (10:18–22)? Why would God create at all if he was only going to destroy later? **6.** From his description of it, is Job eagerly awaiting the joy of life after death, as his one hope of escaping the pain of this life? Or does his "moment's joy" lie somewhere, sometime only on this side of the grave?

1. Job saw himself in 10:14–17 as, we might say, "caught between a rock and a hard place." When have you felt likewise? How did you solve the riddle of your dilemma? **2.** In the future, how is Christ to be the answer to the questions raised by Job? How has Christ the Mediator solved the unsolvable dilemmas of your life?

if I were blameless, it would pronounce me
    guilty.
21"Although I am blameless,
    I have no concern for myself;
    I despise my own life.
22It is all the same; that is why I say,
    'He destroys both the blameless and the
        wicked.'
23When a scourge brings sudden death,
    he mocks the despair of the innocent.
24When a land falls into the hands of the wicked,
    he blindfolds its judges.
    If it is not he, then who is it?

25"My days are swifter than a runner;
    they fly away without a glimpse of joy.
26They skim past like boats of papyrus,
    like eagles swooping down on their prey.
27If I say, 'I will forget my complaint,
    I will change my expression, and smile,'
28I still dread all my sufferings,
    for I know you will not hold me innocent.
29Since I am already found guilty,
    why should I struggle in vain?
30Even if I washed myself with soap[a]
    and my hands with washing soda,
31you would plunge me into a slime pit
    so that even my clothes would detest me.

32"He is not a man like me that I might answer
        him,
    that we might confront each other in court.
33If only there were someone to arbitrate between
        us,
    to lay his hand upon us both,
34someone to remove God's rod from me,
    so that his terror would frighten me no more.
35Then I would speak up without fear of him,
    but as it now stands with me, I cannot.

10   "I loathe my very life;
    therefore I will give free rein to my complaint
    and speak out in the bitterness of my soul.
2I will say to God: Do not condemn me,
    but tell me what charges you have against me.
3Does it please you to oppress me,
    to spurn the work of your hands,
    while you smile on the schemes of the wicked?
4Do you have eyes of flesh?
    Do you see as a mortal sees?
5Are your days like those of a mortal
    or your years like those of a man,
6that you must search out my faults
    and probe after my sin—
7though you know that I am not guilty
    and that no one can rescue me from your hand?

8"Your hands shaped me and made me.
    Will you now turn and destroy me?

[a]30 Or snow

⁹Remember that you molded me like clay.
  Will you now turn me to dust again?
¹⁰Did you not pour me out like milk
  and curdle me like cheese,
¹¹clothe me with skin and flesh
  and knit me together with bones and sinews?
¹²You gave me life and showed me kindness,
  and in your providence watched over my spirit.

¹³"But this is what you concealed in your heart,
  and I know that this was in your mind:
¹⁴If I sinned, you would be watching me
  and would not let my offense go unpunished.
¹⁵If I am guilty—woe to me!
  Even if I am innocent, I cannot lift my head,
for I am full of shame
  and drowned in*ᵃ* my affliction.
¹⁶If I hold my head high, you stalk me like a lion
  and again display your awesome power against
    me.
¹⁷You bring new witnesses against me
  and increase your anger toward me;
  your forces come against me wave upon wave.

¹⁸"Why then did you bring me out of the womb?
  I wish I had died before any eye saw me.
¹⁹If only I had never come into being,
  or had been carried straight from the womb to
    the grave!
²⁰Are not my few days almost over?
  Turn away from me so I can have a moment's
    joy
²¹before I go to the place of no return,
  to the land of gloom and deep shadow,ᵇ
²²to the land of deepest night,
  of deep shadow and disorder,
  where even the light is like darkness."

Zophar

11 Then Zophar the Naamathite replied:

²"Are all these words to go unanswered?
  Is this talker to be vindicated?
³Will your idle talk reduce men to silence?
  Will no one rebuke you when you mock?
⁴You say to God, 'My beliefs are flawless
  and I am pure in your sight.'
⁵Oh, how I wish that God would speak,
  that he would open his lips against you
⁶and disclose to you the secrets of wisdom,
  for true wisdom has two sides.
  Know this: God has even forgotten some of
    your sin.

⁷"Can you fathom the mysteries of God?
  Can you probe the limits of the Almighty?
⁸They are higher than the heavens—what can you
  do?

3. When have you simply laid out your miserable options before God in a "complaint"? What happened as a result?

1. What favorite saying in your family (e.g., "Time heals all wounds") is quoted to those who hit bottom and need a pick-me-up? **2.** What do you do when you want to wipe out the memory of a bad day: (a) Sleep? (b) Play music? (c) Eat? (d) Talk to God? (e) Read a book? (f) Write a book? (g) Work out? (h) Call a friend? (i) Other?

1. Which theological formula of Eliphaz and Bildad does Zophar now carry forward, even more forcefully? Is Zophar "all wet" in this thinking, or is he right in some respects? At what points do you think he is right? And wrong? **2.** Compared to the other two, what tone of voice do you hear in Zophar's speech? Why does Zophar seem more eager to rebuke Job? **3.** What presumptions does he make about Job (vv. 3–4,13–20)? When has Job ever mocked God?

ᵃ15 Or and aware of   ᵇ21 Or and the shadow of death; also in verse 22

Or claimed "flawless" beliefs and "pure" behavior? **4.** In what ways does Zophar misrepresent God (vv. 6,17,19; compare Ps 73, where the psalmist disagrees with Zophar's "bed of roses" theology)?

1. How do you explain situations in life that you don't understand? Is the "Why" question something which nags at you? **2.** How much do you want to know about the behind-the-scenes drama going on between God and Satan in the battle for *your* obedience of faith? Would you rather not know all there is to know? **3.** What is the proper role of faith and reason in solving the mysteries of life, such as the one faced by Job? Does prayer reveal answers to the otherwise "unexplainable"? Or is prayer itself a mystery? Explain.

---

1. Describe the counselor or pastor who has been the most help to you over the years. What about that person was most helpful? **2.** When have you been more helped by the counsel of friends, not professionals? What about their friendship meant the most?

1. What tone of voice do you hear in Job's reply here? Where is sarcasm most evident? **2.** What superior knowledge do the three friends claim to have, that Job and all of creation know as well (vv. 2–3,7–12; 13:1–2)? **3.** On what basis does Job make this claim to know as much as they (vv. 3,22; 13:1)? **4.** What distinguishes Job from criminals and idolaters (vv. 4–6)? **5.** What does Job hope his three friends will learn from God's random activity in creation (vv. 7–10,14–25)? **6.** In creation and history, is there a *moral* pattern: Do the righteous suffer, regardless of God's presence? Does the punishment always fit the crime? **7.** In verses 17–25, who parades forth in Job's view of human history? What disasters befall each? Why? (Or is there no rea-

They are deeper than the depths of the
 grave*ᵃ*—what can you know?
⁹Their measure is longer than the earth
 and wider than the sea.

¹⁰"If he comes along and confines you in prison
 and convenes a court, who can oppose him?
¹¹Surely he recognizes deceitful men;
 and when he sees evil, does he not take note?
¹²But a witless man can no more become wise
 than a wild donkey's colt can be born a man.*ᵇ*

¹³"Yet if you devote your heart to him
 and stretch out your hands to him,
¹⁴if you put away the sin that is in your hand
 and allow no evil to dwell in your tent,
¹⁵then you will lift up your face without shame;
 you will stand firm and without fear.
¹⁶You will surely forget your trouble,
 recalling it only as waters gone by.
¹⁷Life will be brighter than noonday,
 and darkness will become like morning.
¹⁸You will be secure, because there is hope;
 you will look about you and take your rest in safety.
¹⁹You will lie down, with no one to make you afraid,
 and many will court your favor.
²⁰But the eyes of the wicked will fail,
 and escape will elude them;
 their hope will become a dying gasp."

Job 12

Then Job replied:

²"Doubtless you are the people,
 and wisdom will die with you!
³But I have a mind as well as you;
 I am not inferior to you.
 Who does not know all these things?

⁴"I have become a laughingstock to my friends,
 though I called upon God and he answered—
 a mere laughingstock, though righteous and blameless!
⁵Men at ease have contempt for misfortune
 as the fate of those whose feet are slipping.
⁶The tents of marauders are undisturbed,
 and those who provoke God are secure—
 those who carry their god in their hands.*ᶜ*

⁷"But ask the animals, and they will teach you,
 or the birds of the air, and they will tell you;
⁸or speak to the earth, and it will teach you,
 or let the fish of the sea inform you.
⁹Which of all these does not know
 that the hand of the LORD has done this?
¹⁰In his hand is the life of every creature
 and the breath of all mankind.

ᵃ8 Hebrew *than Sheol*   *ᵇ12* Or *wild donkey can be born tame*   *ᶜ6* Or *secure /
in what God's hand brings them*

11Does not the ear test words
	as the tongue tastes food?
12Is not wisdom found among the aged?
	Does not long life bring understanding?

13"To God belong wisdom and power;
	counsel and understanding are his.
14What he tears down cannot be rebuilt;
	the man he imprisons cannot be released.
15If he holds back the waters, there is drought;
	if he lets them loose, they devastate the land.
16To him belong strength and victory;
	both deceived and deceiver are his.
17He leads counselors away stripped
	and makes fools of judges.
18He takes off the shackles put on by kings
	and ties a loinclotha around their waist.
19He leads priests away stripped
	and overthrows men long established.
20He silences the lips of trusted advisers
	and takes away the discernment of elders.
21He pours contempt on nobles
	and disarms the mighty.
22He reveals the deep things of darkness
	and brings deep shadows into the light.
23He makes nations great, and destroys them;
	he enlarges nations, and disperses them.
24He deprives the leaders of the earth of their
		reason;
	he sends them wandering through a trackless
		waste.
25They grope in darkness with no light;
	he makes them stagger like drunkards.

13   "My eyes have seen all this,
	my ears have heard and understood it.
2What you know, I also know;
	I am not inferior to you.
3But I desire to speak to the Almighty
	and to argue my case with God.
4You, however, smear me with lies;
	you are worthless physicians, all of you!
5If only you would be altogether silent!
	For you, that would be wisdom.
6Hear now my argument;
	listen to the plea of my lips.
7Will you speak wickedly on God's behalf?
	Will you speak deceitfully for him?
8Will you show him partiality?
	Will you argue the case for God?
9Would it turn out well if he examined you?
	Could you deceive him as you might deceive
		men?
10He would surely rebuke you
	if you secretly showed partiality.
11Would not his splendor terrify you?
	Would not the dread of him fall on you?

a 18 Or shackles of kings / and ties a belt

son?) **8.** Is God whimsical or arbitrary? Is God seen as detached from it all, or responsible for it all? What does Job say to either defend, or indict, God's nature? **9.** How does this contrast with Eliphaz's "simple" understanding of the way God works in nature and history (see 5:10–16)? **10.** Is merely "knowing" the ways of God enough to satisfy Job (13:1–5)? Why or why not? What more does he want from God? From his "wise" friends (see Pr 17:28)?

1. To what source do you attribute most of your knowledge? What is common to the rest of humanity? What is unique to you? **2.** What does it mean to "know" God, as Job does? How is that different than knowing "about" God, as Eliphaz does? Which knowledge do you possess? **3.** If you only had "general revelation" (creation and history) to learn from, and no "special revelation" (the Bible and Jesus Christ), what could you deduce about God's character? How does that compare with Romans 1:18–23?

1. When you were a child, what was on the very top of your wish list? **2.** When you became an adult, how did that wish list change?

1. In verses 6–12, how does Job, the defendant, turn the tables on the three friends? **2.** What is so wrong with the way they have been arguing the case for God (vv. 7–8)? By what standards will they in turn be judged (vv. 9–12)? **3.** What risks is Job taking in bypassing his friends and appealing his case directly to God (vv. 13–19)? Of what is he most certain? Why? **4.** What do you see here in Job's character: Spunk? Spite? Courage? Arrogance? Hope? Foolishness? **5.** Of the many issues he takes up with God (vv. 20–27), what are the "two things" Job desires most from him? **6.** In what ways does Job lay himself wide open for yet more "bitter things" from God? With what mistaken notion about sins and suffering is Job still burdened?

1. If you could make two requests of God, with the prospect of them both coming true, what would they be? How might they change if you were facing extreme hardship? **2.** Compared to Job, with what attitudes do you approach God? When does seeking after God become "risky" for you? Are you willing to take that risk, now? Why or why not?

In tending your garden (if you have one), do you prefer annuals (which bloom all summer long, but then die forever) or perennials (which bloom only briefly, but spring to life again the next year)? Which of each are your favorites?

1. What are the four major poetic images in this chapter (vv. 1–6, 7–13, 14–17, 18–22)? What mixed metaphors do you see here? **2.** What do these poems say about the human condition? About God's link to humankind? **3.** What mood swings in Job do you detect as he moves through the various stanzas? Where do you see waves of despair? Renewal of hope? Certainty of faith? **4.** What is the movement here: Is Job regressing? Or progressing? What is the "bottom line" for him? (Note: Job is speaking *poetically*, often circling around

¹²Your maxims are proverbs of ashes;
    your defenses are defenses of clay.

¹³"Keep silent and let me speak;
    then let come to me what may.
¹⁴Why do I put myself in jeopardy
    and take my life in my hands?
¹⁵Though he slay me, yet will I hope in him;
    I will surelyᵃ defend my ways to his face.
¹⁶Indeed, this will turn out for my deliverance,
    for no godless man would dare come before
        him!
¹⁷Listen carefully to my words;
    let your ears take in what I say.
¹⁸Now that I have prepared my case,
    I know I will be vindicated.
¹⁹Can anyone bring charges against me?
    If so, I will be silent and die.

²⁰"Only grant me these two things, O God,
    and then I will not hide from you:
²¹Withdraw your hand far from me,
    and stop frightening me with your terrors.
²²Then summon me and I will answer,
    or let me speak, and you reply.
²³How many wrongs and sins have I committed?
    Show me my offense and my sin.
²⁴Why do you hide your face
    and consider me your enemy?
²⁵Will you torment a windblown leaf?
    Will you chase after dry chaff?
²⁶For you write down bitter things against me
    and make me inherit the sins of my youth.
²⁷You fasten my feet in shackles;
    you keep close watch on all my paths
    by putting marks on the soles of my feet.

²⁸"So man wastes away like something rotten,
    like a garment eaten by moths.

14 "Man born of woman
    is of few days and full of trouble.
²He springs up like a flower and withers away;
    like a fleeting shadow, he does not endure.
³Do you fix your eye on such a one?
    Will you bring himᵇ before you for judgment?
⁴Who can bring what is pure from the impure?
    No one!
⁵Man's days are determined;
    you have decreed the number of his months
    and have set limits he cannot exceed.
⁶So look away from him and let him alone,
    till he has put in his time like a hired man.

⁷"At least there is hope for a tree:
    If it is cut down, it will sprout again,
    and its new shoots will not fail.
⁸Its roots may grow old in the ground
    and its stump die in the soil,

ᵃ15 Or *He will surely slay me; I have no hope — / yet I will*   ᵇ3 Septuagint, Vulgate and Syriac; Hebrew *me*

⁹yet at the scent of water it will bud
  and put forth shoots like a plant.
¹⁰But man dies and is laid low;
  he breathes his last and is no more.
¹¹As water disappears from the sea
  or a riverbed becomes parched and dry,
¹²so man lies down and does not rise;
  till the heavens are no more, men will not
    awake
  or be roused from their sleep.

¹³"If only you would hide me in the grave[a]
  and conceal me till your anger has passed!
If only you would set me a time
  and then remember me!
¹⁴If a man dies, will he live again?
  All the days of my hard service
  I will wait for my renewal[b] to come.
¹⁵You will call and I will answer you;
  you will long for the creature your hands have
    made.
¹⁶Surely then you will count my steps
  but not keep track of my sin.
¹⁷My offenses will be sealed up in a bag;
  you will cover over my sin.

¹⁸"But as a mountain erodes and crumbles
  and as a rock is moved from its place,
¹⁹as water wears away stones
  and torrents wash away the soil,
  so you destroy man's hope.
²⁰You overpower him once for all, and he is gone;
  you change his countenance and send him
    away.
²¹If his sons are honored, he does not know it;
  if they are brought low, he does not see it.
²²He feels but the pain of his own body
  and mourns only for himself."

Eliphaz

15 Then Eliphaz the Temanite replied:

²"Would a wise man answer with empty notions
  or fill his belly with the hot east wind?
³Would he argue with useless words,
  with speeches that have no value?
⁴But you even undermine piety
  and hinder devotion to God.
⁵Your sin prompts your mouth;
  you adopt the tongue of the crafty.
⁶Your own mouth condemns you, not mine;
  your own lips testify against you.

⁷"Are you the first man ever born?
  Were you brought forth before the hills?
⁸Do you listen in on God's council?
  Do you limit wisdom to yourself?
⁹What do you know that we do not know?

a 13 Hebrew *Sheol*   *b 14* Or *release*

the main point, *not logically*, in step-wise sequence, as if each new line of thought built upon or superseded the previous one.) **5.** What will God do with Job's sin (vv. 13–17)? When? To what does Job owe his continued existence, now and hereafter: To some immortal element intrinsic to his soul? Or some act and gift of God?

1. Which of the poems best captures your present mood? **2.** Where on the continuum between suicidal despair and resurrection hope are you? Where are most of your friends? How might Job speak to their condition? **3.** Chapter 14 ends the first round of three debates between Job and his friends. What impressions do you have of them, as friends? As theologians? **4.** What impression has Job made on you so far? Would you want him for a dinner guest? A missionary project? A best friend in time of need? **5.** Has Job cursed God yet, as Satan says he surely will? If so where? If not, how close does he come?

1. Who was voted "Most Likely to Succeed" in your graduating class? Who is the most successful person you have ever met since? How would you account for their success: (a) Born great? (b) Achieved greatness? (c) Greatness was thrust upon them? **2.** At what age did you first say, "I know more than my teachers (or parents)"? In what areas do you now think of yourself as knowledgeable? As ignorant?

1. How does this scene compare with the scene where the four men sat together on a dunghill, in silence (see 2:11–13). What is happening to the sympathy which Eliphaz used to express to Job (see 4:3–4; 5:17–19)? **2.** Why is he so offended with Job? Of what is he accusing Job (vv. 7–9)? **3.** What does Job "know" that his friends don't know? What type of knowledge do they possess (v. 10)? Whose words do they claim to be speaking? **4.** What is Eliphaz' view of humanity (vv. 14–16)? How does that compare with Job's view (see 10:12–13)? **5.** How does Eliphaz describe the plight of the evil man in verses 20–35? In what ways do evil people suffer? (And are they aware of it?) In what ways do they prosper? **6.** In denying that the evil always prosper, is Eliphaz answering Job's real question, or avoiding it? How so? **7.** Is Eliphaz accurate in his view of the human plight? How does Eliphaz compare to the psalmist in his views on the prosperity of the wicked (see Ps 73)? How do you reconcile the two descriptions of the plight of the evil person?

1. Who do you consider "evil" in the world today? How aware do you think they are of their evil? Are they tormented or unfeeling? **2.** Why do *you* think the wicked prosper? Why aren't good people honored and evil persons shown for who they really are? **3.** In your experience, have you seen the rich get richer and the poor get poorer? How do you account for that? Is God to blame? Why or why not?

What insights do you have that we do not have?

¹⁰The gray-haired and the aged are on our side,
    men even older than your father.
¹¹Are God's consolations not enough for you,
    words spoken gently to you?
¹²Why has your heart carried you away,
    and why do your eyes flash,
¹³so that you vent your rage against God
    and pour out such words from your mouth?

¹⁴"What is man, that he could be pure,
    or one born of woman, that he could be righteous?
¹⁵If God places no trust in his holy ones,
    if even the heavens are not pure in his eyes,
¹⁶how much less man, who is vile and corrupt,
    who drinks up evil like water!

¹⁷"Listen to me and I will explain to you;
    let me tell you what I have seen,
¹⁸what wise men have declared,
    hiding nothing received from their fathers
¹⁹(to whom alone the land was given
    when no alien passed among them):
²⁰All his days the wicked man suffers torment,
    the ruthless through all the years stored up for him.
²¹Terrifying sounds fill his ears;
    when all seems well, marauders attack him.
²²He despairs of escaping the darkness;
    he is marked for the sword.
²³He wanders about—food for vultures[a];
    he knows the day of darkness is at hand.
²⁴Distress and anguish fill him with terror;
    they overwhelm him, like a king poised to attack,
²⁵because he shakes his fist at God
    and vaunts himself against the Almighty,
²⁶defiantly charging against him
    with a thick, strong shield.

²⁷"Though his face is covered with fat
    and his waist bulges with flesh,
²⁸he will inhabit ruined towns
    and houses where no one lives,
    houses crumbling to rubble.
²⁹He will no longer be rich and his wealth will not endure,
    nor will his possessions spread over the land.
³⁰He will not escape the darkness;
    a flame will wither his shoots,
    and the breath of God's mouth will carry him away.
³¹Let him not deceive himself by trusting what is worthless,
    for he will get nothing in return.
³²Before his time he will be paid in full,
    and his branches will not flourish.

a23 Or about, looking for food

³³He will be like a vine stripped of its unripe
　　grapes,
　　like an olive tree shedding its blossoms.
³⁴For the company of the godless will be barren,
　　and fire will consume the tents of those who
　　love bribes.
³⁵They conceive trouble and give birth to evil;
　　their womb fashions deceit."

Job
16

Then Job replied:

²"I have heard many things like these;
　　miserable comforters are you all!
³Will your long-winded speeches never end?
　　What ails you that you keep on arguing?
⁴I also could speak like you,
　　if you were in my place;
　I could make fine speeches against you
　　and shake my head at you.
⁵But my mouth would encourage you;
　　comfort from my lips would bring you relief.

⁶"Yet if I speak, my pain is not relieved;
　　and if I refrain, it does not go away.
⁷Surely, O God, you have worn me out;
　　you have devastated my entire household.
⁸You have bound me—and it has become a
　　witness;
　　my gauntness rises up and testifies against me.
⁹God assails me and tears me in his anger
　　and gnashes his teeth at me;
　　my opponent fastens on me his piercing eyes.
¹⁰Men open their mouths to jeer at me;
　　they strike my cheek in scorn
　　and unite together against me.
¹¹God has turned me over to evil men
　　and thrown me into the clutches of the wicked.
¹²All was well with me, but he shattered me;
　　he seized me by the neck and crushed me.
　He has made me his target;
¹³　his archers surround me.
　Without pity, he pierces my kidneys
　　and spills my gall on the ground.
¹⁴Again and again he bursts upon me;
　　he rushes at me like a warrior.

¹⁵"I have sewed sackcloth over my skin
　　and buried my brow in the dust.
¹⁶My face is red with weeping,
　　deep shadows ring my eyes;
¹⁷yet my hands have been free of violence
　　and my prayer is pure.

¹⁸"O earth, do not cover my blood;
　　may my cry never be laid to rest!
¹⁹Even now my witness is in heaven;
　　my advocate is on high.
²⁰My intercessor is my friend[a]

1. Which role best describes the image of God you had as you were growing up: Grandfather? Executioner? Benefactor? Politician? Coach? Lifeguard? Spy? Scrooge? Other? 2. Today, what roles would you use to describe God to a non-Christian friend? 3. How would your unchurched friend depict God?

1. How does Job feel about his friends now (vv. 1–5). What kind of comforters have they proven to be? Could he do any better? 2. Who does Job see as his real enemy and why (vv. 7–8)? What four pictures of God does he paint in verses 8–14? What is his attitude toward God: Irreverent? Hateful? Bitter? 3. Is there any question in Job's mind who is the source of his suffering? Is Job cursing God here? Why or why not? 4. What picture does Job paint of himself in verses 15–17? Does he admit guilt? Does he feel the need to perform sacrifices to God as he does in 1:5? Why or why not? 5. What does he want in 16:18–17:1: Death? Heavenly intercession? Human comfort? Vindication before his peers while there's still time?

1. When have you blamed God for something in your life? What were the circumstances? Were you justified in your accusations, or was your case "thrown out of court"? On what grounds? 2. When have you felt accused by God? Were you feeling real, objective guilt, or was it self-inflicted, psychological guilt? How so?

---

a20 Or *My friends treat me with scorn*

as my eyes pour out tears to God;
²¹on behalf of a man he pleads with God
    as a man pleads for his friend.

²²"Only a few years will pass
    before I go on the journey of no return.

17 ¹My spirit is broken,
    my days are cut short,
    the grave awaits me.
²Surely mockers surround me;
    my eyes must dwell on their hostility.

³"Give me, O God, the pledge you demand.
    Who else will put up security for me?
⁴You have closed their minds to understanding;
    therefore you will not let them triumph.
⁵If a man denounces his friends for reward,
    the eyes of his children will fail.

⁶"God has made me a byword to everyone,
    a man in whose face people spit.
⁷My eyes have grown dim with grief;
    my whole frame is but a shadow.
⁸Upright men are appalled at this;
    the innocent are aroused against the ungodly.
⁹Nevertheless, the righteous will hold to their
    ways,
    and those with clean hands will grow stronger.

¹⁰"But come on, all of you, try again!
    I will not find a wise man among you.
¹¹My days have passed, my plans are shattered,
    and so are the desires of my heart.
¹²These men turn night into day;
    in the face of darkness they say, 'Light is near.'
¹³If the only home I hope for is the grave,ᵃ
    if I spread out my bed in darkness,
¹⁴if I say to corruption, 'You are my father,'
    and to the worm, 'My mother' or 'My sister,'
¹⁵where then is my hope?
    Who can see any hope for me?
¹⁶Will it go down to the gates of deathᵃ?
    Will we descend together into the dust?"

Bildad

18 Then Bildad the Shuhite replied:

²"When will you end these speeches?
    Be sensible, and then we can talk.
³Why are we regarded as cattle
    and considered stupid in your sight?
⁴You who tear yourself to pieces in your anger,
    is the earth to be abandoned for your sake?
    Or must the rocks be moved from their place?

⁵"The lamp of the wicked is snuffed out;
    the flame of his fire stops burning.
⁶The light in his tent becomes dark;
    the lamp beside him goes out.
⁷The vigor of his step is weakened;

We all have our moments when we fly so high with hope "we scrape the ceiling" or feel so sad someone has to "scrape us off the floor." What two such scraping experiences have you had most recently?

1. What tone of voice do you hear in verse 3? 6? 8–10? 12–16? **2.** Who are the mockers (v. 2), the denouncing man (v. 5), the upright and innocent (v. 8), the righteous (v. 9), and the worm (v. 14)? **3.** Does Job's claim to righteousness provide genuine hope or wishful thinking during his suffering? How can he be so sure he's right?

1. How low is Job here? Can he get any lower? Is this a case of it always being "darkest before the dawn"? Or is darkness alone the end in view? Explain. **2.** When someone demands from you an assurance that they are right, how do you react? **3.** What do you think of Job's odd bedfellows in verses 13–16? Have you (or anyone you know) ever felt that suicide was an option? What kept you going? **4.** How would you intercede for a person this close to hitting rock bottom? Where would you turn for help?

Think of a time in your childhood when you did wrong and got away with it. How did you feel about it then? How do you feel about it now?

1. In what ways has Bildad's mood changed from his first speech (ch. 8)? Who does he now view as wicked? Why? **2.** How does Bildad respond to Job's words in 12:7–10? What is he suggesting that Job is trying to do (vv. 3–4)? **3.** What is so wrong with Bildad's theology in verses 5–21? Which of his assertions is tainted: (a) Evil persons have to live with the consequences of their sin? (b) Evil is a trap? (c) Evil brings calamity? (d) The wages of sin is death

---

ᵃ *13,16 Hebrew* Sheol

his own schemes throw him down.
8His feet thrust him into a net
   and he wanders into its mesh.
9A trap seizes him by the heel;
   a snare holds him fast.
10A noose is hidden for him on the ground;
   a trap lies in his path.
11Terrors startle him on every side
   and dog his every step.
12Calamity is hungry for him;
   disaster is ready for him when he falls.
13It eats away parts of his skin;
   death's firstborn devours his limbs.
14He is torn from the security of his tent
   and marched off to the king of terrors.
15Fire resides*a* in his tent;
   burning sulfur is scattered over his dwelling.
16His roots dry up below
   and his branches wither above.
17The memory of him perishes from the earth;
   he has no name in the land.
18He is driven from light into darkness
   and is banished from the world.
19He has no offspring or descendants among his
     people,
   no survivor where once he lived.
20Men of the west are appalled at his fate;
   men of the east are seized with horror.
21Surely such is the dwelling of an evil man;
   such is the place of one who knows not God."

Job
19   Then Job replied:

2"How long will you torment me
   and crush me with words?
3Ten times now you have reproached me;
   shamelessly you attack me.
4If it is true that I have gone astray,
   my error remains my concern alone.
5If indeed you would exalt yourselves above me
   and use my humiliation against me,
6then know that God has wronged me
   and drawn his net around me.

7"Though I cry, 'I've been wronged!' I get no
     response;
   though I call for help, there is no justice.
8He has blocked my way so I cannot pass;
   he has shrouded my paths in darkness.
9He has stripped me of my honor
   and removed the crown from my head.
10He tears me down on every side till I am gone;
   he uproots my hope like a tree.
11His anger burns against me;
   he counts me among his enemies.
12His troops advance in force;

a 15 Or *Nothing he had remains*

(see Ro 6:23)? **4.** But to whom is Bildad applying this theology? In what circumstances? What is of primary concern to Bildad, the traditionalist? Can one be right in theory and wrong in practice? How so?

1. When have you caught yourself saying "they are only living with the consequences of their sin"? What were the circumstances? When have you been right in applying this concept to others? When have you been wrong? Upon what grounds did you judge? **2.** Is there an exact correlation between a person's suffering and his or her sin? How is this concept of "suffering equals sin" different from the concept of "living with the consequences of your sin"?

---

1. If you were poised over your own tombstone with chisel in hand, what words would you inscribe to summarize your life? How would you want people to remember you? **2.** What are your favorite lines from Handel's *Messiah*?

1. Surely now (vv. 6–20) Job has cursed God, or has he? What does cursing God mean for Job: (a) To claim righteousness for himself (vv. 4–9)? (b) To blame God as his enemy (v. 6)? (c) To be lonely, rejected by loved ones and in despair rather than to "trust" God (vv. 13–20)? (d) Other? **2.** Could it be that God has cursed or "wronged" Job? How so? Is Job here refuting Bildad's notion that man brings evil on himself (see 18:8–10)? Or is he only denying that in his case, suffering is not the consequence of evil? And if not Job, then who else but God can he blame? **3.** In contrast to friends and family who are all alienated from him, to whom does Job turn in verses 23–27? What is it that Job wants inscribed and for what reason? For what does he yearn? **4.**

God has wronged, struck and alienated Job (vv. 6–22). How can he also be Job's "Redeemer" (v. 25)? (a) Job is speaking of Christ who redeems from guilt and sin. (b) Job wants someone to plead his case before God. (c) Job thinks of God alone as his "Kinsman-redeemer" (akin to Boaz in the story of Ruth). What else could Job have in mind here?

1. Is there a sharper pain than rejection by your loved ones? When have you been a parent in pain? A spouse in pain? A child in pain? 2. When have you found it easier to depend upon your good works rather than to hope in a Redeemer who lives and cares for his own? How could you use a living Redeemer right now?

they build a siege ramp against me
and encamp around my tent.

13"He has alienated my brothers from me;
my acquaintances are completely estranged from me.
14My kinsmen have gone away;
my friends have forgotten me.
15My guests and my maidservants count me a stranger;
they look upon me as an alien.
16I summon my servant, but he does not answer,
though I beg him with my own mouth.
17My breath is offensive to my wife;
I am loathsome to my own brothers.
18Even the little boys scorn me;
when I appear, they ridicule me.
19All my intimate friends detest me;
those I love have turned against me.
20I am nothing but skin and bones;
I have escaped with only the skin of my teeth.ᵃ

21"Have pity on me, my friends, have pity,
for the hand of God has struck me.
22Why do you pursue me as God does?
Will you never get enough of my flesh?

23"Oh, that my words were recorded,
that they were written on a scroll,
24that they were inscribed with an iron tool onᵇ lead,
or engraved in rock forever!
25I know that my Redeemerᶜ lives,
and that in the end he will stand upon the earth.ᵈ
26And after my skin has been destroyed,
yetᵉ inᶠ my flesh I will see God;
27I myself will see him
with my own eyes—I, and not another.
How my heart yearns within me!

28"If you say, 'How we will hound him,
since the root of the trouble lies in him,ᵍ'
29you should fear the sword yourselves;
for wrath will bring punishment by the sword,
and then you will know that there is judgment.ʰ"

Zophar

20 Then Zophar the Naamathite replied:

2"My troubled thoughts prompt me to answer
because I am greatly disturbed.
3I hear a rebuke that dishonors me,
and my understanding inspires me to reply.

4"Surely you know how it has been from of old,

What is the "sure-fire" way of starting an argument in your home (or on the job, with your in-laws, your best friend)? What is your "sure-fire" way of ending one?

1. What seems to bother Zophar the most about Job's earlier remarks (19:28–29), as reflected here (vv. 1–3)? Are Zophar's arguments (vv. 4–11) now just theoretical? What else is at stake for him and his source of authority? 2. According to Zophar,

ᵃ20 Or only my gums   ᵇ24 Or and   ᶜ25 Or defender   ᵈ25 Or upon my grave   ᵉ26 Or And after I awake, / though this ⌊body⌋ has been destroyed, / then   ᶠ26 Or / apart from   ᵍ28 Many Hebrew manuscripts, Septuagint and Vulgate; most Hebrew manuscripts me   ʰ29 Or / that you may come to know the Almighty

ever since man[a] was placed on the earth,
⁵that the mirth of the wicked is brief,
    the joy of the godless lasts but a moment.
⁶Though his pride reaches to the heavens
    and his head touches the clouds,
⁷he will perish forever, like his own dung;
    those who have seen him will say, 'Where is
        he?'
⁸Like a dream he flies away, no more to be found,
    banished like a vision of the night.
⁹The eye that saw him will not see him again;
    his place will look on him no more.
¹⁰His children must make amends to the poor;
    his own hands must give back his wealth.
¹¹The youthful vigor that fills his bones
    will lie with him in the dust.

¹²"Though evil is sweet in his mouth
    and he hides it under his tongue,
¹³though he cannot bear to let it go
    and keeps it in his mouth,
¹⁴yet his food will turn sour in his stomach;
    it will become the venom of serpents within
        him.
¹⁵He will spit out the riches he swallowed;
    God will make his stomach vomit them up.
¹⁶He will suck the poison of serpents;
    the fangs of an adder will kill him.
¹⁷He will not enjoy the streams,
    the rivers flowing with honey and cream.
¹⁸What he toiled for he must give back uneaten;
    he will not enjoy the profit from his trading.
¹⁹For he has oppressed the poor and left them
        destitute;
    he has seized houses he did not build.

²⁰"Surely he will have no respite from his craving;
    he cannot save himself by his treasure.
²¹Nothing is left for him to devour;
    his prosperity will not endure.
²²In the midst of his plenty, distress will overtake
        him;
    the full force of misery will come upon him.
²³When he has filled his belly,
    God will vent his burning anger against him
    and rain down his blows upon him.
²⁴Though he flees from an iron weapon,
    a bronze-tipped arrow pierces him.
²⁵He pulls it out of his back,
    the gleaming point out of his liver.
    Terrors will come over him;
²⁶   total darkness lies in wait for his treasures.
    A fire unfanned will consume him
        and devour what is left in his tent.
²⁷The heavens will expose his guilt;
    the earth will rise up against him.
²⁸A flood will carry off his house,
    rushing waters[b] on the day of God's wrath.

what immediate consequences befall the wicked (vv. 4–11)? What images help to make his point? What disasters are prepared for the wicked (vv. 23–29)? **3.** According to standards for "orthodoxy," what flaws, if any, can you find in Zophar's theology of what happens to the wicked? Can there be any escaping the "logic" of what he's saying?

1. When was the last time a sweet, healthy family discussion turned into a sour, vicious argument? Did it start with good intentions? What went wrong? Why did it turn personal? What drama was going on beneath the spoken words? How did the discussion end? **2.** What was going on in your own mouth and stomach as you chewed on what Zophar had to say in verses 12–23?

a4 Or *Adam*   b28 Or *The possessions in his house will be carried off, / washed away*

²⁹Such is the fate God allots the wicked,
the heritage appointed for them by God."

Job 21

Then Job replied:

²"Listen carefully to my words;
let this be the consolation you give me.
³Bear with me while I speak,
and after I have spoken, mock on.

⁴"Is my complaint directed to man?
Why should I not be impatient?
⁵Look at me and be astonished;
clap your hand over your mouth.
⁶When I think about this, I am terrified;
trembling seizes my body.
⁷Why do the wicked live on,
growing old and increasing in power?
⁸They see their children established around them,
their offspring before their eyes.
⁹Their homes are safe and free from fear;
the rod of God is not upon them.
¹⁰Their bulls never fail to breed;
their cows calve and do not miscarry.
¹¹They send forth their children as a flock;
their little ones dance about.
¹²They sing to the music of tambourine and harp;
they make merry to the sound of the flute.
¹³They spend their years in prosperity
and go down to the grave^a in peace.^b
¹⁴Yet they say to God, 'Leave us alone!
We have no desire to know your ways.
¹⁵Who is the Almighty, that we should serve him?
What would we gain by praying to him?'
¹⁶But their prosperity is not in their own hands,
so I stand aloof from the counsel of the wicked.

¹⁷"Yet how often is the lamp of the wicked snuffed out?
How often does calamity come upon them,
the fate God allots in his anger?
¹⁸How often are they like straw before the wind,
like chaff swept away by a gale?
¹⁹⌊It is said,⌋ 'God stores up a man's punishment for his sons.'
Let him repay the man himself, so that he will know it!
²⁰Let his own eyes see his destruction;
let him drink of the wrath of the Almighty.^c
²¹For what does he care about the family he leaves behind
when his allotted months come to an end?

²²"Can anyone teach knowledge to God,
since he judges even the highest?
²³One man dies in full vigor,
completely secure and at ease,

---

1. What best describes your ideas on prosperity: (a) "The one with the most toys in the end wins"? (b) "You can't take it with you"? (c) "Eat, drink and be merry, for tomorrow we die(t)"? (d) "Everything that goes around, comes around," so no one gets away with anything? (e) "God sends rain on the just and the unjust," so both their parades get wet? (f) "The righteous shall prosper"? (g) "Everyone gets what they deserve," nothing more, nothing less? (h) "What the mind can conceive and the will believe, you can and will achieve, so think and grow rich"?

1. To whom is Job directing his complaint in verse 4 and why? *2.* How does Job view the happiness of the wicked (vv. 7–16)? How does it compare to Eliphaz' account of the happiness of the righteous in 5:17–27? *3.* How does Job perceive the fate of the wicked (vv. 17–21)? How does Job's view compare to his friend's (8:11–19; 15:20–35; 18:5–21; 20)? In what ways is Job right? In what ways are his three friends right? *4.* In contrast to his friends, what is Job saying in verses 22–26? In what ways is God bigger than the teaching of his three friends (see Isa 40:14; Mt 5:45)? Is Job focussing here on a principle of equality, fickleness, absurdity, mystery, or what? Explain. *5.* What nonsense and falsehood is Job speaking of in verse 34? How does that relate to his opening remarks in verses 2–3?

1. How do you respond to someone who has an answer for everything? Do they, really? *2.* Relative to your parents, are you more, or less, prosperous than they? Are you paying your dues and getting "just deserts," or being "short-changed"? In general, is life fairly predictable to you or is it "sloppy business"? How do you make sense out of the exceptions in *your* life? *3.* To what extent do you allow God to make sense out of your life? Does he explain every detail? What do you do with all the "loose ends"? *4.* If no one can instruct God (v. 22), then why does the Church try to neatly define its dogma? Why do we say God adheres to certain inviolable spiritual laws of the universe?

---

^a13 Hebrew *Sheol*   ^b13 Or *in an instant*   ^c17-20 Verses 17 and 18 may be taken as exclamations and 19 and 20 as declarations.

²⁴his body*ᵃ* well nourished,
  his bones rich with marrow.
²⁵Another man dies in bitterness of soul,
  never having enjoyed anything good.
²⁶Side by side they lie in the dust,
  and worms cover them both.

²⁷"I know full well what you are thinking,
  the schemes by which you would wrong me.
²⁸You say, 'Where now is the great man's house,
  the tents where wicked men lived?'
²⁹Have you never questioned those who travel?
  Have you paid no regard to their accounts—
³⁰that the evil man is spared from the day of
    calamity,
  that he is delivered from*ᵇ* the day of wrath?
³¹Who denounces his conduct to his face?
  Who repays him for what he has done?
³²He is carried to the grave,
  and watch is kept over his tomb.
³³The soil in the valley is sweet to him;
  all men follow after him,
  and a countless throng goes*ᶜ* before him.

³⁴"So how can you console me with your nonsense?
  Nothing is left of your answers but falsehood!"

Eliphaz

22 Then Eliphaz the Temanite replied:

²"Can a man be of benefit to God?
  Can even a wise man benefit him?
³What pleasure would it give the Almighty if you
    were righteous?
  What would he gain if your ways were
    blameless?

⁴"Is it for your piety that he rebukes you
  and brings charges against you?
⁵Is not your wickedness great?
  Are not your sins endless?
⁶You demanded security from your brothers for no
    reason;
  you stripped men of their clothing, leaving
    them naked.
⁷You gave no water to the weary
  and you withheld food from the hungry,
⁸though you were a powerful man, owning land—
  an honored man, living on it.
⁹And you sent widows away empty-handed
  and broke the strength of the fatherless.
¹⁰That is why snares are all around you,
  why sudden peril terrifies you,
¹¹why it is so dark you cannot see,
  and why a flood of water covers you.

¹²"Is not God in the heights of heaven?
  And see how lofty are the highest stars!

ᵃ24 The meaning of the Hebrew for this word is uncertain.   *ᵇ30* Or *man is reserved
for the day of calamity, / that he is brought forth to*   *ᶜ33* Or / *as a countless throng
went*

---

1. Do you pay attention to advice columnists like Ann Landers and Dr. Ruth? If you did submit a problem to them, what do you fear might happen? How would you have to qualify their counsel? **2.** Likewise, with applying the case studies from self-help books, when have you misapplied truth that didn't really fit your situation?

1. Chapters 22:1–26:14 constitute the third cycle of dialogue. Compared with Eliphaz' first speech (see 4:3–6; 5:17–19, for example), what kind of friend has he become? Why the change? **2.** What is Eliphaz saying about the character of God and humanity in verses 2–4? What irony is Eliphaz unwittingly contributing to the story of Job (see 1:8–12; 2:3–6)? **3.** In verses 5–11, why is he claiming Job is evil? Is he being fair, or libelous? (For Job's reputation, see 1:1–5; for Job's refutation, see 29:11–17.) What concerns do they share in common? **4.** In verses 12–20, in what ways has Eliphaz overstated his case? **5.** In verses 21–30, in what ways is he theologically "correct" in his last attempt to reach Job? How does this speech of Eliphaz compare with the song of David in 2 Samuel 22:20–28? **6.** Good theology can be harmful if applied to the wrong situation. How are the situations different for David and Job?

1. When have you misapplied truth in counseling another? 2. What does it mean to "walk a mile in the moccasins of another"? Have you? When and with whom? How did it change you or your attitude toward the other person? How did it affect the other person? 3. Eliphaz and Job agree on at least this much—the appalling treatment received by the fatherless, the widowed, the hungry. How can you help the single-parent household in your neighborhood?

¹³Yet you say, 'What does God know?
    Does he judge through such darkness?
¹⁴Thick clouds veil him, so he does not see us
    as he goes about in the vaulted heavens.'
¹⁵Will you keep to the old path
    that evil men have trod?
¹⁶They were carried off before their time,
    their foundations washed away by a flood.
¹⁷They said to God, 'Leave us alone!
    What can the Almighty do to us?'
¹⁸Yet it was he who filled their houses with good
      things,
    so I stand aloof from the counsel of the wicked.

¹⁹"The righteous see their ruin and rejoice;
    the innocent mock them, saying,
²⁰'Surely our foes are destroyed,
    and fire devours their wealth.'

²¹"Submit to God and be at peace with him;
    in this way prosperity will come to you.
²²Accept instruction from his mouth
    and lay up his words in your heart.
²³If you return to the Almighty, you will be
      restored:
    If you remove wickedness far from your tent
²⁴and assign your nuggets to the dust,
    your gold of Ophir to the rocks in the ravines,
²⁵then the Almighty will be your gold,
    the choicest silver for you.
²⁶Surely then you will find delight in the Almighty
    and will lift up your face to God.
²⁷You will pray to him, and he will hear you,
    and you will fulfill your vows.
²⁸What you decide on will be done,
    and light will shine on your ways.
²⁹When men are brought low and you say, 'Lift
      them up!'
    then he will save the downcast.
³⁰He will deliver even one who is not innocent,
    who will be delivered through the cleanness of
      your hands."

1. Did you enjoy playing "hide-and-seek" as a child (or as a parent with a child)? Which did you like more—hiding or seeking? If you were "it," what motivated you to keep seeking? 2. If you were to bring a malpractice suit against God for the bad way things turned out one particular day, what would be the charges? What compensation would you want?

1. Job dares seek a day in court with God. What would he do in God's presence (vv. 3–7)? What does he wish from God in return? 2. Why can't Job find God (vv. 8–9; compare Ps 139:7–10): (a) Looking in the wrong places? (b) Not looking with faith or humili-

Job

23 Then Job replied:

²"Even today my complaint is bitter;
    his hand^a is heavy in spite of^b my groaning.
³If only I knew where to find him;
    if only I could go to his dwelling!
⁴I would state my case before him
    and fill my mouth with arguments.
⁵I would find out what he would answer me,
    and consider what he would say.
⁶Would he oppose me with great power?
    No, he would not press charges against me.
⁷There an upright man could present his case
    before him,

a2 Septuagint and Syriac; Hebrew */ the hand on me*   *b2* Or *heavy on me in*

and I would be delivered forever from my judge.

8"But if I go to the east, he is not there;
    if I go to the west, I do not find him.
9When he is at work in the north, I do not see him;
    when he turns to the south, I catch no glimpse of him.
10But he knows the way that I take;
    when he has tested me, I will come forth as gold.
11My feet have closely followed his steps;
    I have kept to his way without turning aside.
12I have not departed from the commands of his lips;
    I have treasured the words of his mouth more than my daily bread.

13"But he stands alone, and who can oppose him?
    He does whatever he pleases.
14He carries out his decree against me,
    and many such plans he still has in store.
15That is why I am terrified before him;
    when I think of all this, I fear him.
16God has made my heart faint;
    the Almighty has terrified me.
17Yet I am not silenced by the darkness,
    by the thick darkness that covers my face.

24 "Why does the Almighty not set times for judgment?
    Why must those who know him look in vain for such days?
2Men move boundary stones;
    they pasture flocks they have stolen.
3They drive away the orphan's donkey
    and take the widow's ox in pledge.
4They thrust the needy from the path
    and force all the poor of the land into hiding.
5Like wild donkeys in the desert,
    the poor go about their labor of foraging food;
    the wasteland provides food for their children.
6They gather fodder in the fields
    and glean in the vineyards of the wicked.
7Lacking clothes, they spend the night naked;
    they have nothing to cover themselves in the cold.
8They are drenched by mountain rains
    and hug the rocks for lack of shelter.
9The fatherless child is snatched from the breast;
    the infant of the poor is seized for a debt.
10Lacking clothes, they go about naked;
    they carry the sheaves, but still go hungry.
11They crush olives among the terraces *a*;
    they tread the winepresses, yet suffer thirst.
12The groans of the dying rise from the city,
    and the souls of the wounded cry out for help.
    But God charges no one with wrongdoing.

a 11 Or *olives between the millstones*; the meaning of the Hebrew for this word is uncertain.

---

ty? (c) Veiled from seeing what we readers of the Prologue can see? (d) God can stay in hiding as long as he pleases? **3.** How do verses 10–12 resolve this paradox of God's silence? How does Job contradict Eliphaz' advice in 22:22? What does it mean to be "tested" by God? **4.** In verses 13–17, what does Job fear? What does he hope?

♥ **1.** When you, like Job, can't sense God in your life, what do you feel most: Disorientation? Guilt? Loneliness? Alienation? Explain. **2.** Why does God sometimes choose to "hide"? What can you do to make God reveal himself? **3.** At such times, is he hiding from you, or are you hiding from him? **4.** How does God take the initiative in finding *you?*

---

1. Desk tops can be quite revealing (e.g., "Clean desks are the province of a sick mind"). What does yours say about you: "Creative clutter" or "Well-ordered paranoia"? What would your closest family member say and why? **2.** Would you want Judgment Day to come *sooner* (while everything is still in order) or *later* (to give you time to clean house)?

1. Job still wants to know where in the world God is when it hurts. What is the implication behind his questions in verse 1? **2.** What does the prosperity of the wicked say about God's system of justice (vv. 1–12)? What does Job think God is doing about crimes committed against the poor (vv. 2–4)? The unfulfilled needs of the poor and oppressed (vv. 5–12)? The crimes of the wicked (vv. 13–17)? **3.** Does Job seem more concerned about the victims of crime, the perpetrators of crime, or the God who seemingly does nothing about either? In questioning him in this manner, is Job cursing God now? **4.** Does it please Job (and his friends) that the wicked do get their due (vv. 18–25), or does that only exacerbate Job's dilemma? How so? **5.** How is Job limited by *time* (vv. 1, 21–24)? How is God unlimited by this constraint?

♡ **1.** When you look at the condition of the world today, do you ever wonder whether God is in control? Explain. **2.** What is your answer to why the evil person prospers? To why poverty and social injustice persist? To why murder, theft, adultery are on the rise? **3.** If justice is served only after you pass from the scene, what satisfaction do you derive from that? Are you willing to wait until then for justice to be done? What moral deterrent is that to those who don't care what happens to them in the next life?

13"There are those who rebel against the light,
   who do not know its ways
   or stay in its paths.
14When daylight is gone, the murderer rises up
   and kills the poor and needy;
   in the night he steals forth like a thief.
15The eye of the adulterer watches for dusk;
   he thinks, 'No eye will see me,'
   and he keeps his face concealed.
16In the dark, men break into houses,
   but by day they shut themselves in;
   they want nothing to do with the light.
17For all of them, deep darkness is their morning*a*;
   they make friends with the terrors of
      darkness.*b*

18"Yet they are foam on the surface of the water;
   their portion of the land is cursed,
   so that no one goes to the vineyards.
19As heat and drought snatch away the melted
      snow,
   so the grave*c* snatches away those who have
      sinned.
20The womb forgets them,
   the worm feasts on them;
   evil men are no longer remembered
   but are broken like a tree.
21They prey on the barren and childless woman,
   and to the widow show no kindness.
22But God drags away the mighty by his power;
   though they become established, they have no
      assurance of life.
23He may let them rest in a feeling of security,
   but his eyes are on their ways.
24For a little while they are exalted, and then they
      are gone;
   they are brought low and gathered up like all
      others;
   they are cut off like heads of grain.

25"If this is not so, who can prove me false
   and reduce my words to nothing?"

🍵 What worm-like qualities do you exhibit? Which worm-like qualities are repugnant to you?

📖 Bildad echoes the traditional view of human sin and impurity and God's righteousness (see 4:17–19; 15:14–16). Would Job agree or disagree with Bildad? How so?

♡ **1.** What does it mean to be basically good or evil? Is mankind basically good or evil? Or both? Support your view from your own experience, history and Scripture. **2.** What is the place of "worm theology" for the Christian? Is it a healthy or a dangerous corrective?

Bildad

25 Then Bildad the Shuhite replied:

2"Dominion and awe belong to God;
   he establishes order in the heights of heaven.
3Can his forces be numbered?
   Upon whom does his light not rise?
4How then can a man be righteous before God?
   How can one born of woman be pure?
5If even the moon is not bright
   and the stars are not pure in his eyes,
6how much less man, who is but a maggot—
   a son of man, who is only a worm!"

a17 Or *them, their morning is like the shadow of death*   *b17* Or *of the shadow of death*   *c19* Hebrew *Sheol*

Job

26

Then Job replied:

2"How you have helped the powerless!
  How you have saved the arm that is feeble!
3What advice you have offered to one without
      wisdom!
  And what great insight you have displayed!
4Who has helped you utter these words?
  And whose spirit spoke from your mouth?

5"The dead are in deep anguish,
  those beneath the waters and all that live in
      them.
6Death[a] is naked before God;
  Destruction[b] lies uncovered.
7He spreads out the northern ⌊skies⌋ over empty
      space;
  he suspends the earth over nothing.
8He wraps up the waters in his clouds,
  yet the clouds do not burst under their weight.
9He covers the face of the full moon,
  spreading his clouds over it.
10He marks out the horizon on the face of the
      waters
  for a boundary between light and darkness.
11The pillars of the heavens quake,
  aghast at his rebuke.
12By his power he churned up the sea;
  by his wisdom he cut Rahab to pieces.
13By his breath the skies became fair;
  his hand pierced the gliding serpent.
14And these are but the outer fringe of his works;
  how faint the whisper we hear of him!
  Who then can understand the thunder of his
      power?"

27

And Job continued his discourse:

2"As surely as God lives, who has denied me
      justice,
  the Almighty, who has made me taste bitterness
      of soul,
3as long as I have life within me,
  the breath of God in my nostrils,
4my lips will not speak wickedness,
  and my tongue will utter no deceit.
5I will never admit you are in the right;
  till I die, I will not deny my integrity.
6I will maintain my righteousness and never let go
      of it;
  my conscience will not reproach me as long as I
      live.

7"May my enemies be like the wicked,
  my adversaries like the unjust!
8For what hope has the godless when he is cut off,
  when God takes away his life?
9Does God listen to his cry

Were you ever fascinated with dinosaurs and monsters of the deep? Who did you picture as able to slay them?

1. How does this speech relate to Bildad's speech (ch. 25)? To what his friends said earlier in 11:7–9? 2. Why the sarcasm? Why the colorful images? 3. Review the figures of speech: What pictures do they paint for you of God in relation to his creation? 4. What attributes of God are plainly evident in creation? Which can only be faintly discerned (v. 14)?

1. What is your response to this hymn of praise? 2. Imagine yourself praising God in this manner while in Job's condition. Can you? How can a man who once looked futilely in all directions for God (in ch. 23) now describe God like this? What does it say about Job? About God? 3. With *words only* (no pictures, analogies or figurative language), try to describe God, as if to a child. What words do you use? Are words alone adequate? Why or why not?

1. In disputed matters, how easy is it for you to admit someone else is in the right: During the first round of the conflict? Second? Fifteenth? 2. Ever lock horns in a never-ending dispute? What was it like?

1. Is Job appealing to his own rights or to God's justice (vv. 2–6)? If he were appealing to his rights what would be his case? 2. How far has Job come here from his response to his wife in 2:9–10? Has he compromised an inch? A foot? A mile? What is still most important to him? What does hanging onto his integrity have to do with cursing or not cursing God? 3. Who are Job's enemies? What does he wish for them? What are the implications? 4. What is the fate of the wicked (vv. 13–23)? How does this description compare with Zophar's description in chapter 20? To what extent does Job fit this description?

*a*6 Hebrew *Sheol*   *b*6 Hebrew *Abaddon*

♡ **1.** When have you wanted something so much that you were willing to come to blows in order to receive it? How might the saying, "No pain, no gain," fit Job? How might that describe your last year? **2.** Was it wrong for Job to complain to God? Why or why not? What does the believer's apparent freedom to question or argue with God say about the character of God?

when distress comes upon him?
¹⁰Will he find delight in the Almighty?
Will he call upon God at all times?

¹¹"I will teach you about the power of God;
the ways of the Almighty I will not conceal.
¹²You have all seen this yourselves.
Why then this meaningless talk?

¹³"Here is the fate God allots to the wicked,
the heritage a ruthless man receives from the Almighty:
¹⁴However many his children, their fate is the sword;
his offspring will never have enough to eat.
¹⁵The plague will bury those who survive him,
and their widows will not weep for them.
¹⁶Though he heaps up silver like dust
and clothes like piles of clay,
¹⁷what he lays up the righteous will wear,
and the innocent will divide his silver.
¹⁸The house he builds is like a moth's cocoon,
like a hut made by a watchman.
¹⁹He lies down wealthy, but will do so no more;
when he opens his eyes, all is gone.
²⁰Terrors overtake him like a flood;
a tempest snatches him away in the night.
²¹The east wind carries him off, and he is gone;
it sweeps him out of his place.
²²It hurls itself against him without mercy
as he flees headlong from its power.
²³It claps its hands in derision
and hisses him out of his place.

☕ **1.** If you were looking for "wisdom" in your hometown, where would you look first: (a) The community college? (b) The den of your house? (c) The bar scene? (d) Your relatives? (e) Sunday School class? How would you know when you found it? **2.** Recall a time when you were looking to master a certain subject matter in school. Where did you go to find what you were looking for?

📖 **1.** Where, if anywhere, has Job found wisdom in the words of his friends: (a) Through mystical experience? (b) Theology and historical precedent? (c) Common sense? Why not just call God's actions a mystery and leave it at that? **2.** If a monetary figure could assess how precious wisdom and understanding are to Job (vv. 13–19), what figure would you pick? **3.** How does one answer Job's question, "Where then does wisdom come from?" (vv. 12,20)? Does it appear to be easily available? Plainly seen? Mysteriously hidden? Divinely revealed? Spiritually discerned? Commonly over-

28 "There is a mine for silver
and a place where gold is refined.
²Iron is taken from the earth,
and copper is smelted from ore.
³Man puts an end to the darkness;
he searches the farthest recesses
for ore in the blackest darkness.
⁴Far from where people dwell he cuts a shaft,
in places forgotten by the foot of man;
far from men he dangles and sways.
⁵The earth, from which food comes,
is transformed below as by fire;
⁶sapphires*ᵃ* come from its rocks,
and its dust contains nuggets of gold.
⁷No bird of prey knows that hidden path,
no falcon's eye has seen it.
⁸Proud beasts do not set foot on it,
and no lion prowls there.
⁹Man's hand assaults the flinty rock
and lays bare the roots of the mountains.
¹⁰He tunnels through the rock;
his eyes see all its treasures.
¹¹He searches*ᵇ* the sources of the rivers
and brings hidden things to light.

ᵃ6 Or *lapis lazuli*; also in verse 16   *ᵇ11* Septuagint, Aquila and Vulgate; Hebrew *He dams up*

¹²"But where can wisdom be found?
    Where does understanding dwell?
¹³Man does not comprehend its worth;
    it cannot be found in the land of the living.
¹⁴The deep says, 'It is not in me';
    the sea says, 'It is not with me.'
¹⁵It cannot be bought with the finest gold,
    nor can its price be weighed in silver.
¹⁶It cannot be bought with the gold of Ophir,
    with precious onyx or sapphires.
¹⁷Neither gold nor crystal can compare with it,
    nor can it be had for jewels of gold.
¹⁸Coral and jasper are not worthy of mention;
    the price of wisdom is beyond rubies.
¹⁹The topaz of Cush cannot compare with it;
    it cannot be bought with pure gold.

²⁰"Where then does wisdom come from?
    Where does understanding dwell?
²¹It is hidden from the eyes of every living thing,
    concealed even from the birds of the air.
²²Destruction^a and Death say,
    'Only a rumor of it has reached our ears.'
²³God understands the way to it
    and he alone knows where it dwells,
²⁴for he views the ends of the earth
    and sees everything under the heavens.
²⁵When he established the force of the wind
    and measured out the waters,
²⁶when he made a decree for the rain
    and a path for the thunderstorm,
²⁷then he looked at wisdom and appraised it;
    he confirmed it and tested it.
²⁸And he said to man,
    'The fear of the Lord—that is wisdom,
    and to shun evil is understanding.'"

29

Job continued his discourse:

²"How I long for the months gone by,
    for the days when God watched over me,
³when his lamp shone upon my head
    and by his light I walked through darkness!
⁴Oh, for the days when I was in my prime,
    when God's intimate friendship blessed my
      house,
⁵when the Almighty was still with me
    and my children were around me,
⁶when my path was drenched with cream
    and the rock poured out for me streams of olive
      oil.

⁷"When I went to the gate of the city
    and took my seat in the public square,
⁸the young men saw me and stepped aside
    and the old men rose to their feet;
⁹the chief men refrained from speaking
    and covered their mouths with their hands;
¹⁰the voices of the nobles were hushed,

^a22 Hebrew *Abaddon*

looked? **4.** With what price tag does wisdom come (vv. 15–19)? **5.** What does it mean that God *looked, appraised, confirmed* and *tested* wisdom (v. 27)? How is wisdom apparent in one's life (v. 28)?

1. How understanding are you of the way God is working in your life? If you could see behind heaven's curtain to behold the purpose and rationale behind all the things happening to you, would you keep your eyes open, or would you turn away? **2.** All modesty aside, are you considered a wise person? In what ways? How will you strive to be a wiser and more understanding person this month?

"Oh, for the good ol' days!" What slice of life in your past are you yearning to taste once again? What made it so good? Was it really all that good?

1. How does Job characterize his past relationship with God (vv. 1–6)? How does his memory of the "good ol' days" compare with what was said of him back then (1:1–5)? Has God's relationship with Job changed? How so? **2.** How would you portray Job's role in the community: (a) Wealthy banker? (b) Civic-minded mayor? (c) Benevolent physician? (d) Community activist? (e) Pious preacher? In a word, characterize his reputation. Is Job being boastful here, or just realistic? **3.** What were Job's expectations and goals in life (vv. 18–20)? Did he have every right to hold these expectations? What right did Job have to expect anything good from God?

♡ 1. What memories of your past are especially meaningful to you? Why? How have these memories sustained you in difficult times? In what ways can memories be viewed as gifts from God? 2. Looking to the future, what right do we have to expect only good things from God? Doesn't God always give us "the desires of our heart" (see Ps 20:4)? What does God promise that we can expect? What doesn't he promise?

and their tongues stuck to the roof of their
        mouths.
¹¹Whoever heard me spoke well of me,
    and those who saw me commended me,
¹²because I rescued the poor who cried for help,
    and the fatherless who had none to assist him.
¹³The man who was dying blessed me;
    I made the widow's heart sing.
¹⁴I put on righteousness as my clothing;
    justice was my robe and my turban.
¹⁵I was eyes to the blind
    and feet to the lame.
¹⁶I was a father to the needy;
    I took up the case of the stranger.
¹⁷I broke the fangs of the wicked
    and snatched the victims from their teeth.

¹⁸"I thought, 'I will die in my own house,
    my days as numerous as the grains of sand.
¹⁹My roots will reach to the water,
    and the dew will lie all night on my branches.
²⁰My glory will remain fresh in me,
    the bow ever new in my hand.'

²¹"Men listened to me expectantly,
    waiting in silence for my counsel.
²²After I had spoken, they spoke no more;
    my words fell gently on their ears.
²³They waited for me as for showers
    and drank in my words as the spring rain.
²⁴When I smiled at them, they scarcely believed it;
    the light of my face was precious to them.[a]
²⁵I chose the way for them and sat as their chief;
    I dwelt as a king among his troops;
    I was like one who comforts mourners.

30 "But now they mock me,
        men younger than I,
    whose fathers I would have disdained
        to put with my sheep dogs.
²Of what use was the strength of their hands to
        me,
    since their vigor had gone from them?
³Haggard from want and hunger,
    they roamed[b] the parched land
        in desolate wastelands at night.
⁴In the brush they gathered salt herbs,
    and their food[c] was the root of the broom
        tree.
⁵They were banished from their fellow men,
    shouted at as if they were thieves.
⁶They were forced to live in the dry stream beds,
    among the rocks and in holes in the ground.
⁷They brayed among the bushes
    and huddled in the undergrowth.
⁸A base and nameless brood,
    they were driven out of the land.

⁹"And now their sons mock me in song;

☕ The before-and-after picture that best describes your life would involve: (a) The loss of poundage? (b) The loss of hair? (c) Your mortgage payments in lieu of rent? (d) A picture of you wearing far more polyester than any person should have been allowed to wear? (e) Other?

📖 1. Demonstrating the truth of 1:21, "the Lord gave" (ch. 29) and "the Lord has taken away" (ch. 30). In chapter 30, what has been taken away? What was Job most concerned about losing? What about his children, his possessions, his health? Why is his reputation so important (vv. 9–15) to him? 2. As those who understand the events of chapters 1–2, how do you respond to Job's comments in verses 16–23? What is Job claiming God has done with his divine power? Is he right? 3. Why doesn't God answer Job when he calls (v. 20)? Is Job being ignored by God? Why aren't Job's sincerity and righteousness enough (vv.

a24 The meaning of the Hebrew for this clause is uncertain.   b3 Or *gnawed*
c4 Or *fuel*

I have become a byword among them.
¹⁰They detest me and keep their distance;
    they do not hesitate to spit in my face.
¹¹Now that God has unstrung my bow and afflicted me,
    they throw off restraint in my presence.
¹²On my right the tribe[a] attacks;
    they lay snares for my feet,
    they build their siege ramps against me.
¹³They break up my road;
    they succeed in destroying me—
    without anyone's helping them.[b]
¹⁴They advance as through a gaping breach;
    amid the ruins they come rolling in.
¹⁵Terrors overwhelm me;
    my dignity is driven away as by the wind,
    my safety vanishes like a cloud.

¹⁶"And now my life ebbs away;
    days of suffering grip me.
¹⁷Night pierces my bones;
    my gnawing pains never rest.
¹⁸In his great power ⌞God⌟ becomes like clothing to me[c];
    he binds me like the neck of my garment.
¹⁹He throws me into the mud,
    and I am reduced to dust and ashes.

²⁰"I cry out to you, O God, but you do not answer;
    I stand up, but you merely look at me.
²¹You turn on me ruthlessly;
    with the might of your hand you attack me.
²²You snatch me up and drive me before the wind;
    you toss me about in the storm.
²³I know you will bring me down to death,
    to the place appointed for all the living.

²⁴"Surely no one lays a hand on a broken man
    when he cries for help in his distress.
²⁵Have I not wept for those in trouble?
    Has not my soul grieved for the poor?
²⁶Yet when I hoped for good, evil came;
    when I looked for light, then came darkness.
²⁷The churning inside me never stops;
    days of suffering confront me.
²⁸I go about blackened, but not by the sun;
    I stand up in the assembly and cry for help.
²⁹I have become a brother of jackals,
    a companion of owls.
³⁰My skin grows black and peels;
    my body burns with fever.
³¹My harp is tuned to mourning,
    and my flute to the sound of wailing.

31

"I made a covenant with my eyes
    not to look lustfully at a girl.
²For what is man's lot from God above,
    his heritage from the Almighty on high?
³Is it not ruin for the wicked,

24–25)? Is it a matter of praying harder? **4.** What larger "celestial" issues are at stake here of which Job is not aware? How would the cause-and-effects of Job's life make more sense if he, too, had the bigger picture? **5.** Didn't Job show a great lack of faith by not simply trusting that God had a bigger plan and that he needn't worry? Explain.

1. If you had access to the "larger picture" in your life how would it affect your attitude heading into next week? How would it affect your relationship with God? What one corner of the larger picture would you like to know? **2.** What would you guess are the larger issues going on between God and Satan that are presently shaping the cause-and-effects of your life and your world right now? **3.** Does questioning God mean you are lacking in faith, or exercising faith? Do problems in your life result from lack of faith on your part, or because your faith is deemed worthy? In light of Job, what else could be the cause of problems in your life?

Forgetting all the good things you have done, in a probationary court of law, what would be the most impressive thing you could tell the judge that you *have not* done? Is there anyone in your group who can truthfully say they have never tried to be anyone else,

---

[a]12 The meaning of the Hebrew for this word is uncertain.   [b]13 Or *me.* / *'No one can help him,'* ⌞*they say*⌟.   [c]18 Hebrew; Septuagint ⌞*God*⌟ *grasps my clothing*

but have always been truly themselves?

1. In Job's final claim to uphold his integrity, before
whom is he making his defense?
Who is his adversary at law
(v. 35)? What kind of courtroom is
this, in Job's mind, where the
Judge and the prosecutor are the
same person (v. 35)? Is this true
justice or blind perception? Explain. 2. Who would you guess is
standing silently on one side of the
courtroom and why? 3. Upon what
basis does Job claim his innocence
in verses 5–7? In verses 1,9? In
verses 13–21? In verses 24–27?
In verses 29–33? In verses
38–39? 4. What is the implicit answer to each of these "if-clauses"?
How can Job be so confident before God? What can you assume
from this about Job's understanding of God's character? 5. What
strategy does Job use for his defense? Is he claiming sinless perfection? If not, what? 6. How does
Job wish to confirm his oath-taking.
How is this oath related to his wish
of 19:23? 7. In the end, what has
Job claimed in this chapter that has
already been claimed for him by
God in 1:3? From the perspective
of chapters 1–2, is Job right in his
defense of himself? If so, upon
what grounds?

1. How will you claim your innocence before God when
your "day in court" comes? Of what
sins will you quickly claim yourself
innocent? What sins (of omission
or commission) will you, more than
likely, not want to bring up? 2. How
confident will you be before the divine Judge? Who will be your accuser? Upon what ground can anyone come confidently before the
throne of Judgment? Who will be at
your side? In this matter, how is our
situation different from Job's?

disaster for those who do wrong?
⁴Does he not see my ways
　　and count my every step?

⁵"If I have walked in falsehood
　　or my foot has hurried after deceit—
⁶let God weigh me in honest scales
　　and he will know that I am blameless—
⁷if my steps have turned from the path,
　　if my heart has been led by my eyes,
　　or if my hands have been defiled,
⁸then may others eat what I have sown,
　　and may my crops be uprooted.

⁹"If my heart has been enticed by a woman,
　　or if I have lurked at my neighbor's door,
¹⁰then may my wife grind another man's grain,
　　and may other men sleep with her.
¹¹For that would have been shameful,
　　a sin to be judged.
¹²It is a fire that burns to Destruction*a*;
　　it would have uprooted my harvest.

¹³"If I have denied justice to my menservants and
　　　maidservants
　　when they had a grievance against me,
¹⁴what will I do when God confronts me?
　　What will I answer when called to account?
¹⁵Did not he who made me in the womb make
　　　them?
　　Did not the same one form us both within our
　　　mothers?

¹⁶"If I have denied the desires of the poor
　　or let the eyes of the widow grow weary,
¹⁷if I have kept my bread to myself,
　　not sharing it with the fatherless—
¹⁸but from my youth I reared him as would a father,
　　and from my birth I guided the widow—
¹⁹if I have seen anyone perishing for lack of
　　　clothing,
　　or a needy man without a garment,
²⁰and his heart did not bless me
　　for warming him with the fleece from my
　　　sheep,
²¹if I have raised my hand against the fatherless,
　　knowing that I had influence in court,
²²then let my arm fall from the shoulder,
　　let it be broken off at the joint.
²³For I dreaded destruction from God,
　　and for fear of his splendor I could not do such
　　　things.

²⁴"If I have put my trust in gold
　　or said to pure gold, 'You are my security,'
²⁵if I have rejoiced over my great wealth,
　　the fortune my hands had gained,
²⁶if I have regarded the sun in its radiance
　　or the moon moving in splendor,
²⁷so that my heart was secretly enticed

a 12 Hebrew *Abaddon*

and my hand offered them a kiss of homage,
28then these also would be sins to be judged,
    for I would have been unfaithful to God on
      high.

29"If I have rejoiced at my enemy's misfortune
    or gloated over the trouble that came to him—
30I have not allowed my mouth to sin
    by invoking a curse against his life—
31if the men of my household have never said,
    'Who has not had his fill of Job's meat?'—
32but no stranger had to spend the night in the
      street,
    for my door was always open to the traveler—
33if I have concealed my sin as men do,*a*
    by hiding my guilt in my heart
34because I so feared the crowd
    and so dreaded the contempt of the clans
    that I kept silent and would not go outside

35("Oh, that I had someone to hear me!
    I sign now my defense—let the Almighty
      answer me;
    let my accuser put his indictment in writing.
36Surely I would wear it on my shoulder,
    I would put it on like a crown.
37I would give him an account of my every step;
    like a prince I would approach him.)—

38"if my land cries out against me
    and all its furrows are wet with tears,
39if I have devoured its yield without payment
    or broken the spirit of its tenants,
40then let briers come up instead of wheat
    and weeds instead of barley."

The words of Job are ended.

Elihu

32 So these three men stopped answering Job, because he was
righteous in his own eyes. 2But Elihu son of Barakel the
Buzite, of the family of Ram, became very angry with Job for justify-
ing himself rather than God. 3He was also angry with the three
friends, because they had found no way to refute Job, and yet had
condemned him.*b* 4Now Elihu had waited before speaking to Job
because they were older than he. 5But when he saw that the three
men had nothing more to say, his anger was aroused.
6So Elihu son of Barakel the Buzite said:

    "I am young in years,
      and you are old;
    that is why I was fearful,
      not daring to tell you what I know.
7I thought, 'Age should speak;
    advanced years should teach wisdom.'
8But it is the spirit*c* in a man,
    the breath of the Almighty, that gives him
      understanding.
9It is not only the old*d* who are wise,

---

a33 Or as Adam did *b3 Masoretic Text; an ancient Hebrew scribal tradition Job, and*
so had condemned God *c8 Or Spirit; also in verse 18* *d9 Or many; or great*

ever claimed to be "pure and without sin" (7:21; 13:26)? Does he think God never speaks to man? Or that God is his enemy? What has Job claimed? **4.** In what ways does Elihu show that God speaks (33:14–22)? Which of these ways seems most intelligible and credible to you? **5.** What does Elihu view as the benefits of suffering (33:23–28)? How can something good come from something evil? **6.** How can sinful humanity be spared from going to the pit or grave (33:18,24,30)? What does he claim God promises, even in the midst of sin? **7.** Why should Job listen to Elihu (33:31,33)? According to Elihu, what will it take for Job to be cleared (33:32)?

♡ **1.** In your group life together, how have you heard God speak—"now one way, now another" (33:14)? How do you account for the variety of ways each of you hears God? **2.** What has God used to catch your attention: 2x4 between the eyes? Bouts with suffering? Prophetic rebukes? Group Bible study? Other? **3.** Do you agree with Elihu that God speaks to us especially through suffering? How can illness be considered a message from God? How can God (who desires the very best for us) allow us to experience pain? If that is the case, are we right in saying, "Bring on the pain, I want to learn more about God"? **4.** Think of a time in your life when you have suffered. In what ways did it change you? How did it affect your relationship with God? Were you ultimately "a better person for it" or were you devastated by it?

not only the aged who understand what is right.

10 "Therefore I say: Listen to me;
    I too will tell you what I know.
11 I waited while you spoke,
    I listened to your reasoning;
  while you were searching for words,
12   I gave you my full attention.
  But not one of you has proved Job wrong;
    none of you has answered his arguments.
13 Do not say, 'We have found wisdom;
    let God refute him, not man.'
14 But Job has not marshaled his words against me,
    and I will not answer him with your arguments.

15 "They are dismayed and have no more to say;
    words have failed them.
16 Must I wait, now that they are silent,
    now that they stand there with no reply?
17 I too will have my say;
    I too will tell what I know.
18 For I am full of words,
    and the spirit within me compels me;
19 inside I am like bottled-up wine,
    like new wineskins ready to burst.
20 I must speak and find relief;
    I must open my lips and reply.
21 I will show partiality to no one,
    nor will I flatter any man;
22 for if I were skilled in flattery,
    my Maker would soon take me away.

33 "But now, Job, listen to my words;
    pay attention to everything I say.
2 I am about to open my mouth;
    my words are on the tip of my tongue.
3 My words come from an upright heart;
    my lips sincerely speak what I know.
4 The Spirit of God has made me;
    the breath of the Almighty gives me life.
5 Answer me then, if you can;
    prepare yourself and confront me.
6 I am just like you before God;
    I too have been taken from clay.
7 No fear of me should alarm you,
    nor should my hand be heavy upon you.

8 "But you have said in my hearing—
    I heard the very words—
9 'I am pure and without sin;
    I am clean and free from guilt.
10 Yet God has found fault with me;
    he considers me his enemy.
11 He fastens my feet in shackles;
    he keeps close watch on all my paths.'

12 "But I tell you, in this you are not right,
    for God is greater than man.
13 Why do you complain to him

that he answers none of man's words*a*?
[14] For God does speak—now one way, now
          another—
     though man may not perceive it.
[15] In a dream, in a vision of the night,
     when deep sleep falls on men
          as they slumber in their beds,
[16] he may speak in their ears
     and terrify them with warnings,
[17] to turn man from wrongdoing
     and keep him from pride,
[18] to preserve his soul from the pit,*b*
     his life from perishing by the sword.*c*
[19] Or a man may be chastened on a bed of pain
     with constant distress in his bones,
[20] so that his very being finds food repulsive
     and his soul loathes the choicest meal.
[21] His flesh wastes away to nothing,
     and his bones, once hidden, now stick out.
[22] His soul draws near to the pit,*d*
     and his life to the messengers of death.*e*

[23] "Yet if there is an angel on his side
     as a mediator, one out of a thousand,
          to tell a man what is right for him,
[24] to be gracious to him and say,
     'Spare him from going down to the pit*f*;
          I have found a ransom for him'—
[25] then his flesh is renewed like a child's;
     it is restored as in the days of his youth.
[26] He prays to God and finds favor with him,
     he sees God's face and shouts for joy;
          he is restored by God to his righteous state.
[27] Then he comes to men and says,
     'I sinned, and perverted what was right,
          but I did not get what I deserved.
[28] He redeemed my soul from going down to the
          pit,*g*
     and I will live to enjoy the light.'

[29] "God does all these things to a man—
     twice, even three times—
[30] to turn back his soul from the pit,*h*
     that the light of life may shine on him.

[31] "Pay attention, Job, and listen to me;
     be silent, and I will speak.
[32] If you have anything to say, answer me;
     speak up, for I want you to be cleared.
[33] But if not, then listen to me;
     be silent, and I will teach you wisdom."

34

Then Elihu said:

[2] "Hear my words, you wise men;
     listen to me, you men of learning.
[3] For the ear tests words

---

a13 Or *that he does not answer for any of his actions*   *b18* Or *preserve him from the grave*   *c18* Or *from crossing the River*   *d22* Or *He draws near to the grave*   *e22* Or *to the dead*   *f24* Or *grave*   *g28* Or *redeemed me from going down to the grave*   *h30* Or *turn him back from the grave*

1. Who owes us "life, liberty, and the pursuit of happiness": (a) Our Creator? (b) Our country? (c) Our community? (d) Our family? Where do you go to find these things, especially happiness? 2. What do you say to the person whose life motto is: "My rights, right or wrong!"

1. The self-appointed arbitra-
tor, Elihu, summons Job to
an earthly court to judge what is
justice (v. 4). Since it is not appropriate for God to appear in a human court (v. 23), who does he use
as judges? What are the charges
brought against Job (vv. 5–9)? And
the verdict (vv. 34–37)? 2. Why
does Elihu rush to God's defense
(vv. 10–15)? From Elihu's perspective, who sets the ground rules for
justice? Upon what basis does God
determine what is just? According
to Elihu, does man have an "inalienable right" to God's justice, or
is it a divine gift? 3. How does Elihu
characterize the way that God ad-
ministers justice in this world (vv.
16–30): As democratic leader?
Totalitarian tyrant? Enlightened
despot? Human rights activist? To
what extent does man have an active part in administering God's justice? 4. What "right" does man
have to experience the presence of
God? From Elihu's perspective, if
God so chooses to hide himself,
what does his silence say about
God? About man? Does God's silence mean judgment? What else
could it mean?

1. Nowadays, we treasure
certain "inalienable rights."
What rights do we have before
God? Does God "owe" us anything:
Good health? Prosperity? Freedom
from suffering unusual punishment? Sense of his presence? 2. If
we do have rights before God, how
do we demand justice from him? If
God's justice is not based upon our
rights, upon what is it based? 3. In
what specific ways does a biblical
view of justice (where the unrivaled
God is the standard) come in conflict with our civil view of justice
(where equality under the law is the
standard)?

as the tongue tastes food.
⁴Let us discern for ourselves what is right;
let us learn together what is good.

⁵"Job says, 'I am innocent,
but God denies me justice.
⁶Although I am right,
I am considered a liar;
although I am guiltless,
his arrow inflicts an incurable wound.'
⁷What man is like Job,
who drinks scorn like water?
⁸He keeps company with evildoers;
he associates with wicked men.
⁹For he says, 'It profits a man nothing
when he tries to please God.'

¹⁰"So listen to me, you men of understanding.
Far be it from God to do evil,
from the Almighty to do wrong.
¹¹He repays a man for what he has done;
he brings upon him what his conduct deserves.
¹²It is unthinkable that God would do wrong,
that the Almighty would pervert justice.
¹³Who appointed him over the earth?
Who put him in charge of the whole world?
¹⁴If it were his intention
and he withdrew his spirit ᵃ and breath,
¹⁵all mankind would perish together
and man would return to the dust.

¹⁶"If you have understanding, hear this;
listen to what I say.
¹⁷Can he who hates justice govern?
Will you condemn the just and mighty One?
¹⁸Is he not the One who says to kings, 'You are
worthless,'
and to nobles, 'You are wicked,'
¹⁹who shows no partiality to princes
and does not favor the rich over the poor,
for they are all the work of his hands?
²⁰They die in an instant, in the middle of the night;
the people are shaken and they pass away;
the mighty are removed without human hand.

²¹"His eyes are on the ways of men;
he sees their every step.
²²There is no dark place, no deep shadow,
where evildoers can hide.
²³God has no need to examine men further,
that they should come before him for judgment.
²⁴Without inquiry he shatters the mighty
and sets up others in their place.
²⁵Because he takes note of their deeds,
he overthrows them in the night and they are
crushed.
²⁶He punishes them for their wickedness
where everyone can see them,
²⁷because they turned from following him

and had no regard for any of his ways.
²⁸They caused the cry of the poor to come before
    him,
    so that he heard the cry of the needy.
²⁹But if he remains silent, who can condemn him?
    If he hides his face, who can see him?
  Yet he is over man and nation alike,
³⁰ to keep a godless man from ruling,
    from laying snares for the people.

³¹"Suppose a man says to God,
    'I am guilty but will offend no more.
³²Teach me what I cannot see;
    if I have done wrong, I will not do so again.'
³³Should God then reward you on your terms,
    when you refuse to repent?
  You must decide, not I;
    so tell me what you know.

³⁴"Men of understanding declare,
    wise men who hear me say to me,
³⁵'Job speaks without knowledge;
    his words lack insight.'
³⁶Oh, that Job might be tested to the utmost
    for answering like a wicked man!
³⁷To his sin he adds rebellion;
    scornfully he claps his hands among us
    and multiplies his words against God."

35
Then Elihu said:

²"Do you think this is just?
  You say, 'I will be cleared by God.^a'
³Yet you ask him, 'What profit is it to me,^b
  and what do I gain by not sinning?'

⁴"I would like to reply to you
    and to your friends with you.
⁵Look up at the heavens and see;
    gaze at the clouds so high above you.
⁶If you sin, how does that affect him?
    If your sins are many, what does that do to
      him?
⁷If you are righteous, what do you give to him,
    or what does he receive from your hand?
⁸Your wickedness affects only a man like yourself,
    and your righteousness only the sons of men.

⁹"Men cry out under a load of oppression;
    they plead for relief from the arm of the
      powerful.
¹⁰But no one says, 'Where is God my Maker,
    who gives songs in the night,
¹¹who teaches more to us than to^c the beasts of
    the earth
    and makes us wiser than^d the birds of the air?'
¹²He does not answer when men cry out
    because of the arrogance of the wicked.
¹³Indeed, God does not listen to their empty plea;

^a2 Or *My righteousness is more than God's*   ^b3 Or *you*   ^c11 Or *teaches us by*
^d11 Or *us wise by*

---

1. In conversation, when do you end up using more words without making any more sense: When more sure of your position or less so? When angry and upset or when happy and joyous? 2. In prayer, when do you end up using a lot of words: When feeling righteous? When you feel God has not heard yet? When you feel someone in the group is listening? When you feel someone is *not* listening?

1. God is seen by some as familiar and personal and by others as transcendent and detached. According to Elihu, why is that? 2. How does sin affect our relationship and righteousness with God (vv. 5–7)? What difference does it make whether we sin or not (v. 3)? 3. Why does Elihu say that God hasn't answered some prayers (vv. 12–15)? 4. Does his description of God strike you as quite intimately involved, or does Elihu's God detach himself from Job? Why no answers to prayer?

1. What tells you that you've "made contact" with God? When in your life has it seemed that God was just not answering a prayer of yours? What did you do then? What reasons were you given? 2. Have you ever thought that

God didn't care, or that he was judging you for some sin or lack of faith in your life? What was that period of silence like?

---

1. If it is true that "to spare the rod is to spoil the child," how did you make it through your childhood: (a) By the skin of your teeth? (b) With flying colors and a sore bottom? (c) Counting your blessings? (d) Spoiled and thankful? 2. Would you discipline your children (if any) differently than you were punished and rewarded? How so?

1. Is Elihu being virtuous or presumptuous in claiming to speak for God, and to speak for him so perfectly (vv. 2–4)? Upon what grounds does he defend God? Why is he striving to prove God innocent? 2. From Elihu's perspective (vv. 5–21), why is humanity endowed with the divine rights of kings? Why are we treated as captains of our own fate, getting exactly what we deserve, even what we choose? 3. Elihu says that the righteous are rewarded and sinners are punished (vv. 11–12). How does that contrast with what Job has been claiming? 4. What are the benefits of God's discipline? What is the fate of those who respond positively to God's correction? Likewise, to those who ignore God's correction? 5. What new reason, hope and warning with regard to suffering does Elihu introduce in this section (vv. 16–21)? What does Elihu say here that distinguishes him from the other three friends who have given up on Job? What does he say here that contradicts God's view of Job (see 1:8; 2:3)? 6. In verses 22–33, what does Elihu say about God that is true and worthy of full acceptance?

1. Is the discipline of Job at all like the discipline of other believers, as in Hebrews 12:7–13? How do you see that NT passage relating to Job's situation? If Job is being disciplined, what does that suggest about his value in God's eyes? 2. When have you been in a situation where you have felt stretched by God in order to learn something from him? What were

the Almighty pays no attention to it.
¹⁴How much less, then, will he listen
    when you say that you do not see him,
    that your case is before him
    and you must wait for him,
¹⁵and further, that his anger never punishes
    and he does not take the least notice of
        wickedness.ᵃ
¹⁶So Job opens his mouth with empty talk;
    without knowledge he multiplies words."

36 Elihu continued:

²"Bear with me a little longer and I will show you
    that there is more to be said in God's behalf.
³I get my knowledge from afar;
    I will ascribe justice to my Maker.
⁴Be assured that my words are not false;
    one perfect in knowledge is with you.

⁵"God is mighty, but does not despise men;
    he is mighty, and firm in his purpose.
⁶He does not keep the wicked alive
    but gives the afflicted their rights.
⁷He does not take his eyes off the righteous;
    he enthrones them with kings
    and exalts them forever.
⁸But if men are bound in chains,
    held fast by cords of affliction,
⁹he tells them what they have done—
    that they have sinned arrogantly.
¹⁰He makes them listen to correction
    and commands them to repent of their evil.
¹¹If they obey and serve him,
    they will spend the rest of their days in
        prosperity
    and their years in contentment.
¹²But if they do not listen,
    they will perish by the swordᵇ
    and die without knowledge.

¹³"The godless in heart harbor resentment;
    even when he fetters them, they do not cry for
        help.
¹⁴They die in their youth,
    among male prostitutes of the shrines.
¹⁵But those who suffer he delivers in their suffering;
    he speaks to them in their affliction.

¹⁶"He is wooing you from the jaws of distress
    to a spacious place free from restriction,
    to the comfort of your table laden with choice
        food.
¹⁷But now you are laden with the judgment due the
        wicked;
    judgment and justice have taken hold of you.
¹⁸Be careful that no one entices you by riches;
    do not let a large bribe turn you aside.

ᵃ15 Symmachus, Theodotion and Vulgate; the meaning of the Hebrew for this word is uncertain.   ᵇ12 Or *will cross the River*

¹⁹Would your wealth
　　or even all your mighty efforts
　　sustain you so you would not be in distress?
²⁰Do not long for the night,
　　to drag people away from their homes.ª
²¹Beware of turning to evil,
　　which you seem to prefer to affliction.

²²"God is exalted in his power.
　　Who is a teacher like him?
²³Who has prescribed his ways for him,
　　or said to him, 'You have done wrong'?
²⁴Remember to extol his work,
　　which men have praised in song.
²⁵All mankind has seen it;
　　men gaze on it from afar.
²⁶How great is God—beyond our understanding!
　　The number of his years is past finding out.

²⁷"He draws up the drops of water,
　　which distill as rain to the streams ᵇ;
²⁸the clouds pour down their moisture
　　and abundant showers fall on mankind.
²⁹Who can understand how he spreads out the
　　　clouds,
　　how he thunders from his pavilion?
³⁰See how he scatters his lightning about him,
　　bathing the depths of the sea.
³¹This is the way he governs ᶜ the nations
　　and provides food in abundance.
³²He fills his hands with lightning
　　and commands it to strike its mark.
³³His thunder announces the coming storm;
　　even the cattle make known its approach. ᵈ

37 "At this my heart pounds
　　and leaps from its place.
²Listen! Listen to the roar of his voice,
　　to the rumbling that comes from his mouth.
³He unleashes his lightning beneath the whole
　　　heaven
　　and sends it to the ends of the earth.
⁴After that comes the sound of his roar;
　　he thunders with his majestic voice.
　When his voice resounds,
　　he holds nothing back.
⁵God's voice thunders in marvelous ways;
　　he does great things beyond our understanding.
⁶He says to the snow, 'Fall on the earth,'
　　and to the rain shower, 'Be a mighty
　　　downpour.'
⁷So that all men he has made may know his work,
　　he stops every man from his labor. ᵉ
⁸The animals take cover;
　　they remain in their dens.
⁹The tempest comes out from its chamber,
　　the cold from the driving winds.

the circumstances and what did you learn? Was the pain worth the gain? Why didn't God just "tell" you what he wanted you to know and leave the agony to those who aren't listening anyway?

🍵 **1.** What motivates you more: (a) A well-timed whisper full of wisdom? (b) A mighty shout that gets you off your feet? (c) A radical change in circumstances? **2.** Are you more of a fall, winter, spring or summer person? Why?

📖 **1.** Why does Elihu's heart "leap"? How does he describe God's voice? **2.** How does God grab our attention here (vv. 6–13)? How does God "show his love" (v. 13)? **3.** In what condition is Job now as Elihu addresses him (vv. 14–18)? Could Job use a chilling north wind (v. 10) or a warm southerly (v. 17) right about now? **4.** According to Elihu, is God oppressing Job (v. 23)? Why or why not? **5.** Why do people worship God (v. 24)? How does that fit Job's situation?

❤️ **1.** On a scale of one to 10, how would you describe your "LQ" (listening quotient) in your relationship with God? What needs to happen for you to become a better

---

ª20 The meaning of the Hebrew for verses 18-20 is uncertain.　　ᵇ27 Or *distill from the mist as rain*　　ᶜ31 Or *nourishes*　　ᵈ33 Or *announces his coming—/ the One zealous against evil*　　ᵉ7 Or */ he fills all men with fear by his power*

listener to God in nature? To God in his Word? **2.** Paraphrase "awesome majesty" (v. 22) in terms of something non-theological. Is this inspiring power of God beyond the reach of all believers (v. 23), even those who know God through Jesus Christ? When, where and how will we humans come close to "awesome majesty"?

[10]The breath of God produces ice,
  and the broad waters become frozen.
[11]He loads the clouds with moisture;
  he scatters his lightning through them.
[12]At his direction they swirl around
  over the face of the whole earth
  to do whatever he commands them.
[13]He brings the clouds to punish men,
  or to water his earth[a] and show his love.

[14]"Listen to this, Job;
  stop and consider God's wonders.
[15]Do you know how God controls the clouds
  and makes his lightning flash?
[16]Do you know how the clouds hang poised,
  those wonders of him who is perfect in
    knowledge?
[17]You who swelter in your clothes
  when the land lies hushed under the south
    wind,
[18]can you join him in spreading out the skies,
  hard as a mirror of cast bronze?

[19]"Tell us what we should say to him;
  we cannot draw up our case because of our
    darkness.
[20]Should he be told that I want to speak?
  Would any man ask to be swallowed up?
[21]Now no one can look at the sun,
  bright as it is in the skies
  after the wind has swept them clean.
[22]Out of the north he comes in golden splendor;
  God comes in awesome majesty.
[23]The Almighty is beyond our reach and exalted in
    power;
  in his justice and great righteousness, he does
    not oppress.
[24]Therefore, men revere him,
  for does he not have regard for all the wise in
    heart?[b]"

The LORD Speaks

38 Then the LORD answered Job out of the storm. He said:

[2]"Who is this that darkens my counsel
  with words without knowledge?
[3]Brace yourself like a man;
  I will question you,
  and you shall answer me.

[4]"Where were you when I laid the earth's
    foundation?
  Tell me, if you understand.
[5]Who marked off its dimensions? Surely you know!
  Who stretched a measuring line across it?
[6]On what were its footings set,
  or who laid its cornerstone—
[7]while the morning stars sang together
  and all the angels[c] shouted for joy?

1. Think of a time in your life when you have gotten the wrong answer because you asked the wrong question. Silly you, what happened? When did you finally wake up and fly right? **2.** What about the natural world is for you a most awesome experience: Scary things, like snow storms? Tall things, like mountain peaks? Powerful things, like waterfalls? Little things, like sprouting grass? Vast things, like the starry constellations? Give one example of being overwhelmed by God's creation.

1. Does God reveal himself here as a distant, transcendent entity under whom Job should cower, or as a personal God who is willing to reveal himself? What does it mean for Job to meet God in the storm? Is this what either Job

---

[a]13 Or *to favor them*   [b]24 Or *for he does not have regard for any who think they are wise.*   [c]7 Hebrew *the sons of God*

8"Who shut up the sea behind doors
    when it burst forth from the womb,
9when I made the clouds its garment
    and wrapped it in thick darkness,
10when I fixed limits for it
    and set its doors and bars in place,
11when I said, 'This far you may come and no
        farther;
    here is where your proud waves halt'?

12"Have you ever given orders to the morning,
    or shown the dawn its place,
13that it might take the earth by the edges
    and shake the wicked out of it?
14The earth takes shape like clay under a seal;
    its features stand out like those of a garment.
15The wicked are denied their light,
    and their upraised arm is broken.

16"Have you journeyed to the springs of the sea
    or walked in the recesses of the deep?
17Have the gates of death been shown to you?
    Have you seen the gates of the shadow of
        death[a]?
18Have you comprehended the vast expanses of the
        earth?
    Tell me, if you know all this.

19"What is the way to the abode of light?
    And where does darkness reside?
20Can you take them to their places?
    Do you know the paths to their dwellings?
21Surely you know, for you were already born!
    You have lived so many years!

22"Have you entered the storehouses of the snow
    or seen the storehouses of the hail,
23which I reserve for times of trouble,
    for days of war and battle?
24What is the way to the place where the lightning
        is dispersed,
    or the place where the east winds are scattered
        over the earth?
25Who cuts a channel for the torrents of rain,
    and a path for the thunderstorm,
26to water a land where no man lives,
    a desert with no one in it,
27to satisfy a desolate wasteland
    and make it sprout with grass?
28Does the rain have a father?
    Who fathers the drops of dew?
29From whose womb comes the ice?
    Who gives birth to the frost from the heavens
30when the waters become hard as stone,
    when the surface of the deep is frozen?

31"Can you bind the beautiful[b] Pleiades?
    Can you loose the cords of Orion?

(see 31:35) or Elihu expected (see 37:22)? How is Job proven wrong about what would happen if he were to meet God face-to-face (see 9:14–20)? **2.** From the peculiar way that God chooses to answer Job, who really is on trial? Which, if any, of Job's charges against God does God choose to answer? **3.** Is God skirting the issues, or getting to the main point? Is God trying to humiliate Job with a list of his grave sins or of God's great accomplishments? Explain. **4.** What do you think is the net effect on Job of God's dumfounding questions? Pick a few of these ponderous questions and see how Job would have answered them. **5.** What is God trying to teach Job about his divine nature? What does it say about human nature in general, and the nature of Job in particular, that God is communicating with him in this manner? **6.** Does God reveal the specific answers for why Job suffered? What does he reveal? **7.** How does God's response to Job reflect Job's concerns throughout? Has Job ever asked for specific answers to the "whys" behind the loss of children, possessions, health? What has always been his concern instead? To what extent are God's concerns here the same concerns Job has had all along?

1. What kind of questions do you ask God when you don't understand circumstances in your life? What do you pray for? Does God always give you solutions to your problems or answers to your questions? **2.** What else might God want to be revealing to you? Any "reasons why" certain things happen to you? Or is it enough to know God is good and God is great?

---

[a]17 Or gates of deep shadows   [b]31 Or the twinkling; or the chains of the

³²Can you bring forth the constellations in their
    seasons^a
or lead out the Bear^b with its cubs?
³³Do you know the laws of the heavens?
Can you set up ⌊God's^c⌋ dominion over the
    earth?

³⁴"Can you raise your voice to the clouds
and cover yourself with a flood of water?
³⁵Do you send the lightning bolts on their way?
Do they report to you, 'Here we are'?
³⁶Who endowed the heart^d with wisdom
or gave understanding to the mind^d?
³⁷Who has the wisdom to count the clouds?
Who can tip over the water jars of the heavens
³⁸when the dust becomes hard
and the clods of earth stick together?

³⁹"Do you hunt the prey for the lioness
and satisfy the hunger of the lions
⁴⁰when they crouch in their dens
or lie in wait in a thicket?
⁴¹Who provides food for the raven
when its young cry out to God
and wander about for lack of food?

39 "Do you know when the mountain goats give birth?
Do you watch when the doe bears her fawn?
²Do you count the months till they bear?
Do you know the time they give birth?
³They crouch down and bring forth their young;
their labor pains are ended.
⁴Their young thrive and grow strong in the wilds;
they leave and do not return.

⁵"Who let the wild donkey go free?
Who untied his ropes?
⁶I gave him the wasteland as his home,
the salt flats as his habitat.
⁷He laughs at the commotion in the town;
he does not hear a driver's shout.
⁸He ranges the hills for his pasture
and searches for any green thing.

⁹"Will the wild ox consent to serve you?
Will he stay by your manger at night?
¹⁰Can you hold him to the furrow with a harness?
Will he till the valleys behind you?
¹¹Will you rely on him for his great strength?
Will you leave your heavy work to him?
¹²Can you trust him to bring in your grain
and gather it to your threshing floor?

¹³"The wings of the ostrich flap joyfully,
but they cannot compare with the pinions and
    feathers of the stork.
¹⁴She lays her eggs on the ground
and lets them warm in the sand,
¹⁵unmindful that a foot may crush them,
that some wild animal may trample them.

1. Which animals do you have more fascination for—those on a farm, in a zoo or in a wilderness? Of those animals, which is your favorite? What details of that animal's behavior have you most enjoyed observing? 2. Would you make a better zookeeper, veterinarian or forest ranger? Why?

1. How does the animal imagery in this chapter affect you? Which of these miracles of nature have you personally witnessed? What effect did that have on you at the time? 2. In looking at both the intricate order and balance of creation, as well as its mystery and paradox, what can be said about the Creator? About the similar ways God may govern both the animal kingdom and humanity? 3. What, if anything, does God say here about Job's suffering? About divine justice? About Job's innocence or guilt? Why is that?

1. How does God's active involvement with creation redefine our Job-like questions? What questions does this chapter raise for you? For example, what is said here about the *calamities* of nature wrought by earth, wind, fire and water run amok? 2. In light of who God is, who are we? What are our problems as creature relating to our Creator? 3. Does knowing God is sovereign comfort you or scare you? Why? Knowing God is always

^a32 Or *the morning star in its season*   ^b32 Or *out Leo*   ^c33 Or *his*; or *their*
^d36 The meaning of the Hebrew for this word is uncertain.

16She treats her young harshly, as if they were not
    hers;
  she cares not that her labor was in vain,
17for God did not endow her with wisdom
  or give her a share of good sense.
18Yet when she spreads her feathers to run,
  she laughs at horse and rider.

19"Do you give the horse his strength
  or clothe his neck with a flowing mane?
20Do you make him leap like a locust,
  striking terror with his proud snorting?
21He paws fiercely, rejoicing in his strength,
  and charges into the fray.
22He laughs at fear, afraid of nothing;
  he does not shy away from the sword.
23The quiver rattles against his side,
  along with the flashing spear and lance.
24In frenzied excitement he eats up the ground;
  he cannot stand still when the trumpet sounds.
25At the blast of the trumpet he snorts, 'Aha!'
  He catches the scent of battle from afar,
  the shout of commanders and the battle cry.

26"Does the hawk take flight by your wisdom
  and spread his wings toward the south?
27Does the eagle soar at your command
  and build his nest on high?
28He dwells on a cliff and stays there at night;
  a rocky crag is his stronghold.
29From there he seeks out his food;
  his eyes detect it from afar.
30His young ones feast on blood,
  and where the slain are, there is he."

40

The LORD said to Job:

2"Will the one who contends with the Almighty
    correct him?
  Let him who accuses God answer him!"

3Then Job answered the LORD:

4"I am unworthy—how can I reply to you?
  I put my hand over my mouth.
5I spoke once, but I have no answer—
  twice, but I will say no more."

6Then the LORD spoke to Job out of the storm:

7"Brace yourself like a man;
  I will question you,
  and you shall answer me.

8"Would you discredit my justice?
  Would you condemn me to justify yourself?
9Do you have an arm like God's,
  and can your voice thunder like his?
10Then adorn yourself with glory and splendor,
  and clothe yourself in honor and majesty.
11Unleash the fury of your wrath,
  look at every proud man and bring him low,
12look at every proud man and humble him,

at work, do you relax more or work harder? Why? Knowing God controls every circumstance of life, how does that affect your planning for the future? Your praying for needs and wants?

What animal do you think God had the most fun designing? What features about this animal strike you as funny?

1. In God's second speech, who is on trial? What common refrains link this speech to the first one (38:1–40:2)? Once again, how does God reverse the roles of prosecutor and defendant in this trial? 2. What else do you learn about God's character from the manner in which he answers Job? Is God being coy? Caring? Abrasive? Just? 3. In the prologue to this speech (vv. 8–14), what does God say about Job's suffering or God's justice? 4. *Justice* can mean both "claim or right" on man's part and "sovereign rule" on God's part. Depending on which way one uses the term *justice*, the problem of Job's suffering looks very different. Which way do you see the problem? As the term is used in verse 8, is God's justice an inalienable right for Job, or a sovereign act for God? In either event, who needs justification—God or Job?

Why? **5.** In the follow-up question (v. 9), what is God saying to Job about Job's ability to comprehend the suffering and evil that is around him? **6.** In verses 15–24, what is the point about the behemoth?

🫶 **1.** We live life on the back side of a woven tapestry, from which we can see only knots, loose ends and a faint, obscured outline of the picture on the front side. What picture is God weaving for Job in these last three chapters? **2.** What new insights does that give you into the place of suffering in your own life? How can the events of your life be used by God for reasons you might not be aware of? From what perspective can you say, "the pain is worth the gain?" **3.** Because evil and its consequences has some limited control in our lives, does that mean that God is not ultimately in control? Does it mean we are all being tested like Job depending on what God knows we can handle?

☕ **1.** As a child, or as a parent-reading-to-children, what is your favorite monster story? Were you raised to believe in any particular monsters of mythical proportions—hiding under your bed or in your closet? **2.** Did (or do) you have much interest in dinosaurs? Reptiles? Snakes? The Loch Ness monster in Scotland?

📖 **1.** Look closely at the behemoth (40:15–24) and especially the leviathan here (vv. 1–34). What mental images of each come to mind? What points of similarity do you see? **2.** What sections of the leviathan's portrait seem literal enough to refer to a large marine animal (as in Ps 104:26)? Which references here are obviously figurative (as in 3:8 and Isa 27:1)? How did you make that distinction between literal and figurative language? **3.** Nowhere after chapter 2 is Satan the Accuser mentioned. Does this seem strange to you? In what ways can you see Satan symbolized in the figurative language describing the leviathan? What characteristics do Satan and this leviathan possess in common? How do they rate in power? To what extent can humanity control them? **4.** What is God saying here

crush the wicked where they stand.
¹³Bury them all in the dust together;
shroud their faces in the grave.
¹⁴Then I myself will admit to you
that your own right hand can save you.

¹⁵"Look at the behemoth,ᵃ
which I made along with you
and which feeds on grass like an ox.
¹⁶What strength he has in his loins,
what power in the muscles of his belly!
¹⁷His tailᵇ sways like a cedar;
the sinews of his thighs are close-knit.
¹⁸His bones are tubes of bronze,
his limbs like rods of iron.
¹⁹He ranks first among the works of God,
yet his Maker can approach him with his sword.
²⁰The hills bring him their produce,
and all the wild animals play nearby.
²¹Under the lotus plants he lies,
hidden among the reeds in the marsh.
²²The lotuses conceal him in their shadow;
the poplars by the stream surround him.
²³When the river rages, he is not alarmed;
he is secure, though the Jordan should surge against his mouth.
²⁴Can anyone capture him by the eyes,ᶜ
or trap him and pierce his nose?

41 "Can you pull in the leviathanᵈ with a fishhook
or tie down his tongue with a rope?
²Can you put a cord through his nose
or pierce his jaw with a hook?
³Will he keep begging you for mercy?
Will he speak to you with gentle words?
⁴Will he make an agreement with you
for you to take him as your slave for life?
⁵Can you make a pet of him like a bird
or put him on a leash for your girls?
⁶Will traders barter for him?
Will they divide him up among the merchants?
⁷Can you fill his hide with harpoons
or his head with fishing spears?
⁸If you lay a hand on him,
you will remember the struggle and never do it again!
⁹Any hope of subduing him is false;
the mere sight of him is overpowering.
¹⁰No one is fierce enough to rouse him.
Who then is able to stand against me?
¹¹Who has a claim against me that I must pay?
Everything under heaven belongs to me.

¹²"I will not fail to speak of his limbs,
his strength and his graceful form.
¹³Who can strip off his outer coat?
Who would approach him with a bridle?

ᵃ15 Possibly the hippopotamus or the elephant   ᵇ17 Possibly trunk   ᶜ24 Or by a water hole   ᵈ1 Possibly the crocodile

¹⁴Who dares open the doors of his mouth,
    ringed about with his fearsome teeth?
¹⁵His back has*ª* rows of shields
    tightly sealed together;
¹⁶each is so close to the next
    that no air can pass between.
¹⁷They are joined fast to one another;
    they cling together and cannot be parted.
¹⁸His snorting throws out flashes of light;
    his eyes are like the rays of dawn.
¹⁹Firebrands stream from his mouth;
    sparks of fire shoot out.
²⁰Smoke pours from his nostrils
    as from a boiling pot over a fire of reeds.
²¹His breath sets coals ablaze,
    and flames dart from his mouth.
²²Strength resides in his neck;
    dismay goes before him.
²³The folds of his flesh are tightly joined;
    they are firm and immovable.
²⁴His chest is hard as rock,
    hard as a lower millstone.
²⁵When he rises up, the mighty are terrified;
    they retreat before his thrashing.
²⁶The sword that reaches him has no effect,
    nor does the spear or the dart or the javelin.
²⁷Iron he treats like straw
    and bronze like rotten wood.
²⁸Arrows do not make him flee;
    slingstones are like chaff to him.
²⁹A club seems to him but a piece of straw;
    he laughs at the rattling of the lance.
³⁰His undersides are jagged potsherds,
    leaving a trail in the mud like a threshing
        sledge.
³¹He makes the depths churn like a boiling caldron
    and stirs up the sea like a pot of ointment.
³²Behind him he leaves a glistening wake;
    one would think the deep had white hair.
³³Nothing on earth is his equal—
    a creature without fear.
³⁴He looks down on all that are haughty;
    he is king over all that are proud."

Job
42

Then Job replied to the LORD:

²"I know that you can do all things;
    no plan of yours can be thwarted.
³ ⌊You asked,⌋ 'Who is this that obscures my
        counsel without knowledge?'
    Surely I spoke of things I did not understand,
    things too wonderful for me to know.

⁴ "⌊You said,⌋ 'Listen now, and I will speak;
    I will question you,
    and you shall answer me.'
⁵My ears had heard of you

ª15 Or His pride is his

about Job's ability to control the Accuser and to comprehend evil, as typified by this leviathan? **5.** Job is allowed the privilege of participating in the heavenly battle between good and evil. What does that say about God's view of Job?

1. In what ways has God called us to spiritual warfare? What is your mental picture of what that is all about? Anything like Job 41? **2.** How does God defeat evil with goodness? Can you illustrate that from your own life? **3.** In similar fashion, how can the serpent in your life be subdued and conquered?

If you, like the readers of Robert Frost's classic lines, faced the two roads that "diverged in a yellow wood," what road would you have taken: The road better claimed or the road not taken? Looking back on your life, what is the road better claimed? What is the road not taken?

1. If Job were deemed "blameless and upright" before his time of suffering (1:1), in what ways has he become a changed person after? What "wonderful things" (v. 3) does he understand now that he didn't before? **2.** Of what is Job repenting? Is igno-

rance a sin? How so? What do the
"eyes" have that the "ears" never
did? **3.** From the epilogue (vv.
7–17), how would you characterize
Job? **4.** What irony is there in the
fact that Job becomes the necessary mediator for his friends? **5.**
How complete is Job's restoration
by God, materially and spiritually?
Why then did he still need to be
comforted by others (v. 11)? **6.** Is
Job's restoration the result of his
repentance in verse 6 or his intercession in verses 8–9? Explain the
difference. **7.** Does this ending tend
to reinforce the theology of the
three friends (that the righteous are
blessed and the wicked suffer)?
Why or why not? **8.** How does this
epilogue tie in with the prologue
(ch. 1) for Job? For the reader?

♡ **1.** Does God always promise
happy endings to the stories
of his people? Why or why not? **2.**
How else would you have ended
this classic story and kept the
same punch line? Would any other
ending but this one have had the
same punch line? **3.** What would
you say is the primary theme of
Job: Suffering? Justice? Patience?

but now my eyes have seen you.
⁶Therefore I despise myself
and repent in dust and ashes."

Epilogue

⁷After the LORD had said these things to Job, he said to Eliphaz
the Temanite, "I am angry with you and your two friends, because
you have not spoken of me what is right, as my servant Job has. ⁸So
now take seven bulls and seven rams and go to my servant Job and
sacrifice a burnt offering for yourselves. My servant Job will pray
for you, and I will accept his prayer and not deal with you according to your folly. You have not spoken of me what is right, as my
servant Job has." ⁹So Eliphaz the Temanite, Bildad the Shuhite and
Zophar the Naamathite did what the LORD told them; and the LORD
accepted Job's prayer.

¹⁰After Job had prayed for his friends, the LORD made him prosperous again and gave him twice as much as he had before. ¹¹All
his brothers and sisters and everyone who had known him before
came and ate with him in his house. They comforted and consoled
him over all the trouble the LORD had brought upon him, and each
one gave him a piece of silver*a* and a gold ring.

¹²The LORD blessed the latter part of Job's life more than the first.
He had fourteen thousand sheep, six thousand camels, a thousand
yoke of oxen and a thousand donkeys. ¹³And he also had seven
sons and three daughters. ¹⁴The first daughter he named Jemimah,
the second Keziah and the third Keren-Happuch. ¹⁵Nowhere in all

a 11 Hebrew *him a kesitah*; a kesitah was a unit of money of unknown weight and value.

  Job 42:7–17   **JOB IS RESTORED**

After God allowed Satan to destroy
Job's heath, wealth and children, forlorn Job was visited by three friends—
who insisted Job must be guilty of some
sin. Though Job angrily complained
and questioned the Lord, he still didn't
curse the Lord. As the book nears its
end, God speaks and makes judgment
concerning Job and his "comforters."

1. Why did Job's friends need to go to
Job and offer a sacrifice?
   a. because they were wrong
   b. because God was angry with
      them
   c. because they had sinned
   d. because they violated Job

2. Why was Job restored?
   a. because he repented (v. 6) of his
      doubts and complaints
   b. because he forgave his friends
   c. because he prayed for his friends
   d. because of God's grace
   e. because he was righteous
   f. because it was God's plan

3. Why did Job's family and friends,
   from whom he had been alienated,

come to comfort him now?
   a. because he didn't get everything
      back overnight
   b. to relieve their guilt
   c. to get back on his good side
   d. because it's easier to comfort
      someone after things get better

4. Why did Job receive twice as much
   as he had before?
   a. for good measure
   b. as compensation for his "pain and
      suffering"
   c. to provide a storybook ending
   d. to vindicate Job clearly and fully
   e. God loves to bless people.

5. Does God always promise a happy
   ending? What does "acceptance"
   mean when things *don't* get better?

6. Are you aware of anything that could
   interfere with you receiving God's
   blessings? Do you have a need to
   make amends? Is there anyone you
   need to forgive?

7. ✚✚ How do you think Job would
   have answered the question,

"Where is God when it hurts?" Would
his answer be different now than it
was after he lost everything? How
would *you* answer the question?

8. ✚✚ How can you keep your
   hope that "things can
   change"? How does the Bible's perspective of God's ultimate and eternal justice encourage you?

9. 💲 In your involvement in the
   business world, what would
   the rewards of integrity be?
   a. doubling of my assets
   b. beating out the competition
   c. a prospering business
   d. supportive family and friends
   e. a nice inheritance for my children
   f. a long and healthy life

10. In the end Job was affirmed by God
    and comforted by others. What have
    you appreciated about this group?
    Focusing on one member at a time,
    how can you affirm or encourage
    that person? Close by thanking God
    in prayer for each other.

the land were there found women as beautiful as Job's daughters, and their father granted them an inheritance along with their brothers.

[16]After this, Job lived a hundred and forty years; he saw his children and their children to the fourth generation. [17]And so he died, old and full of years.

Sovereignty? Faith? Other? 4. How does your choice of theme best summarize the book?

INTRODUCTION to
PSALMS

Book Study Outline: If you are using Psalms for a study course, here is a 7- or 13-week outline. Use the questions in the margin for your group agenda:

🍵 start meeting / 15 min.

📖 read & discuss Bible / 30 min.

♡ close meeting / 15–45 min.

Refer to the Questions and Answers in the front of this Bible for more information.

7-week plan	13-week plan	Personal Reading	Group Study Passage
1	1	32,34,65,84	1/True Happiness
	2	13,69,88,143	22/Suffering
2	3	3,31,39,142	42–43/Discouragement
	4	11,23,27,107	63/Trust
3	5	25,90,102,106	51/Confession
	6	35,59,129,137	58/Anger
4	7	2,21,45,110	72/The King's Glory
	8	10,55,74,77	73/Despair and Hope
5	9	16,18,31,112	91/Security
	10	93–98	99/God's Universal Reign
6	11	6,38,103,123	130/Forgiveness
	12	8,19,37,89	139/God's Sovereignty
7	13	146–150	145/Praise the Lord!

Author: King David (e.g. Ps 3), King Solomon (Ps 72; 127), the sons of Korah (Ps 42–49; 84–85; 87–88), Asaph (Ps 50; 73–83), the Ezrahite Heman (Ps 88), Ethan (Ps 89), and Moses (Ps 90) all have psalms attributed to them. Many psalms are anonymous.

Date: Although composed over centuries (c. 1400–400 B.C.), the Psalms may well have been collected and arranged in their present form as the "hymn book" of Israel sometime in the fourth or third century B.C.

TYPES OF PSALMS

Prayers of the Individual
Ps 3; 7–8

Praise From the Individual for God's Saving Help
Ps 30; 34

Prayers of the Community
Ps 12; 44; 79

Praise From the Community for God's Saving Help
Ps 66; 75

Confessions of Confidence in the Lord
Ps 11; 16; 52

Hymns in Praise of God's Majesty and Virtues
Ps 8; 19; 29; 65

Hymns Celebrating God's Universal Reign
Ps 47; 93–99

Songs of Zion, the City of God
Ps 46; 48; 76; 84; 122; 126; 129; 137

Royal Psalms: by, for or Concerning the King, the Lord's Anointed
Ps 2; 18; 20; 45; 72; 89; 110

Pilgrimage Songs
Ps 120–134

Liturgical Songs
Ps 15; 24; 68

Didactic (Instructional) Songs
Ps 1; 34; 37; 73; 112; 119; 128; 133

Theme: Range of human response to God and his world.

Historical Background: The Book of Psalms is a collection of various smaller groupings of psalms that were used in Israel's worship over the centuries. Some psalms were associated with certain feasts (Ps 130, Yom Kippur; Ps 135, Passover), others with the Sabbath (Ps 92–100), and others for confession (Ps 32; 51) or praise (Ps 111–118; 146–150).

Characteristics: The Psalms reflect the stylistic characteristics of Hebrew poetry, i.e., repetition, parallelism and vivid imagery. The moods of the psalms embrace the whole range of human experience from exuberant praise (Ps 145) to despair (Ps 42); from intense anger (Ps 137) and doubt about God's care (Ps 73) to hope for a future based precisely upon God's care (Ps 23). They can help us express emotions that otherwise we might not have words for, or feel right about. The Psalms catch the reality of our up-and-down-relationship to God, but they also move us steadily along the path of knowing God.

Responsive Readings: For most of the psalms, instructions are given in the margin to start off the meeting with two or three people or groups reading the psalm out loud like a responsive reading, with verses assigned to Reader(s) A, Reader(s) B, etc.

Psalms

BOOK I

Psalms 1–41

Psalm 1

¹Blessed is the man
  who does not walk in the counsel of the wicked
or stand in the way of sinners
  or sit in the seat of mockers.
²But his delight is in the law of the LORD,
  and on his law he meditates day and night.
³He is like a tree planted by streams of water,
  which yields its fruit in season
and whose leaf does not wither.
  Whatever he does prospers.

⁴Not so the wicked!
  They are like chaff
  that the wind blows away.
⁵Therefore the wicked will not stand in the
      judgment,
  nor sinners in the assembly of the righteous.

⁶For the LORD watches over the way of the
      righteous,
  but the way of the wicked will perish.

Psalm 2

¹Why do the nations conspire*a*
  and the peoples plot in vain?
²The kings of the earth take their stand
  and the rulers gather together
against the LORD
  and against his Anointed One.*b*
³"Let us break their chains," they say,
  "and throw off their fetters."

⁴The One enthroned in heaven laughs;
  the Lord scoffs at them.
⁵Then he rebukes them in his anger
  and terrifies them in his wrath, saying,
⁶"I have installed my King*c*
  on Zion, my holy hill."

⁷I will proclaim the decree of the LORD:

  He said to me, "You are my Son*d*;
    today I have become your Father.*e*
⁸Ask of me,
  and I will make the nations your inheritance,
    the ends of the earth your possession.

a 1 Hebrew; Septuagint *rage*   b 2 Or *anointed one*   c 6 Or *king*   d 7 Or *son;*
also in verse 12   e 7 Or *have begotten you*

---

1. What makes you happy?
2. *Read aloud*—Reader(s) A:
1–3; B: 4–5; C:6

1. What are the "blessed" like
and not like? 2. What is the
point of the tree comparison? 3.
What are the "wicked" like and
why? 4. What was the "law of the
Lord" in David's day (v. 2)? How
could one meditate on it so long?
5. Do you feel a tension between
the two "ways"? Is there a third
way? Why or why not?

1. How should people today
find happiness, according to
TV, music and ads? 2. Where have
you searched for happiness?
Where do you find it? 3. What is
the "law of the Lord" for you? How
would you find time to meditate as
this blessed man does?

---

1. When you were young,
how did you try to plot, conspire or weasel your way out of a
jam with your folks? How did they
react? 2. As "king for a day," what
law would you first abolish? Why?
3. *Read aloud*—Reader(s) A: 1–5,
odd; Reader(s) B: 2–6, even.

1. As a song about the king,
what do verses 1–3 indicate
is happening? What are the "chains
and fetters"? 2. "Messiah" is Hebrew for "anointed one." Who is the
"messiah" of verse 2? How is opposition to Israel's king (vv. 2,3,10)
also opposition to God? 3. What
comforting news does the psalmist
proclaim in the face of warring
neighbors (vv. 4–6)? Who is God's
"son" in verses 7 and 12 (see 2Sa
7:12–16)? Why would the Jews pin
their messianic hopes on the king?
4. Who are the "nations" and "ends
of the earth"? What is God asking
these nations to do?

1. The New Testament fre-
quently applies this psalm to
Jesus (see Mt 3:17; Ac 4:25–27,

13:33; Heb 1:5; 5:5). How are Jesus and the "anointed one" similar as "sons of God"? How do they differ? **2.** How does God deal with you: (a) Iron rod? (b) Pottery repair? (c) A kiss? (d) A flare up? Give an example? **3.** How do you "kiss the Son"? How can the group express homage to King Jesus?

---

1. How much sleep have you "lost" this week? Why? **2.** Which parent could you more easily cry with? Why? **3.** *Read aloud*—Reader(s) A: 1–6; Reader(s) B: 7–12.

1. Who are David's "foes" (see 2Sa 15:13–30)? Why does he flee the city rather than fight? **2.** What must have happened to transform David's "weeping" eyes and bowed head (vv. 3–5)? **3.** From where does his peace, victory and blessing come (vv. 6–8)? Likewise, his anger and anxiety?

1. When did you last feel abandoned by friends? By God? What happened? **2.** What "foes" are you facing? From what are you praying for deliverance? How will you know when that prayer is answered? Will it look like verse 7?

---

1. Which are you: Defeatist? Optimist? Realist? Why? **2.** *Read aloud*—Reader(s) A: 1–7, odd; Reader(s) B: 2–8, even.

1. What four things does David ask of God in verse 1? What might be causing him this distress and shame (v. 2)? **2.** What outcome does David expect? Why is he so confident? Why is he "set apart"? **3.** While wavering loyalty grieves David (v. 2), what counsel does he give those whose loyalty burns too fierce (vv. 4–5)? **4.** What's his answer to the defeatist (vv. 6b–8)? **5.** Given his prior mood (vv. 1–2), why is David now joyful, peaceful and secure?

1. Does your anger flash hot or burn slow? Is Paul asking too much when he quotes "in your anger do not sin" (see Eph 4:26)? How do you manage it? **2.** What is

[9]You will rule them with an iron scepter[a];
you will dash them to pieces like pottery."

[10]Therefore, you kings, be wise;
be warned, you rulers of the earth.
[11]Serve the LORD with fear
and rejoice with trembling.
[12]Kiss the Son, lest he be angry
and you be destroyed in your way,
for his wrath can flare up in a moment.
Blessed are all who take refuge in him.

Psalm 3

A psalm of David. When he fled from his son Absalom.

[1]O LORD, how many are my foes!
How many rise up against me!
[2]Many are saying of me,
"God will not deliver him."　　　*Selah*[b]

[3]But you are a shield around me, O LORD;
you bestow glory on me and lift[c] up my head.
[4]To the LORD I cry aloud,
and he answers me from his holy hill.　*Selah*

[5]I lie down and sleep;
I wake again, because the LORD sustains me.
[6]I will not fear the tens of thousands
drawn up against me on every side.

[7]Arise, O LORD!
Deliver me, O my God!
Strike all my enemies on the jaw;
break the teeth of the wicked.

[8]From the LORD comes deliverance.
May your blessing be on your people.　*Selah*

Psalm 4

For the director of music. With stringed instruments. A psalm of David.

[1]Answer me when I call to you,
O my righteous God.
Give me relief from my distress;
be merciful to me and hear my prayer.

[2]How long, O men, will you turn my glory into shame[d]?
How long will you love delusions and seek false gods[e]?　*Selah*
[3]Know that the LORD has set apart the godly for himself;
the LORD will hear when I call to him.

[4]In your anger do not sin;
when you are on your beds,

---

[a]9 Or *will break them with a rod of iron*　[b]2 A word of uncertain meaning, occurring frequently in the Psalms; possibly a musical term　[c]3 Or *LORD, / my Glorious One, who lifts*　[d]2 Or *you dishonor my Glorious One*　[e]2 Or *seek lies*

search your hearts and be silent.   *Selah*
[5]Offer right sacrifices
    and trust in the LORD.

[6]Many are asking, "Who can show us any good?"
    Let the light of your face shine upon us,
      O LORD.
[7]You have filled my heart with greater joy
    than when their grain and new wine abound.
[8]I will lie down and sleep in peace,
    for you alone, O LORD,
    make me dwell in safety.

Psalm 5

For the director of music. For flutes. A psalm
of David.

[1]Give ear to my words, O LORD,
    consider my sighing.
[2]Listen to my cry for help,
    my King and my God,
    for to you I pray.
[3]In the morning, O LORD, you hear my voice;
    in the morning I lay my requests before you
    and wait in expectation.

[4]You are not a God who takes pleasure in evil;
    with you the wicked cannot dwell.
[5]The arrogant cannot stand in your presence;
    you hate all who do wrong.
[6]You destroy those who tell lies;
    bloodthirsty and deceitful men
    the LORD abhors.

[7]But I, by your great mercy,
    will come into your house;
in reverence will I bow down
    toward your holy temple.
[8]Lead me, O LORD, in your righteousness
    because of my enemies—
    make straight your way before me.

[9]Not a word from their mouth can be trusted;
    their heart is filled with destruction.
Their throat is an open grave;
    with their tongue they speak deceit.
[10]Declare them guilty, O God!
    Let their intrigues be their downfall.
Banish them for their many sins,
    for they have rebelled against you.

[11]But let all who take refuge in you be glad;
    let them ever sing for joy.
Spread your protection over them,
    that those who love your name may rejoice in
      you.
[12]For surely, O LORD, you bless the righteous;
    you surround them with your favor as with a
      shield.

your biggest source of stress? Where lies your confidence? **3.** Do disloyal people get you down? What does it mean to yield your rights, needs and feelings to God?

1. Who gave you the most comfort growing up: Mom? Dad? Grandparent? Siblings? Your pets or stuffed toys? Your pastor? The telephone? Why? **2.** What schoolyard bully did you just hate? **3.** *Read aloud*—Reader(s) A: 1–8; Reader(s) B: 9–12.

1. What do verses 1–3 sound like? Look like? Feel like? What is David losing sleep over? **2.** What is the focus of verses 4–6? Where does the focus shift in the next stanza (vv. 7–8)? Verses 9–10? **3.** Why does David plea for justice one minute and mercy the next? What does it say about his guilt? How dare he come before God after the violence and deceit regarding Bathsheba, for instance (see 2Sa 11–12)? Given that, how can he consider himself "the righteous" (v. 12)? **4.** What contrasts are drawn between "rebels" against God (v. 10) and "refugees" who come to God (v. 11)? Is David out of danger yet? Why?

1. Paul applies verse 9 to everyone (see Ro 3:13). Do you deserve such an indictment? Considering your own wrongdoing, deceit and violence, what are you praying for: Justice or mercy? Why? **2.** Why pray for the same thing day after day? How can you tell if God is answering "Wait" or "No"? Why do you persist? **3.** How (when? where?) could you build this "morning watch" into your daily routine? Is a routine for everyone? **4.** What situation are you now facing, where you could use help from God and your group?

1. Did (or does) your family express negative emotions very well? How so? 2. *Read aloud*—Reader(s) A: 1–9, odd; Reader(s) B: 2–10, even.

1. Why is David so sick with grief? Is God punishing him for sin, or is David just afraid that God is against him (vv. 1–2)? Why has God not answered him? 2. What does David believe about death (v. 5)? 3. Why do David's eyes fail (v. 7): (a) He's in the dark? (b) Justice is blind? (c) No end in sight? (d) Seeing is believing? 4. Why the different tone in verses 8–10? How does he know God has answered him?

1. Have you ever worried about your health, prayed for healing and not received it, or been sick with grief? How so? 2. What in your life makes you cry out "How long, O Lord"? Why is God waiting? 3. Do you ever see God as an "angry judge"? Does this psalm add to your despair or your hope? How can you turn your pain over to God?

---

1. In school, were you more likely the one picking on others or the one getting picked on? How did that feel? 2. It's 3:00 AM. You are being pursued or caught in a jam. Who do you call first? Second? Why? 3. *Read aloud*—Reader(s) A: 1–5; Reader(s) B: 6–13; Leader: 14–17.

1. Why was the tribe of Benjamin hostile to David (see 2Sa 16:5–8; 20:1–2)? What is David accused of in verses 3–4? Why? 2. In verses 6–11, how does David broaden his appeal for personal vindication? With what images of God? 3. What is meant by "my righteousness" (v. 8): (a) David is sinless? (b) Right? (c) Sincere? 4. Does David's appeal stand (or fall) on his righteousness, or on God's? Why is that? 5. From verses 11–12, how is evil done in: (a) By a personal Judge? (b) By self-destruction? (c) In a purely anonymous way? Compare this with verses 14–16. Why the difference, if any?

1. Have you felt falsely accused? How did you appeal your case? Like David? 2. If the content of your prayers from the last month were analyzed, how

Psalm 6

For the director of music. With stringed instruments. According to *sheminith.* [a]
A psalm of David.

[1]O Lord, do not rebuke me in your anger
  or discipline me in your wrath.
[2]Be merciful to me, Lord, for I am faint;
  O Lord, heal me, for my bones are in agony.
[3]My soul is in anguish.
  How long, O Lord, how long?

[4]Turn, O Lord, and deliver me;
  save me because of your unfailing love.
[5]No one remembers you when he is dead.
  Who praises you from the grave[b]?

[6]I am worn out from groaning;
  all night long I flood my bed with weeping
  and drench my couch with tears.
[7]My eyes grow weak with sorrow;
  they fail because of all my foes.

[8]Away from me, all you who do evil,
  for the Lord has heard my weeping.
[9]The Lord has heard my cry for mercy;
  the Lord accepts my prayer.
[10]All my enemies will be ashamed and dismayed;
  they will turn back in sudden disgrace.

Psalm 7

A *shiggaion* [c] of David, which he sang to the
  Lord concerning Cush, a Benjamite.

[1]O Lord my God, I take refuge in you;
  save and deliver me from all who pursue me,
[2]or they will tear me like a lion
  and rip me to pieces with no one to rescue me.

[3]O Lord my God, if I have done this
  and there is guilt on my hands—
[4]if I have done evil to him who is at peace with
    me
  or without cause have robbed my foe—
[5]then let my enemy pursue and overtake me;
  let him trample my life to the ground
  and make me sleep in the dust.   *Selah*

[6]Arise, O Lord, in your anger;
  rise up against the rage of my enemies.
  Awake, my God; decree justice.
[7]Let the assembled peoples gather around you.
  Rule over them from on high;
[8] let the Lord judge the peoples.
  Judge me, O Lord, according to my righteousness,
    according to my integrity, O Most High.
[9]O righteous God,
  who searches minds and hearts,

---

[a]Title: Probably a musical term   [b]5 Hebrew *Sheol*   [c]Title: Probably a literary or musical term

bring to an end the violence of the wicked
and make the righteous secure.
¹⁰My shield*a* is God Most High,
who saves the upright in heart.
¹¹God is a righteous judge,
a God who expresses his wrath every day.
¹²If he does not relent,
he*b* will sharpen his sword;
he will bend and string his bow.
¹³He has prepared his deadly weapons;
he makes ready his flaming arrows.
¹⁴He who is pregnant with evil
and conceives trouble gives birth to
disillusionment.
¹⁵He who digs a hole and scoops it out
falls into the pit he has made.
¹⁶The trouble he causes recoils on himself;
his violence comes down on his own head.
¹⁷I will give thanks to the LORD because of his
righteousness
and will sing praise to the name of the LORD
Most High.

Psalm 8

For the director of music. According to
*gittith.*c A psalm of David.

¹O LORD, our Lord,
how majestic is your name in all the earth!
You have set your glory
above the heavens.
²From the lips of children and infants
you have ordained praise*d*
because of your enemies,
to silence the foe and the avenger.
³When I consider your heavens,
the work of your fingers,
the moon and the stars,
which you have set in place,
⁴what is man that you are mindful of him,
the son of man that you care for him?
⁵You made him a little lower than the heavenly
beings*e*
and crowned him with glory and honor.
⁶You made him ruler over the works of your
hands;
you put everything under his feet:
⁷all flocks and herds,
and the beasts of the field,
⁸the birds of the air,
and the fish of the sea,
all that swim the paths of the seas.
⁹O LORD, our Lord,
how majestic is your name in all the earth!

much concern for injustice would we find? **3.** Would you want God to judge you according to your righteousness or the integrity of your heart? Why? **4.** What "pit" of your own making have you fallen into lately? Are you digging out? Or piling it down on your head? **5.** For what aspect of God's character are you especially thankful today?

1. Rank the following as to which you'd most (1) and least (7) prefer to be: Starry-eyed lover? Zookeeper? Children's choir director? Environmentalist? King of _____? Astronaut? Angel? **2.** *Read aloud*—Reader(s) A: 1–9, odd; Reader(s) B: 2–8, even.

1. Where is "above the heavens" (see Ge 1:6–8)? What is David saying about God? **2.** How might "majestic name" be linked to "infant praise" (v. 2)? How does "baby talk" silence God's foes? **3.** How are humans a "little lower" than heavenly beings (v. 5)? **4.** What is the job of the "ruler" (v. 6; see Ge 1:28; 2:15)?

1. Can we do anything we want to God's creation? What are our limits? Responsibilities? **2.** What is man, according to the pessimist? The optimist? Sinner? Sufferer? Which are you today? **3.** Have you ever wondered, gazing at a starry sky, how God could be "mindful" of your little life? Do you feel important to God?

---

a10 Or *sovereign*   b12 Or *If a man does not repent, / God*   cTitle: Probably a musical term   d2 Or *strength*   e5 Or *than God*

1. If you were a judge, which crime would you punish more severely than is usual? Which crime would you go easier on than usual? 2. Digging a pit for someone else and then falling in it yourself can be embarrassing. When has that happened to you? 3. *Read aloud*—Reader(s) A: 1–6; Reader(s) B: 7–12; All: 13–20.

1. What might be some of the "wonders" David refers to in verse 1 (v. 3; see 2Sa 8:1–14)? 2. David sings of God dispensing justice for "the world" and for "ever and ever." Has God already brought justice or is David just confident his prayer will be answered (v. 7)? In what sense does God reign? 3. How are worship and witness related for David (v. 11)? For you? 4. Who are the "wicked" (vv. 5,16,17)? What three names are given in contrast (vv. 9,12,18)? 5. In what way is the Lord "known by his justice" (v. 16)? Does God bring justice by divine intervention or by "the work of our hands"? 6. Skim the next psalm to see how Psalm 10 once may have been an extension of Psalm 9. Why might it have been later separated into the two Psalms we now have?

1. Which of God's wonders have you felt like singing about this week? Or are you still distracted from enjoying God's wonders by the pursuit of "enemies"? 2. What word best describes you: (a) Oppressed? (b) Afflicted? (c) Needy? (d) Wicked? (e) Wonderful? Why? 3. Does your private worship affect your public witness? How has your public witness affected your desire to pray, plead and sing? 4. What hope does this psalm give people suffering injustice? What is your advice to them? 5. Does God carry out judgments in this life or does he wait for a future "Judgment Day"? Why has God waited so long?

Psalm 9[a]

For the director of music. To ⌊the tune of⌋
"The Death of the Son." A psalm of David.

¹I will praise you, O LORD, with all my heart;
    I will tell of all your wonders.
²I will be glad and rejoice in you;
    I will sing praise to your name, O Most High.

³My enemies turn back;
    they stumble and perish before you.
⁴For you have upheld my right and my cause;
    you have sat on your throne, judging
      righteously.
⁵You have rebuked the nations and destroyed the
      wicked;
    you have blotted out their name for ever and
      ever.
⁶Endless ruin has overtaken the enemy,
    you have uprooted their cities;
    even the memory of them has perished.

⁷The LORD reigns forever;
    he has established his throne for judgment.
⁸He will judge the world in righteousness;
    he will govern the peoples with justice.
⁹The LORD is a refuge for the oppressed,
    a stronghold in times of trouble.
¹⁰Those who know your name will trust in you,
    for you, LORD, have never forsaken those who
      seek you.

¹¹Sing praises to the LORD, enthroned in Zion;
    proclaim among the nations what he has done.
¹²For he who avenges blood remembers;
    he does not ignore the cry of the afflicted.

¹³O LORD, see how my enemies persecute me!
    Have mercy and lift me up from the gates of
      death,
¹⁴that I may declare your praises
    in the gates of the Daughter of Zion
    and there rejoice in your salvation.
¹⁵The nations have fallen into the pit they have
      dug;
    their feet are caught in the net they have
      hidden.
¹⁶The LORD is known by his justice;
    the wicked are ensnared by the work of their
      hands.   *Higgaion.*[b] Selah
¹⁷The wicked return to the grave,[c]
    all the nations that forget God.
¹⁸But the needy will not always be forgotten,
    nor the hope of the afflicted ever perish.

¹⁹Arise, O LORD, let not man triumph;

[a] Psalms 9 and 10 may have been originally a single acrostic poem, the stanzas of which begin with the successive letters of the Hebrew alphabet. In the Septuagint they constitute one psalm.   [b] *16* Or *Meditation*; possibly a musical notation   [c] *17* Hebrew *Sheol*

let the nations be judged in your presence.
²⁰Strike them with terror, O Lᴏʀᴅ;
    let the nations know they are but men.   *Selah*

Psalm 10 ᵃ

¹Why, O Lᴏʀᴅ, do you stand far off?
    Why do you hide yourself in times of trouble?

²In his arrogance the wicked man hunts down the
      weak,
    who are caught in the schemes he devises.
³He boasts of the cravings of his heart;
    he blesses the greedy and reviles the Lᴏʀᴅ.
⁴In his pride the wicked does not seek him;
    in all his thoughts there is no room for God.
⁵His ways are always prosperous;
    he is haughty and your laws are far from him;
    he sneers at all his enemies.
⁶He says to himself, "Nothing will shake me;
    I'll always be happy and never have trouble."
⁷His mouth is full of curses and lies and threats;
    trouble and evil are under his tongue.
⁸He lies in wait near the villages;
    from ambush he murders the innocent,
    watching in secret for his victims.
⁹He lies in wait like a lion in cover;
    he lies in wait to catch the helpless;
    he catches the helpless and drags them off in
      his net.
¹⁰His victims are crushed, they collapse;
    they fall under his strength.
¹¹He says to himself, "God has forgotten;
    he covers his face and never sees."

¹²Arise, Lᴏʀᴅ! Lift up your hand, O God.
    Do not forget the helpless.
¹³Why does the wicked man revile God?
    Why does he say to himself,
    "He won't call me to account"?
¹⁴But you, O God, do see trouble and grief;
    you consider it to take it in hand.
The victim commits himself to you;
    you are the helper of the fatherless.
¹⁵Break the arm of the wicked and evil man;
    call him to account for his wickedness
    that would not be found out.

¹⁶The Lᴏʀᴅ is King for ever and ever;
    the nations will perish from his land.
¹⁷You hear, O Lᴏʀᴅ, the desire of the afflicted;
    you encourage them, and you listen to their
      cry,
¹⁸defending the fatherless and the oppressed,
    in order that man, who is of the earth, may
      terrify no more.

---

1. Where do you hide in times of trouble: Under the bed covers? Behind a smoke screen? Behind a veil of humor? With face covered ("hear no evil, see no evil")? Explain. **2.** When you were young, did your friends (or enemies) boast about picking on others? How did that make you feel? **3.** *Read aloud*—Reader(s) A: 1–15, odd; Reader(s) B: 2–14, even; All:16–18.

1. This continuation of Psalm 9 seems to make contradictory statements within itself: How can both verses 1 and 14 be true? Or verses 11 and 17? **2.** What is the basis for this wicked man's practical atheism? Does he sound "far away" from God, or is God far removed from him? Or is God actually "too close for comfort" (vv. 6,11,13)? Why do you think so? **3.** How does this man victimize his prey? Who does he remind you of? Does he arouse your compassion or revulsion? Why? **4.** When, if ever, does justice catch up with him? Why or why not? **5.** What does the helpless victim want God to do (vv. 12,15)? What does God do instead? Why?

1. Have you ever felt like the king does here? What happened? Why is God sometimes so silent in the face of great needs? **2.** When God does not appear to answer your prayers, as in this psalmist's plight, do you persevere in faith anyway? If so, how? If not, why not? **3.** Who in the world today seems similar to the wicked man in this psalm? What would you like to say to him or her? What do you think God wants to say? **4.** Paul applies verse 7 to all of us (see Ro 3:14)? What's his point? How does the image fit you? Might anyone be praying this psalm "against you"? Are you part of the problem or the solution?

ᵃ Psalms 9 and 10 may have been originally a single acrostic poem, the stanzas of which begin with the successive letters of the Hebrew alphabet. In the Septuagint they constitute one psalm.

1. What made you feel secure as a child? As an adult, do you have a "getaway" place? When do you go there? 2. *Read aloud*—Reader(s) A: 1–3; Reader(s) B: 4–7.

1. What advice is David receiving here (vv. 1–3)? What attitudes does such advice reflect? 2. What is David's response (vv. 4–6)? Was he wrong to "head for the hills" at other times (see 1Sa 23:14)? 3. "Fire and brimstone" is an enduring image. What do you see as the lot of the wicked (v. 6)?

1. What hiding places or "getaways" does the world urge upon you? How do you seek refuge in the Lord instead? 2. Do you feel like "the foundations are being destroyed"? Which ones? What can your small group do about it?

1. When something important must be said, do you write, call or visit in person? Why? 2. *Read aloud*—Reader(s) A: 1–7, odd; Reader(s) B: 2–8, even.

1. What three types of "lip service" does David lament in verses 2–4? 2. How do these hurt the weak (v. 5)? 3. What is meant by "the words of the Lord" (v. 6)? Who wins this battle of words? Why? How?

1. What is your biggest "speech impediment": Withholding the truth? Flattery? Boasting? Not listening? 2. Do you consider yourself a good communicator? What do your friends think? 3. When did a small word hurt a lot? Encourage a lot? 4. How do you rate on Paul's view of speech (see Eph 4:15,25,29)?

Psalm 11

For the director of music. Of David.

[1]In the LORD I take refuge.
How then can you say to me:
"Flee like a bird to your mountain.
[2]For look, the wicked bend their bows;
they set their arrows against the strings
to shoot from the shadows
at the upright in heart.
[3]When the foundations are being destroyed,
what can the righteous do[a]?"

[4]The LORD is in his holy temple;
the LORD is on his heavenly throne.
He observes the sons of men;
his eyes examine them.
[5]The LORD examines the righteous,
but the wicked[b] and those who love violence
his soul hates.
[6]On the wicked he will rain
fiery coals and burning sulfur;
a scorching wind will be their lot.

[7]For the LORD is righteous,
he loves justice;
upright men will see his face.

Psalm 12

For the director of music. According to
sheminith.[c] A psalm of David.

[1]Help, LORD, for the godly are no more;
the faithful have vanished from among men.
[2]Everyone lies to his neighbor;
their flattering lips speak with deception.

[3]May the LORD cut off all flattering lips
and every boastful tongue
[4]that says, "We will triumph with our tongues;
we own our lips[d]—who is our master?"

[5]"Because of the oppression of the weak
and the groaning of the needy,
I will now arise," says the LORD.
"I will protect them from those who malign
them."
[6]And the words of the LORD are flawless,
like silver refined in a furnace of clay,
purified seven times.

[7]O LORD, you will keep us safe
and protect us from such people forever.
[8]The wicked freely strut about
when what is vile is honored among men.

---

*a3 Or what is the Righteous One doing   b5 Or The LORD, the Righteous One,
examines the wicked, /   cTitle: Probably a musical term   d4 Or / our lips are
our plowshares*

Psalm 13

For the director of music. A psalm of David.

¹How long, O LORD? Will you forget me forever?
  How long will you hide your face from me?
²How long must I wrestle with my thoughts
  and every day have sorrow in my heart?
  How long will my enemy triumph over me?

³Look on me and answer, O LORD my God.
  Give light to my eyes, or I will sleep in death;
⁴my enemy will say, "I have overcome him,"
  and my foes will rejoice when I fall.

⁵But I trust in your unfailing love;
  my heart rejoices in your salvation.
⁶I will sing to the LORD,
  for he has been good to me.

Psalm 14

For the director of music. Of David.

¹The fool*ᵃ* says in his heart,
  "There is no God."
They are corrupt, their deeds are vile;
  there is no one who does good.

²The LORD looks down from heaven
  on the sons of men
to see if there are any who understand,
  any who seek God.
³All have turned aside,
  they have together become corrupt;
there is no one who does good,
  not even one.

⁴Will evildoers never learn—
  those who devour my people as men eat bread
  and who do not call on the LORD?
⁵There they are, overwhelmed with dread,
  for God is present in the company of the
    righteous.
⁶You evildoers frustrate the plans of the poor,
  but the LORD is their refuge.

⁷Oh, that salvation for Israel would come out of
    Zion!
When the LORD restores the fortunes of his
    people,
  let Jacob rejoice and Israel be glad!

Psalm 15

A psalm of David.

¹LORD, who may dwell in your sanctuary?
  Who may live on your holy hill?

²He whose walk is blameless

---

1. Have you ever been forgotten by someone who was supposed to pick you up? How did you feel? What were you thinking? 2. *Read aloud*—Reader(s) A: 1–2; Reader(s) B: 3–4; Leader: 5–6.

1. What are the three stages in this uphill prayer? What makes David so low? So high? 2. What is David's tension? Why does he become hopeful at the end of his prayer?

1. Have you felt anger or despair like David does here? For how long? Did praying help? Where do you seek relief today? 2. When do you feel like singing? When is God's goodness most real?

1. Who played the "fool" in your senior class? What antics of your class clown were outrageous? 2. *Read aloud*—Reader(s) A: 1–7, odd; Reader(s) B: 2–6, even.

1. Why is it "foolish" to say "there is no God"? In what way is this fool an atheist (vv. 1–3)? 2. Is David's sweeping indictment a bit exaggerated? Or exceptionally accurate? Explain. 3. What does this psalm say about God's view of evil? What does God plan to do about it?

1. Have you ever been one of these fools: (a) The intellectual seeker? (b) The practical atheist? (c) Self-destructive? (d) Ravenous in relationships? 2. What tempts you to think "there is no God"? Does distance from God affect your behavior? 3. What part of your life runs without regard to God? How will you put your faith to work here today?

1. Where would your dream house be? What feature would have to be present? 2. *Read aloud*—Reader(s) A: 1–5, odd; Reader(s) B: 2–4, even.

1. Who gets to live on God's "holy hill"? Why isn't God's dwelling available on an "equal housing opportunity" basis? 2. Why

---

ᵃ 1 The Hebrew words rendered *fool* in Psalms denote one who is morally deficient.

"despise" the vile (v. 4)? **3.** What is "usury" (v. 5; see Ex 22:25)?

♡ **1.** In applying for God's dwelling, would your references say you have the required good character? Words? Works? Dealings? Why or why not? **2.** Does Paul have a different Landlord than David (see Eph 2:8–10)? Explain.

——————

☕ **1.** Have you inherited anything from a relative? What do you wish would be left to you? **2.** Are you a night person? If so, what do you do late at night? **3.** *Read aloud*—Reader(s) A: 1–3; Reader(s) B: 4–6; Leader: 7–8; All: 9–11.

📖 **1.** What two types of Israelites did David see (vv. 3–4)? **2.** For what blessings does he praise God (vv. 5–8)? What exactly do you think he means by each? **3.** Did David's hope come true (v. 10)? In what way?

♡ **1.** Judging from your appointment calendar or your daydreams this past week, what do you "delight" in? **2.** What "gods" are you tempted to pursue? What sorrows do they bring? **3.** In this psalm, David moves from refugee to an heir of God's kingdom: Which do you feel more like now? Why?

and who does what is righteous,
who speaks the truth from his heart
3   and has no slander on his tongue,
who does his neighbor no wrong
and casts no slur on his fellowman,
⁴who despises a vile man
but honors those who fear the LORD,
who keeps his oath
even when it hurts,
⁵who lends his money without usury
and does not accept a bribe against the
innocent.

He who does these things
will never be shaken.

Psalm 16

*A miktam*ᵃ *of David.*

¹Keep me safe, O God,
for in you I take refuge.

²I said to the LORD, "You are my Lord;
apart from you I have no good thing."
³As for the saints who are in the land,
they are the glorious ones in whom is all my
delight.ᵇ
⁴The sorrows of those will increase
who run after other gods.
I will not pour out their libations of blood
or take up their names on my lips.

⁵LORD, you have assigned me my portion and my
cup;
you have made my lot secure.
⁶The boundary lines have fallen for me in pleasant
places;
surely I have a delightful inheritance.

⁷I will praise the LORD, who counsels me;
even at night my heart instructs me.
⁸I have set the LORD always before me.
Because he is at my right hand,
I will not be shaken.

⁹Therefore my heart is glad and my tongue
rejoices;
my body also will rest secure,
¹⁰because you will not abandon me to the
grave,ᶜ
nor will you let your Holy Oneᵈ see
decay.

ᵃTitle: Probably a literary or musical term   ᵇ3 Or *As for the pagan priests who are in the land / and the nobles in whom all delight, I said:*   ᶜ10 Hebrew *Sheol*   ᵈ10 Or *your faithful one*

[11]You have made[a] known to me the path of life;
  you will fill me with joy in your presence,
  with eternal pleasures at your right hand.

Psalm 17

A prayer of David.

[1]Hear, O LORD, my righteous plea;
  listen to my cry.
Give ear to my prayer—
  it does not rise from deceitful lips.
[2]May my vindication come from you;
  may your eyes see what is right.

[3]Though you probe my heart and examine me at
    night,
  though you test me, you will find nothing;
  I have resolved that my mouth will not sin.
[4]As for the deeds of men—
  by the word of your lips
I have kept myself
  from the ways of the violent.
[5]My steps have held to your paths;
  my feet have not slipped.

[6]I call on you, O God, for you will answer me;
  give ear to me and hear my prayer.
[7]Show the wonder of your great love,
  you who save by your right hand
  those who take refuge in you from their foes.
[8]Keep me as the apple of your eye;
  hide me in the shadow of your wings
[9]from the wicked who assail me,
  from my mortal enemies who surround me.

[10]They close up their callous hearts,
  and their mouths speak with arrogance.
[11]They have tracked me down, they now surround
    me,
  with eyes alert, to throw me to the ground.
[12]They are like a lion hungry for prey,
  like a great lion crouching in cover.

[13]Rise up, O LORD, confront them, bring them down;
  rescue me from the wicked by your sword.
[14]O LORD, by your hand save me from such men,
  from men of this world whose reward is in this
    life.

You still the hunger of those you cherish;
  their sons have plenty,
  and they store up wealth for their children.
[15]And I—in righteousness I will see your face;
  when I awake, I will be satisfied with seeing
    your likeness.

1. When have you felt singled out for punishment by your parents, teacher or boss? Was it ever for something you didn't do? How did you feel then? 2. When did you feel really terrified? Did your worst fears come true? 3. Read aloud—Reader(s) A: 1–15, odd; Reader(s) B: 2–14, even.

1. Does David think he is without sin (vv. 3–5)? Or is he merely contrasting himself with his enemies (vv. 9–12)? What else might he be saying? 2. Although he calls on God as a judge (vv. 1–5), how does David relate to him (vv. 6–9)? 3. Of the three things that he prays for—justice (vv. 1–5), protection (vv. 6–9) and God's fellowship (v. 15)—what does David desire most? Why do you think so? 4. "When I awake" (v. 15) may be a metaphor for resurrection (see Isa 26:19; Da 12:2). What reward does David wish for his enemies (v. 14)?

1. On what basis do you make your plea before God: Your integrity? The heartlessness of your enemies? God's love? Some combination? Or do you rarely see God as Judge? 2. What makes the biggest difference in how and why you live compared with people who do not know God: (a) God's love? (b) God's righteousness? (c) God's reward? 3. In what situation now do you need deliverance from people or forces that seem out to get you?

a 11 Or You will make

1. Picture God as you did when you were a child. What did the face look like? The body? Did God hold anything? What color was God? What words did God say? 2. What images do you have of God today? What colors? Emotions? Sounds? 3. Would you make a good soldier? Why? 4. *Read aloud*—Reader(s) A: 1–45, odd; Reader(s) B: 2–44, even; All: 46–50.

1. If you had to express the emotions of this psalm in music, what types of music would you choose? What refrains would you dramatize? What solo parts stand out? Where would you signal the musical crescendo? 2. This psalm appears at the end of 2 Samuel as a summary of David's life. How accurate a summary is it? Does it gloss over some of David's less noble deeds? 3. David spent much time hiding from Saul in rocks and caves. What insight does this give you into the meaning of God as "fortress" or "stronghold" or "rock"? What names could you give God based on your experiences? 4. Nowhere in 1 or 2 Samuel are the cosmic events of verses 4–19 recorded. Why does David use such dramatic language to describe God saving him? To what other redemptive experiences in Israel's history is he alluding (vv. 16–17)? 5. What does the linking of God's rescue of David to God's actions for Israel at the Red Sea or Mt. Sinai say about God's love for the individual? What else does this dramatic picture say about God's justice? 6. In several psalms David speaks as though he were sinless (vv. 20–24). In others he is very aware of his failure (see 32:5). How do you account for this? 7. Is David boasting or praising God in verses 20–29? What "decrees" had God given him? How did David perform? How much of his appeal is based on God's promises and peculiar delight in him? Why do you think so? 8. What image of God is most prominent in the eyes of David, according to verses 30–36 and 46–50? Do we tend to "make God" in our own image?

1. Much religion is the honoring, fearing or appeasing of God. Is it easy or hard for you to say "I love you, Lord"? When are you most aware of God's love for you? 2. Would God shake heaven and earth to save you? Do you think God would even lift a finger to

Psalm 18

For the director of music. Of David the servant of the LORD. He sang to the LORD the words of this song when the LORD delivered him from the hand of all his enemies and from the hand of Saul. He said:

¹I love you, O LORD, my strength.

²The LORD is my rock, my fortress and my
    deliverer;
  my God is my rock, in whom I take refuge.
  He is my shield and the horn[a] of my salvation,
    my stronghold.
³I call to the LORD, who is worthy of praise,
  and I am saved from my enemies.

⁴The cords of death entangled me;
  the torrents of destruction overwhelmed me.
⁵The cords of the grave[b] coiled around me;
  the snares of death confronted me.
⁶In my distress I called to the LORD;
  I cried to my God for help.
From his temple he heard my voice;
  my cry came before him, into his ears.

⁷The earth trembled and quaked,
  and the foundations of the mountains shook;
  they trembled because he was angry.
⁸Smoke rose from his nostrils;
  consuming fire came from his mouth,
  burning coals blazed out of it.
⁹He parted the heavens and came down;
  dark clouds were under his feet.
¹⁰He mounted the cherubim and flew;
  he soared on the wings of the wind.
¹¹He made darkness his covering, his canopy around
    him—
  the dark rain clouds of the sky.
¹²Out of the brightness of his presence clouds
    advanced,
  with hailstones and bolts of lightning.
¹³The LORD thundered from heaven;
  the voice of the Most High resounded.[c]
¹⁴He shot his arrows and scattered ⌊the enemies⌋,
  great bolts of lightning and routed them.
¹⁵The valleys of the sea were exposed
  and the foundations of the earth laid bare
at your rebuke, O LORD,
  at the blast of breath from your nostrils.

¹⁶He reached down from on high and took hold of
    me;
  he drew me out of deep waters.
¹⁷He rescued me from my powerful enemy,
  from my foes, who were too strong for me.
¹⁸They confronted me in the day of my disaster,
  but the LORD was my support.

[a]2 *Horn* here symbolizes strength.   [b]5 Hebrew *Sheol*   [c]13 Some Hebrew manuscripts and Septuagint (see also 2 Samuel 22:14); most Hebrew manuscripts *resounded, / amid hailstones and bolts of lightning*

¹⁹He brought me out into a spacious place;
    he rescued me because he delighted in me.

²⁰The LORD has dealt with me according to my
        righteousness;
    according to the cleanness of my hands he has
        rewarded me.
²¹For I have kept the ways of the LORD;
    I have not done evil by turning from my God.
²²All his laws are before me;
    I have not turned away from his decrees.
²³I have been blameless before him
    and have kept myself from sin.
²⁴The LORD has rewarded me according to my
        righteousness,
    according to the cleanness of my hands in his
        sight.

²⁵To the faithful you show yourself faithful,
    to the blameless you show yourself blameless,
²⁶to the pure you show yourself pure,
    but to the crooked you show yourself shrewd.
²⁷You save the humble
    but bring low those whose eyes are haughty.
²⁸You, O LORD, keep my lamp burning;
    my God turns my darkness into light.
²⁹With your help I can advance against a troop*a*;
    with my God I can scale a wall.

³⁰As for God, his way is perfect;
    the word of the LORD is flawless.
He is a shield
    for all who take refuge in him.
³¹For who is God besides the LORD?
    And who is the Rock except our God?
³²It is God who arms me with strength
    and makes my way perfect.
³³He makes my feet like the feet of a deer;
    he enables me to stand on the heights.
³⁴He trains my hands for battle;
    my arms can bend a bow of bronze.
³⁵You give me your shield of victory,
    and your right hand sustains me;
    you stoop down to make me great.
³⁶You broaden the path beneath me,
    so that my ankles do not turn.

³⁷I pursued my enemies and overtook them;
    I did not turn back till they were destroyed.
³⁸I crushed them so that they could not rise;
    they fell beneath my feet.
³⁹You armed me with strength for battle;
    you made my adversaries bow at my feet.
⁴⁰You made my enemies turn their backs in flight,
    and I destroyed my foes.
⁴¹They cried for help, but there was no one to save
        them—
    to the LORD, but he did not answer.

save you? Why? Why doesn't God save his many children dying of hunger and war? **3.** Who fights your battles, you or God? What is the balance? **4.** Habakkuk 3:19 quotes verse 33 to build up hope in the face of a national crisis. What verse would you choose to describe how you want to see God work in your own crisis? In your nation's crisis? Why that verse? **5.** The group members may hold a short time of praise, offering short prayers beginning like this psalm: "I love you, O Lord, because …"

a29 Or can run through a barricade

⁴²I beat them as fine as dust borne on the wind;
    I poured them out like mud in the streets.

⁴³You have delivered me from the attacks of the
        people;
    you have made me the head of nations;
    people I did not know are subject to me.
⁴⁴As soon as they hear me, they obey me;
    foreigners cringe before me.
⁴⁵They all lose heart;
    they come trembling from their strongholds.

⁴⁶The LORD lives! Praise be to my Rock!
    Exalted be God my Savior!
⁴⁷He is the God who avenges me,
    who subdues nations under me,
⁴⁸ who saves me from my enemies.
  You exalted me above my foes;
    from violent men you rescued me.
⁴⁹Therefore I will praise you among the nations,
        O LORD;
    I will sing praises to your name.
⁵⁰He gives his king great victories;
    he shows unfailing kindness to his anointed,
    to David and his descendants forever.

Psalm 19

For the director of music. A psalm of David.

¹The heavens declare the glory of God;
    the skies proclaim the work of his hands.
²Day after day they pour forth speech;
    night after night they display knowledge.
³There is no speech or language
    where their voice is not heard.ᵃ
⁴Their voiceᵇ goes out into all the earth,
    their words to the ends of the world.

  In the heavens he has pitched a tent for the sun,
⁵ which is like a bridegroom coming forth from
        his pavilion,
    like a champion rejoicing to run his course.
⁶It rises at one end of the heavens
    and makes its circuit to the other;
    nothing is hidden from its heat.

⁷The law of the LORD is perfect,
    reviving the soul.
  The statutes of the LORD are trustworthy,
    making wise the simple.
⁸The precepts of the LORD are right,
    giving joy to the heart.
  The commands of the LORD are radiant,
    giving light to the eyes.
⁹The fear of the LORD is pure,
    enduring forever.
  The ordinances of the LORD are sure
    and altogether righteous.

1. What's your favorite dessert? When's the last time you had it? 2. Do you like to read? What would you rather do? 3. *Read aloud*—Reader(s) A: 1–6; Reader(s) B: 7–13; All: 14.

1. Who speaks in verses 1–4? What do "they" say? Is the truth about God in nature obvious to everyone? Why don't some people "hear" it? 2. David believed the sun moved across the sky (v. 6). Is this psalm art or science? 3. What six names does David give the Jewish law (vv. 7–10)? What eight words describe this law? What phrases describe its effect on our lives? 4. What does the revelation through Scripture do for us that the revelation in creation does not (v. 11)? 5. David uses the name "God" ("El") in verse 1, then switches to "the Lord" ("Yahweh") in verses 7–9. Why the change? Note: "El" is the least specific Hebrew word for God, whereas "Yahweh" is God's personal name (see Ex 3:14–15). 6. How does David's confession and prayer (vv. 12–14) square with his claims to blamelessness in the previous psalm (18:20–24)?

1. What in creation fills you most with a sense of God's glory? Can you see God "creating" in so-called "natural disasters"? 2. Which of David's "one-liners" about God's law best matches your expe-

ᵃ3 Or *They have no speech, there are no words; / no sound is heard from them*
ᵇ4 Septuagint, Jerome and Syriac; Hebrew *line*

¹⁰They are more precious than gold,
  than much pure gold;
they are sweeter than honey,
  than honey from the comb.
¹¹By them is your servant warned;
  in keeping them there is great reward.

¹²Who can discern his errors?
  Forgive my hidden faults.
¹³Keep your servant also from willful sins;
  may they not rule over me.
Then will I be blameless,
  innocent of great transgression.

¹⁴May the words of my mouth and the meditation
    of my heart
  be pleasing in your sight,
  O Lord, my Rock and my Redeemer.

Psalm 20

For the director of music. A psalm of David.

¹May the Lord answer you when you are in
    distress;
  may the name of the God of Jacob protect you.
²May he send you help from the sanctuary
  and grant you support from Zion.
³May he remember all your sacrifices
  and accept your burnt offerings.   *Selah*
⁴May he give you the desire of your heart
  and make all your plans succeed.
⁵We will shout for joy when you are victorious
  and will lift up our banners in the name of our
    God.
May the Lord grant all your requests.

⁶Now I know that the Lord saves his anointed;
  he answers him from his holy heaven
  with the saving power of his right hand.
⁷Some trust in chariots and some in horses,
  but we trust in the name of the Lord our God.
⁸They are brought to their knees and fall,
  but we rise up and stand firm.

⁹O Lord, save the king!
  Answer*ᵃ* us when we call!

Psalm 21

For the director of music. A psalm of David.

¹O Lord, the king rejoices in your strength.
  How great is his joy in the victories you give!
²You have granted him the desire of his heart
  and have not withheld the request of his lips.
                                                   Selah

³You welcomed him with rich blessings
  and placed a crown of pure gold on his head.
⁴He asked you for life, and you gave it to him—

rience with Scripture? Or should you write your own? How does your sense of its value translate into the time you spend reading it? **3.** Which would nurture your faith most: (a) Meditation on creation? (b) Meditation on the Word? (c) A combination? (d) Other? Why? **4.** What "hidden faults" or "willful sins" come to mind today? Is it hard to share these with the group? Why or why not?

---

1. What are you looking forward to least in the upcoming week? Why? **2.** How do you psych yourself for a challenge? A conflict? **3.** *Read aloud*—Reader(s) A: 1–9, odd; Reader(s) B: 2–8, even.

1. This psalm is a prayer before war (see 1Ki 8:44–45). Picture the scene in verses 1–5, people gathered around their army. How can they be so confident? **2.** "Chariots and horses" were the potent technology at the time: What is the equivalent today?

1. What does it mean to trust the Lord instead of weapons in our modern world? How does this apply to our prayers? To our political commitments? **2.** What challenge are you facing today for which you need group prayer? State your requests specifically.

---

1. What is the biggest victory you've ever won? The most recent? Do you feel exhilarated, exhausted or what? **2.** How do you celebrate your victories? With whom? **3.** *Read aloud*—Reader(s) A: read the first half of the verse; Reader(s) B: read the second half of the verse.

1. This psalm is the "morning after" complement to Psalm 20. What must have happened meanwhile? Does God take sides in war (vv. 1, 5)? **2.** What has

ᵃ9 Or save! / O King, answer

God done for the king (vv. 3–6)? What does this tell you about what God will do for those who trust in him? **3.** Do verses 8–12 strike you as a realistic picture of the battle past? Is the psalmist referring to more than just David (v. 10)?

1. The last time you overcame a major obstacle, what were you inclined to do: Give yourself a pat on the back? Give thanks to God? Rally the troops who prayed for you? Why? **2.** When have you prayed and not received the victory? How did it affect the way you prayed and faced your big test the next time? **3.** What difference does it make, knowing ultimate victory belongs to God?

1. What close encounter with a ferocious dog or animal would you sooner forget? **2.** Anyone ever call you a worm? Why? Because you are sluggish? Like to play in the dirt? You're a slippery character? **3.** Do you have an older brother? Did someone play that role for you? **4.** *Read aloud*— Reader(s) A: 1–31, odd; Reader(s) B: 2–30, even.

1. What is David's basic struggle (vv. 1–2,6–8)? What seems worse: God's distance or people's mocking? **2.** Where is David's faith in the midst of these struggles (vv. 3–5)? What does he recall about God's past action that leads to the words of verses 1 and 11? **3.** What is David's claim in verse 10? How is this true? **4.** How would you describe the mood shift between verses 1–21 and verses 22–31? What may have happened between verses 21 and 22? **5.** Who is invited to David's assembly (vv. 26–29)? Why does he want to host this world-wide feast? **6.** Jesus quoted the first line of this psalm on the cross (Mt 27:46). What other details of this psalm turn up in the crucifixion narratives (see Mt 27, Mk 14, Lk 23 and Jn 19)? How do these help you to understand this psalm?

length of days, for ever and ever.
⁵Through the victories you gave, his glory is great;
  you have bestowed on him splendor and
    majesty.
⁶Surely you have granted him eternal blessings
  and made him glad with the joy of your
    presence.
⁷For the king trusts in the LORD;
  through the unfailing love of the Most High
  he will not be shaken.

⁸Your hand will lay hold on all your enemies;
  your right hand will seize your foes.
⁹At the time of your appearing
  you will make them like a fiery furnace.
  In his wrath the LORD will swallow them up,
    and his fire will consume them.
¹⁰You will destroy their descendants from the earth,
  their posterity from mankind.
¹¹Though they plot evil against you
  and devise wicked schemes, they cannot
    succeed;
¹²for you will make them turn their backs
  when you aim at them with drawn bow.

¹³Be exalted, O LORD, in your strength;
  we will sing and praise your might.

Psalm 22

For the director of music. To ⌊the tune of⌋
"The Doe of the Morning." A psalm of David.

¹My God, my God, why have you forsaken me?
  Why are you so far from saving me,
  so far from the words of my groaning?
²O my God, I cry out by day, but you do not
    answer,
  by night, and am not silent.

³Yet you are enthroned as the Holy One;
  you are the praise of Israel.ᵃ
⁴In you our fathers put their trust;
  they trusted and you delivered them.
⁵They cried to you and were saved;
  in you they trusted and were not disappointed.

⁶But I am a worm and not a man,
  scorned by men and despised by the people.
⁷All who see me mock me;
  they hurl insults, shaking their heads:
⁸"He trusts in the LORD;
  let the LORD rescue him.
  Let him deliver him,
  since he delights in him."

⁹Yet you brought me out of the womb;
  you made me trust in you
  even at my mother's breast.
¹⁰From birth I was cast upon you;

ᵃ3 Or *Yet you are holy, / enthroned on the praises of Israel*

from my mother's womb you have been my
    God.
[11]Do not be far from me,
    for trouble is near
    and there is no one to help.

[12]Many bulls surround me;
    strong bulls of Bashan encircle me.
[13]Roaring lions tearing their prey
    open their mouths wide against me.
[14]I am poured out like water,
    and all my bones are out of joint.
My heart has turned to wax;
    it has melted away within me.
[15]My strength is dried up like a potsherd,
    and my tongue sticks to the roof of my mouth;
    you lay me[a] in the dust of death.
[16]Dogs have surrounded me;
    a band of evil men has encircled me,
    they have pierced[b] my hands and my feet.
[17]I can count all my bones;
    people stare and gloat over me.
[18]They divide my garments among them
    and cast lots for my clothing.

[19]But you, O LORD, be not far off;
    O my Strength, come quickly to help me.
[20]Deliver my life from the sword,
    my precious life from the power of the dogs.
[21]Rescue me from the mouth of the lions;
    save[c] me from the horns of the wild oxen.

[22]I will declare your name to my brothers;
    in the congregation I will praise you.
[23]You who fear the LORD, praise him!
    All you descendants of Jacob, honor him!
    Revere him, all you descendants of Israel!
[24]For he has not despised or disdained
    the suffering of the afflicted one;
he has not hidden his face from him
    but has listened to his cry for help.

[25]From you comes the theme of my praise in the
    great assembly;
before those who fear you[d] will I fulfill my
    vows.
[26]The poor will eat and be satisfied;
    they who seek the LORD will praise him—
    may your hearts live forever!
[27]All the ends of the earth
    will remember and turn to the LORD,
and all the families of the nations
    will bow down before him,
[28]for dominion belongs to the LORD
    and he rules over the nations.

[29]All the rich of the earth will feast and worship;

1. When you are stricken with grief, feeling abandoned even by God, how do you express yourself: Disbelief? Tears? Anger? Woe is me? Wanting to crawl back into the womb? Thinking about your death? Bargaining with God? Faith in spite of a bleak outlook? 2. At such times, does it help to know that Jesus experienced despair and felt the same way? 3. Verses 1–21 shift between faith and despair. If "Faith" was on the wall to your right, "Despair" on the wall to your left, where would you position yourself in the room to show where you are spiritually? Why? 4. Does it help you to recall the past in times of desperation? How would you rephrase verses 3–5 or 9–11? 5. If you were to host a feast to celebrate God's grace to you, what's one thing you'd say in proposing a toast to your King? 6. Since Jews, Gentiles, the poor, the rich, people present and people future are all invited to Jesus' feast (vv. 22–31), how then will you reach out to others? Whom could you invite to Jesus' feast this week? 7. The author of Hebrews quotes verse 22, saying Jesus is "not ashamed to call them brothers" (Heb 2:11–12). Do you ever think of Jesus as "brother"? What does this kind of relationship mean to you?

---

[a]15 Or / I am laid   [b]16 Some Hebrew manuscripts, Septuagint and Syriac; most Hebrew manuscripts / like the lion,   [c]21 Or / you have heard   [d]25 Hebrew him

all who go down to the dust will kneel before
him—
those who cannot keep themselves alive.
³⁰Posterity will serve him;
future generations will be told about the Lord.
³¹They will proclaim his righteousness
to a people yet unborn—
for he has done it.

Psalm 23

A psalm of David.

¹The LORD is my shepherd, I shall not be in want.
² He makes me lie down in green pastures,
he leads me beside quiet waters,
³ he restores my soul.
He guides me in paths of righteousness
for his name's sake.
⁴Even though I walk
through the valley of the shadow of death,ᵃ
I will fear no evil,
for you are with me;
your rod and your staff,
they comfort me.

⁵You prepare a table before me
in the presence of my enemies.
You anoint my head with oil;
my cup overflows.
⁶Surely goodness and love will follow me
all the days of my life,
and I will dwell in the house of the LORD
forever.

Psalm 24

Of David. A psalm.

¹The earth is the LORD's, and everything in it,
the world, and all who live in it;
²for he founded it upon the seas
and established it upon the waters.

³Who may ascend the hill of the LORD?
Who may stand in his holy place?
⁴He who has clean hands and a pure heart,
who does not lift up his soul to an idol
or swear by what is false.ᵇ
⁵He will receive blessing from the LORD
and vindication from God his Savior.
⁶Such is the generation of those who seek him,
who seek your face, O God of Jacob.ᶜ   *Selah*

⁷Lift up your heads, O you gates;
be lifted up, you ancient doors,
that the King of glory may come in.
⁸Who is this King of glory?
The LORD strong and mighty,

---

1. With what formulas for dealing with stress were you raised? "Forget it"? "Pray about it"? "Sleep on it"? **2.** *Read aloud*—Reader(s) A: 1–5, odd; Reader(s) B: 2–6, even.

1. David now departs from the "rock" and "stronghold" images of God. From what part of his life does this psalm come (see 1Sa 16:10–12)? **2.** What second image is used (vv. 5–6)? What are the possible meanings of "anointment" (see 1Sa 16:13; Lk 7:46)?

1. Read this psalm again in the negative ("The Lord is not my shepherd ..."). What verse is most disturbing? **2.** What dark valley do you walk now? Has God rescued or protected you with his "rod and staff"? What "green pastures and still waters" has he brought your way? **3.** Who are your "enemies" today? What would you like your cup to overflow with?

---

1. What was the toughest hike or climb you ever made? How did you prepare for it? **2.** Do you like telephone answering machines? What message do you like best? **3.** *Read aloud*—Reader(s) A: 1–2; Reader(s) B: 3–6; All: 7–10.

1. What lines of this psalm indicate a procession into the city (see 1Ch 15:25–29)? **2.** What does David stress about God in verses 1–2? How does that relate to his question and answer (vv. 3–4)? **3.** What is meant by "clean hands and a pure heart"? **4.** What is stressed about God in verses 7–10? What three names would you give God from this psalm?

1. How does Paul apply this psalm to freedom in Christ (v. 1; see 1Co 10:25–26)? **2.** How do you prepare for Sunday worship? What might help you prepare this week? **3.** What modern "idols" tempt us to live for them instead of

---

ᵃ4 Or *through the darkest valley*   ᵇ4 Or *swear falsely*   ᶜ6 Two Hebrew manuscripts and Syriac (see also Septuagint); most Hebrew manuscripts *face, Jacob*

the LORD mighty in battle.
⁹Lift up your heads, O you gates;
lift them up, you ancient doors,
that the King of glory may come in.
¹⁰Who is he, this King of glory?
The LORD Almighty—
he is the King of glory.   *Selah*

Psalm 25ᵃ

Of David.

¹To you, O LORD, I lift up my soul;
² in you I trust, O my God.
Do not let me be put to shame,
nor let my enemies triumph over me.
³No one whose hope is in you
will ever be put to shame,
but they will be put to shame
who are treacherous without excuse.

⁴Show me your ways, O LORD,
teach me your paths;
⁵guide me in your truth and teach me,
for you are God my Savior,
and my hope is in you all day long.
⁶Remember, O LORD, your great mercy and love,
for they are from of old.
⁷Remember not the sins of my youth
and my rebellious ways;
according to your love remember me,
for you are good, O LORD.

⁸Good and upright is the LORD;
therefore he instructs sinners in his ways.
⁹He guides the humble in what is right
and teaches them his way.
¹⁰All the ways of the LORD are loving and faithful
for those who keep the demands of his
covenant.
¹¹For the sake of your name, O LORD,
forgive my iniquity, though it is great.
¹²Who, then, is the man that fears the LORD?
He will instruct him in the way chosen for him.
¹³He will spend his days in prosperity,
and his descendants will inherit the land.
¹⁴The LORD confides in those who fear him;
he makes his covenant known to them.
¹⁵My eyes are ever on the LORD,
for only he will release my feet from the snare.

¹⁶Turn to me and be gracious to me,
for I am lonely and afflicted.
¹⁷The troubles of my heart have multiplied;
free me from my anguish.
¹⁸Look upon my affliction and my distress
and take away all my sins.
¹⁹See how my enemies have increased

the true God? What does God's reign call you to be and do?

1. When lost in a strange city or new store, do you: (a) Ask for help? (b) Consult the map? (c) Find your own way? 2. Were you a rebel as a child? Teenager? Adult? Senior? What did you do? 3. *Read aloud*—Reader(s) A: 1–21, odd; Reader(s) B: 2–20, even; All: 22.

1. In which verses does David ask God for protection from his enemies? What sort of enemies did he face? 2. In which verses does David ask for guidance? What characterizes God's "path" (v. 5)? Who will God guide? 3. In which verses does David ask for forgiveness? Does God have a bad memory (v. 7)? To what aspect of God does David make his appeal? 4. How is David's personal plea also a congregational prayer (v. 22)?

1. What are you most in need of today: protection, guidance or forgiveness? Do you feel you will receive it? Why or why not? 2. God promises to guide those who admit their sin, humble themselves, obey his covenant, and live in awe of him. Can anyone hope to be guided? How does such guidance come: (a) The "green lights" of circumstance? (b) A billboard along the road? (c) A new "road map"? (d) State trooper to the rescue? (e) Joining a "carpool"? How has it worked for you? 3. With what is God's guidance more concerned: Ethics or geography? Character or direction? Morals or prosperity? 4. What quality needed for finding God's guidance will you work to develop this week? How could this psalm answer the question, "How can I know God's will"? 5. If someone says "my hope is in you," how should they act? What about God's character gives you the most hope as you face tough times ahead?

ᵃThis psalm is an acrostic poem, the verses of which begin with the successive letters of the Hebrew alphabet.

and how fiercely they hate me!
²⁰Guard my life and rescue me;
   let me not be put to shame,
   for I take refuge in you.
²¹May integrity and uprightness protect me,
   because my hope is in you.

²²Redeem Israel, O God,
   from all their troubles!

Psalm 26

Of David.

¹Vindicate me, O LORD,
   for I have led a blameless life;
I have trusted in the LORD
   without wavering.
²Test me, O LORD, and try me,
   examine my heart and my mind;
³for your love is ever before me,
   and I walk continually in your truth.
⁴I do not sit with deceitful men,
   nor do I consort with hypocrites;
⁵I abhor the assembly of evildoers
   and refuse to sit with the wicked.
⁶I wash my hands in innocence,
   and go about your altar, O LORD,
⁷proclaiming aloud your praise
   and telling of all your wonderful deeds.
⁸I love the house where you live, O LORD,
   the place where your glory dwells.

⁹Do not take away my soul along with sinners,
   my life with bloodthirsty men,
¹⁰in whose hands are wicked schemes,
   whose right hands are full of bribes.
¹¹But I lead a blameless life;
   redeem me and be merciful to me.

¹²My feet stand on level ground;
   in the great assembly I will praise the LORD.

Psalm 27

Of David.

¹The LORD is my light and my salvation—
   whom shall I fear?
The LORD is the stronghold of my life—
   of whom shall I be afraid?
²When evil men advance against me
   to devour my flesh,ᵃ
when my enemies and my foes attack me,
   they will stumble and fall.
³Though an army besiege me,
   my heart will not fear;
though war break out against me,
   even then will I be confident.

---

1. Do you tend to sit in the same place at the dinner table? In class? Church? In this group? Next to whom? Why? 2. Read aloud—Reader(s) A: 1–11, odd; Reader(s) B: 2–12, even.

1. What does "blameless" mean (vv. 1,11)? Faultless? Sincere? How does David's life contrast with those pictured here (vv. 4–5,9–10)? 2. How does "love" motivate David (vv. 3,8)? How is that love expressed? 3. From what you know of David, what "grade" would you give him on the Lord's "test" (v. 2)? Why would you grant his request (vv. 1,9,11)?

1. Given a "sincerity scale" of 1 to 10, how would you score on the Lord's test? Why? 2. David's "crib sheet" (it helped him pass the test) was God's love and truth: What "crib sheet" do you rely on? How can you follow David's example to improve your "grade"? 3. What changes in your "seating preferences" would help you conform with verses 4–5, without becoming proud or pompous?

1. If you could ask "one thing" of the Lord, and have it granted, what would it be? Why don't you ask? 2. How good are you at remembering faces? Why? 3. Read aloud—Reader(s) A: 1–13, odd; Reader(s) B: 2–14, even.

1. What three qualities of God does David recall in verse 1? What do you think he means by each? How does each relate to David's confidence (vv. 2–3)? In what ways might these verses reflect David's life experiences? 2. What clue does the oft-repeated "seek" (vv. 4,8) give you into David's deepest desire: Does he desire to be a priest? Receive

---

ᵃ2 Or to slander me

⁴One thing I ask of the LORD,
  this is what I seek:
that I may dwell in the house of the LORD
  all the days of my life,
to gaze upon the beauty of the LORD
  and to seek him in his temple.
⁵For in the day of trouble
  he will keep me safe in his dwelling;
he will hide me in the shelter of his tabernacle
  and set me high upon a rock.
⁶Then my head will be exalted
  above the enemies who surround me;
at his tabernacle will I sacrifice with shouts of joy;
  I will sing and make music to the LORD.

⁷Hear my voice when I call, O LORD;
  be merciful to me and answer me.
⁸My heart says of you, "Seek hisᵃ face!"
  Your face, LORD, I will seek.
⁹Do not hide your face from me,
  do not turn your servant away in anger;
  you have been my helper.
Do not reject me or forsake me,
  O God my Savior.
¹⁰Though my father and mother forsake me,
  the LORD will receive me.
¹¹Teach me your way, O LORD;
  lead me in a straight path
  because of my oppressors.
¹²Do not turn me over to the desire of my foes,
  for false witnesses rise up against me,
  breathing out violence.

¹³I am still confident of this:
  I will see the goodness of the LORD
  in the land of the living.
¹⁴Wait for the LORD;
  be strong and take heart
  and wait for the LORD.

Psalm 28

Of David.

¹To you I call, O LORD my Rock;
  do not turn a deaf ear to me.
For if you remain silent,
  I will be like those who have gone down to the
    pit.
²Hear my cry for mercy
  as I call to you for help,
as I lift up my hands
  toward your Most Holy Place.

³Do not drag me away with the wicked,
  with those who do evil,
who speak cordially with their neighbors
  but harbor malice in their hearts.

sanctuary? Do God's will? What does it mean to you to seek God's face? **3.** What is the relationship between "seeking" and "waiting" for God (v. 14)? What does this tell you about the Christian life? **4.** Given David's experience with rejection, what seems to be most comforting about God's presence?

1. How has the Lord been like a "light" or a "stronghold" in your life this past month? What situation has driven you to him to find shelter? What words describe your sense of his presence at the point of need? **2.** "Seek his face" is echoed by Jesus: "Seek first his kingdom and his righteousness and all these other things will be given to you as well" (Mt 6:33). Is seeking God's face (or kingdom) first for you? Second or third? What gives you your greatest sense of security? What distracts you from "putting first things first"? How will you deal with this competition? **3.** In your love life with God, where does he stand: (a) Closer to you than your own parents? (b) More like a distant relative you've only heard about? (c) Somewhere in between? Why? **4.** What will it take for you to get better acquainted: More seeking? More waiting? Both? Explain.

1. When you call on your best friend for help, what do you need most: A listening ear? A certain voice? A handout? A detailed game plan? Companionship? Why? **2.** *Read aloud*—Reader(s) A: 1–9, odd; Reader(s) B: 2–8, even.

1. What is David's main concern (vv. 1–5): A premature death? A miscarriage of justice? A plea for mercy? Why do you think so? **2.** What images does he associate with God? Why? What experiences do they reflect upon? What meaning do they convey for you? **3.** What must have happened for David to turn his personal plea (vv. 1–7) into a prayer for the people as a whole (vv. 8–9)?

ᵃ8 Or *To you, O my heart, he has said, "Seek my*

1. When have you been as desperate as David (vv. 1–5)? As confident as David (vv. 6–7)? 2. Music helps David better express his feelings to God (28:7; 27:6; 26:7). How about for you? What words, song or poetry best sums up how you are feeling about God now? 3. Which image means more to you now: God as your fortress? Or God as your shepherd? Why?

1. How does a thunderstorm make you feel? Does it make you think of God? 2. *Read aloud*—Reader(s) A: 1–11, odd; Reader(s) B: 2–10, even.

1. What is the impact of this thunderous Lord on nature? On the people? On you? 2. What path does the storm take (vv. 5–8)? Trace it on a map. 3. Why is the name Yahweh ("the Lord") repeated 18 times? 4. When the storm passes (v. 10), what then?

1. What storm blows through your life now? Are you responding like the people—giving glory to God for ruling over the storm? Or are you like nature—in uproar? Why? 2. Would you find peace by recognizing the Lord of the storm? Why or why not?

⁴Repay them for their deeds
  and for their evil work;
repay them for what their hands have done
  and bring back upon them what they deserve.
⁵Since they show no regard for the works of the
    LORD
  and what his hands have done,
he will tear them down
  and never build them up again.

⁶Praise be to the LORD,
  for he has heard my cry for mercy.
⁷The LORD is my strength and my shield;
  my heart trusts in him, and I am helped.
My heart leaps for joy
  and I will give thanks to him in song.

⁸The LORD is the strength of his people,
  a fortress of salvation for his anointed one.
⁹Save your people and bless your inheritance;
  be their shepherd and carry them forever.

Psalm 29

A psalm of David.

¹Ascribe to the LORD, O mighty ones,
  ascribe to the LORD glory and strength.
²Ascribe to the LORD the glory due his name;
  worship the LORD in the splendor of hisᵃ
    holiness.

³The voice of the LORD is over the waters;
  the God of glory thunders,
  the LORD thunders over the mighty waters.
⁴The voice of the LORD is powerful;
  the voice of the LORD is majestic.
⁵The voice of the LORD breaks the cedars;
  the LORD breaks in pieces the cedars of
    Lebanon.
⁶He makes Lebanon skip like a calf,
  Sirionᵇ like a young wild ox.
⁷The voice of the LORD strikes
  with flashes of lightning.
⁸The voice of the LORD shakes the desert;
  the LORD shakes the Desert of Kadesh.
⁹The voice of the LORD twists the oaksᶜ
  and strips the forests bare.
And in his temple all cry, "Glory!"

¹⁰The LORD sitsᵈ enthroned over the flood;
  the LORD is enthroned as King forever.
¹¹The LORD gives strength to his people;
  the LORD blesses his people with peace.

ᵃ2 Or LORD with the splendor of   ᵇ6 That is, Mount Hermon   ᶜ9 Or LORD makes
the deer give birth   ᵈ10 Or sat

Psalm 30

A psalm. A song. For the dedication of the temple.[a] Of David.

[1]I will exalt you, O LORD,
  for you lifted me out of the depths
  and did not let my enemies gloat over me.
[2]O LORD my God, I called to you for help
  and you healed me.
[3]O LORD, you brought me up from the grave[b];
  you spared me from going down into the pit.

[4]Sing to the LORD, you saints of his;
  praise his holy name.
[5]For his anger lasts only a moment,
  but his favor lasts a lifetime;
weeping may remain for a night,
  but rejoicing comes in the morning.

[6]When I felt secure, I said,
  "I will never be shaken."
[7]O LORD, when you favored me,
  you made my mountain[c] stand firm;
but when you hid your face,
  I was dismayed.

[8]To you, O LORD, I called;
  to the Lord I cried for mercy:
[9]"What gain is there in my destruction,[d]
  in my going down into the pit?
Will the dust praise you?
  Will it proclaim your faithfulness?
[10]Hear, O LORD, and be merciful to me;
  O LORD, be my help."

[11]You turned my wailing into dancing;
  you removed my sackcloth and clothed me with
    joy,
[12]that my heart may sing to you and not be silent.
  O LORD my God, I will give you thanks forever.

Psalm 31

For the director of music. A psalm of David.

[1]In you, O LORD, I have taken refuge;
  let me never be put to shame;
  deliver me in your righteousness.
[2]Turn your ear to me,
  come quickly to my rescue;
  be my rock of refuge,
  a strong fortress to save me.
[3]Since you are my rock and my fortress,
  for the sake of your name lead and guide me.
[4]Free me from the trap that is set for me,
  for you are my refuge.
[5]Into your hands I commit my spirit;
  redeem me, O LORD, the God of truth.

1. Do you like roller-coast-
ers? Is your life like a roller-
coaster? A ferris wheel? Slow-
moving train? **2.** *Read aloud*
—Reader(s) A: 1–3; Reader(s)
B: 4–7; Leader: 8–10; All: 11–12.

1. For what reasons does
David praise God (vv. 1–3)?
How does he account for why the
Lord allowed these hard times to
come upon him? **2.** What do you
learn about the Lord's anger (v. 5)?
About his favor? **3.** What error did
David make (vv. 6–7)? Is it wrong
to feel secure? **4.** How does David
argue that God should spare him
(v. 9)? What does this indicate
about his view of the afterlife? **5.**
Why would this psalm be written for
the dedication of the temple (see
1Ch 22)?

1. Is security important to
you? How much of your money goes toward buying a house?
Medical and life insurance? Savings? Where does security lie? **2.**
Has God turned a time of wailing
into a time of dancing for you? Was
it "overnight," surprising you with
joy? Or did your mood swings level
out more gradually? **3.** How is the
theme of "sorrow producing joy"
developed in the New Testament
(see Jn 16:19–22; 2Co 4:16–18)?
For what are you "mourning"? How
long has your "night" been? How
long until "morning" comes?

1. In your family, when did
you feel most "trapped" or
stuck at home: (a) Sick in bed? (b)
Sent to your room for "time out"?
(c) Left with a baby-sitter? (d) No
one called for a Saturday night
date? (e) Somebody called, but
you had no baby-sitter? **2.** Is there
someone you would hide from if
you saw him or her on the street
today? Why? **3.** *Read aloud*—
Reader(s) A: 1–23, odd; Reader(s)
B: 2–24, even.

1. How do you picture Da-
vid's "trap" (vv. 1–5)? **2.**
What turn do verses 6–8 take?
How is David's trust rewarded? **3.**
What causes David's sorrow in
verses 9–18? Hasn't God rescued
him (v. 8)? What might have happened to cause such fluctuations in

---

a Title: Or *palace* b 3 Hebrew *Sheol* c 7 Or *hill country* d 9 Or *there if I am*
silenced

his feelings? **4.** What feelings are expressed in verses 9–18 which are not present in verses 1–5? What new situation is David likely facing? **5.** This time, how does David break through in faith (vv. 14–18) and praise (vv. 19–24)? What words and acts prove this faith? How is God's goodness evident? To whom?

♡ **1.** Both Jesus and Stephen quoted verse 5 as they were about to die (see Lk 23:46; Ac 7:59). Were their situations similar to David's? What would you like your "famous last words" to be? **2.** Where are you feeling "trapped": By your enemies? By your desires? By loneliness? How will you "escape"? **3.** Can you express feelings of abandonment or rejection by God? Does it show a lack of faith? Why or why not? **4.** Like David, have you ever felt joy in God, then felt the joy ebb and flow unpredictably? **5.** What does the phrase "My times are in your hands," mean to you: (a) Time's up? (b) Time's a-wasting? (c) Fighting time? (d) Killing time? (e) God's timing? **6.** What action from verses 19–24 do you most need to take: Fear God? Take refuge in God? Call out to God? Be faithful? Place hope in God? How will you do so? **7.** In what situation now do you need to "be strong and take heart"? What from this psalm can help you do just that?

⁶I hate those who cling to worthless idols;
  I trust in the LORD.
⁷I will be glad and rejoice in your love,
  for you saw my affliction
  and knew the anguish of my soul.
⁸You have not handed me over to the enemy
  but have set my feet in a spacious place.

⁹Be merciful to me, O LORD, for I am in distress;
  my eyes grow weak with sorrow,
  my soul and my body with grief.
¹⁰My life is consumed by anguish
  and my years by groaning;
  my strength fails because of my affliction,ᵃ
  and my bones grow weak.
¹¹Because of all my enemies,
  I am the utter contempt of my neighbors;
  I am a dread to my friends—
  those who see me on the street flee from me.
¹²I am forgotten by them as though I were dead;
  I have become like broken pottery.
¹³For I hear the slander of many;
  there is terror on every side;
  they conspire against me
  and plot to take my life.

¹⁴But I trust in you, O LORD;
  I say, "You are my God."
¹⁵My times are in your hands;
  deliver me from my enemies
  and from those who pursue me.
¹⁶Let your face shine on your servant;
  save me in your unfailing love.
¹⁷Let me not be put to shame, O LORD,
  for I have cried out to you;
  but let the wicked be put to shame
  and lie silent in the grave.ᵇ
¹⁸Let their lying lips be silenced,
  for with pride and contempt
  they speak arrogantly against the righteous.

¹⁹How great is your goodness,
  which you have stored up for those who fear
    you,
  which you bestow in the sight of men
  on those who take refuge in you.
²⁰In the shelter of your presence you hide them
  from the intrigues of men;
  in your dwelling you keep them safe
  from accusing tongues.

²¹Praise be to the LORD,
  for he showed his wonderful love to me
  when I was in a besieged city.
²²In my alarm I said,
  "I am cut off from your sight!"
  Yet you heard my cry for mercy
  when I called to you for help.

²³Love the LORD, all his saints!

ᵃ10 Or *guilt*   *ᵇ17* Hebrew *Sheol*

The LORD preserves the faithful,
  but the proud he pays back in full.
²⁴Be strong and take heart,
  all you who hope in the LORD.

Psalm 32

Of David. A *maskil.* ᵃ

¹Blessed is he
  whose transgressions are forgiven,
  whose sins are covered.
²Blessed is the man
  whose sin the LORD does not count against him
  and in whose spirit is no deceit.

³When I kept silent,
  my bones wasted away
  through my groaning all day long.
⁴For day and night
  your hand was heavy upon me;
  my strength was sapped
  as in the heat of summer.   *Selah*
⁵Then I acknowledged my sin to you
  and did not cover up my iniquity.
I said, "I will confess
  my transgressions to the LORD"—
and you forgave
  the guilt of my sin.   *Selah*

⁶Therefore let everyone who is godly pray to you
  while you may be found;
surely when the mighty waters rise,
  they will not reach him.
⁷You are my hiding place;
  you will protect me from trouble
  and surround me with songs of deliverance.   *Selah*

⁸I will instruct you and teach you in the way you
    should go;
  I will counsel you and watch over you.
⁹Do not be like the horse or the mule,
  which have no understanding
but must be controlled by bit and bridle
  or they will not come to you.
¹⁰Many are the woes of the wicked,
  but the LORD's unfailing love
  surrounds the man who trusts in him.

¹¹Rejoice in the LORD and be glad, you righteous;
  sing, all you who are upright in heart!

Psalm 33

¹Sing joyfully to the LORD, you righteous;
  it is fitting for the upright to praise him.
²Praise the LORD with the harp;
  make music to him on the ten-stringed lyre.

ᵃTitle: Probably a literary or musical term

1. How do you compare to a horse: (a) Not much understanding, but lots of horse sense? (b) Hot-tempered, must be broken in? (c) Lazy and stubborn, must be led by bit and bridle? (d) Love to take people for a ride? Why are you that way? 2. *Read aloud*—Reader(s) A: 1–5; Reader(s) B: 6–10; Leader: 11.

1. What is the source of blessedness or happiness in this psalm? How does this compare with Psalm 1:1? 2. What does "in whose spirit is no deceit" mean? How does it relate to the struggle expressed in verses 3–5? Why do you think he would refuse to confess his sin for so long? What happened when he did? 3. What has David realized about God (vv. 6–7)? 4. How does the Lord's counsel (vv. 8–9) relate to David's struggle (vv. 3–4)? How is he like a mule? 5. What's the punch line of this psalm for you?

1. What does Paul try to prove with this psalm (see Ro 4:7–8)? 2. Unconfessed sin sapped David's strength like the summer heat. What picture would you use to describe forfeiting God's blessing by covering up your own sin? 3. God freely forgives those who trust him: How has that message been driven home to you recently? How has that forgiveness spilled over into your other relationships? How do you see yourself differently? 4. Have you felt like God is not to be found? What "waters" rise and obscure God?

1. What helps you worship best: Music? Loud shouts? Nature? Silence? Ritual? Why? 2. *Read aloud*—Reader(s) A: 1–19, odd; Reader(s) B: 2–18, even; All: 20–22.

1. What aids to worship do you see employed in this psalm? **2.** For what reasons is the psalmist praising God (vv. 4–11)? Where does God seem most active to him: In creation? History? The future? **3.** How are both the love and the power of God evident in creation? If verses 4–9 focus on God's creative power, what is the focus of verses 10–19? How might verses 16–19 bring hope to people in hard times? **4.** What response does the Lord expect from all the earth (v. 8)? From all nations, especially his own people (v. 12)? What is incompatible about trust in "horses" and trust in God (vv. 16–18)? **5.** How does God's "unfailing love" apply to justice (v. 5)? Worship (v. 18)? Hope (v. 22)?

1. What are two things about creation that have impressed you about God's power? About his love? Do these things help you to worship God? **2.** What modern equivalents would you substitute for the images in verses 16–19? Is this psalm true in today's world of immense military force? **3.** Do you believe that God controls even "the plans of the nations"? In what sense? Does that comfort you? **4.** In what would an outside observer conclude that you place your hope: "horses" or the Lord?

---

1. What commercial could you rewrite to recommend God? **2.** Do your grudges last long? How do you get rid of them? **3.** *Read aloud*—Reader(s) A: 1–21, odd; Reader(s) B: 2–22, even.

1. Read 1 Samuel 21:10–15 to see what prompted this psalm ("Abimelech" may be a title used by King Achish). If you were David, would you write a psalm praising God for deliverance, or one congratulating yourself for a clever ploy? **2.** This psalm has two

³Sing to him a new song;
    play skillfully, and shout for joy.

⁴For the word of the LORD is right and true;
    he is faithful in all he does.
⁵The LORD loves righteousness and justice;
    the earth is full of his unfailing love.

⁶By the word of the LORD were the heavens made,
    their starry host by the breath of his mouth.
⁷He gathers the waters of the sea into jarsᵃ;
    he puts the deep into storehouses.
⁸Let all the earth fear the LORD;
    let all the people of the world revere him.
⁹For he spoke, and it came to be;
    he commanded, and it stood firm.
¹⁰The LORD foils the plans of the nations;
    he thwarts the purposes of the peoples.
¹¹But the plans of the LORD stand firm forever,
    the purposes of his heart through all
       generations.

¹²Blessed is the nation whose God is the LORD,
    the people he chose for his inheritance.
¹³From heaven the LORD looks down
    and sees all mankind;
¹⁴from his dwelling place he watches
    all who live on earth—
¹⁵he who forms the hearts of all,
    who considers everything they do.
¹⁶No king is saved by the size of his army;
    no warrior escapes by his great strength.
¹⁷A horse is a vain hope for deliverance;
    despite all its great strength it cannot save.
¹⁸But the eyes of the LORD are on those who fear
      him,
    on those whose hope is in his unfailing love,
¹⁹to deliver them from death
    and keep them alive in famine.

²⁰We wait in hope for the LORD;
    he is our help and our shield.
²¹In him our hearts rejoice,
    for we trust in his holy name.
²²May your unfailing love rest upon us, O LORD,
    even as we put our hope in you.

Psalm 34ᵇ

Of David. When he pretended to be insane
before Abimelech, who drove him away, and
he left.

¹I will extol the LORD at all times;
    his praise will always be on my lips.
²My soul will boast in the LORD;
    let the afflicted hear and rejoice.
³Glorify the LORD with me;
    let us exalt his name together.

ᵃ7 Or *sea as into a heap*   ᵇThis psalm is an acrostic poem, the verses of which begin with the successive letters of the Hebrew alphabet.

[4]I sought the LORD, and he answered me;
  he delivered me from all my fears.
[5]Those who look to him are radiant;
  their faces are never covered with shame.
[6]This poor man called, and the LORD heard him;
  he saved him out of all his troubles.
[7]The angel of the LORD encamps around those who
    fear him,
  and he delivers them.

[8]Taste and see that the LORD is good;
  blessed is the man who takes refuge in him.
[9]Fear the LORD, you his saints,
  for those who fear him lack nothing.
[10]The lions may grow weak and hungry,
  but those who seek the LORD lack no good
    thing.

[11]Come, my children, listen to me;
  I will teach you the fear of the LORD.
[12]Whoever of you loves life
  and desires to see many good days,
[13]keep your tongue from evil
  and your lips from speaking lies.
[14]Turn from evil and do good;
  seek peace and pursue it.

[15]The eyes of the LORD are on the righteous
  and his ears are attentive to their cry;
[16]the face of the LORD is against those who do evil,
  to cut off the memory of them from the earth.

[17]The righteous cry out, and the LORD hears them;
  he delivers them from all their troubles.
[18]The LORD is close to the brokenhearted
  and saves those who are crushed in spirit.

[19]A righteous man may have many troubles,
  but the LORD delivers him from them all;
[20]he protects all his bones,
  not one of them will be broken.

[21]Evil will slay the wicked;
  the foes of the righteous will be condemned.
[22]The LORD redeems his servants;
  no one will be condemned who takes refuge in
    him.

Psalm 35

Of David.

[1]Contend, O LORD, with those who contend with
    me;
  fight against those who fight against me.
[2]Take up shield and buckler;
  arise and come to my aid.
[3]Brandish spear and javelin[a]
  against those who pursue me.
  Say to my soul,
    "I am your salvation."

a3 Or and block the way

parts. Where do you think the dividing line is? What subtitle would you give the first half? The rest? **3.** How could David "taste and see" that the Lord is good? Is he saying the righteous will never die of hunger (v. 10)? **4.** What promises do you see in this psalm? Which one has your name on it? **5.** What destroys the wicked (v. 21)? Why doesn't God intervene?

1. Peter uses this psalm to comfort those who suffer for doing good (v. 8, see 1Pe 2:3; vv. 12–16, see 1Pe 3:10–12). How do you reconcile the "good things" the Lord promises with the acute suffering experienced by some Christians? **2.** How does the Christian life "taste" to you: Sweet? Sour? Spicy? Salty? Bitter? Bland? Why? Or have you only sampled God? Why is that? **3.** John saw verse 20 fulfilled in Jesus (see Jn 19:36). What was significant about the bones (see Ex 12:46)? How might this psalm be Jesus' testimony, as well as David's? **4.** In what way is this psalm also your testimony (v. 22, see Ro 8:1)? **5.** What does it mean to "seek peace and pursue it" (v. 14)? How does it apply to God? Others? Society? Would "casual" or "relentless" better describe your pursuit of peace this week? Why?

1. Salt on the tail catches the bird, but what catches a person? If you wanted to "trap" somebody who has tried to do you in, how would you do it? **2.** If "spear throwing" were your sport, which enemy of yours would you want to be your "spear catcher"? **3.** Read aloud—Reader(s) A: read the first half of the verse; Reader(s) B: read the second half of the verse.

1. What seems to be the occasion for this psalm? How might his plea be related to the events of David's life? **2.** What hurts David the most: The pain of injustice? The one-sidedness of it all? The Lord's delay in judgment? **3.** What does he want the Lord to do to these people? What do you think of the "poetic justice" in David's plea (v. 8)? **4.** How will David respond when God acts (vv. 9–10)? How do you account for his rejoicing at another's downfall? **5.** Is David recalling accurately his record of behavior (vv. 13–14)? Is he justified in praying "against" Saul and his advisors? **6.** What is the significance of a "wink" (v. 19; see Pr 6:13)?

♡ **1.** How do you respond when people treat you unfairly? In what situation do you wish the Lord would fight for you? **2.** Are you comfortable with David's many cries for vengeance? How might a Christian pray "against" enemies? **3.** When we pray "Thy kingdom come," what are we asking God to do to those who oppose him? How does that relate to David's plea? **4.** What injustice around you hurts enough to move you to pray against it? If nothing does, what does that say about your compassion and concern for justice for other people?

4May those who seek my life
   be disgraced and put to shame;
may those who plot my ruin
   be turned back in dismay.
5May they be like chaff before the wind,
   with the angel of the LORD driving them away;
6may their path be dark and slippery,
   with the angel of the LORD pursuing them.
7Since they hid their net for me without cause
   and without cause dug a pit for me,
8may ruin overtake them by surprise—
   may the net they hid entangle them,
   may they fall into the pit, to their ruin.
9Then my soul will rejoice in the LORD
   and delight in his salvation.
10My whole being will exclaim,
   "Who is like you, O LORD?
You rescue the poor from those too strong for them,
   the poor and needy from those who rob them."

11Ruthless witnesses come forward;
   they question me on things I know nothing about.
12They repay me evil for good
   and leave my soul forlorn.
13Yet when they were ill, I put on sackcloth
   and humbled myself with fasting.
When my prayers returned to me unanswered,
14   I went about mourning
      as though for my friend or brother.
   I bowed my head in grief
      as though weeping for my mother.
15But when I stumbled, they gathered in glee;
   attackers gathered against me when I was unaware.
They slandered me without ceasing.
16Like the ungodly they maliciously mocked*a*;
   they gnashed their teeth at me.
17O Lord, how long will you look on?
   Rescue my life from their ravages,
   my precious life from these lions.
18I will give you thanks in the great assembly;
   among throngs of people I will praise you.

19Let not those gloat over me
   who are my enemies without cause;
let not those who hate me without reason
   maliciously wink the eye.
20They do not speak peaceably,
   but devise false accusations
   against those who live quietly in the land.
21They gape at me and say, "Aha! Aha!
   With our own eyes we have seen it."

22O LORD, you have seen this; be not silent.
   Do not be far from me, O Lord.
23Awake, and rise to my defense!
   Contend for me, my God and Lord.

---

a 16 Septuagint; Hebrew may mean *ungodly circle of mockers.*

²⁴Vindicate me in your righteousness, O LORD my
    God;
  do not let them gloat over me.
²⁵Do not let them think, "Aha, just what we
    wanted!"
  or say, "We have swallowed him up."

²⁶May all who gloat over my distress
    be put to shame and confusion;
  may all who exalt themselves over me
    be clothed with shame and disgrace.
²⁷May those who delight in my vindication
    shout for joy and gladness;
  may they always say, "The LORD be exalted,
    who delights in the well-being of his servant."
²⁸My tongue will speak of your righteousness
    and of your praises all day long.

Psalm 36

For the director of music. Of David the
servant of the LORD.

¹An oracle is within my heart
    concerning the sinfulness of the wicked:ᵃ
  There is no fear of God
    before his eyes.
²For in his own eyes he flatters himself
    too much to detect or hate his sin.
³The words of his mouth are wicked and deceitful;
    he has ceased to be wise and to do good.
⁴Even on his bed he plots evil;
    he commits himself to a sinful course
    and does not reject what is wrong.

⁵Your love, O LORD, reaches to the heavens,
    your faithfulness to the skies.
⁶Your righteousness is like the mighty mountains,
    your justice like the great deep.
  O LORD, you preserve both man and beast.
⁷ How priceless is your unfailing love!
  Both high and low among men
    findᵇ refuge in the shadow of your wings.
⁸They feast on the abundance of your house;
    you give them drink from your river of delights.
⁹For with you is the fountain of life;
    in your light we see light.

¹⁰Continue your love to those who know you,
    your righteousness to the upright in heart.
¹¹May the foot of the proud not come against me,
    nor the hand of the wicked drive me away.
¹²See how the evildoers lie fallen—
    thrown down, not able to rise!

1. Where do you go to get refreshed or live it up? 2. *Read aloud*—Reader(s) A: 1–4; Reader(s) B: 5–9; All: 10–12.

1. From verses 1–4, what qualities characterize the wicked? What is meant by verse 2? 2. What difference do you see in the thoughts of the "wicked" and the "righteous"? How do thoughts give birth to actions? 3. David's thoughts about the wicked (vv. 1–4) suddenly move him to reflect upon God's character: Why is that? What is the point of each word picture in verses 5–9? 4. How does verse 12 flow out of verses 10–11? Is this a fitting end to the psalm? Why or why not?

1. In the Psalms the "righteous" seem to be those who may do evil but are generally seeking to please God. The "wicked" are those who, despite good they may do, are generally rejecting God's ways. What aspects of each do you see in your own life? 2. Using your own literary license, rewrite verses 5–6 in terms of your own experience of God. To what can you compare God's love? His faithfulness? His justice? 3. What have you tasted of God's "feast" recently? How has he refreshed or enlivened you?

ᵃ1 Or *heart: / Sin proceeds from the wicked.*   ᵇ7 Or *love, O God! / Men find*; or
love! / Both heavenly beings and men / find

1. What do you consider your "home turf"? Why? 2. What do you worry about the most? 3. *Read aloud*—Reader(s) A: 1–39, odd; Reader(s) B: 2–40, even.

1. Is the psalmist addressing himself, God or man? What problem is David addressing (v. 7)? 2. What different answers does David give to the fact that the wicked often go unpunished (vv. 2,9, 13,15,17)? 3. Instead of worrying about the short-lived success of evil, what qualities should shape their lives (vv. 3–8)? What is meant by "be still ... and wait patiently for the Lord" (v. 7)? 4. What does David mean by "the meek" (v. 11)? Why do you think "inheriting" or "dwelling in" the land is mentioned eight times in this psalm? How would that comfort disenfranchised or dispossessed people? 5. The wicked being "cut off" is mentioned five times. What other images portray how they will be frustrated eventually in their plans (vv. 2, 9–10,12–17,20,35–36)? 6. What proverbial wisdom do you see here with regard to money matters (vv. 16–21,25–26)? How is generosity with money an indicator of trust and waiting on the Lord to uphold?

1. What do you secretly want to see happen to those who do evil and enjoy momentary success? How does their success and your reaction to it make you feel about God? 2. Give an example of how you are postponing an immediate good for a greater, future gain? Does society encourage "delayed gratification"? 3. Is verse 25 always true? Or was this just David's experience, for which there are many exceptions? Why do you think so? 4. How does Jesus use the idea that the meek will inherit the land (see Mt 5:5)? 5. Are you currently frustrated because "evil" people are getting their way? How can you apply verses 3–8 this week? Which of those biblical qualities would a best friend tell you to work on? 6. Righteousness affects a person's pocketbook (vv. 21, 26), speech (v. 30) and thoughts (v. 31): In which of these areas have you grown the most during the past year? 7. Since Job, good people have been asking why bad things happen to them. How would you sensitively encourage Christians who suffer oppression? How does the suffering of Jesus relate to these times?

Psalm 37[a]

Of David.

¹Do not fret because of evil men
    or be envious of those who do wrong;
²for like the grass they will soon wither,
    like green plants they will soon die away.

³Trust in the Lord and do good;
    dwell in the land and enjoy safe pasture.
⁴Delight yourself in the Lord
    and he will give you the desires of your heart.

⁵Commit your way to the Lord;
    trust in him and he will do this:
⁶He will make your righteousness shine like the
    dawn,
    the justice of your cause like the noonday sun.

⁷Be still before the Lord and wait patiently for him;
    do not fret when men succeed in their ways,
    when they carry out their wicked schemes.

⁸Refrain from anger and turn from wrath;
    do not fret—it leads only to evil.
⁹For evil men will be cut off,
    but those who hope in the Lord will inherit the
    land.

¹⁰A little while, and the wicked will be no more;
    though you look for them, they will not be
    found.
¹¹But the meek will inherit the land
    and enjoy great peace.

¹²The wicked plot against the righteous
    and gnash their teeth at them;
¹³but the Lord laughs at the wicked,
    for he knows their day is coming.

¹⁴The wicked draw the sword
    and bend the bow
to bring down the poor and needy,
    to slay those whose ways are upright.
¹⁵But their swords will pierce their own hearts,
    and their bows will be broken.

¹⁶Better the little that the righteous have
    than the wealth of many wicked;
¹⁷for the power of the wicked will be broken,
    but the Lord upholds the righteous.

¹⁸The days of the blameless are known to the Lord,
    and their inheritance will endure forever.
¹⁹In times of disaster they will not wither;
    in days of famine they will enjoy plenty.

²⁰But the wicked will perish:
    The Lord's enemies will be like the beauty of
    the fields,
    they will vanish—vanish like smoke.

[a] This psalm is an acrostic poem, the stanzas of which begin with the successive letters of the Hebrew alphabet.

²¹The wicked borrow and do not repay,
  but the righteous give generously;
²²those the LORD blesses will inherit the land,
  but those he curses will be cut off.

²³If the LORD delights in a man's way,
  he makes his steps firm;
²⁴though he stumble, he will not fall,
  for the LORD upholds him with his hand.

²⁵I was young and now I am old,
  yet I have never seen the righteous forsaken
  or their children begging bread.
²⁶They are always generous and lend freely;
  their children will be blessed.

²⁷Turn from evil and do good;
  then you will dwell in the land forever.
²⁸For the LORD loves the just
  and will not forsake his faithful ones.

  They will be protected forever,
  but the offspring of the wicked will be cut off;
²⁹the righteous will inherit the land
  and dwell in it forever.

³⁰The mouth of the righteous man utters wisdom,
  and his tongue speaks what is just.
³¹The law of his God is in his heart;
  his feet do not slip.

³²The wicked lie in wait for the righteous,
  seeking their very lives;
³³but the LORD will not leave them in their power
  or let them be condemned when brought to
    trial.

³⁴Wait for the LORD
  and keep his way.
He will exalt you to inherit the land;
  when the wicked are cut off, you will see it.

³⁵I have seen a wicked and ruthless man
  flourishing like a green tree in its native soil,
³⁶but he soon passed away and was no more;
  though I looked for him, he could not be found.

³⁷Consider the blameless, observe the upright;
  there is a future[a] for the man of peace.
³⁸But all sinners will be destroyed;
  the future[b] of the wicked will be cut off.

³⁹The salvation of the righteous comes from the
    LORD;
  he is their stronghold in time of trouble.
⁴⁰The LORD helps them and delivers them;
  he delivers them from the wicked and saves
    them,
  because they take refuge in him.

---

a37 Or *there will be posterity*   *b38* Or *posterity*

1. What is the first part of your body to serve as an alarm clock that "something's wrong"? 2. How do you get rid of hiccups? 3. *Read aloud*—Reader(s) A: 1–21, odd; Reader(s) B: 2–22, even.

1. How has God's hand come down on David (vv. 1–8)? What did people believe caused illness in David's day (v. 3)? Why does it follow that friends avoid him (v. 11)? 2. What adds insult to injury for David (vv. 9–12)? In light of his compounded suffering, how do you account for David's continued trust in God: A placid or stoic disposition? Does he enjoy a pleasant turn of events? 3. Who does David feel is responsible for his suffering? If this same God is seen as the one who punishes sin, why trust him for future deliverance?

1. Think of this psalm as written at a time of great illness. What illnesses are caused by ignoring God's laws? What did Jesus say to the notion of illness as punishment (see Jn 9:1–3)? 2. Think of this psalm as written at a time of great awareness of sin. Is David's guilt healthy? Why or why not? 3. When have you felt punished by God? What happened at that time of crisis? How did you relate to God then? 4. What part of David's faith can you relate to from your own experience? How so? Where do you need to exert such faith now?

Psalm 38

A psalm of David. A petition.

¹O LORD, do not rebuke me in your anger
    or discipline me in your wrath.
²For your arrows have pierced me,
    and your hand has come down upon me.
³Because of your wrath there is no health in my
        body;
    my bones have no soundness because of my
        sin.
⁴My guilt has overwhelmed me
    like a burden too heavy to bear.

⁵My wounds fester and are loathsome
    because of my sinful folly.
⁶I am bowed down and brought very low;
    all day long I go about mourning.
⁷My back is filled with searing pain;
    there is no health in my body.
⁸I am feeble and utterly crushed;
    I groan in anguish of heart.

⁹All my longings lie open before you, O Lord;
    my sighing is not hidden from you.
¹⁰My heart pounds, my strength fails me;
    even the light has gone from my eyes.
¹¹My friends and companions avoid me because of
        my wounds;
    my neighbors stay far away.
¹²Those who seek my life set their traps,
    those who would harm me talk of my ruin;
    all day long they plot deception.

¹³I am like a deaf man, who cannot hear,
    like a mute, who cannot open his mouth;
¹⁴I have become like a man who does not hear,
    whose mouth can offer no reply.
¹⁵I wait for you, O LORD;
    you will answer, O Lord my God.
¹⁶For I said, "Do not let them gloat
    or exalt themselves over me when my foot
        slips."

¹⁷For I am about to fall,
    and my pain is ever with me.
¹⁸I confess my iniquity;
    I am troubled by my sin.
¹⁹Many are those who are my vigorous enemies;
    those who hate me without reason are
        numerous.
²⁰Those who repay my good with evil
    slander me when I pursue what is good.

²¹O LORD, do not forsake me;
    be not far from me, O my God.
²²Come quickly to help me,
    O Lord my Savior.

Psalm 39

For the director of music. For Jeduthun.
A psalm of David.

¹I said, "I will watch my ways
  and keep my tongue from sin;
I will put a muzzle on my mouth
  as long as the wicked are in my presence."
²But when I was silent and still,
  not even saying anything good,
  my anguish increased.
³My heart grew hot within me,
  and as I meditated, the fire burned;
  then I spoke with my tongue:

⁴"Show me, O LORD, my life's end
  and the number of my days;
  let me know how fleeting is my life.
⁵You have made my days a mere handbreadth;
  the span of my years is as nothing before you.
  Each man's life is but a breath.   Selah
⁶Man is a mere phantom as he goes to and fro:
  He bustles about, but only in vain;
  he heaps up wealth, not knowing who will get
    it.

⁷"But now, Lord, what do I look for?
  My hope is in you.
⁸Save me from all my transgressions;
  do not make me the scorn of fools.
⁹I was silent; I would not open my mouth,
  for you are the one who has done this.
¹⁰Remove your scourge from me;
  I am overcome by the blow of your hand.
¹¹You rebuke and discipline men for their sin;
  you consume their wealth like a moth—
  each man is but a breath.   Selah

¹²"Hear my prayer, O LORD,
  listen to my cry for help;
  be not deaf to my weeping.
For I dwell with you as an alien,
  a stranger, as all my fathers were.
¹³Look away from me, that I may rejoice again
  before I depart and am no more."

Psalm 40

For the director of music. Of David. A psalm.

¹I waited patiently for the LORD;
  he turned to me and heard my cry.
²He lifted me out of the slimy pit,
  out of the mud and mire;
he set my feet on a rock
  and gave me a firm place to stand.
³He put a new song in my mouth,
  a hymn of praise to our God.
Many will see and fear
  and put their trust in the LORD.

1. Would you want to know the exact date you'll die? Why or why not? 2. If you had only two weeks to live, what is one thing you must do? Why that one? 3. Read aloud—Reader(s) A: 1–13, odd; Reader(s) B: 2–12, even.

1. Why does David ask to know the "number of my days" (v. 4)? What does this say about his mood? 2. Who imposes the silence: David (vv. 1–3) or God (vv. 9–11)? Both? Why? 3. What are David's burdens (vv. 6,8)? What would he prefer from God, silence or severity? 4. Why does David ask God to "look away from me" (v. 13)? What does he think the Lord's "departure" will do for him?

1. How is David's shame like Peter's "Depart from me" (Lk 5:8)? Have you ever felt ashamed before God? 2. Perhaps David is angry when God seems unfair. Do you ever feel like God "gangs up" on you? Can you express hard questions or doubts about what God is doing? 3. Does life sometimes seem short and empty? How does that awareness affect your priorities? 4. Compare verse 13 with Job 7:16–20: When have you felt God was demanding "too much" from you? What happened to push you to the brink? Will this psalm give you hope in God when hard times next occur?

1. As a child, what "big deal" do you remember waiting for Dad to do with you or for you? How did you feel when the planned event actually happened? 2. Are you good at waiting? How long do you wait before giving up? 3. Read aloud—Reader(s) A: 1–17, odd; Reader(s) B: 2–16, even.

1. Compare the first and last verses. What subtitle would you give the first half of the psalm (vv. 1–10)? The last half? Why the two moods? Do you suppose these were written at the same time or at

different times? **2.** From what "slimy pit" has the psalmist been rescued: Sickness? Sin? Peril? Or does it matter? **3.** What sacrifice does God desire (vv. 6–8)? Then why did God command burnt offerings? What is David referring to as "your law"? **4.** How do you account for David's recurring problems? For David's renewed waiting? Wherein lies his hope?

♡ **1.** When God seems to take too long to help you, what "false gods" offer tempting alternative solutions? What happened the last time you relied on one of those gods? **2.** What in your life feels like a "slimy pit"? Where are you: (a) Knee-deep? (b) "Waisted" (c) One foot out? (d) Standing up to it? **3.** Which helps you most with present troubles: Remembering God's actions in the past? Or claiming God's promises for the future? Why? **4.** The New Testament puts verses 6–8 into the mouth of Jesus (see Heb 10:5–9). Do you see any other foretastes of Jesus in the psalm? What sacrifice does God require from you? **5.** Which is the greater pressure on you right now: The external opposition of others? Or the internal weight of your sin? What from this psalm most helps you in dealing with this pressure?

[4]Blessed is the man
who makes the LORD his trust,
who does not look to the proud,
to those who turn aside to false gods.[a]
[5]Many, O LORD my God,
are the wonders you have done.
The things you planned for us
no one can recount to you;
were I to speak and tell of them,
they would be too many to declare.

[6]Sacrifice and offering you did not desire,
but my ears you have pierced[b,c];
burnt offerings and sin offerings
you did not require.
[7]Then I said, "Here I am, I have come—
it is written about me in the scroll.[d]
[8]I desire to do your will, O my God;
your law is within my heart."

[9]I proclaim righteousness in the great assembly;
I do not seal my lips,
as you know, O LORD.
[10]I do not hide your righteousness in my heart;
I speak of your faithfulness and salvation.
I do not conceal your love and your truth
from the great assembly.

[11]Do not withhold your mercy from me, O LORD;
may your love and your truth always protect
me.
[12]For troubles without number surround me;
my sins have overtaken me, and I cannot see.
They are more than the hairs of my head,
and my heart fails within me.

[13]Be pleased, O LORD, to save me;
O LORD, come quickly to help me.
[14]May all who seek to take my life
be put to shame and confusion;
may all who desire my ruin
be turned back in disgrace.
[15]May those who say to me, "Aha! Aha!"
be appalled at their own shame.
[16]But may all who seek you
rejoice and be glad in you;
may those who love your salvation always say,
"The LORD be exalted!"

[17]Yet I am poor and needy;
may the Lord think of me.
You are my help and my deliverer;
O my God, do not delay.

---

[a]4 Or *to falsehood*   [b]6 Hebrew; Septuagint *but a body you have prepared for me* (see also Symmachus and Theodotion)   [c]6 Or *opened*   [d]7 Or *come / with the scroll written for me*

Psalm 41

For the director of music. A psalm of David.

¹Blessed is he who has regard for the weak;
   the Lord delivers him in times of trouble.
²The Lord will protect him and preserve his life;
   he will bless him in the land
   and not surrender him to the desire of his foes.
³The Lord will sustain him on his sickbed
   and restore him from his bed of illness.

⁴I said, "O Lord, have mercy on me;
   heal me, for I have sinned against you."
⁵My enemies say of me in malice,
   "When will he die and his name perish?"
⁶Whenever one comes to see me,
   he speaks falsely, while his heart gathers
      slander;
   then he goes out and spreads it abroad.

⁷All my enemies whisper together against me;
   they imagine the worst for me, saying,
⁸"A vile disease has beset him;
   he will never get up from the place where he
      lies."
⁹Even my close friend, whom I trusted,
   he who shared my bread,
   has lifted up his heel against me.

¹⁰But you, O Lord, have mercy on me;
   raise me up, that I may repay them.
¹¹I know that you are pleased with me,
   for my enemy does not triumph over me.
¹²In my integrity you uphold me
   and set me in your presence forever.

¹³Praise be to the Lord, the God of Israel,
   from everlasting to everlasting.
      Amen and Amen.

BOOK II

Psalms 42–72

Psalm 42ᵃ

For the director of music. A *maskil*ᵇ of the
Sons of Korah.

¹As the deer pants for streams of water,
   so my soul pants for you, O God.
²My soul thirsts for God, for the living God.
   When can I go and meet with God?
³My tears have been my food
   day and night,
while men say to me all day long,
   "Where is your God?"
⁴These things I remember

ᵃIn many Hebrew manuscripts Psalms 42 and 43 constitute one psalm.   ᵇTitle: Probably a literary or musical term

1. Are you sick and tired of being sick and tired? Do you tend to be sick or tired? What is your most recurrent illness? The most effective cure? 2. *Read aloud*—Reader(s) A: read first half of verse; Reader(s) B: read second half of verse.

1. What's promised in verses 1–3? Why is David's experience so different (vv. 4–9)? 2. The "close friend" of verse 9 may be David's counselor, Ahithophel (see 2Sa 16:23–17:4). What light does this throw on the psalm? 3. What hope sustains David through his trials? Given his confession of sin (v. 4), what does he mean by invoking his "integrity" (v. 13)? How does he know he is "right"?

1. Do you consider yourself strong or weak? What does it mean to you to show regard for the weak? 2. Have you secretly rejoiced at another's trouble? What does that say about you? What will Judas be forever remembered as? 3. What one word describes your life in relation to God's promises: Incongruity? Integrity? Blessed? Never-say-die? Illustrate with an experience.

1. What do you find best quenches your thirst? 2. When were you homesick? What would your correspondence from that time reveal about your innermost yearnings and fears? 3. *Read aloud*—Reader(s) A: 1–11, odd; Reader(s) B: 2–10, even.

1. These two psalms form one unified whole: What refrains and themes are common to each? 2. From 2 Kings 14:11–14, we see hostages being taken captive from Judah: How might such a situation give birth to these psalms (42:1–3)? 3. From the descriptive words and phrases, what diagnosis best fits this psalmist's condition: (a) Thirsty? (b) Depressed? (c) Exiled? (d) Homesick? (e) Hopeful? (f) Plagued by spiritual doubts? 4.

What prescription does the psalmist recommend (vv. 5,11)? Is this a realistic way to handle grief? Why or why not? **5.** Although the psalmist asks the same question in 42:9 that his foes ask in 42:3 and 42:10, what is the difference in how these questions are put? What does this say about the dark side of faith and the sunny side of doubt? **6.** He wants to be back in God's house in Jerusalem, but what is he learning about God from where he is right now? (What does the difference between what's happening "day and night" in 42:3 and 42:8 tell you)? **7.** What progression of faith or mood swing do you see in Psalm 43? Does his prayer in 43:3–4 express a conviction that he will soon be released by his enemies? Or is this a spiritual homecoming?

♡ **1.** What causes God to seem far away at times? Who moved, God or you? How might these two psalms help you in times when you wonder where God is? **2.** In dealing with his depression, this man freely cried (42:3), talked to himself (42:5,11; 43:5), reminded himself of God's nature (42:6,8) and prayed honestly (42:9; 43:2). By comparison, how do you deal with depression? What from this man's example might help you face times of spiritual dryness in your life? **3.** Of the adjectives and titles which this man ascribed to God, which ones best describe your relationship with God? Is the possessive pronoun "my" one that you readily use in relation to God? Why or why not? How has God been "yours" in recent weeks?

as I pour out my soul:
how I used to go with the multitude,
    leading the procession to the house of God,
with shouts of joy and thanksgiving
    among the festive throng.

⁵Why are you downcast, O my soul?
    Why so disturbed within me?
Put your hope in God,
    for I will yet praise him,
    my Savior and ⁶my God.

My*ᵃ* soul is downcast within me;
    therefore I will remember you
from the land of the Jordan,
    the heights of Hermon—from Mount Mizar.
⁷Deep calls to deep
    in the roar of your waterfalls;
all your waves and breakers
    have swept over me.

⁸By day the LORD directs his love,
    at night his song is with me—
    a prayer to the God of my life.

⁹I say to God my Rock,
    "Why have you forgotten me?
Why must I go about mourning,
    oppressed by the enemy?"
¹⁰My bones suffer mortal agony
    as my foes taunt me,
saying to me all day long,
    "Where is your God?"

¹¹Why are you downcast, O my soul?
    Why so disturbed within me?
Put your hope in God,
    for I will yet praise him,
    my Savior and my God.

Psalm 43 *ᵇ*

¹Vindicate me, O God,
    and plead my cause against an ungodly nation;
    rescue me from deceitful and wicked men.
²You are God my stronghold.
    Why have you rejected me?
Why must I go about mourning,
    oppressed by the enemy?
³Send forth your light and your truth,
    let them guide me;
let them bring me to your holy mountain,
    to the place where you dwell.
⁴Then will I go to the altar of God,
    to God, my joy and my delight.
I will praise you with the harp,
    O God, my God.

⁵Why are you downcast, O my soul?

ᵃ5,6 A few Hebrew manuscripts, Septuagint and Syriac; most Hebrew manuscripts praise him for his saving help. / ᵇ6 O my God, my   ᵇIn many Hebrew manuscripts Psalms 42 and 43 constitute one psalm.

Why so disturbed within me?
Put your hope in God,
   for I will yet praise him,
   my Savior and my God.

Psalm 44

For the director of music. Of the Sons of
   Korah. A *maskil*. [a]

[1]We have heard with our ears, O God;
   our fathers have told us
what you did in their days,
   in days long ago.
[2]With your hand you drove out the nations
   and planted our fathers;
you crushed the peoples
   and made our fathers flourish.
[3]It was not by their sword that they won the land,
   nor did their arm bring them victory;
it was your right hand, your arm,
   and the light of your face, for you loved them.

[4]You are my King and my God,
   who decrees [b] victories for Jacob.
[5]Through you we push back our enemies;
   through your name we trample our foes.
[6]I do not trust in my bow,
   my sword does not bring me victory;
[7]but you give us victory over our enemies,
   you put our adversaries to shame.
[8]In God we make our boast all day long,
   and we will praise your name forever.   *Selah*

[9]But now you have rejected and humbled us;
   you no longer go out with our armies.
[10]You made us retreat before the enemy,
   and our adversaries have plundered us.
[11]You gave us up to be devoured like sheep
   and have scattered us among the nations.
[12]You sold your people for a pittance,
   gaining nothing from their sale.

[13]You have made us a reproach to our neighbors,
   the scorn and derision of those around us.
[14]You have made us a byword among the nations;
   the peoples shake their heads at us.
[15]My disgrace is before me all day long,
   and my face is covered with shame
[16]at the taunts of those who reproach and revile
   me,
because of the enemy, who is bent on revenge.

[17]All this happened to us,
   though we had not forgotten you
   or been false to your covenant.
[18]Our hearts had not turned back;
   our feet had not strayed from your path.

1. What does it take to rouse you from sleep: (a) Noisy termites? (b) Noisy neighbors? (c) A train going through your living room? 2. *Read aloud*—Reader(s) A: 1–21, odd; Reader(s) B: 2–22, even; All: 23–26.

1. This might be the prayer of a Judean king. What about God does he recall in verses 1–8? What does this king realize about his own limitations? 2. What problem is the king facing (vv. 9–16)? How does he see God related to this problem? 3. Beyond the physical pain, the social stigma and the emotional turmoil lies the real problem bothering the psalmist (vv. 17–22): What is it? 4. Compare verse 22 with Romans 8:31–39. Might Paul see the sufferings of the king as a battle scar resulting from loyalty? A punishment for sin? Why?

1. What is one "bad thing" that has happened to you recently that you didn't deserve? 2. This king felt like God was sleeping on the job, as did Jesus' disciples (see Mk 4:35–38). Have you felt like this? What did you do to rouse God? What does God's apparent neglect of your situation do to your faith in God's justice and love? 3. Write a group "psalm of distress" about unanswered questions facing you. Follow the shape of this psalm: (a) You have helped us in the past, (b) but you seem to be asleep now. (c) We're not aware we have sinned, (d) so please help us again now!

---

[a]Title: Probably a literary or musical term   [b]4 Septuagint, Aquila and Syriac; Hebrew *King, O God; / command*

¹⁹But you crushed us and made us a haunt for
jackals
and covered us over with deep darkness.

²⁰If we had forgotten the name of our God
or spread out our hands to a foreign god,
²¹would not God have discovered it,
since he knows the secrets of the heart?
²²Yet for your sake we face death all day long;
we are considered as sheep to be slaughtered.

²³Awake, O Lord! Why do you sleep?
Rouse yourself! Do not reject us forever.
²⁴Why do you hide your face
and forget our misery and oppression?

²⁵We are brought down to the dust;
our bodies cling to the ground.
²⁶Rise up and help us;
redeem us because of your unfailing love.

Psalm 45

For the director of music. To ⌊the tune of⌋
"Lilies." Of the Sons of Korah. A *maskil.* ᵃ
A wedding song.

¹My heart is stirred by a noble theme
as I recite my verses for the king;
my tongue is the pen of a skillful writer.

²You are the most excellent of men
and your lips have been anointed with grace,
since God has blessed you forever.
³Gird your sword upon your side, O mighty one;
clothe yourself with splendor and majesty.
⁴In your majesty ride forth victoriously
in behalf of truth, humility and righteousness;
let your right hand display awesome deeds.
⁵Let your sharp arrows pierce the hearts of the
king's enemies;
let the nations fall beneath your feet.
⁶Your throne, O God, will last for ever and ever;
a scepter of justice will be the scepter of your
kingdom.
⁷You love righteousness and hate wickedness;
therefore God, your God, has set you above
your companions
by anointing you with the oil of joy.
⁸All your robes are fragrant with myrrh and aloes
and cassia;
from palaces adorned with ivory
the music of the strings makes you glad.
⁹Daughters of kings are among your honored
women;
at your right hand is the royal bride in gold of
Ophir.

¹⁰Listen, O daughter, consider and give ear:
Forget your people and your father's house.

1. Who was one of your favorite comic book or TV super-heroes? Why? **2.** What was the most extravagant wedding you ever attended or witnessed? **3.** *Read aloud*—Reader(s) A: 1–17, odd; Reader(s) B: 2–16, even.

1. This is a royal wedding song which celebrates the groom (vv. 1–9), the bride (vv. 10–15) and their future (vv. 16–17). For what is the groom praised? **2.** What are the most appealing qualities of the bride? Do these two sound like a good match? **3.** The king is called "God" in verses 6–7. Who else is likened to God (see Ex 7:1; Zec 12:8; Isa 9:6)? What is being said? **4.** What does the "daughter of Tyre" represent (v. 12)? What future did the Jews hope for the Gentiles (see Isa 60:3)?

1. How does the New Testament make sense out of verses 6–7 (see Heb 1:8–9)? What is being said about Jesus and the Church (see Eph 5:25–27)? **2.** Taking verses 2–7 as applying to Jesus, which royal qualities about him mean the most to you now? Why? **3.** What place does "truth, humility and righteousness" have in your life? Where do white lies, false humility and self-justification still hold sway? **4.** Do you believe King Jesus is "enthralled by your beauty"? Why or why not? **5.** How does someone truly loving you help you "forget" all other relationships? What are some of the things in your past that you must "forget" in order to truly honor Jesus as Lord?

ᵃTitle: Probably a literary or musical term

¹¹The king is enthralled by your beauty;
  honor him, for he is your lord.
¹²The Daughter of Tyre will come with a gift,ᵃ
  men of wealth will seek your favor.

¹³All glorious is the princess within ⌊her chamber⌋;
  her gown is interwoven with gold.
¹⁴In embroidered garments she is led to the king;
  her virgin companions follow her
  and are brought to you.
¹⁵They are led in with joy and gladness;
  they enter the palace of the king.

¹⁶Your sons will take the place of your fathers;
  you will make them princes throughout the
  land.
¹⁷I will perpetuate your memory through all
  generations;
  therefore the nations will praise you for ever
  and ever.

Psalm 46

For the director of music. Of the Sons of
Korah. According to *alamoth*.ᵇ A song.

¹God is our refuge and strength,
  an ever-present help in trouble.
²Therefore we will not fear, though the earth give
  way
  and the mountains fall into the heart of the sea,
³though its waters roar and foam
  and the mountains quake with their surging.
                                          Selah

⁴There is a river whose streams make glad the city
  of God,
  the holy place where the Most High dwells.
⁵God is within her, she will not fall;
  God will help her at break of day.
⁶Nations are in uproar, kingdoms fall;
  he lifts his voice, the earth melts.

⁷The LORD Almighty is with us;
  the God of Jacob is our fortress.   *Selah*

⁸Come and see the works of the LORD,
  the desolations he has brought on the earth.
⁹He makes wars cease to the ends of the earth;
  he breaks the bow and shatters the spear,
  he burns the shieldsᶜ with fire.
¹⁰"Be still, and know that I am God;
  I will be exalted among the nations,
  I will be exalted in the earth."

¹¹The LORD Almighty is with us;
  the God of Jacob is our fortress.   *Selah*

1. What cooking experience of yours sent you back to frozen foods? 2. *Read aloud*—Reader(s) A: 1–6; Leader: 7; Reader(s) B: 8–10; All: 11.

1. Biblical writers often used apocalyptic pictures to describe a national crisis. What might be happening to Israel here (vv. 2,3,6)? 2. Why does the writer feel immune to disaster (vv. 4–5)? Did Israel prove to be immune? 3. What seven phrases describe God? Which of these have proven true?

1. The New Testament usually applies promises originally meant for Israel to the Church. What forces threaten the Church today? 2. Could verses 2–3 and 5–6 portray any crisis in your life? How did you respond to that crisis? 3. What difference does it make to you to know Jesus is Lord over all those chaotic events? How is he a fortress to you? Where do you feel a need for his special protection right now? 4. Spend some time in prayer. As each group member shares a trouble, one member can read verse 10 in response.

ᵃ12 Or *A Tyrian robe is among the gifts*   ᵇTitle: Probably a musical term   ᶜ9 Or
chariots

1. Have you ever seen a famous person in the flesh? Did he or she seem different than you imagined? **2.** How often do you clap your hands or shout for joy in church: Always? Sometimes? Never? **3.** *Read aloud*—Reader(s) A: 1–9, odd; Reader(s) B: 2–8, even.

1. "Nations" and "all the earth" are repeated 7 times here. Who are the "nations"? What's the psalmist saying about them? **2.** What might verse 5 refer to (see 2Sa 6:12–15)? **3.** What Jewish hope is expressed in verse 9 (see Ge 12:3)?

1. In what way is God King of all the earth when so many people ignore and disobey him? **2.** Judaism does not teach that all should become Jews. Do you think God wants everyone to become a Christian? Even Jews? What is your vision of the messianic assembly (v. 9)? **3.** Do you enjoy loud singing, clapping and praises? How often do your church services give you a sense of awe?

---

1. What part of the city best symbolizes your life: (a) Downtown? (b) Central park? (c) Skid row? (d) The outskirts? (e) The mall? **2.** *Read aloud*—Reader(s) A: 1–13, odd; Reader(s) B: 2–14, even.

1. Mount Zion (Jerusalem) is idealized in verse 2. What verses are "down to earth"? How must the people be feeling? **2.** How was the city delivered (see 2Ki 18:17–36; 19:35–37)? Was it "secure forever" (v. 8)? **3.** How did the Jews recall God's deeds to the "next generation"? What methods has the Church used to hand on the story of Jesus? **4.** What wider conflict or "war of kings" does the sweeping language of this psalm anticipate? How might the Church sing this psalm of the Gospel and the final rout by its Great King?

1. How have you seen God guide you through a crisis which threatened your city? **2.** A lot of money is spent on church buildings. How can you avoid being enamored with the "citadels" of power and the "ramparts" of a building fund drive, and keep God's work in focus? **3.** Who was significant in passing God's love on to you? How can *you* pass God's love on?

Psalm 47

For the director of music. Of the Sons of Korah. A psalm.

¹Clap your hands, all you nations;
    shout to God with cries of joy.
²How awesome is the LORD Most High,
    the great King over all the earth!
³He subdued nations under us,
    peoples under our feet.
⁴He chose our inheritance for us,
    the pride of Jacob, whom he loved.   *Selah*

⁵God has ascended amid shouts of joy,
    the LORD amid the sounding of trumpets.
⁶Sing praises to God, sing praises;
    sing praises to our King, sing praises.

⁷For God is the King of all the earth;
    sing to him a psalm*ᵃ* of praise.
⁸God reigns over the nations;
    God is seated on his holy throne.
⁹The nobles of the nations assemble
    as the people of the God of Abraham,
for the kings*ᵇ* of the earth belong to God;
    he is greatly exalted.

Psalm 48

A song. A psalm of the Sons of Korah.

¹Great is the LORD, and most worthy of praise,
    in the city of our God, his holy mountain.
²It is beautiful in its loftiness,
    the joy of the whole earth.
Like the utmost heights of Zaphon*ᶜ* is Mount Zion,
    the*ᵈ* city of the Great King.
³God is in her citadels;
    he has shown himself to be her fortress.

⁴When the kings joined forces,
    when they advanced together,
⁵they saw ⌊her⌋ and were astounded;
    they fled in terror.
⁶Trembling seized them there,
    pain like that of a woman in labor.
⁷You destroyed them like ships of Tarshish
    shattered by an east wind.

⁸As we have heard,
    so have we seen
in the city of the LORD Almighty,
    in the city of our God:
    God makes her secure forever.   *Selah*

⁹Within your temple, O God,
    we meditate on your unfailing love.

ᵃ7 Or *a maskil* (probably a literary or musical term)   *ᵇ9* Or *shields*   *ᶜ2 Zaphon* can refer to a sacred mountain or the direction north.   *ᵈ2* Or *earth,* / *Mount Zion, on the northern side* / *of the*

¹⁰Like your name, O God,
   your praise reaches to the ends of the earth;
   your right hand is filled with righteousness.
¹¹Mount Zion rejoices,
   the villages of Judah are glad
   because of your judgments.

¹²Walk about Zion, go around her,
   count her towers,
¹³consider well her ramparts,
   view her citadels,
   that you may tell of them to the next
      generation.
¹⁴For this God is our God for ever and ever;
   he will be our guide even to the end.

Psalm 49

For the director of music. Of the Sons of
Korah. A psalm.

¹Hear this, all you peoples;
   listen, all who live in this world,
²both low and high,
   rich and poor alike:
³My mouth will speak words of wisdom;
   the utterance from my heart will give
      understanding.
⁴I will turn my ear to a proverb;
   with the harp I will expound my riddle:

⁵Why should I fear when evil days come,
   when wicked deceivers surround me—
⁶those who trust in their wealth
   and boast of their great riches?
⁷No man can redeem the life of another
   or give to God a ransom for him—
⁸the ransom for a life is costly,
   no payment is ever enough—
⁹that he should live on forever
   and not see decay.

¹⁰For all can see that wise men die;
   the foolish and the senseless alike perish
   and leave their wealth to others.
¹¹Their tombs will remain their houses*a* forever,
   their dwellings for endless generations,
   though they had*b* named lands after
      themselves.

¹²But man, despite his riches, does not endure;
   he is*c* like the beasts that perish.

¹³This is the fate of those who trust in themselves,
   and of their followers, who approve their
      sayings.   Selah
¹⁴Like sheep they are destined for the grave,*d*
   and death will feed on them.
   The upright will rule over them in the morning;

1. How would you complete the phrase: "Man is the only animal that ..."? 2. What would you want named after you: (a) Children or grandchildren? (b) Town? (c) Park or building? (d) Scholarship fund? (e) Scientific discovery? What would others associate with your name? 3. *Read aloud*—Reader(s) A: 1–19, odd; Reader(s) B: 2–18, even; All: 20.

1. How does the psalmist get your attention in verses 1–4? What is his "riddle"? 2. Is the message for the rich alone? In what things do these people trust (vv. 6,11)? What reality do they refuse to see? How is that world view expressed today? 3. How does the psalmist account for the unfairness in life (v. 15)? What is the basis for his viewing reality that way? How can God solve the problem stated in verses 7–9? 4. What picture does the psalmist paint of the hereafter (vv. 16–19)? What verses indicate a heaven and hell? What verses indicate no afterlife at all? 5. How is mankind different from the animal world (v. 20)?

1. Do you believe the best things in life are free? Give some examples of great things money can't buy. 2. If there were no heaven or hell, would you agree with modern sentiments like "Just do it," or "He who dies with the most toys, wins." What world view would attract you most if there was no Christianity? 3. Has the death of a loved one caused a "big chill" on your or your friends' world views? 4. This psalm is echoed in Jesus' teaching (see Mt 6:25–34). How do both teachings challenge your current lifestyle and priorities? How can you avoid being "like the beasts"?

a 11 Septuagint and Syriac; Hebrew *In their thoughts their houses will remain*
b 11 Or */ for they have*   *c 12* Hebrew; Septuagint and Syriac read verse 12 the same as verse 20.   *d 14* Hebrew *Sheol*; also in verse 15

their forms will decay in the grave,[a]
   far from their princely mansions.
¹⁵But God will redeem my life[b] from the grave;
   he will surely take me to himself.   *Selah*

¹⁶Do not be overawed when a man grows rich,
   when the splendor of his house increases;
¹⁷for he will take nothing with him when he dies,
   his splendor will not descend with him.
¹⁸Though while he lived he counted himself
      blessed—
   and men praise you when you prosper—
¹⁹he will join the generation of his fathers,
   who will never see the light ˻of life˼.

²⁰A man who has riches without understanding
   is like the beasts that perish.

Psalm 50

A psalm of Asaph.

¹The Mighty One, God, the LORD,
   speaks and summons the earth
   from the rising of the sun to the place where it
      sets.
²From Zion, perfect in beauty,
   God shines forth.
³Our God comes and will not be silent;
   a fire devours before him,
   and around him a tempest rages.
⁴He summons the heavens above,
   and the earth, that he may judge his people:
⁵"Gather to me my consecrated ones,
   who made a covenant with me by sacrifice."
⁶And the heavens proclaim his righteousness,
   for God himself is judge.   *Selah*

⁷"Hear, O my people, and I will speak,
   O Israel, and I will testify against you:
   I am God, your God.
⁸I do not rebuke you for your sacrifices
   or your burnt offerings, which are ever before
      me.
⁹I have no need of a bull from your stall
   or of goats from your pens,
¹⁰for every animal of the forest is mine,
   and the cattle on a thousand hills.
¹¹I know every bird in the mountains,
   and the creatures of the field are mine.
¹²If I were hungry I would not tell you,
   for the world is mine, and all that is in it.
¹³Do I eat the flesh of bulls
   or drink the blood of goats?
¹⁴Sacrifice thank offerings to God,
   fulfill your vows to the Most High,
¹⁵and call upon me in the day of trouble;
   I will deliver you, and you will honor me."

¹⁶But to the wicked, God says:

☕ **1.** Does your mind wander during church? At what part of the service do you daydream the most? **2.** Have you ever heard God speak like a voice in your head? An audible voice outside your head? What did God say? **3.** *Read aloud*—Reader(s) A: 1–23, odd; Reader(s) B: 2–22, even.

📖 **1.** What picture of God is drawn in verses 1–6? Whom is he addressing and judging here? Why summon the heavens and the earth to witness this trial? **2.** What is God's message to the religious in verses 7–15? Is it wrong to offer sacrifices as decreed in the Law? For whose benefit were they decreed? God's? **3.** Why is God so harsh with his own people (see Am 3:2)? What does God want (vv. 14–15)? **4.** What is God's message to the "wicked" (vv. 16–21)? How do they differ from the first group? Who has the right words? The right actions? What does each group lack? **5.** What is the threat and promise in verses 22–23? Why is God so fierce?

♥ **1.** Do you ever picture God as an angry judge? How does it make you feel? Did your parents give you this image? **2.** If God were to address your church today through this psalm, what would he more likely attack: mindless ritualism or lip service? Why? What forms of empty religion would he rail against? What forms of hypocrisy? **3.** What comes first in your spirituality: (a) Action? (b) Sacrifice? (c) Prayer? (d) Talk? Why? What comes second? What does the small group emphasize? **4.** In this psalm, God first warned the people, then re-issued his call to follow him: How has he done

---

a14 Hebrew *Sheol*; also in verse 15   b15 Or *soul*

"What right have you to recite my laws
    or take my covenant on your lips?
17You hate my instruction
    and cast my words behind you.
18When you see a thief, you join with him;
    you throw in your lot with adulterers.
19You use your mouth for evil
    and harness your tongue to deceit.
20You speak continually against your brother
    and slander your own mother's son.
21These things you have done and I kept silent;
    you thought I was altogether*a* like you.
But I will rebuke you
    and accuse you to your face.

22"Consider this, you who forget God,
    or I will tear you to pieces, with none to
      rescue:
23He who sacrifices thank offerings honors me,
    and he prepares the way
    so that I may show him*b* the salvation of
      God."

Psalm 51

For the director of music. A psalm of David.
When the prophet Nathan came to him after
David had committed adultery with
Bathsheba.

1Have mercy on me, O God,
    according to your unfailing love;
according to your great compassion
    blot out my transgressions.
2Wash away all my iniquity
    and cleanse me from my sin.

3For I know my transgressions,
    and my sin is always before me.
4Against you, you only, have I sinned
    and done what is evil in your sight,
so that you are proved right when you speak
    and justified when you judge.
5Surely I was sinful at birth,
    sinful from the time my mother conceived me.
6Surely you desire truth in the inner parts*c*;
    you teach*d* me wisdom in the inmost place.

7Cleanse me with hyssop, and I will be clean;
    wash me, and I will be whiter than snow.
8Let me hear joy and gladness;
    let the bones you have crushed rejoice.
9Hide your face from my sins
    and blot out all my iniquity.

10Create in me a pure heart, O God,
    and renew a steadfast spirit within me.
11Do not cast me from your presence

that for you? **5.** What "thank offerings" do you give to God? Brainstorm on ideas. Can this group give
a "thank offering"?

---

1. Do you recall getting
caught with your "hand in the
cookie jar" as a child? As an adult?
What happened each time? **2.**
Read aloud—Reader(s) A: 1–19,
odd; Reader(s) B: 2–15, even.

1. In how many ways did David sin in the Bathsheba af-
fair (see 2Sa 11:1–27)? **2.** In light
of his arrogance, adultery, deception and murder, how does he dare
approach God? What does he
feel? **3.** Murder is a capital crime
under Jewish law. Why also adultery (see Dt 22:22)? **4.** Since such
sins involve others, what is the
meaning of verse 4? What does
this show about the nature of sin?
5. How can an unborn child be considered "sinful" (v. 5)? If God created all things "good," why does
mankind tend to sin (see Ro
5:12–14)? **6.** In light of all this,
what does David ask God to do (vv.
7–12)? What is "cleansing with
hyssop" (see Lev 14:4–7)? Why
does David request this? **7.** How
does David hope to escape God's
wrath (vv. 13–17)? On what basis
does he hope for a restored relationship? **8.** Why does David gen-
eralize his prayer to include the
whole nation (vv. 18–19)? What
does this say about the nature of
sin? **9.** What kinds of sacrifices
does the Lord desire in verses
16–17? In verse 19? When is a
broken spirit or contrite heart
enough? When are acts of sacrifice
due?

a21 Or thought the 'I AM' was   *b23 Or and to him who considers his way / I will show*   *c6 The meaning of the Hebrew for this phrase is uncertain.*   *d6 Or you desired . . . ; / you taught*

1. Has covering up sin back-fired in your life? How have you seen God's mercy when you owned up to your sin? 2. Are there really any victimless crimes? How do personal failings affect God? Others? Self? Society? 3. Are you more sensitive to sin and broken-ness in yourself as a Christian than beforehand? Why?

or take your Holy Spirit from me.
¹²Restore to me the joy of your salvation
and grant me a willing spirit, to sustain me.

¹³Then I will teach transgressors your ways,
and sinners will turn back to you.
¹⁴Save me from bloodguilt, O God,
the God who saves me,
and my tongue will sing of your righteousness.
¹⁵O Lord, open my lips,
and my mouth will declare your praise.
¹⁶You do not delight in sacrifice, or I would bring it;
you do not take pleasure in burnt offerings.
¹⁷The sacrifices of God are[a] a broken spirit;
a broken and contrite heart,
O God, you will not despise.

¹⁸In your good pleasure make Zion prosper;
build up the walls of Jerusalem.
¹⁹Then there will be righteous sacrifices,
whole burnt offerings to delight you;
then bulls will be offered on your altar.

1. When you were a child, did any three words strike more terror than "I'm gonna tell"? Did you tend to get told on or were you the tattler? 2. *Read aloud*—Reader(s) A: read the first line of each verse; Reader(s) B: read the second and third line of each verse.

1. What type of man was Doeg the Edomite (see 1Sa 22:6–23)? What was he willing to do that Jewish soldiers were not? 2. What was Doeg's boast (v. 1)? How does David account for Doeg's success (v. 7)? 3. Why are the righteous often compared to trees (v. 8; also 1:3)? What did ol-ive trees provide in David's time? 4. What does David trust (vv. 8–9)? How is that trust in God evi-dent in what David does?

1. Doeg was someone who used people and loved things. Where do you see that atti-tude in others or in yourself today? 2. Has anyone ever suffered for helping or taking a risk for you? What happened? What did you feel: Guilt? Regret? Shame? Non-chalance? 3. Are you "flourishing in the house of God"? What is lacking in your spiritual commitment? What helps you flourish?

Psalm 52

For the director of music. A *maskil*[b]
of David. When Doeg the Edomite had gone
to Saul and told him: "David has gone to the
house of Ahimelech."

¹Why do you boast of evil, you mighty man?
Why do you boast all day long,
you who are a disgrace in the eyes of God?
²Your tongue plots destruction;
it is like a sharpened razor,
you who practice deceit.
³You love evil rather than good,
falsehood rather than speaking the truth.   *Selah*
⁴You love every harmful word,
O you deceitful tongue!

⁵Surely God will bring you down to everlasting
ruin:
He will snatch you up and tear you from your
tent;
he will uproot you from the land of the living.
Selah
⁶The righteous will see and fear;
they will laugh at him, saying,
⁷"Here now is the man
who did not make God his stronghold
but trusted in his great wealth
and grew strong by destroying others!"

⁸But I am like an olive tree
flourishing in the house of God;
I trust in God's unfailing love
for ever and ever.
⁹I will praise you forever for what you have done;

in your name I will hope, for your name is
        good.
I will praise you in the presence of your saints.

Psalm 53

For the director of music. According to
mahalath.[a] A *maskil*[b] of David.

[1]The fool says in his heart,
        "There is no God."
They are corrupt, and their ways are vile;
        there is no one who does good.

[2]God looks down from heaven
        on the sons of men
to see if there are any who understand,
        any who seek God.
[3]Everyone has turned away,
        they have together become corrupt;
there is no one who does good,
        not even one.

[4]Will the evildoers never learn—
        those who devour my people as men eat bread
and who do not call on God?
[5]There they were, overwhelmed with dread,
        where there was nothing to dread.
God scattered the bones of those who attacked
        you;
        you put them to shame, for God despised them.

[6]Oh, that salvation for Israel would come out of
        Zion!
When God restores the fortunes of his people,
        let Jacob rejoice and Israel be glad!

Psalm 54

For the director of music. With stringed
instruments. A *maskil*[b] of David. When the
Ziphites had gone to Saul and said, "Is not
David hiding among us?"

[1]Save me, O God, by your name;
        vindicate me by your might.
[2]Hear my prayer, O God;
        listen to the words of my mouth.

[3]Strangers are attacking me;
        ruthless men seek my life—
        men without regard for God.   *Selah*

[4]Surely God is my help;
        the Lord is the one who sustains me.

[5]Let evil recoil on those who slander me;
        in your faithfulness destroy them.

[6]I will sacrifice a freewill offering to you;
        I will praise your name, O LORD,
        for it is good.

---

1. Who is your favorite TV, movie or fictional "fool"? What makes him or her foolish? 2. *Read aloud*—Reader(s) A: 1–5, odd; Reader(s) B: 2–6, even.

1. Does this psalm seem familiar (see Ps 14)? What accounts for this? 2. Why is it foolish to say "there is no God"? In what way is this fool an atheist (vv. 1–3)? 3. Is David's sweeping indictment a bit exaggerated? Or exceptionally accurate? Explain. 4. What does this psalm say about God's view of evil? What does God plan to do about it?

1. Have you ever been one of these fools: (a) The intellectual seeker? (b) The practical atheist? (c) Self-destructive? (d) Unhealthy in relationships? 2. What tempts you to think "there is no God"? Does distance from God affect your behavior? 3. What part of your life runs without regard to God? How will you put your faith to work today?

---

1. How do you feel when members of a strange religious sect come to your door? Do you invite them in or hide? 2. *Read aloud*—Reader(s) A: 1–3; Reader(s) B: 4–5; All: 6–7.

1. What strangers (v. 3) attack David (see 1Sa 23:1–20)? Why do they betray the man who saved them from the Philistines? 2. How does David feel? How do you account for the switch in tone in verses 6–7 (see 1Sa 23:26–29)?

1. Has your faith ever been attacked? Was the attack: (a) Intellectual? (b) Theological? (c) Emotional? (d) Social? How do you respond? 2. Have you seen evil recoil back on those who promote it? When has this happened to you?

---

*a*Title: Probably a musical term   *b*Title: Probably a literary or musical term

7For he has delivered me from all my troubles,
and my eyes have looked in triumph on my
foes.

Psalm 55

For the director of music. With stringed
instruments. A *maskil*[a] of David.

1Listen to my prayer, O God,
do not ignore my plea;
2 hear me and answer me.
My thoughts trouble me and I am distraught
3 at the voice of the enemy,
at the stares of the wicked;
for they bring down suffering upon me
and revile me in their anger.

4My heart is in anguish within me;
the terrors of death assail me.
5Fear and trembling have beset me;
horror has overwhelmed me.
6I said, "Oh, that I had the wings of a dove!
I would fly away and be at rest—
7I would flee far away
and stay in the desert;   *Selah*
8I would hurry to my place of shelter,
far from the tempest and storm."

9Confuse the wicked, O Lord, confound their
speech,
for I see violence and strife in the city.
10Day and night they prowl about on its walls;
malice and abuse are within it.
11Destructive forces are at work in the city;
threats and lies never leave its streets.

12If an enemy were insulting me,
I could endure it;
if a foe were raising himself against me,
I could hide from him.
13But it is you, a man like myself,
my companion, my close friend,
14with whom I once enjoyed sweet fellowship
as we walked with the throng at the house of
God.

15Let death take my enemies by surprise;
let them go down alive to the grave,[b]
for evil finds lodging among them.

16But I call to God,
and the LORD saves me.
17Evening, morning and noon
I cry out in distress,
and he hears my voice.
18He ransoms me unharmed
from the battle waged against me,
even though many oppose me.
19God, who is enthroned forever,

---

1. Where would you fly if you
had the "wings of a dove"?
How far south? With what other
love bird? Where would you nest?
2. What age do you figure was (or
will be) your halfway point in
life: 17? 27? 37? 47? 3. *Read
aloud*—Reader(s) A: 1–23, odd;
Reader(s) B: 2–22, even.

1. Is David troubled by internal or external strife (vv.
1–3)? What is he afraid of (vv.
5–6)? 2. Does David feel like facing his problems head on (vv.
6–8)? He has had "escapist" feelings before (11:1). Why not fight
his enemies (vv. 9–11)? What
does he want God to do? 3. What
makes David's present trouble terrifying (vv. 12–14)? Do you think
this psalm fits Ahitophel's defection
to Saul (2Sa 15:12–31)? 4. What
fate does David wish on his enemies beyond mere "confusion"
(v. 15)? What do you think of his
other curses (vv. 19,23)? 5. David's
betrayer is a good speaker (vv.
20–21). What do his words hide?
What else do words often hide? 6.
Faced with open rebellion, what
does it mean for David to be "sustained" by God?

1. How do you tend to re-
spond to troubles: (a) Deny
they exist? (b) Blame someone
else? (c) Avoid the problem or person? (d) Escape? (e) Tackle them
head on? (f) Pray? How are you
handling your biggest problem today? 2. To whom would you like to
pass the message of verse 22
(also 1Pe 5:7)? 3. Do the streets of
your city resemble verses 10–11?
How do you handle the increasing
deterioration of urban life? Where
lies hope? 4. When do you use
speech as described in verse 21?
What feelings do you cover up with
deceitful words: Anger? Hatred?
Jealousy? Envy? Love? Praise?
Sexual interest? What does that do
to your sense of who you are?

---

a Title: Probably a literary or musical term   b 15 Hebrew *Sheol*

will hear them and afflict them—   *Selah*
men who never change their ways
   and have no fear of God.

20My companion attacks his friends;
   he violates his covenant.
21His speech is smooth as butter,
   yet war is in his heart;
his words are more soothing than oil,
   yet they are drawn swords.

22Cast your cares on the LORD
   and he will sustain you;
he will never let the righteous fall.
23But you, O God, will bring down the wicked
   into the pit of corruption;
bloodthirsty and deceitful men
   will not live out half their days.

But as for me, I trust in you.

Psalm 56

For the director of music. To ⌊the tune of⌋ "A
   Dove on Distant Oaks." Of David. A
miktam. [a] When the Philistines had seized
   him in Gath.

1Be merciful to me, O God, for men hotly pursue
   me;
   all day long they press their attack.
2My slanderers pursue me all day long;
   many are attacking me in their pride.

3When I am afraid,
   I will trust in you.
4In God, whose word I praise,
   in God I trust; I will not be afraid.
   What can mortal man do to me?

5All day long they twist my words;
   they are always plotting to harm me.
6They conspire, they lurk,
   they watch my steps,
   eager to take my life.

7On no account let them escape;
   in your anger, O God, bring down the nations.
8Record my lament;
   list my tears on your scroll[b]—
   are they not in your record?

9Then my enemies will turn back
   when I call for help.
   By this I will know that God is for me.
10In God, whose word I praise,
   in the LORD, whose word I praise—
11in God I trust; I will not be afraid.
   What can man do to me?

12I am under vows to you, O God;
   I will present my thank offerings to you.

1. If you collected all the tears you shed in recent years, how much water would you have: A glass? Bucket? Swimming pool? Niagara Falls? 2. What is the silliest thing you are afraid of? 3. *Read aloud*—Reader(s) A: 1–4; Reader(s) B: 5–9; Leader: 10–11; All: 12–13.

1. This psalm reflects 1 Samuel 21:10–15, where David flees Saul by escaping to Gath, Goliath's hometown. How desperate must David be to jump out of the frying pan into the fire? Where do you see that despair reflected in this psalm? 2. What's happening to David (vv. 5–6)? How would you feel in his place, hunted by your former friends? 3. What does it mean that God "records your tears" (v. 8)? 4. Is David invincible (vv. 4,11)? What does it mean to trust God in fearful circumstances? How is such trust demonstrated? How is it rewarded?

1. Does being afraid lead you to trust God more, or less? Conversely, does not trusting God lead you to be more afraid? Less? Why? How can you choose faith when you are afraid? 2. Which gets more notice from God: Your tears? Sins? Praises? Petitions? Why? If not God, in front of whom can you cry openly? 3. If God is with us, why do we fear human threats so much? Can head knowledge of God alleviate fears, which are emotional? How do you overcome fear?

---

aTitle: Probably a literary or musical term   b8 Or / *put my tears in your wineskin*

¹³For you have delivered me*a* from death
    and my feet from stumbling,
  that I may walk before God
    in the light of life.*b*

Psalm 57

For the director of music. ⌊To the tune of⌋
"Do Not Destroy." Of David. A *miktam.*ᶜ
When he had fled from Saul into the cave.

¹Have mercy on me, O God, have mercy on me,
    for in you my soul takes refuge.
  I will take refuge in the shadow of your wings
    until the disaster has passed.

²I cry out to God Most High,
    to God, who fulfills ⌊his purpose⌋ for me.
³He sends from heaven and saves me,
    rebuking those who hotly pursue me;   *Selah*
  God sends his love and his faithfulness.

⁴I am in the midst of lions;
    I lie among ravenous beasts—
  men whose teeth are spears and arrows,
    whose tongues are sharp swords.

⁵Be exalted, O God, above the heavens;
    let your glory be over all the earth.

⁶They spread a net for my feet—
    I was bowed down in distress.
  They dug a pit in my path—
    but they have fallen into it themselves.   *Selah*

⁷My heart is steadfast, O God,
    my heart is steadfast;
  I will sing and make music.
⁸Awake, my soul!
    Awake, harp and lyre!
  I will awaken the dawn.

⁹I will praise you, O Lord, among the nations;
    I will sing of you among the peoples.
¹⁰For great is your love, reaching to the heavens;
    your faithfulness reaches to the skies.

¹¹Be exalted, O God, above the heavens;
    let your glory be over all the earth.

Psalm 58

For the director of music. ⌊To the tune of⌋
"Do Not Destroy." Of David. A *miktam.*ᶜ

¹Do you rulers indeed speak justly?
    Do you judge uprightly among men?
²No, in your heart you devise injustice,
    and your hands mete out violence on the earth.
³Even from birth the wicked go astray;

---

1. When you were a child, what did you want to be when you grew up? Now what do you want to be when you grow up? **2.** *Read aloud*—Reader(s) A: 1–7, odd; Reader(s) B: 2–8, even; All: 9–10; Leader: 11.

1. To which cave hide-out does this psalm heading refer? Form two groups: one read 1 Samuel 21:10–22:2, the other 1 Samuel 24. Present a case for your cave. **2.** David cries to God to fulfill "his purpose for me" (v. 2). What is God's purpose (see 1 Sa 16:1–13)? As one hated and hunted by Saul, the Lord's current "anointed one," how might David come to view that job? Is David deterred from, or spurred on, to see that purpose fulfilled? Why do you think so? **3.** Where do you see an abrupt change in mood in this psalm? What must have occurred?

1. What promises of God do you lean on in hard times? Can you expect God's protection from every disaster? Why or why not? **2.** What do you feel is God's purpose for you? How far along are you in seeing God's purpose fulfilled: (a) In the research stage? (b) Stalled in a production snag? (c) Back to the drawing boards? (d) Already useful in the marketplace? **3.** Verses 5 and 11 are the same except for their context: 5 expresses faith in hard times, 11 expresses joy after deliverance. Which context is yours right now?

1. Can you stand the sight of blood? Your own? **2.** What methods did your parents use to extract your baby teeth? **3.** *Read aloud*—Reader(s) A: read the first half of each verse; Reader(s) B: read the second half of each verse.

1. With whom is David angry (v. 1–2)? What is their problem? **2.** Are the wicked predestined to evil (vv. 3–5)? Who are the "charmers and enchanters" of life? **3.** What does David wish for unjust

---

*a*13 Or *my soul*   *b*13 Or *the land of the living*   *c*Title: Probably a literary or musical term

from the womb they are wayward and speak
  lies.
⁴Their venom is like the venom of a snake,
  like that of a cobra that has stopped its ears,
⁵that will not heed the tune of the charmer,
  however skillful the enchanter may be.

⁶Break the teeth in their mouths, O God;
  tear out, O LORD, the fangs of the lions!
⁷Let them vanish like water that flows away;
  when they draw the bow, let their arrows be
    blunted.
⁸Like a slug melting away as it moves along,
  like a stillborn child, may they not see the sun.

⁹Before your pots can feel ⌊the heat of⌋ the
    thorns—
  whether they be green or dry—the wicked will
    be swept away.ᵃ
¹⁰The righteous will be glad when they are
    avenged,
  when they bathe their feet in the blood of the
    wicked.
¹¹Then men will say,
  "Surely the righteous still are rewarded;
  surely there is a God who judges the earth."

Psalm 59

For the director of music. ⌊To the tune of⌋
"Do Not Destroy." Of David. A *miktam.*ᵇ
When Saul had sent men to watch David's
  house in order to kill him.

¹Deliver me from my enemies, O God;
  protect me from those who rise up against me.
²Deliver me from evildoers
  and save me from bloodthirsty men.

³See how they lie in wait for me!
  Fierce men conspire against me
  for no offense or sin of mine, O LORD.
⁴I have done no wrong, yet they are ready to
    attack me.
  Arise to help me; look on my plight!
⁵O LORD God Almighty, the God of Israel,
  rouse yourself to punish all the nations;
  show no mercy to wicked traitors.   *Selah*

⁶They return at evening,
  snarling like dogs,
  and prowl about the city.
⁷See what they spew from their mouths—
  they spew out swords from their lips,
  and they say, "Who can hear us?"
⁸But you, O LORD, laugh at them;
  you scoff at all those nations.

⁹O my Strength, I watch for you;
  you, O God, are my fortress, ¹⁰my loving God.

rulers (vv. 6–8)? What does this say about God's abhorrence of injustice? **4.** What do people say about God when injustice and cruelty continually occur? What would David like us to believe (v. 11)?

1. What social injustice or tyranny gets you stirred up? Why? How is that reflected in your prayers? **2.** Could you use the cries for vengeance in verses 6–9 as your own? Why or why not? **3.** Compare this psalm with Jesus' words in Matthew 23:33–36. When are such words appropriate today? **4.** What can this group do to help bring justice in the community?

1. Did you ever write a letter in the heat of the moment and then choose not to mail it? Why? Did you send a revised version instead? **2.** Have people thrown a surprise party for you? Did you suspect? Did you play into it? **3.** *Read aloud*—Reader(s) A: 1–15, odd; Reader(s) B: 2–14, even; All: 16; Leader: 17.

1. Who does David credit for his escape (vv. 1–2; see 1Sa 19:11–18)? Is he out of danger yet? **2.** Why does David include all Gentiles in his plea (vv. 5,8)? Is he getting paranoid? **3.** What are his enemies like (vv. 6–7)? What is their attitude towards God? **4.** In verses 11–13, what does David pray for "my people"? For the "ends of the earth"? What does "consume them" mean? Is this David the fugitive praying, or David the king? Why do you think so? **5.** What comfort and hope does David draw from the promise of God's personal and world-wide judgment? What does judgment show about God's view of injustice in the world? What would it mean if God did not judge evil? **6.** What words change in verses 9 and 17? What does this show about David's progression in faith between then and now? **7.** How did God answer David's prayer (see 1Sa 19:19–24)? Is this what David had in mind?

ᵃ9 The meaning of the Hebrew for this verse is uncertain.   ᵇTitle: Probably a literary or musical term

1. How should we pray for criminals or those who persecute God's people? How do you balance hatred of evil with love for enemies? 2. How would you relate this psalm to the New Testament teaching that suffering is redemptive (see 1Pe 4:12–13; Col 1:24)? 3. David could easily have become a cynic: Why didn't he? How could David's use of joyful worship be your freedom from cynicism?

1. Were you ever in a fist fight at school? What happened? Who won? 2. Can you recall a pep talk from a teacher, parent or coach that deeply affected you? 3. *Read aloud*—Reader(s) A: every third verse starting with 1; Reader(s) B; every third verse starting with 2; Leader: every third verse starting with 3.

1. While David was securing his borders on the far NE corner of his kingdom, Edom attacked on the far south (see 2Sa 8:2,3,13). How did David respond to this behind-the-back blow? Does this psalm paint as glorious a picture as the Samuel account (vv. 1–3)? Why does he blame God? 2. Armies "raised a banner" to regroup fleeing, disorganized soldiers. For whom does God raise a banner (v. 4)? Why? 3. How do you account for the confident tone of verse 5? How did God promise (vv. 6–8)? 4. Why David's growing sense of hope (vv. 9–12)? What is David's part and God's part in this upcoming battle?

1. Have you ever felt in "retreat" (scattered, unorganized)? What serves as God's rallying banner for you? 2. What "Edom" is attacking you now from

God will go before me
    and will let me gloat over those who slander me.
[11]But do not kill them, O Lord our shield,[a]
    or my people will forget.
In your might make them wander about,
    and bring them down.
[12]For the sins of their mouths,
    for the words of their lips,
    let them be caught in their pride.
For the curses and lies they utter,
[13]   consume them in wrath,
    consume them till they are no more.
Then it will be known to the ends of the earth
    that God rules over Jacob.   *Selah*

[14]They return at evening,
    snarling like dogs,
    and prowl about the city.
[15]They wander about for food
    and howl if not satisfied.
[16]But I will sing of your strength,
    in the morning I will sing of your love;
for you are my fortress,
    my refuge in times of trouble.

[17]O my Strength, I sing praise to you;
    you, O God, are my fortress, my loving God.

Psalm 60

For the director of music. To ⌊the tune of⌋ "The Lily of the Covenant." A *miktam*[b] of David. For teaching. When he fought Aram Naharaim[c] and Aram Zobah,[d] and when Joab returned and struck down twelve thousand Edomites in the Valley of Salt.

[1]You have rejected us, O God, and burst forth upon us;
    you have been angry—now restore us!
[2]You have shaken the land and torn it open;
    mend its fractures, for it is quaking.
[3]You have shown your people desperate times;
    you have given us wine that makes us stagger.

[4]But for those who fear you, you have raised a banner
    to be unfurled against the bow.   *Selah*

[5]Save us and help us with your right hand,
    that those you love may be delivered.
[6]God has spoken from his sanctuary:
    "In triumph I will parcel out Shechem
    and measure off the Valley of Succoth.
[7]Gilead is mine, and Manasseh is mine;
    Ephraim is my helmet,
    Judah my scepter.
[8]Moab is my washbasin,

[a] 11 Or *sovereign*   [b]Title: Probably a literary or musical term   [c]Title: That is, Arameans of Northwest Mesopotamia   [d]Title: That is, Arameans of central Syria

upon Edom I toss my sandal;
over Philistia I shout in triumph."

⁹Who will bring me to the fortified city?
Who will lead me to Edom?
¹⁰Is it not you, O God, you who have rejected us
and no longer go out with our armies?
¹¹Give us aid against the enemy,
for the help of man is worthless.
¹²With God we will gain the victory,
and he will trample down our enemies.

Psalm 61

For the director of music. With stringed
instruments. Of David.

¹Hear my cry, O God;
listen to my prayer.

²From the ends of the earth I call to you,
I call as my heart grows faint;
lead me to the rock that is higher than I.
³For you have been my refuge,
a strong tower against the foe.

⁴I long to dwell in your tent forever
and take refuge in the shelter of your wings.
Selah

⁵For you have heard my vows, O God;
you have given me the heritage of those who
fear your name.

⁶Increase the days of the king's life,
his years for many generations.
⁷May he be enthroned in God's presence forever;
appoint your love and faithfulness to protect
him.

⁸Then will I ever sing praise to your name
and fulfill my vows day after day.

Psalm 62

For the director of music. For Jeduthun.
A psalm of David.

¹My soul finds rest in God alone;
my salvation comes from him.
²He alone is my rock and my salvation;
he is my fortress, I will never be shaken.

³How long will you assault a man?
Would all of you throw him down—
this leaning wall, this tottering fence?
⁴They fully intend to topple him
from his lofty place;
they take delight in lies.
With their mouths they bless,
but in their hearts they curse.
Selah

⁵Find rest, O my soul, in God alone;
my hope comes from him.

your blind side? What lesson in this psalm can help you face problems head on? **3.** When you pray, do you address God indirectly or as "You"? **4.** How are the battles that Christians have to face different from the wars of God's Old Testament people? How are they similar?

---

1. Which parent gave you rock-like security? How so? **2.** What is the longest long-distance phone call you've ever made? **3.** *Read aloud*—Reader(s) A: 1–3; Reader(s) B: 4–5; Leader: 6–8.

1. How far away from home is David (v. 2)? In what state of health? **2.** What kind of fellowship with God does David want (vv. 3–5)? What vows has he taken? What does he inherit? **3.** Is David praying for himself (vv. 6–7)? What else is he thinking about (see 2Sa 7:8–16)?

1. When have you felt exiled? How do you pray when faint from exhaustion? **2.** Do Christians inherit anything like David (see Eph 1:3–6)? What vow could you make this coming week to help you grow stronger in faith?

---

1. What is the most restful vacation you have taken in the last 10 years? What made it so? **2.** What is the best reward someone could give you for a job well done? **3.** *Read aloud*—Reader(s) A: 1–11, odd; Reader(s) B: 2–12, even.

1. What two evils prompt David to write this psalm (vv. 3–4)? **2.** What is the refrain of the song? What is the difference between "salvation" and "honor" (v. 7)? **3.** In what does David urge us to "trust" and "not trust" (vv. 8–10)? How can people know if they are trusting in God, people or money? **4.** What two things has David heard about God? (vv. 11–12)? How will God judge?

1. What circumstances, people or forces are pressuring you now? What are you learning from their pressure? 2. Who do you bless with your lips but curse in your heart? Is this hypocrisy? What can you most readily change, lips or heart? 3. In what do you trust first: God, yourself, people or money? What do you trust second? Third? 4. What kind of God would you prefer: strong or loving? Does it help you to know God is both? 5. How does it feel to know you will be rewarded according to what you have done (see Ro 2:6–8; 2Co 5:10; Mt 16:27)? To what hope do you hold?

1. Describe the object, person or activity you were most devoted to as a teenager. How has your obsession or first love changed since then? 2. When your mind starts to wander from what you're doing, where does it go? What do your daydreams zero in on? 3. *Read aloud*—All: 1; Reader(s) A: 2–6; Reader(s) B: 7–11.

1. Why is David in the desert (see 2Sa 15:13–14, 23–25)? What dangers wait there (vv. 1,6–7,10)? 2. What memories keep David going (vv. 2–5)? What is better than life? How can David devote himself to the love of God at a time and place like this? 3. What does it mean to "swear by God's name" (v. 11)?

1. What "desert" have you been through recently? What did you long for the most? Did you find it? 2. Which verse of this psalm best fits your relationship with God? How might you deepen your first love with God? 3. Are you a clinger in relationships? How tight is your grasp on God? 4. St. John Chrysostom advised reading this psalm daily. Try it for the next week and share any impact.

⁶He alone is my rock and my salvation;
    he is my fortress, I will not be shaken.
⁷My salvation and my honor depend on God[a];
    he is my mighty rock, my refuge.
⁸Trust in him at all times, O people;
    pour out your hearts to him,
    for God is our refuge.   *Selah*

⁹Lowborn men are but a breath,
    the highborn are but a lie;
if weighed on a balance, they are nothing;
    together they are only a breath.
¹⁰Do not trust in extortion
    or take pride in stolen goods;
though your riches increase,
    do not set your heart on them.

¹¹One thing God has spoken,
    two things have I heard:
that you, O God, are strong,
¹²   and that you, O Lord, are loving.
Surely you will reward each person
    according to what he has done.

Psalm 63

A psalm of David. When he was in the
Desert of Judah.

¹O God, you are my God,
    earnestly I seek you;
my soul thirsts for you,
    my body longs for you,
in a dry and weary land
    where there is no water.

²I have seen you in the sanctuary
    and beheld your power and your glory.
³Because your love is better than life,
    my lips will glorify you.
⁴I will praise you as long as I live,
    and in your name I will lift up my hands.
⁵My soul will be satisfied as with the richest of
        foods;
    with singing lips my mouth will praise you.

⁶On my bed I remember you;
    I think of you through the watches of the night.
⁷Because you are my help,
    I sing in the shadow of your wings.
⁸My soul clings to you;
    your right hand upholds me.

⁹They who seek my life will be destroyed;
    they will go down to the depths of the earth.
¹⁰They will be given over to the sword
    and become food for jackals.

¹¹But the king will rejoice in God;
    all who swear by God's name will praise him,
    while the mouths of liars will be silenced.

a7 Or / *God Most High is my salvation and my honor*

Psalm 64

For the director of music. A psalm of David.

¹Hear me, O God, as I voice my complaint;
 protect my life from the threat of the enemy.
²Hide me from the conspiracy of the wicked,
 from that noisy crowd of evildoers.

³They sharpen their tongues like swords
 and aim their words like deadly arrows.
⁴They shoot from ambush at the innocent man;
 they shoot at him suddenly, without fear.

⁵They encourage each other in evil plans,
 they talk about hiding their snares;
 they say, "Who will see them*ᵃ*?"
⁶They plot injustice and say,
 "We have devised a perfect plan!"
 Surely the mind and heart of man are cunning.

⁷But God will shoot them with arrows;
 suddenly they will be struck down.
⁸He will turn their own tongues against them
 and bring them to ruin;
 all who see them will shake their heads in
 scorn.

⁹All mankind will fear;
 they will proclaim the works of God
 and ponder what he has done.
¹⁰Let the righteous rejoice in the LORD
 and take refuge in him;
 let all the upright in heart praise him!

Psalm 65

For the director of music. A psalm of David.
A song.

¹Praise awaits*ᵇ* you, O God, in Zion;
 to you our vows will be fulfilled.
²O you who hear prayer,
 to you all men will come.
³When we were overwhelmed by sins,
 you forgave*ᶜ* our transgressions.
⁴Blessed are those you choose
 and bring near to live in your courts!
We are filled with the good things of your house,
 of your holy temple.

⁵You answer us with awesome deeds of
 righteousness,
 O God our Savior,
the hope of all the ends of the earth
 and of the farthest seas,
⁶who formed the mountains by your power,
 having armed yourself with strength,
⁷who stilled the roaring of the seas,
 the roaring of their waves,

1. What is your biggest complaint about work or school? With whom are you most free to share? 2. *Read aloud*—Leader: 1–2; Reader(s) A: 3–6; Reader(s) B: 7–8; All: 9–10.

1. While Psalm 63 focused almost exclusively on God, what does this one focus on? 2. What are the weapons and tactics of David's opponents (vv. 2–6)? Are people really as bad as he makes them out here? Do you know anyone this wicked? 3. How will God judge evil (vv. 7–8)? What will others think (vv. 8–9)? Does this happen, then or now?

1. Do you feel ambushed? Threatened? How so? Does anyone think of you as "the enemy"? 2. Have you seen evil turn back on those who planned it? 3. What is most important to you about God's judgment: (a) Its certainty? (b) Swiftness? (c) "Tit-for-tat" fairness? (d) It foils the cleverest of plans? 4. Which is more sinful: thoughts or actions? Why do you think so?

1. Which season brings out the best in you? Why? 2. What would you want on the menu of your last meal? 3. *Read aloud*— Reader(s) A: 1–13, odd; Reader(s) B: 2–12, even.

1. List the verbs associated with God in this psalm. Which describe God as Creator? As Redeemer? As Provider? 2. Which verses support the possible origins of the psalm: (a) Harvest festival? (b) Spring celebration of first fruits? (c) National deliverance from draught or famine? (d) God's forgiveness? 3. How did the Israelites see their God, Yahweh, as different than other tribal or national gods (vv. 5–8)? In what sense is God the "hope of all the ends of the earth"? 4. If this psalm was first written after an abundant harvest, what did such plenty signify to David (v. 3)?

1. What aspect of God is most exciting to you today: Creator? Provider? Redeemer? What does it mean to you that God not only forgives your sin but brings

---

ᵃ5 Or *us*   *ᵇ1* Or *befits*; the meaning of the Hebrew for this word is uncertain.
ᶜ3 Or *made atonement for*

you near to "live in his courts" (vv. 3–4)? **2.** David expressed God's provision in terms of a harvest: How would you re-write verses 9–13 to praise God's provision for you? **3.** How would you explain these verses to a people living in drought or famine? Why doesn't God provide for them? What can the group do to help them?

1. What feelings does a noisy child stir up within you: Irritation? Attention? Affection? **2.** Have you ever been in prison, either as a resident or visitor? What was it like? **3.** *Read aloud*—All: 1–4; Reader(s) A: 5–12; Reader(s) B: 13–20.

1. Who does the psalmist call to worship (vv. 1,4)? What types of things can mankind "come and see" (v. 5)? **2.** On what event does he reflect (vv. 6–7)? What does it reveal about God? In what ways have Jews and Christians memorialized it? **3.** What tests did the people go through (vv. 10–12)? What is the purpose of "refining"? **4.** What kind of vows did the psalmist make (vv. 13–14)? **5.** Why does the psalmist think God answered his prayers (vv. 18–19)?

1. What could you say God has done for you lately? What about God and his ways of dealing with all people would we learn from your testimony? **2.** Have you ever made a deal with God? Did God do his part? What about your part? **3.** All the earth does not bow to God. What is the point of saying so (v. 4)? What is your vision of a world at peace with God? **4.** Do you feel God is testing you? How? Why? What "abundant place" do you hope for? **5.** What sacrifices should you make this week for the Lord? What would be your equivalent to "bulls and goats"?

and the turmoil of the nations.
⁸Those living far away fear your wonders;
  where morning dawns and evening fades
  you call forth songs of joy.

⁹You care for the land and water it;
  you enrich it abundantly.
 The streams of God are filled with water
  to provide the people with grain,
  for so you have ordained it.ᵃ
¹⁰You drench its furrows
  and level its ridges;
 you soften it with showers
  and bless its crops.
¹¹You crown the year with your bounty,
  and your carts overflow with abundance.
¹²The grasslands of the desert overflow;
  the hills are clothed with gladness.
¹³The meadows are covered with flocks
  and the valleys are mantled with grain;
  they shout for joy and sing.

Psalm 66

For the director of music. A song. A psalm.

¹Shout with joy to God, all the earth!
² Sing the glory of his name;
  make his praise glorious!
³Say to God, "How awesome are your deeds!
  So great is your power
  that your enemies cringe before you.
⁴All the earth bows down to you;
  they sing praise to you,
  they sing praise to your name."   *Selah*

⁵Come and see what God has done,
  how awesome his works in man's behalf!
⁶He turned the sea into dry land,
  they passed through the waters on foot—
  come, let us rejoice in him.
⁷He rules forever by his power,
  his eyes watch the nations—
  let not the rebellious rise up against him.   *Selah*

⁸Praise our God, O peoples,
  let the sound of his praise be heard;
⁹he has preserved our lives
  and kept our feet from slipping.
¹⁰For you, O God, tested us;
  you refined us like silver.
¹¹You brought us into prison
  and laid burdens on our backs.
¹²You let men ride over our heads;
  we went through fire and water,
  but you brought us to a place of abundance.

¹³I will come to your temple with burnt offerings
  and fulfill my vows to you—
¹⁴vows my lips promised and my mouth spoke

ᵃ9 Or *for that is how you prepare the land*

when I was in trouble.
¹⁵I will sacrifice fat animals to you
   and an offering of rams;
I will offer bulls and goats.   *Selah*

¹⁶Come and listen, all you who fear God;
   let me tell you what he has done for me.
¹⁷I cried out to him with my mouth;
   his praise was on my tongue.
¹⁸If I had cherished sin in my heart,
   the Lord would not have listened;
¹⁹but God has surely listened
   and heard my voice in prayer.
²⁰Praise be to God,
   who has not rejected my prayer
   or withheld his love from me!

Psalm 67

For the director of music. With stringed
instruments. A psalm. A song.

¹May God be gracious to us and bless us
   and make his face shine upon us,   *Selah*
²that your ways may be known on earth,
   your salvation among all nations.

³May the peoples praise you, O God;
   may all the peoples praise you.
⁴May the nations be glad and sing for joy,
   for you rule the peoples justly
   and guide the nations of the earth.   *Selah*
⁵May the peoples praise you, O God;
   may all the peoples praise you.

⁶Then the land will yield its harvest,
   and God, our God, will bless us.
⁷God will bless us,
   and all the ends of the earth will fear him.

Psalm 68

For the director of music. Of David. A psalm.
A song.

¹May God arise, may his enemies be scattered;
   may his foes flee before him.
²As smoke is blown away by the wind,
   may you blow them away;
as wax melts before the fire,
   may the wicked perish before God.
³But may the righteous be glad
   and rejoice before God;
   may they be happy and joyful.

⁴Sing to God, sing praise to his name,
   extol him who rides on the clouds^a—
his name is the LORD—
   and rejoice before him.
⁵A father to the fatherless, a defender of widows,

---

^a4 Or / *prepare the way for him who rides through the deserts*

1. Do you recite the Lord's Prayer? What's your favorite line? Do you say "trespasses," "debts" or "sins"? Why? 2. *Read aloud*—Leader: 1–2; Reader(s) A: 3–4; Reader(s) B: 5–6; All: 7.

1. What famous blessing has shaped this psalm (see Nu 6:24–26)? 2. Israel seeks God's blessing (vv. 1–2) for what reasons (vv. 6–7)? 3. What vision of a Messiah is echoed in this psalm (see Isa 66:18–23)? Will all embrace Judaism one day (v. 7)?

What blessings has God brought into your life? For whose benefit? For what wider purpose?

1. In your choice of churches, do you prefer a large congregation for its resources, or a small one for its intimacy? What do you like most about the church you are in now? 2. On a scale of 1–10, how much do you like parades? Do you watch them at street level, or from your living room? Why? 3. *Read aloud*—Reader(s) A: 1–35, odd; Reader(s) B: 2–34, even.

1. This psalm may be based on the return of the Ark to Jerusalem (see 1Ch 15). Why did poets and preachers recount Israel's history at such events? 2. Which phrases in the prelude (vv. 1–6) sing of God as Judge? Creator? Redeemer? Parent? 3. What event is referred to in verse 7? When did the "earth shake" (see Ex 19:16–19)? What miracles occurred in the wilderness (vv. 9–10)? 4. The

periods of Joshua and the Judges are covered in verses 11–14. What kings fled (see Jdg 5:19)? What plunder did the Israelites divide besides silver and gold (see Jdg 5:30)? What happened at Mt Zalmon (see Jdg 9:48–49)? **5.** Israel eventually wanted a king instead of judges. What mountain did David acquire for God's dwelling (vv. 15–16)? Is it high or rugged? Can you think of other times when God chose the unimpressive to show his glory? **6.** What were the "chariots of God" (v. 17; see 2Ki 6:15–17; 7:5–6)? What king "received gifts from men" (v. 18) for God's dwelling (see 1Ki 10)? **7.** What would this rapid review of their redemption by God do for the worshippers as they draw near to Jerusalem with the ark of God? From your reviewing stand (vv. 24–27), what in this parade do you see? Hear? Feel? **8.** What is significant about Zebulun and Naphtali joining the ceremonies (see Isa 9:1; also Mt 4:13–16)? **9.** The psalmist expands his vision from the renegade Galileans to the neighboring pagans (vv. 28–31). What does he want God to do? How big is his vision (vv. 32–34)?

♡ **1.** Give a brief review of your personal salvation history. What was your Egypt? Your Exodus? Desert? Promised land? Kingdom expansion? What evil had to be rooted out of your life? **2.** Who or what are some mighty "mountains of Bashan" that threaten or intimidate you? What does it mean to you that God chooses the "weak and the small" (such as Zion) to confound the strong and accomplish his purpose? **3.** Why do you think God works that way? What will that encourage you to go out and do next week for him? **4.** Paul applies verse 18 to Jesus (see Eph 4:8). How does Christ's ascension demonstrate God's power and care? How do verses 19–20 express what Christ has done for you? **5.** Do you experience an awesome God in your church sanctuary? Is the building inspirational? The people? The ceremony? How does worship affect your mission in life?

is God in his holy dwelling.
⁶God sets the lonely in families,ᵃ
  he leads forth the prisoners with singing;
  but the rebellious live in a sun-scorched land.

⁷When you went out before your people, O God,
  when you marched through the wasteland,
                                              Selah
⁸the earth shook,
  the heavens poured down rain,
before God, the One of Sinai,
  before God, the God of Israel.
⁹You gave abundant showers, O God;
  you refreshed your weary inheritance.
¹⁰Your people settled in it,
  and from your bounty, O God, you provided for
    the poor.

¹¹The Lord announced the word,
  and great was the company of those who
    proclaimed it:
¹²"Kings and armies flee in haste;
  in the camps men divide the plunder.
¹³Even while you sleep among the campfires,ᵇ
  the wings of ⌊my⌋ dove are sheathed with
    silver,
  its feathers with shining gold."
¹⁴When the Almightyᶜ scattered the kings in the
    land,
  it was like snow fallen on Zalmon.

¹⁵The mountains of Bashan are majestic mountains;
  rugged are the mountains of Bashan.
¹⁶Why gaze in envy, O rugged mountains,
  at the mountain where God chooses to reign,
  where the LORD himself will dwell forever?
¹⁷The chariots of God are tens of thousands
  and thousands of thousands;
  the Lord ⌊has come⌋ from Sinai into his
    sanctuary.
¹⁸When you ascended on high,
  you led captives in your train;
  you received gifts from men,
even fromᵈ the rebellious—
  that you,ᵉ O LORD God, might dwell there.

¹⁹Praise be to the Lord, to God our Savior,
  who daily bears our burdens.   *Selah*
²⁰Our God is a God who saves;
  from the Sovereign LORD comes escape from
    death.

²¹Surely God will crush the heads of his enemies,
  the hairy crowns of those who go on in their
    sins.
²²The Lord says, "I will bring them from Bashan;
  I will bring them from the depths of the sea,
²³that you may plunge your feet in the blood of
    your foes,

ᵃ6 Or *the desolate in a homeland*   ᵇ13 Or *saddlebags*   ᶜ14 Hebrew *Shaddai*
ᵈ18 Or *gifts for men, / even*   ᵉ18 Or *they*

while the tongues of your dogs have their
    share."

²⁴Your procession has come into view, O God,
    the procession of my God and King into the
        sanctuary.
²⁵In front are the singers, after them the musicians;
    with them are the maidens playing
        tambourines.
²⁶Praise God in the great congregation;
    praise the LORD in the assembly of Israel.
²⁷There is the little tribe of Benjamin, leading them,
    there the great throng of Judah's princes,
    and there the princes of Zebulun and of
        Naphtali.

²⁸Summon your power, O God[a];
    show us your strength, O God, as you have
        done before.
²⁹Because of your temple at Jerusalem
    kings will bring you gifts.
³⁰Rebuke the beast among the reeds,
    the herd of bulls among the calves of the
        nations.
Humbled, may it bring bars of silver.
Scatter the nations who delight in war.
³¹Envoys will come from Egypt;
    Cush[b] will submit herself to God.

³²Sing to God, O kingdoms of the earth,
    sing praise to the Lord,   *Selah*
³³to him who rides the ancient skies above,
    who thunders with mighty voice.
³⁴Proclaim the power of God,
    whose majesty is over Israel,
    whose power is in the skies.
³⁵You are awesome, O God, in your sanctuary;
    the God of Israel gives power and strength to
        his people.

Praise be to God!

Psalm 69

For the director of music. To ⌊the tune of⌋
"Lilies." Of David.

¹Save me, O God,
    for the waters have come up to my neck.
²I sink in the miry depths,
    where there is no foothold.
I have come into the deep waters;
    the floods engulf me.
³I am worn out calling for help;
    my throat is parched.
My eyes fail,
    looking for my God.
⁴Those who hate me without reason
    outnumber the hairs of my head;

[1. If your life were the subject of a political cartoon, what traits (physical, clothing, mannerisms) would be exaggerated to make sport of you or to make a humorous point? 2. What's your favorite thirst-quencher? Are you thirsty now? Are there any of your favorite thirst-quenchers on hand? 3. *Read aloud*—Reader(s) A: 1–35, odd; Reader(s) B: 2–36, even.]

[1. David has become the butt of jokes in Israel. Why do people hate him (v. 4)? Is David over-stating his innocence or is all the trouble really unjustified (v. 5)? What groups of people opposing David can you identify in verses 4–12? 2. What does David fear might happen to those who look up]

^a*28* Many Hebrew manuscripts, Septuagint and Syriac; most Hebrew manuscripts *Your God has summoned power for you*   ^b*31* That is, the upper Nile region

to him (v. 6)? **3.** Why does David think he is being subjected to such abuse in the media (vv. 7–11)? Who has written a song about him (v. 12)? **4.** "Help!" seems to sum up David's prayer in verses 13–18. Where do flashfloods occur? What must be David's spiritual condition? On what basis does he appeal to God for help? **5.** What does David wish for his enemies (vv. 22–28)? Do such prayers shock you? Why does he feel this way (vv. 19–21)? **6.** Verse 29 serves as a hinge to this psalm: How so? From the context, what must have happened to turn David's curse of men into praise of God? **7.** What does the phrase "captive people" tell us about when this psalm was composed (v. 33)? What does the psalmist hope for the exiles (v. 35)? Without a temple, what sacrifices can the people make (vv. 30–31)? **8.** How might recalling the experiences of David help the people at such a time of exile?

♡ **1.** When you feel up to your neck in hot water, do you keep it to yourself? Do you cry on someone's shoulder? Do you tell everybody in sight? What response do you want from others: (a) Good biblical answers? (b) Advice? (c) "I know how you feel?" (d) No response, just a listening ear? **2.** The New Testament applies three verses in this psalm to Jesus (vv. 4,9,21). In what ways might Jesus have felt like David? Why wouldn't Jesus drink the wine he was offered, knowing it would ease his pain (v. 21; see Mt 27:34,48)? **3.** Jesus never cursed his accusers as David did; instead, Jesus forgave his persecutors from the cross (Lk 23:34) and urged us to do the same (Mt 5:10–12). How are you like David? Like Jesus? **4.** How do people today substitute formal religion ("an ox and bull") for heartfelt gratitude? What tips you off when this is happening to you? What can you do to keep the heart in your worship?

many are my enemies without cause,
    those who seek to destroy me.
I am forced to restore
    what I did not steal.

⁵You know my folly, O God;
    my guilt is not hidden from you.

⁶May those who hope in you
    not be disgraced because of me,
    O Lord, the LORD Almighty;
may those who seek you
    not be put to shame because of me,
    O God of Israel.
⁷For I endure scorn for your sake,
    and shame covers my face.
⁸I am a stranger to my brothers,
    an alien to my own mother's sons;
⁹for zeal for your house consumes me,
    and the insults of those who insult you fall on
      me.
¹⁰When I weep and fast,
    I must endure scorn;
¹¹when I put on sackcloth,
    people make sport of me.
¹²Those who sit at the gate mock me,
    and I am the song of the drunkards.

¹³But I pray to you, O LORD,
    in the time of your favor;
in your great love, O God,
    answer me with your sure salvation.
¹⁴Rescue me from the mire,
    do not let me sink;
deliver me from those who hate me,
    from the deep waters.
¹⁵Do not let the floodwaters engulf me
    or the depths swallow me up
    or the pit close its mouth over me.
¹⁶Answer me, O LORD, out of the goodness of your
      love;
    in your great mercy turn to me.
¹⁷Do not hide your face from your servant;
    answer me quickly, for I am in trouble.
¹⁸Come near and rescue me;
    redeem me because of my foes.

¹⁹You know how I am scorned, disgraced and
      shamed;
    all my enemies are before you.
²⁰Scorn has broken my heart
    and has left me helpless;
I looked for sympathy, but there was none,
    for comforters, but I found none.
²¹They put gall in my food
    and gave me vinegar for my thirst.

²²May the table set before them become a snare;
    may it become retribution andᵃ a trap.
²³May their eyes be darkened so they cannot see,

ᵃ22 Or *snare / and their fellowship become*

and their backs be bent forever.
²⁴Pour out your wrath on them;
   let your fierce anger overtake them.
²⁵May their place be deserted;
   let there be no one to dwell in their tents.
²⁶For they persecute those you wound
   and talk about the pain of those you hurt.
²⁷Charge them with crime upon crime;
   do not let them share in your salvation.
²⁸May they be blotted out of the book of life
   and not be listed with the righteous.

²⁹I am in pain and distress;
   may your salvation, O God, protect me.

³⁰I will praise God's name in song
   and glorify him with thanksgiving.
³¹This will please the LORD more than an ox,
   more than a bull with its horns and hoofs.
³²The poor will see and be glad—
   you who seek God, may your hearts live!
³³The LORD hears the needy
   and does not despise his captive people.

³⁴Let heaven and earth praise him,
   the seas and all that move in them,
³⁵for God will save Zion
   and rebuild the cities of Judah.
Then people will settle there and possess it;
³⁶   the children of his servants will inherit it,
   and those who love his name will dwell there.

Psalm 70

For the director of music. Of David.
A petition.

¹Hasten, O God, to save me;
   O LORD, come quickly to help me.
²May those who seek my life
   be put to shame and confusion;
may all who desire my ruin
   be turned back in disgrace.
³May those who say to me, "Aha! Aha!"
   turn back because of their shame.
⁴But may all who seek you
   rejoice and be glad in you;
may those who love your salvation always say,
   "Let God be exalted!"

⁵Yet I am poor and needy;
   come quickly to me, O God.
You are my help and my deliverer;
   O LORD, do not delay.

Psalm 71

¹In you, O LORD, I have taken refuge;
   let me never be put to shame.
²Rescue me and deliver me in your righteousness;
   turn your ear to me and save me.
³Be my rock of refuge,

1. Are you a poor loser or good one? Under what situations have you recently found out? 2. *Read aloud*—Reader(s) A: 1–3; Reader(s) B: 4–5.

1. This psalm also appears at the end of Psalm 40. Why make it a separate song? 2. David's enemies are poor losers, seeking his ruin and belittling God: How does David counteract them? 3. How can King David see himself as "poor and needy" (v. 5)? Is he a bit of a whiner, or what?

What prayers of yours are marked "rush order"? Why? Is God obliging you? If not, do you yet exalt him, or do you grow impatient, even spiteful?

1. Which would you rather keep and why: (a) The mind of a 20-year-old, while your body ages? (b) The body of a 20-year-old, while your mind ages? 2. What gets better with age? What gets worse? 3. *Read aloud*—All: 1–4;

Reader(s) A: 5–23, odd; Reader(s)
B: 6–24, even.

1. An elder statesman, perhaps David, wrote this psalm.
What was his upbringing like (vv.
5–6,17)? What other circumstances sound similar to David's
life? 2. What does he now fear (vv.
9,18)? Why? How might he be a
"portent" (v. 7), a foreboding sign?
3. What is the center of the psalmist's life (vv. 8,14–16, 22–24)?
How does he hope God will reward
him for this (vv. 13,21)? 4. How can
God "restore" the life of the old
man?

1. What do you fear most
about growing older: (a) Failing health? (b) Failing mind? (c)
Becoming dependent? (d) Death of
family members? (e) Your own
death? 2. Were you raised a Christian, or did you come to faith later
in life? What are the advantages
and disadvantages of either experience? 3. What experience with
God in the past gives you confidence now that he will be with you
in the future? 4. What would you
like to declare to "the next generation"? Why not start this week? 5.
What elderly Christian in your
church can you seek out to learn
from? What would you hope to
learn? 6. From this psalmist's experience and faith, what do you
still need to work on so that others
may learn from you when you are
elderly?

to which I can always go;
give the command to save me,
for you are my rock and my fortress.
⁴Deliver me, O my God, from the hand of the
wicked,
from the grasp of evil and cruel men.

⁵For you have been my hope, O Sovereign LORD,
my confidence since my youth.
⁶From birth I have relied on you;
you brought me forth from my mother's womb.
I will ever praise you.
⁷I have become like a portent to many,
but you are my strong refuge.
⁸My mouth is filled with your praise,
declaring your splendor all day long.

⁹Do not cast me away when I am old;
do not forsake me when my strength is gone.
¹⁰For my enemies speak against me;
those who wait to kill me conspire together.
¹¹They say, "God has forsaken him;
pursue him and seize him,
for no one will rescue him."
¹²Be not far from me, O God;
come quickly, O my God, to help me.
¹³May my accusers perish in shame;
may those who want to harm me
be covered with scorn and disgrace.

¹⁴But as for me, I will always have hope;
I will praise you more and more.
¹⁵My mouth will tell of your righteousness,
of your salvation all day long,
though I know not its measure.
¹⁶I will come and proclaim your mighty acts,
O Sovereign LORD;
I will proclaim your righteousness, yours alone.
¹⁷Since my youth, O God, you have taught me,
and to this day I declare your marvelous deeds.
¹⁸Even when I am old and gray,
do not forsake me, O God,
till I declare your power to the next generation,
your might to all who are to come.

¹⁹Your righteousness reaches to the skies, O God,
you who have done great things.
Who, O God, is like you?
²⁰Though you have made me see troubles, many
and bitter,
you will restore my life again;
from the depths of the earth
you will again bring me up.
²¹You will increase my honor
and comfort me once again.

²²I will praise you with the harp
for your faithfulness, O my God;
I will sing praise to you with the lyre,
O Holy One of Israel.
²³My lips will shout for joy
when I sing praise to you—

I, whom you have redeemed.
²⁴My tongue will tell of your righteous acts
all day long,
for those who wanted to harm me
have been put to shame and confusion.

Psalm 72

Of Solomon.

¹Endow the king with your justice, O God,
the royal son with your righteousness.
²He will[a] judge your people in righteousness,
your afflicted ones with justice.
³The mountains will bring prosperity to the people,
the hills the fruit of righteousness.
⁴He will defend the afflicted among the people
and save the children of the needy;
he will crush the oppressor.

⁵He will endure[b] as long as the sun,
as long as the moon, through all generations.
⁶He will be like rain falling on a mown field,
like showers watering the earth.
⁷In his days the righteous will flourish;
prosperity will abound till the moon is no more.

⁸He will rule from sea to sea
and from the River[c] to the ends of the
earth.[d]
⁹The desert tribes will bow before him
and his enemies will lick the dust.
¹⁰The kings of Tarshish and of distant shores
will bring tribute to him;
the kings of Sheba and Seba
will present him gifts.
¹¹All kings will bow down to him
and all nations will serve him.

¹²For he will deliver the needy who cry out,
the afflicted who have no one to help.
¹³He will take pity on the weak and the needy
and save the needy from death.
¹⁴He will rescue them from oppression and
violence,
for precious is their blood in his sight.

¹⁵Long may he live!
May gold from Sheba be given him.
May people ever pray for him
and bless him all day long.
¹⁶Let grain abound throughout the land;
on the tops of the hills may it sway.
Let its fruit flourish like Lebanon;
let it thrive like the grass of the field.
¹⁷May his name endure forever;
may it continue as long as the sun.

1. To get your vote, what one characteristic must a candidate for the highest office in the land exhibit? What second trait? Third? **2.** Do you like your national anthem? With what lines do you agree or disagree most strongly? **3.** *Read aloud*—Leader: 1–4; Reader(s) A: 5–11; Reader(s) B: 12–17; All: 18–19.

1. This psalm is dedicated to Solomon. To what other king does it allude (see Isa 9:6–7; Zec 9:9–10)? **2.** What three qualities will the king bring his people (vv. 1–4)? What should he do about oppression? Why aren't middle or upper classes mentioned? **3.** How long will he rule (vv. 5–7)? Over what boundaries (v. 8)? How will the nations respond (vv. 9–11)? Since no Israelite king ever ruled such vast territory, what is the author saying in this royal extravagance? **4.** How does verse 17 relate to Abraham (see Ge 12:3)? To Christ?

1. This psalm is regarded in Jewish and Christian tradition as "messianic." Given only this psalm to work with, how would you explain the Messiah to someone else? Can you see why Jews from Jesus' time to the present fail to see it fulfilled in Jesus? How does it fit your view of Jesus? **2.** How do you feel about nationalism? Who rules you? Why have human government? Does God approve of all world leaders and their actions? **3.** Could you honestly say that God is your ruler? If not, who is? If so, what about your life reveals God's rule? What does it mean to have God as King of your life?

ᵃ2 Or *May he*; similarly in verses 3-11 and 17   ᵇ5 Septuagint; Hebrew *You will be feared*   ᶜ8 That is, the Euphrates   ᵈ8 Or *the end of the land*

All nations will be blessed through him,
and they will call him blessed.

[18]Praise be to the LORD God, the God of Israel,
who alone does marvelous deeds.
[19]Praise be to his glorious name forever;
may the whole earth be filled with his glory.
Amen and Amen.

[20]This concludes the prayers of David son of Jesse.

BOOK III
Psalms 73–89

Psalm 73

A psalm of Asaph.

[1]Surely God is good to Israel,
to those who are pure in heart.

[2]But as for me, my feet had almost slipped;
I had nearly lost my foothold.
[3]For I envied the arrogant
when I saw the prosperity of the wicked.

[4]They have no struggles;
their bodies are healthy and strong.[a]
[5]They are free from the burdens common to man;
they are not plagued by human ills.
[6]Therefore pride is their necklace;
they clothe themselves with violence.
[7]From their callous hearts comes iniquity[b];
the evil conceits of their minds know no limits.
[8]They scoff, and speak with malice;
in their arrogance they threaten oppression.
[9]Their mouths lay claim to heaven,
and their tongues take possession of the earth.
[10]Therefore their people turn to them
and drink up waters in abundance.[c]
[11]They say, "How can God know?
Does the Most High have knowledge?"

[12]This is what the wicked are like—
always carefree, they increase in wealth.

[13]Surely in vain have I kept my heart pure;
in vain have I washed my hands in innocence.
[14]All day long I have been plagued;
I have been punished every morning.

[15]If I had said, "I will speak thus,"
I would have betrayed your children.
[16]When I tried to understand all this,
it was oppressive to me
[17]till I entered the sanctuary of God;
then I understood their final destiny.

[18]Surely you place them on slippery ground;

---

1. If you had to choose between being (a) prosperous and wicked, or (b) poverty-stricken and pure in heart, what would you be? Why? 2. *Read aloud*—Reader(s) A: 1–27, odd; Reader(s) B: 2–28, even.

1. Asaph is credited with Psalms 50 and 73–83. He was most likely a poet associated with the Temple. What is his nagging doubt in this psalm (vv. 2–3)? 2. What has he seen (vv. 4–12)? What attitudes may be undermining his faith? 3. Do you think Asaph is objective in what he sees? Why or why not? What does he find both attractive and negative in the lifestyle, world-view and agnosticism of the rich? 4. What was he hoping his "pure heart" would get him (vv. 13–14)? What causes him to change his mind (vv. 15–17)? To what might the "sanctuary of God" refer? What new insight does he gain? Why does Asaph feel like God sleeps (v. 20; see 35:23; 44:23)? 5. What "glory" does Asaph have in mind (vv. 24–25; see 16:9–11)? What path will he take toward it (vv. 23–28)? 6. What constant hope literally surrounds Asaph's envy and despair (vv. 1,28)?

1. Imagine your life now is just a dream (or a nightmare), and when you awake, all will return to normal. What heavy burden, human ill or gross injustice would you like to wish away, as if it were but a dream? Do you ever share Asaph's envy? Does his insight satisfy you? Why or why not? 2. Name some rich and famous people who have committed suicide, gone through a string of unhappy marriages or lost fortunes to drugs and alcohol? What comes first: the problems or the money? What problems does money create? If you were suddenly rich and famous, would you be free of these problems? 3. When your feet have stumbled in this area, how have

---

a4 With a different word division of the Hebrew; Masoretic Text *struggles at their death;*
/ their bodies are healthy   b7 Syriac (see also Septuagint); Hebrew *Their eyes bulge
with fat*   c10 The meaning of the Hebrew for this verse is uncertain.

you cast them down to ruin.
¹⁹How suddenly are they destroyed,
    completely swept away by terrors!
²⁰As a dream when one awakes,
    so when you arise, O Lord,
    you will despise them as fantasies.

²¹When my heart was grieved
    and my spirit embittered,
²²I was senseless and ignorant;
    I was a brute beast before you.

²³Yet I am always with you;
    you hold me by my right hand.
²⁴You guide me with your counsel,
    and afterward you will take me into glory.
²⁵Whom have I in heaven but you?
    And earth has nothing I desire besides you.
²⁶My flesh and my heart may fail,
    but God is the strength of my heart
    and my portion forever.

²⁷Those who are far from you will perish;
    you destroy all who are unfaithful to you.
²⁸But as for me, it is good to be near God.
    I have made the Sovereign Lord my refuge;
    I will tell of all your deeds.

Psalm 74

A *maskil*[a] of Asaph.

¹Why have you rejected us forever, O God?
    Why does your anger smolder against the sheep
        of your pasture?
²Remember the people you purchased of old,
    the tribe of your inheritance, whom you
        redeemed—
    Mount Zion, where you dwelt.
³Turn your steps toward these everlasting ruins,
    all this destruction the enemy has brought on
        the sanctuary.

⁴Your foes roared in the place where you met with
        us;
    they set up their standards as signs.
⁵They behaved like men wielding axes
    to cut through a thicket of trees.
⁶They smashed all the carved paneling
    with their axes and hatchets.
⁷They burned your sanctuary to the ground;
    they defiled the dwelling place of your Name.
⁸They said in their hearts, "We will crush them
        completely!"
    They burned every place where God was
        worshiped in the land.
⁹We are given no miraculous signs;
    no prophets are left,
    and none of us knows how long this will be.

[a] Title: Probably a literary or musical term

you recovered your balance? Can the group help? **4.** Have you had a "sanctuary" experience? When? Where? What happened? What are you doing to keep that faith perspective alive? **5.** How would you explain to a child why God does not knock down bullies and trouble-makers at school?

1. How is it appropriate to use your hands at your church: (a) Praying? (b) Greeting? (c) Raised in worship? (d) Asking "why" with raised hands? **2.** Would you say you are a "summer" or "winter" person? In what way? What does the group think? **3.** *Read aloud*—Reader(s) A: 1–23, odd; Reader(s) B: 2–22, even.

1. Where in history must we place this psalm (vv. 3,7)? What crisis of faith does Jerusalem's destruction bring (vv. 1–2)? **2.** Why is this so perplexing to the "sheep of God's pasture"? What had the prophets said (v. 9; see Jer 6:6–8)? What "sign" proved them right (see 2Ki 25:1–21)? **3.** Why does the destruction of Jerusalem bring mockery to God (v. 10)? What do the people want God to do? **4.** Which verse serves as the "watershed" verse, on either side of which flow the two major streams of thought in this psalm? **5.** What event in Israel's history does the psalmist cite as evidence for his case (vv. 13–15)? What event in world history (vv. 16–17)? If God is so powerful, why doesn't he save the people from their enemies? **6.** To what does the psalmist appeal in the end? What does he think God cares about (vv. 19–21)?

What "clamor" does he think God
will want to silence (vv. 18,22–23)?

1. On which side of the "watershed" are you: Focused on
the "they" who ruined life for you?
Or the "you" who can do something
about it? 2. Have you ever felt like
God had forgotten you or your
cause forever? What triggered your
tears? Your anger? Or do you keep
all such emotion inside? 3. Can
you be yourself with the group?
With God? What would God do in
your situation now if you freely expressed your feelings? What is
God likely to do if you're not honest? 4. What event in your lifetime
caused a crisis in faith? Did you
have any warning? What about
God was called into question? Is
the problem resolved? Could it
ever be? Can the group help?

1. Which best describes you:
Stiff neck? Rubber neck?
Long neck? Stick your neck out?
No neck? 2. Read aloud—All: 1;
Reader(s) A: 2–5; Reader(s) B:
6–8; All: 9–10.

1. What is the mood of this
psalm: Triumphant? Desperate? Impatient? Other? 2. When
will the proud and defiant get their
due (vv. 2–5)? Why not now? How
bad does it have to get before God
acts? What purpose of God could
possibly be served by waiting any
longer? 3. Why does verse 6 leave
out the "mountains" or "north"?
Who was located to the north (see
2Ki 19:32–36)? 4. For what does
the psalmist praise God (v. 9)?

10How long will the enemy mock you, O God?
　　Will the foe revile your name forever?
11Why do you hold back your hand, your right
　　hand?
　　Take it from the folds of your garment and
　　destroy them!

12But you, O God, are my king from of old;
　　you bring salvation upon the earth.
13It was you who split open the sea by your power;
　　you broke the heads of the monster in the
　　waters.
14It was you who crushed the heads of Leviathan
　　and gave him as food to the creatures of the
　　desert.
15It was you who opened up springs and streams;
　　you dried up the ever flowing rivers.
16The day is yours, and yours also the night;
　　you established the sun and moon.
17It was you who set all the boundaries of the
　　earth;
　　you made both summer and winter.

18Remember how the enemy has mocked you,
　　O LORD,
　　how foolish people have reviled your name.
19Do not hand over the life of your dove to wild
　　beasts;
　　do not forget the lives of your afflicted people
　　forever.
20Have regard for your covenant,
　　because haunts of violence fill the dark places
　　of the land.
21Do not let the oppressed retreat in disgrace;
　　may the poor and needy praise your name.

22Rise up, O God, and defend your cause;
　　remember how fools mock you all day long.
23Do not ignore the clamor of your adversaries,
　　the uproar of your enemies, which rises
　　continually.

Psalm 75

For the director of music. To the tune of
"Do Not Destroy." A psalm of Asaph. A song.

1We give thanks to you, O God,
　　we give thanks, for your Name is near;
　　men tell of your wonderful deeds.

2You say, "I choose the appointed time;
　　it is I who judge uprightly.
3When the earth and all its people quake,
　　it is I who hold its pillars firm.　　　　　*Selah*
4To the arrogant I say, 'Boast no more,'
　　and to the wicked, 'Do not lift up your horns.
5Do not lift your horns against heaven;
　　do not speak with outstretched neck.'"

6No one from the east or the west
　　or from the desert can exalt a man.

⁷But it is God who judges:
   He brings one down, he exalts another.
⁸In the hand of the LORD is a cup
   full of foaming wine mixed with spices;
he pours it out, and all the wicked of the earth
   drink it down to its very dregs.

⁹As for me, I will declare this forever;
   I will sing praise to the God of Jacob.
¹⁰I will cut off the horns of all the wicked,
   but the horns of the righteous will be lifted up.

Psalm 76

For the director of music. With stringed
instruments. A psalm of Asaph. A song.

¹In Judah God is known;
   his name is great in Israel.
²His tent is in Salem,
   his dwelling place in Zion.
³There he broke the flashing arrows,
   the shields and the swords, the weapons of
      war.   *Selah*

⁴You are resplendent with light,
   more majestic than mountains rich with game.
⁵Valiant men lie plundered,
   they sleep their last sleep;
not one of the warriors
   can lift his hands.
⁶At your rebuke, O God of Jacob,
   both horse and chariot lie still.
⁷You alone are to be feared.
   Who can stand before you when you are angry?
⁸From heaven you pronounced judgment,
   and the land feared and was quiet—
⁹when you, O God, rose up to judge,
   to save all the afflicted of the land.   *Selah*
¹⁰Surely your wrath against men brings you praise,
   and the survivors of your wrath are
      restrained. [a]

¹¹Make vows to the LORD your God and fulfill them;
   let all the neighboring lands
bring gifts to the One to be feared.
¹²He breaks the spirit of rulers;
   he is feared by the kings of the earth.

Psalm 77

For the director of music. For Jeduthun.
Of Asaph. A psalm.

¹I cried out to God for help;
   I cried out to God to hear me.
²When I was in distress, I sought the Lord;
   at night I stretched out untiring hands
and my soul refused to be comforted.

[a] 10 Or *Surely the wrath of men brings you praise, / and with the remainder of wrath you arm yourself*

1. What has held the world together for you in hard times? Give an example. 2. Does "because I said so" satisfy you? How do you deal with the mysteries of God's relationship to life's events? 3. For what do you praise God today? Wondrous deeds? Upright judgment? Firm hold on the world? Uplifting righteousness? Other?

1. How did your parents show anger: (a) A protruding vein? (b) Invoking your full name? (c) Invoking God's name? (d) Giving a talking to? (e) A spanking? 2. *Read aloud*—Reader(s) A: 1–9, odd; Reader(s) B: 2–10, even; All: 11–12.

1. What local judgment has God just performed (vv. 3–6)? Does verse 5 fit Assyria's retreat (see 2Ki 19:35–36)? 2. What does this show Israel about God (vv. 7–9)? Who does God judge? For what purpose? 3. How does "wrath against men" bring God praise? Who are the "survivors"? 4. What do particular judgments imply of God's wrath to come?

1. Does God prevent wars today? Why or why not? Does God care about those who suffer from invading armies? 2. How well do you know God as an angry Judge: (a) All too well? (b) Casually? (c) Never met on that basis? What does it mean to "fear God"? 3. What vows have you taken? What vow do you want to make to the Lord today? Should it be private or should this group know and hold you to it?

1. What song always seems to bring back memories? Are they pleasant memories of fulfilled promise? Or painful memories of a failed one? 2. *Read aloud*—Reader(s) A: 1–19, odd; Reader(s) B: 2–20, even.

1. What modern titles could describe the psalmist's condition (vv. 1–4)? 2. What question is at the bottom of his despair (vv. 7–9)? What do you think he remembers about God (vv. 3,6)?

What "promise" seems to have failed? **3.** Where do his thoughts wander (vv. 10–12)? What are the "years of the right hand" (see 18:35; 139:10)? How can a meditation on the past help him? How does it answer his questions (vv. 7–9)? **4.** What specific acts of God does the poet recall (vv. 13–20)? What hints can you find of: (a) The Exodus? (b) Moses at Sinai? (c) Seven years of famine? (d) The Flood? (e) Creation? **5.** What is the difference between the remembering in verses 3–6 and verses 11–15? In this renewal of his faith, what new affirmations about God does he make?

♡ **1.** Are you feeling close to God, or do you long for "the good old days"? Could these days someday seem like the "good old days"? How do you keep your relationship with God fresh? **2.** How would you try to comfort someone feeling like Asaph does? Would you point to the past, present or future? **3.** Ritual has always been used in Jewish and Christian worship to "remember" God's acts. What specific events do you recall in a given Sunday service? In church holidays? **4.** What does this poet's experience suggest is the interplay between physical, emotional and spiritual forces in managing stress? **5.** What event in your past do you call to mind in times of trouble? How often do you think of past things? Do you tend to live in the past?

☕ **1.** What were your favorite stories when you were young: Mother Goose? Aesop's Fables? Grimm's Fairy Tales? Home-spun stories? Bible stories? Others? What are the favorite stories for any children you may have (at home, in school, in church)? **2.** Who is the keeper of your family stories and traditions? Do you ever hear of times when your folks or grandparents were young? What warning to future generations is implicit in their oft-repeated stories? **3.** *Read aloud*—Reader(s) A:

³I remembered you, O God, and I groaned;
  I mused, and my spirit grew faint. *Selah*
⁴You kept my eyes from closing;
  I was too troubled to speak.
⁵I thought about the former days,
  the years of long ago;
⁶I remembered my songs in the night.
  My heart mused and my spirit inquired:

⁷"Will the Lord reject forever?
  Will he never show his favor again?
⁸Has his unfailing love vanished forever?
  Has his promise failed for all time?
⁹Has God forgotten to be merciful?
  Has he in anger withheld his compassion?" *Selah*

¹⁰Then I thought, "To this I will appeal:
  the years of the right hand of the Most High."
¹¹I will remember the deeds of the LORD;
  yes, I will remember your miracles of long ago.
¹²I will meditate on all your works
  and consider all your mighty deeds.

¹³Your ways, O God, are holy.
  What god is so great as our God?
¹⁴You are the God who performs miracles;
  you display your power among the peoples.
¹⁵With your mighty arm you redeemed your people,
  the descendants of Jacob and Joseph. *Selah*

¹⁶The waters saw you, O God,
  the waters saw you and writhed;
  the very depths were convulsed.
¹⁷The clouds poured down water,
  the skies resounded with thunder;
  your arrows flashed back and forth.
¹⁸Your thunder was heard in the whirlwind,
  your lightning lit up the world;
  the earth trembled and quaked.
¹⁹Your path led through the sea,
  your way through the mighty waters,
  though your footprints were not seen.

²⁰You led your people like a flock
  by the hand of Moses and Aaron.

Psalm 78

A *maskil*[a] of Asaph.

¹O my people, hear my teaching;
  listen to the words of my mouth.
²I will open my mouth in parables,
  I will utter hidden things, things from of old—
³what we have heard and known,
  what our fathers have told us.
⁴We will not hide them from their children;
  we will tell the next generation
the praiseworthy deeds of the LORD,

[a]Title: Probably a literary or musical term

his power, and the wonders he has done.
⁵He decreed statutes for Jacob
　　and established the law in Israel,
which he commanded our forefathers
　　to teach their children,
⁶so the next generation would know them,
　　even the children yet to be born,
　　and they in turn would tell their children.
⁷Then they would put their trust in God
　　and would not forget his deeds
　　but would keep his commands.
⁸They would not be like their forefathers—
　　a stubborn and rebellious generation,
whose hearts were not loyal to God,
　　whose spirits were not faithful to him.

⁹The men of Ephraim, though armed with bows,
　　turned back on the day of battle;
¹⁰they did not keep God's covenant
　　and refused to live by his law.
¹¹They forgot what he had done,
　　the wonders he had shown them.
¹²He did miracles in the sight of their fathers
　　in the land of Egypt, in the region of Zoan.
¹³He divided the sea and led them through;
　　he made the water stand firm like a wall.
¹⁴He guided them with the cloud by day
　　and with light from the fire all night.
¹⁵He split the rocks in the desert
　　and gave them water as abundant as the seas;
¹⁶he brought streams out of a rocky crag
　　and made water flow down like rivers.

¹⁷But they continued to sin against him,
　　rebelling in the desert against the Most High.
¹⁸They willfully put God to the test
　　by demanding the food they craved.
¹⁹They spoke against God, saying,
　　"Can God spread a table in the desert?
²⁰When he struck the rock, water gushed out,
　　and streams flowed abundantly.
But can he also give us food?
　　Can he supply meat for his people?"
²¹When the LORD heard them, he was very angry;
　　his fire broke out against Jacob,
　　and his wrath rose against Israel,
²²for they did not believe in God
　　or trust in his deliverance.
²³Yet he gave a command to the skies above
　　and opened the doors of the heavens;
²⁴he rained down manna for the people to eat,
　　he gave them the grain of heaven.
²⁵Men ate the bread of angels;
　　he sent them all the food they could eat.
²⁶He let loose the east wind from the heavens
　　and led forth the south wind by his power.
²⁷He rained meat down on them like dust,
　　flying birds like sand on the seashore.
²⁸He made them come down inside their camp,
　　all around their tents.

1–71, odd; Reader(s) B: 2–72, even.

📖 **1.** People in Biblical times did not have universal access to scripture. What took the place of history books, schools and seminaries (vv. 1–8)? What does this believer want future believers to know and not forget about God? What would happen if the next generation forgets? Whose responsibility is it to see that they remember (see also Dt 6:6–9)? **2.** Who are the men of Ephraim (vv. 9–11; see Jer 31:5–6)? Who does Ephraim come to symbolize as the list of sins grows (vv. 8–11)? How could anyone forget such acts of God? What difference should these miracles of the past make in their present lives? **3.** What test do they put to God (vv. 18–20)? What test does God put to them (see Ex 16:16–20)? Why do they demand further proofs of God's covenant love? What moods does God alternate between (vv. 21–24,30–31)? Why does God save them only to kill them (see Nu 11:33–34)? What limits to divine patience do you see here? **4.** How would you characterize the role Israel relegated to God (vv. 32–39)? What name would you give to the "game" Israel plays with God: (a) The spirit is willing, the flesh is weak? (b) Flattery will get you anywhere? (c) Lip service only? (d) Insincerity? (e) Let's buy some time? (f) Good start, but no follow through? (g) All head, no heart? **5.** Why does God have mercy on humans (vv. 38–39)? Is it fair for God to expect more from "a passing breeze"? **6.** What is Israel urged to remember (vv. 40–55)? What plagues of Egypt underscore the psalmist's point? **7.** What events from the times of Joshua and Samuel are recalled (vv. 54–66)? Why does the psalmist say the Lord "abandoned the tabernacle of Shiloh" (v. 60; see 1Sa 4:1–11)? How did God put the Philistines "to everlasting shame" (v. 66; see 1Sa 5:6–10)? **8.** In the psalmist's mind, why did God have the Temple built in Judah (vv. 67–69)? Since the Temple was built by Solomon, why does the psalmist sing the praises of David? **9.** What is Asaph's message to Ephraim? To Judah? Will his generation avoid the mistakes of the past? **10.** What portion of this long poem is devoted to: (a) The sins of the people? (b) God's judgment? (c) God's forgiveness?

1. Does this psalm leave you hanging? How did the New Testament writers pick up where Asaph left off (see Mt 2:6; Jn 10:1–18; Rev 7:17)? 2. How do you feel about God's involvement in the staging of your own continuing story: (a) God has written every chapter? (b) God is seen between the lines only? (c) God is the audience? (d) God is the director? (e) God is hogging center stage? 3. Would you like your part or God's part in that script to be re-written? What ending would you prefer? Does the group play a part in it? 4. What lesson would you like to pass along to the next generation? What historical example would you use to make your point? Optional: Try writing another stanza to Psalm 78 for all children to read and heed. 5. Since all people as a group create the environment in which children grow up, should parents be solely responsible for their nurturing? How can you take a more active role in helping the children in your neighborhood? In your church? 6. Why doesn't God perform the same miraculous deeds as in Bible times? Is God sleeping? What deeds could you point to as evidence to the young that God is "awake"? 7. When does your patience run out? When do you feel like "abandoning your people"? How do you resolve the problem of your people going "the wrong way": (a) Let the people go? (b) Increase the consequences? (c) Withdraw your blessing? (d) Keep forgiving? (e) Begin again? (f) No good resolution yet? 8. What story of God's past dealings with you can you "remember" in times of temptation, forgetfulness and doubt you still face?

²⁹They ate till they had more than enough,
    for he had given them what they craved.
³⁰But before they turned from the food they craved,
    even while it was still in their mouths,
³¹God's anger rose against them;
    he put to death the sturdiest among them,
    cutting down the young men of Israel.

³²In spite of all this, they kept on sinning;
    in spite of his wonders, they did not believe.
³³So he ended their days in futility
    and their years in terror.
³⁴Whenever God slew them, they would seek him;
    they eagerly turned to him again.
³⁵They remembered that God was their Rock,
    that God Most High was their Redeemer.
³⁶But then they would flatter him with their
        mouths,
    lying to him with their tongues;
³⁷their hearts were not loyal to him,
    they were not faithful to his covenant.
³⁸Yet he was merciful;
    he forgave their iniquities
    and did not destroy them.
    Time after time he restrained his anger
    and did not stir up his full wrath.
³⁹He remembered that they were but flesh,
    a passing breeze that does not return.

⁴⁰How often they rebelled against him in the desert
    and grieved him in the wasteland!
⁴¹Again and again they put God to the test;
    they vexed the Holy One of Israel.
⁴²They did not remember his power—
    the day he redeemed them from the oppressor,
⁴³the day he displayed his miraculous signs in
        Egypt,
    his wonders in the region of Zoan.
⁴⁴He turned their rivers to blood;
    they could not drink from their streams.
⁴⁵He sent swarms of flies that devoured them,
    and frogs that devastated them.
⁴⁶He gave their crops to the grasshopper,
    their produce to the locust.
⁴⁷He destroyed their vines with hail
    and their sycamore-figs with sleet.
⁴⁸He gave over their cattle to the hail,
    their livestock to bolts of lightning.
⁴⁹He unleashed against them his hot anger,
    his wrath, indignation and hostility—
    a band of destroying angels.
⁵⁰He prepared a path for his anger;
    he did not spare them from death
    but gave them over to the plague.
⁵¹He struck down all the firstborn of Egypt,
    the firstfruits of manhood in the tents of Ham.
⁵²But he brought his people out like a flock;
    he led them like sheep through the desert.
⁵³He guided them safely, so they were unafraid;
    but the sea engulfed their enemies.

⁵⁴Thus he brought them to the border of his holy
    land,
  to the hill country his right hand had taken.
⁵⁵He drove out nations before them
  and allotted their lands to them as an
      inheritance;
  he settled the tribes of Israel in their homes.

⁵⁶But they put God to the test
  and rebelled against the Most High;
  they did not keep his statutes.
⁵⁷Like their fathers they were disloyal and faithless,
  as unreliable as a faulty bow.
⁵⁸They angered him with their high places;
  they aroused his jealousy with their idols.
⁵⁹When God heard them, he was very angry;
  he rejected Israel completely.
⁶⁰He abandoned the tabernacle of Shiloh,
  the tent he had set up among men.
⁶¹He sent ⌊the ark of⌋ his might into captivity,
  his splendor into the hands of the enemy.
⁶²He gave his people over to the sword;
  he was very angry with his inheritance.
⁶³Fire consumed their young men,
  and their maidens had no wedding songs;
⁶⁴their priests were put to the sword,
  and their widows could not weep.

⁶⁵Then the Lord awoke as from sleep,
  as a man wakes from the stupor of wine.
⁶⁶He beat back his enemies;
  he put them to everlasting shame.
⁶⁷Then he rejected the tents of Joseph,
  he did not choose the tribe of Ephraim;
⁶⁸but he chose the tribe of Judah,
  Mount Zion, which he loved.
⁶⁹He built his sanctuary like the heights,
  like the earth that he established forever.
⁷⁰He chose David his servant
  and took him from the sheep pens;
⁷¹from tending the sheep he brought him
  to be the shepherd of his people Jacob,
  of Israel his inheritance.
⁷²And David shepherded them with integrity of
      heart;
  with skillful hands he led them.

Psalm 79

A psalm of Asaph.

¹O God, the nations have invaded your
      inheritance;
  they have defiled your holy temple,
  they have reduced Jerusalem to rubble.
²They have given the dead bodies of your servants
  as food to the birds of the air,
  the flesh of your saints to the beasts of the
      earth.
³They have poured out blood like water

1. If your house were on fire,
   what one possession would
you save? What would you make
sure got left behind? 2. Before facing a firing squad, what would be
your last request? 3. Read aloud—
Reader(s) A: 1–11, odd; Reader(s)
B: 2–12, even; All: 13.

1. What does this psalm lament (vv. 1–4; see 2Ki
25:8–12)? 2. Did God feel like the
people of Jerusalem had been
"servants" (v. 10; see Jer 5:1–2)?
How did the exile make the God of

the Jews look (v. 4)? **3.** Is the people's plea, "How long, O Lord" an
expression of trust or self-pity
(v. 5)? **4.** What two things do they
ask God to do (vv. 6–8)? Are they
responsible for what has happened
(vv. 8–9)? Who is? **5.** What is an
"avenger of blood" (v. 10; see Nu
35:19–21)? In Israel's view, how
would avenging their blood be in
God's best interest (v. 12)? **6.** How
much space is given to repentance? Praising God? Seeking
vengeance? How would you react
to such prayers if you were God?

1. How would you react if the
events recorded in verses
1–4 were happening in your
church or community? Has distress
ever given your church, family or
friends the opportunity to pull together? **2.** In what ways does the
world ask "Where is your God?"
What answer can you give? Where
can you point to the power of God?
3. Are you asking "How long?" right
now? What makes you impatient?
Can the group step in for you? **4.**
Do you have a responsibility to preserve those "condemned to die"?

---

1. If you were sinking in quick
sand, would you: (a) Pray for
help? (b) Yell at God? (c) Figure
out an escape? (d) Give up? (e)
Look for help? **2.** *Read aloud—*
Reader(s) A: 1–2; All: 3; Reader(s)
B: 4–6; All: 7; Reader(s) A: 8–13;
Reader(s) B: 14–18; All: 19.

1. Why is Joseph mentioned
(v. 1–2; see Gen 46:19–21)?
Who do these names represent?
From what do they need to be
saved (see 2Ki 17:6)? **2.** What
does "make your face shine upon
us" mean (v. 3; see Nu 6:24–26)?
3. What is their affliction? What do
you think is most painful about their
trial of faith (vv. 4–6)? **4.** How do
you read the symbols in the allegory of the vine (vv. 8–16)? Is the
"vine" the northern kingdom? What
does its great size mean? What is
the removal of the walls (see Isa
5:5–6)? The boar (v. 13)? The son

all around Jerusalem,
and there is no one to bury the dead.
⁴We are objects of reproach to our neighbors,
of scorn and derision to those around us.

⁵How long, O Lᴏʀᴅ? Will you be angry forever?
How long will your jealousy burn like fire?
⁶Pour out your wrath on the nations
that do not acknowledge you,
on the kingdoms
that do not call on your name;
⁷for they have devoured Jacob
and destroyed his homeland.
⁸Do not hold against us the sins of the fathers;
may your mercy come quickly to meet us,
for we are in desperate need.

⁹Help us, O God our Savior,
for the glory of your name;
deliver us and forgive our sins
for your name's sake.
¹⁰Why should the nations say,
"Where is their God?"
Before our eyes, make known among the nations
that you avenge the outpoured blood of your
servants.
¹¹May the groans of the prisoners come before you;
by the strength of your arm
preserve those condemned to die.

¹²Pay back into the laps of our neighbors seven
times
the reproach they have hurled at you, O Lord.
¹³Then we your people, the sheep of your pasture,
will praise you forever;
from generation to generation
we will recount your praise.

Psalm 80

For the director of music. To ˎthe tune ofˏ
"The Lilies of the Covenant." Of Asaph.
A psalm.

¹Hear us, O Shepherd of Israel,
you who lead Joseph like a flock;
you who sit enthroned between the cherubim,
shine forth
²   before Ephraim, Benjamin and Manasseh.
Awaken your might;
come and save us.

³Restore us, O God;
make your face shine upon us,
that we may be saved.

⁴O Lᴏʀᴅ God Almighty,
how long will your anger smolder
against the prayers of your people?
⁵You have fed them with the bread of tears;
you have made them drink tears by the bowlful.

⁶You have made us a source of contention to our
    neighbors,
  and our enemies mock us.

⁷Restore us, O God Almighty;
  make your face shine upon us,
  that we may be saved.

⁸You brought a vine out of Egypt;
  you drove out the nations and planted it.
⁹You cleared the ground for it,
  and it took root and filled the land.
¹⁰The mountains were covered with its shade,
  the mighty cedars with its branches.
¹¹It sent out its boughs to the Sea,ᵃ
  its shoots as far as the River.ᵇ

¹²Why have you broken down its walls
  so that all who pass by pick its grapes?
¹³Boars from the forest ravage it
  and the creatures of the field feed on it.
¹⁴Return to us, O God Almighty!
  Look down from heaven and see!
  Watch over this vine,
¹⁵ the root your right hand has planted,
  the sonᶜ you have raised up for yourself.

¹⁶Your vine is cut down, it is burned with fire;
  at your rebuke your people perish.
¹⁷Let your hand rest on the man at your right hand,
  the son of man you have raised up for yourself.
¹⁸Then we will not turn away from you;
  revive us, and we will call on your name.

¹⁹Restore us, O LORD God Almighty;
  make your face shine upon us,
  that we may be saved.

Psalm 81

For the director of music. According to
    *gittith.*ᵈ Of Asaph.

¹Sing for joy to God our strength;
  shout aloud to the God of Jacob!
²Begin the music, strike the tambourine,
  play the melodious harp and lyre.

³Sound the ram's horn at the New Moon,
  and when the moon is full, on the day of our
    Feast;
⁴this is a decree for Israel,
  an ordinance of the God of Jacob.
⁵He established it as a statute for Joseph
  when he went out against Egypt,
  where we heard a language we did not
    understand.ᵉ

⁶He says, "I removed the burden from their
    shoulders;
  their hands were set free from the basket.

(v. 15)? **5.** How is the change in the refrain significant (v. 14)? Is this psalm saying that only God can close the distance the people feel? **6.** Who is the "son of man" mentioned in verse 17: (a) The nation of Israel (see Ex 4:22)? (b) The king of the returning exiles? (c) A future Davidic king? What three images in this psalm did Jesus apply to himself (see Jn 10:11; 15:1; 17:1)?

1. What do you do in times of trouble and need: (a) Pray for God's restoration? (b) Turn to other people? (c) Go it on your own? (d) Retreat in frustration? Does God want you to respond differently? **2.** What is your "bowl of tears"? Is there any relief in sight? How can you keep from being overwhelmed? Can the group help? **3.** Can you talk when you're angry? How do you work through conflicts when you are angry at someone? Do you let anger out or hide it inside? Do you prefer to act like nothing happened?

1. What food or drink would really "hit the spot" after the group meeting? Will you have to go out for it? **2.** How do you feel about going to the dentist: Fear? Jaw clenches? Mouth quivers? You're glad someone is taking care of you? **3.** *Read aloud*—Reader(s) A: 1–11, odd; Reader(s) B: 2–12, even; All: 13–16.

1. What festival begins after the first full moon of the Jewish New Year (vv. 1–3; see Lev 23:34–36)? What is the purpose of the celebration (see Lev 23:42–43)? **2.** From what "basket" are the people free (v. 6)? What test did God give them at Meribah (v. 7; see Nu 20:1–13)? **3.** Does God's mood fit the party spirit (vv. 8–12)? What does God want the people to do? How should reliving the past for seven days help get the message through? **4.** How else would Israel benefit by listening to the Lord (vv. 13–16)? What is

---

ᵃ*11* Probably the Mediterranean   ᵇ*11* That is, the Euphrates   ᶜ*15* Or *branch*
ᵈTitle: Probably a musical term   ᵉ*5* Or */ and we heard a voice we had not known*

"honey from the rock" (v. 16; see Dt 32:13–14)?

1. What excites you about your relationship with God? Have you experienced the freedom and spontaneity expressed in this psalm? If so, how? If not, why not? 2. Does your church have festivals that commemorate or even act out events of the past? What such festivals are coming up? What truths is God trying to teach in them? 3. Has God ever lifted a burden from your shoulders? What was it? What happened? Are you carrying a burden now? 4. Are you stubborn? Is it a good quality or does it trap you in "your own devices"? How do stubbornness and persistence differ?

1. What trial is making the news right now? Is the accused guilty as far as you can tell? 2. Read aloud—Reader(s) A: 1–4; Reader(s) B: 5–7; All: 8.

1. Who are the "gods" (v. 1)? Angels and devils (see 1Ki 22:19; Job 1:6)? Rulers and judges in Israel (see Ex 21:6, 22:8–9,28)? 2. Of what does God accuse them (vv. 2–4)? Why is God so concerned about those with the least power? 3. Why does God call them "gods" when he thinks so little of them (v. 5)? 4. Why do the "gods" misuse power (vv. 6–7)? What incorrect assumption have they made?

1. How did Jesus use this psalm when he was "on trial" (see Jn 10:30–39)? 2. What responsibility do you have to the weak and needy? Can the group help?

1. What war, past or present, do you follow? Why does it interest you? Why are wars intriguing? 2. Read aloud—Reader(s) A: 1–8; Reader(s) B: 9–17; All: 18.

1. What is Asaph's problem (v. 2–4)? How does he try to interest God in his cause (vv. 2,5)? 2. Why are these enemies so ruthless? What could Israel have done

7In your distress you called and I rescued you,
　I answered you out of a thundercloud;
　I tested you at the waters of Meribah. 　　*Selah*

8"Hear, O my people, and I will warn you—
　if you would but listen to me, O Israel!
9You shall have no foreign god among you;
　you shall not bow down to an alien god.
10I am the LORD your God,
　who brought you up out of Egypt.
　Open wide your mouth and I will fill it.

11"But my people would not listen to me;
　Israel would not submit to me.
12So I gave them over to their stubborn hearts
　to follow their own devices.

13"If my people would but listen to me,
　if Israel would follow my ways,
14how quickly would I subdue their enemies
　and turn my hand against their foes!
15Those who hate the LORD would cringe before him,
　and their punishment would last forever.
16But you would be fed with the finest of wheat;
　with honey from the rock I would satisfy you."

Psalm 82

A psalm of Asaph.

1God presides in the great assembly;
　he gives judgment among the "gods":

2"How long will youᵃ defend the unjust
　and show partiality to the wicked? 　　*Selah*
3Defend the cause of the weak and fatherless;
　maintain the rights of the poor and oppressed.
4Rescue the weak and needy;
　deliver them from the hand of the wicked.

5"They know nothing, they understand nothing.
　They walk about in darkness;
　all the foundations of the earth are shaken.

6"I said, 'You are "gods";
　you are all sons of the Most High.'
7But you will die like mere men;
　you will fall like every other ruler."

8Rise up, O God, judge the earth,
　for all the nations are your inheritance.

Psalm 83

A song. A psalm of Asaph.

1O God, do not keep silent;
　be not quiet, O God, be not still.
2See how your enemies are astir,
　how your foes rear their heads.

ᵃ2 The Hebrew is plural.

³With cunning they conspire against your people;
   they plot against those you cherish.
⁴"Come," they say, "let us destroy them as a
      nation,
   that the name of Israel be remembered no
      more."

⁵With one mind they plot together;
   they form an alliance against you—
⁶the tents of Edom and the Ishmaelites,
   of Moab and the Hagrites,
⁷Gebal,ᵃ Ammon and Amalek,
   Philistia, with the people of Tyre.
⁸Even Assyria has joined them
   to lend strength to the descendants of Lot.
                                         Selah

⁹Do to them as you did to Midian,
   as you did to Sisera and Jabin at the river
      Kishon,
¹⁰who perished at Endor
   and became like refuse on the ground.
¹¹Make their nobles like Oreb and Zeeb,
   all their princes like Zebah and Zalmunna,
¹²who said, "Let us take possession
   of the pasturelands of God."

¹³Make them like tumbleweed, O my God,
   like chaff before the wind.
¹⁴As fire consumes the forest
   or a flame sets the mountains ablaze,
¹⁵so pursue them with your tempest
   and terrify them with your storm.
¹⁶Cover their faces with shame
   so that men will seek your name, O LORD.

¹⁷May they ever be ashamed and dismayed;
   may they perish in disgrace.
¹⁸Let them know that you, whose name is the
      LORD—
   that you alone are the Most High over all the
      earth.

Psalm 84

For the director of music. According to
gittith.ᵇ Of the Sons of Korah. A psalm.

¹How lovely is your dwelling place,
   O LORD Almighty!
²My soul yearns, even faints,
   for the courts of the LORD;
my heart and my flesh cry out
   for the living God.

³Even the sparrow has found a home,
   and the swallow a nest for herself,
   where she may have her young—
a place near your altar,
   O LORD Almighty, my King and my God.

ᵃ7 That is, Byblos   ᵇTitle: Probably a musical term

to make them want to wipe out their memory? **3.** What happened to the Hagrites (v. 6; see 1Ch 5:10)? To Gebal, Philistia and Tyre (v. 7; see Jos 13:1–7)? Who now fuels the wave of revenge (v. 8)? **4.** From what did the Judges protect the people of Israel (vv. 9–12; see Jdg 4:1–7; 7:19–8:21)? Who are these people and why were they punished? **5.** What does the psalmist want God to do to enemies present (vv. 9–18)? How does this cry for vengeance sit with Jesus' belief about loving enemies?

1. Are you generally quiet or talkative? When do you go against your norm: speaking out for once or finally shutting up? How do you feel about periods of silence in conversations? **2.** When have you wanted God to be more "talkative" in your life? How do you communicate your desire to God to "break the silence"? **3.** Who are your opponents in the "game of life" right now? Your church's? Are your enemies also God's? Do you pray for vengeance or the grace to love your enemy?

1. Do you like "roughing it"? Backpacks and tents? Or do you prefer hotels and bathrooms? **2.** With whom do you feel "at home"? Why? What do you like to do to make someone feel "at home" with you? **3.** *Read aloud—* Reader(s) A: 1–11, odd; Reader(s) B: 2–12, even.

1. Who were the sons of Korah, to whom this psalm is attributed (see 1Ch 26:1–19)? With what are they enamored (vv. 1–2)? **2.** Why does the psalmist mention birds in verse 3? Why do the Korahites love their job (v. 4)? **3.** Verses 5–7 describe one of the three annual pilgrimages to the Jerusalem Temple. Which one might meet with "autumn rains" (see Lev

23:39–43)? **4.** "Baca" is Hebrew for "balsam tree" and also comes from the root "to weep." What happened to David in this valley (see 2Sa 5:22–25)? What image does the poet give you of the pilgrims (vv. 6–7)? **5.** What do they pray in the Temple (vv. 8–9)? Who is the "shield" or "anointed one"? **6.** What could be so good about being in the Temple courts (vv. 10–12)? What keeps it from getting repetitious? **7.** Whose walk is "blameless" (v. 11)?

1. What makes worship either dull or exciting for you? **2.** Why did God command three pilgrimages a year for the Jews? Why couldn't they thank God in their hometowns? What is the difference between private and corporate worship? **3.** Are you more of a "settler" or a "pilgrim"? Why? What does insecurity do to you? How does this Psalm make you feel about God's role in your life choices?

---

1. Relatives excepted, who gave you your first kiss? Was it what you expected? Did you try again? **2.** *Read aloud*—Leader: 1–3; Reader(s) A: 4–7; Reader(s) B: 8–13.

1. Which verses are about the past? The present? The future? What are the restored fortunes of Jacob (v. 1)? **2.** How is the present going? What tension do verses 1–3 and 4–7 create? How would you explain the word "revive" in verse 6? **3.** What do verses 4–7 give as the cause of God's anger? What is a sign of revival, both personal and corporate (v. 6)? **4.** What is dangerous about a crisis of faith (v. 8)? What does it mean for God's glory to dwell in the land (v. 9; see Eze 11:22–24)? **5.** What truth is expressed in verses 10–12? What is God's part of the deal? What is the people's? **6.** What's the meaning of verse 13? How might this be a messianic promise?

1. How can "believing backward" help you "believe forward"? **2.** Are you disappointed that something didn't turn out the way you hoped it would? How might this psalm help you? **3.** What are some "national laments" of today? Does God show favor to certain nations? Why or why not? How

[4]Blessed are those who dwell in your house;
    they are ever praising you.   *Selah*

[5]Blessed are those whose strength is in you,
    who have set their hearts on pilgrimage.
[6]As they pass through the Valley of Baca,
    they make it a place of springs;
    the autumn rains also cover it with pools.[a]
[7]They go from strength to strength,
    till each appears before God in Zion.

[8]Hear my prayer, O LORD God Almighty;
    listen to me, O God of Jacob.   *Selah*
[9]Look upon our shield,[b] O God;
    look with favor on your anointed one.

[10]Better is one day in your courts
    than a thousand elsewhere;
I would rather be a doorkeeper in the house of
    my God
    than dwell in the tents of the wicked.
[11]For the LORD God is a sun and shield;
    the LORD bestows favor and honor;
no good thing does he withhold
    from those whose walk is blameless.

[12]O LORD Almighty,
    blessed is the man who trusts in you.

Psalm 85

For the director of music. Of the Sons of
Korah. A psalm.

[1]You showed favor to your land, O LORD;
    you restored the fortunes of Jacob.
[2]You forgave the iniquity of your people
    and covered all their sins.   *Selah*
[3]You set aside all your wrath
    and turned from your fierce anger.

[4]Restore us again, O God our Savior,
    and put away your displeasure toward us.
[5]Will you be angry with us forever?
    Will you prolong your anger through all
    generations?
[6]Will you not revive us again,
    that your people may rejoice in you?
[7]Show us your unfailing love, O LORD,
    and grant us your salvation.

[8]I will listen to what God the LORD will say;
    he promises peace to his people, his saints—
    but let them not return to folly.
[9]Surely his salvation is near those who fear him,
    that his glory may dwell in our land.

[10]Love and faithfulness meet together;
    righteousness and peace kiss each other.
[11]Faithfulness springs forth from the earth,
    and righteousness looks down from heaven.

---

[a]6 Or *blessings*   [b]9 Or *sovereign*

¹²The LORD will indeed give what is good,
  and our land will yield its harvest.
¹³Righteousness goes before him
  and prepares the way for his steps.

Psalm 86

A prayer of David.

¹Hear, O LORD, and answer me,
  for I am poor and needy.
²Guard my life, for I am devoted to you.
  You are my God; save your servant
  who trusts in you.
³Have mercy on me, O Lord,
  for I call to you all day long.
⁴Bring joy to your servant,
  for to you, O Lord,
  I lift up my soul.

⁵You are forgiving and good, O Lord,
  abounding in love to all who call to you.
⁶Hear my prayer, O LORD;
  listen to my cry for mercy.
⁷In the day of my trouble I will call to you,
  for you will answer me.

⁸Among the gods there is none like you, O Lord;
  no deeds can compare with yours.
⁹All the nations you have made
  will come and worship before you, O Lord;
  they will bring glory to your name.
¹⁰For you are great and do marvelous deeds;
  you alone are God.

¹¹Teach me your way, O LORD,
  and I will walk in your truth;
  give me an undivided heart,
  that I may fear your name.
¹²I will praise you, O Lord my God, with all my
    heart;
  I will glorify your name forever.
¹³For great is your love toward me;
  you have delivered me from the depths of the
    grave.ᵃ

¹⁴The arrogant are attacking me, O God;
  a band of ruthless men seeks my life—
  men without regard for you.
¹⁵But you, O Lord, are a compassionate and gracious
    God,
  slow to anger, abounding in love and
    faithfulness.
¹⁶Turn to me and have mercy on me;
  grant your strength to your servant
  and save the son of your maidservant.ᵇ
¹⁷Give me a sign of your goodness,

can we express our corporate laments? **4.** What pattern of faith unfolds in this psalm? In your life? **5.** What does it mean to let God's glory dwell in your life?

---

1. What "sign of goodness" do you look forward to receiving from your parents that lets you know you are special? **2.** Did you ever need a lifeguard? Ever wish you could be one? Any lifeguards you'd like to meet in a non-life-threatening situation? **3.** *Read aloud*—Reader(s) A: 1–7; All: 8–10; Reader(s) B: 11–17.

1. What four reasons does David give for God to answer him (vv. 1–4)? Is he boasting in his own piety? Why or why not? Which reason do you think would be most convincing to God? **2.** What fifth reason does he give (v. 7)? Does he sound confident or wishful? **3.** What do verses 8–10 affirm about God? On what basis does David say all nations will worship Yahweh? Has this ever been the case? **4.** Why is David now moved to make promises to God (vv. 11–13)? What does he pledge? What is an undivided heart? What feeling underlies his praise (v. 13)? **5.** Why is he still bothered (v. 14)? What kind of "sign" is he asking for (v. 17)?

1. Does God answer all of your prayers? What would you say is the biggest reason God should answer them? **2.** On a scale of 1 to 10, how do you rate on self-esteem: "I am a worm" (1) to "I am God's gift to the world" (10)? How would you complete the phrase, "I am ..."? How would you rate the attitude in this psalm? **3.** Can God's character really be separated from God's action? What action does not reflect character? What character trait exists but is not embodied in action? **4.** How is God the Lord of modern day affairs? Of your life? What personal demands does God's lordship make on you? **5.** Do you have an undivided heart? What divides it? How many "pieces" of heart do you carry inside? What can restore your internal unity?

ᵃ13 Hebrew *Sheol*   ᵇ16 Or *save your faithful son*

that my enemies may see it and be put to
shame,
for you, O LORD, have helped me and comforted
me.

Psalm 87

Of the Sons of Korah. A psalm. A song.

¹He has set his foundation on the holy mountain;
²   the LORD loves the gates of Zion
more than all the dwellings of Jacob.
³Glorious things are said of you,
O city of God: Selah
⁴"I will record Rahab*a* and Babylon
among those who acknowledge me—
Philistia too, and Tyre, along with Cush*b*—
and will say, 'This*c* one was born in Zion.'"

⁵Indeed, of Zion it will be said,
"This one and that one were born in her,
and the Most High himself will establish her."
⁶The LORD will write in the register of the peoples:
"This one was born in Zion."   Selah
⁷As they make music they will sing,
"All my fountains are in you."

Psalm 88

A song. A psalm of the Sons of Korah. For the
director of music. According to *mahalath
leannoth.* *d* A *maskil*e* of Heman the
Ezrahite.

¹O LORD, the God who saves me,
day and night I cry out before you.
²May my prayer come before you;
turn your ear to my cry.

³For my soul is full of trouble
and my life draws near the grave.*f*
⁴I am counted among those who go down to the
pit;
I am like a man without strength.
⁵I am set apart with the dead,
like the slain who lie in the grave,
whom you remember no more,
who are cut off from your care.

⁶You have put me in the lowest pit,
in the darkest depths.
⁷Your wrath lies heavily upon me;
you have overwhelmed me with all your waves.
Selah
⁸You have taken from me my closest friends
and have made me repulsive to them.

1. How do you feel about that part of the country or world where you were born? 2. *Read aloud*—Reader(s) A: 1–4; Reader(s) B: 5–7.

1. Why is Jerusalem the center of the world for the psalmist (vv. 1–2)? 2. What future does he see for Israel's former enemies (vv. 3–4)? Will Jews and Gentiles be treated differently (vv. 5–6)? 3. How would this idea strike nationalists?

Even Jesus sometimes overlooked pagans in his thinking (see Mt 15:21–28). How inclusive or exclusive do you think God's kingdom is? Who will be left out?

1. Can you think of a movie that made you cry? Was it sad or happy? Were you glad to be in a dark theatre? 2. Did you ever "ditch" a friend? How did you feel about playing the game? How does it feel to be the "ditchee"? 3. *Read aloud*—Reader(s) A: 1–11, odd; Reader(s) B: 2–12, even.

1. With what glimmer of hope does the sick and discouraged psalmist begin (vv. 1–2)? 2. What hints do we have that the psalmist, Heman, has leprosy (vv. 5–9,15)? How has illness affected his spirits? Has God been very comforting? How might his experiences in prayer be the source of his deepest frustration? Why? 3. What kind of place is Sheol? What is Heman's argument in verses 10–12? What does he want God to do? 4. Who does he blame for his afflictions (vv. 6–9)? Why does he think God is angry with him? 5. How does the psalmist experience God (vv. 13–14)? 6. On what note does the psalm end? Has there been any development or growth? Why or why not?

1. Is it possible for devoted believers to be in perpetual trouble? Depressed? Feel forsaken? 2. Do you fear or suffer from illness? Do you see God as a heal-

---

a4 A poetic name for Egypt   *b4* That is, the upper Nile region   *c4* Or *"O Rahab and Babylon, / Philistia, Tyre and Cush, / I will record concerning those who acknowledge me: / 'This*   *d*Title: Possibly a tune, "The Suffering of Affliction"
*e*Title: Probably a literary or musical term   *f3* Hebrew *Sheol*

I am confined and cannot escape;
9 my eyes are dim with grief.

I call to you, O LORD, every day;
   I spread out my hands to you.
10Do you show your wonders to the dead?
   Do those who are dead rise up and praise you?
                         Selah

11Is your love declared in the grave,
   your faithfulness in Destruction*a*?
12Are your wonders known in the place of darkness,
   or your righteous deeds in the land of oblivion?

13But I cry to you for help, O LORD;
   in the morning my prayer comes before you.
14Why, O LORD, do you reject me
   and hide your face from me?

15From my youth I have been afflicted and close to
     death;
   I have suffered your terrors and am in despair.
16Your wrath has swept over me;
   your terrors have destroyed me.
17All day long they surround me like a flood;
   they have completely engulfed me.
18You have taken my companions and loved ones
     from me;
   the darkness is my closest friend.

Psalm 89

A *maskil*b of Ethan the Ezrahite.

1I will sing of the LORD's great love forever;
   with my mouth I will make your faithfulness
     known through all generations.
2I will declare that your love stands firm forever,
   that you established your faithfulness in heaven
     itself.
3You said, "I have made a covenant with my
     chosen one,
   I have sworn to David my servant,
4'I will establish your line forever
   and make your throne firm through all
     generations.'"   *Selah*

5The heavens praise your wonders, O LORD,
   your faithfulness too, in the assembly of the
     holy ones.
6For who in the skies above can compare with the
     LORD?
   Who is like the LORD among the heavenly
     beings?
7In the council of the holy ones God is greatly
     feared;
   he is more awesome than all who surround
     him.
8O LORD God Almighty, who is like you?

er? Why are some healed and others not? Of what would you like to be healed? **3.** Have you ever been treated like a "leper"? Have you treated someone like that? Who are the lepers in your life? Society? Church? Family? What can you do to help them? As a group? **4.** Why do you suppose this psalm is in the Psalter? What good are unanswered questions about suffering? Can comfort be found here? **5.** Can a Christian be both a committed realist and optimist? Which do you tend to be? Do you feel the need to grow in one area? What steps can you take?

1. Have you ever been forced to break an important promise? How was it taken by the "promisee"? **2.** What part of yourself was most mature in your early teenage years: body, soul or spirit? **3.** *Read aloud*—Reader(s) A: 1–29; Reader(s) B: 30–51; All: 52.

1. How does Ethan define love in this psalm (vv. 1–2)? To what covenant is he referring (vv. 3–4; see 2Sa 7:8–17)? **2.** Why do you think Ethan launches into a lengthy hymn to the Creator at this point (vv. 5–18)? Who are "the holy ones" (see Da 4:13; Job 15:15–16)? What is the connection between God's faithfulness and might? **3.** Are verses 9–13 about creation? What battle is hinted at (v. 10)? Do you think "Rahab" refers to the mythical sea monster or Egypt (see 87:4; Job 7:12)? **4.** The psalmist's God has power to create and defend. What other power does Yahweh wield (vv. 14–16)? How is the Jewish God different from the pagan gods (see Ex 34:6–7)? **5.** To what theme does the psalmist finally return (vv. 19–29)? To whom did God speak in a vision (v. 19; see 2Sa 7:16–17)? What promises were made to David? How did he respond (v. 26)? What position would Israel hold among the peoples of

a 11 Hebrew *Abaddon*   bTitle: Probably a literary or musical term

the world (v. 27)? **6.** What conditions were on the agreement (vv. 30–31)? How could God be "faithful" and still reserve the right to correct the erring king? What is the psalmist thinking has happened (v. 38)? **7.** What event has shattered the psalmist's faith (vv. 40–45)? What are the neighboring people saying (v. 50)? Has the covenant really been broken? What would a modern Jew conclude from this psalm, knowing that the Davidic line disappeared thousands of years ago? **8.** Does the closing of Book III fit with this psalm (v. 52)?

1. Does God seem to keep promises with you or have you felt misled or confused? What situation of life has called God's promises into question? **2.** When you experience setbacks what is your first reaction: (a) Become overwhelmed by feelings? (b) Focus on the problem? (c) Affirm God's control? What is the psalmist's approach? **3.** Do you see God at work in the adversities you face now? Do you feel free to go to God in the "hard times" or do you think you have to "be at your best"? How do you keep yourself hidden from God? **4.** What has God created in your life? What battles has God won for you? Your church? Your group? **5.** Does God's faithfulness excite you? Why or why not? Do you make the Lord's faithfulness known "through all generations"? What do you want others to know? How can you become a more effective witness? **6.** How did the early Christians feel God solved the problem of the lost Davidic line (see Rev 1:5)? How is God's covenant to Israel alive in the church today? **7.** Have you ever felt that God didn't come through on a promise? What happened? To what divine quality would you appeal to guarantee God keeps his promise? **8.** What does this psalm say about our ability to resolve contradictions by ourselves? How does this keep us "hanging on" in crisis?

You are mighty, O LORD, and your faithfulness
　　surrounds you.

⁹You rule over the surging sea;
　　when its waves mount up, you still them.
¹⁰You crushed Rahab like one of the slain;
　　with your strong arm you scattered your
　　　enemies.
¹¹The heavens are yours, and yours also the earth;
　　you founded the world and all that is in it.
¹²You created the north and the south;
　　Tabor and Hermon sing for joy at your name.
¹³Your arm is endued with power;
　　your hand is strong, your right hand exalted.

¹⁴Righteousness and justice are the foundation of
　　　your throne;
　　love and faithfulness go before you.
¹⁵Blessed are those who have learned to acclaim
　　you,
　　who walk in the light of your presence, O LORD.
¹⁶They rejoice in your name all day long;
　　they exult in your righteousness.
¹⁷For you are their glory and strength,
　　and by your favor you exalt our horn.ᵃ
¹⁸Indeed, our shieldᵇ belongs to the LORD,
　　our king to the Holy One of Israel.

¹⁹Once you spoke in a vision,
　　to your faithful people you said:
"I have bestowed strength on a warrior;
　　I have exalted a young man from among the
　　　people.
²⁰I have found David my servant;
　　with my sacred oil I have anointed him.
²¹My hand will sustain him;
　　surely my arm will strengthen him.
²²No enemy will subject him to tribute;
　　no wicked man will oppress him.
²³I will crush his foes before him
　　and strike down his adversaries.
²⁴My faithful love will be with him,
　　and through my name his hornᶜ will be
　　　exalted.
²⁵I will set his hand over the sea,
　　his right hand over the rivers.
²⁶He will call out to me, 'You are my Father,
　　my God, the Rock my Savior.'
²⁷I will also appoint him my firstborn,
　　the most exalted of the kings of the earth.
²⁸I will maintain my love to him forever,
　　and my covenant with him will never fail.
²⁹I will establish his line forever,
　　his throne as long as the heavens endure.

³⁰"If his sons forsake my law
　　and do not follow my statutes,

ᵃ17 *Horn* here symbolizes strong one.　　ᵇ18 Or *sovereign*　　ᶜ24 *Horn* here symbolizes strength.

³¹if they violate my decrees
    and fail to keep my commands,
³²I will punish their sin with the rod,
    their iniquity with flogging;
³³but I will not take my love from him,
    nor will I ever betray my faithfulness.
³⁴I will not violate my covenant
    or alter what my lips have uttered.
³⁵Once for all, I have sworn by my holiness—
    and I will not lie to David—
³⁶that his line will continue forever
    and his throne endure before me like the sun;
³⁷it will be established forever like the moon,
    the faithful witness in the sky."   *Selah*

³⁸But you have rejected, you have spurned,
    you have been very angry with your anointed
        one.
³⁹You have renounced the covenant with your
        servant
    and have defiled his crown in the dust.
⁴⁰You have broken through all his walls
    and reduced his strongholds to ruins.
⁴¹All who pass by have plundered him;
    he has become the scorn of his neighbors.
⁴²You have exalted the right hand of his foes;
    you have made all his enemies rejoice.
⁴³You have turned back the edge of his sword
    and have not supported him in battle.
⁴⁴You have put an end to his splendor
    and cast his throne to the ground.
⁴⁵You have cut short the days of his youth;
    you have covered him with a mantle of shame.   *Selah*

⁴⁶How long, O Lord? Will you hide yourself forever?
    How long will your wrath burn like fire?
⁴⁷Remember how fleeting is my life.
    For what futility you have created all men!
⁴⁸What man can live and not see death,
    or save himself from the power of the grave^a?   *Selah*
⁴⁹O Lord, where is your former great love,
    which in your faithfulness you swore to David?
⁵⁰Remember, Lord, how your servant has^b been
        mocked,
    how I bear in my heart the taunts of all the
        nations,
⁵¹the taunts with which your enemies have
        mocked, O Lord,
    with which they have mocked every step of
        your anointed one.

⁵²Praise be to the Lord forever!
    Amen and Amen.

a48 Hebrew *Sheol*   *b50* Or *your servants have*

BOOK IV

Psalms 90–106

Psalm 90

A prayer of Moses the man of God.

¹Lord, you have been our dwelling place
　throughout all generations.
²Before the mountains were born
　or you brought forth the earth and the world,
　from everlasting to everlasting you are God.

³You turn men back to dust,
　saying, "Return to dust, O sons of men."
⁴For a thousand years in your sight
　are like a day that has just gone by,
　or like a watch in the night.
⁵You sweep men away in the sleep of death;
　they are like the new grass of the morning—
⁶though in the morning it springs up new,
　by evening it is dry and withered.

⁷We are consumed by your anger
　and terrified by your indignation.
⁸You have set our iniquities before you,
　our secret sins in the light of your presence.
⁹All our days pass away under your wrath;
　we finish our years with a moan.
¹⁰The length of our days is seventy years—
　or eighty, if we have the strength;
　yet their span^a is but trouble and sorrow,
　for they quickly pass, and we fly away.

¹¹Who knows the power of your anger?
　For your wrath is as great as the fear that is
　　due you.
¹²Teach us to number our days aright,
　that we may gain a heart of wisdom.

¹³Relent, O LORD! How long will it be?
　Have compassion on your servants.
¹⁴Satisfy us in the morning with your unfailing love,
　that we may sing for joy and be glad all our
　　days.
¹⁵Make us glad for as many days as you have
　　afflicted us,
　for as many years as we have seen trouble.
¹⁶May your deeds be shown to your servants,
　your splendor to their children.

¹⁷May the favor^b of the Lord our God rest upon
　　us;
　establish the work of our hands for us—
　yes, establish the work of our hands.

Psalm 91

¹He who dwells in the shelter of the Most High
　will rest in the shadow of the Almighty.^{c}

---

1. What is your earliest memory? Why do you think this incident has stuck in your mind? **2.** Who do you consider a wise person? Who do you think is just a "wise guy"? What's the difference? **3.** *Read aloud*—Reader(s) A: 1–8; Reader(s) B: 9–16; All: 17.

1. At what point in his life do you think Moses wrote this psalm? What country did he consider home (v. 1)? **2.** How do God and humans differ (vv. 3–6)? **3.** Life is short. What else is wrong with it (vv. 7–9)? What picture of God comes in verse 7? Why is humanity full of "trouble and sorrow"? **4.** Why is God so angry (v. 11)? How should Moses feel, being barred from the Promised Land (see Dt 32:50–52; Nu 20:6–13)? Do you think his mood would be different if he knew of the resurrection and afterlife? **5.** What does it mean to "number our days aright"? **6.** What different requests are made of God (vv. 13–17)? Does the final request remove the futility? What gives ultimate purpose to our endeavors?

1. What do you think is the biggest difference between God and people? What difference is hardest to understand? Hardest to accept? **2.** Would you call this psalm pessimistic? Realistic? Encouraging? Why? Do you consider life something God has "afflicted" you with? **3.** Are you "teachable"? When are you most able to receive instruction? When are you most resistant? **4.** How do you "number your days": (a) One day at a time? (b) Make each one count? (c) On a scale of 1 to 10? (d) With a clock and calendar? (e) Lost count?

1. How do you feel when someone gives you a hug? What kind of "hugger" are you: (a) "Bear hugger"? (b) "Three-light-pats-on-the-back" hugger? (c) Non-hugger? **2.** What does the word

---

a 10 Or *yet the best of them*　　b 17 Or *beauty*　　c 1 Hebrew *Shaddai*

2I will say[a] of the LORD, "He is my refuge and my
        fortress,
    my God, in whom I trust."

3Surely he will save you from the fowler's snare
        and from the deadly pestilence.
4He will cover you with his feathers,
        and under his wings you will find refuge;
    his faithfulness will be your shield and rampart.
5You will not fear the terror of night,
        nor the arrow that flies by day,
6nor the pestilence that stalks in the darkness,
        nor the plague that destroys at midday.
7A thousand may fall at your side,
        ten thousand at your right hand,
    but it will not come near you.
8You will only observe with your eyes
        and see the punishment of the wicked.

9If you make the Most High your dwelling—
        even the LORD, who is my refuge—
10then no harm will befall you,
        no disaster will come near your tent.
11For he will command his angels concerning you
        to guard you in all your ways;
12they will lift you up in their hands,
        so that you will not strike your foot against a
            stone.
13You will tread upon the lion and the cobra;
        you will trample the great lion and the serpent.

14"Because he loves me," says the LORD, "I will
        rescue him;
    I will protect him, for he acknowledges my
        name.
15He will call upon me, and I will answer him;
        I will be with him in trouble,
    I will deliver him and honor him.
16With long life will I satisfy him
        and show him my salvation."

Psalm 92

A psalm. A song. For the Sabbath day.

1It is good to praise the LORD
        and make music to your name, O Most High,
2to proclaim your love in the morning
        and your faithfulness at night,
3to the music of the ten-stringed lyre
        and the melody of the harp.

4For you make me glad by your deeds, O LORD;
        I sing for joy at the works of your hands.
5How great are your works, O LORD,
        how profound your thoughts!
6The senseless man does not know,
        fools do not understand,
7that though the wicked spring up like grass

a2 Or He says

"shelter" bring to mind? What person, place, thing or institution is shelter for you? 3. *Read aloud—* Reader(s) A: 1–15, odd; Reader(s) B: 2–16, even.

1. What four names of God does the psalmist use (vv. 1–2)? What other names can you think of? 2. What types of disasters are discussed (vv. 3–8)? What image of God do you prefer: (a) Mother hen? (b) Shield? (c) Fortress? (d) Immune system? (e) Force field? 3. What is the "terror of the night" (v. 5)? 4. Is God's protection available to everyone (vv. 9–10)? Who does all the work (v. 11)? How do they show motherly care (v. 12)? 5. Is God's favor shown by spiritual blessing or material (vv. 14–16)?

1. If God promises such perfect protection, why does evil befall believers? Didn't it befall Jesus? The Apostles? The early church? Why does this psalm follow Moses' "we finish our years with a moan" (see Ps 90)? 2. What does it mean to make God your refuge? 3. Think about all the potential for harm in your life. Could angels be guarding you? Can you think of an instance when you were miraculously delivered or protected "against all odds"? What did you learn from this? 4. Is God calling you to take some risks? How can you avail yourself of God's protection?

1. What's your idea of an ideal Sunday? When's the last time it happened? 2. What is your favorite movie "good guy"? Your favorite "bad guy"? Who do you like to see triumph? Why? 3. *Read aloud—*Reader(s) A: 1–7; All: 8; Reader(s) B: 9–15.

1. What kind of day does the psalmist have on a sabbath (vv. 1–3)? Since he cannot work, what "work" becomes the focus (vv. 4–5)? 2. Although he praises God's deeds, what does he find most profound? What thought do fools fail to grasp (vv. 6–7)? Are they victims of low I.Q., or are they responsible for their ignorance (see Pr 1:7)? Why could we say God's greatest deed is justice? 3. How does the psalmist express faith in

the future (vv. 8–9)? How has the Lord blessed him (v. 10)? **4.** What promises are made to the "righteous" (vv. 12–14)? What does it mean to be "planted in the house of the Lord"?

1. Which of God's deeds brings you joy? How do you express spiritual joy? **2.** Do Sundays help you grow spiritually? If so, how? If not, what is lacking for you? **3.** How can you stay "fresh and green" as the years go by? What "fruit" can you bear? **4.** Does the prosperity of the wicked bother you? Do you want what they have? What do you have that they might envy?

Read aloud—Reader(s) A: 1–2; Reader(s) B: 3–4; All: 5.

1. For what, other than creation, does the psalmist praise God (v. 5)? How did the Jewish concept of God differ from neighboring countries? **2.** Is God "mightier than the breakers" through creative or moral power? Why does the psalm end with praise for God's statutes?

1. What is most important to you: might or right? Do you believe because you gain power or because you seek truth? Both? Neither? **2.** Is it sometimes hard to believe that God controls nature and history? What does this belief imply? What might obscure it?

---

1. Were your parents strict or easy-going? How do you feel about the kind and amount of discipline you received as a child? **2.** Are you sure-footed or a bit of a "klutz"? What is the most clumsy thing you've ever done? **3.** Read aloud—Leader: 1–3; Reader(s) A: 4–11; Reader(s) B: 12–23.

1. How would you describe the tone of verses 1–3: (a) Vengeful and bitter? (b) Self-righteous? (c) Pleading? (d) Confident and direct? Why? **2.** What is the psalmist's complaint (v. 3)? What is the sin of the wicked (vv. 4–7)? How do they misuse power? Why

and all evildoers flourish,
　　they will be forever destroyed.

⁸But you, O LORD, are exalted forever.

⁹For surely your enemies, O LORD,
　　surely your enemies will perish;
　　all evildoers will be scattered.
¹⁰You have exalted my horn*ᵃ* like that of a wild
　　　ox;
　　fine oils have been poured upon me.
¹¹My eyes have seen the defeat of my adversaries;
　　my ears have heard the rout of my wicked foes.

¹²The righteous will flourish like a palm tree,
　　they will grow like a cedar of Lebanon;
¹³planted in the house of the LORD,
　　they will flourish in the courts of our God.
¹⁴They will still bear fruit in old age,
　　they will stay fresh and green,
¹⁵proclaiming, "The LORD is upright;
　　he is my Rock, and there is no wickedness in
　　　him."

Psalm 93

¹The LORD reigns, he is robed in majesty;
　　the LORD is robed in majesty
　　and is armed with strength.
The world is firmly established;
　　it cannot be moved.
²Your throne was established long ago;
　　you are from all eternity.

³The seas have lifted up, O LORD,
　　the seas have lifted up their voice;
　　the seas have lifted up their pounding waves.
⁴Mightier than the thunder of the great waters,
　　mightier than the breakers of the sea—
　　the LORD on high is mighty.

⁵Your statutes stand firm;
　　holiness adorns your house
　　for endless days, O LORD.

Psalm 94

¹O LORD, the God who avenges,
　　O God who avenges, shine forth.
²Rise up, O Judge of the earth;
　　pay back to the proud what they deserve.
³How long will the wicked, O LORD,
　　how long will the wicked be jubilant?

⁴They pour out arrogant words;
　　all the evildoers are full of boasting.
⁵They crush your people, O LORD;
　　they oppress your inheritance.
⁶They slay the widow and the alien;
　　they murder the fatherless.

ᵃ10 Horn here symbolizes strength.

[7]They say, "The LORD does not see;
the God of Jacob pays no heed."

[8]Take heed, you senseless ones among the people;
you fools, when will you become wise?
[9]Does he who implanted the ear not hear?
Does he who formed the eye not see?
[10]Does he who disciplines nations not punish?
Does he who teaches man lack knowledge?
[11]The LORD knows the thoughts of man;
he knows that they are futile.

[12]Blessed is the man you discipline, O LORD,
the man you teach from your law;
[13]you grant him relief from days of trouble,
till a pit is dug for the wicked.
[14]For the LORD will not reject his people;
he will never forsake his inheritance.
[15]Judgment will again be founded on righteousness,
and all the upright in heart will follow it.

[16]Who will rise up for me against the wicked?
Who will take a stand for me against evildoers?
[17]Unless the LORD had given me help,
I would soon have dwelt in the silence of
death.
[18]When I said, "My foot is slipping,"
your love, O LORD, supported me.
[19]When anxiety was great within me,
your consolation brought joy to my soul.

[20]Can a corrupt throne be allied with you—
one that brings on misery by its decrees?
[21]They band together against the righteous
and condemn the innocent to death.
[22]But the LORD has become my fortress,
and my God the rock in whom I take refuge.
[23]He will repay them for their sins
and destroy them for their wickedness;
the LORD our God will destroy them.

Psalm 95

[1]Come, let us sing for joy to the LORD;
let us shout aloud to the Rock of our salvation.
[2]Let us come before him with thanksgiving
and extol him with music and song.

[3]For the LORD is the great God,
the great King above all gods.
[4]In his hand are the depths of the earth,
and the mountain peaks belong to him.
[5]The sea is his, for he made it,
and his hands formed the dry land.

[6]Come, let us bow down in worship,
let us kneel before the LORD our Maker;
[7]for he is our God
and we are the people of his pasture,
the flock under his care.

Today, if you hear his voice,

do they oppress the powerless (v. 7)? **3.** What is the psalmist's warning (vv. 8–11)? What is his argument? If God created man, what can we deduce about God? About man? Has the psalmist found an answer for verse 3? **4.** How does the focus change in verse 12? How is God addressed differently? Why? If wickedness goes unpunished, what can the psalmist hope for the righteous (vv. 12–13)? **5.** What kind of "run in" has this writer had with the wicked (vv. 16–21)? Is he poor? Siding with the poor? A victim of politics? What keeps him going? Has he found peace of mind yet?

1. Have you ever continued doing wrong because no punishment or ill consequences seemed to come? How did you become aware of your misdeeds? Should the group help keep you accountable? **2.** What is your feeling about injustice? Why doesn't God just end it? Is it our job or do we wait for God to intervene and "set the record straight"? **3.** When does God seem to come to your rescue: (a) When the wave of trouble is approaching? (b) When your feet get wet? (c) When you're shivering and worn out? (d) When you're just about to drown? How has God rescued you?

1. Complete this sentence: "I belong to the _____ generation." Why give your generation that title? **2.** *Read aloud*—All: 1–2; Reader(s) A: 3–5; All: 6–7; Reader(s) B: 8–11.

1. Why use music to rejoice (vv. 1–2)? What dimension does music add to words? **2.** What does bowing or kneeling represent (v. 6)? **3.** What happened at Meribah and Massah (v. 8; see Ex 17:1–7)? How was God on trial? **4.** What is God's response (vv. 10–11)? What is the meaning of "rest" (see Eze 20:15–16)?

1. What is the New Testament notion of "entering God's rest" (see Heb 4:1–3)? Does your relationship with God feel like rest or is there more work to be done? **2.** Is your heart "hard" to-day? How can it be softened? **3.** How do you live like "your fathers"? Or have you left the beliefs of your parents?

1. What's your favorite new song on the radio? From church? Where else do you hear new material? **2.** When is the last time you changed a long-held opinion of yours? What do you now believe? **3.** *Read aloud*—Reader(s) A: 1–3; All: 4–6; Reader(s) B: 7–9; All: 10–13.

1. Why does this psalm appear in the Book of Chronicles (see 1Ch 16:8–33)? Why do you think one version is longer? **2.** To whom are verses 1–6 directed? Verses 7–10? Verses 11–13? **3.** Why is "new" important (v. 1; see Isa 43:18–19)? What "new thing" is God doing? **4.** What 10 things does the psalmist want the Israelites to include in their worship of God (vv. 1–10)? What does "ascribe" mean (vv. 7–8)? **5.** What's the importance of the international appeal? What is the psalmist's vision of the One to come? Why is that? Why is "for he comes" a cause of joy (v. 13)?

1. What new thing would you like God to do in your life? How do old habits, limitations or people interfere with your singing a new song? How could it start today? **2.** Does it seem to you that God reigns? Why hasn't the just Judge come?

1. If you were "king for a day," how would you speed up justice? **2.** What was the last party you really liked? Who, besides yourself, was the life of the party? **3.** *Read aloud*—Reader(s) A: 1–11, odd; Reader(s) B: 2–12, even.

1. In the psalmist's opinion, how far-reaching is the power of the Lord (v. 1)? Why does he

8   do not harden your hearts as you did at
         Meribah,[a]
      as you did that day at Massah[b] in the desert,
9 where your fathers tested and tried me,
      though they had seen what I did.
10 For forty years I was angry with that generation;
      I said, "They are a people whose hearts go
         astray,
      and they have not known my ways."
11 So I declared on oath in my anger,
      "They shall never enter my rest."

Psalm 96

1 Sing to the LORD a new song;
      sing to the LORD, all the earth.
2 Sing to the LORD, praise his name;
      proclaim his salvation day after day.
3 Declare his glory among the nations,
      his marvelous deeds among all peoples.

4 For great is the LORD and most worthy of praise;
      he is to be feared above all gods.
5 For all the gods of the nations are idols,
      but the LORD made the heavens.
6 Splendor and majesty are before him;
      strength and glory are in his sanctuary.

7 Ascribe to the LORD, O families of nations,
      ascribe to the LORD glory and strength.
8 Ascribe to the LORD the glory due his name;
      bring an offering and come into his courts.
9 Worship the LORD in the splendor of his[c]
         holiness;
      tremble before him, all the earth.

10 Say among the nations, "The LORD reigns."
      The world is firmly established, it cannot be
         moved;
      he will judge the peoples with equity.
11 Let the heavens rejoice, let the earth be glad;
      let the sea resound, and all that is in it;
12   let the fields be jubilant, and everything in
         them.
      Then all the trees of the forest will sing for joy;
13   they will sing before the LORD, for he comes,
      he comes to judge the earth.
      He will judge the world in righteousness
         and the peoples in his truth.

Psalm 97

1 The LORD reigns, let the earth be glad;
      let the distant shores rejoice.

2 Clouds and thick darkness surround him;
      righteousness and justice are the foundation of
         his throne.
3 Fire goes before him

---

[a]8 *Meribah* means *quarreling.*   [b]8 *Massah* means *testing.*   [c]9 Or *LORD with the splendor of*

and consumes his foes on every side.
[4]His lightning lights up the world;
   the earth sees and trembles.
[5]The mountains melt like wax before the LORD,
   before the Lord of all the earth.
[6]The heavens proclaim his righteousness,
   and all the peoples see his glory.

[7]All who worship images are put to shame,
   those who boast in idols—
   worship him, all you gods!

[8]Zion hears and rejoices
   and the villages of Judah are glad
   because of your judgments, O LORD.
[9]For you, O LORD, are the Most High over all the
   earth;
   you are exalted far above all gods.

[10]Let those who love the LORD hate evil,
   for he guards the lives of his faithful ones
   and delivers them from the hand of the wicked.
[11]Light is shed upon the righteous
   and joy on the upright in heart.
[12]Rejoice in the LORD, you who are righteous,
   and praise his holy name.

Psalm 98

A psalm.

[1]Sing to the LORD a new song,
   for he has done marvelous things;
his right hand and his holy arm
   have worked salvation for him.
[2]The LORD has made his salvation known
   and revealed his righteousness to the nations.
[3]He has remembered his love
   and his faithfulness to the house of Israel;
all the ends of the earth have seen
   the salvation of our God.

[4]Shout for joy to the LORD, all the earth,
   burst into jubilant song with music;
[5]make music to the LORD with the harp,
   with the harp and the sound of singing,
[6]with trumpets and the blast of the ram's horn—
   shout for joy before the LORD, the King.

[7]Let the sea resound, and everything in it,
   the world, and all who live in it.
[8]Let the rivers clap their hands,
   let the mountains sing together for joy;
[9]let them sing before the LORD,
   for he comes to judge the earth.
He will judge the world in righteousness
   and the peoples with equity.

Psalm 99

[1]The LORD reigns,
   let the nations tremble;

think the God of the Jews is so powerful (vv. 3–6)? When did God make such fantastic appearances (see 1Ki 8:10–12; Jdg 5:5)? **2.** Why are the Gentiles ashamed at God's appearance (v. 7)? Why does Judah rejoice (vv. 8–9)? **3.** How does one keep on receiving God's blessings (vv. 10–12)? What blessings are promised?

1. Can rejoicing be commanded? Why or why not? **2.** What word pictures describe God's presence in your life? **3.** Which describes you the closest: (a) Hater of evil? (b) Faithful? (c) Righteous? (d) Upright in heart? Which would you like to be?

1. Who is your favorite singer, musician or group? Why? **2.** *Read aloud*—Reader(s) A: 1–3; All: 4–6; Reader(s) B: 7–9.

1. Why should we sing a new song: don't the old ones apply (v. 1)? **2.** What three titles for God could you derive from this psalm (vv. 3,6,9)? **3.** What do "his right hand and his holy arm" say about God's need for assistance (see Ps 44:3)? **4.** How is Israel's salvation an opportunity for the nations (vv. 3,9)? **5.** Can creation praise God, or is this just a poetic metaphor (vv. 7–9; see Lk 19:39–40)?

1. Do you expect God to do new things in your life? Or do you think a lot about how God should change the next person? **2.** Do you ever "cut loose" in joyful expression? Or do you sing your songs to God like a quiet ballad? **3.** You might want to sing some favorite praise songs together. How might homemade instruments join in?

1. If someone called you "holy," would you assume: (a) Your clothes have holes? (b) You come across as pious? (c)

You are a holistic person? (d) You are pure and righteous? (e) Something else? **2.** *Read aloud*—All: 1–3; Reader(s) A: 4–5; Reader(s) B: 6–7; All: 8–9.

1. What does it mean to call God "holy" (v. 3)? Why would this lead someone to worship God? **2.** How is God's holiness expressed in verses 1–3? In verses 4–5? How has God's righteousness been worked out "in Jacob" (v. 4)? **3.** How can a holy God get his "hands dirty" dealing with humans (vv. 6–7)? How did God respond to intercessors (v. 8)? In what way is God more than just a mighty being?

1. How can God forgive and still punish us for our misdeeds? What actions and attitudes deserve punishment? What would it mean to you to love justice more? **2.** "God knows, we're only human." True enough, but does that really excuse us (see Lev 19:2; also Mt 5:48)? How can love for holiness be seen in your life?

---

1. For what are you most thankful? **2.** *Read aloud*—Reader(s) A: 1–2; All: 3; Reader(s) B: 4–5.

1. What six reasons does the psalmist give to praise God? Do these apply to "all the earth" or just to "his people"? **2.** What responsibilities are involved in knowing that the Lord is God (v. 3)? **3.** What attitude characterizes God's people (vv. 4–5)? Why is thanksgiving a public, communal event?

1. Which reason most motivates you to praise God? **2.** Is your expression of joy too limited? Too private? Do you need the freedom to have a more joyful life?

---

1. Name a New Year's resolution you actually made and kept? Why that one? **2.** What do you like to daydream about? **3.** *Read aloud*—Reader(s) A: 1–4; Reader(s) B: 5–8.

he sits enthroned between the cherubim,
   let the earth shake.
[2]Great is the LORD in Zion;
   he is exalted over all the nations.
[3]Let them praise your great and awesome name—
   he is holy.

[4]The King is mighty, he loves justice—
   you have established equity;
in Jacob you have done
   what is just and right.
[5]Exalt the LORD our God
   and worship at his footstool;
   he is holy.

[6]Moses and Aaron were among his priests,
   Samuel was among those who called on his name;
they called on the LORD
   and he answered them.
[7]He spoke to them from the pillar of cloud;
   they kept his statutes and the decrees he gave them.

[8]O LORD our God,
   you answered them;
you were to Israel[a] a forgiving God,
   though you punished their misdeeds.[b]
[9]Exalt the LORD our God
   and worship at his holy mountain,
   for the LORD our God is holy.

Psalm 100

A psalm. For giving thanks.

[1]Shout for joy to the LORD, all the earth.
[2]   Worship the LORD with gladness;
   come before him with joyful songs.
[3]Know that the LORD is God.
   It is he who made us, and we are his[c];
   we are his people, the sheep of his pasture.

[4]Enter his gates with thanksgiving
   and his courts with praise;
   give thanks to him and praise his name.
[5]For the LORD is good and his love endures forever;
   his faithfulness continues through all generations.

Psalm 101

Of David. A psalm.

[1]I will sing of your love and justice;
   to you, O LORD, I will sing praise.
[2]I will be careful to lead a blameless life—
   when will you come to me?

I will walk in my house

a8 Hebrew *them*   *b8* Or / *an avenger of the wrongs done to them*   *c3* Or *and*
not we ourselves

with blameless heart.
³I will set before my eyes
    no vile thing.

The deeds of faithless men I hate;
    they will not cling to me.
⁴Men of perverse heart shall be far from me;
    I will have nothing to do with evil.

⁵Whoever slanders his neighbor in secret,
    him will I put to silence;
whoever has haughty eyes and a proud heart,
    him will I not endure.

⁶My eyes will be on the faithful in the land,
    that they may dwell with me;
he whose walk is blameless
    will minister to me.

⁷No one who practices deceit
    will dwell in my house;
no one who speaks falsely
    will stand in my presence.

⁸Every morning I will put to silence
    all the wicked in the land;
I will cut off every evildoer
    from the city of the LORD.

Psalm 102

A prayer of an afflicted man. When he is faint
and pours out his lament before the LORD.

¹Hear my prayer, O LORD;
    let my cry for help come to you.
²Do not hide your face from me
    when I am in distress.
Turn your ear to me;
    when I call, answer me quickly.

³For my days vanish like smoke;
    my bones burn like glowing embers.
⁴My heart is blighted and withered like grass;
    I forget to eat my food.
⁵Because of my loud groaning
    I am reduced to skin and bones.
⁶I am like a desert owl,
    like an owl among the ruins.
⁷I lie awake; I have become
    like a bird alone on a roof.
⁸All day long my enemies taunt me;
    those who rail against me use my name as a
        curse.
⁹For I eat ashes as my food
    and mingle my drink with tears
¹⁰because of your great wrath,
    for you have taken me up and thrown me aside.
¹¹My days are like the evening shadow;
    I wither away like grass.

¹²But you, O LORD, sit enthroned forever;
    your renown endures through all generations.

---

1. What is David's resolution (v. 2)? Why must he be careful? Are rulers known for their blameless lives? 2. Where does purity of heart begin (v. 3)? Is conscious effort involved? 3. What public standards grow from a blameless heart (vv. 5–7)? What kind of advisors will lose their jobs?

1. How do you feel about the level of ethics in the government of your country? How would you feel if this psalm were adopted as a credo and lived? 2. Where do your ethics need a boost: (a) Talking about others? (b) Looking at others with respect? (c) Speaking less than the truth? 3. What makes an effective leader according to this psalm? How does one earn the right to lead? In what ways are you a leader? What did Jesus have to say about leadership (see Lk 22:24–26)?

---

1. What is your favorite cure for the blues: TV? Sleep? Food? Exercise? Talk? How does it help? 2. What two books (besides the Bible) would you want to pass on to the next generation? 3. Read aloud—Reader(s) A: 1–27, odd; Reader(s) B: 2–28, even.

1. What hint can you find that this psalm was written during the Exile in Babylon (v. 16)? 2. List the psalmist's afflictions (vv. 3–11). What modern diagnoses would you give? What ailments are physical? Psychological? 3. Why does he liken himself to a desert owl (v. 6; see Lev 11:13–18)? What feeling does this and verse 7 underscore? What ails him socially (v. 8)? 4. Who does he think is responsible for the trouble (v. 10)? What is the meaning of "evening shadow" (v. 11; see 109:23)? What is the tone of this section? 5. How does the tone and content change in verses 12–17? Why does he bring up God's immortality? What is his argument? 6. What is his messianic vision for Jerusalem (v. 15)? 7. If this poet has had it so bad, why does he recommend telling future generations about God (v. 18)? Why does he continue his lament in verses 23 and 24? What role has God played in his affliction? 8. How is God different from creation? What promise is reiterated in the closing verse?

1. Would the story of your spiritual life be beneficial to future generations? Or should you be forgotten? Why? 2. Are you afflicted, depressed, alone or distressed in any way? Do you feel free to express it to God? A special friend? The group? Or do you bear it all alone? How can this group help you keep your faith alive? What is your prayer request? 3. Does the group know of someone whose physical suffering has been worsened by the sting of loneliness? By feeling punished by God? What could you do to alleviate that situation?

1. Do you like your job? Why or why not? Would you keep it if you inherited a million dollars? 2. Do you talk to yourself? Why? When is the last time you answered back? 3. *Read aloud*—All: 1–5; Reader(s) A: 6–12; Reader(s) 13–19; All: 20–22.

1. Who does David address in verses 1–5? How has he benefited from God's favor? Why does he say the eagle's youth is renewed (v. 5)? Where is the David who is constantly complaining about disease and death (see 38:2–8)? 2. To where does the focus shift in verses 6–14? What

13You will arise and have compassion on Zion,
    for it is time to show favor to her;
    the appointed time has come.
14For her stones are dear to your servants;
    her very dust moves them to pity.
15The nations will fear the name of the LORD,
    all the kings of the earth will revere your glory.
16For the LORD will rebuild Zion
    and appear in his glory.
17He will respond to the prayer of the destitute;
    he will not despise their plea.

18Let this be written for a future generation,
    that a people not yet created may praise the
      LORD:
19"The LORD looked down from his sanctuary on
      high,
    from heaven he viewed the earth,
20to hear the groans of the prisoners
    and release those condemned to death."
21So the name of the LORD will be declared in Zion
    and his praise in Jerusalem
22when the peoples and the kingdoms
    assemble to worship the LORD.

23In the course of my life[a] he broke my strength;
    he cut short my days.
24So I said:
    "Do not take me away, O my God, in the midst
      of my days;
    your years go on through all generations.
25In the beginning you laid the foundations of the
      earth,
    and the heavens are the work of your hands.
26They will perish, but you remain;
    they will all wear out like a garment.
Like clothing you will change them
    and they will be discarded.
27But you remain the same,
    and your years will never end.
28The children of your servants will live in your
      presence;
    their descendants will be established before
      you."

Psalm 103

Of David.

1Praise the LORD, O my soul;
    all my inmost being, praise his holy name.
2Praise the LORD, O my soul,
    and forget not all his benefits—
3who forgives all your sins
    and heals all your diseases,
4who redeems your life from the pit
    and crowns you with love and compassion,
5who satisfies your desires with good things
    so that your youth is renewed like the eagle's.

a23 Or *By his power*

⁶The LORD works righteousness
and justice for all the oppressed.

⁷He made known his ways to Moses,
his deeds to the people of Israel:
⁸The LORD is compassionate and gracious,
slow to anger, abounding in love.
⁹He will not always accuse,
nor will he harbor his anger forever;
¹⁰he does not treat us as our sins deserve
or repay us according to our iniquities.
¹¹For as high as the heavens are above the earth,
so great is his love for those who fear him;
¹²as far as the east is from the west,
so far has he removed our transgressions from
us.
¹³As a father has compassion on his children,
so the LORD has compassion on those who fear
him;
¹⁴for he knows how we are formed,
he remembers that we are dust.
¹⁵As for man, his days are like grass,
he flourishes like a flower of the field;
¹⁶the wind blows over it and it is gone,
and its place remembers it no more.
¹⁷But from everlasting to everlasting
the LORD's love is with those who fear him,
and his righteousness with their children's
children—
¹⁸with those who keep his covenant
and remember to obey his precepts.

¹⁹The LORD has established his throne in heaven,
and his kingdom rules over all.

²⁰Praise the LORD, you his angels,
you mighty ones who do his bidding,
who obey his word.
²¹Praise the LORD, all his heavenly hosts,
you his servants who do his will.
²²Praise the LORD, all his works
everywhere in his dominion.

Praise the LORD, O my soul.

Psalm 104

¹Praise the LORD, O my soul.

O LORD my God, you are very great;
you are clothed with splendor and majesty.
²He wraps himself in light as with a garment;
he stretches out the heavens like a tent
³   and lays the beams of his upper chambers on
their waters.
He makes the clouds his chariot
and rides on the wings of the wind.
⁴He makes winds his messengers,ᵃ
flames of fire his servants.

⁵He set the earth on its foundations;

"ways" were made known to Moses
and Israel? Is a loving and forgiving
God known only from the New Testament (v. 8; see Ex 34:6–7)? **3.**
Which word picture of forgiveness
do you like best (vv. 11–13)? Why
does God bother with such temporary beings as humans? What
seems to be most important: personal souls or impersonal principles (vv. 17–18)? Is God "talking to
himself" somehow? **4.** What is the
focus of verses 19–22? What
takes "center stage": God's will or
God's creation? What do you think
of the last line?

♡ **1.** Which do you tend to be: a
complainer or a praiser? Satisfied or dissatisfied? Why? Has affliction made you positive or negative? Why? **2.** Like other ancient
Jews, David believed prosperity to
be a sign of God's favor and illness
a sign of personal sin (see Jn
5:5–15). Do you think healing is a
sign of forgiveness? Is disease a
result of unconfessed sin? Why or
why not? **3.** Does your experience
with your father or mother resemble the picture of God in verse 13?
Does this image help you? Can
God's knowing how you are formed
comfort you (v. 14)? **4.** When have
you experienced God's grace firsthand? How have you benefited
from it? **5.** Whom do you treat as
he or she deserves? What would it
mean to bring God's grace into that
situation?

☕ **1.** Are you a "detail person"
or a "big picture thinker"?
What evidence do you have to support this claim? **2.** Do you like
books or documentaries on nature? What part of nature interests
you the most? **3.** *Read aloud*—
Reader(s) A: 1–35, odd; Reader(s)
B: 2–34, even.

📖 **1.** How closely does this
psalm follow the creation sequence in Genesis 1? What segments correspond to which "days"
of creation? **2.** What's the psalmist's picture of the heavens (see Isa
40:22)? What are the "upper chambers" (see Am 9:6)? How are they
held up? What's the purpose of the

ᵃ4 Or *angels*

clouds, wind, and fire (vv. 3–4)? **3.** What holds up the flat, table-like earth (v. 5; see 75:3)? What waters "stood above the mountains" (v. 6; see Ge 1:6–9)? How did God harness the waters (vv. 7–9; see Job 38:8–11)? **4.** For what four things does water set the stage (vv. 10–14)? What are three fruits of the earth (v. 15)? How have these become enduring religious symbols? Does God seem concerned about the small things? How does this give confidence in God's ability to sustain creation? **5.** Why do you think the sun and moon are created on the "fourth day" (vv. 19–23; see Ge 1:16–19)? How does God's wise control of space and time affect the world? How are man and beast able to coexist? **6.** Why is "in wisdom you made them all" a pivotal phrase (v. 24; see Pr 3:19)? What other part of nature displays God's handiwork (vv. 25–26)? **7.** What do all creatures have in common (vv. 27–30)? How does God provide? Is God's food steaming hot or has it cooled off? Does God give it all or keep some for tomorrow's leftovers? Does God give healthy or diet size portions? How total is God's care (vv. 29–30)? What's the creature's greatest fear? **8.** What is the ultimate purpose of creation and the writing of this psalm (v. 31)? **9.** What does God's wise creation inspire the psalmist to do (vv. 33–34)? What commitment does it arouse? What motivates the strong statement in verse 35?

♡ **1.** What do you make of David's elaboration on the creation story? Does it sound primitive and simplistic? Grand and holy? Has science added or subtracted from the wonder of the natural order? **2.** What is the ultimate purpose of nature? What is mankind's role? Should Christians take on a special role in preserving creation? How so? **3.** What does the infinite variety of creation say about God? **4.** How does God provide for you physically? Spiritually? Emotionally? Is it enough or are you left wanting more? Is it good or mixed with bad? Why? **5.** When has God's provision come at just the right time? In the nick of time? Have you thought God was tardy? Could your watch have been running a few minutes fast? **6.** Is dependence on God a happy state? Is it frightening to be distant from God? Is it possible to benefit from God's care without a total de-

it can never be moved.
⁶You covered it with the deep as with a garment;
the waters stood above the mountains.
⁷But at your rebuke the waters fled,
at the sound of your thunder they took to flight;
⁸they flowed over the mountains,
they went down into the valleys,
to the place you assigned for them.
⁹You set a boundary they cannot cross;
never again will they cover the earth.

¹⁰He makes springs pour water into the ravines;
it flows between the mountains.
¹¹They give water to all the beasts of the field;
the wild donkeys quench their thirst.
¹²The birds of the air nest by the waters;
they sing among the branches.
¹³He waters the mountains from his upper chambers;
the earth is satisfied by the fruit of his work.
¹⁴He makes grass grow for the cattle,
and plants for man to cultivate—
bringing forth food from the earth:
¹⁵wine that gladdens the heart of man,
oil to make his face shine,
and bread that sustains his heart.
¹⁶The trees of the LORD are well watered,
the cedars of Lebanon that he planted.
¹⁷There the birds make their nests;
the stork has its home in the pine trees.
¹⁸The high mountains belong to the wild goats;
the crags are a refuge for the coneys.ᵃ

¹⁹The moon marks off the seasons,
and the sun knows when to go down.
²⁰You bring darkness, it becomes night,
and all the beasts of the forest prowl.
²¹The lions roar for their prey
and seek their food from God.
²²The sun rises, and they steal away;
they return and lie down in their dens.
²³Then man goes out to his work,
to his labor until evening.

²⁴How many are your works, O LORD!
In wisdom you made them all;
the earth is full of your creatures.
²⁵There is the sea, vast and spacious,
teeming with creatures beyond number—
living things both large and small.
²⁶There the ships go to and fro,
and the leviathan, which you formed to frolic there.

²⁷These all look to you
to give them their food at the proper time.
²⁸When you give it to them,
they gather it up;
when you open your hand,

ᵃ18 That is, the hyrax or rock badger

they are satisfied with good things.
²⁹When you hide your face,
    they are terrified;
when you take away their breath,
    they die and return to the dust.
³⁰When you send your Spirit,
    they are created,
    and you renew the face of the earth.

³¹May the glory of the LORD endure forever;
    may the LORD rejoice in his works—
³²he who looks at the earth, and it trembles,
    who touches the mountains, and they smoke.

³³I will sing to the LORD all my life;
    I will sing praise to my God as long as I live.
³⁴May my meditation be pleasing to him,
    as I rejoice in the LORD.
³⁵But may sinners vanish from the earth
    and the wicked be no more.

Praise the LORD, O my soul.

Praise the LORD.ᵃ

Psalm 105

¹Give thanks to the LORD, call on his name;
    make known among the nations what he has
        done.
²Sing to him, sing praise to him;
    tell of all his wonderful acts.
³Glory in his holy name;
    let the hearts of those who seek the LORD
        rejoice.
⁴Look to the LORD and his strength;
    seek his face always.

⁵Remember the wonders he has done,
    his miracles, and the judgments he pronounced,
⁶O descendants of Abraham his servant,
    O sons of Jacob, his chosen ones.
⁷He is the LORD our God;
    his judgments are in all the earth.

⁸He remembers his covenant forever,
    the word he commanded, for a thousand
        generations,
⁹the covenant he made with Abraham,
    the oath he swore to Isaac.
¹⁰He confirmed it to Jacob as a decree,
    to Israel as an everlasting covenant:
¹¹"To you I will give the land of Canaan
    as the portion you will inherit."

¹²When they were but few in number,
    few indeed, and strangers in it,
¹³they wandered from nation to nation,
    from one kingdom to another.
¹⁴He allowed no one to oppress them;
    for their sake he rebuked kings:

ᵃ35 Hebrew *Hallelu Yah*; in the Septuagint this line stands at the beginning of Psalm 105.

pendence on his provisions? What does "total dependence" mean? How does it relate to self-reliance or reliance upon others?

1. What period of history interests you most? What about it attracts you? 2. Test yourself: what did you do two days ago? Five years ago this month? Which was easier to recall? 3. *Read aloud*—All: 1–4; Reader(s) A: 5–45, odd; Reader(s) B: 6–44, even.

1. Like Psalm 78, this psalm is a lengthy run-down of Israel's ancient history. Why are the Jewish people frequently called to "remember" (vv. 1–7)? 2. What is the gist of God's covenant with Abraham (vv. 5–11; see Ge 15:18–21)? Why would the promise of land be so important? Why didn't God promise spiritual blessings such as great enlightenment or grace? 3. When they were a small and insignificant group of nomads, how did God esteem them (vv. 12–15)? In what nations did they wander (see Ge 12:1,10; 13:1,18; 20:1; 21:34; 28:10; 33:18–19; 35:1)? Why does God call them "prophets" (v. 15)? 4. Who does the psalmist think is responsible for the famine (v. 16)? Who planned Joseph's slavery? Who made the Egyptians "hate" the Israelites (vv. 23–25)? Do you think God really controls all this? Do humans have no choices? 5. What plagues of Egypt are not mentioned in this psalm (see Ex 7–11)? What ultimate purpose did the plagues serve? What was Egypt's response to the Exodus (v. 38)? 6. Why did God make a

covenant with Abraham about some land (vv. 42–45)? What is God's higher purpose? What did God want to do for all people through Israel?

♡ **1.** Is it right to trace God's hand in the history of a country? Is God planning and executing every detail? Or do people of faith simply "see" God in retrospect? To what extent does God control the politics of the modern world? **2.** How can focusing your thoughts on God positively affect your attitude? Your emotions? How can it give you a sense of control over your life? Do you find comfort in remembering God's wonders? What are one or two recent wonders in your life? **3.** If God's promise to Israel is everlasting, what's your understanding of Israel today? Is the State of Israel part of God's plan? Do the Israelis obey God's precepts as an example to the world? Or is "Israel" now the Church? If so, what does the covenant mean? How is God's purpose served in the Church? **4.** What does God think about those to whom he extends the covenant promise? Is anyone insignificant to God? What causes you to feel unimportant at times? Can this psalm help? **5.** How has God come through for you when you saw no way out? What has turned out for good? What did you learn? **6.** How does the Lord take care of your basic needs? How does God provide beyond your expectations? Are you a gracious recipient? Or do you feel you have to pay God back for the kindness? Are your expectations too narrow? Too restricted?

¹⁵"Do not touch my anointed ones;
  do my prophets no harm."

¹⁶He called down famine on the land
  and destroyed all their supplies of food;
¹⁷and he sent a man before them—
  Joseph, sold as a slave.
¹⁸They bruised his feet with shackles,
  his neck was put in irons,
¹⁹till what he foretold came to pass,
  till the word of the Lord proved him true.
²⁰The king sent and released him,
  the ruler of peoples set him free.
²¹He made him master of his household,
  ruler over all he possessed,
²²to instruct his princes as he pleased
  and teach his elders wisdom.

²³Then Israel entered Egypt;
  Jacob lived as an alien in the land of Ham.
²⁴The Lord made his people very fruitful;
  he made them too numerous for their foes,
²⁵whose hearts he turned to hate his people,
  to conspire against his servants.
²⁶He sent Moses his servant,
  and Aaron, whom he had chosen.
²⁷They performed his miraculous signs among them,
  his wonders in the land of Ham.
²⁸He sent darkness and made the land dark—
  for had they not rebelled against his words?
²⁹He turned their waters into blood,
  causing their fish to die.
³⁰Their land teemed with frogs,
  which went up into the bedrooms of their
    rulers.
³¹He spoke, and there came swarms of flies,
  and gnats throughout their country.
³²He turned their rain into hail,
  with lightning throughout their land;
³³he struck down their vines and fig trees
  and shattered the trees of their country.
³⁴He spoke, and the locusts came,
  grasshoppers without number;
³⁵they ate up every green thing in their land,
  ate up the produce of their soil.
³⁶Then he struck down all the firstborn in their
    land,
  the firstfruits of all their manhood.

³⁷He brought out Israel, laden with silver and gold,
  and from among their tribes no one faltered.
³⁸Egypt was glad when they left,
  because dread of Israel had fallen on them.
³⁹He spread out a cloud as a covering,
  and a fire to give light at night.
⁴⁰They asked, and he brought them quail
  and satisfied them with the bread of heaven.
⁴¹He opened the rock, and water gushed out;
  like a river it flowed in the desert.

⁴²For he remembered his holy promise

given to his servant Abraham.
⁴³He brought out his people with rejoicing,
      his chosen ones with shouts of joy;
⁴⁴he gave them the lands of the nations,
      and they fell heir to what others had toiled
         for—
⁴⁵that they might keep his precepts
      and observe his laws.

   Praise the LORD.ᵃ

Psalm 106

¹Praise the LORD.ᵇ

Give thanks to the LORD, for he is good;
   his love endures forever.
²Who can proclaim the mighty acts of the LORD
   or fully declare his praise?
³Blessed are they who maintain justice,
   who constantly do what is right.
⁴Remember me, O LORD, when you show favor to
      your people,
   come to my aid when you save them,
⁵that I may enjoy the prosperity of your chosen
      ones,
   that I may share in the joy of your nation
   and join your inheritance in giving praise.

⁶We have sinned, even as our fathers did;
   we have done wrong and acted wickedly.
⁷When our fathers were in Egypt,
      they gave no thought to your miracles;
   they did not remember your many kindnesses,
      and they rebelled by the sea, the Red Sea.ᶜ
⁸Yet he saved them for his name's sake,
   to make his mighty power known.
⁹He rebuked the Red Sea, and it dried up;
   he led them through the depths as through a
      desert.
¹⁰He saved them from the hand of the foe;
   from the hand of the enemy he redeemed
      them.
¹¹The waters covered their adversaries;
   not one of them survived.
¹²Then they believed his promises
   and sang his praise.

¹³But they soon forgot what he had done
   and did not wait for his counsel.
¹⁴In the desert they gave in to their craving;
   in the wasteland they put God to the test.
¹⁵So he gave them what they asked for,
   but sent a wasting disease upon them.

¹⁶In the camp they grew envious of Moses
   and of Aaron, who was consecrated to the LORD.
¹⁷The earth opened up and swallowed Dathan;
   it buried the company of Abiram.

1. What period of history are you glad you weren't around for? Why was it so bad? 2. Did you never rebel as teenager? As a preteen? Young adult? Older adult? What was or is the issue that most concerns you with regard to this? 3. *Read aloud*—Reader(s) A: 1–47, odd; Reader(s) B: 2–48, even.

1. The long, historical Psalm 105 focused on God's covenant. What does this one bring to light (v. 6)? For what "salvation" is the psalmist waiting (vv. 4–5)? At what point in time was this written (v. 41)? 2. Eight examples of rebellion are given. Is the psalmist taking responsibility for his sins (v. 6)? Why does he link himself up with the sins of his ancestors? What sin comes first (v. 7; see Ex 14:10–12)? Why did God save them (v. 8)? Does their opposition hinder God's power in any way? 3. Why is Israel so forgetful (v. 13)? How could anyone doubt God after having passed through the Red Sea? 4. What did the people crave (vv. 14–15; see Nu 11:4–5, 32–34)? Why do people get cravings? Are they wrong? Why did God punish them for this one? 5. Who were Dathan and Abiram (vv. 16–18; see Nu 16:12–14, 26–33)? What sin deserved so severe a punishment? 6. What rebellion led God to say he would destroy the people (vv. 19–23)? Why does the psalmist locate this at Horeb? What is at the heart of Moses' intercession (see Ex 32:11–13)? What difference does it make? 7. What report did 10 of the 12 spies give on the land of Canaan (see Nu 13:25–29)? In what sense was the land filled with "giants" or was this a metaphor? What is so wrong about believing the majority report (vv. 25–27)? 8. What started Baal-worship during the wilderness wandering (vv. 28–31; see Nu 25:1–13)? How can women so easily turn the hearts of men (see 1Ki 11:4–6)? Why don't the men seem to turn

ᵃ45 Hebrew *Hallelu Yah*   ᵇ1 Hebrew *Hallelu Yah*; also in verse 48   ᶜ7 Hebrew *Yam Suph*; that is, Sea of Reeds; also in verses 9 and 22

the pagan women toward God? **9.** What "trouble" came to Moses because of the rebellion at Meribah (vv. 32–33; see Dt 32:48–52)? What happened (see Nu 20:2–13)? **10.** Over the course of 600 years in Canaan, what did the Israelites fail to do (vv. 34–39)? How did they "sacrifice" their children (see Jer 7:30–31)? **11.** What punishment befits their disobedience (vv. 40–43)? Where was God during the sentence of judgment? How is Yahweh's loyalty and love contrasted with Israel's? How does God's love prevail? **12.** How does this full confession of sin give the psalmist confidence in God's power to save (vv. 47–48)? What attitude comes after confession?

♡ **1.** How can you "maintain justice" in your part of the world? **2.** Are you experiencing God's favor now? Is unconfessed sin standing in the way? Do you have a time for confession at church? In the group? Why is it important to confess sins to other believers (see Jas 5:16)? **3.** Is it hard for you to take full responsibility for your mistakes and failures? Are other people, things or circumstances usually to blame? Is it easier at work? At home? In what area are you avoiding responsibility right now? **4.** Are you responsible for the sins of your parents? Are your parents' sins passed on in you? In what ways? **5.** Does forgiveness ever remove the consequences of sin? Why or why not? When have you suffered serious consequences even after being forgiven? **6.** Has impatience ever yielded harmful and lasting results? When did you think your solution was the only one? Has the desire to fix the problem blinded you to reality? What happened? Could you have waited for God's counsel? **7.** How do you feel about making mistakes? Do you "rake yourself over the coals," or do you see them as opportunities to grow? What's good about taking your share of the blame? How can it influence your children and others around you?

¹⁸Fire blazed among their followers;
    a flame consumed the wicked.

¹⁹At Horeb they made a calf
    and worshiped an idol cast from metal.
²⁰They exchanged their Glory
    for an image of a bull, which eats grass.
²¹They forgot the God who saved them,
    who had done great things in Egypt,
²²miracles in the land of Ham
    and awesome deeds by the Red Sea.
²³So he said he would destroy them—
    had not Moses, his chosen one,
  stood in the breach before him
    to keep his wrath from destroying them.

²⁴Then they despised the pleasant land;
    they did not believe his promise.
²⁵They grumbled in their tents
    and did not obey the LORD.
²⁶So he swore to them with uplifted hand
    that he would make them fall in the desert,
²⁷make their descendants fall among the nations
    and scatter them throughout the lands.

²⁸They yoked themselves to the Baal of Peor
    and ate sacrifices offered to lifeless gods;
²⁹they provoked the LORD to anger by their wicked deeds,
    and a plague broke out among them.
³⁰But Phinehas stood up and intervened,
    and the plague was checked.
³¹This was credited to him as righteousness
    for endless generations to come.

³²By the waters of Meribah they angered the LORD,
    and trouble came to Moses because of them;
³³for they rebelled against the Spirit of God,
    and rash words came from Moses' lips.ᵃ

³⁴They did not destroy the peoples
    as the LORD had commanded them,
³⁵but they mingled with the nations
    and adopted their customs.
³⁶They worshiped their idols,
    which became a snare to them.
³⁷They sacrificed their sons
    and their daughters to demons.
³⁸They shed innocent blood,
    the blood of their sons and daughters,
  whom they sacrificed to the idols of Canaan,
    and the land was desecrated by their blood.
³⁹They defiled themselves by what they did;
    by their deeds they prostituted themselves.

⁴⁰Therefore the LORD was angry with his people
    and abhorred his inheritance.
⁴¹He handed them over to the nations,
    and their foes ruled over them.
⁴²Their enemies oppressed them

ᵃ33 Or *against his spirit, / and rash words came from his lips*

and subjected them to their power.
⁴³Many times he delivered them,
    but they were bent on rebellion
    and they wasted away in their sin.

⁴⁴But he took note of their distress
    when he heard their cry;
⁴⁵for their sake he remembered his covenant
    and out of his great love he relented.
⁴⁶He caused them to be pitied
    by all who held them captive.

⁴⁷Save us, O LORD our God,
    and gather us from the nations,
that we may give thanks to your holy name
    and glory in your praise.

⁴⁸Praise be to the LORD, the God of Israel,
    from everlasting to everlasting.
Let all the people say, "Amen!"

Praise the LORD.

BOOK V

Psalms 107–150

Psalm 107

¹Give thanks to the LORD, for he is good;
    his love endures forever.
²Let the redeemed of the LORD say this—
    those he redeemed from the hand of the foe,
³those he gathered from the lands,
    from east and west, from north and south.^a

⁴Some wandered in desert wastelands,
    finding no way to a city where they could
      settle.
⁵They were hungry and thirsty,
    and their lives ebbed away.
⁶Then they cried out to the LORD in their trouble,
    and he delivered them from their distress.
⁷He led them by a straight way
    to a city where they could settle.
⁸Let them give thanks to the LORD for his unfailing
    love
    and his wonderful deeds for men,
⁹for he satisfies the thirsty
    and fills the hungry with good things.

¹⁰Some sat in darkness and the deepest gloom,
    prisoners suffering in iron chains,
¹¹for they had rebelled against the words of God
    and despised the counsel of the Most High.
¹²So he subjected them to bitter labor;
    they stumbled, and there was no one to help.
¹³Then they cried to the LORD in their trouble,
    and he saved them from their distress.
¹⁴He brought them out of darkness and the deepest
    gloom

1. What do you do when you get lost while driving: (a) Stop at a gas station? (b) Ask people on the street for directions? (c) Drive around in hope of finding your destination? (d) Panic? (e) Make a phone call? 2. Have you attended some kind of reunion? What was it like seeing old friends? Do you avoid reunions? Why? 3. *Read aloud*—Reader(s) A: 1–43, odd; Reader(s) B: 2–42, even.

1. Who is invited to thank God (vv. 1–3)? What four groups of "redeemed" people are mentioned? How should each group respond to God's unfailing love (vv. 8,15,21,31)? 2. Of what time in Israel's history do the lost travelers remind you (vv. 4–9)? What do they symbolize? What is their basic problem (v. 5)? 3. What is the plight of the prisoners (vv. 10–16)? Of what time in Judah's history do they remind you (see Isa 45:2)? Why are they subjected to this plight? What belief of the times undergirds the reason given (see Job 36:8–9)? 4. In the same way, how are the physically ill viewed (v. 17)? What are their symptoms? How does the Lord answer their cry (vv. 19–20)? 5. What is the sailor's greatest need (vv. 23–30)? What kind of seas are described (v. 26)? Who seems to be in charge of calm seas? 6. What events are being described in the reversals of verses 33,34,38 and 39? When does God destroy? When does God build up?

^{a3} Hebrew *north and the sea*

and broke away their chains.
¹⁵Let them give thanks to the LORD for his unfailing
　　love
　and his wonderful deeds for men,
¹⁶for he breaks down gates of bronze
　and cuts through bars of iron.

¹⁷Some became fools through their rebellious ways
　and suffered affliction because of their
　　iniquities.
¹⁸They loathed all food
　and drew near the gates of death.
¹⁹Then they cried to the LORD in their trouble,
　and he saved them from their distress.
²⁰He sent forth his word and healed them;
　he rescued them from the grave.
²¹Let them give thanks to the LORD for his unfailing
　　love
　and his wonderful deeds for men.
²²Let them sacrifice thank offerings
　and tell of his works with songs of joy.

²³Others went out on the sea in ships;
　they were merchants on the mighty waters.
²⁴They saw the works of the LORD,
　his wonderful deeds in the deep.
²⁵For he spoke and stirred up a tempest
　that lifted high the waves.
²⁶They mounted up to the heavens and went down
　　to the depths;
　in their peril their courage melted away.
²⁷They reeled and staggered like drunken men;
　they were at their wits' end.
²⁸Then they cried out to the LORD in their trouble,
　and he brought them out of their distress.
²⁹He stilled the storm to a whisper;
　the waves of the sea were hushed.
³⁰They were glad when it grew calm,
　and he guided them to their desired haven.
³¹Let them give thanks to the LORD for his unfailing
　　love
　and his wonderful deeds for men.
³²Let them exalt him in the assembly of the people
　and praise him in the council of the elders.

³³He turned rivers into a desert,
　flowing springs into thirsty ground,
³⁴and fruitful land into a salt waste,
　because of the wickedness of those who lived
　　there.
³⁵He turned the desert into pools of water
　and the parched ground into flowing springs;
³⁶there he brought the hungry to live,
　and they founded a city where they could
　　settle.
³⁷They sowed fields and planted vineyards
　that yielded a fruitful harvest;
³⁸he blessed them, and their numbers greatly
　　increased,
　and he did not let their herds diminish.

³⁹Then their numbers decreased, and they were
      humbled
   by oppression, calamity and sorrow;
⁴⁰he who pours contempt on nobles
   made them wander in a trackless waste.
⁴¹But he lifted the needy out of their affliction
   and increased their families like flocks.
⁴²The upright see and rejoice,
   but all the wicked shut their mouths.

⁴³Whoever is wise, let him heed these things
   and consider the great love of the LORD.

Psalm 108

A song. A psalm of David.

¹My heart is steadfast, O God;
   I will sing and make music with all my soul.
²Awake, harp and lyre!
   I will awaken the dawn.
³I will praise you, O LORD, among the nations;
   I will sing of you among the peoples.
⁴For great is your love, higher than the heavens;
   your faithfulness reaches to the skies.
⁵Be exalted, O God, above the heavens,
   and let your glory be over all the earth.

⁶Save us and help us with your right hand,
   that those you love may be delivered.
⁷God has spoken from his sanctuary:
   "In triumph I will parcel out Shechem
   and measure off the Valley of Succoth.
⁸Gilead is mine, Manasseh is mine;
   Ephraim is my helmet,
   Judah my scepter.
⁹Moab is my washbasin,
   upon Edom I toss my sandal;
   over Philistia I shout in triumph."

¹⁰Who will bring me to the fortified city?
   Who will lead me to Edom?
¹¹Is it not you, O God, you who have rejected us
   and no longer go out with our armies?
¹²Give us aid against the enemy,
   for the help of man is worthless.
¹³With God we will gain the victory,
   and he will trample down our enemies.

Psalm 109

For the director of music. Of David. A psalm.

¹O God, whom I praise,
   do not remain silent,
²for wicked and deceitful men
   have opened their mouths against me;
   they have spoken against me with lying
      tongues.
³With words of hatred they surround me;
   they attack me without cause.

1. What do you do to relax after a long day out of the house? How often do you get time to unwind? 2. What CD, group or piece of music would you want to have if you were marooned on a desert island? 3. *Read aloud*— Leader: 1–5; Reader(s) A: 6–9; Reader(s) B: 10–13.

1. Verses 1–5 can be found in Psalm 57, while verses 6–13 are in Psalm 60. Look briefly at these other two psalms which stem from different but similarly harsh situations. Why do you think these two segments were placed together here? 2. How can David's heart be so steadfast in the midst of adverse circumstances? Is he escapist? Stoic? Trusting? Blind? 3. How do you explain David's growing sense of hope from verses 10–13? What is God's part and what is David's part in this upcoming battle?

How does the memory of God's provision for you in the past give you hope for the future?

1. On a scale of 1 to 10, rate your impulsiveness/caution: "Hey, go for it" (1) to "Let's set up a committee" (10)? What would your rule of thumb be? 2. If someone gave you $200 to satisfy an urgent personal need, how would you spend it? 3. *Read aloud*—Reader(s) A:1–31, odd; Reader(s) B: 2–30, even.

1. What motivates these attacks on David as far as he's concerned (v. 3)? Do you think he's completely innocent? How well do they know him (v. 5)? How is David different from them (v. 4)? 2. What is the tone of verses 6–19? Is David: (a) Cursing his enemies? (b) Quoting their accusations against him (see footnote, v. 6; Dt 19:16–21)? 3. What do you think was the water that brings a curse (v. 18; see Nu 5:23–31)? 4. How could David, the king, claim to be "poor and needy" (vv. 22–25)? Why would people "shake their heads" when they saw him? 5. Does David lighten up at the end (vv. 28–29)? How will God "bless" these accusers? Why does he conclude with a vow (vv. 30–31)?

1. How does this psalm agree with Jesus' attitude toward false persecution (see Mt 5:11–12)? Which verse of the psalm seems closest to his teaching? 2. Have you ever been a victim in an intense conflict? What hurt did you sustain? What did you do with your feelings? 3. Do you tend to feel guilty: (a) Too much? (b) Only when you're wrong? (c) Not enough? (d) Even when it's mostly someone else's responsibility? 4. Are you responsible for your parents' mistakes? Has God "visited" the sins of the past generation on you and your family? What role does confession and self-awareness play? 5. Peter saw verse 8 of this psalm fulfilled in Judas (see Ac 1:20). What does this psalm have to do with choosing an apostolic replacement for Judas? What irony do you see in Judas receiving this curse he intended for Jesus? 6. How do you wrongly accuse yourself? How does the "accuser" take over God's place at your right hand? How can you let God have his rightful place there? Can the group help?

⁴In return for my friendship they accuse me,
    but I am a man of prayer.
⁵They repay me evil for good,
    and hatred for my friendship.

⁶Appoint[a] an evil man[b] to oppose him;
    let an accuser[c] stand at his right hand.
⁷When he is tried, let him be found guilty,
    and may his prayers condemn him.
⁸May his days be few;
    may another take his place of leadership.
⁹May his children be fatherless
    and his wife a widow.
¹⁰May his children be wandering beggars;
    may they be driven[d] from their ruined homes.
¹¹May a creditor seize all he has;
    may strangers plunder the fruits of his labor.
¹²May no one extend kindness to him
    or take pity on his fatherless children.
¹³May his descendants be cut off,
    their names blotted out from the next
      generation.
¹⁴May the iniquity of his fathers be remembered
    before the LORD;
    may the sin of his mother never be blotted out.
¹⁵May their sins always remain before the LORD,
    that he may cut off the memory of them from
      the earth.

¹⁶For he never thought of doing a kindness,
    but hounded to death the poor
    and the needy and the brokenhearted.
¹⁷He loved to pronounce a curse—
    may it[e] come on him;
    he found no pleasure in blessing—
    may it be[f] far from him.
¹⁸He wore cursing as his garment;
    it entered into his body like water,
    into his bones like oil.
¹⁹May it be like a cloak wrapped about him,
    like a belt tied forever around him.
²⁰May this be the LORD's payment to my accusers,
    to those who speak evil of me.

²¹But you, O Sovereign LORD,
    deal well with me for your name's sake;
    out of the goodness of your love, deliver me.
²²For I am poor and needy,
    and my heart is wounded within me.
²³I fade away like an evening shadow;
    I am shaken off like a locust.
²⁴My knees give way from fasting;
    my body is thin and gaunt.
²⁵I am an object of scorn to my accusers;
    when they see me, they shake their heads.

²⁶Help me, O LORD my God;
    save me in accordance with your love.

a6 Or ⌊They say:⌋ "Appoint (with quotation marks at the end of verse 19)   b6 Or the
Evil One   c6 Or let Satan   d10 Septuagint; Hebrew sought   e17 Or curse, /
and it has   f17 Or blessing, / and it is

²⁷Let them know that it is your hand,
　　that you, O LORD, have done it.
²⁸They may curse, but you will bless;
　　when they attack they will be put to shame,
　　but your servant will rejoice.
²⁹My accusers will be clothed with disgrace
　　and wrapped in shame as in a cloak.

³⁰With my mouth I will greatly extol the LORD;
　　in the great throng I will praise him.
³¹For he stands at the right hand of the needy one,
　　to save his life from those who condemn him.

Psalm 110

Of David. A psalm.

¹The LORD says to my Lord:
　　"Sit at my right hand
until I make your enemies
　　a footstool for your feet."

²The LORD will extend your mighty scepter from
　　Zion;
　　you will rule in the midst of your enemies.
³Your troops will be willing
　　on your day of battle.
Arrayed in holy majesty,
　　from the womb of the dawn
　　you will receive the dew of your youth.ᵃ

⁴The LORD has sworn
　　and will not change his mind:
"You are a priest forever,
　　in the order of Melchizedek."

⁵The Lord is at your right hand;
　　he will crush kings on the day of his wrath.
⁶He will judge the nations, heaping up the dead
　　and crushing the rulers of the whole earth.
⁷He will drink from a brook beside the wayᵇ;
　　therefore he will lift up his head.

Psalm 111ᶜ

¹Praise the LORD.ᵈ

I will extol the LORD with all my heart
　　in the council of the upright and in the
　　assembly.

²Great are the works of the LORD;
　　they are pondered by all who delight in them.
³Glorious and majestic are his deeds,
　　and his righteousness endures forever.
⁴He has caused his wonders to be remembered;
　　the LORD is gracious and compassionate.
⁵He provides food for those who fear him;
　　he remembers his covenant forever.

---

1. What is the most unusual first name you've ever heard? 2. *Read aloud*—Reader(s) A: 1–3; Reader(s) B: 4–7.

1. The New Testament applies this psalm to Jesus. If you lived in David's day, what sense would it make? Who is the first "Lord" in verse 1? The second? What will the first Lord do while the second Lord waits? 2. Who is Melchizedek (v. 4; see Ge 14:17–20)? Was he a Hebrew? What two offices did he combine? Why are these roles conferred on the Davidic line (see Heb 7:1–19)? 3. Would you apply verses 5–7 to David? What do you make of verse 7?

1. What point did Jesus make with this psalm (see Lk 20:41–44)? 2. How did Jesus say nations would be judged (see Mt 25:31–46)? How do you think your country will fare?

1. What job or career looks pretty good compared to your present one? Why is it attractive? What's wrong with the one you've got? 2. *Read aloud*—Reader(s) A:1–9, odd; Reader(s) B: 2–8, even; All: 10.

1. Why is the author praising the Lord (v. 2)? How did God cause his works to be "remembered" (v. 4; see Ex 23:14–17)? 2. When did God provide food (v. 5)? How did God show power (v. 6)? What "works" of God show faithfulness and justice (v. 7)? 3. What does the psalmist mean by the term "redemption" (v. 9)?

1. How has God worked your recent personal hist… Can you think of any "works"

ᵃ3 Or / *your young men will come to you like the dew*　　ᵇ7 Or / *The One who grants succession will set him in authority*　　ᶜThis psalm is an acrostic poem, the lines of which begin with the successive letters of the Hebrew alphabet.　　ᵈ1 Hebrew *Hallelu Yah*

could ponder? **2.** The Hebrew acrostic starts each line with the next letter in the alphabet. Try writing your own acrostic psalm, using the letters of the words WORKS, FEAR or WISDOM to start the lines.

---

1. What were you afraid of when you were a child? Dogs? Big trucks? Big kids? The doctor? Did you outgrow it? **2.** *Read aloud*—All: 1; Reader(s) A: 2–10, even; Reader(s) B: 3–9, odd.

1. Using the same acrostic device as the previous one, how does this psalm flow out of the last one? To what "commands" does the psalmist refer (v. 1)? What does fearing God mean? **2.** What external signs point to the righteous man being blessed (vv. 2–3)? What kind of blessing is implied in verse 4a? **3.** What two traits characterize his dealings with people (vv. 4–5)? **4.** What internal blessings are available (vv. 7–8)? Why does disastrous news fail to shake him?

1. Do any of the lines in this psalm fit someone you admire? Do any fit yourself? Which one do you wish fit you? **2.** Is life really this smooth for the "nice guy"? Do you know any good people who aren't rich and carefree? Do you know any bad people who are? Why bother with this simplistic poem? **3.** Would you say you are generous? Give a recent example.

---

1. Do you ever give money to strangers on the street? Who would most likely get your money? **2.** *Read aloud*—Reader(s) A: 1–9, odd; Reader(s) B: 2–8, even.

1. Why praise the Lord's name (vv. 1–3)? **2.** What two extremes does God bridge? Where is God in relation to the heavens and the earth? **3.** Why do verses 8 appear on Hannah's lips (see ?:8)? On Mary's (see Lk

⁶He has shown his people the power of his works,
    giving them the lands of other nations.
⁷The works of his hands are faithful and just;
    all his precepts are trustworthy.
⁸They are steadfast for ever and ever,
    done in faithfulness and uprightness.
⁹He provided redemption for his people;
    he ordained his covenant forever—
    holy and awesome is his name.

¹⁰The fear of the Lord is the beginning of wisdom;
    all who follow his precepts have good
      understanding.
    To him belongs eternal praise.

Psalm 112 [a]

¹Praise the Lord. [b]

Blessed is the man who fears the Lord,
    who finds great delight in his commands.

²His children will be mighty in the land;
    the generation of the upright will be blessed.
³Wealth and riches are in his house,
    and his righteousness endures forever.
⁴Even in darkness light dawns for the upright,
    for the gracious and compassionate and
      righteous man. [c]
⁵Good will come to him who is generous and lends
      freely,
    who conducts his affairs with justice.
⁶Surely he will never be shaken;
    a righteous man will be remembered forever.
⁷He will have no fear of bad news;
    his heart is steadfast, trusting in the Lord.
⁸His heart is secure, he will have no fear;
    in the end he will look in triumph on his foes.
⁹He has scattered abroad his gifts to the poor,
    his righteousness endures forever;
    his horn [d] will be lifted high in honor.

¹⁰The wicked man will see and be vexed,
    he will gnash his teeth and waste away;
    the longings of the wicked will come to
      nothing.

Psalm 113

¹Praise the Lord. [e]

Praise, O servants of the Lord,
    praise the name of the Lord.
²Let the name of the Lord be praised,
    both now and forevermore.
³From the rising of the sun to the place where it
      sets,
    the name of the Lord is to be praised.

---

a This psalm is an acrostic poem, the lines of which begin with the successive letters of the Hebrew alphabet.   *b1* Hebrew *Hallelu Yah*   *c4* Or */ for ⌊the Lord⌋ is gracious and compassionate and righteous*   *d9* *Horn* here symbolizes dignity.   *e1* Hebrew *Hallelu Yah*; also in verse 9

4The LORD is exalted over all the nations,
  his glory above the heavens.
5Who is like the LORD our God,
  the One who sits enthroned on high,
6who stoops down to look
  on the heavens and the earth?
7He raises the poor from the dust
  and lifts the needy from the ash heap;
8he seats them with princes,
  with the princes of their people.
9He settles the barren woman in her home
  as a happy mother of children.

Praise the LORD.

Psalm 114

1When Israel came out of Egypt,
  the house of Jacob from a people of foreign
    tongue,
2Judah became God's sanctuary,
  Israel his dominion.

3The sea looked and fled,
  the Jordan turned back;
4the mountains skipped like rams,
  the hills like lambs.

5Why was it, O sea, that you fled,
  O Jordan, that you turned back,
6you mountains, that you skipped like rams,
  you hills, like lambs?

7Tremble, O earth, at the presence of the Lord,
  at the presence of the God of Jacob,
8who turned the rock into a pool,
  the hard rock into springs of water.

Psalm 115

1Not to us, O LORD, not to us
  but to your name be the glory,
  because of your love and faithfulness.

2Why do the nations say,
  "Where is their God?"
3Our God is in heaven;
  he does whatever pleases him.
4But their idols are silver and gold,
  made by the hands of men.
5They have mouths, but cannot speak,
  eyes, but they cannot see;
6they have ears, but cannot hear,
  noses, but they cannot smell;
7they have hands, but cannot feel,
  feet, but they cannot walk;
  nor can they utter a sound with their throats.
8Those who make them will be like them,
  and so will all who trust in them.

9O house of Israel, trust in the LORD—
  he is their help and shield.

1:52)? Were they like the woman of verse 9?

♡ 1. What name of God means the most to you? Why? Based on your life, what name could be added to the biblical ones? 2. If God always exalts the poor and needy, why are they so dishonored in society? How should the Christian act toward them? How can you develop this trait?

—————

☕ 1. Ever forded or waded across a river? What happened? 2. *Read aloud*—Reader(s) A: 1–7, odd; Reader(s) B: 2–8, even.

📖 1. What ripple effect do you notice in the structure of the psalm? 2. Why are events at the Red Sea and the Jordan associated (v. 3; see Jos 4:23–24)? 3. How is Sinai depicted? How does the poet's approach to events differ from the approach in Moses' song (see Ex 15)?

♡ 1. Where does your salvation history begin? What main events would you retell in a personal psalm? 2. What in your life was: (a) Egypt? (b) The Red Sea? (c) The Jordan? (d) Sinai? (e) Water from the rock?

—————

☕ 1. What brings out the artist in you? What kind of art do you appreciate? 2. What modern gadget is conspicuously missing from your house? Why? Or do you have everything you need? 3. *Read aloud*—All: 1; Reader(s) A: 2–14, even; Reader(s) B: 3–15, odd; All: 16–18.

📖 1. What trouble is written between the lines (vv. 1–2)? Why do the pagans ask where Yahweh is? 2. What kind of gods are the pagans used to (vv. 4–7)? Why do they worship idols if they have no power? Why do the Jews refuse to represent God in sculpture or painting (see Ex 20:4–5)? What would be wrong with making an image of Yahweh? 3. Why do idolaters receive the fate in verse 8? 4. Who are the three groups addressed in verses 9–11? Who are "those who fear the Lord" (v. 13)? 5. What kinds of blessings are promised (vv. 14–15)? **6.** What view of the afterlife does the psalmist hold (vv. 16–18)?

1. Have you ever been asked "where is your God?" Has your faith been ridiculed? Not taken seriously? How did you respond? **2.** What are some modern idols? Christian idols? In what sense do you become what you worship? Are there any ideas, things, people that you trust more readily than God? **3.** What do you think of religious statues and paintings? Is it wrong to depict Jesus in art? Why do you think the early church departed from the Jewish interpretation of the Second Commandment? **4.** What behaviors and attitudes characterize trust in God?

---

1. Has your experience in dating or business made you feel people cannot be trusted? If not, what percentage would you say are honest? **2.** Do you owe anyone a lot of money? How do you plan to pay it off? **3.** *Read aloud*—Reader(s) A: 1–19, odd; Reader(s) B: 2–18, even.

1. Why is the psalmist so devoted to God (vv. 1–2)? Is this a good reason? What trouble had apparently befallen him (vv. 3–4)? **2.** What does the psalmist mean by "simplehearted" (v. 6; see 19:7; Pr 1:4)? Who was perhaps responsible for his "great need"? **3.** What clues do you find in verses 8–11 about the psalmist's problems? What did he "believe" (v. 10)? **4.** How will the psalmist try to repay the Lord (vv. 12–14,17–19)? What is the "cup of salvation" (v. 13; see Ge 14:18; 1Co 10:16)? What vows are fulfilled in public (vv. 14,18; see Lev 7:12–15)? **5.** What do you make of verse 15 (see 72:14)? Why do you think the psalmist put it here? **6.** What choices were given to slaves upon release (v. 16; see Dt 15:12–17)? What choice does the psalmist make?

1. Is your devotion to God based on what God has done for you? What personal needs does God supply for you? **2.** What does God's "turned ear" (v. 2) say about how he feels about you? How can you strive to imitate God's

¹⁰O house of Aaron, trust in the LORD—
  he is their help and shield.
¹¹You who fear him, trust in the LORD—
  he is their help and shield.

¹²The LORD remembers us and will bless us:
  He will bless the house of Israel,
  he will bless the house of Aaron,
¹³he will bless those who fear the LORD—
  small and great alike.

¹⁴May the LORD make you increase,
  both you and your children.
¹⁵May you be blessed by the LORD,
  the Maker of heaven and earth.

¹⁶The highest heavens belong to the LORD,
  but the earth he has given to man.
¹⁷It is not the dead who praise the LORD,
  those who go down to silence;
¹⁸it is we who extol the LORD,
  both now and forevermore.

Praise the LORD.ᵃ

Psalm 116

¹I love the LORD, for he heard my voice;
  he heard my cry for mercy.
²Because he turned his ear to me,
  I will call on him as long as I live.

³The cords of death entangled me,
  the anguish of the graveᵇ came upon me;
  I was overcome by trouble and sorrow.
⁴Then I called on the name of the LORD:
  "O LORD, save me!"

⁵The LORD is gracious and righteous;
  our God is full of compassion.
⁶The LORD protects the simplehearted;
  when I was in great need, he saved me.

⁷Be at rest once more, O my soul,
  for the LORD has been good to you.

⁸For you, O LORD, have delivered my soul from
    death,
  my eyes from tears,
  my feet from stumbling,
⁹that I may walk before the LORD
  in the land of the living.
¹⁰I believed; thereforeᶜ I said,
  "I am greatly afflicted."
¹¹And in my dismay I said,
  "All men are liars."

¹²How can I repay the LORD
  for all his goodness to me?
¹³I will lift up the cup of salvation
  and call on the name of the LORD.

ᵃ18 Hebrew *Hallelu Yah*   ᵇ3 Hebrew *Sheol*   ᶜ10 Or *believed even when*

¹⁴I will fulfill my vows to the LORD
    in the presence of all his people.

¹⁵Precious in the sight of the LORD
    is the death of his saints.
¹⁶O LORD, truly I am your servant;
    I am your servant, the son of your
        maidservant*ᵃ*;
    you have freed me from my chains.

¹⁷I will sacrifice a thank offering to you
    and call on the name of the LORD.
¹⁸I will fulfill my vows to the LORD
    in the presence of all his people,
¹⁹in the courts of the house of the LORD—
    in your midst, O Jerusalem.

Praise the LORD.ᵇ

Psalm 117

¹Praise the LORD, all you nations;
    extol him, all you peoples.
²For great is his love toward us,
    and the faithfulness of the LORD endures forever.

Praise the LORD.ᵇ

Psalm 118

¹Give thanks to the LORD, for he is good;
    his love endures forever.

²Let Israel say:
    "His love endures forever."
³Let the house of Aaron say:
    "His love endures forever."
⁴Let those who fear the LORD say:
    "His love endures forever."

⁵In my anguish I cried to the LORD,
    and he answered by setting me free.
⁶The LORD is with me; I will not be afraid.
    What can man do to me?
⁷The LORD is with me; he is my helper.
    I will look in triumph on my enemies.

⁸It is better to take refuge in the LORD
    than to trust in man.
⁹It is better to take refuge in the LORD
    than to trust in princes.

¹⁰All the nations surrounded me,
    but in the name of the LORD I cut them off.
¹¹They surrounded me on every side,
    but in the name of the LORD I cut them off.
¹²They swarmed around me like bees,
    but they died out as quickly as burning thorns;
    in the name of the LORD I cut them off.

¹³I was pushed back and about to fall,
    but the LORD helped me.

readiness to listen? **3.** When has God rescued you from serious danger or distress? **4.** Have you ever been naive, much to your regret? Has life made you cynical in any way? For what past innocence or simplicity do you long? **5.** What thank offerings could you give to God?

1. Why is this psalm so short? **2.** Who are the "nations"?

What outsiders need to be included in your life? Give examples of broken barriers.

1. Who was your favorite childhood hero? What did you admire about him or her? **2.** What is your favorite holiday? What makes it special? Which holiday would you rather drop? **3.** *Read aloud*—Reader(s) A: 1–27, odd; Reader(s) B: 2–26, even; All: 28–29.

1. What clues can you find that this psalm describes the Feast of Tabernacles (vv. 19–20,27; see Lev 23:33–36, 39–44)? What do these three groups represent (vv. 1–4)? What do they mean by "love"? **2.** What has the Lord done for the psalmist (v. 5)? Based on the attitude in verses 6–7, from what do you think he is free? **3.** In verses 10–12, what does it mean to cut off the nations? Is this the psalmist's personal story, or the story of the whole people? **4.** What do you make of verse 14? Is there a process being described, or simply two ways of saying the same thing? **5.** What is the psalmist's mood about being chastened (vv. 17–18)? **6.** Why does the psalmist call himself "righteous" (vv. 19–20)? Why does he feel worthy to enter the "gates of righteousness"? **7.** Who are the "builders" (v. 22)? What "stone" do they reject? What is a capstone (see Zec 4:7–9)? Who did the New Testament writers see in this alle-

---

ᵃ16 Or *servant, your faithful son*   *ᵇ19,2* Hebrew *Hallelu Yah*

gory (see Ac 4:8–11)? **8.** "Hosanna" is Hebrew for "O grant salvation." Who do you think is "he who comes in the name of the Lord" (vv. 25–26)? How does this thanksgiving procession end (v. 27; see Ne 8:15–18)?

♡ **1.** Have you ever felt like a "stone the builders rejected"? How did you handle it? Why do you suppose Martin Luther called this his favorite psalm? **2.** Do you feel part of a spiritual community that has gone through "chastening"? Or must you "go it alone" spiritually? Who is the "us" in your "Lord, save us"? **3.** Where do you need help right now? Joy? Victory? Success? What promise do you hold on to? **4.** Read verse 24. On a scale of 1 to 10, how much are you rejoicing today? What's keeping you from rejoicing more?

📖 **1.** What teacher or friend helped you enjoy a subject of study you once disliked? How did this person encourage you? **2.** In how many languages do you know your A,B,Cs?

📖 **1.** What is the positive intention of God's law? What promise is implied in seeking the Lord wholeheartedly? Can only "perfect" people be blessed? Why or why not? **2.** What deeper devotion underlies devotion to the law? How is such commitment shown? What is the law's final purpose?

♡ What or whom do you love so much that no language adequately expresses your devotion?

¹⁴The LORD is my strength and my song;
　　he has become my salvation.

¹⁵Shouts of joy and victory
　　resound in the tents of the righteous:
　"The LORD's right hand has done mighty things!
¹⁶　The LORD's right hand is lifted high;
　　the LORD's right hand has done mighty things!"

¹⁷I will not die but live,
　　and will proclaim what the LORD has done.
¹⁸The LORD has chastened me severely,
　　but he has not given me over to death.

¹⁹Open for me the gates of righteousness;
　　I will enter and give thanks to the LORD.
²⁰This is the gate of the LORD
　　through which the righteous may enter.
²¹I will give you thanks, for you answered me;
　　you have become my salvation.

²²The stone the builders rejected
　　has become the capstone;
²³the LORD has done this,
　　and it is marvelous in our eyes.
²⁴This is the day the LORD has made;
　　let us rejoice and be glad in it.

²⁵O LORD, save us;
　　O LORD, grant us success.
²⁶Blessed is he who comes in the name of the LORD.
　　From the house of the LORD we bless you.ᵃ
²⁷The LORD is God,
　　and he has made his light shine upon us.
　With boughs in hand, join in the festal procession
　　upᵇ to the horns of the altar.

²⁸You are my God, and I will give you thanks;
　　you are my God, and I will exalt you.

²⁹Give thanks to the LORD, for he is good;
　　his love endures forever.

Psalm 119ᶜ

א Aleph

¹Blessed are they whose ways are blameless,
　　who walk according to the law of the LORD.
²Blessed are they who keep his statutes
　　and seek him with all their heart.
³They do nothing wrong;
　　they walk in his ways.
⁴You have laid down precepts
　　that are to be fully obeyed.
⁵Oh, that my ways were steadfast
　　in obeying your decrees!
⁶Then I would not be put to shame
　　when I consider all your commands.
⁷I will praise you with an upright heart

ᵃ26 The Hebrew is plural.　　ᵇ27 Or *Bind the festal sacrifice with ropes / and take it*
ᶜThis psalm is an acrostic poem; the verses of each stanza begin with the same letter of the Hebrew alphabet.

as I learn your righteous laws.
⁸I will obey your decrees;
do not utterly forsake me.

ב Beth

⁹How can a young man keep his way pure?
By living according to your word.
¹⁰I seek you with all my heart;
do not let me stray from your commands.
¹¹I have hidden your word in my heart
that I might not sin against you.
¹²Praise be to you, O LORD;
teach me your decrees.
¹³With my lips I recount
all the laws that come from your mouth.
¹⁴I rejoice in following your statutes
as one rejoices in great riches.
¹⁵I meditate on your precepts
and consider your ways.
¹⁶I delight in your decrees;
I will not neglect your word.

ג Gimel

¹⁷Do good to your servant, and I will live;
I will obey your word.
¹⁸Open my eyes that I may see
wonderful things in your law.
¹⁹I am a stranger on earth;
do not hide your commands from me.
²⁰My soul is consumed with longing
for your laws at all times.
²¹You rebuke the arrogant, who are cursed
and who stray from your commands.
²²Remove from me scorn and contempt,
for I keep your statutes.
²³Though rulers sit together and slander me,
your servant will meditate on your decrees.
²⁴Your statutes are my delight;
they are my counselors.

ד Daleth

²⁵I am laid low in the dust;
preserve my life according to your word.
²⁶I recounted my ways and you answered me;
teach me your decrees.
²⁷Let me understand the teaching of your precepts;
then I will meditate on your wonders.
²⁸My soul is weary with sorrow;
strengthen me according to your word.
²⁹Keep me from deceitful ways;
be gracious to me through your law.
³⁰I have chosen the way of truth;
I have set my heart on your laws.
³¹I hold fast to your statutes, O LORD;
do not let me be put to shame.
³²I run in the path of your commands,
for you have set my heart free.

What do teenage boys you know do for fun?

1. Can youthful indiscretion be avoided? If so, how much of yourself is involved? How can you do this? 2. What practical steps can you take to pattern your life after God's word? 3. What attitude is a hallmark of following the law? What does this say about the psalmist's perception of the law?

In each eight-verse stanza of this psalm, the verses all begin with the Hebrew letter shown at the top of the stanza. What eight "B-words" describe your group's spiritual life?

What is your idea of something good?

1. Why does the psalmist's life depend on God's word? What does it mean to be a "stranger on earth"? 2. When have you longed to know God's will? Are you longing for it now? 3. How can you be in a position to have your eyes opened by God? Are good people immune from slander? 4. What is your comfort when others have turned against you?

What eight "G-words" describe your group's spiritual life?

When were you last feeling down in the dumps?

1. Are those who follow God's word exempt from stress? Depression? What does suffering motivate the psalmist to do? 2. Is God willing to hear his list of troubles? 3. What is your attitude toward those around you who suffer? 4. What three things does he ask God to supply (vv. 27–29)? How has he prepared himself to receive God's help?

What eight "D-words" describe your group's spiritual life?

What do you desire with all your heart?

1. What teaching does the psalmist want from God: theory or practice? To what might "selfish gain" refer? **2.** What "worthless things" distract you from following God? **3.** Although he longs for God's law, what "disgrace" threatens him? How does his poverty or disease make God look? Can he expect longevity and wealth from obeying God?

What eight "H-words" describe your group's spiritual life?

How would you describe your attempts at witnessing?

1. To what "promise" does the psalmist refer? What commitment is necessary to effectively speak God's truth? **2.** Does the Jewish law seem like a burden to him (v. 45)? Can anyone dispute the justice of God's law? **3.** Does the psalmist actually worship the law (v. 48)? Can God's person really be separated from God's will?

What eight "W-words" describe your group's spiritual life?

What zoo animal best describes your personality?

1. What "promise" keeps the psalmist going in crisis? **2.** What two irritants threaten his hope (vv. 51,53)? **3.** Does he seem to have a permanent home (v. 54)? **4.** What's the theme of his song? What's your song? How do you practice it?

What eight "Z-words" (or Z-sounding words) describe your group's spiritual life?

ה   He

33Teach me, O LORD, to follow your decrees;
    then I will keep them to the end.
34Give me understanding, and I will keep your law
    and obey it with all my heart.
35Direct me in the path of your commands,
    for there I find delight.
36Turn my heart toward your statutes
    and not toward selfish gain.
37Turn my eyes away from worthless things;
    preserve my life according to your word.ᵃ
38Fulfill your promise to your servant,
    so that you may be feared.
39Take away the disgrace I dread,
    for your laws are good.
40How I long for your precepts!
    Preserve my life in your righteousness.

ו   Waw

41May your unfailing love come to me, O LORD,
    your salvation according to your promise;
42then I will answer the one who taunts me,
    for I trust in your word.
43Do not snatch the word of truth from my mouth,
    for I have put my hope in your laws.
44I will always obey your law,
    for ever and ever.
45I will walk about in freedom,
    for I have sought out your precepts.
46I will speak of your statutes before kings
    and will not be put to shame,
47for I delight in your commands
    because I love them.
48I lift up my hands toᵇ your commands, which I love,
    and I meditate on your decrees.

ז   Zayin

49Remember your word to your servant,
    for you have given me hope.
50My comfort in my suffering is this:
    Your promise preserves my life.
51The arrogant mock me without restraint,
    but I do not turn from your law.
52I remember your ancient laws, O LORD,
    and I find comfort in them.
53Indignation grips me because of the wicked,
    who have forsaken your law.
54Your decrees are the theme of my song
    wherever I lodge.
55In the night I remember your name, O LORD,
    and I will keep your law.
56This has been my practice:
    I obey your precepts.

ᵃ37 Two manuscripts of the Masoretic Text and Dead Sea Scrolls; most manuscripts of the Masoretic Text *life in your way*   ᵇ48 Or *for*

ה   Heth

57You are my portion, O Lord;
    I have promised to obey your words.
58I have sought your face with all my heart;
    be gracious to me according to your promise.
59I have considered my ways
    and have turned my steps to your statutes.
60I will hasten and not delay
    to obey your commands.
61Though the wicked bind me with ropes,
    I will not forget your law.
62At midnight I rise to give you thanks
    for your righteous laws.
63I am a friend to all who fear you,
    to all who follow your precepts.
64The earth is filled with your love, O Lord;
    teach me your decrees.

ט   Teth

65Do good to your servant
    according to your word, O Lord.
66Teach me knowledge and good judgment,
    for I believe in your commands.
67Before I was afflicted I went astray,
    but now I obey your word.
68You are good, and what you do is good;
    teach me your decrees.
69Though the arrogant have smeared me with lies,
    I keep your precepts with all my heart.
70Their hearts are callous and unfeeling,
    but I delight in your law.
71It was good for me to be afflicted
    so that I might learn your decrees.
72The law from your mouth is more precious to me
    than thousands of pieces of silver and gold.

י   Yodh

73Your hands made me and formed me;
    give me understanding to learn your commands.
74May those who fear you rejoice when they see
        me,
    for I have put my hope in your word.
75I know, O Lord, that your laws are righteous,
    and in faithfulness you have afflicted me.
76May your unfailing love be my comfort,
    according to your promise to your servant.
77Let your compassion come to me that I may live,
    for your law is my delight.
78May the arrogant be put to shame for wronging
        me without cause;
    but I will meditate on your precepts.
79May those who fear you turn to me,
    those who understand your statutes.
80May my heart be blameless toward your decrees,
    that I may not be put to shame.

What about the church do you most cherish?

1. To what did "portion" refer for the Israelite (see 16:5–6)? What does it mean to have the Lord as your portion? How might introspection help? 2. Is the psalmist bound with physical "ropes"? What in society "ties you up"? 3. How involved is the commitment to remember God's law? How involved are you? 4. Who lends support to the psalmist? Who supports you?

What eight "CH-words" describe your group's spiritual life?

What is it that you do, collect or say by the thousands?

1. How many times does the psalmist use the word "good"? 2. What does he assume about God's discipline? What character changes are evident? How does he assess the law's value? 3. Which would you take today: $10,000 or a good Bible study? 4. Do you welcome God's discipline? How about "constructive criticism" from others?

What eight "TH-words" describe your group's spiritual life?

Describe a time when you were wrongly judged.

1. What is the purpose of the intellect? With whom does the psalmist hope to be popular? Why? 2. Against whom will they be his allies (vv. 78–79)? 3. Do people light up when you come in the room? Should they? 4. Is it realistic to try to be "blameless"? What happens if you set a lower goal?

What eight "J-words" describe your group's spiritual life?

When have you been shown kindness by someone not of your own kind?

1. What mood is the psalmist in? Why does he feel blind? Have you ever felt this way? 2. What is a "wineskin in the smoke" (v. 83)? Is his resolve fading? 3. What does he still hope obedience will bring him? 4. What bargain does he offer God (v. 88)? Have you ever made a deal with God? Did God come through? Did you keep your part?

What eight "K-words" describe your group's spiritual life?

What was most *limiting* about your growing up years? Do you live by these limits now?

1. Is the "eternal word" referring to the Jewish Law (see Pr 8:22–23)? From what do the commandments flow? 2. What enables a person to be saved? What parts of your life do you hold back? 3. Is it important to see a limit to "all perfection"? How does it affect your search for excellence?

What eight "L-words" describe your group's spiritual life?

With nothing to do, what do you tend to meditate on or mull over in your *mind*?

1. What attests to the psalmist's love of God's law? 2. What do his enemies, teachers and elders have in common? What is the heart of his boast? 3. How do you tell the difference between "right" and "wrong" paths? What role does the law play? 4. Has acting in a just but unpopular way ever left a sweet taste in your mouth? A bitter one?

What eight "M-words" describe your group's spiritual life?

כ   Kaph

81My soul faints with longing for your salvation,
  but I have put my hope in your word.
82My eyes fail, looking for your promise;
  I say, "When will you comfort me?"
83Though I am like a wineskin in the smoke,
  I do not forget your decrees.
84How long must your servant wait?
  When will you punish my persecutors?
85The arrogant dig pitfalls for me,
  contrary to your law.
86All your commands are trustworthy;
  help me, for men persecute me without cause.
87They almost wiped me from the earth,
  but I have not forsaken your precepts.
88Preserve my life according to your love,
  and I will obey the statutes of your mouth.

ל   Lamedh

89Your word, O LORD, is eternal;
  it stands firm in the heavens.
90Your faithfulness continues through all
    generations;
  you established the earth, and it endures.
91Your laws endure to this day,
  for all things serve you.
92If your law had not been my delight,
  I would have perished in my affliction.
93I will never forget your precepts,
  for by them you have preserved my life.
94Save me, for I am yours;
  I have sought out your precepts.
95The wicked are waiting to destroy me,
  but I will ponder your statutes.
96To all perfection I see a limit;
  but your commands are boundless.

מ   Mem

97Oh, how I love your law!
  I meditate on it all day long.
98Your commands make me wiser than my enemies,
  for they are ever with me.
99I have more insight than all my teachers,
  for I meditate on your statutes.
100I have more understanding than the elders,
  for I obey your precepts.
101I have kept my feet from every evil path
  so that I might obey your word.
102I have not departed from your laws,
  for you yourself have taught me.
103How sweet are your words to my taste,
  sweeter than honey to my mouth!
104I gain understanding from your precepts;
  therefore I hate every wrong path.

נ   Nun

105Your word is a lamp to my feet
  and a light for my path.

106I have taken an oath and confirmed it,
    that I will follow your righteous laws.
107I have suffered much;
    preserve my life, O LORD, according to your
        word.
108Accept, O LORD, the willing praise of my mouth,
    and teach me your laws.
109Though I constantly take my life in my hands,
    I will not forget your law.
110The wicked have set a snare for me,
    but I have not strayed from your precepts.
111Your statutes are my heritage forever;
    they are the joy of my heart.
112My heart is set on keeping your decrees
    to the very end.

ם   Samekh

113I hate double-minded men,
    but I love your law.
114You are my refuge and my shield;
    I have put my hope in your word.
115Away from me, you evildoers,
    that I may keep the commands of my God!
116Sustain me according to your promise, and I will live;
    do not let my hopes be dashed.
117Uphold me, and I will be delivered;
    I will always have regard for your decrees.
118You reject all who stray from your decrees,
    for their deceitfulness is in vain.
119All the wicked of the earth you discard like dross;
    therefore I love your statutes.
120My flesh trembles in fear of you;
    I stand in awe of your laws.

ע   Ayin

121I have done what is righteous and just;
    do not leave me to my oppressors.
122Ensure your servant's well-being;
    let not the arrogant oppress me.
123My eyes fail, looking for your salvation,
    looking for your righteous promise.
124Deal with your servant according to your love
    and teach me your decrees.
125I am your servant; give me discernment
    that I may understand your statutes.
126It is time for you to act, O LORD;
    your law is being broken.
127Because I love your commands
    more than gold, more than pure gold,
128and because I consider all your precepts right,
    I hate every wrong path.

פ   Pe

129Your statutes are wonderful;
    therefore I obey them.
130The unfolding of your words gives light;
    it gives understanding to the simple.
131I open my mouth and pant,
    longing for your commands.

What *needs* did you bring with you to the study?

1. What are the functions and images in the word "lamp"? What does it illuminate? How does it direct us? 2. With what oil does the psalmist keep it burning? What threatens to extinguish it? 3. For what would he risk his life (v. 109)? How do you keep your lamp on? Have you gotten "burned out"?

What eight "N-words" describe your group's spiritual life?

Apart from God's Word, what most *sustains* you?

1. Who are "double-minded" men (see 1Ki 18:21)? Have you ever wanted "the best of both worlds"? 2. What gives the psalmist peace of mind in his struggles with evildoers? What "hope" is he afraid might be dashed (v. 116)? 3. How does the tension between belief and uncertainty leave him feeling? How well do you handle uncertainty?

What eight "S-words" describe your group's spiritual life?

When do you feel most *oppressed* or *overwhelmed*?

1. What situation has thrown the psalmist into confusion? What does he seek to understand or discern (v. 126)? Does his plea sound confident? 2. On what does he rest his case: in his own merit or something else? 3. What do you seek when the wicked around you prosper: more money or better insight?

What eight "O-words" describe your group's spiritual life?

If you had to throw away all but three child-raising *precepts*, which three would you keep?

1. Why does the psalmist obey God's law? What kind of world would we have if everyone

acted in love and mercy? **2.** What name does he give those who ignore God's law (v. 118–119)? Why are their deeds especially painful for the psalmist? **3.** Does injustice and inhumanity ever bring you to tears? Give an example.

What eight "P-words" describe your group's spiritual life?

What is the most outlandish T-shirt design you've seen? Which is the wildest one you dare wear?

1. Why does the psalmist grow weary (v. 139)? Is he trying too hard to change other people? Is he sensitive to people being treated unjustly? Is he too interested in being proven right? Has his zeal for the law faded? Is he stubborn? Trusting? **2.** Have you persevered in an unpopular cause because you felt it was right?

What "T-shirt" best conveys your zeal for God and his Word?

What quest or questions would keep you up at night?

1. What deal does the psalmist make with God? Does it seem like a fair bargain? Why is he having a hard time sleeping? What does he do with the insomnia? **2.** What do you do with time spent waiting in lines and traffic? **3.** Who is closer: the wicked or God (vv. 150–151)? Why will God prevail?

What eight "Q-words" describe your group's spiritual life?

When have you experienced rejection for something other than the cause of Christ? Likewise, when have you experienced redemption?

1. What does the psalmist hope obeying God's law will bring him? **2.** Why does the poet "loathe" the faithless? Is it right to hate anyone? Is the lack of visible rewards getting to him?

¹³²Turn to me and have mercy on me,
  as you always do to those who love your name.
¹³³Direct my footsteps according to your word;
  let no sin rule over me.
¹³⁴Redeem me from the oppression of men,
  that I may obey your precepts.
¹³⁵Make your face shine upon your servant
  and teach me your decrees.
¹³⁶Streams of tears flow from my eyes,
  for your law is not obeyed.

צ   **Tsadhe**

¹³⁷Righteous are you, O LORD,
  and your laws are right.
¹³⁸The statutes you have laid down are righteous;
  they are fully trustworthy.
¹³⁹My zeal wears me out,
  for my enemies ignore your words.
¹⁴⁰Your promises have been thoroughly tested,
  and your servant loves them.
¹⁴¹Though I am lowly and despised,
  I do not forget your precepts.
¹⁴²Your righteousness is everlasting
  and your law is true.
¹⁴³Trouble and distress have come upon me,
  but your commands are my delight.
¹⁴⁴Your statutes are forever right;
  give me understanding that I may live.

ק   **Qoph**

¹⁴⁵I call with all my heart; answer me, O LORD,
  and I will obey your decrees.
¹⁴⁶I call out to you; save me
  and I will keep your statutes.
¹⁴⁷I rise before dawn and cry for help;
  I have put my hope in your word.
¹⁴⁸My eyes stay open through the watches of the night,
  that I may meditate on your promises.
¹⁴⁹Hear my voice in accordance with your love;
  preserve my life, O LORD, according to your
    laws.
¹⁵⁰Those who devise wicked schemes are near,
  but they are far from your law.
¹⁵¹Yet you are near, O LORD,
  and all your commands are true.
¹⁵²Long ago I learned from your statutes
  that you established them to last forever.

ר   **Resh**

¹⁵³Look upon my suffering and deliver me,
  for I have not forgotten your law.
¹⁵⁴Defend my cause and redeem me;
  preserve my life according to your promise.
¹⁵⁵Salvation is far from the wicked,
  for they do not seek out your decrees.
¹⁵⁶Your compassion is great, O LORD;
  preserve my life according to your laws.
¹⁵⁷Many are the foes who persecute me,
  but I have not turned from your statutes.

¹⁵⁸I look on the faithless with loathing,
　　for they do not obey your word.
¹⁵⁹See how I love your precepts;
　　preserve my life, O LORD, according to your
　　　love.
¹⁶⁰All your words are true;
　　all your righteous laws are eternal.

‫שׂ‬　Sin and Shin

¹⁶¹Rulers persecute me without cause,
　　but my heart trembles at your word.
¹⁶²I rejoice in your promise
　　like one who finds great spoil.
¹⁶³I hate and abhor falsehood
　　but I love your law.
¹⁶⁴Seven times a day I praise you
　　for your righteous laws.
¹⁶⁵Great peace have they who love your law,
　　and nothing can make them stumble.
¹⁶⁶I wait for your salvation, O LORD,
　　and I follow your commands.
¹⁶⁷I obey your statutes,
　　for I love them greatly.
¹⁶⁸I obey your precepts and your statutes,
　　for all my ways are known to you.

‫ת‬　Taw

¹⁶⁹May my cry come before you, O LORD;
　　give me understanding according to your word.
¹⁷⁰May my supplication come before you;
　　deliver me according to your promise.
¹⁷¹May my lips overflow with praise,
　　for you teach me your decrees.
¹⁷²May my tongue sing of your word,
　　for all your commands are righteous.
¹⁷³May your hand be ready to help me,
　　for I have chosen your precepts.
¹⁷⁴I long for your salvation, O LORD,
　　and your law is my delight.
¹⁷⁵Let me live that I may praise you,
　　and may your laws sustain me.
¹⁷⁶I have strayed like a lost sheep.
　　Seek your servant,
　　for I have not forgotten your commands.

Psalm 120

A song of ascents.

¹I call on the LORD in my distress,
　　and he answers me.
²Save me, O LORD, from lying lips
　　and from deceitful tongues.

³What will he do to you,
　　and what more besides, O deceitful tongue?
⁴He will punish you with a warrior's sharp arrows,
　　with burning coals of the broom tree.

⁵Woe to me that I dwell in Meshech,

What eight "R-words" describe your group's spiritual life?

At whose word might you shake? Why?

1. How much stake in earthly society does the psalmist have? 2. Is it important to remember the Lord "seven times a day"? What benefit does the psalmist find in it (v. 164–165)? Where do you need God's peace now? Are you waiting for the Lord's salvation? 3. How honest are you with God about "all your ways"? With yourself? Others?

What eight "SH-words" describe your group's spiritual life?

When was the last time your tongue got you in trouble?

1. God gave a specific code of law to the Jews. How can God's "laws" actively guide your day? What does it mean to delight in God's laws? What doesn't it mean? 2. How can you follow God's word without "living by the book"? 3. Do you find the end of this psalm a surprise (v. 176)? Is the psalmist satisfied yet? Do you think he ever will be?

What eight "T-words" describe your group's spiritual life?

---

1. What "peace pipe" has helped you get back in the graces of an offended one? 2. *Read aloud*—Reader(s) A: 1–4; Reader(s) B: 5–7.

1. Called "ascents," Psalms 120–134 were sung as pilgrims climbed to Jerusalem. Of what is the psalmist a victim (vv. 1–2)? 2. How powerful is the tongue (vv. 3–4; see Jas 3:6)? 3. Among what kind of people have the pilgrims lived (vv. 5–6; see Isa 21:16–17)?

1. Do you "wear your heart on your sleeve"? Or do you keep your emotional guard up? Why? 2. Do you approve of violence as a means of resolving conflict? When?

---

1. Are you more of a "night owl" or a "morning lark"? What are your most creative hours 2. *Read aloud*—Leader: 1–2; Reader(s) A: 3–4; Reader(s) B: 5–6; Leader: 7–8.

1. What is the mood of pilgrims on a winding road through hills? To what are they vulnerable (vv. 1–3)? How much more after nightfall? 2. What comfort does the traveler receive for the journey (vv. 3,5–8)?

1. Do you like to travel or dread it? What dangers lie on the road on inward journeys? 2. Does God protect you? Do you feel invincible? What form has God's protection taken for you? 3. When do you feel most vulnerable? How do you protect yourself?

1. In what way, small or large, did you "make peace" with someone this past week? 2. *Read aloud*—Reader(s) A: 1–9, odd; Reader(s) B: 2–8, even.

1. Why does David rejoice (v. 1)? What is the mood of the pilgrim crowd (vv. 3–5)? 2. What does it mean that Jerusalem is "compacted" (v. 3; see Ne 7:4)? 3. For what two reasons do the tribes come here (vv. 4–5; see Dt 16:16–17, 17:8)? 4. How are the pilgrims asked to show concern for Jerusalem (vv. 6–9)?

1. What is the mood or atmosphere prior to worship in the church? In the parking lot? The hall? What do you like or dislike about it? 2. How can you seek the prosperity of all who suffer war and oppression? Can the group help people of special interest to you?

that I live among the tents of Kedar!
⁶Too long have I lived
    among those who hate peace.
⁷I am a man of peace;
    but when I speak, they are for war.

Psalm 121

A song of ascents.

¹I lift up my eyes to the hills—
    where does my help come from?
²My help comes from the LORD,
    the Maker of heaven and earth.

³He will not let your foot slip—
    he who watches over you will not slumber;
⁴indeed, he who watches over Israel
    will neither slumber nor sleep.

⁵The LORD watches over you—
    the LORD is your shade at your right hand;
⁶the sun will not harm you by day,
    nor the moon by night.

⁷The LORD will keep you from all harm—
    he will watch over your life;
⁸the LORD will watch over your coming and going
    both now and forevermore.

Psalm 122

A song of ascents. Of David.

¹I rejoiced with those who said to me,
    "Let us go to the house of the LORD."
²Our feet are standing
    in your gates, O Jerusalem.

³Jerusalem is built like a city
    that is closely compacted together.
⁴That is where the tribes go up,
    the tribes of the LORD,
  to praise the name of the LORD
    according to the statute given to Israel.
⁵There the thrones for judgment stand,
    the thrones of the house of David.

⁶Pray for the peace of Jerusalem:
    "May those who love you be secure.
⁷May there be peace within your walls
    and security within your citadels."
⁸For the sake of my brothers and friends,
    I will say, "Peace be within you."
⁹For the sake of the house of the LORD our God,
    I will seek your prosperity.

Psalm 123

A song of ascents.

[1]I lift up my eyes to you,
   to you whose throne is in heaven.
[2]As the eyes of slaves look to the hand of their
      master,
   as the eyes of a maid look to the hand of her
      mistress,
 so our eyes look to the LORD our God,
   till he shows us his mercy.

[3]Have mercy on us, O LORD, have mercy on us,
   for we have endured much contempt.
[4]We have endured much ridicule from the proud,
   much contempt from the arrogant.

1. What kind of servant are you? 2. *Read aloud*—Reader(s) A: 1–2; Reader(s) B: 3–4.

1. What "contempt" have the pilgrims faced (v. 3; see Ne 4:1–3)? 2. For what do slaves look to their masters? The psalmist to God? 3. Why do the proud ridicule? Superiority or hidden inferiority?

1. What task did you successfully finish despite the doomsaying of observers? 2. Has God shown mercy when you've said "I've had it"?

Psalm 124

A song of ascents. Of David.

[1]If the LORD had not been on our side—
   let Israel say—
[2]if the LORD had not been on our side
   when men attacked us,
[3]when their anger flared against us,
   they would have swallowed us alive;
[4]the flood would have engulfed us,
   the torrent would have swept over us,
[5]the raging waters
   would have swept us away.

[6]Praise be to the LORD,
   who has not let us be torn by their teeth.
[7]We have escaped like a bird
   out of the fowler's snare;
 the snare has been broken,
   and we have escaped.
[8]Our help is in the name of the LORD,
   the Maker of heaven and earth.

1. What's the closest you've come to being a "dare devil"? 2. *Read aloud*—Reader(s) A: 1–7, odd; Reader(s) B: 2–8, even.

1. Jerusalem has never been threatened by flood. What foes might David be describing (vv. 1–5)? Who are "they"? 2. What realization leads to praise (v. 6)? 3. How do verses 7 and 8 further underscore Israel's helplessness and God's helpfulness?

1. If Israel had lost this battle, would David have written a psalm about God's wrath for their sin? Does God take sides? 2. From what external or internal enemy is God saving you?

Psalm 125

A song of ascents.

[1]Those who trust in the LORD are like Mount Zion,
   which cannot be shaken but endures forever.
[2]As the mountains surround Jerusalem,
   so the LORD surrounds his people
   both now and forevermore.

[3]The scepter of the wicked will not remain
      over the land allotted to the righteous,
 for then the righteous might use
   their hands to do evil.

[4]Do good, O LORD, to those who are good,
   to those who are upright in heart.

1. What has been one of your wisest purchases in terms of durability and quality? 2. *Read aloud*—Reader(s) A: 1–3, Reader(s) B: 4–5.

1. How do these pilgrims feel going up the mountain pass (vv. 1–2)? Are the trusting immune from "shaking"? 2. What does the poet fear might happen if foreign domination isn't removed (v. 3)?

1. What non-Christian influences tempt you at home, work, school or in society? How do you stay "true"? 2. When is it hardest for you to trust the Lord? Why is that?

5But those who turn to crooked ways
  the LORD will banish with the evildoers.

Peace be upon Israel.

Psalm 126

A song of ascents.

1When the LORD brought back the captives to*a*
    Zion,
  we were like men who dreamed. *b*
2Our mouths were filled with laughter,
  our tongues with songs of joy.
Then it was said among the nations,
  "The LORD has done great things for them."
3The LORD has done great things for us,
  and we are filled with joy.

4Restore our fortunes,*c* O LORD,
  like streams in the Negev.
5Those who sow in tears
  will reap with songs of joy.
6He who goes out weeping,
  carrying seed to sow,
will return with songs of joy,
  carrying sheaves with him.

Psalm 127

A song of ascents. Of Solomon.

1Unless the LORD builds the house,
  its builders labor in vain.
Unless the LORD watches over the city,
  the watchmen stand guard in vain.
2In vain you rise early
  and stay up late,
toiling for food to eat—
  for he grants sleep to*d* those he loves.

3Sons are a heritage from the LORD,
  children a reward from him.
4Like arrows in the hands of a warrior
  are sons born in one's youth.
5Blessed is the man
  whose quiver is full of them.
They will not be put to shame
  when they contend with their enemies in the
    gate.

Psalm 128

A song of ascents.

1Blessed are all who fear the LORD,
  who walk in his ways.
2You will eat the fruit of your labor;
  blessings and prosperity will be yours.

1. What period could you describe as your "golden years"? Why? 2. Read aloud—Reader(s) A: 1–5, odd; Reader(s) B: 2–6, even.

1. What mood does "we were like men who dreamed" capture? What verses show the exiles have mixed feelings? 2. On what do they agree (vv. 2–3)? 3. What problems do they still face (vv. 4–6; see Ne 5:1–5)? How do the two parables of God answering prayer differ?

1. Has God ever done something so great you had to pinch yourself to see if you were dreaming? 2. How does God tend to answer your prayers: A flash flood or a long growing season?

1. Have you ever been called a "workaholic"? Why? 2. Read aloud—Reader(s) A: 1–2; Reader(s) B: 3–5.

1. What work does Solomon renounce (v. 1)? How do those who rely on their own efforts see their work (v. 2)? 2. Is the beginning tied to the end? What is said about large families? What happens "in the gate" (v. 5)?

1. Is God building your business? Family? Support systems? Or are you? 2. Jewish law promoted big families. Are they obsolete today? Does society help or hurt family unity?

1. Describe your domestic happiness from a fruit picker's perspective: (a) Out of season? (b) Ripening? (c) Ripe and juicy? (d) Rotting? 2. Read aloud—Reader(s) A: 1–5, odd; Reader(s) B: 2–6a, even; All: 6b.

1. What type of blessings are promised the "man who fears the Lord"? Why not blessings of a more spiritual nature? 2. How are

3Your wife will be like a fruitful vine
    within your house;
your sons will be like olive shoots
    around your table.
4Thus is the man blessed
    who fears the LORD.

5May the LORD bless you from Zion
    all the days of your life;
may you see the prosperity of Jerusalem,
6   and may you live to see your children's
        children.

Peace be upon Israel.

Psalm 129

A song of ascents.

1They have greatly oppressed me from my youth—
    let Israel say—
2they have greatly oppressed me from my youth,
    but they have not gained the victory over me.
3Plowmen have plowed my back
    and made their furrows long.
4But the LORD is righteous;
    he has cut me free from the cords of the
        wicked.

5May all who hate Zion
    be turned back in shame.
6May they be like grass on the roof,
    which withers before it can grow;
7with it the reaper cannot fill his hands,
    nor the one who gathers fill his arms.
8May those who pass by not say,
    "The blessing of the LORD be upon you;
    we bless you in the name of the LORD."

Psalm 130

A song of ascents.

1Out of the depths I cry to you, O LORD;
2   O Lord, hear my voice.
    Let your ears be attentive
        to my cry for mercy.

3If you, O LORD, kept a record of sins,
    O Lord, who could stand?
4But with you there is forgiveness;
    therefore you are feared.

5I wait for the LORD, my soul waits,
    and in his word I put my hope.
6My soul waits for the Lord
    more than watchmen wait for the morning,
    more than watchmen wait for the morning.

7O Israel, put your hope in the LORD,
    for with the LORD is unfailing love
    and with him is full redemption.

---

the individual blessings bound up with national prosperity (vv. 5–6)?

1. Do you believe that God rewards good in this life? Why or why not? How or how not? 2. Will happy, godly families lead to a prosperous, peaceful nation? Why or why not? How or how not?

---

1. What chore would you prefer: mowing the lawn, putting on a new roof or cleaning house? 2. *Read aloud*—Reader(s) A: 1–4; Reader(s) B: 5–8.

1. Why has Israel been oppressed and hated throughout history (vv. 1–3)? How have the Jews managed to outlive every oppressor (v. 4)? 2. What does the psalmist wish for the "haters of Zion" (vv. 5–8)? Do you like this attitude?

1. What is freedom? Does it lie in political sovereignty? What internal menace always plagued Israel? 2. Have you ever suffered harsh treatment? Are you emotionally tied up? How? Has God cut the cords for you before? Can this group become "freedom fighters" for you?

---

1. Have you ever lost sleep anticipating the next day's events? Did it turn out like you hoped? 2. *Read aloud*—Reader(s) A: 1–7, odd; Reader(s) B: 2–8, even.

1. Where are "the depths" (v. 1)? 2. What disrupted his relationship with God (v. 3)? How does forgiveness lead to revering God (v. 4)? 3. With what attitude does he await forgiveness (vv. 5–6)? What is God's attitude?

1. Why do you think this psalm is a standard for Christian funerals? 2. Has sin ever cut a rift between you and God? Was a closeness restored? How? 3. Have you been waiting for something a long time? Why don't you give up? How long will you wait?

1. When does a child sit still? **2.** *Read aloud*—Reader(s) A: 1–2; Reader(s) B: 3.

1. What does David avoid (v. 1)? Why? **2.** What does the "weaned child" image suggest? **3.** What's important to David?

1. How do you "still your soul"? **2.** To what "weaning" has spiritual growth called you?

---

1. Who are your two closest friends? Why are you close? Is your time together prearranged or does it "just happen"? **2.** Have you ever had to spend the night in a car? Airport or train station? Out in the brush or on a hillside? Why? **3.** *Read aloud*—Reader(s) A: 1–17, odd; Reader(s) B: 2–18, even.

1. What "hardships" has David endured (v. 1; see 2Sa 7:1)? What does he promise Yahweh? Does God need an earthly "dwelling"? **2.** Where was the Ark of the Covenant prior to David's conquest of Jerusalem (v. 6; see 1Sa 6:21–7:2)? Why does he want it in his city? **3.** What does the Lord swear to David (v. 11; see 2Sa 7:16)? What condition is placed on the promise (v. 12)? Based on what happened to Israel, how would you say his sons did? **4.** On what is the permanence of David's dynasty based (v. 13)? How will Israel be blessed (vv. 14–18)?

1. What human needs are fulfilled in the building of churches and shrines? In the anointing of human leaders? Should we get beyond such needs? **2.** Do you give yourself deadlines? Is it good to put time limits on goals? What is the relationship between human and divine effort? **3.** What need does God want you to fill in your church? At home? At work? In the neighborhood? How committed are you to the project(s)? Have you made so many promises, you can't fulfill them all? **4.** What do you make of the fact that there is no longer a king in Israel and that Jerusalem was conquered? Is God unable to keep his promises? Or did the peo-

---

[8]He himself will redeem Israel
from all their sins.

Psalm 131

A song of ascents. Of David.

[1]My heart is not proud, O LORD,
my eyes are not haughty;
I do not concern myself with great matters
or things too wonderful for me.
[2]But I have stilled and quieted my soul;
like a weaned child with its mother,
like a weaned child is my soul within me.

[3]O Israel, put your hope in the LORD
both now and forevermore.

Psalm 132

A song of ascents.

[1]O LORD, remember David
and all the hardships he endured.

[2]He swore an oath to the LORD
and made a vow to the Mighty One of Jacob:
[3]"I will not enter my house
or go to my bed—
[4]I will allow no sleep to my eyes,
no slumber to my eyelids,
[5]till I find a place for the LORD,
a dwelling for the Mighty One of Jacob."

[6]We heard it in Ephrathah,
we came upon it in the fields of Jaar[a]:[b]
[7]"Let us go to his dwelling place;
let us worship at his footstool—
[8]arise, O LORD, and come to your resting place,
you and the ark of your might.
[9]May your priests be clothed with righteousness;
may your saints sing for joy."

[10]For the sake of David your servant,
do not reject your anointed one.

[11]The LORD swore an oath to David,
a sure oath that he will not revoke:
"One of your own descendants
I will place on your throne—
[12]if your sons keep my covenant
and the statutes I teach them,
then their sons will sit
on your throne for ever and ever."

[13]For the LORD has chosen Zion,
he has desired it for his dwelling:
[14]"This is my resting place for ever and ever;
here I will sit enthroned, for I have desired it—
[15]I will bless her with abundant provisions;

---

[a]6 That is, Kiriath Jearim   [b]6 Or *heard of it in Ephrathah, / we found it in the fields of Jaar.* (And no quotes around verses 7-9)

her poor will I satisfy with food.
¹⁶I will clothe her priests with salvation,
and her saints will ever sing for joy.

¹⁷"Here I will make a horn^a grow for David
and set up a lamp for my anointed one.
¹⁸I will clothe his enemies with shame,
but the crown on his head will be resplendent."

Psalm 133

A song of ascents. Of David.

¹How good and pleasant it is
when brothers live together in unity!
²It is like precious oil poured on the head,
running down on the beard,
running down on Aaron's beard,
down upon the collar of his robes.
³It is as if the dew of Hermon
were falling on Mount Zion.
For there the LORD bestows his blessing,
even life forevermore.

Psalm 134

A song of ascents.

¹Praise the LORD, all you servants of the LORD
who minister by night in the house of the LORD.
²Lift up your hands in the sanctuary
and praise the LORD.

³May the LORD, the Maker of heaven and earth,
bless you from Zion.

Psalm 135

¹Praise the LORD.^b

Praise the name of the LORD;
praise him, you servants of the LORD,
²you who minister in the house of the LORD,
in the courts of the house of our God.

³Praise the LORD, for the LORD is good;
sing praise to his name, for that is pleasant.
⁴For the LORD has chosen Jacob to be his own,
Israel to be his treasured possession.

⁵I know that the LORD is great,
that our Lord is greater than all gods.
⁶The LORD does whatever pleases him,
in the heavens and on the earth,
in the seas and all their depths.
⁷He makes clouds rise from the ends of the earth;
he sends lightning with the rain
and brings out the wind from his storehouses.

⁸He struck down the firstborn of Egypt,

---

ple bring it on themselves? 5. How has Israel become the most dangerous place for Jews today?

---

1. Are you easy to live with? Why? 2. *Read aloud*—Reader(s) A: 1–2; Reader(s) B: 3.

1. How is unity like the oil used to anoint priests (see Ex 30:22–30)? Like a morning dew? 2. What does "life forevermore" mean here?

1. Do we really need separate, competing institutional churches? 2. Where do you find Christian community? What hinders it?

Read aloud—All: 1–2; Leader: 3.

What night workers does the poet have in mind (see Isa 30:29)? Why minister at night?

1. What is the last thing you do before going to sleep? 2. Do you ever "bless" others? Take group time to bless each other.

---

1. Have you ever inherited anything? What would you like to inherit some day? 2. What great person, alive or dead, do you admire? Why? 3. *Read aloud*—Leader: 1; Reader(s) A:2–20, even; Reader(s) B: 3–19, odd.

1. This psalm borrows verses from several other psalms. To whom is the call of worship addressed (vv. 1–2)? What three reasons are given for praising the Lord (vv. 3–4)? 2. What title for God would you draw from verses 5–7? From verses 8–12? Why does the psalmist praise God for the slaughter of Egyptians and Canaanites? How do you feel praising God for such events? 3. What does it mean to "vindicate his people" (v. 14; see Dt 32:36)? 4. What is the difference between the Lord and idols (vv. 15–17)? If idols are so impotent, why would anyone worship them? How does the worshipper—of God or idol—become like the object of worship? 5. What is the signifi-

---

^a*17 Horn* here symbolizes strong one, that is, king.   ^b*1* Hebrew *Hallelu Yah*; also in verses 3 and 21

cance of the four groups called to praise God (vv. 19–20)?

1. In your prayers, are you generally God's servant or is God yours? What does it mean for you to be a servant of the Lord? **2.** What's pleasant about praising God? Does this mean you always have to feel like doing it? Can worship be pleasant when you're not in the mood for it? Why or why not? **3.** Do you feel like one of God's chosen ones? Why or why not? How could you come to view yourself as a treasure in God's eyes? Would a stronger assurance of God's high esteem of you give you new attitudes and behavior? **4.** How do ancient and modern day idols differ? How are they alike? In what do you place your trust? How have you become like that in which you trust? **5.** How would you rewrite verses 15–18 to mock modern idols? Brainstorm some ideas in the group.

1. Who was your childhood hero? Teen idol? What attracted you: Strength? Beauty? Smarts? Cool? Other? **2.** What skill would you like to acquire in your sleep tonight? How would you use this ability? What would be the disadvantages of having this gift? **3.** *Read aloud*—Reader(s) A: read the first half of the verse; Reader(s) B: read the second half of the verse.

1. This psalm is called "the Great Hallel" and is recited at Jewish Passover meals. What is the purpose of a "call and response" prayer? **2.** What types of "wonders" are listed? In what different spheres of life has the Lord been actively involved? **3.** How are the acts of verse 10 and 17–20 signs of God's enduring love? **4.** Is the refrain monotonous or does it center your thoughts?

1. What are some modern day "gods" and "lords"? How do they vie for your attention from

the firstborn of men and animals.
⁹He sent his signs and wonders into your midst, O Egypt,
against Pharaoh and all his servants.
¹⁰He struck down many nations and killed mighty kings—
¹¹Sihon king of the Amorites, Og king of Bashan and all the kings of Canaan—
¹²and he gave their land as an inheritance, an inheritance to his people Israel.

¹³Your name, O Lord, endures forever, your renown, O Lord, through all generations.
¹⁴For the Lord will vindicate his people and have compassion on his servants.

¹⁵The idols of the nations are silver and gold, made by the hands of men.
¹⁶They have mouths, but cannot speak, eyes, but they cannot see;
¹⁷they have ears, but cannot hear, nor is there breath in their mouths.
¹⁸Those who make them will be like them, and so will all who trust in them.

¹⁹O house of Israel, praise the Lord; O house of Aaron, praise the Lord;
²⁰O house of Levi, praise the Lord; you who fear him, praise the Lord.
²¹Praise be to the Lord from Zion, to him who dwells in Jerusalem.

Praise the Lord.

Psalm 136

¹Give thanks to the Lord, for he is good.
His love endures forever.
²Give thanks to the God of gods.
His love endures forever.
³Give thanks to the Lord of lords:
His love endures forever.

⁴to him who alone does great wonders,
His love endures forever.
⁵who by his understanding made the heavens,
His love endures forever.
⁶who spread out the earth upon the waters,
His love endures forever.
⁷who made the great lights—
His love endures forever.
⁸the sun to govern the day,
His love endures forever.
⁹the moon and stars to govern the night;
His love endures forever.

¹⁰to him who struck down the firstborn of Egypt
His love endures forever.
¹¹and brought Israel out from among them
His love endures forever.

¹²with a mighty hand and outstretched arm;
> *His love endures forever.*

¹³to him who divided the Red Sea[a] asunder
> *His love endures forever.*

¹⁴and brought Israel through the midst of it,
> *His love endures forever.*

¹⁵but swept Pharaoh and his army into the Red Sea;
> *His love endures forever.*

¹⁶to him who led his people through the desert,
> *His love endures forever.*

¹⁷who struck down great kings,
> *His love endures forever.*

¹⁸and killed mighty kings—
> *His love endures forever.*

¹⁹Sihon king of the Amorites
> *His love endures forever.*

²⁰and Og king of Bashan—
> *His love endures forever.*

²¹and gave their land as an inheritance,
> *His love endures forever.*

²²an inheritance to his servant Israel;
> *His love endures forever.*

²³to the One who remembered us in our low estate
> *His love endures forever.*

²⁴and freed us from our enemies,
> *His love endures forever.*

²⁵and who gives food to every creature.
> *His love endures forever.*

²⁶Give thanks to the God of heaven.
> *His love endures forever.*

Psalm 137

¹By the rivers of Babylon we sat and wept
  when we remembered Zion.
²There on the poplars
  we hung our harps,
³for there our captors asked us for songs,
  our tormentors demanded songs of joy;
  they said, "Sing us one of the songs of Zion!"

⁴How can we sing the songs of the LORD
  while in a foreign land?
⁵If I forget you, O Jerusalem,
  may my right hand forget ⌞its skill⌟.
⁶May my tongue cling to the roof of my mouth
  if I do not remember you,
 if I do not consider Jerusalem
  my highest joy.

⁷Remember, O LORD, what the Edomites did
  on the day Jerusalem fell.
"Tear it down," they cried,
  "tear it down to its foundations!"

⁸O Daughter of Babylon, doomed to destruction,
  happy is he who repays you

[a] 13 Hebrew *Yam Suph*; that is, Sea of Reeds; also in verse 15

time to time? **2.** Which of the wonders listed especially moves you to thanksgiving? What wonder from your own life would you add to the litany? **3.** Why do you suppose God so earnestly calls us to give thanks in this and other psalms? Is there anything you don't want to thank God for? Why? Is it possible that you have stopped believing in God's ability to do "great wonders" there? **4.** Do you consciously or unconsciously tell yourself that God's love for you is conditional, limited or dependent upon your performance? How can you hold the reality of God's love in the forefront of your mind? What practical difference would it make? **5.** How do you feel when those who are evil suffer? Do you rejoice that justice is done? Are you sad when anyone suffers? Do you have mixed feelings?

1. Have you ever sung a solo? Is it harder to sing in front of a group of people or speak to them? Why? **2.** *Read aloud—* Reader(s) A: 1–3; Reader(s) B: 4–6; Reader(s) A: 7–9.

1. When does this psalm take place? What is the mood of the exiled musicians (vv. 1–3)? **2.** Why do their captors demand songs (v. 3)? Why is this an offensive request? Why is remembering Jerusalem so important to the psalmist? **3.** What had Edom done (v. 7; see Ob 8–14)? What does he wish for them in return? What does he wish for Babylon? What must the Babylonians have done to the Jews?

1. Have you or a loved one experienced deep grief? Did you "hang your harps"? Or were you pressured to keep playing and singing as before? When is it okay to hang our harps? **2.** Do you feel a sense of belonging in this group, or are you in a "foreign land"? How could you feel at home?

for what you have done to us—
⁹he who seizes your infants
and dashes them against the rocks.

Psalm 138

Of David.

¹I will praise you, O LORD, with all my heart;
before the "gods" I will sing your praise.
²I will bow down toward your holy temple
and will praise your name
for your love and your faithfulness,
for you have exalted above all things
your name and your word.
³When I called, you answered me;
you made me bold and stouthearted.

⁴May all the kings of the earth praise you, O LORD,
when they hear the words of your mouth.
⁵May they sing of the ways of the LORD,
for the glory of the LORD is great.

⁶Though the LORD is on high, he looks upon the
lowly,
but the proud he knows from afar.
⁷Though I walk in the midst of trouble,
you preserve my life;
you stretch out your hand against the anger of my
foes,
with your right hand you save me.
⁸The LORD will fulfill ⌐his purpose⌐ for me;
your love, O LORD, endures forever—
do not abandon the works of your hands.

Psalm 139

For the director of music. Of David. A psalm.

¹O LORD, you have searched me
and you know me.
²You know when I sit and when I rise;
you perceive my thoughts from afar.
³You discern my going out and my lying down;
you are familiar with all my ways.
⁴Before a word is on my tongue
you know it completely, O LORD.

⁵You hem me in—behind and before;
you have laid your hand upon me.
⁶Such knowledge is too wonderful for me,
too lofty for me to attain.

⁷Where can I go from your Spirit?
Where can I flee from your presence?
⁸If I go up to the heavens, you are there;
if I make my bed in the depths,ᵃ you are
there.
⁹If I rise on the wings of the dawn,
if I settle on the far side of the sea,

---

1. Who was the best friend you ever had? What was special about him or her? **2.** *Read aloud*—Reader(s) A: 1–3; Reader(s) B: 4–6; Leader: 7–8.

1. In the context of the psalm, before what "gods" does David sing (v. 1): Angels? Idols? Earthly rulers? What "word" has God exalted (v. 2)? **2.** How does David tie his own life into something greater (vv. 4–5)? What possible picture captures his attention (see Isa 40:5)? **3.** What mood underlies the thanksgiving (vv. 6–8)? How does God help the "lowly"? **4.** How does God's cause become the psalmist's own (v. 8)?

1. What exterior factors encourage you to praise God? What interior ones? **2.** Why is humility a prerequisite for asking God to grant a request? How do humility and weakness differ? **3.** Do you feel that God is fulfilling a purpose in you? What? How do you find it? Can the group help?

---

1. If you found out the government was bugging your home, what would you immediately stop saying or doing? **2.** Break into pairs and jot down as many positive facts about your partner as you can in three minutes. Then tell your partner something he or she doesn't already know. **3.** *Read aloud*—Reader(s) A: 1–21, odd; Reader(s) B: 2–22, even; All: 23–24.

1. How does David feel about God's total knowledge of him (vv. 1–6)? Is he restricted or protected? Free or oppressed? Why does he bother to pray (v. 4)? Is he free to choose his own actions (v. 6)? **2.** Why does David think about escaping God (vv. 7–12)? What directions are mentioned (vv. 8–9)? What do verses 11 and 12 say about God's ability to transform the most hopeless situations? **3.** The ancients spoke of child-bearing in mysterious terms (vv. 13–16). Has science added or subtracted from the mystery of life?

ᵃ8 Hebrew *Sheol*

¹⁰even there your hand will guide me,
   your right hand will hold me fast.

¹¹If I say, "Surely the darkness will hide me
   and the light become night around me,"
¹²even the darkness will not be dark to you;
   the night will shine like the day,
   for darkness is as light to you.

¹³For you created my inmost being;
   you knit me together in my mother's womb.
¹⁴I praise you because I am fearfully and
     wonderfully made;
   your works are wonderful,
   I know that full well.
¹⁵My frame was not hidden from you
   when I was made in the secret place.
   When I was woven together in the depths of the
     earth,
¹⁶ your eyes saw my unformed body.
  All the days ordained for me
   were written in your book
   before one of them came to be.

¹⁷How precious to[a] me are your thoughts, O God!
   How vast is the sum of them!
¹⁸Were I to count them,
   they would outnumber the grains of sand.
  When I awake,
   I am still with you.

¹⁹If only you would slay the wicked, O God!
   Away from me, you bloodthirsty men!
²⁰They speak of you with evil intent;
   your adversaries misuse your name.
²¹Do I not hate those who hate you, O Lord,
   and abhor those who rise up against you?
²²I have nothing but hatred for them;
   I count them my enemies.

²³Search me, O God, and know my heart;
   test me and know my anxious thoughts.
²⁴See if there is any offensive way in me,
   and lead me in the way everlasting.

Psalm 140

For the director of music. A psalm of David.

¹Rescue me, O Lord, from evil men;
   protect me from men of violence,
²who devise evil plans in their hearts
   and stir up war every day.
³They make their tongues as sharp as a serpent's;
   the poison of vipers is on their lips.   *Selah*

⁴Keep me, O Lord, from the hands of the wicked;
   protect me from men of violence
   who plan to trip my feet.
⁵Proud men have hidden a snare for me;

a17 Or *concerning*

What do you think of David's conclusion (v. 16)? **4.** To what "thoughts" do you think David refers (vv. 17–18)? What thought plagues him in particular (v. 19)? **5.** What do you think of David's "hatred" (vv. 21–22)? Is the mood of personal animosity or concern for God's honor? **6.** Why does he ask God to search his thoughts? How does he show an awareness of his own limitations (vv. 23–24)?

1. How does this Psalm make you feel about yourself and your value to God? **2.** What does it say to you about people with various disabilities? **3.** If God is so omnipresent, why do so many people not believe in God? Can non-believers escape God more easily than believers? **4.** Is there a "dark" situation in your life? How can it be brought into God's light? **5.** Has God "ordained" all your days (see Jer 1:5)? What does this mean? What doesn't it mean? **6.** Do you ask God to check your motives? Does God correct you with an internal voice or do you need the feedback of others? **7.** Does any human relationship in some way resemble your relationship with God? How?

1. Do you like action movies with lots of fighting and gore? Why or why not? What is attractive about violence? **2.** If you were elected King or Queen of the World for a day, what one thing would you do to promote peace? Why? **3.** *Read aloud*—Reader(s) A: 1–5; Reader(s) B: 6–8; Leader: 9–11; All: 12–13.

1. What characterizes "evil men" (vv. 1–3)? Is David opposed to violence in general or just when it's aimed at him (vv. 4–5)? **2.** How does David contrast his character with his enemies' (vv. 6–7)? What argument does he make (v. 8)? Why would the wicked become proud? **3.** What does David want God to do (vv. 9–11)? Should God answer such a prayer? **4.** Why the change in mood between verses 11 and 12? What might God have said to David to change his tone?

1. Who or what is your greatest enemy? What ensnares you, keeping you from following the path God has set out for you? From reaching your own goals and dreams? What would you like God to do? **2.** In what circumstances is violence appropriate? What do you make of Jesus' refusal to defend himself (see Mt 26:51–52)? Why was Peter out of line?

1. From whom can you accept constructive criticism gracefully? Why that person? Why not others? **2.** Read aloud—Reader(s) A: 1–4; Reader(s) B: 5–7; All: 8–10.

1. What clues do we have that David wrote this "on the run" (vv. 1–2)? What does he need (vv. 3–4)? Why? What awareness undergirds the request (see Pr 13:3)? **2.** Why would a righteous man "strike" David (v. 5)? What would be kind about it (see Pr 9:8)? **3.** What do you think verse 6 means? **4.** Of what is David most afraid (v. 8)? Where does he focus his attention to overcome temptation?

1. What temptations are hard for you to overcome? Can God actually "guard" you and "keep watch" over you? Or do you tend to go it alone? Who else can help you keep your heart from being drawn to evil? **2.** Do you get defensive easily? How can you receive good feedback on your spiritual growth?

they have spread out the cords of their net
and have set traps for me along my path. *Selah*

⁶O Lord, I say to you, "You are my God."
Hear, O Lord, my cry for mercy.
⁷O Sovereign Lord, my strong deliverer,
who shields my head in the day of battle—
⁸do not grant the wicked their desires, O Lord;
do not let their plans succeed,
or they will become proud. *Selah*

⁹Let the heads of those who surround me
be covered with the trouble their lips have
caused.
¹⁰Let burning coals fall upon them;
may they be thrown into the fire,
into miry pits, never to rise.
¹¹Let slanderers not be established in the land;
may disaster hunt down men of violence.

¹²I know that the Lord secures justice for the poor
and upholds the cause of the needy.
¹³Surely the righteous will praise your name
and the upright will live before you.

Psalm 141

A psalm of David.

¹O Lord, I call to you; come quickly to me.
Hear my voice when I call to you.
²May my prayer be set before you like incense;
may the lifting up of my hands be like the
evening sacrifice.

³Set a guard over my mouth, O Lord;
keep watch over the door of my lips.
⁴Let not my heart be drawn to what is evil,
to take part in wicked deeds
with men who are evildoers;
let me not eat of their delicacies.

⁵Let a righteous man^a strike me—it is a kindness;
let him rebuke me—it is oil on my head.
My head will not refuse it.

Yet my prayer is ever against the deeds of
evildoers;
⁶ their rulers will be thrown down from the cliffs,
and the wicked will learn that my words were
well spoken.
⁷They will say, "As one plows and breaks up the
earth,
so our bones have been scattered at the mouth
of the grave.^b"

⁸But my eyes are fixed on you, O Sovereign Lord;
in you I take refuge—do not give me over to
death.
⁹Keep me from the snares they have laid for me,
from the traps set by evildoers.

^a5 Or *Let the Righteous One*   ^b7 Hebrew *Sheol*

[10]Let the wicked fall into their own nets,
while I pass by in safety.

Psalm 142

A *maskil*[a] of David. When he was in the
cave. A prayer.

[1]I cry aloud to the LORD;
I lift up my voice to the LORD for mercy.
[2]I pour out my complaint before him;
before him I tell my trouble.

[3]When my spirit grows faint within me,
it is you who know my way.
In the path where I walk
men have hidden a snare for me.
[4]Look to my right and see;
no one is concerned for me.
I have no refuge;
no one cares for my life.

[5]I cry to you, O LORD;
I say, "You are my refuge,
my portion in the land of the living."
[6]Listen to my cry,
for I am in desperate need;
rescue me from those who pursue me,
for they are too strong for me.
[7]Set me free from my prison,
that I may praise your name.

Then the righteous will gather about me
because of your goodness to me.

Psalm 143

A psalm of David.

[1]O LORD, hear my prayer,
listen to my cry for mercy;
in your faithfulness and righteousness
come to my relief.
[2]Do not bring your servant into judgment,
for no one living is righteous before you.

[3]The enemy pursues me,
he crushes me to the ground;
he makes me dwell in darkness
like those long dead.
[4]So my spirit grows faint within me;
my heart within me is dismayed.
[5]I remember the days of long ago;
I meditate on all your works
and consider what your hands have done.
[6]I spread out my hands to you;
my soul thirsts for you like a parched land.

Selah

[7]Answer me quickly, O LORD;

[a]Title: Probably a literary or musical term

1. If God kept a complaint box, what grievance would you put in it? 2. *Read aloud*— Reader(s) A: 1–7, odd; Reader(s) B: 2–6, even.

1. In which cave do you think this psalm was written (see 1Sa 22:1–2 and 1Sa 24:1–7)? What is the tone of this lament (vv. 1–3)? How free is David to express his true feelings? 2. What's painful about the immediate circumstances (v. 4)? Is this an exaggeration? 3. What does David mean by "portion" (v. 5; see Nu 18:20)? 4. Why will the righteous "gather about" (v. 7)? What do the righteous tend to do and say when the chips are down (see Job 36: 8–9)?

1. Are there complaints you keep from God? Feelings you consider inappropriate to bring up? Do you feel this group is a safe place to speak your true feelings? Or only the positive ones? 2. Is the Lord your portion? Or are you seeking an earthly inheritance? Both? Where do you want to be?

1. How old were you when you got your first job? What was it? How are peons treated? 2. Have you ever fainted? What happened? How did you feel when you came to again? 3. *Read aloud*— Reader(s) A: 1–6; Reader(s) B: 7–12.

1. What kind of calamity do you think David faces (vv. 1–4)? Is he making excuses by saying "I'm only human" in verse 2? 2. What brings a glimmer of hope into his dark days (vv. 5–6)? What attitude motivates him? 3. Who are "those who go down to the pit" (v. 7)? Is David afraid of dying? 4. What "deal" does he strike with God (vv. 8–10)? What's his concluding argument to "persuade" God to hear his plea?

1. Is mankind all that bad? Are people really "sinful" or just ignorant? Irrational? Who made us this way, anyway? 2. When you experience calamity, can you direct your thoughts to

God and keep from becoming despondent? What do you focus on? **3.** Do you consider yourself teachable? When did you last change your mind on an important matter? **4.** When's the last time you felt you were walking on "level ground"? Are you usually climbing upwards or going "downhill"?

---

1. Did you ever protect a childhood friend? How? Did you need defending as a child? **2.** Do you like war films? Which war? Why do you find it intriguing? **3.** *Read aloud*—Reader(s) A: 1–15, odd; Reader(s) B: 2–14, even.

1. For what does David give thanks (vv. 1–2)? Why does he rejoice in war-making abilities? **2.** Why do David's thoughts turn to his insignificance (vv. 3–4)? If he is feeling so puny, why does he launch into a string of requests (vv. 5–8)? Is his humility genuine? Or is he "buttering God up"? What promise does he make (vv. 9–10)? **3.** What hints can you find that this psalm was written after the Exile in Babylon (vv. 11,14)? Did David live before or after the Exile? **4.** What kind of prosperity does David desire for the people (vv. 12–14)? Why not ask for great wisdom and spiritual strength? What view of the afterlife is implied here?

1. Do you think a country has to be strongly defended in order to enjoy safety and peace? Do you train your hands for war or endorse others to do so? Under what conditions would you go to battle? **2.** Why do you think God cares about fleeting "shadows"? Do you ever feel so small as to be insignificant to God? **3.** Does humility lead you to greater confidence before God? When do you feel most confident? Least? Can this group help? **4.** Do you see yourself as a fighter, well-nurtured plant or carved pillar? What one blessing would you seek

my spirit fails.
Do not hide your face from me
  or I will be like those who go down to the pit.
[8]Let the morning bring me word of your unfailing
    love,
  for I have put my trust in you.
Show me the way I should go,
  for to you I lift up my soul.
[9]Rescue me from my enemies, O LORD,
  for I hide myself in you.
[10]Teach me to do your will,
  for you are my God;
may your good Spirit
  lead me on level ground.

[11]For your name's sake, O LORD, preserve my life;
  in your righteousness, bring me out of trouble.
[12]In your unfailing love, silence my enemies;
  destroy all my foes,
  for I am your servant.

Psalm 144

Of David.

[1]Praise be to the LORD my Rock,
  who trains my hands for war,
  my fingers for battle.
[2]He is my loving God and my fortress,
  my stronghold and my deliverer,
my shield, in whom I take refuge,
  who subdues peoples[a] under me.

[3]O LORD, what is man that you care for him,
  the son of man that you think of him?
[4]Man is like a breath;
  his days are like a fleeting shadow.

[5]Part your heavens, O LORD, and come down;
  touch the mountains, so that they smoke.
[6]Send forth lightning and scatter ⌞the enemies⌟;
  shoot your arrows and rout them.
[7]Reach down your hand from on high;
  deliver me and rescue me
from the mighty waters,
  from the hands of foreigners
[8]whose mouths are full of lies,
  whose right hands are deceitful.

[9]I will sing a new song to you, O God;
  on the ten-stringed lyre I will make music to
    you,
[10]to the One who gives victory to kings,
  who delivers his servant David from the deadly
    sword.

[11]Deliver me and rescue me
  from the hands of foreigners

---

a2 Many manuscripts of the Masoretic Text, Dead Sea Scrolls, Aquila, Jerome and Syriac; most manuscripts of the Masoretic Text *subdues my people*

whose mouths are full of lies,
whose right hands are deceitful.
¹²Then our sons in their youth
will be like well-nurtured plants,
and our daughters will be like pillars
carved to adorn a palace.
¹³Our barns will be filled
with every kind of provision.
Our sheep will increase by thousands,
by tens of thousands in our fields;
¹⁴ our oxen will draw heavy loads.ª
There will be no breaching of walls,
no going into captivity,
no cry of distress in our streets.

¹⁵Blessed are the people of whom this is true;
blessed are the people whose God is the LORD.

Psalm 145ᵇ

A psalm of praise. Of David.

¹I will exalt you, my God the King;
I will praise your name for ever and ever.
²Every day I will praise you
and extol your name for ever and ever.

³Great is the LORD and most worthy of praise;
his greatness no one can fathom.
⁴One generation will commend your works to
another;
they will tell of your mighty acts.
⁵They will speak of the glorious splendor of your
majesty,
and I will meditate on your wonderful works.ᶜ
⁶They will tell of the power of your awesome
works,
and I will proclaim your great deeds.
⁷They will celebrate your abundant goodness
and joyfully sing of your righteousness.

⁸The LORD is gracious and compassionate,
slow to anger and rich in love.
⁹The LORD is good to all;
he has compassion on all he has made.
¹⁰All you have made will praise you, O LORD;
your saints will extol you.
¹¹They will tell of the glory of your kingdom
and speak of your might,
¹²so that all men may know of your mighty acts
and the glorious splendor of your kingdom.
¹³Your kingdom is an everlasting kingdom,
and your dominion endures through all
generations.

The LORD is faithful to all his promises

ª14 Or our chieftains will be firmly established   ᵇThis psalm is an acrostic poem, the
verses of which (including verse 13b) begin with the successive letters of the Hebrew
alphabet.   ᶜ5 Dead Sea Scrolls and Syriac (see also Septuagint); Masoretic Text On the
glorious splendor of your majesty / and on your wonderful works I will meditate

for yourself? **5.** Are Christians the only "people whose God is the Lord"? Who can expect God's favor today?

1. Have you ever seen a modern day monarch? What is the purpose of royalty? How do they differ from presidents or prime ministers? **2.** *Read aloud*—Reader(s) A: 1–21, odd; Reader(s) B: 2–20, even.

1. Why does God deserve praise (vv. 1–3)? What method will be used to spread the divine King's fame (vv. 4–7)? Won't it be obvious to everyone? **2.** Is the King's good repute merely the result of effective propaganda or is there more substance to it? List all the reasons given for praising God. Which is most exciting to you? What is the divine King's true greatness (v. 8)? **3.** How does God treat subjects (v. 9)? And the subjects treat God (v. 10)? Do all subjects respond equally (vv. 10–13)? **4.** How does the Lord return the loyalty given (vv. 13–16)? What kind of king is this? What two characteristics does the Lord hold in balance (v. 17)? **5.** What does the divine King promise to give those who call on him earnestly (vv. 18–20)? What can one's only response to these gifts be (v. 21)?

1. What kind of ruler is God to you: (a) Benevolent king? (b) Harsh dictator? (c) Ceremonial monarch? (d) Democratic leader? (e) Prime minister? What has influenced your picture of God? Does it need adjusting? **2.** Picture yourself as one of the divine King's subjects. What's good about living in this Kingdom? Why would spending time with the King one-on-one within the palace walls be the greatest reward for a citizen? **3.** What does God want to give you? How do your eyes look to God the

King? What promise is contained in the phrase "at the proper time"? **4.** Has God fulfilled your desires? Which ones? If you are unfulfilled in some way, does this indicate you are not right with God? What does it mean to call on God "in truth"?

1. Apart from eating, drinking and sleeping, what can you look back and say you've done "all your life"? **2.** *Read aloud*—Reader(s) A: 1–9, odd; Reader(s) B: 2–8, even; All: 10.

1. Is the psalmist being pious or is this really his daily experience (vv. 1–2)? **2.** What is "trust in princes" (vv. 3–4)? Is it wrong to seek human help? Is the psalmist plagued by a low view of himself or is he blessed with realism and courage? How so? **3.** At what two types of power does the psalmist marvel (vv. 5–9)? Who does God seem to be most concerned about?

1. Ask the members of your group to comment on what they think makes you tick. What two or three goals are evident from how you spend your time and talents? What do they see in your life that glorifies God? **2.** Does God step in where human help stops? Or is God's will performed strictly through human action? Who should the oppressed trust: Princes? Divine intervention? Human intervention inspired by God? Their own actions? **3.** How does this psalm speak to you when you're feeling betrayed or on your own?

and loving toward all he has made.[a]

¹⁴The LORD upholds all those who fall
and lifts up all who are bowed down.
¹⁵The eyes of all look to you,
and you give them their food at the proper time.
¹⁶You open your hand
and satisfy the desires of every living thing.

¹⁷The LORD is righteous in all his ways
and loving toward all he has made.
¹⁸The LORD is near to all who call on him,
to all who call on him in truth.
¹⁹He fulfills the desires of those who fear him;
he hears their cry and saves them.
²⁰The LORD watches over all who love him,
but all the wicked he will destroy.

²¹My mouth will speak in praise of the LORD.
Let every creature praise his holy name
for ever and ever.

Psalm 146

¹Praise the LORD.[b]

Praise the LORD, O my soul.
² I will praise the LORD all my life;
I will sing praise to my God as long as I live.

³Do not put your trust in princes,
in mortal men, who cannot save.
⁴When their spirit departs, they return to the ground;
on that very day their plans come to nothing.

⁵Blessed is he whose help is the God of Jacob,
whose hope is in the LORD his God,
⁶the Maker of heaven and earth,
the sea, and everything in them—
the LORD, who remains faithful forever.
⁷He upholds the cause of the oppressed
and gives food to the hungry.
The LORD sets prisoners free,
⁸ the LORD gives sight to the blind,
the LORD lifts up those who are bowed down,
the LORD loves the righteous.
⁹The LORD watches over the alien
and sustains the fatherless and the widow,
but he frustrates the ways of the wicked.

¹⁰The LORD reigns forever,
your God, O Zion, for all generations.

Praise the LORD.

a13 One manuscript of the Masoretic Text, Dead Sea Scrolls and Syriac (see also Septuagint); most manuscripts of the Masoretic Text do not have the last two lines of verse 13.   b1 Hebrew *Hallelu Yah*; also in verse 10

Psalm 147

[1]Praise the LORD. [a]

How good it is to sing praises to our God,
  how pleasant and fitting to praise him!

[2]The LORD builds up Jerusalem;
  he gathers the exiles of Israel.
[3]He heals the brokenhearted
  and binds up their wounds.

[4]He determines the number of the stars
  and calls them each by name.
[5]Great is our Lord and mighty in power;
  his understanding has no limit.
[6]The LORD sustains the humble
  but casts the wicked to the ground.

[7]Sing to the LORD with thanksgiving;
  make music to our God on the harp.

[8]He covers the sky with clouds;
  he supplies the earth with rain
  and makes grass grow on the hills.
[9]He provides food for the cattle
  and for the young ravens when they call.

[10]His pleasure is not in the strength of the horse,
  nor his delight in the legs of a man;
[11]the LORD delights in those who fear him,
  who put their hope in his unfailing love.

[12]Extol the LORD, O Jerusalem;
  praise your God, O Zion,
[13]for he strengthens the bars of your gates
  and blesses your people within you.
[14]He grants peace to your borders
  and satisfies you with the finest of wheat.

[15]He sends his command to the earth;
  his word runs swiftly.
[16]He spreads the snow like wool
  and scatters the frost like ashes.
[17]He hurls down his hail like pebbles.
  Who can withstand his icy blast?
[18]He sends his word and melts them;
  he stirs up his breezes, and the waters flow.

[19]He has revealed his word to Jacob,
  his laws and decrees to Israel.
[20]He has done this for no other nation;
  they do not know his laws.

Praise the LORD.

Psalm 148

[1]Praise the LORD. [b]

Praise the LORD from the heavens,
  praise him in the heights above.
[2]Praise him, all his angels,
  praise him, all his heavenly hosts.

1. Do you prefer thinking, talking or doing? Demonstrate from your activities today. 2. How do you express creativity? What squelches it? What inspires it? 3. *Read aloud*—Reader(s) A: 1–19, odd; Reader(s) B: 2–20, even.

1. List the verbs describing God's activity. Which are thinking? Speaking? Doing? 2. When was this psalm probably written (vv. 2–3)? How has God chosen to respond to the needs at hand? On what two qualities is our attention focused (vv. 5–6)? 3. What's the cause of thanksgiving in verses 7 through 9? Why do we need to be reminded to give thanks? What does God see as strength (vv. 10–11)? 4. What two blessings are in store for Jerusalem (vv. 12–14)? What is this "word" that "runs swiftly" (v. 15)? 5. Does the poet sound burdened by the Jewish Law here (vv. 19–20)? Why is the law so important to Jews?

1. What comes to mind when you think of power: (a) Physical strength? (b) Beauty? (c) Ability to influence events? (d) Moral truth? (e) Compassion? (f) Other? Do you feel powerful in any way? 2. Has God ever surprised you with a creative alternative to an "impossible" situation? Is a new creation waiting to be born in your life now? Or are you empty, infertile, running up against the limits of your understanding? How can God's might and understanding penetrate these barriers? 3. Do you sometimes delight in the strength of the horse? The legs of a man? The legs of a woman? Why is fearing God the better choice?

1. Who is your favorite composer, song writer, conductor or group? 2. What color seems to go best with praising God? What taste? Kind of weather? 3. *Read aloud*—Reader(s) A: read the first half of the verse; Reader(s) B: read the second half of the verse.

---

[a]1 Hebrew *Hallelu Yah*; also in verse 20   [b]1 Hebrew *Hallelu Yah*; also in verse 14

1. Can you trace the psalmist's call to worship from the "top down"? Where are the "highest heavens" (see 1Ki 8:27; 2Cor 12:2)? What different parts of creation join in this symphony of praise? 2. Are any instructions given on how to play your instrument? Who gets the attention and applause? Why (vv. 5–6,13)? 3. What do all creatures have in common? 4. What is the "horn" raised up (v. 14)?

1. It is taken for granted in the psalm that creation knows "how to" praise God. How do inanimate objects praise God? Animals and plants? How do you praise God? 2. What songs, liturgy or activity has helped you praise God in the past? How could your church or group explore new and different avenues of worship? 3. Do you enjoy nature? What is your response to man's slow destruction of it? Do you feel this is a problem for God to solve?

1. Do you like to dance? What kind of dance? Or do you prefer to watch others do it? 2. Read aloud—Reader(s) A: 1–5; Reader(s) B: 6–9.

1. What four activities are done to praise God (vv. 1–3)? What is God doing to praise the people (v. 4)? 2. What is meant by singing for joy "on their beds" (v. 5; see 63:6)? In a land with few private bedrooms, wouldn't this be a nuisance? 3. What's the flipside of this kingdom of joy (vv. 6–9)? Why vengeance? How is this type of activity "the glory" of all saints?

1. In your church's worship, can you see God joining in with delight and spontaneity or nodding off in boredom? How about you? What kind of celebration does God delight in? 2. What "double-edged sword" do you wield against the "kings" of this world? Are you binding the evil in the world or are you bound yourself?

³Praise him, sun and moon,
  praise him, all you shining stars.
⁴Praise him, you highest heavens
  and you waters above the skies.
⁵Let them praise the name of the LORD,
  for he commanded and they were created.
⁶He set them in place for ever and ever;
  he gave a decree that will never pass away.

⁷Praise the LORD from the earth,
  you great sea creatures and all ocean depths,
⁸lightning and hail, snow and clouds,
  stormy winds that do his bidding,
⁹you mountains and all hills,
  fruit trees and all cedars,
¹⁰wild animals and all cattle,
  small creatures and flying birds,
¹¹kings of the earth and all nations,
  you princes and all rulers on earth,
¹²young men and maidens,
  old men and children.

¹³Let them praise the name of the LORD,
  for his name alone is exalted;
  his splendor is above the earth and the heavens.
¹⁴He has raised up for his people a horn,ᵃ
  the praise of all his saints,
  of Israel, the people close to his heart.

Praise the LORD.

Psalm 149

¹Praise the LORD.ᵇ

Sing to the LORD a new song,
  his praise in the assembly of the saints.

²Let Israel rejoice in their Maker;
  let the people of Zion be glad in their King.
³Let them praise his name with dancing
  and make music to him with tambourine and harp.
⁴For the LORD takes delight in his people;
  he crowns the humble with salvation.
⁵Let the saints rejoice in this honor
  and sing for joy on their beds.

⁶May the praise of God be in their mouths
  and a double-edged sword in their hands,
⁷to inflict vengeance on the nations
  and punishment on the peoples,
⁸to bind their kings with fetters,
  their nobles with shackles of iron,
⁹to carry out the sentence written against them.
  This is the glory of all his saints.

Praise the LORD.

ᵃ14 *Horn* here symbolizes strong one, that is, king.   ᵇ1 Hebrew *Hallelu Yah*; also in verse 9

Psalm 150

[1]Praise the LORD.[a]

Praise God in his sanctuary;
  praise him in his mighty heavens.
[2]Praise him for his acts of power;
  praise him for his surpassing greatness.
[3]Praise him with the sounding of the trumpet,
  praise him with the harp and lyre,
[4]praise him with tambourine and dancing,
  praise him with the strings and flute,
[5]praise him with the clash of cymbals,
  praise him with resounding cymbals.

[6]Let everything that has breath praise the LORD.

Praise the LORD.

1. Do you play a musical instrument? 2. *Read aloud*—Reader(s) A: 1–5, odd; Reader(s) B: 2–4, even; All: 6.

1. Of what is the Temple an earthly symbol (v. 1)? 2. What instruments provide the rhythm? Melody? Chords? Do people sit politely? 3. What is significant about "breath" (v. 6; see Ge 2:7)?

1. Is your worship mostly mental appreciation? Emotion? 2. Spend some time praising God aloud for each other.

a 1 Hebrew *Hallelu Yah*; also in verse 6

INTRODUCTION to
PROVERBS

Book Study Outline: If you are using Proverbs for a study course, here is a 7- or 13-week outline. Use the questions in the margin for your group agenda:

🍵 start meeting / 15 min.

📖 read & discuss Bible / 30 min.

♡ close meeting / 15–45 min.

Refer to the Questions and Answers in the front of this Bible for more information.

7-week plan	13-week plan	Personal Reading	Group Study Passage
1	1	1:1–2:22	1:1–7/Purpose and Theme
	2	3:1–4:27	4:1–27/Wisdom Is Supreme
2	3	5:1–7:27	6:1–19/Warnings Against Folly
	4	8:1–9:18	8:1–36/Wisdom Personified
3	5	10:1–11:31	11:1–31/Consequences of Life
	6	12:1–14:35	14:1–35/Power of Words
4	7	15:1–16:33	16:1–33/Sovereignty of God
	8	17:1–19:29	17:1–28/Relationships
5	9	20:1–22:16	22:1–16/Worthy Advice
	10	22:17–24:34	23:1–35/Social Climbing
6	11	25:1–26:28	25:1–28/More Power of Words
	12	27:1–29:27	27:1–27/More Relationships
7	13	30:1–31:31	31:10–31/Virtuous Woman

Author: Proverbs has multiple authors and compilers who are named in the section subtitles. Solomon (1:1–22:16; 25:1–29:27) is the most prominent of these, and the introduction to the entire work is attributed to him. The group of authors entitled "the wise" (22:17–24:34) may have been royal scribes. The sayings of Agur (ch. 30) and Lemuel (ch. 31) conclude the book.

Date: Solomon reigned in Israel c. 970–930 B.C. During that time he wrote thousands of proverbs and songs (1Ki 4:32). The final compilation of this work occurred after Hezekiah's time (25:1), more than 200 years later, and very possibly as late as 500 B.C.

Theme: To impart moral wisdom and uncommon sense for right living.

Historical Background: Following Solomon's ascension to the throne of Israel, Yahweh appeared to him in a dream and offered him the desire of his heart (1Ki 3:1–28; 4:29–34)—wisdom. The Book of Proverbs collects this God-given wisdom in poetic figures of speech, along with the trusted sayings of wise men, accumulated over 200-plus years. Given the international nature of Solomon's court and Israel's mixing with its neighbors, it is not surprising that many parallels to the Proverbs have been found in extra-biblical texts.

Characteristics: Proverbs, consisting of short, pithy sayings with a very practical point, are a part of the Wisdom Literature of the Hebrews. Drawn from the everyday life of common people, these proverbs are couched in figurative, poetic speech laced with analogies and similes. Therefore, proverbs leave a visual as well as verbal impact upon the reader.

STRUCTURE OF THE OLD TESTAMENT			
39 Books in the Old Testament + **27** Books in the New Testament = **66** Books in the Bible			
Historical Books	**Poetical Books**	**Prophetical Books**	
THE PENTATEUCH: *HISTORICAL:*		*THE MAJOR PROPHETS:*	*THE MINOR PROPHETS:*
Genesis Joshua	Job	Isaiah	Hosea
Exodus Judges	Psalms	Jeremiah	Joel
Leviticus Ruth	Proverbs	Lamentations	Amos
Numbers 1 Samuel	Ecclesiastes	Ezekiel	Obadiah
Deuteronomy 2 Samuel	Song of Songs	Daniel	Jonah
1 Kings			Micah
2 Kings			Nahum
1 Chronicles			Habakkuk
2 Chronicles			Zephaniah
Ezra			Haggai
Nehemiah			Zechariah
Esther			Malachi

Proverbs

Prologue: Purpose and Theme

1 The proverbs of Solomon son of David, king of Israel:

²for attaining wisdom and discipline;
    for understanding words of insight;
³for acquiring a disciplined and prudent life,
    doing what is right and just and fair;
⁴for giving prudence to the simple,
    knowledge and discretion to the young—
⁵let the wise listen and add to their learning,
    and let the discerning get guidance—
⁶for understanding proverbs and parables,
    the sayings and riddles of the wise.

⁷The fear of the LORD is the beginning of
    knowledge,
but fools*ᵃ* despise wisdom and discipline.

Exhortations to Embrace Wisdom

Warning Against Enticement

⁸Listen, my son, to your father's instruction
    and do not forsake your mother's teaching.
⁹They will be a garland to grace your head
    and a chain to adorn your neck.

¹⁰My son, if sinners entice you,
    do not give in to them.
¹¹If they say, "Come along with us;
    let's lie in wait for someone's blood,
    let's waylay some harmless soul;
¹²let's swallow them alive, like the grave,*ᵇ*
    and whole, like those who go down to the pit;
¹³we will get all sorts of valuable things
    and fill our houses with plunder;
¹⁴throw in your lot with us,
    and we will share a common purse"—
¹⁵my son, do not go along with them,
    do not set foot on their paths;
¹⁶for their feet rush into sin,
    they are swift to shed blood.
¹⁷How useless to spread a net
    in full view of all the birds!
¹⁸These men lie in wait for their own blood;
    they waylay only themselves!
¹⁹Such is the end of all who go after ill-gotten gain;
    it takes away the lives of those who get it.

Warning Against Rejecting Wisdom

²⁰Wisdom calls aloud in the street,
    she raises her voice in the public squares;

What is on your mind in the mornings? What do you read, listen to, watch or eat?

1. What greets you in this prologue? What grips you? Why? **2.** What does "fear of the Lord" mean? Why is that the controlling principle of all knowledge?

1. Where are you on this road to wisdom: Stuck in traffic? Backtracking? Fast lane? Fool's alley? Why? **2.** How can this group help you? Where are you needing wisdom now?

---

1. How does your mom usually greet you? What does she say before you leave? **2.** What favorite sayings do you recall of your dad's?

1. How is heeding parental instruction (vv. 8–9) related to verse 7? How does it stand in contrast with the way of sinners (vv. 10–19)? **2.** What is appealing about the get-rich-quick schemes and peer acceptance? What is wrong with them? **3.** Would this advice *keep* a son out of trouble, or get him out of trouble? Why? **4.** To whom is verse 17 addressed? What kind of person walks into their own trap? Who should warn them? **5.** What is the end of all wrongdoing? What does Jesus say about gaining the world but losing one's soul (Mk 8:36)?

1. How did you handle peer pressure the first time you took the car out with friends? The first time you could drink? With what results? What counsel would you give your own children in these areas? **2.** To what get-rich-quick schemes and peer pressure are you most susceptible today?

You've been nominated to preach on Laity Sunday. What do you feel qualified to preach on? Would you warn people, or comfort them? Why?

ᵃ7 The Hebrew words rendered *fool* in Proverbs, and often elsewhere in the Old Testament, denote one who is morally deficient.   *ᵇ12* Hebrew *Sheol*

1. If you were a reporter covering "Wisdom's" speech in the town square, what would you say about the *content*? About the *tone*? About the *impact*? Would your report be approving or disapproving? 2. How will God laugh (vv. 26–27; also Ps 2:4; 14:1–4): With tears? Smiles? Vindication? 3. What is the result of rejecting wisdom (v. 32)? Of receiving wisdom (v. 33)? Does that seem fair? Why or why not?

1. When, if ever, have you been a Town Crier? For what? 2. What press coverage would this proverbial town crier be given where you live? Why? Would you tune in or turn off? Why? What would get your attention? 3. When have you heard "wisdom crying" to you recently? How did you respond? How did you discern that what you heard was truly wisdom? 4. If wisdom is so publicly available, why are so many so foolish? What will you do to get wise?

1. What collectible item do you treasure the most? Why that one? 2. What do you keep that your parents or spouse would rather you threw out?

1. If in Proverbs 1:20ff it was wisdom who was clamoring to be heard, who must clamor now? Why? If not "clamorous," what tone of voice do you now hear this father using? 2. By what means and in what order does this wisdom come to us? (Note the verbs.) Why begin with God's words and commandments? 3. What is the goal of this treasure hunt (vv. 5–6): Head knowledge? Moral knowledge? Change in behavior? Conversion? Why do you think so? 4. Is such a relationship with God discovered or given? Why? 5. How does God help you in this (vv. 7–8)? What further benefits attend the awe and intimacy of knowing God (vv. 9–11)? 6. Verses 12–19 are in couplets, each half mirroring the other, even

21at the head of the noisy streets*a* she cries out,
   in the gateways of the city she makes her
     speech:

22"How long will you simple ones*b* love your
     simple ways?
   How long will mockers delight in mockery
   and fools hate knowledge?
23If you had responded to my rebuke,
   I would have poured out my heart to you
   and made my thoughts known to you.
24But since you rejected me when I called
   and no one gave heed when I stretched out my
     hand,
25since you ignored all my advice
   and would not accept my rebuke,
26I in turn will laugh at your disaster;
   I will mock when calamity overtakes you—
27when calamity overtakes you like a storm,
   when disaster sweeps over you like a
     whirlwind,
   when distress and trouble overwhelm you.

28"Then they will call to me but I will not answer;
   they will look for me but will not find me.
29Since they hated knowledge
   and did not choose to fear the LORD,
30since they would not accept my advice
   and spurned my rebuke,
31they will eat the fruit of their ways
   and be filled with the fruit of their schemes.
32For the waywardness of the simple will kill them,
   and the complacency of fools will destroy them;
33but whoever listens to me will live in safety
   and be at ease, without fear of harm."

Moral Benefits of Wisdom

2   My son, if you accept my words
     and store up my commands within you,
2turning your ear to wisdom
   and applying your heart to understanding,
3and if you call out for insight
   and cry aloud for understanding,
4and if you look for it as for silver
   and search for it as for hidden treasure,
5then you will understand the fear of the LORD
   and find the knowledge of God.
6For the LORD gives wisdom,
   and from his mouth come knowledge and
     understanding.
7He holds victory in store for the upright,
   he is a shield to those whose walk is blameless,
8for he guards the course of the just
   and protects the way of his faithful ones.

9Then you will understand what is right and just
   and fair—every good path.
10For wisdom will enter your heart,

a21 Hebrew; Septuagint / *on the tops of the walls*   *b22* The Hebrew word rendered *simple* in Proverbs generally denotes one without moral direction and inclined to evil.

and knowledge will be pleasant to your soul.
[11]Discretion will protect you,
  and understanding will guard you.

[12]Wisdom will save you from the ways of wicked
    men,
  from men whose words are perverse,
[13]who leave the straight paths
  to walk in dark ways,
[14]who delight in doing wrong
  and rejoice in the perverseness of evil,
[15]whose paths are crooked
  and who are devious in their ways.

[16]It will save you also from the adulteress,
  from the wayward wife with her seductive
    words,
[17]who has left the partner of her youth
  and ignored the covenant she made before
    God.[a]
[18]For her house leads down to death
  and her paths to the spirits of the dead.
[19]None who go to her return
  or attain the paths of life.

[20]Thus you will walk in the ways of good men
  and keep to the paths of the righteous.
[21]For the upright will live in the land,
  and the blameless will remain in it;
[22]but the wicked will be cut off from the land,
  and the unfaithful will be torn from it.

Further Benefits of Wisdom

3 My son, do not forget my teaching,
    but keep my commands in your heart,
  [2]for they will prolong your life many years
    and bring you prosperity.

  [3]Let love and faithfulness never leave you;
    bind them around your neck,
    write them on the tablet of your heart.
  [4]Then you will win favor and a good name
    in the sight of God and man.

  [5]Trust in the LORD with all your heart
    and lean not on your own understanding;
  [6]in all your ways acknowledge him,
    and he will make your paths straight.[b]

  [7]Do not be wise in your own eyes;
    fear the LORD and shun evil.
  [8]This will bring health to your body
    and nourishment to your bones.

  [9]Honor the LORD with your wealth,
    with the firstfruits of all your crops;
  [10]then your barns will be filled to overflowing,
    and your vats will brim over with new wine.

  [11]My son, do not despise the LORD's discipline
    and do not resent his rebuke,

in key words: What other poetic parallelism do you see? **7.** What protection (vv. 12–19) and provision (vv. 20–22) can you expect from wisdom?

1. How's your search for wisdom coming along: "I found it"? "I lost it"? Or "I give up, where is it"? What two clues from this passage can help you find the source and benefits of wisdom? **2.** What attracts you about the "ways of good men" (v. 20): Their looks? Their means? Results (vv. 21–22)? Why? **3.** Since pleasures of sin are compelling, what must righteousness and wisdom counter-offer for you to follow them instead? **4.** Is the path of your life taking you where you've always dreamed of going? Or are you off-course somewhere? How can knowing God better help get you back on track? Likewise, how can your group help?

1. What nicknames were you given as a child? How did you get them? **2.** How do you gauge success: Earnings? Education? Toys? Good name? Leisure-time?

1. How does this passage strike you: (a) The ramblings of an old man? (b) The insight of a philosopher? (c) The logic of a scholar? (d) The warm entreaty of a concerned father? Why? **2.** What three sections do you observe (introduced by "My son")? What instructions, benefits and exhortation accompany that lead-in address? Within each section, what verses best sum up what the teaching is all about? **3.** How does one *know* if God is trustworthy (vv. 5–6)? Does such faith involve a "blind leap"? Or is faith predicated on understanding based on sound teaching (vv. 1–4)? Why is that? **4.** Who makes it possible to have wisdom (see 2Co 3:5–6)? Why is this the only trustworthy wisdom? **5.** "Poetic parallelism" is a literary device wherein the second line or verse repeats, extends or contrasts with the first. What evidence of each kind of parallelism can you find here? **6.** A

---

[a]17 Or *covenant of her God*   [b]6 Or *will direct your paths*

good name (honor and reputation) is highly prized in our culture. How does this chapter suggest you gain it (vv. 4,32,35)? How might you lose it? **7.** This chapter introduces us to the first use of short, isolated, seemingly unrelated bits of wisdom called "proverbs." We tend to seize on these "promise" verses, either hopefully or critically, but often out of context. Verse 10 is a case in point: What is this promise based on? What does it mean to honor the Lord with your finances: Gratitude? Trust (v. 5)? Tithing from the cream of the crops? Investing in the Lord's work? **8.** How does the Lord's discipline (vv. 11–12) relate to his blessing? What other blessing is to be prized besides the material one (vv. 13ff)?

1. Which one of the promises and warnings seem to have "your name" on it (whether you be "my son" or a daughter)? Why that one? **2.** With verses 1–2 in mind, what would you say to the saddened parents of a Christian 8-year-old who was killed by a drunk driver? How might your Christian understanding of life help? **3.** Whose name comes to mind as you read verses 27–28: Which charitable organization? Any political action committees? Any unemployed neighbors? Anyone in your small group or church? **4.** How can verses 5–6 help if a skeptic asked you, "How can you believe all those fantasies in the Bible"? **5.** Where have you experienced the leading of the Lord (as in vv. 5–6)? Let someone in your group share their story of God's leading: How does that make you feel? At what points can you relate to it? **6.** What kind of person does the Lord "take into his confidence" (v. 26)? Would you like to be that person? At what price? For whose benefit? How are you doing at not betraying the confidences of your group?

¹²because the LORD disciplines those he loves,
  as a father*a* the son he delights in.

¹³Blessed is the man who finds wisdom,
  the man who gains understanding,
¹⁴for she is more profitable than silver
  and yields better returns than gold.
¹⁵She is more precious than rubies;
  nothing you desire can compare with her.
¹⁶Long life is in her right hand;
  in her left hand are riches and honor.
¹⁷Her ways are pleasant ways,
  and all her paths are peace.
¹⁸She is a tree of life to those who embrace her;
  those who lay hold of her will be blessed.

¹⁹By wisdom the LORD laid the earth's foundations,
  by understanding he set the heavens in place;
²⁰by his knowledge the deeps were divided,
  and the clouds let drop the dew.

²¹My son, preserve sound judgment and discernment,
  do not let them out of your sight;
²²they will be life for you,
  an ornament to grace your neck.
²³Then you will go on your way in safety,
  and your foot will not stumble;
²⁴when you lie down, you will not be afraid;
  when you lie down, your sleep will be sweet.
²⁵Have no fear of sudden disaster
  or of the ruin that overtakes the wicked,
²⁶for the LORD will be your confidence
  and will keep your foot from being snared.

²⁷Do not withhold good from those who deserve it,
  when it is in your power to act.
²⁸Do not say to your neighbor,
  "Come back later; I'll give it tomorrow"—
  when you now have it with you.

²⁹Do not plot harm against your neighbor,
  who lives trustfully near you.
³⁰Do not accuse a man for no reason—
  when he has done you no harm.

³¹Do not envy a violent man
  or choose any of his ways,
³²for the LORD detests a perverse man
  but takes the upright into his confidence.

³³The LORD's curse is on the house of the wicked,
  but he blesses the home of the righteous.
³⁴He mocks proud mockers
  but gives grace to the humble.
³⁵The wise inherit honor,
  but fools he holds up to shame.

a 12 Hebrew; Septuagint / *and he punishes*

Wisdom Is Supreme

4 Listen, my sons, to a father's instruction;
pay attention and gain understanding.
[2]I give you sound learning,
so do not forsake my teaching.
[3]When I was a boy in my father's house,
still tender, and an only child of my mother,
[4]he taught me and said,
"Lay hold of my words with all your heart;
keep my commands and you will live.
[5]Get wisdom, get understanding;
do not forget my words or swerve from them.
[6]Do not forsake wisdom, and she will protect you;
love her, and she will watch over you.
[7]Wisdom is supreme; therefore get wisdom.
Though it cost all you have,[a] get
understanding.
[8]Esteem her, and she will exalt you;
embrace her, and she will honor you.
[9]She will set a garland of grace on your head
and present you with a crown of splendor."

[10]Listen, my son, accept what I say,
and the years of your life will be many.
[11]I guide you in the way of wisdom
and lead you along straight paths.
[12]When you walk, your steps will not be hampered;
when you run, you will not stumble.
[13]Hold on to instruction, do not let it go;
guard it well, for it is your life.
[14]Do not set foot on the path of the wicked
or walk in the way of evil men.
[15]Avoid it, do not travel on it;
turn from it and go on your way.
[16]For they cannot sleep till they do evil;
they are robbed of slumber till they make
someone fall.
[17]They eat the bread of wickedness
and drink the wine of violence.
[18]The path of the righteous is like the first gleam of
dawn,
shining ever brighter till the full light of day.
[19]But the way of the wicked is like deep darkness;
they do not know what makes them stumble.

[20]My son, pay attention to what I say;
listen closely to my words.
[21]Do not let them out of your sight,
keep them within your heart;
[22]for they are life to those who find them
and health to a man's whole body.
[23]Above all else, guard your heart,
for it is the wellspring of life.
[24]Put away perversity from your mouth;
keep corrupt talk far from your lips.
[25]Let your eyes look straight ahead,
fix your gaze directly before you.
[26]Make level[b] paths for your feet

What one thing can you recall being true of granddad, which was true of your father, which is now also true of you?

1. It is commonly agreed that Solomon was the author/compiler of most of Proverbs. This particular passage draws from his family background (see 1Ki 1:28–30; 2:1–4): Who was his dad? His mom? What do you suppose their father-son talks were like: Monologue? Dialogue? Q & A? What was David's charge to Solomon? How is that reflected here (vv. 4–9)? **2.** In passing along wisdom from one generation to another (vv. 1,3–4), what's involved: Setting a good example? Being good with words? Minding your "P's and Q's"? Long lists of *"Dos and Don'ts"*? **3.** In this proverb are there more *"Dos,* or more *Don'ts"?* Why might that be? How is Solomon able to sell his "sons" on the value of wisdom? **4.** What does the travel motif imply about the nature of biblical wisdom? Is the way to wisdom well-traveled, or is it less-traveled? Can you stay at home or in your "ivory tower" and still learn it? Do you dare leave home without it? Why or why not?

1. Using the travel motif as it applies to your pursuit of biblical wisdom these days, what would you say you are: (a) Lonely trailblazer? (b) Crazy "off-road" driver? (c) Sleepless over-the-road 18-wheeler? (d) Teenage hot rodder? (e) Demolition derby buff? (f) Chugging along in your compact car? (g) Touring the USA in your Chevrolet? (h) Strictly thumbing and bumming? Why is that? **2.** What common path or vehicle can your group agree on for the remainder of your Proverbs study? What path or vehicle would you want to use on life's highways? **3.** In what area of your life do you need the counsel of verses 25–27? How can your group help you to do this? What are you willing to do to help straighten out or make level someone else's path? **4.** Of all the father-son or mother-daughter talks you've had, which one stands out as the most helpful in the long run? Have you passed that wisdom along to another (child or friend)? Why not now?

---

[a]7 Or *Whatever else you get*   [b]26 Or *Consider the*

and take only ways that are firm.
²⁷Do not swerve to the right or the left;
   keep your foot from evil.

Warning Against Adultery

5 My son, pay attention to my wisdom,
   listen well to my words of insight,
²that you may maintain discretion
   and your lips may preserve knowledge.
³For the lips of an adulteress drip honey,
   and her speech is smoother than oil;
⁴but in the end she is bitter as gall,
   sharp as a double-edged sword.
⁵Her feet go down to death;
   her steps lead straight to the grave.ᵃ
⁶She gives no thought to the way of life;
   her paths are crooked, but she knows it not.

⁷Now then, my sons, listen to me;
   do not turn aside from what I say.
⁸Keep to a path far from her,
   do not go near the door of her house,
⁹lest you give your best strength to others
   and your years to one who is cruel,
¹⁰lest strangers feast on your wealth
   and your toil enrich another man's house.
¹¹At the end of your life you will groan,
   when your flesh and body are spent.
¹²You will say, "How I hated discipline!
   How my heart spurned correction!
¹³I would not obey my teachers
   or listen to my instructors.
¹⁴I have come to the brink of utter ruin
   in the midst of the whole assembly."

¹⁵Drink water from your own cistern,
   running water from your own well.
¹⁶Should your springs overflow in the streets,
   your streams of water in the public squares?
¹⁷Let them be yours alone,
   never to be shared with strangers.
¹⁸May your fountain be blessed,
   and may you rejoice in the wife of your youth.
¹⁹A loving doe, a graceful deer—
   may her breasts satisfy you always,
   may you ever be captivated by her love.
²⁰Why be captivated, my son, by an adulteress?
   Why embrace the bosom of another man's
     wife?

²¹For a man's ways are in full view of the LORD,
   and he examines all his paths.
²²The evil deeds of a wicked man ensnare him;
   the cords of his sin hold him fast.
²³He will die for lack of discipline,
   led astray by his own great folly.

What advice have your parents given you on marriage?

1. What bells and whistles ring in your ears after reading this? Can you hear the police bullhorn? The ambulance siren? The cheated spouse blowing the whistle? 2. This chapter is filled with picture words. Do they enhance the point of the passage for you, or detract from it? What is the main point here? 3. Why does adultery appeal (vv. 3–4,7–8,12–13,20–22)? What helps him resist? 4. What consequences does this permissive lifestyle reap (vv. 9–11,14)? What benefits accrue to those who "drink from their own cistern" (vv. 15ff)?

1. What has been most influential in your understanding of sexual *Dos* and *Don'ts*: TV sitcoms? Real life sit-coms? Classroom courses? Locker room discussions? Bull sessions? AIDS? Pop love songs? Porno mags? Parents? Scripture? What was lacking in your sexual education as a youth? 2. What causes a man to think "the grass is greener on the other side"? Are wives tempted by the same things as husbands? Why? 3. Martin Luther said of sexual temptation: "We can't do anything about the birds flying over our head, but we can prevent them building a nest in our hair." How does that metaphor fit your experience and Proverbs 5? 4. "If only I knew then what I know now": What sexual advice have you once rejected but later discovered was sound? What happened? What problem remains unresolved? Where can you get help? 5. The adulteress does not even realize that "her paths are crooked" (v. 6). If you were going down the wrong path would you want someone to correct you? Who? How? 6. Given verse 21, what difference will that make in your future thoughts and decisions regarding sex?

ᵃ5 Hebrew *Sheol*

Warnings Against Folly

6 My son, if you have put up security for your
neighbor,
if you have struck hands in pledge for another,
[2] if you have been trapped by what you said,
ensnared by the words of your mouth,
[3] then do this, my son, to free yourself,
since you have fallen into your neighbor's
hands:
Go and humble yourself;
press your plea with your neighbor!
[4] Allow no sleep to your eyes,
no slumber to your eyelids.
[5] Free yourself, like a gazelle from the hand of the
hunter,
like a bird from the snare of the fowler.

[6] Go to the ant, you sluggard;
consider its ways and be wise!
[7] It has no commander,
no overseer or ruler,
[8] yet it stores its provisions in summer
and gathers its food at harvest.

[9] How long will you lie there, you sluggard?
When will you get up from your sleep?
[10] A little sleep, a little slumber,
a little folding of the hands to rest—
[11] and poverty will come on you like a bandit
and scarcity like an armed man. [a]

[12] A scoundrel and villain,
who goes about with a corrupt mouth,
[13]   who winks with his eye,
signals with his feet
and motions with his fingers,
[14]   who plots evil with deceit in his heart—
he always stirs up dissension.
[15] Therefore disaster will overtake him in an instant;
he will suddenly be destroyed—without
remedy.

[16] There are six things the LORD hates,
seven that are detestable to him:
[17]   haughty eyes,
a lying tongue,
hands that shed innocent blood,
[18]   a heart that devises wicked schemes,
feet that are quick to rush into evil,
[19]   a false witness who pours out lies
and a man who stirs up dissension among
brothers.

Warning Against Adultery

[20] My son, keep your father's commands
and do not forsake your mother's teaching.
[21] Bind them upon your heart forever;
fasten them around your neck.
[22] When you walk, they will guide you;

---

a 11 Or like a vagrant / and scarcity like a beggar

1. What is your favorite animal? Why? 2. Who is the person you most admire? What is it about their personality that you admire?

1. How would you describe the "intensity" of this passage: Fireside chat? Fiery sermon? Political filibuster? Ad for a TV mini-series? Or what? 2. What is Solomon's point? How well does he present it? How effective are his figures of speech? 3. If he were writing for a modern audience, would he have to change anything? If so, what? Why? 4. From verses 1–5 (also Ps 15:4b), what are the dangers of "co-signing for a loan"? Why? 5. From verses 6–11, why work? Why use an ant to make this point? 6. What is the final end of the "scoundrel and villain" (vv. 12ff)? Is this a natural consequence? Or the judgment of God? Why do you think so?

1. When have you pledged yourself to something you later regretted? How does humility (v. 3) work to get you out of difficult situations? 2. What does sluggard-like and ant-like behavior look like in your friends? In yourself? In what one way can you be more like the ant this week? 3. If all your material needs were met without *having* to work, would you still work? Why? 4. Where have you seen the character described in verses 12–14: In a TV melodrama? In church? In the mirror? How do you deal with the villain within you? Likewise, the villain in your fellowship? 5. Solomon gives a checklist (vv. 16–19) to evaluate our relationship to the Lord: How do you measure up? How would your closest friend rate you? How can your small group help you improve in one of these areas?

---

1. Which of your dad's or mom's sayings can you recall? Which do you use? 2. What were you disciplined for most often? How were you disciplined?

1. What do you suppose this "father-son" (or mother-daughter) talk involved: Mono-

logue? Q & A? Trial and error? Bedtime prayers? **2.** What images help picture what the "commands" and "teaching" are like? And what sexual sin is like? What does it mean that a "prostitute reduces you to a loaf of bread"? **3.** How does the use of poetry (exaggerated language, parallelism, emotional pull) help to make the point vividly? **4.** What do you see in verses 30–31: Situation ethics? Moral relativity? Justice? Or what? **5.** Do you think God's judgment (vv. 32–35) is brought on by ourselves, or exacted by others? Why?

♡ **1.** How have your parents' instructions actually guided, watched or spoken to you? *If their instruction is wrong or not of God, must you still obey?* Why? What experience of parental discipline illustrates your point? **2.** When in your life, past or present, have you been burned when "playing with fire" (vv. 27f)? How does this passage suggest you keep your life pure?

🍵 **1.** For a fun night out on the town, what would you do? Where would you go? With whom? **2.** Where do you go to have fun *without* "wine, women or song"? Why there? **3.** Which TV ads get your attention and why? What sales pitch jingle rings in your mind most often?

📖 **1.** If you were to set this chapter to music, what would you underscore? Where would you introduce dissonance? Cymbals? Harp? Drum roll? Resolution? **2.** What is meant by the "apple of your eye"? Why is it used here (v. 2)? **3.** What is meant by "write them on the tablet of your heart" (v. 3; see Jer 31:33)? How do you write on it? What do you write? Why (see Ps 119:9,11)? **4.** Solomon seems to be quite concerned about adultery and prostitution (ch. 2; 5; 6; 7). Why? How has sexual sin affected Solomon's own life, heritage, integrity and parenting? What is the result of marital disloyalty which causes biblical writers to speak so forcefully against it? **5.** Can adultery and prostitution also be sym-

when you sleep, they will watch over you;
when you awake, they will speak to you.
²³For these commands are a lamp,
this teaching is a light,
and the corrections of discipline
are the way to life,
²⁴keeping you from the immoral woman,
from the smooth tongue of the wayward wife.
²⁵Do not lust in your heart after her beauty
or let her captivate you with her eyes,
²⁶for the prostitute reduces you to a loaf of bread,
and the adulteress preys upon your very life.
²⁷Can a man scoop fire into his lap
without his clothes being burned?
²⁸Can a man walk on hot coals
without his feet being scorched?
²⁹So is he who sleeps with another man's wife;
no one who touches her will go unpunished.

³⁰Men do not despise a thief if he steals
to satisfy his hunger when he is starving.
³¹Yet if he is caught, he must pay sevenfold,
though it costs him all the wealth of his house.
³²But a man who commits adultery lacks judgment;
whoever does so destroys himself.
³³Blows and disgrace are his lot,
and his shame will never be wiped away;
³⁴for jealousy arouses a husband's fury,
and he will show no mercy when he takes
revenge.
³⁵He will not accept any compensation;
he will refuse the bribe, however great it is.

Warning Against the Adulteress

7 My son, keep my words
and store up my commands within you.
²Keep my commands and you will live;
guard my teachings as the apple of your eye.
³Bind them on your fingers;
write them on the tablet of your heart.
⁴Say to wisdom, "You are my sister,"
and call understanding your kinsman;
⁵they will keep you from the adulteress,
from the wayward wife with her seductive
words.

⁶At the window of my house
I looked out through the lattice.
⁷I saw among the simple,
I noticed among the young men,
a youth who lacked judgment.
⁸He was going down the street near her corner,
walking along in the direction of her house
⁹at twilight, as the day was fading,
as the dark of night set in.

¹⁰Then out came a woman to meet him,
dressed like a prostitute and with crafty intent.
¹¹(She is loud and defiant,
her feet never stay at home;
¹²now in the street, now in the squares,

at every corner she lurks.)

¹³She took hold of him and kissed him
  and with a brazen face she said:

¹⁴"I have fellowship offerings[a] at home;
  today I fulfilled my vows.
¹⁵So I came out to meet you;
  I looked for you and have found you!
¹⁶I have covered my bed
  with colored linens from Egypt.
¹⁷I have perfumed my bed
  with myrrh, aloes and cinnamon.
¹⁸Come, let's drink deep of love till morning;
  let's enjoy ourselves with love!
¹⁹My husband is not at home;
  he has gone on a long journey.
²⁰He took his purse filled with money
  and will not be home till full moon."

²¹With persuasive words she led him astray;
  she seduced him with her smooth talk.
²²All at once he followed her
  like an ox going to the slaughter,
  like a deer[b] stepping into a noose[c]
²³   till an arrow pierces his liver,
  like a bird darting into a snare,
  little knowing it will cost him his life.

²⁴Now then, my sons, listen to me;
  pay attention to what I say.
²⁵Do not let your heart turn to her ways
  or stray into her paths.
²⁶Many are the victims she has brought down;
  her slain are a mighty throng.
²⁷Her house is a highway to the grave,[d]
  leading down to the chambers of death.

Wisdom's Call

8 Does not wisdom call out?
  Does not understanding raise her voice?
²On the heights along the way,
  where the paths meet, she takes her stand;
³beside the gates leading into the city,
  at the entrances, she cries aloud:
⁴"To you, O men, I call out;
  I raise my voice to all mankind.
⁵You who are simple, gain prudence;
  you who are foolish, gain understanding.
⁶Listen, for I have worthy things to say;
  I open my lips to speak what is right.
⁷My mouth speaks what is true,
  for my lips detest wickedness.
⁸All the words of my mouth are just;
  none of them is crooked or perverse.
⁹To the discerning all of them are right;
  they are faultless to those who have knowledge.
¹⁰Choose my instruction instead of silver,
  knowledge rather than choice gold,

1. When was the last time some smooth talker convinced you to do or buy something that was against your better judgment? What did you learn from the experience? What did the lesson learned really cost you? 2. In shopping for a church, do you always ask up front what membership will cost you in the end? Or do you "buy now and pay later," little knowing what the full cost will be? Why? 3. In seeking God's will, by what means does he divert your attention from a wrong course of action? Or do you usually find out only after it's too late? 4. How then does God "advertise" his will and persuade you to buy into it: (a) He abides by "full disclosure" standards? (b) God wants you to "buy first and pay later," as otherwise you might never buy? (c) God wants you to fully count the cost first before making any decision of faith? (d) Fully trusting, in a childlike way? 5. In which of these areas can you use this group's help?

---

1. In the last major debate between political candidates, what is one memorable campaign promise you paid attention to? Did it come true? Why or why not? 2. Rank order these "pillars of trust" according to your experience of them: (a) Political candidates? (b) MDs? (c) Police officers? (d) Doomsday prophets? (e) News editors? (f) TV evangelists?

1. As you listen to "Wisdom" call out, what does she sound like: (a) Talk show host? (b) Football coach? (c) TV evangelist? (d) Kindly grandma? (e) Barker at a carnival? (f) Other? 2. "Parallelism" is where the second line of a couplet repeats, enhances, or contrasts with the first, in order to enrich the idea. What examples of each form do you find in this passage? Is this poetry confusing, or convincing, for you? Why? Is this poetic way of speaking simply a quaint oriental custom to you? Or

do you see God's purpose in it? What purpose is that? **3.** With what is wisdom equated or likened? How many different comparisons can you find here? **4.** From verses 12–21, what results from finding wisdom? Which fruit of wisdom do you most want? **5.** Verses 22–31 are a hymn personifying wisdom as an attribute of God, active in creation (see 1:20–33; 3:15–18; and 9:1–12). Later, biblical writers used this as a background for portraying Christ as the Word of God (see Jn 1:1–3) and the wisdom of God (see 1Co 1:24,30; Col 2:3). What connection do you see between this hymn to wisdom and hymns you sing about Christ (on whom all wisdom is focused)? **6.** Verses 32–36 drive home the appeal of wisdom with the ultimate sanctions of life and death. It's as if the Lord Jesus himself were talking. How might these be considered a promise of the Savior?

♡ **1.** "Listen, for I have worthy things to say"—how many times have you heard that line before? From whom? Was it worthy? How did you discern that for sure? In this Scripture, "Wisdom" is begging you to listen: Are you? Why or why not? What first grabs your attention? What keeps you listening for more? **2.** Would wisdom make your list of "Ten Most Precious Things in the World"? Why? Solomon says wisdom is "more precious than rubies": Is jewelry, money or possessions on your "Top Ten" list? What, if anything, could buy wisdom? On the other hand, what could wisdom buy? **3.** If "Christ" could be substituted for "wisdom" in this chapter, how would that affect your view or application of its main points? For example, what then would be the meaning of "finds life" (v. 35)? How can you find "wisdom" or "life" without Christ? **4.** How is your personal search for wisdom progressing? Wisdom intended for all mankind includes your group, as well. Ask them for help.

[11]for wisdom is more precious than rubies,
  and nothing you desire can compare with her.

[12]"I, wisdom, dwell together with prudence;
  I possess knowledge and discretion.
[13]To fear the LORD is to hate evil;
  I hate pride and arrogance,
  evil behavior and perverse speech.
[14]Counsel and sound judgment are mine;
  I have understanding and power.
[15]By me kings reign
  and rulers make laws that are just;
[16]by me princes govern,
  and all nobles who rule on earth.[a]
[17]I love those who love me,
  and those who seek me find me.
[18]With me are riches and honor,
  enduring wealth and prosperity.
[19]My fruit is better than fine gold;
  what I yield surpasses choice silver.
[20]I walk in the way of righteousness,
  along the paths of justice,
[21]bestowing wealth on those who love me
  and making their treasuries full.

[22]"The LORD brought me forth as the first of his
    works,[b,c]
  before his deeds of old;
[23]I was appointed[d] from eternity,
  from the beginning, before the world began.
[24]When there were no oceans, I was given birth,
  when there were no springs abounding with
    water;
[25]before the mountains were settled in place,
  before the hills, I was given birth,
[26]before he made the earth or its fields
  or any of the dust of the world.
[27]I was there when he set the heavens in place,
  when he marked out the horizon on the face of
    the deep,
[28]when he established the clouds above
  and fixed securely the fountains of the deep,
[29]when he gave the sea its boundary
  so the waters would not overstep his command,
  and when he marked out the foundations of the
    earth.
[30]   Then I was the craftsman at his side.
  I was filled with delight day after day,
  rejoicing always in his presence,
[31]rejoicing in his whole world
  and delighting in mankind.

[32]"Now then, my sons, listen to me;
  blessed are those who keep my ways.
[33]Listen to my instruction and be wise;
  do not ignore it.
[34]Blessed is the man who listens to me,

a 16 Many Hebrew manuscripts and Septuagint; most Hebrew manuscripts *and nobles—all righteous rulers*   b 22 Or *way*; or *dominion*   c 22 Or *The LORD possessed me at the beginning of his work*; or *The LORD brought me forth at the beginning of his work*   d 23 Or *fashioned*

watching daily at my doors,
    waiting at my doorway.
³⁵For whoever finds me finds life
    and receives favor from the LORD.
³⁶But whoever fails to find me harms himself;
    all who hate me love death."

Invitations of Wisdom and of Folly

9 Wisdom has built her house;
    she has hewn out its seven pillars.
²She has prepared her meat and mixed her wine;
    she has also set her table.
³She has sent out her maids, and she calls
    from the highest point of the city.
⁴"Let all who are simple come in here!"
    she says to those who lack judgment.
⁵"Come, eat my food
    and drink the wine I have mixed.
⁶Leave your simple ways and you will live;
    walk in the way of understanding.

⁷"Whoever corrects a mocker invites insult;
    whoever rebukes a wicked man incurs abuse.
⁸Do not rebuke a mocker or he will hate you;
    rebuke a wise man and he will love you.
⁹Instruct a wise man and he will be wiser still;
    teach a righteous man and he will add to his
        learning.
¹⁰"The fear of the LORD is the beginning of wisdom,
    and knowledge of the Holy One is
        understanding.
¹¹For through me your days will be many,
    and years will be added to your life.
¹²If you are wise, your wisdom will reward you;
    if you are a mocker, you alone will suffer."

¹³The woman Folly is loud;
    she is undisciplined and without knowledge.
¹⁴She sits at the door of her house,
    on a seat at the highest point of the city,
¹⁵calling out to those who pass by,
    who go straight on their way.
¹⁶"Let all who are simple come in here!"
    she says to those who lack judgment.
¹⁷"Stolen water is sweet;
    food eaten in secret is delicious!"
¹⁸But little do they know that the dead are there,
    that her guests are in the depths of the grave.^a

Proverbs of Solomon

10 The proverbs of Solomon:

A wise son brings joy to his father,
    but a foolish son grief to his mother.

²Ill-gotten treasures are of no value,
    but righteousness delivers from death.

^a18 Hebrew *Sheol*

☕ 1. Describe a memorable dinner you've attended. What made it memorable: The food? The people? The gifts exchanged? The lobbying or prospecting that went on? **2.** Who in your family is the loudest, lacking any volume control?

📖 1. If this poem were set to music and sung, how many stanzas would there be? Where is the chorus? (Note the structure and repetition of key phrases and concepts.) What instruments would underscore the major and minor themes? What parts would a soloist sing? **2.** Compare and contrast *Wisdom* (ch. 8) and *Folly*: What are their personalities? Lifestyles? Residences? Messages? Results?

♡ 1. In practical terms, what is the difference between a "mocker" and a "wise man" (vv. 7–9)? When have you tried to correct one or the other? What happened? **2.** How easy is it for someone to correct you? Why is that? What would make it easier for you to hear the input your critics have to offer? **3.** How do you feel being around loud, undisciplined people? What does this say about you? About the person you want to become? What can your group do to help? **4.** The first nine chapters of Proverbs serve as an introduction to the whole book (see 10:1). Why do you think Solomon closes his introduction as he does? Why is choice so important in a person's life?

☕ 1. What was your first "real job"? What made it so "real": Money? Career advancement? Friendships? Locale? Hard work? **2.** What did you do with the money you made: Room and board? Fun in the sun? College expenses? Car? Clothes?

1. According to Webster, a proverb is a "short, pithy, popular wise saying or precept, often in picturesque language." How do these proverbs of Solomon fit that definition? How else would you define what you see here? 2. What do you see here that relates to *hard work*? What is its reward? Its opposite? 3. What aspects of the "righteous" and the "wicked" are conveyed here by the images of head? Of memory? Mouth or lips? Wages? Desires? Destinies? 4. We usually reserve *discipline* for children or people who do bad things. What here suggests otherwise (vv. 8,13,17,25; see Heb 12:4–13)? 5. Literary doublets tell us as much by the converse truth they imply as by plain truth they affirm, as in verse 19. What is Solomon affirming there? What does the alternative imply? How does this relate to the "chattering fool" (vv. 8,10, 14,18)? 6. What do you learn here about the material and spiritual results of righteousness? What is long-term? Immediate? Temporary? How can you "nourish many" (v. 21) with your righteousness?

1. Which proverbs here have a New Testament ring to them? For example, what proverb is the equivalent of James 5:20? Romans 6:23? Matthew 7:24–27? 2. Which of these Proverbs would your parents want to read to you? Which of these are written with you in mind? What kind of wages have you been earning lately: Joy or grief? Life or punishment? When has God's rod disciplined you? What were the results? Where does it still hurt? 3. Are you desiring what God may grant? Or dreading something else may overtake you (see v. 14)? 4. How do you understand verses 6b and 11b: (a) The tongue conceals violence? (b) The tongue gets us in trouble? (c) The tongue only reflects what enters through the eyes and ears, as in "garbage in, garbage out"? Illustrate from your experience. 5. How can "love cover up all wrongs" (v. 12): Is love blind, innocent, forgiving, or what? How has this happened to you? 6. What storms are passing through your life right now? How are you holding up? Where are you seeking refuge? How can your small group help?

³The Lord does not let the righteous go hungry
　but he thwarts the craving of the wicked.

⁴Lazy hands make a man poor,
　but diligent hands bring wealth.

⁵He who gathers crops in summer is a wise son,
　but he who sleeps during harvest is a disgraceful son.

⁶Blessings crown the head of the righteous,
　but violence overwhelms the mouth of the wicked. ^a

⁷The memory of the righteous will be a blessing,
　but the name of the wicked will rot.

⁸The wise in heart accept commands,
　but a chattering fool comes to ruin.

⁹The man of integrity walks securely,
　but he who takes crooked paths will be found out.

¹⁰He who winks maliciously causes grief,
　and a chattering fool comes to ruin.

¹¹The mouth of the righteous is a fountain of life,
　but violence overwhelms the mouth of the wicked.

¹²Hatred stirs up dissension,
　but love covers over all wrongs.

¹³Wisdom is found on the lips of the discerning,
　but a rod is for the back of him who lacks judgment.

¹⁴Wise men store up knowledge,
　but the mouth of a fool invites ruin.

¹⁵The wealth of the rich is their fortified city,
　but poverty is the ruin of the poor.

¹⁶The wages of the righteous bring them life,
　but the income of the wicked brings them punishment.

¹⁷He who heeds discipline shows the way to life,
　but whoever ignores correction leads others astray.

¹⁸He who conceals his hatred has lying lips,
　and whoever spreads slander is a fool.

¹⁹When words are many, sin is not absent,
　but he who holds his tongue is wise.

²⁰The tongue of the righteous is choice silver,
　but the heart of the wicked is of little value.

²¹The lips of the righteous nourish many,
　but fools die for lack of judgment.

²²The blessing of the Lord brings wealth,
　and he adds no trouble to it.

a6 Or *but the mouth of the wicked conceals violence*; also in verse 11

23A fool finds pleasure in evil conduct,
  but a man of understanding delights in wisdom.

24What the wicked dreads will overtake him;
  what the righteous desire will be granted.

25When the storm has swept by, the wicked are
    gone,
  but the righteous stand firm forever.

26As vinegar to the teeth and smoke to the eyes,
  so is a sluggard to those who send him.

27The fear of the LORD adds length to life,
  but the years of the wicked are cut short.

28The prospect of the righteous is joy,
  but the hopes of the wicked come to nothing.

29The way of the LORD is a refuge for the righteous,
  but it is the ruin of those who do evil.

30The righteous will never be uprooted,
  but the wicked will not remain in the land.

31The mouth of the righteous brings forth wisdom,
  but a perverse tongue will be cut out.

32The lips of the righteous know what is fitting,
  but the mouth of the wicked only what is
    perverse.

11 The LORD abhors dishonest scales,
  but accurate weights are his delight.

2When pride comes, then comes disgrace,
  but with humility comes wisdom.

3The integrity of the upright guides them,
  but the unfaithful are destroyed by their
    duplicity.

4Wealth is worthless in the day of wrath,
  but righteousness delivers from death.

5The righteousness of the blameless makes a
    straight way for them,
  but the wicked are brought down by their own
    wickedness.

6The righteousness of the upright delivers them,
  but the unfaithful are trapped by evil desires.

7When a wicked man dies, his hope perishes;
  all he expected from his power comes to
    nothing.

8The righteous man is rescued from trouble,
  and it comes on the wicked instead.

9With his mouth the godless destroys his neighbor,
  but through knowledge the righteous escape.

10When the righteous prosper, the city rejoices;
  when the wicked perish, there are shouts of
    joy.

1. Which modern proverb sums up your philosophy of money management: (a) "A penny saved is a penny earned"? (b) "Don't be penny wise and pound foolish"? (c) "You can't take it with you"? (d) "Eat, drink and be merry, for tomorrow we die(t)"? (e) "He who dies with the most toys wins"? (f) Other? 2. What is one of the smarter things you've done with your money? What is one of the more foolish things?

1. What proverbs do you see here that develop the theme of *generosity*? Taken together, how do they shape Solomon's view of giving: (a) Generosity pays? (b) Money misers are miserable? (c) Neither a borrower, nor a lender be? (d) I got mine the good old fashioned way—I earned it? (e) God helps him who helps himself? 2. What is the end result of those who trust in their wealth (vv. 4,7,28)? Who benefits from the prosperity of the righteous (vv. 10,11,17,24,25)? 3. What's wrong with using your prosperity to alleviate someone else's debts (v. 15; see 6:1; 22:26–27)? How does the story of Joseph and his brothers illustrate both aspects of this truth? 4. What proverbs do you see here that develop the theme of *honesty*?

Taken together, how do they shape Solomon's view of honesty: (a) Scales never lie, even if people do? (b) Honesty hurts, but it's the best policy? (c) Honesty does not always pay, but it's still worth it? (d) It doesn't matter what you believe as long as you have integrity? (e) The heart is exceedingly corrupt? **5.** What is the end of those who betray truth (vv. 3,6,11,19,21,31)? How can one be sure the wicked *will* get their due?

♡ **1.** How does *Solomon's view* of riches and stewardship compare with *Jesus' view* (What we are unwilling to part with will keep us from the kingdom of God)? And with *Paul's view* (A generous sower will reap likewise)? **2.** How satisfied are you with the way you handle money? Of the many proverbs here dealing with money matters, pick one to apply: How might its wisdom bring about the change you (and God) desire with respect to money matters? **3.** What do you learn here about admitting your mistakes (v. 2)? About keeping secrets (v. 13)? Seeking guidance (v. 14)? Seeking "good" (vv. 23, 27)? Pig-like behavior (v. 22)? **4.** What does it mean here to "win souls" (v. 30): Winning pagans to Jesus? Getting fools to adopt the ways of the wise and righteous? Or what? How are you attempting to do this? What must you do to win more? How can your small group help in this? **5.** How might verse 4 be construed as a "life insurance policy"? What kind of "life" is in view here? How does one receive "righteousness" and thus be delivered from "death" (see Jn 5:24)?

11Through the blessing of the upright a city is
    exalted,
  but by the mouth of the wicked it is destroyed.

12A man who lacks judgment derides his neighbor,
  but a man of understanding holds his tongue.

13A gossip betrays a confidence,
  but a trustworthy man keeps a secret.

14For lack of guidance a nation falls,
  but many advisers make victory sure.

15He who puts up security for another will surely
    suffer,
  but whoever refuses to strike hands in pledge is
    safe.

16A kindhearted woman gains respect,
  but ruthless men gain only wealth.

17A kind man benefits himself,
  but a cruel man brings trouble on himself.

18The wicked man earns deceptive wages,
  but he who sows righteousness reaps a sure
    reward.

19The truly righteous man attains life,
  but he who pursues evil goes to his death.

20The LORD detests men of perverse heart
  but he delights in those whose ways are
    blameless.

21Be sure of this: The wicked will not go
    unpunished,
  but those who are righteous will go free.

22Like a gold ring in a pig's snout
  is a beautiful woman who shows no discretion.

23The desire of the righteous ends only in good,
  but the hope of the wicked only in wrath.

24One man gives freely, yet gains even more;
  another withholds unduly, but comes to
    poverty.

25A generous man will prosper;
  he who refreshes others will himself be
    refreshed.

26People curse the man who hoards grain,
  but blessing crowns him who is willing to sell.

27He who seeks good finds goodwill,
  but evil comes to him who searches for it.

28Whoever trusts in his riches will fall,
  but the righteous will thrive like a green leaf.

29He who brings trouble on his family will inherit
    only wind,
  and the fool will be servant to the wise.

30The fruit of the righteous is a tree of life,
  and he who wins souls is wise.

³¹If the righteous receive their due on earth,
how much more the ungodly and the sinner!

12

Whoever loves discipline loves knowledge,
but he who hates correction is stupid.

²A good man obtains favor from the LORD,
but the LORD condemns a crafty man.

³A man cannot be established through wickedness,
but the righteous cannot be uprooted.

⁴A wife of noble character is her husband's crown,
but a disgraceful wife is like decay in his bones.

⁵The plans of the righteous are just,
but the advice of the wicked is deceitful.

⁶The words of the wicked lie in wait for blood,
but the speech of the upright rescues them.

⁷Wicked men are overthrown and are no more,
but the house of the righteous stands firm.

⁸A man is praised according to his wisdom,
but men with warped minds are despised.

⁹Better to be a nobody and yet have a servant
than pretend to be somebody and have no food.

¹⁰A righteous man cares for the needs of his animal,
but the kindest acts of the wicked are cruel.

¹¹He who works his land will have abundant food,
but he who chases fantasies lacks judgment.

¹²The wicked desire the plunder of evil men,
but the root of the righteous flourishes.

¹³An evil man is trapped by his sinful talk,
but a righteous man escapes trouble.

¹⁴From the fruit of his lips a man is filled with good
things
as surely as the work of his hands rewards him.

¹⁵The way of a fool seems right to him,
but a wise man listens to advice.

¹⁶A fool shows his annoyance at once,
but a prudent man overlooks an insult.

¹⁷A truthful witness gives honest testimony,
but a false witness tells lies.

¹⁸Reckless words pierce like a sword,
but the tongue of the wise brings healing.

¹⁹Truthful lips endure forever,
but a lying tongue lasts only a moment.

²⁰There is deceit in the hearts of those who plot
evil,
but joy for those who promote peace.

²¹No harm befalls the righteous,
but the wicked have their fill of trouble.

²²The LORD detests lying lips,
but he delights in men who are truthful.

1. In meeting someone new, do you: (a) Shake hands? (b) Fill the void with small talk? (c) Think first, speak later? (d) Wear your feelings on your sleeve? 2. If your use of words were compared to the way you drive a car, what kind of "talker" are you: (a) *Cautious,* looking both ways? (b) *Fast,* running the stop lights, cutting corners? (c) *Egocentric,* tooting your own horn? (d) *Distracted,* watching the girls or guys go by? (e) *Reckless,* with a few fender-benders?

1. How many proverbs can you find here which refer to *speech?* Why is one's speech so important in marriage? In counseling? In civil justice? In peace-making? In befriending? 2. All together, what do these proverbs say positively and negatively about the power of mere words? About the value of true talk? The venom of sinful talk? Who reaps more of the consequences for good? For evil? 3. Verse 14 links *words* to the theme of *work* (also 14:23). What is the point of this connection? How might a career built on lies and one built on honesty illustrate this point? 4. How are we to handle advice (v. 15), insults (v. 16) and anxiety (v. 25)? How would that approach work on the job? In the home? 5. If generosity or helping others is a virtue, what does verse 23 mean (see 10:14)? 6. "Working hard" and "diligence" contrast with "chasing fantasies" and "laziness" (vv. 11,24,27; see 28:19; 10:4; 19:24). What's the point of each contrast? When is it okay to rest from our labors? When is it okay to let our money or our employees work in our stead? When is it okay to enjoy our possessions?

1. Regarding this theme of work, what does Solomon say to your culture about: (a) Dreamers who don't do the actual labor but chase "fantastic" ideas? (b) Get-rich-quick schemers vs. sound financial planners, both of whom would sooner let their money work for them? (c) Welfare recipients and the roots of poverty? (d) "Workaholics" and the roots of their disease? 2. Subject the proverbs in verses 1,3,13–19 and 21 to a "True-False" test. According to you, which proverbs ring true "always," "sometimes" and "never"? 3. As in 12:9 and 13:7, when have you pre-

tended to be somebody you are not? How were you found out? **4.** What "favor from the Lord" (v. 2) are you thankful for? What other favor do you seek? Why?

----

1. Judging by the people you spent time with last month, what kind of company do you keep? By contrast, who did you used to hang around with? **2.** (Parents) If you could pick friends for your kids, who would you pick and why? (Children) How does your choice of friends vary from your parents' choice? Why?

1. What recurring themes do you see here? Which proverbs pick up themes from previous chapters? **2.** What does this chapter sound like to you: (a) Sweet pillow talk? (b) Tough parent-kid talk? (c) Teacher-parent-student talk? (d) Grandfather-teenager talk? (e) Smooth life insurance talk? Where do you see examples of each? **3.** On the *riches/poverty* theme (see vv. 7,8,11,18,21,22,23), what point of contrast does each verse make? Why do rich and poor alike pretend to be what they are not (v. 7)? **4.** In the face of robbers, blackmail or big fiscal commitments, what edge do the poor have over the rich (v. 8)? In terms of the best justice money can buy, how is that advantage reversed (v. 23)? **5.** What happens to the "get-rich-quick" scheme or the unjust person (v. 11)? What profit do diligence and discipline bring (vv. 4,11,18)? **6.** Proverbs stresses the *general rule* that righteous living leads to prosperity. What Bible book is concerned with the *exceptions* to that rule? What exceptions are noteworthy? **7.** *Discipline* links the material and spiritual aspects of prosperity and poverty. How is that evident in verses 4,13,18,25? How many "sluggards" (v. 4) or "wicked stomachs" (v. 25) do you see go hungry? What kind of hunger is Solomon referring to? What does "prospering" mean here? What results do "scorning" and "respecting"

²³A prudent man keeps his knowledge to himself,
   but the heart of fools blurts out folly.

²⁴Diligent hands will rule,
   but laziness ends in slave labor.

²⁵An anxious heart weighs a man down,
   but a kind word cheers him up.

²⁶A righteous man is cautious in friendship,[a]
   but the way of the wicked leads them astray.

²⁷The lazy man does not roast[b] his game,
   but the diligent man prizes his possessions.

²⁸In the way of righteousness there is life;
   along that path is immortality.

13 A wise son heeds his father's instruction,
   but a mocker does not listen to rebuke.

²From the fruit of his lips a man enjoys good things,
   but the unfaithful have a craving for violence.

³He who guards his lips guards his life,
   but he who speaks rashly will come to ruin.

⁴The sluggard craves and gets nothing,
   but the desires of the diligent are fully satisfied.

⁵The righteous hate what is false,
   but the wicked bring shame and disgrace.

⁶Righteousness guards the man of integrity,
   but wickedness overthrows the sinner.

⁷One man pretends to be rich, yet has nothing;
   another pretends to be poor, yet has great wealth.

⁸A man's riches may ransom his life,
   but a poor man hears no threat.

⁹The light of the righteous shines brightly,
   but the lamp of the wicked is snuffed out.

¹⁰Pride only breeds quarrels,
   but wisdom is found in those who take advice.

¹¹Dishonest money dwindles away,
   but he who gathers money little by little makes it grow.

¹²Hope deferred makes the heart sick,
   but a longing fulfilled is a tree of life.

¹³He who scorns instruction will pay for it,
   but he who respects a command is rewarded.

¹⁴The teaching of the wise is a fountain of life,
   turning a man from the snares of death.

¹⁵Good understanding wins favor,
   but the way of the unfaithful is hard.[c]

----

a26 Or *man is a guide to his neighbor*   b27 The meaning of the Hebrew for this word is uncertain.   c15 Or *unfaithful does not endure*

¹⁶Every prudent man acts out of knowledge,
  but a fool exposes his folly.

¹⁷A wicked messenger falls into trouble,
  but a trustworthy envoy brings healing.

¹⁸He who ignores discipline comes to poverty and
    shame,
  but whoever heeds correction is honored.

¹⁹A longing fulfilled is sweet to the soul,
  but fools detest turning from evil.

²⁰He who walks with the wise grows wise,
  but a companion of fools suffers harm.

²¹Misfortune pursues the sinner,
  but prosperity is the reward of the righteous.

²²A good man leaves an inheritance for his
    children's children,
  but a sinner's wealth is stored up for the
    righteous.

²³A poor man's field may produce abundant food,
  but injustice sweeps it away.

²⁴He who spares the rod hates his son,
  but he who loves him is careful to discipline
    him.

²⁵The righteous eat to their hearts' content,
  but the stomach of the wicked goes hungry.

14 The wise woman builds her house,
      but with her own hands the foolish one tears
        hers down.

²He whose walk is upright fears the LORD,
  but he whose ways are devious despises him.

³A fool's talk brings a rod to his back,
  but the lips of the wise protect them.

⁴Where there are no oxen, the manger is empty,
  but from the strength of an ox comes an
    abundant harvest.

⁵A truthful witness does not deceive,
  but a false witness pours out lies.

⁶The mocker seeks wisdom and finds none,
  but knowledge comes easily to the discerning.

⁷Stay away from a foolish man,
  for you will not find knowledge on his lips.

⁸The wisdom of the prudent is to give thought to
    their ways,
  but the folly of fools is deception.

⁹Fools mock at making amends for sin,
  but goodwill is found among the upright.

¹⁰Each heart knows its own bitterness,
  and no one else can share its joy.

¹¹The house of the wicked will be destroyed,
  but the tent of the upright will flourish.

godly and wise instruction each
bring (v. 13)?

1. How does the company
you keep (v. 20) affect you?
Why? 2. What is your "hope deferred" or "longing fulfilled" (vv.
12–19)? What comfort do you find
as you wait for Jesus to fulfill that
hope? 3. What do you believe
about leaving large inheritances to
your children or grandchildren: (a)
Let them earn it the hard way? (b)
Spend it all on your retirement? (c)
Leave as much as possible for others? (d) Giving money creates
more problems than it solves? 4.
How would your view on large inheritances differ if you were the
recipient? 5. You are a talk-show
host discussing spanking children.
How does your three-generation
panel each react to verse 24?

1. When building a house of
sand, wooden blocks, Lin-
coln logs or cards, how did you
make sure it stood up? How much
easier was it to tear down? Why is
that? 2. If forced to choose, which
lot in life would you prefer and why:
(a) Farmer without oxen to plow?
(b) Museum curator without artifacts to display? (c) King without
subjects to rule? (d) Love life without bitterness or joy?

1. How might verse 1 serve
as a good "subtitle" for this
chapter? Compare 9:1–12, for the
house built by wisdom. What building blocks of wisdom do you see
here in chapter 14 that would help
ensure that one's "house" flourishes? What stumbling blocks of
the foolish would you avoid for that
same reason? 2. Some proverbs
arrest our attention due to a figure
of speech that is ambiguous. Such
is the case with verse 4. What
could it mean: (a) Growth (corporate and spiritual) is never neat, but
often messy—like an ox? (b) Take
care of your means of production if
you want a rich harvest? (c) Be
kind to animals and they'll be kind
to you? 3. What does the "fear of
the Lord" imply for living today (vv.
2,26,27)? What will future retribu-

tion for present inequality look like (vv. 14,18,19,24,32)? **4.** How should we relate to our neighbors in need (vv. 21,31)? What happens if we follow this advice? How does shabby treatment of the unfortunate reflect on one's relationship with God? How does the good we do for the poor honor God and exalt one's nation as morally righteous? Why is that?

1. Comparing your life to a "house," what condition is it in: (a) Crumbling foundation, but good soil? (b) Good foundation, but tacky additions? (c) Fancy exterior, but shabby interior? (d) Underpriced fixer-upper? (e) Well lived in? (f) Ready for sale? **2.** If you had a choice of the following, which would you like to work on and why? (a) Strong back? (b) Wise lips? (c) Rich friends? (d) Caring heart? (e) Discerning heart? (f) Quick temper? (g) King's delight? (h) Nation's righteousness? How can your group study of Proverbs help you in this one area? **3.** To what extent do you and your church practice shunning the "fool," as in verse 7? How do you avoid worshipping, socializing or working with a "fool"? **4.** Where do you find security? Job? Money? Home? Family? Friends? Possessions? What could happen to each of these in time? What alone provides true security (v. 26)? Have you found your security there? Why or why not? **5.** Are you experiencing "body life," or "bone rot" (v. 30) these days? What causes the two conditions? What cures them? Where does the heartfelt peace come from? **6.** Is yours an exalted nation, or a disgraced one (v. 34)? Why do you think so? What is your contribution or solution to that? **7.** If, after making a bad decision, someone quoted verse 12 to you, how would you feel? What is a proper context for "the way leading to death" (see 7:21–27)? **8.** When have you had laughter and joy turn to grief and sadness (v. 13; see Mt 5:4)?

[12]There is a way that seems right to a man,
    but in the end it leads to death.

[13]Even in laughter the heart may ache,
    and joy may end in grief.

[14]The faithless will be fully repaid for their ways,
    and the good man rewarded for his.

[15]A simple man believes anything,
    but a prudent man gives thought to his steps.

[16]A wise man fears the LORD and shuns evil,
    but a fool is hotheaded and reckless.

[17]A quick-tempered man does foolish things,
    and a crafty man is hated.

[18]The simple inherit folly,
    but the prudent are crowned with knowledge.

[19]Evil men will bow down in the presence of the good,
    and the wicked at the gates of the righteous.

[20]The poor are shunned even by their neighbors,
    but the rich have many friends.

[21]He who despises his neighbor sins,
    but blessed is he who is kind to the needy.

[22]Do not those who plot evil go astray?
    But those who plan what is good find[a] love
      and faithfulness.

[23]All hard work brings a profit,
    but mere talk leads only to poverty.

[24]The wealth of the wise is their crown,
    but the folly of fools yields folly.

[25]A truthful witness saves lives,
    but a false witness is deceitful.

[26]He who fears the LORD has a secure fortress,
    and for his children it will be a refuge.

[27]The fear of the LORD is a fountain of life,
    turning a man from the snares of death.

[28]A large population is a king's glory,
    but without subjects a prince is ruined.

[29]A patient man has great understanding,
    but a quick-tempered man displays folly.

[30]A heart at peace gives life to the body,
    but envy rots the bones.

[31]He who oppresses the poor shows contempt for their Maker,
    but whoever is kind to the needy honors God.

[32]When calamity comes, the wicked are brought down,
    but even in death the righteous have a refuge.

[33]Wisdom reposes in the heart of the discerning

a22 Or *show*

and even among fools she lets herself be
    known.^a

³⁴Righteousness exalts a nation,
    but sin is a disgrace to any people.

³⁵A king delights in a wise servant,
    but a shameful servant incurs his wrath.

15

A gentle answer turns away wrath,
    but a harsh word stirs up anger.

²The tongue of the wise commends knowledge,
    but the mouth of the fool gushes folly.

³The eyes of the LORD are everywhere,
    keeping watch on the wicked and the good.

⁴The tongue that brings healing is a tree of life,
    but a deceitful tongue crushes the spirit.

⁵A fool spurns his father's discipline,
    but whoever heeds correction shows prudence.

⁶The house of the righteous contains great
        treasure,
    but the income of the wicked brings them
        trouble.

⁷The lips of the wise spread knowledge;
    not so the hearts of fools.

⁸The LORD detests the sacrifice of the wicked,
    but the prayer of the upright pleases him.

⁹The LORD detests the way of the wicked
    but he loves those who pursue righteousness.

¹⁰Stern discipline awaits him who leaves the path;
    he who hates correction will die.

¹¹Death and Destruction^b lie open before the
        LORD—
    how much more the hearts of men!

¹²A mocker resents correction;
    he will not consult the wise.

¹³A happy heart makes the face cheerful,
    but heartache crushes the spirit.

¹⁴The discerning heart seeks knowledge,
    but the mouth of a fool feeds on folly.

¹⁵All the days of the oppressed are wretched,
    but the cheerful heart has a continual feast.

¹⁶Better a little with the fear of the LORD
    than great wealth with turmoil.

¹⁷Better a meal of vegetables where there is love
    than a fattened calf with hatred.

¹⁸A hot-tempered man stirs up dissension,
    but a patient man calms a quarrel.

1. Who would get the prize for best peace-making efforts in your family? Why did you select that person? 2. What is your "Achilles' heel" that, when hit, will ignite your anger every time? What have you learned that might help you next time in turning away your wrath, as well as your opponent's?

1. As a key is used to unlock the door to a house, what key words unlock the meaning and main points of this chapter? What is the key to "joy"? To "success"? To "keeping peace"? To "healing hurts"? What key words carry over from previous chapters? Which are unique to this chapter? Which seems to be a master key? 2. "Talk is cheap." Would Solomon agree or disagree with that? Why do you think so? What value does he place on the tongue, lips, mouth, words? 3. What do the "eyes of the Lord" symbolize (v. 3; see 2Ch 16:9)? What does he see (vv. 8,9,11)? 4. What does the Lord "detest" about the wicked (vv. 8,9,26)? What is their sacrifice (see 21:3,27): Pagan idolatry? Child-sacrificing? Insincerity? Malice? Ignorance? Injustice? Or what (see Ecc 5:1; Isa 1:11–15; Mic 6:7–8)? 5. What is the interplay between the "heart" and the other aspects of the personality mentioned here (vv. 7,11,13–15, 28,30)? Does what's on the inside come through to the outside (as in v. 13)? Or does seeing and putting on a cheerful face determine how the heart feels (as in v. 30)? Why do you think so? 6. What is to be our response to correction or rebuke (vv. 5,10,12,31,32)? If we listen to it, what happens? If we don't, what happens? Do you believe it's that simple? Why or why not? 7. If this chapter were a book for sale, which verse would be on the cover as a "come on" to persuade you to buy it? Why?

1. In what sense is your "sacrifice" detestable? Could something as good as going to church and saying your prayers actually be offensive to God? How so? What does please the Lord? 2.

---

^a33 Hebrew; Septuagint and Syriac / *but in the heart of fools she is not known*
^b11 Hebrew *Sheol and Abaddon*

How does it make you feel to know God is always, everywhere "keeping watch" (v. 3): Uneasy? Naked? Relieved? Secure? Scared? **3.** Share a time when you rejected your parent's discipline or when your children spurned yours? What happened? What did you (or they) learn? In what sense do you (and your kids) relate to God as to your earthly father? **4.** What doors have you opened lately using the keys found here in proverbs? What doors remain shut? What keys seem not to work for you? Whose wrath seems "unturned," in spite of your "gentle answer"? **5.** Given your economic standard of living and family status, do verses 16–17 still present viable options today? Which option would you prefer and why? **6.** For whose heart can you show a cheerful face? Whose look are you trying to catch for your own heart-felt joy? Have you looked to the Lord to provide that elusive joy?

---

1. Who plans most of the trips in your family? What does this involve: Family consensus? Long-range commitments? Prayer? Winning a lottery? Flying by the seat of your pants? Paralysis of indecision? Getting lost? **2.** At work, what is your usual role: Active initiator? Reliable respondent? Delegated to implement? Just along for the ride? Foot-dragger? Antagonist?

1. What proverbial wisdom recurs from previous chapters? What new themes are introduced here? Which one raises the most questions for you? **2.** What does this chapter sound like to you: (a) Personal testimony? (b) History lesson? (c) Philosophy class? (d) Father-son chat? (e) Career coun-

¹⁹The way of the sluggard is blocked with thorns,
  but the path of the upright is a highway.

²⁰A wise son brings joy to his father,
  but a foolish man despises his mother.

²¹Folly delights a man who lacks judgment,
  but a man of understanding keeps a straight course.

²²Plans fail for lack of counsel,
  but with many advisers they succeed.

²³A man finds joy in giving an apt reply—
  and how good is a timely word!

²⁴The path of life leads upward for the wise
  to keep him from going down to the grave.^a

²⁵The LORD tears down the proud man's house
  but he keeps the widow's boundaries intact.

²⁶The LORD detests the thoughts of the wicked,
  but those of the pure are pleasing to him.

²⁷A greedy man brings trouble to his family,
  but he who hates bribes will live.

²⁸The heart of the righteous weighs its answers,
  but the mouth of the wicked gushes evil.

²⁹The LORD is far from the wicked
  but he hears the prayer of the righteous.

³⁰A cheerful look brings joy to the heart,
  and good news gives health to the bones.

³¹He who listens to a life-giving rebuke
  will be at home among the wise.

³²He who ignores discipline despises himself,
  but whoever heeds correction gains understanding.

³³The fear of the LORD teaches a man wisdom,^b
  and humility comes before honor.

16 To man belong the plans of the heart,
  but from the LORD comes the reply of the tongue.

²All a man's ways seem innocent to him,
  but motives are weighed by the LORD.

³Commit to the LORD whatever you do,
  and your plans will succeed.

⁴The LORD works out everything for his own ends—
  even the wicked for a day of disaster.

⁵The LORD detests all the proud of heart.
  Be sure of this: They will not go unpunished.

⁶Through love and faithfulness sin is atoned for;
  through the fear of the LORD a man avoids evil.

⁷When a man's ways are pleasing to the LORD,

^a24 Hebrew *Sheol*   ^b33 Or *Wisdom teaches the fear of the LORD*

he makes even his enemies live at peace with
him.

[8]Better a little with righteousness
than much gain with injustice.

[9]In his heart a man plans his course,
but the LORD determines his steps.

[10]The lips of a king speak as an oracle,
and his mouth should not betray justice.

[11]Honest scales and balances are from the LORD;
all the weights in the bag are of his making.

[12]Kings detest wrongdoing,
for a throne is established through
righteousness.

[13]Kings take pleasure in honest lips;
they value a man who speaks the truth.

[14]A king's wrath is a messenger of death,
but a wise man will appease it.

[15]When a king's face brightens, it means life;
his favor is like a rain cloud in spring.

[16]How much better to get wisdom than gold,
to choose understanding rather than silver!

[17]The highway of the upright avoids evil;
he who guards his way guards his life.

[18]Pride goes before destruction,
a haughty spirit before a fall.

[19]Better to be lowly in spirit and among the
oppressed
than to share plunder with the proud.

[20]Whoever gives heed to instruction prospers,
and blessed is he who trusts in the LORD.

[21]The wise in heart are called discerning,
and pleasant words promote instruction.[a]

[22]Understanding is a fountain of life to those who
have it,
but folly brings punishment to fools.

[23]A wise man's heart guides his mouth,
and his lips promote instruction.[b]

[24]Pleasant words are a honeycomb,
sweet to the soul and healing to the bones.

[25]There is a way that seems right to a man,
but in the end it leads to death.

[26]The laborer's appetite works for him;
his hunger drives him on.

[27]A scoundrel plots evil,
and his speech is like a scorching fire.

seling? (f) Money matters? What
elements of each do you see here?
3. Compare verses 1–9 with
10–15. What are the roles and
character of the Lord? Of the king?
How do they compare? **4.** By
whose love and faithfulness is sin
atoned for in this context (v. 6)? Is
this a denial of God's grace, or a
demand for fruits that befit repentance? How is it possible to avoid
evil (vv. 6,17)? Does that mean
avoiding the evil mischief-makers
in verses 27–30? When is that not
possible? **5.** What principles for decision-making, goal-setting and
knowing God's will do you see here
(vv. 1–4,9–10,17,20,25,33)? **6.** It
has been said, "Man proposes,
God disposes." How is that viewpoint supported here? Likewise, to
what extent does Solomon say we
are "free" to set goals and reach
them? **7.** If "God works out everything for his own ends" (v. 4), does
that make him responsible for evil?
If not, then does evil function outside his control? If so, then does
evil always serve God's purposes
(e.g., the Pharaoh of Egypt; the
brothers of Joseph)? How so?

1. What role should feelings,
circumstances, counsel, conscience, Scripture, casting lots
(v. 33), oracles (v. 10) and law of
the land each play, in knowing and
doing God's will? Which one
should be determinative? Sugges-
tive? Confirming? Suspect? Subordinate? **2.** It has been said, "Don't
let the good get in the way of the
better." What "good" and "better"
opportunities and options do you
see laid out here (vv. 8,16,32)?
Would you choose (or have you
chosen) the "better" in each case?
Why or why not? How would your
life be different tomorrow if you
didn't "go for the gold," but pursued
wisdom instead? **3.** Which aspect
of God seems to be uppermost in
these proverbs: Just? Sovereign?
Caring? Judging? Guiding? Blessing? Which aspect is God showing
you these days? **4.** Do "disaster,"
"destruction" and "death" (vv. 4,18,
25) await the wayward person by
God's design or by man's default? **5.** Who are some of the other
"kings" in your life to whom you listen? Do they speak "the very words
of God" (see 1Pe 4:11)? What
checks and balances on human
authority does King Solomon suggest?

[a]21 Or *words make a man persuasive*   [b]23 Or *mouth / and makes his lips*
persuasive

²⁸A perverse man stirs up dissension,
and a gossip separates close friends.

²⁹A violent man entices his neighbor
and leads him down a path that is not good.

³⁰He who winks with his eye is plotting perversity;
he who purses his lips is bent on evil.

³¹Gray hair is a crown of splendor;
it is attained by a righteous life.

³²Better a patient man than a warrior,
a man who controls his temper than one who
takes a city.

³³The lot is cast into the lap,
but its every decision is from the LORD.

17 Better a dry crust with peace and quiet
than a house full of feasting,^a with strife.

²A wise servant will rule over a disgraceful son,
and will share the inheritance as one of the
brothers.

³The crucible for silver and the furnace for gold,
but the LORD tests the heart.

⁴A wicked man listens to evil lips;
a liar pays attention to a malicious tongue.

⁵He who mocks the poor shows contempt for their
Maker;
whoever gloats over disaster will not go
unpunished.

⁶Children's children are a crown to the aged,
and parents are the pride of their children.

⁷Arrogant^b lips are unsuited to a fool—
how much worse lying lips to a ruler!

⁸A bribe is a charm to the one who gives it;
wherever he turns, he succeeds.

⁹He who covers over an offense promotes love,
but whoever repeats the matter separates close
friends.

¹⁰A rebuke impresses a man of discernment
more than a hundred lashes a fool.

¹¹An evil man is bent only on rebellion;
a merciless official will be sent against him.

¹²Better to meet a bear robbed of her cubs
than a fool in his folly.

¹³If a man pays back evil for good,
evil will never leave his house.

¹⁴Starting a quarrel is like breaching a dam;
so drop the matter before a dispute breaks out.

---

1. If money and time were no object, what would you do for "peace and quiet"? 2. With the resources you actually have, what gives you "peace and quiet"?

1. From this chapter, do you get the idea the author was: (a) Poor but peaceful? (b) Rich and resentful? (c) Young and restless? (d) A grief-stricken parent? (e) A proud grandparent? Why do you think so? Where in these proverbs do you see elements of each? 2. What conflict management ideas do you see in verses 1,4,9,11, 14,17 and 19? What insight do get from these images: (a) Dry crust vs. feasting? (b) Malicious tongue? (c) Repeating an offense? (d) Breaching a dam? (e) Building a high gate? 3. In what sense is verse 2 true? How did this come true for Solomon's servant and son (see 1Ki 11:28ff)? 4. In what sense is verse 22 true (see 15:13,30)? What about the grief-stricken "father of a fool" (vv. 21,25)? How does he get a cheerful heart (see Jas 1:2ff)? 5. What principles for justice and justification do you see here (vv. 8,13,15,23,26)? In what ways are "bribes," "flogging," "paying back evil for good" practiced today? How does the Lord deal with the perpetrators and victims of injustice? How should we?

1. If the Lord detests the injustice of acquitting the guilty, why does he acquit you of your sin (see Ro 3:26; 4:5)? How does God remain just in doing that? 2. With what crucible has the Lord been testing your heart: Rebel child? Relationship end? Job loss? How do you know it is the Lord testing you and not you falling into temptation (see Jas 1:3,12–15)? Can you

a 1 Hebrew *sacrifices*   *b 7* Or *Eloquent*

¹⁵Acquitting the guilty and condemning the
   innocent—
   the Lord detests them both.

¹⁶Of what use is money in the hand of a fool,
   since he has no desire to get wisdom?

¹⁷A friend loves at all times,
   and a brother is born for adversity.

¹⁸A man lacking in judgment strikes hands in
   pledge
   and puts up security for his neighbor.

¹⁹He who loves a quarrel loves sin;
   he who builds a high gate invites destruction.

²⁰A man of perverse heart does not prosper;
   he whose tongue is deceitful falls into trouble.

²¹To have a fool for a son brings grief;
   there is no joy for the father of a fool.

²²A cheerful heart is good medicine,
   but a crushed spirit dries up the bones.

²³A wicked man accepts a bribe in secret
   to pervert the course of justice.

²⁴A discerning man keeps wisdom in view,
   but a fool's eyes wander to the ends of the
   earth.

²⁵A foolish son brings grief to his father
   and bitterness to the one who bore him.

²⁶It is not good to punish an innocent man,
   or to flog officials for their integrity.

²⁷A man of knowledge uses words with restraint,
   and a man of understanding is even-tempered.

²⁸Even a fool is thought wise if he keeps silent,
   and discerning if he holds his tongue.

18 An unfriendly man pursues selfish ends;
   he defies all sound judgment.

²A fool finds no pleasure in understanding
   but delights in airing his own opinions.

³When wickedness comes, so does contempt,
   and with shame comes disgrace.

⁴The words of a man's mouth are deep waters,
   but the fountain of wisdom is a bubbling brook.

⁵It is not good to be partial to the wicked
   or to deprive the innocent of justice.

⁶A fool's lips bring him strife,
   and his mouth invites a beating.

⁷A fool's mouth is his undoing,
   and his lips are a snare to his soul.

⁸The words of a gossip are like choice morsels;
   they go down to a man's inmost parts.

think of a self-administered lab test for your heart-felt motives? **3.** What recent crucible experience tried your true friends? How has a test separated your close friends? Which "brother" (or sister) proved in adversity to love you at all times? **4.** When you are wrong, how do you like to be corrected: 100 lashes with a tongue, whip or wet noodle? On the other hand, what kind of correction only provokes you or stiffens your neck? Why? **5.** When corrected by the Lord, how does it feel? Are you ever in his doghouse very long? What does it take to get you back on the "path of righteousness"? **6.** Money talks (v. 8). How have you seen this work in your life with friends? With parents? At work? At school? **7.** In what ways can you identify with the author's experience of family strife (v. 1), grief (vv. 21,25), disgrace (v. 2) and pride (v. 6)? What would you want your group to pray concerning your family ties? **8.** Who in your group deserves the "Appearance of Wisdom" award (vv. 27–28)? Don't all speak up at once! This is best done by silent ballot.

1. What is your favorite proverb or witty saying? From whom did you learn it? Where does it apply? **2.** In forming your own opinion of political candidates and officeholders, what sources do you listen to and why? Which do you ignore and why?

1. Following 17:27–28, what does this chapter say about a fool's tongue, lips, mouth? How do these proverbs relate to the forming and articulating of opinions? Which three relate to eating? Which one best sums up all the others? **2.** What is the meaning of "deep waters" (v. 4; see 20:5)? How does the "bubbling brook" of wisdom differ from the profundity, obscurity or secrecy of "deep waters"? **3.** Which proverbs convey principles of justice for rich and poor alike (see vv. 5,16,17,19,23)? Why do you think favoritism of any kind is uniformly condemned in the Scriptures? How might the Lord deal justly with the "fortified cities" of verses 11 and 19? **4.** What does this chapter say about finding and keeping your brothers, friends, even your life mate? **5.** What is the main point of verses 13 and 17, taken together? As a guiding principle, how would you apply this to raising children? To formulating doctrine? Deliberating legal cases? Conducting scientific experiments? Making public policy?

♡ **1.** Where in your life does this guiding principle apply? What use of this proverbial wisdom does James 1:19–27 make? What difference would "listening before speaking" make in your group Bible study? In personal relationships? In your righteous living and pure religion? **2.** How can you tell a closed mind from an open mind (vv. 2,13,17)? How do you feel around such people? Which is more typical of you? **3.** Could your spirit sustain you in sickness? Or does it crush you? Why (v. 14)? How might you strengthen your spirit so that it can sustain you, and so that you are a source of life to others? **4.** The tongue (speech) has "the power of life and death" (v. 21). What are some examples of life? Of death? **5.** What kind of friend or brother are you?

☕ **1.** What great cause has really pumped you up? How have you demonstrated this excitement? **2.** What cause were you once zealous for, but no longer actively engage in? Why? **3.** Do you support causes now more with your head, heart or checkbook? Explain.

📖 **1.** What recurring themes and key words are highlighted here? **2.** One of Solomon's highlighting devices is the use of thesis and antithesis in his couplets. In which proverbs is this contrast most pronounced? How does this literary device add to under-

⁹One who is slack in his work
   is brother to one who destroys.

¹⁰The name of the Lᴏʀᴅ is a strong tower;
   the righteous run to it and are safe.

¹¹The wealth of the rich is their fortified city;
   they imagine it an unscalable wall.

¹²Before his downfall a man's heart is proud,
   but humility comes before honor.

¹³He who answers before listening—
   that is his folly and his shame.

¹⁴A man's spirit sustains him in sickness,
   but a crushed spirit who can bear?

¹⁵The heart of the discerning acquires knowledge;
   the ears of the wise seek it out.

¹⁶A gift opens the way for the giver
   and ushers him into the presence of the great.

¹⁷The first to present his case seems right,
   till another comes forward and questions him.

¹⁸Casting the lot settles disputes
   and keeps strong opponents apart.

¹⁹An offended brother is more unyielding than a fortified city,
   and disputes are like the barred gates of a citadel.

²⁰From the fruit of his mouth a man's stomach is filled;
   with the harvest from his lips he is satisfied.

²¹The tongue has the power of life and death,
   and those who love it will eat its fruit.

²²He who finds a wife finds what is good
   and receives favor from the Lᴏʀᴅ.

²³A poor man pleads for mercy,
   but a rich man answers harshly.

²⁴A man of many companions may come to ruin,
   but there is a friend who sticks closer than a brother.

19 Better a poor man whose walk is blameless
   than a fool whose lips are perverse.

²It is not good to have zeal without knowledge,
   nor to be hasty and miss the way.

³A man's own folly ruins his life,
   yet his heart rages against the Lᴏʀᴅ.

⁴Wealth brings many friends,
   but a poor man's friend deserts him.

⁵A false witness will not go unpunished,
   and he who pours out lies will not go free.

⁶Many curry favor with a ruler,
   and everyone is the friend of a man who gives gifts.

⁷A poor man is shunned by all his relatives—
    how much more do his friends avoid him!
Though he pursues them with pleading,
    they are nowhere to be found.ᵃ

⁸He who gets wisdom loves his own soul;
    he who cherishes understanding prospers.

⁹A false witness will not go unpunished,
    and he who pours out lies will perish.

¹⁰It is not fitting for a fool to live in luxury—
    how much worse for a slave to rule over
        princes!

¹¹A man's wisdom gives him patience;
    it is to his glory to overlook an offense.

¹²A king's rage is like the roar of a lion,
    but his favor is like dew on the grass.

¹³A foolish son is his father's ruin,
    and a quarrelsome wife is like a constant
        dripping.

¹⁴Houses and wealth are inherited from parents,
    but a prudent wife is from the LORD.

¹⁵Laziness brings on deep sleep,
    and the shiftless man goes hungry.

¹⁶He who obeys instructions guards his life,
    but he who is contemptuous of his ways will
        die.

¹⁷He who is kind to the poor lends to the LORD,
    and he will reward him for what he has done.

¹⁸Discipline your son, for in that there is hope;
    do not be a willing party to his death.

¹⁹A hot-tempered man must pay the penalty;
    if you rescue him, you will have to do it again.

²⁰Listen to advice and accept instruction,
    and in the end you will be wise.

²¹Many are the plans in a man's heart,
    but it is the LORD's purpose that prevails.

²²What a man desires is unfailing loveᵇ;
    better to be poor than a liar.

²³The fear of the LORD leads to life:
    Then one rests content, untouched by trouble.

²⁴The sluggard buries his hand in the dish;
    he will not even bring it back to his mouth!

²⁵Flog a mocker, and the simple will learn
        prudence;
    rebuke a discerning man, and he will gain
        knowledge.

²⁶He who robs his father and drives out his mother
    is a son who brings shame and disgrace.

standing of the main point? **3.** Some couplets use comparison more than contrast to make their point. What examples do you see of this? What point is made by these comparisons using "better than," "worse than" and "like"? **4.** Some contrasts are set up by cross-referencing proverbs. What do you see here contrasting ruining and guarding one's life? Between ignoring the special pleading of the poor and giving to them, as unto the Lord? **5.** What contrasts fall under the "Different Strokes for Different Folks" category? What distinctions do you see here between treatment of the mocker, the simple, the hot-tempered person, the son, the discerning and the fools? **6.** What do the jarring absurdities and metaphors in verses 10,13,24 and 26 tell you about the practical difference wisdom should make in one's lifestyle?

1. In your life, how have you experienced the truth of verses 5,9,28? How have you been hurt by a "false witness"? What was the net result for them? **2.** What experience have you had with a raging heart (vv. 3,12) and a patient one (v. 11)? When have you been tempted to blame God for some ruinous situation? How do you treat those who offend you with a false witness? **3.** What experience have you had with drippy faucets or leaky roofs in your home (v. 13)? What was your plumber's solution? Did that shut it off? If not, what will? Who is the wisest plumber you know? **4.** What discipline or instruction are you under now? What do you think is the reason or goal? What does that say about the Lord's prevailing purpose (v. 21)?

ᵃ7 The meaning of the Hebrew for this sentence is uncertain.   ᵇ22 Or *A man's greed is his shame*

²⁷Stop listening to instruction, my son,
and you will stray from the words of
knowledge.

²⁸A corrupt witness mocks at justice,
and the mouth of the wicked gulps down evil.

²⁹Penalties are prepared for mockers,
and beatings for the backs of fools.

20 Wine is a mocker and beer a brawler;
whoever is led astray by them is not wise.

²A king's wrath is like the roar of a lion;
he who angers him forfeits his life.

³It is to a man's honor to avoid strife,
but every fool is quick to quarrel.

⁴A sluggard does not plow in season;
so at harvest time he looks but finds nothing.

⁵The purposes of a man's heart are deep waters,
but a man of understanding draws them out.

⁶Many a man claims to have unfailing love,
but a faithful man who can find?

⁷The righteous man leads a blameless life;
blessed are his children after him.

⁸When a king sits on his throne to judge,
he winnows out all evil with his eyes.

⁹Who can say, "I have kept my heart pure;
I am clean and without sin"?

¹⁰Differing weights and differing measures—
the LORD detests them both.

¹¹Even a child is known by his actions,
by whether his conduct is pure and right.

¹²Ears that hear and eyes that see—
the LORD has made them both.

¹³Do not love sleep or you will grow poor;
stay awake and you will have food to spare.

¹⁴"It's no good, it's no good!" says the buyer;
then off he goes and boasts about his purchase.

¹⁵Gold there is, and rubies in abundance,
but lips that speak knowledge are a rare jewel.

¹⁶Take the garment of one who puts up security for
a stranger;
hold it in pledge if he does it for a wayward
woman.

¹⁷Food gained by fraud tastes sweet to a man,
but he ends up with a mouth full of gravel.

¹⁸Make plans by seeking advice;
if you wage war, obtain guidance.

¹⁹A gossip betrays a confidence;
so avoid a man who talks too much.

When you were a child, what was one forbidden activity? By whom were you caught? Why do you suppose you were always found out? Who told?

1. If you were promoting this chapter during a 10-second sneak preview TV commercial, which verse(s) would you use as a tease to attract an audience? Why? 2. "Personification" (where a thing is spoken of as a person) is another figure of speech we find in the proverbs. Where do you see it? What is meant by a lamp being snuffed out (v. 20) or searching out (v. 27)? 3. Wisdom often gives insight into the deepest recesses of human nature, as in verses 5,8–9,11–12,25–27,30. How is it that wisdom is able to do this? What is it about inner secrets, guilty consciences, evil motives, and rash vows that is susceptible to wisdom? 4. The moral wisdom of Proverbs not only permeates our inmost being, it directs us into the future. Where is this evident in this chapter? What is the end in view for the sluggard (v. 4)? The children of the righteous (v. 7)? The fraud (vv. 10,17)? The disrespectful son (v. 20)? The prodigal son (v. 21; see Lk 15:12–13)? The one who does not avenge himself (v. 22)? 5. How important is it to the Lord (and you) to keep a vow once it is made (vv. 6,16,25)? What will happen in each instance if you keep the vow? And if you don't?

1. Who in your society draws out understanding (v. 24): Clergy? Reporters? Lawyers? Counselors? TV talk show hosts? Bartenders? Wise kings? Who in your life draws out understanding? To whom can you be this kind of person? 2. What kind of "security" is love (vv. 6,28)? Why would it work for a king or other leaders? Has it worked for you? 3. How would you answer the rhetorical question in verse 9? How does Job (see Job 14:4)? The psalmist (see Ps 24:4; 119:9,11)? The apostle Paul (see Ro 3:23)? 4. In our society, talk is cheap and jewels are

²⁰If a man curses his father or mother,
  his lamp will be snuffed out in pitch darkness.

²¹An inheritance quickly gained at the beginning
  will not be blessed at the end.

²²Do not say, "I'll pay you back for this wrong!"
  Wait for the LORD, and he will deliver you.

²³The LORD detests differing weights,
  and dishonest scales do not please him.

²⁴A man's steps are directed by the LORD.
  How then can anyone understand his own way?

²⁵It is a trap for a man to dedicate something rashly
  and only later to consider his vows.

²⁶A wise king winnows out the wicked;
  he drives the threshing wheel over them.

²⁷The lamp of the LORD searches the spirit of a
    man*ᵃ*;
  it searches out his inmost being.

²⁸Love and faithfulness keep a king safe;
  through love his throne is made secure.

²⁹The glory of young men is their strength,
  gray hair the splendor of the old.

³⁰Blows and wounds cleanse away evil,
  and beatings purge the inmost being.

21 The king's heart is in the hand of the LORD;
  he directs it like a watercourse wherever he
    pleases.

²All a man's ways seem right to him,
  but the LORD weighs the heart.

³To do what is right and just
  is more acceptable to the LORD than sacrifice.

⁴Haughty eyes and a proud heart,
  the lamp of the wicked, are sin!

⁵The plans of the diligent lead to profit
  as surely as haste leads to poverty.

⁶A fortune made by a lying tongue
  is a fleeting vapor and a deadly snare.ᵇ

⁷The violence of the wicked will drag them away,
  for they refuse to do what is right.

⁸The way of the guilty is devious,
  but the conduct of the innocent is upright.

⁹Better to live on a corner of the roof
  than share a house with a quarrelsome wife.

¹⁰The wicked man craves evil;
  his neighbor gets no mercy from him.

¹¹When a mocker is punished, the simple gain
    wisdom;

expensive, so how do you react to verse 15? Which would you honestly prefer: Jewels or knowledge? Why? What could you do with each? What can't you do (see 17:16)? **5.** If even "a child is known by his actions" (v. 11), what does that say about a child's character? About God's character? Likewise, what can be known about you, and the child within? **6.** When does seeking advice (v. 18) become gossip (v. 19)? How do you decide just who you will trust? Who alone is worthy of your trust? **7.** What is your "glory" (v. 29)? Or what glory do you covet: Gray hair? Strength? Cover-girl beauty? Olympic medal? Club trophy? Kids? How do you plan to attain your goal in this life (see vv. 24,27)?

———————————

What kind of character do you think you'd most enjoy portraying in a play? Why? How are you like, or unlike, that character?

1. If this chapter were a play, what would the cast of characters look like? Who has the lead role? Does Solomon have in mind real people, or is his cast of characters largely symbolic? Symbolic of what? **2.** How are the first eight verses linked thematically to one another? How are the themes of heart attitude and right behavior linked? What do the images of "haughty eyes" and "lying tongue" have in common? Likewise, what is the contrast linking "watercourse" with "fleeting vapor"? **3.** Knowing that kings are subject to the King of kings (v 1), what does that say about what a subject can expect from a king and vice versa? **4.** Why does the Lord regard "sacrifice" (vv. 3,27) as unacceptable, even detestable? What does he want instead (see 15:8; Mic 6:7–8)? What does this say about mere religious ritual or orthodox belief? Why are spiritual reality and practical justice more acceptable? **5.** The pursuit of justice brings "joy" (v. 15) among other blessings (v. 21), but the di-

---

ᵃ27 Or *The spirit of man is the LORD's lamp*   ᵇ6 Some Hebrew manuscripts,
Septuagint and Vulgate; most Hebrew manuscripts *vapor for those who seek death*

rect pursuit of "pleasure" leads to poverty (v. 17). How do you explain that paradox? **6.** As for the poor, what happens when we ignore and when we heed their cry for justice and mercy (v. 13; see 14,21,31)? Positively restated, what does this proverb and related ones suggest we do for the poor (see 22:9; 28:8; 31:9)? **7.** What do verses 14,20 and 26 add to this subject of stewardship?

♡ **1.** If the proverbial types in this chapter were characters in a play, which one(s) would get your standing ovation? Why? With whom would you feel the most empathy? Why? **2.** Verse 1 expresses the truth proverbially what Tiglath-pileser (Isa 10:6–7), Cyrus (Isa 41:2–4) and Artaxerxes (Ezr 7:21) exemplify historically. Where do you see this principle in force today? How does that affect your view of those in authority, even pagan leaders? How are pagan leaders subservient to God? **3.** We tend to exert authority as kings in our own right, but in reality we are subject to God's heart-searching authority (vv. 2,30,31; see 16:2; Heb 4:12). How have you tried to prevail against the Lord? What was the result? What victory did you experience with the Lord? **4.** What does it mean for God's people to make sacrifices with "evil intent" (v. 27; see Isa 1:11–15 on "evil assemblies")? What is the result to God? To us? To others? **5.** What different feelings do verses 9 and 19 arouse in the men and women of your group? Why? Where are you living these days? Why there?

when a wise man is instructed, he gets
    knowledge.

¹²The Righteous One[a] takes note of the house of
        the wicked
    and brings the wicked to ruin.

¹³If a man shuts his ears to the cry of the poor,
    he too will cry out and not be answered.

¹⁴A gift given in secret soothes anger,
    and a bribe concealed in the cloak pacifies great
        wrath.

¹⁵When justice is done, it brings joy to the
        righteous
    but terror to evildoers.

¹⁶A man who strays from the path of understanding
    comes to rest in the company of the dead.

¹⁷He who loves pleasure will become poor;
    whoever loves wine and oil will never be rich.

¹⁸The wicked become a ransom for the righteous,
    and the unfaithful for the upright.

¹⁹Better to live in a desert
    than with a quarrelsome and ill-tempered wife.

²⁰In the house of the wise are stores of choice food
        and oil,
    but a foolish man devours all he has.

²¹He who pursues righteousness and love
    finds life, prosperity[b] and honor.

²²A wise man attacks the city of the mighty
    and pulls down the stronghold in which they
        trust.

²³He who guards his mouth and his tongue
    keeps himself from calamity.

²⁴The proud and arrogant man—"Mocker" is his
        name;
    he behaves with overweening pride.

²⁵The sluggard's craving will be the death of him,
    because his hands refuse to work.

²⁶All day long he craves for more,
    but the righteous give without sparing.

²⁷The sacrifice of the wicked is detestable—
    how much more so when brought with evil
        intent!

²⁸A false witness will perish,
    and whoever listens to him will be destroyed
        forever.[c]

²⁹A wicked man puts up a bold front,
    but an upright man gives thought to his ways.

³⁰There is no wisdom, no insight, no plan
    that can succeed against the LORD.

---

a12 Or *The righteous man*   b21 Or *righteousness*   c28 Or / *but the words of an obedient man will live on*

³¹The horse is made ready for the day of battle,
  but victory rests with the LORD.

22

A good name is more desirable than great riches;
  to be esteemed is better than silver or gold.

²Rich and poor have this in common:
  The LORD is the Maker of them all.

³A prudent man sees danger and takes refuge,
  but the simple keep going and suffer for it.

⁴Humility and the fear of the LORD
  bring wealth and honor and life.

⁵In the paths of the wicked lie thorns and snares,
  but he who guards his soul stays far from them.

⁶Train*a* a child in the way he should go,
  and when he is old he will not turn from it.

⁷The rich rule over the poor,
  and the borrower is servant to the lender.

⁸He who sows wickedness reaps trouble,
  and the rod of his fury will be destroyed.

⁹A generous man will himself be blessed,
  for he shares his food with the poor.

¹⁰Drive out the mocker, and out goes strife;
  quarrels and insults are ended.

¹¹He who loves a pure heart and whose speech is
    gracious
  will have the king for his friend.

¹²The eyes of the LORD keep watch over knowledge,
  but he frustrates the words of the unfaithful.

¹³The sluggard says, "There is a lion outside!"
  or, "I will be murdered in the streets!"

¹⁴The mouth of an adulteress is a deep pit;
  he who is under the LORD's wrath will fall into
    it.

¹⁵Folly is bound up in the heart of a child,
  but the rod of discipline will drive it far from
    him.

¹⁶He who oppresses the poor to increase his wealth
  and he who gives gifts to the rich—both come
    to poverty.

Sayings of the Wise

¹⁷Pay attention and listen to the sayings of the wise;
  apply your heart to what I teach,
¹⁸for it is pleasing when you keep them in your
    heart
  and have all of them ready on your lips.
¹⁹So that your trust may be in the LORD,
  I teach you today, even you.
²⁰Have I not written thirty*b* sayings for you,
  sayings of counsel and knowledge,

What inherited meaning does your name have? What other names do you go by?

1. How can a good name be more valuable than riches? 2. How should we view the rich and poor (vv. 2,7,9,16)? What do they have in common? How do they differ? How might they depend on each other? Who does God bless and why? 3. What distinguishes the "wicked," the "simple," the "mocker," the "sluggard" and "adulteress" from the "prudent" and "pure in heart"? 4. What child-rearing principle and promise do you see in verses 6 and 15? Does this general rule offer an absolute guarantee? What about the child's freedom to choose, despite perfect parenting?

1. What have you done (or could you do) to make—or unmake—a "good name" for yourself, your family, your profession? 2. Someone has said of verse 6 and related texts: "You can't raise a Christian, only sinners exposed to the Gospel." And … "Before, I had three sure-fire child-rearing principles but no kids; now I have three kids but no sure-fire principles." What do such statements assume about human nature? Sin? Parenting? God's grace? Do you agree or disagree? Why? 3. What kind of child to your Heavenly Father have you proven to be? Whose faith do you have now: Your own? Your parents? No faith at all? Why? 4. Verse 13 smacks of "Excuses, Excuses." How do you procrastinate in your relationship with God? How can your group help you?

Which grade school or high school teacher did you have a crush on? Which one swayed your character or career? How so? Which one would you seek out at a school reunion? Why?

1. What do these "sayings of the wise" sound like: Empathy? Game rules? Parent talk? Candid confessions? 2. Why do they strike you that way: Tone? Context? Or what? 3. Toward what end is this instruction in wisdom

a6 Or Start   *b20* Or not formerly written; or not written excellent

given (vv. 17–21)? What three-step process gets you there? By whom is one held accountable for this? **4.** What is the wise course of action with regard to the poor and needy? Your friends and associates? Your vows and debts? **5.** What do verses 28–29 say about getting ahead honestly?

♡ **1.** Where are you in the 3-step process of verses 17–21? How prepared are you to "give sound answers"? **2.** What works for you in handling an angry associate or roommate? What does this chapter suggest (v. 24)? **3.** If you are (or want to be) skilled at some work (v. 29), who would you want to work for? What people would you want to serve? Why?

———————

☕ **1.** At what age do you think you became (or will become) an adult? What telltale signs, privileges or rites of passage marked the occasion? **2.** Can you recall your first major Father-Son or Mother-Daughter talk about what it means to be an adult? What prompted it: Concern about driving? Drinking? Smoking? College? Voting rights? Mom's apron strings too tight?

📖 **1.** Where do you think the conversation of this chapter took place: Family dinner? Son's 21st birthday? Father-son woodshed chat? Or what? **2.** How many don'ts are in this chapter? What positive alternatives are given for someone who chooses "not to"? **3.** What is it about the king's fare, a stingy man's offering or strong drink which we are to avoid (vv. 1–8,30–34)? What is the point of such abstinence? **4.** How are we to regard the fool? The poor and fatherless? "Sinners"? Drunkards? Wayward persons? **5.** Who is this Defender of those who lose property and lose their fathers (vv. 10–11; see the kinsman-redeemer in Lev 25:25; Ru 3:12–13; 4:1ff and the Deliverer in Ge 48:16; Ex 6:6)? **6.** What is the rod of discipline (vv. 13–14; also 13:24)? Is it stoning (see Dt 21:18–21)? What is the result of using "it"? Of not doing so? **7.** What makes a parent happy (vv. 15,16,24–25)? Which of those three happy events would make you most glad?

²¹teaching you true and reliable words,
 so that you can give sound answers
 to him who sent you?

²²Do not exploit the poor because they are poor
 and do not crush the needy in court,
²³for the LORD will take up their case
 and will plunder those who plunder them.

²⁴Do not make friends with a hot-tempered man,
 do not associate with one easily angered,
²⁵or you may learn his ways
 and get yourself ensnared.

²⁶Do not be a man who strikes hands in pledge
 or puts up security for debts;
²⁷if you lack the means to pay,
 your very bed will be snatched from under you.

²⁸Do not move an ancient boundary stone
 set up by your forefathers.

²⁹Do you see a man skilled in his work?
 He will serve before kings;
 he will not serve before obscure men.

23 When you sit to dine with a ruler,
 note well whatª is before you,
²and put a knife to your throat
 if you are given to gluttony.
³Do not crave his delicacies,
 for that food is deceptive.

⁴Do not wear yourself out to get rich;
 have the wisdom to show restraint.
⁵Cast but a glance at riches, and they are gone,
 for they will surely sprout wings
 and fly off to the sky like an eagle.

⁶Do not eat the food of a stingy man,
 do not crave his delicacies;
⁷for he is the kind of man
 who is always thinking about the cost.ᵇ
 "Eat and drink," he says to you,
 but his heart is not with you.
⁸You will vomit up the little you have eaten
 and will have wasted your compliments.

⁹Do not speak to a fool,
 for he will scorn the wisdom of your words.

¹⁰Do not move an ancient boundary stone
 or encroach on the fields of the fatherless,
¹¹for their Defender is strong;
 he will take up their case against you.

¹²Apply your heart to instruction
 and your ears to words of knowledge.

¹³Do not withhold discipline from a child;
 if you punish him with the rod, he will not die.
¹⁴Punish him with the rod
 and save his soul from death.ᶜ

ª1 Or *who feast, / so he is*   ᵇ7 Or *for as he thinks within himself, / so he is*; or *for as he puts on a*   ᶜ14 Hebrew *Sheol*

¹⁵My son, if your heart is wise,
  then my heart will be glad;
¹⁶my inmost being will rejoice
  when your lips speak what is right.

¹⁷Do not let your heart envy sinners,
  but always be zealous for the fear of the LORD.
¹⁸There is surely a future hope for you,
  and your hope will not be cut off.

¹⁹Listen, my son, and be wise,
  and keep your heart on the right path.
²⁰Do not join those who drink too much wine
  or gorge themselves on meat,
²¹for drunkards and gluttons become poor,
  and drowsiness clothes them in rags.

²²Listen to your father, who gave you life,
  and do not despise your mother when she is
    old.
²³Buy the truth and do not sell it;
  get wisdom, discipline and understanding.
²⁴The father of a righteous man has great joy;
  he who has a wise son delights in him.
²⁵May your father and mother be glad;
  may she who gave you birth rejoice!

²⁶My son, give me your heart
  and let your eyes keep to my ways,
²⁷for a prostitute is a deep pit
  and a wayward wife is a narrow well.
²⁸Like a bandit she lies in wait,
  and multiplies the unfaithful among men.

²⁹Who has woe? Who has sorrow?
  Who has strife? Who has complaints?
  Who has needless bruises? Who has bloodshot
    eyes?
³⁰Those who linger over wine,
  who go to sample bowls of mixed wine.
³¹Do not gaze at wine when it is red,
  when it sparkles in the cup,
  when it goes down smoothly!
³²In the end it bites like a snake
  and poisons like a viper.
³³Your eyes will see strange sights
  and your mind imagine confusing things.
³⁴You will be like one sleeping on the high seas,
  lying on top of the rigging.
³⁵"They hit me," you will say, "but I'm not hurt!
  They beat me, but I don't feel it!
  When will I wake up
    so I can find another drink?"

24 Do not envy wicked men,
  do not desire their company;
²for their hearts plot violence,
  and their lips talk about making trouble.

³By wisdom a house is built,
  and through understanding it is established;
⁴through knowledge its rooms are filled
  with rare and beautiful treasures.

1. If getting "wisdom, discipline and understanding" were compared to a football game, where are you: (a) Still in the locker room, getting suited up? (b) On the bench, resting from your turn on defense? (c) Stopping for a Gatorade break? (d) Running with the ball on offense? 2. What does this "future hope" depend upon (v. 18; see 24:14,20; Ps 37:37)? To what extent are you sharing in that hope for yourself? For others? 3. What effect do all the negative words ("do not …") have on you? Do they make you feel negative? How so? 4. If you were advising abstinence to your child, or a friend, how would you word it? Where would you put the accent? 5. On a scale of 1–10, how much do you agree with verses 13 and 14? If less than 5, what practical alternative to the rod do you suggest? How does your alternative compare with how you were raised? What uses and abuses of rod-like discipline are you concerned about? 6. To what extent do you identify with this father's other concerns (vv. 19–35)? With his wisdom? His joy? What advice, given here, have you found most relevant to your family situation? 7. In Solomon's day, it was the duty of a relative to take care of widows and children who lost their husband/father. Who would take care of you in a similar situation?

1. You've been given a box of Lego blocks or Lincoln logs for a present. What's the first object you will build? How large? Will you follow directions, or make it up as you go along? 2. About the first house you lived in, where was it? What color? How many rooms? Your favorite room?

1. The "wise" man compares honey and wisdom (vv. 13–14). How are they alike? How do they differ? 2. Advertising encourages us to envy. What does this chapter imply about envy (vv. 1,19,20)? What or who should we follow instead? 3. How are we to wield power wisely (vv. 5–7)? Compassionately (vv. 11–12)? How are the two related? 4. What is meant by defeating evil powers and deferring to the Lord's justice (vv. 17–22)? 5. What happens when God's people seem to be defeated (vv. 10,16)? What is their hope?

1. Re-read verse 10. With what would you compare your strength in times of trouble: A pea? A hatbox? A bookshelf? A brick building? Or a huge mountain? 2. What is your typical reaction when drug thugs, rapists or terrorists get their due? How can you not gloat (vv. 17–18)? 3. What does it mean to you that the Lord God knows all your secret thoughts—your faltering, your gloating, your ignorance? 4. Do God's people "fall"? What difference is there then between God's people falling and the ungodly falling (v. 16)? 5. What compassionate rescuing effort do verses 11–12 bring to mind? Who reached out to you in that way as your lifesaver? How can your small group join hands to rescue the perishing? When will you begin? 6. If your life were a house built by wisdom, what "rare and beautiful treasures" would be housed there?

1. If you were judging a beauty contest, would you emphasize looks, talent, or poise? 2. What do you remember about your first kiss on the lips: Who? When? What were you feeling at the time?

⁵A wise man has great power,
  and a man of knowledge increases strength;
⁶for waging war you need guidance,
  and for victory many advisers.

⁷Wisdom is too high for a fool;
  in the assembly at the gate he has nothing to
    say.

⁸He who plots evil
  will be known as a schemer.
⁹The schemes of folly are sin,
  and men detest a mocker.

¹⁰If you falter in times of trouble,
  how small is your strength!

¹¹Rescue those being led away to death;
  hold back those staggering toward slaughter.
¹²If you say, "But we knew nothing about this,"
  does not he who weighs the heart perceive it?
Does not he who guards your life know it?
  Will he not repay each person according to
    what he has done?

¹³Eat honey, my son, for it is good;
  honey from the comb is sweet to your taste.
¹⁴Know also that wisdom is sweet to your soul;
  if you find it, there is a future hope for you,
  and your hope will not be cut off.

¹⁵Do not lie in wait like an outlaw against a
    righteous man's house,
  do not raid his dwelling place;
¹⁶for though a righteous man falls seven times, he
    rises again,
  but the wicked are brought down by calamity.

¹⁷Do not gloat when your enemy falls;
  when he stumbles, do not let your heart
    rejoice,
¹⁸or the LORD will see and disapprove
  and turn his wrath away from him.

¹⁹Do not fret because of evil men
  or be envious of the wicked,
²⁰for the evil man has no future hope,
  and the lamp of the wicked will be snuffed out.

²¹Fear the LORD and the king, my son,
  and do not join with the rebellious,
²²for those two will send sudden destruction upon
    them,
  and who knows what calamities they can bring?

Further Sayings of the Wise
²³These also are sayings of the wise:

To show partiality in judging is not good:
²⁴Whoever says to the guilty, "You are innocent"—
  peoples will curse him and nations denounce
    him.

²⁵But it will go well with those who convict the
guilty,
and rich blessing will come upon them.

²⁶An honest answer
is like a kiss on the lips.

²⁷Finish your outdoor work
and get your fields ready;
after that, build your house.

²⁸Do not testify against your neighbor without
cause,
or use your lips to deceive.

²⁹Do not say, "I'll do to him as he has done to me;
I'll pay that man back for what he did."

³⁰I went past the field of the sluggard,
past the vineyard of the man who lacks
judgment;

³¹thorns had come up everywhere,
the ground was covered with weeds,
and the stone wall was in ruins.

³²I applied my heart to what I observed
and learned a lesson from what I saw:

³³A little sleep, a little slumber,
a little folding of the hands to rest—

³⁴and poverty will come on you like a bandit
and scarcity like an armed man.[a]

More Proverbs of Solomon

25 These are more proverbs of Solomon, copied by the men of
Hezekiah king of Judah:

²It is the glory of God to conceal a matter;
to search out a matter is the glory of kings.

³As the heavens are high and the earth is deep,
so the hearts of kings are unsearchable.

⁴Remove the dross from the silver,
and out comes material for[b] the silversmith;

⁵remove the wicked from the king's presence,
and his throne will be established through
righteousness.

⁶Do not exalt yourself in the king's presence,
and do not claim a place among great men;

⁷it is better for him to say to you, "Come up
here,"
than for him to humiliate you before a
nobleman.

What you have seen with your eyes
8   do not bring[c] hastily to court,
for what will you do in the end
if your neighbor puts you to shame?

⁹If you argue your case with a neighbor,
do not betray another man's confidence,

---

1. How do these "sayings of the wise" extend the themes set forth in the preceding chapter? How do the wise approach their life and learning (v. 32)? 2. What is the difference between judging rightly and wrongly? 3. What does verse 27 imply about priorities for work? For marriage?

1. What was once your strong suit ("stone wall," v. 31), but is no longer, due to neglect ("thorns" and "weeds")? What would it take to rebuild that neglected area of your life to what it once was? 2. What do "outdoor work," "fields," "your house" (v. 27), each typify in your life? Has the nesting instinct taken over? What must be done first? How willing are you to do that? 3. What areas of your life are wide awake to the Lord? What areas are still asleep? How might you become more awake?

---

1. Have you ever watched the Emmy, Oscar or Tony awards program on TV? What interests you most? 2. If you were to receive a prestigious award, would you: (a) Run to the front? (b) Casually saunter? (c) Delay your move? (d) Walk slowly with dignity? (e) Boycott the program? What would prompt this reaction?

1. Many of Solomon's proverbs are but "variations on a theme." What major themes do you see? What variations are significant in this chapter? How do they affect his message? 2. In what ways are kings like, and unlike, God and the silversmith (vv. 2–5)? What would it be like for you to stand in the presence of each? What does Jesus say about this in his parable (see Lk 14:7–14)? 3. How do leaders "remove wickedness from their presence" (vv. 4–5,26)? What does that achieve? Why does that seem so hard to do? 4. Why is it crucial to settle out of court (v. 8)? To keep a confidence (vv. 9–10)? 5. What variations do you see here on the power of the spoken word, for good and evil (vv. 9–15,20,23,25)? 6. When does quiet persistence win out? What other actions speak louder

---

ᵃ34 Or like a vagrant / and scarcity like a beggar   ᵇ4 Or comes a vessel from
ᶜ7,8 Or nobleman / on whom you had set your eyes. / ⁸Do not go

than words (see Ro 12:20)? What does it mean (v. 22) to "heap coals on his head"? What faith in God does this method of revenge presuppose? **7.** What variation on the "honey" theme do you see here (vv. 16,27; see 24:13)? What rules of thumb does this suggest for any who wish not to overstay their welcome, or not indulge in too much of a good thing?

1. What do the repeated themes in Proverbs do for you: (a) Drive home a point I may have missed? (b) Suggest new areas for application? (c) Bore me to tears? (d) Develop a habit from reinforced ideas? **2.** What things do you think God has concealed from you (v. 2)? What is your attitude toward this? Is finding the answer an obtainable goal, a worthy pursuit, a matter of trust, or like eating from the "tree of the knowledge of good and evil" (Ge 2:17)? **3.** If you practiced the principle of humility set forth in verses 6–7, what would happen at work? At home? At church? To what would you like to be elevated? **4.** From the integrity and humility theme, what hits you like a "club, a sword, or a sharp arrow"(v. 18)? Why? **5.** What area of your life would you compare to a "broken down wall" (v. 28)? What will you do to regain that missing measure of self-control? How might others in your small group help you shore up those weaker areas? **6.** What "good news from a distant land" (v. 25) would be refreshing to your soul right now?

1. The last time you dressed up for a costume party, what did you go as? Why that get-up? **2.** What character would you like to

---

¹⁰or he who hears it may shame you
  and you will never lose your bad reputation.

¹¹A word aptly spoken
  is like apples of gold in settings of silver.

¹²Like an earring of gold or an ornament of fine
    gold
  is a wise man's rebuke to a listening ear.

¹³Like the coolness of snow at harvest time
  is a trustworthy messenger to those who send
    him;
  he refreshes the spirit of his masters.

¹⁴Like clouds and wind without rain
  is a man who boasts of gifts he does not give.

¹⁵Through patience a ruler can be persuaded,
  and a gentle tongue can break a bone.

¹⁶If you find honey, eat just enough—
  too much of it, and you will vomit.

¹⁷Seldom set foot in your neighbor's house—
  too much of you, and he will hate you.

¹⁸Like a club or a sword or a sharp arrow
  is the man who gives false testimony against his
    neighbor.

¹⁹Like a bad tooth or a lame foot
  is reliance on the unfaithful in times of trouble.

²⁰Like one who takes away a garment on a cold day,
  or like vinegar poured on soda,
  is one who sings songs to a heavy heart.

²¹If your enemy is hungry, give him food to eat;
  if he is thirsty, give him water to drink.

²²In doing this, you will heap burning coals on his
    head,
  and the LORD will reward you.

²³As a north wind brings rain,
  so a sly tongue brings angry looks.

²⁴Better to live on a corner of the roof
  than share a house with a quarrelsome wife.

²⁵Like cold water to a weary soul
  is good news from a distant land.

²⁶Like a muddied spring or a polluted well
  is a righteous man who gives way to the
    wicked.

²⁷It is not good to eat too much honey,
  nor is it honorable to seek one's own honor.

²⁸Like a city whose walls are broken down
  is a man who lacks self-control.

26

  Like snow in summer or rain in harvest,
    honor is not fitting for a fool.

²Like a fluttering sparrow or a darting swallow,
    an undeserved curse does not come to rest.

³A whip for the horse, a halter for the donkey,
  and a rod for the backs of fools!

⁴Do not answer a fool according to his folly,
  or you will be like him yourself.

⁵Answer a fool according to his folly,
  or he will be wise in his own eyes.

⁶Like cutting off one's feet or drinking violence
  is the sending of a message by the hand of a
  fool.

⁷Like a lame man's legs that hang limp
  is a proverb in the mouth of a fool.

⁸Like tying a stone in a sling
  is the giving of honor to a fool.

⁹Like a thornbush in a drunkard's hand
  is a proverb in the mouth of a fool.

¹⁰Like an archer who wounds at random
  is he who hires a fool or any passer-by.

¹¹As a dog returns to its vomit,
  so a fool repeats his folly.

¹²Do you see a man wise in his own eyes?
  There is more hope for a fool than for him.

¹³The sluggard says, "There is a lion in the road,
  a fierce lion roaming the streets!"

¹⁴As a door turns on its hinges,
  so a sluggard turns on his bed.

¹⁵The sluggard buries his hand in the dish;
  he is too lazy to bring it back to his mouth.

¹⁶The sluggard is wiser in his own eyes
  than seven men who answer discreetly.

¹⁷Like one who seizes a dog by the ears
  is a passer-by who meddles in a quarrel not his
  own.

¹⁸Like a madman shooting
  firebrands or deadly arrows
¹⁹is a man who deceives his neighbor
  and says, "I was only joking!"

²⁰Without wood a fire goes out;
  without gossip a quarrel dies down.

²¹As charcoal to embers and as wood to fire,
  so is a quarrelsome man for kindling strife.

²²The words of a gossip are like choice morsels;
  they go down to a man's inmost parts.

²³Like a coating of glaze ᵃ over earthenware
  are fervent lips with an evil heart.

²⁴A malicious man disguises himself with his lips,
  but in his heart he harbors deceit.

impersonate the next time you go to a masquerade party?

1. What three one-word titles can your group come up with to fit the three main divisions of this chapter? What three summary verses amplify your subject themes? 2. What examples of an "undeserved curse" come to mind (v. 2; see Nu 23:8; 2Sa 16:5–12)? 3. Verses 4–5 seem self-contradictory. What is Solomon's point? What good might result from not arguing with a fool? What bad might come from not arguing? 4. To what is a "proverb in the mouth of a fool" compared (v. 9)? Why this analogy? What would be a modern equivalent? 5. What does verse 10 tell an employer about hiring practices? What general principle is at work here? 6. The "sluggard" has suffered some bad press, but who in your group would not see themselves in this mirror: Verse 13, the sluggard as realist? Verse 14, the sluggard as not a morning person? Verse 15, the one who objects to being hustled? Verse 16, the one who sticks to his guns? 7. What is the point of the observations in verses 17–28 about mischief-making? Which of the actions described here seem innocent, but are not? What "life principle" is implied by verse 27?

1. How does this chapter leave you: Uplifted? Slapped down? Laughing at yourself in a mirror? What lies behind that feeling? 2. Which proverb hits closest to home? How so? 3. Solomon might well say today, "A fool opens mouth, inserts foot" (compare vv. 6–7). How might such a fool fit something you've done recently? When you meet someone you want to impress, how do you "put your best foot forward"? What about you is considered your best foot? 4. Have you been "cursed" before, as in verse 2? What did it feel like? With this verse in mind, how will you reply next time at work? At home? 5. If a malicious person can disguise himself (vv. 24–26), how can he be "exposed"? 6. In the mirror of verses 13–16, what made you laugh the hardest? In what areas or circumstances of your life have you been like a sluggard? Why? What can you do to change?

ᵃ23 With a different word division of the Hebrew; Masoretic Text *of silver dross*

²⁵Though his speech is charming, do not believe him,
for seven abominations fill his heart.
²⁶His malice may be concealed by deception,
but his wickedness will be exposed in the assembly.
²⁷If a man digs a pit, he will fall into it;
if a man rolls a stone, it will roll back on him.
²⁸A lying tongue hates those it hurts,
and a flattering mouth works ruin.

27

Do not boast about tomorrow,
for you do not know what a day may bring forth.
²Let another praise you, and not your own mouth;
someone else, and not your own lips.
³Stone is heavy and sand a burden,
but provocation by a fool is heavier than both.
⁴Anger is cruel and fury overwhelming,
but who can stand before jealousy?
⁵Better is open rebuke
than hidden love.
⁶Wounds from a friend can be trusted,
but an enemy multiplies kisses.
⁷He who is full loathes honey,
but to the hungry even what is bitter tastes sweet.
⁸Like a bird that strays from its nest
is a man who strays from his home.
⁹Perfume and incense bring joy to the heart,
and the pleasantness of one's friend springs from his earnest counsel.
¹⁰Do not forsake your friend and the friend of your father,
and do not go to your brother's house when disaster strikes you—
better a neighbor nearby than a brother far away.
¹¹Be wise, my son, and bring joy to my heart;
then I can answer anyone who treats me with contempt.
¹²The prudent see danger and take refuge,
but the simple keep going and suffer for it.
¹³Take the garment of one who puts up security for a stranger;
hold it in pledge if he does it for a wayward woman.
¹⁴If a man loudly blesses his neighbor early in the morning,
it will be taken as a curse.
¹⁵A quarrelsome wife is like
a constant dripping on a rainy day;

1. Do you work best with people, things or ideas? Give an example. 2. Suppose you had a fan club (with Mom and Dad as charter members). What would they say is your key contribution to your family life, work setting or field of study?

1. Some proverbs are simple observations of life, some are advice on living. How can you tell the difference? From this chapter, what key concepts distinguish them both? 2. What's the point of boasting or praising (vv. 1–2,21)? How does the New Testament expand that (see Mt 6:34; Lk 12:19–20; Jn 12:43; 2Co 10:12,18; Jas 4:13–16)? 3. What choices are implicit in each of the comparisons in verses 3–6? 4. What distinguishes true friends (vv. 5–6, 9–10,14,17)? 5. What do verses 7–8 condemn: Food or possessiveness? Fugitives, pilgrims, or wanderlust? 6. What reveals true character (vv. 19–22)? What can de done to satisfy a person's restlessness or change a fool's character? 7. What is the proper balance between hard work and God's provision (vv. 23–27)?

1. Your local high school has invited you to be a guest lecturer on "friendship," and you have chosen this chapter as your text. How would you start? What illustrations would you use? What stories from personal experience come to mind of someone who has openly rebuked you, sharpened you like iron, earnestly counseled you, or been a good neighbor? What clincher would you close? 2. How well do you "know the condition of your flocks" (v. 23)? Do you have a laid back ("What, me worry?") attitude? 3. Where do you put more stock: (a) Long-term financial plans? (b) Get-rich-quick schemes? (c) Just living for today with no thought of tomorrow? (d) Armageddon will come soon, so no need to plan ahead? 4. What per-

¹⁶restraining her is like restraining the wind
    or grasping oil with the hand.

¹⁷As iron sharpens iron,
    so one man sharpens another.

¹⁸He who tends a fig tree will eat its fruit,
    and he who looks after his master will be
        honored.

¹⁹As water reflects a face,
    so a man's heart reflects the man.

²⁰Death and Destruction*a* are never satisfied,
    and neither are the eyes of man.

²¹The crucible for silver and the furnace for gold,
    but man is tested by the praise he receives.

²²Though you grind a fool in a mortar,
    grinding him like grain with a pestle,
    you will not remove his folly from him.

²³Be sure you know the condition of your flocks,
    give careful attention to your herds;
²⁴for riches do not endure forever,
    and a crown is not secure for all generations.
²⁵When the hay is removed and new growth
        appears
    and the grass from the hills is gathered in,
²⁶the lambs will provide you with clothing,
    and the goats with the price of a field.
²⁷You will have plenty of goats' milk
    to feed you and your family
    and to nourish your servant girls.

28 The wicked man flees though no one pursues,
    but the righteous are as bold as a lion.

²When a country is rebellious, it has many rulers,
    but a man of understanding and knowledge
        maintains order.

³A ruler*b* who oppresses the poor
    is like a driving rain that leaves no crops.

⁴Those who forsake the law praise the wicked,
    but those who keep the law resist them.

⁵Evil men do not understand justice,
    but those who seek the LORD understand it fully.

⁶Better a poor man whose walk is blameless
    than a rich man whose ways are perverse.

⁷He who keeps the law is a discerning son,
    but a companion of gluttons disgraces his
        father.

⁸He who increases his wealth by exorbitant
        interest
    amasses it for another, who will be kind to the
        poor.

sonal or national "danger" lurks on
the horizon (v. 12)? What will it cost
to take refuge? To forsake refuge?
So, what prudent thing will you do?
5. Who in your life "sharpens you
like iron" (v. 17)? What kind of relationship do you expect from a person like this? Are you that to anyone else? Does this idea make you
feel good, or cause a little fear?
Why? **6.** If verse 22 is true, what
hope is there for a fool?

---

1. In your present position,
over what domain do you
rule? What appeals to you about
ruling your roost: Are you like the
fox in charge of the hen house or a
roaring lion, king of all beasts? **2.** In
tackling anything new (friends, job,
sport, investments, etc.) are you a
high risk-taker or a steady plodder
toward your goal? Cite an example.

1. What does the rambling of
this chapter sound like: (a)
Angry street corner preacher? (b)
Learned political science prof? (c)
Wise grandma? (d) Police captain?
(e) Other? **2.** What is the point of all
this "law and order" talk? Who is
the intended audience: Top brass?
The ruling class? The under class?
Victims of injustice? Teachers?
Parents? Why do you think so? **3.**
What law is to be upheld? How is it
to be applied? What abuses of that
law and their victims are singled
out here? **4.** What point is made
more vivid by the "lion" figure of
speech (vv. 1,15)? By the "driving
rain" (v. 3)? **5.** Who are the
"wicked"? What is their behavior

a20 Hebrew *Sheol and Abaddon*   *b3* Or *A poor man*

like? What impact do they have on others (vv. 1,4–5,12,15,28)? What will be their comeuppance (vv. 8–11, 13–15, 17–18, 22, 27)? **6.** When this justice prevails, what will the poor be and do (vv. 6,8,11,19–20)? **7.** What is the message in all this for rulers, teachers, parents, pastors and for those who follow them (vv. 2,7,10, 13,16,18,20,24)? **8.** Why confess or renounce sins? Why not cover them up (vv. 13,14,17)? Why not wait for someone to expose or rebuke the sin (v. 23), in the hope that will buy time or save face?

♡ **1.** What is the difference between (a) trusting in self (v. 26), (b) self-confidence and (c) trusting in the Lord (v. 25)? Which trust is foolish? Commendable? Prosperous? Which trust level is higher for you: (a), (b) or (c)? **2.** Which half of verses 6,19 and 20 are true for you? In what way is it "better" to be poor? In what way can one be rich and blameless, or rich and unpunished? **3.** How is verse 17 a commentary on these Bible stories: Cain and Abel? Saul and David? Judas and Jesus? Saul and the early Christians? How were these characters tormented by their guilt? How can one be rid of this torment? **4.** Of what do we "rob" parents (v. 24): Their life savings? Dignity? Their jobs? What kind of parent robbery is tantamount to "murder" (as in v. 17)? **5.** Whose favor is to be gained in verse 23? What will this favor gain you and when? Is it worth waiting for in the situation facing you? **6.** Ruling and leading occur frequently in this chapter. Of the many "rulers" (v. 2) you have (at work, home, church, state), how do you make sense or maintain order in all that? Who is it that you are following and obeying? Are you sure of where you're being led (v. 10)? Do you really want to go "there"? What allegiance for you is the integrating one?

⁹If anyone turns a deaf ear to the law,
  even his prayers are detestable.

¹⁰He who leads the upright along an evil path
  will fall into his own trap,
  but the blameless will receive a good
    inheritance.

¹¹A rich man may be wise in his own eyes,
  but a poor man who has discernment sees
    through him.

¹²When the righteous triumph, there is great
    elation;
  but when the wicked rise to power, men go
    into hiding.

¹³He who conceals his sins does not prosper,
  but whoever confesses and renounces them
    finds mercy.

¹⁴Blessed is the man who always fears the LORD,
  but he who hardens his heart falls into trouble.

¹⁵Like a roaring lion or a charging bear
  is a wicked man ruling over a helpless people.

¹⁶A tyrannical ruler lacks judgment,
  but he who hates ill-gotten gain will enjoy a
    long life.

¹⁷A man tormented by the guilt of murder
  will be a fugitive till death;
  let no one support him.

¹⁸He whose walk is blameless is kept safe,
  but he whose ways are perverse will suddenly
    fall.

¹⁹He who works his land will have abundant food,
  but the one who chases fantasies will have his
    fill of poverty.

²⁰A faithful man will be richly blessed,
  but one eager to get rich will not go
    unpunished.

²¹To show partiality is not good—
  yet a man will do wrong for a piece of bread.

²²A stingy man is eager to get rich
  and is unaware that poverty awaits him.

²³He who rebukes a man will in the end gain more
    favor
  than he who has a flattering tongue.

²⁴He who robs his father or mother
  and says, "It's not wrong"—
  he is partner to him who destroys.

²⁵A greedy man stirs up dissension,
  but he who trusts in the LORD will prosper.

²⁶He who trusts in himself is a fool,
  but he who walks in wisdom is kept safe.

²⁷He who gives to the poor will lack nothing,

but he who closes his eyes to them receives
    many curses.

²⁸When the wicked rise to power, people go into
    hiding;
  but when the wicked perish, the righteous
    thrive.

29 A man who remains stiff-necked after many rebukes
    will suddenly be destroyed—without remedy.

²When the righteous thrive, the people rejoice;
  when the wicked rule, the people groan.

³A man who loves wisdom brings joy to his father,
  but a companion of prostitutes squanders his
    wealth.

⁴By justice a king gives a country stability,
  but one who is greedy for bribes tears it down.

⁵Whoever flatters his neighbor
  is spreading a net for his feet.

⁶An evil man is snared by his own sin,
  but a righteous one can sing and be glad.

⁷The righteous care about justice for the poor,
  but the wicked have no such concern.

⁸Mockers stir up a city,
  but wise men turn away anger.

⁹If a wise man goes to court with a fool,
  the fool rages and scoffs, and there is no peace.

¹⁰Bloodthirsty men hate a man of integrity
  and seek to kill the upright.

¹¹A fool gives full vent to his anger,
  but a wise man keeps himself under control.

¹²If a ruler listens to lies,
  all his officials become wicked.

¹³The poor man and the oppressor have this in
    common:
  The Lord gives sight to the eyes of both.

¹⁴If a king judges the poor with fairness,
  his throne will always be secure.

¹⁵The rod of correction imparts wisdom,
  but a child left to himself disgraces his mother.

¹⁶When the wicked thrive, so does sin,
  but the righteous will see their downfall.

¹⁷Discipline your son, and he will give you peace;
  he will bring delight to your soul.

¹⁸Where there is no revelation, the people cast off
    restraint;
  but blessed is he who keeps the law.

¹⁹A servant cannot be corrected by mere words;
  though he understands, he will not respond.

²⁰Do you see a man who speaks in haste?
  There is more hope for a fool than for him.

1. When do you break into melody to yourself: (a) With the radio? (b) In the shower? (c) After church? (d) Never? 2. As for your ability to sing, are you a Johnny one-note, a joyful noise, or a one-man barbershop quartet? 3. What song is part of your bedtime ritual or teaching method with your children?

1. If you were to put mood music to the reading of this chapter, would it be classical, upbeat or just old fashioned? In a major or a minor key? 2. What might the righteous person of verse 6 choose to sing about? 3. What else marks the righteous (vv. 2,7,16,27)? What notes would they be singing? 4. Verses 8–9,11,20, 22 again raise the twin issues of anger and fools. How do you deal with the temperament of a fool? What hope does Solomon offer here? 5. Who are "stiff-necked" folk (v. 1)? How and when do you think such irrevocable destruction occurs? 6. What is the result of dishonesty in leadership (v. 12)? Are "lies" (v. 12) more powerful than "rebukes" (v. 1) or "mere words" (v. 19)? Why might that be? 7. How might "discipline" give meaning to "words" (v. 19)? 8. Of what value is a "revelation" (v. 18)? Why is that? What incident in Israel's early history might be in mind here? What is significant about this convergence of law, the prophets and wisdom literature in one verse?

1. Which proverb here penetrates an area of your life? 2. If "mere words" (v. 19) or "rebukes" (v. 1) are not enough to correct someone, but only make one "stiff-necked" (v. 2), what else is needed? What does this say about nagging mates? Stem-winding preachers? Self-help books? The Bible itself? Why are flesh and blood examples and multi-image shows more forceful than mere words? 3. These proverbs seem to suggest that lasting change is not externally imposed but internally motivated. When is "leaving a child to himself" (v. 15) a healthy corrective? And when is that too permissive? 4. If "from the Lord we get

justice" (v. 26), what does this say about courts of appeal (civil and church)? Does one judicial process exclude the other? Or reflect the other? How will you handle your next disagreement with someone with regard to this truth? **5.** What threats do righteous people face (v. 10)? What threats do you fear most?

²¹If a man pampers his servant from youth,
　he will bring grief[a] in the end.

²²An angry man stirs up dissension,
　and a hot-tempered one commits many sins.

²³A man's pride brings him low,
　but a man of lowly spirit gains honor.

²⁴The accomplice of a thief is his own enemy;
　he is put under oath and dare not testify.

²⁵Fear of man will prove to be a snare,
　but whoever trusts in the LORD is kept safe.

²⁶Many seek an audience with a ruler,
　but it is from the LORD that man gets justice.

²⁷The righteous detest the dishonest;
　the wicked detest the upright.

Sayings of Agur

30 The sayings of Agur son of Jakeh—an oracle[b]:

This man declared to Ithiel,
　to Ithiel and to Ucal:[c]

²"I am the most ignorant of men;
　I do not have a man's understanding.
³I have not learned wisdom,
　nor have I knowledge of the Holy One.
⁴Who has gone up to heaven and come down?
　Who has gathered up the wind in the hollow of
　　his hands?
Who has wrapped up the waters in his cloak?
　Who has established all the ends of the earth?
What is his name, and the name of his son?
　Tell me if you know!

⁵"Every word of God is flawless;
　he is a shield to those who take refuge in him.
⁶Do not add to his words,
　or he will rebuke you and prove you a liar.

⁷"Two things I ask of you, O LORD;
　do not refuse me before I die:
⁸Keep falsehood and lies far from me;
　give me neither poverty nor riches,
　but give me only my daily bread.
⁹Otherwise, I may have too much and disown you
　and say, 'Who is the LORD?'
Or I may become poor and steal,
　and so dishonor the name of my God.

¹⁰"Do not slander a servant to his master,
　or he will curse you, and you will pay for it.

¹¹"There are those who curse their fathers
　and do not bless their mothers;
¹²those who are pure in their own eyes
　and yet are not cleansed of their filth;

1. To what vehicle would you compare yourself or your lifestyle: Four-wheel drive truck? Nine-passenger van? Speedy sports car? Classic roadster? Comfort sedan? Economy car? All terrain vehicle? Chauffeur-driven limo? Ambulance? With what features of that car do you identify? **2.** Where would you like to take you and yours for a day's drive in this vehicle?

1. In what ways are the "Sayings of Agur" like Solomon's proverbs? How are they different? Which ones are more like the Psalms, addressed to God? **2.** What is the point of the literary style and device which compares three and four items with one another? In using this device, is Agur: (a) Losing track of his sermon outline? (b) Stuttering in his speech? (c) Trying to be cute, witty or chatty? (d) Painting a picture without making his point explicit? **3.** How does that style affect the content and impact of the chapter? Is his main point to observe, to suggest, or to preach? Why do you think so? **4.** What do you learn about Agur from verses 2–4? From verses 7–9? What assumptions about human nature and money underlie his two-fold request? Why doesn't he pray to use poverty and riches rightly? **5.** What do you learn of God from the agnostic's questions in verse 4? From the answer in verses 5–6? From Agur's prayer in verses 7–9? From the arrogant "eyes" of verses 11–14? **6.** How does the character of "those" pictured in verses 11–14 contrast with Agur at prayer? What will happen

---

^a21 The meaning of the Hebrew for this word is uncertain.　　^b1 Or *Jakeh of Massa*
^c1 Masoretic Text; with a different word division of the Hebrew *declared, "I am weary, O God; / I am weary, O God, and faint.*

13those whose eyes are ever so haughty,
     whose glances are so disdainful;
14those whose teeth are swords
     and whose jaws are set with knives
to devour the poor from the earth,
     the needy from among mankind.

15"The leech has two daughters.
     'Give! Give!' they cry.

"There are three things that are never satisfied,
     four that never say, 'Enough!':
16the grave,*a* the barren womb,
     land, which is never satisfied with water,
     and fire, which never says, 'Enough!'

17"The eye that mocks a father,
     that scorns obedience to a mother,
will be pecked out by the ravens of the valley,
     will be eaten by the vultures.

18"There are three things that are too amazing for
     me,
     four that I do not understand:
19the way of an eagle in the sky,
     the way of a snake on a rock,
the way of a ship on the high seas,
     and the way of a man with a maiden.

20"This is the way of an adulteress:
     She eats and wipes her mouth
     and says, 'I've done nothing wrong.'

21"Under three things the earth trembles,
     under four it cannot bear up:
22a servant who becomes king,
     a fool who is full of food,
23an unloved woman who is married,
     and a maidservant who displaces her mistress.

24"Four things on earth are small,
     yet they are extremely wise:
25Ants are creatures of little strength,
     yet they store up their food in the summer;
26coneys*b* are creatures of little power,
     yet they make their home in the crags;
27locusts have no king,
     yet they advance together in ranks;
28a lizard can be caught with the hand,
     yet it is found in kings' palaces.

29"There are three things that are stately in their
     stride,
     four that move with stately bearing:
30a lion, mighty among beasts,
     who retreats before nothing;
31a strutting rooster, a he-goat,
     and a king with his army around him.*c*

32"If you have played the fool and exalted yourself,
     or if you have planned evil,

to the "eyes" of those who arrogantly leech off others (vv. 15–17)? 7. What is "amazing" about the "ways" and the fifth way (vv. 18–20)? 8. What is "unbearable" about the next four things (vv. 21–23)? 9. What is so "wise" about the four "small" creatures (vv. 24–28)? 10. What is "stately" about the next four things (vv. 29–31)? 11. How do verses 32–33 tie together all the other sayings about humility?

♡ 1. After viewing Agur's humble, artistic impressions, how do you feel: (a) "I know where this guy's comin' from"? (b) "I'm totally confused"? (c) "But for the grace of God, there go I"? (d) "I wish he would not be poetic." 2. Which gives you more grief: Not enough money or too much money? Explain. 3. What childhood or childlike cravings of yours are still unsatisfied? What can you take to heart from these sayings which will help you crave things less? 4. What does it mean to "play the fool" (v. 32)? Where have you "played the fool and exalted yourself" (vv. 32–33)? What can you take to heart from these sayings? 5. How are you tempted to add to God's words (v. 6)? What principles of inductive group Bible study help to avoid that? 6. Of these ways, things and creatures in this chapter, with which can you most easily identify? Is the comparison at all flattering, humbling or what? How so?

---

a16 Hebrew *Sheol*   *b26* That is, the hyrax or rock badger   *c31* Or *king secure against revolt*

clap your hand over your mouth!
33For as churning the milk produces butter,
and as twisting the nose produces blood,
so stirring up anger produces strife."

Sayings of King Lemuel

31 The sayings of King Lemuel—an oracle*a* his mother taught him:

2"O my son, O son of my womb,
O son of my vows,*b*
3do not spend your strength on women,
your vigor on those who ruin kings.

4"It is not for kings, O Lemuel—
not for kings to drink wine,
not for rulers to crave beer,
5lest they drink and forget what the law decrees,
and deprive all the oppressed of their rights.
6Give beer to those who are perishing,
wine to those who are in anguish;
7let them drink and forget their poverty
and remember their misery no more.

8"Speak up for those who cannot speak for
themselves,
for the rights of all who are destitute.
9Speak up and judge fairly;
defend the rights of the poor and needy."

Epilogue: The Wife of Noble Character

10*c*A wife of noble character who can find?
She is worth far more than rubies.
11Her husband has full confidence in her
and lacks nothing of value.
12She brings him good, not harm,
all the days of her life.
13She selects wool and flax
and works with eager hands.
14She is like the merchant ships,
bringing her food from afar.
15She gets up while it is still dark;
she provides food for her family
and portions for her servant girls.
16She considers a field and buys it;
out of her earnings she plants a vineyard.
17She sets about her work vigorously;
her arms are strong for her tasks.
18She sees that her trading is profitable,
and her lamp does not go out at night.
19In her hand she holds the distaff
and grasps the spindle with her fingers.
20She opens her arms to the poor
and extends her hands to the needy.
21When it snows, she has no fear for her
household;

What favorite saying of your mother's can you still recite?

1. How is this king brought to his mother? To the Lord? To his senses? And to his people? **2.** If the *Jerusalem Times* decided to print each of these paragraphs (vv. 2–3,4–7,8–9) as separate articles, with you as its editor, what headline would you give each one? What accompanying pictures do they bring to mind? What section of the paper do they fit in best?

1. In what ways can you "speak up for those who cannot speak for themselves" (v. 8)? **2.** Other than women (v. 3), who are "those who ruin kings"? How so? What should be your attitude to them? **3.** What is your reaction to these sayings of this unknown king?

1. (Women) Of all the TV sitcom women, with whom do you identify most: June Cleaver? Jill Taylor? Roseanne? Claire Huxtable? Elaine (Seinfeld)? Other? What features of those women do you admire? **2.** (Men) To which of these women would you prefer to be married? Why? **3.** Both complete and compare: "A woman's place is in the _____." What feelings does this slogan evoke?

1. Verses 10–31 form an "acrostic"; that is, each verse in succession begins with the next letter of the 22–character Hebrew alphabet. How might this carefully crafted epilogue and personification of wisdom relate to the prologue (1:1–7)? **2.** Would the author of this epilogue be applauded by feminists or traditionalists? Would he or she (perhaps Lemuel's mother, see 31:1) support equal rights for women? Or sex-defined roles? What makes you think so? Which verses support which view? **3.** From this chapter, how would this ideal woman define her "place": (a) The house, making meals and clothes? (b) The House and Senate, making decisions? (c) City market, on a shopping spree? (d)

a1 Or *of Lemuel king of Massa, which*   *b2* Or / the answer to my prayers
c10 Verses 10-31 are an acrostic, each verse beginning with a successive letter of the Hebrew alphabet.

for all of them are clothed in scarlet.
²²She makes coverings for her bed;
   she is clothed in fine linen and purple.
²³Her husband is respected at the city gate,
   where he takes his seat among the elders of the
      land.
²⁴She makes linen garments and sells them,
   and supplies the merchants with sashes.
²⁵She is clothed with strength and dignity;
   she can laugh at the days to come.
²⁶She speaks with wisdom,
   and faithful instruction is on her tongue.
²⁷She watches over the affairs of her household
   and does not eat the bread of idleness.
²⁸Her children arise and call her blessed;
   her husband also, and he praises her:
²⁹"Many women do noble things,
   but you surpass them all."
³⁰Charm is deceptive, and beauty is fleeting;
   but a woman who fears the LORD is to be
      praised.
³¹Give her the reward she has earned,
   and let her works bring her praise at the city
      gate.

City market, as an entrepreneur, selling? **4.** What does she manage: Kids? Domestic help? Property? Money? Business partnership? All of the above? Which of these roles do you see as the primary one for her? Why? **5.** What abilities make her praise-worthy in the eyes of her husband? Her children? The city fathers? The poor and needy? **6.** What is her spiritual life like? Her appointment calendar? Her work pace? Her personal temperament?

1. How could anyone become like this woman? What does verse 10 imply? Is she just a symbol for some spiritual quality? A flesh and blood woman? Or both? **2.** If she represents "God's ideal woman," should an "average" woman (single or married) aspire to her qualities? Likewise, should a man? Why or why not? **3.** What would you think of a person who aspired to these qualities, but came up "a buck short"? What if she came up "woefully short"? **4.** Which of the domains managed by this ideal woman are also things you are involved in? Which of those roles energize you? Which ones drain energy from you? **5.** How does this woman who "does it all" compare with your image of the woman today who "does it all"? What are the differences? The similarities? How can women today follow her example without wearing themselves out and compromising their role as wife and mother? **6.** She spent her expertise and resources on the poor and needy (v. 20). To whom or what mission do you give yourself? **7.** She both feared the Lord and received the praise of children, husband and co-workers. Apart from the Lord's favor, whose opinion or praise matters most to you? Who is it harder to please—your family members or your co-workers? Why? **8.** (Women) What do you think is "the reward she has earned" (v. 31)? What reward do you think you deserve? **9.** (Men) In what way could you best reward the work of the woman in your life? How do you expect the woman to respond? **10.** (Group) You've finished your study of Proverbs. What stands out? What changes are you still praying about? In what ways are you wiser now than when you started? What disturbed you most?

INTRODUCTION to
ECCLESIASTES

Book Study Outline: If you are using Ecclesiastes for a study course, here is a 7- or 13-week outline. Use the questions in the margin for your group agenda:

☕ start meeting / 15 min.

📖 read & discuss Bible / 30 min.

♡ close meeting / 15–45 min.

Refer to the Questions and Answers in the front of this Bible for more information.

7-week plan	13-week plan	Personal Reading	Group Study Passage
1	1	1:1–18	1:1–11/Life's Meaninglessness
	2	2:1–26	2:1–16/Wealth's Passing Value
2	3	3:1–22	3:1–15/God's Sovereignty
	4	4:1–5:7	4:13–5:7/Change and Honesty
3	5	5:8–6:9	5:8–6:9/Riches
	6	6:10–7:14	6:10–7:14/The Truly Good
4	7	7:15–8:1	7:15–8:1/Extremism and Sin
	8	8:2–17	8:2–17/Response to Injustice
5	9	9:1–12	9:1–12/Chance and Destiny
	10	9:13–10:15	9:13–10:15/Wisdom and Folly
6	11	10:16–11:6	11:1–6/Investing Wisely
	12	11:7–12:8	11:7–12:8/Life's Backside
7	13	12:9–14	12:9–14/Conclusion

Author: Traditionally attributed to Solomon, though no writer is named in the book (see 1:1,12). However, Ecclesiastes may have been the product of a writer from a later period who felt that his teaching was akin to the great wisdom which Solomon possessed.

Date: Perhaps after the return from exile, in the fifth century B.C. If Solomon is the author, the book would date from c. 950 B.C.

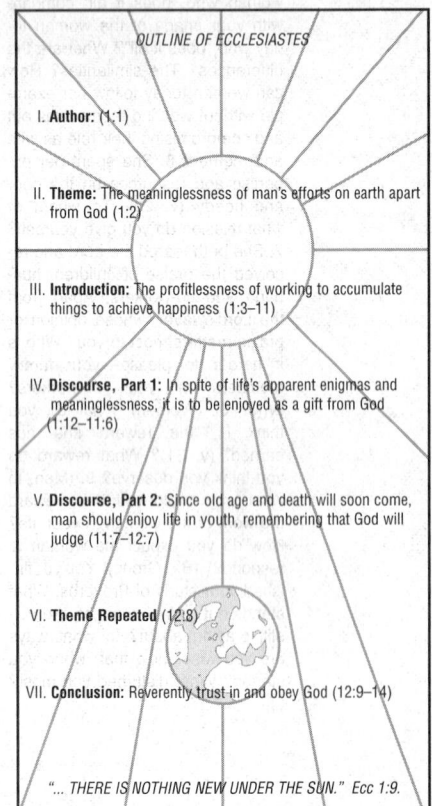

OUTLINE OF ECCLESIASTES

I. **Author:** (1:1)

II. **Theme:** The meaninglessness of man's efforts on earth apart from God (1:2)

III. **Introduction:** The profitlessness of working to accumulate things to achieve happiness (1:3–11)

IV. **Discourse, Part 1:** In spite of life's apparent enigmas and meaninglessness, it is to be enjoyed as a gift from God (1:12–11:6)

V. **Discourse, Part 2:** Since old age and death will soon come, man should enjoy life in youth, remembering that God will judge (11:7–12:7)

VI. **Theme Repeated** (12:8)

VII. **Conclusion:** Reverently trust in and obey God (12:9–14)

"... THERE IS NOTHING NEW UNDER THE SUN." Ecc 1:9.

Theme: Life not focused on God is purposeless and meaningless. Without him, nothing can satisfy (2:25). With him, all of life is to be enjoyed to the full (2:26; 11:9).

Historical Background: With so little information available about the author or date, it is difficult to place Ecclesiastes into a historical context. One possibility is that it was produced by a wisdom movement in Judaism that was responsible for collecting stories and sayings.

Characteristics: This book has always raised questions concerning its appropriateness in the OT canon. Its apparent pessimism and questioning of beliefs that are central to Judaism and Christianity has led many to reject or ignore it. Others have tried to explain it as what Solomon would have said on an "off" day, or suggest that it clearly demonstrates the futility of the agnostic and therefore acts as a warning against such a position. It may be, however, that the work is a foil against which we discern our tendency to overestimate or overspiritualize our relationship with God. The book is unsparingly forthright in recording the author's desperate search for meaning. While he might be accused of overstating his case, hints of his true piety are evident (see 7:29), and the conclusion challenges the reader to obey God (12:13–14).

Ecclesiastes

Everything Is Meaningless

1 The words of the Teacher,[a] son of David, king in Jerusalem:

²"Meaningless! Meaningless!"
  says the Teacher.
"Utterly meaningless!
  Everything is meaningless."

³What does man gain from all his labor
  at which he toils under the sun?
⁴Generations come and generations go,
  but the earth remains forever.
⁵The sun rises and the sun sets,
  and hurries back to where it rises.
⁶The wind blows to the south
  and turns to the north;
round and round it goes,
  ever returning on its course.
⁷All streams flow into the sea,
  yet the sea is never full.
To the place the streams come from,
  there they return again.
⁸All things are wearisome,
  more than one can say.
The eye never has enough of seeing,
  nor the ear its fill of hearing.
⁹What has been will be again,
  what has been done will be done again;
  there is nothing new under the sun.
¹⁰Is there anything of which one can say,
  "Look! This is something new"?
It was here already, long ago;
  it was here before our time.
¹¹There is no remembrance of men of old,
  and even those who are yet to come
will not be remembered
  by those who follow.

Wisdom Is Meaningless

¹²I, the Teacher, was king over Israel in Jerusalem. ¹³I devoted myself to study and to explore by wisdom all that is done under heaven. What a heavy burden God has laid on men! ¹⁴I have seen all the things that are done under the sun; all of them are meaningless, a chasing after the wind.

¹⁵What is twisted cannot be straightened;
  what is lacking cannot be counted.

¹⁶I thought to myself, "Look, I have grown and increased in wisdom more than anyone who has ruled over Jerusalem before me; I have experienced much of wisdom and knowledge." ¹⁷Then I applied myself to the understanding of wisdom, and also of mad-

a 1 Or *leader of the assembly*; also in verses 2 and 12

1. What clothing was in style when you were 13? Would you be "caught dead" in it today? 2. What was the first large thing you saved your pennies for?

1. The word for "meaningless" (v. 1) can also mean "breath" or "vapor." What, then, is meant by the motto, "everything is meaningless"? 2. What does the phrase "under the sun" (vv. 3,9) tell you about the perspective of this thesis? 3. How does mankind's labor compare with the earth's cycle (vv. 3–7)? 4. What problem does verse 8 point out? 5. What's the theme of verses 9–10? What qualifies as "something new" by this Teacher's definition? 6. In verse 11, what tone of voice do you hear? What logic do you see? Is verse 11 the logical extension or inevitable conclusion of careful reasoning? Or is this an emotional lament of an embittered old man?

1. What areas of life do you take too seriously? 2. What parallel do you see between this passage and Christ's saying, "What does it profit a man ..." (Mk 8:36)? 3. For what have you spent your life laboring? What do you have to show for it? 4. For what would you like to be remembered after you are long gone?

1. In which subject did (or do) you get the best grades? 2. At what age did you first say, "I know more than my teachers (or parents)"?

1. Where has the Teacher searched for wisdom? 2. What is the "burden" in verse 13? Why is God blamed for it? 3. Why does wisdom bring sorrow and knowledge bring grief?

1. Where "under heaven" have you searched for meaning? Where have you found it? 2. In what instances has knowledge caused you sorrow?

ness and folly, but I learned that this, too, is a chasing after the wind.

> [18]For with much wisdom comes much sorrow;
> the more knowledge, the more grief.

Pleasures Are Meaningless

2 I thought in my heart, "Come now, I will test you with pleasure to find out what is good." But that also proved to be meaningless. [2]"Laughter," I said, "is foolish. And what does pleasure accomplish?" [3]I tried cheering myself with wine, and embracing folly—my mind still guiding me with wisdom. I wanted to see what was worthwhile for men to do under heaven during the few days of their lives.

[4]I undertook great projects: I built houses for myself and planted vineyards. [5]I made gardens and parks and planted all kinds of fruit trees in them. [6]I made reservoirs to water groves of flourishing trees. [7]I bought male and female slaves and had other slaves who were born in my house. I also owned more herds and flocks than anyone in Jerusalem before me. [8]I amassed silver and gold for myself, and the treasure of kings and provinces. I acquired men and women singers, and a harem[a] as well—the delights of the heart of man. [9]I became greater by far than anyone in Jerusalem before me. In all this my wisdom stayed with me.

> [10]I denied myself nothing my eyes desired;
> I refused my heart no pleasure.
> My heart took delight in all my work,
> and this was the reward for all my labor.
> [11]Yet when I surveyed all that my hands had done
> and what I had toiled to achieve,
> everything was meaningless, a chasing after the wind;
> nothing was gained under the sun.

Wisdom and Folly Are Meaningless

> [12]Then I turned my thoughts to consider wisdom,
> and also madness and folly.
> What more can the king's successor do
> than what has already been done?
> [13]I saw that wisdom is better than folly,
> just as light is better than darkness.
> [14]The wise man has eyes in his head,
> while the fool walks in the darkness;
> but I came to realize
> that the same fate overtakes them both.

[15]Then I thought in my heart,

> "The fate of the fool will overtake me also.
> What then do I gain by being wise?"
> I said in my heart,
> "This too is meaningless."
> [16]For the wise man, like the fool, will not be long remembered;
> in days to come both will be forgotten.
> Like the fool, the wise man too must die!

a8 The meaning of the Hebrew for this phrase is uncertain.

1. What crazy stunt in high school are you remembered for? 2. What creative science project do you remember from those days? 3. What material goods are on your all-time wish list?

1. What paradox does the teacher find in hedonism (vv. 1–3)? 2. What do these key phrases tell you about the perspective of this passage: (a) "During the few days of their lives" (v. 3)? (b) "Under the sun" (v. 11)? (c) "In days to come" (v. 16)? 3. What "great projects" does he undertake (vv. 4–8)? What desires were such projects meant to satisfy? 4. During these projects, what is the Teacher's relation to wisdom (vv. 3,9,12–13)? 5. In verses 12–16, to what does "wisdom" refer: Spiritual insight? Street smarts? Survival skills? Upright behavior? 6. Does "folly" here mean something similar to wisdom, or something opposite? 7. How is light better than darkness? What does this say about the difference between wisdom and folly? 8. Why is this Teacher so unhappy with what so many would call success?

1. What is the most important project you have undertaken in the last year? How do you measure your success in that? 2. Do you see yourself as more led by your heart, or by your head? In what areas do you find yourself controlled more by your desires than by wisdom? 3. Do you regard death as the final tragedy or the final triumph? Is the death of the fool different from that of the wise? How can you prepare yourself for death? 4. How does a passage like this help you focus on the truly important things in life? What are they?

Toil Is Meaningless

[17]So I hated life, because the work that is done under the sun was grievous to me. All of it is meaningless, a chasing after the wind. [18]I hated all the things I had toiled for under the sun, because I must leave them to the one who comes after me. [19]And who knows whether he will be a wise man or a fool? Yet he will have control over all the work into which I have poured my effort and skill under the sun. This too is meaningless. [20]So my heart began to despair over all my toilsome labor under the sun. [21]For a man may do his work with wisdom, knowledge and skill, and then he must leave all he owns to someone who has not worked for it. This too is meaningless and a great misfortune. [22]What does a man get for all the toil and anxious striving with which he labors under the sun? [23]All his days his work is pain and grief; even at night his mind does not rest. This too is meaningless.

[24]A man can do nothing better than to eat and drink and find satisfaction in his work. This too, I see, is from the hand of God, [25]for without him, who can eat or find enjoyment? [26]To the man who pleases him, God gives wisdom, knowledge and happiness, but to the sinner he gives the task of gathering and storing up wealth to hand it over to the one who pleases God. This too is meaningless, a chasing after the wind.

A Time for Everything

3 There is a time for everything,
   and a season for every activity under heaven:

[2]   a time to be born and a time to die,
      a time to plant and a time to uproot,
[3]   a time to kill and a time to heal,
      a time to tear down and a time to build,
[4]   a time to weep and a time to laugh,
      a time to mourn and a time to dance,
[5]   a time to scatter stones and a time to gather
         them,
      a time to embrace and a time to refrain,
[6]   a time to search and a time to give up,
      a time to keep and a time to throw away,
[7]   a time to tear and a time to mend,
      a time to be silent and a time to speak,
[8]   a time to love and a time to hate,
      a time for war and a time for peace.

[9]What does the worker gain from his toil? [10]I have seen the burden God has laid on men. [11]He has made everything beautiful in its time. He has also set eternity in the hearts of men; yet they cannot fathom what God has done from beginning to end. [12]I know that there is nothing better for men than to be happy and do good while they live. [13]That everyone may eat and drink, and find satisfaction in all his toil—this is the gift of God. [14]I know that everything God does will endure forever; nothing can be added to it and nothing taken from it. God does it so that men will revere him.

[15]Whatever is has already been,
   and what will be has been before;
   and God will call the past to account.[a]

[16]And I saw something else under the sun:

---

[a]15 Or *God calls back the past*

1. What is your most valued possession? Who would you like to leave it to when you die?

1. Why did the Teacher hate life? 2. Who is said to be the real beneficiary of someone's work (vv. 18–21)? Why is that? 3. How do verses 24–26 contrast with the preceding? 4. What does it mean to "please God" in this context? 5. What does God have to do with satisfaction in work? 6. Who is the "sinner"? Why does God favor the one over the other?

1. Why do you work? When do you most feel like not working? 2. Do you see your work as a gift from God, as drudgery, or both? Does that make you grateful, even for the drudgery, or hateful? Why?

1. What is the most important date you ever forgot? 2. Which are you like at a party: (a) Party animal? (b) Party pooper? (c) Hostess helper? (d) Wall flower? 3. What was your favorite season as a child? Why? Which is your favorite now?

1. In the list of opposites (vv. 1–8), is the Teacher describing what is, or prescribing what one should do? Why do you think so? 2. What is "the burden God has laid on man" (v. 10)? 3. What does it mean to "set eternity in the hearts of men" (v. 11)? 4. What is the Teacher encouraging in verses 12–13: Hedonism? Gratitude? Or what? 5. Toward what end does all of this point (vv. 14–15)? 6. What is meant by "God will call the past to account" (v. 15)?

1. What "time" is it for you? At what "times" (vv. 1–8) do you doubt that God is in control? 2. Would you rather spend your time fathoming God's work (v. 11), doing good (v. 12), or eating and drinking (v. 13)? Why? 3. How do you differentiate enjoying yourself from going too far? 4. Does belief in God's sovereignty free you to enjoy life? How so?

Which childhood pet do you miss most? Is your dead pet in the ground or in "animal heaven"? Why do you think so?

1. How does the theme of this passage (vv. 16–17) relate to the previous one? 2. How are humans like, and unlike, animals? 3. How does the "wickedness" in verse 16 relate to this comparison with animals? 4. What does this passage teach concerning the destiny of humans? Or animals?

1. How do you respond to those who act as if there is no God or final judgment? 2. How does the promise of eternal life (Jn 5:24) help you deal with injustice?

---

1. When in life were you most in need of a friend? Did one come? 2. Which of your neighbor's possessions do you most covet?

1. Who are the "oppressed" in verse 1? The "oppressors"? 2. Why does the Teacher say that the dead are happier than the living? 3. What does he say is the primary motivation for mankind (v. 4)? 4. What is the meaning of each of the proverbs in verses 5–6? What do they imply is the Teacher's view of labor and competition?

1. Do you see yourself more often in the role of the "oppressed" or the "oppressor"? How so? 2. How much does someone's wealth or status affect the way you treat him? 3. Do you presently have "one handful" or "two" (v. 6)?

What job have you tackled by yourself that you should have asked someone to help you do?

1. What is the status of the man in verse 8a? How materially successful is he? At what cost? What is he questioning? 2. Why does the Teacher see the "business" in verse 8 as "meaningless"? 3. What are the benefits of "two" in verses 9–12? How is the proverb in 12b a fitting conclusion?

In the place of judgment—wickedness was there,
in the place of justice—wickedness was there.

[17] I thought in my heart,

"God will bring to judgment
both the righteous and the wicked,
for there will be a time for every activity,
a time for every deed."

[18] I also thought, "As for men, God tests them so that they may see that they are like the animals. [19] Man's fate is like that of the animals; the same fate awaits them both: As one dies, so dies the other. All have the same breath[a]; man has no advantage over the animal. Everything is meaningless. [20] All go to the same place; all come from dust, and to dust all return. [21] Who knows if the spirit of man rises upward and if the spirit of the animal[b] goes down into the earth?"

[22] So I saw that there is nothing better for a man than to enjoy his work, because that is his lot. For who can bring him to see what will happen after him?

Oppression, Toil, Friendlessness

4 Again I looked and saw all the oppression that was taking place under the sun:

I saw the tears of the oppressed—
and they have no comforter;
power was on the side of their oppressors—
and they have no comforter.
[2] And I declared that the dead,
who had already died,
are happier than the living,
who are still alive.
[3] But better than both
is he who has not yet been,
who has not seen the evil
that is done under the sun.

[4] And I saw that all labor and all achievement spring from man's envy of his neighbor. This too is meaningless, a chasing after the wind.

[5] The fool folds his hands
and ruins himself.
[6] Better one handful with tranquillity
than two handfuls with toil
and chasing after the wind.

[7] Again I saw something meaningless under the sun:

[8] There was a man all alone;
he had neither son nor brother.
There was no end to his toil,
yet his eyes were not content with his wealth.
"For whom am I toiling," he asked,
"and why am I depriving myself of enjoyment?"
This too is meaningless—
a miserable business!

[9] Two are better than one,

a19 Or *spirit*   b21 Or *Who knows the spirit of man, which rises upward, or the spirit of the animal, which*

because they have a good return for their work:
10If one falls down,
  his friend can help him up.
But pity the man who falls
  and has no one to help him up!
11Also, if two lie down together, they will keep
    warm.
  But how can one keep warm alone?
12Though one may be overpowered,
  two can defend themselves.
A cord of three strands is not quickly broken.

Advancement Is Meaningless

13Better a poor but wise youth than an old but foolish king who no longer knows how to take warning. 14The youth may have come from prison to the kingship, or he may have been born in poverty within his kingdom. 15I saw that all who lived and walked under the sun followed the youth, the king's successor. 16There was no end to all the people who were before them. But those who came later were not pleased with the successor. This too is meaningless, a chasing after the wind.

Stand in Awe of God

5 Guard your steps when you go to the house of God. Go near to listen rather than to offer the sacrifice of fools, who do not know that they do wrong.

2Do not be quick with your mouth,
  do not be hasty in your heart
    to utter anything before God.
God is in heaven
  and you are on earth,
    so let your words be few.
3As a dream comes when there are many cares,
  so the speech of a fool when there are many
    words.

4When you make a vow to God, do not delay in fulfilling it. He has no pleasure in fools; fulfill your vow. 5It is better not to vow than to make a vow and not fulfill it. 6Do not let your mouth lead you into sin. And do not protest to the ⌊temple⌋ messenger, "My vow was a mistake." Why should God be angry at what you say and destroy the work of your hands? 7Much dreaming and many words are meaningless. Therefore stand in awe of God.

Riches Are Meaningless

8If you see the poor oppressed in a district, and justice and rights denied, do not be surprised at such things; for one official is eyed by a higher one, and over them both are others higher still. 9The increase from the land is taken by all; the king himself profits from the fields.

10Whoever loves money never has money enough;
  whoever loves wealth is never satisfied with his
    income.
  This too is meaningless.

11As goods increase,
  so do those who consume them.
And what benefit are they to the owner
  except to feast his eyes on them?

1. For whom (yourself, God, others) do you toil in the different areas of life (work, home, school, church)? How much satisfaction do you derive from your toil and your companions? 2. How easy is it for you to allow someone to help you? Or, to let someone know that you need help? 3. Where would you be spiritually were it not for the help of others?

1. How do you react to a guest preacher (vs. the regular pastor)? 2. What "hasty promise" did you later regret making?

1. These two passages (4:13–16; 5:1–7) focus on our relationship to lordship. What type of lordship is the focus in the first? In the second? 2. In 4:13–16, why is the old king so unpopular? The successor so popular? Why are those who come "later" displeased with the successor (4:16)? 3. In 5:1–7, what is the fool's error? What is meant by the exhortations to "listen," "keep silent," and "not delay"? What are the potential results of "quick" mouths? 4. How does verse 7 summarize the message of 5:1–7? Of 4:13–16?

1. Facing poor or evil leadership in a particular group, when are you most patient? Most prayerful? Most pushy for change? Most "quick with your mouth"? 2. How do you become part of its solution instead of the problem? 3. What do you do when you make a hasty promise you cannot keep?

1. What was the most physically exhausting job you ever did? 2. What effect does your work have on you: (a) Invigoration? (b) Frustration? (c) Exhaustion? (d) Boredom? 3. What pleasure in life do you not get enough time for?

1. What is the reason for the oppression in 5:8–9? Why should we not be surprised by this? 2. Why do the three proverbs (5:10,11,12) prove to be meaningless? 3. What about money is he bemoaning here: (a) The addiction to money? (b) Its emptiness? (c) The swarm of hangers-on? (d) The indulgence of money? 4. What is

the "grievous evil" of 5:13–15? Of 5:16–17? How do "wealth hoarded" and "wealth lost" (5:13–14) fit into this observation? **5.** What isn't "right" about going out as naked as we arrive? Is the Teacher asking of life more than it can ever give? **6.** In 5:18–20, what does the Teacher conclude is "good and proper"? Why (see 2:24–26)? **7.** Why is it a blessing not to "reflect" with the mind but to "enjoy" with the heart? What might the Teacher be saying about himself here? **8.** What is the other evil in 6:1–2 and 3–6? What belief influences the Teacher's conclusions (v. 6b)? **9.** How does 6:7–9 continue the thought of the preceding? What is "better" (v. 9)? Why is that?

1. Do you view the person at the top of your organization as getting rich off the others down below? Where are you on that corporate ladder—getting richer or getting poorer? **2.** What priority does the pursuit of wealth and work have in your life? Is this necessary? What are you expecting your life's work will give you in the end? **3.** Are you more inclined to help the poor and needy when your situation is similar, or when you have more money to make a bigger difference? **4.** How much "gladness of heart" do you presently experience in your "labor under the sun" (5:20)? What would help you enjoy your work more? **5.** In the Old Testament, the "dream of a lifetime" was hundreds of children and thousands of years on earth (6:3,6). What is your life's dream? When might you most enjoy your life's attainments?

---

1. If you compared your life to a product in a Sears catalogue, which item is it most like: (a) Power tool? (b) Sofa? (c) Lawn ornament? (d) Grey flannel pajamas

12The sleep of a laborer is sweet,
  whether he eats little or much,
but the abundance of a rich man
  permits him no sleep.

13I have seen a grievous evil under the sun:

  wealth hoarded to the harm of its owner,
14 or wealth lost through some misfortune,
  so that when he has a son
    there is nothing left for him.
15Naked a man comes from his mother's womb,
  and as he comes, so he departs.
He takes nothing from his labor
  that he can carry in his hand.

16This too is a grievous evil:

  As a man comes, so he departs,
    and what does he gain,
  since he toils for the wind?
17All his days he eats in darkness,
  with great frustration, affliction and anger.

18Then I realized that it is good and proper for a man to eat and drink, and to find satisfaction in his toilsome labor under the sun during the few days of life God has given him—for this is his lot. 19Moreover, when God gives any man wealth and possessions, and enables him to enjoy them, to accept his lot and be happy in his work—this is a gift of God. 20He seldom reflects on the days of his life, because God keeps him occupied with gladness of heart.

6 I have seen another evil under the sun, and it weighs heavily on men: 2God gives a man wealth, possessions and honor, so that he lacks nothing his heart desires, but God does not enable him to enjoy them, and a stranger enjoys them instead. This is meaningless, a grievous evil.

3A man may have a hundred children and live many years; yet no matter how long he lives, if he cannot enjoy his prosperity and does not receive proper burial, I say that a stillborn child is better off than he. 4It comes without meaning, it departs in darkness, and in darkness its name is shrouded. 5Though it never saw the sun or knew anything, it has more rest than does that man— 6even if he lives a thousand years twice over but fails to enjoy his prosperity. Do not all go to the same place?

  7All man's efforts are for his mouth,
    yet his appetite is never satisfied.
  8What advantage has a wise man
    over a fool?
  What does a poor man gain
    by knowing how to conduct himself before
      others?
  9Better what the eye sees
    than the roving of the appetite.
  This too is meaningless,
    a chasing after the wind.

  10Whatever exists has already been named,
    and what man is has been known;
  no man can contend
    with one who is stronger than he.
  11The more the words,

the less the meaning,
and how does that profit anyone?

12For who knows what is good for a man in life, during the few and meaningless days he passes through like a shadow? Who can tell him what will happen under the sun after he is gone?

Wisdom

7 A good name is better than fine perfume,
and the day of death better than the day of birth.
2It is better to go to a house of mourning
than to go to a house of feasting,
for death is the destiny of every man;
the living should take this to heart.
3Sorrow is better than laughter,
because a sad face is good for the heart.
4The heart of the wise is in the house of mourning,
but the heart of fools is in the house of pleasure.
5It is better to heed a wise man's rebuke
than to listen to the song of fools.
6Like the crackling of thorns under the pot,
so is the laughter of fools.
This too is meaningless.

7Extortion turns a wise man into a fool,
and a bribe corrupts the heart.

8The end of a matter is better than its beginning,
and patience is better than pride.
9Do not be quickly provoked in your spirit,
for anger resides in the lap of fools.

10Do not say, "Why were the old days better than these?"
For it is not wise to ask such questions.

11Wisdom, like an inheritance, is a good thing
and benefits those who see the sun.
12Wisdom is a shelter
as money is a shelter,
but the advantage of knowledge is this:
that wisdom preserves the life of its possessor.

13Consider what God has done:

Who can straighten
what he has made crooked?
14When times are good, be happy;
but when times are bad, consider:
God has made the one
as well as the other.
Therefore, a man cannot discover
anything about his future.

15In this meaningless life of mine I have seen both of these:

a righteous man perishing in his righteousness,
and a wicked man living long in his wickedness.
16Do not be overrighteous,
neither be overwise—

(e) Other? Would you be the good, better or best model? **2.** Who in your family is the most accomplished funeral-goer? What sets him or her apart? **3.** Who was the last person to "tell you off"? Why? How did you react? **4.** Dream a bit: If all goes well, what do you predict for yourself next year?

1. In 6:10–12, the Teacher gives some observations and questions that introduce the next section. What are the observations? The questions? **2.** In 7:1–12, how does the Teacher go about searching for answers to his question, "What is good"? Is anything absolutely good, or are some things only relatively better? **3.** In each of the couplets or comparisons in 7:1–4, which is the better thing and why? **4.** What is the reason behind the advice given in verses 5–7? **5.** Why is the question in verse 10 so unwise (see 7:8–10; 1:9)? **6.** In 7:11–12, what is meant by comparing wisdom to "an inheritance"? To a "shelter"? How does wisdom preserve life?

1. How sincere is your quest for the "good" things God provides in life? How do you recognize them? **2.** When you are confused, how do you decide who to listen to? How do you know when to give advice? Rebuke? Praise? **3.** As compared to dwelling on the past or longing for the future, how much do you live in the present? How much do you enjoy it? What can you do to enjoy the "here and now" more? **4.** Would you say these days are good times or bad times for you? Is your answer based on nostalgia (for the past) or hope (for the future)?

1. What gossip about yourself got back to you and made your blood boil? How did you react? **2.** In trying new things, which are you: (a) Cautious? (b) Venturesome? (c) Uninterested? In what areas are you most likely to experiment?

1. What observations inspire these warnings (vv. 15–18)? What is meant by "over-righteous" (v. 16)? By "over-wicked" (v. 17)? 2. Would the Teacher ever say, "Nothing to excess, everything in moderation"? How does such a view square with genuine fear of God (v. 18)? 3. Is verse 20 a confession, an excuse or an accusation? What light does verse 20 shed on verse 19? 4. What is the danger in paying attention to gossip or hearsay (v. 21)? What theme unites verses 19–22? 5. In verses 23 and 25, what are the Teacher's goals? How do they differ? What does he conclude about these goals? What is meant by "the scheme of things" (vv. 25,27)? 6. How do the two stories about "woman" (vv. 26,28–29) differ? What is the basis for his pessimism: (a) Sampling of "a thousand" wives (v. 28; see 1Ki 11:3)? (b) Experience with human nature (v. 20)? (c) Revealed truth of Creation and the Fall (v. 29)? 7. Is the "search of many schemes" (v. 29) our fault or our fate? Why? 8. In light of 7:24, how is 8:1 best understood? What is the advantage of wisdom in this verse?

1. Who sees you as an "extremist"? In what? Has such extremism helped, or hindered, your ability to minister? How so? 2. What do you do when you find sin in your life? How does this affect your self-image? 3. When might you "curse" others (v. 22)? How can you break that habit? 4. Are you ignorant of the scheme of things, or all too aware? In what positive ways can you increase in such wisdom? 5. Are you a "snare" to others (v. 26), or an "uprighter" (vv. 28–29)? How so?

1. Who was the first "bully" you stood up against? With what results? 2. When you hear the

why destroy yourself?
17Do not be overwicked,
and do not be a fool—
why die before your time?
18It is good to grasp the one
and not let go of the other.
The man who fears God will avoid all
⌊extremes⌋.[a]

19Wisdom makes one wise man more powerful
than ten rulers in a city.

20There is not a righteous man on earth
who does what is right and never sins.

21Do not pay attention to every word people say,
or you may hear your servant cursing you—
22for you know in your heart
that many times you yourself have cursed
others.

23All this I tested by wisdom and I said,

"I am determined to be wise"—
but this was beyond me.
24Whatever wisdom may be,
it is far off and most profound—
who can discover it?
25So I turned my mind to understand,
to investigate and to search out wisdom and the
scheme of things
and to understand the stupidity of wickedness
and the madness of folly.

26I find more bitter than death
the woman who is a snare,
whose heart is a trap
and whose hands are chains.
The man who pleases God will escape her,
but the sinner she will ensnare.

27"Look," says the Teacher,[b] "this is what I have discovered:

"Adding one thing to another to discover the
scheme of things—
28 while I was still searching
but not finding—
I found one ⌊upright⌋ man among a thousand,
but not one ⌊upright⌋ woman among them all.
29This only have I found:
God made mankind upright,
but men have gone in search of many
schemes."

8 Who is like the wise man?
Who knows the explanation of things?
Wisdom brightens a man's face
and changes its hard appearance.

Obey the King

2Obey the king's command, I say, because you took an oath before God. 3Do not be in a hurry to leave the king's presence. Do

a18 Or will follow them both   b27 Or leader of the assembly

not stand up for a bad cause, for he will do whatever he pleases.
⁴Since a king's word is supreme, who can say to him, "What are you doing?"

⁵Whoever obeys his command will come to no
        harm,
    and the wise heart will know the proper time
        and procedure.
⁶For there is a proper time and procedure for every
        matter,
    though a man's misery weighs heavily upon
        him.
⁷Since no man knows the future,
    who can tell him what is to come?
⁸No man has power over the wind to contain it*ᵃ*;
    so no one has power over the day of his death.
As no one is discharged in time of war,
    so wickedness will not release those who
        practice it.

⁹All this I saw, as I applied my mind to everything done under the sun. There is a time when a man lords it over others to his own*ᵇ* hurt. ¹⁰Then too, I saw the wicked buried—those who used to come and go from the holy place and receive praise*ᶜ* in the city where they did this. This too is meaningless.

¹¹When the sentence for a crime is not quickly carried out, the hearts of the people are filled with schemes to do wrong. ¹²Although a wicked man commits a hundred crimes and still lives a long time, I know that it will go better with God-fearing men, who are reverent before God. ¹³Yet because the wicked do not fear God, it will not go well with them, and their days will not lengthen like a shadow.

¹⁴There is something else meaningless that occurs on earth: righteous men who get what the wicked deserve, and wicked men who get what the righteous deserve. This too, I say, is meaningless. ¹⁵So I commend the enjoyment of life, because nothing is better for a man under the sun than to eat and drink and be glad. Then joy will accompany him in his work all the days of the life God has given him under the sun.

¹⁶When I applied my mind to know wisdom and to observe man's labor on earth—his eyes not seeing sleep day or night— ¹⁷then I saw all that God has done. No one can comprehend what goes on under the sun. Despite all his efforts to search it out, man cannot discover its meaning. Even if a wise man claims he knows, he cannot really comprehend it.

A Common Destiny for All

9 So I reflected on all this and concluded that the righteous and the wise and what they do are in God's hands, but no man knows whether love or hate awaits him. ²All share a common destiny—the righteous and the wicked, the good and the bad,*ᵈ* the clean and the unclean, those who offer sacrifices and those who do not.

As it is with the good man,
    so with the sinner;

ᵃ8 Or *over his spirit to retain it*   *ᵇ9* Or *to their*   *ᶜ10* Some Hebrew manuscripts and Septuagint (Aquila); most Hebrew manuscripts *and are forgotten*   *ᵈ2* Septuagint (Aquila), Vulgate and Syriac; Hebrew does not have *and the bad.*

---

phrase "the good die young," whom do you think of? At such times, are you: (a) Sorrowful? (b) Angry? (c) Disgusted? (d) Disillusioned?

1. What reasons are given for obedience in verses 2–5? How will the "wise heart" know "the proper time and procedure" (vv. 5–6; see 3:1–15)? **2.** Who would you substitute for "no man" in verses 7–8? In every sentence? **3.** Who seems to be the subject in verses 9–10? How does the "lording it over" in verse 9 contrast to having "power over" in verse 8? **4.** What is the problem in verse 11, and who is to blame for it? In verses 12–13, what injustice does the Teacher see? In what ways will it "go better" for the God-fearer (vv. 12–13)? Why? **5.** How is the injustice depicted in verse 14 meaningless? How does verse 15 strike you: (a) Realistic? (b) Sarcastic? (c) Cop-out? (d) Joyful? What is the link between verses 15 and 14? **6.** What is the difference between seeing "all that God has done" and grasping "what goes on" (v. 17)? What advice is implied in the Teacher's realization (vv. 16–17)?

1. What sort of injustices (personal, family, global) are most likely to arouse you to act? Where do you draw the line ("To here, and no further")? **2.** How does your search for answers to life's problems affect your relationship with God? How easy is it for you to trust him when the answers are unattainable? What can be done to develop such trust?

1. Everyone knows the phrase, "You can't take it with you." If you could, what one exception to this rule would you like, when your time comes? **2.** What oaths or vows have you ever taken (scouts, marriage, secrecy, etc.)? How easy is it for you to keep them?

1. What does the Teacher conclude about human destiny (vv. 1–2)? What people "take oaths" and who are "afraid to" (v. 2)? **2.** What theme unifies verses 3–6? How is death described here? In this context, what is the "madness in their hearts" (v. 3): Evil? Craziness? Aliveness? Hope? Love? Hate? Jealousy? **3.** To whom is this madness ascribed? In this context, are you "mad"? **4.** To what actions does the Teacher exhort us in verses 7–10? To what attitude? What motivation does he suggest for such a lifestyle? What does it mean to be "clothed in white" (v. 8)? **5.** What explanation is offered for the apparent contradictions in verse 11? How does this relate to the "evil times" in verse 12?

♡ **1.** Do you feel you deserve a reward in life for your righteousness? Or would some kick-in-the-pants be more appropriate? What trophy, booby prize or punishment do you feel you deserve? **2.** In what ways do you feel you receive the benefits of faith in this life? Are there benefits that you have ignored or rejected? Why? What are they? **3.** Given the unexpected nature of life (vv. 11–12), how do you prepare yourself for such disruptions? How can you best help others through them?

☕ **1.** In games of strategy, how would you rate yourself: (a) Ruthless? (b) Reluctant? (c) First one out? **2.** If you could learn any instrument, what would it be? What song would you like to play on it? **3.** What was the last time you got lost? Where were you going? Did you ever get there?

📖 **1.** The Teacher derives two morals from the example story in 9:13–16. What are they? **2.** How does the first pair of proverbs (9:17–18) correspond to the preceding example story? What themes are similar? Do they agree with, or take issue with, the story? Why doesn't wisdom win out? **3.** What two things are contrasted in

as it is with those who take oaths,
so with those who are afraid to take them.

3This is the evil in everything that happens under the sun: The same destiny overtakes all. The hearts of men, moreover, are full of evil and there is madness in their hearts while they live, and afterward they join the dead. **4**Anyone who is among the living has hope[a]—even a live dog is better off than a dead lion!

5For the living know that they will die,
but the dead know nothing;
they have no further reward,
and even the memory of them is forgotten.
6Their love, their hate
and their jealousy have long since vanished;
never again will they have a part
in anything that happens under the sun.

7Go, eat your food with gladness, and drink your wine with a joyful heart, for it is now that God favors what you do. **8**Always be clothed in white, and always anoint your head with oil. **9**Enjoy life with your wife, whom you love, all the days of this meaningless life that God has given you under the sun— all your meaningless days. For this is your lot in life and in your toilsome labor under the sun. **10**Whatever your hand finds to do, do it with all your might, for in the grave,[b] where you are going, there is neither working nor planning nor knowledge nor wisdom.

11I have seen something else under the sun:

The race is not to the swift
or the battle to the strong,
nor does food come to the wise
or wealth to the brilliant
or favor to the learned;
but time and chance happen to them all.

12Moreover, no man knows when his hour will come:

As fish are caught in a cruel net,
or birds are taken in a snare,
so men are trapped by evil times
that fall unexpectedly upon them.

Wisdom Better Than Folly

13I also saw under the sun this example of wisdom that greatly impressed me: **14**There was once a small city with only a few people in it. And a powerful king came against it, surrounded it and built huge siegeworks against it. **15**Now there lived in that city a man poor but wise, and he saved the city by his wisdom. But nobody remembered that poor man. **16**So I said, "Wisdom is better than strength." But the poor man's wisdom is despised, and his words are no longer heeded.

17The quiet words of the wise are more to be heeded
than the shouts of a ruler of fools.
18Wisdom is better than weapons of war,
but one sinner destroys much good.

*a*4 Or *What then is to be chosen? With all who live, there is hope*   *b*10 Hebrew *Sheol*

10

As dead flies give perfume a bad smell,
  so a little folly outweighs wisdom and honor.
[2]The heart of the wise inclines to the right,
  but the heart of the fool to the left.
[3]Even as he walks along the road,
  the fool lacks sense
  and shows everyone how stupid he is.
[4]If a ruler's anger rises against you,
  do not leave your post;
  calmness can lay great errors to rest.

[5]There is an evil I have seen under the sun,
  the sort of error that arises from a ruler:
[6]Fools are put in many high positions,
  while the rich occupy the low ones.
[7]I have seen slaves on horseback,
  while princes go on foot like slaves.

[8]Whoever digs a pit may fall into it;
  whoever breaks through a wall may be bitten
  by a snake.
[9]Whoever quarries stones may be injured by them;
  whoever splits logs may be endangered by
  them.

[10]If the ax is dull
  and its edge unsharpened,
more strength is needed
  but skill will bring success.

[11]If a snake bites before it is charmed,
  there is no profit for the charmer.

[12]Words from a wise man's mouth are gracious,
  but a fool is consumed by his own lips.
[13]At the beginning his words are folly;
  at the end they are wicked madness—
[14] and the fool multiplies words.

No one knows what is coming—
  who can tell him what will happen after him?

[15]A fool's work wearies him;
  he does not know the way to town.

[16]Woe to you, O land whose king was a servant[a]
  and whose princes feast in the morning.
[17]Blessed are you, O land whose king is of noble
  birth
  and whose princes eat at a proper time—
  for strength and not for drunkenness.

[18]If a man is lazy, the rafters sag;
  if his hands are idle, the house leaks.

[19]A feast is made for laughter,
  and wine makes life merry,
  but money is the answer for everything.

[20]Do not revile the king even in your thoughts,
  or curse the rich in your bedroom,
  because a bird of the air may carry your words,

---

a 16 Or *king is a child*

10:1–3? What is the main point here? **4.** In this context (vv. 3–5), what's wrong with leaving your post? **5.** What is the "evil" in 10:5–7? Where is it found? **6.** In 10:6–11, where do you see poetic justice? Random events? Cause and effect? Dry humor? How does the "skill" in verse 10 relate to wisdom? **7.** What topic is addressed in 10:12–15? What progression is evident in 10:12–14a? How does the contention in 10:14b add to the problem of the fool? What hope, if any, is there for the lost fool?

1. How does someone's social position affect your respect for his opinions? In what ways could that person's "wisdom" help you? **2.** How "skilled" are you in the various areas of life (family, friendships, work, ministry)? In which areas do you need to develop greater skills? How can this best be done? How can your small group help in this? **3.** How has something foolish you said affected others and yourself? To whom do you need to apologize because of it (no names)? What practical steps can you take to avoid such "foolish" conversation?

Ever quit a job due to the boss? What made the boss hard to work for?

1. What makes a leader good or bad (vv. 16–17)? **2.** What do verses 18–19 say about government? How is money the "answer" (v. 19)? **3.** Why should we not revile those in power?

1. As a leader, how conscientious are you? How generous? **2.** What is your duty to those over you? Under you?

and a bird on the wing may report what you
say.

Bread Upon the Waters

11 Cast your bread upon the waters,
    for after many days you will find it again.
²Give portions to seven, yes to eight,
    for you do not know what disaster may come
        upon the land.

³If clouds are full of water,
    they pour rain upon the earth.
Whether a tree falls to the south or to the north,
    in the place where it falls, there will it lie.
⁴Whoever watches the wind will not plant;
    whoever looks at the clouds will not reap.

⁵As you do not know the path of the wind,
    or how the body is formed*a* in a mother's
        womb,
so you cannot understand the work of God,
    the Maker of all things.

⁶Sow your seed in the morning,
    and at evening let not your hands be idle,
for you do not know which will succeed,
    whether this or that,
    or whether both will do equally well.

Remember Your Creator While Young

⁷Light is sweet,
    and it pleases the eyes to see the sun.
⁸However many years a man may live,
    let him enjoy them all.
But let him remember the days of darkness,
    for they will be many.
    Everything to come is meaningless.

⁹Be happy, young man, while you are young,
    and let your heart give you joy in the days of
        your youth.
Follow the ways of your heart
    and whatever your eyes see,
but know that for all these things
    God will bring you to judgment.
¹⁰So then, banish anxiety from your heart
    and cast off the troubles of your body,
    for youth and vigor are meaningless.

12 Remember your Creator
    in the days of your youth,
before the days of trouble come
    and the years approach when you will say,
        "I find no pleasure in them"—
²before the sun and the light
    and the moon and the stars grow dark,
    and the clouds return after the rain;
³when the keepers of the house tremble,
    and the strong men stoop,
when the grinders cease because they are few,

☕ What is the worst investment (of time, money, etc.) you ever made? Why?

📖 **1.** What does "bread" symbolize? What happens when you "cast your bread" (v. 1)? How will the giving of "portions" help in a time of disaster (v. 2)? **2.** What do the matter-of-fact observations in verse 3 imply? **3.** Why are those who just "watch" so unproductive and ignorant (vv. 4–5)? **4.** How do the observations in verses 3–5 lead to the concluding advice (v. 6)? How does this relate to the advice in verse 1?

♡ **1.** How well do you manage your time? Money? Emotions? **2.** In what areas of life are your "investments" too concentrated? Spread too thin?

☕ **1.** Who was the wildest classmate when you were growing up? What has happened to that person? **2.** On the scale of 1 (blissfully ignorant) to 10 (painfully aware), how well do you see the consequences of your actions? Give an example of underestimating the consequences. **3.** As you grow older, which do you want to hold on to most: (a) Youthful body? (b) Youthful mind? (c) Youthful heart? **4.** What do you imagine you'll be like at age 100?

📖 **1.** What are "the days of darkness" (11:8) and why does the Teacher want us to "remember" them? What light do the other exhortations to "remember" (12:1,6) shed on this? **2.** What does the Teacher encourage in 11:9–10? What qualifies the joy we experience? How are youth and vigor "meaningless"? **3.** What does the long sentence in 12:1–5a describe? What sort of description is this: Positive, negative, or neutral? Realistic or imaginary? Vain regrets or pipe dreams? **4.** What event is described in 12:5b–7? Is this akin to the Christian hope of eternal life? Or is he speaking merely of finality? Which fits the book as a whole? **5.** In 12:8 the motto is repeated (see 1:2). What does this signal? What does it re-

---

a5 Or know how life (or *the spirit*) / *enters the body being formed*

and those looking through the windows grow
    dim;
[4]when the doors to the street are closed
    and the sound of grinding fades;
when men rise up at the sound of birds,
    but all their songs grow faint;
[5]when men are afraid of heights
    and of dangers in the streets;
when the almond tree blossoms
    and the grasshopper drags himself along
    and desire no longer is stirred.
Then man goes to his eternal home
    and mourners go about the streets.

[6]Remember him—before the silver cord is severed,
    or the golden bowl is broken;
before the pitcher is shattered at the spring,
    or the wheel broken at the well,
[7]and the dust returns to the ground it came from,
    and the spirit returns to God who gave it.

[8]"Meaningless! Meaningless!" says the Teacher.[a]
    "Everything is meaningless!"

The Conclusion of the Matter

[9]Not only was the Teacher wise, but also he imparted knowledge to the people. He pondered and searched out and set in order many proverbs. [10]The Teacher searched to find just the right words, and what he wrote was upright and true.

[11]The words of the wise are like goads, their collected sayings like firmly embedded nails—given by one Shepherd. [12]Be warned, my son, of anything in addition to them.

Of making many books there is no end, and much study wearies the body.

[13]Now all has been heard;
    here is the conclusion of the matter:
Fear God and keep his commandments,
    for this is the whole ⌊duty⌋ of man.
[14]For God will bring every deed into judgment,
    including every hidden thing,
    whether it is good or evil.

veal about any change of perspective by the Teacher?

1. How much do "eternal concerns" affect your daily decisions? Which areas of your life are least influenced by your faith in God? Which are most? 2. How free do you feel to "be happy" and enjoy life? 3. How can you "remember your Creator in the days of your youth"? How can you help children to do so? 4. How has your faith in God affected your outlook on aging? On dying? On death? Which do you fear most? Or do you truly yearn for one of these? Why?

Name one of the best books you ever read. Why did you enjoy it? What is one of the worst?

1. Who is speaking in 12:9–14? 2. How is the Teacher described (vv. 9–10)? What work has he done? 3. What do verses 11–12 warn against? Who is the "Shepherd" in verse 11? 4. How does the speaker summarize his interpretation of the book (vv. 13–14)? How does this compare to the teachings in the rest of the book?

1. In retrospect, how do you respond to the reflections in this book? What do you feel about its author? 2. Which discussion had the most impact on your thinking? How do you think its author would want you to apply his work to your life? How do you think God would?

[a]8 Or *the leader of the assembly*; also in verses 9 and 10

INTRODUCTION to
SONG OF SONGS

Book Study Outline: If you are using Song of Songs for a study course, here is a 7-week outline. Use the questions in the margin for your group agenda:

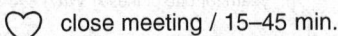 start meeting / 15 min.

read & discuss Bible / 30 min.

close meeting / 15–45 min.

7-week plan	Group Study Passage
1	1:1–2:7/The First Meeting: "The Bud of Romance"
2	2:8–3:5/The Second Meeting: "The Blossom of Courtship"
3	3:6–11/The Third Meeting: "The Wedding Song"
4	4:1–5:1/The Fourth Meeting: "Some Enchanted Evening"
5	5:2–6:3/The Fifth Meeting: "The Absence of the Lover"
6	6:4–7:9a/The Sixth Meeting: "The Return of Love"
7	7:9b–8:14/The Climactic Meeting: "A Romp in the Woods"

Refer to the Questions and Answers in the front of this Bible for more information.

Author: Traditionally, King Solomon is thought to be the author of this book. However, its title, "Solomon's Song of Songs" (1:1), can mean a song *by, for* or *about* Solomon. For this and other reasons, the identity of the author remains an open question.

Date: Perhaps during Solomon's reign, c. 970–930 B.C., but the presence of Persian loan-words suggests a later date for the final editing.

Theme: A celebration of love between a man and woman which is akin to God's love for his people.

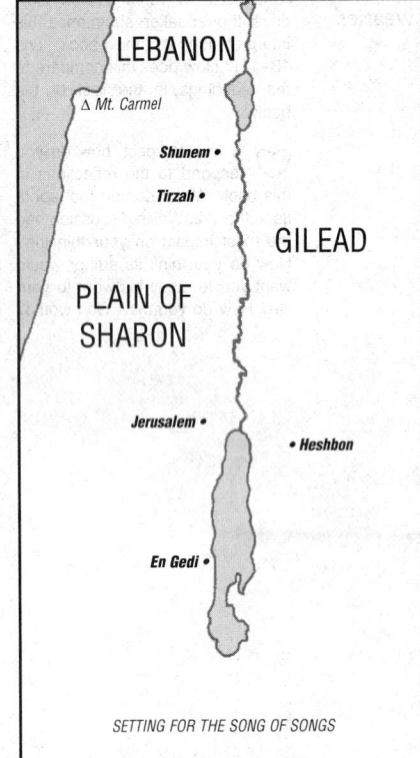

SETTING FOR THE SONG OF SONGS

Historical Background: Solomon's dynasty, his unsurpassed wisdom and wealth, and his many wives and concubines are perplexing contrasts to the simple rustic purity of the Song of Songs.

Characteristics: Interpretations of this "best of all songs" vary widely. Some view it literally, as a human love poem about King Solomon and his bride. Others see a third character in a triangle of relationships: a shepherd figure who is the true lover and who wins the Shulammite girl's hand over against the advances of Solomon. Some understand the book to be an anthology of unrelated love poems, with no overall story to tell. Many interpret this lovers' song as an allegory, depicting either God's love for Israel or Christ's love for his bride, the Church. Still others think that the song makes no such connection to God's love, but that it is only natural that the wonders of human love inspire thoughts of its divine source. Readers are sometimes surprised to find an explicit love song in the Bible, hence the many attempts to spiritualize away its occasionally erotic lyrics. Still other readers who try singing these same lines to their lovers will be disappointed to find that the eroticism gets lost in the translation. Another problem in understanding the Song of Songs has to do with the frequent change of voice and scene. Questions in the margin, along with the captions in the text, are designed to help follow the lovers' dialogue.

Song of Songs

1 Solomon's Song of Songs.

Beloved[a]

2Let him kiss me with the kisses of his mouth—
   for your love is more delightful than wine.
3Pleasing is the fragrance of your perfumes;
   your name is like perfume poured out.
   No wonder the maidens love you!
4Take me away with you—let us hurry!
   Let the king bring me into his chambers.

Friends

We rejoice and delight in you[b];
   we will praise your love more than wine.

---

[a]Primarily on the basis of the gender of the Hebrew pronouns used, male and female speakers are indicated in the margins by the captions *Lover* and *Beloved* respectively. The words of others are marked *Friends*. In some instances the divisions and their captions are debatable.   [b]4 The Hebrew is masculine singular.

1. In your experience, would you say: (a) Romance is best left to teenagers? (b) Life begins at 40? (c) Still counting the ways of love at 60? Explain. 2. What is your first or most romantic moment? 3. What snapshot of your dating or courtship days typifies your relationship: (a) Painting in bib overalls? (b) Sharing a candlelit dinner? (c) Staring bleary-eyed from a stack of school books? (d) Holding hands at the senior prom? (e) Dancing the night away at a fraternity party? (f) Holding hands at an office coffee break? (g) Bundled up in ski wear? (h) Decked out in fancy formal wear? Tell the story behind the picture.

1. Just as a few choice snapshots can capture the flavor of your relationship, so also with the courtship of this king and his beloved. In this first snapshot of the king (vv. 2–4), taken by the bride,

---

 Song of Songs 1:1–14   **DELIGHTING IN LOVE**

Here are three considerations for leaders of groups studying Song of Songs for the course on sexual intimacy in marriage: (1) Ask each couple to bring to the next session a few snapshots—of their dating days, wedding, honeymoon, etc.; (2) Use different voices to read the Scripture, such as women for the "Beloved," men for the "Lover," and everyone for the "Friends"; (3) Be sensitive to the group's preference to discuss some questions only with their spouses—particularly those questions marked with the Marriage Logo.

1. Why do you think God included a book about sex in the Bible?
   a. It was "sweeps week" and he wanted to increase his audience share.
   b. It must be symbolic for something more spiritual.
   c. God wanted to give a prototype for Christian romance novels.
   d. God wanted to affirm the beauty of human sexual love.
   e. God didn't want to include it—people slipped it in by mistake.

2. How is King Solomon portrayed in this passage?
   a. as a good kisser
   b. popular with women
   c. worthy of respect
   d. generous

3. How is his bride portrayed?
   a. swept off her feet   c. exquisite
   b. self-conscious   d. ordinary

4. How did your parents handle the subject of sex?
   a. They avoided the subject.
   b. They stumbled their way through the subject with me.
   c. They were open and helpful.
   d. They left it to the school.
   e. They left it to the church.

5. How did you and your spouse meet? How long did it take your relationship to become romantic?

6. What first struck you about your future mate?
   a. striking good looks
   b. dashing wit
   c. brilliant mind

d. shared values
e. money (or lack of it)
f. personality (or lack of it)
g. other:_____

7. What would be your definition of sex?
   a. a gift from God
   b. a gift I give my spouse
   c. an obligation
   d. a celebration of love
   e. not all it's cracked up to be
   f. the glue of a marriage
   g. none of your business

8. What brought you to this group?
   a. My spouse dragged me here.
   b. This is my favorite subject.
   c. I want to know more about what the Bible says about sex.
   d. Our marriage could use more sizzle and excitement.
   e. I'm expecting to have lots of fun.
   f. other:_____

9. How do you feel about discussing sexual intimacy in this group?

how is he portrayed? What tells you he is affectionate? A leader? With pleasing character? Worthy of respect? Popular with women? **2.** In the next snapshot (vv. 5–8), what does the bride look like? Why does this sun-darkened peasant girl feel self-conscious around the fair-skinned palace girls? How does she distinguish herself from a "veiled woman" (loose girl)? What does she fancy her lover doing? **3.** In the third snapshot (vv. 9–11), how does the king see her differently? How does he attend to her insecure feelings and neglected appearance? **4.** In the fourth snapshot (vv. 12–14), what fragrant, refreshing memories does she have of him? What does this aromatic myrrh signify for these lovers? **5.** In the next series of snapshots (1:15–2:3), the scene shifts from the palace to a quiet walk and talk in the woods. What do you make of their exchange of compliments? What makes such dialogue possible? How has her self-image changed from 1:6? Is their love blinding or enabling them to see truly? Why? **6.** Back at the palace (2:4–7), what tells you the beloved woman is feeling more and more secure in her man's love? What does the banner (used to signal large troop movements in battle) signify here? What does she do with her aroused feelings?

♥ **1.** What image reflects the relationship you have to your partner: (a) King and queen? (b) Shepherd and peasant girl? (c) Hero and heroine? (d) Nurse and patient? (e) Father and daughter? (f) Cat and mouse? (g) Other? What elements of each image do you see in the roles you play with one another? **2.** (Women) Early on, how did your spouse cater to your needs, deal with insecurity or boost a poor self-image? How do you keep fond memories of your man always before you? (With a sachet of perfume around your neck?) How can you deepen what you give to all your friendships, not only marriage? **3.** (Men) How can you be the leader without making your wife feel subservient? How can you help her feel more secure in your love? When did you last give her unsolicited affirmation? **4.** (Both) What quality of the one you courted is still true today? **5.** The friends play a vital role in this courtship, as they do in all marriages that work. Are you a true friend to couples you know? How so? **6.** How are

Beloved

How right they are to adore you!

[5]Dark am I, yet lovely,
  O daughters of Jerusalem,
  dark like the tents of Kedar,
  like the tent curtains of Solomon.[a]
[6]Do not stare at me because I am dark,
  because I am darkened by the sun.
My mother's sons were angry with me
  and made me take care of the vineyards;
  my own vineyard I have neglected.
[7]Tell me, you whom I love, where you graze your
    flock
  and where you rest your sheep at midday.
Why should I be like a veiled woman
  beside the flocks of your friends?

Friends

[8]If you do not know, most beautiful of women,
  follow the tracks of the sheep
and graze your young goats
  by the tents of the shepherds.

Lover

[9]I liken you, my darling, to a mare
  harnessed to one of the chariots of Pharaoh.
[10]Your cheeks are beautiful with earrings,
  your neck with strings of jewels.
[11]We will make you earrings of gold,
  studded with silver.

Beloved

[12]While the king was at his table,
  my perfume spread its fragrance.
[13]My lover is to me a sachet of myrrh
  resting between my breasts.
[14]My lover is to me a cluster of henna blossoms
  from the vineyards of En Gedi.

Lover

[15]How beautiful you are, my darling!
  Oh, how beautiful!
  Your eyes are doves.

Beloved

[16]How handsome you are, my lover!
  Oh, how charming!
  And our bed is verdant.

Lover

[17]The beams of our house are cedars;
  our rafters are firs.

a 5 Or *Salma*

Beloved[a]

2

I am a rose[b] of Sharon,
    a lily of the valleys.

Lover

[2]Like a lily among thorns
    is my darling among the maidens.

Beloved

[3]Like an apple tree among the trees of the forest
    is my lover among the young men.
I delight to sit in his shade,
    and his fruit is sweet to my taste.
[4]He has taken me to the banquet hall,
    and his banner over me is love.
[5]Strengthen me with raisins,
    refresh me with apples,
    for I am faint with love.
[6]His left arm is under my head,
    and his right arm embraces me.
[7]Daughters of Jerusalem, I charge you
    by the gazelles and by the does of the field:
Do not arouse or awaken love
    until it so desires.

[8]Listen! My lover!
    Look! Here he comes,

a 1 Or *Lover*   b 1 Possibly a member of the crocus family

sexual desire *and* self-restraint (2:6–7) both healthy and beneficial to any couple growing in love toward marriage? What happens if love-making occurs too soon? **7.** If this lover's song were an allegory, what image of God and Israel, or Christ and the church, do you see here? Are you currently camped under his banner of love (2:4)?

1. With what time of the year and time of your life do you associate romantic love? Why then? **2.** Describe the when, the

---

Song of Songs 1:15–2:15   WOOING WORDS

1. What do you think of this couple's exchange of compliments?
   a. They had a severe case of spring fever.
   b. They had ulterior motives.
   c. They were still in the "honeymoon" stage of their relationship.
   d. This is the way every marriage should be.
   e. This is poetry—not real life.

2. What does the "banner" (used to direct troops in battle) in 2:4 signify?
   a. She feels secure.
   b. She feels proud.
   c. His love for her is obvious.
   d. His love for her is both private and public.

3. Which image in the passage do you find most romantic or exciting?
   a. lying together in a verdant field
   b. sampling each other's "fruit"
   c. his left arm under her head and his right arm embracing her
   d. her watching him leap toward her
   e. him trying to catch a glimpse of her through the window

4. The king and his bride obviously felt attractive to each other. Which of the following does your spouse do most?
   a. tells me how nice I look
   b. tells me with his/her eyes how nice I look
   c. brings me romantic gifts
   d. brags about me to others
   e. displays affection for me
   f. writes me love notes or cards

5. Which of the actions in the previous question would you like your spouse to do more often?

6. What would you say is your mate's most attractive physical feature?

7. What would you say is your mate's most attractive personality trait?

8. This couple was in the springtime of their love relationship. Where are you in your relationship with Christ?
   a. Where have all the flowers gone?
   b. Everything is coming up roses.
   c. I need to stop and smell the roses.
   d. I'm trying to force open the buds.
   e. other:_____

9. How would you characterize you and your spouse's communication about sex?
   a. What communication?
   b. We'd rather do it than talk about it.
   c. We talk when there's a problem.
   d. Communicating about sex is an important part of our sex life.

10. This couple was aware of the "little foxes" (2:15) that can ruin love. What problems do couples face today when it comes to sexual intimacy?
    a. overly busy
    b. puritanical views and inhibitions
    c. bad experiences in the past
    d. false expectations
    e. physical problems
    f. difficulty talking about sex
    g. too much stress, too little energy

11. What are the "little foxes" — the hindrances to sexual intimacy in *your* marriage? What can you and your spouse agree on to make your relationship more satisfying for both of you?

where and the voice of your first *heart-throb* (perhaps one from grade school or high school). Why do you suppose those memories linger? **3.** If married: What did mom or dad say on the eve of your wedding to calm your fear?

📖 **1.** What season is it now (2:11–12)? What effect has their "winter past" had on the flowering of their love? Like the changing seasons, how do they appear transformed? **2.** As their relationship grows, how do they protect and preserve their love from anything that might ruin it (2:15)? How does she express the mutuality of their love (vv. 16–17)? How does their mutuality strike you: Possessive? Lustful? Stifling? Freeing? Enviable? **3.** As she dreams of her lover, what hopes and fears are aroused (3:1–5)? Why is she afraid of losing her lover? **4.** What happens when she's apart from him? What does this say about true married love? **5.** Why can't her love wait for fulfillment? Where does she go for security once she finds and hugs her man again? Why there? **6.** Why *must* love wait as a flower to blossom in season?

♡ **1.** What season of your love life are you in right now? How is it flowering? (a) Everything is coming up roses? (b) I can't even smell the flowers? (c) I am forcing open the buds? (d) Pulling up my budding romance by the roots? **2.** What do you need in your love life now: More space? More time? More sizzle? More sharing? Fewer foxes? **3.** What ruinous "foxes" must be caught before your love can grow: Pride? Unbridled desire? Unforgiving spirit? **4.** How can you help younger friends (and yourself) not to arouse or waken love until its time? **5.** What aspect of your courting days do you still carry forward? Why is it important to rekindle the fire of that first love? What new realities must set in to deepen that first love and keep it forever alive? **6.** Fiery passions are hard to maintain. Even our passion for Christ can dwindle over time. What does this passage suggest to you, allegorically, about rekindling that fellowship? Does absence from Christ make your heart grow fonder or colder? Why?

leaping across the mountains,
  bounding over the hills.
[9]My lover is like a gazelle or a young stag.
  Look! There he stands behind our wall,
gazing through the windows,
  peering through the lattice.
[10]My lover spoke and said to me,
  "Arise, my darling,
  my beautiful one, and come with me.
[11]See! The winter is past;
  the rains are over and gone.
[12]Flowers appear on the earth;
  the season of singing has come,
  the cooing of doves
  is heard in our land.
[13]The fig tree forms its early fruit;
  the blossoming vines spread their fragrance.
Arise, come, my darling;
  my beautiful one, come with me."

Lover

[14]My dove in the clefts of the rock,
  in the hiding places on the mountainside,
show me your face,
  let me hear your voice;
for your voice is sweet,
  and your face is lovely.
[15]Catch for us the foxes,
  the little foxes
that ruin the vineyards,
  our vineyards that are in bloom.

Beloved

[16]My lover is mine and I am his;
  he browses among the lilies.
[17]Until the day breaks
  and the shadows flee,
turn, my lover,
  and be like a gazelle
or like a young stag
  on the rugged hills.[a]

3 All night long on my bed
  I looked for the one my heart loves;
  I looked for him but did not find him.
[2]I will get up now and go about the city,
  through its streets and squares;
I will search for the one my heart loves.
  So I looked for him but did not find him.
[3]The watchmen found me
  as they made their rounds in the city.
  "Have you seen the one my heart loves?"
[4]Scarcely had I passed them
  when I found the one my heart loves.
I held him and would not let him go
  till I had brought him to my mother's house,
  to the room of the one who conceived me.
[5]Daughters of Jerusalem, I charge you

a 17 Or *the hills of Bether*

by the gazelles and by the does of the field:
Do not arouse or awaken love
   until it so desires.

⁶Who is this coming up from the desert
   like a column of smoke,
perfumed with myrrh and incense
   made from all the spices of the merchant?
⁷Look! It is Solomon's carriage,
   escorted by sixty warriors,
   the noblest of Israel,
⁸all of them wearing the sword,
   all experienced in battle,
each with his sword at his side,
   prepared for the terrors of the night.
⁹King Solomon made for himself the carriage;
   he made it of wood from Lebanon.
¹⁰Its posts he made of silver,
   its base of gold.
Its seat was upholstered with purple,
   its interior lovingly inlaid
   by^a the daughters of Jerusalem.
¹¹Come out, you daughters of Zion,
   and look at King Solomon wearing the crown,
   the crown with which his mother crowned him

^a10 Or *its inlaid interior a gift of love / from*

---

1. If married: on your wedding day, what was the most unconventional thing you did? The funniest thing that happened? What was your gift to each other? Share a "snapshot" of the wedding party. 2. If single or single again, what do you hope to experience on your wedding day?

1. In this wedding snapshot (vv. 6–11), where is the focus: (a) On the bridal procession? (b) The king's wedding crown? (c) The royal wedding? Why do you think so? 2. Note the number and purpose of the groomsmen: If the groom wanted to back out now, how could he?

1. What factors enter into an engaged couple's decision about how BIG to make their wedding? What was (or would be) the determining factor in your case? 2. If married: On your wedding day, what made your heart skip? Do you still feel that way? Why?

Song of Songs 2:16–3:11

THE RHYTHM OF ROMANCE

1. Which do you value most in a romantic relationship?
   a. flowers (or other gifts)
   b. special dates
   c. verbal affection
   d. physical affection
   e. quality time together
   f. thoughtful acts of service
   g. open communication

2. How does the bride react when she and her lover are apart?
   a. petrified   c. aroused
   b. insecure   d. unable to sleep

3. What do you think the woman meant when she said, "Daughters of Jerusalem ... Do not arouse or awaken love until it so desires" (3:5)?
   a. Love and desire go together.
   b. Don't try to make love happen— be patient until you know it's right.
   c. Don't put yourself in a compromising position.
   d. Keep yourself pure until married.

4. How are sexual desire *and* self-restraint both healthy and beneficial to a married couple growing in love?
   a. Lack of desire kills romance.

   b. Abstinence makes the heart grow fonder.
   c. Occasional self-restraint heightens sexual desire and satisfaction.
   d. Self-control for your spouse's sake is an important part of sexuality.
   e. I don't see that self-restraint is in any way beneficial.

5. Assuming the last part of chapter 3 refers to their wedding day, how do you think Solomon's bride felt as she saw the wedding party approaching?

6. What made your heart skip a beat on your wedding day and on your honeymoon? Is it important to rekindle that kind of spark? Why?

7. When you were first married, how would you compare your relationship to the couple's in Song of Songs?
   a. Ours was every bit as romantic as this couple's.
   b. We had some of the same feelings, but didn't know how to put them into words.
   c. Our relationship was much more subdued.
   d. Our relationship is still this way.

8. What are some ways you have discovered to create "marriage time" (apart from "family time")?

9. How do you handle times of separation from your spouse? Do you agree with the saying, "Absence makes the heart grow fonder"?

10. Does absence from Christ make your heart grow fonder or colder? Why is that?

11. Like the couple in this story, what keeps your love alive?
    a. playful teasing
    b. dreaming together
    c. times apart
    d. having caring friends
    e. private rendezvous

12. What positive steps can you take to insure time and privacy to nurture your love life?
    a. Establish a day or a weekend alone every _____.
    b. Go on a "date" every _____.
    c. Experience some creative romance by _____.
    d. Plan a trip just for us to _____.

on the day of his wedding,
　the day his heart rejoiced.

Lover

4

How beautiful you are, my darling!
　Oh, how beautiful!
　Your eyes behind your veil are doves.
Your hair is like a flock of goats
　descending from Mount Gilead.
2Your teeth are like a flock of sheep just shorn,
　coming up from the washing.
Each has its twin;
　not one of them is alone.
3Your lips are like a scarlet ribbon;
　your mouth is lovely.
Your temples behind your veil
　are like the halves of a pomegranate.
4Your neck is like the tower of David,
　built with elegance*a*;
on it hang a thousand shields,
　all of them shields of warriors.
5Your two breasts are like two fawns,
　like twin fawns of a gazelle
　that browse among the lilies.
6Until the day breaks
　and the shadows flee,
I will go to the mountain of myrrh
　and to the hill of incense.
7All beautiful you are, my darling;
　there is no flaw in you.

8Come with me from Lebanon, my bride,
　come with me from Lebanon.
Descend from the crest of Amana,
　from the top of Senir, the summit of Hermon,
from the lions' dens
　and the mountain haunts of the leopards.
9You have stolen my heart, my sister, my bride;
　you have stolen my heart
with one glance of your eyes,
　with one jewel of your necklace.
10How delightful is your love, my sister, my bride!
How much more pleasing is your love than
　wine,
　and the fragrance of your perfume than any
　spice!
11Your lips drop sweetness as the honeycomb, my
　bride;
　milk and honey are under your tongue.
The fragrance of your garments is like that of
　Lebanon.
12You are a garden locked up, my sister, my bride;
　you are a spring enclosed, a sealed fountain.
13Your plants are an orchard of pomegranates
　with choice fruits,
　with henna and nard,
14　nard and saffron,
　calamus and cinnamon,

a4 The meaning of the Hebrew for this word is uncertain.

Where did you go on your honeymoon? (Or, where would you like to go?) Why there?

1. Assuming this section refers to the couple's wedding night, what is memorable about it (4:1–5:1)? What do you make of these compliments? Do you ever compliment someone you adore? How does your beloved react? 2. The husband praises seven different aspects of his wife's beauty. What makes her beauty and personality flawless to him? In the long run, what will bring out all the wife's beauty: Praise or Criticism? Why? 3. What effect does his intimate foreplay have on his wife? How does she reciprocate (vv. 10–11, 16)? 4. How does the king deal with her fears about marriage and thoughts of home (v. 8)? What role does such reassurance and foreplay serve in the love-making which follows? 5. How is the extended metaphor of the garden used here? Where do you see restraint and freedom expressed? 6. What choral benediction is given this married couple (5:1c), as if from God? What is the meaning here for those who question the beauty, playfulness and joy of sex?

1. If God's view of sex in marriage is conveyed here, then why do so many couples experience nothing like it? What does this Song have to say to a divorced person? To macho men? To prudish women? 2. If single: How might a beautiful courtship, like the one here, better equip you for marriage? What about God's wonderful creation (you!) and your (hoped for) courtship can you give thanks for (or pray for)? 3. If married: Using the garden metaphor as it applies to love-making, what are you now growing: Nothing? Weeds? Desert? Annuals? Perennials? A new garden? 4. Reflecting on the winds of change since your wedding day, what is now blowing your way: A cold northerly or warm southerly wind? Breezy or gusty? Clearing up or clouding over? Why? 5. Applying this lovers' poem allegorically to Christ and the church, what might this story say about the second coming and the great wedding feast that will be? How does Christ's royal love for the church inspire your devotion and

with every kind of incense tree,
with myrrh and aloes
and all the finest spices.
¹⁵You are[a] a garden fountain,
a well of flowing water
streaming down from Lebanon.

Beloved

¹⁶Awake, north wind,
and come, south wind!
Blow on my garden,
that its fragrance may spread abroad.
Let my lover come into his garden
and taste its choice fruits.

Lover

5

I have come into my garden, my sister, my bride;
I have gathered my myrrh with my spice.
I have eaten my honeycomb and my honey;
I have drunk my wine and my milk.

Friends

Eat, O friends, and drink;
drink your fill, O lovers.

Beloved

²I slept but my heart was awake.
Listen! My lover is knocking:
"Open to me, my sister, my darling,
my dove, my flawless one.
My head is drenched with dew,
my hair with the dampness of the night."
³I have taken off my robe—
must I put it on again?
I have washed my feet—
must I soil them again?
⁴My lover thrust his hand through the
latch-opening;
my heart began to pound for him.
⁵I arose to open for my lover,
and my hands dripped with myrrh,
my fingers with flowing myrrh,
on the handles of the lock.
⁶I opened for my lover,
but my lover had left; he was gone.
My heart sank at his departure.[b]
I looked for him but did not find him.
I called him but he did not answer.
⁷The watchmen found me
as they made their rounds in the city.
They beat me, they bruised me;
they took away my cloak,
those watchmen of the walls!
⁸O daughters of Jerusalem, I charge you—
if you find my lover,
what will you tell him?
Tell him I am faint with love.

---

a15 Or *I am* (spoken by the *Beloved*)   b6 Or *heart had gone out to him when he*
spoke

If married: How long did your honeymoon last: 7 days? 7 weeks? 7 years? How did you know that your honeymoon had ended and new realities had set in? Who do you know who seems to have enjoyed a perpetual honeymoon?

1. The next significant event is either a dream or reality. In 5:2–8, what support can you find for each view? 2. How do you account for the wife not rushing to the door at her lover's knock (5:2–3): (a) Playful? (b) Sleepy? (c) Lethargic? 3. In either event, how does her lover respond (5: 6): (a) Hurt by the rebuff? (b) Playing hide and seek? (c) Realizes sex on demand was wrong? (d) Respects the principle that love, even with one's wife, should not be roused until it pleases? 4. What impact do you suppose her run-away lover and run-in with "police" (5:6–8) had on her: (a) Roused her from a nightmare? (b) Brought her back to her senses? (c) Made her heart grow fonder? 5. What is the spirit behind the friends' first question (v. 9): (a) To replace her apathy with gratitude? (b) To coax him out of his wounded ego or pouting? (c) To calm their fear of love and the agony of parting? 6. How much does he evidently mean to her, after all (5:10–16)? What strikes you about her sensuous desire for her "lover and friend"? 7. If the friends' first

question prepares her attitude, to what does the second question lead (6:1–3)? What paves the way for reunion with her beloved: (a) A place to talk privately? (b) A sense of mutual belonging? (c) A time to make love after making up?

 1. What person would you describe as both your lover and your friend? Are you your mate's *best* friend? Was your love first based in friendship, or did friendship really develop only after the fires of passion settled down? **2.** How are you ensuring that neither friendship nor love-making will be neglected in the future? What is the next date on the calendar for just the two of you? **3.** With your beloved, as with the two in this story, what keeps your love alive: (a) Playful teasing? (b) Dreaming together? (c) Times apart? (d) Caring friends? (e) Private reunion times? **4.** What would a reminder list of his or her attributes do for your relationship? What three things about your mate do you most appreciate? Write them down and exchange lists. **5.** Rank in order the following needs for yourself and your mate: Admiration, affection, attractive spouse, honesty and trust, family commitment, open conversation, domestic support, financial security, recreational companionship, sexual fulfillment. Which needs are the top five on both lists? **6.** Knowing this, how can you better meet each other's needs to celebrate what God has given you and to strengthen your marriage?

1. Was *sex* a wholesome word, or a dirty word, for you growing up? Who embarrasses more easily about questions of sex: You, your parents or your kids? Why is that? **2.** How did your parents resolve conflicts? (a) An eye for an eye? (b) Repetitive round robins? (c) Mount Vesuvius temper tantrums? (d) Hit-and-run attacks? (e) Peace at any price? (f) No fights allowed? (g) Fighting fair? How did you feel when they fought?

Friends

⁹How is your beloved better than others,
    most beautiful of women?
How is your beloved better than others,
    that you charge us so?

Beloved

¹⁰My lover is radiant and ruddy,
    outstanding among ten thousand.
¹¹His head is purest gold;
    his hair is wavy
    and black as a raven.
¹²His eyes are like doves
    by the water streams,
washed in milk,
    mounted like jewels.
¹³His cheeks are like beds of spice
    yielding perfume.
His lips are like lilies
    dripping with myrrh.
¹⁴His arms are rods of gold
    set with chrysolite.
His body is like polished ivory
    decorated with sapphires.[a]
¹⁵His legs are pillars of marble
    set on bases of pure gold.
His appearance is like Lebanon,
    choice as its cedars.
¹⁶His mouth is sweetness itself;
    he is altogether lovely.
This is my lover, this my friend,
    O daughters of Jerusalem.

Friends

6 Where has your lover gone,
    most beautiful of women?
Which way did your lover turn,
    that we may look for him with you?

Beloved

²My lover has gone down to his garden,
    to the beds of spices,
to browse in the gardens
    and to gather lilies.
³I am my lover's and my lover is mine;
    he browses among the lilies.

Lover

⁴You are beautiful, my darling, as Tirzah,
    lovely as Jerusalem,
    majestic as troops with banners.
⁵Turn your eyes from me;
    they overwhelm me.
Your hair is like a flock of goats
    descending from Gilead.
⁶Your teeth are like a flock of sheep
    coming up from the washing.

a 14 Or *lapis lazuli*

Each has its twin,
    not one of them is alone.
[7]Your temples behind your veil
    are like the halves of a pomegranate.
[8]Sixty queens there may be,
    and eighty concubines,
    and virgins beyond number;
[9]but my dove, my perfect one, is unique,
    the only daughter of her mother,
    the favorite of the one who bore her.
The maidens saw her and called her blessed;
    the queens and concubines praised her.

Friends

[10]Who is this that appears like the dawn,
    fair as the moon, bright as the sun,
    majestic as the stars in procession?

Lover

[11]I went down to the grove of nut trees
    to look at the new growth in the valley,
    to see if the vines had budded
    or the pomegranates were in bloom.
[12]Before I realized it,
    my desire set me among the royal chariots of
    my people.[a]

[a]12 Or *among the chariots of Amminadab; or among the chariots of the people of the prince*

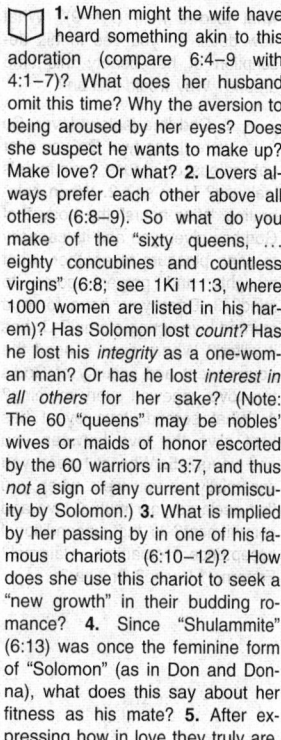

1. When might the wife have heard something akin to this adoration (compare 6:4–9 with 4:1–7)? What does her husband omit this time? Why the aversion to being aroused by her eyes? Does she suspect he wants to make up? Make love? Or what? 2. Lovers always prefer each other above all others (6:8–9). So what do you make of the "sixty queens, ... eighty concubines and countless virgins" (6:8; see 1Ki 11:3, where 1000 women are listed in his harem)? Has Solomon lost *count*? Has he lost his *integrity* as a one-woman man? Or has he lost *interest in all others* for her sake? (Note: The 60 "queens" may be nobles' wives or maids of honor escorted by the 60 warriors in 3:7, and thus *not* a sign of any current promiscuity by Solomon.) 3. What is implied by her passing by in one of his famous chariots (6:10–12)? How does she use this chariot to seek a "new growth" in their budding romance? 4. Since "Shulammite" (6:13) was once the feminine form of "Solomon" (as in Don and Donna), what does this say about her fitness as his mate? 5. After expressing how in love they truly are,

---

 Song of Songs 5:9–6:9   **ONLY YOU**

1. MEN: If your wife described you like Solomon's wife did in 5:10–16, how would you respond?
   a. I would blush.
   b. I would feel honored.
   c. I would faint.
   d. I would expect it.
   e. I would wonder what she wants.

2. WOMEN: If your husband described you like Solomon did in 6:4–9, how would you respond?
   a. I would blush.
   b. I would feel honored.
   c. I would faint.
   d. I would expect it.
   e. I would know exactly what he wants—sex!

3. How do you react to the woman calling Solomon "outstanding among ten thousand" (5:10) and him calling her "my perfect one" (6:9)?
   a. They hadn't been married long!
   b. They had ulterior motives.
   c. They looked at each other through eyes of love.
   d. They wanted their partner to feel good about himself/herself.

e. Complimenting your mate makes you feel good about yourself.

4. What do you make of Solomon's words here in light of the fact he had *many* wives (hundreds eventually)?
   a. She was his favorite.
   b. He had enough love to go around.
   c. He flattered all his wives this way.
   d. His feelings didn't last.
   e. This was the only real romance he ever experienced.

5. What point does the statement, "I am my lover's and my lover is mine; he browses among the lilies" (6:3) illustrate about sex?
   a. mutuality—a mutually shared and enjoyed experience
   b. exclusiveness—giving ourselves solely to one another
   c. uninhibited—giving ourselves to each other freely
   d. intimacy—knowing my mate fully
   e. security—in each other's love

6. The wife referred to her husband as "my lover, my friend." Was your relationship first based in friendship, or

did friendship not really develop until the fires of passion settled down?

7. Why is friendship an important part of a healthy sexual relationship? Are you and your spouse best friends?

8. What do you think causes adultery?
   a. It happens on an impulse.
   b. It happens to weak marriages.
   c. The guilty spouse is sexually unfulfilled.
   d. Our society encourages it.
   e. Our sin nature encourages it.
   f. other:_____

9. How are you guarding against marital unfaithfulness? How are you ensuring that neither lovemaking nor friendship is neglected in your marriage? What is the next date on the calendar for just the two of you?

10. What would a "reminder list" of your mate's attributes do for your relationship? Write down three things and share them with your spouse.

what follows next (7:1–9)? What new detail do you see in his description of her beauty this time around? Why would that be?

 1. God is a jealous lover. So were these two. Do *you* ever get jealous or arouse your mate's jealousy? How so? **2.** When celebrating "after hours" the body that God has given you and its capacity to bring pleasure to another, what thoughts and prayers come to mind? **3.** Does your hope for true married love spring eternal? Or has it wilted? Where does it need the nourishment and security of God's true love, renewed every morning? **4.** What serendipitous event has kept alive the love between you and yours? **5.** Who still sees you essentially as you were when you first declared your mutual love and commitment? Is that unconditional acceptance romantic? Paternal? Fraternal? Divine? Or what?

Friends

13Come back, come back, O Shulammite;
　come back, come back, that we may gaze on
　　you!

Lover

Why would you gaze on the Shulammite
　as on the dance of Mahanaim?

7 How beautiful your sandaled feet,
　O prince's daughter!
Your graceful legs are like jewels,
　the work of a craftsman's hands.
2Your navel is a rounded goblet
　that never lacks blended wine.
Your waist is a mound of wheat
　encircled by lilies.
3Your breasts are like two fawns,
　twins of a gazelle.
4Your neck is like an ivory tower.
Your eyes are the pools of Heshbon
　by the gate of Bath Rabbim.
Your nose is like the tower of Lebanon
　looking toward Damascus.
5Your head crowns you like Mount Carmel.
Your hair is like royal tapestry;
　the king is held captive by its tresses.
6How beautiful you are and how pleasing,
　O love, with your delights!

Song of Songs 6:13–8:4   VIVA LA DIFFERENCE!

1. What surprises you the most—and the least—about this passage?
   a. Solomon's romantic nature
   b. his wife's romantic nature
   c. Solomon's focus on her body
   d. her sexual initiative
   e. the Bible's recording this couple's playful and creative sex life

2. Which of the lovers' suggestions do you find most powerful?
   a. I will climb the palm tree and take hold of its (your) fruit.
   b. Let's go to the countryside and spend the night in a village inn.
   c. I will give you my love beside the blossoming trees.
   d. I have stored up for you every delicacy, both new and old.
   e. Your left arm is under my head and your right arm embraces me.

3. Which aspect of this passage is most important to you?
   a. the attractive physical descriptions
   b. the sense of belonging
   c. the feeling of being desirable
   d. the sensual experiences

4. What do you think is the major difference between men's and women's perspectives about sex?

5. How are your sexual expectations different than your spouse's?

6. The beloved regrets that her culture prohibited public expression of her love for her husband, as opposed to her brother (8:1). What do you wish was different about our culture's sexual expectations, and their effects on you?

7. Which of the following best captures your idea of sex in marriage?
   a. the supreme moment of human celebration
   b. the one experience a couple shares only with each other
   c. a movement toward intimacy
   d. an exciting desire to give and receive from the one we love

8. As in virtually all successful marriages, the "friends" play a part in this love story. How have the couples in this group (or other friends) contributed to your marriage? How has being together in this course helped you be a better friend and lover to your spouse?

9. Using the sense of taste as a sexual symbol, which this book often does, how would you describe you and your mate's sex life—and how would you like it to change? (You may prefer to answer this alone with your spouse.)
   a. full-course dinners
   b. snacks on the run
   c. gourmet extravaganzas
   d. meat and potatoes
   e. feast or famine
   f. well-balanced diet
   g. mystery meals

10. The beloved had stored up both new and old delights for her lover (7:13). Get alone with your spouse and share with each other: (1) good memories you have about past romance and lovemaking; and (2) your hopes and dreams for new "delights" yet to be enjoyed.

⁷Your stature is like that of the palm,
  and your breasts like clusters of fruit.
⁸I said, "I will climb the palm tree;
  I will take hold of its fruit."
May your breasts be like the clusters of the vine,
  the fragrance of your breath like apples,
⁹ and your mouth like the best wine.

Beloved

May the wine go straight to my lover,
  flowing gently over lips and teeth.*ᵃ*
¹⁰I belong to my lover,
  and his desire is for me.
¹¹Come, my lover, let us go to the countryside,
  let us spend the night in the villages.*ᵇ*
¹²Let us go early to the vineyards
  to see if the vines have budded,
if their blossoms have opened,
  and if the pomegranates are in bloom—
  there I will give you my love.
¹³The mandrakes send out their fragrance,
  and at our door is every delicacy,
both new and old,
  that I have stored up for you, my lover.

8 If only you were to me like a brother,
  who was nursed at my mother's breasts!
Then, if I found you outside,
  I would kiss you,
  and no one would despise me.
²I would lead you
  and bring you to my mother's house—
  she who has taught me.
I would give you spiced wine to drink,
  the nectar of my pomegranates.
³His left arm is under my head
  and his right arm embraces me.
⁴Daughters of Jerusalem, I charge you:
  Do not arouse or awaken love
  until it so desires.

Friends

⁵Who is this coming up from the desert
  leaning on her lover?

Beloved

Under the apple tree I roused you;
  there your mother conceived you,
  there she who was in labor gave you birth.
⁶Place me like a seal over your heart,
  like a seal on your arm;
for love is as strong as death,
  its jealousy*ᶜ* unyielding as the grave.*ᵈ*
It burns like blazing fire,
  like a mighty flame.*ᵉ*
⁷Many waters cannot quench love;

---

1. Where did you first meet your "one and only"? 2. Complete this sentence: "Love is ...." Compare your definitions for what they have in common.

1. What "love potion" seems to be a favorite of this couple? Is their marriage any less sacred for their playfulness at sex? Why do you think so? 2. What does it tell you that the woman has an equal role in the dance of love and sex (7:11–13)? 3. Why the repeated charge to the daughters of Jerusalem (8:4; also 2:7; 3:5)? Is this meant to warn any who may have prurient interests aroused by this candid love story? 4. Many of the lovers' metaphors deserve a second look (8:6–7). How is married love like an owner's *seal*? Like *death*? Or like *fire*? (For example, would a death-like love be a fatal attraction, or unbearable, or irreversible? Like-wise, would a fire-like love be dangerous, or unquenchable, or capable of burning hot and then dying out?) 5. What is the point about the price of love (8:7)? (a) The one with the most toys wins the girl? (b) Sex can be cheaply bought? (c) Love must be freely given? (d) Other? 6. In 8:8–14, we have a series of flashbacks to bring closure to this story. How does her family both encourage and discipline her to save herself for marriage? 7. What lover's freedom does she assert in the end? What is memorable about their last words to each other?

1. Take time to think about the degree of exclusiveness in your relationship with the one you love. Do you actively and openly prefer your beloved to all others? Do you work to make yourself preferable? How so? When were you last jealous for the good of your beloved? Ask the Author of love for the gift of single-minded love today. 2. What makes sexual freedom within marriage possible? (a) Time spent together. (b) Reassurances from each other. (c) Environmental factors. (d) Internal factors. Explain. 3. How important is

---

ᵃ9 Septuagint, Aquila, Vulgate and Syriac; Hebrew *lips of sleepers*   *ᵇ11* Or *henna bushes*   *ᶜ6* Or *ardor*   *ᵈ6* Hebrew *Sheol*   *ᵉ6* Or */ like the very flame of the* LORD

the *sizzle factor* in friendship that leads to marriage? Even if *all* other systems indicate "Go for it," should two friends marry who do *not* have irresistible physical chemistry? What's wrong with experimenting beforehand to see if the sexual compatibility is there? Would such an experiment even be valid without a *commitment factor* secured only in marriage blessed by God? **4.** This story only speaks of the woman saving herself for marriage (8:8–9). Isn't sexual purity equally incumbent upon men? Why or why not? **5.** How would you compare the Song of Songs in its approach to love, sex and marriage with today's culture? What healthy antidotes to casual sex, emotional insecurity and self-destructive thinking does this Song offer? **6.** What aspects of this love poem were for you erotic? Which were romantic? Why then do you think this Song is in the Bible? **7.** Using the allegorical approach, how is Christ's love for you like the king's love for his bride? Where have you experienced his painful, possessive, persevering and priceless love? **8.** Who would you recommend this book to? Why?

rivers cannot wash it away.
If one were to give
all the wealth of his house for love,
it[a] would be utterly scorned.

Friends

[8]We have a young sister,
and her breasts are not yet grown.
What shall we do for our sister
for the day she is spoken for?
[9]If she is a wall,
we will build towers of silver on her.
If she is a door,
we will enclose her with panels of cedar.

Beloved

[10]I am a wall,
and my breasts are like towers.
Thus I have become in his eyes
like one bringing contentment.
[11]Solomon had a vineyard in Baal Hamon;
he let out his vineyard to tenants.
Each was to bring for its fruit
a thousand shekels[b] of silver.
[12]But my own vineyard is mine to give;
the thousand shekels are for you, O Solomon,

a7 Or *he*   *b11* That is, about 25 pounds (about 11.5 kilograms); also in verse 12

 Song of Songs 8:5–14   **THE POWER OF LOVE**

1. Why do you believe this couple's love relationship is going to last?
   a. They are physically attracted to each other.
   b. They "belong" to each other.
   c. They are incurable romantics.
   d. They have supportive friends.
   e. Their love is as strong as death.

2. What do the beloved's words in 8:6–7 mean?
   a. Don't let me go.
   b. I won't let you go.
   c. Love is the strongest of emotions.
   d. Passionate love is out of control.
   e. Sex can be bought, but love can only be given.

3. What is the strongest ending note of the Song of Songs for you?
   a. What matters is the intensity of my feelings for my spouse (8:6–7).
   b. What matters is my commitment to my spouse (8:6–7).
   c. What matters is how my spouse sees me (8:10).
   d. What matters is that my love is freely given (8:12).

   e. What matters is that we're together and in love (8:13–14).

4. If God's view of sex in marriage is conveyed in the Song of Songs, then why do so many couples experience nothing like it?
   a. because sex has been distorted in our culture
   b. because they have hang-ups from the church
   c. because they have hang-ups from their past
   d. because they don't work at it
   e. other:_____

5. How is God's love for you like this couple's love for each other?

6. How do you see your spirituality relating to your sexuality?
   a. It doesn't.
   b. Sexuality and spirituality are opposites that tug at me from both ends.
   c. Sexuality and spirituality are opposites that keep me balanced.
   d. Sexuality and spirituality both connect me with others.

   e. Spirituality helps me express my sexuality in ways that affirm God's lordship of life.

7. What have you most appreciated about this course and this group?

8. What is your greatest need regarding your sexuality?
   a. expressing my sexual needs
   b. feeling good about myself
   c. receiving forgiveness for the past
   d. controlling my impulses
   e. the security of physical closeness
   f. other:_____

9. Rank from 1 to 6 the respective strengths of your marriage, 1 being the highest, then get together alone with your spouse to discuss your answers.
   a. romance
   b. sexual passion
   c. communication about sex
   d. companionship
   e. spiritual intimacy
   f. commitment

and two hundred[a] are for those who tend its
fruit.

Lover

¹³You who dwell in the gardens
with friends in attendance,
let me hear your voice!

Beloved

¹⁴Come away, my lover,
and be like a gazelle
or like a young stag
on the spice-laden mountains.

INTRODUCTION to
ISAIAH

Book Study Outline: If you are using Isaiah for a study course, here is a 7- or 13-week outline. Use the questions in the margin for your group agenda:

🥛 start meeting / 15 min.

📖 read & discuss Bible / 30 min.

♡ close meeting / 15–45 min.

Refer to the Questions and Answers in the front of this Bible for more information.

7-week plan	13-week plan	Personal Reading	Group Study Passage
1	1	1:1–5:30	1:1–31/True and False Faith
	2	6:1–10:34	6:1–13/Call of Isaiah
2	3	11:1–12:6	11:1–16/Kingdom of Peace
	4	13:1–21:17	15:1–16:13/People in Pain
3	5	22:1–26:21	26:1–21/Song of Praise
	6	27:1–33:24	29:1–24/Woes on Jerusalem
4	7	34:1–39:8	37:1–38/Salvation From God
	8	40:1–44:5	40:1–31/The Comfort of God
5	9	44:6–48:22	44:6–23/God and Idols
	10	49:1–55:13	55:1–13/God's Invitation
6	11	42,49,50,53	Review the Four "Servant Songs"
	12	56:1–59:21	58:1–14/True and False Fasting
7	13	60:1–66:24	60:1–22/The Coming Glory

Author: In the opening verse of the book, the author is declared to be Isaiah son of Amoz (see also 2:1; 13:1). Chapters 1–39 ("The Book of Judgment") reflect for the most part the kingdom of Isaiah's day, but chapters 40–66 ("The Book of Comfort") envision the return from exile (536 B.C.) and the coming kingdom of God. Some believe that these visionary chapters may have been written later by others following in Isaiah's steps.

Date: Isaiah ministered in Judah c. 740–681 B.C.

Theme: The sovereign Lord, judging and redeeming the whole earth.

Historical Background: Assyria, the invincible superpower of the day, was threatening Jerusalem with conquest (2Ki 15–20; 2Ch 26–32). Isaiah saw in this the culmination of God's judgment against the widespread apostasy of Judah under King Ahaz. He predicted the fall of Jerusalem (which happened in 586 B.C.). The only hope for escape, Isaiah declared, was God's intervention, not political alliances, material wealth, or religious pretense. Chapters 40–66 focus on events 150–200 years after Isaiah's day, foretelling God's deliverance of his people from their Babylonian captors (in 538 B.C.) and prefiguring the greater deliverance from sin through Christ.

Characteristics: As a prophet, poet and politician, Isaiah was a giant in his day, respected in royal circles despite his unpopular message. Known for his beautiful images and profound insights into the nature of God (whom Isaiah calls "The Holy One of Israel"), the prophet Isaiah is quoted in the New Testament more than all other prophets combined.

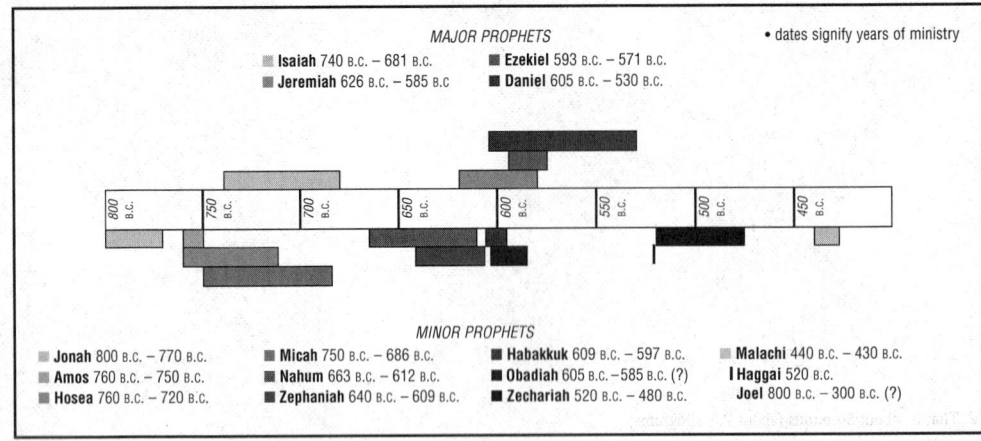

MAJOR PROPHETS • dates signify years of ministry

Isaiah 740 B.C. – 681 B.C.   Ezekiel 593 B.C. – 571 B.C.
Jeremiah 626 B.C. – 585 B.C   Daniel 605 B.C. – 530 B.C.

800 B.C.   750 B.C.   700 B.C.   650 B.C.   600 B.C.   550 B.C.   500 B.C.   450 B.C.

MINOR PROPHETS

Jonah 800 B.C. – 770 B.C.   Micah 750 B.C. – 686 B.C.   Habakkuk 609 B.C. – 597 B.C.   Malachi 440 B.C. – 430 B.C.
Amos 760 B.C. – 750 B.C.   Nahum 663 B.C. – 612 B.C.   Obadiah 605 B.C. –585 B.C. (?)   I Haggai 520 B.C.
Hosea 760 B.C. – 720 B.C.   Zephaniah 640 B.C. – 609 B.C.   Zechariah 520 B.C. – 480 B.C.   Joel 800 B.C. – 300 B.C. (?)

Isaiah

1 The vision concerning Judah and Jerusalem that Isaiah son of Amoz saw during the reigns of Uzziah, Jotham, Ahaz and Hezekiah, kings of Judah.

A Rebellious Nation

²Hear, O heavens! Listen, O earth!
  For the LORD has spoken:
"I reared children and brought them up,
  but they have rebelled against me.
³The ox knows his master,
  the donkey his owner's manger,
but Israel does not know,
  my people do not understand."

⁴Ah, sinful nation,
  a people loaded with guilt,
a brood of evildoers,
  children given to corruption!
They have forsaken the LORD;
  they have spurned the Holy One of Israel
  and turned their backs on him.

⁵Why should you be beaten anymore?
  Why do you persist in rebellion?
Your whole head is injured,
  your whole heart afflicted.
⁶From the sole of your foot to the top of your head
  there is no soundness—
only wounds and welts
  and open sores,
not cleansed or bandaged
  or soothed with oil.

⁷Your country is desolate,
  your cities burned with fire;
your fields are being stripped by foreigners
  right before you,
  laid waste as when overthrown by strangers.
⁸The Daughter of Zion is left
  like a shelter in a vineyard,
like a hut in a field of melons,
  like a city under siege.
⁹Unless the LORD Almighty
  had left us some survivors,
we would have become like Sodom,
  we would have been like Gomorrah.

¹⁰Hear the word of the LORD,
  you rulers of Sodom;
listen to the law of our God,
  you people of Gomorrah!
¹¹"The multitude of your sacrifices—
  what are they to me?" says the LORD.
"I have more than enough of burnt offerings,
  of rams and the fat of fattened animals;

1. Who was president or prime minister of your country when you were born? What were your mom and dad doing for a living then? 2. As a teenager, over what issues would you rebel against your parents: Curfew? Car? Phone? Dates? Church? Money? How long did your rebellion last? When did you grow out of it? (Or did you ever?)

1. Isaiah's ministry spanned the reigns of four kings of Judah, almost 50 years. What do you know about the reign of Uzziah (see 2Ch 26:3–5,16–20)? Of Jotham (see 2Ch 27:1–9)? Of Ahaz (see 2Ch 28:1–8,22–25)? Of Hezekiah (see 2Ch 29:1–11; 31:20–21; 32:24–26)? How would you sum up what was going on in Judah during their reigns? 2. Chapters 1–5 contain sermons that at some time Isaiah preached to the people. Though not arranged chronologically, they introduce major themes to be developed throughout the book, as when Isaiah begins (v. 2) and ends (66:24) by condemning rebels against God. What is the purpose of God calling heaven and earth to witness his complaint against his covenant people? What is his case against them (vv. 2–4)? 3. What is their pitiable condition like? What sympathy do they get (vv. 5–6)? What is going on in their country (vv. 7–9; see 2Ki 16:5–6; 18:9–16)? 4. God compares the people of Judah with Sodom and Gomorrah (vv. 9–20). What is the point of the comparison? 5. The Jews loved the feasts, ceremonies and sacrifices (such as Passover). Then how come God took no pleasure in their sacrifices? Why are they "meaningless" and "evil"? 6. What does God call the people to do (vv. 16–17)? What does God promise in accordance with their repentance? What's happening in Judah that accounts for this call and promise (vv. 15b,21–23)? 7. Given their religious rituals (vv. 11–15), how does the secular image of adultery (v. 21) fit their spiritual state? Likewise, how do "scarlet" and "red" fit? What is the condition upon which the forgiveness of their sins rests?

8. What is the purpose of the judgment awaiting those who forsake the Lord (vv. 24–31)? What is the future for those who are penitent? How will it be different from their present situation?

♡ **1.** Was there a time in your life when religion was meaningless? What changed your mind, or does it tend to be that way now? Why? **2.** Is mere sincerity what counts with God (see Ro 2:17–24,28–29)? What could make your worship more meaningful? **3.** Karl Marx said that religion is "the opiate of the masses" to numb them to the evils going on around them. In what sense is Isaiah saying something similar? What should be the result of worshiping God? **4.** Some define spirituality in personal moral terms, while others see it as a matter of working for social justice. Which better reflects your background? Your present church affiliation? How are both these concerns interrelated in this chapter? **5.** How is your church seeking justice and encouraging the oppressed in your community? What situations ought it to address? What risks would that entail? **6.** Someone has said, "Justice is finding out what belongs to whom and returning it to them." Another, "Justice is the act of instituting love for those people you don't know." How do you respond to these statements? How would you define justice? **7.** Why is Isaiah so hard-hitting in his message? How do you know when to use *shock treatment* as he does, or a *gentle word* without skirting the main issue, as does Jesus with the Samaritan woman (see Jn 4)?

I have no pleasure
  in the blood of bulls and lambs and goats.
¹²When you come to appear before me,
  who has asked this of you,
  this trampling of my courts?
¹³Stop bringing meaningless offerings!
  Your incense is detestable to me.
New Moons, Sabbaths and convocations—
  I cannot bear your evil assemblies.
¹⁴Your New Moon festivals and your appointed feasts
  my soul hates.
They have become a burden to me;
  I am weary of bearing them.
¹⁵When you spread out your hands in prayer,
  I will hide my eyes from you;
even if you offer many prayers,
  I will not listen.
Your hands are full of blood;
¹⁶ wash and make yourselves clean.
Take your evil deeds
  out of my sight!
Stop doing wrong,
¹⁷ learn to do right!
Seek justice,
  encourage the oppressed.ᵃ
Defend the cause of the fatherless,
  plead the case of the widow.

¹⁸"Come now, let us reason together,"
  says the LORD.
"Though your sins are like scarlet,
  they shall be as white as snow;
though they are red as crimson,
  they shall be like wool.
¹⁹If you are willing and obedient,
  you will eat the best from the land;
²⁰but if you resist and rebel,
  you will be devoured by the sword."
          For the mouth of the LORD has spoken.

²¹See how the faithful city
  has become a harlot!
She once was full of justice;
  righteousness used to dwell in her—
  but now murderers!
²²Your silver has become dross,
  your choice wine is diluted with water.
²³Your rulers are rebels,
  companions of thieves;
they all love bribes
  and chase after gifts.
They do not defend the cause of the fatherless;
  the widow's case does not come before them.
²⁴Therefore the Lord, the LORD Almighty,
  the Mighty One of Israel, declares:
"Ah, I will get relief from my foes
  and avenge myself on my enemies.

ᵃ 17 Or / rebuke the oppressor

²⁵I will turn my hand against you;
  I will thoroughly purge away your dross
    and remove all your impurities.
²⁶I will restore your judges as in days of old,
  your counselors as at the beginning.
    Afterward you will be called
      the City of Righteousness,
      the Faithful City."

²⁷Zion will be redeemed with justice,
  her penitent ones with righteousness.
²⁸But rebels and sinners will both be broken,
  and those who forsake the LORD will perish.

²⁹"You will be ashamed because of the sacred oaks
  in which you have delighted;
you will be disgraced because of the gardens
  that you have chosen.
³⁰You will be like an oak with fading leaves,
  like a garden without water.
³¹The mighty man will become tinder
  and his work a spark;
both will burn together,
  with no one to quench the fire."

The Mountain of the LORD

2 This is what Isaiah son of Amoz saw concerning Judah and Jerusalem:

²In the last days

  the mountain of the LORD's temple will be
    established
  as chief among the mountains;
it will be raised above the hills,
  and all nations will stream to it.

³Many peoples will come and say,

  "Come, let us go up to the mountain of the LORD,
    to the house of the God of Jacob.
He will teach us his ways,
  so that we may walk in his paths."
The law will go out from Zion,
  the word of the LORD from Jerusalem.
⁴He will judge between the nations
  and will settle disputes for many peoples.
They will beat their swords into plowshares
  and their spears into pruning hooks.
Nation will not take up sword against nation,
  nor will they train for war anymore.

⁵Come, O house of Jacob,
  let us walk in the light of the LORD.

The Day of the LORD

⁶You have abandoned your people,
  the house of Jacob.
They are full of superstitions from the East;
  they practice divination like the Philistines
  and clasp hands with pagans.
⁷Their land is full of silver and gold;
  there is no end to their treasures.

In your family, who is the explorer? The warrior? Peacemaker? Idealist? Realist?

1. "The mountain of the Lord" refers to the site upon which the temple in Jerusalem was built (11:9; 24:23; 27:13; 56:6–7). What picture does Isaiah envision? 2. Why are so many coming to the temple? What will God do for them? 3. What is meant by "the last days" (v. 2; see Ac 2:17; Heb 1:2)? Why does Isaiah call Judah to come to the temple *at this time*?

1. Which of your *swords and spears* (i.e., mean streak? angry outbursts? cutting tongue?) has God transformed into *tools for peace*? 2. What does the New Testament make of Isaiah's vision? Did, or will, Jesus inaugurate this era of peace? If so, when will it be fulfilled? Why do you think so? 3. How might this vision of God's kingdom shape your hope? Prayers? Values?

1. Of what "all by myself" project were you most proud as a child? Of what trophies are you most proud? Which ones are still on display? 2. Did you have a favorite hiding place in the house you grew up in? Or a getaway place now? Under what circumstances would you go there?

1. Isaiah returns from the vision of the future (vv. 1–5), to the reality of the present. What do verses 6–8 add to Isaiah's catalogue of sins in 1:21–23? 2. What makes the pagan practices (v. 6b) so awful to God? (See Dt 7:1–6; 18:9–13 and 2Ki 16:7–18, where King Ahaz is guilty of clasping hands with pagans.) What's wrong with kings accumulating horses, silver or gold (v. 7; see Dt 17:16–20)? 3. What is significant about Judah prostrating themselves before idols (vv. 8–9; see Dt 31:16–18)? 4. Verses 10–21 are a song of judgment against the people described in verses 6–8. What is the root cause of their sin? 5. What will the "Day of the Lord" be like for the proud (vv. 10,19,21)? What is their essential problem (v. 22)?

1. Despite the rise of the New Age movement, (occultism, witchcraft, etc.), what should be a Christian's response to these things? Why does God consider them so dangerous for us? 2. Some live as if "the one with the most toys in the end wins." What would Isaiah say to that slogan? In the conflict between serving God or money (v. 7; see Mt 6:24), which seems to be winning in your life this week? Why? 3. The proud, arrogant people are condemned in powerful images relevant to Isaiah's day (vv. 13–16). If Isaiah wrote this prophecy today, what symbols would he use? How do we "trust in man" today? 4. Isaiah anticipated that God's judgment would come via Assyria and, later, Babylon. John (in Rev 6:15–17) alludes to Isaiah's imagery as an apt description of the coming worldwide judgment of God. What do you need to change, so that you will not be one who is trying to hide from the Lord on that judgment day?

1. Tell three characteristics you look for in a political leader? 2. What effect has the "dress for success" mentality had on you? Are you dressing upscale or downscale as compared to several years ago?

Their land is full of horses;
   there is no end to their chariots.
[8]Their land is full of idols;
   they bow down to the work of their hands,
   to what their fingers have made.
[9]So man will be brought low
   and mankind humbled—
   do not forgive them.[a]

[10]Go into the rocks,
   hide in the ground
from dread of the LORD
   and the splendor of his majesty!
[11]The eyes of the arrogant man will be humbled
   and the pride of men brought low;
the LORD alone will be exalted in that day.

[12]The LORD Almighty has a day in store
   for all the proud and lofty,
   for all that is exalted
   (and they will be humbled),
[13]for all the cedars of Lebanon, tall and lofty,
   and all the oaks of Bashan,
[14]for all the towering mountains
   and all the high hills,
[15]for every lofty tower
   and every fortified wall,
[16]for every trading ship[b]
   and every stately vessel.
[17]The arrogance of man will be brought low
   and the pride of men humbled;
the LORD alone will be exalted in that day,
[18]   and the idols will totally disappear.

[19]Men will flee to caves in the rocks
   and to holes in the ground
from dread of the LORD
   and the splendor of his majesty,
   when he rises to shake the earth.
[20]In that day men will throw away
   to the rodents and bats
their idols of silver and idols of gold,
   which they made to worship.
[21]They will flee to caverns in the rocks
   and to the overhanging crags
from dread of the LORD
   and the splendor of his majesty,
   when he rises to shake the earth.

[22]Stop trusting in man,
   who has but a breath in his nostrils.
   Of what account is he?

Judgment on Jerusalem and Judah

3 See now, the Lord,
   the LORD Almighty,
is about to take from Jerusalem and Judah
   both supply and support:
all supplies of food and all supplies of water,

---

[a]9 Or *not raise them up*   [b]16 Hebrew *every ship of Tarshish*

² the hero and warrior,
  the judge and prophet,
    the soothsayer and elder,
³the captain of fifty and man of rank,
  the counselor, skilled craftsman and clever
    enchanter.

⁴I will make boys their officials;
  mere children will govern them.
⁵People will oppress each other—
  man against man, neighbor against neighbor.
The young will rise up against the old,
  the base against the honorable.

⁶A man will seize one of his brothers
  at his father's home, and say,
"You have a cloak, you be our leader;
  take charge of this heap of ruins!"
⁷But in that day he will cry out,
  "I have no remedy.
I have no food or clothing in my house;
  do not make me the leader of the people."

⁸Jerusalem staggers,
  Judah is falling;
their words and deeds are against the LORD,
  defying his glorious presence.
⁹The look on their faces testifies against them;
  they parade their sin like Sodom;
  they do not hide it.
Woe to them!
  They have brought disaster upon themselves.

¹⁰Tell the righteous it will be well with them,
  for they will enjoy the fruit of their deeds.
¹¹Woe to the wicked! Disaster is upon them!
  They will be paid back for what their hands have
    done.

¹²Youths oppress my people,
  women rule over them.
O my people, your guides lead you astray;
  they turn you from the path.

¹³The LORD takes his place in court;
  he rises to judge the people.
¹⁴The LORD enters into judgment
  against the elders and leaders of his people:
"It is you who have ruined my vineyard;
  the plunder from the poor is in your houses.
¹⁵What do you mean by crushing my people
  and grinding the faces of the poor?"
                declares the Lord, the LORD Almighty.

¹⁶The LORD says,
  "The women of Zion are haughty,
walking along with outstretched necks,
  flirting with their eyes,
tripping along with mincing steps,
  with ornaments jingling on their ankles.
¹⁷Therefore the Lord will bring sores on the heads
  of the women of Zion;
  the LORD will make their scalps bald."

1. The first part of this sermon is a more specific prophecy of the judgment that is coming upon Judah. What things make up their "supply and support" that the Lord is going to take away? 2. The soothsayer and clever enchanter should never have existed in a faithful Judah. What would happen to a society where all their partners in crime (3:2–3) were removed as well? 3. What types of social chaos would come about as a result of God's judgment (3:4–7)? If you lived during a time like this, what would you expect to see around you? How would you feel about your future? Your family? Your money? 4. What attitudes and actions precipitate God's judgment (3:8–15)? By what "legal" means might the leaders "plunder the poor"? 5. How are the women pictured in 3:16–24? What reference to their captivity do you see here? What judgment upon the men is really meant for the women (3:25–4:1)? How do you account for this (3:9)? Since being unmarried and childless was considered a disgrace, how is God's judgment appropriate to their sin? What contrasts do you see between 3:16; 3:24 and 4:1? 6. The "Branch of the Lord" (4:2–6) is the remnant of people who survive God's judgment. How does the remnant contrast with the leaders and women described in chapter 3? What will the Lord do for them? What does this show about God's purpose in judgment? 7. What is meant by "cloud … fire … shelter" (4:5–6; see Ex 13:21–22; 40:34–38)? What is the purpose of the canopy God will spread over those who come to him? What does Isaiah mean by being safe from "the heat of the day" and the "storm and rain"?

1. What examples come to mind of how poor people in your world are oppressed by "legal" means? For example, is it fair that inner city schools are generally inferior to suburban schools? Is busing the answer? Why or why not? 2. How do you see the haughty, self-centered attitudes (3:16ff) reflected in men and women around you? How does their idea of beauty compare with that of 1 Peter 3:3–4? Do you think such inner beauty applies to men, as well? 3. How have you tried to develop this inner beauty on your own? How has God's discipline of you led to growth and purity? 4. The "Branch

of the Lord" theme is used by Jesus (see Jn 15:1–8), as well as by other prophets (see Jer 23:5; 33:15; Zec 3:8; 6:12). How does Jesus' use of it differ from the way Isaiah uses it here? What does that say about who the true Branch of the Lord is? How do we become part of this Branch?

---

1. When you start a project (term paper, remodeling a house) with high hopes but it fails repeatedly, what do you do: Give up? Try again? Wait 'til next year? Why? **2.** What does your garden grow?

1. Put yourself in the place of the gardener in this song: What do you expect from your labors (v. 2)? How do you feel about the results? What would you do next year? **2.** If you were a gardener with an annual crop, how long would it take you to give up on that plot of land? What is God's purpose in asking the people to judge for themselves what he should do to the vineyard (vv. 3–4)? **3.** Verse 7 explains the song. What are some of the ways God cultivated and cared for Judah, the garden of his delight? What is one chief quality God expects to see in his people (see also 1:17)? How is the

18In that day the Lord will snatch away their finery: the bangles
and headbands and crescent necklaces, 19the earrings and bracelets
and veils, 20the headdresses and ankle chains and sashes, the perfume bottles and charms, 21the signet rings and nose rings, 22the
fine robes and the capes and cloaks, the purses 23and mirrors, and
the linen garments and tiaras and shawls.

24Instead of fragrance there will be a stench;
instead of a sash, a rope;
instead of well-dressed hair, baldness;
instead of fine clothing, sackcloth;
instead of beauty, branding.
25Your men will fall by the sword,
your warriors in battle.
26The gates of Zion will lament and mourn;
destitute, she will sit on the ground.

4 In that day seven women
will take hold of one man
and say, "We will eat our own food
and provide our own clothes;
only let us be called by your name.
Take away our disgrace!"

The Branch of the LORD

2In that day the Branch of the LORD will be beautiful and glorious,
and the fruit of the land will be the pride and glory of the survivors
in Israel. 3Those who are left in Zion, who remain in Jerusalem,
will be called holy, all who are recorded among the living in Jerusalem. 4The Lord will wash away the filth of the women of Zion; he
will cleanse the bloodstains from Jerusalem by a spirit[a] of judgment and a spirit[a] of fire. 5Then the LORD will create over all of
Mount Zion and over those who assemble there a cloud of smoke
by day and a glow of flaming fire by night; over all the glory will be
a canopy. 6It will be a shelter and shade from the heat of the day,
and a refuge and hiding place from the storm and rain.

The Song of the Vineyard

5 I will sing for the one I love
a song about his vineyard:
My loved one had a vineyard
on a fertile hillside.
2He dug it up and cleared it of stones
and planted it with the choicest vines.
He built a watchtower in it
and cut out a winepress as well.
Then he looked for a crop of good grapes,
but it yielded only bad fruit.

3"Now you dwellers in Jerusalem and men of
Judah,
judge between me and my vineyard.
4What more could have been done for my vineyard
than I have done for it?
When I looked for good grapes,
why did it yield only bad?
5Now I will tell you
what I am going to do to my vineyard:
I will take away its hedge,

a4 Or *the Spirit*

and it will be destroyed;
I will break down its wall,
    and it will be trampled.
[6]I will make it a wasteland,
    neither pruned nor cultivated,
    and briers and thorns will grow there.
I will command the clouds
    not to rain on it."

[7]The vineyard of the LORD Almighty
    is the house of Israel,
and the men of Judah
    are the garden of his delight.
And he looked for justice, but saw bloodshed;
    for righteousness, but heard cries of distress.

Woes and Judgments

[8]Woe to you who add house to house
    and join field to field
till no space is left
    and you live alone in the land.

[9]The LORD Almighty has declared in my hearing:

"Surely the great houses will become desolate,
    the fine mansions left without occupants.
[10]A ten-acre[a] vineyard will produce only a bath[b]
    of wine,
    a homer[c] of seed only an ephah[d] of grain."

[11]Woe to those who rise early in the morning
    to run after their drinks,
who stay up late at night
    till they are inflamed with wine.
[12]They have harps and lyres at their banquets,
    tambourines and flutes and wine,
but they have no regard for the deeds of the LORD,
    no respect for the work of his hands.
[13]Therefore my people will go into exile
    for lack of understanding;
their men of rank will die of hunger
    and their masses will be parched with thirst.
[14]Therefore the grave[e] enlarges its appetite
    and opens its mouth without limit;
into it will descend their nobles and masses
    with all their brawlers and revelers.
[15]So man will be brought low
    and mankind humbled,
    the eyes of the arrogant humbled.
[16]But the LORD Almighty will be exalted by his
    justice,
    and the holy God will show himself holy by his
    righteousness.
[17]Then sheep will graze as in their own pasture;
    lambs will feed[f] among the ruins of the rich.

[18]Woe to those who draw sin along with cords of
    deceit,

"fruit" that has grown different from
what he expected?

1. What are some of the
"fruits" people use today to
evaluate how spiritual a person is?
How do these compare with what
God looks for in a growing church
(see Mt 21:33–44; Jn 15:1–3; Gal
5:22–23)? 2. How would you assess the
"fruit" in your life: (a) Just
budding? (b) Still premature? (c)
Developing on schedule? (d) Ripe
for enjoyment? (e) Diseased?

1. When someone "let you
have it" for all the things they
held against you, how did you feel?
What did you do? 2. Where you live
and work, are you among the "nobles"
or the "masses"? Why?

1. This sermon elaborates
what God said about the condition
of the people in verse 7.
What have the people in the first
woe (v. 8) done that is so offensive
to the Lord (see also 3:14–15)? 2.
How would you react if you reaped
only a tenth of what you had sown
(v. 10)? How does this curse contrast
with the promise of blessing in
Amos 9:13–15? Why will judgment
come upon these people? 3. Who
gets hit with the second woe and
why (vv. 11–17)? How contemporary
does their lifestyle sound to
you? What are their offenses?
Does their judgment seem appropriate?
4. What role reversal do
you see in the fate of the "arrogant"
(v. 15) and that of the "lambs" and
"sheep" (v. 17)? Who's who in this
portrait of justice? 5. Who gets hit
with the third woe and why (vv.
18–19)? In today's images, how
would you describe what they are
doing with these "cords of deceit"?
What sarcasm do you hear between
the lines? 6. How would you
describe the sin of those deserving
the fourth woe (v. 20)? The fifth
woe (v. 21)? How do they relate?
What effect would these woeful
people have on others who tried to
follow after God's ways? 7. Although
the sixth woe (vv. 22–24)
starts off in a similar way to that in
verses 11–17, what is the focus of
God's judgment here? How does
Isaiah emphasize the completeness
of the judgment they will
face? On what grounds will that
judgment come? 8. Verse 25 sums
up God's anger against all the "bad
fruit" described so far. If judgment

---

[a]10 Hebrew *ten-yoke,* that is, the land plowed by 10 yoke of oxen in one day
[b]10 That is, probably about 6 gallons (about 22 liters)   [c]10 That is, probably about 6
bushels (about 220 liters)   [d]10 That is, probably about 3/5 bushel (about 22 liters)
[e]14 Hebrew *Sheol*   [f]17 Septuagint; Hebrew / *strangers will eat*

has already come to Judah (1:5–7), why is yet more punishment necessary? What will be the climactic judgment they have to face (vv. 26–30)? What are these invaders like? **9.** How will this prophecy be fulfilled by Assyria during Isaiah's lifetime (see 2Ki 18:17–25) and later by Babylon (see 2Ki 25:1–7)?

1. Which one of these woes gets you cheering, "Hit 'em again, harder … harder!"? Is there any particular person or group where you live or work whom you would like to see get their due punishment? **2.** Which of these woes could make *you* say, "Woe is me!"? Why that one? **3.** "Trading places" is a common fantasy many poor people have in their view of the rich. Are there any rich in whose "pasture" you'd love to graze, as do the sheep and lambs in God's great reversal (v. 17)? In your society, what are some compelling examples of evil which others call good and vice versa (v. 20): Pornography? Abortion? Cheating on your spouse? Cheating on your taxes? On exams? Getting rich at the expense of the poor? **4.** What lessons from war do you think God wants you to learn? **5.** Does the woeful reality of chapter 5 make you hunger all the more for the hopeful vision of 2:1–4? Why is it some people never appreciate the good news of peace without first hearing the bad news of war?

and wickedness as with cart ropes,
[19]to those who say, "Let God hurry,
    let him hasten his work
    so we may see it.
Let it approach,
    let the plan of the Holy One of Israel come,
    so we may know it."

[20]Woe to those who call evil good
    and good evil,
who put darkness for light
    and light for darkness,
who put bitter for sweet
    and sweet for bitter.

[21]Woe to those who are wise in their own eyes
    and clever in their own sight.

[22]Woe to those who are heroes at drinking wine
    and champions at mixing drinks,
[23]who acquit the guilty for a bribe,
    but deny justice to the innocent.
[24]Therefore, as tongues of fire lick up straw
    and as dry grass sinks down in the flames,
so their roots will decay
    and their flowers blow away like dust;
for they have rejected the law of the LORD Almighty
    and spurned the word of the Holy One of Israel.
[25]Therefore the LORD's anger burns against his people;
    his hand is raised and he strikes them down.
The mountains shake,
    and the dead bodies are like refuse in the streets.

Yet for all this, his anger is not turned away,
    his hand is still upraised.

[26]He lifts up a banner for the distant nations,
    he whistles for those at the ends of the earth.
Here they come,
    swiftly and speedily!
[27]Not one of them grows tired or stumbles,
    not one slumbers or sleeps;
not a belt is loosened at the waist,
    not a sandal thong is broken.
[28]Their arrows are sharp,
    all their bows are strung;
their horses' hoofs seem like flint,
    their chariot wheels like a whirlwind.
[29]Their roar is like that of the lion,
    they roar like young lions;
they growl as they seize their prey
    and carry it off with no one to rescue.
[30]In that day they will roar over it
    like the roaring of the sea.
And if one looks at the land,
    he will see darkness and distress;
    even the light will be darkened by the clouds.

Isaiah's Commission

6 In the year that King Uzziah died, I saw the Lord seated on a throne, high and exalted, and the train of his robe filled the temple. ²Above him were seraphs, each with six wings: With two wings they covered their faces, with two they covered their feet, and with two they were flying. ³And they were calling to one another:

> "Holy, holy, holy is the LORD Almighty;
>   the whole earth is full of his glory."

⁴At the sound of their voices the doorposts and thresholds shook and the temple was filled with smoke.

⁵"Woe to me!" I cried. "I am ruined! For I am a man of unclean lips, and I live among a people of unclean lips, and my eyes have seen the King, the LORD Almighty."

⁶Then one of the seraphs flew to me with a live coal in his hand, which he had taken with tongs from the altar. ⁷With it he touched my mouth and said, "See, this has touched your lips; your guilt is taken away and your sin atoned for."

⁸Then I heard the voice of the Lord saying, "Whom shall I send? And who will go for us?"

And I said, "Here am I. Send me!"

⁹He said, "Go and tell this people:

> "'Be ever hearing, but never understanding;
>   be ever seeing, but never perceiving.'
> ¹⁰Make the heart of this people calloused;
>   make their ears dull
>   and close their eyes.ᵃ
> Otherwise they might see with their eyes,
>   hear with their ears,
>   understand with their hearts,
>   and turn and be healed."

¹¹Then I said, "For how long, O Lord?"

And he answered:

> "Until the cities lie ruined
>   and without inhabitant,
> until the houses are left deserted
>   and the fields ruined and ravaged,
> ¹²until the LORD has sent everyone far away
>   and the land is utterly forsaken.
> ¹³And though a tenth remains in the land,
>   it will again be laid waste.
> But as the terebinth and oak
>   leave stumps when they are cut down,
>   so the holy seed will be the stump in the land."

The Sign of Immanuel

7 When Ahaz son of Jotham, the son of Uzziah, was king of Judah, King Rezin of Aram and Pekah son of Remaliah king of Israel marched up to fight against Jerusalem, but they could not overpower it.

²Now the house of David was told, "Aram has allied itself withᵇ

ᵃ9,10 Hebrew; Septuagint *'You will be ever hearing, but never understanding; / you will be ever seeing, but never perceiving.' / ¹⁰This people's heart has become calloused; / they hardly hear with their ears, / and they have closed their eyes*   ᵇ2 Or *has set up camp in*

---

1. When were you last called into the office of your chief principal or boss's boss? What for? How did that affect you? 2. What volunteer ministries have you been involved with? How were you recruited?

1. If King Uzziah represents stability to Judah, what does his death mean? Why does God choose this time to reveal himself to Isaiah? 2. Imagine you are Isaiah. What do you tell a friend about what you saw, heard, felt and smelled in verses 1–4? 3. What questions about God's nature and purpose does this encounter raise for you? 4. What makes Isaiah despair for his life and confess his sin (v. 5; see Ex 20:19; 33:20)? 5. Animals were burned on the altar as a substitute for the death of the sinner. What is the significance of Isaiah's lips being touched with a coal from this altar? 6. Compare Isaiah's response in verse 8 with verse 5. What is significant about that? 7. What is Isaiah's new mission (vv. 9–10). What effect will it have on Judah? Is this what God *wants* to happen? Or an ironic statement of what God knows *will* happen? 8. What does "But" (v. 13b) signify? How does the stump in verse 13 relate to the Branch (4:2–6)?

1. How is your experience with God like Isaiah's: Awestruck? Guilt-ridden? Cleansed? Are you willing to serve anywhere, anytime? 2. God's holiness and universal reign awed Isaiah. Which of God's attributes most impresses you? Why? 3. John 12:40–41 relates this vision to Jesus. How is Jesus' glory like the suffering and healing Isaiah saw? 4. Why has God sent *you* to your world?

---

1. Picture yourself at age 12–13: Where were you living? Who were your heroes? 2. What experience, if any, have you had with special diets? K-rations? Dorm food? Foraging for food? Surviving without much food?

1. The events here occur in Ahaz' reign, some 10–16 years after those of chapter 6 (see 2Ki 16:5–18)? What danger was

threatening him now (vv. 1–6)? (Note: this is known in history books as the Syro-Ephraimite War of 735/734 B.C.) **2.** What is the point of discussing the various "heads" (vv. 8–9) in relation to the head of Judah (v. 14)? Is this a cause for alarm or comfort? **3.** Ahaz was known as an evil king, so what do you make of his response here (v. 12)? Was this unbelief or humility? What was his alternative plan (see 2Ki 16:7–9)? **4.** What is the sign that the Lord will give to Ahaz anyway? How does this sign fit the crisis? Can a *comforting* sign also *warn*? Instead of peace, what will happen once Israel and Aram are out of the picture? **5.** What images does Isaiah use in verses 18–25 to show what Assyria will do to Judah? Which one is the most graphic to you? What do you make of the "curds and honey" imagery?

1. What situation are you facing that frightens you now? What forces are involved? How trusting of God are you in that situation? What makes it difficult for you to trust God in such fearful times? **2.** When have you found that following *your* solution to a problem, rather than God's, only made the problem worse? **3.** Ahaz masked his lack of trust in God with false humility. What examples have you seen of people covering up their sin with a veneer of virtue? When was the last time you did this? **4.** Since Ahaz was a bad king all along, what does it mean to you that God would still desire to give him a sign of his mercy? How does Ahaz' refusal serve as a warning to you? **5.** Matthew 1:23 shows that Jesus fulfilled the prophecy in verse 14 far more than any child in Ahaz' day could have. When facing a challenging crisis, how have you seen Jesus as "Immanuel" ("God with us")?

Ephraim"; so the hearts of Ahaz and his people were shaken, as the trees of the forest are shaken by the wind.

³Then the LORD said to Isaiah, "Go out, you and your son Shear-Jashub,ᵃ to meet Ahaz at the end of the aqueduct of the Upper Pool, on the road to the Washerman's Field. ⁴Say to him, 'Be careful, keep calm and don't be afraid. Do not lose heart because of these two smoldering stubs of firewood—because of the fierce anger of Rezin and Aram and of the son of Remaliah. ⁵Aram, Ephraim and Remaliah's son have plotted your ruin, saying, ⁶"Let us invade Judah; let us tear it apart and divide it among ourselves, and make the son of Tabeel king over it." ⁷Yet this is what the Sovereign LORD says:

> " 'It will not take place,
>   it will not happen,
> ⁸for the head of Aram is Damascus,
>   and the head of Damascus is only Rezin.
> Within sixty-five years
>   Ephraim will be too shattered to be a people.
> ⁹The head of Ephraim is Samaria,
>   and the head of Samaria is only Remaliah's son.
> If you do not stand firm in your faith,
>   you will not stand at all.' "

¹⁰Again the LORD spoke to Ahaz, ¹¹"Ask the LORD your God for a sign, whether in the deepest depths or in the highest heights."

¹²But Ahaz said, "I will not ask; I will not put the LORD to the test."

¹³Then Isaiah said, "Hear now, you house of David! Is it not enough to try the patience of men? Will you try the patience of my God also? ¹⁴Therefore the Lord himself will give youᵇ a sign: The virgin will be with child and will give birth to a son, andᶜ will call him Immanuel.ᵈ ¹⁵He will eat curds and honey when he knows enough to reject the wrong and choose the right. ¹⁶But before the boy knows enough to reject the wrong and choose the right, the land of the two kings you dread will be laid waste. ¹⁷The LORD will bring on you and on your people and on the house of your father a time unlike any since Ephraim broke away from Judah—he will bring the king of Assyria."

¹⁸In that day the LORD will whistle for flies from the distant streams of Egypt and for bees from the land of Assyria. ¹⁹They will all come and settle in the steep ravines and in the crevices in the rocks, on all the thornbushes and at all the water holes. ²⁰In that day the Lord will use a razor hired from beyond the Riverᵉ—the king of Assyria—to shave your head and the hair of your legs, and to take off your beards also. ²¹In that day, a man will keep alive a young cow and two goats. ²²And because of the abundance of the milk they give, he will have curds to eat. All who remain in the land will eat curds and honey. ²³In that day, in every place where there were a thousand vines worth a thousand silver shekels,ᶠ there will be only briers and thorns. ²⁴Men will go there with bow and arrow, for the land will be covered with briers and thorns. ²⁵As for all the hills once cultivated by the hoe, you will no longer go there for fear of the briers and thorns; they will become places where cattle are turned loose and where sheep run.

ᵃ3 *Shear-Jashub* means *a remnant will return.*   ᵇ14 The Hebrew is plural.   ᶜ14 Masoretic Text; Dead Sea Scrolls *and he* or *and they*   ᵈ14 *Immanuel* means *God with us.*   ᵉ20 That is, the Euphrates   ᶠ23 That is, about 25 pounds (about 11.5 kilograms)

Assyria, the LORD's Instrument

8 The LORD said to me, "Take a large scroll and write on it with an ordinary pen: Maher-Shalal-Hash-Baz.*a* ²And I will call in Uriah the priest and Zechariah son of Jeberekiah as reliable witnesses for me."

³Then I went to the prophetess, and she conceived and gave birth to a son. And the LORD said to me, "Name him Maher-Shalal-Hash-Baz. ⁴Before the boy knows how to say 'My father' or 'My mother,' the wealth of Damascus and the plunder of Samaria will be carried off by the king of Assyria."

⁵The LORD spoke to me again:

⁶"Because this people has rejected
    the gently flowing waters of Shiloah
and rejoices over Rezin
    and the son of Remaliah,
⁷therefore the Lord is about to bring against them
    the mighty floodwaters of the River*b*—
    the king of Assyria with all his pomp.
It will overflow all its channels,
    run over all its banks
⁸and sweep on into Judah, swirling over it,
    passing through it and reaching up to the neck.
Its outspread wings will cover the breadth of your
    land,
    O Immanuel*c*!"

⁹Raise the war cry,*d* you nations, and be
    shattered!
    Listen, all you distant lands.
Prepare for battle, and be shattered!
Prepare for battle, and be shattered!
¹⁰Devise your strategy, but it will be thwarted;
    propose your plan, but it will not stand,
    for God is with us.*e*

Fear God

¹¹The LORD spoke to me with his strong hand upon me, warning me not to follow the way of this people. He said:

¹²"Do not call conspiracy
    everything that these people call conspiracy*f*;
do not fear what they fear,
    and do not dread it.
¹³The LORD Almighty is the one you are to regard as
    holy,
he is the one you are to fear,
    he is the one you are to dread,
¹⁴and he will be a sanctuary;
    but for both houses of Israel he will be
    a stone that causes men to stumble
    and a rock that makes them fall.
And for the people of Jerusalem he will be
    a trap and a snare.
¹⁵Many of them will stumble;

a1 Maher-Shalal-Hash-Baz means *quick to the plunder, swift to the spoil*; also in verse 3.
b7 That is, the Euphrates   *c8 Immanuel* means *God with us.*   *d9* Or *Do your worst*   *e10* Hebrew *Immanuel*   *f12* Or *Do not call for a treaty / every time these people call for a treaty*

---

1. Whom were you named after? What does your full name mean? 2. When have you been afraid of water and why?

1. What do the names of Isaiah's two sons (7:3 and 8:3) symbolize in the context of chapters 7–8? 2. What do the "waters of Shiloah" in Jerusalem and the river Euphrates in Assyria represent? What then is the meaning of Judah "rejecting" Shiloah and "rejoicing" over Rezin (vv. 6–7; see 7:1), resulting in a sweeping flood? Why does Judah prefer Assyrian help over God's as they face this crisis (see 2Ki 16:7–9)? Why would idolatry lead to destructive political alliances? 3. Is "O Immanuel" (vv. 8,10) a cry of *despair* or of *hope*? Why? What is the prophet's hope for Judah, even as he considers the coming siege from Assyria (see ch. 36–37)?

1. How has the Lord been like a gently flowing stream to you? When has your choice of allies resulted in a flood of overwhelming trouble? When has God stopped the flood of wrong choices from overwhelming you? 2. What "Rezin's" and overflowing "Rivers" do people today flee from? Which affect you?

---

1. When have you been afraid of the dark and why? How did you get over that fear? 2. What funny or fearful experience have you had with blackouts?

1. From 7:2–4 and 8:6, what is the "way of this people" God told Isaiah not to follow? What do they fear contrasted with what Isaiah fears? 2. What effects do these fears have on the way each acts? On God's response? 3. How does Isaiah respond to Judah's rejection of his message? How is his family a *sign* and *symbol* from the Lord (v. 18; see v. 3; 7:3,14)? 4. How does Isaiah bring out the contrast between mediums and spiritists and God? What should the people be seeking? What "blackout" will result from their refusal to do so?

1. What fears could motivate your agnostic friends to consider God: Job loss? Stock loss?

Emotional blackout? Serious illness? If you have no agnostic friends, why is that? **2.** From watching your life this week, what would someone say it means for you to fear God? What does it really mean to fear God? **3.** How is Jesus both a "sanctuary" and a "stumbling block" (v. 14; see Ro 9:33; 1Pe 2:6–8)? Which is he to you right now? **4.** What does the rise of the New Age movement (occultism and spiritism) tell you about people's spiritual hunger today? What would Isaiah say to those involved?

1. When were you most in need of, or grateful for, a flashlight? **2.** When have you gotten up early to greet the sunrise? What "dawn of a new day" are you anticipating on this year's calendar?

1. From 8:19–22, what do you think Isaiah meant by the "darkness" in which the people walk (v. 2)? What suffering had Zebulun and Naphtali (in Israel) experienced? **2.** How does Isaiah describe the effects of the dawning light (vv. 3–5; see Jdg 7:19–25 for Midian's defeat)? In the context of the Assyrian threat, what does this light mean (see 10:26–27)? **3.** What will be the light? How is he defined in verses 6–7? **4.** What expectations would this arouse in you if you had first heard Isaiah pronounce it? What type of son or ruler would you expect to arise? How would his future rule and counsel compare with past alliances and plans (see 8:7–10)? How would this make you feel?

1. How does the New Testament interpret what this prophecy means (see Mt 4:12–17; Lk 1:32; Jn 8:12)? Of the titles given in verse 6, which fit Jesus as you know him? **2.** What is the purpose of his reign in your life? In the world? What does it mean that there will be no end to the "increase and peace" of his reign? **3.** How has he shattered some of the "yokes that burden" you? What is one yoke that you desire to have him shatter now?

they will fall and be broken,
　they will be snared and captured."

[16]Bind up the testimony
　and seal up the law among my disciples.
[17]I will wait for the LORD,
　who is hiding his face from the house of Jacob.
　I will put my trust in him.

[18]Here am I, and the children the LORD has given me. We are signs and symbols in Israel from the LORD Almighty, who dwells on Mount Zion.

[19]When men tell you to consult mediums and spiritists, who whisper and mutter, should not a people inquire of their God? Why consult the dead on behalf of the living? [20]To the law and to the testimony! If they do not speak according to this word, they have no light of dawn. [21]Distressed and hungry, they will roam through the land; when they are famished, they will become enraged and, looking upward, will curse their king and their God. [22]Then they will look toward the earth and see only distress and darkness and fearful gloom, and they will be thrust into utter darkness.

To Us a Child Is Born

9 Nevertheless, there will be no more gloom for those who were in distress. In the past he humbled the land of Zebulun and the land of Naphtali, but in the future he will honor Galilee of the Gentiles, by the way of the sea, along the Jordan—

[2]The people walking in darkness
　have seen a great light;
on those living in the land of the shadow of
　　death[a]
　a light has dawned.
[3]You have enlarged the nation
　and increased their joy;
they rejoice before you
　as people rejoice at the harvest,
as men rejoice
　when dividing the plunder.
[4]For as in the day of Midian's defeat,
　you have shattered
the yoke that burdens them,
　the bar across their shoulders,
　the rod of their oppressor.
[5]Every warrior's boot used in battle
　and every garment rolled in blood
will be destined for burning,
　will be fuel for the fire.
[6]For to us a child is born,
　to us a son is given,
　and the government will be on his shoulders.
And he will be called
　Wonderful Counselor,[b] Mighty God,
　Everlasting Father, Prince of Peace.
[7]Of the increase of his government and peace
　there will be no end.
He will reign on David's throne
　and over his kingdom,
establishing and upholding it

---

[a]2 Or *land of darkness*　　[b]6 Or *Wonderful, Counselor*

with justice and righteousness
  from that time on and forever.
The zeal of the LORD Almighty
  will accomplish this.

The LORD's Anger Against Israel

[8]The Lord has sent a message against Jacob;
  it will fall on Israel.
[9]All the people will know it—
  Ephraim and the inhabitants of Samaria—
who say with pride
  and arrogance of heart,
[10]"The bricks have fallen down,
  but we will rebuild with dressed stone;
the fig trees have been felled,
  but we will replace them with cedars."
[11]But the LORD has strengthened Rezin's foes against
      them
  and has spurred their enemies on.
[12]Arameans from the east and Philistines from the
      west
  have devoured Israel with open mouth.

Yet for all this, his anger is not turned away,
  his hand is still upraised.

[13]But the people have not returned to him who
      struck them,
  nor have they sought the LORD Almighty.
[14]So the LORD will cut off from Israel both head and
      tail,
  both palm branch and reed in a single day;
[15]the elders and prominent men are the head,
  the prophets who teach lies are the tail.
[16]Those who guide this people mislead them,
  and those who are guided are led astray.
[17]Therefore the Lord will take no pleasure in the
      young men,
  nor will he pity the fatherless and widows,
for everyone is ungodly and wicked,
  every mouth speaks vileness.

Yet for all this, his anger is not turned away,
  his hand is still upraised.

[18]Surely wickedness burns like a fire;
  it consumes briers and thorns,
it sets the forest thickets ablaze,
  so that it rolls upward in a column of smoke.
[19]By the wrath of the LORD Almighty
  the land will be scorched
and the people will be fuel for the fire;
  no one will spare his brother.
[20]On the right they will devour,
  but still be hungry;
on the left they will eat,
  but not be satisfied.
Each will feed on the flesh of his own offspring[a]:

[a]20 Or arm

1. When have you boastfully thought something would turn out fine, but it didn't? 2. Have you ever felt a decision was rigged against you: "Heads I win, tails you lose"?

1. The repetition in 9:12,17,21, and 10:4 shows that this is a poem or song. From this refrain, what do you think the song is about? 2. From verses 10–11 (with 7:1), what must have happened in Israel? (Note: The opposition of King Rezin of Aram in vv. 11–12 indicates this prophecy was given *prior* to the alliance described in 7:1.) How *did* the people of Israel (Ephraim and Samaria) respond to these attacks (9:9,10,13)? How *should* they have responded? 3. Hence, what will God do to their leaders (9:14–17)? With what result? 4. What pictures come to mind as Isaiah describes the wickedness of the people (9:18–20)? What is the point of comparing their wickedness to a raging forest fire or people eating up their own family? 5. What are the specific charges God lays against the leaders of Israel (10:1–2)? What will be the result of refusing to provide justice and peace for the people? How is the finality of this judgment emphasized? (See 2Ki 17, where in 722 B.C., Israel as a nation was totally destroyed by Assyria.)

1. From this song, what attitudes and actions do you see that are particularly offensive to God? Which ones do you feel are evident in your life? In the life of your nation? 2. God's final judgment came only after many attempts to warn the people about the consequences of their deeds. How has God tried to warn you in the past of the consequences of where you were heading? How did you respond to those warnings? 3. What signs do you see today that God still cleans house, beginning with his own people? How might allowing the effects of wickedness to grow actually serve as part of God's judgment upon that evil (compare Ro 1:21–27)? 4. What is one area of injustice or neglect of the poor in your community or nation that you could work on correcting: Tax reform? Housing? Health

care? Race relations? Abuse victims? Or what? What keeps you from doing so?

²¹ Manasseh will feed on Ephraim, and Ephraim
　　on Manasseh;
　　together they will turn against Judah.

Yet for all this, his anger is not turned away,
　　his hand is still upraised.

10 Woe to those who make unjust laws,
　　to those who issue oppressive decrees,
²to deprive the poor of their rights
　　and withhold justice from the oppressed of my
　　　　people,
making widows their prey
　　and robbing the fatherless.
³What will you do on the day of reckoning,
　　when disaster comes from afar?
To whom will you run for help?
　　Where will you leave your riches?
⁴Nothing will remain but to cringe among the
　　　　captives
or fall among the slain.

Yet for all this, his anger is not turned away,
　　his hand is still upraised.

God's Judgment on Assyria

⁵"Woe to the Assyrian, the rod of my anger,
　　in whose hand is the club of my wrath!
⁶I send him against a godless nation,
　　I dispatch him against a people who anger me,
to seize loot and snatch plunder,
　　and to trample them down like mud in the
　　　　streets.
⁷But this is not what he intends,
　　this is not what he has in mind;
his purpose is to destroy,
　　to put an end to many nations.
⁸'Are not my commanders all kings?' he says.
⁹　'Has not Calno fared like Carchemish?
Is not Hamath like Arpad,
　　and Samaria like Damascus?
¹⁰As my hand seized the kingdoms of the idols,
　　kingdoms whose images excelled those of
　　　　Jerusalem and Samaria—
¹¹shall I not deal with Jerusalem and her images
　　as I dealt with Samaria and her idols?' "

¹²When the Lord has finished all his work against Mount Zion
and Jerusalem, he will say, "I will punish the king of Assyria for the
willful pride of his heart and the haughty look in his eyes. ¹³For he
says:

" 'By the strength of my hand I have done this,
　　and by my wisdom, because I have
　　　　understanding.
I removed the boundaries of nations,
　　I plundered their treasures;
like a mighty one I subdued^a their kings.
¹⁴As one reaches into a nest,

Who was the bully in your grade school, neighborhood or family who pushed you around with apparent impunity? How did you feel about that? Whatever became of that person?

1. While 9:8–10:4 conveys God's judgment against Israel, what is the focus of his judgment here? What was God's purpose in allowing Assyria to overrun Israel and Judah (vv. 5–6; see 7:17)? 2. The cities listed in verse 9 are all conquered by the Assyrian army en route to Jerusalem. What attitudes have these victories produced in the Assyrian leaders (vv. 10–11)? Why do they think Jerusalem ought to be an easy victory? What does this show about their deep misunderstanding of the Lord? 3. Read aloud verses 13–14, accenting the tone of voice and attitude expressed in the many times "I" and "my" are used. What root problem does this reveal? According to the absurd picture in verse 15, what have they got backwards? 4. What is the Lord's response to their pride? Compare verse 16 with 37:36. What do you think happened here? 5. How is God both like a *light* and a *fire* (vv. 16–19)? What truth about God is expressed in each idea?

1. When have you taken the credit for what was really God's work and you were merely his instrument? How do you prac-

so my hand reached for the wealth of the
nations;
as men gather abandoned eggs,
so I gathered all the countries;
not one flapped a wing,
or opened its mouth to chirp.' "

[15]Does the ax raise itself above him who swings it,
or the saw boast against him who uses it?
As if a rod were to wield him who lifts it up,
or a club brandish him who is not wood!
[16]Therefore, the Lord, the LORD Almighty,
will send a wasting disease upon his sturdy
warriors;
under his pomp a fire will be kindled
like a blazing flame.
[17]The Light of Israel will become a fire,
their Holy One a flame;
in a single day it will burn and consume
his thorns and his briers.
[18]The splendor of his forests and fertile fields
it will completely destroy,
as when a sick man wastes away.
[19]And the remaining trees of his forests will be so
few
that a child could write them down.

The Remnant of Israel

[20]In that day the remnant of Israel,
the survivors of the house of Jacob,
will no longer rely on him
who struck them down
but will truly rely on the LORD,
the Holy One of Israel.
[21]A remnant will return,[a] a remnant of Jacob
will return to the Mighty God.
[22]Though your people, O Israel, be like the sand by
the sea,
only a remnant will return.
Destruction has been decreed,
overwhelming and righteous.
[23]The Lord, the LORD Almighty, will carry out
the destruction decreed upon the whole land.

[24]Therefore, this is what the Lord, the LORD Almighty, says:

"O my people who live in Zion,
do not be afraid of the Assyrians,
who beat you with a rod
and lift up a club against you, as Egypt did.
[25]Very soon my anger against you will end
and my wrath will be directed to their
destruction."

[26]The LORD Almighty will lash them with a whip,
as when he struck down Midian at the rock of
Oreb;
and he will raise his staff over the waters,
as he did in Egypt.

[a]21 Hebrew shear-jashub; also in verse 22

tice giving credit where credit is due? Would you rather judge or be judged? Why? **2.** What are the "Assyrian armies" in which people today place their trust instead of God? How have you seen that trust backfire in betrayal? Where are you now finding it easier to trust an "Assyrian army" rather than God? **3.** Does God seem more like a guiding *Light*, or a consuming *Fire* to you right now? How so? When have you experienced him in the other way? What have you learned about God from these experiences?

1. What remnants do you have more of in your house: Food? Carpets? Clothing? Other? What do you plan on doing with them? **2.** What do you fear might happen on that "Day of Reckoning": Job loss? Market crash? Marriage failure? Other? What is the basis for your fears?

1. Judah originally looked to Assyria to help them (2Ki 16:7). What will result from this experience? What price is paid for this object lesson? **2.** The "remnant" theme has appeared before (see 1:9; 4:3; 6:13). How does this theme show both God's judgment and his mercy? What attitudes characterize the "remnant of Israel"? **3.** In verses 24–27, what hope does Isaiah provide for the people even before these events occur? How do the stories of Gideon (Jdg 7) and Moses (Ex 14:21ff) boost their hope? **4.** Verses 28–32 recount an army's hypothetical approach from a point about 10 miles north of Jerusalem. Substitute names of cities and towns near you. How does this help you to understand what the author wants the people of Jerusalem to feel? To do? **5.** What will God do to this army (vv. 33–34)? How do you feel after God's intervention?

♡ Isaiah looked back to the stories of Moses and Gideon to provide hope for the people. What stories of God's grace and deliverance—both Biblical and contemporary—can you look back upon to find hope in times when it is hard to trust God? How have you seen God cut down an "Assyrian army" that has threatened to overwhelm you? What "army" seems to be breathing down your neck now?

☕ 1. Who was your hero when you were 10 years old? Was he or she fictional or real? What was your hero able to do that you couldn't? 2. What do you like most about coming home after being away a long time?

📖 1. Whereas the *mighty tree of Assyria* was destroyed (10:33–34), what will happen to the *roots of Jesse* (Israel)? How is this "Branch" different from that mentioned in 4:2? 2. What does it mean that "the Spirit of the Lord will rest on him" (vv. 2–3a; see 2Ki 2:15)? What supernatural knowledge, ability or motivation do you see here? 3. What will his reign be like (vv. 3b–5; compare 9:6–7; contrast 1:17–23 and 5:12–23)? 4. Verses 6–9 figuratively portray the peaceable kingdom. What types of people or situations may Isaiah have in mind here (see 19:23–25)? What does this scene tell you about human relationships under the rule of this King? About the cause and extent of his reign? 5. Armies rally round a raised banner. Who will rally here? What will be the result (v. 12; see 32:16–18)? Once before, God saved his people by the Exodus. How will this happen a second time? 6. How might verses 11–12 relate to the imagery of

²⁷In that day their burden will be lifted from your shoulders,
    their yoke from your neck;
the yoke will be broken
    because you have grown so fat.ᵃ

²⁸They enter Aiath;
    they pass through Migron;
    they store supplies at Micmash.
²⁹They go over the pass, and say,
    "We will camp overnight at Geba."
Ramah trembles;
    Gibeah of Saul flees.
³⁰Cry out, O Daughter of Gallim!
    Listen, O Laishah!
    Poor Anathoth!
³¹Madmenah is in flight;
    the people of Gebim take cover.
³²This day they will halt at Nob;
    they will shake their fist
at the mount of the Daughter of Zion,
    at the hill of Jerusalem.

³³See, the Lord, the LORD Almighty,
    will lop off the boughs with great power.
The lofty trees will be felled,
    the tall ones will be brought low.
³⁴He will cut down the forest thickets with an ax;
    Lebanon will fall before the Mighty One.

The Branch From Jesse

11 A shoot will come up from the stump of Jesse;
    from his roots a Branch will bear fruit.
²The Spirit of the LORD will rest on him—
    the Spirit of wisdom and of understanding,
    the Spirit of counsel and of power,
    the Spirit of knowledge and of the fear of the
    LORD—
³and he will delight in the fear of the LORD.

He will not judge by what he sees with his eyes,
    or decide by what he hears with his ears;
⁴but with righteousness he will judge the needy,
    with justice he will give decisions for the poor
    of the earth.
He will strike the earth with the rod of his
    mouth;
    with the breath of his lips he will slay the
    wicked.
⁵Righteousness will be his belt
    and faithfulness the sash around his waist.

⁶The wolf will live with the lamb,
    the leopard will lie down with the goat,
the calf and the lion and the yearlingᵇ together;
    and a little child will lead them.
⁷The cow will feed with the bear,
    their young will lie down together,
    and the lion will eat straw like the ox.

ᵃ27 Hebrew; Septuagint *broken / from your shoulders*   ᵇ6 Hebrew; Septuagint *lion will feed*

⁸The infant will play near the hole of the cobra,
  and the young child put his hand into the
    viper's nest.
⁹They will neither harm nor destroy
  on all my holy mountain,
for the earth will be full of the knowledge of the
    LORD
  as the waters cover the sea.

¹⁰In that day the Root of Jesse will stand as a banner for the peoples; the nations will rally to him, and his place of rest will be glorious. ¹¹In that day the Lord will reach out his hand a second time to reclaim the remnant that is left of his people from Assyria, from Lower Egypt, from Upper Egypt,ᵃ from Cush,ᵇ from Elam, from Babylonia,ᶜ from Hamath and from the islands of the sea.

¹²He will raise a banner for the nations
    and gather the exiles of Israel;
  he will assemble the scattered people of Judah
    from the four quarters of the earth.
¹³Ephraim's jealousy will vanish,
    and Judah's enemiesᵈ will be cut off;
  Ephraim will not be jealous of Judah,
    nor Judah hostile toward Ephraim.
¹⁴They will swoop down on the slopes of Philistia to
      the west;
    together they will plunder the people to the
      east.
  They will lay hands on Edom and Moab,
    and the Ammonites will be subject to them.
¹⁵The LORD will dry up
    the gulf of the Egyptian sea;
  with a scorching wind he will sweep his hand
    over the Euphrates River.ᵉ
He will break it up into seven streams
  so that men can cross over in sandals.
¹⁶There will be a highway for the remnant of his
      people
    that is left from Assyria,
  as there was for Israel
    when they came up from Egypt.

Songs of Praise

12 In that day you will say:

  "I will praise you, O LORD.
    Although you were angry with me,
  your anger has turned away
    and you have comforted me.
²Surely God is my salvation;
    I will trust and not be afraid.
  The LORD, the LORD, is my strength and my song;
    he has become my salvation."
³With joy you will draw water
    from the wells of salvation.

⁴In that day you will say:

  "Give thanks to the LORD, call on his name;

verses 6–9? To the promise of 19:24–25? How certain will all this be (see 9:7)? Why?

♡ **1.** The New Testament interprets the "Branch" as the Messiah, Jesus (see Ro 15:12; Rev 5:5). What stories, teachings or sayings about Jesus come to mind as you consider the qualities described in verses 2–5? Which of these qualities of Jesus has particularly made a difference in your life? **2.** Comparing verse 12 with John 12:32, could it be that the "banner" raised by the promised Messiah is ultimately the cross of Christ? Why do you think so? **3.** Do you see yourself at this time more like a *wolf* or a *lamb*? Who do you see as your opposite in this regard? Why? What does it mean for the two of you that God does not change wolves into sheep, or vice versa, but transforms them so they can live in peace with one another? **4.** This picture of the Messiah's reign is both deeply personal and social. What would a new society look like under the Messiah's reign (be specific)? **5.** How would you like to grow under the Lordship of Christ?

☕ **1.** How would you share good news with a loved one: Phone? Write a letter? Sing a song? **2.** What is the best thing that happened to you last week?

📖 **1.** How does this song of God's deliverance from Assyria compare with the way Israel celebrated God's deliverance from Egypt (see Ex 15)? **2.** How deeply does Israel respond to the Lord's salvation in verses 1–3? In verses 4–6? **3.** What is the real deliverance—of which Assyria is only an example—that God has in view here? What is the ultimate reason for Israel's joy?

♡ **1.** How well does your joy match your walk and your talk for God? **2.** When have you

---

ᵃ11 Hebrew *from Pathros*   ᵇ11 That is, the upper Nile region   ᶜ11 Hebrew
Shinar   ᵈ13 Or *hostility*   ᵉ15 Hebrew *the River*

most keenly felt God's *anger*?
God's *goodness*?

⚬ **1.** What was the most dramatic or true-to-life war movie you ever saw? How did it affect you as you watched it? **2.** What warring nation in real life gets your "Evil Empire" award and why?

📖 Chapters 13–23 bring together several prophetic judgments against the nations surrounding Judah. This new section, together with the world-visions in chapters 24–27, serves as an interlude between the promised Assyrian crisis (ch. 1–12) and its onset (ch. 28–39). **1.** What is the intended audience of these prophecies? Why might God lead Isaiah to pronounce judgment upon all these nations if *only Judah*, and not the nations themselves, would have heard them? What does this say about Judah's tendency to trust in alliances with lesser nations for protection against greater enemies? **2.** Since Babylon was not the dominant world power until a century after this prophecy in chapters 13–14, what does this city symbolize that is timeless and bigger than itself (13:5,9,11)? What characterizes this Babylon (13:11,19; 14:13–14)? **3.** What is the "Day of the Lord" like for Babylon (13:6,9; see 2:11,17,20)? What poetic and cosmic images in 13:4–16 graphically communicate its power to you? **4.** What should the Judeans have learned about God from this prophecy against such a powerful nation? **5.** The Medes (13:17), from what is today part of Iran, had a reputation as fighters even in the days of the Assyrian dominance. How will they be used as God's agents against Babylon (an event which happened, definitively, in 539 B.C.)? What is the ultimate destiny of any endeavor built upon human pride (13:19–22)? **6.** What is the positive side and real purpose of this judgment (14:1–2)? What is the basis for God acting on Israel's behalf (12:1; see 40:1–2)? On the Gentiles' behalf? What do you think this imagery of tables turned actually means (13:2; see 2:3–4; 11:11; 19:24–25)?

make known among the nations what he has
    done,
  and proclaim that his name is exalted.
⁵Sing to the LORD, for he has done glorious things;
  let this be known to all the world.
⁶Shout aloud and sing for joy, people of Zion,
  for great is the Holy One of Israel among you."

A Prophecy Against Babylon

13 An oracle concerning Babylon that Isaiah son of Amoz saw:

²Raise a banner on a bare hilltop,
  shout to them;
beckon to them
  to enter the gates of the nobles.
³I have commanded my holy ones;
  I have summoned my warriors to carry out my
    wrath—
  those who rejoice in my triumph.

⁴Listen, a noise on the mountains,
  like that of a great multitude!
Listen, an uproar among the kingdoms,
  like nations massing together!
The LORD Almighty is mustering
  an army for war.
⁵They come from faraway lands,
  from the ends of the heavens—
the LORD and the weapons of his wrath—
  to destroy the whole country.

⁶Wail, for the day of the LORD is near;
  it will come like destruction from the
    Almighty.ᵃ
⁷Because of this, all hands will go limp,
  every man's heart will melt.
⁸Terror will seize them,
  pain and anguish will grip them;
  they will writhe like a woman in labor.
They will look aghast at each other,
  their faces aflame.

⁹See, the day of the LORD is coming
  —a cruel day, with wrath and fierce anger—
to make the land desolate
  and destroy the sinners within it.
¹⁰The stars of heaven and their constellations
  will not show their light.
The rising sun will be darkened
  and the moon will not give its light.
¹¹I will punish the world for its evil,
  the wicked for their sins.
I will put an end to the arrogance of the haughty
  and will humble the pride of the ruthless.
¹²I will make man scarcer than pure gold,
  more rare than the gold of Ophir.
¹³Therefore I will make the heavens tremble;
  and the earth will shake from its place

ᵃ6 Hebrew *Shaddai*

at the wrath of the LORD Almighty,
   in the day of his burning anger.
¹⁴Like a hunted gazelle,
   like sheep without a shepherd,
each will return to his own people,
   each will flee to his native land.
¹⁵Whoever is captured will be thrust through;
   all who are caught will fall by the sword.
¹⁶Their infants will be dashed to pieces before their
      eyes;
   their houses will be looted and their wives
      ravished.

¹⁷See, I will stir up against them the Medes,
   who do not care for silver
   and have no delight in gold.
¹⁸Their bows will strike down the young men;
   they will have no mercy on infants
   nor will they look with compassion on children.
¹⁹Babylon, the jewel of kingdoms,
   the glory of the Babylonians'^a pride,
will be overthrown by God
   like Sodom and Gomorrah.
²⁰She will never be inhabited
   or lived in through all generations;
no Arab will pitch his tent there,
   no shepherd will rest his flocks there.
²¹But desert creatures will lie there,
   jackals will fill her houses;
there the owls will dwell,
   and there the wild goats will leap about.
²²Hyenas will howl in her strongholds,
   jackals in her luxurious palaces.
Her time is at hand,
   and her days will not be prolonged.

14

The LORD will have compassion on Jacob;
   once again he will choose Israel
   and will settle them in their own land.
Aliens will join them
   and unite with the house of Jacob.
²Nations will take them
   and bring them to their own place.
And the house of Israel will possess the nations
   as menservants and maidservants in the LORD's
      land.
They will make captives of their captors
   and rule over their oppressors.

³On the day the LORD gives you relief from suffering and turmoil
and cruel bondage, ⁴you will take up this taunt against the king of
Babylon:

How the oppressor has come to an end!
   How his fury^b has ended!
⁵The LORD has broken the rod of the wicked,
   the scepter of the rulers,
⁶which in anger struck down peoples

1. Where in our culture, and in your life, do you see the attitudes typified by Babylon? What do you learn about God's response to these attitudes from this prophecy? What parallels do you see between the destruction of Babylon and the judgment God will bring upon the whole earth in the last days (see Rev 6:12–13; 18:2, where "Babylon" represents human pride)? 2. Babylon stood for wealth, refined culture and political power. What 20th century culture holds these values as the most important ones? How have you seen these values blind people to the reality of God's values such as truth, justice and love? How are you experiencing the tension between this dual set of values today? 3. What helps you keep God's values primary? In what area is that especially hard for you right now? How can your small group help in this regard?

In your childhood relationships, what taunts used to anger you? Which of your taunts used to get the best of others? Which taunts among your children (if any) are most mischievous or upsetting?

The taunt song here (vv. 4–21) is comprised of four stanzas which celebrate the overthrow of the ruler of Babylon who

^a19 Or *Chaldeans'*   ^b4 Dead Sea Scrolls, Septuagint and Syriac; the meaning of the word in the Masoretic Text is uncertain.

personifies the pride that marked the nation as a whole. **1.** In the first stanza (vv. 4–8), how is this king described? What was his rule like? What happens now that his rule is ended? **2.** In the second stanza (vv. 9–11), what grave matter should concern this king but doesn't? How does this stanza demonstrate the folly of laying up treasure on earth? **3.** In the third stanza (vv. 12–15), Isaiah makes use of pagan mythology to ridicule the king. What primarily motivates this king? How does his *destiny* compare with his *ambition*? The "morning star" is probably Venus, which appears bright on the horizon until the sun rises and it disappears from view. What does this tell you about human pride that asserts itself against God? **4.** In the final stanza (vv. 16–21), what is the contrast between the king's *early power* and *final condition*? Unable to have his power endure, what is the final judgment upon this king? **5.** There is no known Babylonian or Assyrian king who suffered this type of disgrace. What then is the idea which verses 22–23 reinforce? Is all that is said about this king really a symbol for God's judgment upon the *people of Babylon* as a whole? Upon *human pride* as a whole? Or what?

1. How does this song taunt you? Is there any sense in which you have experienced pride going before the fall? What is the "pomp" and "noise of your harps" that distracts you from living for God instead of yourself? **2.** What historical and contemporary events exemplify God's judgment upon a people (or leaders) caught up in their pride and superiority: Hitler and WW II? Saddam Hussein in Iraq? Idi Amin in Uganda? Other? What does this imply about what a believer's attitude ought to be about in situations where these forces seem to be in control? Do you think it's right to rejoice over their destruction as Isaiah does here? Why or why not? **3.** From your experience, what is the relationship between pride in yourself and cruelty towards others? Why is that so? What is the difference in purpose between (a) the fear of God's judgment and (b) the terror the Babylonians inspired in others? **4.** What does it mean to you that God has absolute power over all who would try to exercise or usurp power? How does that challenge you? How

with unceasing blows,
 and in fury subdued nations
 with relentless aggression.
⁷All the lands are at rest and at peace;
 they break into singing.
⁸Even the pine trees and the cedars of Lebanon
 exult over you and say,
 "Now that you have been laid low,
 no woodsman comes to cut us down."

⁹The grave*ᵃ* below is all astir
 to meet you at your coming;
it rouses the spirits of the departed to greet you—
 all those who were leaders in the world;
it makes them rise from their thrones—
 all those who were kings over the nations.
¹⁰They will all respond,
 they will say to you,
 "You also have become weak, as we are;
 you have become like us."
¹¹All your pomp has been brought down to the grave,
 along with the noise of your harps;
maggots are spread out beneath you
 and worms cover you.

¹²How you have fallen from heaven,
 O morning star, son of the dawn!
You have been cast down to the earth,
 you who once laid low the nations!
¹³You said in your heart,
 "I will ascend to heaven;
I will raise my throne
 above the stars of God;
I will sit enthroned on the mount of assembly,
 on the utmost heights of the sacred
 mountain.*ᵇ*
¹⁴I will ascend above the tops of the clouds;
 I will make myself like the Most High."
¹⁵But you are brought down to the grave,
 to the depths of the pit.

¹⁶Those who see you stare at you,
 they ponder your fate:
"Is this the man who shook the earth
 and made kingdoms tremble,
¹⁷the man who made the world a desert,
 who overthrew its cities
 and would not let his captives go home?"

¹⁸All the kings of the nations lie in state,
 each in his own tomb.
¹⁹But you are cast out of your tomb
 like a rejected branch;
you are covered with the slain,
 with those pierced by the sword,
 those who descend to the stones of the pit.
Like a corpse trampled underfoot,
²⁰ you will not join them in burial,

ᵃ9 Hebrew *Sheol*; also in verses 11 and 15   *ᵇ13* Or *the north*; Hebrew *Zaphon*

for you have destroyed your land
   and killed your people.

The offspring of the wicked
   will never be mentioned again.
21Prepare a place to slaughter his sons
   for the sins of their forefathers;
they are not to rise to inherit the land
   and cover the earth with their cities.

22"I will rise up against them,"
   declares the LORD Almighty.
"I will cut off from Babylon her name and
     survivors,
   her offspring and descendants,"
           declares the LORD.
23"I will turn her into a place for owls
   and into swampland;
I will sweep her with the broom of destruction,"
   declares the LORD Almighty.

A Prophecy Against Assyria
24The LORD Almighty has sworn,

   "Surely, as I have planned, so it will be,
     and as I have purposed, so it will stand.
25I will crush the Assyrian in my land;
   on my mountains I will trample him down.
His yoke will be taken from my people,
   and his burden removed from their shoulders."

26This is the plan determined for the whole world;
   this is the hand stretched out over all nations.
27For the LORD Almighty has purposed, and who can
     thwart him?
His hand is stretched out, and who can turn it
     back?

A Prophecy Against the Philistines
28This oracle came in the year King Ahaz died:

29Do not rejoice, all you Philistines,
   that the rod that struck you is broken;
from the root of that snake will spring up a viper,
   its fruit will be a darting, venomous serpent.
30The poorest of the poor will find pasture,
   and the needy will lie down in safety.
But your root I will destroy by famine;
   it will slay your survivors.

31Wail, O gate! Howl, O city!
   Melt away, all you Philistines!
A cloud of smoke comes from the north,
   and there is not a straggler in its ranks.
32What answer shall be given
   to the envoys of that nation?
"The LORD has established Zion,
   and in her his afflicted people will find refuge."

does it encourage and strengthen you?

1. Here the previous taunt song is applied to Judah's immediate enemy, Assyria, of which Babylon is the capital city. What aspects of Babylon's judgment will be validated by Assyria's overthrow (see 10:5–34)? 2. What qualities of God are stressed here? How does God's planning and counsel stand over "the whole world"?

In view of this, how should Israel respond to God? How should the world? How then should you?

What experience have you had with snakes?

1. One tradition says Ahaz died in 715 B.C., when Assyria's control was weak and Philistia rebelled. What will result from this revolt (vv. 29,30b,31)? 2. Philistia wanted Judah as an ally against Assyria. Why would this message against Philistia be given to Judah? Where should Judah look for safety (vv. 30a,32)?

What alliances (getting in with the "right" people, hoarding wealth, etc.) might keep you from fully trusting God? What does this prophecy tell you about those alliances?

1. If you had to flee on foot from your home tonight because of the sudden invasion of an alien force, what three things would you grab to take with you? Why those three? 2. From what you have seen of modern refugees, what strikes you most about their lot?

1. Ar, Kir, Dibon, Nebo, Medeba, Heshbon, Elealeh and Jahaz are all cities or mountains in Moab, a country to the immediate east of Judah. What do you imagine Isaiah foresees happening to these places that accounts for such wailing and mourning (15:1–4)? 2. What do you imagine the scene was like for these refugees fleeing the warfare in Moab (15:5–8)? What do they look like? What are they carrying? What are they feeling? What future prospects do they have (15:9)? 3. Sending lambs to a ruler was a common sign of submission to his authority. To whom are the Moabites to send these lambs (16:1–4a)? What need prompts them to do so? What is their request of Judah? 4. What hope is held out to them (16:4b–5)? How is this related to the prophecy in 11:1–5? 5. From God's perspective, what is the reason for Moab's destruction? What does it tell you about God that he, through Isaiah, weeps for their destruction even as he ordains it to occur (16:9–11)? 6. Why is it futile for the Moabites to go to their "high place" or "shrine" (16:12) in Dibon, where they worshiped the god Chemosh (see 44:17–20)? 7. From 16:13–14, this prophecy may be dated c. 714 B.C., three years before Moab was destroyed. Since Judah would be tempted to look to Moab as an ally against Assyria, what would God desire them to learn from this prophecy?

1. What part of your world suffers most because of political chaos and war? When you hear of the oppression and suffering people experience due to these situations, what do you feel? Say? Do? How do you think God responds to such misery? 2. Isaiah held out the Messiah as the only real hope for his hearers and readers. In what way is the reign of Jesus Christ the only real hope for people suffering in the world? How does his rule serve as a model for how believers ought to respond now toward the poor, the homeless and the hungry? 3. In what ways

A Prophecy Against Moab

15 An oracle concerning Moab:

Ar in Moab is ruined,
    destroyed in a night!
Kir in Moab is ruined,
    destroyed in a night!
²Dibon goes up to its temple,
    to its high places to weep;
Moab wails over Nebo and Medeba.
Every head is shaved
    and every beard cut off.
³In the streets they wear sackcloth;
    on the roofs and in the public squares
they all wail,
    prostrate with weeping.
⁴Heshbon and Elealeh cry out,
    their voices are heard all the way to Jahaz.
Therefore the armed men of Moab cry out,
    and their hearts are faint.

⁵My heart cries out over Moab;
    her fugitives flee as far as Zoar,
    as far as Eglath Shelishiyah.
They go up the way to Luhith,
    weeping as they go;
on the road to Horonaim
    they lament their destruction.
⁶The waters of Nimrim are dried up
    and the grass is withered;
the vegetation is gone
    and nothing green is left.
⁷So the wealth they have acquired and stored up
    they carry away over the Ravine of the Poplars.
⁸Their outcry echoes along the border of Moab;
    their wailing reaches as far as Eglaim,
    their lamentation as far as Beer Elim.
⁹Dimon'sᵃ waters are full of blood,
    but I will bring still more upon Dimonᵃ—
a lion upon the fugitives of Moab
    and upon those who remain in the land.

16 Send lambs as tribute
    to the ruler of the land,
from Sela, across the desert,
    to the mount of the Daughter of Zion.
²Like fluttering birds
    pushed from the nest,
so are the women of Moab
    at the fords of the Arnon.

³"Give us counsel,
    render a decision.
Make your shadow like night—
    at high noon.
Hide the fugitives,
    do not betray the refugees.

ᵃ9 Masoretic Text; Dead Sea Scrolls, some Septuagint manuscripts and Vulgate *Dibon*

⁴Let the Moabite fugitives stay with you;
    be their shelter from the destroyer."

The oppressor will come to an end,
    and destruction will cease;
    the aggressor will vanish from the land.
⁵In love a throne will be established;
    in faithfulness a man will sit on it—
    one from the house[a] of David—
one who in judging seeks justice
    and speeds the cause of righteousness.

⁶We have heard of Moab's pride—
    her overweening pride and conceit,
her pride and her insolence—
    but her boasts are empty.
⁷Therefore the Moabites wail,
    they wail together for Moab.
Lament and grieve
    for the men[b] of Kir Hareseth.
⁸The fields of Heshbon wither,
    the vines of Sibmah also.
The rulers of the nations
    have trampled down the choicest vines,
which once reached Jazer
    and spread toward the desert.
Their shoots spread out
    and went as far as the sea.
⁹So I weep, as Jazer weeps,
    for the vines of Sibmah.
O Heshbon, O Elealeh,
    I drench you with tears!
The shouts of joy over your ripened fruit
    and over your harvests have been stilled.
¹⁰Joy and gladness are taken away from the
        orchards;
    no one sings or shouts in the vineyards;
no one treads out wine at the presses,
    for I have put an end to the shouting.
¹¹My heart laments for Moab like a harp,
    my inmost being for Kir Hareseth.
¹²When Moab appears at her high place,
    she only wears herself out;
when she goes to her shrine to pray,
    it is to no avail.

¹³This is the word the LORD has already spoken concerning Moab. ¹⁴But now the LORD says: "Within three years, as a servant bound by contract would count them, Moab's splendor and all her many people will be despised, and her survivors will be very few and feeble."

An Oracle Against Damascus

17 An oracle concerning Damascus:

    "See, Damascus will no longer be a city
        but will become a heap of ruins.
²The cities of Aroer will be deserted
    and left to flocks, which will lie down,

---

might "today's necessities" become "tomorrow's luxuries"? What is a false god you once trusted in? How did that god serve only to wear you out? How does that god look to you now, compared to the King described in 16:5?

What experience, if any, have you had with harvesting? What fascinates you about what grows in your garden and in the fields, and what retards or kills that growth?

1. Whereas the previous two prophecies were dated c. 715 B.C., this one refers to events

---

a5 Hebrew *tent*   b7 Or "*raisin cakes*," a wordplay

c. 735 B.C., when the northern kingdom of Israel was allied with Aram (or Syria, of which Damascus was the leading city) against Assyria (see ch. 7). Comparing verses 1–3 with 7:4–9, what will be the future of Damascus and Israel (Ephraim)? **2.** What do verses 7–8 and 10a imply about Israel's spiritual condition during this time (see also 2Ki 17:7–18)? Since Israel still worshiped the Lord (as well as other gods), what does it mean to "have forgotten God" (v. 10a)? **3.** Verses 10–11 refer to a pagan fertility rite whereby plants were force-bloomed in hopes of persuading the gods to bless the harvest. How will this practice backfire on Israel? **4.** What does the farmer's image of harvesting and gleaning (vv. 4–6,9–11) mean for the cities of Israel? What will be the result of this destruction? **5.** What does the *sailor's* image ("raging sea") and the *desert* image ("chaff" and "tumbleweed") mean for the future of "many nations" (vv. 12–14)? What does such imagery mean for the future of Israel? **6.** Where else have you seen Israel's powerful enemies so quickly cut down, as in verse 14? How is this depicted in 10:28–34 and 37:36–37?

♡ **1.** In this section, God is described as the Maker, the Holy One, the Savior and the Rock. Which of these aspects do you tend to forget? What leads you to do so? Instead, what do you find yourself trusting in? What practices can help you remember God and live out your life accordingly? **2.** Compare verses 12–13 with Psalm 2:1–6. What truth about God emerges from these descriptions? **3.** How might the story of Jesus calming the sea (Mk 4:35–41), together with the image of verse 13, affect you as you face a world full of confusion and tumult?

with no one to make them afraid.
³The fortified city will disappear from Ephraim,
    and royal power from Damascus;
the remnant of Aram will be
    like the glory of the Israelites,"
                 declares the LORD Almighty.

⁴"In that day the glory of Jacob will fade;
    the fat of his body will waste away.
⁵It will be as when a reaper gathers the standing
       grain
    and harvests the grain with his arm—
as when a man gleans heads of grain
    in the Valley of Rephaim.
⁶Yet some gleanings will remain,
    as when an olive tree is beaten,
leaving two or three olives on the topmost
       branches,
four or five on the fruitful boughs,"
         declares the LORD, the God of Israel.

⁷In that day men will look to their Maker
    and turn their eyes to the Holy One of Israel.
⁸They will not look to the altars,
    the work of their hands,
and they will have no regard for the Asherah
    poles*a*
and the incense altars their fingers have made.

⁹In that day their strong cities, which they left because of the Israelites, will be like places abandoned to thickets and undergrowth. And all will be desolation.

¹⁰You have forgotten God your Savior;
    you have not remembered the Rock, your
       fortress.
Therefore, though you set out the finest plants
    and plant imported vines,
¹¹though on the day you set them out, you make
       them grow,
    and on the morning when you plant them, you
       bring them to bud,
yet the harvest will be as nothing
    in the day of disease and incurable pain.

¹²Oh, the raging of many nations—
    they rage like the raging sea!
Oh, the uproar of the peoples—
    they roar like the roaring of great waters!
¹³Although the peoples roar like the roar of surging
       waters,
when he rebukes them they flee far away,
driven before the wind like chaff on the hills,
    like tumbleweed before a gale.
¹⁴In the evening, sudden terror!
    Before the morning, they are gone!
This is the portion of those who loot us,
    the lot of those who plunder us.

    a8 That is, symbols of the goddess Asherah

A Prophecy Against Cush

18 Woe to the land of whirring wings[a]
      along the rivers of Cush,[b]
[2] which sends envoys by sea
      in papyrus boats over the water.

Go, swift messengers,
  to a people tall and smooth-skinned,
  to a people feared far and wide,
an aggressive nation of strange speech,
  whose land is divided by rivers.

[3] All you people of the world,
  you who live on the earth,
when a banner is raised on the mountains,
  you will see it,
and when a trumpet sounds,
  you will hear it.
[4] This is what the LORD says to me:
  "I will remain quiet and will look on from my
    dwelling place,
like shimmering heat in the sunshine,
  like a cloud of dew in the heat of harvest."
[5] For, before the harvest, when the blossom is gone
  and the flower becomes a ripening grape,
he will cut off the shoots with pruning knives,
  and cut down and take away the spreading
    branches.
[6] They will all be left to the mountain birds of prey
  and to the wild animals;
the birds will feed on them all summer,
  the wild animals all winter.

[7] At that time gifts will be brought to the LORD Almighty

from a people tall and smooth-skinned,
  from a people feared far and wide,
an aggressive nation of strange speech,
  whose land is divided by rivers—

the gifts will be brought to Mount Zion, the place of the Name of
the LORD Almighty.

A Prophecy About Egypt

19 An oracle concerning Egypt:

See, the LORD rides on a swift cloud
  and is coming to Egypt.
The idols of Egypt tremble before him,
  and the hearts of the Egyptians melt within
    them.
[2] "I will stir up Egyptian against Egyptian—
  brother will fight against brother,
  neighbor against neighbor,
  city against city,
  kingdom against kingdom.
[3] The Egyptians will lose heart,
  and I will bring their plans to nothing;

---

a 1 Or *of locusts*   b 1 That is, the upper Nile region

1. What would your life be like if you were a head taller? A head shorter? 2. On hot summer days, how do you beat the heat?

1. During 715 B.C., envoys of Cush (Ethiopia) tried to persuade Jerusalem to align with them against Assyria. How would you sum up God's answer (vv. 3–6), which they are to bring to the "aggressive nation" (likely Assyria)? 2. What do the images of the summer heat, morning dew and the farmer pruning his garden show about the way God will work with Assyria? How do the events of 37:36–38 illustrate the lesson of verses 5–6? 3. How does this message broadly apply to all the world (v. 3)? What banner will God raise (see 5:26; 11:10,12)? 4. Beyond the Assyrian crisis, what ultimately will result from God's work among the nations (v. 7; see 2:2–4; 9:6–7; 11:10–12; 14:1–2; 16:4–5; Ps 68:31)?

1. If God's purpose for the nations is unchanged, how does this affect the way you pray for countries that seem most fearsome to you? 2. How has the "banner" of the cross transformed someone feared far and wide into someone close to Christ? The Ethiopian Eunuch (Ac 8:26ff) is one example. Who else comes to mind? 3. In your life, who has been God's "heat" and "dew"? How might you be like that to someone you know who is feared far and wide? What would it take for you to do so?

1. Who is the most unlikely convert you know? 2. What would you miss most if there were no interstate highway system or paved roads? 3. What has sibling rivalry done for you?

1. Egypt was the most likely ally for Judah against Assyria (see ch. 30–31). Why is that so foolish (vv. 1–4)? What about the Exodus might account for the idols trembling (see Ex 7:10–12; 8:16–18; 9:10–11)? 2. Zoan and Memphis were major cities in Upper and Lower Egypt. Compared to the Lord's power and wisdom, what are their famed wise men like? What effect has their leadership had upon the country? How is this

related to their wayward spiritual ties (v. 3)? **3.** Since Egypt's plans (v. 3), natural resources (vv. 5–7) and leadership (vv. 11–12) are all dependent upon God, what should that have said to the Judeans who were looking to Egypt instead of God for help? **4.** Isaiah anticipates a tremendous change in Egypt (vv. 16–25). How and why will Egypt's sense of superiority over Judah change? What do you think is meant by the image of the five Egyptian cities? What could Isaiah have meant by that one city, the center for the worship of the chief Egyptian god, adopting the very language of the Jews (v. 18)? **5.** Compare verses 19–20 with Exodus 3:7–10. What does that tell you about God's judgments? **6.** What does the "highway" motif indicate about restored fellowship between Egypt, Assyria and Israel (v. 23; also 11:16; 40:3–4)? How would Isaiah's fellow Jews feel about Assyrians? What effect would hearing verse 25 have on them? What does that show about God's attitude toward other nations?

1. Someone has said, "Whatever we trust in place of God will eventually turn on us and destroy us." How have you seen that to be true so far in Isaiah? How about in your own experience? Where are you struggling with that now? **2.** Since the steady flow of the Nile River accounts for Egypt's prosperity, what would happen if that river should be dried up by God? Why would God do a thing like that? Could God's judgment in verses 1–15 be intended to bring about the events of verses 16–25? How so? **3.** In verses 16–22, Egypt moves from (a) fearing God, to (b) calling upon him for help, to (c) joyfully worshiping him. How far along are you on that a-b-c highway? **4.** Egypt and Assyria represent all nations (see 2:2–4; Rev 7:9–10). What then do verses 23–25 imply about God's relationship to the world? Hence, how will you pray for the world? **5.** What most excites you about what it will be like when the promise of verse 19 is fulfilled? How will the "altar in the heart of Egypt" (v. 19), in turn, alter your heart of hearts? **6.** What "pagan Assyrian" in your life do you presently disdain, much as a Jew in Isaiah's day would? What will you do about changing your heart in this area? Can this group help?

they will consult the idols and the spirits of the
  dead,
  the mediums and the spiritists.
⁴I will hand the Egyptians over
  to the power of a cruel master,
and a fierce king will rule over them,"
  declares the Lord, the LORD Almighty.

⁵The waters of the river will dry up,
  and the riverbed will be parched and dry.
⁶The canals will stink;
  the streams of Egypt will dwindle and dry up.
The reeds and rushes will wither,
⁷ also the plants along the Nile,
  at the mouth of the river.
Every sown field along the Nile
  will become parched, will blow away and be no
    more.
⁸The fishermen will groan and lament,
  all who cast hooks into the Nile;
those who throw nets on the water
  will pine away.
⁹Those who work with combed flax will despair,
  the weavers of fine linen will lose hope.
¹⁰The workers in cloth will be dejected,
  and all the wage earners will be sick at heart.

¹¹The officials of Zoan are nothing but fools;
  the wise counselors of Pharaoh give senseless
    advice.
How can you say to Pharaoh,
  "I am one of the wise men,
  a disciple of the ancient kings"?

¹²Where are your wise men now?
  Let them show you and make known
what the LORD Almighty
  has planned against Egypt.
¹³The officials of Zoan have become fools,
  the leaders of Memphis*ᵃ* are deceived;
the cornerstones of her peoples
  have led Egypt astray.
¹⁴The LORD has poured into them
  a spirit of dizziness;
they make Egypt stagger in all that she does,
  as a drunkard staggers around in his vomit.
¹⁵There is nothing Egypt can do—
  head or tail, palm branch or reed.

¹⁶In that day the Egyptians will be like women. They will shudder with fear at the uplifted hand that the LORD Almighty raises against them. ¹⁷And the land of Judah will bring terror to the Egyptians; everyone to whom Judah is mentioned will be terrified, because of what the LORD Almighty is planning against them.

¹⁸In that day five cities in Egypt will speak the language of Canaan and swear allegiance to the LORD Almighty. One of them will be called the City of Destruction.*ᵇ*

¹⁹In that day there will be an altar to the LORD in the heart of Egypt, and a monument to the LORD at its border. ²⁰It will be a sign

ᵃ13 Hebrew *Noph*   ᵇ18 Most manuscripts of the Masoretic Text; some manuscripts of the Masoretic Text, Dead Sea Scrolls and Vulgate *City of the Sun* (that is, Heliopolis)

and witness to the LORD Almighty in the land of Egypt. When they cry out to the LORD because of their oppressors, he will send them a savior and defender, and he will rescue them. ²¹So the LORD will make himself known to the Egyptians, and in that day they will acknowledge the LORD. They will worship with sacrifices and grain offerings; they will make vows to the LORD and keep them. ²²The LORD will strike Egypt with a plague; he will strike them and heal them. They will turn to the LORD, and he will respond to their pleas and heal them.

²³In that day there will be a highway from Egypt to Assyria. The Assyrians will go to Egypt and the Egyptians to Assyria. The Egyptians and Assyrians will worship together. ²⁴In that day Israel will be the third, along with Egypt and Assyria, a blessing on the earth. ²⁵The LORD Almighty will bless them, saying, "Blessed be Egypt my people, Assyria my handiwork, and Israel my inheritance."

A Prophecy Against Egypt and Cush

20 In the year that the supreme commander, sent by Sargon king of Assyria, came to Ashdod and attacked and captured it— ²at that time the LORD spoke through Isaiah son of Amoz. He said to him, "Take off the sackcloth from your body and the sandals from your feet." And he did so, going around stripped and barefoot.

³Then the LORD said, "Just as my servant Isaiah has gone stripped and barefoot for three years, as a sign and portent against Egypt and Cush,ᵃ ⁴so the king of Assyria will lead away stripped and barefoot the Egyptian captives and Cushite exiles, young and old, with buttocks bared—to Egypt's shame. ⁵Those who trusted in Cush and boasted in Egypt will be afraid and put to shame. ⁶In that day the people who live on this coast will say, 'See what has happened to those we relied on, those we fled to for help and deliverance from the king of Assyria! How then can we escape?'"

A Prophecy Against Babylon

21 An oracle concerning the Desert by the Sea:

> Like whirlwinds sweeping through the southland,
>   an invader comes from the desert,
>   from a land of terror.

²A dire vision has been shown to me:
  The traitor betrays, the looter takes loot.
Elam, attack! Media, lay siege!
  I will bring to an end all the groaning she
    caused.

³At this my body is racked with pain,
  pangs seize me, like those of a woman in labor;
I am staggered by what I hear,
  I am bewildered by what I see.
⁴My heart falters,
  fear makes me tremble;
the twilight I longed for
  has become a horror to me.

⁵They set the tables,
  they spread the rugs,
    they eat, they drink!
Get up, you officers,
  oil the shields!

ᵃ3 That is, the upper Nile region; also in verse 5

1. Ashdod, a city in revolt against Assyria, was destroyed by Sargon in 711 B.C. What object lesson was that meant to teach Judah? 2. Nudity was culturally unacceptable, so what was Isaiah likely wearing? How would that, plus his message, take on new meaning when Assyria triumphs?

1. What object lesson has God provided for you that has contributed to your trusting God more? 2. What is the "Assyria" that seems unstoppable in your life? What "Egypt" are you tempted to rely upon for help?

1. What scary theme recurs in your dreams: Bad school? Car accident? War casualties? End times? Other? How do you feel when you wake up from a bad dream? 2. When have you been a lookout?

1. What might these three prophecies refer to, historically: (a) The temporary defeat of the Babylonians by the Assyrians in 710 and 689 B.C.? (b) Their ultimate defeat by the Persians in 539 B.C.? (c) Both? (d) Primarily that "fall of Babylon" associated with the end times? Why do you think so? 2. In Isaiah's day, Babylon sought allies among the other nations, including Judah (see ch. 39), to help her resist Assyria. Why is that a faulty, even fatal hope? 3. How does this "dire vision" affect Isaiah? Why is he so upset? What does that show you about him? 4. Though verse 5 may refer to events just prior to an Assyrian attack, compare it as well with Daniel 5:1–30. What were the leaders of Babylon doing the very night of

their final overthrow? **5.** Why post a watchman (vv. 6–10)? If Judah in Isaiah's day hoped that Babylon might protect them from Assyria, how would they react to the news "Babylon has fallen!" (v. 9)? **6.** Dumah, invaded by the Assyrians when they came against Babylon, was an oasis on a major trade route to Seir (Edom) and an ally of Babylon. In calling to the watchman (Isaiah?) regarding these events (vv. 11–12), what are the Edomites really asking? What's behind their question? And Isaiah's puzzling answer? How do you think Edom responds to this divine call in verse 12b (see 34:5–15 and the book of Obadiah)? **7.** What are the Arabian cities of Dedan and Tema told to do (vv. 13–14)? Which fugitives (or refugees) are they to care for? From verses 16–17 (also Jer 49:28–33), what does the future hold for Arabia (Kedar)? **8.** How might these three prophecies affect Judah's sense of hope as they consider the Assyrian threat? Why do you think God revealed these things to Judah?

♡ **1.** What "Babylon" are you betting on to shelter you from the uncertainties of life? Knowing that such temporal security will be swept away, like Babylon, how do you feel? What can you do to fill that God-shaped void of insecurity? **2.** When Isaiah envisions a suffering Babylon, even though it was a direct judgment by God, he is moved with God's compassion. What model does that give you for how to respond to the sufferings of others? Does your television help you identify with the suffering of others, or does it harden you against it? Why? **3.** Babylon's leaders feast and party, unaware of their impending doom. Is that typical of people under God's judgment? How is the fall of this Babylon typical of the final judgment on human pride (see Rev 18:2ff)? What is the lesson for you regarding in whom or what you trust?

[6] This is what the Lord says to me:

"Go, post a lookout
  and have him report what he sees.
[7] When he sees chariots
  with teams of horses,
riders on donkeys
  or riders on camels,
let him be alert,
  fully alert."

[8] And the lookout[a] shouted,

"Day after day, my lord, I stand on the
    watchtower;
  every night I stay at my post.
[9] Look, here comes a man in a chariot
  with a team of horses.
And he gives back the answer:
  'Babylon has fallen, has fallen!
All the images of its gods
  lie shattered on the ground!'"

[10] O my people, crushed on the threshing floor,
  I tell you what I have heard
from the LORD Almighty,
  from the God of Israel.

A Prophecy Against Edom

[11] An oracle concerning Dumah[b]:

Someone calls to me from Seir,
  "Watchman, what is left of the night?
  Watchman, what is left of the night?"
[12] The watchman replies,
  "Morning is coming, but also the night.
If you would ask, then ask;
  and come back yet again."

A Prophecy Against Arabia

[13] An oracle concerning Arabia:

You caravans of Dedanites,
  who camp in the thickets of Arabia,
[14] bring water for the thirsty;
you who live in Tema,
  bring food for the fugitives.
[15] They flee from the sword,
  from the drawn sword,
from the bent bow
  and from the heat of battle.

[16] This is what the Lord says to me: "Within one year, as a servant bound by contract would count it, all the pomp of Kedar will come to an end. [17] The survivors of the bowmen, the warriors of Kedar, will be few." The LORD, the God of Israel, has spoken.

[a]8 Dead Sea Scrolls and Syriac; Masoretic Text *A lion*   [b]11 *Dumah* means *silence* or *stillness*, a wordplay on *Edom*.

A Prophecy About Jerusalem

22

An oracle concerning the Valley of Vision:

What troubles you now,
    that you have all gone up on the roofs,
²O town full of commotion,
    O city of tumult and revelry?
Your slain were not killed by the sword,
    nor did they die in battle.
³All your leaders have fled together;
    they have been captured without using the
      bow.
All you who were caught were taken prisoner
    together,
    having fled while the enemy was still far away.
⁴Therefore I said, "Turn away from me;
    let me weep bitterly.
Do not try to console me
    over the destruction of my people."

⁵The Lord, the LORD Almighty, has a day
    of tumult and trampling and terror
    in the Valley of Vision,
a day of battering down walls
    and of crying out to the mountains.
⁶Elam takes up the quiver,
    with her charioteers and horses;
Kir uncovers the shield.
⁷Your choicest valleys are full of chariots,
    and horsemen are posted at the city gates;
⁸   the defenses of Judah are stripped away.

And you looked in that day
    to the weapons in the Palace of the Forest;
⁹you saw that the City of David
    had many breaches in its defenses;
you stored up water
    in the Lower Pool.
¹⁰You counted the buildings in Jerusalem
    and tore down houses to strengthen the wall.
¹¹You built a reservoir between the two walls
    for the water of the Old Pool,
but you did not look to the One who made it,
    or have regard for the One who planned it long
    ago.

¹²The Lord, the LORD Almighty,
    called you on that day
to weep and to wail,
    to tear out your hair and put on sackcloth.
¹³But see, there is joy and revelry,
    slaughtering of cattle and killing of sheep,
    eating of meat and drinking of wine!
"Let us eat and drink," you say,
    "for tomorrow we die!"

¹⁴The LORD Almighty has revealed this in my hearing: "Till your dying day this sin will not be atoned for," says the Lord, the LORD Almighty.

¹⁵This is what the Lord, the LORD Almighty, says:

1. When have you felt like crying even though everyone around you was partying? **2.** What might prompt you to tear your hair out? **3.** In your planning, are you near-sighted or far-sighted? Telescopic or microscopic? When have you failed to see what lay ahead because you kept looking down?

1. In light of Judah's searching for worldly allies while rejecting God, what is the irony in how Isaiah addresses Jerusalem (vv. 1, 8b–11)? **2.** Judging from verses 2–3 and 6–8a, what do you think had happened or would soon happen to Jerusalem? How would you describe the quality of leadership Jerusalem had? **3.** How would the people respond to the threat of enemy attack (vv. 8b–11)? (Note: The Palace of the Forest was an armory in Jerusalem constructed of fine woods.) What is wrong with such stock-piling for war? **4.** With danger around them, why their "eat drink and be merry" attitude (v. 13)? What does such revelry show about their trust in God? Their hope for the future? Their inner character? Why are they no different than the people of Babylon (see 21:5)? **5.** How would their attitudes and actions be different if they had responded as God desired (v. 12)? What does God's final word on the matter indicate about the depth of their hard-heartedness? How does their hard-heartedness illustrate the dynamics foreseen in 6:9–13? **6.** What is the shameful example of what Isaiah has been denouncing in verses 1–14 (vv. 15–25)? In view of impending national disaster, what is Shebna, the steward (a high administrative position in government), preoccupied with? How will God deal with such egocentric leadership? **7.** Eliakim had replaced Shebna as steward at least by the time of the Assyrian invasion of 701 B.C. (see 36:3). How do his qualities contrast with those of Shebna? In spite of his good leadership, what will ultimately happen?

1. What evil regimes in your society seem ripe for judgment today? Would you weep over their callousness as Isaiah did (v. 4)? Or would you inwardly cheer that they finally "got what was coming to them"? Why? What does that reveal about you? **2.** When have you experienced such stress that your response was like that of the people in 8b–11? What would it mean for you to look to God instead? What could help you develop that trust? **3.** Consider how popular music, movies and politicians react to threats like nuclear war, political instability and an uncertain future. Where do you see the revelry (v. 13) reflected in those signs of the times? **4.** Consider your own response to such stressful issues. Are you any less cynical? Less apathetic? Are you more prayerful? Or pro-active? Why do you respond as you do? **5.** What leadership positions (in the home, work, church, community) do you have? When, if ever, have you acted like a *Shebna* in that position? If Isaiah spoke to *you*, as you were busy glorifying your name, how would you react? How can you be more like an *Eliakim*?

☕ **1.** What loss would be most devastating to you and why: (a) Your home? (b) Your business? (c) Your job? (d) Your ability to communicate? (e) Your car? **2.** How do you feel when introduced to one far more powerful and wealthy than you? Why do you react that way?

📖 **1.** Tyre was the main city of Phoenicia, a prosperous trading country on the Mediterranean Sea. What role did Tyre play in the economy of the surrounding nations (vv. 1–3)? What was the city like before the events of this prophecy (vv. 7–8)? **2.** Ships of Tarshish were capable of sailing to the ends of the known world. What message was given to their sailors as they were returning home? How did this message affect Tyre's trading partners? **3.** Isaiah may be anticipating here one of the Assyrian attacks upon Tyre (c. 705–701 and 679–671 B.C.), or its final destruction by the Greeks (c. 332 B.C.). In either event, whom does he credit with planning the

"Go, say to this steward,
  to Shebna, who is in charge of the palace:
[16]What are you doing here and who gave you permission
  to cut out a grave for yourself here,
hewing your grave on the height
  and chiseling your resting place in the rock?

[17]"Beware, the LORD is about to take firm hold of you
  and hurl you away, O you mighty man.
[18]He will roll you up tightly like a ball
  and throw you into a large country.
There you will die
  and there your splendid chariots will remain—
  you disgrace to your master's house!
[19]I will depose you from your office,
  and you will be ousted from your position.

[20]"In that day I will summon my servant, Eliakim son of Hilkiah. [21]I will clothe him with your robe and fasten your sash around him and hand your authority over to him. He will be a father to those who live in Jerusalem and to the house of Judah. [22]I will place on his shoulder the key to the house of David; what he opens no one can shut, and what he shuts no one can open. [23]I will drive him like a peg into a firm place; he will be a seat[a] of honor for the house of his father. [24]All the glory of his family will hang on him: its offspring and offshoots—all its lesser vessels, from the bowls to all the jars.

[25]"In that day," declares the LORD Almighty, "the peg driven into the firm place will give way; it will be sheared off and will fall, and the load hanging on it will be cut down." The LORD has spoken.

A Prophecy About Tyre

23 An oracle concerning Tyre:

Wail, O ships of Tarshish!
  For Tyre is destroyed
  and left without house or harbor.
From the land of Cyprus[b]
  word has come to them.

[2]Be silent, you people of the island
  and you merchants of Sidon,
  whom the seafarers have enriched.
[3]On the great waters
  came the grain of the Shihor;
the harvest of the Nile[c] was the revenue of Tyre,
  and she became the marketplace of the nations.

[4]Be ashamed, O Sidon, and you, O fortress of the sea,
  for the sea has spoken:
"I have neither been in labor nor given birth;
  I have neither reared sons nor brought up daughters."

---

[a]23 Or *throne*   [b]1 Hebrew *Kittim*   [c]2,3 Masoretic Text; one Dead Sea Scroll *Sidon, / who cross over the sea; / your envoys* [3]*are on the great waters. / The grain of the Shihor, / the harvest of the Nile,*

[5]When word comes to Egypt,
   they will be in anguish at the report from Tyre.

[6]Cross over to Tarshish;
   wail, you people of the island.
[7]Is this your city of revelry,
   the old, old city,
whose feet have taken her
   to settle in far-off lands?
[8]Who planned this against Tyre,
   the bestower of crowns,
whose merchants are princes,
   whose traders are renowned in the earth?
[9]The LORD Almighty planned it,
   to bring low the pride of all glory
and to humble all who are renowned on the
   earth.

[10]Till[a] your land as along the Nile,
   O Daughter of Tarshish,
for you no longer have a harbor.
[11]The LORD has stretched out his hand over the sea
   and made its kingdoms tremble.
He has given an order concerning Phoenicia[b]
   that her fortresses be destroyed.
[12]He said, "No more of your reveling,
   O Virgin Daughter of Sidon, now crushed!

"Up, cross over to Cyprus[c];
   even there you will find no rest."
[13]Look at the land of the Babylonians,[d]
   this people that is now of no account!
The Assyrians have made it
   a place for desert creatures;
they raised up their siege towers,
   they stripped its fortresses bare
and turned it into a ruin.

[14]Wail, you ships of Tarshish;
   your fortress is destroyed!

[15]At that time Tyre will be forgotten for seventy years, the span of a king's life. But at the end of these seventy years, it will happen to Tyre as in the song of the prostitute:

[16]"Take up a harp, walk through the city,
   O prostitute forgotten;
play the harp well, sing many a song,
   so that you will be remembered."

[17]At the end of seventy years, the LORD will deal with Tyre. She will return to her hire as a prostitute and will ply her trade with all the kingdoms on the face of the earth. [18]Yet her profit and her earnings will be set apart for the LORD; they will not be stored up or hoarded. Her profits will go to those who live before the LORD, for abundant food and fine clothes.

[a]10 Dead Sea Scrolls and some Septuagint manuscripts; Masoretic Text *Go through*
[b]11 Hebrew *Canaan*   [c]12 Hebrew *Kittim*   [d]13 Or *Chaldeans*

downfall of Tyre, the king-maker? How is God's control over the kings and nations evident (vv. 9–12)? **4.** Babylon, the symbol of strength and prestige in the East, was beaten by Assyria in 710 B.C. and again in 689 B.C. What effect would recalling the destruction of both Babylon in the East and Tyre on the West have on Judah as they faced the Assyrians? What would they associate with the "70 years" (v. 15)? **5.** In what sense will the Lord "deal with" Tyre (vv. 17–18)? What will happen as a result of Tyre's restoration? How does this compare with what Isaiah said of Egypt and Assyria (see 19:23–25)? Since verse 18 has never happened literally, what is the figurative meaning behind this passage? What does it imply about God's plan for the world (see Rev 18:3)?

1. Chapters 13–23 reflect upon the foolishness of Judah depending upon alliances with the other nations rather than upon God to protect her from Assyria. What do you see as one implication of that loyalty principle for your life today? To what or to whom have you looked to fill that God-shaped void of insecurity in your life? **2.** If *Babylon* represented the height of the world's culture, and *Tyre* the apex of its wealth, how would you use Isaiah's message to challenge people dedicated to power and money? Does this mean power and wealth in themselves are wrong? Why or why not? How does this message serve as an ongoing warning to the church in every age? To your church in particular? **3.** How does the promise in verse 18 (see also 19:23–25) relate to Jesus' promise in Matthew 5:5? How would you picture the hope stirred up by these pictures and promises? What specific action will you take to embody that hope for a reconciled world loyal to God?

1. Have you ever visited a ghost town? Where? What was it like? 2. Have you ever been to a party that came to a crashing halt? (Was that when your parents came home?) What happened?

Chapters 24–27 present in universal terms the blessings and judgments prophesied for specific nations in 13–23. 1. What is the scope of the judgment in verses 1–6? Who gets hit? Who is left? 2. What is the reason for this total devastation that is to come (vv. 5–6)? What "everlasting covenant" (from God's viewpoint) might the people have broken (see Ge 9:8–17)? What subsequent "curse" have the people brought on themselves? How has this been illustrated by some of the specific judgments (see 14:12–14; 16:6; 17:10; 22:11)? 3. What will be the impact of this future judgment on the rural and urban sectors (vv. 7–13)? What images does this bring to mind for you? If you walked through such a ghost town (as in vv. 10–12) how would you feel? 4. Who are "they" who rejoice in verses 14–16? How does their "song of glory" (v. 16a) differ from the "sounds of silence" (v. 8)? How do you account for this flip-side of judgment in verses 14–16 (see 14:7; 16:5; 17:7–8; 18:7; 19:23–25; 23:18)? 5. Verses 16b–20 return to the theme of judgment. What is the point of the dilemma that Isaiah presents here? Who is wasting away? Under whose treachery? How would you feel under such persecution? 6. Pretend these pictures of the earth (vv. 18b–20) are literal descriptions. What do you see happening? When has something like this happened before? What is the reality these pictures are meant to convey? What effect does that have upon you? 7. What cosmic realities does God battle and bind "in that day" (v. 21)? What is the ultimate purpose of this judgment? Why, in spite of all the destruction foreseen here, is this really good news? How does your answer relate to 11:10?

1. How does this prospect of universal judgment strike you: (a) An archaic view of a Zionist Jew? (b) Vindictive action on God's part? (c) Source of hope and joy conveyed by God's control? (d) A day to be feared by all, regardless of social or religious distinction? (e) Other? 2. How would your view of "that day" change if you

The LORD's Devastation of the Earth

24 See, the LORD is going to lay waste the earth
and devastate it;
he will ruin its face
and scatter its inhabitants—
²it will be the same
for priest as for people,
for master as for servant,
for mistress as for maid,
for seller as for buyer,
for borrower as for lender,
for debtor as for creditor.
³The earth will be completely laid waste
and totally plundered.
    The LORD has spoken this word.

⁴The earth dries up and withers,
the world languishes and withers,
the exalted of the earth languish.
⁵The earth is defiled by its people;
they have disobeyed the laws,
violated the statutes
and broken the everlasting covenant.
⁶Therefore a curse consumes the earth;
its people must bear their guilt.
Therefore earth's inhabitants are burned up,
and very few are left.
⁷The new wine dries up and the vine withers;
all the merrymakers groan.
⁸The gaiety of the tambourines is stilled,
the noise of the revelers has stopped,
the joyful harp is silent.
⁹No longer do they drink wine with a song;
the beer is bitter to its drinkers.
¹⁰The ruined city lies desolate;
the entrance to every house is barred.
¹¹In the streets they cry out for wine;
all joy turns to gloom,
all gaiety is banished from the earth.
¹²The city is left in ruins,
its gate is battered to pieces.
¹³So will it be on the earth
and among the nations,
as when an olive tree is beaten,
or as when gleanings are left after the grape
harvest.

¹⁴They raise their voices, they shout for joy;
from the west they acclaim the LORD's majesty.
¹⁵Therefore in the east give glory to the LORD;
exalt the name of the LORD, the God of Israel,
in the islands of the sea.
¹⁶From the ends of the earth we hear singing:
"Glory to the Righteous One."

But I said, "I waste away, I waste away!
Woe to me!
The treacherous betray!
With treachery the treacherous betray!"
¹⁷Terror and pit and snare await you,

O people of the earth.
¹⁸Whoever flees at the sound of terror
    will fall into a pit;
whoever climbs out of the pit
    will be caught in a snare.

The floodgates of the heavens are opened,
    the foundations of the earth shake.
¹⁹The earth is broken up,
    the earth is split asunder,
    the earth is thoroughly shaken.
²⁰The earth reels like a drunkard,
    it sways like a hut in the wind;
so heavy upon it is the guilt of its rebellion
    that it falls—never to rise again.

²¹In that day the LORD will punish
    the powers in the heavens above
    and the kings on the earth below.
²²They will be herded together
    like prisoners bound in a dungeon;
they will be shut up in prison
    and be punished[a] after many days.
²³The moon will be abashed, the sun ashamed;
    for the LORD Almighty will reign
on Mount Zion and in Jerusalem,
    and before its elders, gloriously.

Praise to the LORD

25 O LORD, you are my God;
    I will exalt you and praise your name,
for in perfect faithfulness
    you have done marvelous things,
    things planned long ago.
²You have made the city a heap of rubble,
    the fortified town a ruin,
the foreigners' stronghold a city no more;
    it will never be rebuilt.
³Therefore strong peoples will honor you;
    cities of ruthless nations will revere you.
⁴You have been a refuge for the poor,
    a refuge for the needy in his distress,
a shelter from the storm
    and a shade from the heat.
For the breath of the ruthless
    is like a storm driving against a wall
⁵   and like the heat of the desert.
You silence the uproar of foreigners;
    as heat is reduced by the shadow of a cloud,
    so the song of the ruthless is stilled.

⁶On this mountain the LORD Almighty will prepare
    a feast of rich food for all peoples,
a banquet of aged wine—
    the best of meats and the finest of wines.
⁷On this mountain he will destroy
    the shroud that enfolds all peoples,
the sheet that covers all nations;
⁸   he will swallow up death forever.

a22 Or released

were a powerful, corrupt king? If you were a victim of his oppressive rule? **3.** Both joy (v. 14) and sorrow (v. 16b) will be the experience of the godly remnant who survive this judgment. When you see or hear about current disaster striking those who don't deserve it what do you feel? **4.** When have you tried getting "out of the frying pan" only to find yourself "in the fire"? What did you learn about yourself in that situation? Did that experience drive you toward God, or away from God? Why? **5.** What do you learn about God from considering his past judgments (such as Noah's flood, or the fall of specific nations)? In comparison, what do you learn when you consider God's future glory, which will eclipse even the sun and stars above?

1. As a child, where was the "heap of rubble" that you used to play on? What was one of the more useful pieces of junk you brought home? **2.** What was your safe place when a severe storm was brewing? Where was your *emotional* shelter when things were stormy? **3.** What annual feast do you always overeat at?

1. What mood shift do you sense in this new chapter? What leads Isaiah (and his people) to exclaim, "O Lord, you are my God!"? **2.** The "city" and "fortified town" in verse 2 symbolize all the things in which people have placed their pride and confidence. What will be the result of God's judgment upon these things? How does this relate to 19:23–25? **3.** How is God's relationship to the poor and the needy pictured here? **4.** Kings would often hold inaugural and wedding feasts for their subjects. For whom is this feast on Mt. Zion given? Who will be excluded from this feast? Why? **5.** What will be the effects of the Lord's reign on those who submit and those who don't?

1. What applications does the New Testament make of this great feast (v. 6; see 1Co 15:54; Rev 19:9; 21:4)? What will be the effect of Christ's coming in that day? **2.** What are some of the "cities" (seats of power, feats or accomplishments) in which people place their pride and confidence today? To which of these things do you find yourself drawn? Why? **3.** What is the "storm" or "heat of the desert" that is affecting you right now? How has God sheltered you from that? Where do you need a shelter or cloud cover now? **4.** In coping with death, disappointment or disgrace, what does the promise of verses 7–8 mean to you? When has that promise been made real to you? Or does it seem so distant in its fulfillment that it is not much help to you, here and now?

---

1. Are you more of a "day dreamer," "worry wart" or "book worm"? Last week, did you day dream more, worry more, or read more? **2.** What do you do that keeps your mind sharp and glowing? Rested and peaceful?

1. How does this "city of God" contrast with the "cities of the world" mentioned in 24:10–12 and 25:2–3? What characterizes the inhabitants of God's city (vv. 3–4,7–9)? What qualities mark those upon whom judgment comes (vv. 5,10–11)? **2.** What makes the Lord worthy of trust (vv. 4–6)? Does this reversal of human fortune underscore, or undermine, either God's justice or his love? How so? **3.** What do you learn about faith from the images of the ramparts (v. 1), the gates (v. 2), the steadfast mind (v. 3), the Rock (v. 4), level paths (v. 7), walking, waiting and yearning (vv. 8–9)? **4.** With these images in mind, is faith active, passive or both? How so? **5.** How is God contrasted to the "other lords" (Assyria and Egypt) (vv. 12–15)? What image of faith is projected over against these foreign powers? **6.** What does the pain of childbirth imagery add to your understanding of faith—its pain and purpose (vv. 16–18)? **7.** In her failure to give birth and bring salvation to others, Israel has failed in her divine calling. Still, what hope is she given here (vv. 4–6,19; also 25:7–8; Eze 37:11–12; contrast v. 14 with Da 12:2)? **8.** What

The Sovereign Lord will wipe away the tears
　　from all faces;
he will remove the disgrace of his people
　　from all the earth.
　　　　　　　The Lord has spoken.

⁹In that day they will say,

"Surely this is our God;
　　we trusted in him, and he saved us.
This is the Lord, we trusted in him;
　　let us rejoice and be glad in his salvation."

¹⁰The hand of the Lord will rest on this mountain;
　　but Moab will be trampled under him
　　as straw is trampled down in the manure.
¹¹They will spread out their hands in it,
　　as a swimmer spreads out his hands to swim.
God will bring down their pride
　　despite the cleverness*ᵃ* of their hands.
¹²He will bring down your high fortified walls
　　and lay them low;
he will bring them down to the ground,
　　to the very dust.

A Song of Praise

26 In that day this song will be sung in the land of Judah:

We have a strong city;
　　God makes salvation
　　its walls and ramparts.
²Open the gates
　　that the righteous nation may enter,
　　the nation that keeps faith.
³You will keep in perfect peace
　　him whose mind is steadfast,
　　because he trusts in you.
⁴Trust in the Lord forever,
　　for the Lord, the Lord, is the Rock eternal.
⁵He humbles those who dwell on high,
　　he lays the lofty city low;
he levels it to the ground
　　and casts it down to the dust.
⁶Feet trample it down—
　　the feet of the oppressed,
　　the footsteps of the poor.

⁷The path of the righteous is level;
　　O upright One, you make the way of the
　　　　righteous smooth.
⁸Yes, Lord, walking in the way of your laws,ᵇ
　　we wait for you;
your name and renown
　　are the desire of our hearts.
⁹My soul yearns for you in the night;
　　in the morning my spirit longs for you.
When your judgments come upon the earth,
　　the people of the world learn righteousness.
¹⁰Though grace is shown to the wicked,
　　they do not learn righteousness;

ᵃ11 The meaning of the Hebrew for this word is uncertain.　　*ᵇ8* Or *judgments*

even in a land of uprightness they go on doing
    evil
and regard not the majesty of the LORD.
[11]O LORD, your hand is lifted high,
    but they do not see it.
Let them see your zeal for your people and be put
    to shame;
let the fire reserved for your enemies consume
    them.

[12]LORD, you establish peace for us;
    all that we have accomplished you have done
    for us.
[13]O LORD, our God, other lords besides you have
    ruled over us,
but your name alone do we honor.
[14]They are now dead, they live no more;
    those departed spirits do not rise.
You punished them and brought them to ruin;
    you wiped out all memory of them.
[15]You have enlarged the nation, O LORD;
    you have enlarged the nation.
You have gained glory for yourself;
    you have extended all the borders of the land.

[16]LORD, they came to you in their distress;
    when you disciplined them,
    they could barely whisper a prayer.[a]
[17]As a woman with child and about to give birth
    writhes and cries out in her pain,
so were we in your presence, O LORD.
[18]We were with child, we writhed in pain,
    but we gave birth to wind.
We have not brought salvation to the earth;
    we have not given birth to people of the world.

[19]But your dead will live;
    their bodies will rise.
You who dwell in the dust,
    wake up and shout for joy.
Your dew is like the dew of the morning;
    the earth will give birth to her dead.

[20]Go, my people, enter your rooms
    and shut the doors behind you;
hide yourselves for a little while
    until his wrath has passed by.
[21]See, the LORD is coming out of his dwelling
    to punish the people of the earth for their sins.
The earth will disclose the blood shed upon her;
    she will conceal her slain no longer.

Deliverance of Israel

27 In that day,

the LORD will punish with his sword,
    his fierce, great and powerful sword,

---

[a]16 The meaning of the Hebrew for this clause is uncertain.

does Isaiah mean by his advice in verse 20? What are they to hide from (see 24:21–22)? How long will the oppressor's tyranny and Judah's exile last? How is that related to "waiting on the Lord" (v.8)?

1. Of the qualities of God's people (vv. 3–4,7–9), what one or two do you yearn for now? **2.** What would it be like to always be a credit to God's name and reputation? What things do you do that you'd just as soon not have God's name dragged into. **3.** What are some 20th century examples of the reversal in verses 5–6? Why are such case studies in judgment ultimately a cause for joy? **4.** How might this prophecy serve as a model for how you could pray for oppressive governments today? When you pray the Lord's Prayer ("Thy kingdom come"), do such judgments come to mind? Why or why not? How would you feel about God if he did *not* answer prayer in that way? **5.** What hope is held out to you in verse 19 as you consider your failures in life? How might this hope *affect* your view of yourself? Your willingness to take risks? Your sense of God's call and courage?

1. As a child, did you love or fear monsters? Were any "hidden" in your room? Where? **2.** Tell about your garden. Do you grow food or flowers? How much do you lavish on it?

1. The Leviathan was an evil monster in ancient Near Eastern mythology. What would God's slaying this familiar symbol accomplish (see 24:1–3, 21–23; 26:20–21)? 2. As God sings about his garden (vv. 2–6), what chords does he strike: Major or minor? Harmony or discord? High notes or low notes? 3. How does this song of God's vineyard harmonize with that in 5:1–7? What accounts for the change in tune? 4. How fruitful has Israel been? What is the "fruit" that will eventually "fill all the world" (see 2:1–5; 19:23–25; 26:18)? 5. What has been the cause and purpose of God's judgments against Judah (vv. 7–11; compare 11:11)? 6. Whether "the city" (v. 10) is Jerusalem, or is symbolic of any human endeavor pursued without regard for God (as in 24:10–12; 25:2–3), what is the future of all such plans?

1. What "sea monsters" (pressures, temptations, opposing forces) seem to be chasing after you these days? How do you cope with them? Which one do you want God to slay first? 2. Is the fruit of your life mostly *taking root* (present, but unseen)? Or is your fruit *budding and blossoming* (it's beginning to show its God-given potential)? 3. This past year, have you sensed God singing about your garden (as in vv. 2–6)? Or have you felt God was disciplining you in some way (as in vv. 7–9)? Why? In retrospect (and in view of Jn 15), what do you see as the purpose of such discipline? What is your part, and God's part, in being fruitful and multiplying for God? 4. "Asherah poles" and "incense altars" (v. 9) were idolatrous; even so, they were used by Judah. What things have possibly taken the place of God as "the desire of *your* heart" (26:8)?

Leviathan the gliding serpent,
Leviathan the coiling serpent;
he will slay the monster of the sea.

²In that day—

"Sing about a fruitful vineyard:
³ I, the LORD, watch over it;
I water it continually.
I guard it day and night
so that no one may harm it.
⁴ I am not angry.
If only there were briers and thorns confronting
me!
I would march against them in battle;
I would set them all on fire.
⁵Or else let them come to me for refuge;
let them make peace with me,
yes, let them make peace with me."

⁶In days to come Jacob will take root,
Israel will bud and blossom
and fill all the world with fruit.

⁷Has ⌊the LORD⌋ struck her
as he struck down those who struck her?
Has she been killed
as those were killed who killed her?
⁸By warfare^a and exile you contend with her—
with his fierce blast he drives her out,
as on a day the east wind blows.
⁹By this, then, will Jacob's guilt be atoned for,
and this will be the full fruitage of the removal
of his sin:
When he makes all the altar stones
to be like chalk stones crushed to pieces,
no Asherah poles^b or incense altars
will be left standing.
¹⁰The fortified city stands desolate,
an abandoned settlement, forsaken like the
desert;
there the calves graze,
there they lie down;
they strip its branches bare.
¹¹When its twigs are dry, they are broken off
and women come and make fires with them.
For this is a people without understanding;
so their Maker has no compassion on them,
and their Creator shows them no favor.

¹²In that day the LORD will thresh from the flowing Euphrates^c to the Wadi of Egypt, and you, O Israelites, will be gathered up one by one. ¹³And in that day a great trumpet will sound. Those who were perishing in Assyria and those who were exiled in Egypt will come and worship the LORD on the holy mountain in Jerusalem.

---

a8 See Septuagint; the meaning of the Hebrew for this word is uncertain.   b9 That is, symbols of the goddess Asherah   c12 Hebrew *River*

Woe to Ephraim

28 Woe to that wreath, the pride of Ephraim's
        drunkards,
to the fading flower, his glorious beauty,
set on the head of a fertile valley—
        to that city, the pride of those laid low by wine!
²See, the Lord has one who is powerful and strong.
        Like a hailstorm and a destructive wind,
like a driving rain and a flooding downpour,
        he will throw it forcefully to the ground.
³That wreath, the pride of Ephraim's drunkards,
        will be trampled underfoot.
⁴That fading flower, his glorious beauty,
        set on the head of a fertile valley,
will be like a fig ripe before harvest—
        as soon as someone sees it and takes it in his
            hand,
        he swallows it.

⁵In that day the LORD Almighty
        will be a glorious crown,
a beautiful wreath
        for the remnant of his people.
⁶He will be a spirit of justice
        to him who sits in judgment,
a source of strength
        to those who turn back the battle at the gate.

⁷And these also stagger from wine
        and reel from beer:
Priests and prophets stagger from beer
        and are befuddled with wine;
they reel from beer,
        they stagger when seeing visions,
        they stumble when rendering decisions.
⁸All the tables are covered with vomit
        and there is not a spot without filth.

⁹"Who is it he is trying to teach?
        To whom is he explaining his message?
To children weaned from their milk,
        to those just taken from the breast?
¹⁰For it is:
        Do and do, do and do,
        rule on rule, rule on rule ª;
        a little here, a little there."

¹¹Very well then, with foreign lips and strange
            tongues
God will speak to this people,
¹²to whom he said,
        "This is the resting place, let the weary rest";
and, "This is the place of repose"—
        but they would not listen.
¹³So then, the word of the LORD to them will
            become:
        Do and do, do and do,
        rule on rule, rule on rule;

ª 10 Hebrew / *sav lasav sav lasav / kav lakav kav lakav* (possibly meaningless sounds;
perhaps a mimicking of the prophet's words); also in verse 13

---

1. What household chore stands out as one that your parent or spouse keeps saying, "Do and do, do and do"? Why did you have to be nagged or coerced into doing that chore? Did you ever get away with waiting until someone else did it? In either event, how did that affect your relationship with your parent or spouse? **2.** Do you feel your parents set down "rule on rule"? Or were they lax when it came to rules? Which would you have preferred?

While chapters 13–27 deal with God's authority over the nations in general, chapters 28–33 consist of six "woes" detailing God's judgment (ch. 28–31) and restoration (ch. 32–33) of Judah in particular. **1.** In verses 1–4, Isaiah singles out Samaria (a luxurious and decadent city in Israel at this time) as an example of God's judgment, comparing her to a head-wreath of flowers that party goers would wear. What will happen to this "wreath" in which the Israelites have taken such pride? What are the reasons for God's judgment upon Israel (see also 1:12–17; 10:1–4)? **2.** What light does 2 Kings 17:1–6 shed on the fulfillment of this prophecy against Samaria? **3.** What will be different when God is truly the "crown" of his people (vv. 5–6)? **4.** What is Isaiah saying about the "visions" and "decisions" of the religious leadership of Israel by the severe way he describes them (vv. 7–8)? What is the effect on Israel of their drunken excesses? To what spiritual reality does this vivid imagery point? **5.** How do these leaders receive Isaiah's message (vv. 9–10)? Why would they mock him and his warnings, much like a rebel teenager does his parents? **6.** How will they be forced to eat their mocking words (v. 13; see 6:9–13)? **7.** What is God's basic message to Israel which they are ignoring to their detriment (v. 12)? What is meant by this "resting place" (see 30:15; 40:31; Jos 1:13)? **8.** Isaiah now applies the lesson of Israel to Judah. What is their "covenant with death" (v. 15): (a) Invoking the gods of the underworld, as in 8:19? (b) Political alliance with Egypt, as in 30:1–2? (c) Isaiah's mocking view of their hope to escape death? **9.** In contrast to lies and falsehood (v. 15), what is the "sure foundation" of God's kingdom (vv. 16–19)? What promise is given to those who will trust in that cornerstone? What is the warning given to those who do not? **10.** How will their covenant prove "too short" (vv. 20–22)? What was God's work at Mount Perazim and at Gibeon (see 1Ch 14:8–11; Jos 10:10f)? **11.** What is the point of the farmer parable (vv. 23–29)? What picture of God's ways do we get by appreciating the seemingly strange ways of this farmer? If Judah's leaders do not stop their mocking, what "strange" and yet "wonderful" work will God do (vv. 21–22)?

1. What examples from national news stories can you think of where a person's pride, arrogance and self-indulgence have ultimately destroyed his or her plans? Do you tend to react to these stories more by scoffing or by examining your own life? Why? What have you learned about yourself from considering one of these stories? **2.** Judah's kings often lacked strength to oppose evil. Where do you need, like Israel did (vv. 5–6), the Spirit of the Lord to strengthen you to "turn back the battle at the gate" of your life? **3.** Have you ever responded to the Lord's message as the leaders did in verses 9–10? How long did that rebellious phase last? With what result? How did God break through your cynicism? **4.** In what "dead-end covenant" (money, relationships, power, etc.) do people today try to find refuge? From what "overwhelming scourge" (poverty, loneliness, insecurity) are they hiding? What is the good news for them in this passage? What is the accompanying warning? **5.** What would it take for you to learn to trust God as your resting place instead of these things? **6.** What use has the New Testament made of verse 16 (see 1Co 3:11; 1Pe 2:4–8)? What are some of the implications of saying that Jesus is the foundation stone for your life? How will you demonstrate that in a practical way this week?

a little here, a little there—
so that they will go and fall backward,
be injured and snared and captured.

¹⁴Therefore hear the word of the LORD, you scoffers
who rule this people in Jerusalem.
¹⁵You boast, "We have entered into a covenant with death,
with the grave^a we have made an agreement.
When an overwhelming scourge sweeps by,
it cannot touch us,
for we have made a lie our refuge
and falsehood^b our hiding place."

¹⁶So this is what the Sovereign LORD says:

"See, I lay a stone in Zion,
a tested stone,
a precious cornerstone for a sure foundation;
the one who trusts will never be dismayed.
¹⁷I will make justice the measuring line
and righteousness the plumb line;
hail will sweep away your refuge, the lie,
and water will overflow your hiding place.
¹⁸Your covenant with death will be annulled;
your agreement with the grave will not stand.
When the overwhelming scourge sweeps by,
you will be beaten down by it.
¹⁹As often as it comes it will carry you away;
morning after morning, by day and by night,
it will sweep through."

The understanding of this message
will bring sheer terror.
²⁰The bed is too short to stretch out on,
the blanket too narrow to wrap around you.
²¹The LORD will rise up as he did at Mount Perazim,
he will rouse himself as in the Valley of Gibeon—
to do his work, his strange work,
and perform his task, his alien task.
²²Now stop your mocking,
or your chains will become heavier;
the Lord, the LORD Almighty, has told me
of the destruction decreed against the whole land.

²³Listen and hear my voice;
pay attention and hear what I say.
²⁴When a farmer plows for planting, does he plow continually?
Does he keep on breaking up and harrowing the soil?
²⁵When he has leveled the surface,
does he not sow caraway and scatter cummin?
Does he not plant wheat in its place,^c
barley in its plot,^c
and spelt in its field?

---

^a15 Hebrew *Sheol*; also in verse 18   ^b15 Or *false gods*   ^c25 The meaning of the Hebrew for this word is uncertain.

²⁶His God instructs him
　　and teaches him the right way.

²⁷Caraway is not threshed with a sledge,
　　nor is a cartwheel rolled over cummin;
caraway is beaten out with a rod,
　　and cummin with a stick.
²⁸Grain must be ground to make bread,
　　so one does not go on threshing it forever.
Though he drives the wheels of his threshing cart
　　over it,
　　his horses do not grind it.
²⁹All this also comes from the LORD Almighty,
　　wonderful in counsel and magnificent in
　　　wisdom.

Woe to David's City

29 Woe to you, Ariel, Ariel,
　　the city where David settled!
Add year to year
　　and let your cycle of festivals go on.
²Yet I will besiege Ariel;
　　she will mourn and lament,
　　she will be to me like an altar hearth. ᵃ
³I will encamp against you all around;
　　I will encircle you with towers
　　and set up my siege works against you.
⁴Brought low, you will speak from the ground;
　　your speech will mumble out of the dust.
Your voice will come ghostlike from the earth;
　　out of the dust your speech will whisper.

⁵But your many enemies will become like fine
　　　dust,
　　the ruthless hordes like blown chaff.
Suddenly, in an instant,
⁶　the LORD Almighty will come
with thunder and earthquake and great noise,
　　with windstorm and tempest and flames of a
　　　devouring fire.
⁷Then the hordes of all the nations that fight
　　　against Ariel,
　　that attack her and her fortress and besiege her,
will be as it is with a dream,
　　with a vision in the night—
⁸as when a hungry man dreams that he is eating,
　　but he awakens, and his hunger remains;
as when a thirsty man dreams that he is drinking,
　　but he awakens faint, with his thirst
　　　unquenched.
So will it be with the hordes of all the nations
　　that fight against Mount Zion.

⁹Be stunned and amazed,
　　blind yourselves and be sightless;
be drunk, but not from wine,
　　stagger, but not from beer.
¹⁰The LORD has brought over you a deep sleep:

ᵃ2 The Hebrew for *altar hearth* sounds like the Hebrew for *Ariel*.

1. In what part of your family heritage do you take special pride? What part is less flattering, even embarrassing, to talk about? **2.** What things do you display around the house (or on the refrigerator) that you once made with your hands (out of clay, wood, metal, etc.)? Which creation do you treasure most?

1. In calling David's city "Ariel" (which sounds like "altar hearth" in Hebrew), what word play is Isaiah making here (vv. 1,2,7)? What happened regularly on the temple's altar that Isaiah is warning is mere lip service and unintelligible at that (vv. 4,13)? Who is being criticized in this mockery of the city's unwarranted hope in their immunity from God's judgment? **2.** Although it will be the Assyrian army outside their gates, who is really encamped against Jerusalem (v. 3; also 28:21)? How would this realization affect the city's proud leaders (v. 4; compare 28:14–15)? What might they expect to happen next? **3.** Instead, what serendipity will God bring about, "in an instant" (vv. 5–8)? What will happen, like a dream in the night, to those who have been devastating Jerusalem (see 10:5–19 and 27:1, which refer to the destruction of Assyria's army in 701 B.C.)? **4.** Even though the 11th hour defeat of Judah's enemies has been foretold, what effect will these events have on the people (vv. 9–14)? What will the impact be, specifically, on the prophets and seers? On the uneducated? On the literate? On the wise and intelligent? **5.** How do you account for why they are so unable to grasp what Isaiah is saying to them (vv. 10–13; compare 26:8)? **6.** Verses 15–24 comprise another "woe" to the leaders of Jerusalem. What hidden agenda do

you think was going on in their hearts or behind closed doors to bring on this woe (vv. 15–16)? What does such secrecy show about their view of God? **7.** What will be the future of these unjust leaders (vv. 20–21)? By contrast, what will become of their victims (vv. 17–19)? What irony do you see here (compare vv. 10–12)? **8.** What will be the net result of all that the Lord promises to do (vv. 22–24)?

♡ **1.** What spiritual high (v. 9), man-made rules (v. 13) or hidden agenda (v. 15) do those in political and religious circles today use to try to keep God "on their side," regardless of what is going on in their hearts? What such rituals or routines do you see in your church? **2.** Which of these traps do you fall into at times? When was the last time you tried to sneak something past God so he wouldn't notice? What did the "Potter" then say to the "clay"? What else would it take to break you out of such presumptuous thinking (that the Potter is just like the clay)? **3.** Tell the group about a time when God turned things around for you "in an instant" (v. 5). What were you doing at the time you were "surprised by joy"? How did God show his love to you in a special, personal way? What does such a serendipity show you about God's grace? **4.** The apostle Paul echoes Isaiah in saying that the "wisdom of the wise," which advocates that people find spiritual reality in some other way than Christ, will perish (see 1Co 1:19). Have you found Christ to be a more reliable ally in your spiritual life than the other alternatives people turn to? How so? What other ally still seems to appeal to you? Why? What does this ally do to your faith in God? **5.** How has Jesus opened your ears and eyes to learn his message in a way you never could before? In what ways do you still feel like you can't quite hear or see what's going on in Isaiah? What hope do the promises in verses 17–24 give you even in that situation?

He has sealed your eyes (the prophets);
he has covered your heads (the seers).

[11] For you this whole vision is nothing but words sealed in a scroll. And if you give the scroll to someone who can read, and say to him, "Read this, please," he will answer, "I can't; it is sealed." [12] Or if you give the scroll to someone who cannot read, and say, "Read this, please," he will answer, "I don't know how to read."

[13] The Lord says:

"These people come near to me with their mouth
and honor me with their lips,
but their hearts are far from me.
Their worship of me
is made up only of rules taught by men.[a]
[14] Therefore once more I will astound these people
with wonder upon wonder;
the wisdom of the wise will perish,
the intelligence of the intelligent will vanish."
[15] Woe to those who go to great depths
to hide their plans from the Lord,
who do their work in darkness and think,
"Who sees us? Who will know?"
[16] You turn things upside down,
as if the potter were thought to be like the clay!
Shall what is formed say to him who formed it,
"He did not make me"?
Can the pot say of the potter,
"He knows nothing"?

[17] In a very short time, will not Lebanon be turned
into a fertile field
and the fertile field seem like a forest?
[18] In that day the deaf will hear the words of the
scroll,
and out of gloom and darkness
the eyes of the blind will see.
[19] Once more the humble will rejoice in the Lord;
the needy will rejoice in the Holy One of Israel.
[20] The ruthless will vanish,
the mockers will disappear,
and all who have an eye for evil will be cut
down—
[21] those who with a word make a man out to be
guilty,
who ensnare the defender in court
and with false testimony deprive the innocent
of justice.

[22] Therefore this is what the Lord, who redeemed Abraham, says to the house of Jacob:

"No longer will Jacob be ashamed;
no longer will their faces grow pale.
[23] When they see among them their children,
the work of my hands,
they will keep my name holy;
they will acknowledge the holiness of the Holy
One of Jacob,

---

[a] 13 Hebrew; Septuagint *They worship me in vain; / their teachings are but rules taught by men*

and will stand in awe of the God of Israel.
²⁴Those who are wayward in spirit will gain
  understanding;
  those who complain will accept instruction."

Woe to the Obstinate Nation

30 "Woe to the obstinate children,"
      declares the LORD,
"to those who carry out plans that are not mine,
  forming an alliance, but not by my Spirit,
  heaping sin upon sin;
²who go down to Egypt
  without consulting me;
who look for help to Pharaoh's protection,
  to Egypt's shade for refuge.
³But Pharaoh's protection will be to your shame,
  Egypt's shade will bring you disgrace.
⁴Though they have officials in Zoan
  and their envoys have arrived in Hanes,
⁵everyone will be put to shame
  because of a people useless to them,
who bring neither help nor advantage,
  but only shame and disgrace."

⁶An oracle concerning the animals of the Negev:

  Through a land of hardship and distress,
    of lions and lionesses,
    of adders and darting snakes,
  the envoys carry their riches on donkeys' backs,
    their treasures on the humps of camels,
    to that unprofitable nation,
⁷ to Egypt, whose help is utterly useless.
  Therefore I call her
    Rahab the Do-Nothing.

⁸Go now, write it on a tablet for them,
  inscribe it on a scroll,
that for the days to come
  it may be an everlasting witness.
⁹These are rebellious people, deceitful children,
  children unwilling to listen to the LORD's
    instruction.
¹⁰They say to the seers,
  "See no more visions!"
and to the prophets,
  "Give us no more visions of what is right!
Tell us pleasant things,
  prophesy illusions.
¹¹Leave this way,
  get off this path,
and stop confronting us
  with the Holy One of Israel!"

¹²Therefore, this is what the Holy One of Israel says:

"Because you have rejected this message,
  relied on oppression
  and depended on deceit,
¹³this sin will become for you
  like a high wall, cracked and bulging,
  that collapses suddenly, in an instant.

1. When you are in need of a good rest, what do you like to do? 2. Would your parents have ever called you obstinate or a "do-nothing"? For what reason? 3. What was an embarrassing nickname for you? How did you get it?

1. This is Isaiah's fourth "woe" message since 28:1. For what is he pronouncing God's judgment here? What is the basic problem with their desire to form an alliance with Egypt against Assyria (vv. 1–7)? 2. How would you feel as one of the envoys to Egypt when Isaiah approaches your caravan and gives this oracle? How does the nickname for Egypt ("Rahab the Do-Nothing") contrast with the description of God throughout these chapters? (Note: "Rahab" is a mythical sea dragon; its name means "storm" or "arrogance.") 3. What was the "official" response to Isaiah (vv. 8–11)? What inescapable logic do you see in God's judgment here? What does Isaiah mean by the image of the wall (vv. 13–14)? 4. In contrast to their alliance with Egypt, what is Isaiah's plan for their deliverance (v. 15)? What will happen as a result of Israel rejecting this plan? 5. In light of all the warnings throughout chapters 28–30, how do you account for the promises of God's grace (vv. 18–26)? 6. What do the agricultural images convey about God's grace? What would be equivalent industrial or technological images to convey the same idea today? What is the condition for this outpouring of grace? 7. Are salvation (vv. 18–26) and judgment (vv. 27–33) flip sides of the same action on God's part? How do they work together to achieve the same divine purpose? 8. Some songs teach theology. This song of God's imminent judgment over Assyria is a case in point. What images, names and verbs are associated with God? What do these teach you about who God is, what he does and why? 9. What will happen to Assyria at Topheth? (Note: For a pungent account of how this garbage dump or burning place outside Jerusalem came to be associated with what the New Testament called Gehenna or hell, see Jer 7:31–32; 19:6,11–14.)

♡ **1.** Judah's shame is repeated three times in verses 3–5. Judah looked for the right thing (security) but in the wrong place (Egypt instead of God). What are some of the wrong places *you* have hoped to find the right things (security, love, acceptance)? As a result of your search, did you find what you were looking for? Or did your search ultimately lead to the building up of shame in your inner life? What is the antidote to dealing with shame? **2.** Israel was tired of hearing the Word of God, and wished to be left alone or listen to others as well. What in your life are the "pleasant things" or "illusions" (v. 10) you would rather listen to at times? How have they resulted in "high walls" (v. 13), fencing out God? **3.** Have you experienced this wall of illusion eventually "cracking, bulging and collapsing" down on you (as in vv. 9–14)? What effect has that had upon you? With what are you building a new wall? **4.** Comparing 28:12 and 30:15 with Matthew 11:28–30, what differences do you see? What similarities? What thoughts or pictures come to mind as you consider the Lord as a "resting place"? **5.** If you are a workaholic, reliant on "swift horses," how would you begin to apply verse 15? How does a busybody or workaholic find rest and quietness? What is there to repent of? How might the small group help in this regard? **6.** When we pray "thy kingdom come," what does that imply about those who resist God and are not part of his kingdom? Should one rejoice at the thought of God's judgment? Why or why not? **7.** What does this passage say to severely oppressed people (Jewish prisoners in a Nazi concentration camp, or American Blacks marching for civil rights in the 1960s, or the Arab Palestinians in the 1980s)? Knowing God's judgment is certain, how does that strengthen you to keep on following him?

¹⁴It will break in pieces like pottery,
shattered so mercilessly
that among its pieces not a fragment will be found
for taking coals from a hearth
or scooping water out of a cistern."

¹⁵This is what the Sovereign Lord, the Holy One of Israel, says:

"In repentance and rest is your salvation,
in quietness and trust is your strength,
but you would have none of it.
¹⁶You said, 'No, we will flee on horses.'
Therefore you will flee!
You said, 'We will ride off on swift horses.'
Therefore your pursuers will be swift!
¹⁷A thousand will flee
at the threat of one;
at the threat of five
you will all flee away,
till you are left
like a flagstaff on a mountaintop,
like a banner on a hill."

¹⁸Yet the Lord longs to be gracious to you;
he rises to show you compassion.
For the Lord is a God of justice.
Blessed are all who wait for him!

¹⁹O people of Zion, who live in Jerusalem, you will weep no more. How gracious he will be when you cry for help! As soon as he hears, he will answer you. ²⁰Although the Lord gives you the bread of adversity and the water of affliction, your teachers will be hidden no more; with your own eyes you will see them. ²¹Whether you turn to the right or to the left, your ears will hear a voice behind you, saying, "This is the way; walk in it." ²²Then you will defile your idols overlaid with silver and your images covered with gold; you will throw them away like a menstrual cloth and say to them, "Away with you!"

²³He will also send you rain for the seed you sow in the ground, and the food that comes from the land will be rich and plentiful. In that day your cattle will graze in broad meadows. ²⁴The oxen and donkeys that work the soil will eat fodder and mash, spread out with fork and shovel. ²⁵In the day of great slaughter, when the towers fall, streams of water will flow on every high mountain and every lofty hill. ²⁶The moon will shine like the sun, and the sunlight will be seven times brighter, like the light of seven full days, when the Lord binds up the bruises of his people and heals the wounds he inflicted.

²⁷See, the Name of the Lord comes from afar,
with burning anger and dense clouds of smoke;
his lips are full of wrath,
and his tongue is a consuming fire.
²⁸His breath is like a rushing torrent,
rising up to the neck.
He shakes the nations in the sieve of destruction;
he places in the jaws of the peoples
a bit that leads them astray.
²⁹And you will sing
as on the night you celebrate a holy festival;
your hearts will rejoice

as when people go up with flutes
  to the mountain of the LORD,
  to the Rock of Israel.
[30]The LORD will cause men to hear his majestic
     voice
  and will make them see his arm coming down
with raging anger and consuming fire,
  with cloudburst, thunderstorm and hail.
[31]The voice of the LORD will shatter Assyria;
  with his scepter he will strike them down.
[32]Every stroke the LORD lays on them
  with his punishing rod
will be to the music of tambourines and harps,
  as he fights them in battle with the blows of his
     arm.
[33]Topheth has long been prepared;
  it has been made ready for the king.
Its fire pit has been made deep and wide,
  with an abundance of fire and wood;
the breath of the LORD,
  like a stream of burning sulfur,
  sets it ablaze.

Woe to Those Who Rely on Egypt

31 Woe to those who go down to Egypt for help,
    who rely on horses,
who trust in the multitude of their chariots
  and in the great strength of their horsemen,
but do not look to the Holy One of Israel,
  or seek help from the LORD.
[2]Yet he too is wise and can bring disaster;
  he does not take back his words.
He will rise up against the house of the wicked,
  against those who help evildoers.
[3]But the Egyptians are men and not God;
  their horses are flesh and not spirit.
When the LORD stretches out his hand,
  he who helps will stumble,
  he who is helped will fall;
  both will perish together.

[4]This is what the LORD says to me:

"As a lion growls,
  a great lion over his prey—
and though a whole band of shepherds
  is called together against him,
he is not frightened by their shouts
  or disturbed by their clamor—
so the LORD Almighty will come down
  to do battle on Mount Zion and on its heights.
[5]Like birds hovering overhead,
  the LORD Almighty will shield Jerusalem;
he will shield it and deliver it,
  he will 'pass over' it and will rescue it."

[6]Return to him you have so greatly revolted against, O Israelites. [7]For in that day every one of you will reject the idols of silver and gold your sinful hands have made.

[8]"Assyria will fall by a sword that is not of man;

If you had to be a horse, lion or bird, which one would you choose and why? Which of their assets (speed, strength, appetite, quickness) would you like to have?

1. How is this "woe" related to the one in chapter 30? What similarities do you see? What differences? What reasoning is given here for the warning in the previous "woe"? **2.** If you were a leader in Judah, why would you be seeking this alliance? What have these leaders overlooked as they have formed this alliance? **3.** In contrast to the stumbling of the Egyptians, how will God help Judah during the Assyrian attack (vv. 4–9)? How will God be like a lion? Like a mother bird? Like a fire? **4.** How will this event be like another Passover for Judah (v. 5; see Ex 12:12–13)? What will be the result for the Assyrians? For the Jews? **5.** What does it mean that this deliverance doesn't depend upon whether they "return to him" first (v. 6)? What will happen as a result of this deliverance?

1. What pressures have you felt lately? In practical terms, does relying on God in such times mean not involving the help of anyone else? How can you tell when it is wise and right to rely on others, or when that shows independence from God? **2.** God intended to deliver Judah even while she persisted in rebellion. What hope does that offer you (see Ro 5:8)? **3.** When have you actually lived as though God didn't matter? What did matter at that time? What difference does it make to you to realize that even in those times God is protecting you as a lion or a mother bird? What other images of God help you to embrace him?

What are you thirsty or hungry for, right now?

1. What conditions marked the reign of the leaders who did not trust God (see 28:7–10, 14–15; 29:13,20–21)? 2. By contrast, what will this kingdom of righteousness look like (vv. 2–4)? 3. What will happen to the ways of the fool and the unjust? Why does foolishness flourish when there's no justice?

1. When you need someone to be a shelter for you, to whom do you turn? Why? How is Jesus presented in this passage? 2. For whom could you be like a shelter or a stream of water today? How? What example can you think of where a person's power has been mistaken for true greatness? Is your culture more influenced by a leader's style or by substance? Why do you think so? 3. What marks of true greatness (v. 8) do you want to see growing in you? How can you cultivate that fruit (see Mt 6:33)?

In the morning, are you easy to wake up? Or do you need two alarms, a dog with a cold nose and someone to pull the covers off of you?

1. Up to this point, how have the men responded to Isaiah's message (see 28:7–10)? Why might he be turning to the women at this juncture? What does he anticipate for them? 2. What does he mean by the "thorns and briers" (v. 13; see 5:6; 7:23; 27:4)? What is wrong with the revelry and merriment over which he calls the women to mourn (see 22:12–13)? 3. What will restore Judah (vv. 15–20)? What will the restored kingdom look like? 4. How do these promises of God compare with those given earlier (see 28:16; 29:17–24; 30:19–26; 32:1–8;

a sword, not of mortals, will devour them.
They will flee before the sword
    and their young men will be put to forced labor.
9Their stronghold will fall because of terror;
    at sight of the battle standard their commanders will panic,"
declares the LORD,
    whose fire is in Zion,
    whose furnace is in Jerusalem.

The Kingdom of Righteousness

32 See, a king will reign in righteousness
    and rulers will rule with justice.
2Each man will be like a shelter from the wind
    and a refuge from the storm,
like streams of water in the desert
    and the shadow of a great rock in a thirsty land.

3Then the eyes of those who see will no longer be closed,
    and the ears of those who hear will listen.
4The mind of the rash will know and understand,
    and the stammering tongue will be fluent and clear.
5No longer will the fool be called noble
    nor the scoundrel be highly respected.
6For the fool speaks folly,
    his mind is busy with evil:
He practices ungodliness
    and spreads error concerning the LORD;
the hungry he leaves empty
    and from the thirsty he withholds water.
7The scoundrel's methods are wicked,
    he makes up evil schemes
to destroy the poor with lies,
    even when the plea of the needy is just.
8But the noble man makes noble plans,
    and by noble deeds he stands.

The Women of Jerusalem

9You women who are so complacent,
    rise up and listen to me;
you daughters who feel secure,
    hear what I have to say!
10In little more than a year
    you who feel secure will tremble;
the grape harvest will fail,
    and the harvest of fruit will not come.
11Tremble, you complacent women;
    shudder, you daughters who feel secure!
Strip off your clothes,
    put sackcloth around your waists.
12Beat your breasts for the pleasant fields,
    for the fruitful vines
13and for the land of my people,
    a land overgrown with thorns and briers—
yes, mourn for all houses of merriment
    and for this city of revelry.
14The fortress will be abandoned,

the noisy city deserted;
citadel and watchtower will become a wasteland
forever,
the delight of donkeys, a pasture for flocks,
¹⁵till the Spirit is poured upon us from on high,
and the desert becomes a fertile field,
and the fertile field seems like a forest.
¹⁶Justice will dwell in the desert
and righteousness live in the fertile field.
¹⁷The fruit of righteousness will be peace;
the effect of righteousness will be quietness and
confidence forever.
¹⁸My people will live in peaceful dwelling places,
in secure homes,
in undisturbed places of rest.
¹⁹Though hail flattens the forest
and the city is leveled completely,
²⁰how blessed you will be,
sowing your seed by every stream,
and letting your cattle and donkeys range free.

Distress and Help

33 Woe to you, O destroyer,
you who have not been destroyed!
Woe to you, O traitor,
you who have not been betrayed!
When you stop destroying,
you will be destroyed;
when you stop betraying,
you will be betrayed.

²O Lord, be gracious to us;
we long for you.
Be our strength every morning,
our salvation in time of distress.
³At the thunder of your voice, the peoples flee;
when you rise up, the nations scatter.
⁴Your plunder, O nations, is harvested as by young
locusts;
like a swarm of locusts men pounce on it.

⁵The Lord is exalted, for he dwells on high;
he will fill Zion with justice and righteousness.
⁶He will be the sure foundation for your times,
a rich store of salvation and wisdom and
knowledge;
the fear of the Lord is the key to this
treasure.ᵃ

⁷Look, their brave men cry aloud in the streets;
the envoys of peace weep bitterly.
⁸The highways are deserted,
no travelers are on the roads.
The treaty is broken,
its witnessesᵇ are despised,
no one is respected.
⁹The land mournsᶜ and wastes away,
Lebanon is ashamed and withers;

ᵃ6 Or *is a treasure from him*   ᵇ8 Dead Sea Scrolls; Masoretic Text / *the cities*
ᶜ9 Or *dries up*

33:20–24). What is distinctive about the imagery Isaiah uses to convey his message?

1. What is the difference between security in God's love and complacency that you are on the right side? 2. What does Isaiah feel the outpouring of the Spirit will be like on God's people? How does that compare to the disciples' question in Acts 1:5–6? 3. Which is closer to your own view of what it means to be filled with the Spirit? Is it more an individual or corporate experience? How so? 4. Are you experiencing the fullness of the Spirit in your life? In your church's life? How so? 5. What does Isaiah say about God's ultimate desire for you?

1. "When the cat is away the mice will play." What playful thing do you try to get away with when the boss (parent, teacher, pastor) is gone? 2. Recall the three monkeys who "hear no evil, see no evil, and speak no evil." What contemporary issues do you wish someone in office would notice and speak against?

1. Although the earlier "woes" in chapters 28–32 were directed toward Judah in light of the Assyrian invasion, to whom is this one addressed? In verses 1–9, what four shifts in mood and speaker do you sense? 2. How are the Jerusalem leaders reacting to the news that Egypt will not help in the fight against Assyria? What does it matter that Assyria rebuffs the envoys of peace with their payments of tribute (v. 7; 2Ki 18:14–16)? 3. As their city is besieged, how does Israel respond (vv. 2–3)? How does that compare with earlier responses in a national emergency (see 28:14–15; 31:1)? Are they any closer to demonstrating what God desired for them all along (see 30:15; 31:6)? How will they find in God what they have been mistakenly looking for in their alliance with Egypt? 4. What will occur "now" that it is God's time to act (vv. 10–12)? How will the people of Jerusalem react to this outpouring of God's power in the defeat of her enemy? How does their reaction to God's holiness and power (v. 14) compare to Isaiah's reaction (see 6:5)? 5. What is it that is heard, seen and spoken in God's answer (vv. 15–16; see Ps 15), in

contrast to the proverbial deaf, blind and dumb monkeys? How does God's answer reflect both personal and social righteousness? **6.** Verses 17–24 conclude the series of prophecies begun in 28:1. What does this final picture of God's grace to Judah emphasize about God's plan for his people? Who do you think "the king in his beauty" (v. 17) refers to: (a) Hezekiah (who was the king of Judah at this time)? (b) Some Davidic king still to come? Or (c) God as king? Why do you think so? Might this also be a picture of what the Gospel of Christ is all about? How so?

1. When was one time God's power was so evident to you that by contrast your weakness was highlighted? In your experience of God now, does he seem more like a consuming fire or a fading candle? How can you keep on experiencing the fire? **2.** If you had to answer the question of verse 14, how would you relate faith in Jesus to the lifestyle commanded in verses 15–16? **3.** From what former "terror" has God delivered you? How? What effect has that had upon your view of God? On the way you worship or live? **4.** Of the kingdom traits described in verses 17–24, which ones do you most yearn to see with your own eyes? Which one do you desire to see take root in your life more and more? **5.** What does it mean to you that the Lord Jesus is the fulfillment of verse 22? What aspects of his earthly and future ministry come to mind when you picture Jesus as Judge? Lawgiver? King? Savior?

Sharon is like the Arabah,
    and Bashan and Carmel drop their leaves.

¹⁰"Now will I arise," says the LORD.
    "Now will I be exalted;
    now will I be lifted up.
¹¹You conceive chaff,
    you give birth to straw;
    your breath is a fire that consumes you.
¹²The peoples will be burned as if to lime;
    like cut thornbushes they will be set ablaze."

¹³You who are far away, hear what I have done;
    you who are near, acknowledge my power!
¹⁴The sinners in Zion are terrified;
    trembling grips the godless:
"Who of us can dwell with the consuming fire?
    Who of us can dwell with everlasting burning?"
¹⁵He who walks righteously
    and speaks what is right,
who rejects gain from extortion
    and keeps his hand from accepting bribes,
who stops his ears against plots of murder
    and shuts his eyes against contemplating evil—
¹⁶this is the man who will dwell on the heights,
    whose refuge will be the mountain fortress.
His bread will be supplied,
    and water will not fail him.

¹⁷Your eyes will see the king in his beauty
    and view a land that stretches afar.
¹⁸In your thoughts you will ponder the former
      terror:
    "Where is that chief officer?
    Where is the one who took the revenue?
    Where is the officer in charge of the towers?"
¹⁹You will see those arrogant people no more,
    those people of an obscure speech,
    with their strange, incomprehensible tongue.

²⁰Look upon Zion, the city of our festivals;
    your eyes will see Jerusalem,
    a peaceful abode, a tent that will not be moved;
its stakes will never be pulled up,
    nor any of its ropes broken.
²¹There the LORD will be our Mighty One.
    It will be like a place of broad rivers and
      streams.
No galley with oars will ride them,
    no mighty ship will sail them.
²²For the LORD is our judge,
    the LORD is our lawgiver,
    the LORD is our king;
    it is he who will save us.

²³Your rigging hangs loose:
    The mast is not held secure,
    the sail is not spread.
Then an abundance of spoils will be divided
    and even the lame will carry off plunder.
²⁴No one living in Zion will say, "I am ill";

and the sins of those who dwell there will be
  forgiven.

Judgment Against the Nations

34 Come near, you nations, and listen;
  pay attention, you peoples!
Let the earth hear, and all that is in it,
  the world, and all that comes out of it!
²The LORD is angry with all nations;
  his wrath is upon all their armies.
He will totally destroy*ᵃ* them,
  he will give them over to slaughter.
³Their slain will be thrown out,
  their dead bodies will send up a stench;
  the mountains will be soaked with their blood.
⁴All the stars of the heavens will be dissolved
  and the sky rolled up like a scroll;
all the starry host will fall
  like withered leaves from the vine,
  like shriveled figs from the fig tree.

⁵My sword has drunk its fill in the heavens;
  see, it descends in judgment on Edom,
  the people I have totally destroyed.
⁶The sword of the LORD is bathed in blood,
  it is covered with fat—
the blood of lambs and goats,
  fat from the kidneys of rams.
For the LORD has a sacrifice in Bozrah
  and a great slaughter in Edom.
⁷And the wild oxen will fall with them,
  the bull calves and the great bulls.
Their land will be drenched with blood,
  and the dust will be soaked with fat.

⁸For the LORD has a day of vengeance,
  a year of retribution, to uphold Zion's cause.
⁹Edom's streams will be turned into pitch,
  her dust into burning sulfur;
  her land will become blazing pitch!
¹⁰It will not be quenched night and day;
  its smoke will rise forever.
From generation to generation it will lie desolate;
  no one will ever pass through it again.
¹¹The desert owlᵇ and screech owlᵇ will possess
    it;
  the great owlᵇ and the raven will nest there.
God will stretch out over Edom
  the measuring line of chaos
  and the plumb line of desolation.
¹²Her nobles will have nothing there to be called a
    kingdom,
  all her princes will vanish away.
¹³Thorns will overrun her citadels,
  nettles and brambles her strongholds.
She will become a haunt for jackals,
  a home for owls.

1. What do you associate with the following words: War? Massacre? Meat slaughter house? Red Cross blood drive? Hospital surgery? Other? **2.** What's the bloodiest thing that's ever happened to you? What does the sight of lots of blood do to you? Have you ever fainted?

Chapters 34 and 35 together conclude the series of prophecies in chapters 13–33 about God's rule over the nations. **1.** If special effects recreated the cosmic and gory scenes depicted here for a movie, what would God's anger look like? Feel like? **2.** As music director, where would you place the drum roll? The crescendo? The discordant notes? The resolution? **3.** Why is the Lord this angry with "all nations" (v. 2; see 10:5–19, for the example of Assyria)? What modern political and military leaders does that example bring to mind? What is Isaiah's purpose in doing so in such graphic detail? **4.** How is God's vengeance related to his saving purpose (v. 8; see 35:4)? **5.** Edom, a traditional enemy of Judah, represents all the nations as an object lesson here. What is the object lesson meted out to Edom for having refused to willingly offer sacrifice to the Lord (vv. 4–7)? **6.** After making them give their own blood in sacrifice to him, what will the resulting population and landscape be like for Edom (and all nations under judgment)? Are these images meant to be understood literally, figuratively or both? Explain.

1. How do you feel about God after reading this passage? How might you feel if you read it from the viewpoint of an oppressed person reflecting on the fact that justice would one day overtake your oppressor? **2.** What do you think it would mean to have the "measuring line of chaos" and the "plumb line of desolation" stretched out over your country (v. 11)? **3.** How would you explain God's justice to someone if there was no prospect of judgment? How is his wrath related to his love? What does it mean to you that God will fight this hard in order to save you?

ᵃ2 The Hebrew term refers to the irrevocable giving over of things or persons to the LORD, often by totally destroying them; also in verse 5.   *ᵇ11* The precise identification of these birds is uncertain.

¹⁴Desert creatures will meet with hyenas,
   and wild goats will bleat to each other;
there the night creatures will also repose
   and find for themselves places of rest.
¹⁵The owl will nest there and lay eggs,
   she will hatch them, and care for her young
      under the shadow of her wings;
there also the falcons will gather,
   each with its mate.

¹⁶Look in the scroll of the LORD and read:

None of these will be missing,
   not one will lack her mate.
For it is his mouth that has given the order,
   and his Spirit will gather them together.
¹⁷He allots their portions;
   his hand distributes them by measure.
They will possess it forever
   and dwell there from generation to generation.

Joy of the Redeemed

35 The desert and the parched land will be glad;
   the wilderness will rejoice and blossom.
Like the crocus, ²it will burst into bloom;
   it will rejoice greatly and shout for joy.
The glory of Lebanon will be given to it,
   the splendor of Carmel and Sharon;
they will see the glory of the LORD,
   the splendor of our God.

³Strengthen the feeble hands,
   steady the knees that give way;
⁴say to those with fearful hearts,
   "Be strong, do not fear;
your God will come,
   he will come with vengeance;
with divine retribution
   he will come to save you."

⁵Then will the eyes of the blind be opened
   and the ears of the deaf unstopped.
⁶Then will the lame leap like a deer,
   and the mute tongue shout for joy.
Water will gush forth in the wilderness
   and streams in the desert.
⁷The burning sand will become a pool,
   the thirsty ground bubbling springs.
In the haunts where jackals once lay,
   grass and reeds and papyrus will grow.

⁸And a highway will be there;
   it will be called the Way of Holiness.
The unclean will not journey on it;
   it will be for those who walk in that Way;
   wicked fools will not go about on it. ^a
⁹No lion will be there,
   nor will any ferocious beast get up on it;
   they will not be found there.
But only the redeemed will walk there,

1. After a long, cold winter, what is the first spring flower that you watch for? How do you feel when you see it? 2. What was the last time you or your city "danced in the streets for joy"?

1. In contrast to those God destroys (see ch. 34), what will happen to the land and people he saves? What does the image of the crocus bursting into bloom convey to you? What does this show you about the ultimate purpose of God's judgment? 2. What effect will this spring-like salvation have on the people (vv. 5–10)? When do you think such everlasting joy will come? 3. Are such physical transformations meant to be taken literally, or figuratively (see 6:9f; 32:3–4)? If figuratively, then what does each mean? Might Isaiah have in view the work of the Messiah (see Lk 7:22; Jn 14:6) and the Holy Spirit (Jn 7:38–39)?

1. What pressures are "causing your hands and knees to tremble" now? How might the message of verse 4 bring strength to you? When you have given up trying to reach God, how has he come to you? 2. Is the water of God's Spirit more like a flooded spring or a plugged faucet in your life now? Why? What will it take to release all the joy of the redeemed in your life? 3. Jesus claims to be "the Way" (Jn 14:6). What insight does that give you into the meaning of verse 8? How are you doing on this "Highway to Holiness": (a) Cruising on auto-pilot? (b) Running out of gas? (c) Stuck in the breakdown lane? (d) Still trying to find

^a8 Or / the simple will not stray from it

10 and the ransomed of the LORD will return.
    They will enter Zion with singing;
        everlasting joy will crown their heads.
    Gladness and joy will overtake them,
        and sorrow and sighing will flee away.

Sennacherib Threatens Jerusalem

36 In the fourteenth year of King Hezekiah's reign, Sennacherib king of Assyria attacked all the fortified cities of Judah and captured them. [2]Then the king of Assyria sent his field commander with a large army from Lachish to King Hezekiah at Jerusalem. When the commander stopped at the aqueduct of the Upper Pool, on the road to the Washerman's Field, [3]Eliakim son of Hilkiah the palace administrator, Shebna the secretary, and Joah son of Asaph the recorder went out to him.

[4]The field commander said to them, "Tell Hezekiah,

" 'This is what the great king, the king of Assyria, says: On what are you basing this confidence of yours? [5]You say you have strategy and military strength—but you speak only empty words. On whom are you depending, that you rebel against me? [6]Look now, you are depending on Egypt, that splintered reed of a staff, which pierces a man's hand and wounds him if he leans on it! Such is Pharaoh king of Egypt to all who depend on him. [7]And if you say to me, "We are depending on the LORD our God"—isn't he the one whose high places and altars Hezekiah removed, saying to Judah and Jerusalem, "You must worship before this altar"?

[8]" 'Come now, make a bargain with my master, the king of Assyria: I will give you two thousand horses—if you can put riders on them! [9]How then can you repulse one officer of the least of my master's officials, even though you are depending on Egypt for chariots and horsemen? [10]Furthermore, have I come to attack and destroy this land without the LORD? The LORD himself told me to march against this country and destroy it.' "

[11]Then Eliakim, Shebna and Joah said to the field commander, "Please speak to your servants in Aramaic, since we understand it. Don't speak to us in Hebrew in the hearing of the people on the wall."

[12]But the commander replied, "Was it only to your master and you that my master sent me to say these things, and not to the men sitting on the wall—who, like you, will have to eat their own filth and drink their own urine?"

[13]Then the commander stood and called out in Hebrew, "Hear the words of the great king, the king of Assyria! [14]This is what the king says: Do not let Hezekiah deceive you. He cannot deliver you! [15]Do not let Hezekiah persuade you to trust in the LORD when he says, 'The LORD will surely deliver us; this city will not be given into the hand of the king of Assyria.'

[16]"Do not listen to Hezekiah. This is what the king of Assyria says: Make peace with me and come out to me. Then every one of you will eat from his own vine and fig tree and drink water from his own cistern, [17]until I come and take you to a land like your own—a land of grain and new wine, a land of bread and vineyards.

[18]"Do not let Hezekiah mislead you when he says, 'The LORD will deliver us.' Has the god of any nation ever delivered his land from the hand of the king of Assyria? [19]Where are the gods of Hamath and Arpad? Where are the gods of Sepharvaim? Have they rescued

---

the entrance ramp? How can others in the group help you get on and stay on that Way?

---

1. When approached by solicitors with "an offer too good to refuse" are you an easy sell or a hard sell? **2.** When have you bought something "hook, line and sinker," only to regret it?

Chapters 36–37 climax all that has been foretold up to this point. **1.** The Assyrian army had already routed Egyptian forces 20 miles west of Jerusalem, and were fighting at Lachish, some 20 miles southwest. What would the people in Jerusalem feel as they saw this Assyrian army pincer movement? **2.** How does this event fulfill what Isaiah warned in 7:3,18–25 and 8:6–8? **3.** What arguments does the field commander offer for why Jerusalem should surrender (vv. 4–10)? Do you find them persuasive? Or can you see through them? What do you see? What tone of voice do you hear? **4.** How do Assyria and Isaiah compare in their view of Judah's alliance with Egypt (see 19:14–15; 30:3–5)? As a Judean leader, how would you feel, hearing this Assyrian commander repeat the same things Isaiah has been saying for years? **5.** How does the Assyrian king's account of Hezekiah's reforms (v. 7) differ from the account in 2 Kings 18:3–4? What is the purpose of such misrepresentation? **6.** What is the meaning of his sarcastic offer in verse 8? What is he implying by his final statement in verse 10 (see 10:6–7,12)? **7.** Why does the king speak in Hebrew to people on the city wall (vv. 13–20)? What alternatives does he offer them? Compared to the "gods," where is the Lord in all this? **8.** Do the people respond as expected? Why not panic in the face of such a clear threat from Assyria?

1. How must the faith of Hezekiah have appeared to the Assyrians? In what situation has your faith in God's promises appeared equally foolish? **2.** Given your level of faith now, would you have clung to Isaiah's prophecies at this point, or would you have caved in to "reality"? Why? What "Assyrian threat" faces you now? To what promises of God are you clinging?

Samaria from my hand? ²⁰Who of all the gods of these countries has been able to save his land from me? How then can the LORD deliver Jerusalem from my hand?"

²¹But the people remained silent and said nothing in reply, because the king had commanded, "Do not answer him."

²²Then Eliakim son of Hilkiah the palace administrator, Shebna the secretary, and Joah son of Asaph the recorder went to Hezekiah, with their clothes torn, and told him what the field commander had said.

Jerusalem's Deliverance Foretold

37 When King Hezekiah heard this, he tore his clothes and put on sackcloth and went into the temple of the LORD. ²He sent Eliakim the palace administrator, Shebna the secretary, and the leading priests, all wearing sackcloth, to the prophet Isaiah son of Amoz. ³They told him, "This is what Hezekiah says: This day is a day of distress and rebuke and disgrace, as when children come to the point of birth and there is no strength to deliver them. ⁴It may be that the LORD your God will hear the words of the field commander, whom his master, the king of Assyria, has sent to ridicule the living God, and that he will rebuke him for the words the LORD your God has heard. Therefore pray for the remnant that still survives."

⁵When King Hezekiah's officials came to Isaiah, ⁶Isaiah said to them, "Tell your master, 'This is what the LORD says: Do not be afraid of what you have heard—those words with which the underlings of the king of Assyria have blasphemed me. ⁷Listen! I am going to put a spirit in him so that when he hears a certain report, he will return to his own country, and there I will have him cut down with the sword.'"

⁸When the field commander heard that the king of Assyria had left Lachish, he withdrew and found the king fighting against Libnah.

⁹Now Sennacherib received a report that Tirhakah, the Cushite[a] king ⌊of Egypt⌋, was marching out to fight against him. When he heard it, he sent messengers to Hezekiah with this word: ¹⁰"Say to Hezekiah king of Judah: Do not let the god you depend on deceive you when he says, 'Jerusalem will not be handed over to the king of Assyria.' ¹¹Surely you have heard what the kings of Assyria have done to all the countries, destroying them completely. And will you be delivered? ¹²Did the gods of the nations that were destroyed by my forefathers deliver them—the gods of Gozan, Haran, Rezeph and the people of Eden who were in Tel Assar? ¹³Where is the king of Hamath, the king of Arpad, the king of the city of Sepharvaim, or of Hena or Ivvah?"

Hezekiah's Prayer

¹⁴Hezekiah received the letter from the messengers and read it. Then he went up to the temple of the LORD and spread it out before the LORD. ¹⁵And Hezekiah prayed to the LORD: ¹⁶"O LORD Almighty, God of Israel, enthroned between the cherubim, you alone are God over all the kingdoms of the earth. You have made heaven and earth. ¹⁷Give ear, O LORD, and hear; open your eyes, O LORD, and see; listen to all the words Sennacherib has sent to insult the living God.

¹⁸"It is true, O LORD, that the Assyrian kings have laid waste all these peoples and their lands. ¹⁹They have thrown their gods into

---

1. What is one of the most memorable reports you have ever received? 2. What report, yet to come, would "make your day"?

1. What is the significance of Hezekiah tearing his clothes and wearing burlap? How would you react if a leader you revered did anything like that? 2. How does his response to this threat differ from that of his father Ahaz (see 7:2–13)? On what basis does Hezekiah believe God will help him (see 2Ch 32:6–8)? 3. What work is God doing to control events and undermine the smug king of Assyria (see 36:16–20)? 4. What changes Sennacherib's plans: (a) Spirit of compulsion from the Lord? (b) News from abroad? (c) Outflanked army? How might his withdrawal affect those in Jerusalem? 5. In terms of mocking God, how does Sennacherib outdo his field commander (vv. 10–13)? What's the point of reminding Hezekiah of the other kings' fates? 6. How does Hezekiah's prayer compare to what God has been calling Judean leaders to do all along (see 1:15)? 7. What truths about God does Hezekiah grasp? Why does he dwell on these? 8. How is the point of his prayer like that of the Exodus (see Ex 15:14–16)?

1. Hezekiah models how to respond to intimidation. What big threat to the Christian faith do you worry about? Is the threat real or imagined? How does Hezekiah's example help you deal with that threat? 2. What does this prayer have in common with that of the disciples in Acts 4:23–31? What do these prayers show about God's and Hezekiah's character? What do you see here as the proper focus of prayer?

---

^a 9 That is, from the upper Nile region

the fire and destroyed them, for they were not gods but only wood and stone, fashioned by human hands. [20]Now, O LORD our God, deliver us from his hand, so that all kingdoms on earth may know that you alone, O LORD, are God.[a]"

Sennacherib's Fall

[21]Then Isaiah son of Amoz sent a message to Hezekiah: "This is what the LORD, the God of Israel, says: Because you have prayed to me concerning Sennacherib king of Assyria, [22]this is the word the LORD has spoken against him:

"The Virgin Daughter of Zion
    despises and mocks you.
The Daughter of Jerusalem
    tosses her head as you flee.
[23]Who is it you have insulted and blasphemed?
    Against whom have you raised your voice
and lifted your eyes in pride?
    Against the Holy One of Israel!
[24]By your messengers
    you have heaped insults on the Lord.
And you have said,
    'With my many chariots
I have ascended the heights of the mountains,
    the utmost heights of Lebanon.
I have cut down its tallest cedars,
    the choicest of its pines.
I have reached its remotest heights,
    the finest of its forests.
[25]I have dug wells in foreign lands[b]
    and drunk the water there.
With the soles of my feet
    I have dried up all the streams of Egypt.'

[26]"Have you not heard?
    Long ago I ordained it.
In days of old I planned it;
    now I have brought it to pass,
that you have turned fortified cities
    into piles of stone.
[27]Their people, drained of power,
    are dismayed and put to shame.
They are like plants in the field,
    like tender green shoots,
like grass sprouting on the roof,
    scorched[c] before it grows up.

[28]"But I know where you stay
    and when you come and go
    and how you rage against me.
[29]Because you rage against me
    and because your insolence has reached my
        ears,
    I will put my hook in your nose
    and my bit in your mouth,

---

[a]20 Dead Sea Scrolls (see also 2 Kings 19:19); Masoretic Text *alone are the LORD*   [b]25 Dead Sea Scrolls (see also 2 Kings 19:24); Masoretic Text does not have *in foreign lands.*   [c]27 Some manuscripts of the Masoretic Text, Dead Sea Scrolls and some Septuagint manuscripts (see also 2 Kings 19:26); most manuscripts of the Masoretic Text *roof / and terraced fields*

1. How did you feel as a child when you played "king of the hill" and got to the top? What did you do to stay there? How did you feel when you were knocked off? **2.** What version of this same game do you play at work or in society? Have you reached the top yet? Have you fallen yet?

1. What is the intended impact of this woman taunting her attacker (v. 22)? How does this taunt song suit the occasion? What is Isaiah asserting about God's relationship to Jerusalem by portraying him as the woman's defender? **2.** What insults have the Assyrians made against God (vv. 24–25; see 36:18–20; 37:10–12)? How will they end up eating their own words? In what way has Sennacherib misunderstood the reason for his past success (see 10:12–19)? **3.** In response to Hezekiah's prayer, by what images does God convey his authority over all nations (vv. 26–29)? What lesson is in this event for Assyria? For Judah? How might it pave the way for 19:23–25 to be fulfilled? **4.** What sign does God give Hezekiah (vv. 30–32)? Why give a sign that will be fulfilled only after the event it is meant to show? How does this sign relate to the promises of restoration (as in 10:20–23)? **5.** In what sense is God saving Jerusalem for his sake? For David's sake? **6.** Other ancient writings speak of Sennacherib's army being decimated by fear and panic perhaps because of a plague. How does this fulfill the earlier prophecies (see 10:33–34; 29:5–8; 30:31)? If you were living in Jerusalem, how would you react when you heard that 185,000 Assyrian soldiers had died? Would you be more likely to respond like those described in 33:14–15, or in 35:10? Why? **7.** Verse 38 records an event that occurred 20 years after the events of verses 36–37. What irony do you see in Sennacherib's death as he enters the temple (see 37:1,7,14, where Hezekiah goes into the temple of his God)? **8.** Considering that every city in Judah, except Jerusalem, was destroyed, thousands of innocent people were killed and Judah was plunged into poverty for decades following this attack, do you think this is really a victory for Judah and a defeat for Assyria? Why or why not?

♡ 1. What is the difference between spiritual pride and a rightful sense of accomplishment? What are the indications of each? 2. Since all we have comes from God, what is the place for human planning, preparing and hard work? How have you taken credit for something that was in reality far more than you could possibly have pulled off by yourself? What did it take to wake you up to that fact? 3. When have you felt like Hezekiah—backed up against a wall with no recourse but to pray? How have you seen God's affirmation of his love for you? 4. Although Jerusalem was spared, Lachish, a city only 20 miles away was destroyed. How would you explain God's ways to a resident of Lachish? 5. Lachish wanted "last-minute salvation" from God, but it didn't happen that way. When "11th hour" appeals to God seem to fall on deaf ears, how do you cope? What could be God's purpose in delaying or saying "No"?

☕ 1. Would you like to know the exact date when you will die? What difference would it make in how you lived now: Buy more life insurance? Save more money for retirement? Spend more time with the children or grandchildren? Other? 2. What premonition do you have about when or how you will die: Burn out in the prime of life? Worn out in old age? Or what?

📖 Chapters 38–39 serve as a transition to chapters 40–66, which deal with the period, 115 years later, when Jerusalem is destroyed and its people are captives in Babylon. 1. Why is Hezekiah so distressed by the message from Isaiah? (a) His house is messy. (b) He hadn't made out his will yet. (c) He objects to bad things happening to good people. (d) He objects to his father Ahaz, who had been a

and I will make you return
by the way you came.

³⁰"This will be the sign for you, O Hezekiah:

"This year you will eat what grows by itself,
and the second year what springs from that.
But in the third year sow and reap,
plant vineyards and eat their fruit.
³¹Once more a remnant of the house of Judah
will take root below and bear fruit above.
³²For out of Jerusalem will come a remnant,
and out of Mount Zion a band of survivors.
The zeal of the LORD Almighty
will accomplish this.

³³"Therefore this is what the LORD says concerning the king of Assyria:

"He will not enter this city
or shoot an arrow here.
He will not come before it with shield
or build a siege ramp against it.
³⁴By the way that he came he will return;
he will not enter this city,"
declares the LORD.
³⁵"I will defend this city and save it,
for my sake and for the sake of David my
servant!"

³⁶Then the angel of the LORD went out and put to death a hundred and eighty-five thousand men in the Assyrian camp. When the people got up the next morning—there were all the dead bodies! ³⁷So Sennacherib king of Assyria broke camp and withdrew. He returned to Nineveh and stayed there.

³⁸One day, while he was worshiping in the temple of his god Nisroch, his sons Adrammelech and Sharezer cut him down with the sword, and they escaped to the land of Ararat. And Esarhaddon his son succeeded him as king.

Hezekiah's Illness

38 In those days Hezekiah became ill and was at the point of death. The prophet Isaiah son of Amoz went to him and said, "This is what the LORD says: Put your house in order, because you are going to die; you will not recover."

²Hezekiah turned his face to the wall and prayed to the LORD, ³"Remember, O LORD, how I have walked before you faithfully and with wholehearted devotion and have done what is good in your eyes." And Hezekiah wept bitterly.

⁴Then the word of the LORD came to Isaiah: ⁵"Go and tell Hezekiah, 'This is what the LORD, the God of your father David, says: I have heard your prayer and seen your tears; I will add fifteen years to your life. ⁶And I will deliver you and this city from the hand of the king of Assyria. I will defend this city.

⁷"'This is the LORD's sign to you that the LORD will do what he has promised: ⁸I will make the shadow cast by the sun go back the ten steps it has gone down on the stairway of Ahaz.'" So the sunlight went back the ten steps it had gone down.

⁹A writing of Hezekiah king of Judah after his illness and recovery:

¹⁰I said, "In the prime of my life
     must I go through the gates of death[a]
     and be robbed of the rest of my years?"
¹¹I said, "I will not again see the LORD,
     the LORD, in the land of the living;
  no longer will I look on mankind,
     or be with those who now dwell in this
        world.[b]
¹²Like a shepherd's tent my house
     has been pulled down and taken from me.
  Like a weaver I have rolled up my life,
     and he has cut me off from the loom;
     day and night you made an end of me.
¹³I waited patiently till dawn,
     but like a lion he broke all my bones;
     day and night you made an end of me.
¹⁴I cried like a swift or thrush,
     I moaned like a mourning dove.
  My eyes grew weak as I looked to the heavens.
  I am troubled; O Lord, come to my aid!"

¹⁵But what can I say?
  He has spoken to me, and he himself has done
        this.
  I will walk humbly all my years
     because of this anguish of my soul.
¹⁶Lord, by such things men live;
     and my spirit finds life in them too.
  You restored me to health
     and let me live.
¹⁷Surely it was for my benefit
     that I suffered such anguish.
  In your love you kept me
     from the pit of destruction;
  you have put all my sins
     behind your back.
¹⁸For the grave[a] cannot praise you,
     death cannot sing your praise;
  those who go down to the pit
     cannot hope for your faithfulness.
¹⁹The living, the living—they praise you,
     as I am doing today;
  fathers tell their children
     about your faithfulness.

²⁰The LORD will save me,
     and we will sing with stringed instruments
  all the days of our lives
     in the temple of the LORD.

²¹Isaiah had said, "Prepare a poultice of figs and apply it to the boil, and he will recover."
²²Hezekiah had asked, "What will be the sign that I will go up to the temple of the LORD?"

terrible king, getting to reign longer than him. (e) His whole relationship with God is thrown into question by such premature death. (f) He needs more time to complete some reforms he only started. (g) He'd like more time with his children and grandchildren. **2.** What is the track record of "whole-hearted devotion" (v. 3) on which he appeals to the Lord to spare his life (see 2Ki 18:1–8)? **3.** Hezekiah asked Isaiah for a sign that his healing would occur (vv. 7–8; also 2Ki 20:8–11). How does this contrast with Ahaz' response to Isaiah in 7:11–14, when Ahaz was told to ask for a sign but refused to do so? Which man—Ahaz or Hezekiah—demonstrates more faith? How so? What does God's response tell you about God and his mysterious ways? **4.** In the song (vv. 10–20), what images does Hezekiah use to talk about death? What aspect of death and dying do they each convey? To what does he credit his temporary deliverance from death? What part has divine forgiveness played in his healing? What resolve does he make in light of that deliverance?

♡ **1.** Wicked people often live easy lives, or long lives, whereas those serving God often experience great hardships. How do you deal with the seeming unfairness? What might be God's perspective on the matter? **2.** What do you fear about death? What hope does the gospel give you that was unknown to Hezekiah? **3.** Hezekiah realized his illness and his deliverance were both from God (vv. 15–17). What does it mean to you that suffering is part of God's plan for you? What role does suffering serve in your life? **4.** Hezekiah viewed life as a gift from God to be used for his purposes. How would this affect how you will live out your numbered days?

---

a 10,18 Hebrew *Sheol*   *b 11* A few Hebrew manuscripts; most Hebrew manuscripts *in the place of cessation*

1. What treasure do you show off when you can: Trophy? Car? House? Kids? 2. How do you feel towards someone whose treasures outshine yours?

1. What treasure is Hezekiah showing off? Why is he strutting his stuff (see 2Ch 32:22–25)? 2. How does this puffed-up Hezekiah compare with the Hezekiah in 38:15–19? What happened in the meantime? 3. What hopes might such wealth stir up among patronizing people of Judah and Babylon? Could Hezekiah be the deliverer foreseen in 9:1–7 and 11:1–11? 4. How does Isaiah dash these hopes?

1. What hero (religious or political) have you idolized? How has seeing his or her faults forced you to look again to Jesus as the model for your life? 2. Is it harder for you to be faithful during times of hardship or times of success? Why?

---

1. What was the most exciting news you ever received? Why was it so welcome? 2. What is the farthest distance you have ever run or walked? How did you feel at the end?

Jerusalem's deliverance in 701 B.C. from the Assyrian king Sennacherib (Isa 37) climaxes the prophecies of chapters 1–39. Chapters 40–48 deal with events that occur some 150 years later. 1. In 587 B.C. Jerusalem is sacked and its people deported by Babylon, the new world power (see 2Ki 25). Given this situation, what does Isaiah's emphatic "comfort" mean to Israel? What word of comfort do the three "voices" bring (vv. 3,6,9)? What images does the Lord use to assure his people of their forgiveness? 2. In Isaiah's time the coming of a king is announced by a herald. People literally leveled the roads the king would travel. What king is in view in verses 3–5? What does it mean to prepare the way for him? 3. How would this message affect you if you were one of these defeated people torn away from your home, your faith, and your way of life? After all you'd been through at the hands of foreign kings, how would you feel toward the coming King? 4. What then would the eternal word of God (vv. 6–8) mean to you? What promises from Israel's history might

Envoys From Babylon

39 At that time Merodach-Baladan son of Baladan king of Babylon sent Hezekiah letters and a gift, because he had heard of his illness and recovery. ²Hezekiah received the envoys gladly and showed them what was in his storehouses—the silver, the gold, the spices, the fine oil, his entire armory and everything found among his treasures. There was nothing in his palace or in all his kingdom that Hezekiah did not show them.

³Then Isaiah the prophet went to King Hezekiah and asked, "What did those men say, and where did they come from?"

"From a distant land," Hezekiah replied. "They came to me from Babylon."

⁴The prophet asked, "What did they see in your palace?"

"They saw everything in my palace," Hezekiah said. "There is nothing among my treasures that I did not show them."

⁵Then Isaiah said to Hezekiah, "Hear the word of the Lord Almighty: ⁶The time will surely come when everything in your palace, and all that your fathers have stored up until this day, will be carried off to Babylon. Nothing will be left, says the Lord. ⁷And some of your descendants, your own flesh and blood who will be born to you, will be taken away, and they will become eunuchs in the palace of the king of Babylon."

⁸"The word of the Lord you have spoken is good," Hezekiah replied. For he thought, "There will be peace and security in my lifetime."

Comfort for God's People

40 Comfort, comfort my people,
    says your God.
²Speak tenderly to Jerusalem,
    and proclaim to her
that her hard service has been completed,
    that her sin has been paid for,
that she has received from the Lord's hand
    double for all her sins.

³A voice of one calling:
"In the desert prepare
    the way for the Lord ª;
make straight in the wilderness
    a highway for our God. ᵇ
⁴Every valley shall be raised up,
    every mountain and hill made low;
the rough ground shall become level,
    the rugged places a plain.
⁵And the glory of the Lord will be revealed,
    and all mankind together will see it.
        For the mouth of the Lord has spoken."

⁶A voice says, "Cry out."
    And I said, "What shall I cry?"

"All men are like grass,
    and all their glory is like the flowers of the
        field.
⁷The grass withers and the flowers fall,
    because the breath of the Lord blows on them.
    Surely the people are grass.

ª3 Or *A voice of one calling in the desert: / "Prepare the way for the Lord*
ᵇ3 Hebrew; Septuagint *make straight the paths of our God*

⁸The grass withers and the flowers fall,
　　but the word of our God stands forever."

⁹You who bring good tidings to Zion,
　　go up on a high mountain.
　You who bring good tidings to Jerusalem,ᵃ
　　lift up your voice with a shout,
　lift it up, do not be afraid;
　　say to the towns of Judah,
　　"Here is your God!"
¹⁰See, the Sovereign LORD comes with power,
　　and his arm rules for him.
　See, his reward is with him,
　　and his recompense accompanies him.
¹¹He tends his flock like a shepherd:
　　He gathers the lambs in his arms
　and carries them close to his heart;
　　he gently leads those that have young.

¹²Who has measured the waters in the hollow of his
　　hand,
　　or with the breadth of his hand marked off the
　　　heavens?
　Who has held the dust of the earth in a basket,
　　or weighed the mountains on the scales
　　and the hills in a balance?
¹³Who has understood the mindᵇ of the LORD,
　　or instructed him as his counselor?
¹⁴Whom did the LORD consult to enlighten him,
　　and who taught him the right way?
　Who was it that taught him knowledge
　　or showed him the path of understanding?

¹⁵Surely the nations are like a drop in a bucket;
　　they are regarded as dust on the scales;
　he weighs the islands as though they were fine
　　dust.
¹⁶Lebanon is not sufficient for altar fires,
　　nor its animals enough for burnt offerings.
¹⁷Before him all the nations are as nothing;
　　they are regarded by him as worthless
　　and less than nothing.

¹⁸To whom, then, will you compare God?
　　What image will you compare him to?
¹⁹As for an idol, a craftsman casts it,
　　and a goldsmith overlays it with gold
　　and fashions silver chains for it.
²⁰A man too poor to present such an offering
　　selects wood that will not rot.
　He looks for a skilled craftsman
　　to set up an idol that will not topple.

²¹Do you not know?
　Have you not heard?
　Has it not been told you from the beginning?
　Have you not understood since the earth was
　　founded?
²²He sits enthroned above the circle of the earth,

ᵃ9 Or O Zion, bringer of good tidings, / go up on a high mountain. / O Jerusalem,
bringer of good tidings　　ᵇ13 Or Spirit; or spirit

be in view here (see Ge 12:1–3;
2Sa 7:8–16)?

1. The Gospels quote
verse 3 in reference to John
the Baptist preparing the way for
Jesus. What does that imply about
the identity of Jesus? 2. How can
you "prepare the way" in your life
for Jesus? What needs leveling or
shoring up? 3. Jesus comes as
Shepherd (v. 11) as well as King.
What sort of sheep do you feel like:
Cradled? Content? Wandering?
Caught? Lost? Why?

1. When you are down in the
dumps, what favorite things
do you like to think about to lift your
spirits? Does it help? 2. In your
group, who has the largest hand
breadth (the distance from thumb
to little finger as the hand is
stretched out)? Who has the smallest breadth?

1. What is the intended effect
of all these rhetorical questions? In each comparison (creation, knowledge, the nations), how
does God fare? 2. How do the
works of our hands compare with
those of God (vv. 12,19–20)?
When do our own works become
idols? 3. How does God regard the
power of nations, even today's superpowers (vv. 15–17,23–24)? 4.
Is any image or standard of comparison adequate to measure
God's worth (vv. 18–25)? Why or
why not? 5. What is the complaint
of the exiles (v. 27)? What must
they still learn about God before
they can be restored to their homeland (vv. 21,28)? 6. As a weary exile, which of these promises would
you find most uplifting?

1. What "grass and flowers"
(v. 6) or "idols" (v. 19) of this
world today seem awfully powerful
to you? How much do you depend
on them? By comparison, do the
promises of God just seem like
words right now, or do they provide
you with hope? Why? 2. What sort
of complaints do you hear today
from non-Christians? From Christians? How might you answer them
from the truths of this chapter? 3.
When have you most recently felt
like God must have lost your address or phone number? What
fears and thoughts arose in your

mind? How might the truths of this chapter help restore strength to you? **4.** Practically and theologically, how does one "soar like an eagle?" Compare verse 31 with Exodus 19:4 and Deuteronomy 32:10–11. How is learning to hope in God (v. 31) like a fledgling bird learning to fly? How has God "caught" you when you have fallen instead of flown? In what way is he teaching you to fly now?

1. When you were afraid as a child, who would hold your hand? **2.** Have you ever won a game when the odds looked like it was impossible for you to do so? How did your opponent react?

1. Having reassured the exiled Jews in chapter 40, whom does God address in verses 1–7? What do you picture is happening to these nations? **2.** The "one from the east" (v. 2) was Cyrus, the Persian king who overthrew Babylon in 538 B.C. (see 45:1ff). What is God asserting about himself by claiming that he is the one behind Cyrus' success? **3.** Why was the victory of Cyrus good news for the Jewish exiles in Babylon? (See 2Ch 36:22–23.) How are the other nations reacting to this onward march of Cyrus' army (vv. 5–7)? How is their response

and its people are like grasshoppers.
He stretches out the heavens like a canopy,
   and spreads them out like a tent to live in.
²³He brings princes to naught
   and reduces the rulers of this world to nothing.
²⁴No sooner are they planted,
   no sooner are they sown,
   no sooner do they take root in the ground,
than he blows on them and they wither,
   and a whirlwind sweeps them away like chaff.

²⁵"To whom will you compare me?
   Or who is my equal?" says the Holy One.
²⁶Lift your eyes and look to the heavens:
   Who created all these?
He who brings out the starry host one by one,
   and calls them each by name.
Because of his great power and mighty strength,
   not one of them is missing.

²⁷Why do you say, O Jacob,
   and complain, O Israel,
"My way is hidden from the LORD;
   my cause is disregarded by my God"?
²⁸Do you not know?
   Have you not heard?
The LORD is the everlasting God,
   the Creator of the ends of the earth.
He will not grow tired or weary,
   and his understanding no one can fathom.
²⁹He gives strength to the weary
   and increases the power of the weak.
³⁰Even youths grow tired and weary,
   and young men stumble and fall;
³¹but those who hope in the LORD
   will renew their strength.
They will soar on wings like eagles;
   they will run and not grow weary,
   they will walk and not be faint.

The Helper of Israel

41 "Be silent before me, you islands!
   Let the nations renew their strength!
Let them come forward and speak;
   let us meet together at the place of judgment.

²"Who has stirred up one from the east,
   calling him in righteousness to his service?ᵃ
He hands nations over to him
   and subdues kings before him.
He turns them to dust with his sword,
   to windblown chaff with his bow.
³He pursues them and moves on unscathed,
   by a path his feet have not traveled before.
⁴Who has done this and carried it through,
   calling forth the generations from the
      beginning?
I, the LORD—with the first of them
   and with the last—I am he."

ᵃ2 Or / whom victory meets at every step

[5]The islands have seen it and fear;
  the ends of the earth tremble.
They approach and come forward;
[6] each helps the other
  and says to his brother, "Be strong!"
[7]The craftsman encourages the goldsmith,
  and he who smooths with the hammer
  spurs on him who strikes the anvil.
He says of the welding, "It is good."
  He nails down the idol so it will not topple.

[8]"But you, O Israel, my servant,
  Jacob, whom I have chosen,
  you descendants of Abraham my friend,
[9]I took you from the ends of the earth,
  from its farthest corners I called you.
I said, 'You are my servant';
  I have chosen you and have not rejected you.
[10]So do not fear, for I am with you;
  do not be dismayed, for I am your God.
I will strengthen you and help you;
  I will uphold you with my righteous right hand.

[11]"All who rage against you
  will surely be ashamed and disgraced;
those who oppose you
  will be as nothing and perish.
[12]Though you search for your enemies,
  you will not find them.
Those who wage war against you
  will be as nothing at all.
[13]For I am the LORD, your God,
  who takes hold of your right hand
and says to you, Do not fear;
  I will help you.
[14]Do not be afraid, O worm Jacob,
  O little Israel,
for I myself will help you," declares the LORD,
  your Redeemer, the Holy One of Israel.
[15]"See, I will make you into a threshing sledge,
  new and sharp, with many teeth.
You will thresh the mountains and crush them,
  and reduce the hills to chaff.
[16]You will winnow them, the wind will pick them
  up,
  and a gale will blow them away.
But you will rejoice in the LORD
  and glory in the Holy One of Israel.

[17]"The poor and needy search for water,
  but there is none;
  their tongues are parched with thirst.
But I the LORD will answer them;
  I, the God of Israel, will not forsake them.
[18]I will make rivers flow on barren heights,
  and springs within the valleys.
I will turn the desert into pools of water,
  and the parched ground into springs.
[19]I will put in the desert
  the cedar and the acacia, the myrtle and the
  olive.

different from the one God urges upon the Jews in verses 8–10? **4.** What terms does he use to address the exiles in verses 8–10? What do these terms reveal about God's relationship with them? About his plans for them? How would these terms calm their fears? **5.** Why does God address the exiles as "worm Jacob" and "little Israel" (v. 14)? **6.** What is to be the fate of Babylon (vv. 11–16)? How would you react to these statements as you considered all the power and might of Babylon which was all around you? What would it mean to these humiliated exiles to consider that God was influencing all of world history in order to bring about their deliverance? **7.** What type of thirst is Isaiah referring to in verse 17 (see also Ps 42:1–2)? How will their situation soon change? Why will the Lord restore his people (v. 20)? **8.** Of all the peoples conquered by Babylon, only the Jews retained their religious, ethnic and political identity. How might this be a witness to the other nations (v. 20)? How does this relate to Israel's call to be his servant?

♡ **1.** What world problems today seem to be beyond solution? What forces appear to be in control? Do you react to these problems with: Helplessness? Cynicism? Sorrow? Disgust? Hope? Why? **2.** What does this chapter show us of God's involvement in human history? How should this affect our attitude toward world problems? **3.** If God moves heaven and earth in order to protect and save his people, how should that knowledge affect your prayers? Your worship? Your attitude in hard times? Your priorities and purpose in life? How might meditating upon the picture of God in chapters 40–41 help you grasp this truth? **4.** What "mountains" and "hills" are there in your life today? If you compare your faith to Israel's threshing sledge, how "new," "sharp" and "many" are your "teeth"?

I will set pines in the wasteland,
    the fir and the cypress together,
20so that people may see and know,
    may consider and understand,
that the hand of the LORD has done this,
    that the Holy One of Israel has created it.

21"Present your case," says the LORD.
    "Set forth your arguments," says Jacob's King.
22"Bring in ⌊ your idols ⌋ to tell us
    what is going to happen.
Tell us what the former things were,
    so that we may consider them
    and know their final outcome.
Or declare to us the things to come,
23   tell us what the future holds,
    so we may know that you are gods.
Do something, whether good or bad,
    so that we will be dismayed and filled with
      fear.
24But you are less than nothing
    and your works are utterly worthless;
    he who chooses you is detestable.

25"I have stirred up one from the north, and he
      comes—
    one from the rising sun who calls on my name.
He treads on rulers as if they were mortar,
    as if he were a potter treading the clay.
26Who told of this from the beginning, so we could
      know,
    or beforehand, so we could say, 'He was right'?
No one told of this,
    no one foretold it,
    no one heard any words from you.
27I was the first to tell Zion, 'Look, here they are!'
    I gave to Jerusalem a messenger of good tidings.
28I look but there is no one—
    no one among them to give counsel,
    no one to give answer when I ask them.
29See, they are all false!
    Their deeds amount to nothing;
    their images are but wind and confusion.

The Servant of the LORD

42 "Here is my servant, whom I uphold,
    my chosen one in whom I delight;
I will put my Spirit on him
    and he will bring justice to the nations.
2He will not shout or cry out,
    or raise his voice in the streets.
3A bruised reed he will not break,
    and a smoldering wick he will not snuff out.
In faithfulness he will bring forth justice;
4   he will not falter or be discouraged
till he establishes justice on earth.
    In his law the islands will put their hope."

5This is what God the LORD says—
he who created the heavens and stretched them
    out,

Have you ever predicted something would happen and nobody listened? Were you correct? How did you feel?

1. Verses 21–29 resume God's address to the nations. To what competition does the Lord challenge the idols? Why do the idols fail when the Lord succeeds? What will be the outcome for those who had placed their trust in the idols? In the Lord? 2. Cyrus is also called the "one from the north" (v. 25). Persia was to the east of Babylon, yet Cyrus marched against her from the north. Although Cyrus credited his victories to many "gods," what was the real truth about this period of history? How do the military conquests of Cyrus stand in contrast to those of Assyria (see 10:12–13)?

1. In whose predictions of the future do you place your faith? Are there any "idols" in your life whose wisdom or advice you credit above God's? What will you do to change that attitude? 2. Where do you see God at work in history? In your own life? What new perspective have you gained from this chapter on God's wisdom? On his dependability?

As a kid, were you ever disciplined by having to remain in the house or in your bedroom for a period of time? How did you feel when you got out again?

1. This is the first of four "Servant Songs" (see also 49:1–6; 50:4–9; 52:13–53:12). In Isaiah's time, a king's servant stood in a position of great importance. What terms express this servant's relationship to God (vv. 1–7)? His mission? His character? 2. Who is the servant referred to here (see 41:9)? What kind of servant has he been (see 26:17–18)? Why is the Lord singing to honor the servant? 3. Why will God's ser-

who spread out the earth and all that comes out
    of it,
who gives breath to its people,
    and life to those who walk on it:
6"I, the LORD, have called you in righteousness;
    I will take hold of your hand.
I will keep you and will make you
    to be a covenant for the people
    and a light for the Gentiles,
7to open eyes that are blind,
    to free captives from prison
    and to release from the dungeon those who sit
        in darkness.

8"I am the LORD; that is my name!
    I will not give my glory to another
    or my praise to idols.
9See, the former things have taken place,
    and new things I declare;
before they spring into being
    I announce them to you."

Song of Praise to the LORD

10Sing to the LORD a new song,
    his praise from the ends of the earth,
you who go down to the sea, and all that is in it,
    you islands, and all who live in them.
11Let the desert and its towns raise their voices;
    let the settlements where Kedar lives rejoice.
Let the people of Sela sing for joy;
    let them shout from the mountaintops.
12Let them give glory to the LORD
    and proclaim his praise in the islands.
13The LORD will march out like a mighty man,
    like a warrior he will stir up his zeal;
with a shout he will raise the battle cry
    and will triumph over his enemies.

14"For a long time I have kept silent,
    I have been quiet and held myself back.
But now, like a woman in childbirth,
    I cry out, I gasp and pant.
15I will lay waste the mountains and hills
    and dry up all their vegetation;
I will turn rivers into islands
    and dry up the pools.
16I will lead the blind by ways they have not
        known,
    along unfamiliar paths I will guide them;
I will turn the darkness into light before them
    and make the rough places smooth.
These are the things I will do;
    I will not forsake them.
17But those who trust in idols,
    who say to images, 'You are our gods,'
    will be turned back in utter shame.

Israel Blind and Deaf

18"Hear, you deaf;
    look, you blind, and see!

vant "not shout or cry out" (v. 2)?
(See Pr 8:1–4; 9:13ff.) What is
meant by a bruised reed and smoldering wick (v. 3; see 36:6)?

1. In what ways does Jesus
fulfill this picture of God's
servant? 2. Acts 13:47 and 2 Timothy 2:24–26 extend this image of
"the servant" to apply to all believers. In light of that, what does this
passage say about your mission?
Your family? Your work? Your priorities? Your character? How does
this encourage and challenge you?

What new song has been
running through your head
lately? Why that one?

1. What places does the
prophet call upon here? How
does this widespread call relate to
the mission of the servant in verses
6–7? 2. How is God "like a mighty
man" (v. 13)? How is he "like a
woman in childbirth" (v. 14)? Why
does he first "shout" the battle cry,
then "gasp and pant"? 3. Why does
Isaiah finish the good promises of
verses 14–16 with the warning of
verse 17?

1. How are we called to imitate God's actions in this
song (see Ac 26:18 and 1Pe 2:9)?
Who has helped you to see the
light in the darkness? How can you
help others turn from darkness to
light? 2. What "idols" are you
tempted to look to in your life? How
might this passage help you? 3.
Create a "new song" (v. 10) of
praise to God, each person adding
a verse or stanza based upon this
section.

Have you ever misplaced
something, only to discover it
"right under your nose"? What and

where was it? Why did you fail to see it right away?

📖 1. What things have the exiles seen and heard but failed to notice? What was the result? 2. What did God originally plan that Israel should be? How have they failed to live up to this? What have they become instead? 3. If you were an exile, what comfort would you find in this passage? What lesson for the future would you learn?

♡ 1. Are there times in your past when you were deaf or blind to the obvious will of God? How was it obvious, now that you look back? Did God give up on you? 2. If God needed to gain your attention today, where would you place yourself on the scale of 1 (deaf) to 5 (all ears)? Are there any areas of your life where you might still be turning a deaf ear or an intentional blind eye?

🍵 If your house were on fire, what three things would you save and why?

📖 1. If you were an exile, how would you feel if the prophet stopped with chapter 42? What would be your reaction to 43:1–7? 2. Persia, under Cyrus, conquered Egypt, Cush and Seba. Based on Cyrus' treatment of the exiles, what might the Lord mean in verses 3 and 4? Why will he give "men in exchange" (v. 4) for Israel? 3. Why are the exiles told not to fear (vv. 1,5)? How will they know that God is with them? What effect will this have upon them? 4. Although Israel has been blind and deaf to God in the past (42:18–20), what is the purpose for which he will lead them out of Babylon (44:10,12; see 41:20)? What will that act of deliverance communicate to the nations? With what attitude do you imagine this witness will be carried out?

♡ 1. Compare 42:23–43:2 with Romans 3:19–24 and Ephesians 2:11–13. What does the "but now" in each of these passages

¹⁹Who is blind but my servant,
    and deaf like the messenger I send?
Who is blind like the one committed to me,
    blind like the servant of the LORD?
²⁰You have seen many things, but have paid no
        attention;
    your ears are open, but you hear nothing."
²¹It pleased the LORD
    for the sake of his righteousness
    to make his law great and glorious.
²²But this is a people plundered and looted,
    all of them trapped in pits
    or hidden away in prisons.
They have become plunder,
    with no one to rescue them;
they have been made loot,
    with no one to say, "Send them back."

²³Which of you will listen to this
    or pay close attention in time to come?
²⁴Who handed Jacob over to become loot,
    and Israel to the plunderers?
Was it not the LORD,
    against whom we have sinned?
For they would not follow his ways;
    they did not obey his law.
²⁵So he poured out on them his burning anger,
    the violence of war.
It enveloped them in flames, yet they did not
        understand;
    it consumed them, but they did not take it to
        heart.

Israel's Only Savior

43 But now, this is what the LORD says—
    he who created you, O Jacob,
    he who formed you, O Israel:
"Fear not, for I have redeemed you;
    I have summoned you by name; you are mine.
²When you pass through the waters,
    I will be with you;
and when you pass through the rivers,
    they will not sweep over you.
When you walk through the fire,
    you will not be burned;
    the flames will not set you ablaze.
³For I am the LORD, your God,
    the Holy One of Israel, your Savior;
I give Egypt for your ransom,
    Cush[a] and Seba in your stead.
⁴Since you are precious and honored in my sight,
    and because I love you,
I will give men in exchange for you,
    and people in exchange for your life.
⁵Do not be afraid, for I am with you;
    I will bring your children from the east
    and gather you from the west.
⁶I will say to the north, 'Give them up!'

a3 That is, the upper Nile region

and to the south, 'Do not hold them back.'
Bring my sons from afar
    and my daughters from the ends of the earth—
[7]everyone who is called by my name,
    whom I created for my glory,
    whom I formed and made."

[8]Lead out those who have eyes but are blind,
    who have ears but are deaf.
[9]All the nations gather together
    and the peoples assemble.
Which of them foretold this
    and proclaimed to us the former things?
Let them bring in their witnesses to prove they
        were right,
    so that others may hear and say, "It is true."
[10]"You are my witnesses," declares the LORD,
    "and my servant whom I have chosen,
so that you may know and believe me
    and understand that I am he.
Before me no god was formed,
    nor will there be one after me.
[11]I, even I, am the LORD,
    and apart from me there is no savior.
[12]I have revealed and saved and proclaimed—
    I, and not some foreign god among you.
You are my witnesses," declares the LORD, "that I
        am God.
[13] Yes, and from ancient days I am he.
No one can deliver out of my hand.
    When I act, who can reverse it?"

God's Mercy and Israel's Unfaithfulness

[14]This is what the LORD says—
    your Redeemer, the Holy One of Israel:
"For your sake I will send to Babylon
    and bring down as fugitives all the
        Babylonians,[a]
    in the ships in which they took pride.
[15]I am the LORD, your Holy One,
    Israel's Creator, your King."

[16]This is what the LORD says—
    he who made a way through the sea,
    a path through the mighty waters,
[17]who drew out the chariots and horses,
    the army and reinforcements together,
and they lay there, never to rise again,
    extinguished, snuffed out like a wick:
[18]"Forget the former things;
    do not dwell on the past.
[19]See, I am doing a new thing!
    Now it springs up; do you not perceive it?
I am making a way in the desert
    and streams in the wasteland.
[20]The wild animals honor me,
    the jackals and the owls,
because I provide water in the desert

[a] 14 Or Chaldeans

emphasize about your relationship with God? Which side of the "but" are you presently on? **2.** If you were to set these passages to music, what type of music would you use for the lyrics before the "but now"? For the lyrics afterwards? **3.** What "waters" or "fire" (v. 2) seem to be fearfully close to you at the moment? What does it mean to you that God says he will be with his people through these things? How have you experienced that in the past? How come he doesn't just let us avoid them? **4.** During the "unromantic" times in your life, when life and relationships have lost their sparkle, how does this passage help you to put things in perspective? **5.** When has God worked good in your life despite your blindness and deafness? How would you explain to a non-Christian what God has done for you? What should be our motivation in witnessing to others of God's grace in our lives?

Have you ever fallen asleep in church? Was it out of tiredness or boredom? What woke you up?

1. What contrasting attitudes has God found in the Babylonians, in the wild animals, and in Israel (vv. 14,20,22)? **2.** With what attitude do you imagine the exiles carried out their religious practices (vv. 22–28)? What does that show about their view of God? Although God has not wearied them with his demands, how have they wearied him? **3.** In spite of their attitudes, what has God done for them? What does God say about himself in these verses? **4.** What does God mean by blotting out sins "for my own sake" (v. 25)?

1. When has God seemed like a dusty memory to you? At those times, what helps you get in touch with him? How might recalling the acts of God in your past give you courage to face the present and future? **2.** What has God done in your past that you especially can look to as evidence of his presence with you? What "stream in the desert" is bubbling up for you now? **3.** In your worship life, are you lavishly giving yourself to God or callously wearying him with meaningless rituals? When has it been different? What accounts for the change? **4.** In your service to God, are you wearying yourself for him or are you wearying him? **5.** What "new thing" (v. 19) has the Lord done in your life? What is he doing now? **6.** What "former things" (v. 18) from your past do you have difficulty forgetting? How might verse 25 help?

and streams in the wasteland,
to give drink to my people, my chosen,
21 the people I formed for myself
that they may proclaim my praise.

22"Yet you have not called upon me, O Jacob,
you have not wearied yourselves for me,
O Israel.
23You have not brought me sheep for burnt offerings,
nor honored me with your sacrifices.
I have not burdened you with grain offerings
nor wearied you with demands for incense.
24You have not bought any fragrant calamus for me,
or lavished on me the fat of your sacrifices.
But you have burdened me with your sins
and wearied me with your offenses.

25"I, even I, am he who blots out
your transgressions, for my own sake,
and remembers your sins no more.
26Review the past for me,
let us argue the matter together;
state the case for your innocence.
27Your first father sinned;
your spokesmen rebelled against me.
28So I will disgrace the dignitaries of your temple,
and I will consign Jacob to destruction*a*
and Israel to scorn.*

Israel the Chosen

44 "But now listen, O Jacob, my servant,
Israel, whom I have chosen.
2This is what the LORD says—
he who made you, who formed you in the womb,
and who will help you:
Do not be afraid, O Jacob, my servant,
Jeshurun, whom I have chosen.
3For I will pour water on the thirsty land,
and streams on the dry ground;
I will pour out my Spirit on your offspring,
and my blessing on your descendants.
4They will spring up like grass in a meadow,
like poplar trees by flowing streams.
5One will say, 'I belong to the LORD';
another will call himself by the name of Jacob;
still another will write on his hand, 'The LORD's,'
and will take the name Israel.

The LORD, Not Idols

6"This is what the LORD says—
Israel's King and Redeemer, the LORD Almighty:
I am the first and I am the last;
apart from me there is no God.
7Who then is like me? Let him proclaim it.
Let him declare and lay out before me

What affectionate nicknames do you have for people you care about?

1. What is the prophet emphasizing by saying "but now" (v. 1)? **2.** Since the Spirit seems to have been given only to Israel's *leaders* in the past, what is the significance and hope of the promise in verse 3?

1. Is the "flower" of your spiritual life still a seed? Breaking ground? In full bloom? How so? **2.** How do you typically let others know that you are a Christian? What new idea does verse 5 suggest?

1. What is one thing that you made as a child that you were really proud of? **2.** Have you ever worked hard toward a goal, only to discover that it wasn't worth the work? How did you feel then?

1. In verses 6–8, what are the ways that God claims to be unique? What titles and descriptions does God use of himself?

a28 The Hebrew term refers to the irrevocable giving over of things or persons to the LORD, often by totally destroying them.

what has happened since I established my ancient
   people,
   and what is yet to come—
yes, let him foretell what will come.
⁸Do not tremble, do not be afraid.
   Did I not proclaim this and foretell it long ago?
You are my witnesses. Is there any God besides
   me?
   No, there is no other Rock; I know not one."

⁹All who make idols are nothing,
   and the things they treasure are worthless.
Those who would speak up for them are blind;
   they are ignorant, to their own shame.
¹⁰Who shapes a god and casts an idol,
   which can profit him nothing?
¹¹He and his kind will be put to shame;
   craftsmen are nothing but men.
Let them all come together and take their stand;
   they will be brought down to terror and infamy.

¹²The blacksmith takes a tool
   and works with it in the coals;
he shapes an idol with hammers,
   he forges it with the might of his arm.
He gets hungry and loses his strength;
   he drinks no water and grows faint.
¹³The carpenter measures with a line
   and makes an outline with a marker;
he roughs it out with chisels
   and marks it with compasses.
He shapes it in the form of man,
   of man in all his glory,
   that it may dwell in a shrine.
¹⁴He cut down cedars,
   or perhaps took a cypress or oak.
He let it grow among the trees of the forest,
   or planted a pine, and the rain made it grow.
¹⁵It is man's fuel for burning;
   some of it he takes and warms himself,
   he kindles a fire and bakes bread.
But he also fashions a god and worships it;
   he makes an idol and bows down to it.
¹⁶Half of the wood he burns in the fire;
   over it he prepares his meal,
   he roasts his meat and eats his fill.
He also warms himself and says,
   "Ah! I am warm; I see the fire."
¹⁷From the rest he makes a god, his idol;
   he bows down to it and worships.
He prays to it and says,
   "Save me; you are my god."
¹⁸They know nothing, they understand nothing;
   their eyes are plastered over so they cannot see,
   and their minds closed so they cannot
      understand.
¹⁹No one stops to think,
   no one has the knowledge or understanding to
      say,
   "Half of it I used for fuel;

What does each mean? In what
ways is he different from the idols
in verses 12–20? **2.** For what reasons is idolatry mocked in verses
9–20? In what ways do those who
worship idols end up like the idols
(vv. 18–20)? **3.** In contrast to the
idols that can do nothing, what
things has God done for Israel (vv.
21–23)? In turn, what does he call
upon the people to do? What does
he mean by it? **4.** God redeemed
Israel before they returned to him.
What does this show of God's nature?

1. What "gods" have people
in our culture shaped for
themselves? Why are people attracted to these false gods? With
which ones do you struggle? How
have you seen these false gods
end up oppressing those who
make them? **2.** How do modern
forms of idolatry help people ignore
reality? How might Christianity itself end up being an idol? How is
true worship of God different? **3.**
How is the irony of verses 15–17
reflected in modern forms of idolatry? In what way have you experienced that following these modern
idols is nothing but "feeding on
ashes"? **4.** Is your worship life
more characterized by singing and
joy, or ritual and dullness? Why?
What helps you move toward joyful
worship?

I even baked bread over its coals,
   I roasted meat and I ate.
Shall I make a detestable thing from what is left?
   Shall I bow down to a block of wood?"
²⁰He feeds on ashes, a deluded heart misleads him;
   he cannot save himself, or say,
   "Is not this thing in my right hand a lie?"

²¹"Remember these things, O Jacob,
   for you are my servant, O Israel.
I have made you, you are my servant;
   O Israel, I will not forget you.
²²I have swept away your offenses like a cloud,
   your sins like the morning mist.
Return to me,
   for I have redeemed you."

²³Sing for joy, O heavens, for the LORD has done
     this;
   shout aloud, O earth beneath.
Burst into song, you mountains,
   you forests and all your trees,
for the LORD has redeemed Jacob,
   he displays his glory in Israel.

Jerusalem to Be Inhabited

²⁴"This is what the LORD says—
   your Redeemer, who formed you in the womb:

I am the LORD,
   who has made all things,
   who alone stretched out the heavens,
   who spread out the earth by myself,

²⁵who foils the signs of false prophets
   and makes fools of diviners,
who overthrows the learning of the wise
   and turns it into nonsense,
²⁶who carries out the words of his servants
   and fulfills the predictions of his messengers,

who says of Jerusalem, 'It shall be inhabited,'
   of the towns of Judah, 'They shall be built,'
   and of their ruins, 'I will restore them,'
²⁷who says to the watery deep, 'Be dry,
   and I will dry up your streams,'
²⁸who says of Cyrus, 'He is my shepherd
   and will accomplish all that I please;
he will say of Jerusalem, "Let it be rebuilt,"
   and of the temple, "Let its foundations be
     laid." '

45 "This is what the LORD says to his anointed,
   to Cyrus, whose right hand I take hold of
to subdue nations before him
   and to strip kings of their armor,
to open doors before him
   so that gates will not be shut:
²I will go before you

☕ **1.** Reflecting on your high school graduating class, was there anyone whom you thought would never amount to much? What became of that person? What has become of those thought "most likely to succeed"? **2.** What outrageous success have you experienced which led you to say, "There must be a God!"?

📖 **1.** What truth about God is stressed in 44:24? In 44:25–26a? How do these truths confirm the promises given in 44:26b–28? As an exile who had no freedom to leave Babylon, much less consider rebuilding Jerusalem, would you have responded to these promises with hope or with cynicism? Why? **2.** In light of this prophecy, how might the exiles feel as they heard rumors of Cyrus' conquests and approach to Babylon? Cyrus entered Babylon by diverting the flow of the Euphrates River, which flowed through the city, so that his army could enter via the river bed. How does 44:27 interpret this action? What does that imply about the relationship between God's actions and Cyrus' plans? **3.** Although "the servant" in 42:1–7 does not refer only to Cyrus, what aspects of this servant does he represent (see 42:6–7)? **4.** In the past, only Israelite kings were called God's anointed. What is the significance of God's using this title for a pagan king? **5.** Why

and will level the mountains[a];
I will break down gates of bronze
and cut through bars of iron.
³I will give you the treasures of darkness,
riches stored in secret places,
so that you may know that I am the LORD,
the God of Israel, who summons you by name.
⁴For the sake of Jacob my servant,
of Israel my chosen,
I summon you by name
and bestow on you a title of honor,
though you do not acknowledge me.
⁵I am the LORD, and there is no other;
apart from me there is no God.
I will strengthen you,
though you have not acknowledged me,
⁶so that from the rising of the sun
to the place of its setting
men may know there is none besides me.
I am the LORD, and there is no other.
⁷I form the light and create darkness,
I bring prosperity and create disaster;
I, the LORD, do all these things.

⁸"You heavens above, rain down righteousness;
let the clouds shower it down.
Let the earth open wide,
let salvation spring up,
let righteousness grow with it;
I, the LORD, have created it.

⁹"Woe to him who quarrels with his Maker,
to him who is but a potsherd among the
potsherds on the ground.
Does the clay say to the potter,
'What are you making?'
Does your work say,
'He has no hands'?
¹⁰Woe to him who says to his father,
'What have you begotten?'
or to his mother,
'What have you brought to birth?'

¹¹"This is what the LORD says—
the Holy One of Israel, and its Maker:
Concerning things to come,
do you question me about my children,
or give me orders about the work of my hands?
¹²It is I who made the earth
and created mankind upon it.
My own hands stretched out the heavens;
I marshaled their starry hosts.
¹³I will raise up Cyrus[b] in my righteousness:
I will make all his ways straight.
He will rebuild my city
and set my exiles free,
but not for a price or reward,
says the LORD Almighty."

does God give victory after victory to Cyrus (45:3–6)? Since no other deported people ever maintained their ethnic and religious heritage, how will the re-establishment of the Jews fulfill these purposes? (45:6–8) **6.** Several times in this section God repeats that there is no god but him. Why is this being stressed? Does God's deliverance of the Jews from Babylon by the hand of a Persian prove this claim? How so? What does this communicate to the Jews? To the nations? **7.** Persian religion taught that a god of light and a god of darkness were in perpetual warfare with each other. What light does this shed on 45:7? Why does God bring about these judgments and blessings (45:6)? **8.** Evidently, some people objected to the prophet's declaration that God would use a pagan as the means of deliverance. How does God refute that objection (45:11–13)?

♡ **1.** Do you think that God still shapes all of history around the purpose of saving his people? What are the implications of saying yes to that? Of saying no? **2.** How might the purpose of God be traced in some recent world event? What current event especially disturbs you because you cannot see any sense in it? From this passage, what should be your response to that event? **3.** What does the continued existence of the Jews, despite their long history of persecution and oppression, show us about God? **4.** In what ways are the actions of Cyrus like the work of Christ? What other Christ-like figures today do you think God might be using to accomplish his purposes? **5.** Do you have any outstanding quarrels with your "Maker"? What are they? What should you do to resolve them?

---

[a]2 Dead Sea Scrolls and Septuagint; the meaning of the word in the Masoretic Text is uncertain.   [b]13 Hebrew *him*

Can you remember a political speech that impressed you? Why? Did any of the hopes and promises expressed come true?

1. Verse 14 describes a defeated people being led in chains to the land of their conquerors. Since Israel never even tried to conquer these people, what type of conquest is in view here? What "forces" are involved in the battle (vv. 15–17)? What effect will this deliverance have even upon nations that are far away? (Note: Egypt, Cush and Seba—all in Africa—were considered the farthest nations.) 2. What lessons from 44:24–26 are repeated here? What is the purpose of this continual contrast between God and idols (45:22–25)? 3. From this passage alone, what does God say about his character? His purposes? His desires?

1. How do verses 22–25 form the backdrop for Philippians 2:10–11? Accordingly, who are the "descendants of Israel" (see also Gal 3:29)? What do these verses indicate about the ultimate purpose of God's judgments and acts in history? 2. God calls all types of people to come to him. How does that affect your prayers? Your priorities? Your sense of purpose? Your hope? 3. Verse 15 should read, "God is hidden among you." If a non-believer visited your church or small group this past month, what evidence would show that God is in your midst? What types of evidence does God want us to show forth in our lives?

¹⁴This is what the LORD says:

"The products of Egypt and the merchandise of
    Cush,ª
and those tall Sabeans—
they will come over to you
    and will be yours;
they will trudge behind you,
    coming over to you in chains.
They will bow down before you
    and plead with you, saying,
'Surely God is with you, and there is no other;
    there is no other god.'"

¹⁵Truly you are a God who hides himself,
    O God and Savior of Israel.
¹⁶All the makers of idols will be put to shame and
    disgraced;
    they will go off into disgrace together.
¹⁷But Israel will be saved by the LORD
    with an everlasting salvation;
you will never be put to shame or disgraced,
    to ages everlasting.

¹⁸For this is what the LORD says—
he who created the heavens,
    he is God;
he who fashioned and made the earth,
    he founded it;
he did not create it to be empty,
    but formed it to be inhabited—
he says:
"I am the LORD,
    and there is no other.
¹⁹I have not spoken in secret,
    from somewhere in a land of darkness;
I have not said to Jacob's descendants,
    'Seek me in vain.'
I, the LORD, speak the truth;
    I declare what is right.

²⁰"Gather together and come;
    assemble, you fugitives from the nations.
Ignorant are those who carry about idols of wood,
    who pray to gods that cannot save.
²¹Declare what is to be, present it—
    let them take counsel together.
Who foretold this long ago,
    who declared it from the distant past?
Was it not I, the LORD?
    And there is no God apart from me,
a righteous God and a Savior;
    there is none but me.

²²"Turn to me and be saved,
    all you ends of the earth;
    for I am God, and there is no other.
²³By myself I have sworn,
    my mouth has uttered in all integrity
    a word that will not be revoked:

ª14 That is, the upper Nile region

Before me every knee will bow;
    by me every tongue will swear.
²⁴They will say of me, 'In the LORD alone
    are righteousness and strength.'"
All who have raged against him
    will come to him and be put to shame.
²⁵But in the LORD all the descendants of Israel
    will be found righteous and will exult.

Gods of Babylon

46 Bel bows down, Nebo stoops low;
    their idols are borne by beasts of burden.ᵃ
The images that are carried about are
    burdensome,
    a burden for the weary.
²They stoop and bow down together;
    unable to rescue the burden,
    they themselves go off into captivity.

³"Listen to me, O house of Jacob,
    all you who remain of the house of Israel,
you whom I have upheld since you were
    conceived,
    and have carried since your birth.
⁴Even to your old age and gray hairs
    I am he, I am he who will sustain you.
I have made you and I will carry you;
    I will sustain you and I will rescue you.

⁵"To whom will you compare me or count me
    equal?
To whom will you liken me that we may be
    compared?
⁶Some pour out gold from their bags
    and weigh out silver on the scales;
they hire a goldsmith to make it into a god,
    and they bow down and worship it.
⁷They lift it to their shoulders and carry it;
    they set it up in its place, and there it stands.
    From that spot it cannot move.
Though one cries out to it, it does not answer;
    it cannot save him from his troubles.

⁸"Remember this, fix it in mind,
    take it to heart, you rebels.
⁹Remember the former things, those of long ago;
    I am God, and there is no other;
    I am God, and there is none like me.
¹⁰I make known the end from the beginning,
    from ancient times, what is still to come.
I say: My purpose will stand,
    and I will do all that I please.
¹¹From the east I summon a bird of prey;
    from a far-off land, a man to fulfill my purpose.
What I have said, that will I bring about;
    what I have planned, that will I do.
¹²Listen to me, you stubborn-hearted,
    you who are far from righteousness.
¹³I am bringing my righteousness near,

Have you ever walked a long distance carrying a heavy load: In a backpack? Wheelbarrow? Appliance dolly? Describe the scene.

1. Bel and Nebo were the names of the two principal gods in Babylon (v. 1). What burden are they carrying? What happens to them? How does this compare with the Lord (vv. 3–4)? What do they do for the people that worship and carry them? What things does God say here that "I" have done and will do for Israel? **2.** Who are the "rebels" and the "stubborn-hearted" (vv. 8,12; see 42:18–25)? How does this relate to the promises in verses 3 and 4? What will the people learn once more through the events that are soon to occur? **3.** The man in verse 11 is Cyrus. Although Israel is currently "far from righteousness" (v. 12) how will God use Cyrus (whose standard was an eagle) to bring "righteousness near" to them? Why is God doing this?

1. Have you seen people today worn out and let down by the very "idols" to which they have devoted themselves? How so? When has this happened to you? **2.** By contrast, how have you experienced God as a father carrying you when you were weak? Or as a strong man sustaining you when you were tired? Or as a warrior rescuing you when you were trapped? **3.** Isaiah concludes "there is none like God" (v. 9). Based on your sampling of modern idols, what would you say comes closest to, or is even equal to, God (v. 5)? If someone were to observe your lifestyle this past week, what would he think about your answer? **4.** How has God brought righteousness near to you (v. 13; see Ro 3:21–24; Eph 2:13)? Why?

ᵃ *1 Or are but beasts and cattle*

it is not far away;
and my salvation will not be delayed.
I will grant salvation to Zion,
my splendor to Israel.

The Fall of Babylon

47 "Go down, sit in the dust,
Virgin Daughter of Babylon;
sit on the ground without a throne,
Daughter of the Babylonians. [a]
No more will you be called
tender or delicate.
²Take millstones and grind flour;
take off your veil.
Lift up your skirts, bare your legs,
and wade through the streams.
³Your nakedness will be exposed
and your shame uncovered.
I will take vengeance;
I will spare no one."

⁴Our Redeemer—the LORD Almighty is his name—
is the Holy One of Israel.

⁵"Sit in silence, go into darkness,
Daughter of the Babylonians;
no more will you be called
queen of kingdoms.
⁶I was angry with my people
and desecrated my inheritance;
I gave them into your hand,
and you showed them no mercy.
Even on the aged
you laid a very heavy yoke.
⁷You said, 'I will continue forever—
the eternal queen!'
But you did not consider these things
or reflect on what might happen.

⁸"Now then, listen, you wanton creature,
lounging in your security
and saying to yourself,
'I am, and there is none besides me.
I will never be a widow
or suffer the loss of children.'
⁹Both of these will overtake you
in a moment, on a single day:
loss of children and widowhood.
They will come upon you in full measure,
in spite of your many sorceries
and all your potent spells.
¹⁰You have trusted in your wickedness
and have said, 'No one sees me.'
Your wisdom and knowledge mislead you
when you say to yourself,
'I am, and there is none besides me.'
¹¹Disaster will come upon you,
and you will not know how to conjure it away.
A calamity will fall upon you

In your lifetime what famous person, who seemed to have it all, ended up in sorrow and tragedy? What did you learn from that situation?

1. What does the picture of a queen reduced to slavery tell you about Babylon's past and future? Since Babylon was not destroyed, though literally conquered by Cyrus in a single day, what is the meaning of this image? What is the reason for this judgment (see also 10:12)? What does this say about God? 2. What do you learn about the spiritual beliefs and practices of Babylon (vv. 9b–15)? What do you imagine they were doing as Cyrus came closer and closer? 3. What will they inherit for all their activity? How does this highlight the truth proclaimed since chapter 40, that there is no other god but the Lord? Of what value would this truth be for the exiles?

1. In our sophisticated and cynical age, why do you think most major newspapers faithfully print astrological information day after day? Have you ever been drawn to astrology or any other occult practices? Why? Do you think it is appropriate for Christians to be involved in these things? Why or why not? 2. During the 50s and 60s, many predicted that the rise of science would lead to a decline in people's interest in the supernatural, yet the sales and use of occult books and devices has risen dramatically since then. How do you account for that? What does that show about people? What would it take to have an effective witness to someone involved in these practices? 3. The Babylonians ignored God, justice and mercy by hiding behind pride, wealth and magic. How do people today try hiding from God? What helped you to see that these things are not to be trusted? Might they still tempt you? How so?

---

a 1 Or *Chaldeans*; also in verse 5

that you cannot ward off with a ransom;
a catastrophe you cannot foresee
    will suddenly come upon you.

12"Keep on, then, with your magic spells
    and with your many sorceries,
    which you have labored at since childhood.
Perhaps you will succeed,
    perhaps you will cause terror.
13All the counsel you have received has only worn
        you out!
Let your astrologers come forward,
those stargazers who make predictions month by
        month,
    let them save you from what is coming upon
        you.
14Surely they are like stubble;
    the fire will burn them up.
They cannot even save themselves
    from the power of the flame.
Here are no coals to warm anyone;
    here is no fire to sit by.
15That is all they can do for you—
    these you have labored with
    and trafficked with since childhood.
Each of them goes on in his error;
    there is not one that can save you.

Stubborn Israel

48

"Listen to this, O house of Jacob,
    you who are called by the name of Israel
    and come from the line of Judah,
you who take oaths in the name of the LORD
    and invoke the God of Israel—
    but not in truth or righteousness—
2you who call yourselves citizens of the holy city
    and rely on the God of Israel—
    the LORD Almighty is his name:
3I foretold the former things long ago,
    my mouth announced them and I made them
        known;
    then suddenly I acted, and they came to pass.
4For I knew how stubborn you were;
    the sinews of your neck were iron,
    your forehead was bronze.
5Therefore I told you these things long ago;
    before they happened I announced them to you
so that you could not say,
    'My idols did them;
    my wooden image and metal god ordained
        them.'
6You have heard these things; look at them all.
    Will you not admit them?

"From now on I will tell you of new things,
    of hidden things unknown to you.
7They are created now, and not long ago;
    you have not heard of them before today.
So you cannot say,
    'Yes, I knew of them.'

Have you ever obstinately refused to do something merely because a certain person suggested it? What did that do for your
relationship?

1. For what does the prophet
rebuke the nation here? How
might this attitude account for the
Lord's ridicule of idolatry in chapters 40–48? 2. Why has God gone
to such lengths to announce this
deliverance ahead of time (vv.
5–6)? 3. Why does he bother to
save them, anyway (see 44:8;
45:14)? If he had cut them off, what
would the nations assume about
God compared to the gods of Babylon?

1. The Jews, both before and
during the captivity, never
gave up the worship of the Lord,
but many added idolatrous practices to their Judaism. Where do
you feel caught between relying on
Christian doctrines yet living by the
values of modern idols? How might
God be getting across the message to you that you can't have it
both ways? What, if anything, do
you want to change in order to honestly call upon the Lord in "truth
and righteousness"? 2. How have
you been influenced by the rebellious attitude of other Christians?
How has your rebellion at times af-

fected others? What has it cost you in terms of God's peace and blessing in your life? **3.** Since God saved the exiles anyway, does it really matter whether we try to obey God? How so?

As a teen, did you pay more attention to your driving teacher or to your English teacher? Why?

1. Who are the two people God has specifically "called" (vv. 12,15)? What has each been given to do? **2.** What message has God been communicating to the exiles (vv. 14–16)? In what way is Cyrus the Lord's chosen ally? **3.** What has their history of rebellion and ignoring God cost the people (vv. 18–19)? How might history have been different if Israel had followed God's original plan? **4.** What have God's people lost through their exile in Babylon (vv. 18–22)? **5.** Chapters 40–48 reach their climax in 48:20–21. If you were reading these words to the people, would you sob with tears of joy? Shout in victory? Whisper? Why? What about God will this deliverance communicate to all the nations? **6.** How does this show that God's concern for his people has not changed since the Exodus?

1. In what ways is Cyrus' deliverance of the Jews from Babylon like the deliverance from sin that Jesus has won for his people? How did you *first* respond to the news that, because of what Jesus has done, you are free from enslavement to sin (Ro 8:1–3)? How do you respond *now*? Why? **2.** What are some *bad* reasons people witness to others about Christ? What is the one *good* reason (v. 20)? How might grasping the goodness of the Gospel encourage others to listen? What will help you grasp that goodness afresh? **3.** Paul compares the water from the rock (v. 21; Ex 17:6) to the life of the Spirit that flows from Christ (1Co 10:3). In your life, is the water of the Spirit gushing, trickling, dripping or turned off? Why? What would help increase the flow?

⁸You have neither heard nor understood;
  from of old your ear has not been open.
Well do I know how treacherous you are;
  you were called a rebel from birth.
⁹For my own name's sake I delay my wrath;
  for the sake of my praise I hold it back from
    you,
  so as not to cut you off.
¹⁰See, I have refined you, though not as silver;
  I have tested you in the furnace of affliction.
¹¹For my own sake, for my own sake, I do this.
  How can I let myself be defamed?
  I will not yield my glory to another.

Israel Freed

¹²"Listen to me, O Jacob,
  Israel, whom I have called:
I am he;
  I am the first and I am the last.
¹³My own hand laid the foundations of the earth,
  and my right hand spread out the heavens;
when I summon them,
  they all stand up together.

¹⁴"Come together, all of you, and listen:
  Which of ⌊the idols⌋ has foretold these things?
The LORD's chosen ally
  will carry out his purpose against Babylon;
  his arm will be against the Babylonians.ᵃ
¹⁵I, even I, have spoken;
  yes, I have called him.
I will bring him,
  and he will succeed in his mission.

¹⁶"Come near me and listen to this:

"From the first announcement I have not spoken
    in secret;
  at the time it happens, I am there."

And now the Sovereign LORD has sent me,
  with his Spirit.

¹⁷This is what the LORD says—
  your Redeemer, the Holy One of Israel:
"I am the LORD your God,
  who teaches you what is best for you,
  who directs you in the way you should go.
¹⁸If only you had paid attention to my commands,
  your peace would have been like a river,
  your righteousness like the waves of the sea.
¹⁹Your descendants would have been like the sand,
  your children like its numberless grains;
  their name would never be cut off
  nor destroyed from before me."

²⁰Leave Babylon,
  flee from the Babylonians!
Announce this with shouts of joy
  and proclaim it.

ᵃ14 Or *Chaldeans*; also in verse 20

Send it out to the ends of the earth;
    say, "The LORD has redeemed his servant
        Jacob."
21They did not thirst when he led them through the
        deserts;
    he made water flow for them from the rock;
he split the rock
    and water gushed out.

22"There is no peace," says the LORD, "for the
        wicked."

The Servant of the LORD

49 Listen to me, you islands;
    hear this, you distant nations:
Before I was born the LORD called me;
    from my birth he has made mention of my
        name.
2He made my mouth like a sharpened sword,
    in the shadow of his hand he hid me;
he made me into a polished arrow
    and concealed me in his quiver.
3He said to me, "You are my servant,
    Israel, in whom I will display my splendor."
4But I said, "I have labored to no purpose;
    I have spent my strength in vain and for
        nothing.
Yet what is due me is in the LORD's hand,
    and my reward is with my God."

5And now the LORD says—
    he who formed me in the womb to be his
        servant
to bring Jacob back to him
    and gather Israel to himself,
for I am honored in the eyes of the LORD
    and my God has been my strength—
6he says:
"It is too small a thing for you to be my servant
    to restore the tribes of Jacob
    and bring back those of Israel I have kept.
I will also make you a light for the Gentiles,
    that you may bring my salvation to the ends of
        the earth."

7This is what the LORD says—
    the Redeemer and Holy One of Israel—
to him who was despised and abhorred by the
        nation,
    to the servant of rulers:
"Kings will see you and rise up,
    princes will see and bow down,
because of the LORD, who is faithful,
    the Holy One of Israel, who has chosen you."

Restoration of Israel

8This is what the LORD says:

"In the time of my favor I will answer you,
    and in the day of salvation I will help you;
I will keep you and will make you

During your childhood, who was your favorite hero? How did you show it?

1. How might this servant speak to the people (v. 2a)? How does that contrast with the servant's type of speech in 42:2? **2.** Why does the Lord call his servant by the name Israel (v. 3), if he is speaking to an individual with a mission to Israel (v. 5; see 26:18)? **3.** How do you think the servant was received by Israel, the nation (vv. 4,7)? How does this reflect the experience of Isaiah (30:9–11)? Of Jeremiah (Jer 26:7–8)? Of Jesus? **4.** In his discouragement, what promises does the servant receive from God? How is this related to the prophecy of 11:10? What does this imply about the identity of the servant?

1. What examples can you think of in Jesus' life when his speech was gentle (as in 42:2)? When it was cutting like a sword? Why the difference? When is it best to speak gently with people? To be strong and cutting? **2.** Jesus said that believers were "the light of the world" (Mt 5:14). From this passage, what did he mean by that image? How might the promises in this passage apply to you when you feel as though your efforts to follow God have little effect on others? **3.** Which of these traits of the servant seem beyond you? Which are within your grasp?

When hurt as a child, did you normally run to mom, to dad or to whom? Why? What was the best way they could help you feel better?

1. What will happen for the exiles "in the day of salvation"? How will the nations learn of God's covenant promises (see 45:14, 22–24)? How does Israel reflect the mission of "the Servant" (42:6)? 2. If the exiles are to return on a "highway" to Jerusalem (see 35:5–10; 43:19–20), what will the trip be like (vv. 9–12)? 3. What are Israel's doubts (vv. 14,24)? How does this passage answer them? 4. Having children was important, both as a sign of God's blessing and for provision for the future. What then does it mean that the people feel like a barren and widowed woman? What images does God use to respond to that feeling? 5. Verses 22 and 23 present a military image where the conquered bring their spoil and bow down before the victor. How does that fit in with God's work in the world (see also 45:22–23)? 6. The grotesque description in verse 26 describes civil strife within a nation (as in 9:20–21). How does this apply to the coming conquest of Babylon by Cyrus (45:1–7)? What is the ultimate purpose of it all (vv. 23b, 26b)? 7. What response is God looking for in Israel (v. 23)? What exactly do you think it means?

1. Emotionally and spiritually, what does it mean to be a forsaken captive? What can cause you to feel that way? Right now, do you feel more like that or like a person coming home to a long-awaited reunion? Why? 2. Jesus' mission was unique, yet it sets a pattern for ours as well. Did the Lord ever use another person to extend his "covenant of the people" (v. 8) to you? How? How might you be part of this process to someone else this week? 3. Although we normally think of God as "our Father," what insight do you gain about him from considering the image of God as a mother (v. 15)? How have you experienced this type of maternal care from God? 4. How does verse 25 illuminate Jesus' comment about "binding the strong man" (Mt 12:29)? How have you been "retrieved from the fierce"? 5. Is the freeing of the exiles from Babylon by Cyrus (vv. 22–23) at all like what Jesus has done for you? How so? 6. What is one thing that convinces you that the Lord, and not some other god or force, is indeed the one you can trust?

to be a covenant for the people,
to restore the land
and to reassign its desolate inheritances,
⁹to say to the captives, 'Come out,'
and to those in darkness, 'Be free!'

"They will feed beside the roads
and find pasture on every barren hill.
¹⁰They will neither hunger nor thirst,
nor will the desert heat or the sun beat upon
them.
He who has compassion on them will guide them
and lead them beside springs of water.
¹¹I will turn all my mountains into roads,
and my highways will be raised up.
¹²See, they will come from afar—
some from the north, some from the west,
some from the region of Aswan.ᵃ"

¹³Shout for joy, O heavens;
rejoice, O earth;
burst into song, O mountains!
For the LORD comforts his people
and will have compassion on his afflicted ones.

¹⁴But Zion said, "The LORD has forsaken me,
the Lord has forgotten me."

¹⁵"Can a mother forget the baby at her breast
and have no compassion on the child she has
borne?
Though she may forget,
I will not forget you!
¹⁶See, I have engraved you on the palms of my
hands;
your walls are ever before me.
¹⁷Your sons hasten back,
and those who laid you waste depart from you.
¹⁸Lift up your eyes and look around;
all your sons gather and come to you.
As surely as I live," declares the LORD,
"you will wear them all as ornaments;
you will put them on, like a bride.

¹⁹"Though you were ruined and made desolate
and your land laid waste,
now you will be too small for your people,
and those who devoured you will be far away.
²⁰The children born during your bereavement
will yet say in your hearing,
'This place is too small for us;
give us more space to live in.'
²¹Then you will say in your heart,
'Who bore me these?
I was bereaved and barren;
I was exiled and rejected.
Who brought these up?
I was left all alone,
but these—where have they come from?'"

ᵃ12 Dead Sea Scrolls; Masoretic Text *Sinim*

22This is what the Sovereign LORD says:

"See, I will beckon to the Gentiles,
  I will lift up my banner to the peoples;
they will bring your sons in their arms
  and carry your daughters on their shoulders.
23Kings will be your foster fathers,
  and their queens your nursing mothers.
They will bow down before you with their faces
    to the ground;
  they will lick the dust at your feet.
Then you will know that I am the LORD;
  those who hope in me will not be
    disappointed."

24Can plunder be taken from warriors,
  or captives rescued from the fierce*a*?

25But this is what the LORD says:

"Yes, captives will be taken from warriors,
  and plunder retrieved from the fierce;
I will contend with those who contend with you,
  and your children I will save.
26I will make your oppressors eat their own flesh;
  they will be drunk on their own blood, as with
    wine.
Then all mankind will know
  that I, the LORD, am your Savior,
  your Redeemer, the Mighty One of Jacob."

Israel's Sin and the Servant's Obedience

50

This is what the LORD says:

"Where is your mother's certificate of divorce
  with which I sent her away?
Or to which of my creditors
  did I sell you?
Because of your sins you were sold;
  because of your transgressions your mother was
    sent away.
2When I came, why was there no one?
  When I called, why was there no one to
    answer?
Was my arm too short to ransom you?
  Do I lack the strength to rescue you?
By a mere rebuke I dry up the sea,
  I turn rivers into a desert;
their fish rot for lack of water
  and die of thirst.
3I clothe the sky with darkness
  and make sackcloth its covering."

4The Sovereign LORD has given me an instructed
    tongue,
  to know the word that sustains the weary.
He wakens me morning by morning,
  wakens my ear to listen like one being taught.
5The Sovereign LORD has opened my ears,

a24 Dead Sea Scrolls, Vulgate and Syriac (see also Septuagint and verse 25); Masoretic Text *righteous*

What is the first thing you hear in the morning: Alarm? Radio? Kids? Dog? How do you respond?

1. What is the Lord emphasizing with the rhetorical questions in verses 1–2? Has he in fact divorced Israel (see 49:14ff)? 2. Verses 4–9 present the third of four "Servant songs" (see 42:1–7; 49:1–7; 52:13–53:12). How would you describe the servant's mission? His relationship to God? How does he differ from the nation of Israel (see 48:8)? 3. What new element about the servant, not found in the previous two songs, is added in verses 6–9? Consider the response of the people to Isaiah in 28:9–10 and 30:9–11. What might cause the servant to be mistreated like this? What gives the servant confidence and hope in spite of such ill-treatment? 4. What might the prophet mean by those "in the dark" (v. 10; see 49:14)? What are they to do? How might the example of the servant encourage them? 5. In view of the many rebukes against idolatry in chapters 40–48, what does he mean by those who "provide themselves with flaming torches"? What will happen to

those who try to find solutions apart from God?

♡ **1.** How would you describe your current relationship with God: (a) Casual date? (b) Going steady? (c) Engaged? (d) Married? (e) Divorced? Why? **2.** What would it mean for you to start your day by listening to God? How might you do so? **3.** Recently, has the voice of Jesus to you been one that sustains you when weary (50:4a), or one that cuts like a sharp sword (49:2)? Why? How is that related to your attitude of love and obedience to him? **4.** Have you ever been verbally or physically abused because of your faith? How did you respond? What did your relationship to God feel like at that time? How does Paul apply verses 8–9 to us in Romans 8:31–39? In what situation do you need to lay hold of that confidence today?

☕ Who is your favorite Bible character? Why? When do you find the most encouragement from that person's biography?

📖 **1.** Chapters 51:1–52:12 are an extended poem, summing up God's intent for the exiles. How is their current situation like that of Abraham and Sarah (vv. 1–3)? Since Abraham was old and his wife, Sarah, was barren, why would God use this example for the exiles? **2.** If verses 1–3 were meant to give hope to the exiles, what would verses 4–6 do for them? What effect will their deliverance have upon the other nations? What does this indicate about God's purpose in restoring Jerusalem? **3.** Compare verse 6 with Genesis 15:5. How does the "starry" lesson of the exiles compare with that of Abraham? What does this stress about God? **4.** How are the people here (vv. 1,7) different from those addressed in 48:1–4? What effect should the heavenly vision (v. 6) have upon these exiles as they face their oppressors (vv. 7–8)? **5.** Who is speaking in verses 9–11?

and I have not been rebellious;
    I have not drawn back.
⁶I offered my back to those who beat me,
    my cheeks to those who pulled out my beard;
I did not hide my face
    from mocking and spitting.
⁷Because the Sovereign LORD helps me,
    I will not be disgraced.
Therefore have I set my face like flint,
    and I know I will not be put to shame.
⁸He who vindicates me is near.
    Who then will bring charges against me?
    Let us face each other!
Who is my accuser?
    Let him confront me!
⁹It is the Sovereign LORD who helps me.
    Who is he that will condemn me?
They will all wear out like a garment;
    the moths will eat them up.

¹⁰Who among you fears the LORD
    and obeys the word of his servant?
Let him who walks in the dark,
    who has no light,
trust in the name of the LORD
    and rely on his God.
¹¹But now, all you who light fires
    and provide yourselves with flaming torches,
go, walk in the light of your fires
    and of the torches you have set ablaze.
This is what you shall receive from my hand:
    You will lie down in torment.

Everlasting Salvation for Zion

51 "Listen to me, you who pursue righteousness
    and who seek the LORD:
Look to the rock from which you were cut
    and to the quarry from which you were hewn;
²look to Abraham, your father,
    and to Sarah, who gave you birth.
When I called him he was but one,
    and I blessed him and made him many.
³The LORD will surely comfort Zion
    and will look with compassion on all her ruins;
he will make her deserts like Eden,
    her wastelands like the garden of the LORD.
Joy and gladness will be found in her,
    thanksgiving and the sound of singing.

⁴"Listen to me, my people;
    hear me, my nation:
The law will go out from me;
    my justice will become a light to the nations.
⁵My righteousness draws near speedily,
    my salvation is on the way,
    and my arm will bring justice to the nations.
The islands will look to me
    and wait in hope for my arm.
⁶Lift up your eyes to the heavens,
    look at the earth beneath;

the heavens will vanish like smoke,
    the earth will wear out like a garment
    and its inhabitants die like flies.
But my salvation will last forever,
    my righteousness will never fail.

7"Hear me, you who know what is right,
    you people who have my law in your hearts:
Do not fear the reproach of men
    or be terrified by their insults.
8For the moth will eat them up like a garment;
    the worm will devour them like wool.
But my righteousness will last forever,
    my salvation through all generations."

9Awake, awake! Clothe yourself with strength,
    O arm of the LORD;
awake, as in days gone by,
    as in generations of old.
Was it not you who cut Rahab to pieces,
    who pierced that monster through?
10Was it not you who dried up the sea,
    the waters of the great deep,
who made a road in the depths of the sea
    so that the redeemed might cross over?
11The ransomed of the LORD will return.
    They will enter Zion with singing;
    everlasting joy will crown their heads.
Gladness and joy will overtake them,
    and sorrow and sighing will flee away.

12"I, even I, am he who comforts you.
    Who are you that you fear mortal men,
    the sons of men, who are but grass,
13that you forget the LORD your Maker,
    who stretched out the heavens
    and laid the foundations of the earth,
that you live in constant terror every day
    because of the wrath of the oppressor,
    who is bent on destruction?
For where is the wrath of the oppressor?
14   The cowering prisoners will soon be set free;
they will not die in their dungeon,
    nor will they lack bread.
15For I am the LORD your God,
    who churns up the sea so that its waves roar—
    the LORD Almighty is his name.
16I have put my words in your mouth
    and covered you with the shadow of my
        hand—
I who set the heavens in place,
    who laid the foundations of the earth,
    and who say to Zion, 'You are my people.'"

The Cup of the LORD's Wrath

17Awake, awake!
    Rise up, O Jerusalem,
you who have drunk from the hand of the LORD
    the cup of his wrath,
you who have drained to its dregs
    the goblet that makes men stagger.

For what nation was Rahab the nickname (see 30:7)? To what event is the speaker referring? What does the speaker mean by calling upon God to "do it again"? What effect would recalling this event have upon the exiles? **6.** What words or pictures are used to describe what the exile felt like to those people who loved God (vv. 12–16)? How would you sum up God's message to these people? What would that word do for you if you were a discouraged exile?

1. When have God's promises seemed to you like mere words? At those times, what forces seem to be stronger to you than God? When you feel like that, how might the faith of Abraham, who waited 25 years to see one child born, encourage you? **2.** If you were an exile, what would it mean to you that God's promises are more enduring than the stars or the earth around you? How might meditating upon the lesson of the stars give you a new perspective on the problems that you face today? **3.** When feeling discouraged, what event in your personal history can you look back upon and call on God to do again? **4.** What promises of God especially encourage you to keep on following him even when things get hard? Why do they mean so much to you?

Drawing either upon personal experience or empathy for others, what is one of the most unpleasant things about being drunk?

1. Who is responsible for making Jerusalem drunk (51:17–23)? What would such a portrait of herself teach Israel? **2.** What six things does Zion need to do to change this picture (52: 1–2)? What does each mean? What is God going to do to change it? **3.** This section continues the long poem begun in 51:1. Whereas in 51:9, God was called upon to awake, who is called upon in 51:17–23? What has been the effect of God's punishment upon the people? What promise is given to them now? Why is God's anger turning upon the Babylonians (see 45:5–7)? What does this judgment show about God? **4.** In the third "awake" section (52:1–10), what promises are given to the exiles? **5.** What have the watchmen been faithfully saying? What will be their reward for this? Who are the watchmen?

♡ **1.** The rulers of Egypt, Assyria and Babylon only saw themselves as working to build up their power, yet they were actually accomplishing God's plan to reach all types of people. Do you think it is legitimate to view political movements and upheavals in our day from a similar perspective? Why or why not? What examples might you use as evidence for your position? What cautions need to be observed? **2.** What does Paul say about the "beautiful feet" of verse 7 (see Ro 10:14–15)? When you share your faith with others what image fits best: (a) Messenger clicking your heels with joy? (b) Messenger dragging your feet? (c) Operator of travel booth just passing out information? (d) Doomsday prophet? **3.** If your "feet" were judged in a "Gospel beauty contest," how would they appear: Full of warts? Well-calloused? Smelly? Shapely? **4.** When have you sensed and conveyed real joy and peace in witnessing? How could you share more of the "good tidings" of the Gospel next week? **5.** When is it helpful for a non-Christian to be confronted with a portrait of how he appears to God? When might it be harmful? What can we learn from this passage about proclaiming the Gospel?

¹⁸Of all the sons she bore
  there was none to guide her;
of all the sons she reared
  there was none to take her by the hand.
¹⁹These double calamities have come upon you—
  who can comfort you?—
ruin and destruction, famine and sword—
  who can*a* console you?
²⁰Your sons have fainted;
  they lie at the head of every street,
  like antelope caught in a net.
They are filled with the wrath of the Lord
  and the rebuke of your God.

²¹Therefore hear this, you afflicted one,
  made drunk, but not with wine.
²²This is what your Sovereign Lord says,
  your God, who defends his people:
"See, I have taken out of your hand
  the cup that made you stagger;
from that cup, the goblet of my wrath,
  you will never drink again.
²³I will put it into the hands of your tormentors,
  who said to you,
'Fall prostrate that we may walk over you.'
And you made your back like the ground,
  like a street to be walked over."

52 Awake, awake, O Zion,
  clothe yourself with strength.
Put on your garments of splendor,
  O Jerusalem, the holy city.
The uncircumcised and defiled
  will not enter you again.
²Shake off your dust;
  rise up, sit enthroned, O Jerusalem.
Free yourself from the chains on your neck,
  O captive Daughter of Zion.

³For this is what the Lord says:

"You were sold for nothing,
  and without money you will be redeemed."

⁴For this is what the Sovereign Lord says:

"At first my people went down to Egypt to live;
  lately, Assyria has oppressed them.

⁵"And now what do I have here?" declares the Lord.

"For my people have been taken away for
    nothing,
  and those who rule them mock,*b*"
              declares the Lord.
"And all day long
  my name is constantly blasphemed.
⁶Therefore my people will know my name;
  therefore in that day they will know

a19 Dead Sea Scrolls, Septuagint, Vulgate and Syriac; Masoretic Text / *how can I*
b5 Dead Sea Scrolls and Vulgate; Masoretic Text *wail*

that it is I who foretold it.
    Yes, it is I."

7How beautiful on the mountains
    are the feet of those who bring good news,
who proclaim peace,
    who bring good tidings,
    who proclaim salvation,
who say to Zion,
    "Your God reigns!"
8Listen! Your watchmen lift up their voices;
    together they shout for joy.
When the LORD returns to Zion,
    they will see it with their own eyes.
9Burst into songs of joy together,
    you ruins of Jerusalem,
for the LORD has comforted his people,
    he has redeemed Jerusalem.
10The LORD will lay bare his holy arm
    in the sight of all the nations,
and all the ends of the earth will see
    the salvation of our God.

11Depart, depart, go out from there!
    Touch no unclean thing!
Come out from it and be pure,
    you who carry the vessels of the LORD.
12But you will not leave in haste
    or go in flight;
for the LORD will go before you,
    the God of Israel will be your rear guard.

The Suffering and Glory of the Servant

13See, my servant will act wisely[a];
    he will be raised and lifted up and highly
       exalted.
14Just as there were many who were appalled at
       him[b]—
    his appearance was so disfigured beyond that of
       any man
    and his form marred beyond human likeness—
15so will he sprinkle many nations,[c]
    and kings will shut their mouths because of
       him.
For what they were not told, they will see,
    and what they have not heard, they will
       understand.

53 Who has believed our message
    and to whom has the arm of the LORD been
       revealed?
2He grew up before him like a tender shoot,
    and like a root out of dry ground.
He had no beauty or majesty to attract us to him,
    nothing in his appearance that we should desire
       him.
3He was despised and rejected by men,
    a man of sorrows, and familiar with suffering.

a 13 Or *will prosper*   b 14 Hebrew *you*   c 15 Hebrew; Septuagint *so will many nations marvel at him*

1. When you were growing up, who was the kid in school who everyone picked on? Why? Did you join in? How do you feel about that now? 2. In what circumstances might you consider giving up a body organ or even your life for another person?

1. This is the last of the four "Servant songs" (see 42:1–7; 49:1–6; 50:4–9). If all we had were 52:13–15, what would you imagine happened to this one that so many were appalled by? 2. The songs in chapters 42 and 49 indicated that the servant would "be a light to the Gentiles." How is that idea communicated in these opening lines? 3. If you had grown up next door to "the Servant," how would you describe his childhood to a newspaper reporter who interviewed you about him (53:2–3)? How does that contrast with God's perspective of him (53:2a)? 4. If all you knew about the Servant's adult life was summed up in 53:7–9, what would you assume must have happened to him? How does this relate to the picture of the servant in 50:6? 5. What was the purpose of the Servant's suffering (53:4–6)? What

was the nature of his suffering? What benefits come to others because of his suffering and death? **6.** How do you account for the paradox between his death (v. 9) and his seeing the "light of life" (v. 11)? **7.** Verses 7,10 and 12 use sacrificial imagery to speak of the Servant. How does that make his death more than a mere martyr's death?

♡ **1.** The New Testament freely applies this song to Jesus (Mt 27:38,57–60; Jn 1:29; Ac 8:32–34; 1Pe 2:22–23). From this song, how would you explain to someone else the meaning of Jesus' death and resurrection? How does it bring reassurance to you of God's forgiveness and love? **2.** Paul applies 53:1 to the ministry of the Christian (see Ro 10:16). How have you experienced rejection from others because of your faith? Has obedience to God ever left you feeling "cut off from the land of the living" (v. 8)? **3.** Does knowing of God's approval give you courage to serve, even when others turn against you? How so?

Like one from whom men hide their faces
    he was despised, and we esteemed him not.

⁴Surely he took up our infirmities
    and carried our sorrows,
yet we considered him stricken by God,
    smitten by him, and afflicted.
⁵But he was pierced for our transgressions,
    he was crushed for our iniquities;
the punishment that brought us peace was upon
    him,
    and by his wounds we are healed.
⁶We all, like sheep, have gone astray,
    each of us has turned to his own way;
and the LORD has laid on him
    the iniquity of us all.

⁷He was oppressed and afflicted,
    yet he did not open his mouth;
he was led like a lamb to the slaughter,
    and as a sheep before her shearers is silent,
    so he did not open his mouth.
⁸By oppression*ᵃ* and judgment he was taken away.
    And who can speak of his descendants?
For he was cut off from the land of the living;
    for the transgression of my people he was
      stricken.*ᵇ*
⁹He was assigned a grave with the wicked,
    and with the rich in his death,
though he had done no violence,
    nor was any deceit in his mouth.

¹⁰Yet it was the LORD's will to crush him and cause
    him to suffer,
and though the LORD makes*ᶜ* his life a guilt
    offering,
he will see his offspring and prolong his days,
    and the will of the LORD will prosper in his
      hand.
¹¹After the suffering of his soul,
    he will see the light ⌊of life⌋*ᵈ* and be
      satisfied*ᵉ*;
by his knowledge*ᶠ* my righteous servant will
    justify many,
    and he will bear their iniquities.
¹²Therefore I will give him a portion among the
    great,*ᵍ*
and he will divide the spoils with the strong,*ʰ*
because he poured out his life unto death,
    and was numbered with the transgressors.
For he bore the sin of many,
    and made intercession for the transgressors.

ᵃ8 Or *From arrest*   *ᵇ8* Or *away. / Yet who of his generation considered / that he was cut off from the land of the living / for the transgression of my people, / to whom the blow was due?*   *ᶜ10* Hebrew *though you make*   *ᵈ11* Dead Sea Scrolls (see also Septuagint); Masoretic Text does not have *the light ⌊of life⌋*   *ᵉ11* Or (with Masoretic Text) *¹¹He will see the result of the suffering of his soul / and be satisfied*   *ᶠ11* Or *by knowledge of him*   *ᵍ12* Or *many*   *ʰ12* Or *numerous*

The Future Glory of Zion

54 "Sing, O barren woman,
you who never bore a child;
burst into song, shout for joy,
you who were never in labor;
because more are the children of the desolate
woman
than of her who has a husband,"
says the LORD.

2"Enlarge the place of your tent,
stretch your tent curtains wide,
do not hold back;
lengthen your cords,
strengthen your stakes.
3For you will spread out to the right and to the
left;
your descendants will dispossess nations
and settle in their desolate cities.

4"Do not be afraid; you will not suffer shame.
Do not fear disgrace; you will not be
humiliated.
You will forget the shame of your youth
and remember no more the reproach of your
widowhood.
5For your Maker is your husband—
the LORD Almighty is his name—
the Holy One of Israel is your Redeemer;
he is called the God of all the earth.
6The LORD will call you back
as if you were a wife deserted and distressed in
spirit—
a wife who married young,
only to be rejected," says your God.
7"For a brief moment I abandoned you,
but with deep compassion I will bring you back.
8In a surge of anger
I hid my face from you for a moment,
but with everlasting kindness
I will have compassion on you,"
says the LORD your Redeemer.

9"To me this is like the days of Noah,
when I swore that the waters of Noah would
never again cover the earth.
So now I have sworn not to be angry with you,
never to rebuke you again.
10Though the mountains be shaken
and the hills be removed,
yet my unfailing love for you will not be shaken
nor my covenant of peace be removed,"
says the LORD, who has compassion on you.

11"O afflicted city, lashed by storms and not
comforted,
I will build you with stones of turquoise,ᵃ
your foundations with sapphires.ᵇ
12I will make your battlements of rubies,
your gates of sparkling jewels,

1. If you discovered you were going to be the proud parent of quintuplets, what changes would that force on your budget? Your housing situation? Your emotions? 2. Ever witness an earthquake? When? What was it like?

1. In 51:2 Sarah was used as an example of faith for the exiles. How is her experience reflected in verses 1–3 as well (see Ge 18:9–14; 21:6–7)? What does the prophet mean by using this image? 2. Since singleness and barrenness were causes of shame for a woman, how would that exemplify the experience of the exiles? How does this picture differ from that seen in Jeremiah 3:6–10? What is the point of each analogy? 3. How was the captivity in Babylon like "the days of Noah" for the exiles? For God?

1. Although Jerusalem was rebuilt, it had not regained the influence and status pictured in verses 11–15. In light of that, what does the prophet really mean? How does this relate to John's description of "the new Jerusalem" seen in Revelation 21:11–21? What promises are associated with it? 2. What point is Isaiah making in verses 10,16 and 17? Have you felt the "ground" under your spiritual life quake? Can you trace God's control of events in your own life which seemed out of control? 3. What circumstances have caused you to feel abandoned by God? At those times, how might you be helped by the picture of God as a husband renewing his vows? 4. Of the promises in verses 11–17, which one means the most to you now? Why? How will that hope make a difference in the way you live today?

ᵃ11 The meaning of the Hebrew for this word is uncertain.   ᵇ11 Or *lapis lazuli*

and all your walls of precious stones.
¹³All your sons will be taught by the LORD,
    and great will be your children's peace.
¹⁴In righteousness you will be established:
    Tyranny will be far from you;
      you will have nothing to fear.
    Terror will be far removed;
      it will not come near you.
¹⁵If anyone does attack you, it will not be my doing;
    whoever attacks you will surrender to you.

¹⁶"See, it is I who created the blacksmith
    who fans the coals into flame
    and forges a weapon fit for its work.
And it is I who have created the destroyer to
    work havoc;
¹⁷ no weapon forged against you will prevail,
    and you will refute every tongue that accuses
      you.
This is the heritage of the servants of the LORD,
    and this is their vindication from me,"
                    declares the LORD.

Invitation to the Thirsty

55 "Come, all you who are thirsty,
    come to the waters;
and you who have no money,
    come, buy and eat!
Come, buy wine and milk
    without money and without cost.
²Why spend money on what is not bread,
    and your labor on what does not satisfy?
Listen, listen to me, and eat what is good,
    and your soul will delight in the richest of fare.
³Give ear and come to me;
    hear me, that your soul may live.
I will make an everlasting covenant with you,
    my faithful love promised to David.
⁴See, I have made him a witness to the peoples,
    a leader and commander of the peoples.
⁵Surely you will summon nations you know not,
    and nations that do not know you will hasten to
      you,
because of the LORD your God,
    the Holy One of Israel,
    for he has endowed you with splendor."

⁶Seek the LORD while he may be found;
    call on him while he is near.
⁷Let the wicked forsake his way
    and the evil man his thoughts.
Let him turn to the LORD, and he will have mercy
    on him,
    and to our God, for he will freely pardon.

⁸"For my thoughts are not your thoughts,
    neither are your ways my ways,"
                    declares the LORD.
⁹"As the heavens are higher than the earth,
    so are my ways higher than your ways
    and my thoughts than your thoughts.

What is your favorite junk food? How would you feel if that were all you had available to eat?

1. What is God's message to poor exiles (v. 1) and rich exiles (v. 2)? How will this "class" distinction be removed? What is required of the exiles to receive this blessing from God? 2. How would the exiles respond to the disparity in verses 8 and 9? How might they have felt if the Lord had not reminded them of this? 3. What is the expiration date of the covenant God is making with the exiles (v. 3)? What is its purpose (vv. 4–5)? What other sections from Isaiah 40–55 have stressed this same theme? What does that tell you about God's purpose for the world? 4. What does it mean to "seek the Lord" (vv. 6–7)? What hopeful promise is associated with doing so?

1. How does the question in verse 2 strike you? What things have you spent your money or labor on that have ultimately proven to be unfulfilling? 2. How does God's word taste to you: (a) Awful, but good for you, like medicine? (b) Too watered down, like soggy cereal? (c) Too out-dated, like stale bread? (d) Very rich, like gourmet food? 3. How does Isaiah's invitation relate to Jesus' words in John 6:35? What does it mean to "feed" upon Jesus? This past week, would you say you have been living on spiritual junk food or

¹⁰As the rain and the snow
    come down from heaven,
and do not return to it
    without watering the earth
and making it bud and flourish,
    so that it yields seed for the sower and bread
      for the eater,
¹¹so is my word that goes out from my mouth:
    It will not return to me empty,
but will accomplish what I desire
    and achieve the purpose for which I sent it.
¹²You will go out in joy
    and be led forth in peace;
the mountains and hills
    will burst into song before you,
and all the trees of the field
    will clap their hands.
¹³Instead of the thornbush will grow the pine tree,
    and instead of briers the myrtle will grow.
This will be for the LORD's renown,
    for an everlasting sign,
    which will not be destroyed."

Salvation for Others

56 This is what the LORD says:

"Maintain justice
    and do what is right,
for my salvation is close at hand
    and my righteousness will soon be revealed.
²Blessed is the man who does this,
    the man who holds it fast,
who keeps the Sabbath without desecrating it,
    and keeps his hand from doing any evil."

³Let no foreigner who has bound himself to the
    LORD say,
    "The LORD will surely exclude me from his
      people."
And let not any eunuch complain,
    "I am only a dry tree."

⁴For this is what the LORD says:

"To the eunuchs who keep my Sabbaths,
    who choose what pleases me
    and hold fast to my covenant—
⁵to them I will give within my temple and its walls
    a memorial and a name
    better than sons and daughters;
I will give them an everlasting name
    that will not be cut off.
⁶And foreigners who bind themselves to the LORD
    to serve him,
to love the name of the LORD,
    and to worship him,
all who keep the Sabbath without desecrating it
    and who hold fast to my covenant—
⁷these I will bring to my holy mountain
    and give them joy in my house of prayer.
Their burnt offerings and sacrifices

God's healthy, low-fat meals? Why? **4.** In light of verses 6–7, would you say you have been seeking the Lord or hiding from him this week? Why? **5.** Joy and peace are the fruit God's Word produces (vv. 11–12). At what stage of development is this fruit in your life: Buried seed? Just starting to sprout? Ripening fruit? In need of weeding? How might you be "fertilized" by the commands in verses 1–3 and 6–7? **6.** What is the most impressive mountain range you have ever seen? How do you imagine they would sound if suddenly they burst into song: Like rock? Opera? The Symphony? How would you feel as you realized they were singing for joy over what God has done in and for *you*? What does that imply about your importance to God?

Have you ever moved into a new neighborhood? How long did it take to settle down and become a full member of the community?

1. In light of the impending deliverance (55:12), what type of lifestyle ought to characterize the exiles? **2.** Given the fact that family life was central to Jewish identity, what types of losses would those Jewish men suffer who were castrated by the Babylonians (vv. 3–5; see Dt 23:1–3, where eunuchs are barred from worship)? What hope is God extending to them? What must they do to receive it? **3.** What is God's purpose in restoring Jerusalem (vv. 7–8)?

1. How do the attitudes and actions of verses 1–8 apply to us today? Why are these so crucial to God? **2.** How might you pursue justice and love this week in your family? Your work place? In an area of social concern? **3.** Would you describe your church as a gathering place for sinners, or a fortress to protect those "inside" from those "outside"? Why? **4.** Try seeing your church services from the viewpoint of someone from a totally different background. What "inside" practices or beliefs might prevent outsiders from regarding it as a place for them to meet God? What might you do to help change this? What "outsider" will you befriend this week?

Who is your favorite dog hero: Rin Tin Tin? Lassie? Benji? Snoopy? Oliver? Why? What in yourself do you see in your hero?

It is uncertain whether this section is addressed to the Jews *before* or *during* the exile. **1.** In what ways are the leaders as useless as gluttonous, sleeping watchdogs that can't even bark? What are their primary concerns (56:11–12)? In a situation like this, why is the death of a good person an act of mercy? **2.** How is the people's idolatry like adultery (57:3–10)? What is his point in using that image? Why has this happened? **3.** What is meant by the prophet's harsh words in 57:9? **4.** How will their fate contrast with the future of those who have taken refuge in God (57:11–13)?

1. From your nation's history, what leaders can you think of who seemed to be more concerned with their own status than with fulfilling their responsibilities to the people? How did that affect the nation as a whole? How can you best help your nation's "watchmen" to stay awake? **2.** In the positions of leadership you have held (at home, work, school, in the community or church), how have you felt the temptation to pursue your own goals regardless of the effects it could have on others? **3.** Are you spiritually awake to the subtle invasions of the world? How so? **4.** How are people today still "burning with lust" and "sacrificing their children" (57:5)? How are they "sending ambassadors far away" (57:9)? **5.** Why are they "wearied with all their ways," yet do not say, "It is hopeless" (57:10)? In what things do they "find renewal of their strength"? What things have helped you when you really needed help? In contrast, how do these very things end up separating us from the help God gives? **6.** Accordingly, how would you explain to someone what it means to take refuge in God? What pressures are directing you to God's protection today?

will be accepted on my altar;
for my house will be called
a house of prayer for all nations."
⁸The Sovereign LORD declares—
he who gathers the exiles of Israel:
"I will gather still others to them
besides those already gathered."

God's Accusation Against the Wicked

⁹Come, all you beasts of the field,
come and devour, all you beasts of the forest!
¹⁰Israel's watchmen are blind,
they all lack knowledge;
they are all mute dogs,
they cannot bark;
they lie around and dream,
they love to sleep.
¹¹They are dogs with mighty appetites;
they never have enough.
They are shepherds who lack understanding;
they all turn to their own way,
each seeks his own gain.
¹²"Come," each one cries, "let me get wine!
Let us drink our fill of beer!
And tomorrow will be like today,
or even far better."

57 The righteous perish,
and no one ponders it in his heart;
devout men are taken away,
and no one understands
that the righteous are taken away
to be spared from evil.
²Those who walk uprightly
enter into peace;
they find rest as they lie in death.

³"But you—come here, you sons of a sorceress,
you offspring of adulterers and prostitutes!
⁴Whom are you mocking?
At whom do you sneer
and stick out your tongue?
Are you not a brood of rebels,
the offspring of liars?
⁵You burn with lust among the oaks
and under every spreading tree;
you sacrifice your children in the ravines
and under the overhanging crags.
⁶ ⌞The idols⌟ among the smooth stones of the
ravines are your portion;
they, they are your lot.
Yes, to them you have poured out drink offerings
and offered grain offerings.
In the light of these things, should I relent?
⁷You have made your bed on a high and lofty hill;
there you went up to offer your sacrifices.
⁸Behind your doors and your doorposts
you have put your pagan symbols.
Forsaking me, you uncovered your bed,
you climbed into it and opened it wide;

you made a pact with those whose beds you love,
  and you looked on their nakedness.
9You went to Molech*a* with olive oil
  and increased your perfumes.
You sent your ambassadors*b* far away;
  you descended to the grave*c* itself!
10You were wearied by all your ways,
  but you would not say, 'It is hopeless.'
You found renewal of your strength,
  and so you did not faint.

11"Whom have you so dreaded and feared
  that you have been false to me,
and have neither remembered me
  nor pondered this in your hearts?
Is it not because I have long been silent
  that you do not fear me?
12I will expose your righteousness and your works,
  and they will not benefit you.
13When you cry out for help,
  let your collection ⌊of idols⌋ save you!
The wind will carry all of them off,
  a mere breath will blow them away.
But the man who makes me his refuge
  will inherit the land
  and possess my holy mountain."

Comfort for the Contrite

14And it will be said:

  "Build up, build up, prepare the road!
  Remove the obstacles out of the way of my
    people."
15For this is what the high and lofty One says—
  he who lives forever, whose name is holy:
"I live in a high and holy place,
  but also with him who is contrite and lowly in
    spirit,
to revive the spirit of the lowly
  and to revive the heart of the contrite.
16I will not accuse forever,
  nor will I always be angry,
for then the spirit of man would grow faint before
    me—
  the breath of man that I have created.
17I was enraged by his sinful greed;
  I punished him, and hid my face in anger,
  yet he kept on in his willful ways.
18I have seen his ways, but I will heal him;
  I will guide him and restore comfort to him,
19   creating praise on the lips of the mourners in
    Israel.
  Peace, peace, to those far and near,"
    says the LORD. "And I will heal them."
20But the wicked are like the tossing sea,
  which cannot rest,
  whose waves cast up mire and mud.

If the President or the Queen were coming to visit you, what repair jobs would you suddenly find time to do?

1. What does God promise in verses 15,18 and 19? What must the people do first? 2. What does it mean to be lowly and contrite (v. 15)? 3. What "obstacles" did the people need to clear out of God's way? What "road" needed building up (v. 14)?

1. If the wicked are like the tossing sea, how would you picture those at peace with God? Which do you feel like? Why? What might you need to do to quiet things down? What word of peace might Jesus speak to calm you? 2. Are you "lowly and contrite," or "high and lofty" (v. 15)? 3. What "obstacles" (v. 14) are hindering God's work in your life? What areas of your spiritual walk are in need of repair?

a9 Or *to the king*   *b9* Or *idols*   *c9* Hebrew *Sheol*

21"There is no peace," says my God, "for the
       wicked."

True Fasting

58 "Shout it aloud, do not hold back.
       Raise your voice like a trumpet.
Declare to my people their rebellion
       and to the house of Jacob their sins.
2For day after day they seek me out;
       they seem eager to know my ways,
as if they were a nation that does what is right
       and has not forsaken the commands of its God.
They ask me for just decisions
       and seem eager for God to come near them.
3'Why have we fasted,' they say,
       'and you have not seen it?
Why have we humbled ourselves,
       and you have not noticed?'

"Yet on the day of your fasting, you do as you
              please
       and exploit all your workers.
4Your fasting ends in quarreling and strife,
       and in striking each other with wicked fists.
You cannot fast as you do today
       and expect your voice to be heard on high.
5Is this the kind of fast I have chosen,
       only a day for a man to humble himself?
Is it only for bowing one's head like a reed
       and for lying on sackcloth and ashes?
Is that what you call a fast,
       a day acceptable to the LORD?

6"Is not this the kind of fasting I have chosen:
to loose the chains of injustice
       and untie the cords of the yoke,
to set the oppressed free
       and break every yoke?
7Is it not to share your food with the hungry
       and to provide the poor wanderer with
              shelter—
when you see the naked, to clothe him,
       and not to turn away from your own flesh and
              blood?
8Then your light will break forth like the dawn,
       and your healing will quickly appear;
then your righteousness[a] will go before you,
       and the glory of the LORD will be your rear
              guard.
9Then you will call, and the LORD will answer;
       you will cry for help, and he will say:
              Here am I.

"If you do away with the yoke of oppression,
       with the pointing finger and malicious talk,
10and if you spend yourselves in behalf of the
              hungry
       and satisfy the needs of the oppressed,
then your light will rise in the darkness,

---

1. Have you ever fasted? Why or why not? What benefits did you experience? 2. What is your first reaction to TV or newspaper reports of homeless people: "They probably are just too lazy to work"? or "We ought to do something to help"? Why?

1. In what ways did God's people seem to do the right thing (vv. 1–3a)? How did they spoil it (vv. 3b–5)? 2. How did their view of fasting differ from God's? If their fasting were sincere, what would be different about their relationships with others? Their concern for the poor? 3. What is the connection between religious exercises like this and a concern for justice (58:13; see 56:1–2)? How is personal spiritual renewal related to seeking justice for the poor (vv. 8–14)? Which do you think comes first? Although expressed in physical terms, what do these promises mean spiritually? 4. Note the relationship between the "yoke of oppression" and the "pointing finger" (v. 9). Where should God's people be looking to discover and remove oppression?

1. In which religious activities do you find yourself just going through the motions: Attending church? Reading the Bible? Prayer? Communion services? Fasting? 2. How should these activities impact us individually and as a community? How are they affecting you now? What attitudes are needed for these activities to be acceptable to the Lord? 3. If we direct an attitude of self-denial (or fasting) toward social action, where will our "pointing finger" be likely to point first? Are you guilty of any forms of oppression to others at work, church or socially? 4. When should God's people fast? When should we act? Would you be willing to fast from food and other forms of self-fulfillment for one day this week? How can you use that spiritual activity to help satisfy the needs of the oppressed and hungry? 5. Do you know any role models of this combination of piety and practical concern for others? How has their example affected you? How could you imitate their example this week?

---

a8 Or your righteous One

and your night will become like the noonday.
¹¹The LORD will guide you always;
    he will satisfy your needs in a sun-scorched
        land
    and will strengthen your frame.
You will be like a well-watered garden,
    like a spring whose waters never fail.
¹²Your people will rebuild the ancient ruins
    and will raise up the age-old foundations;
you will be called Repairer of Broken Walls,
    Restorer of Streets with Dwellings.

¹³"If you keep your feet from breaking the Sabbath
    and from doing as you please on my holy day,
if you call the Sabbath a delight
    and the LORD's holy day honorable,
and if you honor it by not going your own way
    and not doing as you please or speaking idle
        words,
¹⁴then you will find your joy in the LORD,
    and I will cause you to ride on the heights of
        the land
    and to feast on the inheritance of your father
        Jacob."
           The mouth of the LORD has spoken.

Sin, Confession and Redemption

59 Surely the arm of the LORD is not too short to save,
    nor his ear too dull to hear.
²But your iniquities have separated
    you from your God;
your sins have hidden his face from you,
    so that he will not hear.
³For your hands are stained with blood,
    your fingers with guilt.
Your lips have spoken lies,
    and your tongue mutters wicked things.
⁴No one calls for justice;
    no one pleads his case with integrity.
They rely on empty arguments and speak lies;
    they conceive trouble and give birth to evil.
⁵They hatch the eggs of vipers
    and spin a spider's web.
Whoever eats their eggs will die,
    and when one is broken, an adder is hatched.
⁶Their cobwebs are useless for clothing;
    they cannot cover themselves with what they
        make.
Their deeds are evil deeds,
    and acts of violence are in their hands.
⁷Their feet rush into sin;
    they are swift to shed innocent blood.
Their thoughts are evil thoughts;
    ruin and destruction mark their ways.
⁸The way of peace they do not know;
    there is no justice in their paths.
They have turned them into crooked roads;
    no one who walks in them will know peace.

⁹So justice is far from us,

1. Have you ever cracked open a bad egg or brushed up against a spider's web in the dark? How did you feel? 2. As a child, did you feel authority figures were there to help and protect you or to spoil your fun? How have your opinions changed? 3. Have you ever been lost or had trouble finding your way in the dark? What was your response?

1. From 58:2–3 and verses 1–2, what question is on the minds of the people? How does their perception of the problem compare with God's? 2. Of what sins does God accuse them (vv. 3–8)? What would life in this community be like? What does the image of the adder's eggs and spider's web say about the effect of all their sin? 3. What does each image in verses 9–11 add to your understanding of what has happened as a result of the people's sins? 4. What will God do about this situation? How does that relate to their confession in verses 12–15? How do you reconcile the picture of God as a warrior (vv. 15b–19) with that of the redeemer (v. 20)? 5. What will be the results of God's action on those who have opposed him? On those who repent? On the nations? 6. What is the covenant Isaiah speaks of in verse 21? What is required of the people?

1. How did you feel as you read the description of sin (vv. 3–8)? How does that compare with Romans 3:9–17? What does it mean to you that this is the situation within the heart of all people, including you? What wrong action or inaction, words or silence, thoughts or thoughtlessness was yours this week? **2.** When have you experienced blindness like that described in verse 10? What effective aids or artificial props did you use to grope through life's darkness? Did God break through to you in that dark time? How? **3.** What New Testament passages come to mind that emphasize Jesus' role as the Redeemer and the Judge in Isaiah's prophecy? (See Jn 3:16–21 and Ro 11:22–27, for example.) What determines which way he will relate to you? **4.** Paul exhorts Christians to wear the armor that God wears (v. 17; see Eph 6:13–17). How might this help you face evil and injustice? What is one way you can suit up and be God's instrument in bringing salvation to others this week?

and righteousness does not reach us.
We look for light, but all is darkness;
   for brightness, but we walk in deep shadows.
[10]Like the blind we grope along the wall,
   feeling our way like men without eyes.
At midday we stumble as if it were twilight;
   among the strong, we are like the dead.
[11]We all growl like bears;
   we moan mournfully like doves.
We look for justice, but find none;
   for deliverance, but it is far away.

[12]For our offenses are many in your sight,
   and our sins testify against us.
Our offenses are ever with us,
   and we acknowledge our iniquities:
[13]rebellion and treachery against the LORD,
   turning our backs on our God,
fomenting oppression and revolt,
   uttering lies our hearts have conceived.
[14]So justice is driven back,
   and righteousness stands at a distance;
truth has stumbled in the streets,
   honesty cannot enter.
[15]Truth is nowhere to be found,
   and whoever shuns evil becomes a prey.

The LORD looked and was displeased
   that there was no justice.
[16]He saw that there was no one,
   he was appalled that there was no one to
     intervene;
so his own arm worked salvation for him,
   and his own righteousness sustained him.
[17]He put on righteousness as his breastplate,
   and the helmet of salvation on his head;
he put on the garments of vengeance
   and wrapped himself in zeal as in a cloak.
[18]According to what they have done,
   so will he repay
wrath to his enemies
   and retribution to his foes;
   he will repay the islands their due.
[19]From the west, men will fear the name of the
   LORD,
   and from the rising of the sun, they will revere
     his glory.
For he will come like a pent-up flood
   that the breath of the LORD drives along.[a]

[20]"The Redeemer will come to Zion,
   to those in Jacob who repent of their sins,"
               declares the LORD.

[21]"As for me, this is my covenant with them," says the LORD. "My Spirit, who is on you, and my words that I have put in your mouth will not depart from your mouth, or from the mouths of your children, or from the mouths of their descendants from this time on and forever," says the LORD.

---

[a]19 Or *When the enemy comes in like a flood, / the Spirit of the LORD will put him to flight*

The Glory of Zion

60 "Arise, shine, for your light has come,
and the glory of the LORD rises upon you.
[2] See, darkness covers the earth
and thick darkness is over the peoples,
but the LORD rises upon you
and his glory appears over you.
[3] Nations will come to your light,
and kings to the brightness of your dawn.

[4] "Lift up your eyes and look about you:
All assemble and come to you;
your sons come from afar,
and your daughters are carried on the arm.
[5] Then you will look and be radiant,
your heart will throb and swell with joy;
the wealth on the seas will be brought to you,
to you the riches of the nations will come.
[6] Herds of camels will cover your land,
young camels of Midian and Ephah.
And all from Sheba will come,
bearing gold and incense
and proclaiming the praise of the LORD.
[7] All Kedar's flocks will be gathered to you,
the rams of Nebaioth will serve you;
they will be accepted as offerings on my altar,
and I will adorn my glorious temple.

[8] "Who are these that fly along like clouds,
like doves to their nests?
[9] Surely the islands look to me;
in the lead are the ships of Tarshish,[a]
bringing your sons from afar,
with their silver and gold,
to the honor of the LORD your God,
the Holy One of Israel,
for he has endowed you with splendor.

[10] "Foreigners will rebuild your walls,
and their kings will serve you.
Though in anger I struck you,
in favor I will show you compassion.
[11] Your gates will always stand open,
they will never be shut, day or night,
so that men may bring you the wealth of the
nations—
their kings led in triumphal procession.
[12] For the nation or kingdom that will not serve you
will perish;
it will be utterly ruined.

[13] "The glory of Lebanon will come to you,
the pine, the fir and the cypress together,
to adorn the place of my sanctuary;
and I will glorify the place of my feet.
[14] The sons of your oppressors will come bowing
before you;
all who despise you will bow down at your feet

[a] 9 Or the trading ships

1. What do you like best about a parade: Bands? Floats? Military displays? Have you ever felt tingles down your spine of pride or joy during such an event? Describe it. 2. Have you ever witnessed a total eclipse of the sun or moon? How did you feel?

1. How do you understand verses 1–3 in light of 59:10? In light of 9:1–2? How intense will that coming light be (verses 19–20)? What does the prophet mean by this? 2. What are some of the major themes seen throughout Isaiah which this song ties together (see 2:2–3; 9:1; 14:1–2; 27:12; 30:26; 49:22–23)? 3. From what directions will people come to Jerusalem? How will they do so? Why will they do so? What will change as a result for Jerusalem? For the nations? 4. Since a city's gates were normally closed at night as a defense against enemies, what does verse 11 say about the new situation God will bring about? 5. What does the Lord mean by "in its time I will do this swiftly" (v. 22)? When and how will this come to pass?

1. How does this song parallel the whole movement of the Christian's experience from conversion, to spiritual growth, to eternity with Christ? 2. Where in the range of "darkness" (v. 2) to "radiance" (v. 5) are you this week? What aspects of the Christian life have lost their shine since your salvation? Which have gained new sparkle? What can help you shine more brightly? 3. Is the light prophesied by Isaiah a future hope, a present reality or both? Why do you think so (see Jn 4:23; Rev 21:23–25)? 4. What is the relationship between peace and righteousness? What would be different if those qualities dominated in your community's civic life? In your church life? In your family life? 5. How can this song encourage you at a time when peace and righteousness do not dominate in any of those spheres (v. 2)? What can you do to help nurture peace and righteousness within yourself and those around you? 6. Daydream, as a group, about what it would be like if Jesus returned tomorrow and set up his throne in Jerusalem. Would you go there? How? What would it be like? What would it be like to see Jesus in person? How would you feel then about the important and urgent matters of your

daily life? Spend some time together in praise and worship.

and will call you the City of the LORD,
Zion of the Holy One of Israel.
15"Although you have been forsaken and hated,
with no one traveling through,
I will make you the everlasting pride
and the joy of all generations.
16You will drink the milk of nations
and be nursed at royal breasts.
Then you will know that I, the LORD, am your
Savior,
your Redeemer, the Mighty One of Jacob.
17Instead of bronze I will bring you gold,
and silver in place of iron.
Instead of wood I will bring you bronze,
and iron in place of stones.
I will make peace your governor
and righteousness your ruler.
18No longer will violence be heard in your land,
nor ruin or destruction within your borders,
but you will call your walls Salvation
and your gates Praise.
19The sun will no more be your light by day,
nor will the brightness of the moon shine on
you,
for the LORD will be your everlasting light,
and your God will be your glory.
20Your sun will never set again,
and your moon will wane no more;
the LORD will be your everlasting light,
and your days of sorrow will end.
21Then will all your people be righteous
and they will possess the land forever.
They are the shoot I have planted,
the work of my hands,
for the display of my splendor.
22The least of you will become a thousand,
the smallest a mighty nation.
I am the LORD;
in its time I will do this swiftly."

The Year of the LORD's Favor

61 The Spirit of the Sovereign LORD is on me,
because the LORD has anointed me
to preach good news to the poor.
He has sent me to bind up the brokenhearted,
to proclaim freedom for the captives
and release from darkness for the prisoners,[a]
2to proclaim the year of the LORD's favor
and the day of vengeance of our God,
to comfort all who mourn,
3   and provide for those who grieve in Zion—
to bestow on them a crown of beauty
instead of ashes,
the oil of gladness
instead of mourning,
and a garment of praise
instead of a spirit of despair.

☕ 1. In your family chores or in your work situation, what is the dirtiest job you have to do? What clothes do you wear to do it? 2. When you celebrate special occasions, what clothes do you wear? How do these clothes affect your mood? 3. When you were very young, what did you expect adulthood would be like?

📖 1. What good news is the prophet bringing to the poor, broken-hearted and grief-stricken? 2. During times of grief, people would put on sackcloth and cover themselves with ashes as a sign of their mourning. With what will God replace these garments? 3. Are the promises in verses 4–7 primarily material or spiritual in nature? Why? Priests were supported by

a 1 Hebrew; Septuagint the blind

They will be called oaks of righteousness,
    a planting of the LORD
    for the display of his splendor.

[4]They will rebuild the ancient ruins
    and restore the places long devastated;
they will renew the ruined cities
    that have been devastated for generations.
[5]Aliens will shepherd your flocks;
    foreigners will work your fields and vineyards.
[6]And you will be called priests of the LORD,
    you will be named ministers of our God.
You will feed on the wealth of nations,
    and in their riches you will boast.

[7]Instead of their shame
    my people will receive a double portion,
and instead of disgrace
    they will rejoice in their inheritance;
and so they will inherit a double portion in their
      land,
    and everlasting joy will be theirs.

[8]"For I, the LORD, love justice;
    I hate robbery and iniquity.
In my faithfulness I will reward them
    and make an everlasting covenant with them.
[9]Their descendants will be known among the
      nations
    and their offspring among the peoples.
All who see them will acknowledge
    that they are a people the LORD has blessed."

[10]I delight greatly in the LORD;
    my soul rejoices in my God.
For he has clothed me with garments of salvation
    and arrayed me in a robe of righteousness,
as a bridegroom adorns his head like a priest,
    and as a bride adorns herself with her jewels.
[11]For as the soil makes the sprout come up
    and a garden causes seeds to grow,
so the Sovereign LORD will make righteousness and
      praise
    spring up before all nations.

Zion's New Name

62 For Zion's sake I will not keep silent,
    for Jerusalem's sake I will not remain quiet,
till her righteousness shines out like the dawn,
    her salvation like a blazing torch.
[2]The nations will see your righteousness,
    and all kings your glory;
you will be called by a new name
    that the mouth of the LORD will bestow.
[3]You will be a crown of splendor in the LORD's
      hand,
    a royal diadem in the hand of your God.
[4]No longer will they call you Deserted,
    or name your land Desolate.

the gifts of the worshippers, so what is the implication in verse 6? **4.** How extensive is this priesthood? Who are the worshippers? Why is God going to do this for the people (vv. 8–9)? **5.** Verses 10–11 present the people's response to the Lord's promises. In what way are they like a bride? A garden? What emotions are these images meant to convey?

1. Who does "me" refer to in verse 1? **2.** What stories from the Gospels portray Jesus' ministry in terms of verses 1–3? (See Lk 4:18–19, for example.) How do those verses relate to your experience upon hearing the good news? **3.** Do you feel as though you are "wearing ashes" or are you "trying on new clothes"? Why? In what way do you especially want to see God bring this freedom to you? **4.** How do you feel about being called a priest? What would it mean for you to live like a priest this week? What is one specific way the group could pray for you in this regard? **5.** In your response to God's promises, are you like a person preparing for marriage, or one wondering whether to go out on a second date? Why?

1. Do you know the meanings of your names? For what reason were you given your first and middle names? What did they mean to your parents? What do they mean to you? **2.** What was one of the more exuberant weddings you have attended? What made it so much fun? **3.** What is one "blood and gore" movie you have seen? How did you feel during it? How do you feel about fairy tales or movies where the heroes kill all the bad guys?

1. What is God's intent for his people (62:1–2)? What is the relationship between God's plan for the nations and the restoration of his people (62:2; see 61:6,9,11)? 2. What does each new name indicate about God's new relationship with his people (62:4,12; see 60:14,18)? Why is a new name so important for Zion? What names and words have been associated with her in the past? Why? Why will they no longer be appropriate? 3. What things does the picture of marriage communicate about God's relationship to his people (62:5; compare 61:10)? 4. Normally, watchmen were guards who kept a lookout for enemies approaching the city, but what is the purpose of the watchmen in this new Jerusalem? 5. What are these watchmen like (62:6–7; compare 56:10)? What are they calling to God for? Why give him "no rest"? 6. "Edom" (symbol for God's enemies) means red. What might the symbols used in 63:1–6 mean? How is this the flip side of the salvation coming to Jerusalem? 7. What does this picture of God as a warrior add to the other images of God in 62:1–12?

1. Of the new names God gives to the people he saves, which one means the most to you right now? Why? 2. Do you normally tend to think of God's relationship with you as that of a bride to her waiting bridegroom? Or a judge to a criminal? Why? How does each picture affect your view of God? Of yourself? What does it mean to you that the bride and bridegroom image is the one he invites us to consider in his relationship with us? 3. Is there anything you want so much that you will neither rest, nor give God rest, until you see it come to pass? What does this mean for your prayer life? 4. How might the prayer to establish Jerusalem relate to the request in the Lord's prayer, "Thy Kingdom come, thy will be done"? If you prayed that consistently and sincerely, how might that begin to affect your priorities? Your perspective on life? Your plans? How might it lead you to "prepare the way" for God's kingdom? 5. Many think God's wrath is an Old Testament idea. How would you respond to that in light of Revelation 19:11–16? How do you feel about this as a description of Jesus (see also Ro 2:5–11; 2Th 1:6–10)? 6. Isaiah 60:1–63:6 portrays what the

But you will be called Hephzibah,[a]
and your land Beulah[b];
for the LORD will take delight in you,
and your land will be married.
[5]As a young man marries a maiden,
so will your sons[c] marry you;
as a bridegroom rejoices over his bride,
so will your God rejoice over you.

[6]I have posted watchmen on your walls,
O Jerusalem;
they will never be silent day or night.
You who call on the LORD,
give yourselves no rest,
[7]and give him no rest till he establishes Jerusalem
and makes her the praise of the earth.

[8]The LORD has sworn by his right hand
and by his mighty arm:
"Never again will I give your grain
as food for your enemies,
and never again will foreigners drink the new wine
for which you have toiled;
[9]but those who harvest it will eat it
and praise the LORD,
and those who gather the grapes will drink it
in the courts of my sanctuary."

[10]Pass through, pass through the gates!
Prepare the way for the people.
Build up, build up the highway!
Remove the stones.
Raise a banner for the nations.

[11]The LORD has made proclamation
to the ends of the earth:
"Say to the Daughter of Zion,
'See, your Savior comes!
See, his reward is with him,
and his recompense accompanies him.'"
[12]They will be called the Holy People,
the Redeemed of the LORD;
and you will be called Sought After,
the City No Longer Deserted.

God's Day of Vengeance and Redemption

63 Who is this coming from Edom,
from Bozrah, with his garments stained crimson?
Who is this, robed in splendor,
striding forward in the greatness of his strength?

"It is I, speaking in righteousness,
mighty to save."

[2]Why are your garments red,
like those of one treading the winepress?

a4 *Hephzibah* means *my delight is in her.*   b4 *Beulah* means *married.*   c5 Or *Builder*

3"I have trodden the winepress alone;
  from the nations no one was with me.
I trampled them in my anger
  and trod them down in my wrath;
their blood spattered my garments,
  and I stained all my clothing.
4For the day of vengeance was in my heart,
  and the year of my redemption has come.
5I looked, but there was no one to help,
  I was appalled that no one gave support;
so my own arm worked salvation for me,
  and my own wrath sustained me.
6I trampled the nations in my anger;
  in my wrath I made them drunk
  and poured their blood on the ground."

Praise and Prayer

7I will tell of the kindnesses of the LORD,
  the deeds for which he is to be praised,
  according to all the LORD has done for us—
yes, the many good things he has done
  for the house of Israel,
according to his compassion and many
  kindnesses.
8He said, "Surely they are my people,
  sons who will not be false to me";
  and so he became their Savior.
9In all their distress he too was distressed,
  and the angel of his presence saved them.
In his love and mercy he redeemed them;
  he lifted them up and carried them
  all the days of old.
10Yet they rebelled
  and grieved his Holy Spirit.
So he turned and became their enemy
  and he himself fought against them.

11Then his people recalled[a] the days of old,
  the days of Moses and his people—
where is he who brought them through the sea,
  with the shepherd of his flock?
Where is he who set
  his Holy Spirit among them,
12who sent his glorious arm of power
  to be at Moses' right hand,
who divided the waters before them,
  to gain for himself everlasting renown,
13who led them through the depths?
Like a horse in open country,
  they did not stumble;
14like cattle that go down to the plain,
  they were given rest by the Spirit of the LORD.
This is how you guided your people
  to make for yourself a glorious name.

15Look down from heaven and see
  from your lofty throne, holy and glorious.
Where are your zeal and your might?

coming kingdom of God will be like. He will include judgment of those who rebelled against him. Is this what you are praying for when you pray, "Thy Kingdom come"? Why or why not?

1. What are the three most common emotions you feel when you come to God in prayer? 2. When you were a teenager, did you ever get in trouble trying to rebel against your parents' authority? How did they respond? (If you could have switched roles and been the parent, how would you have responded to this teenage rebellion?)

This long prayer sums up the desires of the prophet as he anticipates the salvation God has promised. 1. What things might the prophet be recalling as he considers "the many good things God has done for the house of Israel" (63:7–9)? What do these verses express about God's relationship to Israel? 2. What might the prophet mean in 63:10 (see Ps 78:17–22)? 3. In 63:11–19, the prophet moves from recalling the past to considering the present. What questions must be on the minds of the exiles as they face their present suffering? What does this prayer tell you about their emotional state? What things upset them? Do you see this as more a prayer of confession, or of complaint? Why? 4. How would you compare the tone of the prayer in 64:1–4 to that in 63:15–19? What does that tell you about the emotional state of the prophet? About his real desire? 5. In those days, women used strips of old cloth to catch their menstrual flow. What does that image (64:6) illustrate about the spiritual state of the exiles? What does the shriveled leaf illustrate? 6. In view of their spiritual bankruptcy, to what truths does the prophet appeal as he asks for God's help (64:8–12)? Why does he think that now is the time for God to act?

a 11 Or But may he recall

1. What is the "exodus event" that you fondly recall in your life when it was clear that God was working in you? How do you feel now when times of spiritual emptiness occur? Does it encourage or discourage you to recall the past? Why? 2. When have you felt that God must need new glasses because he just doesn't seem to see what you are going through? How do you account for his silence in those times? How do you pray then? 3. When you pray, do you express to God the full range and intensity of your emotions (joy, anger, sorrow, doubt, fear) or just a narrow band of them? Why? How does your church tradition affect the emotional range present in your prayers? Have you ever wanted to say something like 63:17 or 64:12 to God? Why? 4. Where in your life now do you wish God would do something? How does that affect your prayers? 5. Was there a time when all your righteous acts became as dry leaves or menstrual rags because you lacked humility or did not call on God's name? What did that do to you? What hope do you have that God will still relate to you with mercy and grace (see Ro 3:21–26)? 6. Learning from the prophet, choose one area of your own prayer life which might benefit from attention: repentance, faith, zeal, relationship, boldness, humility, contentedness, concern for God's honor. How will you strengthen this area?

Your tenderness and compassion are withheld
  from us.
¹⁶But you are our Father,
  though Abraham does not know us
  or Israel acknowledge us;
you, O LORD, are our Father,
  our Redeemer from of old is your name.
¹⁷Why, O LORD, do you make us wander from your
    ways
  and harden our hearts so we do not revere you?
Return for the sake of your servants,
  the tribes that are your inheritance.
¹⁸For a little while your people possessed your holy
    place,
  but now our enemies have trampled down your
    sanctuary.
¹⁹We are yours from of old;
  but you have not ruled over them,
  they have not been called by your name.ᵃ

64
Oh, that you would rend the heavens and come
    down,
  that the mountains would tremble before you!
²As when fire sets twigs ablaze
  and causes water to boil,
come down to make your name known to your
    enemies
  and cause the nations to quake before you!
³For when you did awesome things that we did not
    expect,
  you came down, and the mountains trembled
    before you.
⁴Since ancient times no one has heard,
  no ear has perceived,
no eye has seen any God besides you,
  who acts on behalf of those who wait for him.
⁵You come to the help of those who gladly do
    right,
  who remember your ways.
But when we continued to sin against them,
  you were angry.
  How then can we be saved?
⁶All of us have become like one who is unclean,
  and all our righteous acts are like filthy rags;
we all shrivel up like a leaf,
  and like the wind our sins sweep us away.
⁷No one calls on your name
  or strives to lay hold of you;
for you have hidden your face from us
  and made us waste away because of our sins.

⁸Yet, O LORD, you are our Father.
  We are the clay, you are the potter;
  we are all the work of your hand.
⁹Do not be angry beyond measure, O LORD;
  do not remember our sins forever.
Oh, look upon us, we pray,
  for we are all your people.

ᵃ 19 Or *We are like those you have never ruled, / like those never called by your name*

¹⁰Your sacred cities have become a desert;
    even Zion is a desert, Jerusalem a desolation.
¹¹Our holy and glorious temple, where our fathers
      praised you,
    has been burned with fire,
    and all that we treasured lies in ruins.
¹²After all this, O LORD, will you hold yourself back?
    Will you keep silent and punish us beyond
      measure?

Judgment and Salvation

65   "I revealed myself to those who did not ask for me;
    I was found by those who did not seek me.
To a nation that did not call on my name,
    I said, 'Here am I, here am I.'
²All day long I have held out my hands
    to an obstinate people,
who walk in ways not good,
    pursuing their own imaginations—
³a people who continually provoke me
    to my very face,
offering sacrifices in gardens
    and burning incense on altars of brick;
⁴who sit among the graves
    and spend their nights keeping secret vigil;
who eat the flesh of pigs,
    and whose pots hold broth of unclean meat;
⁵who say, 'Keep away; don't come near me,
    for I am too sacred for you!'
Such people are smoke in my nostrils,
    a fire that keeps burning all day.

⁶"See, it stands written before me:
    I will not keep silent but will pay back in full;
    I will pay it back into their laps—
⁷both your sins and the sins of your fathers,"
    says the LORD.
"Because they burned sacrifices on the mountains
    and defied me on the hills,
I will measure into their laps
    the full payment for their former deeds."

⁸This is what the LORD says:

"As when juice is still found in a cluster of grapes
    and men say, 'Don't destroy it,
    there is yet some good in it,'
so will I do in behalf of my servants;
    I will not destroy them all.
⁹I will bring forth descendants from Jacob,
    and from Judah those who will possess my
      mountains;
my chosen people will inherit them,
    and there will my servants live.
¹⁰Sharon will become a pasture for flocks,
    and the Valley of Achor a resting place for
      herds,
    for my people who seek me.

¹¹"But as for you who forsake the LORD
    and forget my holy mountain,

1. Have you had a cherished possession that was broken, lost or stolen? How did you feel? How would you have felt if you had given it away? 2. When you were a kid playing hide-and-seek, did you prefer being the hider or the seeker? Where was a favorite hiding place?

This section is God's reply to the prayer of chapter 64. 1. What has been God's frustration in his relationship with Israel? How would he answer the questions of the people in 64:11–12? 2. Verses 3–5 and 11 depict practices associated with idolatry. How does God react to these practices? Why did judgment have to come upon Israel (vv. 1–5)? 3. Although their sin of idolatry is the focus here, what other sins have led up to judgment (see 56:9–12; 58:3–4; 59:3–4)? How might these sins all stem from the practice of idolatry? 4. Compare 65:8–12 with 10:20–23. What do they have in common? How is the emphasis of each different? What promises are here for those who have not followed the way of idolatry? 5. What do the contrasts in verses 13–16 show about the quality of life God intends for his people (compare Lk 6:20–26)? What will happen to those who have placed their hope in other gods?

1. When have you been so caught up with chasing after modern "idols" that you have been unable to hear God calling you? What did it take for him to finally break through? 2. What qualities mark the people who receive the curses pronounced by Isaiah? Where do you see that in evidence today? Or will this only be manifested in the distant future? Why do you think so? 3. How can the promises of verses 13–16 be of help when you feel spiritually hungry, thirsty and ashamed? 4. In terms of "hide and seek," do you see God in your own life as more the hider or the seeker? Is there any area in your life today where God is hold-

ing out his hands (v. 2) or calling, "Here am I" (v. 1)? How will you respond?

who spread a table for Fortune
  and fill bowls of mixed wine for Destiny,
[12]I will destine you for the sword,
  and you will all bend down for the slaughter;
for I called but you did not answer,
  I spoke but you did not listen.
You did evil in my sight
  and chose what displeases me."

[13]Therefore this is what the Sovereign LORD says:

"My servants will eat,
  but you will go hungry;
my servants will drink,
  but you will go thirsty;
my servants will rejoice,
  but you will be put to shame.
[14]My servants will sing
  out of the joy of their hearts,
but you will cry out
  from anguish of heart
  and wail in brokenness of spirit.
[15]You will leave your name
  to my chosen ones as a curse;
the Sovereign LORD will put you to death,
  but to his servants he will give another name.
[16]Whoever invokes a blessing in the land
  will do so by the God of truth;
he who takes an oath in the land
  will swear by the God of truth.
For the past troubles will be forgotten
  and hidden from my eyes.

New Heavens and a New Earth

[17]"Behold, I will create
  new heavens and a new earth.
The former things will not be remembered,
  nor will they come to mind.
[18]But be glad and rejoice forever
  in what I will create,
for I will create Jerusalem to be a delight
  and its people a joy.
[19]I will rejoice over Jerusalem
  and take delight in my people;
the sound of weeping and of crying
  will be heard in it no more.

[20]"Never again will there be in it
  an infant who lives but a few days,
  or an old man who does not live out his years;
he who dies at a hundred
  will be thought a mere youth;
he who fails to reach[a] a hundred
  will be considered accursed.
[21]They will build houses and dwell in them;
  they will plant vineyards and eat their fruit.
[22]No longer will they build houses and others live
  in them,
  or plant and others eat.

1. Who is the oldest person you have ever known? What insight into life did you pick up from him or her? 2. As a child, how did you picture what heaven must be like?

1. What emotion will typify the relationship of the restored people to God? Of God to them? What accounts for this new state of affairs? 2. What will life be like when the exiles are freed? What is the reality that lies behind each figure of speech? 3. What promises, echoed elsewhere in Isaiah, are summed up in this section (see 2:4; 11:6–9; 14:1; 30:19; 32:18)? 4. How does the account of the creation and fall figure as background to this passage? What do we learn here about God's purposes and plans?

1. How does this new creation come into being for us (see 2Co 5:17)? What will be the impact of this truth on our lifestyle (see 2Pe 3:11–13)? What does this vision ultimately mean to us (see Rev 21:1–5)? 2. Which of these New Testament applications

a20 Or / the sinner who reaches

For as the days of a tree,
    so will be the days of my people;
my chosen ones will long enjoy
    the works of their hands.
[23]They will not toil in vain
    or bear children doomed to misfortune;
for they will be a people blessed by the LORD,
    they and their descendants with them.
[24]Before they call I will answer;
    while they are still speaking I will hear.
[25]The wolf and the lamb will feed together,
    and the lion will eat straw like the ox,
    but dust will be the serpent's food.
They will neither harm nor destroy
    on all my holy mountain,"

                        says the LORD.

Judgment and Hope

66 This is what the LORD says:

"Heaven is my throne,
    and the earth is my footstool.
Where is the house you will build for me?
    Where will my resting place be?
[2]Has not my hand made all these things,
    and so they came into being?"

                    declares the LORD.

"This is the one I esteem:
    he who is humble and contrite in spirit,
    and trembles at my word.
[3]But whoever sacrifices a bull
    is like one who kills a man,
and whoever offers a lamb,
    like one who breaks a dog's neck;
whoever makes a grain offering
    is like one who presents pig's blood,
and whoever burns memorial incense,
    like one who worships an idol.
They have chosen their own ways,
    and their souls delight in their abominations;
[4]so I also will choose harsh treatment for them
    and will bring upon them what they dread.
For when I called, no one answered,
    when I spoke, no one listened.
They did evil in my sight
    and chose what displeases me."

[5]Hear the word of the LORD,
    you who tremble at his word:
"Your brothers who hate you,
    and exclude you because of my name, have
        said,
'Let the LORD be glorified,
    that we may see your joy!'
    Yet they will be put to shame.
[6]Hear that uproar from the city,
    hear that noise from the temple!
It is the sound of the LORD
    repaying his enemies all they deserve.

---

of this heavenly vision especially strikes you now? Why? **3.** Try to picture your life without any of the causes or results of grief, sin and pain. What would that free you to do? How might this vision of what God will bring about affect the way you deal with the struggles you face now?

☕ **1.** What is one of the most beautiful churches or cathedrals you have seen? What emotions did it evoke as you walked in? As you joined in the worship service? **2.** Did you ever do something to please your parents or teachers which invoked their displeasure instead? Tell about it. How did you feel?

📖 **1.** Before the exile, the temple of Jerusalem was viewed as the proof of God's dwelling in the midst of Israel. The returning exiles were anxious to rebuild the temple that had been destroyed by the Babylonians. Hence, what is the significance of verses 1–2 as God's final word to the people? What would they mean to you as you signed on to work in the temple reconstruction program? **2.** Verses 3–6 indicate that the exiles looked forward to being able to resume offering the sacrifices commanded under the Mosaic law. Why would God choose to disavow their cherished temple practices at this time? How does this relate to the warnings given much earlier (see 1:10–17)? Why does Isaiah warn them again at this point? **3.** The image of a *mother* is used here (vv. 7–13) to describe the new Jerusalem and the Lord giving birth and nursing their respective children. This contrasts with an earlier picture of Zion as barren (54:1) and with our usual view of God as Father. Who are these *sons* and *daughters*? Are they the same ones as in 49:18–22? Or as in 60:4–5? Why do you think so? **4.** What does the image of God as a mother convey about the renewed relationship God will establish with these people? **5.** Verses 14–18 and 24 focus on God's judgment.

To whom is this directed (vv. 17–18,24)? What is God's purpose in ending this book with this final warning? **6.** Throughout Isaiah, God's ultimate concern has been for all nations. How does that come to its final expression in verses 19–22? Looking at a map, in what directions will God's representatives be sent? (Note: Tubal was an area near the Black Sea.) Why? How is this prophecy to be fulfilled (see Ezr 6:8–9; Mt 24:30; 28:18–20; Ac 1:8; Rev 21)?

♡ **1.** In your background, what religious traditions do you especially value: Communion? Certain holidays? Certain mode of baptism? Saying the creeds? Special type of building? The Scriptures? Other? How important are these things to you now? **2.** How would you feel if you were suddenly forced (or asked by God) to stop practicing these traditions? How would you feel if, like the sons and daughters in this chapter, you were once again free to do so? **3.** When have you found yourself focusing on the forms of worship and missing the reality of what it's all about? What *is* worship all about (vv. 2–5)? **4.** What might help *public* worship become more in line with the ideal? How does your *private* worship compare to the ideal? What have you found helpful in cultivating a spirit of worship? **5.** Although normally God is pictured as a father, Isaiah has used feminine images to describe God (see also 42:14; 49:15). What does the picture of God as a mother tell you about the type of relationship God desires to have with you? What shades of meaning does it represent to you that seeing God as a father does not? In what way do you need to be drawn close and comforted by God as your mother now? **6.** What types of people do you find it hard to reach out to or care about? Why? What does the final vision (of the glory of God being declared among the nations) say to you about the loving purposes of God for those hard-to-love people? How might you reflect that love for them this week at home? In your work place? In your church? In your community? What hope is held out to you that such efforts are blessed?

⁷"Before she goes into labor,
    she gives birth;
before the pains come upon her,
    she delivers a son.
⁸Who has ever heard of such a thing?
    Who has ever seen such things?
Can a country be born in a day
    or a nation be brought forth in a moment?
Yet no sooner is Zion in labor
    than she gives birth to her children.
⁹Do I bring to the moment of birth
    and not give delivery?" says the LORD.
"Do I close up the womb
    when I bring to delivery?" says your God.
¹⁰"Rejoice with Jerusalem and be glad for her,
    all you who love her;
rejoice greatly with her,
    all you who mourn over her.
¹¹For you will nurse and be satisfied
    at her comforting breasts;
you will drink deeply
    and delight in her overflowing abundance."

¹²For this is what the LORD says:

"I will extend peace to her like a river,
    and the wealth of nations like a flooding
        stream;
you will nurse and be carried on her arm
    and dandled on her knees.
¹³As a mother comforts her child,
    so will I comfort you;
and you will be comforted over Jerusalem."

¹⁴When you see this, your heart will rejoice
    and you will flourish like grass;
the hand of the LORD will be made known to his
        servants,
    but his fury will be shown to his foes.
¹⁵See, the LORD is coming with fire,
    and his chariots are like a whirlwind;
he will bring down his anger with fury,
    and his rebuke with flames of fire.
¹⁶For with fire and with his sword
    the LORD will execute judgment upon all men,
    and many will be those slain by the LORD.

¹⁷"Those who consecrate and purify themselves to go into the gardens, following the one in the midst of*ᵃ* those who eat the flesh of pigs and rats and other abominable things—they will meet their end together," declares the LORD.

¹⁸"And I, because of their actions and their imaginations, am about to come*ᵇ* and gather all nations and tongues, and they will come and see my glory.

¹⁹"I will set a sign among them, and I will send some of those who survive to the nations—to Tarshish, to the Libyans*ᶜ* and Lydians (famous as archers), to Tubal and Greece, and to the distant islands that have not heard of my fame or seen my glory. They

---

ᵃ17 Or *gardens behind one of your temples, and*   *ᵇ18* The meaning of the Hebrew for this clause is uncertain.   *ᶜ19* Some Septuagint manuscripts *Put* (Libyans); Hebrew *Pul*

will proclaim my glory among the nations. ²⁰And they will bring all your brothers, from all the nations, to my holy mountain in Jerusalem as an offering to the LORD—on horses, in chariots and wagons, and on mules and camels," says the LORD. "They will bring them, as the Israelites bring their grain offerings, to the temple of the LORD in ceremonially clean vessels. ²¹And I will select some of them also to be priests and Levites," says the LORD.

²²"As the new heavens and the new earth that I make will endure before me," declares the LORD, "so will your name and descendants endure. ²³From one New Moon to another and from one Sabbath to another, all mankind will come and bow down before me," says the LORD. ²⁴"And they will go out and look upon the dead bodies of those who rebelled against me; their worm will not die, nor will their fire be quenched, and they will be loathsome to all mankind."

INTRODUCTION to
JEREMIAH

Book Study Outline: If you are using Jeremiah for a study course, here is a 7- or 13-week outline. Use the questions in the margin for your group agenda:

7-week plan	13-week plan	Personal Reading	Group Study Passage
1	1	1–2	1:1–19/Call of Jeremiah
	2	3–4	3:6–4:4/Unfaithful Israel
2	3	5–7	7:1–29/Worthless Religion
	4	8–11	8:4–9:1/Fountain of Tears
3	5	12–17	12:1–17/Jeremiah's Complaint
	6	18–19	18:1–19:15/Potter and Clay
4	7	20–25	20:1–18/Pashur and Jeremiah
	8	26–29	26:1–24/Jeremiah Threatened
5	9	30–32	30:1–24/Restoration of Israel
	10	33–35	33:1–26/Promise of Renewal
6	11	36–38	37:1–21/Jeremiah in Prison
	12	39–45	44:1–30/Jeremiah's Last Word
7	13	46–52	52:1–30/Fall of Jerusalem

☕ start meeting / 15 min.

📖 read & discuss Bible / 30 min.

♡ close meeting / 15–45 min.

Refer to the Questions and Answers in the front of this Bible for more information.

Author: These are the words of Jeremiah, who was both a prophet and a priest. They were written down by his secretary Baruch (36:4–32) who may have been the one to put the book in its final form.

Date: Events recorded here span the years 626–585 B.C. The book was compiled sometime later.

Theme: God is just and must punish sin. But God in his grace promises Israel restoration and covenant renewal.

Historical Background: The prophet Jeremiah ministered in the context of three major kings. Under King Josiah (640–609 B.C.), Jeremiah was free to preach and join in Josiah's reform movement. Under King Jehoiakim (609–598 B.C.), Jeremiah fell out of royal favor and experienced frequent imprisonments. Under King Zedekiah (597–586 B.C.), Jeremiah was treated more kindly but still had to fear for his life. The judgment that Jeremiah announced was brought about by King Nebuchadnezzar of Babylon. He besieged Jerusalem three times, culminating in the sacking of Jerusalem in 586 B.C. and a full-scale exile of Jews to Babylon.

Characteristics: The book is constructed thematically, not chronologically. In it Jeremiah speaks his mind—a most disturbed and distressed mind. He complains to God about the job allotted to him more than any other prophet. Jeremiah denounces Judah's kings for their folly and weakness and the people for going their own way. Equally a part of his message, however, is a God of love who is determined to make a people worthy of his name.

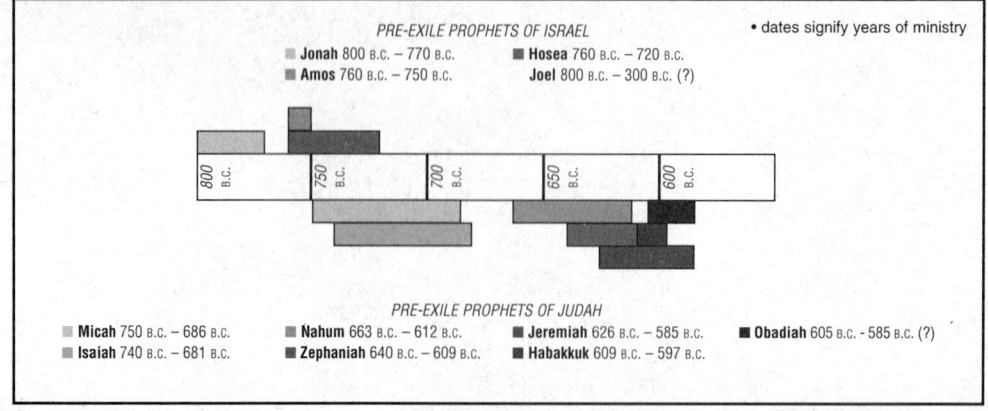

PRE-EXILE PROPHETS OF ISRAEL   • dates signify years of ministry

■ **Jonah** 800 B.C. – 770 B.C.   ■ **Hosea** 760 B.C. – 720 B.C.
■ **Amos** 760 B.C. – 750 B.C.   **Joel** 800 B.C. – 300 B.C. (?)

800 B.C.   750 B.C.   700 B.C.   650 B.C.   600 B.C.

PRE-EXILE PROPHETS OF JUDAH

■ **Micah** 750 B.C. – 686 B.C.   ■ **Nahum** 663 B.C. – 612 B.C.   ■ **Jeremiah** 626 B.C. – 585 B.C.   ■ **Obadiah** 605 B.C. - 585 B.C. (?)
■ **Isaiah** 740 B.C. – 681 B.C.   ■ **Zephaniah** 640 B.C. – 609 B.C.   ■ **Habakkuk** 609 B.C. – 597 B.C.

Jeremiah

1 The words of Jeremiah son of Hilkiah, one of the priests at Anathoth in the territory of Benjamin. ²The word of the LORD came to him in the thirteenth year of the reign of Josiah son of Amon king of Judah, ³and through the reign of Jehoiakim son of Josiah king of Judah, down to the fifth month of the eleventh year of Zedekiah son of Josiah king of Judah, when the people of Jerusalem went into exile.

The Call of Jeremiah

⁴The word of the LORD came to me, saying,

⁵"Before I formed you in the womb I knew*ᵃ* you,
before you were born I set you apart;
I appointed you as a prophet to the nations."

⁶"Ah, Sovereign LORD," I said, "I do not know how to speak; I am only a child."

⁷But the LORD said to me, "Do not say, 'I am only a child.' You must go to everyone I send you to and say whatever I command you. ⁸Do not be afraid of them, for I am with you and will rescue you," declares the LORD.

⁹Then the LORD reached out his hand and touched my mouth and said to me, "Now, I have put my words in your mouth. ¹⁰See, today I appoint you over nations and kingdoms to uproot and tear down, to destroy and overthrow, to build and to plant."

¹¹The word of the LORD came to me: "What do you see, Jeremiah?"

"I see the branch of an almond tree," I replied.

¹²The LORD said to me, "You have seen correctly, for I am watching*ᵇ* to see that my word is fulfilled."

¹³The word of the LORD came to me again: "What do you see?"

"I see a boiling pot, tilting away from the north," I answered.

¹⁴The LORD said to me, "From the north disaster will be poured out on all who live in the land. ¹⁵I am about to summon all the peoples of the northern kingdoms," declares the LORD.

"Their kings will come and set up their thrones
in the entrance of the gates of Jerusalem;
they will come against all her surrounding walls
and against all the towns of Judah.
¹⁶I will pronounce my judgments on my people
because of their wickedness in forsaking me,
in burning incense to other gods
and in worshiping what their hands have made.

¹⁷"Get yourself ready! Stand up and say to them whatever I command you. Do not be terrified by them, or I will terrify you before them. ¹⁸Today I have made you a fortified city, an iron pillar and a bronze wall to stand against the whole land—against the kings of Judah, its officials, its priests and the people of the land. ¹⁹They will fight against you but will not overcome you, for I am with you and will rescue you," declares the LORD.

1. Where were you born: At home? Hospital? Taxi? What stories about the event have you been told? **2.** Which relative made you feel wanted and safe as a child?

1. What was Jeremiah's occupation (v. 1)? What can you deduce about his family and heritage? **2.** When did Josiah rule? When did Zedekiah? How long did Jeremiah prophesy? Through the reigns of which five kings? **3.** What kind of king was Josiah (see 2Ki 22:1–2)? What did he do to renew the worship of the Lord (see 2Ki 23:1–5,20–21,24)? **4.** How do you think the "word of the Lord" came to Jeremiah: (a) Voice from the clouds? (b) Human-sounding voice? (c) Inner voice? **5.** How far back does God's relationship with Jeremiah go (v. 5)? How involved was God in preparing Jeremiah? **6.** How does God's call make Jeremiah feel (v. 6)? How old is Jeremiah? What does God say to Jeremiah to confirm his call (vv. 7–8)? What does he do to him (vv. 9–10)? **7.** What two object lessons does God give him (vv. 11–15)? Upon what pun does the first depend (see footnote)? What does the second mean? Why is God going to punish his people (v. 16)? **8.** What opposition will Jeremiah face in his ministry (vv. 17–19)? What does he need to do to overcome it? What things does God promise to do for him?

1. Do you trust that God has a wonderful plan for your life? Or do you feel somewhat like Jeremiah—dubious and fearful? **2.** When you were little, what did you want to be when you grew up? Which future plans did your parents encourage? Discourage? **3.** How does the Lord communicate with you: Are his plans for you always clear, sometimes clear or never clear? What role does Scripture play? What about advice, hunches, prayer, circumstances?

ᵃ5 Or *chose*   *ᵇ12* The Hebrew for *watching* sounds like the Hebrew for *almond tree.*

1. For the never-married: Describe the perfect honeymoon. When, where and with whom? If you have married: Where did you go on your honeymoon? How were the travel arrangements? Lodging? Weather? What snapshot helps you best remember this time? 2. Is it hard to maintain "friendship" with past loves? Why or why not?

Chapters 2–6 of Jeremiah's prophecy are considered to be among his earliest (c. 626 B.C.) and were delivered midway during the reign of Josiah (3:6), who was the most favorable of all kings to Jeremiah's radical message. These chapters deal with the near total apostasy of Judah and the inevitable foreign invasion which serves as God's retribution. 1. God pictures Israel as a bride. How did the marriage start out (vv. 2–3)? To what "desert" does he refer (vv. 2,6–7)? 2. What went wrong (v. 5)? What did the powerful do that was so contrary to God's intent (vv. 6–8)? Where was the Lord all this time? 3. What effect does Israel's behavior have on the natural world (vv. 7,10–12)? Do you think these descriptions are literal or metaphorical? Why? 4. What charges does God bring? What is so impossible about changing gods or lovers (v. 11)? 5. "Baal" is Hebrew for "master" or "lord." Who is Baal (see Jdg 2:11–13)? In what way is Baal-worship or idolatry really two sins in one (v. 13)? 6. What role do "lions" (symbolic of Assyria) and the Egyptians (v. 16; see 44:1) play in humiliating and destroying Israel? What role does Israel play in this (vv. 17–19)? What role does God play in sealing Israel's fate (see 2:36–37)?

1. What emotions do you think God is trying to convey through these vivid pictures? How does God feel: Hurt? Betrayed? Outraged? Jilted? Jealous? Or what? 2. What was wrong with worshipping a few other gods as long as the Lord was included? Or making military alliances with the major powers of the day? Why do you think God takes these things so personally? 3. As reflected in this passage, is sin breaking rules or hurting a person? Which way of thinking about it better motivates you to avoid it? Why?

Israel Forsakes God

2 The word of the LORD came to me: [2]"Go and proclaim in the hearing of Jerusalem:

> " 'I remember the devotion of your youth,
>   how as a bride you loved me
> and followed me through the desert,
>   through a land not sown.
> [3]Israel was holy to the LORD,
>   the firstfruits of his harvest;
> all who devoured her were held guilty,
>   and disaster overtook them,' "

declares the LORD.

[4]Hear the word of the LORD, O house of Jacob,
  all you clans of the house of Israel.

[5]This is what the LORD says:

> "What fault did your fathers find in me,
>   that they strayed so far from me?
> They followed worthless idols
>   and became worthless themselves.
> [6]They did not ask, 'Where is the LORD,
>   who brought us up out of Egypt
> and led us through the barren wilderness,
>   through a land of deserts and rifts,
> a land of drought and darkness,[a]
>   a land where no one travels and no one lives?'
> [7]I brought you into a fertile land
>   to eat its fruit and rich produce.
> But you came and defiled my land
>   and made my inheritance detestable.
> [8]The priests did not ask,
>   'Where is the LORD?'
> Those who deal with the law did not know me;
>   the leaders rebelled against me.
> The prophets prophesied by Baal,
>   following worthless idols.

> [9]"Therefore I bring charges against you again,"

declares the LORD.

> "And I will bring charges against your
>   children's children.
> [10]Cross over to the coasts of Kittim[b] and look,
>   send to Kedar[c] and observe closely;
>   see if there has ever been anything like this:
> [11]Has a nation ever changed its gods?
>   (Yet they are not gods at all.)
> But my people have exchanged their[d] Glory
>   for worthless idols.
> [12]Be appalled at this, O heavens,
>   and shudder with great horror,"

declares the LORD.

> [13]"My people have committed two sins:
> They have forsaken me,
>   the spring of living water,
> and have dug their own cisterns,

---

[a]6 Or *and the shadow of death*   [b]10 That is, Cyprus and western coastlands
[c]10 The home of Bedouin tribes in the Syro-Arabian desert   [d]11 Masoretic Text; an ancient Hebrew scribal tradition *my*

broken cisterns that cannot hold water.
¹⁴Is Israel a servant, a slave by birth?
    Why then has he become plunder?
¹⁵Lions have roared;
    they have growled at him.
They have laid waste his land;
    his towns are burned and deserted.
¹⁶Also, the men of Memphis^a and Tahpanhes
    have shaved the crown of your head.^b
¹⁷Have you not brought this on yourselves
    by forsaking the LORD your God
    when he led you in the way?
¹⁸Now why go to Egypt
    to drink water from the Shihor^c?
And why go to Assyria
    to drink water from the River^d?
¹⁹Your wickedness will punish you;
    your backsliding will rebuke you.
Consider then and realize
    how evil and bitter it is for you
when you forsake the LORD your God
    and have no awe of me,"
        declares the Lord, the LORD Almighty.

²⁰"Long ago you broke off your yoke
    and tore off your bonds;
    you said, 'I will not serve you!'
Indeed, on every high hill
    and under every spreading tree
    you lay down as a prostitute.
²¹I had planted you like a choice vine
    of sound and reliable stock.
How then did you turn against me
    into a corrupt, wild vine?
²²Although you wash yourself with soda
    and use an abundance of soap,
    the stain of your guilt is still before me,"
        declares the Sovereign LORD.
²³"How can you say, 'I am not defiled;
    I have not run after the Baals'?
See how you behaved in the valley;
    consider what you have done.
You are a swift she-camel
    running here and there,
²⁴a wild donkey accustomed to the desert,
    sniffing the wind in her craving—
    in her heat who can restrain her?
Any males that pursue her need not tire
    themselves;
    at mating time they will find her.
²⁵Do not run until your feet are bare
    and your throat is dry.
But you said, 'It's no use!
    I love foreign gods,
    and I must go after them.'

²⁶"As a thief is disgraced when he is caught,
    so the house of Israel is disgraced—

^a16 Hebrew *Noph*   ^b16 Or *have cracked your skull*   ^c18 That is, a branch of the
Nile   ^d18 That is, the Euphrates

1. Who is considered the "black sheep" or "wild vine" of your family? How and why did he or she become that way? **2.** Have you ever been accused of something and thought you were innocent? What happened? Did you later discover you were wrong?

1. What word-pictures does Jeremiah paint to describe Israel? How is Israel like a stubborn mule? Like a prostitute? A wild vine? A she-camel? A disgraced thief? A ravenous lion? **2.** How does this picture of prostitutes and animals in heat differ from the earlier one of Israel as bride (see 2:2–3)? **3.** What answers does Jeremiah expect to his rhetorical questions and sarcasm in 2:31–34? **4.** How has Israel treated the poor (v. 34)? Did Jewish law permit killing burglars in defense of property (see Ex 22:2–3)? **5.** What punishment of Israel is indicated in 2:35–37? For what reasons? By what means? **6.** What does the analogy of divorce mean in this context (3:1–5)? Who is the one properly entitled to seek divorce: God or Israel? **7.** Who is the one seeking reconciliation? Who is the one likely to reject that effort? Why is that?

1. Not many people bow down before or converse with gods of wood and stone in our society. Do you think we've licked the sin of idolatry? What kinds of things do people worship today? What

things are you tempted to worship?
2. Do you think God regards you as
a "bride" or a "prostitute"? Why?
How do you show your loyalty to
God as your first love? How do you
handle conflicts of loyalty between
God and other loves (such as Israel found herself in)? **3.** How important is loyalty to you in your relationships apart from God? To what
or whom do you feel most loyal?
Why? How loyal do you feel towards your small group? In what
ways can you show your loyalty to
them?

they, their kings and their officials,
    their priests and their prophets.
²⁷They say to wood, 'You are my father,'
    and to stone, 'You gave me birth.'
They have turned their backs to me
    and not their faces;
yet when they are in trouble, they say,
    'Come and save us!'
²⁸Where then are the gods you made for
        yourselves?
    Let them come if they can save you
        when you are in trouble!
For you have as many gods
    as you have towns, O Judah.

²⁹"Why do you bring charges against me?
    You have all rebelled against me,"
                    declares the LORD.
³⁰"In vain I punished your people;
    they did not respond to correction.
Your sword has devoured your prophets
    like a ravening lion.

³¹"You of this generation, consider the word of the LORD:

"Have I been a desert to Israel
    or a land of great darkness?
Why do my people say, 'We are free to roam;
    we will come to you no more'?
³²Does a maiden forget her jewelry,
    a bride her wedding ornaments?
Yet my people have forgotten me,
    days without number.
³³How skilled you are at pursuing love!
    Even the worst of women can learn from your
        ways.
³⁴On your clothes men find
    the lifeblood of the innocent poor,
    though you did not catch them breaking in.
Yet in spite of all this
³⁵   you say, 'I am innocent;
    he is not angry with me.'
But I will pass judgment on you
    because you say, 'I have not sinned.'
³⁶Why do you go about so much,
    changing your ways?
You will be disappointed by Egypt
    as you were by Assyria.
³⁷You will also leave that place
    with your hands on your head,
for the LORD has rejected those you trust;
    you will not be helped by them.

3

"If a man divorces his wife
    and she leaves him and marries another man,
should he return to her again?
    Would not the land be completely defiled?
But you have lived as a prostitute with many
        lovers—
    would you now return to me?"
                    declares the LORD.

²"Look up to the barren heights and see.
  Is there any place where you have not been
    ravished?
By the roadside you sat waiting for lovers,
  sat like a nomad[a] in the desert.
You have defiled the land
  with your prostitution and wickedness.
³Therefore the showers have been withheld,
  and no spring rains have fallen.
Yet you have the brazen look of a prostitute;
  you refuse to blush with shame.
⁴Have you not just called to me:
  'My Father, my friend from my youth,
⁵will you always be angry?
  Will your wrath continue forever?'
This is how you talk,
  but you do all the evil you can."

Unfaithful Israel

⁶During the reign of King Josiah, the LORD said to me, "Have you seen what faithless Israel has done? She has gone up on every high hill and under every spreading tree and has committed adultery there. ⁷I thought that after she had done all this she would return to me but she did not, and her unfaithful sister Judah saw it. ⁸I gave faithless Israel her certificate of divorce and sent her away because of all her adulteries. Yet I saw that her unfaithful sister Judah had no fear; she also went out and committed adultery. ⁹Because Israel's immorality mattered so little to her, she defiled the land and committed adultery with stone and wood. ¹⁰In spite of all this, her unfaithful sister Judah did not return to me with all her heart, but only in pretense," declares the LORD.

¹¹The LORD said to me, "Faithless Israel is more righteous than unfaithful Judah. ¹²Go, proclaim this message toward the north:

" 'Return, faithless Israel,' declares the LORD,
  'I will frown on you no longer,
for I am merciful,' declares the LORD,
  'I will not be angry forever.
¹³Only acknowledge your guilt—
  you have rebelled against the LORD your God,
you have scattered your favors to foreign gods
  under every spreading tree,
  and have not obeyed me,' "
                                     declares the LORD.

¹⁴"Return, faithless people," declares the LORD, "for I am your husband. I will choose you—one from a town and two from a clan—and bring you to Zion. ¹⁵Then I will give you shepherds after my own heart, who will lead you with knowledge and understanding. ¹⁶In those days, when your numbers have increased greatly in the land," declares the LORD, "men will no longer say, 'The ark of the covenant of the LORD.' It will never enter their minds or be remembered; it will not be missed, nor will another one be made. ¹⁷At that time they will call Jerusalem The Throne of the LORD, and all nations will gather in Jerusalem to honor the name of the LORD. No longer will they follow the stubbornness of their evil hearts. ¹⁸In those days the house of Judah will join the house of Israel, and

[a]2 Or an Arab

Sometimes we must learn the hard way, by ourselves. Sometimes we learn from an elder sibling. What lesson do you remember learning "the hard way" for which you wish you had had an older brother or sister to learn from? What lesson did you spare a younger sibling from having to learn the hard way?

1. To what does God compare the northern kingdom of Israel and the southern kingdom of Judah (3:6–7)? The people of the north were attacked and deported by the Assyrians c. 721 B.C., a century before Jeremiah. Why did God allow that to happen (3:8–10)? 2. What did God hope the people of Judah would do when they saw what happened to Israel? What did Judah do? 3. Why was Israel "more righteous" (3:11)? What is Jeremiah's message to the north (3:12–14)? What do the "one ... two" represent? 4. How does Jeremiah envision the future for all Israel (3:16–18)? Why will the ark of the covenant be irrelevant "in those days"? 5. In what sense has Israel become like a disenfranchised firstborn son (3:19)? Like an unfaithful woman (3:20)? 6. Under what conditions would God find Israel acceptable again (3:22–25)? 7. The northern tribes were never regathered, becoming the "lost 10 tribes of Israel." What could we guess about their answer to God's call (4:1–2)? 8. What should Judah do now (4:3–4; see Hos 10:12; Mt 4:7,22)? What is a "circumcised heart" (see Dt 30:6)?

1. Consider silently how you would feel and react if a sweetheart or spouse were unfaith-

ful to you. As a group, what does it tell you about God's love that he wants to take Israel back? **2.** Do you have trouble forgiving yourself for something you've done? Does it help knowing that God forgives you? Is something more needed? How can the group help? **3.** Did you feel like the preferred child in your family, or was another sibling preferred? How did that make you feel about your parents? Yourself? The preferred sibling? **4.** Is it easy for you to feel responsible when things go wrong? Or do you feel most problems in your life are caused by other people? When is the last time you admitted you were wrong? How did it go over? **5.** When have you experienced honesty and trust? What can the group do to encourage a sense of openness?

together they will come from a northern land to the land I gave your forefathers as an inheritance.

¹⁹"I myself said,

    " 'How gladly would I treat you like sons
      and give you a desirable land,
      the most beautiful inheritance of any nation.'
    I thought you would call me 'Father'
      and not turn away from following me.
²⁰But like a woman unfaithful to her husband,
      so you have been unfaithful to me, O house of
        Israel,"
                                    declares the LORD.

²¹A cry is heard on the barren heights,
      the weeping and pleading of the people of
        Israel,
    because they have perverted their ways
      and have forgotten the LORD their God.

²²"Return, faithless people;
    I will cure you of backsliding."

    "Yes, we will come to you,
      for you are the LORD our God.
²³Surely the ⌊idolatrous⌋ commotion on the hills
      and mountains is a deception;
    surely in the LORD our God
      is the salvation of Israel.
²⁴From our youth shameful gods have consumed
      the fruits of our fathers' labor—
    their flocks and herds,
      their sons and daughters.
²⁵Let us lie down in our shame,
      and let our disgrace cover us.
    We have sinned against the LORD our God,
      both we and our fathers;
    from our youth till this day
      we have not obeyed the LORD our God."

4   "If you will return, O Israel,
      return to me,"
                              declares the LORD.
    "If you put your detestable idols out of my sight
      and no longer go astray,
²and if in a truthful, just and righteous way
      you swear, 'As surely as the LORD lives,'
    then the nations will be blessed by him
      and in him they will glory."

³This is what the LORD says to the men of Judah and to Jerusalem:

    "Break up your unplowed ground
      and do not sow among thorns.
⁴Circumcise yourselves to the LORD,
      circumcise your hearts,
      you men of Judah and people of Jerusalem,
    or my wrath will break out and burn like fire
      because of the evil you have done—
      burn with no one to quench it.

Disaster From the North

5"Announce in Judah and proclaim in Jerusalem
and say:
'Sound the trumpet throughout the land!'
Cry aloud and say:
'Gather together!
Let us flee to the fortified cities!'
6Raise the signal to go to Zion!
Flee for safety without delay!
For I am bringing disaster from the north,
even terrible destruction."

7A lion has come out of his lair;
a destroyer of nations has set out.
He has left his place
to lay waste your land.
Your towns will lie in ruins
without inhabitant.
8So put on sackcloth,
lament and wail,
for the fierce anger of the LORD
has not turned away from us.

9"In that day," declares the LORD,
"the king and the officials will lose heart,
the priests will be horrified,
and the prophets will be appalled."

10Then I said, "Ah, Sovereign LORD, how completely you have deceived this people and Jerusalem by saying, 'You will have peace,' when the sword is at our throats."

11At that time this people and Jerusalem will be told, "A scorching wind from the barren heights in the desert blows toward my people, but not to winnow or cleanse; 12a wind too strong for that comes from me.ᵃ Now I pronounce my judgments against them."

13Look! He advances like the clouds,
his chariots come like a whirlwind,
his horses are swifter than eagles.
Woe to us! We are ruined!
14O Jerusalem, wash the evil from your heart and
be saved.
How long will you harbor wicked thoughts?
15A voice is announcing from Dan,
proclaiming disaster from the hills of Ephraim.
16"Tell this to the nations,
proclaim it to Jerusalem:
'A besieging army is coming from a distant land,
raising a war cry against the cities of Judah.
17They surround her like men guarding a field,
because she has rebelled against me,'"
declares the LORD.
18"Your own conduct and actions
have brought this upon you.
This is your punishment.
How bitter it is!
How it pierces to the heart!"

19Oh, my anguish, my anguish!
I writhe in pain.

ᵃ12 Or comes at my command

1. If you were warned that a nuclear strike would hit your area in 25 minutes, where would you go for safety? What would you take with you? What would you spend the time doing? 2. What skill do you keep telling yourself you'll learn when you get a little extra time? Do you think you will ever acquire it? 3. What was your birthing experience like for your mom? When have you witnessed a woman giving birth? Was it what you expected? Better or worse? Would you like to have that experience again?

1. From where comes the disaster about to befall Judah (vv. 5–6; see 6:1)? Who will be affected by the invasion (vv. 7–9)? 2. When did God "deceive" the people (v. 10; see 14:13–14)? What do the people think will happen to them? 3. What five word-pictures does Jeremiah use to describe the Babylonians (vv. 11–17)? Why has God brought them to attack his people (v. 18)? Can Jerusalem be saved (v. 14)? How so (see 3:23; 4:1–2)? 4. How does Jeremiah feel when he learns his nation will be destroyed (vv. 18–21)? What does his pain reveal about him? 5. What excuse, if any do the people have (v. 22)? Did they not know any better, or did they know only too well what they were doing? If they were ignorant, would you say it is right to punish people for that? 6. What vision does Jeremiah now have of life after the Babylonian invasion (vv. 23–26)? To what does Jeremiah compare the aftermath? 7. Verses 29–31 depict three different responses to the invasion. What are they? What do the images represent?

1. The false prophets told the people of Judah that they need not change because God would never punish them (3:10). What was in it for them and their listeners? Who tends to profit from such "prophets"? 2. Do you know of any situations where trouble is coming unless people change? What, if anything, can you do to help them? 3. How do you feel when you hear that a wicked person has suffered? How does your response compare to Jeremiah's? If your feelings are different, why do you feel that way? How should you feel? 4. Do you ever see people reacting to God's judgment in one of the ways described in 4:29–31? How should they re-

spond instead? **5.** Have you experienced God as Judge or Avenger? How did the experience affect you? How do you square the pictures of God the loving parent with God the avenging judge? **6.** Think of a place that has been devastated recently by war or disaster. Do you ever experience something like Jeremiah's concern and agony when you learn of people's suffering? Why or why not?

Oh, the agony of my heart!
  My heart pounds within me,
  I cannot keep silent.
For I have heard the sound of the trumpet;
  I have heard the battle cry.
²⁰Disaster follows disaster;
  the whole land lies in ruins.
In an instant my tents are destroyed,
  my shelter in a moment.
²¹How long must I see the battle standard
  and hear the sound of the trumpet?

²²"My people are fools;
  they do not know me.
They are senseless children;
  they have no understanding.
They are skilled in doing evil;
  they know not how to do good."

²³I looked at the earth,
  and it was formless and empty;
and at the heavens,
  and their light was gone.
²⁴I looked at the mountains,
  and they were quaking;
  all the hills were swaying.
²⁵I looked, and there were no people;
  every bird in the sky had flown away.
²⁶I looked, and the fruitful land was a desert;
  all its towns lay in ruins
  before the LORD, before his fierce anger.

²⁷This is what the LORD says:

"The whole land will be ruined,
  though I will not destroy it completely.
²⁸Therefore the earth will mourn
  and the heavens above grow dark,
because I have spoken and will not relent,
  I have decided and will not turn back."

²⁹At the sound of horsemen and archers
  every town takes to flight.
Some go into the thickets;
  some climb up among the rocks.
All the towns are deserted;
  no one lives in them.

³⁰What are you doing, O devastated one?
  Why dress yourself in scarlet
  and put on jewels of gold?
Why shade your eyes with paint?
  You adorn yourself in vain.
Your lovers despise you;
  they seek your life.

³¹I hear a cry as of a woman in labor,
  a groan as of one bearing her first child—
the cry of the Daughter of Zion gasping for breath,
  stretching out her hands and saying,
"Alas! I am fainting;
  my life is given over to murderers."

Not One Is Upright

5 "Go up and down the streets of Jerusalem,
    look around and consider,
    search through her squares.
If you can find but one person
    who deals honestly and seeks the truth,
    I will forgive this city.
²Although they say, 'As surely as the LORD lives,'
    still they are swearing falsely."

³O LORD, do not your eyes look for truth?
    You struck them, but they felt no pain;
    you crushed them, but they refused correction.
They made their faces harder than stone
    and refused to repent.
⁴I thought, "These are only the poor;
    they are foolish,
for they do not know the way of the LORD,
    the requirements of their God.
⁵So I will go to the leaders
    and speak to them;
surely they know the way of the LORD,
    the requirements of their God."
But with one accord they too had broken off the
    yoke
    and torn off the bonds.
⁶Therefore a lion from the forest will attack them,
    a wolf from the desert will ravage them,
a leopard will lie in wait near their towns
    to tear to pieces any who venture out,
for their rebellion is great
    and their backslidings many.

⁷"Why should I forgive you?
    Your children have forsaken me
    and sworn by gods that are not gods.
I supplied all their needs,
    yet they committed adultery
    and thronged to the houses of prostitutes.
⁸They are well-fed, lusty stallions,
    each neighing for another man's wife.
⁹Should I not punish them for this?"
    declares the LORD.
"Should I not avenge myself
    on such a nation as this?

¹⁰"Go through her vineyards and ravage them,
    but do not destroy them completely.
Strip off her branches,
    for these people do not belong to the LORD.
¹¹The house of Israel and the house of Judah
    have been utterly unfaithful to me,"
                            declares the LORD.

¹²They have lied about the LORD;
    they said, "He will do nothing!
No harm will come to us;
    we will never see sword or famine.
¹³The prophets are but wind
    and the word is not in them;
    so let what they say be done to them."

1. What section of the newspaper do you read first or most attentively? What part of the TV news grips you? Where in your reading or viewing priorities is the report on violent crimes? 2. Why might you be more fascinated with crime: Empathy for victims? Fear it might happen to you? Fantasy wish that you could get away with something similar? 3. Who are your favorite fictional or cartoon villains? Why do you like them? Do you ever find yourself rooting for the bad guy?

1. What is Jeremiah's quest (v. 1)? How will he know one when he sees one? What will God do if Jeremiah succeeds? How does that compare to God's response to Abraham's plea for Sodom (see Ge 18:16–32)? 2. Jeremiah finds a city full of evil. What evil actions does he find (vv. 2,7–8,19,23,26–27,31)? What evil attitudes does he find (vv. 3,5,11–13,21–24)? What sinful omission (v. 28)? 3. Is Jeremiah inclined to excuse the poor and blame the upper class (vv. 4–6)? Or are they equally at fault? Why do you think so? 4. How would you answer Jeremiah's rhetorical questions in verses 7 and 9 (also v. 29)? What answer is provided in verse 10? 5. How is God going to punish Judah (vv. 10,13–18)? How will the words of God differ from the words of the false prophets? Why won't the destruction be final? 6. What has become the prevailing attitude about God (vv. 12,22–24)? Why should people fear God when the wicked grow rich? 7. Which of Judah's failings do you think angers God the most? Do you think God gets as angry as Jeremiah tells it?

1. If Jeremiah walked your neighborhood, what would he find? What are peoples' relationships to God like in your neighborhood, town or city? Would your "truth rating" save the city? 2. Is honesty that hard to practice? Why? When is it easy to be truthful? When is it hardest? In what area of life do you need to raise the level of honesty? 3. Who are the "fatherless" and "poor" in today's society? Do you know any of these people? How are they treated? What can the group do to defend the rights of the poor? 4. Who do you think are false prophets today? What is their lie? How do they profit? 5. People in Jeremiah's day

were blind to their faults and easily led to presume their innocence. What accountability mechanisms do you have in place to help detect spiritual blindspots in your life? How can your group or family help in this?

¹⁴Therefore this is what the LORD God Almighty says:

"Because the people have spoken these words,
I will make my words in your mouth a fire
and these people the wood it consumes.
¹⁵O house of Israel," declares the LORD,
"I am bringing a distant nation against you—
an ancient and enduring nation,
a people whose language you do not know,
whose speech you do not understand.
¹⁶Their quivers are like an open grave;
all of them are mighty warriors.
¹⁷They will devour your harvests and food,
devour your sons and daughters;
they will devour your flocks and herds,
devour your vines and fig trees.
With the sword they will destroy
the fortified cities in which you trust.

¹⁸"Yet even in those days," declares the LORD, "I will not destroy you completely. ¹⁹And when the people ask, 'Why has the LORD our God done all this to us?' you will tell them, 'As you have forsaken me and served foreign gods in your own land, so now you will serve foreigners in a land not your own.'

²⁰"Announce this to the house of Jacob
and proclaim it in Judah:
²¹Hear this, you foolish and senseless people,
who have eyes but do not see,
who have ears but do not hear:
²²Should you not fear me?" declares the LORD.
"Should you not tremble in my presence?
I made the sand a boundary for the sea,
an everlasting barrier it cannot cross.
The waves may roll, but they cannot prevail;
they may roar, but they cannot cross it.
²³But these people have stubborn and rebellious
hearts;
they have turned aside and gone away.
²⁴They do not say to themselves,
'Let us fear the LORD our God,
who gives autumn and spring rains in season,
who assures us of the regular weeks of harvest.'
²⁵Your wrongdoings have kept these away;
your sins have deprived you of good.

²⁶"Among my people are wicked men
who lie in wait like men who snare birds
and like those who set traps to catch men.
²⁷Like cages full of birds,
their houses are full of deceit;
they have become rich and powerful
²⁸   and have grown fat and sleek.
Their evil deeds have no limit;
they do not plead the case of the fatherless to
win it,
they do not defend the rights of the poor.
²⁹Should I not punish them for this?"
declares the LORD.
"Should I not avenge myself
on such a nation as this?

³⁰"A horrible and shocking thing
    has happened in the land:
³¹The prophets prophesy lies,
    the priests rule by their own authority,
and my people love it this way.
    But what will you do in the end?

Jerusalem Under Siege

6   "Flee for safety, people of Benjamin!
      Flee from Jerusalem!
Sound the trumpet in Tekoa!
    Raise the signal over Beth Hakkerem!
For disaster looms out of the north,
    even terrible destruction.
²I will destroy the Daughter of Zion,
    so beautiful and delicate.
³Shepherds with their flocks will come against her;
    they will pitch their tents around her,
    each tending his own portion."

⁴"Prepare for battle against her!
    Arise, let us attack at noon!
But, alas, the daylight is fading,
    and the shadows of evening grow long.
⁵So arise, let us attack at night
    and destroy her fortresses!"

⁶This is what the LORD Almighty says:

"Cut down the trees
    and build siege ramps against Jerusalem.
This city must be punished;
    it is filled with oppression.
⁷As a well pours out its water,
    so she pours out her wickedness.
Violence and destruction resound in her;
    her sickness and wounds are ever before me.
⁸Take warning, O Jerusalem,
    or I will turn away from you
and make your land desolate
    so no one can live in it."

⁹This is what the LORD Almighty says:

"Let them glean the remnant of Israel
    as thoroughly as a vine;
pass your hand over the branches again,
    like one gathering grapes."

¹⁰To whom can I speak and give warning?
    Who will listen to me?
Their ears are closed*ᵃ*
    so they cannot hear.
The word of the LORD is offensive to them;
    they find no pleasure in it.
¹¹But I am full of the wrath of the LORD,
    and I cannot hold it in.

"Pour it out on the children in the street
    and on the young men gathered together;
both husband and wife will be caught in it,

ᵃ10 Hebrew *uncircumcised*

---

1. How would you rate yourself as an optimist on a scale of 1 ("Everything that can go wrong will go wrong") to 10 ("Every cloud has a silver lining")? 2. When you go on trips, are you a plan-it-for-months type, or a pick-up-and-go type? Is the rest of your family like you? Does this make travel easy or hard?

1. Who is speaking to whom in verses 1–3? In verses 4–5? 6? 8? 10–11a? 11b–23? 24–26? 27–30? Look for this change of speaker and audience throughout Jeremiah's prophecy. 2. Why should people flee the walled city of Jerusalem (vv. 1–5; compare 4:6, where they are told to go to Zion/Jerusalem)? Why is it safer outside? What happens in a siege (v. 6)? 3. Why does God want Jeremiah to warn Jerusalem (v. 8)? How eager is the city to hear God's word (v. 10)? What role have the religious leaders played in delivering the warning (vv. 13–15)? 4. What are the "ancient paths" to Jeremiah's audience (v. 16)? Who are the "watchmen" (v. 17)? Why does God call the earth and the nations to witness the disaster (vv. 18–20)? 5. What has Judah offered God instead of obedience (v. 20)? How do they respond to God's warning (vv. 24–25)? What response would God prefer? 6. What is Jeremiah's role now (v. 27; see Mal 3:2–3)? Smelters purify silver ore by throwing it into molten lead: The pure silver floats, the dross sinks. What does Jeremiah observe as Jerusalem goes into the fire?

1. What do you think was God's purpose in this warning? What does this tell you about God's character? 2. Smokers know cigarettes cause cancer; Californians know an earthquake will come eventually. Why do people frequently ignore warnings? What warnings does God have for your society? Are you paying attention or ignoring them? 3. If material gifts and burnt offerings were unacceptable to the Lord (v. 20), What kind of gifts or offerings do you think would have been acceptable to the

Lord? **4.** If presents are not good substitutes for time and attention spent on our children, what does that say about what we should be giving to the church and charities? Do you know anyone who tries to buy God off with gifts instead of obedience (no names)? Are you ever tempted to do this? **5.** Have you experienced God's refining fire? What "silver" came to the surface? What dross remains to be burnt away?

and the old, those weighed down with years.
¹²Their houses will be turned over to others,
   together with their fields and their wives,
when I stretch out my hand
   against those who live in the land,"
                                          declares the LORD.
¹³"From the least to the greatest,
   all are greedy for gain;
prophets and priests alike,
   all practice deceit.
¹⁴They dress the wound of my people
   as though it were not serious.
'Peace, peace,' they say,
   when there is no peace.
¹⁵Are they ashamed of their loathsome conduct?
   No, they have no shame at all;
   they do not even know how to blush.
So they will fall among the fallen;
   they will be brought down when I punish
      them,"
                                          says the LORD.

¹⁶This is what the LORD says:

"Stand at the crossroads and look;
   ask for the ancient paths,
ask where the good way is, and walk in it,
   and you will find rest for your souls.
   But you said, 'We will not walk in it.'
¹⁷I appointed watchmen over you and said,
   'Listen to the sound of the trumpet!'
   But you said, 'We will not listen.'
¹⁸Therefore hear, O nations;
   observe, O witnesses,
   what will happen to them.
¹⁹Hear, O earth:
I am bringing disaster on this people,
   the fruit of their schemes,
because they have not listened to my words
   and have rejected my law.
²⁰What do I care about incense from Sheba
   or sweet calamus from a distant land?
Your burnt offerings are not acceptable;
   your sacrifices do not please me."

²¹Therefore this is what the LORD says:

"I will put obstacles before this people.
   Fathers and sons alike will stumble over them;
   neighbors and friends will perish."

²²This is what the LORD says:

"Look, an army is coming
   from the land of the north;
a great nation is being stirred up
   from the ends of the earth.
²³They are armed with bow and spear;
   they are cruel and show no mercy.
They sound like the roaring sea
   as they ride on their horses;

they come like men in battle formation
  to attack you, O Daughter of Zion.”

²⁴We have heard reports about them,
  and our hands hang limp.
Anguish has gripped us,
  pain like that of a woman in labor.
²⁵Do not go out to the fields
  or walk on the roads,
for the enemy has a sword,
  and there is terror on every side.
²⁶O my people, put on sackcloth
  and roll in ashes;
mourn with bitter wailing
  as for an only son,
for suddenly the destroyer
  will come upon us.

²⁷“I have made you a tester of metals
  and my people the ore,
that you may observe
  and test their ways.
²⁸They are all hardened rebels,
  going about to slander.
They are bronze and iron;
  they all act corruptly.
²⁹The bellows blow fiercely
  to burn away the lead with fire,
but the refining goes on in vain;
  the wicked are not purged out.
³⁰They are called rejected silver,
  because the LORD has rejected them.”

False Religion Worthless

7 This is the word that came to Jeremiah from the LORD: ²“Stand at the gate of the LORD’s house and there proclaim this message:

“ ‘Hear the word of the LORD, all you people of Judah who come through these gates to worship the LORD. ³This is what the LORD Almighty, the God of Israel, says: Reform your ways and your actions, and I will let you live in this place. ⁴Do not trust in deceptive words and say, “This is the temple of the LORD, the temple of the LORD, the temple of the LORD!” ⁵If you really change your ways and your actions and deal with each other justly, ⁶if you do not oppress the alien, the fatherless or the widow and do not shed innocent blood in this place, and if you do not follow other gods to your own harm, ⁷then I will let you live in this place, in the land I gave your forefathers for ever and ever. ⁸But look, you are trusting in deceptive words that are worthless.

⁹“ ‘Will you steal and murder, commit adultery and perjury,^a burn incense to Baal and follow other gods you have not known, ¹⁰and then come and stand before me in this house, which bears my Name, and say, “We are safe”—safe to do all these detestable things? ¹¹Has this house, which bears my Name, become a den of robbers to you? But I have been watching! declares the LORD.

¹²“ ‘Go now to the place in Shiloh where I first made a dwelling for my Name, and see what I did to it because of the wickedness of my people Israel. ¹³While you were doing all these things, declares

---

^a9 Or *and swear by false gods*

1. Have you ever seen abandoned farms, a ghost town or ancient ruins? Where? How did it make you feel? 2. Have you ever seen a 1960s-style protest or a labor strike? What was the issue? How did it make you feel?

This series of temple prophecies (ch. 7–10) may be dated to Jehoiakim’s reign (c. 609–598 B.C.), due to similarities between chapters 7 and 26. 1. How did Jehoiakim come to be king (2Ki 23:29–37)? What kind of king was he? 2. Where does the prophet go to proclaim this message (v. 2)? Who would hear it there? 3. How can Judah remain in the land (vv. 5–7)? What kind of crimes have the people committed? 4. What have they done to the temple (vv. 8–11)? What happened a century earlier that makes them feel safe (2Ki 19:32–36)? But are they safe, despite what the other prophets say in verse 4? 5. Israel had a tabernacle at Shiloh long before David conquered Jerusalem and Solomon built the temple. What happened to it (see Ps 78:60–64; 1Sa

4:3–11)? What lesson does God want Judah to learn from that (vv. 12–15)? **6.** Why do you think God forbids Jeremiah to pray for Judah (v. 16)? What is the point of mentioning men, women and children involved in this idolatrous worship (vv. 18–19)? Who is really being hurt by this practice? **7.** How are they trying to appease God now (v. 21)? What's being neglected (vv. 22–24)? **8.** Will Jeremiah fare any better than the other prophets (vv. 25–27)? What will happen then (vv. 28–29)?

1. Where are you in your spiritual journey: (a) Egypt? (b) Going forward? (c) Backward? (d) At the temple gate? **2.** Do people in your church substitute being religious for being obedient? Do you? How can you make sure you're not fooling yourself? **3.** What does God have to do to get the attention of people today? What message does he want to send to you? **4.** How did Jesus see Jeremiah's words fulfilled in his day (see Mt 21:12–13)? What would Jeremiah and Jesus say about what goes on in churches today? In what ways is your church "doing business"? Who are the paying customers? What's the product?

1. What song would you like sung at your funeral? **2.** What is the most exciting thing you have seen in the heavens: UFO? Eclipse? Northern lights? Meteors?

1. What two crimes have the people committed (7:30–31)? Is child sacrifice new to Palestine (see Ge 22:1–2)? Why did God forbid it (see Lev 18:21; Ex 13:13–16)? **2.** Why will God rename the Hinnom Valley (7:32)? How is this ironic? **3.** What disgrace will the powerful face (8:1–2)? What punishment will the living suffer?

In what ways do parents hinder the religious growth of their children today? How will this affect the church? What do you think of "consulting the stars"? How

the LORD, I spoke to you again and again, but you did not listen; I called you, but you did not answer. [14]Therefore, what I did to Shiloh I will now do to the house that bears my Name, the temple you trust in, the place I gave to you and your fathers. [15]I will thrust you from my presence, just as I did all your brothers, the people of Ephraim.'

[16]"So do not pray for this people nor offer any plea or petition for them; do not plead with me, for I will not listen to you. [17]Do you not see what they are doing in the towns of Judah and in the streets of Jerusalem? [18]The children gather wood, the fathers light the fire, and the women knead the dough and make cakes of bread for the Queen of Heaven. They pour out drink offerings to other gods to provoke me to anger. [19]But am I the one they are provoking? declares the LORD. Are they not rather harming themselves, to their own shame?

[20]"'Therefore this is what the Sovereign LORD says: My anger and my wrath will be poured out on this place, on man and beast, on the trees of the field and on the fruit of the ground, and it will burn and not be quenched.

[21]"'This is what the LORD Almighty, the God of Israel, says: Go ahead, add your burnt offerings to your other sacrifices and eat the meat yourselves! [22]For when I brought your forefathers out of Egypt and spoke to them, I did not just give them commands about burnt offerings and sacrifices, [23]but I gave them this command: Obey me, and I will be your God and you will be my people. Walk in all the ways I command you, that it may go well with you. [24]But they did not listen or pay attention; instead, they followed the stubborn inclinations of their evil hearts. They went backward and not forward. [25]From the time your forefathers left Egypt until now, day after day, again and again I sent you my servants the prophets. [26]But they did not listen to me or pay attention. They were stiff-necked and did more evil than their forefathers.'

[27]"When you tell them all this, they will not listen to you; when you call to them, they will not answer. [28]Therefore say to them, 'This is the nation that has not obeyed the LORD its God or responded to correction. Truth has perished; it has vanished from their lips. [29]Cut off your hair and throw it away; take up a lament on the barren heights, for the LORD has rejected and abandoned this generation that is under his wrath.

The Valley of Slaughter

[30]"'The people of Judah have done evil in my eyes, declares the LORD. They have set up their detestable idols in the house that bears my Name and have defiled it. [31]They have built the high places of Topheth in the Valley of Ben Hinnom to burn their sons and daughters in the fire—something I did not command, nor did it enter my mind. [32]So beware, the days are coming, declares the LORD, when people will no longer call it Topheth or the Valley of Ben Hinnom, but the Valley of Slaughter, for they will bury the dead in Topheth until there is no more room. [33]Then the carcasses of this people will become food for the birds of the air and the beasts of the earth, and there will be no one to frighten them away. [34]I will bring an end to the sounds of joy and gladness and to the voices of bride and bridegroom in the towns of Judah and the streets of Jerusalem, for the land will become desolate.

8 "'At that time, declares the LORD, the bones of the kings and officials of Judah, the bones of the priests and prophets, and the bones of the people of Jerusalem will be removed from their graves. [2]They will be exposed to the sun and the moon and all the stars of the heavens, which they have loved and served and which they have followed and consulted and worshiped. They will not be gathered up or buried, but will be like refuse lying on the ground. ³Wherever I banish them, all the survivors of this evil nation will prefer death to life, declares the LORD Almighty.'

Sin and Punishment

⁴"Say to them, 'This is what the LORD says:

"'When men fall down, do they not get up?
    When a man turns away, does he not return?
⁵Why then have these people turned away?
    Why does Jerusalem always turn away?
They cling to deceit;
    they refuse to return.
⁶I have listened attentively,
    but they do not say what is right.
No one repents of his wickedness,
    saying, "What have I done?"
Each pursues his own course
    like a horse charging into battle.
⁷Even the stork in the sky
    knows her appointed seasons,
and the dove, the swift and the thrush
    observe the time of their migration.
But my people do not know
    the requirements of the LORD.

⁸"'How can you say, "We are wise,
    for we have the law of the LORD,"
when actually the lying pen of the scribes
    has handled it falsely?
⁹The wise will be put to shame;
    they will be dismayed and trapped.
Since they have rejected the word of the LORD,
    what kind of wisdom do they have?
¹⁰Therefore I will give their wives to other men
    and their fields to new owners.
From the least to the greatest,
    all are greedy for gain;
prophets and priests alike,
    all practice deceit.
¹¹They dress the wound of my people
    as though it were not serious.
"Peace, peace," they say,
    when there is no peace.
¹²Are they ashamed of their loathsome conduct?
    No, they have no shame at all;
    they do not even know how to blush.
So they will fall among the fallen;
    they will be brought down when they are
        punished,
                            says the LORD.

¹³"'I will take away their harvest,
                            declares the LORD.
There will be no grapes on the vine.
There will be no figs on the tree,
    and their leaves will wither.

might God frustrate those who trust their daily horoscope?

———

1. What is your greatest accomplishment so far? How long did it take you to do it? What was so hard about it? 2. If you were a migratory bird, where would you like to spend your winters? 3. Are your trips to the doctor frequent or rare? Does the doctor usually know what's wrong, or could you have taken care of it yourself? What advice do you find easiest, and hardest, to obey?

1. What about the people of Jerusalem amazes God (vv. 4–7)? How are even the birds smarter than they? 2. Who preserved the written Law of the Lord (vv. 8–12)? What have they done to deceive the people? What were their motives? How will God punish them? 3. Is verse 13 a threat of physical destruction, or is the figless tree the spiritual condition God finds in Judah? 4. How would you describe the people's feeling about the coming invasion (vv. 14–16): (a) Frightened? (b) Resolved? (c) Nonchalant? (d) Resigned? (e) Mad at God? 5. How does Jeremiah feel (8:18–9:1)? What seems to bother him the most? Where does he hope to find healing (see 46:11; 51:8)? Does his fountain of tears seem genuine to you, or is this for show?

1. What "social sins" prevail today, as in Jeremiah's day? What other parallels do you see between the people and the leadership of Judah and those of your country? 2. How do you respond to them: (a) Moral outrage? (b) Self-denial? (c) Genuine sorrow? (d) Do-nothing resignation? (e) Flight to warmer, safer climates? (f) Determination to change things? 3. Jeremiah deserved his reputation as the "weeping prophet." Who in your society has that reputation of intensely and extensively grieving over the social sins of the nation? 4. How might you learn to be more genuinely anxious over the welfare of others, even to point of weeping? 5. Upon what human institutions do people pin their hopes for "peace now"? What might Jeremiah say at one of their conferences?

What I have given them
   will be taken from them.*' ”

¹⁴“Why are we sitting here?
   Gather together!
Let us flee to the fortified cities
   and perish there!
For the LORD our God has doomed us to perish
   and given us poisoned water to drink,
     because we have sinned against him.
¹⁵We hoped for peace
   but no good has come,
for a time of healing
   but there was only terror.
¹⁶The snorting of the enemy's horses
   is heard from Dan;
at the neighing of their stallions
   the whole land trembles.
They have come to devour
   the land and everything in it,
   the city and all who live there.”

¹⁷“See, I will send venomous snakes among you,
   vipers that cannot be charmed,
   and they will bite you,”
                declares the LORD.

¹⁸O my Comforter*ᵇ* in sorrow,
   my heart is faint within me.
¹⁹Listen to the cry of my people
   from a land far away:
“Is the LORD not in Zion?
   Is her King no longer there?”

“Why have they provoked me to anger with their
     images,
   with their worthless foreign idols?”

²⁰“The harvest is past,
   the summer has ended,
   and we are not saved.”

²¹Since my people are crushed, I am crushed;
   I mourn, and horror grips me.
²²Is there no balm in Gilead?
   Is there no physician there?
Why then is there no healing
   for the wound of my people?

9 ¹Oh, that my head were a spring of water
   and my eyes a fountain of tears!
I would weep day and night
   for the slain of my people.
²Oh, that I had in the desert
   a lodging place for travelers,
so that I might leave my people
   and go away from them;
for they are all adulterers,
   a crowd of unfaithful people.

³“They make ready their tongue

1. What is your favorite place to get away from it all? How often do you go there? 2. Who in your group can twist their tongue or touch their nose with it? Try it and see.

1. Having wept continuously (9:1), what does Jeremiah now want to do? Why? 2. What are their tongues capable of doing (vv.

ᵃ13 The meaning of the Hebrew for this sentence is uncertain.   *ᵇ18* The meaning of the Hebrew for this word is uncertain.

like a bow, to shoot lies;
it is not by truth
 that they triumph[a] in the land.
They go from one sin to another;
 they do not acknowledge me,"
       declares the LORD.
4"Beware of your friends;
 do not trust your brothers.
For every brother is a deceiver,[b]
 and every friend a slanderer.
5Friend deceives friend,
 and no one speaks the truth.
They have taught their tongues to lie;
 they weary themselves with sinning.
6You[c] live in the midst of deception;
 in their deceit they refuse to acknowledge me,"
       declares the LORD.

7Therefore this is what the LORD Almighty says:

"See, I will refine and test them,
 for what else can I do
 because of the sin of my people?
8Their tongue is a deadly arrow;
 it speaks with deceit.
With his mouth each speaks cordially to his
  neighbor,
but in his heart he sets a trap for him.
9Should I not punish them for this?"
 declares the LORD.
"Should I not avenge myself
 on such a nation as this?"

10I will weep and wail for the mountains
 and take up a lament concerning the desert
  pastures.
They are desolate and untraveled,
 and the lowing of cattle is not heard.
The birds of the air have fled
 and the animals are gone.

11"I will make Jerusalem a heap of ruins,
 a haunt of jackals;
and I will lay waste the towns of Judah
 so no one can live there."

12What man is wise enough to understand this? Who has been
instructed by the LORD and can explain it? Why has the land been
ruined and laid waste like a desert that no one can cross?

13The LORD said, "It is because they have forsaken my law, which
I set before them; they have not obeyed me or followed my law.
14Instead, they have followed the stubbornness of their hearts; they
have followed the Baals, as their fathers taught them." 15Therefore,
this is what the LORD Almighty, the God of Israel, says: "See, I will
make this people eat bitter food and drink poisoned water. 16I will
scatter them among nations that neither they nor their fathers have
known, and I will pursue them with the sword until I have destroyed them."

17This is what the LORD Almighty says:

3,8)? In what situations does deception prove effective? **3.** What
does the prophet weep over in
verse 10? What seems to bother
Jeremiah the most about God
bringing Jerusalem to ruins (vv.
11–12)? **4.** How does the Lord answer him (vv. 13–19)? Who are
"wailing women" (vv. 17–20; see
2Ch 35:25 and Mt 9:23, for a tradition instituted by Jeremiah)? Why
will this become a booming profession? **5.** In what sense is death the
"grim reaper" (v. 22)? **6.** What do
the wise, the strong and the rich
stand to lose from the invasion?
What does it mean to "boast" in
wisdom, strength or riches? In what
should one boast instead (v. 24;
compare 1Co 1:31)? **7.** Was circumcision the sole property of the
Israelites (vv. 25–26)? What kind
of circumcision matters to God and
why (see 4:4; also 6:10 and NIV
text footnote; Ge 17:10; Dt 10:16)?

♡ **1.** What kinds of things do
people today "boast" or take
pride in? What do you tend to
boast about? **2.** What has been a
great sadness in your life? Would it
feel good to have someone "wail"
with you about it? How do people
respond to your feelings of loss or
sorrow? How has God treated you?
3. Even in circumcision, Judah had
become like the surrounding countries. In what ways is the Church
today indistinguishable from the
society it is in? In what ways is the
Church distinct from any other social group? **4.** Do you make friends
easily, or are you a loner? Did betrayal by a friend or sibling make it
hard for you to trust? How do you
protect yourself from being hurt by
people important to you?

---

a3 Or lies; / they are not valiant for truth b4 Or a deceiving Jacob c6 That is,
Jeremiah (the Hebrew is singular)

"Consider now! Call for the wailing women to
    come;
  send for the most skillful of them.
[18]Let them come quickly
  and wail over us
till our eyes overflow with tears
  and water streams from our eyelids.
[19]The sound of wailing is heard from Zion:
  'How ruined we are!
  How great is our shame!
We must leave our land
  because our houses are in ruins.'"

[20]Now, O women, hear the word of the LORD;
  open your ears to the words of his mouth.
Teach your daughters how to wail;
  teach one another a lament.
[21]Death has climbed in through our windows
  and has entered our fortresses;
it has cut off the children from the streets
  and the young men from the public squares.

[22]Say, "This is what the LORD declares:

"'The dead bodies of men will lie
  like refuse on the open field,
like cut grain behind the reaper,
  with no one to gather them.'"

[23]This is what the LORD says:

"Let not the wise man boast of his wisdom
  or the strong man boast of his strength
  or the rich man boast of his riches,
[24]but let him who boasts boast about this:
  that he understands and knows me,
that I am the LORD, who exercises kindness,
  justice and righteousness on earth,
  for in these I delight,"
                declares the LORD.

[25]"The days are coming," declares the LORD, "when I will punish
all who are circumcised only in the flesh— [26]Egypt, Judah, Edom,
Ammon, Moab and all who live in the desert in distant places.[a]
For all these nations are really uncircumcised, and even the whole
house of Israel is uncircumcised in heart."

God and Idols

10 Hear what the LORD says to you, O house of Israel. [2]This is
what the LORD says:

"Do not learn the ways of the nations
  or be terrified by signs in the sky,
  though the nations are terrified by them.
[3]For the customs of the peoples are worthless;
  they cut a tree out of the forest,
  and a craftsman shapes it with his chisel.
[4]They adorn it with silver and gold;
  they fasten it with hammer and nails
  so it will not totter.
[5]Like a scarecrow in a melon patch,

1. In choosing your Christ-mas tree, do you prefer it natural or artificial? Large or small? Big needle or small needle? 2. In adorning your tree, do you prefer lots of bulbs and glitter? Only natural, handmade items? Only lights? 3. Describe one of your favorite ornaments that gets hung on your Christmas tree every year, or the special one you made or received last year.

1. The word "nations" is from the Hebrew "Goyim," meaning "Gentiles" or non-Jews. From what two Gentile customs does God discourage Israel (vv. 2–3)?

a26 Or *desert and who clip the hair by their foreheads*

their idols cannot speak;
>they must be carried
>because they cannot walk.
Do not fear them;
>they can do no harm
>nor can they do any good."

6No one is like you, O LORD;
>you are great,
>and your name is mighty in power.
7Who should not revere you,
>O King of the nations?
>This is your due.
Among all the wise men of the nations
>and in all their kingdoms,
>there is no one like you.
8They are all senseless and foolish;
>they are taught by worthless wooden idols.
9Hammered silver is brought from Tarshish
>and gold from Uphaz.
What the craftsman and goldsmith have made
>is then dressed in blue and purple—
>all made by skilled workers.
10But the LORD is the true God;
>he is the living God, the eternal King.
When he is angry, the earth trembles;
>the nations cannot endure his wrath.

11"Tell them this: 'These gods, who did not make the heavens and the earth, will perish from the earth and from under the heavens.'"[a]

12But God made the earth by his power;
>he founded the world by his wisdom
>and stretched out the heavens by his
>understanding.
13When he thunders, the waters in the heavens
>roar;
>he makes clouds rise from the ends of the
>earth.
He sends lightning with the rain
>and brings out the wind from his storehouses.

14Everyone is senseless and without knowledge;
>every goldsmith is shamed by his idols.
His images are a fraud;
>they have no breath in them.
15They are worthless, the objects of mockery;
>when their judgment comes, they will perish.
16He who is the Portion of Jacob is not like these,
>for he is the Maker of all things,
including Israel, the tribe of his inheritance—
>the LORD Almighty is his name.

Coming Destruction

17Gather up your belongings to leave the land,
>you who live under siege.
18For this is what the LORD says:
>"At this time I will hurl out

[a]11 The text of this verse is in Aramaic.

What feeling lies beneath these words about idols (vv. 4–5)? 2. If idols are so impotent and worthless (see also Ps 115:4–7), why do you think God's people constantly turn to them? Did idol worship play a part in the social and economic fabric of Palestine (v. 9; see Ac 19:23–27)? 3. How was the Jewish concept of God different from that of the pagans (vv. 10–13)? How easy would it be to combine the monotheism of Israel with worship of local cultic deities? Who ultimately is mocked by this attempt? 4. The words "portion" and "inheritance" are equated in verse 16. What does it mean that Israel's inheritance is God? That God's portion is Israel?

1. Jeremiah 10 has been used to condemn the tradition of making Christmas trees. Using this passage, can you support that idea? How do you know Jeremiah is talking about something else? 2. Idolatry has always been big business. Can you think of any modern industries that depend upon our homage? To what images must we bow in order to participate in the social and economic system around us? 3. What kinds of things do people idolize today—things that they are counting on to speak to them, carry them or do good for them, as only God can? 4. How much time do you take to meditate on God's creation and power? What aspect of nature speaks most clearly to you of God's power? 5. In what sense might verse 5 apply to you: Is there anything you fear that you need not? Do your work or your purchases "do good" for others? Is there a better way you could spend your prime waking hours and disposable income?

1. What is the most time away from school or work which you have missed because of an illness or injury? How did you make up for the lost time? 2. If you had to vacate your house before dawn, how many carloads would it take to move your belongings?

Truckloads? What would you take if you could keep only what you could carry?

📖 1. What will happen to those who stay under siege? To those who flee the city? If Jeremiah's name means "the Lord throws," what possible pun do you see here? 2. Who speaks in verses 19–22? What is the "incurable wound"? What happened to the leaders? 3. How does Jeremiah feel about himself in this time of crisis (vv. 23–24)? For what two reasons is he angry with Judah's enemies (v. 25)? 4. Is this prayer (also in Ps 79:6–7) vengeful, or is it an appeal for God's justice? Why do you think so?

❤ 1. In what circumstances might God allow his people to endure an illness or injury that is curable or preventable? 2. Have you ever met a refugee? How would you feel if your home was destroyed and your country at war? 3. Which would you rather receive: God's justice or anger? What determines who gets what? 4. Do you believe the fate of your country depends on whether the political leaders look to God for guidance? Why?

━━━━━━━━

☕ 1. Think of one promise you have kept for a long time and one promise that was broken. Why is it important to you to keep a promise? How did (or do) you feel about a broken promise? 2. Where would you live if you could choose anywhere in the world? What would you want there that would be the modern equivalent of the "milk and honey" promised to the ancient Israelites?

📖 1. When did God and Israel make "the terms of this covenant," especially those dealing with "cursed is the man" (vv. 1–5; see Dt 27:15–26)? What happened in the reign of Josiah to renew such interest in the covenant (see 2Ki 22:8–13; 23:1–3)? 2. What did God promise to do for Israel (vv. 4–8)? What was their land of "milk and honey" (see Ex 3:8)? 3. What was their part of the bargain? How are the people of Judah responding to Josiah's and Jeremiah's call (vv. 9–13)? 4. Again, Jeremiah is forbidden to pray for Israel (see

those who live in this land;
I will bring distress on them
so that they may be captured."

¹⁹Woe to me because of my injury!
My wound is incurable!
Yet I said to myself,
"This is my sickness, and I must endure it."
²⁰My tent is destroyed;
all its ropes are snapped.
My sons are gone from me and are no more;
no one is left now to pitch my tent
or to set up my shelter.
²¹The shepherds are senseless
and do not inquire of the LORD;
so they do not prosper
and all their flock is scattered.
²²Listen! The report is coming—
a great commotion from the land of the north!
It will make the towns of Judah desolate,
a haunt of jackals.

Jeremiah's Prayer

²³I know, O LORD, that a man's life is not his own;
it is not for man to direct his steps.
²⁴Correct me, LORD, but only with justice—
not in your anger,
lest you reduce me to nothing.
²⁵Pour out your wrath on the nations
that do not acknowledge you,
on the peoples who do not call on your name.
For they have devoured Jacob;
they have devoured him completely
and destroyed his homeland.

The Covenant Is Broken

11 This is the word that came to Jeremiah from the LORD: ²"Listen to the terms of this covenant and tell them to the people of Judah and to those who live in Jerusalem. ³Tell them that this is what the LORD, the God of Israel, says: 'Cursed is the man who does not obey the terms of this covenant— ⁴the terms I commanded your forefathers when I brought them out of Egypt, out of the iron-smelting furnace.' I said, 'Obey me and do everything I command you, and you will be my people, and I will be your God. ⁵Then I will fulfill the oath I swore to your forefathers, to give them a land flowing with milk and honey'—the land you possess today."

I answered, "Amen, LORD."

⁶The LORD said to me, "Proclaim all these words in the towns of Judah and in the streets of Jerusalem: 'Listen to the terms of this covenant and follow them. ⁷From the time I brought your forefathers up from Egypt until today, I warned them again and again, saying, "Obey me." ⁸But they did not listen or pay attention; instead, they followed the stubbornness of their evil hearts. So I brought on them all the curses of the covenant I had commanded them to follow but that they did not keep.'"

⁹Then the LORD said to me, "There is a conspiracy among the people of Judah and those who live in Jerusalem. ¹⁰They have returned to the sins of their forefathers, who refused to listen to my words. They have followed other gods to serve them. Both the

house of Israel and the house of Judah have broken the covenant I made with their forefathers. [11]Therefore this is what the LORD says: 'I will bring on them a disaster they cannot escape. Although they cry out to me, I will not listen to them. [12]The towns of Judah and the people of Jerusalem will go and cry out to the gods to whom they burn incense, but they will not help them at all when disaster strikes. [13]You have as many gods as you have towns, O Judah; and the altars you have set up to burn incense to that shameful god Baal are as many as the streets of Jerusalem.'

[14]"Do not pray for this people nor offer any plea or petition for them, because I will not listen when they call to me in the time of their distress.

[15]"What is my beloved doing in my temple
    as she works out her evil schemes with many?
  Can consecrated meat avert ⌞your punishment⌟?
  When you engage in your wickedness,
    then you rejoice. [a]"

[16]The LORD called you a thriving olive tree
    with fruit beautiful in form.
  But with the roar of a mighty storm
    he will set it on fire,
    and its branches will be broken.

[17]The LORD Almighty, who planted you, has decreed disaster for you, because the house of Israel and the house of Judah have done evil and provoked me to anger by burning incense to Baal.

Plot Against Jeremiah

[18]Because the LORD revealed their plot to me, I knew it, for at that time he showed me what they were doing. [19]I had been like a gentle lamb led to the slaughter; I did not realize that they had plotted against me, saying,

"Let us destroy the tree and its fruit;
    let us cut him off from the land of the living,
    that his name be remembered no more."
  [20]But, O LORD Almighty, you who judge righteously
    and test the heart and mind,
  let me see your vengeance upon them,
    for to you I have committed my cause.

[21]"Therefore this is what the LORD says about the men of Anathoth who are seeking your life and saying, 'Do not prophesy in the name of the LORD or you will die by our hands'— [22]therefore this is what the LORD Almighty says: 'I will punish them. Their young men will die by the sword, their sons and daughters by famine. [23]Not even a remnant will be left to them, because I will bring disaster on the men of Anathoth in the year of their punishment.'"

Jeremiah's Complaint

12 You are always righteous, O LORD,
    when I bring a case before you.
  Yet I would speak with you about your justice:
    Why does the way of the wicked prosper?
    Why do all the faithless live at ease?
  [2]You have planted them, and they have taken root;
    they grow and bear fruit.
  You are always on their lips

7:16)? Why (see 1Jn 5:16–17)? **5.** What is the point of the covenant when Israel never keeps it? What curses are coming if they don't (see Dt 28:15–68)? **6.** What is Judah doing to win God's favor (v. 15; see 7:10–11,21–24)? Can anything change God's mind at this point (vv. 11,14)? Is this fair?

1. Is it ever too late with God? When might God's patience run out for you? For your country? The world? **2.** Does your group have a covenant with God? With each other? What promises need to be restated in the group? **3.** Who do you think raises the voice of reform today? Are you listening? What is being asked of you? Of the church?

1. What were you noted for in your hometown? **2.** Tom Wolfe wrote, "You can't go home again." Has this been true for you?

1. Jeremiah helps Josiah close local shrines. Does this play well in his hometown of Anathoth? Why does this distress him (see 12:2)? **2.** How does he discover the plot? Why did it take him so long to realize his peril? **3.** Why was the plot revealed?

1. Jesus also had a "bad homecoming" (see Mt 13:53–58). Has obeying God ever alienated those closest to you? What happened? **2.** Are you comfortable in seeking God's vengeance? What would you request if you were Jeremiah?

1. If you were a lawyer, would you prefer to prosecute or defend? Would you prosecute someone you felt was innocent? Defend someone you thought was guilty? **2.** In your experience, do nice guys always finish last? Do bad guys always finish first? **3.** What member of your family or small group would you nominate as "King of the World" for a day? What do you think he or she

---

[a]15 Or *Could consecrated meat avert your punishment? / Then you would rejoice*

could do that other world leaders can't or won't?

📖 **1.** What is his bone of contention (v. 2)? Has this thought ever crossed your mind? **2.** What does Jeremiah want God to do (v. 3)? Why is Jeremiah so brutal? Why are the faithless so carefree (v. 4)? **3.** In Jeremiah's complaint, on what is he basing his appeal: (a) Good guys always win in the end? (b) Divine justice? (c) Prophetic license? **4.** What is the point of the comparison in verses 5–6? What comfort can Jeremiah take in that? **5.** What is God's warning to Judah (vv. 7–13)? How does he seem to feel? How is this an answer for Jeremiah? **6.** What is God's warning to Judah's marauding neighbors (vv. 14–17; see 2Ki 24:1–2)? **7.** What good news do you see here for the exiles, both Jewish and Gentile (compare Isa 2:2–4; 56:6–7)? What will determine how God treats them (vv. 16–17)?

♡ **1.** Have you ever felt the unfairness of life as keenly as Jeremiah? In your experience, have the wicked prospered? How so? For how long? Why does God delay in executing justice? **2.** How would you describe God's response to Jeremiah's honesty: Angry? Glad? Disturbed? Sympathetic? Puzzled? Matter-of-fact? Other? Have you ever complained to God as honestly as Jeremiah did? What was God's response? **3.** What would our world be like if God instantly punished every sin? What would your life be like? **4.** Are you "on foot … competing with horses" (v. 5)? Or are you "stumbling in safe country"? How do you prepare for tougher times? How can your group assist?

but far from their hearts.
³Yet you know me, O LORD;
    you see me and test my thoughts about you.
Drag them off like sheep to be butchered!
    Set them apart for the day of slaughter!
⁴How long will the land lie parched*a*
    and the grass in every field be withered?
Because those who live in it are wicked,
    the animals and birds have perished.
Moreover, the people are saying,
    "He will not see what happens to us."

God's Answer

⁵"If you have raced with men on foot
    and they have worn you out,
    how can you compete with horses?
If you stumble in safe country,*b*
    how will you manage in the thickets by*c* the Jordan?
⁶Your brothers, your own family—
    even they have betrayed you;
    they have raised a loud cry against you.
Do not trust them,
    though they speak well of you.

⁷"I will forsake my house,
    abandon my inheritance;
I will give the one I love
    into the hands of her enemies.
⁸My inheritance has become to me
    like a lion in the forest.
She roars at me;
    therefore I hate her.
⁹Has not my inheritance become to me
    like a speckled bird of prey
    that other birds of prey surround and attack?
Go and gather all the wild beasts;
    bring them to devour.
¹⁰Many shepherds will ruin my vineyard
    and trample down my field;
they will turn my pleasant field
    into a desolate wasteland.
¹¹It will be made a wasteland,
    parched and desolate before me;
the whole land will be laid waste
    because there is no one who cares.
¹²Over all the barren heights in the desert
    destroyers will swarm,
for the sword of the LORD will devour
    from one end of the land to the other;
    no one will be safe.
¹³They will sow wheat but reap thorns;
    they will wear themselves out but gain nothing.
So bear the shame of your harvest
    because of the LORD's fierce anger."

¹⁴This is what the LORD says: "As for all my wicked neighbors who seize the inheritance I gave my people Israel, I will uproot

---

a4 Or *land mourn*   *b5* Or *If you put your trust in a land of safety*   *c5* Or *the flooding of* them from their lands and I will uproot the house of Judah from among them. ¹⁵But after I uproot them, I will again have compassion and will bring each of them back to his own inheritance and his own country. ¹⁶And if they learn well the ways of my people and swear by my name, saying, 'As surely as the LORD lives'—even as they once taught my people to swear by Baal—then they will be established among my people. ¹⁷But if any nation does not listen, I will completely uproot and destroy it," declares the LORD.

A Linen Belt

13 This is what the LORD said to me: "Go and buy a linen belt and put it around your waist, but do not let it touch water." ²So I bought a belt, as the LORD directed, and put it around my waist.

³Then the word of the LORD came to me a second time: ⁴"Take the belt you bought and are wearing around your waist, and go now to Perath[a] and hide it there in a crevice in the rocks." ⁵So I went and hid it at Perath, as the LORD told me.

⁶Many days later the LORD said to me, "Go now to Perath and get the belt I told you to hide there." ⁷So I went to Perath and dug up the belt and took it from the place where I had hidden it, but now it was ruined and completely useless.

⁸Then the word of the LORD came to me: ⁹"This is what the LORD says: 'In the same way I will ruin the pride of Judah and the great pride of Jerusalem. ¹⁰These wicked people, who refuse to listen to my words, who follow the stubbornness of their hearts and go after other gods to serve and worship them, will be like this belt—completely useless! ¹¹For as a belt is bound around a man's waist, so I bound the whole house of Israel and the whole house of Judah to me,' declares the LORD, 'to be my people for my renown and praise and honor. But they have not listened.'

Wineskins

¹²"Say to them: 'This is what the LORD, the God of Israel, says: Every wineskin should be filled with wine.' And if they say to you, 'Don't we know that every wineskin should be filled with wine?' ¹³then tell them, 'This is what the LORD says: I am going to fill with drunkenness all who live in this land, including the kings who sit on David's throne, the priests, the prophets and all those living in Jerusalem. ¹⁴I will smash them one against the other, fathers and sons alike, declares the LORD. I will allow no pity or mercy or compassion to keep me from destroying them.'"

Threat of Captivity

¹⁵Hear and pay attention,
    do not be arrogant,
    for the LORD has spoken.
¹⁶Give glory to the LORD your God
    before he brings the darkness,
before your feet stumble
    on the darkening hills.
You hope for light,
    but he will turn it to thick darkness
    and change it to deep gloom.
¹⁷But if you do not listen,
    I will weep in secret
    because of your pride;

a4 Or possibly *the Euphrates*; also in verses 5-7

What are some of the more creative uses for a belt which you have come up with?

1. What metaphors do you see in this allegory (vv. 1–6)? Why a linen belt? The hiding? The spoiling? 2. What does the allegory mean (vv. 6–11)? Why does God use an object lesson? 3. What is the meaning of the wineskin metaphor (v. 12)? Why belabor the obvious? What should be obvious to Judah? 4. Is Judah's drunkenness literal or spiritual (v. 13; see 25:15–29)? What's the message in this for Judah to hear? For you?

1. Have there been times in your life when God used actions, even a "belting," to speak louder than words? What happened? How did the message get through? 2. Jeremiah obeyed God instantly, without questioning. How willing are you to go along with things that you don't understand? 3. We try to convey God's message through words and deeds. Which is easier for you? In what ways might one without the other confuse people? How can you share God's message more clearly and openly?

1. What precautions do you take when traveling at night, alone? When darkness falls, what do you fear might happen to you? 2. When was the last time you were lost? What happened?

1. Is there any hope for Judah, or is captivity inevitable (vv. 15–17)? Why would Jeremiah weep secretly (see 9:1)? 2. Who are the "king and ... queen mother" (v. 18; see 2Ki 24:8–12, which dates this prophecy c. 597 B.C.)? 3. The defeated were often led naked into captivity. What sense of shame does this fate convey (vv. 22,26; see Eze 16:36–38)? 4. Is

Judah unable to stop sinning (v. 23)? Is it fair to punish people for acts that Jeremiah seems to consider beyond their control? 5. What had Judah done to deserve this fate (vv. 24–25)?

1. How do you think Jeremiah felt delivering this kind of message again and again? Why didn't God just warn Judah once and then lower the boom? What do these repeated warnings tell you about God? 2. How easily do you cry? What was the cause of your last tears? Has the state of the church or humanity ever upset you enough to weep? 3. Why did God liken the worship of other gods to adultery? What does that tell you about the way he thinks of his relationship with us? Imagining God as your spouse, do you feel: (a) Head over heels? (b) The honeymoon's over? (c) All work, no play? (d) Separation? (e) Still going strong? (f) Divorced? 4. Can a leopard change its spots? Is that true of people in general? Of you? Is this verse "hopeless" or do you see it differently?

my eyes will weep bitterly,
overflowing with tears,
because the LORD's flock will be taken captive.

¹⁸Say to the king and to the queen mother,
"Come down from your thrones,
for your glorious crowns
will fall from your heads."
¹⁹The cities in the Negev will be shut up,
and there will be no one to open them.
All Judah will be carried into exile,
carried completely away.

²⁰Lift up your eyes and see
those who are coming from the north.
Where is the flock that was entrusted to you,
the sheep of which you boasted?
²¹What will you say when ⌊the LORD⌋ sets over you
those you cultivated as your special allies?
Will not pain grip you
like that of a woman in labor?
²²And if you ask yourself,
"Why has this happened to me?"—
it is because of your many sins
that your skirts have been torn off
and your body mistreated.
²³Can the Ethiopian^a change his skin
or the leopard its spots?
Neither can you do good
who are accustomed to doing evil.

²⁴"I will scatter you like chaff
driven by the desert wind.
²⁵This is your lot,
the portion I have decreed for you,"
                                        declares the LORD,
"because you have forgotten me
and trusted in false gods.
²⁶I will pull up your skirts over your face
that your shame may be seen—
²⁷your adulteries and lustful neighings,
your shameless prostitution!
I have seen your detestable acts
on the hills and in the fields.
Woe to you, O Jerusalem!
How long will you be unclean?"

1. Are you usually early, on-time or late for appointments or meetings? Why? Would you consider breaking the mold by being the opposite (early for once, or late)? 2. When was the last time you were too late for something? What happened? How did you feel? 3. If you had to pick a torturous "fate worse than death," what would it be?

1. What "triple whammy" from God finally gets Judah's attention (14:1–6)? How do you

Drought, Famine, Sword

14 This is the word of the LORD to Jeremiah concerning the drought:

²"Judah mourns,
her cities languish;
they wail for the land,
and a cry goes up from Jerusalem.
³The nobles send their servants for water;
they go to the cisterns
but find no water.
They return with their jars unfilled;

^a23 Hebrew Cushite (probably a person from the upper Nile region)

dismayed and despairing,
  they cover their heads.
4The ground is cracked
  because there is no rain in the land;
the farmers are dismayed
  and cover their heads.
5Even the doe in the field
  deserts her newborn fawn
  because there is no grass.
6Wild donkeys stand on the barren heights
  and pant like jackals;
their eyesight fails
  for lack of pasture."

7Although our sins testify against us,
  O Lord, do something for the sake of your
    name.
For our backsliding is great;
  we have sinned against you.
8O Hope of Israel,
  its Savior in times of distress,
why are you like a stranger in the land,
  like a traveler who stays only a night?
9Why are you like a man taken by surprise,
  like a warrior powerless to save?
You are among us, O Lord,
  and we bear your name;
  do not forsake us!

10This is what the Lord says about this people:

"They greatly love to wander;
  they do not restrain their feet.
So the Lord does not accept them;
  he will now remember their wickedness
  and punish them for their sins."

11Then the Lord said to me, "Do not pray for the well-being of this people. 12Although they fast, I will not listen to their cry; though they offer burnt offerings and grain offerings, I will not accept them. Instead, I will destroy them with the sword, famine and plague."

13But I said, "Ah, Sovereign Lord, the prophets keep telling them, 'You will not see the sword or suffer famine. Indeed, I will give you lasting peace in this place.'"

14Then the Lord said to me, "The prophets are prophesying lies in my name. I have not sent them or appointed them or spoken to them. They are prophesying to you false visions, divinations, idolatriesa and the delusions of their own minds. 15Therefore, this is what the Lord says about the prophets who are prophesying in my name: I did not send them, yet they are saying, 'No sword or famine will touch this land.' Those same prophets will perish by sword and famine. 16And the people they are prophesying to will be thrown out into the streets of Jerusalem because of the famine and sword. There will be no one to bury them or their wives, their sons or their daughters. I will pour out on them the calamity they deserve.

17"Speak this word to them:

a 14 Or visions, worthless divinations

---

imagine this "drought, famine and sword" would come about: All at once? In shifts of successive years? Or what? **2.** On what basis do the people hope God will rescue them (14:7–9)? What do you think was the most effective part of their appeal? **3.** Why is God fed up with them and their cries (14:10–13)? Why should Jeremiah pray for them, as a true prophet would (see 1Sa 7:8; 12:23)? **4.** What will happen to the false prophets (14:14–18)? What irony do you see here? **5.** Though told not to pray for the people, what is Jeremiah doing in 14:19–22? What is the basis of Jeremiah's appeal on behalf of the rejected people (see Lev 26:44–45)? **6.** Does God soften up (15:1–4)? What sins did King Manasseh commit (see 2Ki 21:1–18)? **7.** What is the focus of the poem in 15:5–9? What irony and tragedy do you see here?

1. Do you think God's patience finally wears out? At what point? Does patience have to have a time limit? What becomes of limitless patience? **2.** The false prophets told the kings what they wanted to hear. Do you know someone who says "yes" to avoid rocking the boat? Are you ever a "yes-sayer" in your family? At work? At church? Has it ever gotten you or the church in trouble? What troubles do you see stemming from people who only tell others what they want to hear? **3.** On the other hand, some people like to make waves. Do you? What is one thing you have said that greatly upset some people's presumptuous thinking? What happened as a result? **4.** When have you reacted with scorn or persecution against someone who rocked your boat?

" 'Let my eyes overflow with tears
 night and day without ceasing;
for my virgin daughter—my people—
 has suffered a grievous wound,
 a crushing blow.
¹⁸If I go into the country,
 I see those slain by the sword;
if I go into the city,
 I see the ravages of famine.
Both prophet and priest
 have gone to a land they know not.' "

¹⁹Have you rejected Judah completely?
 Do you despise Zion?
Why have you afflicted us
 so that we cannot be healed?
We hoped for peace
 but no good has come,
for a time of healing
 but there is only terror.
²⁰O LORD, we acknowledge our wickedness
 and the guilt of our fathers;
 we have indeed sinned against you.
²¹For the sake of your name do not despise us;
 do not dishonor your glorious throne.
Remember your covenant with us
 and do not break it.
²²Do any of the worthless idols of the nations bring
  rain?
 Do the skies themselves send down showers?
No, it is you, O LORD our God.
 Therefore our hope is in you,
 for you are the one who does all this.

15 Then the LORD said to me: "Even if Moses and Samuel were to stand before me, my heart would not go out to this people. Send them away from my presence! Let them go! ²And if they ask you, 'Where shall we go?' tell them, 'This is what the LORD says:

" 'Those destined for death, to death;
 those for the sword, to the sword;
 those for starvation, to starvation;
 those for captivity, to captivity.'

³"I will send four kinds of destroyers against them," declares the LORD, "the sword to kill and the dogs to drag away and the birds of the air and the beasts of the earth to devour and destroy. ⁴I will make them abhorrent to all the kingdoms of the earth because of what Manasseh son of Hezekiah king of Judah did in Jerusalem.

⁵"Who will have pity on you, O Jerusalem?
 Who will mourn for you?
 Who will stop to ask how you are?
⁶You have rejected me," declares the LORD.
 "You keep on backsliding.
So I will lay hands on you and destroy you;
 I can no longer show compassion.
⁷I will winnow them with a winnowing fork
 at the city gates of the land.
I will bring bereavement and destruction on my
  people,

for they have not changed their ways.
⁸I will make their widows more numerous
    than the sand of the sea.
At midday I will bring a destroyer
    against the mothers of their young men;
suddenly I will bring down on them
    anguish and terror.
⁹The mother of seven will grow faint
    and breathe her last.
Her sun will set while it is still day;
    she will be disgraced and humiliated.
I will put the survivors to the sword
    before their enemies,"

> declares the LORD.

¹⁰Alas, my mother, that you gave me birth,
    a man with whom the whole land strives and
        contends!
I have neither lent nor borrowed,
    yet everyone curses me.

¹¹The LORD said,

> "Surely I will deliver you for a good purpose;
>   surely I will make your enemies plead with you
>   in times of disaster and times of distress.

¹²"Can a man break iron—
    iron from the north—or bronze?
¹³Your wealth and your treasures
    I will give as plunder, without charge,
because of all your sins
    throughout your country.
¹⁴I will enslave you to your enemies
    in^a a land you do not know,
for my anger will kindle a fire
    that will burn against you."

¹⁵You understand, O LORD;
    remember me and care for me.
Avenge me on my persecutors.
You are long-suffering—do not take me away;
    think of how I suffer reproach for your sake.
¹⁶When your words came, I ate them;
    they were my joy and my heart's delight,
for I bear your name,
    O LORD God Almighty.
¹⁷I never sat in the company of revelers,
    never made merry with them;
I sat alone because your hand was on me
    and you had filled me with indignation.
¹⁸Why is my pain unending
    and my wound grievous and incurable?
Will you be to me like a deceptive brook,
    like a spring that fails?

¹⁹Therefore this is what the LORD says:

> "If you repent, I will restore you
>   that you may serve me;

Have you ever wished you had not been born? If so, when and why? Did your parents ever say they wished you'd never been born? How did such words affect your outlook on life?

1. Why does Jeremiah think God is being unfair (15:10,15–18)? Would you agree? Why does Jeremiah wish he'd never been born? What other reward for his dedication to God was he expecting? **2.** Does God console him or punish him in verses 11–14? In verses 16–18? Of what does Jeremiah need to repent (v. 19)? How does God use both the "carrot" and the "stick" with him?

1. If you could go back and change anything in your life, what would you change? What do you wish could have happened instead? **2.** Do you think serving the Lord was a pleasant task for Jeremiah? Would you have liked his job? Do you ever feel unrewarded for your dedication? Unappreciated by God? By others? How does God equip you for the role you play? **3.** Do you receive enough encouragement and support from this group? How could the group provide more of what you need?

---

^a14 Some Hebrew manuscripts, Septuagint and Syriac (see also Jer. 17:4); most Hebrew manuscripts *I will cause your enemies to bring you / into*

if you utter worthy, not worthless, words,
    you will be my spokesman.
Let this people turn to you,
    but you must not turn to them.
[20]I will make you a wall to this people,
    a fortified wall of bronze;
they will fight against you
    but will not overcome you,
for I am with you
    to rescue and save you,"
                            declares the LORD.
[21]"I will save you from the hands of the wicked
    and redeem you from the grasp of the cruel."

Day of Disaster

16 Then the word of the LORD came to me: [2]"You must not marry and have sons or daughters in this place." [3]For this is what the LORD says about the sons and daughters born in this land and about the women who are their mothers and the men who are their fathers: [4]"They will die of deadly diseases. They will not be mourned or buried but will be like refuse lying on the ground. They will perish by sword and famine, and their dead bodies will become food for the birds of the air and the beasts of the earth."

[5]For this is what the LORD says: "Do not enter a house where there is a funeral meal; do not go to mourn or show sympathy, because I have withdrawn my blessing, my love and my pity from this people," declares the LORD. [6]"Both high and low will die in this land. They will not be buried or mourned, and no one will cut himself or shave his head for them. [7]No one will offer food to comfort those who mourn for the dead—not even for a father or a mother—nor will anyone give them a drink to console them.

[8]"And do not enter a house where there is feasting and sit down to eat and drink. [9]For this is what the LORD Almighty, the God of Israel, says: Before your eyes and in your days I will bring an end to the sounds of joy and gladness and to the voices of bride and bridegroom in this place.

[10]"When you tell these people all this and they ask you, 'Why has the LORD decreed such a great disaster against us? What wrong have we done? What sin have we committed against the LORD our God?' [11]then say to them, 'It is because your fathers forsook me,' declares the LORD, 'and followed other gods and served and worshiped them. They forsook me and did not keep my law. [12]But you have behaved more wickedly than your fathers. See how each of you is following the stubbornness of his evil heart instead of obeying me. [13]So I will throw you out of this land into a land neither you nor your fathers have known, and there you will serve other gods day and night, for I will show you no favor.'

[14]"However, the days are coming," declares the LORD, "when men will no longer say, 'As surely as the LORD lives, who brought the Israelites up out of Egypt,' [15]but they will say, 'As surely as the LORD lives, who brought the Israelites up out of the land of the north and out of all the countries where he had banished them.' For I will restore them to the land I gave their forefathers.

[16]"But now I will send for many fishermen," declares the LORD, "and they will catch them. After that I will send for many hunters, and they will hunt them down on every mountain and hill and from the crevices of the rocks. [17]My eyes are on all their ways; they are not hidden from me, nor is their sin concealed from my eyes. [18]I will repay them double for their wickedness and their sin,

---

1. Recall a really good wedding you have attended. What made it great? 2. What was (or what do you imagine might be) the best part of your wedding? 3. When was the last time you were invited to a celebration but could not go? Did the others miss you? How did you feel? 4. For you, what is the best part of fishing or hunting? What is the worst part?

1. What three activities of normal human life does God forbid to Jeremiah (vv. 1–9)? Why? What is his abstinence from these things supposed to convey to the people? How do you suppose Jeremiah coped with the loneliness that came with his particular calling? 2. How do verses 6 and 7 make you feel about the desolation in store for Judah? In what way will the people "serve other gods" (v. 13)? 3. What rays of hope do you see in this otherwise dismal picture? What event will outshine the Exodus? 4. What is so doubly detestable to God about idol worship, that "fisherman" and "hunters" were sent in after them (vv. 16–18)?

1. Have you made sacrifices to serve God? Give an example. 2. Have you gone to the funeral of someone in your church whom you did not know? The wedding of a stranger? Are these events strictly private or do they belong to the entire community of faith? 3. When did a condemnation of society's failing last pass your lips? A prayer of compassion for a sick world? Set some time aside this week to pray for the world.

because they have defiled my land with the lifeless forms of their vile images and have filled my inheritance with their detestable idols."

¹⁹O Lord, my strength and my fortress,
　　my refuge in time of distress,
to you the nations will come
　　from the ends of the earth and say,
"Our fathers possessed nothing but false gods,
　　worthless idols that did them no good.
²⁰Do men make their own gods?
　　Yes, but they are not gods!"

²¹"Therefore I will teach them—
　　this time I will teach them
　　my power and might.
Then they will know
　　that my name is the Lord.

17 "Judah's sin is engraved with an iron tool,
　　inscribed with a flint point,
on the tablets of their hearts
　　and on the horns of their altars.
²Even their children remember
　　their altars and Asherah poles^a
beside the spreading trees
　　and on the high hills.
³My mountain in the land
　　and your^b wealth and all your treasures
I will give away as plunder,
　　together with your high places,
　　because of sin throughout your country.
⁴Through your own fault you will lose
　　the inheritance I gave you.
I will enslave you to your enemies
　　in a land you do not know,
for you have kindled my anger,
　　and it will burn forever."

⁵This is what the Lord says:

"Cursed is the one who trusts in man,
　　who depends on flesh for his strength
　　and whose heart turns away from the Lord.
⁶He will be like a bush in the wastelands;
　　he will not see prosperity when it comes.
He will dwell in the parched places of the desert,
　　in a salt land where no one lives.
⁷"But blessed is the man who trusts in the Lord,
　　whose confidence is in him.
⁸He will be like a tree planted by the water
　　that sends out its roots by the stream.
It does not fear when heat comes;
　　its leaves are always green.
It has no worries in a year of drought
　　and never fails to bear fruit."

⁹The heart is deceitful above all things

To what tree or plant would you compare your life: (a) Evergreen tree, tall and majestic? (b) Weeping willow, bending with the wind? (c) Desert cactus, a sole survivor? (d) Oak tree, a bit nutty? (e) Other?

1. Upon what is Jeremiah relying? How does this contrast with the gods of other nations, "their altars and Asherah poles" (v. 2; see Ex 34:12–14)? 2. In contrast to the cursed drought conditions that prevail, what blessed hope does Jeremiah cling to and hold forth for others (vv. 5–8)? 3. Why does Jeremiah call the human heart "deceitful above all things" (v. 9)? What is the relationship between mind and action (v. 10)? What is the point of the related parable (v. 11)? 4. What are Jeremiah's countrymen saying about his ability to prophesy (vv. 14–15)? How will the coming disaster bring both hope and terror to the prophet? 5. Of what does Jeremiah need healing? How might he be confused with a false prophet? (Hint: What has not yet happened that he is predicting will?)

1. What times of spiritual "drought" have you experienced? What keeps you going during those dry times? 2. At present, are you felling more like a "bush in the wastelands" (v. 6) or a "tree planted by the water" (v. 8)? Why? 3. How honest are you with yourself? Could your heart be deceiving you about the motives of some of your actions at work? At home? In relationships?

---

^a2 That is, symbols of the goddess Asherah　　^b2,3 Or hills / ³and the mountains of the land. / Your

and beyond cure.
Who can understand it?

10"I the LORD search the heart
    and examine the mind,
to reward a man according to his conduct,
    according to what his deeds deserve."

11Like a partridge that hatches eggs it did not lay
    is the man who gains riches by unjust means.
When his life is half gone, they will desert him,
    and in the end he will prove to be a fool.

12A glorious throne, exalted from the beginning,
    is the place of our sanctuary.
13O LORD, the hope of Israel,
    all who forsake you will be put to shame.
Those who turn away from you will be written in
        the dust
    because they have forsaken the LORD,
        the spring of living water.

14Heal me, O LORD, and I will be healed;
    save me and I will be saved,
    for you are the one I praise.
15They keep saying to me,
    "Where is the word of the LORD?
    Let it now be fulfilled!"
16I have not run away from being your shepherd;
    you know I have not desired the day of despair.
    What passes my lips is open before you.
17Do not be a terror to me;
    you are my refuge in the day of disaster.
18Let my persecutors be put to shame,
    but keep me from shame;
let them be terrified,
    but keep me from terror.
Bring on them the day of disaster;
    destroy them with double destruction.

Keeping the Sabbath Holy

19This is what the LORD said to me: "Go and stand at the gate of the people, through which the kings of Judah go in and out; stand also at all the other gates of Jerusalem. 20Say to them, 'Hear the word of the LORD, O kings of Judah and all people of Judah and everyone living in Jerusalem who come through these gates. 21This is what the LORD says: Be careful not to carry a load on the Sabbath day or bring it through the gates of Jerusalem. 22Do not bring a load out of your houses or do any work on the Sabbath, but keep the Sabbath day holy, as I commanded your forefathers. 23Yet they did not listen or pay attention; they were stiff-necked and would not listen or respond to discipline. 24But if you are careful to obey me, declares the LORD, and bring no load through the gates of this city on the Sabbath, but keep the Sabbath day holy by not doing any work on it, 25then kings who sit on David's throne will come through the gates of this city with their officials. They and their officials will come riding in chariots and on horses, accompanied by the men of Judah and those living in Jerusalem, and this city will be inhabited forever. 26People will come from the towns of Judah and the villages around Jerusalem, from the territory of Benjamin and the western foothills, from the hill country and the Negev,

---

1. What was your favorite Sunday activity as a kid? What sounds like an ideal Sunday to you now? 2. Would you keep your job if you inherited a fortune?

1. Why doesn't Jeremiah make this announcement at the gates of the temple (vv. 20–22)? What does the Sabbath rank in Jewish law (see Ex 20:3–8)? Why is it important (see Ex 31:12–17)? Why is "work" forbidden (v. 24; see Nu 15:32–36; Ne 13:15)? 3. Why is God now demanding a formal religious practice (vv. 24–27)?

1. Orthodox Jews do not drive, cook or carry money on Saturday. Would you like the Christian Sunday to be like the Orthodox Jewish Sabbath? 2. Do you need to put more worship, more leisure, or more spiritual growth into

bringing burnt offerings and sacrifices, grain offerings, incense and thank offerings to the house of the LORD. ²⁷But if you do not obey me to keep the Sabbath day holy by not carrying any load as you come through the gates of Jerusalem on the Sabbath day, then I will kindle an unquenchable fire in the gates of Jerusalem that will consume her fortresses.' "

At the Potter's House

18 This is the word that came to Jeremiah from the LORD: ²"Go down to the potter's house, and there I will give you my message." ³So I went down to the potter's house, and I saw him working at the wheel. ⁴But the pot he was shaping from the clay was marred in his hands; so the potter formed it into another pot, shaping it as seemed best to him.

⁵Then the word of the LORD came to me: ⁶"O house of Israel, can I not do with you as this potter does?" declares the LORD. "Like clay in the hand of the potter, so are you in my hand, O house of Israel. ⁷If at any time I announce that a nation or kingdom is to be uprooted, torn down and destroyed, ⁸and if that nation I warned repents of its evil, then I will relent and not inflict on it the disaster I had planned. ⁹And if at another time I announce that a nation or kingdom is to be built up and planted, ¹⁰and if it does evil in my sight and does not obey me, then I will reconsider the good I had intended to do for it.

¹¹"Now therefore say to the people of Judah and those living in Jerusalem, 'This is what the LORD says: Look! I am preparing a disaster for you and devising a plan against you. So turn from your evil ways, each one of you, and reform your ways and your actions.' ¹²But they will reply, 'It's no use. We will continue with our own plans; each of us will follow the stubbornness of his evil heart.' "

¹³Therefore this is what the LORD says:

"Inquire among the nations:
　　Who has ever heard anything like this?
A most horrible thing has been done
　　by Virgin Israel.
¹⁴Does the snow of Lebanon
　　ever vanish from its rocky slopes?
Do its cool waters from distant sources
　　ever cease to flow?^a
¹⁵Yet my people have forgotten me;
　　they burn incense to worthless idols,
which made them stumble in their ways
　　and in the ancient paths.
They made them walk in bypaths
　　and on roads not built up.
¹⁶Their land will be laid waste,
　　an object of lasting scorn;
all who pass by will be appalled
　　and will shake their heads.
¹⁷Like a wind from the east,
　　I will scatter them before their enemies;
I will show them my back and not my face
　　in the day of their disaster."

¹⁸They said, "Come, let's make plans against Jeremiah; for the teaching of the law by the priest will not be lost, nor will counsel

---

^a14 The meaning of the Hebrew for this sentence is uncertain.

---

your Sundays? How can you begin doing that next week?

1. Are you any good at making things or doing crafts? What have you made? What would you like to make? 2. What "pot" best describes you: Kettle? Crack pot? Frying pan? Cast-iron? Flower pot? Fine china? Other?

1. What does Jeremiah see at the potter's house (18:2–4)? 2. How does the nature of the clay determine the quality of the pot and what it is used for? What point is God trying to make about the conditional nature of his promises and threats? (18:5–10) 3. What is Judah's decision regarding God's warning (18:11–12)? Why do the people continually ignore God? What sense does Jeremiah try to make of their stubbornness (18:13–17)? 4. What do the people want to do with Jeremiah and why (18:18)? In Jeremiah's confession (18:19–23), how does he come to terms with what is happening to him? Can you fault Jeremiah for wanting to dish out punishment equal to what he has had to take from his accusers? 5. Who is supposed to see the lesson of the jar first (19:1–3)? Why do you suppose he goes to the Hinnom Valley near the Potsherd Gate? What would be happening there (19:4–9)? 6. What does Jeremiah's action symbolize (19:10–11)? Do you think such cannibalism was merely symbolic, or could it actually have happened that way? (For some historical precedents, see 2Ki 6:28–29; La 2:20; 4:10; Eze 5:10.) 7. What does Jerusalem have in common with Topheth (19:12–13), that her fate will be similar (see 19:5–6; 2Ki 23:10)? 8. Why does Jeremiah repeat the warning in the Temple court (19:14–15)? Do you think Judah deserves another spin on God's "potter's wheel," or does Judah deserve the scrap heap or total destruction?

1. Are God's plans set in "concrete" or "wet clay"? How much does he mold people, and how much do people mold themselves (see Ro 9:19–23)? 2. The prophets often dramatized their messages. What message do you

want the world to hear today? How could you make the point through a symbolic action or dramatized parable? Could you see it being covered on national TV news? **3.** Why did the people of these ancient cultures kill their children? For what reasons are children killed today? **4.** Do you suppose God saved the mold when he first created you, so that he could create more people like you? If God were to re-create you, what chip, crack or bulge in your life's jar would you like God to fix the second time around?

from the wise, nor the word from the prophets. So come, let's attack him with our tongues and pay no attention to anything he says."

> [19]Listen to me, O LORD;
>   hear what my accusers are saying!
> [20]Should good be repaid with evil?
>   Yet they have dug a pit for me.
> Remember that I stood before you
>   and spoke in their behalf
>   to turn your wrath away from them.
> [21]So give their children over to famine;
>   hand them over to the power of the sword.
> Let their wives be made childless and widows;
>   let their men be put to death,
>   their young men slain by the sword in battle.
> [22]Let a cry be heard from their houses
>   when you suddenly bring invaders against
>   them,
> for they have dug a pit to capture me
>   and have hidden snares for my feet.
> [23]But you know, O LORD,
>   all their plots to kill me.
> Do not forgive their crimes
>   or blot out their sins from your sight.
> Let them be overthrown before you;
>   deal with them in the time of your anger.

19 This is what the LORD says: "Go and buy a clay jar from a potter. Take along some of the elders of the people and of the priests [2]and go out to the Valley of Ben Hinnom, near the entrance of the Potsherd Gate. There proclaim the words I tell you, [3]and say, 'Hear the word of the LORD, O kings of Judah and people of Jerusalem. This is what the LORD Almighty, the God of Israel, says: Listen! I am going to bring a disaster on this place that will make the ears of everyone who hears of it tingle. [4]For they have forsaken me and made this a place of foreign gods; they have burned sacrifices in it to gods that neither they nor their fathers nor the kings of Judah ever knew, and they have filled this place with the blood of the innocent. [5]They have built the high places of Baal to burn their sons in the fire as offerings to Baal—something I did not command or mention, nor did it enter my mind. [6]So beware, the days are coming, declares the LORD, when people will no longer call this place Topheth or the Valley of Ben Hinnom, but the Valley of Slaughter.

[7]"'In this place I will ruin[a] the plans of Judah and Jerusalem. I will make them fall by the sword before their enemies, at the hands of those who seek their lives, and I will give their carcasses as food to the birds of the air and the beasts of the earth. [8]I will devastate this city and make it an object of scorn; all who pass by will be appalled and will scoff because of all its wounds. [9]I will make them eat the flesh of their sons and daughters, and they will eat one another's flesh during the stress of the siege imposed on them by the enemies who seek their lives.'

[10]"Then break the jar while those who go with you are watching, [11]and say to them, 'This is what the LORD Almighty says: I will smash this nation and this city just as this potter's jar is smashed and cannot be repaired. They will bury the dead in Topheth until

---

[a]7 The Hebrew for *ruin* sounds like the Hebrew for *jar* (see verses 1 and 10).

there is no more room. ¹²This is what I will do to this place and to those who live here, declares the LORD. I will make this city like Topheth. ¹³The houses in Jerusalem and those of the kings of Judah will be defiled like this place, Topheth—all the houses where they burned incense on the roofs to all the starry hosts and poured out drink offerings to other gods.'"

¹⁴Jeremiah then returned from Topheth, where the LORD had sent him to prophesy, and stood in the court of the LORD's temple and said to all the people, ¹⁵"This is what the LORD Almighty, the God of Israel, says: 'Listen! I am going to bring on this city and the villages around it every disaster I pronounced against them, because they were stiff-necked and would not listen to my words.'"

Jeremiah and Pashhur

20 When the priest Pashhur son of Immer, the chief officer in the temple of the LORD, heard Jeremiah prophesying these things, ²he had Jeremiah the prophet beaten and put in the stocks at the Upper Gate of Benjamin at the LORD's temple. ³The next day, when Pashhur released him from the stocks, Jeremiah said to him, "The LORD's name for you is not Pashhur, but Magor-Missabib.ᵃ ⁴For this is what the LORD says: 'I will make you a terror to yourself and to all your friends; with your own eyes you will see them fall by the sword of their enemies. I will hand all Judah over to the king of Babylon, who will carry them away to Babylon or put them to the sword. ⁵I will hand over to their enemies all the wealth of this city—all its products, all its valuables and all the treasures of the kings of Judah. They will take it away as plunder and carry it off to Babylon. ⁶And you, Pashhur, and all who live in your house will go into exile to Babylon. There you will die and be buried, you and all your friends to whom you have prophesied lies.'"

Jeremiah's Complaint

⁷O LORD, you deceivedᵇ me, and I was
        deceivedᵇ;
    you overpowered me and prevailed.
I am ridiculed all day long;
    everyone mocks me.
⁸Whenever I speak, I cry out
    proclaiming violence and destruction.
So the word of the LORD has brought me
    insult and reproach all day long.
⁹But if I say, "I will not mention him
    or speak any more in his name,"
his word is in my heart like a fire,
    a fire shut up in my bones.
I am weary of holding it in;
    indeed, I cannot.
¹⁰I hear many whispering,
    "Terror on every side!
    Report him! Let's report him!"
All my friends
    are waiting for me to slip, saying,
"Perhaps he will be deceived;
    then we will prevail over him
    and take our revenge on him."

¹¹But the LORD is with me like a mighty warrior;
    so my persecutors will stumble and not prevail.

---

1. If you could rename yourself, what new name would you pick? Why? 2. Why did you pick the names you did for your children? Or, what are your favorite names for children? 3. What's the first thing you want to know when you've heard someone has just had a baby?

1. Jeremiah's cracked pot lands him in what kind of trouble (vv. 1–2)? How does he react to the disciplinary action of Pashur, his superior (vv. 3–6)? 2. To whom will the renamed Pashur be a terror and why? (Note: These events were fulfilled in 597 B.C. [see 2Ki 24:13] and 586 B.C. [see 2Ki 25:13–17].) 3. What happens to Jeremiah the day he is confined to prison (vv. 2–3,7,10)? What blame does Jeremiah dare shift to God (v. 8)? What internal tension does that create? Which seems more dominant at this point: Personal bitterness or divine compulsion? 4. What totally opposing emotions take turns gripping him (vv. 13–18)? Which feeling do you think is winning at this juncture? Why is he so despairing of the day of his birth (see 1:5; compare Job 3)? 5. Why doesn't God answer his outburst? Has God been very consoling to him in the past?

1. Have you ever done the right thing and then suffered for it? How did it make you feel? What did you say to God? 2. Where in your life are you facing a "no-win" situation? How can the group help you find a "win-win" solution to it? 3. Is your way of handling anger and depression anything like Jeremiah's way: Have you ever wished you were never born? Do you keep violence inside or let it out? How often do you ride an emotional roller coaster—up one moment, down the next?

ᵃ3 *Magor-Missabib* means *terror on every side.*   ᵇ7 Or *persuaded*

> They will fail and be thoroughly disgraced;
>   their dishonor will never be forgotten.
> ¹²O Lord Almighty, you who examine the righteous
>   and probe the heart and mind,
> let me see your vengeance upon them,
>   for to you I have committed my cause.
>
> ¹³Sing to the Lord!
>   Give praise to the Lord!
> He rescues the life of the needy
>   from the hands of the wicked.
>
> ¹⁴Cursed be the day I was born!
>   May the day my mother bore me not be
>   blessed!
> ¹⁵Cursed be the man who brought my father the
>   news,
>   who made him very glad, saying,
>   "A child is born to you—a son!"
> ¹⁶May that man be like the towns
>   the Lord overthrew without pity.
> May he hear wailing in the morning,
>   a battle cry at noon.
> ¹⁷For he did not kill me in the womb,
>   with my mother as my grave,
>   her womb enlarged forever.
> ¹⁸Why did I ever come out of the womb
>   to see trouble and sorrow
>   and to end my days in shame?

God Rejects Zedekiah's Request

21 The word came to Jeremiah from the Lord when King Zedekiah sent to him Pashhur son of Malkijah and the priest Zephaniah son of Maaseiah. They said: ²"Inquire now of the Lord for us because Nebuchadnezzarᵃ king of Babylon is attacking us. Perhaps the Lord will perform wonders for us as in times past so that he will withdraw from us."

³But Jeremiah answered them, "Tell Zedekiah, ⁴'This is what the Lord, the God of Israel, says: I am about to turn against you the weapons of war that are in your hands, which you are using to fight the king of Babylon and the Babyloniansᵇ who are outside the wall besieging you. And I will gather them inside this city. ⁵I myself will fight against you with an outstretched hand and a mighty arm in anger and fury and great wrath. ⁶I will strike down those who live in this city—both men and animals—and they will die of a terrible plague. ⁷After that, declares the Lord, I will hand over Zedekiah king of Judah, his officials and the people in this city who survive the plague, sword and famine, to Nebuchadnezzar king of Babylon and to their enemies who seek their lives. He will put them to the sword; he will show them no mercy or pity or compassion.'

⁸"Furthermore, tell the people, 'This is what the Lord says: See, I am setting before you the way of life and the way of death. ⁹Whoever stays in this city will die by the sword, famine or plague. But whoever goes out and surrenders to the Babylonians who are besieging you will live; he will escape with his life. ¹⁰I have determined to do this city harm and not good, declares the Lord. It will

1. How do you imagine you might die: (a) Struck down in the prime of life? (b) Rust out from old age? (c) Burn out in your youth from lack of balance and sustenance? 2. Once you die, what do you think you will miss most about life?

1. What kind of a king was Zedekiah (see 2Ki 24:18–20)? Does he consult Jeremiah before or after he makes the decision to stop paying tribute to Babylon (v. 2)? 2. What good news/bad news does Jeremiah give the two priests of Zedekiah (vv. 3–7)? What radical survival tip does Jeremiah give them? 3. For saying this, would you brand Jeremiah a traitor, or salute him as a patriot? Would this news sit well, or upset the soldiers defending Jerusalem? 4. What crisis of faith does Judah now face (vv. 8–10; compare Dt 30:15)? What does God want Zedekiah to do (vv. 11–12)? 5. Is it ever too late for God's people to repent, or is there always time to make peace with God?

1. Why do some people never learn? Are you a slow learner? Is there some growing edge in your life that you refuse to

ᵃ2 Hebrew *Nebuchadrezzar*, of which *Nebuchadnezzar* is a variant; here and often in Jeremiah and Ezekiel   ᵇ4 Or *Chaldeans*; also in verse 9

be given into the hands of the king of Babylon, and he will destroy it with fire.'

[11]"Moreover, say to the royal house of Judah, 'Hear the word of the LORD; [12]O house of David, this is what the LORD says:

> " 'Administer justice every morning;
>   rescue from the hand of his oppressor
>   the one who has been robbed,
> or my wrath will break out and burn like fire
>   because of the evil you have done—
>   burn with no one to quench it.
> [13]I am against you, ⌊Jerusalem,⌋
>   you who live above this valley
>   on the rocky plateau,
>   declares the LORD—
> you who say, "Who can come against us?
>   Who can enter our refuge?"
> [14]I will punish you as your deeds deserve,
>   declares the LORD.
> I will kindle a fire in your forests
>   that will consume everything around you.' "

Judgment Against Evil Kings

22 This is what the LORD says: "Go down to the palace of the king of Judah and proclaim this message there: [2]'Hear the word of the LORD, O king of Judah, you who sit on David's throne—you, your officials and your people who come through these gates. [3]This is what the LORD says: Do what is just and right. Rescue from the hand of his oppressor the one who has been robbed. Do no wrong or violence to the alien, the fatherless or the widow, and do not shed innocent blood in this place. [4]For if you are careful to carry out these commands, then kings who sit on David's throne will come through the gates of this palace, riding in chariots and on horses, accompanied by their officials and their people. [5]But if you do not obey these commands, declares the LORD, I swear by myself that this palace will become a ruin.' "

[6]For this is what the LORD says about the palace of the king of Judah:

> "Though you are like Gilead to me,
>   like the summit of Lebanon,
> I will surely make you like a desert,
>   like towns not inhabited.
> [7]I will send destroyers against you,
>   each man with his weapons,
> and they will cut up your fine cedar beams
>   and throw them into the fire.

[8]"People from many nations will pass by this city and will ask one another, 'Why has the LORD done such a thing to this great city?' [9]And the answer will be: 'Because they have forsaken the covenant of the LORD their God and have worshiped and served other gods.' "

> [10]Do not weep for the dead ⌊king⌋ or mourn his
>   loss;
> rather, weep bitterly for him who is exiled,
> because he will never return
>   nor see his native land again.

attend to? A warning you refuse to heed? A conflict you refuse to resolve? Why? How can the group help? 2. Would you have deserted the city, as Jeremiah advised? What would it have cost you to flee? What would it have cost you to remain? 3. How might leaving Jerusalem be an allegory for becoming a committed Christian? What would you need to leave behind to become more committed to Christ? 4. Who in your world are "oppressors" and who are the "robbed"? How can you help bring justice to the oppressed? How can the group help?

---

1. Where are most of your ancestors and family buried? Where would you like to be buried? 2. What kind of funeral would you like: Loud and brassy? Quiet and somber? Short and sweet? Well-attended or family only?

1. What message does Jeremiah repeat to the rulers (vv. 1–3)? Does this message seem like one addressed to a particular king, or a timeless message, applicable to all those in David's royal line? Why? 2. What three oppressed groups of people are mentioned? What do they have in common (see Ex 22:21–24)? Why does the king's security depend upon how he treats them? 3. Why is King Shallum, also called Jehoahaz, to be pitied more than his father, Josiah (vv. 10–12)? What happened to Jehoahaz (see 2Ki 23:34, an event dated c. 609 B.C.)? 4. After his brother was deposed, Jehoiakim became king. For what did he use slave labor (vv. 13–14)? What was his father, Josiah, like (vv. 15–17)? How could such a good king have such nasty sons? 5. Jehoiachin next ruled as king. What will happen to him (vv. 24–27)? Did any of his descendants sit on the throne (vv. 28–30; see 2Ki 24:15–17)? 6. If you were Zedekiah, what would you conclude from this sad replay of your family history? Through how many reigns has God been patient? Why does God wait so long to end the line?

♡ **1.** Does God care about how governments rule? How did the early Christians feel about pagan kings (see 1Ti 2:1–2; Ro 13:1–5)? How do you feel about the "kings" of today? **2.** Which leader (church, civic or world) has made a great impact on you by their life? By their death? **3.** How did you feel when a public champion of peace and justice (Gandhi, JFK, Martin Luther King, Yitzhak Rabin) was assassinated? Do you hold any real hope that love is stronger than bullets? **4.** As in Jeremiah's time, leaders today usually set a tone for others. What positive tone or atmosphere are you setting in your home, job, school or church? Where might you have a negative impact?

11For this is what the LORD says about Shallum[a] son of Josiah, who succeeded his father as king of Judah but has gone from this place: "He will never return. 12He will die in the place where they have led him captive; he will not see this land again."

13"Woe to him who builds his palace by
      unrighteousness,
   his upper rooms by injustice,
making his countrymen work for nothing,
   not paying them for their labor.
14He says, 'I will build myself a great palace
   with spacious upper rooms.'
So he makes large windows in it,
   panels it with cedar
   and decorates it in red.

15"Does it make you a king
   to have more and more cedar?
Did not your father have food and drink?
   He did what was right and just,
   so all went well with him.
16He defended the cause of the poor and needy,
   and so all went well.
Is that not what it means to know me?"
   declares the LORD.
17"But your eyes and your heart
   are set only on dishonest gain,
on shedding innocent blood
   and on oppression and extortion."

18Therefore this is what the LORD says about Jehoiakim son of Josiah king of Judah:

"They will not mourn for him:
   'Alas, my brother! Alas, my sister!'
They will not mourn for him:
   'Alas, my master! Alas, his splendor!'
19He will have the burial of a donkey—
   dragged away and thrown
   outside the gates of Jerusalem."

20"Go up to Lebanon and cry out,
   let your voice be heard in Bashan,
cry out from Abarim,
   for all your allies are crushed.
21I warned you when you felt secure,
   but you said, 'I will not listen!'
This has been your way from your youth;
   you have not obeyed me.
22The wind will drive all your shepherds away,
   and your allies will go into exile.
Then you will be ashamed and disgraced
   because of all your wickedness.
23You who live in 'Lebanon,'[b]
   who are nestled in cedar buildings,
how you will groan when pangs come upon you,
   pain like that of a woman in labor!

24"As surely as I live," declares the LORD, "even if you, Jehoiachin[c] son of Jehoiakim king of Judah, were a signet ring on my

a11 Also called Jehoahaz   b23 That is, the palace in Jerusalem (see 1 Kings 7:2)
c24 Hebrew Coniah, a variant of Jehoiachin; also in verse 28

right hand, I would still pull you off. ²⁵I will hand you over to those who seek your life, those you fear—to Nebuchadnezzar king of Babylon and to the Babylonians.ᵃ ²⁶I will hurl you and the mother who gave you birth into another country, where neither of you was born, and there you both will die. ²⁷You will never come back to the land you long to return to."

²⁸Is this man Jehoiachin a despised, broken pot,
   an object no one wants?
Why will he and his children be hurled out,
   cast into a land they do not know?
²⁹O land, land, land,
   hear the word of the LORD!
³⁰This is what the LORD says:
"Record this man as if childless,
   a man who will not prosper in his lifetime,
for none of his offspring will prosper,
   none will sit on the throne of David
   or rule anymore in Judah."

The Righteous Branch

23 "Woe to the shepherds who are destroying and scattering the sheep of my pasture!" declares the LORD. ²Therefore this is what the LORD, the God of Israel, says to the shepherds who tend my people: "Because you have scattered my flock and driven them away and have not bestowed care on them, I will bestow punishment on you for the evil you have done," declares the LORD. ³"I myself will gather the remnant of my flock out of all the countries where I have driven them and will bring them back to their pasture, where they will be fruitful and increase in number. ⁴I will place shepherds over them who will tend them, and they will no longer be afraid or terrified, nor will any be missing," declares the LORD.

⁵"The days are coming," declares the LORD,
   "when I will raise up to Davidᵇ a righteous
   Branch,
a King who will reign wisely
   and do what is just and right in the land.
⁶In his days Judah will be saved
   and Israel will live in safety.
This is the name by which he will be called:
   The LORD Our Righteousness.

⁷"So then, the days are coming," declares the LORD, "when people will no longer say, 'As surely as the LORD lives, who brought the Israelites up out of Egypt,' ⁸but they will say, 'As surely as the LORD lives, who brought the descendants of Israel up out of the land of the north and out of all the countries where he had banished them.' Then they will live in their own land."

Lying Prophets

⁹Concerning the prophets:

My heart is broken within me;
   all my bones tremble.
I am like a drunken man,
   like a man overcome by wine,
because of the LORD

Which would you rather be and why: Politician, church leader or shepherd? Who is more likely to get their flock to follow their lead?

1. Who are the "shepherds" (v. 1)? How are they scattering the "flock"? What will God do to them? 2. What new shepherds and "righteous Branch" will God appoint (vv. 4–5; see Isa 11:1–2)? 3. "Zedekiah" is Hebrew for "The Lord my righteousness." What is the significance of the future king's title in verse 6? 4. What historical bench marks define Israel as a nation (vv. 7–8)? Why is one more significant?

1. Jesus applied this shepherd imagery to himself (see Jn 10:7–16). How does he fulfill this promise for you? Which title, name or role of Jesus is most special to you? 2. Hope shines in even the most difficult chapters of Israel's history. How does hope shine for you?

1. List all the professions you can think of—from palm reader to weatherman—whose job it is to predict the future. Which of them can you trust? Why? 2. Do you remember your dreams? Describe a dream you had recently. Why does it stick in your memory? 3. Do you ever read the horoscope

ᵃ25 Or Chaldeans   ᵇ5 Or up from David's line

section of the newspaper? Why or why not?

📖 **1.** Why would Jeremiah feel "like a drunken man" upon finding out that the court prophets are false (v. 9)? What does God mean by calling the prophets "adulterers" (vv. 10,14; see Ge 19, for the story of Sodom and Gomorrah)? **2.** What distinguishes the false prophet (vv. 13–17,21,27,32; see Dt 13:1–5)? How are Judah's prophets measuring up to these criteria? What false image of God do they project (vv. 23–24)? **3.** Compared to the source of the false prophet's word, where does a true prophet get God's word (vv. 18,22)? **4.** How will both the false and true prophets be exposed for what they are (vv. 25–32)? **5.** What catch-phrases did the religious people use in Jeremiah's day (vv. 33–38)? What would be a modern equivalent of this language, often heard in churches today? **6.** Who has become a "burden" to God (see footnote to v. 33)? Why is he weary of all this? What will God do to unburden his people (vv. 39–40; see 20:11)?

💟 **1.** Are there "prophets" (false or true) today? If not, why not? If so, how does one discern the modern true prophet? What is the message of the modern false prophet? **2.** Regarding "the Lord's council" (vv. 18,22) and the shape of the future, do you think God: (a) Knows all? (b) Controls all? (c) Both? (d) Neither? What difference does it make to you? **3.** What does it mean for you to "stand" in that council of the Lord (see 1Co 2:16): What is involved, where, when, with whom? **4.** For what do you have a burden today? Do you have a message to give? An action to take? A situation to remedy? In what way is that burdensome? Can the group help?

and his holy words.

¹⁰The land is full of adulterers;
    because of the curse[a] the land lies parched[b]
    and the pastures in the desert are withered.
The ⌐prophets⌐ follow an evil course
    and use their power unjustly.

¹¹"Both prophet and priest are godless;
    even in my temple I find their wickedness,"
                    declares the LORD.
¹²"Therefore their path will become slippery;
    they will be banished to darkness
    and there they will fall.
I will bring disaster on them
    in the year they are punished,"
                    declares the LORD.

¹³"Among the prophets of Samaria
    I saw this repulsive thing:
They prophesied by Baal
    and led my people Israel astray.
¹⁴And among the prophets of Jerusalem
    I have seen something horrible:
They commit adultery and live a lie.
They strengthen the hands of evildoers,
    so that no one turns from his wickedness.
They are all like Sodom to me;
    the people of Jerusalem are like Gomorrah."

¹⁵Therefore, this is what the LORD Almighty says concerning the prophets:

"I will make them eat bitter food
    and drink poisoned water,
because from the prophets of Jerusalem
    ungodliness has spread throughout the land."

¹⁶This is what the LORD Almighty says:

"Do not listen to what the prophets are
        prophesying to you;
    they fill you with false hopes.
They speak visions from their own minds,
    not from the mouth of the LORD.
¹⁷They keep saying to those who despise me,
    'The LORD says: You will have peace.'
And to all who follow the stubbornness of their
        hearts
    they say, 'No harm will come to you.'
¹⁸But which of them has stood in the council of the
    LORD
    to see or to hear his word?
    Who has listened and heard his word?
¹⁹See, the storm of the LORD
    will burst out in wrath,
a whirlwind swirling down
    on the heads of the wicked.
²⁰The anger of the LORD will not turn back
    until he fully accomplishes
    the purposes of his heart.

a 10 Or because of these things   *b 10 Or land mourns*

In days to come
    you will understand it clearly.
21I did not send these prophets,
    yet they have run with their message;
I did not speak to them,
    yet they have prophesied.
22But if they had stood in my council,
    they would have proclaimed my words to my
        people
    and would have turned them from their evil ways
    and from their evil deeds.

23"Am I only a God nearby,"
                      declares the LORD,
    "and not a God far away?
24Can anyone hide in secret places
    so that I cannot see him?"
                      declares the LORD.
    "Do not I fill heaven and earth?"
                      declares the LORD.

25"I have heard what the prophets say who prophesy lies in my name. They say, 'I had a dream! I had a dream!' 26How long will this continue in the hearts of these lying prophets, who prophesy the delusions of their own minds? 27They think the dreams they tell one another will make my people forget my name, just as their fathers forgot my name through Baal worship. 28Let the prophet who has a dream tell his dream, but let the one who has my word speak it faithfully. For what has straw to do with grain?" declares the LORD. 29"Is not my word like fire," declares the LORD, "and like a hammer that breaks a rock in pieces?

30"Therefore," declares the LORD, "I am against the prophets who steal from one another words supposedly from me. 31Yes," declares the LORD, "I am against the prophets who wag their own tongues and yet declare, 'The LORD declares.' 32Indeed, I am against those who prophesy false dreams," declares the LORD. "They tell them and lead my people astray with their reckless lies, yet I did not send or appoint them. They do not benefit these people in the least," declares the LORD.

False Oracles and False Prophets

33"When these people, or a prophet or a priest, ask you, 'What is the oracle*a* of the LORD?' say to them, 'What oracle?*b* I will forsake you, declares the LORD.' 34If a prophet or a priest or anyone else claims, 'This is the oracle of the LORD,' I will punish that man and his household. 35This is what each of you keeps on saying to his friend or relative: 'What is the LORD's answer?' or 'What has the LORD spoken?' 36But you must not mention 'the oracle of the LORD' again, because every man's own word becomes his oracle and so you distort the words of the living God, the LORD Almighty, our God. 37This is what you keep saying to a prophet: 'What is the LORD's answer to you?' or 'What has the LORD spoken?' 38Although you claim, 'This is the oracle of the LORD,' this is what the LORD says: You used the words, 'This is the oracle of the LORD,' even though I told you that you must not claim, 'This is the oracle of the LORD.' 39Therefore, I will surely forget you and cast you out of my presence along with the city I gave to you and your fathers. 40I will

---

a33 Or *burden* (see Septuagint and Vulgate)   *b33* Hebrew; Septuagint and Vulgate
'You are the burden. (The Hebrew for *oracle* and *burden* is the same.)

bring upon you everlasting disgrace—everlasting shame that will not be forgotten."

Two Baskets of Figs

24 After Jehoiachin[a] son of Jehoiakim king of Judah and the officials, the craftsmen and the artisans of Judah were carried into exile from Jerusalem to Babylon by Nebuchadnezzar king of Babylon, the LORD showed me two baskets of figs placed in front of the temple of the LORD. ²One basket had very good figs, like those that ripen early; the other basket had very poor figs, so bad they could not be eaten.

³Then the LORD asked me, "What do you see, Jeremiah?"

"Figs," I answered. "The good ones are very good, but the poor ones are so bad they cannot be eaten."

⁴Then the word of the LORD came to me: ⁵"This is what the LORD, the God of Israel, says: 'Like these good figs, I regard as good the exiles from Judah, whom I sent away from this place to the land of the Babylonians.[b] ⁶My eyes will watch over them for their good, and I will bring them back to this land. I will build them up and not tear them down; I will plant them and not uproot them. ⁷I will give them a heart to know me, that I am the LORD. They will be my people, and I will be their God, for they will return to me with all their heart.

⁸"'But like the poor figs, which are so bad they cannot be eaten,' says the LORD, 'so will I deal with Zedekiah king of Judah, his officials and the survivors from Jerusalem, whether they remain in this land or live in Egypt. ⁹I will make them abhorrent and an offense to all the kingdoms of the earth, a reproach and a byword, an object of ridicule and cursing, wherever I banish them. ¹⁰I will send the sword, famine and plague against them until they are destroyed from the land I gave to them and their fathers.'"

Seventy Years of Captivity

25 The word came to Jeremiah concerning all the people of Judah in the fourth year of Jehoiakim son of Josiah king of Judah, which was the first year of Nebuchadnezzar king of Babylon. ²So Jeremiah the prophet said to all the people of Judah and to all those living in Jerusalem: ³For twenty-three years—from the thirteenth year of Josiah son of Amon king of Judah until this very day—the word of the LORD has come to me and I have spoken to you again and again, but you have not listened.

⁴And though the LORD has sent all his servants the prophets to you again and again, you have not listened or paid any attention. ⁵They said, "Turn now, each of you, from your evil ways and your evil practices, and you can stay in the land the LORD gave to you and your fathers for ever and ever. ⁶Do not follow other gods to serve and worship them; do not provoke me to anger with what your hands have made. Then I will not harm you."

⁷"But you did not listen to me," declares the LORD, "and you have provoked me with what your hands have made, and you have brought harm to yourselves."

⁸Therefore the LORD Almighty says this: "Because you have not listened to my words, ⁹I will summon all the peoples of the north and my servant Nebuchadnezzar king of Babylon," declares the LORD, "and I will bring them against this land and its inhabitants and against all the surrounding nations. I will completely destroy[c]

Do you have anything in your refrigerator that has gone bad? Why is it still there?

1. The Babylonians under Nebuchadnezzar threatened Judah in 597 B.C. and deported many in the reign of Jehoachin. Who was left in Judah for Zedekiah to rule (vv. 1–3,8; see 2Ki 24:14–20)? What would their world look like? **2.** What does each basket of figs symbolize (vv. 5–8)? What is God going to do with the exiles, why and when? What is he going to do with those left behind (vv. 9–10)? **3.** Why would God favor one group over another (see 1Ch 36:11–16)?

1. If you lived in Jeremiah's day, would you prefer exile in Babylon, or life in your homeland? **2.** How "at home" should the church be in this world? **3.** Can what appears to be harsh judgment turn into good (see Jas 1:2–3)? When has that happened for you?

---

1. When was the last time someone said to you: "I told you so"? Did you appreciate it? **2.** What title would you give your autobiography? What kind of movie would your life story make?

1. The dovetailing of the two events in verse one dates this prophesy c. 605 B.C. How long has God been speaking through Jeremiah? Through other prophets (v. 4; see 7:25)? How must Jeremiah and God be feeling at this point? **2.** Why does God call a pagan king his "servant" (v. 8)? What purpose will he serve? **3.** Is it fair to punish Babylon for performing God's will (v. 12)? What principle is at work here? What do you suppose was their crime (vv. 13–14)? **4.** In retrospect, which of Jeremiah's predictions have come true? Why does God reveal the length of the coming exile?

1. Why did God warn the people for so long before taking action? Why did God's patience finally run out? **2.** How long would you persist in a task without seeing any success? Do you ever wonder

---

a1 Hebrew *Jeconiah,* a variant of *Jehoiachin*   *b5* Or *Chaldeans*   *c9* The Hebrew term refers to the irrevocable giving over of things or persons to the LORD, often by totally destroying them.

them and make them an object of horror and scorn, and an ever-lasting ruin. [10]I will banish from them the sounds of joy and gladness, the voices of bride and bridegroom, the sound of millstones and the light of the lamp. [11]This whole country will become a desolate wasteland, and these nations will serve the king of Babylon seventy years.

[12]"But when the seventy years are fulfilled, I will punish the king of Babylon and his nation, the land of the Babylonians,[a] for their guilt," declares the LORD, "and will make it desolate forever. [13]I will bring upon that land all the things I have spoken against it, all that are written in this book and prophesied by Jeremiah against all the nations. [14]They themselves will be enslaved by many nations and great kings; I will repay them according to their deeds and the work of their hands."

The Cup of God's Wrath

[15]This is what the LORD, the God of Israel, said to me: "Take from my hand this cup filled with the wine of my wrath and make all the nations to whom I send you drink it. [16]When they drink it, they will stagger and go mad because of the sword I will send among them."

[17]So I took the cup from the LORD's hand and made all the nations to whom he sent me drink it: [18]Jerusalem and the towns of Judah, its kings and officials, to make them a ruin and an object of horror and scorn and cursing, as they are today; [19]Pharaoh king of Egypt, his attendants, his officials and all his people, [20]and all the foreign people there; all the kings of Uz; all the kings of the Philistines (those of Ashkelon, Gaza, Ekron, and the people left at Ashdod); [21]Edom, Moab and Ammon; [22]all the kings of Tyre and Sidon; the kings of the coastlands across the sea; [23]Dedan, Tema, Buz and all who are in distant places[b]; [24]all the kings of Arabia and all the kings of the foreign people who live in the desert; [25]all the kings of Zimri, Elam and Media; [26]and all the kings of the north, near and far, one after the other—all the kingdoms on the face of the earth. And after all of them, the king of Sheshach[c] will drink it too.

[27]"Then tell them, 'This is what the LORD Almighty, the God of Israel, says: Drink, get drunk and vomit, and fall to rise no more because of the sword I will send among you.' [28]But if they refuse to take the cup from your hand and drink, tell them, 'This is what the LORD Almighty says: You must drink it! [29]See, I am beginning to bring disaster on the city that bears my Name, and will you indeed go unpunished? You will not go unpunished, for I am calling down a sword upon all who live on the earth, declares the LORD Almighty.'

[30]"Now prophesy all these words against them and say to them:

"'The LORD will roar from on high;
　　he will thunder from his holy dwelling
　　and roar mightily against his land.
He will shout like those who tread the grapes,
　　shout against all who live on the earth.
[31]The tumult will resound to the ends of the earth,
　　for the LORD will bring charges against the
　　　　nations;
he will bring judgment on all mankind
　　and put the wicked to the sword,'"

declares the LORD.

---

about a direction you once took but abandoned? **3.** Is God warning you about anything? Are you paying more attention than Judah did? How so?

1. Have you ever been caught doing something that others got away with? What happened? How did it make you feel? **2.** Imagine you want some grape juice, but the grapes need to be trod first. Name one person you wouldn't mind treading the grapes for you. Why would you choose that person?

1. Why is God's wrath likened to a cup of wine (vv. 15–16; see Isa 51:17–23; Rev 14:8; 18:6)? What effect will it have on those who drink it? Is this what they would suspect? **2.** Who drinks from the cup first and why (v. 18)? Who next (v. 19)? Who last (v. 26; see text footnote)? Try to locate the other nations on a map of ancient Palestine. **3.** Why will God punish the nations (vv. 27–33) with the "sword" and "mighty storm" of the Babylonian invasion? What "charges" will God bring (see 2:5–9,35)? **4.** What will happen to the world leaders (vv. 34–38)? How is their fate like that of Judah's leaders (see 21:1–23:7)?

1. If you were compiling a list of nations to punish, which ones would top the list? Who would not have to "drink the cup"? **2.** Is God's treatment of Judah and the nations appropriate? How will God in Christ judge the world (see Mt 25:31–46; Ro 2:6–16)? **3.** How does it feel to know God is hardest on his own people (see 1Pe 4:17–18)? Why? **4.** Does the fact that God will someday avenge every evil deed and punish all evildoers comfort you, or scare you?

---

a12 Or *Chaldeans*　　b23 Or *who clip the hair by their foreheads*　　c26 *Sheshach* is a cryptogram for Babylon.

32This is what the LORD Almighty says:

> "Look! Disaster is spreading
>   from nation to nation;
> a mighty storm is rising
>   from the ends of the earth."

33At that time those slain by the LORD will be everywhere—from one end of the earth to the other. They will not be mourned or gathered up or buried, but will be like refuse lying on the ground.

> **34**Weep and wail, you shepherds;
>   roll in the dust, you leaders of the flock.
> For your time to be slaughtered has come;
>   you will fall and be shattered like fine pottery.
> **35**The shepherds will have nowhere to flee,
>   the leaders of the flock no place to escape.
> **36**Hear the cry of the shepherds,
>   the wailing of the leaders of the flock,
>   for the LORD is destroying their pasture.
> **37**The peaceful meadows will be laid waste
>   because of the fierce anger of the LORD.
> **38**Like a lion he will leave his lair,
>   and their land will become desolate
> because of the sword*a* of the oppressor
>   and because of the LORD's fierce anger.

Jeremiah Threatened With Death

26 Early in the reign of Jehoiakim son of Josiah king of Judah, this word came from the LORD: **2**"This is what the LORD says: Stand in the courtyard of the LORD's house and speak to all the people of the towns of Judah who come to worship in the house of the LORD. Tell them everything I command you; do not omit a word. **3**Perhaps they will listen and each will turn from his evil way. Then I will relent and not bring on them the disaster I was planning because of the evil they have done. **4**Say to them, 'This is what the LORD says: If you do not listen to me and follow my law, which I have set before you, **5**and if you do not listen to the words of my servants the prophets, whom I have sent to you again and again (though you have not listened), **6**then I will make this house like Shiloh and this city an object of cursing among all the nations of the earth.'"

7The priests, the prophets and all the people heard Jeremiah speak these words in the house of the LORD. **8**But as soon as Jeremiah finished telling all the people everything the LORD had commanded him to say, the priests, the prophets and all the people seized him and said, "You must die! **9**Why do you prophesy in the LORD's name that this house will be like Shiloh and this city will be desolate and deserted?" And all the people crowded around Jeremiah in the house of the LORD.

10When the officials of Judah heard about these things, they went up from the royal palace to the house of the LORD and took their places at the entrance of the New Gate of the LORD's house. **11**Then the priests and the prophets said to the officials and all the people, "This man should be sentenced to death because he has prophesied against this city. You have heard it with your own ears!"

12Then Jeremiah said to all the officials and all the people: "The

1. What is the closest brush with death you ever had? How did it make you feel? 2. Are you at ease speaking in front of groups? How about large or hostile audiences? Give an example of when you were able to win friends and influence people initially opposed to your viewpoint.

1. Verses 2–6 and 12–15 correlate closely with the temple message of chapter 7. What new details, provided here, expand on that previous chapter in Jeremiah's life? (For example, whose "innocent blood" is it in 7:6 and 26:15?) 2. Why do the other priests and prophets want Jeremiah sentenced to death (vv. 7–11)? 3. In defending his case, how does Jeremiah distinguish himself from the other prophets who would justly deserve death (v. 12; see 23:21; Dt 13:5)? 4. Who takes his side and why (vv. 16–19,24)? Who is Micah of Moresheth and what impact did he have on King Hezekiah (see Mic 1:1; 3:12; 2Ki 28:1–6)? What parallel does that suggest? Who is this Shaphan and family (see 2Ki 22:8–13)? 5. How does the argument of these Jewish elders compare with that of Gamaliel in a similar situation (see Ac 5:33–40)? What principle of interpreting Scripture and signs of the times is at work here? 6. Why do you think the

a38 Some Hebrew manuscripts and Septuagint (see also Jer. 46:16 and 50:16); most Hebrew manuscripts *anger*

LORD sent me to prophesy against this house and this city all the things you have heard. 13Now reform your ways and your actions and obey the LORD your God. Then the LORD will relent and not bring the disaster he has pronounced against you. 14As for me, I am in your hands; do with me whatever you think is good and right. 15Be assured, however, that if you put me to death, you will bring the guilt of innocent blood on yourselves and on this city and on those who live in it, for in truth the LORD has sent me to you to speak all these words in your hearing."

16Then the officials and all the people said to the priests and the prophets, "This man should not be sentenced to death! He has spoken to us in the name of the LORD our God."

17Some of the elders of the land stepped forward and said to the entire assembly of people, 18"Micah of Moresheth prophesied in the days of Hezekiah king of Judah. He told all the people of Judah, 'This is what the LORD Almighty says:

> "'Zion will be plowed like a field,
> Jerusalem will become a heap of rubble,
>   the temple hill a mound overgrown with
>   thickets.'ª

19"Did Hezekiah king of Judah or anyone else in Judah put him to death? Did not Hezekiah fear the LORD and seek his favor? And did not the LORD relent, so that he did not bring the disaster he pronounced against them? We are about to bring a terrible disaster on ourselves!"

20(Now Uriah son of Shemaiah from Kiriath Jearim was another man who prophesied in the name of the LORD; he prophesied the same things against this city and this land as Jeremiah did. 21When King Jehoiakim and all his officers and officials heard his words, the king sought to put him to death. But Uriah heard of it and fled in fear to Egypt. 22King Jehoiakim, however, sent Elnathan son of Acbor to Egypt, along with some other men. 23They brought Uriah out of Egypt and took him to King Jehoiakim, who had him struck down with a sword and his body thrown into the burial place of the common people.)

24Furthermore, Ahikam son of Shaphan supported Jeremiah, and so he was not handed over to the people to be put to death.

Judah to Serve Nebuchadnezzar

27 Early in the reign of Zedekiahᵇ son of Josiah king of Judah, this word came to Jeremiah from the LORD: 2This is what the LORD said to me: "Make a yoke out of straps and crossbars and put it on your neck. 3Then send word to the kings of Edom, Moab, Ammon, Tyre and Sidon through the envoys who have come to Jerusalem to Zedekiah king of Judah. 4Give them a message for their masters and say, 'This is what the LORD Almighty, the God of Israel, says: "Tell this to your masters: 5With my great power and outstretched arm I made the earth and its people and the animals that are on it, and I give it to anyone I please. 6Now I will hand all your countries over to my servant Nebuchadnezzar king of Babylon; I will make even the wild animals subject to him. 7All nations will serve him and his son and his grandson until the time for his land comes; then many nations and great kings will subjugate him.

8" 'If, however, any nation or kingdom will not serve Nebuchadnezzar king of Babylon or bow its neck under his yoke, I will

---

rulers killed Uriah but not Jeremiah (vv. 20–24)?

♡ 1. Why does God seem so indifferent to the earthly fate of his servants (see Heb 11:32–38)? Does God oppose torture, death and unjust imprisonment? Should we? 2. Why do you think Jeremiah was so calm facing death? Does the fear of the Lord make you immune to the fear of men? Should it? 3. What do you fear the most? How can you overcome it? 4. Are you at ease taking sides in a debate before all the votes are counted? Or do you usually hedge your bets by waiting to see how things will pan out? Give an example. 5. When was the last time you stuck up for someone unpopular? Why did you do it? How were you treated? 6. How might the principle of interpretation evident in Jeremiah 26:16–19 (and Ac 5:34–40) be used today in deciding who speaks for God?

---

1. Have you ever arrived somewhere without your luggage? How did that feel? 2. Have you ever camped out in an empty house, devoid of its furnishings? What was it like? 3. Ever try taming a wild animal? What kind?

1. What does Jeremiah's hand-made yoke mean (vv. 2,8,11–12; see Lev 26:13)? How might he feel wearing this through Jerusalem? Whose neck was meant to be yoked? 2. Babylon controls Palestine and has just deported King Jehoachin (v. 20). Why then do the small nations meet in Jerusalem and consult mediums (vv. 3–11)? What does God think of their consultation (see also Dt 18:10–11)? What does Jeremiah advise? 3. Why does he give the same message to Zedekiah (vv. 12–15)? How are court prophets

---

ª18 Micah 3:12   ᵇ1 A few Hebrew manuscripts and Syriac (see also Jer. 27:3, 12 and 28:1); most Hebrew manuscripts *Jehoiakim* (Most Septuagint manuscripts do not have this verse.)

different than pagan mediums, if at all? **4.** The deportation of exiles and the temple articles began in 605 B.C. and did not end until 586 B.C. From 28:1, we know it's now 593 B.C. What does that tell you about the false hope of these prophets and the people who listened to them? **5.** What hope does Jeremiah hold out for them instead (vv. 7,16–22)? **6.** What sacrilegious use would Nebuchadnezzar and his heirs have for the temple gold (see 2Ki 24:12–13; Da 5:1–4)? **7.** Why does Jeremiah recommend surrender to a pagan, sacrilegious king? Why shouldn't Zedekiah and the other rulers band together against him?

1. Ancient cultures saw the world run by many gods, each exercising power over a certain territory. In your world, how is God's sphere of influence limited? Do you look to God to reign over certain areas but not others? Explain. **2.** When have you experienced the fight-or-flight dilemma faced by Judah in this chapter? When do you know when to fight and when to surrender? **3.** Do you think nations today can avoid war by obeying God? What kind of national behavior leads to God's blessing? What can be done to promote it?

1. Do you like to argue, or do you avoid conflict? When was the last time you went against your natural tendency? **2.** On a scale of 1 ("It'll never work") to 10 ("Go for it!"), how do you rate on optimism?

1. When does Hananiah predict that Babylon will fall (vv. 1–4)? Do you hear sincerity or sarcasm? Optimism or opportunism? **2.** Likewise, what tone in Jeremiah's voice do you hear in verse 6? Why is it easier to be a prophet of doom than a prophet of peace (vv. 7–9)? **3.** What does Hananiah do to illustrate his prophecy (vv. 10–11)? How long has Jeremiah been wearing it (v. 1; see 27:1)? Why do you think he leaves rather than argue his case? **4.** What

punish that nation with the sword, famine and plague, declares the LORD, until I destroy it by his hand. 9So do not listen to your prophets, your diviners, your interpreters of dreams, your mediums or your sorcerers who tell you, 'You will not serve the king of Babylon.' 10They prophesy lies to you that will only serve to remove you far from your lands; I will banish you and you will perish. 11But if any nation will bow its neck under the yoke of the king of Babylon and serve him, I will let that nation remain in its own land to till it and to live there, declares the LORD." '"

12I gave the same message to Zedekiah king of Judah. I said, "Bow your neck under the yoke of the king of Babylon; serve him and his people, and you will live. 13Why will you and your people die by the sword, famine and plague with which the LORD has threatened any nation that will not serve the king of Babylon? 14Do not listen to the words of the prophets who say to you, 'You will not serve the king of Babylon,' for they are prophesying lies to you. 15'I have not sent them,' declares the LORD. 'They are prophesying lies in my name. Therefore, I will banish you and you will perish, both you and the prophets who prophesy to you.' "

16Then I said to the priests and all these people, "This is what the LORD says: Do not listen to the prophets who say, 'Very soon now the articles from the LORD's house will be brought back from Babylon.' They are prophesying lies to you. 17Do not listen to them. Serve the king of Babylon, and you will live. Why should this city become a ruin? 18If they are prophets and have the word of the LORD, let them plead with the LORD Almighty that the furnishings remaining in the house of the LORD and in the palace of the king of Judah and in Jerusalem not be taken to Babylon. 19For this is what the LORD Almighty says about the pillars, the Sea, the movable stands and the other furnishings that are left in this city, 20which Nebuchadnezzar king of Babylon did not take away when he carried Jehoiachin[a] son of Jehoiakim king of Judah into exile from Jerusalem to Babylon, along with all the nobles of Judah and Jerusalem— 21yes, this is what the LORD Almighty, the God of Israel, says about the things that are left in the house of the LORD and in the palace of the king of Judah and in Jerusalem: 22'They will be taken to Babylon and there they will remain until the day I come for them,' declares the LORD. 'Then I will bring them back and restore them to this place.' "

The False Prophet Hananiah

28 In the fifth month of that same year, the fourth year, early in the reign of Zedekiah king of Judah, the prophet Hananiah son of Azzur, who was from Gibeon, said to me in the house of the LORD in the presence of the priests and all the people: 2"This is what the LORD Almighty, the God of Israel, says: 'I will break the yoke of the king of Babylon. 3Within two years I will bring back to this place all the articles of the LORD's house that Nebuchadnezzar king of Babylon removed from here and took to Babylon. 4I will also bring back to this place Jehoiachin[a] son of Jehoiakim king of Judah and all the other exiles from Judah who went to Babylon,' declares the LORD, 'for I will break the yoke of the king of Babylon.' "

5Then the prophet Jeremiah replied to the prophet Hananiah before the priests and all the people who were standing in the house of the LORD. 6He said, "Amen! May the LORD do so! May the LORD fulfill the words you have prophesied by bringing the articles

---

a20,4 Hebrew *Jeconiah*, a variant of *Jehoiachin*

of the Lord's house and all the exiles back to this place from Babylon. 7Nevertheless, listen to what I have to say in your hearing and in the hearing of all the people: 8From early times the prophets who preceded you and me have prophesied war, disaster and plague against many countries and great kingdoms. 9But the prophet who prophesies peace will be recognized as one truly sent by the Lord only if his prediction comes true."

10Then the prophet Hananiah took the yoke off the neck of the prophet Jeremiah and broke it, 11and he said before all the people, "This is what the Lord says: 'In the same way will I break the yoke of Nebuchadnezzar king of Babylon off the neck of all the nations within two years.'" At this, the prophet Jeremiah went on his way.

12Shortly after the prophet Hananiah had broken the yoke off the neck of the prophet Jeremiah, the word of the Lord came to Jeremiah: 13"Go and tell Hananiah, 'This is what the Lord says: You have broken a wooden yoke, but in its place you will get a yoke of iron. 14This is what the Lord Almighty, the God of Israel, says: I will put an iron yoke on the necks of all these nations to make them serve Nebuchadnezzar king of Babylon, and they will serve him. I will even give him control over the wild animals.'"

15Then the prophet Jeremiah said to Hananiah the prophet, "Listen, Hananiah! The Lord has not sent you, yet you have persuaded this nation to trust in lies. 16Therefore, this is what the Lord says: 'I am about to remove you from the face of the earth. This very year you are going to die, because you have preached rebellion against the Lord.'"

17In the seventh month of that same year, Hananiah the prophet died.

A Letter to the Exiles

29 This is the text of the letter that the prophet Jeremiah sent from Jerusalem to the surviving elders among the exiles and to the priests, the prophets and all the other people Nebuchadnezzar had carried into exile from Jerusalem to Babylon. 2(This was after King Jehoiachin[a] and the queen mother, the court officials and the leaders of Judah and Jerusalem, the craftsmen and the artisans had gone into exile from Jerusalem.) 3He entrusted the letter to Elasah son of Shaphan and to Gemariah son of Hilkiah, whom Zedekiah king of Judah sent to King Nebuchadnezzar in Babylon. It said:

4This is what the Lord Almighty, the God of Israel, says to all those I carried into exile from Jerusalem to Babylon: 5"Build houses and settle down; plant gardens and eat what they produce. 6Marry and have sons and daughters; find wives for your sons and give your daughters in marriage, so that they too may have sons and daughters. Increase in number there; do not decrease. 7Also, seek the peace and prosperity of the city to which I have carried you into exile. Pray to the Lord for it, because if it prospers, you too will prosper." 8Yes, this is what the Lord Almighty, the God of Israel, says: "Do not let the prophets and diviners among you deceive you. Do not listen to the dreams you encourage them to have. 9They are prophesying lies to you in my name. I have not sent them," declares the Lord.

10This is what the Lord says: "When seventy years are completed for Babylon, I will come to you and fulfill my gracious promise to bring you back to this place. 11For I know the plans

does the new message to Hananiah mean (vv. 12–14)? How does Jeremiah show he is a true prophet (vv. 15–17)?

1. As with alleged prophets for ancient Israel, today's political advisors also give opposing advice, often to protect their vested interest. How do you know who to believe? What political opinion have you recently changed? 2. "If you can't say something nice, don't say anything at all," the saying goes. Do you agree? Why is it often easier to say something good (as did Hananiah) rather than the truth (as did Jeremiah)? 3. Are you optimistic or pessimistic about prospects for a lasting international peace? What shapes your outlook? What role does your faith play? 4. Are you having trouble deciding something important right now? How can the group help out?

Are you a good letter writer? To how many people do you owe letters right now? Which correspondent of yours lives the farthest away?

1. What do you think of the postal system in Jeremiah's day (vv. 1–3,25)? What effect do you think this written Word of God will have on the exiles, as compared with Jeremiah's other words from God, which were usually spoken, sometimes acted out? How should they pay heed to it (vv. 4,19)? 2. What question does Jeremiah answer for the exiles (vv. 5–9,15)? How would this radical concept sound to the Jews living in refugee camps in Babylon? Would you have prayed for the welfare of your captors? 3. Why does Jeremiah debunk those prophesying an early return (vv. 8–9)? What seems to be God's reason for both extending and ending the exile (vv. 10–14)? Is there a catch to this wonderful promise? If so, what? 4. What must the exiles be feeling about those trapped in Jerusalem (vv. 15–19), as well as the false prophets Ahab and Zedekiah (vv. 20–23): (a) "I told you so"? (b) "Serves 'em right"? (c) But for the grace of God, there go I? (d)

---

a2 Hebrew Jeconiah, *a variant of* Jehoiachin

"What—me too!"? 5. How do Jeremiah's superiors learn of his letter to the exiles (vv. 25–28)? Why was Jeremiah regarded a madman if his prophecies had finally come true? Should Shemaiah's letter come as any surprise to Zephaniah the priest? 6. What do the two prophets—Hananiah in Palestine and Shemaiah in Babylon—have in common (vv. 31–32; see 28:15–16)? What clues do you see as to how to spot false prophets?

1. Do you think God uses evil to accomplish good: (a) Never, at least not in my life? (b) Sometimes, as in Jeremiah's life? (c) Always, as in ancient Israel and the early Church? What support for your answer do you find in Scripture? In personal observation? 2. Is there any randomness in life as Jeremiah has experienced it? As you have experienced it? Explain. 3. Have you ever seen God bring good out of bad situations in your life, as in verses 11–14? What happened? Could there have been an easier way to learn that lesson? 4. As a "wonderful plan for life," what do you think of verses 5–7? Do you aspire to something else? What? 5. Who might think of you in any sense as a "madman"? Or do you blend in pretty good? 6. Is criticism hard to take? What makes it easier? When's the last time you gave criticism successfully?

I have for you," declares the LORD, "plans to prosper you and not to harm you, plans to give you hope and a future. [12]Then you will call upon me and come and pray to me, and I will listen to you. [13]You will seek me and find me when you seek me with all your heart. [14]I will be found by you," declares the LORD, "and will bring you back from captivity.[a] I will gather you from all the nations and places where I have banished you," declares the LORD, "and will bring you back to the place from which I carried you into exile."

[15]You may say, "The LORD has raised up prophets for us in Babylon," [16]but this is what the LORD says about the king who sits on David's throne and all the people who remain in this city, your countrymen who did not go with you into exile— [17]yes, this is what the LORD Almighty says: "I will send the sword, famine and plague against them and I will make them like poor figs that are so bad they cannot be eaten. [18]I will pursue them with the sword, famine and plague and will make them abhorrent to all the kingdoms of the earth and an object of cursing and horror, of scorn and reproach, among all the nations where I drive them. [19]For they have not listened to my words," declares the LORD, "words that I sent to them again and again by my servants the prophets. And you exiles have not listened either," declares the LORD.

[20]Therefore, hear the word of the LORD, all you exiles whom I have sent away from Jerusalem to Babylon. [21]This is what the LORD Almighty, the God of Israel, says about Ahab son of Kolaiah and Zedekiah son of Maaseiah, who are prophesying lies to you in my name: "I will hand them over to Nebuchadnezzar king of Babylon, and he will put them to death before your very eyes. [22]Because of them, all the exiles from Judah who are in Babylon will use this curse: 'The LORD treat you like Zedekiah and Ahab, whom the king of Babylon burned in the fire.' [23]For they have done outrageous things in Israel; they have committed adultery with their neighbors' wives and in my name have spoken lies, which I did not tell them to do. I know it and am a witness to it," declares the LORD.

Message to Shemaiah

[24]Tell Shemaiah the Nehelamite, [25]"This is what the LORD Almighty, the God of Israel, says: You sent letters in your own name to all the people in Jerusalem, to Zephaniah son of Maaseiah the priest, and to all the other priests. You said to Zephaniah, [26]'The LORD has appointed you priest in place of Jehoiada to be in charge of the house of the LORD; you should put any madman who acts like a prophet into the stocks and neck-irons. [27]So why have you not reprimanded Jeremiah from Anathoth, who poses as a prophet among you? [28]He has sent this message to us in Babylon: It will be a long time. Therefore build houses and settle down; plant gardens and eat what they produce.'"

[29]Zephaniah the priest, however, read the letter to Jeremiah the prophet. [30]Then the word of the LORD came to Jeremiah: [31]"Send this message to all the exiles: 'This is what the LORD says about Shemaiah the Nehelamite: Because Shemaiah has prophesied to you, even though I did not send him, and has led you to believe a lie, [32]this is what the LORD says: I will surely punish Shemaiah the Nehelamite and his descendants. He will have no one left among

---

a14 Or will restore your fortunes

this people, nor will he see the good things I will do for my people, declares the LORD, because he has preached rebellion against me.'"

Restoration of Israel

30 This is the word that came to Jeremiah from the LORD: ²"This is what the LORD, the God of Israel, says: 'Write in a book all the words I have spoken to you. ³The days are coming,' declares the LORD, 'when I will bring my people Israel and Judah back from captivity*a* and restore them to the land I gave their forefathers to possess,' says the LORD."

⁴These are the words the LORD spoke concerning Israel and Judah: ⁵"This is what the LORD says:

"'Cries of fear are heard—
    terror, not peace.
⁶Ask and see:
    Can a man bear children?
Then why do I see every strong man
    with his hands on his stomach like a woman in
        labor,
    every face turned deathly pale?
⁷How awful that day will be!
    None will be like it.
It will be a time of trouble for Jacob,
    but he will be saved out of it.

⁸"'In that day,' declares the LORD Almighty,
    'I will break the yoke off their necks
and will tear off their bonds;
    no longer will foreigners enslave them.
⁹Instead, they will serve the LORD their God
    and David their king,
    whom I will raise up for them.

¹⁰"'So do not fear, O Jacob my servant;
    do not be dismayed, O Israel,'
                                    declares the LORD.
    'I will surely save you out of a distant place,
    your descendants from the land of their exile.
Jacob will again have peace and security,
    and no one will make him afraid.
¹¹I am with you and will save you,'
    declares the LORD.
    'Though I completely destroy all the nations
        among which I scatter you,
    I will not completely destroy you.
I will discipline you but only with justice;
    I will not let you go entirely unpunished.'

¹²"This is what the LORD says:

"'Your wound is incurable,
    your injury beyond healing.
¹³There is no one to plead your cause,
    no remedy for your sore,
    no healing for you.
¹⁴All your allies have forgotten you;
    they care nothing for you.
I have struck you as an enemy would
    and punished you as would the cruel,

a3 Or will restore the fortunes of my people Israel and Judah

1. What is your favorite book of the Bible? What is your favorite book apart from the Bible? How do each of your favorites turn out in the end? 2. How far back do you date your "days of old"? Is that a past you would sooner forget, or are they the "good ol' days"?

1. Chapters 30–31 (mostly in poetry) and perhaps, as well, chapters 32–33 (almost all prose) were originally one "book of consolation" (vv. 1–3), which can be dated c. 587 B.C., the year before the fall of Jerusalem (see 32:1). How do you suppose God conveyed this message to Jeremiah: By messenger? Audibly, giving dictation? In a dream (see 31:26)? 2. What clues tell you this Book of Consolation is largely directed to the northern tribes of Israel (vv. 7,10,18; also 31:1–22)? 3. What had happened to Israel a century before Jeremiah (v. 8; see 2Ki 17:5–6, 24–33), a situation which would soon be rectified (vv. 16–18)? 4. Who is "David their king" (vv. 8–9)? What will he be like (v. 21; see 23:5)? What had King Josiah of Judah done for the northerners early in Jeremiah's career (see 2Ki 23:15–20) to serve as a prototype for this righteous King to come? 5. What were the "days of old" (v. 20) like for Israel, under the reign of David? What fortunes, songs of praise and covenant promises would be restored (vv. 18–22)? What will accomplish this turnabout?

1. Is it easy for you to detach yourself emotionally from people who were once important to you? After a falling out, does "out of sight, out of mind" come naturally? Would you like a "restoration" with someone from your past? How could it happen? 2. What and how could your fortunes be restored: (a) More money, for less work? (b) More friends, for less energy? (c) More knowledge, for less time? (d) Other? Explain how you are truly fortunate.

because your guilt is so great
and your sins so many.
¹⁵Why do you cry out over your wound,
your pain that has no cure?
Because of your great guilt and many sins
I have done these things to you.

¹⁶"'But all who devour you will be devoured;
all your enemies will go into exile.
Those who plunder you will be plundered;
all who make spoil of you I will despoil.
¹⁷But I will restore you to health
and heal your wounds,'

declares the LORD,

'because you are called an outcast,
Zion for whom no one cares.'

¹⁸"This is what the LORD says:

"'I will restore the fortunes of Jacob's tents
and have compassion on his dwellings;
the city will be rebuilt on her ruins,
and the palace will stand in its proper place.
¹⁹From them will come songs of thanksgiving
and the sound of rejoicing.
I will add to their numbers,
and they will not be decreased;
I will bring them honor,
and they will not be disdained.
²⁰Their children will be as in days of old,
and their community will be established before
me;
I will punish all who oppress them.
²¹Their leader will be one of their own;
their ruler will arise from among them.
I will bring him near and he will come close to
me,
for who is he who will devote himself
to be close to me?'

declares the LORD.

²²"'So you will be my people,
and I will be your God.'"

²³See, the storm of the LORD
will burst out in wrath,
a driving wind swirling down
on the heads of the wicked.
²⁴The fierce anger of the LORD will not turn back
until he fully accomplishes
the purposes of his heart.
In days to come
you will understand this.

31 "At that time," declares the LORD, "I will be the God of all
the clans of Israel, and they will be my people."
²This is what the LORD says:

"The people who survive the sword
will find favor in the desert;
I will come to give rest to Israel."

1. Right now, would you say
your spiritual life is closer to a
sunrise or a sunset? Is a new day
dawning in your life? How so? 2.
"It's always darkest before the
dawn," the saying goes. How has
this been true for you? 3. What is

[3]The LORD appeared to us in the past,[a] saying:

"I have loved you with an everlasting love;
  I have drawn you with loving-kindness.
[4]I will build you up again
  and you will be rebuilt, O Virgin Israel.
Again you will take up your tambourines
  and go out to dance with the joyful.
[5]Again you will plant vineyards
  on the hills of Samaria;
the farmers will plant them
  and enjoy their fruit.
[6]There will be a day when watchmen cry out
  on the hills of Ephraim,
'Come, let us go up to Zion,
  to the LORD our God.'"

[7]This is what the LORD says:

"Sing with joy for Jacob;
  shout for the foremost of the nations.
Make your praises heard, and say,
  'O LORD, save your people,
  the remnant of Israel.'
[8]See, I will bring them from the land of the north
  and gather them from the ends of the earth.
Among them will be the blind and the lame,
  expectant mothers and women in labor;
  a great throng will return.
[9]They will come with weeping;
  they will pray as I bring them back.
I will lead them beside streams of water
  on a level path where they will not stumble,
because I am Israel's father,
  and Ephraim is my firstborn son.

[10]"Hear the word of the LORD, O nations;
  proclaim it in distant coastlands:
'He who scattered Israel will gather them
  and will watch over his flock like a shepherd.'
[11]For the LORD will ransom Jacob
  and redeem them from the hand of those
  stronger than they.
[12]They will come and shout for joy on the heights
  of Zion;
they will rejoice in the bounty of the LORD—
  the grain, the new wine and the oil,
  the young of the flocks and herds.
They will be like a well-watered garden,
  and they will sorrow no more.
[13]Then maidens will dance and be glad,
  young men and old as well.
I will turn their mourning into gladness;
  I will give them comfort and joy instead of
  sorrow.
[14]I will satisfy the priests with abundance,
  and my people will be filled with my bounty,"
  declares the LORD.

[15]This is what the LORD says:

[a]3 Or LORD has appeared to us from afar

the best news you heard last week? What made it so special?

1. Chapter 32:1–22 continues the consolation for Israel. By what other names is Israel called in this section (vv. 7,10,17–18)? 2. What evidence do you see here that the promise of restoration is extended to the southern kingdom of Judah, as well (vv. 1,23–40)? 3. What political vision does Jeremiah have of the restored nation (vv. 5–8)? Why would Israel be considered the "foremost of nations" (see Dt 7:6–8)? Why will they come "with weeping" (v. 9)? 4. Who else is included in this vision and why (vv. 10–14)? 5. Who are Rachel and her children (v. 15; see Ge 29:18,30; 46:19–20)? How and why does Jeremiah use the image of "Rachel weeping"? (Note: Babylon turned Ramah, north of Jerusalem, into a detainment camp for Jews being led into captivity.) What use of this image does the early church make (see Mt 2:8)? 6. What other images of grieving and consolation give hope to the readers (vv. 16–20,23–25,27–28)? 7. What relationship does God want to restore between himself and Israel (vv. 21–22; see Hos 2:18–20)? How can adulterous Israel become a "virgin" again? 8. What is the meaning of the proverb quoted in verse 29 (see Eze 18:2–4)? Is God changing the rules (e.g., Ex 20:5; Nu 14:18) by which many thought of themselves as guilty (v. 30; see Dt 24:16)? 9. What was the covenant God made with Israel's forefathers (vv. 31–32; see Ge 17:1–14; Ex 19:1–6)? What was "wrong" or obsolete about this old or first covenant (see Heb 8:6–13; 9:13–15; 10:11–18, where Jeremiah is quoted)? 10. How will the new covenant supersede or fulfill the old one (vv. 33–34)? In what way will it be a covenant? What seals or secures the covenant from God's side (vv. 35–37)? 11. The exiles rebuilt Jerusalem after 70 years. The city did not prove invincible, but was sacked again, most notably by the Romans in A.D. 70 (see Lk 21:6). What then does God's promise of eternal security for Jerusalem really mean (vv. 38–40)?

1. How and when is the promise of the new covenant put into effect (see Mt 26:28; Heb 9:16–18)? How would you explain the difference between the old and new covenants to a friend? 2.

Which covenant are you living under: Law or grace? How do you
know for sure? What does it mean
to you to truly know the Lord as
Jeremiah intended? What is God's
part? What is yours? 3. Jeremiah's
new covenant promises: (a) Ready
forgiveness of sins (30:34)? (b)
Freedom from the sins of the parents (30:29)? (c) Internal working
of the Spirit (31:33–34)? (d) All of
the above? (e) Other? Which aspect means the most to your spiritual walk? Why?

"A voice is heard in Ramah,
    mourning and great weeping,
Rachel weeping for her children
    and refusing to be comforted,
    because her children are no more."

¹⁶This is what the LORD says:

"Restrain your voice from weeping
    and your eyes from tears,
for your work will be rewarded,"
                                    declares the LORD.
"They will return from the land of the enemy.
¹⁷So there is hope for your future,"
                                    declares the LORD.
"Your children will return to their own land.

¹⁸"I have surely heard Ephraim's moaning:
    'You disciplined me like an unruly calf,
    and I have been disciplined.
Restore me, and I will return,
    because you are the LORD my God.
¹⁹After I strayed,
    I repented;
after I came to understand,
    I beat my breast.
I was ashamed and humiliated
    because I bore the disgrace of my youth.'
²⁰Is not Ephraim my dear son,
    the child in whom I delight?
Though I often speak against him,
    I still remember him.
Therefore my heart yearns for him;
    I have great compassion for him,"
                                    declares the LORD.

²¹"Set up road signs;
    put up guideposts.
Take note of the highway,
    the road that you take.
Return, O Virgin Israel,
    return to your towns.
²²How long will you wander,
    O unfaithful daughter?
The LORD will create a new thing on earth—
    a woman will surround^a a man."

²³This is what the LORD Almighty, the God of Israel, says: "When
I bring them back from captivity,^{b} the people in the land of Judah
and in its towns will once again use these words: 'The LORD bless
you, O righteous dwelling, O sacred mountain.' ²⁴People will live
together in Judah and all its towns—farmers and those who move
about with their flocks. ²⁵I will refresh the weary and satisfy the
faint."

²⁶At this I awoke and looked around. My sleep had been pleasant
to me.

²⁷"The days are coming," declares the LORD, "when I will plant
the house of Israel and the house of Judah with the offspring of
men and of animals. ²⁸Just as I watched over them to uproot and
tear down, and to overthrow, destroy and bring disaster, so I will

^{a}22 Or will go about ⌊seeking⌋; or will protect ^{b}23 Or I restore their fortunes

watch over them to build and to plant," declares the LORD. ²⁹"In those days people will no longer say,

'The fathers have eaten sour grapes,
    and the children's teeth are set on edge.'

³⁰Instead, everyone will die for his own sin; whoever eats sour grapes—his own teeth will be set on edge.

³¹"The time is coming," declares the LORD,
    "when I will make a new covenant
    with the house of Israel
    and with the house of Judah.
³²It will not be like the covenant
    I made with their forefathers
    when I took them by the hand
    to lead them out of Egypt,
    because they broke my covenant,
    though I was a husband to*ᵃ* them,*ᵇ*"
                        declares the LORD.
³³"This is the covenant I will make with the house
        of Israel
    after that time," declares the LORD.
    "I will put my law in their minds
    and write it on their hearts.
    I will be their God,
    and they will be my people.
³⁴No longer will a man teach his neighbor,
    or a man his brother, saying, 'Know the LORD,'
    because they will all know me,
    from the least of them to the greatest,"
                        declares the LORD.
    "For I will forgive their wickedness
    and will remember their sins no more."

³⁵This is what the LORD says,

    he who appoints the sun
        to shine by day,
    who decrees the moon and stars
        to shine by night,
    who stirs up the sea
        so that its waves roar—
        the LORD Almighty is his name:
³⁶"Only if these decrees vanish from my sight,"
        declares the LORD,
    "will the descendants of Israel ever cease
        to be a nation before me."

³⁷This is what the LORD says:

    "Only if the heavens above can be measured
        and the foundations of the earth below be
            searched out
    will I reject all the descendants of Israel
        because of all they have done,"
                        declares the LORD.

³⁸"The days are coming," declares the LORD, "when this city will be rebuilt for me from the Tower of Hananel to the Corner Gate. ³⁹The measuring line will stretch from there straight to the hill of

---

ᵃ32 Hebrew; Septuagint and Syriac / *and I turned away from*   *ᵇ32* Or *was their master*

Gareb and then turn to Goah. 40The whole valley where dead bodies and ashes are thrown, and all the terraces out to the Kidron Valley on the east as far as the corner of the Horse Gate, will be holy to the LORD. The city will never again be uprooted or demolished."

Jeremiah Buys a Field

32 This is the word that came to Jeremiah from the LORD in the tenth year of Zedekiah king of Judah, which was the eighteenth year of Nebuchadnezzar. 2The army of the king of Babylon was then besieging Jerusalem, and Jeremiah the prophet was confined in the courtyard of the guard in the royal palace of Judah.

3Now Zedekiah king of Judah had imprisoned him there, saying, "Why do you prophesy as you do? You say, 'This is what the LORD says: I am about to hand this city over to the king of Babylon, and he will capture it. 4Zedekiah king of Judah will not escape out of the hands of the Babylonians[a] but will certainly be handed over to the king of Babylon, and will speak with him face to face and see him with his own eyes. 5He will take Zedekiah to Babylon, where he will remain until I deal with him, declares the LORD. If you fight against the Babylonians, you will not succeed.'"

6Jeremiah said, "The word of the LORD came to me: 7Hanamel son of Shallum your uncle is going to come to you and say, 'Buy my field at Anathoth, because as nearest relative it is your right and duty to buy it.'

8"Then, just as the LORD had said, my cousin Hanamel came to me in the courtyard of the guard and said, 'Buy my field at Anathoth in the territory of Benjamin. Since it is your right to redeem it and possess it, buy it for yourself.'

"I knew that this was the word of the LORD; 9so I bought the field at Anathoth from my cousin Hanamel and weighed out for him seventeen shekels[b] of silver. 10I signed and sealed the deed, had it witnessed, and weighed out the silver on the scales. 11I took the deed of purchase—the sealed copy containing the terms and conditions, as well as the unsealed copy— 12and I gave this deed to Baruch son of Neriah, the son of Mahseiah, in the presence of my cousin Hanamel and of the witnesses who had signed the deed and of all the Jews sitting in the courtyard of the guard.

13"In their presence I gave Baruch these instructions: 14'This is what the LORD Almighty, the God of Israel, says: Take these documents, both the sealed and unsealed copies of the deed of purchase, and put them in a clay jar so they will last a long time. 15For this is what the LORD Almighty, the God of Israel, says: Houses, fields and vineyards will again be bought in this land.'

16"After I had given the deed of purchase to Baruch son of Neriah, I prayed to the LORD:

17"Ah, Sovereign LORD, you have made the heavens and the earth by your great power and outstretched arm. Nothing is too hard for you. 18You show love to thousands but bring the punishment for the fathers' sins into the laps of their children after them. O great and powerful God, whose name is the LORD Almighty, 19great are your purposes and mighty are your deeds. Your eyes are open to all the ways of men; you reward everyone according to his conduct and as his deeds deserve. 20You performed miraculous signs and wonders in Egypt and have continued them to this day, both in Israel and among all

---

1. On a scale of 1 ("A fool and his money are soon parted") to 10 ("Midas touch"), how would you rate your business acumen? Are you better at spending money or making money? 2. Have you ever bought any real estate? Was it easier or harder than you thought it would be? Would you do it again? 3. What is the dumbest purchase you've made?

1. This chapter resumes stories from Jeremiah's history. How might it also be an extension of his Book of Consolation (ch. 31–32)? 2. At the end of chapter 26, Jeremiah was last seen under arrest for preaching in the temple. As this chapter opens in 587 B.C. (vv. 1–5), what is happening to the city and to Jeremiah? Why? 3. How then do you account for the intrusion and seeming irrelevance of Jeremiah's cousin and God's confirming word (vv. 6–8)? At this time is the real estate market a buyer's market, or a seller's market? 4. Why does Jeremiah have the "right and duty" to buy it (see Lev 25:23–25; Ru 4:1–4)? Does he think it's a good deal, or does he feel stuck (vv. 24–25)? 5. Why then does he purchase the field (vv. 8–12)? What proof did he have that it was the right thing to do? 6. How do the parts played by Hanamel, the witnesses and Baruch serve the overall point of this passage? 7. How does Jeremiah's prayer (vv. 17–25) serve that overall purpose? What themes from chapters 31–32 does he bring before God? Is this a prayer of affirmation or resignation? Why do you think so? 8. What comfort does God offer in verses 26–29? In verses 36–41? In verses 42–44? 9. If the spiritual health of Anathoth is at all like the other Israelite towns (vv. 30–35), what will probably be the fate of Jeremiah's newly-acquired property (see 11:21–23)? Why then does God ask Jeremiah to buy the field (vv. 42–44)? What do you think the rest of the city would have thought about this crazy real estate transaction?

1. Of what comfort to you are long-range assurances of prosperity, when your present fi-

---

a4 Or *Chaldeans*; also in verses 5, 24, 25, 28, 29 and 43   b9 That is, about 7 ounces (about 200 grams)

mankind, and have gained the renown that is still yours. ²¹You brought your people Israel out of Egypt with signs and wonders, by a mighty hand and an outstretched arm and with great terror. ²²You gave them this land you had sworn to give their forefathers, a land flowing with milk and honey. ²³They came in and took possession of it, but they did not obey you or follow your law; they did not do what you commanded them to do. So you brought all this disaster upon them.

²⁴"See how the siege ramps are built up to take the city. Because of the sword, famine and plague, the city will be handed over to the Babylonians who are attacking it. What you said has happened, as you now see. ²⁵And though the city will be handed over to the Babylonians, you, O Sovereign LORD, say to me, 'Buy the field with silver and have the transaction witnessed.'"

²⁶Then the word of the LORD came to Jeremiah: ²⁷"I am the LORD, the God of all mankind. Is anything too hard for me? ²⁸Therefore, this is what the LORD says: I am about to hand this city over to the Babylonians and to Nebuchadnezzar king of Babylon, who will capture it. ²⁹The Babylonians who are attacking this city will come in and set it on fire; they will burn it down, along with the houses where the people provoked me to anger by burning incense on the roofs to Baal and by pouring out drink offerings to other gods.

³⁰"The people of Israel and Judah have done nothing but evil in my sight from their youth; indeed, the people of Israel have done nothing but provoke me with what their hands have made, declares the LORD. ³¹From the day it was built until now, this city has so aroused my anger and wrath that I must remove it from my sight. ³²The people of Israel and Judah have provoked me by all the evil they have done—they, their kings and officials, their priests and prophets, the men of Judah and the people of Jerusalem. ³³They turned their backs to me and not their faces; though I taught them again and again, they would not listen or respond to discipline. ³⁴They set up their abominable idols in the house that bears my Name and defiled it. ³⁵They built high places for Baal in the Valley of Ben Hinnom to sacrifice their sons and daughters*a* to Molech, though I never commanded, nor did it enter my mind, that they should do such a detestable thing and so make Judah sin.

³⁶"You are saying about this city, 'By the sword, famine and plague it will be handed over to the king of Babylon'; but this is what the LORD, the God of Israel, says: ³⁷I will surely gather them from all the lands where I banish them in my furious anger and great wrath; I will bring them back to this place and let them live in safety. ³⁸They will be my people, and I will be their God. ³⁹I will give them singleness of heart and action, so that they will always fear me for their own good and the good of their children after them. ⁴⁰I will make an everlasting covenant with them: I will never stop doing good to them, and I will inspire them to fear me, so that they will never turn away from me. ⁴¹I will rejoice in doing them good and will assuredly plant them in this land with all my heart and soul.

⁴²"This is what the LORD says: As I have brought all this great calamity on this people, so I will give them all the prosperity I have promised them. ⁴³Once more fields will be bought in this land of which you say, 'It is a desolate waste, without men or animals, for it has been handed over to the Babylonians.' ⁴⁴Fields will be bought for silver, and deeds will be signed, sealed and witnessed in

nancial outlook is precarious (at best) or bankrupt (at worst)? **2.** What lessons of hope have you learned that could only have been taught you through adversity, doom and gloom? **3.** God gave Jeremiah advance confirmation of his will regarding Jeremiah's purchase of the field from his cousin. Has God ever told you in advance what he wants you to do when a certain situation arises? What role does God have in your decision-making process? **4.** Where do you think the world will be in 70 years? Is it hard for you to put stock in the present when the world looks so grim? What investment would God want you to make in the future of your world, as a testimony of your faith in God? **5.** When have you stepped out on faith and then seriously reconsidered, even rescinded, your actions? If you ever challenge God about the way things work out for you, how does God answer? What kind of answers do you expect?

---

a35 Or to make their sons and daughters pass through ⌊the fire⌋

the territory of Benjamin, in the villages around Jerusalem, in the towns of Judah and in the towns of the hill country, of the western foothills and of the Negev, because I will restore their fortunes,[a] declares the LORD."

Promise of Restoration

33 While Jeremiah was still confined in the courtyard of the guard, the word of the LORD came to him a second time: [2]"This is what the LORD says, he who made the earth, the LORD who formed it and established it—the LORD is his name: [3]'Call to me and I will answer you and tell you great and unsearchable things you do not know.' [4]For this is what the LORD, the God of Israel, says about the houses in this city and the royal palaces of Judah that have been torn down to be used against the siege ramps and the sword [5]in the fight with the Babylonians[b]: 'They will be filled with the dead bodies of the men I will slay in my anger and wrath. I will hide my face from this city because of all its wickedness.

[6]'Nevertheless, I will bring health and healing to it; I will heal my people and will let them enjoy abundant peace and security. [7]I will bring Judah and Israel back from captivity[c] and will rebuild them as they were before. [8]I will cleanse them from all the sin they have committed against me and will forgive all their sins of rebellion against me. [9]Then this city will bring me renown, joy, praise and honor before all nations on earth that hear of all the good things I do for it; and they will be in awe and will tremble at the abundant prosperity and peace I provide for it.'

[10]"This is what the LORD says: 'You say about this place, "It is a desolate waste, without men or animals." Yet in the towns of Judah and the streets of Jerusalem that are deserted, inhabited by neither men nor animals, there will be heard once more [11]the sounds of joy and gladness, the voices of bride and bridegroom, and the voices of those who bring thank offerings to the house of the LORD, saying,

> "Give thanks to the LORD Almighty,
>   for the LORD is good;
>   his love endures forever."

For I will restore the fortunes of the land as they were before,' says the LORD.

[12]"This is what the LORD Almighty says: 'In this place, desolate and without men or animals—in all its towns there will again be pastures for shepherds to rest their flocks. [13]In the towns of the hill country, of the western foothills and of the Negev, in the territory of Benjamin, in the villages around Jerusalem and in the towns of Judah, flocks will again pass under the hand of the one who counts them,' says the LORD.

[14]"'The days are coming,' declares the LORD, 'when I will fulfill the gracious promise I made to the house of Israel and to the house of Judah.

[15]"'In those days and at that time
   I will make a righteous Branch sprout from
      David's line;
   he will do what is just and right in the land.
[16]In those days Judah will be saved
   and Jerusalem will live in safety.

---

1. When were you most homesick? When were you most sick of home? What happened? **2.** What current situations come to mind for you as you picture these fragments of dialogue expressing concern about promises made and not yet fulfilled: (a) "But you said _____" ... "When did I say that?" (b) "Here it is in writing." ... "Ah, that contract has been superseded by a new one." (c) "I can't trust you." ... "What do I have to do, sign in blood?"

1. This chapter summarizes some themes from earlier in Jeremiah's life. How might it also be an extension of his Book of Consolation (ch. 31–32)? (Hint: Why does Jeremiah say a "second time," v. 1)? **2.** With the siege of Jerusalem still underway (vv. 4–5), what must have happened to their hope, necessitating this second word? **3.** What three things does the Lord promise to do in and for his people (vv. 6–8)? Toward what end does God bless them (v. 9)? **4.** What signs of hope are conveyed by the sights and sounds of verses 10–11 (compare 7:34; 16:9; 25:10)? What other activities would you use to express the same hope? **5.** What two offices does God once again promise to establish (vv. 15–18; see 23:5–6)? When were these promises first made (see Nu 25:13; 2Sa 7:12–16; Ge 22:17)? Why might the people need reassurance that God will still keep his word as always? **6.** Who will ultimately fulfill both offices? How so (see Lk 1:32–33; Heb 7:11–25)? **7.** Are the people justified in saying God has rejected Israel and Judah (vv. 23–24)? Who rejected who?

1. Have you ever doubted God's faithfulness? Why? What hope do you have in the times when you are unfaithful to God? **2.** Jewish people through the ages have had mixed thoughts on these promises of a Messiah. Do you wonder why God seems to wait so long to act? What answers seem to satisfy you for the time being? **3.** Israel needed constant reassurance. Do you need to be reminded of God's promises? Which

---

This is the name by which it*a* will be called:
The LORD Our Righteousness.'

17For this is what the LORD says: 'David will never fail to have a man to sit on the throne of the house of Israel, 18nor will the priests, who are Levites, ever fail to have a man to stand before me continually to offer burnt offerings, to burn grain offerings and to present sacrifices.'"

19The word of the LORD came to Jeremiah: 20"This is what the LORD says: 'If you can break my covenant with the day and my covenant with the night, so that day and night no longer come at their appointed time, 21then my covenant with David my servant—and my covenant with the Levites who are priests ministering before me—can be broken and David will no longer have a descendant to reign on his throne. 22I will make the descendants of David my servant and the Levites who minister before me as countless as the stars of the sky and as measureless as the sand on the seashore.'"

23The word of the LORD came to Jeremiah: 24"Have you not noticed that these people are saying, 'The LORD has rejected the two kingdoms*b* he chose'? So they despise my people and no longer regard them as a nation. 25This is what the LORD says: 'If I have not established my covenant with day and night and the fixed laws of heaven and earth, 26then I will reject the descendants of Jacob and David my servant and will not choose one of his sons to rule over the descendants of Abraham, Isaac and Jacob. For I will restore their fortunes*c* and have compassion on them.'"

Warning to Zedekiah

34 While Nebuchadnezzar king of Babylon and all his army and all the kingdoms and peoples in the empire he ruled were fighting against Jerusalem and all its surrounding towns, this word came to Jeremiah from the LORD: 2"This is what the LORD, the God of Israel, says: Go to Zedekiah king of Judah and tell him, 'This is what the LORD says: I am about to hand this city over to the king of Babylon, and he will burn it down. 3You will not escape from his grasp but will surely be captured and handed over to him. You will see the king of Babylon with your own eyes, and he will speak with you face to face. And you will go to Babylon.

4" 'Yet hear the promise of the LORD, O Zedekiah king of Judah. This is what the LORD says concerning you: You will not die by the sword; 5you will die peacefully. As people made a funeral fire in honor of your fathers, the former kings who preceded you, so they will make a fire in your honor and lament, "Alas, O master!" I myself make this promise, declares the LORD.' "

6Then Jeremiah the prophet told all this to Zedekiah king of Judah, in Jerusalem, 7while the army of the king of Babylon was fighting against Jerusalem and the other cities of Judah that were still holding out—Lachish and Azekah. These were the only fortified cities left in Judah.

Freedom for Slaves

8The word came to Jeremiah from the LORD after King Zedekiah had made a covenant with all the people in Jerusalem to proclaim freedom for the slaves. 9Everyone was to free his Hebrew slaves, both male and female; no one was to hold a fellow Jew in bondage. 10So all the officials and people who entered into this covenant agreed that they would free their male and female slaves and no

promise, recorded in Jeremiah, do you need to remember now?

1. What totally unexpected gift (or serendipity!) did you once receive? From whom? What for? 2. How would you rather die: By famine, sword or plague? Why?

1. How is Judah able to hold out so long under a four-year seige (v. 7; see 2Ki 25:1–3)? 2. What has God already told Zedekiah about the war (see 21:1–10)? What has Zedekiah done to deserve a break (vv. 4–5)?

1. What blessing has God given you recently that you did not deserve? How do you respond to unmerited goodness? 2. Are you "between a rock and a hard place," as was Zedekiah? How so? How can your group help?

1. Has anyone gone back on a promise to you? When? How did it make you feel? 2. What freedoms were you granted upon reaching the age of 16? 18? 21? 40? 65?

1. Who became slaves in ancient Israel and why (vv. 8–9; see Lev 25:39–46)? Why was a

a16 Or he   b24 Or families   c26 Or will bring them back from captivity limit set for the servitude of a fellow Jew (vv. 13–14)? **2.** Why do you think Zedekiah declares freedom for the slaves (vv. 8–10)? Why do the slave-holders renege on this (vv. 11,16; see 34:21–22 and 37:5)? **3.** One ancient rite to "cut" a covenant had partners cut a calf in two and walk between the pieces. What might have been the significance of this (vv. 18–20; see Ge 15:8–11,17)? **4.** Why fuss over the slaves? How would it feel to be freed, then enslaved again? How will God "free" those who break their vow (vv. 17–22)?

1. If this were your only biblical basis for learning how God cares for the poor, what would you conclude about God? About the poor? About rich land-owners and office-holders? **2.** If your CEO or government leader reneges on a pledge to your people, what happens? **3.** Who are the "slaves" in your country today? Is your church proclaiming their freedom, as did Isaiah and Jesus (see Isa 61:1–2; Lk 4:18)? How can your group become involved? **4.** Do you feel "enslaved" in any way? What would freedom mean to you? What can you do for those enslaved as you once were (or still are)?

1. When it comes to parties, are you: (a) A party animal? (b) A party pooper? (c) A wall flower? (d) Prudish with food and drink? (e) Enough food and drink to satisfy an army? **2.** What famous people would you invite to an "ideal" dinner party? What does your guest list (or last year's social calendar) say about you?

1. Chapters 35–36 flash back to the reign of Jehoiakim (v. 1), nearly 25 years earlier. What is the relationship between Judah and Babylon at this time (see 2Ki 24:1–2)? **2.** Why did God tell Jeremiah to offer the Recabites wine (vv. 2–5)? What two things made them different from other Israelites (vv. 6–10)? Why do you think they had been told to live so radically different (see 2Ki 10:15–23; compare the Nazirite's vow, Nu 6:2–4,20)? **3.** Why had they moved into Jerusalem (v. 11)? Why might they feel uneasy about the situation? **4.** What about the

longer hold them in bondage. They agreed, and set them free. [11]But afterward they changed their minds and took back the slaves they had freed and enslaved them again.

[12]Then the word of the LORD came to Jeremiah: [13]"This is what the LORD, the God of Israel, says: I made a covenant with your forefathers when I brought them out of Egypt, out of the land of slavery. I said, [14]'Every seventh year each of you must free any fellow Hebrew who has sold himself to you. After he has served you six years, you must let him go free.'[a] Your fathers, however, did not listen to me or pay attention to me. [15]Recently you repented and did what is right in my sight: Each of you proclaimed freedom to his countrymen. You even made a covenant before me in the house that bears my Name. [16]But now you have turned around and profaned my name; each of you has taken back the male and female slaves you had set free to go where they wished. You have forced them to become your slaves again.

[17]"Therefore, this is what the LORD says: You have not obeyed me; you have not proclaimed freedom for your fellow countrymen. So I now proclaim 'freedom' for you, declares the LORD—'freedom' to fall by the sword, plague and famine. I will make you abhorrent to all the kingdoms of the earth. [18]The men who have violated my covenant and have not fulfilled the terms of the covenant they made before me, I will treat like the calf they cut in two and then walked between its pieces. [19]The leaders of Judah and Jerusalem, the court officials, the priests and all the people of the land who walked between the pieces of the calf, [20]I will hand over to their enemies who seek their lives. Their dead bodies will become food for the birds of the air and the beasts of the earth.

[21]"I will hand Zedekiah king of Judah and his officials over to their enemies who seek their lives, to the army of the king of Babylon, which has withdrawn from you. [22]I am going to give the order, declares the LORD, and I will bring them back to this city. They will fight against it, take it and burn it down. And I will lay waste the towns of Judah so no one can live there."

The Recabites

35 This is the word that came to Jeremiah from the LORD during the reign of Jehoiakim son of Josiah king of Judah: [2]"Go to the Recabite family and invite them to come to one of the side rooms of the house of the LORD and give them wine to drink."

[3]So I went to get Jaazaniah son of Jeremiah, the son of Habazziniah, and his brothers and all his sons—the whole family of the Recabites. [4]I brought them into the house of the LORD, into the room of the sons of Hanan son of Igdaliah the man of God. It was next to the room of the officials, which was over that of Maaseiah son of Shallum the doorkeeper. [5]Then I set bowls full of wine and some cups before the men of the Recabite family and said to them, "Drink some wine."

[6]But they replied, "We do not drink wine, because our forefather Jonadab son of Recab gave us this command: 'Neither you nor your descendants must ever drink wine. [7]Also you must never build houses, sow seed or plant vineyards; you must never have any of these things, but must always live in tents. Then you will live a long time in the land where you are nomads.' [8]We have obeyed everything our forefather Jonadab son of Recab commanded us. Neither we nor our wives nor our sons and daughters have ever drunk wine [9]or built houses to live in or had vineyards, fields or

[a]14 Deut. 15:12

crops. [10]We have lived in tents and have fully obeyed everything our forefather Jonadab commanded us. [11]But when Nebuchadnezzar king of Babylon invaded this land, we said, 'Come, we must go to Jerusalem to escape the Babylonian[a] and Aramean armies.' So we have remained in Jerusalem."

[12]Then the word of the LORD came to Jeremiah, saying: [13]"This is what the LORD Almighty, the God of Israel, says: Go and tell the men of Judah and the people of Jerusalem, 'Will you not learn a lesson and obey my words?' declares the LORD. [14]'Jonadab son of Recab ordered his sons not to drink wine and this command has been kept. To this day they do not drink wine, because they obey their forefather's command. But I have spoken to you again and again, yet you have not obeyed me. [15]Again and again I sent all my servants the prophets to you. They said, "Each of you must turn from your wicked ways and reform your actions; do not follow other gods to serve them. Then you will live in the land I have given to you and your fathers." But you have not paid attention or listened to me. [16]The descendants of Jonadab son of Recab have carried out the command their forefather gave them, but these people have not obeyed me.'

[17]"Therefore, this is what the LORD God Almighty, the God of Israel, says: 'Listen! I am going to bring on Judah and on everyone living in Jerusalem every disaster I pronounced against them. I spoke to them, but they did not listen; I called to them, but they did not answer.'"

[18]Then Jeremiah said to the family of the Recabites, "This is what the LORD Almighty, the God of Israel, says: 'You have obeyed the command of your forefather Jonadab and have followed all his instructions and have done everything he ordered.' [19]Therefore, this is what the LORD Almighty, the God of Israel, says: 'Jonadab son of Recab will never fail to have a man to serve me.'"

Jehoiakim Burns Jeremiah's Scroll

36 In the fourth year of Jehoiakim son of Josiah king of Judah, this word came to Jeremiah from the LORD: [2]"Take a scroll and write on it all the words I have spoken to you concerning Israel, Judah and all the other nations from the time I began speaking to you in the reign of Josiah till now. [3]Perhaps when the people of Judah hear about every disaster I plan to inflict on them, each of them will turn from his wicked way; then I will forgive their wickedness and their sin."

[4]So Jeremiah called Baruch son of Neriah, and while Jeremiah dictated all the words the LORD had spoken to him, Baruch wrote them on the scroll. [5]Then Jeremiah told Baruch, "I am restricted; I cannot go to the LORD's temple. [6]So you go to the house of the LORD on a day of fasting and read to the people from the scroll the words of the LORD that you wrote as I dictated. Read them to all the people of Judah who come in from their towns. [7]Perhaps they will bring their petition before the LORD, and each will turn from his wicked ways, for the anger and wrath pronounced against this people by the LORD are great."

[8]Baruch son of Neriah did everything Jeremiah the prophet told him to do; at the LORD's temple he read the words of the LORD from the scroll. [9]In the ninth month of the fifth year of Jehoiakim son of Josiah king of Judah, a time of fasting before the LORD was proclaimed for all the people in Jerusalem and those who had come from the towns of Judah. [10]From the room of Gemariah son of

Recabites pleases God (vv. 13–16)? How will they be rewarded (vv. 18–19)? What is the object lesson in this for Judah (see 33:18)? For you?

1. The Recabites refused to take the "modern way" of Judah. Who in your world is like these Recabites: Any "communal nomads"? Any "puritan reformers"? Any "Christian radicals"? Any "loyal traditionalists"? What can you and your church learn from such steadfast pace-setters? 2. Is yours an alternative lifestyle—distinct from that of your peers at work, school or neighborhood? What one thing distinguishes you? 3. How should Christians be separate from the rest of society, yet live close enough so that others can tell what motivates us? In what respect is your small group a pace-setter for those around you?

1. Have you ever been vandalized? What happened? How did it make you feel? 2. If you wrote a book, who would be the last person you'd want to read it? Who is your harshest critic? Your easiest? 3. How often have you tried excusing yourself for not turning in a paper by saying something like, "My dog ate it!"? Did that ever really happen?

1. What roles did Jeremiah, Baruch and the Lord each play in producing the first version of the Book of Jeremiah (vv. 1–4,17–18)? Why might a written account fare better than nearly 20 years of preaching? 2. Why do you think Jeremiah is banned from the temple area (vv. 5–7; see 26:7–11)? Who might have called the time of fasting (v. 9): The king? The priests? The Lord? 3. Why do the officials tell Baruch and Jeremiah to hide (vv. 16–19)? How has the family of Shaphan treated Jeremiah in the past (see 26:24)? Why must they tell the king? 4. What review does the king give Jeremiah's book (vv. 22–24)? How would you

compare Jehoiakim's "critique" with what King Josiah did upon rediscovering God's word (see 2Ki 22:11–23:3)? **5.** How must Jeremiah have felt when he heard the fate of the scroll? How did the Lord address that felt need and the cockiness of Jehoiakim (vv. 27–31; see 2Ki 24:1)? **6.** What is the point of writing it all down again (vv. 28,32; compare Ex 34:1)? What extra words might have appeared in the second version of the book of Jeremiah?

1. Have you ever persisted in a task for years despite legal opposition and a total lack of visible success? What would motivate you (or anyone) to persist? **2.** Why do you think officials sympathetic to Jeremiah did not stand up to the king? What would decisive action have cost them? Ever "look the other way" when something unjust or unethical was going on? **3.** How do people today show disdain for God's word? Do you honor it? How so? **4.** How do the events of this chapter account for the patch-work quilt shape and non-chronological order of the current Book of Jeremiah? (For instance, if this book were in chronological order, chapter 45 would come in between 36:8 and 36:9.) **5.** What is your explanation, based in part on this chapter, of *how* the Word of God came to be written in the words of men?

Shaphan the secretary, which was in the upper courtyard at the entrance of the New Gate of the temple, Baruch read to all the people at the LORD's temple the words of Jeremiah from the scroll.

[11]When Micaiah son of Gemariah, the son of Shaphan, heard all the words of the LORD from the scroll, [12]he went down to the secretary's room in the royal palace, where all the officials were sitting: Elishama the secretary, Delaiah son of Shemaiah, Elnathan son of Acbor, Gemariah son of Shaphan, Zedekiah son of Hananiah, and all the other officials. [13]After Micaiah told them everything he had heard Baruch read to the people from the scroll, [14]all the officials sent Jehudi son of Nethaniah, the son of Shelemiah, the son of Cushi, to say to Baruch, "Bring the scroll from which you have read to the people and come." So Baruch son of Neriah went to them with the scroll in his hand. [15]They said to him, "Sit down, please, and read it to us."

So Baruch read it to them. [16]When they heard all these words, they looked at each other in fear and said to Baruch, "We must report all these words to the king." [17]Then they asked Baruch, "Tell us, how did you come to write all this? Did Jeremiah dictate it?"

[18]"Yes," Baruch replied, "he dictated all these words to me, and I wrote them in ink on the scroll."

[19]Then the officials said to Baruch, "You and Jeremiah, go and hide. Don't let anyone know where you are."

[20]After they put the scroll in the room of Elishama the secretary, they went to the king in the courtyard and reported everything to him. [21]The king sent Jehudi to get the scroll, and Jehudi brought it from the room of Elishama the secretary and read it to the king and all the officials standing beside him. [22]It was the ninth month and the king was sitting in the winter apartment, with a fire burning in the firepot in front of him. [23]Whenever Jehudi had read three or four columns of the scroll, the king cut them off with a scribe's knife and threw them into the firepot, until the entire scroll was burned in the fire. [24]The king and all his attendants who heard all these words showed no fear, nor did they tear their clothes. [25]Even though Elnathan, Delaiah and Gemariah urged the king not to burn the scroll, he would not listen to them. [26]Instead, the king commanded Jerahmeel, a son of the king, Seraiah son of Azriel and Shelemiah son of Abdeel to arrest Baruch the scribe and Jeremiah the prophet. But the LORD had hidden them.

[27]After the king burned the scroll containing the words that Baruch had written at Jeremiah's dictation, the word of the LORD came to Jeremiah: [28]"Take another scroll and write on it all the words that were on the first scroll, which Jehoiakim king of Judah burned up. [29]Also tell Jehoiakim king of Judah, 'This is what the LORD says: You burned that scroll and said, "Why did you write on it that the king of Babylon would certainly come and destroy this land and cut off both men and animals from it?" [30]Therefore, this is what the LORD says about Jehoiakim king of Judah: He will have no one to sit on the throne of David; his body will be thrown out and exposed to the heat by day and the frost by night. [31]I will punish him and his children and his attendants for their wickedness; I will bring on them and those living in Jerusalem and the people of Judah every disaster I pronounced against them, because they have not listened.'"

[32]So Jeremiah took another scroll and gave it to the scribe Baruch son of Neriah, and as Jeremiah dictated, Baruch wrote on it all the words of the scroll that Jehoiakim king of Judah had burned in the fire. And many similar words were added to them.

Jeremiah in Prison

37 Zedekiah son of Josiah was made king of Judah by Nebuchadnezzar king of Babylon; he reigned in place of Jehoiachin[a] son of Jehoiakim. ²Neither he nor his attendants nor the people of the land paid any attention to the words the LORD had spoken through Jeremiah the prophet.

³King Zedekiah, however, sent Jehucal son of Shelemiah with the priest Zephaniah son of Maaseiah to Jeremiah the prophet with this message: "Please pray to the LORD our God for us."

⁴Now Jeremiah was free to come and go among the people, for he had not yet been put in prison. ⁵Pharaoh's army had marched out of Egypt, and when the Babylonians[b] who were besieging Jerusalem heard the report about them, they withdrew from Jerusalem.

⁶Then the word of the LORD came to Jeremiah the prophet: ⁷"This is what the LORD, the God of Israel, says: Tell the king of Judah, who sent you to inquire of me, 'Pharaoh's army, which has marched out to support you, will go back to its own land, to Egypt. ⁸Then the Babylonians will return and attack this city; they will capture it and burn it down.'

⁹"This is what the LORD says: Do not deceive yourselves, thinking, 'The Babylonians will surely leave us.' They will not! ¹⁰Even if you were to defeat the entire Babylonian[c] army that is attacking you and only wounded men were left in their tents, they would come out and burn this city down."

¹¹After the Babylonian army had withdrawn from Jerusalem because of Pharaoh's army, ¹²Jeremiah started to leave the city to go to the territory of Benjamin to get his share of the property among the people there. ¹³But when he reached the Benjamin Gate, the captain of the guard, whose name was Irijah son of Shelemiah, the son of Hananiah, arrested him and said, "You are deserting to the Babylonians!"

¹⁴"That's not true!" Jeremiah said. "I am not deserting to the Babylonians." But Irijah would not listen to him; instead, he arrested Jeremiah and brought him to the officials. ¹⁵They were angry with Jeremiah and had him beaten and imprisoned in the house of Jonathan the secretary, which they had made into a prison.

¹⁶Jeremiah was put into a vaulted cell in a dungeon, where he remained a long time. ¹⁷Then King Zedekiah sent for him and had him brought to the palace, where he asked him privately, "Is there any word from the LORD?"

"Yes," Jeremiah replied, "you will be handed over to the king of Babylon."

¹⁸Then Jeremiah said to King Zedekiah, "What crime have I committed against you or your officials or this people, that you have put me in prison? ¹⁹Where are your prophets who prophesied to you, 'The king of Babylon will not attack you or this land'? ²⁰But now, my lord the king, please listen. Let me bring my petition before you: Do not send me back to the house of Jonathan the secretary, or I will die there."

²¹King Zedekiah then gave orders for Jeremiah to be placed in the courtyard of the guard and given bread from the street of the bakers each day until all the bread in the city was gone. So Jeremiah remained in the courtyard of the guard.

---

1. Have you ever been to jail or a prison? As a tourist, visitor or resident? How long were you "in for"? How did the place make you feel? 2. What makes someone your best friend? How many best friends have you had?

---

1. Chapter 37 moves forward 20 years, once again (see 20:2), to Jeremiah's sufferings under Zedekiah. What fulfilled prophecy links this chapter with the previous one (v. 1; see 36:30; 2Ki 24:17–20)? 2. What events led to the siege and later withdrawal by Babylon (vv. 5,7,11; see 2Ki 25:1–2)? Where do you think Jeremiah stands in the public opinion polls of that day? 3. How would you make sense of Zedekiah's feelings about the prophet (vv. 2–3,16–17)? Why does he respect him at times and ignore him at others? 4. Why does Jeremiah try leaving the city (vv. 11–13; 32:8)? Why doesn't Irijah believe him (see 21:8–10)? Would you have been suspicious, or trusting, of Jeremiah? 5. How does God use evil events (recorded in vv. 14–21) for Jeremiah's welfare and Zedekiah's downfall? How does Jeremiah show his ability to think on his feet? Why is he persuasive?

---

1. At what points can you empathize with the main characters in this story: (a) I predicted doom that did not come to pass? (b) I warned people against a course of action, only to find them ignoring me and prospering to boot? (c) I once hoped someone would suffer so that I could be proved right? (d) I feel my motives are often mistrusted? Choose one to explain further. 2. Do you know people who only want to hear the "God's will" that matches their own (no names)? Do you waver on God sometimes yourself? What did Jesus say about such behavior (see Rev 3:15–16)? 3. Jeremiah had a trust problem, not altogether of his making. How is trust built and broken? How can trust be rebuilt?

---

a1 Hebrew *Coniah*, a variant of *Jehoiachin*   b5 Or *Chaldeans*; also in verses 8, 9, 13 and 14   c10 Or *Chaldean*; also in verse 11

1. Has your car ever gotten stuck in the mud or snow? How did you get out? 2. What is your favorite odd item of clothing? Why are you attached to it?

1. Why does this "gang of four" have it in for Jeremiah (vv. 1–4; 21:1; 37:3)? 2. How and why does Zedekiah appear "wimpish" (vv. 5–6,10)? Why not just kill Jeremiah outright? In using a cistern so publicly accessible (v. 6), what might the king be secretly hoping? 3. Who stands up for Jeremiah and why (vv. 7–9; see 39:18)? Why the details about the 30 men and the old rags? 4. Is this a retelling of the same story recorded in 37:16–21? Has Jeremiah been thrown in different cisterns, or the same one twice? Why do you think so?

1. Are you "stuck in the mud" or "climbing the walls" right now? Is it from: (a) An accident? (b) All work, no play? (c) Enemy? (d) No friends? What would be solid ground to you? 2. What has been your spiritual low point? Where did you receive help? Were any "old rags" or trusted friends used in your rescue? 3. Like King Zedekiah, do you come off as "everyone's friend," even "wishy-washy"? Explain. 4. What are you (your group or your church) doing for the human rights of political prisoners and detainees?

1. Do you find it easier to give or to receive advice? Why? What advice do you have on giving or asking for advice? 2. Have you ever been entrusted with a secret which you (accidentally) passed on to others? Are there secrets you've never told? (Don't start now.) Any secrets of yours you hope someone else is keeping?

1. Is Jeremiah reluctant to answer Zedekiah, or is he simply negotiating (vv. 14–15; compare Jesus' predicament, Lk 22:66–67)? Why has Zedekiah neither killed him nor heeded his advice? What does he stand to lose either way? 2. What question does the king actually ask (vv. 16–19)? What question do you deduce from Jeremiah's answer? Is this message different from others in the past (see 21:9–10; 32:3–5;

Jeremiah Thrown Into a Cistern

38 Shephatiah son of Mattan, Gedaliah son of Pashhur, Jehucal[a] son of Shelemiah, and Pashhur son of Malkijah heard what Jeremiah was telling all the people when he said, [2]"This is what the LORD says: 'Whoever stays in this city will die by the sword, famine or plague, but whoever goes over to the Babylonians[b] will live. He will escape with his life; he will live.' [3]And this is what the LORD says: 'This city will certainly be handed over to the army of the king of Babylon, who will capture it.'"

[4]Then the officials said to the king, "This man should be put to death. He is discouraging the soldiers who are left in this city, as well as all the people, by the things he is saying to them. This man is not seeking the good of these people but their ruin."

[5]"He is in your hands," King Zedekiah answered. "The king can do nothing to oppose you."

[6]So they took Jeremiah and put him into the cistern of Malkijah, the king's son, which was in the courtyard of the guard. They lowered Jeremiah by ropes into the cistern; it had no water in it, only mud, and Jeremiah sank down into the mud.

[7]But Ebed-Melech, a Cushite,[c] an official[d] in the royal palace, heard that they had put Jeremiah into the cistern. While the king was sitting in the Benjamin Gate, [8]Ebed-Melech went out of the palace and said to him, [9]"My lord the king, these men have acted wickedly in all they have done to Jeremiah the prophet. They have thrown him into a cistern, where he will starve to death when there is no longer any bread in the city."

[10]Then the king commanded Ebed-Melech the Cushite, "Take thirty men from here with you and lift Jeremiah the prophet out of the cistern before he dies."

[11]So Ebed-Melech took the men with him and went to a room under the treasury in the palace. He took some old rags and worn-out clothes from there and let them down with ropes to Jeremiah in the cistern. [12]Ebed-Melech the Cushite said to Jeremiah, "Put these old rags and worn-out clothes under your arms to pad the ropes." Jeremiah did so, [13]and they pulled him up with the ropes and lifted him out of the cistern. And Jeremiah remained in the courtyard of the guard.

Zedekiah Questions Jeremiah Again

[14]Then King Zedekiah sent for Jeremiah the prophet and had him brought to the third entrance to the temple of the LORD. "I am going to ask you something," the king said to Jeremiah. "Do not hide anything from me."

[15]Jeremiah said to Zedekiah, "If I give you an answer, will you not kill me? Even if I did give you counsel, you would not listen to me."

[16]But King Zedekiah swore this oath secretly to Jeremiah: "As surely as the LORD lives, who has given us breath, I will neither kill you nor hand you over to those who are seeking your life."

[17]Then Jeremiah said to Zedekiah, "This is what the LORD God Almighty, the God of Israel, says: 'If you surrender to the officers of the king of Babylon, your life will be spared and this city will not be burned down; you and your family will live. [18]But if you will not surrender to the officers of the king of Babylon, this city will be handed over to the Babylonians and they will burn it down; you yourself will not escape from their hands.'"

a1 Hebrew *Jucal,* a variant of *Jehucal*   b2 Or *Chaldeans;* also in verses 18, 19 and 23
c7 Probably from the upper Nile region   d7 Or *a eunuch*

[19]King Zedekiah said to Jeremiah, "I am afraid of the Jews who have gone over to the Babylonians, for the Babylonians may hand me over to them and they will mistreat me."

[20]"They will not hand you over," Jeremiah replied. "Obey the LORD by doing what I tell you. Then it will go well with you, and your life will be spared. [21]But if you refuse to surrender, this is what the LORD has revealed to me: [22]All the women left in the palace of the king of Judah will be brought out to the officials of the king of Babylon. Those women will say to you:

> "'They misled you and overcame you—
>   those trusted friends of yours.
> Your feet are sunk in the mud;
>   your friends have deserted you.'

[23]"All your wives and children will be brought out to the Babylonians. You yourself will not escape from their hands but will be captured by the king of Babylon; and this city will[a] be burned down."

[24]Then Zedekiah said to Jeremiah, "Do not let anyone know about this conversation, or you may die. [25]If the officials hear that I talked with you, and they come to you and say, 'Tell us what you said to the king and what the king said to you; do not hide it from us or we will kill you,' [26]then tell them, 'I was pleading with the king not to send me back to Jonathan's house to die there.'"

[27]All the officials did come to Jeremiah and question him, and he told him everything the king had ordered him to say. So they said no more to him, for no one had heard his conversation with the king.

[28]And Jeremiah remained in the courtyard of the guard until the day Jerusalem was captured.

The Fall of Jerusalem

39 This is how Jerusalem was taken: [1]In the ninth year of Zedekiah king of Judah, in the tenth month, Nebuchadnezzar king of Babylon marched against Jerusalem with his whole army and laid siege to it. [2]And on the ninth day of the fourth month of Zedekiah's eleventh year, the city wall was broken through. [3]Then all the officials of the king of Babylon came and took seats in the Middle Gate: Nergal-Sharezer of Samgar, Nebo-Sarsekim[b] a chief officer, Nergal-Sharezer a high official and all the other officials of the king of Babylon. [4]When Zedekiah king of Judah and all the soldiers saw them, they fled; they left the city at night by way of the king's garden, through the gate between the two walls, and headed toward the Arabah.[c]

[5]But the Babylonian[d] army pursued them and overtook Zedekiah in the plains of Jericho. They captured him and took him to Nebuchadnezzar king of Babylon at Riblah in the land of Hamath, where he pronounced sentence on him. [6]There at Riblah the king of Babylon slaughtered the sons of Zedekiah before his eyes and also killed all the nobles of Judah. [7]Then he put out Zedekiah's eyes and bound him with bronze shackles to take him to Babylon.

[8]The Babylonians[e] set fire to the royal palace and the houses of the people and broke down the walls of Jerusalem. [9]Nebuzaradan commander of the imperial guard carried into exile to Babylon the people who remained in the city, along with those who had gone over to him, and the rest of the people. [10]But Nebuzaradan the commander of the guard left behind in the land of Judah some of

34:2–5; 38:2–3)? **3.** Why is the king afraid to surrender (v. 19)? Who else is he afraid of (vv. 16,24–26)? What word fits Zedekiah's situation? **4.** Jeremiah says there is only one path to save the city (vv. 17–18,20–23). Which path do you think he'll take? **5.** Was it right for Jeremiah to tell the officials a half-truth (vv. 26–27)? What would you have done here?

1. Have you ever been in a no-win situation? If it looked like you'd be "damned if you did and damned if you didn't," how did you decide the best way to lose? **2.** Who do you know who shows interest in Christ time after time but never really takes the step of faith? What fears lie behind the mixed feelings? Do you have any mixed feelings about following God all the way? Explain. **3.** Is the omission of true and relevant facts the same as lying? Do you always try to tell the whole truth, or is there a time for misleading silence, as in Jeremiah's case?

1. What "family" movie have you seen recently that had far too much violence in your opinion? What about violence attracts (and repels) you? **2.** What is the longest you have gone without eating? Was it planned or forced on you? How did you "break fast"?

1. Imagine living in Jerusalem during the two-year Babylonian siege (vv. 1–2; also 2Ki 25:1–3). What would you fear the most: (a) Giving up the stones in my house to buttress the walls? (b) Not knowing when the end would come? (c) Sure death by sword? (d) Slow death by famine? **2.** Jeremiah has been predicting the fall of Jerusalem ever since he was first called by the Lord some 40 years earlier (vv. 1–3; compare 1:14–16). How many kings have heard his message since then (see 1:2–3; 2Ki 22:1; 23:31,36; 24:8,18)? **3.** What violence is Zedekiah forced to endure, which he would sooner have not seen (vv. 5–9)? Do you feel sympathy for him? Why or why not? **4.** Who does Nebuchadnezzar (and the Lord) spare and why (vv. 9–10,12–14,16–18)? Why does

---

a23 Or and you will cause this city to Sarsekim   *b3 Or Nergal-Sharezer, Samgar-Nebo,*   *c4 Or the Jordan Valley*   *d5 Or Chaldean*   *e8 Or Chaldeans*

Babylon deport the ruling class and leave the poor people to tend the land (see 2Ki 24:12–14)? **5.** Why does Nebuchadnezzar treat Jeremiah so well? Has Jeremiah sold out (see 27:12; 37:13)? Or is he in debt only to the Shaphan family (v. 14; see 27:24)? **6.** Why is God sparing Ebed-Melech (vv. 15–18; see 38:10)?

1. When have you been in a no-win situation, as was Jeremiah? Whom did God use to get you out of this tough spot? **2.** How do you think Jeremiah (and God) felt when the city finally fell? **3.** To whom could you show kindness and help out of a tough spot?

Ever wish you could start over with a clean slate? Did you ever try it? What happened?

1. What "word" comes to Jeremiah (v. 1; see 39:11–14)? **2.** How has Jeremiah's prediction about Ramah (see 31:15) come true in his day? In Jesus' day (see Mt 2:18)? **3.** Why does Nebuzaradan grasp what no Judean king ever did (vv. 2–3)? Why would he host Jeremiah in Babylon (v. 4)? **4.** Why does Jeremiah say "no" (vv. 5–6)?

1. How do you respond to unexpected setbacks: Complain? Fight? Rebound? Give up? Give a recent example. **2.** Ever been freed by a non-believer to pursue God's will? How did that feel?

1. Which assassination do you remember most clearly: Gandhi? Kennedy? Martin Luther King? Anwar Sadat? Other? Which affected you most deeply? Why? **2.** Do you have any hobby collections? What lengths do you go to get these? **3.** Are you a "pack-rat," collecting everything? If you had to suddenly clear out all your stuff, what would be the last to go?

1. What sort of governor was Gedaliah (40:7)? What were the Jewish guerrilla commanders concerned about (40:8–10)? **2.** Why do the Jewish refugees from the war return to Judah

the poor people, who owned nothing; and at that time he gave them vineyards and fields.

[11]Now Nebuchadnezzar king of Babylon had given these orders about Jeremiah through Nebuzaradan commander of the imperial guard: [12]"Take him and look after him; don't harm him but do for him whatever he asks." [13]So Nebuzaradan the commander of the guard, Nebushazban a chief officer, Nergal-Sharezer a high official and all the other officers of the king of Babylon [14]sent and had Jeremiah taken out of the courtyard of the guard. They turned him over to Gedaliah son of Ahikam, the son of Shaphan, to take him back to his home. So he remained among his own people.

[15]While Jeremiah had been confined in the courtyard of the guard, the word of the LORD came to him: [16]"Go and tell Ebed-Melech the Cushite, 'This is what the LORD Almighty, the God of Israel, says: I am about to fulfill my words against this city through disaster, not prosperity. At that time they will be fulfilled before your eyes. [17]But I will rescue you on that day, declares the LORD; you will not be handed over to those you fear. [18]I will save you; you will not fall by the sword but will escape with your life, because you trust in me, declares the LORD.'"

Jeremiah Freed

40 The word came to Jeremiah from the LORD after Nebuzaradan commander of the imperial guard had released him at Ramah. He had found Jeremiah bound in chains among all the captives from Jerusalem and Judah who were being carried into exile to Babylon. [2]When the commander of the guard found Jeremiah, he said to him, "The LORD your God decreed this disaster for this place. [3]And now the LORD has brought it about; he has done just as he said he would. All this happened because you people sinned against the LORD and did not obey him. [4]But today I am freeing you from the chains on your wrists. Come with me to Babylon, if you like, and I will look after you; but if you do not want to, then don't come. Look, the whole country lies before you; go wherever you please." [5]However, before Jeremiah turned to go,[a] Nebuzaradan added, "Go back to Gedaliah son of Ahikam, the son of Shaphan, whom the king of Babylon has appointed over the towns of Judah, and live with him among the people, or go anywhere else you please."

Then the commander gave him provisions and a present and let him go. [6]So Jeremiah went to Gedaliah son of Ahikam at Mizpah and stayed with him among the people who were left behind in the land.

Gedaliah Assassinated

[7]When all the army officers and their men who were still in the open country heard that the king of Babylon had appointed Gedaliah son of Ahikam as governor over the land and had put him in charge of the men, women and children who were the poorest in the land and who had not been carried into exile to Babylon, [8]they came to Gedaliah at Mizpah—Ishmael son of Nethaniah, Johanan and Jonathan the sons of Kareah, Seraiah son of Tanhumeth, the sons of Ephai the Netophathite, and Jaazaniah[b] the son of the Maacathite, and their men. [9]Gedaliah son of Ahikam, the son of Shaphan, took an oath to reassure them and their men. "Do not be afraid to serve the Babylonians,[c]" he said. "Settle down in the land and serve the king of Babylon, and it will go well with you. [10]I

[a]5 Or *Jeremiah answered*   [b]8 Hebrew *Jezaniah*, a variant of *Jaazaniah*   [c]9 Or *Chaldeans*; also in verse 10

myself will stay at Mizpah to represent you before the Babylonians who come to us, but you are to harvest the wine, summer fruit and oil, and put them in your storage jars, and live in the towns you have taken over."

¹¹When all the Jews in Moab, Ammon, Edom and all the other countries heard that the king of Babylon had left a remnant in Judah and had appointed Gedaliah son of Ahikam, the son of Shaphan, as governor over them, ¹²they all came back to the land of Judah, to Gedaliah at Mizpah, from all the countries where they had been scattered. And they harvested an abundance of wine and summer fruit.

¹³Johanan son of Kareah and all the army officers still in the open country came to Gedaliah at Mizpah ¹⁴and said to him, "Don't you know that Baalis king of the Ammonites has sent Ishmael son of Nethaniah to take your life?" But Gedaliah son of Ahikam did not believe them.

¹⁵Then Johanan son of Kareah said privately to Gedaliah in Mizpah, "Let me go and kill Ishmael son of Nethaniah, and no one will know it. Why should he take your life and cause all the Jews who are gathered around you to be scattered and the remnant of Judah to perish?"

¹⁶But Gedaliah son of Ahikam said to Johanan son of Kareah, "Don't do such a thing! What you are saying about Ishmael is not true."

41 In the seventh month Ishmael son of Nethaniah, the son of Elishama, who was of royal blood and had been one of the king's officers, came with ten men to Gedaliah son of Ahikam at Mizpah. While they were eating together there, ²Ishmael son of Nethaniah and the ten men who were with him got up and struck down Gedaliah son of Ahikam, the son of Shaphan, with the sword, killing the one whom the king of Babylon had appointed as governor over the land. ³Ishmael also killed all the Jews who were with Gedaliah at Mizpah, as well as the Babylonian*a* soldiers who were there.

⁴The day after Gedaliah's assassination, before anyone knew about it, ⁵eighty men who had shaved off their beards, torn their clothes and cut themselves came from Shechem, Shiloh and Samaria, bringing grain offerings and incense with them to the house of the LORD. ⁶Ishmael son of Nethaniah went out from Mizpah to meet them, weeping as he went. When he met them, he said, "Come to Gedaliah son of Ahikam." ⁷When they went into the city, Ishmael son of Nethaniah and the men who were with him slaughtered them and threw them into a cistern. ⁸But ten of them said to Ishmael, "Don't kill us! We have wheat and barley, oil and honey, hidden in a field." So he let them alone and did not kill them with the others. ⁹Now the cistern where he threw all the bodies of the men he had killed along with Gedaliah was the one King Asa had made as part of his defense against Baasha king of Israel. Ishmael son of Nethaniah filled it with the dead.

¹⁰Ishmael made captives of all the rest of the people who were in Mizpah—the king's daughters along with all the others who were left there, over whom Nebuzaradan commander of the imperial guard had appointed Gedaliah son of Ahikam. Ishmael son of Nethaniah took them captive and set out to cross over to the Ammonites.

¹¹When Johanan son of Kareah and all the army officers who were with him heard about all the crimes Ishmael son of Nethani-

(40:11–12)? What are their alternatives? What alternative is Ishmael pursuing and why (40:14–41:1)? **3.** Why would Baalis support this assassination plot? Why does Gedaliah find such a plot incredible? What is Gedaliah's "fatal flaw"? **4.** Why do the 80 Samaritans come to Judah (41:5; see 16:6–7)? Why does Ishmael ambush them (41:7–8)? What political statement is made in filling King Asa's cistern with the dead (41:9; see 1Ki 15:16–22)? **5.** Ishmael could set up rule at Mizpah and declare war on Babylon. Why doesn't he (41:10–12)? Why is his leadership divided? **6.** To this day, Jews commemorate the assassination of Gedaliah with a day of fasting. Why do you think this event was so significant?

♡ **1.** Do you think Gedaliah was right not to make a preemptive strike at Ishmael? Why or why not? What else could he have done to protect himself? **2.** Are you a good judge of character? What sorts of things influence your impressions? Have you ever seriously misjudged someone's intentions towards you? **3.** Is there any situation in which you are tempted to take matters into your own hands and rid yourself of the person you can't get along with? If violence only begets more violence, why do you do it? If running away from your problems or striking first doesn't solve your problems, what does?

*a*3 Or *Chaldean*

ah had committed, [12]they took all their men and went to fight Ishmael son of Nethaniah. They caught up with him near the great pool in Gibeon. [13]When all the people Ishmael had with him saw Johanan son of Kareah and the army officers who were with him, they were glad. [14]All the people Ishmael had taken captive at Mizpah turned and went over to Johanan son of Kareah. [15]But Ishmael son of Nethaniah and eight of his men escaped from Johanan and fled to the Ammonites.

Flight to Egypt

[16]Then Johanan son of Kareah and all the army officers who were with him led away all the survivors from Mizpah whom he had recovered from Ishmael son of Nethaniah after he had assassinated Gedaliah son of Ahikam: the soldiers, women, children and court officials he had brought from Gibeon. [17]And they went on, stopping at Geruth Kimham near Bethlehem on their way to Egypt [18]to escape the Babylonians.[a] They were afraid of them because Ishmael son of Nethaniah had killed Gedaliah son of Ahikam, whom the king of Babylon had appointed as governor over the land.

42 Then all the army officers, including Johanan son of Kareah and Jezaniah[b] son of Hoshaiah, and all the people from the least to the greatest approached [2]Jeremiah the prophet and said to him, "Please hear our petition and pray to the LORD your God for this entire remnant. For as you now see, though we were once many, now only a few are left. [3]Pray that the LORD your God will tell us where we should go and what we should do."

[4]"I have heard you," replied Jeremiah the prophet. "I will certainly pray to the LORD your God as you have requested; I will tell you everything the LORD says and will keep nothing back from you."

[5]Then they said to Jeremiah, "May the LORD be a true and faithful witness against us if we do not act in accordance with everything the LORD your God sends you to tell us. [6]Whether it is favorable or unfavorable, we will obey the LORD our God, to whom we are sending you, so that it will go well with us, for we will obey the LORD our God."

[7]Ten days later the word of the LORD came to Jeremiah. [8]So he called together Johanan son of Kareah and all the army officers who were with him and all the people from the least to the greatest. [9]He said to them, "This is what the LORD, the God of Israel, to whom you sent me to present your petition, says: [10]'If you stay in this land, I will build you up and not tear you down; I will plant you and not uproot you, for I am grieved over the disaster I have inflicted on you. [11]Do not be afraid of the king of Babylon, whom you now fear. Do not be afraid of him, declares the LORD, for I am with you and will save you and deliver you from his hands. [12]I will show you compassion so that he will have compassion on you and restore you to your land.'

[13]"However, if you say, 'We will not stay in this land,' and so disobey the LORD your God, [14]and if you say, 'No, we will go and live in Egypt, where we will not see war or hear the trumpet or be hungry for bread,' [15]then hear the word of the LORD, O remnant of Judah. This is what the LORD Almighty, the God of Israel, says: 'If you are determined to go to Egypt and you do go to settle there, [16]then the sword you fear will overtake you there, and the famine you dread will follow you into Egypt, and there you will die. [17]In-

1. When lost, do you just keep driving, or do you stop to ask for directions? How long have you been lost before you finally decided to consult a map? 2. What type of stone best describes you: Hefty boulder in the way? Diamond in the rough? Bedrock that can't be penetrated? Brick for building? Pebble for a sling shot? Other? Explain.

1. Why are the army officers afraid, even though they had nothing to do with Gedaliah's murder (41:16–18; see 2Ki 25:25–26)? How might Nebuchadnezzar interpret the act? What are their options? What is "Plan A"? 2. Are the people sincere in seeking guidance (42:2–6)? Why ask Jeremiah, if their minds are already made up? 3. What do you suppose they were thinking about during the 10 day delay, waiting to hear from God (42:7)? What do you think Jeremiah did during those 10 days? 4. What does God tell them and why (42:8–18)? What is wrong with the Jews following their natural instincts and "getting out of the kitchen if you can't stand the heat (the Babylonians)"? Why would they want to live in Egypt anyway? 5. How does Jeremiah's counsel go over (43:2–3)? Does this surprise you after hearing all their promises? Or could you tell that their minds were already made up? How so? Why would they accuse Baruch of manipulating him? What do they think the Babylonians will do to them (43:3)? Why might they suspect Jeremiah and Baruch are not afraid? 6. Do you suppose Jeremiah and Baruch go along to Egypt willingly or unwillingly (43:4–6)? What was Egypt's relationship with Babylon (see 37:5; 2Ki 24:7)? How would Nebuchadnezzar interpret a flight to Egypt? 7. What message does God give Jeremiah at the Egyptian border and why (43:8–13)?

1. Review the dialogue this past week between you and others. When were your questions really statements? When were your

deed, all who are determined to go to Egypt to settle there will die by the sword, famine and plague; not one of them will survive or escape the disaster I will bring on them.' [18]This is what the LORD Almighty, the God of Israel, says: 'As my anger and wrath have been poured out on those who lived in Jerusalem, so will my wrath be poured out on you when you go to Egypt. You will be an object of cursing and horror, of condemnation and reproach; you will never see this place again.'

[19]"O remnant of Judah, the LORD has told you, 'Do not go to Egypt.' Be sure of this: I warn you today [20]that you made a fatal mistake[a] when you sent me to the LORD your God and said, 'Pray to the LORD our God for us; tell us everything he says and we will do it.' [21]I have told you today, but you still have not obeyed the LORD your God in all he sent me to tell you. [22]So now, be sure of this: You will die by the sword, famine and plague in the place where you want to go to settle."

43 When Jeremiah finished telling the people all the words of the LORD their God—everything the LORD had sent him to tell them— [2]Azariah son of Hoshaiah and Johanan son of Kareah and all the arrogant men said to Jeremiah, "You are lying! The LORD our God has not sent you to say, 'You must not go to Egypt to settle there.' [3]But Baruch son of Neriah is inciting you against us to hand us over to the Babylonians,[b] so they may kill us or carry us into exile to Babylon."

[4]So Johanan son of Kareah and all the army officers and all the people disobeyed the LORD's command to stay in the land of Judah. [5]Instead, Johanan son of Kareah and all the army officers led away all the remnant of Judah who had come back to live in the land of Judah from all the nations where they had been scattered. [6]They also led away all the men, women and children and the king's daughters whom Nebuzaradan commander of the imperial guard had left with Gedaliah son of Ahikam, the son of Shaphan, and Jeremiah the prophet and Baruch son of Neriah. [7]So they entered Egypt in disobedience to the LORD and went as far as Tahpanhes.

[8]In Tahpanhes the word of the LORD came to Jeremiah: [9]"While the Jews are watching, take some large stones with you and bury them in clay in the brick pavement at the entrance to Pharaoh's palace in Tahpanhes. [10]Then say to them, 'This is what the LORD Almighty, the God of Israel, says: I will send for my servant Nebuchadnezzar king of Babylon, and I will set his throne over these stones I have buried here; he will spread his royal canopy above them. [11]He will come and attack Egypt, bringing death to those destined for death, captivity to those destined for captivity, and the sword to those destined for the sword. [12]He[c] will set fire to the temples of the gods of Egypt; he will burn their temples and take their gods captive. As a shepherd wraps his garment around him, so will he wrap Egypt around himself and depart from there unscathed. [13]There in the temple of the sun[d] in Egypt he will demolish the sacred pillars and will burn down the temples of the gods of Egypt.'"

Disaster Because of Idolatry

44 This word came to Jeremiah concerning all the Jews living in Lower Egypt—in Migdol, Tahpanhes and Memphis[e]— and in Upper Egypt[f]: [2]"This is what the LORD Almighty, the God of Israel, says: You saw the great disaster I brought on Jerusalem and on all the towns of Judah. Today they lie deserted and in ruins

---

statements really questions? Do you have trouble being direct? When is it toughest to ask what you really want to know or say how you really feel? **2.** In your decision-making process this past week, at what point did you seek God's counsel? The input of others? Did you truly want advice, or simply a blessing on your plans? **3.** Have you ever obeyed God's word to you at a time when all your gut instincts said "no"? What happened as a result of your obedience? **4.** When in doubt about someone's intentions, do you assume the best or the worst? Are you naturally trusting or skeptical? Has anyone ever doubted your integrity, as they did Jeremiah's? Why? **5.** Do you prefer to call the shots in work situations? In relationships? What do you find objectionable about submitting to someone? When was the last time you deliberately surrendered control? What happened? **6.** Have you ever felt beyond God's reach? Did God reach you, after all? How so? Do you know anyone who feels "out of touch" with God? How can you help?

---

1. What "famous last words" have you had to eat recently? How did you feel when the other person got the last laugh? **2.** When have you crowed, "I told you so," over a similar fate happening to someone else? **3.** Do you picture God as King or Queen? Is it possible to visualize God as neither male nor female?

---

[a]20 Or you erred in your hearts   [b]3 Or Chaldeans   [c]12 Or I   [d]13 Or in Heliopolis   [e]1 Hebrew Noph   [f]1 Hebrew in Pathros

📖 **1.** The Jews fleeing the scene of the crime (Gedaliah's murder) plus any who had been deported earlier (see 2Ki 23:34) make up the "large assembly" (vv. 1,15) to hear what would be Jeremiah's last recorded prophecy. In this word of the Lord, what does Jeremiah try to explain (vv. 2–6)? **2.** What have the Jews in Egypt done (vv. 7–10)? Does this surprise you, in light of all Judah has suffered? Why are they honoring Ishtar or the "Queen of Heaven" (vv. 17–18; compare 7:17–19)? What must their opinion of Yahweh be? **3.** What does God promise in return (vv. 11–14)? Who will the "few fugitives" be? Does Jeremiah's prophecy surprise you? **4.** Why do you think this story of apostasy keeps playing over and over, with only the names or places changing? **5.** What prophecy does Jeremiah make as a sign (vv. 29–30)? Hophra was deposed and executed a few years later. What impact do you think Jeremiah's accurate prediction would have on the Jews? Would that impact be any different than a current prediction of some astrologer coming true within a few years? **6.** This chapter gives the end of Jeremiah's story as we know it. Was his 40-odd years of prophecy a failure? How would you gauge success as a prophet?

❤️ **1.** How can people hear God's word, see God's power and yet still misunderstand the message? In what sense were you like that with your parents? In what sense are you like that with your Parent in Heaven? **2.** Would you say your life has been a success so far? On what basis? What constitutes a failure: (a) Falling short of a goal? (b) Not seeing any results for all your effort? (c) Not trying hard enough? (d) Making mistakes? (e) Not making any mistakes? **3.** Looking at our world's often sordid and bloody history, would you say God has been a success? Can God fail, or can he only succeed? **4.** Martin Luther examined his conscience by contemplating the "regrets" in his life. What do you regret? Do you have a lot of regrets? How do "regrets" point to sin? What do you do with "regrets"?

³because of the evil they have done. They provoked me to anger by burning incense and by worshiping other gods that neither they nor you nor your fathers ever knew. ⁴Again and again I sent my servants the prophets, who said, 'Do not do this detestable thing that I hate!' ⁵But they did not listen or pay attention; they did not turn from their wickedness or stop burning incense to other gods. ⁶Therefore, my fierce anger was poured out; it raged against the towns of Judah and the streets of Jerusalem and made them the desolate ruins they are today.

⁷"Now this is what the LORD God Almighty, the God of Israel, says: Why bring such great disaster on yourselves by cutting off from Judah the men and women, the children and infants, and so leave yourselves without a remnant? ⁸Why provoke me to anger with what your hands have made, burning incense to other gods in Egypt, where you have come to live? You will destroy yourselves and make yourselves an object of cursing and reproach among all the nations on earth. ⁹Have you forgotten the wickedness committed by your fathers and by the kings and queens of Judah and the wickedness committed by you and your wives in the land of Judah and the streets of Jerusalem? ¹⁰To this day they have not humbled themselves or shown reverence, nor have they followed my law and the decrees I set before you and your fathers.

¹¹"Therefore, this is what the LORD Almighty, the God of Israel, says: I am determined to bring disaster on you and to destroy all Judah. ¹²I will take away the remnant of Judah who were determined to go to Egypt to settle there. They will all perish in Egypt; they will fall by the sword or die from famine. From the least to the greatest, they will die by sword or famine. They will become an object of cursing and horror, of condemnation and reproach. ¹³I will punish those who live in Egypt with the sword, famine and plague, as I punished Jerusalem. ¹⁴None of the remnant of Judah who have gone to live in Egypt will escape or survive to return to the land of Judah, to which they long to return and live; none will return except a few fugitives."

¹⁵Then all the men who knew that their wives were burning incense to other gods, along with all the women who were present—a large assembly—and all the people living in Lower and Upper Egypt,ᵃ said to Jeremiah, ¹⁶"We will not listen to the message you have spoken to us in the name of the LORD! ¹⁷We will certainly do everything we said we would: We will burn incense to the Queen of Heaven and will pour out drink offerings to her just as we and our fathers, our kings and our officials did in the towns of Judah and in the streets of Jerusalem. At that time we had plenty of food and were well off and suffered no harm. ¹⁸But ever since we stopped burning incense to the Queen of Heaven and pouring out drink offerings to her, we have had nothing and have been perishing by sword and famine."

¹⁹The women added, "When we burned incense to the Queen of Heaven and poured out drink offerings to her, did not our husbands know that we were making cakes like her image and pouring out drink offerings to her?"

²⁰Then Jeremiah said to all the people, both men and women, who were answering him, ²¹"Did not the LORD remember and think about the incense burned in the towns of Judah and the streets of Jerusalem by you and your fathers, your kings and your officials and the people of the land? ²²When the LORD could no longer endure your wicked actions and the detestable things you

ᵃ15 Hebrew *in Egypt and Pathros*

did, your land became an object of cursing and a desolate waste without inhabitants, as it is today. [23]Because you have burned incense and have sinned against the LORD and have not obeyed him or followed his law or his decrees or his stipulations, this disaster has come upon you, as you now see."

[24]Then Jeremiah said to all the people, including the women, "Hear the word of the LORD, all you people of Judah in Egypt. [25]This is what the LORD Almighty, the God of Israel, says: You and your wives have shown by your actions what you promised when you said, 'We will certainly carry out the vows we made to burn incense and pour out drink offerings to the Queen of Heaven.'

"Go ahead then, do what you promised! Keep your vows! [26]But hear the word of the LORD, all Jews living in Egypt: 'I swear by my great name,' says the LORD, 'that no one from Judah living anywhere in Egypt will ever again invoke my name or swear, "As surely as the Sovereign LORD lives." [27]For I am watching over them for harm, not for good; the Jews in Egypt will perish by sword and famine until they are all destroyed. [28]Those who escape the sword and return to the land of Judah from Egypt will be very few. Then the whole remnant of Judah who came to live in Egypt will know whose word will stand—mine or theirs.

[29]" 'This will be the sign to you that I will punish you in this place,' declares the LORD, 'so that you will know that my threats of harm against you will surely stand.' [30]This is what the LORD says: 'I am going to hand Pharaoh Hophra king of Egypt over to his enemies who seek his life, just as I handed Zedekiah king of Judah over to Nebuchadnezzar king of Babylon, the enemy who was seeking his life.' "

A Message to Baruch

45 This is what Jeremiah the prophet told Baruch son of Neriah in the fourth year of Jehoiakim son of Josiah king of Judah, after Baruch had written on a scroll the words Jeremiah was then dictating: [2]"This is what the LORD, the God of Israel, says to you, Baruch: [3]You said, 'Woe to me! The LORD has added sorrow to my pain; I am worn out with groaning and find no rest.' "

[4]⌊The LORD said,⌋ "Say this to him: 'This is what the LORD says: I will overthrow what I have built and uproot what I have planted, throughout the land. [5]Should you then seek great things for yourself? Seek them not. For I will bring disaster on all people, declares the LORD, but wherever you go I will let you escape with your life.' "

A Message About Egypt

46 This is the word of the LORD that came to Jeremiah the prophet concerning the nations:

[2]Concerning Egypt:

This is the message against the army of Pharaoh Neco king of Egypt, which was defeated at Carchemish on the Euphrates River by Nebuchadnezzar king of Babylon in the fourth year of Jehoiakim son of Josiah king of Judah:

[3]"Prepare your shields, both large and small,
    and march out for battle!
[4]Harness the horses,
    mount the steeds!
Take your positions
    with helmets on!

---

1. Why is Baruch so tired (see 36:4,27–28)? **2.** Is God very consoling to him? What "great things" might Baruch want? What "great thing" does God promise? **3.** Why this post-script here?

Are you ambitious for great things, or satisfied with very little? Illustrate.

---

1. What image comes to mind at the word "Egypt"? Do you have any desire to visit there? **2.** How do you relate to a horse: (a) Like horsing around? (b) Could eat a horse? (c) Work horse? (d) Other? **3.** How long does it take you to get ready for a night out? What takes the most time? What does this say about you?

---

1. This chapter resumes the oracles against the nations first introduced in chapter 25. Why does Neco march against Nebuchadnezzar (v. 8; see 37:5–7)? Who would the people of Judah want to win and why? **2.** Why does Jeremiah prophesy defeat for

Egypt? What is Egypt's problem (vv. 15,25)? Why does God favor the pagan Babylonians (see Eze 29:19–20)? **3.** Apart from the immediate participants, who comes out the winner in this prophecy (compare Isa 19:23–25)? Who stands to lose the most? **4.** Thirty years later Nebuchadnezzar carries the war back into Egypt (vv. 13–17,19–21)? Why do many soldiers desert? **5.** Will Egypt be different after the dust settles (v. 26)? **6.** What does disciplined "only with justice" mean (v. 28)? What other types of discipline are there?

♡ **1.** Do you think God is as involved with world affairs today? Is God only involved with Christian nations? Do you think Nebuchadnezzar attacked Egypt out of conscious obedience to the Lord? Why or why not? **2.** How visible is God's plan and power, apart from the eyes of faith? Where do you see God's activity in your world, or don't you? **3.** Are you troubled by the direction of the world or concerned about humanity's future? What is your role in our fate? What is God's role? The church's? World government's? **4.** Have you lived through a trying time, learned lots of lessons and then gone to ways "as in times past" when the dust settled? How can you make a lesson once learned stick for all time? Can the group help? **5.** Do you "stumble repeatedly" (v. 16) over the same problem? Why is it hard to get up and walk straight? Is God the one "pushing you down" (v. 15; see Jas 1:12–15, for the difference between a trial and a temptation)? **6.** Have you ever missed your opportunity (v. 17) when its time finally came? Why did you hesitate to follow through? Was it something you really didn't want, or something you thought you might not deserve?

Polish your spears,
  put on your armor!
5What do I see?
  They are terrified,
  they are retreating,
    their warriors are defeated.
They flee in haste
  without looking back,
  and there is terror on every side,"
                        declares the LORD.
6"The swift cannot flee
  nor the strong escape.
In the north by the River Euphrates
  they stumble and fall.

7"Who is this that rises like the Nile,
  like rivers of surging waters?
8Egypt rises like the Nile,
  like rivers of surging waters.
She says, 'I will rise and cover the earth;
  I will destroy cities and their people.'
9Charge, O horses!
  Drive furiously, O charioteers!
March on, O warriors—
  men of Cush[a] and Put who carry shields,
  men of Lydia who draw the bow.
10But that day belongs to the Lord, the LORD
    Almighty—
  a day of vengeance, for vengeance on his foes.
The sword will devour till it is satisfied,
  till it has quenched its thirst with blood.
For the Lord, the LORD Almighty, will offer
    sacrifice
  in the land of the north by the River Euphrates.

11"Go up to Gilead and get balm,
  O Virgin Daughter of Egypt.
But you multiply remedies in vain;
  there is no healing for you.
12The nations will hear of your shame;
  your cries will fill the earth.
One warrior will stumble over another;
  both will fall down together."

13This is the message the LORD spoke to Jeremiah the prophet about the coming of Nebuchadnezzar king of Babylon to attack Egypt:

14"Announce this in Egypt, and proclaim it in
    Migdol;
  proclaim it also in Memphis[b] and Tahpanhes:
'Take your positions and get ready,
  for the sword devours those around you.'
15Why will your warriors be laid low?
  They cannot stand, for the LORD will push them
    down.
16They will stumble repeatedly;
  they will fall over each other.
They will say, 'Get up, let us go back

---

[a]9 That is, the upper Nile region   [b]14 Hebrew *Noph*; also in verse 19

to our own people and our native lands,
    away from the sword of the oppressor.'
[17]There they will exclaim,
    'Pharaoh king of Egypt is only a loud noise;
    he has missed his opportunity.'

[18]"As surely as I live," declares the King,
    whose name is the LORD Almighty,
"one will come who is like Tabor among the
      mountains,
    like Carmel by the sea.
[19]Pack your belongings for exile,
    you who live in Egypt,
for Memphis will be laid waste
    and lie in ruins without inhabitant.

[20]"Egypt is a beautiful heifer,
    but a gadfly is coming
    against her from the north.
[21]The mercenaries in her ranks
    are like fattened calves.
They too will turn and flee together,
    they will not stand their ground,
for the day of disaster is coming upon them,
    the time for them to be punished.
[22]Egypt will hiss like a fleeing serpent
    as the enemy advances in force;
they will come against her with axes,
    like men who cut down trees.
[23]They will chop down her forest,"
                declares the LORD,
    "dense though it be.
They are more numerous than locusts,
    they cannot be counted.
[24]The Daughter of Egypt will be put to shame,
    handed over to the people of the north."

[25]The LORD Almighty, the God of Israel, says: "I am about to
bring punishment on Amon god of Thebes,[a] on Pharaoh, on Egypt
and her gods and her kings, and on those who rely on Pharaoh. [26]I
will hand them over to those who seek their lives, to Nebuchadnezzar king of Babylon and his officers. Later, however, Egypt will
be inhabited as in times past," declares the LORD.

[27]"Do not fear, O Jacob my servant;
    do not be dismayed, O Israel.
I will surely save you out of a distant place,
    your descendants from the land of their exile.
Jacob will again have peace and security,
    and no one will make him afraid.
[28]Do not fear, O Jacob my servant,
    for I am with you," declares the LORD.
"Though I completely destroy all the nations
    among which I scatter you,
    I will not completely destroy you.
I will discipline you but only with justice;
    I will not let you go entirely unpunished."

[a]25 Hebrew No

1. If you could have traded fathers when you were a kid, whose dad would you have taken? Why? **2.** What war interests you the most? Why is war intriguing?

1. What do your five senses tell you is happening in this prophecy? **2.** How were relations between Judah and Philistia in the past (see Jdg 13:1; 1Sa 18:25–27)? **3.** Why has God ordered the sword against the Philistines (vv. 6–7; see Eze 25:15–17)? (Note: Ashkelon was attacked by Nebuchadnezzar in 604 B.C., in partial fulfillment of this prophecy.)

1. What determines who wins battles: Superior equipment? Stronger forces? Better strategy? Something else? **2.** What would you call an "overflowing torrent" (v. 2) on today's scene? What can be done about it? **3.** Do you know anyone who has fought in a war or lived in a war zone? What do wars accomplish? Are they acts of God's wrath, or the results of man's folly? Explain.

---

1. Where do you keep your family records: With a relative? In a family Bible? Safe deposit box? Museum of Natural History? **2.** What one fact or story do you think would distinguish your family tree from the others in your small group? **3.** In school, did you ever study much about this country's bordering neighbors? What can you recall about their population? GNP? History? Geography? **4.** If you were a news reporter, which "beat" would you like to be assigned: Foreign War? Government intrigue? Movies & TV? Business? Sports? Love life? Other? Explain.

1. How are Judah and Moab related (see Ge 19:36–37)? Where is Moab located? How many towns does Jeremiah mention (vv. 1–5,21–24)? Why do you think he knows so much? **2.** Who is the "local god" of the Moabites (v. 7; see 1Ki 11:7,33)? Although

A Message About the Philistines

47 This is the word of the LORD that came to Jeremiah the prophet concerning the Philistines before Pharaoh attacked Gaza:

²This is what the LORD says:

"See how the waters are rising in the north;
they will become an overflowing torrent.
They will overflow the land and everything in it,
the towns and those who live in them.
The people will cry out;
all who dwell in the land will wail
³at the sound of the hoofs of galloping steeds,
at the noise of enemy chariots
and the rumble of their wheels.
Fathers will not turn to help their children;
their hands will hang limp.
⁴For the day has come
to destroy all the Philistines
and to cut off all survivors
who could help Tyre and Sidon.
The LORD is about to destroy the Philistines,
the remnant from the coasts of Caphtor.ᵃ
⁵Gaza will shave her head in mourning;
Ashkelon will be silenced.
O remnant on the plain,
how long will you cut yourselves?

⁶" 'Ah, sword of the LORD,' ⌐you cry,⌐
'how long till you rest?
Return to your scabbard;
cease and be still.'
⁷But how can it rest
when the LORD has commanded it,
when he has ordered it
to attack Ashkelon and the coast?"

A Message About Moab

48 Concerning Moab:

This is what the LORD Almighty, the God of Israel, says:

"Woe to Nebo, for it will be ruined.
Kiriathaim will be disgraced and captured;
the strongholdᵇ will be disgraced and
shattered.
²Moab will be praised no more;
in Heshbonᶜ men will plot her downfall:
'Come, let us put an end to that nation.'
You too, O Madmen,ᵈ will be silenced;
the sword will pursue you.
³Listen to the cries from Horonaim,
cries of great havoc and destruction.
⁴Moab will be broken;
her little ones will cry out.ᵉ
⁵They go up the way to Luhith,
weeping bitterly as they go;

ᵃ4 That is, Crete   ᵇ1 Or / Misgab   ᶜ2 The Hebrew for *Heshbon* sounds like the Hebrew for *plot*.   ᵈ2 The name of the Moabite town Madmen sounds like the Hebrew for *be silenced*.   ᵉ4 Hebrew; Septuagint / *proclaim it to Zoar*

on the road down to Horonaim
   anguished cries over the destruction are heard.
⁶Flee! Run for your lives;
   become like a bush*a* in the desert.
⁷Since you trust in your deeds and riches,
   you too will be taken captive,
and Chemosh will go into exile,
   together with his priests and officials.
⁸The destroyer will come against every town,
   and not a town will escape.
The valley will be ruined
   and the plateau destroyed,
   because the LORD has spoken.
⁹Put salt on Moab,
   for she will be laid waste*b*;
her towns will become desolate,
   with no one to live in them.

¹⁰"A curse on him who is lax in doing the LORD's
   work!
A curse on him who keeps his sword from
   bloodshed!

¹¹"Moab has been at rest from youth,
   like wine left on its dregs,
not poured from one jar to another—
   she has not gone into exile.
So she tastes as she did,
   and her aroma is unchanged.
¹²But days are coming,"
   declares the LORD,
"when I will send men who pour from jars,
   and they will pour her out;
they will empty her jars
   and smash her jugs.
¹³Then Moab will be ashamed of Chemosh,
   as the house of Israel was ashamed
   when they trusted in Bethel.

¹⁴"How can you say, 'We are warriors,
   men valiant in battle'?
¹⁵Moab will be destroyed and her towns invaded;
   her finest young men will go down in the
     slaughter,"
   declares the King, whose name is the LORD
     Almighty.
¹⁶"The fall of Moab is at hand;
   her calamity will come quickly.
¹⁷Mourn for her, all who live around her,
   all who know her fame;
say, 'How broken is the mighty scepter,
   how broken the glorious staff!'

¹⁸"Come down from your glory
   and sit on the parched ground,
   O inhabitants of the Daughter of Dibon,
for he who destroys Moab
   will come up against you
   and ruin your fortified cities.

Yahweh has not given them the Jewish Law, what does he expect from Moab (v. 13; see 1Ki 12:26–30)? **3.** Besides worshiping Chemosh, what has Moab done to Judah (vv. 26–27; see 2Ki 24:1–2)? What was the prevailing attitude about Judah's plight (v. 29)? **4.** What product was Moab particularly famous for (vv. 11–12,32–33)? What form of political domination is Moab going to suffer for the first time? When Moab was invaded by the Babylonians soon after the fall of Judah, who occupied their land (see Eze 25:10)? **5.** Verses 36–38 describe an ancient Middle Eastern funeral. Why do you think these things were done? **6.** Around 150 years earlier, Isaiah prophesied against Moab (see Isa 15). Why do you think Jeremiah's language is so similar? **7.** How final does Moab's defeat sound to you?

♡ **1.** Are there any long-standing feuds in your family? What issues do relatives fight over? What punishments do they exact? Why is it so easy for family members to be so hard on each other? **2.** Why does God condemn pride and arrogance so severely? What is evil about them? Where do they turn up in your life? **3.** The Moabites no longer exist as a national group. What do you make of God's promise to "restore their fortunes"? **4.** Does seeing and hearing about disasters from the media affect you anymore? What is the affect of broadcasting disaster after disaster every day? How can you keep from being hardened to the suffering of others in the world? **5.** Have you ever had the last laugh on a boss? Parent? Schoolyard bully? How did it feel? Has anyone had the last laugh on you? Is there ever a last laugh?

*a*6 Or *like Aroer*   *b*9 Or *Give wings to Moab, / for she will fly away*

¹⁹Stand by the road and watch,
　you who live in Aroer.
Ask the man fleeing and the woman escaping,
　ask them, 'What has happened?'
²⁰Moab is disgraced, for she is shattered.
　Wail and cry out!
Announce by the Arnon
　that Moab is destroyed.
²¹Judgment has come to the plateau—
　to Holon, Jahzah and Mephaath,
²² 　to Dibon, Nebo and Beth Diblathaim,
²³ 　to Kiriathaim, Beth Gamul and Beth Meon,
²⁴ 　to Kerioth and Bozrah—
to all the towns of Moab, far and near.
²⁵Moab's horn[a] is cut off;
　her arm is broken,"

declares the LORD.

²⁶"Make her drunk,
　for she has defied the LORD.
Let Moab wallow in her vomit;
　let her be an object of ridicule.
²⁷Was not Israel the object of your ridicule?
　Was she caught among thieves,
that you shake your head in scorn
　whenever you speak of her?
²⁸Abandon your towns and dwell among the rocks,
　you who live in Moab.
Be like a dove that makes its nest
　at the mouth of a cave.

²⁹"We have heard of Moab's pride—
　her overweening pride and conceit,
her pride and arrogance
　and the haughtiness of her heart.
³⁰I know her insolence but it is futile,"

declares the LORD,

　"and her boasts accomplish nothing.
³¹Therefore I wail over Moab,
　for all Moab I cry out,
I moan for the men of Kir Hareseth.
³²I weep for you, as Jazer weeps,
　O vines of Sibmah.
Your branches spread as far as the sea;
　they reached as far as the sea of Jazer.
The destroyer has fallen
　on your ripened fruit and grapes.
³³Joy and gladness are gone
　from the orchards and fields of Moab.
I have stopped the flow of wine from the presses;
　no one treads them with shouts of joy.
Although there are shouts,
　they are not shouts of joy.

³⁴"The sound of their cry rises
　from Heshbon to Elealeh and Jahaz,
from Zoar as far as Horonaim and Eglath
　　Shelishiyah,
　for even the waters of Nimrim are dried up.

---

a25 *Horn* here symbolizes strength.

³⁵In Moab I will put an end
    to those who make offerings on the high places
    and burn incense to their gods,"
                        declares the LORD.
³⁶"So my heart laments for Moab like a flute;
    it laments like a flute for the men of Kir
        Hareseth.
    The wealth they acquired is gone.
³⁷Every head is shaved
    and every beard cut off;
    every hand is slashed
    and every waist is covered with sackcloth.
³⁸On all the roofs in Moab
    and in the public squares
    there is nothing but mourning,
    for I have broken Moab
    like a jar that no one wants,"
                        declares the LORD.
³⁹"How shattered she is! How they wail!
    How Moab turns her back in shame!
    Moab has become an object of ridicule,
    an object of horror to all those around her."

⁴⁰This is what the LORD says:

"Look! An eagle is swooping down,
    spreading its wings over Moab.
⁴¹Kerioth*ᵃ* will be captured
    and the strongholds taken.
In that day the hearts of Moab's warriors
    will be like the heart of a woman in labor.
⁴²Moab will be destroyed as a nation
    because she defied the LORD.
⁴³Terror and pit and snare await you,
    O people of Moab,"
                        declares the LORD.
⁴⁴"Whoever flees from the terror
    will fall into a pit,
    whoever climbs out of the pit
    will be caught in a snare;
    for I will bring upon Moab
    the year of her punishment,"
                        declares the LORD.

⁴⁵"In the shadow of Heshbon
    the fugitives stand helpless,
    for a fire has gone out from Heshbon,
    a blaze from the midst of Sihon;
    it burns the foreheads of Moab,
    the skulls of the noisy boasters.
⁴⁶Woe to you, O Moab!
    The people of Chemosh are destroyed;
    your sons are taken into exile
    and your daughters into captivity.

⁴⁷"Yet I will restore the fortunes of Moab
    in days to come,"
                        declares the LORD.

Here ends the judgment on Moab.

ᵃ41 Or The cities

1. Are you a world traveler or a homebody? Why? 2. If you could learn instantly, what new language would you learn? Why?

1. Where is Ammon? And Gad? How are Judah, Moab and Ammon related (see Ge 19:36–38)? 2. What do you make of verse 1? Who is Molech (vv. 1,3; see 2Ki 23:13–14)? Why do the Ammonites trust him (v. 4)? How much are riches and prosperity the basis of military strength today? 3. Is the promised restoration an afterthought (v. 6; see Eze 25:7) or the highlight?

1. Ammon enjoyed the "fruits" of land that belonged to someone else. Of which countries is that true today? Is it true of this country? 2. Do you benefit from cheap land and labor in another country? What can you do to make the distribution of goods more equitable? Can the group help?

1. If you could painlessly learn a foreign language and cheaply travel in a foreign country, where would you go? Which countries might you consider living in as a foreign ambassador? Which ones, due to their naked violence, would you be sure to avoid? 2. What is your favorite way of acquainting yourself with a foreign culture: Movies? Gourmet clubs? Host International students? Travel abroad? National Geographic specials? In this way which countries do you know best?

1. From whom do the Edomites descend (see Ge 25:29–30; 36:6–8)? Where is their country? What kind of land is it? For what quality are they known (v. 7; see Ob 8; also Job 2:11, where this quality is typified in Job's friends)? 2. The crimes of

A Message About Ammon

49 Concerning the Ammonites:

This is what the LORD says:

"Has Israel no sons?
  Has she no heirs?
Why then has Molech[a] taken possession of Gad?
  Why do his people live in its towns?
²But the days are coming,"
  declares the LORD,
"when I will sound the battle cry
  against Rabbah of the Ammonites;
it will become a mound of ruins,
  and its surrounding villages will be set on fire.
Then Israel will drive out
  those who drove her out,"
                                 says the LORD.
³"Wail, O Heshbon, for Ai is destroyed!
  Cry out, O inhabitants of Rabbah!
Put on sackcloth and mourn;
  rush here and there inside the walls,
for Molech will go into exile,
  together with his priests and officials.
⁴Why do you boast of your valleys,
  boast of your valleys so fruitful?
O unfaithful daughter,
  you trust in your riches and say,
  'Who will attack me?'
⁵I will bring terror on you
  from all those around you,"
                  declares the Lord, the LORD Almighty.
"Every one of you will be driven away,
  and no one will gather the fugitives.

⁶"Yet afterward, I will restore the fortunes of the
  Ammonites,"
                                 declares the LORD.

A Message About Edom

⁷Concerning Edom:

This is what the LORD Almighty says:

"Is there no longer wisdom in Teman?
  Has counsel perished from the prudent?
  Has their wisdom decayed?
⁸Turn and flee, hide in deep caves,
  you who live in Dedan,
for I will bring disaster on Esau
  at the time I punish him.
⁹If grape pickers came to you,
  would they not leave a few grapes?
If thieves came during the night,
  would they not steal only as much as they
    wanted?
¹⁰But I will strip Esau bare;
  I will uncover his hiding places,
  so that he cannot conceal himself.

a 1 Or their king; Hebrew malcam; also in verse 3

His children, relatives and neighbors will perish,
   and he will be no more.
[11]Leave your orphans; I will protect their lives.
   Your widows too can trust in me."

[12]This is what the LORD says: "If those who do not deserve to drink the cup must drink it, why should you go unpunished? You will not go unpunished, but must drink it. [13]I swear by myself," declares the LORD, "that Bozrah will become a ruin and an object of horror, of reproach and of cursing; and all its towns will be in ruins forever."

[14]I have heard a message from the LORD:
   An envoy was sent to the nations to say,
   "Assemble yourselves to attack it!
   Rise up for battle!"

[15]"Now I will make you small among the nations,
   despised among men.
[16]The terror you inspire
   and the pride of your heart have deceived you,
   you who live in the clefts of the rocks,
   who occupy the heights of the hill.
Though you build your nest as high as the eagle's,
   from there I will bring you down,"
                              declares the LORD.
[17]"Edom will become an object of horror;
   all who pass by will be appalled and will scoff
   because of all its wounds.
[18]As Sodom and Gomorrah were overthrown,
   along with their neighboring towns,"
                              says the LORD,
"so no one will live there;
   no man will dwell in it.

[19]"Like a lion coming up from Jordan's thickets
   to a rich pastureland,
I will chase Edom from its land in an instant.
   Who is the chosen one I will appoint for this?
Who is like me and who can challenge me?
   And what shepherd can stand against me?"
[20]Therefore, hear what the LORD has planned against Edom,
   what he has purposed against those who live in Teman:
The young of the flock will be dragged away;
   he will completely destroy their pasture because of them.
[21]At the sound of their fall the earth will tremble;
   their cry will resound to the Red Sea.[a]
[22]Look! An eagle will soar and swoop down,
   spreading its wings over Bozrah.
In that day the hearts of Edom's warriors
   will be like the heart of a woman in labor.

A Message About Damascus

[23]Concerning Damascus:

   "Hamath and Arpad are dismayed,
   for they have heard bad news.

[a]21 Hebrew *Yam Suph*; that is, Sea of Reeds

Edom are well known to Jeremiah's hearers, but they are only hinted at here. What have they done (vv. 12,16; see Eze 25:12; Am 1:11; Ob 10–14)? **3.** How extensive would God's wrath be (see Eze 25:13–14)? Why are orphans and widows exempt from this wrath (v. 11)? **4.** God is compared to a lion and an eagle (vv. 19,22). Which image do you think fits God best? **5.** Why do you think God makes the people no promise of restoration, as he does for the Egyptians, Moabites and Ammonites (see 46:26; 48:47; 49:6)?

1. Have you ever been afraid of God? When and why? What does it mean to "fear God" in the way Jeremiah advises? **2.** The flip side of every virtue is a vice, and so it was with Edom's wisdom. How can intellect hinder spiritual growth? How can it help? What is the role of intelligence in your spiritual life? **3.** Of the "orphans and widows" in your world, for whom can you be an instrument of God's mercy? **4.** What "eagle's nest" (fortress mentality) have you built to feel secure in your private world? How secure are you, really? How has God broken through that to bring you to himself?

Ever sail the open seas? Ever get seasick? Are you pretty much a "landlubber"? Why?

1. Where is Damascus? In what state does Jeremiah see the cities of Syria? **2.** Who is

They are disheartened,
  troubled like[a] the restless sea.
²⁴Damascus has become feeble,
  she has turned to flee
  and panic has gripped her;
anguish and pain have seized her,
  pain like that of a woman in labor.
²⁵Why has the city of renown not been abandoned,
  the town in which I delight?
²⁶Surely, her young men will fall in the streets;
  all her soldiers will be silenced in that day,"
        declares the Lord Almighty.
²⁷"I will set fire to the walls of Damascus;
  it will consume the fortresses of Ben-Hadad."

A Message About Kedar and Hazor

²⁸Concerning Kedar and the kingdoms of Hazor, which Nebuchadnezzar king of Babylon attacked:

This is what the Lord says:

  "Arise, and attack Kedar
    and destroy the people of the East.
²⁹Their tents and their flocks will be taken;
    their shelters will be carried off
    with all their goods and camels.
Men will shout to them,
  'Terror on every side!'

³⁰"Flee quickly away!
  Stay in deep caves, you who live in Hazor,"
        declares the Lord.
"Nebuchadnezzar king of Babylon has plotted
    against you;
  he has devised a plan against you.

³¹"Arise and attack a nation at ease,
  which lives in confidence,"
        declares the Lord,
  "a nation that has neither gates nor bars;
    its people live alone.
³²Their camels will become plunder,
  and their large herds will be booty.
I will scatter to the winds those who are in
    distant places[b]
  and will bring disaster on them from every
    side,"
        declares the Lord.

³³"Hazor will become a haunt of jackals,
  a desolate place forever.
No one will live there;
  no man will dwell in it."

A Message About Elam

³⁴This is the word of the Lord that came to Jeremiah the prophet concerning Elam, early in the reign of Zedekiah king of Judah:

³⁵This is what the Lord Almighty says:

  "See, I will break the bow of Elam,

a23 Hebrew *on* or *by*   b32 Or *who clip the hair by their foreheads*

the mainstay of their might.
36 I will bring against Elam the four winds
   from the four quarters of the heavens;
I will scatter them to the four winds,
   and there will not be a nation
   where Elam's exiles do not go.
37 I will shatter Elam before their foes,
   before those who seek their lives;
I will bring disaster upon them,
   even my fierce anger,"

declares the LORD.

"I will pursue them with the sword
   until I have made an end of them.
38 I will set my throne in Elam
   and destroy her king and officials,"

declares the LORD.

39 "Yet I will restore the fortunes of Elam
   in days to come,"

declares the LORD.

A Message About Babylon

50 This is the word the LORD spoke through Jeremiah the
prophet concerning Babylon and the land of the Babylonians[a]:

2 "Announce and proclaim among the nations,
   lift up a banner and proclaim it;
   keep nothing back, but say,
'Babylon will be captured;
   Bel will be put to shame,
   Marduk filled with terror.
Her images will be put to shame
   and her idols filled with terror.'
3 A nation from the north will attack her
   and lay waste her land.
No one will live in it;
   both men and animals will flee away.

4 "In those days, at that time,"
   declares the LORD,
"the people of Israel and the people of Judah
      together
   will go in tears to seek the LORD their God.
5 They will ask the way to Zion
   and turn their faces toward it.
They will come and bind themselves to the LORD
   in an everlasting covenant
   that will not be forgotten.

6 "My people have been lost sheep;
   their shepherds have led them astray
   and caused them to roam on the mountains.
They wandered over mountain and hill
   and forgot their own resting place.
7 Whoever found them devoured them;
   their enemies said, 'We are not guilty,

Their fate (also 9:16)? Who is to blame (see Eze 32:24–25)? **3.** Why do you think God promises to restore them, but not the people of Edom, Damascus, Kedar and Hazor? Is restoration only for those nations specified (see 46:26; 48:47; 49:6), or is it implied for the others as well (see Isa 11:11–12)?

1. What is your "claim to fame"? How would life look if God took that away from you? **2.** Did these nations ever hear Jeremiah's prophecies? For whose benefit were they intended? **3.** Do you learn from the hardships of others? What lesson did you pick up recently?

1. Who is the meanest looking person you know: Hulk Hogan (pro wrestler)? Sylvester Stallone (Rambo)? Other? **2.** Is your nominee more like a velvet-covered brick (soft on the outside, tough on the inside), or like a pretty tough cookie (with a soft, creamy inside)? **3.** Did you see the "Star Wars" movies? What impression do you have of Darth Vadar and the Empire? Does that evil empire remind you of any contemporary nations?

This is by far the longest of Jeremiah's oracles of judgment against foreign nations. To make it possible to complete this study in your usual allotted time, assign different readers to each major grouping of verses: 50:1–20; 50:21–46; 51:1–26; 51:27–39; 51:40–64; then answer the following questions from your respective sections. **1.** Just as he said in chapter 25, Jeremiah holds out the "cup of wrath" to Babylon. For what sins will they "drink the cup" (50:2,11,15,24,29,32,36; 51:9,24, 44,47,49,52; see Hab 1:6–11)? Which sins seem most foul-tasting to you? **2.** Who will God use to punish Babylon (50:3,9,41; 51:11, 14,27–28,53)? What does that tell you about what it will take to knock out this evil empire for good? **3.** What will be the effect on the Babylonians themselves (50:2–3,9–16, 21–27, 30–32, 35–40, 43–45; 51:1–4, 13–14, 20–23, 25–26, 29–33,36–44,52–58)? How can God punish Babylon for invading

---

a 1 Or *Chaldeans*; also in verses 8, 25, 35 and 45

Judah when he approved the invasion for his own purposes? What principle of retribution should any person or nation keep in mind when they go to war? **4.** What will be the effect on the nations of the world (50:2; 51:9,27,44,48)? How do you account for the different responses? **5.** What will be the effect on the Jews (50:4–8, 17–20, 28,33–34; 51:5–6,9–10,45–47, 50–51)? Why is it crucial that Israel and Judah take the initiative in seeking God? **6.** What is to be done with this message (51:59–63)? How would it comfort the exiles in Babylon? How is the fate of this scroll like the fate of Babylon (51:64)? **7.** How has God used the Babylonians to punish Judah (21:1–7)? Should the Jews have fought against them (21:8–10)? **8.** If a fall is imminent, why did Jeremiah tell the exiles earlier to settle into society? Why no mention of the 70 years (25:12)? How and why were they supposed to pray about the Babylonians (29:7)? **9.** What overall picture of God do you get from this prophecy and the preceding ones? **10.** Why do you think Jeremiah's prophecy ends with God's judgment on Babylon? How is this a fitting conclusion to the book?

1. Just because God uses a nation or a person to carry out his plan, does that mean God is pleased with them? Can you think of any other instances where God uses bad people to accomplish his will? What do these incidents tell you about God's power and plan? **2.** Does Babylon stand for anything else in prophecy, besides itself (see Rev 17–18)? If so, to what future event might these chapters point? **3.** What feelings and actions do you think God wanted these chapters to inspire in the Jews in exile? What feelings and actions does he want them to inspire in you? **4.** What do you need most in your life: (a) Destruction of enemies? (b) Restoration of fortunes? (c) Raised banner in the field? What would you like to see happen in one of these areas? **5.** If God did to you as you have done to others, what would be your fate? Do you sense a basic fairness in life: "What goes around comes around"? Or does life seem unfair or unpredictable?

for they sinned against the LORD, their true
        pasture,
    the LORD, the hope of their fathers.'

8"Flee out of Babylon;
    leave the land of the Babylonians,
    and be like the goats that lead the flock.
9For I will stir up and bring against Babylon
    an alliance of great nations from the land of the
        north.
They will take up their positions against her,
    and from the north she will be captured.
Their arrows will be like skilled warriors
    who do not return empty-handed.
10So Babylonia[a] will be plundered;
    all who plunder her will have their fill,"
                                    declares the LORD.

11"Because you rejoice and are glad,
    you who pillage my inheritance,
because you frolic like a heifer threshing grain
    and neigh like stallions,
12your mother will be greatly ashamed;
    she who gave you birth will be disgraced.
She will be the least of the nations—
    a wilderness, a dry land, a desert.
13Because of the LORD's anger she will not be
        inhabited
    but will be completely desolate.
All who pass Babylon will be horrified and scoff
    because of all her wounds.

14"Take up your positions around Babylon,
    all you who draw the bow.
Shoot at her! Spare no arrows,
    for she has sinned against the LORD.
15Shout against her on every side!
    She surrenders, her towers fall,
    her walls are torn down.
Since this is the vengeance of the LORD,
    take vengeance on her;
    do to her as she has done to others.
16Cut off from Babylon the sower,
    and the reaper with his sickle at harvest.
Because of the sword of the oppressor
    let everyone return to his own people,
    let everyone flee to his own land.

17"Israel is a scattered flock
    that lions have chased away.
The first to devour him
    was the king of Assyria;
the last to crush his bones
    was Nebuchadnezzar king of Babylon."

18Therefore this is what the LORD Almighty, the God of Israel, says:

"I will punish the king of Babylon and his land
    as I punished the king of Assyria.

a 10 Or *Chaldea*

¹⁹But I will bring Israel back to his own pasture
  and he will graze on Carmel and Bashan;
his appetite will be satisfied
  on the hills of Ephraim and Gilead.
²⁰In those days, at that time,"
  declares the LORD,
"search will be made for Israel's guilt,
  but there will be none,
and for the sins of Judah,
  but none will be found,
  for I will forgive the remnant I spare.

²¹"Attack the land of Merathaim
  and those who live in Pekod.
Pursue, kill and completely destroy*ᵃ them,"
                    declares the LORD.
  "Do everything I have commanded you.
²²The noise of battle is in the land,
  the noise of great destruction!
²³How broken and shattered
  is the hammer of the whole earth!
How desolate is Babylon
  among the nations!
²⁴I set a trap for you, O Babylon,
  and you were caught before you knew it;
you were found and captured
  because you opposed the LORD.
²⁵The LORD has opened his arsenal
  and brought out the weapons of his wrath,
for the Sovereign LORD Almighty has work to do
  in the land of the Babylonians.
²⁶Come against her from afar.
  Break open her granaries;
  pile her up like heaps of grain.
Completely destroy her
  and leave her no remnant.
²⁷Kill all her young bulls;
  let them go down to the slaughter!
Woe to them! For their day has come,
  the time for them to be punished.
²⁸Listen to the fugitives and refugees from Babylon
  declaring in Zion
how the LORD our God has taken vengeance,
  vengeance for his temple.

²⁹"Summon archers against Babylon,
  all those who draw the bow.
Encamp all around her;
  let no one escape.
Repay her for her deeds;
  do to her as she has done.
For she has defied the LORD,
  the Holy One of Israel.
³⁰Therefore, her young men will fall in the streets;
  all her soldiers will be silenced in that day,"
                    declares the LORD.
³¹"See, I am against you, O arrogant one,"
  declares the Lord, the LORD Almighty,

ᵃ21 The Hebrew term refers to the irrevocable giving over of things or persons to the
LORD, often by totally destroying them; also in verse 26.

"for your day has come,
     the time for you to be punished.
³²The arrogant one will stumble and fall
     and no one will help her up;
I will kindle a fire in her towns
     that will consume all who are around her."

³³This is what the LORD Almighty says:

"The people of Israel are oppressed,
     and the people of Judah as well.
All their captors hold them fast,
     refusing to let them go.
³⁴Yet their Redeemer is strong;
     the LORD Almighty is his name.
He will vigorously defend their cause
     so that he may bring rest to their land,
     but unrest to those who live in Babylon.

³⁵"A sword against the Babylonians!"
     declares the LORD—
"against those who live in Babylon
     and against her officials and wise men!
³⁶A sword against her false prophets!
     They will become fools.
A sword against her warriors!
     They will be filled with terror.
³⁷A sword against her horses and chariots
     and all the foreigners in her ranks!
     They will become women.
A sword against her treasures!
     They will be plundered.
³⁸A drought on^a her waters!
     They will dry up.
For it is a land of idols,
     idols that will go mad with terror.

³⁹"So desert creatures and hyenas will live there,
     and there the owl will dwell.
It will never again be inhabited
     or lived in from generation to generation.
⁴⁰As God overthrew Sodom and Gomorrah
     along with their neighboring towns,"
                                        declares the LORD,
"so no one will live there;
     no man will dwell in it.

⁴¹"Look! An army is coming from the north;
     a great nation and many kings
     are being stirred up from the ends of the earth.
⁴²They are armed with bows and spears;
     they are cruel and without mercy.
They sound like the roaring sea
     as they ride on their horses;
they come like men in battle formation
     to attack you, O Daughter of Babylon.
⁴³The king of Babylon has heard reports about
          them,
     and his hands hang limp.
Anguish has gripped him,

^a38 Or A sword against

pain like that of a woman in labor.
⁴⁴Like a lion coming up from Jordan's thickets
    to a rich pastureland,
I will chase Babylon from its land in an instant.
    Who is the chosen one I will appoint for this?
Who is like me and who can challenge me?
    And what shepherd can stand against me?"
⁴⁵Therefore, hear what the LORD has planned against
        Babylon,
    what he has purposed against the land of the
        Babylonians:
The young of the flock will be dragged away;
    he will completely destroy their pasture because
        of them.
⁴⁶At the sound of Babylon's capture the earth will
        tremble;
    its cry will resound among the nations.

51

This is what the LORD says:

"See, I will stir up the spirit of a destroyer
    against Babylon and the people of Leb Kamai.ᵃ
²I will send foreigners to Babylon
    to winnow her and to devastate her land;
they will oppose her on every side
    in the day of her disaster.
³Let not the archer string his bow,
    nor let him put on his armor.
Do not spare her young men;
    completely destroyᵇ her army.
⁴They will fall down slain in Babylon,ᶜ
    fatally wounded in her streets.
⁵For Israel and Judah have not been forsaken
    by their God, the LORD Almighty,
though their landᵈ is full of guilt
    before the Holy One of Israel.

⁶"Flee from Babylon!
    Run for your lives!
    Do not be destroyed because of her sins.
It is time for the LORD's vengeance;
    he will pay her what she deserves.
⁷Babylon was a gold cup in the LORD's hand;
    she made the whole earth drunk.
The nations drank her wine;
    therefore they have now gone mad.
⁸Babylon will suddenly fall and be broken.
    Wail over her!
Get balm for her pain;
    perhaps she can be healed.

⁹" 'We would have healed Babylon,
    but she cannot be healed;
let us leave her and each go to his own land,
    for her judgment reaches to the skies,
    it rises as high as the clouds.'

ᵃ1 Leb Kamai is a cryptogram for Chaldea, that is, Babylonia.   ᵇ3 The Hebrew term
refers to the irrevocable giving over of things or persons to the LORD, often by totally
destroying them.   ᶜ4 Or Chaldea   ᵈ5 Or / and the land ⌊of the Babylonians⌋

10 " 'The LORD has vindicated us;
    come, let us tell in Zion
    what the LORD our God has done.'

11 "Sharpen the arrows,
    take up the shields!
The LORD has stirred up the kings of the Medes,
    because his purpose is to destroy Babylon.
The LORD will take vengeance,
    vengeance for his temple.
12 Lift up a banner against the walls of Babylon!
    Reinforce the guard,
station the watchmen,
    prepare an ambush!
The LORD will carry out his purpose,
    his decree against the people of Babylon.
13 You who live by many waters
    and are rich in treasures,
your end has come,
    the time for you to be cut off.
14 The LORD Almighty has sworn by himself:
    I will surely fill you with men, as with a swarm
        of locusts,
    and they will shout in triumph over you.

15 "He made the earth by his power;
    he founded the world by his wisdom
    and stretched out the heavens by his
        understanding.
16 When he thunders, the waters in the heavens
        roar;
    he makes clouds rise from the ends of the
        earth.
He sends lightning with the rain
    and brings out the wind from his storehouses.

17 "Every man is senseless and without knowledge;
    every goldsmith is shamed by his idols.
His images are a fraud;
    they have no breath in them.
18 They are worthless, the objects of mockery;
    when their judgment comes, they will perish.
19 He who is the Portion of Jacob is not like these,
    for he is the Maker of all things,
including the tribe of his inheritance—
    the LORD Almighty is his name.

20 "You are my war club,
    my weapon for battle—
with you I shatter nations,
    with you I destroy kingdoms,
21 with you I shatter horse and rider,
    with you I shatter chariot and driver,
22 with you I shatter man and woman,
    with you I shatter old man and youth,
    with you I shatter young man and maiden,
23 with you I shatter shepherd and flock,
    with you I shatter farmer and oxen,
    with you I shatter governors and officials.

24 "Before your eyes I will repay Babylon and all who live in

Babylonia*a* for all the wrong they have done in Zion," declares the
LORD.

> ²⁵"I am against you, O destroying mountain,
>   you who destroy the whole earth,"
>   declares the LORD.
> "I will stretch out my hand against you,
>   roll you off the cliffs,
>   and make you a burned-out mountain.
> ²⁶No rock will be taken from you for a cornerstone,
>   nor any stone for a foundation,
>   for you will be desolate forever,"
>   declares the LORD.

> ²⁷"Lift up a banner in the land!
>   Blow the trumpet among the nations!
> Prepare the nations for battle against her;
>   summon against her these kingdoms:
>   Ararat, Minni and Ashkenaz.
> Appoint a commander against her;
>   send up horses like a swarm of locusts.
> ²⁸Prepare the nations for battle against her—
>   the kings of the Medes,
> their governors and all their officials,
>   and all the countries they rule.
> ²⁹The land trembles and writhes,
>   for the LORD's purposes against Babylon stand—
> to lay waste the land of Babylon
>   so that no one will live there.
> ³⁰Babylon's warriors have stopped fighting;
>   they remain in their strongholds.
> Their strength is exhausted;
>   they have become like women.
> Her dwellings are set on fire;
>   the bars of her gates are broken.
> ³¹One courier follows another
>   and messenger follows messenger
> to announce to the king of Babylon
>   that his entire city is captured,
> ³²the river crossings seized,
>   the marshes set on fire,
>   and the soldiers terrified."

³³This is what the LORD Almighty, the God of Israel, says:

> "The Daughter of Babylon is like a threshing floor
>   at the time it is trampled;
>   the time to harvest her will soon come."

> ³⁴"Nebuchadnezzar king of Babylon has devoured
>   us,
>   he has thrown us into confusion,
>   he has made us an empty jar.
> Like a serpent he has swallowed us
>   and filled his stomach with our delicacies,
>   and then has spewed us out.
> ³⁵May the violence done to our flesh*b* be upon
>   Babylon,"
>   say the inhabitants of Zion.

a24 Or *Chaldea*; also in verse 35   *b35* Or *done to us and to our children*

"May our blood be on those who live in
    Babylonia,"
says Jerusalem.

³⁶Therefore, this is what the LORD says:

"See, I will defend your cause
    and avenge you;
I will dry up her sea
    and make her springs dry.
³⁷Babylon will be a heap of ruins,
    a haunt of jackals,
an object of horror and scorn,
    a place where no one lives.
³⁸Her people all roar like young lions,
    they growl like lion cubs.
³⁹But while they are aroused,
    I will set out a feast for them
    and make them drunk,
so that they shout with laughter—
    then sleep forever and not awake,"
                    declares the LORD.
⁴⁰"I will bring them down
    like lambs to the slaughter,
    like rams and goats.

⁴¹"How Sheshach^a will be captured,
    the boast of the whole earth seized!
What a horror Babylon will be
    among the nations!
⁴²The sea will rise over Babylon;
    its roaring waves will cover her.
⁴³Her towns will be desolate,
    a dry and desert land,
a land where no one lives,
    through which no man travels.
⁴⁴I will punish Bel in Babylon
    and make him spew out what he has
    swallowed.
The nations will no longer stream to him.
    And the wall of Babylon will fall.

⁴⁵"Come out of her, my people!
    Run for your lives!
    Run from the fierce anger of the LORD.
⁴⁶Do not lose heart or be afraid
    when rumors are heard in the land;
one rumor comes this year, another the next,
    rumors of violence in the land
    and of ruler against ruler.
⁴⁷For the time will surely come
    when I will punish the idols of Babylon;
her whole land will be disgraced
    and her slain will all lie fallen within her.
⁴⁸Then heaven and earth and all that is in them
    will shout for joy over Babylon,
for out of the north
    destroyers will attack her,"
                    declares the LORD.

_{a41 *Sheshach* is a cryptogram for Babylon.}

49"Babylon must fall because of Israel's slain,
　　just as the slain in all the earth
　　have fallen because of Babylon.
50You who have escaped the sword,
　　leave and do not linger!
Remember the LORD in a distant land,
　　and think on Jerusalem."

51"We are disgraced,
　　for we have been insulted
　　and shame covers our faces,
because foreigners have entered
　　the holy places of the LORD's house."

52"But days are coming," declares the LORD,
　　"when I will punish her idols,
and throughout her land
　　the wounded will groan.
53Even if Babylon reaches the sky
　　and fortifies her lofty stronghold,
　　I will send destroyers against her,"
　　　　　　　　　　　　　declares the LORD.

54"The sound of a cry comes from Babylon,
　　the sound of great destruction
　　from the land of the Babylonians.*a*
55The LORD will destroy Babylon;
　　he will silence her noisy din.
Waves ⌞of enemies⌟ will rage like great waters;
　　the roar of their voices will resound.
56A destroyer will come against Babylon;
　　her warriors will be captured,
　　and their bows will be broken.
For the LORD is a God of retribution;
　　he will repay in full.
57I will make her officials and wise men drunk,
　　her governors, officers and warriors as well;
they will sleep forever and not awake,"
　　declares the King, whose name is the LORD
　　　　Almighty.

58This is what the LORD Almighty says:

"Babylon's thick wall will be leveled
　　and her high gates set on fire;
the peoples exhaust themselves for nothing,
　　the nations' labor is only fuel for the flames."

59This is the message Jeremiah gave to the staff officer Seraiah son of Neriah, the son of Mahseiah, when he went to Babylon with Zedekiah king of Judah in the fourth year of his reign. 60Jeremiah had written on a scroll about all the disasters that would come upon Babylon—all that had been recorded concerning Babylon. 61He said to Seraiah, "When you get to Babylon, see that you read all these words aloud. 62Then say, 'O LORD, you have said you will destroy this place, so that neither man nor animal will live in it; it will be desolate forever.' 63When you finish reading this scroll, tie a stone to it and throw it into the Euphrates. 64Then say, 'So will

a 54 Or Chaldeans

Babylon sink to rise no more because of the disaster I will bring upon her. And her people will fall.' "

The words of Jeremiah end here.

The Fall of Jerusalem

52 Zedekiah was twenty-one years old when he became king, and he reigned in Jerusalem eleven years. His mother's name was Hamutal daughter of Jeremiah; she was from Libnah. ²He did evil in the eyes of the Lord, just as Jehoiakim had done. ³It was because of the Lord's anger that all this happened to Jerusalem and Judah, and in the end he thrust them from his presence.

Now Zedekiah rebelled against the king of Babylon.

⁴So in the ninth year of Zedekiah's reign, on the tenth day of the tenth month, Nebuchadnezzar king of Babylon marched against Jerusalem with his whole army. They camped outside the city and built siege works all around it. ⁵The city was kept under siege until the eleventh year of King Zedekiah.

⁶By the ninth day of the fourth month the famine in the city had become so severe that there was no food for the people to eat. ⁷Then the city wall was broken through, and the whole army fled. They left the city at night through the gate between the two walls near the king's garden, though the Babylonians[a] were surrounding the city. They fled toward the Arabah,[b] ⁸but the Babylonian[c] army pursued King Zedekiah and overtook him in the plains of Jericho. All his soldiers were separated from him and scattered, ⁹and he was captured.

He was taken to the king of Babylon at Riblah in the land of Hamath, where he pronounced sentence on him. ¹⁰There at Riblah the king of Babylon slaughtered the sons of Zedekiah before his eyes; he also killed all the officials of Judah. ¹¹Then he put out Zedekiah's eyes, bound him with bronze shackles and took him to Babylon, where he put him in prison till the day of his death.

¹²On the tenth day of the fifth month, in the nineteenth year of Nebuchadnezzar king of Babylon, Nebuzaradan commander of the imperial guard, who served the king of Babylon, came to Jerusalem. ¹³He set fire to the temple of the Lord, the royal palace and all the houses of Jerusalem. Every important building he burned down. ¹⁴The whole Babylonian army under the commander of the imperial guard broke down all the walls around Jerusalem. ¹⁵Nebuzaradan the commander of the guard carried into exile some of the poorest people and those who remained in the city, along with the rest of the craftsmen[d] and those who had gone over to the king of Babylon. ¹⁶But Nebuzaradan left behind the rest of the poorest people of the land to work the vineyards and fields.

¹⁷The Babylonians broke up the bronze pillars, the movable stands and the bronze Sea that were at the temple of the Lord and they carried all the bronze to Babylon. ¹⁸They also took away the pots, shovels, wick trimmers, sprinkling bowls, dishes and all the bronze articles used in the temple service. ¹⁹The commander of the imperial guard took away the basins, censers, sprinkling bowls, pots, lampstands, dishes and bowls used for drink offerings—all that were made of pure gold or silver.

²⁰The bronze from the two pillars, the Sea and the twelve bronze bulls under it, and the movable stands, which King Solomon had made for the temple of the Lord, was more than could be weighed. ²¹Each of the pillars was eighteen cubits high and twelve cubits in

a7 Or *Chaldeans*; also in verse 17   b7 Or *the Jordan Valley*   c8 Or *Chaldean*; also in verse 14   d15 Or *populace*

circumference[a]; each was four fingers thick, and hollow. 22The bronze capital on top of the one pillar was five cubits[b] high and was decorated with a network and pomegranates of bronze all around. The other pillar, with its pomegranates, was similar. 23There were ninety-six pomegranates on the sides; the total number of pomegranates above the surrounding network was a hundred.

24The commander of the guard took as prisoners Seraiah the chief priest, Zephaniah the priest next in rank and the three doorkeepers. 25Of those still in the city, he took the officer in charge of the fighting men, and seven royal advisers. He also took the secretary who was chief officer in charge of conscripting the people of the land and sixty of his men who were found in the city. 26Nebuzaradan the commander took them all and brought them to the king of Babylon at Riblah. 27There at Riblah, in the land of Hamath, the king had them executed.

So Judah went into captivity, away from her land. 28This is the number of the people Nebuchadnezzar carried into exile:

in the seventh year, 3,023 Jews;
29in Nebuchadnezzar's eighteenth year,
    832 people from Jerusalem;
30in his twenty-third year,
    745 Jews taken into exile by Nebuzaradan the commander
        of the imperial guard.
There were 4,600 people in all.

Jehoiachin Released

31In the thirty-seventh year of the exile of Jehoiachin king of Judah, in the year Evil-Merodach[c] became king of Babylon, he released Jehoiachin king of Judah and freed him from prison on the twenty-fifth day of the twelfth month. 32He spoke kindly to him and gave him a seat of honor higher than those of the other kings who were with him in Babylon. 33So Jehoiachin put aside his prison clothes and for the rest of his life ate regularly at the king's table. 34Day by day the king of Babylon gave Jehoiachin a regular allowance as long as he lived, till the day of his death.

ing? Or do you feel satisfied that the punishment fit the crime?

If you could award honors or medals to other members of your group, what would you give them and why?

1. After building throughout the book to God's judgment upon Israel and Judah, are you surprised by the way in which the book ends? Why or why not? 2. Why do you think this happier note of Jehoiachin's elevation follows the previous passage about Hezekiah's rebellion and imprisonment? 3. What is the significance of eating at the king's table? What does this say about how God rewards faithful people, even those who wait 37 years for answered prayer?

1. When have you had to wait a long time for an answer to prayer? What did you feel about God while you waited? How did you recognize the answer when it finally came? 2. The King of kings has asked you to put off your old clothes and come to eat with him at his table (see Col 3:5–12; Rev 3:20). What is your response? 3. As you review the book, which promises of God did Jeremiah live to see fulfilled? Which were still to come?

a21 That is, about 27 feet (about 8.1 meters) high and 18 feet (about 5.4 meters) in circumference   b22 That is, about 7 1/2 feet (about 2.3 meters)   c31 Also called Amel-Marduk

INTRODUCTION to
LAMENTATIONS

Book Study Outline: If you are using Lamentations for a study course, here is a 5-week outline. Use the questions in the margin for your group agenda:

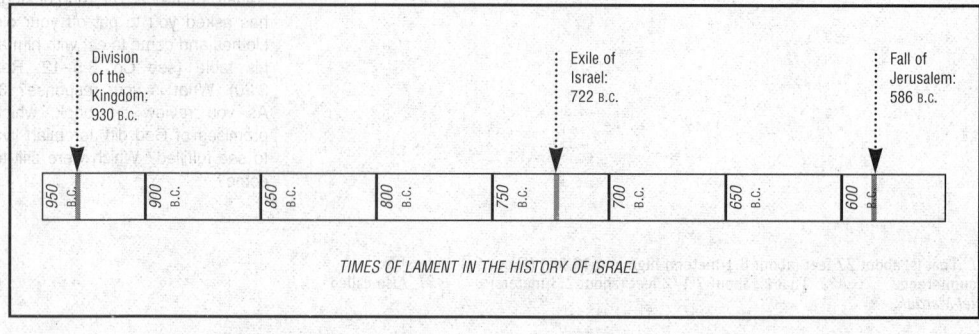 start meeting / 15 min.

read & discuss Bible / 30 min.

close meeting / 15–45 min.

5-week plan	Personal Reading	Group Study Passage
1	1:1–22	Jerusalem: Unconsoled and Unconsolable
2	2:1–22	The Desolate Daughter of Zion
3	3:1–66	Crushed, but Not Consumed
4	4:1–22	The Precious Has Become Profane
5	5:1–22	Lord, Remember and Restore

Refer to the Questions and Answers in the front of this Bible for more information.

Author: Early Jewish and Christian tradition ascribes this anonymous book to Jeremiah. Although plausible, the evidence for this view is not certain. It is clear, however, that the author was an eye witness to the fall of Jerusalem and Judah's forced exile to Babylon.

Date: The book was probably written between 586 B.C. (the fall of Jerusalem) and 516 B.C. (the dedication of the rebuilt temple).

Theme: Grief over Judah's fall and Jerusalem's destruction.

Historical Background: Jerusalem has lain under siege by Babylon for 18 months. Outside the city, the Babylonians have captured and slain the people of Judah. Inside the city, disease and famine have claimed many more.

Characteristics: Lamentations is a good example of ancient Near Eastern "dirge" poetry which was read aloud at funerals. It is used by Jews wailing at the Western Wall, even to this day. The author of this book crafted his theological lessons and channeled his emotions to fit his lament into an "acrostic" poem. (An acrostic poem is one in which the verses each begin with the successive 22 letters of the Hebrew alphabet.) An interesting thematic parallel to Lamentations is the book of Job (see the introduction page for Job). Job grieves over the calamity which has struck him on a personal level, while the author of Lamentations pours out his grief over the destruction of the city of Jerusalem. Whereas Job has done nothing to deserve his disaster and thus wonders how God can be just, the poet of Lamentations readily confesses that Judah is guilty and that God is just. Lamentations provides a sad "post-mortem" on the prophetic warnings that Judah had repeatedly (and fatally) ignored. Though appalled at the severity of the national destruction, the poet still trusts God. Having confessed the people's sin, the poet desperately hopes that the God who brings grief will also renew mercy (see 3:21–33; 5:21–22). Because of its profound reflection on the problem of suffering (which finds no easy answers, but is content to trust God's mercy), Lamentations, like Job, has inspired Christian devotion and hymnody.

Division of the Kingdom: 930 B.C.				Exile of Israel: 722 B.C.			Fall of Jerusalem: 586 B.C.
950 B.C.	900 B.C.	850 B.C.	800 B.C.	750 B.C.	700 B.C.	650 B.C.	600 B.C.

TIMES OF LAMENT IN THE HISTORY OF ISRAEL

Lamentations

1 ^a

How deserted lies the city,
    once so full of people!
How like a widow is she,
    who once was great among the nations!
She who was queen among the provinces
    has now become a slave.

²Bitterly she weeps at night,
    tears are upon her cheeks.
Among all her lovers
    there is none to comfort her.
All her friends have betrayed her;
    they have become her enemies.

³After affliction and harsh labor,
    Judah has gone into exile.
She dwells among the nations;
    she finds no resting place.
All who pursue her have overtaken her
    in the midst of her distress.

⁴The roads to Zion mourn,
    for no one comes to her appointed feasts.
All her gateways are desolate,
    her priests groan,
her maidens grieve,
    and she is in bitter anguish.

⁵Her foes have become her masters;
    her enemies are at ease.
The LORD has brought her grief
    because of her many sins.
Her children have gone into exile,
    captive before the foe.

⁶All the splendor has departed
    from the Daughter of Zion.
Her princes are like deer
    that find no pasture;
in weakness they have fled
    before the pursuer.

⁷In the days of her affliction and wandering
    Jerusalem remembers all the treasures
    that were hers in days of old.
When her people fell into enemy hands,
    there was no one to help her.
Her enemies looked at her
    and laughed at her destruction.

⁸Jerusalem has sinned greatly
    and so has become unclean.
All who honored her despise her,
    for they have seen her nakedness;

---

^aThis chapter is an acrostic poem, the verses of which begin with the successive letters of the Hebrew alphabet.

---

1. What do you consider the darkest hour in your country's history? Why? If you were alive then, how did you feel? What public reaction best expressed the nation's sorrow? **2.** Think of one humiliation or tragedy you have suffered. What kinds of emotions toward God did you feel? How did you deal with those feelings? How did you try to make sense out of what had happened?

1. What does the title Lamentations suggest to you? Is this the grief of an individual or of a nation? Can you think of similar outpourings of grief in Scripture? **2.** From this, what overall picture of Judah comes to mind? What phrase repeatedly sounds like a refrain (see vv. 2,9,16,17,21)? What one word would you use to describe her situation? **3.** What has happened to Judah and her "lovers" (v. 2; see Jer 52:4–30 for background details of Jerusalem's fall)? What irony do you see here? What do you imagine Jerusalem looked like after these events? Compare this to her "glory days" (1Ch 14:17; 1Ki 10:1–9,23–25). **4.** What "reversals" of her fortunes has she suffered (vv. 1–7)? Why? What were some of her sins (see 2Ki 21:1–9,16)? **5.** How had Judah failed to "consider her future" (v. 9)? What warnings had she received as part of the covenant (see Dt 28:58–68)? How did she respond to the warnings of the prophets? What is especially tragic about this failure? **6.** What has happened to the sanctuary (v. 10)? Why is this "rape" so devastating? What does it suggest about God's attitude toward Judah? **7.** Does the poet consider the Lord's treatment unjust (v. 18)? What lesson is here for the "peoples"? What resources or securities have proven futile against the Lord's anger? **8.** Jerusalem was under siege for about a year and a half (Jer 52:4–6). What do you think life was like during the siege (vv. 20–21)? **9.** In his distress, to whom does the poet appeal? For what does he pray (vv. 21–22)? On what basis does he make this request?

1. Could this disaster have been averted? How so? What do you think made Judah so "blind" and "deaf"? 2. How do people presume upon God's favor and goodness? How do nations do the same? 3. If God in his righteousness brought Judah low, what warning is here for us? 4. Judah fell because "she did not consider her future." Are you, as a nation or as individual, guilty of the same error? How so? How can you consider the future more effectively? 5. What warnings has God given you that you've failed to heed? With what result? Could you be living now on "borrowed time"? 6. Could there be a "sin of presumption" in your life that threatens your prosperity? How is the psalmist's attitude in Psalm 139:23–24 a necessary safeguard? Can you pray that prayer today and mean it?

she herself groans
and turns away.

9Her filthiness clung to her skirts;
she did not consider her future.
Her fall was astounding;
there was none to comfort her.
"Look, O LORD, on my affliction,
for the enemy has triumphed."

10The enemy laid hands
on all her treasures;
she saw pagan nations
enter her sanctuary—
those you had forbidden
to enter your assembly.

11All her people groan
as they search for bread;
they barter their treasures for food
to keep themselves alive.
"Look, O LORD, and consider,
for I am despised."

12"Is it nothing to you, all you who pass by?
Look around and see.
Is any suffering like my suffering
that was inflicted on me,
that the LORD brought on me
in the day of his fierce anger?

13"From on high he sent fire,
sent it down into my bones.
He spread a net for my feet
and turned me back.
He made me desolate,
faint all the day long.

14"My sins have been bound into a yoke*a*;
by his hands they were woven together.
They have come upon my neck
and the Lord has sapped my strength.
He has handed me over
to those I cannot withstand.

15"The Lord has rejected
all the warriors in my midst;
he has summoned an army against me
to*b* crush my young men.
In his winepress the Lord has trampled
the Virgin Daughter of Judah.

16"This is why I weep
and my eyes overflow with tears.
No one is near to comfort me,
no one to restore my spirit.
My children are destitute
because the enemy has prevailed."

17Zion stretches out her hands,
but there is no one to comfort her.

a 14 Most Hebrew manuscripts; Septuagint *He kept watch over my sins*   b 15 Or *has set a time for me / when he will*

The LORD has decreed for Jacob
    that his neighbors become his foes;
Jerusalem has become
    an unclean thing among them.

18"The LORD is righteous,
    yet I rebelled against his command.
Listen, all you peoples;
    look upon my suffering.
My young men and maidens
    have gone into exile.

19"I called to my allies
    but they betrayed me.
My priests and my elders
    perished in the city
while they searched for food
    to keep themselves alive.

20"See, O LORD, how distressed I am!
    I am in torment within,
and in my heart I am disturbed,
    for I have been most rebellious.
Outside, the sword bereaves;
    inside, there is only death.

21"People have heard my groaning,
    but there is no one to comfort me.
All my enemies have heard of my distress;
    they rejoice at what you have done.
May you bring the day you have announced
    so they may become like me.

22"Let all their wickedness come before you;
    deal with them
as you have dealt with me
    because of all my sins.
My groans are many
    and my heart is faint."

2^a How the Lord has covered the Daughter of Zion
    with the cloud of his anger^b!
He has hurled down the splendor of Israel
    from heaven to earth;
he has not remembered his footstool
    in the day of his anger.

2Without pity the Lord has swallowed up
    all the dwellings of Jacob;
in his wrath he has torn down
    the strongholds of the Daughter of Judah.
He has brought her kingdom and its princes
    down to the ground in dishonor.

3In fierce anger he has cut off
    every horn^c of Israel.
He has withdrawn his right hand
    at the approach of the enemy.

---

1. How would you feel if you organized a party or group activity, only to have nobody come? Has that ever happened to you or your friends? How did you feel? 2. Have you ever seen a person or group get "what was coming to them"? What happened? Why did they deserve it? How would you have felt if they did not get their "just desserts"?

1. Compare 1:1 with 2:1. What is similar? What is different? 2. In verses 1–8, who is the main actor? What verbs are used to describe his actions? What emotions does the poet attribute to God? What images does he use to describe God's treatment of the "Daughter of Zion" (vv. 4–5,8)? 3. How extensive has the calamity been? List the things "torn down," "swallowed up" or "destroyed". 4. In

---

^aThis chapter is an acrostic poem, the verses of which begin with the successive letters of the Hebrew alphabet.   ^b1 Or *How the Lord in his anger / has treated the Daughter of Zion with contempt*   ^c3 Or / *all the strength*; or *every king*; horn here symbolizes strength.

verses 6–7, what has the Lord done to "his dwelling"? Why would he treat his own things this way? **5.** What images of helplessness and hopelessness does the poet paint in verses 9–12? What do the gates and bars represent: The kings and princes? The law? The prophets? Or what? What is significant of the posture of the elders and young women (v. 10)? **6.** What emotions does the poet express when he sees the suffering of the children? Who has escaped the judgment of the Lord? Why? **7.** Why is the poet without words of comfort for Judah (v. 13)? Had anything like this happened in her history before? **8.** Where does the poet lay much of the blame for Judah's destruction (v. 14)? What "false and misleading" oracles have the prophets spoken (see Jer 14:13–16)? Why? **9.** What does Judah's downfall bring about in onlookers? In her enemies? What do both groups seem to forget about her punishment (v. 17)? **10.** Judah's punishment had been decreed by God much earlier, as recorded in Leviticus 26:27–46. How is God just in sending this calamity? How is he merciful? **11.** Why is Judah encouraged to "pour out" her heart to the Lord (vv. 18–19)? As she pleads her case, is she asking for justice or mercy (vv. 20–21)? **12.** What questions are especially troubling for Judah (v. 20)? What is she ultimately looking for (v. 22)? To whom?

1. What characteristic of God is most strikingly displayed by his treatment of the "Daughter of Zion"? What does it mean to lose the "ear of the Lord"? In what ways have you become casual about sin? **2.** Does God seem like an "enemy" to you right now? Are there any sins with which you have "made friends"? **3.** In this chapter, the poet indicts the false prophets who did not expose the sins of Judah. Who are the false prophets we tend to "give ear" to: Politicians? University profs? Entertainers? Our peer group? Psychologists? "Health and wealth" evangelists? **4.** What do the people around you think when prominent ministers or ministries fail? Is God's reputation tarnished, or polished, when such ministries are put through the fire? Or is God's reputation separate from the reputation of men and their institutions? How should we react when Christianity receives such bad press? **5.** If Ju-

He has burned in Jacob like a flaming fire
    that consumes everything around it.

[4]Like an enemy he has strung his bow;
    his right hand is ready.
Like a foe he has slain
    all who were pleasing to the eye;
he has poured out his wrath like fire
    on the tent of the Daughter of Zion.

[5]The Lord is like an enemy;
    he has swallowed up Israel.
He has swallowed up all her palaces
    and destroyed her strongholds.
He has multiplied mourning and lamentation
    for the Daughter of Judah.

[6]He has laid waste his dwelling like a garden;
    he has destroyed his place of meeting.
The LORD has made Zion forget
    her appointed feasts and her Sabbaths;
in his fierce anger he has spurned
    both king and priest.

[7]The Lord has rejected his altar
    and abandoned his sanctuary.
He has handed over to the enemy
    the walls of her palaces;
they have raised a shout in the house of the LORD
    as on the day of an appointed feast.

[8]The LORD determined to tear down
    the wall around the Daughter of Zion.
He stretched out a measuring line
    and did not withhold his hand from destroying.
He made ramparts and walls lament;
    together they wasted away.

[9]Her gates have sunk into the ground;
    their bars he has broken and destroyed.
Her king and her princes are exiled among the
    nations,
    the law is no more,
and her prophets no longer find
    visions from the LORD.

[10]The elders of the Daughter of Zion
    sit on the ground in silence;
they have sprinkled dust on their heads
    and put on sackcloth.
The young women of Jerusalem
    have bowed their heads to the ground.

[11]My eyes fail from weeping,
    I am in torment within,
my heart is poured out on the ground
    because my people are destroyed,
because children and infants faint
    in the streets of the city.

[12]They say to their mothers,
    "Where is bread and wine?"
as they faint like wounded men
    in the streets of the city,

as their lives ebb away
  in their mothers' arms.

13What can I say for you?
  With what can I compare you,
  O Daughter of Jerusalem?
To what can I liken you,
  that I may comfort you,
  O Virgin Daughter of Zion?
Your wound is as deep as the sea.
  Who can heal you?

14The visions of your prophets
  were false and worthless;
they did not expose your sin
  to ward off your captivity.
The oracles they gave you
  were false and misleading.

15All who pass your way
  clap their hands at you;
they scoff and shake their heads
  at the Daughter of Jerusalem:
"Is this the city that was called
  the perfection of beauty,
  the joy of the whole earth?"

16All your enemies open their mouths
  wide against you;
they scoff and gnash their teeth
  and say, "We have swallowed her up.
This is the day we have waited for;
  we have lived to see it."

17The LORD has done what he planned;
  he has fulfilled his word,
  which he decreed long ago.
He has overthrown you without pity,
  he has let the enemy gloat over you,
  he has exalted the horn*a* of your foes.

18The hearts of the people
  cry out to the Lord.
O wall of the Daughter of Zion,
  let your tears flow like a river
  day and night;
give yourself no relief,
  your eyes no rest.

19Arise, cry out in the night,
  as the watches of the night begin;
pour out your heart like water
  in the presence of the Lord.
Lift up your hands to him
  for the lives of your children,
who faint from hunger
  at the head of every street.

20"Look, O LORD, and consider:
  Whom have you ever treated like this?
  Should women eat their offspring,

dah returns to the Lord, of what
can she be confident? What comfort can this give you the next time
you feel his "rod of correction"? **6.**
God's discipline is a "severe mercy." What evidence of mercy can
you see in his past discipline of
you? Can you trust that his present
discipline of you is merciful?

---

a17 Horn here symbolizes strength.

the children they have cared for?
Should priest and prophet be killed
in the sanctuary of the Lord?

²¹"Young and old lie together
in the dust of the streets;
my young men and maidens
have fallen by the sword.
You have slain them in the day of your anger;
you have slaughtered them without pity.

²²"As you summon to a feast day,
so you summoned against me terrors on every
side.
In the day of the LORD's anger
no one escaped or survived;
those I cared for and reared,
my enemy has destroyed."

3 ᵃ

I am the man who has seen affliction
by the rod of his wrath.
²He has driven me away and made me walk
in darkness rather than light;
³indeed, he has turned his hand against me
again and again, all day long.

⁴He has made my skin and my flesh grow old
and has broken my bones.
⁵He has besieged me and surrounded me
with bitterness and hardship.
⁶He has made me dwell in darkness
like those long dead.

⁷He has walled me in so I cannot escape;
he has weighed me down with chains.
⁸Even when I call out or cry for help,
he shuts out my prayer.
⁹He has barred my way with blocks of stone;
he has made my paths crooked.

¹⁰Like a bear lying in wait,
like a lion in hiding,
¹¹he dragged me from the path and mangled me
and left me without help.
¹²He drew his bow
and made me the target for his arrows.

¹³He pierced my heart
with arrows from his quiver.
¹⁴I became the laughingstock of all my people;
they mock me in song all day long.
¹⁵He has filled me with bitter herbs
and sated me with gall.

¹⁶He has broken my teeth with gravel;
he has trampled me in the dust.
¹⁷I have been deprived of peace;
I have forgotten what prosperity is.

🍵 **1.** What sayings or home-spun wisdom can you still hear your mom or dad reciting? How do these still affect you? **2.** How do you pass the time in a dentist's waiting room? What feelings do you experience there? **3.** What do you do to get an hour's reprieve from the hectic pace of your day? Where do you go to get away for a weekend?

📖 **1.** For whom is the poet speaking in the opening verses? How has God treated him (vv. 1–18)? How is he feeling? What benefits are there in making such a frank lament? What dangers? **2.** What has Judah focused her attention on (vv. 17,19)? What are the consequences of forgetting her past prosperity? **3.** How does the poet stem the tide of grief and despair (v. 21)? Is this an easy or natural thing to do in the midst of sorrow? What is the secret of redirecting one's focus this way? **4.** Where does the poet look to find hope (vv. 22–27)? Given the situation, do these words seem hollow? Insane? Unreal? Courageous? Noble? Explain. **5.** These phrases (in vv. 22–27) come from Psalms and Isaiah. Why were they familiar to the poet? How must he have prepared himself in the past to deal with his current depression? **6.** What attributes of the Lord are recalled in verses 22–33? How does this picture contrast with that in verses 1–18? Why is it necessary to balance both feelings (vv. 1–18) and faith (vv. 22–33)? **7.** To whom does the poet address his rhetorical questions in verses 34–39? What attributes of God do they establish? **8.** To what logical conclu-

---

ᵃThis chapter is an acrostic poem; the verses of each stanza begin with the successive letters of the Hebrew alphabet, and the verses within each stanza begin with the same letter.

¹⁸So I say, "My splendor is gone
and all that I had hoped from the LORD."

¹⁹I remember my affliction and my wandering,
the bitterness and the gall.

²⁰I well remember them,
and my soul is downcast within me.

²¹Yet this I call to mind
and therefore I have hope:

²²Because of the LORD's great love we are not
consumed,
for his compassions never fail.

²³They are new every morning;
great is your faithfulness.

²⁴I say to myself, "The LORD is my portion;
therefore I will wait for him."

²⁵The LORD is good to those whose hope is in him,
to the one who seeks him;

²⁶it is good to wait quietly
for the salvation of the LORD.

²⁷It is good for a man to bear the yoke
while he is young.

²⁸Let him sit alone in silence,
for the LORD has laid it on him.

²⁹Let him bury his face in the dust—
there may yet be hope.

³⁰Let him offer his cheek to one who would strike
him,
and let him be filled with disgrace.

³¹For men are not cast off
by the Lord forever.

³²Though he brings grief, he will show compassion,
so great is his unfailing love.

³³For he does not willingly bring affliction
or grief to the children of men.

³⁴To crush underfoot
all prisoners in the land,

³⁵to deny a man his rights
before the Most High,

³⁶to deprive a man of justice—
would not the Lord see such things?

³⁷Who can speak and have it happen
if the Lord has not decreed it?

³⁸Is it not from the mouth of the Most High
that both calamities and good things come?

³⁹Why should any living man complain
when punished for his sins?

⁴⁰Let us examine our ways and test them,
and let us return to the LORD.

⁴¹Let us lift up our hearts and our hands
to God in heaven, and say:

⁴²"We have sinned and rebelled
and you have not forgiven.

⁴³"You have covered yourself with anger and
pursued us;
you have slain without pity.

sion is the poet brought (vv. 40–42)? How was this conclusion arrived at? How does this begin to make sense out of Judah's suffering? **9.** Why does the poet list the sufferings of the people (vv. 43–54)? **10.** For what does the poet pray (vv. 55–66)? What hope of an answer does his own punishment give him? When and how had God heard and answered their plea in the past? What did the covenant and the prophets say about God's hearing (see Dt 30:1–8; Jer 30: 10–11)? **11.** Briefly review the chapter. What kind of psychological and emotional progress has the poet made from the beginning to the end of this dirge? What have been the steps in that process? What spiritual "weapons" has the poet used to fight his way back to God?

1. Have you ever felt like the poet in the opening section of this chapter (vv. 1–18)? Were you able to express those feelings to God? If so, how? If not, why? What kept you from giving up completely at that time? **2.** What portions of Scripture are especially helpful to you in difficult times? What hymns are especially meaningful to you? Why? Do you know them by heart? What benefit might there be in memorizing them? **3.** When you're feeling forsaken and chastened how do you express your feelings? How do you avoid wallowing in self-pity? What is the danger of being too stoic or unemotional? What can you do to balance these two extremes? **4.** Do you grow more during easy times or during tough times? What help does verse 33 (also Ro 5:3–5; Jas 1:2–4) teach you about affliction? **5.** In what ways do we lift up our hands, but not our hearts, when we are in trouble (v. 41)? What does true repentance look like? What do truly repentant people do? What will happen if you dare to embrace the Lord's discipline as does this poet (see also Heb 12:11)? **6.** Based on Judah's experience, how seriously does God take the issue of sin? What does Jesus' death on the cross add to this picture? How then should we treat sin in our own lives? **7.** What "compassions" or "faithfulness" (vv. 22–23) has the Lord shown you this week? How have you shown your love and gratitude to God?

⁴⁴You have covered yourself with a cloud
    so that no prayer can get through.
⁴⁵You have made us scum and refuse
    among the nations.

⁴⁶"All our enemies have opened their mouths
    wide against us.
⁴⁷We have suffered terror and pitfalls,
    ruin and destruction."
⁴⁸Streams of tears flow from my eyes
    because my people are destroyed.

⁴⁹My eyes will flow unceasingly,
    without relief,
⁵⁰until the LORD looks down
    from heaven and sees.
⁵¹What I see brings grief to my soul
    because of all the women of my city.

⁵²Those who were my enemies without cause
    hunted me like a bird.
⁵³They tried to end my life in a pit
    and threw stones at me;
⁵⁴the waters closed over my head,
    and I thought I was about to be cut off.

⁵⁵I called on your name, O LORD,
    from the depths of the pit.
⁵⁶You heard my plea: "Do not close your ears
    to my cry for relief."
⁵⁷You came near when I called you,
    and you said, "Do not fear."

⁵⁸O Lord, you took up my case;
    you redeemed my life.
⁵⁹You have seen, O LORD, the wrong done to me.
    Uphold my cause!
⁶⁰You have seen the depth of their vengeance,
    all their plots against me.

⁶¹O LORD, you have heard their insults,
    all their plots against me—
⁶²what my enemies whisper and mutter
    against me all day long.
⁶³Look at them! Sitting or standing,
    they mock me in their songs.

⁶⁴Pay them back what they deserve, O LORD,
    for what their hands have done.
⁶⁵Put a veil over their hearts,
    and may your curse be on them!
⁶⁶Pursue them in anger and destroy them
    from under the heavens of the LORD.

4 ᵃ

How the gold has lost its luster,
    the fine gold become dull!
The sacred gems are scattered
    at the head of every street.

²How the precious sons of Zion,
    once worth their weight in gold,

1. Are the stories from your parents' past "the good old days," or are they "those hard times"? What experiences of satisfaction and suffering do you recall from those stories? 2. Have you ever dressed up in your "Sunday best," only to find yourself doing some dirty job? What was the job?

ᵃThis chapter is an acrostic poem, the verses of which begin with the successive letters of the Hebrew alphabet.

are now considered as pots of clay,
the work of a potter's hands!

³Even jackals offer their breasts
to nurse their young,
but my people have become heartless
like ostriches in the desert.

⁴Because of thirst the infant's tongue
sticks to the roof of its mouth;
the children beg for bread,
but no one gives it to them.

⁵Those who once ate delicacies
are destitute in the streets.
Those nurtured in purple
now lie on ash heaps.

⁶The punishment of my people
is greater than that of Sodom,
which was overthrown in a moment
without a hand turned to help her.

⁷Their princes were brighter than snow
and whiter than milk,
their bodies more ruddy than rubies,
their appearance like sapphires.ᵃ

⁸But now they are blacker than soot;
they are not recognized in the streets.
Their skin has shriveled on their bones;
it has become as dry as a stick.

⁹Those killed by the sword are better off
than those who die of famine;
racked with hunger, they waste away
for lack of food from the field.

¹⁰With their own hands compassionate women
have cooked their own children,
who became their food
when my people were destroyed.

¹¹The LORD has given full vent to his wrath;
he has poured out his fierce anger.
He kindled a fire in Zion
that consumed her foundations.

¹²The kings of the earth did not believe,
nor did any of the world's people,
that enemies and foes could enter
the gates of Jerusalem.

¹³But it happened because of the sins of her
prophets
and the iniquities of her priests,
who shed within her
the blood of the righteous.

¹⁴Now they grope through the streets
like men who are blind.
They are so defiled with blood
that no one dares to touch their garments.

ᵃ7 Or lapis lazuli

Did you keep your clothes clean? 3. What is the hungriest or thirstiest you have ever been? How did you get that way? How did it feel? 4. Have you ever visited an old castle or fortress which was once considered impregnable? What was it like in its glory? What is it like now?

1. What are the "gold" and "sacred gems" of verses 1–2? What is the difference between these items and the clay pots? What modern image is the equivalent of this comparison? 2. What is the difference in child-rearing responsibility between the jackal and the ostrich? (Ostriches will abandon their eggs when confronted with danger.) What have the people of Judah done to deserve this comparison? 3. How is Judah's punishment worse than that of Sodom (vv. 6–10)? 4. Why did everyone assume that Jerusalem's gates were impregnable (see Jer 7:1–8)? What made the gates vulnerable (vv. 12–13)? How might these false prophets have been guilty of shedding innocent blood (see Jer 23:16–19)? How could these people have so great an effect on the whole nation? 5. Even as destruction approached, where did Judah look for help (v. 17)? Who is probably responsible for this "looking in vain"? 6. Have the people lost confidence in their king (v. 20)? Why or why not (see 2Ki 25:1–7)? 7. Why does the poet's attention shift to "the Daughter of Edom" in verses 21–22? Why is she rejoicing (see Ps 137:7)? What will be her end (see Jer 49:17–22)? 8. What hope is given to the "Daughter of Zion" in verse 22? If you were one of the people of Judah, how would you feel at the end of this dirge?

1. What are the "gold and sacred gems" in your life? If these were suddenly taken away, how would you feel? Where would you look for a sense of self-worth? 2. Jerusalem's gates were, for Judah, a symbol of security. What are the symbols of security for your nation: NATO alliance? Nuclear arsenal? Technological superiority? Fort Knox? Other? 3. Has national pride or presumption of safety actually made your country vulnerable? By the same token, are you spiritually vulnerable? 4. Does your country, like Judah, have prophets and priests who prophesy false visions? Who are they: (a) Advertisers? (b) Political "image makers"? (c)

School textbook publishers? (d) "Health and wealth" evangelists? (e) New Age advocates? (f) Other? What makes their visions so attractive? So dangerous? **5.** Are you or your nation guilty of being an "ostrich" toward the children in your life? How so? What can be done to stop this? **6.** If an individual does not resist the Lord's discipline, but submits to it, what can he hope for? Is that your hope? Your church's hope? By contrast, what is your nation's hope? Explain the difference.

1. Were you ever lured into wrongdoing, caught and punished while the ones who led you astray got away clean? What were the circumstances? How did you feel? **2.** Have you ever found yourself under the authority of someone who wasn't entitled to that authority? Summarize the situation and your reactions.

1. Who is responsible for the punishment Judah is suffering (v. 7)? Is this a realistic view or blame-shifting (see v. 16)? **2.** Who are the different groups mentioned in verses 11–14? What is said of each? What is the total impact of these verses? **3.** Describe the emotion you hear in verses 15–18. What is the climactic line of verses 1–18? How is this the beginning of Judah's return? **4.** What attribute of God does the poet mention (v. 19)? Why is that significant? **5.** For what

15"Go away! You are unclean!" men cry to them.
  "Away! Away! Don't touch us!"
When they flee and wander about,
  people among the nations say,
  "They can stay here no longer."

16The LORD himself has scattered them;
  he no longer watches over them.
The priests are shown no honor,
  the elders no favor.

17Moreover, our eyes failed,
  looking in vain for help;
from our towers we watched
  for a nation that could not save us.

18Men stalked us at every step,
  so we could not walk in our streets.
Our end was near, our days were numbered,
  for our end had come.

19Our pursuers were swifter
  than eagles in the sky;
they chased us over the mountains
  and lay in wait for us in the desert.

20The LORD's anointed, our very life breath,
  was caught in their traps.
We thought that under his shadow
  we would live among the nations.

21Rejoice and be glad, O Daughter of Edom,
  you who live in the land of Uz.
But to you also the cup will be passed;
  you will be drunk and stripped naked.

22O Daughter of Zion, your punishment will end;
  he will not prolong your exile.
But, O Daughter of Edom, he will punish your sin
  and expose your wickedness.

5

Remember, O LORD, what has happened to us;
  look, and see our disgrace.
2Our inheritance has been turned over to aliens,
  our homes to foreigners.
3We have become orphans and fatherless,
  our mothers like widows.
4We must buy the water we drink;
  our wood can be had only at a price.
5Those who pursue us are at our heels;
  we are weary and find no rest.
6We submitted to Egypt and Assyria
  to get enough bread.
7Our fathers sinned and are no more,
  and we bear their punishment.
8Slaves rule over us,
  and there is none to free us from their hands.
9We get our bread at the risk of our lives
  because of the sword in the desert.
10Our skin is hot as an oven,
  feverish from hunger.
11Women have been ravished in Zion,
  and virgins in the towns of Judah.

¹²Princes have been hung up by their hands;
  elders are shown no respect.
¹³Young men toil at the millstones;
  boys stagger under loads of wood.
¹⁴The elders are gone from the city gate;
  the young men have stopped their music.
¹⁵Joy is gone from our hearts;
  our dancing has turned to mourning.
¹⁶The crown has fallen from our head.
  Woe to us, for we have sinned!
¹⁷Because of this our hearts are faint,
  because of these things our eyes grow dim
¹⁸for Mount Zion, which lies desolate,
  with jackals prowling over it.

¹⁹You, O LORD, reign forever;
  your throne endures from generation to
  generation.
²⁰Why do you always forget us?
  Why do you forsake us so long?
²¹Restore us to yourself, O LORD, that we may
  return;
  renew our days as of old
²²unless you have utterly rejected us
  and are angry with us beyond measure.

does the poet pray throughout this chapter? Has God abandoned Judah or has Judah abandoned God? Both? Neither? Does the book end on a hopeful note or a despairing one? Why do you think so?

1. When are we most apt to "consider our ways": During smooth sailing? In the midst of the storm? When we're going nowhere? 2. In what sense are you bearing the punishment for the sins of your fathers? In what ways are you laying up punishment for your children? How can the cycle be broken? 3. As a nation, are we storing up judgment for the next generation? Explain. 4. If repentance is the first step in returning to God's favor, why is it so difficult for us? Where in your life is it most difficult to admit your failure and ask for God's help? What incentive does this book give you to do that?

INTRODUCTION to
EZEKIEL

Book Study Outline: If you are using Ezekiel for a study course, here is a 7- or 13-week outline. Use the questions in the margin for your group agenda:

start meeting / 15 min.

read & discuss Bible / 30 min.

close meeting / 15–45 min.

Refer to the Questions and Answers in the front of this Bible for more information.

Author: Ezekiel, a Jewish priest-prophet, exiled in Babylon.

7-week plan	13-week plan	Personal Reading	Group Study Passage
1	1	1	1:1–28/Glory of the Lord
	2	2–3	2:1–3:15/Ezekiel's Call
2	3	4–5	4:1–5:17/Siege of Jerusalem
	4	6–8	8:1–18/Idolatry in the Temple
3	5	9–16	16:1–63/Unfaithful Jerusalem
	6	17–18	18:1–32/Sin and Death
4	7	19–22	22:1–31/Jerusalem's Sins
	8	23–28	25:1–17/Nations in Prophecy
5	9	29–34	34:1–31/Shepherds and Sheep
	10	35–36	36:1–38/Mountains of Israel
6	11	37–39	37:1–14/The Dry Bones
	12	40–43	40:1–43:27/The New Temple
7	13	44–48	47:1–12/River From the Temple

Date: Ezekiel's prophecies can be dated with precision, more than any other prophet. His first dates from 593 B.C., seven years before the fall of Jerusalem; his last from 571 B.C.

Theme: God acts in the events of human history so that everyone may come to know him and find new life in him.

Historical Background: Like his contemporary Jeremiah, Ezekiel prophesied in politically volatile times. After Israel was destroyed by the Assyrians in 722 B.C., only the southern kingdom of Judah was left. Assyria lost its ascendancy in 612 B.C. and was replaced as a world power by Babylon. Judah was a vassal state of Babylon, but rebelled, hoping for Egypt's support. Egypt proved unreliable and Judah was subdued by King Nebuchadnezzar of Babylon in 605 and again in 598–597 B.C. He took thousands of Jews captive each time. Among those in the second wave of exiles was Ezekiel.

Characteristics: Ezekiel is a book of unearthly visions, poems, parables and comic street-theater. However, to get the people's attention, God uses more than Ezekiel's vivid images and symbolic actions. He allows the people to suffer. But Ezekiel's message of imminent doom turns to ultimate hope in the end. There is symmetry in the book with the vision of the desecrated temple balanced by that of the restored temple, the message of God's anger balanced by the truth of God's mercy, and the appointment of Ezekiel as a watchman of judgment balanced by his role as a watchman of consolation.

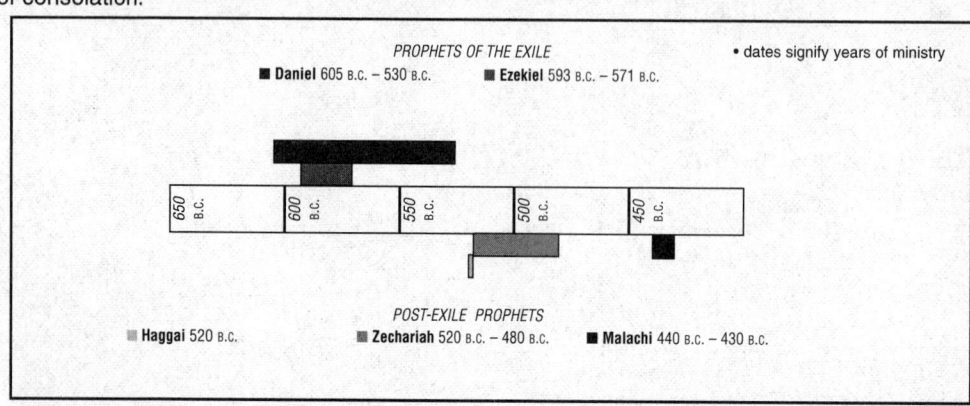

PROPHETS OF THE EXILE   • dates signify years of ministry

■ Daniel 605 B.C. – 530 B.C.   ■ Ezekiel 593 B.C. – 571 B.C.

650 B.C.   600 B.C.   550 B.C.   500 B.C.   450 B.C.

POST-EXILE PROPHETS

■ Haggai 520 B.C.   ■ Zechariah 520 B.C. – 480 B.C.   ■ Malachi 440 B.C. – 430 B.C.

Ezekiel

The Living Creatures and the Glory of the LORD

1 In the[a] thirtieth year, in the fourth month on the fifth day, while I was among the exiles by the Kebar River, the heavens were opened and I saw visions of God.

²On the fifth of the month—it was the fifth year of the exile of King Jehoiachin— ³the word of the LORD came to Ezekiel the priest, the son of Buzi,[b] by the Kebar River in the land of the Babylonians.[c] There the hand of the LORD was upon him.

⁴I looked, and I saw a windstorm coming out of the north—an immense cloud with flashing lightning and surrounded by brilliant light. The center of the fire looked like glowing metal, ⁵and in the fire was what looked like four living creatures. In appearance their form was that of a man, ⁶but each of them had four faces and four wings. ⁷Their legs were straight; their feet were like those of a calf and gleamed like burnished bronze. ⁸Under their wings on their four sides they had the hands of a man. All four of them had faces and wings, ⁹and their wings touched one another. Each one went straight ahead; they did not turn as they moved.

¹⁰Their faces looked like this: Each of the four had the face of a man, and on the right side each had the face of a lion, and on the left the face of an ox; each also had the face of an eagle. ¹¹Such were their faces. Their wings were spread out upward; each had two wings, one touching the wing of another creature on either side, and two wings covering its body. ¹²Each one went straight ahead. Wherever the spirit would go, they would go, without turning as they went. ¹³The appearance of the living creatures was like burning coals of fire or like torches. Fire moved back and forth among the creatures; it was bright, and lightning flashed out of it. ¹⁴The creatures sped back and forth like flashes of lightning.

¹⁵As I looked at the living creatures, I saw a wheel on the ground beside each creature with its four faces. ¹⁶This was the appearance and structure of the wheels: They sparkled like chrysolite, and all four looked alike. Each appeared to be made like a wheel intersecting a wheel. ¹⁷As they moved, they would go in any one of the four directions the creatures faced; the wheels did not turn about[d] as the creatures went. ¹⁸Their rims were high and awesome, and all four rims were full of eyes all around.

¹⁹When the living creatures moved, the wheels beside them moved; and when the living creatures rose from the ground, the wheels also rose. ²⁰Wherever the spirit would go, they would go, and the wheels would rise along with them, because the spirit of the living creatures was in the wheels. ²¹When the creatures moved, they also moved; when the creatures stood still, they also stood still; and when the creatures rose from the ground, the wheels rose along with them, because the spirit of the living creatures was in the wheels.

²²Spread out above the heads of the living creatures was what looked like an expanse, sparkling like ice, and awesome. ²³Under the expanse their wings were stretched out one toward the other, and each had two wings covering its body. ²⁴When the creatures

1. Think back to the time when you were age 30 (or project yourself into that time frame): Where are you living? Who with? What are you doing for a living? What lies ahead for you, five years down the road? **2.** When and where have you felt the closest to God? **3.** If you were the special effects director for a movie and had to portray God, how would you do it?

1. When Ezekiel sees this vision, where is he (v. 1)? Why is he there? How old is he now? How long has he been there (v. 2)? **2.** What career might Ezekiel have entered at age 30 (v. 3; see Nu 4:3), had it not been for exile? What new career has opened up to him instead (see 2:5)? How do you think the last five years in exile have prepared Ezekiel, emotionally and spiritually, for his new role? **3.** List the different elements which comprise Ezekiel's two-part vision. What does he see? Hear? **4.** Pretend you are playing the "Pictionary" game. Take one minute to sketch Ezekiel's vision without using words or numbers. Then share your drawings with each other, or even someone outside the group. **5.** To what does he liken the four attendants to the throne? Likewise, the UFO-type object? What aspects of God's nature are revealed in such other-worldly images? **6.** How does Ezekiel react to this multi-sensory experience (v. 28b)? What must he be feeling on the inside?

1. God obviously has Ezekiel's attention: What does God have to do to get yours? **2.** The way God reveals himself to your group will probably differ radically from Ezekiel's "special effects" vision. Why is that? Why does God seem to appear that way only to certain Old Testament prophets? **3.** What aspects of God's nature revealed here most appeal to you? Which most disturb you? Why? What is your bottom-line response to Ezekiel's God?

---

a1 Or my, aside   b3 Or Ezekiel son of Buzi the priest   c3 Or Chaldeans   d17 Or

moved, I heard the sound of their wings, like the roar of rushing waters, like the voice of the Almighty,[a] like the tumult of an army. When they stood still, they lowered their wings.

²⁵Then there came a voice from above the expanse over their heads as they stood with lowered wings. ²⁶Above the expanse over their heads was what looked like a throne of sapphire,[b] and high above on the throne was a figure like that of a man. ²⁷I saw that from what appeared to be his waist up he looked like glowing metal, as if full of fire, and that from there down he looked like fire; and brilliant light surrounded him. ²⁸Like the appearance of a rainbow in the clouds on a rainy day, so was the radiance around him.

This was the appearance of the likeness of the glory of the LORD. When I saw it, I fell facedown, and I heard the voice of one speaking.

Ezekiel's Call

2 He said to me, "Son of man, stand up on your feet and I will speak to you." ²As he spoke, the Spirit came into me and raised me to my feet, and I heard him speaking to me.

³He said: "Son of man, I am sending you to the Israelites, to a rebellious nation that has rebelled against me; they and their fathers have been in revolt against me to this very day. ⁴The people to whom I am sending you are obstinate and stubborn. Say to them, 'This is what the Sovereign LORD says.' ⁵And whether they listen or fail to listen—for they are a rebellious house—they will know that a prophet has been among them. ⁶And you, son of man, do not be afraid of them or their words. Do not be afraid, though briers and thorns are all around you and you live among scorpions. Do not be afraid of what they say or terrified by them, though they are a rebellious house. ⁷You must speak my words to them, whether they listen or fail to listen, for they are rebellious. ⁸But you, son of man, listen to what I say to you. Do not rebel like that rebellious house; open your mouth and eat what I give you."

⁹Then I looked, and I saw a hand stretched out to me. In it was a scroll, ¹⁰which he unrolled before me. On both sides of it were written words of lament and mourning and woe.

3 And he said to me, "Son of man, eat what is before you, eat this scroll; then go and speak to the house of Israel." ²So I opened my mouth, and he gave me the scroll to eat.

³Then he said to me, "Son of man, eat this scroll I am giving you and fill your stomach with it." So I ate it, and it tasted as sweet as honey in my mouth.

⁴He then said to me: "Son of man, go now to the house of Israel and speak my words to them. ⁵You are not being sent to a people of obscure speech and difficult language, but to the house of Israel— ⁶not to many peoples of obscure speech and difficult language, whose words you cannot understand. Surely if I had sent you to them, they would have listened to you. ⁷But the house of Israel is not willing to listen to you because they are not willing to listen to me, for the whole house of Israel is hardened and obstinate. ⁸But I will make you as unyielding and hardened as they are. ⁹I will make your forehead like the hardest stone, harder than flint. Do not be afraid of them or terrified by them, though they are a rebellious house."

¹⁰And he said to me, "Son of man, listen carefully and take to heart all the words I speak to you. ¹¹Go now to your countrymen in

1. What does your tax form say you do for a living? How does your professional resume amplify that "one word"? 2. What parts of your job do you tackle first? What parts are still left undone at the end of the week (month or year)? 3. If you could have any other job, what would you pick and why?

1. What is significant about Ezekiel's current posture (1:28) and the position God wants him to assume (2:1–2)? 2. What do you think God intends by repeatedly (93 times) calling him "son of man"? Addressed in his human weakness, where does Ezekiel get the strength to comply with God's request (2:2; also 3:8,12,14)? 3. To whom does God send Ezekiel to speak (2:3–8; 3:5–9)? What are they like? Why might Ezekiel be afraid to take on this "mission impossible" (3:6–7)? 4. How does God console him (2:6–7; 3:1–3,8–12)? What seems to be required to get this job done: (a) Thick skin? (b) Strong stomach? (c) Hard hat? (d) Big ears? (e) Soft heart? (f) Foreign language? (g) Flying machine? 5. What is on the scroll that Ezekiel has to eat (2:10)? How does it taste to him (3:3)? What he thought would be sour or "bitter" (3:14) actually wasn't. What lesson do you think God is trying to teach him in shaking up his taste buds (a lesson also taught to John, see Rev 10:9–10)? 6. Ezekiel returns to his home in Tel Abib (3:14–15): How does he get there? How does he feel at first? And seven days later? How might his sitting among his fellow exiles compare with his having stood before the Lord? What is the net impact on him?

exile and speak to them. Say to them, 'This is what the Sovereign LORD says,' whether they listen or fail to listen."

¹²Then the Spirit lifted me up, and I heard behind me a loud rumbling sound—May the glory of the LORD be praised in his dwelling place!— ¹³the sound of the wings of the living creatures brushing against each other and the sound of the wheels beside them, a loud rumbling sound. ¹⁴The Spirit then lifted me up and took me away, and I went in bitterness and in the anger of my spirit, with the strong hand of the LORD upon me. ¹⁵I came to the exiles who lived at Tel Abib near the Kebar River. And there, where they were living, I sat among them for seven days—overwhelmed.

Warning to Israel

¹⁶At the end of seven days the word of the LORD came to me: ¹⁷"Son of man, I have made you a watchman for the house of Israel; so hear the word I speak and give them warning from me. ¹⁸When I say to a wicked man, 'You will surely die,' and you do not warn him or speak out to dissuade him from his evil ways in order to save his life, that wicked man will die for[a] his sin, and I will hold you accountable for his blood. ¹⁹But if you do warn the wicked man and he does not turn from his wickedness or from his evil ways, he will die for his sin; but you will have saved yourself.

²⁰"Again, when a righteous man turns from his righteousness and does evil, and I put a stumbling block before him, he will die. Since you did not warn him, he will die for his sin. The righteous things he did will not be remembered, and I will hold you accountable for his blood. ²¹But if you do warn the righteous man not to sin and he does not sin, he will surely live because he took warning, and you will have saved yourself."

²²The hand of the LORD was upon me there, and he said to me, "Get up and go out to the plain, and there I will speak to you." ²³So I got up and went out to the plain. And the glory of the LORD was standing there, like the glory I had seen by the Kebar River, and I fell facedown.

²⁴Then the Spirit came into me and raised me to my feet. He spoke to me and said: "Go, shut yourself inside your house. ²⁵And you, son of man, they will tie with ropes; you will be bound so that you cannot go out among the people. ²⁶I will make your tongue stick to the roof of your mouth so that you will be silent and unable to rebuke them, though they are a rebellious house. ²⁷But when I speak to you, I will open your mouth and you shall say to them, 'This is what the Sovereign LORD says.' Whoever will listen let him listen, and whoever will refuse let him refuse; for they are a rebellious house.

Siege of Jerusalem Symbolized

4 "Now, son of man, take a clay tablet, put it in front of you and draw the city of Jerusalem on it. ²Then lay siege to it: Erect siege works against it, build a ramp up to it, set up camps against it and put battering rams around it. ³Then take an iron pan, place it as an iron wall between you and the city and turn your face toward it. It will be under siege, and you shall besiege it. This will be a sign to the house of Israel.

⁴"Then lie on your left side and put the sin of the house of Israel upon yourself.[b] You are to bear their sin for the number of days you lie on your side. ⁵I have assigned you the same number of days

---

1. As you review your life's work, have you ever been aware of any special calling or "overwhelming" task from the Lord? 2. What about God stands out to you in the call to Ezekiel?

---

1. Do you read the warning labels on the products you buy? What warning labels do you read, but choose to ignore as silly or "that couldn't happen to me"? 2. Recall a time when you were quite "tongue-tied" or speechless. What happened? How did you recover?

1. What is the main point of God's warning to Ezekiel (vv. 18–21,24– 26)? Of Ezekiel's warning to Israel (vv. 17,27)? Why is Ezekiel held accountable for their response? 2. "Watchmen" were posted on farm and town walls to warn of thieves or attackers. What then does it mean for Ezekiel to be made a spiritual watchman? 3. How does the hand of the Lord feel to Ezekiel (vv. 22–27)? What restraints does God impose on him? How does this show God is serious?

1. What message do you think God has for the people where you live? What is your role: To tell everyone, or only those who come to you? 2. What would help them take you more seriously?

---

1. What do you recall about 1968, the year of many civil rights and anti-Vietnam protests? Were you in school then, or not even born yet, or part of that "don't-trust-anyone-over-30" group? 2. From what you've read or seen of that era, what did you think of those who staged pickets, boycotts, "sit-ins" or "sleep-ins" at your university campus or state capitol? Did you mimic or condemn their long hair and "radical lifestyle"? 3. When have you "put your body on the line" to protest some social evil?

---

a18 Or *in*; also in verses 19 and 20   *b4* Or *your side*

1. For each object lesson Ezekiel was to act out, answer the following: What equipment or props did he need for it? What were the lines scripted for him to speak? How long would it take? What did each prop or action or time span symbolize? 2. What was the object lesson the audience was intended to learn? Do you think Israel got the point and repented? Or did they likely get angry and take out revenge on Ezekiel for "offending community standards of decency" by his outrageous street theatre? 3. Given his priestly training, what object lesson was too offensive even for brazen Ezekiel to do (vv. 12–15)? What other object lessons would you have found tough to do? Which would you, as an Israelite, find too much to stomach? Why? 4. In one column list all the things God says he will do in his wrath; in the other column list all of Israel's sins. How are the two lists related? 5. The particular judgments listed here represent God's anger "fully spent" (5:13; see 6:12; 7:8; 13:15; 20:8, 21). Why would God want to spend all of his anger on his chosen people? Doesn't he have better places to spend it? How do you feel about this?

1. How would you react if your pastor did any of the things God required Ezekiel to do? 2. From your list of Israel's sins, which ones bring to mind a modern equivalent? How does the moral condition of your country compare to that of ancient Israel? What do you think will be God's certain eventual response? 3. God says he will do some terrible things to Israel. In wrath, where will he remember mercy? In punishment, where do you see his love? How will renewal come out of such stinging rebukes?

as the years of their sin. So for 390 days you will bear the sin of the house of Israel.

⁶"After you have finished this, lie down again, this time on your right side, and bear the sin of the house of Judah. I have assigned you 40 days, a day for each year. ⁷Turn your face toward the siege of Jerusalem and with bared arm prophesy against her. ⁸I will tie you up with ropes so that you cannot turn from one side to the other until you have finished the days of your siege.

⁹"Take wheat and barley, beans and lentils, millet and spelt; put them in a storage jar and use them to make bread for yourself. You are to eat it during the 390 days you lie on your side. ¹⁰Weigh out twenty shekels[a] of food to eat each day and eat it at set times. ¹¹Also measure out a sixth of a hin[b] of water and drink it at set times. ¹²Eat the food as you would a barley cake; bake it in the sight of the people, using human excrement for fuel." ¹³The LORD said, "In this way the people of Israel will eat defiled food among the nations where I will drive them."

¹⁴Then I said, "Not so, Sovereign LORD! I have never defiled myself. From my youth until now I have never eaten anything found dead or torn by wild animals. No unclean meat has ever entered my mouth."

¹⁵"Very well," he said, "I will let you bake your bread over cow manure instead of human excrement."

¹⁶He then said to me: "Son of man, I will cut off the supply of food in Jerusalem. The people will eat rationed food in anxiety and drink rationed water in despair, ¹⁷for food and water will be scarce. They will be appalled at the sight of each other and will waste away because of[c] their sin.

5 "Now, son of man, take a sharp sword and use it as a barber's razor to shave your head and your beard. Then take a set of scales and divide up the hair. ²When the days of your siege come to an end, burn a third of the hair with fire inside the city. Take a third and strike it with the sword all around the city. And scatter a third to the wind. For I will pursue them with drawn sword. ³But take a few strands of hair and tuck them away in the folds of your garment. ⁴Again, take a few of these and throw them into the fire and burn them up. A fire will spread from there to the whole house of Israel.

⁵"This is what the Sovereign LORD says: This is Jerusalem, which I have set in the center of the nations, with countries all around her. ⁶Yet in her wickedness she has rebelled against my laws and decrees more than the nations and countries around her. She has rejected my laws and has not followed my decrees.

⁷"Therefore this is what the Sovereign LORD says: You have been more unruly than the nations around you and have not followed my decrees or kept my laws. You have not even[d] conformed to the standards of the nations around you.

⁸"Therefore this is what the Sovereign LORD says: I myself am against you, Jerusalem, and I will inflict punishment on you in the sight of the nations. ⁹Because of all your detestable idols, I will do to you what I have never done before and will never do again. ¹⁰Therefore in your midst fathers will eat their children, and children will eat their fathers. I will inflict punishment on you and will scatter all your survivors to the winds. ¹¹Therefore as surely as I live, declares the Sovereign LORD, because you have defiled my sanctuary with all your vile images and detestable practices, I my-

---

a10 That is, about 8 ounces (about 0.2 kilogram)   b11 That is, about 2/3 quart (about 0.6 liter)   c17 Or away in   d7 Most Hebrew manuscripts; some Hebrew manuscripts and Syriac You have

self will withdraw my favor; I will not look on you with pity or spare you. ¹²A third of your people will die of the plague or perish by famine inside you; a third will fall by the sword outside your walls; and a third I will scatter to the winds and pursue with drawn sword.

¹³"Then my anger will cease and my wrath against them will subside, and I will be avenged. And when I have spent my wrath upon them, they will know that I the LORD have spoken in my zeal.

¹⁴"I will make you a ruin and a reproach among the nations around you, in the sight of all who pass by. ¹⁵You will be a reproach and a taunt, a warning and an object of horror to the nations around you when I inflict punishment on you in anger and in wrath and with stinging rebuke. I the LORD have spoken. ¹⁶When I shoot at you with my deadly and destructive arrows of famine, I will shoot to destroy you. I will bring more and more famine upon you and cut off your supply of food. ¹⁷I will send famine and wild beasts against you, and they will leave you childless. Plague and bloodshed will sweep through you, and I will bring the sword against you. I the LORD have spoken."

A Prophecy Against the Mountains of Israel

6 The word of the LORD came to me: ²"Son of man, set your face against the mountains of Israel; prophesy against them ³and say: 'O mountains of Israel, hear the word of the Sovereign LORD. This is what the Sovereign LORD says to the mountains and hills, to the ravines and valleys: I am about to bring a sword against you, and I will destroy your high places. ⁴Your altars will be demolished and your incense altars will be smashed; and I will slay your people in front of your idols. ⁵I will lay the dead bodies of the Israelites in front of their idols, and I will scatter your bones around your altars. ⁶Wherever you live, the towns will be laid waste and the high places demolished, so that your altars will be laid waste and devastated, your idols smashed and ruined, your incense altars broken down, and what you have made wiped out. ⁷Your people will fall slain among you, and you will know that I am the LORD.

⁸"But I will spare some, for some of you will escape the sword when you are scattered among the lands and nations. ⁹Then in the nations where they have been carried captive, those who escape will remember me—how I have been grieved by their adulterous hearts, which have turned away from me, and by their eyes, which have lusted after their idols. They will loathe themselves for the evil they have done and for all their detestable practices. ¹⁰And they will know that I am the LORD; I did not threaten in vain to bring this calamity on them.

¹¹"This is what the Sovereign LORD says: Strike your hands together and stamp your feet and cry out "Alas!" because of all the wicked and detestable practices of the house of Israel, for they will fall by the sword, famine and plague. ¹²He that is far away will die of the plague, and he that is near will fall by the sword, and he that survives and is spared will die of famine. So will I spend my wrath upon them. ¹³And they will know that I am the LORD, when their people lie slain among their idols around their altars, on every high hill and on all the mountaintops, under every spreading tree and every leafy oak—places where they offered fragrant incense to all their idols. ¹⁴And I will stretch out my hand against them and make the land a desolate waste from the desert to Diblah*ᵃ*—wherever they live. Then they will know that I am the LORD.'"

1. For a vacation, would you rather go to the mountains or the seashore? Why? 2. When you get really angry, does it show in your face, arms, legs or body? How so? Demonstrate.

1. Why does God want Ezekiel to prophesy against the mountains (see Dt 12:2–7)? What had happened on those "high places" that so displeased the Lord? What was so evil about burning incense to "idols" (a derisive term, meaning literally "dung pellets")? 2. What are the different punishments God says he will bring against Israel? What effect will these punishments have on those who survive them? 3. What do you think is implied by: "You will know that I am the Lord"? (God is unique? Universal? Jealous? Sovereign?) 4. Why do you think Ezekiel talks so much about God's judgment?

1. What is the ultimate purpose of God's judgment? Why is it sometimes selective? Why are people hit differently? 2. Have you ever seen the effects of "sword, famine and plague," or other forms of God's judgment? How did it affect you? 3. How do those around you view God's wrath? What do you say in response?

ᵃ14 Most Hebrew manuscripts; a few Hebrew manuscripts *Riblah*

1. What things from last week did you put off until another day: School work? Home work? Office work? Relationships? Promised time with spouse or kids? 2. What does such procrastination tell you about yourself? 3. What would you do with the rest of today if you knew the world would end at midnight?

1. What specifically has come to an end for Israel? What is "The end!" all about? 2. What effect will God's punishment have on Israel militarily, financially, emotionally and spiritually? How will the whole world be affected (vv. 2,21,24)? 3. What actions and attitudes of Israel have brought God's wrath upon them? What loop-hole or escape clause is provided? 4. What end-time advice will the people be looking for? Where will they turn (vv. 25–26)? 5. What does God say about the fairness of his actions against Israel?

1. Would you like to be judged by the standards you use to evaluate others? Why or why not? 2. In the context of relating to people you love, where is your patience being stretched the thinnest? How much more patience do you have left? What will happen when you run out? How might limiting your patience be the more loving thing to do? 3. Does it surprise you that God's patience has an end? Why or why not? If God's patience were limitless, what would his justice look like?

The End Has Come

7 The word of the LORD came to me: 2"Son of man, this is what the Sovereign LORD says to the land of Israel: The end! The end has come upon the four corners of the land. 3The end is now upon you and I will unleash my anger against you. I will judge you according to your conduct and repay you for all your detestable practices. 4I will not look on you with pity or spare you; I will surely repay you for your conduct and the detestable practices among you. Then you will know that I am the LORD.

5"This is what the Sovereign LORD says: Disaster! An unheard-of[a] disaster is coming. 6The end has come! The end has come! It has roused itself against you. It has come! 7Doom has come upon you—you who dwell in the land. The time has come, the day is near; there is panic, not joy, upon the mountains. 8I am about to pour out my wrath on you and spend my anger against you; I will judge you according to your conduct and repay you for all your detestable practices. 9I will not look on you with pity or spare you; I will repay you in accordance with your conduct and the detestable practices among you. Then you will know that it is I the LORD who strikes the blow.

10"The day is here! It has come! Doom has burst forth, the rod has budded, arrogance has blossomed! 11Violence has grown into[b] a rod to punish wickedness; none of the people will be left, none of that crowd—no wealth, nothing of value. 12The time has come, the day has arrived. Let not the buyer rejoice nor the seller grieve, for wrath is upon the whole crowd. 13The seller will not recover the land he has sold as long as both of them live, for the vision concerning the whole crowd will not be reversed. Because of their sins, not one of them will preserve his life. 14Though they blow the trumpet and get everything ready, no one will go into battle, for my wrath is upon the whole crowd.

15"Outside is the sword, inside are plague and famine; those in the country will die by the sword, and those in the city will be devoured by famine and plague. 16All who survive and escape will be in the mountains, moaning like doves of the valleys, each because of his sins. 17Every hand will go limp, and every knee will become as weak as water. 18They will put on sackcloth and be clothed with terror. Their faces will be covered with shame and their heads will be shaved. 19They will throw their silver into the streets, and their gold will be an unclean thing. Their silver and gold will not be able to save them in the day of the LORD's wrath. They will not satisfy their hunger or fill their stomachs with it, for it has made them stumble into sin. 20They were proud of their beautiful jewelry and used it to make their detestable idols and vile images. Therefore I will turn these into an unclean thing for them. 21I will hand it all over as plunder to foreigners and as loot to the wicked of the earth, and they will defile it. 22I will turn my face away from them, and they will desecrate my treasured place; robbers will enter it and desecrate it.

23"Prepare chains, because the land is full of bloodshed and the city is full of violence. 24I will bring the most wicked of the nations to take possession of their houses; I will put an end to the pride of the mighty, and their sanctuaries will be desecrated. 25When terror comes, they will seek peace, but there will be none. 26Calamity upon calamity will come, and rumor upon rumor. They will try to get a vision from the prophet; the teaching of the law by the priest

---

a5 Most Hebrew manuscripts; some Hebrew manuscripts and Syriac *Disaster after*
b11 Or *The violent one has become*

will be lost, as will the counsel of the elders. [27]The king will mourn, the prince will be clothed with despair, and the hands of the people of the land will tremble. I will deal with them according to their conduct, and by their own standards I will judge them. Then they will know that I am the LORD."

Idolatry in the Temple

8 In the sixth year, in the sixth month on the fifth day, while I was sitting in my house and the elders of Judah were sitting before me, the hand of the Sovereign LORD came upon me there. [2]I looked, and I saw a figure like that of a man.[a] From what appeared to be his waist down he was like fire, and from there up his appearance was as bright as glowing metal. [3]He stretched out what looked like a hand and took me by the hair of my head. The Spirit lifted me up between earth and heaven and in visions of God he took me to Jerusalem, to the entrance to the north gate of the inner court, where the idol that provokes to jealousy stood. [4]And there before me was the glory of the God of Israel, as in the vision I had seen in the plain.

[5]Then he said to me, "Son of man, look toward the north." So I looked, and in the entrance north of the gate of the altar I saw this idol of jealousy.

[6]And he said to me, "Son of man, do you see what they are doing—the utterly detestable things the house of Israel is doing here, things that will drive me far from my sanctuary? But you will see things that are even more detestable."

[7]Then he brought me to the entrance to the court. I looked, and I saw a hole in the wall. [8]He said to me, "Son of man, now dig into the wall." So I dug into the wall and saw a doorway there.

[9]And he said to me, "Go in and see the wicked and detestable things they are doing here." [10]So I went in and looked, and I saw portrayed all over the walls all kinds of crawling things and detestable animals and all the idols of the house of Israel. [11]In front of them stood seventy elders of the house of Israel, and Jaazaniah son of Shaphan was standing among them. Each had a censer in his hand, and a fragrant cloud of incense was rising.

[12]He said to me, "Son of man, have you seen what the elders of the house of Israel are doing in the darkness, each at the shrine of his own idol? They say, 'The LORD does not see us; the LORD has forsaken the land.'" [13]Again, he said, "You will see them doing things that are even more detestable."

[14]Then he brought me to the entrance to the north gate of the house of the LORD, and I saw women sitting there, mourning for Tammuz. [15]He said to me, "Do you see this, son of man? You will see things that are even more detestable than this."

[16]He then brought me into the inner court of the house of the LORD, and there at the entrance to the temple, between the portico and the altar, were about twenty-five men. With their backs toward the temple of the LORD and their faces toward the east, they were bowing down to the sun in the east.

[17]He said to me, "Have you seen this, son of man? Is it a trivial matter for the house of Judah to do the detestable things they are doing here? Must they also fill the land with violence and continually provoke me to anger? Look at them putting the branch to their nose! [18]Therefore I will deal with them in anger; I will not look on them with pity or spare them. Although they shout in my ears, I will not listen to them."

a2 Or saw a fiery figure

1. If you saw a hole in a wall, what would arouse your curiosity? 2. Recall the parody of three monkeys whose hands cover their eyes, ears and mouth so that they "see no evil, hear no evil, speak no evil." What neglected issues concern you, that you wish more people would see, hear or speak up about? 3. Which monkey are you?

1. Where is Ezekiel when the vision begins? To what city is he taken? By whom? 2. In each of Ezekiel's four visions he is shown a part of the temple. What about each vision is "more detestable" than the one before? Like the blind, deaf-mute monkey with its eyes opened and ears unplugged, what evil does he sense, as if for the first time? 3. When else has Ezekiel seen a fiery "figure like that of a man" (v. 2; see 1:26–27)? What is the prior history of the "idol of jealousy" (vv. 3,5; see 2Ki 21:7; 23:6; 2Ch 33:15). 4. Tammuz (v. 14) is a Babylonian fertility god, and smelling branches (v. 17) was a form of nature worship. What do the peoples' actions reveal about what some Israelites really believed?

1. The idol that made God jealous kept reappearing in the temple. What idol has the tendency to reappear in your heart? What can you do to keep it out? 2. The actions Ezekiel saw were typical of Israel's neighbors. Which actions of the people around you do you tend to imitate if you don't watch out? 3. If Ezekiel were allowed to peep through "a hole in the wall" of your heart and mind, what would he see there? 4. What can you do about anything there that displeases God?

1. When have you been sin-gled out from a group for dis-tinguished service? 2. Have you ever joined a group with a special mark, badge or uniform signifying membership?

1. Where is Ezekiel in this vi-sion and who is his guide (see ch. 8)? 2. Ezekiel sees seven men. What are they given to do and with what tools? 3. Who gets the special "mark" and why? What do you think the people are like who do not get marks? 4. When the men begin killing unmarked people (vv. 5–8), what does Ezek-iel do? Say? What is God's an-swer? Do you think that satisfies Ezekiel? Why?

1. If you had lived in Jerusa-lem, would you have been marked? Why or why not? 2. How do you think you are different from the people around you? If seven of your neighbors and co-workers were interviewed, what would they say is different about you? 3. From John 13:35, 1 Corinthians 13 and Galatians 5:22–23, what is sup-posed to "mark" the Christian? What can you do to make your mark more visible?

1. Have you ever been part of a group where a well-liked leader has resigned or retired? How did the people who remained feel? 2. Have you lived through any climactic transitions, either in your nation's life or in your own life? Which decade for you was the cli-max or turning point? Why? As a witness to history in the making, how did you feel about it?

1. As in chapter 1, Ezekiel sees a vision of God's glory. From where has the glory of the Lord come (see 1Ki 8:10–11)? To where has Ezekiel seen the glory move (see 8:4; 9:3; 10:18,19; 11:23)? What do you think was symbolized by this departing, hov-ering glory? 2. What order does the Lord give to "the man clothed in lin-en"? What do you think the coals represent (see Ge 19:24; Am 7:4)? What do you think his action ac-complishes? 3. How does Ezekiel react this time around to this deja vu experience (compare 1:28)? How do you account for his rela-tively tranquil, matter-of-fact re-sponse?

Idolaters Killed

9 Then I heard him call out in a loud voice, "Bring the guards of the city here, each with a weapon in his hand." ²And I saw six men coming from the direction of the upper gate, which faces north, each with a deadly weapon in his hand. With them was a man clothed in linen who had a writing kit at his side. They came in and stood beside the bronze altar.

³Now the glory of the God of Israel went up from above the cherubim, where it had been, and moved to the threshold of the temple. Then the LORD called to the man clothed in linen who had the writing kit at his side ⁴and said to him, "Go throughout the city of Jerusalem and put a mark on the foreheads of those who grieve and lament over all the detestable things that are done in it."

⁵As I listened, he said to the others, "Follow him through the city and kill, without showing pity or compassion. ⁶Slaughter old men, young men and maidens, women and children, but do not touch anyone who has the mark. Begin at my sanctuary." So they began with the elders who were in front of the temple.

⁷Then he said to them, "Defile the temple and fill the courts with the slain. Go!" So they went out and began killing throughout the city. ⁸While they were killing and I was left alone, I fell face-down, crying out, "Ah, Sovereign LORD! Are you going to destroy the entire remnant of Israel in this outpouring of your wrath on Jerusalem?"

⁹He answered me, "The sin of the house of Israel and Judah is exceedingly great; the land is full of bloodshed and the city is full of injustice. They say, 'The LORD has forsaken the land; the LORD does not see.' ¹⁰So I will not look on them with pity or spare them, but I will bring down on their own heads what they have done."

¹¹Then the man in linen with the writing kit at his side brought back word, saying, "I have done as you commanded."

The Glory Departs From the Temple

10 I looked, and I saw the likeness of a throne of sapphire*ᵃ* above the expanse that was over the heads of the cherubim. ²The LORD said to the man clothed in linen, "Go in among the wheels beneath the cherubim. Fill your hands with burning coals from among the cherubim and scatter them over the city." And as I watched, he went in.

³Now the cherubim were standing on the south side of the temple when the man went in, and a cloud filled the inner court. ⁴Then the glory of the LORD rose from above the cherubim and moved to the threshold of the temple. The cloud filled the temple, and the court was full of the radiance of the glory of the LORD. ⁵The sound of the wings of the cherubim could be heard as far away as the outer court, like the voice of God Almighty*ᵇ* when he speaks.

⁶When the LORD commanded the man in linen, "Take fire from among the wheels, from among the cherubim," the man went in and stood beside a wheel. ⁷Then one of the cherubim reached out his hand to the fire that was among them. He took up some of it and put it into the hands of the man in linen, who took it and went out. ⁸(Under the wings of the cherubim could be seen what looked like the hands of a man.)

⁹I looked, and I saw beside the cherubim four wheels, one be-side each of the cherubim; the wheels sparkled like chrysolite. ¹⁰As for their appearance, the four of them looked alike; each was like a wheel intersecting a wheel. ¹¹As they moved, they would go in any

ᵃ1 Or lapis lazuli   ᵇ5 Hebrew El-Shaddai

one of the four directions the cherubim faced; the wheels did not turn about[a] as the cherubim went. The cherubim went in whatever direction the head faced, without turning as they went. [12]Their entire bodies, including their backs, their hands and their wings, were completely full of eyes, as were their four wheels. [13]I heard the wheels being called "the whirling wheels." [14]Each of the cherubim had four faces: One face was that of a cherub, the second the face of a man, the third the face of a lion, and the fourth the face of an eagle.

[15]Then the cherubim rose upward. These were the living creatures I had seen by the Kebar River. [16]When the cherubim moved, the wheels beside them moved; and when the cherubim spread their wings to rise from the ground, the wheels did not leave their side. [17]When the cherubim stood still, they also stood still; and when the cherubim rose, they rose with them, because the spirit of the living creatures was in them.

[18]Then the glory of the LORD departed from over the threshold of the temple and stopped above the cherubim. [19]While I watched, the cherubim spread their wings and rose from the ground, and as they went, the wheels went with them. They stopped at the entrance to the east gate of the LORD's house, and the glory of the God of Israel was above them.

[20]These were the living creatures I had seen beneath the God of Israel by the Kebar River, and I realized that they were cherubim. [21]Each had four faces and four wings, and under their wings was what looked like the hands of a man. [22]Their faces had the same appearance as those I had seen by the Kebar River. Each one went straight ahead.

Judgment on Israel's Leaders

11 Then the Spirit lifted me up and brought me to the gate of the house of the LORD that faces east. There at the entrance to the gate were twenty-five men, and I saw among them Jaazaniah son of Azzur and Pelatiah son of Benaiah, leaders of the people. [2]The LORD said to me, "Son of man, these are the men who are plotting evil and giving wicked advice in this city. [3]They say, 'Will it not soon be time to build houses?[b] This city is a cooking pot, and we are the meat.' [4]Therefore prophesy against them; prophesy, son of man."

[5]Then the Spirit of the LORD came upon me, and he told me to say: "This is what the LORD says: That is what you are saying, O house of Israel, but I know what is going through your mind. [6]You have killed many people in this city and filled its streets with the dead.

[7]"Therefore this is what the Sovereign LORD says: The bodies you have thrown there are the meat and this city is the pot, but I will drive you out of it. [8]You fear the sword, and the sword is what I will bring against you, declares the Sovereign LORD. [9]I will drive you out of the city and hand you over to foreigners and inflict punishment on you. [10]You will fall by the sword, and I will execute judgment on you at the borders of Israel. Then you will know that I am the LORD. [11]This city will not be a pot for you, nor will you be the meat in it; I will execute judgment on you at the borders of Israel. [12]And you will know that I am the LORD, for you have not followed my decrees or kept my laws but have conformed to the standards of the nations around you."

[13]Now as I was prophesying, Pelatiah son of Benaiah died. Then

1. How do you reconcile the teaching of this chapter, that God is *not* always present with his people, with the promise of Jesus that he *is* always with us (see Mt 28:20)? What is *conditional*, and what is *unconditional*, about God's presence? 2. If it is conditional, what might be the conditions? What might cause the glory of the Lord to withdraw from a person's life? 3. Do you sense the presence of God in your life now? How might your life be more welcoming of him? How would you react if told, "God has left your church"?

1. How do you like your meat done? If not cooked that way, do you send it back? Why or why not? 2. In renting, buying or building your own place, what's the best advice you've heard? What's the worst advice—information which proved bad or unreliable?

1. Where is Ezekiel and who does he see? What role do these 25 men play in Jerusalem? 2. What kind of leadership have they been offering? What is their advice? What effect has their leadership had (v. 6)? 3. If the "cooking pot" implies security for Israel's top chefs (leaders), what does that say about how well the Lord's message has gotten through to them? 4. If they view themselves as choice meat (v. 3), who do they think are the discarded bones (v. 15)? How does Ezekiel (and God) turn the tables on them to help them eat their own words (vv. 7–13; see ch. 24)? 5. How will they then *know* God is sovereign?

1. Have you ever misunderstood or misapplied a word from God? What happened? Whose fault was it? 2. What word is God giving you now?

---

a 11 Or *aside*   *b 3* Or *This is not the time to build houses.*

I fell facedown and cried out in a loud voice, "Ah, Sovereign LORD! Will you completely destroy the remnant of Israel?"

[14] The word of the LORD came to me: [15] "Son of man, your brothers—your brothers who are your blood relatives[a] and the whole house of Israel—are those of whom the people of Jerusalem have said, 'They are[b] far away from the LORD; this land was given to us as our possession.'

Promised Return of Israel

[16] "Therefore say: 'This is what the Sovereign LORD says: Although I sent them far away among the nations and scattered them among the countries, yet for a little while I have been a sanctuary for them in the countries where they have gone.'

[17] "Therefore say: 'This is what the Sovereign LORD says: I will gather you from the nations and bring you back from the countries where you have been scattered, and I will give you back the land of Israel again.'

[18] "They will return to it and remove all its vile images and detestable idols. [19] I will give them an undivided heart and put a new spirit in them; I will remove from them their heart of stone and give them a heart of flesh. [20] Then they will follow my decrees and be careful to keep my laws. They will be my people, and I will be their God. [21] But as for those whose hearts are devoted to their vile images and detestable idols, I will bring down on their own heads what they have done, declares the Sovereign LORD."

[22] Then the cherubim, with the wheels beside them, spread their wings, and the glory of the God of Israel was above them. [23] The glory of the LORD went up from within the city and stopped above the mountain east of it. [24] The Spirit lifted me up and brought me to the exiles in Babylonia[c] in the vision given by the Spirit of God.

Then the vision I had seen went up from me, [25] and I told the exiles everything the LORD had shown me.

The Exile Symbolized

12 The word of the LORD came to me: [2] "Son of man, you are living among a rebellious people. They have eyes to see but do not see and ears to hear but do not hear, for they are a rebellious people.

[3] "Therefore, son of man, pack your belongings for exile and in the daytime, as they watch, set out and go from where you are to another place. Perhaps they will understand, though they are a rebellious house. [4] During the daytime, while they watch, bring out your belongings packed for exile. Then in the evening, while they are watching, go out like those who go into exile. [5] While they watch, dig through the wall and take your belongings out through it. [6] Put them on your shoulder as they are watching and carry them out at dusk. Cover your face so that you cannot see the land, for I have made you a sign to the house of Israel."

[7] So I did as I was commanded. During the day I brought out my things packed for exile. Then in the evening I dug through the wall with my hands. I took my belongings out at dusk, carrying them on my shoulders while they watched.

[8] In the morning the word of the LORD came to me: [9] "Son of man, did not that rebellious house of Israel ask you, 'What are you doing?'

[10] "Say to them, 'This is what the Sovereign LORD says: This

---

Where do you consider "home"? What's the longest you've been away? What did it feel like to return?

1. In chapter 11, how does the fate of those who stayed in Jerusalem compare with those who were taken into exile? How is God himself a "sanctuary" (v. 16) for people who have always believed God's presence is linked to the temple? 2. What changes does God promise to make in the hearts of his people (vv. 18–21)? 3. How will their behavior change as a result? Will all be changed? Why not?

1. Have you had this "sanctuary" experience? Where? When? What happened? Are you different? 2. What was Christ's role in providing "a substitute temple" while you were in "exile"?

1. Where do you go when you just want to get away from it all for a day? Why there? What or who do you take with you? 2. Who in your family packs for a week, even though it's just an overnite trip? 3. What big trips have you taken recently?

1. What are the people like to whom Ezekiel prophesies (vv. 1–2; also Isa 6:9–10)? 2. Because they don't listen or see, in what way does God use to communicate his message? Do you think such *sign*-language will work? Why or why not? 3. In the timing and sequence of this unfolding revelation, what is significant about (a) "The word of the Lord " coming to Ezekiel? (b) Ezekiel's unquestioning obedience? (c) Israel's questioning response (v. 9)? How are (a) (b) and (c) related? 4. Of all the things God tells Ezekiel to do in verses 3–16, what part seems most eye-catching or poignant? What is its symbolic meaning? Read Jeremiah 39:1–10 to see to what extent Ezekiel's words came true. 5. What

---

[a] 15 Or *are in exile with you* (see Septuagint and Syriac)   [b] 15 Or *those to whom the people of Jerusalem have said, 'Stay*   [c] 24 Or *Chaldea*

oracle concerns the prince in Jerusalem and the whole house of Israel who are there.' [11]Say to them, 'I am a sign to you.'

"As I have done, so it will be done to them. They will go into exile as captives.

[12]"The prince among them will put his things on his shoulder at dusk and leave, and a hole will be dug in the wall for him to go through. He will cover his face so that he cannot see the land. [13]I will spread my net for him, and he will be caught in my snare; I will bring him to Babylonia, the land of the Chaldeans, but he will not see it, and there he will die. [14]I will scatter to the winds all those around him—his staff and all his troops—and I will pursue them with drawn sword.

[15]"They will know that I am the LORD, when I disperse them among the nations and scatter them through the countries. [16]But I will spare a few of them from the sword, famine and plague, so that in the nations where they go they may acknowledge all their detestable practices. Then they will know that I am the LORD."

[17]The word of the LORD came to me: [18]"Son of man, tremble as you eat your food, and shudder in fear as you drink your water. [19]Say to the people of the land: 'This is what the Sovereign LORD says about those living in Jerusalem and in the land of Israel: They will eat their food in anxiety and drink their water in despair, for their land will be stripped of everything in it because of the violence of all who live there. [20]The inhabited towns will be laid waste and the land will be desolate. Then you will know that I am the LORD.'"

[21]The word of the LORD came to me: [22]"Son of man, what is this proverb you have in the land of Israel: 'The days go by and every vision comes to nothing'? [23]Say to them, 'This is what the Sovereign LORD says: I am going to put an end to this proverb, and they will no longer quote it in Israel.' Say to them, 'The days are near when every vision will be fulfilled. [24]For there will be no more false visions or flattering divinations among the people of Israel. [25]But I the LORD will speak what I will, and it shall be fulfilled without delay. For in your days, you rebellious house, I will fulfill whatever I say, declares the Sovereign LORD.'"

[26]The word of the LORD came to me: [27]"Son of man, the house of Israel is saying, 'The vision he sees is for many years from now, and he prophesies about the distant future.'

[28]"Therefore say to them, 'This is what the Sovereign LORD says: None of my words will be delayed any longer; whatever I say will be fulfilled, declares the Sovereign LORD.'"

False Prophets Condemned

13 The word of the LORD came to me: [2]"Son of man, prophesy against the prophets of Israel who are now prophesying. Say to those who prophesy out of their own imagination: 'Hear the word of the LORD! [3]This is what the Sovereign LORD says: Woe to the foolish[a] prophets who follow their own spirit and have seen nothing! [4]Your prophets, O Israel, are like jackals among ruins. [5]You have not gone up to the breaks in the wall to repair it for the house of Israel so that it will stand firm in the battle on the day of the LORD. [6]Their visions are false and their divinations a lie. They say, "The LORD declares," when the LORD has not sent them; yet they expect their words to be fulfilled. [7]Have you not seen false visions and uttered lying divinations when you say, "The LORD declares," though I have not spoken?

[a] 3 Or *wicked*

revelation unfolds next in verses 17–20? What do Ezekiel's symbolic acts mean this time? **6.** What proverbs does God say are popular in Israel (vv. 22,27)? What do they mean? How will God put an end to such false visions and human procrastination? How does this prove God is the Sovereign Lord?

1. Why do you think God cares so much that his people understand what he is going to do before he does it? What if God's revelation consisted of only events without any interpretation? As it is, what part does human response play in the unfolding of divine revelation? **2.** Read 2 Peter 3:3–13 for another answer to the problem mentioned in verses 22 and 27. Do you find it hard to wait for God to fulfill his promises? Why do you think he delays? **3.** Evidently, prophetic signs of the future are meant to grab our attention and prompt us to ask questions. What questions do you have so far about what on earth God is doing (or not doing) to bring about his kingdom? **4.** In what ways do Christians play down what God is trying to say to the church in the late 20th and early 21st century? What modern prophets do you think speak God's words but whose message is ignored?

1. List all the professions that your group can think of—from palm readers to economic forecasters to weathermen—whose job it is to predict the future. **2.** Which of them can't you trust? Why? Whose advice or warnings do you pay most attention to? Why? **3.** Have you ever had someone's prediction for you come true? On what was that prediction based?

1. What is the basic message of the false prophets? How does it differ from Ezekiel's message? **2.** God uses a number of powerful images or metaphors to condemn the false prophets. What is meant here by "whitewashed walls" and "torrential rains" (vv. 10–16)? **3.** What props do the female false prophets use in their occult practices? What is the random effect of their evil actions (vv. 19,22)? **4.** Why would anyone listen to "lies" of false prophets? In Deuteronomy 18:14–22, what criteria does God give for distinguishing true from false prophets? **5.** What will God do to intervene and put a stop to this (vv. 20–23)? How will this prove that God is the sovereign Lord?

1. How did Jesus distinguish between true and false prophets (see Mt 7:15–23; 23:13–32; 24:23–27)? How do his warnings compare with Ezekiel's? **2.** Can you think of any false prophets who are operating today? What is their message? How do you know they are false? **3.** Judging by your reading habits and whom you consult with, are you more concerned with "what the future holds" or "who holds the future"? What are you doing to reduce your anxiety level?

Ever had a speaking part in a play? What did you like best about it? And least? Ever stumble over your lines? What happened?

1. Who comes to see Ezekiel? What do you think they want? Why is God angry with them? **2.** What do you think is meant by the "idols in their hearts"? By "wicked stumbling blocks before their faces" (vv. 3,4,7; see 3:20; 7:19)? **3.** What's so wrong with

8" 'Therefore this is what the Sovereign Lord says: Because of your false words and lying visions, I am against you, declares the Sovereign Lord. 9My hand will be against the prophets who see false visions and utter lying divinations. They will not belong to the council of my people or be listed in the records of the house of Israel, nor will they enter the land of Israel. Then you will know that I am the Sovereign Lord.

10" 'Because they lead my people astray, saying, "Peace," when there is no peace, and because, when a flimsy wall is built, they cover it with whitewash, 11therefore tell those who cover it with whitewash that it is going to fall. Rain will come in torrents, and I will send hailstones hurtling down, and violent winds will burst forth. 12When the wall collapses, will people not ask you, "Where is the whitewash you covered it with?"

13" 'Therefore this is what the Sovereign Lord says: In my wrath I will unleash a violent wind, and in my anger hailstones and torrents of rain will fall with destructive fury. 14I will tear down the wall you have covered with whitewash and will level it to the ground so that its foundation will be laid bare. When it*a* falls, you will be destroyed in it; and you will know that I am the Lord. 15So I will spend my wrath against the wall and against those who covered it with whitewash. I will say to you, "The wall is gone and so are those who whitewashed it, 16those prophets of Israel who prophesied to Jerusalem and saw visions of peace for her when there was no peace, declares the Sovereign Lord." '

17"Now, son of man, set your face against the daughters of your people who prophesy out of their own imagination. Prophesy against them 18and say, 'This is what the Sovereign Lord says: Woe to the women who sew magic charms on all their wrists and make veils of various lengths for their heads in order to ensnare people. Will you ensnare the lives of my people but preserve your own? 19You have profaned me among my people for a few handfuls of barley and scraps of bread. By lying to my people, who listen to lies, you have killed those who should not have died and have spared those who should not live.

20" 'Therefore this is what the Sovereign Lord says: I am against your magic charms with which you ensnare people like birds and I will tear them from your arms; I will set free the people that you ensnare like birds. 21I will tear off your veils and save my people from your hands, and they will no longer fall prey to your power. Then you will know that I am the Lord. 22Because you disheartened the righteous with your lies, when I had brought them no grief, and because you encouraged the wicked not to turn from their evil ways and so save their lives, 23therefore you will no longer see false visions or practice divination. I will save my people from your hands. And then you will know that I am the Lord.' "

Idolaters Condemned

14 Some of the elders of Israel came to me and sat down in front of me. 2Then the word of the Lord came to me: 3"Son of man, these men have set up idols in their hearts and put wicked stumbling blocks before their faces. Should I let them inquire of me at all? 4Therefore speak to them and tell them, 'This is what the Sovereign Lord says: When any Israelite sets up idols in his heart and puts a wicked stumbling block before his face and then goes to a prophet, I the Lord will answer him myself in keeping with his

a 14 Or the city

great idolatry. [5]I will do this to recapture the hearts of the people of Israel, who have all deserted me for their idols.'

[6]"Therefore say to the house of Israel, 'This is what the Sovereign LORD says: Repent! Turn from your idols and renounce all your detestable practices!

[7]" 'When any Israelite or any alien living in Israel separates himself from me and sets up idols in his heart and puts a wicked stumbling block before his face and then goes to a prophet to inquire of me, I the LORD will answer him myself. [8]I will set my face against that man and make him an example and a byword. I will cut him off from my people. Then you will know that I am the LORD.

[9]" 'And if the prophet is enticed to utter a prophecy, I the LORD have enticed that prophet, and I will stretch out my hand against him and destroy him from among my people Israel. [10]They will bear their guilt—the prophet will be as guilty as the one who consults him. [11]Then the people of Israel will no longer stray from me, nor will they defile themselves anymore with all their sins. They will be my people, and I will be their God, declares the Sovereign LORD.' "

Judgment Inescapable

[12]The word of the LORD came to me: [13]"Son of man, if a country sins against me by being unfaithful and I stretch out my hand against it to cut off its food supply and send famine upon it and kill its men and their animals, [14]even if these three men—Noah, Daniel[a] and Job—were in it, they could save only themselves by their righteousness, declares the Sovereign LORD.

[15]"Or if I send wild beasts through that country and they leave it childless and it becomes desolate so that no one can pass through it because of the beasts, [16]as surely as I live, declares the Sovereign LORD, even if these three men were in it, they could not save their own sons or daughters. They alone would be saved, but the land would be desolate.

[17]"Or if I bring a sword against that country and say, 'Let the sword pass throughout the land,' and I kill its men and their animals, [18]as surely as I live, declares the Sovereign LORD, even if these three men were in it, they could not save their own sons or daughters. They alone would be saved.

[19]"Or if I send a plague into that land and pour out my wrath upon it through bloodshed, killing its men and their animals, [20]as surely as I live, declares the Sovereign LORD, even if Noah, Daniel and Job were in it, they could save neither son nor daughter. They would save only themselves by their righteousness.

[21]"For this is what the Sovereign LORD says: How much worse will it be when I send against Jerusalem my four dreadful judgments—sword and famine and wild beasts and plague—to kill its men and their animals! [22]Yet there will be some survivors—sons and daughters who will be brought out of it. They will come to you, and when you see their conduct and their actions, you will be consoled regarding the disaster I have brought upon Jerusalem—every disaster I have brought upon it. [23]You will be consoled when you see their conduct and their actions, for you will know that I have done nothing in it without cause, declares the Sovereign LORD."

---

[a]14 Or *Daniel*; the Hebrew spelling may suggest a person other than the prophet Daniel; also in verse 20.

---

consulting the Lord's prophet when you also worship idols (vv. 4–5,7–8)? **4.** Why is the prophet who is consulted also liable? If God would never speak to an idolater, who then is the prophecy for? **5.** What then is significant about this first warning to "Repent!"?

♡ **1.** What kind of idols might people have in their hearts today? What stumbling block might you be fixating upon? **2.** What effect will mixed loyalties have on one's relationship with God? What action does God want you to take in this regard?

☕ Who is your favorite hero from modern history? Why? How are you like that person?

📖 **1.** Why do you suppose God picks these three heroes from Israel's history? What did each one do to become famous? **2.** What point does God make by mentioning Noah, Daniel and Job in this context? What had the people in Jerusalem evidently thought would spare them from God's judgment? On what similar hope did Abraham base his plea for Sodom (see Ge 18:16–33)? **3.** Will everyone in Jerusalem be killed? If not, where will the survivors go? **4.** What will those who see them say about the mercy and justice of God's punishment? Why? How will this object lesson prove God is the Sovereign Lord?

♡ **1.** Have you ever been tempted to think that, because of family or church ties, you were right with God? What does God say about such an idea? **2.** Of these three—Noah, Daniel and Job—who seems more heroic to you? Why? **3.** On what hero in the political or religious arena are you pinning your hopes? Or, are you captain of your own ship? **4.** In this chapter, what hope does God give you for surviving his future judgment?

☕ Have you built anything out of wood? Did it last?

📖 **1.** What is vine wood good for? Why is that so shocking? How else are God's people like a "vine" (see Ps 80:8–11; Hos 14:5–8) or a "peg" (see Isa 22:23–25)? **2.** Though they survived the fire of 597 B.C. (see 2Ki 24:10–17), what "fire will yet consume them"? How will this prove God is sovereign?

♡ How can you keep from becoming mere firewood?

☕ **1.** What recent book or magazine have you bought, mostly because of its cover appeal? Any romance novels or tabloids? **2.** Of the TV personalities you know, which ones would you like to meet in person to see what beauty lies beneath the surface? **3.** If married: How did you and your mate get engaged? If single: How do you imagine making or receiving the marriage proposal?

📖 **1.** Who are the characters in this allegorical love story? Who do they represent? **2.** What about this woman's "ancestry and birth" is significant (v. 3)? (Has Jerusalem always been Israelite territory? Who possessed it before David finally conquered it?) **3.** What does the man do for the woman in the beginning of this story? What reference do you see here to childbirth? Puberty? Marriage? What one word sums up his desire for her (and God's desire for all people)? **4.** Beginning with verse 15, the focus shifts from "I" to "You," signaling what shift in emphasis? **5.** How does the woman respond to the man? What does she do now (vv. 15–19) with all the gifts he once gave her (vv. 10–14)? To what physical involvement (with fertility gods) and spiritual attitude does the man's accusation refer? **6.** How does she treat his children (vv. 20–21)? Is this act literal or figurative? Why do you think so (see 2Ki 17:17)? **7.** What does she do (physically and spiritually) with her neighbors and strangers (vv. 25–34)? What does she do this for? **8.** How will the husband punish his wife for her deeds (vv. 35–42; see Dt 22:20–24)? How will these actions make him feel? **9.** What kind of a relationship will they

Jerusalem, A Useless Vine

15 The word of the LORD came to me: ²"Son of man, how is the wood of a vine better than that of a branch on any of the trees in the forest? ³Is wood ever taken from it to make anything useful? Do they make pegs from it to hang things on? ⁴And after it is thrown on the fire as fuel and the fire burns both ends and chars the middle, is it then useful for anything? ⁵If it was not useful for anything when it was whole, how much less can it be made into something useful when the fire has burned it and it is charred?

⁶"Therefore this is what the Sovereign LORD says: As I have given the wood of the vine among the trees of the forest as fuel for the fire, so will I treat the people living in Jerusalem. ⁷I will set my face against them. Although they have come out of the fire, the fire will yet consume them. And when I set my face against them, you will know that I am the LORD. ⁸I will make the land desolate because they have been unfaithful, declares the Sovereign LORD."

An Allegory of Unfaithful Jerusalem

16 The word of the LORD came to me: ²"Son of man, confront Jerusalem with her detestable practices ³and say, 'This is what the Sovereign LORD says to Jerusalem: Your ancestry and birth were in the land of the Canaanites; your father was an Amorite and your mother a Hittite. ⁴On the day you were born your cord was not cut, nor were you washed with water to make you clean, nor were you rubbed with salt or wrapped in cloths. ⁵No one looked on you with pity or had compassion enough to do any of these things for you. Rather, you were thrown out into the open field, for on the day you were born you were despised.

⁶"'Then I passed by and saw you kicking about in your blood, and as you lay there in your blood I said to you, "Live!"ᵃ ⁷I made you grow like a plant of the field. You grew up and developed and became the most beautiful of jewels.ᵇ Your breasts were formed and your hair grew, you who were naked and bare.

⁸"'Later I passed by, and when I looked at you and saw that you were old enough for love, I spread the corner of my garment over you and covered your nakedness. I gave you my solemn oath and entered into a covenant with you, declares the Sovereign LORD, and you became mine.

⁹"'I bathedᶜ you with water and washed the blood from you and put ointments on you. ¹⁰I clothed you with an embroidered dress and put leather sandals on you. I dressed you in fine linen and covered you with costly garments. ¹¹I adorned you with jewelry: I put bracelets on your arms and a necklace around your neck, ¹²and I put a ring on your nose, earrings on your ears and a beautiful crown on your head. ¹³So you were adorned with gold and silver; your clothes were of fine linen and costly fabric and embroidered cloth. Your food was fine flour, honey and olive oil. You became very beautiful and rose to be a queen. ¹⁴And your fame spread among the nations on account of your beauty, because the splendor I had given you made your beauty perfect, declares the Sovereign LORD.

¹⁵"'But you trusted in your beauty and used your fame to become a prostitute. You lavished your favors on anyone who passed by and your beauty became his.ᵈ ¹⁶You took some of your garments to make gaudy high places, where you carried on your pros-

---

ᵃ6 A few Hebrew manuscripts, Septuagint and Syriac; most Hebrew manuscripts *"Live!" And as you lay there in your blood I said to you, "Live!"*   ᵇ7 Or *became mature*   ᶜ9 Or *I had bathed*   ᵈ15 Most Hebrew manuscripts; one Hebrew manuscript (see some Septuagint manuscripts) *by. Such a thing should not happen*

titution. Such things should not happen, nor should they ever occur. ¹⁷You also took the fine jewelry I gave you, the jewelry made of my gold and silver, and you made for yourself male idols and engaged in prostitution with them. ¹⁸And you took your embroidered clothes to put on them, and you offered my oil and incense before them. ¹⁹Also the food I provided for you—the fine flour, olive oil and honey I gave you to eat—you offered as fragrant incense before them. That is what happened, declares the Sovereign LORD.

²⁰ 'And you took your sons and daughters whom you bore to me and sacrificed them as food to the idols. Was your prostitution not enough? ²¹You slaughtered my children and sacrificed them*ᵃ* to the idols. ²²In all your detestable practices and your prostitution you did not remember the days of your youth, when you were naked and bare, kicking about in your blood.

²³ 'Woe! Woe to you, declares the Sovereign LORD. In addition to all your other wickedness, ²⁴you built a mound for yourself and made a lofty shrine in every public square. ²⁵At the head of every street you built your lofty shrines and degraded your beauty, offering your body with increasing promiscuity to anyone who passed by. ²⁶You engaged in prostitution with the Egyptians, your lustful neighbors, and provoked me to anger with your increasing promiscuity. ²⁷So I stretched out my hand against you and reduced your territory; I gave you over to the greed of your enemies, the daughters of the Philistines, who were shocked by your lewd conduct. ²⁸You engaged in prostitution with the Assyrians too, because you were insatiable; and even after that, you still were not satisfied. ²⁹Then you increased your promiscuity to include Babylonia,ᵇ a land of merchants, but even with this you were not satisfied.

³⁰ 'How weak-willed you are, declares the Sovereign LORD, when you do all these things, acting like a brazen prostitute! ³¹When you built your mounds at the head of every street and made your lofty shrines in every public square, you were unlike a prostitute, because you scorned payment.

³² 'You adulterous wife! You prefer strangers to your own husband! ³³Every prostitute receives a fee, but you give gifts to all your lovers, bribing them to come to you from everywhere for your illicit favors. ³⁴So in your prostitution you are the opposite of others; no one runs after you for your favors. You are the very opposite, for you give payment and none is given to you.

³⁵ 'Therefore, you prostitute, hear the word of the LORD! ³⁶This is what the Sovereign LORD says: Because you poured out your wealthᶜ and exposed your nakedness in your promiscuity with your lovers, and because of all your detestable idols, and because you gave them your children's blood, ³⁷therefore I am going to gather all your lovers, with whom you found pleasure, those you loved as well as those you hated. I will gather them against you from all around and will strip you in front of them, and they will see all your nakedness. ³⁸I will sentence you to the punishment of women who commit adultery and who shed blood; I will bring upon you the blood vengeance of my wrath and jealous anger. ³⁹Then I will hand you over to your lovers, and they will tear down your mounds and destroy your lofty shrines. They will strip you of your clothes and take your fine jewelry and leave you naked and bare. ⁴⁰They will bring a mob against you, who will stone you and hack you to pieces with their swords. ⁴¹They will burn down your houses and inflict punishment on you in the sight of many women.

have in the future? Why do you think the "Like mother, like daughter" illustration is an apt one (vv. 3,44–48)? What does she have in common with her "sisters"? How is she worse off? **10.** Does all this mean the woman (Jerusalem) will never again remember, much less recover, the "days of her youth"? Who has the last laugh and why? **11.** Does this story have a happy ending or a sad one? How so? What hope is there that the love of her youth, if not her innocence, will be restored to this woman (vv. 53–58)? **12.** How does this extended parable show God is the Sovereign Lord?

1. How would you treat a wife who behaved like the woman in this story? Does God's response surprise you? Why or why not? **2.** Compare *Ezekiel's God*—"giving over" Jerusalem to her "enemies" (v. 27) or her "lovers" (v. 39)—with *Paul's God*—"giving over" all mankind to "sinful desires … shameful lusts … a depraved mind" (Ro 1:24–32). What similarities do you see? **3.** What does this story tell you about God's jealous love? His long-suffering patience? His righteous anger? His ultimately redemptive covenant? **4.** What does this story say about God's father-like relationship to Israel? To her "lustful neighbors"? To you? **5.** What would an updated allegory directed at today's church have to say about sexual perversion, abortion, secular humanism, social injustice and other scornful and idolatrous behavior? What "lustful neighbors" would you include? What punishment to fit the crime would you dish out? Why? What final hope would you offer? Why?

ᵃ21 Or *and made them pass through ⌊the fire⌋*　　ᵇ29 Or *Chaldea*　　ᶜ36 Or *lust*

I will put a stop to your prostitution, and you will no longer pay your lovers. [42]Then my wrath against you will subside and my jealous anger will turn away from you; I will be calm and no longer angry.

[43]" 'Because you did not remember the days of your youth but enraged me with all these things, I will surely bring down on your head what you have done, declares the Sovereign LORD. Did you not add lewdness to all your other detestable practices?

[44]" 'Everyone who quotes proverbs will quote this proverb about you: "Like mother, like daughter." [45]You are a true daughter of your mother, who despised her husband and her children; and you are a true sister of your sisters, who despised their husbands and their children. Your mother was a Hittite and your father an Amorite. [46]Your older sister was Samaria, who lived to the north of you with her daughters; and your younger sister, who lived to the south of you with her daughters, was Sodom. [47]You not only walked in their ways and copied their detestable practices, but in all your ways you soon became more depraved than they. [48]As surely as I live, declares the Sovereign LORD, your sister Sodom and her daughters never did what you and your daughters have done.

[49]" 'Now this was the sin of your sister Sodom: She and her daughters were arrogant, overfed and unconcerned; they did not help the poor and needy. [50]They were haughty and did detestable things before me. Therefore I did away with them as you have seen. [51]Samaria did not commit half the sins you did. You have done more detestable things than they, and have made your sisters seem righteous by all these things you have done. [52]Bear your disgrace, for you have furnished some justification for your sisters. Because your sins were more vile than theirs, they appear more righteous than you. So then, be ashamed and bear your disgrace, for you have made your sisters appear righteous.

[53]" 'However, I will restore the fortunes of Sodom and her daughters and of Samaria and her daughters, and your fortunes along with them, [54]so that you may bear your disgrace and be ashamed of all you have done in giving them comfort. [55]And your sisters, Sodom with her daughters and Samaria with her daughters, will return to what they were before; and you and your daughters will return to what you were before. [56]You would not even mention your sister Sodom in the day of your pride, [57]before your wickedness was uncovered. Even so, you are now scorned by the daughters of Edom[a] and all her neighbors and the daughters of the Philistines—all those around you who despise you. [58]You will bear the consequences of your lewdness and your detestable practices, declares the LORD.

[59]" 'This is what the Sovereign LORD says: I will deal with you as you deserve, because you have despised my oath by breaking the covenant. [60]Yet I will remember the covenant I made with you in the days of your youth, and I will establish an everlasting covenant with you. [61]Then you will remember your ways and be ashamed when you receive your sisters, both those who are older than you and those who are younger. I will give them to you as daughters, but not on the basis of my covenant with you. [62]So I will establish my covenant with you, and you will know that I am the LORD. [63]Then, when I make atonement for you for all you have done, you will remember and be ashamed and never again open your mouth because of your humiliation, declares the Sovereign LORD.' "

[a]57 Many Hebrew manuscripts and Syriac; most Hebrew manuscripts, Septuagint and Vulgate *Aram*

Two Eagles and a Vine

17 The word of the LORD came to me: [2]"Son of man, set forth an allegory and tell the house of Israel a parable. [3]Say to them, 'This is what the Sovereign LORD says: A great eagle with powerful wings, long feathers and full plumage of varied colors came to Lebanon. Taking hold of the top of a cedar, [4]he broke off its topmost shoot and carried it away to a land of merchants, where he planted it in a city of traders.

[5]" 'He took some of the seed of your land and put it in fertile soil. He planted it like a willow by abundant water, [6]and it sprouted and became a low, spreading vine. Its branches turned toward him, but its roots remained under it. So it became a vine and produced branches and put out leafy boughs.

[7]" 'But there was another great eagle with powerful wings and full plumage. The vine now sent out its roots toward him from the plot where it was planted and stretched out its branches to him for water. [8]It had been planted in good soil by abundant water so that it would produce branches, bear fruit and become a splendid vine.'

[9]"Say to them, 'This is what the Sovereign LORD says: Will it thrive? Will it not be uprooted and stripped of its fruit so that it withers? All its new growth will wither. It will not take a strong arm or many people to pull it up by the roots. [10]Even if it is transplanted, will it thrive? Will it not wither completely when the east wind strikes it—wither away in the plot where it grew?' "

[11]Then the word of the LORD came to me: [12]"Say to this rebellious house, 'Do you not know what these things mean?' Say to them: 'The king of Babylon went to Jerusalem and carried off her king and her nobles, bringing them back with him to Babylon. [13]Then he took a member of the royal family and made a treaty with him, putting him under oath. He also carried away the leading men of the land, [14]so that the kingdom would be brought low, unable to rise again, surviving only by keeping his treaty. [15]But the king rebelled against him by sending his envoys to Egypt to get horses and a large army. Will he succeed? Will he who does such things escape? Will he break the treaty and yet escape?

[16]" 'As surely as I live, declares the Sovereign LORD, he shall die in Babylon, in the land of the king who put him on the throne, whose oath he despised and whose treaty he broke. [17]Pharaoh with his mighty army and great horde will be of no help to him in war, when ramps are built and siege works erected to destroy many lives. [18]He despised the oath by breaking the covenant. Because he had given his hand in pledge and yet did all these things, he shall not escape.

[19]" 'Therefore this is what the Sovereign LORD says: As surely as I live, I will bring down on his head my oath that he despised and my covenant that he broke. [20]I will spread my net for him, and he will be caught in my snare. I will bring him to Babylon and execute judgment upon him there because he was unfaithful to me. [21]All his fleeing troops will fall by the sword, and the survivors will be scattered to the winds. Then you will know that I the LORD have spoken.

[22]" 'This is what the Sovereign LORD says: I myself will take a shoot from the very top of a cedar and plant it; I will break off a tender sprig from its topmost shoots and plant it on a high and lofty mountain. [23]On the mountain heights of Israel I will plant it; it will produce branches and bear fruit and become a splendid cedar. Birds of every kind will nest in it; they will find shelter in the shade of its branches. [24]All the trees of the field will know that I

1. What's your favorite fable of Aesop? Why do you like it? 2. If you had to liken yourself to an animal to tell a fable about yourself, what animal would you pick and why?

1. Retell the fable of the two eagles and the vine in your own words. What does each element represent: Great eagle (vv. 3,12)? Lebanon (vv. 3,12)? Cedar (v. 3)? Topmost shoot (vv. 4,12)? Land of merchants (vv. 4,12; 16:29)? Seed planted (vv. 5,13; 2Ki 24:17)? Low spreading vine (vv. 6,14; 15:2)? Another great eagle (vv. 7,17)? Sent out its roots toward him (vv. 7,15)? East wind (vv. 10,21)? 2. What is the punch line of this fable? Read 2 Chronicles 36 for another account of what happened. What was wrong with Zedekiah's actions? 3. What *new* allegory does God develop from the elements of the previous story (vv. 22–24)? What does he promise to do with the very top of the cedar tree? What does this mean for Israel? 4. What do you think Jesus meant by similar imagery in his parables (see Mt 13:31–32)?

1. As you consider the forces at work in the world today, what hope do you find in this parable? How might this help you deal with fear, cynicism and discouragement? 2. Why do you think God cares about how various political leaders treat each other? Why does he care about treaties and agreements? 3. What agreements are you party to that God might care about? Are you fulfilling them or forgetting them? How so? 4. Why should Christians be people you can inherently trust?

the LORD bring down the tall tree and make the low tree grow tall. I dry up the green tree and make the dry tree flourish.

"'I the LORD have spoken, and I will do it.'"

The Soul Who Sins Will Die

18 The word of the LORD came to me: [2]"What do you people mean by quoting this proverb about the land of Israel:

> "'The fathers eat sour grapes,
>   and the children's teeth are set on edge'?

[3]"As surely as I live, declares the Sovereign LORD, you will no longer quote this proverb in Israel. [4]For every living soul belongs to me, the father as well as the son—both alike belong to me. The soul who sins is the one who will die.

> [5]"Suppose there is a righteous man
>   who does what is just and right.
> [6]He does not eat at the mountain shrines
>   or look to the idols of the house of Israel.
> He does not defile his neighbor's wife
>   or lie with a woman during her period.
> [7]He does not oppress anyone,
>   but returns what he took in pledge for a loan.
> He does not commit robbery
>   but gives his food to the hungry
>   and provides clothing for the naked.
> [8]He does not lend at usury
>   or take excessive interest.[a]
> He withholds his hand from doing wrong
>   and judges fairly between man and man.
> [9]He follows my decrees
>   and faithfully keeps my laws.
> That man is righteous;
>   he will surely live,
>   declares the Sovereign LORD.

[10]"Suppose he has a violent son, who sheds blood or does any of these other things[b] [11](though the father has done none of them):

> "He eats at the mountain shrines.
> He defiles his neighbor's wife.
> [12]He oppresses the poor and needy.
> He commits robbery.
> He does not return what he took in pledge.
> He looks to the idols.
> He does detestable things.
> [13]He lends at usury and takes excessive interest.

Will such a man live? He will not! Because he has done all these detestable things, he will surely be put to death and his blood will be on his own head.

[14]"But suppose this son has a son who sees all the sins his father commits, and though he sees them, he does not do such things:

> [15]"He does not eat at the mountain shrines
>   or look to the idols of the house of Israel.
> He does not defile his neighbor's wife.
> [16]He does not oppress anyone
>   or require a pledge for a loan.
> He does not commit robbery

---

1. What quotable quote or favorite saying do (or did) your parents live by? What did it mean? 2. If your philosophy of life were likewise summed up in a favorite slogan or saying of yours, what would that be? What do you like about it? 3. In what two ways (proverbial or otherwise) are you like, and unlike, your dad or mom?

---

1. What was the original meaning of this (still popular) saying about "eating sour grapes" and "setting your teeth on edge"? Why do you suppose that saying was so popular in Israel (see Jer 31:29)? 2. How does this saying compare or contrast to an earlier one, "Like mother, like daughter" (16:44)? 3. How might it relate to the people whose way of thinking is expressed in chapter 14? 4. What false ideas put forth in this three-generation pattern does the Lord oppose with a divine oath (vv. 3–4)? 5. What alternative standard for judgment does the Sovereign Lord swear by? (Note: "Soul," as used here, connotes "life" or "person," not something distinct from the body.) 6. What point does listing both the deeds of the righteous and the wicked *affirm*? What point does it *refute*? Would a different listing of actions God rewards and punishes accomplish the same purpose? Why do you think so? 7. In the lists given here, what is particularly germane to the thrust of Ezekiel's prophecy so far? 8. What *guilt* does God want each party to assume? Why? What *action* does God want each party to take? Why? 9. To what criticism is this principle of judgment susceptible (vv. 25–29)? How does God remain just in forgiving sinners who repent? Instead, who is truly "unjust"? (Is *God* in the dock, having to defend himself and his just standards? Or are *you*?) 10. How do you think God feels when someone dies in his or her sins?

---

1. Does it seem unfair to you that God would pardon those who have been wicked all their lives? Why or why not? How did Jesus speak to this question of "eleventh hour" conversions (see Mt 20:1–16)? How did Jesus speak to the question of inherited guilt (see Jn 9)? 2. If your good and bad works were weighed in the bal-

---

a8 Or *take interest*; similarly in verses 13 and 17   b10 Or *things to a brother*

but gives his food to the hungry
and provides clothing for the naked.
¹⁷He withholds his hand from sin[a]
and takes no usury or excessive interest.
He keeps my laws and follows my decrees.

He will not die for his father's sin; he will surely live. ¹⁸But his father will die for his own sin, because he practiced extortion, robbed his brother and did what was wrong among his people.

¹⁹"Yet you ask, 'Why does the son not share the guilt of his father?' Since the son has done what is just and right and has been careful to keep all my decrees, he will surely live. ²⁰The soul who sins is the one who will die. The son will not share the guilt of the father, nor will the father share the guilt of the son. The righteousness of the righteous man will be credited to him, and the wickedness of the wicked will be charged against him.

²¹"But if a wicked man turns away from all the sins he has committed and keeps all my decrees and does what is just and right, he will surely live; he will not die. ²²None of the offenses he has committed will be remembered against him. Because of the righteous things he has done, he will live. ²³Do I take any pleasure in the death of the wicked? declares the Sovereign LORD. Rather, am I not pleased when they turn from their ways and live?

²⁴"But if a righteous man turns from his righteousness and commits sin and does the same detestable things the wicked man does, will he live? None of the righteous things he has done will be remembered. Because of the unfaithfulness he is guilty of and because of the sins he has committed, he will die.

²⁵"Yet you say, 'The way of the Lord is not just.' Hear, O house of Israel: Is my way unjust? Is it not your ways that are unjust? ²⁶If a righteous man turns from his righteousness and commits sin, he will die for it; because of the sin he has committed he will die. ²⁷But if a wicked man turns away from the wickedness he has committed and does what is just and right, he will save his life. ²⁸Because he considers all the offenses he has committed and turns away from them, he will surely live; he will not die. ²⁹Yet the house of Israel says, 'The way of the Lord is not just.' Are my ways unjust, O house of Israel? Is it not your ways that are unjust?

³⁰"Therefore, O house of Israel, I will judge you, each one according to his ways, declares the Sovereign LORD. Repent! Turn away from all your offenses; then sin will not be your downfall. ³¹Rid yourselves of all the offenses you have committed, and get a new heart and a new spirit. Why will you die, O house of Israel? ³²For I take no pleasure in the death of anyone, declares the Sovereign LORD. Repent and live!

A Lament for Israel's Princes

19 "Take up a lament concerning the princes of Israel ²and say:

" 'What a lioness was your mother
among the lions!
She lay down among the young lions
and reared her cubs.
³She brought up one of her cubs,
and he became a strong lion.
He learned to tear the prey
and he devoured men.

[a] 17 Septuagint (see also verse 8); Hebrew *from the poor*

ance, which way would the scales tip? How do such weights and measures miss the point of this extended parable? Are sins and good deeds even *quantifiable*? Is not the one who is forgiven much able to love much, as in Luke 7:36–50? **3.** How does Ezekiel 18 square with Joshua 7 or Romans 5? That is, if Ezekiel's point about individual accountability is true, then how come *all* Israel suffered for Achan's sin? And how come *all* humanity is guilty for Adam's sin? **4.** Is repentance hard or easy for you? Why? What can you think of now for which you should repent?

1. Of all the stories you've heard your parents or grandparents tell about "the good ol' days," which one sticks in your mind? Were "the days gone by," which they lament, really that much better than the present? Why? **2.** Who is you favorite political cartoonist? What satirical cartoon lamenting the signs of the times still sticks in your mind? Why?

1. What is a "lament"? How might its use in funeral dirges apply here? **2.** This chapter is also an allegory, similar in content to

chapter 17, with an interpretation in 2 Kings 23:31–24:20. What then is your best guess at the meaning of these symbolic elements: Lioness ... your mother ... a vine (vv. 2,10; 15:2; 17:7)? One of her cubs ... devoured men ... brought to Egypt (vv. 3–4; 2Ki 23:31–34)? Another of her cubs ... brought to Babylon (vv. 5–9; 2Ki 24:8,15)? East wind (v. 12; 17:10)? Desert (v. 13; 20:25)? Fire ... one of its main branches (v. 14; 2Ki 24:20)? **3.** Putting these puzzle pieces all together, is the picture you get just a sad funeral song about the destruction of Jerusalem and its last kings? Or does this puzzling lament contain any hints that the tragedy was their fault and came as God's judgment on them?

1. Why do you think God inspires a lament for a few evil kings? How might this lament be a particular illustration of the general teaching in chapter 18? **2.** How would you update the political cartoon or allegorical lament of Ezekiel 19, so that it fits your current situation? **3.** What do *you* lament? What does God lament? What difference do you see between what breaks your heart and what breaks his? What can you do to be more a person "after God's own heart," even in your laments?

1. How far back do you know your family tree? Who is your favorite ancestor? Why? **2.** What incident from your family history tells us what you'd like your family name to be noted for? **3.** How did you spend last Sunday? How do you typically spend your day off?

⁴The nations heard about him,
    and he was trapped in their pit.
They led him with hooks
    to the land of Egypt.

⁵ " 'When she saw her hope unfulfilled,
    her expectation gone,
she took another of her cubs
    and made him a strong lion.
⁶He prowled among the lions,
    for he was now a strong lion.
He learned to tear the prey
    and he devoured men.
⁷He broke down*a* their strongholds
    and devastated their towns.
The land and all who were in it
    were terrified by his roaring.
⁸Then the nations came against him,
    those from regions round about.
They spread their net for him,
    and he was trapped in their pit.
⁹With hooks they pulled him into a cage
    and brought him to the king of Babylon.
They put him in prison,
    so his roar was heard no longer
    on the mountains of Israel.

¹⁰ " 'Your mother was like a vine in your vineyard*b*
    planted by the water;
it was fruitful and full of branches
    because of abundant water.
¹¹Its branches were strong,
    fit for a ruler's scepter.
It towered high
    above the thick foliage,
conspicuous for its height
    and for its many branches.
¹²But it was uprooted in fury
    and thrown to the ground.
The east wind made it shrivel,
    it was stripped of its fruit;
its strong branches withered
    and fire consumed them.
¹³Now it is planted in the desert,
    in a dry and thirsty land.
¹⁴Fire spread from one of its main*c* branches
    and consumed its fruit.
No strong branch is left on it
    fit for a ruler's scepter.' "

This is a lament and is to be used as a lament."

Rebellious Israel

20 In the seventh year, in the fifth month on the tenth day, some of the elders of Israel came to inquire of the LORD, and they sat down in front of me.

²Then the word of the LORD came to me: ³"Son of man, speak to the elders of Israel and say to them, 'This is what the Sovereign

---

a7 Targum (see Septuagint); Hebrew *He knew*   *b10* Two Hebrew manuscripts; most Hebrew manuscripts *your blood*   *c14* Or *from under its*

LORD says: Have you come to inquire of me? As surely as I live, I will not let you inquire of me, declares the Sovereign LORD.'

⁴"Will you judge them? Will you judge them, son of man? Then confront them with the detestable practices of their fathers ⁵and say to them: 'This is what the Sovereign LORD says: On the day I chose Israel, I swore with uplifted hand to the descendants of the house of Jacob and revealed myself to them in Egypt. With uplifted hand I said to them, "I am the LORD your God." ⁶On that day I swore to them that I would bring them out of Egypt into a land I had searched out for them, a land flowing with milk and honey, the most beautiful of all lands. ⁷And I said to them, "Each of you, get rid of the vile images you have set your eyes on, and do not defile yourselves with the idols of Egypt. I am the LORD your God."

⁸" 'But they rebelled against me and would not listen to me; they did not get rid of the vile images they had set their eyes on, nor did they forsake the idols of Egypt. So I said I would pour out my wrath on them and spend my anger against them in Egypt. ⁹But for the sake of my name I did what would keep it from being profaned in the eyes of the nations they lived among and in whose sight I had revealed myself to the Israelites by bringing them out of Egypt. ¹⁰Therefore I led them out of Egypt and brought them into the desert. ¹¹I gave them my decrees and made known to them my laws, for the man who obeys them will live by them. ¹²Also I gave them my Sabbaths as a sign between us, so they would know that I the LORD made them holy.

¹³" 'Yet the people of Israel rebelled against me in the desert. They did not follow my decrees but rejected my laws—although the man who obeys them will live by them—and they utterly desecrated my Sabbaths. So I said I would pour out my wrath on them and destroy them in the desert. ¹⁴But for the sake of my name I did what would keep it from being profaned in the eyes of the nations in whose sight I had brought them out. ¹⁵Also with uplifted hand I swore to them in the desert that I would not bring them into the land I had given them—a land flowing with milk and honey, most beautiful of all lands— ¹⁶because they rejected my laws and did not follow my decrees and desecrated my Sabbaths. For their hearts were devoted to their idols. ¹⁷Yet I looked on them with pity and did not destroy them or put an end to them in the desert. ¹⁸I said to their children in the desert, "Do not follow the statutes of your fathers or keep their laws or defile yourselves with their idols. ¹⁹I am the LORD your God; follow my decrees and be careful to keep my laws. ²⁰Keep my Sabbaths holy, that they may be a sign between us. Then you will know that I am the LORD your God."

²¹" 'But the children rebelled against me: They did not follow my decrees, they were not careful to keep my laws—although the man who obeys them will live by them—and they desecrated my Sabbaths. So I said I would pour out my wrath on them and spend my anger against them in the desert. ²²But I withheld my hand, and for the sake of my name I did what would keep it from being profaned in the eyes of the nations in whose sight I had brought them out. ²³Also with uplifted hand I swore to them in the desert that I would disperse them among the nations and scatter them through the countries, ²⁴because they had not obeyed my laws but had rejected my decrees and desecrated my Sabbaths, and their eyes ⌊lusted⌋ after their fathers' idols. ²⁵I also gave them over to statutes that were not good and laws they could not live by; ²⁶I let them become defiled through their gifts—the sacrifice of every first-

1. What sets this chapter up as distinct from the five previous ones? As similar to chapters 1 and 8? 2. Imagine this unfolding revelation as a four-act play: "Curtain rise" (vv. 1–4); "Act I" (vv. 5–9); "Act II" (vv. 10–17); "Act III" (vv. 18–26); "Act IV" (vv. 27–29). What titles would you give to each act? 3. A full cycle of four "scenes" or seasons may be seen in all but the fourth act. What repeated pattern do you see in the first three acts? 4. When they were in Egypt (vv. 5–9), how did God reveal himself to Israel? How did they rebel? What display of wrath resulted? Why didn't God destroy them there? 5. Likewise in the desert (vv. 10–26), what did God do for Israel? How did they treat him? What was God's response? Why did he reconsider pouring out his wrath? 6. Were the children of that desert generation any different from their parents? How did God treat them? Why? 7. What does it mean that those who keep or obey God's laws "will live by them" (vv. 11,13,21)? Is law-keeping a *way of salvation* for the *lost* (see Ro 10:5; Gal 3:12)? Or is law-keeping *a way of life* for the *redeemed* (see Ex 19:6; Lev 18:2–5)? 8. In practical terms, what does it mean to "desecrate the Sabbath" (vv. 13,16, 21,24)? What is the point of keeping the Sabbath? 9. How does this timeless revelation prove God is sovereign?

1. Why do you think God is so concerned for his name and reputation? How is God's name dragged through the mud every time his people rebel? 2. If a later generation of believers only had stories of your experience with God to go by, would they say your life story *enhances* or *detracts* from God's reputation? How so? 3. Do you think God minds as much now, as he did in the Old Testament era, if we do not keep the Sabbath holy and as a day of rest? Why or why not?

born[a]—that I might fill them with horror so they would know that I am the LORD.'

27"Therefore, son of man, speak to the people of Israel and say to them, 'This is what the Sovereign LORD says: In this also your fathers blasphemed me by forsaking me: 28When I brought them into the land I had sworn to give them and they saw any high hill or any leafy tree, there they offered their sacrifices, made offerings that provoked me to anger, presented their fragrant incense and poured out their drink offerings. 29Then I said to them: What is this high place you go to?' " (It is called Bamah[b] to this day.)

Judgment and Restoration

30"Therefore say to the house of Israel: 'This is what the Sovereign LORD says: Will you defile yourselves the way your fathers did and lust after their vile images? 31When you offer your gifts—the sacrifice of your sons in[c] the fire—you continue to defile yourselves with all your idols to this day. Am I to let you inquire of me, O house of Israel? As surely as I live, declares the Sovereign LORD, I will not let you inquire of me.

32" 'You say, "We want to be like the nations, like the peoples of the world, who serve wood and stone." But what you have in mind will never happen. 33As surely as I live, declares the Sovereign LORD, I will rule over you with a mighty hand and an outstretched arm and with outpoured wrath. 34I will bring you from the nations and gather you from the countries where you have been scattered—with a mighty hand and an outstretched arm and with outpoured wrath. 35I will bring you into the desert of the nations and there, face to face, I will execute judgment upon you. 36As I judged your fathers in the desert of the land of Egypt, so I will judge you, declares the Sovereign LORD. 37I will take note of you as you pass under my rod, and I will bring you into the bond of the covenant. 38I will purge you of those who revolt and rebel against me. Although I will bring them out of the land where they are living, yet they will not enter the land of Israel. Then you will know that I am the LORD.

39" 'As for you, O house of Israel, this is what the Sovereign LORD says: Go and serve your idols, every one of you! But afterward you will surely listen to me and no longer profane my holy name with your gifts and idols. 40For on my holy mountain, the high mountain of Israel, declares the Sovereign LORD, there in the land the entire house of Israel will serve me, and there I will accept them. There I will require your offerings and your choice gifts,[d] along with all your holy sacrifices. 41I will accept you as fragrant incense when I bring you out from the nations and gather you from the countries where you have been scattered, and I will show myself holy among you in the sight of the nations. 42Then you will know that I am the LORD, when I bring you into the land of Israel, the land I had sworn with uplifted hand to give to your fathers. 43There you will remember your conduct and all the actions by which you have defiled yourselves, and you will loathe yourselves for all the evil you have done. 44You will know that I am the LORD, when I deal with you for my name's sake and not according to your evil ways and your corrupt practices, O house of Israel, declares the Sovereign LORD.' "

---

1. What wears out your patience more: (a) Training a dog to obey? (b) Training your child to obey? (c) Learning yourself to obey? 2. After you've been impatient, how do you calm down?

1. What is the point of the comparisons in verses 30–32 and the irony in verse 39: How is Israel like (or unlike) her "fathers"? And "the nations"? What sins of this generation truly provoke the Lord? 2. In what ways will the future judgment of God be reminiscent of the Exodus (vv. 33–38)? 3. Who is God telling, "Go and serve your idols" (v. 39): (a) The rebels of verse 38? (b) The purified Israel of verse 40? (c) Both (a) and (b)? Why do you think so? 4. What will be different about the way God treats this generation from the ones that have gone before (vv. 40–44)? 5. What, ultimately, will result from God's punishment? 6. How will God's particular way of restoring Israel show him to be the Sovereign Lord?

1. What do you learn from this passage about God's character and plan of salvation? About God's *permissive* will and his *perfect* will? 2. How do you think God's mercy and his wrath work together toward the same purpose? Do you see them working together for good in your particular generation? How so? 3. Which could you use more of now: God's "carrot" or "stick"? Why?

---

a26 Or —making every firstborn pass through ⌊the fire⌋ place.   c31 Or —making your sons pass through firstfruits   *b29 Bamah means high*   *d40 Or and the gifts of your*

Prophecy Against the South

45The word of the LORD came to me: **46**"Son of man, set your face toward the south; preach against the south and prophesy against the forest of the southland. **47**Say to the southern forest: 'Hear the word of the LORD. This is what the Sovereign LORD says: I am about to set fire to you, and it will consume all your trees, both green and dry. The blazing flame will not be quenched, and every face from south to north will be scorched by it. **48**Everyone will see that I the LORD have kindled it; it will not be quenched.'"

49Then I said, "Ah, Sovereign LORD! They are saying of me, 'Isn't he just telling parables?'"

Babylon, God's Sword of Judgment

21 The word of the LORD came to me: **2**"Son of man, set your face against Jerusalem and .preach against the sanctuary. Prophesy against the land of Israel **3**and say to her: 'This is what the LORD says: I am against you. I will draw my sword from its scabbard and cut off from you both the righteous and the wicked. **4**Because I am going to cut off the righteous and the wicked, my sword will be unsheathed against everyone from south to north. **5**Then all people will know that I the LORD have drawn my sword from its scabbard; it will not return again.'

6"Therefore groan, son of man! Groan before them with broken heart and bitter grief. **7**And when they ask you, 'Why are you groaning?' you shall say, 'Because of the news that is coming. Every heart will melt and every hand go limp; every spirit will become faint and every knee become as weak as water.' It is coming! It will surely take place, declares the Sovereign LORD."

8The word of the LORD came to me: **9**"Son of man, prophesy and say, 'This is what the Lord says:

> "'A sword, a sword,
>   sharpened and polished—
> **10**sharpened for the slaughter,
>   polished to flash like lightning!

"'Shall we rejoice in the scepter of my son ⌞Judah⌟? The sword despises every such stick.

> **11**"'The sword is appointed to be polished,
>   to be grasped with the hand;
> it is sharpened and polished,
>   made ready for the hand of the slayer.
> **12**Cry out and wail, son of man,
>   for it is against my people;
>   it is against all the princes of Israel.
> They are thrown to the sword
>   along with my people.
> Therefore beat your breast.

13"'Testing will surely come. And what if the scepter ⌞of Judah⌟, which the sword despises, does not continue? declares the Sovereign LORD.'

> **14**"So then, son of man, prophesy
>   and strike your hands together.
> Let the sword strike twice,
>   even three times.
> It is a sword for slaughter—
>   a sword for great slaughter,
>   closing in on them from every side.

1. As "fire" commonly refers to an invading enemy, and "forest" refers to Judah in the south, what is God saying here? How do "green" and "dry" trees fare (see 17:24)? **2.** Do the hearers heed this warning? Why not?

What was God's purpose in this warning? In the NT, what is the "unquenchable (or eternal) fire" (see Lk 3:17; Mt 25:41)?

1. As a child, what was your favorite cowboy western? When you played "gun fights" and "sword fights," who were you imitating? How many pretend bullets or stab wounds did it take before you fell dead? What do you think of such "play" now? **2.** What kind of things make you cry more: Birthdays, weddings or funerals? Saying good-bye or saying hello? Seeing bad news on TV or hearing good news? **3.** What accidents have you had with a sharp cutting instrument? What stitches do you have to show for it? Which show-and-tell story leaves you all in stitches?

1. In these five "sword oracles," what is the overall intent and impact of this sharp metaphor on Ezekiel? On his audience? On God himself? **2.** To what or whom does the sword refer (vv. 3,19)? What does this tell you about God's use of human instruments to execute his divine purpose? **3.** Why will both the righteous and the wicked die in this invasion (v. 4)? How does this square with the teaching of chapter 18? How does John 11:25–26 help Christian believers resolve this apparent contradiction? **4.** How will people respond to news of this invasion (vv. 6–7,12,15)? Compare their response to God's (see 18:23)? **5.** What symbols of royalty do you see (vv. 10,13,16)? What will the sword do to them? What do these actions represent? **6.** In verses 18–32, Ezekiel is supposed to make a model of a road with a fork in it. What lies at the end of each road? How will the king of Babylon decide which fork to take? What false hope do those in Judah loyal to Nebuchadnezzar cling to (vv. 10b,23; see 17:14–15)? Why are they guilty (v. 24)? **7.** What ruinous reversal will happen later (586 B.C.) to the "prince" (vv. 25–27)? When will this Davidic kingship be restored? **8.** What will happen later to those Ammonites on the other fork (vv. 28–32)? By whom? Why at this time (see 25:1–7)?

1. What do you think of God's "sword dance"? Was this an effective way to get his point across? How so? 2. God controlled the military and political destiny of Babylon and Israel. Do you think he is as involved with today's nations? What evidence do you have for your answer: Any events from modern history? Or current events? What nations do you think will see God's wrath somewhere down the road? 3. Have you ever experienced a punishment from God? Or are you hoping God's sword took the other turn at the fork in the road, never to return your way again? What is your basis for hoping that? 4. God's Word still cuts "sharper than any double-edged sword" (Heb 4:12–13), even though it hurts him to do so, as well as us. How do you account for that ambivalence in God? How does he want you to respond to his "sword"? How did you respond the last time? 5. Are you responsible for training or supervising others at home or work? What "sword" (pen or tongue) do you wield in your correction of them? How do you feel when you do this? What would likely happen if you kept your sword always in its scabbard?

15So that hearts may melt
    and the fallen be many,
I have stationed the sword for slaughter[a]
    at all their gates.
Oh! It is made to flash like lightning,
    it is grasped for slaughter.
16O sword, slash to the right,
    then to the left,
    wherever your blade is turned.
17I too will strike my hands together,
    and my wrath will subside.
I the LORD have spoken."

18The word of the LORD came to me: 19"Son of man, mark out two roads for the sword of the king of Babylon to take, both starting from the same country. Make a signpost where the road branches off to the city. 20Mark out one road for the sword to come against Rabbah of the Ammonites and another against Judah and fortified Jerusalem. 21For the king of Babylon will stop at the fork in the road, at the junction of the two roads, to seek an omen: He will cast lots with arrows, he will consult his idols, he will examine the liver. 22Into his right hand will come the lot for Jerusalem, where he is to set up battering rams, to give the command to slaughter, to sound the battle cry, to set battering rams against the gates, to build a ramp and to erect siege works. 23It will seem like a false omen to those who have sworn allegiance to him, but he will remind them of their guilt and take them captive.

24"Therefore this is what the Sovereign LORD says: 'Because you people have brought to mind your guilt by your open rebellion, revealing your sins in all that you do—because you have done this, you will be taken captive.

25" 'O profane and wicked prince of Israel, whose day has come, whose time of punishment has reached its climax, 26this is what the Sovereign LORD says: Take off the turban, remove the crown. It will not be as it was: The lowly will be exalted and the exalted will be brought low. 27A ruin! A ruin! I will make it a ruin! It will not be restored until he comes to whom it rightfully belongs; to him I will give it.'

28"And you, son of man, prophesy and say, 'This is what the Sovereign LORD says about the Ammonites and their insults:

" 'A sword, a sword,
    drawn for the slaughter,
polished to consume
    and to flash like lightning!
29Despite false visions concerning you
    and lying divinations about you,
it will be laid on the necks
    of the wicked who are to be slain,
whose day has come,
    whose time of punishment has reached its
        climax.
30Return the sword to its scabbard.
    In the place where you were created,
in the land of your ancestry,
    I will judge you.
31I will pour out my wrath upon you
    and breathe out my fiery anger against you;

a 15 Septuagint; the meaning of the Hebrew for this word is uncertain.

I will hand you over to brutal men,
   men skilled in destruction.
³²You will be fuel for the fire,
   your blood will be shed in your land,
   you will be remembered no more;
for I the LORD have spoken.' "

Jerusalem's Sins

22 The word of the LORD came to me: ²"Son of man, will you judge her? Will you judge this city of bloodshed? Then confront her with all her detestable practices ³and say: 'This is what the Sovereign LORD says: O city that brings on herself doom by shedding blood in her midst and defiles herself by making idols, ⁴you have become guilty because of the blood you have shed and have become defiled by the idols you have made. You have brought your days to a close, and the end of your years has come. Therefore I will make you an object of scorn to the nations and a laughing-stock to all the countries. ⁵Those who are near and those who are far away will mock you, O infamous city, full of turmoil.

⁶" 'See how each of the princes of Israel who are in you uses his power to shed blood. ⁷In you they have treated father and mother with contempt; in you they have oppressed the alien and mistreated the fatherless and the widow. ⁸You have despised my holy things and desecrated my Sabbaths. ⁹In you are slanderous men bent on shedding blood; in you are those who eat at the mountain shrines and commit lewd acts. ¹⁰In you are those who dishonor their fathers' bed; in you are those who violate women during their period, when they are ceremonially unclean. ¹¹In you one man commits a detestable offense with his neighbor's wife, another shamefully defiles his daughter-in-law, and another violates his sister, his own father's daughter. ¹²In you men accept bribes to shed blood; you take usury and excessive interest*a* and make unjust gain from your neighbors by extortion. And you have forgotten me, declares the Sovereign LORD.

¹³" 'I will surely strike my hands together at the unjust gain you have made and at the blood you have shed in your midst. ¹⁴Will your courage endure or your hands be strong in the day I deal with you? I the LORD have spoken, and I will do it. ¹⁵I will disperse you among the nations and scatter you through the countries; and I will put an end to your uncleanness. ¹⁶When you have been defiled*b* in the eyes of the nations, you will know that I am the LORD.' "

¹⁷Then the word of the LORD came to me: ¹⁸"Son of man, the house of Israel has become dross to me; all of them are the copper, tin, iron and lead left inside a furnace. They are but the dross of silver. ¹⁹Therefore this is what the Sovereign LORD says: 'Because you have all become dross, I will gather you into Jerusalem. ²⁰As men gather silver, copper, iron, lead and tin into a furnace to melt it with a fiery blast, so will I gather you in my anger and my wrath and put you inside the city and melt you. ²¹I will gather you and I will blow on you with my fiery wrath, and you will be melted inside her. ²²As silver is melted in a furnace, so you will be melted inside her, and you will know that I the LORD have poured out my wrath upon you.' "

²³Again the word of the LORD came to me: ²⁴"Son of man, say to the land, 'You are a land that has had no rain or showers*c* in the day of wrath.' ²⁵There is a conspiracy of her princes*d* within her

---

1. If you wanted to read all about the latest sins of the "rich and infamous," what gossip column or tabloid would you turn to? What's one of the more laughable "scoops" you've seen in one of those? 2. If you wanted to read an expose on sins of today's religious "clerics and quacks," where would you go? What news has recently embarrassed you in that regard?

1. This chapter reads like a gossip column or scandal sheet pre-dating the *National Enquirer.* Here God is cataloguing the sins of ancient Israel for everyone to mock. In verses 3–4, he provides an apparent "table of contents," dividing sins into social crimes ("shedding blood") and religious ones ("making idols"). Using these two broad categories, make a table of contents page for Israel's sins listed here. 2. As managing editor of this *Jerusalem Tabloid,* which sins would you highlight on the front page with lurid photos? What ones would you bury in the back pages? Which sin would get your centerfold coverage? 3. What pictures does Ezekiel give of God's judgment in verse 17–22? In verses 25–29? What meaningful caption would you give each symbolic snapshot? 4. On the weather page of your tabloid, what is your prognosis (v. 24)? Why so bleak? 5. What kind of person is Ezekiel's Editor-in-Chief looking for in verse 30? Write a catchy advertisement to appear in the classified section of this paper. If no one responds to the ad, what will Ezekiel's Editor-in-Chief do?

1. Look at the two lists of sins. Which would bring the most derision from your neighbors, co-workers or fellow church-goers? Which sins are common to those people? Do you think they are more guilty, or less guilty, than Israel? Why? Unless things change, what do you think God will do with your nation? 2. Which sins on the two lists embarrass *you?* Did you see your name anywhere in the *Jerusalem Tabloid?* Are you suing for libel? Or are you guilty as charged? 3. In either case, what sentence

---

a 12 Or *usury and interest*   *b 16* Or *When I have allotted you your inheritance*
c 24 Septuagint; Hebrew *has not been cleansed or rained on*   *d 25* Septuagint; Hebrew *prophets*

will God likely hand out? What or who could possibly stay God's hand of judgment? **4.** How would you answer the ad in the classified section for the person God is looking for to stand in the gap? Do you know anyone else who's qualified to stand in the gap? What can you do to become more qualified?

___

1. What about the "days of your youth" do you yearn for? If you could turn the clock back for one day, which day in your youth would you like to relive? Why? **2.** What about the days of your youth do you find disgusting (so much so, you can't imagine why you did any of those crazy things)? Why then did you? How do you account for your change of heart? **3.** Where would you expect to find a frank discussion about sex: (a) Around the dinner table? (b) In the locker room? (c) In the bedroom? (d) In adult bookstores? (e) In Christian bookstores? (f) In the pulpit? (g) In the schools? (h) In the halls of government? (i) In Ezekiel?

1. The i's have it: You answered correctly, if you said "Ezekiel." In this frank story about Israel and Judah, the sexual language is vivid, but figurative, implying political alliances not idolatrous worship (as in ch. 16). How is each people represented? Who is the true husband? **2.** Where do the adulterous sins begin for each sister (vv. 5–13)? What other partners are involved? **3.** What happens to each woman, figuratively and historically? What do their sins represent? Why is Oholibah's sin worse than that of Oholah? **4.** How does Oholibah "carry her prostitution still further" (vv. 14–21)? With what cruel and unusual punishment (vv. 22–28)? **5.** What is the "cup" that the two sisters share (vv. 31–34)? What will happen if and when they drink it? **6.** What word of instruction and explanation does God give Ezekiel privately (vv. 36–45)? **7.** What "mob-related" and "terrorist" activ-

like a roaring lion tearing its prey; they devour people, take treasures and precious things and make many widows within her. ²⁶Her priests do violence to my law and profane my holy things; they do not distinguish between the holy and the common; they teach that there is no difference between the unclean and the clean; and they shut their eyes to the keeping of my Sabbaths, so that I am profaned among them. ²⁷Her officials within her are like wolves tearing their prey; they shed blood and kill people to make unjust gain. ²⁸Her prophets whitewash these deeds for them by false visions and lying divinations. They say, 'This is what the Sovereign LORD says'—when the LORD has not spoken. ²⁹The people of the land practice extortion and commit robbery; they oppress the poor and needy and mistreat the alien, denying them justice.

³⁰"I looked for a man among them who would build up the wall and stand before me in the gap on behalf of the land so I would not have to destroy it, but I found none. ³¹So I will pour out my wrath on them and consume them with my fiery anger, bringing down on their own heads all they have done, declares the Sovereign LORD."

Two Adulterous Sisters

23 The word of the LORD came to me: ²"Son of man, there were two women, daughters of the same mother. ³They became prostitutes in Egypt, engaging in prostitution from their youth. In that land their breasts were fondled and their virgin bosoms caressed. ⁴The older was named Oholah, and her sister was Oholibah. They were mine and gave birth to sons and daughters. Oholah is Samaria, and Oholibah is Jerusalem.

⁵"Oholah engaged in prostitution while she was still mine; and she lusted after her lovers, the Assyrians—warriors ⁶clothed in blue, governors and commanders, all of them handsome young men, and mounted horsemen. ⁷She gave herself as a prostitute to all the elite of the Assyrians and defiled herself with all the idols of everyone she lusted after. ⁸She did not give up the prostitution she began in Egypt, when during her youth men slept with her, caressed her virgin bosom and poured out their lust upon her.

⁹"Therefore I handed her over to her lovers, the Assyrians, for whom she lusted. ¹⁰They stripped her naked, took away her sons and daughters and killed her with the sword. She became a byword among women, and punishment was inflicted on her.

¹¹"Her sister Oholibah saw this, yet in her lust and prostitution she was more depraved than her sister. ¹²She too lusted after the Assyrians—governors and commanders, warriors in full dress, mounted horsemen, all handsome young men. ¹³I saw that she too defiled herself; both of them went the same way.

¹⁴"But she carried her prostitution still further. She saw men portrayed on a wall, figures of Chaldeans*a* portrayed in red, ¹⁵with belts around their waists and flowing turbans on their heads; all of them looked like Babylonian chariot officers, natives of Chaldea.*b* ¹⁶As soon as she saw them, she lusted after them and sent messengers to them in Chaldea. ¹⁷Then the Babylonians came to her, to the bed of love, and in their lust they defiled her. After she had been defiled by them, she turned away from them in disgust. ¹⁸When she carried on her prostitution openly and exposed her nakedness, I turned away from her in disgust, just as I had turned away from her sister. ¹⁹Yet she became more and more promiscuous as she recalled the days of her youth, when she was a prostitute in Egypt. ²⁰There she lusted after her lovers, whose genitals

a 14 Or *Babylonians*   *b 15* Or *Babylonia*; also in verse 16

were like those of donkeys and whose emission was like that of horses. **21**So you longed for the lewdness of your youth, when in Egypt your bosom was caressed and your young breasts fondled.*a*

22"Therefore, Oholibah, this is what the Sovereign LORD says: I will stir up your lovers against you, those you turned away from in disgust, and I will bring them against you from every side— **23**the Babylonians and all the Chaldeans, the men of Pekod and Shoa and Koa, and all the Assyrians with them, handsome young men, all of them governors and commanders, chariot officers and men of high rank, all mounted on horses. **24**They will come against you with weapons,*b* chariots and wagons and with a throng of people; they will take up positions against you on every side with large and small shields and with helmets. I will turn you over to them for punishment, and they will punish you according to their standards. **25**I will direct my jealous anger against you, and they will deal with you in fury. They will cut off your noses and your ears, and those of you who are left will fall by the sword. They will take away your sons and daughters, and those of you who are left will be consumed by fire. **26**They will also strip you of your clothes and take your fine jewelry. **27**So I will put a stop to the lewdness and prostitution you began in Egypt. You will not look on these things with longing or remember Egypt anymore.

28"For this is what the Sovereign LORD says: I am about to hand you over to those you hate, to those you turned away from in disgust. **29**They will deal with you in hatred and take away everything you have worked for. They will leave you naked and bare, and the shame of your prostitution will be exposed. Your lewdness and promiscuity **30**have brought this upon you, because you lusted after the nations and defiled yourself with their idols. **31**You have gone the way of your sister; so I will put her cup into your hand.

32"This is what the Sovereign LORD says:

"You will drink your sister's cup,
    a cup large and deep;
it will bring scorn and derision,
    for it holds so much.
33You will be filled with drunkenness and sorrow,
    the cup of ruin and desolation,
    the cup of your sister Samaria.
34You will drink it and drain it dry;
    you will dash it to pieces
    and tear your breasts.

I have spoken, declares the Sovereign LORD.

35"Therefore this is what the Sovereign LORD says: Since you have forgotten me and thrust me behind your back, you must bear the consequences of your lewdness and prostitution."

36The LORD said to me: "Son of man, will you judge Oholah and Oholibah? Then confront them with their detestable practices, **37**for they have committed adultery and blood is on their hands. They committed adultery with their idols; they even sacrificed their children, whom they bore to me,*c* as food for them. **38**They have also done this to me: At that same time they defiled my sanctuary and desecrated my Sabbaths. **39**On the very day they sacrificed their children to their idols, they entered my sanctuary and desecrated it. That is what they did in my house.

ities is Ezekiel associated with? What will be the ultimate result of God's punishment (v. 49)? How will this prove God is the Sovereign Lord?

1. Have you ever heard a sermon on this passage? Why are ministers reluctant to talk about "promiscuous sex" in public? Then why do you think God uses such a disgusting story with such revolting language? How would you make the language of Ezekiel 23 more palatable to your Sunday school class? **2.** Do you ever get disgusted by sin? Yours or someone else's? Why is that? What makes you both calloused toward sin and sensitive to sin? **3.** Is there anything about your personal life or your nation's life which would come under the scrutiny of Ezekiel's indiscreet prophecy? What is it about the game of international politics that God is so dead set against it? **4.** If Ezekiel were your country's minister of foreign relations, what would he have to say about what's going on today? **5.** What would you do if you were one of the "mob" or "terrorist" groups under the direction of Ezekiel? Could you go through with your violent assignment? Why or why not?

---

a21 Syriac (see also verse 3); Hebrew *caressed because of your young breasts*
b24 The meaning of the Hebrew for this word is uncertain.   *c37* Or *even made the children they bore to me pass through ⸤the fire⸥*

⁴⁰"They even sent messengers for men who came from far away, and when they arrived you bathed yourself for them, painted your eyes and put on your jewelry. ⁴¹You sat on an elegant couch, with a table spread before it on which you had placed the incense and oil that belonged to me.

⁴²"The noise of a carefree crowd was around her; Sabeans[a] were brought from the desert along with men from the rabble, and they put bracelets on the arms of the woman and her sister and beautiful crowns on their heads. ⁴³Then I said about the one worn out by adultery, 'Now let them use her as a prostitute, for that is all she is.' ⁴⁴And they slept with her. As men sleep with a prostitute, so they slept with those lewd women, Oholah and Oholibah. ⁴⁵But righteous men will sentence them to the punishment of women who commit adultery and shed blood, because they are adulterous and blood is on their hands.

⁴⁶"This is what the Sovereign LORD says: Bring a mob against them and give them over to terror and plunder. ⁴⁷The mob will stone them and cut them down with their swords; they will kill their sons and daughters and burn down their houses.

⁴⁸"So I will put an end to lewdness in the land, that all women may take warning and not imitate you. ⁴⁹You will suffer the penalty for your lewdness and bear the consequences of your sins of idolatry. Then you will know that I am the Sovereign LORD."

The Cooking Pot

24 In the ninth year, in the tenth month on the tenth day, the word of the LORD came to me: ²"Son of man, record this date, this very date, because the king of Babylon has laid siege to Jerusalem this very day. ³Tell this rebellious house a parable and say to them: 'This is what the Sovereign LORD says:

> " 'Put on the cooking pot; put it on
> and pour water into it.
> ⁴Put into it the pieces of meat,
> all the choice pieces—the leg and the shoulder.
> Fill it with the best of these bones;
> ⁵   take the pick of the flock.
> Pile wood beneath it for the bones;
> bring it to a boil
> and cook the bones in it.

⁶" 'For this is what the Sovereign LORD says:

> " 'Woe to the city of bloodshed,
> to the pot now encrusted,
> whose deposit will not go away!
> Empty it piece by piece
> without casting lots for them.

⁷" 'For the blood she shed is in her midst:
> She poured it on the bare rock;
> she did not pour it on the ground,
> where the dust would cover it.
> ⁸To stir up wrath and take revenge
> I put her blood on the bare rock,
> so that it would not be covered.

⁹" 'Therefore this is what the Sovereign LORD says:

> " 'Woe to the city of bloodshed!

1. Who's the best cook in your family? What's your favorite dish? (Be descriptive!) **2.** When was the last time someone burned something in your kitchen? What happened? **3.** Suppose you get an over-cooked fortune cookie that says, "You are about to jump from the frying pan into the fire." To what in your life situation might that saying refer?

1. What sets this chapter up as conveying a revelation worth noting? What happens in Jerusalem on the same day this word comes to Ezekiel? **2.** What figures of speech does Ezekiel use to describe the city and its leadership? What does each part represent: The cooking pot (vv. 3,6; 11:3)? The choice pieces of meat (v. 4; 11:3)? The dirty deposit that has encrusted the pot (vv. 6,11–13)? **3.** What will happen to the city (vv. 9–13)? Why did the "choice pieces" mistakenly think their names would be omitted from this "pot-boiler" (see 11:1–8)? **4.** What does their uncovered blood represent (vv. 7–8; see Isa 3:9; 26:21; Ge 4:10)? **5.** Here, as in the story of Jonah, God sometimes does not carry out his threats. What is God's reason for threatening Jerusalem (v. 13)? How do they respond? Can they hope for a similar change of heart on God's part this time (v. 14)?

a42 Or *drunkards*

I, too, will pile the wood high.
¹⁰So heap on the wood
    and kindle the fire.
Cook the meat well,
    mixing in the spices;
    and let the bones be charred.
¹¹Then set the empty pot on the coals
    till it becomes hot and its copper glows
so its impurities may be melted
    and its deposit burned away.
¹²It has frustrated all efforts;
    its heavy deposit has not been removed,
    not even by fire.

¹³" 'Now your impurity is lewdness. Because I tried to cleanse you but you would not be cleansed from your impurity, you will not be clean again until my wrath against you has subsided.

¹⁴" 'I the LORD have spoken. The time has come for me to act. I will not hold back; I will not have pity, nor will I relent. You will be judged according to your conduct and your actions, declares the Sovereign LORD.' "

Ezekiel's Wife Dies

¹⁵The word of the LORD came to me: ¹⁶"Son of man, with one blow I am about to take away from you the delight of your eyes. Yet do not lament or weep or shed any tears. ¹⁷Groan quietly; do not mourn for the dead. Keep your turban fastened and your sandals on your feet; do not cover the lower part of your face or eat the customary food ⌊of mourners⌋."

¹⁸So I spoke to the people in the morning, and in the evening my wife died. The next morning I did as I had been commanded.

¹⁹Then the people asked me, "Won't you tell us what these things have to do with us?"

²⁰So I said to them, "The word of the LORD came to me: ²¹Say to the house of Israel, 'This is what the Sovereign LORD says: I am about to desecrate my sanctuary—the stronghold in which you take pride, the delight of your eyes, the object of your affection. The sons and daughters you left behind will fall by the sword. ²²And you will do as I have done. You will not cover the lower part of your face or eat the customary food ⌊of mourners⌋. ²³You will keep your turbans on your heads and your sandals on your feet. You will not mourn or weep but will waste away because of ᵃ your sins and groan among yourselves. ²⁴Ezekiel will be a sign to you; you will do just as he has done. When this happens, you will know that I am the Sovereign LORD.'

²⁵"And you, son of man, on the day I take away their stronghold, their joy and glory, the delight of their eyes, their heart's desire, and their sons and daughters as well— ²⁶on that day a fugitive will come to tell you the news. ²⁷At that time your mouth will be opened; you will speak with him and will no longer be silent. So you will be a sign to them, and they will know that I am the LORD."

A Prophecy Against Ammon

25 The word of the LORD came to me: ²"Son of man, set your face against the Ammonites and prophesy against them. ³Say to them, 'Hear the word of the Sovereign LORD. This is what the Sovereign LORD says: Because you said "Aha!" over my sanctu-

ᵃ23 Or away in

---

1. Why does God warn about his punishments beforehand? What does he hope will happen? 2. Are you feeling the heat anywhere? Is God warning you about anything? If you are on God's hot seat or in his cooking pot, what does he want you to do about that? 3. As for the corruption of city government officials in your area, what are some "back-burner issues" which Ezekiel might be prompting you to bring to the front burner and "pile on the wood"?

---

1. What is the saddest day of your life you can still recall with feeling? 2. Who is your "heart's desire"? What would life be like without him or her?

1. How does Ezekiel seem to react to his wife's death? 2. What was Ezekiel's "grief" meant to signal by analogy? How does this analogy extend to God losing his "eye's delight" and "heart's desire"? 3. By contrast, how would the Jews in Babylon react to their Temple's destruction and their children's captivity? Why does God not want them to grieve? 4. What happens to Ezekiel here (v. 27; see 33:21–22; compare in 3:26 when God silenced Ezekiel)?

1. Of all that God calls Ezekiel to do, what do you think is the hardest? Why? 2. If obeying God sometimes made Ezekiel suffer, what about us? By obeying God, can you hope to escape Ezekiel's loss? 3. How can you cultivate "his heart's desire"?

---

1. Do you like "put down" jokes? Do you find them rude? (Is that your nose or are you eating a banana?) 2. Is your family tightly knit or spread out all over geographically? Socially? Religiously?

1. Where were Ammon, Moab, Edom and Philistia? From whom did these nations descend (see Ge 36:6–9; 19:36–38)? Were the Philistines related to Israel? (see Ge 10:13) **2.** For what crime is each nation being punished? Had any of them been given the Ten Commandments or any part of God's law? **3.** How will God punish each nation? **4.** What will be the effect of the punishments (vv. 7,11,14,17)?

1. Do you recall a time when you learned "the Lord is God" through hard knocks? Does your faith grow best in good times or adversity? Is God really putting down those he punishes (18:23)? **2.** What is your attitude when you hear bad things are happening to bad people? What should it be? **3.** Does God punish the modern foes of Christianity to reveal his glory? **4.** If God did not give Israel's neighbors biblical revelation, how do you think he made his will known? How does God communicate today? With whom does God communicate?

1. Have you ever come close to drowning? Have you ever saved somebody from drowning? What was it like? **2.** Have you ever been in an earthquake? Did it move buildings or furniture? Did it move you?

1. Tyre was about 100 miles north of Jerusalem. How would Tyre prosper from Israel's destruction (v. 2)? How was Tyre's response like those of the nations back in chapter 25? **2.** What will Tyre's punishment be? Who will inflict it (v. 7)? Will it be thorough (vv.

ary when it was desecrated and over the land of Israel when it was laid waste and over the people of Judah when they went into exile, ⁴therefore I am going to give you to the people of the East as a possession. They will set up their camps and pitch their tents among you; they will eat your fruit and drink your milk. ⁵I will turn Rabbah into a pasture for camels and Ammon into a resting place for sheep. Then you will know that I am the LORD. ⁶For this is what the Sovereign LORD says: Because you have clapped your hands and stamped your feet, rejoicing with all the malice of your heart against the land of Israel, ⁷therefore I will stretch out my hand against you and give you as plunder to the nations. I will cut you off from the nations and exterminate you from the countries. I will destroy you, and you will know that I am the LORD.'"

A Prophecy Against Moab

⁸"This is what the Sovereign LORD says: 'Because Moab and Seir said, "Look, the house of Judah has become like all the other nations," ⁹therefore I will expose the flank of Moab, beginning at its frontier towns—Beth Jeshimoth, Baal Meon and Kiriathaim—the glory of that land. ¹⁰I will give Moab along with the Ammonites to the people of the East as a possession, so that the Ammonites will not be remembered among the nations; ¹¹and I will inflict punishment on Moab. Then they will know that I am the LORD.'"

A Prophecy Against Edom

¹²"This is what the Sovereign LORD says: 'Because Edom took revenge on the house of Judah and became very guilty by doing so, ¹³therefore this is what the Sovereign LORD says: I will stretch out my hand against Edom and kill its men and their animals. I will lay it waste, and from Teman to Dedan they will fall by the sword. ¹⁴I will take vengeance on Edom by the hand of my people Israel, and they will deal with Edom in accordance with my anger and my wrath; they will know my vengeance, declares the Sovereign LORD.'"

A Prophecy Against Philistia

¹⁵"This is what the Sovereign LORD says: 'Because the Philistines acted in vengeance and took revenge with malice in their hearts, and with ancient hostility sought to destroy Judah, ¹⁶therefore this is what the Sovereign LORD says: I am about to stretch out my hand against the Philistines, and I will cut off the Kerethites and destroy those remaining along the coast. ¹⁷I will carry out great vengeance on them and punish them in my wrath. Then they will know that I am the LORD, when I take vengeance on them.'"

A Prophecy Against Tyre

26 In the eleventh year, on the first day of the month, the word of the LORD came to me: ²"Son of man, because Tyre has said of Jerusalem, 'Aha! The gate to the nations is broken, and its doors have swung open to me; now that she lies in ruins I will prosper,' ³therefore this is what the Sovereign LORD says: I am against you, O Tyre, and I will bring many nations against you, like the sea casting up its waves. ⁴They will destroy the walls of Tyre and pull down her towers; I will scrape away her rubble and make her a bare rock. ⁵Out in the sea she will become a place to spread fishnets, for I have spoken, declares the Sovereign LORD. She will become plunder for the nations, ⁶and her settlements on the mainland will be ravaged by the sword. Then they will know that I am the LORD.

7"For this is what the Sovereign LORD says: From the north I am going to bring against Tyre Nebuchadnezzar[a] king of Babylon, king of kings, with horses and chariots, with horsemen and a great army. 8He will ravage your settlements on the mainland with the sword; he will set up siege works against you, build a ramp up to your walls and raise his shields against you. 9He will direct the blows of his battering rams against your walls and demolish your towers with his weapons. 10His horses will be so many that they will cover you with dust. Your walls will tremble at the noise of the war horses, wagons and chariots when he enters your gates as men enter a city whose walls have been broken through. 11The hoofs of his horses will trample all your streets; he will kill your people with the sword, and your strong pillars will fall to the ground. 12They will plunder your wealth and loot your merchandise; they will break down your walls and demolish your fine houses and throw your stones, timber and rubble into the sea. 13I will put an end to your noisy songs, and the music of your harps will be heard no more. 14I will make you a bare rock, and you will become a place to spread fishnets. You will never be rebuilt, for I the LORD have spoken, declares the Sovereign LORD.

15"This is what the Sovereign LORD says to Tyre: Will not the coastlands tremble at the sound of your fall, when the wounded groan and the slaughter takes place in you? 16Then all the princes of the coast will step down from their thrones and lay aside their robes and take off their embroidered garments. Clothed with terror, they will sit on the ground, trembling every moment, appalled at you. 17Then they will take up a lament concerning you and say to you:

> "'How you are destroyed, O city of renown,
>   peopled by men of the sea!
> You were a power on the seas,
>   you and your citizens;
> you put your terror
>   on all who lived there.
> 18Now the coastlands tremble
>   on the day of your fall;
> the islands in the sea
>   are terrified at your collapse.'

19"This is what the Sovereign LORD says: When I make you a desolate city, like cities no longer inhabited, and when I bring the ocean depths over you and its vast waters cover you, 20then I will bring you down with those who go down to the pit, to the people of long ago. I will make you dwell in the earth below, as in ancient ruins, with those who go down to the pit, and you will not return or take your place[b] in the land of the living. 21I will bring you to a horrible end and you will be no more. You will be sought, but you will never again be found, declares the Sovereign LORD."

A Lament for Tyre

27 The word of the LORD came to me: 2"Son of man, take up a lament concerning Tyre. 3Say to Tyre, situated at the gateway to the sea, merchant of peoples on many coasts, 'This is what the Sovereign LORD says:

> "'You say, O Tyre,
>   "I am perfect in beauty."

[a]7 Hebrew Nebuchadrezzar, of which Nebuchadnezzar is a variant; here and often in Ezekiel and Jeremiah   [b]20 Septuagint; Hebrew return, and I will give glory

9–14)? 3. If God knows disaster is coming, what is the point of warning Tyre? Why not just let it happen? 4. The "coastlands" are the countries and islands of the Mediterranean that Tyre engaged in trade. Why will they be so "shaken up" (vv. 15–18)?

1. Is God going overboard in punishing those who rejoice in Israel's misfortune so harshly? What does this say about God's commitment to Israel? 2. What does this chapter do to the ancient belief that gods only have power within territorial borders? Was Yahweh "washed-up" when Israel was destroyed? 3. Do you rejoice or lament over the current political situation in your country? Is God working out a plan or wringing his hands? Should your small group be involved in national and international politics?

1. What is the most beautiful city you've ever visited? What impressed you the most? Have you been in a city you could describe as "clean"? 2. Have you ever had anything beautiful which was ruined? How did it happen? How did you feel?

1. To what is Tyre likened in this poem (vv. 4–9)? Do you find the image fitting? What parts of

it are mentioned? From where did the supplies come? What words reveal the elegance of its construction? **2.** Where did this ship travel? Can you find the limits of its trade in each direction on a map? What were some of the goods it exchanged? Do you think Tyre had good reasons to be proud? **3.** What will happen to this great luxury ship (vv. 25–36)? What will cause the accident? What will happen to the ship and crew? **4.** What different groups will hear of the mishap (vv. 30–36)? Who is most upset? Why?

♡ **1.** Is it wrong to feel pride in your achievements or attributes? What's wrong with a realistic appraisal? Do you find a lot of "humility" rings falsely? **2.** Who would be upset if you were broke? Friends? Family? Church members? Creditors? Would anyone even know? **3.** What is the mood of this lament: (a) Joy over a fallen foe? (b) Regret over something lovely destroyed? (c) Sorrow over a people crushed? What does this lament tell you about God's feelings? About God's regard for beauty? **4.** If you were writing a lament for your city, what items might appear in the verses? **5.** Would people in other nations lament the destruction of your country? Who might not?

⁴Your domain was on the high seas;
    your builders brought your beauty to perfection.
⁵They made all your timbers
    of pine trees from Senir*a*;
    they took a cedar from Lebanon
    to make a mast for you.
⁶Of oaks from Bashan
    they made your oars;
    of cypress wood*b* from the coasts of Cyprus*c*
    they made your deck, inlaid with ivory.
⁷Fine embroidered linen from Egypt was your sail
    and served as your banner;
    your awnings were of blue and purple
    from the coasts of Elishah.
⁸Men of Sidon and Arvad were your oarsmen;
    your skilled men, O Tyre, were aboard as your
        seamen.
⁹Veteran craftsmen of Gebal*d* were on board
    as shipwrights to caulk your seams.
All the ships of the sea and their sailors
    came alongside to trade for your wares.

¹⁰ 'Men of Persia, Lydia and Put
    served as soldiers in your army.
They hung their shields and helmets on your
        walls,
    bringing you splendor.
¹¹Men of Arvad and Helech
    manned your walls on every side;
men of Gammad
    were in your towers.
They hung their shields around your walls;
    they brought your beauty to perfection.

¹² 'Tarshish did business with you because of your great wealth of goods; they exchanged silver, iron, tin and lead for your merchandise.
¹³ 'Greece, Tubal and Meshech traded with you; they exchanged slaves and articles of bronze for your wares.
¹⁴ 'Men of Beth Togarmah exchanged work horses, war horses and mules for your merchandise.
¹⁵ 'The men of Rhodes*e* traded with you, and many coastlands were your customers; they paid you with ivory tusks and ebony.
¹⁶ 'Aram*f* did business with you because of your many products; they exchanged turquoise, purple fabric, embroidered work, fine linen, coral and rubies for your merchandise.
¹⁷ 'Judah and Israel traded with you; they exchanged wheat from Minnith and confections,*g* honey, oil and balm for your wares.
¹⁸ 'Damascus, because of your many products and great wealth of goods, did business with you in wine from Helbon and wool from Zahar.
¹⁹ 'Danites and Greeks from Uzal bought your merchandise; they exchanged wrought iron, cassia and calamus for your wares.
²⁰ 'Dedan traded in saddle blankets with you.

---

a5 That is, Hermon   *b6* Targum; the Masoretic Text has a different division of the consonants.   *c6* Hebrew *Kittim*   *d9* That is, Byblos   *e15* Septuagint; Hebrew *Dedan*   *f16* Most Hebrew manuscripts; some Hebrew manuscripts and Syriac *Edom*   *g17* The meaning of the Hebrew for this word is uncertain.

21" 'Arabia and all the princes of Kedar were your customers; they did business with you in lambs, rams and goats.

22" 'The merchants of Sheba and Raamah traded with you; for your merchandise they exchanged the finest of all kinds of spices and precious stones, and gold.

23" 'Haran, Canneh and Eden and merchants of Sheba, Asshur and Kilmad traded with you. 24In your marketplace they traded with you beautiful garments, blue fabric, embroidered work and multicolored rugs with cords twisted and tightly knotted.

25" 'The ships of Tarshish serve
    as carriers for your wares.
You are filled with heavy cargo
    in the heart of the sea.
26Your oarsmen take you
    out to the high seas.
But the east wind will break you to pieces
    in the heart of the sea.
27Your wealth, merchandise and wares,
    your mariners, seamen and shipwrights,
    your merchants and all your soldiers,
    and everyone else on board
will sink into the heart of the sea
    on the day of your shipwreck.
28The shorelands will quake
    when your seamen cry out.
29All who handle the oars
    will abandon their ships;
the mariners and all the seamen
    will stand on the shore.
30They will raise their voice
    and cry bitterly over you;
they will sprinkle dust on their heads
    and roll in ashes.
31They will shave their heads because of you
    and will put on sackcloth.
They will weep over you with anguish of soul
    and with bitter mourning.
32As they wail and mourn over you,
    they will take up a lament concerning you:
"Who was ever silenced like Tyre,
    surrounded by the sea?"
33When your merchandise went out on the seas,
    you satisfied many nations;
with your great wealth and your wares
    you enriched the kings of the earth.
34Now you are shattered by the sea
    in the depths of the waters;
your wares and all your company
    have gone down with you.
35All who live in the coastlands
    are appalled at you;
their kings shudder with horror
    and their faces are distorted with fear.
36The merchants among the nations hiss at you;
    you have come to a horrible end
    and will be no more.' "

1. What's your favorite status symbol? How do you let people know you are successful? Do you prefer to appear unsuccessful? 2. To which celebrity would you give the "Most Conceited Person in the World Award"? What did he or she do to earn it?

1. Why did the king consider himself wise (vv. 2–5)? How did he show it? 2. Do you think other countries admired the king's "great skill in trading" (v. 5)? Did such skill help or hurt them? 3. Who will God use to punish him (v. 7)? What will they do to him? 4. In what exaggerated terms does Ezekiel describe the king's character, adornment, location and role (vv. 13–15)? What biblical character does this remind you of? 5. How does the lament describe his sin (vv. 15–18)? Do you think the king mattered to God?

1. Why do you think God hates pride so much? Why is he so jealous of his role as the only God in the universe? 2. Do you ever "play god" in your words, actions or attitudes? Who in your life would know? Have you asked them about your "pride status"? 3. Who sits on the throne in your heart? Has the issue been decided or is there sometimes a struggle for power? Are there some areas in which your surrender is less than complete? How can your small group help you change attitudes or actions?

A Prophecy Against the King of Tyre

28 The word of the LORD came to me: [2]"Son of man, say to the ruler of Tyre, 'This is what the Sovereign LORD says:

" 'In the pride of your heart
    you say, "I am a god;
I sit on the throne of a god
    in the heart of the seas."
But you are a man and not a god,
    though you think you are as wise as a god.
[3]Are you wiser than Daniel[a]?
    Is no secret hidden from you?
[4]By your wisdom and understanding
    you have gained wealth for yourself
and amassed gold and silver
    in your treasuries.
[5]By your great skill in trading
    you have increased your wealth,
and because of your wealth
    your heart has grown proud.

[6]" 'Therefore this is what the Sovereign LORD says:

" 'Because you think you are wise,
    as wise as a god,
[7]I am going to bring foreigners against you,
    the most ruthless of nations;
they will draw their swords against your beauty
    and wisdom
    and pierce your shining splendor.
[8]They will bring you down to the pit,
    and you will die a violent death
    in the heart of the seas.
[9]Will you then say, "I am a god,"
    in the presence of those who kill you?
You will be but a man, not a god,
    in the hands of those who slay you.
[10]You will die the death of the uncircumcised
    at the hands of foreigners.

I have spoken, declares the Sovereign LORD.' "

[11]The word of the LORD came to me: [12]"Son of man, take up a lament concerning the king of Tyre and say to him: 'This is what the Sovereign LORD says:

" 'You were the model of perfection,
    full of wisdom and perfect in beauty.
[13]You were in Eden,
    the garden of God;
every precious stone adorned you:
    ruby, topaz and emerald,
    chrysolite, onyx and jasper,
    sapphire,[b] turquoise and beryl.[c]
Your settings and mountings[d] were made of gold;
    on the day you were created they were
        prepared.

[a]3 Or Danel; the Hebrew spelling may suggest a person other than the prophet Daniel.
[b]13 Or lapis lazuli   [c]13 The precise identification of some of these precious stones is uncertain.   [d]13 The meaning of the Hebrew for this phrase is uncertain.

14You were anointed as a guardian cherub,
　for so I ordained you.
You were on the holy mount of God;
　you walked among the fiery stones.
15You were blameless in your ways
　from the day you were created
　till wickedness was found in you.
16Through your widespread trade
　you were filled with violence,
　and you sinned.
So I drove you in disgrace from the mount of God,
　and I expelled you, O guardian cherub,
　from among the fiery stones.
17Your heart became proud
　on account of your beauty,
and you corrupted your wisdom
　because of your splendor.
So I threw you to the earth;
　I made a spectacle of you before kings.
18By your many sins and dishonest trade
　you have desecrated your sanctuaries.
So I made a fire come out from you,
　and it consumed you,
and I reduced you to ashes on the ground
　in the sight of all who were watching.
19All the nations who knew you
　are appalled at you;
you have come to a horrible end
　and will be no more.' "

A Prophecy Against Sidon

20The word of the LORD came to me: **21**"Son of man, set your face against Sidon; prophesy against her **22**and say: 'This is what the Sovereign LORD says:

" 'I am against you, O Sidon,
　and I will gain glory within you.
They will know that I am the LORD,
　when I inflict punishment on her
　and show myself holy within her.
23I will send a plague upon her
　and make blood flow in her streets.
The slain will fall within her,
　with the sword against her on every side.
Then they will know that I am the LORD.

24" 'No longer will the people of Israel have malicious neighbors who are painful briers and sharp thorns. Then they will know that I am the Sovereign LORD.

25" 'This is what the Sovereign LORD says: When I gather the people of Israel from the nations where they have been scattered, I will show myself holy among them in the sight of the nations. Then they will live in their own land, which I gave to my servant Jacob. **26**They will live there in safety and will build houses and plant vineyards; they will live in safety when I inflict punishment on all their neighbors who maligned them. Then they will know that I am the LORD their God.' "

1. Who is the best next-door neighbor you've ever had? The worst? 2. Was there ever a time when you got some really good news after a long period of bad news? What happened?

1. What is God going to do to Sidon (v. 23)? Why are neighbors often "briers and sharp thorns"? 2. What is God going to do for Israel (vv. 24–26)? Why? 3. What does God mean when he says both Sidon and Israel will know that he is the Lord? Will they both know him in the same way?

1. There are two ways of knowing God: by wrath or mercy. Why do you think some know the merciful God and some know the wrathful God? Which God do you know? 2. Do you know any of your neighbors? How do you treat them?

1. Which barnyard animal best describes this country? Which jungle animal? Is the world more like a barnyard or jungle? 2. Has a good friend ever let you down? What happened? How did it feel?

1. God depicted Tyre as a ship. How does he depict Egypt? Why is it appropriate? 2. For what two things does God punish Pharaoh (vv. 3,6–7)? How reliable was Egypt as a military ally (see 2Ki 18:19–21)? 3. How will God punish Egypt? When will God regather her? How does this compare with the fate of Ammon (25:7)? Tyre (26:14)? Israel (20:36–38)? 4. Why might the "horn" in verse 21 symbolize strength (see 1Sa 2:1; Ps 92:10)?

1. Does God work in your life without your knowing it? On hindsight, when do you recall this happening? 2. How does God reveal his actions and plans? How can you better understand and fit in with his purposes? 3. Is it good to rely on others or is it wiser to be as independent as possible? How would you define: (a) Dependence? (b) Independence? (c) Interdependence? 4. Do you think Nebuchadnezzar attacked Tyre and Egypt out of conscious obedience to the Lord? What is the significance of your answer as you consider international conflicts today?

A Prophecy Against Egypt

29 In the tenth year, in the tenth month on the twelfth day, the word of the LORD came to me: [2]"Son of man, set your face against Pharaoh king of Egypt and prophesy against him and against all Egypt. [3]Speak to him and say: 'This is what the Sovereign LORD says:

> " 'I am against you, Pharaoh king of Egypt,
>   you great monster lying among your streams.
> You say, "The Nile is mine;
>   I made it for myself."
> [4]But I will put hooks in your jaws
>   and make the fish of your streams stick to your
>   scales.
> I will pull you out from among your streams,
>   with all the fish sticking to your scales.
> [5]I will leave you in the desert,
>   you and all the fish of your streams.
> You will fall on the open field
>   and not be gathered or picked up.
> I will give you as food
>   to the beasts of the earth and the birds of the
>   air.

[6]Then all who live in Egypt will know that I am the LORD.

" 'You have been a staff of reed for the house of Israel. [7]When they grasped you with their hands, you splintered and you tore open their shoulders; when they leaned on you, you broke and their backs were wrenched.[a]

[8]"'Therefore this is what the Sovereign LORD says: I will bring a sword against you and kill your men and their animals. [9]Egypt will become a desolate wasteland. Then they will know that I am the LORD.

"'Because you said, "The Nile is mine; I made it," [10]therefore I am against you and against your streams, and I will make the land of Egypt a ruin and a desolate waste from Migdol to Aswan, as far as the border of Cush.[b] [11]No foot of man or animal will pass through it; no one will live there for forty years. [12]I will make the land of Egypt desolate among devastated lands, and her cities will lie desolate forty years among ruined cities. And I will disperse the Egyptians among the nations and scatter them through the countries.

[13]"'Yet this is what the Sovereign LORD says: At the end of forty years I will gather the Egyptians from the nations where they were scattered. [14]I will bring them back from captivity and return them to Upper Egypt,[c] the land of their ancestry. There they will be a lowly kingdom. [15]It will be the lowliest of kingdoms and will never again exalt itself above the other nations. I will make it so weak that it will never again rule over the nations. [16]Egypt will no longer be a source of confidence for the people of Israel but will be a reminder of their sin in turning to her for help. Then they will know that I am the Sovereign LORD.' "

[17]In the twenty-seventh year, in the first month on the first day, the word of the LORD came to me: [18]"Son of man, Nebuchadnezzar king of Babylon drove his army in a hard campaign against Tyre; every head was rubbed bare and every shoulder made raw. Yet he

a7 Syriac (see also Septuagint and Vulgate); Hebrew *and you caused their backs to stand*
b10 That is, the upper Nile region   c14 Hebrew *to Pathros*

and his army got no reward from the campaign he led against Tyre. [19]Therefore this is what the Sovereign LORD says: I am going to give Egypt to Nebuchadnezzar king of Babylon, and he will carry off its wealth. He will loot and plunder the land as pay for his army. [20]I have given him Egypt as a reward for his efforts because he and his army did it for me, declares the Sovereign LORD.

[21]"On that day I will make a horn[a] grow for the house of Israel, and I will open your mouth among them. Then they will know that I am the LORD."

A Lament for Egypt

30 The word of the LORD came to me: [2]"Son of man, prophesy and say: 'This is what the Sovereign LORD says:

" 'Wail and say,
"Alas for that day!"
[3]For the day is near,
the day of the LORD is near—
a day of clouds,
a time of doom for the nations.
[4]A sword will come against Egypt,
and anguish will come upon Cush.[b]
When the slain fall in Egypt,
her wealth will be carried away
and her foundations torn down.

[5]Cush and Put, Lydia and all Arabia, Libya[c] and the people of the covenant land will fall by the sword along with Egypt.

[6]"This is what the LORD says:

" 'The allies of Egypt will fall
and her proud strength will fail.
From Migdol to Aswan
they will fall by the sword within her,
declares the Sovereign LORD.
[7]"They will be desolate
among desolate lands,
and their cities will lie
among ruined cities.
[8]Then they will know that I am the LORD,
when I set fire to Egypt
and all her helpers are crushed.

[9]"On that day messengers will go out from me in ships to frighten Cush out of her complacency. Anguish will take hold of them on the day of Egypt's doom, for it is sure to come.

[10]"This is what the Sovereign LORD says:

" 'I will put an end to the hordes of Egypt
by the hand of Nebuchadnezzar king of
Babylon.
[11]He and his army—the most ruthless of nations—
will be brought in to destroy the land.
They will draw their swords against Egypt
and fill the land with the slain.
[12]I will dry up the streams of the Nile
and sell the land to evil men;
by the hand of foreigners
I will lay waste the land and everything in it.

---

1. Have you ever broken a bone? Did it heal, good as new? 2. Have you ever had to "break the news" to a friend? How do you approach a friend with criticism or bad news? 3. What is your favorite form of escapism? How many times a week do you have to escape reality?

1. What does the Lord say he is going to do to Egypt (v. 4)? What will be the effect on all its military allies (vv. 5–6)? 2. Who will God use to punish Egypt (v. 10)? What kind of nation are they (v. 11)? 3. What are some of the specific things God promises to do to Egypt (vv. 13–19)? 4. While Ezekiel chanted this lament, the Babylonians laid siege to Jerusalem. Did Egypt save the day (see Jer 37:6–8)? Does God have a "bone to pick" with Pharaoh (vv. 21–22)? Why do you think the Lord did not want the people to depend on Egypt for deliverance? Could the city be saved from God's judgment anyway?

1. The people in Jerusalem hoped that Ezekiel was wrong about the Babylonians and that Egypt would come to their rescue. Do you find yourself waiting for someone to rescue you? How do you feel broken and helpless? 2. God had to take away Israel's false hope before he could help them. Is God doing this in any area to you? How are you responding? Are you listening or gripping your hopes more tightly? 3. Do you know anyone with false hopes? How can you help him or her: (a) Confrontation? (b) A gentle question? (c) "Break the news"? (d) Say nothing and pray?

---

[a]21 *Horn* here symbolizes strength.   [b]4 That is, the upper Nile region; also in verses 5 and 9   [c]5 Hebrew *Cub*

I the Lord have spoken.

13 " 'This is what the Sovereign Lord says:

" 'I will destroy the idols
  and put an end to the images in Memphis.[a]
No longer will there be a prince in Egypt,
  and I will spread fear throughout the land.
14 I will lay waste Upper Egypt,[b]
  set fire to Zoan
  and inflict punishment on Thebes.[c]
15 I will pour out my wrath on Pelusium,[d]
  the stronghold of Egypt,
  and cut off the hordes of Thebes.
16 I will set fire to Egypt;
  Pelusium will writhe in agony.
Thebes will be taken by storm;
  Memphis will be in constant distress.
17 The young men of Heliopolis[e] and Bubastis[f]
  will fall by the sword,
  and the cities themselves will go into captivity.
18 Dark will be the day at Tahpanhes
  when I break the yoke of Egypt;
  there her proud strength will come to an end.
She will be covered with clouds,
  and her villages will go into captivity.
19 So I will inflict punishment on Egypt,
  and they will know that I am the Lord.' "

20 In the eleventh year, in the first month on the seventh day, the word of the Lord came to me: 21 "Son of man, I have broken the arm of Pharaoh king of Egypt. It has not been bound up for healing or put in a splint so as to become strong enough to hold a sword. 22 Therefore this is what the Sovereign Lord says: I am against Pharaoh king of Egypt. I will break both his arms, the good arm as well as the broken one, and make the sword fall from his hand. 23 I will disperse the Egyptians among the nations and scatter them through the countries. 24 I will strengthen the arms of the king of Babylon and put my sword in his hand, but I will break the arms of Pharaoh, and he will groan before him like a mortally wounded man. 25 I will strengthen the arms of the king of Babylon, but the arms of Pharaoh will fall limp. Then they will know that I am the Lord, when I put my sword into the hand of the king of Babylon and he brandishes it against Egypt. 26 I will disperse the Egyptians among the nations and scatter them through the countries. Then they will know that I am the Lord."

A Cedar in Lebanon

31 In the eleventh year, in the third month on the first day, the word of the Lord came to me: 2 "Son of man, say to Pharaoh king of Egypt and to his hordes:

" 'Who can be compared with you in majesty?
3 Consider Assyria, once a cedar in Lebanon,
  with beautiful branches overshadowing the
    forest;
  it towered on high,
  its top above the thick foliage.

1. When was the last time you were in a forest? Why were you there? How did you feel? 2. Who is the most successful person you know? What impresses you most about him or her?

1. Who does God tell Pharaoh to consider (v. 3)? To what does God compare this country? How does God describe it? 2. What was the sin of the cedar? How was it punished? By whom (v. 12; see 30:10–11)? What will be the impact on other trees (vv. 14,16–17)? 3. What lesson does

a 13 Hebrew Noph; also in verse 16   b 14 Hebrew waste Pathros   c 14 Hebrew No; also in verses 15 and 16   d 15 Hebrew Sin; also in verse 16   e 17 Hebrew Awen (or On)   f 17 Hebrew Pi Beseth

⁴The waters nourished it,
    deep springs made it grow tall;
their streams flowed
    all around its base
and sent their channels
    to all the trees of the field.
⁵So it towered higher
    than all the trees of the field;
its boughs increased
    and its branches grew long,
    spreading because of abundant waters.
⁶All the birds of the air
    nested in its boughs,
all the beasts of the field
    gave birth under its branches;
all the great nations
    lived in its shade.
⁷It was majestic in beauty,
    with its spreading boughs,
for its roots went down
    to abundant waters.
⁸The cedars in the garden of God
    could not rival it,
nor could the pine trees
    equal its boughs,
nor could the plane trees
    compare with its branches—
no tree in the garden of God
    could match its beauty.
⁹I made it beautiful
    with abundant branches,
the envy of all the trees of Eden
    in the garden of God.

¹⁰"'Therefore this is what the Sovereign LORD says: Because it towered on high, lifting its top above the thick foliage, and because it was proud of its height, ¹¹I handed it over to the ruler of the nations, for him to deal with according to its wickedness. I cast it aside, ¹²and the most ruthless of foreign nations cut it down and left it. Its boughs fell on the mountains and in all the valleys; its branches lay broken in all the ravines of the land. All the nations of the earth came out from under its shade and left it. ¹³All the birds of the air settled on the fallen tree, and all the beasts of the field were among its branches. ¹⁴Therefore no other trees by the waters are ever to tower proudly on high, lifting their tops above the thick foliage. No other trees so well-watered are ever to reach such a height; they are all destined for death, for the earth below, among mortal men, with those who go down to the pit.

¹⁵"'This is what the Sovereign LORD says: On the day it was brought down to the grave[a] I covered the deep springs with mourning for it; I held back its streams, and its abundant waters were restrained. Because of it I clothed Lebanon with gloom, and all the trees of the field withered away. ¹⁶I made the nations tremble at the sound of its fall when I brought it down to the grave with those who go down to the pit. Then all the trees of Eden, the choicest and best of Lebanon, all the trees that were well-watered, were consoled in the earth below. ¹⁷Those who lived in its shade,

God want Pharaoh to learn from this allegory of the cedar tree?

♡ **1.** Has God ever acted in blessing or judgment in the life of someone you know? What did you learn from that experience? Can you really learn from other peoples' mistakes, or must you make your own? **2.** Everyone can't have it "made in the shade" in Beverly Hills (or Aspen). Is it always true that for one person to have abundance, others must have less? **3.** If the world were a forest, how much of the water would you say you get? How much does your nation take? **4.** How does God measure success? In what area of life do you feel you are "branching out"?

ª15 Hebrew *Sheol*; also in verses 16 and 17

its allies among the nations, had also gone down to the grave with it, joining those killed by the sword.

¹⁸ " 'Which of the trees of Eden can be compared with you in splendor and majesty? Yet you, too, will be brought down with the trees of Eden to the earth below; you will lie among the uncircumcised, with those killed by the sword.

" 'This is Pharaoh and all his hordes, declares the Sovereign LORD.' "

A Lament for Pharaoh

32 In the twelfth year, in the twelfth month on the first day, the word of the LORD came to me: ²"Son of man, take up a lament concerning Pharaoh king of Egypt and say to him:

> " 'You are like a lion among the nations;
>   you are like a monster in the seas
> thrashing about in your streams,
>   churning the water with your feet
>   and muddying the streams.

³" 'This is what the Sovereign LORD says:

> " 'With a great throng of people
>   I will cast my net over you,
>   and they will haul you up in my net.
> ⁴I will throw you on the land
>   and hurl you on the open field.
> I will let all the birds of the air settle on you
>   and all the beasts of the earth gorge themselves
>   on you.
> ⁵I will spread your flesh on the mountains
>   and fill the valleys with your remains.
> ⁶I will drench the land with your flowing blood
>   all the way to the mountains,
>   and the ravines will be filled with your flesh.
> ⁷When I snuff you out, I will cover the heavens
>   and darken their stars;
> I will cover the sun with a cloud,
>   and the moon will not give its light.
> ⁸All the shining lights in the heavens
>   I will darken over you;
> I will bring darkness over your land,
>   declares the Sovereign LORD.
> ⁹I will trouble the hearts of many peoples
>   when I bring about your destruction among the
>   nations,
>   amongᵃ lands you have not known.
> ¹⁰I will cause many peoples to be appalled at you,
>   and their kings will shudder with horror
>   because of you
>   when I brandish my sword before them.
> On the day of your downfall
>   each of them will tremble
>   every moment for his life.

¹¹" 'For this is what the Sovereign LORD says:

> " 'The sword of the king of Babylon
>   will come against you.
> ¹²I will cause your hordes to fall

---

1. What countries do you think will be world superpowers 50 years from now? Is your answer a hunch or do you have reasons? **2.** If you could live some time in the past, when and where would you choose? Why?

1. What animals join the list of metaphors for Egypt and Pharaoh? What will God do to Pharaoh (vv. 3–8)? How will the "birds and beasts" react? The "moon and stars"? **2.** What is the ultimate destination of Pharaoh and his mighty army (v. 18)? Who will share this fate? What had these other nations been like in their prime? **3.** How would you define "terrorists"? How are they different than "freedom fighters"? **4.** Circumcision was thought to be a rite of purification. Why would it be particularly shameful to be buried with the uncircumcised? With those who had been killed by the sword? **5.** Why would Pharaoh "console" himself when he saw that his fate was the same as the great nations of the past (v. 31)?

1. Would you bother being a Christian if there was no afterlife? Why or why not? **2.** Judaism has no concept of an eternal hell. What temporal sins do you think deserve eternal punishment? What do you fear most about dying? Why? What hope do you have about facing death? What hope does God want you to have? **3.** All world powers have eventually fallen. What might help a mighty nation survive God's judgment?

by the swords of mighty men—
the most ruthless of all nations.
They will shatter the pride of Egypt,
and all her hordes will be overthrown.
¹³I will destroy all her cattle
from beside abundant waters
no longer to be stirred by the foot of man
or muddied by the hoofs of cattle.
¹⁴Then I will let her waters settle
and make her streams flow like oil,
declares the Sovereign LORD.
¹⁵When I make Egypt desolate
and strip the land of everything in it,
when I strike down all who live there,
then they will know that I am the LORD.'

¹⁶"This is the lament they will chant for her. The daughters of the nations will chant it; for Egypt and all her hordes they will chant it, declares the Sovereign LORD."

¹⁷In the twelfth year, on the fifteenth day of the month, the word of the LORD came to me: ¹⁸"Son of man, wail for the hordes of Egypt and consign to the earth below both her and the daughters of mighty nations, with those who go down to the pit. ¹⁹Say to them, 'Are you more favored than others? Go down and be laid among the uncircumcised.' ²⁰They will fall among those killed by the sword. The sword is drawn; let her be dragged off with all her hordes. ²¹From within the grave*ᵃ* the mighty leaders will say of Egypt and her allies, 'They have come down and they lie with the uncircumcised, with those killed by the sword.'

²²"Assyria is there with her whole army; she is surrounded by the graves of all her slain, all who have fallen by the sword. ²³Their graves are in the depths of the pit and her army lies around her grave. All who had spread terror in the land of the living are slain, fallen by the sword.

²⁴"Elam is there, with all her hordes around her grave. All of them are slain, fallen by the sword. All who had spread terror in the land of the living went down uncircumcised to the earth below. They bear their shame with those who go down to the pit. ²⁵A bed is made for her among the slain, with all her hordes around her grave. All of them are uncircumcised, killed by the sword. Because their terror had spread in the land of the living, they bear their shame with those who go down to the pit; they are laid among the slain.

²⁶"Meshech and Tubal are there, with all their hordes around their graves. All of them are uncircumcised, killed by the sword because they spread their terror in the land of the living. ²⁷Do they not lie with the other uncircumcised warriors who have fallen, who went down to the grave with their weapons of war, whose swords were placed under their heads? The punishment for their sins rested on their bones, though the terror of these warriors had stalked through the land of the living.

²⁸"You too, O Pharaoh, will be broken and will lie among the uncircumcised, with those killed by the sword.

²⁹"Edom is there, her kings and all her princes; despite their power, they are laid with those killed by the sword. They lie with the uncircumcised, with those who go down to the pit.

³⁰"All the princes of the north and all the Sidonians are there;

ᵃ21 Hebrew Sheol; also in verse 27

they went down with the slain in disgrace despite the terror caused by their power. They lie uncircumcised with those killed by the sword and bear their shame with those who go down to the pit.

³¹"Pharaoh—he and all his army—will see them and he will be consoled for all his hordes that were killed by the sword, declares the Sovereign LORD. ³²Although I had him spread terror in the land of the living, Pharaoh and all his hordes will be laid among the uncircumcised, with those killed by the sword, declares the Sovereign LORD."

Ezekiel a Watchman

33 The word of the LORD came to me: ²"Son of man, speak to your countrymen and say to them: 'When I bring the sword against a land, and the people of the land choose one of their men and make him their watchman, ³and he sees the sword coming against the land and blows the trumpet to warn the people, ⁴then if anyone hears the trumpet but does not take warning and the sword comes and takes his life, his blood will be on his own head. ⁵Since he heard the sound of the trumpet but did not take warning, his blood will be on his own head. If he had taken warning, he would have saved himself. ⁶But if the watchman sees the sword coming and does not blow the trumpet to warn the people and the sword comes and takes the life of one of them, that man will be taken away because of his sin, but I will hold the watchman accountable for his blood.'

⁷"Son of man, I have made you a watchman for the house of Israel; so hear the word I speak and give them warning from me. ⁸When I say to the wicked, 'O wicked man, you will surely die,' and you do not speak out to dissuade him from his ways, that wicked man will die for*ᵃ* his sin, and I will hold you accountable for his blood. ⁹But if you do warn the wicked man to turn from his ways and he does not do so, he will die for his sin, but you will have saved yourself.

¹⁰"Son of man, say to the house of Israel, 'This is what you are saying: "Our offenses and sins weigh us down, and we are wasting away because of*ᵇ* them. How then can we live?" ' ¹¹Say to them, 'As surely as I live, declares the Sovereign LORD, I take no pleasure in the death of the wicked, but rather that they turn from their ways and live. Turn! Turn from your evil ways! Why will you die, O house of Israel?'

¹²"Therefore, son of man, say to your countrymen, 'The righteousness of the righteous man will not save him when he disobeys, and the wickedness of the wicked man will not cause him to fall when he turns from it. The righteous man, if he sins, will not be allowed to live because of his former righteousness.' ¹³If I tell the righteous man that he will surely live, but then he trusts in his righteousness and does evil, none of the righteous things he has done will be remembered; he will die for the evil he has done. ¹⁴And if I say to the wicked man, 'You will surely die,' but he then turns away from his sin and does what is just and right— ¹⁵if he gives back what he took in pledge for a loan, returns what he has stolen, follows the decrees that give life, and does no evil, he will surely live; he will not die. ¹⁶None of the sins he has committed will be remembered against him. He has done what is just and right; he will surely live.

¹⁷"Yet your countrymen say, 'The way of the Lord is not just.' But it is their way that is not just. ¹⁸If a righteous man turns from

---

1. Who is your favorite newscaster? What channel is he or she on? Why do you like him or her? 2. Do you have an alarm system on your house or car? Has it ever scared away a crook? Does it ever give false alarms?

1. What is the one way the watchman can fail in his job (v. 6)? What are those who hear the warning supposed to do? What will happen if people ignore the warning? 2. What problem do the people of Israel have besides their sins (v. 10)? What does God say to encourage them (v. 11)? 3. Verses 12–20 echo chapter 18's declaration of individual responsibility. Which actions will cause the righteous to die? Which will cause the wicked to live? By what standards will God judge each person's life (v. 20)?

1. The word "gospel" literally means "good news." What bad news is part of the good news? Why do people need to hear the bad news? Are you generally a "good newscaster" or a "bad newscaster"? 2. People often get discouraged when they hear the bad news. Do you get discouraged when you fail the Lord? Does God want you to punish yourself or to do something else? What does 2 Corinthians 7:10 say about your attitudes and actions in response to sin? 3. Is God calling every Christian to be a watchman like Ezekiel? What are you watching for? Will he hold you accountable for not warning your people? 4. What concerns you most about the current scene in your country? What are you doing about it? Is there any project the group could work on to help?

ᵃ8 Or *in*; also in verse 9　　*ᵇ10* Or *away in*

his righteousness and does evil, he will die for it. ¹⁹And if a wicked man turns away from his wickedness and does what is just and right, he will live by doing so. ²⁰Yet, O house of Israel, you say, 'The way of the Lord is not just.' But I will judge each of you according to his own ways."

Jerusalem's Fall Explained

²¹In the twelfth year of our exile, in the tenth month on the fifth day, a man who had escaped from Jerusalem came to me and said, "The city has fallen!" ²²Now the evening before the man arrived, the hand of the LORD was upon me, and he opened my mouth before the man came to me in the morning. So my mouth was opened and I was no longer silent.

²³Then the word of the LORD came to me: ²⁴"Son of man, the people living in those ruins in the land of Israel are saying, 'Abraham was only one man, yet he possessed the land. But we are many; surely the land has been given to us as our possession.' ²⁵Therefore say to them, 'This is what the Sovereign LORD says: Since you eat meat with the blood still in it and look to your idols and shed blood, should you then possess the land? ²⁶You rely on your sword, you do detestable things, and each of you defiles his neighbor's wife. Should you then possess the land?'

²⁷"Say this to them: 'This is what the Sovereign LORD says: As surely as I live, those who are left in the ruins will fall by the sword, those out in the country I will give to the wild animals to be devoured, and those in strongholds and caves will die of a plague. ²⁸I will make the land a desolate waste, and her proud strength will come to an end, and the mountains of Israel will become desolate so that no one will cross them. ²⁹Then they will know that I am the LORD, when I have made the land a desolate waste because of all the detestable things they have done.'

³⁰"As for you, son of man, your countrymen are talking together about you by the walls and at the doors of the houses, saying to each other, 'Come and hear the message that has come from the LORD.' ³¹My people come to you, as they usually do, and sit before you to listen to your words, but they do not put them into practice. With their mouths they express devotion, but their hearts are greedy for unjust gain. ³²Indeed, to them you are nothing more than one who sings love songs with a beautiful voice and plays an instrument well, for they hear your words but do not put them into practice.

³³"When all this comes true—and it surely will—then they will know that a prophet has been among them."

Shepherds and Sheep

34 The word of the LORD came to me: ²"Son of man, prophesy against the shepherds of Israel; prophesy and say to them: 'This is what the Sovereign LORD says: Woe to the shepherds of Israel who only take care of themselves! Should not shepherds take care of the flock? ³You eat the curds, clothe yourselves with the wool and slaughter the choice animals, but you do not take care of the flock. ⁴You have not strengthened the weak or healed the sick or bound up the injured. You have not brought back the strays or searched for the lost. You have ruled them harshly and brutally. ⁵So they were scattered because there was no shepherd, and when they were scattered they became food for all the wild animals. ⁶My sheep wandered over all the mountains and on every high hill. They were scattered over the whole earth, and no one searched or looked for them.

What part of the body best describes you? Why?

1. What news comes from Jerusalem? How many years had Ezekiel waited for this (Compare 1:2 with v. 21)? 2. Why was Ezekiel dumb (3:26–27; 24:27)? 3. What false hope did the Jerusalemites entertain in comparing themselves to Abraham (v. 24)? Why wouldn't they possess the land (vv. 25–26)? 4. What three groups remained in the Jerusalem area (v. 27)? What will happen to each? What will the effect be on those who witness the desolation (v. 29)? 5. Did the exiles take Ezekiel seriously (vv. 30–32)? If they were no more serious than those in Jerusalem, why was their fate so different?

1. Are you, like the Israelites, ever tempted to think you can get God's blessing without obeying his commands? Does God require obedience? 2. The exiles liked to listen to Ezekiel but didn't do what he said. What does Jesus say about such people (see Mt 7:24–27)? How would you describe yourself: (a) All listen but no action? (b) Easier said than done? (c) A procrastinating doer? (d) Not even a listener?

---

1. Have you ever taken a bunch of kids to a zoo, fair, circus or similar place? What happened? Did anyone get lost? Was it a restful experience? 2. When was the last time you saw a sheep? Was it cute and cuddly or dirty and stupid? Was it by itself or in a flock?

1. What were the shepherds doing (vv. 2–3)? Five different groups of sheep are mentioned. What care was needed by each? 2. What has happened to the sheep because of the bad shepherds (vv. 5–8)? What will God do to the shepherds for this

malpractice (v. 10)? **3.** What will God himself do for the sheep (vv. 11–16)? What will God do for those who have been scattered? How will God provide food and safety for them? **4.** After God rounds up the flock, what groups will be found among them (vv. 16–22)? How do the sheep treat one another? How will God treat each group? Who will be as a shepherd over them (vv. 23–24)? **5.** What will God do to the land on which he pastures his flock? How will this affect the sheep (vv. 25–31)? **6.** In the allegory of the sheep: Who are the sheep? The shepherds? What is God promising to do? Who is the coming Shepherd?

♡ **1.** In this parable, what do you learn about the mission of Jesus? **2.** What kind of sheep are you: Weak? Sick? Injured? Lost? Does it feel like God is taking care of you? **3.** The word "pastor" literally means "a shepherd." Are you getting good shepherding? Do you follow where your shepherd leads you or are you always running away? Are you growing in your ability to shepherd others? **4.** What sorts of sheep come to your small group: Tramplers? Drinkers? Muddy? Fat? Lean? How can you treat each other better? **5.** Do you feel sufficiently herded or does it seem you do all the herding? How can the small group help?

7 " 'Therefore, you shepherds, hear the word of the LORD: 8As surely as I live, declares the Sovereign LORD, because my flock lacks a shepherd and so has been plundered and has become food for all the wild animals, and because my shepherds did not search for my flock but cared for themselves rather than for my flock, 9therefore, O shepherds, hear the word of the LORD: 10This is what the Sovereign LORD says: I am against the shepherds and will hold them accountable for my flock. I will remove them from tending the flock so that the shepherds can no longer feed themselves. I will rescue my flock from their mouths, and it will no longer be food for them.

11 " 'For this is what the Sovereign LORD says: I myself will search for my sheep and look after them. 12As a shepherd looks after his scattered flock when he is with them, so will I look after my sheep. I will rescue them from all the places where they were scattered on a day of clouds and darkness. 13I will bring them out from the nations and gather them from the countries, and I will bring them into their own land. I will pasture them on the mountains of Israel, in the ravines and in all the settlements in the land. 14I will tend them in a good pasture, and the mountain heights of Israel will be their grazing land. There they will lie down in good grazing land, and there they will feed in a rich pasture on the mountains of Israel. 15I myself will tend my sheep and have them lie down, declares the Sovereign LORD. 16I will search for the lost and bring back the strays. I will bind up the injured and strengthen the weak, but the sleek and the strong I will destroy. I will shepherd the flock with justice.

17 " 'As for you, my flock, this is what the Sovereign LORD says: I will judge between one sheep and another, and between rams and goats. 18Is it not enough for you to feed on the good pasture? Must you also trample the rest of your pasture with your feet? Is it not enough for you to drink clear water? Must you also muddy the rest with your feet? 19Must my flock feed on what you have trampled and drink what you have muddied with your feet?

20 " 'Therefore this is what the Sovereign LORD says to them: See, I myself will judge between the fat sheep and the lean sheep. 21Because you shove with flank and shoulder, butting all the weak sheep with your horns until you have driven them away, 22I will save my flock, and they will no longer be plundered. I will judge between one sheep and another. 23I will place over them one shepherd, my servant David, and he will tend them; he will tend them and be their shepherd. 24I the LORD will be their God, and my servant David will be prince among them. I the LORD have spoken.

25 " 'I will make a covenant of peace with them and rid the land of wild beasts so that they may live in the desert and sleep in the forests in safety. 26I will bless them and the places surrounding my hill.ª I will send down showers in season; there will be showers of blessing. 27The trees of the field will yield their fruit and the ground will yield its crops; the people will be secure in their land. They will know that I am the LORD, when I break the bars of their yoke and rescue them from the hands of those who enslaved them. 28They will no longer be plundered by the nations, nor will wild animals devour them. They will live in safety, and no one will make them afraid. 29I will provide for them a land renowned for its crops, and they will no longer be victims of famine in the land or bear the scorn of the nations. 30Then they will know that I, the LORD their God, am with them and that they, the house of Israel,

ª26 Or *I will make them and the places surrounding my hill a blessing*

are my people, declares the Sovereign LORD. 31You my sheep, the sheep of my pasture, are people, and I am your God, declares the Sovereign LORD.'"

A Prophecy Against Edom

35 The word of the LORD came to me: 2"Son of man, set your face against Mount Seir; prophesy against it 3and say: 'This is what the Sovereign LORD says: I am against you, Mount Seir, and I will stretch out my hand against you and make you a desolate waste. 4I will turn your towns into ruins and you will be desolate. Then you will know that I am the LORD.

5"'Because you harbored an ancient hostility and delivered the Israelites over to the sword at the time of their calamity, the time their punishment reached its climax, 6therefore as surely as I live, declares the Sovereign LORD, I will give you over to bloodshed and it will pursue you. Since you did not hate bloodshed, bloodshed will pursue you. 7I will make Mount Seir a desolate waste and cut off from it all who come and go. 8I will fill your mountains with the slain; those killed by the sword will fall on your hills and in your valleys and in all your ravines. 9I will make you desolate forever; your towns will not be inhabited. Then you will know that I am the LORD.

10"'Because you have said, "These two nations and countries will be ours and we will take possession of them," even though I the LORD was there, 11therefore as surely as I live, declares the Sovereign LORD, I will treat you in accordance with the anger and jealousy you showed in your hatred of them and I will make myself known among them when I judge you. 12Then you will know that I the LORD have heard all the contemptible things you have said against the mountains of Israel. You said, "They have been laid waste and have been given over to us to devour." 13You boasted against me and spoke against me without restraint, and I heard it. 14This is what the Sovereign LORD says: While the whole earth rejoices, I will make you desolate. 15Because you rejoiced when the inheritance of the house of Israel became desolate, that is how I will treat you. You will be desolate, O Mount Seir, you and all of Edom. Then they will know that I am the LORD.'"

A Prophecy to the Mountains of Israel

36 "Son of man, prophesy to the mountains of Israel and say, 'O mountains of Israel, hear the word of the LORD. 2This is what the Sovereign LORD says: The enemy said of you, "Aha! The ancient heights have become our possession." ' 3Therefore prophesy and say, 'This is what the Sovereign LORD says: Because they ravaged and hounded you from every side so that you became the possession of the rest of the nations and the object of people's malicious talk and slander, 4therefore, O mountains of Israel, hear the word of the Sovereign LORD: This is what the Sovereign LORD says to the mountains and hills, to the ravines and valleys, to the desolate ruins and the deserted towns that have been plundered and ridiculed by the rest of the nations around you— 5this is what the Sovereign LORD says: In my burning zeal I have spoken against the rest of the nations, and against all Edom, for with glee and with malice in their hearts they made my land their own possession so that they might plunder its pastureland.' 6Therefore prophesy concerning the land of Israel and say to the mountains and hills, to the ravines and valleys: 'This is what the Sovereign LORD says: I speak in my jealous wrath because you have suffered the scorn of the nations. 7Therefore this is what the Sovereign LORD says: I swear

---

☕ **1.** Is there a certain sports team or politician you really dislike? How do you feel when they lose? **2.** Were you ever envious of anyone when you were young? Who? Why?

📖 **1.** What does the capital Mt. Seir represent? (vv. 2–3,7–8,15)? **2.** Who were the Edomites (Ge 36:6–9)? How far back does their "ancient hostility" go (see Ge 25:19–34, Esau is also called Edom; Ob 11–14)? **3.** Why is God angry with the way Edom responded to Israel's calamity (vv. 5–6,10–13,15)? What will the Lord do to them? **4.** What will be the effect on the people of Edom and of Israel when they see the Lord's punishment (vv. 4,15)?

❤️ **1.** Why do you think it was wrong for Edom to rejoice when God punished Israel? When has someone laughed when you were crying? **2.** What is your attitude when you see nasty people get what they deserve? What should it be? **3.** Once again, two different groups of people will know the Lord in two different ways. What kind of person do you need to be to know the Lord in the good sense?

☕ **1.** Are you afraid of heights? What is the highest spot you've visited? Was it man-made or natural? **2.** Have you or anyone you know had heart surgery? Was it a long ordeal or a quick operation? **3.** Which institution do you hate to deal with the most: Bank? Post office? Motor vehicles? IRS? Supermarket? Social security? Which bureaucrat gets the "Heart of Stone Award"?

📖 **1.** Ezekiel 6 was also directed to the mountains of Israel. What was the earlier message? What had happened in the mountains of Israel (6:13)? **2.** In light of the history of God's actions, why would the Israelites bother with idols in the "high places"? Why was idolatry a constant temptation? **3.** How would you summarize Ezekiel's new message to the mountains? Why did he use the same metaphor for both the good and bad news? **4.** What had Israel's enemies done (vv. 2–3)? What will God do to the nations which plundered Israel (vv. 6–7)? Wasn't this God's will (vv. 17–19)? Is God being fair to Israel's enemies? **5.** What did the nations say about God (vv. 20–21)? What motivated God to restore Israel (vv. 21–22)? What's in a name? **6.** Where will God perform "surgery" on the people of Israel (vv. 24–26)? What changes are "on the table"? What will happen to their land (vv. 29–30)? What will they remember (v. 31)? What did the people do to deserve God's actions (v. 32)? **7.** Would Israel become the kind of place you'd want to visit (vv. 35–38)? **8.** How do verses 24–27 shed light on the mission of Jesus (see Jer 31:33; Heb 10:11–16)?

♡ **1.** Does God treat you better than you deserve? Worse? Pretty fair? What does this show you about God's character? **2.** Have you experienced any of God's promises to Israel: (a) Cleansing? (b) Stony heart transplant? (c) Power to obey? (d) Plentiful harvest? How did it happen? Which would you like to see happen? **3.** What shape is your heart in right now: (a) Like a piece of granite? (b) Being broken up by some hard blows? (c) Being softened by the steady "rain" of the Spirit? (d) Other? Why do you describe yourself like this? **4.** What fear keeps you from "climbing mountains"? Do you find the small group a safe place to express your fears? Do the members: Listen and accept? Try to fix it? Analyze you? Approve or disapprove? What do you need when you're being vulnerable?

with uplifted hand that the nations around you will also suffer scorn.

⁸"'But you, O mountains of Israel, will produce branches and fruit for my people Israel, for they will soon come home. ⁹I am concerned for you and will look on you with favor; you will be plowed and sown, ¹⁰and I will multiply the number of people upon you, even the whole house of Israel. The towns will be inhabited and the ruins rebuilt. ¹¹I will increase the number of men and animals upon you, and they will be fruitful and become numerous. I will settle people on you as in the past and will make you prosper more than before. Then you will know that I am the LORD. ¹²I will cause people, my people Israel, to walk upon you. They will possess you, and you will be their inheritance; you will never again deprive them of their children.

¹³"'This is what the Sovereign LORD says: Because people say to you, "You devour men and deprive your nation of its children," ¹⁴therefore you will no longer devour men or make your nation childless, declares the Sovereign LORD. ¹⁵No longer will I make you hear the taunts of the nations, and no longer will you suffer the scorn of the peoples or cause your nation to fall, declares the Sovereign LORD.'"

¹⁶Again the word of the LORD came to me: ¹⁷"Son of man, when the people of Israel were living in their own land, they defiled it by their conduct and their actions. Their conduct was like a woman's monthly uncleanness in my sight. ¹⁸So I poured out my wrath on them because they had shed blood in the land and because they had defiled it with their idols. ¹⁹I dispersed them among the nations, and they were scattered through the countries; I judged them according to their conduct and their actions. ²⁰And wherever they went among the nations they profaned my holy name, for it was said of them, 'These are the LORD's people, and yet they had to leave his land.' ²¹I had concern for my holy name, which the house of Israel profaned among the nations where they had gone.

²²"Therefore say to the house of Israel, 'This is what the Sovereign LORD says: It is not for your sake, O house of Israel, that I am going to do these things, but for the sake of my holy name, which you have profaned among the nations where you have gone. ²³I will show the holiness of my great name, which has been profaned among the nations, the name you have profaned among them. Then the nations will know that I am the LORD, declares the Sovereign LORD, when I show myself holy through you before their eyes.

²⁴"'For I will take you out of the nations; I will gather you from all the countries and bring you back into your own land. ²⁵I will sprinkle clean water on you, and you will be clean; I will cleanse you from all your impurities and from all your idols. ²⁶I will give you a new heart and put a new spirit in you; I will remove from you your heart of stone and give you a heart of flesh. ²⁷And I will put my Spirit in you and move you to follow my decrees and be careful to keep my laws. ²⁸You will live in the land I gave your forefathers; you will be my people, and I will be your God. ²⁹I will save you from all your uncleanness. I will call for the grain and make it plentiful and will not bring famine upon you. ³⁰I will increase the fruit of the trees and the crops of the field, so that you will no longer suffer disgrace among the nations because of famine. ³¹Then you will remember your evil ways and wicked deeds, and you will loathe yourselves for your sins and detestable practices. ³²I want you to know that I am not doing this for your sake, declares the Sovereign LORD. Be ashamed and disgraced for your conduct, O house of Israel!

³³" 'This is what the Sovereign LORD says: On the day I cleanse you from all your sins, I will resettle your towns, and the ruins will be rebuilt. ³⁴The desolate land will be cultivated instead of lying desolate in the sight of all who pass through it. ³⁵They will say, "This land that was laid waste has become like the garden of Eden; the cities that were lying in ruins, desolate and destroyed, are now fortified and inhabited." ³⁶Then the nations around you that remain will know that I the LORD have rebuilt what was destroyed and have replanted what was desolate. I the LORD have spoken, and I will do it.'

³⁷"This is what the Sovereign LORD says: Once again I will yield to the plea of the house of Israel and do this for them: I will make their people as numerous as sheep, ³⁸as numerous as the flocks for offerings at Jerusalem during her appointed feasts. So will the ruined cities be filled with flocks of people. Then they will know that I am the LORD."

The Valley of Dry Bones

37 The hand of the LORD was upon me, and he brought me out by the Spirit of the LORD and set me in the middle of a valley; it was full of bones. ²He led me back and forth among them, and I saw a great many bones on the floor of the valley, bones that were very dry. ³He asked me, "Son of man, can these bones live?"

I said, "O Sovereign LORD, you alone know."

⁴Then he said to me, "Prophesy to these bones and say to them, 'Dry bones, hear the word of the LORD! ⁵This is what the Sovereign LORD says to these bones: I will make breath[a] enter you, and you will come to life. ⁶I will attach tendons to you and make flesh come upon you and cover you with skin; I will put breath in you, and you will come to life. Then you will know that I am the LORD.' "

⁷So I prophesied as I was commanded. And as I was prophesying, there was a noise, a rattling sound, and the bones came together, bone to bone. ⁸I looked, and tendons and flesh appeared on them and skin covered them, but there was no breath in them.

⁹Then he said to me, "Prophesy to the breath; prophesy, son of man, and say to it, 'This is what the Sovereign LORD says: Come from the four winds, O breath, and breathe into these slain, that they may live.' " ¹⁰So I prophesied as he commanded me, and breath entered them; they came to life and stood up on their feet—a vast army.

¹¹Then he said to me: "Son of man, these bones are the whole house of Israel. They say, 'Our bones are dried up and our hope is gone; we are cut off.' ¹²Therefore prophesy and say to them: 'This is what the Sovereign LORD says: O my people, I am going to open your graves and bring you up from them; I will bring you back to the land of Israel. ¹³Then you, my people, will know that I am the LORD, when I open your graves and bring you up from them. ¹⁴I will put my Spirit in you and you will live, and I will settle you in your own land. Then you will know that I the LORD have spoken, and I have done it, declares the LORD.' "

One Nation Under One King

¹⁵The word of the LORD came to me: ¹⁶"Son of man, take a stick of wood and write on it, 'Belonging to Judah and the Israelites associated with him.' Then take another stick of wood, and write on it, 'Ephraim's stick, belonging to Joseph and all the house of

---

1. Have you ever seen a skeleton? Where? Was it real bone or imitation? How did it make you feel? 2. What little things can raise your spirits on a gloomy day? Where do you go when you're depressed?

1. Imagine a valley full of bones. Why might their dryness be significant (vv. 2,4)? 2. Hebrews uses the word "ruach" for "wind," "breath" and "spirit." How are these three related (vv. 5, 9,14)? 3. What are the two steps in raising these dead (vv. 7–8,10)? Why not do it all at once? 4. How are the exiles feeling (v. 11)? What is God telling them about the future of: Israel? The individual? Humanity?

1. How would you describe your life currently: (a) Dry bones? (b) No backbone? (c) Into the flesh? (d) Full of hot air? (e) Standing tall? 2. Has God raised you from "the dead"? When and how did it happen? 3. Are you "filled with the Spirit"? What does this mean? How does it happen? 4. How can group members help to raise each others' spirits?

1. Do you learn best by hearing, seeing or doing? Give an example. 2. Did you ever break something as a child and try to fix it without your parents finding out? Did it work?

---

a5 The Hebrew for this word can also mean *wind* or *spirit* (see verses 6-14).

1. The people of Israel split into northern and southern kingdoms after the death of Solomon. Which kingdom is the "stick of Judah" (see 1Ki 12:21–25)? Where was "Ephraim" (see 2Ki 17:5–6)? 2. What is the "point" of Ezekiel's stick lesson to Israel? (vv. 22–23)? 3. Who will be king of the united land (v. 24)? How long will his reign last? Who might this "David" represent? 4. Do you think this prophecy has ever been fulfilled?

1. What object lesson has illustrated God's truth to you recently? Have you been paying attention? 2. Has your family been divided by: (a) Sibling rivalry? (b) Divorce? (c) Long-standing feuds? (d) Death? Can this brokenness be healed? How? 3. Christendom is currently divided into hundreds of rival groups. Do you think God approves? What would it take to restore the unity of all believers as God intended (see Jn 17:20–26)? Is your small group open to Christians of different perspectives?

1. Have you ever been given a nickname you couldn't stand? Would it embarrass you to tell the group? How does the name make you feel? 2. Are your hunches about the future very reliable? Give an example of one that was either exactly right or laughably wrong. 3. If you knew you were going to win, would that make playing a game more or less fun for you? Why?

1. Gog is unknown to us outside this reference. Magog is Hebrew for "the place where Gog lives." What was the fate of Meshech and Tubal in Ezekiel 32:26? 2. When will the invasion by Gog occur (38:8,14)? Is this an upcoming event or the distant future? Will it come soon after the regathering of Israel predicted in 37:24–28? 3. What does Gog stand to gain from the attack (38:11–13)? Why is Israel "unwalled"? Who is really behind the attack (38:16–17)? Is God always behind wars? 4. Will Gog win this war (38:18–22)? What will Israel do with Gog's weapons (39:9–10)? Wouldn't you keep a few for yourself? How long will it

Israel associated with him.' 17Join them together into one stick so that they will become one in your hand.

18"When your countrymen ask you, 'Won't you tell us what you mean by this?' 19say to them, 'This is what the Sovereign LORD says: I am going to take the stick of Joseph—which is in Ephraim's hand—and of the Israelite tribes associated with him, and join it to Judah's stick, making them a single stick of wood, and they will become one in my hand.' 20Hold before their eyes the sticks you have written on 21and say to them, 'This is what the Sovereign LORD says: I will take the Israelites out of the nations where they have gone. I will gather them from all around and bring them back into their own land. 22I will make them one nation in the land, on the mountains of Israel. There will be one king over all of them and they will never again be two nations or be divided into two kingdoms. 23They will no longer defile themselves with their idols and vile images or with any of their offenses, for I will save them from all their sinful backsliding,a and I will cleanse them. They will be my people, and I will be their God.

24"'My servant David will be king over them, and they will all have one shepherd. They will follow my laws and be careful to keep my decrees. 25They will live in the land I gave to my servant Jacob, the land where your fathers lived. They and their children and their children's children will live there forever, and David my servant will be their prince forever. 26I will make a covenant of peace with them; it will be an everlasting covenant. I will establish them and increase their numbers, and I will put my sanctuary among them forever. 27My dwelling place will be with them; I will be their God, and they will be my people. 28Then the nations will know that I the LORD make Israel holy, when my sanctuary is among them forever.'"

A Prophecy Against Gog

38 The word of the LORD came to me: 2"Son of man, set your face against Gog, of the land of Magog, the chief prince ofb Meshech and Tubal; prophesy against him 3and say: 'This is what the Sovereign LORD says: I am against you, O Gog, chief prince ofc Meshech and Tubal. 4I will turn you around, put hooks in your jaws and bring you out with your whole army—your horses, your horsemen fully armed, and a great horde with large and small shields, all of them brandishing their swords. 5Persia, Cushd and Put will be with them, all with shields and helmets, 6also Gomer with all its troops, and Beth Togarmah from the far north with all its troops—the many nations with you.

7"'Get ready; be prepared, you and all the hordes gathered about you, and take command of them. 8After many days you will be called to arms. In future years you will invade a land that has recovered from war, whose people were gathered from many nations to the mountains of Israel, which had long been desolate. They had been brought out from the nations, and now all of them live in safety. 9You and all your troops and the many nations with you will go up, advancing like a storm; you will be like a cloud covering the land.

10"'This is what the Sovereign LORD says: On that day thoughts will come into your mind and you will devise an evil scheme. 11You will say, "I will invade a land of unwalled villages; I will

a23 Many Hebrew manuscripts (see also Septuagint); most Hebrew manuscripts *all their dwelling places where they sinned*　　b2 Or *the prince of Rosh,*　　c3 Or *Gog, prince of Rosh,*　　d5 That is, the upper Nile region

attack a peaceful and unsuspecting people—all of them living without walls and without gates and bars. ¹²I will plunder and loot and turn my hand against the resettled ruins and the people gathered from the nations, rich in livestock and goods, living at the center of the land." ¹³Sheba and Dedan and the merchants of Tarshish and all her villages*a* will say to you, "Have you come to plunder? Have you gathered your hordes to loot, to carry off silver and gold, to take away livestock and goods and to seize much plunder?" '

¹⁴"Therefore, son of man, prophesy and say to Gog: 'This is what the Sovereign LORD says: In that day, when my people Israel are living in safety, will you not take notice of it? ¹⁵You will come from your place in the far north, you and many nations with you, all of them riding on horses, a great horde, a mighty army. ¹⁶You will advance against my people Israel like a cloud that covers the land. In days to come, O Gog, I will bring you against my land, so that the nations may know me when I show myself holy through you before their eyes.

¹⁷" 'This is what the Sovereign LORD says: Are you not the one I spoke of in former days by my servants the prophets of Israel? At that time they prophesied for years that I would bring you against them. ¹⁸This is what will happen in that day: When Gog attacks the land of Israel, my hot anger will be aroused, declares the Sovereign LORD. ¹⁹In my zeal and fiery wrath I declare that at that time there shall be a great earthquake in the land of Israel. ²⁰The fish of the sea, the birds of the air, the beasts of the field, every creature that moves along the ground, and all the people on the face of the earth will tremble at my presence. The mountains will be overturned, the cliffs will crumble and every wall will fall to the ground. ²¹I will summon a sword against Gog on all my mountains, declares the Sovereign LORD. Every man's sword will be against his brother. ²²I will execute judgment upon him with plague and bloodshed; I will pour down torrents of rain, hailstones and burning sulfur on him and on his troops and on the many nations with him. ²³And so I will show my greatness and my holiness, and I will make myself known in the sight of many nations. Then they will know that I am the LORD.'

39 "Son of man, prophesy against Gog and say: 'This is what the Sovereign LORD says: I am against you, O Gog, chief prince of*b* Meshech and Tubal. ²I will turn you around and drag you along. I will bring you from the far north and send you against the mountains of Israel. ³Then I will strike your bow from your left hand and make your arrows drop from your right hand. ⁴On the mountains of Israel you will fall, you and all your troops and the nations with you. I will give you as food to all kinds of carrion birds and to the wild animals. ⁵You will fall in the open field, for I have spoken, declares the Sovereign LORD. ⁶I will send fire on Magog and on those who live in safety in the coastlands, and they will know that I am the LORD.

⁷" 'I will make known my holy name among my people Israel. I will no longer let my holy name be profaned, and the nations will know that I the LORD am the Holy One in Israel. ⁸It is coming! It will surely take place, declares the Sovereign LORD. This is the day I have spoken of.

⁹" 'Then those who live in the towns of Israel will go out and use the weapons for fuel and burn them up—the small and large

take to bury the dead (39:12)? Who do you think should spring for all the cemetery plots? **5.** What will God accomplish through this war? What will the whole world learn from it (39:21)? What will Israel learn (39:22)? **6.** What does Revelation 20:8–9 say about Gog? Do you think Ezekiel and the Revelation are describing the same event? Two events with similar characters? Is it all symbolic? Of what?

♡ **1.** How does the idea that God will ultimately destroy all evil make you feel? Sorry for those who are punished? Relieved? Vindicated? Scared? Expectant? Confident? Something else? All of the above? **2.** In the real world, does good always triumph over evil? Can we humans eliminate evil, or is that something only God can do? Why is it taking so long? **3.** Do you think prophecies concerning Israel in the "last days" refer to the Jewish people or the Christian church? How do you take them: (a) Literally, complete with horses, shields and swords? (b) Allegorically, with Gog and Magog representing actual countries? (c) Symbolically, reflecting spiritual realities in Christian lives? **4.** Do you feel that God is in control of your life? Your country? World destiny? How much depends on our human choices?

a 13 Or *her strong lions*   *b 1* Or *Gog, prince of Rosh,*

shields, the bows and arrows, the war clubs and spears. For seven years they will use them for fuel. [10]They will not need to gather wood from the fields or cut it from the forests, because they will use the weapons for fuel. And they will plunder those who plundered them and loot those who looted them, declares the Sovereign LORD.

[11]"'On that day I will give Gog a burial place in Israel, in the valley of those who travel east toward[a] the Sea.[b] It will block the way of travelers, because Gog and all his hordes will be buried there. So it will be called the Valley of Hamon Gog.[c]

[12]"'For seven months the house of Israel will be burying them in order to cleanse the land. [13]All the people of the land will bury them, and the day I am glorified will be a memorable day for them, declares the Sovereign LORD.

[14]"'Men will be regularly employed to cleanse the land. Some will go throughout the land and, in addition to them, others will bury those that remain on the ground. At the end of the seven months they will begin their search. [15]As they go through the land and one of them sees a human bone, he will set up a marker beside it until the gravediggers have buried it in the Valley of Hamon Gog. [16](Also a town called Hamonah[d] will be there.) And so they will cleanse the land.'

[17]"Son of man, this is what the Sovereign LORD says: Call out to every kind of bird and all the wild animals: 'Assemble and come together from all around to the sacrifice I am preparing for you, the great sacrifice on the mountains of Israel. There you will eat flesh and drink blood. [18]You will eat the flesh of mighty men and drink the blood of the princes of the earth as if they were rams and lambs, goats and bulls—all of them fattened animals from Bashan. [19]At the sacrifice I am preparing for you, you will eat fat till you are glutted and drink blood till you are drunk. [20]At my table you will eat your fill of horses and riders, mighty men and soldiers of every kind,' declares the Sovereign LORD.

[21]"I will display my glory among the nations, and all the nations will see the punishment I inflict and the hand I lay upon them. [22]From that day forward the house of Israel will know that I am the LORD their God. [23]And the nations will know that the people of Israel went into exile for their sin, because they were unfaithful to me. So I hid my face from them and handed them over to their enemies, and they all fell by the sword. [24]I dealt with them according to their uncleanness and their offenses, and I hid my face from them.

[25]"Therefore this is what the Sovereign LORD says: I will now bring Jacob back from captivity[e] and will have compassion on all the people of Israel, and I will be zealous for my holy name. [26]They will forget their shame and all the unfaithfulness they showed toward me when they lived in safety in their land with no one to make them afraid. [27]When I have brought them back from the nations and have gathered them from the countries of their enemies, I will show myself holy through them in the sight of many nations. [28]Then they will know that I am the LORD their God, for though I sent them into exile among the nations, I will gather them to their own land, not leaving any behind. [29]I will no longer hide my face from them, for I will pour out my Spirit on the house of Israel, declares the Sovereign LORD."

---

[a]11 Or of   [b]11 That is, the Dead Sea   [c]11 Hamon Gog means hordes of Gog.
[d]16 Hamonah means horde.   [e]25 Or now restore the fortunes of Jacob

The New Temple Area

40 In the twenty-fifth year of our exile, at the beginning of the year, on the tenth of the month, in the fourteenth year after the fall of the city—on that very day the hand of the LORD was upon me and he took me there. ²In visions of God he took me to the land of Israel and set me on a very high mountain, on whose south side were some buildings that looked like a city. ³He took me there, and I saw a man whose appearance was like bronze; he was standing in the gateway with a linen cord and a measuring rod in his hand. ⁴The man said to me, "Son of man, look with your eyes and hear with your ears and pay attention to everything I am going to show you, for that is why you have been brought here. Tell the house of Israel everything you see."

The East Gate to the Outer Court

⁵I saw a wall completely surrounding the temple area. The length of the measuring rod in the man's hand was six long cubits, each of which was a cubit*ᵃ* and a handbreadth.*ᵇ* He measured the wall; it was one measuring rod thick and one rod high.

⁶Then he went to the gate facing east. He climbed its steps and measured the threshold of the gate; it was one rod deep.*ᶜ* ⁷The alcoves for the guards were one rod long and one rod wide, and the projecting walls between the alcoves were five cubits thick. And the threshold of the gate next to the portico facing the temple was one rod deep.

⁸Then he measured the portico of the gateway; ⁹it*ᵈ* was eight cubits deep and its jambs were two cubits thick. The portico of the gateway faced the temple.

¹⁰Inside the east gate were three alcoves on each side; the three had the same measurements, and the faces of the projecting walls on each side had the same measurements. ¹¹Then he measured the width of the entrance to the gateway; it was ten cubits and its length was thirteen cubits. ¹²In front of each alcove was a wall one cubit high, and the alcoves were six cubits square. ¹³Then he measured the gateway from the top of the rear wall of one alcove to the top of the opposite one; the distance was twenty-five cubits from one parapet opening to the opposite one. ¹⁴He measured along the faces of the projecting walls all around the inside of the gateway—sixty cubits. The measurement was up to the portico*ᵉ* facing the courtyard.*ᶠ* ¹⁵The distance from the entrance of the gateway to the far end of its portico was fifty cubits. ¹⁶The alcoves and the projecting walls inside the gateway were surmounted by narrow parapet openings all around, as was the portico; the openings all around faced inward. The faces of the projecting walls were decorated with palm trees.

The Outer Court

¹⁷Then he brought me into the outer court. There I saw some rooms and a pavement that had been constructed all around the court; there were thirty rooms along the pavement. ¹⁸It abutted the sides of the gateways and was as wide as they were long; this was the lower pavement. ¹⁹Then he measured the distance from the

---

ᵃ5 The common cubit was about 1 1/2 feet (about 0.5 meter).   *ᵇ5* That is, about 3 inches (about 8 centimeters)   *ᶜ6* Septuagint; Hebrew *deep, the first threshold, one rod deep*   *ᵈ8,9* Many Hebrew manuscripts, Septuagint, Vulgate and Syriac; most Hebrew manuscripts *gateway facing the temple; it was one rod deep.* ⁹*Then he measured the portico of the gateway; it*   *ᵉ14* Septuagint; Hebrew *projecting wall*   *ᶠ14* The meaning of the Hebrew for this verse is uncertain.

🥣 **1.** Have you been in on the planning for any construction? Did you have your house built or were you part of a group that built or remodeled a church? What was the part you liked best? Least? **2.** When somebody "gives you the grand tour" through his or her new house, what do you notice? Are you usually envious of what they have? Smug that yours is better? Simply glad that they're happy?

📖 **1.** How many years passed between the fall of Jerusalem (33:21) and Ezekiel's vision of the temple (v. 1)? **2.** Solomon built the original temple around 950 BC. The Babylonians destroyed it in 586 BC. The exiles finished rebuilding it in 515 BC. Why do you think the temple was so important to the Jewish people? **3.** Where will the new temple be located? In relation to the city (v. 2)? **4.** The long cubit was about 21 inches, making the man's measuring rod about 10 feet long. How high and thick is the outer wall (v. 5)? Why do you think Ezekiel records every "nook and cranny"? Is God this concerned about modern buildings of worship? **5.** Ezekiel can enter the outer court from three sides. How are these outer gates decorated (v. 16)? What does this suggest about Hebrew religious art? **6.** There are three entrances to the inner court. What is the purpose of the rooms at the north and south inner gates (v. 38)? How are they furnished (vv. 39–43)? What profession could the priests fall back on during an exile? **7.** What two groups of priests get the rooms inside the inner gates (vv. 45–46)? Who was Zadok (see 1Ki 1:39)?

❤️ **1.** What physical place best draws you into worship? Is place or setting irrelevant to you? How much are the senses of sight and hearing involved? Smell? Taste? Touch? **2.** How much of your church's annual budget do you think is devoted to: (a) Building programs? (b) Mortgage payments? (c) Landscaping and maintenance? (d) Church music? (e) Pastor's salary and housing? (f) Staff salaries? (g) Overseas missions? (h) The local poor? Is a copy of this year's budget readily available to the small group for inspection? What do you think the economic priorities should be? **3.** What percentage of your annual family budget goes to housing, furniture, kitchen gadgets, home improvements? Do you count owning a home as an important life goal? Why or why not? **4.** Imagine you are a temple. The outer court is your public life with casual friends, the inner court your private heart. Who are the "faithful few" who see that inner court? What "sacrifice" did they make to gain entrance? When do you feel you can "open the gates" in safety?

inside of the lower gateway to the outside of the inner court; it was a hundred cubits on the east side as well as on the north.

The North Gate

²⁰Then he measured the length and width of the gate facing north, leading into the outer court. ²¹Its alcoves—three on each side—its projecting walls and its portico had the same measurements as those of the first gateway. It was fifty cubits long and twenty-five cubits wide. ²²Its openings, its portico and its palm tree decorations had the same measurements as those of the gate facing east. Seven steps led up to it, with its portico opposite them. ²³There was a gate to the inner court facing the north gate, just as there was on the east. He measured from one gate to the opposite one; it was a hundred cubits.

The South Gate

²⁴Then he led me to the south side and I saw a gate facing south. He measured its jambs and its portico, and they had the same measurements as the others. ²⁵The gateway and its portico had narrow openings all around, like the openings of the others. It was fifty cubits long and twenty-five cubits wide. ²⁶Seven steps led up to it, with its portico opposite them; it had palm tree decorations on the faces of the projecting walls on each side. ²⁷The inner court also had a gate facing south, and he measured from this gate to the outer gate on the south side; it was a hundred cubits.

Gates to the Inner Court

²⁸Then he brought me into the inner court through the south gate, and he measured the south gate; it had the same measurements as the others. ²⁹Its alcoves, its projecting walls and its portico had the same measurements as the others. The gateway and its portico had openings all around. It was fifty cubits long and twenty-five cubits wide. ³⁰(The porticoes of the gateways around the inner court were twenty-five cubits wide and five cubits deep.) ³¹Its portico faced the outer court; palm trees decorated its jambs, and eight steps led up to it.

³²Then he brought me to the inner court on the east side, and he measured the gateway; it had the same measurements as the others. ³³Its alcoves, its projecting walls and its portico had the same measurements as the others. The gateway and its portico had openings all around. It was fifty cubits long and twenty-five cubits wide. ³⁴Its portico faced the outer court; palm trees decorated the jambs on either side, and eight steps led up to it.

³⁵Then he brought me to the north gate and measured it. It had the same measurements as the others, ³⁶as did its alcoves, its projecting walls and its portico, and it had openings all around. It was fifty cubits long and twenty-five cubits wide. ³⁷Its portico[a] faced the outer court; palm trees decorated the jambs on either side, and eight steps led up to it.

The Rooms for Preparing Sacrifices

³⁸A room with a doorway was by the portico in each of the inner gateways, where the burnt offerings were washed. ³⁹In the portico of the gateway were two tables on each side, on which the burnt offerings, sin offerings and guilt offerings were slaughtered. ⁴⁰By the outside wall of the portico of the gateway, near the steps at the entrance to the north gateway were two tables, and on the other

---

a37 Septuagint (see also verses 31 and 34); Hebrew *jambs*

side of the steps were two tables. ⁴¹So there were four tables on one side of the gateway and four on the other—eight tables in all—on which the sacrifices were slaughtered. ⁴²There were also four tables of dressed stone for the burnt offerings, each a cubit and a half long, a cubit and a half wide and a cubit high. On them were placed the utensils for slaughtering the burnt offerings and the other sacrifices. ⁴³And double-pronged hooks, each a handbreadth long, were attached to the wall all around. The tables were for the flesh of the offerings.

Rooms for the Priests

⁴⁴Outside the inner gate, within the inner court, were two rooms, one*a* at the side of the north gate and facing south, and another at the side of the south*b* gate and facing north. ⁴⁵He said to me, "The room facing south is for the priests who have charge of the temple, ⁴⁶and the room facing north is for the priests who have charge of the altar. These are the sons of Zadok, who are the only Levites who may draw near to the LORD to minister before him."

⁴⁷Then he measured the court: It was square—a hundred cubits long and a hundred cubits wide. And the altar was in front of the temple.

The Temple

⁴⁸He brought me to the portico of the temple and measured the jambs of the portico; they were five cubits wide on either side. The width of the entrance was fourteen cubits and its projecting walls were*c* three cubits wide on either side. ⁴⁹The portico was twenty cubits wide, and twelve*d* cubits from front to back. It was reached by a flight of stairs,*e* and there were pillars on each side of the jambs.

41 Then the man brought me to the outer sanctuary and measured the jambs; the width of the jambs was six cubits*f* on each side.*g* ²The entrance was ten cubits wide, and the projecting walls on each side of it were five cubits wide. He also measured the outer sanctuary; it was forty cubits long and twenty cubits wide. ³Then he went into the inner sanctuary and measured the jambs of the entrance; each was two cubits wide. The entrance was six cubits wide, and the projecting walls on each side of it were seven cubits wide. ⁴And he measured the length of the inner sanctuary; it was twenty cubits, and its width was twenty cubits across the end of the outer sanctuary. He said to me, "This is the Most Holy Place."

⁵Then he measured the wall of the temple; it was six cubits thick, and each side room around the temple was four cubits wide. ⁶The side rooms were on three levels, one above another, thirty on each level. There were ledges all around the wall of the temple to serve as supports for the side rooms, so that the supports were not inserted into the wall of the temple. ⁷The side rooms all around the temple were wider at each successive level. The structure surrounding the temple was built in ascending stages, so that the rooms widened as one went upward. A stairway went up from the lowest floor to the top floor through the middle floor.

⁸I saw that the temple had a raised base all around it, forming the foundation of the side rooms. It was the length of the rod, six

1. Have you ever visited a cathedral? What impressed you the most? What didn't impress you? 2. Do you know anyone who is two-faced? How did he or she earn such a description?

1. Inside the inner court is the temple proper, consisting of an entrance portico, an outer sanctuary and an inner sanctuary. What is the inner sanctuary called (v. 4)? How big is it? 2. What are dimensions of the entire temple (vv. 13–14)? Did you expect it to be this size? 3. What kind of wall covering was inside the temple (vv. 15–16)? What figures adorn the wood (vv. 18–19)? How does this differ from Solomon's original decor (see 1Ki 6:29–30)? What's a cherub (see 11:22; also Ge 3:24, Ps 18:10)? What might be the significance of these "two-faced" creatures? 4. What are the dimensions of the wooden altar (v. 22)? Do you find this impressive? 5. Why do you think it was so important for Israel to know the temple would be rebuilt? What did it symbolize to them?

1. Today there is no temple in Jerusalem. Does that mean God has abandoned Israel? 2. Do we need holy places? What symbolizes the presence of God to you? How can you be more aware of his nearness in your life? 3. How would you design the ideal place for you to worship? Where would it be? What would have to be present? 4. Imagine you are a tem-

---

*a*44 Septuagint; Hebrew *were rooms for singers, which were* *b*44 Septuagint; Hebrew *east* *c*48 Septuagint; Hebrew *entrance was* *d*49 Septuagint; Hebrew *eleven* *e*49 Hebrew; Septuagint *Ten steps led up to it* *f*1 The common cubit was about 1 1/2 feet (about 0.5 meter). *g*1 One Hebrew manuscript and Septuagint; most Hebrew manuscripts *side, the width of the tent*

ple. In the "most holy place" are the thoughts, feelings or parts of your life you would never dream of revealing to another person. Do you have a right to privacy or should we be open about everything? Under what conditions might you open your "inner sanctuary"? Is it possible to hide things from yourself?

long cubits. ⁹The outer wall of the side rooms was five cubits thick. The open area between the side rooms of the temple ¹⁰and the ⌐ priests'⌐ rooms was twenty cubits wide all around the temple. ¹¹There were entrances to the side rooms from the open area, one on the north and another on the south; and the base adjoining the open area was five cubits wide all around.

¹²The building facing the temple courtyard on the west side was seventy cubits wide. The wall of the building was five cubits thick all around, and its length was ninety cubits.

¹³Then he measured the temple; it was a hundred cubits long, and the temple courtyard and the building with its walls were also a hundred cubits long. ¹⁴The width of the temple courtyard on the east, including the front of the temple, was a hundred cubits.

¹⁵Then he measured the length of the building facing the courtyard at the rear of the temple, including its galleries on each side; it was a hundred cubits.

The outer sanctuary, the inner sanctuary and the portico facing the court, ¹⁶as well as the thresholds and the narrow windows and galleries around the three of them—everything beyond and including the threshold was covered with wood. The floor, the wall up to the windows, and the windows were covered. ¹⁷In the space above the outside of the entrance to the inner sanctuary and on the walls at regular intervals all around the inner and outer sanctuary ¹⁸were carved cherubim and palm trees. Palm trees alternated with cherubim. Each cherub had two faces: ¹⁹the face of a man toward the palm tree on one side and the face of a lion toward the palm tree on the other. They were carved all around the whole temple. ²⁰From the floor to the area above the entrance, cherubim and palm trees were carved on the wall of the outer sanctuary.

²¹The outer sanctuary had a rectangular doorframe, and the one at the front of the Most Holy Place was similar. ²²There was a wooden altar three cubits high and two cubits square*a*; its corners, its base*b* and its sides were of wood. The man said to me, "This is the table that is before the LORD." ²³Both the outer sanctuary and the Most Holy Place had double doors. ²⁴Each door had two leaves—two hinged leaves for each door. ²⁵And on the doors of the outer sanctuary were carved cherubim and palm trees like those carved on the walls, and there was a wooden overhang on the front of the portico. ²⁶On the sidewalls of the portico were narrow windows with palm trees carved on each side. The side rooms of the temple also had overhangs.

Rooms for the Priests

42 Then the man led me northward into the outer court and brought me to the rooms opposite the temple courtyard and opposite the outer wall on the north side. ²The building whose door faced north was a hundred cubits*c* long and fifty cubits wide. ³Both in the section twenty cubits from the inner court and in the section opposite the pavement of the outer court, gallery faced gallery at the three levels. ⁴In front of the rooms was an inner passageway ten cubits wide and a hundred cubits*d* long. Their doors were on the north. ⁵Now the upper rooms were narrower, for the galleries took more space from them than from the rooms on the lower and middle floors of the building. ⁶The rooms on the third floor had no pillars, as the courts had; so they were smaller in

1. Have you ever visited a monastery? Met a monk? What are the common stereotypes of monks? 2. Do you dress up special for church? Why or why not? Are Sundays often "fashion shows"? Or is your congregation casual?

1. What did the priests do with the sacrifices of the people (v. 13)? What was the function of the three offerings: (a) Grain (see Nu 15:2–4)? (b) Sin (Lev 4:27–31)? (c) Guilt (Lev 5:14–16)? 2. What garments did the priests have to wear in the sanctuary (see Ex 28:4)? Why couldn't they wear them home (v. 14)? How can

*a*22 Septuagint; Hebrew *long*   *b*22 Septuagint; Hebrew *length*   *c*2 The common cubit was about 1 1/2 feet (about 0.5 meter).   *d*4 Septuagint and Syriac; Hebrew *and one cubit*

floor space than those on the lower and middle floors. [7]There was an outer wall parallel to the rooms and the outer court; it extended in front of the rooms for fifty cubits. [8]While the row of rooms on the side next to the outer court was fifty cubits long, the row on the side nearest the sanctuary was a hundred cubits long. [9]The lower rooms had an entrance on the east side as one enters them from the outer court.

[10]On the south side[a] along the length of the wall of the outer court, adjoining the temple courtyard and opposite the outer wall, were rooms [11]with a passageway in front of them. These were like the rooms on the north; they had the same length and width, with similar exits and dimensions. Similar to the doorways on the north [12]were the doorways of the rooms on the south. There was a doorway at the beginning of the passageway that was parallel to the corresponding wall extending eastward, by which one enters the rooms.

[13]Then he said to me, "The north and south rooms facing the temple courtyard are the priests' rooms, where the priests who approach the LORD will eat the most holy offerings. There they will put the most holy offerings—the grain offerings, the sin offerings and the guilt offerings—for the place is holy. [14]Once the priests enter the holy precincts, they are not to go into the outer court until they leave behind the garments in which they minister, for these are holy. They are to put on other clothes before they go near the places that are for the people."

[15]When he had finished measuring what was inside the temple area, he led me out by the east gate and measured the area all around: [16]He measured the east side with the measuring rod; it was five hundred cubits.[b] [17]He measured the north side; it was five hundred cubits[c] by the measuring rod. [18]He measured the south side; it was five hundred cubits by the measuring rod. [19]Then he turned to the west side and measured; it was five hundred cubits by the measuring rod. [20]So he measured the area on all four sides. It had a wall around it, five hundred cubits long and five hundred cubits wide, to separate the holy from the common.

The Glory Returns to the Temple

43 Then the man brought me to the gate facing east, [2]and I saw the glory of the God of Israel coming from the east. His voice was like the roar of rushing waters, and the land was radiant with his glory. [3]The vision I saw was like the vision I had seen when he[d] came to destroy the city and like the visions I had seen by the Kebar River, and I fell facedown. [4]The glory of the LORD entered the temple through the gate facing east. [5]Then the Spirit lifted me up and brought me into the inner court, and the glory of the LORD filled the temple.

[6]While the man was standing beside me, I heard someone speaking to me from inside the temple. [7]He said: "Son of man, this is the place of my throne and the place for the soles of my feet. This is where I will live among the Israelites forever. The house of Israel will never again defile my holy name—neither they nor their kings—by their prostitution[e] and the lifeless idols[f] of their kings at their high places. [8]When they placed their threshold next to my

clothes be holy? 3. What is the purpose of the outside temple wall (v. 20)? What makes a place holy? Common? Why separate them?

1. During the exile, Judaism was forced to develop new institutions, such as rabbis, synagogues, formal prayers, etc., as temporary substitutes for the temple, sacrifices, priests, etc. Many of the new institutions survive today within Judaism. In what ways have these institutions influenced Christianity (remember that Jesus and many of the early believers were rabbis)? Why bother reading about Jewish temple regulations? 2. Priests acted as bridges between God and Israel. Do any of the following act as a bridge for God's love to you: (a) The Bible? (b) Other believers? (c) A preacher? (d) The Lord's Supper? (e) Nature? What else has been your "priest"? When were you a priest for someone else? What happened? 3. In your life, do you have holy places? Times? People? Objects? What makes something holy?

1. What favorite entertainer of yours has made a big comeback? Who should make a "go-away"? 2. What should never be next door to a church? A liquor store? Movie theatre? Fast food? City hall?

1. Why did the glory of the Lord depart from the temple? Where did the Lord go (10:18–19; 11:22–23)? 2. Where does Ezekiel encounter God (v. 5)? Can he see God? 3. Why does God need to "put his feet up" (see Isa 66:1)? Why is the image of God at rest important? 4. Solomon built his palace adjacent to the temple. What kind of neighbors were the Judean kings (v. 8)? 5. Why would the exiles feel ashamed upon hearing of the new temple plan (vv. 10–11)? 6. What is the law of the temple?

1. How do you experience the "glory of the Lord?" 2.

---

[a]10 Septuagint; Hebrew *Eastward*　　[b]16 See Septuagint of verse 17; Hebrew *rods*; also in verses 18 and 19.　　[c]17 Septuagint; Hebrew *rods*　　[d]3 Some Hebrew manuscripts and Vulgate; most Hebrew manuscripts *I*　　[e]7 Or *their spiritual adultery*; also in verse 9　　[f]7 Or *the corpses*; also in verse 9

When did God seem far away? Has God made a comeback or are you still feeling distant? **3.** Think of someone you were once close to but no longer have a relationship with. How would you renew it if you could?

---

1. Have you served on a jury? What verdict did you give? Or did you arrange to be relieved from jury duty? **2.** What bad habit could you quit anytime? What habit would be harder to quit?

1. Compare the altar dimensions in verses 13–17 with the description of 41:22. Why the difference? How was the small altar in the Most Holy Place used (see Ex 30:1,9–10)? How was the large altar used (1 Ki 8:64)? **2.** What sacrifices were required the first week (vv. 18–26)? Why do you think this was necessary? **3.** What sacrifices were offered after the eighth day (v. 27)? What did these ceremonies mean to the people? **4.** List the three types of "fellowship offerings" (see Lev 7:12,16). Why couldn't some parts be eaten (Lev 3:14–17)? **5.** Ezekiel says that animal sacrifices will make Israel acceptable. Why do other prophets disagree (see Ps 40:6–8; 1Sa 15:22; Am 5:21–22)?

1. Hebrews 10:12 says Jesus made "for all time one sacrifice." Why do churches have altars? **2.** What is Paul's concept of a "living sacrifice" (see Ro 12:1)? **3.** What do you need to give up to be closer to God? Why has it been hard to make the sacrifice? Can the small group help?

threshold and their doorposts beside my doorposts, with only a wall between me and them, they defiled my holy name by their detestable practices. So I destroyed them in my anger. ⁹Now let them put away from me their prostitution and the lifeless idols of their kings, and I will live among them forever.

¹⁰"Son of man, describe the temple to the people of Israel, that they may be ashamed of their sins. Let them consider the plan, ¹¹and if they are ashamed of all they have done, make known to them the design of the temple—its arrangement, its exits and entrances—its whole design and all its regulations*a* and laws. Write these down before them so that they may be faithful to its design and follow all its regulations.

¹²"This is the law of the temple: All the surrounding area on top of the mountain will be most holy. Such is the law of the temple.

The Altar

¹³"These are the measurements of the altar in long cubits, that cubit being a cubit*b* and a handbreadth*c*: Its gutter is a cubit deep and a cubit wide, with a rim of one span*d* around the edge. And this is the height of the altar: ¹⁴From the gutter on the ground up to the lower ledge it is two cubits high and a cubit wide, and from the smaller ledge up to the larger ledge it is four cubits high and a cubit wide. ¹⁵The altar hearth is four cubits high, and four horns project upward from the hearth. ¹⁶The altar hearth is square, twelve cubits long and twelve cubits wide. ¹⁷The upper ledge also is square, fourteen cubits long and fourteen cubits wide, with a rim of half a cubit and a gutter of a cubit all around. The steps of the altar face east."

¹⁸Then he said to me, "Son of man, this is what the Sovereign LORD says: These will be the regulations for sacrificing burnt offerings and sprinkling blood upon the altar when it is built: ¹⁹You are to give a young bull as a sin offering to the priests, who are Levites, of the family of Zadok, who come near to minister before me, declares the Sovereign LORD. ²⁰You are to take some of its blood and put it on the four horns of the altar and on the four corners of the upper ledge and all around the rim, and so purify the altar and make atonement for it. ²¹You are to take the bull for the sin offering and burn it in the designated part of the temple area outside the sanctuary.

²²"On the second day you are to offer a male goat without defect for a sin offering, and the altar is to be purified as it was purified with the bull. ²³When you have finished purifying it, you are to offer a young bull and a ram from the flock, both without defect. ²⁴You are to offer them before the LORD, and the priests are to sprinkle salt on them and sacrifice them as a burnt offering to the LORD.

²⁵"For seven days you are to provide a male goat daily for a sin offering; you are also to provide a young bull and a ram from the flock, both without defect. ²⁶For seven days they are to make atonement for the altar and cleanse it; thus they will dedicate it. ²⁷At the end of these days, from the eighth day on, the priests are to present your burnt offerings and fellowship offerings*e* on the altar. Then I will accept you, declares the Sovereign LORD."

---

a11 Some Hebrew manuscripts and Septuagint; most Hebrew manuscripts *regulations and its whole design*   *b13* The common cubit was about 1 1/2 feet (about 0.5 meter).   *c13* That is, about 3 inches (about 8 centimeters)   *d13* That is, about 9 inches (about 22 centimeters)   *e27* Traditionally *peace offerings*

The Prince, the Levites, the Priests

44 Then the man brought me back to the outer gate of the sanctuary, the one facing east, and it was shut. ²The LORD said to me, "This gate is to remain shut. It must not be opened; no one may enter through it. It is to remain shut because the LORD, the God of Israel, has entered through it. ³The prince himself is the only one who may sit inside the gateway to eat in the presence of the LORD. He is to enter by way of the portico of the gateway and go out the same way."

⁴Then the man brought me by way of the north gate to the front of the temple. I looked and saw the glory of the LORD filling the temple of the LORD, and I fell facedown.

⁵The LORD said to me, "Son of man, look carefully, listen closely and give attention to everything I tell you concerning all the regulations regarding the temple of the LORD. Give attention to the entrance of the temple and all the exits of the sanctuary. ⁶Say to the rebellious house of Israel, 'This is what the Sovereign LORD says: Enough of your detestable practices, O house of Israel! ⁷In addition to all your other detestable practices, you brought foreigners uncircumcised in heart and flesh into my sanctuary, desecrating my temple while you offered me food, fat and blood, and you broke my covenant. ⁸Instead of carrying out your duty in regard to my holy things, you put others in charge of my sanctuary. ⁹This is what the Sovereign LORD says: No foreigner uncircumcised in heart and flesh is to enter my sanctuary, not even the foreigners who live among the Israelites.

¹⁰" 'The Levites who went far from me when Israel went astray and who wandered from me after their idols must bear the consequences of their sin. ¹¹They may serve in my sanctuary, having charge of the gates of the temple and serving in it; they may slaughter the burnt offerings and sacrifices for the people and stand before the people and serve them. ¹²But because they served them in the presence of their idols and made the house of Israel fall into sin, therefore I have sworn with uplifted hand that they must bear the consequences of their sin, declares the Sovereign LORD. ¹³They are not to come near to serve me as priests or come near any of my holy things or my most holy offerings; they must bear the shame of their detestable practices. ¹⁴Yet I will put them in charge of the duties of the temple and all the work that is to be done in it.

¹⁵" 'But the priests, who are Levites and descendants of Zadok and who faithfully carried out the duties of my sanctuary when the Israelites went astray from me, are to come near to minister before me; they are to stand before me to offer sacrifices of fat and blood, declares the Sovereign LORD. ¹⁶They alone are to enter my sanctuary; they alone are to come near my table to minister before me and perform my service.

¹⁷" 'When they enter the gates of the inner court, they are to wear linen clothes; they must not wear any woolen garment while ministering at the gates of the inner court or inside the temple. ¹⁸They are to wear linen turbans on their heads and linen undergarments around their waists. They must not wear anything that makes them perspire. ¹⁹When they go out into the outer court where the people are, they are to take off the clothes they have been ministering in and are to leave them in the sacred rooms, and put on other clothes, so that they do not consecrate the people by means of their garments.

²⁰" 'They must not shave their heads or let their hair grow long, but they are to keep the hair of their heads trimmed. ²¹No priest is to drink wine when he enters the inner court. ²²They must not

1. Have you ever known a leader or teacher who didn't "practice what he preached"? What effect did it have on you? **2.** Would you bother to pick up a penny from the gutter? Three pennies? A nickel? Dollar bill? What amount is worth the effort?

1. Why is the eastern gateway sealed (vv. 1–3)? Why do you think the prince is the only person allowed to eat sacrifices in this area? **2.** Besides all the other sins mentioned in previous chapters, what had Israel done to dishonor the Lord (vv. 5–9)? What do you think it means to be uncircumcised in heart? **3.** Who were some famous members of the tribe of Levi (see Ex 2:1,10; 4:14)? What "put food on the table" in a Levite home (Dt 18:1–5)? How had some of the Levites strayed from the Lord (v. 12)? How does their job description read (vv. 11,13–14)? How will the faithful Levites serve (vv. 15–16)? **4.** What might be wrong with wearing wool (vv. 17–18)? In what ways were the priests in the new temple to sanctify themselves (vv. 20–23,25)? What was the point of these regulations? **5.** Was Israel to have courts of law (v. 24)? Do you think any dispute in Israel could be considered a secular issue?

1. Circumcision made a male a Jew. Why did God exclude non-Jews from his temple? What slang word for "Gentile" did Jesus use (see Mk 7:26–27)? Is there any type of person you'd just as soon not speak to? **2.** What rite makes a person a Christian? Ezekiel spoke of those whose hearts weren't circumcised. Can there be Christians whose hearts aren't baptized? **3.** Why is the Lord so concerned with the cleanness of his representatives? Have prominent figures who claim to represent God been known for cleanness in our society? How has this affected God's reputation? Does your life show the cleanness or holiness of God? **4.** What characterizes your tithes and offerings: (a) Prime rib? (b) Rump roast? (c) Leftovers? How can you give God your first fruits? Is money the only acceptable sacrifice? **5.** What do you think of Ezekiel's system for paying priests? Is this how modern ministers should be paid or compensated?

marry widows or divorced women; they may marry only virgins of Israelite descent or widows of priests. 23They are to teach my people the difference between the holy and the common and show them how to distinguish between the unclean and the clean.

24" 'In any dispute, the priests are to serve as judges and decide it according to my ordinances. They are to keep my laws and my decrees for all my appointed feasts, and they are to keep my Sabbaths holy.

25" 'A priest must not defile himself by going near a dead person; however, if the dead person was his father or mother, son or daughter, brother or unmarried sister, then he may defile himself. 26After he is cleansed, he must wait seven days. 27On the day he goes into the inner court of the sanctuary to minister in the sanctuary, he is to offer a sin offering for himself, declares the Sovereign LORD.

28" 'I am to be the only inheritance the priests have. You are to give them no possession in Israel; I will be their possession. 29They will eat the grain offerings, the sin offerings and the guilt offerings; and everything in Israel devoted[a] to the LORD will belong to them. 30The best of all the firstfruits and of all your special gifts will belong to the priests. You are to give them the first portion of your ground meal so that a blessing may rest on your household. 31The priests must not eat anything, bird or animal, found dead or torn by wild animals.

Division of the Land

45 " 'When you allot the land as an inheritance, you are to present to the LORD a portion of the land as a sacred district, 25,000 cubits long and 20,000[b] cubits wide; the entire area will be holy. 2Of this, a section 500 cubits square is to be for the sanctuary, with 50 cubits around it for open land. 3In the sacred district, measure off a section 25,000 cubits[c] long and 10,000 cubits[d] wide. In it will be the sanctuary, the Most Holy Place. 4It will be the sacred portion of the land for the priests, who minister in the sanctuary and who draw near to minister before the LORD. It will be a place for their houses as well as a holy place for the sanctuary. 5An area 25,000 cubits long and 10,000 cubits wide will belong to the Levites, who serve in the temple, as their possession for towns to live in.[e]

6" 'You are to give the city as its property an area 5,000 cubits wide and 25,000 cubits long, adjoining the sacred portion; it will belong to the whole house of Israel.

7" 'The prince will have the land bordering each side of the area formed by the sacred district and the property of the city. It will extend westward from the west side and eastward from the east side, running lengthwise from the western to the eastern border parallel to one of the tribal portions. 8This land will be his possession in Israel. And my princes will no longer oppress my people but will allow the house of Israel to possess the land according to their tribes.

9" 'This is what the Sovereign LORD says: You have gone far enough, O princes of Israel! Give up your violence and oppression and do what is just and right. Stop dispossessing my people, declares the Sovereign LORD. 10You are to use accurate scales, an

a29 The Hebrew term refers to the irrevocable giving over of things or persons to the LORD.   *b1* Septuagint (see also verses 3 and 5 and 48:9); Hebrew *10,000*
c3 That is, about 7 miles (about 12 kilometers)   *d3* That is, about 3 miles (about 5 kilometers)   *e5* Septuagint; Hebrew *temple; they will have as their possession 20 rooms*

---

1. Would you invest in real estate if you had the money? Why or why not? 2. Have you ever been cheated by a service or sales person? What did you do?

1. Palestine is to be redivided when the tribes return. How many square miles belong to the Lord (v. 1)? 2. Why the "open land" surrounding the temple square (v. 2; also 42:20)? Had the Levites ever owned land before (vv. 4–5; see Jos 13:33)? 3. How does Ezekiel's plan keep the palace away from the temple (v. 7)? Why the separation of church and state (vv. 8–9; also 43:8)? 4. What other injustice does God prevent by assigning official values to weights and measures (vv. 10–12)? What was the state of money changing at the time of Jesus?

1. Why does God care about land distribution, weights and measures? Should Christians be more concerned about people's "spiritual" needs? 2. How do people in your line of work commonly "bend the rules"? Have you ever done this? 3. Do people in power face more temptation than others, or does power simply attract corruptible people?

accurate ephah[a] and an accurate bath.[b] [11]The ephah and the bath are to be the same size, the bath containing a tenth of a homer[c] and the ephah a tenth of a homer; the homer is to be the standard measure for both. [12]The shekel[d] is to consist of twenty gerahs. Twenty shekels plus twenty-five shekels plus fifteen shekels equal one mina.[e]

Offerings and Holy Days

[13]" 'This is the special gift you are to offer: a sixth of an ephah from each homer of wheat and a sixth of an ephah from each homer of barley. [14]The prescribed portion of oil, measured by the bath, is a tenth of a bath from each cor (which consists of ten baths or one homer, for ten baths are equivalent to a homer). [15]Also one sheep is to be taken from every flock of two hundred from the well-watered pastures of Israel. These will be used for the grain offerings, burnt offerings and fellowship offerings[f] to make atonement for the people, declares the Sovereign LORD. [16]All the people of the land will participate in this special gift for the use of the prince in Israel. [17]It will be the duty of the prince to provide the burnt offerings, grain offerings and drink offerings at the festivals, the New Moons and the Sabbaths—at all the appointed feasts of the house of Israel. He will provide the sin offerings, grain offerings, burnt offerings and fellowship offerings to make atonement for the house of Israel.

[18]" 'This is what the Sovereign LORD says: In the first month on the first day you are to take a young bull without defect and purify the sanctuary. [19]The priest is to take some of the blood of the sin offering and put it on the doorposts of the temple, on the four corners of the upper ledge of the altar and on the gateposts of the inner court. [20]You are to do the same on the seventh day of the month for anyone who sins unintentionally or through ignorance; so you are to make atonement for the temple.

[21]" 'In the first month on the fourteenth day you are to observe the Passover, a feast lasting seven days, during which you shall eat bread made without yeast. [22]On that day the prince is to provide a bull as a sin offering for himself and for all the people of the land. [23]Every day during the seven days of the Feast he is to provide seven bulls and seven rams without defect as a burnt offering to the LORD, and a male goat for a sin offering. [24]He is to provide as a grain offering an ephah for each bull and an ephah for each ram, along with a hin[g] of oil for each ephah.

[25]" 'During the seven days of the Feast, which begins in the seventh month on the fifteenth day, he is to make the same provision for sin offerings, burnt offerings, grain offerings and oil.

46 " 'This is what the Sovereign LORD says: The gate of the inner court facing east is to be shut on the six working days, but on the Sabbath day and on the day of the New Moon it is to be opened. [2]The prince is to enter from the outside through the portico of the gateway and stand by the gatepost. The priests are to sacrifice his burnt offering and his fellowship offerings.[h] He is to worship at the threshold of the gateway and then go out, but the gate will not be shut until evening. [3]On the Sabbaths and New Moons the people of the land are to worship in the presence of the LORD at the entrance to that gateway. [4]The burnt offering the prince

1. What was your favorite holiday as a child? Now that you're older, has it changed? Why? 2. If you had to lose one of your physical senses, which would be the hardest one to give up? Which would be the easiest? Why?

1. What kinds of things are offered to the Lord (45:13–15)? On what occasions does the prince pay for the sacrifices (45:17)? What were the three public "festivals" in Israel (see Ex 23:14–16)? 2. What had to be done every New Moon, the first day of Israel's lunar month (45:18)? How often are Sabbaths celebrated? How do they celebrate Passover (45:21–24)? What Feast falls in the seventh month (45:25; see Nu 29:12)? 3. Why do you think the east gate is open only on Sabbaths and New Moons (46:1)? Why is the prince given special treatment (46:2–3)? Is it fair for him to "foot the bill" for so many animals (46:4–7)? In what way is he humbled (46:10)? 4. Why do you think the animals had to be without defect (46:13)? What was the lesson to Israel? 5. What rules does God give the prince about giving away land (46:16–17)? What is the "year of freedom" (see Lev 25:10)? Is it fair to force a poor servant to give land back to the children of kings? What had the kings tended to do (46:18)? 6. Why did the priests cook the offerings (46:23–24)?

1. Imagine you are an Israelite worshipping in the temple. What do you see, hear, smell and taste? What effect does such a service have on you? What effect do you think the Lord wants to produce? How does this effect compare to the one at your church? 2. Israel worshiped the Lord by offering him things. What can we offer him? Could you afford one-tenth of your time every day (2.4 hours)? 3. Can you think of Christian equivalents to: (a) Passover? (b) Feast of Harvest (or "Weeks")? (c) Feast of Ingathering (or "Booths")? (d) Sabbath? (e) New Moon? 4. Does your relationship with God contain as much celebration as Israel's did?

[a]10 An ephah was a dry measure.   [b]10 A bath was a liquid measure.   [c]11 A homer was a dry measure.   [d]12 A shekel weighed about 2/5 ounce (about 11.5 grams).   [e]12 That is, 60 shekels; the common mina was 50 shekels.
[f]15 Traditionally *peace offerings*; also in verse 17   [g]24 That is, probably about 4 quarts (about 4 liters)   [h]2 Traditionally *peace offerings*; also in verse 12

Should it? Do you have an idea for a special "small group festival" you can celebrate together?

brings to the LORD on the Sabbath day is to be six male lambs and a ram, all without defect. 5The grain offering given with the ram is to be an ephah,[a] and the grain offering with the lambs is to be as much as he pleases, along with a hin[b] of oil for each ephah. 6On the day of the New Moon he is to offer a young bull, six lambs and a ram, all without defect. 7He is to provide as a grain offering one ephah with the bull, one ephah with the ram, and with the lambs as much as he wants to give, along with a hin of oil with each ephah. 8When the prince enters, he is to go in through the portico of the gateway, and he is to come out the same way.

9" 'When the people of the land come before the LORD at the appointed feasts, whoever enters by the north gate to worship is to go out the south gate; and whoever enters by the south gate is to go out the north gate. No one is to return through the gate by which he entered, but each is to go out the opposite gate. 10The prince is to be among them, going in when they go in and going out when they go out.

11" 'At the festivals and the appointed feasts, the grain offering is to be an ephah with a bull, an ephah with a ram, and with the lambs as much as one pleases, along with a hin of oil for each ephah. 12When the prince provides a freewill offering to the LORD—whether a burnt offering or fellowship offerings—the gate facing east is to be opened for him. He shall offer his burnt offering or his fellowship offerings as he does on the Sabbath day. Then he shall go out, and after he has gone out, the gate will be shut.

13" 'Every day you are to provide a year-old lamb without defect for a burnt offering to the LORD; morning by morning you shall provide it. 14You are also to provide with it morning by morning a grain offering, consisting of a sixth of an ephah with a third of a hin of oil to moisten the flour. The presenting of this grain offering to the LORD is a lasting ordinance. 15So the lamb and the grain offering and the oil shall be provided morning by morning for a regular burnt offering.

16" 'This is what the Sovereign LORD says: If the prince makes a gift from his inheritance to one of his sons, it will also belong to his descendants; it is to be their property by inheritance. 17If, however, he makes a gift from his inheritance to one of his servants, the servant may keep it until the year of freedom; then it will revert to the prince. His inheritance belongs to his sons only; it is theirs. 18The prince must not take any of the inheritance of the people, driving them off their property. He is to give his sons their inheritance out of his own property, so that none of my people will be separated from his property.' "

19Then the man brought me through the entrance at the side of the gate to the sacred rooms facing north, which belonged to the priests, and showed me a place at the western end. 20He said to me, "This is the place where the priests will cook the guilt offering and the sin offering and bake the grain offering, to avoid bringing them into the outer court and consecrating the people."

21He then brought me to the outer court and led me around to its four corners, and I saw in each corner another court. 22In the four corners of the outer court were enclosed[c] courts, forty cubits long and thirty cubits wide; each of the courts in the four corners was the same size. 23Around the inside of each of the four courts was a ledge of stone, with places for fire built all around under the ledge. 24He said to me, "These are the kitchens where those who minister at the temple will cook the sacrifices of the people."

a5 That is, probably about 3/5 bushel (about 22 liters)   b5 That is, probably about 4 quarts (about 4 liters)   c22 The meaning of the Hebrew for this word is uncertain.

The River From the Temple

47 The man brought me back to the entrance of the temple, and I saw water coming out from under the threshold of the temple toward the east (for the temple faced east). The water was coming down from under the south side of the temple, south of the altar. [2]He then brought me out through the north gate and led me around the outside to the outer gate facing east, and the water was flowing from the south side.

[3]As the man went eastward with a measuring line in his hand, he measured off a thousand cubits[a] and then led me through water that was ankle-deep. [4]He measured off another thousand cubits and led me through water that was knee-deep. He measured off another thousand and led me through water that was up to the waist. [5]He measured off another thousand, but now it was a river that I could not cross, because the water had risen and was deep enough to swim in—a river that no one could cross. [6]He asked me, "Son of man, do you see this?"

Then he led me back to the bank of the river. [7]When I arrived there, I saw a great number of trees on each side of the river. [8]He said to me, "This water flows toward the eastern region and goes down into the Arabah,[b] where it enters the Sea.[c] When it empties into the Sea,[c] the water there becomes fresh. [9]Swarms of living creatures will live wherever the river flows. There will be large numbers of fish, because this water flows there and makes the salt water fresh; so where the river flows everything will live. [10]Fishermen will stand along the shore; from En Gedi to En Eglaim there will be places for spreading nets. The fish will be of many kinds—like the fish of the Great Sea.[d] [11]But the swamps and marshes will not become fresh; they will be left for salt. [12]Fruit trees of all kinds will grow on both banks of the river. Their leaves will not wither, nor will their fruit fail. Every month they will bear, because the water from the sanctuary flows to them. Their fruit will serve for food and their leaves for healing."

The Boundaries of the Land

[13]This is what the Sovereign LORD says: "These are the boundaries by which you are to divide the land for an inheritance among the twelve tribes of Israel, with two portions for Joseph. [14]You are to divide it equally among them. Because I swore with uplifted hand to give it to your forefathers, this land will become your inheritance.

[15]"This is to be the boundary of the land:

"On the north side it will run from the Great Sea by the Hethlon road past Lebo[e] Hamath to Zedad, [16]Berothah[f] and Sibraim (which lies on the border between Damascus and Hamath), as far as Hazer Hatticon, which is on the border of Hauran. [17]The boundary will extend from the sea to Hazar Enan,[g] along the northern border of Damascus, with the border of Hamath to the north. This will be the north boundary.
[18]"On the east side the boundary will run between Hauran and Damascus, along the Jordan between Gilead and the land of Israel, to the eastern sea and as far as Tamar.[h] This will be the east boundary.

---

[a]3 That is, about 1,500 feet (about 450 meters)   [b]8 Or the Jordan Valley
[c]8 That is, the Dead Sea   [d]10 That is, the Mediterranean; also in verses 15, 19 and 20   [e]15 Or past the entrance to   [f]15,16 See Septuagint and Ezekiel 48:1; Hebrew road to go into Zedad, [16]Hamath, Berothah   [g]17 Hebrew Enon, a variant of Enan   [h]18 Septuagint and Syriac; Hebrew Israel. You will measure to the eastern sea

1. Do you like swimming? Do you prefer an ocean, lake or swimming pool? **2.** What's your favorite drink on a hot day?

1. Where does the river start? Which direction does it flow (vv. 1–2)? **2.** What happens to the river as it gets farther from the temple (vv. 3–6)? **3.** As it flows into the Dead Sea, what happens to the animals, fish, trees and people of the region (vv. 7–12)? What would the river mean to a people dependent on wells and cisterns for water?

1. What might Ezekiel's river represent? How do Jesus and the NT writers use the image of the river (Jn 4:14, Rev 22:2)? **2.** What best describes your relationship with God: (a) Dying of thirst? (b) Man overboard? (c) Treading water? (d) Overflowing? (e) Waterlogged? (f) Smooth sailing? **3.** Does some part of your life feel like a parched desert? What could happen that would be like living water in the desert? **4.** Picture the spiritual life as a river that keeps getting deeper and deeper. Are you testing the waters? Ankle deep? Up to your waist? What is the next step? Can the small group help you take it?

1. Would you ever live in a foreign country? Why or why not? Which one, if any, might attract you? **2.** Do you get along with your next-door neighbors? Why did Robert Frost say "good fences make good neighbors"?

1. These boundaries resemble the boundaries of Solomon's golden age. Why is God so concerned to return the land to Israel (v. 14)? **2.** Can you locate the boundaries on a map (vv. 15–20)? **3.** Why is God concerned about the non-Jewish inhabitants (vv. 22–23; see Ex 22:21)? What is the meaning of "inheritance" if aliens are entitled?

1. How important is "settling down" to you? Do you need land? A house? An army to protect you? **2.** What people in your area are regarded as "aliens"? Is there prejudice in your town? Does your church have the racial and social mix of the surrounding population? Does the small group? **3.** Has God given you an inheritance or were you "left out of the will"? What is your inheritance? What would you like it to be?

---

1. How many children did your parents have? Did any of your relatives have 10–12 children? How did they manage? 2. What are your most prized earthly assets? If you died tonight, who would you want to get them?

1. Does God redistribute the land evenly (vv. 1–7, 23–29)? Will some of the land be more fertile? More mountainous? Is this fair? 2. There are 13 tribes listed here. Which son of Jacob sired two tribes (Ge 48:5–6)? Which tribe gets land for the first time (vv. 13–14)? How does this land rank? Why can't they sell it? 3. How does God treat the Zadokites differently from the rest of the Levites (vv. 10–13)? Why? 4. Who will share the arable pastureland near the city (vv. 15–20)? In Ezekiel's vision, is land owned by private individuals or by the community?

1. When you picture God's kingdom coming to this world, do you see economic justice as a central feature? Why or why not? Should it be? What do you imagine it will look like? 2. Should individual rights suffer for the good of the community, or should the community suffer to protect individual rights? What prevails in this country? 3. What are the biggest barriers to community in your neighborhood? How can you promote community in the world?

---

[19]"On the south side it will run from Tamar as far as the waters of Meribah Kadesh, then along the Wadi ⌊of Egypt⌋ to the Great Sea. This will be the south boundary. [20]"On the west side, the Great Sea will be the boundary to a point opposite Lebo[a] Hamath. This will be the west boundary.

[21]"You are to distribute this land among yourselves according to the tribes of Israel. [22]You are to allot it as an inheritance for yourselves and for the aliens who have settled among you and who have children. You are to consider them as native-born Israelites; along with you they are to be allotted an inheritance among the tribes of Israel. [23]In whatever tribe the alien settles, there you are to give him his inheritance," declares the Sovereign LORD.

The Division of the Land

48 "These are the tribes, listed by name: At the northern frontier, Dan will have one portion; it will follow the Hethlon road to Lebo[b] Hamath; Hazar Enan and the northern border of Damascus next to Hamath will be part of its border from the east side to the west side.

[2]"Asher will have one portion; it will border the territory of Dan from east to west.

[3]"Naphtali will have one portion; it will border the territory of Asher from east to west.

[4]"Manasseh will have one portion; it will border the territory of Naphtali from east to west.

[5]"Ephraim will have one portion; it will border the territory of Manasseh from east to west.

[6]"Reuben will have one portion; it will border the territory of Ephraim from east to west.

[7]"Judah will have one portion; it will border the territory of Reuben from east to west.

[8]"Bordering the territory of Judah from east to west will be the portion you are to present as a special gift. It will be 25,000 cubits[c] wide, and its length from east to west will equal one of the tribal portions; the sanctuary will be in the center of it.

[9]"The special portion you are to offer to the LORD will be 25,000 cubits long and 10,000 cubits[d] wide. [10]This will be the sacred portion for the priests. It will be 25,000 cubits long on the north side, 10,000 cubits wide on the west side, 10,000 cubits wide on the east side and 25,000 cubits long on the south side. In the center of it will be the sanctuary of the LORD. [11]This will be for the consecrated priests, the Zadokites, who were faithful in serving me and did not go astray as the Levites did when the Israelites went astray. [12]It will be a special gift to them from the sacred portion of the land, a most holy portion, bordering the territory of the Levites.

[13]"Alongside the territory of the priests, the Levites will have an allotment 25,000 cubits long and 10,000 cubits wide. Its total length will be 25,000 cubits and its width 10,000 cubits. [14]They must not sell or exchange any of it. This is the best of the land and must not pass into other hands, because it is holy to the LORD.

[15]"The remaining area, 5,000 cubits wide and 25,000 cubits long, will be for the common use of the city, for houses and for pastureland. The city will be in the center of it [16]and will have these measurements: the north side 4,500 cubits, the south side 4,500 cubits, the east side 4,500 cubits, and the west side 4,500 cubits. [17]The pastureland for the city will be 250 cubits on the

---

a20 Or opposite the entrance to　　*b1 Or to the entrance to*　　*c8 That is, about 7 miles (about 12 kilometers)*　　*d9 That is, about 3 miles (about 5 kilometers)*

north, 250 cubits on the south, 250 cubits on the east, and 250 cubits on the west. ¹⁸What remains of the area, bordering on the sacred portion and running the length of it, will be 10,000 cubits on the east side and 10,000 cubits on the west side. Its produce will supply food for the workers of the city. ¹⁹The workers from the city who farm it will come from all the tribes of Israel. ²⁰The entire portion will be a square, 25,000 cubits on each side. As a special gift you will set aside the sacred portion, along with the property of the city.

²¹"What remains on both sides of the area formed by the sacred portion and the city property will belong to the prince. It will extend eastward from the 25,000 cubits of the sacred portion to the eastern border, and westward from the 25,000 cubits to the western border. Both these areas running the length of the tribal portions will belong to the prince, and the sacred portion with the temple sanctuary will be in the center of them. ²²So the property of the Levites and the property of the city will lie in the center of the area that belongs to the prince. The area belonging to the prince will lie between the border of Judah and the border of Benjamin.

²³"As for the rest of the tribes: Benjamin will have one portion; it will extend from the east side to the west side.

²⁴"Simeon will have one portion; it will border the territory of Benjamin from east to west.

²⁵"Issachar will have one portion; it will border the territory of Simeon from east to west.

²⁶"Zebulun will have one portion; it will border the territory of Issachar from east to west.

²⁷"Gad will have one portion; it will border the territory of Zebulun from east to west.

²⁸"The southern boundary of Gad will run south from Tamar to the waters of Meribah Kadesh, then along the Wadi ⌊of Egypt⌋ to the Great Sea.^a

²⁹"This is the land you are to allot as an inheritance to the tribes of Israel, and these will be their portions," declares the Sovereign L<small>ORD</small>.

The Gates of the City

³⁰"These will be the exits of the city: Beginning on the north side, which is 4,500 cubits long, ³¹the gates of the city will be named after the tribes of Israel. The three gates on the north side will be the gate of Reuben, the gate of Judah and the gate of Levi.

³²"On the east side, which is 4,500 cubits long, will be three gates: the gate of Joseph, the gate of Benjamin and the gate of Dan.

³³"On the south side, which measures 4,500 cubits, will be three gates: the gate of Simeon, the gate of Issachar and the gate of Zebulun.

³⁴"On the west side, which is 4,500 cubits long, will be three gates: the gate of Gad, the gate of Asher and the gate of Naphtali.

³⁵"The distance all around will be 18,000 cubits.

"And the name of the city from that time on will be:

T<small>HE</small> L<small>ORD</small> I<small>S</small> T<small>HERE</small>."

---

1. How many gates are there? Where are they located? What are they named after (vv. 30–34)? Which two tribes share one gate (v. 32; see Ge 48:5–6)? **2.** What is the name of the city (v. 35)? Given the nature of this book, why is this name especially significant? Do you think the Jerusalem envisioned by Ezekiel ever came to be? Was the name ever changed? **3.** Do you think the book of Ezekiel ends abruptly? How would you have ended it? Considering the way it ends, what is especially important about Ezekiel's prophecy?

1. The prophets often see the image of God living in the midst of a peaceful city. Why hasn't it come to pass? Do you think we humans are called to build the "beautiful city," or is that a job only for God? **2.** In John's vision of the "New Jerusalem" (see Rev 21–22), what kind of person will live there? Are you one of its citizens?

---

^a28 That is, the Mediterranean

INTRODUCTION to
DANIEL

Book Study Outline: If you are using Daniel for a study course, here is a 6- or 11-week outline. Use the questions in the margin for your group agenda:

6-week plan	11-week plan	Personal Reading	Group Study Passage
1	1	1:1–21	1:1–21/Daniel's Training
	2	2:1–49	2:24–49/Dream Interpreted
2	3	3:1–30	3:1–30/The Fiery Furnace
	4	4:1–5:31	5:1–31/Handwriting on Wall
3	5	6:1–28	6:1–24/In the Den of Lions
	6	7:1–28	7:1–14/Four Beasts
4	7	8:1–27	8:1–27/Ram and a Goat
	8	9:1–27	9:1–19/Daniel's Prayer
5	9	10:1–11:1	10:1–11:1/Heavenly Visitor
	10	11:2–45	11:2–35/History Prophesied
6	11	12:1–13	12:1–13/Victory Promised

🕭 start meeting / 15 min.

📖 read & discuss Bible / 30 min.

♡ close meeting / 15–45 min.

Refer to the Questions and Answers in the front of this Bible for more information.

Author: Daniel (whose name means "God is my judge") was a statesman in the alien court of Babylon.

Date: The date for the writing of this book has been vigorously debated. Scholars who regard the book as genuine predictive prophecy date it c. 530 B.C., near the end of Daniel's life. The events depicted in the life of Daniel and his friends (ch. 1–6) are set in the time of the Babylonian captivity (605–538 B.C.) and the onset of the Persian Empire. The visions (ch. 7–12) look ahead to succeeding history, at least to 160 B.C., and perhaps to events that are still in the future even today.

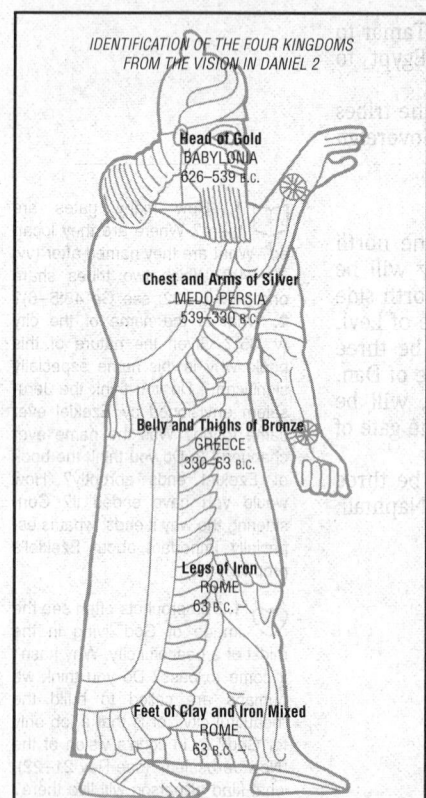

IDENTIFICATION OF THE FOUR KINGDOMS FROM THE VISION IN DANIEL 2

Head of Gold
BABYLONIA
626–539 B.C.

Chest and Arms of Silver
MEDO/PERSIA
539–330 B.C.

Belly and Thighs of Bronze
GREECE
330–63 B.C.

Legs of Iron
ROME
63 B.C. –

Feet of Clay and Iron Mixed
ROME
63 B.C. –

Theme: God is sovereign over the kingdoms of men (2:21; 5:21).

Historical Background: In 605 B.C. Nebuchadnezzar took Daniel and other captives to Babylon. Daniel rose quickly to prominence under Nebuchadnezzar. After the king's death, Daniel seems to have fallen from favor only to regain it by interpreting the handwriting on the wall at Belshazzar's feast (5:13–29). With the capture of Babylon by Darius, Daniel maintained his official position, serving under both Darius and Cyrus, the king of Persia.

Characteristics: Daniel is written in the context of the exile. It seeks to evoke a commitment to God's law amongst the people of God who are suffering persecution (even unto death). Daniel beckons them to awaken and prepare for the unexpected intervention of God into world affairs. Jesus refers to Daniel in his teachings (Mt 24:15) and quotes from 9:27; 11:31 and 12:11. John's Revelation draws heavily from Daniel's enigmatic apocalyptic imagery (in ch. 7–12).

Daniel

Daniel's Training in Babylon

1 In the third year of the reign of Jehoiakim king of Judah, Nebuchadnezzar king of Babylon came to Jerusalem and besieged it. ²And the Lord delivered Jehoiakim king of Judah into his hand, along with some of the articles from the temple of God. These he carried off to the temple of his god in Babylonia*ᵃ* and put in the treasure house of his god.

³Then the king ordered Ashpenaz, chief of his court officials, to bring in some of the Israelites from the royal family and the nobility— ⁴young men without any physical defect, handsome, showing aptitude for every kind of learning, well informed, quick to understand, and qualified to serve in the king's palace. He was to teach them the language and literature of the Babylonians.*ᵇ* ⁵The king assigned them a daily amount of food and wine from the king's table. They were to be trained for three years, and after that they were to enter the king's service.

⁶Among these were some from Judah: Daniel, Hananiah, Mishael and Azariah. ⁷The chief official gave them new names: to Daniel, the name Belteshazzar; to Hananiah, Shadrach; to Mishael, Meshach; and to Azariah, Abednego.

ᵃ2 Hebrew *Shinar*   *ᵇ4* Or *Chaldeans*

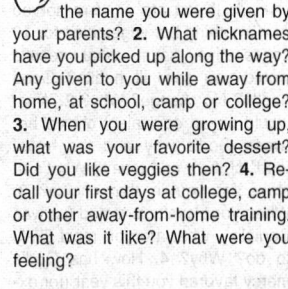

1. What is the story behind the name you were given by your parents? **2.** What nicknames have you picked up along the way? Any given to you while away from home, at school, camp or college? **3.** When you were growing up, what was your favorite dessert? Did you like veggies then? **4.** Recall your first days at college, camp or other away-from-home training. What was it like? What were you feeling?

1. How were these Israelites chosen and trained for the king's special service (vv. 3–7)? How did the king seek to capture their mind? Their body? Their loyalty? **2.** What is conveyed by giving a new name to another (person or pet)? **3.** Why does Daniel resist these attempts by the foreign king (v. 8)? To whom and on what grounds does Daniel make his ap-

---

     Daniel 1:1–21   **DANIEL'S TRAINING IN BABYLON**

Because of breaking their covenant with God, the people of Judah were taken into exile in Babylon. Among the deported Israelites was young Daniel.

1. What purpose did the king have for bringing the young Israelites to the palace?
   a. company   d. slavery
   b. training   e. brainwashing
   c. consultation services

2. How do you think the four young men felt about being selected?
   a. proud of being chosen over others
   b. insecure about what was expected
   c. disgusted, like bodies on display
   d. confident, like a commando team

3. Why did Daniel ask for different food?
   a. religious reasons
   b. physical reasons
   c. cultural reasons
   d. He missed "down home cookin'."

4. What would you call Daniel and his friends' resolve to maintain their diet?
   a. easy   c. spiritual
   b. traumatic d. risky

5. What impressed the king about the four young Israelites?
   a. their faith
   b. their appearance
   c. their courage
   d. their wisdom

6. What message does this story have for today?
   a. Christians should be vegetarians.
   b. Christians shouldn't drink.
   c. We should look for God's direction for what goes into our bodies.
   d. When it comes to our bodies, we shouldn't just do what others do.
   e. If God is on your side, it doesn't matter what you eat or drink.

7. The Israelites likely considered the royal food and wine defiled because it included animals declared "unclean" by the Law of Moses, and because a portion of it was first offered to idols. What practices in your life could be displeasing to God?

8. ✠ Which of the following do you need to work on to be a "whole person" physically?
   a. less food
   b. better food
   c. more exercise
   d. not so much exercise
   e. stop smoking, drinking, etc.
   f. better sleeping habits

9. ◉ Which of Daniel's attributes would help you most in your quest for healthy habits?
   a. wisdom   d. discipline
   b. conviction   e. youthful energy
   c. attractive appearance

10. Y How would kids today feel about Daniel saying no to alcohol?
   a. They would think he was a wimp.
   b. They would respect him for it.
   c. He better be good at sports.
   d. Some would laugh at him, but some would admire him.

11. Y What have you found helpful when confronted with alcohol or drugs?
   a. leave   d. explain myself
   b. just say "no" e. turn them in
   c. I haven't been in that situation.

peals for an exception to the king's edict (vv. 8–14)? **4.** Why does Daniel end up passing his first "entrance exam" with "flying colors" (vv. 15–21)? **5.** How does Daniel end up showing his true loyalty is to God? And to his three fellow believers?

♡ **1.** If you ate or were served nothing but vegetables for 10 consecutive days, what results would you see: Ill health? Good health? No change? Why? **2.** What would be an equivalent choice between God's way and the "royal food" of the world today? What's at stake for you in that choice? **3.** When your loyalty is tested (as was Daniel's), what are you most likely to do? Why? **4.** How has God's mercy favored you this year (for example, in your efforts toward excellence or in your service to others)?

<hr/>

🍵 **1.** What is one of the most memorable or unusual dreams you have ever had? **2.** What kinds of dreams most disturb you: (a) Daydreams? (b) Nightmares? (c) Sleep-walking? Give examples. **3.** How many ways can you think of that help people interpret their dreams?

📖 **1.** What does the king ask of the astrologers (vv. 1–3)? Why is he testing their competence (vv. 4–13)? Why is he so firm? So angry? **2.** In his fury, what does the king decide to do (vv. 12–13)? How does Daniel respond to this edict? **3.** Embracing the death-defying dare to interpret the dream, what role is played by Daniel's personal faith? Group prayer? God's special revelation? **4.** Does Daniel's psalm (vv. 20–23) express personal faith, or corporate worship? Why do you think so? **5.** What gifts does he praise God for? Why? What does that say about God? About Daniel? About intercession, thanksgiving and counting our blessings? **6.** Why does Daniel particularly praise God's "wisdom and might"? How does this relate to the king's and astrologers' claim? **7.** Compare Daniel and this king to

8But Daniel resolved not to defile himself with the royal food and wine, and he asked the chief official for permission not to defile himself this way. **9**Now God had caused the official to show favor and sympathy to Daniel, **10**but the official told Daniel, "I am afraid of my lord the king, who has assigned your[a] food and drink. Why should he see you looking worse than the other young men your age? The king would then have my head because of you."

11Daniel then said to the guard whom the chief official had appointed over Daniel, Hananiah, Mishael and Azariah, **12**"Please test your servants for ten days: Give us nothing but vegetables to eat and water to drink. **13**Then compare our appearance with that of the young men who eat the royal food, and treat your servants in accordance with what you see." **14**So he agreed to this and tested them for ten days.

15At the end of the ten days they looked healthier and better nourished than any of the young men who ate the royal food. **16**So the guard took away their choice food and the wine they were to drink and gave them vegetables instead.

17To these four young men God gave knowledge and understanding of all kinds of literature and learning. And Daniel could understand visions and dreams of all kinds.

18At the end of the time set by the king to bring them in, the chief official presented them to Nebuchadnezzar. **19**The king talked with them, and he found none equal to Daniel, Hananiah, Mishael and Azariah; so they entered the king's service. **20**In every matter of wisdom and understanding about which the king questioned them, he found them ten times better than all the magicians and enchanters in his whole kingdom.

21And Daniel remained there until the first year of King Cyrus.

Nebuchadnezzar's Dream

2 In the second year of his reign, Nebuchadnezzar had dreams; his mind was troubled and he could not sleep. **2**So the king summoned the magicians, enchanters, sorcerers and astrologers[b] to tell him what he had dreamed. When they came in and stood before the king, **3**he said to them, "I have had a dream that troubles me and I want to know what it means.[c]"

4Then the astrologers answered the king in Aramaic,[d] "O king, live forever! Tell your servants the dream, and we will interpret it."

5The king replied to the astrologers, "This is what I have firmly decided: If you do not tell me what my dream was and interpret it, I will have you cut into pieces and your houses turned into piles of rubble. **6**But if you tell me the dream and explain it, you will receive from me gifts and rewards and great honor. So tell me the dream and interpret it for me."

7Once more they replied, "Let the king tell his servants the dream, and we will interpret it."

8Then the king answered, "I am certain that you are trying to gain time, because you realize that this is what I have firmly decided: **9**If you do not tell me the dream, there is just one penalty for you. You have conspired to tell me misleading and wicked things, hoping the situation will change. So then, tell me the dream, and I will know that you can interpret it for me."

10The astrologers answered the king, "There is not a man on earth who can do what the king asks! No king, however great and

<hr/>

a10 The Hebrew for *your* and *you* in this verse is plural.　　*b2* Or *Chaldeans*; also in verses 4, 5 and 10　　*c3* Or *was*　　*d4* The text from here through chapter 7 is in Aramaic.

mighty, has ever asked such a thing of any magician or enchanter or astrologer. [11]What the king asks is too difficult. No one can reveal it to the king except the gods, and they do not live among men."

[12]This made the king so angry and furious that he ordered the execution of all the wise men of Babylon. [13]So the decree was issued to put the wise men to death, and men were sent to look for Daniel and his friends to put them to death.

[14]When Arioch, the commander of the king's guard, had gone out to put to death the wise men of Babylon, Daniel spoke to him with wisdom and tact. [15]He asked the king's officer, "Why did the king issue such a harsh decree?" Arioch then explained the matter to Daniel. [16]At this, Daniel went in to the king and asked for time, so that he might interpret the dream for him.

[17]Then Daniel returned to his house and explained the matter to his friends Hananiah, Mishael and Azariah. [18]He urged them to plead for mercy from the God of heaven concerning this mystery, so that he and his friends might not be executed with the rest of the wise men of Babylon. [19]During the night the mystery was revealed to Daniel in a vision. Then Daniel praised the God of heaven [20]and said:

> "Praise be to the name of God for ever and ever;
>   wisdom and power are his.
> [21]He changes times and seasons;
>   he sets up kings and deposes them.
> He gives wisdom to the wise
>   and knowledge to the discerning.
> [22]He reveals deep and hidden things;
>   he knows what lies in darkness,
>   and light dwells with him.
> [23]I thank and praise you, O God of my fathers:
>   You have given me wisdom and power,
> you have made known to me what we asked of
>   you,
> you have made known to us the dream of the
>   king."

Daniel Interprets the Dream

[24]Then Daniel went to Arioch, whom the king had appointed to execute the wise men of Babylon, and said to him, "Do not execute the wise men of Babylon. Take me to the king, and I will interpret his dream for him."

[25]Arioch took Daniel to the king at once and said, "I have found a man among the exiles from Judah who can tell the king what his dream means."

[26]The king asked Daniel (also called Belteshazzar), "Are you able to tell me what I saw in my dream and interpret it?"

[27]Daniel replied, "No wise man, enchanter, magician or diviner can explain to the king the mystery he has asked about, [28]but there is a God in heaven who reveals mysteries. He has shown King Nebuchadnezzar what will happen in days to come. Your dream and the visions that passed through your mind as you lay on your bed are these:

[29]"As you were lying there, O king, your mind turned to things to come, and the revealer of mysteries showed you what is going to happen. [30]As for me, this mystery has been revealed to me, not because I have greater wisdom than other living men, but so that you, O king, may know the interpretation and that you may understand what went through your mind.

Joseph and the Pharaoh (Ge 41): How are they alike? Not alike?

♡ **1.** Who (or what) drives you up the wall with demands? How do you decide when to give in and when to say no? **2.** What influences you more: Daily horoscope? Church or workplace grapevine? Editorial page? Your boss? Other? **3.** Daniel was given wisdom. Nebuchadnezzar had power. Who in your life or society claims to have wisdom or power? How do their claims compare to God's gifts to us? **4.** How may your prayer life reflect Daniel's praise and thanksgiving? And his friends' powerful intercession?

☕ **1.** Were you ever told a big secret? How did you feel? Did you have to keep it "secret," or could you share it with others? **2.** Recall when you shaped clay people or made sand castles or snowmen. Did it work? What or who destroyed your creation?

📖 **1.** What Messiah-like action by Daniel saves the day for the other wise men (v. 24)? **2.** As Daniel unfolds the meaning of the king's dream, how does he put the other wise men in their place (v. 27; as did Joseph, Ge 41:16)? **3.** How does he picture the large statue? How does Daniel put the king in his place (vv. 36–39)? The other kingdoms in their place (vv. 39–45)? **4.** How does Daniel testify to God by name (vv. 28,37,44–45)? **5.** How does the king honor Daniel and his God (vv. 46–49)? How does Daniel in turn share the wealth and give God his due? **6.** The word "interpret" appears 30 times in this Aramaic section of Daniel (ch. 2–7): Why is it so decisive to interpret God's mysteries? **7.** In what time frame do you place the kingdom of God as prophesied by Daniel?

1. In the face of seemingly weak church influence and strong secular and military forces, how does the promised kingdom-rule encourage *you?* **2.** What signs of the end times does this passage encourage you to look for? In what sense are *you* a sign of God's kingly rule in your life? **3.** What unstable "iron and clay" unions do *you* see in our broken world? Which do you feel more like these days: Iron or clay? Why? **4.** This polytheistic king falls prostrate in public, but confesses the true God only as "your God." Isaiah predicts many such kings will likewise bow down before God's people. Paul points to that time at Christ's return, when "every knee shall bow ... and every tongue confess that Jesus ... is Lord" (Php 2:10–11). What would it mean for you to make or reaffirm that confession today?

31"You looked, O king, and there before you stood a large statue—an enormous, dazzling statue, awesome in appearance. 32The head of the statue was made of pure gold, its chest and arms of silver, its belly and thighs of bronze, 33its legs of iron, its feet partly of iron and partly of baked clay. 34While you were watching, a rock was cut out, but not by human hands. It struck the statue on its feet of iron and clay and smashed them. 35Then the iron, the clay, the bronze, the silver and the gold were broken to pieces at the same time and became like chaff on a threshing floor in the summer. The wind swept them away without leaving a trace. But the rock that struck the statue became a huge mountain and filled the whole earth.

36"This was the dream, and now we will interpret it to the king. 37You, O king, are the king of kings. The God of heaven has given you dominion and power and might and glory; 38in your hands he has placed mankind and the beasts of the field and the birds of the air. Wherever they live, he has made you ruler over them all. You are that head of gold.

39"After you, another kingdom will rise, inferior to yours. Next, a third kingdom, one of bronze, will rule over the whole earth. 40Finally, there will be a fourth kingdom, strong as iron—for iron breaks and smashes everything—and as iron breaks things to pieces, so it will crush and break all the others. 41Just as you saw that the feet and toes were partly of baked clay and partly of iron, so this will be a divided kingdom; yet it will have some of the strength of iron in it, even as you saw iron mixed with clay. 42As the toes were partly iron and partly clay, so this kingdom will be partly strong and partly brittle. 43And just as you saw the iron mixed with baked clay, so the people will be a mixture and will not remain united, any more than iron mixes with clay.

44"In the time of those kings, the God of heaven will set up a kingdom that will never be destroyed, nor will it be left to another people. It will crush all those kingdoms and bring them to an end, but it will itself endure forever. 45This is the meaning of the vision of the rock cut out of a mountain, but not by human hands—a rock that broke the iron, the bronze, the clay, the silver and the gold to pieces.

"The great God has shown the king what will take place in the future. The dream is true and the interpretation is trustworthy."

46Then King Nebuchadnezzar fell prostrate before Daniel and paid him honor and ordered that an offering and incense be presented to him. 47The king said to Daniel, "Surely your God is the God of gods and the Lord of kings and a revealer of mysteries, for you were able to reveal this mystery."

48Then the king placed Daniel in a high position and lavished many gifts on him. He made him ruler over the entire province of Babylon and placed him in charge of all its wise men. 49Moreover, at Daniel's request the king appointed Shadrach, Meshach and Abednego administrators over the province of Babylon, while Daniel himself remained at the royal court.

The Image of Gold and the Fiery Furnace

3 King Nebuchadnezzar made an image of gold, ninety feet high and nine feet[a] wide, and set it up on the plain of Dura in the province of Babylon. 2He then summoned the satraps, prefects, governors, advisers, treasurers, judges, magistrates and all the other provincial officials to come to the dedication of the image he had

1. What is the hottest you can remember being? **2.** What things seem threatening to you? Fire? Accident? Height? **3.** What has been your closest brush with death or disaster?

1. What does King Nebuchadnezzar do and why (vv. 1–3)? The king's huge statue and

---

a1 Aramaic *sixty cubits high and six cubits wide* (about 27 meters high and 2.7 meters wide)

set up. [3]So the satraps, prefects, governors, advisers, treasurers, judges, magistrates and all the other provincial officials assembled for the dedication of the image that King Nebuchadnezzar had set up, and they stood before it.

[4]Then the herald loudly proclaimed, "This is what you are commanded to do, O peoples, nations and men of every language: [5]As soon as you hear the sound of the horn, flute, zither, lyre, harp, pipes and all kinds of music, you must fall down and worship the image of gold that King Nebuchadnezzar has set up. [6]Whoever does not fall down and worship will immediately be thrown into a blazing furnace."

[7]Therefore, as soon as they heard the sound of the horn, flute, zither, lyre, harp and all kinds of music, all the peoples, nations and men of every language fell down and worshiped the image of gold that King Nebuchadnezzar had set up.

[8]At this time some astrologers[a] came forward and denounced the Jews. [9]They said to King Nebuchadnezzar, "O king, live forever! [10]You have issued a decree, O king, that everyone who hears the sound of the horn, flute, zither, lyre, harp, pipes and all kinds of music must fall down and worship the image of gold, [11]and that whoever does not fall down and worship will be thrown into a blazing furnace. [12]But there are some Jews whom you have set over the affairs of the province of Babylon—Shadrach, Meshach and Abednego—who pay no attention to you, O king. They neither serve your gods nor worship the image of gold you have set up."

[13]Furious with rage, Nebuchadnezzar summoned Shadrach, Meshach and Abednego. So these men were brought before the king,

[a]8 Or *Chaldeans*

invited guests speaks to what tendency in people? **2.** At the dedication ceremony for this statue (vv. 4–7), what was the king's audience commanded to do? By whom? With what result? **3.** What exception to this universal decree is duly noted (vv. 8–12)? By whom? Why would these people tip off the king? **4.** Why is the king furious? What test does the king propose? Who is he really testing? **5.** How does this relate to Daniel's theme of God's authority vs. worldly authority? To the Fall (Ge 3)? The Ten Commandments (Ex 20)? **6.** For you, what is the bottom line or climax in the classic testimony by Shadrach, Meshach and Abednego (vv.16–18)? What were they sure about? What were they unsure about? What does this say about how martyrs for the faith ought to face their divine Maker and their human executioner? **7.** What is remarkable about the fiery furnace? Who is killed? Why? Who manages to survive? How? **8.** How do you explain the mysterious fourth figure: (a) An "angel," as does a Jewish tradition (see Ps 91:9–12)? (b) A "son of the gods," as does Nebuchadnezzar (who, as a pagan king,

---

 Daniel 3:1–30   **THE IMAGE OF GOLD AND THE FIERY FURNACE**

Daniel and three other young Jewish exiles were chosen to enter the service of the king of Babylon. Now King Nebuchadnezzar makes a large image of gold—probably a statue representing the god Nabu, for whom Nebuchadnezzar was named.

1. Why did Nebuchadnezzar insist everyone worship the golden image?
   a. He wanted to control them.
   b. He was committed to his god.
   c. He was insecure.
   d. He wanted to unite his people.

2. How would you describe the king's officials?
   a. yes-men   d. loyal
   b. fearful   e. idolatrous
   c. politically pragmatic

3. Who or what was the fourth figure in the furnace?
   a. an optical illusion
   b. an angel
   c. "a son of the gods"
   d. the Son of God
   e. a mystery

4. Nebuchadnezzar's response to the miracle indicated that he:
   a. believed their God was powerful.
   b. believed their God was the only true God.
   c. wanted to serve their God.
   d. wanted their God on his side.

5. What do you most admire about these three young Jews?
   a. their courage to defy authority
   b. their witness for the Lord
   c. their faith in God for a miracle
   d. their trust in God no matter what would happen

6. Which of the qualities in the previous question do you most need right now? For what reason?

7. Who has been—like the three young men—an example of trust that has drawn you to the Lord?

8. When did you come to have a faith in God that caused someone (like Nebuchadnezzar) to notice God working in your life?

9. Where do you feel God wants you to take a stand because of your faith?
   a. family relationships
   b. breaking a bad habit
   c. my business practices
   d. a public issue
   e. setting priorities
   f. being open about my faith

10. What is your greatest resource for taking a stand?
    a. supportive family
    b. supportive friends
    c. financial resources
    d. God's power
    e. the Christian community
    f. encouragement from Scripture

11. In what area of life are you facing the greatest pressure?
    a. work   d. fathering
    b. finances   e. time demands
    c. marriage   f. other:_____

12. When in the past have you felt God's presence with you in the "fiery furnace"? Whether or not you can see him, how might God be with you in the heat now?

affirms "polytheism" or many gods)? (c) "Son of God," as does an ancient Christian tradition? Why do you think so? **9.** What does Nebuchadnezzar make of the "God Most High" and his three undying servants (vv. 26–30)? Why? Do you think this experience made a believer out of him or not? Why?

♡ **1.** In what ways do you identify, or not identify, with each of the following egos: (a) The colossal ego of the pagan king? (b) The subservient ego of the king's officials? (c) The jealous ego of the astrologers? (d) The obedient ego of the near-martyrs? **2.** How is God with you in your sufferings? What have your sufferings to do with standing up for what you believe about God? How do you remain faithful "if he does not" rescue you? **3.** How does the king's affirming the Most High God relate to the Christian belief concerning Jesus (see Php 2:6–11)? **4.** How much are you willing to risk in order to obey a clear commandment of God?

☕ **1.** Remember the school or team braggart? How did you feel being around such braggarts? How do you feel when people brag about you or yours? **2.** What have you dreamed or daydreamed about your future? Were your dreams ex-

[14]and Nebuchadnezzar said to them, "Is it true, Shadrach, Meshach and Abednego, that you do not serve my gods or worship the image of gold I have set up? [15]Now when you hear the sound of the horn, flute, zither, lyre, harp, pipes and all kinds of music, if you are ready to fall down and worship the image I made, very good. But if you do not worship it, you will be thrown immediately into a blazing furnace. Then what god will be able to rescue you from my hand?"

[16]Shadrach, Meshach and Abednego replied to the king, "O Nebuchadnezzar, we do not need to defend ourselves before you in this matter. [17]If we are thrown into the blazing furnace, the God we serve is able to save us from it, and he will rescue us from your hand, O king. [18]But even if he does not, we want you to know, O king, that we will not serve your gods or worship the image of gold you have set up."

[19]Then Nebuchadnezzar was furious with Shadrach, Meshach and Abednego, and his attitude toward them changed. He ordered the furnace heated seven times hotter than usual [20]and commanded some of the strongest soldiers in his army to tie up Shadrach, Meshach and Abednego and throw them into the blazing furnace. [21]So these men, wearing their robes, trousers, turbans and other clothes, were bound and thrown into the blazing furnace. [22]The king's command was so urgent and the furnace so hot that the flames of the fire killed the soldiers who took up Shadrach, Meshach and Abednego, [23]and these three men, firmly tied, fell into the blazing furnace.

[24]Then King Nebuchadnezzar leaped to his feet in amazement and asked his advisers, "Weren't there three men that we tied up and threw into the fire?"

They replied, "Certainly, O king."

[25]He said, "Look! I see four men walking around in the fire, unbound and unharmed, and the fourth looks like a son of the gods."

[26]Nebuchadnezzar then approached the opening of the blazing furnace and shouted, "Shadrach, Meshach and Abednego, servants of the Most High God, come out! Come here!"

So Shadrach, Meshach and Abednego came out of the fire, [27]and the satraps, prefects, governors and royal advisers crowded around them. They saw that the fire had not harmed their bodies, nor was a hair of their heads singed; their robes were not scorched, and there was no smell of fire on them.

[28]Then Nebuchadnezzar said, "Praise be to the God of Shadrach, Meshach and Abednego, who has sent his angel and rescued his servants! They trusted in him and defied the king's command and were willing to give up their lives rather than serve or worship any god except their own God. [29]Therefore I decree that the people of any nation or language who say anything against the God of Shadrach, Meshach and Abednego be cut into pieces and their houses be turned into piles of rubble, for no other god can save in this way."

[30]Then the king promoted Shadrach, Meshach and Abednego in the province of Babylon.

Nebuchadnezzar's Dream of a Tree

4 King Nebuchadnezzar,

To the peoples, nations and men of every language, who live in all the world:

May you prosper greatly!

²It is my pleasure to tell you about the miraculous signs and wonders that the Most High God has performed for me.

³How great are his signs,
how mighty his wonders!
His kingdom is an eternal kingdom;
his dominion endures from generation to
generation.

⁴I, Nebuchadnezzar, was at home in my palace, contented and prosperous. ⁵I had a dream that made me afraid. As I was lying in my bed, the images and visions that passed through my mind terrified me. ⁶So I commanded that all the wise men of Babylon be brought before me to interpret the dream for me. ⁷When the magicians, enchanters, astrologers*ᵃ* and diviners came, I told them the dream, but they could not interpret it for me. ⁸Finally, Daniel came into my presence and I told him the dream. (He is called Belteshazzar, after the name of my god, and the spirit of the holy gods is in him.)

⁹I said, "Belteshazzar, chief of the magicians, I know that the spirit of the holy gods is in you, and no mystery is too difficult for you. Here is my dream; interpret it for me. ¹⁰These are the visions I saw while lying in my bed: I looked, and there before me stood a tree in the middle of the land. Its height was enormous. ¹¹The tree grew large and strong and its top touched the sky; it was visible to the ends of the earth. ¹²Its leaves were beautiful, its fruit abundant, and on it was food for all. Under it the beasts of the field found shelter, and the birds of the air lived in its branches; from it every creature was fed.

¹³"In the visions I saw while lying in my bed, I looked, and there before me was a messenger,*ᵇ* a holy one, coming down from heaven. ¹⁴He called in a loud voice: 'Cut down the tree and trim off its branches; strip off its leaves and scatter its fruit. Let the animals flee from under it and the birds from its branches. ¹⁵But let the stump and its roots, bound with iron and bronze, remain in the ground, in the grass of the field.

"'Let him be drenched with the dew of heaven, and let him live with the animals among the plants of the earth. ¹⁶Let his mind be changed from that of a man and let him be given the mind of an animal, till seven times*ᶜ* pass by for him.

¹⁷"'The decision is announced by messengers, the holy ones declare the verdict, so that the living may know that the Most High is sovereign over the kingdoms of men and gives them to anyone he wishes and sets over them the lowliest of men.'

¹⁸"This is the dream that I, King Nebuchadnezzar, had. Now, Belteshazzar, tell me what it means, for none of the wise men in my kingdom can interpret it for me. But you can, because the spirit of the holy gods is in you."

Daniel Interprets the Dream

¹⁹Then Daniel (also called Belteshazzar) was greatly perplexed for a time, and his thoughts terrified him. So the king said, "Belteshazzar, do not let the dream or its meaning alarm you."

Belteshazzar answered, "My lord, if only the dream applied to your enemies and its meaning to your adversaries! ²⁰The

citing? Ho hum? Morbid? What dreams have come true?

1. What position regarding "all the world" and the "Most High God" is Nebuchadnezzar assuming (vv. 1–3)? If people do "prosper greatly," who would like to take the credit? What does that say about this king? 2. How does the king's handling of this dream (vv. 4–9) differ from his handling of the earlier one (2:1–13)? How and why does he flatter Daniel this time? 3. How does the tree seem to fit the king (vv. 10–12): In size? Appearance? Visibility? In ability to prosper others? In comparison to the gold statue of chapter 3? How would you interpret the tree if you were Nebuchadnezzar? If you were Daniel? 4. Where does the messenger fit into the dream of the tree? What hope is conveyed by letting the stump remain (vv. 15,26)? 5. How does the king's being "given the mind of an animal" (v. 16) relate to God's message in verse 17 about authority? Power? Pride? Humility? 6. Are God's plans set in concrete or are they somewhat contingent upon our actions? What are the implications of verse 27 in this regard?

1. How can you appreciate your accomplishments without bragging or putting yourself down? Whom do you credit for your prosperity? 2. What "tree" of yours has been cut down to size? To what do you attribute that? 3. How has God changed your mind regarding his authority or power? 4. How do you feel about God speaking via dreams in the past? How about now?

1. What tactful way have you found to break bad news to someone? 2. How would you like to receive news: Bad news first? Good news last? 3. Share a time when you delayed doing something urgent or needful only to regret it. What were the results? How did you feel?

ᵃ7 Or *Chaldeans*　*ᵇ13* Or *watchman*; also in verses 17 and 23　*ᶜ16* Or *years*; also in verses 23, 25 and 32

1. How does Daniel break his bad news tactfully? What does he do and say at the outset (v. 19) and at the end (v. 27) which would increase the likelihood that Nebuchadnezzar would listen? What hope does he hold out for the king? 2. Daniel's use of "Heaven" (v. 26) is the first and only time the word is inserted for God in the Old Testament. What does it imply: Reverence for God's name? Deference to the king's polytheistic beliefs? Or what? 3. The Aramaic word for righteous or "what is right" (v. 27) links human responsibility to both God and neighbor. Why does Daniel stress both? (How is "being kind to the oppressed" a witness to God?) 4. How does his interpretation of the king's dream relate to issues of pride, arrogance and humility? 5. Has "all this happened" to the king by chance? By decree? By default? What clue does "twelve months later" provide? 6. How is the voice from heaven shown to be powerful (vv. 31–33)? How does the immediacy and power of God's word relate to Genesis 1? 7. With his sanity restored, what does the king conclude about "the Most High"? How does his testimony strike you: (a) Sincerely penitent? (b) Coaxed or coached by Daniel? (c) Sanely rational? (d) Miraculous turn-about? 8. How do you account for the king's restored greatness and prosperity: (a) Humility pays? (b) Daniel's prophecy is fulfilled? (c) God has a sense of humor? (d) The king's dream of the tree and stump comes true? (e) Other?

1. How have you shown courage in declaring God's word to others, both the good and the bad news? 2. What "stump" signals for you what God still wants to do? How might that be fully restored by "Heaven's rule"? 3. At this time Babylon, with its hanging gardens, is a "great" nation. Why does such success make change or repentance difficult? How does this relate to Jesus' word about the rich entering the kingdom of God (see Mt 19:24)?

tree you saw, which grew large and strong, with its top touching the sky, visible to the whole earth, 21with beautiful leaves and abundant fruit, providing food for all, giving shelter to the beasts of the field, and having nesting places in its branches for the birds of the air— 22you, O king, are that tree! You have become great and strong; your greatness has grown until it reaches the sky, and your dominion extends to distant parts of the earth.

23"You, O king, saw a messenger, a holy one, coming down from heaven and saying, 'Cut down the tree and destroy it, but leave the stump, bound with iron and bronze, in the grass of the field, while its roots remain in the ground. Let him be drenched with the dew of heaven; let him live like the wild animals, until seven times pass by for him.'

24"This is the interpretation, O king, and this is the decree the Most High has issued against my lord the king: 25You will be driven away from people and will live with the wild animals; you will eat grass like cattle and be drenched with the dew of heaven. Seven times will pass by for you until you acknowledge that the Most High is sovereign over the kingdoms of men and gives them to anyone he wishes. 26The command to leave the stump of the tree with its roots means that your kingdom will be restored to you when you acknowledge that Heaven rules. 27Therefore, O king, be pleased to accept my advice: Renounce your sins by doing what is right, and your wickedness by being kind to the oppressed. It may be that then your prosperity will continue."

The Dream Is Fulfilled

28All this happened to King Nebuchadnezzar. 29Twelve months later, as the king was walking on the roof of the royal palace of Babylon, 30he said, "Is not this the great Babylon I have built as the royal residence, by my mighty power and for the glory of my majesty?"

31The words were still on his lips when a voice came from heaven, "This is what is decreed for you, King Nebuchadnezzar: Your royal authority has been taken from you. 32You will be driven away from people and will live with the wild animals; you will eat grass like cattle. Seven times will pass by for you until you acknowledge that the Most High is sovereign over the kingdoms of men and gives them to anyone he wishes."

33Immediately what had been said about Nebuchadnezzar was fulfilled. He was driven away from people and ate grass like cattle. His body was drenched with the dew of heaven until his hair grew like the feathers of an eagle and his nails like the claws of a bird.

34At the end of that time, I, Nebuchadnezzar, raised my eyes toward heaven, and my sanity was restored. Then I praised the Most High; I honored and glorified him who lives forever.

His dominion is an eternal dominion;
  his kingdom endures from generation to
    generation.
35All the peoples of the earth
  are regarded as nothing.
He does as he pleases
  with the powers of heaven

and the peoples of the earth.
No one can hold back his hand
    or say to him: "What have you done?"

[36] At the same time that my sanity was restored, my honor and splendor were returned to me for the glory of my kingdom. My advisers and nobles sought me out, and I was restored to my throne and became even greater than before. [37] Now I, Nebuchadnezzar, praise and exalt and glorify the King of heaven, because everything he does is right and all his ways are just. And those who walk in pride he is able to humble.

The Writing on the Wall

5 King Belshazzar gave a great banquet for a thousand of his nobles and drank wine with them. [2] While Belshazzar was drinking his wine, he gave orders to bring in the gold and silver goblets that Nebuchadnezzar his father[a] had taken from the temple in Jerusalem, so that the king and his nobles, his wives and his concubines might drink from them. [3] So they brought in the gold goblets that had been taken from the temple of God in Jerusalem, and the king and his nobles, his wives and his concubines drank from them. [4] As they drank the wine, they praised the gods of gold and silver, of bronze, iron, wood and stone.

[5] Suddenly the fingers of a human hand appeared and wrote on the plaster of the wall, near the lampstand in the royal palace. The king watched the hand as it wrote. [6] His face turned pale and he was so frightened that his knees knocked together and his legs gave way.

[7] The king called out for the enchanters, astrologers[b] and diviners to be brought and said to these wise men of Babylon, "Whoever reads this writing and tells me what it means will be clothed in purple and have a gold chain placed around his neck, and he will be made the third highest ruler in the kingdom."

[8] Then all the king's wise men came in, but they could not read the writing or tell the king what it meant. [9] So King Belshazzar became even more terrified and his face grew more pale. His nobles were baffled.

[10] The queen,[c] hearing the voices of the king and his nobles, came into the banquet hall. "O king, live forever!" she said. "Don't be alarmed! Don't look so pale! [11] There is a man in your kingdom who has the spirit of the holy gods in him. In the time of your father he was found to have insight and intelligence and wisdom like that of the gods. King Nebuchadnezzar your father—your father the king, I say—appointed him chief of the magicians, enchanters, astrologers and diviners. [12] This man Daniel, whom the king called Belteshazzar, was found to have a keen mind and knowledge and understanding, and also the ability to interpret dreams, explain riddles and solve difficult problems. Call for Daniel, and he will tell you what the writing means."

[13] So Daniel was brought before the king, and the king said to him, "Are you Daniel, one of the exiles my father the king brought from Judah? [14] I have heard that the spirit of the gods is in you and that you have insight, intelligence and outstanding wisdom. [15] The wise men and enchanters were brought before me to read this writing and tell me what it means, but they could not explain it. [16] Now I have heard that you are able to give interpretations and to

1. Recall one of your most scary, hair-raising, goose-bumpy, heart-thumping experiences. What was so frightening? **2.** Whom do you know who is good at solving puzzles, riddles, rubic cubes, crosswords, etc.? **3.** Tell about a time you saw "the handwriting on the wall." How did you feel? What did you do? What happened?

1. Given this script for a scene in a mystery thriller to be developed by you as the movie director, how would you underscore the drama, musically? (Where would you place the minor and major keys in dissonance, and in resolution? Where would you place the drum roll, crescendo, cymbals and taps?) **2.** As the movie director, how would you set the stage? What special effects would you use for the mysterious handwriting on the wall? What close-cropped visuals and panning shots of the audience would you weave in for maximum effect? **3.** What flashbacks to Nebuchadnezzar's reign would provide contrasting relief and background insight to the drama here? What sin has Belshazzar added to his father's (vv. 2–4)? How is this an insult to God? How is this even worse than his father's sin (vv. 22–23)? **4.** What does Belshazzar's reaction to the mysterious hand (vv. 6–9) disclose about him? About his little secure world? His guilt? Fear? **5.** What does the king learn that money, things and promotions cannot buy, but only Daniel can supply? How is that point made by the queen (vv. 10–12)? By Daniel (v. 17)? **6.** What does Daniel's rejection of flattery and rewards say about the authenticity of this man and his message? **7.** What does the handwriting on the wall mean (vv. 26–28)? How is that prophecy fulfilled (v. 30)? In accord with what prediction (see 2:36–39)? **8.** Compare the two

a2 Or *ancestor;* or *predecessor;* also in verses 11, 13 and 18   *b7* Or *Chaldeans;* also in verse 11   *c10* Or *queen mother*

kings' portraits in 5:29–30 and 4:34–37. Whom do they praise? What does that tell you about them? From their contrasting fates, what do you learn about God's mercy and justice, power and authority?

♡ 1. What contemporary examples come to mind of people mocking God by demeaning sacred things, as Belshazzar did with the temple goblets? Does it seem God is quick, or slow, to judge sacrilegious behavior? Why? 2. What have you learned from your parents or predecessors? Why do people often fail, as does Belshazzar, to learn from the past? 3. What would you do if you were offered position and/or power as a way to buy your vote or pre-determine your thinking?

solve difficult problems. If you can read this writing and tell me what it means, you will be clothed in purple and have a gold chain placed around your neck, and you will be made the third highest ruler in the kingdom."

[17]Then Daniel answered the king, "You may keep your gifts for yourself and give your rewards to someone else. Nevertheless, I will read the writing for the king and tell him what it means.

[18]"O king, the Most High God gave your father Nebuchadnezzar sovereignty and greatness and glory and splendor. [19]Because of the high position he gave him, all the peoples and nations and men of every language dreaded and feared him. Those the king wanted to put to death, he put to death; those he wanted to spare, he spared; those he wanted to promote, he promoted; and those he wanted to humble, he humbled. [20]But when his heart became arrogant and hardened with pride, he was deposed from his royal throne and stripped of his glory. [21]He was driven away from people and given the mind of an animal; he lived with the wild donkeys and ate grass like cattle; and his body was drenched with the dew of heaven, until he acknowledged that the Most High God is sovereign over the kingdoms of men and sets over them anyone he wishes.

[22]"But you his son,[a] O Belshazzar, have not humbled yourself, though you knew all this. [23]Instead, you have set yourself up against the Lord of heaven. You had the goblets from his temple brought to you, and you and your nobles, your wives and your concubines drank wine from them. You praised the gods of silver and gold, of bronze, iron, wood and stone, which cannot see or hear or understand. But you did not honor the God who holds in his hand your life and all your ways. [24]Therefore he sent the hand that wrote the inscription.

[25]"This is the inscription that was written:

MENE, MENE, TEKEL, PARSIN[b]

[26]"This is what these words mean:

Mene[c]: God has numbered the days of your reign and brought it to an end.
[27]*Tekel*[d]: You have been weighed on the scales and found wanting.
[28]*Peres*[e]: Your kingdom is divided and given to the Medes and Persians."

[29]Then at Belshazzar's command, Daniel was clothed in purple, a gold chain was placed around his neck, and he was proclaimed the third highest ruler in the kingdom.

[30]That very night Belshazzar, king of the Babylonians,[f] was slain, [31]and Darius the Mede took over the kingdom, at the age of sixty-two.

Daniel in the Den of Lions

6 It pleased Darius to appoint 120 satraps to rule throughout the kingdom, [2]with three administrators over them, one of whom was Daniel. The satraps were made accountable to them so that the king might not suffer loss. [3]Now Daniel so distinguished himself among the administrators and the satraps by his exceptional qualities that the king planned to set him over the whole kingdom. [4]At this, the administrators and the satraps tried to find grounds for

☕ 1. Share a time when you were done-in by having the rug pulled out from under you? How were you set up, betrayed or falsely accused? 2. When have you felt really good about something you did, only to have someone else be jealous or unhappy?

📖 1. What stirs up the jealousy of the administrators and satraps? When their jealous fault-finding campaign (or special investigative unit) runs free of any

a22 Or *descendant*; or *successor*   b25 Aramaic *UPARSIN* (that is, *AND PARSIN*)
c26 *Mene* can mean *numbered* or *mina* (a unit of money).   d27 *Tekel* can mean *weighed* or *shekel*.   e28 *Peres* (the singular of *Parsin*) can mean *divided* or *Persia* or a *half mina* or a *half shekel*.   f30 Or *Chaldeans*

charges against Daniel in his conduct of government affairs, but they were unable to do so. They could find no corruption in him, because he was trustworthy and neither corrupt nor negligent. [5]Finally these men said, "We will never find any basis for charges against this man Daniel unless it has something to do with the law of his God."

[6]So the administrators and the satraps went as a group to the king and said: "O King Darius, live forever! [7]The royal administrators, prefects, satraps, advisers and governors have all agreed that the king should issue an edict and enforce the decree that anyone who prays to any god or man during the next thirty days, except to you, O king, shall be thrown into the lions' den. [8]Now, O king, issue the decree and put it in writing so that it cannot be altered—in accordance with the laws of the Medes and Persians, which cannot be repealed." [9]So King Darius put the decree in writing.

[10]Now when Daniel learned that the decree had been published, he went home to his upstairs room where the windows opened toward Jerusalem. Three times a day he got down on his knees and prayed, giving thanks to his God, just as he had done before. [11]Then these men went as a group and found Daniel praying and asking God for help. [12]So they went to the king and spoke to him about his royal decree: "Did you not publish a decree that during the next thirty days anyone who prays to any god or man except to you, O king, would be thrown into the lions' den?"

The king answered, "The decree stands—in accordance with the laws of the Medes and Persians, which cannot be repealed."

[13]Then they said to the king, "Daniel, who is one of the exiles from Judah, pays no attention to you, O king, or to the decree you put in writing. He still prays three times a day." [14]When the king

ethical guidelines, where does it stop (vv. 1–5)? **2.** What trap do the satraps set for Daniel? Why has Daniel's private life become an issue for public policy and the public's right to know? **3.** How do the satraps manage to get their way with the king (vv. 6–7,12–13,15)? Why are appeals to vanity so powerful? **4.** Why is the king so distressed (vv. 14–18)? Is he just being a "wimp," favoring whoever he happens to be with at the moment? Or is he sincerely siding with Daniel and his God? Why do you think so? **5.** What do you think really happened in the lions' den to Daniel? To the lions? To the satraps and their families? What about this do you have problems with? **6.** What role does the "laws of the Medes and the Persians" play here (vv. 8,12,15,17,24)? Likewise, what role does the law of God play (vv. 5,10; see 2Ch 6:38–39; Ps 55:17)? Likewise, the faith of Daniel (vv. 4,11,16,20–23; see Heb 11:33)? **7.** As part of Daniel's complete vindication, his accusers receive the same punishment they had demanded that the accused receive (v. 24). Is this Persian custom of vindication and limited ("eye for

 Daniel 6:1–24   **DANIEL IN THE DEN OF LIONS**

Daniel, the exiled Israelite, has faithfully served the kings of Babylon. Now, after the Babylonians were conquered by the Medes and Persians, Daniel continues to be a faithful servant.

1. What would you call King Darius' advisers?
   a. schemers   c. political sharks
   b. spiteful   d. snitches

2. Why did the king issue his decree?
   a. He was outnumbered.
   b. He was naive.
   c. He had an inflated ego.
   d. He thought everyone would obey.

3. How would you describe Daniel's response to the edict?
   a. rebellion   d. faithfulness
   b. perseverance   e. disregard
   c. a plea for help

4. Upon discovering the implications of his decree, how did Darius feel?
   a. angry   d. despairing
   b. stupid   e. trapped
   c. frustrated   f. repentant

5. What saved Daniel?
   a. his faith
   b. his prayers
   c. his innocence
   d. the king's prayers
   e. God's faithfulness
   f. lethargic lions

6. When have you been betrayed or falsely accused? Do strong values make you more or less vulnerable to others? What can you learn from Daniel about how to respond in such situations?

7. What often keeps you from standing up for something you believe in?
   a. apathy   d. time
   b. ignorance   e. peer pressure
   c. fear   f. consequences

8. What do you feel when you do take a stand?
   a. confidence   d. elation
   b. power   e. fear
   c. peace   f. freedom

9. If you were on trial for being a Christian, what verdict would the

evidence most likely require?
   a. not guilty
   b. guilty in the second degree
   c. guilty in the first degree
   d. deserving of capital punishment

10. Where is the most difficult place for you to maintain your identity as a Christian?
   a. at home
   b. at work
   c. at school
   d. at play (ball games, etc.)
   e. among my non-Christian friends
   f. other:_____

11. What "hot issue" feels like a den of lions to you? How have you experienced God in the midst of a lions' den in the past?

12. How has this course and group helped you see the hot issues of your life in a different light, and helped you take a stand regarding them? To conclude, focus on one person at a time and have others share how he or she has contributed to your group.

eye," "life for life") retribution supported anywhere in the Bible (see Ex 21:24; Lev 24:20; Dt 21; Mt 5:38)? But when, if ever, might it be okay to punish innocent family members of false accusers? **8.** How does King Darius respond to all this? Has he himself become a believer? Why do you think so?

♡ **1.** Besides jealousy, what might cause people to be interested in the private lives of public figures, especially incorruptible ones? **2.** What stirs up your jealousy: (a) The success of others? (b) Desire for material things? (c) The devil? (d) When someone else gets what is coming to you? (e) Other? Does having strong principles and values cause you to be more or less vulnerable to others? Why? **3.** Daniel shows us that the law of one's God supersedes the law of the land. How do you reconcile what Daniel did with Romans 13:1? How does this square with your view of church and state issues? (See also Mt 22:21; Lk 20:25; Ac 5:29) **4.** What parallels do you see between Daniel's betrayal (vv. 3–18) and Jesus'? Between Daniel's vindication (vv. 19–28) and Jesus'? What do you make of those obvious parallels? **5.** When in your life have you experienced God in the midst of a "lions' den" of skeptics, critics, etc.? How has God alone been your lifeline?

🍵 **1.** What animals or birds represent: (a) USA? (b) England? (c) France? (d) Russia? (e) Your favorite ball team? **2.** What are your favorite animals, wild or tame? **3.** What are your favorite animal cartoon characters? **4.** What animal scares you to pieces?

heard this, he was greatly distressed; he was determined to rescue Daniel and made every effort until sundown to save him.

¹⁵Then the men went as a group to the king and said to him, "Remember, O king, that according to the law of the Medes and Persians no decree or edict that the king issues can be changed."

¹⁶So the king gave the order, and they brought Daniel and threw him into the lions' den. The king said to Daniel, "May your God, whom you serve continually, rescue you!"

¹⁷A stone was brought and placed over the mouth of the den, and the king sealed it with his own signet ring and with the rings of his nobles, so that Daniel's situation might not be changed. ¹⁸Then the king returned to his palace and spent the night without eating and without any entertainment being brought to him. And he could not sleep.

¹⁹At the first light of dawn, the king got up and hurried to the lions' den. ²⁰When he came near the den, he called to Daniel in an anguished voice, "Daniel, servant of the living God, has your God, whom you serve continually, been able to rescue you from the lions?"

²¹Daniel answered, "O king, live forever! ²²My God sent his angel, and he shut the mouths of the lions. They have not hurt me, because I was found innocent in his sight. Nor have I ever done any wrong before you, O king."

²³The king was overjoyed and gave orders to lift Daniel out of the den. And when Daniel was lifted from the den, no wound was found on him, because he had trusted in his God.

²⁴At the king's command, the men who had falsely accused Daniel were brought in and thrown into the lions' den, along with their wives and children. And before they reached the floor of the den, the lions overpowered them and crushed all their bones.

²⁵Then King Darius wrote to all the peoples, nations and men of every language throughout the land:

"May you prosper greatly!

²⁶"I issue a decree that in every part of my kingdom people must fear and reverence the God of Daniel.

"For he is the living God
   and he endures forever;
his kingdom will not be destroyed,
   his dominion will never end.
²⁷He rescues and he saves;
   he performs signs and wonders
   in the heavens and on the earth.
He has rescued Daniel
   from the power of the lions."

²⁸So Daniel prospered during the reign of Darius and the reign of Cyrus*a* the Persian.

Daniel's Dream of Four Beasts

7 In the first year of Belshazzar king of Babylon, Daniel had a dream, and visions passed through his mind as he was lying on his bed. He wrote down the substance of his dream.

²Daniel said: "In my vision at night I looked, and there before me were the four winds of heaven churning up the great sea. ³Four great beasts, each different from the others, came up out of the sea.

⁴"The first was like a lion, and it had the wings of an eagle. I

a28 Or *Darius, that is, the reign of Cyrus*

watched until its wings were torn off and it was lifted from the ground so that it stood on two feet like a man, and the heart of a man was given to it.

⁵"And there before me was a second beast, which looked like a bear. It was raised up on one of its sides, and it had three ribs in its mouth between its teeth. It was told, 'Get up and eat your fill of flesh!'

⁶"After that, I looked, and there before me was another beast, one that looked like a leopard. And on its back it had four wings like those of a bird. This beast had four heads, and it was given authority to rule.

⁷"After that, in my vision at night I looked, and there before me was a fourth beast—terrifying and frightening and very powerful. It had large iron teeth; it crushed and devoured its victims and trampled underfoot whatever was left. It was different from all the former beasts, and it had ten horns.

⁸"While I was thinking about the horns, there before me was another horn, a little one, which came up among them; and three of the first horns were uprooted before it. This horn had eyes like the eyes of a man and a mouth that spoke boastfully.

⁹"As I looked,

"thrones were set in place,
    and the Ancient of Days took his seat.
His clothing was as white as snow;
    the hair of his head was white like wool.
His throne was flaming with fire,
    and its wheels were all ablaze.
¹⁰A river of fire was flowing,
    coming out from before him.
Thousands upon thousands attended him;
    ten thousand times ten thousand stood before
        him.
The court was seated,
    and the books were opened.

¹¹"Then I continued to watch because of the boastful words the horn was speaking. I kept looking until the beast was slain and its body destroyed and thrown into the blazing fire. ¹²(The other beasts had been stripped of their authority, but were allowed to live for a period of time.)

¹³"In my vision at night I looked, and there before me was one like a son of man, coming with the clouds of heaven. He approached the Ancient of Days and was led into his presence. ¹⁴He was given authority, glory and sovereign power; all peoples, nations and men of every language worshiped him. His dominion is an everlasting dominion that will not pass away, and his kingdom is one that will never be destroyed.

The Interpretation of the Dream

¹⁵"I, Daniel, was troubled in spirit, and the visions that passed through my mind disturbed me. ¹⁶I approached one of those standing there and asked him the true meaning of all this.

"So he told me and gave me the interpretation of these things: ¹⁷'The four great beasts are four kingdoms that will rise from the earth. ¹⁸But the saints of the Most High will receive the kingdom and will possess it forever—yes, for ever and ever.'

¹⁹"Then I wanted to know the true meaning of the fourth beast, which was different from all the others and most terrifying, with its iron teeth and bronze claws—the beast that crushed and devoured

1. Jesus takes Daniel's royal "Son of Man" title as his own, but fuses it with a suffering motif (see Isa 53). What aspect of Christ and his kingdom, then, is Daniel predicting in verses 13–14? How does this compare to the other four kingdoms? 2. How has Daniel's relation to dreams changed in this chapter? (Note: The events here may precede those in ch. 5.) Are these dreams humanly concocted or divinely given? Why do you think so? 3. To what does Daniel liken the four beasts? What's distinctive about each? What do you make of the 10 horns? The "little horn" with the big mouth? (Does it imply a man, government, a coalition of states, an ideology?) 4. What picture does the "Ancient of Days" bring to mind: Wisdom or senility? Venerability or vulnerability? Sentimental softy or moral purity? Why? 5. What do you think is implied by "the books were opened" (v. 10)? Does your answer say more about God's control or human freedom? 6. How does Daniel convey transcendent and earthly aspects of God (vv. 9–14)? What is the coming kingdom and its heavenly leader like?

1. How do you react to "wild, scary and beastly" forces within your world? Within your life? What reason does Daniel give you to trust that God "has the whole world in his hands"? 2. Take a minute to draw the scene in verses 13–14 in your imagination. What does this emphasize to you about Jesus Christ? Why is it significant to you that he like this?

1. Share about a time your favorite team was the underdog and they won. 2. Share about when you were in an underdog role and came out on top. 3. When have you gone through tough times, only to awaken and find out things came out okay?

1. How is Daniel affected by this vision (vv. 15,19,28)? How does he learn its true meaning? 2. How might you go about

cracking the code of the four king-doms? (Modern attempts to do so are based on comparisons among the visions of Daniel in chapters 2, 7 and 9, with a chronology of major empires we know in retrospect from secular history.) **3.** In judg-ment, what role is played by the "saints" (vv. 18,21–22,25,27)? By "the Most High"? **4.** How does Dan-iel's view on saints in judgment compare with that of Jesus and John (see Mt 19:28–29; Lk 22:29–30; Rev 1:6; 20:4–6)?

♡ **1.** What will kingdom posses-sion by the saints mean, now and in the future, for the arrogant? The meek? For you? **2.** Daniel shows us that God doesn't always side with the strong or victorious (athletes, candidates or military) but with the defeated, oppressed and exiled. How might this relate to you?

☕ When you think of people butting heads like two rams, what sport comes to mind? What do you like, and not like, about con-tact sports?

📖 **1.** What does it matter when (before the events of ch. 5) and where (in the mind of Daniel) this vision actually takes place? **2.** What about this vision makes you wince and rub your forehead? **3.** What does the two-horned ram represent (vv. 3,20)? The goat and its prominent horn (vv. 5,21)? What do the charging animals, the shat-tering of the two horns, and the breaking off of the large horn repre-sent (vv. 7–8)? **4.** What other "little horn" does the emerging horn in verse 9 bring to mind (see 7:8,11)? How is this one different in origin, nature and destiny? How is it simi-lar in its overwhelming pride? **5.** What do you make of Daniel speci-fying the time frame for the fulfill-ment of his vision (vv. 13,26)? Why do you think God allows the trans-gression of his moral law for such a long time? **6.** Verses 20–25 (also Da 7 with Rev 12 and 13) are the background for the Christian belief in an Antichrist, the last days and God's doing battle for us. What do you see here? How will "he" be de-stroyed? **7.** What impact does all this have on Daniel (vv. 15,17,27)?

its victims and trampled underfoot whatever was left. ²⁰I also want-ed to know about the ten horns on its head and about the other horn that came up, before which three of them fell—the horn that looked more imposing than the others and that had eyes and a mouth that spoke boastfully. ²¹As I watched, this horn was waging war against the saints and defeating them, ²²until the Ancient of Days came and pronounced judgment in favor of the saints of the Most High, and the time came when they possessed the kingdom.

²³"He gave me this explanation: 'The fourth beast is a fourth kingdom that will appear on earth. It will be different from all the other kingdoms and will devour the whole earth, trampling it down and crushing it. ²⁴The ten horns are ten kings who will come from this kingdom. After them another king will arise, different from the earlier ones; he will subdue three kings. ²⁵He will speak against the Most High and oppress his saints and try to change the set times and the laws. The saints will be handed over to him for a time, times and half a time.ᵃ

²⁶"'But the court will sit, and his power will be taken away and completely destroyed forever. ²⁷Then the sovereignty, power and greatness of the kingdoms under the whole heaven will be handed over to the saints, the people of the Most High. His kingdom will be an everlasting kingdom, and all rulers will worship and obey him.'

²⁸"This is the end of the matter. I, Daniel, was deeply troubled by my thoughts, and my face turned pale, but I kept the matter to myself."

Daniel's Vision of a Ram and a Goat

8 In the third year of King Belshazzar's reign, I, Daniel, had a vision, after the one that had already appeared to me. ²In my vision I saw myself in the citadel of Susa in the province of Elam; in the vision I was beside the Ulai Canal. ³I looked up, and there before me was a ram with two horns, standing beside the canal, and the horns were long. One of the horns was longer than the other but grew up later. ⁴I watched the ram as he charged toward the west and the north and the south. No animal could stand against him, and none could rescue from his power. He did as he pleased and became great.

⁵As I was thinking about this, suddenly a goat with a prominent horn between his eyes came from the west, crossing the whole earth without touching the ground. ⁶He came toward the two-horned ram I had seen standing beside the canal and charged at him in great rage. ⁷I saw him attack the ram furiously, striking the ram and shattering his two horns. The ram was powerless to stand against him; the goat knocked him to the ground and trampled on him, and none could rescue the ram from his power. ⁸The goat became very great, but at the height of his power his large horn was broken off, and in its place four prominent horns grew up toward the four winds of heaven.

⁹Out of one of them came another horn, which started small but grew in power to the south and to the east and toward the Beauti-ful Land. ¹⁰It grew until it reached the host of the heavens, and it threw some of the starry host down to the earth and trampled on them. ¹¹It set itself up to be as great as the Prince of the host; it took away the daily sacrifice from him, and the place of his sanctu-ary was brought low. ¹²Because of rebellion, the host ⌊of the

ᵃ25 Or *for a year, two years and half a year*

saints,ᵃ and the daily sacrifice were given over to it. It prospered in everything it did, and truth was thrown to the ground.

¹³Then I heard a holy one speaking, and another holy one said to him, "How long will it take for the vision to be fulfilled—the vision concerning the daily sacrifice, the rebellion that causes desolation, and the surrender of the sanctuary and of the host that will be trampled underfoot?"

¹⁴He said to me, "It will take 2,300 evenings and mornings; then the sanctuary will be reconsecrated."

The Interpretation of the Vision

¹⁵While I, Daniel, was watching the vision and trying to understand it, there before me stood one who looked like a man. ¹⁶And I heard a man's voice from the Ulai calling, "Gabriel, tell this man the meaning of the vision."

¹⁷As he came near the place where I was standing, I was terrified and fell prostrate. "Son of man," he said to me, "understand that the vision concerns the time of the end."

¹⁸While he was speaking to me, I was in a deep sleep, with my face to the ground. Then he touched me and raised me to my feet.

¹⁹He said: "I am going to tell you what will happen later in the time of wrath, because the vision concerns the appointed time of the end.ᵇ ²⁰The two-horned ram that you saw represents the kings of Media and Persia. ²¹The shaggy goat is the king of Greece, and the large horn between his eyes is the first king. ²²The four horns that replaced the one that was broken off represent four kingdoms that will emerge from his nation but will not have the same power.

²³"In the latter part of their reign, when rebels have become completely wicked, a stern-faced king, a master of intrigue, will arise. ²⁴He will become very strong, but not by his own power. He will cause astounding devastation and will succeed in whatever he does. He will destroy the mighty men and the holy people. ²⁵He will cause deceit to prosper, and he will consider himself superior. When they feel secure, he will destroy many and take his stand against the Prince of princes. Yet he will be destroyed, but not by human power.

²⁶"The vision of the evenings and mornings that has been given you is true, but seal up the vision, for it concerns the distant future."

²⁷I, Daniel, was exhausted and lay ill for several days. Then I got up and went about the king's business. I was appalled by the vision; it was beyond understanding.

Daniel's Prayer

9 In the first year of Darius son of Xerxesᶜ (a Mede by descent), who was made ruler over the Babylonianᵈ kingdom— ²in the first year of his reign, I, Daniel, understood from the Scriptures, according to the word of the LORD given to Jeremiah the prophet, that the desolation of Jerusalem would last seventy years. ³So I turned to the Lord God and pleaded with him in prayer and petition, in fasting, and in sackcloth and ashes.

⁴I prayed to the LORD my God and confessed:

"O Lord, the great and awesome God, who keeps his covenant of love with all who love him and obey his commands, ⁵we have sinned and done wrong. We have been wicked and

---

ᵃ12 Or rebellion, the armies   ᵇ19 Or because the end will be at the appointed time
ᶜ1 Hebrew Ahasuerus   ᵈ1 Or Chaldean

---

8. Does Daniel's prophecy strike you as history written *beforehand* or *after the fact*? Why? **9.** If the horn that "started small" but "grew in power" toward the "Beautiful Land" of Israel (v. 9) *was* Antiochus IV Epiphanes, who set up a pagan altar in the temple in 168 B.C., *then* the rededication of the temple was three years later by Judas Maccabeus in 165 B.C. *If* this horn also prefigures the world-wide ecumenical movement or a merger of East-West religions (as some say), *then* *when* will verse 13 take place? What do such multiple fulfillments say about the nature of biblical prophecy?

1. When have you been dismayed over: (a) Something God revealed to you? (b) Some triumph of evil or good? **2.** The study of Daniel's prophecies often produces more heat than light. How do you relate to other Christians who favor an interpretation that differs from yours? **3.** How might one reach for the stars, desecrate the temple, or trample truth underfoot, as in verses 10–12: (a) Disregard biblical truth? (b) Deny Jesus is God? (c) "Play God"? (d) Other? How long can your society get away with that? **4.** Where have you seen God active in violent world affairs?

What's the longest prayer you have ever timed? Who first said prayers with you at night and taught you how to pray? When did prayer first become your own conversation with God?

1. What moves Daniel to pray as he does? What clues do Jeremiah 25:1–14 and 29:10–14 provide? If the "70-year" period begins with the onset of Jehoiakim's reign (608 B.C.) or Nebuchadnezzar's reign (605 B.C.), what then happens almost 70 years later (in 538 B.C.)? **2.** How does Daniel prepare himself for this divine encounter? Who is Daniel speaking for as he prays? What elements of common prayer do you see here? **3.** How does each aspect of God prompt a round of Daniel's confession: (a) God is great and awesome? (b) Faithful to his covenant? (c) Righteous in bringing judgment? (d) Merciful and forgiving? (e) Jealous for his Name? **4.** Why will God answer his prayer (vv. 16–19)? **5.** What does this prayer say about God's covenant: Based on grace or works, his character or ours? Conveys love or justice? Forever binding or always renegotiable?

♥ **1.** Daniel's study of the Scriptures drove him to pray a prayer filled with Scripture. How could you use Scripture in your prayers? **2.** Judging from the content of your recent prayers, what concerns you most these days? **3.** Daniel humbled himself before meeting his God in prayer (v. 3). How do you prepare to meet your God? How do you keep from viewing God as a celestial butler? **4.** What aspects of God move you to pray? Why? Who do you pray for most frequently? What prayer agenda for you and your group does Daniel 9 suggest? Try it.

What's it like to do a jigsaw puzzle that has missing pieces? Whose handwriting do you find near impossible to decipher?

1. What does this enigma imply about God's "answering service" (vv. 20–23)? **2.** What six things happen within "seventy sevens"? Which events may refer to the time of Ezra and Nehemiah (c. 458–430 B.C.)? Which to Jesus as the Anointed One? Which results seem yet to be? (Hint: What do the "seven sevens", the "62 sevens," the "one seven" mean?) **3.** What is

have rebelled; we have turned away from your commands and laws. 6We have not listened to your servants the prophets, who spoke in your name to our kings, our princes and our fathers, and to all the people of the land.

7"Lord, you are righteous, but this day we are covered with shame—the men of Judah and people of Jerusalem and all Israel, both near and far, in all the countries where you have scattered us because of our unfaithfulness to you. 8O LORD, we and our kings, our princes and our fathers are covered with shame because we have sinned against you. 9The Lord our God is merciful and forgiving, even though we have rebelled against him; 10we have not obeyed the LORD our God or kept the laws he gave us through his servants the prophets. 11All Israel has transgressed your law and turned away, refusing to obey you.

"Therefore the curses and sworn judgments written in the Law of Moses, the servant of God, have been poured out on us, because we have sinned against you. 12You have fulfilled the words spoken against us and against our rulers by bringing upon us great disaster. Under the whole heaven nothing has ever been done like what has been done to Jerusalem. 13Just as it is written in the Law of Moses, all this disaster has come upon us, yet we have not sought the favor of the LORD our God by turning from our sins and giving attention to your truth. 14The LORD did not hesitate to bring the disaster upon us, for the LORD our God is righteous in everything he does; yet we have not obeyed him.

15"Now, O Lord our God, who brought your people out of Egypt with a mighty hand and who made for yourself a name that endures to this day, we have sinned, we have done wrong. 16O Lord, in keeping with all your righteous acts, turn away your anger and your wrath from Jerusalem, your city, your holy hill. Our sins and the iniquities of our fathers have made Jerusalem and your people an object of scorn to all those around us.

17"Now, our God, hear the prayers and petitions of your servant. For your sake, O Lord, look with favor on your desolate sanctuary. 18Give ear, O God, and hear; open your eyes and see the desolation of the city that bears your Name. We do not make requests of you because we are righteous, but because of your great mercy. 19O Lord, listen! O Lord, forgive! O Lord, hear and act! For your sake, O my God, do not delay, because your city and your people bear your Name."

The Seventy "Sevens"

20While I was speaking and praying, confessing my sin and the sin of my people Israel and making my request to the LORD my God for his holy hill— 21while I was still in prayer, Gabriel, the man I had seen in the earlier vision, came to me in swift flight about the time of the evening sacrifice. 22He instructed me and said to me, "Daniel, I have now come to give you insight and understanding. 23As soon as you began to pray, an answer was given, which I have come to tell you, for you are highly esteemed. Therefore, consider the message and understand the vision:

24"Seventy 'sevens'ᵃ are decreed for your people and your holy city to finishᵇ transgression, to put an end to sin, to atone for

ᵃ24 Or 'weeks'; also in verses 25 and 26   ᵇ24 Or restrain wickedness, to bring in everlasting righteousness, to seal up vision and prophecy and to anoint the most holy.*a*

25"Know and understand this: From the issuing of the decree*b* to restore and rebuild Jerusalem until the Anointed One,*c* the ruler, comes, there will be seven 'sevens,' and sixty-two 'sevens.' It will be rebuilt with streets and a trench, but in times of trouble. **26**After the sixty-two 'sevens,' the Anointed One will be cut off and will have nothing.*d* The people of the ruler who will come will destroy the city and the sanctuary. The end will come like a flood: War will continue until the end, and desolations have been decreed. **27**He will confirm a covenant with many for one 'seven.'*e* In the middle of the 'seven'*e* he will put an end to sacrifice and offering. And on a wing ⌐of the temple⌐ he will set up an abomination that causes desolation, until the end that is decreed is poured out on him.*f*" *g*

Daniel's Vision of a Man

10 In the third year of Cyrus king of Persia, a revelation was given to Daniel (who was called Belteshazzar). Its message was true and it concerned a great war.*h* The understanding of the message came to him in a vision.

2At that time I, Daniel, mourned for three weeks. **3**I ate no choice food; no meat or wine touched my lips; and I used no lotions at all until the three weeks were over.

4On the twenty-fourth day of the first month, as I was standing on the bank of the great river, the Tigris, **5**I looked up and there before me was a man dressed in linen, with a belt of the finest gold around his waist. **6**His body was like chrysolite, his face like lightning, his eyes like flaming torches, his arms and legs like the gleam of burnished bronze, and his voice like the sound of a multitude.

7I, Daniel, was the only one who saw the vision; the men with me did not see it, but such terror overwhelmed them that they fled and hid themselves. **8**So I was left alone, gazing at this great vision; I had no strength left, my face turned deathly pale and I was helpless. **9**Then I heard him speaking, and as I listened to him, I fell into a deep sleep, my face to the ground.

10A hand touched me and set me trembling on my hands and knees. **11**He said, "Daniel, you who are highly esteemed, consider carefully the words I am about to speak to you, and stand up, for I have now been sent to you." And when he said this to me, I stood up trembling.

12Then he continued, "Do not be afraid, Daniel. Since the first day that you set your mind to gain understanding and to humble yourself before your God, your words were heard, and I have come in response to them. **13**But the prince of the Persian kingdom resisted me twenty-one days. Then Michael, one of the chief princes, came to help me, because I was detained there with the king of Persia. **14**Now I have come to explain to you what will happen to your people in the future, for the vision concerns a time yet to come."

15While he was saying this to me, I bowed with my face toward the ground and was speechless. **16**Then one who looked like a man*i* touched my lips, and I opened my mouth and began to

the "abomination that causes desolation" (v. 27; 11:31; 12:11): Idolmaking? State-church war? Armageddon? In the Gospels, what is it (see Mt 24:15; Mk 13:14)?

1. For Daniel and Jesus, is the emphasis on what the future holds? Or on who holds the future? **2.** For you, what is the Gospel in this passage?

1. When have you been scared stiff? What experiences have left you drained? How did someone help you through? **2.** How do you feel when touched physically by your spouse? Sweetheart? Parent? Child? A friend? A stranger?

1. Daniel's Babylonian name links him with the past. What other links orient the reader in these opening verses? **2.** Some see Christ in verses 5–6. How is this fantastic image like the one in Ezekiel 1 or Revelation 1:12–16? Do you think these are different images of the same divine figure? Why? Do these images fit your picture of Jesus? Why or why not? **3.** If Daniel's companions did not see this figure, what caused them to become terrified (v. 7)? How did they "know" something they did not "see"? How does their experience compare with Saul's Damascus road experience (see Ac 9:7)? **4.** What impact does this rendezvous have on Daniel (vv. 8–10)? What brings him to his feet? **5.** What in this continuing encounter (vv. 12–19) would you find comforting? Scary? Why? **6.** How many times do God's messengers "touch" Daniel (vv. 10–18)? What does the progression of these touching moments say about Daniel? About God's means of self-revelation?

1. Repeatedly Daniel is told he is "highly esteemed" (vv. 11,19; see 9:23)? Is it as tough for you to trust such good news from God? How so? Who in your circles needs to hear this good news? **2.** How has God "touched" your life? What new strength and resources can you now embrace due to his touch? **3.** Daniel finds that messengers from God are friendly (vv. 10–19), though at first terrifying

a24 Or *Most Holy Place;* or *most holy One*   *b25* Or *word*   *c25* Or *an anointed one;* also in verse 26   *d26* Or *off and will have no one;* or *off, but not for himself*   *e27* Or *'week'*   *f27* Or *it*   *g27* Or *And one who causes desolation will come upon the pinnacle of the abominable* ⌐*temple*⌐*, until the end that is decreed is poured out on the desolated* ⌐*city*⌐   *h1* Or *true and burdensome*   *i16* Most manuscripts of the Masoretic Text; one manuscript of the Masoretic Text, Dead Sea Scrolls and Septuagint *Then something that looked like a man's hand*

and draining (vv. 5–9). What does this mean for you? Other Christians? **4.** Daniel's prayer seems to have been opposed by an evil power. When has this happened to you? How did you persevere?

1. What war experience have you had: (a) As a veteran? (b) a friend, relative or spouse of a As a veteran? (c) As a victim? (d) As a protester? (e) From books and movies? (f) As a war buff, collecting relics, memorabilia? (g) As a kid, playing war games? (h) Other? **2.** If you could relive any of those wars as a war hero or commanding general, which war would you choose and why? **3.** What feelings arise within when you sing *Onward Christian Soldiers*?

1. Would it matter to you that these kings and their successors can be positively identified from secular history? What would that add to your appreciation of this passage? **2.** They are: in verse 2, the Persian kings (reigning 530–465 B.C.), among them, Xerxes who attempted to conquer Greece in 480 B.C.; in verses 3–4, Alexander the Great (336–323 B.C.); in verses 5–9, the kingdoms of Ptolemy and Seleucus (323–223 B.C.); in verses 10–19, Antiochus the Great (223–187 B.C.) at war with various Egyptian kings; in verses 21–35, Antiochus IV Epiphanes (175–164 B.C.). Which king would you consider the most important for Daniel? Why? **3.** In describing the wars of the kings, what does Daniel have to say about such pitfalls as: Pride going before the fall? The fault of alliances? Abuse of power? Lack of honor among thieves? Futility of war? Illusion of security? Principle of just desserts? Rebel in the ranks? Spoils of war? Authority corrupts, and absolute authority corrupts absolutely? **4.** What happens "at the appointed time" (vv. 27,29,35)? (Note: Many think this specific "abomination that causes desolation" is the altar honoring

speak. I said to the one standing before me, "I am overcome with anguish because of the vision, my lord, and I am helpless. [17]How can I, your servant, talk with you, my lord? My strength is gone and I can hardly breathe."

[18]Again the one who looked like a man touched me and gave me strength. [19]"Do not be afraid, O man highly esteemed," he said. "Peace! Be strong now; be strong."

When he spoke to me, I was strengthened and said, "Speak, my lord, since you have given me strength."

[20]So he said, "Do you know why I have come to you? Soon I will return to fight against the prince of Persia, and when I go, the prince of Greece will come; [21]but first I will tell you what is written in the Book of Truth. (No one supports me against them except Michael, your prince. [1]And in the first year of Darius the Mede, I took my stand to support and protect him.)

The Kings of the South and the North

[2]"Now then, I tell you the truth: Three more kings will appear in Persia, and then a fourth, who will be far richer than all the others. When he has gained power by his wealth, he will stir up everyone against the kingdom of Greece. [3]Then a mighty king will appear, who will rule with great power and do as he pleases. [4]After he has appeared, his empire will be broken up and parceled out toward the four winds of heaven. It will not go to his descendants, nor will it have the power he exercised, because his empire will be uprooted and given to others.

[5]"The king of the South will become strong, but one of his commanders will become even stronger than he and will rule his own kingdom with great power. [6]After some years, they will become allies. The daughter of the king of the South will go to the king of the North to make an alliance, but she will not retain her power, and he and his power[a] will not last. In those days she will be handed over, together with her royal escort and her father[b] and the one who supported her.

[7]"One from her family line will arise to take her place. He will attack the forces of the king of the North and enter his fortress; he will fight against them and be victorious. [8]He will also seize their gods, their metal images and their valuable articles of silver and gold and carry them off to Egypt. For some years he will leave the king of the North alone. [9]Then the king of the North will invade the realm of the king of the South but will retreat to his own country. [10]His sons will prepare for war and assemble a great army, which will sweep on like an irresistible flood and carry the battle as far as his fortress.

[11]"Then the king of the South will march out in a rage and fight against the king of the North, who will raise a large army, but it will be defeated. [12]When the army is carried off, the king of the South will be filled with pride and will slaughter many thousands, yet he will not remain triumphant. [13]For the king of the North will muster another army, larger than the first; and after several years, he will advance with a huge army fully equipped.

[14]"In those times many will rise against the king of the South. The violent men among your own people will rebel in fulfillment of the vision, but without success. [15]Then the king of the North will come and build up siege ramps and will capture a fortified city. The

[a]6 Or *offspring*   [b]6 Or *child* (see Vulgate and Syriac)

forces of the South will be powerless to resist; even their best troops will not have the strength to stand. ¹⁶The invader will do as he pleases; no one will be able to stand against him. He will establish himself in the Beautiful Land and will have the power to destroy it. ¹⁷He will determine to come with the might of his entire kingdom and will make an alliance with the king of the South. And he will give him a daughter in marriage in order to overthrow the kingdom, but his plans*ᵃ* will not succeed or help him. ¹⁸Then he will turn his attention to the coastlands and will take many of them, but a commander will put an end to his insolence and will turn his insolence back upon him. ¹⁹After this, he will turn back toward the fortresses of his own country but will stumble and fall, to be seen no more.

²⁰"His successor will send out a tax collector to maintain the royal splendor. In a few years, however, he will be destroyed, yet not in anger or in battle.

²¹"He will be succeeded by a contemptible person who has not been given the honor of royalty. He will invade the kingdom when its people feel secure, and he will seize it through intrigue. ²²Then an overwhelming army will be swept away before him; both it and a prince of the covenant will be destroyed. ²³After coming to an agreement with him, he will act deceitfully, and with only a few people he will rise to power. ²⁴When the richest provinces feel secure, he will invade them and will achieve what neither his fathers nor his forefathers did. He will distribute plunder, loot and wealth among his followers. He will plot the overthrow of fortresses—but only for a time.

²⁵"With a large army he will stir up his strength and courage against the king of the South. The king of the South will wage war with a large and very powerful army, but he will not be able to stand because of the plots devised against him. ²⁶Those who eat from the king's provisions will try to destroy him; his army will be swept away, and many will fall in battle. ²⁷The two kings, with their hearts bent on evil, will sit at the same table and lie to each other, but to no avail, because an end will still come at the appointed time. ²⁸The king of the North will return to his own country with great wealth, but his heart will be set against the holy covenant. He will take action against it and then return to his own country.

²⁹"At the appointed time he will invade the South again, but this time the outcome will be different from what it was before. ³⁰Ships of the western coastlands*ᵇ* will oppose him, and he will lose heart. Then he will turn back and vent his fury against the holy covenant. He will return and show favor to those who forsake the holy covenant.

³¹"His armed forces will rise up to desecrate the temple fortress and will abolish the daily sacrifice. Then they will set up the abomination that causes desolation. ³²With flattery he will corrupt those who have violated the covenant, but the people who know their God will firmly resist him.

³³"Those who are wise will instruct many, though for a time they will fall by the sword or be burned or captured or plundered. ³⁴When they fall, they will receive a little help, and many who are not sincere will join them. ³⁵Some of the wise will stumble, so that they may be refined, purified and made spotless until the time of the end, for it will still come at the appointed time.

Zeus, set up by Antiochus IV Epiphanes in 168 B.C., typical of a later one Jesus warned of [see Mt 24:15; Mk 13:14] foreshadowing the Antichrist.) What does this imply about God's control of history, even heathen nations and kings? **5.** Which wars sound like "holy wars"? Why do you think so? What faith and wisdom do these Jewish resistance leaders display? With what "success" (vv. 32–35)? What precedent do they set for suffering Christians who "know God" and are martyred for it? **6.** From what vantage point does Daniel purport to be "telling the truth" (v. 2) concerning these kingdoms? How do you account for his accuracy: Prophecy written with remarkable foreknowledge? Or after the fact? What from this passage supports your view?

♡ **1.** From what you know of secular and religious history, what impresses you about someone's sudden rise to power and equally precipitous fall (from grace)? **2.** What is the place of political ambition for the Christian who wants to avoid the pitfalls described by Daniel? **3.** What are your feelings about "sons preparing for war" (v. 10)? What is your view on the call to Christians to defend, with force, certain human rights or freedoms? **4.** Daniel's portrayal of what it's like to be a "king's kid" is a bleak scene of betrayal and tragedy. By contrast, how do you see life as an heir to the victorious King?

ᵃ17 Or *but she*   *ᵇ30* Hebrew *of Kittim*

If you were able to do as you pleased next year, what might you do?

1. How do you see verses 36–45: (a) Continuing the description of Antiochus? (b) Prophesying about the coming Antichrist (of which Antiochus is a prototype)? (c) A "both-and" situation? Support your view from the text. **2.** In what will this Antichrist trust (vv. 38–39)? What fierce conflicts does this evil figure wage (vv. 40–45)? **3.** To what extent will he succeed? How will he meet his demise?

1. What assumptions do the arrogant have about God? Where in your life are these assumptions at work? **2.** How do Christians, churches and nations "honor a god of fortresses"? How do you rid yourself of such a fortress-mentality? **3.** Daniel proclaims a relevant word from God for his current crisis. What is your relevant word from God?

Which do you like better: Starting a task or ending it? Why?

1. For Daniel and his readers, what is the good news in verses 1–4? What is the bad news? **2.** This is the first and only use of the term "everlasting life" in the Old Testament. What does that tell you about what most Jews in Daniel's day believed (or didn't believe) about life after death? **3.** How does Daniel's embryonic doctrine of the Resurrection compare with the New Testament view that we are saved "by grace alone"? In this regard, what does it mean to be "wise"? To "lead many to righteousness" (v. 3)? **4.** Verses 1–4 imply that the kingdom of God is assured to the faithful and wise, but that destiny is born out of tribulation and soul-searching. How does that relate to the faith of Jesus (see Mk 13; Mt 24:8; Rev 12:1–6)? How does Daniel's view compare with Jesus' view of the Resurrection of the righteous and the wicked (see Jn 5:24–30)? **5.** Compare verse 9 with Revelation 22:10. How do you account for the difference? **6.** Did Daniel have all his questions answered (vv. 4,8–10)? What is left unanswered for Daniel (and you)?

The King Who Exalts Himself

36"The king will do as he pleases. He will exalt and magnify himself above every god and will say unheard-of things against the God of gods. He will be successful until the time of wrath is completed, for what has been determined must take place. 37He will show no regard for the gods of his fathers or for the one desired by women, nor will he regard any god, but will exalt himself above them all. 38Instead of them, he will honor a god of fortresses; a god unknown to his fathers he will honor with gold and silver, with precious stones and costly gifts. 39He will attack the mightiest fortresses with the help of a foreign god and will greatly honor those who acknowledge him. He will make them rulers over many people and will distribute the land at a price.ᵃ

40"At the time of the end the king of the South will engage him in battle, and the king of the North will storm out against him with chariots and cavalry and a great fleet of ships. He will invade many countries and sweep through them like a flood. 41He will also invade the Beautiful Land. Many countries will fall, but Edom, Moab and the leaders of Ammon will be delivered from his hand. 42He will extend his power over many countries; Egypt will not escape. 43He will gain control of the treasures of gold and silver and all the riches of Egypt, with the Libyans and Nubians in submission. 44But reports from the east and the north will alarm him, and he will set out in a great rage to destroy and annihilate many. 45He will pitch his royal tents between the seas atᵇ the beautiful holy mountain. Yet he will come to his end, and no one will help him.

The End Times

12 "At that time Michael, the great prince who protects your people, will arise. There will be a time of distress such as has not happened from the beginning of nations until then. But at that time your people—everyone whose name is found written in the book—will be delivered. 2Multitudes who sleep in the dust of the earth will awake: some to everlasting life, others to shame and everlasting contempt. 3Those who are wiseᶜ will shine like the brightness of the heavens, and those who lead many to righteousness, like the stars for ever and ever. 4But you, Daniel, close up and seal the words of the scroll until the time of the end. Many will go here and there to increase knowledge."

5Then I, Daniel, looked, and there before me stood two others, one on this bank of the river and one on the opposite bank. 6One of them said to the man clothed in linen, who was above the waters of the river, "How long will it be before these astonishing things are fulfilled?"

7The man clothed in linen, who was above the waters of the river, lifted his right hand and his left hand toward heaven, and I heard him swear by him who lives forever, saying, "It will be for a time, times and half a time.ᵈ When the power of the holy people has been finally broken, all these things will be completed."

8I heard, but I did not understand. So I asked, "My lord, what will the outcome of all this be?"

9He replied, "Go your way, Daniel, because the words are closed up and sealed until the time of the end. 10Many will be purified, made spotless and refined, but the wicked will continue to be

---

ᵃ39 Or *land for a reward*   ᵇ45 Or *the sea and*   ᶜ3 Or *who impart wisdom*
ᵈ7 Or *a year, two years and half a year*

wicked. None of the wicked will understand, but those who are wise will understand.

11"From the time that the daily sacrifice is abolished and the abomination that causes desolation is set up, there will be 1,290 days. 12Blessed is the one who waits for and reaches the end of the 1,335 days.

13"As for you, go your way till the end. You will rest, and then at the end of the days you will rise to receive your allotted inheritance."

What does this say about the basis of faith for a believer?

1. Do you expect to find your name "written in the Book"? 2. Daniel was told to go on with life even if he didn't understand. When have you had to cope in faith with the perplexities of life? 3. The bottom line for Daniel is that the royal power of the Most High God always triumphs over the kingdoms of men (7:11,26–27; 8:25; 9:27; 10:13; 11:45; 12:13). How is that evident for Daniel personally? For the kings and subjects he treats? For the readers he comforts? For you and your small group?

INTRODUCTION to
HOSEA

Book Study Outline: If you are using Hosea for a study course, here is a 7- or 14-week outline. Use the questions in the margin for your group agenda:

🍵 start meeting / 15 min.

📖 read & discuss Bible / 30 min.

♡ close meeting / 15–45 min.

Refer to the Questions and Answers in the front of this Bible for more information.

7-week plan	14-week plan	Personal Reading	Group Study Passage
1	1	1:1–2:1	Hosea's Prophetic Progeny
	2	2:2–23	Israel Ruined and Restored
2	3	3:1–5	Gomer Re-loved and Redeemed
	4	4:1–19	God's Case Against Israel
3	5	5:1–15	God's Wrath, Israel's Remorse
	6	6:1–11	Israel's Fickleness
4	7	7:1–16	God's Frustration
	8	8:1–14	Israel Warned, yet Wandering
5	9	9:1–17	From the Pinnacle ...
	10	10:1–15	... To the Pit
6	11	11:1–11	Israel In and Out of Egypt
	12	11:12–12:14	Israel Deceives, God Despairs
7	13	13:1–16	God's Anger, Israel's Arrogance
	14	14:1–9	Israel Confesses, God Blesses

Author: A prophet to the northern kingdom—Hosea, son of Beeri.

Date: Hosea's prophetic career spanned four decades, from the prosperous latter years of Jeroboam II (793–753 B.C.), to the 720s shortly before the fall of Samaria and the exile of Israel.

Theme: God's undying love for his people.

OLD TESTAMENT PROPHECIES FULFILLED

OLD TESTAMENT	NEW TESTAMENT
Immanuel's virgin birth	
Isaiah 7:14	Matthew 1:23
Messiah will come from Bethlehem in Judah	
Micah 5:2	John 7:42
Messenger (John the Baptist) who will prepare the way for the Messiah	
Malachi 3:1	Matthew 11:10
The Messiah's Triumphal Entry into Jerusalem	
Zechariah 9:9	Matthew 21:4–5
Christ will be abandoned by his disciples	
Zechariah 13:7	Mark 14:27,49–50
The Lord lays upon Christ "the iniquity of us all"	
Isaiah 53:4–12	1 Peter 2:21–25
Israel "will look on the one they have pierced"	
(Jesus's side pierced by a soldier's spear at the crucifixion)	
Zechariah 12:10	John 19:37
Christ will usher in the "new covenant"	
Jeremiah 31:31–34	Hebrews 8:7–13
The outpouring of God's Spirit at the Day of Pentecost	
Joel 2:28–32	Acts 2:16–21
Gentiles will be included in the people of God	
Hosea 2:23	Romans 9:25
The Messiah's kingdom will last forever	
Daniel 7:14,27	Revelation 11:15

Historical Background: The dominant faith of Israel during Hosea's time was not Mosaic Judaism but a mixture of the worship of Yahweh and the local polytheistic Baal religions. Israel was prosperous and complacent under Jeroboam II, but after his death, and a succession of six kings in 30 years, life became increasingly insecure and the nation's resources weakened. Israel stubbornly sought help from other nations instead of from the Lord.

Characteristics: Hosea's language relies heavily upon the covenant stipulations of blessings and curses (see Lev 26; Dt 28–32). While reciting the case against Israel and the consequential curses she will face, Hosea interjects God's promise ultimately to restore her to the land and to himself in covenant faithfulness. The question of Gomer (ch. 1–3) is intriguing. Is the story allegorical or is it meant to be taken literally? The precise nature of Gomer's relationship to Hosea cannot be established with certainty. Yahweh's purpose in this "enacted" prophecy is clear, however. Bound to the Lord by covenant, Israel still prostitutes herself and bears "children of harlotry." In word and deed, Hosea says that despite Israel's faithlessness, God remains faithful.

Hosea

1 The word of the LORD that came to Hosea son of Beeri during the reigns of Uzziah, Jotham, Ahaz and Hezekiah, kings of Judah, and during the reign of Jeroboam son of Jehoash*a* king of Israel:

Hosea's Wife and Children

²When the LORD began to speak through Hosea, the LORD said to him, "Go, take to yourself an adulterous wife and children of unfaithfulness, because the land is guilty of the vilest adultery in departing from the LORD." ³So he married Gomer daughter of Diblaim, and she conceived and bore him a son.

⁴Then the LORD said to Hosea, "Call him Jezreel, because I will soon punish the house of Jehu for the massacre at Jezreel, and I will put an end to the kingdom of Israel. ⁵In that day I will break Israel's bow in the Valley of Jezreel."

⁶Gomer conceived again and gave birth to a daughter. Then the LORD said to Hosea, "Call her Lo-Ruhamah,*b* for I will no longer show love to the house of Israel, that I should at all forgive them. ⁷Yet I will show love to the house of Judah; and I will save them— not by bow, sword or battle, or by horses and horsemen, but by the LORD their God."

⁸After she had weaned Lo-Ruhamah, Gomer had another son. ⁹Then the LORD said, "Call him Lo-Ammi,*c* for you are not my people, and I am not your God.

¹⁰"Yet the Israelites will be like the sand on the seashore, which cannot be measured or counted. In the place where it was said to them, 'You are not my people,' they will be called 'sons of the living God.' ¹¹The people of Judah and the people of Israel will be reunited, and they will appoint one leader and will come up out of the land, for great will be the day of Jezreel.

2 "Say of your brothers, 'My people,' and of your sisters, 'My loved one.'

Israel Punished and Restored

²"Rebuke your mother, rebuke her,
 for she is not my wife,
 and I am not her husband.
Let her remove the adulterous look from her face
 and the unfaithfulness from between her
  breasts.
³Otherwise I will strip her naked
 and make her as bare as on the day she was
  born;
 I will make her like a desert,
 turn her into a parched land,
 and slay her with thirst.
⁴I will not show my love to her children,
 because they are the children of adultery.
⁵Their mother has been unfaithful
 and has conceived them in disgrace.

---

a1 Hebrew *Joash*, a variant of *Jehoash*   *b6* *Lo-Ruhamah* means *not loved.*
c9 *Lo-Ammi* means *not my people.*

---

1. Are you named after someone? Who? What nicknames have you had? 2. What loyal friend sticks even closer to you than a brother or sister?

1. Why does God have Hosea marry an adulteress? How is God's covenant with Israel like that? 2. Do you think Gomer was loyal to Hosea at first? Why? Then what happened? (Who fathers her second and third children?) 3. What do the names of Gomer's three children mean? What would have been the reaction by local Jews to their births? 4. What hope is given (1:10–2:1)? What is meant by Israel being: (a) as "the sand on the seashore"? (b) "sons of the living God"? (c) "reunited" under "one leader"? (d) "brothers … sisters … loved one"?

1. Using the marriage metaphor, describe your relation to God, now and in the past. Have you ever left or "cheated" on God? Was God faithful anyway? 2. Where in your life could you use the hope of restoration Hosea offers?

---

1. Who's your favorite poet? Your favorite poem? Why? 2. Have you ever become engaged? When? How? If not, how might you imagine that event? 3. How would your feelings for your betrothed compare to any who may have betrayed you? How do you express your love or hate? By poetry?

1. How does Hosea feel about Gomer (vv. 2–13)? What will he do about that? Why does he deny their marriage? 2. Why does he want to expose and thwart her adultery (vv. 3–8)? What effect would further punishment (vv. 9–13) have on her? 3. What "adultery" is she guilty of (vv. 8,13)? Who then are her "lovers" (v. 5)? Her "husband" (v. 7)? Her "children" (vv. 4,23)? 4. Though the marriage was broken by adultery,

is divorce or reconciliation sought? Why do you think so? **5.** How do you account for the contrast between punishment and allurement (vv. 13–14)? What "desert" experience is Hosea referring to? What effect will this have and why? When and where had God "betrothed" Israel to himself initially? **6.** What changes will occur "in that day" (vv. 16–19)? What play on words do you see here and in the NIV text footnote (v. 16)? How might that explain the confusion of Israel's worship of Yahweh with the pagan Baal rituals? **7.** How will Israel respond to the Lord's marriage proposal (vv. 19–20)? How will the skies, earth and its resources then respond (vv. 21–23)? **8.** What is significant about Jezreel (v. 22) and the other name reversals? What does this reveal about the Lord's purpose in disciplining his own?

♡ **1.** Since we become slaves of whatever we yield ourselves to (see Ro 6:16), what are the "baals" (or masters) in your life? In what ways might you be serving them instead of God? What promise do these masters make to lure you into their service? **2.** How is the Lord's authority in your life different from these other masters? (Is God less demanding, or more so? Less forgiving, or more so?) **3.** When, if ever, have you outgrown your need for God? Have you ever felt rejected by him? What for? **4.** What "desert experience" or other trying circumstance brought you back to him? If you are *not* looking for God (as Gomer was not), how do you know if God *is* still pursuing you (as he did Gomer)? **5.** Using the marriage metaphor, how would you describe your present relationship with God: (a) Getting acquainted? (b) Good friends? (c) Engaged couple? (d) Newlyweds, still honeymooning? (e) On the rocks or unfaithful? (f) Growing old together? **6.** What "adulterous wife" or "prodigal son" are you burdened for these days? How could you be God's instrument of discipline and restoration in their lives? What impact would this have on you? On them?

She said, 'I will go after my lovers,
  who give me my food and my water,
  my wool and my linen, my oil and my drink.'
⁶Therefore I will block her path with thornbushes;
  I will wall her in so that she cannot find her way.
⁷She will chase after her lovers but not catch them;
  she will look for them but not find them.
Then she will say,
  'I will go back to my husband as at first,
  for then I was better off than now.'
⁸She has not acknowledged that I was the one
  who gave her the grain, the new wine and oil,
  who lavished on her the silver and gold—
  which they used for Baal.

⁹"Therefore I will take away my grain when it ripens,
  and my new wine when it is ready.
I will take back my wool and my linen,
  intended to cover her nakedness.
¹⁰So now I will expose her lewdness
  before the eyes of her lovers;
  no one will take her out of my hands.
¹¹I will stop all her celebrations:
  her yearly festivals, her New Moons,
  her Sabbath days—all her appointed feasts.
¹²I will ruin her vines and her fig trees,
  which she said were her pay from her lovers;
I will make them a thicket,
  and wild animals will devour them.
¹³I will punish her for the days
  she burned incense to the Baals;
she decked herself with rings and jewelry,
  and went after her lovers,
  but me she forgot,"

declares the LORD.

¹⁴"Therefore I am now going to allure her;
  I will lead her into the desert
  and speak tenderly to her.
¹⁵There I will give her back her vineyards,
  and will make the Valley of Achor[a] a door of hope.
There she will sing[b] as in the days of her youth,
  as in the day she came up out of Egypt.

¹⁶"In that day," declares the LORD,
  "you will call me 'my husband';
  you will no longer call me 'my master.'[c]
¹⁷I will remove the names of the Baals from her lips;
  no longer will their names be invoked.
¹⁸In that day I will make a covenant for them
  with the beasts of the field and the birds of the air
  and the creatures that move along the ground.
Bow and sword and battle

---

a 15 Achor means *trouble*.   b 15 Or *respond*   c 16 Hebrew *baal*

I will abolish from the land,
so that all may lie down in safety.
¹⁹I will betroth you to me forever;
I will betroth you in*a* righteousness and
justice,
in*b* love and compassion.
²⁰I will betroth you in faithfulness,
and you will acknowledge the Lᴏʀᴅ.

²¹"In that day I will respond,"
declares the Lᴏʀᴅ—
"I will respond to the skies,
and they will respond to the earth;
²²and the earth will respond to the grain,
the new wine and oil,
and they will respond to Jezreel.*c*
²³I will plant her for myself in the land;
I will show my love to the one I called 'Not my
loved one.*d*'
I will say to those called 'Not my people,*e*' 'You
are my people';
and they will say, 'You are my God.'"

Hosea's Reconciliation With His Wife

3 The Lᴏʀᴅ said to me, "Go, show your love to your wife again,
though she is loved by another and is an adulteress. Love her
as the Lᴏʀᴅ loves the Israelites, though they turn to other gods and
love the sacred raisin cakes."

²So I bought her for fifteen shekels*f* of silver and about a homer
and a lethek*g* of barley. ³Then I told her, "You are to live with*h*
me many days; you must not be a prostitute or be intimate with
any man, and I will live with*h* you."

⁴For the Israelites will live many days without king or prince,
without sacrifice or sacred stones, without ephod or idol. ⁵Afterward the Israelites will return and seek the Lᴏʀᴅ their God and
David their king. They will come trembling to the Lᴏʀᴅ and to his
blessings in the last days.

The Charge Against Israel

4 Hear the word of the Lᴏʀᴅ, you Israelites,
because the Lᴏʀᴅ has a charge to bring
against you who live in the land:
"There is no faithfulness, no love,
no acknowledgment of God in the land.
²There is only cursing,*i* lying and murder,
stealing and adultery;
they break all bounds,
and bloodshed follows bloodshed.
³Because of this the land mourns,*j*
and all who live in it waste away;
the beasts of the field and the birds of the air
and the fish of the sea are dying.

⁴"But let no man bring a charge,
let no man accuse another,
for your people are like those

Recall a broken relationship (with spouse, kids, boss). Were you able to fix it? How difficult was it?

1. What is the toughest part of what Hosea has to do? 2. Why must he buy Gomer? 3. What does Gomer's waiting have to do with Israel? 4. When does Israel return to seek God? Has this occurred?

When did God "buy" you back to himself? How so?

1. When has an injustice hit close to home for you? How did you express your opposition to it: Voted someone out of office? Wrote a letter to the editor? Boycotted? Pressed charges? 2. What was your adolescent rebellion like? Was it similar to that of your siblings? How so? 3. Did your folks ever urge you to avoid the same mistake an older brother or sister had made? Did you listen?

1. What does the Lord claim is lacking in Israel (v. 1)? How do these virtues relate to self, to others, to God? 2. What does God find instead (v. 2)? How do these virtues and vices compare with the Ten Commandments? What are the consequences of such a climate of evil? 3. Do you think the land and animals "wasting away" (v. 3) is merely poetic language? Why or why not? Is the

a19 Or *with;* also in verse 20　　*b19* Or *with*　　*c22 Jezreel* means *God plants.*
d23 Hebrew *Lo-Ruhamah*　　*e23* Hebrew *Lo-Ammi*　　*f2* That is, about 6 ounces
(about 170 grams)　　*g2* That is, probably about 10 bushels (about 330 liters)
h3 Or *wait for*　　*i2* That is, to pronounce a curse upon　　*j3* Or *dries up*

who bring charges against a priest.
⁵You stumble day and night,
and the prophets stumble with you.
So I will destroy your mother—
⁶ my people are destroyed from lack of
knowledge.

"Because you have rejected knowledge,
I also reject you as my priests;
because you have ignored the law of your God,
I also will ignore your children.
⁷The more the priests increased,
the more they sinned against me;
they exchanged^a their^b Glory for something
disgraceful.
⁸They feed on the sins of my people
and relish their wickedness.
⁹And it will be: Like people, like priests.
I will punish both of them for their ways
and repay them for their deeds.

¹⁰"They will eat but not have enough;
they will engage in prostitution but not
increase,
because they have deserted the LORD
to give themselves ¹¹to prostitution,
to old wine and new,
which take away the understanding ¹²of my
people.
They consult a wooden idol
and are answered by a stick of wood.
A spirit of prostitution leads them astray;
they are unfaithful to their God.
¹³They sacrifice on the mountaintops
and burn offerings on the hills,
under oak, poplar and terebinth,
where the shade is pleasant.
Therefore your daughters turn to prostitution
and your daughters-in-law to adultery.

¹⁴"I will not punish your daughters
when they turn to prostitution,
nor your daughters-in-law
when they commit adultery,
because the men themselves consort with harlots
and sacrifice with shrine prostitutes—
a people without understanding will come to
ruin!

¹⁵"Though you commit adultery, O Israel,
let not Judah become guilty.

"Do not go to Gilgal;
do not go up to Beth Aven.^c
And do not swear, 'As surely as the LORD lives!'
¹⁶The Israelites are stubborn,
like a stubborn heifer.
How then can the LORD pasture them

same thing true in your culture? How so? **4.** Why do you suppose "no man is to accuse another" (v. 4)? Who are "your people" and "your mother" (vv. 4–5)? **5.** What effect does their behavior have on the priests? Of what are the priests guilty (vv. 6–8)? How might they profit from the people's sins? **6.** What "wages of sin" will the people receive (vv. 9–11)? Are they personal or social? Limited or contagious? Why? **7.** Does the laxity of the priests excuse the people? Conversely, does their behavior indict the priests? Who does God hold accountable for the sexual immorality that is rampant (v. 14)? Why? **8.** What directed them in these paths and eroded their understanding (v. 12)? What is a "spirit of prostitution"? How does it hook its victim? What is its seductive impact on succeeding generations (v. 13)? **9.** What is God's concern for Judah? What does he urge them to avoid? How do the Israelites prove "stubborn" (vv. 16–18)? What future can Ephraim (Israel) expect (vv. 17–19)?

♡ **1.** Are you a "heifer" or a "lamb" (v. 16)? Give an example of your stubbornness or meekness. **2.** What causes moral or spiritual decline in individuals and in society? What knowledge or understanding is crucial in this regard (vv. 1,6,10,14)? Where do you see this situation paralleled today? How can you avoid being swept along? **3.** The priests were particularly responsible for Israel's moral decline (vv. 6,14). In your society, who are the people Hosea would hold responsible: (a) Rock stars? (b) Ad agencies? (c) TV evangelists? (d) College profs? (e) Counselors? (f) Government officials? (g) Other? Who profits from society's sins and sicknesses? **4.** Who is more successful in passing on wisdom to the next generation: The church, the family or the schools? Why is the passing on of wisdom and values such a crucial task? **5.** Israel's idolatry was obvious. Is ours more subtle? What idols do we tend to "give" ourselves to: (a) Careers? (b) Status symbols? (c) Relationships? (d) New age mysticism? (e) Wealth? (f) Military power? (g) Other? Do our idols make us more enlightened than Israel was back then? How do they erode understanding? **6.** What potential idol in *your* life might lure you away from God?

---

^a7 Syriac and an ancient Hebrew scribal tradition; Masoretic Text *I will exchange*
^b7 Masoretic Text; an ancient Hebrew scribal tradition *my*   ^c15 *Beth Aven* means *house of wickedness* (a name for Bethel, which means *house of God*).

like lambs in a meadow?
17Ephraim is joined to idols;
    leave him alone!
18Even when their drinks are gone,
    they continue their prostitution;
    their rulers dearly love shameful ways.
19A whirlwind will sweep them away,
    and their sacrifices will bring them shame.

Judgment Against Israel

5 "Hear this, you priests!
    Pay attention, you Israelites!
Listen, O royal house!
    This judgment is against you:
You have been a snare at Mizpah,
    a net spread out on Tabor.
2The rebels are deep in slaughter.
    I will discipline all of them.
3I know all about Ephraim;
    Israel is not hidden from me.
Ephraim, you have now turned to prostitution;
    Israel is corrupt.

4"Their deeds do not permit them
    to return to their God.
A spirit of prostitution is in their heart;
    they do not acknowledge the LORD.
5Israel's arrogance testifies against them;
    the Israelites, even Ephraim, stumble in their
        sin;
    Judah also stumbles with them.
6When they go with their flocks and herds
    to seek the LORD,
they will not find him;
    he has withdrawn himself from them.
7They are unfaithful to the LORD;
    they give birth to illegitimate children.
Now their New Moon festivals
    will devour them and their fields.

8"Sound the trumpet in Gibeah,
    the horn in Ramah.
Raise the battle cry in Beth Aven a;
    lead on, O Benjamin.
9Ephraim will be laid waste
    on the day of reckoning.
Among the tribes of Israel
    I proclaim what is certain.
10Judah's leaders are like those
    who move boundary stones.
I will pour out my wrath on them
    like a flood of water.
11Ephraim is oppressed,
    trampled in judgment,
    intent on pursuing idols. b
12I am like a moth to Ephraim,
    like rot to the people of Judah.

1. When you are betrayed or hurt by a close friend, what is your natural response: (a) Break off the relationship? (b) Forgive and bless, thereby "heaping burning coals on their head"? (c) Give them the "silent treatment"? (d) Give them a one-way ticket on a guilt trip? (e) Other? 2. When did you first learn the benefits of discipline: As a child or a parent? Illustrate.

1. What three groups are indicted here? To whom have they been a snare? Why does the Lord promise to discipline all of them? How had Israel (Ephraim) played the harlot? 2. How far have his people sunk in their corruption (vv. 4–7)? What is their root problem? 3. Hosea pictures God as being married to his people. What would it mean for Israel to acknowledge the Lord as her husband? What would it mean for her (and her children) to "adulterate" that relationship (v. 7)? With what results? 4. In "seeking the Lord" (v. 6) do they view him as a: (a) Husband? (b) Lover? (c) Local deity? (d) "John" or "pimp"? (e) Bothersome duty? How does this compare with their seeking him later (v. 15)? 5. What does Hosea envision for Israel (vv. 8–9)? Why use trumpets and horns? What's wrong with moving boundary stones (v. 10; see Dt 19:14)? 6. How is the Lord like a "moth and rot" to Israel and Judah (v. 12)? When consumed by the Lord, where do they turn for help? How is this like Gomer (see ch. 2)? Why is it so futile? 7. How does God intend to deal with Israel and Judah (v. 14)? Why such harsh treatment? When in their history did this actually happen (see 2Ki 17:5ff)? With what result (v. 15)?

1. How do you picture the God of Hosea: (a) Angry bully? (b) Jealous husband? (c) Frustrated father? (d) Jilted lover? (e) Determined dad? 2. What people in your life are close enough for you to influence by your actions? What consequences for them might your disloyalty to God have? 3. Have

---

a8 Beth Aven means house of wickedness (a name for Bethel, which means house of God).   b11 The meaning of the Hebrew for this word is uncertain.

you ever "taken your flocks and herds to seek the Lord," only to pursue other "lovers" at the same time? Could you be doing this now and be blind to it? **4.** God's discipline here is patient, progressive and purposeful (vv. 2,6–7, 9–10,14–15). How did Israel experience his discipline at each point? **5.** When the Lord disciplines, what are some of the early warning signals? What are the consequences of failing to heed these? **6.** Why must we hit bottom, like Israel, before we begin to look up? When have you, in your misery, earnestly sought the Lord? What did God have to take you through to restore you? Did you sense his love in that?

---

1. As a child, parent, boss or employee, when have you made or received an "empty promise"? Which one really hurt? **2.** Have you ever "let someone off easy," only to have them take advantage of you? How did you feel? What would be your response "the next time"?

1. Who appears to be speaking in these verses? What is curiously lacking in this "confession"? On what is their hope for a light sentence based? **2.** How does God view Israel's love and worship (vv. 4–6)? What does it mean to truly "acknowledge God" in our dealings with others? **3.** Who is charged with breaking the covenant (vv. 7–11)? What covenant could this be (see Ex 19:5–6 and Jos 24:16–27, for examples)? **4.** How might the priests be "ambushing" the people (v. 9; see 4:8)? **5.** Has Israel really sincerely repented (compare v. 10 with 5:3)?

1. Have you ever tried to hide from God behind an easy act of repentance? What sacrifices or "burnt offerings" did you try to please God with: (a) Church attendance? (b) Giving a larger tithe? (c) Praying more? (d) Fasting? (e) Other? **2.** Have you ever become frustrated or indignant when these actions didn't seem to work? What did you do then? What *does* make the Lord return like the "winter and spring rains"? **3.** On a scale of 1 (morning mist) to 5 (rock of Gibraltar), how would you rate the staying power of your love for the Lord?

---

[13]"When Ephraim saw his sickness,
  and Judah his sores,
 then Ephraim turned to Assyria,
  and sent to the great king for help.
 But he is not able to cure you,
  not able to heal your sores.
[14]For I will be like a lion to Ephraim,
  like a great lion to Judah.
 I will tear them to pieces and go away;
  I will carry them off, with no one to rescue
   them.
[15]Then I will go back to my place
  until they admit their guilt.
 And they will seek my face;
  in their misery they will earnestly seek me."

Israel Unrepentant

6 "Come, let us return to the LORD.
 He has torn us to pieces
  but he will heal us;
 he has injured us
  but he will bind up our wounds.
[2]After two days he will revive us;
  on the third day he will restore us,
  that we may live in his presence.
[3]Let us acknowledge the LORD;
  let us press on to acknowledge him.
 As surely as the sun rises,
  he will appear;
 he will come to us like the winter rains,
  like the spring rains that water the earth."

[4]"What can I do with you, Ephraim?
  What can I do with you, Judah?
 Your love is like the morning mist,
  like the early dew that disappears.
[5]Therefore I cut you in pieces with my prophets,
  I killed you with the words of my mouth;
  my judgments flashed like lightning upon you.
[6]For I desire mercy, not sacrifice,
  and acknowledgment of God rather than burnt
   offerings.
[7]Like Adam,[a] they have broken the covenant—
  they were unfaithful to me there.
[8]Gilead is a city of wicked men,
  stained with footprints of blood.
[9]As marauders lie in ambush for a man,
  so do bands of priests;
 they murder on the road to Shechem,
  committing shameful crimes.
[10]I have seen a horrible thing
  in the house of Israel.
 There Ephraim is given to prostitution
  and Israel is defiled.

[11]"Also for you, Judah,
  a harvest is appointed.

---

[a]7 Or *As at Adam*; or *Like men*

7 "Whenever I would restore the fortunes of my
people,
¹whenever I would heal Israel,
the sins of Ephraim are exposed
and the crimes of Samaria revealed.
They practice deceit,
thieves break into houses,
bandits rob in the streets;
²but they do not realize
that I remember all their evil deeds.
Their sins engulf them;
they are always before me.

³"They delight the king with their wickedness,
the princes with their lies.
⁴They are all adulterers,
burning like an oven
whose fire the baker need not stir
from the kneading of the dough till it rises.
⁵On the day of the festival of our king
the princes become inflamed with wine,
and he joins hands with the mockers.
⁶Their hearts are like an oven;
they approach him with intrigue.
Their passion smolders all night;
in the morning it blazes like a flaming fire.
⁷All of them are hot as an oven;
they devour their rulers.
All their kings fall,
and none of them calls on me.

⁸"Ephraim mixes with the nations;
Ephraim is a flat cake not turned over.
⁹Foreigners sap his strength,
but he does not realize it.
His hair is sprinkled with gray,
but he does not notice.
¹⁰Israel's arrogance testifies against him,
but despite all this
he does not return to the Lord his God
or search for him.

¹¹"Ephraim is like a dove,
easily deceived and senseless—
now calling to Egypt,
now turning to Assyria.
¹²When they go, I will throw my net over them;
I will pull them down like birds of the air.
When I hear them flocking together,
I will catch them.
¹³Woe to them,
because they have strayed from me!
Destruction to them,
because they have rebelled against me!
I long to redeem them
but they speak lies against me.
¹⁴They do not cry out to me from their hearts
but wail upon their beds.

1. When caught red-handed, what is your favorite defense plea: (a) Guilty, with an excuse? (b) Guilty, with no excuse? (c) Run from your accuser? (d) Pin the blame elsewhere? (e) Obscure the issue with irrelevancies? (f) Other? Cite a case in point. 2. Bread is a fascinating food. Have you ever made any or watched it being made? What do you associate with the smells of baking bread?

1. Why is God frustrated in his desire to pardon Israel? How widespread is the disease he would heal (v. 1)? What is wrong with Israel's view of God (v. 2)? 2. What does the oven image tell you about the people's conspiracy (vv. 3–7; compare 2Ki 15:8–30 for the historical basis of Hosea's image)? When and how does their passion blaze into open flame? What guilt do the kings share for their downfall? 3. What was wrong with Israel mixing with the nations (vv. 8–10)? What happens to a pancake cooked on one side only? What price were they paying for their failure to remain pure? What do the sapping of strength and graying hair indicate? Were the Israelites doing anything to stop the decay? Why not? 4. How and why is Ephraim (Israel) like a dove (vv. 11–12)? How will God deal with them? 5. How has Israel repaid God evil for good (vv. 13–15)? How will their confidence in Egypt come back to haunt them?

1. What's wrong with food, fun and fellowship as the basis for one's church group? In God's eyes what would be missing, as with Ephraim? 2. On what basis do you try to win God's favor: (a) His past goodness? (b) Your good behavior? (c) Your promise to do better? (d) His forgiving character? (e) His promise to bless his own? (f) On Christ's behalf? Which is the only adequate basis? 3. Like Ephraim, are there areas you have compromised (by "paying" for continued loyalty of friends) in your personal life? Church life? National life? What effect would you expect this to have in your life, church or nation, if you continued as though it didn't matter? 4. When you hear the Lord say, "I long to redeem you" (v. 13), what *verbal response* do you have: (a) Disbelief? (b) Self-deprecation? (c) Repentance? 5. Consider one specific need for repentance which this chapter

brings to your attention. What *action steps* will you take this week in response to the Lord's desire to redeem you?

---

1. Have you ever been awakened by trumpet blasts—perhaps during a worship service or morning reveille? What was your first thought? What did you do? 2. What do you do "like a whirlwind": Clean house? Mow the lawn? Do dishes? Race home from school or work? Or are you laid back, letting the whirlwind pass you by?

1. Why does Hosea sound the alarm? What is the danger? Why do eagles, or "vultures," hover? 2. What evidence is there that Israel's loyalty to God is shallow? Why do they forget God? How did men become kings in Israel at this time (see 2Ki 15:10,14, 25,30)? 3. When and why was the calf idol made (vv. 5–6; see 1Ki 12:26–30)? What resulted? 4. How will Israel reap what she sows (vv. 3,7; see Ge 6:7)? What is this "whirlwind"? In selling herself to her lovers, what hidden price does she pay (v. 8)? 5. Despite such infidelity, what is God's intent for Israel? What must be the first step in that redemption (v. 10)? Why? 6. What "sacred" objects does Israel possess (vv. 11–14)? In each case, how have they been misused? 7. What does "return to Egypt" (v. 13) mean for Israel? Does God's punishment fit the crime? How so? 8. What do Israel and Judah expect from their palaces and forts? Is that wrong? Where does true security come from?

1. Despite professions of loyalty to God, are you "rejecting what is good" (vv. 2–3) with: (a) Spouse? (b) Family? (c) Business? (d) Money? (e) Leisure? How might errors in these areas lead to an addiction or idolatry? 2. As a nation, do we worship "calves" (laws, buildings, weapons, etc.) of our own making? What sacrifices do we give to them? From this passage, what consequences can we expect if we continue? 3. Consider the "sacred objects" in your life. Are you in danger of worshiping what inspires you (creation, spiritual

---

They gather together[a] for grain and new wine
    but turn away from me.
[15]I trained them and strengthened them,
    but they plot evil against me.
[16]They do not turn to the Most High;
    they are like a faulty bow.
Their leaders will fall by the sword
    because of their insolent words.
For this they will be ridiculed
    in the land of Egypt.

Israel to Reap the Whirlwind

8 "Put the trumpet to your lips!
    An eagle is over the house of the LORD
because the people have broken my covenant
    and rebelled against my law.
[2]Israel cries out to me,
    'O our God, we acknowledge you!'
[3]But Israel has rejected what is good;
    an enemy will pursue him.
[4]They set up kings without my consent;
    they choose princes without my approval.
With their silver and gold
    they make idols for themselves
    to their own destruction.
[5]Throw out your calf-idol, O Samaria!
    My anger burns against them.
How long will they be incapable of purity?
[6] They are from Israel!
This calf—a craftsman has made it;
    it is not God.
It will be broken in pieces,
    that calf of Samaria.

[7]"They sow the wind
    and reap the whirlwind.
The stalk has no head;
    it will produce no flour.
Were it to yield grain,
    foreigners would swallow it up.
[8]Israel is swallowed up;
    now she is among the nations
    like a worthless thing.
[9]For they have gone up to Assyria
    like a wild donkey wandering alone.
Ephraim has sold herself to lovers.
[10]Although they have sold themselves among the
    nations,
    I will now gather them together.
They will begin to waste away
    under the oppression of the mighty king.

[11]"Though Ephraim built many altars for sin
    offerings,
    these have become altars for sinning.
[12]I wrote for them the many things of my law,
    but they regarded them as something alien.
[13]They offer sacrifices given to me

---

[a]*14* Most Hebrew manuscripts; some Hebrew manuscripts and Septuagint *They slash themselves*

and they eat the meat,
　but the LORD is not pleased with them.
Now he will remember their wickedness
　and punish their sins:
　They will return to Egypt.
¹⁴Israel has forgotten his Maker
　and built palaces;
Judah has fortified many towns.
But I will send fire upon their cities
　that will consume their fortresses."

Punishment for Israel

9 Do not rejoice, O Israel;
　do not be jubilant like the other nations.
For you have been unfaithful to your God;
　you love the wages of a prostitute
　at every threshing floor.
²Threshing floors and winepresses will not feed the
　　people;
　the new wine will fail them.
³They will not remain in the LORD's land;
　Ephraim will return to Egypt
　and eat unclean* food in Assyria.
⁴They will not pour out wine offerings to the LORD,
　nor will their sacrifices please him.
Such sacrifices will be to them like the bread of
　　mourners;
　all who eat them will be unclean.
This food will be for themselves;
　it will not come into the temple of the LORD.

⁵What will you do on the day of your appointed
　　feasts,
　on the festival days of the LORD?
⁶Even if they escape from destruction,
　Egypt will gather them,
　and Memphis will bury them.
Their treasures of silver will be taken over by
　　briers,
　and thorns will overrun their tents.
⁷The days of punishment are coming,
　the days of reckoning are at hand.
　Let Israel know this.
Because your sins are so many
　and your hostility so great,
the prophet is considered a fool,
　the inspired man a maniac.
⁸The prophet, along with my God,
　is the watchman over Ephraim,ᵇ
yet snares await him on all his paths,
　and hostility in the house of his God.
⁹They have sunk deep into corruption,
　as in the days of Gibeah.
God will remember their wickedness
　and punish them for their sins.

¹⁰"When I found Israel,
　it was like finding grapes in the desert;

1. Recall a time when you were sufficiently warned (about drugs, drinking, driving, etc.), but had to learn the hard way. What happened? What did you ultimately learn? Has it changed how you respond to "warnings"? **2.** Back then, what did you think of the person who warned you: (a) Fool? (b) Meddler? (c) Kill-joy? (d) Self-righteous prude? (e) Over-protective nanny? Now, how do you view that person's intent?

1. Various fertility cults were common among the people of this region. What link do you see here (also 10:12) between these cults and the harvest? What do these fertility rites say about who owned the land? About who gave the increase? How then does God regard their sacrifices and offerings to him (vv. 1–4)? **2.** What has happened to Israel in verses 5–7? Who (or what) has taken over the land (see 8:14)? **3.** What does Hosea cite as evidence of their perverse condition (vv. 7–8)? What are the "days of Gibeah" like (v. 9; see Jdg 19–20)? What impact would this comparison have on Hosea's audience? **4.** Compare God's feeling for Israel *then* (v. 10) and *now* (vv. 12–13, 15–16). When did their relationship with God begin to turn sour (see Nu 25:1–3)? How long has God been patient? How are they now reaping what their fathers sowed? Is God unjust in this? Why or why not? **5.** What was Ephraim's "glory" (v. 11; see Ge 41:52; 48:16,19)? How is the punishment related to her sin? How had Hosea's treatment of Gomer set the stage for this? **6.** In verse 14, is Hosea asking for *compassion* or *vengeance*? How so? **7.** What emotion do you hear in Hosea's prediction (v.17): Horror? Anger? Sadness? Despair? Smugness?

1. During this period, Israel made a show of worshiping God while observing the fertility cults to ensure a healthy harvest.

ᵃ3 That is, ceremonially unclean　　ᵇ8 Or *The prophet is the watchman over Ephraim,*
/ *the people of my God*

What are some standard practices for ensuring success today: (a) Cheating on a test? (b) Cutting corners? (c) "Greasing" a client's palm? (d) Taking a "cut"? (e) Undercutting the competition? (f) Searching for "loopholes"? (g) Other? How is your allegiance to God "supplemented" by keeping today's cultural "fertility cults"? **2.** What do these practices say about who we really think is responsible for our prosperity? What kind of "bondage" can these things lead us into? How is it people become "as vile as the thing they love" (v. 10)? **3.** In what ways is the person who upholds God's standard in your culture considered a "fool" or a "maniac" (v. 7)? Have you ever felt this way about pro-lifers? TV evangelists? Nuclear freeze-niks? Conscientious objectors? Social prophets? Creationists? **4.** Have you ever been treated badly, like Hosea, because of some radical expression of your Christian faith? What happened?

1. Who was voted "most likely to succeed" in your graduating class? Did their "product" match their "promise"? What do you think is the reason for that? **2.** If you have been away from home for a while (summer camp or overseas trip), what do you dream of doing when you get back?

1. What had Israel done all these years with the blessing of God (v. 1)? What should they have done with the "sacred stones" present in the land (see Dt 16:21–22)? As a result, what happened? What will God do now? In addition to their idols, what had Israel been trusting in (v. 3)? What will happen to both of these "security blankets" (vv. 5–8)? **2.** What were the "evildoers" in Gibeah: Jewish or Gentile (see Jdg 19–20)? What was the lesson for

when I saw your fathers,
    it was like seeing the early fruit on the fig tree.
But when they came to Baal Peor,
    they consecrated themselves to that shameful idol
and became as vile as the thing they loved.
11Ephraim's glory will fly away like a bird—
    no birth, no pregnancy, no conception.
12Even if they rear children,
    I will bereave them of every one.
Woe to them
    when I turn away from them!
13I have seen Ephraim, like Tyre,
    planted in a pleasant place.
But Ephraim will bring out
    their children to the slayer."

14Give them, O LORD—
    what will you give them?
Give them wombs that miscarry
    and breasts that are dry.

15"Because of all their wickedness in Gilgal,
    I hated them there.
Because of their sinful deeds,
    I will drive them out of my house.
I will no longer love them;
    all their leaders are rebellious.
16Ephraim is blighted,
    their root is withered,
    they yield no fruit.
Even if they bear children,
    I will slay their cherished offspring."

17My God will reject them
    because they have not obeyed him;
    they will be wanderers among the nations.

10 Israel was a spreading vine;
    he brought forth fruit for himself.
As his fruit increased,
    he built more altars;
as his land prospered,
    he adorned his sacred stones.
2Their heart is deceitful,
    and now they must bear their guilt.
The LORD will demolish their altars
    and destroy their sacred stones.

3Then they will say, "We have no king
    because we did not revere the LORD.
But even if we had a king,
    what could he do for us?"
4They make many promises,
    take false oaths
    and make agreements;
therefore lawsuits spring up
    like poisonous weeds in a plowed field.
5The people who live in Samaria fear

for the calf-idol of Beth Aven. [a]
Its people will mourn over it,
and so will its idolatrous priests,
those who had rejoiced over its splendor,
because it is taken from them into exile.
[6]It will be carried to Assyria
as tribute for the great king.
Ephraim will be disgraced;
Israel will be ashamed of its wooden idols. [b]
[7]Samaria and its king will float away
like a twig on the surface of the waters.
[8]The high places of wickedness[c] will be
destroyed—
it is the sin of Israel.
Thorns and thistles will grow up
and cover their altars.
Then they will say to the mountains, "Cover us!"
and to the hills, "Fall on us!"

[9]"Since the days of Gibeah, you have sinned,
O Israel,
and there you have remained. [d]
Did not war overtake
the evildoers in Gibeah?
[10]When I please, I will punish them;
nations will be gathered against them
to put them in bonds for their double sin.
[11]Ephraim is a trained heifer
that loves to thresh;
so I will put a yoke
on her fair neck.
I will drive Ephraim,
Judah must plow,
and Jacob must break up the ground.
[12]Sow for yourselves righteousness,
reap the fruit of unfailing love,
and break up your unplowed ground;
for it is time to seek the LORD,
until he comes
and showers righteousness on you.
[13]But you have planted wickedness,
you have reaped evil,
you have eaten the fruit of deception.
Because you have depended on your own strength
and on your many warriors,
[14]the roar of battle will rise against your people,
so that all your fortresses will be devastated—
as Shalman devastated Beth Arbel on the day of
battle,
when mothers were dashed to the ground with
their children.
[15]Thus will it happen to you, O Bethel,
because your wickedness is great.
When that day dawns,
the king of Israel will be completely destroyed.

all of Israel? How is Hosea applying this lesson in the present circumstance? What is the "double sin" of Israel (v. 10)? What is the "yoke" she can expect (v. 11)? **3.** What laws of sowing and reaping do you see here (vv. 12–13)? Which has Israel chosen? What crop can she expect to reap? Was there no other way? Why do you suppose Israel didn't take it? **4.** Despite the certainty of Israel's punishment, what hope might Hosea's treatment of Gomer have given to Hosea's listeners?

1. What is the "spirit" behind the idols that are popular in our society: Power? Material prosperity? Status? Pleasure? **2.** How has God blessed you and allowed your harvest to prosper? Are you using these blessings to honor him and further his work, or to satisfy and enhance your own ends? **3.** Where do you look for help when in need: Self? Others? God? Have you made any "unholy alliances"? How can you begin to break them in the next week? **4.** What is the "unplowed ground" in your life that must be "turned over"? Is there some area in which you are not allowing God to be Master? Take a moment now and give this area to him. What result can you expect if you continue to commit this area to his Lordship (v. 12)?

[a]5 Beth Aven means house of wickedness (a name for Bethel, which means house of God).   [b]6 Or its counsel   [c]8 Hebrew aven, a reference to Beth Aven (a derogatory name for Bethel)   [d]9 Or there a stand was taken

1. Were you more compliant or strong-willed as a child? How are your children like you? 2. At what age are children the most adorable to you? Most aggravating? Why those ages? 3. What is your earliest memory of Mom or Dad helping you master some activity?

1. What images describe God's relationship to Israel (vv. 1–4)? Which image seems particularly female? Have you ever thought of God as female, as well as male? 2. What impact did that parental love have on Israel (vv. 2–7; compare Dt 21:18–21; Isa 1:2–20)? Why will they return to bondage (v. 5)? 3. Why won't God deliver them, even if they call to him (v. 7)? What is God's dilemma in verses 8–9? (For the history of Admah and Zeboiim, see Dt 29:23.) 4. What in God's character and covenant prompt him to turn from his plan to destroy Israel (v. 9; see Dt 4:27–31)? 5. How will God restore them (vv. 10–11)? What hope would this promise give to the faithful?

1. When have you found painful discipline necessary? How did you feel, carrying out the sentence? Did you ever change your mind about doing so? Why? 2. How has God shown a parent's love to you? In what ways have you spurned that love? 3. How is Hosea's story like Abram's, who reasoned with God to spare Sodom (see Ge 18:16–33)? Like the father who waited for the prodigal son (see Lk 15:11–31)? 4. How are God's justice and mercy reconciled in each case? How has God reconciled his justice and mercy toward you, in Christ? What is the only pre-condition in order to be restored to him? 5. What comfort do you take in God's enduring love? How will you share that with those who have yet to "come home"?

What stories about your ancestors convey values (the value of thrift, completing your education, etc.)? Whom do you identify with most in your family tree?

1. How does Hosea picture Ephraim's (Israel's) dealings with Assyria and Egypt? What was Israel trying to do in her diplomacy with both powers (v. 1; see 2Ki 17:3–4)? What deceit was involved in these political dealings? 2. In

God's Love for Israel

11

"When Israel was a child, I loved him,
   and out of Egypt I called my son.
²But the more I[a] called Israel,
   the further they went from me.[b]
They sacrificed to the Baals
   and they burned incense to images.
³It was I who taught Ephraim to walk,
   taking them by the arms;
but they did not realize
   it was I who healed them.
⁴I led them with cords of human kindness,
   with ties of love;
I lifted the yoke from their neck
   and bent down to feed them.

⁵"Will they not return to Egypt
   and will not Assyria rule over them
   because they refuse to repent?
⁶Swords will flash in their cities,
   will destroy the bars of their gates
   and put an end to their plans.
⁷My people are determined to turn from me.
   Even if they call to the Most High,
   he will by no means exalt them.

⁸"How can I give you up, Ephraim?
   How can I hand you over, Israel?
How can I treat you like Admah?
   How can I make you like Zeboiim?
My heart is changed within me;
   all my compassion is aroused.
⁹I will not carry out my fierce anger,
   nor will I turn and devastate Ephraim.
For I am God, and not man—
   the Holy One among you.
I will not come in wrath.[c]
¹⁰They will follow the LORD;
   he will roar like a lion.
When he roars,
   his children will come trembling from the west.
¹¹They will come trembling
   like birds from Egypt,
   like doves from Assyria.
I will settle them in their homes,"
   declares the LORD.

Israel's Sin

¹²Ephraim has surrounded me with lies,
   the house of Israel with deceit.
And Judah is unruly against God,
   even against the faithful Holy One.

12

¹Ephraim feeds on the wind;
   he pursues the east wind all day
   and multiplies lies and violence.
He makes a treaty with Assyria
   and sends olive oil to Egypt.

[a]2 Some Septuagint manuscripts; Hebrew *they*   [b]2 Septuagint; Hebrew *them*
[c]9 Or *come against any city*

²The Lord has a charge to bring against Judah;
  he will punish Jacob*a* according to his ways
  and repay him according to his deeds.
³In the womb he grasped his brother's heel;
  as a man he struggled with God.
⁴He struggled with the angel and overcame him;
  he wept and begged for his favor.
He found him at Bethel
  and talked with him there—
⁵the Lord God Almighty,
  the Lord is his name of renown!
⁶But you must return to your God;
  maintain love and justice,
  and wait for your God always.

⁷The merchant uses dishonest scales;
  he loves to defraud.
⁸Ephraim boasts,
  "I am very rich; I have become wealthy.
With all my wealth they will not find in me
  any iniquity or sin."

⁹"I am the Lord your God,
  ⌊who brought you⌋ out of*b* Egypt;
I will make you live in tents again,
  as in the days of your appointed feasts.
¹⁰I spoke to the prophets,
  gave them many visions
  and told parables through them."

¹¹Is Gilead wicked?
  Its people are worthless!
Do they sacrifice bulls in Gilgal?
  Their altars will be like piles of stones
  on a plowed field.
¹²Jacob fled to the country of Aram*c*;
  Israel served to get a wife,
  and to pay for her he tended sheep.
¹³The Lord used a prophet to bring Israel up from
    Egypt,
  by a prophet he cared for him.
¹⁴But Ephraim has bitterly provoked him to anger;
  his Lord will leave upon him the guilt of his
    bloodshed
  and will repay him for his contempt.

The Lord's Anger Against Israel

13 When Ephraim spoke, men trembled;
  he was exalted in Israel.
  But he became guilty of Baal worship and died.
²Now they sin more and more;
  they make idols for themselves from their
    silver,
  cleverly fashioned images,
  all of them the work of craftsmen.
It is said of these people,
  "They offer human sacrifice

a2 Jacob means he grasps the heel (figuratively, he deceives). since you were in   c12 That is, Northwest Mesopotamia   b9 Or God / ever

making his case against Judah (and Israel), how does Hosea use the well-known stories about Jacob (vv. 2–5,12)? What did Jacob's name mean? How had he lived up to it in his dealings with Esau (Ge 25:24–34)? With Isaac (Ge 27)? With Laban (Ge 30:25–43)? What finally turned him around (Ge 32:24–30)? How was that change symbolized (see Ge 35:10–12)? 3. What is the punch line of this history for Israel (v. 6)? 4. How is Israel (Ephraim) "self-deceived" and "deaf" to God's overtures (vv. 8–10)? What would "living in tents again" bring to mind? 5. What analogy is drawn in verses 12–13? Why refer to "a prophet" rather than naming Moses? What hope does this analogy give to Israel in her situation? 6. Does Hosea foresee any escape from God's wrath (v. 14)? Is God rejecting, or fulfilling, his covenant (see Dt 4:25–31)?

1. Do you or your church try to live off your history or reputation in any way? How so? 2. Are Jacob's tactics (clever alliances, self-reliance and lip-service to God) a part of your life at all? How so? 3. Jacob, after years of scheming, was finally changed by a direct encounter with God. How are you being changed by knowing Christ? 4. Do you think the rich have more problems being Christians than the poor? How? 5. How has God cared for you by disciplining you? 6. Is God calling attention to something now, but you're ignoring him? What is it?

1. About what things are you jealous? Why? What are you likely to do to someone who threatens or steals that "precious possession"? 2. When have you greeted the sunrise? Have you ever tried capturing the morning mist or the morning dew? What happened?

1. What had made Ephraim (Israel) once so feared (v. 1; see Jos 2:9–11)? What does Hosea see as absurd and ironic about Israel's idol worship? How will they be like the four things in verse 3? 2.

What in God's character and covenant-keeping has Israel forgotten
(vv. 4–6)? How do they bite the
hand that feeds them (vv. 1,6,9;
see 12:8; Ex 20:1–3)? **3.** What
does God intend to do about that
(vv. 7–9)? Is this consistent with
his covenant? Why or why not (see
Dt 4:25–31)? **4.** How did Israel's
desire for a king deceive them (see
1Sa 8:6–9,20; 2Ki 17:4)? What
have they done to the One who
could save them? **5.** How is Ephraim a "child without wisdom" (v. 13)?
What desired effect did the birth
pangs *not* produce? What is the result for a child "unwilling" or unable
to be born? **6.** If the first two lines
of verse 14 were a rhetorical question (i.e., "Shall I ...?"), what would
Hosea's audience have understood
this to mean? What would it do to
their presumption of God's forgiveness and love (see 6:1–2; compare 1:6)? **7.** What devastation
does Hosea foresee (vv. 15–16)?
Does God's covenant and character demand it? How so?

1. Have your own desires
ever been self-destructive?
Any addictive behaviors, sub-
stances or relationships? How did
you treat those who tried to help
you? What saved you from completely destroying yourself with
these "hand-made idols"? **2.** What
warning is there for those individuals and churches who let success
go to their heads (v. 6)? **3.** What
makes you feel secure: (a) Job? (b)
Home? (c) Pension? (d) Spouse or
friends? (e) Health? (f) Other?
What would you rely on if these
were taken away? **4.** How might we
falsely presume upon God's forgiveness and favor: (a) "Serve" him
with time and money? (b) "Claim"
his promises? (c) Cry "crocodile
tears"? (d) Make plans and ask him
to bless them? (e) Other? **5.** When
you have experienced God's "rod,"
how have you felt his love?

and kiss[a] the calf-idols.' "
[3]Therefore they will be like the morning mist,
like the early dew that disappears,
like chaff swirling from a threshing floor,
like smoke escaping through a window.

[4]"But I am the LORD your God,
⌊who brought you⌋ out of[b] Egypt.
You shall acknowledge no God but me,
no Savior except me.
[5]I cared for you in the desert,
in the land of burning heat.
[6]When I fed them, they were satisfied;
when they were satisfied, they became proud;
then they forgot me.
[7]So I will come upon them like a lion,
like a leopard I will lurk by the path.
[8]Like a bear robbed of her cubs,
I will attack them and rip them open.
Like a lion I will devour them;
a wild animal will tear them apart.

[9]"You are destroyed, O Israel,
because you are against me, against your
helper.
[10]Where is your king, that he may save you?
Where are your rulers in all your towns,
of whom you said,
'Give me a king and princes'?
[11]So in my anger I gave you a king,
and in my wrath I took him away.
[12]The guilt of Ephraim is stored up,
his sins are kept on record.
[13]Pains as of a woman in childbirth come to him,
but he is a child without wisdom;
when the time arrives,
he does not come to the opening of the womb.

[14]"I will ransom them from the power of the
grave[c];
I will redeem them from death.
Where, O death, are your plagues?
Where, O grave,[c] is your destruction?

"I will have no compassion,
15   even though he thrives among his brothers.
An east wind from the LORD will come,
blowing in from the desert;
his spring will fail
and his well dry up.
His storehouse will be plundered
of all its treasures.
[16]The people of Samaria must bear their guilt,
because they have rebelled against their God.
They will fall by the sword;
their little ones will be dashed to the ground,
their pregnant women ripped open."

---

a2 Or "Men who sacrifice / kiss   *b4 Or God / ever since you were in*
c14 Hebrew Sheol

Repentance to Bring Blessing

14 Return, O Israel, to the LORD your God.
　　Your sins have been your downfall!
²Take words with you
　　and return to the LORD.
Say to him:
"Forgive all our sins
and receive us graciously,
　　that we may offer the fruit of our lips.ᵃ
³Assyria cannot save us;
　　we will not mount war-horses.
We will never again say 'Our gods'
　　to what our own hands have made,
　　for in you the fatherless find compassion."

⁴"I will heal their waywardness
　　and love them freely,
　　for my anger has turned away from them.
⁵I will be like the dew to Israel;
　　he will blossom like a lily.
Like a cedar of Lebanon
　　he will send down his roots;
⁶　his young shoots will grow.
His splendor will be like an olive tree,
　　his fragrance like a cedar of Lebanon.
⁷Men will dwell again in his shade.
　　He will flourish like the grain.
He will blossom like a vine,
　　and his fame will be like the wine from
　　　　Lebanon.
⁸O Ephraim, what more have Iᵇ to do with idols?
　　I will answer him and care for him.
I am like a green pine tree;
　　your fruitfulness comes from me."

⁹Who is wise? He will realize these things.
　　Who is discerning? He will understand them.
The ways of the LORD are right;
　　the righteous walk in them,
　　but the rebellious stumble in them.

1. If someone were to call you "fruitful," to what would they be referring: (a) Your garden? (b) Children? (c) Good deeds? 2. What do you like best about trees: Climbing? Swinging? Shade? Lumber? Fruit? Birds? What is your favorite tree?

1. What is different about the "return" pictured here (vv. 1–3; compare 5:6; 6:1–3)? What is the "fruit of our lips" (v. 2)? How will Israel show true repentance (v. 3)? 2. What does God promise to do and be for Israel (vv. 4–8)? What will Israel's future be like? 3. How does this relate to Hosea's daughter and second son (1:6–9)? How has God's anger been turned away? 4. When will this restoration to glory occur? Will Israel avoid exile (see Lev 26:40–45)? 5. Where had Israel sought prosperity (see 2:5)? What had she forgotten (v. 8; also 2:8)? 6. What does the name "Ephraim" mean (see Ge 41:52)? What is the source of that fruitfulness? 7. What does the wise person know (v. 9)? The wise society? What influence does it have on how they live?

1. What condition and promise does true repentance involve (see 1Jn 1:9; Lk 15:11–24)? 2. How has God's anger toward your sin been turned away (see Eph 2:3–5)? Can the consequences of sin always be avoided? What can we look forward to if we walk in covenant faithfulness with him (vv. 5–8)? 3. How are you wiser from your study of Hosea? 4. Has your health, your job or a broken relationship ever been "restored" to you? How? How did you feel? 5. What restoration project can you and your group take on, with the compassion of Hosea for Gomer?

ᵃ2 Or offer our lips as sacrifices of bulls   ᵇ8 Or What more has Ephraim

INTRODUCTION to
JOEL

Book Study Outline: If you are using Joel for a study course, here is a 4-week outline. Use the questions in the margin for your group agenda:

☕ start meeting / 15 min.

📖 read & discuss Bible / 30 min.

♡ close meeting / 15–45 min.

4-week plan	Personal Reading	Group Study Passage
1	1:1–20	1:1–12/Land-Eating Locusts
2	2:1–17	2:12–17/Heart-Rending Call
3	2:18–32	2:28–32/Promised Spirit
4	3:1–21	3:17–21/Blessed Zion

Refer to the Questions and Answers in the front of this Bible for more information.

Author: The prophet Joel, son of Pethuel (1:1). While there are 12 other Old Testament characters with this name, none of them can be identified with this prophet.

Date: The date is uncertain. Joel could have been written as early as the ninth and as late as the fourth century B.C. Since Joel uses quotes or paraphrases from several other prophets and does not refer to either the Babylonian or Assyrian Empire, a later date seems probable—sometime during the Persian period (539–331 B.C.).

Theme: A plague of locusts portends the Day of the Lord.

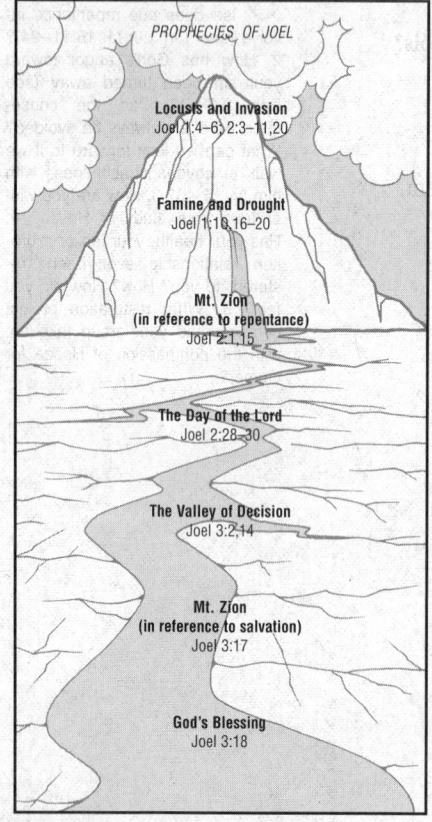

PROPHECIES OF JOEL

Locusts and Invasion
Joel 1:4–6; 2:3–11,20

Famine and Drought
Joel 1:10,16–20

Mt. Zion
(in reference to repentance)
Joel 2:1,15

The Day of the Lord
Joel 2:28–30

The Valley of Decision
Joel 3:2,14

Mt. Zion
(in reference to salvation)
Joel 3:17

God's Blessing
Joel 3:18

Historical Background: The occasion for Joel's prophetic ministry was a plague of locusts which was consuming Judah. The fact that no historical record of such a plague has endured does not mean this event was simply an allegorical device of the writer. Rather, this underscores the truth that even the worst natural or national disasters fade from memory when attention is turned to something that endures forever—an eternal God and his future kingdom (see 2:28–3:21).

Characteristics: The literary genius of Joel shines through in the book's structure, which flows smoothly from start to finish. Each section relates to what precedes it and what follows it. Hence, it helps to read the whole book in one sitting before studying its parts. The focus of the book is twofold: (1) The ever-present, practical problem of what to do about the locust plague (1:1–2:27); and (2) The future Day of the Lord, of which the current plague is a sign (2:28–3:21). In combining the two—event plus interpretation—Joel is performing the classic function of an Old Testament prophet, that of conveying God's revelation. Likewise, the borrowing of phrases from other prophets to speak a "new word" from the Lord in a new setting shows that Joel was probably an educated person, and had heard, if not read, the prophecies of Micah, Jeremiah and Isaiah. In 2:28–3:21, Joel expands the apocalyptic dimensions of these prophets. In Acts 2, the apostle Peter expounds the meaning of Joel's prophecy.

Joel

1

The word of the LORD that came to Joel son of Pethuel.

An Invasion of Locusts

²Hear this, you elders;
   listen, all who live in the land.
Has anything like this ever happened in your days
   or in the days of your forefathers?
³Tell it to your children,
   and let your children tell it to their children,
   and their children to the next generation.
⁴What the locust swarm has left
   the great locusts have eaten;
what the great locusts have left
   the young locusts have eaten;
what the young locusts have left
   other locusts*ᵃ* have eaten.

⁵Wake up, you drunkards, and weep!
   Wail, all you drinkers of wine;
wail because of the new wine,
   for it has been snatched from your lips.
⁶A nation has invaded my land,
   powerful and without number;
it has the teeth of a lion,
   the fangs of a lioness.
⁷It has laid waste my vines
   and ruined my fig trees.
It has stripped off their bark
   and thrown it away,
   leaving their branches white.

⁸Mourn like a virgin*ᵇ* in sackcloth
   grieving for the husband*ᶜ* of her youth.
⁹Grain offerings and drink offerings
   are cut off from the house of the LORD.
The priests are in mourning,
   those who minister before the LORD.
¹⁰The fields are ruined,
   the ground is dried up*ᵈ*;
the grain is destroyed,
   the new wine is dried up,
   the oil fails.
¹¹Despair, you farmers,
   wail, you vine growers;
grieve for the wheat and the barley,
   because the harvest of the field is destroyed.
¹²The vine is dried up
   and the fig tree is withered;
the pomegranate, the palm and the apple tree—
   all the trees of the field—are dried up.

1. What weather conditions (hot and humid, cold and windy, storm brewing) might depict the week you've just had? What weather forecast might fit the week ahead? 2. What is the closest you've come to experiencing famine or plague conditions?

1. What various groups does Joel address? What event has come to them? How does it affect them? 2. Why does Joel emphasize hearing and retelling (vv. 2–3)? What does that say about how faith is born and nurtured? 3. What famous plague in their recital of God's mighty acts would Joel's hearers have recalled (see Ex 10:13–15)? Since that other plague of locusts happened to God's foes, what makes this one especially unpalatable? 4. How does Joel describe this disastrous event? How complete is it? How do you respond to his vivid, poetic images? 5. What drama and progressive mood do you observe in the text? In Joel himself? What does the change in verbs tell you (vv. 3,5,8,11)? Where is the musical crescendo or literary climax in this section? (How final is "withered," v. 12?) 6. Is this plague a punishment for sin, or a test of faith?

1. How would the local TV or newspaper have covered these events? Pointing fingers at whom? Suggesting what remedies? 2. Do you respond to personal calamity as Joel's original hearers did? How so? Describe your response to one current or recent experience. 3. The joy of this nation was linked to external circumstances. On a scale of 1 (Never) to 10 (Always), how often is that true of you? 4. When your joy withers, what or who has God used to renew it?

ᵃ4 The precise meaning of the four Hebrew words used here for locusts is uncertain.
ᵇ8 Or *young woman*   *ᶜ8* Or *betrothed*   *ᵈ10* Or *ground mourns*

Surely the joy of mankind
   is withered away.

A Call to Repentance

[13] Put on sackcloth, O priests, and mourn;
   wail, you who minister before the altar.
Come, spend the night in sackcloth,
   you who minister before my God;
for the grain offerings and drink offerings
   are withheld from the house of your God.
[14] Declare a holy fast;
   call a sacred assembly.
Summon the elders
   and all who live in the land
to the house of the LORD your God,
   and cry out to the LORD.

[15] Alas for that day!
   For the day of the LORD is near;
   it will come like destruction from the
      Almighty.[a]

[16] Has not the food been cut off
   before our very eyes—
joy and gladness
   from the house of our God?
[17] The seeds are shriveled
   beneath the clods.[b]
The storehouses are in ruins,
   the granaries have been broken down,
   for the grain has dried up.
[18] How the cattle moan!
   The herds mill about
because they have no pasture;
   even the flocks of sheep are suffering.

[19] To you, O LORD, I call,
   for fire has devoured the open pastures
   and flames have burned up all the trees of the
      field.
[20] Even the wild animals pant for you;
   the streams of water have dried up
   and fire has devoured the open pastures.

An Army of Locusts

2
Blow the trumpet in Zion;
   sound the alarm on my holy hill.
Let all who live in the land tremble,
   for the day of the LORD is coming.
It is close at hand—
[2]   a day of darkness and gloom,
   a day of clouds and blackness.
Like dawn spreading across the mountains
   a large and mighty army comes,
such as never was of old
   nor ever will be in ages to come.

[3] Before them fire devours,
   behind them a flame blazes.

---

1. What social statement are you making with the clothes you wear: (a) Out of it? (b) In charge? (c) Dressed to kill? 2. If the clothes you have on were all made of burlap, how would you feel?

1. What is Joel calling the priests to do? Likewise, the elders? Why fast and pray (see Lev 16:29)? 2. What is the link between their current famine and the future "Day of the Lord" (vv. 14–15)? From Amos 5:18ff, what else might Joel be associating with this day when the Lord is clearly vindicated and manifest in earthly history? What does "the Lord's Day" mean nowadays? 3. How does Joel depict this drought-stricken land (vv. 16–20)? What is the point of picturing God as the Lord of plants and animals, land and water? 4. If locusts consume all that's edible, and fire destroys what remains, where then is hope (vv. 16,19)?

1. Do you know of any community or church gathering to cry out to God when resources have dried up? What purposes do such gatherings fulfill? 2. When have you felt like your resources (spiritual, financial, physical) were drying up or burnt out? Did you or could you cry out to God? Why or why not? What happened?

---

1. What does it take to rouse you from sleep: Two alarms? Three trumpets? Four jolts? 2. What memories of waking up do you have from camping days: Reveille? Calisthenics? Cold showers? 3. What is the funniest or most embarrassing consequence of your sleeping through an alarm?

1. How are the images of this army like, and unlike, the army of locusts that previously invaded the land (ch. 1)? How are these images like human invaders? How are they larger than life, taking on theological meaning? 2. How do these poetic images engage and exhaust all five senses to under-

---

a15 Hebrew *Shaddai*   *b17* The meaning of the Hebrew for this word is uncertain.

Before them the land is like the garden of Eden,
  behind them, a desert waste—
  nothing escapes them.
[4]They have the appearance of horses;
  they gallop along like cavalry.
[5]With a noise like that of chariots
  they leap over the mountaintops,
like a crackling fire consuming stubble,
  like a mighty army drawn up for battle.

[6]At the sight of them, nations are in anguish;
  every face turns pale.
[7]They charge like warriors;
  they scale walls like soldiers.
They all march in line,
  not swerving from their course.
[8]They do not jostle each other;
  each marches straight ahead.
They plunge through defenses
  without breaking ranks.
[9]They rush upon the city;
  they run along the wall.
They climb into the houses;
  like thieves they enter through the windows.

[10]Before them the earth shakes,
  the sky trembles,
the sun and moon are darkened,
  and the stars no longer shine.
[11]The LORD thunders
  at the head of his army;
his forces are beyond number,
  and mighty are those who obey his command.
The day of the LORD is great;
  it is dreadful.
  Who can endure it?

Rend Your Heart

[12]"Even now," declares the LORD,
  "return to me with all your heart,
  with fasting and weeping and mourning."

[13]Rend your heart
  and not your garments.
Return to the LORD your God,
  for he is gracious and compassionate,
slow to anger and abounding in love,
  and he relents from sending calamity.
[14]Who knows? He may turn and have pity
  and leave behind a blessing—
grain offerings and drink offerings
  for the LORD your God.

[15]Blow the trumpet in Zion,
  declare a holy fast,
  call a sacred assembly.
[16]Gather the people,
  consecrate the assembly;
bring together the elders,
  gather the children,
  those nursing at the breast.

stand them? 3. What might the trumpet (v. 1) signify: The call to fast? The call to action? The call of the Lord's coming? Or what? 4. Since his people have just experienced a locust plague and ensuing famine, why do you think Joel is dwelling on this theme of the coming "Day of the Lord"? 5. Who is at the head of this army? What does that mean?

1. How do you respond to the image of the Lord as the head of a destructive army? What jolts your senses about that? 2. If Joel were a street preacher in your community trumpeting this message about the coming "Day of the Lord," what would be the response from the people? From you? 3. Each of us may be part of the Lord's army (maybe not in the way described here); when, if ever, have you sensed God's call to do battle? With what or whom? 4. How does one endure the coming Day of the Lord (v. 11)? What feelings do you have about that day? Are they mixed?

1. When, if ever, have you fasted from food? Drink? Dates? TV? 2. What was your incentive? Results? 3. Would you do it again?

1. With destruction at the Lord's hand near, what does Joel expect? 2. What is meant by "rend your heart and not your garments" (v. 13)? What else should prompt them to return to God (see Ex 34:6–7; Ne 9:16–17)? 3. Why are daily temple offerings so key (v. 14; see Da 8:11–13)? For what blessing does Joel hope? 4. Who is this event for? Why "everyone"? Why does a bridal party "never" fast (v. 16; see Mk 2:19–20)? 5. What's the point in the priests' prayer for Israel (v. 17)?

1. Can repentance of heart be true without "fasting and mourning"? How? What would a spiritual fast include today? How would that differ from a spiritual

diet? **2.** What would corporate repentance require for your group? For the church? For the nation? What role should clergy take? **3.** Do others ask, "Where is your God" of your nation or you? When was that said of Christ (see Mt 27:43–46)?

---

1. Are your parents or spouse the "jealous" kind? What are they jealous about? When does their jealousy seem redemptive? **2.** What people or situations arouse your pity? Why? **3.** When have you seen nature "rejoice"? What thing in "the wild" brings you the most joy?

1. To what time does "then" in verse 18 refer? Do verses 18–27 assume the "Day of the Lord" has come already? Or was that day averted and still to be expected? Or both? Why do you think so? **2.** What does it mean that God is "jealous" for or takes "pity" on his people (see Ex 20:5)? How can God claim and enforce such an exclusive relationship with us? **3.** What specific "great things" does God do which correspond to the concrete situation of Israel (in 1:1–20 and 2:1–11)? What does this correspondence say about the effectiveness and completeness of God's restoration? **4.** What are some of the resulting changes in God's people which he brings about by his zealous restoration? What is the end result (v. 27) intended by God's answer to the priests' prayer (2:17)? **5.** What does this tell you about God's love, power and uniqueness? About God's care for creation? For his covenant people? **6.** Why do you think God responds so specifically to his people's needs and prayers?

1. Very few want to be objects of someone else's pity. Why would you or your church want God's pity? Describe a time when you believe God took pity on you or your church. What current situation might call for God's pity? **2.** In your prayer life, when has God granted you a deeper "knowledge" of himself? **3.** When and why have you felt a sense of shame: (a) Not knowing God was working in your life? (b) Enduring personal calamity? (c) Not living as a Christian? (d) Giving up too soon on God? On others? On self? **4.** In

Let the bridegroom leave his room
and the bride her chamber.
[17]Let the priests, who minister before the LORD,
weep between the temple porch and the altar.
Let them say, "Spare your people, O LORD.
Do not make your inheritance an object of
scorn,
a byword among the nations.
Why should they say among the peoples,
'Where is their God?' "

The LORD's Answer

[18]Then the LORD will be jealous for his land
and take pity on his people.

[19]The LORD will reply[a] to them:

"I am sending you grain, new wine and oil,
enough to satisfy you fully;
never again will I make you
an object of scorn to the nations.

[20]"I will drive the northern army far from you,
pushing it into a parched and barren land,
with its front columns going into the eastern
sea[b]
and those in the rear into the western sea.[c]
And its stench will go up;
its smell will rise."

Surely he has done great things.[d]
[21]   Be not afraid, O land;
be glad and rejoice.
Surely the LORD has done great things.
[22]   Be not afraid, O wild animals,
for the open pastures are becoming green.
The trees are bearing their fruit;
the fig tree and the vine yield their riches.
[23]Be glad, O people of Zion,
rejoice in the LORD your God,
for he has given you
the autumn rains in righteousness.[e]
He sends you abundant showers,
both autumn and spring rains, as before.
[24]The threshing floors will be filled with grain;
the vats will overflow with new wine and oil.

[25]"I will repay you for the years the locusts have
eaten—
the great locust and the young locust,
the other locusts and the locust swarm[f]—
my great army that I sent among you.
[26]You will have plenty to eat, until you are full,
and you will praise the name of the LORD your
God,
who has worked wonders for you;
never again will my people be shamed.
[27]Then you will know that I am in Israel,

---

[a]18,19 Or LORD was jealous . . . / and took pity . . . / [19]The LORD replied   [b]20 That is, the Dead Sea   [c]20 That is, the Mediterranean   [d]20 Or rise. / Surely it has done great things."   [e]23 Or / the teacher for righteousness: [f]25 The precise meaning of the four Hebrew words used here for locusts is uncertain.

that I am the LORD your God,
and that there is no other;
never again will my people be shamed.

The Day of the LORD

28"And afterward,
I will pour out my Spirit on all people.
Your sons and daughters will prophesy,
your old men will dream dreams,
your young men will see visions.
29Even on my servants, both men and women,
I will pour out my Spirit in those days.
30I will show wonders in the heavens
and on the earth,
blood and fire and billows of smoke.
31The sun will be turned to darkness
and the moon to blood
before the coming of the great and dreadful day
of the LORD.
32And everyone who calls
on the name of the LORD will be saved;
for on Mount Zion and in Jerusalem
there will be deliverance,
as the LORD has said,
among the survivors
whom the LORD calls.

The Nations Judged

3 "In those days and at that time,
when I restore the fortunes of Judah and
Jerusalem,
2I will gather all nations
and bring them down to the Valley of
Jehoshaphat.a
There I will enter into judgment against them
concerning my inheritance, my people Israel,
for they scattered my people among the nations
and divided up my land.
3They cast lots for my people
and traded boys for prostitutes;
they sold girls for wine
that they might drink.

4"Now what have you against me, O Tyre and Sidon and all you regions of Philistia? Are you repaying me for something I have done? If you are paying me back, I will swiftly and speedily return on your own heads what you have done. 5For you took my silver and my gold and carried off my finest treasures to your temples. 6You sold the people of Judah and Jerusalem to the Greeks, that you might send them far from their homeland.

7"See, I am going to rouse them out of the places to which you sold them, and I will return on your own heads what you have done. 8I will sell your sons and daughters to the people of Judah, and they will sell them to the Sabeans, a nation far away." The LORD has spoken.

9Proclaim this among the nations:
Prepare for war!

a2 *Jehoshaphat* means *the LORD judges*; also in verse 12.

---

these experiences, what do the promises given in verses 19 and 27 mean to you?

Can you keep a secret about love? Gifts? Birthdays? (Share about one.)

1. When is "afterward" (v. 28; see Ac 2:16ff)? Could these "last days" also include "today"? Why? 2. To Joel's people, what is unusual about the Spirit coming upon men and women? Likewise, to Peter's mixed audience (Ac 2:16ff)? What is unusual to you about Joel's prophecy? Why? 3. What does the Spirit do: Reveal God's will? Renew our energy? Recast the cosmos? Redeem the survivors? 4. How does this picture of the "Day of the Lord" differ from the previous one (2:1–11)?

What is the promise here for spiritual dryness? For spiritual exclusiveness and pride? For fear? For your group? Your church? Your world?

1. What "lost fortune" would you like to see returned to you? How might you get it back? 2. What is your favorite anti-war slogan: (a) "Peace is disarming"? (b) "Arms are for hugging, not war"? (c) "One nuclear bomb could ruin your whole day"? (d) "Make love not war"? (e) Joel 3:10a? (f) Other? 3. Which slogan fits how you maintain peace in your life?

1. "In those days" (v. 1) refers to when: (a) Sometime after Joel but before Christ? (b) After Christ but before now? (c) A time yet to come? (d) All of the above? (e) Nothing specific? Explain. 2. For what five things will the nations be judged (vv. 2–3)? How will they be "repaid"? 3. The "valley where the Lord judges" (vv. 3,12) is not a known geographical site. What then might Joel intend by naming such a place? 4. Why are the nations to be judged called to prepare for war (vv. 9–11), only to meet the Lord's warriors? What is the outcome of that war (v. 13)? 5. Is that outcome determined more by human decision "in the valley"? Or by divine fiat from where God sits? 6. Compare 3:10a with Isaiah 2:4 and Micah 4:3. Why do you think Joel reversed that traditional prophetic vision of peace? 7. If not peace, what promise from Joel can God's people count on (v. 16c)?

1. Reflect how people might be "sold" or "traded"? Is prostitution or child pornography a problem in your community? Likewise, refugee relocation and prisoners of conscience? What do you suppose God thinks of this? 2. How do you respond to Joel saying, "God will return on your heads what you have done"? 3. Does Joel disturb your image of God? How so? Does your image of God allow, preclude or demand this kind of judgment on sinful nations or persons? 4. What "payback" schedule are you on with creditors? With God? 5. When, if ever, have you felt slain in the "Valley of Decision"? When have you felt secure in the Lord's stronghold? What would get you out of the valley into the stronghold?

1. How does the word "then" ("so") relate this passage to the previous ones? How are God's judgment and salvation linked? Justice and mercy? Hope and despair? 2. What message does Joel intend with the contrasting images of 3:18–19? How is one like "Paradise lost," the other "Paradise regained"? How can one event pronounce both irrevocable doom and promise such abundant blessing (see Ps 107:33–36)? 3. How does the last promise (v. 21, offering forgiveness and fellowship) relate to the specific situation of Israel which prompted these oracles (ch. 1–2) in the first place?

1. If the presence of the Lord in Jerusalem made it holy (v. 17), then what does the Lord's presence in your life mean? What evidence is there of this? 2. If your privacy or property has been invaded one or more times, as with Israel, what comfort do you draw from Joel? How can the fountain of God's blessing heal the wounds inflicted by those invaders? 3. How can you imitate Joel today?

Rouse the warriors!
Let all the fighting men draw near and attack.
¹⁰Beat your plowshares into swords
and your pruning hooks into spears.
Let the weakling say,
"I am strong!"
¹¹Come quickly, all you nations from every side,
and assemble there.

Bring down your warriors, O LORD!

¹²"Let the nations be roused;
let them advance into the Valley of
Jehoshaphat,
for there I will sit
to judge all the nations on every side.
¹³Swing the sickle,
for the harvest is ripe.
Come, trample the grapes,
for the winepress is full
and the vats overflow—
so great is their wickedness!"

¹⁴Multitudes, multitudes
in the valley of decision!
For the day of the LORD is near
in the valley of decision.
¹⁵The sun and moon will be darkened,
and the stars no longer shine.
¹⁶The LORD will roar from Zion
and thunder from Jerusalem;
the earth and the sky will tremble.
But the LORD will be a refuge for his people,
a stronghold for the people of Israel.

Blessings for God's People

¹⁷"Then you will know that I, the LORD your God,
dwell in Zion, my holy hill.
Jerusalem will be holy;
never again will foreigners invade her.

¹⁸"In that day the mountains will drip new wine,
and the hills will flow with milk;
all the ravines of Judah will run with water.
A fountain will flow out of the LORD's house
and will water the valley of acacias.[a]
¹⁹But Egypt will be desolate,
Edom a desert waste,
because of violence done to the people of Judah,
in whose land they shed innocent blood.
²⁰Judah will be inhabited forever
and Jerusalem through all generations.
²¹Their bloodguilt, which I have not pardoned,
I will pardon."

The LORD dwells in Zion!

a 18 Or *Valley of Shittim*

INTRODUCTION to
AMOS

Book Study Outline: If you are using Amos for a study course, here is a 4- or 8-week outline. Use the questions in the margin for your group agenda:

start meeting / 15 min.

read & discuss Bible / 30 min.

close meeting / 15–45 min.

4-week plan	8-week plan	Personal Reading	Group Study Passage
1	1	1–2	2:6–16/Judgment on Israel
	2	3	3:1–15/Witness Against Israel
2	3	4	4:1–13/Cows of Bashan
	4	5	5:18–27/Justice Like a River
3	5	6	6:8–14/Perversion of Justice
	6	7	7:10–17/Amos Refutes Amaziah
4	7	8	8:1–14/Fruit Basket Upset
	8	9	9:11–15/Good News, Finally!

Refer to the Questions and Answers in the front of this Bible for more information.

Author: Amos, who came from the small town of Tekoa, was a citizen of the southern state of Judah, but ministered in the northern state of Israel, alongside the prophet Hosea. Amos was a shepherd (1:1) and fruit farmer (7:14), not a professional prophet.

Date: Amos ministered during the reigns of Uzziah, king of Judah (783–742 B.C.), and Jeroboam II, king of Israel (786–746 B.C.), possibly c. 760–750 B.C.

Theme: God's judgment on injustice.

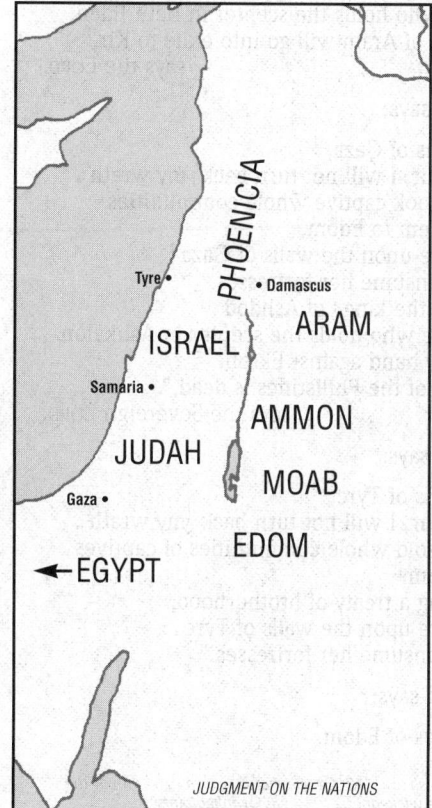

JUDGMENT ON THE NATIONS

Historical Background: By 800 B.C. both the northern kingdom (Israel) and the southern kingdom (Judah) had reached new political and military heights. Peace reigned and business was booming. Even religion was on the rise. However, the exterior calm belied Israel's inner disease. Idolatry, extravagant indulgence, and a corrupt judicial system ran beneath the surface. In this context, Amos calls for social justice as the foundation for true piety (5:24).

Characteristics: Whereas his contemporary, Hosea, focuses on the love of God and spiritual adultery, Amos focuses on the righteousness of God and social injustice. He often makes his points by use of a simple rhetorical question (e.g., 5:25). Amos speaks as a simple Judean farmer burdened for the materialistic nation of Israel. His prayer averts the total destruction of Israel (7:1–6), and yet his message was most unpopular. However, social acceptance didn't matter to one whose job was not on the line (7:12–15). In Amos, God roars like a lion (1:2) and brings hope only at the end (9:11–15). The book of Amos is constantly shadowed by clouds of judgment as the Lord reacts to the cruel social events in the land. Amos' message is an uncomfortable one in any age. Amos challenges us to examine ourselves and our society and to confront injustice wherever we find it.

Amos

1 The words of Amos, one of the shepherds of Tekoa—what he saw concerning Israel two years before the earthquake, when Uzziah was king of Judah and Jeroboam son of Jehoash*a* was king of Israel.

²He said:

> "The LORD roars from Zion
>   and thunders from Jerusalem;
> the pastures of the shepherds dry up,*b*
>   and the top of Carmel withers."

Judgment on Israel's Neighbors

³This is what the LORD says:

> "For three sins of Damascus,
>   even for four, I will not turn back ⌊my wrath⌋.
> Because she threshed Gilead
>   with sledges having iron teeth,
> ⁴I will send fire upon the house of Hazael
>   that will consume the fortresses of Ben-Hadad.
> ⁵I will break down the gate of Damascus;
>   I will destroy the king who is in*c* the Valley of
>   Aven*d*
> and the one who holds the scepter in Beth Eden.
>   The people of Aram will go into exile to Kir,"
>   says the LORD.

⁶This is what the LORD says:

> "For three sins of Gaza,
>   even for four, I will not turn back ⌊my wrath⌋.
> Because she took captive whole communities
>   and sold them to Edom,
> ⁷I will send fire upon the walls of Gaza
>   that will consume her fortresses.
> ⁸I will destroy the king*e* of Ashdod
>   and the one who holds the scepter in Ashkelon.
> I will turn my hand against Ekron,
>   till the last of the Philistines is dead,"
>   says the Sovereign LORD.

⁹This is what the LORD says:

> "For three sins of Tyre,
>   even for four, I will not turn back ⌊my wrath⌋.
> Because she sold whole communities of captives
>   to Edom,
> disregarding a treaty of brotherhood,
> ¹⁰I will send fire upon the walls of Tyre
>   that will consume her fortresses."

¹¹This is what the LORD says:

> "For three sins of Edom,

---

1. What is your vocation? If you could change vocations for a week, what would you try? 2. What "earth-shaking" event has happened to you within the last two years? How are you a different person today because of it? 3. This week, have the circumstances in your life been as gentle as a lamb or fierce as a lion?

1. Does Amos have the proper credentials to speak for God? Why should the people listen to him? 2. How might the people have reacted as the shepherd began preaching: (a) Hushed silence? (b) Joyous welcome? (c) Curious? (d) Concerned? 3. Verse 2 has been called Amos' theme verse. Hence, what do we have in store? 4. What do you suppose the people said among themselves as Amos spoke against their neighbors: (a) "They have it coming"? (b) "We are better than they are"? (c) "Whew! For a minute I thought it was us!"? (d) "Can we help in the destruction"? 5. How might they have reacted to the prophecy against Judah (2:4–5)? Is Judah's sin as grievous as those of Israel's foreign neighbors? If so, why? 6. Why would Amos say, "For three sins ... even for four"? Is he losing track of his sermon outline, stuttering, driving home a final point, or what? 7. How are the sins of Israel's neighbors similar? How are they different? Which of these sins are prevalent today? 8. By what standard will the nations be judged: (a) God's law? (b) The law of brotherly love? (c) The law of conscience? (d) The law of the land? What does this reveal about God's role in international affairs? Do you think Israel would have been surprised by this? Why or why not? 9. If you were to describe the God portrayed here in one word, would it be: (a) Loving? (b) Consistent? (c) Patient? (d) Mean? (e) Judgmental? (f) Angry? (g) Other?

1. When have you felt unqualified to do something for God (e.g., give an extemporaneous speech or teach a class of Junior High students), but did it anyway? How did you get past the fear?

---

a1 Hebrew *Joash,* a variant of *Jehoash*   *b2* Or *shepherds mourn*   *c5* Or *the inhabitants of*   *d5 Aven* means *wickedness.*   *e8* Or *inhabitants*

even for four, I will not turn back ⌞my wrath⌟.
Because he pursued his brother with a sword,
    stifling all compassion,ᵃ
because his anger raged continually
    and his fury flamed unchecked,
¹²I will send fire upon Teman
    that will consume the fortresses of Bozrah."

¹³This is what the LORD says:

"For three sins of Ammon,
    even for four, I will not turn back ⌞my wrath⌟.
Because he ripped open the pregnant women of
        Gilead
    in order to extend his borders,
¹⁴I will set fire to the walls of Rabbah
    that will consume her fortresses
amid war cries on the day of battle,
    amid violent winds on a stormy day.
¹⁵Her kingᵇ will go into exile,
    he and his officials together,"
                                        says the LORD.

2 This is what the LORD says:

"For three sins of Moab,
    even for four, I will not turn back ⌞my wrath⌟.
Because he burned, as if to lime,
    the bones of Edom's king,
²I will send fire upon Moab
    that will consume the fortresses of Kerioth.ᶜ
Moab will go down in great tumult
    amid war cries and the blast of the trumpet.
³I will destroy her ruler
    and kill all her officials with him,"
                                        says the LORD.

⁴This is what the LORD says:

"For three sins of Judah,
    even for four, I will not turn back ⌞my wrath⌟.
Because they have rejected the law of the LORD
    and have not kept his decrees,
because they have been led astray by false gods,ᵈ
    the godsᵉ their ancestors followed,
⁵I will send fire upon Judah
    that will consume the fortresses of Jerusalem."

Judgment on Israel

⁶This is what the LORD says:

"For three sins of Israel,
    even for four, I will not turn back ⌞my wrath⌟.
They sell the righteous for silver,
    and the needy for a pair of sandals.
⁷They trample on the heads of the poor
    as upon the dust of the ground
    and deny justice to the oppressed.
Father and son use the same girl
    and so profane my holy name.

ᵃ11 Or sword / and destroyed his allies   ᵇ15 Or / Molech; Hebrew malcam
ᶜ2 Or of her cities   ᵈ4 Or by lies   ᵉ4 Or lies

What challenge is facing you now that you can't handle alone? **2.** Speaking for God, instead of shepherding sheep, Amos leveled his guns at enemies of Israel and Israel itself. How do you respond when enemies are criticized: (a) If I'm honest, I enjoy it? (b) I add more? (c) I secretly set myself above them? (d) I'm reminded of my own sin? **3.** How do you respond when friends are criticized: (a) Sit in silence? (b) Jump to their rescue? (c) Try to be objective? (d) Express friend's perspective? (e) Agree that friend is wrong? **4.** How do you feel when you are criticized: (a) Defensive? (b) Embarrassed? (c) Accepting? (d) Smug? **5.** What sort of issues do you sense God is pointing out as wrong today? Are they personal, individual sins or do they delve into the way society treats other people and other nations? **6.** Can a whole country or political system be sinful? How so? **7.** What issue could you "roar" against today? What else could you do to facilitate change: (a) Pray? (b) Organize a group? (c) Organize a boycott? (d) Work within the system? (e) Contact the right people in the right places? (f) Gather ideas from others?

---

1. Where does God speak to you most clearly: (a) In nature? (b) In friendships? (c) In art? (d) In worship? (e) In Scripture? (f) In prayer? 2. Recall a time when you deserved to be disciplined, but weren't. What happened? 3. What money-making venture did you enjoy as a child?

1. The shepherd from Judah now turns to Israel. What do you imagine was the Israelites' response: (a) Shock? (b) Anger? (c) Humility? (d) Bewilderment? 2. What do the six sins listed in

verses 6–8 have in common? **3.** What purpose does bringing up the Amorites, the Exodus, the prophets and the Nazirites serve in Amos' argument (vv. 9–12)? **4.** What kind of person would travel in social circles of those indicted here? Is Amos' indictment of them like a class action suit today? Why or why not? **5.** Which statement comes closest to this crowd's motto: (a) Get while the gettin's good? (b) God helps those who help themselves? (c) Do unto others before they do unto you? (d) Some of us have it, some of us don't? **6.** What will happen to the Israelites in turn (vv. 13–16)?

♡ **1.** If you were given the task of judging Israel's sins listed here, which would you go easiest on? Which would you judge more harshly? Why? **2.** How would you know that a nation was repenting of its sins? What may God be calling you to do about these sins? What person or group is addressing the sins that concern you? **3.** What will happen without repentance in Israel's case? In your case?

☕ **1.** If you could choose one relative, living or dead, to spend a day with, who would it be? Why? **2.** If your possessions make one statement about you, what do they say: (a) Middle class? (b) Frugal? (c) Extravagant? (d) Misfit? **3.** Where would you enjoy having a winter house? A summer house?

📖 **1.** Israel is called "family" and "chosen" (vv. 1–2). What is implied by these names? **2.** What is the purpose of Amos' rhetorical questions in 3:3–6? What kind of answers is Amos expecting from these examples of cause and effect? Why is this a good method of preaching? **3.** How many in your group agree with the statement in verse 7? How many disagree? Support your positions. **4.** What moves Amos (or anyone else) to prophesy (3:7–8; see 1:1–2)? **5.** What do their households and furnishings tell you about the lifestyle of these people? What contemporary images does this bring to mind? **6.** Pagan nations are summoned to be witnesses (v. 9). What would this reveal to Israel? To the pagan nations? **7.** How could "chosen" people come to the point

---

⁸They lie down beside every altar
　　on garments taken in pledge.
In the house of their god
　　they drink wine taken as fines.

⁹"I destroyed the Amorite before them,
　　though he was tall as the cedars
　　and strong as the oaks.
I destroyed his fruit above
　　and his roots below.

¹⁰"I brought you up out of Egypt,
　　and I led you forty years in the desert
　　to give you the land of the Amorites.
¹¹I also raised up prophets from among your sons
　　and Nazirites from among your young men.
Is this not true, people of Israel?"
　　　　　　　　　　　　declares the LORD.
¹²"But you made the Nazirites drink wine
　　and commanded the prophets not to prophesy.

¹³"Now then, I will crush you
　　as a cart crushes when loaded with grain.
¹⁴The swift will not escape,
　　the strong will not muster their strength,
　　and the warrior will not save his life.
¹⁵The archer will not stand his ground,
　　the fleet-footed soldier will not get away,
　　and the horseman will not save his life.
¹⁶Even the bravest warriors
　　will flee naked on that day,"
　　　　　　　　　　　　declares the LORD.

Witnesses Summoned Against Israel

3 Hear this word the LORD has spoken against you, O people of Israel—against the whole family I brought up out of Egypt:

²"You only have I chosen
　　of all the families of the earth;
therefore I will punish you
　　for all your sins."

³Do two walk together
　　unless they have agreed to do so?
⁴Does a lion roar in the thicket
　　when he has no prey?
Does he growl in his den
　　when he has caught nothing?
⁵Does a bird fall into a trap on the ground
　　where no snare has been set?
Does a trap spring up from the earth
　　when there is nothing to catch?
⁶When a trumpet sounds in a city,
　　do not the people tremble?
When disaster comes to a city,
　　has not the LORD caused it?

⁷Surely the Sovereign LORD does nothing
　　without revealing his plan
　　to his servants the prophets.

⁸The lion has roared—
　　who will not fear?

The Sovereign LORD has spoken—
who can but prophesy?

⁹Proclaim to the fortresses of Ashdod
and to the fortresses of Egypt:
"Assemble yourselves on the mountains of
Samaria;
see the great unrest within her
and the oppression among her people."

¹⁰"They do not know how to do right," declares the
LORD,
"who hoard plunder and loot in their
fortresses."

¹¹Therefore this is what the Sovereign LORD says:

"An enemy will overrun the land;
he will pull down your strongholds
and plunder your fortresses."

¹²This is what the LORD says:

"As a shepherd saves from the lion's mouth
only two leg bones or a piece of an ear,
so will the Israelites be saved,
those who sit in Samaria
on the edge of their beds
and in Damascus on their couches.ᵃ"

¹³"Hear this and testify against the house of Jacob," declares the
Lord, the LORD God Almighty.

¹⁴"On the day I punish Israel for her sins,
I will destroy the altars of Bethel;
the horns of the altar will be cut off
and fall to the ground.
¹⁵I will tear down the winter house
along with the summer house;
the houses adorned with ivory will be destroyed
and the mansions will be demolished,"
declares the LORD.

Israel Has Not Returned to God

4 Hear this word, you cows of Bashan on Mount
Samaria,
you women who oppress the poor and crush
the needy
and say to your husbands, "Bring us some
drinks!"
²The Sovereign LORD has sworn by his holiness:
"The time will surely come
when you will be taken away with hooks,
the last of you with fishhooks.
³You will each go straight out
through breaks in the wall,
and you will be cast out toward Harmon,ᵇ"
declares the LORD.
⁴"Go to Bethel and sin;
go to Gilgal and sin yet more.
Bring your sacrifices every morning,

ᵃ12 The meaning of the Hebrew for this line is uncertain.   ᵇ3 Masoretic Text; with a
different word division of the Hebrew (see Septuagint) out, O mountain of oppression

where "they do not know how to do
right" (v. 10)? **8.** The remains of an
animal were often kept as evidence
of the slaughter. The corner of the
couch was the place of honor. How
many will be rescued from God's
punishment? What social level is
Amos talking about in verse 12?

1. If your behavior is going to
cause you or others prob-
lems, how would you prefer to be
warned: (a) Face to face? (b) By
letter? (c) By phone? (d) In a support group? **2.** Do you think that being a Christian will mean that God
is more lenient, or more severe, in
speaking to you about your possessions? **3.** How might you become more free *from* your possessions, so that you might become
more free *with* your possessions?
4. In terms of your life right now
would you say: (a) I'm in the lion's
mouth? (b) I see the lion? (c) I just
got out of the lion's mouth? (d) I
didn't even know I was in the jungle? **5.** God still snatches "burning
sticks from the fire" (4:11). Are you
one of the ones so blessed? Amos
saw that his world would be on fire
and in need of someone to rescue
the perishing. Are you inclined to
get involved in that life-saving effort?

---

1. What situations make you
the most angry? Have you
ever been angry enough to call
someone an animal name? **2.**
Which "cow" do you most identify
with right now: (a) Newborn calf?
(b) Milk cow? (c) Angry bull? (d)
Rodeo steer? (e) Prize heifer? (f)
Fatted calf ready for slaughter?

1. Bashan was an area
known for its "fatted" cattle. Is
verse 1 a sexist statement? What
would a contemporary slur sound
like? **2.** What is the attitude of
these women: (a) "I wear the pants
in this house"? (b) "The world exists to serve me"? (c) "I deserve a
break today"? (d) "My needs come
first"? **3.** What will be the fate of the
women? Why does Amos use ex-
amples such as cow and meat
hooks? **4.** Verses 4–5 speak of going to worship centers and sinning.

How is that possible? How would you describe this worship: (a) Style without substance? (b) Ceremony without faith? (c) Faith without action? (d) The right words with the wrong spirit? **5.** Amos is angry and sarcastic in verses 1–5, but what about God? In verses 6–11, what emotional quality is attributed to him? How is his divine wrath expressed in a way different from human anger? **6.** We see here five unsuccessful attempts by God to get Israel's attention. As a stubborn Israelite, which of these divine acts would you have ignored? Which would you have heeded? **7.** What might the people have thought when Egypt, Sodom and Gomorrah were brought up: (a) "But we are God's chosen"? (b) "We're a cut above them"? (c) "Maybe we should listen to this shepherd"? (d) "Now we're afraid"? (e) "What does he know anyway"? **8.** What does it mean to "prepare to meet your God" (v. 12)? Would this instill fear, joy, apathy or what? Why?

♡ **1.** For Amos, the way we treat the needy is the area by which we are judged. What is the Christian church doing for the needy? **2.** To what extent do you get involved in trying to alleviate poverty and oppression? Why don't you do more: (a) Selfishness? (b) Ignorance? (c) Politics? (d) Caught up in "church work"? Other? **3.** What would it mean for you to prepare to meet your God? Would that instill in you fear or joy? **4.** Speaking of meeting God, how would you describe your relationship with him: (a) We met long ago and have been friends ever since? (b) We've met, and our friendship is growing daily? (c) We just met? (d) I am still waiting to be introduced?

your tithes every three years.ᵃ
⁵Burn leavened bread as a thank offering
    and brag about your freewill offerings—
boast about them, you Israelites,
    for this is what you love to do,"
                declares the Sovereign LORD.

⁶"I gave you empty stomachsᵇ in every city
    and lack of bread in every town,
    yet you have not returned to me,"
                declares the LORD.

⁷"I also withheld rain from you
    when the harvest was still three months away.
I sent rain on one town,
    but withheld it from another.
One field had rain;
    another had none and dried up.
⁸People staggered from town to town for water
    but did not get enough to drink,
    yet you have not returned to me,"
                declares the LORD.

⁹"Many times I struck your gardens and vineyards,
    I struck them with blight and mildew.
Locusts devoured your fig and olive trees,
    yet you have not returned to me,"
                declares the LORD.

¹⁰"I sent plagues among you
    as I did to Egypt.
I killed your young men with the sword,
    along with your captured horses.
I filled your nostrils with the stench of your
        camps,
    yet you have not returned to me,"
                declares the LORD.

¹¹"I overthrew some of you
    as Iᶜ overthrew Sodom and Gomorrah.
You were like a burning stick snatched from the
        fire,
    yet you have not returned to me,"
                declares the LORD.

¹²"Therefore this is what I will do to you, Israel,
    and because I will do this to you,
    prepare to meet your God, O Israel."

¹³He who forms the mountains,
    creates the wind,
    and reveals his thoughts to man,
he who turns dawn to darkness,
    and treads the high places of the earth—
    the LORD God Almighty is his name.

ᵃ4 Or *tithes on the third day*   ᵇ6 Hebrew *you cleanness of teeth*   ᶜ11 Hebrew *God*

A Lament and Call to Repentance

5 Hear this word, O house of Israel, this lament I take up concerning you:

2"Fallen is Virgin Israel,
>   never to rise again,
> deserted in her own land,
>   with no one to lift her up."

3This is what the Sovereign LORD says:

> "The city that marches out a thousand strong for
>   Israel
>   will have only a hundred left;
> the town that marches out a hundred strong
>   will have only ten left."

4This is what the LORD says to the house of Israel:

> "Seek me and live;
>   5 do not seek Bethel,
> do not go to Gilgal,
>   do not journey to Beersheba.
> For Gilgal will surely go into exile,
>   and Bethel will be reduced to nothing.[a]"
> 6Seek the LORD and live,
>   or he will sweep through the house of Joseph
>   like a fire;
> it will devour,
>   and Bethel will have no one to quench it.

> 7You who turn justice into bitterness
>   and cast righteousness to the ground
> 8(he who made the Pleiades and Orion,
>   who turns blackness into dawn
>   and darkens day into night,
> who calls for the waters of the sea
>   and pours them out over the face of the land—
>   the LORD is his name—
> 9he flashes destruction on the stronghold
>   and brings the fortified city to ruin),
> 10you hate the one who reproves in court
>   and despise him who tells the truth.

> 11You trample on the poor
>   and force him to give you grain.
> Therefore, though you have built stone mansions,
>   you will not live in them;
> though you have planted lush vineyards,
>   you will not drink their wine.
> 12For I know how many are your offenses
>   and how great your sins.

> You oppress the righteous and take bribes
>   and you deprive the poor of justice in the
>   courts.
> 13Therefore the prudent man keeps quiet in such
>   times,
>   for the times are evil.

> 14Seek good, not evil,

a 5 Or *grief*; or *wickedness*; Hebrew *aven*, a reference to Beth Aven (a derogatory name for Bethel)

1. As a child, what places were you told not to go? Why were they off limits? Did you secretly go there anyway? 2. When did you feel the most "alive" this week?

1. A lament is a poem, or song, of grief. What emotions and thoughts are associated with the various stages of grieving? 2. Why does Amos call Israel "Virgin" (v. 2)? What is he lamenting? What ideal and what people seem, from the rest of the passage, to have been the main victims of life in Israel? 3. The people would have come to Gilgal and Bethel for religious services. They would have been a happy crowd. How would they feel after Amos' message: (a) Angry? (b) Appreciative? (c) Apathetic? 4. What kind of ratings would you give Amos for tact? For courage? For integrity? 5. To "seek the Lord" (vv. 4,6) usually means to go to a quiet, holy place to meet with God. What does it mean here to "seek": (a) Casually look for? (b) Intently look for? (c) Desperately look for? (d) Run after? 6. Why were people urged not to seek where they worshiped (v. 5)? 7. How could the people "turn justice into bitterness and cast the righteousness to the ground" (v. 7)? What does this have to do with their temple activity? With their daily lifestyle? 8. How is their "turning" (v. 7) different than God's "turning" (v. 8)? What is the point of this contrast? 9. How does this list of wrongdoing (vv. 11–12) compare with the list in Amos 2:6–16? What is the effect on the poor financially? Socially? Legally? Spiritually? Emotionally? 10. Having built mansions and planted vineyards, how would the people feel after being told they would never drink the wine or live in the mansions: (a) Disgusted? (b) Enraged? (c) Bitter? (d) Hopeless? (e) Helpless? (f) Quietly penitent? 11. What rays of hope do you sense in this lament? 12. After all the warnings, why does the Lord say, "There will be wailing ..." (vv. 16–17)? Does this imply a second chance to seek good? Or is their fate sealed?

1. Recall a time you wanted, even prayed, for someone you loved to make a positive change in their life, and they didn't. What happened? How did you feel? 2. The Lord says, "Seek me and live" (v. 4). How will you do that this week? What spiritual disci-

plines help you feel more alive in the Lord? **3.** Amos preaches both bad news and good news to Israel. Does his message to you bring to mind more things to lament, or more rays of hope? Choose one negative and one positive to pray about and share with the group. **4.** To what extent does money equal power in the world today? As much as in Amos' day, or more?

1. Complete this sentence: When the Lord comes again I will probably be found _____. **2.** In the next three months, what one day are you anticipating the most?

1. The ancient Jews long for the day of the Lord's coming (v. 18). What do you think they expect to happen? Why is Amos warning them not to be so eager? **2.** Why does God despise their religious practices? **3.** Verse 24 speaks of water being poured out forever. Elsewhere, water symbolizes life consecrated to God. Together, what does this water symbol imply for their worship? Their mission? **4.** What is the "bottom line" for Israel?

1. Are you yearning for the "Day of the Lord"? Why or why not? **2.** What do you think God would say about your worship: (a) Keep it up? (b) Wake up? (c) Shape up? (d) Ship out? (e) Other? **3.** If Amos were preaching in your church, what would he speak on: (a) Fellowship? (b) Worship? (c) Budget? (d) Justice for the poor? (e) False gods? What contemporary illustrations would he use?

that you may live.
Then the Lord God Almighty will be with you,
just as you say he is.
¹⁵Hate evil, love good;
maintain justice in the courts.
Perhaps the Lord God Almighty will have mercy
on the remnant of Joseph.

¹⁶Therefore this is what the Lord, the Lord God Almighty, says:

"There will be wailing in all the streets
and cries of anguish in every public square.
The farmers will be summoned to weep
and the mourners to wail.
¹⁷There will be wailing in all the vineyards,
for I will pass through your midst,"
says the Lord.

The Day of the Lord

¹⁸Woe to you who long
for the day of the Lord!
Why do you long for the day of the Lord?
That day will be darkness, not light.
¹⁹It will be as though a man fled from a lion
only to meet a bear,
as though he entered his house
and rested his hand on the wall
only to have a snake bite him.
²⁰Will not the day of the Lord be darkness, not
light—
pitch-dark, without a ray of brightness?

²¹"I hate, I despise your religious feasts;
I cannot stand your assemblies.
²²Even though you bring me burnt offerings and
grain offerings,
I will not accept them.
Though you bring choice fellowship offerings,ᵃ
I will have no regard for them.
²³Away with the noise of your songs!
I will not listen to the music of your harps.
²⁴But let justice roll on like a river,
righteousness like a never-failing stream!

²⁵"Did you bring me sacrifices and offerings
forty years in the desert, O house of Israel?
²⁶You have lifted up the shrine of your king,
the pedestal of your idols,
the star of your godᵇ—
which you made for yourselves.
²⁷Therefore I will send you into exile beyond
Damascus,"
says the Lord, whose name is God Almighty.

ᵃ22 Traditionally *peace offerings*   ᵇ26 Or *lifted up Sakkuth your king / and Kaiwan your idols, / your star-gods*; Septuagint *lifted up the shrine of Molech / and the star of your god Rephan, / their idols*

Woe to the Complacent

6 Woe to you who are complacent in Zion,
and to you who feel secure on Mount Samaria,
you notable men of the foremost nation,
to whom the people of Israel come!

²Go to Calneh and look at it;
go from there to great Hamath,
and then go down to Gath in Philistia.
Are they better off than your two kingdoms?
Is their land larger than yours?

³You put off the evil day
and bring near a reign of terror.

⁴You lie on beds inlaid with ivory
and lounge on your couches.
You dine on choice lambs
and fattened calves.

⁵You strum away on your harps like David
and improvise on musical instruments.

⁶You drink wine by the bowlful
and use the finest lotions,
but you do not grieve over the ruin of Joseph.

⁷Therefore you will be among the first to go into
exile;
your feasting and lounging will end.

The Lord Abhors the Pride of Israel

⁸The Sovereign Lord has sworn by himself—the Lord God Almighty declares:

"I abhor the pride of Jacob
and detest his fortresses;
I will deliver up the city
and everything in it."

⁹If ten men are left in one house, they too will die. ¹⁰And if a relative who is to burn the bodies comes to carry them out of the house and asks anyone still hiding there, "Is anyone with you?" and he says, "No," then he will say, "Hush! We must not mention the name of the Lord."

¹¹For the Lord has given the command,
and he will smash the great house into pieces
and the small house into bits.

¹²Do horses run on the rocky crags?
Does one plow there with oxen?
But you have turned justice into poison
and the fruit of righteousness into bitterness—

¹³you who rejoice in the conquest of Lo Debar*a*
and say, "Did we not take Karnaim*b* by our
own strength?"

¹⁴For the Lord God Almighty declares,
"I will stir up a nation against you, O house of
Israel,
that will oppress you all the way
from Lebo*c* Hamath to the valley of the
Arabah."

---

a13 Lo Debar means *nothing.*   *b13* Karnaim means *horns; horn* here symbolizes strength.   *c14* Or *from the entrance to*

What three things give you a secure feeling? When was the last time you had everything going for you?

1. Who does Amos go after in this section of his prophecy? What is their sin? 2. How is "security" related to "complacency" (v. 1)? Where should these people have found their security? 3. Is Amos condemning a life of luxury, or something more? 4. What will happen to those who have the most prosperity and privilege and yet abuse it (v. 7; see Lk 12:48)?

1. Tell three areas of your life in which you feel somewhat insecure. 2. Where might you be complacent: At home? With friends? At church? 3. The more secure you are in relation to God, are you more, or less, eager to serve him? 4. Is God a God of the rich (blessing them), or of the poor (defending them)? Explain.

What is one thing you said you'd never do again, but ended up doing anyway?

1. What has the Lord sworn to do? Could he have expressed himself any more strongly? 2. How extensive will the coming judgment be? 3. What futile activities did the people take pride in (vv. 11–13)? 4. How did they turn "justice into poison" and "the fruit of righteousness into bitterness" (v. 12)? 5. Does the punishment fit the crime (v. 14)?

1. What is the difference between pride and confidence? How can you develop confidence without pride? 2. If you were "The Little Engine That Could," what would you be saying about your life right now: (a) I don't think I can? (b) I think I can? (c) I know I can? (d) I thought I could? 3. What "poisonous" or "bitter" place (v. 12) might be in your life today? How can it become just or fruitful?

Have you given testimony or spoken up in another's defense? What happened? Was that easy or hard for you to do?

1. Who in your group has any experience with swarming locusts, consuming fire or a plumb line? 2. What do the three visions of Amos have in common (vv. 1–9)? How do they differ? Is the judgment conveyed here total? Partial? Universal? Inescapable? Exacting? 3. What do these visions say about the purpose and character of God? Of Amos? 4. What would be unusual about a person from Judah speaking up on behalf of Israel? Do prayers for mercy change God's mind (see Ge 18, where Abraham interceded likewise for Sodom and Gomorrah)? Explain. 5. Why would God relent on the first two judgments but not on the third? Why doesn't Amos object to God's action in the third?

When have you prayed, as Amos, "God, I beg you to stop"? How did God answer?

1. What did your father do for a living? What impact did that have on your development? 2. What are the most and least favorite jobs you have held?

1. How does Amaziah's accusation (vv. 10–11) compare with the Lord's message given to Amos (5:27; 7:9)? 2. Why would Amaziah want Amos out of Israel? 3. Why would Amaziah keep Amos from speaking God's word when Amos' office identified him as being a servant of the Lord? 4. What were Amos' credentials to be a prophet? Would Amos rather be farming in Judah or prophesying in Israel? 5. Do you hear pity or anger in Amos' voice as he utters the words of verse 17? Why?

1. How many ministers are in your group? What credentials (academic, spiritual, other) do you have to be in ministry? 2. If there is one thing out of the ordinary that God is calling you to do, what is it?

Locusts, Fire and a Plumb Line

7 This is what the Sovereign LORD showed me: He was preparing swarms of locusts after the king's share had been harvested and just as the second crop was coming up. ²When they had stripped the land clean, I cried out, "Sovereign LORD, forgive! How can Jacob survive? He is so small!"

³So the LORD relented.

"This will not happen," the LORD said.

⁴This is what the Sovereign LORD showed me: The Sovereign LORD was calling for judgment by fire; it dried up the great deep and devoured the land. ⁵Then I cried out, "Sovereign LORD, I beg you, stop! How can Jacob survive? He is so small!"

⁶So the LORD relented.

"This will not happen either," the Sovereign LORD said.

⁷This is what he showed me: The Lord was standing by a wall that had been built true to plumb, with a plumb line in his hand. ⁸And the LORD asked me, "What do you see, Amos?"

"A plumb line," I replied.

Then the Lord said, "Look, I am setting a plumb line among my people Israel; I will spare them no longer.

⁹"The high places of Isaac will be destroyed
and the sanctuaries of Israel will be ruined;
with my sword I will rise against the house of
Jeroboam."

Amos and Amaziah

¹⁰Then Amaziah the priest of Bethel sent a message to Jeroboam king of Israel: "Amos is raising a conspiracy against you in the very heart of Israel. The land cannot bear all his words. ¹¹For this is what Amos is saying:

" 'Jeroboam will die by the sword,
and Israel will surely go into exile,
away from their native land.' "

¹²Then Amaziah said to Amos, "Get out, you seer! Go back to the land of Judah. Earn your bread there and do your prophesying there. ¹³Don't prophesy anymore at Bethel, because this is the king's sanctuary and the temple of the kingdom."

¹⁴Amos answered Amaziah, "I was neither a prophet nor a prophet's son, but I was a shepherd, and I also took care of sycamore-fig trees. ¹⁵But the LORD took me from tending the flock and said to me, 'Go, prophesy to my people Israel.' ¹⁶Now then, hear the word of the LORD. You say,

" 'Do not prophesy against Israel,
and stop preaching against the house of Isaac.'

¹⁷"Therefore this is what the LORD says:

" 'Your wife will become a prostitute in the city,
and your sons and daughters will fall by the
sword.
Your land will be measured and divided up,
and you yourself will die in a pagan^a country.
And Israel will certainly go into exile,
away from their native land.' "

^{a}17 Hebrew an unclean

A Basket of Ripe Fruit

8 This is what the Sovereign Lord showed me: a basket of ripe fruit. [2]"What do you see, Amos?" he asked.

"A basket of ripe fruit," I answered.

Then the Lord said to me, "The time is ripe for my people Israel; I will spare them no longer.

[3]"In that day," declares the Sovereign Lord, "the songs in the temple will turn to wailing.[a] Many, many bodies—flung everywhere! Silence!"

> [4]Hear this, you who trample the needy
>   and do away with the poor of the land,
>
> [5]saying,
>
> "When will the New Moon be over
>   that we may sell grain,
> and the Sabbath be ended
>   that we may market wheat?"—
> skimping the measure,
>   boosting the price
>   and cheating with dishonest scales,
> [6]buying the poor with silver
>   and the needy for a pair of sandals,
>   selling even the sweepings with the wheat.

[7]The Lord has sworn by the Pride of Jacob: "I will never forget anything they have done.

> [8]"Will not the land tremble for this,
>   and all who live in it mourn?
> The whole land will rise like the Nile;
>   it will be stirred up and then sink
>   like the river of Egypt.

[9]"In that day," declares the Sovereign Lord,

> "I will make the sun go down at noon
>   and darken the earth in broad daylight.
> [10]I will turn your religious feasts into mourning
>   and all your singing into weeping.
> I will make all of you wear sackcloth
>   and shave your heads.
> I will make that time like mourning for an only
>   son
>   and the end of it like a bitter day.
>
> [11]"The days are coming," declares the Sovereign
>   Lord,
>   "when I will send a famine through the land—
> not a famine of food or a thirst for water,
>   but a famine of hearing the words of the Lord.
> [12]Men will stagger from sea to sea
>   and wander from north to east,
> searching for the word of the Lord,
>   but they will not find it.
>
> [13]"In that day
>
> "the lovely young women and strong young men
>   will faint because of thirst.
> [14]They who swear by the shame[b] of Samaria,

---

1. What is some bad news you have had to deliver: Accident? Death? Failing grades? Job loss? Jury vote? How did you prepare yourself to deliver the news? 2. Have you received bad news recently? How did you deal with it after you heard it? 3. If a famine swept the land, what food would you miss most?

1. This is Amos' fourth vision (see 7:1–9 for the others). How is this vision like and unlike the last one? 2. Consider the look, smell and taste of fruit that is overripe. What does this say about the condition Israel was in? 3. Is this coming judgment seen as inevitable, postponable or avoidable? How so? Can God relent, as in the first two visions? 4. What sins is Amos condemning in verses 4–6? Where else have you heard Amos sound this familiar theme? What could that repetition mean? 5. Is this "God who won't forget" (v. 7) consistent, or inconsistent, with what you know of God? 6. The coming doom is described as an earthquake, eclipse, famine and drought. Of these, which would be most frightening to you? Why? 7. What lesson learned in fasting is learned the hard way in famine? 8. What would a "famine of hearing the words of the Lord" (v. 11) entail? In such a time, what would be missing? What would run rampant?

1. Comparing your church to a tree, what do you see: (a) Baby seedling? (b) Full blossoms? (c) Green fruit? (d) Good fruit? (e) Overripe fruit? Explain. 2. When it comes to hearing the Word of God in your church, are you in a time of feast or famine? Why? 3. If there is a strange silence of the Bible in the churches, how would you account for that? What makes us deaf to God? If we were closer to the poor and oppressed, might that help us better hear God? 4. From this passage, how do you view the temptations affecting church and state leaders? How can you support those in leadership who fall, that they might thirst again for God and find him?

---

a3 Or *"the temple singers will wail*   *b14* Or *by Ashima; or by the idol*

or say, 'As surely as your god lives, O Dan,'
or, 'As surely as the god^a of Beersheba
    lives'—
they will fall,
    never to rise again."

Israel to Be Destroyed

9 I saw the Lord standing by the altar, and he said:

"Strike the tops of the pillars
    so that the thresholds shake.
Bring them down on the heads of all the people;
    those who are left I will kill with the sword.
Not one will get away,
    none will escape.
²Though they dig down to the depths of the
    grave,^b
from there my hand will take them.
Though they climb up to the heavens,
    from there I will bring them down.
³Though they hide themselves on the top of
    Carmel,
there I will hunt them down and seize them.
Though they hide from me at the bottom of the
    sea,
there I will command the serpent to bite them.
⁴Though they are driven into exile by their
    enemies,
there I will command the sword to slay them.
I will fix my eyes upon them
    for evil and not for good."

⁵The Lord, the LORD Almighty,
    he who touches the earth and it melts,
    and all who live in it mourn—
the whole land rises like the Nile,
    then sinks like the river of Egypt—
⁶he who builds his lofty palace^c in the heavens
    and sets its foundation^d on the earth,
who calls for the waters of the sea
    and pours them out over the face of the land—
    the LORD is his name.

⁷"Are not you Israelites
    the same to me as the Cushites^e?"
                   declares the LORD.
"Did I not bring Israel up from Egypt,
    the Philistines from Caphtor^f
    and the Arameans from Kir?

⁸"Surely the eyes of the Sovereign LORD
    are on the sinful kingdom.
I will destroy it
    from the face of the earth—
yet I will not totally destroy
    the house of Jacob,"
                   declares the LORD.
⁹"For I will give the command,

---

1. Who do you admire for: (a) Telling it like it is? (b) Taking criticism and making positive improvements? 2. Do you prefer to face up to a problem and get it over with, or do you tend to put it off as long as possible?

1. What is meant by Amos seeing the Lord "standing by the altar" and the temple sanctuary coming down on their heads (v. 1)? 2. How does this vision compare to the ones that preceded it? Are things getting better? Staying the same? Getting worse? 3. How does this vision expand, confirm or contradict what you know of God? 4. Is the Exodus of no more significance than the migration of other peoples the world over? Or what does verse 7 imply? 5. What is the main message in verses 1–4: (a) It is useless to run from God? (b) You can't hide from God? (c) Sin marks you for life? (d) God is out to get you? (e) Other? 6. If you were an original recipient of this prophecy, how would you feel: (a) Hunted? (b) Haunted? (c) Trapped? (d) Terrified? 7. Why would God not destroy all of Judah (v. 8)? How would Israelites know if they were one of the few not to be overtaken by disaster? What must life have been like for these shaken people? 8. Who would dare say, "Disaster will not overtake or meet us" (v. 10): (a) Optimist Club president? (b) Irrational sentimentalist? (c) Spiritually blind person? (d) Other?

1. How do you attempt to hide from God: (a) Ignore certain pressing issues? (b) Skip church? (c) Keep on moving and don't slow down? (d) Stop praying and reading the Bible? (e) Other? 2. If God shook the church today, what would fall out? Would you? When have you experienced God shaking you? 3. How do you accept critical news: (a) Shoot the messenger? (b) Pull the covers over your head? (c) Grin and bear it? (d) Praise the Lord, anyway? (e) Act on it?

---

^a14 Or *power*   ^b2 Hebrew *to Sheol*   ^c6 The meaning of the Hebrew for this phrase is uncertain.   ^d6 The meaning of the Hebrew for this word is uncertain.
^e7 That is, people from the upper Nile region   ^f7 That is, Crete

and I will shake the house of Israel
    among all the nations
as grain is shaken in a sieve,
    and not a pebble will reach the ground.
[10]All the sinners among my people
    will die by the sword,
all those who say,
    'Disaster will not overtake or meet us.'

Israel's Restoration

[11]"In that day I will restore
    David's fallen tent.
I will repair its broken places,
    restore its ruins,
    and build it as it used to be,
[12]so that they may possess the remnant of Edom
    and all the nations that bear my name,[a]"
                    declares the LORD, who will
                            do these things.

[13]"The days are coming," declares the LORD,

"when the reaper will be overtaken by the
        plowman
    and the planter by the one treading grapes.
New wine will drip from the mountains
    and flow from all the hills.
[14]I will bring back my exiled[b] people Israel;
    they will rebuild the ruined cities and live in
        them.
They will plant vineyards and drink their wine;
    they will make gardens and eat their fruit.
[15]I will plant Israel in their own land,
    never again to be uprooted
    from the land I have given them,"

                    says the LORD your God.

1. When it comes to gardening, do you have a green thumb or a brown one? How so? 2. When it comes to repairing broken relationships or growing new ones, are you a green thumb or brown?

1. To what does "in that day" and "David's fallen tent" (v. 11) refer? 2. What promises does the Lord make (vv. 11–15)? 3. What have the people endured to receive these promises (see 4:6–11)? 4. How do the last words of Amos compare with his other words? Are these words in or out of character for Amos? 5. Do you think verse 15 has come true? When?

1. When have you felt as though you were back in the promised land after a long exile? 2. Which area of your life needs a fresh touch of God's spirit today? 3. In silent review and prayer, ask God to use Amos to reveal any sin that needs to be addressed. Jot that on paper. Pair up and share Amos' promise of renewal with each other. (Share what's on the paper, only as you wish.) As a group, destroy the slips of paper (i.e. tear up or burn), thus symbolizing that God forgives and forgets our sin.

[a]12 Hebrew; Septuagint *so that the remnant of men / and all the nations that bear my
name may seek the Lord*   [b]14 Or *will restore the fortunes of my*

INTRODUCTION to

OBADIAH

Book Study Outline: If you are using Obadiah for a study course, spend one to two meetings on this short book. Use the questions in the margin for your group agenda:

start meeting / 15 min.	read & discuss Bible / 30 min.	close meeting / 15–45 min.

Refer to the Questions and Answers in the front of this Bible for more information.

Author: A prophet named Obadiah, whose name means "the servant of the Lord." While there are 11 other Old Testament characters with this name, none of them can be identified with this prophet.

Date: The date of composition is uncertain, depending upon which of two events in Israel's history correlates with verses 11–14: (1) The Philistine invasion of Jerusalem during the reign of Jehoram (853–841 B.C.; see 2Ch 21:8–20), in which case, Obadiah would be a ninth century contemporary of Elisha; or, (2) The Babylonian campaign against Jerusalem (605–585 B.C.), in which case, Obadiah would be a sixth century contemporary of Jeremiah. The latter seems more likely.

Theme: God's judgment of proud Edom and the restoration of Israel.

Historical Background: The Edomites apparently took advantage of the fall of Jerusalem to Babylon in 586 B.C. They plundered the land and pillaged the homes of survivors. Obadiah speaks God's judgment on Edom for the way they took advantage of "brother Jacob" in his moment of weakness. The term "Edom" is used in the Old Testament for the name of Esau (the brother of Jacob) and for the race made up of his descendants. The area this tribe occupied was originally the land of Seir. It was a rugged, mountainous region that extended from the Dead Sea south to the Gulf of Aqabah. The enmity between Edom and Israel was long-standing. The history of the blood feud between the two peoples can be traced by a study of the relevant Old Testament passages (see adjoining map for references). Edom was known for sitting smugly in her fortified cities atop rocky clefts, and Obadiah prophesies against her for relying on this for her sense of security. In the fifth century the Edomites were driven out of their own land by the Nabateans. After this many Edomites moved into southern Palestine.

JUDGMENT ON EDOM

The Edomites were the descendants of Esau, the twin brother of Jacob.

ISRAEL

The following biblical references are helpful in understanding the relation of Israel and Edom:
Ge 27:41–45; 32:1–21; 33; 36;
Ex 15:15;
Nu 20:14–21;
Dt 2:1–6; 23:7;

JUDAH

1Sa 21 with Ps 52;
2Sa 8:13–14;
2Ki 8:20–22; 14:7;
Ps 83;
Eze 35;
Joel 3:18–19;
Am 1:11–12; 9:12.

EDOM

Characteristics: Obadiah is the shortest book in the Old Testament. While other prophets often announced oracles directed at other nations (along with their words for Israel), nearly the whole of Obadiah consists of the words of a Jewish prophet to another country. In this respect Obadiah is like Nahum, who preached against Nineveh. With respect to language, Obadiah is like Jeremiah (compare vv. 1–9 with Jer 49:7–22), which suggests interdependence or mutual reliance on an unknown third source. The language of this book is characterized by vivid and striking metaphors (see vv. 4,5,16,18).

Obadiah

¹The vision of Obadiah.

This is what the Sovereign LORD says about Edom—

> We have heard a message from the LORD:
>   An envoy was sent to the nations to say,
>   "Rise, and let us go against her for battle"—

²"See, I will make you small among the nations;
  you will be utterly despised.
³The pride of your heart has deceived you,
  you who live in the clefts of the rocksᵃ
  and make your home on the heights,
you who say to yourself,
  'Who can bring me down to the ground?'
⁴Though you soar like the eagle
  and make your nest among the stars,
  from there I will bring you down,"
>   declares the LORD.

⁵"If thieves came to you,
  if robbers in the night—
Oh, what a disaster awaits you—
  would they not steal only as much as they
    wanted?
If grape pickers came to you,
  would they not leave a few grapes?
⁶But how Esau will be ransacked,
  his hidden treasures pillaged!
⁷All your allies will force you to the border;
  your friends will deceive and overpower you;
  those who eat your bread will set a trap for
    you,ᵇ
  but you will not detect it.

⁸"In that day," declares the LORD,
  "will I not destroy the wise men of Edom,
  men of understanding in the mountains of
    Esau?
⁹Your warriors, O Teman, will be terrified,
  and everyone in Esau's mountains
  will be cut down in the slaughter.
¹⁰Because of the violence against your brother
    Jacob,
  you will be covered with shame;
  you will be destroyed forever.
¹¹On the day you stood aloof
  while strangers carried off his wealth
and foreigners entered his gates
  and cast lots for Jerusalem,
  you were like one of them.
¹²You should not look down on your brother
  in the day of his misfortune,

ᵃ3 Or *of Sela*   ᵇ7 The meaning of the Hebrew for this clause is uncertain.

---

1. Where was your safe place of retreat as a child? Why there? Where is such a place for you now? **2.** Is there one day that stands out as a day of disaster for your family? For your nation? What happened that day: Flood? Fire? Stock market crash? Serious accident? What good came of it?

1. This prophecy about Edom is drawn from the words of an earlier prophet (see Jer 49:7–22). What, if anything, does Obadiah's introduction (v. 1a) tell you about the historical context of this writing or the event it portends (contrast Am 1:1, for a more informative prologue)? **2.** Who are the Edomites named after (see Ge 36:1,8–9)? What was the relationship like between Jacob and Esau (see Ge 27:41–44; 33:4,16–17a)? What does Hebrews 12:15–17 say about this brotherly relationship? About the bitterness and godlessness of Esau? **3.** What natural fortifications give Edom an illusion of security (v. 3)? To whom are they still vulnerable (vv. 4,7)? **4.** What is the point of Obadiah's eagle imagery (v. 4; compare Isa 40:30–31)? What message is intended by the poetic imagery in verses 5–6? **5.** What happens "in that day" of the Lord's judgment (vv. 8ff)? Why is this judgment coming upon Edom? Do you find Edom's bad attitude toward Judah surprising? Why or why not? What does this tell you about the history of relations between these nations? **6.** How do you think Israel responded to this message of doom for Edom, their enemy?

1. Upon what *rock-like* structures might you be basing your security: An insurance policy? A church? A family inheritance? How might this "pride of your heart" be deceiving you? **2.** Has that security been shaken by God? How so? **3.** How do you respond when disaster befalls someone you know: (a) *Avoid* the disaster, lest you also get hit? (b) *Rescue* the perishing? (c) *Comfort* the bereaved? (d) Do what you can to *prevent* the disaster from happening again? (e) Give an example. **4.** Edom was judged for not serving brother Jacob when Jacob was down and out. What down-and-out persons should you be serving? How might you begin to serve them this week?

1. Where is your "spiritual home"? How long have you been away from there? What was your reunion like the last time you went there? 2. What experience, if any, have you or your church had in helping to relocate "exiles"?

1. What new parameters do you see in "the day of the Lord," as used in verse 15? By what logic will it come upon Edom? 2. To whom is this word addressed? How are the house of Esau and the house of Jacob contrasted here? 3. What would Edom have drunk on Mt. Zion (v. 16)? Is this drinking language meant literally or figuratively? Why do you think so (see Jer 25:15–16)? What is the message intended by this language? 4. If Edom's allies will defeat her (v. 7), who will finish the job (vv. 19–21)? How total will be their ultimate defeat? 5. In what ways would the return of the exiles (vv. 19ff) be a social event? A political event? A theological event?

1. Just as Judah waited for the "Day of the Lord" in this passage, what "Day of the Lord" do you await? 2. In your opinion, is that day too far away to be concerned about? Or is it "right around the corner," on this month's calendar? In either event, what are you doing and "drinking" (v. 16) in preparation for that day? 3. Who are some displaced persons today? What hope might Obadiah offer them? What would Obadiah say to those who encouraged their displacement? 4. How would you respond if God called you to share a message like Obadiah's with some people today? What audience might be ripe for that message? How do you think they would respond?

nor rejoice over the people of Judah
in the day of their destruction,
nor boast so much
in the day of their trouble.
13You should not march through the gates of my people
in the day of their disaster,
nor look down on them in their calamity
in the day of their disaster,
nor seize their wealth
in the day of their disaster.
14You should not wait at the crossroads
to cut down their fugitives,
nor hand over their survivors
in the day of their trouble.

15"The day of the LORD is near
for all nations.
As you have done, it will be done to you;
your deeds will return upon your own head.
16Just as you drank on my holy hill,
so all the nations will drink continually;
they will drink and drink
and be as if they had never been.
17But on Mount Zion will be deliverance;
it will be holy,
and the house of Jacob
will possess its inheritance.
18The house of Jacob will be a fire
and the house of Joseph a flame;
the house of Esau will be stubble,
and they will set it on fire and consume it.
There will be no survivors
from the house of Esau."
The LORD has spoken.

19People from the Negev will occupy
the mountains of Esau,
and people from the foothills will possess
the land of the Philistines.
They will occupy the fields of Ephraim and Samaria,
and Benjamin will possess Gilead.
20This company of Israelite exiles who are in Canaan
will possess ˌthe landˌ as far as Zarephath;
the exiles from Jerusalem who are in Sepharad
will possess the towns of the Negev.
21Deliverers will go up onᵃ Mount Zion
to govern the mountains of Esau.
And the kingdom will be the LORD's.

a21 Or *from*

INTRODUCTION to

JONAH

Book Study Outline: If you are using Jonah for a study course, here is a 3-week outline. Use the questions in the margin for your group agenda:

☕ start meeting / 15 min.

📖 read & discuss Bible / 30 min.

♡ close meeting / 15–45 min.

3-week plan	Personal Reading	Group Study Passage
1	1:1–17	Jonah Flees From the Lord
2	2:1–3:10	Jonah Goes to Nineveh
3	4:1–11	Jonah's Anger at God's Compassion

Refer to the Questions and Answers in the front of this Bible for more information.

Author: Originally told by Jonah, though others may have written it down. The author is not identified in the text.

Date: Sometime after Jonah's ministry c. 800–770 B.C., before Nineveh's destruction (612 B.C.) and Samaria's fall (722–721 B.C.).

Theme: God's love for the Gentiles, even Nineveh.

Historical Background: Israel had just restored her northern borders under King Jeroboam II (793–753 B.C.), as Jonah had prophesied (2Ki 14:25). At this time, Israel was politically secure, spiritually smug and morally corrupt. Nineveh, the city to which Jonah was sent by God, was the capital of Assyria. Assyria was a ruthless empire which threatened tiny Israel, and eventually conquered it in 722 B.C. Nineveh was 500 miles east of Joppa, but Jonah boarded a ship heading 2000 miles west, revealing how far and fast Jonah wanted to get away from a people he dreaded. Israelites had many reasons to hate the proud Ninevites, as Nahum points out in a prophecy dedicated exclusively to the Ninevites (see the introduction page for Nahum). Nineveh's repentance and revival under Jonah was short-lived. The second time around for proud, cruel Nineveh resulted in her fall in 612 B.C. She was never heard from again.

Characteristics: Unlike most other Old Testament prophetic books, Jonah gives an account of a single incident in the life of the prophet. The story is briefly told in some 40 verses. His prayer consumes the remaining eight verses. The Jews accepted this book as reflecting the experience of the actual prophet Jonah (2Ki 14:25). However, some regard this book as an imaginative tale, akin to a modern "fish story." Others view Jonah as an allegory or parable, teaching God's universal love. Jonah's missionary message finds later parallels in the message of Peter (see Ac 10:1–11:18) and Paul (see Ro 9–11). Jesus also referred to Jonah (Mt 12:38–41). The theological emphasis in Jonah (on God's universal love, sovereignty and redemption) are equally applicable today.

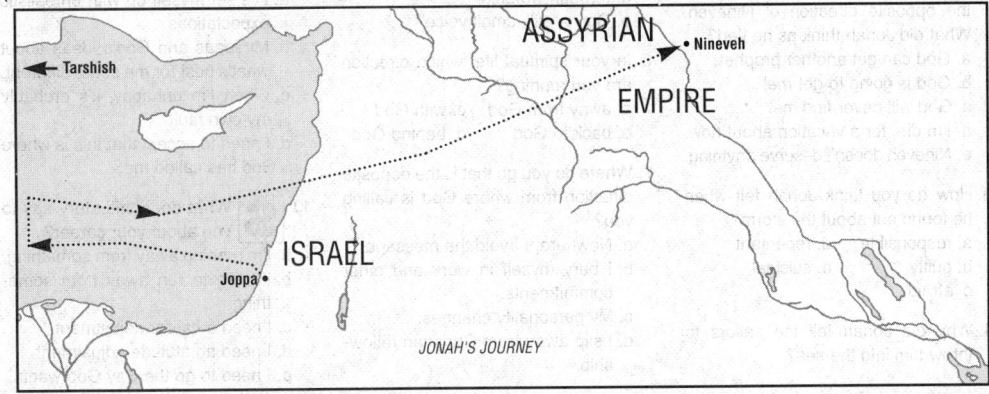

JONAH'S JOURNEY

Jonah

Jonah Flees From the LORD

1 The word of the LORD came to Jonah son of Amittai: ²"Go to the great city of Nineveh and preach against it, because its wickedness has come up before me."

³But Jonah ran away from the LORD and headed for Tarshish. He went down to Joppa, where he found a ship bound for that port. After paying the fare, he went aboard and sailed for Tarshish to flee from the LORD.

⁴Then the LORD sent a great wind on the sea, and such a violent storm arose that the ship threatened to break up. ⁵All the sailors were afraid and each cried out to his own god. And they threw the cargo into the sea to lighten the ship.

But Jonah had gone below deck, where he lay down and fell into a deep sleep. ⁶The captain went to him and said, "How can you sleep? Get up and call on your god! Maybe he will take notice of us, and we will not perish."

⁷Then the sailors said to each other, "Come, let us cast lots to find out who is responsible for this calamity." They cast lots and the lot fell on Jonah.

⁸So they asked him, "Tell us, who is responsible for making all

---

(margin, top)

1. If you had a chance to go on a cruise anywhere in the world, where would you go and why? 2. What role has "distance from mom and dad" played in your choice of school? Career? Mate? Residence? Faith? Have you ever been caught in a terrible storm while traveling? Describe it.

1. What seems both *fitting* and *surprising* about God's command (v. 2)? About Jonah's evasive effort? Why do you think Jonah disobeyed? 2. Jonah runs away in response to God's call. How does that compare to how other prophets responded (see 1Ki 17:1–6; Jer 1:4–10)? 3. What effect did God stirring and stilling the storm have on the sailors? In what sense are they saved (compare vv. 5,16)? Likewise, how is Jonah saved?

   Jonah 1:1–17   **JONAH FLEES FROM THE LORD**

Nineveh was the capital of Assyria, the ruthless empire which threatened (and eventually conquered) tiny Israel.

1. How do you think the prophet Jonah felt when he heard the "word of the Lord"?
   a. overwhelmed
   b. afraid
   c. confused
   d. enraged

2. Tarshish was about 2,000 miles in the opposite direction of Nineveh. What did Jonah think as he fled?
   a. God can get another prophet.
   b. God is going to get *me*!
   c. God will never find me.
   d. I'm due for a vacation about now.
   e. Nineveh doesn't deserve anything.

3. How do you think Jonah felt when he found out about the storm?
   a. responsible
   b. guilty
   c. afraid
   d. repentant
   e. suicidal

4. Why did Jonah tell the sailors to throw him into the sea?

a. He still hadn't "hit bottom."
b. He still thought he could get away.
c. He felt guilty about causing the sailors to perish.
d. He regarded going to Nineveh as worse than death.

5. How do you hear the "word of the Lord" most clearly?
   a. in nature
   b. reading Scripture
   c. through others
   d. through worship
   e. God's "still, small voice"

6. In your spiritual life, which direction are you running?
   a. away from God   c. with God
   b. back to God   d. behind God

7. Where do you go that is the opposite direction from where God is calling you?
   a. Nowhere, I avoid the message.
   b. I bury myself in work and other commitments.
   c. My personality changes.
   d. I slip away from Christian fellowship.

8. What keeps you from doing something you believe God is calling you to do?
   a. I'm comfortable where I am.
   b. I don't want to make waves.
   c. I'm not qualified.
   d. I care too much what others think.
   e. I'm afraid I might not be hearing God correctly.

9. How does this story relate to your outlook on life?
   a. I've set myself up with unrealistic expectations.
   b. My ideas and God's ideas about what's best for me seem different.
   c. When I'm unhappy, it's probably my own fault.
   d. I need to accept that this is where God has called me.

10. What does this story say to you about your career?
    a. I'm running away from something.
    b. I'd like to run away from something.
    c. I need a career adjustment.
    d. I need an attitude adjustment.
    e. I need to go the way God wants.

this trouble for us? What do you do? Where do you come from? What is your country? From what people are you?"

9He answered, "I am a Hebrew and I worship the LORD, the God of heaven, who made the sea and the land."

10This terrified them and they asked, "What have you done?" (They knew he was running away from the LORD, because he had already told them so.)

11The sea was getting rougher and rougher. So they asked him, "What should we do to you to make the sea calm down for us?"

12"Pick me up and throw me into the sea," he replied, "and it will become calm. I know that it is my fault that this great storm has come upon you."

13Instead, the men did their best to row back to land. But they could not, for the sea grew even wilder than before. 14Then they cried to the LORD, "O LORD, please do not let us die for taking this man's life. Do not hold us accountable for killing an innocent man, for you, O LORD, have done as you pleased." 15Then they took Jonah and threw him overboard, and the raging sea grew calm. 16At this the men greatly feared the LORD, and they offered a sacrifice to the LORD and made vows to him.

17But the LORD provided a great fish to swallow Jonah, and Jonah was inside the fish three days and three nights.

Jonah's Prayer

2 From inside the fish Jonah prayed to the LORD his God. 2He said:

"In my distress I called to the LORD,
    and he answered me.
From the depths of the grave*a* I called for help,
    and you listened to my cry.
3You hurled me into the deep,
    into the very heart of the seas,
    and the currents swirled about me;
all your waves and breakers
    swept over me.
4I said, 'I have been banished
    from your sight;
yet I will look again
    toward your holy temple.'
5The engulfing waters threatened me,*b*
    the deep surrounded me;
    seaweed was wrapped around my head.
6To the roots of the mountains I sank down;
    the earth beneath barred me in forever.
But you brought my life up from the pit,
    O LORD my God.

7"When my life was ebbing away,
    I remembered you, LORD,
and my prayer rose to you,
    to your holy temple.

8"Those who cling to worthless idols
    forfeit the grace that could be theirs.
9But I, with a song of thanksgiving,
    will sacrifice to you.
What I have vowed I will make good.
    Salvation comes from the LORD."

1. God's pursuit of Jonah is quite revealing. What does it reveal about: (a) The justice and mercy of God? (b) The gifts and call of God? (c) Human fear and faith? (d) God's claim to judge all the earth? 2. When have you "run away" from God—refusing to do something you know he's telling you to do? Where can you escape him (see Ps 139:7–12)? What "storms," then and now, bring you back? 3. Could God intervene in the world in a miraculous way more often? Why doesn't he? What kind of Christians would that create? 4. What's the meaning of Jonah's entombment for Jesus (Mt 12:40–41)? For you?

1. What was your favorite small hiding place as a child? How long could you stay there before you started feeling claustrophobic? 2. When have you ever felt, "My whole life passed before my eyes"? What happened? 3. In the ebb and flow of your life last year, when were you at "low tide"? At "high tide"? Why the big mood swing?

1. What do you see in this prayer: A psalm of thanksgiving? A call for help? Recommitment? What do you make of the fact that Jonah prays "inside the fish" (v. 1), and uses verbs in the *past tense*, as though God had already answered prayer? 2. While Jonah may be safe for the moment, how is he still in deep trouble? Where does he show assurance of deliverance in spite of appearances to the contrary (vv. 4, 6–7,9)? 3. Compare verse 3 with 1:15: How does Jonah view circumstances? God's control? God's purposes?

1. When have you felt like Jonah—far from God, enmeshed in a situation beyond your control? How then was your life brought "up from the pit"? 2. Where in your life are you desperate enough to pray *with hope*, as Jonah does?

a2 Hebrew *Sheol*   *b5* Or *waters were at my throat*

¹⁰And the LORD commanded the fish, and it vomited Jonah onto dry land.

Jonah Goes to Nineveh

3 Then the word of the LORD came to Jonah a second time: ²"Go to the great city of Nineveh and proclaim to it the message I give you."

³Jonah obeyed the word of the LORD and went to Nineveh. Now Nineveh was a very important city—a visit required three days. ⁴On the first day, Jonah started into the city. He proclaimed: "Forty more days and Nineveh will be overturned." ⁵The Ninevites believed God. They declared a fast, and all of them, from the greatest to the least, put on sackcloth.

⁶When the news reached the king of Nineveh, he rose from his throne, took off his royal robes, covered himself with sackcloth and sat down in the dust. ⁷Then he issued a proclamation in Nineveh:

"By the decree of the king and his nobles:

Do not let any man or beast, herd or flock, taste anything; do not let them eat or drink. ⁸But let man and beast be covered with sackcloth. Let everyone call urgently on God. Let them give up their evil ways and their violence. ⁹Who knows? God may yet relent and with compassion turn from his fierce anger so that we will not perish."

¹⁰When God saw what they did and how they turned from their evil ways, he had compassion and did not bring upon them the destruction he had threatened.

Side column (left)

What is the largest city you have ever visited at street level? How did you feel about the street people and their future?

1. What evidence do you see here that God is the God of "a second chance"? 2. In response to God's word, what does Jonah do? The Ninevites? Their king? 3. How do you account for their response to Jonah's message? For God's change of heart (v. 10)? What does this say about God's will? What does it say about God's use of us to achieve his will?

1. When has God given you two chances? To be or do what? To witness where? When have you ignored a second chance? Why? 2. If God gave you "Mission Impossible," 40 days after which the object of the mission would be destroyed, would you do it? Why or why not? 3. When would you consider "fasting" and "putting on a sackcloth," as the Ninevites did? What is a "spiritual fast"?

 Jonah 2:1–3:10   **JONAH GOES TO NINEVEH**

When God told Jonah to preach to Nineveh—capital of the evil Assyrian empire—Jonah fled the other way. When a storm came up, Jonah told the sailors to throw him overboard, then was swallowed by a great fish.

1. What song title best describes the book of Jonah?
a. "Stop—in the Name of Love"
b. "Slip Sliding Away"
c. "On the Road Again"
d. "I've Learned My Lesson Well" ("Garden Party")
e. "Amazing Grace"

2. What would you call Jonah's prayer from inside the fish?
a. a cry for help
b. a psalm of thanksgiving
c. spiritual recommitment
d. a confession of hope

3. Why did the fish vomit Jonah onto dry land?
a. He was sick of Jonah.
b. God told him to.
c. God wasn't finished with Jonah.
d. Jonah had learned his lesson.

4. How do you think Jonah felt as he headed toward Nineveh?
a. grateful to be alive
b. anxious to preach
c. afraid of what the Ninevites would do to him
d. afraid the Ninevites would repent

5. How would you describe Nineveh's reaction to Jonah's message?
a. radical
b. sincere
c. too little too late
d. appropriate
e. humble
f. just what Jonah feared
g. just what God wanted

6. What is your "Nineveh"?
a. an unfriendly place
b. a difficult person
c. an unpleasant emotion
d. a personal bondage
e. God's call in my life

7. How do you feel when you know you have responded to God's call?
a. free as a bird
b. deeply satisfied

c. relieved
d. close to God
e. still confused

8. Share a time when God gave you a second chance? Have you ever ignored God's second chance?

9. When have you felt like Jonah—far from God and enmeshed in a situation beyond your control? How were you rescued?

10. How does this story relate to your spiritual pilgrimage?
a. I've been in "the pit" (2:6).
b. I'm *in* the pit.
c. I'm trying to fulfill a vow I made to the Lord (2:9).
d. I've recently recognized that "salvation comes from the Lord" alone (2:9).
e. I've made a complete 180-degree turn (3:3).
f. I'm afraid if I don't return to God, I'm headed for disaster (3:4).
g. I need to get really serious about my faith (3:5–8).

Jonah's Anger at the LORD's Compassion

4 But Jonah was greatly displeased and became angry. [2]He prayed to the LORD, "O LORD, is this not what I said when I was still at home? That is why I was so quick to flee to Tarshish. I knew that you are a gracious and compassionate God, slow to anger and abounding in love, a God who relents from sending calamity. [3]Now, O LORD, take away my life, for it is better for me to die than to live."

[4]But the LORD replied, "Have you any right to be angry?"

[5]Jonah went out and sat down at a place east of the city. There he made himself a shelter, sat in its shade and waited to see what would happen to the city. [6]Then the LORD God provided a vine and made it grow up over Jonah to give shade for his head to ease his discomfort, and Jonah was very happy about the vine. [7]But at dawn the next day God provided a worm, which chewed the vine so that it withered. [8]When the sun rose, God provided a scorching east wind, and the sun blazed on Jonah's head so that he grew faint. He wanted to die, and said, "It would be better for me to die than to live."

[9]But God said to Jonah, "Do you have a right to be angry about the vine?"

"I do," he said. "I am angry enough to die."

[10]But the LORD said, "You have been concerned about this vine, though you did not tend it or make it grow. It sprang up overnight and died overnight. [11]But Nineveh has more than a hundred and twenty thousand people who cannot tell their right hand from their left, and many cattle as well. Should I not be concerned about that great city?"

How do you usually express anger?

1. Why did Jonah run from God earlier (v. 2)? Why is he depressed and angry now? What is the history of relations between the Israelites and the Assyrians? 2. Given the size of the city (v. 11; see also 3:3), the message to be proclaimed (3:4), and what you know about God (v. 2; see Ex 34:6–7), how would you have felt? Like Jonah (vv. 1–3)? Why? 3. What three things does God provide Jonah? Why? What do the vine, worm and hot sun reveal about God? About Jonah? 4. How would you end this dangling story? 5. Compare Elijah's encounter with Baal-worship in 1 Kings 17–19 with Jonah's relation to these heathens. What peak religious experiences, depressions, provisions, and rebuke from God do they have in common with each other? With you and your life?

1. When have you tried limiting God's mercy to others? To yourself? To whom is God wanting you to show mercy? 2. How has God challenged you in your study of Jonah?

Jonah 4:1–11   **JONAH'S ANGER AT GOD'S COMPASSION**

1. What was the reason for Jonah's anger?
   a. God backed out on his promise to destroy Nineveh.
   b. God robbed Jonah of seeing the destruction of these evil Gentiles.
   c. Jonah was angry that God would be merciful to Israel's enemies.
   d. Jonah thought God's favor was limited to Israel and excluded Gentiles.

2. Why did Jonah ask the Lord to take his life?
   a. He was just spouting off.
   b. He was deeply depressed.
   c. If the Ninevites were going to live, Jonah prefered to die.
   d. Jonah's reputation as a Jewish prophet was at stake.
   e. Jonah forgot that God had just spared his life.

3. How did God deal with Jonah?
   a. God toyed with Jonah.
   b. God showed that he's in charge.
   c. God exposed Jonah's selfishness.
   d. God used a parable to make his point.

4. How does the book of Jonah end?
   a. like something is missing
   b. like it began—God has the first and last word
   c. emphasizing God's compassion
   d. emphasizing Jonah's (and our) need to have compassion

5. What was Jonah's biggest problem?
   a. prejudice   f. disobedience
   b. pouting   g. jealousy
   c. pride   h. burnout
   d. procrastination   i. depression
   e. being "hot-headed"

6. Which characteristic in the last question are you most vulnerable to? What can you do to avoid it?

7. How do you express anger in general, and anger toward God in particular? How prone are you to pout?

8. How willing are you to go to others with a message of repentance toward God and faith in Christ?
   a. Count me out, I'll be out of town.
   b. Count me out, I don't know enough about the Bible.
   c. Count me out, I admit that I don't care enough about other people.
   d. Count me in, but only if I don't have to take much heat.
   e. Count me in, with God's help I'll give it a shot.

9. Who are the "Ninevites" to whom God might be calling you to go?
   a. the unchurched in my community
   b. my neighbors next door
   c. my coworkers
   d. my classmates
   e. my "enemies"

10. What feelings do you have toward these people?
    a. apathy   d. fear
    b. anger   e. pity
    c. jealousy   f. compassion

11. What moral from Jonah will you apply to your "missionary vision"?
    a. Don't start what you can't finish.
    b. Get rid of your prejudice.
    c. Show mercy where you've been shown mercy.
    d. Be willing to go anywhere, anytime, to anyone with a message from God.

INTRODUCTION to
MICAH

Book Study Outline: If you are using Micah for a study course, here is a 7-week outline. Use the questions in the margin for your group agenda:

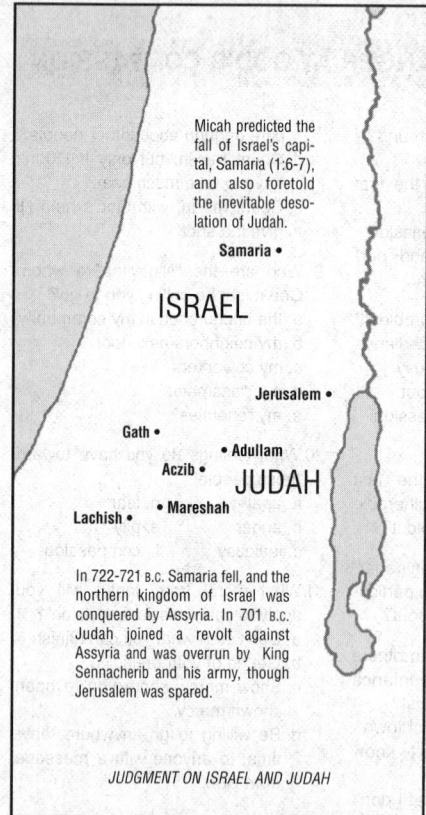

start meeting / 15 min.

read & discuss Bible / 30 min.

close meeting / 15–45 min.

7-week plan	Personal Reading	Group Study Passage
1	1:1–16	1:1–7/Judgment and Shame
2	2:1–13	2:6–13/False Prophets
3	3:1–12	3:1–12/True Prophets
4	4:1–13	4:6–13/God's Future Reign
5	5:1–15	5:1–5a/God's Future Ruler
6	6:1–16	6:1–8/God's Accusation
7	7:1–20	7:14–20/Israel's Restoration

Refer to the Questions and Answers in the front of this Bible for more information.

Author: Micah, a contemporary of Isaiah and Hosea.

Date: These prophecies were given during the reigns of Jotham, Ahaz and Hezekiah (1:1)—kings of Judah who reigned c. 750–686 B.C. Since Micah predicted the fall of Samaria (1:6–7), which occurred in c. 722 B.C., these prophecies would date from before then.

Theme: A just and merciful God delivers his people from darkness. The lives of God's covenant people should reflect God's standards.

Micah predicted the fall of Israel's capital, Samaria (1:6-7), and also foretold the inevitable desolation of Judah.

Samaria •

ISRAEL

Jerusalem •

Gath •
Aczib •   • Adullam
    JUDAH
Lachish •   • Mareshah

In 722-721 B.C. Samaria fell, and the northern kingdom of Israel was conquered by Assyria. In 701 B.C. Judah joined a revolt against Assyria and was overrun by King Sennacherib and his army, though Jerusalem was spared.

JUDGMENT ON ISRAEL AND JUDAH

Historical Background: It is helpful to understand the life and times during which Micah prophesied (1:1; see 2Ki 15:32–20:21). During this dark time when the sins of the nothern kingdom of Israel were being punished by Assyrian invaders, Micah could see that these same activities (idolatry, Baal worship, child sacrifice, sorcery) were creeping south to Judah and Jerusalem. As in the northern kingdom, this led to an increasing gap between the rich and the poor. The poor were oppressed with no recourse to the courts, because of corrupt judges, so Micah champions their cause. Religious life flourished but had little depth or reality. Micah draws a sharp contrast between this "pop religion" and true faith, which involves justice, mercy and walking with God (6:8).

Characteristics: Against this background, judgment is inevitable, says Micah. However, it will be followed by restoration, which will prepare the way for a new future. Micah emphasizes God's undeserved grace and unstoppable initiative. Micah had a big view of history, taking in several thousand years at a glance. One moment he is talking about the promised Messiah; in the next fragment of verses he may focus on the imminent invasion of Assyria. Reading these short speeches with their rapid shifts of focus can be confusing. Furthermore, Micah shifts voices frequently—from God to Micah to the rebellious people and back again. Micah also has a passion for punning, as in 1:10–15 (see NIV text footnotes).

Micah

1 The word of the LORD that came to Micah of Moresheth during the reigns of Jotham, Ahaz and Hezekiah, kings of Judah—the vision he saw concerning Samaria and Jerusalem.

> ²Hear, O peoples, all of you,
>> listen, O earth and all who are in it,
> that the Sovereign LORD may witness against you,
>> the Lord from his holy temple.

Judgment Against Samaria and Jerusalem

> ³Look! The LORD is coming from his dwelling place;
>> he comes down and treads the high places of
>> the earth.
> ⁴The mountains melt beneath him
>> and the valleys split apart,
> like wax before the fire,
>> like water rushing down a slope.
> ⁵All this is because of Jacob's transgression,
>> because of the sins of the house of Israel.
> What is Jacob's transgression?
>> Is it not Samaria?
> What is Judah's high place?
>> Is it not Jerusalem?

> ⁶"Therefore I will make Samaria a heap of rubble,
>> a place for planting vineyards.
> I will pour her stones into the valley
>> and lay bare her foundations.
> ⁷All her idols will be broken to pieces;
>> all her temple gifts will be burned with fire;
>> I will destroy all her images.
> Since she gathered her gifts from the wages of
>> prostitutes,
>> as the wages of prostitutes they will again be
>> used."

Weeping and Mourning

> ⁸Because of this I will weep and wail;
>> I will go about barefoot and naked.
> I will howl like a jackal
>> and moan like an owl.
> ⁹For her wound is incurable;
>> it has come to Judah.
> It[a] has reached the very gate of my people,
>> even to Jerusalem itself.
> ¹⁰Tell it not in Gath[b];
>> weep not at all.[c]
> In Beth Ophrah[d]
>> roll in the dust.
> ¹¹Pass on in nakedness and shame,

---

1. When have you seen one of your parents get really angry? Over what issues? How is your anger like, and unlike, his or hers? 2. What is your favorite city? Why do you like it?

1. Just as Washington and Moscow represent countries, what kingdoms do Samaria and Jerusalem here represent? 2. What's happening in the divided kingdoms under Jotham (see 2Ki 15:32–35)? Under Ahaz (see 2Ki 16)? Under Hezekiah (see 2Ki 18)? 3. While Micah's ministry and the kings' reign are localized (v. 1), is God's rule restricted (vv. 2–3)? Why is God coming out of his dwelling place? 4. To what does Micah compare God's wrath? How does God's holy, perfect wrath differ from human wrath?

1. Does your capital city represent what is wrong with your country? How so? Do your rulers ever acknowledge God's rule over them? How? 2. How big is your God? When have you tried confining him to heaven? To church? To civic life? 3. What would God's wrath feel like to you? To someone you know?

What hometowns do you still connect with? Do you still read the local news? Hear the town gossip? What concerns you most about changes in this town(s)?

1. How widespread is the sacking of the Southern Kingdom by the Assyrians as prophesied here? As reported in 2 Kings 18–19? 2. How does this message affect the messenger (v. 8)? Why would Micah go naked or imitate a jackal? What does he feel for these hometowns in the path of an invader? 3. What is the diagnosis and prognosis of Judah's spiritual disease (vv. 9–15)? What puns do you see here on the town names (see footnotes)? 4. Is Micah

---

a9 Or *He*   b10 *Gath* sounds like the Hebrew for *tell.*   c10 Hebrew; Septuagint may suggest *not in Acco.* The Hebrew for *in Acco* sounds like the Hebrew for *weep.* d10 *Beth Ophrah* means *house of dust.*

saying there's no hope of avoiding imminent destruction? Or is he condemning false hope? Why do you think so? **5.** How do you explain that this "disaster has come from the Lord" (v. 12): (a) Assyria's gods were stronger? (b) God was powerless to stop it? (c) God didn't care enough to stop it? (d) It simply happened? (e) God was somehow behind it all, punishing and restraining evil? (f) All common disasters come from God? Explain.

1. People shave heads for different reasons. What would it mean to an Israelite (v. 16)? To a Hare Krishna devotee? To a punk rocker? To you? **2.** Micah's very personal lament is a model. The last time you criticized someone, did it hurt you as much as them? Was there "weeping and mourning" in your communication? How did it come through? **3.** If we are commanded not to judge, seek revenge, or burn with rage, how can God? Does he have rights that we don't?

Have you received family heirlooms from other generations? How do you feel about such relics?

1. What do the idle rich plan day and night? With what result? Who are these idle rich: Landowners? Moneylenders? Insurance agents? Politicians? **2.** How does God here demonstrate his concern for the poor and defrauded (compare 1Ki 21)? Why does God respond to pride with taunts and traitors? **3.** Does God's justice, as portrayed here, disturb you? How? Is God just in planning disaster (vv. 3–5) against his people? How so? **4.** What is the link here between justice and other-centered humility? Between injustice and self-seeking pride?

1. Today, many people have lost property or possessions because of fraudulent or illegal schemes. When was something that belonged to you taken from you unjustly? How did you feel toward the person who took it? **2.** If you were among Micah's hearers, would you feel envious? Defrauded? Proud? Ridiculed? Betrayed? Humbled? **3.** If you had no one "in the Lord's assembly" (v. 5), what would you fear losing?

you who live in Shaphir.[a]
Those who live in Zaanan[b]
  will not come out.
Beth Ezel is in mourning;
  its protection is taken from you.
[12]Those who live in Maroth[c] writhe in pain,
  waiting for relief,
because disaster has come from the LORD,
  even to the gate of Jerusalem.
[13]You who live in Lachish,[d]
  harness the team to the chariot.
You were the beginning of sin
  to the Daughter of Zion,
for the transgressions of Israel
  were found in you.
[14]Therefore you will give parting gifts
  to Moresheth Gath.
The town of Aczib[e] will prove deceptive
  to the kings of Israel.
[15]I will bring a conqueror against you
  who live in Mareshah.[f]
He who is the glory of Israel
  will come to Adullam.
[16]Shave your heads in mourning
  for the children in whom you delight;
make yourselves as bald as the vulture,
  for they will go from you into exile.

Man's Plans and God's

2 Woe to those who plan iniquity,
  to those who plot evil on their beds!
At morning's light they carry it out
  because it is in their power to do it.
[2]They covet fields and seize them,
  and houses, and take them.
They defraud a man of his home,
  a fellowman of his inheritance.

[3]Therefore, the LORD says:

"I am planning disaster against this people,
  from which you cannot save yourselves.
You will no longer walk proudly,
  for it will be a time of calamity.
[4]In that day men will ridicule you;
  they will taunt you with this mournful song:
'We are utterly ruined;
  my people's possession is divided up.
He takes it from me!
  He assigns our fields to traitors.'"

[5]Therefore you will have no one in the assembly of
  the LORD
  to divide the land by lot.

---

a11 Shaphir means pleasant.   *b11 Zaanan sounds like the Hebrew for come out.*
c12 Maroth sounds like the Hebrew for bitter.   *d13 Lachish sounds like the Hebrew for team.*   *e14 Aczib means deception.*   *f15 Mareshah sounds like the Hebrew for conqueror.*

False Prophets

⁶"Do not prophesy," their prophets say.
  "Do not prophesy about these things;
  disgrace will not overtake us."
⁷Should it be said, O house of Jacob:
  "Is the Spirit of the LORD angry?
  Does he do such things?"

"Do not my words do good
  to him whose ways are upright?
⁸Lately my people have risen up
  like an enemy.
You strip off the rich robe
  from those who pass by without a care,
  like men returning from battle.
⁹You drive the women of my people
  from their pleasant homes.
You take away my blessing
  from their children forever.
¹⁰Get up, go away!
  For this is not your resting place,
because it is defiled,
  it is ruined, beyond all remedy.
¹¹If a liar and deceiver comes and says,
  'I will prophesy for you plenty of wine and
    beer,'
  he would be just the prophet for this people!

Deliverance Promised

¹²"I will surely gather all of you, O Jacob;
  I will surely bring together the remnant of
    Israel.
I will bring them together like sheep in a pen,
  like a flock in its pasture;
  the place will throng with people.
¹³One who breaks open the way will go up before
    them;
  they will break through the gate and go out.
Their king will pass through before them,
  the LORD at their head."

Leaders and Prophets Rebuked

3 Then I said,

"Listen, you leaders of Jacob,
  you rulers of the house of Israel.
Should you not know justice,
² you who hate good and love evil;
who tear the skin from my people
  and the flesh from their bones;
³who eat my people's flesh,
  strip off their skin
  and break their bones in pieces;
who chop them up like meat for the pan,
  like flesh for the pot?"

⁴Then they will cry out to the LORD,
  but he will not answer them.
At that time he will hide his face from them
  because of the evil they have done.

---

1. What most disturbs you: Raising taxes? Speaking for God? False, misleading advertising? Impersonations? Give an example. 2. In your experience, when is good news most appreciated and welcomed? Why?

1. How do the false prophets try to silence Micah (vv. 6–7a,11)? Why? 2. What tones of voice do you hear in Micah's response (vv. 7b–11)? Why this rhetoric? How would it be received? 3. What has made God's people an "enemy" (vv. 8–9)? What are they doing to themselves? How do you account for this? What is God's response to people who are bent on self-destruction? 4. Are the people aware of their wrongdoing? Or do they see themselves as fairly pious? How so? 5. The oracle in verses 12–13 refers to a later time. Why do you suppose it was inserted into this context? 6. What is the good news here? Who is "their king"? How can God love the very people he judges?

1. Were you ever not believed when you were telling the truth? Why weren't you believed? 2. Who in your world says, "You can have it all"? What is your honest reaction to such a sales pitch? If you were Micah, what would be your retort? 3. If God were showing wrath to you, how might he also be merciful?

---

1. If the phone doesn't ring and there's no mail for days, how does that make you feel? 2. Have you ever felt like the plug was pulled out of your life? How did you cope with the power failure?

1. Why is Micah doubly hard on these leaders? What three groups of leaders does he rebuke? 2. When someone calls another person a cannibal, what does that usually mean? Of what "cannibalistic," self-serving concept of justice are these leaders guilty (vv. 2–3,5)? Why should they know better? 3. On what basis were they presuming God would rubber-stamp their unjust decisions? How does Micah feed hungry prophets their just desserts? What does the Lord's silence look like? Sound

like? Feel like? **4.** How is Micah empowered by God and at odds with the state religion (vv. 8–9)? **5.** What misunderstanding of God (v. 11, see also Dt 16:18–20) distorts their prophecy and destroys the people (vv. 9–12)?

1. What does this chapter imply about God's expectations of those in your country and community who are entrusted with faithfully upholding justice for all? Are there any current legislators, executives or judges where you live who might fail by Micah's standards? **2.** What would Micah say today about those who carry on religious ritual or preach peace, yet oppress the poor? **3.** What is the more popular notion of God today: The God of mercy? Or the God of wrath? Why is that? How does Micah balance your image of God? **4.** Have you ever felt like your prayers went no higher than the ceiling? How do you know God is there, especially when he is silent? **5.** In response to earthquakes, terrorist bombings, highway deaths, the AIDS epidemic, etc., people often say, "How can God allow this?" For what kinds of disasters do you lay the blame on civil leaders? On church leaders? On victims? Chance? God?

---

1. What do you like most about mountains? Trees? Which mountain is "chief" for you? Why? What is your tree of choice? Why? **2.** What is your favorite antiwar slogan? Why that one?

1. Which mountain will be "chief" for God's people? What exalts it above the rest? **2.** In this prophecy, what changes will be accomplished? By whom? When (v. 1)? **3.** What time frame do you think "the last days" refers to in this context: In this world? In the next? Or when the Messiah returns? Why? **4.** How does this prophecy of "swords beaten into plowshares" (v. 3) square with the one just before it of Zion "plowed like a field" by the sword (3:12)? How does this

⁵This is what the LORD says:

> "As for the prophets
>   who lead my people astray,
> if one feeds them,
>   they proclaim 'peace';
> if he does not,
>   they prepare to wage war against him.
> ⁶Therefore night will come over you, without
>   visions,
>   and darkness, without divination.
> The sun will set for the prophets,
>   and the day will go dark for them.
> ⁷The seers will be ashamed
>   and the diviners disgraced.
> They will all cover their faces
>   because there is no answer from God."

> ⁸But as for me, I am filled with power,
>   with the Spirit of the LORD,
>   and with justice and might,
> to declare to Jacob his transgression,
>   to Israel his sin.
> ⁹Hear this, you leaders of the house of Jacob,
>   you rulers of the house of Israel,
> who despise justice
>   and distort all that is right;
> ¹⁰who build Zion with bloodshed,
>   and Jerusalem with wickedness.
> ¹¹Her leaders judge for a bribe,
>   her priests teach for a price,
>   and her prophets tell fortunes for money.
> Yet they lean upon the LORD and say,
>   "Is not the LORD among us?
>   No disaster will come upon us."
> ¹²Therefore because of you,
>   Zion will be plowed like a field,
> Jerusalem will become a heap of rubble,
>   the temple hill a mound overgrown with
>   thickets.

The Mountain of the LORD

4 In the last days

> the mountain of the LORD's temple will be
>   established
>   as chief among the mountains;
> it will be raised above the hills,
>   and peoples will stream to it.

²Many nations will come and say,

> "Come, let us go up to the mountain of the LORD,
>   to the house of the God of Jacob.
> He will teach us his ways,
>   so that we may walk in his paths."
> The law will go out from Zion,
>   the word of the LORD from Jerusalem.
> ³He will judge between many peoples
>   and will settle disputes for strong nations far
>   and wide.

They will beat their swords into plowshares
     and their spears into pruning hooks.
Nation will not take up sword against nation,
     nor will they train for war anymore.
⁴Every man will sit under his own vine
     and under his own fig tree,
and no one will make them afraid,
     for the LORD Almighty has spoken.
⁵All the nations may walk
     in the name of their gods;
we will walk in the name of the LORD
     our God for ever and ever.

The LORD's Plan

⁶"In that day," declares the LORD,

"I will gather the lame;
     I will assemble the exiles
and those I have brought to grief.
⁷I will make the lame a remnant,
     those driven away a strong nation.
The LORD will rule over them in Mount Zion
     from that day and forever.
⁸As for you, O watchtower of the flock,
     O strongholdᵃ of the Daughter of Zion,
the former dominion will be restored to you;
     kingship will come to the Daughter of
          Jerusalem."

⁹Why do you now cry aloud—
     have you no king?
Has your counselor perished,
     that pain seizes you like that of a woman in
          labor?
¹⁰Writhe in agony, O Daughter of Zion,
     like a woman in labor,
for now you must leave the city
     to camp in the open field.
You will go to Babylon;
     there you will be rescued.
There the LORD will redeem you
     out of the hand of your enemies.

¹¹But now many nations
     are gathered against you.
They say, "Let her be defiled,
     let our eyes gloat over Zion!"
¹²But they do not know
     the thoughts of the LORD;
they do not understand his plan,
     he who gathers them like sheaves to the
          threshing floor.

¹³"Rise and thresh, O Daughter of Zion,
     for I will give you horns of iron;
I will give you hoofs of bronze
     and you will break to pieces many nations."

You will devote their ill-gotten gains to the LORD,
     their wealth to the Lord of all the earth.

vision of united nations under God
fit Isaiah 19:23–25?

What is your vision of perfect peace? Should Christians take the lead in the disarmament movement? How else, by God's grace, will you plan, work and pray toward your peace project?

---

1. What do you like to gather, collect or assemble? What project have you recently completed with your children (or parents)? 2. What was your longest time away from home? How did you feel coming home?

1. What will the Lord do for the lame, the exiled and grief-stricken? What has happened to bring you to this point of need? 2. What is the "remnant" here (v. 7; see Isa 10:20–23; Jer 23:1–8)? What is the equivalent of that remnant today? 3. How is this future kingdom (vv. 7–8) a comfort to those who would suffer the fall of Jerusalem (130 years hence, in 586 B.C.)? What comfort does that kingdom bring to those who suffer "now" (v. 11)? 4. The nations now gloating over Zion are in for a rude awakening. What? What don't they understand about their role in God's plan of punishment (vv. 11–13; see Isa 10:5–19)? What is to be the role of the remnant in this spiritual warfare?

1. Pain and joy are intermingled in birth (v. 10) and in the Christian life. How has this been true for you this past year? How is hope in God's kingdom helping you with a painful situation? Would you be a believer if it were not for pain? Why? 2. Who are the lame, the exiled and the grief-stricken where you live? With whom can you share this hope? 3. Would a country's refusal to arm itself (as in 4:3) increase its vulnerability or power (4:6–7a, 11–13)? Do you have faith to believe pacifism is God's way for you? Enough to persuade others?

ᵃ8 Or *hill*

1. Compare the hopelessness in verse 1 with the security and peace in verses 4–5: What does that contrast mean? Who (v. 2) makes the big difference? What will his reign of peace look like? Feel like? 2. Who is this ruler from Bethlehem: King David (see 1Sa 16:1–13)? Christ Jesus (see Mt 2:6)? Or both? What will he do for his people? 3. How might such humble, ancient roots shape the way he rules?

1. What makes you feel like a besieged city, or a secure flock? What "rules" you in each case? 2. When have you seen despair give birth to hope? What "midwife" made the difference? 3. How far can and should a country go in relying on God's Messiah as its only national defense?

1. Complete this prayer: "Lord, deliver us from …"? Why is that your chief concern? 2. What do you like about carpet, clothing or food remnants? What redemptive purpose can they serve?

1. How is the vision of universal peace (4:1–5a) like, and unlike, this picture (5b–9)? 2. The Assyrian invasion takes place in 587 B.C. How will the redemption of God's remnant then take place (vv. 6–9)? 3. While this prophecy refers primarily to the release of the captives in 538 B.C., to what future deliverance can this prophecy also point? 4. What will this restoration of the remnant look like? How can the remnant be both morning dew which refreshes (v. 7) and roaring lion which devours (v. 8)? 5. What does God have against horses, chariots, strongholds, witchcraft, carved images, cities and the like (vv. 10–14)? What do they all have in common against God (v. 15)?

1. In what sense is your church like a spiritual remnant? Remnant of what? How is it like dew? A lion? 2. What would Micah say about modern empire-building in politics? In church life? Our superstitions, horoscopes and the occult? 3. What modern forms of rebellion and pride could you list beside the ones rebuked by Micah,

A Promised Ruler From Bethlehem

5 Marshal your troops, O city of troops,[a]
for a siege is laid against us.
They will strike Israel's ruler
on the cheek with a rod.

2"But you, Bethlehem Ephrathah,
though you are small among the clans[b] of
Judah,
out of you will come for me
one who will be ruler over Israel,
whose origins[c] are from of old,
from ancient times.[d]"

3Therefore Israel will be abandoned
until the time when she who is in labor gives
birth
and the rest of his brothers return
to join the Israelites.

4He will stand and shepherd his flock
in the strength of the LORD,
in the majesty of the name of the LORD his God.
And they will live securely, for then his greatness
will reach to the ends of the earth.
5   And he will be their peace.

Deliverance and Destruction

When the Assyrian invades our land
and marches through our fortresses,
we will raise against him seven shepherds,
even eight leaders of men.
6They will rule[e] the land of Assyria with the
sword,
the land of Nimrod with drawn sword.[f]
He will deliver us from the Assyrian
when he invades our land
and marches into our borders.

7The remnant of Jacob will be
in the midst of many peoples
like dew from the LORD,
like showers on the grass,
which do not wait for man
or linger for mankind.
8The remnant of Jacob will be among the nations,
in the midst of many peoples,
like a lion among the beasts of the forest,
like a young lion among flocks of sheep,
which mauls and mangles as it goes,
and no one can rescue.
9Your hand will be lifted up in triumph over your
enemies,
and all your foes will be destroyed.

10"In that day," declares the LORD,

"I will destroy your horses from among you
and demolish your chariots.

a1 Or *Strengthen your walls, O walled city*   b2 Or *rulers*   c2 Hebrew *goings out*
d2 Or *from days of eternity*   e6 Or *crush*   f6 Or *Nimrod in its gates*

11I will destroy the cities of your land
 and tear down all your strongholds.
12I will destroy your witchcraft
 and you will no longer cast spells.
13I will destroy your carved images
 and your sacred stones from among you;
 you will no longer bow down
 to the work of your hands.
14I will uproot from among you your Asherah
 poles*a*
 and demolish your cities.
15I will take vengeance in anger and wrath
 upon the nations that have not obeyed me."

The LORD's Case Against Israel

6 Listen to what the LORD says:

 "Stand up, plead your case before the mountains;
 let the hills hear what you have to say.
2Hear, O mountains, the LORD's accusation;
 listen, you everlasting foundations of the earth.
For the LORD has a case against his people;
 he is lodging a charge against Israel.

3"My people, what have I done to you?
 How have I burdened you? Answer me.
4I brought you up out of Egypt
 and redeemed you from the land of slavery.
I sent Moses to lead you,
 also Aaron and Miriam.
5My people, remember
 what Balak king of Moab counseled
 and what Balaam son of Beor answered.
Remember ∟your journey⌐ from Shittim to Gilgal,
 that you may know the righteous acts of the
 LORD."

6With what shall I come before the LORD
 and bow down before the exalted God?
Shall I come before him with burnt offerings,
 with calves a year old?
7Will the LORD be pleased with thousands of rams,
 with ten thousand rivers of oil?
Shall I offer my firstborn for my transgression,
 the fruit of my body for the sin of my soul?
8He has showed you, O man, what is good.
 And what does the LORD require of you?
To act justly and to love mercy
 and to walk humbly with your God.

Israel's Guilt and Punishment

9Listen! The LORD is calling to the city—
 and to fear your name is wisdom—
 "Heed the rod and the One who appointed it.*b*
10Am I still to forget, O wicked house,
 your ill-gotten treasures
 and the short ephah,*c* which is accursed?
11Shall I acquit a man with dishonest scales,

to be destroyed by the Lord "in that day"? Compare lists as a group. **4.** What might God want to destroy in your life? Why that? Would God be both loving and just to perform that spiritual "cancer surgery"? How so? **5.** To Micah, it was more important to be obedient (v. 15) than to be victorious. What does that way mean to our success-oriented society? How can you be sure you desire God, not success?

When, if ever, have you tried bribing your parents for a favor?

1. In this trial scene, who is the accused? The prosecutor? Chief witnesses? Judge and jury? **2.** What makes God's case against Israel so convincing (vv. 2–5)? What evidence do Moses, Aaron and Miriam provide? What did Balak counsel and Balaam answer (see Nu 22–24)? How does the "journey from Shittim to Gilgal" (see Jos 2–4) strengthen God's case? **3.** Under cross-examination, what does the accused have to say (vv. 6–8)? What does their silence imply? Are they guilty as charged? Why? **4.** What recompense can the accused offer? Why is such up-to-date religion inadequate? **5.** What will the Lord accept instead? Why?

1. On what would you base a case against God (v. 1)? Would it hold up in his court of justice and mercy? **2.** What does it mean to "act justly" and "love mercy" and "walk humbly"? Are you obeying? What requirements have *you* added to verse 8 in your own view of "what is good" for your life? Are these really from God?

1. Ever seen produce carefully weighed and packaged before your eyes? Describe such a store—its sights, sounds, smells, service. **2.** Where do you do most of your shopping? Why there?

1. How is the "fear" of God's name the source of wisdom (v. 9; see Pr 1:7)? What does it mean to "heed the rod"? **2.** How does God uphold the moral law (vv.

a 14 That is, symbols of the goddess Asherah   *b 9* The meaning of the Hebrew for this line is uncertain.   *c 10* An ephah was a dry measure.

10–16)? **3.** How will God's punishment fit the crime: (a) Sinners reap what they sow? (b) Sin afflicts undeserving victims? (c) Evil triumphs, but only for a day? (d) Others get the last laugh? (e) God is a scrooge? Explain. **4.** What sins of Northern kings, Omri and Ahab, are imitated by those in the South (v. 16; see 1Ki 16:21–33)?

1. In God's discipline of Israel, what view of sin does that encourage you to adopt? Knowing God loves you and hates your sin, how will you be weighed in the balance? **2.** Where do you find dishonest traders today? Does the punishment still fit the crime? Is that as effective as in Micah's day?

---

1. What food do you crave, even now? When deprived of that, what are you like? **2.** For what visitor will you clean house: The boss? Your parents? Neighbor? Your first date? (Why that one?)

1. Who is Micah speaking for here in chapter 7: himself or the repentant remnant of Israel? Is he miserable (v. 1) or hopeful (v. 7)? Why do you think so? What is the figurative food he desires? **2.** If God restrains sin, what happens when people block him out of their lives (vv. 2–6)? How bad does it get in government? In the streets? In the home? **3.** Overcome by such misery, corruption and brokenness, what gives "me" (the repentant remnant) hope (v. 7)? What does "watching" and "waiting" for the Lord entail?

1. Where are you just now on the misery-hope index? Why? What spiritual hunger does that leave you with? **2.** On a large-scale misery-hope index, how would you rate your country compared to early Israel? Why that rating? What can be done about that?

with a bag of false weights?
[12]Her rich men are violent;
    her people are liars
    and their tongues speak deceitfully.
[13]Therefore, I have begun to destroy you,
    to ruin you because of your sins.
[14]You will eat but not be satisfied;
    your stomach will still be empty.[a]
You will store up but save nothing,
    because what you save I will give to the sword.
[15]You will plant but not harvest;
    you will press olives but not use the oil on
      yourselves,
    you will crush grapes but not drink the wine.
[16]You have observed the statutes of Omri
    and all the practices of Ahab's house,
    and you have followed their traditions.
Therefore I will give you over to ruin
    and your people to derision;
    you will bear the scorn of the nations.[b]"

Israel's Misery

7 What misery is mine!
I am like one who gathers summer fruit
    at the gleaning of the vineyard;
there is no cluster of grapes to eat,
    none of the early figs that I crave.
[2]The godly have been swept from the land;
    not one upright man remains.
All men lie in wait to shed blood;
    each hunts his brother with a net.
[3]Both hands are skilled in doing evil;
    the ruler demands gifts,
    the judge accepts bribes,
    the powerful dictate what they desire—
    they all conspire together.
[4]The best of them is like a brier,
    the most upright worse than a thorn hedge.
The day of your watchmen has come,
    the day God visits you.
Now is the time of their confusion.
[5]Do not trust a neighbor;
    put no confidence in a friend.
Even with her who lies in your embrace
    be careful of your words.
[6]For a son dishonors his father,
    a daughter rises up against her mother,
a daughter-in-law against her mother-in-law—
    a man's enemies are the members of his own
      household.

[7]But as for me, I watch in hope for the LORD,
    I wait for God my Savior;
    my God will hear me.

---

[a]14 The meaning of the Hebrew for this word is uncertain.   [b]16 Septuagint; Hebrew *scorn due my people*

Israel Will Rise

⁸Do not gloat over me, my enemy!
  Though I have fallen, I will rise.
Though I sit in darkness,
  the LORD will be my light.
⁹Because I have sinned against him,
  I will bear the LORD's wrath,
until he pleads my case
  and establishes my right.
He will bring me out into the light;
  I will see his righteousness.
¹⁰Then my enemy will see it
  and will be covered with shame,
she who said to me,
  "Where is the LORD your God?"
My eyes will see her downfall;
  even now she will be trampled underfoot
  like mire in the streets.

¹¹The day for building your walls will come,
  the day for extending your boundaries.
¹²In that day people will come to you
  from Assyria and the cities of Egypt,
  even from Egypt to the Euphrates
  and from sea to sea
  and from mountain to mountain.
¹³The earth will become desolate because of its
      inhabitants,
  as the result of their deeds.

Prayer and Praise

¹⁴Shepherd your people with your staff,
  the flock of your inheritance,
which lives by itself in a forest,
  in fertile pasturelands.ᵃ
Let them feed in Bashan and Gilead
  as in days long ago.

¹⁵"As in the days when you came out of Egypt,
  I will show them my wonders."

¹⁶Nations will see and be ashamed,
  deprived of all their power.
They will lay their hands on their mouths
  and their ears will become deaf.
¹⁷They will lick dust like a snake,
  like creatures that crawl on the ground.
They will come trembling out of their dens;
  they will turn in fear to the LORD our God
  and will be afraid of you.
¹⁸Who is a God like you,
  who pardons sin and forgives the transgression
  of the remnant of his inheritance?
You do not stay angry forever
  but delight to show mercy.
¹⁹You will again have compassion on us;
  you will tread our sins underfoot

ᵃ14 Or *in the middle of Carmel*

What helps you to see light at the end of the tunnel?

1. Who seems to be speaking in verses 8–10? In verses 11–13? What is each saying? **2.** Why will the gloating nations feel shame instead (v. 10)? **3.** What out-of-the-darkness and into-the-light experience does fallen Israel anticipate? How does this prove the mercy and justice of the Lord (v. 9)? **4.** What world-wide "desolation" and "deeds" are expected (v. 13)? **5.** How will this fix attention on spiritual Israel (v. 12)? Why will that mean wrath for some, but salvation for others?

1. How does God answer the enemy's question in verse 10? When your enemy (or the Enemy) asks you the same, how do you answer? Based on what? **2.** At what points do you identify with Israel and her enemies: (a) Gloating over others? (b) Sitting in darkness? (c) Covered with shame? (d) Seeing righteousness prevail? (e) Trampled underfoot? (f) Secure in your salvation? (g) Extending your boundaries?

---

1. Can you communicate without using your hands? How well? **2.** When was the last time you felt like the proverbial three monkeys: "See-no-evil" (hands over eyes), "Hear-no-evil" (hands in ears) and "Speak-no-evil" (hands on mouth)? **3.** Which monkey are you like?

1. What restoration is here pictured for Israel's (and your) prayer and praise? What picture of God do you see? **2.** What is the basis in antiquity for these "wonders from God" (v. 15)? **3.** How will God confound the once proud, powerful nations (vv. 16–17)? Can you see this happening today?

1. Which aspect of Micah's God most endears him to you? Which aspect of God might cause you and others to repent in fear? To rebel in anger? **2.** From your study of Micah, do you believe God loves you because you are so good? Or because he is so good? Why? **3.** From your study of this book, how could this prophet have such a clear understanding of grace and hold forth the greatest hope, if he had not also the most serious view of sin? How are these three concepts related in the Gospel you present to others? **4.** What else have you appreciated from your group study of Micah? How will you remain true to Micah's God? **5.** Is there anything about you or your group which would inspire in outsiders a reverence and awe of your God (as in vv. 16–17)? Why or why not? **6.** What song might your group close with which affirms this God of wonders?

and hurl all our iniquities into the depths of the
    sea.
20You will be true to Jacob,
    and show mercy to Abraham,
as you pledged on oath to our fathers
    in days long ago.

INTRODUCTION to
NAHUM

Book Study Outline: If you are using Nahum for a study course, here is a 3-week outline. Use the questions in the margin for your group agenda:

☕ start meeting / 15 min.

📖 read & discuss Bible / 30 min.

♡ close meeting / 15–45 min.

3-week plan	Personal Reading	Group Study Passage
1	1:1–15	Proclaiming God's Anger Against Nineveh
2	2:1–13	Predicting the Fall of Nineveh
3	3:1–19	Portraying the Woe to Nineveh

Refer to the Questions and Answers in the front of this Bible for more information.

Author: Nahum, "the Elkoshite," who was probably from Judah.

Date: Nahum's oracle is dated between the overthrow of Thebes (in 663 B.C.; see 3:8–10) and the fall of Nineveh (in 612 B.C.).

Theme: The Lord's judgment of Nineveh.

Historical Background: Samaria had fallen at the hands of the Assyrians c. 722 B.C. About 700 B.C., the Assyrian king Sennacherib made Nineveh, which was the greatest city of its day, the capital of the empire. Jonah had announced Nineveh's doom, but the people repented and were given a "stay of execution" (see the Introduction to Jonah). However, they quickly returned to their evil ways. Poetic justice and Nineveh's destruction are the focus of Nahum's prophecy. Within a few years, Nahum's prophecies came true. Proud Nineveh fell so hard that it never rose again. Its site was obliterated; it was only rediscovered some 2500 years later!

Characteristics: Like Obadiah, but unlike other minor prophets, Nahum does not address his homeland at all, but a foreign city—Nineveh. Still, the book was intended for Jewish readers. While the style of Nahum is that of traditional judgment oracles, the language is poetic, with many metaphors and similes, as well as other vivid images. Each of the three chapters in Nahum is a complete unit in itself. Chapter 1 is in the form of an acrostic poem in which Nahum declares the judgment that is to come. Chapter 2 describes the siege and subsequent sack of Nineveh. In chapter 3, Nineveh is described and compared to Thebes. Thebes, the capital of Upper Egypt, was a city like Nineveh that was strong and proud and yet its destruction had come. Thus Nahum shows that the God of Israel is, in fact, the God who controls the fate of all the nations. Nahum's purpose is to lift up the great God of Israel, and thus bring comfort to his people. (The name "Nahum" means "comfort.") This book is a powerful indictment of a nation that seeks glory by aggression and oppression. God hates violence and pride and "will not leave the guilty unpunished" (1:3).

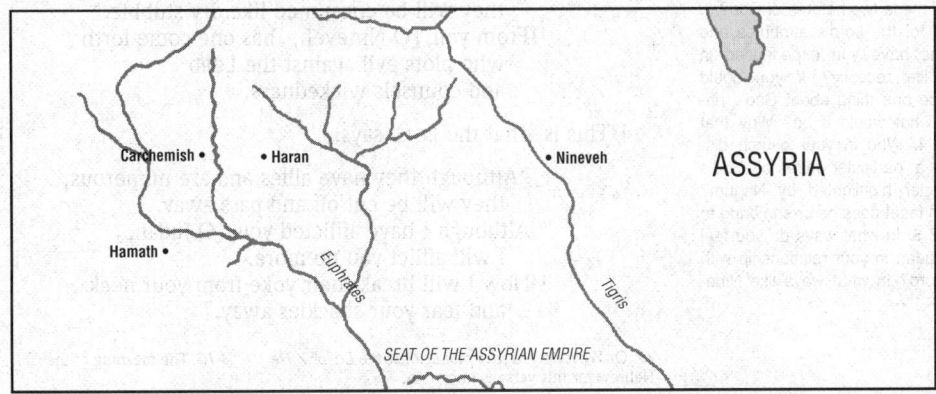

SEAT OF THE ASSYRIAN EMPIRE

Nahum

☕ **1.** If your patience were likened to a keg of dynamite, would you have a: (a) Short fuse? (b) Long fuse? (c) No fuse? (d) No powder? (e) No keg? (f) Other? **2.** What pet peeve gives you a "pain in the neck"? Why is this a particular irritation to you? **3.** If, during this past week, your feet were dragging or you had a lilt or bounce in your step, what do you think was the reason?

📖 **1.** What do we learn about the attributes and actions of the Lord in verses 2–8? What characteristic of God demonstrated here surprises you? Why? **2.** What has Nineveh done to kindle the Lord's wrath (v. 2; see Jnh 1:2)? What images are used to depict Nineveh's end? **3.** Do you think verse 7 is part of Nahum's vision or his own personal opinion? Why? **4.** What words of comfort are meant only for Judah? What good news are they to take to the mountains and proclaim? Why are they now free to attend to their festivals and vows? **5.** What is the point of contrasting the futures of Nineveh and Judah? Why is God treating the two nations so differently?

♡ **1.** Does the fierce anger of God shock or distress you? In your opinion could God's anger be best likened to: (a) A keg of dynamite? (b) Mt. St. Helen's volcano? (c) Old Faithful? Explain. **2.** How do you reconcile God's wrath with God's love? Is one primary and the other secondary? Are they flip sides of the same coin? Or is there no way to bring consistency out of these two natures of God? **3.** Which of the Lord's attributes and actions have you experienced in your life recently? *If you could change one thing about God's nature, what would it be? Why that one?* **4.** Who in your church displays a particular facet of God's character highlighted by Nahum? Which facet does he or she bring to mind? **5.** In what ways do you feel like Judah in your relationship with the Lord? In what ways like Nineveh?

1 An oracle concerning Nineveh. The book of the vision of Nahum the Elkoshite.

The LORD's Anger Against Nineveh

²The LORD is a jealous and avenging God;
　the LORD takes vengeance and is filled with
　　wrath.
The LORD takes vengeance on his foes
　and maintains his wrath against his enemies.
³The LORD is slow to anger and great in power;
　the LORD will not leave the guilty unpunished.
His way is in the whirlwind and the storm,
　and clouds are the dust of his feet.
⁴He rebukes the sea and dries it up;
　he makes all the rivers run dry.
Bashan and Carmel wither
　and the blossoms of Lebanon fade.
⁵The mountains quake before him
　and the hills melt away.
The earth trembles at his presence,
　the world and all who live in it.
⁶Who can withstand his indignation?
　Who can endure his fierce anger?
His wrath is poured out like fire;
　the rocks are shattered before him.

⁷The LORD is good,
　a refuge in times of trouble.
He cares for those who trust in him,
⁸　but with an overwhelming flood
he will make an end of ⌐Nineveh⌐;
　he will pursue his foes into darkness.

⁹Whatever they plot against the LORD
　he*ᵃ* will bring to an end;
　trouble will not come a second time.
¹⁰They will be entangled among thorns
　and drunk from their wine;
　they will be consumed like dry stubble.*ᵇ*
¹¹From you, ⌐O Nineveh,⌐ has one come forth
　who plots evil against the LORD
　and counsels wickedness.

¹²This is what the LORD says:

"Although they have allies and are numerous,
　they will be cut off and pass away.
Although I have afflicted you, ⌐O Judah,⌐
　I will afflict you no more.
¹³Now I will break their yoke from your neck
　and tear your shackles away."

ᵃ9 Or *What do you foes plot against the LORD? / He*　　*ᵇ10* The meaning of the Hebrew for this verse is uncertain.

¹⁴The LORD has given a command concerning you,
  ˌNinevehˌ:
  "You will have no descendants to bear your
    name.
  I will destroy the carved images and cast idols
    that are in the temple of your gods.
  I will prepare your grave,
    for you are vile."

¹⁵Look, there on the mountains,
  the feet of one who brings good news,
  who proclaims peace!
  Celebrate your festivals, O Judah,
    and fulfill your vows.
  No more will the wicked invade you;
    they will be completely destroyed.

Nineveh to Fall

2   An attacker advances against you, ˌNinevehˌ.
  Guard the fortress,
  watch the road,
  brace yourselves,
  marshal all your strength!

²The LORD will restore the splendor of Jacob
  like the splendor of Israel,
  though destroyers have laid them waste
    and have ruined their vines.

³The shields of his soldiers are red;
  the warriors are clad in scarlet.
  The metal on the chariots flashes
    on the day they are made ready;
  the spears of pine are brandished.^a
⁴The chariots storm through the streets,
  rushing back and forth through the squares.
  They look like flaming torches;
    they dart about like lightning.

⁵He summons his picked troops,
  yet they stumble on their way.
  They dash to the city wall;
    the protective shield is put in place.
⁶The river gates are thrown open
    and the palace collapses.
⁷It is decreed^b that ˌthe cityˌ
    be exiled and carried away.
  Its slave girls moan like doves
    and beat upon their breasts.
⁸Nineveh is like a pool,
    and its water is draining away.
  "Stop! Stop!" they cry,
    but no one turns back.
⁹Plunder the silver!
  Plunder the gold!
  The supply is endless,
    the wealth from all its treasures!
¹⁰She is pillaged, plundered, stripped!

^a3 Hebrew; Septuagint and Syriac / the horsemen rush to and fro   ^b7 The meaning
of the Hebrew for this word is uncertain.

1. "Big cats" are a fascination in our zoos. Why do they interest you? 2. When was the last time you went to a history museum to see the chariots of old and knights in shining armor? Why might they interest you?

1. In what does Nineveh put her confidence? Why does the Lord encourage her to prepare for battle? 2. How do Nineveh's elite forces perform in the end? What comfort is this to Israel, a frequent victim of their cruelty (v. 2; see 1:12–13)? 3. Of Nahum's highly pictorial language, what images seem literal to you? Which seem figurative? 4. What is meant by the imagery of the pool (v. 8)? Of plundered wealth (v. 9)? How is Nineveh's humiliation and shame pictured? 5. The lion was this nation's symbol. In what ways had Nineveh lived up to the symbol in the past? How is it used to taunt her in defeat (vv. 11–13)? What irony do you see here? 6. Lest Nineveh gets the idea her downfall will be caused by merely natural disaster or superior fire power, what bottom line underscores that this is an act of God? 7. What specifically is the Lord dead set "against"?

1. Israel experienced God's restoring strength and power in the face of the enemy's attack. How have you seen God work this way in your own life? 2. God dealt convincingly with Nineveh's pride, as he always does (see Jas 4:6; Pr 3:34). What lessons do you learn about God from this story? How do you go about humbling yourself? 3. The Lord Almighty declares to Nineveh, "I am against you." To what extent is your nation guilty of the sins of Nineveh, such as cruelty and warmongering? What can be

done to bring repentance? **4.** How would you judge yourself based on God's standard regarding pride, cruelty or selfishness? Would your friends and others agree? Would you want to be held accountable for this?

---

1. Recall an embarrassing moment of your childhood. What happened that brought on such a red face? **2.** What best describes your parents' discipline of you as a child: (a) "I'm warning you"? (b) "Boys will be boys"? (c) "Face the music"? (d) Other? **3.** Recall a severe childhood (or adult) punishment you received that was the result of your deliberate disobedience. How did it make you feel? Did it alter your life in any way?

1. How does God discipline Nineveh? How do you view God's harshness? Why was such severity necessary? **2.** What impression do the staccato phrases in verses 2–3 make on you? Is this Nineveh's fate or that of her victims? Why does Nahum leave this unclear? **3.** In what ways has Nineveh "played the harlot" in relation to God (v. 4)? In what ways is she "ripe" for judgment? Why would the metaphorical punishment of verses 5 and 6 be especially appropriate to her? **4.** In what specific people and things does Nineveh put her trust? What images does Nahum use to describe these "trustworthy" sources? Which do you think is most striking? What is the end of each? **5.** What great sin of Nineveh is graphically addressed in verses 16–17? How does the image of the locust fit the actions of the Ninevites? **6.** "Nahum" means comfort. For whom is the comfort of Nahum's message? Why does God send comfort to one group and wrath to another?

1. Nineveh's first great sin (3:13–15) and second great sin (3:16–17) are combined in 3:1.

Hearts melt, knees give way,
   bodies tremble, every face grows pale.

¹¹Where now is the lions' den,
   the place where they fed their young,
where the lion and lioness went,
   and the cubs, with nothing to fear?
¹²The lion killed enough for his cubs
   and strangled the prey for his mate,
filling his lairs with the kill
   and his dens with the prey.

¹³"I am against you,"
   declares the LORD Almighty.
"I will burn up your chariots in smoke,
   and the sword will devour your young lions.
I will leave you no prey on the earth.
The voices of your messengers
   will no longer be heard."

Woe to Nineveh

3 Woe to the city of blood,
   full of lies,
full of plunder,
   never without victims!
²The crack of whips,
   the clatter of wheels,
galloping horses
   and jolting chariots!
³Charging cavalry,
   flashing swords
   and glittering spears!
Many casualties,
   piles of dead,
bodies without number,
   people stumbling over the corpses—
⁴all because of the wanton lust of a harlot,
   alluring, the mistress of sorceries,
who enslaved nations by her prostitution
   and peoples by her witchcraft.

⁵"I am against you," declares the LORD Almighty.
   "I will lift your skirts over your face.
I will show the nations your nakedness
   and the kingdoms your shame.
⁶I will pelt you with filth,
   I will treat you with contempt
   and make you a spectacle.
⁷All who see you will flee from you and say,
   'Nineveh is in ruins—who will mourn for her?'
Where can I find anyone to comfort you?"

⁸Are you better than Thebes,ᵃ
   situated on the Nile,
with water around her?
The river was her defense,
   the waters her wall.
⁹Cushᵇ and Egypt were her boundless strength;
   Put and Libya were among her allies.

ᵃ8 Hebrew *No Amon*   ᵇ9 That is, the upper Nile region

¹⁰Yet she was taken captive
    and went into exile.
Her infants were dashed to pieces
    at the head of every street.
Lots were cast for her nobles,
    and all her great men were put in chains.
¹¹You too will become drunk;
    you will go into hiding
    and seek refuge from the enemy.

¹²All your fortresses are like fig trees
    with their first ripe fruit;
when they are shaken,
    the figs fall into the mouth of the eater.
¹³Look at your troops—
    they are all women!
The gates of your land
    are wide open to your enemies;
fire has consumed their bars.

¹⁴Draw water for the siege,
    strengthen your defenses!
Work the clay,
    tread the mortar,
    repair the brickwork!
¹⁵There the fire will devour you;
    the sword will cut you down
    and, like grasshoppers, consume you.
Multiply like grasshoppers,
    multiply like locusts!
¹⁶You have increased the number of your merchants
    till they are more than the stars of the sky,
but like locusts they strip the land
    and then fly away.
¹⁷Your guards are like locusts,
    your officials like swarms of locusts
    that settle in the walls on a cold day—
but when the sun appears they fly away,
    and no one knows where.

¹⁸O king of Assyria, your shepherdsᵃ slumber;
    your nobles lie down to rest.
Your people are scattered on the mountains
    with no one to gather them.
¹⁹Nothing can heal your wound;
    your injury is fatal.
Everyone who hears the news about you
    claps his hands at your fall,
for who has not felt
    your endless cruelty?

What parallels are you aware of in our nation today? Could your nation's capitol be as liable as Nineveh for bloody massacres? For lies? For making money at the expense of others? 2. What personal responsibility do you consider yourself to have in giving warning to our nation today? What would this warning look like to others? Would that make a difference? 3. In what circumstances did the Lord seem to be against you? Can you share a "pressed up against the wall" or a "hiding from God" experience in your own life? Are other "gods" in your life trying to compete for your allegiance or worship? Which ones? 4. When in your life have you felt God's comfort? Any "down and out" experience you care to share? 5. What promise of God's comfort (in Nahum) means the most to you now? How do you intend to apply this to your life? 6. Try writing a song or poem of woe to any nation or group you feel are in danger of God's judgment, citing specific Scripture verses as "proof." Then write a song or poem of joy and encouragement to those who serve the Lord.

ᵃ18 Or rulers

INTRODUCTION to
HABAKKUK

Book Study Outline: If you are using Habakkuk for a study course, here is a 3- or 5-week outline. Use the questions in the margin for your group agenda:

start meeting / 15 min.

read & discuss Bible / 30 min.

close meeting / 15–45 min.

3-week plan	5-week plan	Group Study Passage
1	1	1:1–4/Habakkuk Complains, "Do Something"
	2	1:5–11/God Answers, "Babylon Is My Instrument"
2	3	1:12–2:1/Habakkuk Complains, "That's Not Fair"
	4	2:2–20/God Answers, "Faith Will Be Rewarded"
3	5	3:1–19/Habakkuk Prays, "Yet Will I Rejoice"

Refer to the Questions and Answers in the front of this Bible for more information.

Author: A prophet (likely at the temple) named Habakkuk, a contemporary of Jeremiah and Nahum.

Date: The latter part of the seventh century B.C., probably c. 610–605 B.C.

Theme: Faith triumphs over doubt. Habakkuk wrestles with a problem that faces every age: Why does God seem inactive in the face of evil and injustice?

Historical Background: The northern kingdom (Israel) had fallen to Assyria c. 722 B.C. and now the rising Chaldean Empire (i.e., the second Babylonian Empire) was on the horizon. In Habakkuk's day, the rulers of the southern kingdom (Judah) were known to "do evil in the eyes of the Lord" (see 2Ki 23:31–24:7). As an agent of judgment in God's hand, the Chaldeans invaded Judah in 605 B.C. The king of Babylon, Nebuchadnezzar, made the Judean king, Jehoiakim, his vassal. Chapters one and two of Habakkuk are historically rooted in the events preceding and following the 605 B.C. invasion under Nebuchadnezzar's leadership. While 3:1 contains Habakkuk's name, it is less certain as to whether this chapter should be dated at the time of the invasion, or later in the prophet's life.

Characteristics: Habakkuk is unusual in that it contains no prophecy directed to Israel. Instead, it is a dialogue between the prophet and God. The book shares some of the structural and thematic traits of the psalms of lament (e.g. Ps 13,44,74,80). Complaint and petition are followed by the divine perspective on the problem. Like the psalmist, Habakkuk uses stark poetic images to color and convey his message. Like the psalmist, and unlike all other prophets (who mostly speak on God's behalf to the people), Habakkuk speaks for himself and on behalf of his people directly and only to God. Like Job he receives no answer except that God is God. God is holy, does care and will act as he sees fit, but only in his time. Habakkuk 2:4 is quoted by several New Testament authors who use it in speaking of faith (see Ro 1:17; Gal 3:11; Heb 10:38).

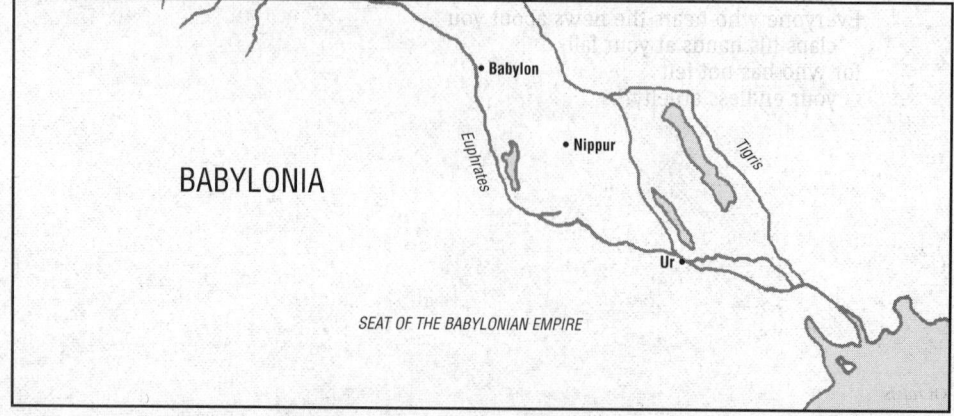

SEAT OF THE BABYLONIAN EMPIRE

Habakkuk

1 The oracle that Habakkuk the prophet received.

Habakkuk's Complaint

2How long, O LORD, must I call for help,
  but you do not listen?
Or cry out to you, "Violence!"
  but you do not save?
3Why do you make me look at injustice?
  Why do you tolerate wrong?
Destruction and violence are before me;
  there is strife, and conflict abounds.
4Therefore the law is paralyzed,
  and justice never prevails.
The wicked hem in the righteous,
  so that justice is perverted.

The LORD's Answer

5"Look at the nations and watch—
  and be utterly amazed.
For I am going to do something in your days
  that you would not believe,
  even if you were told.
6I am raising up the Babylonians,ᵃ
  that ruthless and impetuous people,
who sweep across the whole earth
  to seize dwelling places not their own.
7They are a feared and dreaded people;
  they are a law to themselves
  and promote their own honor.
8Their horses are swifter than leopards,
  fiercer than wolves at dusk.
Their cavalry gallops headlong;
  their horsemen come from afar.
They fly like a vulture swooping to devour;
9 they all come bent on violence.
Their hordesᵇ advance like a desert wind
  and gather prisoners like sand.
10They deride kings
  and scoff at rulers.
They laugh at all fortified cities;
  they build earthen ramps and capture them.
11Then they sweep past like the wind and go on—
  guilty men, whose own strength is their god."

Habakkuk's Second Complaint

12O LORD, are you not from everlasting?
  My God, my Holy One, we will not die.
O LORD, you have appointed them to execute
    judgment;
O Rock, you have ordained them to punish.

ᵃ6 Or Chaldeans   ᵇ9 The meaning of the Hebrew for this word is uncertain.

this new situation? **2.** To whom does he address this second complaint? How does his "voice" change in 2:1? **3.** How is the character issue related to the problem of evil (1:12–13)? How will that change God's mind? **4.** Who are the "treacherous" and the "more righteous" (1:13)? What is the "net" (see 1:14–17)? **5.** What would it mean for the wicked to sacrifice to the "net"? How does the "net" support luxurious living? **6.** What is the punch of 1:17 and 2:1? Is Habakkuk resigning himself to fate? Or casting himself on God?

♡ **1.** What symbols of power do we worship in our culture? How so? **2.** When else in history have the righteous been "swallowed up" by the wicked? Why? **3.** Share a yet-to-be-answered prayer with the group.

☕ **1.** When told, "Wait for it," how do you respond? What's tough about waiting for dinner? For a bus? For a buyer? For Christmas? **2.** When are you "exhausted for nothing"? What was it you were striving after at the time?

📖 **1.** What "revelation" is Habakkuk to write down? What aspects of it are described here (vv. 2–3)? **2.** Within the context of the book, who is "he" in verses 4–5? How are the righteous to live in contrast to "him"? In context, does this "living by faith" imply *national deliverance* or *spiritual salvation*? Explain. **3.** Find the five "woes" in verses 6–20. In verse 6a, who are "all of them" and who is "him"? What is the larger context for these woes (vv. 14,20)? How does this oracle answer Habakkuk's original concern (1:12–17)? **4.** What is the content of the first woe (vv. 6–8)? What metaphor is used of Babylon? How has Habakkuk's view changed? **5.** What is announced in the second woe (vv. 9–11)? What metaphor is used of Babylon? **6.** Paraphrase the third woe (vv. 12–14). What is the climax to the first three woes (v. 14)? How will destroying Babylon spread God's glory? **7.** How is the fourth woe different from the first three (contrast vv. 6b,9a,12a with 15a)? Do you read "drink" literally, or might this also refer to the drunkenness of power? What example of this do you see in Babylon's on-

13Your eyes are too pure to look on evil;
    you cannot tolerate wrong.
Why then do you tolerate the treacherous?
    Why are you silent while the wicked
    swallow up those more righteous than
        themselves?
14You have made men like fish in the sea,
    like sea creatures that have no ruler.
15The wicked foe pulls all of them up with hooks,
    he catches them in his net,
he gathers them up in his dragnet;
    and so he rejoices and is glad.
16Therefore he sacrifices to his net
    and burns incense to his dragnet,
for by his net he lives in luxury
    and enjoys the choicest food.
17Is he to keep on emptying his net,
    destroying nations without mercy?

2   I will stand at my watch
    and station myself on the ramparts;
I will look to see what he will say to me,
    and what answer I am to give to this
        complaint. *a*

The LORD's Answer

2Then the LORD replied:

  "Write down the revelation
    and make it plain on tablets
    so that a herald *b* may run with it.
3For the revelation awaits an appointed time;
    it speaks of the end
    and will not prove false.
Though it linger, wait for it;
    it *c* will certainly come and will not delay.

4"See, he is puffed up;
    his desires are not upright—
    but the righteous will live by his faith *d*—
5indeed, wine betrays him;
    he is arrogant and never at rest.
Because he is as greedy as the grave *e*
    and like death is never satisfied,
he gathers to himself all the nations
    and takes captive all the peoples.

6"Will not all of them taunt him with ridicule and scorn, saying,

   "'Woe to him who piles up stolen goods
    and makes himself wealthy by extortion!
    How long must this go on?'
7Will not your debtors *f* suddenly arise?
    Will they not wake up and make you tremble?
    Then you will become their victim.
8Because you have plundered many nations,
    the peoples who are left will plunder you.
For you have shed man's blood;

---

*a*1 Or *and what to answer when I am rebuked*   *b*2 Or *so that whoever reads it*
*c*3 Or *Though he linger, wait for him; / he*   *d*4 Or *faithfulness*   *e*5 Hebrew
Sheol   *f*7 Or *creditors*

you have destroyed lands and cities and
  everyone in them.

9"Woe to him who builds his realm by unjust gain
  to set his nest on high,
  to escape the clutches of ruin!
10You have plotted the ruin of many peoples,
  shaming your own house and forfeiting your
    life.
11The stones of the wall will cry out,
  and the beams of the woodwork will echo it.

12"Woe to him who builds a city with bloodshed
  and establishes a town by crime!
13Has not the LORD Almighty determined
  that the people's labor is only fuel for the fire,
  that the nations exhaust themselves for
    nothing?
14For the earth will be filled with the knowledge of
    the glory of the LORD,
  as the waters cover the sea.

15"Woe to him who gives drink to his neighbors,
  pouring it from the wineskin till they are
    drunk,
  so that he can gaze on their naked bodies.
16You will be filled with shame instead of glory.
  Now it is your turn! Drink and be exposed[a]!
  The cup from the LORD's right hand is coming
    around to you,
  and disgrace will cover your glory.
17The violence you have done to Lebanon will
    overwhelm you,
  and your destruction of animals will terrify you.
  For you have shed man's blood;
  you have destroyed lands and cities and
    everyone in them.

18"Of what value is an idol, since a man has carved
    it?
  Or an image that teaches lies?
  For he who makes it trusts in his own creation;
  he makes idols that cannot speak.
19Woe to him who says to wood, 'Come to life!'
  Or to lifeless stone, 'Wake up!'
  Can it give guidance?
  It is covered with gold and silver;
    there is no breath in it.
20But the LORD is in his holy temple;
  let all the earth be silent before him."

Habakkuk's Prayer

3 A prayer of Habakkuk the prophet. On *shigionoth*.[b]

2LORD, I have heard of your fame;
  I stand in awe of your deeds, O LORD.
  Renew them in our day,
    in our time make them known;
  in wrath remember mercy.

slaught of Jerusalem in 586 B.C. (see 2Ki 25:8–21)? **8.** What new theme does verse 18 introduce? How is that related to the fifth woe (vv. 19–20)? What ironic point do you see here in idols silent before people and people silent before God? What is the climax of the whole "woe" section (v. 20) and of the "end" for which Israel is to wait?

1. Compare 2:4 with Romans 1:16–18 and Galatians 3:10–14. What use does Paul make of this famous passage to speak a new word to a new generation? How is Paul's emphasis like and unlike Habakkuk's? **2.** "God may seem to be *late*, but is invariably *on time*"—Would Habakkuk say that? Would you? How does God measure "time"? **3.** Do you know someone who is "puffed up"? How can you "live by your faith" in his or her presence without also becoming "puffed up"? **4.** What or who builds an empire today like Babylon—with stolen goods, unjust gain, bloodshed, is drunk with power and encourages others to do likewise? What would Habakkuk say to such a person or organization? What can *you* do to impact a world in which such things happen? **5.** What help are the affirmations in verses 14 and 20 to you? What other "waters covered the sea" to God's glory (see Ex 14)? When will the Lord do this a "second time" (see Isa 11:9–11)? What final fulfillment of this prophecy do you see in Babylon's fall at the end of history (see Rev 17–18)?

1. What's your favorite spot from which to view the sunrise? How often do you go there? What do sunrises bring to mind for you? **2.** "It's always darkest before the dawn"—To what would that saying refer in your life these days? **3.** What popular song typified your teenage years? What memory does your favorite song bring to mind?

---

a16 Masoretic Text; Dead Sea Scrolls, Aquila, Vulgate and Syriac (see also Septuagint) *and* stagger   *b1* Probably a literary or musical term

1. Why can the once woeful Habakkuk afford to be so joyful? How has his situation changed? How long after chapters 1 and 2 do you suppose it was written? 2. How is verse 2 related to the rest of this psalm-like prayer? How is verse 2 related to the promise of 2:2–4? How are wrath and mercy related? 3. How does reciting God's marvelous deeds in the past anticipate God's future deliverance "in our day" (v. 2)? 4. To what historical events do the poetic allusions refer in verses 3–5 (see Ex 7–12)? In verses 6–7 (see Ex 19:16)? 5. In verses 8–10, what do you see poetically depicted: (a) Creation of the world? (b) Parting of the Red Sea (see Ex 14:15–31)? (c) Crossing the Jordan (see Jos 3:15–17)? 6. Compare verses 8–10 with Psalms 74:12–17 and 77:16–19. What similar images do these prayers use to evoke awe for God's mighty works? What other images (from nature, warfare or whatever) have a similar impact on you? 7. What is Habakkuk's response to the poetic and dramatic vision of verses 3–15? Why is his heart racing? What evidence does he have for rejoicing? How does he get his sure-footed confidence? 8. What does Habakkuk's irrepressible joy (vv. 17–19) mean in the context of injustice (1:2–4)? Of God's use of wicked Babylon (1:12–17)? Of expectation (2:2–4)?

1. This hymn-like chapter stirred up vivid memories in Israel of God's might and mercy. When has God worked mightily and mercifully in your past? In your present, where do you want God to renew his mercy and work mightily again? 2. What new meaning would Habakkuk bring to the belief "It's always darkest before the dawn"? In what area of your life is God's power dawning? Where are you still waiting in the twilight for the sun to rise? 3. What things are barren in your life, as in Habakkuk's day (v. 17)? Are you ready to yet rejoice in the Lord, anyway? Why or why not? 4. What promise does verse 19 hold for your present situation? For your future? 5. What other key verse(s) are you prepared to "write down," "run with" or "wait for" (2:2–3)? 6. Do you write down any of your prayers? Try it as a group. 7. Do you really believe God has the power described in this poem? Or is this just poetic exaggeration?

³God came from Teman,
  the Holy One from Mount Paran.   *Selah*ᵃ
His glory covered the heavens
  and his praise filled the earth.
⁴His splendor was like the sunrise;
  rays flashed from his hand,
  where his power was hidden.
⁵Plague went before him;
  pestilence followed his steps.
⁶He stood, and shook the earth;
  he looked, and made the nations tremble.
The ancient mountains crumbled
  and the age-old hills collapsed.
  His ways are eternal.
⁷I saw the tents of Cushan in distress,
  the dwellings of Midian in anguish.

⁸Were you angry with the rivers, O LORD?
  Was your wrath against the streams?
Did you rage against the sea
  when you rode with your horses
  and your victorious chariots?
⁹You uncovered your bow,
  you called for many arrows.   *Selah*
You split the earth with rivers;
¹⁰ the mountains saw you and writhed.
Torrents of water swept by;
  the deep roared
  and lifted its waves on high.

¹¹Sun and moon stood still in the heavens
  at the glint of your flying arrows,
  at the lightning of your flashing spear.
¹²In wrath you strode through the earth
  and in anger you threshed the nations.
¹³You came out to deliver your people,
  to save your anointed one.
You crushed the leader of the land of wickedness,
  you stripped him from head to foot.   *Selah*
¹⁴With his own spear you pierced his head
  when his warriors stormed out to scatter us,
  gloating as though about to devour
  the wretched who were in hiding.
¹⁵You trampled the sea with your horses,
  churning the great waters.

¹⁶I heard and my heart pounded,
  my lips quivered at the sound;
decay crept into my bones,
  and my legs trembled.
Yet I will wait patiently for the day of calamity
  to come on the nation invading us.
¹⁷Though the fig tree does not bud
  and there are no grapes on the vines,
though the olive crop fails
  and the fields produce no food,
though there are no sheep in the pen
  and no cattle in the stalls,

ᵃ3 A word of uncertain meaning; possibly a musical term; also in verses 9 and 13

¹⁸yet I will rejoice in the L<small>ORD</small>,
  I will be joyful in God my Savior.

¹⁹The Sovereign L<small>ORD</small> is my strength;
  he makes my feet like the feet of a deer,
  he enables me to go on the heights.

For the director of music. On my stringed
instruments.

INTRODUCTION to
ZEPHANIAH

Book Study Outline: If you are using Zephaniah for a study course, here is a 3-week outline. Use the questions in the margin for your group agenda:

☕ start meeting / 15 min.

📖 read & discuss Bible / 30 min.

♡ close meeting / 15–45 min.

3-week plan	Personal Reading	Group Study Passage
1	1:1–2:3	The Day of the Lord Announced
2	2:4–15	The Day of the Lord Implemented
3	3:1–20	The Redemption of the Lord Promised

Refer to the Questions and Answers in the front of this Bible for more information.

Author: Zephaniah was an aristocrat, a great-great grandson of Hezekiah, the king of Judah from 715 to 686 B.C. (see 1:1).

Date: Zephaniah prophesied during the reign of Josiah (640–609 B.C.). His preaching as record-ed here may have contributed to Josiah's reforms, which took place in 621 B.C. This makes Zephaniah an older contemporary and kindred spirit of Jeremiah.

Theme: The coming Day of the Lord.

Historical Background: Zephaniah's twofold message—"gloom and doom" for Judah and its neighbors (1:1–3:8), then the Lord's purging and purifying of a faithful remnant (3:9–20)—is best appreciated within the context of what necessitated this spiritual house cleaning. The historical sit-uation which he addressed is the same pervasive decadence that triggered King Josiah's reform movement (see 2Ch 34–35). Josiah was spurred on by the evils of King Manasseh and King Amon, by the rediscovery of Moses' Law, by hearing Jeremiah's early preaching, and quite possibly by Zephaniah's preaching as well. Thus it was that Josiah removed the pagan centers of idol worship. The immediate occasion for Zephaniah's prophecy may have been a century-long invasion of Canaan by the Scythians (a fierce nomadic people). Fulfillment of Zephaniah's prophecy (destruc-tion of Judah) came at the hands of King Nebuchadnezzar of Babylon. He defeated the Assyrians in 612 B.C., thus establishing Babylonian supremacy in the Near East.

Characteristics: Zephaniah consists of several brief oracles or utterances, many heavy with gloom. The prophet foresaw a world-wide catastrophe, but he also saw beyond it. In the prophet-ic tradition, Zephaniah delivers his message with lament, exhortation, invective and hope. Zephaniah presents a beautiful picture of a God who delights in his people (3:14–20).

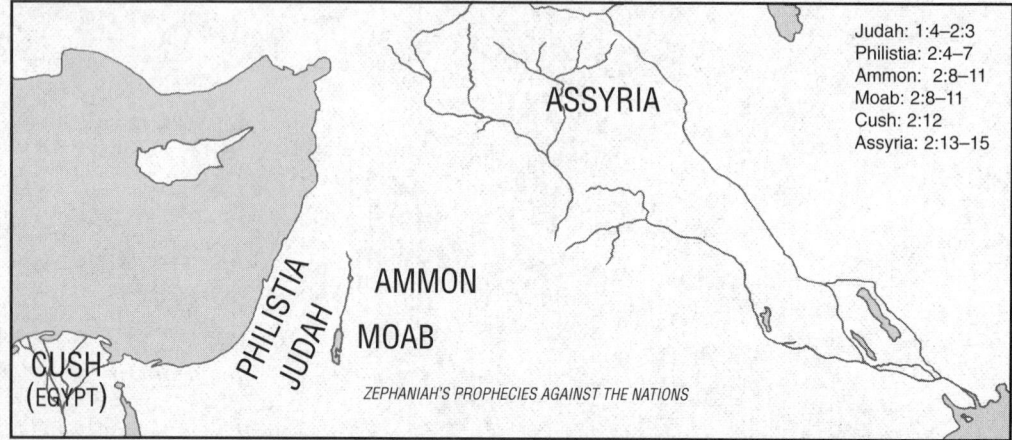

Judah: 1:4–2:3
Philistia: 2:4–7
Ammon: 2:8–11
Moab: 2:8–11
Cush: 2:12
Assyria: 2:13–15

ASSYRIA

AMMON

MOAB

PHILISTIA

JUDAH

CUSH (EGYPT)

ZEPHANIAH'S PROPHECIES AGAINST THE NATIONS

Zephaniah

1 The word of the LORD that came to Zephaniah son of Cushi, the son of Gedaliah, the son of Amariah, the son of Hezekiah, during the reign of Josiah son of Amon king of Judah:

Warning of Coming Destruction

²"I will sweep away everything
    from the face of the earth,"
                    declares the LORD.
³"I will sweep away both men and animals;
    I will sweep away the birds of the air
    and the fish of the sea.
The wicked will have only heaps of rubble^a
    when I cut off man from the face of the earth,"
                    declares the LORD.

Against Judah

⁴"I will stretch out my hand against Judah
    and against all who live in Jerusalem.
I will cut off from this place every remnant of
        Baal,
    the names of the pagan and the idolatrous
        priests—
⁵those who bow down on the roofs
    to worship the starry host,
those who bow down and swear by the LORD
    and who also swear by Molech,^b
⁶those who turn back from following the LORD
    and neither seek the LORD nor inquire of him.
⁷Be silent before the Sovereign LORD,
    for the day of the LORD is near.
The LORD has prepared a sacrifice;
    he has consecrated those he has invited.
⁸On the day of the LORD's sacrifice
    I will punish the princes
    and the king's sons
and all those clad
    in foreign clothes.
⁹On that day I will punish
    all who avoid stepping on the threshold,^c
who fill the temple of their gods
    with violence and deceit.
¹⁰"On that day," declares the LORD,
    "a cry will go up from the Fish Gate,
    wailing from the New Quarter,
    and a loud crash from the hills.
¹¹Wail, you who live in the market district^d;
    all your merchants will be wiped out,
    all who trade with^e silver will be ruined.
¹²At that time I will search Jerusalem with lamps
    and punish those who are complacent,

---

^a3 The meaning of the Hebrew for this line is uncertain.   ^b5 Hebrew *Malcam,* that is, Milcom   ^c9 See 1 Samuel 5:5.   ^d11 Or *the Mortar*   ^e11 Or *in*

☕ **1.** For what was your great-grandfather noted? Your granddad? Your dad? Any royal blood? Or bad blood? **2.** "Wait until your father gets home"—What did that mean for you: (a) Court of appeal? (b) D-day? (c) Wailing? (d) Goodies? What went through your mind as you awaited that "appointed" time?

📖 **1.** What is noteworthy about Zephaniah's background? What social circles did he likely move in? What situation did he inherit (vv. 4–6), following the reigns of two bad kings—Manasseh and Amon (see 2Ki 21)—before Josiah's reform and renewal (see 2Ki 23:4–16; 2Ch 34:1–7)? **2.** What "word of the Lord" does Zephaniah bring, after a long period of prophetic silence? What universal judgment does this house-cleaning imagery bring to mind (vv. 2–3)? **3.** What are five specific religious actions that have brought on this judgment (vv. 4–6)? What does it mean to "swear by Molech" (see Lev 18:21; 20:1–5; 2Ch 33:6)? **4.** What five groups are indicted for their social practices (vv. 8–9)? What has each done? What does it mean to "step on the threshold" (see 1Sa 5:1–5)? **5.** How thorough and unsuspecting will God's judgment be "on that day" (vv. 8–13)? Who will suffer most? Why?

❤️ **1.** Judah seems to want her own cake (Yahweh) and eat someone else's (Molech), too. What is the danger of such syncretism, then and now? How might we become like who or what we worship? **2.** Gross pagan idolatry (v. 4) may not be your thing. But are you "caught up in the rat race" of high finance, bigger homes and fruitless labor (vv. 11–13)? How so? How do you tell the difference between *honorable* wealth and *unjust* riches? **3.** When told, "Just wait until *God your Father* comes home," what would that elicit in Judah and in *you*: Hope of deliverance? Fear of wrath? A vow of repentance? A lull of complacency? **4.** Then and now, people "worship the starry host" (v. 2) or read their horoscope. Do you? Why? What's wrong with that?

who are like wine left on its dregs,
who think, 'The LORD will do nothing,
    either good or bad.'
¹³Their wealth will be plundered,
    their houses demolished.
They will build houses
    but not live in them;
they will plant vineyards
    but not drink the wine.

The Great Day of the LORD

¹⁴"The great day of the LORD is near—
    near and coming quickly.
Listen! The cry on the day of the LORD will be
    bitter,
    the shouting of the warrior there.
¹⁵That day will be a day of wrath,
    a day of distress and anguish,
a day of trouble and ruin,
    a day of darkness and gloom,
    a day of clouds and blackness,
¹⁶a day of trumpet and battle cry
    against the fortified cities
    and against the corner towers.
¹⁷I will bring distress on the people
    and they will walk like blind men,
    because they have sinned against the LORD.
Their blood will be poured out like dust
    and their entrails like filth.
¹⁸Neither their silver nor their gold
    will be able to save them
    on the day of the LORD's wrath.
In the fire of his jealousy
    the whole world will be consumed,
for he will make a sudden end
    of all who live in the earth."

2 Gather together, gather together,
    O shameful nation,
²before the appointed time arrives
    and that day sweeps on like chaff,
before the fierce anger of the LORD comes upon
       you,
    before the day of the LORD's wrath comes upon
       you.
³Seek the LORD, all you humble of the land,
    you who do what he commands.
Seek righteousness, seek humility;
    perhaps you will be sheltered
    on the day of the LORD's anger.

Against Philistia

⁴Gaza will be abandoned
    and Ashkelon left in ruins.
At midday Ashdod will be emptied
    and Ekron uprooted.
⁵Woe to you who live by the sea,
    O Kerethite people;
the word of the LORD is against you,
    O Canaan, land of the Philistines.

☕ From your year-at-a-glance calendar, what "appointed time" are you eagerly *anticipating*? Which scheduled appointment are you *dreading*? Are you good at waiting? How so?

📖 **1.** How close does Zephaniah say the people are to "the great Day of the Lord?" Is that day inked, penciled, or not even on their appointment calendars? Why or why not? **2.** Amid prosperity, how bright is Judah's future? What will "that day" be like? Is there any escape, or are God's consequences universal? What escape routes are dead ends (1:18)? **3.** What hope does God offer to any who gather together contritely before him (2:1–3)? What attitudes and actions please the Lord? What will be the final result?

❤️ **1.** What do these judgments reveal about God's view of sin and its consequences? About God's view of the oppressor and the oppressed? **2.** Why is it harder to hear God's warnings during prosperity, when things are going well? Do you "shine" in *suffering* or in *prosperity*? Why is that? **3.** What contemporary "signs" (dark clouds and social distress) do you see as God's warning to the nation? To the Church? To *you*? **4.** In what ways are you and your group seeking the Lord? His righteousness? With what promise?

☕ **1.** What is your favorite sport? Your favorite ball team? When have you seen your team trail badly throughout a game, only to rally late and win? What did it feel like to have your team's "fortune" restored? **2.** Have you ever visited a ghost town, ancient ruins or once-famous building, long

"I will destroy you,
and none will be left."

6The land by the sea, where the Kerethites*a*
dwell,
will be a place for shepherds and sheep pens.
7It will belong to the remnant of the house of
Judah;
there they will find pasture.
In the evening they will lie down
in the houses of Ashkelon.
The LORD their God will care for them;
he will restore their fortunes.*b*

Against Moab and Ammon

8"I have heard the insults of Moab
and the taunts of the Ammonites,
who insulted my people
and made threats against their land.
9Therefore, as surely as I live,"
declares the LORD Almighty, the God of Israel,
"surely Moab will become like Sodom,
the Ammonites like Gomorrah—
a place of weeds and salt pits,
a wasteland forever.
The remnant of my people will plunder them;
the survivors of my nation will inherit their
land."

10This is what they will get in return for their
pride,
for insulting and mocking the people of the
LORD Almighty.
11The LORD will be awesome to them
when he destroys all the gods of the land.
The nations on every shore will worship him,
every one in its own land.

Against Cush

12"You too, O Cushites,*c*
will be slain by my sword."

Against Assyria

13He will stretch out his hand against the north
and destroy Assyria,
leaving Nineveh utterly desolate
and dry as the desert.
14Flocks and herds will lie down there,
creatures of every kind.
The desert owl and the screech owl
will roost on her columns.
Their calls will echo through the windows,
rubble will be in the doorways,
the beams of cedar will be exposed.
15This is the carefree city
that lived in safety.
She said to herself,
"I am, and there is none besides me."

since abandoned? What was it like, then and now?

1. What desolation will God bring against the cities and land of Philistia? How extensive will this destruction be? What will this land be good for, after God finishes with it? 2. In what ways will God's punishment fall on Moab and Ammon as it did on their ancestor Lot (v. 9; see Ge 18–19)? Will they be as fortunate? What will they get in return for their pride and arrogance? What will happen to the gods they chose to serve? 3. What is God's verdict against the Cushites (Ethiopians, Egyptians)? Why would this be just, in light of their supposed power? 4. What irony do you see in the way God will ruin impregnable Nineveh (compare vv. 15b and 5c, with Isa 45:5–6, 18,21)? See the books of Jonah and Nahum for how exact and true God's vengeance against Nineveh would be in 612 B.C. at the hands of the Babylonians.

1. In what ways are your and your nation's attitudes and actions like and unlike Philistia, Moab, Ammon, Cush or Nineveh? What can be the outcome of overzealous pride in "God and country"? 2. In what sense do you act like "there's none besides me"? In that case, how does this implementation of the Day of the Lord hit home with you? 3. What inner motives for God's wrath do you see revealed against these nations: (a) Wrath is the just reward for sinful pride? (b) Wrath vindicates God's chosen people? (c) Wrath pursues "all the gods" who vie for what is God's alone? (d) Wrath is designed to bring "every nation" to worship him? 4. God's *wrath* has its flip side—*restoration*. What one quality above all others do you think God wants restored in the nation, church, or individual who worships him? How could you and your group model that quality? 5. If all nations will end up worshiping God, "every one in its own land" (v. 11), what do you imagine that to be like? Will that include worship of the one true God by various names?

*a*6 The meaning of the Hebrew for this word is uncertain.   *b*7 Or *will bring back
their captives*   *c*12 That is, people from the upper Nile region

What a ruin she has become,
  a lair for wild beasts!
All who pass by her scoff
  and shake their fists.

The Future of Jerusalem

3 Woe to the city of oppressors,
  rebellious and defiled!
²She obeys no one,
  she accepts no correction.
She does not trust in the LORD,
  she does not draw near to her God.
³Her officials are roaring lions,
  her rulers are evening wolves,
  who leave nothing for the morning.
⁴Her prophets are arrogant;
  they are treacherous men.
Her priests profane the sanctuary
  and do violence to the law.
⁵The LORD within her is righteous;
  he does no wrong.
Morning by morning he dispenses his justice,
  and every new day he does not fail,
  yet the unrighteous know no shame.

⁶"I have cut off nations;
  their strongholds are demolished.
I have left their streets deserted,
  with no one passing through.
Their cities are destroyed;
  no one will be left—no one at all.
⁷I said to the city,
  'Surely you will fear me
  and accept correction!'
Then her dwelling would not be cut off,
  nor all my punishments come upon her.
But they were still eager
  to act corruptly in all they did.
⁸Therefore wait for me," declares the LORD,
  "for the day I will stand up to testify.ᵃ
I have decided to assemble the nations,
  to gather the kingdoms
and to pour out my wrath on them—
  all my fierce anger.
The whole world will be consumed
  by the fire of my jealous anger.

⁹"Then will I purify the lips of the peoples,
  that all of them may call on the name of the
    LORD
  and serve him shoulder to shoulder.
¹⁰From beyond the rivers of Cushᵇ
  my worshipers, my scattered people,
  will bring me offerings.
¹¹On that day you will not be put to shame
  for all the wrongs you have done to me,
because I will remove from this city
  those who rejoice in their pride.

---

1. Share an anecdote about when you "took a short cut" after being told by a parent or other adult exactly how to do something. What happened as a result? How did you feel about being corrected? What lesson did you learn from that experience? 2. Which typifies your stance as a youth relating to that heavenly parent Yahweh: (a) "My way is Yahweh"? (b) "Any way but Yahweh"? (c) "Have it your way, Yahweh"? Illustrate.

1. After announcing God's judgment against Judah and her neighbors, upon what city does Zephaniah finally focus? What words does he use to describe her? 2. What four specific actions highlight her insensitivity to sin? What four leadership groups are singled out (vv. 3–4)? In each case, for what? 3. What qualities of God does Zephaniah hold up as a standard for the people? How well have they modeled these qualities and held to this standard? 4. With their history and the destruction of neighboring nations, why does Jerusalem ignore God's gracious warning (vv. 6–8)? What's so hard about "accepting correction" (see 2:1–3)? 5. How is God's redemption (vv. 9–20) consistent with his righteousness and wrath (vv. 5,8)? Has God changed his mind? Or is there some cause-and-effect link operating here? How does this compare with what is happening in Matthew 5:5 and Luke 1:52? 6. What will God do for his scattered people to make them more like himself (v. 19)? What will be the cause for their rejoicing "on that day"? How does that compare with why they were once weeping "on that day" (1:10–13)? 7. Which of God's actions do you believe would make the people most *glad*, but seem "too good to be true"? Which aspects of God's deliverance might be *shrugged off* as "too little, too late"? Which reassurance would sound most *convincing* to Israel?

1. Try reading this chapter from the perspective of a poor peasant in Latin America or a starving person in sub-Saharan Africa. What does the promised Second Coming mean to *them*? To their oppressors? Does it mean anything different to *you*? If so,

---

ᵃ8 Septuagint and Syriac; Hebrew *will rise up to plunder*   ᵇ10 That is, the upper Nile region

Never again will you be haughty
  on my holy hill.
12But I will leave within you
  the meek and humble,
  who trust in the name of the LORD.
13The remnant of Israel will do no wrong;
  they will speak no lies,
  nor will deceit be found in their mouths.
They will eat and lie down
  and no one will make them afraid."

14Sing, O Daughter of Zion;
  shout aloud, O Israel!
Be glad and rejoice with all your heart,
  O Daughter of Jerusalem!
15The LORD has taken away your punishment,
  he has turned back your enemy.
The LORD, the King of Israel, is with you;
  never again will you fear any harm.
16On that day they will say to Jerusalem,
  "Do not fear, O Zion;
  do not let your hands hang limp.
17The LORD your God is with you,
  he is mighty to save.
He will take great delight in you,
  he will quiet you with his love,
  he will rejoice over you with singing."

18"The sorrows for the appointed feasts
  I will remove from you;
  they are a burden and a reproach to you.a
19At that time I will deal
  with all who oppressed you;
  I will rescue the lame
  and gather those who have been scattered.
I will give them praise and honor
  in every land where they were put to shame.
20At that time I will gather you;
  at that time I will bring you home.
I will give you honor and praise
  among all the peoples of the earth
when I restore your fortunesb
  before your very eyes,"
                                        says the LORD.

what? Will you be classed with the rejoicers (v. 11), or with those who trust (v. 12)? **2.** Throughout Zephaniah there is a pattern of *rebellion*, *restoration* and *rejoicing*. If this book were the story of your life, in which of those three stages do you find yourself in relation to God? Why? **3.** *Joy* will displace mourning and *calm* will follow the storms of God's refining fire. How does that square with your experience of God? **4.** What is the most important thing you learned from Zephaniah? What life-changing application are you making? **5.** What application would you like God to favorably "remember?" How can the group help you remember to follow through?

---

a18 Or "I will gather you who mourn for the appointed feasts; / your reproach is a burden to you   b20 Or I bring back your captives

INTRODUCTION to
HAGGAI

Book Study Outline: If you are using Haggai for a study course, here is a 2- or 4-week outline. Use the margin questions for your group agenda:

2-week plan	4-week plan	Group Study Passage
1	1	1:1–15/From Indifference to Rebuilding
	2	2:1–9/From Discouragement to Rebuilding
2	3	2:10–19/From Defilement to Blessing
	4	2:20–23/A Signet Ring Signals the Lord's Day

start meeting / 15 min.

read & discuss Bible / 30 min.

close meeting / 15–45 min.

Refer to the Questions and Answers in the front of this Bible for more information.

Author: Not identifed, though the book tells of Haggai's ministry and records his oracles.

Date: Haggai is quite specific as to the year, month and day of his messages: August 29 (1:1); September 15 (1:15); October 17 (2:1); December 18 (2:10 and 2:20), 520 B.C.

Theme: Rebuilding for results—the blessing is in the doing.

Historical Background: This book is set in the context of the return of the Jews from the Babylonian exile and the subsequent rebuilding of Jerusalem and the temple (see the Introductions to Ezra and Nehemiah). It was through the ministry of Haggai (along with Zechariah) that the rebuilding of the temple began (see Ezr 5:1–2). The problem with getting the building started, it seems, was not just with the neighboring Samaritans who opposed the rebuilding projects (fearing that this would lead to a renewed and politically powerful Jewish state). The real problem had to do with the lethargy of the people. Haggai's aim was to get the people moving on the project. The temple was completed and dedicated four years later in 516 B.C. No other prophet had results as direct, immediate and identifiable as Haggai!

Characteristics: There is only one book in the Old Testament that is shorter than Haggai (Obadiah). Yet in just 38 verses Haggai is able to show the differing consequences of disobedience vs. obedience, as well as point to the coming of the Messiah. Haggai was an older contemporary of Zechariah. Both dealt with the same themes, although in quite different ways (see the Introduction to Zechariah). Haggai was a practical doer, while Zechariah was an apocalyptic visionary. Haggai did not mince words but went right to the point, while Zechariah mixed metaphors in a memorable way. Haggai exhorted the people to get to work on the project at hand (the rebuilding of the temple), while Zechariah encouraged them to put their hope in what lay ahead for them in the distant future (which also served to motivate the people to rebuild the temple, though in a different way). The book records not only his oracles, but also his ministry and the response of the people to it, while in Zechariah the emphasis is on his prophecies (with no indication of response).

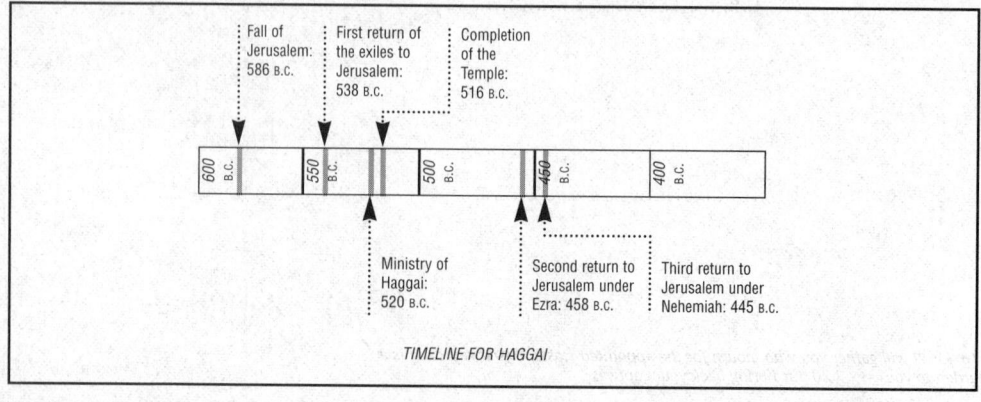

Fall of Jerusalem: 586 B.C.
First return of the exiles to Jerusalem: 538 B.C.
Completion of the Temple: 516 B.C.

600 B.C. 550 B.C. 500 B.C. 450 B.C. 400 B.C.

Ministry of Haggai: 520 B.C.
Second return to Jerusalem under Ezra: 458 B.C.
Third return to Jerusalem under Nehemiah: 445 B.C.

TIMELINE FOR HAGGAI

Haggai

A Call to Build the House of the LORD

1 In the second year of King Darius, on the first day of the sixth month, the word of the LORD came through the prophet Haggai to Zerubbabel son of Shealtiel, governor of Judah, and to Joshua[a] son of Jehozadak, the high priest:

²This is what the LORD Almighty says: "These people say, 'The time has not yet come for the LORD's house to be built.'"

³Then the word of the LORD came through the prophet Haggai: ⁴"Is it a time for you yourselves to be living in your paneled houses, while this house remains a ruin?"

⁵Now this is what the LORD Almighty says: "Give careful thought to your ways. ⁶You have planted much, but have harvested little. You eat, but never have enough. You drink, but never have your fill. You put on clothes, but are not warm. You earn wages, only to put them in a purse with holes in it."

⁷This is what the LORD Almighty says: "Give careful thought to your ways. ⁸Go up into the mountains and bring down timber and build the house, so that I may take pleasure in it and be honored," says the LORD. ⁹"You expected much, but see, it turned out to be little. What you brought home, I blew away. Why?" declares the LORD Almighty. "Because of my house, which remains a ruin, while each of you is busy with his own house. ¹⁰Therefore, because of you the heavens have withheld their dew and the earth its crops. ¹¹I called for a drought on the fields and the mountains, on the grain, the new wine, the oil and whatever the ground produces, on men and cattle, and on the labor of your hands."

¹²Then Zerubbabel son of Shealtiel, Joshua son of Jehozadak, the high priest, and the whole remnant of the people obeyed the voice of the LORD their God and the message of the prophet Haggai, because the LORD their God had sent him. And the people feared the LORD.

¹³Then Haggai, the LORD's messenger, gave this message of the LORD to the people: "I am with you," declares the LORD. ¹⁴So the LORD stirred up the spirit of Zerubbabel son of Shealtiel, governor of Judah, and the spirit of Joshua son of Jehozadak, the high priest, and the spirit of the whole remnant of the people. They came and began to work on the house of the LORD Almighty, their God, ¹⁵on the twenty-fourth day of the sixth month in the second year of King Darius.

The Promised Glory of the New House

2 On the twenty-first day of the seventh month, the word of the LORD came through the prophet Haggai: ²"Speak to Zerubbabel son of Shealtiel, governor of Judah, to Joshua son of Jehozadak, the high priest, and to the remnant of the people. Ask them, ³'Who of you is left who saw this house in its former glory? How does it look to you now? Does it not seem to you like nothing? ⁴But now be strong, O Zerubbabel,' declares the LORD. 'Be strong, O Joshua son of Jehozadak, the high priest. Be strong, all you people of the land,'

---

1. As a child, what did you enjoy building: Train sets? Tinker toys? Model cars? Tree houses? Igloos? **2.** Who were your teammates in this? **3.** As a child, where did you store your allowance? Today, are you a saver or a big spender?

1. Why do you think Haggai chose to speak to both the civil and religious leaders? And why on "the first day" of that particular month and year (Aug 29, 520 B.C.)? **2.** After 18 years of starts and stops in rebuilding the temple since returning from Exile, "this house remains a ruin" (v. 4). Why is that? To what are the people to "give careful thought" (vv. 5–8)? **3.** How did the Lord force their consideration of Haggai's alternative (vv. 9ff)? **4.** How did they respond to Haggai's call (v. 12)? Who led their response? How soon did they begin (v. 15)? **5.** How did God enable this (vv. 12–14)?

1. When have you been part of a communal building project: Church? Village? Barn-raising? What part did you play? How was the community built up at the same time? How did God move during the project? **2.** How has God spoken to you about your financial priorities and spending habits? Have you seen "famines" or fruitlessness in your personal finances? **3.** When have you put your wages into "a purse with holes in it"? How did that feel? What will you do about that hole?

What great expectations of yours have fallen short?

1. How long have the people been working (1:15; 2:1)? What have the people been doing during this seventh month (see Lev 23:23–43)? **2.** Why does Haggai speak now? **3.** What feelings does Solomon's temple evoke (vv. 3–5)? How does God's command and covenant relate to this? **4.** God "shaking heavens, earth ... nations" refers to what events (vv. 6–7; see Ex 8ff; Heb 12:26–27)?

---

a 1 A variant of *Jeshua*; here and elsewhere in Haggai

5. "The desired of all nations" refers to what? When will this be (vv. 7ff)?

What dream of yours has shattered recently? Do comparisons with past successes help? How might God be building you into a temple of His glory?

———

In your home, what spreads by itself: Cleanliness or messes? Give an example.

1. At winter planting time (v. 10), what does Haggai have to say? **2.** *Consecration* does *not* rub off, but defilement does (vv. 10,13). What *holy* work were the people trusting in that would *not* rub off on their fruitfulness or moral character, much to their chagrin (vv. 14ff)? **3.** Who is "this people" whom Haggai accuses (v. 14; see Ezr 4:1–5)? (With friends like these Samaritans, who needs enemies?) **4.** What thematic ties do you see between 2:15–19 and 1:10–11? Between 2:15–19 and 2:10–14? **5.** Since crops have only just been planted (vv. 10,19), how can Haggai assure Judah of God's blessing?

When have you been tempted to trust in a holy work, as did Judah?

———

1. How much time has elapsed (v. 20; compare 1:1)? How much longer before the job is done (see Ezr 6:15)? **2.** In this last oracle, what will happen? When? Why? **3.** What biblical events does this day recall (see Ge 19:25; Ex 15:1,4,19,21; Jdg 7:22)?

1. What does Haggai say here about God's power over world governments? **2.** What part of your spiritual life has God begun to rebuild? How can your small group figure in that? How long will this rebuilding take place? **3.** As the son of David and of Zerubbabel (see Mt 1:1,12), how is Christ "like God's signet ring" (v. 23)? As a follower of Jesus, how are you also like God's signet ring? **4.** From Haggai, what can you apply to growing your church?

declares the LORD, 'and work. For I am with you,' declares the LORD Almighty. 5"This is what I covenanted with you when you came out of Egypt. And my Spirit remains among you. Do not fear.'

6"This is what the LORD Almighty says: 'In a little while I will once more shake the heavens and the earth, the sea and the dry land. 7I will shake all nations, and the desired of all nations will come, and I will fill this house with glory,' says the LORD Almighty. 8'The silver is mine and the gold is mine,' declares the LORD Almighty. 9'The glory of this present house will be greater than the glory of the former house,' says the LORD Almighty. 'And in this place I will grant peace,' declares the LORD Almighty."

Blessings for a Defiled People

10On the twenty-fourth day of the ninth month, in the second year of Darius, the word of the LORD came to the prophet Haggai: 11"This is what the LORD Almighty says: 'Ask the priests what the law says: 12If a person carries consecrated meat in the fold of his garment, and that fold touches some bread or stew, some wine, oil or other food, does it become consecrated?'"

The priests answered, "No."

13Then Haggai said, "If a person defiled by contact with a dead body touches one of these things, does it become defiled?"

"Yes," the priests replied, "it becomes defiled."

14Then Haggai said, "'So it is with this people and this nation in my sight,' declares the LORD. 'Whatever they do and whatever they offer there is defiled.

15"'Now give careful thought to this from this day on[a]—consider how things were before one stone was laid on another in the LORD's temple. 16When anyone came to a heap of twenty measures, there were only ten. When anyone went to a wine vat to draw fifty measures, there were only twenty. 17I struck all the work of your hands with blight, mildew and hail, yet you did not turn to me,' declares the LORD. 18'From this day on, from this twenty-fourth day of the ninth month, give careful thought to the day when the foundation of the LORD's temple was laid. Give careful thought: 19Is there yet any seed left in the barn? Until now, the vine and the fig tree, the pomegranate and the olive tree have not borne fruit.

"'From this day on I will bless you.'"

Zerubbabel the LORD's Signet Ring

20The word of the LORD came to Haggai a second time on the twenty-fourth day of the month: 21"Tell Zerubbabel governor of Judah that I will shake the heavens and the earth. 22I will overturn royal thrones and shatter the power of the foreign kingdoms. I will overthrow chariots and their drivers; horses and their riders will fall, each by the sword of his brother.

23"'On that day,' declares the LORD Almighty, 'I will take you, my servant Zerubbabel son of Shealtiel,' declares the LORD, 'and I will make you like my signet ring, for I have chosen you,' declares the LORD Almighty."

a15 Or to the days past

INTRODUCTION to
ZECHARIAH

Book Study Outline: If you are using Zechariah for a study course, here is a 6- or 11-week outline. Use the questions in the margin for your group agenda:

🍵 start meeting / 15 min.

📖 read & discuss Bible / 30 min.

❤️ close meeting / 15–45 min.

Refer to the Questions and Answers in the front of this Bible for more information.

6-week plan	11-week plan	Personal Reading	Group Study Passage
1	1	1:1–17	1:1–17/Call to Repent
	2	1:18–2:13	1:18–2:13/Surveyor's Line
2	3	3:1–10	3:1–10/Priest's Garments
	4	4:1–14	4:1–14/Lampstand and Trees
3	5	5:1–6:8	5:5–6:8/Wicked Basket Case
	6	6:9–15	6:9–15/Crown for Joshua
4	7	7:1–8:23	7:1–14/True Justice
	8	9:1–17	9:9–13/New King for a New Day
5	9	10:1–11:17	11:4–17/Two Shepherds
	10	12:1–13:6	12:10–13:6/God Purges His Own
6	11	13:7–14:21	14:1–21/God Punishes Nations

Author: Zechariah, the prophet and priest who was born in exile and returned from Babylon to Judah in 538 B.C. (1:1; see Ezr 5:1; 6:14).

Date: Zechariah is specific as to the year, month and day of the messages recorded in chapters 1–8. They span the years from 520 to 518 B.C. The date of his final prophecy (ch. 9–14) is uncertain, though it was probably not given until some 40 years later (e.g., after 480 B.C.).

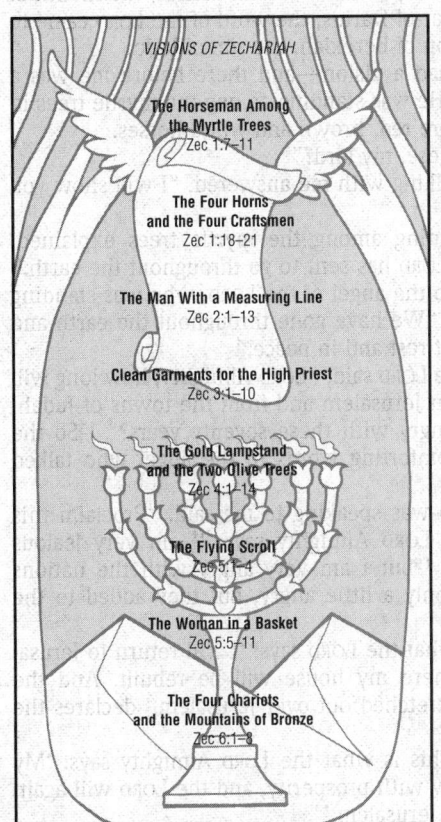

VISIONS OF ZECHARIAH

The Horseman Among the Myrtle Trees
Zec 1:7–11

The Four Horns and the Four Craftsmen
Zec 1:18–21

The Man With a Measuring Line
Zec 2:1–13

Clean Garments for the High Priest
Zec 3:1–10

The Gold Lampstand and the Two Olive Trees
Zec 4:1–14

The Flying Scroll
Zec 5:1–4

The Woman in a Basket
Zec 5:5–11

The Four Chariots and the Mountains of Bronze
Zec 6:1–8

Theme: Rebuilding the temple and the nation of Judah; the Lord's return.

Historical Background: This book is set in the context of the return of the Jews from the Babylonian exile and the subsequent rebuilding of Jerusalem and the temple (see the Introductions to Ezra and Nehemiah). It was through the ministry of Zechariah (along with Haggai) that the rebuilding of the temple began (see Ezr 5:1–2). The temple was completed and dedicated four years later in 516 B.C.

Characteristics: Zechariah was a younger contemporary of Haggai, with a ministry extending well beyond Haggai's, possibly into the reign of Artaxerxes I (465–424 B.C.). Both prophets dealt with the same theme (rebuilding the temple) but in contrasting ways (see the Introduction to Haggai). Zechariah was an apocalyptic visionary, while Haggai was a practical doer. The Book of Zechariah poses a study in contrast between its Part I (ch. 1–8) and Part II (ch. 9–14) written some 40 years later. In Part I Zechariah conveys that when the people of his day see how things ultimately result in their deliverance and God's greater glory, they will be encouraged to take up the temple rebuilding project. In Part II he proclaims that rebuilding the temple will point them to the future transformation of God's people into a holy nation.

Zechariah

1. What physical traits (eyes, hair coloring, etc.) did you inherit from your ancestors. What traits seem to have skipped a generation? 2. What social skills (outgoing-type, shy-type, etc.) were passed along to you? 3. In what one respect are you most like your parents?

1. What "word of the Lord" came to Zechariah in Oct–Nov, 520 B.C.? What word came three months later? 2. Why is God so angry with Israel's forefathers? What were they like (vv. 4–6)? What impact did the call to repentance have on them? What's the object lesson in that? 3. The second word came three months later in audio-visual form (vv. 7–17). What did Zechariah see? Hear? Ask? 4. Are the horsemen's words alarming or comforting? 5. What connects the Lord's mercy, jealousy and anger? What is he most angry about "these seventy years" (v. 12)? 6. What is meant by the "measuring line" in God's plans for Jerusalem?

1. What does Zechariah say about the consequences of returning and of disobedience for God's people, then and now? 2. In matters of faith, what did you inherit from your ancestors? How have you rebelled? Returned? 3. What vision for your life have you received through studying God's word? How does that affect your day-to-day decisions? Your long-term decisions? 4. How is your life similar to Jerusalem: (a) Feeling the pressure of the enemy? (b) Dry or desolate like a desert? (c) Needing restoration and comfort? (d) Restful and peaceful?

A Call to Return to the LORD

1 In the eighth month of the second year of Darius, the word of the LORD came to the prophet Zechariah son of Berekiah, the son of Iddo:

2"The LORD was very angry with your forefathers. 3Therefore tell the people: This is what the LORD Almighty says: 'Return to me,' declares the LORD Almighty, 'and I will return to you,' says the LORD Almighty. 4Do not be like your forefathers, to whom the earlier prophets proclaimed: This is what the LORD Almighty says: 'Turn from your evil ways and your evil practices.' But they would not listen or pay attention to me, declares the LORD. 5Where are your forefathers now? And the prophets, do they live forever? 6But did not my words and my decrees, which I commanded my servants the prophets, overtake your forefathers?

"Then they repented and said, 'The LORD Almighty has done to us what our ways and practices deserve, just as he determined to do.'"

The Man Among the Myrtle Trees

7On the twenty-fourth day of the eleventh month, the month of Shebat, in the second year of Darius, the word of the LORD came to the prophet Zechariah son of Berekiah, the son of Iddo.

8During the night I had a vision—and there before me was a man riding a red horse! He was standing among the myrtle trees in a ravine. Behind him were red, brown and white horses.

9I asked, "What are these, my lord?"

The angel who was talking with me answered, "I will show you what they are."

10Then the man standing among the myrtle trees explained, "They are the ones the LORD has sent to go throughout the earth."

11And they reported to the angel of the LORD, who was standing among the myrtle trees, "We have gone throughout the earth and found the whole world at rest and in peace."

12Then the angel of the LORD said, "LORD Almighty, how long will you withhold mercy from Jerusalem and from the towns of Judah, which you have been angry with these seventy years?" 13So the LORD spoke kind and comforting words to the angel who talked with me.

14Then the angel who was speaking to me said, "Proclaim this word: This is what the LORD Almighty says: 'I am very jealous for Jerusalem and Zion, 15but I am very angry with the nations that feel secure. I was only a little angry, but they added to the calamity.'

16"Therefore, this is what the LORD says: 'I will return to Jerusalem with mercy, and there my house will be rebuilt. And the measuring line will be stretched out over Jerusalem,' declares the LORD Almighty.

17"Proclaim further: This is what the LORD Almighty says: 'My towns will again overflow with prosperity, and the LORD will again comfort Zion and choose Jerusalem.'"

Four Horns and Four Craftsmen

[18]Then I looked up—and there before me were four horns! [19]I asked the angel who was speaking to me, "What are these?"

He answered me, "These are the horns that scattered Judah, Israel and Jerusalem."

[20]Then the LORD showed me four craftsmen. [21]I asked, "What are these coming to do?"

He answered, "These are the horns that scattered Judah so that no one could raise his head, but the craftsmen have come to terrify them and throw down these horns of the nations who lifted up their horns against the land of Judah to scatter its people."

A Man With a Measuring Line

2 Then I looked up—and there before me was a man with a measuring line in his hand! [2]I asked, "Where are you going?"

He answered me, "To measure Jerusalem, to find out how wide and how long it is."

[3]Then the angel who was speaking to me left, and another angel came to meet him [4]and said to him: "Run, tell that young man, 'Jerusalem will be a city without walls because of the great number of men and livestock in it. [5]And I myself will be a wall of fire around it,' declares the LORD, 'and I will be its glory within.'

[6]"Come! Come! Flee from the land of the north," declares the LORD, "for I have scattered you to the four winds of heaven," declares the LORD.

[7]"Come, O Zion! Escape, you who live in the Daughter of Babylon!" [8]For this is what the LORD Almighty says: "After he has honored me and has sent me against the nations that have plundered you—for whoever touches you touches the apple of his eye— [9]I will surely raise my hand against them so that their slaves will plunder them.[a] Then you will know that the LORD Almighty has sent me.

[10]"Shout and be glad, O Daughter of Zion. For I am coming, and I will live among you," declares the LORD. [11]"Many nations will be joined with the LORD in that day and will become my people. I will live among you and you will know that the LORD Almighty has sent me to you. [12]The LORD will inherit Judah as his portion in the holy land and will again choose Jerusalem. [13]Be still before the LORD, all mankind, because he has roused himself from his holy dwelling."

Clean Garments for the High Priest

3 Then he showed me Joshua[b] the high priest standing before the angel of the LORD, and Satan[c] standing at his right side to accuse him. [2]The LORD said to Satan, "The LORD rebuke you, Satan! The LORD, who has chosen Jerusalem, rebuke you! Is not this man a burning stick snatched from the fire?"

[3]Now Joshua was dressed in filthy clothes as he stood before the angel. [4]The angel said to those who were standing before him, "Take off his filthy clothes."

Then he said to Joshua, "See, I have taken away your sin, and I will put rich garments on you."

[5]Then I said, "Put a clean turban on his head." So they put a clean turban on his head and clothed him, while the angel of the LORD stood by.

[6]The angel of the LORD gave this charge to Joshua: [7]"This is what the LORD Almighty says: 'If you will walk in my ways and keep my

1. From your childhood, what do you remember about the neighborhood or grade school bully? What eventually happened to the bully? 2. When a remodeling job must be done at home, do you: (a) Get right to it? (b) Read a book first? (c) Hire a pro?

1. What effect did the horns of strength have on Judah (1:19; see Eze 6:8; 36:19)? 2. Is the coming of the craftsmen good or bad news to the horns? To Judah? How so? 3. What remodeling job has God planned for Jerusalem? What boundaries and measurements have been set for the project? 4. How does the Lord guarantee the safety and security of its inhabitants (2:5; see Ex 14:19–20; 40:34)? 5. What is the future for the "Daughter of Babylon" (2:7–9)? For the "Daughter of Zion" (2:10–12)? 6. How important is Jerusalem to the Lord as the center of worship, learning and judgment?

1. Who are the bullies or "horns" that you fear? 2. In what ways has God helped defeat and subdue them in your life? 3. The measuring line is a very powerful symbol in Zechariah's vision for Jerusalem. What remodeling would the Lord like to do in your life? 4. Are you living in the "Daughter of Babylon," or the "Daughter of Zion"? What is the Lord telling you to do about that, so you can be more "in Zion" (or in Christ)?

For the first day of school after summer vacation, what did your parents do for you: (a) Bubble bath the night before? (b) New set of clothes? (c) New paper and pens? (d) Haircut? (e) Clean fingernails? (f) All of the above? What did cleanliness have to do with life and learning?

1. How many characters are in this fourth vision of Zechariah? What part does each play? Who or what does Joshua represent? 2. How will their guilt be removed, initially? Ultimately? 3. What are the things to come: The Branch? The stone with seven eyes? That single day? 4. What promise is given to Joshua (v. 7)? To Israel (v. 10)? What present

---

[a]8,9 Or says after . . . eye: [9]"I . . . plunder them."   [b]1 A variant of Jeshua; here and elsewhere in Zechariah   [c]1 Satan means accuser.

duty and future prosperity does it involve?

♥ 1. As for *your* laundry and clothing situation, *how* is it: (a) All dirty? (b) All clean? (c) Still in the wash? 2. What does it mean to "walk in God's ways and keep his requirements" for Joshua? For your church leaders? For you?

◔ 1. What are you like when just awakened? 2. What one project at home or work do you most want to complete?

▥ 1. What do you think each object in Zechariah's vision represents: Gold lampstand? Bowl of oil? Channels? Two olive trees (vv. 3,14; see Rev 11:4)? The sevens? Mountain? Capstone? Plumb line? 2. Is this vision meant to encourage or warn the people? How so? 3. What will it take for Zerubbabel to rebuild the temple (vv. 6–7)? At the time, what stood in his way (v. 10; see Ezr 4:1–5,24; Hag 1:14; 2:1–5)? 4. How will Zerubbabel and Joshua utilize God's resources?

♥ 1. How does God's glory and blessing come into your life? Does it come more in day-to-day work (Zerubbabel) or in worship (Joshua)? 2. Into whose life will you carry blessing and renewal? 3. When told your smarts and strength alone will not get you through life or glorify God (v. 6), how do you respond? How does your life compare to the Master Builder's plumb line? What will you do today to bring your life back into line?

◔ In discipline, did your parents ever tell you (or did you ever tell your children), "Some day you'll thank me for this"? What for?

▥ 1. What message does the unfurled scroll bring? Why is it so big? 2. Who is this curse meant for (v. 3; see Ex 20:7,15; Dt 27:26; Gal 3:10)? 3. How effective will the curse or warning be?

♥ 1. Do you think God's warnings are as severe today? Or does God judge on a sliding scale? 2. How does God bring warning

requirements, then you will govern my house and have charge of my courts, and I will give you a place among these standing here. 8 "'Listen, O high priest Joshua and your associates seated before you, who are men symbolic of things to come: I am going to bring my servant, the Branch. 9See, the stone I have set in front of Joshua! There are seven eyes[a] on that one stone, and I will engrave an inscription on it,' says the LORD Almighty, 'and I will remove the sin of this land in a single day.

10 "'In that day each of you will invite his neighbor to sit under his vine and fig tree,' declares the LORD Almighty."

The Gold Lampstand and the Two Olive Trees

4 Then the angel who talked with me returned and wakened me, as a man is wakened from his sleep. 2He asked me, "What do you see?"

I answered, "I see a solid gold lampstand with a bowl at the top and seven lights on it, with seven channels to the lights. 3Also there are two olive trees by it, one on the right of the bowl and the other on its left."

4I asked the angel who talked with me, "What are these, my lord?"

5He answered, "Do you not know what these are?"

"No, my lord," I replied.

6So he said to me, "This is the word of the LORD to Zerubbabel: 'Not by might nor by power, but by my Spirit,' says the LORD Almighty.

7 "What[b] are you, O mighty mountain? Before Zerubbabel you will become level ground. Then he will bring out the capstone to shouts of 'God bless it! God bless it!' "

8Then the word of the LORD came to me: 9"The hands of Zerubbabel have laid the foundation of this temple; his hands will also complete it. Then you will know that the LORD Almighty has sent me to you.

10"Who despises the day of small things? Men will rejoice when they see the plumb line in the hand of Zerubbabel.

"(These seven are the eyes of the LORD, which range throughout the earth.)"

11Then I asked the angel, "What are these two olive trees on the right and the left of the lampstand?"

12Again I asked him, "What are these two olive branches beside the two gold pipes that pour out golden oil?"

13He replied, "Do you not know what these are?"

"No, my lord," I said.

14So he said, "These are the two who are anointed to[c] serve the Lord of all the earth."

The Flying Scroll

5 I looked again—and there before me was a flying scroll! 2He asked me, "What do you see?"

I answered, "I see a flying scroll, thirty feet long and fifteen feet wide.[d]"

3And he said to me, "This is the curse that is going out over the whole land; for according to what it says on one side, every thief will be banished, and according to what it says on the other, everyone who swears falsely will be banished. 4The LORD Almighty declares, 'I will send it out, and it will enter the house of the thief and the house of him who swears falsely by my name. It will

---

[a]9 Or *facets*   [b]7 Or *Who*   [c]14 Or *two who bring oil and*   [d]2 Hebrew *twenty cubits long and ten cubits wide* (about 9 meters long and 4.5 meters wide)

remain in his house and destroy it, both its timbers and its stones.' "

The Woman in a Basket

[5] Then the angel who was speaking to me came forward and said to me, "Look up and see what this is that is appearing."

[6] I asked, "What is it?"

He replied, "It is a measuring basket.[a]" And he added, "This is the iniquity[b] of the people throughout the land."

[7] Then the cover of lead was raised, and there in the basket sat a woman! [8] He said, "This is wickedness," and he pushed her back into the basket and pushed the lead cover down over its mouth.

[9] Then I looked up—and there before me were two women, with the wind in their wings! They had wings like those of a stork, and they lifted up the basket between heaven and earth.

[10] "Where are they taking the basket?" I asked the angel who was speaking to me.

[11] He replied, "To the country of Babylonia[c] to build a house for it. When it is ready, the basket will be set there in its place."

Four Chariots

6 I looked up again—and there before me were four chariots coming out from between two mountains—mountains of bronze! [2] The first chariot had red horses, the second black, [3] the third white, and the fourth dappled—all of them powerful. [4] I asked the angel who was speaking to me, "What are these, my lord?"

[5] The angel answered me, "These are the four spirits[d] of heaven, going out from standing in the presence of the Lord of the whole world. [6] The one with the black horses is going toward the north country, the one with the white horses toward the west,[e] and the one with the dappled horses toward the south."

[7] When the powerful horses went out, they were straining to go throughout the earth. And he said, "Go throughout the earth!" So they went throughout the earth.

[8] Then he called to me, "Look, those going toward the north country have given my Spirit[f] rest in the land of the north."

A Crown for Joshua

[9] The word of the LORD came to me: [10] "Take ⌊silver and gold⌋ from the exiles Heldai, Tobijah and Jedaiah, who have arrived from Babylon. Go the same day to the house of Josiah son of Zephaniah. [11] Take the silver and gold and make a crown, and set it on the head of the high priest, Joshua son of Jehozadak. [12] Tell him this is what the LORD Almighty says: 'Here is the man whose name is the Branch, and he will branch out from his place and build the temple of the LORD. [13] It is he who will build the temple of the LORD, and he will be clothed with majesty and will sit and rule on his throne. And he will be a priest on his throne. And there will be harmony between the two.' [14] The crown will be given to Heldai,[g] Tobijah, Jedaiah and Hen[h] son of Zephaniah as a memorial in the temple of the LORD. [15] Those who are far away will come and help to build the temple of the LORD, and you will know that the LORD Almighty has sent me to you. This will happen if you diligently obey the LORD your God."

---

into your life? Does he have to put it on a billboard to catch your attention? How sensitive are you to God's promptings?

1. As a kid, how did you picture Satan? Now, how do you envision him? Why the change? 2. From your family background, what images does "horse" bring to mind: (a) Horse and buggy days? (b) Equestrian events? (c) Betting on races? (d) Merry-go-round? (e) Cowboy westerns on TV? (f) Mr. Ed, the talking horse? What would you do with a horse now?

1. How big must this "measuring basket" have been (5:6)? 2. Whose "wickedness" did the woman represent: People? Government? Priests? Satan? 3. Who removed it from the land? Why take it to Babylonia (see Rev 17–18)? What does all this mean? 4. How does Zechariah's eighth and last vision (6:1–8) compare with 1:7–17? With Revelation 6:1–8? 5. What mission are these four chariots on? 6. What does this vision say about judgment? About God's rest?

1. Where does evil rear its ugly head today? In what disguises? Places? 2. Is the lid on evil (5:8) open or shut in your life? 3. What do horses have to do with judgment? What vehicle of judgment does God use in your life? 4. When have you known God's "rest" (v. 8)?

1. Here Zechariah receives a direct command rather than an interactive vision. Why? What exactly was the prophet to do? 2. What is meant by crowning Joshua? By the prophecy about the royal Branch (vv. 11–13; see Jer 23:5; 33:15–16; Jn 19:5; Ps 110; Heb 7:1–3,15–17)? 3. Which temple will those who "are far away" build (v. 15; see Hag 2:6–9; Eph 2:13)? What else will happen then?

1. What is it like to be a child of Christ the King? 2. What kind of Christian life are you building for your King: Shack? Condo? Cathedral? Temple? 3. If you are God's temple (see 1Co 3:16), what building materials are you using? What craftsmanship?

---

a6 Hebrew *an ephah*; also in verses 7-11   b6 Or *appearance*   c11 Hebrew *Shinar*   d5 Or *winds*   e6 Or *horses after them*   f8 Or *spirit*   g14 Syriac; Hebrew *Helem*   h14 Or *and the gracious one, the*

1. How did you impress your spouse, or the one you hope to marry, on your first date: (a) With flowers? (b) Make-up? (c) Clothes? (d) Car? (e) Dieting? (f) Great meal? 2. What actually impressed your date most?

1. What question did the Bethel delegation ask Zechariah? How did he reply? What was so wrong with their fasting and feasting these 70 years? 2. Instead, what should they have done to show "justice and mercy" in practice (vv. 9–10)? 3. What attitude was in their heart (see 1Co 10:31)? How was that obvious? How did God react? Why?

1. How does the worship at your church or in your group compare with that of Zechariah's day? Is your heart in it? How so? 2. How can you obey Zechariah 7:9–10? What do your heart-felt actions of justice and mercy say to God? To the world? 3. Do you ever feel like the Bethel group in your response toward God's Word? How so? As a result, is your life scattered or desolate? In what way?

Did you ever fall out of favor with a good friend or break up with your boy/girlfriend? Over what issue? Did you ever get back together? Who made the first move? What did you gain by mending the relationship?

1. Zechariah foresees countless benefits concerning Jerusalem getting back together with her Lord. Can you find 10 of them? 2. What moral force is given to each blessing by the constant refrain, "the Lord Almighty says"? 3. What will it take to restore the people to covenant favor and be given these blessings (vv. 14–17)? What gap lies between promise and fulfillment? Between desire and delivery? 4. What is God's answer to the Bethel group's question concerning fasts (vv. 18–19; see 7:2–3)? What does this indicate about the health of the relationship between God and the people? 5. What role will a restored Israel play in the worship of God and his witness among the nations (vv. 20–23)? How will other nations express their desire to know God?

Justice and Mercy, Not Fasting

7 In the fourth year of King Darius, the word of the LORD came to Zechariah on the fourth day of the ninth month, the month of Kislev. ²The people of Bethel had sent Sharezer and Regem-Melech, together with their men, to entreat the LORD ³by asking the priests of the house of the LORD Almighty and the prophets, "Should I mourn and fast in the fifth month, as I have done for so many years?"

⁴Then the word of the LORD Almighty came to me: ⁵"Ask all the people of the land and the priests, 'When you fasted and mourned in the fifth and seventh months for the past seventy years, was it really for me that you fasted? ⁶And when you were eating and drinking, were you not just feasting for yourselves? ⁷Are these not the words the LORD proclaimed through the earlier prophets when Jerusalem and its surrounding towns were at rest and prosperous, and the Negev and the western foothills were settled?'"

⁸And the word of the LORD came again to Zechariah: ⁹"This is what the LORD Almighty says: 'Administer true justice; show mercy and compassion to one another. ¹⁰Do not oppress the widow or the fatherless, the alien or the poor. In your hearts do not think evil of each other.'

¹¹"But they refused to pay attention; stubbornly they turned their backs and stopped up their ears. ¹²They made their hearts as hard as flint and would not listen to the law or to the words that the LORD Almighty had sent by his Spirit through the earlier prophets. So the LORD Almighty was very angry.

¹³"'When I called, they did not listen; so when they called, I would not listen,' says the LORD Almighty. ¹⁴'I scattered them with a whirlwind among all the nations, where they were strangers. The land was left so desolate behind them that no one could come or go. This is how they made the pleasant land desolate.'"

The LORD Promises to Bless Jerusalem

8 Again the word of the LORD Almighty came to me. ²This is what the LORD Almighty says: "I am very jealous for Zion; I am burning with jealousy for her."

³This is what the LORD says: "I will return to Zion and dwell in Jerusalem. Then Jerusalem will be called the City of Truth, and the mountain of the LORD Almighty will be called the Holy Mountain."

⁴This is what the LORD Almighty says: "Once again men and women of ripe old age will sit in the streets of Jerusalem, each with cane in hand because of his age. ⁵The city streets will be filled with boys and girls playing there."

⁶This is what the LORD Almighty says: "It may seem marvelous to the remnant of this people at that time, but will it seem marvelous to me?" declares the LORD Almighty.

⁷This is what the LORD Almighty says: "I will save my people from the countries of the east and the west. ⁸I will bring them back to live in Jerusalem; they will be my people, and I will be faithful and righteous to them as their God."

⁹This is what the LORD Almighty says: "You who now hear these words spoken by the prophets who were there when the foundation was laid for the house of the LORD Almighty, let your hands be strong so that the temple may be built. ¹⁰Before that time there were no wages for man or beast. No one could go about his business safely because of his enemy, for I had turned every man against his neighbor. ¹¹But now I will not deal with the remnant of this people as I did in the past," declares the LORD Almighty.

¹²"The seed will grow well, the vine will yield its fruit, the

ground will produce its crops, and the heavens will drop their dew. I will give all these things as an inheritance to the remnant of this people. ¹³As you have been an object of cursing among the nations, O Judah and Israel, so will I save you, and you will be a blessing. Do not be afraid, but let your hands be strong."

¹⁴This is what the LORD Almighty says: "Just as I had determined to bring disaster upon you and showed no pity when your fathers angered me," says the LORD Almighty, ¹⁵"so now I have determined to do good again to Jerusalem and Judah. Do not be afraid. ¹⁶These are the things you are to do: Speak the truth to each other, and render true and sound judgment in your courts; ¹⁷do not plot evil against your neighbor, and do not love to swear falsely. I hate all this," declares the LORD.

¹⁸Again the word of the LORD Almighty came to me. ¹⁹This is what the LORD Almighty says: "The fasts of the fourth, fifth, seventh and tenth months will become joyful and glad occasions and happy festivals for Judah. Therefore love truth and peace."

²⁰This is what the LORD Almighty says: "Many peoples and the inhabitants of many cities will yet come, ²¹and the inhabitants of one city will go to another and say, 'Let us go at once to entreat the LORD and seek the LORD Almighty. I myself am going.' ²²And many peoples and powerful nations will come to Jerusalem to seek the LORD Almighty and to entreat him."

²³This is what the LORD Almighty says: "In those days ten men from all languages and nations will take firm hold of one Jew by the hem of his robe and say, 'Let us go with you, because we have heard that God is with you.'"

Judgment on Israel's Enemies

An Oracle

9 The word of the LORD is against the land of Hadrach
    and will rest upon Damascus—
for the eyes of men and all the tribes of Israel
    are on the LORD—ᵃ
²and upon Hamath too, which borders on it,
    and upon Tyre and Sidon, though they are very
        skillful.
³Tyre has built herself a stronghold;
    she has heaped up silver like dust,
    and gold like the dirt of the streets.
⁴But the Lord will take away her possessions
    and destroy her power on the sea,
    and she will be consumed by fire.
⁵Ashkelon will see it and fear;
    Gaza will writhe in agony,
    and Ekron too, for her hope will wither.
  Gaza will lose her king
    and Ashkelon will be deserted.
⁶Foreigners will occupy Ashdod,
    and I will cut off the pride of the Philistines.
⁷I will take the blood from their mouths,
    the forbidden food from between their teeth.
  Those who are left will belong to our God
    and become leaders in Judah,
    and Ekron will be like the Jebusites.
⁸But I will defend my house

ᵃ1 Or Damascus. / For the eye of the LORD is on all mankind, / as well as on the tribes of Israel,

1. When parents, preachers, salespeople or politicians make too-good-to-be-true promises, are you initially trusting or are you mostly skeptical? What does your response depend on? 2. What difference does it make when God promises you something? Which of the blessings promised in Zechariah have you seen come true for spiritual Israel and the Christian Church? Which promises are yet to be fulfilled? 3. Right now does your relationship with God feel like "fast" or "feast" (v. 19)? Explain. 4. One sign of a restored Israel is that people the world over will say, "Let us go with you, because we have heard that God is with you" (v. 23). What does this say about the need for you or your church to grow in worship and witness? In your community, who else has a worship service or outreach program that attracts you?

1. What have you lost that you once took great pride in: (a) Academic standing? (b) Car? (c) House? (d) Houseful of kids? (e) Athletic ability? (f) Nest egg? (g) Other? 2. How did it feel to be without your claim to fun, fame or fortune? 3. How did you deal with your loss?

1. What fate does Zechariah envision for Syria, Phoenicia and Philistia (vv. 3–6)? What have they done to deserve this fate? 2. Are Syria, Phoenicia and Philistia the real targets of this prophecy? What about Jerusalem (v. 9)? 3. Who is being destroyed and who is being preserved? For what purpose?

1. In history (c. 333 B.C.) God used Alexander the Great to deal convincingly with those who opposed his will. Thus was this oracle fulfilled. What lessons does that teach you about God's love and holiness? About the authority of God's word spoken through prophets? 2. Are you doing any of the things targeted in this oracle for judgment: Hoarding wealth? Victimizing others? Trusting in your own strength? How has God dealt with you in this area? 3. Unlike the Syrians, Phoenicians,

Philistines or the Jebusites, what can you legitimately take pride in that is of eternal value, knowing that it will never be taken away?

☕ What would be the three top qualities you would look for in a leader: (a) Vision? (b) Integrity? (c) Service record? (d) Promises made? (e) Looks? (f) Other?

📖 1. What qualities will Zion's King possess? Describe the scene at his coming. How will the people respond? Why the donkey (v. 9; see Mt 21:5, for Jesus' use of it), instead of the war-horse (v. 10)? 2. On what basis will restoration be given to prisoners or exiles?

♡ 1. Describe the King's advent in your life. 2. God's intention for exiles and prisoners is peace. How have you experienced that wholeness, health and harmony in your life? In your group life? 3. What projects or actions have you taken to promote peace within your church, community or world?

☕ When were you most celebrated or showered with gifts?

📖 1. What will the victory banquet of God's people be like? How will the Sovereign Lord make his entry? 2. What blessings does God as Shepherd (v. 16) bring?

♡ 1. When have you or your church had a foretaste of the victory celebration described here? What victory do you want to celebrate when the Lord returns? 2. Do you feel much like a crown jewel in God's possession? Where do you sparkle? What rough spots need polishing?

☕ Try a "What's-my-line?" group exercise where you make three statements about yourself. Two are elaborately truthful and one is a well-disguised "line" (deceit or lie). Then have the group guess which was the false line. The object of the game is to fool everyone with the best line.

against marauding forces.
Never again will an oppressor overrun my people,
for now I am keeping watch.

The Coming of Zion's King

⁹Rejoice greatly, O Daughter of Zion!
Shout, Daughter of Jerusalem!
See, your king*a* comes to you,
righteous and having salvation,
gentle and riding on a donkey,
on a colt, the foal of a donkey.
¹⁰I will take away the chariots from Ephraim
and the war-horses from Jerusalem,
and the battle bow will be broken.
He will proclaim peace to the nations.
His rule will extend from sea to sea
and from the River*b* to the ends of the
earth.*c*
¹¹As for you, because of the blood of my covenant
with you,
I will free your prisoners from the waterless pit.
¹²Return to your fortress, O prisoners of hope;
even now I announce that I will restore twice
as much to you.
¹³I will bend Judah as I bend my bow
and fill it with Ephraim.
I will rouse your sons, O Zion,
against your sons, O Greece,
and make you like a warrior's sword.

The Lord Will Appear

¹⁴Then the Lord will appear over them;
his arrow will flash like lightning.
The Sovereign Lord will sound the trumpet;
he will march in the storms of the south,
15 and the Lord Almighty will shield them.
They will destroy
and overcome with slingstones.
They will drink and roar as with wine;
they will be full like a bowl
used for sprinkling*d* the corners of the altar.
¹⁶The Lord their God will save them on that day
as the flock of his people.
They will sparkle in his land
like jewels in a crown.
¹⁷How attractive and beautiful they will be!
Grain will make the young men thrive,
and new wine the young women.

The Lord Will Care for Judah

10 Ask the Lord for rain in the springtime;
it is the Lord who makes the storm clouds.
He gives showers of rain to men,
and plants of the field to everyone.
²The idols speak deceit,
diviners see visions that lie;
they tell dreams that are false,

---

*a*9 Or *King*   *b*10 That is, the Euphrates   *c*10 Or *the end of the land*
*d*15 Or *bowl, / like*

they give comfort in vain.
Therefore the people wander like sheep
    oppressed for lack of a shepherd.

³"My anger burns against the shepherds,
    and I will punish the leaders;
for the Lord Almighty will care
    for his flock, the house of Judah,
    and make them like a proud horse in battle.
⁴From Judah will come the cornerstone,
    from him the tent peg,
    from him the battle bow,
    from him every ruler.
⁵Together theyª will be like mighty men
    trampling the muddy streets in battle.
Because the Lord is with them,
    they will fight and overthrow the horsemen.

⁶"I will strengthen the house of Judah
    and save the house of Joseph.
I will restore them
    because I have compassion on them.
They will be as though
    I had not rejected them,
for I am the Lord their God
    and I will answer them.
⁷The Ephraimites will become like mighty men,
    and their hearts will be glad as with wine.
Their children will see it and be joyful;
    their hearts will rejoice in the Lord.
⁸I will signal for them
    and gather them in.
Surely I will redeem them;
    they will be as numerous as before.
⁹Though I scatter them among the peoples,
    yet in distant lands they will remember me.
They and their children will survive,
    and they will return.
¹⁰I will bring them back from Egypt
    and gather them from Assyria.
I will bring them to Gilead and Lebanon,
    and there will not be room enough for them.
¹¹They will pass through the sea of trouble;
    the surging sea will be subdued
    and all the depths of the Nile will dry up.
Assyria's pride will be brought down
    and Egypt's scepter will pass away.
¹²I will strengthen them in the Lord
    and in his name they will walk,"
                declares the Lord.

11

Open your doors, O Lebanon,
    so that fire may devour your cedars!
²Wail, O pine tree, for the cedar has fallen;
    the stately trees are ruined!
Wail, oaks of Bashan;
    the dense forest has been cut down!
³Listen to the wail of the shepherds;
    their rich pastures are destroyed!

1. In what ways were the Israelites to distinguish between Yahweh and the gods of other nations? What are some good lines that these pretenders might have used to dupe Israel into worshipping a false god? 2. How will God deal with the false shepherds who have exploited his flock and allowed them to wander (10:3a; 11:1–3)? 3. What images are used to denote the strength and stability God will restore to his flock (10:3b–7)? Why will God do this? 4. How is the theme of restoration, promise and fulfillment developed further in verses 8–12? 5. Which line here plays on the true meaning of Zechariah's name (the Lord remembers)? What will God do on behalf of his covenant promises and people?

1. What are the false gods or idols in your world? How can you discern their well-disguised lines? How can your small group help you not to fall for their deceit? 2. As a member of God's flock, are you: (a) Wandering aimlessly? (b) Looking in vain for greener pastures or still waters? (c) Listening to the voices of many shepherds? (d) Grazing in the land of promise? (e) Getting fleeced? Is it time to get back to the strength and security of the sheepfold? 3. Zechariah's name means "the Lord remembers." What of your needs has the Lord remembered to care for? Which of your needs are you still waiting on the Lord to remember? 4. The citizens of Lebanon, Bashan and Jordan (11:1–3) probably wished the Lord had not remembered their sin. Do you sometimes feel that way? When he does remember, and you are punished, what does that teach you to remember the next time around?

ª4,5 Or ruler, all of them together. / ⁵They

Listen to the roar of the lions;
　the lush thicket of the Jordan is ruined!

Two Shepherds

4This is what the LORD my God says: "Pasture the flock marked for slaughter. 5Their buyers slaughter them and go unpunished. Those who sell them say, 'Praise the LORD, I am rich!' Their own shepherds do not spare them. 6For I will no longer have pity on the people of the land," declares the LORD. "I will hand everyone over to his neighbor and his king. They will oppress the land, and I will not rescue them from their hands."

7So I pastured the flock marked for slaughter, particularly the oppressed of the flock. Then I took two staffs and called one Favor and the other Union, and I pastured the flock. 8In one month I got rid of the three shepherds.

The flock detested me, and I grew weary of them 9and said, "I will not be your shepherd. Let the dying die, and the perishing perish. Let those who are left eat one another's flesh."

10Then I took my staff called Favor and broke it, revoking the covenant I had made with all the nations. 11It was revoked on that day, and so the afflicted of the flock who were watching me knew it was the word of the LORD.

12I told them, "If you think it best, give me my pay; but if not, keep it." So they paid me thirty pieces of silver.

13And the LORD said to me, "Throw it to the potter"—the handsome price at which they priced me! So I took the thirty pieces of silver and threw them into the house of the LORD to the potter.

14Then I broke my second staff called Union, breaking the brotherhood between Judah and Israel.

15Then the LORD said to me, "Take again the equipment of a foolish shepherd. 16For I am going to raise up a shepherd over the land who will not care for the lost, or seek the young, or heal the injured, or feed the healthy, but will eat the meat of the choice sheep, tearing off their hoofs.

17"Woe to the worthless shepherd,
　who deserts the flock!
May the sword strike his arm and his right eye!
　May his arm be completely withered,
　his right eye totally blinded!"

Jerusalem's Enemies to Be Destroyed
An Oracle

12 This is the word of the LORD concerning Israel. The LORD, who stretches out the heavens, who lays the foundation of the earth, and who forms the spirit of man within him, declares: 2"I am going to make Jerusalem a cup that sends all the surrounding peoples reeling. Judah will be besieged as well as Jerusalem. 3On that day, when all the nations of the earth are gathered against her, I will make Jerusalem an immovable rock for all the nations. All who try to move it will injure themselves. 4On that day I will strike every horse with panic and its rider with madness," declares the LORD. "I will keep a watchful eye over the house of Judah, but I will blind all the horses of the nations. 5Then the leaders of Judah will say in their hearts, 'The people of Jerusalem are strong, because the LORD Almighty is their God.'

6"On that day I will make the leaders of Judah like a firepot in a woodpile, like a flaming torch among sheaves. They will consume

---

When have you broken your favorite club, bat, racket or garden tool? At the time, did you feel like cursing or blessing? How did you compensate for your loss?

1. Who is this cast of characters: The "flock marked for slaughter"? Their "buyers"? "They" (v. 6)? "I" (v. 7)? 2. What roles are scripted here? What is meant by their rejecting the prototype Good Shepherd (vv. 7–8)? What then happened? 3. How are the props used here: "Favor" (v. 10)? "thirty pieces of silver" (v. 13)? "Union" (v. 14)? 4. What insight does this give us into Zechariah as "a shepherd"? The Messiah as Good Shepherd (compare Jn 10:1–18)? The anti-Christ as false shepherd?

1. Have you ever rejected a good shepherd? And later regretted it? What did the experience teach you? 2. Zechariah's staffs suggest that his mission was to ensure divine favor on the flock by binding them into one. How far does this parallel the experience of your group and your church in relation to the Good Shepherd? 3. Breaking the staffs signifies the breaking of Israel into two hostile parties. In what ways are members of your church broken up into factions? 4. When do you envision the fulfillment of this prophecy?

1. Who was your childhood hero? Was your hero fictional or real? 2. What did you admire most about your hero? Did you ever dress up like your hero? Belong to a fan club? Explain.

1. What graphic images are used here to describe God's people? What does this tell you about the covenant relationship? 2. How will Jerusalem survive the attacks of "all the nations"? What is the secret of their strength? How will they dispatch their enemies? 3. Who will be delivered first? Why? On that day, what hero will the feeblest soldiers be like? What will be God's mission?

right and left all the surrounding peoples, but Jerusalem will remain intact in her place.

7"The LORD will save the dwellings of Judah first, so that the honor of the house of David and of Jerusalem's inhabitants may not be greater than that of Judah. 8On that day the LORD will shield those who live in Jerusalem, so that the feeblest among them will be like David, and the house of David will be like God, like the Angel of the LORD going before them. 9On that day I will set out to destroy all the nations that attack Jerusalem.

Mourning for the One They Pierced

10"And I will pour out on the house of David and the inhabitants of Jerusalem a spirit*a* of grace and supplication. They will look on*b* me, the one they have pierced, and they will mourn for him as one mourns for an only child, and grieve bitterly for him as one grieves for a firstborn son. 11On that day the weeping in Jerusalem will be great, like the weeping of Hadad Rimmon in the plain of Megiddo. 12The land will mourn, each clan by itself, with their wives by themselves: the clan of the house of David and their wives, the clan of the house of Nathan and their wives, 13the clan of the house of Levi and their wives, the clan of Shimei and their wives, 14and all the rest of the clans and their wives.

Cleansing From Sin

13 "On that day a fountain will be opened to the house of David and the inhabitants of Jerusalem, to cleanse them from sin and impurity.

2"On that day, I will banish the names of the idols from the land, and they will be remembered no more," declares the LORD Almighty. "I will remove both the prophets and the spirit of impurity from the land. 3And if anyone still prophesies, his father and mother, to whom he was born, will say to him, 'You must die, because you have told lies in the LORD's name.' When he prophesies, his own parents will stab him.

4"On that day every prophet will be ashamed of his prophetic vision. He will not put on a prophet's garment of hair in order to deceive. 5He will say, 'I am not a prophet. I am a farmer; the land has been my livelihood since my youth.*c'* 6If someone asks him, 'What are these wounds on your body*d*?' he will answer, 'The wounds I was given at the house of my friends.'

The Shepherd Struck, the Sheep Scattered

7"Awake, O sword, against my shepherd,
　　against the man who is close to me!"
　　declares the LORD Almighty.
"Strike the shepherd,
　　and the sheep will be scattered,
　　and I will turn my hand against the little ones.
8In the whole land," declares the LORD,
　　"two-thirds will be struck down and perish;
　　yet one-third will be left in it.
9This third I will bring into the fire;
　　I will refine them like silver
　　and test them like gold.

1. When you or your group feel like feeble foot soldiers, what is God's promise to you? 2. When do you feel most like a hero? Why? What's your secret?

1. What sad day do you recall from your childhood? How did that event affect you growing up? 2. If forced to choose between the two, would you rather be a prophet or a farmer? Why?

1. Who's crying here? Why? How extensively (12:11; see 2Ch 35:22–25)? 2. The word for "stab" (13:3) is the same in Hebrew as "pierced" (12:10). What might that say about the fate of those who killed the Messiah? 3. Why would these prophets prefer to be farmers (vv. 4–6)? 4. What is the good news in all this (13:1–2)?

1. In what ways has a "spirit of grace and supplication" (v. 10) lead to conviction and repentance for you? Your church? Your nation? 2. What false prophets today fit the description here? 3. When asked if you are a Christian, what do you say? How do others know without asking? What masks do you wear to avoid detection? What shameful things in church history and in today's church have caused you to hide?

Have you ever been singled out or summoned to the office of your principal or boss? How did you feel?

1. Which shepherd is slain: The Good Shepherd (11:4–14; 12:10)? Or the foolish one (11:15–17)? 2. What will happen when the shepherd is struck (v. 7b; see Mt 26:31,56)? 3. Will all be lost? What will happen to the remnant? 4. How will the "one-third" be refined and tested (vv. 8–9; see Isa 48:10)? With what results on their covenant relationship with God (also 8:8)?

---

*a*10 Or *the Spirit*　　*b*10 Or *to*　　*c*5 Or *farmer; a man sold me in my youth*
*d*6 Or *wounds between your hands*

They will call on my name
　　and I will answer them;
I will say, 'They are my people,'
　　and they will say, 'The LORD is our God.'"

The LORD Comes and Reigns

14 A day of the LORD is coming when your plunder will be
divided among you.

²I will gather all the nations to Jerusalem to fight against it; the city will be captured, the houses ransacked, and the women raped. Half of the city will go into exile, but the rest of the people will not be taken from the city.

³Then the LORD will go out and fight against those nations, as he fights in the day of battle. ⁴On that day his feet will stand on the Mount of Olives, east of Jerusalem, and the Mount of Olives will be split in two from east to west, forming a great valley, with half of the mountain moving north and half moving south. ⁵You will flee by my mountain valley, for it will extend to Azel. You will flee as you fled from the earthquake*a* in the days of Uzziah king of Judah. Then the LORD my God will come, and all the holy ones with him.

⁶On that day there will be no light, no cold or frost. ⁷It will be a unique day, without daytime or nighttime—a day known to the LORD. When evening comes, there will be light.

⁸On that day living water will flow out from Jerusalem, half to the eastern sea*b* and half to the western sea,*c* in summer and in winter.

⁹The LORD will be king over the whole earth. On that day there will be one LORD, and his name the only name.

¹⁰The whole land, from Geba to Rimmon, south of Jerusalem, will become like the Arabah. But Jerusalem will be raised up and remain in its place, from the Benjamin Gate to the site of the First Gate, to the Corner Gate, and from the Tower of Hananel to the royal winepresses. ¹¹It will be inhabited; never again will it be destroyed. Jerusalem will be secure.

¹²This is the plague with which the LORD will strike all the nations that fought against Jerusalem: Their flesh will rot while they are still standing on their feet, their eyes will rot in their sockets, and their tongues will rot in their mouths. ¹³On that day men will be stricken by the LORD with great panic. Each man will seize the hand of another, and they will attack each other. ¹⁴Judah too will fight at Jerusalem. The wealth of all the surrounding nations will be collected—great quantities of gold and silver and clothing. ¹⁵A similar plague will strike the horses and mules, the camels and donkeys, and all the animals in those camps.

¹⁶Then the survivors from all the nations that have attacked Jerusalem will go up year after year to worship the King, the LORD Almighty, and to celebrate the Feast of Tabernacles. ¹⁷If any of the peoples of the earth do not go up to Jerusalem to worship the King, the LORD Almighty, they will have no rain. ¹⁸If the Egyptian people do not go up and take part, they will have no rain. The LORD*d* will bring on them the plague he inflicts on the nations that do not go up to celebrate the Feast of Tabernacles. ¹⁹This will be the punishment of Egypt and the punishment of all the nations that do not go up to celebrate the Feast of Tabernacles.

---

a5 Or *⁵My mountain valley will be blocked and will extend to Azel. It will be blocked as it was blocked because of the earthquake*　　*b8* That is, the Dead Sea　　*c8* That is, the Mediterranean　　*d18* Or *part, then the LORD*

Side column (study notes):

♥ Which "third" do you find yourself in? How does God refine and test your character? What part does your small group play in this process?

☕ If you could bequeath the group member to your right with a gift from your kitchen, symbolic of what he or she means to you, what would it be? Exchange gift ideas.

📖 **1.** How will God remember Jerusalem? What will the "Day of the Lord" be like? **2.** Who will fight against the city? What is the inhabitants' fate (vv. 1–2,10–11)? The attackers' fate (vv. 3–5,12–19)? **3.** What irony, mercy and justice do you see here? **4.** What will mark the advent of the Lord? What "holy ones" will accompany him (v. 5): Saints? Angels? The fleeing host coming to recapture their city? **5.** Why would Zechariah repeat "on that day" over and over again? What is unique about it? **6.** What might the "living water" imply (v. 8; see Ps 46:4; Jer 2:13; 17:13; Joel 3:18; Jn 4:11; 7:38–39)? **7.** Who will join the pilgrimage to worship the one God (vv. 9,16)? Why is special mention given here to the Feast of Tabernacles (see Lev 23:39–43; Neh 8:16–18)? And to Egypt? **8.** How transformed will this new city be (vv. 20–21)? "Holy to the Lord" is the fulfillment of which intention of God (see Ex 19:6; 28:36)? What does it mean that even "cooking pots" will be sacred? **9.** How does this vision in verses 9,16,20–21 compare with Isaiah's (see Isa 2:2–4) or Paul's (see Php 2:9–11)? What time frame is likely in view here?

♥ **1.** How will God remember you "on that day"? What promise from God are you counting on? In what area of your life do you need to make special preparations? **2.** Are you feeling attacked on every side, like Jerusalem? By what? Are you fleeing or surviving? **3.** Through this conflict and the tribulation to come, do you sense God's love shining through the darkness? Or do you find it hard to believe that there will ever be an evening with only light? **4.** Is worship a special part of your day? Of your group? How so? **5.** The High Priest wore an inscription which said: "Holy to the Lord." Which

20On that day HOLY TO THE LORD will be inscribed on the bells of the horses, and the cooking pots in the LORD's house will be like the sacred bowls in front of the altar. 21Every pot in Jerusalem and Judah will be holy to the LORD Almighty, and all who come to sacrifice will take some of the pots and cook in them. And on that day there will no longer be a Canaanite^a in the house of the LORD Almighty.

INTRODUCTION to
MALACHI

Book Study Outline: If you are using Malachi for a study course, here is a 3- or 6-week outline. Use the questions in the margin for your group agenda:

	3-week plan	6-week plan	Group Study Passage
	1	1	1:1–14/A Loving and Great God
		2	2:1–9/Profane Priests
	2	3	2:10–16/Unfaithful Judah
		4	2:17–3:5/Purifying the People
	3	5	3:6–17/Robbing the Lord
		6	4:1–6/The Last Word

start meeting / 15 min.

read & discuss Bible / 30 min.

close meeting / 15–45 min.

Refer to the Questions and Answers in the front of this Bible for more information.

Author: This book is ascribed to Malachi, a contemporary of Ezra and Nehemiah. Since the word "Malachi" means "my messenger," some think that this is a title rather than the name of a person. The Greek translation of the OT (the Septuagint) renders "Malachi" in 1:1 as "my messenger." However, the evidence is not conclusive, and there may well have been a specific prophet by this name.

Date: The sins denounced by Nehemiah (see Ne 13:6–31) correspond closely to the denunciation of Malachi (see 1:6–14; 2:14–16; 3:8–11). Hence, a date may be inferred anytime after Nehemiah returned to Jerusalem the second time, i.e., some time later than 433 B.C.

Theme: Repentance and information as prescription to cure the spirit of skepticism and indifference.

Historical Background: In the face of stern opposition, the exiles finished the temple in 516 B.C. under the leadership of Zerubbabel and the prophecy of Haggai. The community was strengthened through the restoration of temple worship by Ezra in 458 B.C. In 445 B.C., Nehemiah returned to Jerusalem, rebuilt the walls, and brought many religious reforms. Twelve years later, Nehemiah returned to serve the Persian king. With success behind them, the people lapsed into religious indifference. Malachi addresses the sins of a people "just going through the motions" of their faith, doubting the love and justice of God. Malachi was most likely the last prophet until the time of Christ, some 400 years later.

Characteristics: Malachi uses a question-answer form of dialogue to develop his themes. Seven questions or complaints raised by the people are recorded. However, the book is dominated by God's voice, the voice of an effective father (1:6) having to dish out "tough love" to his children. Malachi is written in forceful, lofty prose. He uses repetition and vivid images to help the people he is addressing (and his readers) to sense the attitudes of God.

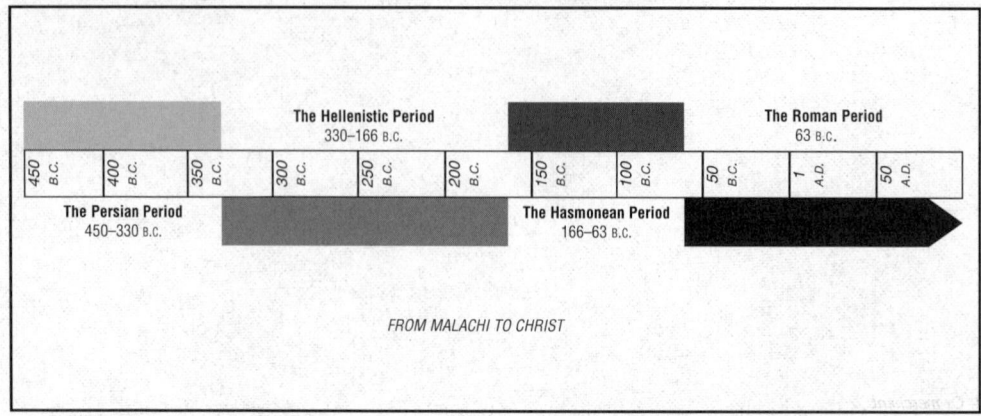

		The Hellenistic Period 330–166 B.C.					The Roman Period 63 B.C.		

450 B.C. | 400 B.C. | 350 B.C. | 300 B.C. | 250 B.C. | 200 B.C. | 150 B.C. | 100 B.C. | 50 B.C. | 1 A.D. | 50 A.D.

The Persian Period 450–330 B.C.

The Hasmonean Period 166–63 B.C.

FROM MALACHI TO CHRIST

Malachi

1 An oracle: The word of the Lord to Israel through Malachi.[a]

Jacob Loved, Esau Hated

2"I have loved you," says the Lord.

"But you ask, 'How have you loved us?'

"Was not Esau Jacob's brother?" the Lord says. "Yet I have loved Jacob, 3but Esau I have hated, and I have turned his mountains into a wasteland and left his inheritance to the desert jackals."

4Edom may say, "Though we have been crushed, we will rebuild the ruins."

But this is what the Lord Almighty says: "They may build, but I will demolish. They will be called the Wicked Land, a people always under the wrath of the Lord. 5You will see it with your own eyes and say, 'Great is the Lord—even beyond the borders of Israel!'

Blemished Sacrifices

6"A son honors his father, and a servant his master. If I am a father, where is the honor due me? If I am a master, where is the respect due me?" says the Lord Almighty. "It is you, O priests, who show contempt for my name.

"But you ask, 'How have we shown contempt for your name?'

7"You place defiled food on my altar.

"But you ask, 'How have we defiled you?'

"By saying that the Lord's table is contemptible. 8When you bring blind animals for sacrifice, is that not wrong? When you sacrifice crippled or diseased animals, is that not wrong? Try offering them to your governor! Would he be pleased with you? Would he accept you?" says the Lord Almighty.

9"Now implore God to be gracious to us. With such offerings from your hands, will he accept you?"—says the Lord Almighty.

10"Oh, that one of you would shut the temple doors, so that you would not light useless fires on my altar! I am not pleased with you," says the Lord Almighty, "and I will accept no offering from your hands. 11My name will be great among the nations, from the rising to the setting of the sun. In every place incense and pure offerings will be brought to my name, because my name will be great among the nations," says the Lord Almighty.

12"But you profane it by saying of the Lord's table, 'It is defiled,' and of its food, 'It is contemptible.' 13And you say, 'What a burden!' and you sniff at it contemptuously," says the Lord Almighty.

"When you bring injured, crippled or diseased animals and offer them as sacrifices, should I accept them from your hands?" says the Lord. 14"Cursed is the cheat who has an acceptable male in his flock and vows to give it, but then sacrifices a blemished animal to the Lord. For I am a great king," says the Lord Almighty, "and my name is to be feared among the nations.

---

1. As a teen, who was your first love? How did that person demonstrate their love? Did that puppy love ever turn into dogfights or hate? 2. What care do you take in giving gifts at Christmas time: (a) Most anything will do, within a certain price range? (b) Only gifts from a want list will do? (c) Used gifts or hand-me-downs are just fine? (d) Only new items will do, preferably deluxe editions? (e) Most any gift covering will do? (f) Each gift must be carefully wrapped, with ribbons, bows and cute tags?

1. How did the Lord show his love to the people of Israel? What happened to that love? 2. What attitude is expressed by Edom/Esau in verse 4? What is the Lord's response? 3. Who is the target of the Lord's probing questions in verses 6–8? What is wrong with their gift-giving? 4. Why are these people just going through the motions: (a) Didn't care any more? (b) Couldn't afford any better? (c) Didn't think the Lord was that picky? (d) Wanted to defy him openly? (e) Tried to fool him covertly? 5. How does this chapter affirm the smallness of the priests? The greatness of the Lord?

1. When have you asked the Lord to prove his love for you? What was his response? 2. Is it ever constructive to defy the Lord and do what you believe is right, no matter what? Explain. 3. In what ways are contemporary spiritual leaders like or unlike the priests in Malachi's day? 4. How might your attitude or actions honor or dishonor the Lord? In what ways are God's requirements a "burden" to you? 5. How has the Lord shown his greatness to you? Did you have to feel small before you knew he was great? Explain.

---

a 1 Malachi means my messenger.

As a child, when did you refuse to do what someone
asked? Over what issue? Why was
that so crucial? Is it now?

1. Why is the Lord so tough
on the priests? What have
they done to deserve this? 2. What
is a covenant? What did the Lord's
covenant with Levi require? (vv.
1–7; see Nu 3:12–13; 25:10–13)
3. How have these priests altered
the Lord's description for them?
What has been the effect of their
actions on others?

1. Has anyone ever stumbled
in their faith due to what you
did or didn't do? Explain. 2. What
would "life and peace" (v. 5) mean
for your church? For your family?
For your society? 3. How can your
spiritual leaders help, not hinder,
peacemaking?

In dating, have you ever
been jilted by anyone? What
made you most jealous or hurt?

1. How had Judah broken
faith? With whom? What has
this to do with creation and covenant? 2. What sin was separating
them and the Lord? 3. What does
"divorce" (v. 16) mean in the context of breaking faith, intermarriage
and violence? Why does the God
of Israel hate divorce? What are we
urged to do?

1. In your experience, how
often is unanswered prayer
due to unconfessed sin or a wrong
heart attitude toward the Lord or
others? 2. How could you "guard
yourself in your spirit," and not
"break faith" (v. 15)? In what situations are you most on guard? Most
vulnerable?

Of your *telephone, writing,
prayer* and *speaking* style,
which is most to the point? Which
requires a prologue? A postscript?
Which seems to go on and on?

1. How have the people wearied the Lord in word? In
deed? What is the Lord's re-

Admonition for the Priests

2 "And now this admonition is for you, O priests. [2]If you do not listen, and if you do not set your heart to honor my name," says the Lord Almighty, "I will send a curse upon you, and I will curse your blessings. Yes, I have already cursed them, because you have not set your heart to honor me.

[3]"Because of you I will rebuke[a] your descendants[b]; I will spread on your faces the offal from your festival sacrifices, and you will be carried off with it. [4]And you will know that I have sent you this admonition so that my covenant with Levi may continue," says the Lord Almighty. [5]"My covenant was with him, a covenant of life and peace, and I gave them to him; this called for reverence and he revered me and stood in awe of my name. [6]True instruction was in his mouth and nothing false was found on his lips. He walked with me in peace and uprightness, and turned many from sin.

[7]"For the lips of a priest ought to preserve knowledge, and from his mouth men should seek instruction—because he is the messenger of the Lord Almighty. [8]But you have turned from the way and by your teaching have caused many to stumble; you have violated the covenant with Levi," says the Lord Almighty. [9]"So I have caused you to be despised and humiliated before all the people, because you have not followed my ways but have shown partiality in matters of the law."

Judah Unfaithful

[10]Have we not all one Father[c]? Did not one God create us? Why do we profane the covenant of our fathers by breaking faith with one another?

[11]Judah has broken faith. A detestable thing has been committed in Israel and in Jerusalem: Judah has desecrated the sanctuary the Lord loves, by marrying the daughter of a foreign god. [12]As for the man who does this, whoever he may be, may the Lord cut him off from the tents of Jacob[d]—even though he brings offerings to the Lord Almighty.

[13]Another thing you do: You flood the Lord's altar with tears. You weep and wail because he no longer pays attention to your offerings or accepts them with pleasure from your hands. [14]You ask, "Why?" It is because the Lord is acting as the witness between you and the wife of your youth, because you have broken faith with her, though she is your partner, the wife of your marriage covenant.

[15]Has not ˌthe Lordˌ made them one? In flesh and spirit they are his. And why one? Because he was seeking godly offspring.[e] So guard yourself in your spirit, and do not break faith with the wife of your youth.

[16]"I hate divorce," says the Lord God of Israel, "and I hate a man's covering himself[f] with violence as well as with his garment," says the Lord Almighty.

So guard yourself in your spirit, and do not break faith.

The Day of Judgment

[17]You have wearied the Lord with your words.

"How have we wearied him?" you ask.

---

a3 Or *cut off* (see Septuagint)   b3 Or *will blight your grain*   c10 Or *father*
d12 Or [12]*May the Lord cut off from the tents of Jacob anyone who gives testimony in behalf of the man who does this*   e15 Or [15]*But the one ˌwho is our fatherˌ did not do this, not as long as life remained in him. And what was he seeking? An offspring from God*   f16 Or *his wife*

By saying, "All who do evil are good in the eyes of the LORD, and he is pleased with them" or "Where is the God of justice?"

3 "See, I will send my messenger, who will prepare the way before me. Then suddenly the Lord you are seeking will come to his temple; the messenger of the covenant, whom you desire, will come," says the LORD Almighty.

²But who can endure the day of his coming? Who can stand when he appears? For he will be like a refiner's fire or a launderer's soap. ³He will sit as a refiner and purifier of silver; he will purify the Levites and refine them like gold and silver. Then the LORD will have men who will bring offerings in righteousness, ⁴and the offerings of Judah and Jerusalem will be acceptable to the LORD, as in days gone by, as in former years.

⁵"So I will come near to you for judgment. I will be quick to testify against sorcerers, adulterers and perjurers, against those who defraud laborers of their wages, who oppress the widows and the fatherless, and deprive aliens of justice, but do not fear me," says the LORD Almighty.

Robbing God

⁶"I the LORD do not change. So you, O descendants of Jacob, are not destroyed. ⁷Ever since the time of your forefathers you have turned away from my decrees and have not kept them. Return to me, and I will return to you," says the LORD Almighty.

"But you ask, 'How are we to return?'

⁸"Will a man rob God? Yet you rob me.

"But you ask, 'How do we rob you?'

"In tithes and offerings. ⁹You are under a curse—the whole nation of you—because you are robbing me. ¹⁰Bring the whole tithe into the storehouse, that there may be food in my house. Test me in this," says the LORD Almighty, "and see if I will not throw open the floodgates of heaven and pour out so much blessing that you will not have room enough for it. ¹¹I will prevent pests from devouring your crops, and the vines in your fields will not cast their fruit," says the LORD Almighty. ¹²"Then all the nations will call you blessed, for yours will be a delightful land," says the LORD Almighty.

¹³"You have said harsh things against me," says the LORD.

"Yet you ask, 'What have we said against you?'

¹⁴"You have said, 'It is futile to serve God. What did we gain by carrying out his requirements and going about like mourners before the LORD Almighty? ¹⁵But now we call the arrogant blessed. Certainly the evildoers prosper, and even those who challenge God escape.'"

¹⁶Then those who feared the LORD talked with each other, and the LORD listened and heard. A scroll of remembrance was written in his presence concerning those who feared the LORD and honored his name.

¹⁷"They will be mine," says the LORD Almighty, "in the day when I make up my treasured possession.ᵃ I will spare them, just as in compassion a man spares his son who serves him. ¹⁸And you will again see the distinction between the righteous and the wicked, between those who serve God and those who do not.

sponse? **2.** Who is the Lord's messenger (3:1): Malachi ("my messenger" in Hebrew)? John the Baptist (see Mt 11:10)? A second Elijah (4:5)? What will he (they) do (see Isa 40:3–4)? **3.** What will the Day of the Lord's coming be like? **4.** What does the Lord's judgment process entail? Who, if any, endures?

1. Have you "wearied" the Lord? Do you "fear" him? How so? How has the Lord responded? **2.** If given the chance next Sunday to declare war on sin, what sins would make it into your 3-point sermon? Why those three?

1. When told, "Eat whatever food you find in the house," what do you look for? What is your reaction if it's not there? **2.** When caught with your hand in the cookie jar, how do you react?

1. How had Malachi's peers robbed God? With what results? **2.** How does the Lord challenge the people to put him to the test (vv. 10–12)? **3.** What was futile about their worshipping God with a "what's-in-this-for-me" attitude? **4.** How will everyone get their just desserts in the end (vv. 16–18)? **5.** What distinguishes the righteous from the wicked?

1. When have you struggled with bad things happening to good people? With good things happening to bad people? **2.** What does it feel like to be in relationship with such a God who "does not change"? *If you could change one thing about God, what would it be?* **3.** In what ways do you rob God everyday? What tithe do you need to offer? Accordingly, rewrite verses 10–12 as personal promises to you from God.

ᵃ17 Or Almighty, "my treasured possession, in the day when I act

From your appointment book, what are you eagerly anticipating three months from now? What are you dreading? How are you preparing for these due dates?

1. Is the Day of the Lord inked, penciled or not even on their calendars? Why or why not? 2. As Malachi is the last prophet until the New Testament, what is the importance of verses 4–5?

1. Reread the Q & A portions of Malachi. Rewrite them for your church. What images and issues would a modern Malachi hit home with? 2. What one thing have you learned from Malachi? What one application are you making? How can the group help you do this?

The Day of the LORD

4 "Surely the day is coming; it will burn like a furnace. All the arrogant and every evildoer will be stubble, and that day that is coming will set them on fire," says the LORD Almighty. "Not a root or a branch will be left to them. ²But for you who revere my name, the sun of righteousness will rise with healing in its wings. And you will go out and leap like calves released from the stall. ³Then you will trample down the wicked; they will be ashes under the soles of your feet on the day when I do these things," says the LORD Almighty.

⁴"Remember the law of my servant Moses, the decrees and laws I gave him at Horeb for all Israel.

⁵"See, I will send you the prophet Elijah before that great and dreadful day of the LORD comes. ⁶He will turn the hearts of the fathers to their children, and the hearts of the children to their fathers; or else I will come and strike the land with a curse."

The
New Testament

INTRODUCTION to
MATTHEW

Book Study Outline: If you are using Matthew for a study course, here is a 7- or 13-week outline. Use the margin questions for your group agenda:

☕ start meeting / 15 min.

📖 read & discuss Bible / 30 min.

♡ close meeting / 15–45 min.

Refer to the Questions and Answers in front of Bible for more information.

7-week plan	13-week plan	Personal Reading	Group Study Passage
1	1	1:1–25	1:18–25/Angel Appears to Joseph
	2	3:1–4:25	3:13–4:11/Baptism &Temptation
2	3	5:1–6:34	5:1–12/The Beatitudes
	4	7:1–9:34	7:24–29/Wise & Foolish Builders
3	5	9:35–11:30	10:1–42/Jesus Sends Out 12
	6	12:1–13:52	13:1–23/Parable of Sower
4	7	13:53–16:12	14:22–33/Walking on Water
	8	16:13–17:27	16:13–28/Christ Must Die
5	9	18:1–35	18:21–35/Unmerciful Servant
	10	19:1–20:34	20:1–16/Workers in Vineyard
6	11	21:1–25:46	25:14–30/Parable of Talents
	12	26:1–75	26:47–56/Jesus Arrested
7	13	27:1–28:20	28:1–20/Jesus' Resurrection

Author: Although not named, a long tradition has assigned it to Matthew, the tax collector who became an apostle.

Date: Uncertain, but probably between A.D. 50–70.

Theme: Jesus, the long-promised Messiah and authoritative teacher.

Historical Background: The first three Gospels cover many of the same events in Jesus' life in the same way. For that reason they are often called the "synoptic Gospels" meaning that they are "able to be seen together." It is generally assumed that Matthew and Luke used Mark as their prime source in compiling their writings. In Matthew nearly 90 percent of the material in Mark is reproduced. These similarities, however, do not mean that the Gospels are merely a restatement of each other. Matthew adds many teaching sections and other details not found in Mark. Matthew slants his material to a Jewish readership as he cites numerous Old Testament prophecies that were fulfilled in Jesus' life and ministry. His purpose was to show that Jesus is the promised Son of David, the Messiah, come to establish the kingdom of God.

Characteristics: Matthew is built around five teaching sections (ch. 5–7; 10; 13; 18; 24–25) which illustrate what life in the kingdom of heaven is all about. Matthew's frequent citation of Old Testament prophecies makes it the perfect book to bridge the Old Testament and the New Testament. While strongly oriented to be a witness to the Jews, Matthew also makes it clear that the Messiah has come for all peoples.

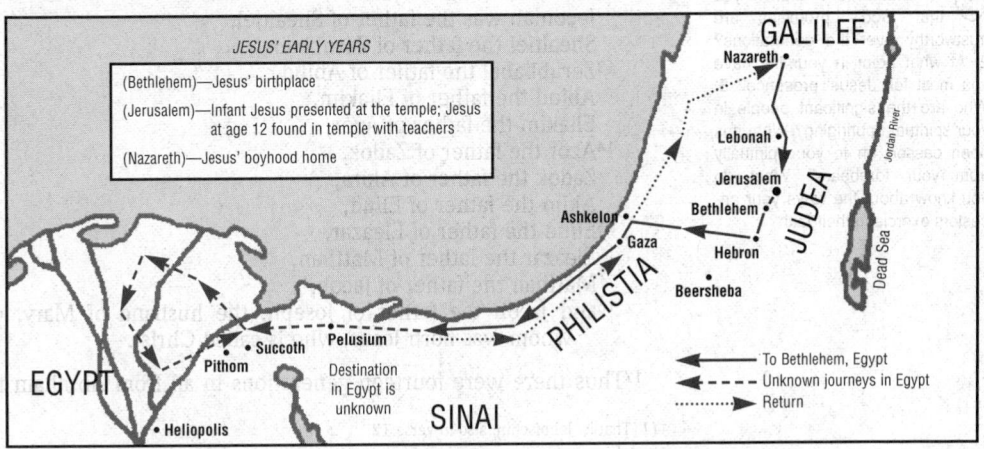

JESUS' EARLY YEARS

(Bethlehem)—Jesus' birthplace

(Jerusalem)—Infant Jesus presented at the temple; Jesus at age 12 found in temple with teachers

(Nazareth)—Jesus' boyhood home

GALILEE
Nazareth
Lebonah
Jerusalem
Bethlehem
Ashkelon
Gaza
Hebron
Beersheba
JUDEA
PHILISTIA
Pelusium
Succoth
Pithom
Destination in Egypt is unknown
EGYPT
Heliopolis
SINAI
Jordan River
Dead Sea

→ To Bethlehem, Egypt
---▶ Unknown journeys in Egypt
········▶ Return

Matthew

The Genealogy of Jesus

1. When you were a child, what did you like best about your grandparents? What is your most vivid memory of any great-grandparents? **2.** What do you know about your genealogy? What would you like to discover about it? **3.** If you could design a coat of arms for your family, what symbols would you choose? Why?

1. What titles does Matthew assign Jesus in verses 1 and 16? What is the meaning of each title? **2.** Which people do you recognize in this genealogy? What do you remember about each of these people? Which people on the list are the most significant in establishing who Jesus is? **3.** Why do you think some women were named when it was not the Jewish custom to include women's names in genealogies? What do you know about these women? **4.** Into what three sections does Matthew divide his genealogical table? What great event climaxes each section? From the promises to Abraham (Ge 12:2–3; 17:6–8), why is it significant that Jesus is Abraham's son (Gal 3:16–18)? From 2 Samuel 7:11–16, why is it significant that he is David's son as well? Of what does that assure us? **5.** If Luke's genealogy (Lk 3:23–38) goes back to Adam to emphasize the universality of the Gospel, what is Matthew's point in beginning with Abraham? What does Matthew's lineage say to Jewish readers?

1. What does it mean to you that God's promises are trustworthy over the generations? **2.** At what point in your life have you most felt Jesus' presence? **3.** Who are the significant people in your spiritual upbringing? What has been passed on to you spiritually from your forebears? What do you know about the ways your ancestors exercised their faith?

1 A record of the genealogy of Jesus Christ the son of David, the son of Abraham:

²Abraham was the father of Isaac,
Isaac the father of Jacob,
Jacob the father of Judah and his brothers,
³Judah the father of Perez and Zerah, whose mother was Tamar,
Perez the father of Hezron,
Hezron the father of Ram,
⁴Ram the father of Amminadab,
Amminadab the father of Nahshon,
Nahshon the father of Salmon,
⁵Salmon the father of Boaz, whose mother was Rahab,
Boaz the father of Obed, whose mother was Ruth,
Obed the father of Jesse,
⁶and Jesse the father of King David.

David was the father of Solomon, whose mother had been Uriah's wife,
⁷Solomon the father of Rehoboam,
Rehoboam the father of Abijah,
Abijah the father of Asa,
⁸Asa the father of Jehoshaphat,
Jehoshaphat the father of Jehoram,
Jehoram the father of Uzziah,
⁹Uzziah the father of Jotham,
Jotham the father of Ahaz,
Ahaz the father of Hezekiah,
¹⁰Hezekiah the father of Manasseh,
Manasseh the father of Amon,
Amon the father of Josiah,
¹¹and Josiah the father of Jeconiah[a] and his brothers at the time of the exile to Babylon.

¹²After the exile to Babylon:
Jeconiah was the father of Shealtiel,
Shealtiel the father of Zerubbabel,
¹³Zerubbabel the father of Abiud,
Abiud the father of Eliakim,
Eliakim the father of Azor,
¹⁴Azor the father of Zadok,
Zadok the father of Akim,
Akim the father of Eliud,
¹⁵Eliud the father of Eleazar,
Eleazar the father of Matthan,
Matthan the father of Jacob,
¹⁶and Jacob the father of Joseph, the husband of Mary, of whom was born Jesus, who is called Christ.

¹⁷Thus there were fourteen generations in all from Abraham to

---

a 11 That is, Jehoiachin; also in verse 12

David, fourteen from David to the exile to Babylon, and fourteen from the exile to the Christ.[a]

The Birth of Jesus Christ

18This is how the birth of Jesus Christ came about: His mother Mary was pledged to be married to Joseph, but before they came together, she was found to be with child through the Holy Spirit. 19Because Joseph her husband was a righteous man and did not want to expose her to public disgrace, he had in mind to divorce her quietly.

20But after he had considered this, an angel of the Lord appeared to him in a dream and said, "Joseph son of David, do not be afraid to take Mary home as your wife, because what is conceived in her is from the Holy Spirit. 21She will give birth to a son, and you are to give him the name Jesus,[b] because he will save his people from their sins."

22All this took place to fulfill what the Lord had said through the prophet: 23"The virgin will be with child and will give birth to a son, and they will call him Immanuel"[c]—which means, "God with us."

24When Joseph woke up, he did what the angel of the Lord had commanded him and took Mary home as his wife. 25But he had no

a17 Or Messiah. "The Christ" (Greek) and "the Messiah" (Hebrew) both mean "the Anointed One."   b21 Jesus is the Greek form of Joshua, which means the LORD saves.
c23 Isaiah 7:14

What two positive qualities about your mom or dad come to mind as you recall your childhood?

1. How would you feel in Joseph's place in verse 19? In verses 20–21? What would you say to family and friends? To God? 2. What reason does Matthew give as to why Jesus was born (v. 21)?

1. What is most striking to you in this story of Jesus' conception? How have you experienced Jesus as Immanuel in your life lately? 2. What do you learn about faith from Joseph?

  Matthew 1:18–25   **AN ANGEL APPEARS TO JOSEPH**

Though a Jewish couple were forbidden to have sexual relations during engagement, they were referred to as "husband and wife," and their relationship could be broken only by divorce.

1. If you had been in Joseph or Mary's sandals, what would have been the most difficult aspect of this situation?
a. telling Joseph I was pregnant
b. trusting Mary, and the angel, that no other man was involved
c. trying to explain the pregnancy to our families
d. facing the gossip of neighbors because of this early pregnancy

2. What effect do you think these incidents had on Joseph and Mary's future marriage relationship?
a. It strengthened their mutual trust.
b. It strained their relationship.
c. Knowing God had a special task for them brought them closer.
d. Dealing with a child so soon put a lot of pressure on their marriage.

3. How do you think Joseph and Mary felt about being parents to a child who would "save his people from their sins"?

4. What is the most miraculous aspect of this story to you?
a. that a virgin could have a baby
b. that an angel appeared to Joseph
c. that God came to earth in the person of a baby
d. that this baby would save people from their sins

5. When did Jesus really become your "Immanuel"—God with you? How are you experiencing Jesus "with you" in your life now?

6. What caused most of the strain early in your marriage relationship?
a. financial struggles
b. vocational struggles
c. relational struggles—between us
d. relational struggles—with others
e. a pregnancy early in our marriage

7. What "angel" or special person came along to help you when you had trouble as a couple?

8. The hard times in our marriage have brought us greater commitment as a couple because they helped us:

a. realize what is important in life.
b. appreciate each other's strengths.
c. see that our love is strong enough to last.
d. be less self-focused.
e. depend more on God.

9. When you were growing up, who were your most significant masculine role models?
a. my father
b. another relative or family friend
c. a sports or entertainment celebrity
d. a teacher or coach
e. a church leader
f. Jesus Christ
g. other:_____

10. How do you feel about viewing Jesus as a model of masculinity?
a. His divine nature makes him too different from me.
b. His divine nature keeps me from identifying with his human nature.
c. His divine nature makes him the ultimate masculine role model.
d. He's the Savior, not a male role model.
e. He's as much a role model for women as men.

union with her until she gave birth to a son. And he gave him the name Jesus.

The Visit of the Magi

2 After Jesus was born in Bethlehem in Judea, during the time of King Herod, Magi[a] from the east came to Jerusalem ²and asked, "Where is the one who has been born king of the Jews? We saw his star in the east[b] and have come to worship him."

³When King Herod heard this he was disturbed, and all Jerusalem with him. ⁴When he had called together all the people's chief priests and teachers of the law, he asked them where the Christ[c] was to be born. ⁵"In Bethlehem in Judea," they replied, "for this is what the prophet has written:

⁶" 'But you, Bethlehem, in the land of Judah,
      are by no means least among the rulers of
         Judah;
   for out of you will come a ruler
      who will be the shepherd of my people
         Israel.'[d]"

⁷Then Herod called the Magi secretly and found out from them the exact time the star had appeared. ⁸He sent them to Bethlehem and said, "Go and make a careful search for the child. As soon as you find him, report to me, so that I too may go and worship him."

⁹After they had heard the king, they went on their way, and the star they had seen in the east[e] went ahead of them until it stopped over the place where the child was. ¹⁰When they saw the star, they were overjoyed. ¹¹On coming to the house, they saw the child with his mother Mary, and they bowed down and worshiped him. Then they opened their treasures and presented him with gifts of gold and of incense and of myrrh. ¹²And having been warned in a dream not to go back to Herod, they returned to their country by another route.

The Escape to Egypt

¹³When they had gone, an angel of the Lord appeared to Joseph in a dream. "Get up," he said, "take the child and his mother and escape to Egypt. Stay there until I tell you, for Herod is going to search for the child to kill him."

¹⁴So he got up, took the child and his mother during the night and left for Egypt, ¹⁵where he stayed until the death of Herod. And so was fulfilled what the Lord had said through the prophet: "Out of Egypt I called my son."[f]

¹⁶When Herod realized that he had been outwitted by the Magi, he was furious, and he gave orders to kill all the boys in Bethlehem and its vicinity who were two years old and under, in accordance with the time he had learned from the Magi. ¹⁷Then what was said through the prophet Jeremiah was fulfilled:

¹⁸"A voice is heard in Ramah,
      weeping and great mourning,
   Rachel weeping for her children
      and refusing to be comforted,
         because they are no more."[g]

---

1. What is your favorite tradition related to Christmas? 2. Who are three "Magi" or wise men you look to for advice?

1. Why was it important that Jesus be born in Bethlehem? 2. Since the Magi were pagan astrologers, why would they leave everything in order to follow that star? 3. Note the responses of the Magi upon seeing Jesus. How is that similar to the response that Christians make to Jesus? How is it different? 4. What do the star, the Magi, the gifts, the homage, the hostility and the prophecy teach about the significance of Jesus?

1. In your journey toward God, how are you like the Magi? Unlike them? Have you had to leave anything to follow Jesus? 2. What is the "gold, incense, and myrrh" in your life? How have you offered this to Jesus?

1. If you or your parent(s) decided to move to another country to work or retire, how would you feel? 2. How far away from where you were born do you now live? Would you go back to your birthplace to live (or retire later)? Why?

1. Based on Herod's response to the news of the coming Messiah, what kind of person do you think he was? What does his response say about his view of the Messiah? 2. What is Matthew's point in emphasizing God's watchfulness over Jesus? In fulfillment of Hosea's and Jeremiah's prophecies (vv. 17–18,23)? 3. What relocation options face Joseph? How did God use prophecy, dreams, faith and circumstances to guide him?

1. When, like Herod, have you felt threatened by Jesus' Kingship? How do you react? 2.

---

a1 Traditionally *Wise Men*   *b2* Or *star when it rose*   *c4* Or *Messiah*
d6 Micah 5:2   *e9* Or *seen when it rose*   *f15* Hosea 11:1   *g18* Jer. 31:15

The Return to Nazareth

[19]After Herod died, an angel of the Lord appeared in a dream to Joseph in Egypt [20]and said, "Get up, take the child and his mother and go to the land of Israel, for those who were trying to take the child's life are dead."

[21]So he got up, took the child and his mother and went to the land of Israel. [22]But when he heard that Archelaus was reigning in Judea in place of his father Herod, he was afraid to go there. Having been warned in a dream, he withdrew to the district of Galilee, [23]and he went and lived in a town called Nazareth. So was fulfilled what was said through the prophets: "He will be called a Nazarene."

John the Baptist Prepares the Way

3 In those days John the Baptist came, preaching in the Desert of Judea [2]and saying, "Repent, for the kingdom of heaven is near." [3]This is he who was spoken of through the prophet Isaiah:

"A voice of one calling in the desert,
'Prepare the way for the Lord,
make straight paths for him.'"[a]

[4]John's clothes were made of camel's hair, and he had a leather belt around his waist. His food was locusts and wild honey. [5]People went out to him from Jerusalem and all Judea and the whole region of the Jordan. [6]Confessing their sins, they were baptized by him in the Jordan River.

[7]But when he saw many of the Pharisees and Sadducees coming to where he was baptizing, he said to them: "You brood of vipers! Who warned you to flee from the coming wrath? [8]Produce fruit in keeping with repentance. [9]And do not think you can say to yourselves, 'We have Abraham as our father.' I tell you that out of these stones God can raise up children for Abraham. [10]The ax is already at the root of the trees, and every tree that does not produce good fruit will be cut down and thrown into the fire.

[11]"I baptize you with[b] water for repentance. But after me will come one who is more powerful than I, whose sandals I am not fit to carry. He will baptize you with the Holy Spirit and with fire. [12]His winnowing fork is in his hand, and he will clear his threshing floor, gathering his wheat into the barn and burning up the chaff with unquenchable fire."

The Baptism of Jesus

[13]Then Jesus came from Galilee to the Jordan to be baptized by John. [14]But John tried to deter him, saying, "I need to be baptized by you, and do you come to me?"

[15]Jesus replied, "Let it be so now; it is proper for us to do this to fulfill all righteousness." Then John consented.

[16]As soon as Jesus was baptized, he went up out of the water. At that moment heaven was opened, and he saw the Spirit of God descending like a dove and lighting on him. [17]And a voice from heaven said, "This is my Son, whom I love; with him I am well pleased."

[a]3 Isaiah 40:3   [b]11 Or in

From Joseph's responsiveness, what do you learn about faith and obedience? How long would it take you to say "yes" if God asked you to relocate?

1. What was the longest period of time you spent in the wilderness or away from civilization? What was it like? 2. When you were baptized, how much water did it take?

1. What was John the Baptist like? Why would anyone go out of their way to hear this radical preacher (v. 7)? Who did they think he was (see 2Ki 1:8)? 2. How would you paraphrase John's message (v. 2) for people today? What is the "kingdom of heaven"? 3. What angered John so much about the Pharisees and Sadducees? 4. What do the images of judgment mean: The coming wrath? The ax? The fire? His winnowing fork? 5. How do John's and Jesus' ministries compare? 6. Why did Jesus, who was without sin, come to John to be baptized? What "righteousness" did he fulfill (see Isa 53:12)? 7. What do you think verse 17 meant to Jesus? How does this set the stage for his ministry to begin?

1. Who has been a John the Baptist in your life? How did he or she prepare you to meet Jesus? 2. Who are today's Pharisees and Sadducees? 3. How is repentance linked to your experience of salvation: In the past? Now? Where does repentance, to God and/or others, still need to happen in your life? 4. How has God affirmed you as his child in Christ?

What is the longest you ever went without eating? How did it feel?

1. For each of the three temptations: (a) What is its nature? (b) What potentially might appeal to Jesus? (c) What price would there be were he to yield? (d) How does Jesus respond? **2.** What links these temptations with the baptism of Jesus (vv. 1,3,6)? **3.** Of these three, which temptation appears most legitimate? Which one is most shrewd?

1. What human need is at the heart of each temptation? How are these needs evident in your life? How does Satan use these to tempt you? **2.** What is your greatest temptation right now? How can others help?

1. When did you leave home to be on your own for the first time? **2.** Have you ever been fishing? Tell a story about your adventures.

The Temptation of Jesus

4 Then Jesus was led by the Spirit into the desert to be tempted by the devil. ²After fasting forty days and forty nights, he was hungry. ³The tempter came to him and said, "If you are the Son of God, tell these stones to become bread."

⁴Jesus answered, "It is written: 'Man does not live on bread alone, but on every word that comes from the mouth of God.'ᵃ"

⁵Then the devil took him to the holy city and had him stand on the highest point of the temple. ⁶"If you are the Son of God," he said, "throw yourself down. For it is written:

"'He will command his angels concerning you,
and they will lift you up in their hands,
so that you will not strike your foot against a
stone.'ᵇ"

⁷Jesus answered him, "It is also written: 'Do not put the Lord your God to the test.'ᶜ"

⁸Again, the devil took him to a very high mountain and showed him all the kingdoms of the world and their splendor. ⁹"All this I will give you," he said, "if you will bow down and worship me."

¹⁰Jesus said to him, "Away from me, Satan! For it is written: 'Worship the Lord your God, and serve him only.'ᵈ"

¹¹Then the devil left him, and angels came and attended him.

Jesus Begins to Preach

¹²When Jesus heard that John had been put in prison, he returned to Galilee. ¹³Leaving Nazareth, he went and lived in Caper-

ᵃ4 Deut. 8:3   ᵇ6 Psalm 91:11,12   ᶜ7 Deut. 6:16   ᵈ10 Deut. 6:13

Mt 3:13–4:11 BAPTISM AND TEMPTATION OF JESUS

1. What was the purpose of Jesus coming to John to be baptized?
   a. to commit himself to God
   b. to get God's approval
   c. to kick off his public ministry
   d. to be free of sin
   e. to identify with our sin
   f. to set an example for his followers
   g. to be equipped by the Holy Spirit

2. Do you think Jesus needed this affirmation from God (3:16–17) when he began his ministry?
   a. No—it was for the crowd.
   b. Maybe—because of the skeptics.
   c. Yes—just like anyone else.

3. How important was it for Jesus to be tempted by Satan?
   a. Not very important—the Son of God couldn't *really* be tempted.
   b. Somewhat—to toughen him up.
   c. Very important—just like any other "rookie."

4. How would you describe the power struggle going on in this story?
   a. This is the ultimate struggle between good and evil.

   b. Satan is trying to conquer Jesus when he seems weak.
   c. Jesus is being tempted to use his power as God's Son for himself.
   d. This power struggle is no different than those we face daily.
   e. This power struggle is greater than anything we could face.

5. What do you think was appealing to Jesus about the three temptations?

6. What does Jesus' encounter with temptation teach us?
   a. Fasting and prayer make us vulnerable to temptation.
   b. Fasting and prayer enable us to overcome temptation.
   c. It's best to be armed with Scripture when temptation comes.
   d. Satan knows Scripture too.
   e. We need to tell Satan to get lost.
   f. When you resist, God sends help.

7. When do you find yourself most vulnerable to the tempter?
   a. when I'm tired or under stress
   b. when I'm alone or away from home
   c. after a spiritual high

   d. when I'm not expecting it
   e. when I let my mind dwell on certain things

8. What has helped you overcome temptation when it comes?
   a. Scripture (such as:_____)
   b. prayer
   c. telling someone about it
   d. talking myself out of it
   e. running away

9. When have you been alone in the "desert"? How can it help to know Jesus has been there? What is the difference between being *lonely* and being *alone*?

10. How do kids open themselves up to the occult? What other kinds of temptations do kids face today? Which of these temptations presses in on *you* the hardest?

11. What is the closest you have come to a time of initiation into manhood? Who was there for you—affirming you and cheering you on?

naum, which was by the lake in the area of Zebulun and Naphtali— [14]to fulfill what was said through the prophet Isaiah:

> [15]"Land of Zebulun and land of Naphtali,
> the way to the sea, along the Jordan,
> Galilee of the Gentiles—
> [16]the people living in darkness
> have seen a great light;
> on those living in the land of the shadow of death
> a light has dawned."[a]

[17]From that time on Jesus began to preach, "Repent, for the kingdom of heaven is near."

The Calling of the First Disciples

[18]As Jesus was walking beside the Sea of Galilee, he saw two brothers, Simon called Peter and his brother Andrew. They were casting a net into the lake, for they were fishermen. [19]"Come, follow me," Jesus said, "and I will make you fishers of men." [20]At once they left their nets and followed him.

[21]Going on from there, he saw two other brothers, James son of Zebedee and his brother John. They were in a boat with their father Zebedee, preparing their nets. Jesus called them, [22]and immediately they left the boat and their father and followed him.

Jesus Heals the Sick

[23]Jesus went throughout Galilee, teaching in their synagogues, preaching the good news of the kingdom, and healing every disease and sickness among the people. [24]News about him spread all over Syria, and people brought to him all who were ill with various diseases, those suffering severe pain, the demon-possessed, those having seizures, and the paralyzed, and he healed them. [25]Large crowds from Galilee, the Decapolis,[b] Jerusalem, Judea and the region across the Jordan followed him.

The Beatitudes

5 Now when he saw the crowds, he went up on a mountainside and sat down. His disciples came to him, [2]and he began to teach them, saying:

> [3]"Blessed are the poor in spirit,
> for theirs is the kingdom of heaven.
> [4]Blessed are those who mourn,
> for they will be comforted.
> [5]Blessed are the meek,
> for they will inherit the earth.
> [6]Blessed are those who hunger and thirst for
> righteousness,
> for they will be filled.
> [7]Blessed are the merciful,
> for they will be shown mercy.
> [8]Blessed are the pure in heart,
> for they will see God.
> [9]Blessed are the peacemakers,
> for they will be called sons of God.
> [10]Blessed are those who are persecuted because of
> righteousness,
> for theirs is the kingdom of heaven.

[a]16 Isaiah 9:1,2   [b]25 That is, the Ten Cities

1. How does Jesus react to John's imprisonment? 2. How had they been living in darkness (v. 16)? What was Jesus' message? What is the relation between repentance, the kingdom of heaven, and the light? 3. What invitations does Jesus give to these fishermen? What seems unusual about their response? What prior knowledge of Jesus do you think they had (vv. 13,17)? How might Zebedee have felt (v. 22)? 4. From how far away are the crowds coming (vv. 23–25; see map on page 1337)? What needs do they have? What are they learning about God's kingdom?

1. How has coming to know Jesus been like moving from darkness to light for you? 2. In what ways does God's kingdom seem present now for you? In what ways does it seem "not yet"? 3. Spiritually, are you still preparing the nets? Leaving the boat? Following hard after Jesus? Feeling left behind? 4. If you were in the crowds (vv. 23–25), what would you ask Jesus to heal for you? Why not pray about that as a group?

1. When you want to get away from people, where do you go and what do you do? 2. What saying or bumper sticker do you keep on your desk or car?

1. How do the eight qualities that describe "kingdom people" relate to the promises that follow them? How do they relate to each other? How would you describe the opposite of each quality? 2. Is Jesus *describing* who his followers *are*? Or *prescribing* what they must *do*? Why do you think so? 3. How does this "sermonette" explain the nature of the kingdom? How are these Beatitudes related to being salt and light (vv. 13–16)? How are Christians to penetrate society?

1. How do these promised blessings compare with what most people in the world prize? Would "kingdom people" be admired in your society? Why or why not? 2. Of these eight qualities, which two do you desire most in

your life? Why? Who in your group or family do you associate with each? **3.** Which of these qualities are you most tempted to avoid? **4.** Based on the beatitudes, is the light of your life shining like a 300-watt bulb? A 100-watt? A night light? Why? How can Jesus enable you to "shine brighter"?

As a child, what family rule did you love to break? Why?

1. How does Jesus "fulfill" the Prophets and "accomplish everything" in the Law? **2.** What is Jesus' point about the "least" and the "great"? **3.** How do we obtain a righteousness that surpasses the Pharisees?

Consider the Ten Commandments (Ex 20:1–17). Which commandments are most difficult for you? Why?

11"Blessed are you when people insult you, persecute you and falsely say all kinds of evil against you because of me. 12Rejoice and be glad, because great is your reward in heaven, for in the same way they persecuted the prophets who were before you.

Salt and Light

13"You are the salt of the earth. But if the salt loses its saltiness, how can it be made salty again? It is no longer good for anything, except to be thrown out and trampled by men.

14"You are the light of the world. A city on a hill cannot be hidden. 15Neither do people light a lamp and put it under a bowl. Instead they put it on its stand, and it gives light to everyone in the house. 16In the same way, let your light shine before men, that they may see your good deeds and praise your Father in heaven.

The Fulfillment of the Law

17"Do not think that I have come to abolish the Law or the Prophets; I have not come to abolish them but to fulfill them. 18I tell you the truth, until heaven and earth disappear, not the smallest letter, not the least stroke of a pen, will by any means disappear from the Law until everything is accomplished. 19Anyone who breaks one of the least of these commandments and teaches others to do the same will be called least in the kingdom of heaven, but whoever practices and teaches these commands will be called great in the kingdom of heaven. 20For I tell you that unless your righteousness surpasses that of the Pharisees and the teachers of the law, you will certainly not enter the kingdom of heaven.

Matthew 5:1–12	THE BEATITUDES

1. Imagine that you were sitting on the hillside that day with the disciples. What would be your first impression after hearing Jesus' words?
   a. What on earth is he talking about?
   b. This guy doesn't live in the real world.
   c. Jesus had better change his message, or he won't get very far.
   d. I've been searching for this.

2. The Beatitudes are important because they:
   a. are true words spoken by Jesus.
   b. will make me happy.
   c. will help me "get ahead."
   d. are marks of spiritual maturity.
   e. are in the Bible (though they seem unrealistic to me in daily life).

3. Silently rate yourself from 1 (very low) to 4 (very high) on each of the following qualities of the Beatitudes:

POOR IN SPIRIT: I recognize my spiritual bankruptcy and my need for God. Because my relationship with God depends on his grace, I know I'm incapable of earning God's love on my own.

MOURN: I feel the pain that sin, including my own, causes. I can let others know when I am hurting without embarrassment. I can weep like Jesus did.

MEEK: I don't have to be the strong one who is always in control. I can be tender and gentle. I've given control of my life to God and I don't always have to win.

SPIRITUAL HUNGER: I want to know God and his will for my life more than anything—including my own pleasure, status or success. My heart truly longs for God.

MERCIFUL: I can share the feelings of people who are hurting, lonely or distressed, and walk alongside them in their pain. God has given me a sensitivity for the suffering of others.

PURE IN HEART: I am completely honest with God and others. I don't have to put on a false front or pretend to be something I'm not. My life is marked with openness and integrity.

PEACEMAKER: I work hard to keep channels of communication open with others. Rather than allowing anger and conflict to fester, I deal with them constructively. I help those around me work out their differences without hurting one another.

PERSECUTION: I know for whom and for what I am living. And for this I am willing to suffer and (if need be) stand alone for what is right. I can take criticism without reacting defensively or feeling self-pity.

4. Share with the group where you scored yourself the *highest* and where you scored yourself the *lowest*. How can you work on this area?

5. Have one person in your group sit in silence while others share which of the Beatitudes they see most clearly in that person. Go around the group and do this for each member. End with a prayer of thanks for the character qualities God gives and for God's gift of each other.

Murder

21"You have heard that it was said to the people long ago, 'Do not murder,*a* and anyone who murders will be subject to judgment.' 22But I tell you that anyone who is angry with his brother*b* will be subject to judgment. Again, anyone who says to his brother, 'Raca,*c*' is answerable to the Sanhedrin. But anyone who says, 'You fool!' will be in danger of the fire of hell.

23"Therefore, if you are offering your gift at the altar and there remember that your brother has something against you, 24leave your gift there in front of the altar. First go and be reconciled to your brother; then come and offer your gift.

25"Settle matters quickly with your adversary who is taking you to court. Do it while you are still with him on the way, or he may hand you over to the judge, and the judge may hand you over to the officer, and you may be thrown into prison. 26I tell you the truth, you will not get out until you have paid the last penny.*d*

Adultery

27"You have heard that it was said, 'Do not commit adultery.'*e* 28But I tell you that anyone who looks at a woman lustfully has already committed adultery with her in his heart. 29If your right eye causes you to sin, gouge it out and throw it away. It is better for you to lose one part of your body than for your whole body to be thrown into hell. 30And if your right hand causes you to sin, cut it off and throw it away. It is better for you to lose one part of your body than for your whole body to go into hell.

Divorce

31"It has been said, 'Anyone who divorces his wife must give her a certificate of divorce.'*f* 32But I tell you that anyone who divorces his wife, except for marital unfaithfulness, causes her to become an adulteress, and anyone who marries the divorced woman commits adultery.

Oaths

33"Again, you have heard that it was said to the people long ago, 'Do not break your oath, but keep the oaths you have made to the Lord.' 34But I tell you, Do not swear at all: either by heaven, for it is God's throne; 35or by the earth, for it is his footstool; or by Jerusalem, for it is the city of the Great King. 36And do not swear by your head, for you cannot make even one hair white or black. 37Simply let your 'Yes' be 'Yes,' and your 'No,' 'No'; anything beyond this comes from the evil one.

An Eye for an Eye

38"You have heard that it was said, 'Eye for eye, and tooth for tooth.'*g* 39But I tell you, Do not resist an evil person. If someone strikes you on the right cheek, turn to him the other also. 40And if someone wants to sue you and take your tunic, let him have your cloak as well. 41If someone forces you to go one mile, go with him two miles. 42Give to the one who asks you, and do not turn away from the one who wants to borrow from you.

---

a21 Exodus 20:13   *b22* Some manuscripts *brother without cause*   *c22* An Aramaic term of contempt   *d26* Greek *kodrantes*   *e27* Exodus 20:14 *f31* Deut. 24:1   *g38* Exodus 21:24; Lev. 24:20; Deut. 19:21

---

1. How did your parents settle disputes between you and your brother/sister? 2. What's the best advice you have been given for dealing with anger?

1. What new standard of right and wrong is Jesus creating (vv. 21–26)? How does he link anger and murder? Why? What inner attitudes is he stressing? 2. How does Jesus apply the principle in verses 21–26 to the commandment about adultery? What is Jesus' point in using such exaggerated language (vv. 29–30)? 3. Some rabbis allowed divorce for nearly any reason if a husband wanted it. What was their casual attitude toward divorce promoting? How are they misusing Moses' allowance for divorce (see Dt 24:1–4)? What inner quality is Jesus seeking instead? 4. How do you imagine the OT teaching about oaths is being misapplied (vv. 33–37)? What ought always be true about our speech? 5. What was the original intent of "eye for eye" and "tooth for tooth" (see Ex 21:24; Lev 24:17–20)? How is this law being perverted? What qualities ought to replace those desires for revenge? 6. Only the first part of the quote in verse 43 is from the OT. What does this show about the common use of Scripture at this time? In this context, what does the type of love Jesus calls for involve?

1. When it comes to making things right with others, or reconciling, who in your life do you think of? How do verses 21–26 and 43–48 speak to you? 2. How do you think God wants you to apply verses 29–30 in your life? 3. Since all of us experience something of anger, lust, divorce, duplicity, revenge, selfishness and hate, what is Jesus saying to us here? Which illustration gets to you the most? 4. If these standards are like a doctor's thermometer to show us how sick we are, what is the medicine needed to heal us? How does that relate to the Beatitudes (vv. 3–10)? What is the hope for us here? 5. Although these standards are not a new law that we must attain *before* God will have mercy on us, what do they suggest about the direction in which God wants us to grow *after* we have received his mercy? Which of these qualities do you want to cultivate most right now? How would your life be different as God helps you to put this quality into action?

Love for Enemies

43"You have heard that it was said, 'Love your neighbor[a] and hate your enemy.' **44**But I tell you: Love your enemies[b] and pray for those who persecute you, **45**that you may be sons of your Father in heaven. He causes his sun to rise on the evil and the good, and sends rain on the righteous and the unrighteous. **46**If you love those who love you, what reward will you get? Are not even the tax collectors doing that? **47**And if you greet only your brothers, what are you doing more than others? Do not even pagans do that? **48**Be perfect, therefore, as your heavenly Father is perfect.

Giving to the Needy

6 "Be careful not to do your 'acts of righteousness' before men, to be seen by them. If you do, you will have no reward from your Father in heaven.

2"So when you give to the needy, do not announce it with trumpets, as the hypocrites do in the synagogues and on the streets, to be honored by men. I tell you the truth, they have received their reward in full. **3**But when you give to the needy, do not let your left hand know what your right hand is doing, **4**so that your giving may be in secret. Then your Father, who sees what is done in secret, will reward you.

Prayer

5"And when you pray, do not be like the hypocrites, for they love to pray standing in the synagogues and on the street corners to be seen by men. I tell you the truth, they have received their reward in full. **6**But when you pray, go into your room, close the door and pray to your Father, who is unseen. Then your Father, who sees what is done in secret, will reward you. **7**And when you pray, do not keep on babbling like pagans, for they think they will be heard because of their many words. **8**Do not be like them, for your Father knows what you need before you ask him.

9"This, then, is how you should pray:

> " 'Our Father in heaven,
> hallowed be your name,
> **10**your kingdom come,
> your will be done
>   on earth as it is in heaven.
> **11**Give us today our daily bread.
> **12**Forgive us our debts,
>   as we also have forgiven our debtors.
> **13**And lead us not into temptation,
>   but deliver us from the evil one.[c]'

14For if you forgive men when they sin against you, your heavenly Father will also forgive you. **15**But if you do not forgive men their sins, your Father will not forgive your sins.

Fasting

16"When you fast, do not look somber as the hypocrites do, for they disfigure their faces to show men they are fasting. I tell you the truth, they have received their reward in full. **17**But when you fast, put oil on your head and wash your face, **18**so that it will not be obvious to men that you are fasting, but only to your Father,

---

1. Did you grow up in an openly "religious" home? Or was religion a private matter, unseen by you until later years? **2.** Were you taught any prayers as a child? What was one of the earliest ones you can recall?

1. Jesus continues to describe a righteousness surpassing that of the Scribes and Pharisees (5:20). How have they corrupted giving to the poor? What is their motivation? Their reward? How does their hypocrisy contrast with genuine compassion for the poor? **2.** How does their hypocrisy affect their prayer? How does their reward contrast with that of those who pray sincerely? Why did Jesus warn his followers to avoid wordiness? **3.** In Jesus' model prayer (vv. 9–13), what three concerns related to God did he pray about first? What personal concerns follow? What is the relationship between forgiveness and prayer? **4.** If our Father knows what we need before we ask, why pray? **5.** How does the fasting of Jesus' disciples contrast with that of the religious leaders? Why? Why fast?

1. What "religious disciplines" are valued in your circles? In what way can they be used to impress others? When have you given in to that temptation? Why? **2.** Do you tend to join in with public religious displays, or do you avoid such disciplines as fasting, praying or giving altogether? What attitudes does it take to practice these disciplines? How does that relate to the attitudes expressed in 5:3–11? When used properly, what is the value of religious discipline?

---

a43 Lev. 19:18   b44 Some late manuscripts *enemies, bless those who curse you, do good to those who hate you*   c13 Or *from evil*; some late manuscripts *one, / for yours is the kingdom and the power and the glory forever. Amen.*

saw this, they were filled with awe; and they praised God, who had given such authority to men.

The Calling of Matthew

9As Jesus went on from there, he saw a man named Matthew sitting at the tax collector's booth. "Follow me," he told him, and Matthew got up and followed him.

10While Jesus was having dinner at Matthew's house, many tax collectors and "sinners" came and ate with him and his disciples. 11When the Pharisees saw this, they asked his disciples, "Why does your teacher eat with tax collectors and 'sinners'?"

12On hearing this, Jesus said, "It is not the healthy who need a doctor, but the sick. 13But go and learn what this means: 'I desire mercy, not sacrifice.'ᵃ For I have not come to call the righteous, but sinners."

Jesus Questioned About Fasting

14Then John's disciples came and asked him, "How is it that we and the Pharisees fast, but your disciples do not fast?"

15Jesus answered, "How can the guests of the bridegroom mourn while he is with them? The time will come when the bridegroom will be taken from them; then they will fast.

16"No one sews a patch of unshrunk cloth on an old garment, for the patch will pull away from the garment, making the tear worse. 17Neither do men pour new wine into old wineskins. If they do, the skins will burst, the wine will run out and the wineskins will be ruined. No, they pour new wine into new wineskins, and both are preserved."

A Dead Girl and a Sick Woman

18While he was saying this, a ruler came and knelt before him and said, "My daughter has just died. But come and put your hand on her, and she will live." 19Jesus got up and went with him, and so did his disciples.

20Just then a woman who had been subject to bleeding for twelve years came up behind him and touched the edge of his cloak. 21She said to herself, "If I only touch his cloak, I will be healed."

22Jesus turned and saw her. "Take heart, daughter," he said, "your faith has healed you." And the woman was healed from that moment.

23When Jesus entered the ruler's house and saw the flute players and the noisy crowd, 24he said, "Go away. The girl is not dead but asleep." But they laughed at him. 25After the crowd had been put outside, he went in and took the girl by the hand, and she got up. 26News of this spread through all that region.

Jesus Heals the Blind and Mute

27As Jesus went on from there, two blind men followed him, calling out, "Have mercy on us, Son of David!"

28When he had gone indoors, the blind men came to him, and he asked them, "Do you believe that I am able to do this?"

"Yes, Lord," they replied.

29Then he touched their eyes and said, "According to your faith will it be done to you"; 30and their sight was restored. Jesus warned them sternly, "See that no one knows about this." 31But they went out and spread the news about him all over that region.

ᵃ13 Hosea 6:6

---

in Jesus' response to the Pharisees' criticism?

1. If Jesus really does forgive sin, why do many Christians struggle so with their forgiveness? 2. What is more valuable to you: physical healing or forgiveness? Why? 3. Who are the "Matthews" around you?

As a kid, did you outgrow your clothes or wear them out?

1. Why don't Jesus' disciples fast now? When will they? 2. How do unshrunk cloth and new wine relate to fasting, the bridegroom and the kingdom?

What is your "new wine"? Your "old wineskins"?

What are you like when you wake up: (a) Rarin' to go when my feet hit the floor? (b) Give me coffee, and leave me alone?

1. What feelings prompted the ruler to approach Jesus? How about the woman? How would you feel as you reached out to touch Jesus? Just afterward? 2. Compare the ruler and the woman. What does Jesus' response to both show about the kingdom? 3. What part does faith play in these healings?

The ruler and the woman were desperate. What is the relationship between desperation and faith? What does this story encourage you to do as you face desperate situations?

Would you describe yourself as gullible or cynical? Why?

1. What is the meaning of the title the blind men use for Jesus (v. 27)? How do they show faith? Why does Jesus want them to keep quiet? 2. How did the crowds react to Jesus' power? How did the Pharisees react? Why the difference? 3. How do Jesus' ac-

If you had a year's wages to blow on one special gift, what would you buy and for whom?

1. Why was Passover an appropriate time for the events of verses 1–5 to unfold? Why might the timing be risky? 2. What is significant about the setting for this woman's gift to Jesus? 3. What context in Jesus' life (v. 12) justifies this woman's act? Why are the disciples indignant? 4. What is Jesus trying to teach his disciples about priorities? 5. How could this scene relate to what happens in verses 14–16?

1. What "beautiful" thing could you do this week for Jesus (or "the least of these")? 2. Whereas the woman (v. 7) gave lavishly *for* Jesus, Judas wanted to see what he could get *from* him. In what ways are you like the woman? Like Judas?

As a kid, what were mealtimes like in your family? Where did everyone sit around the table? What behavior was not allowed?

1. What do you know about the Feast of Unleavened Bread (see Ex 12:1–30)? 2. Why do you think Jesus was so secretive about his arrangements for the Passover meal? 3. In what stages does Jesus reveal his betrayer (vv. 21,23,25)? Why does he do this? 4. In what ways do the bread and wine relate to his body and blood?

1. What does Communion mean to you? 2. How deeply do you know God's forgiveness of your sins? Why do many Christians struggle with guilt if Jesus provides the forgiveness of sins? 3. What impresses you most about Jesus at the Last Supper?

The Plot Against Jesus

26 When Jesus had finished saying all these things, he said to his disciples, [2]"As you know, the Passover is two days away—and the Son of Man will be handed over to be crucified."

[3]Then the chief priests and the elders of the people assembled in the palace of the high priest, whose name was Caiaphas, [4]and they plotted to arrest Jesus in some sly way and kill him. [5]"But not during the Feast," they said, "or there may be a riot among the people."

Jesus Anointed at Bethany

[6]While Jesus was in Bethany in the home of a man known as Simon the Leper, [7]a woman came to him with an alabaster jar of very expensive perfume, which she poured on his head as he was reclining at the table.

[8]When the disciples saw this, they were indignant. "Why this waste?" they asked. [9]"This perfume could have been sold at a high price and the money given to the poor."

[10]Aware of this, Jesus said to them, "Why are you bothering this woman? She has done a beautiful thing to me. [11]The poor you will always have with you, but you will not always have me. [12]When she poured this perfume on my body, she did it to prepare me for burial. [13]I tell you the truth, wherever this gospel is preached throughout the world, what she has done will also be told, in memory of her."

Judas Agrees to Betray Jesus

[14]Then one of the Twelve—the one called Judas Iscariot—went to the chief priests [15]and asked, "What are you willing to give me if I hand him over to you?" So they counted out for him thirty silver coins. [16]From then on Judas watched for an opportunity to hand him over.

The Lord's Supper

[17]On the first day of the Feast of Unleavened Bread, the disciples came to Jesus and asked, "Where do you want us to make preparations for you to eat the Passover?"

[18]He replied, "Go into the city to a certain man and tell him, 'The Teacher says: My appointed time is near. I am going to celebrate the Passover with my disciples at your house.'" [19]So the disciples did as Jesus had directed them and prepared the Passover.

[20]When evening came, Jesus was reclining at the table with the Twelve. [21]And while they were eating, he said, "I tell you the truth, one of you will betray me."

[22]They were very sad and began to say to him one after the other, "Surely not I, Lord?"

[23]Jesus replied, "The one who has dipped his hand into the bowl with me will betray me. [24]The Son of Man will go just as it is written about him. But woe to that man who betrays the Son of Man! It would be better for him if he had not been born."

[25]Then Judas, the one who would betray him, said, "Surely not I, Rabbi?"

Jesus answered, "Yes, it is you." [a]

[26]While they were eating, Jesus took bread, gave thanks and broke it, and gave it to his disciples, saying, "Take and eat; this is my body."

[27]Then he took the cup, gave thanks and offered it to them,

---

[a]25 Or *"You yourself have said it"*

saying, "Drink from it, all of you. ²⁸This is my blood of the^a covenant, which is poured out for many for the forgiveness of sins. ²⁹I tell you, I will not drink of this fruit of the vine from now on until that day when I drink it anew with you in my Father's kingdom."

³⁰When they had sung a hymn, they went out to the Mount of Olives.

Jesus Predicts Peter's Denial

³¹Then Jesus told them, "This very night you will all fall away on account of me, for it is written:

" 'I will strike the shepherd,
    and the sheep of the flock will be scattered.'^b

³²But after I have risen, I will go ahead of you into Galilee."

³³Peter replied, "Even if all fall away on account of you, I never will."

³⁴"I tell you the truth," Jesus answered, "this very night, before the rooster crows, you will disown me three times."

³⁵But Peter declared, "Even if I have to die with you, I will never disown you." And all the other disciples said the same.

Gethsemane

³⁶Then Jesus went with his disciples to a place called Gethsemane, and he said to them, "Sit here while I go over there and pray." ³⁷He took Peter and the two sons of Zebedee along with him, and he began to be sorrowful and troubled. ³⁸Then he said to them, "My soul is overwhelmed with sorrow to the point of death. Stay here and keep watch with me."

³⁹Going a little farther, he fell with his face to the ground and prayed, "My Father, if it is possible, may this cup be taken from me. Yet not as I will, but as you will."

⁴⁰Then he returned to his disciples and found them sleeping. "Could you men not keep watch with me for one hour?" he asked Peter. ⁴¹"Watch and pray so that you will not fall into temptation. The spirit is willing, but the body is weak."

⁴²He went away a second time and prayed, "My Father, if it is not possible for this cup to be taken away unless I drink it, may your will be done."

⁴³When he came back, he again found them sleeping, because their eyes were heavy. ⁴⁴So he left them and went away once more and prayed the third time, saying the same thing.

⁴⁵Then he returned to the disciples and said to them, "Are you still sleeping and resting? Look, the hour is near, and the Son of Man is betrayed into the hands of sinners. ⁴⁶Rise, let us go! Here comes my betrayer!"

Jesus Arrested

⁴⁷While he was still speaking, Judas, one of the Twelve, arrived. With him was a large crowd armed with swords and clubs, sent from the chief priests and the elders of the people. ⁴⁸Now the betrayer had arranged a signal with them: "The one I kiss is the man; arrest him." ⁴⁹Going at once to Jesus, Judas said, "Greetings, Rabbi!" and kissed him.

⁵⁰Jesus replied, "Friend, do what you came for."^c

Then the men stepped forward, seized Jesus and arrested him. ⁵¹With that, one of Jesus' companions reached for his sword, drew

a28 Some manuscripts *the new*   *b31* Zech. 13:7   *c50* Or *"Friend, why have you come?"*

What very sincere promise did you once make but failed to deliver on?

What emotions and motives accompany Jesus' next prediction? Peter's vow? Jesus' reply? Peter's follow-up vow?

1. When have you felt betrayed? How did you deal with it? 2. When, if ever, have you had the rooster crow in your relationship with Jesus? How did you and Jesus resolve that issue?

What was the longest night of your life: Delivering your first child? Waiting up for your teenager? Making a major decision?

1. What are the various emotions Jesus must have felt in Gethsemane? What does he ask of his disciples? What does he ask of God? 2. What is God's will (vv. 39, 42)? What model for our prayers does Jesus provide here?

1. What has been your "Gethsemane"—a place where you really wrestled with God? What was the issue? What do you learn from Jesus' example about praying at those times? 2. Who would you want to "watch and pray" with you next time you face a "Gethsemane"? 3. What do you appreciate most about Jesus' emotions in this story?

How did your favorite adventure hero respond to danger?

1. What kind of Messiah was the large, armed crowd expecting to arrest? Was the sword-wielding disciple's expectation essentially the same as theirs? Why or why not? 2. What does Jesus' response to Judas, the crowd and the disciple show about the type of Messiah he is?

INTRODUCTION to
MARK

Book Study Outline: If you are using Mark for a study course, here is a 7- or 13-week outline. Use the questions in the margin for your group agenda:

📖 start meeting / 15 min.

📖 read & discuss Bible / 30 min.

♡ close meeting / 15–45 min.

Refer to the Questions and Answers in the front of this Bible for more information.

Author: No author is named in the text. However, an early tradition ascribes this Gospel to Mark, the son of Mary (Ac 12:12) and the companion of both Paul (Ac 12:25; Col 4:10; Phm 24) and Peter (1Pe 5:13).

7-week plan	13-week plan	Personal Reading	Group Study Passage
1	1	1:1–45	1:29–39/Jesus Heals
	2	2:1–3:6	2:1–12/Paralytic Healed
2	3	3:7–35	3:20–35/Facing Criticism
	4	4:1–41	4:35–41/Jesus Calms Storm
3	5	5:1–43	5:24–34/A Bleeding Woman
	6	6:1–30	6:14–29/John Beheaded
4	7	6:31–7:37	6:30–44/Feeding 5000
	8	8:1–9:13	9:2–13/The Transfiguration
5	9	9:14–10:16	9:14–29/Boy's Evil Spirit
	10	10:17–34	10:17–31/Rich Young Man
6	11	10:35–11:19	11:12–19/Jesus Clears Temple
	12	11:20–14:42	14:32–42/Gethsemane
7	13	14:43–16:20	15:1–15/Jesus and Pilate

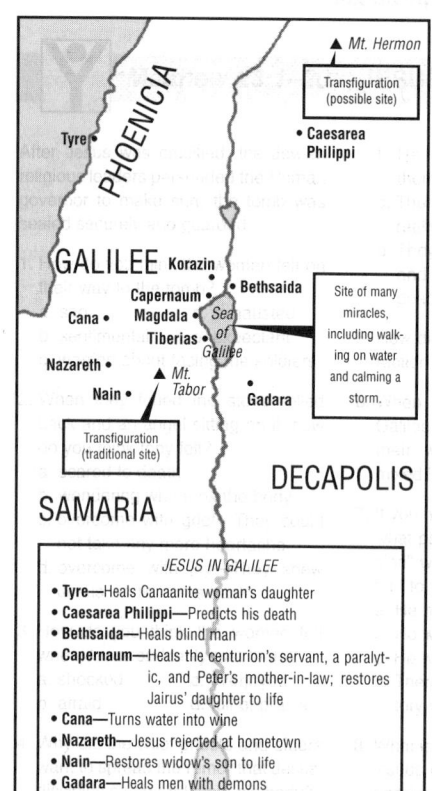

▲ Mt. Hermon

Transfiguration (possible site)

PHOENICIA

Tyre •

• Caesarea Philippi

GALILEE Korazin •

Capernaum • • Bethsaida

Cana • Magdala • Sea of Galilee

Tiberias •

Nazareth • ▲ Mt. Tabor

Nain • Gadara •

Site of many miracles, including walking on water and calming a storm.

Transfiguration (traditional site)

SAMARIA

DECAPOLIS

JESUS IN GALILEE
- **Tyre**—Heals Canaanite woman's daughter
- **Caesarea Philippi**—Predicts his death
- **Bethsaida**—Heals blind man
- **Capernaum**—Heals the centurion's servant, a paralytic, and Peter's mother-in-law; restores Jairus' daughter to life
- **Cana**—Turns water into wine
- **Nazareth**—Jesus rejected at hometown
- **Nain**—Restores widow's son to life
- **Gadara**—Heals men with demons

Date: Mark was written somewhere between A.D. 50–70; probably in the mid-60s.

Theme: Jesus the Messiah, the Son of God.

Historical Background: Mark was written for a Gentile audience; traditionally, the church at Rome. It may have been occasioned by the great fire which devastated much of Rome in A.D. 64. Despite his efforts at rebuilding the city, many people believed the Emperor Nero himself had arranged for this fire. To shift the focus off himself, Nero placed the blame for this tragedy on the Christians. This led to an outbreak of severe persecution which tested the faith of many. It was to people in this situation that Mark may have written this Gospel. This book would encourage these suffering believers by showing them Jesus' authority over all types of opposing forces. At the same time, Mark called on them to serve Christ faithfully even as they shared in his sufferings. Mark was probably the first Gospel written, forming the basis for much of Matthew and Luke.

Characteristics: Mark is not so much a biography of Jesus as it is a character sketch. Without any introduction or infancy narrative, Jesus bursts onto the scene as a fully grown man. Three years of ministry are packed into chapters 1–10, while Jesus' final week stretches out through chapters 11–16.

Mark

John the Baptist Prepares the Way

1 The beginning of the gospel about Jesus Christ, the Son of God.[a]

[2] It is written in Isaiah the prophet:

"I will send my messenger ahead of you,
    who will prepare your way"[b]—
[3] "a voice of one calling in the desert,
    'Prepare the way for the Lord,
    make straight paths for him.'"[c]

[4] And so John came, baptizing in the desert region and preaching a baptism of repentance for the forgiveness of sins. [5] The whole Judean countryside and all the people of Jerusalem went out to him. Confessing their sins, they were baptized by him in the Jordan River. [6] John wore clothing made of camel's hair, with a leather belt around his waist, and he ate locusts and wild honey. [7] And this was his message: "After me will come one more powerful than I, the thongs of whose sandals I am not worthy to stoop down and untie. [8] I baptize you with[d] water, but he will baptize you with the Holy Spirit."

The Baptism and Temptation of Jesus

[9] At that time Jesus came from Nazareth in Galilee and was baptized by John in the Jordan. [10] As Jesus was coming up out of the water, he saw heaven being torn open and the Spirit descending on him like a dove. [11] And a voice came from heaven: "You are my Son, whom I love; with you I am well pleased."

[12] At once the Spirit sent him out into the desert, [13] and he was in the desert forty days, being tempted by Satan. He was with the wild animals, and angels attended him.

The Calling of the First Disciples

[14] After John was put in prison, Jesus went into Galilee, proclaiming the good news of God. [15] "The time has come," he said. "The kingdom of God is near. Repent and believe the good news!"

[16] As Jesus walked beside the Sea of Galilee, he saw Simon and his brother Andrew casting a net into the lake, for they were fishermen. [17] "Come, follow me," Jesus said, "and I will make you fishers of men." [18] At once they left their nets and followed him.

[19] When he had gone a little farther, he saw James son of Zebedee and his brother John in a boat, preparing their nets. [20] Without delay he called them, and they left their father Zebedee in the boat with the hired men and followed him.

Jesus Drives Out an Evil Spirit

[21] They went to Capernaum, and when the Sabbath came, Jesus went into the synagogue and began to teach. [22] The people were amazed at his teaching, because he taught them as one who had authority, not as the teachers of the law. [23] Just then a man in

---

1. When the mail comes, what do you open and read first? 2. What is the strangest thing you have ever eaten?

1. What do the contexts of the quotes (Mal 3:1; Isa 40:3) teach about the "coming one"? 2. Why is John's ministry so popular (vv. 4–5)? 3. Given John's message (vv. 7–8), what type of person is the crowd anticipating (see Isa 32:15–20)? 4. What do you think the dove and voice (vv. 10–11) meant to Jesus as he came out of the water? As he entered the desert? During his temptations? How would all this prepare him?

1. What from your life illustrates what it means to repent? 2. John the Baptist prepared "the way for the Lord." Who prepared the way for the Lord in your life? 3. As Jesus came out of the water as he was being baptized, what did the voice from heaven say? What would you like to hear God say to you? 4. What do you think would happen if you went away by yourself for 40 days to face your particular temptations?

What is the "good news" according to Jesus? What might this kingdom mean to the disciples?

1. What is it about Jesus that makes you follow him? 2. Different types of fishermen need different skills: sailing, casting, maintaining nets, reading charts, etc. If Jesus asked you to be a "fisher of men," what skills could you bring?

Who was one of your best teachers? What made that teacher so good?

1. Why do you suppose Jesus started his public ministry in a synagogue? What two things about Jesus amazed the people? Why? 2. What does it

---

a1 Some manuscripts do not have *the Son of God.*   *b2* Mal. 3:1   *c3* Isaiah 40:3
d8 Or *in*

mean to teach "with authority"? What was the nature and source of Jesus' authority?

 1. Why do you think Jesus healed people? **2.** On a scale of 1 to 10, how much authority does Jesus have in your life? What would you have to cast out to rate a 10?

---

 1. As a child, were you sickly or robust? **2.** What is your solitary place?

 1. How does Jesus' healing (vv. 30–31) compare with his exorcism (v. 25)? What new realm of authority is seen here? **2.** How do you picture the scene in verses 32–34? Why does he silence the demons? **3.** After a day like this (vv. 29–34), what pressures could Jesus feel as a new day dawns? What might he pray about? How might this relate to his decision to move on (v. 38)?

 1. What do you do when you need to get away and be with

their synagogue who was possessed by an evil[a] spirit cried out, **24**"What do you want with us, Jesus of Nazareth? Have you come to destroy us? I know who you are—the Holy One of God!"

25"Be quiet!" said Jesus sternly. "Come out of him!" **26**The evil spirit shook the man violently and came out of him with a shriek.

27The people were all so amazed that they asked each other, "What is this? A new teaching—and with authority! He even gives orders to evil spirits and they obey him." **28**News about him spread quickly over the whole region of Galilee.

Jesus Heals Many

29As soon as they left the synagogue, they went with James and John to the home of Simon and Andrew. **30**Simon's mother-in-law was in bed with a fever, and they told Jesus about her. **31**So he went to her, took her hand and helped her up. The fever left her and she began to wait on them.

32That evening after sunset the people brought to Jesus all the sick and demon-possessed. **33**The whole town gathered at the door, **34**and Jesus healed many who had various diseases. He also drove out many demons, but he would not let the demons speak because they knew who he was.

Jesus Prays in a Solitary Place

35Very early in the morning, while it was still dark, Jesus got up, left the house and went off to a solitary place, where he prayed.

[a]23 Greek *unclean*; also in verses 26 and 27

 Mark 1:29–39   **JESUS HEALS AND PRAYS**

After Jesus' baptism and temptation, he immediately launched into his public ministry. As his base of operations during his ministry in Galilee, Jesus uses the Capernaum home of Simon Peter, one of the first disciples.

1. If you were having a private prayer time and the disciples came looking for you, how would you feel?
   a. angry I couldn't have time alone
   b. like telling the disciples to leave so I could keep praying
   c. like inviting the disciples to join me
   d. gratified that I was so needed
   e. guilty that I wasn't around when I was needed
   f. torn between my need to be alone and my desire to help others

2. What do you think the crowds were looking for in Jesus?
   a. a quick fix
   b. a miracle-worker
   c. a teacher of truth
   d. a spiritual leader to follow
   e. a better way to live

3. What do you think Jesus was looking for in the people?

   a. appreciation and applause
   b. faith
   c. followers
   d. He gave with no strings attached.

4. Which of the things Jesus faced cause you the most stress?
   a. being physically crowded (v. 33)
   b. short nights (v. 35)
   c. having routines disrupted (v. 37)
   d. constant demands (v. 37)
   e. always on the go (v. 39)

5. When you need time alone, where do you go and what do you do?

6. What is the greatest obstacle in your personal devotional life?
   a. finding time
   b. finding somewhere quiet
   c. being consistent
   d. staying awake
   e. keeping my concentration
   f. knowing what to do
   g. having the desire

7. What goals would you like to set for your "quiet time"—for example, amount of time, or a Scripture-reading plan?

8. How does this Scripture speak to your life?
   a. Being alone at times is good.
   b. I need more balance between activity and prayer.
   c. I need more balance between being with others and being alone.
   d. I shouldn't stay constantly busy just to keep from being lonely.

9. Which of the following ways do you typically manage stress? Which of these ways could you and your spouse do together to manage stress better?
   a. ignore it
   b. rant and rave
   c. exercise regularly
   d. get out into nature
   e. go out for an evening
   f. take vacations
   g. have quality devotional time
   h. relax with a book or TV
   i. participate in a hobby
   j. draw support from others

10. What difference has getting alone to pray made (or could it make) in handling the stress of being a caregiver?

³⁶Simon and his companions went to look for him, ³⁷and when they found him, they exclaimed: "Everyone is looking for you!"

³⁸Jesus replied, "Let us go somewhere else—to the nearby villages—so I can preach there also. That is why I have come." ³⁹So he traveled throughout Galilee, preaching in their synagogues and driving out demons.

A Man With Leprosy

⁴⁰A man with leprosy^a came to him and begged him on his knees, "If you are willing, you can make me clean."

⁴¹Filled with compassion, Jesus reached out his hand and touched the man. "I am willing," he said. "Be clean!" ⁴²Immediately the leprosy left him and he was cured.

⁴³Jesus sent him away at once with a strong warning: ⁴⁴"See that you don't tell this to anyone. But go, show yourself to the priest and offer the sacrifices that Moses commanded for your cleansing, as a testimony to them." ⁴⁵Instead he went out and began to talk freely, spreading the news. As a result, Jesus could no longer enter a town openly but stayed outside in lonely places. Yet the people still came to him from everywhere.

Jesus Heals a Paralytic

2 A few days later, when Jesus again entered Capernaum, the people heard that he had come home. ²So many gathered that there was no room left, not even outside the door, and he preached the word to them. ³Some men came, bringing to him a paralytic,

^a40 The Greek word was used for various diseases affecting the skin—not necessarily leprosy.

God? **2.** What insight do you see in these stories about Jesus and the kingdom?

When caught in a crowd (rush hour, Christmas crunch, etc.), what do you do?

Why is the leper unsure of Jesus' desire to help (see Lev 13)? What is significant about Jesus touching the leper prior to healing him? What do the crowds expect?

Where do you need his special touch this week? How can you "touch lepers" in your community?

If in a crisis, even at 3 a.m., which four friends would you call?

1. What would you be seeing and feeling if you were in this crowd (vv. 1–4)? **2.** Why are the teachers so upset? In their minds, how are sin and the authority of

Mark 2:1–12   JESUS HEALS A PARALYTIC

1. If you were one of the paralytic's four friends and saw the crowd where Jesus was, what would you do?
   a. suggest we come back later
   b. politely wait in line
   c. make a hole in the roof
   d. go along with the hole in the roof, but make clear it wasn't my idea

2. How would you feel if you were the paralytic when your friends decided to help you "drop in on Jesus"?
   a. reluctant—You will embarrass me.
   b. scared—You're going to drop me.
   c. grateful—Thanks for your concern.
   d. apprehensive—They are going to throw us out!
   e. mixed—I don't think this is going to work, but I will trust you guys.

3. When the crowd heard the commotion and saw the man lowered into the room, how do you think they felt?
   a. annoyed—Where's their respect?
   b. amused—This is the best show in town!
   c. angry—Throw them out!
   d. admiring—They are really concerned for their friend.

4. Why were the teachers of the Law so upset with Jesus?
   a. They were worried about the roof.
   b. They didn't believe Jesus was the Son of God.
   c. They didn't accept the connection of spiritual and physical healing.
   d. They thought Jesus was being disrespectful to God.

5. What quality do the four men possess that impresses you most?
   a. faith   d. determination
   b. ingenuity   e. boldness
   c. concern for their friend

6. How do you need to change to receive more support from friends?
   a. stop trying to be so self-sufficient
   b. learn to take the risk of asking
   c. be more supportive of others
   d. recruit some different friends
   e. I'm doing fine as is.

7. If you had friends who would take you to Jesus for healing today, what kind of healing would you ask for?
   a. physical   c. emotional
   b. spiritual   d. relational

8. What is the closest you have come to having a supportive community who cared for you when you were hurting? How have you felt cared for by this group?

9. As your friends help you find healing or comfort, what is the biggest obstacle they may have to help you overcome?
   a. my self-pity
   b. my anger
   c. some family members or friends who don't understand my pain
   d. the distance I feel from God
   e. I'm afraid I don't have friends like that.

10. As you begin this accountability group, in what specific ways would you like the group to hold you accountable?

11. What do you think it takes to be a true friend? Conclude this course by having each person listen silently while others share what qualities that person has that make him or her a good friend.

God linked (see Jn 9:1–3)? **3.** Why didn't Jesus just heal the man like everyone expected? What new insight about the kingdom and himself is he revealing?

♡ **1.** In what ways is sin like paralysis? What freedoms has Jesus' word of forgiveness given to you? Where do you need to hear that word again? **2.** In this story, do you identify more with the paralytic, his friends or the teachers? Why?

_____

☕ If your salary was suddenly tripled, what would you do with the extra money?

📖 The disciples who were fishermen (1:16–19) may have paid inflated taxes to Levi for years. How would they feel when Jesus called him? Why did he do so?

♡ **1.** Describe a time in your life when you felt like you were at odds with the religious establishment. **2.** When have you resented Jesus calling a particular person?

_____

☕ Do you fix and mend or toss and replace? Why?

📖 **1.** Why did John's disciples and the Pharisees fast (see Lev 16:29,31; 23:27,29,31)? Why did Jesus' disciples not fast? **2.** How do the three mini-parables (vv. 19–22) answer the question? What is the new wine? The old wineskins?

♡ How has the "wine" of Jesus burst some of your "old wineskins"?

_____

☕ Who in your family was (or is) always checking up on you to see if you "do it right"?

📖 **1.** What is the complaint about Jesus here? **2.** How does David's story apply to Jesus' situation (see 1Sa 21:1–6)? **3.** What causes the tension in the synagogue (3:1–6)? What concerns are shared by the leaders? By Jesus? By the man with the

carried by four of them. ⁴Since they could not get him to Jesus because of the crowd, they made an opening in the roof above Jesus and, after digging through it, lowered the mat the paralyzed man was lying on. ⁵When Jesus saw their faith, he said to the paralytic, "Son, your sins are forgiven."

⁶Now some teachers of the law were sitting there, thinking to themselves, ⁷"Why does this fellow talk like that? He's blaspheming! Who can forgive sins but God alone?"

⁸Immediately Jesus knew in his spirit that this was what they were thinking in their hearts, and he said to them, "Why are you thinking these things? ⁹Which is easier: to say to the paralytic, 'Your sins are forgiven,' or to say, 'Get up, take your mat and walk'? ¹⁰But that you may know that the Son of Man has authority on earth to forgive sins . . . ." He said to the paralytic, ¹¹"I tell you, get up, take your mat and go home." ¹²He got up, took his mat and walked out in full view of them all. This amazed everyone and they praised God, saying, "We have never seen anything like this!"

The Calling of Levi

¹³Once again Jesus went out beside the lake. A large crowd came to him, and he began to teach them. ¹⁴As he walked along, he saw Levi son of Alphaeus sitting at the tax collector's booth. "Follow me," Jesus told him, and Levi got up and followed him.

¹⁵While Jesus was having dinner at Levi's house, many tax collectors and "sinners" were eating with him and his disciples, for there were many who followed him. ¹⁶When the teachers of the law who were Pharisees saw him eating with the "sinners" and tax collectors, they asked his disciples: "Why does he eat with tax collectors and 'sinners'?"

¹⁷On hearing this, Jesus said to them, "It is not the healthy who need a doctor, but the sick. I have not come to call the righteous, but sinners."

Jesus Questioned About Fasting

¹⁸Now John's disciples and the Pharisees were fasting. Some people came and asked Jesus, "How is it that John's disciples and the disciples of the Pharisees are fasting, but yours are not?"

¹⁹Jesus answered, "How can the guests of the bridegroom fast while he is with them? They cannot, so long as they have him with them. ²⁰But the time will come when the bridegroom will be taken from them, and on that day they will fast.

²¹"No one sews a patch of unshrunk cloth on an old garment. If he does, the new piece will pull away from the old, making the tear worse. ²²And no one pours new wine into old wineskins. If he does, the wine will burst the skins, and both the wine and the wineskins will be ruined. No, he pours new wine into new wineskins."

Lord of the Sabbath

²³One Sabbath Jesus was going through the grainfields, and as his disciples walked along, they began to pick some heads of grain. ²⁴The Pharisees said to him, "Look, why are they doing what is unlawful on the Sabbath?"

²⁵He answered, "Have you never read what David did when he and his companions were hungry and in need? ²⁶In the days of Abiathar the high priest, he entered the house of God and ate the consecrated bread, which is lawful only for priests to eat. And he also gave some to his companions."

²⁷Then he said to them, "The Sabbath was made for man, not

man for the Sabbath. [28]So the Son of Man is Lord even of the Sabbath."

3 Another time he went into the synagogue, and a man with a shriveled hand was there. [2]Some of them were looking for a reason to accuse Jesus, so they watched him closely to see if he would heal him on the Sabbath. [3]Jesus said to the man with the shriveled hand, "Stand up in front of everyone."

[4]Then Jesus asked them, "Which is lawful on the Sabbath: to do good or to do evil, to save life or to kill?" But they remained silent.

[5]He looked around at them in anger and, deeply distressed at their stubborn hearts, said to the man, "Stretch out your hand." He stretched it out, and his hand was completely restored. [6]Then the Pharisees went out and began to plot with the Herodians how they might kill Jesus.

Crowds Follow Jesus

[7]Jesus withdrew with his disciples to the lake, and a large crowd from Galilee followed. [8]When they heard all he was doing, many people came to him from Judea, Jerusalem, Idumea, and the regions across the Jordan and around Tyre and Sidon. [9]Because of the crowd he told his disciples to have a small boat ready for him, to keep the people from crowding him. [10]For he had healed many, so that those with diseases were pushing forward to touch him. [11]Whenever the evil[a] spirits saw him, they fell down before him and cried out, "You are the Son of God." [12]But he gave them strict orders not to tell who he was.

[a] 11 Greek unclean; also in verse 30

shriveled hand? **4.** What prompts Jesus' anger?

1. How have you seen religious rules or institutions hurt people? What causes that? **2.** Have you ever felt angry at a church or religious institution? Why? How has that experience affected you?

_____

1. When have you been attracted to or repelled by large crowds (sporting events, rock concerts, political rallies, opening day at a new mall)? **2.** What do you do to get away from the maddening crowd?

1. From what places were people traveling to see and hear Jesus? What would have motivated you to go? What motives would have pleased Jesus? Why? **2.** What qualities did the 12 disciples possess which might have

---

Mark 2:23–3:6   **LORD OF THE SABBATH**

The conflict in these two stories arose from the Pharisees' adherence to traditional interpretations of Old Testament Sabbath laws: "harvesting" of any kind was forbidden, and aid could be given the sick only when the person's life was threatened.

1. How would the _Galilee Gazette_ headline these two stories?
   a. New Rules for New Rabbi
   b. Jesus and Pharisees Square Off in Sabbath Spat
   c. Controversial Miracle Occurs in Local Synagogue
   d. Jesus' Popularity Growing ... But Not With Everyone

2. What reasoning did Jesus use to answer the Pharisees' accusation of the disciples breaking the Sabbath?
   a. Lighten up, it's a small infraction.
   b. I'm reinterpreting the Law.
   c. You're concentrating on the letter of the Law, and I'm concerned with the spirit behind it.
   d. The Sabbath should be a help to people, not a burden.

3. What made Jesus so upset with the Pharisees in the synagogue (3:5)?
   a. their refusal to answer his question
   b. their disbelief
   c. their suspicion of him
   d. their lack of compassion
   e. their putting principles over people

4. What made the Pharisees so upset with Jesus?
   a. intolerance   d. jealousy
   b. spiritual blindness   e. legalism
   c. righteous indignation

5. Why did Jesus heal the man on the Sabbath?
   a. because there was no reason to wait until the next day
   b. to spite the Pharisees
   c. because he had compassion upon the man
   d. to demonstrate he was Lord of the Sabbath

6. These two confrontations show that Jesus:
   a. liked to stir up trouble.
   b. didn't care what the religious elite thought.

c. was above Old Testament Law.
d. came to abolish the Law.
e. came to restore the Law's intent.

7. How have you seen religious rules or institutions hurt people? How might you be guilty of that yourself?

8. What does "Sabbath" mean for you?
   a. worship   d. no work
   b. physical rest   e. no anxiety
   c. inner peace   f. other:_____

9. What do you regularly give up your Sabbath for? What are the difficult things for you to set aside?

10. God's intent for the Sabbath was our restoration. Complete the following sentences:
    a. I find physical rest/recuperation when I _____.
    b. I find mental rest/recuperation when I _____.
    c. I find emotional rest/recuperation when I _____.
    d. I find spiritual rest/recuperation when I _____.

caused Jesus to select them? What is their purpose? Why such ordinary guys?

What motivates you to seek Jesus? What does it mean to you to be "with him"? To be "sent out" by him?

What crazy stunt or notorious behavior from your high school days are your classmates likely to remember you by?

1. Why was Jesus' family worried about him? What type of conversation might they have had before deciding to "take charge of him?" 2. What tensions might these people feel when they hear what the Pharisees say about Jesus? 3. How do Jesus' parables answer the "teachers of the law"? How do they relate to verse 29? 4. What did the crowd expect in verses 31–32? What did Jesus say is the basis for a family relationship with him (v. 35)? Is doing God's will

The Appointing of the Twelve Apostles

¹³Jesus went up on a mountainside and called to him those he wanted, and they came to him. ¹⁴He appointed twelve—designating them apostles*ᵃ*—that they might be with him and that he might send them out to preach ¹⁵and to have authority to drive out demons. ¹⁶These are the twelve he appointed: Simon (to whom he gave the name Peter); ¹⁷James son of Zebedee and his brother John (to them he gave the name Boanerges, which means Sons of Thunder); ¹⁸Andrew, Philip, Bartholomew, Matthew, Thomas, James son of Alphaeus, Thaddaeus, Simon the Zealot ¹⁹and Judas Iscariot, who betrayed him.

Jesus and Beelzebub

²⁰Then Jesus entered a house, and again a crowd gathered, so that he and his disciples were not even able to eat. ²¹When his family heard about this, they went to take charge of him, for they said, "He is out of his mind."

²²And the teachers of the law who came down from Jerusalem said, "He is possessed by Beelzebub*ᵇ*! By the prince of demons he is driving out demons."

²³So Jesus called them and spoke to them in parables: "How can Satan drive out Satan? ²⁴If a kingdom is divided against itself, that kingdom cannot stand. ²⁵If a house is divided against itself, that house cannot stand. ²⁶And if Satan opposes himself and is divided, he cannot stand; his end has come. ²⁷In fact, no one can enter a strong man's house and carry off his possessions unless he first ties up the strong man. Then he can rob his house. ²⁸I tell you the

ᵃ14 Some manuscripts do not have *designating them apostles.*   *ᵇ22* Greek *Beezeboul* or *Beelzeboul*

Mark 3:20–35   JESUS FACES CRITICISM

1. If you were Jesus, what would be the hardest for you to handle?
   a. not getting to eat
   b. my family thinking I was crazy
   c. rejection by religious authorities
   d. accusations of being possessed

2. Why did Jesus' family think he was out of his mind?
   a. No normal person would act the way he did.
   b. They thought he was under excessive stress.
   c. They thought he had "delusions of grandeur."
   d. They really didn't understand who he was.
   e. They were swayed by others.

3. Why did Jesus' family want to "take charge of him"?
   a. They were afraid he would overwork himself.
   b. They were afraid of what his opponents might do to him.
   c. They wanted to teach him proper behavior.
   d. He was embarrassing them.

4. What does it mean to "blaspheme against the Holy Spirit"?
   a. to ridicule the Holy Spirit
   b. to sin repeatedly
   c. to refuse to accept God's forgiveness
   d. to attribute Jesus' works to Satan

5. What would you have thought if you were listening to Jesus when he spoke about his "family"?
   a. Jesus is anti-family.
   b. Jesus sees himself as belonging to the family of all humanity.
   c. I can belong to Jesus' family.
   d. Membership in God's spiritual family is more important than membership in my biological family.
   e. I have to turn my back on my natural family.
   f. I have to obey the will of God.

6. Which of the following statements describe your relationship with the family of God?
   a. I've been in the family a long time.
   b. I'm just a baby in the family.
   c. I'm a "black sheep" in the family.

   d. I generally don't get along with other family members.
   e. I generally get along great with other family members.

7. How can you improve the way you relate to your "brothers and sisters" in the family of God?

8. How can you improve the way you relate to your "Heavenly Father"?

9. Which of the following is *most* true of your family? Which of the following is *least* true?
   a. My parents think I'm weird.
   b. I don't feel very accepted by my parents.
   c. I don't feel like I can do anything right in my parents' eyes.
   d. I feel closer to other people than to my own family.
   e. Our family life is full of tension.

10. How do you think God wants you to deal with the frustrations you feel toward your parents? What *can* you change? What *can't* you change?

truth, all the sins and blasphemies of men will be forgiven them. ²⁹But whoever blasphemes against the Holy Spirit will never be forgiven; he is guilty of an eternal sin."

³⁰He said this because they were saying, "He has an evil spirit."

Jesus' Mother and Brothers

³¹Then Jesus' mother and brothers arrived. Standing outside, they sent someone in to call him. ³²A crowd was sitting around him, and they told him, "Your mother and brothers are outside looking for you."

³³"Who are my mother and my brothers?" he asked.

³⁴Then he looked at those seated in a circle around him and said, "Here are my mother and my brothers! ³⁵Whoever does God's will is my brother and sister and mother."

The Parable of the Sower

4 Again Jesus began to teach by the lake. The crowd that gathered around him was so large that he got into a boat and sat in it out on the lake, while all the people were along the shore at the water's edge. ²He taught them many things by parables, and in his teaching said: ³"Listen! A farmer went out to sow his seed. ⁴As he was scattering the seed, some fell along the path, and the birds came and ate it up. ⁵Some fell on rocky places, where it did not have much soil. It sprang up quickly, because the soil was shallow. ⁶But when the sun came up, the plants were scorched, and they withered because they had no root. ⁷Other seed fell among thorns, which grew up and choked the plants, so that they did not bear grain. ⁸Still other seed fell on good soil. It came up, grew and produced a crop, multiplying thirty, sixty, or even a hundred times."

⁹Then Jesus said, "He who has ears to hear, let him hear."

¹⁰When he was alone, the Twelve and the others around him asked him about the parables. ¹¹He told them, "The secret of the kingdom of God has been given to you. But to those on the outside everything is said in parables ¹²so that,

> " 'they may be ever seeing but never perceiving,
>   and ever hearing but never understanding;
> otherwise they might turn and be forgiven!' ^a "

¹³Then Jesus said to them, "Don't you understand this parable? How then will you understand any parable? ¹⁴The farmer sows the word. ¹⁵Some people are like seed along the path, where the word is sown. As soon as they hear it, Satan comes and takes away the word that was sown in them. ¹⁶Others, like seed sown on rocky places, hear the word and at once receive it with joy. ¹⁷But since they have no root, they last only a short time. When trouble or persecution comes because of the word, they quickly fall away. ¹⁸Still others, like seed sown among thorns, hear the word; ¹⁹but the worries of this life, the deceitfulness of wealth and the desires for other things come in and choke the word, making it unfruitful. ²⁰Others, like seed sown on good soil, hear the word, accept it, and produce a crop—thirty, sixty or even a hundred times what was sown."

A Lamp on a Stand

²¹He said to them, "Do you bring in a lamp to put it under a bowl or a bed? Instead, don't you put it on its stand? ²²For what-

a 12 Isaiah 6:9,10

---

an action or a belief (see Lk 6:46; Jn 6:29)?

1. What do you need to do with your life before Jesus can more fully be the Master of your life? 2. Have you ever experienced a conflict between what God wanted for you and what your family expected of you? 3. What differences can you identify between the members of your biological family and your spiritual brothers and sisters? 4. Of the responses to Jesus in this chapter (3:6,8, 21–22,34–35), which best describes your relationship to him now? Why?

1. If you were to change careers and become a farmer, what kind of crops would you like to raise? Why? 2. What is the oldest house plant you own? What is the shortest time you have kept a house plant living?

1. What are the four types of ground on which these seeds fall? What kind of growth occurred in each soil type? 2. How might this crowd have responded to such a parable? How are the parables like a spiritual hearing test? What blocks understanding? What distinguishes those who are told "the secret of the kingdom" from those "outside"? 3. Why does the word not take root at all in some people? What causes the second plant to wither? What things choked off the third plant? 4. What modern analogy would you use to explain this parable to city kids who have never seen a farm?

1. Which soil would best describe your response to the Gospel when you first heard it? What kind of crop have you been producing lately? 2. What "worries of life, deceitfulness of wealth and desires for other things" might hinder your ability to produce a bountiful crop? 3. What do you need to do so your spiritual life is producing an abundant crop?

Of all the different types of lights (such as desk lamps, night lights, torches, candelabras, florescent lights, etc.), which one best describes you?

1. If Jesus is the lamp (v. 21), what is he revealing (see also vv. 11–12)? 2. What is the secret of receiving more from Jesus? 3. In verses 26–29, what part (if any) do people play in the growing kingdom? How does this parable com-plement the one in verses 3–20? 4. What does the contrasting seed and bush teach about the kingdom (vv. 30–32)?

1. In terms of the light of Christ that you shed, are you a 20-, 75-, or 200-watt light bulb? Or a burned out bulb? Why? 2. How comfortable do you feel about everything you've ever concealed being disclosed? 3. How would you live your life differently if you wanted to live it without worrying what was disclosed? 4. Does knowing that the growth of the kingdom is ultimately in God's hands cause you to rest or to work more? Why? 5. At what stage is the kingdom in your life now: Still a seed? Sprouting? Outgrowing the "weeds"? Producing a harvest?

Have you ever been in a natural disaster? What happened?

1. How do you picture the disciples' faces in verses 39–41? Which would frighten you more—the storm or Jesus? 2. What was Jesus showing them about himself in all this?

1. How do you react to Jesus when he seems to be asleep in your life? 2. What is the worst personal "storm" you have faced? How did Jesus help?

1. When did a vacation turn into something unpleasant you never expected? 2. What is the most dramatic change you have ever seen in someone's behavior?

1. After a nerve-wracking ride across a lake, how would you react to being accosted by an escapee from a cemetery? 2. What do we learn about demons from the actions of the possessed man? 3. How does his healing take place? What is the man like afterwards? 4. Why do you think the people reacted as they did? Why were they afraid (v. 15) after seeing the man "dressed and in his right mind"? What does this story say

ever is hidden is meant to be disclosed, and whatever is concealed is meant to be brought out into the open. [23]If anyone has ears to hear, let him hear."

[24]"Consider carefully what you hear," he continued. "With the measure you use, it will be measured to you—and even more. [25]Whoever has will be given more; whoever does not have, even what he has will be taken from him."

The Parable of the Growing Seed

[26]He also said, "This is what the kingdom of God is like. A man scatters seed on the ground. [27]Night and day, whether he sleeps or gets up, the seed sprouts and grows, though he does not know how. [28]All by itself the soil produces grain—first the stalk, then the head, then the full kernel in the head. [29]As soon as the grain is ripe, he puts the sickle to it, because the harvest has come."

The Parable of the Mustard Seed

[30]Again he said, "What shall we say the kingdom of God is like, or what parable shall we use to describe it? [31]It is like a mustard seed, which is the smallest seed you plant in the ground. [32]Yet when planted, it grows and becomes the largest of all garden plants, with such big branches that the birds of the air can perch in its shade."

[33]With many similar parables Jesus spoke the word to them, as much as they could understand. [34]He did not say anything to them without using a parable. But when he was alone with his own disciples, he explained everything.

Jesus Calms the Storm

[35]That day when evening came, he said to his disciples, "Let us go over to the other side." [36]Leaving the crowd behind, they took him along, just as he was, in the boat. There were also other boats with him. [37]A furious squall came up, and the waves broke over the boat, so that it was nearly swamped. [38]Jesus was in the stern, sleeping on a cushion. The disciples woke him and said to him, "Teacher, don't you care if we drown?"

[39]He got up, rebuked the wind and said to the waves, "Quiet! Be still!" Then the wind died down and it was completely calm.

[40]He said to his disciples, "Why are you so afraid? Do you still have no faith?"

[41]They were terrified and asked each other, "Who is this? Even the wind and the waves obey him!"

The Healing of a Demon-possessed Man

5 They went across the lake to the region of the Gerasenes.[a] [2]When Jesus got out of the boat, a man with an evil[b] spirit came from the tombs to meet him. [3]This man lived in the tombs, and no one could bind him any more, not even with a chain. [4]For he had often been chained hand and foot, but he tore the chains apart and broke the irons on his feet. No one was strong enough to subdue him. [5]Night and day among the tombs and in the hills he would cry out and cut himself with stones.

[6]When he saw Jesus from a distance, he ran and fell on his knees in front of him. [7]He shouted at the top of his voice, "What do you want with me, Jesus, Son of the Most High God? Swear to God that you won't torture me!" [8]For Jesus had said to him, "Come out of this man, you evil spirit!"

[a]1 Some manuscripts *Gadarenes*; other manuscripts *Gergesenes*   [b]2 Greek *unclean*; also in verses 8 and 13

⁹Then Jesus asked him, "What is your name?"

"My name is Legion," he replied, "for we are many." ¹⁰And he begged Jesus again and again not to send them out of the area.

¹¹A large herd of pigs was feeding on the nearby hillside. ¹²The demons begged Jesus, "Send us among the pigs; allow us to go into them." ¹³He gave them permission, and the evil spirits came out and went into the pigs. The herd, about two thousand in number, rushed down the steep bank into the lake and were drowned.

¹⁴Those tending the pigs ran off and reported this in the town and countryside, and the people went out to see what had happened. ¹⁵When they came to Jesus, they saw the man who had been possessed by the legion of demons, sitting there, dressed and in his right mind; and they were afraid. ¹⁶Those who had seen it told the people what had happened to the demon-possessed man— and told about the pigs as well. ¹⁷Then the people began to plead with Jesus to leave their region.

¹⁸As Jesus was getting into the boat, the man who had been demon-possessed begged to go with him. ¹⁹Jesus did not let him, but said, "Go home to your family and tell them how much the Lord has done for you, and how he has had mercy on you." ²⁰So the man went away and began to tell in the Decapolis*ᵃ* how much Jesus had done for him. And all the people were amazed.

A Dead Girl and a Sick Woman

²¹When Jesus had again crossed over by boat to the other side of the lake, a large crowd gathered around him while he was by the lake. ²²Then one of the synagogue rulers, named Jairus, came

ᵃ20 That is, the Ten Cities

about their values? **5.** What do you suppose the demoniac said to his family? **6.** What did the disciples learn about Jesus on this day (4:35–5:20)?

1. When have you felt torn by many conflicting voices and feelings? How did Jesus bring peace to you? How do you need to hear his word of peace right now? **2.** Have you ever told your family how Jesus has shown mercy on you? If so, what happened? If not, why? What would you like to tell them?

1. What would you do if the phone rang, the doorbell chimed, your child called for help, and the oven alarm went off all at the same time? **2.** If you could raise

---

  Mark 4:35–41   **JESUS CALMS THE STORM**

1. If you had been one of the disciples when the boat was about to sink, what would you have done?
   a. started bailing water
   b. jumped overboard
   c. taken command
   d. woken up Jesus

2. Why do you think the disciples awakened Jesus?
   a. They were afraid for his life.
   b. They were afraid for *their* lives.
   c. They wanted help bailing water.
   d. They wanted a miracle.
   e. They were mad that Jesus was sleeping through their crisis.

3. What was the tone in Jesus' voice when he said, "Why are you afraid? Do you still have no faith?"
   a. angry   c. disappointed
   b. scolding   d. compassionate

4. Why did Jesus allow a storm to come up in the first place?
   a. He didn't—storms are natural.
   b. He was asleep at the switch.
   c. He wanted to test them.
   d. He wanted to stretch their faith.

5. If you had been there, what would you have told your friends afterward?
   a. "I just about got killed!"
   b. "Jesus sure is a sound sleeper."
   c. "I can't figure Jesus out."
   d. "Only God can do what I just saw."

6. What do you do when "storms" come up in your life?
   a. turn to a person I can trust
   b. turn to God
   c. act like nothing is wrong
   d. get touchy and irritable
   e. take charge of things
   f. panic

7. What brings on most of the storms in your life?
   a. financial difficulties
   b. hassles with relationships
   c. overwhelming demands
   d. insecurity: worry about job/future
   e. disappointment: feelings of failure
   f. tragedy: sickness/death

8. As time goes on, have you seen improvement in the way you handle storms? What difference does your faith in Christ make?

9. How would you compare your life right now to the storm in this story?
   a. smooth sailing—enjoying the ride
   b. choppy water—a storm is brewing
   c. furious squall—sinking fast
   d. storm is over—clearing up

10. "Quiet! Be still!" If Jesus were to speak these words to you today, what would they mean?

11. What is the most stressful recurring storm you face?
    a. making the grade in school
    b. getting along with my parents
    c. making friends
    d. getting along with friends
    e. other:_____

12. On a scale of 1 to 10, how would you rate each of the following?
    a. the amount of time and emotional energy you give to work
    b. the amount of meaning you get from work
    c. the amount of stress you get from work

someone from the dead, who would it be? Why?

1. Of all the people pressing for Jesus' attention, two get through to him in this story? Why?
2. What impressions do you get of the sick woman (vv. 25–26)? This illness made her ritually unclean and thus unable to have contact with other people. What do you think it took for her to touch Jesus? Why do you think Jesus makes the sick woman reveal herself? How was her faith obvious to Jesus? 3. What impressions do you get of Jairus (vv. 22–23)? How is his situation similar to that of the sick woman? How is it different? 4. What is Jesus' reaction to the news that the child is dead? Jairus' reaction? Why did Jesus say the child was asleep? As Jairus, what would you say to the crowd outside your house after Jesus left?

1. Jairus, the synagogue ruler, fell at Jesus' feet and begged him to heal his 12-year-old daughter. When was the last time you "fell at Jesus' feet" and begged

there. Seeing Jesus, he fell at his feet 23and pleaded earnestly with him, "My little daughter is dying. Please come and put your hands on her so that she will be healed and live." 24So Jesus went with him.

A large crowd followed and pressed around him. 25And a woman was there who had been subject to bleeding for twelve years. 26She had suffered a great deal under the care of many doctors and had spent all she had, yet instead of getting better she grew worse. 27When she heard about Jesus, she came up behind him in the crowd and touched his cloak, 28because she thought, "If I just touch his clothes, I will be healed." 29Immediately her bleeding stopped and she felt in her body that she was freed from her suffering.

30At once Jesus realized that power had gone out from him. He turned around in the crowd and asked, "Who touched my clothes?"

31"You see the people crowding against you," his disciples answered, "and yet you can ask, 'Who touched me?' "

32But Jesus kept looking around to see who had done it. 33Then the woman, knowing what had happened to her, came and fell at his feet and, trembling with fear, told him the whole truth. 34He said to her, "Daughter, your faith has healed you. Go in peace and be freed from your suffering."

35While Jesus was still speaking, some men came from the house of Jairus, the synagogue ruler. "Your daughter is dead," they said. "Why bother the teacher any more?"

   Mark 5:24–34 **JESUS HEALS A BLEEDING WOMAN**

Jesus had just agreed to go to the home of a man whose young daughter was dying. On the way he encounters a woman who most likely suffered from steady menstrual bleeding. Her affliction was social as well as physical since, according to Old Testament ritual laws, both her and anyone touching her were "unclean."

1. What would you consider to be the worst of this woman's problems?
   a. her physical suffering
   b. spending all her money in vain
   c. being a social outcast
   d. always being religiously impure
   e. guilt and low self-esteem

2. What do you think gave her the courage to touch Jesus' clothes?
   a. She didn't have anything to lose.
   b. She was desperate.
   c. She believed she'd be healed.
   d. She thought she could slip away unnoticed.

3. Why was it so important to Jesus that the person who touched him be identified?
   a. so Jesus could see who it was
   b. so the crowd would know a miracle had taken place

c. so he could point out that the woman's faith had healed her
d. so the woman could know she was accepted and given God's peace
e. so it would be clear her physical healing included social healing

4. What would have caused the woman's fearful reaction in verse 33?
   a. fear of what the crowd would do
   b. fear of Jesus shaming her
   c. fear her healing would be revoked
   d. years of failure and rejection

5. In what way does this woman most remind you of yourself?
   a. having pain that no one can heal
   b. struggling with finances
   c. feeling emotionally alone
   d. feeling spiritually impure
   e. being shy about asking for help
   f. being shy about sharing what Christ has done for me

6. When do you remember being the most desperate for God's help? How did Jesus "touch" you?

7. 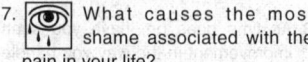 What causes the most shame associated with the pain in your life?
   a. the guilt I feel just for being sick

b. that my prayers aren't working
c. all the money my illness has cost
d. being such a burden to others
e. relying on medicine/pain relievers

8. What obstacles do you (or did you) need to "push through" to bring yourself in contact with the healing power of Jesus?
   a. anger toward those who hurt me
   b. fear of rejection
   c. the pain of broken trust
   d. feelings of guilt
   e. doubts that I really can be healed
   f. the stigma of a shameful identity

9. What does this story say about recovery from abuse?
   a. Jesus always has time and compassion for the abused.
   b. Jesus can help the abused become whole.
   c. Jesus understands how one kind of pain causes another.
   d. No one is too shameful for Jesus' touch.

10. What have you appreciated about this course? Is there anything you still want or need to share? What would you like the group to do now?

[36]Ignoring what they said, Jesus told the synagogue ruler, "Don't be afraid; just believe."

[37]He did not let anyone follow him except Peter, James and John the brother of James. [38]When they came to the home of the synagogue ruler, Jesus saw a commotion, with people crying and wailing loudly. [39]He went in and said to them, "Why all this commotion and wailing? The child is not dead but asleep." [40]But they laughed at him.

After he put them all out, he took the child's father and mother and the disciples who were with him, and went in where the child was. [41]He took her by the hand and said to her, *"Talitha koum!"* (which means, "Little girl, I say to you, get up!"). [42]Immediately the girl stood up and walked around (she was twelve years old). At this they were completely astonished. [43]He gave strict orders not to let anyone know about this, and told them to give her something to eat.

A Prophet Without Honor

6 Jesus left there and went to his hometown, accompanied by his disciples. [2]When the Sabbath came, he began to teach in the synagogue, and many who heard him were amazed.

"Where did this man get these things?" they asked. "What's this wisdom that has been given him, that he even does miracles! [3]Isn't this the carpenter? Isn't this Mary's son and the brother of James, Joseph,[a] Judas and Simon? Aren't his sisters here with us?" And they took offense at him.

[4]Jesus said to them, "Only in his hometown, among his relatives and in his own house is a prophet without honor." [5]He could not do any miracles there, except lay his hands on a few sick people and heal them. [6]And he was amazed at their lack of faith.

Jesus Sends Out the Twelve

Then Jesus went around teaching from village to village. [7]Calling the Twelve to him, he sent them out two by two and gave them authority over evil[b] spirits.

[8]These were his instructions: "Take nothing for the journey except a staff—no bread, no bag, no money in your belts. [9]Wear sandals but not an extra tunic. [10]Whenever you enter a house, stay there until you leave that town. [11]And if any place will not welcome you or listen to you, shake the dust off your feet when you leave, as a testimony against them."

[12]They went out and preached that people should repent. [13]They drove out many demons and anointed many sick people with oil and healed them.

John the Baptist Beheaded

[14]King Herod heard about this, for Jesus' name had become well known. Some were saying,[c] "John the Baptist has been raised from the dead, and that is why miraculous powers are at work in him."

[15]Others said, "He is Elijah."

And still others claimed, "He is a prophet, like one of the prophets of long ago."

[16]But when Herod heard this, he said, "John, the man I beheaded, has been raised from the dead!"

[17]For Herod himself had given orders to have John arrested, and he had him bound and put in prison. He did this because of Herodi-

---

for help? **2.** The woman with the bleeding problem spent all her money and a great deal of effort to find a solution for her suffering. How likely are you to try every other option before you take your problem to God?

What childhood escapade of yours do you hear about most often when you visit family?

After these two power draining miracles, what happens when Jesus goes home? Why?

1. How has familiarity with Jesus blocked you from really seeing who he is? What helps you get a fresh look? **2.** How does your family react to your faith in Christ? How does that affect you?

Who in your family overpacks for a trip?

1. What does the disciples' assignment tell you about the kingdom of God? What impact would this have on the villages? **2.** How is the disciples' message like that of John (1:4) and Jesus (1:14–15)?

Where has God sent you to tell about the kingdom? How is it going?

---

1. If you were granted one wish for your next birthday, what would it be? **2.** What quality do you have that your family does not fully appreciate?

1. Why include this flashback to Herod between sending out the disciples (vv. 6–13) and their return (vv. 30–31)? **2.** What drew Herod's attention to Jesus? What was the significance of Elijah and John the Baptist to the people of Jesus' day (see Mt 17:9–13)? Why might people mistake Jesus for one of them? **3.** Why does Herod jail John? What does that reveal

---

[a]3 Greek *Joses*, a variant of *Joseph*   [b]7 Greek *unclean*   [c]14 Some early manuscripts *He was saying*

about Herod? About John? About Herodias? **4.** How do the two "kings"—Jesus and Herod—differ in terms of their kingdoms, character, popularity and use of power?

1. What do you do when God's message leaves you puzzled? **2.** Would you consider John's ministry as a success or a tragedy? **3.** What would the story say to someone facing persecution, then and now? **4.** Do you feel like you deserve a first place ribbon for your spiritual life or a consolation prize?

as, his brother Philip's wife, whom he had married. [18]For John had been saying to Herod, "It is not lawful for you to have your brother's wife." [19]So Herodias nursed a grudge against John and wanted to kill him. But she was not able to, [20]because Herod feared John and protected him, knowing him to be a righteous and holy man. When Herod heard John, he was greatly puzzled[a]; yet he liked to listen to him.

[21]Finally the opportune time came. On his birthday Herod gave a banquet for his high officials and military commanders and the leading men of Galilee. [22]When the daughter of Herodias came in and danced, she pleased Herod and his dinner guests.

The king said to the girl, "Ask me for anything you want, and I'll give it to you." [23]And he promised her with an oath, "Whatever you ask I will give you, up to half my kingdom."

[24]She went out and said to her mother, "What shall I ask for?"

"The head of John the Baptist," she answered.

[25]At once the girl hurried in to the king with the request: "I want you to give me right now the head of John the Baptist on a platter."

[26]The king was greatly distressed, but because of his oaths and his dinner guests, he did not want to refuse her. [27]So he immediately sent an executioner with orders to bring John's head. The man went, beheaded John in the prison, [28]and brought back his head on a platter. He presented it to the girl, and she gave it to her mother. [29]On hearing of this, John's disciples came and took his body and laid it in a tomb.

[a]20 Some early manuscripts he did many things

 *Mark 6:14–29* **JOHN THE BAPTIST BEHEADED**

Though subject to Rome, Herod ruled over Galilee. In this story, Herod faces a dilemma after his step-daughter (Salome) performs what was surely a highly sensual dance.

1. If tabloids existed back then, what would the headlines be?
   a. "Prophet Loses Head Over Girl"
   b. "First Lady in Charge at Palace"
   c. "Popular Preacher Pays the Price for Exotic Dancer"
   d. "John the Baptist Returns From the Dead to Haunt Herod"

2. Of the people involved in the death of John the Baptist, whom do you hold most responsible?
   a. Herodias—because she set up the king out of her spite for John
   b. Herodias' daughter—because she let her mother use her "dirty dancing" to ask for John's head
   c. Herod—because he took his brother's wife, and gave the order to have John beheaded

3. What bothered Herod the most about killing John the Baptist?

   a. his conscience
   b. his fear of a revolt by the people
   c. his fear of insulting his guests
   d. his awareness that John was a righteous man
   e. his being forced to do it by his wife

4. Whom have you hurt so badly in the past that it still bothers your conscience?

5. How important is it to you to please others? When does your desire to please others lead you, like Herod, to do wrong?

6.  Which of the following statements do you agree with, and which do you disagree with?
   a. Sexuality is feeling good about being a guy/girl.
   b. Sexuality brings a great deal of pressure to life.
   c. Sexuality is overly identified with sexual activity.
   d. Sexuality is not overemphasized in our society.
   e. You cannot express your sexuality without being sexually active.

   f. When you have sex apart from marriage, you get used and hurt.

7.  Whom do you see today as an unhealthy role model of sex and sexuality (like Herod and Herodias were)? Whom do you admire as a role model for a healthy view of sex and sexuality?

8. In what way is your "dark side" like Herod's?
   a. I've been tempted to have an affair.
   b. I struggle with being drawn to images like sexy female dancers.
   c. Sometimes I think I'd do anything to please a particular person.
   d. I've acted violently, and regret it.

9. What do you think you need to do about your "dark side"?
   a. ignore it
   b. admit it
   c. enjoy it
   d. exert more effort to suppress it
   e. ask God to forgive my indulging it
   f. invite God's Spirit to empower me
   g. avoid certain tempting situations

Jesus Feeds the Five Thousand

30The apostles gathered around Jesus and reported to him all they had done and taught. **31**Then, because so many people were coming and going that they did not even have a chance to eat, he said to them, "Come with me by yourselves to a quiet place and get some rest."

32So they went away by themselves in a boat to a solitary place. **33**But many who saw them leaving recognized them and ran on foot from all the towns and got there ahead of them. **34**When Jesus landed and saw a large crowd, he had compassion on them, because they were like sheep without a shepherd. So he began teaching them many things.

35By this time it was late in the day, so his disciples came to him. "This is a remote place," they said, "and it's already very late. **36**Send the people away so they can go to the surrounding countryside and villages and buy themselves something to eat."

37But he answered, "You give them something to eat."

They said to him, "That would take eight months of a man's wages[a]! Are we to go and spend that much on bread and give it to them to eat?"

38"How many loaves do you have?" he asked. "Go and see."

When they found out, they said, "Five—and two fish."

39Then Jesus directed them to have all the people sit down in groups on the green grass. **40**So they sat down in groups of hundreds and fifties. **41**Taking the five loaves and the two fish and looking up to heaven, he gave thanks and broke the loaves. Then

a37 Greek *take two hundred denarii*

What was the largest dinner party you ever had? What did you serve? Did everyone have enough to eat?

1. Why did Jesus decide to take the disciples away (v. 31)? What happened as soon as they left? How did the disciples and Jesus differ in the way they viewed the problem? How would you have felt about this intrusion? **2.** What emotions might have been expressed by the disciples in verse 37? **3.** What would you feel as a disciple when you gathered the leftovers? What was the lesson to be learned?

1. How has Jesus fed you when you've been spiritually hungry lately? When you sense that hunger, do you come searching for him, or do you usually try to fill up on something else first? If so, what? Why? **2.** If you went to a solitary place with Jesus, what would you talk about?

    Mark 6:30–44   **JESUS FEEDS THE 5,000**

Jesus had sent the disciples on a ministry trip. After hearing their reports, he now leads them to sail to a different point on the small Sea of Galilee.

1. "Come with me by yourselves to a quiet place and get some rest." If you were one of the disciples, what would you expect?
   a. a quiet little vacation
   b. time to be with Jesus
   c. fun and recreation
   d. anything but people

2. Surprise! There are 5,000 men, plus women and children, waiting on the shore. Now how do you feel?
   a. delighted   d. angry
   b. overwhelmed   e. whipped
   c. compassionate   f. frustrated

3. "You give them something to eat." How would you have reacted to Jesus' statement?
   a. Are you serious?!
   b. We don't have that much "bread"!
   c. I don't believe in giving handouts.
   d. What happened to our vacation?!
   e. Whatever you say, Lord.

4. "How many loaves do you have?" What was Jesus asking the disciples to do?
   a. take inventory of their resources
   b. see how impossible it really was
   c. start with what they had
   d. trust that he had a plan
   e. learn how to give
   f. exercise their faith

5. How do you react when you are faced with an overwhelming sense of need? When do you feel most inadequate and short of resources as you look at the needs around you?

6. Jesus had compassion on the crowd because "they were like sheep without a shepherd." What group of people do you feel the most compassion for? What could you do to act on that compassion? How could this group help you do that?

7. How have you noticed compassion among the people in your group?

8. **$** What is the biggest reason you work hard?

a. to feel good about myself
b. to please others
c. to be successful
d. to fulfill a calling
e. I don't know how to slow down.
f. I was brought up this way.
g. I don't work all that hard.

9. **$** Do you think you get enough rest? What would your family say? What would God say? What could you do to have a healthier balance between work and rest?

10. What is sure to ruin a restful family vacation for you?
a. mosquitoes/jellyfish/ants
b. car trouble
c. seven straight days of rain
d. unfinished business at work/home
e. standing in long lines
f. tight time schedules
g. cranky/misbehaved kids

11. What was the best vacation your family ever took? How can you begin planning for a vacation that will honor the Lord by producing great memories for your children?

he gave them to his disciples to set before the people. He also divided the two fish among them all. ⁴²They all ate and were satisfied, ⁴³and the disciples picked up twelve basketfuls of broken pieces of bread and fish. ⁴⁴The number of the men who had eaten was five thousand.

Jesus Walks on the Water

⁴⁵Immediately Jesus made his disciples get into the boat and go on ahead of him to Bethsaida, while he dismissed the crowd. ⁴⁶After leaving them, he went up on a mountainside to pray.

⁴⁷When evening came, the boat was in the middle of the lake, and he was alone on land. ⁴⁸He saw the disciples straining at the oars, because the wind was against them. About the fourth watch of the night he went out to them, walking on the lake. He was about to pass by them, ⁴⁹but when they saw him walking on the lake, they thought he was a ghost. They cried out, ⁵⁰because they all saw him and were terrified.

Immediately he spoke to them and said, "Take courage! It is I. Don't be afraid." ⁵¹Then he climbed into the boat with them, and the wind died down. They were completely amazed, ⁵²for they had not understood about the loaves; their hearts were hardened.

⁵³When they had crossed over, they landed at Gennesaret and anchored there. ⁵⁴As soon as they got out of the boat, people recognized Jesus. ⁵⁵They ran throughout that whole region and carried the sick on mats to wherever they heard he was. ⁵⁶And wherever he went—into villages, towns or countryside—they placed the sick in the marketplaces. They begged him to let them touch even the edge of his cloak, and all who touched him were healed.

Clean and Unclean

7 The Pharisees and some of the teachers of the law who had come from Jerusalem gathered around Jesus and ²saw some of his disciples eating food with hands that were "unclean," that is, unwashed. ³(The Pharisees and all the Jews do not eat unless they give their hands a ceremonial washing, holding to the tradition of the elders. ⁴When they come from the marketplace they do not eat unless they wash. And they observe many other traditions, such as the washing of cups, pitchers and kettles.ᵃ)

⁵So the Pharisees and teachers of the law asked Jesus, "Why don't your disciples live according to the tradition of the elders instead of eating their food with 'unclean' hands?"

⁶He replied, "Isaiah was right when he prophesied about you hypocrites; as it is written:

> " 'These people honor me with their lips,
>> but their hearts are far from me.
> ⁷They worship me in vain;
>> their teachings are but rules taught by men.'ᵇ

⁸You have let go of the commands of God and are holding on to the traditions of men."

⁹And he said to them: "You have a fine way of setting aside the commands of God in order to observeᶜ your own traditions! ¹⁰For Moses said, 'Honor your father and your mother,'ᵈ and, 'Anyone who curses his father or mother must be put to death.'ᵉ ¹¹But you say that if a man says to his father or mother: 'Whatever help you

---

Do you know how to ice-skate? Windsurf? Water-ski? Float on an inner tube? Have you ever had any memorable experiences while doing any of these things?

1. What is the significance of Jesus' walking on the water and his response to the disciples' terror? How do you think they understood it (see Mt 8:23–27)? 2. What should they have perceived in the lesson of the loaves that would have prepared them for this? Who is Jesus revealing himself to be?

1. How do Jesus' words (v. 50) speak to that storm? 2. The disciples did not understand about the loaves and fish because "their hearts were hardened." What in your life needs to be softened?

---

1. What is the messiest food that you enjoy the most (fried chicken, cotton candy, sloppy joes, tacos, etc.)? 2. What is the most fun you ever had getting dirty?

1. What is the issue debated by the Pharisees and Jesus (v. 15)? Given this debate, how would each define what it means to be spiritual? How does the quote from Isaiah address the issue at hand? 2. Although the traditions were established to help people obey the law, how is it that they ended up overshadowing that law (vv. 8–9)? 3. Something declared "Corban" meant it was dedicated to God, thus it was no longer able to be given away. What does this illustration show about how traditions twisted the law? 4. How does Jesus' idea of being unclean differ from that of the Pharisees? Why doesn't Jesus offer any solution to the problem at this time?

1. Jesus told the Pharisees that fulfilling human traditions can interfere with obeying the commands of God. Have you ever felt like a victim of human, religious traditions in your efforts to obey God? 2. How do you avoid hypocrisy in

---

ᵃ4 Some early manuscripts *pitchers, kettles and dining couches*   ᵇ6,7 Isaiah 29:13
ᶜ9 Some manuscripts *set up*   ᵈ10 Exodus 20:12; Deut. 5:16   ᵉ10 Exodus 21:17; Lev. 20:9

might otherwise have received from me is Corban' (that is, a gift devoted to God), ¹²then you no longer let him do anything for his father or mother. ¹³Thus you nullify the word of God by your tradition that you have handed down. And you do many things like that."

¹⁴Again Jesus called the crowd to him and said, "Listen to me, everyone, and understand this. ¹⁵Nothing outside a man can make him 'unclean' by going into him. Rather, it is what comes out of a man that makes him 'unclean.'ᵃ"

¹⁷After he had left the crowd and entered the house, his disciples asked him about this parable. ¹⁸"Are you so dull?" he asked. "Don't you see that nothing that enters a man from the outside can make him 'unclean'? ¹⁹For it doesn't go into his heart but into his stomach, and then out of his body." (In saying this, Jesus declared all foods "clean.")

²⁰He went on: "What comes out of a man is what makes him 'unclean.' ²¹For from within, out of men's hearts, come evil thoughts, sexual immorality, theft, murder, adultery, ²²greed, malice, deceit, lewdness, envy, slander, arrogance and folly. ²³All these evils come from inside and make a man 'unclean.'"

The Faith of a Syrophoenician Woman

²⁴Jesus left that place and went to the vicinity of Tyre.ᵇ He entered a house and did not want anyone to know it; yet he could not keep his presence secret. ²⁵In fact, as soon as she heard about him, a woman whose little daughter was possessed by an evilᶜ spirit came and fell at his feet. ²⁶The woman was a Greek, born in Syrian Phoenicia. She begged Jesus to drive the demon out of her daughter.

²⁷"First let the children eat all they want," he told her, "for it is not right to take the children's bread and toss it to their dogs."

²⁸"Yes, Lord," she replied, "but even the dogs under the table eat the children's crumbs."

²⁹Then he told her, "For such a reply, you may go; the demon has left your daughter."

³⁰She went home and found her child lying on the bed, and the demon gone.

The Healing of a Deaf and Mute Man

³¹Then Jesus left the vicinity of Tyre and went through Sidon, down to the Sea of Galilee and into the region of the Decapolis.ᵈ ³²There some people brought to him a man who was deaf and could hardly talk, and they begged him to place his hand on the man.

³³After he took him aside, away from the crowd, Jesus put his fingers into the man's ears. Then he spit and touched the man's tongue. ³⁴He looked up to heaven and with a deep sigh said to him, "Ephphatha!" (which means, "Be opened!"). ³⁵At this, the man's ears were opened, his tongue was loosened and he began to speak plainly.

³⁶Jesus commanded them not to tell anyone. But the more he did so, the more they kept talking about it. ³⁷People were overwhelmed with amazement. "He has done everything well," they said. "He even makes the deaf hear and the mute speak."

your life? 3. What changes would you make in your own church to more effectively embrace the commands of God? 4. Have you experienced a conflict between your religious obligations and your obligations to your loved ones? What happened? 5. What is the nicest thing you have ever done for your parents or guardians?

For what would you walk 100 miles out of your way? Why?

1. What is Jesus' point in going to Tyre (a Gentile area) after the discussion in 7:1–23? 2. Were Jesus' words overly harsh? How does this woman respond? How does her reply show faith? 3. What message is Jesus giving by this healing?

How does Jesus care for the "unclean" in your community? How might you be his hands and feet for them?

1. If you were to become deaf, what sound would you miss hearing the most? 2. If you were to become unable to speak, what would you miss saying?

1. Why do you think Jesus used this method to heal the man? 2. How is the response of these Gentiles (v. 37) like that of the Jews (1:27; 2:12) and the disciples (4:41)? What is Mark's point in emphasizing this?

1. How has your grasp of who Jesus is changed over the past five years? 2. What can you do this week to show friendship to someone who is alone? 3. What would you like Jesus to help you hear or say?

ᵃ15 Some early manuscripts 'unclean.' ¹⁶If anyone has ears to hear, let him hear. ᵇ24 Many early manuscripts Tyre and Sidon   ᶜ25 Greek unclean   ᵈ31 That is, the Ten Cities

How did your parents complete this sentence when you were a child: "How many times do I have to tell you ..."?

1. How does this feeding compare and contrast with that of 6:30–44? 2. In light of all the miracles that Jesus had already done, why would the Pharisees "demand a sign from heaven"? How would they have responded if Jesus had provided one? 3. From what you have seen of the Pharisees and Herod so far, what does Jesus mean by his warning in verse 15? How does their "yeast" differ from Jesus' "bread"? How do the disciples interpret Jesus' comments here? 4. With what tone of voice do you hear Jesus saying verses 17–21? Why? 5. What is Jesus' point in highlighting the numbers "12" and "7"? What should the disciples understand about Jesus from these numbers? How are they like and unlike the Pharisees (vv. 11–12)?

1. Do you sometimes doubt Jesus' ability to meet your needs? How so? How are you discovering that he really can shepherd you? In what areas are you still unsure about that? 2. How can you recognize where the "yeast of the Pharisees and Herod" is still active today? How does it show in the way people relate to God? To one another? 3. What does "hardness of heart" mean to you? How has Jesus made your heart softer? What part is still hard?

If you lost your sight, what would you miss seeing the most?

1. Why does Jesus take the man outside the city to heal him? 2. What is Jesus' point in healing him in stages, not all at once?

As for understanding Jesus, are you: (a) Almost blind? (b) Seeing blurred shapes? (c) Enjoying 20/20 vision? Explain.

Jesus Feeds the Four Thousand

8 During those days another large crowd gathered. Since they had nothing to eat, Jesus called his disciples to him and said, 2"I have compassion for these people; they have already been with me three days and have nothing to eat. 3If I send them home hungry, they will collapse on the way, because some of them have come a long distance."

4His disciples answered, "But where in this remote place can anyone get enough bread to feed them?"

5"How many loaves do you have?" Jesus asked.

"Seven," they replied.

6He told the crowd to sit down on the ground. When he had taken the seven loaves and given thanks, he broke them and gave them to his disciples to set before the people, and they did so. 7They had a few small fish as well; he gave thanks for them also and told the disciples to distribute them. 8The people ate and were satisfied. Afterward the disciples picked up seven basketfuls of broken pieces that were left over. 9About four thousand men were present. And having sent them away, 10he got into the boat with his disciples and went to the region of Dalmanutha.

11The Pharisees came and began to question Jesus. To test him, they asked him for a sign from heaven. 12He sighed deeply and said, "Why does this generation ask for a miraculous sign? I tell you the truth, no sign will be given to it." 13Then he left them, got back into the boat and crossed to the other side.

The Yeast of the Pharisees and Herod

14The disciples had forgotten to bring bread, except for one loaf they had with them in the boat. 15"Be careful," Jesus warned them. "Watch out for the yeast of the Pharisees and that of Herod."

16They discussed this with one another and said, "It is because we have no bread."

17Aware of their discussion, Jesus asked them: "Why are you talking about having no bread? Do you still not see or understand? Are your hearts hardened? 18Do you have eyes but fail to see, and ears but fail to hear? And don't you remember? 19When I broke the five loaves for the five thousand, how many basketfuls of pieces did you pick up?"

"Twelve," they replied.

20"And when I broke the seven loaves for the four thousand, how many basketfuls of pieces did you pick up?"

They answered, "Seven."

21He said to them, "Do you still not understand?"

The Healing of a Blind Man at Bethsaida

22They came to Bethsaida, and some people brought a blind man and begged Jesus to touch him. 23He took the blind man by the hand and led him outside the village. When he had spit on the man's eyes and put his hands on him, Jesus asked, "Do you see anything?"

24He looked up and said, "I see people; they look like trees walking around."

25Once more Jesus put his hands on the man's eyes. Then his eyes were opened, his sight was restored, and he saw everything clearly. 26Jesus sent him home, saying, "Don't go into the village.ᵃ"

ᵃ26 Some manuscripts *Don't go and tell anyone in the village*

Peter's Confession of Christ

²⁷Jesus and his disciples went on to the villages around Caesarea Philippi. On the way he asked them, "Who do people say I am?" ²⁸They replied, "Some say John the Baptist; others say Elijah; and still others, one of the prophets."

²⁹"But what about you?" he asked. "Who do you say I am?" Peter answered, "You are the Christ.^a"

³⁰Jesus warned them not to tell anyone about him.

Jesus Predicts His Death

³¹He then began to teach them that the Son of Man must suffer many things and be rejected by the elders, chief priests and teachers of the law, and that he must be killed and after three days rise again. ³²He spoke plainly about this, and Peter took him aside and began to rebuke him.

³³But when Jesus turned and looked at his disciples, he rebuked Peter. "Get behind me, Satan!" he said. "You do not have in mind the things of God, but the things of men."

³⁴Then he called the crowd to him along with his disciples and said: "If anyone would come after me, he must deny himself and take up his cross and follow me. ³⁵For whoever wants to save his life^b will lose it, but whoever loses his life for me and for the gospel will save it. ³⁶What good is it for a man to gain the whole world, yet forfeit his soul? ³⁷Or what can a man give in exchange for his soul? ³⁸If anyone is ashamed of me and my words in this adulterous and sinful generation, the Son of Man will be ashamed of him when he comes in his Father's glory with the holy angels."

9 And he said to them, "I tell you the truth, some who are standing here will not taste death before they see the kingdom of God come with power."

The Transfiguration

²After six days Jesus took Peter, James and John with him and led them up a high mountain, where they were all alone. There he was transfigured before them. ³His clothes became dazzling white, whiter than anyone in the world could bleach them. ⁴And there appeared before them Elijah and Moses, who were talking with Jesus.

⁵Peter said to Jesus, "Rabbi, it is good for us to be here. Let us put up three shelters—one for you, one for Moses and one for Elijah." ⁶(He did not know what to say, they were so frightened.)

⁷Then a cloud appeared and enveloped them, and a voice came from the cloud: "This is my Son, whom I love. Listen to him!"

⁸Suddenly, when they looked around, they no longer saw anyone with them except Jesus.

⁹As they were coming down the mountain, Jesus gave them orders not to tell anyone what they had seen until the Son of Man had risen from the dead. ¹⁰They kept the matter to themselves, discussing what "rising from the dead" meant.

¹¹And they asked him, "Why do the teachers of the law say that Elijah must come first?"

¹²Jesus replied, "To be sure, Elijah does come first, and restores all things. Why then is it written that the Son of Man must suffer much and be rejected? ¹³But I tell you, Elijah has come, and they have done to him everything they wished, just as it is written about him."

---

1. What was your nickname in school? 2. What do you do when someone says something you do not want to hear?

1. Thus far, what answers have been given to Jesus' poll (v. 27; see 3:21–22; 4:41; 6:3, 14–15)? 2. How and why does the tone of the Gospel shift after Peter's declaration? 3. What title does Jesus take on, and why (see Da 7:13–14)? What four things does he prophesy about the Son of Man? Why does Jesus react so strongly to Peter? 4. How would you paraphrase what Jesus says in verse 34? How do Herod and John (6:14–29) display the "life-saving" principle (vv. 35–36)? What does it really mean to believe in Jesus?

1. What do you do when you are angry at God? 2. How has your relationship with Jesus affected your lifestyle? Relationships? Priorities? Politics? 3. Where does Jesus' way conflict with your way? What do you stand to lose by following Christ? What do you stand to gain?

---

1. If you could take three people up a mountain to meet God, whom would you take and why? 2. Where is one outdoor location you feel especially close to God?

1. What is the connection between 9:1 and this event? 2. What do you imagine this scene was like? What is the significance of Moses' and Elijah's presence? Of the voice (see 1:11)? Why would this event be important for the disciples? 3. Who played the role of Elijah (see Mt 17:10–13)? With what result (6:14–29)? How could John the Baptist's experience help the disciples understand the nature of Jesus' Messiahship?

1. Where have you grasped a bit of Jesus' glory in a special way? 2. How does the picture of a suffering Messiah shape your view of what the Christian life is all about?

---

^a29 Or *Messiah.* "The Christ" (Greek) and "the Messiah" (Hebrew) both mean "the Anointed One."   *^b35* The Greek word means either *life* or *soul*; also in verse 36.

When you were a child, what issues were most likely to trigger an argument within your family?

1. While the three disciples were up on the mountain, what problem were the other nine having? How did they deal with it? What do you think the argument was about in verse 14? **2.** As the boy's father, how would you feel during this argument? **3.** How do the contrasts between this story and the transfiguration account for Jesus' response (v. 19)? **4.** What is the major difference between Jesus' teaching in 8:31 and 9:30–32? What is significant about this difference?

1. Whom do you identify with in the story of the demon-possessed boy: Someone watching from the crowd? The Pharisees? The disciples? The little boy? The boy's father? **2.** When have you felt like the father in verse 24? How do prayer and faith relate for you at those times? **3.** Where do you learn more—during spiritual highs or lows? **4.** How can you live with the full reality of evil and yet with strong awareness of

The Healing of a Boy With an Evil Spirit

¹⁴When they came to the other disciples, they saw a large crowd around them and the teachers of the law arguing with them. ¹⁵As soon as all the people saw Jesus, they were overwhelmed with wonder and ran to greet him.

¹⁶"What are you arguing with them about?" he asked.

¹⁷A man in the crowd answered, "Teacher, I brought you my son, who is possessed by a spirit that has robbed him of speech. ¹⁸Whenever it seizes him, it throws him to the ground. He foams at the mouth, gnashes his teeth and becomes rigid. I asked your disciples to drive out the spirit, but they could not."

¹⁹"O unbelieving generation," Jesus replied, "how long shall I stay with you? How long shall I put up with you? Bring the boy to me."

²⁰So they brought him. When the spirit saw Jesus, it immediately threw the boy into a convulsion. He fell to the ground and rolled around, foaming at the mouth.

²¹Jesus asked the boy's father, "How long has he been like this?"

"From childhood," he answered. ²²"It has often thrown him into fire or water to kill him. But if you can do anything, take pity on us and help us."

²³"'If you can'?" said Jesus. "Everything is possible for him who believes."

²⁴Immediately the boy's father exclaimed, "I do believe; help me overcome my unbelief!"

²⁵When Jesus saw that a crowd was running to the scene, he

 Mark 9:2–13   **THE TRANSFIGURATION**

1. Why do you think Jesus took time for a trip to the mountains not long before his death?
   a. to get away from people
   b. to spend time with God
   c. to prepare for what was ahead
   d. to reveal himself in his glorified state to his three closest disciples
   e. to receive Moses' and Elijah's encouragement
   f. for these two great Old Testament characters to bear witness that Jesus was the Messiah

2. How would you have felt if you had been there when Jesus' form changed and Elijah and Moses appeared?
   a. totally awed   d. on a high
   b. out of place   e. like hiding
   c. scared spitless

3. Why did Peter suggest building three shelters?
   a. to honor Elijah, Moses and Jesus
   b. to memorialize the occasion
   c. to keep the mountaintop feeling
   d. He enjoyed camping.
   e. He had "foot in mouth disease."

f. He hoped this meant Jesus had come into his kingdom without the suffering he had told them about.

4. What is the meaning of the words, "This is my Son, whom I love. Listen to him"?
   a. Shut up a minute.
   b. Forget about building anything.
   c. The splendor you have seen is proof that Jesus is my Son.
   d. My Son has all my authority.

5. As they came down the mountain, what do you think the disciples concluded about Jesus' words regarding his suffering and death?
   a. It makes sense.
   b. It doesn't make sense.
   c. We need more information.
   d. It conflicts with what we know about the Messiah.

6. How did you come to realize that Jesus was the one above all others you should listen to? What keeps you from being a better listener?

7. What spot for you is like the Mount of

Transfiguration—where you grasped Jesus' glory in a special way?

8. When was your most recent mountaintop experience with God?
   a. a long time ago
   b. recently
   c. right now
   d. I've never had one.

9. How would you describe your relationship with God now?
   a. in the valley
   b. climbing the mountain
   c. on the mountaintop
   d. on the rocks

10. Jesus was perfect and complete in and of himself. What needs to happen for you to feel like a "whole in one" as a single person? How has this course helped you in that process?

11. Have each person listen in silence as other group members affirm how that person demonstrates one aspect of personal "wholeness."

rebuked the evil*a* spirit. "You deaf and mute spirit," he said, "I command you, come out of him and never enter him again."

26The spirit shrieked, convulsed him violently and came out. The boy looked so much like a corpse that many said, "He's dead." **27**But Jesus took him by the hand and lifted him to his feet, and he stood up.

28After Jesus had gone indoors, his disciples asked him privately, "Why couldn't we drive it out?"

29He replied, "This kind can come out only by prayer.*b*"

30They left that place and passed through Galilee. Jesus did not want anyone to know where they were, **31**because he was teaching his disciples. He said to them, "The Son of Man is going to be betrayed into the hands of men. They will kill him, and after three days he will rise." **32**But they did not understand what he meant and were afraid to ask him about it.

Who Is the Greatest?

33They came to Capernaum. When he was in the house, he asked them, "What were you arguing about on the road?" **34**But they kept quiet because on the way they had argued about who was the greatest.

35Sitting down, Jesus called the Twelve and said, "If anyone wants to be first, he must be the very last, and the servant of all."

36He took a little child and had him stand among them. Taking him in his arms, he said to them, **37**"Whoever welcomes one of these little children in my name welcomes me; and whoever welcomes me does not welcome me but the one who sent me."

a25 Greek *unclean*   *b29* Some manuscripts *prayer and fasting*

God's transforming power? In what way do you feel that tension now? **5.** What possibilities and what abuses come to mind when you ponder the fact that "everything is possible for him who believes" (v. 23)?

What one childhood quality would you like to recapture?

1. As a disciple, how would you feel when Jesus asked about the argument? Why does Jesus use the child as an object lesson on true greatness in the kingdom? **2.** What does it mean to do something "in Jesus' name"?

1. What can you do in Jesus' name? **2.** How does Jesus' idea of success differ from success portrayed by television or pursued

---

 Mark 9:14–29   **THE HEALING OF A BOY WITH AN EVIL SPIRIT**

1. How would you describe the father in this story?
   a. a parent who had been disappointed a few too many times
   b. a skeptic who had little faith
   c. a man who was doing his best to have faith
   d. a person of faith who was honest enough to admit his doubts

2. Whom do you identify with most in this story?
   a. the disciples—because I never seem to give people the help they need
   b. the boy—because I often feel like I'm controlled by evil
   c. the father—because I find it hard to believe sometimes
   d. Jesus—because I get called in to fix things when others mess up

3. What do you learn about evil spirits from this story?
   a. I think there must be some other explanation.
   b. They are very real.
   c. They are very powerful.
   d. Jesus has authority over them.

e. Some are harder to cast out than others.
   f. Confronting them should be done with prayer.

4. What would you call the father's statement, "I do believe; help me overcome my unbelief"?
   a. contradictory
   b. wishy-washy
   c. an honest statement, because no one is entirely without doubt
   d. a good example, for we all need God's help to overcome unbelief
   e. encouraging, because it shows that healing from God is not dependent on our having perfect faith

5. When Jesus tells you, "Everything is possible for him who believes," which aspect of the father's response is closer to your own: "I believe" or "Help me overcome my unbelief"?

6. What do you have the hardest time believing?
   a. that God exists at all
   b. that Jesus is God's Son

c. that a good God controls the world
   d. that there is life after death
   e. that God loves me
   f. that miracles can occur today
   g. other:_____

7. What do you believe that you wish you could believe more intensely?

8. What kind of doubts hit you the hardest?
   a. spiritual—questions like "Can my life please God?"
   b. family—questions like "Am I failing as a husband/father?"
   c. vocational—questions like "Will I make it in my work life?"
   d. personal—questions like "Will I always have these weaknesses and struggles?"

9. What would help silence the doubts you feel?
   a. admit that I have them
   b. more Bible study and prayer
   c. gleaning from those who can share how God helped them
   d. some miracle, like in the Bible
   e. people who will pray for me

by most people? Have you ever let your relationship with Christ get polluted by using your relationship with him for status, power or earthly success? What happened? **3.** What Christian groups do you tend to bad-mouth because they are "not one of us"? Why? What is Jesus' point for you here?

If you had to give up a hand, a foot or an eye, which would you give up and why?

1. What four things does Jesus say are "better"? What is his point in using this hyperbole? **2.** How does the admonition to be at peace (v. 50) relate to verses 42–49?

1. Short of amputating body parts, what do you need to cut out of your life in order to avoid sin? **2.** What can you do to "salt" your relationships with peace this week?

Who had the best marriage you have ever seen? Why was it so special?

1. How were the Pharisees trying to test Jesus by their question? What was their view on divorce (see Dt 24:1,3)? **2.** Instead of answering their question, how does Jesus test them by emphasizing God's intent for marriage (see Mt 19:1–12)?

1. How can you apply the principles of marriage underlined here? **2.** Do you think Jesus would respond the same to someone in a troubled marriage who was sincerely asking the question in verse 2? Why or why not?

---

1. When are you most likely to lose patience with little children? When do you really like them? **2.** Did you choose the job you are in for (a) money, (b) fulfillment, or (c) the chance to make a contribution?

1. Why would the disciples want to keep the children away from Jesus? What childlike qualities was Jesus encouraging

Whoever Is Not Against Us Is for Us

38"Teacher," said John, "we saw a man driving out demons in your name and we told him to stop, because he was not one of us."

39"Do not stop him," Jesus said. "No one who does a miracle in my name can in the next moment say anything bad about me, **40**for whoever is not against us is for us. **41**I tell you the truth, anyone who gives you a cup of water in my name because you belong to Christ will certainly not lose his reward.

Causing to Sin

42"And if anyone causes one of these little ones who believe in me to sin, it would be better for him to be thrown into the sea with a large millstone tied around his neck. **43**If your hand causes you to sin, cut it off. It is better for you to enter life maimed than with two hands to go into hell, where the fire never goes out.[a] **45**And if your foot causes you to sin, cut it off. It is better for you to enter life crippled than to have two feet and be thrown into hell.[b] **47**And if your eye causes you to sin, pluck it out. It is better for you to enter the kingdom of God with one eye than to have two eyes and be thrown into hell, **48**where

> " 'their worm does not die,
> and the fire is not quenched.'[c]

49Everyone will be salted with fire.

50"Salt is good, but if it loses its saltiness, how can you make it salty again? Have salt in yourselves, and be at peace with each other."

Divorce

10 Jesus then left that place and went into the region of Judea and across the Jordan. Again crowds of people came to him, and as was his custom, he taught them.

2Some Pharisees came and tested him by asking, "Is it lawful for a man to divorce his wife?"

3"What did Moses command you?" he replied.

4They said, "Moses permitted a man to write a certificate of divorce and send her away."

5"It was because your hearts were hard that Moses wrote you this law," Jesus replied. **6**"But at the beginning of creation God 'made them male and female.'[d] **7**'For this reason a man will leave his father and mother and be united to his wife,[e] **8**and the two will become one flesh.'[f] So they are no longer two, but one. **9**Therefore what God has joined together, let man not separate."

10When they were in the house again, the disciples asked Jesus about this. **11**He answered, "Anyone who divorces his wife and marries another woman commits adultery against her. **12**And if she divorces her husband and marries another man, she commits adultery."

The Little Children and Jesus

13People were bringing little children to Jesus to have him touch them, but the disciples rebuked them. **14**When Jesus saw this, he was indignant. He said to them, "Let the little children come to me, and do not hinder them, for the kingdom of God belongs to such as these. **15**I tell you the truth, anyone who will not receive

---

[a]43 Some manuscripts *out,* 44*where / " 'their worm does not die, / and the fire is not quenched.'* [b]45 Some manuscripts *hell,* 46*where / " 'their worm does not die, / and the fire is not quenched.'* [c]48 Isaiah 66:24 [d]6 Gen. 1:27 [e]7 Some early manuscripts do not have *and be united to his wife.* [f]8 Gen. 2:24

the kingdom of God like a little child will never enter it." ¹⁶And he took the children in his arms, put his hands on them and blessed them.

The Rich Young Man

¹⁷As Jesus started on his way, a man ran up to him and fell on his knees before him. "Good teacher," he asked, "what must I do to inherit eternal life?"

¹⁸"Why do you call me good?" Jesus answered. "No one is good—except God alone. ¹⁹You know the commandments: 'Do not murder, do not commit adultery, do not steal, do not give false testimony, do not defraud, honor your father and mother.'ᵃ"

²⁰"Teacher," he declared, "all these I have kept since I was a boy."

²¹Jesus looked at him and loved him. "One thing you lack," he said. "Go, sell everything you have and give to the poor, and you will have treasure in heaven. Then come, follow me."

²²At this the man's face fell. He went away sad, because he had great wealth.

²³Jesus looked around and said to his disciples, "How hard it is for the rich to enter the kingdom of God!"

²⁴The disciples were amazed at his words. But Jesus said again, "Children, how hard it isᵇ to enter the kingdom of God! ²⁵It is easier for a camel to go through the eye of a needle than for a rich man to enter the kingdom of God."

²⁶The disciples were even more amazed, and said to each other, "Who then can be saved?"

ᵃ19 Exodus 20:12-16; Deut. 5:16-20   ᵇ24 Some manuscripts is for those who trust in riches

(vv. 13–16)? **2.** How does the man's question (v. 17) compare with what Jesus had just taught about the kingdom (v. 15)? What was his assumption about how one gains the kingdom? **3.** What is Jesus trying to drive home by responding to the way the man addressed him? **4.** Jesus quizzes the man on only a partial list of the Ten Commandments (see Ex 20). How well might the man have obeyed the ones relating directly to God? **5.** Why does Jesus command the man as he does (v. 21; see also 8:34)? What does his response reveal which had been hidden by his good works? **6.** What does the disciples' shock reveal about them? On what basis is it possible for anyone to receive the kingdom? **7.** How is the promise (vv. 29–30) to come true for believers?

♡ **1.** Are you more like the rich young man or the children (vv. 13–16) in terms of the way you approach God? Why? **2.** What has helped you to see the impossibility of earning the kingdom? As a result, how have you experienced the gift of the kingdom as described in verses 29–30? **3.** What in your life could Jesus point to as something

---

 Mark 10:17–31   **THE RICH YOUNG MAN**

1. What do you think motivated the man to ask Jesus his question?
   a. He was testing Jesus' knowledge as a teacher.
   b. He was sincerely searching to know spiritual truth.
   c. He was feeling self-righteous and wanted affirmation from Jesus.
   d. He had everything, except an "eternal life insurance policy."

2. What did Jesus mean by his reply, "Why do you call me good? No one is good—except God alone"?
   a. Take a close look at who I am.
   b. I'm not "good."
   c. I'm not on God's level.
   d. Your only hope for goodness is to rely on God.

3. Jesus asked the man to sell all his possessions and give the money to the poor because Jesus knew:
   a. the poor needed the money.
   b. the man was greedy.
   c. as long as the man was rich he wouldn't be able to trust God.
   d. the man's money was his god.

4. By choosing his wealth over a relationship with Jesus, what was the rich man gaining? What was he losing?

5. According to verses 29–31, what might you lose by following Christ? What will you gain? Which carries the greater sacrifice?

6. What is Jesus teaching us in this passage?
   a. Commitment to him must be total.
   b. Wealth is evil.
   c. Following Jesus means sacrifice.
   d. Eternal life is more important than earthly life.
   e. Giving is part of discipleship.
   f. We can only be saved by God's doing, not our own.

7. What would you do if Jesus asked you to sell everything you had and give the proceeds to the poor?
   a. have my hearing checked
   b. compute my net worth and think about it
   c. hold a garage sale this Saturday
   d. increase my pledge to the church
   e. sadly walk away

8. Jesus "looked at him and loved him" and invited the man to follow him. Have you ever had to choose between material comforts and Christ's love?

9. Name one thing you can do this week to let go of material things and embrace God's kingdom more fully.

10. If Jesus were to evaluate your life and say, "One thing you lack"—what do you think that one thing would be?

11. What does this story say about "success"? What would you say is your greatest success unrelated to your profession (or making money)?

12. What holds you back from being totally committed to Christ?
    a. wealth
    b. apathy
    c. pride
    d. habits or temptations
    e. doubts about issues of faith
    f. fear of being labeled a fanatic

that is preventing you from receiving the kingdom?

1. If you had one week to live, how would you spend your time? **2.** What did your parents want you to be when you grew up?

1. Why would going to Jerusalem cause the disciples to be astonished and afraid? **2.** When Jesus said, "What do you want me to do for you?" to James and John, what tone of voice do you think he used? **3.** What view of the kingdom are James and John still clinging to? How could they respond like this in light of verses 33–34? **4.** What is the *cup*, the *baptism* and the *glory* as each applies to Jesus? As each applies to the disciples? **5.** What made the other disciples indignant? **6.** How does Jesus use

²⁷Jesus looked at them and said, "With man this is impossible, but not with God; all things are possible with God."

²⁸Peter said to him, "We have left everything to follow you!"

²⁹"I tell you the truth," Jesus replied, "no one who has left home or brothers or sisters or mother or father or children or fields for me and the gospel ³⁰will fail to receive a hundred times as much in this present age (homes, brothers, sisters, mothers, children and fields—and with them, persecutions) and in the age to come, eternal life. ³¹But many who are first will be last, and the last first."

Jesus Again Predicts His Death

³²They were on their way up to Jerusalem, with Jesus leading the way, and the disciples were astonished, while those who followed were afraid. Again he took the Twelve aside and told them what was going to happen to him. ³³"We are going up to Jerusalem," he said, "and the Son of Man will be betrayed to the chief priests and teachers of the law. They will condemn him to death and will hand him over to the Gentiles, ³⁴who will mock him and spit on him, flog him and kill him. Three days later he will rise."

The Request of James and John

³⁵Then James and John, the sons of Zebedee, came to him. "Teacher," they said, "we want you to do for us whatever we ask."

³⁶"What do you want me to do for you?" he asked.

³⁷They replied, "Let one of us sit at your right and the other at your left in your glory."

³⁸"You don't know what you are asking," Jesus said. "Can you

$ 👤   Mark 10:35–45   THE REQUEST OF JAMES AND JOHN

Jesus has just taken the 12 disciples aside to tell them about his approaching death. Now two of the disciples, James and his brother John, come to Jesus with a request.

1. What were James and John really wanting in their request?
a. a close relationship with God
b. power and position
c. special recognition
d. spiritual security
e. parental approval

2. "You don't know what you are asking?" What did Jesus' reply mean?
a. You've got to be kidding!
b. What you ask is impossible.
c. You don't deserve it.
d. It's not my decision to make.
e. You don't understand what following me is all about.

3. What was Jesus referring to when he asked, "Can you drink the cup I am going to drink?"
a. royal dinnerware
b. divine authority
c. suffering and death
d. future glory

4. Why were the other 10 disciples upset with James and John? How did Jesus use this uproar to convey new insights about the meaning of true greatness?

5. Which of the following is typical of people in positions of authority?
a. expecting others to serve them
b. taking advantage of other people
c. using their position to serve
d. using their position to get ahead
e. not caring about other people

6. What does being a "slave of all" mean?
a. doing menial tasks for everyone
b. following the example of Christ
c. allowing others to treat you poorly
d. considering others' interests over your own

7. Who has been an example to you of a Christlike servant? What effect has that person had on your life?

8. How does Jesus practice what he preached—as the ultimate servant? When and how have you responded to Christ as your "ransom"?

9. **$** What is the *best* thing about your relationships at work?
a. Say what?!
b. humor and camaraderie
c. accomplishing goals together
d. spending time together after hours
e. working with other Christians
f. other:_____

10. **$** What is the *worst* thing about your relationships at work?
a. employer/employee tensions
b. backbiting and gossip
c. jealousy and competition
d. authority issues
e. personality clashes
f. clashes regarding faith or values
g. other:_____

11. 👤 What advantages does being single have when it comes to serving God and others? Would getting married have a positive or negative effect on your servanthood?

12. 👤 How have you experienced Christlike servanthood in this group?

drink the cup I drink or be baptized with the baptism I am baptized with?"

³⁹"We can," they answered.

Jesus said to them, "You will drink the cup I drink and be baptized with the baptism I am baptized with, ⁴⁰but to sit at my right or left is not for me to grant. These places belong to those for whom they have been prepared."

⁴¹When the ten heard about this, they became indignant with James and John. ⁴²Jesus called them together and said, "You know that those who are regarded as rulers of the Gentiles lord it over them, and their high officials exercise authority over them. ⁴³Not so with you. Instead, whoever wants to become great among you must be your servant, ⁴⁴and whoever wants to be first must be slave of all. ⁴⁵For even the Son of Man did not come to be served, but to serve, and to give his life as a ransom for many."

Blind Bartimaeus Receives His Sight

⁴⁶Then they came to Jericho. As Jesus and his disciples, together with a large crowd, were leaving the city, a blind man, Bartimaeus (that is, the Son of Timaeus), was sitting by the roadside begging. ⁴⁷When he heard that it was Jesus of Nazareth, he began to shout, "Jesus, Son of David, have mercy on me!"

⁴⁸Many rebuked him and told him to be quiet, but he shouted all the more, "Son of David, have mercy on me!"

⁴⁹Jesus stopped and said, "Call him."

So they called to the blind man, "Cheer up! On your feet! He's calling you." ⁵⁰Throwing his cloak aside, he jumped to his feet and came to Jesus.

⁵¹"What do you want me to do for you?" Jesus asked him.

The blind man said, "Rabbi, I want to see."

⁵²"Go," said Jesus, "your faith has healed you." Immediately he received his sight and followed Jesus along the road.

The Triumphal Entry

11 As they approached Jerusalem and came to Bethphage and Bethany at the Mount of Olives, Jesus sent two of his disciples, ²saying to them, "Go to the village ahead of you, and just as you enter it, you will find a colt tied there, which no one has ever ridden. Untie it and bring it here. ³If anyone asks you, 'Why are you doing this?' tell him, 'The Lord needs it and will send it back here shortly.'"

⁴They went and found a colt outside in the street, tied at a doorway. As they untied it, ⁵some people standing there asked, "What are you doing, untying that colt?" ⁶They answered as Jesus had told them to, and the people let them go. ⁷When they brought the colt to Jesus and threw their cloaks over it, he sat on it. ⁸Many people spread their cloaks on the road, while others spread branches they had cut in the fields. ⁹Those who went ahead and those who followed shouted,

"Hosanna!ᵃ"

"Blessed is he who comes in the name of the Lord!"ᵇ

¹⁰"Blessed is the coming kingdom of our father David!"

"Hosanna in the highest!"

ᵃ9 A Hebrew expression meaning "Save!" which became an exclamation of praise; also in verse 10   ᵇ9 Psalm 118:25,26

this uproar to convey new insights into his greatness? 7. How does Jesus practice what he preached? In this context, what is a "ransom for many"? How is the death of Christ the ultimate service to all?

1. Do you find yourself desiring to sit next to God? 2. Do you resist following the servant's path to greatness? Why? 3. What one way could you serve this week?

How do you respond when a beggar approaches you on the street? Why?

1. What is significant about the way Bartimaeus addresses Jesus? How does Bartimaeus show his faith (while the crowd does not)? 2. How is Bartimaeus different from the rich young man in 10:17–22? 3. Why is there no "order of silence" here (as in 7:36)?

If Jesus asked you, "What do you want me to do for you?" what would you say?

What is the closest you have come to meeting a world leader or celebrity?

1. Jesus always does the unexpected. What was unexpected about the way he entered Jerusalem? 2. In light of the response he received, what were the expectations of the crowd? The disciples (see 10:37)? Jesus? 3. What do you find most significant about the triumphal entry into Jerusalem?

1. How did Jesus ride into your life: As a Conquering Hero forcing you into submission? As a Gentle King bearing peace? As a White Knight rescuing you? How about now? 2. Have you ever misunderstood Jesus' purposes, praising him one day and despairing the next?

¹¹Jesus entered Jerusalem and went to the temple. He looked around at everything, but since it was already late, he went out to Bethany with the Twelve.

Jesus Clears the Temple

¹²The next day as they were leaving Bethany, Jesus was hungry. ¹³Seeing in the distance a fig tree in leaf, he went to find out if it had any fruit. When he reached it, he found nothing but leaves, because it was not the season for figs. ¹⁴Then he said to the tree, "May no one ever eat fruit from you again." And his disciples heard him say it.

¹⁵On reaching Jerusalem, Jesus entered the temple area and began driving out those who were buying and selling there. He overturned the tables of the money changers and the benches of those selling doves, ¹⁶and would not allow anyone to carry merchandise through the temple courts. ¹⁷And as he taught them, he said, "Is it not written:

> " 'My house will be called
> a house of prayer for all nations'^a?

But you have made it 'a den of robbers.'^b"

¹⁸The chief priests and the teachers of the law heard this and began looking for a way to kill him, for they feared him, because the whole crowd was amazed at his teaching. ¹⁹When evening came, they^c went out of the city.

a17 Isaiah 56:7   *b17* Jer. 7:11   *c19* Some early manuscripts *he*

If you could change one thing about modern Christianity, what would it be?

1. How does the story of the fig tree relate to the clearing of the temple (vv. 13–14, 20–21)? In what ways did the Pharisees cover their fruitlessness with flashy foliage? **2.** This profiteering on the sale of sacrificial animals took place in the only area where Gentiles could worship. Why would that especially anger Jesus (see Isa 56:6–8)? What was Jesus threatening when he called the temple a "den of robbers" (see Jer 7:9–15)? **3.** Why was Peter amazed (vv. 20–21)? Should he have been? What conditions for effective prayer are upheld here?

1. If you were a tree, what would help you produce more fruit: Pruning? Watering? Staking? Transplanting? Fertilizing? Why? **2.** Like the temple, no church is perfect. What have you

---

Mark 11:12–19   **JESUS CLEARS THE TEMPLE**

As Passover approaches, Jesus confronts abuses in the temple. Pilgrims needed to buy animals approved for sacrifice and have their money changed into the local currency for the annual temple tax. They were grossly cheated in both transactions. In addition, these chaotic activities took place in the court of the Gentiles, the only part of the temple in which God-fearing non-Jews could worship and pray.

1. What does Jesus resemble here?
   a. bouncer
   b. fiery prophet
   c. Marine sergeant
   d. political activist
   e. bull in a china shop

2. What were the temple merchants doing that made Jesus so upset?
   a. not paying rent to use the temple
   b. mixing worship and business
   c. ripping off the people
   d. robbing the temple of its holiness
   e. ruining the Gentiles' area of prayer

3. Why did the religious authorities of the time want to kill Jesus?

4. What does this story tell you about anger?
   a. Even Jesus expressed anger.
   b. At times it's okay to throw things.
   c. After you get angry, it's best to leave town.
   d. The reason for your anger should always be clearly expressed.

5. When was the last time something happened that aroused "righteous anger" within you?

6. On a scale of 1 ("peace at any price") to 10 ("let's have it out"), how would you rate yourself on taking a stand that could lead to conflict?

7. If Jesus came to clean up your community, where would he start?
   a. crime district   d. the media
   b. city hall   e. the churches
   c. the schools   f. my house

8. How is God calling you now to get involved?
   a. to overturn a few tables
   b. to reach leaders in my community

c. to win people to Christ
d. to get involved politically
e. to get involved in programs helping those in need
f. to bring change to my church

9. What keeps you from making your life more of a "house of prayer"?

10. What is your biggest problem regarding anger?
   a. being argumentative
   b. swearing—either out loud or under my breath
   c. dwelling on revenge
   d. hurting someone else verbally
   e. hurting someone else physically
   f. hurting myself by holding it in

11. In what way do you need to be more of a "tough guy"?
   a. more assertive/open with anger
   b. more courage to share my faith
   c. more tolerance for pain or stress
   d. more disciplined devotional life
   e. more resistant of temptation
   f. more spiritual leadership at home
   g. more involved in disciplining and directing my children

The Withered Fig Tree

20In the morning, as they went along, they saw the fig tree withered from the roots. **21**Peter remembered and said to Jesus, "Rabbi, look! The fig tree you cursed has withered!"

22"Have*a* faith in God," Jesus answered. **23**"I tell you the truth, if anyone says to this mountain, 'Go, throw yourself into the sea,' and does not doubt in his heart but believes that what he says will happen, it will be done for him. **24**Therefore I tell you, whatever you ask for in prayer, believe that you have received it, and it will be yours. **25**And when you stand praying, if you hold anything against anyone, forgive him, so that your Father in heaven may forgive you your sins.*b*"

The Authority of Jesus Questioned

27They arrived again in Jerusalem, and while Jesus was walking in the temple courts, the chief priests, the teachers of the law and the elders came to him. **28**"By what authority are you doing these things?" they asked. "And who gave you authority to do this?"

29Jesus replied, "I will ask you one question. Answer me, and I will tell you by what authority I am doing these things. **30**John's baptism—was it from heaven, or from men? Tell me!"

31They discussed it among themselves and said, "If we say, 'From heaven,' he will ask, 'Then why didn't you believe him?' **32**But if we say, 'From men' . . . ." (They feared the people, for everyone held that John really was a prophet.)

33So they answered Jesus, "We don't know."

Jesus said, "Neither will I tell you by what authority I am doing these things."

The Parable of the Tenants

12 He then began to speak to them in parables: "A man planted a vineyard. He put a wall around it, dug a pit for the winepress and built a watchtower. Then he rented the vineyard to some farmers and went away on a journey. **2**At harvest time he sent a servant to the tenants to collect from them some of the fruit of the vineyard. **3**But they seized him, beat him and sent him away empty-handed. **4**Then he sent another servant to them; they struck this man on the head and treated him shamefully. **5**He sent still another, and that one they killed. He sent many others; some of them they beat, others they killed.

6"He had one left to send, a son, whom he loved. He sent him last of all, saying, 'They will respect my son.'

7"But the tenants said to one another, 'This is the heir. Come, let's kill him, and the inheritance will be ours.' **8**So they took him and killed him, and threw him out of the vineyard.

9"What then will the owner of the vineyard do? He will come and kill those tenants and give the vineyard to others. **10**Haven't you read this scripture:

" 'The stone the builders rejected
    has become the capstone*c*;
11the Lord has done this,
    and it is marvelous in our eyes'*d*?"

12Then they looked for a way to arrest him because they knew he had spoken the parable against them. But they were afraid of the crowd; so they left him and went away.

What authority figures do you still trust completely? Which do you distrust? Why?

1. Why were the leaders concerned about authority? Who had legitimate authority? 2. What dilemma does this pose for Jesus? Why doesn't he answer them directly? How does he cause the leaders' trickery to backfire?

The religious leaders in Jerusalem considered Jesus a threat. Have you ever felt like Jesus was a threat to you? Why?

1. If you owned a garden or an orchard, what would you grow? 2. If you had to entrust your business or belongings to someone outside your family, whom would you choose? Why?

1. What does the vineyard represent? Who is the owner? The son? Who are the tenants? The servants? The "others"? What was Jesus prophesying by telling this story? 2. How does the Scripture Jesus quotes relate to the parable? Who is the capstone? 3. How did this parable answer the question about Jesus' authority (11:28)?

1. How do you make Jesus feel welcome in your life each day? What actions of yours might make him feel unwelcome? 2. In what ways is Jesus the capstone in your life? In what ways is he not?

done to make your church a better place? 3. How do you feel about expressing anger? Have you ever expressed righteous anger? What happened? 4. What amazing answer to prayer can you remember receiving? How much faith did it take?

a22 Some early manuscripts *If you have*   *b25* Some manuscripts *sins.* *26But if you do not forgive, neither will your Father who is in heaven forgive your sins.*   *c10* Or *cornerstone*   *d11* Psalm 118:22,23

Which taxes do you hate paying the most? Which ones are you less bothered by paying?

1. What was dangerous about this trap? Why do the Herodians (allied to Rome) and the Pharisees make strange partners? How was Jesus a threat to each? **2.** What if Jesus had just said yes? If he had said no?

What do you give to Caesar? What do you give to God? What prevents you from giving to God what is God's?

No one knows exactly what heaven is like, but what would make heaven especially "heavenly" for you?

1. What was odd about the Sadducees' question? Why ask it? **2.** What is the source of the Sadducees' false assumption (v. 24)? **3.** How does Exodus 3:6 (quoted in v. 26) demonstrate the fact of the resurrection?

Paying Taxes to Caesar

¹³Later they sent some of the Pharisees and Herodians to Jesus to catch him in his words. ¹⁴They came to him and said, "Teacher, we know you are a man of integrity. You aren't swayed by men, because you pay no attention to who they are; but you teach the way of God in accordance with the truth. Is it right to pay taxes to Caesar or not? ¹⁵Should we pay or shouldn't we?"

But Jesus knew their hypocrisy. "Why are you trying to trap me?" he asked. "Bring me a denarius and let me look at it." ¹⁶They brought the coin, and he asked them, "Whose portrait is this? And whose inscription?"

"Caesar's," they replied.

¹⁷Then Jesus said to them, "Give to Caesar what is Caesar's and to God what is God's."

And they were amazed at him.

Marriage at the Resurrection

¹⁸Then the Sadducees, who say there is no resurrection, came to him with a question. ¹⁹"Teacher," they said, "Moses wrote for us that if a man's brother dies and leaves a wife but no children, the man must marry the widow and have children for his brother. ²⁰Now there were seven brothers. The first one married and died without leaving any children. ²¹The second one married the widow, but he also died, leaving no child. It was the same with the third. ²²In fact, none of the seven left any children. Last of all, the woman died too. ²³At the resurrection[a] whose wife will she be, since the seven were married to her?"

a23 Some manuscripts resurrection, when men rise from the dead,

---

$ Mark 12:13–17   **PAYING TAXES TO CAESAR**

In their disdain for Jesus, the Pharisees (religious conservatives) and the Herodians (supporters of Rome) had become strange allies. If Jesus answered their explosive question by saying the Jews should *not* pay taxes to Caesar, he could be arrested. If he said they *should* pay, he could lose his popular support.

1. What would you call the Pharisees' and Herodians' approach to Jesus?
   a. sneaky   c. flattering
   b. respectful   d. hypocritical

2. How would you describe Jesus' response to their question?
   a. evasive   c. compromising
   b. smart   d. balanced

3. What is implied in Jesus saying, "Give to Caesar what is Caesar's and to God what is God's"?
   a. Both God and the government should be given their due.
   b. Government has rightful authority, but final authority must be to God.
   c. Paying taxes is a spiritual as well as a political obligation.

   d. Don't do any more for the government than you have to do.

4. Which of the following do you think Jesus would encourage or condone?
   a. cheating on income taxes
   b. minimizing taxes with "loopholes"
   c. refusing to pay taxes because of an unjust war or program
   d. protesting a government policy
   e. disobeying what you believe is an unchristian law
   f. disrespecting government officials

5. What do you have the most trouble with in giving "Caesar" what is his?
   a. submitting to authority—I don't like to be told what to do.
   b. paying so much money in taxes
   c. supporting a government I don't agree with

6. How did you demonstrate rebellion in your younger days? What is your attitude toward authority now?
   a. highly obedient/compliant
   b. moderately obedient/compliant
   c. moderately rebellious
   d. highly rebellious

7. What can you give to God that you cannot give to the government? What often prevents you from doing so?

8. **$** Which of the following do you think would violate Jesus' teaching in this story?
   a. avoiding government safety or environmental regulations
   b. inaccurately completing required reports to the government
   c. overcharging on government contracts
   d. disobeying a government policy which is bad for business

9. **$** In your business dealings, when have you been in trouble due to rebelliousness? Were there times you felt it was *good* to be a little rebellious?

10. **$** Rank the following in order of the loyalty you believe you should give them (1 being highest and 6 being lowest).
    a. country   d. God
    b. family   e. my business
    c. self   f. people in general

24Jesus replied, "Are you not in error because you do not know the Scriptures or the power of God? 25When the dead rise, they will neither marry nor be given in marriage; they will be like the angels in heaven. 26Now about the dead rising—have you not read in the book of Moses, in the account of the bush, how God said to him, 'I am the God of Abraham, the God of Isaac, and the God of Jacob'*a*? 27He is not the God of the dead, but of the living. You are badly mistaken!"

The Greatest Commandment

28One of the teachers of the law came and heard them debating. Noticing that Jesus had given them a good answer, he asked him, "Of all the commandments, which is the most important?"

29"The most important one," answered Jesus, "is this: 'Hear, O Israel, the Lord our God, the Lord is one.*b* 30Love the Lord your God with all your heart and with all your soul and with all your mind and with all your strength.'*c* 31The second is this: 'Love your neighbor as yourself.'*d* There is no commandment greater than these."

32"Well said, teacher," the man replied. "You are right in saying that God is one and there is no other but him. 33To love him with all your heart, with all your understanding and with all your strength, and to love your neighbor as yourself is more important than all burnt offerings and sacrifices."

34When Jesus saw that he had answered wisely, he said to him, "You are not far from the kingdom of God." And from then on no one dared ask him any more questions.

Whose Son Is the Christ?

35While Jesus was teaching in the temple courts, he asked, "How is it that the teachers of the law say that the Christ*e* is the son of David? 36David himself, speaking by the Holy Spirit, declared:

> " 'The Lord said to my Lord:
> "Sit at my right hand
> until I put your enemies
> under your feet." '*f*

37David himself calls him 'Lord.' How then can he be his son?"
The large crowd listened to him with delight.

38As he taught, Jesus said, "Watch out for the teachers of the law. They like to walk around in flowing robes and be greeted in the marketplaces, 39and have the most important seats in the synagogues and the places of honor at banquets. 40They devour widows' houses and for a show make lengthy prayers. Such men will be punished most severely."

The Widow's Offering

41Jesus sat down opposite the place where the offerings were put and watched the crowd putting their money into the temple treasury. Many rich people threw in large amounts. 42But a poor widow came and put in two very small copper coins,*g* worth only a fraction of a penny.*h*

43Calling his disciples to him, Jesus said, "I tell you the truth, this poor widow has put more into the treasury than all the others. 44They all gave out of their wealth; but she, out of her poverty, put in everything—all she had to live on."

Which do you know more about—the Scriptures or the power of God? What are your hopes for growing in the other area?

What subject is guaranteed to spark a debate in your house? Sports? Politics? Religion? Other?

1. Why are these two commandments the greatest? How do the Ten Commandments relate to these two? 2. How was this teacher's attitude different from that of many others who questioned Jesus (11:28; 12:13–14; 12:18–19)? What does Jesus' response to this man teach you about Jesus? About the kingdom of God?

1. In the three possibilities of love relationships (with God, neighbors and self), where are you the strongest? The weakest? 2. How do you show your love for God?

---

1. Whom did your parents tell you to avoid? 2. Do you know more rich uncles or more poor widows? Do you treat them any differently? If so, how?

1. What issue lies behind Jesus' question (vv. 35–37)? How will the answer to this question answer all the others directed at Jesus in 11:27–12:34? 2. How would you describe the lifestyle of these teachers of the Law (vv. 38–40)? By contrast, what should the attitude of a Christian leader look like (see 10:42–45)? 3. What is Jesus' point in contrasting their situation with that of the poor widow? 4. When is "more" actually "less"? When is a "little" a "lot"?

1. How do people use religion to make themselves look good? How have you been tempted to do so? 2. Why do you give to God's work? What do you give besides money?

a26 Exodus 3:6   *b29* Or *the Lord our God is one Lord*   *c30* Deut. 6:4,5
d31 Lev. 19:18   *e35* Or *Messiah*   *f36* Psalm 110:1   *g42* Greek *two lepta*
h42 Greek *kodrantes*

1. If you could take two things with you to heaven, what would they be? 2. In school or at work, did you ever get burned because you stood for the truth or refused to go along with the crowd? Was it worth it? Why or why not?

1. Why do you think that Jesus used the discussion about the temple to begin his discourse about the end of the age? What made the temple so significant for the disciples? What would its destruction symbolize for them? 2. Upon hearing this bombshell, what two questions do the disciples ask (v. 4)? What events might deceive them into thinking the end times had come (vv. 5–8)? Of what will these events be a sign? 3. After that, what things will happen to the disciples and the early church (vv. 9–13)? What comfort and advocate will aid them to endure their trials? 4. What dreadful event (v. 14; see Da 9:26; 11:31; 12:11) will bring "days of distress" unequalled in human history? What deceptive signs will accompany that distress (vv. 21–22)? 5. How

Signs of the End of the Age

13 As he was leaving the temple, one of his disciples said to him, "Look, Teacher! What massive stones! What magnificent buildings!"

2"Do you see all these great buildings?" replied Jesus. "Not one stone here will be left on another; every one will be thrown down."

3As Jesus was sitting on the Mount of Olives opposite the temple, Peter, James, John and Andrew asked him privately, 4"Tell us, when will these things happen? And what will be the sign that they are all about to be fulfilled?"

5Jesus said to them: "Watch out that no one deceives you. 6Many will come in my name, claiming, 'I am he,' and will deceive many. 7When you hear of wars and rumors of wars, do not be alarmed. Such things must happen, but the end is still to come. 8Nation will rise against nation, and kingdom against kingdom. There will be earthquakes in various places, and famines. These are the beginning of birth pains.

9"You must be on your guard. You will be handed over to the local councils and flogged in the synagogues. On account of me you will stand before governors and kings as witnesses to them. 10And the gospel must first be preached to all nations. 11Whenever you are arrested and brought to trial, do not worry beforehand about what to say. Just say whatever is given you at the time, for it is not you speaking, but the Holy Spirit.

12"Brother will betray brother to death, and a father his child. Children will rebel against their parents and have them put to

Mark 12:41–44   **THE WIDOW'S OFFERING**

This story takes place in the temple in the court of women, where the treasury was located. It contained 13 trumpet-shaped receptacles used to collect donations for the temple.

1. Why do you think Jesus was watching people give to the temple?
   a. He was just killing time.
   b. He was curious.
   c. He was rating the givers.
   d. He was setting up a teaching situation for his disciples.

2. What do you think motivated the widow to give all she had?
   a. She was senile.
   b. She loved God very deeply.
   c. She was grateful for what she did have.
   d. She thought it would earn her some "brownie points" with God.

3. What was Jesus trying to teach the disciples?
   a. Poor people are better than rich people.
   b. Everyone should give to God.
   c. You should give your all to God.
   d. Your giving should be sacrificial.

4. What is your opinion of the widow's actions?
   a. Her actions were admirable, but I wouldn't do it.
   b. She was foolhardy and not using common sense.
   c. She was doing exactly what God wanted her to do.
   d. She should have talked to a financial planner.

5. What is the message of this story?
   a. We should be completely "sold-out" to God.
   b. A willing attitude, not a large amount, is all that matters.
   c. You don't need a big bank balance to be a big giver.
   d. It's not how much you give, but how much is left over, that counts with God.

6. In your opinion, why do most people give money to churches?

7. What kind of faith did the widow possess in order to give the way she did? How does the way you give financial offerings reflect your faith?

8. Why do you give to God's work? What do you give besides money?

9. Imagine yourself in this woman's place—surrounded by people who were vastly out-giving her. How do you think she felt about herself? How would it affect her view of herself to hear Jesus' affirmation of her offering?

10. What does this story have to say about self-esteem?
   a. God's opinion of who we are and what we do is the one that counts.
   b. God doesn't judge our worth by assets, abilities or appearances.
   c. Anyone can make an important contribution to God's kingdom.
   d. God is aware of what we do for him, no matter how insignificant it seems to others or ourselves.

11. What have you appreciated about this course? Go around your group and tell each person one thing you have appreciated about their giving to God or their contribution to the group.

death. [13]All men will hate you because of me, but he who stands firm to the end will be saved.

[14]"When you see 'the abomination that causes desolation'[a] standing where it[b] does not belong—let the reader understand—then let those who are in Judea flee to the mountains. [15]Let no one on the roof of his house go down or enter the house to take anything out. [16]Let no one in the field go back to get his cloak. [17]How dreadful it will be in those days for pregnant women and nursing mothers! [18]Pray that this will not take place in winter, [19]because those will be days of distress unequaled from the beginning, when God created the world, until now—and never to be equaled again. [20]If the Lord had not cut short those days, no one would survive. But for the sake of the elect, whom he has chosen, he has shortened them. [21]At that time if anyone says to you, 'Look, here is the Christ[c]!' or, 'Look, there he is!' do not believe it. [22]For false Christs and false prophets will appear and perform signs and miracles to deceive the elect—if that were possible. [23]So be on your guard; I have told you everything ahead of time.

[24]"But in those days, following that distress,

> "'the sun will be darkened,
>   and the moon will not give its light;
> [25]the stars will fall from the sky,
>   and the heavenly bodies will be shaken.'[d]

[26]"At that time men will see the Son of Man coming in clouds with great power and glory. [27]And he will send his angels and gather his elect from the four winds, from the ends of the earth to the ends of the heavens.

[28]"Now learn this lesson from the fig tree: As soon as its twigs get tender and its leaves come out, you know that summer is near. [29]Even so, when you see these things happening, you know that it is near, right at the door. [30]I tell you the truth, this generation[e] will certainly not pass away until all these things have happened. [31]Heaven and earth will pass away, but my words will never pass away.

The Day and Hour Unknown

[32]"No one knows about that day or hour, not even the angels in heaven, nor the Son, but only the Father. [33]Be on guard! Be alert[f]! You do not know when that time will come. [34]It's like a man going away: He leaves his house and puts his servants in charge, each with his assigned task, and tells the one at the door to keep watch.

[35]"Therefore keep watch because you do not know when the owner of the house will come back—whether in the evening, or at midnight, or when the rooster crows, or at dawn. [36]If he comes suddenly, do not let him find you sleeping. [37]What I say to you, I say to everyone: 'Watch!'"

Jesus Anointed at Bethany

14 Now the Passover and the Feast of Unleavened Bread were only two days away, and the chief priests and the teachers of the law were looking for some sly way to arrest Jesus and kill him. [2]"But not during the Feast," they said, "or the people may riot."

[3]While he was in Bethany, reclining at the table in the home of a man known as Simon the Leper, a woman came with an alabaster

---

will the Son of Man come (vv. 24–27)? **6.** How does the "fig tree" lesson (vv. 28–29) answer the disciples' questions from verse 4 (also 11:12–14,20–21)? **7.** What promises does Jesus give in verses 30–31? How would this comfort (or discomfort) the disciples? What impact do these promises have on you, 21 centuries later? **8.** How do you reconcile Jesus' predictions of the destruction of Jerusalem with his predictions of his return? **9.** Why do you think the Father has kept the time secret (v. 32)? What is the responsibility of believers in the meantime?

1. Have you ever faced persecution for your faith? What happened? **2.** When you see the forces of evil apparently winning, do you feel like withdrawing from the battle and perching on the rooftop? Or rolling up your sleeves and getting into the fray? **3.** What is the most exciting thing to you about the Second Coming? The most distressing? What questions would you like to ask Jesus about it? **4.** Specifically, how can you fulfill verses 33 and 37: "Be on guard! Be alert ... Watch!"?

If you had a year's wages to blow on friends, which would you choose: (a) Big party for all? (b) Glorious trip for a few? or (c) Extravagant gift for one?

1. How does this woman's action (v. 3) strike you: Thoughtful, but misguided? Tasteful, but extravagant? Wasteful, no buts about it? Honoring to the Nth degree? **2.** Do you think the per-

---

a14 Daniel 9:27; 11:31; 12:11   b14 Or *he*; also in verse 29   c21 Or *Messiah*   d25 Isaiah 13:10; 34:4   e30 Or *race*   f33 Some manuscripts *alert and pray*

fume could have been better used? Why? How was her action justified by Jesus (vv. 6–9) and used by Judas (vv. 10–11)?

1. What "beautiful thing" (v. 6) would you like to do for Jesus that some might see as wasteful? 2. What is the most beautiful, touching thing you have ever seen one person do for another? What is the most beautiful, touching thing another person has ever done for you?

1. What is one of your favorite places to eat? What makes it special? 2. What favorite meal does Mom prepare on your special days?

1. How does this meal relate to the Passover (see Ex 12)? 2. Why would secrecy be needed as this meal was planned? What risk was involved? 3. What does Jesus say about his betrayer? How do the disciples react to that bombshell? 4. What new meaning did Jesus give to the Passover bread? The wine? What vow did he make? 5. How much do you think the disciples understood when Jesus spoke about his body and blood?

1. How would you have felt if you had been at that meal? 2. What is your focus when you partake of Communion? Why is Communion important to a body of believers? 3. What do you think the disciples were thinking when Jesus said, "this is my body" and "this is my blood"?

Where do you go (or what do you do) when you're facing difficult situations? Do you prefer to be alone at these times, or in the company of close friends?

jar of very expensive perfume, made of pure nard. She broke the jar and poured the perfume on his head.

⁴Some of those present were saying indignantly to one another, "Why this waste of perfume? ⁵It could have been sold for more than a year's wages[a] and the money given to the poor." And they rebuked her harshly.

⁶"Leave her alone," said Jesus. "Why are you bothering her? She has done a beautiful thing to me. ⁷The poor you will always have with you, and you can help them any time you want. But you will not always have me. ⁸She did what she could. She poured perfume on my body beforehand to prepare for my burial. ⁹I tell you the truth, wherever the gospel is preached throughout the world, what she has done will also be told, in memory of her."

¹⁰Then Judas Iscariot, one of the Twelve, went to the chief priests to betray Jesus to them. ¹¹They were delighted to hear this and promised to give him money. So he watched for an opportunity to hand him over.

The Lord's Supper

¹²On the first day of the Feast of Unleavened Bread, when it was customary to sacrifice the Passover lamb, Jesus' disciples asked him, "Where do you want us to go and make preparations for you to eat the Passover?"

¹³So he sent two of his disciples, telling them, "Go into the city, and a man carrying a jar of water will meet you. Follow him. ¹⁴Say to the owner of the house he enters, 'The Teacher asks: Where is my guest room, where I may eat the Passover with my disciples?' ¹⁵He will show you a large upper room, furnished and ready. Make preparations for us there."

¹⁶The disciples left, went into the city and found things just as Jesus had told them. So they prepared the Passover.

¹⁷When evening came, Jesus arrived with the Twelve. ¹⁸While they were reclining at the table eating, he said, "I tell you the truth, one of you will betray me—one who is eating with me."

¹⁹They were saddened, and one by one they said to him, "Surely not I?"

²⁰"It is one of the Twelve," he replied, "one who dips bread into the bowl with me. ²¹The Son of Man will go just as it is written about him. But woe to that man who betrays the Son of Man! It would be better for him if he had not been born."

²²While they were eating, Jesus took bread, gave thanks and broke it, and gave it to his disciples, saying, "Take it; this is my body."

²³Then he took the cup, gave thanks and offered it to them, and they all drank from it.

²⁴"This is my blood of the[b] covenant, which is poured out for many," he said to them. ²⁵"I tell you the truth, I will not drink again of the fruit of the vine until that day when I drink it anew in the kingdom of God."

²⁶When they had sung a hymn, they went out to the Mount of Olives.

Jesus Predicts Peter's Denial

²⁷"You will all fall away," Jesus told them, "for it is written:

" 'I will strike the shepherd,
and the sheep will be scattered.'[c]

---

a5 Greek *than three hundred denarii*   b24 Some manuscripts *the new*
c27 Zech. 13:7

²⁸But after I have risen, I will go ahead of you into Galilee."

²⁹Peter declared, "Even if all fall away, I will not."

³⁰"I tell you the truth," Jesus answered, "today—yes, tonight—before the rooster crows twice*ᵃ* you yourself will disown me three times."

³¹But Peter insisted emphatically, "Even if I have to die with you, I will never disown you." And all the others said the same.

Gethsemane

³²They went to a place called Gethsemane, and Jesus said to his disciples, "Sit here while I pray." ³³He took Peter, James and John along with him, and he began to be deeply distressed and troubled. ³⁴"My soul is overwhelmed with sorrow to the point of death," he said to them. "Stay here and keep watch."

³⁵Going a little farther, he fell to the ground and prayed that if possible the hour might pass from him. ³⁶"Abba,*ᵇ* Father," he said, "everything is possible for you. Take this cup from me. Yet not what I will, but what you will."

³⁷Then he returned to his disciples and found them sleeping. "Simon," he said to Peter, "are you asleep? Could you not keep watch for one hour? ³⁸Watch and pray so that you will not fall into temptation. The spirit is willing, but the body is weak."

³⁹Once more he went away and prayed the same thing. ⁴⁰When he came back, he again found them sleeping, because their eyes were heavy. They did not know what to say to him.

⁴¹Returning the third time, he said to them, "Are you still sleep-

1. How does Peter see himself in relation to the other disciples? Was Peter sincere in verse 29? **2.** Why do you think Jesus warned the disciples (especially Peter) of their upcoming denial? **3.** Why did Jesus take Peter, James and John with him to pray (v. 33)? **4.** Why don't the disciples share Jesus' sense of urgency? How does this relate to their statements in the previous passage? **5.** Why did this woman know to prepare Jesus for his burial when the disciples did not? **6.** Why did Jesus urge Peter specifically to "watch and pray" (v. 34)?

1. How do you feel, realizing that Jesus knows your weaknesses and failures? **2.** When, if ever, have you faced a Gethsemane? What happened? **3.** What determines for whom and what you pray? How will the Gethsemane story change the way you pray this week?

ᵃ30 Some early manuscripts do not have *twice.*　　　*ᵇ36* Aramaic for *Father*

  　　Mark 14:32–42　　　　　　　　　**JESUS IN GETHSEMANE**

Just after the Last Supper and before his arrest, Jesus goes to a garden (or orchard) outside Jerusalem to pray.

1. Why do you think Jesus went to Gethsemane to pray?
   a. It was part of his routine.
   b. He was stressed out and knew he needed strength and guidance.
   c. He wanted to provide a good example for his disciples.
   d. It was his last chance to ask God for a plan other than the cross.

2. Why did Jesus take Peter, James and John along with him?
   a. He wanted them on the lookout.
   b. He needed their support.
   c. He was testing their endurance.
   d. He wanted them to pray for him.
   e. He knew they needed to pray for themselves.

3. If Jesus knew his mission was to go to the cross, why was he flinching at doing God's will?
   a. Being human, he was scared.
   b. He faced the same battle we face—submitting to God's will.
   c. He knew the cross was painful.

d. He dreaded taking the sins of the world upon himself.
e. The closer he got to the cross, the worse the pressure became.

4. How do you think Jesus felt when he said to his disciples, "Could you not keep watch for one hour?"
   a. let down　　　d. angry
   b. sympathetic　e. lonely
   c. unimportant　f. sad

5. What is more of a struggle for you?
   a. finding God's will for my life
   b. doing what I know God wants
   c. standing alone without the support of others
   d. watching someone I love struggle

6. What is the closest you have come to going through a time of stress and soul-searching like Jesus did here?

7. When has there been a time you felt you relied on friends and they "fell asleep on you"? How did you react?

8. If you were to go through a time of agony like Jesus did in this story, what three people (not in this group) would you choose to be with you?

9. 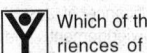 Which of the following experiences of loneliness have you had in the last month?
   a. feeling alone in a crowd
   b. feeling abandoned by friends
   c. feeling desperate for close friends
   d. feeling nobody understands me
   e. feeling everyone was out to get me
   f. having no one just to have fun with

10. How does this story relate to your situation in life?
    a. It's not wrong for me to ask God for my situation to change.
    b. Part of prayer is becoming willing to submit to God's plan for my life.
    c. God's will for my life may not be easy, but it is best.
    d. God can give me strength and grace to be alone.
    e. My "spirit" is willing to be single, but my "body" would rather not.

11. When it comes to your physical lifestyle and habits, how do you experience a spirit that is willing but a body that is weak? How do you feel about sharing those frustrations with this group? How can the group support you in your struggles?

ing and resting? Enough! The hour has come. Look, the Son of Man is betrayed into the hands of sinners. 42Rise! Let us go! Here comes my betrayer!"

Jesus Arrested

43Just as he was speaking, Judas, one of the Twelve, appeared. With him was a crowd armed with swords and clubs, sent from the chief priests, the teachers of the law, and the elders. 44Now the betrayer had arranged a signal with them: "The one I kiss is the man; arrest him and lead him away under guard." 45Going at once to Jesus, Judas said, "Rabbi!" and kissed him. 46The men seized Jesus and arrested him. 47Then one of those standing near drew his sword and struck the servant of the high priest, cutting off his ear.

48"Am I leading a rebellion," said Jesus, "that you have come out with swords and clubs to capture me? 49Every day I was with you, teaching in the temple courts, and you did not arrest me. But the Scriptures must be fulfilled." 50Then everyone deserted him and fled.

51A young man, wearing nothing but a linen garment, was following Jesus. When they seized him, 52he fled naked, leaving his garment behind.

Before the Sanhedrin

53They took Jesus to the high priest, and all the chief priests, elders and teachers of the law came together. 54Peter followed him at a distance, right into the courtyard of the high priest. There he sat with the guards and warmed himself at the fire.

55The chief priests and the whole Sanhedrin were looking for evidence against Jesus so that they could put him to death, but they did not find any. 56Many testified falsely against him, but their statements did not agree.

57Then some stood up and gave this false testimony against him: 58"We heard him say, 'I will destroy this man-made temple and in three days will build another, not made by man.'" 59Yet even then their testimony did not agree.

60Then the high priest stood up before them and asked Jesus, "Are you not going to answer? What is this testimony that these men are bringing against you?" 61But Jesus remained silent and gave no answer.

Again the high priest asked him, "Are you the Christ,[a] the Son of the Blessed One?"

62"I am," said Jesus. "And you will see the Son of Man sitting at the right hand of the Mighty One and coming on the clouds of heaven."

63The high priest tore his clothes. "Why do we need any more witnesses?" he asked. 64"You have heard the blasphemy. What do you think?"

They all condemned him as worthy of death. 65Then some began to spit at him; they blindfolded him, struck him with their fists, and said, "Prophesy!" And the guards took him and beat him.

Peter Disowns Jesus

66While Peter was below in the courtyard, one of the servant girls of the high priest came by. 67When she saw Peter warming himself, she looked closely at him.

"You also were with that Nazarene, Jesus," she said.

a61 Or Messiah

How would you react if one of your kids (or parents!) was arrested?

1. Why is the crowd armed (v. 48)? What does this tell you about Judas' misunderstanding of Jesus' mission? 2. How do you account for the disciples' reactions (vv. 47,50,51)?

In times of crisis, how do you respond: Like the impulsive disciple? Like Judas? Like the naked disciple? What would help you respond like Jesus did?

Have you ever gotten a bad deal from a judge or a policeman? How did it make you feel?

1. What does the fact that Peter has followed Jesus (at a distance) tell you about Peter's character? 2. What perversions of justice do you find in Jesus' trial? Why do you think that Jesus, for the most part, remains silent? 3. What is the significance of Jesus' messianic acknowledgment, the first direct confession recorded in Mark (v. 62; see Ps 110:1 and Da 7:13)? 4. If the high priest, chief priests, elders and teachers of the law were waiting for the Messiah, why would they consider it blasphemy when the actual Messiah, who is right in front of them, identifies himself?

1. How does Jesus' behavior differ from that of the priests, elders and teachers? What does this say about the character of each? 2. What would your reaction be to seeing Jesus spit on, blindfolded, struck and mocked?

When in your life were you most disappointed with yourself?

1. Peter is brave enough to follow Jesus to the high priest's house. Why do you think he now denies Christ (v. 68)? Do

[68]But he denied it. "I don't know or understand what you're talking about," he said, and went out into the entryway.[a]

[69]When the servant girl saw him there, she said again to those standing around, "This fellow is one of them." [70]Again he denied it.

After a little while, those standing near said to Peter, "Surely you are one of them, for you are a Galilean."

[71]He began to call down curses on himself, and he swore to them, "I don't know this man you're talking about."

[72]Immediately the rooster crowed the second time.[b] Then Peter remembered the word Jesus had spoken to him: "Before the rooster crows twice[c] you will disown me three times." And he broke down and wept.

Jesus Before Pilate

15 Very early in the morning, the chief priests, with the elders, the teachers of the law and the whole Sanhedrin, reached a decision. They bound Jesus, led him away and handed him over to Pilate.

[2]"Are you the king of the Jews?" asked Pilate.

"Yes, it is as you say," Jesus replied.

[3]The chief priests accused him of many things. [4]So again Pilate asked him, "Aren't you going to answer? See how many things they are accusing you of."

[5]But Jesus still made no reply, and Pilate was amazed.

---

[a]68 Some early manuscripts *entryway and the rooster crowed*   [b]72 Some early manuscripts do not have *the second time.*   [c]72 Some early manuscripts do not have *twice.*

---

you think he realized what he was doing? Why? **2.** How were the three denials similar? Different?

1. When, if ever, have you felt that your failures had made it impossible for Christ to use you again? **2.** What "rooster" reminds you of failure and guilt? What helps then?

---

1. As a child, would you rather have been punished by Mom or by Dad? Why? **2.** Were you ever bullied as a child? What happened? How did it feel?

1. What insights into Pilate's and Jesus' character does this story offer? Why is Pilate indecisive (v. 12)? Why is Jesus silent? **2.** Why do the people, after witnessing Jesus' miracles, hearing his teachings, and praising him with hosannas, now demand that Jesus be crucified? **3.** Why does Pilate grant their request? **4.** What insights into the Gospel do you see

---

 Mark 15:1–15   **JESUS BEFORE PILATE**

The night before this, Jesus had been arrested and brought before the Sanhedrin (Jewish high court consisting of 71 religious leaders). He was found guilty of blasphemy—a crime punishable by death. However, the Sanhedrin's power was limited by Roman rule; so now they bring Jesus to Pilate, the Roman governor, with a request for his execution.

1. If you were a film director, how would you portray Pilate?
   a. a smooth politician
   b. a wimp
   c. a victim of circumstances
   d. a pragmatist—going with the flow

2. Why was Jesus so silent throughout his trials?
   a. His words had been so twisted against him, there was no point in speaking.
   b. He trusted God's plan.
   c. The ears of his accusers were sealed against him.
   d. The Old Testament prophesied the Messiah's silence before his accusers.

3. Do you think the Roman governor knew Jesus was innocent?
   a. absolutely
   b. probably
   c. It's hard to say.
   d. If he didn't, he was blind.

4. Why did Pilate offer to release a prisoner chosen by the crowd?
   a. to check out their motives
   b. to expose their hypocrisy
   c. to get Jesus off the hook
   d. to keep everybody happy
   e. to avoid making a decision

5. Who ended up the biggest winner and who ended up the biggest loser in Jesus' sentence of crucifixion?
   a. Pilate   d. Jesus
   b. Sanhedrin   e. the crowd
   c. Barabbas   f. me

6. How can you relate to each of the following?
   a. Pilate—selling short my convictions in exchange for "peace"
   b. Jesus—acting on my convictions and suffering the consequences
   c. Barabbas—guilty, yet released

7. What do you find most amazing about this story?
   a. that Jesus was so silent
   b. that the people turned on Jesus
   c. that Jesus was so misunderstood
   d. that Jesus was so mistreated
   e. that a murderer was released instead of the Messiah
   f. that Jesus took my place so my sins could be forgiven
   g. that Jesus allowed all this to happen when he could have used his great powers to escape

8. At what point in your life did you ask Jesus to forgive your sins, realizing he died as your substitute?
   a. as a child
   b. years ago
   c. just recently
   d. I don't know that I have.

9. Close with a time of silent prayer—thanking Christ for his sacrifice, confessing your need for forgiveness, and committing/recommitting your life to him.

in the release of Barabbas in exchange for Jesus (see 8:37; 10:45)? **5.** What mental, physical and emotional brutality do the soldiers inflict on Jesus? Why? Does their mockery stem from fear, anger, unbelief or what?

♡ **1.** Why did Jesus go through this trial and torture when he could easily have used his great powers and escaped? How does this make you feel? What does it make you want to do? **2.** If you were the only person in the world, would Jesus have done the same thing? **3.** Have your actions ever mocked the name of Jesus? What can you do to resist this kind of behavior?

☕ **1.** Have you ever sat with someone who was dying? What was it like? **2.** How do you feel deep down when you attend funerals and burials?

📖 **1.** Why is Simon needed to carry Jesus' cross (see 14:65; 15:15,19)? How might that affect him? **2.** What kinds of people were usually crucified (v. 27)? How is Jesus like them? **3.** What further insults are added to injury (vv. 29–32)? **4.** What ironies do you see here: In the places occupied by the robbers (see 10:37)? In the call for Jesus to save himself by coming down from the cross? In the officially posted reason for Jesus' death? **5.** What aspect of the crucifixion was the worst for Jesus: The physical pain? Feeling forsaken by God? What does this say about our part in his crucifixion? **6.** How are the cry of Jesus (v. 34; also Ps 22:1), the tearing of the temple curtain (v. 38; see Mt 27:51–53; Heb 10:19–22), and the faith of the centurion (v. 39) all related? **7.** What do you learn about Joseph (vv. 43–46)? What risks does a man of his status take by this action? **8.** What is significant about the centurion's confirmation of Jesus' death? About the eyewitnesses of his burial (Mt 28:11–15)?

⁶Now it was the custom at the Feast to release a prisoner whom the people requested. ⁷A man called Barabbas was in prison with the insurrectionists who had committed murder in the uprising. ⁸The crowd came up and asked Pilate to do for them what he usually did.

⁹"Do you want me to release to you the king of the Jews?" asked Pilate, ¹⁰knowing it was out of envy that the chief priests had handed Jesus over to him. ¹¹But the chief priests stirred up the crowd to have Pilate release Barabbas instead.

¹²"What shall I do, then, with the one you call the king of the Jews?" Pilate asked them.

¹³"Crucify him!" they shouted.

¹⁴"Why? What crime has he committed?" asked Pilate.

But they shouted all the louder, "Crucify him!"

¹⁵Wanting to satisfy the crowd, Pilate released Barabbas to them. He had Jesus flogged, and handed him over to be crucified.

The Soldiers Mock Jesus

¹⁶The soldiers led Jesus away into the palace (that is, the Praetorium) and called together the whole company of soldiers. ¹⁷They put a purple robe on him, then twisted together a crown of thorns and set it on him. ¹⁸And they began to call out to him, "Hail, king of the Jews!" ¹⁹Again and again they struck him on the head with a staff and spit on him. Falling on their knees, they paid homage to him. ²⁰And when they had mocked him, they took off the purple robe and put his own clothes on him. Then they led him out to crucify him.

The Crucifixion

²¹A certain man from Cyrene, Simon, the father of Alexander and Rufus, was passing by on his way in from the country, and they forced him to carry the cross. ²²They brought Jesus to the place called Golgotha (which means The Place of the Skull). ²³Then they offered him wine mixed with myrrh, but he did not take it. ²⁴And they crucified him. Dividing up his clothes, they cast lots to see what each would get.

²⁵It was the third hour when they crucified him. ²⁶The written notice of the charge against him read: THE KING OF THE JEWS. ²⁷They crucified two robbers with him, one on his right and one on his left.ᵃ ²⁹Those who passed by hurled insults at him, shaking their heads and saying, "So! You who are going to destroy the temple and build it in three days, ³⁰come down from the cross and save yourself!"

³¹In the same way the chief priests and the teachers of the law mocked him among themselves. "He saved others," they said, "but he can't save himself! ³²Let this Christ,ᵇ this King of Israel, come down now from the cross, that we may see and believe." Those crucified with him also heaped insults on him.

The Death of Jesus

³³At the sixth hour darkness came over the whole land until the ninth hour. ³⁴And at the ninth hour Jesus cried out in a loud voice, *"Eloi, Eloi, lama sabachthani?"*—which means, "My God, my God, why have you forsaken me?"ᶜ

³⁵When some of those standing near heard this, they said, "Listen, he's calling Elijah."

³⁶One man ran, filled a sponge with wine vinegar, put it on a

ᵃ27 Some manuscripts *left,* ²⁸*and the scripture was fulfilled which says, "He was counted with the lawless ones"* (Isaiah 53:12)　　ᵇ32 Or *Messiah*　　ᶜ34 Psalm 22:1

stick, and offered it to Jesus to drink. "Now leave him alone. Let's see if Elijah comes to take him down," he said.

³⁷With a loud cry, Jesus breathed his last.

³⁸The curtain of the temple was torn in two from top to bottom. ³⁹And when the centurion, who stood there in front of Jesus, heard his cry and*ᵃ* saw how he died, he said, "Surely this man was the Son*ᵇ* of God!"

⁴⁰Some women were watching from a distance. Among them were Mary Magdalene, Mary the mother of James the younger and of Joses, and Salome. ⁴¹In Galilee these women had followed him and cared for his needs. Many other women who had come up with him to Jerusalem were also there.

The Burial of Jesus

⁴²It was Preparation Day (that is, the day before the Sabbath). So as evening approached, ⁴³Joseph of Arimathea, a prominent member of the Council, who was himself waiting for the kingdom of God, went boldly to Pilate and asked for Jesus' body. ⁴⁴Pilate was surprised to hear that he was already dead. Summoning the centurion, he asked him if Jesus had already died. ⁴⁵When he learned from the centurion that it was so, he gave the body to Joseph. ⁴⁶So Joseph bought some linen cloth, took down the body, wrapped it in the linen, and placed it in a tomb cut out of rock. Then he rolled a stone against the entrance of the tomb. ⁴⁷Mary Magdalene and Mary the mother of Joses saw where he was laid.

The Resurrection

16 When the Sabbath was over, Mary Magdalene, Mary the mother of James, and Salome bought spices so that they might go to anoint Jesus' body. ²Very early on the first day of the week, just after sunrise, they were on their way to the tomb ³and they asked each other, "Who will roll the stone away from the entrance of the tomb?"

⁴But when they looked up, they saw that the stone, which was very large, had been rolled away. ⁵As they entered the tomb, they saw a young man dressed in a white robe sitting on the right side, and they were alarmed.

⁶"Don't be alarmed," he said. "You are looking for Jesus the Nazarene, who was crucified. He has risen! He is not here. See the place where they laid him. ⁷But go, tell his disciples and Peter, 'He is going ahead of you into Galilee. There you will see him, just as he told you.'"

⁸Trembling and bewildered, the women went out and fled from the tomb. They said nothing to anyone, because they were afraid.

[The earliest manuscripts and some other ancient witnesses do not have Mark 16:9–20.]

⁹When Jesus rose early on the first day of the week, he appeared first to Mary Magdalene, out of whom he had driven seven demons. ¹⁰She went and told those who had been with him and who were mourning and weeping. ¹¹When they heard that Jesus was alive and that she had seen him, they did not believe it.

¹²Afterward Jesus appeared in a different form to two of them

---

1. Read Isaiah 53:12. How would you paraphrase it to explain what Jesus' death was all about? 2. What curtain do you feel still separates you from God? How does Jesus' death relate to that? 3. What is the riskiest thing you have ever done because of your faith in Jesus? Why did you do it? 4. When did the crucifixion begin to make a difference in your own life?

---

1. What do you like to do on Sunday mornings? 2. What was the most incredible event you have ever seen? Convince your small group it really happened. What difficulties do you experience in the retelling of your eyewitness account?

---

1. Mary Magdalene and Mary, the mother of James and Salome, were never very far away during the crucifixion and entombment of Christ (see 15:40–41). What does this tell you about the faith of these women? What does this tell you about the role of women in Jesus' life? 2. What potential problem looms ahead (v. 3)? What do they find instead? What do they fear? Seeing the empty tomb and the man sitting beside it, what thoughts are racing through their heads? 3. Do you think they believed the man (v. 8)? How do their actions support your answer? 4. Why do you think the angel asked them specifically to speak to Peter? What does this tell you about Jesus' plans for Peter?

---

1. Would you have had trouble believing the angel's words? Why or why not? 2. Who did Jesus send to you to tell you he had risen? Did you have trouble believing that person? How were you finally convinced of Jesus' res-

---

ᵃ39 Some manuscripts do not have *heard his cry and*   *ᵇ39* Or *a son*

urrection? **3.** To whom is Jesus sending you with this message? How will you accomplish this mission? **4.** Where is your spiritual life focused these days: On Good Friday? Easter Sunday? Or in between? **5.** How would your life be different if Jesus was not risen from the dead? **6.** What will you remember most from the Gospel of Mark to sharpen your focus of who Jesus really is?

while they were walking in the country. [13]These returned and reported it to the rest; but they did not believe them either.

[14]Later Jesus appeared to the Eleven as they were eating; he rebuked them for their lack of faith and their stubborn refusal to believe those who had seen him after he had risen.

[15]He said to them, "Go into all the world and preach the good news to all creation. [16]Whoever believes and is baptized will be saved, but whoever does not believe will be condemned. [17]And these signs will accompany those who believe: In my name they will drive out demons; they will speak in new tongues; [18]they will pick up snakes with their hands; and when they drink deadly poison, it will not hurt them at all; they will place their hands on sick people, and they will get well."

[19]After the Lord Jesus had spoken to them, he was taken up into heaven and he sat at the right hand of God. [20]Then the disciples went out and preached everywhere, and the Lord worked with them and confirmed his word by the signs that accompanied it.

INTRODUCTION to
LUKE

Book Study Outline: If you are using Luke for a study course, here is a 7- or 13-week outline. Use the margin questions for your group agenda:

☕ start meeting / 15 min.

📖 read & discuss Bible / 30 min.

♡ close meeting / 15–45 min.

Refer to the Questions and Answers in front of Bible for more information.

7-week plan	13-week plan	Personal Reading	Group Study Passage
	1	1:1–38	1:26–38/Jesus Foretold
1	2	1:39–2:20	2:1–20/Birth of Jesus
	3	2:21–4:30	4:14–30/Jesus Rejected
2	4	4:31–7:50	5:27–39/Levi; Wineskins
	5	8:1–10:37	10:25–37/Good Samaritan
3	6	10:38–12:12	10:38–42/Martha and Mary
	7	12:13–15:10	12:13–21/The Rich Fool
4	8	15:11–16:18	15:11–32/The Prodigal Son
	9	16:19–18:8	16:19–31/Heaven and Hell
5	10	18:9–22:6	18:9–14/Two Prayers
	11	22:7–23:43	22:7–34/Last Supper
6	12	23:44–24:12	23:44–49/Jesus' Death
7	13	24:13–53	24:13–35/Road to Emmaus

Author: While the book itself is anonymous, traditionally it is thought to be the work of Luke the physician, Paul's coworker and companion (Col 4:14; 2Ti 4:11). Luke is the only non-Jewish author in the New Testament. The Gospel of Luke is Volume I ("The Story of Jesus") in Luke's two-part account. The Acts of the Apostles is Volume II ("The Story of the Church").

Date: Uncertain, probably sometime after the fall of Jerusalem in A.D. 70.

Theme: Jesus is the Savior of the whole world.

Historical Background: Luke wrote this record of Jesus' life for a Gentile audience. In 1:3 he addresses the book to Theophilus, an unknown but probably wealthy Roman aristocrat.

Characteristics: Luke is the longest book in the NT. While using much of the same material as Mark and Matthew, Luke adds his own distinctive flavor to the story. This Gospel is marked by joy (1:46–47; 15:8–32; 24:52–53), songs of praise (1:46–55,68–79; 2:14,29–32), and an interest in the relationship of Jesus with people considered outcasts by his fellow countrymen (e.g., women, children, the poor, tax collectors and Samaritans). Luke's Gentile orientation is seen in the fact that Jesus' genealogy is traced back to Adam, the founder of the human race, rather than back to Abraham, the founder of the Jewish race (as Matthew does). Luke seldom quotes the OT, and he translates Hebrew words into their Greek equivalents. This is a book that tells how the promised Jewish Messiah is indeed the Savior of the whole world.

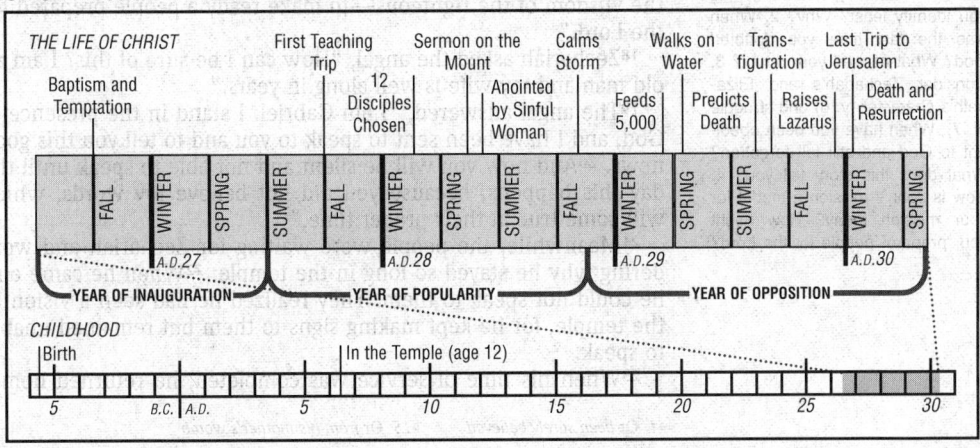

Luke

Introduction

1 Many have undertaken to draw up an account of the things that have been fulfilled[a] among us, 2just as they were handed down to us by those who from the first were eyewitnesses and servants of the word. 3Therefore, since I myself have carefully investigated everything from the beginning, it seemed good also to me to write an orderly account for you, most excellent Theophilus, 4so that you may know the certainty of the things you have been taught.

The Birth of John the Baptist Foretold

5In the time of Herod king of Judea there was a priest named Zechariah, who belonged to the priestly division of Abijah; his wife Elizabeth was also a descendant of Aaron. 6Both of them were upright in the sight of God, observing all the Lord's commandments and regulations blamelessly. 7But they had no children, because Elizabeth was barren; and they were both well along in years.

8Once when Zechariah's division was on duty and he was serving as priest before God, 9he was chosen by lot, according to the custom of the priesthood, to go into the temple of the Lord and burn incense. 10And when the time for the burning of incense came, all the assembled worshipers were praying outside.

11Then an angel of the Lord appeared to him, standing at the right side of the altar of incense. 12When Zechariah saw him, he was startled and was gripped with fear. 13But the angel said to him: "Do not be afraid, Zechariah; your prayer has been heard. Your wife Elizabeth will bear you a son, and you are to give him the name John. 14He will be a joy and delight to you, and many will rejoice because of his birth, 15for he will be great in the sight of the Lord. He is never to take wine or other fermented drink, and he will be filled with the Holy Spirit even from birth.[b] 16Many of the people of Israel will he bring back to the Lord their God. 17And he will go on before the Lord, in the spirit and power of Elijah, to turn the hearts of the fathers to their children and the disobedient to the wisdom of the righteous—to make ready a people prepared for the Lord."

18Zechariah asked the angel, "How can I be sure of this? I am an old man and my wife is well along in years."

19The angel answered, "I am Gabriel. I stand in the presence of God, and I have been sent to speak to you and to tell you this good news. 20And now you will be silent and not able to speak until the day this happens, because you did not believe my words, which will come true at their proper time."

21Meanwhile, the people were waiting for Zechariah and wondering why he stayed so long in the temple. 22When he came out, he could not speak to them. They realized he had seen a vision in the temple, for he kept making signs to them but remained unable to speak.

23When his time of service was completed, he returned home.

---

1. Have you drawn up your last will and testament? What important facts did you include? Who would you choose as the biographer of your life story, and why? **2.** What is a recent surprise that your family has experienced: A job promotion? A new addition to the family? Your child earned all "A's"? You joined this Bible study?

1. What do you learn from verses 1–4 about Luke? About the reason he wrote this Gospel? About his sources? **2.** What stands out to you about Zechariah and Elizabeth (vv. 5–7)? What feelings might the couple have had in light of their barrenness? **3.** What was the significance of the task for which Zechariah was chosen (see 1Ch 23:13)? Since many priests never had the chance to go into the temple and burn incense, what might he be feeling as he prepares for it? How about when the angel appears? **4.** What is the connection between alcohol and the Holy Spirit (see Eph 5:18)? **5.** How would the birth of this son affect Zechariah and Elizabeth? Describe the child's mission in your own words. Why would Zechariah doubt? **6.** In the meantime, how were the people feeling (v. 21)? What did they think when Zechariah emerged from the temple, mute?

1. Of the major characters in this story—Zechariah, Elizabeth, John—with whom do you identify most? Why? With whom do you identify least? Why? **2.** When was the last time you doubted God? What caused your doubt? **3.** Consider Zechariah's and Elizabeth's character (v. 6) and struggle (v. 7). When have you been obedient to God and still felt forgotten? What does this story tell you? **4.** How is John's mission a model for your mission today? How might you "prepare" people for the Lord?

---

a1 Or been surely believed   b15 Or from his mother's womb

²⁴After this his wife Elizabeth became pregnant and for five months remained in seclusion. ²⁵"The Lord has done this for me," she said. "In these days he has shown his favor and taken away my disgrace among the people."

The Birth of Jesus Foretold

²⁶In the sixth month, God sent the angel Gabriel to Nazareth, a town in Galilee, ²⁷to a virgin pledged to be married to a man named Joseph, a descendant of David. The virgin's name was Mary. ²⁸The angel went to her and said, "Greetings, you who are highly favored! The Lord is with you."

²⁹Mary was greatly troubled at his words and wondered what kind of greeting this might be. ³⁰But the angel said to her, "Do not be afraid, Mary, you have found favor with God. ³¹You will be with child and give birth to a son, and you are to give him the name Jesus. ³²He will be great and will be called the Son of the Most High. The Lord God will give him the throne of his father David, ³³and he will reign over the house of Jacob forever; his kingdom will never end."

³⁴"How will this be," Mary asked the angel, "since I am a virgin?"

³⁵The angel answered, "The Holy Spirit will come upon you, and the power of the Most High will overshadow you. So the holy one to be born will be called[a] the Son of God. ³⁶Even Elizabeth your relative is going to have a child in her old age, and she who was said to be barren is in her sixth month. ³⁷For nothing is impossible with God."

a35 Or So the child to be born will be called holy,

☕ If told that you (or your parents) were to have a child this year, how would you react?

📖 **1.** How does Gabriel's word to Mary compare with his word to Zechariah (1:13–17)? **2.** How does Mary (vv. 34,38) respond differently than Zechariah (vv. 12,18)? **3.** What truths about Jesus are emphasized here? What expectations must have been raised in Mary?

❤ **1.** What would it mean to doubt and fear God? When were you recently fearful but believing? How did God meet you? **2.** In what area of your life do you need to believe that nothing is impossible with God? What keeps you from believing this?

 *Luke 1:26–38*　　　　**THE BIRTH OF JESUS FORETOLD**

1. What was Mary's initial reaction to the appearance of the angel?
   a. fear　　　　d. doubt
   b. curiosity　　e. faith
   c. confusion　　f. concern

2. If you had been Mary, what would have been hardest to comprehend?
   a. being favored by God
   b. getting pregnant as a virgin
   c. who her child was going to be
   d. how to explain this to others, especially Joseph and her family

3. How do you think Mary felt about giving birth to the Messiah?
   a. scared　　　d. overjoyed
   b. honored　　　e. lonely
   c. burdened　　f. clueless

4. If an angel were to reveal God's plan for my life today, I would:
   a. ask a lot of questions.
   b. wonder if I had any say about it.
   c. rejoice that God could use me.
   d. worry about my ability to do it.
   e. run away scared.
   f. tell the angel I would rather not know my future.

5. What point about Jesus sticks out to you the most?
   a. his conception—by the Holy Spirit and a virgin
   b. his nature—God's holy Son
   c. his authority—as an eternal King
   d. his mission—as Savior (*Jesus* means "the Lord saves")

6. My understanding of who Jesus is:
   a. came as an instantaneous insight.
   b. came over time.
   c. has begun and is still coming.
   d. hasn't come very clearly yet.
   e. other:_____

7. Who was the "angel" God sent to help explain the truth about Jesus Christ to you?

8. In what area of your life do you need to believe that "nothing is impossible with God"? What keeps you from believing him?

9. 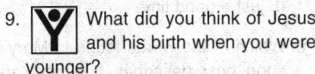 What did you think of Jesus and his birth when you were younger?
   a. Santa Claus was more exciting.

   b. It made for a nice children's play.
   c. Jesus seemed more "spiritual" than real.
   d. I can't remember not wanting Jesus to be first in my life.

10. What do you think of Jesus and his birth *now?*

11. How do you feel about being in a group studying about "becoming a Christian"?
    a. eager　　　d. embarrassed
    b. nervous　　e. cautious
    c. out of place　f. comfortable

12. How would you describe your commitment to Jesus Christ?
    a. I have lots of questions.
    b. I'm still recovering from bad experiences in the past.
    c. I'm drawn to Christ but unsure what that involves.
    d. I'm committed to Christ and want to find out all I need to know.
    e. other:_____

³⁸"I am the Lord's servant," Mary answered. "May it be to me as you have said." Then the angel left her.

Mary Visits Elizabeth

³⁹At that time Mary got ready and hurried to a town in the hill country of Judea, ⁴⁰where she entered Zechariah's home and greeted Elizabeth. ⁴¹When Elizabeth heard Mary's greeting, the baby leaped in her womb, and Elizabeth was filled with the Holy Spirit. ⁴²In a loud voice she exclaimed: "Blessed are you among women, and blessed is the child you will bear! ⁴³But why am I so favored, that the mother of my Lord should come to me? ⁴⁴As soon as the sound of your greeting reached my ears, the baby in my womb leaped for joy. ⁴⁵Blessed is she who has believed that what the Lord has said to her will be accomplished!"

Mary's Song

⁴⁶And Mary said:

"My soul glorifies the Lord
⁴⁷   and my spirit rejoices in God my Savior,
⁴⁸for he has been mindful
    of the humble state of his servant.
From now on all generations will call me blessed,
⁴⁹   for the Mighty One has done great things for
        me—
    holy is his name.
⁵⁰His mercy extends to those who fear him,
    from generation to generation.
⁵¹He has performed mighty deeds with his arm;

Whom do you call first when you have good news to share?

How might Mary have felt when Elizabeth greeted her? How is she "blessed" and encouraged?

How is Mary's faith an example to you?

What song has been playing in your head lately? When has the song in your head annoyed you? Inspired you?

1. For what does Mary praise God in this song? What contrasts does she make in verses 51–53? How do these reflect her feelings about God? About herself?
2. Who are the "proud," the "rulers" and the "rich," whose overthrow she celebrates? How will Jesus fulfill the themes of this song?

Luke 1:39–56

MARY VISITS ELIZABETH

The angel Gabriel appeared to Mary, telling her that, though she was a virgin, she would become the mother of the Messiah. The angel also reported that Mary's relative Elizabeth was pregnant as well. Elizabeth was six months pregnant with the child who would be known as John the Baptist.

1. Why did Mary go to Elizabeth's house?
   a. for a little "female bonding"
   b. to share her exciting news
   c. to share in the joy of another pregnant woman
   d. to get some advice from an older and wiser relative
   e. to get away from the talk about her "illegitimate" pregnancy

2. Why did Elizabeth's baby leap in her womb when Mary arrived?
   a. He was a hyper child.
   b. He was filled with joy.
   c. The Lord was demonstrating how special these babies—especially Mary's—were.
   d. Elizabeth just imagined it.

3. Why did God choose Mary to give birth to his Son?
   a. She was at the right place at the right time.
   b. She earned the honor by her holy life.
   c. God had her in mind from the beginning.
   d. Only God knows why he did.

4. How did Mary envision herself?
   a. a lowly servant
   b. a surrogate mother
   c. an ordinary person
   d. greatly blessed
   e. deserving of her recognition
   f. as someone who would never be forgotten

5. What do you need to share with an "Elizabeth" right now?
   a. a joy I've been wanting to share
   b. a burden I need to talk about
   c. some questions about my faith
   d. just a good time

6. Which of the words found in Mary's song best describes how you are feeling about your spiritual life?

   a. rejoicing   e. lifted up
   b. humble   f. filled
   c. blessed   g. hungry
   d. proud   h. empty

7. What do you appreciate most about Mary?
   a. She had a humble background.
   b. She had a humble spirit.
   c. She gave God all the glory for her blessings.
   d. She had faith to believe that the amazing things she heard would be accomplished.
   e. She didn't let what others would think about her (like getting pregnant out of wedlock) control her.

8. In what way would you like to be more like Mary?

9. What have you really appreciated about this course? Conclude your time together by affirming each other like Elizabeth affirmed Mary: One at a time, have each group member simply listen as others share with them an affirmation or blessing.

he has scattered those who are proud in their
>   inmost thoughts.
52He has brought down rulers from their thrones
>   but has lifted up the humble.
53He has filled the hungry with good things
>   but has sent the rich away empty.
54He has helped his servant Israel,
>   remembering to be merciful
55to Abraham and his descendants forever,
>   even as he said to our fathers."

56Mary stayed with Elizabeth for about three months and then returned home.

The Birth of John the Baptist

57When it was time for Elizabeth to have her baby, she gave birth to a son. **58**Her neighbors and relatives heard that the Lord had shown her great mercy, and they shared her joy.

59On the eighth day they came to circumcise the child, and they were going to name him after his father Zechariah, **60**but his mother spoke up and said, "No! He is to be called John."

61They said to her, "There is no one among your relatives who has that name."

62Then they made signs to his father, to find out what he would like to name the child. **63**He asked for a writing tablet, and to everyone's astonishment he wrote, "His name is John." **64**Immediately his mouth was opened and his tongue was loosed, and he began to speak, praising God. **65**The neighbors were all filled with awe, and throughout the hill country of Judea people were talking about all these things. **66**Everyone who heard this wondered about it, asking, "What then is this child going to be?" For the Lord's hand was with him.

Zechariah's Song

67His father Zechariah was filled with the Holy Spirit and prophesied:

68"Praise be to the Lord, the God of Israel,
>   because he has come and has redeemed his
>   people.
69He has raised up a horn*a* of salvation for us
>   in the house of his servant David
70(as he said through his holy prophets of long ago),
71salvation from our enemies
>   and from the hand of all who hate us—
72to show mercy to our fathers
>   and to remember his holy covenant,
73   the oath he swore to our father Abraham:
74to rescue us from the hand of our enemies,
>   and to enable us to serve him without fear
75   in holiness and righteousness before him all our
>   days.

76And you, my child, will be called a prophet of the
>   Most High;
>   for you will go on before the Lord to prepare
>   the way for him,
77to give his people the knowledge of salvation

a69 Horn here symbolizes strength.

---

1. Of the attributes of God celebrated in Mary's song, which do you appreciate the most? Which challenges you the most? Why? 2. Considering Mary, what level of social status do you need to fulfill God's purposes? Does that encourage you? Why? 3. Would Mary consider you God's humble servant or a proud, rich ruler?

What is your nickname and how did you get it?

1. How did John's birth fulfill the words of the angel in verses 13–17? 2. How did the neighbors and relatives respond to these events? How does all this begin to promote the Gospel? 3. As Zechariah's neighbor, what would you think about his son?

1. Describe a time when you, like Zechariah, took a step of faith and began speaking, praising God. 2. How was "the Lord's hand" seen in John's life? In your life?

How did you (or would you) celebrate the birth of your first child?

1. Make a list of the things for which Zechariah praises God. How does his song compare and contrast with Mary's (vv. 46–55)? 2. What does it mean that Zechariah was "filled with the Holy Spirit"? Is that the same experience with the Spirit that believers experience today? Why or why not? 3. What, according to this song, is the purpose of salvation? How does Zechariah's song show God's unfolding plan from OT days to the coming of the Messiah?

1. Of the promises listed in this song, which one means the most to you? Why? 2. How has God unfolded his plan of salvation in your life? Who helped prepare the way? What were some key events that led you to your commitment to Jesus? 3. Write a verse of praise to God using the special events from your own spiritual journey.

through the forgiveness of their sins,
⁷⁸because of the tender mercy of our God,
by which the rising sun will come to us from
heaven
⁷⁹to shine on those living in darkness
and in the shadow of death,
to guide our feet into the path of peace."

⁸⁰And the child grew and became strong in spirit; and he lived in the desert until he appeared publicly to Israel.

The Birth of Jesus

2 In those days Caesar Augustus issued a decree that a census should be taken of the entire Roman world. ²(This was the first census that took place while Quirinius was governor of Syria.) ³And everyone went to his own town to register.

⁴So Joseph also went up from the town of Nazareth in Galilee to Judea, to Bethlehem the town of David, because he belonged to the house and line of David. ⁵He went there to register with Mary, who was pledged to be married to him and was expecting a child. ⁶While they were there, the time came for the baby to be born, ⁷and she gave birth to her firstborn, a son. She wrapped him in cloths and placed him in a manger, because there was no room for them in the inn.

The Shepherds and the Angels

⁸And there were shepherds living out in the fields nearby, keeping watch over their flocks at night. ⁹An angel of the Lord appeared to them, and the glory of the Lord shone around them, and they

---

What is one way your hometown is different now than when you grew up? Is it still home to you? Why or why not?

In light of the promises of 1:30–35, how might Mary feel as she awaits delivery in a stable? How does this tie into God's plan (Mic 5:2)?

How did God take your "hopeless situation" and use it for good? What does that teach you?

When does your Christmas tree go up? Who trims it? How? What other traditions do you observe from your childhood?

Luke 2:1–20   THE BIRTH OF JESUS

1. Pregnant before marriage. Broke. Homeless. If you were Mary and Joseph's friend, what chance would you have given them?
   a. none
   b. 50/50
   c. uphill all the way
   d. a great way to begin

2. Why do you suppose the Savior of the world was born in an obscure village and laid in a manger?
   a. to fulfill Old Testament prophecy
   b. to show he was an ordinary person
   c. It just happened that way.
   d. He demanded no special favors.
   e. God didn't want to draw attention to his son's birth.
   f. No place would have been as grand as he deserved.

3. What effect did the angelic visit have on the shepherds?
   a. They wondered if they had been dreaming.
   b. They saw God in a new way.
   c. Their lives were changed forever.
   d. It was soon business as usual.

4. What do you think the shepherds were most excited to tell others?
   a. about hearing the angels sing
   b. about seeing the newborn baby
   c. God's plan for their salvation
   d. that the angel's words were true
   e. that the wait for Messiah was over

5. Do you think Mary and Joseph understood the full significance of the child they brought into the world?
   a. probably not
   b. up to a point
   c. Mary could have.
   d. They must have.
   e. They couldn't have.

6. What effect has the news of Christ's birth had on you?
   a. business as usual
   b. spiritual commitment
   c. an awakened sense of joy
   d. hope for the future
   e. thankfulness for God's forgiveness
   f. confusion about God's plan

7. How would you describe your relationship with Jesus Christ now?

8. If you were to spread the word about what Jesus has done for you, with whom would you speak first?

9. How would Mary and Joseph's humble beginnings prepare them for parenting?
   a. It gave them a dose of real life.
   b. It caused them to grow up fast.
   c. It caused them to depend on God.
   d. It showed them that struggle is the best teacher.

10. How would you compare your start to Jesus' parents'?
    a. We were also very young.
    b. We didn't have much either.
    c. We were also under much stress.
    d. Our start was much easier.

11. What was your reaction when you found out you were going to have your first baby? Reflecting back, how prepared were you to be a parent?
    a. I was totally prepared.
    b. I was basically prepared.
    c. I was basically unprepared.
    d. I was totally unprepared.

were terrified. ¹⁰But the angel said to them, "Do not be afraid. I bring you good news of great joy that will be for all the people. ¹¹Today in the town of David a Savior has been born to you; he is Christ*ᵃ* the Lord. ¹²This will be a sign to you: You will find a baby wrapped in cloths and lying in a manger."

¹³Suddenly a great company of the heavenly host appeared with the angel, praising God and saying,

¹⁴"Glory to God in the highest,
    and on earth peace to men on whom his favor
        rests."

¹⁵When the angels had left them and gone into heaven, the shepherds said to one another, "Let's go to Bethlehem and see this thing that has happened, which the Lord has told us about."

¹⁶So they hurried off and found Mary and Joseph, and the baby, who was lying in the manger. ¹⁷When they had seen him, they spread the word concerning what had been told them about this child, ¹⁸and all who heard it were amazed at what the shepherds said to them. ¹⁹But Mary treasured up all these things and pondered them in her heart. ²⁰The shepherds returned, glorifying and praising God for all the things they had heard and seen, which were just as they had been told.

Jesus Presented in the Temple

²¹On the eighth day, when it was time to circumcise him, he was named Jesus, the name the angel had given him before he had been conceived.

²²When the time of their purification according to the Law of Moses had been completed, Joseph and Mary took him to Jerusalem to present him to the Lord ²³(as it is written in the Law of the Lord, "Every firstborn male is to be consecrated to the Lord"*ᵇ*), ²⁴and to offer a sacrifice in keeping with what is said in the Law of the Lord: "a pair of doves or two young pigeons."*ᶜ*

²⁵Now there was a man in Jerusalem called Simeon, who was righteous and devout. He was waiting for the consolation of Israel, and the Holy Spirit was upon him. ²⁶It had been revealed to him by the Holy Spirit that he would not die before he had seen the Lord's Christ. ²⁷Moved by the Spirit, he went into the temple courts. When the parents brought in the child Jesus to do for him what the custom of the Law required, ²⁸Simeon took him in his arms and praised God, saying:

²⁹"Sovereign Lord, as you have promised,
    you now dismiss*ᵈ* your servant in peace.
³⁰For my eyes have seen your salvation,
³¹   which you have prepared in the sight of all
        people,
³²a light for revelation to the Gentiles
    and for glory to your people Israel."

³³The child's father and mother marveled at what was said about him. ³⁴Then Simeon blessed them and said to Mary, his mother: "This child is destined to cause the falling and rising of many in Israel, and to be a sign that will be spoken against, ³⁵so that the thoughts of many hearts will be revealed. And a sword will pierce your own soul too."

³⁶There was also a prophetess, Anna, the daughter of Phanuel, of

1. How does the shepherds' experience with the angels compare to that of Zechariah (1:8–9) and Mary (1:26–27)? 2. Of all the people the angels could have visited, why did God send them to the shepherds? How does that relate to Mary's song (1:46–55)?

1. God appeared to Zechariah, Mary and the shepherds when they were just being themselves. What does that imply about what it means to be "spiritual"? How has God spoken to you in the ordinary flow of life? 2. What precious event has God done that you "treasure in your heart"?

1. When you were growing up, what teacher, coach or relative made you feel special? How did that person make you feel good? 2. Who is the oldest person you know?

1. What Mosaic laws are being fulfilled by this presentation (see Lev 12:1–8, Ex 13:2, 12,13)? How do these events foreshadow Jesus' mission? 2. What does this temple ceremony reveal about the parents of Jesus: They were very poor? Religious? Proud? Dedicated? Fearful of their salvation? 3. In Simeon's two prophecies (vv. 29–32,34–35), what was he predicting about the work of Jesus? His effect on people? The pain of his parents? 4. Do you know anyone like dear old, saintly Anna? How does she complement Simeon's prophecy? 5. What impact would these startling predictions by Simeon and Anna have on all who were listening that day? On the parents of Jesus as they returned home (vv. 33,39)? 6. What do you learn about Mary and Joseph in this passage? About Jesus? About God?

1. How has Christ brought "light" to your life? How is he still the cause of "the falling and rising" of people that you know? 2. Did your parents dedicate you to the Lord? How did they help you mature spiritually? 3. When has God brought along a "Simeon" and "Anna" to confirm something in your life? How did this affect you?

ᵃ11 Or *Messiah*. "The Christ" (Greek) and "the Messiah" (Hebrew) both mean "the Anointed One"; also in verse 26.   *ᵇ23* Exodus 13:2,12   *ᶜ24* Lev. 12:8   *ᵈ29* Or *promised, / now dismiss*

the tribe of Asher. She was very old; she had lived with her husband seven years after her marriage, [37]and then was a widow until she was eighty-four.[a] She never left the temple but worshiped night and day, fasting and praying. [38]Coming up to them at that very moment, she gave thanks to God and spoke about the child to all who were looking forward to the redemption of Jerusalem.

[39]When Joseph and Mary had done everything required by the Law of the Lord, they returned to Galilee to their own town of Nazareth. [40]And the child grew and became strong; he was filled with wisdom, and the grace of God was upon him.

The Boy Jesus at the Temple

[41]Every year his parents went to Jerusalem for the Feast of the Passover. [42]When he was twelve years old, they went up to the Feast, according to the custom. [43]After the Feast was over, while his parents were returning home, the boy Jesus stayed behind in Jerusalem, but they were unaware of it. [44]Thinking he was in their company, they traveled on for a day. Then they began looking for him among their relatives and friends. [45]When they did not find him, they went back to Jerusalem to look for him. [46]After three days they found him in the temple courts, sitting among the teachers, listening to them and asking them questions. [47]Everyone who heard him was amazed at his understanding and his answers. [48]When his parents saw him, they were astonished. His mother said to him, "Son, why have you treated us like this? Your father and I have been anxiously searching for you."

[49]"Why were you searching for me?" he asked. "Didn't you

---

1. What was your best family trip? **2.** Ever get lost as a child? What happened?

1. What was the significance of this feast, which was an annual tradition with Jesus' parents (see Dt 16:1–6)? **2.** What do Jesus' character traits revealed in this passage (vv. 43–51) tell us about him? **3.** How much does he seem to know about his mission? How much do his parents know? **4.** Why do you think Luke included this episode of Jesus' life?

Has your hunger for God ever been misunderstood by your family? How? How do you maintain a balance between daily responsibilities and serving God?

---

a37 Or *widow for eighty-four years*

Luke 2:21–40   **JESUS PRESENTED IN THE TEMPLE**

Joseph and Mary now fulfill three Old Testament requirements for parents: circumcision, the ritual purification of the mother and the dedication of the firstborn.

1. If you were Joseph or Mary and experienced the events in this story, what would have been the first thing you wrote in your diary for that day?
   a. "Everybody loved him—I was so proud!"
   b. "Old people say such strange things sometimes!"
   c. "I never had so much to thank the Lord for as I do now!"
   d. "I wonder what that man meant about a sword piercing my soul."

2. Why do you suppose this was such a meaningful occasion for Simeon?
   a. He had been expecting to see the Christ.
   b. He had waited so long for this moment.
   c. God had not forgotten about his promise of the Messiah.
   d. He marveled at how God could use a baby to bring his salvation.

3. Why do you suppose this was such a meaningful occasion for Anna?
   a. Years of prayer were answered.
   b. Her heart was filled with praise.
   c. God showed her this baby was the Messiah.
   d. She was privileged to introduce the Messiah to others.

4. In Simeon's prophetic words about the child, what was he predicting?
   a. Jesus would bring the light of salvation to both Jews and Gentiles.
   b. Israel would reject their Messiah.
   c. People will respond to Jesus strongly—one way or the other.
   d. Both Jesus and Mary would suffer greatly.

5. How did your parents dedicate you to the Lord (if at all)? How did they help you mature spiritually?

6. How has Christ brought "light" to your life in the past? What is he illuminating about your spiritual life now?

7. Which of the following were or are on your list for doing "everything required" by the Lord?

a. circumcision
b. baptism or dedication
c. taking my child to church
d. praying *for* my child
e. praying *with* my child
f. teaching my child about God
g. disciplining my child
h. spending lots of time with my child

8. Which of those actions are your top two priorities right now? Which of them do you have the hardest time doing?

9. What would be the crowning joy for you in your old age?
a. to see my children's children
b. to see my family serving God
c. to strike it rich
d. to leave the world a better place
e. to feel I have done God's will
f. to know I've spent my days walking with the Lord

10. What family or young person might God want you to "bless"? How will you go about doing that—A letter? A phone call? A personal visit? Your prayers?

know I had to be in my Father's house?" ⁵⁰But they did not understand what he was saying to them.

⁵¹Then he went down to Nazareth with them and was obedient to them. But his mother treasured all these things in her heart. ⁵²And Jesus grew in wisdom and stature, and in favor with God and men.

John the Baptist Prepares the Way

3 In the fifteenth year of the reign of Tiberius Caesar—when Pontius Pilate was governor of Judea, Herod tetrarch of Galilee, his brother Philip tetrarch of Iturea and Traconitis, and Lysanias tetrarch of Abilene— ²during the high priesthood of Annas and Caiaphas, the word of God came to John son of Zechariah in the desert. ³He went into all the country around the Jordan, preaching a baptism of repentance for the forgiveness of sins. ⁴As is written in the book of the words of Isaiah the prophet:

> "A voice of one calling in the desert,
> 'Prepare the way for the Lord,
>   make straight paths for him.
> ⁵Every valley shall be filled in,
>   every mountain and hill made low.
> The crooked roads shall become straight,
>   the rough ways smooth.
> ⁶And all mankind will see God's salvation.'"[a]

[a]6 Isaiah 40:3-5

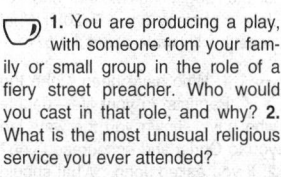

1. You are producing a play, with someone from your family or small group in the role of a fiery street preacher. Who would you cast in that role, and why? **2.** What is the most unusual religious service you ever attended?

1. How much time passes between appearances of John the Baptist here and in 1:80? What was John doing in those intervening years (Mt 3:1–6; Mk 1:4–6)? Why? **2.** Why does Luke list all the political and religious figures in verses 1–2? **3.** How would you describe John's message and style? **4.** What's radical about John's message? What does the "root" and "fruit" signify (v. 9)? Is he advocating social upheaval? Or inner transformation? Is he preaching or meddling? Why? Why would

---

      Luke 2:41–52   **YOUNG JESUS AT THE TEMPLE**

1. What do you think of Jesus' behavior in this story?
   a. He disobeyed his parents.
   b. He was oblivious to his parents.
   c. He behaved like any 12-year-old.
   d. He put his heavenly Father's concerns over his parents' concerns.

2. What do you think of Mary and Joseph's behavior in this story?
   a. They were negligent parents.
   b. They behaved like any parents would.
   c. They gave Jesus more freedom than parents can today.
   d. They were confused about who Jesus really was.

3. If you had been Mary or Joseph, what would you have said to Jesus?
   a. "Why did you run off like that?!"
   b. "You had us worried sick!"
   c. "I'm so sorry we forgot you!"
   d. "You're grounded for a month!"
   e. "I understand why you are here."

4. This event was important in Jesus' development because it showed he:
   a. had become independent.
   b. was choosing to honor his Father.
   c. could now teach his elders.
   d. knew he was God's Son.

5. In what ways are you growing "in wisdom and stature, and in favor with God and men"?

6. What similar tension have you experienced with your parents? (How can you reduce it?)
   a. My parents don't understand me.
   b. I probably confuse my parents too.
   c. My parents don't like some of the places I hang out.
   d. I go through hassles about what time I have to come home.

7. As a parent, how can you relate to this story?
   a. This sounds like my teenager!
   b. My child is a lot like Jesus, except for the "obedient" part!
   c. Like Mary, I often ask or think "Why have you treated us like this?"
   d. It reminds me that my strong-willed child is full of potential.
   e. It illustrates how perplexing my "gifted" child can be.
   f. Like Joseph and Mary must have felt, I feel like nobody else can understand what I go through.

8. What are your biggest anxieties about parenting teens or adolescent-aged children?

9. How does this story give you comfort or insight?
   a. Even Jesus' parents had to go through stress and challenges.
   b. Even Jesus did things that disturbed his parents.
   c. Developing independence is necessary in growing up.
   d. Sometimes we misjudge children.
   e. Sometimes children mature without us really noticing.

10. How much stress have you experienced due to the changes in your children's lives? How do you deal with that stress?

11. What does this story say to you about your relationships?
   a. I need to do what God wants regardless of what others think.
   b. Like Mary, if I'm upset with someone I should voice my concerns.
   c. Like Jesus, if I know I'm doing what's right I shouldn't apologize.
   d. In all my relationships, I have to be at peace with myself.

12. How have you noticed your group growing in wisdom and in relationship with God and each other?

anyone go out of their way to hear such a preacher? **5.** Why is John confused with Christ (v. 15; Jn 1:19–28)? By contrast, how does John differentiate himself and his ministry? What does the "wheat" and "chaff" signify (v. 17)? **6.** What is the beginning of the end for John's ministry (vv. 19–20)? What does this illustrate about John?

1. Who have been "John the Baptists" in your life—people who have shown you the way, led you to Christ and encouraged you? **2.** If you asked John, "What should we do?" how would he answer? **3.** What *one* action will you take this week to produce fruit in keeping with your repentance? **4.** How can you emulate John's attitude toward Jesus as seen in verse 16?

1. Who is the historian in your family? What has he/she done to help you know more about your ancestors? **2.** If you were to explore in more detail the life of one of your ancestors, whose life would you investigate? Why? **3.** Whose life would you prefer not to know about?

1. What is significant about Jesus being baptized at the same time as "all the people"? What three things happen at Jesus' baptism that make it unlike the others' (vv. 21–22)? Was Jesus any different after his baptism? Why or why not? **2.** How does this account of Jesus' baptism compare and contrast with the other accounts (Mt 3:13–17; Mk 1:9–11; Jn 1:32–34)? **3.** If Matthew's genealogy starts with Abraham to demonstrate God's working through the chosen people (Mt 1:1–17), what is Luke's point in going all the way back to Adam (v. 38)? What do Adam and Jesus have in common? Why else might Luke include this genealogy (see 1:27,32,69)? **4.** In this genealogy, which names stand out to you? What do you know about them? What can you conclude about Jesus' earthly ancestry

7John said to the crowds coming out to be baptized by him, "You brood of vipers! Who warned you to flee from the coming wrath? 8Produce fruit in keeping with repentance. And do not begin to say to yourselves, 'We have Abraham as our father.' For I tell you that out of these stones God can raise up children for Abraham. 9The ax is already at the root of the trees, and every tree that does not produce good fruit will be cut down and thrown into the fire."

10"What should we do then?" the crowd asked.

11John answered, "The man with two tunics should share with him who has none, and the one who has food should do the same."

12Tax collectors also came to be baptized. "Teacher," they asked, "what should we do?"

13"Don't collect any more than you are required to," he told them.

14Then some soldiers asked him, "And what should we do?"

He replied, "Don't extort money and don't accuse people falsely—be content with your pay."

15The people were waiting expectantly and were all wondering in their hearts if John might possibly be the Christ.*a* 16John answered them all, "I baptize you with*b* water. But one more powerful than I will come, the thongs of whose sandals I am not worthy to untie. He will baptize you with the Holy Spirit and with fire. 17His winnowing fork is in his hand to clear his threshing floor and to gather the wheat into his barn, but he will burn up the chaff with unquenchable fire." 18And with many other words John exhorted the people and preached the good news to them.

19But when John rebuked Herod the tetrarch because of Herodias, his brother's wife, and all the other evil things he had done, 20Herod added this to them all: He locked John up in prison.

The Baptism and Genealogy of Jesus

21When all the people were being baptized, Jesus was baptized too. And as he was praying, heaven was opened 22and the Holy Spirit descended on him in bodily form like a dove. And a voice came from heaven: "You are my Son, whom I love; with you I am well pleased."

23Now Jesus himself was about thirty years old when he began his ministry. He was the son, so it was thought, of Joseph,

the son of Heli, 24the son of Matthat,
the son of Levi, the son of Melki,
the son of Jannai, the son of Joseph,
25the son of Mattathias, the son of Amos,
the son of Nahum, the son of Esli,
the son of Naggai, 26the son of Maath,
the son of Mattathias, the son of Semein,
the son of Josech, the son of Joda,
27the son of Joanan, the son of Rhesa,
the son of Zerubbabel, the son of Shealtiel,
the son of Neri, 28the son of Melki,
the son of Addi, the son of Cosam,
the son of Elmadam, the son of Er,
29the son of Joshua, the son of Eliezer,
the son of Jorim, the son of Matthat,
the son of Levi, 30the son of Simeon,
the son of Judah, the son of Joseph,
the son of Jonam, the son of Eliakim,
31the son of Melea, the son of Menna,

a15 Or *Messiah*   *b16* Or *in*

the son of Mattatha, the son of Nathan,
the son of David, ³²the son of Jesse,
the son of Obed, the son of Boaz,
the son of Salmon,ᵃ the son of Nahshon,
³³the son of Amminadab, the son of Ram,ᵇ
the son of Hezron, the son of Perez,
the son of Judah, ³⁴the son of Jacob,
the son of Isaac, the son of Abraham,
the son of Terah, the son of Nahor,
³⁵the son of Serug, the son of Reu,
the son of Peleg, the son of Eber,
the son of Shelah, ³⁶the son of Cainan,
the son of Arphaxad, the son of Shem,
the son of Noah, the son of Lamech,
³⁷the son of Methuselah, the son of Enoch,
the son of Jared, the son of Mahalalel,
the son of Kenan, ³⁸the son of Enosh,
the son of Seth, the son of Adam,
the son of God.

The Temptation of Jesus

4 Jesus, full of the Holy Spirit, returned from the Jordan and was led by the Spirit in the desert, ²where for forty days he was tempted by the devil. He ate nothing during those days, and at the end of them he was hungry.

³The devil said to him, "If you are the Son of God, tell this stone to become bread."

⁴Jesus answered, "It is written: 'Man does not live on bread alone.'ᶜ"

⁵The devil led him up to a high place and showed him in an instant all the kingdoms of the world. ⁶And he said to him, "I will give you all their authority and splendor, for it has been given to me, and I can give it to anyone I want to. ⁷So if you worship me, it will all be yours."

⁸Jesus answered, "It is written: 'Worship the Lord your God and serve him only.'ᵈ"

⁹The devil led him to Jerusalem and had him stand on the highest point of the temple. "If you are the Son of God," he said, "throw yourself down from here. ¹⁰For it is written:

" 'He will command his angels concerning you
    to guard you carefully;
¹¹they will lift you up in their hands,
    so that you will not strike your foot against a
    stone.'ᵉ"

¹²Jesus answered, "It says: 'Do not put the Lord your God to the test.'ᶠ"

¹³When the devil had finished all this tempting, he left him until an opportune time.

Jesus Rejected at Nazareth

¹⁴Jesus returned to Galilee in the power of the Spirit, and news about him spread through the whole countryside. ¹⁵He taught in their synagogues, and everyone praised him.

¹⁶He went to Nazareth, where he had been brought up, and on the Sabbath day he went into the synagogue, as was his custom.

from what you know of this genealogy?

1. How has Jesus been like a "new Adam" for you—giving you a fresh start at life? How does Jesus' sonship (v. 22) form the basis for the way the Father sees you? What kinship do you sense with Jesus? 2. What means the most to you about your own baptism? 3. When in your life have you felt God's special touch, as if something new were beginning for you? What happened?

1. What's one of your all-time favorite foods? How often do you eat it? 2. If you were the emperor of the world, what would be your first decree?

1. Under what circumstances (vv. 1–2) was Jesus tempted: After a spiritual high? At a weak moment? At a new stage in life? 2. In each temptation, what was its appeal? Its price? How does Jesus resist them? How does Satan's use of Scripture differ from the way Jesus uses it? 3. How are the three temptations similar? Different? 4. Why were the temptations directed at Jesus immediately after he was affirmed by God at his baptism (3:22)?

1. What does it mean to you that all the authority and splendor of the kingdoms of the world has been given to Satan (vv. 5–6)? 2. If the devil had three shots at you, what three temptations would he use? 3. What can help you resist? What encouragement does this story provide?

1. What do you like best about the hometown where you grew up? 2. What was the symbol or sign of having "made it" in your hometown?

1. Compare 3:21; 4:1,14,18. What is the common element in each of these verses? What does this tell us about the source of Jesus' power? 2. What is signifi-

---

ᵃ32 Some early manuscripts *Sala*   ᵇ33 Some manuscripts *Amminadab, the son of Admin, the son of Arni*; other manuscripts vary widely.   ᶜ4 Deut. 8:3   ᵈ8 Deut. 6:13   ᵉ11 Psalm 91:11,12   ᶠ12 Deut. 6:16

cant about the time, place and posture (vv. 16,21–22) for Jesus' reading from Isaiah? **3.** What is Jesus' five-fold mission (vv. 18–19)? How did Jesus fulfill it then? Now? **4.** What expectations stirred in the people as a result of Jesus' claim (vv. 21–22)? **5.** What is Jesus saying through the proverb (v. 23)? Through the Elijah and Elisha stories (vv. 24–27)? Why does this turn their amazement (v. 22) into anger (vv. 28–29)? How does all this relate to the prophetic statements in 2:14, 2:32 and 3:6?

♡ **1.** If all five areas of Jesus' mission are to be carried on by the church as a whole, which area of concern do you give priority and which do you tend to neglect: (a) Preaching the Gospel? (b) Helping people to be free to live for God? (c) Performing acts of mercy? (d) Working for fair and just social structures? (e) Explaining God's grace to disheartened people? **2.** Who are the "Gentiles" (2:32) God desires you to care for? How might you do so?

And he stood up to read. [17]The scroll of the prophet Isaiah was handed to him. Unrolling it, he found the place where it is written:

> [18]"The Spirit of the Lord is on me,
>   because he has anointed me
>   to preach good news to the poor.
> He has sent me to proclaim freedom for the
>   prisoners
>   and recovery of sight for the blind,
> to release the oppressed,
> [19]   to proclaim the year of the Lord's favor."[a]

[20]Then he rolled up the scroll, gave it back to the attendant and sat down. The eyes of everyone in the synagogue were fastened on him, [21]and he began by saying to them, "Today this scripture is fulfilled in your hearing."

[22]All spoke well of him and were amazed at the gracious words that came from his lips. "Isn't this Joseph's son?" they asked.

[23]Jesus said to them, "Surely you will quote this proverb to me: 'Physician, heal yourself! Do here in your hometown what we have heard that you did in Capernaum.'"

[24]"I tell you the truth," he continued, "no prophet is accepted in his hometown. [25]I assure you that there were many widows in Israel in Elijah's time, when the sky was shut for three and a half years and there was a severe famine throughout the land. [26]Yet Elijah was not sent to any of them, but to a widow in Zarephath in the region of Sidon. [27]And there were many in Israel with lepro-

[a]*19* Isaiah 61:1,2

     Luke 4:14–30   **JESUS REJECTED AT NAZARETH**

Though Jesus was born in the town of Bethlehem, he grew up in the town of Nazareth in Galilee. Now, early in his ministry, he returns to Nazareth.

1. How would you describe the reception Jesus got in his hometown?
   a. thunderous applause
   b. faint praise
   c. mixed reviews
   d. a drastic change in public opinion

2. Why did people in Nazareth have a problem accepting Jesus?
   a. They were spiritually blind.
   b. He was just a carpenter's son.
   c. There were rumors about his "illegitimate birth."
   d. He sounded like a traitor—affirming Gentiles and condemning Israel.

3. In the end, why were Jesus' hometown neighbors so furious?
   a. They felt put down.
   b. They felt he was blasphemous.
   c. He felt he was better than them.
   d. He would rather go to non-Jews who would accept his claims.

4. How was Jesus affected when he was rejected by his hometown?
   a. He anticipated rejection and was not bothered much by it.
   b. He was upset, but didn't show it.
   c. Being human, he was hurt by it.
   d. Being divine, he wasn't affected by it at all.

5. In verses 18–21 Jesus applied five points from an Old Testament passage to his mission. Of these five ministries, which do you have a need for in your life—either literally/physically or symbolically/spiritually?
   a. good news to the poor
   b. freedom for the prisoners
   c. recovery of sight for the blind
   d. release for the oppressed
   e. proclaiming the year of the Lord's favor (celebrating God's grace to "debtors")

6. In which of the five ministries do you feel God is calling you to invest yourself toward serving others?

7. How do you deal with feelings of rejection?

8. Where do you find it hardest to be accepted as a person of value? How do feelings of rejection affect your participation in a group like this?

9. How does this story speak to your financial stress?
   a. I need some "good news."
   b. I have felt a lot of rejection because of my financial problems.
   c. I feel imprisoned and oppressed by financial pressures.
   d. I feel like others are saying, "You made this mess—'heal yourself!'"
   e. I wish I could be like Jesus and "walk right through" my creditors!

10. Do you think Jesus was a real man, with hair on his chest?
    a. I've never really thought about it.
    b. Yes—though he was divine, he was no less a man than I am.
    c. No—I like the stained glass Jesus.

11. What did your father think being a man meant? When you were an adolescent, how did you fare with the "tests of manhood"?

sy[a] in the time of Elisha the prophet, yet not one of them was cleansed—only Naaman the Syrian."

28All the people in the synagogue were furious when they heard this. 29They got up, drove him out of the town, and took him to the brow of the hill on which the town was built, in order to throw him down the cliff. 30But he walked right through the crowd and went on his way.

Jesus Drives Out an Evil Spirit

31Then he went down to Capernaum, a town in Galilee, and on the Sabbath began to teach the people. 32They were amazed at his teaching, because his message had authority.

33In the synagogue there was a man possessed by a demon, an evil[b] spirit. He cried out at the top of his voice, 34"Ha! What do you want with us, Jesus of Nazareth? Have you come to destroy us? I know who you are—the Holy One of God!"

35"Be quiet!" Jesus said sternly. "Come out of him!" Then the demon threw the man down before them all and came out without injuring him.

36All the people were amazed and said to each other, "What is this teaching? With authority and power he gives orders to evil spirits and they come out!" 37And the news about him spread throughout the surrounding area.

Jesus Heals Many

38Jesus left the synagogue and went to the home of Simon. Now Simon's mother-in-law was suffering from a high fever, and they asked Jesus to help her. 39So he bent over her and rebuked the fever, and it left her. She got up at once and began to wait on them.

40When the sun was setting, the people brought to Jesus all who had various kinds of sickness, and laying his hands on each one, he healed them. 41Moreover, demons came out of many people, shouting, "You are the Son of God!" But he rebuked them and would not allow them to speak, because they knew he was the Christ.[c]

42At daybreak Jesus went out to a solitary place. The people were looking for him and when they came to where he was, they tried to keep him from leaving them. 43But he said, "I must preach the good news of the kingdom of God to the other towns also, because that is why I was sent." 44And he kept on preaching in the synagogues of Judea.[d]

The Calling of the First Disciples

5 One day as Jesus was standing by the Lake of Gennesaret,[e] with the people crowding around him and listening to the word of God, 2he saw at the water's edge two boats, left there by the fishermen, who were washing their nets. 3He got into one of the boats, the one belonging to Simon, and asked him to put out a little from shore. Then he sat down and taught the people from the boat.

4When he had finished speaking, he said to Simon, "Put out into deep water, and let down[f] the nets for a catch."

5Simon answered, "Master, we've worked hard all night and haven't caught anything. But because you say so, I will let down the nets."

6When they had done so, they caught such a large number of

Who was your favorite teacher in secondary school?

1. How is this story related to the one before, especially verses 18–19? What similarities and differences do you see? 2. What strikes you most about the behavior of the evil spirit?

1. How has Jesus' authority grabbed your attention recently? 2. How is his authority bringing freedom to you?

When you need a break from pressure, where do you go? What do you do?

1. How has Jesus' life changed since his temptation? What in this section (vv. 38–42) shows that Jesus is beginning to feel the effects of this change? 2. Why does Jesus find it necessary to retreat at this time (vv. 42–44)? What pressure is he facing? What are his priorities?

Jesus is obviously busy, yet he takes time to be alone. How do you discern God's long-range call to you amidst all the shouting of the urgent needs?

What was your first paying job you had?

1. What do you think Simon was thinking and feeling in verse 5? 7? 8? 2. How did this miracle affect Peter? Why does this have a more profound effect on him than the healing of his mother-in-law? What is he beginning to grasp about Jesus? About sin? About belief in himself?

---

a27 The Greek word was used for various diseases affecting the skin—not necessarily leprosy.   b33 Greek unclean; also in verse 36   c41 Or Messiah   d44 Or the land of the Jews; some manuscripts Galilee   e1 That is, Sea of Galilee   f4 The Greek verb is plural.

1. When was the first time, if ever, that you responded to Jesus like Peter did in verse 8? **2.** In *your* "fishing business," how do you see Jesus: (a) Interesting, but a slightly irrelevant teacher? (b) Potentially a great business partner—if you could hire him to work for you? (c) The one who calls all the shots?

What illness are you most afraid of catching? Why?

1. By touching the leper before he heals him, what is Jesus demonstrating? **2.** Why does Jesus try to silence him?

1. When have you felt shunned, like a leper? How did Jesus "touch" you then? **2.** Who are the "lepers" in your life? What would it mean for you to touch them for Christ?

fish that their nets began to break. 7So they signaled their partners in the other boat to come and help them, and they came and filled both boats so full that they began to sink.

8When Simon Peter saw this, he fell at Jesus' knees and said, "Go away from me, Lord; I am a sinful man!" 9For he and all his companions were astonished at the catch of fish they had taken, 10and so were James and John, the sons of Zebedee, Simon's partners.

Then Jesus said to Simon, "Don't be afraid; from now on you will catch men." 11So they pulled their boats up on shore, left everything and followed him.

The Man With Leprosy

12While Jesus was in one of the towns, a man came along who was covered with leprosy.*a* When he saw Jesus, he fell with his face to the ground and begged him, "Lord, if you are willing, you can make me clean."

13Jesus reached out his hand and touched the man. "I am willing," he said. "Be clean!" And immediately the leprosy left him.

14Then Jesus ordered him, "Don't tell anyone, but go, show yourself to the priest and offer the sacrifices that Moses commanded for your cleansing, as a testimony to them."

15Yet the news about him spread all the more, so that crowds of

a12 The Greek word was used for various diseases affecting the skin—not necessarily leprosy.

Luke 5:1–11 CALLING OF THE FIRST DISCIPLES

1. If you had been Simon Peter when Jesus said, "Put out into deep water, and let down the nets for a catch," what would you have done?
   a. wondered who he thought he was
   b. told Jesus I was too tired
   c. suggested another time when the fish were biting
   d. politely told Jesus to stick to his preaching
   e. grudgingly complied with the idea

2. When they caught so many fish that their nets began to break, how do you think Peter felt?
   a. overjoyed
   b. dumfounded
   c. terrible about what he had said
   d. aware of who Jesus was

3. "Go away from me, Lord; I am a sinful man!" What did Peter mean?
   a. "Your power frightens me."
   b. "I feel unworthy to be around you because of my sinful life."
   c. "I know you are all you say you are, but I'm not ready to give up my life and follow you."
   d. "I'm afraid of what you might ask me to do."

4. Compared to Peter, how would you describe your spiritual beginning?
   a. pretty tame
   b. more intellectual
   c. just as confusing
   d. even crazier
   e. different, but just as real

5. What would Jesus have in mind if he asked you right now to launch out into the deep and let down your nets?

6. Of the decisions Peter and his friends made, which do you have the hardest time making?
   a. who to serve or follow
   b. where to live and work
   c. what my mission and role is in life
   d. when to begin something new

7. What gifts do you feel God has given you? How do you think God wants you to use your gifts as you follow Jesus?

8. How do these fishermen's decisions to leave everything strike you?
   a. How silly to give up a respectable career for who knows what.
   b. How exciting to try something new.
   c. It would take a lot more than this to get me to change careers.
   d. Following Jesus is more important than any career.

9. What connection can you see between your career or job and the call to follow Jesus? Can you let God use you more where you're at, or would you be more useful for God's purposes elsewhere?

10. What issues about working or about a career are most unsettling to you?
    a. knowing *if* or *how much* I should work
    b. adjusting to a new job or career
    c. deciding whether I should change jobs or careers
    d. balancing work and family
    e. discerning how work and career issues relate to following Christ

11. In order to "catch" people for Jesus, what do you have going for you to help draw them?
    a. my ability to make friends
    b. my knowledge of the Bible
    c. my willingness to help people
    d. my willingness to take risks
    e. my willingness to "walk my talk"

12. Where have you grown in your understanding of yourself in this course? Where have you seen growth in other members of your group?

people came to hear him and to be healed of their sicknesses. ¹⁶But Jesus often withdrew to lonely places and prayed.

Jesus Heals a Paralytic

¹⁷One day as he was teaching, Pharisees and teachers of the law, who had come from every village of Galilee and from Judea and Jerusalem, were sitting there. And the power of the Lord was present for him to heal the sick. ¹⁸Some men came carrying a paralytic on a mat and tried to take him into the house to lay him before Jesus. ¹⁹When they could not find a way to do this because of the crowd, they went up on the roof and lowered him on his mat through the tiles into the middle of the crowd, right in front of Jesus.

²⁰When Jesus saw their faith, he said, "Friend, your sins are forgiven."

²¹The Pharisees and the teachers of the law began thinking to themselves, "Who is this fellow who speaks blasphemy? Who can forgive sins but God alone?"

²²Jesus knew what they were thinking and asked, "Why are you thinking these things in your hearts? ²³Which is easier: to say, 'Your sins are forgiven,' or to say, 'Get up and walk'? ²⁴But that you may know that the Son of Man has authority on earth to forgive sins. . . ." He said to the paralyzed man, "I tell you, get up, take your mat and go home." ²⁵Immediately he stood up in front of them, took what he had been lying on and went home praising God. ²⁶Everyone was amazed and gave praise to God. They were filled with awe and said, "We have seen remarkable things today."

The Calling of Levi

²⁷After this, Jesus went out and saw a tax collector by the name of Levi sitting at his tax booth. "Follow me," Jesus said to him, ²⁸and Levi got up, left everything and followed him.

²⁹Then Levi held a great banquet for Jesus at his house, and a large crowd of tax collectors and others were eating with them. ³⁰But the Pharisees and the teachers of the law who belonged to their sect complained to his disciples, "Why do you eat and drink with tax collectors and 'sinners'?"

³¹Jesus answered them, "It is not the healthy who need a doctor, but the sick. ³²I have not come to call the righteous, but sinners to repentance."

Jesus Questioned About Fasting

³³They said to him, "John's disciples often fast and pray, and so do the disciples of the Pharisees, but yours go on eating and drinking."

³⁴Jesus answered, "Can you make the guests of the bridegroom fast while he is with them? ³⁵But the time will come when the bridegroom will be taken from them; in those days they will fast."

³⁶He told them this parable: "No one tears a patch from a new garment and sews it on an old one. If he does, he will have torn the new garment, and the patch from the new will not match the old. ³⁷And no one pours new wine into old wineskins. If he does, the new wine will burst the skins, the wine will run out and the wineskins will be ruined. ³⁸No, new wine must be poured into new wineskins. ³⁹And no one after drinking old wine wants the new, for he says, 'The old is better.'"

Who were your four closest friends in high school? What was one memorable prank you pulled off together?

1. How might the Pharisees and teachers have felt in verses 17–19? Verse 20? Verses 21–23? Verses 24–26? 2. The man came for *healing*, so why did Jesus raise the issue of *forgiveness*? How would the friends react to Jesus' words (v. 20)? To his actions (v. 24)? 3. What new realm of Jesus' authority is demonstrated here? 4. What motivates the Pharisees to respond as they do to the situation?

1. Who are you most like in this story? Why? 2. Are you a little paralyzed now—emotionally, spiritually, relationally? What needs to happen for you to "take your mat and go home"?

A famous person you admire is coming to dine with you tomorrow. What would you do to get ready?

1. Tax collectors lined their pockets with money they collected. How might the disciples (5:1–11) feel about Jesus' choice? 2. Why choose Levi? What is the irony here (vv. 31–32)? 3. Why is Jesus questioned about fasting? 4. What is Jesus implying by the parable in verses 34–35? In verses 36–39? How does this relate to Levi's call and to the disciples' not fasting? 5. What is the new cloth? Old garment? New wine? Old wineskins?

1. In this story, what do you have to do to qualify as a disciple? 2. In the way you relate to "undesirable types," are you more like Levi (inviting them to your party), the Pharisees (looking down on them), or the disciples (unsure what to do)? Why?

As a child, what family rules did you consider stupid? How do you view those rules now?

1. How are things developing in the Pharisees' ongoing investigation of Jesus (5:17,30, 33)? What is the main issue here for the Pharisees? For Jesus? 2. How does the story of David (1Sa 21:1–6) apply to Jesus and his disciples? 3. How does Jesus clarify the Sabbath issue (vv. 5,9)? 4. Why does Jesus provoke the Pharisees' wrath by healing on the Sabbath? Why not wait a day? 5. What is Jesus' attitude about formalized religion in 5:27–6:10?

1. When have you felt tension between obeying religious *principles* and helping *people*? What causes that tension? What relieves it? 2. As you try to follow Jesus, are you becoming more free to love others, or becoming more constrained by religious rules? Why?

What was one of the best teams you ever belonged to?

Lord of the Sabbath

6 One Sabbath Jesus was going through the grainfields, and his disciples began to pick some heads of grain, rub them in their hands and eat the kernels. ²Some of the Pharisees asked, "Why are you doing what is unlawful on the Sabbath?"

³Jesus answered them, "Have you never read what David did when he and his companions were hungry? ⁴He entered the house of God, and taking the consecrated bread, he ate what is lawful only for priests to eat. And he also gave some to his companions." ⁵Then Jesus said to them, "The Son of Man is Lord of the Sabbath."

⁶On another Sabbath he went into the synagogue and was teaching, and a man was there whose right hand was shriveled. ⁷The Pharisees and the teachers of the law were looking for a reason to accuse Jesus, so they watched him closely to see if he would heal on the Sabbath. ⁸But Jesus knew what they were thinking and said to the man with the shriveled hand, "Get up and stand in front of everyone." So he got up and stood there.

⁹Then Jesus said to them, "I ask you, which is lawful on the Sabbath: to do good or to do evil, to save life or to destroy it?"

¹⁰He looked around at them all, and then said to the man, "Stretch out your hand." He did so, and his hand was completely restored. ¹¹But they were furious and began to discuss with one another what they might do to Jesus.

The Twelve Apostles

¹²One of those days Jesus went out to a mountainside to pray, and spent the night praying to God. ¹³When morning came, he called his disciples to him and chose twelve of them, whom he also

---

Luke 5:27–39   **THE CALLING OF LEVI; NEW WINESKINS**

This story illustrates the disdain of two groups of people: (1) "sinners"—those who were notoriously evil, as well as those who refused to follow the Pharisees' interpretations of the Law of Moses; (2) tax collectors like Levi (also known as Matthew)—Jewish agents for the Roman government who were detested both by the religious authorities and common people for their disloyalty and cheating.

1. Why did Jesus call a despised tax collector like Levi to follow him?
   a. He saw his potential.
   b. He overlooked his faults.
   c. Levi must have been honest.
   d. He was calling him to repentance.
   e. He was looking for followers from a variety of backgrounds.

2. How do you think the other disciples felt when Jesus asked Levi to join their group?
   a. angry that Jesus did such a thing
   b. embarrassed for Levi to join them
   c. hopeful about their future tax bills
   d. delighted to accept a new recruit

3. Why do you think Jesus attended a dinner party with a bunch of tax collectors and "sinners"?
   a. to show he accepted them
   b. to convert them
   c. to enjoy himself
   d. to offend the self-righteousness of the Pharisees
   e. I'm not sure—I don't think I would have gone.

4. What did Jesus mean when he said, "I have not come to call the righteous, but sinners to repentance"?
   a. The Pharisees didn't need Jesus.
   b. Jesus came for sinners—not for Pharisees.
   c. Jesus came for sinners—anyone recognizing themselves as such.
   d. Only admitted sinners can see their need for salvation.
   e. You can lead a horse to water, but you can't make it drink.

5. Why weren't Jesus' disciples fasting? When would they?

6. Generally, how receptive are you to "new wine"?

a. I like to keep things as they are.
b. I accept change slowly, but with God's help I can handle it.
c. I'm all for change if I'm sure it's God's doing.
d. I'm a revolutionary—let's turn the world upside down!

7. Why do you suppose Levi and the other disciples responded to Jesus' call so readily? If you were in their position, how readily do you think you would have responded?

8. When was the first time you recall feeling Jesus' tug on your heart? What was it about Jesus that first drew you to him?

9. How has (or should) Jesus' "new wine" burst some of your "old wineskins"—your religious rituals or ruts?

10. How do you relate to "undesirable types"? Do you look down on them? Do you invite them to your parties? How can your group reach out to "sinners" and persons considered unacceptable?

designated apostles: [14]Simon (whom he named Peter), his brother Andrew, James, John, Philip, Bartholomew, [15]Matthew, Thomas, James son of Alphaeus, Simon who was called the Zealot, [16]Judas son of James, and Judas Iscariot, who became a traitor.

Blessings and Woes

[17]He went down with them and stood on a level place. A large crowd of his disciples was there and a great number of people from all over Judea, from Jerusalem, and from the coast of Tyre and Sidon, [18]who had come to hear him and to be healed of their diseases. Those troubled by evil[a] spirits were cured, [19]and the people all tried to touch him, because power was coming from him and healing them all.

[20]Looking at his disciples, he said:

> "Blessed are you who are poor,
>   for yours is the kingdom of God.
> [21]Blessed are you who hunger now,
>   for you will be satisfied.
> Blessed are you who weep now,
>   for you will laugh.
> [22]Blessed are you when men hate you,
>   when they exclude you and insult you
>   and reject your name as evil,
>   because of the Son of Man.

[23]"Rejoice in that day and leap for joy, because great is your reward in heaven. For that is how their fathers treated the prophets.

> [24]"But woe to you who are rich,
>   for you have already received your comfort.
> [25]Woe to you who are well fed now,
>   for you will go hungry.
> Woe to you who laugh now,
>   for you will mourn and weep.
> [26]Woe to you when all men speak well of you,
>   for that is how their fathers treated the false
>   prophets.

Love for Enemies

[27]"But I tell you who hear me: Love your enemies, do good to those who hate you, [28]bless those who curse you, pray for those who mistreat you. [29]If someone strikes you on one cheek, turn to him the other also. If someone takes your cloak, do not stop him from taking your tunic. [30]Give to everyone who asks you, and if anyone takes what belongs to you, do not demand it back. [31]Do to others as you would have them do to you.

[32]"If you love those who love you, what credit is that to you? Even 'sinners' love those who love them. [33]And if you do good to those who are good to you, what credit is that to you? Even 'sinners' do that. [34]And if you lend to those from whom you expect repayment, what credit is that to you? Even 'sinners' lend to 'sinners,' expecting to be repaid in full. [35]But love your enemies, do good to them, and lend to them without expecting to get anything back. Then your reward will be great, and you will be sons of the Most High, because he is kind to the ungrateful and wicked. [36]Be merciful, just as your Father is merciful.

[a] 18 Greek *unclean*

In the context of chapter 6, what is significant about Jesus calling these men? What do you know about them? Who are brothers? Buddies? Antagonists?

Describe a time recently when something you dreaded or something you wished for was disappointing.

1. Who is in the crowd? Why have they come? How does Jesus meet their needs? How do his actions (vv. 18–19) relate to his teaching (vv. 20–22)? **2.** What four qualities ought to characterize "kingdom people" (vv. 20–22)? How would you define each of these? What blessing is promised for each? Are these present blessings or future blessings? **3.** Who is Jesus addressing (vv. 24–26)? How would you define each warning he gives here?

1. How do the values Jesus talks about here compare with the values you are sold every day on TV? What values do you and your family accept? Reject? **2.** If you could add another "blessed" and another "woe" to counteract modern values, what would you want to add?

As a child, who were the bad guys on your favorite Saturday morning cartoons or TV show?

1. Why has Jesus made a shift in the object of love (see Lev 19:18)? What specifically are we to do to enemies? **2.** Since applying verses 29–30 literally could reinforce someone's bad behavior, what is Jesus' point (see vv. 31, 36)?

1. How does this description of love challenge you? **2.** How can that be a model for relating to someone you find difficult? **3.** Have you ever shown love to an enemy? How?

1. Would you rather be a movie director or a movie critic? Why? 2. Where would you like to locate your "dream house"? Why?

1. What activities does Jesus condemn and commend (vv. 37–38)? What does the promise (v. 38) mean in this context? 2. Does verse 37 say that we must love others before God will love us? Why or why not? 3. What's the point of this parable (vv. 39–40) in this context? 4. What is the point of the speck and the plank? 5. How does the tree and its fruit (vv. 43–45) help you recognize a "kingdom person"? How does this relate to verses 37–42? 6. Compare the two houses and their owner-builders (vv. 46–49). How does this lesson relate to verses 41–45?

1. In light of this three-fold passage (vv. 41–45), how would you recommend approaching people who need help or correction? 2. What quality of fruit would your acquaintances say you are producing: Grade A–1? So-so? Wormy? Why? What would Jesus need to do to make it good? 3. During the last storm to hit your life, what did you learn about your life's foundation?

What is the most dramatic "near death" experience you've ever had: An accident? Illness? Showing your father a bad report card? Stock market crash?

1. Describe the faith of the centurion in this story. How are Roman centurions portrayed elsewhere (see Mt 27:26,54; 28:4, 11–15; Ac 10:2; 23:17–18; 27:43)? In what way is this related to 6:43–45? 2. On what basis did the elders request Jesus' help? How does their approach differ from the centurion's (vv. 6–8)? How does this relate to Jesus' commandment (v. 9)? 3. What quality of faith is exhibited here?

Describe a time when you let go and let God accomplish his purposes.

Judging Others

37"Do not judge, and you will not be judged. Do not condemn, and you will not be condemned. Forgive, and you will be forgiven. **38**Give, and it will be given to you. A good measure, pressed down, shaken together and running over, will be poured into your lap. For with the measure you use, it will be measured to you."

39He also told them this parable: "Can a blind man lead a blind man? Will they not both fall into a pit? **40**A student is not above his teacher, but everyone who is fully trained will be like his teacher.

41"Why do you look at the speck of sawdust in your brother's eye and pay no attention to the plank in your own eye? **42**How can you say to your brother, 'Brother, let me take the speck out of your eye,' when you yourself fail to see the plank in your own eye? You hypocrite, first take the plank out of your eye, and then you will see clearly to remove the speck from your brother's eye.

A Tree and Its Fruit

43"No good tree bears bad fruit, nor does a bad tree bear good fruit. **44**Each tree is recognized by its own fruit. People do not pick figs from thornbushes, or grapes from briers. **45**The good man brings good things out of the good stored up in his heart, and the evil man brings evil things out of the evil stored up in his heart. For out of the overflow of his heart his mouth speaks.

The Wise and Foolish Builders

46"Why do you call me, 'Lord, Lord,' and do not do what I say? **47**I will show you what he is like who comes to me and hears my words and puts them into practice. **48**He is like a man building a house, who dug down deep and laid the foundation on rock. When a flood came, the torrent struck that house but could not shake it, because it was well built. **49**But the one who hears my words and does not put them into practice is like a man who built a house on the ground without a foundation. The moment the torrent struck that house, it collapsed and its destruction was complete."

The Faith of the Centurion

7 When Jesus had finished saying all this in the hearing of the people, he entered Capernaum. **2**There a centurion's servant, whom his master valued highly, was sick and about to die. **3**The centurion heard of Jesus and sent some elders of the Jews to him, asking him to come and heal his servant. **4**When they came to Jesus, they pleaded earnestly with him, "This man deserves to have you do this, **5**because he loves our nation and has built our synagogue." **6**So Jesus went with them.

He was not far from the house when the centurion sent friends to say to him: "Lord, don't trouble yourself, for I do not deserve to have you come under my roof. **7**That is why I did not even consider myself worthy to come to you. But say the word, and my servant will be healed. **8**For I myself am a man under authority, with soldiers under me. I tell this one, 'Go,' and he goes; and that one, 'Come,' and he comes. I say to my servant, 'Do this,' and he does it."

9When Jesus heard this, he was amazed at him, and turning to the crowd following him, he said, "I tell you, I have not found such great faith even in Israel." **10**Then the men who had been sent returned to the house and found the servant well.

Jesus Raises a Widow's Son

¹¹Soon afterward, Jesus went to a town called Nain, and his disciples and a large crowd went along with him. ¹²As he approached the town gate, a dead person was being carried out—the only son of his mother, and she was a widow. And a large crowd from the town was with her. ¹³When the Lord saw her, his heart went out to her and he said, "Don't cry."

¹⁴Then he went up and touched the coffin, and those carrying it stood still. He said, "Young man, I say to you, get up!" ¹⁵The dead man sat up and began to talk, and Jesus gave him back to his mother.

¹⁶They were all filled with awe and praised God. "A great prophet has appeared among us," they said. "God has come to help his people." ¹⁷This news about Jesus spread throughout Judea*a* and the surrounding country.

Jesus and John the Baptist

¹⁸John's disciples told him about all these things. Calling two of them, ¹⁹he sent them to the Lord to ask, "Are you the one who was to come, or should we expect someone else?"

²⁰When the men came to Jesus, they said, "John the Baptist sent us to you to ask, 'Are you the one who was to come, or should we expect someone else?'"

²¹At that very time Jesus cured many who had diseases, sicknesses and evil spirits, and gave sight to many who were blind. ²²So he replied to the messengers, "Go back and report to John what you have seen and heard: The blind receive sight, the lame walk, those who have leprosy*b* are cured, the deaf hear, the dead are raised, and the good news is preached to the poor. ²³Blessed is the man who does not fall away on account of me."

²⁴After John's messengers left, Jesus began to speak to the crowd about John: "What did you go out into the desert to see? A reed swayed by the wind? ²⁵If not, what did you go out to see? A man dressed in fine clothes? No, those who wear expensive clothes and indulge in luxury are in palaces. ²⁶But what did you go out to see? A prophet? Yes, I tell you, and more than a prophet. ²⁷This is the one about whom it is written:

> "'I will send my messenger ahead of you,
> who will prepare your way before you.'*c*

²⁸I tell you, among those born of women there is no one greater than John; yet the one who is least in the kingdom of God is greater than he."

²⁹(All the people, even the tax collectors, when they heard Jesus' words, acknowledged that God's way was right, because they had been baptized by John. ³⁰But the Pharisees and experts in the law rejected God's purpose for themselves, because they had not been baptized by John.)

³¹"To what, then, can I compare the people of this generation? What are they like? ³²They are like children sitting in the marketplace and calling out to each other:

> "'We played the flute for you,
> and you did not dance;
> we sang a dirge,
> and you did not cry.'

What national hero do you associate with the "good ol' days"?

This story resembles the one in 2 Kings 4:8–37. Why did Jesus perform this miracle in Nain (near Shunem)? What did he reveal about himself? What impact did he have on others?

How does Jesus' power over death affect the way you live your life?

---

1. (For the married:) When did you know that the person you married was "the one"? (For the unmarried:) What is the "sign" you look for as that decisive signal you have found the "right one"? 2. What situation recently has frustrated you because you weren't sure what to do?

1. How does John receive information about Jesus? Why can't he get it firsthand (see 3:20)? What question does John tell his men to ask Jesus (v. 20)? Why? 2. How does Jesus answer the question (vv. 21–23)? Why doesn't he answer directly? What six things characterize Jesus' ministry? 3. From Isaiah 29:18–19; 35:5–6; 61:1, how might John interpret Jesus' reply? How might he take Jesus' added blessing (v. 23)? 4. What questions does Jesus put to the people (vv. 24–28)? How does Jesus affirm John? 5. How does the people's response to John contrast to that of the Pharisees (v. 29)? How are the followers of the Pharisees like children?

1. When did you come to the place in your spiritual pilgrimage when you knew Jesus was "the one" you were looking for? How did you come to this understanding? What difference has it made? 2. Looking at verses 33–34, are you more like John or Jesus in your lifestyle? Would you be more effective if you lived differently? Why or why not? 3. If you could ask Jesus one question today about a decision you are facing, what would it be?

---

a17 Or *the land of the Jews*   *b22* The Greek word was used for various diseases affecting the skin—not necessarily leprosy.   *c27* Mal. 3:1

³³For John the Baptist came neither eating bread nor drinking wine, and you say, 'He has a demon.' ³⁴The Son of Man came eating and drinking, and you say, 'Here is a glutton and a drunkard, a friend of tax collectors and "sinners." ' ³⁵But wisdom is proved right by all her children."

Jesus Anointed by a Sinful Woman

³⁶Now one of the Pharisees invited Jesus to have dinner with him, so he went to the Pharisee's house and reclined at the table. ³⁷When a woman who had lived a sinful life in that town learned that Jesus was eating at the Pharisee's house, she brought an alabaster jar of perfume, ³⁸and as she stood behind him at his feet weeping, she began to wet his feet with her tears. Then she wiped them with her hair, kissed them and poured perfume on them.

³⁹When the Pharisee who had invited him saw this, he said to himself, "If this man were a prophet, he would know who is touching him and what kind of woman she is—that she is a sinner."

⁴⁰Jesus answered him, "Simon, I have something to tell you."

"Tell me, teacher," he said.

⁴¹"Two men owed money to a certain moneylender. One owed him five hundred denarii,ᵃ and the other fifty. ⁴²Neither of them had the money to pay him back, so he canceled the debts of both. Now which of them will love him more?"

ᵃ41 A denarius was a coin worth about a day's wages.

☕ 1. What is one special gift you've received from your children or parents? 2. What parties do you enjoy? Dislike?

📖 1. What risk was this "sinful woman" taking in coming to the house of Simon, the Pharisee? What does this tell you about her state of mind? 2. What is your impression of Simon? What do you think Jesus' purpose was in telling the parable in verses 41–43? Why didn't he just accuse Simon of not loving enough? 3. What does Jesus see in this woman that Simon does not? How does this affect Jesus' actions toward her? In this passage, what seems to be Jesus' main concern? Simon's concern? 4. Who do you think was a greater sinner, the woman or Simon? Why? How important is it to

---

Luke 7:36–50 JESUS ANOINTED BY A SINFUL WOMAN

1. Why do you think this woman, an apparent prostitute, came to the Pharisee's house?
   a. to ruin the party
   b. to upset Simon the Pharisee
   c. to seek forgiveness
   d. to minister to Jesus

2. How do you think Jesus felt when she began crying, wetting his feet with her tears, wiping them with her hair, then kissing his feet and pouring perfume on them?
   a. surprised   d. embarrassed
   b. flattered   e. moved
   c. upset   f. uncomfortable

3. Why do you suppose the woman expressed her repentance and devotion like she did, instead of verbally?

4. What are the implications of Jesus' words and parable?
   a. The more you have sinned the more you will love God.
   b. You can't experience grace until you recognize you are a sinner.
   c. Our love for Christ is the basis of our forgiveness.
   d. Our love for Christ is the evidence of our forgiveness.

5. Whom do you identify with most in this story?
   a. the woman—because I feel bad about my past
   b. the Pharisee—because I have a tendency to be judgmental
   c. Jesus—because hypocritical attitudes make me angry

6. Who in your life has played the role of Simon, questioning your value? Who has played the role of Jesus, believing in and sticking up for you?

7. How has the kindness and caring of others in this group "touched" you?

8. 🔍 When in your life have you most felt like an outsider (like this woman) who didn't belong? How closely can you relate to her ability to be herself regardless of how she appeared to others?

9. 👤 Which of the following expresses your attitude toward touching and being touched?
   a. I want and need to be touched and hugged more.
   b. I'm suspicious of people who want to touch me.
   c. I want to be touched and hugged,

but worry if it's okay.
   d. People should avoid touching—it brings too much temptation.
   e. To be close emotionally, you have to be able to touch physically.

10. ✝️ What needs to happen for you to feel the kind of forgiveness this woman felt?
   a. I need to get my life straightened out first.
   b. I need to find someone to talk to who is as sympathetic as Jesus.
   c. I need to stop listening to the "Pharisees" who condemn me.
   d. I need to accept the forgiveness which Jesus has already offered.

11. ✝️ What have you appreciated about this course? In your journey to come home to God, do you feel you have a clean slate? How can the group pray for you?

12. 👤 Conclude with a time of silent prayer: Do you need to ask God's forgiveness for failures sexually or in other ways in your relationships? Do you need to seek out someone to share with concerning these issues?

43Simon replied, "I suppose the one who had the bigger debt canceled."

"You have judged correctly," Jesus said.

44Then he turned toward the woman and said to Simon, "Do you see this woman? I came into your house. You did not give me any water for my feet, but she wet my feet with her tears and wiped them with her hair. **45**You did not give me a kiss, but this woman, from the time I entered, has not stopped kissing my feet. **46**You did not put oil on my head, but she has poured perfume on my feet. **47**Therefore, I tell you, her many sins have been forgiven—for she loved much. But he who has been forgiven little loves little."

48Then Jesus said to her, "Your sins are forgiven."

49The other guests began to say among themselves, "Who is this who even forgives sins?"

50Jesus said to the woman, "Your faith has saved you; go in peace."

The Parable of the Sower

8 After this, Jesus traveled about from one town and village to another, proclaiming the good news of the kingdom of God. The Twelve were with him, **2**and also some women who had been cured of evil spirits and diseases: Mary (called Magdalene) from whom seven demons had come out; **3**Joanna the wife of Cuza, the manager of Herod's household; Susanna; and many others. These women were helping to support them out of their own means.

4While a large crowd was gathering and people were coming to Jesus from town after town, he told this parable: **5**"A farmer went out to sow his seed. As he was scattering the seed, some fell along the path; it was trampled on, and the birds of the air ate it up. **6**Some fell on rock, and when it came up, the plants withered because they had no moisture. **7**Other seed fell among thorns, which grew up with it and choked the plants. **8**Still other seed fell on good soil. It came up and yielded a crop, a hundred times more than was sown."

When he said this, he called out, "He who has ears to hear, let him hear."

9His disciples asked him what this parable meant. **10**He said, "The knowledge of the secrets of the kingdom of God has been given to you, but to others I speak in parables, so that,

" 'though seeing, they may not see;
though hearing, they may not understand.'*a*

11"This is the meaning of the parable: The seed is the word of God. **12**Those along the path are the ones who hear, and then the devil comes and takes away the word from their hearts, so that they may not believe and be saved. **13**Those on the rock are the ones who receive the word with joy when they hear it, but they have no root. They believe for a while, but in the time of testing they fall away. **14**The seed that fell among thorns stands for those who hear, but as they go on their way they are choked by life's worries, riches and pleasures, and they do not mature. **15**But the seed on good soil stands for those with a noble and good heart, who hear the word, retain it, and by persevering produce a crop.

A Lamp on a Stand

16"No one lights a lamp and hides it in a jar or puts it under a bed. Instead, he puts it on a stand, so that those who come in can

a 10 Isaiah 6:9

this woman that Jesus loves and forgives her?

1. How difficult is it for you to express your love in a relationship with Jesus? 2. What is the most loving thing you have ever done for Jesus? For someone else? How was Jesus part of it? 3. What have you learned from this story that you could apply this week?

What kind of luck have you had with growing things? Are you a "green thumb" or a "brown thumb"? What is your secret of success (or reason for failure)?

1. What is Jesus' ministry style here (v. 1)? Who travels with him? What strikes you about them? 2. What is a parable? Why does Jesus use parables? 3. What is the reason why the disciples receive an explanation, while the others do not? How would the parable help the disciples to better understand what is happening in their ministry? 4. In Jesus' explanation of this parable, what is the seed? The birds? The soils? The fruit? The farmer? 5. What does it really mean to "hear"? How would you explain this parable to children who have never been on a farm? What modern analogy would you use? 6. What does Jesus mean to be "a noble and good heart"?

1. What kind of "soil" best represents you now? Five years ago? 2. When it comes to hearing God right now, are you: (a) Locked in on the station? (b) Getting a lot of static? (c) Barely picking up the signal? Why? The disciples were always asking Jesus questions (even dumb ones). How comfortable are you taking your questions to Jesus? 3. What help do you get from this parable about sharing your faith with others?

If I looked under your bed right now, what would I find? (A suitcase, old socks, dust balls!)

1. If Jesus and his message are the lamp of truth, what is this parable saying about the kingdom of God? What is the promise for those who do and don't listen? 2. How does Jesus expand on this in verses 19–21?

1. How do you feel about verse 17? 2. Are you closer to your church family or your family of origin? Why?

What is the worst storm you remember?

1. What is Jesus teaching his disciples by ignoring and then rebuking the storm? 2. What tone did Jesus use in verse 25?

Comparing your life to a storm, what would it be like right now: Partly cloudy? Lightning? Raging? Clearing up? What do you wish Jesus would do for you?

When did a vacation turn into something you never expected? What happened?

1. After verses 22–25, how might the disciples be feeling: As they arrive on the other side of the lake? Once they realize they are near a graveyard? As the demoniac runs toward them? 2. How does Jesus treat the man differently than the way others have? What is the net result? 3. How do the pig farmers respond? The townspeople? Why are they afraid? 4. Usually doing the opposite, why does Jesus tell this man to tell others what happened?

1. In your life right now, what is the thing that makes you feel like a "legion" (6,000 soldiers) is marching through your head, keeping you awake at night or filled with anxiety? 2. When, if ever, have you wanted Jesus to leave you alone? To get out of your life? To let you hurt yourself? 3. What is the most dramatic transformation you have seen Jesus work in someone's life? 4. When you first met Jesus, how did he treat you? How was this different from the way others treated you?

see the light. [17]For there is nothing hidden that will not be disclosed, and nothing concealed that will not be known or brought out into the open. [18]Therefore consider carefully how you listen. Whoever has will be given more; whoever does not have, even what he thinks he has will be taken from him."

Jesus' Mother and Brothers

[19]Now Jesus' mother and brothers came to see him, but they were not able to get near him because of the crowd. [20]Someone told him, "Your mother and brothers are standing outside, wanting to see you."

[21]He replied, "My mother and brothers are those who hear God's word and put it into practice."

Jesus Calms the Storm

[22]One day Jesus said to his disciples, "Let's go over to the other side of the lake." So they got into a boat and set out. [23]As they sailed, he fell asleep. A squall came down on the lake, so that the boat was being swamped, and they were in great danger.

[24]The disciples went and woke him, saying, "Master, Master, we're going to drown!"

He got up and rebuked the wind and the raging waters; the storm subsided, and all was calm. [25]"Where is your faith?" he asked his disciples.

In fear and amazement they asked one another, "Who is this? He commands even the winds and the water, and they obey him."

The Healing of a Demon-possessed Man

[26]They sailed to the region of the Gerasenes,[a] which is across the lake from Galilee. [27]When Jesus stepped ashore, he was met by a demon-possessed man from the town. For a long time this man had not worn clothes or lived in a house, but had lived in the tombs. [28]When he saw Jesus, he cried out and fell at his feet, shouting at the top of his voice, "What do you want with me, Jesus, Son of the Most High God? I beg you, don't torture me!" [29]For Jesus had commanded the evil[b] spirit to come out of the man. Many times it had seized him, and though he was chained hand and foot and kept under guard, he had broken his chains and had been driven by the demon into solitary places.

[30]Jesus asked him, "What is your name?"

"Legion," he replied, because many demons had gone into him. [31]And they begged him repeatedly not to order them to go into the Abyss.

[32]A large herd of pigs was feeding there on the hillside. The demons begged Jesus to let them go into them, and he gave them permission. [33]When the demons came out of the man, they went into the pigs, and the herd rushed down the steep bank into the lake and was drowned.

[34]When those tending the pigs saw what had happened, they ran off and reported this in the town and countryside, [35]and the people went out to see what had happened. When they came to Jesus, they found the man from whom the demons had gone out, sitting at Jesus' feet, dressed and in his right mind; and they were afraid. [36]Those who had seen it told the people how the demon-possessed man had been cured. [37]Then all the people of the region of the Gerasenes asked Jesus to leave them, because they were overcome with fear. So he got into the boat and left.

[a]26 Some manuscripts Gadarenes; other manuscripts Gergesenes; also in verse 37
[b]29 Greek unclean

38The man from whom the demons had gone out begged to go with him, but Jesus sent him away, saying, **39**"Return home and tell how much God has done for you." So the man went away and told all over town how much Jesus had done for him.

A Dead Girl and a Sick Woman

40Now when Jesus returned, a crowd welcomed him, for they were all expecting him. **41**Then a man named Jairus, a ruler of the synagogue, came and fell at Jesus' feet, pleading with him to come to his house **42**because his only daughter, a girl of about twelve, was dying.

As Jesus was on his way, the crowds almost crushed him. **43**And a woman was there who had been subject to bleeding for twelve years,[a] but no one could heal her. **44**She came up behind him and touched the edge of his cloak, and immediately her bleeding stopped.

45"Who touched me?" Jesus asked.

When they all denied it, Peter said, "Master, the people are crowding and pressing against you."

46But Jesus said, "Someone touched me; I know that power has gone out from me."

47Then the woman, seeing that she could not go unnoticed, came trembling and fell at his feet. In the presence of all the people, she told why she had touched him and how she had been instantly healed. **48**Then he said to her, "Daughter, your faith has healed you. Go in peace."

49While Jesus was still speaking, someone came from the house

a43 Many manuscripts *years, and she had spent all she had on doctors*

What is the most astonishing event you have ever witnessed?

1. Of all the people pressing for Jesus' attention, two get through to him—how so? **2.** Why do you think Jesus makes the sick woman reveal herself? For his sake? Or for her sake (vv. 46–48)? **3.** What else do you learn about her character before and after she touches Jesus' garment? How was her faith obvious to Jesus? **4.** What do you know about Jairus' daughter from verses 41,42,49 and 53? **5.** Why does Jesus say she will be healed, or that she is "only asleep," when the facts speak otherwise? **6.** What part does Jairus' intense desire have in the raising of the dead girl? **7.** Why does Jesus sometimes tell those he healed to be silent (v. 56; also 5:14), but other times orders the healed person to first go home and tell all (see 5:24; 8:39)?

 Luke 8:26–39   **THE HEALING OF A DEMON-POSSESSED MAN**

1. Stepping off the boat, how do you think Jesus reacted to the demon-possessed man?
   a. with kindness
   b. with fear
   c. with authority
   d. with uncertainty about the situation
   e. instantly recognizing the Enemy

2. What impresses you most about "Legion"?
   a. their number
   b. their power
   c. their fear of Jesus
   d. their path to destruction

3. Why do you think Jesus granted the demons' request to be allowed to go into the pigs?
   a. Sometimes you have to compromise with a powerful opponent.
   b. It was a dramatic way to get rid of the demons.
   c. Being a Jew, he didn't like pigs.
   d. The pigs (and demons) rushing into the lake were symbolic of the demons' defeat.
   e. He didn't—it just looked that way.

4. After the demons left him, how did the man feel?
   a. empty
   b. healthy
   c. hopeful
   d. in control of his choices
   e. desiring to belong again
   f. committed to Jesus

5. Why did the people of the region want Jesus to leave town?
   a. They were afraid of his power.
   b. They were afraid he might send more pigs into the lake.
   c. They were afraid he might cast out *their* demons.
   d. They were afraid he might be God.

6. Why did Jesus want the healed man to go home instead of with him?

7. What image from this story best describes you at this time?
   a. in solitary places
   b. crying out to Jesus
   c. experiencing God's healing
   d. sitting at Jesus' feet
   e. telling everyone what Jesus has done for me

8. If you could be freed from one specific thing, what would you choose?

9. In what way do you most identify with this demon-possessed man?
   a. My addiction has ruined my life.
   b. The things that afflict me are many.
   c. Sometimes I feel I am driven by an evil force inside of me.
   d. Sometimes I resist God.
   e. Sometimes I resist the people who are trying to help me.
   f. I can't beat this on my own.
   g. God has had great mercy on me.

10. Which of the following would you name as possible sources of your affliction? And what would you like Jesus to do for you in that area (or areas)?
   a. a poor self-image
   b. inherited tendencies to addiction
   c. trying to rely on myself alone
   d. relational or spiritual loneliness
   e. real demons
   f. a painful childhood or loss
   g. spiritual weakness

of Jairus, the synagogue ruler. "Your daughter is dead," he said. "Don't bother the teacher any more."

⁵⁰Hearing this, Jesus said to Jairus, "Don't be afraid; just believe, and she will be healed."

⁵¹When he arrived at the house of Jairus, he did not let anyone go in with him except Peter, John and James, and the child's father and mother. ⁵²Meanwhile, all the people were wailing and mourning for her. "Stop wailing," Jesus said. "She is not dead but asleep."

⁵³They laughed at him, knowing that she was dead. ⁵⁴But he took her by the hand and said, "My child, get up!" ⁵⁵Her spirit returned, and at once she stood up. Then Jesus told them to give her something to eat. ⁵⁶Her parents were astonished, but he ordered them not to tell anyone what had happened.

Jesus Sends Out the Twelve

9 When Jesus had called the Twelve together, he gave them power and authority to drive out all demons and to cure diseases, ²and he sent them out to preach the kingdom of God and to heal the sick. ³He told them: "Take nothing for the journey—no staff, no bag, no bread, no money, no extra tunic. ⁴Whatever house you enter, stay there until you leave that town. ⁵If people do not welcome you, shake the dust off your feet when you leave their town, as a testimony against them." ⁶So they set out and went from village to village, preaching the gospel and healing people everywhere.

⁷Now Herod the tetrarch heard about all that was going on. And he was perplexed, because some were saying that John had been raised from the dead, ⁸others that Elijah had appeared, and still others that one of the prophets of long ago had come back to life. ⁹But Herod said, "I beheaded John. Who, then, is this I hear such things about?" And he tried to see him.

Jesus Feeds the Five Thousand

¹⁰When the apostles returned, they reported to Jesus what they had done. Then he took them with him and they withdrew by themselves to a town called Bethsaida, ¹¹but the crowds learned about it and followed him. He welcomed them and spoke to them about the kingdom of God, and healed those who needed healing.

¹²Late in the afternoon the Twelve came to him and said, "Send the crowd away so they can go to the surrounding villages and countryside and find food and lodging, because we are in a remote place here."

¹³He replied, "You give them something to eat."

They answered, "We have only five loaves of bread and two fish—unless we go and buy food for all this crowd." ¹⁴(About five thousand men were there.)

But he said to his disciples, "Have them sit down in groups of about fifty each." ¹⁵The disciples did so, and everybody sat down. ¹⁶Taking the five loaves and the two fish and looking up to heaven, he gave thanks and broke them. Then he gave them to the disciples to set before the people. ¹⁷They all ate and were satisfied, and the disciples picked up twelve basketfuls of broken pieces that were left over.

Peter's Confession of Christ

¹⁸Once when Jesus was praying in private and his disciples were with him, he asked them, "Who do the crowds say I am?"

¹⁹They replied, "Some say John the Baptist; others say Elijah;

1. When have you been as desperate as Jairus and the bleeding woman? How did Jesus respond to you? 2. Have you ever been too frightened to come to God with a problem? Why? 3. From the stories in 8:2–56, what stands out to you about Jesus' power? His purposes? How might this make a difference as you face desperate situations?

What is one memorable camping trip you have had?

1. What decision does Jesus make about his ministry? Why? 2. What are the disciples told to do? Why? 3. How does King Herod react (vv. 7–9)? Why?

1. Who is someone you admire because they dared to give their life to a mission? 2. What is your mission in life, other than to keep food on the table? How does God's kingdom fit in?

How do you unwind when you return from work or a trip: Eat? Read? Sleep? Play? TV?

1. Why does Jesus take his disciples away with him upon their return? 2. How do you account for the differences in the way Jesus and the disciples view the crowd? 3. What thoughts must the disciples have as they collect the leftovers?

From what do you need a rest: Work hassles? Family? Church activities? Community activities? School deadlines? How would you cope if God gave you a new challenge instead?

When you were a teenager, how did peer pressure affect your choice of clothes? Music? Friends?

and still others, that one of the prophets of long ago has come back to life."

20"But what about you?" he asked. "Who do you say I am?"

Peter answered, "The Christ*a* of God."

21Jesus strictly warned them not to tell this to anyone. 22And he said, "The Son of Man must suffer many things and be rejected by the elders, chief priests and teachers of the law, and he must be killed and on the third day be raised to life."

23Then he said to them all: "If anyone would come after me, he must deny himself and take up his cross daily and follow me. 24For whoever wants to save his life will lose it, but whoever loses his life for me will save it. 25What good is it for a man to gain the whole world, and yet lose or forfeit his very self? 26If anyone is ashamed of me and my words, the Son of Man will be ashamed of him when he comes in his glory and in the glory of the Father and of the holy angels. 27I tell you the truth, some who are standing here will not taste death before they see the kingdom of God."

The Transfiguration

28About eight days after Jesus said this, he took Peter, John and James with him and went up onto a mountain to pray. 29As he was praying, the appearance of his face changed, and his clothes became as bright as a flash of lightning. 30Two men, Moses and Elijah, 31appeared in glorious splendor, talking with Jesus. They spoke about his departure, which he was about to bring to fulfillment at Jerusalem. 32Peter and his companions were very sleepy, but when they became fully awake, they saw his glory and the two men standing with him. 33As the men were leaving Jesus, Peter said to him, "Master, it is good for us to be here. Let us put up three shelters—one for you, one for Moses and one for Elijah." (He did not know what he was saying.)

34While he was speaking, a cloud appeared and enveloped them, and they were afraid as they entered the cloud. 35A voice came from the cloud, saying, "This is my Son, whom I have chosen; listen to him." 36When the voice had spoken, they found that Jesus was alone. The disciples kept this to themselves, and told no one at that time what they had seen.

The Healing of a Boy With an Evil Spirit

37The next day, when they came down from the mountain, a large crowd met him. 38A man in the crowd called out, "Teacher, I beg you to look at my son, for he is my only child. 39A spirit seizes him and he suddenly screams; it throws him into convulsions so that he foams at the mouth. It scarcely ever leaves him and is destroying him. 40I begged your disciples to drive it out, but they could not."

41"O unbelieving and perverse generation," Jesus replied, "how long shall I stay with you and put up with you? Bring your son here."

42Even while the boy was coming, the demon threw him to the ground in a convulsion. But Jesus rebuked the evil*b* spirit, healed the boy and gave him back to his father. 43And they were all amazed at the greatness of God.

While everyone was marveling at all that Jesus did, he said to his disciples, 44"Listen carefully to what I am about to tell you: The Son of Man is going to be betrayed into the hands of men." 45But they did not understand what this meant. It was hidden from them,

---

1. Why would Jesus be interested in this opinion poll? 2. Why does Jesus ask the follow-up question (v. 20)? 3. Why doesn't Jesus want them to tell anyone he is the Christ? 4. How might the disciples have felt about verse 22? 5. What activities or attitudes are key to following Christ (v. 23)?

1. What does it mean specifically to you to: (a) deny yourself, (b) take up your cross daily, (c) follow Christ, and (d) lose your life? 2. Have you ever been ashamed of Jesus? When? 3. Knowing what you do now, would you reconsider your commitment to Christ? Why or why not?

When did you last say something you regretted?

1. Why would Jesus take these three disciples to witness this event? How is this related to: (a) Peter's confession (vv. 18–20)? (b) Jesus' prophecy (v. 22)? (c) The preceding saying (v. 27)? (d) The radiant face of Moses (Ex 34:29–30)? 2. Why is this event misunderstood by Peter? Underscored by God (vv. 34–35)?

1. When have you experienced God in an unusual way? What happened? 2. When it comes to listening to Jesus, how hard of hearing are you?

Can you remember a tantrum you threw as a child? What happened?

1. What has evidently been going on while Jesus was gone? 2. What feelings are behind Jesus' words in verse 41? 3. After the healing, what does Jesus teach his disciples? What's the significance of this teaching?

1. If you had been one of the disciples who couldn't solve the boy's problem only days after you had been on a *mission* trip, how would you feel? 2. What spiritual low has recently followed a spiritual high for you?

---

*a*20 Or *Messiah*   *b*42 Greek *unclean*

so that they did not grasp it, and they were afraid to ask him about it.

Who Will Be the Greatest?

[46]An argument started among the disciples as to which of them would be the greatest. [47]Jesus, knowing their thoughts, took a little child and had him stand beside him. [48]Then he said to them, "Whoever welcomes this little child in my name welcomes me; and whoever welcomes me welcomes the one who sent me. For he who is least among you all—he is the greatest."

[49]"Master," said John, "we saw a man driving out demons in your name and we tried to stop him, because he is not one of us."

[50]"Do not stop him," Jesus said, "for whoever is not against you is for you."

Samaritan Opposition

[51]As the time approached for him to be taken up to heaven, Jesus resolutely set out for Jerusalem. [52]And he sent messengers on ahead, who went into a Samaritan village to get things ready for him; [53]but the people there did not welcome him, because he was heading for Jerusalem. [54]When the disciples James and John saw this, they asked, "Lord, do you want us to call fire down from heaven to destroy them[a]?" [55]But Jesus turned and rebuked them, [56]and[b] they went to another village.

The Cost of Following Jesus

[57]As they were walking along the road, a man said to him, "I will follow you wherever you go."

[58]Jesus replied, "Foxes have holes and birds of the air have nests, but the Son of Man has no place to lay his head."

[59]He said to another man, "Follow me."

But the man replied, "Lord, first let me go and bury my father."

[60]Jesus said to him, "Let the dead bury their own dead, but you go and proclaim the kingdom of God."

[61]Still another said, "I will follow you, Lord; but first let me go back and say good-by to my family."

[62]Jesus replied, "No one who puts his hand to the plow and looks back is fit for service in the kingdom of God."

Jesus Sends Out the Seventy-two

10 After this the Lord appointed seventy-two[c] others and sent them two by two ahead of him to every town and place where he was about to go. [2]He told them, "The harvest is plentiful, but the workers are few. Ask the Lord of the harvest, therefore, to send out workers into his harvest field. [3]Go! I am sending you out like lambs among wolves. [4]Do not take a purse or bag or sandals; and do not greet anyone on the road.

[5]"When you enter a house, first say, 'Peace to this house.' [6]If a man of peace is there, your peace will rest on him; if not, it will return to you. [7]Stay in that house, eating and drinking whatever they give you, for the worker deserves his wages. Do not move around from house to house.

[8]"When you enter a town and are welcomed, eat what is set before you. [9]Heal the sick who are there and tell them, 'The kingdom of God is near you.' [10]But when you enter a town and are not

---

What is the one thing you are best at doing?

1. In verses 46–50, how are the disciples gauging "greatness"? How does Jesus do so? 2. In John's concern (v. 49), what's the root desire? The irony (see v. 40)? 3. How does Jesus' "timetable" meet further resistance (vv. 51–56)? Why from the Samaritans? Why from his own disciples? How must Jesus be feeling by now?

1. What have you done for someone recently "in Jesus' name"? 2. How can you enact "he who is least among you all ... he is the greatest"? How did you picture "greatness" as a child? As an adult?

What's your favorite excuse for not doing something (e.g., "dog ate my homework")?

How does Jesus respond to the excuses offered by the three men (vv. 57,59,61)? In your own words, what do each of Jesus' sayings mean? What's his point?

Of the issues listed here (comfort, social obligations, family concerns), which one would tempt you to not follow Jesus?

If you had to sell something door to door, what would you choose: Fuller brushes? Encyclopedias? Jewelry? Cosmetics? Subscriptions? Serendipity Bibles? Why?

1. Why does he send the disciples out two-by-two? What are they looking for (v. 2)? 2. How is the Christian disciple like a "worker in the harvest"? A "lamb among wolves"? 3. What was the purpose of traveling light (v. 4)? Of praying first, going later? 4. What kind of household guests are they to be (v. 5)? Why? 5. How are they related to the town of which they are a part (vv. 8–12)? What is their basic message? 6. How do verses 1–12 show the urgency Jesus himself senses for evangelism? What is the reason for this urgency? 7.

---

a54 Some manuscripts them, even as Elijah did   b55,56 Some manuscripts them. And he said, "You do not know what kind of spirit you are of, for the Son of Man did not come to destroy men's lives, but to save them." 56And   c1 Some manuscripts seventy; also in verse 17

welcomed, go into its streets and say, ¹¹'Even the dust of your town that sticks to our feet we wipe off against you. Yet be sure of this: The kingdom of God is near.' ¹²I tell you, it will be more bearable on that day for Sodom than for that town.

¹³"Woe to you, Korazin! Woe to you, Bethsaida! For if the miracles that were performed in you had been performed in Tyre and Sidon, they would have repented long ago, sitting in sackcloth and ashes. ¹⁴But it will be more bearable for Tyre and Sidon at the judgment than for you. ¹⁵And you, Capernaum, will you be lifted up to the skies? No, you will go down to the depths.ᵃ

¹⁶"He who listens to you listens to me; he who rejects you rejects me; but he who rejects me rejects him who sent me."

¹⁷The seventy-two returned with joy and said, "Lord, even the demons submit to us in your name."

¹⁸He replied, "I saw Satan fall like lightning from heaven. ¹⁹I have given you authority to trample on snakes and scorpions and to overcome all the power of the enemy; nothing will harm you. ²⁰However, do not rejoice that the spirits submit to you, but rejoice that your names are written in heaven."

²¹At that time Jesus, full of joy through the Holy Spirit, said, "I praise you, Father, Lord of heaven and earth, because you have hidden these things from the wise and learned, and revealed them to little children. Yes, Father, for this was your good pleasure.

²²"All things have been committed to me by my Father. No one knows who the Son is except the Father, and no one knows who the Father is except the Son and those to whom the Son chooses to reveal him."

²³Then he turned to his disciples and said privately, "Blessed are the eyes that see what you see. ²⁴For I tell you that many prophets and kings wanted to see what you see but did not see it, and to hear what you hear but did not hear it."

The Parable of the Good Samaritan

²⁵On one occasion an expert in the law stood up to test Jesus. "Teacher," he asked, "what must I do to inherit eternal life?"

²⁶"What is written in the Law?" he replied. "How do you read it?"

²⁷He answered: "'Love the Lord your God with all your heart and with all your soul and with all your strength and with all your mind'ᵇ; and, 'Love your neighbor as yourself.'ᶜ"

²⁸"You have answered correctly," Jesus replied. "Do this and you will live."

²⁹But he wanted to justify himself, so he asked Jesus, "And who is my neighbor?"

³⁰In reply Jesus said: "A man was going down from Jerusalem to Jericho, when he fell into the hands of robbers. They stripped him of his clothes, beat him and went away, leaving him half dead. ³¹A priest happened to be going down the same road, and when he saw the man, he passed by on the other side. ³²So too, a Levite, when he came to the place and saw him, passed by on the other side. ³³But a Samaritan, as he traveled, came where the man was; and when he saw him, he took pity on him. ³⁴He went to him and bandaged his wounds, pouring on oil and wine. Then he put the man on his own donkey, took him to an inn and took care of him. ³⁵The next day he took out two silver coinsᵈ and gave them to the innkeeper. 'Look after him,' he said, 'and when I return, I will reimburse you for any extra expense you may have.'

What do you know about Sodom (see Ge 19:24–28)? Korazin and Bethsaida? About Capernaum (see Mt 4:13)? Tyre and Sidon (see Ez 28)? **8.** What is the comfort and the danger of aligning oneself with Jesus (v. 16)? **9.** Upon their return, what does Jesus say to them (vv. 18–20)? What in their report gives Jesus reason for joy (v. 21)? **10.** Consider verse 23. Do you think the disciples appreciate the privilege of being with Jesus? Why or why not?

1. How do you feel about the harvest where you live? Are people ripe for the Gospel? What would it take for you to be more involved in the harvest? **2.** When have you felt like a lamb among wolves? What did you learn from that experience? **3.** What do these verses show you about the privileges you have in Jesus Christ? Of these privileges, which are you experiencing now? **4.** What does verse 22 tell you about those who claim to know God without Christ?

Have you ever helped a stranger in distress? What happened?

1. Who's testing whom in this story? **2.** Does the lawyer seem to think he has passed the test in verse 28? How so? **3.** Why does Jesus answer with a story instead of a straight answer? **4.** How might one justify the actions of the priest and the Levite (see Lev 21:1–3; Nu 19:11–22)? **5.** Given the divisions between Jews and Samaritans (see Jn 4), what's unusual about the plot twist in this story? What is Jesus' point here?

1. What attitude or behavior does God want you to have that is the most difficult to accept? **2.** Who have been Good Samaritans in your life? What makes a Good Samaritan really *good*? **3.** To whom will you be a Good Samaritan this week?

ᵃ15 Greek *Hades*   ᵇ27 Deut. 6:5   ᶜ27 Lev. 19:18   ᵈ35 Greek *two denarii*

³⁶"Which of these three do you think was a neighbor to the man who fell into the hands of robbers?"

³⁷The expert in the law replied, "The one who had mercy on him."

Jesus told him, "Go and do likewise."

At the Home of Martha and Mary

³⁸As Jesus and his disciples were on their way, he came to a village where a woman named Martha opened her home to him. ³⁹She had a sister called Mary, who sat at the Lord's feet listening to what he said. ⁴⁰But Martha was distracted by all the preparations that had to be made. She came to him and asked, "Lord, don't you care that my sister has left me to do the work by myself? Tell her to help me!"

⁴¹"Martha, Martha," the Lord answered, "you are worried and upset about many things, ⁴²but only one thing is needed.*a* Mary has chosen what is better, and it will not be taken away from her."

Jesus' Teaching on Prayer

11 One day Jesus was praying in a certain place. When he finished, one of his disciples said to him, "Lord, teach us to pray, just as John taught his disciples."

²He said to them, "When you pray, say:

"'Father,*b*
hallowed be your name,
your kingdom come.*c*

a42 Some manuscripts but few things are needed—or only one   *b2 Some manuscripts Our Father in heaven*   *c2 Some manuscripts come. May your will be done on earth as it is in heaven.*

How do these two sisters differ? Is Mary's choice better? What about Jesus' call to servanthood? What is Jesus' point?

Describe a time when you used your work responsibilities or social obligations to avoid Jesus. How do you seek to serve while also keeping God-given priorities?

1. Recite a prayer you said as a child. 2. What's the funniest prayer you've heard a child say?

1. What motivates the disciples to ask about prayer at this point (v. 1)? 2. In Jesus' model prayer (vv. 2–4), what two concerns related to God come first? Why? What personal concerns then follow? How do prayer and forgiveness relate? 3. What does the parable in verses 5–8 teach

---

Luke 10:25–37   PARABLE OF THE GOOD SAMARITAN

1. In the parable Jesus told, why do you think the priest and the Levite (an assistant to the priests) refused to stop and help the mugging victim?
   a. They were in a big hurry.
   b. They didn't want to be bothered.
   c. Traveling on a notoriously dangerous road, they were afraid this was a trap to rob them.
   d. They thought the man was already dead.
   e. They were afraid to get too close, because the Law didn't allow them to touch a dead body.

2. Why did the Samaritan—whose people the Jews despised as half-breeds both physically and spiritually—stop and help the man?
   a. He evidently knew the man.
   b. The man was hurt, so it didn't matter to the Samaritan who he was.
   c. He put the wounded man's safety above his own.
   d. He didn't care about the religious problem of touching a corpse.
   e. He knew what it was like to be hurt and have others pass by.

3. Why do you think Jesus told this parable in response to the lawyer's question, "Who is my neighbor"?
   a. to let him answer his own question
   b. to catch him in a moral dilemma
   c. to use the "case study" approach that lawyers use
   d. to show how the expert in the Law failed to practice what he preached
   e. because the real question was, "To whom must I *be* a neighbor?"

4. After reading this parable, whom would you say is your "neighbor"?
   a. any person in need
   b. those I have a reasonable hope of being able to help
   c. those I'm most afraid of helping
   d. everyone—even my enemies

5. With whom do you identify most in this parable right now?
   a. the legal expert—always asking tough questions
   b. Jesus—under great pressure to say or do the right thing
   c. the mugging victim—bruised and bleeding

   d. the priest and Levite—too busy or too afraid
   e. the Good Samaritan—fulfilled by passing on God's love
   f. the innkeeper—constantly being asked to take care of someone

6. How do you feel when your efforts help others? How do you feel when your efforts don't seem to help?

7. Who has been a Good Samaritan in your life? How can you be a Good Samaritan to someone this week?

8. What does this story say about each of the following?
   a. how I should spend my life
   b. in whom I should invest my energy
   c. what kind of risks I should take

9. What would be the costs of doing the risky thing God may be calling you to do with your life?
   a. loss of time
   b. loss of energy
   c. financial sacrifice
   d. strain on relationships
   e. strain on my emotions

³Give us each day our daily bread.
⁴Forgive us our sins,
for we also forgive everyone who sins against
us.ᵃ
And lead us not into temptation.ᵇ' "

⁵Then he said to them, "Suppose one of you has a friend, and he goes to him at midnight and says, 'Friend, lend me three loaves of bread, ⁶because a friend of mine on a journey has come to me, and I have nothing to set before him.'

⁷"Then the one inside answers, 'Don't bother me. The door is already locked, and my children are with me in bed. I can't get up and give you anything.' ⁸I tell you, though he will not get up and give him the bread because he is his friend, yet because of the man's boldnessᶜ he will get up and give him as much as he needs.

⁹"So I say to you: Ask and it will be given to you; seek and you will find; knock and the door will be opened to you. ¹⁰For everyone who asks receives; he who seeks finds; and to him who knocks, the door will be opened.

¹¹"Which of you fathers, if your son asks forᵈ a fish, will give him a snake instead? ¹²Or if he asks for an egg, will give him a scorpion? ¹³If you then, though you are evil, know how to give

ᵃ4 Greek *everyone who is indebted to us*   ᵇ4 Some manuscripts *temptation but*
deliver us from the evil one   ᶜ8 Or *persistence*   ᵈ11 Some manuscripts *for*
bread, will give him a stone; or if he asks for

---

about prayer? How do verses 9–10 relate to the parable? What attitude is implied in verses 9–10? How do verses 11–13 clarify the intent of verses 9–10?

♥ 1. What should be the relationship between this prayer and our own? How do you usually pray? Do you have a set time? A set place? Or are you more spontaneous when you pray? 2. What do you use to prepare for prayer: Read a psalm? A devotional guide? A hymn? 3. What concerns occupy most of your time in prayer: Praise? Confession? Petition? Why? In which area do you want to grow? 4. What is the most valuable gift God can give (v. 13)? How much do you want that gift? Why? 5. What one thing would you like to obtain from the Father?

   **Lk 10:38–42 AT THE HOME OF MARTHA & MARY**

1. How would you describe the difference between Martha and Mary as you meet them in this story?
a. a normal person vs. a lazy bum who lets others do all the work
b. a normal person vs. an over-bearing workaholic who needs to relax
c. a person who values responsibility vs. one who values relationships
d. a person who needs to be needed vs. one who needs to be served

2. If you were Martha, how would you have responded to Jesus' words?
a. flown off the handle
b. thought to myself: "He doesn't have to live with my sister."
c. left the room and pouted
d. accepted the correction, sat down with Mary and forgot about supper

3. If Jesus could take Mary aside, what advice would he likely give her?
a. Be a little more understanding of Martha.
b. You are pushing your sister's buttons by being so laid back.
c. You need to work on some of your own weaknesses—like sharing responsibilities in the kitchen.
d. God made you and your sister different and you need each other.

4. What was Jesus saying to Martha?
a. She should be more like Mary.
b. She had her priorities messed up.
c. People are more important than housework.
d. "Sitting at Jesus' feet" is more important than anything else.

5. From this story, how would you describe the different personalities of Mary and Martha? What are their strengths and weaknesses? Which one are you more like?

6. If Jesus dropped in on you, what might he point out that distracts *you* from the really important things in life like spending time with him?

7. Are you more responsible or carefree? More focused on people or yourself? Should you try to change your personality?

8. Regarding giving to others, how often do you experience each of the following motivations—seldom, sometimes or frequently?
a. to feel in control
b. to feel needed
c. to receive in return
d. to get people to like me
e. out of obligation

9. In light of your answers to the last question, what course of action do you need to take?
a. admit my need to change
b. open my life more to God's love
c. keep in touch with my motivations
d. set limits on what I do for others
e. keep doing what I'm doing

10. Which of the following qualities applies to you?
a. I anticipate the needs of others.
b. I take responsibility for others.
c. I find it hard to relax or play.
d. I'm driven by a desire for approval.
e. I feel my serving is unappreciated.

11. In your role as a caregiver, do you feel a need to set limits? Why? If so, what are those limits and how will you enforce them?

12. In each of the following, which quality is more true of you? Which is more true of your spouse? How can your different personalities bring you together rather than apart?
a. *task* or *relational* oriented
b. *work* or *quality-of-life* oriented
c. *practical* or *idea* oriented
d. *uptight* or *laid-back*
e. *physically* or *spiritually* oriented

good gifts to your children, how much more will your Father in heaven give the Holy Spirit to those who ask him!"

Jesus and Beelzebub

[14]Jesus was driving out a demon that was mute. When the demon left, the man who had been mute spoke, and the crowd was amazed. [15]But some of them said, "By Beelzebub,[a] the prince of demons, he is driving out demons." [16]Others tested him by asking for a sign from heaven.

[17]Jesus knew their thoughts and said to them: "Any kingdom divided against itself will be ruined, and a house divided against itself will fall. [18]If Satan is divided against himself, how can his kingdom stand? I say this because you claim that I drive out demons by Beelzebub. [19]Now if I drive out demons by Beelzebub, by whom do your followers drive them out? So then, they will be your judges. [20]But if I drive out demons by the finger of God, then the kingdom of God has come to you.

[21]"When a strong man, fully armed, guards his own house, his possessions are safe. [22]But when someone stronger attacks and overpowers him, he takes away the armor in which the man trusted and divides up the spoils.

[23]"He who is not with me is against me, and he who does not gather with me, scatters.

[24]"When an evil[b] spirit comes out of a man, it goes through arid places seeking rest and does not find it. Then it says, 'I will return to the house I left.' [25]When it arrives, it finds the house swept clean and put in order. [26]Then it goes and takes seven other spirits more wicked than itself, and they go in and live there. And the final condition of that man is worse than the first."

[27]As Jesus was saying these things, a woman in the crowd called out, "Blessed is the mother who gave you birth and nursed you."

[28]He replied, "Blessed rather are those who hear the word of God and obey it."

The Sign of Jonah

[29]As the crowds increased, Jesus said, "This is a wicked generation. It asks for a miraculous sign, but none will be given it except the sign of Jonah. [30]For as Jonah was a sign to the Ninevites, so also will the Son of Man be to this generation. [31]The Queen of the South will rise at the judgment with the men of this generation and condemn them; for she came from the ends of the earth to listen to Solomon's wisdom, and now one[c] greater than Solomon is here. [32]The men of Nineveh will stand up at the judgment with this generation and condemn it; for they repented at the preaching of Jonah, and now one greater than Jonah is here.

The Lamp of the Body

[33]"No one lights a lamp and puts it in a place where it will be hidden, or under a bowl. Instead he puts it on its stand, so that those who come in may see the light. [34]Your eye is the lamp of your body. When your eyes are good, your whole body also is full of light. But when they are bad, your body also is full of darkness. [35]See to it, then, that the light within you is not darkness. [36]Therefore, if your whole body is full of light, and no part of it dark, it will be completely lighted, as when the light of a lamp shines on you."

How well did you keep your bedroom when you were growing up? How have your habits changed with age?

1. How does the crowd react to Jesus' miracle (vv. 14–16)? 2. How does Jesus show the foolishness of the claim that he drives out demons by Beelzebub? What does Jesus' ability to drive out demons say about the kingdom of God (v. 20)? 3. What is Jesus' point in verses 24–26? To whom is the point addressed? Why is the final condition worse than the first? 4. Why does Jesus turn around the blessing shouted to him in verse 27? What is he emphasizing here?

If you compared your life right now to a fortress, what is it like: (a) The Rock of Gibraltar? (b) Slowly eroding? (c) Quickly crumbling? Are you spiritually on the attack or feeling besieged? How's the battle going?

Who is the wisest person you have ever known?

1. Why is Jesus upset about "this generation"? 2. What is the sign of Jonah (see Jnh 1:17)? How is Jesus like that? 3. Who is this Queen (1Ki 10:1–15)? Who condemns whom? 4. What is Jesus' point?

What sign would it take for your generation to turn to God? What's the problem with relying on "signs" to do the trick?

How many flashlights do you own? How many work?

What does the light represent? The eye? The body? The darkness?

How would you score on a spiritual sight exam: 20/20? 20/80? Colorblind? Why?

---

[a]15 Greek Beezeboul or Beelzeboul; also in verses 18 and 19   [b]24 Greek unclean
[c]31 Or something; also in verse 32

Six Woes

37When Jesus had finished speaking, a Pharisee invited him to eat with him; so he went in and reclined at the table. **38**But the Pharisee, noticing that Jesus did not first wash before the meal, was surprised.

39Then the Lord said to him, "Now then, you Pharisees clean the outside of the cup and dish, but inside you are full of greed and wickedness. **40**You foolish people! Did not the one who made the outside make the inside also? **41**But give what is inside ⌊the dish⌋ᵃ to the poor, and everything will be clean for you.

42"Woe to you Pharisees, because you give God a tenth of your mint, rue and all other kinds of garden herbs, but you neglect justice and the love of God. You should have practiced the latter without leaving the former undone.

43"Woe to you Pharisees, because you love the most important seats in the synagogues and greetings in the marketplaces.

44"Woe to you, because you are like unmarked graves, which men walk over without knowing it."

45One of the experts in the law answered him, "Teacher, when you say these things, you insult us also."

46Jesus replied, "And you experts in the law, woe to you, because you load people down with burdens they can hardly carry, and you yourselves will not lift one finger to help them.

47"Woe to you, because you build tombs for the prophets, and it was your forefathers who killed them. **48**So you testify that you approve of what your forefathers did; they killed the prophets, and you build their tombs. **49**Because of this, God in his wisdom said, 'I will send them prophets and apostles, some of whom they will kill and others they will persecute.' **50**Therefore this generation will be held responsible for the blood of all the prophets that has been shed since the beginning of the world, **51**from the blood of Abel to the blood of Zechariah, who was killed between the altar and the sanctuary. Yes, I tell you, this generation will be held responsible for it all.

52"Woe to you experts in the law, because you have taken away the key to knowledge. You yourselves have not entered, and you have hindered those who were entering."

53When Jesus left there, the Pharisees and the teachers of the law began to oppose him fiercely and to besiege him with questions, **54**waiting to catch him in something he might say.

Warnings and Encouragements

12 Meanwhile, when a crowd of many thousands had gathered, so that they were trampling on one another, Jesus began to speak first to his disciples, saying: "Be on your guard against the yeast of the Pharisees, which is hypocrisy. **2**There is nothing concealed that will not be disclosed, or hidden that will not be made known. **3**What you have said in the dark will be heard in the daylight, and what you have whispered in the ear in the inner rooms will be proclaimed from the roofs.

4"I tell you, my friends, do not be afraid of those who kill the body and after that can do no more. **5**But I will show you whom you should fear: Fear him who, after the killing of the body, has power to throw you into hell. Yes, I tell you, fear him. **6**Are not five sparrows sold for two penniesᵇ? Yet not one of them is forgotten by God. **7**Indeed, the very hairs of your head are all numbered. Don't be afraid; you are worth more than many sparrows.

ᵃ41 Or what you have   ᵇ6 Greek two assaria

When you were a child, who insisted that you wash up before meals? Who insisted that you wear clean clothes? How did you react to this fussing?

1. What is the natural and the surprising thing Jesus does to open this scene (v. 38)? **2.** How does the Lord turn the tables on his host? What is his basic point about the Pharisees (vv. 39–41)? **3.** In your own words, what is the meaning of these three woes directed at the Pharisees (vv. 42–44)? Given the Pharisees' view of tombs and the dead (see Nu 19:16), what is the significance of the unmarked graves (v. 44)? **4.** What is the point of these criticisms? **5.** In your own words, what is the meaning of the next three woes (vv. 46–52)? In the sixth woe (v. 52), what does Jesus mean by the key of knowledge? **6.** How does this Pharisee dinner compare with the one in 7:36–50? Why the difference?

1. Typically, Jesus is thought of as "meek and mild." What is the significance of this passage's presentation of Jesus for you? **2.** Of the three woes directed to the Pharisees, which one is Jesus directing most to you? Why? **3.** Of the three woes directed to the lawyers, which one has your name on it? Why? **4.** How would you like your life to change this week in light of what you've read here?

As a kid, who was the disciplinarian at home? What was the unpardonable sin in terms of breaking the rules?

1. Why does this crowd grow? **2.** What warnings (vv. 1–3) does Jesus issue the disciples? **3.** How does hypocrisy work like yeast (see 11:37–54)? **4.** Why does Jesus encourage his disciples to fear, yet be fearless (vv. 4–7)? **5.** What does it mean to "blaspheme against the Holy Spirit" (v. 10; see Lev 24:16)? How is the contrite person assured of not having done this? **6.** What does Jesus teach about the believer's security when facing human opposition (vv. 11–12)?

1. How do you feel knowing that everything done in secret will someday be revealed? **2.** When have you taken a risk and stood for Jesus in a public way? What happened? What did you learn?

What did you like to collect as a child? Now?

In response to the man's plea, Jesus tells a parable. What is the man's problem? His solution? Why is he a fool? What is the punch line?

1. When have you been like the man in this story? **2.** Advertising is dedicated to making us believe the opposite of verse 15. What differences in lifestyle result from believing Jesus versus advertisements? **3.** In planning an investment portfolio to become "rich toward God," what will you do this week? This year?

8"I tell you, whoever acknowledges me before men, the Son of Man will also acknowledge him before the angels of God. 9But he who disowns me before men will be disowned before the angels of God. 10And everyone who speaks a word against the Son of Man will be forgiven, but anyone who blasphemes against the Holy Spirit will not be forgiven.

11"When you are brought before synagogues, rulers and authorities, do not worry about how you will defend yourselves or what you will say, 12for the Holy Spirit will teach you at that time what you should say."

The Parable of the Rich Fool

13Someone in the crowd said to him, "Teacher, tell my brother to divide the inheritance with me."

14Jesus replied, "Man, who appointed me a judge or an arbiter between you?" 15Then he said to them, "Watch out! Be on your guard against all kinds of greed; a man's life does not consist in the abundance of his possessions."

16And he told them this parable: "The ground of a certain rich man produced a good crop. 17He thought to himself, 'What shall I do? I have no place to store my crops.'

18"Then he said, 'This is what I'll do. I will tear down my barns and build bigger ones, and there I will store all my grain and my goods. 19And I'll say to myself, "You have plenty of good things laid up for many years. Take life easy; eat, drink and be merry." '

20"But God said to him, 'You fool! This very night your life will be demanded from you. Then who will get what you have prepared for yourself?'

  Luke 12:13–21   **PARABLE OF THE RICH FOOL**

1. After Jesus' response, how do you think the man who asked Jesus to settle his dispute with his brother felt?
   a. like slinking back into the crowd
   b. upset his dispute wasn't settled
   c. ashamed of his greed
   d. mad he was used to make a point

2. How would you describe the rich man in the parable?
   a. a show-off   d. content
   b. brilliant   e. unhappy
   c. dumb   f. selfish

3. After dying, how would the local paper describe him in the obituaries?
   a. a tireless worker   c. foolish
   b. a success story   d. enterprising

4. God's response to the rich man was so harsh because God is:
   a. intolerant of self-indulgent people.
   b. compassionate for poor people.
   c. down on rich people.
   d. jealous of all other "gods."

5. How do you react to the idea that a person's "life does not consist in the abundance of his possessions"?

   a. It sounds like the teaching of someone poor and jealous.
   b. It's what a preacher should say.
   c. Yeah, but people with nice houses and cars sure *seem* happy!
   d. Yes, the best things in life are free.

6. What is Jesus saying in this story?
   a. People who try to be a financial success are motivated by greed.
   b. It's okay to be successful, but remember your highest priority.
   c. To really prepare for the future, you have to look beyond finances.
   d. When you think you have it made, think again.
   e. You can't take it with you.
   f. Life is short, so get all the gusto you can.
   g. Material things provide the greatest test of our spiritual devotion.

7. In harvest terms, how is your life going? Are your barns closer to bursting with grain, or empty from drought?

8. What changes would be required for you to be "rich toward God"?

9. How can this group help you make spiritual preparations for your future?

10. What do you value most in life?
    a. my loved ones   e. my faith
    b. my assets   f. my integrity
    c. my good health   g. my memories
    d. my work   h. my time

11. I would like to be remembered as a person who:
    a. had a lot.
    b. gave a lot.
    c. built it all single-handedly.
    d. enjoyed what he/she had.
    e. sacrificed to be rich toward God.

12. What does an investment portfolio guided by a desire to be rich toward God contain in areas like savings, retirement and estate planning? How are you handling these issues?

13. If your life ended "this very night," what would be your biggest regret? What can you do now and in the future to change that?

21"This is how it will be with anyone who stores up things for himself but is not rich toward God."

Do Not Worry

22Then Jesus said to his disciples: "Therefore I tell you, do not worry about your life, what you will eat; or about your body, what you will wear. 23Life is more than food, and the body more than clothes. 24Consider the ravens: They do not sow or reap, they have no storeroom or barn; yet God feeds them. And how much more valuable you are than birds! 25Who of you by worrying can add a single hour to his life*a*? 26Since you cannot do this very little thing, why do you worry about the rest?

27"Consider how the lilies grow. They do not labor or spin. Yet I tell you, not even Solomon in all his splendor was dressed like one of these. 28If that is how God clothes the grass of the field, which is here today, and tomorrow is thrown into the fire, how much more will he clothe you, O you of little faith! 29And do not set your heart on what you will eat or drink; do not worry about it. 30For the pagan world runs after all such things, and your Father knows that you need them. 31But seek his kingdom, and these things will be given to you as well.

32"Do not be afraid, little flock, for your Father has been pleased to give you the kingdom. 33Sell your possessions and give to the poor. Provide purses for yourselves that will not wear out, a treasure in heaven that will not be exhausted, where no thief comes near and no moth destroys. 34For where your treasure is, there your heart will be also.

Watchfulness

35"Be dressed ready for service and keep your lamps burning, 36like men waiting for their master to return from a wedding banquet, so that when he comes and knocks they can immediately open the door for him. 37It will be good for those servants whose master finds them watching when he comes. I tell you the truth, he will dress himself to serve, will have them recline at the table and will come and wait on them. 38It will be good for those servants whose master finds them ready, even if he comes in the second or third watch of the night. 39But understand this: If the owner of the house had known at what hour the thief was coming, he would not have let his house be broken into. 40You also must be ready, because the Son of Man will come at an hour when you do not expect him."

41Peter asked, "Lord, are you telling this parable to us, or to everyone?"

42The Lord answered, "Who then is the faithful and wise manager, whom the master puts in charge of his servants to give them their food allowance at the proper time? 43It will be good for that servant whom the master finds doing so when he returns. 44I tell you the truth, he will put him in charge of all his possessions. 45But suppose the servant says to himself, 'My master is taking a long time in coming,' and he then begins to beat the menservants and maidservants and to eat and drink and get drunk. 46The master of that servant will come on a day when he does not expect him and at an hour he is not aware of. He will cut him to pieces and assign him a place with the unbelievers.

47"That servant who knows his master's will and does not get ready or does not do what his master wants will be beaten with

Which situation is most worrisome to you: Overdrawn at the bank? Gained 10 pounds? Child expelled? Nobody called all weekend? Mother-in-law stays two weeks? Business folds?

1. How does this section relate to the preceding parable about riches? 2. What does Jesus tell the disciples *not* to do (v. 22)? Why? What does Jesus urge them to do instead (v. 33)? Why? What will result? 3. What does Jesus teach here about seeking the kingdom of God?

1. On a scale from 1 ("no sweat") to 10 ("panic"), what is the worry quotient in your life right now? Why? 2. How can you transfer your treasure from Wall Street to Heaven's Gate? 3. How would your life be different if you lived the way Jesus sets forth in this passage?

Are you a night owl or an early bird? Ever fall asleep at the wheel? On a date? On duty?

1. What is the relationship between watchfulness and worry (verses 22–34)? 2. Explain the role reversal described in verse 37. Why does Peter ask the question in verse 41? Why does Jesus answer as he does? 3. Why does Jesus say they should be ready (vv. 39–40)? Who is the thief? 4. What should be the attitude and actions of the faithful and wise manager (vv. 42–43)? What could tempt the servants to do wrong (v. 45)? 5. What is the meaning of verse 48? How would the disciples have interpreted it?

1. Consider verse 37. How do you feel about Jesus serving you? 2. What dangers is Jesus warning you about in this section? Which danger is most likely to be a problem for you? 3. What has God entrusted to you as his manager? If you knew that in 30 days Jesus was returning, what would you do to get things ready for inspection?

*a*25 Or *single cubit to his height*

many blows. ⁴⁸But the one who does not know and does things deserving punishment will be beaten with few blows. From everyone who has been given much, much will be demanded; and from the one who has been entrusted with much, much more will be asked.

Not Peace but Division

⁴⁹"I have come to bring fire on the earth, and how I wish it were already kindled! ⁵⁰But I have a baptism to undergo, and how distressed I am until it is completed! ⁵¹Do you think I came to bring peace on earth? No, I tell you, but division. ⁵²From now on there will be five in one family divided against each other, three against two and two against three. ⁵³They will be divided, father against son and son against father, mother against daughter and daughter against mother, mother-in-law against daughter-in-law and daughter-in-law against mother-in-law."

Interpreting the Times

⁵⁴He said to the crowd: "When you see a cloud rising in the west, immediately you say, 'It's going to rain,' and it does. ⁵⁵And when the south wind blows, you say, 'It's going to be hot,' and it is. ⁵⁶Hypocrites! You know how to interpret the appearance of the earth and the sky. How is it that you don't know how to interpret this present time?

⁵⁷"Why don't you judge for yourselves what is right? ⁵⁸As you are going with your adversary to the magistrate, try hard to be reconciled to him on the way, or he may drag you off to the judge, and the judge turn you over to the officer, and the officer throw you into prison. ⁵⁹I tell you, you will not get out until you have paid the last penny.ᵃ"

Repent or Perish

13 Now there were some present at that time who told Jesus about the Galileans whose blood Pilate had mixed with their sacrifices. ²Jesus answered, "Do you think that these Galileans were worse sinners than all the other Galileans because they suffered this way? ³I tell you, no! But unless you repent, you too will all perish. ⁴Or those eighteen who died when the tower in Siloam fell on them—do you think they were more guilty than all the others living in Jerusalem? ⁵I tell you, no! But unless you repent, you too will all perish."

⁶Then he told this parable: "A man had a fig tree, planted in his vineyard, and he went to look for fruit on it, but did not find any. ⁷So he said to the man who took care of the vineyard, 'For three years now I've been coming to look for fruit on this fig tree and haven't found any. Cut it down! Why should it use up the soil?'

⁸"'Sir,' the man replied, 'leave it alone for one more year, and I'll dig around it and fertilize it. ⁹If it bears fruit next year, fine! If not, then cut it down.'"

A Crippled Woman Healed on the Sabbath

¹⁰On a Sabbath Jesus was teaching in one of the synagogues, ¹¹and a woman was there who had been crippled by a spirit for eighteen years. She was bent over and could not straighten up at all. ¹²When Jesus saw her, he called her forward and said to her, "Woman, you are set free from your infirmity." ¹³Then he put his

ᵃ59 Greek lepton

Sidebar notes (left column):

☕ What discussion topics are taboo at your family table or at family reunions? Why?

📖 1. Of what "fire" is Jesus speaking? What "baptism"? What division? How and why does Jesus bring division? Why do you think Jesus wishes the fire was already kindled? How does this relate to "Peace on Earth, goodwill toward men"? 2. How has the crowd misread Jesus? In verses 54–59, would Jesus speak the same way to a Gentile audience?

❤ 1. What has Christ brought to your family and friends: division or peace? Why? 2. How can you tell if it is your faith that strains a relationship, or the way you live your faith? 3. What signs in your own life indicate how you are doing? Using a weather map to describe your spiritual life, what does it forecast?

☕ What was the worst tragedy in your community last year?

📖 1. What is the danger of associating someone's misfortune with sin? 2. In verses 6–9, who does the tree represent: The owner? Farmer? Why the urgency?

❤ 1. If you had "one more year" like the fig tree to turn your life around, what would you do? 2. What fruit do you want to be producing by this time next year?

☕ Are you more of a "the-rules-are-meant-to-be-broken" or a "play-it-by-the-book" type of person? Why? Give an example.

📖 1. What does verse 11 tell you about Dr. Luke's knowledge of medicine? Of spiritual phe-

hands on her, and immediately she straightened up and praised God.

14Indignant because Jesus had healed on the Sabbath, the synagogue ruler said to the people, "There are six days for work. So come and be healed on those days, not on the Sabbath."

15The Lord answered him, "You hypocrites! Doesn't each of you on the Sabbath untie his ox or donkey from the stall and lead it out to give it water? 16Then should not this woman, a daughter of Abraham, whom Satan has kept bound for eighteen long years, be set free on the Sabbath day from what bound her?"

17When he said this, all his opponents were humiliated, but the people were delighted with all the wonderful things he was doing.

The Parables of the Mustard Seed and the Yeast

18Then Jesus asked, "What is the kingdom of God like? What shall I compare it to? 19It is like a mustard seed, which a man took and planted in his garden. It grew and became a tree, and the birds of the air perched in its branches."

20Again he asked, "What shall I compare the kingdom of God to? 21It is like yeast that a woman took and mixed into a large amount*a* of flour until it worked all through the dough."

The Narrow Door

22Then Jesus went through the towns and villages, teaching as he made his way to Jerusalem. 23Someone asked him, "Lord, are only a few people going to be saved?"

He said to them, 24"Make every effort to enter through the narrow door, because many, I tell you, will try to enter and will not be able to. 25Once the owner of the house gets up and closes the door, you will stand outside knocking and pleading, 'Sir, open the door for us.'

"But he will answer, 'I don't know you or where you come from.'

26"Then you will say, 'We ate and drank with you, and you taught in our streets.'

27"But he will reply, 'I don't know you or where you come from. Away from me, all you evildoers!'

28"There will be weeping there, and gnashing of teeth, when you see Abraham, Isaac and Jacob and all the prophets in the kingdom of God, but you yourselves thrown out. 29People will come from east and west and north and south, and will take their places at the feast in the kingdom of God. 30Indeed there are those who are last who will be first, and first who will be last."

Jesus' Sorrow for Jerusalem

31At that time some Pharisees came to Jesus and said to him, "Leave this place and go somewhere else. Herod wants to kill you."

32He replied, "Go tell that fox, 'I will drive out demons and heal people today and tomorrow, and on the third day I will reach my goal.' 33In any case, I must keep going today and tomorrow and the next day—for surely no prophet can die outside Jerusalem!

34"O Jerusalem, Jerusalem, you who kill the prophets and stone those sent to you, how often I have longed to gather your children together, as a hen gathers her chicks under her wings, but you were not willing! 35Look, your house is left to you desolate. I tell you, you will not see me again until you say, 'Blessed is he who comes in the name of the Lord.'*b*"

nomenon? 2. How does Jesus expose the ruler's hypocrisy?

1. What tensions between caring for *people* and keeping religious *rules* do you experience? 2. How do you reconcile this connection between physical and spiritual healing?

What is your favorite story about someone with humble beginnings who greatly succeeds?

What does the contrast between the seed and bush teach about the power of God's kingdom? What does yeast teach about it?

How can a little faith influence *your* everyday life?

What happened the last time you were locked out of your house or car? How did you get in?

1. According to Jesus, who will make it through the narrow door and who won't (v. 30)? 2. If God loves people, why isn't the door wider? Who are the ones outside? Why isn't eating and drinking with Jesus enough? 3. What do you think Jesus means by "evildoers"? In the end, do you think only a few or many or all people will be saved? Why?

How do you know whether you are inside or outside the kingdom? How can you be sure?

What place do you identify with your spiritual roots?

1. What does Jesus reveal here (vv. 32–33) about his intentions? What does his response reveal about him? 2. What strikes you about Jesus' prophecy?

What would it mean for each of us to gather under Jesus' wings?

a21 Greek *three satas* (probably about 1/2 bushel or 22 liters)   *b35* Psalm 118:26

If you could have the best seats in the house, what would you choose: Super Bowl? A rock concert? Philharmonic orchestra? Indy 500? Royal wedding?

1. What's the situation here: The day? Host? Atmosphere? 2. What does Jesus do to heal the man and to trap the Pharisees (vv. 2–6)? What does their silence mean? 3. How does Jesus' view of honor (vv. 7–11) vary from that held by others at the meal? 4. What does this passage teach you about the differences between kingdom values vs. social values? In verse 7 Jesus observes subtle social behavior. What does that tell you about his ability to observe your behavior?

1. How do things like customs and status get in the way of loving others in your family? Church? Work place? Community? 2. If you threw a party for the "poor," "crippled," "lame" and "blind," who would you invite? How might you do this?

What was one of your best parties? How so?

1. Do you think that the man in verse 15 understood Jesus' teaching and blessing in the previous passage? Why or why not? 2. In this parable, who are the invited guests? Why don't they come? What happens to them? Who eventually comes? 3. On what basis is one invited? How might Jesus' servant fulfill the command of verse 23? What does this parable teach about the kingdom?

From your experience, what excuses do people make to avoid God's "banquet"? What can you say or do to help people overcome their hesitation?

If you were on a TV game show, would you try for the $50,000 grand prize, even though you might lose the $25,000 you had won so far? Why?

Jesus at a Pharisee's House

14 One Sabbath, when Jesus went to eat in the house of a prominent Pharisee, he was being carefully watched. [2]There in front of him was a man suffering from dropsy. [3]Jesus asked the Pharisees and experts in the law, "Is it lawful to heal on the Sabbath or not?" [4]But they remained silent. So taking hold of the man, he healed him and sent him away.

[5]Then he asked them, "If one of you has a son[a] or an ox that falls into a well on the Sabbath day, will you not immediately pull him out?" [6]And they had nothing to say.

[7]When he noticed how the guests picked the places of honor at the table, he told them this parable: [8]"When someone invites you to a wedding feast, do not take the place of honor, for a person more distinguished than you may have been invited. [9]If so, the host who invited both of you will come and say to you, 'Give this man your seat.' Then, humiliated, you will have to take the least important place. [10]But when you are invited, take the lowest place, so that when your host comes, he will say to you, 'Friend, move up to a better place.' Then you will be honored in the presence of all your fellow guests. [11]For everyone who exalts himself will be humbled, and he who humbles himself will be exalted."

[12]Then Jesus said to his host, "When you give a luncheon or dinner, do not invite your friends, your brothers or relatives, or your rich neighbors; if you do, they may invite you back and so you will be repaid. [13]But when you give a banquet, invite the poor, the crippled, the lame, the blind, [14]and you will be blessed. Although they cannot repay you, you will be repaid at the resurrection of the righteous."

The Parable of the Great Banquet

[15]When one of those at the table with him heard this, he said to Jesus, "Blessed is the man who will eat at the feast in the kingdom of God."

[16]Jesus replied: "A certain man was preparing a great banquet and invited many guests. [17]At the time of the banquet he sent his servant to tell those who had been invited, 'Come, for everything is now ready.'

[18]"But they all alike began to make excuses. The first said, 'I have just bought a field, and I must go and see it. Please excuse me.'

[19]"Another said, 'I have just bought five yoke of oxen, and I'm on my way to try them out. Please excuse me.'

[20]"Still another said, 'I just got married, so I can't come.'

[21]"The servant came back and reported this to his master. Then the owner of the house became angry and ordered his servant, 'Go out quickly into the streets and alleys of the town and bring in the poor, the crippled, the blind and the lame.'

[22]"'Sir,' the servant said, 'what you ordered has been done, but there is still room.'

[23]"Then the master told his servant, 'Go out to the roads and country lanes and make them come in, so that my house will be full. [24]I tell you, not one of those men who were invited will get a taste of my banquet.'"

The Cost of Being a Disciple

[25]Large crowds were traveling with Jesus, and turning to them he said: [26]"If anyone comes to me and does not hate his father and

a5 Some manuscripts *donkey*

mother, his wife and children, his brothers and sisters—yes, even his own life—he cannot be my disciple. ²⁷And anyone who does not carry his cross and follow me cannot be my disciple.

²⁸"Suppose one of you wants to build a tower. Will he not first sit down and estimate the cost to see if he has enough money to complete it? ²⁹For if he lays the foundation and is not able to finish it, everyone who sees it will ridicule him, ³⁰saying, 'This fellow began to build and was not able to finish.'

³¹"Or suppose a king is about to go to war against another king. Will he not first sit down and consider whether he is able with ten thousand men to oppose the one coming against him with twenty thousand? ³²If he is not able, he will send a delegation while the other is still a long way off and will ask for terms of peace. ³³In the same way, any of you who does not give up everything he has cannot be my disciple.

³⁴"Salt is good, but if it loses its saltiness, how can it be made salty again? ³⁵It is fit neither for the soil nor for the manure pile; it is thrown out.

"He who has ears to hear, let him hear."

The Parable of the Lost Sheep

15 Now the tax collectors and "sinners" were all gathering around to hear him. ²But the Pharisees and the teachers of the law muttered, "This man welcomes sinners and eats with them."

³Then Jesus told them this parable: ⁴"Suppose one of you has a hundred sheep and loses one of them. Does he not leave the ninety-nine in the open country and go after the lost sheep until he finds it? ⁵And when he finds it, he joyfully puts it on his shoulders

1. What is Jesus saying about family? What does he mean by "hate"? By carrying a cross? **2.** What do each of the three parables tell us about how to give our lives to Jesus? **3.** What does the salt analogy emphasize about discipleship? **4.** In summary, what kingdom values are taught? Why such tough talk from Jesus?

1. When did you realize that following Jesus was costly? How so? **2.** Is it worth it? What keeps you going?

Which of your possessions were recently lost? Recently found?

1. Who is in Jesus' audience? How do they respond to him? **2.** How does Jesus' parable of the sheep relate to the muttering of the Pharisees? What is Jesus' point (v. 7)? **3.** How do you

---

Luke 14:15–24   **PARABLE OF THE GREAT BANQUET**

1. The three people in the parable accepted the initial banquet invitation, then backed out with flimsy excuses the day of the party. How would you have felt if you had been the host?
   a. furious   d. indifferent
   b. hurt   e. understanding
   c. curious about the real reason

2. Why did the three invited guests refuse to come?
   a. They weren't interested.
   b. They were interested, but had more important things to do.
   c. Their relationship with the host was not important to them.
   d. They didn't know how good the party was going to be.

3. Who are the poor, crippled, blind and lame who are invited to take the others' place?
   a. losers and outcasts
   b. the party crowd
   c. people hungry for spiritual things
   d. Gentiles outside of the covenant
   e. everybody who knows they don't deserve God's grace

4. What exactly is this great banquet?
   a. the kingdom of God here and now
   b. deeper spiritual things
   c. Jesus himself
   d. the banquet at the return of Christ

5. What does it take to get into God's banquet? Do you have a personal reservation?

6. Why do so many people say "No" to God's banquet? Who in particular comes to your mind? What can you say or do to help them come in?

7. What is the lesson of this passage for you?
   a. God is throwing a party, and it is for everyone.
   b. God is calling me to go and invite others to feast with him.
   c. God desires my fellowship.
   d. I've got to have an appetite for spiritual things.
   e. I need to get my priorities in line with my commitments.

8. Which of the following "kingdom priorities" do you strug-

gle with the most? Which do you struggle with the least?
   a. personal devotional time
   b. family devotional time
   c. regular church participation
   d. regular small group participation
   e. sharing my gifts and talents
   f. sharing my material resources
   g. sharing my faith

9. What excuses do you use for staying away from God's banquet of fellowship with him and your fellow invited guests?
   a. It's my parents' fault—they gave me a bunch of hang-ups instead of a foundation.
   b. It's my spouse's fault—he/she doesn't give me encouragement.
   c. It's a great idea, but unfortunately I don't have the time.
   d. I am what I am, and I can't help it.
   e. No excuses, I just don't want to go!
   f. No excuses, I'm on the way to the banquet!

10. How would Jesus confront you about your excuses?

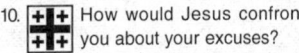

picture the woman searching for her money (vv. 8–9)? What is Jesus' point here?

♡ **1.** Have you ever strayed from the Christian faith? How did God bring you back? **2.** How do these stories make you feel about your value to God? **3.** How could these stories affect your relationships with those you know who wander from the faith?

☕ **1.** Did you ever run away from home? Where did you go? What happened? **2.** Who was (or is) the "obedient type" in your family? The "wild one"? Which were (or are) you? How did (or do) these types get along?

📖 **1.** What stages does the younger son go through on his pilgrimage? What brings him to his senses? What does he realize then? With what sort of attitude does he approach his father? **2.** How does the father receive his son? Why? **3.** How does the older brother feel about his younger brother's return? Why? How does the father answer the older brother's objection? **4.** What's Jesus' point with this parable? What does this story teach about sin, repentance and God's love? **5.** In summary, how do these three parables answer the Pharisee's objection in verse 2? What does Jesus want to teach the Pharisees in verses 25–31? In light of the context (v. 2), why does Jesus leave the story open-ended as to how the older brother responded to his father's plea?

♡ **1.** Comparing yourself to the two brothers in this story, who are you most like? Why? Are you quietly "at home"? Living only for today? Paying the consequences for yesterday? On the way home? Whom would you have identified with 10 years ago, or in your youth? **2.** How have you experienced God as similar to this father? **3.** When have you been like the older brother, quietly resentful of God's lavishness to less deserving people? Why? **4.** Consider verse 31. What does God have to give you that you have not taken?

⁶and goes home. Then he calls his friends and neighbors together and says, 'Rejoice with me; I have found my lost sheep.' ⁷I tell you that in the same way there will be more rejoicing in heaven over one sinner who repents than over ninety-nine righteous persons who do not need to repent.

The Parable of the Lost Coin

⁸"Or suppose a woman has ten silver coins*a* and loses one. Does she not light a lamp, sweep the house and search carefully until she finds it? ⁹And when she finds it, she calls her friends and neighbors together and says, 'Rejoice with me; I have found my lost coin.' ¹⁰In the same way, I tell you, there is rejoicing in the presence of the angels of God over one sinner who repents."

The Parable of the Lost Son

¹¹Jesus continued: "There was a man who had two sons. ¹²The younger one said to his father, 'Father, give me my share of the estate.' So he divided his property between them.

¹³"Not long after that, the younger son got together all he had, set off for a distant country and there squandered his wealth in wild living. ¹⁴After he had spent everything, there was a severe famine in that whole country, and he began to be in need. ¹⁵So he went and hired himself out to a citizen of that country, who sent him to his fields to feed pigs. ¹⁶He longed to fill his stomach with the pods that the pigs were eating, but no one gave him anything.

¹⁷"When he came to his senses, he said, 'How many of my father's hired men have food to spare, and here I am starving to death! ¹⁸I will set out and go back to my father and say to him: Father, I have sinned against heaven and against you. ¹⁹I am no longer worthy to be called your son; make me like one of your hired men.' ²⁰So he got up and went to his father.

"But while he was still a long way off, his father saw him and was filled with compassion for him; he ran to his son, threw his arms around him and kissed him.

²¹"The son said to him, 'Father, I have sinned against heaven and against you. I am no longer worthy to be called your son.*b*'

²²"But the father said to his servants, 'Quick! Bring the best robe and put it on him. Put a ring on his finger and sandals on his feet. ²³Bring the fattened calf and kill it. Let's have a feast and celebrate. ²⁴For this son of mine was dead and is alive again; he was lost and is found.' So they began to celebrate.

²⁵"Meanwhile, the older son was in the field. When he came near the house, he heard music and dancing. ²⁶So he called one of the servants and asked him what was going on. ²⁷'Your brother has come,' he replied, 'and your father has killed the fattened calf because he has him back safe and sound.'

²⁸"The older brother became angry and refused to go in. So his father went out and pleaded with him. ²⁹But he answered his father, 'Look! All these years I've been slaving for you and never disobeyed your orders. Yet you never gave me even a young goat so I could celebrate with my friends. ³⁰But when this son of yours who has squandered your property with prostitutes comes home, you kill the fattened calf for him!'

³¹"'My son,' the father said, 'you are always with me, and everything I have is yours. ³²But we had to celebrate and be glad, because this brother of yours was dead and is alive again; he was lost and is found.'"

---

a8 Greek *ten drachmas,* each worth about a day's wages   *b21* Some early manuscripts *son. Make me like one of your hired men.*

The Parable of the Shrewd Manager

16 Jesus told his disciples: "There was a rich man whose manager was accused of wasting his possessions. ²So he called him in and asked him, 'What is this I hear about you? Give an account of your management, because you cannot be manager any longer.'

³"The manager said to himself, 'What shall I do now? My master is taking away my job. I'm not strong enough to dig, and I'm ashamed to beg— ⁴I know what I'll do so that, when I lose my job here, people will welcome me into their houses.'

⁵"So he called in each one of his master's debtors. He asked the first, 'How much do you owe my master?'

⁶"'Eight hundred gallons*a* of olive oil,' he replied.

"The manager told him, 'Take your bill, sit down quickly, and make it four hundred.'

a6 Greek one hundred batous (probably about 3 kiloliters)

Which job would best fit your personality: Ringmaster at a circus? Movie producer? Sculptor? Librarian? Skydiving instructor? Gourmet chef? Church pastor?

1. Why would it be important for Jesus' disciples to hear this parable? 2. In what crisis does the manager find himself? What plan does he devise? In light of this scheme, why does the owner commend the manager (v. 8)? 3. How does Jesus summarize this parable (v. 9)? What do you think he's commending here? How do verses 10–12 help you understand his point? 4. What's the problem with trying to serve two masters (v. 13)? What characterizes the attitude of

---

      Lk 15:11–32   PRODIGAL SON

1. Why do you think the younger son decided to leave home?
   a. to try to make it on his own
   b. to experience the "fast lane"
   c. to be free of his father's values
   d. to get away from his older brother

2. What made the son come home?
   a. He got homesick.
   b. He got hungry.
   c. He felt sorry for his father.
   d. He felt sorry for himself.
   e. He felt guilty for what he had done.

3. If you were the father, what would have been your attitude when your son returned?
   a. Good to see you—but you're grounded!
   b. You have disgraced the family.
   c. Where's the money?
   d. I don't approve of what you've done, but you're still my son.
   e. Welcome home, son—I love you!

4. If you were the older brother, how would you have felt when you found out your father was throwing a party for your younger brother?
   a. angry   c. happy
   b. confused   d. resentful

5. In your life do you identify most with the father, younger son or older son?

6. Which relationship in your family generates the most conflict? What would need to happen for your family to want to celebrate the way the father did with his son?

7. If you likened your spiritual journey to the younger son's, where are you right now?
   a. never left home
   b. still at home, but itching to leave
   c. in a distant country, having a blast
   d. starting to realize I'm in a pigpen
   e. nervously on my way home
   f. back home and enjoying the party

8. How does this parable remind you of your own story? What are the roadblocks you have faced (or still face) on your way "home"?

9. What is the closest you have come to hitting bottom financially? What have you learned through financial hard times?
   a. that I can fail
   b. that forgiveness awaits when I admit my failure
   c. that I can't control everything that happens in life
   d. that it's never too late to make things right

10. Which of the patterns for resolving family conflict are typical of you and/or your family? (And how would you like things to be different?) I/We usually:
    a. enforce towing the line (because "father knows best").
    b. lovingly let people suffer the consequences of their own decisions.
    c. avoid conflict, and let time heal all wounds.
    d. allow the expression of disappointment and anger.

11. Which of the father's qualities do you most need?
    a. his willingness to let his son make mistakes
    b. his patience in waiting for change
    c. his capacity to forgive
    d. his understanding in dealing with both his children
    e. his ability to celebrate life

12. When should you let your children go their own way even though you know it will probably bring grief? When have you had to make a difficult decision about whether or not to intervene in your child's life?

13. If you were to have a party to celebrate the most positive thing about you and your parents' relationship, what would you celebrate? What can you do to make your relationship better?

14. What in this story is most like your own story?
    a. I have a dream of knowing the joy of reconciliation in a special relationship.
    b. There is a lot of ill-feeling between me and another family member.
    c. Like the younger brother, I had my time of rebellion.
    d. Like the older brother, I have felt cheated or left out.

15. What is your greatest hope regarding your broken relationship(s)? What is your greatest fear?

the Pharisees (v. 14)? How does the parable speak to them?

 1. How do you view your money: (a) It's mine, keep your hands off? (b) It's my creditors'? (c) It's God's—I just manage it? Why? How could you use it for the sake of the kingdom? **2.** Who (or what) are some of the masters you've served in the past? What masters *pull* at you for allegiance now? How do you deal with these pressures in light of your commitment to Christ?

[7]"Then he asked the second, 'And how much do you owe?'

"'A thousand bushels[a] of wheat,' he replied.

"He told him, 'Take your bill and make it eight hundred.'

[8]"The master commended the dishonest manager because he had acted shrewdly. For the people of this world are more shrewd in dealing with their own kind than are the people of the light. [9]I tell you, use worldly wealth to gain friends for yourselves, so that when it is gone, you will be welcomed into eternal dwellings.

[10]"Whoever can be trusted with very little can also be trusted with much, and whoever is dishonest with very little will also be dishonest with much. [11]So if you have not been trustworthy in handling worldly wealth, who will trust you with true riches? [12]And if you have not been trustworthy with someone else's property, who will give you property of your own?

[13]"No servant can serve two masters. Either he will hate the one and love the other, or he will be devoted to the one and despise the other. You cannot serve both God and Money."

[14]The Pharisees, who loved money, heard all this and were sneering at Jesus. [15]He said to them, "You are the ones who justify yourselves in the eyes of men, but God knows your hearts. What is highly valued among men is detestable in God's sight.

 1. How has the coming of the kingdom supplanted the law? Reinforced it? **2.** How is verse 18 to be applied today?

Additional Teachings

[16]"The Law and the Prophets were proclaimed until John. Since that time, the good news of the kingdom of God is being preached, and everyone is forcing his way into it. [17]It is easier for heaven and

[a]7 Greek *one hundred korous* (probably about 35 kiloliters)

$ **👁** *Luke 16:1–15*   **PARABLE OF THE SHREWD MANAGER**

1. What did the manager do when he saw he was about to get fired?
   a. He moved quickly to cut his boss's losses.
   b. He hurried to cover his tracks.
   c. He tried to get even with his boss.
   d. He tried to wheel and deal his way out of trouble.
   e. He created obligations he could "call in" later.

2. Why did the master commend the manager?
   a. because he had given up on collecting the debts
   b. because he admired shrewdness
   c. because some payment was better than none
   d. because the manager had acted quickly and decisively

3. What was Jesus teaching here?
   a. Dishonesty is the best policy.
   b. We should use money shrewdly.
   c. We should use money to buy friends.
   d. We should extend God's kingdom by sharing with those in need.

e. We should be as diligent as unbelievers are in managing money.
   f. Our spiritual growth is directly related to our faithfulness with money.

4. What does it mean to you to be "trustworthy in handling worldly wealth"?
   a. to put profits first
   b. to make smart financial decisions
   c. to implement the decisions of my superiors
   d. to handle wealth with the conviction that God owns it all
   e. to always be honest and ethical
   f. to use money in a way that will reap eternal dividends

5. How do you view your money?
   a. It's mine—keep your hands off!
   b. It's my creditors'.
   c. It's God's—I just manage it.

6. How do you feel about Jesus' black and white words: "You cannot serve both God and Money"? What practical changes can you make in your life to make you less of a servant or slave to money?

7. **$** Have you faced a crisis where, like the manager in this story, you thought you might lose your business or job because of a particular decision or a money management failure? What did you do?

8. **$** What is God calling you to do as a result of this study?
   a. view money management in the business world as an obligation to God to be trustworthy
   b. make wise, but honest, business decisions
   c. stop serving money and start serving God more
   d. give more money to help people

9. **👁** In what way are you currently experiencing the most internal conflict regarding money? How does that conflict affect your relationships with God and others?

10. **👁** What is the toughest decision you need to make concerning your finances? How does this passage speak to that decision? How can this group pray for you?

earth to disappear than for the least stroke of a pen to drop out of the Law.

[18]"Anyone who divorces his wife and marries another woman commits adultery, and the man who marries a divorced woman commits adultery.

The Rich Man and Lazarus

[19]"There was a rich man who was dressed in purple and fine linen and lived in luxury every day. [20]At his gate was laid a beggar named Lazarus, covered with sores [21]and longing to eat what fell from the rich man's table. Even the dogs came and licked his sores.

[22]"The time came when the beggar died and the angels carried him to Abraham's side. The rich man also died and was buried. [23]In hell,[a] where he was in torment, he looked up and saw Abraham far away, with Lazarus by his side. [24]So he called to him, 'Father Abraham, have pity on me and send Lazarus to dip the tip of his finger in water and cool my tongue, because I am in agony in this fire.'

[25]"But Abraham replied, 'Son, remember that in your lifetime you received your good things, while Lazarus received bad things, but now he is comforted here and you are in agony. [26]And besides all this, between us and you a great chasm has been fixed, so that those who want to go from here to you cannot, nor can anyone cross over from there to us.'

[27]"He answered, 'Then I beg you, father, send Lazarus to my

[a]23 Greek *Hades*

1. To clarify this passage, what would you ask Jesus?
2. How have you tried to force your way into the kingdom of heaven?

For what occasions do you feel like dressing to the hilt? When are you permitted and content to dress just in rags?

1. How do the lives of the rich man and Lazarus compare on earth (vv. 19–21)? After death (vv. 22–24)? 2. What determines who enters heaven? Why does this poor man qualify while the rich man is kept out? 3. What does this story teach you about comfort? Suffering? Why is it so difficult for people to be convinced of God's ways? How is verse 31 prophetic? 4. What does this passage teach about the afterlife? 5. What should we do with our lives on earth?

1. On a scale of 1 (the rich man and his brothers) to 10 (Lazarus), where do you stand? Why there? 2. Since lack of knowledge is not the brothers' problem, what is? How do you see that ten-

---

Luke 16:19–31   THE RICH MAN AND LAZARUS

1. Whom do you feel most sorry for?
   a. Lazarus in the beginning of the story
   b. the rich man in the middle of the story
   c. the rich man's brothers in the end of the story

2. What caused the rich man to be condemned?
   a. his great wealth
   b. his luxurious self-indulgence
   c. his oppression of the poor
   d. his hardness of heart toward God
   e. his apathy toward people's needs
   f. his lack of faith
   g. his refusal to listen and submit to Scripture

3. Why do you think Lazarus was qualified for heaven while the rich man was kept out?

4. How do you feel about discussing the subject of hell?

5. If Jesus commented on our view of wealth today, what might he say?
   a. The "Lifestyles of the Rich and Famous" is not the way to go.

   b. You are grabbing for it all, but missing the true meaning of life.
   c. It's difficult to see any difference between Christian values and secular values.
   d. You have so much, but you are spiritually bankrupt.

6. What does this story teach about the dark side of human nature?
   a. People can be very selfish.
   b. People can block out the needs of those around them.
   c. People can shut out God's Word.
   d. People can resist the testimony of miracles.
   e. People can ignore Jesus Christ in general and his resurrection in particular.

7. To which of the preceding offenses are you most vulnerable?

8. If you suddenly came into a great deal of money, what would you do with it?

9. Being totally honest, what are your top three priorities in life right now?
   a. a good time

   b. a good marriage/family
   c. good friendships
   d. making lots of money
   e. having nice things
   f. financial independence/security
   g. greater intimacy with God
   h. developing my spiritual gifts
   i. making a contribution to humanity
   j. being true to myself
   k. other:_____

10. How have your values changed since you gave your life to Christ? How do you think God might want them to change some more?

11. If you died tonight, what could be said about you? Finish the following sentences with the first thing that comes to mind.
    a. Last night (fill in your name) died suddenly.
    b. He/she will always be remembered for his/her ...
    c. He/she always had time for ...
    d. He/she felt possessions were ...
    e. He/she treated people like ...

dency in yourself? **3.** How do you feel about discussing Judgment Day with friends?

As a child, what was a sure-fire way that your siblings or parents could get your goat?

1. What might be an example of Jesus' meaning in verse 1? **2.** How could you practice verses 3–4 without reinforcing someone's bad behavior? **3.** How might the disciples' plea (v. 5) relate to Jesus' statement (vv. 3–4)? What does Jesus' response (v. 6) really mean? **4.** What attitudes should Jesus' followers have in serving him (vv. 7–10)?

Which quality of discipleship do you have the most difficulty with? How might dealing with this affect the other qualities?

When it comes to thank you notes are you: (a) Miss Manners? (b) Sir Sometimes? (c) Father Forgetful? Why?

1. What is it like to be a leper? What would healing mean for them? **2.** As one of the nine, how would you rationalize not going back to Jesus to say thanks? **3.** What is significant about the one being a Samaritan?

How do you express your gratitude to Jesus?

What are you looking forward to or waiting for right now?

1. In answering the Pharisees' question, what does Jesus say about the kingdom—as to when, how or where it is? Does he view the kingdom as an inward, spiritual reality *within* people? Or an outward, social manifestation *among* them? Or is he speaking of their failure to recognize who he is?

father's house, ²⁸for I have five brothers. Let him warn them, so that they will not also come to this place of torment.'

²⁹"Abraham replied, 'They have Moses and the Prophets; let them listen to them.'

³⁰" 'No, father Abraham,' he said, 'but if someone from the dead goes to them, they will repent.'

³¹"He said to him, 'If they do not listen to Moses and the Prophets, they will not be convinced even if someone rises from the dead.' "

Sin, Faith, Duty

17 Jesus said to his disciples: "Things that cause people to sin are bound to come, but woe to that person through whom they come. ²It would be better for him to be thrown into the sea with a millstone tied around his neck than for him to cause one of these little ones to sin. ³So watch yourselves.

"If your brother sins, rebuke him, and if he repents, forgive him. ⁴If he sins against you seven times in a day, and seven times comes back to you and says, 'I repent,' forgive him."

⁵The apostles said to the Lord, "Increase our faith!"

⁶He replied, "If you have faith as small as a mustard seed, you can say to this mulberry tree, 'Be uprooted and planted in the sea,' and it will obey you.

⁷"Suppose one of you had a servant plowing or looking after the sheep. Would he say to the servant when he comes in from the field, 'Come along now and sit down to eat'? ⁸Would he not rather say, 'Prepare my supper, get yourself ready and wait on me while I eat and drink; after that you may eat and drink'? ⁹Would he thank the servant because he did what he was told to do? ¹⁰So you also, when you have done everything you were told to do, should say, 'We are unworthy servants; we have only done our duty.' "

Ten Healed of Leprosy

¹¹Now on his way to Jerusalem, Jesus traveled along the border between Samaria and Galilee. ¹²As he was going into a village, ten men who had leprosy^a met him. They stood at a distance ¹³and called out in a loud voice, "Jesus, Master, have pity on us!"

¹⁴When he saw them, he said, "Go, show yourselves to the priests." And as they went, they were cleansed.

¹⁵One of them, when he saw he was healed, came back, praising God in a loud voice. ¹⁶He threw himself at Jesus' feet and thanked him—and he was a Samaritan.

¹⁷Jesus asked, "Were not all ten cleansed? Where are the other nine? ¹⁸Was no one found to return and give praise to God except this foreigner?" ¹⁹Then he said to him, "Rise and go; your faith has made you well."

The Coming of the Kingdom of God

²⁰Once, having been asked by the Pharisees when the kingdom of God would come, Jesus replied, "The kingdom of God does not come with your careful observation, ²¹nor will people say, 'Here it is,' or 'There it is,' because the kingdom of God is within^b you."

²²Then he said to his disciples, "The time is coming when you will long to see one of the days of the Son of Man, but you will not

^a12 The Greek word was used for various diseases affecting the skin—not necessarily leprosy.   ^b21 Or *among*

see it. ²³Men will tell you, 'There he is!' or 'Here he is!' Do not go running off after them. ²⁴For the Son of Man in his day*ᵃ* will be like the lightning, which flashes and lights up the sky from one end to the other. ²⁵But first he must suffer many things and be rejected by this generation.

²⁶"Just as it was in the days of Noah, so also will it be in the days of the Son of Man. ²⁷People were eating, drinking, marrying and being given in marriage up to the day Noah entered the ark. Then the flood came and destroyed them all.

²⁸"It was the same in the days of Lot. People were eating and drinking, buying and selling, planting and building. ²⁹But the day Lot left Sodom, fire and sulfur rained down from heaven and destroyed them all.

³⁰"It will be just like this on the day the Son of Man is revealed. ³¹On that day no one who is on the roof of his house, with his goods inside, should go down to get them. Likewise, no one in the field should go back for anything. ³²Remember Lot's wife! ³³Whoever tries to keep his life will lose it, and whoever loses his life will preserve it. ³⁴I tell you, on that night two people will be in one bed; one will be taken and the other left. ³⁵Two women will be grinding grain together; one will be taken and the other left.*ᵇ*"

³⁷"Where, Lord?" they asked.

He replied, "Where there is a dead body, there the vultures will gather."

ᵃ24 Some manuscripts do not have in his day.   ᵇ35 Some manuscripts left. ³⁶Two men will be in the field; one will be taken and the other left.

2. What did Jesus mean by "one of the days of the Son of Man"? 3. How will those days be like the days of Noah and Lot? What is so bad about the lives people were living in verses 27–28? What is meant by the warning about Lot's wife (see Ge 19:17–26)? 4. Verse 37 was a common proverb, implying that something will happen in its proper time. Why does Jesus say this?

♡ 1. While you live "in the kingdom" waiting for "the Son of Man" to come, what do you see in this section about the way you ought to apply verses 32–33? 2. Do you ever look back to your pre-Christ lifestyle? In what way?

Luke 17:11–19   TEN HEALED OF LEPROSY

In this story Jesus meets a group of 10 men with leprosy. Because of their disease, lepers were considered "unclean" and were required to keep a distance from others. Only after being declared healed and "clean" by a priest could a leper re-enter society. At least one of the 10 was a Samaritan—whom Jews generally despised as ethnic and religious half-breeds.

1. Why did Jesus send the lepers to the priests rather than healing them on the spot?
   a. He was tired of healing people.
   b. He didn't want to get close enough to them to heal them.
   c. He was testing their obedience.
   d. He wanted them to exercise faith themselves.
   e. He wanted to show that healing doesn't always happen instantly.

2. Why did all but one of the lepers fail to come back and thank Jesus?
   a. They couldn't find him.
   b. They weren't grateful enough to make the effort.
   c. They had what they wanted.
   d. They thought it was time something good happened to them.
   e. They were too busy telling others their good news.
   f. They were too busy getting reunited with their families and friends.
   g. They were only interested in the miracle, not the one providing it.

3. What was significant about the man who did return to thank Jesus?
   a. As a Samaritan, being looked down on made him more grateful.
   b. The others received physical healing, but only he received salvation.
   c. His being a foreigner shows that Jesus came for *all* people.
   d. He provides an example for our attitude toward Jesus.

4. Which of the following can you relate to personally? In what way?
   a. the pain of a physical condition
   b. the pain of social barriers
   c. being more interested in what God can do for me than in God himself
   d. neglecting to thank God or others

5. Whom do you need to thank for what they have done for you? How will you go about conveying your thanks to them?
   a. Jesus   f. a pastor
   b. my parents   g. a doctor
   c. my spouse   h. a teacher
   d. my children   i. a coach/mentor
   e. a friend   j. other:_____

6. The man who was healed praised God in a loud voice and threw himself at Jesus' feet. What keeps you from being that expressive of your thanks to Jesus?
   a. Jesus hasn't done anything that exciting for me.
   b. I'm not the emotional type.
   c. I don't want to look like a fanatic.
   d. Our culture is more restrained.
   e. We aren't like that at my church.
   f. If Jesus were here, I would.
   g. I'd like to, but it's not easy.
   h. Nothing—that's how I am.

7. How has Jesus healed you before?

8. How do you need healing now? How can this group pray for you?

What did you use to do to get your way with your parents: Sulk? Cry? Bribe? Persist? Force? Wit? What worked best?

1. What method did this woman use as she approached the judge? 2. How is God like and unlike the judge?

1. As for prayer, are you more likely to give up or hang tough? Why? 2. Does this story mean you should *keep* praying to get rich or to see the coming of God's kingdom? Why?

1. What group of people would be the Pharisees today? The tax collectors? What would be the "Pharisee's Prayer"? 2. How does this parable complement the one on persistence (vv. 1–8)? How do both demonstrate faith?

1. When have you been like the Pharisee? Like the tax collector? What accounts for the difference? 2. Right now, considering your attitude toward others, who are you most like? 3. How are you humble before God (Mic 6:8)?

The Parable of the Persistent Widow

18 Then Jesus told his disciples a parable to show them that they should always pray and not give up. ²He said: "In a certain town there was a judge who neither feared God nor cared about men. ³And there was a widow in that town who kept coming to him with the plea, 'Grant me justice against my adversary.'

⁴"For some time he refused. But finally he said to himself, 'Even though I don't fear God or care about men, ⁵yet because this widow keeps bothering me, I will see that she gets justice, so that she won't eventually wear me out with her coming!' "

⁶And the Lord said, "Listen to what the unjust judge says. ⁷And will not God bring about justice for his chosen ones, who cry out to him day and night? Will he keep putting them off? ⁸I tell you, he will see that they get justice, and quickly. However, when the Son of Man comes, will he find faith on the earth?"

The Parable of the Pharisee and the Tax Collector

⁹To some who were confident of their own righteousness and looked down on everybody else, Jesus told this parable: ¹⁰"Two men went up to the temple to pray, one a Pharisee and the other a tax collector. ¹¹The Pharisee stood up and prayed about*ᵃ* himself: 'God, I thank you that I am not like other men—robbers, evildoers, adulterers—or even like this tax collector. ¹²I fast twice a week and give a tenth of all I get.'

¹³"But the tax collector stood at a distance. He would not even look up to heaven, but beat his breast and said, 'God, have mercy on me, a sinner.'

ᵃ11 Or to

 Luke 18:1–8   **PARABLE OF THE PERSISTENT WIDOW**

Secular judges in Jesus' time were notoriously corrupt. Without influence or bribe money, plaintiffs might find it impossible to get their case settled.

1. What was this woman's problem?
a. a corrupt judge
b. no husband
c. no lawyer
d. nagging

2. What did she have going for her?
a. not much   e. persistence
b. stubbornness   f. God
c. faith   g. justice
d. power and influence

3. How is God like this judge?
a. God *is* the Judge.
b. God *does* grant justice.
c. Sometimes God *does* take a long time to act.

4. How is God unlike this judge?
a. God *does* care about people.
b. God *doesn't* have to be hounded to bring about justice.
c. God *doesn't* get worn out by our unceasing prayers.

5. What is the point of this parable?
a. If at first you don't succeed—try, try again.
b. If an unjust judge is compelled by persistence to render justice, how much more will God answer justly?
c. If you really love God, you will never get tired of praying.
d. If you really have faith, God will answer all your prayers.

6. For whose sake do you think Jesus spoke this parable?
a. for crooked judges—to clean up their act
b. for Christians in need—to persist in prayer
c. for Christians suffering persecution—to persist in their faith
d. for all Christians—to endure faithfully until "the Son of Man" returns

7. When it comes to prayer, what are you most likely to do?
a. cry out to God day and night
b. worry constantly, rather than pray
c. hang tough
d. give up

8. If you were in desperate need in the middle of the night, whom outside your family would you call?

9. What is your most urgent plea for the Lord right now? How can this group support you and join you in that prayer?

10. As you struggle with pain, what from this story do you need the most?
a. justice
b. faith
c. a persistent prayer life
d. the persistent prayers of others
e. strength not to give up on life
f. strength not to give up hope of getting better
g. strength to cope with my situation

11. What difference has this course made in your ability to cope with pain? Have one person at a time listen silently as others share with them a word of encouragement or affirmation.

[14]"I tell you that this man, rather than the other, went home justified before God. For everyone who exalts himself will be humbled, and he who humbles himself will be exalted."

The Little Children and Jesus

[15]People were also bringing babies to Jesus to have him touch them. When the disciples saw this, they rebuked them. [16]But Jesus called the children to him and said, "Let the little children come to me, and do not hinder them, for the kingdom of God belongs to such as these. [17]I tell you the truth, anyone who will not receive the kingdom of God like a little child will never enter it."

The Rich Ruler

[18]A certain ruler asked him, "Good teacher, what must I do to inherit eternal life?"

[19]"Why do you call me good?" Jesus answered. "No one is good—except God alone. [20]You know the commandments: 'Do not commit adultery, do not murder, do not steal, do not give false testimony, honor your father and mother.'[a]"

[21]"All these I have kept since I was a boy," he said.

[22]When Jesus heard this, he said to him, "You still lack one thing. Sell everything you have and give to the poor, and you will have treasure in heaven. Then come, follow me."

[23]When he heard this, he became very sad, because he was a man of great wealth. [24]Jesus looked at him and said, "How hard it is for the rich to enter the kingdom of God! [25]Indeed, it is easier for

[a]20 Exodus 20:12-16; Deut. 5:16-20

What is the funniest story about you as a child that you cannot remember but others told you?

1. How did the disciples feel about all these parents bringing their babies to Jesus? Why would they try to stop them? **2.** What does the ruler's question (v. 18) imply about his viewpoint on eternal life? What is Jesus' point in his response (v. 19)? Considering the man's religious obedience, what is ironic about verses 23–25? **3.** Since wealth was commonly considered a sign of God's blessing, what was the problem for the disciples (v. 26)? **4.** What is the way into the kingdom (vv. 27–30)? How do the children (vv. 15–17) reflect this attitude better than the rich man?

1. Are you more like the ruler or the children in how you approach God? Why? **2.** What has helped you see the impossibility of

Lk 18:9–14   THE PHARISEE & TAX COLLECTOR

This parable is about two very different men. The Pharisees were a religious sect whose prime concern was keeping the Law of Moses. Tax collectors were considered traitors and thieves, because they collected taxes for the Romans from their fellow Jews—usually with great personal profit.

1. Why do you think the Pharisee acted the way he did?
   a. He was grateful to God.
   b. He was arrogantly self-righteous.
   c. He sincerely wanted to honor God.
   d. He wouldn't be real with others.
   e. He wouldn't be real with himself.

2. Why do you think the tax collector acted the way he did?
   a. He knew he had done wrong.
   b. He wanted sympathy.
   c. He had a poor self-image.
   d. He was plea bargaining with God.
   e. He had hit rock bottom.

3. What is Jesus teaching here?
   a. God hates self-righteous religion.
   b. God loves humble repentance.
   c. Good works can't earn salvation.
   d. God knows what's in our hearts.

4. Which character would you feel more comfortable being around—the Pharisee or the tax collector?

5. Why did you choose that person?
   a. He is more spiritual.
   b. He is more honest.
   c. He is more like me.
   d. He is more like who I want to be.
   e. He could better understand me.

6. How would the Pharisee be accepted in this small group? How about the tax collector?

7. Being really honest, when have you been like the Pharisee—patting yourself on the back for your accomplishments or righteousness?

8. When have you been like the tax collector? When was the first time you cried out, "God, have mercy on me, a sinner"? When was the last time?

9. How did the tax collector demonstrate healthy humility? In each of the following, which is closer to how you view yourself?
   a. I make excuses for my faults or I take responsibility for my faults.

   b. I put myself down or I see myself like God does.
   c. I have a self-defeating attitude or I have a God-confident attitude.
   d. I'm a reject or I'm wanted.

10. Why do you think so many people confess their sins in bars rather than in churches? With whom do you share your problems?

11. How do you feel about opening up with this group?
    a. What did I get myself into?!
    b. I'm nervous, but I know I need it.
    c. I hope things stay confidential.
    d. I'm looking forward to it.
    e. I'll let you know later.

12. In what areas do you most often put yourself down?
    a. grades
    b. looks
    c. athletics
    d. spiritual commitment
    e. physical strength
    f. willpower
    g. coordination

13. What addiction do you battle? How have you tried to deny it? How can you be more like the tax collector on your road to recovery?

earning the kingdom? As a result, how have you experienced the gift of the kingdom (vv. 29–30)?

In light of all the talk about the kingdom of God coming, why is this new teaching misunderstood?

What is the greatest dilemma you have faced in your spiritual life? How did you respond?

Who is the most famous person you have seen up close? What were the circumstances?

1. What do the disciples still fail to see about Jesus (v. 39; compare to 18:15)? About his kingdom? 2. From this story, what do you know of the beggar's handicap? His faith? His intensity?

1. Have you ever felt Jesus was too busy for you? Why? How do we inadvertently communicate that idea to children or people with chronic needs? 2. If Jesus asked, "What do you *want* me to do for you?" what would you say?

If you could pick an ideal height, how tall would you be?

1. How does Zacchaeus compare with the rich, young ruler (18:18–30) in his approach and response to Jesus? 2. Why does Jesus dine with him? Why does this bother others? Do you think Jesus' words (vv. 9–10) stopped the crowd's muttering?

1. Where did Jesus first find you? (Up a tree? Out on a limb?) 2. How did he get you to join him? 3. What wrongs do you need to make right?

a camel to go through the eye of a needle than for a rich man to enter the kingdom of God."

26Those who heard this asked, "Who then can be saved?"

27Jesus replied, "What is impossible with men is possible with God."

28Peter said to him, "We have left all we had to follow you!"

29"I tell you the truth," Jesus said to them, "no one who has left home or wife or brothers or parents or children for the sake of the kingdom of God 30will fail to receive many times as much in this age and, in the age to come, eternal life."

Jesus Again Predicts His Death

31Jesus took the Twelve aside and told them, "We are going up to Jerusalem, and everything that is written by the prophets about the Son of Man will be fulfilled. 32He will be handed over to the Gentiles. They will mock him, insult him, spit on him, flog him and kill him. 33On the third day he will rise again."

34The disciples did not understand any of this. Its meaning was hidden from them, and they did not know what he was talking about.

A Blind Beggar Receives His Sight

35As Jesus approached Jericho, a blind man was sitting by the roadside begging. 36When he heard the crowd going by, he asked what was happening. 37They told him, "Jesus of Nazareth is passing by."

38He called out, "Jesus, Son of David, have mercy on me!"

39Those who led the way rebuked him and told him to be quiet, but he shouted all the more, "Son of David, have mercy on me!"

40Jesus stopped and ordered the man to be brought to him. When he came near, Jesus asked him, 41"What do you want me to do for you?"

"Lord, I want to see," he replied.

42Jesus said to him, "Receive your sight; your faith has healed you." 43Immediately he received his sight and followed Jesus, praising God. When all the people saw it, they also praised God.

Zacchaeus the Tax Collector

19 Jesus entered Jericho and was passing through. 2A man was there by the name of Zacchaeus; he was a chief tax collector and was wealthy. 3He wanted to see who Jesus was, but being a short man he could not, because of the crowd. 4So he ran ahead and climbed a sycamore-fig tree to see him, since Jesus was coming that way.

5When Jesus reached the spot, he looked up and said to him, "Zacchaeus, come down immediately. I must stay at your house today." 6So he came down at once and welcomed him gladly.

7All the people saw this and began to mutter, "He has gone to be the guest of a 'sinner.'"

8But Zacchaeus stood up and said to the Lord, "Look, Lord! Here and now I give half of my possessions to the poor, and if I have cheated anybody out of anything, I will pay back four times the amount."

9Jesus said to him, "Today salvation has come to this house, because this man, too, is a son of Abraham. 10For the Son of Man came to seek and to save what was lost."

The Parable of the Ten Minas

[11]While they were listening to this, he went on to tell them a parable, because he was near Jerusalem and the people thought that the kingdom of God was going to appear at once. [12]He said: "A man of noble birth went to a distant country to have himself appointed king and then to return. [13]So he called ten of his servants and gave them ten minas.[a] 'Put this money to work,' he said, 'until I come back.'

[14]"But his subjects hated him and sent a delegation after him to say, 'We don't want this man to be our king.'

[15]"He was made king, however, and returned home. Then he sent for the servants to whom he had given the money, in order to find out what they had gained with it.

[16]"The first one came and said, 'Sir, your mina has earned ten more.'

[17]"'Well done, my good servant!' his master replied. 'Because you have been trustworthy in a very small matter, take charge of ten cities.'

[18]"The second came and said, 'Sir, your mina has earned five more.'

[19]"His master answered, 'You take charge of five cities.'

[20]"Then another servant came and said, 'Sir, here is your mina; I have kept it laid away in a piece of cloth. [21]I was afraid of you,

[a]13 A mina was about three months' wages.

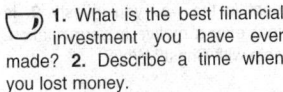

1. What is the best financial investment you have ever made? **2.** Describe a time when you lost money.

1. Where does the man of noble birth go? Why? What are his servants to do in his absence? **2.** What is the meaning of verses 14 and 27? Who are the enemies? **3.** What has happened to the 10 minas given to the first servant? The second servant? How does the master reply to them? How is the third servant's report influenced by a faulty perception of his master? Hence, what is his "reward"? **4.** Does verse 26 contradict Jesus' words to the ruler in 18:18–30? Why or why not? **5.** How does this parable speak to the misconception in verse 11?

1. What talents and resources do you think Jesus has left with you? How do you feel about the way you have invested them? How could you be more pru-

---

     Lk 19:1–10 **ZACCHAEUS THE TAX COLLECTOR**

1. If you had been Zacchaeus when Jesus stopped and told him to come down, how would you have felt?
   a. flabbergasted
   b. embarrassed
   c. overwhelmed with joy
   d. both excited *and* afraid

2. Why did Jesus single him out?
   a. He was wealthy.
   b. He was short.
   c. He was trying to hide.
   d. He was the worst sinner in town.
   e. Jesus could see his potential.

3. Why do you think Jesus invited himself to Zacchaeus' house?
   a. He needed a place to stay.
   b. He wanted to talk to him about his shady business practices.
   c. He wanted to show everyone that Zacchaeus wasn't really a sinner.
   d. He wanted to help this "little guy."
   e. He knew that Zacchaeus was a seeker looking for more in life.

4. "Today salvation has come to this house, because this man, too, is a son of Abraham." What was Jesus saying about Zacchaeus?
   a. He has followed the example of Abraham's faith.
   b. He was "lost" but now is "found."

c. Others see him as an outcast, but God loves and accepts him.
d. His generous decision shows that his heart has changed.

5. How do you think Zacchaeus felt when he and Jesus parted?
   a. clean   d. broke
   b. loved   e. brand new
   c. included in God's family

6. Who was the person early in your life who affirmed you like Jesus did with Zacchaeus? Who is the person who builds you up now?

7. 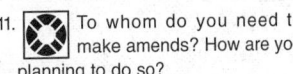 What most helps you to feel good about yourself?
   a. to be treated as a person and not a category (or worse yet, a sinner)
   b. for people to spend time with me
   c. for people to ignore the negative talk about me from the crowd
   d. to be affirmed and encouraged when I make progress
   e. to know that my body or bank account isn't what is important
   f. to be assured and reminded that I am accepted by God

8. Complete each sentence with how that person sees you as special or unique:

a. My parents see me as ...
b. My teachers see me as ...
c. My close friends see me as ...
d. People who don't know me very well see me as ...
e. I see myself as ...

9. What is God calling you to do right now?
   a. stop "watching" Jesus from a safe distance
   b. accept Jesus' invitation to get to know him better
   c. lay claim to God's gift of salvation
   d. celebrate God's acceptance
   e. make restitution for my wrongs

10. Why did Zacchaeus volunteer to make such generous restitution to those he had cheated?
   a. He was already in a 12 Step program.
   b. He felt guilty.
   c. His heart was full of love and gratitude toward Jesus.
   d. He wanted to be accepted by the community.
   e. A miracle had happened in his life.

11. To whom do you need to make amends? How are you planning to do so?

dent in the way you invest? **2.** Is fear ever a motive in your relationship with Christ? Why?

☕ How do you make your grand entry when you come home: With a silent grunt? A big splash? A hug and kiss? Yelling, "What's for dinner?"

📖 **1.** How close is Jesus to Jerusalem now (v. 29)? **2.** What task does he give two of his disciples? Why? What problems might they have encountered in such a job? **3.** How do you picture the scene in verses 35–38? What do you see? Hear? Feel? **4.** What were the people expecting Jesus to do when he reached Jerusalem (v. 11; see Zec 9:9)? How are their expectations different from his? How does this help to explain Jesus' words and emotions in verses 41–44? **5.** What does Jesus' reply to the Pharisees (vv. 39–40) imply about him? **6.** How do verses 45–48 relate to Jesus' concern about Jerusalem? Why does he take such extreme action?

❤️ **1.** What kind of reception would Jesus get: (a) If he rode into your town today? (b) After the people heard the message? **2.** How would he be treated by the local media? By elected officials? The guys in the tavern? The ladies in the bridge club? **3.** What person or group of people do you weep for? **4.** How has Jesus "turned over tables" in your life? What has he been cleaning out recently?

because you are a hard man. You take out what you did not put in and reap what you did not sow.'

²²"His master replied, 'I will judge you by your own words, you wicked servant! You knew, did you, that I am a hard man, taking out what I did not put in, and reaping what I did not sow? ²³Why then didn't you put my money on deposit, so that when I came back, I could have collected it with interest?'

²⁴"Then he said to those standing by, 'Take his mina away from him and give it to the one who has ten minas.'

²⁵"'Sir,' they said, 'he already has ten!'

²⁶"He replied, 'I tell you that to everyone who has, more will be given, but as for the one who has nothing, even what he has will be taken away. ²⁷But those enemies of mine who did not want me to be king over them—bring them here and kill them in front of me.'"

The Triumphal Entry

²⁸After Jesus had said this, he went on ahead, going up to Jerusalem. ²⁹As he approached Bethphage and Bethany at the hill called the Mount of Olives, he sent two of his disciples, saying to them, ³⁰"Go to the village ahead of you, and as you enter it, you will find a colt tied there, which no one has ever ridden. Untie it and bring it here. ³¹If anyone asks you, 'Why are you untying it?' tell him, 'The Lord needs it.'"

³²Those who were sent ahead went and found it just as he had told them. ³³As they were untying the colt, its owners asked them, "Why are you untying the colt?"

³⁴They replied, "The Lord needs it."

³⁵They brought it to Jesus, threw their cloaks on the colt and put Jesus on it. ³⁶As he went along, people spread their cloaks on the road.

³⁷When he came near the place where the road goes down the Mount of Olives, the whole crowd of disciples began joyfully to praise God in loud voices for all the miracles they had seen:

³⁸"Blessed is the king who comes in the name of the Lord!"ᵃ

"Peace in heaven and glory in the highest!"

³⁹Some of the Pharisees in the crowd said to Jesus, "Teacher, rebuke your disciples!"

⁴⁰"I tell you," he replied, "if they keep quiet, the stones will cry out."

⁴¹As he approached Jerusalem and saw the city, he wept over it ⁴²and said, "If you, even you, had only known on this day what would bring you peace—but now it is hidden from your eyes. ⁴³The days will come upon you when your enemies will build an embankment against you and encircle you and hem you in on every side. ⁴⁴They will dash you to the ground, you and the children within your walls. They will not leave one stone on another, because you did not recognize the time of God's coming to you."

Jesus at the Temple

⁴⁵Then he entered the temple area and began driving out those who were selling. ⁴⁶"It is written," he said to them, "'My house will be a house of prayer'ᵇ; but you have made it 'a den of robbers.'ᶜ"

⁴⁷Every day he was teaching at the temple. But the chief priests,

ᵃ38 Psalm 118:26   ᵇ46 Isaiah 56:7   ᶜ46 Jer. 7:11

the teachers of the law and the leaders among the people were trying to kill him. **48**Yet they could not find any way to do it, because all the people hung on his words.

The Authority of Jesus Questioned

20 One day as he was teaching the people in the temple courts and preaching the gospel, the chief priests and the teachers of the law, together with the elders, came up to him. **2**"Tell us by what authority you are doing these things," they said. "Who gave you this authority?"

3He replied, "I will also ask you a question. Tell me, **4**John's baptism—was it from heaven, or from men?"

5They discussed it among themselves and said, "If we say, 'From heaven,' he will ask, 'Why didn't you believe him?' **6**But if we say, 'From men,' all the people will stone us, because they are persuaded that John was a prophet."

7So they answered, "We don't know where it was from."

8Jesus said, "Neither will I tell you by what authority I am doing these things."

The Parable of the Tenants

9He went on to tell the people this parable: "A man planted a vineyard, rented it to some farmers and went away for a long time. **10**At harvest time he sent a servant to the tenants so they would give him some of the fruit of the vineyard. But the tenants beat him and sent him away empty-handed. **11**He sent another servant, but that one also they beat and treated shamefully and sent away empty-handed. **12**He sent still a third, and they wounded him and threw him out.

As a teenager, what authority figure (parent, teacher, minister) upset you most? Why?

1. What "things" (v. 2) has Jesus been doing? What about these things would worry the chief priests? 2. What interests are they trying to protect from Jesus' probing question? Why does Jesus evade their question?

What people, things or events led you to recognize Jesus' authority? What authority does he have (or demand) now?

When have you recently experienced "three-strikes-and-you're-out": Employment? Dating? School? Family? How do you handle rejection?

1. How does this parable relate to the question of authority raised in verses 1–8? 2. What does the landowner do? How do

---

Luke 19:28–44   **THE TRIUMPHAL ENTRY**

With Passover just a few days away, Jerusalem would have been filled with travelers. Jesus makes an entrance into the "holy city" on the first day of this, the last week of his life.

1. What would you have said if you were one of the two disciples Jesus sent to go and get a colt?
   a. "I could get arrested for this!"
   b. "This sounds important."
   c. "This sounds impossible—How will we find this colt?"
   d. "No problem."

2. What would you have said if you owned the colt and saw two men taking it?
   a. "What are you doing?!"
   b. "Who is 'the Lord' who needs my donkey?"
   c. "Quick! Somebody call the police!"
   d. "No problem."

3. Why did Jesus arrange this "triumphal entry"?
   a. to confuse people about his mission and identity
   b. to receive people's praise

   c. to fulfill Old Testament prophecy
   d. to declare openly that he was the Messiah
   e. to start the countdown to the cross

4. Why did the crowd respond the way they did?
   a. because it was Palm Sunday
   b. because of the miracles Jesus did
   c. because they realized Jesus was the Messiah
   d. because they thought Jesus was acting like a deliverer and king
   e. because Jesus deserved their praise and honor

5. What caused Jesus to weep over Jerusalem?
   a. He was angry at the people's hardness of heart.
   b. He was grieved by their rejection.
   c. He foresaw the city's destruction.
   d. He knew that destruction could have been prevented.
   e. He knew how the tide of public opinion would turn against him.
   f. He realized how misunderstood he and his mission were.

   g. He was sad that God's people failed to recognize "God's coming."

6. What kind of king did the crowd think Jesus was? What kind of King do you think Jesus was, and is? When have you had wrong assumptions about how God works?

7. How did Jesus enter your life?
   a. as a knight on a white horse
   b. as a warrior on a chariot
   c. as a rabbi with an armful of scrolls
   d. as an authoritative king with a penetrating gaze
   e. as a humble servant on a colt

8. Has there ever been a "Jerusalem" in your life, when you knew that once you arrived you would be doing God's will at great personal sacrifice?

9. What person or group of people do you yearn to see come to God?

10. If the Pharisees were here now, how much joyful praise would they find to criticize in your church? In your small group? In your own life?

¹³"Then the owner of the vineyard said, 'What shall I do? I will send my son, whom I love; perhaps they will respect him.'

¹⁴"But when the tenants saw him, they talked the matter over. 'This is the heir,' they said. 'Let's kill him, and the inheritance will be ours.' ¹⁵So they threw him out of the vineyard and killed him.

"What then will the owner of the vineyard do to them? ¹⁶He will come and kill those tenants and give the vineyard to others."

When the people heard this, they said, "May this never be!"

¹⁷Jesus looked directly at them and asked, "Then what is the meaning of that which is written:

"'The stone the builders rejected
has become the capstone[a][b]?

¹⁸Everyone who falls on that stone will be broken to pieces, but he on whom it falls will be crushed."

¹⁹The teachers of the law and the chief priests looked for a way to arrest him immediately, because they knew he had spoken this parable against them. But they were afraid of the people.

Paying Taxes to Caesar

²⁰Keeping a close watch on him, they sent spies, who pretended to be honest. They hoped to catch Jesus in something he said so that they might hand him over to the power and authority of the governor. ²¹So the spies questioned him: "Teacher, we know that you speak and teach what is right, and that you do not show partiality but teach the way of God in accordance with the truth. ²²Is it right for us to pay taxes to Caesar or not?"

²³He saw through their duplicity and said to them, ²⁴"Show me a denarius. Whose portrait and inscription are on it?"

²⁵"Caesar's," they replied.

He said to them, "Then give to Caesar what is Caesar's, and to God what is God's."

²⁶They were unable to trap him in what he had said there in public. And astonished by his answer, they became silent.

The Resurrection and Marriage

²⁷Some of the Sadducees, who say there is no resurrection, came to Jesus with a question. ²⁸"Teacher," they said, "Moses wrote for us that if a man's brother dies and leaves a wife but no children, the man must marry the widow and have children for his brother. ²⁹Now there were seven brothers. The first one married a woman and died childless. ³⁰The second ³¹and then the third married her, and in the same way the seven died, leaving no children. ³²Finally, the woman died too. ³³Now then, at the resurrection whose wife will she be, since the seven were married to her?"

³⁴Jesus replied, "The people of this age marry and are given in marriage. ³⁵But those who are considered worthy of taking part in that age and in the resurrection from the dead will neither marry nor be given in marriage, ³⁶and they can no longer die; for they are like the angels. They are God's children, since they are children of the resurrection. ³⁷But in the account of the bush, even Moses showed that the dead rise, for he calls the Lord 'the God of Abraham, and the God of Isaac, and the God of Jacob.'[c] ³⁸He is not the God of the dead, but of the living, for to him all are alive."

³⁹Some of the teachers of the law responded, "Well said, teacher!" ⁴⁰And no one dared to ask him any more questions.

a17 Or *cornerstone*   *b17* Psalm 118:22   *c37* Exodus 3:6

Whose Son Is the Christ?

41Then Jesus said to them, "How is it that they say the Christ[a] is the Son of David? 42David himself declares in the Book of Psalms:

> " 'The Lord said to my Lord:
> "Sit at my right hand
> 43until I make your enemies
>   a footstool for your feet." '[b]

44David calls him 'Lord.' How then can he be his son?"

45While all the people were listening, Jesus said to his disciples, 46"Beware of the teachers of the law. They like to walk around in flowing robes and love to be greeted in the marketplaces and have the most important seats in the synagogues and the places of honor at banquets. 47They devour widows' houses and for a show make lengthy prayers. Such men will be punished most severely."

The Widow's Offering

21 As he looked up, Jesus saw the rich putting their gifts into the temple treasury. 2He also saw a poor widow put in two very small copper coins.[c] 3"I tell you the truth," he said, "this poor widow has put in more than all the others. 4All these people gave their gifts out of their wealth; but she out of her poverty put in all she had to live on."

Signs of the End of the Age

5Some of his disciples were remarking about how the temple was adorned with beautiful stones and with gifts dedicated to God. But Jesus said, 6"As for what you see here, the time will come when not one stone will be left on another; every one of them will be thrown down."

7"Teacher," they asked, "when will these things happen? And what will be the sign that they are about to take place?"

8He replied: "Watch out that you are not deceived. For many will come in my name, claiming, 'I am he,' and, 'The time is near.' Do not follow them. 9When you hear of wars and revolutions, do not be frightened. These things must happen first, but the end will not come right away."

10Then he said to them: "Nation will rise against nation, and kingdom against kingdom. 11There will be great earthquakes, famines and pestilences in various places, and fearful events and great signs from heaven.

12"But before all this, they will lay hands on you and persecute you. They will deliver you to synagogues and prisons, and you will be brought before kings and governors, and all on account of my name. 13This will result in your being witnesses to them. 14But make up your mind not to worry beforehand how you will defend yourselves. 15For I will give you words and wisdom that none of your adversaries will be able to resist or contradict. 16You will be betrayed even by parents, brothers, relatives and friends, and they will put some of you to death. 17All men will hate you because of me. 18But not a hair of your head will perish. 19By standing firm you will gain life.

20"When you see Jerusalem being surrounded by armies, you will know that its desolation is near. 21Then let those who are in Judea flee to the mountains, let those in the city get out, and let those in the country not enter the city. 22For this is the time of punishment in fulfillment of all that has been written. 23How

a41 Or Messiah   b43 Psalm 110:1   c2 Greek two lepta

As a child, what "hot buttons" did you push to make your parents mad?

1. Given the issue of authority in this chapter, why does Jesus continue to challenge traditional values? 2. What undermines the authority of the religious leaders (vv. 45–47)? 3. How does the poor widow differ from these leaders? What is Jesus' point in making this contrast?

1. When have you "used" religion to get something for yourself (attention, respect, good feelings) rather than for love of God? What helps get you back on track? 2. Do you give to God off the top (at the outset of the month), or from what is left over (at month's end)? Explain.

What is the tallest building you have been in? What could you see from the top?

1. What prompts Jesus' next lesson? 2. What bombshell does he drop on his disciples (v. 6)? Considering how the Jews felt about the temple, how must they have felt when they heard Jesus' words? 3. The disciples identified the destruction of the temple with the end times, but Jesus separates them. In verses 8–19, which is he teaching about? 4. What will happen to the disciples and the church during tribulation (v. 10)? What comfort will come in the midst of these trials? 5. In A.D. 70, Jerusalem was destroyed by the Romans. Why would Jesus warn of this event in verses 20–24? Why will Jerusalem be devastated (see 11:49–51; 13:34–35 and 19:41–44)? How does Jesus describe this time (vv. 21–24)? What does he tell the people to do? Why? 6. In verses 25–28, which event (the coming of the end or Jerusalem's destruction) is in view? What do the two events have in common? What is significant about the way the Son of Man will come (v. 27; see Da 7:13–14)? What should be the attitude of believers when they see the Son of Man coming (v. 28)? 7. What is the lesson of the fig tree (vv. 29–31)? How does this lesson answer the disciples' question from verse 7? 8. How would the promises (vv.

32–33) have been a comfort to the disciples? A discomfort? What impact do they have on you? **9.** In the midst of this heavy news, how does Jesus caution his followers (vv. 34–35)?

1. When were you a bold witness for Christ? What happened? How did God give you insight and wisdom? **2.** When reading the parable of the fig tree today, how near is the fig tree to sprouting? What makes you think this? How does this affect the way you live your life? **3.** How well does your life reflect verse 36? What will you do this week to become better at watching and praying?

When you were growing up, what were mealtimes like? Where did everyone sit around the table? What one vivid memory do you have about each family member at that time?

1. What was the significance of Passover? The Passover lamb (see Ex 12:1–13,21–28)? **2.** In light of 19:39–48, why are the priests and teachers so determined to kill Jesus? How does that relate to the roundabout way Jesus has the disciples arrange for the Passover feast? **3.** Besides the desire to be with friends, why might Jesus "eagerly desire" to share this particular Passover feast with the disciples? How will Passover really be "fulfilled" in the kingdom of God (v. 16)? How does Jesus' use of the bread and wine change the emphasis of Passover? What is the meaning of verse 18? Verse 19? From Jeremiah 31:31–33, how would you describe the "new covenant" Jesus brought about? **4.** If you were there, how would you have reacted to the news about Jesus' unnamed betrayer (vv. 21–22)? How might that lead to the argument in verse 24? How does

dreadful it will be in those days for pregnant women and nursing mothers! There will be great distress in the land and wrath against this people. ²⁴They will fall by the sword and will be taken as prisoners to all the nations. Jerusalem will be trampled on by the Gentiles until the times of the Gentiles are fulfilled.

²⁵"There will be signs in the sun, moon and stars. On the earth, nations will be in anguish and perplexity at the roaring and tossing of the sea. ²⁶Men will faint from terror, apprehensive of what is coming on the world, for the heavenly bodies will be shaken. ²⁷At that time they will see the Son of Man coming in a cloud with power and great glory. ²⁸When these things begin to take place, stand up and lift up your heads, because your redemption is drawing near."

²⁹He told them this parable: "Look at the fig tree and all the trees. ³⁰When they sprout leaves, you can see for yourselves and know that summer is near. ³¹Even so, when you see these things happening, you know that the kingdom of God is near.

³²"I tell you the truth, this generation*a* will certainly not pass away until all these things have happened. ³³Heaven and earth will pass away, but my words will never pass away.

³⁴"Be careful, or your hearts will be weighed down with dissipation, drunkenness and the anxieties of life, and that day will close on you unexpectedly like a trap. ³⁵For it will come upon all those who live on the face of the whole earth. ³⁶Be always on the watch, and pray that you may be able to escape all that is about to happen, and that you may be able to stand before the Son of Man."

³⁷Each day Jesus was teaching at the temple, and each evening he went out to spend the night on the hill called the Mount of Olives, ³⁸and all the people came early in the morning to hear him at the temple.

Judas Agrees to Betray Jesus

22 Now the Feast of Unleavened Bread, called the Passover, was approaching, ²and the chief priests and the teachers of the law were looking for some way to get rid of Jesus, for they were afraid of the people. ³Then Satan entered Judas, called Iscariot, one of the Twelve. ⁴And Judas went to the chief priests and the officers of the temple guard and discussed with them how he might betray Jesus. ⁵They were delighted and agreed to give him money. ⁶He consented, and watched for an opportunity to hand Jesus over to them when no crowd was present.

The Last Supper

⁷Then came the day of Unleavened Bread on which the Passover lamb had to be sacrificed. ⁸Jesus sent Peter and John, saying, "Go and make preparations for us to eat the Passover."

⁹"Where do you want us to prepare for it?" they asked.

¹⁰He replied, "As you enter the city, a man carrying a jar of water will meet you. Follow him to the house that he enters, ¹¹and say to the owner of the house, 'The Teacher asks: Where is the guest room, where I may eat the Passover with my disciples?' ¹²He will show you a large upper room, all furnished. Make preparations there."

¹³They left and found things just as Jesus had told them. So they prepared the Passover.

¹⁴When the hour came, Jesus and his apostles reclined at the table. ¹⁵And he said to them, "I have eagerly desired to eat this

a32 Or *race*

Passover with you before I suffer. ¹⁶For I tell you, I will not eat it again until it finds fulfillment in the kingdom of God."

¹⁷After taking the cup, he gave thanks and said, "Take this and divide it among you. ¹⁸For I tell you I will not drink again of the fruit of the vine until the kingdom of God comes."

¹⁹And he took bread, gave thanks and broke it, and gave it to them, saying, "This is my body given for you; do this in remembrance of me."

²⁰In the same way, after the supper he took the cup, saying, "This cup is the new covenant in my blood, which is poured out for you. ²¹But the hand of him who is going to betray me is with mine on the table. ²²The Son of Man will go as it has been decreed, but woe to that man who betrays him." ²³They began to question among themselves which of them it might be who would do this.

²⁴Also a dispute arose among them as to which of them was considered to be greatest. ²⁵Jesus said to them, "The kings of the Gentiles lord it over them; and those who exercise authority over them call themselves Benefactors. ²⁶But you are not to be like that. Instead, the greatest among you should be like the youngest, and the one who rules like the one who serves. ²⁷For who is greater, the one who is at the table or the one who serves? Is it not the one who is at the table? But I am among you as one who serves. ²⁸You are those who have stood by me in my trials. ²⁹And I confer on you a kingdom, just as my Father conferred one on me, ³⁰so that you may eat and drink at my table in my kingdom and sit on thrones, judging the twelve tribes of Israel.

Jesus resolve that argument (vv. 25–27)? What does he mean by the promise in verses 28–30? **5.** How must Peter feel in verses 31–34? What are the differences between Judas (vv. 1–6) and Peter, since both failed Jesus? **6.** What is Jesus trying to impress upon Peter (v. 33) and the others in verses 35–38: (a) They should fight? (b) They really will be left on their own once he's gone? (c) He is indeed going to die, and will not be able to care for them? or (d) Other? Why?

♡ **1.** What does sharing in Communion or the Lord's Supper mean to you? **2.** What would it mean to apply Jesus' words about service (v. 27) in your family life? Work or school relationships? Use of money? Why apply this principle in those areas? Why not? **3.** With which disciple do you identify most and why: (a) Judas— I've sold out on Jesus? (b) Those arguing—I want to follow Jesus, but I still want to be successful in the eyes of others? or (c) Peter—I am passionately committed to

---

Luke 22:7–34   THE LAST SUPPER

1. How do you think Jesus felt at this "last supper"?
   a. nostalgic
   b. sad
   c. relaxed
   d. uptight
   e. anxious to get things over with

2. Rank the following reasons why it was important to Jesus to have this supper with his disciples, from 1 to 5 (most to least significant):
   a. to celebrate the traditional Jewish Passover
   b. to tie his impending death to the Passover and redemption
   c. to share one last time of fellowship
   d. to share some final teaching
   e. to institute the Lord's Supper as an ongoing sacrament/ordinance

3. Probably the hardest thing for the disciples to understand in this passage was what Jesus meant:
   a. by the mysterious preparations.
   b. about eating the Passover again when the kingdom of God comes.
   c. about the bread and the cup.
   d. about one of them betraying him.
   e. about servants being the greatest.

f. about one day "judging," or ruling, the 12 tribes of Israel.
g. about Satan and his sifting.

4. Which of the previous points are hardest for *you* to understand?

5. What do you think is the most striking parallel between Passover and the meaning of the Last Supper?
   a. Both involved a sacrificial "lamb."
   b. God was rescuing his people through both.
   c. Contrary to Passover, Jesus' sacrifice never needs to be repeated.
   d. Passover is a remembrance of deliverance from slavery; the Last Supper is a remembrance of deliverance from sin.

6. What was Jesus' response to the disciples' dispute about which of them was considered to be greatest?
   a. His followers shouldn't argue.
   b. His followers shouldn't compete, unless it's competing to serve.
   c. His followers shouldn't flaunt their authority or position.
   d. His followers should think of themselves as equals.

7. Do you think Peter was sincere when he said, "Lord, I am ready to go with you to prison and to death"? Why can it be so hard for *you* to take a stand for Christ?

8. Why is the Last Supper important to believers? What can you do in preparing for Communion to make it more significant for you?

9. Through both Passover and Christ's death, God brought people freedom. What do you need to be free from?

10. What are you competing for in life?
    a. money—to prove myself a financial success
    b. respect—to prove my competence
    c. my parents' approval—to show them I can make it in life
    d. God's approval—to show I can be God's person in all I do

11. In what relationship(s) or area of life do you find it hardest to be a servant? What is God calling you to do to make your life more service-oriented?

Jesus, but sometimes I fall flat on my face? **4.** Does verse 37 apply to you? Why?

31"Simon, Simon, Satan has asked to sift you*ᵃ* as wheat. **32**But I have prayed for you, Simon, that your faith may not fail. And when you have turned back, strengthen your brothers."

33But he replied, "Lord, I am ready to go with you to prison and to death."

34Jesus answered, "I tell you, Peter, before the rooster crows today, you will deny three times that you know me."

35Then Jesus asked them, "When I sent you without purse, bag or sandals, did you lack anything?"

"Nothing," they answered.

36He said to them, "But now if you have a purse, take it, and also a bag; and if you don't have a sword, sell your cloak and buy one. **37**It is written: 'And he was numbered with the transgressors'*ᵇ*; and I tell you that this must be fulfilled in me. Yes, what is written about me is reaching its fulfillment."

38The disciples said, "See, Lord, here are two swords."

"That is enough," he replied.

Jesus Prays on the Mount of Olives

39Jesus went out as usual to the Mount of Olives, and his disciples followed him. **40**On reaching the place, he said to them, "Pray that you will not fall into temptation." **41**He withdrew about a stone's throw beyond them, knelt down and prayed, **42**"Father, if you are willing, take this cup from me; yet not my will, but yours be done." **43**An angel from heaven appeared to him and strengthened him. **44**And being in anguish, he prayed more earnestly, and his sweat was like drops of blood falling to the ground.*ᶜ*

45When he rose from prayer and went back to the disciples, he found them asleep, exhausted from sorrow. **46**"Why are you sleeping?" he asked them. "Get up and pray so that you will not fall into temptation."

Jesus Arrested

47While he was still speaking a crowd came up, and the man who was called Judas, one of the Twelve, was leading them. He approached Jesus to kiss him, **48**but Jesus asked him, "Judas, are you betraying the Son of Man with a kiss?"

49When Jesus' followers saw what was going to happen, they said, "Lord, should we strike with our swords?" **50**And one of them struck the servant of the high priest, cutting off his right ear.

51But Jesus answered, "No more of this!" And he touched the man's ear and healed him.

52Then Jesus said to the chief priests, the officers of the temple guard, and the elders, who had come for him, "Am I leading a rebellion, that you have come with swords and clubs? **53**Every day I was with you in the temple courts, and you did not lay a hand on me. But this is your hour—when darkness reigns."

Peter Disowns Jesus

54Then seizing him, they led him away and took him into the house of the high priest. Peter followed at a distance. **55**But when they had kindled a fire in the middle of the courtyard and had sat down together, Peter sat down with them. **56**A servant girl saw him seated there in the firelight. She looked closely at him and said, "This man was with him."

57But he denied it. "Woman, I don't know him," he said.

In times of crisis, do you stay cool, get hot, panic or dig in? Where do you go to be alone?

1. What strikes you about Jesus' prayer? In saying, "your will be done," is Jesus: (a) Helplessly submitting to fate? (b) Admitting defeat before a power that beat him? (c) Bitterly resigning himself to the inevitable? or (d) Quietly trusting in God's love? **2.** Why is the crowd so large and armed (v. 52)? What do they fear? Why are their fears unfounded? **3.** What is the irony in Judas' betrayal? How do you reconcile 22:38 and Jesus' behavior in verses 50–51? **4.** What does Jesus mean by "your hour" (v. 53; in contrast to his own, v. 42)?

1. What do *you* mean when you pray, "your will be done"? **2.** How would you compare Jesus' attitudes and actions with those of his disciples? His enemies? What impresses you most about him?

When have you felt like crawling into a hole, never to return: When you gave up the winning run in a baseball game? Hit the wrong note in your orchestra solo? Other?

1. How would you describe Peter's personality? **2.** Given verse 33, what accounts for Peter's actions now? What questions must he have had about himself?

ᵃ31 The Greek is plural.   *ᵇ37* Isaiah 53:12   *ᶜ44* Some early manuscripts do not have verses 43 and 44.

[58]A little later someone else saw him and said, "You also are one of them."

"Man, I am not!" Peter replied.

[59]About an hour later another asserted, "Certainly this fellow was with him, for he is a Galilean."

[60]Peter replied, "Man, I don't know what you're talking about!" Just as he was speaking, the rooster crowed. [61]The Lord turned and looked straight at Peter. Then Peter remembered the word the Lord had spoken to him: "Before the rooster crows today, you will disown me three times." [62]And he went outside and wept bitterly.

The Guards Mock Jesus

[63]The men who were guarding Jesus began mocking and beating him. [64]They blindfolded him and demanded, "Prophesy! Who hit you?" [65]And they said many other insulting things to him.

Jesus Before Pilate and Herod

[66]At daybreak the council of the elders of the people, both the chief priests and teachers of the law, met together, and Jesus was led before them. [67]"If you are the Christ,[a]" they said, "tell us."

Jesus answered, "If I tell you, you will not believe me, [68]and if I asked you, you would not answer. [69]But from now on, the Son of Man will be seated at the right hand of the mighty God."

[70]They all asked, "Are you then the Son of God?"

He replied, "You are right in saying I am."

[a]67 Or *Messiah*

When have you felt like Peter? What "rooster" reminds you of failure? What helps you work through guilt?

When you were a kid, would you rather have been punished by your fourth grade teacher or by your school principal? Why?

1. Why would the guards (22:63–65) treat Jesus as they do? What physical and emotional shape do you think Jesus was in by daybreak (v. 66)? **2.** How is the concern of the elders and priests in verses 67–70 different from the concern which they bring to Pilate (23:2)? Why? **3.** In light of Jesus' condition, with what tone of voice do you picture Pilate asking the question of 23:3? How seriously does he seem to take this claim? **4.** What new charge do the

---

   **Luke 22:54–62**   **PETER DISOWNS JESUS**

1. After Jesus was arrested, what made Peter deny knowing him?
   a. momentary insanity
   b. spiritual weakness
   c. personality weakness
   d. fear for his own life

2. If you could put in a good word for Peter, what would it be?
   a. He meant well.
   b. He was the only disciple to follow Jesus to his trial.
   c. He was only human.
   d. He came back to Christ in the end.
   e. I wouldn't have done any better.

3. How do you think Peter felt when Jesus looked at him?
   a. He realized how stupid he'd been.
   b. He felt ashamed of his behavior.
   c. He was humiliated by his failure.
   d. He was afraid Jesus would never forgive him.

4. The impact this failure had on Peter's future was that it probably:
   a. made him less cocky.
   b. took away all his self-confidence.
   c. made him more sensitive.
   d. helped make him into the man of God he became.

5. How do you usually react to failure, and how would you like to react differently?
   a. kick myself for days
   b. try to be extra good for awhile
   c. shrug it off
   d. admit it and get on with life
   e. become afraid to try again
   f. talk to God about it

6. How has failure changed you?
   a. I'm more caring and empathetic.
   b. I'm more determined.
   c. I'm more humble.
   d. I'm more realistic.
   e. I look out for myself more.
   f. I'm emotionally fragile.
   g. I don't feel I can serve God again.

7. What failure in your life comes closest to hitting you like Peter's failure hit him?
   a. when I went through a divorce
   b. when I lost my job
   c. when I went through bankruptcy or financial failure
   d. when I "fell off the wagon"
   e. when I failed my wife or children
   f. when I had a chance to talk about Christ, but didn't

8. How does this story relate to you and your child?
   a. I have blown it as a parent.
   b. My child has really let me down.
   c. I can sense my child's pain.
   d. I have been in denial about some things in our relationship.
   e. My child has been in denial about some things in our relationship.
   f. One of us has disowned the other.

9. How much pain do you think your strained relationship has brought your child? How can identifying with that pain help you cope with your own pain?

10. Would you give yourself a "plus" or a "minus" for each of the following characteristics:
    a. bouncing back after you blow it
    b. forgiving those who fail you
    c. standing up for Christ
    d. spiritual desire
    e. spiritual consistency

11. How has this course, and especially those in your group, helped you learn to deal better with stress?

elders bring against Jesus in verse 5? What does Pilate's referral of the case to Herod show about the seriousness with which he viewed "the Jesus threat"? **5.** What do you learn about Herod's character from verses 8–11? What do you think he asked Jesus? Why wouldn't Jesus answer him at all? How do you account for the new friendship (v. 12)? **6.** Although Pilate and Herod both found Jesus innocent, why does Pilate finally give in to the leaders? What would you have done in his place? **7.** What ironies do you see in the fact that Barabbas (his name means "son of the father") was released, while Jesus was condemned? What does that show about the leaders? About Pilate?

♡ **1.** In 19:45, Jesus confronted injustice with action, but here he was silent. Why? What particular form of injustice makes your blood boil? How do you decide when to fight for what is right, and when not to? Has that decision faced you recently? **2.** What contrasts do you see between Jesus' kingship and the authority of Pilate and Herod? What difference does it make to you that Jesus is not the type of king they were? **3.** How do you feel as you consider what Jesus experienced during his trial?

🍵 Which childhood chore (cleaning your room, mowing the lawn, caring for pets, doing the dishes), was your least favorite? Most favorite?

📖 **1.** By now, how is Jesus faring (see Mk 14:65; 15:15–19)? Why would someone have to help Jesus carry the cross? **2.** Why would Jesus rather have no one weep for him (vv. 28–31; see 21:20–24)? Does Jesus address these women as his followers or as citizens of Jerusalem? How would you paraphrase what he meant by

⁷¹Then they said, "Why do we need any more testimony? We have heard it from his own lips."

23 Then the whole assembly rose and led him off to Pilate. ²And they began to accuse him, saying, "We have found this man subverting our nation. He opposes payment of taxes to Caesar and claims to be Christ,ᵃ a king."

³So Pilate asked Jesus, "Are you the king of the Jews?"

"Yes, it is as you say," Jesus replied.

⁴Then Pilate announced to the chief priests and the crowd, "I find no basis for a charge against this man."

⁵But they insisted, "He stirs up the people all over Judeaᵇ by his teaching. He started in Galilee and has come all the way here."

⁶On hearing this, Pilate asked if the man was a Galilean. ⁷When he learned that Jesus was under Herod's jurisdiction, he sent him to Herod, who was also in Jerusalem at that time.

⁸When Herod saw Jesus, he was greatly pleased, because for a long time he had been wanting to see him. From what he had heard about him, he hoped to see him perform some miracle. ⁹He plied him with many questions, but Jesus gave him no answer. ¹⁰The chief priests and the teachers of the law were standing there, vehemently accusing him. ¹¹Then Herod and his soldiers ridiculed and mocked him. Dressing him in an elegant robe, they sent him back to Pilate. ¹²That day Herod and Pilate became friends—before this they had been enemies.

¹³Pilate called together the chief priests, the rulers and the people, ¹⁴and said to them, "You brought me this man as one who was inciting the people to rebellion. I have examined him in your presence and have found no basis for your charges against him. ¹⁵Neither has Herod, for he sent him back to us; as you can see, he has done nothing to deserve death. ¹⁶Therefore, I will punish him and then release him.ᶜ"

¹⁸With one voice they cried out, "Away with this man! Release Barabbas to us!" ¹⁹(Barabbas had been thrown into prison for an insurrection in the city, and for murder.)

²⁰Wanting to release Jesus, Pilate appealed to them again. ²¹But they kept shouting, "Crucify him! Crucify him!"

²²For the third time he spoke to them: "Why? What crime has this man committed? I have found in him no grounds for the death penalty. Therefore I will have him punished and then release him."

²³But with loud shouts they insistently demanded that he be crucified, and their shouts prevailed. ²⁴So Pilate decided to grant their demand. ²⁵He released the man who had been thrown into prison for insurrection and murder, the one they asked for, and surrendered Jesus to their will.

The Crucifixion

²⁶As they led him away, they seized Simon from Cyrene, who was on his way in from the country, and put the cross on him and made him carry it behind Jesus. ²⁷A large number of people followed him, including women who mourned and wailed for him. ²⁸Jesus turned and said to them, "Daughters of Jerusalem, do not weep for me; weep for yourselves and for your children. ²⁹For the time will come when you will say, 'Blessed are the barren women, the wombs that never bore and the breasts that never nursed!' ³⁰Then

---

ᵃ2 Or *Messiah*; also in verses 35 and 39   ᵇ5 Or *over the land of the Jews*
ᶜ16 Some manuscripts *him." ¹⁷Now he was obliged to release one man to them at the Feast.*

" 'they will say to the mountains, "Fall on us!"
and to the hills, "Cover us!" ' *a*

31For if men do these things when the tree is green, what will happen when it is dry?"

32Two other men, both criminals, were also led out with him to be executed. 33When they came to the place called the Skull, there they crucified him, along with the criminals—one on his right, the other on his left. 34Jesus said, "Father, forgive them, for they do not know what they are doing."*b* And they divided up his clothes by casting lots.

35The people stood watching, and the rulers even sneered at him. They said, "He saved others; let him save himself if he is the Christ of God, the Chosen One."

36The soldiers also came up and mocked him. They offered him wine vinegar 37and said, "If you are the king of the Jews, save yourself."

38There was a written notice above him, which read: THIS IS THE KING OF THE JEWS.

39One of the criminals who hung there hurled insults at him: "Aren't you the Christ? Save yourself and us!"

40But the other criminal rebuked him. "Don't you fear God," he said, "since you are under the same sentence? 41We are punished justly, for we are getting what our deeds deserve. But this man has done nothing wrong."

42Then he said, "Jesus, remember me when you come into your kingdom.*c*"

43Jesus answered him, "I tell you the truth, today you will be with me in paradise."

Jesus' Death

44It was now about the sixth hour, and darkness came over the whole land until the ninth hour, 45for the sun stopped shining. And the curtain of the temple was torn in two. 46Jesus called out with a loud voice, "Father, into your hands I commit my spirit." When he had said this, he breathed his last.

47The centurion, seeing what had happened, praised God and said, "Surely this was a righteous man." 48When all the people who had gathered to witness this sight saw what took place, they beat their breasts and went away. 49But all those who knew him, including the women who had followed him from Galilee, stood at a distance, watching these things.

Jesus' Burial

50Now there was a man named Joseph, a member of the Council, a good and upright man, 51who had not consented to their decision and action. He came from the Judean town of Arimathea and he was waiting for the kingdom of God. 52Going to Pilate, he asked for Jesus' body. 53Then he took it down, wrapped it in linen cloth and placed it in a tomb cut in the rock, one in which no one had yet been laid. 54It was Preparation Day, and the Sabbath was about to begin.

55The women who had come with Jesus from Galilee followed Joseph and saw the tomb and how his body was laid in it. 56Then they went home and prepared spices and perfumes. But they rested on the Sabbath in obedience to the commandment.

the proverb in verse 31? 3. What attitudes and motives do you see in the crowd following this death-march? In the rulers? The criminals? The soldiers? The sign maker (v. 38)? In Jesus? 4. What aspects of the Gospel message do you see in verses 40–43?

1. How do you view the crucifixion: Necessary evil? Cruel and unusual punishment? Sacrifice for sin? Triumph over injustice? Why? 2. When did the meaning of the death of Christ begin to make sense to you? How would you explain the crucifixion to a non-Christian friend? 3. Who in this story do you identify with most? With least? Why? 4. How do people today similarly reflect the profound misunderstanding expressed in verse 35?

Whose death (family, friend or national figure) has affected you most? Why?

1. What is the meaning of the darkness (see 22:53)? The torn curtain (Heb 9)? Jesus' prayer (Ps 31:5)? The centurion's confession (v. 47)? 2. What do you learn about Joseph of Arimathea? Why would he risk his reputation and status at this point?

1. From the elements here, how would you describe to someone what Jesus' death was all about? How does it make a difference in your view of sin and failure? Your confidence in God's love? 2. Jesus had apparently failed, but Joseph and the women did not abandon him. What do you learn from this for your life? 3. What does Jesus' crucifixion teach you about success, power, wealth and status?

a30 Hosea 10:8   *b34* Some early manuscripts do not have this sentence.
c42 Some manuscripts *come with your kingly power*

Describe a time recently when you woke up very early to do something outside your normal routine.

1. Given what these women experienced in the last few days (19:37ff; 23:26–49, 55), how would they feel as they went to the tomb? When they find it empty? When the two men spoke to them? 2. Why wouldn't the Eleven believe them? What must be going through Peter's mind?

1. How did the meaning of the resurrection first "dawn" upon you? What difference does the resurrection make to you? 2. Where is your spiritual life focused: On Good Friday? Easter Sunday? Or in between?

If you were laid off from work today or your job was terminated, where would you go to get yourself together?

The Resurrection

24 On the first day of the week, very early in the morning, the women took the spices they had prepared and went to the tomb. ²They found the stone rolled away from the tomb, ³but when they entered, they did not find the body of the Lord Jesus. ⁴While they were wondering about this, suddenly two men in clothes that gleamed like lightning stood beside them. ⁵In their fright the women bowed down with their faces to the ground, but the men said to them, "Why do you look for the living among the dead? ⁶He is not here; he has risen! Remember how he told you, while he was still with you in Galilee: ⁷'The Son of Man must be delivered into the hands of sinful men, be crucified and on the third day be raised again.'" ⁸Then they remembered his words.

⁹When they came back from the tomb, they told all these things to the Eleven and to all the others. ¹⁰It was Mary Magdalene, Joanna, Mary the mother of James, and the others with them who told this to the apostles. ¹¹But they did not believe the women, because their words seemed to them like nonsense. ¹²Peter, however, got up and ran to the tomb. Bending over, he saw the strips of linen lying by themselves, and he went away, wondering to himself what had happened.

On the Road to Emmaus

¹³Now that same day two of them were going to a village called Emmaus, about seven miles*a* from Jerusalem. ¹⁴They were talking with each other about everything that had happened. ¹⁵As they

a13 Greek *sixty stadia* (about 11 kilometers)

Luke 23:44–49   JESUS' DEATH

1. How would you illustrate this story?
   a. a black cloud blocking the sun, representing such an ominous day
   b. a sunset, representing the end of an era
   c. a sunrise, representing the hope of the new day to come
   d. the torn curtain of the temple, representing the way to God opened

2. Why did darkness cover the land from about noon until 3 p.m.?
   a. There was probably an eclipse.
   b. The forces of evil were at the height of their power.
   c. God was dealing with the darkness of sin.
   d. God was so upset he didn't want anyone to see these events.
   e. God was mad at the world.

3. What is so significant about the temple curtain (which shielded the Most Holy Place) being torn in two?
   a. The barrier between God and us was removed.
   b. Everyone can approach God directly now.

   c. There's no more need for mystery.
   d. There's no more need for blood sacrifices.
   e. Fellowship between God and people has been restored.

4. What do you think the Roman centurion in charge of the crucifixion, who gave God praise, did the next day?
   a. tried to forget all about this
   b. figured he had let his fears and emotions get the best of him
   c. searched out Jesus' followers to find out more about Jesus
   d. asked God to forgive him for his role in Jesus' death

5. What caused those witnessing the crucifixion (other than Jesus' followers) to leave the cross beating their breasts?
   a. awe at the day's events
   b. guilt for their earlier mocking
   c. grief for Jesus' death
   d. fear for their own future

6. Do you see Jesus' crucifixion as a tragedy or a victory? How does the story of his death make you feel?

7. When did you come to realize that Jesus died for you?

8. How would you describe the way Jesus' death has impacted your lifestyle and value system?
   a. a little bit
   b. a whole lot
   c. not as much as it should
   d. a lot more than it used to
   e. I'm not sure.

9. What kind of man does the story of Jesus' death show him to be?
   a. a *real* man
   b. a righteous man
   c. no ordinary man
   d. a defeated man
   e. a triumphant man

10. How has this course affected your views of masculinity? How can you be more like Jesus?

11. One at a time, listen silently as other group members share what Christlike qualities that person demonstrates.

talked and discussed these things with each other, Jesus himself came up and walked along with them; ¹⁶but they were kept from recognizing him.

¹⁷He asked them, "What are you discussing together as you walk along?"

They stood still, their faces downcast. ¹⁸One of them, named Cleopas, asked him, "Are you only a visitor to Jerusalem and do not know the things that have happened there in these days?"

¹⁹"What things?" he asked.

"About Jesus of Nazareth," they replied. "He was a prophet, powerful in word and deed before God and all the people. ²⁰The chief priests and our rulers handed him over to be sentenced to death, and they crucified him; ²¹but we had hoped that he was the one who was going to redeem Israel. And what is more, it is the third day since all this took place. ²²In addition, some of our women amazed us. They went to the tomb early this morning ²³but didn't find his body. They came and told us that they had seen a vision of angels, who said he was alive. ²⁴Then some of our companions went to the tomb and found it just as the women had said, but him they did not see."

²⁵He said to them, "How foolish you are, and how slow of heart to believe all that the prophets have spoken! ²⁶Did not the Christ*a* have to suffer these things and then enter his glory?" ²⁷And beginning with Moses and all the Prophets, he explained to them what was said in all the Scriptures concerning himself.

²⁸As they approached the village to which they were going, Jesus acted as if he were going farther. ²⁹But they urged him strongly,

a26 Or Messiah; *also in verse 46*

1. What are the two disciples talking about as they walk (see vv. 19–24)? What tones of voice do you hear? What hopes are dashed? What plans might they be making? How do they react to the "stranger"? 2. From your knowledge of OT prophecy, what passages might "the stranger" have discussed with them in verses 25–27 (see list in Introduction to Hosea)? Why did Jesus do a roundabout Bible study rather than just reveal his identity immediately and directly? 3. Why did Jesus act as if he was going further? 4. What has happened to the other disciples that has caused them to change their minds from verse 11? Why a special appearance to Peter?

1. Where is your "Road to Emmaus"—the place where Jesus surprised you recently? What happened? Did you urge him to stay (v. 29)? Why or why not? 2. How well do you think you can explain the life, death and resurrection of Jesus Christ, and the way a person can have a relationship with him? Try rehearsing or role playing

Luke 24:13–35   ON THE ROAD TO EMMAUS

This story happened late in the day in which Jesus rose from the dead.

1. What do you think caused these two disciples to leave town?
   a. fear—They feared for their lives.
   b. disillusionment—They thought they lost their political liberator.
   c. overload—Jesus' suffering and crucifixion had wiped them out.
   d. loneliness—They wanted to get back home.
   e. despair—They lost their hope along with their spiritual leader.

2. Why didn't they recognize Jesus when he joined them?
   a. They were preoccupied.
   b. They refused to believe their eyes.
   c. Jesus wasn't recognizable in his resurrected body.
   d. God supernaturally prevented them from recognizing him.

3. What opened their eyes?
   a. a sudden burst of insight
   b. Jesus taking bread and breaking it
   c. the Holy Spirit
   d. putting two and two together

4. Why did the two disciples want to return to Jerusalem?
   a. to confirm the women's report
   b. to be with their friends
   c. to tell everybody the good news
   d. to rejoin the team they had quit

5. What is the thing that triggers a spiritual crisis for you?
   a. financial panic
   b. anger with God over personal tragedy
   c. disappointment in a relationship
   d. family problems
   e. questions/doubts about my faith
   f. disillusionment with my church
   g. lack of direction from God

6. What is the closest you have come to "throwing in the towel" spiritually?

7. What helps you recognize Jesus alongside you when you are down?
   a. spending time alone with God
   b. talking with someone who cares
   c. getting away from the situation
   d. taking Communion
   e. reading Scripture
   f. fellowshipping with others

8. How would you describe your relationship with Christ right now?
   a. headed the wrong direction
   b. headed the right direction
   c. up and down
   d. a special case of "heartburn" (like the disciples in this story)

9. How are you feeling about your recovery from the pain in your life?
   a. I don't know if I'll ever hope again.
   b. Jesus is making sense of my pain.
   c. I wish that I could see Jesus more clearly.
   d. Jesus has given me hope in the midst of my despair.
   e. I have been looking only at what I've lost and not at what I have.
   f. I am finding hope in Scripture.
   g. The answer to my dashed hopes has been with me all along.

10. The two disciples hurried to share what happened to them with their friends. What have you appreciated about the shared experiences of this group?

this in your group. Who could you communicate these truths with today?

☕ What favorite slogan or pep talk do you recall from your mentors (parents, a coach, music teacher, etc.)? How were you treated when you blew it?

📖 1. How is "Peace be with you" a good summary of the Gospel? 2. Why are the disciples having such difficulty believing: (a) Not using their eyes? (b) Not enough evidence? (c) Not enough faith? (d) Too much excitement? Why was it necessary for them to see that Jesus was not a ghost? 3. What interpretation from Jesus helps them to believe? 4. What task does he give them? With what promise? How must they have felt? 5. Why do the disciples react so differently when Jesus is taken away now (vv. 50–53; compare when he was taken away by the crucifixion, v. 46)?

♡ 1. Why is it important to you that Jesus' mission was anticipated far beforehand in the Old Testament? 2. How would you live differently if Jesus was not currently reigning in heaven, but was only another noble martyr? 3. In light of your circumstances, where is the mission field Jesus has sent you? Who are some of the people you can witness to by your life? By your words? Who are the disciples in your life who encourage your service to Christ? 4. How do you respond to his mission for you: (a) Let's get going!? (b) I couldn't possibly do that!? (c) He didn't mean me? (d) I'm scared, but I'll trust him? Why? 5. What has been the high point for you in this study of Luke?

"Stay with us, for it is nearly evening; the day is almost over." So he went in to stay with them.

³⁰When he was at the table with them, he took bread, gave thanks, broke it and began to give it to them. ³¹Then their eyes were opened and they recognized him, and he disappeared from their sight. ³²They asked each other, "Were not our hearts burning within us while he talked with us on the road and opened the Scriptures to us?"

³³They got up and returned at once to Jerusalem. There they found the Eleven and those with them, assembled together ³⁴and saying, "It is true! The Lord has risen and has appeared to Simon." ³⁵Then the two told what had happened on the way, and how Jesus was recognized by them when he broke the bread.

Jesus Appears to the Disciples

³⁶While they were still talking about this, Jesus himself stood among them and said to them, "Peace be with you."

³⁷They were startled and frightened, thinking they saw a ghost. ³⁸He said to them, "Why are you troubled, and why do doubts rise in your minds? ³⁹Look at my hands and my feet. It is I myself! Touch me and see; a ghost does not have flesh and bones, as you see I have."

⁴⁰When he had said this, he showed them his hands and feet. ⁴¹And while they still did not believe it because of joy and amazement, he asked them, "Do you have anything here to eat?" ⁴²They gave him a piece of broiled fish, ⁴³and he took it and ate it in their presence.

⁴⁴He said to them, "This is what I told you while I was still with you: Everything must be fulfilled that is written about me in the Law of Moses, the Prophets and the Psalms."

⁴⁵Then he opened their minds so they could understand the Scriptures. ⁴⁶He told them, "This is what is written: The Christ will suffer and rise from the dead on the third day, ⁴⁷and repentance and forgiveness of sins will be preached in his name to all nations, beginning at Jerusalem. ⁴⁸You are witnesses of these things. ⁴⁹I am going to send you what my Father has promised; but stay in the city until you have been clothed with power from on high."

The Ascension

⁵⁰When he had led them out to the vicinity of Bethany, he lifted up his hands and blessed them. ⁵¹While he was blessing them, he left them and was taken up into heaven. ⁵²Then they worshiped him and returned to Jerusalem with great joy. ⁵³And they stayed continually at the temple, praising God.

INTRODUCTION to

JOHN

Book Study Outline: If you are using John for a study course, here is a 7- or 13-week outline. Use the margin questions for your group agenda:

☕ start meeting / 15 min.

📖 read & discuss Bible / 30 min.

♡ close meeting / 15–45 min.

Refer to the Questions and Answers in the front of this Bible for more information.

7-week plan	13-week plan	Personal Reading	Group Study Passage
	1	1:1–2:11	2:1–11/Water to Wine
1	2	2:12–3:21	3:1–21/Nicodemus
2	3	3:22–4:30	4:7–30/A Samaritan Woman
	4	4:31–5:15	5:1–15/Healing at the Pool
3	5	5:16–8:11	7:53–8:11/Adulterous Woman
	6	8:12–9:34	9:1–34/Blind Man Healed
4	7	9:35–11:44	11:1–44/Lazarus Raised
5	8	11:45–13:17	13:1–17/Washing of Feet
	9	13:18–16:33	15:1–17/Vine and Branches
6	10	17:1–19:27	19:16–27/The Crucifixion
	11	19:28–20:18	20:1–18/Appearance to Mary
7	12	20:19–31	20:24–31/Thomas Doubts
	13	21:1–25	21:1–25/Peter Reinstated

Author: According to tradition, John, "the beloved disciple" (21:20–24), wrote this Gospel. John was prominent in the early church but is not mentioned by name in this book—which would be natural if he wrote it. For more information about John's long life, see the timeline in the Introduction to 1 John.

Date: Uncertain; estimates range anywhere from the A.D. 50s to 90s.

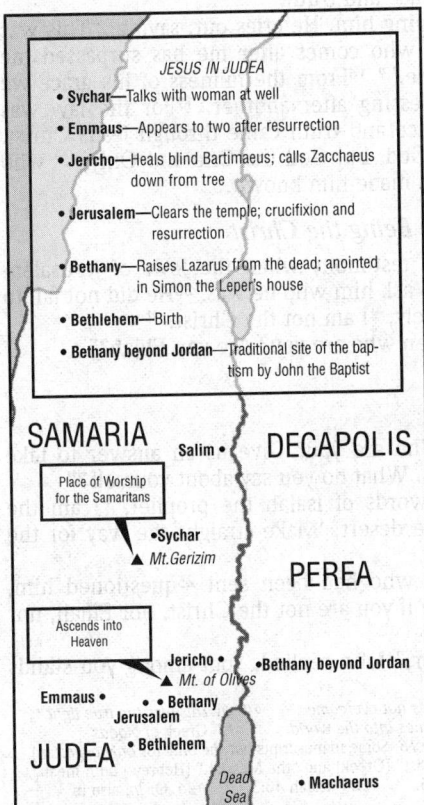

JESUS IN JUDEA

- **Sychar**—Talks with woman at well
- **Emmaus**—Appears to two after resurrection
- **Jericho**—Heals blind Bartimaeus; calls Zacchaeus down from tree
- **Jerusalem**—Clears the temple; crucifixion and resurrection
- **Bethany**—Raises Lazarus from the dead; anointed in Simon the Leper's house
- **Bethlehem**—Birth
- **Bethany beyond Jordan**—Traditional site of the baptism by John the Baptist

SAMARIA   Salim •   DECAPOLIS

Place of Worship for the Samaritans

• Sychar
▲ Mt. Gerizim

PEREA

Ascends into Heaven

Jericho •   • Bethany beyond Jordan
▲ Mt. of Olives
Emmaus •   • • Bethany
Jerusalem

JUDEA   • Bethlehem

Dead Sea   • Machaerus

Theme: Jesus is the giver of life (20:31).

Historical Background: Of all the Gospels, John's is most clearly not meant to be a chronological account of Jesus' life. Instead it is a meditation on the significance of his death—a reality which is present right from the beginning of the Gospel (e.g., 1:29).

Characteristics: One commentator writes that years of studying John "do not leave one with a feeling of having mastered it, but rather with the conviction that it is still strange, restless and unfamiliar" (Morris). In many ways this Gospel is very different from the others. The action centers in Jerusalem rather than in Galilee. Jesus' teaching is given in long discourses instead of pithy parables. The call to faith and the promise of eternal life are repeatedly emphasized. Stories not in the other Gospels about people like Nicodemus, the woman at the well and Lazarus, are highlighted. The "I am" statements of Jesus, as well as the beautiful prologue (1:1–18), are unique. Irony, words with double meanings, and metaphors invite the reader to reflect upon the richness and depth of Jesus. Chapters 1–12 focus on a few public miracles which are expressly meant as "signs" pointing to Jesus' identity, while in chapters 13–21, Jesus is basically alone with his disciples teaching them about his mission, the Holy Spirit and his command to love.

John

🍵 1. What is your full name? 2. What is your nickname? Where did the names come from?

📖 1. Why does this Gospel begin "In the beginning" rather than at Jesus' birth? 2. What facts about "the Word" can you find in verses 1–5? Verses 10–18? 3. What is John the Baptist's role as a witness? 4. Who or what fails to comprehend the light (vv. 5, 10–11)? Why? 5. From the image of "receiving" someone (v. 12), how would you explain what faith is about? What is the result of this type of faith? 6. How would someone "full of grace and truth" treat others? 7. From this passage, how can a person come to know God?

❤️ 1. Are you keeping Jesus at the door? In certain rooms? Why? Or have you given him the keys? 2. What does John's emphasis on the pre-existent, creative Christ mean to you?

🍵 Have you ever been embarrassed for mistaking a stranger for an acquaintance? What happened?

📖 1. What questions do the priests and Levites ask John? What do these questions reveal about the reason why they were sent? 2. Why does John respond so abruptly? What would you have said in his situation? 3. What is John's purpose in life (vv. 22–23,26–27; also Isa 40:3–5)? 4. How does John finally answer their question about his baptism (vv. 30–31)? What does he mean by calling Jesus the "Lamb of God" (v. 29; see Ex 12:1–13; Isa 53:7) and the "Son of God" (v. 34)? What proof supports these claims (Ps 2:7)?

❤️ 1. Who "made straight the way for the Lord" in your life? 2. How could you incorporate the

The Word Became Flesh

1 In the beginning was the Word, and the Word was with God, and the Word was God. ²He was with God in the beginning. ³Through him all things were made; without him nothing was made that has been made. ⁴In him was life, and that life was the light of men. ⁵The light shines in the darkness, but the darkness has not understood[a] it.

⁶There came a man who was sent from God; his name was John. ⁷He came as a witness to testify concerning that light, so that through him all men might believe. ⁸He himself was not the light; he came only as a witness to the light. ⁹The true light that gives light to every man was coming into the world.[b]

¹⁰He was in the world, and though the world was made through him, the world did not recognize him. ¹¹He came to that which was his own, but his own did not receive him. ¹²Yet to all who received him, to those who believed in his name, he gave the right to become children of God— ¹³children born not of natural descent,[c] nor of human decision or a husband's will, but born of God.

¹⁴The Word became flesh and made his dwelling among us. We have seen his glory, the glory of the One and Only,[d] who came from the Father, full of grace and truth.

¹⁵John testifies concerning him. He cries out, saying, "This was he of whom I said, 'He who comes after me has surpassed me because he was before me.'" ¹⁶From the fullness of his grace we have all received one blessing after another. ¹⁷For the law was given through Moses; grace and truth came through Jesus Christ. ¹⁸No one has ever seen God, but God the One and Only,[d,e] who is at the Father's side, has made him known.

John the Baptist Denies Being the Christ

¹⁹Now this was John's testimony when the Jews of Jerusalem sent priests and Levites to ask him who he was. ²⁰He did not fail to confess, but confessed freely, "I am not the Christ.[f]"

²¹They asked him, "Then who are you? Are you Elijah?"

He said, "I am not."

"Are you the Prophet?"

He answered, "No."

²²Finally they said, "Who are you? Give us an answer to take back to those who sent us. What do you say about yourself?"

²³John replied in the words of Isaiah the prophet, "I am the voice of one calling in the desert, 'Make straight the way for the Lord.'"[g]

²⁴Now some Pharisees who had been sent ²⁵questioned him, "Why then do you baptize if you are not the Christ, nor Elijah, nor the Prophet?"

²⁶"I baptize with[h] water," John replied, "but among you stands

---

a5 Or darkness, and the darkness has not overcome   *b9 Or This was the true light that gives light to every man who comes into the world*   *c13 Greek of bloods*
d14,18 Or the Only Begotten   *e18 Some manuscripts but the only (or only begotten) Son*   *f20 Or Messiah.* "The Christ" (Greek) and "the Messiah" (Hebrew) both mean "the Anointed One"; also in verse 25.   *g23 Isaiah 40:3*   *h26 Or in; also in verses 31 and 33*

one you do not know. 27He is the one who comes after me, the thongs of whose sandals I am not worthy to untie."

28This all happened at Bethany on the other side of the Jordan, where John was baptizing.

Jesus the Lamb of God

29The next day John saw Jesus coming toward him and said, "Look, the Lamb of God, who takes away the sin of the world! 30This is the one I meant when I said, 'A man who comes after me has surpassed me because he was before me.' 31I myself did not know him, but the reason I came baptizing with water was that he might be revealed to Israel."

32Then John gave this testimony: "I saw the Spirit come down from heaven as a dove and remain on him. 33I would not have known him, except that the one who sent me to baptize with water told me, 'The man on whom you see the Spirit come down and remain is he who will baptize with the Holy Spirit.' 34I have seen and I testify that this is the Son of God."

Jesus' First Disciples

35The next day John was there again with two of his disciples. 36When he saw Jesus passing by, he said, "Look, the Lamb of God!"

37When the two disciples heard him say this, they followed Jesus. 38Turning around, Jesus saw them following and asked, "What do you want?"

They said, "Rabbi" (which means Teacher), "where are you staying?"

39"Come," he replied, "and you will see."

So they went and saw where he was staying, and spent that day with him. It was about the tenth hour.

40Andrew, Simon Peter's brother, was one of the two who heard what John had said and who had followed Jesus. 41The first thing Andrew did was to find his brother Simon and tell him, "We have found the Messiah" (that is, the Christ). 42And he brought him to Jesus.

Jesus looked at him and said, "You are Simon son of John. You will be called Cephas" (which, when translated, is Peter*a*).

Jesus Calls Philip and Nathanael

43The next day Jesus decided to leave for Galilee. Finding Philip, he said to him, "Follow me."

44Philip, like Andrew and Peter, was from the town of Bethsaida. 45Philip found Nathanael and told him, "We have found the one Moses wrote about in the Law, and about whom the prophets also wrote—Jesus of Nazareth, the son of Joseph."

46"Nazareth! Can anything good come from there?" Nathanael asked.

"Come and see," said Philip.

47When Jesus saw Nathanael approaching, he said of him, "Here is a true Israelite, in whom there is nothing false."

48"How do you know me?" Nathanael asked.

Jesus answered, "I saw you while you were still under the fig tree before Philip called you."

49Then Nathanael declared, "Rabbi, you are the Son of God; you are the King of Israel."

50Jesus said, "You believe*b* because I told you I saw you under the fig tree. You shall see greater things than that." 51He then

submissive, sacrificial lifestyle of the Lamb of God into your own life? Of the titles for Jesus given so far (the Word, the Light, the Christ, the Lamb of God, the Son of God), which means the most to you? Why? **3.** What does baptism mean to you? What about baptism with the Holy Spirit?

---

1. When you get some good news, who is the first person you want to share it with? Why? **2.** As a child, what would it take for you to believe something your brother or sister told you?

1. In light of verses 30–31, how do you think John felt when his disciples left him to follow Jesus? What does this say about John? **2.** What motivated the disciples of John to follow Jesus? What motivated Andrew to tell Simon about him? **3.** How do you think Simon felt when Jesus changed his name to Cephas (meaning "rock")? **4.** What type of person is Nathanael? Why might he find it hard to believe Philip's statement? Why would Jesus call Philip and Nathanael in such different ways? How do you think Nathanael felt when Jesus spoke to him? **5.** Of the five people in verses 35–48 to follow Jesus: (a) How was the contact made for each one? (b) How much did each one know about Jesus when he decided to follow him? (c) How does each decision for Christ illustrate the point of the prologue (vv. 1–17) about the light of John and the true light of Christ?

1. What was your motive for initially following Jesus? What were the circumstances that led you to do so? How much did you know about him? **2.** Consider verse 48. In your life, how has Jesus shown his ability to know all about you?

---

a42 Both *Cephas* (Aramaic) and *Peter* (Greek) mean *rock*.   *b50* Or *Do you believe...?*

added, "I tell you[a] the truth, you[a] shall see heaven open, and the angels of God ascending and descending on the Son of Man."

Jesus Changes Water to Wine

2 On the third day a wedding took place at Cana in Galilee. Jesus' mother was there, [2]and Jesus and his disciples had also been invited to the wedding. [3]When the wine was gone, Jesus' mother said to him, "They have no more wine."

[4]"Dear woman, why do you involve me?" Jesus replied. "My time has not yet come."

[5]His mother said to the servants, "Do whatever he tells you."

[6]Nearby stood six stone water jars, the kind used by the Jews for ceremonial washing, each holding from twenty to thirty gallons.[b]

[7]Jesus said to the servants, "Fill the jars with water"; so they filled them to the brim.

[8]Then he told them, "Now draw some out and take it to the master of the banquet."

They did so, [9]and the master of the banquet tasted the water that had been turned into wine. He did not realize where it had come from, though the servants who had drawn the water knew. Then he called the bridegroom aside [10]and said, "Everyone brings out the choice wine first and then the cheaper wine after the guests have had too much to drink; but you have saved the best till now."

[11]This, the first of his miraculous signs, Jesus performed at Cana in Galilee. He thus revealed his glory, and his disciples put their faith in him.

a51 The Greek is plural.   b6 Greek *two to three metretes* (probably about 75 to 115 liters)

What is the funniest thing you've witnessed at a wedding?

1. Jesus is not known as a miracle-worker, so why does Mary approach him (v. 3)? What do you learn about Jesus and his mother from this story? 2. How does this passage affect your belief in the consumption of alcohol? 3. What part does the function and size of the jars play in this story? How does the quantity and quality of the wine demonstrate Jesus' glory?

Where is the wine level (zest for life) in your life right now: Full? Half full? Empty? What is draining you? What area seems like stale water in an old jug? How could Jesus bring celebration back into your life?

John 2:1–11   JESUS CHANGES WATER TO WINE

Weddings in Jesus' time were important events. Relatives and townspeople would gather to celebrate, often for up to a week! To run out of wine would be a great social embarrassment.

1. Why do you think Jesus went to this wedding?
a. to please his mother
b. to perform a miracle
c. because everyone was invited
d. because weddings are always fun

2. Why did Jesus' mother ask Jesus to do something about the wine?
a. Mothers are that way.
b. She was catering the party.
c. She was concerned for the guests.
d. She wanted to save the bridegroom from embarrassment.
e. She had faith that Jesus could take care of things.
f. She wanted to show what her son could do.

3. How do you think Jesus felt?
a. annoyed   d. honored
b. embarrassed   e. reluctant
c. manipulated   f. willing

4. How do you think the bridegroom felt when he heard about the new wine?
a. perplexed   c. delighted
b. amazed   d. relieved

5. Why do you think Jesus performed his first miracle at a wedding feast?
a. It just happened that way.
b. His mother twisted his arm.
c. He saw a need and met it.
d. Wine had a special significance.
e. Weddings had (and still have) a special significance.

6. In verse 11 what does John, the author of this Gospel, mean by calling Jesus' miracles "signs"?

7. What "sign" led you to put your faith in Jesus?
a. the miracles Jesus did in the Bible
b. a specific miracle Jesus did for me
c. the wrong direction my life was going
d. the resurrection of Jesus and the fact that he is still alive
e. the change in heart I experienced
f. the changes I saw in others
g. Nothing else made sense.

8. What is the "wine" level (zest for living) in your life at the moment?
a. overflowing   c. running out fast
b. half-full   d. empty

9. What is draining you? What in your life feels like stale water in an old jug? How could Jesus change things?

10. How often do your parents pressure you to do something you don't want to do?
a. every day   c. occasionally
b. pretty often   d. rarely/never

11. In what area(s) do your parents ask something of you that really irritates you?
a. chores   i. dating
b. grades   j. manners
c. curfew   k. language
d. clothes   l. music/TV
e. hair   m. using the phone
f. friends   n. driving the car
g. keeping my room clean
h. going to church/youth group

12. What can you do about these hassles with your parents?

Jesus Clears the Temple

¹²After this he went down to Capernaum with his mother and brothers and his disciples. There they stayed for a few days.

¹³When it was almost time for the Jewish Passover, Jesus went up to Jerusalem. ¹⁴In the temple courts he found men selling cattle, sheep and doves, and others sitting at tables exchanging money. ¹⁵So he made a whip out of cords, and drove all from the temple area, both sheep and cattle; he scattered the coins of the money changers and overturned their tables. ¹⁶To those who sold doves he said, "Get these out of here! How dare you turn my Father's house into a market!"

¹⁷His disciples remembered that it is written: "Zeal for your house will consume me."ᵃ

¹⁸Then the Jews demanded of him, "What miraculous sign can you show us to prove your authority to do all this?"

¹⁹Jesus answered them, "Destroy this temple, and I will raise it again in three days."

²⁰The Jews replied, "It has taken forty-six years to build this temple, and you are going to raise it in three days?" ²¹But the temple he had spoken of was his body. ²²After he was raised from the dead, his disciples recalled what he had said. Then they believed the Scripture and the words that Jesus had spoken.

²³Now while he was in Jerusalem at the Passover Feast, many people saw the miraculous signs he was doing and believed in his name.ᵇ ²⁴But Jesus would not entrust himself to them, for he knew all men. ²⁵He did not need man's testimony about man, for he knew what was in a man.

Jesus Teaches Nicodemus

3 Now there was a man of the Pharisees named Nicodemus, a member of the Jewish ruling council. ²He came to Jesus at night and said, "Rabbi, we know you are a teacher who has come from God. For no one could perform the miraculous signs you are doing if God were not with him."

³In reply Jesus declared, "I tell you the truth, no one can see the kingdom of God unless he is born again.ᶜ"

⁴"How can a man be born when he is old?" Nicodemus asked. "Surely he cannot enter a second time into his mother's womb to be born!"

⁵Jesus answered, "I tell you the truth, no one can enter the kingdom of God unless he is born of water and the Spirit. ⁶Flesh gives birth to flesh, but the Spiritᵈ gives birth to spirit. ⁷You should not be surprised at my saying, 'Youᵉ must be born again.' ⁸The wind blows wherever it pleases. You hear its sound, but you cannot tell where it comes from or where it is going. So it is with everyone born of the Spirit."

⁹"How can this be?" Nicodemus asked.

¹⁰"You are Israel's teacher," said Jesus, "and do you not understand these things? ¹¹I tell you the truth, we speak of what we know, and we testify to what we have seen, but still you people do not accept our testimony. ¹²I have spoken to you of earthly things and you do not believe; how then will you believe if I speak of heavenly things? ¹³No one has ever gone into heaven except the one who came from heaven—the Son of Man.ᶠ ¹⁴Just as Moses lifted up the snake in the desert, so the Son of Man must be lifted up, ¹⁵that everyone who believes in him may have eternal life.ᵍ

What room or area of yours is cleanest? Dirtiest?

1. The sellers and money-changers were set up to provide sacrificial animals for sale at the temple as a help to Jews from far away. How might this once useful practice have deteriorated into a racket? Why else was Jesus angry (Ps 69:9)? 2. As one of the sellers, how would you feel about Jesus' actions? As one of the disciples, how would you feel? 3. How is Jesus challenged (v. 19)? Why? What effect does his response have on them? 4. Why doesn't Jesus entrust himself to the crowd in verses 23–25?

If you compare your spiritual life to the rooms of a house, which room do you think Jesus might want to clean up: (a) Library—the reading room? (b) Dining room—appetites, desires? (c) Workshop—where you keep your skills? (d) Recreation room—where you hang out after work? (e) Family room—where most of your relationships are lived out? or (f) Closet—where your hang-ups are?

What were you first told about where babies came from? How old were you when you learned the real story?

1. What can you find out about Nicodemus in verses 1–2? What is significant about his coming to Jesus? Why at night (see vv. 19–20)? Why was Jesus so direct with him? 2. What two ideas about birth are Jesus and Nicodemus thinking of? What point is Jesus making by comparing spiritual birth to the wind? How does Jesus account for Nicodemus' lack of understanding? 3. What does Jesus claim about himself in verses 13–15? 4. From verses 16–18, what stands out to you about God? About what he wants to do? About how a person is condemned? How will belief show itself (vv. 15–21)? 5. How is Jesus' use of the words "born again" similar to and different from the way it is used today? How would you define "born again" in your own words?

1. What first aroused your interest in Jesus? Why? 2. Where are you right now in the birthing process of spiritual life: Not yet conceived? Developing, but not so anyone could tell? Heavy with

---

ᵃ17 Psalm 69:9   ᵇ23 Or and believed in him   ᶜ3 Or born from above; also in verse 7   ᵈ6 Or but spirit   ᵉ7 The Greek is plural.   ᶠ13 Some manuscripts Man, who is in heaven   ᵍ15 Or believes may have eternal life in him

child and waiting? Kicking and screaming like an infant? Growing daily? Explain. **3.** When did you begin to see God as saving you, rather than condemning you?

1. What did you and your brother or sister fight about? How would you try to get your way? **2.** At family reunions, what subject (e.g., politics or religion) is bound to start an argument?

1. Given the different ideas about baptism, what do you think had happened at the river? What do you think the "certain Jew" had said (v. 25)? How would you have felt if you had been one of John's disciples at this point? **2.** How does John the Baptist respond (vv. 27–36)? What is the point of the allegory or story about the bride and bridegroom? What

[16]"For God so loved the world that he gave his one and only Son,[a] that whoever believes in him shall not perish but have eternal life. [17]For God did not send his Son into the world to condemn the world, but to save the world through him. [18]Whoever believes in him is not condemned, but whoever does not believe stands condemned already because he has not believed in the name of God's one and only Son.[b] [19]This is the verdict: Light has come into the world, but men loved darkness instead of light because their deeds were evil. [20]Everyone who does evil hates the light, and will not come into the light for fear that his deeds will be exposed. [21]But whoever lives by the truth comes into the light, so that it may be seen plainly that what he has done has been done through God."[c]

John the Baptist's Testimony About Jesus

[22]After this, Jesus and his disciples went out into the Judean countryside, where he spent some time with them, and baptized. [23]Now John also was baptizing at Aenon near Salim, because there was plenty of water, and people were constantly coming to be baptized. [24](This was before John was put in prison.) [25]An argument developed between some of John's disciples and a certain Jew[d] over the matter of ceremonial washing. [26]They came to John and said to him, "Rabbi, that man who was with you on the other side of the Jordan—the one you testified about—well, he is baptizing, and everyone is going to him."

[27]To this John replied, "A man can receive only what is given

[a]16 Or *his only begotten Son*   [b]18 Or *God's only begotten Son*   [c]21 Some interpreters end the quotation after verse 15.   [d]25 Some manuscripts *and certain Jews*

✠✠ John 3:1–21   JESUS TEACHES NICODEMUS

1. Why did Nicodemus come to Jesus by night?
   a. He worked during the day.
   b. He couldn't wait until morning.
   c. He was afraid of being seen.
   d. He wanted time alone with Jesus.

2. When Jesus brought up the need for a person to be "born again," how did Nicodemus react?
   a. He got curious.
   b. He got defensive.
   c. He got interested.
   d. He got confused.

3. What did Jesus mean when he said you have to be born again to see the kingdom of God?
   a. We have to be able to point to a specific conversion experience.
   b. We can only be accepted into God's kingdom by turning our lives over to him.
   c. Our spirits are destroyed by sin and need God's intervention to be reborn.
   d. Our spiritual lives have a beginning just like our physical lives.

4. How do you think Nicodemus came away from this meeting with Jesus?
   a. turned off
   b. enlightened
   c. totally confused
   d. with a lot to think about
   e. a secret follower of Jesus
   f. convinced in his mind but not in his heart

5. Which of the following describes your openness to the light God might shed on your life?
   a. It's so dark I can't find a light.
   b. There's still a lot of me that I want to hide in the darkness.
   c. I want to leave the darkness, but the light hurts my eyes.
   d. The more I follow the light, the brighter it becomes.
   e. I am completely open to God's light and grateful for it.

6. ✠✠ What is the most important point in this passage for you right now?
   a. Spiritual rebirth is indeed possible (vv. 3–7).

   b. Heaven is waiting for those who believe in Jesus Christ (vv. 14–16).
   c. God loved us enough to give us his only Son (v. 16).
   d. God doesn't desire to condemn us, but to save us (vv. 17–18).
   e. If we are open to being enlightened, light will come (vv. 19–21).

7. ✠✠ To receive Christ's promise of new life, I need to:
   a. stop being so literal and rational.
   b. ask God to forgive me for some things.
   c. forgive myself for some things.
   d. realize I'm not too old to change— to be reborn.
   e. open my heart to Christ.
   f. do nothing—I have already claimed this promise.

8. ✠✠ If you came to Jesus with one question that you were a little embarrassed to ask, what would it be? What other person could you go to with questions about your spiritual journey?

him from heaven. ²⁸You yourselves can testify that I said, 'I am not the Christ[a] but am sent ahead of him.' ²⁹The bride belongs to the bridegroom. The friend who attends the bridegroom waits and listens for him, and is full of joy when he hears the bridegroom's voice. That joy is mine, and it is now complete. ³⁰He must become greater; I must become less.

³¹"The one who comes from above is above all; the one who is from the earth belongs to the earth, and speaks as one from the earth. The one who comes from heaven is above all. ³²He testifies to what he has seen and heard, but no one accepts his testimony. ³³The man who has accepted it has certified that God is truthful. ³⁴For the one whom God has sent speaks the words of God, for God[b] gives the Spirit without limit. ³⁵The Father loves the Son and has placed everything in his hands. ³⁶Whoever believes in the Son has eternal life, but whoever rejects the Son will not see life, for God's wrath remains on him."[c]

Jesus Talks With a Samaritan Woman

4 The Pharisees heard that Jesus was gaining and baptizing more disciples than John, ²although in fact it was not Jesus who baptized, but his disciples. ³When the Lord learned of this, he left Judea and went back once more to Galilee.

⁴Now he had to go through Samaria. ⁵So he came to a town in Samaria called Sychar, near the plot of ground Jacob had given to his son Joseph. ⁶Jacob's well was there, and Jesus, tired as he was from the journey, sat down by the well. It was about the sixth hour.

⁷When a Samaritan woman came to draw water, Jesus said to her, "Will you give me a drink?" ⁸(His disciples had gone into the town to buy food.)

⁹The Samaritan woman said to him, "You are a Jew and I am a Samaritan woman. How can you ask me for a drink?" (For Jews do not associate with Samaritans.[d])

¹⁰Jesus answered her, "If you knew the gift of God and who it is that asks you for a drink, you would have asked him and he would have given you living water."

¹¹"Sir," the woman said, "you have nothing to draw with and the well is deep. Where can you get this living water? ¹²Are you greater than our father Jacob, who gave us the well and drank from it himself, as did also his sons and his flocks and herds?"

¹³Jesus answered, "Everyone who drinks this water will be thirsty again, ¹⁴but whoever drinks the water I give him will never thirst. Indeed, the water I give him will become in him a spring of water welling up to eternal life."

¹⁵The woman said to him, "Sir, give me this water so that I won't get thirsty and have to keep coming here to draw water."

¹⁶He told her, "Go, call your husband and come back."

¹⁷"I have no husband," she replied.

Jesus said to her, "You are right when you say you have no husband. ¹⁸The fact is, you have had five husbands, and the man you now have is not your husband. What you have just said is quite true."

¹⁹"Sir," the woman said, "I can see that you are a prophet. ²⁰Our fathers worshiped on this mountain, but you Jews claim that the place where we must worship is in Jerusalem."

²¹Jesus declared, "Believe me, woman, a time is coming when you will worship the Father neither on this mountain nor in Jerusa-

---

does John's response tell you about him? **3.** What facts about Jesus does John bring out in verses 31–36? **4.** How does the phrase "rejecting the Son" stand in contrast to what belief really means?

1. Consider verse 27. What have you received from heaven? How do you use what you have received? **2.** How can you apply verse 30 in your own life?

When you were growing up, who were the people you were told to avoid? What part of the city or country would you be warned about? What would have happened if you had gone there?

1. What is significant about this story taking place in Samaria? **2.** Since "nice" girls did not come to draw water at noontime ("the sixth hour"), why do you think Jesus risked his reputation to ask a favor of this woman? **3.** How would you describe the woman's response? **4.** How did Jesus turn the tables on her in verse 10? **5.** In the woman's reply, what is she really saying? How is she like Nicodemus (3:1–21)? **6.** Why does Jesus change the topic of conversation so abruptly to her personal life (v. 16–18)? What strikes you about the way he responds to her claim not to have a husband? **7.** Why do you think this woman changed the conversation to focus on a religious controversy? In this story, what does Jesus mean by telling her that God is interested in worshippers who will do so in "spirit and truth"? **8.** What is significant about Jesus choosing this woman as the first person to whom he revealed himself (see vv. 39–42)?

1. What social, ethnic or religious barriers have you overcome in Jesus' name? **2.** What aspects of Jesus' conversation could you use as a model for your own discussions with searching friends? **3.** What are you constantly "thirsting" for? How has Jesus satisfied you?

---

a 28 Or *Messiah*   b 34 Greek *he*   c 36 Some interpreters end the quotation after verse 30.   d 9 Or *do not use dishes Samaritans have used*

lem. [22]You Samaritans worship what you do not know; we worship what we do know, for salvation is from the Jews. [23]Yet a time is coming and has now come when the true worshipers will worship the Father in spirit and truth, for they are the kind of worshipers the Father seeks. [24]God is spirit, and his worshipers must worship in spirit and in truth."

[25]The woman said, "I know that Messiah" (called Christ) "is coming. When he comes, he will explain everything to us."

[26]Then Jesus declared, "I who speak to you am he."

The Disciples Rejoin Jesus

[27]Just then his disciples returned and were surprised to find him talking with a woman. But no one asked, "What do you want?" or "Why are you talking with her?"

[28]Then, leaving her water jar, the woman went back to the town and said to the people, [29]"Come, see a man who told me everything I ever did. Could this be the Christ[a]?" [30]They came out of the town and made their way toward him.

[31]Meanwhile his disciples urged him, "Rabbi, eat something."

[32]But he said to them, "I have food to eat that you know nothing about."

[33]Then his disciples said to each other, "Could someone have brought him food?"

[34]"My food," said Jesus, "is to do the will of him who sent me and to finish his work. [35]Do you not say, 'Four months more and then the harvest'? I tell you, open your eyes and look at the fields!

[a]29 Or Messiah

What causes you to skip a meal? To eat too much unintentionally?

1. Why were the disciples surprised to find Jesus with this woman? 2. What does "leaving her water jar" reveal about Jesus' impact on the woman? How did she affect others? 3. How is Jesus' figurative speech once again misunderstood (see 2:19; 3:3; 4:10)? Why does he continue to speak like this? In what ways is God's will like food for him? 4. How does the parable of harvesting apply to the disciples? 5. Given the social barriers between Jews and Samaritans, what do verses 40–42 teach you about Jesus?

  John 4:7–30   **JESUS TALKS WITH A SAMARITAN WOMAN**

Instead of avoiding Samaria as Jews often did, Jesus passed through this area that Jews considered inhabited by spiritual and ethnic half-breeds.

1. How would you describe this woman's response for most of her conversation with Jesus?
   a. Searching—"Is it possible this is what I've been looking for?"
   b. Avoidance—"I think I'd better try to change the subject."
   c. Skeptical—"Who does this guy think he is?!"

2. What most influenced the woman to consider that the man she was talking to was the Messiah?
   a. what he said about "living water"
   b. the way he knew so much about her without being told
   c. his accepting her though she was a loose-living Samaritan woman
   d. when he claimed, "I who speak to you am he"

3. What was Jesus saying about worshiping God?
   a. The Jews' worship is better than the Samaritans' worship.

b. The object of true worship—the Messiah—comes from the Jews.
   c. Focusing on where to worship misses the point.
   d. True worship is from the heart.

4. What was this woman thirsting for?
   a. intimacy in her relationships
   b. intimacy with God
   c. acceptance of who she was
   d. forgiveness for the life she had led
   e. meaning and purpose in life
   f. basic survival in life

5. What are *you* really thirsting for?

6. What did it take for Jesus and this woman to get past their cultural differences to communicate like this? What can you do to help overcome barriers that exist in your "world"?

7. What have been the most significant changes you have gone through in your spiritual life?
   a. a conversion experience
   b. a spiritual crisis
   c. changes in my beliefs
   d. different choices than my family
   e. switching churches/denominations

8. In what ways have the changes in your spiritual life been stressful or unsettling? How have you worked through that?

9. What differences exist between you as a couple?
   a. religious differences
   b. racial or ethnic differences
   c. political differences
   d. differences about handling money
   e. different ideas about leisure time
   f. different in how we see our roles as husband and wife
   g. other:_____

10. What helps you get past your differences?
    a. willingness to listen and learn
    b. willingness to see past certain controversies between us
    c. determination to make our marriage work
    d. the fact we don't just tolerate our differences—we enjoy them!

11. What do you appreciate about this group? How have the members of your group helped you become refreshed by God's living water?

They are ripe for harvest. [36]Even now the reaper draws his wages, even now he harvests the crop for eternal life, so that the sower and the reaper may be glad together. [37]Thus the saying 'One sows and another reaps' is true. [38]I sent you to reap what you have not worked for. Others have done the hard work, and you have reaped the benefits of their labor."

Many Samaritans Believe

[39]Many of the Samaritans from that town believed in him because of the woman's testimony, "He told me everything I ever did." [40]So when the Samaritans came to him, they urged him to stay with them, and he stayed two days. [41]And because of his words many more became believers.

[42]They said to the woman, "We no longer believe just because of what you said; now we have heard for ourselves, and we know that this man really is the Savior of the world."

Jesus Heals the Official's Son

[43]After the two days he left for Galilee. [44](Now Jesus himself had pointed out that a prophet has no honor in his own country.) [45]When he arrived in Galilee, the Galileans welcomed him. They had seen all that he had done in Jerusalem at the Passover Feast, for they also had been there.

[46]Once more he visited Cana in Galilee, where he had turned the water into wine. And there was a certain royal official whose son lay sick at Capernaum. [47]When this man heard that Jesus had arrived in Galilee from Judea, he went to him and begged him to come and heal his son, who was close to death.

[48]"Unless you people see miraculous signs and wonders," Jesus told him, "you will never believe."

[49]The royal official said, "Sir, come down before my child dies."

[50]Jesus replied, "You may go. Your son will live."

The man took Jesus at his word and departed. [51]While he was still on the way, his servants met him with the news that his boy was living. [52]When he inquired as to the time when his son got better, they said to him, "The fever left him yesterday at the seventh hour."

[53]Then the father realized that this was the exact time at which Jesus had said to him, "Your son will live." So he and all his household believed.

[54]This was the second miraculous sign that Jesus performed, having come from Judea to Galilee.

The Healing at the Pool

5 Some time later, Jesus went up to Jerusalem for a feast of the Jews. [2]Now there is in Jerusalem near the Sheep Gate a pool, which in Aramaic is called Bethesda[a] and which is surrounded by five covered colonnades. [3]Here a great number of disabled people used to lie—the blind, the lame, the paralyzed.[b] [5]One who was there had been an invalid for thirty-eight years. [6]When Jesus saw him lying there and learned that he had been in this condition for a long time, he asked him, "Do you want to get well?"

[7]"Sir," the invalid replied, "I have no one to help me into the pool when the water is stirred. While I am trying to get in, someone else goes down ahead of me."

a2 Some manuscripts Bethzatha; other manuscripts Bethsaida   b3 Some less important manuscripts paralyzed—and they waited for the moving of the waters. 4From time to time an angel of the Lord would come down and stir up the waters. The first one into the pool after each such disturbance would be cured of whatever disease he had.

---

1. Considering your interest in "spiritual things," are you more like the disciples or the woman? Why? 2. Is doing God's will as essential to you as eating food? Why? 3. What do you learn from the woman about telling others about Jesus? From the parable (vv. 35–38)?

When you were a child, what was the most serious illness or injury you ever had?

1. Now that Jesus is home again, what motivates the people to welcome him? 2. How do you account for the contrast between the crowd's welcome (v. 45) and Jesus' comments in verses 44 and 48? How are the Galileans alike and unlike the Samaritans in verses 39–42? 3. What motivates the royal official to travel so far? How would you have responded to what Jesus told him to do? What does this miracle tell you about Jesus?

1. When you bring your problem to God (such as a sickness in the family), do you tend to accept his word or keep fretting and fussing? 2. When have you taken God at his word (even though the circumstances were seemingly impossible), and discovered that he did exactly what was promised?

When you get sick, what are you like: Oscar the Grouch? Superman? Rip Van Winkle?

1. How do you picture the setting of this story (vv. 2–4)? What is the smell? The noises? The atmosphere? 2. How would you picture the invalid (vv. 5–7)? What does Jesus mean by his question in verse 6? What did the invalid hope Jesus might do? 3. As the invalid, what would you feel in verses 8–9? In verses 10–13? In verse 14? 4. Why were the leaders so upset? How do you suppose they responded to the healed man's testimony (v. 15)?

1. In what ways do people to-day try to be healed without Christ? 2. How would you respond to someone who said all sickness is a result of sin? 3. Why would Jesus ask, "Do you want to get well"? Describe a time when you would have said "No." How about "Yes"?

As you get older, do you find yourself becoming more, or less, like your parents? Why?

1. What was the result for Jesus of healing the invalid (vv. 1–15)? 2. How did his response to the Jewish leaders only heighten their opposition? Why would Jesus do this? 3. In what ways is Jesus equal with the Father (vv. 26–27)? What terms are used to show the kind of relation-

⁸Then Jesus said to him, "Get up! Pick up your mat and walk." ⁹At once the man was cured; he picked up his mat and walked.

The day on which this took place was a Sabbath, ¹⁰and so the Jews said to the man who had been healed, "It is the Sabbath; the law forbids you to carry your mat."

¹¹But he replied, "The man who made me well said to me, 'Pick up your mat and walk.' "

¹²So they asked him, "Who is this fellow who told you to pick it up and walk?"

¹³The man who was healed had no idea who it was, for Jesus had slipped away into the crowd that was there.

¹⁴Later Jesus found him at the temple and said to him, "See, you are well again. Stop sinning or something worse may happen to you." ¹⁵The man went away and told the Jews that it was Jesus who had made him well.

Life Through the Son

¹⁶So, because Jesus was doing these things on the Sabbath, the Jews persecuted him. ¹⁷Jesus said to them, "My Father is always at his work to this very day, and I, too, am working." ¹⁸For this reason the Jews tried all the harder to kill him; not only was he breaking the Sabbath, but he was even calling God his own Father, making himself equal with God.

¹⁹Jesus gave them this answer: "I tell you the truth, the Son can do nothing by himself; he can do only what he sees his Father doing, because whatever the Father does the Son also does. ²⁰For the Father loves the Son and shows him all he does. Yes, to your

   John 5:1–15   **THE HEALING AT THE POOL**

This story happened at a pool that evidently had a reputation for bringing healing to the first person to get in when its waters were stirred.

1. How do you think this man felt after being an invalid for 38 years?
   a. bitter and angry
   b. helpless and dependent
   c. discouraged and depressed
   d. comfortable with his condition

2. Jesus asked the man, "Do you want to get well?" because the man:
   a. hadn't asked Jesus for help.
   b. didn't know who Jesus was.
   c. was likely a beggar and could lose his income if he were healed.
   d. may have lost the will to get well.
   e. may have had a psychosomatic illness.

3. What was the man really saying by his response to Jesus' question?
   a. "Are you crazy—Would I be lying here if I didn't want to get well?!"
   b. "I don't know—I'm so helpless."
   c. "If you help me into the pool when the water stirs, I might get well."
   d. "I've been sick for so long I can't take responsibility for my life."

4. What did Jesus mean later when he said to the man: "See, you are well again. Stop sinning or something worse may happen to you"?
   a. "You were sick because of sin."
   b. "You lost 38 years; don't lose any more."
   c. "The eternal consequences of sin are worse than your illness."
   d. "You've got a fresh start in life—don't blow it."

5. What is the closest Jesus has come to saying to you, "Get up! Pick up your mat and walk"?
   a. when I turned my life over to him
   b. when I experienced his healing
   c. when I had a self-pity problem
   d. when I was overly dependent on others
   e. when I lost my will to get better

6. What connection between your physical and spiritual health have you noticed? When have you found yourself getting physically sick over problems in other areas of your life?

7. If Jesus were to stop by the "watering hole" where you hang out, what would he probably ask you?

   a. Do you want to get well?
   b. What are you doing with your life?
   c. Are you satisfied with what you are doing?
   d. Are you looking for the real thing?

8. Briefly share the story of the pain in your life. How often have you asked, "Where is God when I hurt?" What are your hopes and expectations for this group?

9. What about your health causes you the most stress?
   a. battling a chronic condition
   b. dealing with the financial burden
   c. coping with added time pressures, such as missing work
   d. facing health problems alone
   e. other: _____

10. How can you relate to this story in terms of your job and/or career?
    a. I feel like I've been stuck where I'm at for 38 years!
    b. Someone else always seems to get in ahead of me.
    c. I feel powerless to change things.
    d. I'm really not sure why I'm doing what I'm doing.

amazement he will show him even greater things than these. ²¹For just as the Father raises the dead and gives them life, even so the Son gives life to whom he is pleased to give it. ²²Moreover, the Father judges no one, but has entrusted all judgment to the Son, ²³that all may honor the Son just as they honor the Father. He who does not honor the Son does not honor the Father, who sent him.

²⁴"I tell you the truth, whoever hears my word and believes him who sent me has eternal life and will not be condemned; he has crossed over from death to life. ²⁵I tell you the truth, a time is coming and has now come when the dead will hear the voice of the Son of God and those who hear will live. ²⁶For as the Father has life in himself, so he has granted the Son to have life in himself. ²⁷And he has given him authority to judge because he is the Son of Man.

²⁸"Do not be amazed at this, for a time is coming when all who are in their graves will hear his voice ²⁹and come out—those who have done good will rise to live, and those who have done evil will rise to be condemned. ³⁰By myself I can do nothing; I judge only as I hear, and my judgment is just, for I seek not to please myself but him who sent me.

Testimonies About Jesus

³¹"If I testify about myself, my testimony is not valid. ³²There is another who testifies in my favor, and I know that his testimony about me is valid.

³³"You have sent to John and he has testified to the truth. ³⁴Not that I accept human testimony; but I mention it that you may be saved. ³⁵John was a lamp that burned and gave light, and you chose for a time to enjoy his light.

³⁶"I have testimony weightier than that of John. For the very work that the Father has given me to finish, and which I am doing, testifies that the Father has sent me. ³⁷And the Father who sent me has himself testified concerning me. You have never heard his voice nor seen his form, ³⁸nor does his word dwell in you, for you do not believe the one he sent. ³⁹You diligently study*a* the Scriptures because you think that by them you possess eternal life. These are the Scriptures that testify about me, ⁴⁰yet you refuse to come to me to have life.

⁴¹"I do not accept praise from men, ⁴²but I know you. I know that you do not have the love of God in your hearts. ⁴³I have come in my Father's name, and you do not accept me; but if someone else comes in his own name, you will accept him. ⁴⁴How can you believe if you accept praise from one another, yet make no effort to obtain the praise that comes from the only God*b*?

⁴⁵"But do not think I will accuse you before the Father. Your accuser is Moses, on whom your hopes are set. ⁴⁶If you believed Moses, you would believe me, for he wrote about me. ⁴⁷But since you do not believe what he wrote, how are you going to believe what I say?"

Jesus Feeds the Five Thousand

6 Some time after this, Jesus crossed to the far shore of the Sea of Galilee (that is, the Sea of Tiberias), ²and a great crowd of people followed him because they saw the miraculous signs he had performed on the sick. ³Then Jesus went up on a mountainside and sat down with his disciples. ⁴The Jewish Passover Feast was near.

⁵When Jesus looked up and saw a great crowd coming toward

ship between the two? **4.** What claims does Jesus make about himself in verse 24? What is the promise? **5.** What happens to those who hear and believe (vv. 24–30)? To those who do not? **6.** How would you describe the business that God the Father and God the Son are in?

1. If you had to explain to someone what verse 24 means in your own words, how would you put it? **2.** In your own spiritual journey, when did you come to understand this truth? How did it affect your self-image? Your lifestyle? Your life goals?

Whom do you still admire today who was a hero to you as a child? Who was a hero who turned out to be a disappointment?

1. Who or what testifies in favor of Jesus (v. 33)? How do you think the religious leaders felt when Jesus referred to these witnesses (already discounted by the authorities)? **2.** How does Jesus refute the religious leaders with their own Scripture?

1. What witnesses have convinced you that Jesus is indeed the one who gives life? **2.** Have you ever seen anyone put the study of the Scriptures before their love for Christ? Have you ever done this? **3.** Is the love of God in your heart? How can you use Scripture to cultivate the love of God in you?

Do you prefer to socialize at large parties, have a dinner for four, or spend a quiet evening with a friend? Why?

1. Why did the crowd follow Jesus (v. 2)? What did they think about him? **2.** What was the test that Jesus was using on Philip (v. 5)? From their responses, what

a 39 Or *Study diligently* (the imperative)   *b 44* Some early manuscripts *the Only One*

grades would you give Philip and Andrew? **3.** Why was there more food after the feeding than before? **4.** How could the nearness of the Passover feast (when Jews from all over came to Jerusalem) fuel the desires of the people (vv. 14–15)? What does Jesus' response indicate about his idea of his kingship?

1. When has God stretched your limited resources (physically or emotionally) far beyond what you could have imagined? In what way do you need to trust him to do so now? **2.** How are you like Philip and Andrew—failing to remember something about Jesus when you face a difficult situation?

What was one of your greatest childhood fears: Bugs? High places? Darkness? Water?

1. How would you have reacted if you saw Jesus on the water? When he climbed aboard? **2.** What did the disciples fail to see in the feeding of the 5,000 that could have helped them here?

1. Has Jesus ever frightened you? How? **2.** Where in your life do you need Jesus to say "It is I, don't be afraid"?

What type of bread are you today: All natural? Rye? Moldy? Crusty? Fresh? Easy to butter up?

1. Why are the crowds still searching for Jesus (vv. 24–26)? **2.** How does Jesus' response to their question show the difference between his interests and theirs? **3.** How are they to work for the food that leads to eternal life (v. 29)? **4.** What does the crowd ask Jesus to do in order that they can believe him? What is their real interest? **5.** How does Jesus use their interest in food to illustrate what he wants them to understand? What are the similarities and differences between manna (Ex 16) and the "bread of life" (v. 35)? **6.** What claims does Jesus

him, he said to Philip, "Where shall we buy bread for these people to eat?" [6]He asked this only to test him, for he already had in mind what he was going to do.

[7]Philip answered him, "Eight months' wages[a] would not buy enough bread for each one to have a bite!"

[8]Another of his disciples, Andrew, Simon Peter's brother, spoke up, [9]"Here is a boy with five small barley loaves and two small fish, but how far will they go among so many?"

[10]Jesus said, "Have the people sit down." There was plenty of grass in that place, and the men sat down, about five thousand of them. [11]Jesus then took the loaves, gave thanks, and distributed to those who were seated as much as they wanted. He did the same with the fish.

[12]When they had all had enough to eat, he said to his disciples, "Gather the pieces that are left over. Let nothing be wasted." [13]So they gathered them and filled twelve baskets with the pieces of the five barley loaves left over by those who had eaten.

[14]After the people saw the miraculous sign that Jesus did, they began to say, "Surely this is the Prophet who is to come into the world." [15]Jesus, knowing that they intended to come and make him king by force, withdrew again to a mountain by himself.

Jesus Walks on the Water

[16]When evening came, his disciples went down to the lake, [17]where they got into a boat and set off across the lake for Capernaum. By now it was dark, and Jesus had not yet joined them. [18]A strong wind was blowing and the waters grew rough. [19]When they had rowed three or three and a half miles,[b] they saw Jesus approaching the boat, walking on the water; and they were terrified. [20]But he said to them, "It is I; don't be afraid." [21]Then they were willing to take him into the boat, and immediately the boat reached the shore where they were heading.

[22]The next day the crowd that had stayed on the opposite shore of the lake realized that only one boat had been there, and that Jesus had not entered it with his disciples, but that they had gone away alone. [23]Then some boats from Tiberias landed near the place where the people had eaten the bread after the Lord had given thanks. [24]Once the crowd realized that neither Jesus nor his disciples were there, they got into the boats and went to Capernaum in search of Jesus.

Jesus the Bread of Life

[25]When they found him on the other side of the lake, they asked him, "Rabbi, when did you get here?"

[26]Jesus answered, "I tell you the truth, you are looking for me, not because you saw miraculous signs but because you ate the loaves and had your fill. [27]Do not work for food that spoils, but for food that endures to eternal life, which the Son of Man will give you. On him God the Father has placed his seal of approval."

[28]Then they asked him, "What must we do to do the works God requires?"

[29]Jesus answered, "The work of God is this: to believe in the one he has sent."

[30]So they asked him, "What miraculous sign then will you give that we may see it and believe you? What will you do? [31]Our forefathers ate the manna in the desert; as it is written: 'He gave them bread from heaven to eat.'[c]"

---

a7 Greek *two hundred denarii*   b19 Greek *rowed twenty-five or thirty stadia* (about 5 or 6 kilometers)   c31 Exodus 16:4; Neh. 9:15; Psalm 78:24,25

32Jesus said to them, "I tell you the truth, it is not Moses who has given you the bread from heaven, but it is my Father who gives you the true bread from heaven. 33For the bread of God is he who comes down from heaven and gives life to the world."

34"Sir," they said, "from now on give us this bread."

35Then Jesus declared, "I am the bread of life. He who comes to me will never go hungry, and he who believes in me will never be thirsty. 36But as I told you, you have seen me and still you do not believe. 37All that the Father gives me will come to me, and whoever comes to me I will never drive away. 38For I have come down from heaven not to do my will but to do the will of him who sent me. 39And this is the will of him who sent me, that I shall lose none of all that he has given me, but raise them up at the last day. 40For my Father's will is that everyone who looks to the Son and believes in him shall have eternal life, and I will raise him up at the last day."

41At this the Jews began to grumble about him because he said, "I am the bread that came down from heaven." 42They said, "Is this not Jesus, the son of Joseph, whose father and mother we know? How can he now say, 'I came down from heaven'?"

43"Stop grumbling among yourselves," Jesus answered. 44"No one can come to me unless the Father who sent me draws him, and I will raise him up at the last day. 45It is written in the Prophets: 'They will all be taught by God.'a Everyone who listens to the Father and learns from him comes to me. 46No one has seen the Father except the one who is from God; only he has seen the Father. 47I tell you the truth, he who believes has everlasting life. 48I am the bread of life. 49Your forefathers ate the manna in the desert, yet they died. 50But here is the bread that comes down from heaven, which a man may eat and not die. 51I am the living bread that came down from heaven. If anyone eats of this bread, he will live forever. This bread is my flesh, which I will give for the life of the world."

52Then the Jews began to argue sharply among themselves, "How can this man give us his flesh to eat?"

53Jesus said to them, "I tell you the truth, unless you eat the flesh of the Son of Man and drink his blood, you have no life in you. 54Whoever eats my flesh and drinks my blood has eternal life, and I will raise him up at the last day. 55For my flesh is real food and my blood is real drink. 56Whoever eats my flesh and drinks my blood remains in me, and I in him. 57Just as the living Father sent me and I live because of the Father, so the one who feeds on me will live because of me. 58This is the bread that came down from heaven. Your forefathers ate manna and died, but he who feeds on this bread will live forever." 59He said this while teaching in the synagogue in Capernaum.

Many Disciples Desert Jesus

60On hearing it, many of his disciples said, "This is a hard teaching. Who can accept it?"

61Aware that his disciples were grumbling about this, Jesus said to them, "Does this offend you? 62What if you see the Son of Man ascend to where he was before! 63The Spirit gives life; the flesh counts for nothing. The words I have spoken to you are spiritb and they are life. 64Yet there are some of you who do not believe." For Jesus had known from the beginning which of them did not believe and who would betray him. 65He went on to say, "This is

make in verses 35–40? What do these claims emphasize about his being the bread of life? About the will of the Father? **7.** In verses 41–42, how do the crowds respond to his claims? How is the principle of the hometown prophet (see 4:44) played out here? **8.** What part is played by God and by the people in the process of coming to know Jesus (vv. 44–45)? What promise is repeated three times for those who do come to him? Why the emphasis on this? **9.** How is the "bread" he gives greater than that of Moses (vv. 32,49)? **10.** Why does Jesus develop the food analogy even more graphically (vv. 53–58)? **11.** What does Jesus mean by "eating his flesh" and "drinking his blood" (vv. 51–58)?

1. What is the main reason you follow Jesus? **2.** How would you describe your daily spiritual diet: Junk food? Frozen food? Baby food? TV microwave food? Leftovers? Meat and potatoes? Pure bread and wine? **3.** Has your familiarity with Jesus (from Sunday School stories, parochial school, etc.) ever kept you from seeing who he really is? What can remove the blinders? **4.** If someone asked, "How do you hunger and thirst after God," what counsel could you offer?

How did you feel when you were first rejected by a friend or sweetheart?

1. What teaching do Jesus' followers find so unacceptable (6:54–56)? **2.** Why do you think Peter and the others decided to stay? How does this relate to verse 65?

1. What words of Jesus are hard for you to accept? **2.** Have you known anyone who

a45 Isaiah 54:13   b63 Or Spirit

stopped following Jesus? How did their action affect you? **3.** How do people today make Jesus into an errand boy for their own personal agendas? How have you been tempted to do so?

Were you ever dared by your brothers or sisters to do something dangerous? What happened?

1. Why did the religious leaders want to kill Jesus (see 5:18)? **2.** In urging Jesus to attend this feast, are the brothers being wise or worldly (vv. 2–5; see 6:42,66)? **3.** What rumors are circulating about Jesus in Jerusalem (vv. 12–13)? Hence, why do you think he chose to go secretly?

1. Do you face any family opposition to, or ridicule of your faith? How do you deal with it? How does Jesus' situation help? **2.** Are you loved or hated by the world (v. 7)? Why? **3.** Are you more likely to be cautious in sharing your faith with your family? Why?

From your school days, what rule seemed pointless or silly? Did you break it?

1. Given the risk, why did Jesus go to the Passover (v. 16)? How did the people react to Jesus' teaching? Why? **2.** What do Jesus' responses reveal about his authority? **3.** How would you respond if you were in the crowd? **4.** What point are the leaders missing?

1. How does Jesus reveal himself to you today? Are you ever upset by what he says? Why? **2.** When have you seen religious principles put ahead of love?

---

why I told you that no one can come to me unless the Father has enabled him."

⁶⁶From this time many of his disciples turned back and no longer followed him.

⁶⁷"You do not want to leave too, do you?" Jesus asked the Twelve.

⁶⁸Simon Peter answered him, "Lord, to whom shall we go? You have the words of eternal life. ⁶⁹We believe and know that you are the Holy One of God."

⁷⁰Then Jesus replied, "Have I not chosen you, the Twelve? Yet one of you is a devil!" ⁷¹(He meant Judas, the son of Simon Iscariot, who, though one of the Twelve, was later to betray him.)

Jesus Goes to the Feast of Tabernacles

7 After this, Jesus went around in Galilee, purposely staying away from Judea because the Jews there were waiting to take his life. ²But when the Jewish Feast of Tabernacles was near, ³Jesus' brothers said to him, "You ought to leave here and go to Judea, so that your disciples may see the miracles you do. ⁴No one who wants to become a public figure acts in secret. Since you are doing these things, show yourself to the world." ⁵For even his own brothers did not believe in him.

⁶Therefore Jesus told them, "The right time for me has not yet come; for you any time is right. ⁷The world cannot hate you, but it hates me because I testify that what it does is evil. ⁸You go to the Feast. I am not yet*ᵃ* going up to this Feast, because for me the right time has not yet come." ⁹Having said this, he stayed in Galilee.

¹⁰However, after his brothers had left for the Feast, he went also, not publicly, but in secret. ¹¹Now at the Feast the Jews were watching for him and asking, "Where is that man?"

¹²Among the crowds there was widespread whispering about him. Some said, "He is a good man."

Others replied, "No, he deceives the people." ¹³But no one would say anything publicly about him for fear of the Jews.

Jesus Teaches at the Feast

¹⁴Not until halfway through the Feast did Jesus go up to the temple courts and begin to teach. ¹⁵The Jews were amazed and asked, "How did this man get such learning without having studied?"

¹⁶Jesus answered, "My teaching is not my own. It comes from him who sent me. ¹⁷If anyone chooses to do God's will, he will find out whether my teaching comes from God or whether I speak on my own. ¹⁸He who speaks on his own does so to gain honor for himself, but he who works for the honor of the one who sent him is a man of truth; there is nothing false about him. ¹⁹Has not Moses given you the law? Yet not one of you keeps the law. Why are you trying to kill me?"

²⁰"You are demon-possessed," the crowd answered. "Who is trying to kill you?"

²¹Jesus said to them, "I did one miracle, and you are all astonished. ²²Yet, because Moses gave you circumcision (though actually it did not come from Moses, but from the patriarchs), you circumcise a child on the Sabbath. ²³Now if a child can be circumcised on the Sabbath so that the law of Moses may not be broken, why are

---

ᵃ8 Some early manuscripts do not have yet.

you angry with me for healing the whole man on the Sabbath? 24Stop judging by mere appearances, and make a right judgment."

Is Jesus the Christ?

25At that point some of the people of Jerusalem began to ask, "Isn't this the man they are trying to kill? 26Here he is, speaking publicly, and they are not saying a word to him. Have the authorities really concluded that he is the Christ*a*? 27But we know where this man is from; when the Christ comes, no one will know where he is from."

28Then Jesus, still teaching in the temple courts, cried out, "Yes, you know me, and you know where I am from. I am not here on my own, but he who sent me is true. You do not know him, 29but I know him because I am from him and he sent me."

30At this they tried to seize him, but no one laid a hand on him, because his time had not yet come. 31Still, many in the crowd put their faith in him. They said, "When the Christ comes, will he do more miraculous signs than this man?"

32The Pharisees heard the crowd whispering such things about him. Then the chief priests and the Pharisees sent temple guards to arrest him.

33Jesus said, "I am with you for only a short time, and then I go to the one who sent me. 34You will look for me, but you will not find me; and where I am, you cannot come."

35The Jews said to one another, "Where does this man intend to go that we cannot find him? Will he go where our people live scattered among the Greeks, and teach the Greeks? 36What did he mean when he said, 'You will look for me, but you will not find me,' and 'Where I am, you cannot come'?"

37On the last and greatest day of the Feast, Jesus stood and said in a loud voice, "If anyone is thirsty, let him come to me and drink. 38Whoever believes in me, as*b* the Scripture has said, streams of living water will flow from within him." 39By this he meant the Spirit, whom those who believed in him were later to receive. Up to that time the Spirit had not been given, since Jesus had not yet been glorified.

40On hearing his words, some of the people said, "Surely this man is the Prophet."

41Others said, "He is the Christ."

Still others asked, "How can the Christ come from Galilee? 42Does not the Scripture say that the Christ will come from David's family*c* and from Bethlehem, the town where David lived?" 43Thus the people were divided because of Jesus. 44Some wanted to seize him, but no one laid a hand on him.

Unbelief of the Jewish Leaders

45Finally the temple guards went back to the chief priests and Pharisees, who asked them, "Why didn't you bring him in?"

46"No one ever spoke the way this man does," the guards declared.

47"You mean he has deceived you also?" the Pharisees retorted. 48"Has any of the rulers or of the Pharisees believed in him? 49No! But this mob that knows nothing of the law—there is a curse on them."

50Nicodemus, who had gone to Jesus earlier and who was one of

a26 Or Messiah; also in verses 27, 31, 41 and 42   b37,38 Or / If anyone is thirsty, let him come to me. / And let him drink, 38who believes in me. / As   c42 Greek seed

When you played "hide and seek" as a kid (or with your kids), did you prefer hiding or seeking? Where was one of your best hiding spots? Did you stay hidden long, or did you jump out to scare the one seeking you?

1. Who is saying what about Jesus in this passage? What is causing the confusion? 2. Why does Jesus' teaching in verses 14–29 provoke the responses of verses 30–31? How do you account for the wide range of opinions about him? For the timing involved? 3. Every day at this feast, water would be poured out as a symbol of thanks for God's provision. In this context, what does Jesus' statement in verses 37–38 mean? What are some ways that the Spirit's work is like water (compare 4:13–14)? How is the Spirit received? 4. How does the confusion over Jesus' birthplace (vv. 41–42) cloud the issue of his identity?

1. What evidence can you offer of the presence of the Holy Spirit in your life? How is his presence like flowing water? 2. What is the relationship for you between believing the promises of Christ and experiencing the power of the Holy Spirit? 3. What different opinions about Christ do you hear today? Why does that confusion exist?

When has someone jumped to a wrong conclusion about you? How did you feel?

1. Why do the guards keep hands off? What tensions do they feel? 2. What justification do the Pharisees offer in refuting the guards? 3. Why would Nicodemus risk defending Jesus?

When have you been ridiculed because of your faith? What did you do?

their own number, asked, ⁵¹"Does our law condemn anyone without first hearing him to find out what he is doing?"

⁵²They replied, "Are you from Galilee, too? Look into it, and you will find that a prophet*ᵃ* does not come out of Galilee."

[The earliest manuscripts and many other ancient witnesses do not have John 7:53–8:11.]

⁵³Then each went to his own home.

8 But Jesus went to the Mount of Olives. ²At dawn he appeared again in the temple courts, where all the people gathered around him, and he sat down to teach them. ³The teachers of the law and the Pharisees brought in a woman caught in adultery. They made her stand before the group ⁴and said to Jesus, "Teacher, this woman was caught in the act of adultery. ⁵In the Law Moses commanded us to stone such women. Now what do you say?" ⁶They were using this question as a trap, in order to have a basis for accusing him.

But Jesus bent down and started to write on the ground with his finger. ⁷When they kept on questioning him, he straightened up and said to them, "If any one of you is without sin, let him be the first to throw a stone at her." ⁸Again he stooped down and wrote on the ground.

⁹At this, those who heard began to go away one at a time, the

ᵃ52 Two early manuscripts *the Prophet*

Describe a time in your childhood when someone tattled on you.

1. How is this situation a trap for Jesus? What would the Pharisees accuse Jesus of if he told them to let her go? If he told them to stone her? How does he spring the trap (v. 7)? 2. How would the woman just caught in adultery have felt? What was the significance of Jesus' question in verse 10? 3. How does Jesus' response to the woman exemplify "grace and truth" (1:17)?

1. How does the way Jesus treated this woman help you face your sins? 2. Jesus accepts you "as is." Does that free you to

---

John 7:53–8:11   THE WOMAN CAUGHT IN ADULTERY

1. Whom do you feel most sorry for?
a. the woman—for being publicly humiliated
b. Jesus—for being put on the spot
c. the religious leaders—for stooping this low

2. Since adultery was a violation by both parties, why didn't the accusers also bring the man caught in the act?
a. He got away.
b. Men and women were treated differently.
c. He was part of a plot that was staged to trap Jesus.

3. In Jesus' situation, what would you feel most pressured to do?
a. go along with the crowd
b. do what Moses' Law required
c. compromise my moral convictions
d. be compassionate and forgiving

4. Why do you think Jesus bent down and wrote on the ground?
a. to cool off
b. to divert attention from the woman
c. to give himself time to think
d. to force the accusers to think

e. to write something for the accusers to see—maybe *their* sins

5. Why did the accusers slip away?
a. They had all committed adultery.
b. None of them could claim they were without sin.
c. Jesus made them think by asking for one person to step forward.
d. Jesus had their number.

6. What was the tone of Jesus' voice and what did he mean when he said, "Neither do I condemn you. Go now and leave your life of sin"?
a. guilt trip: "You've been bad and I'm ashamed of you."
b. acquittal: "You did nothing wrong."
c. warning: "I'll let you off this time, but don't do it again."
d. encouragement: "You're a beautiful person and you don't have to live like you used to."
e. challenge: "The evidence of forgiveness is a changed life."

7. When did you come to truly believe that Jesus values you as a person?
a. when I committed my life to him

b. when I fully understood what he did for me
c. when I felt his healing or forgiveness during a difficult time
d. when I discovered acceptance in my church
e. when a few close friends really got to know me and still accepted me
f. I'm not sure how to answer that.

8. What do you do when you blow it?
a. crawl into a hole
b. try to be extra good
c. confess it to God and move on
d. confess it to another person
e. shrug it off

9. How could the way Jesus related to this woman help you face the sins you struggle with?

10. Who has affirmed you and helped you recognize your full potential as a woman?

11. How do you struggle the most to measure up in a glitzy world? What woman do you see as a role model for real beauty?

older ones first, until only Jesus was left, with the woman still standing there. [10]Jesus straightened up and asked her, "Woman, where are they? Has no one condemned you?"

[11]"No one, sir," she said.

"Then neither do I condemn you," Jesus declared. "Go now and leave your life of sin."

The Validity of Jesus' Testimony

[12]When Jesus spoke again to the people, he said, "I am the light of the world. Whoever follows me will never walk in darkness, but will have the light of life."

[13]The Pharisees challenged him, "Here you are, appearing as your own witness; your testimony is not valid."

[14]Jesus answered, "Even if I testify on my own behalf, my testimony is valid, for I know where I came from and where I am going. But you have no idea where I come from or where I am going. [15]You judge by human standards; I pass judgment on no one. [16]But if I do judge, my decisions are right, because I am not alone. I stand with the Father, who sent me. [17]In your own Law it is written that the testimony of two men is valid. [18]I am one who testifies for myself; my other witness is the Father, who sent me."

[19]Then they asked him, "Where is your father?"

"You do not know me or my Father," Jesus replied. "If you knew me, you would know my Father also." [20]He spoke these words while teaching in the temple area near the place where the offerings were put. Yet no one seized him, because his time had not yet come.

[21]Once more Jesus said to them, "I am going away, and you will look for me, and you will die in your sin. Where I go, you cannot come."

[22]This made the Jews ask, "Will he kill himself? Is that why he says, 'Where I go, you cannot come'?"

[23]But he continued, "You are from below; I am from above. You are of this world; I am not of this world. [24]I told you that you would die in your sins; if you do not believe that I am ⌊the one I claim to be,⌋[a] you will indeed die in your sins."

[25]"Who are you?" they asked.

"Just what I have been claiming all along," Jesus replied. [26]"I have much to say in judgment of you. But he who sent me is reliable, and what I have heard from him I tell the world."

[27]They did not understand that he was telling them about his Father. [28]So Jesus said, "When you have lifted up the Son of Man, then you will know that I am ⌊the one I claim to be⌋ and that I do nothing on my own but speak just what the Father has taught me. [29]The one who sent me is with me; he has not left me alone, for I always do what pleases him." [30]Even as he spoke, many put their faith in him.

The Children of Abraham

[31]To the Jews who had believed him, Jesus said, "If you hold to my teaching, you are really my disciples. [32]Then you will know the truth, and the truth will set you free."

[33]They answered him, "We are Abraham's descendants[b] and have never been slaves of anyone. How can you say that we shall be set free?"

change, or does it support your bad behavior? How so? **3.** What can you learn from Jesus about helping a friend who has fallen?

What is your most vivid memory as a child in a dark place (cave, tunnel, power blackout)? What feelings do you associate with darkness?

1. What is Jesus really claiming in verse 12? What is the promise? What does Jesus mean by "light" and "darkness"? **2.** With what does Jesus bolster his claim (see 5:31–40)? What does it matter that Jesus knows where he comes from (vv. 14,21–23; see 7:41–42)? **3.** What does the Pharisees' question in verse 19 reveal about their relationship with the Father? **4.** What is at stake in this whole discussion (v. 24)? Why does everything hinge on who Jesus really is (v. 25) and who sent him (vv. 16,18,26,29)? **5.** What does Jesus mean by each phrase in verse 28? How will this show people he is the Christ? **6.** What is the significance of verse 30 in light of the total misunderstanding of the Pharisees? How do the Pharisees exemplify darkness in this scene?

1. How is following Jesus like following someone with a light through a dark place for you? **2.** How do people you know misunderstand Jesus? How do their lives exemplify darkness? How can you be a light-bearer to them?

1. Where did your ancestors come from? How did they get to this country? **2.** Who is one of the more colorful characters in your family tree? **3.** Who, in your family tree, do you look to as a spiritual patriarch or matriarch?

---

[a]24 Or *I am he*; also in verse 28   [b]33 Greek *seed*; also in verse 37

1. What does Jesus want to emphasize to the people who believed him? What does he mean by *disciples*? *Truth*? *Freedom*? 2. What false assumptions confuse the issue of spiritual freedom for Abraham's descendants? How does Jesus undermine their base of confidence? What issues does he force them to confront (vv. 34–41)? 3. How does Jesus undermine their claim in verse 41? What does he say is the ultimate test to show who "belongs to God" (vv. 42–47)? How does he account for their misunderstanding of him (vv. 37,43,45,47)? 4. Why does Jesus continue to address his relationship with the Father? 5. What is the critical question raised by his claim in verse 51 (also v. 24)? How is this issue central to the whole argument in 7:4–8:58? How does Jesus use their loyalty to Abraham against them? Why does Jesus' final claim cause such an outrage (see Ex 3:14)?

1. What are you proud of in your religious heritage? In what ways has it been a handicap? 2. What has knowing the truth set you free to do? How can you be sure that there is room in your life for his Word? What needs to be cleaned out so there is room? 3. Of the four claims Jesus makes in this chapter (vv. 12,32,51,58), which means the most to you? Why? 4. What does Jesus' association between the devil and telling lies mean to you? From this passage, what can you do for someone who is honestly seeking God? What in your spiritual journey might help?

34Jesus replied, "I tell you the truth, everyone who sins is a slave to sin. 35Now a slave has no permanent place in the family, but a son belongs to it forever. 36So if the Son sets you free, you will be free indeed. 37I know you are Abraham's descendants. Yet you are ready to kill me, because you have no room for my word. 38I am telling you what I have seen in the Father's presence, and you do what you have heard from your father.[a]"

39"Abraham is our father," they answered.

"If you were Abraham's children," said Jesus, "then you would[b] do the things Abraham did. 40As it is, you are determined to kill me, a man who has told you the truth that I heard from God. Abraham did not do such things. 41You are doing the things your own father does."

"We are not illegitimate children," they protested. "The only Father we have is God himself."

The Children of the Devil

42Jesus said to them, "If God were your Father, you would love me, for I came from God and now am here. I have not come on my own; but he sent me. 43Why is my language not clear to you? Because you are unable to hear what I say. 44You belong to your father, the devil, and you want to carry out your father's desire. He was a murderer from the beginning, not holding to the truth, for there is no truth in him. When he lies, he speaks his native language, for he is a liar and the father of lies. 45Yet because I tell the truth, you do not believe me! 46Can any of you prove me guilty of sin? If I am telling the truth, why don't you believe me? 47He who belongs to God hears what God says. The reason you do not hear is that you do not belong to God."

The Claims of Jesus About Himself

48The Jews answered him, "Aren't we right in saying that you are a Samaritan and demon-possessed?"

49"I am not possessed by a demon," said Jesus, "but I honor my Father and you dishonor me. 50I am not seeking glory for myself; but there is one who seeks it, and he is the judge. 51I tell you the truth, if anyone keeps my word, he will never see death."

52At this the Jews exclaimed, "Now we know that you are demon-possessed! Abraham died and so did the prophets, yet you say that if anyone keeps your word, he will never taste death. 53Are you greater than our father Abraham? He died, and so did the prophets. Who do you think you are?"

54Jesus replied, "If I glorify myself, my glory means nothing. My Father, whom you claim as your God, is the one who glorifies me. 55Though you do not know him, I know him. If I said I did not, I would be a liar like you, but I do know him and keep his word. 56Your father Abraham rejoiced at the thought of seeing my day; he saw it and was glad."

57"You are not yet fifty years old," the Jews said to him, "and you have seen Abraham!"

58"I tell you the truth," Jesus answered, "before Abraham was born, I am!" 59At this, they picked up stones to stone him, but Jesus hid himself, slipping away from the temple grounds.

[a]38 Or *presence. Therefore do what you have heard from the Father.* [b]39 Some early manuscripts *"If you are Abraham's children," said Jesus, "then*

Jesus Heals a Man Born Blind

9 As he went along, he saw a man blind from birth. [2]His disciples asked him, "Rabbi, who sinned, this man or his parents, that he was born blind?"

[3]"Neither this man nor his parents sinned," said Jesus, "but this happened so that the work of God might be displayed in his life. [4]As long as it is day, we must do the work of him who sent me. Night is coming, when no one can work. [5]While I am in the world, I am the light of the world."

[6]Having said this, he spit on the ground, made some mud with the saliva, and put it on the man's eyes. [7]"Go," he told him, "wash in the Pool of Siloam" (this word means Sent). So the man went and washed, and came home seeing.

[8]His neighbors and those who had formerly seen him begging asked, "Isn't this the same man who used to sit and beg?" [9]Some claimed that he was.

Others said, "No, he only looks like him."

But he himself insisted, "I am the man."

[10]"How then were your eyes opened?" they demanded.

[11]He replied, "The man they call Jesus made some mud and put it on my eyes. He told me to go to Siloam and wash. So I went and washed, and then I could see."

[12]"Where is this man?" they asked him.

"I don't know," he said.

Describe an adventure you had with mud when you were a child.

1. What idea lies behind the disciples' question (v. 1): Curiosity? Guilt-tripping? A trap? Compassion? 2. What does Jesus' answer (vv. 3–5) reveal about how he views the man's suffering? 3. In this story, what is the "work of God" (v. 3)? The "night" that is coming (v. 4)? The "light of the world" (v. 5)? How are sin and suffering related?

1. What physical or emotional misfortune in your life has turned into an opportunity for God to demonstrate his power? 2. When you hear about another person's misfortune, do you react like the disciples or Jesus? Why?

   John 9:1–34   JESUS HEALS A MAN BORN BLIND

1. What was behind the disciples' question, "Who sinned, this man or his parents, that he was born blind?"
   a. judgmentalism   c. curiosity
   b. compassion   d. a trap

2. What did Jesus' reply show about how he viewed the man's affliction?
   a. He and his parents were sinless.
   b. He was an exception to the rule.
   c. The standard theology of the day was full of baloney.
   d. The man was born blind so that Jesus could miraculously heal him.
   e. Suffering like this just happens.
   f. The purpose of the blindness was more important than its cure.

3. Why did Jesus spit and make mud in healing the man?
   a. to add variety to his practices of healing people
   b. to provoke the Pharisees by breaking their Sabbath rules, since treating illness and making mud were considered "work"
   c. to gain the man's confidence since saliva was believed to have healing properties
   d. to give the man a part in the healing process

4. Why did some of the Pharisees take a stand against Jesus?
   a. because he violated their Sabbath restrictions
   b. because he violated their concept of the Messiah
   c. because it never occurred to them their regulations might be wrong
   d. because they started from their own bias instead of the miracle
   e. because *they* were "blind"

5. How does this story illustrate Jesus' statement in verse 5: "I am the light of the world"?

6. The man progressed in his understanding of Jesus: from a man (v. 11), to a prophet (v. 17), to one worthy of following (v. 27), to one "from God" (v. 33), to one who should be worshiped (v. 38). How has your view of Jesus and your commitment to him progressed over time?

7. How would you measure your spiritual vision now (and how could it be corrected)?
   a. 20/20   d. near-sighted
   b. 20/200   e. far-sighted
   c. legally blind f. a few blind spots

8. What hard questions do you have about life, particularly regarding suffering? In spite of them are you able to affirm the basic spiritual reality—"One thing I do know. I was blind but now I see"?

9. How can you relate to the blame this man lived with from a society that said he was blind because of sin? From whom have you felt blame for your pain?
   a. my family   e. myself
   b. my friends   f. God
   c. the church   g. other:_____
   d. the medical community

10. This man's parents feared rejection. How do your child's special needs bring you feelings of fear or rejection?

11. Jesus said the man's blindness "happened so that the work of God might be displayed in his life." How have you seen your child's disabilities turned into an opportunity for God to demonstrate his power—in your child's life? In your life? In the lives of others?

Describe a time when an authority figure (your boss, a
policeman, your pastor) pulled you
over for a talk.

1. What convinces some of
the Pharisees to stand
against Jesus (v. 16; see also
5:9–10,23)? What question bothers others? Why does Jesus keep
healing on the Sabbath when it upsets the Pharisees so much? 2. In
light of their divided opinion, why
do the Pharisees question the
man's parents (vv. 18–23)? How
would you feel if you were his father or mother? 3. Note the conflicting claims to knowledge and certainty on the part of the Pharisees,
the parents and the man born
blind. What is each party sure of?
Not sure of? 4. In the course of this
investigation, what is the man able
to see about Jesus (vv. 12,
17,25,27,30–33,36, 38)? About the
Pharisees? How is his attitude
changing? 5. In contrast to the
man's growing spiritual insight, how
are the Pharisees progressing? 6.
What is the Pharisees' real motive
in questioning the man (vv. 28,34)?
What in the man's response finally
puts them "over the top"?

1. Who has been the toughest person for you to explain
your faith to? Why? What have you
found to be helpful in dealing with
people who ridicule your faith? 2.
Has your faith in Jesus led to your
exclusion from any group? How
has this hurt or helped you? 3.
Have you ever been afraid of religious leaders? Why?

What 24-hour period in your
life had the most ups and
downs?

1. Why does Jesus wait until
now to fully present himself?
How is the man, only now, able to
affirm Jesus as Lord? 2. What
blindness is the result of sin (vv.
39–41)? How do such guilty people see again?

The Pharisees Investigate the Healing

¹³They brought to the Pharisees the man who had been blind.
¹⁴Now the day on which Jesus had made the mud and opened the
man's eyes was a Sabbath. ¹⁵Therefore the Pharisees also asked
him how he had received his sight. "He put mud on my eyes," the
man replied, "and I washed, and now I see."

¹⁶Some of the Pharisees said, "This man is not from God, for he
does not keep the Sabbath."

But others asked, "How can a sinner do such miraculous signs?"
So they were divided.

¹⁷Finally they turned again to the blind man, "What have you to
say about him? It was your eyes he opened."

The man replied, "He is a prophet."

¹⁸The Jews still did not believe that he had been blind and had
received his sight until they sent for the man's parents. ¹⁹"Is this
your son?" they asked. "Is this the one you say was born blind?
How is it that now he can see?"

²⁰"We know he is our son," the parents answered, "and we
know he was born blind. ²¹But how he can see now, or who
opened his eyes, we don't know. Ask him. He is of age; he will
speak for himself." ²²His parents said this because they were afraid
of the Jews, for already the Jews had decided that anyone who
acknowledged that Jesus was the Christᵃ would be put out of the
synagogue. ²³That was why his parents said, "He is of age; ask
him."

²⁴A second time they summoned the man who had been blind.
"Give glory to God,ᵇ" they said. "We know this man is a sinner."

²⁵He replied, "Whether he is a sinner or not, I don't know. One
thing I do know. I was blind but now I see!"

²⁶Then they asked him, "What did he do to you? How did he
open your eyes?"

²⁷He answered, "I have told you already and you did not listen.
Why do you want to hear it again? Do you want to become his
disciples, too?"

²⁸Then they hurled insults at him and said, "You are this fellow's
disciple! We are disciples of Moses! ²⁹We know that God spoke to
Moses, but as for this fellow, we don't even know where he comes
from."

³⁰The man answered, "Now that is remarkable! You don't know
where he comes from, yet he opened my eyes. ³¹We know that
God does not listen to sinners. He listens to the godly man who
does his will. ³²Nobody has ever heard of opening the eyes of a
man born blind. ³³If this man were not from God, he could do
nothing."

³⁴To this they replied, "You were steeped in sin at birth; how
dare you lecture us!" And they threw him out.

Spiritual Blindness

³⁵Jesus heard that they had thrown him out, and when he found
him, he said, "Do you believe in the Son of Man?"

³⁶"Who is he, sir?" the man asked. "Tell me so that I may
believe in him."

³⁷Jesus said, "You have now seen him; in fact, he is the one
speaking with you."

³⁸Then the man said, "Lord, I believe," and he worshiped him.

³⁹Jesus said, "For judgment I have come into this world, so that
the blind will see and those who see will become blind."

ᵃ22 Or Messiah   ᵇ24 A solemn charge to tell the truth (see Joshua 7:19)

40Some Pharisees who were with him heard him say this and asked, "What? Are we blind too?"

41Jesus said, "If you were blind, you would not be guilty of sin; but now that you claim you can see, your guilt remains.

The Shepherd and His Flock

10 "I tell you the truth, the man who does not enter the sheep pen by the gate, but climbs in by some other way, is a thief and a robber. 2The man who enters by the gate is the shepherd of his sheep. 3The watchman opens the gate for him, and the sheep listen to his voice. He calls his own sheep by name and leads them out. 4When he has brought out all his own, he goes on ahead of them, and his sheep follow him because they know his voice. 5But they will never follow a stranger; in fact, they will run away from him because they do not recognize a stranger's voice." 6Jesus used this figure of speech, but they did not understand what he was telling them.

7Therefore Jesus said again, "I tell you the truth, I am the gate for the sheep. 8All who ever came before me were thieves and robbers, but the sheep did not listen to them. 9I am the gate; whoever enters through me will be saved.*a* He will come in and go out, and find pasture. 10The thief comes only to steal and kill and destroy; I have come that they may have life, and have it to the full.

11"I am the good shepherd. The good shepherd lays down his life for the sheep. 12The hired hand is not the shepherd who owns the sheep. So when he sees the wolf coming, he abandons the sheep and runs away. Then the wolf attacks the flock and scatters it. 13The man runs away because he is a hired hand and cares nothing for the sheep.

14"I am the good shepherd; I know my sheep and my sheep know me— 15just as the Father knows me and I know the Father—and I lay down my life for the sheep. 16I have other sheep that are not of this sheep pen. I must bring them also. They too will listen to my voice, and there shall be one flock and one shepherd. 17The reason my Father loves me is that I lay down my life—only to take it up again. 18No one takes it from me, but I lay it down of my own accord. I have authority to lay it down and authority to take it up again. This command I received from my Father."

19At these words the Jews were again divided. 20Many of them said, "He is demon-possessed and raving mad. Why listen to him?" 21But others said, "These are not the sayings of a man possessed by a demon. Can a demon open the eyes of the blind?"

The Unbelief of the Jews

22Then came the Feast of Dedication*b* at Jerusalem. It was winter, 23and Jesus was in the temple area walking in Solomon's Colonnade. 24The Jews gathered around him, saying, "How long will you keep us in suspense? If you are the Christ,*c* tell us plainly."

25Jesus answered, "I did tell you, but you do not believe. The miracles I do in my Father's name speak for me, 26but you do not believe because you are not my sheep. 27My sheep listen to my voice; I know them, and they follow me. 28I give them eternal life, and they shall never perish; no one can snatch them out of my hand. 29My Father, who has given them to me, is greater than all*d*; no one can snatch them out of my Father's hand. 30I and the Father are one."

Describe your own spiritual sight: 20–20? Near-sighted? Far-sighted? A few "blind spots"? Why? What could correct this?

As a child, what was your favorite pet? How did this pet respond when it heard your voice?

1. What do the sheep, shepherd, the sheep pen and stranger represent? How does the story in chapter 9 provide one example of what this parable is about? 2. How do the sheep respond to the shepherd? How does this relate to the Pharisees' difficulty in understanding Jesus? 3. What does Jesus mean by likening himself to a gate for the sheepfold? Who are these "thieves and robbers"? How is Jesus unlike them? 4. How does Jesus identify himself with the "good shepherd" (vv. 11–15)? How does Jesus' death relate to his promise in verse 10? 5. Who are the "other sheep" he must bring also? What characterizes his flock? 6. What final claim does Jesus make (vv. 17–18)? Why do his listeners respond as they do? How would you have responded?

1. What was the turning point for you in terms of hearing "God's voice" and responding? 2. How do you discern his voice from all the voices that vie for your attention? 3. How does it make you feel to think of God caring for you as the Good Shepherd?

---

1. What is the big annual "feast day" for your family? Who usually comes? What is served? What is the big pastime? 2. What family traditions are you going to preserve for your children?

1. Given the meaning of the Feast of Hanukkah (when Jews remember their deliverance during the Maccabean revolt, 168–165 B.C.), what feelings about Rome's authority might surface among the crowds? How would Roman authorities prepare for this feast? What might be the real intent of the Pharisees' question in verse 24? 2. How do the

---

a9 Or *kept safe*   *b22* That is, *Hanukkah*   *c24* Or *Messiah*   *d29* Many early manuscripts *What my Father has given me is greater than all*

leaders interpret Jesus' claim to be one with God? How does Jesus sidetrack them (v. 34; Ps 82:6)? **3.** What could account for the difference in reception Jesus received across the Jordan (vv. 40–42)?

♡ **1.** What has convinced you that Jesus is the Messiah? What "old ways" of looking at Jesus must you overcome by faith? **2.** What difference does it make that Jesus is God and not just a man? Would the promise of verse 28 mean much otherwise?

☕ Describe the sickest you have ever been.

📖 **1.** How would you describe Jesus' relationship with this family (vv. 1–5)? Why does Jesus deliberately delay (v. 6)? **2.** Given his disciples' objection (v. 8), what do you think Jesus means by his parable (vv. 9–10)? **3.** Why is Jesus returning to Lazarus at this time (vv. 11–15)? What do the disciples fear instead (vv. 8,16)?

♡ **1.** Have you ever felt like God was not listening when you prayed? How did you deal with this? How does the way in which Jesus postponed his response to the sisters' request help you in understanding your own prayer life? **2.** Have you, like Thomas (v. 16), ever felt Jesus was calling you to do something very risky? What happened?

☕ If you could raise one person from the dead, who would it be? Why?

📖 **1.** How long had Lazarus been dead by the time Jesus arrived? How would you feel if you were Martha or Mary and you heard that Jesus had finally come? **2.** What do you learn about Martha

³¹Again the Jews picked up stones to stone him, ³²but Jesus said to them, "I have shown you many great miracles from the Father. For which of these do you stone me?"

³³"We are not stoning you for any of these," replied the Jews, "but for blasphemy, because you, a mere man, claim to be God."

³⁴Jesus answered them, "Is it not written in your Law, 'I have said you are gods'ᵃ? ³⁵If he called them 'gods,' to whom the word of God came—and the Scripture cannot be broken— ³⁶what about the one whom the Father set apart as his very own and sent into the world? Why then do you accuse me of blasphemy because I said, 'I am God's Son'? ³⁷Do not believe me unless I do what my Father does. ³⁸But if I do it, even though you do not believe me, believe the miracles, that you may know and understand that the Father is in me, and I in the Father." ³⁹Again they tried to seize him, but he escaped their grasp.

⁴⁰Then Jesus went back across the Jordan to the place where John had been baptizing in the early days. Here he stayed ⁴¹and many people came to him. They said, "Though John never performed a miraculous sign, all that John said about this man was true." ⁴²And in that place many believed in Jesus.

The Death of Lazarus

11 Now a man named Lazarus was sick. He was from Bethany, the village of Mary and her sister Martha. ²This Mary, whose brother Lazarus now lay sick, was the same one who poured perfume on the Lord and wiped his feet with her hair. ³So the sisters sent word to Jesus, "Lord, the one you love is sick."

⁴When he heard this, Jesus said, "This sickness will not end in death. No, it is for God's glory so that God's Son may be glorified through it." ⁵Jesus loved Martha and her sister and Lazarus. ⁶Yet when he heard that Lazarus was sick, he stayed where he was two more days.

⁷Then he said to his disciples, "Let us go back to Judea."

⁸"But Rabbi," they said, "a short while ago the Jews tried to stone you, and yet you are going back there?"

⁹Jesus answered, "Are there not twelve hours of daylight? A man who walks by day will not stumble, for he sees by this world's light. ¹⁰It is when he walks by night that he stumbles, for he has no light."

¹¹After he had said this, he went on to tell them, "Our friend Lazarus has fallen asleep; but I am going there to wake him up."

¹²His disciples replied, "Lord, if he sleeps, he will get better." ¹³Jesus had been speaking of his death, but his disciples thought he meant natural sleep.

¹⁴So then he told them plainly, "Lazarus is dead, ¹⁵and for your sake I am glad I was not there, so that you may believe. But let us go to him."

¹⁶Then Thomas (called Didymus) said to the rest of the disciples, "Let us also go, that we may die with him."

Jesus Comforts the Sisters

¹⁷On his arrival, Jesus found that Lazarus had already been in the tomb for four days. ¹⁸Bethany was less than two milesᵇ from Jerusalem, ¹⁹and many Jews had come to Martha and Mary to comfort them in the loss of their brother. ²⁰When Martha heard that Jesus was coming, she went out to meet him, but Mary stayed at home.

ᵃ34 Psalm 82:6   ᵇ18 Greek *fifteen stadia* (about 3 kilometers)

21"Lord," Martha said to Jesus, "if you had been here, my brother would not have died. 22But I know that even now God will give you whatever you ask."

23Jesus said to her, "Your brother will rise again."

24Martha answered, "I know he will rise again in the resurrection at the last day."

25Jesus said to her, "I am the resurrection and the life. He who believes in me will live, even though he dies; 26and whoever lives and believes in me will never die. Do you believe this?"

27"Yes, Lord," she told him, "I believe that you are the Christ,ᵃ the Son of God, who was to come into the world."

28And after she had said this, she went back and called her sister Mary aside. "The Teacher is here," she said, "and is asking for you." 29When Mary heard this, she got up quickly and went to him. 30Now Jesus had not yet entered the village, but was still at the place where Martha had met him. 31When the Jews who had been with Mary in the house, comforting her, noticed how quickly she got up and went out, they followed her, supposing she was going to the tomb to mourn there.

32When Mary reached the place where Jesus was and saw him,

a27 Or Messiah

from the way she talks with Jesus in verses 21–27? How does Jesus stretch her faith by his claim in verse 25? How does this relate to his claim in 10:9? **3.** What does Martha's statement (v. 27) sound like to you: (a) Stab in the dark? (b) Hope against hope? (c) Intellectual assent? (d) Active commitment? Why do you think so? **4.** How is Mary's greeting (v. 32) like and unlike Martha's? Since Jesus knew he was going to raise Lazarus (11:11), how do you account for his weeping (vv. 33–35)? **5.** What lies behind the comments of the mourners in verses 36–37? **6.** How does Martha's objection in verse 39 contrast with her confidence in verse 22?

1. When have you been faced with a tough situation that ended up stretching your faith? What would have been different for

---

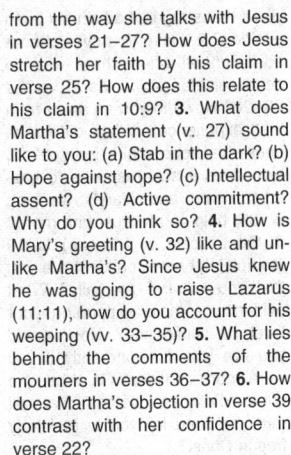

John 11:1–44　　**JESUS RAISES LAZARUS**

1. Why do you think Jesus didn't go immediately to help Lazarus?
   a. He was afraid he would get killed if he went back to Judea.
   b. He didn't always do what people wanted.
   c. He was waiting for the "go ahead" from his Father.
   d. God would receive more glory if Jesus waited until Lazarus died.

2. How would you have felt if you were Mary or Martha and you heard that Jesus was about to arrive?
   a. despondent—It's too late.
   b. angry—It's about time!
   c. consoled—Better late than never.
   d. hopeful—With Jesus, it's never too late.

3. What do you learn about Jesus from his coming to the tomb?
   a. He was a very emotional person.
   b. He was profoundly affected by the reality and power of death.
   c. He empathized with suffering.
   d. He loved people deeply.

4. Why did Jesus raise Lazarus from the dead?
   a. to see his friend again
   b. to relieve Mary and Martha's grief
   c. to demonstrate he was God's Son
   d. to illustrate that he is "the resurrection and the life"
   e. to glorify his Father

5. If you compared your spiritual life to Lazarus, where would you be?
   a. still in the grave
   b. alive but still wrapped with grave clothes
   c. alive and free of the grave clothes

6. What are some old "grave clothes" that still need to be shed for you to feel completely free in Christ?

7. If you had been there and saw Jesus crying, how would you have felt?
   a. embarrassed for him—Grown men don't cry.
   b. relieved—It's okay to cry.
   c. mad—He could have prevented this and now all he can do is bawl.
   d. inspired—He really cared.

8. When you were a child, how tender would you say your mother was? How about your father? How tender are you? What keeps you from being more tender than you are?

9. How has God shown his care for you in the aftermath of your miscarriage?
   a. through a caring spouse
   b. through a caring family or church
   c. through this group
   d. through Scriptures like this
   e. through the comfort of his Spirit
   f. by protecting our marriage

10.  What is your greatest challenge for you related to being assertive? Specifically, how hard is it for you to follow Jesus' example in the following areas?
    a. not dropping everything to answer the requests of others
    b. not feeling like I should be everywhere, meeting every need
    c. not always giving in when there is a difference of opinion

11. What means the most to you concerning your future?
    a. Jesus' promise that believers will "never die"
    b. Jesus' words, "I am the resurrection and the life"
    c. the anticipation of seeing Jesus after I die
    d. the anticipation of seeing my loved ones in heaven

12. How does this story bring hope to your grief and loss? What have you appreciated the most about this course, and particularly the members of your group?

13. What word of hope or encouragement would you like to share with your group or with a particular member? Close in prayer by thanking God for the promises of this Scripture and for Christ's continual comfort and presence with you.

you if that struggle had simply been avoided? **2.** Have you ever attended a funeral where there was no sense of eternal life, as in verses 25–26? How did you go away from that experience? What difference does this hope make for you? **3.** How does Jesus' response to Lazarus' death and Mary's weeping (v. 35) help you to trust him more? **4.** On a scale of 1 (none) to 10 (completely) how confident are you that you will live eternally? What evidence is there supporting your level of confidence? How would you live your life differently if you were more confident? **5.** What are some "old grave clothes" that still must be shed for you to feel truly free in Christ?

When have you challenged company policy? What happened?

1. What responses does the Lazarus miracle produce? Why? **2.** What are the chief concerns of the leaders? How do they misunderstand the role of the Messiah? How does Caiaphas propose to solve "the Jesus problem"? How does Caiaphas' murderous threat unwittingly convey prophetic truth about Jesus' death (see 3:16)? **3.** How does Jesus respond to this new situation?

1. What would you have done if you had been on the Sanhedrin? Would politics or truth win out with you? **2.** In what ways are you most likely to misunderstand who Jesus is? **3.** How have you tried to keep Jesus in line with your religious traditions?

she fell at his feet and said, "Lord, if you had been here, my brother would not have died."

³³When Jesus saw her weeping, and the Jews who had come along with her also weeping, he was deeply moved in spirit and troubled. ³⁴"Where have you laid him?" he asked.

"Come and see, Lord," they replied.

³⁵Jesus wept.

³⁶Then the Jews said, "See how he loved him!"

³⁷But some of them said, "Could not he who opened the eyes of the blind man have kept this man from dying?"

Jesus Raises Lazarus From the Dead

³⁸Jesus, once more deeply moved, came to the tomb. It was a cave with a stone laid across the entrance. ³⁹"Take away the stone," he said.

"But, Lord," said Martha, the sister of the dead man, "by this time there is a bad odor, for he has been there four days."

⁴⁰Then Jesus said, "Did I not tell you that if you believed, you would see the glory of God?"

⁴¹So they took away the stone. Then Jesus looked up and said, "Father, I thank you that you have heard me. ⁴²I knew that you always hear me, but I said this for the benefit of the people standing here, that they may believe that you sent me."

⁴³When he had said this, Jesus called in a loud voice, "Lazarus, come out!" ⁴⁴The dead man came out, his hands and feet wrapped with strips of linen, and a cloth around his face.

Jesus said to them, "Take off the grave clothes and let him go."

The Plot to Kill Jesus

⁴⁵Therefore many of the Jews who had come to visit Mary, and had seen what Jesus did, put their faith in him. ⁴⁶But some of them went to the Pharisees and told them what Jesus had done. ⁴⁷Then the chief priests and the Pharisees called a meeting of the Sanhedrin.

"What are we accomplishing?" they asked. "Here is this man performing many miraculous signs. ⁴⁸If we let him go on like this, everyone will believe in him, and then the Romans will come and take away both our place[a] and our nation."

⁴⁹Then one of them, named Caiaphas, who was high priest that year, spoke up, "You know nothing at all! ⁵⁰You do not realize that it is better for you that one man die for the people than that the whole nation perish."

⁵¹He did not say this on his own, but as high priest that year he prophesied that Jesus would die for the Jewish nation, ⁵²and not only for that nation but also for the scattered children of God, to bring them together and make them one. ⁵³So from that day on they plotted to take his life.

⁵⁴Therefore Jesus no longer moved about publicly among the Jews. Instead he withdrew to a region near the desert, to a village called Ephraim, where he stayed with his disciples.

⁵⁵When it was almost time for the Jewish Passover, many went up from the country to Jerusalem for their ceremonial cleansing before the Passover. ⁵⁶They kept looking for Jesus, and as they stood in the temple area they asked one another, "What do you think? Isn't he coming to the Feast at all?" ⁵⁷But the chief priests and Pharisees had given orders that if anyone found out where Jesus was, he should report it so that they might arrest him.

a48 Or temple

Jesus Anointed at Bethany

12 Six days before the Passover, Jesus arrived at Bethany, where Lazarus lived, whom Jesus had raised from the dead. ²Here a dinner was given in Jesus' honor. Martha served, while Lazarus was among those reclining at the table with him. ³Then Mary took about a pint*ᵃ* of pure nard, an expensive perfume; she poured it on Jesus' feet and wiped his feet with her hair. And the house was filled with the fragrance of the perfume.

⁴But one of his disciples, Judas Iscariot, who was later to betray him, objected, ⁵"Why wasn't this perfume sold and the money given to the poor? It was worth a year's wages.*ᵇ*" ⁶He did not say this because he cared about the poor but because he was a thief; as keeper of the money bag, he used to help himself to what was put into it.

⁷"Leave her alone," Jesus replied. "⌜It was intended⌟ that she should save this perfume for the day of my burial. ⁸You will always have the poor among you, but you will not always have me."

⁹Meanwhile a large crowd of Jews found out that Jesus was there and came, not only because of him but also to see Lazarus, whom he had raised from the dead. ¹⁰So the chief priests made plans to kill Lazarus as well, ¹¹for on account of him many of the Jews were going over to Jesus and putting their faith in him.

The Triumphal Entry

¹²The next day the great crowd that had come for the Feast heard that Jesus was on his way to Jerusalem. ¹³They took palm branches and went out to meet him, shouting,

"Hosanna!*ᶜ*"

"Blessed is he who comes in the name of the
Lord!"*ᵈ*

"Blessed is the King of Israel!"

¹⁴Jesus found a young donkey and sat upon it, as it is written,

¹⁵"Do not be afraid, O Daughter of Zion;
see, your king is coming,
seated on a donkey's colt."*ᵉ*

¹⁶At first his disciples did not understand all this. Only after Jesus was glorified did they realize that these things had been written about him and that they had done these things to him. ¹⁷Now the crowd that was with him when he called Lazarus from the tomb and raised him from the dead continued to spread the word. ¹⁸Many people, because they had heard that he had given this miraculous sign, went out to meet him. ¹⁹So the Pharisees said to one another, "See, this is getting us nowhere. Look how the whole world has gone after him!"

Jesus Predicts His Death

²⁰Now there were some Greeks among those who went up to worship at the Feast. ²¹They came to Philip, who was from Bethsaida in Galilee, with a request. "Sir," they said, "we would like to see Jesus." ²²Philip went to tell Andrew; Andrew and Philip in turn told Jesus.

²³Jesus replied, "The hour has come for the Son of Man to be glorified. ²⁴I tell you the truth, unless a kernel of wheat falls to the

If you had a year's wages to spend on friends, which would you choose: (a) Big party? (b) Glorious trip for a few? (c) Extravagant gift for one?

1. Given the value of the perfume (v. 5), how would you have reacted as you watched Mary? Why? 2. How does Jesus interpret Mary's action? How is his comment in verse 8 especially applicable to Judas? 3. How is the blindness of the priests shown by their reaction to Lazarus?

1. If you had a year's salary or time to use for Christ, how would you use it? How is that reflected in your budget and priorities now? 2. If you gave a dinner in Jesus' honor, whom would you invite?

1. What do you like *best* about parades: Bands? Food Venders? Clowns? 2. What do you like *least*: Traffic? Pickpockets? Tall people?

1. What previous stories stand in contrast to the unity and enthusiasm the people are expressing here? 2. How could you tie in their hope that Jesus will do at *this* Passover what God did at the *first* Passover? 3. Why a lowly donkey for Jesus (see Zec 9:9)? 4. What do you think the crowds, the disciples and the Jewish leaders must be feeling now? One week later? Had you been there, what would you be feeling: Fanaticism, fickleness, faith or fear? Why?

1. What convinced you that Jesus is your King? What is the best thing you've seen about the type of King he is? 2. Is your worship life like a hero's victory or a funeral dirge? Why?

Are you more likely to panic in the *big* crises or the *little* ones? Explain.

1. What brings Gentiles to Jerusalem during a time of a Jewish feast? 2. What was so unique about their request that Philip would first filter it through Andrew? 3. Jesus said several times that "his time had not come" (2:4; 7:6,30). What regarding this request caused him to say that now it

a3 Greek *a litra* (probably about 0.5 liter)   *b5* Greek *three hundred denarii*
c13 A Hebrew expression meaning "Save!" which became an exclamation of praise
d13 Psalm 118:25, 26   *e15* Zech. 9:9

has come? **4.** In Jesus' parable (v. 24), who is the kernel of wheat? How is this related to the Gentiles' request? **5.** What is he calling his disciples to do in verses 25–26? What promise do they receive? **6.** In verses 27–32, what is about to occur "now"? How does this affect Jesus? Why did the crowd deny the reality of Jesus' future death (vv. 32–34)?

1. In what area of your life are you in denial? **2.** Where is Jesus calling you to *die* so that you might *live*? What do you tend to hold on to rather than follow Jesus? **3.** Do you feel like you are walking in the dark, the light, or in some shadowland right now? Why?

Are you more like the salesman who could sell an icebox to an Eskimo, or more like the Eskimo who buys one?

1. What are some of the miraculous signs Jesus has done in this Gospel? How do the prophecies from Isaiah 53:1 and 6:10 account for the people's disbelief in spite of these signs? **2.** What is the author implying about Jesus in verse 41 (see 8:58)? **3.** What inhibits the leaders from speaking? How does this illustrate 12:25–26? **4.** What is Jesus claiming in verses 44–45? How do verses 44–46 relate to 1:1–5? How is Jesus like a light? **5.** What does Jesus emphasize in verses 47–50? As a last public statement, why is this one especially appropriate? How is it that Jesus' words can either judge a person or lead one to life?

1. Where do you find it most difficult to live your faith: At home or work? Why? **2.** If you had to sacrifice social status or certain relationships to follow Jesus, what would you get in return? **3.** How do you let people know where you stand with God?

ground and dies, it remains only a single seed. But if it dies, it produces many seeds. 25The man who loves his life will lose it, while the man who hates his life in this world will keep it for eternal life. 26Whoever serves me must follow me; and where I am, my servant also will be. My Father will honor the one who serves me.

27"Now my heart is troubled, and what shall I say? 'Father, save me from this hour'? No, it was for this very reason I came to this hour. 28Father, glorify your name!"

Then a voice came from heaven, "I have glorified it, and will glorify it again." 29The crowd that was there and heard it said it had thundered; others said an angel had spoken to him.

30Jesus said, "This voice was for your benefit, not mine. 31Now is the time for judgment on this world; now the prince of this world will be driven out. 32But I, when I am lifted up from the earth, will draw all men to myself." 33He said this to show the kind of death he was going to die.

34The crowd spoke up, "We have heard from the Law that the Christ[a] will remain forever, so how can you say, 'The Son of Man must be lifted up'? Who is this 'Son of Man'?"

35Then Jesus told them, "You are going to have the light just a little while longer. Walk while you have the light, before darkness overtakes you. The man who walks in the dark does not know where he is going. 36Put your trust in the light while you have it, so that you may become sons of light." When he had finished speaking, Jesus left and hid himself from them.

The Jews Continue in Their Unbelief

37Even after Jesus had done all these miraculous signs in their presence, they still would not believe in him. 38This was to fulfill the word of Isaiah the prophet:

"Lord, who has believed our message
    and to whom has the arm of the Lord been
        revealed?"[b]

39For this reason they could not believe, because, as Isaiah says elsewhere:

40"He has blinded their eyes
    and deadened their hearts,
so they can neither see with their eyes,
    nor understand with their hearts,
    nor turn—and I would heal them."[c]

41Isaiah said this because he saw Jesus' glory and spoke about him.

42Yet at the same time many even among the leaders believed in him. But because of the Pharisees they would not confess their faith for fear they would be put out of the synagogue; 43for they loved praise from men more than praise from God.

44Then Jesus cried out, "When a man believes in me, he does not believe in me only, but in the one who sent me. 45When he looks at me, he sees the one who sent me. 46I have come into the world as a light, so that no one who believes in me should stay in darkness.

47"As for the person who hears my words but does not keep them, I do not judge him. For I did not come to judge the world, but to save it. 48There is a judge for the one who rejects me and does not accept my words; that very word which I spoke will

---

a34 Or *Messiah*   *b38* Isaiah 53:1   *c40* Isaiah 6:10

condemn him at the last day. ⁴⁹For I did not speak of my own accord, but the Father who sent me commanded me what to say and how to say it. ⁵⁰I know that his command leads to eternal life. So whatever I say is just what the Father has told me to say."

Jesus Washes His Disciples' Feet

13 It was just before the Passover Feast. Jesus knew that the time had come for him to leave this world and go to the Father. Having loved his own who were in the world, he now showed them the full extent of his love.*

²The evening meal was being served, and the devil had already prompted Judas Iscariot, son of Simon, to betray Jesus. ³Jesus knew that the Father had put all things under his power, and that he had come from God and was returning to God; ⁴so he got up from the meal, took off his outer clothing, and wrapped a towel around his waist. ⁵After that, he poured water into a basin and began to wash his disciples' feet, drying them with the towel that was wrapped around him.

⁶He came to Simon Peter, who said to him, "Lord, are you going to wash my feet?"

⁷Jesus replied, "You do not realize now what I am doing, but later you will understand."

⁸"No," said Peter, "you shall never wash my feet."

*1 Or *he loved them to the last*

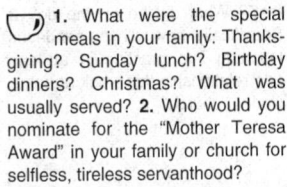

1. What were the special meals in your family: Thanksgiving? Sunday lunch? Birthday dinners? Christmas? What was usually served? **2.** Who would you nominate for the "Mother Teresa Award" in your family or church for selfless, tireless servanthood?

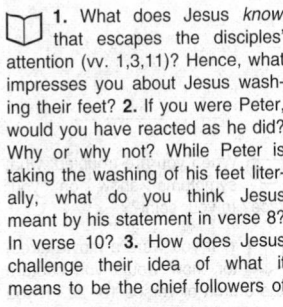

1. What does Jesus *know* that escapes the disciples' attention (vv. 1,3,11)? Hence, what impresses you about Jesus washing their feet? **2.** If you were Peter, would you have reacted as he did? Why or why not? While Peter is taking the washing of his feet literally, what do you think Jesus meant by his statement in verse 8? In verse 10? **3.** How does Jesus challenge their idea of what it means to be the chief followers of

---

   John 13:1–17 **JESUS WASHES THE DISCIPLES' FEET**

It was customary in Jesus' day for people's dusty, sandaled feet to be washed, usually by the lowest ranking servant, before a meal was served.

1. Why didn't the disciples wash their feet before supper?
   a. They forgot.
   b. They were slobs.
   c. It wasn't their job.
   d. There weren't any servants there.

2. What would you have done if Jesus wanted to wash your feet?
   a. left the room
   b. objected like Peter did
   c. insisted that I wash *his* feet
   d. kept quiet but felt uncomfortable
   e. felt honored by his caring act

3. What did Jesus mean when he said, "Unless I wash you, you have no part with me?"
   a. "I don't want to share a room with anyone with dirty feet."
   b. "To be part of me you have to learn to receive."
   c. "You have to let my coming sacrifice cleanse you from your sin."
   d. "As long as you live you will need cleansing and forgiveness."
   e. "Unless you're a servant like I am, you can't be my disciple."

4. Why did Jesus wash his disciples' feet?
   a. to shame them
   b. to be an example of servanthood
   c. to illustrate his whole mission
   d. to show them real leadership
   e. to show his deep love for them before he died

5. How did Jesus expect the disciples to follow his example?
   a. to wash each other's feet literally
   b. to be willing to do the "dirty work"
   c. to take care of each other
   d. to observe footwashing regularly in the church, like Communion

6. Why do you think Christians don't serve each other more than they do?

7. What one thing will you do at home, work or church this week to follow Jesus' example of serving?

8. What would it mean to practice footwashing in your marriage relationship?
   a. to serve my spouse more
   b. to let my spouse serve me
   c. to listen to my spouse more
   d. to show more affection
   e. to show more appreciation
   f. to be more patient and forgiving

g. to serve with no strings attached
h. to do things that aren't "my job"
i. to work at sharing unpleasant tasks

9. Growing up, how often did your family sit down and eat together? How much did you visit around the table? How does that compare to your current lifestyle?

10. How can you better serve your children?
   a. spend more time with them
   b. give them my undivided attention
   c. give them more affection
   d. bless them more with special meals and other fun occasions

11. Which of the following is true about your job?
   a. My job has nothing to do with serving—it's about making money.
   b. Jesus' example of servanthood is what keeps me going in my job.
   c. I have to do many servant tasks, most of which are pleasant.
   d. I have to do many servant tasks, most of which are unpleasant.
   e. Feeling underqualified for my job, I'd welcome more servant tasks.
   f. Feeling overqualified, I do more servant tasks than I would like.

the Messiah (vv. 12–17)? What role reversals do you see here?

♥ 1. In your spiritual life, who is one person who has demonstrated what it means to "wash feet"? What did he or she do? 2. Specifically, how will you put Jesus' teaching into practice in at least one relationship this week at home, work or church?

☕ When you are troubled, what symptoms show on your face? In your spirit?

📖 1. If you were a movie director, how would you capture the drama of verses 18–22? If you had been sitting at this table, what would you be feeling? Saying? 2. In foretelling his betrayal, what do you sense in Jesus: Resolution? Resignation? Restlessness? What do you sense in his disciples? In Judas? 3. Is Judas to be excused or held responsible when "Satan entered into him" (v. 27; also 6:70; 12:4–6; 13:2)?

♥ 1. If you knew ahead of time that someone would stab you in the back, how would you treat that person? How does Jesus show you what love is all about? 2. Given three years of very intimate fellowship with Jesus, how could Judas turn around and betray him? Have you ever betrayed Jesus? If so, how?

☕ What trait do you share with other family members?

📖 1. Why did Jesus wait until Judas had gone to share the message in verses 31–35? 2. What does he call the disciples to do (v. 34)? 3. What type of person is Peter (vv. 6–9,36–37)? How do you think he felt after verse 38?

♥ 1. How do your good intentions compare to Peter's? 2. On a scale from 1 to 10, how does your church rank against the standard of love? How could you increase its score?

Jesus answered, "Unless I wash you, you have no part with me." 9"Then, Lord," Simon Peter replied, "not just my feet but my hands and my head as well!"

10Jesus answered, "A person who has had a bath needs only to wash his feet; his whole body is clean. And you are clean, though not every one of you." 11For he knew who was going to betray him, and that was why he said not every one was clean.

12When he had finished washing their feet, he put on his clothes and returned to his place. "Do you understand what I have done for you?" he asked them. 13"You call me 'Teacher' and 'Lord,' and rightly so, for that is what I am. 14Now that I, your Lord and Teacher, have washed your feet, you also should wash one another's feet. 15I have set you an example that you should do as I have done for you. 16I tell you the truth, no servant is greater than his master, nor is a messenger greater than the one who sent him. 17Now that you know these things, you will be blessed if you do them.

Jesus Predicts His Betrayal

18"I am not referring to all of you; I know those I have chosen. But this is to fulfill the scripture: 'He who shares my bread has lifted up his heel against me.'ᵃ

19"I am telling you now before it happens, so that when it does happen you will believe that I am He. 20I tell you the truth, whoever accepts anyone I send accepts me; and whoever accepts me accepts the one who sent me."

21After he had said this, Jesus was troubled in spirit and testified, "I tell you the truth, one of you is going to betray me."

22His disciples stared at one another, at a loss to know which of them he meant. 23One of them, the disciple whom Jesus loved, was reclining next to him. 24Simon Peter motioned to this disciple and said, "Ask him which one he means."

25Leaning back against Jesus, he asked him, "Lord, who is it?"

26Jesus answered, "It is the one to whom I will give this piece of bread when I have dipped it in the dish." Then, dipping the piece of bread, he gave it to Judas Iscariot, son of Simon. 27As soon as Judas took the bread, Satan entered into him.

"What you are about to do, do quickly," Jesus told him, 28but no one at the meal understood why Jesus said this to him. 29Since Judas had charge of the money, some thought Jesus was telling him to buy what was needed for the Feast, or to give something to the poor. 30As soon as Judas had taken the bread, he went out. And it was night.

Jesus Predicts Peter's Denial

31When he was gone, Jesus said, "Now is the Son of Man glorified and God is glorified in him. 32If God is glorified in him,ᵇ God will glorify the Son in himself, and will glorify him at once.

33"My children, I will be with you only a little longer. You will look for me, and just as I told the Jews, so I tell you now: Where I am going, you cannot come.

34"A new command I give you: Love one another. As I have loved you, so you must love one another. 35By this all men will know that you are my disciples, if you love one another."

36Simon Peter asked him, "Lord, where are you going?"

Jesus replied, "Where I am going, you cannot follow now, but you will follow later."

ᵃ18 Psalm 41:9   ᵇ32 Many early manuscripts do not have *If God is glorified in him.*

³⁷Peter asked, "Lord, why can't I follow you now? I will lay down my life for you."

³⁸Then Jesus answered, "Will you really lay down your life for me? I tell you the truth, before the rooster crows, you will disown me three times!

Jesus Comforts His Disciples

14 "Do not let your hearts be troubled. Trust in God[a]; trust also in me. ²In my Father's house are many rooms; if it were not so, I would have told you. I am going there to prepare a place for you. ³And if I go and prepare a place for you, I will come back and take you to be with me that you also may be where I am. ⁴You know the way to the place where I am going."

Jesus the Way to the Father

⁵Thomas said to him, "Lord, we don't know where you are going, so how can we know the way?"

⁶Jesus answered, "I am the way and the truth and the life. No one comes to the Father except through me. ⁷If you really knew me, you would know[b] my Father as well. From now on, you do know him and have seen him."

⁸Philip said, "Lord, show us the Father and that will be enough for us."

⁹Jesus answered: "Don't you know me, Philip, even after I have been among you such a long time? Anyone who has seen me has seen the Father. How can you say, 'Show us the Father'? ¹⁰Don't you believe that I am in the Father, and that the Father is in me? The words I say to you are not just my own. Rather, it is the Father, living in me, who is doing his work. ¹¹Believe me when I say that I am in the Father and the Father is in me; or at least believe on the evidence of the miracles themselves. ¹²I tell you the truth, anyone who has faith in me will do what I have been doing. He will do even greater things than these, because I am going to the Father. ¹³And I will do whatever you ask in my name, so that the Son may bring glory to the Father. ¹⁴You may ask me for anything in my name, and I will do it.

Jesus Promises the Holy Spirit

¹⁵"If you love me, you will obey what I command. ¹⁶And I will ask the Father, and he will give you another Counselor to be with you forever— ¹⁷the Spirit of truth. The world cannot accept him, because it neither sees him nor knows him. But you know him, for he lives with you and will be[c] in you. ¹⁸I will not leave you as orphans; I will come to you. ¹⁹Before long, the world will not see me anymore, but you will see me. Because I live, you also will live. ²⁰On that day you will realize that I am in my Father, and you are in me, and I am in you. ²¹Whoever has my commands and obeys them, he is the one who loves me. He who loves me will be loved by my Father, and I too will love him and show myself to him."

²²Then Judas (not Judas Iscariot) said, "But, Lord, why do you intend to show yourself to us and not to the world?"

²³Jesus replied, "If anyone loves me, he will obey my teaching. My Father will love him, and we will come to him and make our home with him. ²⁴He who does not love me will not obey my teaching. These words you hear are not my own; they belong to the Father who sent me.

²⁵"All this I have spoken while still with you. ²⁶But the Counsel-

1. What is your favorite room in the house? Why? 2. Can you remember a time when you got lost? What happened?

1. What comfort does Jesus offer his disciples? 2. Look at 13:36, 14:6,8, and 22. What problems are the disciples struggling with? 3. Put Jesus' statement in 14:6–7 in your own words. 4. How does 1:18 relate to what Jesus says in 14:9? With what tone of voice do you imagine Jesus speaking in verses 9–14? What evidence does Jesus give for his claims? 5. Do you think the promises Jesus makes in verses 12–14 are "blank check" promises about prayer? In verse 12, does he mean the church will do works greater in *power*? Greater in *scope*? How could this be?

1. If Jesus is the Way, do you feel you are on a bumpy dead-end street, or on a four-lane highway? Why? 2. In light of 14:6, how would you respond to someone who says, "there are many ways to God"?

Who was the best counselor you ever had? Why was this person so special?

1. How are the disciples to show love to each other (13:34)? To Jesus (14:15)? Why is this idea repeated four times (vv. 15,21,23–24)? 2. What do you learn about the Holy Spirit in verses 16–17 and 25–27? What is the relationship of the Father, Jesus and the Holy Spirit to the believer? To each other? 3. What is the difference between how *Jesus* gives peace and how the *world* does?

1. How at home are the Father, Son and Holy Spirit in your life? Are they more like owners, or temporary guests? 2. On a scale from 1 (smooth sailing) to 10 (furious storm), what is your peace quotient? Why? Where do you need Jesus' peace? Where can you find

hope in this passage? **3.** How
has the Holy Spirit revealed Jesus
in your life? **4.** Of all the promises
made here (vv. 16–18,21,23,26–
27), which one means the most to
you? Why?

or, the Holy Spirit, whom the Father will send in my name, will
teach you all things and will remind you of everything I have said
to you. [27]Peace I leave with you; my peace I give you. I do not give
to you as the world gives. Do not let your hearts be troubled and do
not be afraid.

[28]"You heard me say, 'I am going away and I am coming back to
you.' If you loved me, you would be glad that I am going to the
Father, for the Father is greater than I. [29]I have told you now
before it happens, so that when it does happen you will believe. [30]I
will not speak with you much longer, for the prince of this world is
coming. He has no hold on me, [31]but the world must learn that I
love the Father and that I do exactly what my Father has commanded me.

"Come now; let us leave."

The Vine and the Branches

15 "I am the true vine, and my Father is the gardener. [2]He
cuts off every branch in me that bears no fruit, while every
branch that does bear fruit he prunes[a] so that it will be even more
fruitful. [3]You are already clean because of the word I have spoken
to you. [4]Remain in me, and I will remain in you. No branch can
bear fruit by itself; it must remain in the vine. Neither can you bear
fruit unless you remain in me.

[5]"I am the vine; you are the branches. If a man remains in me
and I in him, he will bear much fruit; apart from me you can do
nothing. [6]If anyone does not remain in me, he is like a branch that
is thrown away and withers; such branches are picked up, thrown
into the fire and burned. [7]If you remain in me and my words
remain in you, ask whatever you wish, and it will be given you.
[8]This is to my Father's glory, that you bear much fruit, showing
yourselves to be my disciples.

[9]"As the Father has loved me, so have I loved you. Now remain
in my love. [10]If you obey my commands, you will remain in my
love, just as I have obeyed my Father's commands and remain in
his love. [11]I have told you this so that my joy may be in you and
that your joy may be complete. [12]My command is this: Love each
other as I have loved you. [13]Greater love has no one than this, that
he lay down his life for his friends. [14]You are my friends if you do
what I command. [15]I no longer call you servants, because a servant
does not know his master's business. Instead, I have called you
friends, for everything that I learned from my Father I have made
known to you. [16]You did not choose me, but I chose you and
appointed you to go and bear fruit—fruit that will last. Then the
Father will give you whatever you ask in my name. [17]This is my
command: Love each other.

The World Hates the Disciples

[18]"If the world hates you, keep in mind that it hated me first. [19]If
you belonged to the world, it would love you as its own. As it is,
you do not belong to the world, but I have chosen you out of the
world. That is why the world hates you. [20]Remember the words I
spoke to you: 'No servant is greater than his master.'[b] If they
persecuted me, they will persecute you also. If they obeyed my
teaching, they will obey yours also. [21]They will treat you this way
because of my name, for they do not know the One who sent me.
[22]If I had not come and spoken to them, they would not be guilty
of sin. Now, however, they have no excuse for their sin. [23]He who

What plant best describes
you now: Towering oak?
Weeping willow? Tumbleweed?
Crab apple tree? Explain.

1. If vine branches were human lives, what pain would
be associated with pruning? What
tools? What fruit? **2.** Jesus repeats
remain in me, *love* and *bear fruit*.
How are these words related?
What is the "fruit that will last"
(v. 16)? **3.** How do verses 9 and 12
tie together? How is love the essential dynamic of the Christian
life? How does your relationship
with Jesus change once you start
practicing his example of love? **4.**
What is the link between obedience and prayer (vv. 7,16; see
14:13–14)?

1. As a branch on Christ's
vine, how would you describe
the fruit in your life: Grade A–1?
Juicy? Green? Wormy? Why? **2.**
Do you feel more like Jesus' servant or his friend? What helps develop the friendship?

Have you ever been to a
large group or reunion of
someone else's family? How did
you feel?

1. Since the emphasis in
15:9–17 was on love, why
does Jesus now talk about hate?
What does Jesus mean here by
"the world"? How is the relationship
of the disciples to the world like that
of Jesus' relationship to it? **2.** What
do you see in the relationship between the Father, Jesus and the
disciples? **3.** How has Jesus' com-

[a]2 The Greek for *prunes* also means *cleans*.   [b]20 John 13:16

hates me hates my Father as well. [24]If I had not done among them what no one else did, they would not be guilty of sin. But now they have seen these miracles, and yet they have hated both me and my Father. [25]But this is to fulfill what is written in their Law: 'They hated me without reason.'[a]

[26]"When the Counselor comes, whom I will send to you from the Father, the Spirit of truth who goes out from the Father, he will testify about me. [27]And you also must testify, for you have been with me from the beginning.

16 "All this I have told you so that you will not go astray. [2]They will put you out of the synagogue; in fact, a time is coming when anyone who kills you will think he is offering a service to God. [3]They will do such things because they have not known the Father or me. [4]I have told you this, so that when the time comes you will remember that I warned you. I did not tell you this at first because I was with you.

The Work of the Holy Spirit

[5]"Now I am going to him who sent me, yet none of you asks me, 'Where are you going?' [6]Because I have said these things, you are filled with grief. [7]But I tell you the truth: It is for your good that I am going away. Unless I go away, the Counselor will not come to you; but if I go, I will send him to you. [8]When he comes, he will convict the world of guilt[b] in regard to sin and righteousness and judgment: [9]in regard to sin, because men do not believe in me; [10]in regard to righteousness, because I am going to the Father, where you can see me no longer; [11]and in regard to judgment, because the prince of this world now stands condemned.

[12]"I have much more to say to you, more than you can now bear. [13]But when he, the Spirit of truth, comes, he will guide you into all truth. He will not speak on his own; he will speak only what he hears, and he will tell you what is yet to come. [14]He will bring glory to me by taking from what is mine and making it known to you. [15]All that belongs to the Father is mine. That is why I said the Spirit will take from what is mine and make it known to you.

[16]"In a little while you will see me no more, and then after a little while you will see me."

The Disciples' Grief Will Turn to Joy

[17]Some of his disciples said to one another, "What does he mean by saying, 'In a little while you will see me no more, and then after a little while you will see me,' and 'Because I am going to the Father'?" [18]They kept asking, "What does he mean by 'a little while'? We don't understand what he is saying."

[19]Jesus saw that they wanted to ask him about this, so he said to them, "Are you asking one another what I meant when I said, 'In a little while you will see me no more, and then after a little while you will see me'? [20]I tell you the truth, you will weep and mourn while the world rejoices. You will grieve, but your grief will turn to joy. [21]A woman giving birth to a child has pain because her time has come; but when her baby is born she forgets the anguish because of her joy that a child is born into the world. [22]So with you: Now is your time of grief, but I will see you again and you will rejoice, and no one will take away your joy. [23]In that day you will no longer ask me anything. I tell you the truth, my Father will give you whatever you ask in my name. [24]Until now you have not asked

ing highlighted the reality and evil of sin (vv. 22,24)?

♥ **1.** When have you found that speaking truth and showing love can lead to hostility from others? How do you explain that? **2.** How do you handle people who are religious but not godly?

How are you at saying "good-bye"? Is it harder for you to be the one leaving home, or the one left behind? Explain.

1. What are the disciples feeling now? What is their grief keeping them from understanding (v. 17)? **2.** How would you paraphrase the three goals of the Spirit's work (vv. 8–11)? Therefore, why is it good that Jesus goes away? **3.** If you were a disciple, how would you feel after hearing verse 16?

♥ **1.** Of the various roles of the Holy Spirit described here, which one have you come to appreciate recently? **2.** Has Jesus ever said things to you that you could hardly bear (v. 12)? What happened?

Did your parents ever tell you about your birth experience? What was it like for them?

1. What tones of voice do you hear in verses 17–18? If you were there, would Jesus' answer encourage you, or confuse you more? **2.** What event is Jesus referring to in verses 20–22? In what ways does the world's "joy" (v. 20) contrast with the joy the disciples will experience (v. 22)? How is this similar to what Jesus said about dying (12:24)? About peace (14:27)? **3.** What characterizes the relationship we can have with the Father because of Jesus (vv. 23–27)? **4.** Do you think the disciples truly grasp what Jesus says in verse 28? Why?

---

a25 Psalms 35:19; 69:4   b8 Or *will expose the guilt of the world*

1. Both Jesus and the world offer a form of peace (14:27; 16:33), joy (15:11; 16:22–24) and love (13:34–35; 15:9–19). How have you experienced each of these? What is different between them? 2. How do you deal with change? Moves? Job transfers? Transitions from one stage of your life to another? How has pain helped you to grow? 3. From your experience, how could you comfort someone going through change? 4. How do you desire joy? How do you experience it?

1. What going-away gift have you received or given that still warms your heart or brings a smile? 2. What is the best reason you have heard for not believing in Jesus as Savior?

1. What event is it now "time" for (v. 1; 12:23–24)? 2. What does it mean to "glorify" someone (vv. 4–5,10,22,24)? How is Jesus' deity emphasized here? 3. Who is the focal point of Jesus' prayer in verses 6–19? Why? If you had to file a report to the Father on Jesus' activities, how would you verify verses 6–8? 4. What is Jesus' concern in verses 11 and 15? What does he mean by "the name you gave me" (see 8:58; Ex 3:14)? What do the events surrounding the original revelation of this name show about its power to save (Ex 3:7–10)? 5. What does he mean by his request in verse 17? What is its purpose? 6. Who is the focus of Jesus' prayer in verses 20–26? Toward what end? What kind of unity exists between God and Jesus that we should copy? 7. What does Jesus' ultimate desire (v. 24) reveal about his love for us? 8. How do verses 25–26 sum up the major concerns of Jesus in chapters 13–16?

1. This week, whom have you glorified by the way you lived? How so? 2. What two phrases sum up your goal for the past year? How does this relate to God's purpose? 3. How are your prayers for others like and unlike Jesus' prayer? Do your prayers re-

for anything in my name. Ask and you will receive, and your joy will be complete.

25"Though I have been speaking figuratively, a time is coming when I will no longer use this kind of language but will tell you plainly about my Father. 26In that day you will ask in my name. I am not saying that I will ask the Father on your behalf. 27No, the Father himself loves you because you have loved me and have believed that I came from God. 28I came from the Father and entered the world; now I am leaving the world and going back to the Father."

29Then Jesus' disciples said, "Now you are speaking clearly and without figures of speech. 30Now we can see that you know all things and that you do not even need to have anyone ask you questions. This makes us believe that you came from God."

31"You believe at last!"[a] Jesus answered. 32"But a time is coming, and has come, when you will be scattered, each to his own home. You will leave me all alone. Yet I am not alone, for my Father is with me.

33"I have told you these things, so that in me you may have peace. In this world you will have trouble. But take heart! I have overcome the world."

Jesus Prays for Himself

17 After Jesus said this, he looked toward heaven and prayed: "Father, the time has come. Glorify your Son, that your Son may glorify you. 2For you granted him authority over all people that he might give eternal life to all those you have given him. 3Now this is eternal life: that they may know you, the only true God, and Jesus Christ, whom you have sent. 4I have brought you glory on earth by completing the work you gave me to do. 5And now, Father, glorify me in your presence with the glory I had with you before the world began.

Jesus Prays for His Disciples

6"I have revealed you[b] to those whom you gave me out of the world. They were yours; you gave them to me and they have obeyed your word. 7Now they know that everything you have given me comes from you. 8For I gave them the words you gave me and they accepted them. They knew with certainty that I came from you, and they believed that you sent me. 9I pray for them. I am not praying for the world, but for those you have given me, for they are yours. 10All I have is yours, and all you have is mine. And glory has come to me through them. 11I will remain in the world no longer, but they are still in the world, and I am coming to you. Holy Father, protect them by the power of your name—the name you gave me—so that they may be one as we are one. 12While I was with them, I protected them and kept them safe by that name you gave me. None has been lost except the one doomed to destruction so that Scripture would be fulfilled.

13"I am coming to you now, but I say these things while I am still in the world, so that they may have the full measure of my joy within them. 14I have given them your word and the world has hated them, for they are not of the world any more than I am of the world. 15My prayer is not that you take them out of the world but that you protect them from the evil one.

a31 Or "Do you now believe?"   b6 Greek your name; also in verse 26

16They are not of the world, even as I am not of it. 17Sanctify[a] them by the truth; your word is truth. 18As you sent me into the world, I have sent them into the world. 19For them I sanctify myself, that they too may be truly sanctified.

Jesus Prays for All Believers

20"My prayer is not for them alone. I pray also for those who will believe in me through their message, 21that all of them may be one, Father, just as you are in me and I am in you. May they also be in us so that the world may believe that you have sent me. 22I have given them the glory that you gave me, that they may be one as we are one: 23I in them and you in me. May they be brought to complete unity to let the world know that you sent me and have loved them even as you have loved me.

24"Father, I want those you have given me to be with me where I am, and to see my glory, the glory you have given me because you loved me before the creation of the world.

25"Righteous Father, though the world does not know you, I know you, and they know that you have sent me. 26I have made you known to them, and will continue to make you known in order that the love you have for me may be in them and that I myself may be in them."

Jesus Arrested

18 When he had finished praying, Jesus left with his disciples and crossed the Kidron Valley. On the other side there was an olive grove, and he and his disciples went into it.

2Now Judas, who betrayed him, knew the place, because Jesus had often met there with his disciples. 3So Judas came to the grove, guiding a detachment of soldiers and some officials from the chief priests and Pharisees. They were carrying torches, lanterns and weapons.

4Jesus, knowing all that was going to happen to him, went out and asked them, "Who is it you want?"

5"Jesus of Nazareth," they replied.

"I am he," Jesus said. (And Judas the traitor was standing there with them.) 6When Jesus said, "I am he," they drew back and fell to the ground.

7Again he asked them, "Who is it you want?"

And they said, "Jesus of Nazareth."

8"I told you that I am he," Jesus answered. "If you are looking for me, then let these men go." 9This happened so that the words he had spoken would be fulfilled: "I have not lost one of those you gave me."[b]

10Then Simon Peter, who had a sword, drew it and struck the high priest's servant, cutting off his right ear. (The servant's name was Malchus.)

11Jesus commanded Peter, "Put your sword away! Shall I not drink the cup the Father has given me?"

Jesus Taken to Annas

12Then the detachment of soldiers with its commander and the Jewish officials arrested Jesus. They bound him 13and brought him first to Annas, who was the father-in-law of Caiaphas, the high priest that year. 14Caiaphas was the one who had advised the Jews that it would be good if one man died for the people.

---

a17 Greek *hagiazo (set apart for sacred use* or *make holy)*; also in verse 19
b9 John 6:39

---

flect the short-term urgent, or the long-term important needs that people have? What can you apply to your prayer skills from this chapter? **4.** How does the fact that Jesus existed before the world began affect the way you live? **5.** How important to you is unity with other believers? With whom do you share this unity? How can you experience more unity?

Where do you go when you need to prepare yourself for a very stressful time?

1. Why do the Pharisees want to take advantage of the night to arrest Jesus (see 3:19–20; 12:35; 13:30)? **2.** How do you think the disciples felt when they saw these menacing-looking people coming? Jesus used many "I am ..." sayings (vine, light, bread). How do you explain verse 6? **3.** Seeing how he deals with the soldiers (vv. 4,8) and Peter (v. 11), what do you learn about Jesus? **4.** How does Peter show he still doesn't grasp what is going on? **5.** What is "the cup" which Jesus must drink (v. 11)? **6.** Given his pacifism, why is Jesus bound (v. 12)? Who's afraid of whom here? Why?

1. Have you ever tried to obey Jesus, only to be overzealous and ending up hurting someone? What happened? **2.** How does Jesus' decision to "drink the cup" (v. 11) help you in your obedience to God? What issue of obedience is challenging you?

1. As a child, what was one "big" thing you really messed up on: Missing the catch for the final out? Forgetting the crucial line in the school play? Leaving something behind, never to be recovered? 2. After forgetting a name or messing up, what did you do?

1. What do you think Peter and the other disciple hoped to do? How do you account for the difference between Peter here (v. 17) and in the garden (18:10)? 2. What is ironic about the high priest's questioning of Jesus? 3. How do Jesus' answers expose this trial as a mockery (v. 23)? If you were there, what would you have done on Jesus' behalf? 4. What feelings must Peter have had after the rooster crowed (v. 27; see 13:37–38)? What do you suppose Peter did at that point?

1. How does the story of Peter both humble and encourage you? When have you felt like Peter? 2. How do you explain the ups and downs in your own spiritual life? 3. When have you dealt with someone whose mind was so made up that the facts didn't matter? How do you deal with this when it relates to your faith?

As a child, were you ever blamed for something you didn't do? How did you react?

1. Where was Jesus taken next? When? Why are the Jewish leaders rushing this trial? 2. What is the irony in verse 28? 3. What reason do they finally give Pilate for bringing Jesus to him (vv. 33–34)? Why would Pilate take this seriously? How are Pilate's fears like those of the Jewish leaders in 11:48? 4. What does Jesus tell Pilate about his kingdom (vv. 36–37)? Who is included in it? What do you think Pilate meant by his concerns in verse 38? 5. In his pursuit of "truth," is Pilate trying to absolve himself, or Jesus? Why do you think so?

1. Since both Peter and Pilate caved in under pressure, why do we tend to scorn Pilate but honor Peter? 2. Do you see any of

Peter's First Denial

15Simon Peter and another disciple were following Jesus. Because this disciple was known to the high priest, he went with Jesus into the high priest's courtyard, 16but Peter had to wait outside at the door. The other disciple, who was known to the high priest, came back, spoke to the girl on duty there and brought Peter in.

17"You are not one of his disciples, are you?" the girl at the door asked Peter.

He replied, "I am not."

18It was cold, and the servants and officials stood around a fire they had made to keep warm. Peter also was standing with them, warming himself.

The High Priest Questions Jesus

19Meanwhile, the high priest questioned Jesus about his disciples and his teaching.

20"I have spoken openly to the world," Jesus replied. "I always taught in synagogues or at the temple, where all the Jews come together. I said nothing in secret. 21Why question me? Ask those who heard me. Surely they know what I said."

22When Jesus said this, one of the officials nearby struck him in the face. "Is this the way you answer the high priest?" he demanded.

23"If I said something wrong," Jesus replied, "testify as to what is wrong. But if I spoke the truth, why did you strike me?" 24Then Annas sent him, still bound, to Caiaphas the high priest.[a]

Peter's Second and Third Denials

25As Simon Peter stood warming himself, he was asked, "You are not one of his disciples, are you?"

He denied it, saying, "I am not."

26One of the high priest's servants, a relative of the man whose ear Peter had cut off, challenged him, "Didn't I see you with him in the olive grove?" 27Again Peter denied it, and at that moment a rooster began to crow.

Jesus Before Pilate

28Then the Jews led Jesus from Caiaphas to the palace of the Roman governor. By now it was early morning, and to avoid ceremonial uncleanness the Jews did not enter the palace; they wanted to be able to eat the Passover. 29So Pilate came out to them and asked, "What charges are you bringing against this man?"

30"If he were not a criminal," they replied, "we would not have handed him over to you."

31Pilate said, "Take him yourselves and judge him by your own law."

"But we have no right to execute anyone," the Jews objected. 32This happened so that the words Jesus had spoken indicating the kind of death he was going to die would be fulfilled.

33Pilate then went back inside the palace, summoned Jesus and asked him, "Are you the king of the Jews?"

34"Is that your own idea," Jesus asked, "or did others talk to you about me?"

35"Am I a Jew?" Pilate replied. "It was your people and your chief priests who handed you over to me. What is it you have done?"

a24 Or (Now Annas had sent him, still bound, to Caiaphas the high priest.)

³⁶Jesus said, "My kingdom is not of this world. If it were, my servants would fight to prevent my arrest by the Jews. But now my kingdom is from another place."

³⁷"You are a king, then!" said Pilate.

Jesus answered, "You are right in saying I am a king. In fact, for this reason I was born, and for this I came into the world, to testify to the truth. Everyone on the side of truth listens to me."

³⁸"What is truth?" Pilate asked. With this he went out again to the Jews and said, "I find no basis for a charge against him. ³⁹But it is your custom for me to release to you one prisoner at the time of the Passover. Do you want me to release 'the king of the Jews'?"

⁴⁰They shouted back, "No, not him! Give us Barabbas!" Now Barabbas had taken part in a rebellion.

Jesus Sentenced to be Crucified

19 Then Pilate took Jesus and had him flogged. ²The soldiers twisted together a crown of thorns and put it on his head. They clothed him in a purple robe ³and went up to him again and again, saying, "Hail, king of the Jews!" And they struck him in the face.

⁴Once more Pilate came out and said to the Jews, "Look, I am bringing him out to you to let you know that I find no basis for a charge against him." ⁵When Jesus came out wearing the crown of thorns and the purple robe, Pilate said to them, "Here is the man!"

⁶As soon as the chief priests and their officials saw him, they shouted, "Crucify! Crucify!"

But Pilate answered, "You take him and crucify him. As for me, I find no basis for a charge against him."

⁷The Jews insisted, "We have a law, and according to that law he must die, because he claimed to be the Son of God."

⁸When Pilate heard this, he was even more afraid, ⁹and he went back inside the palace. "Where do you come from?" he asked Jesus, but Jesus gave him no answer. ¹⁰"Do you refuse to speak to me?" Pilate said. "Don't you realize I have power either to free you or to crucify you?"

¹¹Jesus answered, "You would have no power over me if it were not given to you from above. Therefore the one who handed me over to you is guilty of a greater sin."

¹²From then on, Pilate tried to set Jesus free, but the Jews kept shouting, "If you let this man go, you are no friend of Caesar. Anyone who claims to be a king opposes Caesar."

¹³When Pilate heard this, he brought Jesus out and sat down on the judge's seat at a place known as the Stone Pavement (which in Aramaic is Gabbatha). ¹⁴It was the day of Preparation of Passover Week, about the sixth hour.

"Here is your king," Pilate said to the Jews.

¹⁵But they shouted, "Take him away! Take him away! Crucify him!"

"Shall I crucify your king?" Pilate asked.

"We have no king but Caesar," the chief priests answered.

¹⁶Finally Pilate handed him over to them to be crucified.

The Crucifixion

So the soldiers took charge of Jesus. ¹⁷Carrying his own cross, he went out to the place of the Skull (which in Aramaic is called Golgotha). ¹⁸Here they crucified him, and with him two others—one on each side and Jesus in the middle.

¹⁹Pilate had a notice prepared and fastened to the cross. It read: JESUS OF NAZARETH, THE KING OF THE JEWS. ²⁰Many of the Jews read this

---

Pilate's qualities in yourself? **3.** How does Barabbas' freedom at Christ's expense illustrate the Gospel?

Were you ever bullied as a kid? What happened?

1. In view of Pilate's convictions (see 18:38; 19:4,6), why would he allow Jesus to be struck? Are the soldiers cruel, or are there deeper hates and fears involved? Despite the mock coronation (vv. 2–3), what did Jesus actually deserve? **2.** Why do the Jewish leaders clamor for Jesus to be crucified? What does Pilate's fearful response to that charge show about him? How might his conversation with Jesus in 18:33–37 have influenced him? **3.** What is the implied threat to Pilate in verse 12? **4.** What does the priests' reply (v. 15) indicate about their spiritual condition? Why is this especially ironic (see 8:33,41)? **5.** Pretend you are Pilate. How would you explain to your wife later that night why you finally let Jesus be killed?

When have you made a decision based on fear and ambition, rather than on what is right? How do you feel about that now? How can you guard against it in the future?

What movie or book (such as "Jesus Christ Superstar," "Godspell," or "Jesus of Nazareth") brought home to you most vividly the events of the crucifixion?

1. According to the sign on Jesus' cross, for what "official" reason was he crucified? What meaning does this title have for Pilate (18:33–37)? For the soldiers (19:14–15)? The chief priests (19:14–15)? Is this title being used here sincerely or mockingly? Why is it in all three common languages? **2.** As Jesus may have recited Psalm 22 from the cross (Mt 27:46), how might he have felt as he watched the soldiers take his clothes (vv. 23–24) (Ps 22:18)? **3.** Given Jesus' mother's faith in him at the outset of his public ministry (2:3–5), what must she be feeling now at the end? Why is Old Testament prophecy about Jesus' death (Ex 12:46; Zech 12:10) so important in this chapter? **4.** From here and throughout John's Gospel, we see that Jesus' death has special paradoxical meaning: In what sense was Jesus' death necessary, yet voluntary? Triumphant, yet tragic? Pre-ordained, yet avoidable? Lifted up, yet laid down? Unjust, yet just? Finished, yet ongoing?

 1. If Jesus preached the same Gospel today that he preached in the first century, who might be the "chief priests," the "Peters" and "Pilates"? Who would

sign, for the place where Jesus was crucified was near the city, and the sign was written in Aramaic, Latin and Greek. ²¹The chief priests of the Jews protested to Pilate, "Do not write 'The King of the Jews,' but that this man claimed to be king of the Jews."

²²Pilate answered, "What I have written, I have written."

²³When the soldiers crucified Jesus, they took his clothes, dividing them into four shares, one for each of them, with the undergarment remaining. This garment was seamless, woven in one piece from top to bottom.

²⁴"Let's not tear it," they said to one another. "Let's decide by lot who will get it."

This happened that the scripture might be fulfilled which said,

> "They divided my garments among them
> and cast lots for my clothing." *a*

So this is what the soldiers did.

²⁵Near the cross of Jesus stood his mother, his mother's sister, Mary the wife of Clopas, and Mary Magdalene. ²⁶When Jesus saw his mother there, and the disciple whom he loved standing nearby, he said to his mother, "Dear woman, here is your son," ²⁷and to the disciple, "Here is your mother." From that time on, this disciple took her into his home.

The Death of Jesus

²⁸Later, knowing that all was now completed, and so that the Scripture would be fulfilled, Jesus said, "I am thirsty." ²⁹A jar of wine vinegar was there, so they soaked a sponge in it, put the

a 24 Psalm 22:18

John 19:16–27   THE CRUCIFIXION

1. Why did the chief priests, who plotted Jesus' crucifixion, protest to Pilate about the sign he fastened to the cross: "Jesus of Nazareth, the King of the Jews"?
   a. The sign was too confusing.
   b. They thought Pilate was mocking them.
   c. The truth hurts.
   d. No matter how they tried, they couldn't escape Jesus' claims.

2. How do you think Jesus felt about the soldiers entertaining themselves by gambling for his clothes?
   a. humiliated
   b. angry
   c. forgiving
   d. too distraught to notice
   e. aware that an Old Testament Scripture was being fulfilled
   f. aware that everything happening was somehow part of God's plan

3. What motivated Jesus to go through with this humiliating death when he could have used his tremendous power to avoid it?

4. What feelings do you think Mary had as she watched her son die?
   a. She was confused.
   b. She really wasn't surprised.
   c. She felt incredible anguish.
   d. She realized Jesus' death was necessary, so she was at peace.
   e. She was angry at the injustice.

5. What feelings do you think Jesus had when he saw his mother?
   a. He was in too much agony to be concerned.
   b. He felt helpless.
   c. He felt compassion for her.
   d. He loved her and wanted to look out for her welfare.

6. Why do you think Jesus charged John ("the disciple whom he loved") with taking care of his mother?
   a. Mary's husband Joseph must have been dead.
   b. Jesus' brothers must not have believed in him yet.
   c. John was Jesus' favorite disciple.
   d. Jesus recognized the importance of a "spiritual family."

7. Can you picture the scene of Jesus' crucifixion? What makes Good Friday "good"? For whom?

8. When, and how, did the crucifixion begin to make a difference in your life? How could you explain the need for Jesus' death to someone who really wanted to understand?

9. What does Jesus entrusting his mother and John to each other say to you about being "spiritually single"?
   a. Biological family is important to Jesus.
   b. Spiritual family is important to Jesus.
   c. Our relationships with other Christians are indeed *family* relationships.
   d. My spiritual family can help fill the void of my spouse's lack of spiritual commitment.

10. How have the people in this group become a spiritual family for you? How can they continue to support you in prayer?

sponge on a stalk of the hyssop plant, and lifted it to Jesus' lips. ³⁰When he had received the drink, Jesus said, "It is finished." With that, he bowed his head and gave up his spirit.

³¹Now it was the day of Preparation, and the next day was to be a special Sabbath. Because the Jews did not want the bodies left on the crosses during the Sabbath, they asked Pilate to have the legs broken and the bodies taken down. ³²The soldiers therefore came and broke the legs of the first man who had been crucified with Jesus, and then those of the other. ³³But when they came to Jesus and found that he was already dead, they did not break his legs. ³⁴Instead, one of the soldiers pierced Jesus' side with a spear, bringing a sudden flow of blood and water. ³⁵The man who saw it has given testimony, and his testimony is true. He knows that he tells the truth, and he testifies so that you also may believe. ³⁶These things happened so that the scripture would be fulfilled: "Not one of his bones will be broken,"ᵃ ³⁷and, as another scripture says, "They will look on the one they have pierced."ᵇ

The Burial of Jesus

³⁸Later, Joseph of Arimathea asked Pilate for the body of Jesus. Now Joseph was a disciple of Jesus, but secretly because he feared the Jews. With Pilate's permission, he came and took the body away. ³⁹He was accompanied by Nicodemus, the man who earlier had visited Jesus at night. Nicodemus brought a mixture of myrrh and aloes, about seventy-five pounds.ᶜ ⁴⁰Taking Jesus' body, the two of them wrapped it, with the spices, in strips of linen. This was in accordance with Jewish burial customs. ⁴¹At the place where Jesus was crucified, there was a garden, and in the garden a new tomb, in which no one had ever been laid. ⁴²Because it was the Jewish day of Preparation and since the tomb was nearby, they laid Jesus there.

The Empty Tomb

20 Early on the first day of the week, while it was still dark, Mary Magdalene went to the tomb and saw that the stone had been removed from the entrance. ²So she came running to Simon Peter and the other disciple, the one Jesus loved, and said, "They have taken the Lord out of the tomb, and we don't know where they have put him!"

³So Peter and the other disciple started for the tomb. ⁴Both were running, but the other disciple outran Peter and reached the tomb first. ⁵He bent over and looked in at the strips of linen lying there but did not go in. ⁶Then Simon Peter, who was behind him, arrived and went into the tomb. He saw the strips of linen lying there, ⁷as well as the burial cloth that had been around Jesus' head. The cloth was folded up by itself, separate from the linen. ⁸Finally the other disciple, who had reached the tomb first, also went inside. He saw and believed. ⁹(They still did not understand from Scripture that Jesus had to rise from the dead.)

Jesus Appears to Mary Magdalene

¹⁰Then the disciples went back to their homes, ¹¹but Mary stood outside the tomb crying. As she wept, she bent over to look into the tomb ¹²and saw two angels in white, seated where Jesus' body had been, one at the head and the other at the foot.

¹³They asked her, "Woman, why are you crying?"

"They have taken my Lord away," she said, "and I don't know

---

you be? **2.** How would you explain the need for the crucifixion to someone else? **3.** How is Jesus' death real to you? How have Jesus' "blood" and "water" touched your life? What would your life be like without them?

What kind of burial would you like: Large? Small? Somber? Boisterous? Where would you prefer to be buried? Why?

1. Why did secret believers, Joseph and Nicodemus, risk public exposure now? **2.** Some say Jesus did not really die, but revived in the tomb. How do 19:1,18,32–34 and 40 disprove this notion?

1. How does your fear of others and your love for Jesus sometimes conflict? **2.** In spite of past failures and fears, what will you do this week to show love for Jesus?

When something upsets you, who is the first one you tell?

1. Put yourself in the place of Mary. What is your emotional state two days after the crucifixion? Why do you visit the tomb so early? Realizing the body is gone, how do you react? **2.** If John was "the other disciple," why did he refer to himself as "the one Jesus loved"?

1. When a loved one dies, how does the resurrection of Jesus help you to deal with your pain? **2.** What is your proof that Jesus rose from the dead?

Describe a time when you mistook someone for the wrong person.

1. Would you have responded more like Mary or like the disciples? Why? **2.** Does Mary appear to be quietly grieving, or more hysterical? What finally breaks through her grief and confusion

---

ᵃ36 Exodus 12:46; Num. 9:12; Psalm 34:20   ᵇ37 Zech. 12:10   ᶜ39 Greek *a hundred litrai* (about 34 kilograms)

(v. 16)? **3.** What term (v. 17) does Jesus use for his disciples here? What is new in their relationship from now on (see 15:15)?

1. How has Jesus spoken your name in a time of grief? How did it affect you? **2.** What does it mean to you that Jesus is your brother?

Have you ever gone to your room and locked the door? Why?

1. Why are the disciples fearful now? **2.** Of all the things Jesus must have said, why does John record "peace be with you" three times (vv. 19,21,26)? How does this relate to their fears? To their being sent? **3.** How does Thomas' personality compare to Mary's (v. 13)? To the other disci-

where they have put him." ¹⁴At this, she turned around and saw Jesus standing there, but she did not realize that it was Jesus.

¹⁵"Woman," he said, "why are you crying? Who is it you are looking for?"

Thinking he was the gardener, she said, "Sir, if you have carried him away, tell me where you have put him, and I will get him."

¹⁶Jesus said to her, "Mary."

She turned toward him and cried out in Aramaic, "Rabboni!" (which means Teacher).

¹⁷Jesus said, "Do not hold on to me, for I have not yet returned to the Father. Go instead to my brothers and tell them, 'I am returning to my Father and your Father, to my God and your God.'"

¹⁸Mary Magdalene went to the disciples with the news: "I have seen the Lord!" And she told them that he had said these things to her.

Jesus Appears to His Disciples

¹⁹On the evening of that first day of the week, when the disciples were together, with the doors locked for fear of the Jews, Jesus came and stood among them and said, "Peace be with you!" ²⁰After he said this, he showed them his hands and side. The disciples were overjoyed when they saw the Lord.

²¹Again Jesus said, "Peace be with you! As the Father has sent me, I am sending you." ²²And with that he breathed on them and said, "Receive the Holy Spirit. ²³If you forgive anyone his sins, they are forgiven; if you do not forgive them, they are not forgiven."

John 20:1–18   JESUS APPEARS TO MARY MAGDALENE

Though the other Gospels record that a few women went to the tomb early Easter morning, John's focus is only on Mary Magdalene. One of several women who traveled with Jesus and the disciples, Mary at some point had seven demons cast out of her.

1. What do you think motivated Mary Magdalene to come to the tomb?
   a. grief and loss   d. loyalty
   b. curiosity   e. love
   c. loneliness

2. What would you have thought if you were Mary or one of the disciples and saw that the tomb was empty?
   a. Someone had taken Jesus' body.
   b. Jesus had returned to heaven.
   c. Jesus had risen, but was still on earth.

3. What word would you use to describe Mary's behavior until Jesus appeared to her?
   a. confused
   b. hysterical
   c. impulsive
   d. understandable

4. How did Jesus respond to Mary?
   a. He let her cool off.
   b. He calmed her by using her name.
   c. He opened her eyes.
   d. He spoke to her heart.
   e. He restored her hope.

5. Why did Jesus say to Mary, "Do not hold on to me"?
   a. It was not appropriate for her to touch him after his resurrection.
   b. She would have opportunities to see Jesus again.
   c. She had a message to give.
   d. She would "hold on" to him in an even more personal way when he sent the Holy Spirit.

6. What do you think the disciples said when she told them the news: "I have seen the Lord!"?
   a. "Yeah. Sure!"
   b. "It's that woman again."
   c. "Wait a minute—she could be telling the truth."
   d. "Let's submit this report to a committee for further study."
   e. "Let's get moving."

7. How has Jesus spoken your name in a time of grief or trouble? What effect did that have on you?

8. What do you rely on for evidence that Jesus rose from the dead?

9. What is the evidence that Jesus is alive in your life today?

10. Has your life lately been more like the darkness of Good Friday or the joy of Easter? Or somewhere in between? How can this group support you in your spiritual journey?

11. What have been the hardest "goodbyes" in your life? How can the resurrection of Jesus and the comfort of God's Spirit help you deal with that kind of pain and disappointment?

12. How have the people in this group been a Christ-like model for you in dealing with disappointment? Go around the circle and have each person listen silently while others share their appreciation.

Jesus Appears to Thomas

²⁴Now Thomas (called Didymus), one of the Twelve, was not with the disciples when Jesus came. ²⁵So the other disciples told him, "We have seen the Lord!"

But he said to them, "Unless I see the nail marks in his hands and put my finger where the nails were, and put my hand into his side, I will not believe it."

²⁶A week later his disciples were in the house again, and Thomas was with them. Though the doors were locked, Jesus came and stood among them and said, "Peace be with you!" ²⁷Then he said to Thomas, "Put your finger here; see my hands. Reach out your hand and put it into my side. Stop doubting and believe."

²⁸Thomas said to him, "My Lord and my God!"

²⁹Then Jesus told him, "Because you have seen me, you have believed; blessed are those who have not seen and yet have believed."

³⁰Jesus did many other miraculous signs in the presence of his disciples, which are not recorded in this book. ³¹But these are written that you mayᵃ believe that Jesus is the Christ, the Son of God, and that by believing you may have life in his name.

Jesus and the Miraculous Catch of Fish

21 Afterward Jesus appeared again to his disciples, by the Sea of Tiberias.ᵇ It happened this way: ²Simon Peter, Thomas (called Didymus), Nathanael from Cana in Galilee, the sons of Zebedee, and two other disciples were together. ³"I'm going out to

ᵃ31 Some manuscripts *may continue to*   ᵇ1 That is, Sea of Galilee

---

ples' (vv. 9,19)? **4.** How does Jesus deal with Thomas' doubt (v. 29)? What is significant about the way Thomas responds? How did your first confession of Christ's lordship sound? **5.** What is the author's purpose for writing this Gospel (vv. 30–31; 21:24–25)?

♡ **1.** Where could you use Jesus' "peace" right now: In some relationship? In some inner fear? In your work? **2.** What doubts or questions about God are you struggling with? What have you found helpful in dealing with doubts? **3.** Have you received the gift of the Holy Spirit? How has it changed you?

☕ **1.** What has been your best fishing, hunting or camping? **2.** What is your favorite food on a cookout?

📖 **1.** The seven disciples have returned to the Galilee district, about 90 miles from the place

---

John 20:24–31   JESUS APPEARS TO THOMAS

1. Why do you think Thomas was not with the rest of the disciples Easter night when Jesus appeared to them?
   a. He was a loner.
   b. He was sorting things out.
   c. He thought it was all over.
   d. He just happened to be in the wrong place at the wrong time.

2. "Unless I see the nail marks in his hands and put my finger where the nails were, and put my hand into his side, I will not believe it." What was Thomas saying?
   a. "You guys are crazy."
   b. "I need proof."
   c. "I want to believe, but ..."
   d. "Don't break my heart again."

3. How did Jesus deal with Thomas?
   a. harshly
   b. tenderly
   c. by waiting until Thomas was ready
   d. with the evidence he asked for

4. What do you suppose happened to Thomas' faith after this?
   a. He learned his lesson, and believed from this point on.
   b. He never did get past his doubts.
   c. Voicing his doubts helped him have a stronger faith than those who never admit such things.
   d. He always felt guilty for doubting, which crippled his faith.

5. What did Jesus mean when he said, "Blessed are those who have not seen and yet have believed"?
   a. "You will be happier if you do not doubt."
   b. "You don't have to see me to believe in me."
   c. "God calls you to be faithful even when you can't see clearly."
   d. "You blew it, Thomas."

6. What do you rely upon for spiritual "proof"?
   a. a feeling of peace
   b. simple faith
   c. what my church teaches
   d. what is logical and makes sense
   e. what the Bible says
   f. what my Christian friends say

7. When you have struggles in your faith, what have you found helpful?

8. When you have spiritual doubts, what does that indicate?
   a. My faith is weak.
   b. I need some more information.
   c. I need a spiritual "check up."
   d. Growth may be taking place.

9. ✠ If you could ask God one question about your struggles, what would it be?
   a. How do I deal with doubt?
   b. What if I don't always feel like a Christian?
   c. Why can't I feel closer to Jesus?
   d. Where is God when I'm hurting?

10. ✠ Do you have doubts about being sure you are a Christian? How does it make you feel to know that ...
   a. Jesus invited Thomas to inspect his wounds?
   b. Jesus said those who believe without seeing are "blessed"?
   c. John wrote this so "you may believe that Jesus is the Christ, the Son of God, and that by believing you may have life in his name"?

Jesus was killed and rose again. What might they have discussed on the way? **2.** In fishing all night, using nets, do you think Peter just wanted something to do, or did he return to his old business? **3.** Why did Jesus' followers have difficulty recognizing him after the resurrection? **4.** How would you feel if you had been fishing with the disciples all night? How does Jesus' preparation of breakfast relate to what he did for them in 13:1–17?

1. Where do you go to get away from it all? How does God meet you there? **2.** When was the last time you received a bountiful blessing? Did Jesus get your attention through this blessing?

fish," Simon Peter told them, and they said, "We'll go with you." So they went out and got into the boat, but that night they caught nothing.

⁴Early in the morning, Jesus stood on the shore, but the disciples did not realize that it was Jesus.

⁵He called out to them, "Friends, haven't you any fish?"

"No," they answered.

⁶He said, "Throw your net on the right side of the boat and you will find some." When they did, they were unable to haul the net in because of the large number of fish.

⁷Then the disciple whom Jesus loved said to Peter, "It is the Lord!" As soon as Simon Peter heard him say, "It is the Lord," he wrapped his outer garment around him (for he had taken it off) and jumped into the water. ⁸The other disciples followed in the boat, towing the net full of fish, for they were not far from shore, about a hundred yards.ᵃ ⁹When they landed, they saw a fire of burning coals there with fish on it, and some bread.

¹⁰Jesus said to them, "Bring some of the fish you have just caught."

¹¹Simon Peter climbed aboard and dragged the net ashore. It was full of large fish, 153, but even with so many the net was not torn. ¹²Jesus said to them, "Come and have breakfast." None of the disciples dared ask him, "Who are you?" They knew it was the Lord. ¹³Jesus came, took the bread and gave it to them, and did the same with the fish. ¹⁴This was now the third time Jesus appeared to his disciples after he was raised from the dead.

ᵃ8 Greek *about two hundred cubits* (about 90 meters)

 John 21:1–25   **JESUS REINSTATES PETER**

1. Why do you think Peter and the other disciples went back to Peter's home territory of Galilee?
   a. to relax and do some fishing
   b. to go back to their old occupation
   c. to put their lives back together
   d. to forget about Jesus
   e. to obey Jesus' instructions to go to Galilee and wait for him there

2. Why did Jesus provide a miraculous catch of fish and then make breakfast for the disciples?
   a. to remind them of the miraculous catch of fish that first got them "hooked" as disciples
   b. to assure them they were still called to be "fishers of men"
   c. to show, by eating with them, that he forgave them for failing him
   d. to remind them of the significance of the Last Supper

3. Why do you think Jesus pressed Peter three times with the question, "Do you love me?"
   a. to get Peter's attention
   b. to shame Peter for denying Jesus three times

   c. to make Peter face his failure
   d. to show Peter he had forgiven him
   e. to be sure Peter accepted his love

4. If you had been Peter, how would you have felt by the end of the third question?
   a. angry   d. humiliated
   b. hurt   e. healed
   c. guilty   f. frustrated

5. "Feed my lambs ... Take care of my sheep ... Feed my sheep." What was Jesus saying to Peter?
   a. You would make a better shepherd than fisherman.
   b. Your job is caring for my followers.
   c. Prove that you love me.
   d. I'm still counting on you.
   e. Don't blow it again.
   f. Lay down your life for people— like I did.

6. What is the closest you have come to going back on your promise to follow Jesus? What did you discover about God through that experience? What did you discover about yourself?

7. If Jesus said to you, "Take care of my sheep"—what would he mean?
   a. Pick yourself up and get going.
   b. I need you to carry on my work.
   c. Get your eyes off of yourself.
   d. Do something about others' needs.
   e. Use your gifts.

8. What evidence is there in your life that you truly love Jesus?
   a. I want to spend time with him.
   b. Scripture has come alive to me.
   c. I want to go to church/small group.
   d. It's easier to show love to others.
   e. His joy has been my strength.
   f. My concern for others has grown.
   g. I want to share my faith.

9. How does this story give you hope for a restored relationship with your child? Have you forgiven your child for breaking your heart? Does he/she think you have?

10. What have you appreciated the most about this group? How have you felt the love of those in the group for Jesus *and* for each other?

Jesus Reinstates Peter

[15] When they had finished eating, Jesus said to Simon Peter, "Simon son of John, do you truly love me more than these?"

"Yes, Lord," he said, "you know that I love you."

Jesus said, "Feed my lambs."

[16] Again Jesus said, "Simon son of John, do you truly love me?"

He answered, "Yes, Lord, you know that I love you."

Jesus said, "Take care of my sheep."

[17] The third time he said to him, "Simon son of John, do you love me?"

Peter was hurt because Jesus asked him the third time, "Do you love me?" He said, "Lord, you know all things; you know that I love you."

Jesus said, "Feed my sheep. [18] I tell you the truth, when you were younger you dressed yourself and went where you wanted; but when you are old you will stretch out your hands, and someone else will dress you and lead you where you do not want to go." [19] Jesus said this to indicate the kind of death by which Peter would glorify God. Then he said to him, "Follow me!"

[20] Peter turned and saw that the disciple whom Jesus loved was following them. (This was the one who had leaned back against Jesus at the supper and had said, "Lord, who is going to betray you?") [21] When Peter saw him, he asked, "Lord, what about him?"

[22] Jesus answered, "If I want him to remain alive until I return, what is that to you? You must follow me." [23] Because of this, the rumor spread among the brothers that this disciple would not die. But Jesus did not say that he would not die; he only said, "If I want him to remain alive until I return, what is that to you?"

[24] This is the disciple who testifies to these things and who wrote them down. We know that his testimony is true.

[25] Jesus did many other things as well. If every one of them were written down, I suppose that even the whole world would not have room for the books that would be written.

1. Have you ever been kicked off the team, out of the club, out of the house or out of school? Why? 2. Who was expected to do the most chores around your house when you were a kid? Who got off the easiest?

1. Why do you think Jesus repeated the same question and charge to Peter three times? How is Peter supposed to demonstrate his love and loyalty to Jesus now? In light of 10:15, what would Jesus' shepherd image mean to Peter? 2. What does Jesus mean by his prediction in verse 18? Why did Peter ask about John? 3. What is the crucial issue revealed in Jesus' response to Peter (v. 22)? How is this linked with verses 15–17?

1. What is the closest you have come to blowing it so badly that you thought God was never going to speak to you again? What did you discover about God in that experience? 2. When have you compared yourself with someone else and wondered why his or her life was the way it was? How did that affect your desire to do what you were supposed to do? 3. Whom do you know who needs to feel forgiven by God? What will you do to tell them they are forgiven? 4. If you were writing a book about Jesus' work in your life, what would be some of the chapter titles? 5. What has been brought to light for you through studying John's Gospel?

INTRODUCTION to
ACTS

Book Study Outline: If you are using Acts for a study course, here is a 7- or 13-week outline. Use the margin questions for your group agenda:

☕ start meeting / 15 min.

📖 read & discuss Bible / 30 min.

♡ close meeting / 15–45 min.

Refer to the Questions and Answers in front of Bible for more information.

7-week plan	13-week plan	Personal Reading	Group Study Passage
	1	1:1–26	1:1–11/Jesus Taken
1	2	2:1–41	2:1–24,36–41/Pentecost
2	3	2:42–3:26	2:42–47/Fellowship
	4	4:1–37	4:1–31/Before Sanhedrin
3	5	5:1–8:25	5:1–11/Ananias and Sapphira
	6	8:26–40	8:26–40/The Ethiopian
4	7	9:1–43	9:1–19/Saul's Conversion
5	8	10:1–11:30	10:1–23/Peter's Vision
	9	12:1–16:15	12:1–19/Peter's Escape
6	10	16:16–17:34	16:16–40/In Prison
	11	18:1–21:36	18:5–17/Paul's Vision
	12	21:37–25:27	21:37–22:29/Paul Speaks
7	13	26:1–28:30	26:1–32/Before Agrippa

Author: The writer is unknown; however, because of the "we" passages (e.g., 16:10–17) it seems likely that the author is Luke, the physician who joined Paul on some of his journeys.

Date: The final events recorded here took place in early A.D. 60, so Acts must have been compiled some time after that.

Theme: The spread of the Gospel to all the known world (1:8).

Historical Background: In 30 short years, the church grew from what was considered an insignificant Jewish sect to a major force in the Roman Empire. Luke wrote Acts as a companion piece to his Gospel to show how Christianity was *not* a political threat to Rome, but rather the work of God's Spirit in building up a spiritual "kingdom," one comprised of all who live by faith in Jesus. Luke does this by focusing on the two leading figures in the church: Peter, the apostle to the Jews (ch. 1–12), and Paul, the apostle to the Gentiles (ch. 13–28).

Characteristics: The theme of Acts is defined in 1:8. Luke records the growth of the church in Jerusalem and Judea (1:1–6:7), Galilee and Samaria (6:8–9:31), Antioch, which became a missionary launching pad to the Gentile world (9:32–12:24), Asia (12:25–16:5), Europe (16:6–19:20), and Rome (19:21–28:31). Luke centers in on Paul. By doing so, he affirms Paul's authority as an apostle, as well as his innocence of the charges brought against him. Acts provides essential background information about the churches Paul founded and to whom he wrote his epistles.

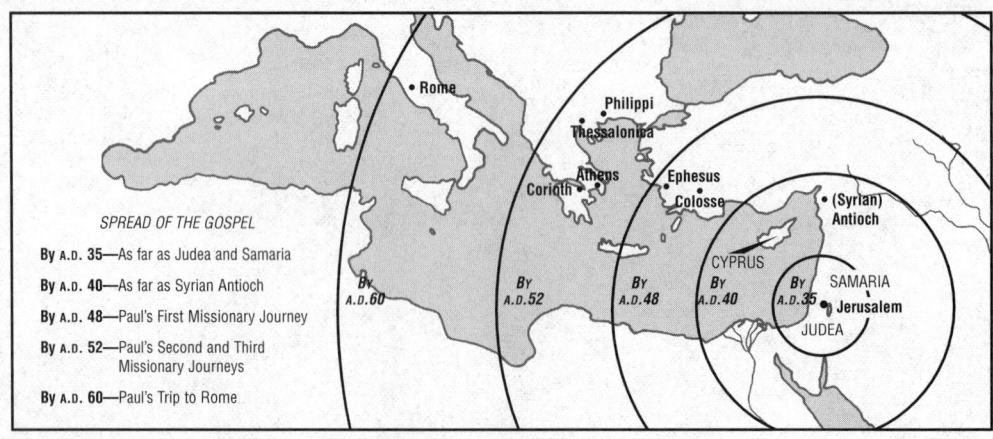

SPREAD OF THE GOSPEL

By A.D. 35—As far as Judea and Samaria

By A.D. 40—As far as Syrian Antioch

By A.D. 48—Paul's First Missionary Journey

By A.D. 52—Paul's Second and Third Missionary Journeys

By A.D. 60—Paul's Trip to Rome

Acts

Jesus Taken Up Into Heaven

1 In my former book, Theophilus, I wrote about all that Jesus began to do and to teach ²until the day he was taken up to heaven, after giving instructions through the Holy Spirit to the apostles he had chosen. ³After his suffering, he showed himself to these men and gave many convincing proofs that he was alive. He appeared to them over a period of forty days and spoke about the kingdom of God. ⁴On one occasion, while he was eating with them, he gave them this command: "Do not leave Jerusalem, but wait for the gift my Father promised, which you have heard me speak about. ⁵For John baptized with*a* water, but in a few days you will be baptized with the Holy Spirit."

⁶So when they met together, they asked him, "Lord, are you at this time going to restore the kingdom to Israel?"

⁷He said to them: "It is not for you to know the times or dates the Father has set by his own authority. ⁸But you will receive power when the Holy Spirit comes on you; and you will be my witnesses in Jerusalem, and in all Judea and Samaria, and to the ends of the earth."

⁹After he said this, he was taken up before their very eyes, and a cloud hid him from their sight.

a5 Or *in*

Who would you want to write the biography of your life? Why that person? What does this person know about you that you would like your group to know?

1. How does this book pick up where Luke 24:45–53 leaves off? **2.** What do the disciples think will happen when they receive the Holy Spirit (v. 6)? How does their idea of the kingdom differ from Jesus' (vv. 7–8)? **3.** As a disciple, what is the impact on you of Jesus' words (v. 8)? Of Jesus' departure (v. 9)? Of the angels' promise (v. 11)?

1. How would you explain the effects of the Resurrection to your non-believing friends? **2.** To which "Jerusalem" are you called to bear witness? How do you need the Spirit to help you?

    Acts 1:1–11   **JESUS TAKEN UP INTO HEAVEN**

1. How do you think the disciples felt about Jesus leaving them?
   a. terrified   d. abandoned
   b. confused   e. angry
   c. excited about what was ahead

2. What would you call Jesus' ascension to heaven?
   a. sad—the end of his ministry
   b. hopeful—the start of a new phase of his ministry
   c. glorious—He will return!

3. What chance would you have given the followers of Jesus at this point to change the world?
   a. a lot   c. a little
   b. some   d. none

4. Why do you think Jesus insisted his followers wait in Jerusalem?
   a. They needed mutual support.
   b. They couldn't make it without the Holy Spirit.
   c. They needed to help each other understand what was going on.
   d. They needed to develop a strategy for spreading the message.

5. What do you think the disciples did during the 10 days of waiting for the Holy Spirit to come?
   a. grieved over the loss of Jesus
   b. praised God with much joy
   c. talked about their mixed-up feelings and encouraged each other
   d. recalled Jesus' teachings and tried to understand what was going on
   e. sat in silence—waiting for something to happen

6. What do you see as the key point of this passage?
   a. God's kingdom isn't a matter of one people's destiny (including Israel's), but a spiritual realm involving the whole world.
   b. Jesus will return, but don't stand around waiting for him.
   c. Jesus continues his mission and ministry through his followers.
   d. The power of the Holy Spirit is crucial to every Christian's life.
   e. Following Jesus and relying on the Spirit leads to both Christian community and evangelism.

7. How was the disciples' idea of the kingdom of God different than Jesus'? When have you been confused about God's plans or ways?

8. What proof do you have of Jesus' resurrection that would make sense to unbelievers? What holds you back from spreading the word about Jesus to them?
   a. lack of knowledge
   b. lack of concern
   c. lack of unbelieving family/friends
   d. lack of courage
   e. nothing—I'm doing it!

9. Where are you called to be Christ's witnesses? How do you sense a need for God's Spirit to help you?

10. How has this course and this group been a witness and testimony to you of God's love, Christ's presence and the Holy Spirit's power? Have one person at a time listen silently while others share how they appreciate him or her.

[10]They were looking intently up into the sky as he was going, when suddenly two men dressed in white stood beside them. [11]"Men of Galilee," they said, "why do you stand here looking into the sky? This same Jesus, who has been taken from you into heaven, will come back in the same way you have seen him go into heaven."

Matthias Chosen to Replace Judas

[12]Then they returned to Jerusalem from the hill called the Mount of Olives, a Sabbath day's walk[a] from the city. [13]When they arrived, they went upstairs to the room where they were staying. Those present were Peter, John, James and Andrew; Philip and Thomas, Bartholomew and Matthew; James son of Alphaeus and Simon the Zealot, and Judas son of James. [14]They all joined together constantly in prayer, along with the women and Mary the mother of Jesus, and with his brothers.

[15]In those days Peter stood up among the believers[b] (a group numbering about a hundred and twenty) [16]and said, "Brothers, the Scripture had to be fulfilled which the Holy Spirit spoke long ago through the mouth of David concerning Judas, who served as guide for those who arrested Jesus— [17]he was one of our number and shared in this ministry."

[18](With the reward he got for his wickedness, Judas bought a field; there he fell headlong, his body burst open and all his intestines spilled out. [19]Everyone in Jerusalem heard about this, so they called that field in their language Akeldama, that is, Field of Blood.)

[20]"For," said Peter, "it is written in the book of Psalms,

> " 'May his place be deserted;
>   let there be no one to dwell in it,'[c]

and,

> " 'May another take his place of leadership.'[d]

[21]Therefore it is necessary to choose one of the men who have been with us the whole time the Lord Jesus went in and out among us, [22]beginning from John's baptism to the time when Jesus was taken up from us. For one of these must become a witness with us of his resurrection."

[23]So they proposed two men: Joseph called Barsabbas (also known as Justus) and Matthias. [24]Then they prayed, "Lord, you know everyone's heart. Show us which of these two you have chosen [25]to take over this apostolic ministry, which Judas left to go where he belongs." [26]Then they cast lots, and the lot fell to Matthias; so he was added to the eleven apostles.

The Holy Spirit Comes at Pentecost

2 When the day of Pentecost came, they were all together in one place. [2]Suddenly a sound like the blowing of a violent wind came from heaven and filled the whole house where they were sitting. [3]They saw what seemed to be tongues of fire that separated and came to rest on each of them. [4]All of them were filled with the Holy Spirit and began to speak in other tongues[e] as the Spirit enabled them.

[5]Now there were staying in Jerusalem God-fearing Jews from every nation under heaven. [6]When they heard this sound, a crowd came together in bewilderment, because each one heard them speaking in his own language. [7]Utterly amazed, they asked: "Are

---

What was your favorite board game as a child? Did it involve luck of the draw, taking risks or strategy? Which is your favorite game now, and why?

1. Who was present at this meeting? From Mark 3:20–21,31–35 and John 7:1–5, how do you account for this change in Jesus' "family"? Why weren't "the women" mentioned by name? **2.** In light of Peter's denial of Jesus, how might the others feel about his leadership? How would the events of John 21:15–19 calm any fears they have? **3.** Given verses 6–8, how would you be praying if you were in this group? What emotions would you express? **4.** What was the role of Scripture, prayer, discussion, qualifications, and trust in God when the disciples selected a replacement for Judas?

1. What have been your best experiences in group prayer? How is praying with others for a common mission (one that is beyond your natural ability) different from private prayer about your individual concerns? **2.** How does the pattern of decision-making here compare with the way you, your family or your church make important decisions? Which of the ingredients listed here do you need to utilize more?

Have you ever traveled where you did not speak the language? What happened?

1. Why did God wait until Pentecost, a Jewish harvest festival (Dt 16:9–10) to give the Holy Spirit? **2.** How far have these pilgrims come (vv. 9–11)? What attracts them to the disciples? How does being filled with the Spirit relate to bearing witness to Jesus?

1. Would you respond more like those in verse 12, or those in verse 13? Why? **2.** Have you ever seen the gift of tongues

---

a12 That is, about 3/4 mile (about 1,100 meters)   b15 Greek *brothers*
c20 Psalm 69:25   d20 Psalm 109:8   e4 Or *languages*; also in verse 11

not all these men who are speaking Galileans? [8]Then how is it that each of us hears them in his own native language? [9]Parthians, Medes and Elamites; residents of Mesopotamia, Judea and Cappadocia, Pontus and Asia, [10]Phrygia and Pamphylia, Egypt and the parts of Libya near Cyrene; visitors from Rome [11](both Jews and converts to Judaism); Cretans and Arabs—we hear them declaring the wonders of God in our own tongues!" [12]Amazed and perplexed, they asked one another, "What does this mean?"

[13]Some, however, made fun of them and said, "They have had too much wine.[a]"

Peter Addresses the Crowd

[14]Then Peter stood up with the Eleven, raised his voice and addressed the crowd: "Fellow Jews and all of you who live in Jerusalem, let me explain this to you; listen carefully to what I say. [15]These men are not drunk, as you suppose. It's only nine in the morning! [16]No, this is what was spoken by the prophet Joel:

[17]" 'In the last days, God says,
    I will pour out my Spirit on all people.
Your sons and daughters will prophesy,
    your young men will see visions,
    your old men will dream dreams.
[18]Even on my servants, both men and women,
    I will pour out my Spirit in those days,
    and they will prophesy.
[19]I will show wonders in the heaven above
    and signs on the earth below,
    blood and fire and billows of smoke.
[20]The sun will be turned to darkness
    and the moon to blood
    before the coming of the great and glorious day
      of the Lord.
[21]And everyone who calls
    on the name of the Lord will be saved.'[b]

[22]"Men of Israel, listen to this: Jesus of Nazareth was a man accredited by God to you by miracles, wonders and signs, which God did among you through him, as you yourselves know. [23]This man was handed over to you by God's set purpose and foreknowledge; and you, with the help of wicked men,[c] put him to death by nailing him to the cross. [24]But God raised him from the dead, freeing him from the agony of death, because it was impossible for death to keep its hold on him. [25]David said about him:

" 'I saw the Lord always before me.
    Because he is at my right hand,
    I will not be shaken.
[26]Therefore my heart is glad and my tongue
    rejoices;
    my body also will live in hope,
[27]because you will not abandon me to the grave,
    nor will you let your Holy One see decay.
[28]You have made known to me the paths of life;
    you will fill me with joy in your presence.'[d]

[29]"Brothers, I can tell you confidently that the patriarch David died and was buried, and his tomb is here to this day. [30]But he was a prophet and knew that God had promised him on oath that he

used this way? Another way? **3.** When have you experienced an empowering from God to witness about Christ?

_____

What are you usually doing at 9:00 in the morning on a Saturday? On Sunday? On a weekday?

1. Compare Peter and the other disciples in John 18:25–27 and 20:19 with their actions here: What accounts for the great difference? **2.** In what way is Luke 24:44–49 reflected in this sermon? Given the audience, why would Peter quote from the Old Testament? **3.** What is the point Peter wants the people to understand about current events (vv. 15, 17–18)? How do you understand verses 19–21? What tells you Joel's prophecy is coming true now? **4.** How familiar were these people with the events of Jesus' life? How might they be dealing with the rumors of the empty tomb? Given that, why does Peter emphasize the resurrection (vv. 24, 31–32)? **5.** What are the implications of the resurrection and ascension for Jesus (vv. 24,30–31,33–36)? For the people? What would it mean to the people that Jesus is a spiritual King far greater than their greatest earthly king (vv. 35–36)? **6.** How would you put Peter's answer (vv. 38–40) in your own words to explain what it means to become a Christian? What is required? What is promised? **7.** How does the resurrection prove that Jesus is the Messiah? Remembering where these 3,000 came from (vv. 8–11), in what way is 1:8 partially fulfilled here? What news will the people bring home with them?

1. To repent and be baptized in Jesus' name means to turn away from all your sin and affirm allegiance to Jesus. Does that present a challenge to you? How have you experienced the reality of God's promises for answering his call? **2.** From Peter's sermon, what facts about Jesus would be key for non-believers to understand (vv. 29–33)? **3.** When did you make your initial commitment to Christ?

---

[a]13 Or *sweet wine*   [b]21 Joel 2:28-32   [c]23 Or *of those not having the law* (that is, Gentiles)   [d]28 Psalm 16:8-11

Who was influential in that process? What convinced you of your need for Christ? **4.** What difference does it make that Jesus truly is the reigning King over all? How does that truth affect your daily life? **5.** When was the last time you seized an opportunity to witness for Jesus? What happened? Who stood with you at that time? How are you like Peter? Unlike him? What encourages you as you watch Peter? Why?

would place one of his descendants on his throne. **31**Seeing what was ahead, he spoke of the resurrection of the Christ,*a* that he was not abandoned to the grave, nor did his body see decay. **32**God has raised this Jesus to life, and we are all witnesses of the fact. **33**Exalted to the right hand of God, he has received from the Father the promised Holy Spirit and has poured out what you now see and hear. **34**For David did not ascend to heaven, and yet he said,

> " 'The Lord said to my Lord:
> "Sit at my right hand
> **35**until I make your enemies
> a footstool for your feet." ' *b*

36"Therefore let all Israel be assured of this: God has made this Jesus, whom you crucified, both Lord and Christ."

37When the people heard this, they were cut to the heart and said to Peter and the other apostles, "Brothers, what shall we do?"

38Peter replied, "Repent and be baptized, every one of you, in the name of Jesus Christ for the forgiveness of your sins. And you will receive the gift of the Holy Spirit. **39**The promise is for you and your children and for all who are far off—for all whom the Lord our God will call."

40With many other words he warned them; and he pleaded with them, "Save yourselves from this corrupt generation." **41**Those who accepted his message were baptized, and about three thousand were added to their number that day.

a31 Or *Messiah.* "The Christ" (Greek) and "the Messiah" (Hebrew) both mean "the Anointed One"; also in verse 36.   *b35* Psalm 110:1

Acts 2:1–24,36–41   **THE HOLY SPIRIT COMES AT PENTECOST**

1. What would you say was the most impressive evidence of the Holy Spirit on the day of Pentecost?
   a. the sudden, mysterious wind
   b. the tongues of fire that came to rest on each of them
   c. the believers all speaking in unknown tongues or languages
   d. the crowd hearing the disciples declaring the wonders of God in their own languages
   e. the giving of prophecies, visions and dreams to all God's people
   f. the response—3,000 converts

2. If you had been there that day, what would have been your strongest feeling afterward?
   a. That was a once-in-a-lifetime experience.
   b. I hope that wasn't a once-in-a-lifetime experience.
   c. If the Spirit is that powerful, there isn't any problem I can't face.
   d. Give us five days and we'll take the world!
   e. I'm keeping quiet about this—people will think I'm crazy.

3. Why did God pour out the gift of the Holy Spirit upon Jesus' followers?
   a. to bless them with a spiritual high
   b. to empower them to be witnesses
   c. to serve as a miraculous sign to draw others
   d. to get the Christian church off to an explosive start

4. What do the wind and fire, symbolic of the Holy Spirit, suggest to you most strongly?
   a. unpredictability—Like wind and fire, you cannot always predict what God will do.
   b. power—The forces of wind and fire remind us of the Spirit's power.
   c. invisibility—Like the wind and the heat of a fire, you cannot always see the Spirit at work.
   d. change—As wind brings change, the Spirit changes the world.
   e. warmth—As fire brings warmth, the Spirit brings loving warmth.

5. From Peter's message to the crowd, especially his conclusion (vv. 36–39), how would you explain to

someone what it means to become a Christian?

6. What preacher or teacher has God used to draw you to Jesus?

7. Compared to the experience of the disciples on the day of Pentecost, how would you describe your initial experience with the Holy Spirit?
   a. rather tame
   b. similar to theirs
   c. quite different, but just as real
   d. something I can't explain

8. How would you describe your experience with the Holy Spirit now?
   a. on fire
   b. up in the air
   c. gone with the wind

9. When have you experienced an empowering from the Holy Spirit to witness about Christ? What are you going to do to be better prepared for God's use?

10. To help add to *your* number, whom can you invite to this group?

The Fellowship of the Believers

⁴²They devoted themselves to the apostles' teaching and to the fellowship, to the breaking of bread and to prayer. ⁴³Everyone was filled with awe, and many wonders and miraculous signs were done by the apostles. ⁴⁴All the believers were together and had everything in common. ⁴⁵Selling their possessions and goods, they gave to anyone as he had need. ⁴⁶Every day they continued to meet together in the temple courts. They broke bread in their homes and ate together with glad and sincere hearts, ⁴⁷praising God and enjoying the favor of all the people. And the Lord added to their number daily those who were being saved.

Peter Heals the Crippled Beggar

3 One day Peter and John were going up to the temple at the time of prayer—at three in the afternoon. ²Now a man crippled from birth was being carried to the temple gate called Beautiful, where he was put every day to beg from those going into the temple courts. ³When he saw Peter and John about to enter, he asked them for money. ⁴Peter looked straight at him, as did John. Then Peter said, "Look at us!" ⁵So the man gave them his attention, expecting to get something from them.

⁶Then Peter said, "Silver or gold I do not have, but what I have I give you. In the name of Jesus Christ of Nazareth, walk." ⁷Taking him by the right hand, he helped him up, and instantly the man's feet and ankles became strong. ⁸He jumped to his feet and began to walk. Then he went with them into the temple courts, walking and jumping, and praising God. ⁹When all the people saw him walking and praising God, ¹⁰they recognized him as the same man who

What do you devote yourself to *daily*? Anything that would pass for a daily devotion?

What did these 3,000 converts end up doing (vv. 42–47)? How is God with them?

How is your church fellowship like and unlike the fellowship here? How could you help your church be more like this? How will this example affect how you get involved in your church?

Describe a time when you found yourself without money.

1. As the cripple, what would you write as a diary entry for a typical day? When Peter grabs your hand? After the healing? **2.** How does this miracle relate to 2:19 and 2:22?

1. How is Jesus healing some crippled area of your life? **2.** Would you do the same thing as Peter did, or would you ask John for a dime? Why? Could God heal through you? Why or why not?

  Acts 2:42–47   THE FELLOWSHIP OF THE BELIEVERS

As a result of the coming of the Holy Spirit on the day of Pentecost, the fellowship of believers described in this passage had grown by about 3,000.

1. Why do you think all these people got together every day?
   a. They loved to eat.
   b. They were excited about their new life and wanted to talk about it.
   c. They had a lot of needs.
   d. They had a lot to learn.
   e. They had nothing else to do.

2. What do you think the atmosphere was like when they got together?
   a. chaotic   e. life-changing
   b. fun   f. exciting
   c. boring   g. claustrophobic
   d. caring   h. unpredictable

3. What made the early church so appealing to others?
   a. their spiritual vitality
   b. their amazing love for each other
   c. their openness to others
   d. miracles
   e. great preaching from the pulpit
   f. advertising

4. Why do you think the Christian community today does not have the early church's depth of relationships?
   a. We don't have time.
   b. We don't know each other.
   c. We don't want to know each other's needs.
   d. It's not okay to have needs.
   e. Our culture is so different.
   f. Caring for one another is not on the church's agenda.

5. On a scale of 1 to 10, how would you rate your small group (and your church) on the following qualities?
   a. spiritual commitment and growth
   b. spiritual healing
   c. caring for one another materially
   d. intimate fellowship
   e. faithfulness in prayer and worship
   f. reaching out/growing in numbers

6. What aspect of the spiritual life and energy found in the early church do you most desire for yourself? For your small group? For your church? How will this example in Acts affect the way you pray?

7. As a single person, what are your two biggest needs?
   a. loneliness
   b. not feeling like a person of worth
   c. sexual frustrations/anxieties
   d. financial problems
   e. single parenting stresses
   f. healing from past relationships
   g. not fitting into the church
   h. lack of someone supportive to communicate with about my needs
   i. other:_____

8. How could a fellowship of believers like that found in this passage make a difference for singles like yourself? What can you do to help your Christian community be more like the early church?

9. How regularly do you go to church as a family? What is the *most* and *least* positive aspect of your family's church involvement?

10. What can you as a parent do to make your family's church experience—and your children's feelings about it—better?

used to sit begging at the temple gate called Beautiful, and they were filled with wonder and amazement at what had happened to him.

Peter Speaks to the Onlookers

¹¹While the beggar held on to Peter and John, all the people were astonished and came running to them in the place called Solomon's Colonnade. ¹²When Peter saw this, he said to them: "Men of Israel, why does this surprise you? Why do you stare at us as if by our own power or godliness we had made this man walk? ¹³The God of Abraham, Isaac and Jacob, the God of our fathers, has glorified his servant Jesus. You handed him over to be killed, and you disowned him before Pilate, though he had decided to let him go. ¹⁴You disowned the Holy and Righteous One and asked that a murderer be released to you. ¹⁵You killed the author of life, but God raised him from the dead. We are witnesses of this. ¹⁶By faith in the name of Jesus, this man whom you see and know was made strong. It is Jesus' name and the faith that comes through him that has given this complete healing to him, as you can all see.

¹⁷"Now, brothers, I know that you acted in ignorance, as did your leaders. ¹⁸But this is how God fulfilled what he had foretold through all the prophets, saying that his Christ[a] would suffer. ¹⁹Repent, then, and turn to God, so that your sins may be wiped out, that times of refreshing may come from the Lord, ²⁰and that he may send the Christ, who has been appointed for you—even Jesus. ²¹He must remain in heaven until the time comes for God to restore everything, as he promised long ago through his holy prophets. ²²For Moses said, 'The Lord your God will raise up for you a prophet like me from among your own people; you must listen to everything he tells you. ²³Anyone who does not listen to him will be completely cut off from among his people.'[b]

²⁴"Indeed, all the prophets from Samuel on, as many as have spoken, have foretold these days. ²⁵And you are heirs of the prophets and of the covenant God made with your fathers. He said to Abraham, 'Through your offspring all peoples on earth will be blessed.'[c] ²⁶When God raised up his servant, he sent him first to you to bless you by turning each of you from your wicked ways."

Peter and John Before the Sanhedrin

4 The priests and the captain of the temple guard and the Saddu-cees came up to Peter and John while they were speaking to the people. ²They were greatly disturbed because the apostles were teaching the people and proclaiming in Jesus the resurrection of the dead. ³They seized Peter and John, and because it was evening, they put them in jail until the next day. ⁴But many who heard the message believed, and the number of men grew to about five thousand.

⁵The next day the rulers, elders and teachers of the law met in Jerusalem. ⁶Annas the high priest was there, and so were Caiaphas, John, Alexander and the other men of the high priest's family. ⁷They had Peter and John brought before them and began to question them: "By what power or what name did you do this?"

⁸Then Peter, filled with the Holy Spirit, said to them: "Rulers and elders of the people! ⁹If we are being called to account today for an act of kindness shown to a cripple and are asked how he was healed, ¹⁰then know this, you and all the people of Israel: It is by the name of Jesus Christ of Nazareth, whom you crucified but

What refreshes you the most? A cool shower? A swim? A glass of lemonade? A massage? Air conditioning?

1. How is this situation like the one in 2:1–12? 2. List all the facts about Jesus which Peter mentions here (vv. 13–16). How does this profile of Jesus compare with the one in 2:22–24? 3. Restate verse 16 in your own words. 4. What does Peter say about the people? How would you feel being accused: "You killed ..." (v. 15)? 5. From Peter's second recorded sermon, how would you sum up what it means to become a Christian? 6. Despite what Peter says about them (vv. 13–15), how does he give the people hope in verses 24–26? How are "blessing" and "turning" related?

1. When is it proper to come on strong against a person's sin, like Peter did in verses 13–15? In coming to Christ, did you need to be hit over the head with your sin first? 2. What does Peter's use of the OT indicate about its benefits to your faith in Christ? How can you start to increase your knowledge of it? 3. How has repentance and turning to God brought "times of refreshing" (v. 19) to you? How can that be used as a means of encouraging others to come to Christ? 4. What does Jesus as "the author of life" (v. 15) mean to you?

Describe a time when you felt right about breaking the rules.

1. What roles did the priest, captain of the guard and the Sadducees play in the ministry of Jesus (see Lk 20:27–40; 22:6,52)? Why would the Sadducees oppose the disciples' preaching (v. 2)? What would you feel if you were one of the believers who saw Peter and John taken away? If you were Peter or John? 2. What is the high priest's family trying to do (v. 7)—seek information or intimidate the disciples? Why (see v. 2; 3:16)? 3. If you were one of the authorities, what would be your reaction to Peter's bold answer? How does Peter "filled with the Holy Spirit" (vv. 8–12) compare with the purpose of the filling in 2:4 (see also Lk

a18 Or *Messiah*; also in verse 20   b23 Deut. 18:15,18,19   c25 Gen. 22:18; 26:4

happened. [8]Peter asked her, "Tell me, is this the price you and Ananias got for the land?"

"Yes," she said, "that is the price."

[9]Peter said to her, "How could you agree to test the Spirit of the Lord? Look! The feet of the men who buried your husband are at the door, and they will carry you out also."

[10]At that moment she fell down at his feet and died. Then the young men came in and, finding her dead, carried her out and buried her beside her husband. [11]Great fear seized the whole church and all who heard about these events.

The Apostles Heal Many

[12]The apostles performed many miraculous signs and wonders among the people. And all the believers used to meet together in Solomon's Colonnade. [13]No one else dared join them, even though they were highly regarded by the people. [14]Nevertheless, more and more men and women believed in the Lord and were added to their number. [15]As a result, people brought the sick into the streets and laid them on beds and mats so that at least Peter's shadow might fall on some of them as he passed by. [16]Crowds gathered also from the towns around Jerusalem, bringing their sick and those tormented by evil[a] spirits, and all of them were healed.

The Apostles Persecuted

[17]Then the high priest and all his associates, who were members of the party of the Sadducees, were filled with jealousy. [18]They arrested the apostles and put them in the public jail. [19]But during

[a]16 Greek *unclean*

13–14? What words might outsiders use to describe this church? **6.** Is coming to Jesus or his disciples for healing the same as giving him your life? Why or why not?

1. When have you tried to fool God? What happened? **2.** How have you experienced the "fear of the Lord"? How has that changed your life?

1. What has been your experience on either side of jail? What sights, sounds and feelings do you associate with jail? **2.** When you leave home or your car unat-

---

Acts 4:32–37   THE BELIEVERS SHARE THEIR POSSESSIONS

1. What would you call the way these first Christians shared their possessions with each other?
   a. radical
   b. ridiculous
   c. exciting
   d. cultish
   e. beautiful
   f. foolish

2. How do you think they felt about their church?
   a. It was really important to them.
   b. It was all they had.
   c. They could take it or leave it.
   d. It felt like family—or even closer.

3. Why did the early church do such a good job of looking after each other?
   a. They were totally committed to it.
   b. They knew each other's needs.
   c. They didn't have government welfare programs, so they had to.
   d. They had the Old Testament model of caring for the poor.
   e. They had small house churches where needs could be shared.

4. How is your church like, and unlike, the fellowship of believers described here? Where does most of the caregiving take place in your church?

5. If you had been invited to join this community, what would your initial reaction have been?
   a. This sounds too much like socialism to me.
   b. This sounds like heaven—where do I sign up?!
   c. I have some things that I wouldn't sell for anyone!
   d. I might try it for awhile.
   e. It's fine for others, but not for me.

6. What is the closest you have come to experiencing the kind of fellowship the early church enjoyed?

7. Whom do you (or your group) know with an urgent need? How can you (or your group) help meet that need?

8. What has the church meant to you?
   a. the Sunday thing to do
   b. a social club
   c. brothers and sisters in the family of God
   d. one more activity to fit in
   e. where my closest friends are
   f. just a building

9. What is necessary for you to feel "one in heart and mind" with a church fellowship?
   a. They can't act super-religious.
   b. It needs to be a place where I can honestly question things.
   c. They have to show they care by their actions.
   d. They need to stand firm for the things I believe.
   e. They have to let me be myself.
   f. They have to be Christ-centered.

10. What questions does this passage raise about your financial stress?
   a. Where is a guy like Barnabas when you need him?!
   b. Why don't Christians do more of this today?
   c. Who determines who is "needy" and how much they should get?
   d. When will I be on the giving end instead of needing to receive?

11. If you had to go to someone with a financial need in your life, to whom would you go?

tended do you always lock it? Why or why not?

 1. How do you account for the jealousy of the Sadducees? **2.** As an apostle, how would you feel during the events of verses 18–21? What would you expect to happen next? **3.** Of what do they accuse the apostles in 5:28? How is this different from what bothered them in 4:2? **4.** What assertions in Peter's response (vv. 29–32) would arouse their fury? Why is Peter being so direct (see 4:1–12; 5:19–20)? **5.** Prior to Jesus, there were many Jewish zealots who led rebellions against Rome. What is Gamaliel's point in recalling two such leaders (vv. 36–37)? Do you think he might be one of the secret believers mentioned in John 12:42? Or a political opportunist not wanting to arouse the public? Why? How do you think Peter's statement in verse 29 (and 4:19) may have influenced Gamaliel? **6.** Flogging sometimes resulted in death. Why do you think the disciples considered it worth rejoicing that they suffered in Jesus' name? **7.** How might proclaiming Jesus as risen Prince and Savior in Jerusalem immediately after his crucifix-

the night an angel of the Lord opened the doors of the jail and brought them out. ²⁰"Go, stand in the temple courts," he said, "and tell the people the full message of this new life."

²¹At daybreak they entered the temple courts, as they had been told, and began to teach the people.

When the high priest and his associates arrived, they called together the Sanhedrin—the full assembly of the elders of Israel—and sent to the jail for the apostles. ²²But on arriving at the jail, the officers did not find them there. So they went back and reported, ²³"We found the jail securely locked, with the guards standing at the doors; but when we opened them, we found no one inside." ²⁴On hearing this report, the captain of the temple guard and the chief priests were puzzled, wondering what would come of this.

²⁵Then someone came and said, "Look! The men you put in jail are standing in the temple courts teaching the people." ²⁶At that, the captain went with his officers and brought the apostles. They did not use force, because they feared that the people would stone them.

²⁷Having brought the apostles, they made them appear before the Sanhedrin to be questioned by the high priest. ²⁸"We gave you strict orders not to teach in this name," he said. "Yet you have filled Jerusalem with your teaching and are determined to make us guilty of this man's blood."

²⁹Peter and the other apostles replied: "We must obey God rather than men! ³⁰The God of our fathers raised Jesus from the dead—whom you had killed by hanging him on a tree. ³¹God exalted him to his own right hand as Prince and Savior that he might give repentance and forgiveness of sins to Israel. ³²We are witnesses of

$ Acts 5:1–11   ANANIAS AND SAPPHIRA

As the previous passage demonstrates, members of the early church cared for each other so much they even sold their possessions and brought the proceeds to the apostles for distribution to those in need.

1. Where did Ananias and Sapphira go wrong?
   a. They shouldn't have sold the land.
   b. They shouldn't have kept part of the proceeds for themselves.
   c. They shouldn't have dishonestly claimed to donate all the proceeds.
   d. They shouldn't have been dishonest about the selling price.

2. What did Ananias and Sapphira have to gain by lying about the amount of money they gave?
   a. enjoyment of the portion they kept
   b. people's praise for their generosity
   c. status in the community
   d. a boost for their egos
   e. nothing, in the long run

3. How would you have felt if you were one of those who carried out and buried Ananias and Sapphira?

   a. shocked   f. saddened
   b. sobered   g. sickened
   c. afraid
   d. full of respect for God
   e. I would have gotten God's point.

4. Why do you think God punished Ananias and Sapphira so severely?
   a. to keep them from continuing in their greed and deceit
   b. to deter others from their sin
   c. to show that, with God, honesty is the *only* policy
   d. to demonstrate that God cannot be deceived
   e. to make it clear at the church's outset that a holy God will not tolerate such hypocrisy and deceit
   f. because the trust and integrity of the fellowship was threatened

5. How have you seen people try to use God and the church to further their own ends?

6. In your personal or professional life, in what situations are you most tempted to be dishonest, unethical or lack integrity in some way?

7. When have you tried to "fool" God? On the other hand, when have you experienced the "fear of the Lord"?

8. $ What do you think is God's attitude toward us "getting ahead"?
   a. He's all for it!
   b. It's okay as long as no one else gets hurt.
   c. It's wrong if it is for selfish reasons.
   d. "Get ahead" for God and not for yourself.
   e. Greater wealth brings greater responsibility.

9. $ Rank the following questions according to how you make business decisions, from 1 (most important) to 6 (least important):
   a. Will it help me realize my dream?
   b. Will I make more money?
   c. Is God calling me to do it?
   d. Will it bring me more respect or prestige?
   e. Does it lack integrity in any way?
   f. How will it affect those with whom I work?

these things, and so is the Holy Spirit, whom God has given to those who obey him."

33When they heard this, they were furious and wanted to put them to death. 34But a Pharisee named Gamaliel, a teacher of the law, who was honored by all the people, stood up in the Sanhedrin and ordered that the men be put outside for a little while. 35Then he addressed them: "Men of Israel, consider carefully what you intend to do to these men. 36Some time ago Theudas appeared, claiming to be somebody, and about four hundred men rallied to him. He was killed, all his followers were dispersed, and it all came to nothing. 37After him, Judas the Galilean appeared in the days of the census and led a band of people in revolt. He too was killed, and all his followers were scattered. 38Therefore, in the present case I advise you: Leave these men alone! Let them go! For if their purpose or activity is of human origin, it will fail. 39But if it is from God, you will not be able to stop these men; you will only find yourselves fighting against God."

40His speech persuaded them. They called the apostles in and had them flogged. Then they ordered them not to speak in the name of Jesus, and let them go.

41The apostles left the Sanhedrin, rejoicing because they had been counted worthy of suffering disgrace for the Name. 42Day after day, in the temple courts and from house to house, they never stopped teaching and proclaiming the good news that Jesus is the Christ.ᵃ

The Choosing of the Seven

6 In those days when the number of disciples was increasing, the Grecian Jews among them complained against the Hebraic Jews because their widows were being overlooked in the daily distribution of food. 2So the Twelve gathered all the disciples together and said, "It would not be right for us to neglect the ministry of the word of God in order to wait on tables. 3Brothers, choose seven men from among you who are known to be full of the Spirit and wisdom. We will turn this responsibility over to them 4and will give our attention to prayer and the ministry of the word."

5This proposal pleased the whole group. They chose Stephen, a man full of faith and of the Holy Spirit; also Philip, Procorus, Nicanor, Timon, Parmenas, and Nicolas from Antioch, a convert to Judaism. 6They presented these men to the apostles, who prayed and laid their hands on them.

7So the word of God spread. The number of disciples in Jerusalem increased rapidly, and a large number of priests became obedient to the faith.

Stephen Seized

8Now Stephen, a man full of God's grace and power, did great wonders and miraculous signs among the people. 9Opposition arose, however, from members of the Synagogue of the Freedmen (as it was called)—Jews of Cyrene and Alexandria as well as the provinces of Cilicia and Asia. These men began to argue with Stephen, 10but they could not stand up against his wisdom or the Spirit by whom he spoke.

11Then they secretly persuaded some men to say, "We have heard Stephen speak words of blasphemy against Moses and against God."

12So they stirred up the people and the elders and the teachers of

ion be different than proclaiming Jesus as risen Prince and Savior over 6000 miles away 2000 years later?

1. How do you think you would feel if you were sent to jail for what you believe? How would your family feel? What would this do for your faith? **2.** In what way has God set you free to honor him more fully? **3.** How do you explain why God sometimes delivers you out of hardships, but at other times he allows you to go through them? **4.** Describe a recent event when you had to choose between God and man (v. 29).

Which responsibility at home or work would you gladly give up? Never give up?

1. Given 2:44–45 and 4:32, how could the widows be neglected? **2.** How do the apostles resolve this problem? **3.** Why did they choose men "full of the Spirit and wisdom"? **4.** Consider verse 6. Why such attention to a seemingly minor task?

1. What secondary issues hinder your church from fulfilling Acts 1:8? **2.** Does your church require high credentials and offer great blessing for the minor tasks? What if it did?

Are you more likely to "rock-the-boat" or keep "peace-at-any-price"?

1. What do you think Stephen was like? **2.** Immigrant Jews often formed their own synagogues in Jerusalem. How is their opposition to Stephen like and unlike the opposition the apostles faced from the Sanhedrin (5:27–28)?

ᵃ42 Or *Messiah*

♡ What two adjectives best describe your spiritual life? What would be different if you were "full of grace and power"?

_____

☕ 1. As a child, who was the best storyteller you ever heard? What made that person so effective? 2. Where did your ancestors come from? Do you have any heroes in your family? Any black sheep? 3. What's the longest speech you've ever listened to? Was it exciting or boring? Why? What makes a speech or sermon interesting to you? 4. In which ways are you "just like your mother" or "just like your father"?

📖 1. From 6:13–14, how would you write up the formal charges against Stephen? 2. What does Stephen's storytelling (in effect a history lesson) reveal about his respect for the Mosaic Law? 3. Why does Stephen spend the bulk of his history lesson talking about Moses? What parallels does he draw between Moses and Jesus? How does this relate to the charges against him in 6:13–14? How does the quote in verse 37 begin to turn the tables on his accusers (regarding who is really rejecting Moses)? 4. From verses 44–50, what is his point about the temple and God's presence? How is he turning the tables against his accusers once again? 5. What does Stephen mean by the phrase "uncircumcised hearts and ears" (v. 51)? In this context, what is Stephen really saying about the Sanhedrin's regard for Moses and the Law? 6. Of what does he accuse them in verses 51–53? How does his charge reveal the reason why he gave them this history lesson? 7. Considering this oppressive situation, what type of person is Stephen?

♡ 1. Since the Sanhedrin knew religious history every bit as well as Stephen, how do you account for their radically different response to Jesus? To fully understand Jesus, what is needed in your life besides well-rehearsed knowledge? 2. How do people hold on to religious rituals and heroes today, while missing the whole point of what those ceremonies and people represent? 3. In what

the law. They seized Stephen and brought him before the Sanhedrin. [13]They produced false witnesses, who testified, "This fellow never stops speaking against this holy place and against the law. [14]For we have heard him say that this Jesus of Nazareth will destroy this place and change the customs Moses handed down to us."

[15]All who were sitting in the Sanhedrin looked intently at Stephen, and they saw that his face was like the face of an angel.

Stephen's Speech to the Sanhedrin

7 Then the high priest asked him, "Are these charges true?" [2]To this he replied: "Brothers and fathers, listen to me! The God of glory appeared to our father Abraham while he was still in Mesopotamia, before he lived in Haran. [3]'Leave your country and your people,' God said, 'and go to the land I will show you.'[a]

[4]"So he left the land of the Chaldeans and settled in Haran. After the death of his father, God sent him to this land where you are now living. [5]He gave him no inheritance here, not even a foot of ground. But God promised him that he and his descendants after him would possess the land, even though at that time Abraham had no child. [6]God spoke to him in this way: 'Your descendants will be strangers in a country not their own, and they will be enslaved and mistreated four hundred years. [7]But I will punish the nation they serve as slaves,' God said, 'and afterward they will come out of that country and worship me in this place.'[b] [8]Then he gave Abraham the covenant of circumcision. And Abraham became the father of Isaac and circumcised him eight days after his birth. Later Isaac became the father of Jacob, and Jacob became the father of the twelve patriarchs.

[9]"Because the patriarchs were jealous of Joseph, they sold him as a slave into Egypt. But God was with him [10]and rescued him from all his troubles. He gave Joseph wisdom and enabled him to gain the goodwill of Pharaoh king of Egypt; so he made him ruler over Egypt and all his palace.

[11]"Then a famine struck all Egypt and Canaan, bringing great suffering, and our fathers could not find food. [12]When Jacob heard that there was grain in Egypt, he sent our fathers on their first visit. [13]On their second visit, Joseph told his brothers who he was, and Pharaoh learned about Joseph's family. [14]After this, Joseph sent for his father Jacob and his whole family, seventy-five in all. [15]Then Jacob went down to Egypt, where he and our fathers died. [16]Their bodies were brought back to Shechem and placed in the tomb that Abraham had bought from the sons of Hamor at Shechem for a certain sum of money.

[17]"As the time drew near for God to fulfill his promise to Abraham, the number of our people in Egypt greatly increased. [18]Then another king, who knew nothing about Joseph, became ruler of Egypt. [19]He dealt treacherously with our people and oppressed our forefathers by forcing them to throw out their newborn babies so that they would die.

[20]"At that time Moses was born, and he was no ordinary child.[c] For three months he was cared for in his father's house. [21]When he was placed outside, Pharaoh's daughter took him and brought him up as her own son. [22]Moses was educated in all the wisdom of the Egyptians and was powerful in speech and action.

[23]"When Moses was forty years old, he decided to visit his fellow Israelites. [24]He saw one of them being mistreated by an Egyp-

a3 Gen. 12:1   b7 Gen. 15:13,14   c20 Or was fair in the sight of God

tian, so he went to his defense and avenged him by killing the Egyptian. [25]Moses thought that his own people would realize that God was using him to rescue them, but they did not. [26]The next day Moses came upon two Israelites who were fighting. He tried to reconcile them by saying, 'Men, you are brothers; why do you want to hurt each other?'

[27]"But the man who was mistreating the other pushed Moses aside and said, 'Who made you ruler and judge over us? [28]Do you want to kill me as you killed the Egyptian yesterday?'[a] [29]When Moses heard this, he fled to Midian, where he settled as a foreigner and had two sons.

[30]"After forty years had passed, an angel appeared to Moses in the flames of a burning bush in the desert near Mount Sinai. [31]When he saw this, he was amazed at the sight. As he went over to look more closely, he heard the Lord's voice: [32]'I am the God of your fathers, the God of Abraham, Isaac and Jacob.'[b] Moses trembled with fear and did not dare to look.

[33]"Then the Lord said to him, 'Take off your sandals; the place where you are standing is holy ground. [34]I have indeed seen the oppression of my people in Egypt. I have heard their groaning and have come down to set them free. Now come, I will send you back to Egypt.'[c]

[35]"This is the same Moses whom they had rejected with the words, 'Who made you ruler and judge?' He was sent to be their ruler and deliverer by God himself, through the angel who appeared to him in the bush. [36]He led them out of Egypt and did wonders and miraculous signs in Egypt, at the Red Sea[d] and for forty years in the desert.

[37]"This is that Moses who told the Israelites, 'God will send you a prophet like me from your own people.'[e] [38]He was in the assembly in the desert, with the angel who spoke to him on Mount Sinai, and with our fathers; and he received living words to pass on to us.

[39]"But our fathers refused to obey him. Instead, they rejected him and in their hearts turned back to Egypt. [40]They told Aaron, 'Make us gods who will go before us. As for this fellow Moses who led us out of Egypt—we don't know what has happened to him!'[f] [41]That was the time they made an idol in the form of a calf. They brought sacrifices to it and held a celebration in honor of what their hands had made. [42]But God turned away and gave them over to the worship of the heavenly bodies. This agrees with what is written in the book of the prophets:

> " 'Did you bring me sacrifices and offerings
>   forty years in the desert, O house of Israel?
> [43]You have lifted up the shrine of Molech
>   and the star of your god Rephan,
>   the idols you made to worship.
> Therefore I will send you into exile'[g] beyond
>   Babylon.

[44]"Our forefathers had the tabernacle of the Testimony with them in the desert. It had been made as God directed Moses, according to the pattern he had seen. [45]Having received the tabernacle, our fathers under Joshua brought it with them when they took the land from the nations God drove out before them. It remained in the land until the time of David, [46]who enjoyed God's

ways could the charges that Stephen makes against the leaders be made against you? How might you be "stiff-necked" this week? How will you begin to bow to God in that area now? **4.** Has Stephen's review of OT history encouraged you? Challenged you? Confused you? Would you say that the OT is more like a stranger or a close friend to you? How does this speech show the importance of the OT to the early Christians? What will you do to let its importance grow for you? **5.** When Jesus was brought to trial, he was basically quiet before the Sanhedrin; yet Stephen spoke very boldly. How do you decide when to speak and when to be quiet before opposition? **6.** What has been your experience with people who seem overly concerned with religious arguments?

---

[a]28 Exodus 2:14   [b]32 Exodus 3:6   [c]34 Exodus 3:5,7,8,10   [d]36 That is, Sea of Reeds   [e]37 Deut. 18:15   [f]40 Exodus 32:1   [g]43 Amos 5:25-27

favor and asked that he might provide a dwelling place for the God of Jacob.[a] 47But it was Solomon who built the house for him.

48"However, the Most High does not live in houses made by men. As the prophet says:

49" 'Heaven is my throne,
and the earth is my footstool.
What kind of house will you build for me?
                              says the Lord.
Or where will my resting place be?
50Has not my hand made all these things?'[b]

51"You stiff-necked people, with uncircumcised hearts and ears! You are just like your fathers: You always resist the Holy Spirit! 52Was there ever a prophet your fathers did not persecute? They even killed those who predicted the coming of the Righteous One. And now you have betrayed and murdered him— 53you who have received the law that was put into effect through angels but have not obeyed it."

The Stoning of Stephen

54When they heard this, they were furious and gnashed their teeth at him. 55But Stephen, full of the Holy Spirit, looked up to heaven and saw the glory of God, and Jesus standing at the right hand of God. 56"Look," he said, "I see heaven open and the Son of Man standing at the right hand of God."

57At this they covered their ears and, yelling at the top of their voices, they all rushed at him, 58dragged him out of the city and began to stone him. Meanwhile, the witnesses laid their clothes at the feet of a young man named Saul.

59While they were stoning him, Stephen prayed, "Lord Jesus, receive my spirit." 60Then he fell on his knees and cried out, "Lord, do not hold this sin against them." When he had said this, he fell asleep.

8 And Saul was there, giving approval to his death.

The Church Persecuted and Scattered

On that day a great persecution broke out against the church at Jerusalem, and all except the apostles were scattered throughout Judea and Samaria. 2Godly men buried Stephen and mourned deeply for him. 3But Saul began to destroy the church. Going from house to house, he dragged off men and women and put them in prison.

Philip in Samaria

4Those who had been scattered preached the word wherever they went. 5Philip went down to a city in Samaria and proclaimed the Christ[c] there. 6When the crowds heard Philip and saw the miraculous signs he did, they all paid close attention to what he said. 7With shrieks, evil[d] spirits came out of many, and many paralytics and cripples were healed. 8So there was great joy in that city.

Simon the Sorcerer

9Now for some time a man named Simon had practiced sorcery in the city and amazed all the people of Samaria. He boasted that he was someone great, 10and all the people, both high and low,

---

What do you do when you feel angry enough to resort to sticks and stones?

1. Why are Stephen's listeners so enraged (see Da 7:13–14)? **2.** Stephen's death was illegal (see Jn 18:31). What does that reveal about the desperation of the Sanhedrin? **3.** This begins phase two ("Judea and Samaria") of God's plan (see 1:8). How would you sum up the "Jerusalem phase" (ch. 2–7)?

1. What is one very traumatic event that happened to you in your formative years? Can you see now how God has used it for good? **2.** Peter's speech led to mass conversion (ch. 2), while Stephen's led to his death. What does that teach about success in one's service to God?

Who was your hero when you were 10? A movie star? An athlete? A comic book character? What ability did they have that you wanted for yourself?

1. What did Simon and Philip have in common (vv. 5–11)? How were they different? How did the crowd respond to both men? **2.** Given that the Samaritans were considered outcasts by the Jews (see Jn 4:9), why would Peter and John come to them? **3.** Why would the Father delay pouring out his Spirit until Peter and John were on the scene? Do you think this was a lesson for the Samaritans or for the

---

[a]46 Some early manuscripts *the house of Jacob*   [b]50 Isaiah 66:1,2   [c]5 Or *Messiah*   [d]7 Greek *unclean*

gave him their attention and exclaimed, "This man is the divine power known as the Great Power." [11]They followed him because he had amazed them for a long time with his magic. [12]But when they believed Philip as he preached the good news of the kingdom of God and the name of Jesus Christ, they were baptized, both men and women. [13]Simon himself believed and was baptized. And he followed Philip everywhere, astonished by the great signs and miracles he saw.

[14]When the apostles in Jerusalem heard that Samaria had accepted the word of God, they sent Peter and John to them. [15]When they arrived, they prayed for them that they might receive the Holy Spirit, [16]because the Holy Spirit had not yet come upon any of them; they had simply been baptized into[a] the name of the Lord Jesus. [17]Then Peter and John placed their hands on them, and they received the Holy Spirit.

[18]When Simon saw that the Spirit was given at the laying on of the apostles' hands, he offered them money [19]and said, "Give me also this ability so that everyone on whom I lay my hands may receive the Holy Spirit."

[20]Peter answered: "May your money perish with you, because you thought you could buy the gift of God with money! [21]You have no part or share in this ministry, because your heart is not right before God. [22]Repent of this wickedness and pray to the Lord. Perhaps he will forgive you for having such a thought in your heart. [23]For I see that you are full of bitterness and captive to sin."

[24]Then Simon answered, "Pray to the Lord for me so that nothing you have said may happen to me."

[25]When they had testified and proclaimed the word of the Lord, Peter and John returned to Jerusalem, preaching the gospel in many Samaritan villages.

Philip and the Ethiopian

[26]Now an angel of the Lord said to Philip, "Go south to the road—the desert road—that goes down from Jerusalem to Gaza." [27]So he started out, and on his way he met an Ethiopian[b] eunuch, an important official in charge of all the treasury of Candace, queen of the Ethiopians. This man had gone to Jerusalem to worship, [28]and on his way home was sitting in his chariot reading the book of Isaiah the prophet. [29]The Spirit told Philip, "Go to that chariot and stay near it."

[30]Then Philip ran up to the chariot and heard the man reading Isaiah the prophet. "Do you understand what you are reading?" Philip asked.

[31]"How can I," he said, "unless someone explains it to me?" So he invited Philip to come up and sit with him.

[32]The eunuch was reading this passage of Scripture:

"He was led like a sheep to the slaughter,
    and as a lamb before the shearer is silent,
        so he did not open his mouth.
[33]In his humiliation he was deprived of justice.
    Who can speak of his descendants?
        For his life was taken from the earth."[c]

[34]The eunuch asked Philip, "Tell me, please, who is the prophet talking about, himself or someone else?" [35]Then Philip began with that very passage of Scripture and told him the good news about Jesus.

apostles? **4.** In what ways does Simon's reaction to the apostles (vv. 18–19) show his deep misunderstanding about the Gospel? **5.** Do you think that Simon's words in verse 24 reveal a change in his heart?

1. What prejudices were you brought up with? How is the Gospel breaking through those prejudices in your life? **2.** What was your primary motivation in first receiving Jesus Christ as Savior? What is your primary motivation for continuing in the faith? **3.** How has jealousy of other Christians affected your faith?

What experience have you had with being tutored, or with tutoring others?

1. Why does the eunuch visit Jerusalem (see 2:1–11)? **2.** The eunuch was reading Isaiah 53. In what ways does Jesus fit the picture of the one described there? **3.** How did God pave the way for his message? What is the relationship between divine preparation and human initiative in this story? **4.** So far, what has been the effect of Stephen's death upon Philip? Upon the church as a whole?

1. From the way God sets up opportunities to witness (vv. 26–40; 2:5–14; 3:6–16), how does that free you from fears in evangelism? **2.** Deep down, do you think successful VIPs really need the Gospel as much as poor beggars do (3:2)? Why or why not? **3.** Would you know the Bible well enough to address the eunuch's questions? How can you grow in faith so you will be prepared for similar opportunities?

_a16_ Or _in_   _b27_ That is, from the upper Nile region   _c33_ Isaiah 53:7,8

36As they traveled along the road, they came to some water and the eunuch said, "Look, here is water. Why shouldn't I be baptized?"*a* 38And he gave orders to stop the chariot. Then both Philip and the eunuch went down into the water and Philip baptized him. 39When they came up out of the water, the Spirit of the Lord suddenly took Philip away, and the eunuch did not see him again, but went on his way rejoicing. 40Philip, however, appeared at Azotus and traveled about, preaching the gospel in all the towns until he reached Caesarea.

Saul's Conversion

9 Meanwhile, Saul was still breathing out murderous threats against the Lord's disciples. He went to the high priest 2and asked him for letters to the synagogues in Damascus, so that if he found any there who belonged to the Way, whether men or women, he might take them as prisoners to Jerusalem. 3As he neared Damascus on his journey, suddenly a light from heaven flashed around him. 4He fell to the ground and heard a voice say to him, "Saul, Saul, why do you persecute me?"

5"Who are you, Lord?" Saul asked.

"I am Jesus, whom you are persecuting," he replied. 6"Now get up and go into the city, and you will be told what you must do."

7The men traveling with Saul stood there speechless; they heard the sound but did not see anyone. 8Saul got up from the ground, but when he opened his eyes he could see nothing. So they led him

a36 Some late manuscripts baptized?" 37Philip said, "If you believe with all your heart, you may." The eunuch answered, "I believe that Jesus Christ is the Son of God."

What is the longest you have been without food or drink: Three days? Three meals? Three hours? Why? How did you feel?

1. What do you know about Saul to this point? **2.** Saul's former teacher was Gamaliel (see 22:3). What had Gamaliel advised the Sanhedrin regarding Christians in 5:34–39? How is Saul responding to this advice? What does this show about him? **3.** Describe what happened in verses 3–9 from the viewpoint of one of Saul's companions? **4.** Was Saul's heart open to Jesus' arrival? Why or why not? **5.** How do you think Saul felt when confronted by Jesus (vv. 4–6)? Given his previous activities, what would he be thinking about during

---

 Acts 8:26–40   **PHILIP AND THE ETHIOPIAN**

1. What is your impression of Philip, one of the church's first evangelists, in this story?
   a. He really got around!
   b. He instantly obeyed the Lord.
   c. He seemed kind of pushy.
   d. I wish I were as bold as he was.
   e. I'm surprised how quick he was to baptize the Ethiopian eunuch.

2. What is your impression of the Ethiopian official in this story?
   a. As a Gentile interested in the Jewish religion, he was a spiritually hungry seeker.
   b. He was fortunate—he found quick answers to his spiritual questions.
   c. He was "ripe" for the Gospel.
   d. He was decisive—when he found what he wanted, he went for it.

3. How would you have reacted if you were the Ethiopian when Philip ran up and asked, "Do you understand what you are reading?"
   a. "Sorry, I don't pick up hitchhikers!"
   b. "Do I know you?"
   c. "I can figure it out myself."
   d. "I'm always open to someone else's opinion."

e. "This stuff is over my head—I'd be glad for your help."
   f. "Who made you an authority?!"

4. Compared to this story, how would you rate yourself with Scripture?
   a. I've never been as interested in Scripture as they were.
   b. I share their strong interest.
   c. I share the Ethiopian's confusion!
   d. I may know a little more than the Ethiopian did, but there is still much I don't understand.
   e. I have questions but, like Philip, I have a good grasp of Scripture and what it says about my faith.
   f. Like Philip, I am fulfilled by helping others understand Scripture.

5. The Ethiopian was traveling along a desert road. How would you describe the "road" you've been traveling?
   a. also a desert road—lonely, with little life around
   b. a scenic mountain road—off the main highway, but beautiful
   c. a highway under construction—smoother some places than others
   d. a freeway—a nice, relaxed trip

6. Who along the road has been like Philip and shown you the way to a more meaningful life? What was the most important spiritual truth that person taught you?

7. $ On a scale of 1 to 10, what degree of meaning have you received from your work (or other main activity) at the following times?
   a. right now
   b. five years ago
   c. 10 years ago
   d. when I was most fulfilled—at the time I was doing _____

8. $ What is it that makes work meaningful or not meaningful for you?
   a. whether I see results
   b. whether I am working mainly with people or not
   c. whether it has lasting value
   d. whether I am using strengths and skills I enjoy using
   e. whether I believe what I do truly helps people
   f. whether the business I am in is operated ethically
   g. other:_____

by the hand into Damascus. ⁹For three days he was blind, and did not eat or drink anything.

¹⁰In Damascus there was a disciple named Ananias. The Lord called to him in a vision, "Ananias!"

"Yes, Lord," he answered.

¹¹The Lord told him, "Go to the house of Judas on Straight Street and ask for a man from Tarsus named Saul, for he is praying. ¹²In a vision he has seen a man named Ananias come and place his hands on him to restore his sight."

¹³"Lord," Ananias answered, "I have heard many reports about this man and all the harm he has done to your saints in Jerusalem. ¹⁴And he has come here with authority from the chief priests to arrest all who call on your name."

¹⁵But the Lord said to Ananias, "Go! This man is my chosen instrument to carry my name before the Gentiles and their kings and before the people of Israel. ¹⁶I will show him how much he must suffer for my name."

¹⁷Then Ananias went to the house and entered it. Placing his hands on Saul, he said, "Brother Saul, the Lord—Jesus, who appeared to you on the road as you were coming here—has sent me so that you may see again and be filled with the Holy Spirit." ¹⁸Immediately, something like scales fell from Saul's eyes, and he could see again. He got up and was baptized, ¹⁹and after taking some food, he regained his strength.

Saul in Damascus and Jerusalem

Saul spent several days with the disciples in Damascus. ²⁰At once he began to preach in the synagogues that Jesus is the Son of

---

those three days of blindness and fasting (v. 9)? **6.** How would you feel in Ananias' place? Since Jesus had already appeared to Saul directly, why this time would he want a person to go to him? What is significant about the way Ananias addresses Saul (v. 17)?

 1. How did the Lord first get your attention? Was it in some dramatic event or something more subtle? Have you had a post-encounter experience like Saul did? **2.** Do you assume some people are beyond God's reach? How does this story challenge those assumptions? **3.** When have you, like Ananias, obeyed the Lord even when you had doubts? What happened? **4.** Who has played the role of Ananias in your life? To whom does the Lord want you to play that part?

Who do people say you look like? Why?

     Acts 9:1–19   **SAUL'S CONVERSION**

While the early church was growing rapidly, Saul the Pharisee—who would become known as the apostle Paul—was trying to destroy it.

1. How might the medical profession today explain what happened to Saul on the road to Damascus?
   a. He was struck by lightning.
   b. He had a physical breakdown.
   c. He had a mental breakdown.
   d. He had a partial stroke that rendered him temporarily blind.
   e. He had a psychological crisis due to an overly-religious personality.
   f. He suffered from repressed guilt for his role in persecuting people.

2. How do you think Saul felt during his three days of blindness?
   a. wiped out   d. humbled
   b. terrified   e. angry
   c. confused   f. repentant

3. If you were Ananias, how would you have reacted when God told you to go and lay hands on Saul?
   a. "I'll lay hands on him all right!"
   b. "This is just a dream, right God?"
   c. "Don't you know who this guy is?"

d. "I love a challenge!"
e. "If you really want me to, I'll do it."

4. What was the most significant thing that happened to Saul after Ananias prayed for him?
   a. His physical vision was restored.
   b. His spiritual vision was corrected.
   c. He believed and was baptized.
   d. He was filled with the Holy Spirit.
   e. He was accepted as a "brother" in God's family.
   f. He was commissioned to represent Christ around the world.

5. How would you compare your conversion to Saul's conversion?
   a. Mine was almost as dramatic.
   b. Mine was a lot more gradual.
   c. I'm still sorting out what has happened to me.
   d. I'm on my way back to God and I still have a lot of questions.

6. Who has played the role of Ananias in your life? To whom might the Lord want you to play the part?

7. In what area of your life have you seen the most change

since you committed your life to Christ? And in what area do you sense God calling you to allow him to bring additional change?
a. priorities   d. beliefs
b. relationships   e. goals
c. attitudes   f. values

8. Why do you think that, as other Scriptures show, Saul (Paul) saw his singleness as a gift?
   a. He probably saw it as a fulfillment of verse 16: "I will show him how much he must *suffer*"!
   b. He realized he could serve God and others more wholeheartedly as a single.
   c. He was such an intense person that he knew it would be better for him to remain single.
   d. He saw it as part of his calling.

9. How do you feel about the possibility that God has given *you* the gift of singleness?
   a. That doesn't sound like a gift!
   b. It makes sense to me.
   c. I'll have to think about it.
   d. If that's what God wants, that's what I want.

1. What would others have expected Saul to say when he came to the synagogue? When he proceeds to preach about Christ, how do they react (v. 23)? Why? **2.** Why would the Jerusalem disciples still fear Saul? What risk is Barnabas taking? **3.** People in Damascus and Jerusalem wanted to kill Saul. What does that say about him? **4.** How is the story of Saul related to 1:8?

1. What changes did people notice when you began following Jesus? How did they react? **2.** Who has been a Barnabas to you? How? Whom have you served as a Barnabas? **3.** What does "living in the fear of the Lord" (v. 31) mean to you?

God. ²¹All those who heard him were astonished and asked, "Isn't he the man who raised havoc in Jerusalem among those who call on this name? And hasn't he come here to take them as prisoners to the chief priests?" ²²Yet Saul grew more and more powerful and baffled the Jews living in Damascus by proving that Jesus is the Christ.ᵃ

²³After many days had gone by, the Jews conspired to kill him, ²⁴but Saul learned of their plan. Day and night they kept close watch on the city gates in order to kill him. ²⁵But his followers took him by night and lowered him in a basket through an opening in the wall.

²⁶When he came to Jerusalem, he tried to join the disciples, but they were all afraid of him, not believing that he really was a disciple. ²⁷But Barnabas took him and brought him to the apostles. He told them how Saul on his journey had seen the Lord and that the Lord had spoken to him, and how in Damascus he had preached fearlessly in the name of Jesus. ²⁸So Saul stayed with them and moved about freely in Jerusalem, speaking boldly in the name of the Lord. ²⁹He talked and debated with the Grecian Jews, but they tried to kill him. ³⁰When the brothers learned of this, they took him down to Caesarea and sent him off to Tarsus.

³¹Then the church throughout Judea, Galilee and Samaria enjoyed a time of peace. It was strengthened; and encouraged by the Holy Spirit, it grew in numbers, living in the fear of the Lord.

Aeneas and Dorcas

³²As Peter traveled about the country, he went to visit the saints in Lydda. ³³There he found a man named Aeneas, a paralytic who

ᵃ22 Or Messiah

Acts 9:20–31   SAUL IN DAMASCUS AND JERUSALEM

As a zealous Pharisee, Saul became a vehement opponent of Christianity. But on his way to Damascus to arrest believers, Saul had a life-changing encounter with the risen Christ. The result was that he not only became a Christian himself, but eventually the renowned "Apostle Paul."

1. What would be the most intriguing scene of a movie about this story?
   a. Jesus suddenly appearing to Saul on the road to Damascus (v. 27)
   b. people's reaction when the persecutor of Christians turned out to be a preacher of Christ (vv. 20–21)
   c. Saul being lowered in a basket to escape the threat on his life (v. 25)
   d. the Jerusalem disciples' fear and distrust of Saul (v. 26)
   e. Barnabas' courage to step forward and speak up for Saul (v. 27)
   f. Saul threatened again, but spared by his new "brothers" (vv. 29–30)

2. How would you have felt if you were part of the church in Jerusalem when Saul wanted to join it?

   a. I would be afraid he was faking a conversion to infiltrate our group.
   b. I would rejoice in his claim to faith and welcome him with open arms.
   c. I would let him in but keep a close eye on him.
   d. I would have required him to make up for his past wrongs.

3. How would you have felt if you met the kind of suspicion Saul did?
   a. I would be hurt.
   b. I would be angry.
   c. I would think I didn't deserve to be accepted.
   d. I would withdraw and give up.
   e. I would take it as a challenge to prove myself.

4. What led Barnabas to help Saul?
   a. He felt sorry for him.
   b. He let Saul tell his story.
   c. He could discern Saul's heart.
   d. He had the gift of encouragement.
   e. He was motivated by love rather than fear.
   f. His belief in Saul outweighed the risks of being rejected himself.

5. Who has been a Barnabas to you—encouraging you or helping you feel accepted? Whom have you, or could you, serve like Barnabas did?

6. How do other people respond to you as a Christian? Have you ever experienced rejection for your faith?

7. Where is it hardest for you to feel accepted?
   a. in my family
   b. at school
   c. at church/youth group
   d. at parties/social gatherings
   e. by the opposite sex
   f. into groups or cliques

8. What do you do when you feel like you don't fit in?
   a. I don't let it bother me.
   b. I *act* like it doesn't bother me.
   c. I try even harder to fit in.
   d. I back off or quit trying.
   e. I find somewhere else to fit in.

9. How accepted do you feel by God? How can God's acceptance help when you don't fit in?

had been bedridden for eight years. ³⁴"Aeneas," Peter said to him, "Jesus Christ heals you. Get up and take care of your mat." Immediately Aeneas got up. ³⁵All those who lived in Lydda and Sharon saw him and turned to the Lord.

³⁶In Joppa there was a disciple named Tabitha (which, when translated, is Dorcas[a]), who was always doing good and helping the poor. ³⁷About that time she became sick and died, and her body was washed and placed in an upstairs room. ³⁸Lydda was near Joppa; so when the disciples heard that Peter was in Lydda, they sent two men to him and urged him, "Please come at once!"

³⁹Peter went with them, and when he arrived he was taken upstairs to the room. All the widows stood around him, crying and showing him the robes and other clothing that Dorcas had made while she was still with them.

⁴⁰Peter sent them all out of the room; then he got down on his knees and prayed. Turning toward the dead woman, he said, "Tabitha, get up." She opened her eyes, and seeing Peter she sat up. ⁴¹He took her by the hand and helped her to her feet. Then he called the believers and the widows and presented her to them alive. ⁴²This became known all over Joppa, and many people believed in the Lord. ⁴³Peter stayed in Joppa for some time with a tanner named Simon.

Cornelius Calls for Peter

10 At Caesarea there was a man named Cornelius, a centurion in what was known as the Italian Regiment. ²He and all his family were devout and God-fearing; he gave generously to those in need and prayed to God regularly. ³One day at about three in the afternoon he had a vision. He distinctly saw an angel of God, who came to him and said, "Cornelius!"

⁴Cornelius stared at him in fear. "What is it, Lord?" he asked.

The angel answered, "Your prayers and gifts to the poor have come up as a memorial offering before God. ⁵Now send men to Joppa to bring back a man named Simon who is called Peter. ⁶He is staying with Simon the tanner, whose house is by the sea."

⁷When the angel who spoke to him had gone, Cornelius called two of his servants and a devout soldier who was one of his attendants. ⁸He told them everything that had happened and sent them to Joppa.

Peter's Vision

⁹About noon the following day as they were on their journey and approaching the city, Peter went up on the roof to pray. ¹⁰He became hungry and wanted something to eat, and while the meal was being prepared, he fell into a trance. ¹¹He saw heaven opened and something like a large sheet being let down to earth by its four corners. ¹²It contained all kinds of four-footed animals, as well as reptiles of the earth and birds of the air. ¹³Then a voice told him, "Get up, Peter. Kill and eat."

¹⁴"Surely not, Lord!" Peter replied. "I have never eaten anything impure or unclean."

¹⁵The voice spoke to him a second time, "Do not call anything impure that God has made clean."

¹⁶This happened three times, and immediately the sheet was taken back to heaven.

¹⁷While Peter was wondering about the meaning of the vision, the men sent by Cornelius found out where Simon's house was and

a36 Both *Tabitha* (Aramaic) and *Dorcas* (Greek) mean *gazelle*.

What does it take to get you out of bed in the morning?

1. What is the purpose of these signs and wonders (vv. 35, 41–42; also 2:22,43; 4:30; 5:12–14)? 2. Although Peter had healed many people, he had never raised anyone from death. What might he be feeling as he goes to Tabitha's home? 3. Which of Jesus' miracles do these two incidents remind you of?

1. Why is it that Tabitha was raised, but Stephen died, even though Peter was there too (8:2)? How would you explain God's ways to Stephen's widow or mother? How does the results of Stephen's death and Tabitha's resurrection help you to understand God's plans? 2. Do miracles like these happen in the same way today? Why or why not?

What dream (or nightmare) has inspired (or haunted) you?

What is Cornelius like (vv. 1–2)? Since he is part of an occupying army, what is unusual about him? About his encounter with God?

1. Are you very "God-fearing"? If evaluated by how you treated others this week, what would they say? 2. How does Cornelius' life challenge you?

As a child, what foods did you refuse to eat? What foods do you still dislike today?

1. Look at Leviticus 11:4–7, 13–19 and 29–30. With these restrictions, how do you think Peter felt when he heard the voice ordering him to eat these animals? Why was it repeated three times? What would the new principle given in verse 15 mean to him? How does it fit with the story of Cornelius (vv. 1–10, 23–34)? 2. How might Peter feel when the men sent by Cornelius showed up?

1. What principles or beliefs do you hold that limit your ability to reach out to people "different" from you? How would others around you feel if you moved be-

yond these limits? **2.** What new relationships has God given you recently? How has he brought these people into your life? How have you influenced each other?

Did you grow up isolated from or associating with other ethnic groups? How much contact do you have with people from other ethnic groups today?

1. Given Peter's experience in verses 9–23 and what you know of Cornelius, how do you think each man was feeling as they greeted one another? **2.** Jews regarded even people like Cornelius as pagans, unless they fully submitted to Jewish practices (see 11:3). Hence, what would verse 28 have meant to Cornelius? Why is

stopped at the gate. ¹⁸They called out, asking if Simon who was known as Peter was staying there.

¹⁹While Peter was still thinking about the vision, the Spirit said to him, "Simon, three*ᵃ* men are looking for you. ²⁰So get up and go downstairs. Do not hesitate to go with them, for I have sent them."

²¹Peter went down and said to the men, "I'm the one you're looking for. Why have you come?"

²²The men replied, "We have come from Cornelius the centurion. He is a righteous and God-fearing man, who is respected by all the Jewish people. A holy angel told him to have you come to his house so that he could hear what you have to say." ²³Then Peter invited the men into the house to be his guests.

Peter at Cornelius' House

The next day Peter started out with them, and some of the brothers from Joppa went along. ²⁴The following day he arrived in Caesarea. Cornelius was expecting them and had called together his relatives and close friends. ²⁵As Peter entered the house, Cornelius met him and fell at his feet in reverence. ²⁶But Peter made him get up. "Stand up," he said, "I am only a man myself."

²⁷Talking with him, Peter went inside and found a large gathering of people. ²⁸He said to them: "You are well aware that it is against our law for a Jew to associate with a Gentile or visit him. But God has shown me that I should not call any man impure or unclean. ²⁹So when I was sent for, I came without raising any objection. May I ask why you sent for me?"

ᵃ19 One early manuscript *two*; other manuscripts do not have the number.

Acts 10:1–23   **PETER'S VISION**

1. Why do you think this story got into the Bible?
   a. It shows that God doesn't care what Christians eat.
   b. It shows that Gentiles are on equal terms as Jews before God.
   c. It teaches Christians not to put limits on God.
   d. Cornelius and his close friends and relatives would be the first Gentiles to become Christians.
   e. It was a turning point in the expansion of the church.

2. Why do you think God gave Peter a vision of "unclean" animals instead of directly telling him what he wanted?
   a. God doesn't like to do things the easy way.
   b. Peter was hungry, so God started where he was at.
   c. God likes to use symbolism.
   d. If God was more direct, Peter might have been more resistant.

3. What do you think Peter's first reaction was to eating animals that "Law-abiding Jews" religiously avoided?

   a. I must be having a crazy dream.
   b. God can't be serious about this.
   c. Why is God changing the rules in midstream?
   d. Is God trying to test my obedience to him?

4. What was God saying through the vision and Cornelius' messengers?
   a. It's okay to eat anything you want.
   b. You can overlook ceremonial laws.
   c. Anybody can become a Christian.
   d. You need to accept non-Jews into the church.

5. Who would it be harder for you to accept into your group or church?
   a. someone like Peter with a very religious mindset
   b. someone like Cornelius with a pagan, unchurched background
   c. We could accept either.
   d. We would have trouble with both.

6. What kind of walls have you permitted between yourself and others?
   a. racial   d. political
   b. religious   e. moral
   c. economic   f. denominational

7. What are some types of people you have written off? What principles or beliefs have limited your ability to reach out to these persons?

8. Considering the makeup of your community and church or small group, would some people assume your church or group is not for them? If so, how can you change that?

9. What does this story say to you about following Christ?
   a. God is pleased by prayer and giving to the poor.
   b. If I were more diligent in prayer, God might speak to me more clearly.
   c. I need to have a teachable spirit.
   d. I need to say no to prejudice.
   e. I need to break down social barriers within my sphere of influence.
   f. other:_____

10. If God gave you a vision or sent an angel to you with a message, what do you think the Spirit would tell you to do? Would you have any hesitation to obey?

30Cornelius answered: "Four days ago I was in my house praying at this hour, at three in the afternoon. Suddenly a man in shining clothes stood before me 31and said, 'Cornelius, God has heard your prayer and remembered your gifts to the poor. 32Send to Joppa for Simon who is called Peter. He is a guest in the home of Simon the tanner, who lives by the sea.' 33So I sent for you immediately, and it was good of you to come. Now we are all here in the presence of God to listen to everything the Lord has commanded you to tell us."

34Then Peter began to speak: "I now realize how true it is that God does not show favoritism 35but accepts men from every nation who fear him and do what is right. 36You know the message God sent to the people of Israel, telling the good news of peace through Jesus Christ, who is Lord of all. 37You know what has happened throughout Judea, beginning in Galilee after the baptism that John preached— 38how God anointed Jesus of Nazareth with the Holy Spirit and power, and how he went around doing good and healing all who were under the power of the devil, because God was with him.

39"We are witnesses of everything he did in the country of the Jews and in Jerusalem. They killed him by hanging him on a tree, 40but God raised him from the dead on the third day and caused him to be seen. 41He was not seen by all the people, but by witnesses whom God had already chosen—by us who ate and drank with him after he rose from the dead. 42He commanded us to preach to the people and to testify that he is the one whom God appointed as judge of the living and the dead. 43All the prophets testify about him that everyone who believes in him receives forgiveness of sins through his name."

44While Peter was still speaking these words, the Holy Spirit came on all who heard the message. 45The circumcised believers who had come with Peter were astonished that the gift of the Holy Spirit had been poured out even on the Gentiles. 46For they heard them speaking in tongues*a* and praising God.

Then Peter said, 47"Can anyone keep these people from being baptized with water? They have received the Holy Spirit just as we have." 48So he ordered that they be baptized in the name of Jesus Christ. Then they asked Peter to stay with them for a few days.

Peter Explains His Actions

11 The apostles and the brothers throughout Judea heard that the Gentiles also had received the word of God. 2So when Peter went up to Jerusalem, the circumcised believers criticized him 3and said, "You went into the house of uncircumcised men and ate with them."

4Peter began and explained everything to them precisely as it had happened: 5"I was in the city of Joppa praying, and in a trance I saw a vision. I saw something like a large sheet being let down from heaven by its four corners, and it came down to where I was. 6I looked into it and saw four-footed animals of the earth, wild beasts, reptiles, and birds of the air. 7Then I heard a voice telling me, 'Get up, Peter. Kill and eat.'

8"I replied, 'Surely not, Lord! Nothing impure or unclean has ever entered my mouth.'

9"The voice spoke from heaven a second time, 'Do not call anything impure that God has made clean.' 10This happened three times, and then it was all pulled up to heaven again.

a46 Or other languages

the story of Cornelius so important in Acts (vv. 28,34–35,43)? **3.** What is the main point in Peter's sermon? How does that compare with his sermons in 2:36–39 and 3:17–23? From these sermons, what do you see as central to the Gospel message? **4.** In light of the astonished reaction of the Jews (v. 45), what did it mean that the Gentiles could speak in tongues? How does this reinforce Peter's private vision in 10:9–23?

♥ **1.** Using this story, how would you respond to the question: "Can people who have never heard the Gospel be saved"? If your answer is "yes," why then did God send Peter to preach (see also 11:14)? If it is "no," how do you explain verses 34–35? **2.** Consider the makeup of your church (ethnically, socially, politically, age-wise, etc.). Are there some people who would just assume that your church is not for them? Are there some forms or practices you could change to remove those barriers? How would you feel about making those changes?

☕ What was the wrong crowd to hang out with when you were in school? Did you anyway?

📖 **1.** Why did Luke take the time and space to record the events of 10:9–46 all over again? **2.** Of what importance is the gift of the Holy Spirit in Peter's argument? Why would this have such a strong effect on the Jerusalem believers? Why is this gift misunderstood (see vv. 5–8)? **3.** Why do you think God chose Peter to be the first to go to the Gentiles? Would any other disciple have been as successful in both Caesarea and Jerusalem? Why or why not? **4.** How do you explain the change in attitudes from verse 2 to verse 18? How does this story relate to 1:8?

1. How can the principle of God bestowing his Spirit on non-Jews affect the way you treat unacceptable people you meet? 2. How have you been criticized for breaking religious traditions? What did you feel was at stake? 3. The lesson of 10:34–35 and 11:18 was not easily learned, even by Peter (see Gal 2:11–14). What might have happened if the early church ignored this principle?

What is the farthest from home you have ever been? Why were you there?

1. Antioch was the third largest city in the Roman empire. What might the apostles feel as they hear the Gospel is taking root there (v. 23)? 2. Write a character reference for Barnabas based on verses 22–26 (also 4:36–37). From this profile, why did Barnabus recruit Saul (9:27–28)?

1. With whom do you associate that no minister would normally contact? How do you share the Gospel with those people? 2. Would these people be comfortable in your church? 3. What is the most unusual thing the Holy Spirit has done in your life?

1. Who was the most surprising person to ever show up at your door? 2. If you were arrested by a dictatorial government for being a Christian, what evidence might they point to as proof of your guilt? What could some "well-meaning" character witnesses point to as proof of your innocence?

1. This Herod is the nephew of the Herod who ruled in Jesus' day. What do you learn about his character in verses 20–23? Why would his choice to arrest (vv. 2–4) Peter please the Jewish leaders? Why do you think

[11]"Right then three men who had been sent to me from Caesarea stopped at the house where I was staying. [12]The Spirit told me to have no hesitation about going with them. These six brothers also went with me, and we entered the man's house. [13]He told us how he had seen an angel appear in his house and say, 'Send to Joppa for Simon who is called Peter. [14]He will bring you a message through which you and all your household will be saved.'

[15]"As I began to speak, the Holy Spirit came on them as he had come on us at the beginning. [16]Then I remembered what the Lord had said: 'John baptized with[a] water, but you will be baptized with the Holy Spirit.' [17]So if God gave them the same gift as he gave us, who believed in the Lord Jesus Christ, who was I to think that I could oppose God?"

[18]When they heard this, they had no further objections and praised God, saying, "So then, God has granted even the Gentiles repentance unto life."

The Church in Antioch

[19]Now those who had been scattered by the persecution in connection with Stephen traveled as far as Phoenicia, Cyprus and Antioch, telling the message only to Jews. [20]Some of them, however, men from Cyprus and Cyrene, went to Antioch and began to speak to Greeks also, telling them the good news about the Lord Jesus. [21]The Lord's hand was with them, and a great number of people believed and turned to the Lord.

[22]News of this reached the ears of the church at Jerusalem, and they sent Barnabas to Antioch. [23]When he arrived and saw the evidence of the grace of God, he was glad and encouraged them all to remain true to the Lord with all their hearts. [24]He was a good man, full of the Holy Spirit and faith, and a great number of people were brought to the Lord.

[25]Then Barnabas went to Tarsus to look for Saul, [26]and when he found him, he brought him to Antioch. So for a whole year Barnabas and Saul met with the church and taught great numbers of people. The disciples were called Christians first at Antioch.

[27]During this time some prophets came down from Jerusalem to Antioch. [28]One of them, named Agabus, stood up and through the Spirit predicted that a severe famine would spread over the entire Roman world. (This happened during the reign of Claudius.) [29]The disciples, each according to his ability, decided to provide help for the brothers living in Judea. [30]This they did, sending their gift to the elders by Barnabas and Saul.

Peter's Miraculous Escape From Prison

12 It was about this time that King Herod arrested some who belonged to the church, intending to persecute them. [2]He had James, the brother of John, put to death with the sword. [3]When he saw that this pleased the Jews, he proceeded to seize Peter also. This happened during the Feast of Unleavened Bread. [4]After arresting him, he put him in prison, handing him over to be guarded by four squads of four soldiers each. Herod intended to bring him out for public trial after the Passover.

[5]So Peter was kept in prison, but the church was earnestly praying to God for him.

[6]The night before Herod was to bring him to trial, Peter was sleeping between two soldiers, bound with two chains, and sentries stood guard at the entrance. [7]Suddenly an angel of the Lord

a16 Or in

appeared and a light shone in the cell. He struck Peter on the side and woke him up. "Quick, get up!" he said, and the chains fell off Peter's wrists.

⁸Then the angel said to him, "Put on your clothes and sandals." And Peter did so. "Wrap your cloak around you and follow me," the angel told him. ⁹Peter followed him out of the prison, but he had no idea that what the angel was doing was really happening; he thought he was seeing a vision. ¹⁰They passed the first and second guards and came to the iron gate leading to the city. It opened for them by itself, and they went through it. When they had walked the length of one street, suddenly the angel left him.

¹¹Then Peter came to himself and said, "Now I know without a doubt that the Lord sent his angel and rescued me from Herod's clutches and from everything the Jewish people were anticipating."

¹²When this had dawned on him, he went to the house of Mary the mother of John, also called Mark, where many people had gathered and were praying. ¹³Peter knocked at the outer entrance, and a servant girl named Rhoda came to answer the door. ¹⁴When she recognized Peter's voice, she was so overjoyed she ran back without opening it and exclaimed, "Peter is at the door!"

¹⁵"You're out of your mind," they told her. When she kept insisting that it was so, they said, "It must be his angel."

¹⁶But Peter kept on knocking, and when they opened the door and saw him, they were astonished. ¹⁷Peter motioned with his hand for them to be quiet and described how the Lord had brought him out of prison. "Tell James and the brothers about this," he said, and then he left for another place.

¹⁸In the morning, there was no small commotion among the soldiers as to what had become of Peter. ¹⁹After Herod had a

Herod, as a Roman official, would now join in the Jewish opposition to the church? **2.** When Rhoda announced who was at the door, what would you have said if you had been there? **3.** How do you feel about the fact that God saved Peter but not James? In light of John 21:18–19, how might Peter respond to this question? **4.** Who is the James of verse 17 (see Gal 1:18–19)? Why do you think he is mentioned? What does this tell you about his importance in the Jerusalem church? **5.** Putting yourself in the place of the soldiers (v. 18), what would you say to each other in the morning? **6.** In verses 20–22, what contrasts do you see between Herod's power and God's? **7.** What do you make of Herod's death (vv. 21–23)? **8.** In this "Judea and Samaria" phase (ch. 8–12) of God's plan (1:8), how has the church fared? What opposition has it faced so far? How far has it expanded?

♡ **1.** Who truly has power here: Herod or the Lord? What does this tell you about how Christians ought to deal with opposition and persecution? What worldly forces seem all-powerful to you?

 Acts 12:1–19   **PETER'S MIRACULOUS ESCAPE FROM PRISON**

Persecution of the first Christians now resumes—at the hands of the Roman representative King, Herod Agrippa I (nephew of Herod Antipas, who questioned Jesus before his death).

1. If one of the people in your group were put to death and another were thrown into jail, what would that do to your group?
   a. It would bring us closer together.
   b. It would cause us to really pray.
   c. We would stand up for our faith.
   d. We would likely go into hiding.
   e. We would likely give up our faith.
   f. I don't know what we would do.

2. Why do you suppose Herod wanted to kill Peter?
   a. Peter was a threat to his authority.
   b. Peter wouldn't stop preaching.
   c. Herod hated Christians.
   d. Herod wanted to stay on the good side of the Jewish leaders.

3. If the Christians were asking God to deliver Peter from jail, why were they so surprised when he showed up at the door?

   a. They knew how tight the security would be.
   b. They didn't really expect God to answer their prayer.
   c. They were afraid it was a trick.
   d. They were caught off guard.
   e. They reacted the same way I probably would have.

4. If you had been present at this prayer meeting, what would this miracle have done for you?
   a. given me courage
   b. boosted my prayer life
   c. made me ashamed for doubting
   d. drawn our group closer together

5. When has God surprised you by intervening in a situation that you thought was hopeless?

6. Where do you find yourself in prison, so to speak, right now?
   a. in my family relationships
   b. to a craving that holds me captive
   c. to a physical limitation that holds me back
   d. to feelings of low self-worth
   e. to a stagnant spiritual life

7. What would most help you to find freedom from this?
   a. an angel rescuing me
   b. some friends praying for me, and really believing it can happen
   c. my own confidence in God's ability to help me
   d. my own desire to change

8. How can this group assist you in your situation?
   a. leave me alone
   b. pray for me
   c. help me deal with the relationship that binds me
   d. call me every now and then
   e. hold me accountable
   f. other:_____

9. ⚭ How do you sense God at work in your marriage? How do you think your prayers are being answered even though you can't clearly or readily see how?

10. ⚭ How would you like the group to join you in prayer—for your spouse? For yourself? For your marriage?

How does this chapter put them in perspective? 2. How are you like the people at the prayer meeting in this story (v. 12)?

thorough search made for him and did not find him, he cross-examined the guards and ordered that they be executed.

Herod's Death

Then Herod went from Judea to Caesarea and stayed there a while. 20He had been quarreling with the people of Tyre and Sidon; they now joined together and sought an audience with him. Having secured the support of Blastus, a trusted personal servant of the king, they asked for peace, because they depended on the king's country for their food supply.

21On the appointed day Herod, wearing his royal robes, sat on his throne and delivered a public address to the people. 22They shouted, "This is the voice of a god, not of a man." 23Immediately, because Herod did not give praise to God, an angel of the Lord struck him down, and he was eaten by worms and died.

24But the word of God continued to increase and spread.

25When Barnabas and Saul had finished their mission, they returned from[a] Jerusalem, taking with them John, also called Mark.

What were you called as a child? Did you ever want a new name besides the one you were given?

Barnabas and Saul Sent Off

13 In the church at Antioch there were prophets and teachers: Barnabas, Simeon called Niger, Lucius of Cyrene, Manaen (who had been brought up with Herod the tetrarch) and Saul. 2While they were worshiping the Lord and fasting, the Holy Spirit said, "Set apart for me Barnabas and Saul for the work to which I have called them." 3So after they had fasted and prayed, they placed their hands on them and sent them off.

1. What was the scene when the Holy Spirit spoke to the leaders at Antioch? How do you think he may have spoken? How does he speak today? 2. Cyprus is a 150-mile sail from Seleucia, and was Barnabas' home (4:36). What might these two men be talking about as they travel? 3. Since Gentiles were already welcome in the church (11:18), why would Barnabas and Saul go to the synagogue? 4. The change of Saul's name to Paul (v. 9) may be related to the beginning of his ministry to the Gentiles. Why do you think names are so important to God?

On Cyprus

4The two of them, sent on their way by the Holy Spirit, went down to Seleucia and sailed from there to Cyprus. 5When they arrived at Salamis, they proclaimed the word of God in the Jewish synagogues. John was with them as their helper.

6They traveled through the whole island until they came to Paphos. There they met a Jewish sorcerer and false prophet named Bar-Jesus, 7who was an attendant of the proconsul, Sergius Paulus. The proconsul, an intelligent man, sent for Barnabas and Saul because he wanted to hear the word of God. 8But Elymas the sorcerer (for that is what his name means) opposed them and tried to turn the proconsul from the faith. 9Then Saul, who was also called Paul, filled with the Holy Spirit, looked straight at Elymas and said, 10"You are a child of the devil and an enemy of everything that is right! You are full of all kinds of deceit and trickery. Will you never stop perverting the right ways of the Lord? 11Now the hand of the Lord is against you. You are going to be blind, and for a time you will be unable to see the light of the sun."

Immediately mist and darkness came over him, and he groped about, seeking someone to lead him by the hand. 12When the proconsul saw what had happened, he believed, for he was amazed at the teaching about the Lord.

1. With what types of people do you feel most comfortable talking about the Lord? Why? 2. When have people tried to turn you from your faith? What happened? How do you deal with such pressures? 3. When should you strongly confront people who oppose Jesus?

In Pisidian Antioch

13From Paphos, Paul and his companions sailed to Perga in Pamphylia, where John left them to return to Jerusalem. 14From Perga they went on to Pisidian Antioch. On the Sabbath they entered the synagogue and sat down. 15After the reading from the Law and the Prophets, the synagogue rulers sent word to them, saying, "Broth-

1. Some great speeches in history are worth committing to memory, at least in part. What famous lines or stanzas from a famous speech can you recall? 2. Are you the kind of person who can commit things (names, birthdates, phone numbers, clothing sizes) to memory easily? Who in your group

a25 Some manuscripts to

ers, if you have a message of encouragement for the people, please speak."

¹⁶Standing up, Paul motioned with his hand and said: "Men of Israel and you Gentiles who worship God, listen to me! ¹⁷The God of the people of Israel chose our fathers; he made the people prosper during their stay in Egypt, with mighty power he led them out of that country, ¹⁸he endured their conduct*a* for about forty years in the desert, ¹⁹he overthrew seven nations in Canaan and gave their land to his people as their inheritance. ²⁰All this took about 450 years.

"After this, God gave them judges until the time of Samuel the prophet. ²¹Then the people asked for a king, and he gave them Saul son of Kish, of the tribe of Benjamin, who ruled forty years. ²²After removing Saul, he made David their king. He testified concerning him: 'I have found David son of Jesse a man after my own heart; he will do everything I want him to do.'

²³"From this man's descendants God has brought to Israel the Savior Jesus, as he promised. ²⁴Before the coming of Jesus, John preached repentance and baptism to all the people of Israel. ²⁵As John was completing his work, he said: 'Who do you think I am? I am not that one. No, but he is coming after me, whose sandals I am not worthy to untie.'

²⁶"Brothers, children of Abraham, and you God-fearing Gentiles, it is to us that this message of salvation has been sent. ²⁷The people of Jerusalem and their rulers did not recognize Jesus, yet in condemning him they fulfilled the words of the prophets that are read every Sabbath. ²⁸Though they found no proper ground for a death sentence, they asked Pilate to have him executed. ²⁹When they had carried out all that was written about him, they took him down from the tree and laid him in a tomb. ³⁰But God raised him from the dead, ³¹and for many days he was seen by those who had traveled with him from Galilee to Jerusalem. They are now his witnesses to our people.

³²"We tell you the good news: What God promised our fathers ³³he has fulfilled for us, their children, by raising up Jesus. As it is written in the second Psalm:

" 'You are my Son;
    today I have become your Father.'*b'c*

³⁴The fact that God raised him from the dead, never to decay, is stated in these words:

" 'I will give you the holy and sure blessings
    promised to David.'*d*

³⁵So it is stated elsewhere:

" 'You will not let your Holy One see decay.'*e*

³⁶"For when David had served God's purpose in his own generation, he fell asleep; he was buried with his fathers and his body decayed. ³⁷But the one whom God raised from the dead did not see decay.

³⁸"Therefore, my brothers, I want you to know that through Jesus the forgiveness of sins is proclaimed to you. ³⁹Through him everyone who believes is justified from everything you could not be justified from by the law of Moses. ⁴⁰Take care that what the prophets have said does not happen to you:

can recall the phone number of a previous residence where you once lived? **3.** What failure of memory is most embarrassing to you?

📖 **1.** From Cyprus to Pisidian Antioch is about 350 miles by sea and land. What does their willingness to travel so far show about Paul and Barnabas? Why do you think John Mark (12:12; 13:5) may have left them to go back to his home? What consequence will this have for Paul and Barnabas later (see 15:36–41)? **2.** What is significant about Paul's audience (v. 15)? **3.** From verses 17–23, list all the things Paul says God has done. How do God's actions prepare the way for Paul to speak about Jesus in verse 23? **4.** Compare verses 22–23 and 36–37 with Romans 1:3 and Acts 2:29–31: What is the connection between David and Jesus? Why is this so important to Paul and Peter? **5.** What things about Jesus is Paul emphasizing by recalling three famous quotes in verses 33–35? The Resurrection is mentioned four times in verses 30–37. How does the Resurrection confirm the meaning of these quotes? **6.** In verses 38–39, what does Paul say is the central meaning of the Resurrection for his listeners? Compare verse 39 with Romans 3:20–24 and 8:3–4. From these verses, how would you explain what Paul means by being "justified"? **7.** Why does Paul end his sermon with this OT quote, "a warning of judgment" (v. 41)? **8.** What feelings and emotions are created by this sermon in the various groups of people mentioned in verses 42–51? How do you explain such a variety of reactions and responses?

♡ **1.** If you were to emphasize one central truth about the Gospel, what would it be? Why? **2.** What difference would it make to your faith if there were no Easter to celebrate, but only Good Friday to remember? **3.** How do you think Paul would respond to a modern-day skeptic who felt Jesus was a noble, but misguided, martyr? What role would the OT play in Paul's answer? How would knowing the OT, even memorizing it, help you to understand and share your faith better? **4.** What kind of opposition have you faced because of your faith? How do you usually respond to opposition? Does it make you stronger? Why? Would it be tougher for you to face opposi-

---

a18 Some manuscripts *and cared for them*   *b33* Or *have begotten you*
c33 Psalm 2:7   *d34* Isaiah 55:3   *e35* Psalm 16:10

41" 'Look, you scoffers,
    wonder and perish,
for I am going to do something in your days
    that you would never believe,
    even if someone told you.'ª"

42As Paul and Barnabas were leaving the synagogue, the people invited them to speak further about these things on the next Sabbath. 43When the congregation was dismissed, many of the Jews and devout converts to Judaism followed Paul and Barnabas, who talked with them and urged them to continue in the grace of God.

44On the next Sabbath almost the whole city gathered to hear the word of the Lord. 45When the Jews saw the crowds, they were filled with jealousy and talked abusively against what Paul was saying.

46Then Paul and Barnabas answered them boldly: "We had to speak the word of God to you first. Since you reject it and do not consider yourselves worthy of eternal life, we now turn to the Gentiles. 47For this is what the Lord has commanded us:

" 'I have made youᵇ a light for the Gentiles,
    that youᵇ may bring salvation to the ends of
    the earth.'ᶜ"

48When the Gentiles heard this, they were glad and honored the word of the Lord; and all who were appointed for eternal life believed.

49The word of the Lord spread through the whole region. 50But the Jews incited the God-fearing women of high standing and the leading men of the city. They stirred up persecution against Paul and Barnabas, and expelled them from their region. 51So they shook the dust from their feet in protest against them and went to Iconium. 52And the disciples were filled with joy and with the Holy Spirit.

In Iconium

14 At Iconium Paul and Barnabas went as usual into the Jewish synagogue. There they spoke so effectively that a great number of Jews and Gentiles believed. 2But the Jews who refused to believe stirred up the Gentiles and poisoned their minds against the brothers. 3So Paul and Barnabas spent considerable time there, speaking boldly for the Lord, who confirmed the message of his grace by enabling them to do miraculous signs and wonders. 4The people of the city were divided; some sided with the Jews, others with the apostles. 5There was a plot afoot among the Gentiles and Jews, together with their leaders, to mistreat them and stone them. 6But they found out about it and fled to the Lycaonian cities of Lystra and Derbe and to the surrounding country, 7where they continued to preach the good news.

In Lystra and Derbe

8In Lystra there sat a man crippled in his feet, who was lame from birth and had never walked. 9He listened to Paul as he was speaking. Paul looked directly at him, saw that he had faith to be healed 10and called out, "Stand up on your feet!" At that, the man jumped up and began to walk.

11When the crowd saw what Paul had done, they shouted in the Lycaonian language, "The gods have come down to us in human form!" 12Barnabas they called Zeus, and Paul they called Hermes

ª41 Hab. 1:5   ᵇ47 The Greek is singular.   ᶜ47 Isaiah 49:6

because he was the chief speaker. [13]The priest of Zeus, whose temple was just outside the city, brought bulls and wreaths to the city gates because he and the crowd wanted to offer sacrifices to them.

[14]But when the apostles Barnabas and Paul heard of this, they tore their clothes and rushed out into the crowd, shouting: [15]"Men, why are you doing this? We too are only men, human like you. We are bringing you good news, telling you to turn from these worthless things to the living God, who made heaven and earth and sea and everything in them. [16]In the past, he let all nations go their own way. [17]Yet he has not left himself without testimony: He has shown kindness by giving you rain from heaven and crops in their seasons; he provides you with plenty of food and fills your hearts with joy." [18]Even with these words, they had difficulty keeping the crowd from sacrificing to them.

[19]Then some Jews came from Antioch and Iconium and won the crowd over. They stoned Paul and dragged him outside the city, thinking he was dead. [20]But after the disciples had gathered around him, he got up and went back into the city. The next day he and Barnabas left for Derbe.

The Return to Antioch in Syria

[21]They preached the good news in that city and won a large number of disciples. Then they returned to Lystra, Iconium and Antioch, [22]strengthening the disciples and encouraging them to remain true to the faith. "We must go through many hardships to enter the kingdom of God," they said. [23]Paul and Barnabas appointed elders[a] for them in each church and, with prayer and fasting, committed them to the Lord, in whom they had put their trust. [24]After going through Pisidia, they came into Pamphylia, [25]and when they had preached the word in Perga, they went down to Attalia.

[26]From Attalia they sailed back to Antioch, where they had been committed to the grace of God for the work they had now completed. [27]On arriving there, they gathered the church together and reported all that God had done through them and how he had opened the door of faith to the Gentiles. [28]And they stayed there a long time with the disciples.

The Council at Jerusalem

15 Some men came down from Judea to Antioch and were teaching the brothers: "Unless you are circumcised, according to the custom taught by Moses, you cannot be saved." [2]This brought Paul and Barnabas into sharp dispute and debate with them. So Paul and Barnabas were appointed, along with some other believers, to go up to Jerusalem to see the apostles and elders about this question. [3]The church sent them on their way, and as they traveled through Phoenicia and Samaria, they told how the Gentiles had been converted. This news made all the brothers very glad. [4]When they came to Jerusalem, they were welcomed by the church and the apostles and elders, to whom they reported everything God had done through them.

[5]Then some of the believers who belonged to the party of the Pharisees stood up and said, "The Gentiles must be circumcised and required to obey the law of Moses."

[6]The apostles and elders met to consider this question. [7]After much discussion, Peter got up and addressed them: "Brothers, you know that some time ago God made a choice among you that the

---

8. Reviewing this journey of about 1100 miles (13:1–14:26), what do you learn about Paul? About the Gospel?

1. Seeing Paul and Barnabas' courage, faith and endurance, how are you challenged to serve the Lord more completely? **2.** What does the difference between Paul's sermon (13:17–41) and his speech in verses 15–17 teach you about sharing your faith with various groups of people? **3.** The people Paul and Barnabas encountered along the way interpreted the Gospel through their own lenses, even calling them Hermes and Zeus. How do people you know interpret the Gospel by their own prejudices and beliefs? **4.** What was one of the biggest misunderstandings about Christianity you had to overcome before you could believe? **5.** How would you share the Gospel differently with a Jewish person than you would a non-Jewish person?

What were some of the expected, extra-biblical rules you were supposed to follow in the church where you grew up? When you became a Christian?

1. What other things would these teachers say the Gentiles must do (vv. 1,5 see Mk 2:16, 18,24; 7:1–5)? **2.** If you were a Gentile hearing that these regulations were required, how would you feel about your new faith? As a strict Jew, why would these rules be important to you? **3.** What is the main issue as Paul sees it (vv. 1–2; see Gal 2:21; 3:5,10–14)? **4.** How would you describe Peter's struggle with this issue (vv. 7–11; see 10:28,34–35; Gal 2:11–13)? How does Paul's teaching in Galatians 2:15–16 show its influence on Peter here? **5.** Knowing Paul's

---

[a]23 Or Barnabas ordained elders; or Barnabas had elders elected

Pharisaic background (26:5) and Peter's desire to keep the law (10:14), how would their testimony carry the day? **6.** What has led James to change his mind? **7.** What is the significance of the council's decision in light of 1:8? Why were the conditions of verse 20 added (see 1Co 8)?

1. What roles do experience, theology and practical considerations play in the decision-making process of this council? What issues, now troubling your church, could be resolved by looking at them with these three perspectives? **2.** Is there some area of your faith where you feel like Peter—going back and forth because you are not sure of what is right? How could verse 11 relate to this concern? **3.** What additions to the Gospel might a new believer encounter in your church? What should you do about that?

What experience have you had in a church with a worship style different than what you were used to?

1. Why would a letter *and* representatives from the Jerusalem church be a good way to communicate the apostles' decision? **2.** What is the tone of the letter? Its main points (vv. 22–29)? **3.** How do Judas and Silas personally add to this letter? What else brings unity to the primarily Jewish church in Jerusalem and the primarily Gentile church in Antioch? **4.** How would things be different if those in 15:5 had been successful?

1. From the debate, the resulting letter, and the way in which it was delivered, what do you learn about the way to solve disagreements among Christians? What conflicts are active in your church? Is your church's style of handling disagreements similar to the way the issue was handled in chapter 15? **2.** In your community's churches, what are the ethnic, social and racial lines of division?

Gentiles might hear from my lips the message of the gospel and believe. [8]God, who knows the heart, showed that he accepted them by giving the Holy Spirit to them, just as he did to us. [9]He made no distinction between us and them, for he purified their hearts by faith. [10]Now then, why do you try to test God by putting on the necks of the disciples a yoke that neither we nor our fathers have been able to bear? [11]No! We believe it is through the grace of our Lord Jesus that we are saved, just as they are."

[12]The whole assembly became silent as they listened to Barnabas and Paul telling about the miraculous signs and wonders God had done among the Gentiles through them. [13]When they finished, James spoke up: "Brothers, listen to me. [14]Simon[a] has described to us how God at first showed his concern by taking from the Gentiles a people for himself. [15]The words of the prophets are in agreement with this, as it is written:

> [16]"'After this I will return
> and rebuild David's fallen tent.
> Its ruins I will rebuild,
> and I will restore it,
> [17]that the remnant of men may seek the Lord,
> and all the Gentiles who bear my name,
> says the Lord, who does these things'[b]
> [18]   that have been known for ages.[c]

[19]"It is my judgment, therefore, that we should not make it difficult for the Gentiles who are turning to God. [20]Instead we should write to them, telling them to abstain from food polluted by idols, from sexual immorality, from the meat of strangled animals and from blood. [21]For Moses has been preached in every city from the earliest times and is read in the synagogues on every Sabbath."

The Council's Letter to Gentile Believers

[22]Then the apostles and elders, with the whole church, decided to choose some of their own men and send them to Antioch with Paul and Barnabas. They chose Judas (called Barsabbas) and Silas, two men who were leaders among the brothers. [23]With them they sent the following letter:

The apostles and elders, your brothers,

To the Gentile believers in Antioch, Syria and Cilicia:

Greetings.

[24]We have heard that some went out from us without our authorization and disturbed you, troubling your minds by what they said. [25]So we all agreed to choose some men and send them to you with our dear friends Barnabas and Paul— [26]men who have risked their lives for the name of our Lord Jesus Christ. [27]Therefore we are sending Judas and Silas to confirm by word of mouth what we are writing. [28]It seemed good to the Holy Spirit and to us not to burden you with anything beyond the following requirements: [29]You are to abstain from food sacrificed to idols, from blood, from the meat of strangled animals and from sexual immorality. You will do well to avoid these things.

Farewell.

---

a14 Greek *Simeon*, a variant of *Simon*; that is, Peter   *b17* Amos 9:11,12
c17,18 Some manuscripts *things'— / [18]known to the Lord for ages is his work*

[30]The men were sent off and went down to Antioch, where they gathered the church together and delivered the letter. [31]The people read it and were glad for its encouraging message. [32]Judas and Silas, who themselves were prophets, said much to encourage and strengthen the brothers. [33]After spending some time there, they were sent off by the brothers with the blessing of peace to return to those who had sent them.[a] [35]But Paul and Barnabas remained in Antioch, where they and many others taught and preached the word of the Lord.

Disagreement Between Paul and Barnabas

[36]Some time later Paul said to Barnabas, "Let us go back and visit the brothers in all the towns where we preached the word of the Lord and see how they are doing." [37]Barnabas wanted to take John, also called Mark, with them, [38]but Paul did not think it wise to take him, because he had deserted them in Pamphylia and had not continued with them in the work. [39]They had such a sharp disagreement that they parted company. Barnabas took Mark and sailed for Cyprus, [40]but Paul chose Silas and left, commended by the brothers to the grace of the Lord. [41]He went through Syria and Cilicia, strengthening the churches.

Timothy Joins Paul and Silas

16 He came to Derbe and then to Lystra, where a disciple named Timothy lived, whose mother was a Jewess and a believer, but whose father was a Greek. [2]The brothers at Lystra and Iconium spoke well of him. [3]Paul wanted to take him along on the journey, so he circumcised him because of the Jews who lived in that area, for they all knew that his father was a Greek. [4]As they traveled from town to town, they delivered the decisions reached by the apostles and elders in Jerusalem for the people to obey. [5]So the churches were strengthened in the faith and grew daily in numbers.

Paul's Vision of the Man of Macedonia

[6]Paul and his companions traveled throughout the region of Phrygia and Galatia, having been kept by the Holy Spirit from preaching the word in the province of Asia. [7]When they came to the border of Mysia, they tried to enter Bithynia, but the Spirit of Jesus would not allow them to. [8]So they passed by Mysia and went down to Troas. [9]During the night Paul had a vision of a man of Macedonia standing and begging him, "Come over to Macedonia and help us." [10]After Paul had seen the vision, we got ready at once to leave for Macedonia, concluding that God had called us to preach the gospel to them.

Lydia's Conversion in Philippi

[11]From Troas we put out to sea and sailed straight for Samothrace, and the next day on to Neapolis. [12]From there we traveled to Philippi, a Roman colony and the leading city of that district of Macedonia. And we stayed there several days.

[13]On the Sabbath we went outside the city gate to the river, where we expected to find a place of prayer. We sat down and began to speak to the women who had gathered there. [14]One of those listening was a woman named Lydia, a dealer in purple cloth from the city of Thyatira, who was a worshiper of God. The Lord

What is your relationship like with believers in these different churches?

What "breakup" was hardest for you and why: Moving? Losing your first girl/boyfriend? Empty nest? Closing shop?

1. Role play how you think Paul and Barnabas split up. With which one would you have sided? Why? 2. Given the decision in Chapter 15, why did Paul circumcise Timothy? How could this be justified (see 1Co 9:19–23)?

1. When have you given up your "rights" in order to better represent Christ to others? How can you do so now? 2. Have you ever lost a friendship because of a religious dispute? What happened?

What was the best idea or invention you ever came up with? How did it turn out?

1. Note the change from "they" (v. 8) to "we" (v. 10): How does this relate to Luke 1:3–4? 2. How does this closed door point to another opportunity? 3. Compare verse 13 with 14:1 and 17:2. What does the lack of a synagogue in Philippi indicate about the Jewish community there? How did that affect Paul's strategy for mission? 4. What do you make of Lydia's career and conversion?

1. How did the Lord open your heart to respond to the Gospel? Who did he use as part of the process? 2. Where do you have an "open door" for ministry now: In your home? School? Work? Community? How will you take advantage of it?

opened her heart to respond to Paul's message. **¹⁵**When she and the members of her household were baptized, she invited us to her home. "If you consider me a believer in the Lord," she said, "come and stay at my house." And she persuaded us.

Paul and Silas in Prison

¹⁶Once when we were going to the place of prayer, we were met by a slave girl who had a spirit by which she predicted the future. She earned a great deal of money for her owners by fortune-telling. **¹⁷**This girl followed Paul and the rest of us, shouting, "These men are servants of the Most High God, who are telling you the way to be saved." **¹⁸**She kept this up for many days. Finally Paul became so troubled that he turned around and said to the spirit, "In the name of Jesus Christ I command you to come out of her!" At that moment the spirit left her.

¹⁹When the owners of the slave girl realized that their hope of making money was gone, they seized Paul and Silas and dragged them into the marketplace to face the authorities. **²⁰**They brought them before the magistrates and said, "These men are Jews, and are throwing our city into an uproar **²¹**by advocating customs unlawful for us Romans to accept or practice."

²²The crowd joined in the attack against Paul and Silas, and the magistrates ordered them to be stripped and beaten. **²³**After they had been severely flogged, they were thrown into prison, and the jailer was commanded to guard them carefully. **²⁴**Upon receiving such orders, he put them in the inner cell and fastened their feet in the stocks.

²⁵About midnight Paul and Silas were praying and singing hymns to God, and the other prisoners were listening to them. **²⁶**Suddenly

---

What type of music lifts your spirits? What music reminds you of the "good ol' days"?

1. How do you think a shouting slave girl affected the apostles' mood? Their goals? **2.** Retell verses 17–21 from the perspective of the owners of the girl: What do you feel about her? About your money? About these missionaries? **3.** Since there was no synagogue in Philippi (v. 13), and since the Gentile missionaries (Luke and Timothy) were not seized, how could racism be a factor in the actions described in verses 19–24? What might be meant by the charge against them? **4.** In light of what happened, how do you think Paul and Silas felt in verse 25? If you were falsely accused, severely beaten and thrown into a dark jail, would you still trust in God's plan (vv. 23–30)? Why or why not? **5.** What does the response of Paul and Silas show about them? If you were the jailer, what would you

---

  Acts 16:11–15   **LYDIA'S CONVERSION**

The apostle Paul's missionary travels brought him to Philippi. Paul's practice was first to preach at each city's synagogue. But there were so few Jews in Philippi that there was no synagogue there. In such cities it was common for the Jews and those Gentiles interested in Judaism ("worshippers of God," like Lydia in this story) to gather outdoors near running water.

1. Which of the following words best describes your impression of Lydia?
   a. persuasive   e. hospitable
   b. spiritual   f. impulsive
   c. trusting   g. naive
   d. industrious   h. friendly

2. Which of the following do you find most impressive about Lydia?
   a. She was a businesswoman at a time when few women were.
   b. Her heart was immediately receptive to the Gospel.
   c. She convinced her household to be baptized.
   d. She was willing to open her home to strangers.

3. Lydia managed to care for her business, her spiritual life and her household. On a scale from 1 to 10, how would you rate yourself in each area:
   a. business/professional life
   b. spiritual life
   c. home life

4. What step do you need to take to put your work life, spiritual life and family life in better balance?

5. Lydia's "place of prayer" was by a river. What is your favorite place to meet God?
   a. in church
   b. with others in a small group
   c. alone in my home
   d. outside in natural surroundings
   e. at special meetings or retreats
   f. other:_____

6. How did the Lord open your heart to respond to the Gospel? What people did God use as part of the process?

7. In comparison, how open to the Lord is your heart right now? What would make it, and keep it, more open?

8. When you were little, what did you want to be when you grew up?

9. Regarding career and family, what are your hopes and dreams now? What would you change about your life if you could?

10. Lydia's status appears to have been "single head of household." What example from her life would you like to apply to your life?
   a. She didn't seem to resent her situation in life.
   b. She made the most of her life both vocationally and spiritually.
   c. She used her situation in life to hospitably serve others.
   d. She avoided loneliness by taking initiative to reach out to people.

11. What have you appreciated about this course, and how has this group served you? Have one person at a time listen silently while others share their thanks or affirmation of that person.

there was such a violent earthquake that the foundations of the prison were shaken. At once all the prison doors flew open, and everybody's chains came loose. ²⁷The jailer woke up, and when he saw the prison doors open, he drew his sword and was about to kill himself because he thought the prisoners had escaped. ²⁸But Paul shouted, "Don't harm yourself! We are all here!"

²⁹The jailer called for lights, rushed in and fell trembling before Paul and Silas. ³⁰He then brought them out and asked, "Sirs, what must I do to be saved?"

³¹They replied, "Believe in the Lord Jesus, and you will be saved—you and your household." ³²Then they spoke the word of the Lord to him and to all the others in his house. ³³At that hour of the night the jailer took them and washed their wounds; then immediately he and all his family were baptized. ³⁴The jailer brought them into his house and set a meal before them; he was filled with joy because he had come to believe in God—he and his whole family.

³⁵When it was daylight, the magistrates sent their officers to the jailer with the order: "Release those men." ³⁶The jailer told Paul, "The magistrates have ordered that you and Silas be released. Now you can leave. Go in peace."

³⁷But Paul said to the officers: "They beat us publicly without a trial, even though we are Roman citizens, and threw us into prison. And now do they want to get rid of us quietly? No! Let them come themselves and escort us out."

³⁸The officers reported this to the magistrates, and when they heard that Paul and Silas were Roman citizens, they were alarmed. ³⁹They came to appease them and escorted them from the prison, requesting them to leave the city. ⁴⁰After Paul and Silas came out of

think of Paul and Silas singing? Remaining? **6.** What kind of man was the jailer before his salvation? In what ways does the jailer express his new faith in Jesus? **7.** Given the charge against them (vv. 20–21), why would Paul insist on his rights as a Roman citizen?

1. The girl's owners rejected the Gospel because it cost them financially. What financial concerns keep some people from faith today? Are any of these a factor for you? **2.** About 12 years later, Paul wrote the letter to the Philippians from another prison. How could the events here be the basis for what Paul said in Philippians 4:4–7,12–13? What can you learn from his example about knowing peace and joy, even in hard times? **3.** If asked, "What must I do to be saved?" how would you answer?

  Acts 16:16–40   **PAUL AND SILAS IN PRISON**

These events take place in the city of Philippi, a Roman colony, during the apostle Paul's second missionary trip.

1. How would you have felt if someone kept shouting, "These men are servants of the Most High God, who are telling you the way to be saved"?
   a. This is good advertising!
   b. This is spooky!
   c. This is driving me crazy!
   d. The words are true, but I'm afraid this is doing more harm than good.

2. What motivated the slave girl's owners to seize Paul and Silas and bring charges against them?
   a. anger   d. greed
   b. legal issues   e. fear
   c. anti-Semitism   f. spite

3. How would you have felt if you were falsely accused, flogged and put in stocks in a dark prison cell?
   a. like getting out of missionary work
   b. like praying and singing hymns
   c. like suing for police brutality
   d. like thanking God for the honor of suffering for him

4. What caused the jailer to want to be saved?
   a. Paul and Silas' example of faith
   b. hearing about their preaching and the slave girl's deliverance
   c. hearing them pray and sing
   d. the earthquake
   e. Paul and Silas' concern that he not take his own life
   f. all of the above

5. In what ways did the jailer demonstrate his new-found faith in the Lord Jesus?

6. How much joy did you have when you first committed your life to Christ? How much joy do you have now?

7. If someone asked you, "What must I do to be saved?"—how would you answer?

8. What does this story say to you about dealing with hard times? How hard is it for you to pray and be thankful in the midst of chaotic or difficult experiences?

9. How does this story relate to the stress in your life?
   a. I feel like I'm constantly hounded by people or demands (v. 18).
   b. I worry about my "hope of making money" disappearing (v. 19).
   c. I'm facing criticism, false accusation or discrimination (vv. 20–21).
   d. I feel trapped ("fastened in the stocks") in a bad situation (v. 24).
   e. I have to take the blame for things out of my control (v. 27).
   f. I need someone to support me and "wash my wounds" (v. 33).
   g. Because God has set me free, I want to encourage others (v. 40).

10. What is the hardest aspect of being married to someone who doesn't share your spiritual commitment? How does this story of a "household conversion" encourage you not to give up?

11. Close your meeting by praying together that you can share the jailer's joy of seeing your whole family come to the Lord.

the prison, they went to Lydia's house, where they met with the brothers and encouraged them. Then they left.

In Thessalonica

17 When they had passed through Amphipolis and Apollonia, they came to Thessalonica, where there was a Jewish synagogue. ²As his custom was, Paul went into the synagogue, and on three Sabbath days he reasoned with them from the Scriptures, ³explaining and proving that the Christ*ᵃ* had to suffer and rise from the dead. "This Jesus I am proclaiming to you is the Christ,*ᵃ*" he said. ⁴Some of the Jews were persuaded and joined Paul and Silas, as did a large number of God-fearing Greeks and not a few prominent women.

⁵But the Jews were jealous; so they rounded up some bad characters from the marketplace, formed a mob and started a riot in the city. They rushed to Jason's house in search of Paul and Silas in order to bring them out to the crowd.*ᵇ* ⁶But when they did not find them, they dragged Jason and some other brothers before the city officials, shouting: "These men who have caused trouble all over the world have now come here, ⁷and Jason has welcomed them into his house. They are all defying Caesar's decrees, saying that there is another king, one called Jesus." ⁸When they heard this, the crowd and the city officials were thrown into turmoil. ⁹Then they made Jason and the others post bond and let them go.

In Berea

¹⁰As soon as it was night, the brothers sent Paul and Silas away to Berea. On arriving there, they went to the Jewish synagogue. ¹¹Now the Bereans were of more noble character than the Thessalonians, for they received the message with great eagerness and examined the Scriptures every day to see if what Paul said was true. ¹²Many of the Jews believed, as did also a number of prominent Greek women and many Greek men.

¹³When the Jews in Thessalonica learned that Paul was preaching the word of God at Berea, they went there too, agitating the crowds and stirring them up. ¹⁴The brothers immediately sent Paul to the coast, but Silas and Timothy stayed at Berea. ¹⁵The men who escorted Paul brought him to Athens and then left with instructions for Silas and Timothy to join him as soon as possible.

In Athens

¹⁶While Paul was waiting for them in Athens, he was greatly distressed to see that the city was full of idols. ¹⁷So he reasoned in the synagogue with the Jews and the God-fearing Greeks, as well as in the marketplace day by day with those who happened to be there. ¹⁸A group of Epicurean and Stoic philosophers began to dispute with him. Some of them asked, "What is this babbler trying to say?" Others remarked, "He seems to be advocating foreign gods." They said this because Paul was preaching the good news about Jesus and the resurrection. ¹⁹Then they took him and brought him to a meeting of the Areopagus, where they said to him, "May we know what this new teaching is that you are presenting? ²⁰You are bringing some strange ideas to our ears, and we want to know what they mean." ²¹(All the Athenians and the foreigners who lived there spent their time doing nothing but talking about and listening to the latest ideas.)

²²Paul then stood up in the meeting of the Areopagus and said:

ᵃ3 Or *Messiah*   *ᵇ5* Or *the assembly of the people*

(Sidebar, left column)

☕ What has been your most exciting experience in a crowd? Your scariest experience?

📖 **1.** Thessalonica was a wealthy trading city on a major road from the Adriatic Sea to the Black Sea (see map in Introduction to Acts). How is Paul received (see 1Th 1:4–10; 3:1–4)? **2.** What accusations has Paul encountered so far (vv. 5–7; also 16:20–21)? What lies behind these accusations? **3.** Since his conversion, this is the sixth time Paul has been forced by persecution to leave an area. How would you view your mission if that happened to you? How does your response compare with Paul's (see 1Th 2:1–6)? **4.** Compared with the Thessalonians (vv. 2–4), how do the Bereans receive the Gospel (vv. 11–12)? **5.** How is Paul's teaching on the diversity of gifts (1Co 12) illustrated here in the functions of Paul, Silas and Timothy?

♡ **1.** Whether Jesus or Caesar was Lord became a real issue for Christians. When has your faith in Christ led to conflict with other authorities claiming your loyalty? **2.** In terms of time, consistency and intensity, how would you rate your Bible study? Is it at all like the Bereans?

☕ If someone made a statue of you, what pose would be most appropriate? What inscription?

📖 **1.** To be noticed by the Greek philosophers of Athens, how extensive was Paul's activity? **2.** What previous understanding of Christianity did these philosophers have? **3.** The Stoics believed in pantheism while the Epicureans had little or no belief in God. What does Paul emphasize about God (vv. 23–30)? How does Paul use their own culture and ideas to help them see the weaknesses in the way they relate to deity? **4.** How is this sermon unlike the one to Jews in 13:16–41? Is not using Scripture here a strength or a weakness? Why? How are the

though he knew only the baptism of John. ²⁶He began to speak boldly in the synagogue. When Priscilla and Aquila heard him, they invited him to their home and explained to him the way of God more adequately.

²⁷When Apollos wanted to go to Achaia, the brothers encouraged him and wrote to the disciples there to welcome him. On arriving, he was a great help to those who by grace had believed. ²⁸For he vigorously refuted the Jews in public debate, proving from the Scriptures that Jesus was the Christ.

Paul in Ephesus

19 While Apollos was at Corinth, Paul took the road through the interior and arrived at Ephesus. There he found some disciples ²and asked them, "Did you receive the Holy Spirit when[a] you believed?"

They answered, "No, we have not even heard that there is a Holy Spirit."

³So Paul asked, "Then what baptism did you receive?"

"John's baptism," they replied.

⁴Paul said, "John's baptism was a baptism of repentance. He told the people to believe in the one coming after him, that is, in Jesus." ⁵On hearing this, they were baptized into[b] the name of the Lord Jesus. ⁶When Paul placed his hands on them, the Holy

[a]2 Or *after*   [b]5 Or *in*

role do women have in your church? How do you feel about that? **4.** How does your church balance evangelism with the strengthening and equipping of believers?

What experiences have you had with religious counterfeits (relics, forgeries, hoaxes, cults and the like)? Any that have really scared you?

1. Why do you think Paul went to Ephesus on his next trip (see 18:19–21)? **2.** Apollos was from Egypt (18:24–25), and these disciples were about 800 miles from Jerusalem. What does the fact that they were followers of John the Baptist tell you about the extent of his influence? How would their awareness of John be good preparation for them to hear the Gospel (see Jn 1:19–34)? **3.** Since

---

 Acts 18:1–4,18–28   PRISCILLA, AQUILA AND APOLLOS

1. What surprises you most?
   a. that the apostle Paul supported himself by making tents (v. 3)
   b. that Paul had his hair cut off because of a vow (v. 18)
   c. that Priscilla, a woman, was so active in ministry, and her name was even mentioned before her husband's (vv. 18–19, 26)
   d. that Apollos with all his fervor and knowledge did not understand Christian baptism (vv. 24–25)

2. What best illustrates Priscilla and Aquila's virtues as servant-leaders?
   a. their tentmaking business partnership with Paul
   b. their invitation and willingness to travel with Paul
   c. Paul's leaving them in Ephesus to start forming a new church there
   d. their ability to teach Apollos
   e. their hospitality toward Paul in Corinth and Apollos in Ephesus

3. How do you envision Apollos?
   a. a silver-tongued orator
   b. an absent-minded professor
   c. a fiery preacher
   d. a sophisticated philosopher
   e. an argumentative bulldog

4. In their lives, Priscilla and Aquila encountered Paul and Apollos—one was a teacher to them and one they taught. Who was one of your early mentors? Whom have you in turn mentored—or could you mentor?

5. What are the primary gifts God has given you for Christian service?

6. On a scale of 1 (totally disagree) to 10 (totally agree), how do you feel about each of the following statements:
   a. Women in leadership was acceptable in the New Testament church.
   b. Women in leadership is acceptable in the church today.
   c. God encourages women to be all that they can be.
   d. Women can realize their full potential in the church.
   e. Gender doesn't matter; what matters is using our gifts for Christ.

7. What type of role do you have in the church? What role would you like to have? What keeps you from that?

8. Priscilla and Aquila were a model of partnership in mar-

riage. Regarding the possibility of discovering a mate, it's important to me to find someone ...
   a. who knows how to make tents.
   b. who shares my faith and values.
   c. whom I find attractive.
   d. who complements my personality and gifts.
   e. with whom I can serve the Lord.
   f. who likes to do everything I like.

9. How can you as a couple use your gifts to serve God and others? How would finding a ministry or service project in which to share affect your marriage?
   a. disastrous—We don't have much free time the way it is.
   b. mostly bad—It would keep our focus off of our marriage.
   c. mostly good—It would force us to spend more time together.
   d. wonderful—A common fulfillment would bind us together.
   e. We are already doing this.

10. How has this course helped strengthen your marriage? Share with the group one word of affirmation for your spouse, then one word for the group.

Paul had to teach these people about Jesus (v. 4), they apparently had not heard about him or the Holy Spirit (v. 2). From 2:38; 10:43–44 and this passage, what do you learn about the relationship between faith in Jesus and receiving the Holy Spirit? **4.** What seems to be the signal throughout Acts for Paul to stop teaching in the synagogues? Why do you think this is so? What do these "stop and go" signals teach you about ministry in general? **5.** Compare verses 8–9 with 13–15: How do these two groups of Jews view Jesus differently? If you were one of Sceva's sons, what would you say about Jesus after being jumped by this evil spirit (v. 16)? **6.** From the reaction of the crowd in verses 17–19, how would you describe the general response to Jesus prior to verses 13–16? Why would those events change people's ideas so much?

♡ **1.** How do people try to use Jesus for their own purposes today? What is the difference between that and real faith in Christ? **2.** What do you need to "burn" in order to live for God? What will it cost you?

_____

☕ What can you make by using your own hands?

📖 **1.** Why would Demetrius rally people against Paul (vv. 25–27; see 17:24–29)? Since this temple was one of the seven wonders of the ancient world, what businesses would Paul be affecting? **2.** Consider the crowd (vv. 32–34). What do they see and hear? Why are they there? Why are the Jews trying to get a speaker to represent them? Why would Alexander be shouted down? **3.** How do the concerns of the city clerk and Demetrius compare?

♡ **1.** Success, money and independence are some cultural idols. What others come to mind? How has your faith affected your relationship to idols? **2.** Could Demetrius have become a Christian _and_ kept his business? Can you think of situations today where someone in a respectable trade would be forced to choose between

Spirit came on them, and they spoke in tongues[a] and prophesied. [7]There were about twelve men in all.

[8]Paul entered the synagogue and spoke boldly there for three months, arguing persuasively about the kingdom of God. [9]But some of them became obstinate; they refused to believe and publicly maligned the Way. So Paul left them. He took the disciples with him and had discussions daily in the lecture hall of Tyrannus. [10]This went on for two years, so that all the Jews and Greeks who lived in the province of Asia heard the word of the Lord.

[11]God did extraordinary miracles through Paul, [12]so that even handkerchiefs and aprons that had touched him were taken to the sick, and their illnesses were cured and the evil spirits left them.

[13]Some Jews who went around driving out evil spirits tried to invoke the name of the Lord Jesus over those who were demon-possessed. They would say, "In the name of Jesus, whom Paul preaches, I command you to come out." [14]Seven sons of Sceva, a Jewish chief priest, were doing this. [15]One day, the evil spirit answered them, "Jesus I know, and I know about Paul, but who are you?" [16]Then the man who had the evil spirit jumped on them and overpowered them all. He gave them such a beating that they ran out of the house naked and bleeding.

[17]When this became known to the Jews and Greeks living in Ephesus, they were all seized with fear, and the name of the Lord Jesus was held in high honor. [18]Many of those who believed now came and openly confessed their evil deeds. [19]A number who had practiced sorcery brought their scrolls together and burned them publicly. When they calculated the value of the scrolls, the total came to fifty thousand drachmas.[b] [20]In this way the word of the Lord spread widely and grew in power.

[21]After all this had happened, Paul decided to go to Jerusalem, passing through Macedonia and Achaia. "After I have been there," he said, "I must visit Rome also." [22]He sent two of his helpers, Timothy and Erastus, to Macedonia, while he stayed in the province of Asia a little longer.

The Riot in Ephesus

[23]About that time there arose a great disturbance about the Way. [24]A silversmith named Demetrius, who made silver shrines of Artemis, brought in no little business for the craftsmen. [25]He called them together, along with the workmen in related trades, and said: "Men, you know we receive a good income from this business. [26]And you see and hear how this fellow Paul has convinced and led astray large numbers of people here in Ephesus and in practically the whole province of Asia. He says that man-made gods are no gods at all. [27]There is danger not only that our trade will lose its good name, but also that the temple of the great goddess Artemis will be discredited, and the goddess herself, who is worshiped throughout the province of Asia and the world, will be robbed of her divine majesty."

[28]When they heard this, they were furious and began shouting: "Great is Artemis of the Ephesians!" [29]Soon the whole city was in an uproar. The people seized Gaius and Aristarchus, Paul's traveling companions from Macedonia, and rushed as one man into the theater. [30]Paul wanted to appear before the crowd, but the disciples would not let him. [31]Even some of the officials of the province, friends of Paul, sent him a message begging him not to venture into the theater.

_a6_ Or _other languages_   _b19_ A drachma was a silver coin worth about a day's wages.

³²The assembly was in confusion: Some were shouting one thing, some another. Most of the people did not even know why they were there. ³³The Jews pushed Alexander to the front, and some of the crowd shouted instructions to him. He motioned for silence in order to make a defense before the people. ³⁴But when they realized he was a Jew, they all shouted in unison for about two hours: "Great is Artemis of the Ephesians!"

³⁵The city clerk quieted the crowd and said: "Men of Ephesus, doesn't all the world know that the city of Ephesus is the guardian of the temple of the great Artemis and of her image, which fell from heaven? ³⁶Therefore, since these facts are undeniable, you ought to be quiet and not do anything rash. ³⁷You have brought these men here, though they have neither robbed temples nor blasphemed our goddess. ³⁸If, then, Demetrius and his fellow craftsmen have a grievance against anybody, the courts are open and there are proconsuls. They can press charges. ³⁹If there is anything further you want to bring up, it must be settled in a legal assembly. ⁴⁰As it is, we are in danger of being charged with rioting because of today's events. In that case we would not be able to account for this commotion, since there is no reason for it." ⁴¹After he had said this, he dismissed the assembly.

Through Macedonia and Greece

20 When the uproar had ended, Paul sent for the disciples and, after encouraging them, said good-by and set out for Macedonia. ²He traveled through that area, speaking many words of encouragement to the people, and finally arrived in Greece, ³where he stayed three months. Because the Jews made a plot against him just as he was about to sail for Syria, he decided to go back through Macedonia. ⁴He was accompanied by Sopater son of Pyrrhus from Berea, Aristarchus and Secundus from Thessalonica, Gaius from Derbe, Timothy also, and Tychicus and Trophimus from the province of Asia. ⁵These men went on ahead and waited for us at Troas. ⁶But we sailed from Philippi after the Feast of Unleavened Bread, and five days later joined the others at Troas, where we stayed seven days.

Eutychus Raised From the Dead at Troas

⁷On the first day of the week we came together to break bread. Paul spoke to the people and, because he intended to leave the next day, kept on talking until midnight. ⁸There were many lamps in the upstairs room where we were meeting. ⁹Seated in a window was a young man named Eutychus, who was sinking into a deep sleep as Paul talked on and on. When he was sound asleep, he fell to the ground from the third story and was picked up dead. ¹⁰Paul went down, threw himself on the young man and put his arms around him. "Don't be alarmed," he said. "He's alive!" ¹¹Then he went upstairs again and broke bread and ate. After talking until daylight, he left. ¹²The people took the young man home alive and were greatly comforted.

Paul's Farewell to the Ephesian Elders

¹³We went on ahead to the ship and sailed for Assos, where we were going to take Paul aboard. He had made this arrangement because he was going there on foot. ¹⁴When he met us at Assos, we took him aboard and went on to Mitylene. ¹⁵The next day we set sail from there and arrived off Kios. The day after that we crossed over to Samos, and on the following day arrived at Miletus. ¹⁶Paul had decided to sail past Ephesus to avoid spending time in

that trade and Christ? How have your business dealings been affected by your faith? 3. Many people, even believers, would find it difficult to do what Paul did. Do you think Paul was happy? Why or why not? 4. What began as Artemis-worship became Artemis-business. How can Christians fall into the same trap and make Jesus-worship into Jesus-business?

Describe a time when, much to your embarrassment, you took a spill or fell "off your rocker."

1. One reason for this trip was to collect money for Christians in Judea (see Ro 15:25–29). Why then would Paul want companions for this task (see 2Co 8:16–23; 1Co 16:1–4)? Why else might Paul want to present these Gentiles to the church in Jerusalem (see ch. 15)? 2. What can you learn about Paul and the church in Troas from this lengthy meeting?

1. Paul's companions protect him from anyone accusing him of misusing funds. How could churches and other ministries today be helped by such accountability? How would this enhance outsiders' opinions of Christian integrity? 2. Are you at all related to Eutychus: Do sermons put you to sleep? Or are you wide awake spiritually? How can you keep from falling flat? 3. What is the role of miracles in God's purposes today?

How do you say goodbye to people you love? Quick and painless? Long or drawn out? Weeping and wailing? Like it's no big deal? Other?

1. Why "sail past" Ephesus to reach Jerusalem for Pentecost (see 2:1)? 2. What has char-

acterized Paul's ministry so far? Why does he emphasize how he lived among them? **3.** What kinds of hardships has Paul already encountered? How would you explain what motivates Paul to keep on (compare 20:24 with Php 3:7–8)? **4.** What does it mean to "keep watch" (v. 28; see 1Ti 4:11–16)? How and why is their appointment as elders divine, humbling and dangerous (vv. 28–31)? **5.** How does the message of grace (v. 32) and the example of Paul (vv. 33–35) protect them from these dangers? Some people viewed the office of elder as a way of gaining power and wealth (see 1Ti 6:6–10; 1Pe 5:3). How does Paul oppose that idea here? **6.** What do you suppose the Ephesians will miss about Paul?

1. Suddenly, Paul is more the loving friend than hard-driving missionary. Has your preoccupation with the task of ministry ever caused you to miss out on loving people? **2.** Who makes up the "flock" for whom you are responsible? In what specific way can you shepherd them? **3.** How would you complete this sentence: "The one thing I must accomplish at any cost is _____?" How does it relate to Paul's goal in verse 24? **4.** In the race of doing God's will, are you in the front of the pack, one of the stragglers, or an onlooker?

What place did your parents have to drag you to, because you were scared to go there: Circus? Dentist's? Elsewhere?

1. How is Paul interpreting these warnings differently than his friends do (vv. 4,10–13; see 20:22–23)? Why doesn't he listen to their advice? **2.** What else do you know about Agabus (see 11:27–29) that gives more credence to his prophecy? Does Paul strike you as courageous or foolish, given this belt-tightening message? Why? **3.** Why does he want to go to Jerusalem?

the province of Asia, for he was in a hurry to reach Jerusalem, if possible, by the day of Pentecost.

[17]From Miletus, Paul sent to Ephesus for the elders of the church. [18]When they arrived, he said to them: "You know how I lived the whole time I was with you, from the first day I came into the province of Asia. [19]I served the Lord with great humility and with tears, although I was severely tested by the plots of the Jews. [20]You know that I have not hesitated to preach anything that would be helpful to you but have taught you publicly and from house to house. [21]I have declared to both Jews and Greeks that they must turn to God in repentance and have faith in our Lord Jesus.

[22]"And now, compelled by the Spirit, I am going to Jerusalem, not knowing what will happen to me there. [23]I only know that in every city the Holy Spirit warns me that prison and hardships are facing me. [24]However, I consider my life worth nothing to me, if only I may finish the race and complete the task the Lord Jesus has given me—the task of testifying to the gospel of God's grace.

[25]"Now I know that none of you among whom I have gone about preaching the kingdom will ever see me again. [26]Therefore, I declare to you today that I am innocent of the blood of all men. [27]For I have not hesitated to proclaim to you the whole will of God. [28]Keep watch over yourselves and all the flock of which the Holy Spirit has made you overseers.[a] Be shepherds of the church of God,[b] which he bought with his own blood. [29]I know that after I leave, savage wolves will come in among you and will not spare the flock. [30]Even from your own number men will arise and distort the truth in order to draw away disciples after them. [31]So be on your guard! Remember that for three years I never stopped warning each of you night and day with tears.

[32]"Now I commit you to God and to the word of his grace, which can build you up and give you an inheritance among all those who are sanctified. [33]I have not coveted anyone's silver or gold or clothing. [34]You yourselves know that these hands of mine have supplied my own needs and the needs of my companions. [35]In everything I did, I showed you that by this kind of hard work we must help the weak, remembering the words the Lord Jesus himself said: 'It is more blessed to give than to receive.'"

[36]When he had said this, he knelt down with all of them and prayed. [37]They all wept as they embraced him and kissed him. [38]What grieved them most was his statement that they would never see his face again. Then they accompanied him to the ship.

On to Jerusalem

21 After we had torn ourselves away from them, we put out to sea and sailed straight to Cos. The next day we went to Rhodes and from there to Patara. [2]We found a ship crossing over to Phoenicia, went on board and set sail. [3]After sighting Cyprus and passing to the south of it, we sailed on to Syria. We landed at Tyre, where our ship was to unload its cargo. [4]Finding the disciples there, we stayed with them seven days. Through the Spirit they urged Paul not to go on to Jerusalem. [5]But when our time was up, we left and continued on our way. All the disciples and their wives and children accompanied us out of the city, and there on the beach we knelt to pray. [6]After saying good-by to each other, we went aboard the ship, and they returned home.

[7]We continued our voyage from Tyre and landed at Ptolemais, where we greeted the brothers and stayed with them for a day.

---

[a]28 Traditionally *bishops*   [b]28 Many manuscripts *of the Lord*

[8]Leaving the next day, we reached Caesarea and stayed at the house of Philip the evangelist, one of the Seven. [9]He had four unmarried daughters who prophesied.

[10]After we had been there a number of days, a prophet named Agabus came down from Judea. [11]Coming over to us, he took Paul's belt, tied his own hands and feet with it and said, "The Holy Spirit says, 'In this way the Jews of Jerusalem will bind the owner of this belt and will hand him over to the Gentiles.'"

[12]When we heard this, we and the people there pleaded with Paul not to go up to Jerusalem. [13]Then Paul answered, "Why are you weeping and breaking my heart? I am ready not only to be bound, but also to die in Jerusalem for the name of the Lord Jesus." [14]When he would not be dissuaded, we gave up and said, "The Lord's will be done."

[15]After this, we got ready and went up to Jerusalem. [16]Some of the disciples from Caesarea accompanied us and brought us to the home of Mnason, where we were to stay. He was a man from Cyprus and one of the early disciples.

Paul's Arrival at Jerusalem

[17]When we arrived at Jerusalem, the brothers received us warmly. [18]The next day Paul and the rest of us went to see James, and all the elders were present. [19]Paul greeted them and reported in detail what God had done among the Gentiles through his ministry.

[20]When they heard this, they praised God. Then they said to Paul: "You see, brother, how many thousands of Jews have believed, and all of them are zealous for the law. [21]They have been informed that you teach all the Jews who live among the Gentiles to turn away from Moses, telling them not to circumcise their children or live according to our customs. [22]What shall we do? They will certainly hear that you have come, [23]so do what we tell you. There are four men with us who have made a vow. [24]Take these men, join in their purification rites and pay their expenses, so that they can have their heads shaved. Then everybody will know there is no truth in these reports about you, but that you yourself are living in obedience to the law. [25]As for the Gentile believers, we have written to them our decision that they should abstain from food sacrificed to idols, from blood, from the meat of strangled animals and from sexual immorality."

[26]The next day Paul took the men and purified himself along with them. Then he went to the temple to give notice of the date when the days of purification would end and the offering would be made for each of them.

Paul Arrested

[27]When the seven days were nearly over, some Jews from the province of Asia saw Paul at the temple. They stirred up the whole crowd and seized him, [28]shouting, "Men of Israel, help us! This is the man who teaches all men everywhere against our people and our law and this place. And besides, he has brought Greeks into the temple area and defiled this holy place." [29](They had previously seen Trophimus the Ephesian in the city with Paul and assumed that Paul had brought him into the temple area.)

[30]The whole city was aroused, and the people came running from all directions. Seizing Paul, they dragged him from the temple, and immediately the gates were shut. [31]While they were trying to kill him, news reached the commander of the Roman troops that the whole city of Jerusalem was in an uproar. [32]He at once took some officers and soldiers and ran down to the crowd. When the

1. In your eyes, did Paul make the right decision to go to Jerusalem, even though godly people through the Spirit urged him not to go? 2. When have you made decisions against the wishes of people you admired and trusted? What happened? In retrospect, were your decisions wise ones? Explain.

What "rites of passage" have been significant for you in maturing in your faith, and why: Baptism/Confirmation? Summer mission project? Ordination? Marriage? Raising your children as believers?

1. What pressure do James and the elders face as Paul comes to Jerusalem? How would Paul's teaching cause strict Jews to be upset (vv. 21–26)? 2. This issue was supposedly settled at least six years earlier (see ch. 15). Why do these tensions still plague Jerusalem believers? 3. How would James' suggestion to Paul solve the problem for both of them (15:19–21)? Why remind the Gentile believers what to do (v. 25; 15:20)?

How do you decide when you should bend for the sake of others, and when you should stand for your principles?

What is the strangest thing you have ever seen done in the name of religion?

1. Why would Asian Jews be especially upset when they saw Paul (19:8–10)? 2. Gentiles were forbidden from entering the temple. How would the accusation of verse 28 fuel the suspicions of James (v. 21)? 3. Compare the reaction against Paul (vv. 30–31) with that against Stephen (6:11–13) 20 years earlier. What does this reveal about Christian-Jewish relationships in Jerusalem during this period?

What group is critical of the church today? How might the church provoke this group? What could be done to lessen this animosity? What can you do to help?

---

1. When have you wished you could understand another language better? How did you do in languages in school? 2. What is one thing you have seen that no one else in your group has seen?

1. From 21:30–36, why would the commander mistake Paul for the Egyptian revolutionary (v. 38)? 2. Under the circumstances, why did Paul think it so important to address this hostile crowd? How would Jewish-Christian relationships erode even further if the charges of 21:28 were left unanswered? 3. Many foreign-born Jews did not speak Aramaic well. How does Paul's use of this language (along with the content of his speech) force these Jews to listen? 4. This speech (22:1–10) recounts the events of 9:1–18. What points of identification does Paul make with his hostile audience? What is he hoping to achieve by this? 5. Why does Paul's reference to the Gentiles (v. 21) upset the crowd (v. 22), whereas they did not react to his speaking about Jesus? What was the real sticking point about the Gospel for the Jews? What does this tell you about them? 6. How was Paul's status as a Roman citizen an asset in his ministry to Gentiles (vv. 25–29; see also 16:37–38)?

1. Paul told his own story instead of preaching a sermon to this crowd. When do you find your story most effective and helpful to others? If you have not already done so, share the story of your relationship with Christ with the small group—in three minutes or less. 2. How has your faith in Jesus redirected your life in a surprising way? How do you struggle with that redirection? In what ways have you embraced some of these changes for yourself? 3. What is one of the hardest things you have had to experience because of your faith? 4. Paul's citizenship became an asset in his efforts to share the

rioters saw the commander and his soldiers, they stopped beating Paul.

³³The commander came up and arrested him and ordered him to be bound with two chains. Then he asked who he was and what he had done. ³⁴Some in the crowd shouted one thing and some another, and since the commander could not get at the truth because of the uproar, he ordered that Paul be taken into the barracks. ³⁵When Paul reached the steps, the violence of the mob was so great he had to be carried by the soldiers. ³⁶The crowd that followed kept shouting, "Away with him!"

Paul Speaks to the Crowd

³⁷As the soldiers were about to take Paul into the barracks, he asked the commander, "May I say something to you?"

"Do you speak Greek?" he replied. ³⁸"Aren't you the Egyptian who started a revolt and led four thousand terrorists out into the desert some time ago?"

³⁹Paul answered, "I am a Jew, from Tarsus in Cilicia, a citizen of no ordinary city. Please let me speak to the people."

⁴⁰Having received the commander's permission, Paul stood on the steps and motioned to the crowd. When they were all silent, he said to them in Aramaic*a*: **22** ¹"Brothers and fathers, listen now to my defense."

²When they heard him speak to them in Aramaic, they became very quiet.

Then Paul said: ³"I am a Jew, born in Tarsus of Cilicia, but brought up in this city. Under Gamaliel I was thoroughly trained in the law of our fathers and was just as zealous for God as any of you are today. ⁴I persecuted the followers of this Way to their death, arresting both men and women and throwing them into prison, ⁵as also the high priest and all the Council can testify. I even obtained letters from them to their brothers in Damascus, and went there to bring these people as prisoners to Jerusalem to be punished.

⁶"About noon as I came near Damascus, suddenly a bright light from heaven flashed around me. ⁷I fell to the ground and heard a voice say to me, 'Saul! Saul! Why do you persecute me?'

⁸"'Who are you, Lord?' I asked.

"'I am Jesus of Nazareth, whom you are persecuting,' he replied. ⁹My companions saw the light, but they did not understand the voice of him who was speaking to me.

¹⁰"'What shall I do, Lord?' I asked.

"'Get up,' the Lord said, 'and go into Damascus. There you will be told all that you have been assigned to do.' ¹¹My companions led me by the hand into Damascus, because the brilliance of the light had blinded me.

¹²"A man named Ananias came to see me. He was a devout observer of the law and highly respected by all the Jews living there. ¹³He stood beside me and said, 'Brother Saul, receive your sight!' And at that very moment I was able to see him.

¹⁴"Then he said: 'The God of our fathers has chosen you to know his will and to see the Righteous One and to hear words from his mouth. ¹⁵You will be his witness to all men of what you have seen and heard. ¹⁶And now what are you waiting for? Get up, be baptized and wash your sins away, calling on his name.'

¹⁷"When I returned to Jerusalem and was praying at the temple, I fell into a trance ¹⁸and saw the Lord speaking. 'Quick!' he said to

a40 Or possibly *Hebrew*; also in 22:2

me. 'Leave Jerusalem immediately, because they will not accept your testimony about me.'

¹⁹" 'Lord,' I replied, 'these men know that I went from one synagogue to another to imprison and beat those who believe in you. ²⁰And when the blood of your martyr[a] Stephen was shed, I stood there giving my approval and guarding the clothes of those who were killing him.'

²¹"Then the Lord said to me, 'Go; I will send you far away to the Gentiles.' "

Paul the Roman Citizen

²²The crowd listened to Paul until he said this. Then they raised their voices and shouted, "Rid the earth of him! He's not fit to live!"

²³As they were shouting and throwing off their cloaks and flinging dust into the air, ²⁴the commander ordered Paul to be taken into the barracks. He directed that he be flogged and questioned in order to find out why the people were shouting at him like this. ²⁵As they stretched him out to flog him, Paul said to the centurion standing there, "Is it legal for you to flog a Roman citizen who hasn't even been found guilty?"

²⁶When the centurion heard this, he went to the commander and reported it. "What are you going to do?" he asked. "This man is a Roman citizen."

²⁷The commander went to Paul and asked, "Tell me, are you a Roman citizen?"

"Yes, I am," he answered.

²⁸Then the commander said, "I had to pay a big price for my citizenship."

"But I was born a citizen," Paul replied.

²⁹Those who were about to question him withdrew immediately. The commander himself was alarmed when he realized that he had put Paul, a Roman citizen, in chains.

Before the Sanhedrin

³⁰The next day, since the commander wanted to find out exactly why Paul was being accused by the Jews, he released him and ordered the chief priests and all the Sanhedrin to assemble. Then he brought Paul and had him stand before them.

23 Paul looked straight at the Sanhedrin and said, "My brothers, I have fulfilled my duty to God in all good conscience to this day." ²At this the high priest Ananias ordered those standing near Paul to strike him on the mouth. ³Then Paul said to him, "God will strike you, you whitewashed wall! You sit there to judge me according to the law, yet you yourself violate the law by commanding that I be struck!"

⁴Those who were standing near Paul said, "You dare to insult God's high priest?"

⁵Paul replied, "Brothers, I did not realize that he was the high priest; for it is written: 'Do not speak evil about the ruler of your people.'[b] "

⁶Then Paul, knowing that some of them were Sadducees and the others Pharisees, called out in the Sanhedrin, "My brothers, I am a Pharisee, the son of a Pharisee. I stand on trial because of my hope in the resurrection of the dead." ⁷When he said this, a dispute broke out between the Pharisees and the Sadducees, and the assembly was divided. ⁸(The Sadducees say that there is no resurrec-

Gospel with Gentiles. What traits, skills or experiences do you have which can help you share the Gospel with others?

What was the most frightening thing that happened to you last week?

1. What sparks this exchange of accusations (see 21:21,28)? **2.** Why (and how) does Paul show his respect for the Jewish Law (vv. 1–5)? **3.** Why does Paul change the focus of attention from keeping the Law to his hope in the Resurrection? Given the tensions between the Pharisees and Sadducees on this issue, describe what you think the next few minutes of the assembly must have been like. **4.** What effect does the split have on Paul's case (vv. 7–10)? **5.** We last heard God speak to Paul in 18:9–10, after he had experienced a series of setbacks. How would the Lord's message here (v. 11) help Paul again? How would this help Paul remember what the Lord said about him to Ananias in 9:15–16?

---

a20 Or witness   *b5 Exodus 22:28*

1. When facing death, what duty do you want to have fulfilled before God? How can you pursue that course this week? 2. How has the Lord encouraged you during hard times? 3. What could be your "Rome"—the next crucial step in your spiritual journey?

Who is your favorite relative? What incident brought the two of you closer?

1. How do you explain the fierce determination of these Jews to kill Paul (see Ro 10:2)? Why do they think he is so dangerous? 2. Given verse 11, how would you feel if you were Paul and you heard this news from your nephew (vv. 12–16)? 3. By sending his nephew to the commander, is Paul showing a lack of faith in God's promise? Why or why not?

1. The Gentile soldier and the Jews take different sides in Paul's situation. When have you seen a non-Christian behave more righteously than a believer? 2. What risks did Paul's nephew take in this story? How might you be called upon this week to take a risk and stand up for someone whom others dislike?

What was the most life-changing letter you ever received?

1. How does the commander's provision for Paul contrast with the way Pilate dealt with Jesus (see Lk 23:1–25)? Why do you think this is the case? 2. What has the commander decided to do with the "Paul problem"? Why the elaborate security precautions and the constant passing the buck? How does this relate to 9:15? 3. How would you feel if you were one of the men in 23:12–13, and you found out the next day that Paul was gone?

tion, and that there are neither angels nor spirits, but the Pharisees acknowledge them all.)

⁹There was a great uproar, and some of the teachers of the law who were Pharisees stood up and argued vigorously. "We find nothing wrong with this man," they said. "What if a spirit or an angel has spoken to him?" ¹⁰The dispute became so violent that the commander was afraid Paul would be torn to pieces by them. He ordered the troops to go down and take him away from them by force and bring him into the barracks.

¹¹The following night the Lord stood near Paul and said, "Take courage! As you have testified about me in Jerusalem, so you must also testify in Rome."

The Plot to Kill Paul

¹²The next morning the Jews formed a conspiracy and bound themselves with an oath not to eat or drink until they had killed Paul. ¹³More than forty men were involved in this plot. ¹⁴They went to the chief priests and elders and said, "We have taken a solemn oath not to eat anything until we have killed Paul. ¹⁵Now then, you and the Sanhedrin petition the commander to bring him before you on the pretext of wanting more accurate information about his case. We are ready to kill him before he gets here."

¹⁶But when the son of Paul's sister heard of this plot, he went into the barracks and told Paul.

¹⁷Then Paul called one of the centurions and said, "Take this young man to the commander; he has something to tell him." ¹⁸So he took him to the commander.

The centurion said, "Paul, the prisoner, sent for me and asked me to bring this young man to you because he has something to tell you."

¹⁹The commander took the young man by the hand, drew him aside and asked, "What is it you want to tell me?"

²⁰He said: "The Jews have agreed to ask you to bring Paul before the Sanhedrin tomorrow on the pretext of wanting more accurate information about him. ²¹Don't give in to them, because more than forty of them are waiting in ambush for him. They have taken an oath not to eat or drink until they have killed him. They are ready now, waiting for your consent to their request."

²²The commander dismissed the young man and cautioned him, "Don't tell anyone that you have reported this to me."

Paul Transferred to Caesarea

²³Then he called two of his centurions and ordered them, "Get ready a detachment of two hundred soldiers, seventy horsemen and two hundred spearmen*ᵃ* to go to Caesarea at nine tonight. ²⁴Provide mounts for Paul so that he may be taken safely to Governor Felix."

²⁵He wrote a letter as follows:

²⁶Claudius Lysias,

To His Excellency, Governor Felix:

Greetings.

²⁷This man was seized by the Jews and they were about to kill him, but I came with my troops and rescued him, for I had learned that he is a Roman citizen. ²⁸I wanted to know why

---

ᵃ23 The meaning of the Greek for this word is uncertain.

they were accusing him, so I brought him to their Sanhedrin. ²⁹I found that the accusation had to do with questions about their law, but there was no charge against him that deserved death or imprisonment. ³⁰When I was informed of a plot to be carried out against the man, I sent him to you at once. I also ordered his accusers to present to you their case against him.

³¹So the soldiers, carrying out their orders, took Paul with them during the night and brought him as far as Antipatris. ³²The next day they let the cavalry go on with him, while they returned to the barracks. ³³When the cavalry arrived in Caesarea, they delivered the letter to the governor and handed Paul over to him. ³⁴The governor read the letter and asked what province he was from. Learning that he was from Cilicia, ³⁵he said, "I will hear your case when your accusers get here." Then he ordered that Paul be kept under guard in Herod's palace.

The Trial Before Felix

24 Five days later the high priest Ananias went down to Caesarea with some of the elders and a lawyer named Tertullus, and they brought their charges against Paul before the governor. ²When Paul was called in, Tertullus presented his case before Felix: "We have enjoyed a long period of peace under you, and your foresight has brought about reforms in this nation. ³Everywhere and in every way, most excellent Felix, we acknowledge this with profound gratitude. ⁴But in order not to weary you further, I would request that you be kind enough to hear us briefly.

⁵"We have found this man to be a troublemaker, stirring up riots among the Jews all over the world. He is a ringleader of the Nazarene sect ⁶and even tried to desecrate the temple; so we seized him. ⁸By[a] examining him yourself you will be able to learn the truth about all these charges we are bringing against him."

⁹The Jews joined in the accusation, asserting that these things were true.

¹⁰When the governor motioned for him to speak, Paul replied: "I know that for a number of years you have been a judge over this nation; so I gladly make my defense. ¹¹You can easily verify that no more than twelve days ago I went up to Jerusalem to worship. ¹²My accusers did not find me arguing with anyone at the temple, or stirring up a crowd in the synagogues or anywhere else in the city. ¹³And they cannot prove to you the charges they are now making against me. ¹⁴However, I admit that I worship the God of our fathers as a follower of the Way, which they call a sect. I believe everything that agrees with the Law and that is written in the Prophets, ¹⁵and I have the same hope in God as these men, that there will be a resurrection of both the righteous and the wicked. ¹⁶So I strive always to keep my conscience clear before God and man.

¹⁷"After an absence of several years, I came to Jerusalem to bring my people gifts for the poor and to present offerings. ¹⁸I was ceremonially clean when they found me in the temple courts doing this. There was no crowd with me, nor was I involved in any disturbance. ¹⁹But there are some Jews from the province of Asia, who ought to be here before you and bring charges if they have anything against me. ²⁰Or these who are here should state what crime they found in me when I stood before the Sanhedrin—

---

a 6-8 Some manuscripts him and wanted to judge him according to our law. ⁷But the commander, Lysias, came and with the use of much force snatched him from our hands ⁸and ordered his accusers to come before you. By

1. How do Paul's experiences with Roman authority here shed light on his comments in Romans 13:1–7? How does this contrast with Peter's experience with the Jewish authorities in Acts 4:8–20? 2. What do these two incidents show you about the Christian's relationship with civil authority? Where should you show your support of government authority? Where should you challenge it?

If someone were to bribe you to do a favor for them, what's the most effective incentive they could use: A return favor? Your favorite meal? Free babysitting? Money? Flattery? Other?

1. Felix had a reputation of violently suppressing rebellions against Rome. How might Tertullus hope that would compensate for the lack of evidence he can offer? 2. What difference can you see in the style Tertullus uses (vv. 2–4) to present his case to Felix compared to Paul's style? 3. How would all the charges in verses 5–6 seem true to Ananias and Tertullus? What does their reference to Christians as the "Nazarene sect" show about their view of Christianity? 4. How then does Paul defend himself (vv. 11–19)? 5. Put yourself in the place of Felix. In light of the riot in Jerusalem over Paul (if you only had Lysias' letter [23:26–30], the accusations of the Jews, and Paul's word to go on), what would you do? 6. What do you learn about Felix from verses 22–26? Why does he merely put Paul under house arrest? 7. In light of Acts 23:11, what must Paul be feeling as time wears on and no progress at all is made?

1. How has your desire to serve Christ been misunderstood by others? How did you feel then? 2. What's the difference between being "well acquainted with the Way" (v. 22) and being a true believer? How long were you "well acquainted" before you became a believer? 3. Have you ever felt there was a period in your life that was "dead time"—when nothing seemed to be happening at all (as seems to be the case with Paul)? Why do you think God allows such

²¹unless it was this one thing I shouted as I stood in their presence: 'It is concerning the resurrection of the dead that I am on trial before you today.'"

²²Then Felix, who was well acquainted with the Way, adjourned the proceedings. "When Lysias the commander comes," he said, "I will decide your case." ²³He ordered the centurion to keep Paul under guard but to give him some freedom and permit his friends to take care of his needs.

²⁴Several days later Felix came with his wife Drusilla, who was a Jewess. He sent for Paul and listened to him as he spoke about faith in Christ Jesus. ²⁵As Paul discoursed on righteousness, self-control and the judgment to come, Felix was afraid and said, "That's enough for now! You may leave. When I find it convenient, I will send for you." ²⁶At the same time he was hoping that Paul would offer him a bribe, so he sent for him frequently and talked with him.

²⁷When two years had passed, Felix was succeeded by Porcius Festus, but because Felix wanted to grant a favor to the Jews, he left Paul in prison.

The Trial Before Festus

25 Three days after arriving in the province, Festus went up from Caesarea to Jerusalem, ²where the chief priests and Jewish leaders appeared before him and presented the charges against Paul. ³They urgently requested Festus, as a favor to them, to have Paul transferred to Jerusalem, for they were preparing an ambush to kill him along the way. ⁴Festus answered, "Paul is being held at Caesarea, and I myself am going there soon. ⁵Let some of your leaders come with me and press charges against the man there, if he has done anything wrong."

⁶After spending eight or ten days with them, he went down to Caesarea, and the next day he convened the court and ordered that Paul be brought before him. ⁷When Paul appeared, the Jews who had come down from Jerusalem stood around him, bringing many serious charges against him, which they could not prove.

⁸Then Paul made his defense: "I have done nothing wrong against the law of the Jews or against the temple or against Caesar."

⁹Festus, wishing to do the Jews a favor, said to Paul, "Are you willing to go up to Jerusalem and stand trial before me there on these charges?"

¹⁰Paul answered: "I am now standing before Caesar's court, where I ought to be tried. I have not done any wrong to the Jews, as you yourself know very well. ¹¹If, however, I am guilty of doing anything deserving death, I do not refuse to die. But if the charges brought against me by these Jews are not true, no one has the right to hand me over to them. I appeal to Caesar!"

¹²After Festus had conferred with his council, he declared: "You have appealed to Caesar. To Caesar you will go!"

Festus Consults King Agrippa

¹³A few days later King Agrippa and Bernice arrived at Caesarea to pay their respects to Festus. ¹⁴Since they were spending many days there, Festus discussed Paul's case with the king. He said: "There is a man here whom Felix left as a prisoner. ¹⁵When I went to Jerusalem, the chief priests and elders of the Jews brought charges against him and asked that he be condemned.

¹⁶"I told them that it is not the Roman custom to hand over any man before he has faced his accusers and has had an opportunity to

---

times in our lives? **4.** Consider verse 25. When have discussions on righteousness, self-control and judgment troubled you? Why?

☕ Name three laws or rules you have never broken.

📖 **1.** Two years have passed since the trial before Felix (24:27). Why hasn't the opposition to Paul by the Jewish leaders dissipated during this time? **2.** Paul has come a long way since the events of 9:1–2. What irony do you see in that? How could 9:1–2 also account in part for their animosity? **3.** How is Paul like a pawn to these Roman officials (v. 9; see 24:27)? How might this account for his decision to appeal to Caesar?

♡ **1.** What laws conflict with your efforts to emulate Jesus Christ? **2.** What was one circumstance that threatened to ambush you in your spiritual life? How did you deal with it? **3.** If someone wanted to prove you were a Christian, what evidence from this past week could they use?

☕ If you could be king or queen for a day, what new law would you enact?

📖 **1.** How fair is Festus in describing the case? How much does he seem to know about Judaism? About Christianity? How would this have affected any decision he would have made in the case? Do you think he is honestly

defend himself against their charges. [17]When they came here with me, I did not delay the case, but convened the court the next day and ordered the man to be brought in. [18]When his accusers got up to speak, they did not charge him with any of the crimes I had expected. [19]Instead, they had some points of dispute with him about their own religion and about a dead man named Jesus who Paul claimed was alive. [20]I was at a loss how to investigate such matters; so I asked if he would be willing to go to Jerusalem and stand trial there on these charges. [21]When Paul made his appeal to be held over for the Emperor's decision, I ordered him held until I could send him to Caesar."

[22]Then Agrippa said to Festus, "I would like to hear this man myself."

He replied, "Tomorrow you will hear him."

Paul Before Agrippa

[23]The next day Agrippa and Bernice came with great pomp and entered the audience room with the high ranking officers and the leading men of the city. At the command of Festus, Paul was brought in. [24]Festus said: "King Agrippa, and all who are present with us, you see this man! The whole Jewish community has petitioned me about him in Jerusalem and here in Caesarea, shouting that he ought not to live any longer. [25]I found he had done nothing deserving of death, but because he made his appeal to the Emperor I decided to send him to Rome. [26]But I have nothing definite to write to His Majesty about him. Therefore I have brought him before all of you, and especially before you, King Agrippa, so that as a result of this investigation I may have something to write. [27]For I think it is unreasonable to send on a prisoner without specifying the charges against him."

26 Then Agrippa said to Paul, "You have permission to speak for yourself."

So Paul motioned with his hand and began his defense: [2]"King Agrippa, I consider myself fortunate to stand before you today as I make my defense against all the accusations of the Jews, [3]and especially so because you are well acquainted with all the Jewish customs and controversies. Therefore, I beg you to listen to me patiently.

[4]"The Jews all know the way I have lived ever since I was a child, from the beginning of my life in my own country, and also in Jerusalem. [5]They have known me for a long time and can testify, if they are willing, that according to the strictest sect of our religion, I lived as a Pharisee. [6]And now it is because of my hope in what God has promised our fathers that I am on trial today. [7]This is the promise our twelve tribes are hoping to see fulfilled as they earnestly serve God day and night. O king, it is because of this hope that the Jews are accusing me. [8]Why should any of you consider it incredible that God raises the dead?

[9]"I too was convinced that I ought to do all that was possible to oppose the name of Jesus of Nazareth. [10]And that is just what I did in Jerusalem. On the authority of the chief priests I put many of the saints in prison, and when they were put to death, I cast my vote against them. [11]Many a time I went from one synagogue to another to have them punished, and I tried to force them to blaspheme. In my obsession against them, I even went to foreign cities to persecute them.

[12]"On one of these journeys I was going to Damascus with the authority and commission of the chief priests. [13]About noon,

trying to find the truth in this matter? Why? **2.** This Agrippa was the son of the Herod in 12:1–23. Why would he be especially interested in hearing from Paul?

When you have questions about your faith, to whom do you turn? Why? How else do you seek input?

1. When have you had to publicly appear before an important or powerful person and put your fate in his/her hands: (a) Defending yourself in a tax audit? (b) Asking for a pay raise or an allowance hike? (c) Asking parents for approval and blessing to marry? (d) Asking for liability damages? (e) Submitting to the dentist or surgeon? **2.** How did you feel as you thought about what to say?

1. What is the problem Festus faces? Why doesn't he simply let Paul go? How could Agrippa be in a position to help (26:3)? **2.** According to Paul, what issue is the real source of his conflict with the Jewish leaders (see 23:6; 24:21; 26:6–8)? Why do you think his adversaries never directly bring this out (see 18:15)? How does his conviction about the Resurrection differ from that of the Pharisees, who in theory believed in a general resurrection as well? **3.** Compare 26:20 with 20:21. How could you tell someone what it means to be a Christian from these two verses? **4.** How does faith in Jesus relate to a repentant change in lifestyle? Would you describe Paul's speech as a legal defense or a personal testimony? How are the two related? Do you think Paul's primary goal in this speech is to convince Agrippa of his innocence, or of the truth of Christianity's claims? Why? **5.** From 25:19 and 26:24, how convinced is Festus regarding the resurrection of Jesus? How might Paul's response in verses 25–27 surprise Festus? **6.** If you were in this hall, what impressions would you have of Paul as he concluded his speech? **7.** Up to this point, the Romans considered Christians and Jews as basically one and the same. From this speech, can the Romans begin to see some differences?

♡ **1.** What difference does it make to you that Jesus truly rose from the dead? What would be different about your faith if that were not the case? **2.** How does verse 18 fit as a description of your spiritual journey? Which other images describe what coming to faith was like for you? **3.** In verse 14, Paul adds a comment not found in his conversion story in chapters 9 or 22. When has God pointed out to you that your struggle has been against him all along? How has he redirected you since then? **4.** Paul considered himself a servant and a witness. In what way is God's call to you similar to or different from his call to Paul? **5.** Paul's obedience to Jesus resulted in a trial very similar to Jesus' trial. How has your obedience to Jesus resulted in similarities to Jesus' experience? **6.** How has Christ brought light into your life? How can you pass on that light to someone else this week?

O king, as I was on the road, I saw a light from heaven, brighter than the sun, blazing around me and my companions. ¹⁴We all fell to the ground, and I heard a voice saying to me in Aramaic,ᵃ 'Saul, Saul, why do you persecute me? It is hard for you to kick against the goads.'

¹⁵"Then I asked, 'Who are you, Lord?'

" 'I am Jesus, whom you are persecuting,' the Lord replied. ¹⁶'Now get up and stand on your feet. I have appeared to you to appoint you as a servant and as a witness of what you have seen of me and what I will show you. ¹⁷I will rescue you from your own people and from the Gentiles. I am sending you to them ¹⁸to open their eyes and turn them from darkness to light, and from the power of Satan to God, so that they may receive forgiveness of sins and a place among those who are sanctified by faith in me.'

¹⁹"So then, King Agrippa, I was not disobedient to the vision from heaven. ²⁰First to those in Damascus, then to those in Jerusalem and in all Judea, and to the Gentiles also, I preached that they should repent and turn to God and prove their repentance by their deeds. ²¹That is why the Jews seized me in the temple courts and tried to kill me. ²²But I have had God's help to this very day, and so I stand here and testify to small and great alike. I am saying nothing beyond what the prophets and Moses said would happen— ²³that the Christᵇ would suffer and, as the first to rise from the dead, would proclaim light to his own people and to the Gentiles."

²⁴At this point Festus interrupted Paul's defense. "You are out of

ᵃ14 Or *Hebrew*   ᵇ23 Or *Messiah*

 Acts 26:1–32   **PAUL BEFORE AGRIPPA**

The apostle Paul's trial before Festus, the Roman governor of Judea, ended with Paul appealing to Caesar. Now Festus has King Herod Agrippa II, himself a Jew, hear Paul to help Festus better understand the case for his report to be sent with Paul to Rome.

1. Why did Paul begin by saying to King Agrippa, "I consider myself fortunate to stand before you today"?
   a. It was just a formality.
   b. Paul was buttering him up.
   c. Since Agrippa should understand the issues, Paul thought he could convince him of his innocence.
   d. Paul wanted to challenge Agrippa to become a Christian.

2. What was the main point Paul wanted to make?
   a. that he was still a faithful Jew
   b. that the real reason he was on trial was his belief that Jesus was the Messiah God raised from the dead
   c. that he was a personal witness to the resurrection of Jesus
   d. that his preaching was doing what God had called him to do

3. If you had been at Paul's defense, how would you describe him?
   a. insane   d. full of passion
   b. logical   e. full of the Spirit
   c. fearful   f. convincing

4. How do you handle situations where your faith is criticized or questioned?
   a. I don't allow myself to get in those situations.
   b. I ask God to give me strength.
   c. I thrive on those situations.
   d. I wilt.

5. Which image from Paul's summary of the Gospel in verse 18 best describes your spiritual journey?
   a. having my eyes opened
   b. turning from darkness to light
   c. turning from Satan's power to God

6. What is the closest you have come to Paul's experience of having your entire focus in life change?

7. Where do you need God's transforming power in your life now?

8. 💲 What is the most important variable in whether or not

you have a passion for what you are doing in life?
   a. believing in God's direction
   b. knowing yourself and your talents
   c. having an ability to focus on something other than yourself
   d. having a purpose greater than the material aspects of life
   e. not being too philosophical, since the purpose of life is survival
   f. other:_____

9. 💲 If you compared where you are right now in your career and sense of calling to Paul's conversion, where would you be?
   a. on the road to Damascus—pursuing my own passion
   b. hearing God call my name and wondering what he's trying to say
   c. starting to sort out God's call on my vocational life
   d. letting God give me *his* passion

10. 💲 How has this course and this group affected your sense of purpose in life? Close by thanking God for the gift of Jesus and for the gift of each other.

your mind, Paul!" he shouted. "Your great learning is driving you insane."

25"I am not insane, most excellent Festus," Paul replied. "What I am saying is true and reasonable. 26The king is familiar with these things, and I can speak freely to him. I am convinced that none of this has escaped his notice, because it was not done in a corner. 27King Agrippa, do you believe the prophets? I know you do."

28Then Agrippa said to Paul, "Do you think that in such a short time you can persuade me to be a Christian?"

29Paul replied, "Short time or long—I pray God that not only you but all who are listening to me today may become what I am, except for these chains."

30The king rose, and with him the governor and Bernice and those sitting with them. 31They left the room, and while talking with one another, they said, "This man is not doing anything that deserves death or imprisonment."

32Agrippa said to Festus, "This man could have been set free if he had not appealed to Caesar."

Paul Sails for Rome

27 When it was decided that we would sail for Italy, Paul and some other prisoners were handed over to a centurion named Julius, who belonged to the Imperial Regiment. 2We boarded a ship from Adramyttium about to sail for ports along the coast of the province of Asia, and we put out to sea. Aristarchus, a Macedonian from Thessalonica, was with us.

3The next day we landed at Sidon; and Julius, in kindness to Paul, allowed him to go to his friends so they might provide for his needs. 4From there we put out to sea again and passed to the lee of Cyprus because the winds were against us. 5When we had sailed across the open sea off the coast of Cilicia and Pamphylia, we landed at Myra in Lycia. 6There the centurion found an Alexandrian ship sailing for Italy and put us on board. 7We made slow headway for many days and had difficulty arriving off Cnidus. When the wind did not allow us to hold our course, we sailed to the lee of Crete, opposite Salmone. 8We moved along the coast with difficulty and came to a place called Fair Havens, near the town of Lasea.

9Much time had been lost, and sailing had already become dangerous because by now it was after the Fast.ᵃ So Paul warned them, 10"Men, I can see that our voyage is going to be disastrous and bring great loss to ship and cargo, and to our own lives also." 11But the centurion, instead of listening to what Paul said, followed the advice of the pilot and of the owner of the ship. 12Since the harbor was unsuitable to winter in, the majority decided that we should sail on, hoping to reach Phoenix and winter there. This was a harbor in Crete, facing both southwest and northwest.

The Storm

13When a gentle south wind began to blow, they thought they had obtained what they wanted; so they weighed anchor and sailed along the shore of Crete. 14Before very long, a wind of hurricane force, called the "northeaster," swept down from the island. 15The ship was caught by the storm and could not head into the wind; so we gave way to it and were driven along. 16As we passed to the lee of a small island called Cauda, we were hardly able to make the lifeboat secure. 17When the men had hoisted it aboard, they passed

ᵃ9 That is, the Day of Atonement (Yom Kippur)

1. If you could take a honeymoon cruise anywhere, where would you go? Why? 2. Have you ever been seasick? What happened? How did you recover?

1. As Paul sets sail for Rome (consult the map in the Introduction to Romans), what points of interest can you locate along the way from Paul's diary? 2. From verses 1–3 and 43, what do you know about the centurion in charge? How does his concern for Paul indicate the way Paul used his time while imprisoned in Caesarea? 3. If you were the ship's owner or pilot, how would you react to Paul's warning about the 50-mile trip they wanted to make (v. 10)? Would you have responded any differently than Julius did to Paul's concern? 4. What in verses 13–20 reveals how severe this storm was? Verse 27 indicates this situation lasted two weeks. How would you be feeling by the end of the first week? What would a page from your ship's diary sound like? 5. As a sailor on board, how would you feel about Paul's message in verses 21–26? As a prisoner? 6. After being in Caesarea for at least two years, why would Paul need to hear the promise of 23:11 repeated (v. 24)? 7. Compare verse 31 with verse 11. How does the centurion feel about Paul now? About the God Paul serves? 8. How do Paul's words and his example serve to encourage the others? How would your estimation of Paul change during the two weeks of the storm? 9. What do you imagine the scene in verses 39–44 was like? What was said? How did people look? Feel? 10. How do Paul's attitudes

and actions compare with those of the sailors? To what would you attribute Paul's ability to remain calm under pressure?

1. When have you felt caught in a "northeaster," driven along by the wind? What happened? What did you learn from the situation? 2. In terms of a weather report, how would you describe your life at present? Your life five years ago? 3. In a crisis, Paul reacted with urgent forewarnings, maintaining hope, counseling, common sense, giving thanks, remaining calm, persevering to the end. In comparison, how do you react to crisis? 4. What is the greatest pressure situation you're facing now? How can Paul's example and the principles you've learned from his experience help you? What is your part and what is God's part in the resolution of your storm? 5. When have you been tempted to bail out of a stormy situation and slip away in a lifeboat? What happened? What did you learn?

ropes under the ship itself to hold it together. Fearing that they would run aground on the sandbars of Syrtis, they lowered the sea anchor and let the ship be driven along. ¹⁸We took such a violent battering from the storm that the next day they began to throw the cargo overboard. ¹⁹On the third day, they threw the ship's tackle overboard with their own hands. ²⁰When neither sun nor stars appeared for many days and the storm continued raging, we finally gave up all hope of being saved.

²¹After the men had gone a long time without food, Paul stood up before them and said: "Men, you should have taken my advice not to sail from Crete; then you would have spared yourselves this damage and loss. ²²But now I urge you to keep up your courage, because not one of you will be lost; only the ship will be destroyed. ²³Last night an angel of the God whose I am and whom I serve stood beside me ²⁴and said, 'Do not be afraid, Paul. You must stand trial before Caesar; and God has graciously given you the lives of all who sail with you.' ²⁵So keep up your courage, men, for I have faith in God that it will happen just as he told me. ²⁶Nevertheless, we must run aground on some island."

The Shipwreck

²⁷On the fourteenth night we were still being driven across the Adriatic[a] Sea, when about midnight the sailors sensed they were approaching land. ²⁸They took soundings and found that the water was a hundred and twenty feet[b] deep. A short time later they took soundings again and found it was ninety feet[c] deep. ²⁹Fearing that we would be dashed against the rocks, they dropped four anchors from the stern and prayed for daylight. ³⁰In an attempt to escape from the ship, the sailors let the lifeboat down into the sea, pretending they were going to lower some anchors from the bow. ³¹Then Paul said to the centurion and the soldiers, "Unless these men stay with the ship, you cannot be saved." ³²So the soldiers cut the ropes that held the lifeboat and let it fall away.

³³Just before dawn Paul urged them all to eat. "For the last fourteen days," he said, "you have been in constant suspense and have gone without food—you haven't eaten anything. ³⁴Now I urge you to take some food. You need it to survive. Not one of you will lose a single hair from his head." ³⁵After he said this, he took some bread and gave thanks to God in front of them all. Then he broke it and began to eat. ³⁶They were all encouraged and ate some food themselves. ³⁷Altogether there were 276 of us on board. ³⁸When they had eaten as much as they wanted, they lightened the ship by throwing the grain into the sea.

³⁹When daylight came, they did not recognize the land, but they saw a bay with a sandy beach, where they decided to run the ship aground if they could. ⁴⁰Cutting loose the anchors, they left them in the sea and at the same time untied the ropes that held the rudders. Then they hoisted the foresail to the wind and made for the beach. ⁴¹But the ship struck a sandbar and ran aground. The bow stuck fast and would not move, and the stern was broken to pieces by the pounding of the surf.

⁴²The soldiers planned to kill the prisoners to prevent any of them from swimming away and escaping. ⁴³But the centurion wanted to spare Paul's life and kept them from carrying out their plan. He ordered those who could swim to jump overboard first

---

[a]27 In ancient times the name referred to an area extending well south of Italy.
[b]28 Greek twenty orguias (about 37 meters)   [c]28 Greek fifteen orguias (about 27 meters)

and get to land. ⁴⁴The rest were to get there on planks or on pieces of the ship. In this way everyone reached land in safety.

Ashore on Malta

28 Once safely on shore, we found out that the island was called Malta. ²The islanders showed us unusual kindness. They built a fire and welcomed us all because it was raining and cold. ³Paul gathered a pile of brushwood and, as he put it on the fire, a viper, driven out by the heat, fastened itself on his hand. ⁴When the islanders saw the snake hanging from his hand, they said to each other, "This man must be a murderer; for though he escaped from the sea, Justice has not allowed him to live." ⁵But Paul shook the snake off into the fire and suffered no ill effects. ⁶The people expected him to swell up or suddenly fall dead, but after waiting a long time and seeing nothing unusual happen to him, they changed their minds and said he was a god.

⁷There was an estate nearby that belonged to Publius, the chief official of the island. He welcomed us to his home and for three days entertained us hospitably. ⁸His father was sick in bed, suffering from fever and dysentery. Paul went in to see him and, after prayer, placed his hands on him and healed him. ⁹When this had happened, the rest of the sick on the island came and were cured. ¹⁰They honored us in many ways and when we were ready to sail, they furnished us with the supplies we needed.

Arrival at Rome

¹¹After three months we put out to sea in a ship that had wintered in the island. It was an Alexandrian ship with the figurehead of the twin gods Castor and Pollux. ¹²We put in at Syracuse and stayed there three days. ¹³From there we set sail and arrived at Rhegium. The next day the south wind came up, and on the following day we reached Puteoli. ¹⁴There we found some brothers who invited us to spend a week with them. And so we came to Rome. ¹⁵The brothers there had heard that we were coming, and they traveled as far as the Forum of Appius and the Three Taverns to meet us. At the sight of these men Paul thanked God and was encouraged. ¹⁶When we got to Rome, Paul was allowed to live by himself, with a soldier to guard him.

Paul Preaches at Rome Under Guard

¹⁷Three days later he called together the leaders of the Jews. When they had assembled, Paul said to them: "My brothers, although I have done nothing against our people or against the customs of our ancestors, I was arrested in Jerusalem and handed over to the Romans. ¹⁸They examined me and wanted to release me, because I was not guilty of any crime deserving death. ¹⁹But when the Jews objected, I was compelled to appeal to Caesar—not that I had any charge to bring against my own people. ²⁰For this reason I have asked to see you and talk with you. It is because of the hope of Israel that I am bound with this chain."

²¹They replied, "We have not received any letters from Judea concerning you, and none of the brothers who have come from there has reported or said anything bad about you. ²²But we want to hear what your views are, for we know that people everywhere are talking against this sect."

²³They arranged to meet Paul on a certain day, and came in even larger numbers to the place where he was staying. From morning till evening he explained and declared to them the kingdom of God and tried to convince them about Jesus from the Law of Moses and

Whom would you elect as "Mr. or Mrs. Hospitality" at work? In your neighborhood? In your church? In your family?

1. In light of the fact God wanted Paul to get to Rome, why do you think he allowed all the events of 27:1–28:9 to happen? What stories would the centurion tell his fellow officers once they arrive? **2.** How could this set the stage for Paul to write about the way his imprisonment at Rome served to advance the Gospel (see Php 1:12–13)? **3.** How do you see Acts 1:8 still being carried out?

How has God used a disaster in your life for ministry? What have you learned from this?

1. As a child, whose visit would you be so excited about that you would wait outside (or by the window) until they arrived? Why? **2.** If in jail, what three items would you want most (a file, saw or key is not permitted!)?

1. Given the long delay, his shipwreck at sea, and his continuing status as a prisoner, how would Paul feel upon finally arriving in Rome? What must the believers' reunion with Paul have been like (vv. 14–15)? **2.** Why might Paul take the initiative to call this meeting with the Jewish leaders in Rome (vv. 17–20)? **3.** How do Paul's statements in 23:6, 24:21; 26:8 and 28:20 illustrate what he means by being a "prisoner for the Lord" (see Eph 4:1; Php 1:13–14; Col 4:3; Phm 1)? How does the existence of these "prison epistles" demonstrate the way Paul made the best of his situation? **4.** In light of all that Paul has been through, how do you think he felt when he heard the Jews' response in verse 21? How is their attitude different from that of the Jews in Jerusalem? How do you account for this difference? **5.** How does Isaiah's "hardening ministry" (vv. 25–28) bridge the gap in perception between those who view Christianity as a narrow Jewish sect (v. 21) and those who view Christianity as a faith for all peoples (v. 28)? How does this thematic bridge relate to 1:8? To 9:15–16? To 26:22–23? **6.** Verse 31 is similar to other summary verses in Acts (see 6:7; 9:31; 12:24; 16:5; 19:20). What does this ending reveal about Luke's central concern in writing this book?

♡ **1.** What bothers your non-Christian friends about the faith? How can you help them overcome those barriers? **2.** When limitations are placed upon you by circumstances beyond your control, how do you react? How can you serve the Lord within these limits? **3.** How does verse 31 set the stage for the way your life could become a continuation of Acts 28? In what way would you like to contribute an "Acts, chapter 29" to this movement of God during the next two years? **4.** Probably within a few years, Paul was killed by the emperor Nero. How would verse 31 serve as a fitting epitaph on Paul's grave? What do you need to build into your life now, so that your faith in Christ will be what people remember about you at death?

from the Prophets. 24Some were convinced by what he said, but others would not believe. 25They disagreed among themselves and began to leave after Paul had made this final statement: "The Holy Spirit spoke the truth to your forefathers when he said through Isaiah the prophet:

26" 'Go to this people and say,
    "You will be ever hearing but never
        understanding;
    you will be ever seeing but never perceiving."
27For this people's heart has become calloused;
    they hardly hear with their ears,
    and they have closed their eyes.
Otherwise they might see with their eyes,
    hear with their ears,
    understand with their hearts
and turn, and I would heal them.' *a*

28"Therefore I want you to know that God's salvation has been sent to the Gentiles, and they will listen!" *b*

30For two whole years Paul stayed there in his own rented house and welcomed all who came to see him. 31Boldly and without hindrance he preached the kingdom of God and taught about the Lord Jesus Christ.

---

*a*27 Isaiah 6:9,10   *b*28 Some manuscripts listen!" 29After he said this, the Jews left, arguing vigorously among themselves.

INTRODUCTION to
ROMANS

Book Study Outline: If you are using Romans for a study course, here is a 7- or 13-week outline. Use the margin questions for your group agenda:

☕ start meeting / 15 min.

📖 read & discuss Bible / 30 min.

♡ close meeting / 15–45 min.

Refer to the Questions and Answers in front of Bible for more information.

Author: The apostle Paul.

Date: Probably A.D. 56–57, but no later than A.D. 59.

7-week plan	13-week plan	Personal Reading	Group Study Passage
1	1	1:1–17	1:1–17/The Gospel of Christ
	2	1:18–2:32	1:18–32/The Bad News
2	3	3:1–31	3:21–31/The Good News
	4	4:1–25	4:1–25/An Example of Faith
3	5	5:1–21	5:12–21/Grace Reigns!
	6	6:1–7:6	6:1–14/Alive in Christ
4	7	7:7–25	7:7–25/The Law of Sin
	8	8:1–39	8:28–39/More Than Conquerors
5	9	9:1–11:36	9:1–29/God's Word Is True
	10	12:1–21	12:1–8/Responding to God
6	11	13:1–14	13:8–14/Love One Another
	12	14:1–15:13	14:1–15:13/Life Together
7	13	15:14–16:27	16:1–27/The Living Church

Theme: Being right with God through faith in Christ.

Historical Background: Paul wrote this letter to introduce himself to the church at Rome. He intended to stop there *en route* to Spain. He was eager to assure the Roman Christians that, in spite of any rumors they might have heard, his message was indeed the Gospel of the grace of God in Christ Jesus. The church at Rome had not been planted by Paul. It may have been started by Roman Jews who were converted on the Day of Pentecost (Ac 2:10–11). The church was a mixture of Jewish and Gentile believers. At that point in time they were experiencing some tensions between these two groups.

Characteristics: The big issue in this letter is how anyone can be right with God on the final Day of Judgment. In his most precise theological statement in the New Testament, Paul asserts that right standing comes only through faith in Jesus Christ who died for us as a sacrifice for sin. In light of the Jewish-Gentile tensions in the church, Paul makes it clear that no one has an "edge" on God; rather, all stand condemned before him because no one has kept his Law. Having driven that truth home, he then declares the good news that forgiveness, acceptance and the new life of the Spirit come to all as God's gift to be received by faith. Chapters 1–11 speak of what God has done for all who believe, while chapters 12–16 show how believers ought to live in response to the lavish grace of God.

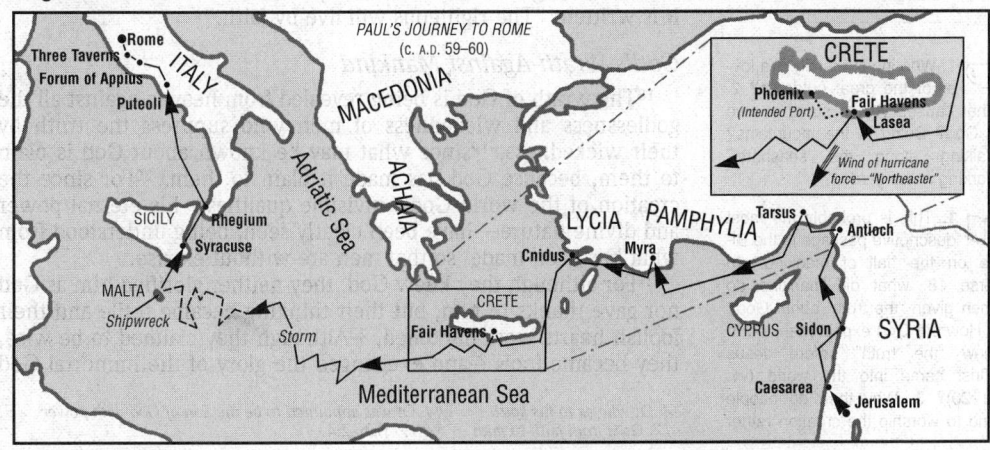

Romans

1. When you write a letter, are you more likely to write until you run out of paper, or keep it short and to the point? 2. What is one place you have never seen that you would like to visit?

1. If you received a letter from Paul (a missionary) saying he wanted to visit your family or small group, how would you react? 2. What do you know about Rome in the first century? What are the circumstances that caused Paul to write this letter? (Read Introduction to Romans.) 3. Note all the "I" statements. What do you learn about Paul in this passage? 4. What do you learn about Jesus Christ in this passage? 5. Reading between the lines, what is the problem in the church in Rome that Paul addresses in this letter?

1. When did you first feel Jesus' call in your life? How has that call changed your goals? Your sense of obligation to others? How is that reflected in your prayers? Your actions? 2. How would you compare your commitment to the Gospel to Paul's in verse 16? 3. Who was the Paul in your life who encouraged you in the rookie year of your spiritual life?

1. Who in your family is a lover of the great outdoors? 2. What causes you to stand in awe of God? Being in the mountains? Walking along the seashore? Working in the garden?

1. This is probably the most descriptive passage in the Bible on the "fall of mankind." In verse 18, what did mankind do when given "the truth" about God? 2. How did God expect mankind to know "the truth" before Jesus Christ came into the world (vv. 19–20)? 3. Why then do people tend to worship the creation rather

1 Paul, a servant of Christ Jesus, called to be an apostle and set apart for the gospel of God— ²the gospel he promised beforehand through his prophets in the Holy Scriptures ³regarding his Son, who as to his human nature was a descendant of David, ⁴and who through the Spirit*a* of holiness was declared with power to be the Son of God*b* by his resurrection from the dead: Jesus Christ our Lord. ⁵Through him and for his name's sake, we received grace and apostleship to call people from among all the Gentiles to obedience that comes from faith. ⁶And you also are among those who are called to belong to Jesus Christ.

⁷To all in Rome who are loved by God and called to be saints:

Grace and peace to you from God our Father and from the Lord Jesus Christ.

Paul's Longing to Visit Rome

⁸First, I thank my God through Jesus Christ for all of you, because your faith is being reported all over the world. ⁹God, whom I serve with my whole heart in preaching the gospel of his Son, is my witness how constantly I remember you ¹⁰in my prayers at all times; and I pray that now at last by God's will the way may be opened for me to come to you.

¹¹I long to see you so that I may impart to you some spiritual gift to make you strong— ¹²that is, that you and I may be mutually encouraged by each other's faith. ¹³I do not want you to be unaware, brothers, that I planned many times to come to you (but have been prevented from doing so until now) in order that I might have a harvest among you, just as I have had among the other Gentiles.

¹⁴I am obligated both to Greeks and non-Greeks, both to the wise and the foolish. ¹⁵That is why I am so eager to preach the gospel also to you who are at Rome.

¹⁶I am not ashamed of the gospel, because it is the power of God for the salvation of everyone who believes: first for the Jew, then for the Gentile. ¹⁷For in the gospel a righteousness from God is revealed, a righteousness that is by faith from first to last,*c* just as it is written: "The righteous will live by faith."*d*

God's Wrath Against Mankind

¹⁸The wrath of God is being revealed from heaven against all the godlessness and wickedness of men who suppress the truth by their wickedness, ¹⁹since what may be known about God is plain to them, because God has made it plain to them. ²⁰For since the creation of the world God's invisible qualities—his eternal power and divine nature—have been clearly seen, being understood from what has been made, so that men are without excuse.

²¹For although they knew God, they neither glorified him as God nor gave thanks to him, but their thinking became futile and their foolish hearts were darkened. ²²Although they claimed to be wise, they became fools ²³and exchanged the glory of the immortal God

---

a4 Or *who as to his spirit*   *b4* Or *was appointed to be the Son of God with power*
c17 Or *is from faith to faith*   *d17* Hab. 2:4

for images made to look like mortal man and birds and animals and reptiles.

²⁴Therefore God gave them over in the sinful desires of their hearts to sexual impurity for the degrading of their bodies with one another. ²⁵They exchanged the truth of God for a lie, and worshiped and served created things rather than the Creator—who is forever praised. Amen.

²⁶Because of this, God gave them over to shameful lusts. Even their women exchanged natural relations for unnatural ones. ²⁷In the same way the men also abandoned natural relations with women and were inflamed with lust for one another. Men committed indecent acts with other men, and received in themselves the due penalty for their perversion.

²⁸Furthermore, since they did not think it worthwhile to retain the knowledge of God, he gave them over to a depraved mind, to do what ought not to be done. ²⁹They have become filled with every kind of wickedness, evil, greed and depravity. They are full of envy, murder, strife, deceit and malice. They are gossips, ³⁰slanderers, God-haters, insolent, arrogant and boastful; they invent ways of doing evil; they disobey their parents; ³¹they are senseless, faithless, heartless, ruthless. ³²Although they know God's righteous decree that those who do such things deserve death, they not only continue to do these very things but also approve of those who practice them.

God's Righteous Judgment

2 You, therefore, have no excuse, you who pass judgment on someone else, for at whatever point you judge the other, you are condemning yourself, because you who pass judgment do the same things. ²Now we know that God's judgment against those who do such things is based on truth. ³So when you, a mere man, pass judgment on them and yet do the same things, do you think you will escape God's judgment? ⁴Or do you show contempt for the riches of his kindness, tolerance and patience, not realizing that God's kindness leads you toward repentance?

⁵But because of your stubbornness and your unrepentant heart, you are storing up wrath against yourself for the day of God's wrath, when his righteous judgment will be revealed. ⁶God "will give to each person according to what he has done."ᵃ ⁷To those who by persistence in doing good seek glory, honor and immortality, he will give eternal life. ⁸But for those who are self-seeking and who reject the truth and follow evil, there will be wrath and anger. ⁹There will be trouble and distress for every human being who does evil: first for the Jew, then for the Gentile; ¹⁰but glory, honor and peace for everyone who does good: first for the Jew, then for the Gentile. ¹¹For God does not show favoritism.

¹²All who sin apart from the law will also perish apart from the law, and all who sin under the law will be judged by the law. ¹³For it is not those who hear the law who are righteous in God's sight, but it is those who obey the law who will be declared righteous. ¹⁴(Indeed, when Gentiles, who do not have the law, do by nature things required by the law, they are a law for themselves, even though they do not have the law, ¹⁵since they show that the requirements of the law are written on their hearts, their consciences also bearing witness, and their thoughts now accusing, now even defending them.) ¹⁶This will take place on the day when

ᵃ6 Psalm 62:12; Prov. 24:12

than the Creator (vv. 21–23,25)? **4.** How does God respond to these evil attitudes? When mankind did not follow the truth, what did God let them do (vv. 24,26,28)?

1. Do you think our society has changed for the better or the worse since Paul wrote this description? **2.** Paul explains in this passage that the root cause for the ills in our society is a "depraved mind" or the sin nature in all of us. How does this view differ from what modern psychology teaches? **3.** If you could take a social psychologist on a tour of your community for a good look at the depraved mind in action, where would you take this person? What would you show this psychologist within your own life?

When you were young, which of your parents was more strict? Merciful? Consistent?

1. Who is Paul talking about in this passage (see v. 17)? **2.** Reading between the lines, what is going on in the church between the Jews and the Gentile converts? Who are the outsiders? Why? **3.** When Paul accuses the readers of doing the "same things" (v. 3), is he referring to the same specific sins, or to the same root causes of sin? **4.** If "the righteous will live by faith" (1:17), why does Paul emphasize doing good (v. 7) and obeying the law (v. 13)?

1. From your experience, is it easier for those who grew up in a Christian home to appreciate God's grace, or someone who had no religious training as a child? **2.** As you grow older in your spiritual life, does your appreciation of God's grace grow stronger ... or is it likely to be taken for granted? **3.** Are you more likely to get upset by the immaturity of new Christians in the gray areas ... or be upset at those who get upset over issues in the gray areas, such as social drinking?

God will judge men's secrets through Jesus Christ, as my gospel declares.

The Jews and the Law

17Now you, if you call yourself a Jew; if you rely on the law and brag about your relationship to God; **18**if you know his will and approve of what is superior because you are instructed by the law; **19**if you are convinced that you are a guide for the blind, a light for those who are in the dark, **20**an instructor of the foolish, a teacher of infants, because you have in the law the embodiment of knowledge and truth— **21**you, then, who teach others, do you not teach yourself? You who preach against stealing, do you steal? **22**You who say that people should not commit adultery, do you commit adultery? You who abhor idols, do you rob temples? **23**You who brag about the law, do you dishonor God by breaking the law? **24**As it is written: "God's name is blasphemed among the Gentiles because of you." *a*

25Circumcision has value if you observe the law, but if you break the law, you have become as though you had not been circumcised. **26**If those who are not circumcised keep the law's requirements, will they not be regarded as though they were circumcised? **27**The one who is not circumcised physically and yet obeys the law will condemn you who, even though you have the *b* written code and circumcision, are a lawbreaker.

28A man is not a Jew if he is only one outwardly, nor is circumcision merely outward and physical. **29**No, a man is a Jew if he is one inwardly; and circumcision is circumcision of the heart, by the Spirit, not by the written code. Such a man's praise is not from men, but from God.

God's Faithfulness

3 What advantage, then, is there in being a Jew, or what value is there in circumcision? **2**Much in every way! First of all, they have been entrusted with the very words of God.

3What if some did not have faith? Will their lack of faith nullify God's faithfulness? **4**Not at all! Let God be true, and every man a liar. As it is written:

> "So that you may be proved right when you speak
> and prevail when you judge." *c*

5But if our unrighteousness brings out God's righteousness more clearly, what shall we say? That God is unjust in bringing his wrath on us? (I am using a human argument.) **6**Certainly not! If that were so, how could God judge the world? **7**Someone might argue, "If my falsehood enhances God's truthfulness and so increases his glory, why am I still condemned as a sinner?" **8**Why not say—as we are being slanderously reported as saying and as some claim that we say—"Let us do evil that good may result"? Their condemnation is deserved.

No One Is Righteous

9What shall we conclude then? Are we any better *d*? Not at all! We have already made the charge that Jews and Gentiles alike are all under sin. **10**As it is written:

> "There is no one righteous, not even one;
> **11**   there is no one who understands,

Does your conscience trouble you when you violate the speed limit?

1. If you were a Christian in the church in Rome and you came from a Jewish background that practiced circumcision, how would you feel about Gentiles if they wanted to come into the church without being circumcised? 2. What was the original intent of the Law and of circumcision (see Ge 17:1–14)? How is that being twisted here? 3. Why is Paul (a Jew) so vocal about Gentiles not having to be circumcised to come into the church? 4. What does Paul mean by "circumcision of the heart" (v. 29; see Dt 10:16; 30:6; Jer 4:4; 9:25–26)? What is the real mark of God's family?

1. How open are you to receiving someone into your own small group or circle of friends who is seeking God but struggling with alcohol? 2. Where might you be hypocritical regarding your spirituality? Bible knowledge? Wisdom? Maturity? Morality? Lack of hypocrisy? Political convictions?

Among your relatives, who comes closest to being the family's spiritual "patriarch"?

1. If you are in a group, have two people read verses 1–8 aloud. Reader #1—verses 1,3,5 and 7. Reader #2—verses 2,4,6 and 8. What are the issues in each question and how does Paul address them? 2. Do you think it is easier for a prodigal who has "hit bottom" to come to God in repentance and faith than it is for someone who has had good religious training? 3. From verses 10–18, list what is said regarding human thought, direction, speech and action. How does this list make you feel? 4. From verse 20, would you say that the law is *descriptive* (more like a doctor's thermometer)? Or *prescriptive* (more like medicine to a sick patient)? What is its purpose?

1. When did you first truly sense your sin and need for God? 2. In raising your own children, what are you going to insist on in their religious training ... and what are you going to let them de-

---

a24 Isaiah 52:5; Ezek. 36:22   *b27* Or *who, by means of a*   *c4* Psalm 51:4
d9 Or *worse*

no one who seeks God.
¹²All have turned away,
   they have together become worthless;
there is no one who does good,
   not even one."ᵃ
¹³"Their throats are open graves;
   their tongues practice deceit."ᵇ
"The poison of vipers is on their lips."ᶜ
¹⁴   "Their mouths are full of cursing and
      bitterness."ᵈ
¹⁵"Their feet are swift to shed blood;
¹⁶   ruin and misery mark their ways,
¹⁷and the way of peace they do not know."ᵉ
¹⁸   "There is no fear of God before their eyes."ᶠ

¹⁹Now we know that whatever the law says, it says to those who are under the law, so that every mouth may be silenced and the whole world held accountable to God. ²⁰Therefore no one will be declared righteous in his sight by observing the law; rather, through the law we become conscious of sin.

Righteousness Through Faith

²¹But now a righteousness from God, apart from law, has been made known, to which the Law and the Prophets testify. ²²This righteousness from God comes through faith in Jesus Christ to all who believe. There is no difference, ²³for all have sinned and fall short of the glory of God, ²⁴and are justified freely by his grace through the redemption that came by Christ Jesus. ²⁵God presented him as a sacrifice of atonement,ᵍ through faith in his blood. He did this to demonstrate his justice, because in his forbearance he had left the sins committed beforehand unpunished— ²⁶he did it to demonstrate his justice at the present time, so as to be just and the one who justifies those who have faith in Jesus.

²⁷Where, then, is boasting? It is excluded. On what principle? On that of observing the law? No, but on that of faith. ²⁸For we maintain that a man is justified by faith apart from observing the law. ²⁹Is God the God of Jews only? Is he not the God of Gentiles too? Yes, of Gentiles too, ³⁰since there is only one God, who will justify the circumcised by faith and the uncircumcised through that same faith. ³¹Do we, then, nullify the law by this faith? Not at all! Rather, we uphold the law.

Abraham Justified by Faith

4 What then shall we say that Abraham, our forefather, discovered in this matter? ²If, in fact, Abraham was justified by works, he had something to boast about—but not before God. ³What does the Scripture say? "Abraham believed God, and it was credited to him as righteousness."ʰ

⁴Now when a man works, his wages are not credited to him as a gift, but as an obligation. ⁵However, to the man who does not work but trusts God who justifies the wicked, his faith is credited as righteousness. ⁶David says the same thing when he speaks of the blessedness of the man to whom God credits righteousness apart from works:

⁷"Blessed are they
   whose transgressions are forgiven,

cide? **3.** Up to this point in Romans, what has Paul been trying to prove? How important is this to a full understanding of the Gospel? **4.** What can you learn about witnessing from Paul's example in chapters 2–3? What kinds of people may need to be approached like this?

How close have you come to getting in trouble with the law?

1. If you were the person who was deserving of the death penalty, what would the word "justify" mean? **2.** If you were a slave, what would the word "redemption" mean to you? **3.** If you were a Jew who brought a yearly sacrifice to "postpone" God's judgment on you, what would the word "atonement" mean to you? **4.** How does this section break down barriers between Jews and Gentiles?

Martin Luther, John Wesley, Karl Barth—This passage, changed their lives ... and world history. How is the message of grace impacting your life?

1. When you were growing up, what chores were you expected to do around the house? Did your parents pay you? **2.** What is the biggest scam or junk mail offer you have fallen for—that promised something for nothing?

1. What is Paul doing when he calls Abraham to the witness stand to testify in his case for "justification by faith," not "by works?" **2.** Why would the example of Abraham be so important to the Jewish people? **3.** Why is circumcision so significant to the church in Rome in Paul's day? **4.** What do you learn about faith from the example in verses 18–21? How would you feel in Abraham's place? **5.** How does Abraham's faith relate

---

ᵃ12 Psalms 14:1-3; 53:1-3; Eccles. 7:20   ᵇ13 Psalm 5:9   ᶜ13 Psalm 140:3
ᵈ14 Psalm 10:7   ᵉ17 Isaiah 59:7,8   ᶠ18 Psalm 36:1   ᵍ25 Or as the one who
would turn aside his wrath, taking away sin   ʰ3 Gen. 15:6; also in verse 22

to what God calls us to believe in verses 23–25? **6.** In some religions, forgiveness or grace as a free gift is a foreign concept. You "earn" your way to heaven by doing good deeds. What would have happened to Christianity if Paul had given in on the issue of circumcision?

1. What does it matter to you—practically or emotionally—whether a right relationship with God is a *gift* to be received or a *prize* to be earned? **2.** In what area of your life do you need to take a lesson from Abraham and focus not on "working" but on "believing"?

whose sins are covered.
[8]Blessed is the man
whose sin the Lord will never count against
him." [a]

[9]Is this blessedness only for the circumcised, or also for the uncircumcised? We have been saying that Abraham's faith was credited to him as righteousness. [10]Under what circumstances was it credited? Was it after he was circumcised, or before? It was not after, but before! [11]And he received the sign of circumcision, a seal of the righteousness that he had by faith while he was still uncircumcised. So then, he is the father of all who believe but have not been circumcised, in order that righteousness might be credited to them. [12]And he is also the father of the circumcised who not only are circumcised but who also walk in the footsteps of the faith that our father Abraham had before he was circumcised.

[13]It was not through law that Abraham and his offspring received the promise that he would be heir of the world, but through the righteousness that comes by faith. [14]For if those who live by law are heirs, faith has no value and the promise is worthless, [15]because law brings wrath. And where there is no law there is no transgression.

[16]Therefore, the promise comes by faith, so that it may be by grace and may be guaranteed to all Abraham's offspring—not only to those who are of the law but also to those who are of the faith of Abraham. He is the father of us all. [17]As it is written: "I have made you a father of many nations." [b] He is our father in the sight of God, in whom he believed—the God who gives life to the dead and calls things that are not as though they were.

[18]Against all hope, Abraham in hope believed and so became the father of many nations, just as it had been said to him, "So shall your offspring be." [c] [19]Without weakening in his faith, he faced the fact that his body was as good as dead—since he was about a hundred years old—and that Sarah's womb was also dead. [20]Yet he did not waver through unbelief regarding the promise of God, but was strengthened in his faith and gave glory to God, [21]being fully persuaded that God had power to do what he had promised. [22]This is why "it was credited to him as righteousness." [23]The words "it was credited to him" were written not for him alone, [24]but also for us, to whom God will credit righteousness—for us who believe in him who raised Jesus our Lord from the dead. [25]He was delivered over to death for our sins and was raised to life for our justification.

Peace and Joy

5 Therefore, since we have been justified through faith, we [d] have peace with God through our Lord Jesus Christ, [2]through whom we have gained access by faith into this grace in which we now stand. And we [d] rejoice in the hope of the glory of God. [3]Not only so, but we [d] also rejoice in our sufferings, because we know that suffering produces perseverance; [4]perseverance, character; and character, hope. [5]And hope does not disappoint us, because God has poured out his love into our hearts by the Holy Spirit, whom he has given us.

[6]You see, at just the right time, when we were still powerless, Christ died for the ungodly. [7]Very rarely will anyone die for a righteous man, though for a good man someone might possibly dare to die. [8]But God demonstrates his own love for us in this: While we were still sinners, Christ died for us.

In your family, who tried to keep the peace? Mom or Dad?

1. How does "justification" change things in our relationship with God? What happened to the wrath of God Paul talked about in verses 9 and 1:18? **2.** How does Paul describe mankind's condition before Christ in verses 6, 8 and 10? How has this changed? **3.** How should a Christian look upon suffering and stress? Upon disappointment?

1. How much of God's peace and hope need to begin with a *feeling* and how much must begin with *head knowledge* and con-

[a]8 Psalm 32:1,2   [b]17 Gen. 17:5   [c]18 Gen. 15:5   [d]1,2,3 Or *let us*

⁹Since we have now been justified by his blood, how much more shall we be saved from God's wrath through him! ¹⁰For if, when we were God's enemies, we were reconciled to him through the death of his Son, how much more, having been reconciled, shall we be saved through his life! ¹¹Not only is this so, but we also rejoice in God through our Lord Jesus Christ, through whom we have now received reconciliation.

Death Through Adam, Life Through Christ

¹²Therefore, just as sin entered the world through one man, and death through sin, and in this way death came to all men, because all sinned— ¹³for before the law was given, sin was in the world. But sin is not taken into account when there is no law. ¹⁴Nevertheless, death reigned from the time of Adam to the time of Moses, even over those who did not sin by breaking a command, as did Adam, who was a pattern of the one to come.

¹⁵But the gift is not like the trespass. For if the many died by the trespass of the one man, how much more did God's grace and the gift that came by the grace of the one man, Jesus Christ, overflow to the many! ¹⁶Again, the gift of God is not like the result of the one man's sin: The judgment followed one sin and brought condemnation, but the gift followed many trespasses and brought justification. ¹⁷For if, by the trespass of the one man, death reigned through that one man, how much more will those who receive God's abundant provision of grace and of the gift of righteousness reign in life through the one man, Jesus Christ.

¹⁸Consequently, just as the result of one trespass was condemnation for all men, so also the result of one act of righteousness was justification that brings life for all men. ¹⁹For just as through the disobedience of the one man the many were made sinners, so also through the obedience of the one man the many will be made righteous.

²⁰The law was added so that the trespass might increase. But where sin increased, grace increased all the more, ²¹so that, just as sin reigned in death, so also grace might reign through righteousness to bring eternal life through Jesus Christ our Lord.

Dead to Sin, Alive in Christ

6 What shall we say, then? Shall we go on sinning so that grace may increase? ²By no means! We died to sin; how can we live in it any longer? ³Or don't you know that all of us who were baptized into Christ Jesus were baptized into his death? ⁴We were therefore buried with him through baptism into death in order that, just as Christ was raised from the dead through the glory of the Father, we too may live a new life.

⁵If we have been united with him like this in his death, we will certainly also be united with him in his resurrection. ⁶For we know that our old self was crucified with him so that the body of sin might be done away with,ᵃ that we should no longer be slaves to sin— ⁷because anyone who has died has been freed from sin.

⁸Now if we died with Christ, we believe that we will also live with him. ⁹For we know that since Christ was raised from the dead, he cannot die again; death no longer has mastery over him. ¹⁰The death he died, he died to sin once for all; but the life he lives, he lives to God. ¹¹In the same way, count yourselves dead to sin but alive to God in Christ Jesus. ¹²Therefore do not let sin reign in your mortal body

ᵃ6 Or be rendered powerless

scious claiming of peace and hope? **2.** What incident in your life can you look back on and see the truth of verses 3–5?

Who do you take after in your temperament, your mother or your father? How about your body build? Your musical ability?

1. Before DNA testing proved the likelihood of a single source for all of mankind, Paul was saying that the disease of sin came from a single source: Adam. What do you remember about the story in the Old Testament of Adam and his "fall" (Ge 3:1–24)? **2.** How has the sin of Adam affected his descendants to the present day? How would you describe this in medical terms? A disease? An epidemic? An infection that attacks the immune system? **3.** From chapter 5, what do you see that God has done through Jesus for us? How does this add to your understanding of God's grace (vv. 1,15, 17, 20–21)? How does this chapter illustrate why "Grace and peace to you" (1:7) is such an appropriate greeting for Christians?

Does the Gospel message excite you as it does Paul? Why or why not? What could help you to experience its life and vitality again?

What is the closest you have come to losing your life?

1. What is Paul's short answer to the addict who says he is a slave to his habit? **2.** The idea of death and resurrection is mentioned 15 times in this passage. What is Paul trying to say? **3.** What do you do with the flashbacks and voices in the night that keep reminding you of your past mistakes? **4.** If we are dead to sin, how is it that Christians still sin? What does it mean to practice the teaching in verses 11–13?

How does the knowledge of your death to sin affect your struggle with sin, or how can it? How can it affect your prayer life?

so that you obey its evil desires. [13]Do not offer the parts of your body to sin, as instruments of wickedness, but rather offer yourselves to God, as those who have been brought from death to life; and offer the parts of your body to him as instruments of righteousness. [14]For sin shall not be your master, because you are not under law, but under grace.

Slaves to Righteousness

[15]What then? Shall we sin because we are not under law but under grace? By no means! [16]Don't you know that when you offer yourselves to someone to obey him as slaves, you are slaves to the one whom you obey—whether you are slaves to sin, which leads to death, or to obedience, which leads to righteousness? [17]But thanks be to God that, though you used to be slaves to sin, you wholeheartedly obeyed the form of teaching to which you were entrusted. [18]You have been set free from sin and have become slaves to righteousness.

[19]I put this in human terms because you are weak in your natural selves. Just as you used to offer the parts of your body in slavery to impurity and to ever-increasing wickedness, so now offer them in slavery to righteousness leading to holiness. [20]When you were slaves to sin, you were free from the control of righteousness. [21]What benefit did you reap at that time from the things you are now ashamed of? Those things result in death! [22]But now that you have been set free from sin and have become slaves to God, the benefit you reap leads to holiness, and the result is eternal life. [23]For the wages of sin is death, but the gift of God is eternal life in[a] Christ Jesus our Lord.

An Illustration From Marriage

7 Do you not know, brothers—for I am speaking to men who know the law—that the law has authority over a man only as long as he lives? [2]For example, by law a married woman is bound to her husband as long as he is alive, but if her husband dies, she is released from the law of marriage. [3]So then, if she marries another man while her husband is still alive, she is called an adulteress. But if her husband dies, she is released from that law and is not an adulteress, even though she marries another man.

[4]So, my brothers, you also died to the law through the body of Christ, that you might belong to another, to him who was raised from the dead, in order that we might bear fruit to God. [5]For when we were controlled by the sinful nature,[b] the sinful passions aroused by the law were at work in our bodies, so that we bore fruit for death. [6]But now, by dying to what once bound us, we have been released from the law so that we serve in the new way of the Spirit, and not in the old way of the written code.

Struggling With Sin

[7]What shall we say, then? Is the law sin? Certainly not! Indeed I would not have known what sin was except through the law. For I would not have known what coveting really was if the law had not said, "Do not covet."[c] [8]But sin, seizing the opportunity afforded by the commandment, produced in me every kind of covetous desire. For apart from law, sin is dead. [9]Once I was alive apart from law; but when the commandment came, sin sprang to life and I died. [10]I found that the very commandment that was intended to bring life actually brought death. [11]For sin, seizing the opportunity

Who was your first "boss"? Was this person easy to work for or a slave driver?

1. If you find yourself once again being a slave to sin, what does this passage ask you to do? 2. From this passage (and also in 1:18–32) what were the members of this church doing before they turned over their lives to Christ? 3. What would Paul say to the modern psychologist who says that you can't change inherited behavior? 4. What is the difference between the pension plan that the old slave owner of your life offered … and the new owner's plan?

1. If Paul were around today, what would he say enslaves our society? What about the Christian community? 2. If you had acted as God's willing servant this week, what would have changed in your attitudes and actions?

When you were dating, did you ever get caught two-timing? Did anyone two-time you?

1. When Paul talks about the "authority" of the law, what does he mean? 2. Using the allegory of marriage, who were you married to originally? How did that marriage work out? 3. When Paul says you are "released" from the obligations of a religious life, is he discouraging spiritual discipline?

1. What were some of the "rules" that were taught in your religious upbringing? 2. Do you feel more "married" to the living Christ, or to some religious code? Explain.

1. When you were a teenager, what was one of your biggest struggles? 2. What New Year's resolution have you started with good intentions only to have it fizzle out?

1. Is the struggle that Paul describes here in verse 18 the struggle *before* he became a Christian … or the struggle *after* he

a23 Or *through*   *b5* Or *the flesh*; also in verse 25   *c7* Exodus 20:17; Deut. 5:21

afforded by the commandment, deceived me, and through the commandment put me to death. ¹²So then, the law is holy, and the commandment is holy, righteous and good.

¹³Did that which is good, then, become death to me? By no means! But in order that sin might be recognized as sin, it produced death in me through what was good, so that through the commandment sin might become utterly sinful.

¹⁴We know that the law is spiritual; but I am unspiritual, sold as a slave to sin. ¹⁵I do not understand what I do. For what I want to do I do not do, but what I hate I do. ¹⁶And if I do what I do not want to do, I agree that the law is good. ¹⁷As it is, it is no longer I myself who do it, but it is sin living in me. ¹⁸I know that nothing good lives in me, that is, in my sinful nature.ᵃ For I have the desire to do what is good, but I cannot carry it out. ¹⁹For what I do is not the good I want to do; no, the evil I do not want to do—this I keep on doing. ²⁰Now if I do what I do not want to do, it is no longer I who do it, but it is sin living in me that does it.

²¹So I find this law at work: When I want to do good, evil is right there with me. ²²For in my inner being I delight in God's law; ²³but I see another law at work in the members of my body, waging war against the law of my mind and making me a prisoner of the law of sin at work within my members. ²⁴What a wretched man I am! Who will rescue me from this body of death? ²⁵Thanks be to God—through Jesus Christ our Lord!

So then, I myself in my mind am a slave to God's law, but in the sinful nature a slave to the law of sin.

Life Through the Spirit

8 Therefore, there is now no condemnation for those who are in Christ Jesus,ᵇ ²because through Christ Jesus the law of the Spirit of life set me free from the law of sin and death. ³For what the law was powerless to do in that it was weakened by the sinful nature,ᶜ God did by sending his own Son in the likeness of sinful man to be a sin offering.ᵈ And so he condemned sin in sinful man,ᵉ ⁴in order that the righteous requirements of the law might be fully met in us, who do not live according to the sinful nature but according to the Spirit.

⁵Those who live according to the sinful nature have their minds set on what that nature desires; but those who live in accordance with the Spirit have their minds set on what the Spirit desires. ⁶The mind of sinful manᶠ is death, but the mind controlled by the Spirit is life and peace; ⁷the sinful mindᵍ is hostile to God. It does not submit to God's law, nor can it do so. ⁸Those controlled by the sinful nature cannot please God.

⁹You, however, are controlled not by the sinful nature but by the Spirit, if the Spirit of God lives in you. And if anyone does not have the Spirit of Christ, he does not belong to Christ. ¹⁰But if Christ is in you, your body is dead because of sin, yet your spirit is alive because of righteousness. ¹¹And if the Spirit of him who raised Jesus from the dead is living in you, he who raised Christ from the dead will also give life to your mortal bodies through his Spirit, who lives in you.

¹²Therefore, brothers, we have an obligation—but it is not to the sinful nature, to live according to it. ¹³For if you live according to the sinful nature, you will die; but if by the Spirit you put to

became a Christian? **2.** If you feel that Paul is talking about his pre-Christian life, where did he get his "desire" to do good? **3.** If you think he is talking about his Christian life, why is he struggling when God is the new owner of his life? **4.** When have you come to the place where you cried out like Paul in verse 24? **5.** Why do you think God's law was given: (a) Means to follow *in order* to be saved? (b) Guide to follow *once we are* saved by grace? (c) Stumbling block, impossible to follow, which only points the sinner to God's grace? How do verses 10, 12 and 22 support your answer?

♡ **1.** In light of your own struggles with sin, how do you feel about Paul's conflict? How is this a model for a healthy, realistic self-image? How is it a model for taking appropriate responsibility? **2.** What is the struggle in your spiritual life right now?

⌒ When you were young, who caused you to change your behavior by their powerful influence?

▯ **1.** The next time the travel agent for your old nature tries to send you on a guilt trip, what does Paul want you to keep in mind? **2.** What do you remember about the Ascension of Jesus Christ and his promise to send the Holy Spirit to indwell his followers at Pentecost (Acts 1)? **3.** In verses 5–11, what does Paul say about the option Christians have in living their life? **4.** Where is the battle for the control of your life going to be fought … and won or lost? **5.** Since we are not set right with God by doing good works, what is the motive for changing our lives? How are we to deal with our sinful nature (vv. 13–14; see 6:13,19)? **6.** What does it mean to be "led by the Spirit" (v. 14)? How does the Spirit help us fight our battles? Give an example.

♡ **1.** If there were a pollution control device on your thoughts right now, what would it register? GREEN (no problem); ORANGE (Warning signs) or RED (Fire alert zone). **2.** What does it mean to you that you are not God's slave, but his child?

ᵃ18 Or *my flesh*   ᵇ1 Some later manuscripts *Jesus, who do not live according to the sinful nature but according to the Spirit,*   ᶜ3 Or *the flesh*; also in verses 4, 5, 8, 9, 12 and 13   ᵈ3 Or *man, for sin*   ᵉ3 Or *in the flesh*   ᶠ6 Or *mind set on the flesh*   ᵍ7 Or *the mind set on the flesh*

death the misdeeds of the body, you will live, [14]because those who are led by the Spirit of God are sons of God. [15]For you did not receive a spirit that makes you a slave again to fear, but you received the Spirit of sonship.[a] And by him we cry, *"Abba,[b]* Father." [16]The Spirit himself testifies with our spirit that we are God's children. [17]Now if we are children, then we are heirs—heirs of God and co-heirs with Christ, if indeed we share in his sufferings in order that we may also share in his glory.

Future Glory

[18]I consider that our present sufferings are not worth comparing with the glory that will be revealed in us. [19]The creation waits in eager expectation for the sons of God to be revealed. [20]For the creation was subjected to frustration, not by its own choice, but by the will of the one who subjected it, in hope [21]that[c] the creation itself will be liberated from its bondage to decay and brought into the glorious freedom of the children of God.

[22]We know that the whole creation has been groaning as in the pains of childbirth right up to the present time. [23]Not only so, but we ourselves, who have the firstfruits of the Spirit, groan inwardly as we wait eagerly for our adoption as sons, the redemption of our bodies. [24]For in this hope we were saved. But hope that is seen is no hope at all. Who hopes for what he already has? [25]But if we hope for what we do not yet have, we wait for it patiently.

[26]In the same way, the Spirit helps us in our weakness. We do not know what we ought to pray for, but the Spirit himself intercedes for us with groans that words cannot express. [27]And he who searches our hearts knows the mind of the Spirit, because the Spirit intercedes for the saints in accordance with God's will.

More Than Conquerors

[28]And we know that in all things God works for the good of those who love him,[d] who[e] have been called according to his purpose. [29]For those God foreknew he also predestined to be conformed to the likeness of his Son, that he might be the firstborn among many brothers. [30]And those he predestined, he also called; those he called, he also justified; those he justified, he also glorified.

[31]What, then, shall we say in response to this? If God is for us, who can be against us? [32]He who did not spare his own Son, but gave him up for us all—how will he not also, along with him, graciously give us all things? [33]Who will bring any charge against those whom God has chosen? It is God who justifies. [34]Who is he that condemns? Christ Jesus, who died—more than that, who was raised to life—is at the right hand of God and is also interceding for us. [35]Who shall separate us from the love of Christ? Shall trouble or hardship or persecution or famine or nakedness or danger or sword? [36]As it is written:

"For your sake we face death all day long;
    we are considered as sheep to be
        slaughtered."[f]

[37]No, in all these things we are more than conquerors through him who loved us. [38]For I am convinced that neither death nor life, neither angels nor demons,[g] neither the present nor the future,

---

What signs of aging or weathering are you starting to feel in your bones?

1. What do you remember about the persecution of Christians in Rome during this time that would help explain Paul's words of comfort in this passage? 2. What is the closest you have come to feeling a "groaning" in your spirit to see the final triumph over sin and death? What would a world like ours be like if there were no decay or death? No expectation or delay? 3. What does the Holy Spirit do for us when we do not know how to pray? When is the last time you did not know how to pray and the Holy Spirit helped and comforted you?

What is the difference between the hope of a Christian and wishful thinking?

Do you tend to see the glass half full or half empty?

1. What confidence does verse 28 give you about events that occur in your life? Do you say the same thing when suffering (v. 18) comes your way? 2. In verses 29–30, what five verbs describe what God has already done for you? 3. If you received this letter and you were facing possible arrest, torture and physical death for your faith in Christ, how would verses 31–39 comfort you? 4. How could the forces in verses 38–39 disrupt your trust in God's love? 5. When has it been hardest for you to believe Romans 8:28?

1. How are you doing in the school of hard knocks right now? 2. What is the closest you have come to feeling the despair and loneliness of being separated from God like Paul describes in verses 31–39?

---

a15 Or *adoption*   b15 Aramaic for *Father*   c20,21 Or *subjected it in hope.* 21For
d28 Some manuscripts *And we know that all things work together for good to those who
love God*   e28 Or *works together with those who love him to bring about what is
good—with those who*   f36 Psalm 44:22   g38 Or *nor heavenly rulers*

nor any powers, **39**neither height nor depth, nor anything else in all creation, will be able to separate us from the love of God that is in Christ Jesus our Lord.

God's Sovereign Choice

9 I speak the truth in Christ—I am not lying, my conscience confirms it in the Holy Spirit— **2**I have great sorrow and unceasing anguish in my heart. **3**For I could wish that I myself were cursed and cut off from Christ for the sake of my brothers, those of my own race, **4**the people of Israel. Theirs is the adoption as sons; theirs the divine glory, the covenants, the receiving of the law, the temple worship and the promises. **5**Theirs are the patriarchs, and from them is traced the human ancestry of Christ, who is God over all, forever praised!*a* Amen.

6It is not as though God's word had failed. For not all who are descended from Israel are Israel. **7**Nor because they are his descendants are they all Abraham's children. On the contrary, "It is through Isaac that your offspring will be reckoned."*b* **8**In other words, it is not the natural children who are God's children, but it is the children of the promise who are regarded as Abraham's offspring. **9**For this was how the promise was stated: "At the appointed time I will return, and Sarah will have a son."*c*

10Not only that, but Rebekah's children had one and the same father, our father Isaac. **11**Yet, before the twins were born or had done anything good or bad—in order that God's purpose in election might stand: **12**not by works but by him who calls—she was told, "The older will serve the younger."*d* **13**Just as it is written: "Jacob I loved, but Esau I hated."*e*

14What then shall we say? Is God unjust? Not at all! **15**For he says to Moses,

> "I will have mercy on whom I have mercy,
>   and I will have compassion on whom I have
>   compassion."*f*

16It does not, therefore, depend on man's desire or effort, but on God's mercy. **17**For the Scripture says to Pharaoh: "I raised you up for this very purpose, that I might display my power in you and that my name might be proclaimed in all the earth."*g* **18**Therefore God has mercy on whom he wants to have mercy, and he hardens whom he wants to harden.

19One of you will say to me: "Then why does God still blame us? For who resists his will?" **20**But who are you, O man, to talk back to God? "Shall what is formed say to him who formed it, 'Why did you make me like this?'"*h* **21**Does not the potter have the right to make out of the same lump of clay some pottery for noble purposes and some for common use?

22What if God, choosing to show his wrath and make his power known, bore with great patience the objects of his wrath—prepared for destruction? **23**What if he did this to make the riches of his glory known to the objects of his mercy, whom he prepared in advance for glory— **24**even us, whom he also called, not only from the Jews but also from the Gentiles? **25**As he says in Hosea:

> "I will call them 'my people' who are not my
>   people;

---

1. What was one thing about which your folks used to say, "Wait 'till you're older, you'll understand then"? **2.** When have you won something unexpected? A trip? Award of achievement? Class officer elections? The big game?

1. How should each of the benefits Paul mentions in verses 4–5 have drawn the Jewish people to Christ? How does he account for their unbelief in spite of such advantages (vv. 6–9; see 4:11–12)? **2.** How would this link to Abraham help resolve conflicts between Jews and Gentiles? **3.** What would be just and fair for each of us to receive from God (see 3:9–20)? **4.** Is God fair? What does Paul says in verses 14–15? How does he respond to further questions about God's fairness in choosing some but not others (v. 19)? What is God's overriding purpose?

1. How deeply do you hurt for unbelievers? As much as Paul? **2.** If you were God, would you choose "you" to be part of your plan for the universe? How do you feel about God's authority to choose who will be "objects of his mercy" (v. 23)? **3.** Who are some non-Christians God has used to help you on your way to spiritual maturity? How so? In light of this passage, how should Christians approach witnessing? Is there any point? **4.** Where are you growing in your understanding of God's will for your life? What questions would you like to ask God about this? **5.** Suppose salvation did depend on human desire and effort. What grade would God give you: "E" for effort? "C" for creativity? "A" for accomplishment? "F" for failure to follow directions? If God graded on a curve, would you have a better chance of passing? Would "crib-sheets" help? How about polishing a few apples and becoming the teacher's pet? How does this passage make you feel about your own salvation?

---

*a*5 Or *Christ, who is over all. God be forever praised!* Or *Christ. God who is over all be forever praised!*   *b*7 Gen. 21:12   *c*9 Gen. 18:10,14   *d*12 Gen. 25:23   *e*13 Mal. 1:2,3   *f*15 Exodus 33:19   *g*17 Exodus 9:16   *h*20 Isaiah 29:16; 45:9

and I will call her 'my loved one' who is not
    my loved one,"[a]

²⁶and,

> "It will happen that in the very place where it
>   was said to them,
>   'You are not my people,'
> they will be called 'sons of the living God.' "[b]

²⁷Isaiah cries out concerning Israel:

> "Though the number of the Israelites be like the
>   sand by the sea,
>   only the remnant will be saved.
> ²⁸For the Lord will carry out
>   his sentence on earth with speed and
>   finality."[c]

²⁹It is just as Isaiah said previously:

> "Unless the Lord Almighty
>   had left us descendants,
> we would have become like Sodom,
> we would have been like Gomorrah."[d]

Israel's Unbelief

³⁰What then shall we say? That the Gentiles, who did not pursue righteousness, have obtained it, a righteousness that is by faith; ³¹but Israel, who pursued a law of righteousness, has not attained it. ³²Why not? Because they pursued it not by faith but as if it were by works. They stumbled over the "stumbling stone." ³³As it is written:

> "See, I lay in Zion a stone that causes men to
>   stumble
> and a rock that makes them fall,
> and the one who trusts in him will never be put
>   to shame."[e]

10

Brothers, my heart's desire and prayer to God for the Israelites is that they may be saved. ²For I can testify about them that they are zealous for God, but their zeal is not based on knowledge. ³Since they did not know the righteousness that comes from God and sought to establish their own, they did not submit to God's righteousness. ⁴Christ is the end of the law so that there may be righteousness for everyone who believes.

⁵Moses describes in this way the righteousness that is by the law: "The man who does these things will live by them."[f] ⁶But the righteousness that is by faith says: "Do not say in your heart, 'Who will ascend into heaven?'[g]" (that is, to bring Christ down) ⁷"or 'Who will descend into the deep?'[h]" (that is, to bring Christ up from the dead). ⁸But what does it say? "The word is near you; it is in your mouth and in your heart,"[i] that is, the word of faith we are proclaiming: ⁹That if you confess with your mouth, "Jesus is Lord," and believe in your heart that God raised him from the dead, you will be saved. ¹⁰For it is with your heart that you believe and are justified, and it is with your mouth that you confess and are saved. ¹¹As the Scripture says, "Anyone who trusts in him will never be put to shame."[j] ¹²For there is no difference between

1. When you were a child, what did you do to earn your allowance? 2. In elementary school, what was your hardest subject? What did you do to try to improve your grades? 3. What were some of the hard and fast rules observed in your house when your were growing up?

1. Is Paul anti-Semitic? What hope does he have for the Israelites in the first verse of Chapter 10? 2. In what characteristic way did Jews seek to be right with God (9:32)? What was the basic problem in this approach (see 3:20; 7:7–11)? 3. On the basis of 10:1–2, how would you respond to someone who said, *"What* you believe doesn't matter as long as you are *sincere"?* How can zeal for God sometimes get in the way of knowing him? 4. What is the only way to be saved according to Paul in 10:9–10? 5. How would the attitude of a person coming to God on the basis of his or her performance (v. 5) be different from that of someone coming to him by faith in Christ (vv. 8–9)? 6. What does it mean to confess "Jesus is Lord"? How does this tie in with belief? 7. What is the purpose of Paul's series of questions in verses 14–17? How does this underscore the importance of evangelism? 8. In general, what is the world's view today of going to heaven?

1. When did you first come to realize that it isn't so much what you do for God, but what he's

a25 Hosea 2:23   *b26* Hosea 1:10   *c28* Isaiah 10:22,23   *d29* Isaiah 1:9
e33 Isaiah 8:14; 28:16   *f5* Lev. 18:5   *g6* Deut. 30:12   *h7* Deut. 30:13
i8 Deut. 30:14   *j11* Isaiah 28:16

Jew and Gentile—the same Lord is Lord of all and richly blesses all who call on him, [13]for, "Everyone who calls on the name of the Lord will be saved."[a]

[14]How, then, can they call on the one they have not believed in? And how can they believe in the one of whom they have not heard? And how can they hear without someone preaching to them? [15]And how can they preach unless they are sent? As it is written, "How beautiful are the feet of those who bring good news!"[b]

[16]But not all the Israelites accepted the good news. For Isaiah says, "Lord, who has believed our message?"[c] [17]Consequently, faith comes from hearing the message, and the message is heard through the word of Christ. [18]But I ask: Did they not hear? Of course they did:

> "Their voice has gone out into all the earth,
>   their words to the ends of the world."[d]

[19]Again I ask: Did Israel not understand? First, Moses says,

> "I will make you envious by those who are not a
>   nation;
> I will make you angry by a nation that has no
>   understanding."[e]

[20]And Isaiah boldly says,

> "I was found by those who did not seek me;
> I revealed myself to those who did not ask for
>   me."[f]

[21]But concerning Israel he says,

> "All day long I have held out my hands
>   to a disobedient and obstinate people."[g]

The Remnant of Israel

11 I ask then: Did God reject his people? By no means! I am an Israelite myself, a descendant of Abraham, from the tribe of Benjamin. [2]God did not reject his people, whom he foreknew. Don't you know what the Scripture says in the passage about Elijah—how he appealed to God against Israel: [3]"Lord, they have killed your prophets and torn down your altars; I am the only one left, and they are trying to kill me"[h]? [4]And what was God's answer to him? "I have reserved for myself seven thousand who have not bowed the knee to Baal."[i] [5]So too, at the present time there is a remnant chosen by grace. [6]And if by grace, then it is no longer by works; if it were, grace would no longer be grace.[j]

[7]What then? What Israel sought so earnestly it did not obtain, but the elect did. The others were hardened, [8]as it is written:

> "God gave them a spirit of stupor,
>   eyes so that they could not see
>   and ears so that they could not hear,
> to this very day."[k]

[9]And David says:

> "May their table become a snare and a trap,
>   a stumbling block and a retribution for them.

done for you? **2.** The central affirmation of the early church was "Jesus is Lord"; everyone else was saying "Caesar is Lord." Who (or what) are some gods that compete with your allegiance to Christ? **3.** How hard is it for you to accept the fact that "the same Lord is Lord of all" (v. 12)? What about rapists and child abusers? What about people of other nations? What about your neighbors?

---

1. As a child, what item did a friend or sibling possess that made you jealous? **2.** What moments of rejection in your teen years do you remember vividly? Getting cut from the team? Not being invited to a big party? Turned down for a date? **3.** What have been the benefits of healthy competition in your life?

1. Has God rejected the Jews (vv. 1,5)? How might Paul's comments in 9:25 and 10:21 lead someone to ask the question in verse 1? **2.** On what basis are Paul and others of the remnant chosen? Why would this be so difficult for his fellow Israelites to grasp (see 10:3)? **3.** What relationships does Paul see between the Gentiles and the Jews in verse 11? **4.** Why does Paul want his Gentile readers to be aware of God's plan (v. 25)? Why would pride become a danger for them? **5.** Does Paul mean in verses 25–32 that every Jewish person will ultimately be saved or that the nation as a whole will experience the salvation of those who believe in faith? **6.** What

a13 Joel 2:32   *b15* Isaiah 52:7   *c16* Isaiah 53:1   *d18* Psalm 19:4
e19 Deut. 32:21   *f20* Isaiah 65:1   *g21* Isaiah 65:2   *h3* 1 Kings 19:10,14
i4 1 Kings 19:18   *j6* Some manuscripts *by grace. But if by works, then it is no longer grace; if it were, work would no longer be work.*   *k8* Deut. 29:4; Isaiah 29:10

is Paul's ultimate hope for Israel (vv. 26–27)? For Gentiles (v. 32)? How does this tie in with Paul's teaching in 3:21–24? **7.** How does the song in verses 33–36 relate to: (a) Paul's argument in verses 25–32? (b) Any questions that may have been raised by chapters 9–11? **8.** Which traits of God does Paul celebrate here? Why these?

♡ **1.** How is it possible for someone to try so hard to please God that they actually resist his love for them? When have you experienced this? **2.** Like the Jews in Paul's day, are churchgoers today relying more on performance of rituals than on God's grace? How? **3.** How does the church itself struggle with works versus grace? In what ways are works still important? **4.** How has arrogance between groups of Christians hurt your church experience? When have you found yourself exhibiting this attitude too? **5.** When someone else receives God's blessing and grace in their life, does that spur you on to seek God all the more, or does it leave you feeling on the short end of the stick? Why? **6.** Why is the end of this chapter a good place for a doxology—Paul's, yours and your group's?

¹⁰May their eyes be darkened so they cannot see,
and their backs be bent forever."ᵃ

Ingrafted Branches

¹¹Again I ask: Did they stumble so as to fall beyond recovery? Not at all! Rather, because of their transgression, salvation has come to the Gentiles to make Israel envious. ¹²But if their transgression means riches for the world, and their loss means riches for the Gentiles, how much greater riches will their fullness bring!

¹³I am talking to you Gentiles. Inasmuch as I am the apostle to the Gentiles, I make much of my ministry ¹⁴in the hope that I may somehow arouse my own people to envy and save some of them. ¹⁵For if their rejection is the reconciliation of the world, what will their acceptance be but life from the dead? ¹⁶If the part of the dough offered as firstfruits is holy, then the whole batch is holy; if the root is holy, so are the branches.

¹⁷If some of the branches have been broken off, and you, though a wild olive shoot, have been grafted in among the others and now share in the nourishing sap from the olive root, ¹⁸do not boast over those branches. If you do, consider this: You do not support the root, but the root supports you. ¹⁹You will say then, "Branches were broken off so that I could be grafted in." ²⁰Granted. But they were broken off because of unbelief, and you stand by faith. Do not be arrogant, but be afraid. ²¹For if God did not spare the natural branches, he will not spare you either.

²²Consider therefore the kindness and sternness of God: sternness to those who fell, but kindness to you, provided that you continue in his kindness. Otherwise, you also will be cut off. ²³And if they do not persist in unbelief, they will be grafted in, for God is able to graft them in again. ²⁴After all, if you were cut out of an olive tree that is wild by nature, and contrary to nature were grafted into a cultivated olive tree, how much more readily will these, the natural branches, be grafted into their own olive tree!

All Israel Will Be Saved

²⁵I do not want you to be ignorant of this mystery, brothers, so that you may not be conceited: Israel has experienced a hardening in part until the full number of the Gentiles has come in. ²⁶And so all Israel will be saved, as it is written:

"The deliverer will come from Zion;
he will turn godlessness away from Jacob.
²⁷And this isᵇ my covenant with them
when I take away their sins."ᶜ

²⁸As far as the gospel is concerned, they are enemies on your account; but as far as election is concerned, they are loved on account of the patriarchs, ²⁹for God's gifts and his call are irrevocable. ³⁰Just as you who were at one time disobedient to God have now received mercy as a result of their disobedience, ³¹so they too have now become disobedient in order that they too may nowᵈ receive mercy as a result of God's mercy to you. ³²For God has bound all men over to disobedience so that he may have mercy on them all.

Doxology

³³Oh, the depth of the riches of the wisdom andᵉ
knowledge of God!

ᵃ10 Psalm 69:22,23   ᵇ27 Or will be   ᶜ27 Isaiah 59:20,21; 27:9; Jer. 31:33,34
ᵈ31 Some manuscripts do not have now.   ᵉ33 Or riches and the wisdom and the

> How unsearchable his judgments,
> and his paths beyond tracing out!
> [34]"Who has known the mind of the Lord?
> Or who has been his counselor?" [a]
> [35]"Who has ever given to God,
> that God should repay him?" [b]
> [36]For from him and through him and to him are all
> things.
> To him be the glory forever! Amen.

Living Sacrifices

12 Therefore, I urge you, brothers, in view of God's mercy, to offer your bodies as living sacrifices, holy and pleasing to God—this is your spiritual[c] act of worship. [2]Do not conform any longer to the pattern of this world, but be transformed by the renewing of your mind. Then you will be able to test and approve what God's will is—his good, pleasing and perfect will.

[3]For by the grace given me I say to every one of you: Do not think of yourself more highly than you ought, but rather think of yourself with sober judgment, in accordance with the measure of faith God has given you. [4]Just as each of us has one body with many members, and these members do not all have the same function, [5]so in Christ we who are many form one body, and each member belongs to all the others. [6]We have different gifts, according to the grace given us. If a man's gift is prophesying, let him use it in proportion to his[d] faith. [7]If it is serving, let him serve; if it is teaching, let him teach; [8]if it is encouraging, let him encourage; if it is contributing to the needs of others, let him give generously; if it is leadership, let him govern diligently; if it is showing mercy, let him do it cheerfully.

Love

[9]Love must be sincere. Hate what is evil; cling to what is good. [10]Be devoted to one another in brotherly love. Honor one another above yourselves. [11]Never be lacking in zeal, but keep your spiritual fervor, serving the Lord. [12]Be joyful in hope, patient in affliction, faithful in prayer. [13]Share with God's people who are in need. Practice hospitality.

[14]Bless those who persecute you; bless and do not curse. [15]Rejoice with those who rejoice; mourn with those who mourn. [16]Live in harmony with one another. Do not be proud, but be willing to associate with people of low position.[e] Do not be conceited.

[17]Do not repay anyone evil for evil. Be careful to do what is right in the eyes of everybody. [18]If it is possible, as far as it depends on you, live at peace with everyone. [19]Do not take revenge, my friends, but leave room for God's wrath, for it is written: "It is mine to avenge; I will repay,"[f] says the Lord. [20]On the contrary:

> "If your enemy is hungry, feed him;
> if he is thirsty, give him something to drink.
> In doing this, you will heap burning coals on his
> head."[g]

[21]Do not be overcome by evil, but overcome evil with good.

As a teen, how did peer pressure affect the way you dressed? How you acted?

1. How can you offer your "body" as a living sacrifice? **2.** What does verse 1 add to your understanding of true worship (see also 6:13; 8:13)? **3.** In what ways do you tend to conform to the world? How does the "renewing of your mind" happen (v. 2)?

1. How clear is your sense of the gifts God has given you? Are you inclined to "think of yourself more highly than you ought" (v. 3) or put yourself down? **2.** What holds you back from using your gifts more fully?

As a child, who was the troublemaker in your family? Who was the peacemaker?

1. How does this section explain what Paul means in verses 1–2? **2.** When is it harder to practice love—when you are hurt by someone close to you? Or by an acquaintance? Why? **3.** How are love (v. 9) and peace (v. 18) the basis for all the other guidelines here?

1. Of the commands listed in these verses, which two are easiest for you to keep? Which two are the most difficult? **2.** Is loving your enemies: (a) nice, but unrealistic; (b) for Jesus and apostle Paul types only; or (c) a result of following Christ? How is Christ helping you to love? **3.** What relationship in your life most needs this lesson? Take a moment in silence to ask for God's forgiveness, understanding, patience and power for this relationship.

---

a34 Isaiah 40:13   *b35* Job 41:11   *c1* Or *reasonable*   *d6* Or *in agreement with the*   *e16* Or *willing to do menial work*   *f19* Deut. 32:35   *g20* Prov. 25:21,22

When was the last time you got a traffic ticket? How did you feel about the police officer?

1. Why does Paul say we should submit to governing authorities? Compare this passage with Acts 5:27–32. What principles do you find for helping you deal with authority? 2. Who are the authorities in your life? How well have you related to them? How could you do better?

What would Paul advise people in a modern democracy who face injustice? Those in countries banning Christianity?

What was the occasion of your first debt or loan?

1. What is the greatest example of love you have ever experienced or observed? How did it make you feel? 2. How does the law help us know what it means to love? How does this differ from popular notions of love? 3. How do you obtain the "clothing" in verse 14? How would you use this section to explain holiness?

How would your life be different if you consciously tried to "wear" Jesus Christ? What must change to ensure a better fit?

1. What, if any, rules did your family have for what you could or could not do on Sunday? 2. What did you, or do you, refuse to eat or drink?

1. Paul is writing about "gray areas"—issues over which equally committed Christians disagree. What are some controversial, gray areas in your life, family, small group or church? 2. Regarding these gray areas, do you need to hear: (a) Paul's challenge not to look down on those who have strict convictions; or (b) his challenge not to condemn those with more lenient convictions? 3. How can both sides stop judging one another and start accepting each other? 4. When you are tempted to judge someone's behavior, is it more out of your own codependency—a need to help the

Submission to the Authorities

13 Everyone must submit himself to the governing authorities, for there is no authority except that which God has established. The authorities that exist have been established by God. [2]Consequently, he who rebels against the authority is rebelling against what God has instituted, and those who do so will bring judgment on themselves. [3]For rulers hold no terror for those who do right, but for those who do wrong. Do you want to be free from fear of the one in authority? Then do what is right and he will commend you. [4]For he is God's servant to do you good. But if you do wrong, be afraid, for he does not bear the sword for nothing. He is God's servant, an agent of wrath to bring punishment on the wrongdoer. [5]Therefore, it is necessary to submit to the authorities, not only because of possible punishment but also because of conscience.

[6]This is also why you pay taxes, for the authorities are God's servants, who give their full time to governing. [7]Give everyone what you owe him: If you owe taxes, pay taxes; if revenue, then revenue; if respect, then respect; if honor, then honor.

Love, for the Day Is Near

[8]Let no debt remain outstanding, except the continuing debt to love one another, for he who loves his fellowman has fulfilled the law. [9]The commandments, "Do not commit adultery," "Do not murder," "Do not steal," "Do not covet,"[a] and whatever other commandment there may be, are summed up in this one rule: "Love your neighbor as yourself."[b] [10]Love does no harm to its neighbor. Therefore love is the fulfillment of the law.

[11]And do this, understanding the present time. The hour has come for you to wake up from your slumber, because our salvation is nearer now than when we first believed. [12]The night is nearly over; the day is almost here. So let us put aside the deeds of darkness and put on the armor of light. [13]Let us behave decently, as in the daytime, not in orgies and drunkenness, not in sexual immorality and debauchery, not in dissension and jealousy. [14]Rather, clothe yourselves with the Lord Jesus Christ, and do not think about how to gratify the desires of the sinful nature.[c]

The Weak and the Strong

14 Accept him whose faith is weak, without passing judgment on disputable matters. [2]One man's faith allows him to eat everything, but another man, whose faith is weak, eats only vegetables. [3]The man who eats everything must not look down on him who does not, and the man who does not eat everything must not condemn the man who does, for God has accepted him. [4]Who are you to judge someone else's servant? To his own master he stands or falls. And he will stand, for the Lord is able to make him stand.

[5]One man considers one day more sacred than another; another man considers every day alike. Each one should be fully convinced in his own mind. [6]He who regards one day as special, does so to the Lord. He who eats meat, eats to the Lord, for he gives thanks to God; and he who abstains, does so to the Lord and gives thanks to God. [7]For none of us lives to himself alone and none of us dies to himself alone. [8]If we live, we live to the Lord; and if we die, we die to the Lord. So, whether we live or die, we belong to the Lord.

[9]For this very reason, Christ died and returned to life so that he might be the Lord of both the dead and the living. [10]You, then,

a9 Exodus 20:13-15,17; Deut. 5:17-19,21   *b9* Lev. 19:18   *c14* Or *the flesh*

why do you judge your brother? Or why do you look down on your brother? For we will all stand before God's judgment seat. ¹¹It is written:

> " 'As surely as I live,' says the Lord,
> 'every knee will bow before me;
>   every tongue will confess to God.' " ª

¹²So then, each of us will give an account of himself to God.

¹³Therefore let us stop passing judgment on one another. Instead, make up your mind not to put any stumbling block or obstacle in your brother's way. ¹⁴As one who is in the Lord Jesus, I am fully convinced that no food ᵇ is unclean in itself. But if anyone regards something as unclean, then for him it is unclean. ¹⁵If your brother is distressed because of what you eat, you are no longer acting in love. Do not by your eating destroy your brother for whom Christ died. ¹⁶Do not allow what you consider good to be spoken of as evil. ¹⁷For the kingdom of God is not a matter of eating and drinking, but of righteousness, peace and joy in the Holy Spirit, ¹⁸because anyone who serves Christ in this way is pleasing to God and approved by men.

¹⁹Let us therefore make every effort to do what leads to peace and to mutual edification. ²⁰Do not destroy the work of God for the sake of food. All food is clean, but it is wrong for a man to eat anything that causes someone else to stumble. ²¹It is better not to eat meat or drink wine or to do anything else that will cause your brother to fall.

²²So whatever you believe about these things keep between yourself and God. Blessed is the man who does not condemn himself by what he approves. ²³But the man who has doubts is condemned if he eats, because his eating is not from faith; and everything that does not come from faith is sin.

15 We who are strong ought to bear with the failings of the weak and not to please ourselves. ²Each of us should please his neighbor for his good, to build him up. ³For even Christ did not please himself but, as it is written: "The insults of those who insult you have fallen on me." ᶜ ⁴For everything that was written in the past was written to teach us, so that through endurance and the encouragement of the Scriptures we might have hope.

⁵May the God who gives endurance and encouragement give you a spirit of unity among yourselves as you follow Christ Jesus, ⁶so that with one heart and mouth you may glorify the God and Father of our Lord Jesus Christ.

⁷Accept one another, then, just as Christ accepted you, in order to bring praise to God. ⁸For I tell you that Christ has become a servant of the Jews ᵈ on behalf of God's truth, to confirm the promises made to the patriarchs ⁹so that the Gentiles may glorify God for his mercy, as it is written:

> "Therefore I will praise you among the Gentiles;
>   I will sing hymns to your name." ᵉ

¹⁰Again, it says,

> "Rejoice, O Gentiles, with his people." ᶠ

other person do it "right"—or out of your own defensiveness—a need to declare your own behavior as "right"? **5.** Instead of judging, what should occupy our energy (14:13,17–18; 15:2)? **6.** What does Paul mean by the words "stumble" and "fall" in 14: 20–21? **7.** What is the essential motivation for this lifestyle of putting others first (15:3,7)? **8.** What should characterize the church (14:17; 15:13)? How would obeying Paul's instructions in this passage free us for this goal? **9.** By instructing the Romans not to judge each other, does Paul mean we are never to judge between right and wrong where others are concerned? Why or why not? Give an example.

1. When has your freedom been a stumbling block to someone else? What happened? **2.** As time has passed, how has your sensitivity to the consciences of other Christians changed? Where do you draw the line on trying to please everyone? **3.** Romans 15:7 states, "Accept one another, then, just as Christ accepted you, in order to bring praise to God." What individual or types of people are you stretching to accept? Can you commit that to the Lord?

ª11 Isaiah 45:23   ᵇ14 Or *that nothing*   ᶜ3 Psalm 69:9   ᵈ8 Greek *circumcision*   ᵉ9 2 Samuel 22:50; Psalm 18:49   ᶠ10 Deut. 32:43

¹¹And again,

> "Praise the Lord, all you Gentiles,
>   and sing praises to him, all you peoples." *a*

¹²And again, Isaiah says,

> "The Root of Jesse will spring up,
>   one who will arise to rule over the nations;
> the Gentiles will hope in him." *b*

¹³May the God of hope fill you with all joy and peace as you trust in him, so that you may overflow with hope by the power of the Holy Spirit.

Paul the Minister to the Gentiles

¹⁴I myself am convinced, my brothers, that you yourselves are full of goodness, complete in knowledge and competent to instruct one another. ¹⁵I have written you quite boldly on some points, as if to remind you of them again, because of the grace God gave me ¹⁶to be a minister of Christ Jesus to the Gentiles with the priestly duty of proclaiming the gospel of God, so that the Gentiles might become an offering acceptable to God, sanctified by the Holy Spirit. ¹⁷Therefore I glory in Christ Jesus in my service to God. ¹⁸I will not venture to speak of anything except what Christ has accomplished through me in leading the Gentiles to obey God by what I have said and done— ¹⁹by the power of signs and miracles, through the power of the Spirit. So from Jerusalem all the way around to Illyricum, I have fully proclaimed the gospel of Christ. ²⁰It has always been my ambition to preach the gospel where Christ was not known, so that I would not be building on someone else's foundation. ²¹Rather, as it is written:

> "Those who were not told about him will see,
>   and those who have not heard will
>   understand." *c*

²²This is why I have often been hindered from coming to you.

Paul's Plan to Visit Rome

²³But now that there is no more place for me to work in these regions, and since I have been longing for many years to see you, ²⁴I plan to do so when I go to Spain. I hope to visit you while passing through and to have you assist me on my journey there, after I have enjoyed your company for a while. ²⁵Now, however, I am on my way to Jerusalem in the service of the saints there. ²⁶For Macedonia and Achaia were pleased to make a contribution for the poor among the saints in Jerusalem. ²⁷They were pleased to do it, and indeed they owe it to them. For if the Gentiles have shared in the Jews' spiritual blessings, they owe it to the Jews to share with them their material blessings. ²⁸So after I have completed this task and have made sure that they have received this fruit, I will go to Spain and visit you on the way. ²⁹I know that when I come to you, I will come in the full measure of the blessing of Christ.

³⁰I urge you, brothers, by our Lord Jesus Christ and by the love of the Spirit, to join me in my struggle by praying to God for me. ³¹Pray that I may be rescued from the unbelievers in Judea and that

1. As a child, what did you want to be when you grew up? 2. What do you remember about the first time you were away from home without a parent?

1. Why would Paul feel the need to write an encouraging word at this point (vv. 14–15)? What are some of the major points Paul has stressed in Romans? 2. Why do you think Paul now switches to writing so much about himself? 3. What motivates and inspires Paul (see vv. 16–22)? 4. Illyricum (v. 19) is in present-day Yugoslavia. How far is that from Jerusalem? Likewise, how far away is Spain (v. 29)? What does this tell you about Paul? 5. Why do you think the collection for the needy believers in Jerusalem was so important to Paul (see also 2Co 8:1–15)? What does he mean when he says that the Gentiles owe this to the Jews (v. 27)?

1. To whom are you indebted for your spiritual blessings? 2. Looking over your schedule and priorities this past month, what would you say is your ambition in life? Is that what you want it to be? How do your ambitions compare with Paul's in terms of clarity? Value? Concern for God's kingdom? 3. What could you begin to work on regarding your ambitions? 4. Where do you sense God calling you in furthering his kingdom? Prayer for the world? Commitment to the poor? Sharing your life of faith with unbelievers you know? Teaching God's values to children?

a11 Psalm 117:1   *b12* Isaiah 11:10   *c21* Isaiah 52:15

my service in Jerusalem may be acceptable to the saints there, ³²so that by God's will I may come to you with joy and together with you be refreshed. ³³The God of peace be with you all. Amen.

Personal Greetings

16 I commend to you our sister Phoebe, a servant*ᵃ* of the church in Cenchrea. ²I ask you to receive her in the Lord in a way worthy of the saints and to give her any help she may need from you, for she has been a great help to many people, including me.

³Greet Priscilla*ᵇ* and Aquila, my fellow workers in Christ Jesus. ⁴They risked their lives for me. Not only I but all the churches of the Gentiles are grateful to them.

⁵Greet also the church that meets at their house.

Greet my dear friend Epenetus, who was the first convert to Christ in the province of Asia.

⁶Greet Mary, who worked very hard for you.

⁷Greet Andronicus and Junias, my relatives who have been in prison with me. They are outstanding among the apostles, and they were in Christ before I was.

⁸Greet Ampliatus, whom I love in the Lord.

⁹Greet Urbanus, our fellow worker in Christ, and my dear friend Stachys.

¹⁰Greet Apelles, tested and approved in Christ.

Greet those who belong to the household of Aristobulus.

¹¹Greet Herodion, my relative.

Greet those in the household of Narcissus who are in the Lord.

¹²Greet Tryphena and Tryphosa, those women who work hard in the Lord.

Greet my dear friend Persis, another woman who has worked very hard in the Lord.

¹³Greet Rufus, chosen in the Lord, and his mother, who has been a mother to me, too.

¹⁴Greet Asyncritus, Phlegon, Hermes, Patrobas, Hermas and the brothers with them.

¹⁵Greet Philologus, Julia, Nereus and his sister, and Olympas and all the saints with them.

¹⁶Greet one another with a holy kiss.

All the churches of Christ send greetings.

¹⁷I urge you, brothers, to watch out for those who cause divisions and put obstacles in your way that are contrary to the teaching you have learned. Keep away from them. ¹⁸For such people are not serving our Lord Christ, but their own appetites. By smooth talk and flattery they deceive the minds of naive people. ¹⁹Everyone has heard about your obedience, so I am full of joy over you; but I want you to be wise about what is good, and innocent about what is evil.

²⁰The God of peace will soon crush Satan under your feet.

The grace of our Lord Jesus be with you.

²¹Timothy, my fellow worker, sends his greetings to you, as do Lucius, Jason and Sosipater, my relatives.

²²I, Tertius, who wrote down this letter, greet you in the Lord.

²³Gaius, whose hospitality I and the whole church here enjoy, sends you his greetings.

1. Describe briefly your first best friend. 2. What "old friends" do you keep in touch with? Why? How often?

1. What kinds of things does Paul commend in the persons mentioned in verses 1–16? What does this say about how we ought to judge "success"? Whom we ought to choose for friends? 2. In your opinion, how close did Paul let people get to him? How close do you let people get to you? 3. Looking at this list, how balanced would you say Paul was in his friendships with both genders? How many women are named here? (In v. 7, "Junias" is most likely "Junia," a woman's name.) What roles do these women have in the church? 4. Although Paul had never been to Rome, what does this greeting show about his perception of the church? 5. What divisions and obstacles are the people to avoid (vv. 17–20; see 3:8; 6:1,15; 7:7; 9:14; also Gal 5:2–6)? Is there a contradiction here when compared with Paul's prior instructions on not passing judgment on disputable matters (14:1–4)?

1. What does it mean to you that in these final chapters, God is described as the "God of hope" (15:13) and the "God of peace" (15:33; 16:20)? How can we know God in this way, especially since Paul began this letter by revealing the God of wrath? 2. What are some of the teachings that divide the church today? How do you work for a balance between the desire for unity and the desire to maintain truth? How do you handle individuals who cause strife and division (vv. 17–18): Avoid them? Talk about them? Confront them? Worry about them? 3. Who are some people you know whom you consider real servants of Christ? What impresses you about them? 4. What can you, or your group, do to increase your participation in God's plan to lead all nations to believe and obey him? Do you view this task more as a grim duty, or as a tremendous privilege? What does this show about your heart attitude toward the Gospel?

ᵃ1 Or *deaconess*   *ᵇ3* Greek *Prisca,* a variant of *Priscilla*

Erastus, who is the city's director of public works, and our brother Quartus send you their greetings.[a]

[25]Now to him who is able to establish you by my gospel and the proclamation of Jesus Christ, according to the revelation of the mystery hidden for long ages past, [26]but now revealed and made known through the prophetic writings by the command of the eternal God, so that all nations might believe and obey him— [27]to the only wise God be glory forever through Jesus Christ! Amen.

---

[a]23 Some manuscripts *their greetings.* [24]*May the grace of our Lord Jesus Christ be with all of you. Amen.*

INTRODUCTION to
1 CORINTHIANS

Book Study Outline: If you are using 1 Corinthians for a study course, here is a 7- or 13-week outline. Use the margin questions for your group agenda:

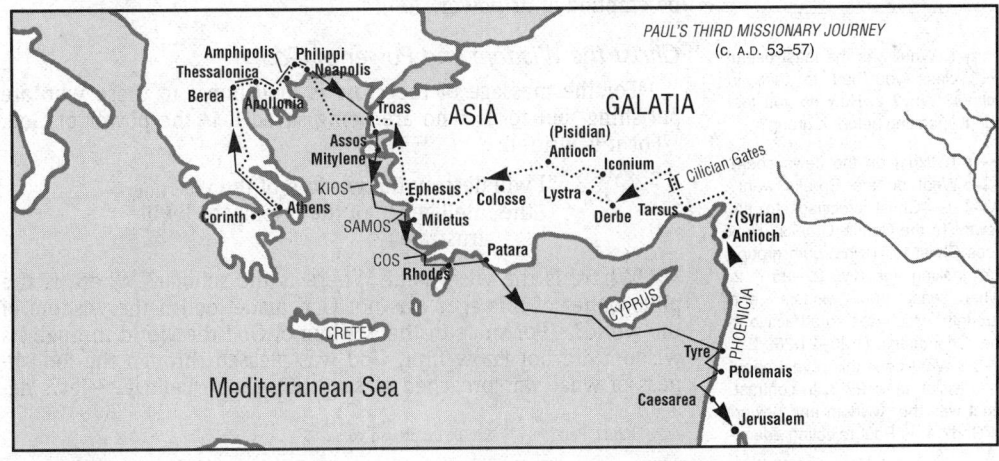

start meeting / 15 min.

read & discuss Bible / 30 min.

close meeting / 15–45 min.

Refer to the Questions and Answers in front of Bible for more information.

Author: The apostle Paul.

Date: A.D. 53–55.

7-week plan	13-week plan	Personal Reading	Group Study Passage
1	1	1:1–2:5	1:18–2:5/True Wisdom
	2	2:6–3:23	3:1–23/God's Temple
2	3	4:1–21	4:1–21/Foolish or Wise?
	4	5:1–13	5:1–13/Proud Immorality
3	5	6:1–20	6:12–20/Sexual Immorality
	6	7:1–40	7:1–40/To Marry or Not?
4	7	8:1–13	8:1–13/Exercising Freedom
	8	9:1–27	9:1–27/Run the Race
5	9	10:1–11:1	10:14–11:1/Glorifying God
	10	11:2–34	11:17–34/Lord's Supper
6	11	12:1–31	12:1–31/Spiritual Gifts
	12	13:1–14:40	13:1–13/Love Is Supreme
7	13	15:1–16:24	15:12–34/The Resurrection

Theme: Christian lifestyle in a pagan society.

Historical Background: Corinth was a large, bustling, wealthy city. Because of its location, goods and people from around the world flowed in and out of its ports. It was a center for art, philosophy and religion. It contained a number of pagan temples including large ones to Apollo and Aphrodite. The city had a reputation for vice, immorality and debauchery. Paul spent 18 months establishing a church in Corinth during his second missionary journey (Ac 18:1–18). This letter, composed three or four years later, was written in response to reports Paul received concerning problems in the church.

Characteristics: The Corinthian church destroys the myth of the early church as the model for us to imitate! Seduction by the surrounding pagan culture and a hyper-spirituality had led this church into a host of problems. As a result, 1 Corinthians is full of information about how a Christian lifestyle differs from that of the culture as a whole. At points, there is difficulty in understanding 1 Corinthians because all we possess are Paul's responses. Thus commentators differ on whether some passages in the letter are meant as Paul's advice, or if he is quoting from their letter before refuting that position (e.g. 7:1; 10:23). Structurally, the letter falls into two parts. Part one (ch. 1–6) deals with four problems reported to Paul (1:11), while part two (ch. 7–16) looks at a variety of issues about which the Corinthians had written to Paul (7:1).

PAUL'S THIRD MISSIONARY JOURNEY
(c. A.D. 53–57)

Amphipolis — Philippi
Thessalonica — Neapolis
Berea
Apollonia — Troas   ASIA   GALATIA
Assos
Mitylene   (Pisidian)
                         Antioch   Iconium   Cilician Gates
KIOS — Ephesus   Colosse   Lystra
Corinth • Athens   Derbe Tarsus   (Syrian)
SAMOS — Miletus   Antioch
COS   Patara
Rhodes   PHOENICIA
CRETE
                            Tyre   Ptolemais
Mediterranean Sea   CYPRUS
                    Caesarea
                    Jerusalem

1 Corinthians

1. When you were 8, who was your hero? **2.** Have you ever felt like you were a part of a close-knit team? When?

1. What kind of place was Corinth? How would life in Corinth affect a young church? (See Introduction to 1 Corinthians.) **2.** Paul spent 18 months in Corinth, his second longest stay with any of the new churches he started. What kind of feelings or emotional connection do you think he had with the people in those churches? **3.** Why would Paul emphasize in verse 1 that he is an apostle? **4.** What divides the church in Corinth (vv. 11–12,15)? Who was Apollos (see Ac 18:24–19:1)?

1. Do you feel like the thanksgiving in verses 4–9 describes you? Why or why not? **2.** Have you ever been a part of a church that was divided? What was it like? Have you ever been a part of a church that was single-minded and unified? What was it like? **3.** Have you been baptized? Did your personal relationship with Christ begin before or after your baptism? Share about that beginning. **4.** Who has been or is your spiritual hero? Why? **5.** Have you ever put your spiritual hero above Christ? Why or why not?

1. What was the least useful class you had to take in school? Why? **2.** How do you feel about speaking before a group?

1. What do the Jews seek? What do the Greeks want? What is "Christ crucified" to the Jews? To the Gentile Greeks? How does Christ fulfill what both groups are looking for (vv. 22–25)? **2.** What was the "wisdom and strength" which was so attractive to the Corinthians (1:20–21,26; 2:1, 4–5)? What does this reveal about the division in 1:12? **3.** In contrast, what was the "wisdom and power" of God? **4.** Is Paul rejecting educa-

1 Paul, called to be an apostle of Christ Jesus by the will of God, and our brother Sosthenes,

²To the church of God in Corinth, to those sanctified in Christ Jesus and called to be holy, together with all those everywhere who call on the name of our Lord Jesus Christ—their Lord and ours:

³Grace and peace to you from God our Father and the Lord Jesus Christ.

Thanksgiving

⁴I always thank God for you because of his grace given you in Christ Jesus. ⁵For in him you have been enriched in every way—in all your speaking and in all your knowledge— ⁶because our testimony about Christ was confirmed in you. ⁷Therefore you do not lack any spiritual gift as you eagerly wait for our Lord Jesus Christ to be revealed. ⁸He will keep you strong to the end, so that you will be blameless on the day of our Lord Jesus Christ. ⁹God, who has called you into fellowship with his Son Jesus Christ our Lord, is faithful.

Divisions in the Church

¹⁰I appeal to you, brothers, in the name of our Lord Jesus Christ, that all of you agree with one another so that there may be no divisions among you and that you may be perfectly united in mind and thought. ¹¹My brothers, some from Chloe's household have informed me that there are quarrels among you. ¹²What I mean is this: One of you says, "I follow Paul"; another, "I follow Apollos"; another, "I follow Cephas*a*"; still another, "I follow Christ."

¹³Is Christ divided? Was Paul crucified for you? Were you baptized into*b* the name of Paul? ¹⁴I am thankful that I did not baptize any of you except Crispus and Gaius, ¹⁵so no one can say that you were baptized into my name. ¹⁶(Yes, I also baptized the household of Stephanas; beyond that, I don't remember if I baptized anyone else.) ¹⁷For Christ did not send me to baptize, but to preach the gospel—not with words of human wisdom, lest the cross of Christ be emptied of its power.

Christ the Wisdom and Power of God

¹⁸For the message of the cross is foolishness to those who are perishing, but to us who are being saved it is the power of God. ¹⁹For it is written:

> "I will destroy the wisdom of the wise;
>   the intelligence of the intelligent I will
>   frustrate."*c*

²⁰Where is the wise man? Where is the scholar? Where is the philosopher of this age? Has not God made foolish the wisdom of the world? ²¹For since in the wisdom of God the world through its wisdom did not know him, God was pleased through the foolishness of what was preached to save those who believe. ²²Jews de-

---

a12 That is, Peter   *b13* Or *in;* also in verse 15   *c19* Isaiah 29:14

mand miraculous signs and Greeks look for wisdom, [23]but we preach Christ crucified: a stumbling block to Jews and foolishness to Gentiles, [24]but to those whom God has called, both Jews and Greeks, Christ the power of God and the wisdom of God. [25]For the foolishness of God is wiser than man's wisdom, and the weakness of God is stronger than man's strength.

[26]Brothers, think of what you were when you were called. Not many of you were wise by human standards; not many were influential; not many were of noble birth. [27]But God chose the foolish things of the world to shame the wise; God chose the weak things of the world to shame the strong. [28]He chose the lowly things of this world and the despised things—and the things that are not— to nullify the things that are, [29]so that no one may boast before him. [30]It is because of him that you are in Christ Jesus, who has become for us wisdom from God—that is, our righteousness, holiness and redemption. [31]Therefore, as it is written: "Let him who boasts boast in the Lord."[a]

2 When I came to you, brothers, I did not come with eloquence or superior wisdom as I proclaimed to you the testimony about God.[b] [2]For I resolved to know nothing while I was with you except Jesus Christ and him crucified. [3]I came to you in weakness and fear, and with much trembling. [4]My message and my preaching were not with wise and persuasive words, but with a demonstration of the Spirit's power, [5]so that your faith might not rest on men's wisdom, but on God's power.

Wisdom From the Spirit

[6]We do, however, speak a message of wisdom among the mature, but not the wisdom of this age or of the rulers of this age, who are coming to nothing. [7]No, we speak of God's secret wisdom, a wisdom that has been hidden and that God destined for our glory before time began. [8]None of the rulers of this age understood it, for if they had, they would not have crucified the Lord of glory. [9]However, as it is written:

> "No eye has seen,
>   no ear has heard,
>   no mind has conceived
>   what God has prepared for those who love
>   him"[c]—

[10]but God has revealed it to us by his Spirit.

The Spirit searches all things, even the deep things of God. [11]For who among men knows the thoughts of a man except the man's spirit within him? In the same way no one knows the thoughts of God except the Spirit of God. [12]We have not received the spirit of the world but the Spirit who is from God, that we may understand what God has freely given us. [13]This is what we speak, not in words taught us by human wisdom but in words taught by the Spirit, expressing spiritual truths in spiritual words.[d] [14]The man without the Spirit does not accept the things that come from the Spirit of God, for they are foolishness to him, and he cannot understand them, because they are spiritually discerned. [15]The spiritual man makes judgments about all things, but he himself is not subject to any man's judgment:

tion itself, or some related and prideful assumptions?

♡ **1.** What pictures come to mind when you think of powerful, successful people? How do these images sometimes conflict with knowing Christ? **2.** How do people today confuse the world's power with God's power? How does that affect you? **3.** What do you think Paul means when he says that the foolish and lowly things will shame the wise and strong? How does your own life reflect this principle?

☕ **1.** How well did you keep secrets when you were a child? How about since then? **2.** What person in your circle of family and friends has the most wisdom?

📖 **1.** From the references to "wisdom" in this passage, what differences do you see between human wisdom and God's? **2.** What is secret about God's wisdom (vv. 7,9)? **3.** How do you feel about verse 9? How is your outlook on life affected by the promises in this verse? **4.** Philosophers were respected as people who could search out deep truths; in contrast, how does Paul say the truth of the Gospel is discovered (vv. 10–13)? Why is that significant for the Corinthians' unity?

♡ **1.** The Corinthians were measuring "truth and success" by how powerful, influential and articulate someone was. How is that idea communicated today? How does it square with the Gospel? **2.** What can you do to exercise "the mind of Christ" (v. 16) more fully in your life?

---

a31 Jer. 9:24   b1 Some manuscripts *as I proclaimed to you God's mystery*
c9 Isaiah 64:4   d13 Or *Spirit, interpreting spiritual truths to spiritual men*

16"For who has known the mind of the Lord
     that he may instruct him?"*a*

But we have the mind of Christ.

On Divisions in the Church

3 Brothers, I could not address you as spiritual but as worldly—mere infants in Christ. 2I gave you milk, not solid food, for you were not yet ready for it. Indeed, you are still not ready. 3You are still worldly. For since there is jealousy and quarreling among you, are you not worldly? Are you not acting like mere men? 4For when one says, "I follow Paul," and another, "I follow Apollos," are you not mere men?

5What, after all, is Apollos? And what is Paul? Only servants, through whom you came to believe—as the Lord has assigned to each his task. 6I planted the seed, Apollos watered it, but God made it grow. 7So neither he who plants nor he who waters is anything, but only God, who makes things grow. 8The man who plants and the man who waters have one purpose, and each will be rewarded according to his own labor. 9For we are God's fellow workers; you are God's field, God's building.

10By the grace God has given me, I laid a foundation as an expert builder, and someone else is building on it. But each one should be careful how he builds. 11For no one can lay any foundation other than the one already laid, which is Jesus Christ. 12If any man builds on this foundation using gold, silver, costly stones, wood, hay or straw, 13his work will be shown for what it is, because the Day will bring it to light. It will be revealed with fire, and the fire will test the quality of each man's work. 14If what he has built survives, he will receive his reward. 15If it is burned up, he will suffer loss; he himself will be saved, but only as one escaping through the flames.

16Don't you know that you yourselves are God's temple and that God's Spirit lives in you? 17If anyone destroys God's temple, God will destroy him; for God's temple is sacred, and you are that temple.

18Do not deceive yourselves. If any one of you thinks he is wise by the standards of this age, he should become a "fool" so that he may become wise. 19For the wisdom of this world is foolishness in God's sight. As it is written: "He catches the wise in their craftiness"*b*; 20and again, "The Lord knows that the thoughts of the wise are futile."*c* 21So then, no more boasting about men! All things are yours, 22whether Paul or Apollos or Cephas*d* or the world or life or death or the present or the future—all are yours, 23and you are of Christ, and Christ is of God.

Apostles of Christ

4 So then, men ought to regard us as servants of Christ and as those entrusted with the secret things of God. 2Now it is required that those who have been given a trust must prove faithful. 3I care very little if I am judged by you or by any human court; indeed, I do not even judge myself. 4My conscience is clear, but that does not make me innocent. It is the Lord who judges me. 5Therefore judge nothing before the appointed time; wait till the Lord comes. He will bring to light what is hidden in darkness and will expose the motives of men's hearts. At that time each will receive his praise from God.

When you were a child, what did you make that you were proud of?

1. What does Paul mean by infants? Milk? Solid food (v. 2)? 2. What were Paul's and Apollos' contributions to the church in Corinth? 3. Who did the planting in your spiritual life? Who did the watering? 4. How do Paul's illustrations help to make his point (vv. 5–15)? 5. What is the wise way to build a foundation for your life? What do the building materials in verse 12 refer to? 6. Paul tells the Corinthians as a church they are "God's temple" (v. 16). What evidence do you have that your church or your body is a dwelling place for God's Spirit?

1. What is the difference between respecting a Christian leader and the problem Paul deals with here? 2. What does it mean to be a "fool" for Christ? What would being a fool for Christ mean in your life? 3. If you could describe your spiritual condition as a building, what kind of building would it be? A cathedral? A health club? A junkyard? A library? A skyscraper? 4. Name one thing you can do this week to build the foundation of your life with "gold, silver and costly stones."

1. What is the most menial job you ever had? What did you like or dislike about it? 2. Who has been a parent figure in your life, outside of your parents?

1. Paul, when talking about judging himself, claims that even his conscience is not dependable (vv. 3–4). Has your conscience ever differed with God's will for you? What happened? 2. How do you feel about the Lord "bringing to light" what is hidden and exposing the motives of our

a16 Isaiah 40:13   *b19* Job 5:13   *c20* Psalm 94:11   *d22* That is, Peter

⁶Now, brothers, I have applied these things to myself and Apollos for your benefit, so that you may learn from us the meaning of the saying, "Do not go beyond what is written." Then you will not take pride in one man over against another. ⁷For who makes you different from anyone else? What do you have that you did not receive? And if you did receive it, why do you boast as though you did not?

⁸Already you have all you want! Already you have become rich! You have become kings—and that without us! How I wish that you really had become kings so that we might be kings with you! ⁹For it seems to me that God has put us apostles on display at the end of the procession, like men condemned to die in the arena. We have been made a spectacle to the whole universe, to angels as well as to men. ¹⁰We are fools for Christ, but you are so wise in Christ! We are weak, but you are strong! You are honored, we are dishonored! ¹¹To this very hour we go hungry and thirsty, we are in rags, we are brutally treated, we are homeless. ¹²We work hard with our own hands. When we are cursed, we bless; when we are persecuted, we endure it; ¹³when we are slandered, we answer kindly. Up to this moment we have become the scum of the earth, the refuse of the world.

¹⁴I am not writing this to shame you, but to warn you, as my dear children. ¹⁵Even though you have ten thousand guardians in Christ, you do not have many fathers, for in Christ Jesus I became your father through the gospel. ¹⁶Therefore I urge you to imitate me. ¹⁷For this reason I am sending to you Timothy, my son whom I love, who is faithful in the Lord. He will remind you of my way of life in Christ Jesus, which agrees with what I teach everywhere in every church.

¹⁸Some of you have become arrogant, as if I were not coming to you. ¹⁹But I will come to you very soon, if the Lord is willing, and then I will find out not only how these arrogant people are talking, but what power they have. ²⁰For the kingdom of God is not a matter of talk but of power. ²¹What do you prefer? Shall I come to you with a whip, or in love and with a gentle spirit?

Expel the Immoral Brother!

5 It is actually reported that there is sexual immorality among you, and of a kind that does not occur even among pagans: A man has his father's wife. ²And you are proud! Shouldn't you rather have been filled with grief and have put out of your fellowship the man who did this? ³Even though I am not physically present, I am with you in spirit. And I have already passed judgment on the one who did this, just as if I were present. ⁴When you are assembled in the name of our Lord Jesus and I am with you in spirit, and the power of our Lord Jesus is present, ⁵hand this man over to Satan, so that the sinful nature*a* may be destroyed and his spirit saved on the day of the Lord.

⁶Your boasting is not good. Don't you know that a little yeast works through the whole batch of dough? ⁷Get rid of the old yeast that you may be a new batch without yeast—as you really are. For Christ, our Passover lamb, has been sacrificed. ⁸Therefore let us keep the Festival, not with the old yeast, the yeast of malice and wickedness, but with bread without yeast, the bread of sincerity and truth.

⁹I have written you in my letter not to associate with sexually

hearts (v. 5)? How can we live so that what is revealed will be less surprising and embarrassing? **3.** Corinthian factions judged one another by the reputation of the leader they followed. What then does Paul mean by the proverb in verse 6? How should they apply it? **4.** Read verse 7. What do you have that you did not receive from God? Of everything God has given you, what do you tend to take credit for yourself? **5.** Paul tells the Corinthians to imitate his way of life. How does this square with not following one leader or another?

1. How would Paul respond to the phrase: "God wants you to be happy, healthy and successful"? **2.** In verses 8–13 Paul rather sarcastically compares his situation with the Corinthians', who have a mistaken idea of wisdom and power. Would you characterize your Christian life as more like the Corinthians' or Paul's? Why? **3.** A role model or mentor is someone you want to emulate. Who has fulfilled these roles in your life? In what ways do you still feel the need? **4.** Reflecting honestly on verse 20, is your Christian life more a matter of talk or of power?

How did your parents, teachers or church leaders talk to you about sex? Openly? Only negatively? Not at all?

1. Why would the Corinthians be proud of such an immoral situation (vv. 1–2)? Have you ever seen a church proud of something typically considered immoral? **2.** How can handing someone over to Satan result in their salvation on the Day of the Lord (v. 5)? **3.** From the yeast imagery (vv. 6–8), what is Paul's concern if this situation is allowed to go on without discipline? **4.** Why does Paul set forth one standard for relating to people in the church who are living in sin, and another for "people of this world" (vv. 9–13)? **5.** How do you reconcile Paul's teaching here with that in 4:3–5? What is the point of each?

a5 Or that his body; or that the flesh

What happens when a church is more concerned with judging those outside the church than evaluating their own behavior and motives?

Have you ever been on jury duty? What was it like?

1. Why is Paul so upset that members of the young church in Corinth are taking their disputes to a civil, secular court? What does Paul mean when he tells the Corinthians that they have been "defeated already" (v. 7)? 2. Why do lawsuits, and other kinds of conflict or indiscretion, cast a shadow over the church? 3. Do you agree with Paul that it is better to be cheated than to go to court against a fellow believer? Why? 4. Does Paul mean that believers who do the things in verses 9–10 will not enter heaven?

What attitudes in conflict situations do you see in yourself: An insistence on "my rights"? A desire for revenge? Peace at any cost? Apathy about my example to non-believers?

What is the best thing you've done for your health?

1. Some of the Corinthians felt that what they did in the "flesh" had no bearing on their spiritual lives (vv. 19–20). What do you think? 2. How does God care for your physical self—your appetites, sexuality, diet, habits? 3. Why would uniting yourself with a prostitute and being "one with him in body" be harmful to a Christian? What other activities would be harmful for similar reasons?

In what ways do you struggle with what is permissible and what is beneficial? How can you keep your "temple" pure?

immoral people— [10]not at all meaning the people of this world who are immoral, or the greedy and swindlers, or idolaters. In that case you would have to leave this world. [11]But now I am writing you that you must not associate with anyone who calls himself a brother but is sexually immoral or greedy, an idolater or a slanderer, a drunkard or a swindler. With such a man do not even eat.

[12]What business is it of mine to judge those outside the church? Are you not to judge those inside? [13]God will judge those outside. "Expel the wicked man from among you."[a]

Lawsuits Among Believers

6 If any of you has a dispute with another, dare he take it before the ungodly for judgment instead of before the saints? [2]Do you not know that the saints will judge the world? And if you are to judge the world, are you not competent to judge trivial cases? [3]Do you not know that we will judge angels? How much more the things of this life! [4]Therefore, if you have disputes about such matters, appoint as judges even men of little account in the church![b] [5]I say this to shame you. Is it possible that there is nobody among you wise enough to judge a dispute between believers? [6]But instead, one brother goes to law against another—and this in front of unbelievers!

[7]The very fact that you have lawsuits among you means you have been completely defeated already. Why not rather be wronged? Why not rather be cheated? [8]Instead, you yourselves cheat and do wrong, and you do this to your brothers.

[9]Do you not know that the wicked will not inherit the kingdom of God? Do not be deceived: Neither the sexually immoral nor idolaters nor adulterers nor male prostitutes nor homosexual offenders [10]nor thieves nor the greedy nor drunkards nor slanderers nor swindlers will inherit the kingdom of God. [11]And that is what some of you were. But you were washed, you were sanctified, you were justified in the name of the Lord Jesus Christ and by the Spirit of our God.

Sexual Immorality

[12]"Everything is permissible for me"—but not everything is beneficial. "Everything is permissible for me"—but I will not be mastered by anything. [13]"Food for the stomach and the stomach for food"—but God will destroy them both. The body is not meant for sexual immorality, but for the Lord, and the Lord for the body. [14]By his power God raised the Lord from the dead, and he will raise us also. [15]Do you not know that your bodies are members of Christ himself? Shall I then take the members of Christ and unite them with a prostitute? Never! [16]Do you not know that he who unites himself with a prostitute is one with her in body? For it is said, "The two will become one flesh."[c] [17]But he who unites himself with the Lord is one with him in spirit.

[18]Flee from sexual immorality. All other sins a man commits are outside his body, but he who sins sexually sins against his own body. [19]Do you not know that your body is a temple of the Holy Spirit, who is in you, whom you have received from God? You are not your own; [20]you were bought at a price. Therefore honor God with your body.

---

[a]13 Deut. 17:7; 19:19; 21:21; 22:21,24; 24:7   [b]4 Or *matters, do you appoint as judges men of little account in the church?*   [c]16 Gen. 2:24

Marriage

7 Now for the matters you wrote about: It is good for a man not to marry.[a] ²But since there is so much immorality, each man should have his own wife, and each woman her own husband. ³The husband should fulfill his marital duty to his wife, and likewise the wife to her husband. ⁴The wife's body does not belong to her alone but also to her husband. In the same way, the husband's body does not belong to him alone but also to his wife. ⁵Do not deprive each other except by mutual consent and for a time, so that you may devote yourselves to prayer. Then come together again so that Satan will not tempt you because of your lack of self-control. ⁶I say this as a concession, not as a command. ⁷I wish that all men were as I am. But each man has his own gift from God; one has this gift, another has that.

⁸Now to the unmarried and the widows I say: It is good for them to stay unmarried, as I am. ⁹But if they cannot control themselves, they should marry, for it is better to marry than to burn with passion.

¹⁰To the married I give this command (not I, but the Lord): A wife must not separate from her husband. ¹¹But if she does, she must remain unmarried or else be reconciled to her husband. And a husband must not divorce his wife.

¹²To the rest I say this (I, not the Lord): If any brother has a wife who is not a believer and she is willing to live with him, he must not divorce her. ¹³And if a woman has a husband who is not a believer and he is willing to live with her, she must not divorce him. ¹⁴For the unbelieving husband has been sanctified through his wife, and the unbelieving wife has been sanctified through her believing husband. Otherwise your children would be unclean, but as it is, they are holy.

¹⁵But if the unbeliever leaves, let him do so. A believing man or woman is not bound in such circumstances; God has called us to live in peace. ¹⁶How do you know, wife, whether you will save your husband? Or, how do you know, husband, whether you will save your wife?

¹⁷Nevertheless, each one should retain the place in life that the Lord assigned to him and to which God has called him. This is the rule I lay down in all the churches. ¹⁸Was a man already circumcised when he was called? He should not become uncircumcised. Was a man uncircumcised when he was called? He should not be circumcised. ¹⁹Circumcision is nothing and uncircumcision is nothing. Keeping God's commands is what counts. ²⁰Each one should remain in the situation which he was in when God called him. ²¹Were you a slave when you were called? Don't let it trouble you—although if you can gain your freedom, do so. ²²For he who was a slave when he was called by the Lord is the Lord's freedman; similarly, he who was a free man when he was called is Christ's slave. ²³You were bought at a price; do not become slaves of men. ²⁴Brothers, each man, as responsible to God, should remain in the situation God called him to.

²⁵Now about virgins: I have no command from the Lord, but I give a judgment as one who by the Lord's mercy is trustworthy. ²⁶Because of the present crisis, I think that it is good for you to remain as you are. ²⁷Are you married? Do not seek a divorce. Are you unmarried? Do not look for a wife. ²⁸But if you do marry, you have not sinned; and if a virgin marries, she has not sinned. But

Are you more like Garfield ("I hate getting up") or Odie ("Life is fun, fun, fun!")?

1. What do verses 3–5 tell you about the role of sex in marriage? Did God create sex to be merely a physical act or a time of mutual edification? **2.** What do verses 5 and 9 say about the human body and sexuality?

Some Corinthian Christians considered sex with their marital partners impure or unspiritual. How have your ideas of sex been skewed? How do you need God's help?

If married, tell your "love story." How did you meet? What attracted you? If single, share what you know about your parents' love story.

1. What obligation does a believing spouse have to an unbelieving mate? What are the limits to this obligation? **2.** What does it mean for an unbeliever to be "sanctified" by their believing spouse (vv. 12–14; see Ro 15:15–16)? **3.** How do verses 12–14 encourage someone who is married to an unbeliever regarding his or her spouse's salvation and that of their children? **4.** In verses 17–24, Paul is saying that Christians should not use their new life in Christ to climb the social ladder or be someone they are not. Have you ever been tempted to do this? What does someone stand to lose by doing this? **5.** Is Paul saying in these verses that a person should not set goals for him or herself?

What questions do you have about these verses? Where do you feel a special need for God's wisdom and power as you seek to "live in peace" (v. 15)?

Whom do you know who has chosen to remain single?

1. Why will those who marry "face many troubles" in life (v. 28)? **2.** What concerns do those who are married have that singles do not? **3.** How does Paul's advice

a 1 Or "It is good for a man not to have sexual relations with a woman."

to the married (v. 29) relate to his teaching in Ephesians 5:21–32.

1. How can an unmarried person find emotional fulfillment and intimacy if they have chosen to remain single in order to be more fully devoted to the Lord? 2. A close look at the Epistles reveals meaningful and touching relationships among believers. Do we expect marriage to bring the kind of intimacy and fulfillment that God intended the church to bring?

1. Paul presents singleness as an option some should consider. What reasons does he give? 2. Whether people marry or not, what is the overriding issue here?

Is singleness more of a calling or a choice? What role does God play? How do you feel about your role?

Have you ever been superstitious? In what ways?

1. Why would eating food sacrificed to idols be difficult for some people? 2. How is it that what is not sin for one group is sin for another? What general principle is Paul applying here (v. 9)? 3. Some of the Corinthian Christians knew that food sacrificed to idols was just that, food. What could those people have done to help those who were not comfortable with eating food sacrificed to idols? 4. In verse 2, Paul points out that if you are focused on what you know, you are likely to exclude empathy and concern for others. Do you ever get focused on knowing something *about* God at the expense of being known *by* God (v. 3)? Explain. 5. What might hinder you from loving new Christians or those believers who do not know something you know?

1. Where in your experience is one person's "freedom" another person's "stumbling block"? Alcohol? Certain styles of clothes? Dance? Music? Lifestyle? Political

those who marry will face many troubles in this life, and I want to spare you this.

²⁹What I mean, brothers, is that the time is short. From now on those who have wives should live as if they had none; ³⁰those who mourn, as if they did not; those who are happy, as if they were not; those who buy something, as if it were not theirs to keep; ³¹those who use the things of the world, as if not engrossed in them. For this world in its present form is passing away.

³²I would like you to be free from concern. An unmarried man is concerned about the Lord's affairs—how he can please the Lord. ³³But a married man is concerned about the affairs of this world— how he can please his wife— ³⁴and his interests are divided. An unmarried woman or virgin is concerned about the Lord's affairs: Her aim is to be devoted to the Lord in both body and spirit. But a married woman is concerned about the affairs of this world—how she can please her husband. ³⁵I am saying this for your own good, not to restrict you, but that you may live in a right way in undivided devotion to the Lord.

³⁶If anyone thinks he is acting improperly toward the virgin he is engaged to, and if she is getting along in years and he feels he ought to marry, he should do as he wants. He is not sinning. They should get married. ³⁷But the man who has settled the matter in his own mind, who is under no compulsion but has control over his own will, and who has made up his mind not to marry the virgin—this man also does the right thing. ³⁸So then, he who marries the virgin does right, but he who does not marry her does even better.[a]

³⁹A woman is bound to her husband as long as he lives. But if her husband dies, she is free to marry anyone she wishes, but he must belong to the Lord. ⁴⁰In my judgment, she is happier if she stays as she is—and I think that I too have the Spirit of God.

Food Sacrificed to Idols

8 Now about food sacrificed to idols: We know that we all possess knowledge.[b] Knowledge puffs up, but love builds up. ²The man who thinks he knows something does not yet know as he ought to know. ³But the man who loves God is known by God.

⁴So then, about eating food sacrificed to idols: We know that an idol is nothing at all in the world and that there is no God but one. ⁵For even if there are so-called gods, whether in heaven or on earth (as indeed there are many "gods" and many "lords"), ⁶yet for us there is but one God, the Father, from whom all things came and for whom we live; and there is but one Lord, Jesus Christ, through whom all things came and through whom we live.

⁷But not everyone knows this. Some people are still so accustomed to idols that when they eat such food they think of it as having been sacrificed to an idol, and since their conscience is weak, it is defiled. ⁸But food does not bring us near to God; we are no worse if we do not eat, and no better if we do.

⁹Be careful, however, that the exercise of your freedom does not become a stumbling block to the weak. ¹⁰For if anyone with a weak conscience sees you who have this knowledge eating in an idol's temple, won't he be emboldened to eat what has been sacrificed to

---

a36-38 Or *36If anyone thinks he is not treating his daughter properly, and if she is getting along in years, and he feels she ought to marry, he should do as he wants. He is not sinning. He should let her get married. 37But the man who has settled the matter in his own mind, who is under no compulsion but has control over his own will, and who has made up his mind to keep the virgin unmarried—this man also does the right thing. 38So then, he who gives his virgin in marriage does right, but he who does not give her in marriage does even better.* *b1* Or *"We all possess knowledge,"* as you say

idols? 11So this weak brother, for whom Christ died, is destroyed by your knowledge. 12When you sin against your brothers in this way and wound their weak conscience, you sin against Christ. 13Therefore, if what I eat causes my brother to fall into sin, I will never eat meat again, so that I will not cause him to fall.

The Rights of an Apostle

9 Am I not free? Am I not an apostle? Have I not seen Jesus our Lord? Are you not the result of my work in the Lord? 2Even though I may not be an apostle to others, surely I am to you! For you are the seal of my apostleship in the Lord.

3This is my defense to those who sit in judgment on me. 4Don't we have the right to food and drink? 5Don't we have the right to take a believing wife along with us, as do the other apostles and the Lord's brothers and Cephas*a*? 6Or is it only I and Barnabas who must work for a living?

7Who serves as a soldier at his own expense? Who plants a vineyard and does not eat of its grapes? Who tends a flock and does not drink of the milk? 8Do I say this merely from a human point of view? Doesn't the Law say the same thing? 9For it is written in the Law of Moses: "Do not muzzle an ox while it is treading out the grain."*b* Is it about oxen that God is concerned? 10Surely he says this for us, doesn't he? Yes, this was written for us, because when the plowman plows and the thresher threshes, they ought to do so in the hope of sharing in the harvest. 11If we have sown spiritual seed among you, is it too much if we reap a material harvest from you? 12If others have this right of support from you, shouldn't we have it all the more?

But we did not use this right. On the contrary, we put up with anything rather than hinder the gospel of Christ. 13Don't you know that those who work in the temple get their food from the temple, and those who serve at the altar share in what is offered on the altar? 14In the same way, the Lord has commanded that those who preach the gospel should receive their living from the gospel.

15But I have not used any of these rights. And I am not writing this in the hope that you will do such things for me. I would rather die than have anyone deprive me of this boast. 16Yet when I preach the gospel, I cannot boast, for I am compelled to preach. Woe to me if I do not preach the gospel! 17If I preach voluntarily, I have a reward; if not voluntarily, I am simply discharging the trust committed to me. 18What then is my reward? Just this: that in preaching the gospel I may offer it free of charge, and so not make use of my rights in preaching it.

19Though I am free and belong to no man, I make myself a slave to everyone, to win as many as possible. 20To the Jews I became like a Jew, to win the Jews. To those under the law I became like one under the law (though I myself am not under the law), so as to win those under the law. 21To those not having the law I became like one not having the law (though I am not free from God's law but am under Christ's law), so as to win those not having the law. 22To the weak I became weak, to win the weak. I have become all things to all men so that by all possible means I might save some. 23I do all this for the sake of the gospel, that I may share in its blessings.

24Do you not know that in a race all the runners run, but only one gets the prize? Run in such a way as to get the prize. 25Everyone who competes in the games goes into strict training. They do

issues? 2. Have you done anything lately to wound the conscience of a fellow believer (v. 12)? How is this sinning against Christ?

————————

1. Describe a time when you were overqualified for a particular job. Describe a time when you felt underqualified. 2. Describe a volunteer position you held which was especially fulfilling.

1. Why would some of the Corinthians try and shed doubt on Paul's authority as an apostle? 2. What is your response when you hear a message from God (i.e. a Bible teacher, a sermon, a wise word from a Christian friend) that you don't want to hear? 3. Some of the rights apostles could claim included monetary payment, bringing a wife along, and eating and drinking with freedom. What was gained by Paul denying himself of these rights? 4. How do you reconcile 8:24 and the principle of integrity with Paul's practice in verses 19–23? 5. Have you ever denied yourself of any basic rights for the sake of the Gospel? Explain your answer. 6. In verses 16–18 Paul refers to his deep passion for preaching the Gospel. What is your passion when it comes to living for God?

1. Consider verses 19–23, what group of people are you especially aware of who need God's love? The poor? The homeless? Homosexuals? Those in nursing homes? Troubled youngsters? What barriers are there between you and these groups? What "rights" would you be willing to discard to love them? 2. Paul summarizes this passage in verses 24–27 by emphasizing the importance of discipline in the Christian life (discipline which includes sacrificing personal rights and comforts for the sake of others). How would you describe your "Gospel readiness" training program? (a) I haven't found the gym; (b) I'm not sure I'm ready to make the necessary sacrifices; (c) I'm ready anytime, if only I had a team of people to train with me; (d) I've run the race and I'm exhausted; (e) I'm rarin' to go!

a5 That is, Peter   *b9* Deut. 25:4

it to get a crown that will not last; but we do it to get a crown that will last forever. 26Therefore I do not run like a man running aimlessly; I do not fight like a man beating the air. 27No, I beat my body and make it my slave so that after I have preached to others, I myself will not be disqualified for the prize.

Warnings From Israel's History

10 For I do not want you to be ignorant of the fact, brothers, that our forefathers were all under the cloud and that they all passed through the sea. 2They were all baptized into Moses in the cloud and in the sea. 3They all ate the same spiritual food 4and drank the same spiritual drink; for they drank from the spiritual rock that accompanied them, and that rock was Christ. 5Nevertheless, God was not pleased with most of them; their bodies were scattered over the desert.

6Now these things occurred as examples[a] to keep us from setting our hearts on evil things as they did. 7Do not be idolaters, as some of them were; as it is written: "The people sat down to eat and drink and got up to indulge in pagan revelry."[b] 8We should not commit sexual immorality, as some of them did—and in one day twenty-three thousand of them died. 9We should not test the Lord, as some of them did—and were killed by snakes. 10And do not grumble, as some of them did—and were killed by the destroying angel.

11These things happened to them as examples and were written down as warnings for us, on whom the fulfillment of the ages has come. 12So, if you think you are standing firm, be careful that you don't fall! 13No temptation has seized you except what is common to man. And God is faithful; he will not let you be tempted beyond what you can bear. But when you are tempted, he will also provide a way out so that you can stand up under it.

Idol Feasts and the Lord's Supper

14Therefore, my dear friends, flee from idolatry. 15I speak to sensible people; judge for yourselves what I say. 16Is not the cup of thanksgiving for which we give thanks a participation in the blood of Christ? And is not the bread that we break a participation in the body of Christ? 17Because there is one loaf, we, who are many, are one body, for we all partake of the one loaf.

18Consider the people of Israel: Do not those who eat the sacrifices participate in the altar? 19Do I mean then that a sacrifice offered to an idol is anything, or that an idol is anything? 20No, but the sacrifices of pagans are offered to demons, not to God, and I do not want you to be participants with demons. 21You cannot drink the cup of the Lord and the cup of demons too; you cannot have a part in both the Lord's table and the table of demons. 22Are we trying to arouse the Lord's jealousy? Are we stronger than he?

The Believer's Freedom

23"Everything is permissible"—but not everything is beneficial. "Everything is permissible"—but not everything is constructive. 24Nobody should seek his own good, but the good of others.

25Eat anything sold in the meat market without raising questions of conscience, 26for, "The earth is the Lord's, and everything in it."[c]

27If some unbeliever invites you to a meal and you want to go, eat whatever is put before you without raising questions of con-

Sidebar

What is the most expensive vacation you've taken?

1. In verses 1–5 Paul asserts that the baptism and spiritual food and drink of the Israelites did not guarantee their protection from God's judgment. What do you tend to look to as your guarantee from God's judgment? 2. In verses 6–10, what four things did the Israelites do that resulted in God's judgment? 3. Which of these four "examples" are you most susceptible to doing? 4. If you think you've "got it together," why do you become vulnerable (v. 12)?

1. What helps satisfy your urges before they grow into temptations and sin? 2. How can the promises in verse 13 help you in your spiritual battles? 3. How can being in this group help you stand up under temptations?

1. What is the strangest food you have ever eaten? 2. Were you raised in a permissive environment or in a strict, but forgiving, one? Give an example.

1. How is drinking the cup of thanksgiving a participation in the blood of Christ? How is breaking the bread a participation in the body of Christ? 2. Why does Paul mention eating the OT sacrifices (v. 18) in this context? 3. When you partake in the body and blood of Christ during Communion, what does it mean to you? 4. How have you been involved in something that God would consider idolatry? 5. In what ways is a Christian free (vv. 23–24)? How do you exercise your freedom in Christ? 6. In verse 24, Paul says, "Nobody should seek his own good, but the good of others." How can you receive the love and care you need if you live by that verse?

1. Is there anything you do that does not bother your conscience but might bother the conscience of someone else? Explain. 2. Verses 27–33 describe

---

a6 Or *types*; also in verse 11   b7 Exodus 32:6   c26 Psalm 24:1

science. **28**But if anyone says to you, "This has been offered in sacrifice," then do not eat it, both for the sake of the man who told you and for conscience' sake*a*— **29**the other man's conscience, I mean, not yours. For why should my freedom be judged by another's conscience? **30**If I take part in the meal with thankfulness, why am I denounced because of something I thank God for?

31So whether you eat or drink or whatever you do, do it all for the glory of God. **32**Do not cause anyone to stumble, whether Jews, Greeks or the church of God— **33**even as I try to please everybody in every way. For I am not seeking my own good but the good of many, so that they may be saved. **1**Follow my example, as I follow the example of Christ.

11

Propriety in Worship

2I praise you for remembering me in everything and for holding to the teachings,*b* just as I passed them on to you.

3Now I want you to realize that the head of every man is Christ, and the head of the woman is man, and the head of Christ is God. **4**Every man who prays or prophesies with his head covered dishonors his head. **5**And every woman who prays or prophesies with her head uncovered dishonors her head—it is just as though her head were shaved. **6**If a woman does not cover her head, she should have her hair cut off; and if it is a disgrace for a woman to have her hair cut or shaved off, she should cover her head. **7**A man ought not to cover his head,*c* since he is the image and glory of God; but the woman is the glory of man. **8**For man did not come from woman, but woman from man; **9**neither was man created for woman, but woman for man. **10**For this reason, and because of the angels, the woman ought to have a sign of authority on her head. **11**In the Lord, however, woman is not independent of man, nor is man independent of woman. **12**For as woman came from man, so also man is born of woman. But everything comes from God. **13**Judge for yourselves: Is it proper for a woman to pray to God with her head uncovered? **14**Does not the very nature of things teach you that if a man has long hair, it is a disgrace to him, **15**but that if a woman has long hair, it is her glory? For long hair is given to her as a covering. **16**If anyone wants to be contentious about this, we have no other practice—nor do the churches of God.

The Lord's Supper

17In the following directives I have no praise for you, for your meetings do more harm than good. **18**In the first place, I hear that when you come together as a church, there are divisions among you, and to some extent I believe it. **19**No doubt there have to be differences among you to show which of you have God's approval. **20**When you come together, it is not the Lord's Supper you eat, **21**for as you eat, each of you goes ahead without waiting for anybody else. One remains hungry, another gets drunk. **22**Don't you have homes to eat and drink in? Or do you despise the church of God and humiliate those who have nothing? What shall I say to you? Shall I praise you for this? Certainly not!

23For I received from the Lord what I also passed on to you: The Lord Jesus, on the night he was betrayed, took bread, **24**and when

---

what a believer should do in a relationship with an unbeliever. Do Paul's instructions sound hypocritical? Do you act differently around Christians and non-Christians? How come?

How did you wear your hair 10 years ago? 20?

1. In Greek, the word "head" (v. 3) means "origin." Why was it important for Paul to state the relationship of women to God, Christ and man? How do verses 11 and 12 fit into your answer? **2.** Paul assumes that women in the Corinthian church will pray and prophesy just as the men do. How do you feel about women leading worship? Have you ever been inspired to worship God because of a woman's efforts? **3.** Pagan cults in Corinth practiced ecstatic worship which frequently involved loose hair and nudity. How does this information shed light on the situation in Corinth?

Concern for the glory of God, the interdependence of men and women, and sensitivity to the culture are three principles here. How do these principles apply in your church? In your marriage?

What is the biggest party you've ever given? What food and drink did you serve?

1. How would you describe the scene if you were observing the Lord's Supper at the Corinthian church? **2.** What changes would the Corinthians need to make to ensure that it really was the "Lord's supper"? **3.** Have you ever been in a church that was affected by divisions among the members? What happened? **4.** How do you respond when you hear the words of verses 23–26 during Communion? **5.** What does Paul mean by eating in "an unworthy manner" (v. 27)? By "not recognizing the body of the Lord" (v. 29)? By self-examination (v. 28)? By judging oneself (v. 31)?

---

a28 Some manuscripts *conscience' sake, for "the earth is the Lord's and everything in it"*
b2 Or *traditions*　　*c4-7* Or *4Every man who prays or prophesies with long hair dishonors his head. 5And every woman who prays or prophesies with no covering ⌊of hair⌋ on her head dishonors her head—she is just like one of the "shorn women." 6If a woman has no covering, let her be for now with short hair, but since it is a disgrace for a woman to have her hair shorn or shaved, she should grow it again. 7A man ought not to have long hair*

he had given thanks, he broke it and said, "This is my body, which is for you; do this in remembrance of me." ²⁵In the same way, after supper he took the cup, saying, "This cup is the new covenant in my blood; do this, whenever you drink it, in remembrance of me." ²⁶For whenever you eat this bread and drink this cup, you proclaim the Lord's death until he comes.

²⁷Therefore, whoever eats the bread or drinks the cup of the Lord in an unworthy manner will be guilty of sinning against the body and blood of the Lord. ²⁸A man ought to examine himself before he eats of the bread and drinks of the cup. ²⁹For anyone who eats and drinks without recognizing the body of the Lord eats and drinks judgment on himself. ³⁰That is why many among you are weak and sick, and a number of you have fallen asleep. ³¹But if we judged ourselves, we would not come under judgment. ³²When we are judged by the Lord, we are being disciplined so that we will not be condemned with the world.

³³So then, my brothers, when you come together to eat, wait for each other. ³⁴If anyone is hungry, he should eat at home, so that when you meet together it may not result in judgment.

And when I come I will give further directions.

Spiritual Gifts

12 Now about spiritual gifts, brothers, I do not want you to be ignorant. ²You know that when you were pagans, somehow or other you were influenced and led astray to mute idols. ³Therefore I tell you that no one who is speaking by the Spirit of God says, "Jesus be cursed," and no one can say, "Jesus is Lord," except by the Holy Spirit.

⁴There are different kinds of gifts, but the same Spirit. ⁵There are different kinds of service, but the same Lord. ⁶There are different kinds of working, but the same God works all of them in all men.

⁷Now to each one the manifestation of the Spirit is given for the common good. ⁸To one there is given through the Spirit the message of wisdom, to another the message of knowledge by means of the same Spirit, ⁹to another faith by the same Spirit, to another gifts of healing by that one Spirit, ¹⁰to another miraculous powers, to another prophecy, to another distinguishing between spirits, to another speaking in different kinds of tongues,ᵃ and to still another the interpretation of tongues.ᵃ ¹¹All these are the work of one and the same Spirit, and he gives them to each one, just as he determines.

One Body, Many Parts

¹²The body is a unit, though it is made up of many parts; and though all its parts are many, they form one body. So it is with Christ. ¹³For we were all baptized byᵇ one Spirit into one body—whether Jews or Greeks, slave or free—and we were all given the one Spirit to drink.

¹⁴Now the body is not made up of one part but of many. ¹⁵If the foot should say, "Because I am not a hand, I do not belong to the body," it would not for that reason cease to be part of the body. ¹⁶And if the ear should say, "Because I am not an eye, I do not belong to the body," it would not for that reason cease to be part of the body. ¹⁷If the whole body were an eye, where would the sense of hearing be? If the whole body were an ear, where would the sense of smell be? ¹⁸But in fact God has arranged the parts in the

Sidebar questions (left column)

♡ 1. When do you tend to approach worship or a part of the worship experience too lightly? 2. The poor in Corinth weren't able to participate fully in the Lord's Supper. How do churches today discriminate? How could your church be more inclusive of the types of people where you live?

☕ What was the most fulfilling job you ever had?

📖 1. What was life like when you first began to believe that "Jesus is Lord"? 2. Verses 4–6 indicate that some Corinthians felt certain spiritual gifts were better than others. Have you ever encountered a similar attitude? In yourself? 3. How is the diversity of the gifts related to the unity of the Father, Son and Holy Spirit?

♡ 1. Of the spiritual gifts listed, which have you received? Is this list all-inclusive? 2. How have you used your gift for the common good? Have you ever seen a spiritual gift not used for the common good?

☕ What is one skill you secretly possess?

📖 1. Why is verse 12 such a good illustration of verse 13? 2. What could be an example of a "weaker" part of the body of Christ (v. 22)? Of a "less honorable" part (v. 23)? Of a "presentable" part (v. 24)? Does each receive the treatment it should in your church? 3. From Paul's rhetorical questions in verses 29–30, what is another problem in this church?

♡ 1. Regardless of your church's doctrinal position, what attitudes toward spiritual gifts dominate: (a) For pastors only? (b)

ᵃ10 Or *languages*; also in verse 28　　ᵇ13 Or *with*; or *in*

body, every one of them, just as he wanted them to be. ¹⁹If they were all one part, where would the body be? ²⁰As it is, there are many parts, but one body.

²¹The eye cannot say to the hand, "I don't need you!" And the head cannot say to the feet, "I don't need you!" ²²On the contrary, those parts of the body that seem to be weaker are indispensable, ²³and the parts that we think are less honorable we treat with special honor. And the parts that are unpresentable are treated with special modesty, ²⁴while our presentable parts need no special treatment. But God has combined the members of the body and has given greater honor to the parts that lacked it, ²⁵so that there should be no division in the body, but that its parts should have equal concern for each other. ²⁶If one part suffers, every part suffers with it; if one part is honored, every part rejoices with it.

²⁷Now you are the body of Christ, and each one of you is a part of it. ²⁸And in the church God has appointed first of all apostles, second prophets, third teachers, then workers of miracles, also those having gifts of healing, those able to help others, those with gifts of administration, and those speaking in different kinds of tongues. ²⁹Are all apostles? Are all prophets? Are all teachers? Do all work miracles? ³⁰Do all have gifts of healing? Do all speak in tongues*a*? Do all interpret? ³¹But eagerly desire*b* the greater gifts.

Love

And now I will show you the most excellent way.

13 If I speak in the tongues*c* of men and of angels, but have not love, I am only a resounding gong or a clanging cymbal. ²If I have the gift of prophecy and can fathom all mysteries and all knowledge, and if I have a faith that can move mountains, but have not love, I am nothing. ³If I give all I possess to the poor and surrender my body to the flames,*d* but have not love, I gain nothing.

⁴Love is patient, love is kind. It does not envy, it does not boast, it is not proud. ⁵It is not rude, it is not self-seeking, it is not easily angered, it keeps no record of wrongs. ⁶Love does not delight in evil but rejoices with the truth. ⁷It always protects, always trusts, always hopes, always perseveres.

⁸Love never fails. But where there are prophecies, they will cease; where there are tongues, they will be stilled; where there is knowledge, it will pass away. ⁹For we know in part and we prophesy in part, ¹⁰but when perfection comes, the imperfect disappears. ¹¹When I was a child, I talked like a child, I thought like a child, I reasoned like a child. When I became a man, I put childish ways behind me. ¹²Now we see but a poor reflection as in a mirror; then we shall see face to face. Now I know in part; then I shall know fully, even as I am fully known.

¹³And now these three remain: faith, hope and love. But the greatest of these is love.

Gifts of Prophecy and Tongues

14 Follow the way of love and eagerly desire spiritual gifts, especially the gift of prophecy. ²For anyone who speaks in a tongue*e* does not speak to men but to God. Indeed, no one understands him; he utters mysteries with his spirit.*f* ³But everyone who prophesies speaks to men for their strengthening, encouragement and comfort. ⁴He who speaks in a tongue edifies himself, but

For all believers? (c) For the good of others? (d) For the first-century church only? (e) For believers who have a post-conversion experience? (f) More spiritual gifts for the more spiritually mature? **2.** How do these verses make you feel about your place in the body of Christ? About your need for others? **3.** Take turns affirming each person in the group with which spiritual gifts and Christ-like qualities you have noticed in them.

1. What was one of your favorite love songs when you were a teenager? **2.** When in your life have you felt the most loved?

1. Given the Corinthians' quest for spiritual gifts and power, what is Paul's point in verses 1–3? What have you *done* that has become a substitute for really loving others? **2.** In what ways has God loved you according to the qualities of love you found in verses 4–8? What have you done lately that is an example of what love is *not*? **3.** Have you ever done a religious act without love? What was it like?

1. In your opinion, what is the best way to develop the ability to love others? **2.** How do verses 8–10 help to put your church in perspective? Your personal life? **3.** What does it mean to you that you will see Jesus face to face?

1. Describe a time when you were in a country or area where you couldn't speak the language. Was it funny? Frustrating? Humbling? **2.** If you could play any musical instrument, what would it be? What songs would you like to play?

1. What is the difference between speaking in tongues and prophesying (vv. 2–4)? **2.** Dur-

a30 Or *other languages*   *b31* Or *But you are eagerly desiring*   *c1* Or *languages*
d3 Some early manuscripts *body that I may boast*   *e2* Or *another language*; also in verses 4, 13, 14, 19, 26 and 27   *f2* Or *by the Spirit*

ing Corinthian worship services far too much time was spent speaking in tongues. The result was chaos. How is this another mark of their immaturity (v. 20; see also 3:1–4)? **3.** What are Paul's corrective instructions to the spiritually proud Corinthians (v. 12)? **4.** What are the values and limits of tongues (vv. 4,9,13–19,21–25)? **5.** What is Paul saying about the need for balance between the mind and the emotions in worship?

1. Have you ever been in a worship service that was chaotic and disorderly? What was it like? **2.** Have you ever seen someone exercise a spiritual gift without regard for "building up the church"? **3.** How does the gift of tongues edify an individual? What do you do that edifies you alone? What do you do to edify others in your church? **4.** The Corinthians presumably were partial to ecstatic or flamboyant spirituality. What exciting experiences do you wish your Christian life could have? Which experiences do you wish your church would tone down? **5.** Whether or not your church practices the gifts of tongues and prophecy, what principles for church life need to be exercised more fully in your church?

What was your favorite song as a child?

1. In verse 26, Paul describes a worship service where everyone seems to have something to offer. How could your church better include the contributions of more people in worship? **2.** Verses 29–33 contain instructions about prophecy. What is prophe-

he who prophesies edifies the church. ⁵I would like every one of you to speak in tongues,ᵃ but I would rather have you prophesy. He who prophesies is greater than one who speaks in tongues,ᵃ unless he interprets, so that the church may be edified.

⁶Now, brothers, if I come to you and speak in tongues, what good will I be to you, unless I bring you some revelation or knowledge or prophecy or word of instruction? ⁷Even in the case of lifeless things that make sounds, such as the flute or harp, how will anyone know what tune is being played unless there is a distinction in the notes? ⁸Again, if the trumpet does not sound a clear call, who will get ready for battle? ⁹So it is with you. Unless you speak intelligible words with your tongue, how will anyone know what you are saying? You will just be speaking into the air. ¹⁰Undoubtedly there are all sorts of languages in the world, yet none of them is without meaning. ¹¹If then I do not grasp the meaning of what someone is saying, I am a foreigner to the speaker, and he is a foreigner to me. ¹²So it is with you. Since you are eager to have spiritual gifts, try to excel in gifts that build up the church.

¹³For this reason anyone who speaks in a tongue should pray that he may interpret what he says. ¹⁴For if I pray in a tongue, my spirit prays, but my mind is unfruitful. ¹⁵So what shall I do? I will pray with my spirit, but I will also pray with my mind; I will sing with my spirit, but I will also sing with my mind. ¹⁶If you are praising God with your spirit, how can one who finds himself among those who do not understandᵇ say "Amen" to your thanksgiving, since he does not know what you are saying? ¹⁷You may be giving thanks well enough, but the other man is not edified.

¹⁸I thank God that I speak in tongues more than all of you. ¹⁹But in the church I would rather speak five intelligible words to instruct others than ten thousand words in a tongue.

²⁰Brothers, stop thinking like children. In regard to evil be infants, but in your thinking be adults. ²¹In the Law it is written:

> "Through men of strange tongues
> and through the lips of foreigners
> I will speak to this people,
> but even then they will not listen to me,"ᶜ

says the Lord.

²²Tongues, then, are a sign, not for believers but for unbelievers; prophecy, however, is for believers, not for unbelievers. ²³So if the whole church comes together and everyone speaks in tongues, and some who do not understandᵈ or some unbelievers come in, will they not say that you are out of your mind? ²⁴But if an unbeliever or someone who does not understandᵉ comes in while everybody is prophesying, he will be convinced by all that he is a sinner and will be judged by all, ²⁵and the secrets of his heart will be laid bare. So he will fall down and worship God, exclaiming, "God is really among you!"

Orderly Worship

²⁶What then shall we say, brothers? When you come together, everyone has a hymn, or a word of instruction, a revelation, a tongue or an interpretation. All of these must be done for the strengthening of the church. ²⁷If anyone speaks in a tongue, two— or at the most three—should speak, one at a time, and someone

ᵃ5 Or *other languages*; also in verses 6, 18, 22, 23 and 39   ᵇ16 Or *among the inquirers*   ᶜ21 Isaiah 28:11,12   ᵈ23 Or *some inquirers*   ᵉ24 Or *or some inquirer*

must interpret. [28]If there is no interpreter, the speaker should keep quiet in the church and speak to himself and God.

[29]Two or three prophets should speak, and the others should weigh carefully what is said. [30]And if a revelation comes to someone who is sitting down, the first speaker should stop. [31]For you can all prophesy in turn so that everyone may be instructed and encouraged. [32]The spirits of prophets are subject to the control of prophets. [33]For God is not a God of disorder but of peace.

As in all the congregations of the saints, [34]women should remain silent in the churches. They are not allowed to speak, but must be in submission, as the Law says. [35]If they want to inquire about something, they should ask their own husbands at home; for it is disgraceful for a woman to speak in the church.

[36]Did the word of God originate with you? Or are you the only people it has reached? [37]If anybody thinks he is a prophet or spiritually gifted, let him acknowledge that what I am writing to you is the Lord's command. [38]If he ignores this, he himself will be ignored.[a]

[39]Therefore, my brothers, be eager to prophesy, and do not forbid speaking in tongues. [40]But everything should be done in a fitting and orderly way.

The Resurrection of Christ

15 Now, brothers, I want to remind you of the gospel I preached to you, which you received and on which you have taken your stand. [2]By this gospel you are saved, if you hold firmly to the word I preached to you. Otherwise, you have believed in vain.

[3]For what I received I passed on to you as of first importance[b]: that Christ died for our sins according to the Scriptures, [4]that he was buried, that he was raised on the third day according to the Scriptures, [5]and that he appeared to Peter,[c] and then to the Twelve. [6]After that, he appeared to more than five hundred of the brothers at the same time, most of whom are still living, though some have fallen asleep. [7]Then he appeared to James, then to all the apostles, [8]and last of all he appeared to me also, as to one abnormally born.

[9]For I am the least of the apostles and do not even deserve to be called an apostle, because I persecuted the church of God. [10]But by the grace of God I am what I am, and his grace to me was not without effect. No, I worked harder than all of them—yet not I, but the grace of God that was with me. [11]Whether, then, it was I or they, this is what we preach, and this is what you believed.

The Resurrection of the Dead

[12]But if it is preached that Christ has been raised from the dead, how can some of you say that there is no resurrection of the dead? [13]If there is no resurrection of the dead, then not even Christ has been raised. [14]And if Christ has not been raised, our preaching is useless and so is your faith. [15]More than that, we are then found to be false witnesses about God, for we have testified about God that he raised Christ from the dead. But he did not raise him if in fact the dead are not raised. [16]For if the dead are not raised, then Christ has not been raised either. [17]And if Christ has not been raised, your faith is futile; you are still in your sins. [18]Then those also who have fallen asleep in Christ are lost. [19]If only for this life we have hope in Christ, we are to be pitied more than all men.

cy? What do you think about two or three prophets speaking during a worship service? Has anything ever popped into your head that you wanted to share with the entire congregation? What would become of your church if that were allowed to happen? **3.** In light of 11:5, verses 34–35 are difficult to understand. What type of talk, contributing to general disorder, might be in view here?

1. What *positive* qualities about public worship could you and your church learn from the Corinthian church's enthusiasm? **2.** What was the most inspiring part of the worship service you attended most recently? The sermon? A prayer? The music? A greeting from someone?

What is one piece of advice you were told as a child that you have never forgotten?

1. How had the Corinthians taken their stand on the Gospel? **2.** In verse 2, what does it mean to "hold firmly to the word I preached to you"? **3.** What do you think it means to "believe in vain"? **4.** Why did Paul go to such detail listing who saw Jesus after he was resurrected?

1. What does "Christ died for our sins" mean to you? How does the Gospel affect your life on a daily basis? **2.** What evidence can you offer that Christ is alive in your life?

When you were a child, what friend or other person was a negative influence on you?

1. What false teaching is being spread among the Corinthians (v. 12)? **2.** How do you connect Christ's resurrection with your own hope of resurrection from death? **3.** Paul puts the Resurrection in perspective with the Second Coming and the end of time. How does it make you feel that in the end Christ will be victorious? **4.** How would your life be different without your hope that you will be resurrected? **5.** It seems that some Corinthians had begun the practice

---

[a]38 Some manuscripts *If he is ignorant of this, let him be ignorant first*   [b]3 Or *you at the first*   [c]5 Greek *Cephas*

of vicarious baptism—the baptism of a living person on behalf of someone who was dead (v. 29). Why does Paul speak of this absurd practice when making his arguments (vv. 30–32)? **6.** Paul says, "I die every day," referring to his willingness to sacrifice his present rights for the salvation of others (knowing he will be raised from the dead). In what ways do you "die every day"?

♡ **1.** Though reaching out to unbelievers is important (v. 33), how can too close an association with unbelievers affect your faith? Have you ever gotten too wrapped up in the lives of unbelievers, to the detriment of your relationship with Christ? How? **2.** What difference has Christ's resurrection and your resulting victory over death made to you in terms of hope and courage? In terms of purpose for life? **3.** What arguments have you found helpful in showing unbelieving friends that Christ did rise from the dead?

☕ During what stage of your life did you change the most? In what ways did you change?

📖 **1.** What practical problem is causing some to question their belief in the Resurrection (v. 35)? **2.** What would Resurrection Day be like if everyone's bodies came back to life without some kind of transformation? How would Hollywood film this scene? **3.** How do the analogies of the seed and the different types of bodies deal with doubts about the Resurrection of the dead (vv. 36–44)? **4.** What is the point of the comparison between Adam and Christ (vv. 45–49; also vv. 21–22)? **5.** Have you ever been face-to-face with death? How did that experience affect you? **6.** How does it make you feel to think of being part of what happens in verses 50–55? **7.** How does the hope of the Resurrection comfort you?

♡ **1.** What is most comforting when you consider the reality of your own death? What is hardest for you to understand? **2.** What can you do now to reveal the likeness of Christ? How can your small group help you do that? **3.** What motivates you to obey God? Fear of judgment? God's anger? Worry about not being resurrected? Love

²⁰But Christ has indeed been raised from the dead, the firstfruits of those who have fallen asleep. ²¹For since death came through a man, the resurrection of the dead comes also through a man. ²²For as in Adam all die, so in Christ all will be made alive. ²³But each in his own turn: Christ, the firstfruits; then, when he comes, those who belong to him. ²⁴Then the end will come, when he hands over the kingdom to God the Father after he has destroyed all dominion, authority and power. ²⁵For he must reign until he has put all his enemies under his feet. ²⁶The last enemy to be destroyed is death. ²⁷For he "has put everything under his feet."ᵃ Now when it says that "everything" has been put under him, it is clear that this does not include God himself, who put everything under Christ. ²⁸When he has done this, then the Son himself will be made subject to him who put everything under him, so that God may be all in all.

²⁹Now if there is no resurrection, what will those do who are baptized for the dead? If the dead are not raised at all, why are people baptized for them? ³⁰And as for us, why do we endanger ourselves every hour? ³¹I die every day—I mean that, brothers—just as surely as I glory over you in Christ Jesus our Lord. ³²If I fought wild beasts in Ephesus for merely human reasons, what have I gained? If the dead are not raised,

> "Let us eat and drink,
> for tomorrow we die."ᵇ

³³Do not be misled: "Bad company corrupts good character." ³⁴Come back to your senses as you ought, and stop sinning; for there are some who are ignorant of God—I say this to your shame.

The Resurrection Body

³⁵But someone may ask, "How are the dead raised? With what kind of body will they come?" ³⁶How foolish! What you sow does not come to life unless it dies. ³⁷When you sow, you do not plant the body that will be, but just a seed, perhaps of wheat or of something else. ³⁸But God gives it a body as he has determined, and to each kind of seed he gives its own body. ³⁹All flesh is not the same: Men have one kind of flesh, animals have another, birds another and fish another. ⁴⁰There are also heavenly bodies and there are earthly bodies; but the splendor of the heavenly bodies is one kind, and the splendor of the earthly bodies is another. ⁴¹The sun has one kind of splendor, the moon another and the stars another; and star differs from star in splendor.

⁴²So will it be with the resurrection of the dead. The body that is sown is perishable, it is raised imperishable; ⁴³it is sown in dishonor, it is raised in glory; it is sown in weakness, it is raised in power; ⁴⁴it is sown a natural body, it is raised a spiritual body.

If there is a natural body, there is also a spiritual body. ⁴⁵So it is written: "The first man Adam became a living being"ᶜ; the last Adam, a life-giving spirit. ⁴⁶The spiritual did not come first, but the natural, and after that the spiritual. ⁴⁷The first man was of the dust of the earth, the second man from heaven. ⁴⁸As was the earthly man, so are those who are of the earth; and as is the man from heaven, so also are those who are of heaven. ⁴⁹And just as we have borne the likeness of the earthly man, so shall weᵈ bear the likeness of the man from heaven.

⁵⁰I declare to you, brothers, that flesh and blood cannot inherit the kingdom of God, nor does the perishable inherit the imperishable. ⁵¹Listen, I tell you a mystery: We will not all sleep, but we

ᵃ27 Psalm 8:6   ᵇ32 Isaiah 22:13   ᶜ45 Gen. 2:7   ᵈ49 Some early manuscripts *so let us* will all be changed— 52in a flash, in the twinkling of an eye, at the last trumpet. For the trumpet will sound, the dead will be raised imperishable, and we will be changed. 53For the perishable must clothe itself with the imperishable, and the mortal with immortality. 54When the perishable has been clothed with the imperishable, and the mortal with immortality, then the saying that is written will come true: "Death has been swallowed up in victory."[a]

> 55"Where, O death, is your victory?
>   Where, O death, is your sting?"[b]

56The sting of death is sin, and the power of sin is the law. 57But thanks be to God! He gives us the victory through our Lord Jesus Christ.

58Therefore, my dear brothers, stand firm. Let nothing move you. Always give yourselves fully to the work of the Lord, because you know that your labor in the Lord is not in vain.

The Collection for God's People

16 Now about the collection for God's people: Do what I told the Galatian churches to do. 2On the first day of every week, each one of you should set aside a sum of money in keeping with his income, saving it up, so that when I come no collections will have to be made. 3Then, when I arrive, I will give letters of introduction to the men you approve and send them with your gift to Jerusalem. 4If it seems advisable for me to go also, they will accompany me.

Personal Requests

5After I go through Macedonia, I will come to you—for I will be going through Macedonia. 6Perhaps I will stay with you awhile, or even spend the winter, so that you can help me on my journey, wherever I go. 7I do not want to see you now and make only a passing visit; I hope to spend some time with you, if the Lord permits. 8But I will stay on at Ephesus until Pentecost, 9because a great door for effective work has opened to me, and there are many who oppose me.

10If Timothy comes, see to it that he has nothing to fear while he is with you, for he is carrying on the work of the Lord, just as I am. 11No one, then, should refuse to accept him. Send him on his way in peace so that he may return to me. I am expecting him along with the brothers.

12Now about our brother Apollos: I strongly urged him to go to you with the brothers. He was quite unwilling to go now, but he will go when he has the opportunity.

13Be on your guard; stand firm in the faith; be men of courage; be strong. 14Do everything in love.

15You know that the household of Stephanas were the first converts in Achaia, and they have devoted themselves to the service of the saints. I urge you, brothers, 16to submit to such as these and to everyone who joins in the work, and labors at it. 17I was glad when Stephanas, Fortunatus and Achaicus arrived, because they have supplied what was lacking from you. 18For they refreshed my spirit and yours also. Such men deserve recognition.

Final Greetings

19The churches in the province of Asia send you greetings. Aquila and Priscilla[c] greet you warmly in the Lord, and so does the

---

from God? Love for God? Hope of being with God? How does verse 58 encourage and motivate you?

---

1. Who is one person you would like to visit? **2.** When you travel, do you like to plan things thoroughly, or just go and see what happens?

1. Why did Paul ask for a collection of money (vv. 1–4; see Ac 11:30; 24:17; Ro 15:25–28; 2Co 8:13–14)? **2.** How do you feel about giving money to your church? What motivates you to give? **3.** What do you think Paul's reunion with the Corinthian church was like (vv. 6–8)? Beneath all his corrective instruction, how do you think Paul felt about the Corinthians? **4.** What was the greatest door of effective work that ever opened for you? What happened? **5.** What should the Corinthians imitate regarding Stephanas and the others (vv. 15–18)? **6.** Who in your life, or in this group, has helped to refresh your spirit?

1. Which of Paul's concluding exhortations in verses 13–14 do you want to apply at this time: (a) "Be on your guard"? (b) "Stand firm in your faith"? (c) "Have courage"? (d) "Be strong"? (e) "Do everything in love"? How will you apply it to your life? **2.** As a member of your church and small group, how has this letter helped you? Challenged you? In what way would you like to grow from here?

---

a54 Isaiah 25:8   b55 Hosea 13:14   c19 Greek *Prisca*, a variant of *Priscilla*

church that meets at their house. ²⁰All the brothers here send you greetings. Greet one another with a holy kiss.

²¹I, Paul, write this greeting in my own hand.

²²If anyone does not love the Lord—a curse be on him. Come, O Lord*a*!

²³The grace of the Lord Jesus be with you.

²⁴My love to all of you in Christ Jesus. Amen.*b*

---

a22 In Aramaic the expression *Come, O Lord* is *Marana tha.*   *b24* Some manuscripts do not have *Amen.*

INTRODUCTION to
2 CORINTHIANS

Book Study Outline: If you are using 2 Corinthians for a study course, here is a 7- or 13-week outline. Use the margin questions for your group agenda:

🍵 start meeting / 15 min.

📖 read & discuss Bible / 30 min.

♡ close meeting / 15–45 min.

Refer to the Questions and Answers in front of Bible for more information.

Author: The apostle Paul.

7-week plan	13-week plan	Personal Reading	Group Study Passage
1	1	1:1–2:4	1:1–11/God's Comfort
	2	2:5–3:6	2:12–3:6/An Aroma of Life
2	3	3:7–18	3:7–18/The New Covenant
	4	4:1–18	4:1–18/Our Treasure
3	5	5:1–6:2	5:11–6:2/Reconciliation
	6	6:3–7:1	6:14–7:1/Be Separate!
4	7	7:2–16	7:2–16/Peace Restored
	8	8:1–24	8:1–15/Our Giving
5	9	9:1–15	9:6–15/God's Giving
	10	10:1–18	10:1–18/Paul's Defense
6	11	11:1–33	11:16–33/Paul's Credentials
	12	12:1–21	12:1–10/Paul's Strength
7	13	13:1–14	13:1–14/True Power

Date: A.D. 55–56.

Theme: The strength of weakness.

Historical Background: Since much of this letter is devoted to explaining Paul's actions since the time he wrote 1 Corinthians, it is important to have a clear idea of what happened in this time period. The problem is that no one really knows! What follows is a "best guess." That Paul promised to visit the Corinthians a second time is clear (1Co 16:5–6). This visit apparently resulted in severe conflict with the "false apostles." Although they attacked Paul vigorously, what really hurt was the fact that the Corinthians did not rally to his support. This letter was written to prepare them for a third visit. The background is further complicated by two factors. First, Paul refers to a "painful letter" he wrote which has not been preserved. Second, because the fierce tone of chapters 10–13 stands in sharp contrast to the reconciling tone of chapters 1–9, 2 Corinthians may actually be a combination of two letters! According to this view, chapters 1–9 were written on the basis of Titus' report that the situation had been rectified (7:6–13). However, when Titus returned to Corinth he found that the "super-apostles" were back in charge. On hearing this, Paul wrote another letter which is chapters 10–13.

Characteristics: This letter, as much as any other, allows us to see inside Paul: his passion for the Gospel, his deep love for his churches, the pain he felt over misunderstanding, rejection and attack, and the cost of his sufferings.

STRUCTURE OF THE NEW TESTAMENT

39 Books in the Old Testament + **27** Books in the New Testament = **66** Books in the Bible

Historical Books	Paul's Epistles	General Letters	Prophetic Books
Matthew	Romans	Hebrews	Revelation
Mark	1 Corinthians	James	
Luke	2 Corinthians	1 Peter	
John	Galatians	2 Peter	
Acts	Ephesians	1 John	
	Philippians	2 John	
	Colossians	3 John	
	1 Thessalonians	Jude	
	2 Thessalonians		
	1 Timothy		
	2 Timothy		
	Titus		
	Philemon		

2 Corinthians

☕ When sick or hurt as a child, what expression of care did you find most comforting?

📖 **1.** What's the relationship between God's ability to comfort us and our ability to comfort others (v. 5)? **2.** When have you been the recipient of this comfort? How are Christ's and Paul's sufferings related to the Corinthians? What pressures is Paul facing that would cause him to despair even of life (see 7:5–7 and Ac 19:23–41)? **3.** What pressures are causing you to despair?

♡ **1.** Paul found that intense pressures led him to depend on God all the more (v. 9). How do you respond to intense pressures? Do they deepen your walk with God or drive you away from him? **2.** Whom do you know who is under intense pressure? How would Paul have you pray for them? **3.** A friend asks, "Why do you have to bother praying, since God knows what's going to happen anyway?" What is your answer?

☕ **1.** What was one accomplishment as a teenager of which you felt proud? If you were permitted to brag a little about your kids or grandkids (if any) what would you boast about? **2.** From which parent could you bank on a "no" reply? A "yes" reply? Which one waffled? Why was that?

📖 **1.** In what does Paul boast (v. 12)? What is the basis for his integrity? **2.** How does a leader who uses his authority according to "worldly wisdom" differ from one who does so by "God's grace" (1:12)? **3.** From 1:15–17, of what may Paul have been accused? How does he account for his change of plans (1:23–2:2)? **4.** What does it mean that Jesus is the "Yes" of God's promise to us? How does this relate to Paul's argument? **5.** Corinth was the commercial center of the region: What do the three trading metaphors in 1:22 indicate that Jesus has done

1 Paul, an apostle of Christ Jesus by the will of God, and Timothy our brother,

To the church of God in Corinth, together with all the saints throughout Achaia:

²Grace and peace to you from God our Father and the Lord Jesus Christ.

The God of All Comfort

³Praise be to the God and Father of our Lord Jesus Christ, the Father of compassion and the God of all comfort, ⁴who comforts us in all our troubles, so that we can comfort those in any trouble with the comfort we ourselves have received from God. ⁵For just as the sufferings of Christ flow over into our lives, so also through Christ our comfort overflows. ⁶If we are distressed, it is for your comfort and salvation; if we are comforted, it is for your comfort, which produces in you patient endurance of the same sufferings we suffer. ⁷And our hope for you is firm, because we know that just as you share in our sufferings, so also you share in our comfort.

⁸We do not want you to be uninformed, brothers, about the hardships we suffered in the province of Asia. We were under great pressure, far beyond our ability to endure, so that we despaired even of life. ⁹Indeed, in our hearts we felt the sentence of death. But this happened that we might not rely on ourselves but on God, who raises the dead. ¹⁰He has delivered us from such a deadly peril, and he will deliver us. On him we have set our hope that he will continue to deliver us, ¹¹as you help us by your prayers. Then many will give thanks on our*a* behalf for the gracious favor granted us in answer to the prayers of many.

Paul's Change of Plans

¹²Now this is our boast: Our conscience testifies that we have conducted ourselves in the world, and especially in our relations with you, in the holiness and sincerity that are from God. We have done so not according to worldly wisdom but according to God's grace. ¹³For we do not write you anything you cannot read or understand. And I hope that, ¹⁴as you have understood us in part, you will come to understand fully that you can boast of us just as we will boast of you in the day of the Lord Jesus.

¹⁵Because I was confident of this, I planned to visit you first so that you might benefit twice. ¹⁶I planned to visit you on my way to Macedonia and to come back to you from Macedonia, and then to have you send me on my way to Judea. ¹⁷When I planned this, did I do it lightly? Or do I make my plans in a worldly manner so that in the same breath I say, "Yes, yes" and "No, no"?

¹⁸But as surely as God is faithful, our message to you is not "Yes" and "No." ¹⁹For the Son of God, Jesus Christ, who was preached among you by me and Silas*b* and Timothy, was not "Yes" and "No," but in him it has always been "Yes." ²⁰For no matter how many promises God has made, they are "Yes" in Christ. And so through him the "Amen" is spoken by us to the glory of God.

a 11 Many manuscripts *your*   *b 19* Greek *Silvanus,* a variant of *Silas*

21Now it is God who makes both us and you stand firm in Christ. He anointed us, 22set his seal of ownership on us, and put his Spirit in our hearts as a deposit, guaranteeing what is to come.

23I call God as my witness that it was in order to spare you that I did not return to Corinth. 24Not that we lord it over your faith, but we work with you for your joy, because it is by faith you stand firm. 1So I made up my mind that I would not make another painful visit to you. 2For if I grieve you, who is left to make me glad but you whom I have grieved? 3I wrote as I did so that when I came I should not be distressed by those who ought to make me rejoice. I had confidence in all of you, that you would all share my joy. 4For I wrote you out of great distress and anguish of heart and with many tears, not to grieve you but to let you know the depth of my love for you.

Forgiveness for the Sinner

5If anyone has caused grief, he has not so much grieved me as he has grieved all of you, to some extent—not to put it too severely. 6The punishment inflicted on him by the majority is sufficient for him. 7Now instead, you ought to forgive and comfort him, so that he will not be overwhelmed by excessive sorrow. 8I urge you, therefore, to reaffirm your love for him. 9The reason I wrote you was to see if you would stand the test and be obedient in everything. 10If you forgive anyone, I also forgive him. And what I have forgiven—if there was anything to forgive—I have forgiven in the sight of Christ for your sake, 11in order that Satan might not outwit us. For we are not unaware of his schemes.

Ministers of the New Covenant

12Now when I went to Troas to preach the gospel of Christ and found that the Lord had opened a door for me, 13I still had no peace of mind, because I did not find my brother Titus there. So I said good-by to them and went on to Macedonia.

14But thanks be to God, who always leads us in triumphal procession in Christ and through us spreads everywhere the fragrance of the knowledge of him. 15For we are to God the aroma of Christ among those who are being saved and those who are perishing. 16To the one we are the smell of death; to the other, the fragrance of life. And who is equal to such a task? 17Unlike so many, we do not peddle the word of God for profit. On the contrary, in Christ we speak before God with sincerity, like men sent from God. 1Are we beginning to commend ourselves again? Or do we need, like some people, letters of recommendation to you or from you? 2You yourselves are our letter, written on our hearts, known and read by everybody. 3You show that you are a letter from Christ, the result of our ministry, written not with ink but with the Spirit of the living God, not on tablets of stone but on tablets of human hearts.

4Such confidence as this is ours through Christ before God. 5Not that we are competent in ourselves to claim anything for ourselves, but our competence comes from God. 6He has made us competent as ministers of a new covenant—not of the letter but of the Spirit; for the letter kills, but the Spirit gives life.

The Glory of the New Covenant

7Now if the ministry that brought death, which was engraved in letters on stone, came with glory, so that the Israelites could not look steadily at the face of Moses because of its glory, fading though

for us? 6. What are the causes of joy and grief for Paul and the Corinthians (1:23–2:5)? 7. What must Paul's grievous letter have been about (see 2:3–9; 7:8–12)? 8. What has happened since the letter was received (2:6–8)? How might their continuation of punishment be a scheme of Satan (vv. 9–11)?

1. What does Paul's example mean for you in terms of how you relate to others? 2. Paraphrase the "business deal" of 1:22 in modern terms. How have you experienced this spiritual "new deal"? 3. How does this passage apply to church discipline and restoration of fallen leaders today? Is there someone you need to forgive and comfort (no names)? Why not now?

What is the most memorable parade you've seen or taken part in?

1. Until Titus returns with "good news" (see 7:6–13), Paul has "no peace of mind" (2:13): What does that say about Paul's concern for this church? 2. How can the same Gospel be either the smell of death or the fragrance of life? 3. What might be happening in Corinth (2:17–3:1)? Although preachers often had letters of recommendation when they traveled to new areas (3Jn 5–8), why does Paul need no such letter? 4. Why should the Corinthians listen to Paul (1:1–3:6)?

1. How can you spread the aroma of Christ in the environment of your home? In your workplace? 2. If you were the only "Bible" someone else had to read, how much of the Gospel would they grasp?

When did you last experience suddenly understanding something that once confused and puzzled you?

1. How does Paul here (also vv. 3,6) contrast the old and new covenants? 2. Compare Exodus 34:27–35 and Jeremiah 32:31–34 with Romans 3:19–24. Why did that once-glorious covenant of Moses have to be replaced by the everlasting covenant of Christ? 3. What then is the basis for Paul's (and our) hope and boldness? 4. What are the practical results of this new covenant (vv. 16–18)?

1. Who or what helped to remove the cobwebs which once veiled your "dull mind"? 2. What changes have you noticed since you "turned to the Lord"?

1. Do you feel more like a disposable cup or a crystal goblet this week? Why? 2. What thought, song or verse encourages you?

1. How does the way Paul *received* his ministry (vv. 1,6) make a difference in the way he *conducts* that ministry (vv. 2–5)? 2. What do you learn from Paul about sharing your faith (vv. 1–6)? About its content? About the lack of response? 3. What about the ministry is most like a struggle (vv. 7–11)? How does Paul's struggle show God's power and reflect Jesus' life? How is this true in your own life? 4. What does "death at work" and "life at work" (v. 12) mean to you? Which is at work in your life? Why? 5. What truths keep Paul going in spite of his hardships? Why does God allow Paul to go through them?

1. How did the light of Christ first break through to you? 2. Why is being a servant to others essential for sharing the Gospel? What is one way you could be more of a servant to someone you are concerned about? 3. How do verses 7–12 and 16–18 help you cope with your present anxieties? 4. How does this section challenge common ideas of "success"?

it was, [8]will not the ministry of the Spirit be even more glorious? [9]If the ministry that condemns men is glorious, how much more glorious is the ministry that brings righteousness! [10]For what was glorious has no glory now in comparison with the surpassing glory. [11]And if what was fading away came with glory, how much greater is the glory of that which lasts!

[12]Therefore, since we have such a hope, we are very bold. [13]We are not like Moses, who would put a veil over his face to keep the Israelites from gazing at it while the radiance was fading away. [14]But their minds were made dull, for to this day the same veil remains when the old covenant is read. It has not been removed, because only in Christ is it taken away. [15]Even to this day when Moses is read, a veil covers their hearts. [16]But whenever anyone turns to the Lord, the veil is taken away. [17]Now the Lord is the Spirit, and where the Spirit of the Lord is, there is freedom. [18]And we, who with unveiled faces all reflect[a] the Lord's glory, are being transformed into his likeness with ever-increasing glory, which comes from the Lord, who is the Spirit.

Treasures in Jars of Clay

4 Therefore, since through God's mercy we have this ministry, we do not lose heart. [2]Rather, we have renounced secret and shameful ways; we do not use deception, nor do we distort the word of God. On the contrary, by setting forth the truth plainly we commend ourselves to every man's conscience in the sight of God. [3]And even if our gospel is veiled, it is veiled to those who are perishing. [4]The god of this age has blinded the minds of unbelievers, so that they cannot see the light of the gospel of the glory of Christ, who is the image of God. [5]For we do not preach ourselves, but Jesus Christ as Lord, and ourselves as your servants for Jesus' sake. [6]For God, who said, "Let light shine out of darkness,"[b] made his light shine in our hearts to give us the light of the knowledge of the glory of God in the face of Christ.

[7]But we have this treasure in jars of clay to show that this all-surpassing power is from God and not from us. [8]We are hard pressed on every side, but not crushed; perplexed, but not in despair; [9]persecuted, but not abandoned; struck down, but not destroyed. [10]We always carry around in our body the death of Jesus, so that the life of Jesus may also be revealed in our body. [11]For we who are alive are always being given over to death for Jesus' sake, so that his life may be revealed in our mortal body. [12]So then, death is at work in us, but life is at work in you.

[13]It is written: "I believed; therefore I have spoken."[c] With that same spirit of faith we also believe and therefore speak, [14]because we know that the one who raised the Lord Jesus from the dead will also raise us with Jesus and present us with you in his presence. [15]All this is for your benefit, so that the grace that is reaching more and more people may cause thanksgiving to overflow to the glory of God.

[16]Therefore we do not lose heart. Though outwardly we are wasting away, yet inwardly we are being renewed day by day. [17]For our light and momentary troubles are achieving for us an eternal glory that far outweighs them all. [18]So we fix our eyes not on what is seen, but on what is unseen. For what is seen is temporary, but what is unseen is eternal.

---

[a]18 Or *contemplate*   [b]6 Gen. 1:3   [c]13 Psalm 116:10

Our Heavenly Dwelling

5 Now we know that if the earthly tent we live in is destroyed, we have a building from God, an eternal house in heaven, not built by human hands. ²Meanwhile we groan, longing to be clothed with our heavenly dwelling, ³because when we are clothed, we will not be found naked. ⁴For while we are in this tent, we groan and are burdened, because we do not wish to be unclothed but to be clothed with our heavenly dwelling, so that what is mortal may be swallowed up by life. ⁵Now it is God who has made us for this very purpose and has given us the Spirit as a deposit, guaranteeing what is to come.

⁶Therefore we are always confident and know that as long as we are at home in the body we are away from the Lord. ⁷We live by faith, not by sight. ⁸We are confident, I say, and would prefer to be away from the body and at home with the Lord. ⁹So we make it our goal to please him, whether we are at home in the body or away from it. ¹⁰For we must all appear before the judgment seat of Christ, that each one may receive what is due him for the things done while in the body, whether good or bad.

The Ministry of Reconciliation

¹¹Since, then, we know what it is to fear the Lord, we try to persuade men. What we are is plain to God, and I hope it is also plain to your conscience. ¹²We are not trying to commend ourselves to you again, but are giving you an opportunity to take pride in us, so that you can answer those who take pride in what is seen rather than in what is in the heart. ¹³If we are out of our mind, it is for the sake of God; if we are in our right mind, it is for you. ¹⁴For Christ's love compels us, because we are convinced that one died for all, and therefore all died. ¹⁵And he died for all, that those who live should no longer live for themselves but for him who died for them and was raised again.

¹⁶So from now on we regard no one from a worldly point of view. Though we once regarded Christ in this way, we do so no longer. ¹⁷Therefore, if anyone is in Christ, he is a new creation; the old has gone, the new has come! ¹⁸All this is from God, who reconciled us to himself through Christ and gave us the ministry of reconciliation: ¹⁹that God was reconciling the world to himself in Christ, not counting men's sins against them. And he has committed to us the message of reconciliation. ²⁰We are therefore Christ's ambassadors, as though God were making his appeal through us. We implore you on Christ's behalf: Be reconciled to God. ²¹God made him who had no sin to be sin*a* for us, so that in him we might become the righteousness of God.

6 As God's fellow workers we urge you not to receive God's grace in vain. ²For he says,

> "In the time of my favor I heard you,
>   and in the day of salvation I helped you."*b*

I tell you, now is the time of God's favor, now is the day of salvation.

Paul's Hardships

³We put no stumbling block in anyone's path, so that our ministry will not be discredited. ⁴Rather, as servants of God we commend ourselves in every way: in great endurance; in troubles, hardships and distresses; ⁵in beatings, imprisonments and riots; in

a21 Or *be a sin offering*   *b2* Isaiah 49:8

Complete this sentence: "Home is where …"

1. How does Paul's confidence in his future relate to 4:16–18? To John 14:1–3? What role does faith play in this? How does Paul's "home" affect his daily living (vv. 6–10)? **2.** What is this "heavenly dwelling" like? **3.** Is Paul motivated more by the desire to be with Christ, or by fear of judgment? Which motivates you?

1. How does God's purpose (v. 5) apply to a current crisis of yours? **2.** How can knowing the location of your ultimate "home" affect your attitude toward aging? How can it encourage you to be more hospitable to others now?

If you were appointed as an ambassador, where would you like to be sent?

1. What is Paul's motive for evangelism in verses 10–11? In verse 14? How do they fit together? How would someone motivated by these values stand in contrast to someone motivated by those mentioned in 2:17 and 5:12? **2.** What does Paul mean by what he says about Christ and our response to him (vv. 15–17; see also Ro 6:5–13)? How does this make you feel about your past life? Your life now? **3.** What does "reconciliation" mean? What story from your life illustrates this? **4.** What does God do through Christ (v. 18)? Through us (v. 20)? For us (vv. 17–18)?

1. What motivation does Paul give to share your faith (see 6:1–2)? What motivates you? What inhibits you? **2.** In light of your experiences of alienation and reconciliation in other relationships, at what stage is your relationship with God: A family feud, a truce or have you made up?

---

1. How does Paul defend the authenticity of his ministry here? How does this differ from the ways those who are challenging him assert their authority (see 3:1; 4:2; 5:12; 11:23–29)? By appealing to these things instead of his supernatural conversion or miracles (Ac 9:3–5; 19:11–12), what is he saying the real test of faith is? **2.** What is Paul asking the Corinthians (and us) to do in verses 11–13 (see 3:2–3; 4:15)?

1. By what standards do you gauge success? Why? How do they compare with verses 4–10? Would Paul be a success by your standards? Would you? **2.** What, from Paul's example, do you want to incorporate into your life? Into your vocational pursuits?

What food are you most likely to spill on yourself? Tell about a "bad spill."

1. What is a yoke? How is *unequal* yoking an apt metaphor in this context? **2.** From verses 16–18, what is necessary if we want to have God as our Father? What does this imply about choosing a spouse? About where we should look for dates and close friends?

1. What does it mean that you are the dwelling place of God? What contaminants can affect your body? Your spirit? Is there something contaminating you now? **2.** How can a believer be a friend and witness to an unbeliever without becoming "yoked"?

1. What does "homecoming" mean to you? **2.** What finally gets your attention: Tough talk? Slammed door? Tears? Letter? Walkout? Give a recent example.

1. Why does Paul want this church to open up to him (vv. 2–4; see 6:11–13)? Hence, do you think Titus' report (v. 7) was entirely positive? Why or why not? **2.** In verse 5, Paul picks up the account of his travels (of which he left off in 2:12–13). How does his account in verses 5–7 illustrate why he began this letter with thanks to God for his comfort (1:3–7)? **3.** What was the result of Paul's previous letter to them (vv. 8–13; see also 2:3–4)? What intentions does Paul clarify here? Practically, how does godly sorrow differ from worldly sorrow? **4.** What tone of voice do you hear in verse 16? In light of his previous hurtful letter, why would he underscore his present joy and confidence? If you were the first to read this, how would you feel?

hard work, sleepless nights and hunger; [6]in purity, understanding, patience and kindness; in the Holy Spirit and in sincere love; [7]in truthful speech and in the power of God; with weapons of righteousness in the right hand and in the left; [8]through glory and dishonor, bad report and good report; genuine, yet regarded as impostors; [9]known, yet regarded as unknown; dying, and yet we live on; beaten, and yet not killed; [10]sorrowful, yet always rejoicing; poor, yet making many rich; having nothing, and yet possessing everything.

[11]We have spoken freely to you, Corinthians, and opened wide our hearts to you. [12]We are not withholding our affection from you, but you are withholding yours from us. [13]As a fair exchange—I speak as to my children—open wide your hearts also.

Do Not Be Yoked With Unbelievers

[14]Do not be yoked together with unbelievers. For what do righteousness and wickedness have in common? Or what fellowship can light have with darkness? [15]What harmony is there between Christ and Belial[a]? What does a believer have in common with an unbeliever? [16]What agreement is there between the temple of God and idols? For we are the temple of the living God. As God has said: "I will live with them and walk among them, and I will be their God, and they will be my people."[b]

[17]"Therefore come out from them
    and be separate,
                            says the Lord.
Touch no unclean thing,
    and I will receive you."[c]
[18]"I will be a Father to you,
    and you will be my sons and daughters,
                    says the Lord Almighty."[d]

7 Since we have these promises, dear friends, let us purify ourselves from everything that contaminates body and spirit, perfecting holiness out of reverence for God.

Paul's Joy

[2]Make room for us in your hearts. We have wronged no one, we have corrupted no one, we have exploited no one. [3]I do not say this to condemn you; I have said before that you have such a place in our hearts that we would live or die with you. [4]I have great confidence in you; I take great pride in you. I am greatly encouraged; in all our troubles my joy knows no bounds.

[5]For when we came into Macedonia, this body of ours had no rest, but we were harassed at every turn—conflicts on the outside, fears within. [6]But God, who comforts the downcast, comforted us by the coming of Titus, [7]and not only by his coming but also by the comfort you had given him. He told us about your longing for me, your deep sorrow, your ardent concern for me, so that my joy was greater than ever.

[8]Even if I caused you sorrow by my letter, I do not regret it. Though I did regret it—I see that my letter hurt you, but only for a little while— [9]yet now I am happy, not because you were made sorry, but because your sorrow led you to repentance. For you became sorrowful as God intended and so were not harmed in any way by us. [10]Godly sorrow brings repentance that leads to salvation and leaves no regret, but worldly sorrow brings death. [11]See what

---

[a]15 Greek *Beliar*, a variant of *Belial*   [b]16 Lev. 26:12; Jer. 32:38; Ezek. 37:27
[c]17 Isaiah 52:11; Ezek. 20:34,41   [d]18 2 Samuel 7:14; 7:8

this godly sorrow has produced in you: what earnestness, what eagerness to clear yourselves, what indignation, what alarm, what longing, what concern, what readiness to see justice done. At every point you have proved yourselves to be innocent in this matter. ¹²So even though I wrote to you, it was not on account of the one who did the wrong or of the injured party, but rather that before God you could see for yourselves how devoted to us you are. ¹³By all this we are encouraged.

In addition to our own encouragement, we were especially delighted to see how happy Titus was, because his spirit has been refreshed by all of you. ¹⁴I had boasted to him about you, and you have not embarrassed me. But just as everything we said to you was true, so our boasting about you to Titus has proved to be true as well. ¹⁵And his affection for you is all the greater when he remembers that you were all obedient, receiving him with fear and trembling. ¹⁶I am glad I can have complete confidence in you.

Generosity Encouraged

8 And now, brothers, we want you to know about the grace that God has given the Macedonian churches. ²Out of the most severe trial, their overflowing joy and their extreme poverty welled up in rich generosity. ³For I testify that they gave as much as they were able, and even beyond their ability. Entirely on their own, ⁴they urgently pleaded with us for the privilege of sharing in this service to the saints. ⁵And they did not do as we expected, but they gave themselves first to the Lord and then to us in keeping with God's will. ⁶So we urged Titus, since he had earlier made a beginning, to bring also to completion this act of grace on your part. ⁷But just as you excel in everything—in faith, in speech, in knowledge, in complete earnestness and in your love for us*a*—see that you also excel in this grace of giving.

⁸I am not commanding you, but I want to test the sincerity of your love by comparing it with the earnestness of others. ⁹For you know the grace of our Lord Jesus Christ, that though he was rich, yet for your sakes he became poor, so that you through his poverty might become rich.

¹⁰And here is my advice about what is best for you in this matter: Last year you were the first not only to give but also to have the desire to do so. ¹¹Now finish the work, so that your eager willingness to do it may be matched by your completion of it, according to your means. ¹²For if the willingness is there, the gift is acceptable according to what one has, not according to what he does not have.

¹³Our desire is not that others might be relieved while you are hard pressed, but that there might be equality. ¹⁴At the present time your plenty will supply what they need, so that in turn their plenty will supply what you need. Then there will be equality, ¹⁵as it is written: "He who gathered much did not have too much, and he who gathered little did not have too little."*b*

Titus Sent to Corinth

¹⁶I thank God, who put into the heart of Titus the same concern I have for you. ¹⁷For Titus not only welcomed our appeal, but he is coming to you with much enthusiasm and on his own initiative. ¹⁸And we are sending along with him the brother who is praised by all the churches for his service to the gospel. ¹⁹What is more, he was chosen by the churches to accompany us as we carry the

1. Have you ever been confronted with a wrong you have done by someone who loves you? How did you feel about that person at the time? 2. When is it more loving to confront someone with their sin than to ignore it? What attitudes are needed to keep loving confrontation from becoming judgmental? How do you see those attitudes in Paul? 3. When did godly sorrow motivate you to make a real change? How do you feel about that change now?

1. With what are you generous? Your money? Time? Talents? Toys? With what are you stingy? 2. What were you doing last year at this time which still needs to be completed?

1. From 1 Corinthians 16:1–4 (written about a year earlier) and Romans 15:25–27 (written either during or shortly after Paul had revisited Corinth), what is this collection all about? 2. What do you learn about the Macedonians from their giving? In light of the struggles in Corinth, why would Paul draw their attention to the Macedonian example? What would this test of generosity reveal? 3. What principles about giving do you observe?

1. If you were to evaluate your zeal for God in light of your checkbook, what grade would you give yourself? 2. What from Jesus' example (v. 9) prompts you to be generous with your money, time and energy? What inhibits you? 3. How can the equality principle (vv. 13–15) help you decide what cause needs your immediate attention? 4. What does this principle say about getting your own needs met?

Whom do you trust with money: (a) Your kids? (b) Bank? (c) Broker? (d) Government? (e) No one but God? (f) What money, I'm broke? Why is that?

---

*a*7 Some manuscripts *in our love for you*   *b*15 Exodus 16:18

offering, which we administer in order to honor the Lord himself and to show our eagerness to help. ²⁰We want to avoid any criticism of the way we administer this liberal gift. ²¹For we are taking pains to do what is right, not only in the eyes of the Lord but also in the eyes of men.

²²In addition, we are sending with them our brother who has often proved to us in many ways that he is zealous, and now even more so because of his great confidence in you. ²³As for Titus, he is my partner and fellow worker among you; as for our brothers, they are representatives of the churches and an honor to Christ. ²⁴Therefore show these men the proof of your love and the reason for our pride in you, so that the churches can see it.

9 There is no need for me to write to you about this service to the saints. ²For I know your eagerness to help, and I have been boasting about it to the Macedonians, telling them that since last year you in Achaia were ready to give; and your enthusiasm has stirred most of them to action. ³But I am sending the brothers in order that our boasting about you in this matter should not prove hollow, but that you may be ready, as I said you would be. ⁴For if any Macedonians come with me and find you unprepared, we— not to say anything about you—would be ashamed of having been so confident. ⁵So I thought it necessary to urge the brothers to visit you in advance and finish the arrangements for the generous gift you had promised. Then it will be ready as a generous gift, not as one grudgingly given.

Sowing Generously

⁶Remember this: Whoever sows sparingly will also reap sparingly, and whoever sows generously will also reap generously. ⁷Each man should give what he has decided in his heart to give, not reluctantly or under compulsion, for God loves a cheerful giver. ⁸And God is able to make all grace abound to you, so that in all things at all times, having all that you need, you will abound in every good work. ⁹As it is written:

"He has scattered abroad his gifts to the poor;
his righteousness endures forever." [a]

¹⁰Now he who supplies seed to the sower and bread for food will also supply and increase your store of seed and will enlarge the harvest of your righteousness. ¹¹You will be made rich in every way so that you can be generous on every occasion, and through us your generosity will result in thanksgiving to God.

¹²This service that you perform is not only supplying the needs of God's people but is also overflowing in many expressions of thanks to God. ¹³Because of the service by which you have proved yourselves, men will praise God for the obedience that accompanies your confession of the gospel of Christ, and for your generosity in sharing with them and with everyone else. ¹⁴And in their prayers for you their hearts will go out to you, because of the surpassing grace God has given you. ¹⁵Thanks be to God for his indescribable gift!

Paul's Defense of His Ministry

10 By the meekness and gentleness of Christ, I appeal to you— I, Paul, who am "timid" when face to face with you, but "bold" when away! ²I beg you that when I come I may not have to be as bold as I expect to be toward some people who think that we

a9 Psalm 112:9

fool, because I would be speaking the truth. But I refrain, so no one will think more of me than is warranted by what I do or say.

[7]To keep me from becoming conceited because of these surpassingly great revelations, there was given me a thorn in my flesh, a messenger of Satan, to torment me. [8]Three times I pleaded with the Lord to take it away from me. [9]But he said to me, "My grace is sufficient for you, for my power is made perfect in weakness." Therefore I will boast all the more gladly about my weaknesses, so that Christ's power may rest on me. [10]That is why, for Christ's sake, I delight in weaknesses, in insults, in hardships, in persecutions, in difficulties. For when I am weak, then I am strong.

Paul's Concern for the Corinthians

[11]I have made a fool of myself, but you drove me to it. I ought to have been commended by you, for I am not in the least inferior to the "super-apostles," even though I am nothing. [12]The things that mark an apostle—signs, wonders and miracles—were done among you with great perseverance. [13]How were you inferior to the other churches, except that I was never a burden to you? Forgive me this wrong!

[14]Now I am ready to visit you for the third time, and I will not be a burden to you, because what I want is not your possessions but you. After all, children should not have to save up for their parents, but parents for their children. [15]So I will very gladly spend for you everything I have and expend myself as well. If I love you more, will you love me less? [16]Be that as it may, I have not been a burden to you. Yet, crafty fellow that I am, I caught you by trickery! [17]Did I exploit you through any of the men I sent you? [18]I urged Titus to go to you and I sent our brother with him. Titus did not exploit you, did he? Did we not act in the same spirit and follow the same course?

[19]Have you been thinking all along that we have been defending ourselves to you? We have been speaking in the sight of God as those in Christ; and everything we do, dear friends, is for your strengthening. [20]For I am afraid that when I come I may not find you as I want you to be, and you may not find me as you want me to be. I fear that there may be quarreling, jealousy, outbursts of anger, factions, slander, gossip, arrogance and disorder. [21]I am afraid that when I come again my God will humble me before you, and I will be grieved over many who have sinned earlier and have not repented of the impurity, sexual sin and debauchery in which they have indulged.

Final Warnings

13 This will be my third visit to you. "Every matter must be established by the testimony of two or three witnesses."[a] [2]I already gave you a warning when I was with you the second time. I now repeat it while absent: On my return I will not spare those who sinned earlier or any of the others, [3]since you are demanding proof that Christ is speaking through me. He is not weak in dealing with you, but is powerful among you. [4]For to be sure, he was crucified in weakness, yet he lives by God's power. Likewise, we are weak in him, yet by God's power we will live with him to serve you.

[5]Examine yourselves to see whether you are in the faith; test yourselves. Do you not realize that Christ Jesus is in you—unless, of course, you fail the test? [6]And I trust that you will discover that

1. How do you react when God appears to be silent in answer to your urgent request? How do you feel about God's promise in verse 9? Why doesn't God simply take the hurt away? 2. How has God worked in and through you during a time of weakness? What will you do to develop trust in God during times of weakness?

What is one way your parents sacrificed for you? How did you feel about that unselfish sacrifice then? Now?

1. What led Paul to write this letter (vv. 11–13)? How have the false "super-apostles" distorted his ministry (see also 2:17; 11:7)? 2. How does Paul distance himself from the superior-sounding leaders (vv. 14–15)? What must he be feeling as he thinks about the Corinthians? 3. What do Paul's rhetorical questions (vv. 17–19) reveal about his intentions versus their perception of him? 4. How would you feel about visiting a ministry you love which is behaving like verses 20–21? How persistent would you be in loving them?

To whom is God leading you to minister? How can you show the spirit of verses 14–15 to them? What will that cost you? How will you prepare for that? How will you keep from being a burden on those to whom God is sending you to minister?

In high school or college, what did you do to prepare yourself for big exams?

1. Acts 18 records Paul's first visit to Corinth, and Acts 20:2–3 alludes to what must have been his third visit. Given that he stayed there three months, what do you think happened as a result of this letter? 2. Paul prefers to come to them in "the gentleness and meekness of Christ" (10:1), and as a loving parent (12:14–15). How will he come, instead, if repentance has not occurred? How does this relate to the ministry of Jesus? 3. While they have been critical of

Paul's "credentials" as an apostle all along, what does he tell them to do in verse 5? Whether or not they approve of him, what does he pray for them in verses 7–9? **4.** What does he hope for as he considers his upcoming visit (vv. 10–11)? **5.** Considering the problems of this church, how would his benediction in verse 14 be appropriate?

♡ **1.** Misunderstanding gentleness and compassion as negative traits was a real problem in Corinth. How is that same problem true in your community? In your church? **2.** If you were searching for a new pastor or new small group leaders, what leadership profile (modeled by Paul) would you look for? How do you fit that profile? **3.** In which area of your spiritual life will you aim for "perfection" (13:9) this week? In which area will you be content with "weakness" (12:9–10)? How can others pray for and encourage you? **4.** As you leave this last study, give a "benediction" to each other, praying specifically for one another's needs.

we have not failed the test. ⁷Now we pray to God that you will not do anything wrong. Not that people will see that we have stood the test but that you will do what is right even though we may seem to have failed. ⁸For we cannot do anything against the truth, but only for the truth. ⁹We are glad whenever we are weak but you are strong; and our prayer is for your perfection. ¹⁰This is why I write these things when I am absent, that when I come I may not have to be harsh in my use of authority—the authority the Lord gave me for building you up, not for tearing you down.

Final Greetings

¹¹Finally, brothers, good-by. Aim for perfection, listen to my appeal, be of one mind, live in peace. And the God of love and peace will be with you.

¹²Greet one another with a holy kiss. ¹³All the saints send their greetings.

¹⁴May the grace of the Lord Jesus Christ, and the love of God, and the fellowship of the Holy Spirit be with you all.

INTRODUCTION to
GALATIANS

Book Study Outline: If you are using Galatians for a study course, here is a 6- or 12-week outline. Use the margin questions for your group agenda:

☕ start meeting / 15 min.

📖 read & discuss Bible / 30 min.

❤ close meeting / 15–45 min.

Refer to the Questions and Answers in front of Bible for more information.

6-week plan	12-week plan	Group Study Passage
1	1	1:1–10/Paul's Passion
	2	1:11–24/Paul's Call
2	3	2:1–10/Paul's Acceptance
	4	2:11–21/Paul's Gospel
3	5	3:1–14/Faith and the Law
	6	3:15–25/Law and Promise
4	7	3:26–4:7/Sonship and Unity
	8	4:8–20/Joy and Zeal
5	9	4:21–31/Hagar and Sarah
	10	5:1–15/Freedom in Christ
6	11	5:16–26/Life by the Spirit
	12	6:1–18/A New Creation

Author: The apostle Paul.

Date: Two possible dates have been proposed depending upon whether Paul is writing to congregations in North or South Galatia. If the first date is correct (between A.D. 48–50) then this is the earliest surviving letter of Paul. The second date, A.D. 51–53, places this work closer to the writing of Romans with which Galatians shares a close thematic connection.

Theme: Justification by faith alone.

Historical Background: Paul founded the churches in Galatia during his first missionary journey (Ac 13–14). After leaving the area, apparently some Jewish Christians arrived. Accusing Paul of omitting crucial parts of the Gospel, they said that the Galatians needed to submit to Jewish law and customs (such as circumcision) in order to be truly Christian (see also Ac 15). Although Paul was willing to accommodate Jewish sensitivities (Ac 16:3), he vehemently opposed this as a requirement. This letter is a ringing declaration that salvation is God's free gift, and a hard-hitting rejection of any hint that it must—or can—somehow be earned.

Characteristics: Paul's passion for Christ and the Gospel are evident in his anger and surprise at the Galatians' acceptance of these false teachers (1:6–9; 3:1; 5:12). Galatians is like a rough-hewn Romans (see the Introduction to Romans). Whereas the argument for justification by faith in that letter is carefully developed and calmly logical, Galatians is an emotionally charged response to a challenge that Paul felt very deeply.

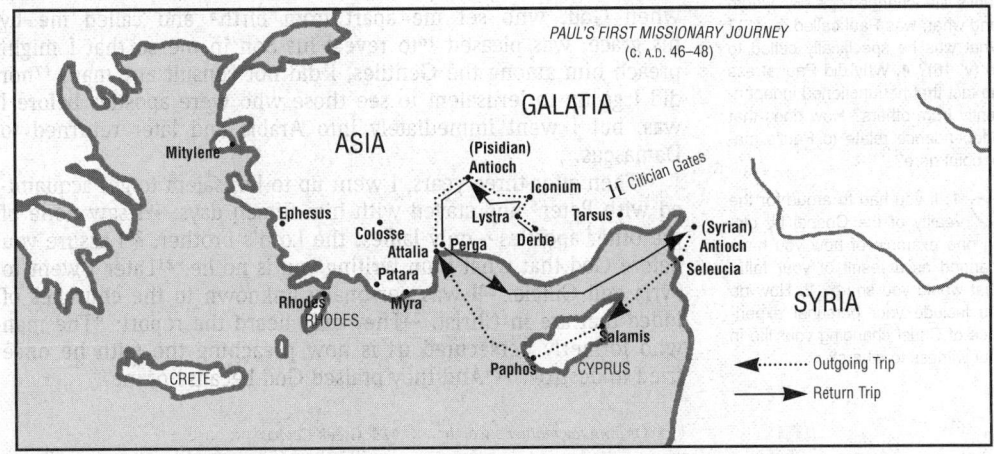

PAUL'S FIRST MISSIONARY JOURNEY
(C. A.D. 46–48)

Galatians

In high school, how loyal were your friends? How loyal were you to them?

1. What, according to Paul's claim in verse 1, gives him the right to be heard? 2. What kind of contrary "gospel" was being preached that led the Galatians astray? (See background in Introduction to Galatians.) How does Paul feel about the Judaizers' message? 3. What does Paul say will happen to anyone who promotes a "gospel" other than that which he preached—the good news of grace (vv. 8–9)? 4. What accusation is Paul refuting in verse 10? How does this reflect Jesus' life? How true would this accusation be of you?

Who has been an "apostle Paul" in your life, contributing to your spiritual growth?

1. At age 18, what career were you preparing for or starting? How does that relate to your life now? 2. How important is it to you to consult others on major decisions you make?

1. In a letter of correction like this, how significant is it that Paul still refers to the Galatians as "brothers" (v. 11)? 2. How was Paul's life changed? By whom (and what) was Paul called (v. 15)? What was he specifically called to do (v. 16)? 4. Why did Paul stress the fact that he functioned independently from others? How does that independence relate to Paul's major point here?

1. If you had to argue for the reality of the Gospel by giving one example of how you have changed as a result of your faith, what would you include and share? 2. How do you include your personal experience of Christ changing your life in your witness to others?

1 Paul, an apostle—sent not from men nor by man, but by Jesus Christ and God the Father, who raised him from the dead— ²and all the brothers with me,

To the churches in Galatia:

³Grace and peace to you from God our Father and the Lord Jesus Christ, ⁴who gave himself for our sins to rescue us from the present evil age, according to the will of our God and Father, ⁵to whom be glory for ever and ever. Amen.

No Other Gospel

⁶I am astonished that you are so quickly deserting the one who called you by the grace of Christ and are turning to a different gospel— ⁷which is really no gospel at all. Evidently some people are throwing you into confusion and are trying to pervert the gospel of Christ. ⁸But even if we or an angel from heaven should preach a gospel other than the one we preached to you, let him be eternally condemned! ⁹As we have already said, so now I say again: If anybody is preaching to you a gospel other than what you accepted, let him be eternally condemned!

¹⁰Am I now trying to win the approval of men, or of God? Or am I trying to please men? If I were still trying to please men, I would not be a servant of Christ.

Paul Called by God

¹¹I want you to know, brothers, that the gospel I preached is not something that man made up. ¹²I did not receive it from any man, nor was I taught it; rather, I received it by revelation from Jesus Christ.

¹³For you have heard of my previous way of life in Judaism, how intensely I persecuted the church of God and tried to destroy it. ¹⁴I was advancing in Judaism beyond many Jews of my own age and was extremely zealous for the traditions of my fathers. ¹⁵But when God, who set me apart from birth*a* and called me by his grace, was pleased ¹⁶to reveal his Son in me so that I might preach him among the Gentiles, I did not consult any man, ¹⁷nor did I go up to Jerusalem to see those who were apostles before I was, but I went immediately into Arabia and later returned to Damascus.

¹⁸Then after three years, I went up to Jerusalem to get acquainted with Peter*b* and stayed with him fifteen days. ¹⁹I saw none of the other apostles—only James, the Lord's brother. ²⁰I assure you before God that what I am writing you is no lie. ²¹Later I went to Syria and Cilicia. ²²I was personally unknown to the churches of Judea that are in Christ. ²³They only heard the report: "The man who formerly persecuted us is now preaching the faith he once tried to destroy." ²⁴And they praised God because of me.

a 15 Or from my mother's womb   b 18 Greek Cephas

Paul Accepted by the Apostles

2 Fourteen years later I went up again to Jerusalem, this time with Barnabas. I took Titus along also. ²I went in response to a revelation and set before them the gospel that I preach among the Gentiles. But I did this privately to those who seemed to be leaders, for fear that I was running or had run my race in vain. ³Yet not even Titus, who was with me, was compelled to be circumcised, even though he was a Greek. ⁴This matter arose┐ because some false brothers had infiltrated our ranks to spy on the freedom we have in Christ Jesus and to make us slaves. ⁵We did not give in to them for a moment, so that the truth of the gospel might remain with you.

⁶As for those who seemed to be important—whatever they were makes no difference to me; God does not judge by external appearance—those men added nothing to my message. ⁷On the contrary, they saw that I had been entrusted with the task of preaching the gospel to the Gentiles,ᵃ just as Peter had been to the Jews.ᵇ ⁸For God, who was at work in the ministry of Peter as an apostle to the Jews, was also at work in my ministry as an apostle to the Gentiles. ⁹James, Peterᶜ and John, those reputed to be pillars, gave me and Barnabas the right hand of fellowship when they recognized the grace given to me. They agreed that we should go to the Gentiles, and they to the Jews. ¹⁰All they asked was that we should continue to remember the poor, the very thing I was eager to do.

Paul Opposes Peter

¹¹When Peter came to Antioch, I opposed him to his face, because he was clearly in the wrong. ¹²Before certain men came from James, he used to eat with the Gentiles. But when they arrived, he began to draw back and separate himself from the Gentiles because he was afraid of those who belonged to the circumcision group. ¹³The other Jews joined him in his hypocrisy, so that by their hypocrisy even Barnabas was led astray.

¹⁴When I saw that they were not acting in line with the truth of the gospel, I said to Peter in front of them all, "You are a Jew, yet you live like a Gentile and not like a Jew. How is it, then, that you force Gentiles to follow Jewish customs?

¹⁵"We who are Jews by birth and not 'Gentile sinners' ¹⁶know that a man is not justified by observing the law, but by faith in Jesus Christ. So we, too, have put our faith in Christ Jesus that we may be justified by faith in Christ and not by observing the law, because by observing the law no one will be justified.

¹⁷"If, while we seek to be justified in Christ, it becomes evident that we ourselves are sinners, does that mean that Christ promotes sin? Absolutely not! ¹⁸If I rebuild what I destroyed, I prove that I am a lawbreaker. ¹⁹For through the law I died to the law so that I might live for God. ²⁰I have been crucified with Christ and I no longer live, but Christ lives in me. The life I live in the body, I live by faith in the Son of God, who loved me and gave himself for me. ²¹I do not set aside the grace of God, for if righteousness could be gained through the law, Christ died for nothing!"ᵈ

Are you the type of person who usually "goes with the crowd" or "does your own thing"?

1. The "false brothers" had caused some believers to become "slaves" (v. 4). To what? 2. What was the outcome of this meeting? What did the leaders add to Paul's message (v. 6)? 3. What did the spiritual "pillars" of the Jerusalem church recognize about Paul (v. 9)? 4. How is grace the critical issue of Galatians, and this passage in particular? 5. How does caring for the poor (v. 10) relate to proclaiming the Gospel of grace?

How do you feel when your beliefs are contrary to popular opinion? On what issue do you need to stand alone? How much was at stake—for Paul, and for you now?

Have you ever "opposed" a boss? What was the outcome?

1. In the past, God had dramatically led Peter to break Jewish custom by fellowshipping and eating with Gentiles (Acts 11:1–18). What causes Peter to reverse course now? 2. How quickly would you stand up and rebuke the leader of the church (v. 14)? What does this incident say about the need for accountability among believers? 3. In the Christian life, what dies and what gets resurrected (vv. 19–20)? How is that made possible? 4. According to verse 21, if you can be in right standing with God through your own efforts—for example, by being a "good person"—what did Christ die for?

1. When are you guilty of double standards? How do you communicate—probably by example—"Do as I say, not as I do"? 2. How would you explain verse 16 to a non-Christian, particularly one with high moral standards? 3. Applying the spiritual concept of verse 20, who is "alive" in your life right now—"I," or "Christ in me"? 4. If you are a self-made person who likes to see everyone pay their own way, how does this Gospel of undeserved grace strike you?

ᵃ7 Greek *uncircumcised*   ᵇ7 Greek *circumcised*; also in verses 8 and 9
ᶜ9 Greek *Cephas*; also in verses 11 and 14   ᵈ21 Some interpreters end the quotation after verse 14.

☕ When you were dating, were you ever dropped for someone else? What did that do to your emotions?

📖 **1.** To what extent was the Galatians' conversion experience related to observing the Law? **2.** Why would anyone revert from a liberating spiritual life of faith to a legalistic spiritual life of works and performance? When have you gone in that direction? What caused it to happen? **3.** Was Abraham considered righteous by God through his faith or through his works (vv. 6–9)? **4.** Who are the true children of Abraham? Who is eligible to be one? **5.** How does Jesus solve the problem that no one can earn their right standing with God (vv. 10–14)?

♡ What "additions" to faith might outsiders sense in your Christian circles regarding what they should do to be approved? How can you help break down these barriers?

☕ When you think of babysitters you had growing up, who comes to mind? How did you feel about that person?

📖 **1.** In what way is a human covenant—a will—like God's covenant-promise with Abraham and his seed (vv. 15–16)? **2.** Who is the Seed through whom the promise to Abraham will be fulfilled? **3.** Since the Law was not to take the place of the promise, what was its purpose? Was it temporary or permanent? **4.** Can the Law give "life" (v. 21)? How (v. 22)? **5.** How is attempting to be right with God through keeping the Law like being in prison (v. 23)? Like having a babysitter (vv. 24–25)?

♡ **1.** How would you share this passage with someone who thinks keeping the Ten Commandments or Golden Rule is enough to be right with God? Or to someone who was brought up believing that keeping rules wins approval? **2.** How has, and is, your faith liberating you from spiritual bondage?

Faith or Observance of the Law

3 You foolish Galatians! Who has bewitched you? Before your very eyes Jesus Christ was clearly portrayed as crucified. ²I would like to learn just one thing from you: Did you receive the Spirit by observing the law, or by believing what you heard? ³Are you so foolish? After beginning with the Spirit, are you now trying to attain your goal by human effort? ⁴Have you suffered so much for nothing—if it really was for nothing? ⁵Does God give you his Spirit and work miracles among you because you observe the law, or because you believe what you heard?

⁶Consider Abraham: "He believed God, and it was credited to him as righteousness."ᵃ ⁷Understand, then, that those who believe are children of Abraham. ⁸The Scripture foresaw that God would justify the Gentiles by faith, and announced the gospel in advance to Abraham: "All nations will be blessed through you."ᵇ ⁹So those who have faith are blessed along with Abraham, the man of faith.

¹⁰All who rely on observing the law are under a curse, for it is written: "Cursed is everyone who does not continue to do everything written in the Book of the Law."ᶜ ¹¹Clearly no one is justified before God by the law, because, "The righteous will live by faith."ᵈ ¹²The law is not based on faith; on the contrary, "The man who does these things will live by them."ᵉ ¹³Christ redeemed us from the curse of the law by becoming a curse for us, for it is written: "Cursed is everyone who is hung on a tree."ᶠ ¹⁴He redeemed us in order that the blessing given to Abraham might come to the Gentiles through Christ Jesus, so that by faith we might receive the promise of the Spirit.

The Law and the Promise

¹⁵Brothers, let me take an example from everyday life. Just as no one can set aside or add to a human covenant that has been duly established, so it is in this case. ¹⁶The promises were spoken to Abraham and to his seed. The Scripture does not say "and to seeds," meaning many people, but "and to your seed,"ᵍ meaning one person, who is Christ. ¹⁷What I mean is this: The law, introduced 430 years later, does not set aside the covenant previously established by God and thus do away with the promise. ¹⁸For if the inheritance depends on the law, then it no longer depends on a promise; but God in his grace gave it to Abraham through a promise.

¹⁹What, then, was the purpose of the law? It was added because of transgressions until the Seed to whom the promise referred had come. The law was put into effect through angels by a mediator. ²⁰A mediator, however, does not represent just one party; but God is one.

²¹Is the law, therefore, opposed to the promises of God? Absolutely not! For if a law had been given that could impart life, then righteousness would certainly have come by the law. ²²But the Scripture declares that the whole world is a prisoner of sin, so that what was promised, being given through faith in Jesus Christ, might be given to those who believe.

²³Before this faith came, we were held prisoners by the law, locked up until faith should be revealed. ²⁴So the law was put in charge to lead us to Christʰ that we might be justified by faith.

ᵃ6 Gen. 15:6   ᵇ8 Gen. 12:3; 18:18; 22:18   ᶜ10 Deut. 27:26   ᵈ11 Hab. 2:4   ᵉ12 Lev. 18:5   ᶠ13 Deut. 21:23   ᵍ16 Gen. 12:7; 13:15; 24:7   ʰ24 Or charge until Christ came

25Now that faith has come, we are no longer under the supervision of the law.

Sons of God

26You are all sons of God through faith in Christ Jesus, 27for all of you who were baptized into Christ have clothed yourselves with Christ. 28There is neither Jew nor Greek, slave nor free, male nor female, for you are all one in Christ Jesus. 29If you belong to Christ, then you are Abraham's seed, and heirs according to the promise.

4 What I am saying is that as long as the heir is a child, he is no different from a slave, although he owns the whole estate. 2He is subject to guardians and trustees until the time set by his father. 3So also, when we were children, we were in slavery under the basic principles of the world. 4But when the time had fully come, God sent his Son, born of a woman, born under law, 5to redeem those under law, that we might receive the full rights of sons. 6Because you are sons, God sent the Spirit of his Son into our hearts, the Spirit who calls out, "Abba,a Father." 7So you are no longer a slave, but a son; and since you are a son, God has made you also an heir.

Paul's Concern for the Galatians

8Formerly, when you did not know God, you were slaves to those who by nature are not gods. 9But now that you know God— or rather are known by God—how is it that you are turning back to those weak and miserable principles? Do you wish to be enslaved by them all over again? 10You are observing special days and months and seasons and years! 11I fear for you, that somehow I have wasted my efforts on you.

12I plead with you, brothers, become like me, for I became like you. You have done me no wrong. 13As you know, it was because of an illness that I first preached the gospel to you. 14Even though my illness was a trial to you, you did not treat me with contempt or scorn. Instead, you welcomed me as if I were an angel of God, as if I were Christ Jesus himself. 15What has happened to all your joy? I can testify that, if you could have done so, you would have torn out your eyes and given them to me. 16Have I now become your enemy by telling you the truth?

17Those people are zealous to win you over, but for no good. What they want is to alienate you ⌊from us⌋, so that you may be zealous for them. 18It is fine to be zealous, provided the purpose is good, and to be so always and not just when I am with you. 19My dear children, for whom I am again in the pains of childbirth until Christ is formed in you, 20how I wish I could be with you now and change my tone, because I am perplexed about you!

Hagar and Sarah

21Tell me, you who want to be under the law, are you not aware of what the law says? 22For it is written that Abraham had two sons, one by the slave woman and the other by the free woman. 23His son by the slave woman was born in the ordinary way; but his son by the free woman was born as the result of a promise.

24These things may be taken figuratively, for the women represent two covenants. One covenant is from Mount Sinai and bears children who are to be slaves: This is Hagar. 25Now Hagar stands for Mount Sinai in Arabia and corresponds to the present city of Jerusalem, because she is in slavery with her children. 26But the

a6 Aramaic for Father

How affectionate was, or is, your relationship with your parents?

1. What effect does being "in Christ" have on relationships among believers (3:28)? 2. How is being under the Law like being an heir who is still a minor (4:1–3)? How has Jesus changed all that?

1. What are some social and cultural barriers in our time? How can you increase the sense of oneness in Christ in your "world"? 2. How affectionate is your relationship with God?

How much joy did you have in the beginning phase of your Christian life?

1. Prior to their conversion, the Galatians worshiped pagan gods. How are they now doing the same with Jewish observances? 2. What is the difference between celebrating religious holidays (Christmas, Easter) and what the Galatians were doing? 3. Overall, was Paul more concerned for himself or the Galatians?

1. How has your relationship with God changed from being one based on zealous love and trust to one based on performance and keeping the rules? 2. Have you slipped back into any bad habits or old ways, from which Christ once delivered you? What can you do about it?

What story do (or did) your parents tell about your birth?

1. What do you remember about the story in Genesis of Hagar and Sarah and their sons— Ishmael and Isaac (Ge 16,17,21)? What was extraordinary about Isaac's birth? 2. Normally, the Jews would regard Sarah as their spiritual mother and Hagar as the mother of the Gentiles. Why does Paul turn the tables and indicate that the Jews are actually the ones in slav-

ery with Hagar (v. 25)? **3.** How does verse 30 give a stern warning to the Judaizers?

Are you living like a "child of the free woman"—liberated from the bondage of trying to win God's approval? How can you live out your "freedom" in Christ, and still please him with your sacrificial obedience?

How do you feel and react when others cut in on you while driving, shopping, speaking, waiting in line, etc.?

1. What does Paul mean by a "yoke of slavery" (v. 1)? **2.** Is circumcision wrong in and of itself, or only if it is a symbol of the "yoke of slavery"? **3.** Since our own efforts and achievements aren't the way to God, what is (vv. 5–6)? **4.** How is Paul's call to serve one another in love (vv. 13–15) reconcilable with his own attitude toward the Judaizers (especially in v. 12)? How good is Paul at demonstrating "tough love"?

1. How have you seen Christian freedom abused? How do verses 6 and 13 address those who think their freedom in Christ allows them to do anything they want? How do they challenge you? **2.** In the past, who or what has cut in and side-tracked you from a child-like faith "expressing itself through love"?

On a scale of 0 to 10, how many "wild oats" did you sow in your youth?

1. Paul has warned the Galatians about being enslaved to legalism. What does he warn them about being enslaved to in this passage? **2.** What two things are in conflict (v. 17)? **3.** If we were made alive by the Spirit, why do we still struggle with sin? How are we "led by" the Spirit? **4.** Is Paul condemning everyone who sins, or those whose sin is part of their lifestyle?

Jerusalem that is above is free, and she is our mother. ²⁷For it is written:

> "Be glad, O barren woman,
>   who bears no children;
> break forth and cry aloud,
>   you who have no labor pains;
> because more are the children of the desolate
>   woman
>   than of her who has a husband." ᵃ

²⁸Now you, brothers, like Isaac, are children of promise. ²⁹At that time the son born in the ordinary way persecuted the son born by the power of the Spirit. It is the same now. ³⁰But what does the Scripture say? "Get rid of the slave woman and her son, for the slave woman's son will never share in the inheritance with the free woman's son." ᵇ ³¹Therefore, brothers, we are not children of the slave woman, but of the free woman.

Freedom in Christ

5 It is for freedom that Christ has set us free. Stand firm, then, and do not let yourselves be burdened again by a yoke of slavery.

²Mark my words! I, Paul, tell you that if you let yourselves be circumcised, Christ will be of no value to you at all. ³Again I declare to every man who lets himself be circumcised that he is obligated to obey the whole law. ⁴You who are trying to be justified by law have been alienated from Christ; you have fallen away from grace. ⁵But by faith we eagerly await through the Spirit the righteousness for which we hope. ⁶For in Christ Jesus neither circumcision nor uncircumcision has any value. The only thing that counts is faith expressing itself through love.

⁷You were running a good race. Who cut in on you and kept you from obeying the truth? ⁸That kind of persuasion does not come from the one who calls you. ⁹"A little yeast works through the whole batch of dough." ¹⁰I am confident in the Lord that you will take no other view. The one who is throwing you into confusion will pay the penalty, whoever he may be. ¹¹Brothers, if I am still preaching circumcision, why am I still being persecuted? In that case the offense of the cross has been abolished. ¹²As for those agitators, I wish they would go the whole way and emasculate themselves!

¹³You, my brothers, were called to be free. But do not use your freedom to indulge the sinful nature ᶜ; rather, serve one another in love. ¹⁴The entire law is summed up in a single command: "Love your neighbor as yourself." ᵈ ¹⁵If you keep on biting and devouring each other, watch out or you will be destroyed by each other.

Life by the Spirit

¹⁶So I say, live by the Spirit, and you will not gratify the desires of the sinful nature. ¹⁷For the sinful nature desires what is contrary to the Spirit, and the Spirit what is contrary to the sinful nature. They are in conflict with each other, so that you do not do what you want. ¹⁸But if you are led by the Spirit, you are not under law.

¹⁹The acts of the sinful nature are obvious: sexual immorality, impurity and debauchery; ²⁰idolatry and witchcraft; hatred, discord, jealousy, fits of rage, selfish ambition, dissensions, factions ²¹and envy; drunkenness, orgies, and the like. I warn you, as I did

ᵃ27 Isaiah 54:1   ᵇ30 Gen. 21:10   ᶜ13 Or *the flesh*; also in verses 16, 17, 19 and 24   ᵈ14 Lev. 19:18

before, that those who live like this will not inherit the kingdom of God. **22**But the fruit of the Spirit is love, joy, peace, patience, kindness, goodness, faithfulness, **23**gentleness and self-control. Against such things there is no law. **24**Those who belong to Christ Jesus have crucified the sinful nature with its passions and desires. **25**Since we live by the Spirit, let us keep in step with the Spirit. **26**Let us not become conceited, provoking and envying each other.

Doing Good to All

6 Brothers, if someone is caught in a sin, you who are spiritual should restore him gently. But watch yourself, or you also may be tempted. **2**Carry each other's burdens, and in this way you will fulfill the law of Christ. **3**If anyone thinks he is something when he is nothing, he deceives himself. **4**Each one should test his own actions. Then he can take pride in himself, without comparing himself to somebody else, **5**for each one should carry his own load.

6Anyone who receives instruction in the word must share all good things with his instructor.

7Do not be deceived: God cannot be mocked. A man reaps what he sows. **8**The one who sows to please his sinful nature, from that nature*a* will reap destruction; the one who sows to please the Spirit, from the Spirit will reap eternal life. **9**Let us not become weary in doing good, for at the proper time we will reap a harvest if we do not give up. **10**Therefore, as we have opportunity, let us do good to all people, especially to those who belong to the family of believers.

Not Circumcision but a New Creation

11See what large letters I use as I write to you with my own hand!

12Those who want to make a good impression outwardly are trying to compel you to be circumcised. The only reason they do this is to avoid being persecuted for the cross of Christ. **13**Not even those who are circumcised obey the law, yet they want you to be circumcised that they may boast about your flesh. **14**May I never boast except in the cross of our Lord Jesus Christ, through which*b* the world has been crucified to me, and I to the world. **15**Neither circumcision nor uncircumcision means anything; what counts is a new creation. **16**Peace and mercy to all who follow this rule, even to the Israel of God.

17Finally, let no one cause me trouble, for I bear on my body the marks of Jesus.

18The grace of our Lord Jesus Christ be with your spirit, brothers. Amen.

1. Is the crucifixion of the sinful nature done *to* or *by* the Christian? **2.** What sinful acts are dead and buried in your life? Alive and well? **3.** Which spiritual fruit is blossoming in your life? Which are still in the bud?

What kind of garden have you tended? What did you enjoy about it? What did you dread?

1. How do verses 1–2 illustrate ways of helping someone to "keep in step with the Spirit" (5:25)? What is the "law of Christ" (see 5:14)? **2.** How can you restore a brother caught in sin, and avoid feeling superior to him or being victimized by it yourself? **3.** How does verse 5 relate to verse 2? Are they contradictory? (The word "load" in verse 5 does not mean a crushing burden, but rather a small, individual pack.) What sort of burdens do your friends or family carry? How do you (or could you) help them with these burdens? **4.** What is the main point of Paul's teaching on the Spirit-filled life (vv. 7–10)? Where in your life do you need to sow to please the Spirit instead of your sinful nature? **5.** How does Paul sum up the motives of the false teachers (vv. 12–13)? His own motives (v. 14)? **6.** Is your concern for creating a good outward impression greater or lesser than it used to be? Why? **7.** Why does Paul call these Gentile Galatians the "Israel of God" (v. 16; see 3:6–9)? How is that a final rebuke to those who would compel these believers to obey Jewish rules? **8.** What does Paul mean by bearing on his body the marks of Jesus (v. 17; see 2Co 11:23–30)? Why would Paul's willingness to suffer be a further rebuke to the false teachers? Do you bear any "marks of Jesus"?

1. As you reflect on what you have sown this year, what harvest are you expecting: Weeds? A bumper crop? Spindly plants? Why? **2.** In what ways do people tamper with the Gospel to make it less offensive to others? Have you been tempted to do so? **3.** In what way has God greatly inspired or convicted you through your study of Galatians? **4.** How has your group contributed to what God has done in your life through this study?

*a*8 Or *his flesh, from the flesh*   *b*14 Or *whom*

INTRODUCTION to
EPHESIANS

Book Study Outline: If you are using Ephesians for a study course, here is a 6- or 11-week outline. Use the margin questions for your group agenda:

start meeting / 15 min.

read & discuss Bible / 30 min.

close meeting / 15–45 min.

Refer to the Questions and Answers in front of Bible for more information.

6-week plan	11-week plan	Group Study Passage
1	1	1:1–14/To God Be the Glory!
	2	1:15–23/Fullness of Christ
2	3	2:1–10/Raised Up With Christ
	4	2:11–22/End of Hostility
3	5	3:1–13/Mystery of Grace
	6	3:14–21/Power to Know Love
4	7	4:1–16/Working Out Our Unity
	8	4:17–32/Children of Light
5	9	5:1–21/Imitators of God
	10	5:22–6:9/Relationships in Christ
6	11	6:10–24/Armor of God

Author: The apostle Paul.

Date: Probably in the early A.D. 60s.

Theme: God's new society.

Historical Background: Ephesians, Colossians and Philemon were all written from prison at about the same time. Because over half of the verses in this letter are found in Colossians, it seems that Paul first developed these themes in that letter while dealing with a local problem, and then expanded them into a more universal setting for this one. It is unclear which imprisonment produced these letters (see 2Co 11:23), but most likely Paul was at Rome (Ac 28).

Characteristics: In this letter, Paul takes us to the mountaintops of Christian truth and invites us to look at the breathtaking view! When we do so, we see that it is Jesus Christ who dominates that view. We see him breaking down the wall between God and humanity. We see him subduing the hostile cosmic powers. We see him creating the church, a new social order of love and unity that transcends the racial, ethnic and social distinctions between people. In conveying this vision, Paul reaches into eternity past and eternity future to demonstrate how God, out of his love and glory, calls people to be reconciled to himself and to one another through the cross of Christ. The cross provides forgiveness of sins, a new life and a new people. Between Paul's greeting (1:1–2) and salutation (6:21–24), the letter divides easily into two parts. Part one (ch. 1–3) focuses on *doctrine*, specifically, the new life and new society God has created through Jesus. Part two (ch. 4–6) focuses on *ethics*, specifically, the new standards and new relationships expected of believers.

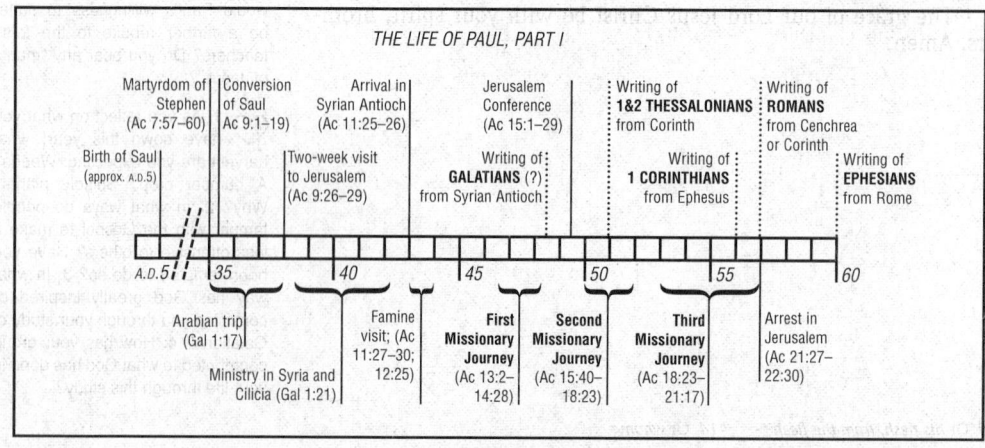

THE LIFE OF PAUL, PART I

Martyrdom of Stephen (Ac 7:57–60)	Conversion of Saul (Ac 9:1–19)	Arrival in Syrian Antioch (Ac 11:25–26)	Jerusalem Conference (Ac 15:1–29)	Writing of **1&2 THESSALONIANS** from Corinth	Writing of **ROMANS** from Cenchrea or Corinth
Birth of Saul (approx. A.D.5)		Two-week visit to Jerusalem (Ac 9:26–29)	Writing of **GALATIANS (?)** from Syrian Antioch	Writing of **1 CORINTHIANS** from Ephesus	Writing of **EPHESIANS** from Rome

A.D.5 35 40 45 50 55 60

Arabian trip (Gal 1:17)	Famine visit; (Ac 11:27–30; 12:25)	First Missionary Journey (Ac 13:2–14:28)	Second Missionary Journey (Ac 15:40–18:23)	Third Missionary Journey (Ac 18:23–21:17)	Arrest in Jerusalem (Ac 21:27–22:30)
Ministry in Syria and Cilicia (Gal 1:21)					

Ephesians

1 Paul, an apostle of Christ Jesus by the will of God,

To the saints in Ephesus,[a] the faithful[b] in Christ Jesus:

[2]Grace and peace to you from God our Father and the Lord Jesus Christ.

Spiritual Blessings in Christ

[3]Praise be to the God and Father of our Lord Jesus Christ, who has blessed us in the heavenly realms with every spiritual blessing in Christ. [4]For he chose us in him before the creation of the world to be holy and blameless in his sight. In love [5]he[c] predestined us to be adopted as his sons through Jesus Christ, in accordance with his pleasure and will— [6]to the praise of his glorious grace, which he has freely given us in the One he loves. [7]In him we have redemption through his blood, the forgiveness of sins, in accordance with the riches of God's grace [8]that he lavished on us with all wisdom and understanding. [9]And he[d] made known to us the mystery of his will according to his good pleasure, which he purposed in Christ, [10]to be put into effect when the times will have reached their fulfillment—to bring all things in heaven and on earth together under one head, even Christ.

[11]In him we were also chosen,[e] having been predestined according to the plan of him who works out everything in conformity with the purpose of his will, [12]in order that we, who were the first to hope in Christ, might be for the praise of his glory. [13]And you also were included in Christ when you heard the word of truth, the gospel of your salvation. Having believed, you were marked in him with a seal, the promised Holy Spirit, [14]who is a deposit guaranteeing our inheritance until the redemption of those who are God's possession—to the praise of his glory.

Thanksgiving and Prayer

[15]For this reason, ever since I heard about your faith in the Lord Jesus and your love for all the saints, [16]I have not stopped giving thanks for you, remembering you in my prayers. [17]I keep asking that the God of our Lord Jesus Christ, the glorious Father, may give you the Spirit[f] of wisdom and revelation, so that you may know him better. [18]I pray also that the eyes of your heart may be enlightened in order that you may know the hope to which he has called you, the riches of his glorious inheritance in the saints, [19]and his incomparably great power for us who believe. That power is like the working of his mighty strength, [20]which he exerted in Christ when he raised him from the dead and seated him at his right hand in the heavenly realms, [21]far above all rule and authority, power and dominion, and every title that can be given, not only in the present age but also in the one to come. [22]And God placed all things under his feet and appointed him to be head over everything for the church, [23]which is his body, the fullness of him who fills everything in every way.

Whom do you know who has been adopted?

1. The large capital city of Ephesus was a center for trade. It featured the renowned Temple of Artemis. In this letter, what does Paul write about that is truly wonderful? **2.** In your words, describe the "blessings in Christ" (vv. 3–9). **3.** What are seven things that God has done for us, starting in verse 4? **4.** How does being chosen by God (v. 4) relate to our believing and salvation (v. 13)?

1. When did you come to appreciate all that God has done for you in Jesus Christ? **2.** How do you know if you are "chosen"? How does knowing you are adopted change your view of yourself and God? **3.** How do you feel about the quality of love of the One who has chosen you? How does this affect your love for others?

What do you remember from your childhood about Thanksgiving Day? Who keeps your family traditions alive now?

1. If the Christians in Ephesus were millionaires in Christ spiritually, what was wrong with them? How were they living? **2.** In your own words, what does Paul pray for the Ephesians? **3.** When a Christian plugs into God's energy source, what kind of power can be expected? **4.** How does Jesus give hope and power?

1. How would you change if your group prayed verses 17–19 every week for each other? Try it and see. **2.** How much of God's energy are you using at the moment? God put into your bank account all of his resources. What is keeping you from transferring them into your checking account?

What special gift have you received recently?

1. Paul divides your life into two periods. What are they? Who owned you in the first period? What was the result? 2. For what purpose did God take over your life? 3. What is the difference between cosmetic surgery (to remove wrinkles) and the surgery God performs? 4. Is a Christian ever completely rid of the cravings of the past—lust, selfishness, pride, etc.?

What in your life is due only to God's presence and goodness?

From where did your ancestors emigrate? What did their new citizenship mean to them?

1. What is the problem in this church? Who are the "in" people? Who are the "out" people? 2. How did God resolve this problem (v. 13)? 3. What is the difference between Hitler's "superior race" and Paul's idea of "one body"? How has your life changed through this "one body"(v. 16)? 4. How do you think the practicing Jews felt when these Gentiles started coming to their church, but didn't want to adopt the Jewish custom of circumcision?

1. If Paul wrote a letter to your church today, what stand would he take on issues that threaten to tear the church apart? 2. What relationship in your life still has walls to be knocked down?

Who is your favorite mystery writer? What is a favorite mystery movie?

1. What exactly is the mystery Paul is talking about? What does Paul have to do with this mystery? Where does the church come in? 2. When did this mystery take on meaning in your life? 3. Is Paul being hard on himself in verse 8, or just appropriately humble? Why? 4. How would you compare Paul's passion to share this mystery to your own passion?

Made Alive in Christ

2 As for you, you were dead in your transgressions and sins, [2]in which you used to live when you followed the ways of this world and of the ruler of the kingdom of the air, the spirit who is now at work in those who are disobedient. [3]All of us also lived among them at one time, gratifying the cravings of our sinful nature[a] and following its desires and thoughts. Like the rest, we were by nature objects of wrath. [4]But because of his great love for us, God, who is rich in mercy, [5]made us alive with Christ even when we were dead in transgressions—it is by grace you have been saved. [6]And God raised us up with Christ and seated us with him in the heavenly realms in Christ Jesus, [7]in order that in the coming ages he might show the incomparable riches of his grace, expressed in his kindness to us in Christ Jesus. [8]For it is by grace you have been saved, through faith—and this not from yourselves, it is the gift of God— [9]not by works, so that no one can boast. [10]For we are God's workmanship, created in Christ Jesus to do good works, which God prepared in advance for us to do.

One in Christ

[11]Therefore, remember that formerly you who are Gentiles by birth and called "uncircumcised" by those who call themselves "the circumcision" (that done in the body by the hands of men)— [12]remember that at that time you were separate from Christ, excluded from citizenship in Israel and foreigners to the covenants of the promise, without hope and without God in the world. [13]But now in Christ Jesus you who once were far away have been brought near through the blood of Christ.

[14]For he himself is our peace, who has made the two one and has destroyed the barrier, the dividing wall of hostility, [15]by abolishing in his flesh the law with its commandments and regulations. His purpose was to create in himself one new man out of the two, thus making peace, [16]and in this one body to reconcile both of them to God through the cross, by which he put to death their hostility. [17]He came and preached peace to you who were far away and peace to those who were near. [18]For through him we both have access to the Father by one Spirit.

[19]Consequently, you are no longer foreigners and aliens, but fellow citizens with God's people and members of God's household, [20]built on the foundation of the apostles and prophets, with Christ Jesus himself as the chief cornerstone. [21]In him the whole building is joined together and rises to become a holy temple in the Lord. [22]And in him you too are being built together to become a dwelling in which God lives by his Spirit.

Paul the Preacher to the Gentiles

3 For this reason I, Paul, the prisoner of Christ Jesus for the sake of you Gentiles—
[2]Surely you have heard about the administration of God's grace that was given to me for you, [3]that is, the mystery made known to me by revelation, as I have already written briefly. [4]In reading this, then, you will be able to understand my insight into the mystery of Christ, [5]which was not made known to men in other generations as it has now been revealed by the Spirit to God's holy apostles and prophets. [6]This mystery is that through the gospel the Gentiles are heirs together with Israel, members together of one body, and sharers together in the promise in Christ Jesus.

a3 Or our flesh

7I became a servant of this gospel by the gift of God's grace given me through the working of his power. **8**Although I am less than the least of all God's people, this grace was given me: to preach to the Gentiles the unsearchable riches of Christ, **9**and to make plain to everyone the administration of this mystery, which for ages past was kept hidden in God, who created all things. **10**His intent was that now, through the church, the manifold wisdom of God should be made known to the rulers and authorities in the heavenly realms, **11**according to his eternal purpose which he accomplished in Christ Jesus our Lord. **12**In him and through faith in him we may approach God with freedom and confidence. **13**I ask you, therefore, not to be discouraged because of my sufferings for you, which are your glory.

A Prayer for the Ephesians

14For this reason I kneel before the Father, **15**from whom his whole family*a* in heaven and on earth derives its name. **16**I pray that out of his glorious riches he may strengthen you with power through his Spirit in your inner being, **17**so that Christ may dwell in your hearts through faith. And I pray that you, being rooted and established in love, **18**may have power, together with all the saints, to grasp how wide and long and high and deep is the love of Christ, **19**and to know this love that surpasses knowledge—that you may be filled to the measure of all the fullness of God.

20Now to him who is able to do immeasurably more than all we ask or imagine, according to his power that is at work within us, **21**to him be glory in the church and in Christ Jesus throughout all generations, for ever and ever! Amen.

Unity in the Body of Christ

4 As a prisoner for the Lord, then, I urge you to live a life worthy of the calling you have received. **2**Be completely humble and gentle; be patient, bearing with one another in love. **3**Make every effort to keep the unity of the Spirit through the bond of peace. **4**There is one body and one Spirit— just as you were called to one hope when you were called— **5**one Lord, one faith, one baptism; **6**one God and Father of all, who is over all and through all and in all.

7But to each one of us grace has been given as Christ apportioned it. **8**This is why it*b* says:

> "When he ascended on high,
> he led captives in his train
> and gave gifts to men."*c*

9(What does "he ascended" mean except that he also descended to the lower, earthly regions*d*? **10**He who descended is the very one who ascended higher than all the heavens, in order to fill the whole universe.) **11**It was he who gave some to be apostles, some to be prophets, some to be evangelists, and some to be pastors and teachers, **12**to prepare God's people for works of service, so that the body of Christ may be built up **13**until we all reach unity in the faith and in the knowledge of the Son of God and become mature, attaining to the whole measure of the fullness of Christ.

14Then we will no longer be infants, tossed back and forth by the waves, and blown here and there by every wind of teaching and by the cunning and craftiness of men in their deceitful scheming.

---

5. How would you explain the way one can know God (2:18; 3:12)?

1. If Paul lived in your community, who in particular would he go after for Christ? 2. Where does the unifying Gospel (v. 6) challenge you: e.g. issues of racism? Sexism? Missions? Concern for the poor and elderly? 3. Where is God calling you to be an ambassador for him? Why has he chosen you?

---

1. What is Paul asking God to do? 2. In this passage, who is the lover? Who is being loved? 3. When have you felt overwhelmed by the love of God?

1. If a person knew only rejection and pain in their relationships, how can this person come to understand the love of God in a personal way? 2. What does the promise in verse 20 mean? How have you seen it to be true?

What is your favorite team sport?

1. Would you say this church has more "servants" or more "masters"? What's wrong? From some of the things that Paul says, what are they doing? Not doing? 2. How do the qualities in verses 2 and 3 promote unity? How does viewing God as our Father add to our unity? 3. What does Paul recommend in verse 11? How would he go about building a successful management team? What would be the goal? 4. If Paul were a management consultant appraising the productivity in the church today, what would he say? How would he go about changing things?

1. Are you living up to the "calling you have received" (v. 1)? In your work? Your home? Your relationships? Why or why not? 2. Of the four jobs he describes for a management team, which job would you choose based on your understanding of your gifts: apostle (pioneer and church planter), prophet (motivator and encourager), evangelist (soul winner) or pastor/teacher (trainer and coach)? How can you develop this

---

a15 Or *whom all fatherhood*   *b8* Or *God*   *c8* Psalm 68:18   *d9* Or *the depths of the earth*

¹⁵Instead, speaking the truth in love, we will in all things grow up into him who is the Head, that is, Christ. ¹⁶From him the whole body, joined and held together by every supporting ligament, grows and builds itself up in love, as each part does its work.

Living as Children of Light

¹⁷So I tell you this, and insist on it in the Lord, that you must no longer live as the Gentiles do, in the futility of their thinking. ¹⁸They are darkened in their understanding and separated from the life of God because of the ignorance that is in them due to the hardening of their hearts. ¹⁹Having lost all sensitivity, they have given themselves over to sensuality so as to indulge in every kind of impurity, with a continual lust for more.

²⁰You, however, did not come to know Christ that way. ²¹Surely you heard of him and were taught in him in accordance with the truth that is in Jesus. ²²You were taught, with regard to your former way of life, to put off your old self, which is being corrupted by its deceitful desires; ²³to be made new in the attitude of your minds; ²⁴and to put on the new self, created to be like God in true righteousness and holiness.

²⁵Therefore each of you must put off falsehood and speak truthfully to his neighbor, for we are all members of one body. ²⁶"In your anger do not sin"ᵃ: Do not let the sun go down while you are still angry, ²⁷and do not give the devil a foothold. ²⁸He who has been stealing must steal no longer, but must work, doing something useful with his own hands, that he may have something to share with those in need.

²⁹Do not let any unwholesome talk come out of your mouths, but only what is helpful for building others up according to their needs, that it may benefit those who listen. ³⁰And do not grieve the Holy Spirit of God, with whom you were sealed for the day of redemption. ³¹Get rid of all bitterness, rage and anger, brawling and slander, along with every form of malice. ³²Be kind and compassionate to one another, forgiving each other, just as in Christ God forgave you.

5 Be imitators of God, therefore, as dearly loved children ²and live a life of love, just as Christ loved us and gave himself up for us as a fragrant offering and sacrifice to God.

³But among you there must not be even a hint of sexual immorality, or of any kind of impurity, or of greed, because these are improper for God's holy people. ⁴Nor should there be obscenity, foolish talk or coarse joking, which are out of place, but rather thanksgiving. ⁵For of this you can be sure: No immoral, impure or greedy person—such a man is an idolater—has any inheritance in the kingdom of Christ and of God.ᵇ ⁶Let no one deceive you with empty words, for because of such things God's wrath comes on those who are disobedient. ⁷Therefore do not be partners with them.

⁸For you were once darkness, but now you are light in the Lord. Live as children of light ⁹(for the fruit of the light consists in all goodness, righteousness and truth) ¹⁰and find out what pleases the Lord. ¹¹Have nothing to do with the fruitless deeds of darkness, but rather expose them. ¹²For it is shameful even to mention what the disobedient do in secret. ¹³But everything exposed by the light becomes visible, ¹⁴for it is light that makes everything visible. This is why it is said:

ᵃ26 Psalm 4:4   ᵇ5 Or *kingdom of the Christ and God*

"Wake up, O sleeper,
    rise from the dead,
and Christ will shine on you."

15Be very careful, then, how you live—not as unwise but as wise, 16making the most of every opportunity, because the days are evil. 17Therefore do not be foolish, but understand what the Lord's will is. 18Do not get drunk on wine, which leads to debauchery. Instead, be filled with the Spirit. 19Speak to one another with psalms, hymns and spiritual songs. Sing and make music in your heart to the Lord, 20always giving thanks to God the Father for everything, in the name of our Lord Jesus Christ.
21Submit to one another out of reverence for Christ.

Wives and Husbands

22Wives, submit to your husbands as to the Lord. 23For the husband is the head of the wife as Christ is the head of the church, his body, of which he is the Savior. 24Now as the church submits to Christ, so also wives should submit to their husbands in everything.
25Husbands, love your wives, just as Christ loved the church and gave himself up for her 26to make her holy, cleansing*a* her by the washing with water through the word, 27and to present her to himself as a radiant church, without stain or wrinkle or any other blemish, but holy and blameless. 28In this same way, husbands ought to love their wives as their own bodies. He who loves his wife loves himself. 29After all, no one ever hated his own body, but he feeds and cares for it, just as Christ does the church— 30for we are members of his body. 31"For this reason a man will leave his father and mother and be united to his wife, and the two will become one flesh."*b* 32This is a profound mystery—but I am talking about Christ and the church. 33However, each one of you also must love his wife as he loves himself, and the wife must respect her husband.

Children and Parents

6 Children, obey your parents in the Lord, for this is right. 2"Honor your father and mother"—which is the first commandment with a promise— 3"that it may go well with you and that you may enjoy long life on the earth."*c*
4Fathers, do not exasperate your children; instead, bring them up in the training and instruction of the Lord.

Slaves and Masters

5Slaves, obey your earthly masters with respect and fear, and with sincerity of heart, just as you would obey Christ. 6Obey them not only to win their favor when their eye is on you, but like slaves of Christ, doing the will of God from your heart. 7Serve wholeheartedly, as if you were serving the Lord, not men, 8because you know that the Lord will reward everyone for whatever good he does, whether he is slave or free.
9And masters, treat your slaves in the same way. Do not threaten them, since you know that he who is both their Master and yours is in heaven, and there is no favoritism with him.

The Armor of God

10Finally, be strong in the Lord and in his mighty power. 11Put on the full armor of God so that you can take your stand against the

---

1. As you look back over your life since becoming a Christian, what positive changes have you seen in your motives and desires? 2. As you compare the life that you lived *before* Christ to the life you live *today*, where have you seen the greatest change? In your language? Your desires? Your values? The way you treat your spouse? Your children?

Which of these TV families reflects your family: Cleavers? Flintstones? Bradys? Huxtables? Waltons? Simpsons?

1. How do verses 18–21, on the Holy Spirit's infilling, affect your attitude toward these verses on submission? 2. In the culture of his day—which addressed women through their husbands, and by Jewish law termed a woman a "thing"—would Paul be considered a "chauvinist" or a "radical feminist"? 3. Christ's love led him to *die* for us. What would it mean for a husband to *live* with his wife with this type of love (vv. 25–33)? How did Christ act out his headship? 4. How did your parents approach marriage? Two masters? Two servants? One master, one servant? What is the goal of Christian marriage (v. 31)? What role does sex play? 5. What does it mean to "honor your parents"? To bring up children in the Lord without exasperating them? 6. If you work for someone, how are you to look upon your job? If you are the boss, how are you to look upon your employees? Can you hold to these principles today in your business and still make it?

1. What does a wife do when the husband does not take spiritual leadership? 2. Whom do you look up to as a good role model for marriage? 3. What is God saying to you about your spouse? Family?

What were some of your (or your kids') favorite dress-up costumes? Why those?

1. From his prison cell awaiting trial, Paul looks up and

---

a26 Or *having cleansed*   *b31* Gen. 2:24   *c3* Deut. 5:16

sees a battle raging (vv. 12–13). What is this battle? What is it over? **2.** What are the six armors for the Christian? Which of these are offensive weapons? Defensive weapons? **3.** What attitude should we have as we face these forces? How does prayer fit into this spiritual battle?

♡ **1.** If you had to compare your spiritual armor to this list, where are you strong? Weak? What do you need to do to prepare for battle? What is at stake if you don't? **2.** What evidence do you see of the battle in your life? Your church? Your community? Your nation? The world? What would it mean for you "to stand" in these particular battlefields?

devil's schemes. ¹²For our struggle is not against flesh and blood, but against the rulers, against the authorities, against the powers of this dark world and against the spiritual forces of evil in the heavenly realms. ¹³Therefore put on the full armor of God, so that when the day of evil comes, you may be able to stand your ground, and after you have done everything, to stand. ¹⁴Stand firm then, with the belt of truth buckled around your waist, with the breastplate of righteousness in place, ¹⁵and with your feet fitted with the readiness that comes from the gospel of peace. ¹⁶In addition to all this, take up the shield of faith, with which you can extinguish all the flaming arrows of the evil one. ¹⁷Take the helmet of salvation and the sword of the Spirit, which is the word of God. ¹⁸And pray in the Spirit on all occasions with all kinds of prayers and requests. With this in mind, be alert and always keep on praying for all the saints.

¹⁹Pray also for me, that whenever I open my mouth, words may be given me so that I will fearlessly make known the mystery of the gospel, ²⁰for which I am an ambassador in chains. Pray that I may declare it fearlessly, as I should.

Final Greetings

²¹Tychicus, the dear brother and faithful servant in the Lord, will tell you everything, so that you also may know how I am and what I am doing. ²²I am sending him to you for this very purpose, that you may know how we are, and that he may encourage you.

²³Peace to the brothers, and love with faith from God the Father and the Lord Jesus Christ. ²⁴Grace to all who love our Lord Jesus Christ with an undying love.

INTRODUCTION to

PHILIPPIANS

Book Study Outline: If you are using Philippians for a study course, here is a 4- or 8-week outline. Use the margin questions for your group agenda:

start meeting / 15 min.

read & discuss Bible / 30 min.

close meeting / 15–45 min.

4-week plan	8-week plan	Group Study Passage
1	1	1:1–11/Partners in Christ's Gospel
	2	1:12–30/Suffering for Christ's Sake
2	3	2:1–11/Imitating Christ's Humility
	4	2:12–30/Examples of Christ's Service
3	5	3:1–11/Knowing Christ's Suffering
	6	3:12–4:1/Pursuing Christ's Call
4	7	4:2–9/Joy in Christ's Nearness
	8	4:10–23/Receiving Christ's Riches

Refer to the Questions and Answers in front of Bible for more information.

Author: The apostle Paul.

Date: Probably around A.D. 61–63, a dozen or so years after Paul had founded the church in Philippi (the first one in Europe; see Ac 16).

Theme: The joy of knowing Jesus.

Historical Background: Paul was in prison (most likely at Rome; see Ac 28:11–31) when Epaphroditus arrived with a gift from the church at Philippi, an important Roman colony in northern Greece. Paul had at least four motives as he wrote this letter in return. For one, it served as a "thank you" to them for their love and partnership in the Gospel (1:5; 4:10–19). Secondly, he wanted them to know he was not discouraged even though he was in prison (1:12–26; 4:10–19). Thirdly, reports of how false teachers were bringing their damaging doctrines into the church prompted him to warn them to stand firm against these errors (1:27–28; 3:2–4,18–19). Finally, he was concerned about a serious clash between two women in the church whose disagreement was apparently affecting the unity of the whole body (4:2–3).

Characteristics: Philippians radiates with joy in the Lord and with love for these old friends and warm supporters. Paul's joy while in prison flows from his awareness of Jesus' presence (1:21–24), his confidence that he is in Christ's hands (1:20; 2:9–13; 3:20–21), his pleasure over the advancement of the Gospel (1:12–14) and his single-minded desire to know Jesus (1:21; 3:7–10). His concern is that the Philippians reflect the same attitudes through a life of mutual service (1:27–2:11), steadfastness in the truth (3:2–4:1) and dedication to the things of Christ (4:4–9).

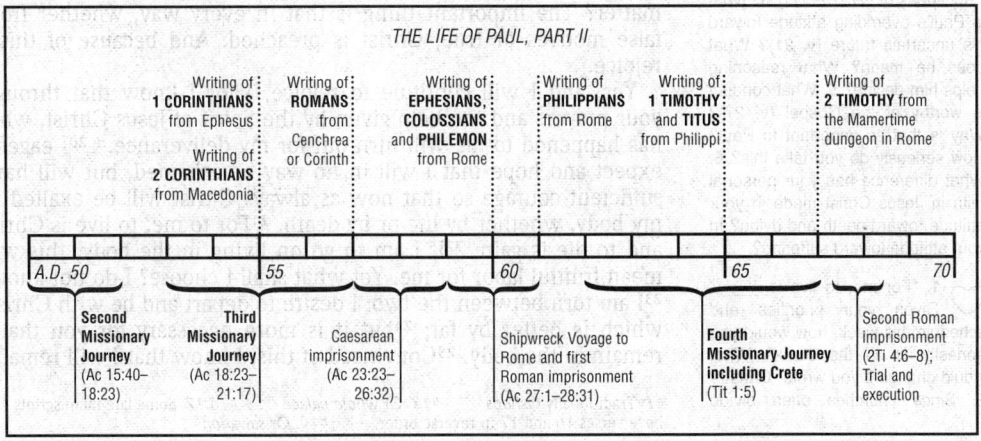

THE LIFE OF PAUL, PART II

Writing of 1 CORINTHIANS from Ephesus	Writing of ROMANS from Cenchrea or Corinth	Writing of EPHESIANS, COLOSSIANS and PHILEMON from Rome	Writing of PHILIPPIANS from Rome	Writing of 1 TIMOTHY and TITUS from Philippi	Writing of 2 TIMOTHY from the Mamertime dungeon in Rome
Writing of 2 CORINTHIANS from Macedonia					

A.D. 50	55	60	65	70

| Second Missionary Journey (Ac 15:40–18:23) | Third Missionary Journey (Ac 18:23–21:17) | Caesarean imprisonment (Ac 23:23–26:32) | Shipwreck Voyage to Rome and first Roman imprisonment (Ac 27:1–28:31) | Fourth Missionary Journey including Crete (Tit 1:5) | Second Roman imprisonment (2Ti 4:6–8); Trial and execution |

Philippians

What mail do you open first: Bills? Official looking stuff? Personal mail? Love letter?

1. Where is Paul writing from? Why? To whom is he writing? (See Introduction to Philippians.) 2. What are Paul's feelings for this church? What does that show about his leadership style? 3. How is God at work in a believer's life according to verses 6 and 9–11? How does this make you feel about uncertainties in your life?

1. Who was the "apostle Paul" in your spiritual life, who introduced you to Jesus Christ and cared about your spiritual growth? 2. Who is your spiritual cheerleader now?

1. When you have had a bad day, what do you do? 2. Are you the kind of person who sees the glass half-empty or half-full?

1. What is the difference between Paul's view of life and the view of the Stoics (grin and bear it) and the Epicureans (eat, drink and be merry)? 2. How does Paul decide if an event (like his jailing) is good or bad? How would this example encourage others? 3. What motives for preaching does Paul speak of (vv. 15–17)? 4. What is Paul's overriding attitude toward his uncertain future (v. 21)? What does he mean? What reasoning helps him decide? 5. What conduct is worthy of the Gospel (v. 27)? Why is that so important to Paul? How seriously do you take this? 6. What difference has your personal faith in Jesus Christ made in your attitude toward death and dying? In your attitude toward suffering?

1. "For me, to live is_____." Given your priorities and schedule this week, how would you honestly fill in the blank? What would change if you wrote "Christ"? 2. Since churches often divide

1 Paul and Timothy, servants of Christ Jesus,

To all the saints in Christ Jesus at Philippi, together with the overseers[a] and deacons:

[2]Grace and peace to you from God our Father and the Lord Jesus Christ.

Thanksgiving and Prayer

[3]I thank my God every time I remember you. [4]In all my prayers for all of you, I always pray with joy [5]because of your partnership in the gospel from the first day until now, [6]being confident of this, that he who began a good work in you will carry it on to completion until the day of Christ Jesus.

[7]It is right for me to feel this way about all of you, since I have you in my heart; for whether I am in chains or defending and confirming the gospel, all of you share in God's grace with me. [8]God can testify how I long for all of you with the affection of Christ Jesus.

[9]And this is my prayer: that your love may abound more and more in knowledge and depth of insight, [10]so that you may be able to discern what is best and may be pure and blameless until the day of Christ, [11]filled with the fruit of righteousness that comes through Jesus Christ—to the glory and praise of God.

Paul's Chains Advance the Gospel

[12]Now I want you to know, brothers, that what has happened to me has really served to advance the gospel. [13]As a result, it has become clear throughout the whole palace guard[b] and to everyone else that I am in chains for Christ. [14]Because of my chains, most of the brothers in the Lord have been encouraged to speak the word of God more courageously and fearlessly.

[15]It is true that some preach Christ out of envy and rivalry, but others out of goodwill. [16]The latter do so in love, knowing that I am put here for the defense of the gospel. [17]The former preach Christ out of selfish ambition, not sincerely, supposing that they can stir up trouble for me while I am in chains.[c] [18]But what does it matter? The important thing is that in every way, whether from false motives or true, Christ is preached. And because of this I rejoice.

Yes, and I will continue to rejoice, [19]for I know that through your prayers and the help given by the Spirit of Jesus Christ, what has happened to me will turn out for my deliverance.[d] [20]I eagerly expect and hope that I will in no way be ashamed, but will have sufficient courage so that now as always Christ will be exalted in my body, whether by life or by death. [21]For to me, to live is Christ and to die is gain. [22]If I am to go on living in the body, this will mean fruitful labor for me. Yet what shall I choose? I do not know! [23]I am torn between the two: I desire to depart and be with Christ, which is better by far; [24]but it is more necessary for you that I remain in the body. [25]Convinced of this, I know that I will remain,

a1 Traditionally *bishops*   b13 Or *whole palace*   c16,17 Some late manuscripts have verses 16 and 17 in reverse order.   d19 Or *salvation*

and I will continue with all of you for your progress and joy in the faith, ²⁶so that through my being with you again your joy in Christ Jesus will overflow on account of me.

²⁷Whatever happens, conduct yourselves in a manner worthy of the gospel of Christ. Then, whether I come and see you or only hear about you in my absence, I will know that you stand firm in one spirit, contending as one man for the faith of the gospel ²⁸without being frightened in any way by those who oppose you. This is a sign to them that they will be destroyed, but that you will be saved—and that by God. ²⁹For it has been granted to you on behalf of Christ not only to believe on him, but also to suffer for him, ³⁰since you are going through the same struggle you saw I had, and now hear that I still have.

Imitating Christ's Humility

2 If you have any encouragement from being united with Christ, if any comfort from his love, if any fellowship with the Spirit, if any tenderness and compassion, ²then make my joy complete by being like-minded, having the same love, being one in spirit and purpose. ³Do nothing out of selfish ambition or vain conceit, but in humility consider others better than yourselves. ⁴Each of you should look not only to your own interests, but also to the interests of others.

⁵Your attitude should be the same as that of Christ Jesus:

> ⁶Who, being in very nature^a God,
>   did not consider equality with God something
>   to be grasped,
> ⁷but made himself nothing,
>   taking the very nature^b of a servant,
>   being made in human likeness.
> ⁸And being found in appearance as a man,
>   he humbled himself
>   and became obedient to death—
>   even death on a cross!
> ⁹Therefore God exalted him to the highest place
>   and gave him the name that is above every
>   name,
> ¹⁰that at the name of Jesus every knee should bow,
>   in heaven and on earth and under the earth,
> ¹¹and every tongue confess that Jesus Christ is Lord,
>   to the glory of God the Father.

Shining as Stars

¹²Therefore, my dear friends, as you have always obeyed—not only in my presence, but now much more in my absence—continue to work out your salvation with fear and trembling, ¹³for it is God who works in you to will and to act according to his good purpose.

¹⁴Do everything without complaining or arguing, ¹⁵so that you may become blameless and pure, children of God without fault in a crooked and depraved generation, in which you shine like stars in the universe ¹⁶as you hold out^c the word of life—in order that I may boast on the day of Christ that I did not run or labor for nothing. ¹⁷But even if I am being poured out like a drink offering on the sacrifice and service coming from your faith, I am glad and rejoice with all of you. ¹⁸So you too should be glad and rejoice with me.

---

a6 Or *in the form of*   *b7* Or *the form*   *c16* Or *hold on to*

---

along denominational, cultural, theological and social lines, what would it mean to apply verse 27 in your community in concrete ways? What would have to change in you to make such unity possible?

---

1. Who takes out the trash in your home? Cleans the toilet? 2. What is your pet peeve at home?

1. Reading between the lines, what was wrong with the church in Philippi? 2. What does it mean to consider someone "better than yourself" (v. 3)? How does humility differ from being a doormat? 3. What do you think it was like for Jesus to leave heaven and become human? To take on himself all of the sin of mankind?

1. How does this passage challenge the Madison Avenue advertising image of success? 2. Who do you admire because they truly put the interests of others ahead of their own interests? 3. What is the closest you have come to being in a fellowship that cared for one another like Paul describes here: Your buddies in the war? Your college sorority? Your sports team? An AA recovery group?

Who are you like in the morning: Big Bird or Oscar the Grouch?

1. Who does Paul sound like in this passage: Your dad? Army sergeant? Coach at halftime? 2. What does it mean to "work out your salvation" (v. 12; see also 2:1–4)? 3. What makes God's people "shine like stars"?

How brightly do you "shine" in your universe?

1. Who would look after your children if something happened to you and your spouse? 2. Who would look after your business or personal affairs?

1. How do Timothy and Epaphroditus illustrate 2:1–4? 2. Consider verses 20–22 and 30. How true is verse 21 today? How rare are people like these two men? Who is one person you know who resembles them?

1. When you were growing up, did your father praise you the way Paul praises Timothy? 2. Who are the people in your life who have helped shape your own self-image by their praise or lack of praise? 3. Do you give praise easily ... or do you find this hard to do? Where do you need to improve?

What skill do you have that you could brag about?

1. Why is Paul so concerned about the influence of the "dogs" on this Christian community? 2. If this problem with those promoting circumcision had gone unchallenged, how would this have hurt the Gospel? 3. Paul lived a "good" life before he became a Christian. Was he trying to put down his religious background?

1. How would you compare your upbringing to Paul's? Your passion for Christ to Paul's? 2. Do you need to walk away from something in your past keeping you from becoming new in Christ?

In your dreams of the ideal life, are you more like the pioneer (always pushing on) or the settler (settling down)?

1. Using the imagery of a track race, where does Paul picture himself in his spiritual life? What prize is he after? How is he going to reach it? 2. From what Paul says in this passage (particu-

Timothy and Epaphroditus

19I hope in the Lord Jesus to send Timothy to you soon, that I also may be cheered when I receive news about you. 20I have no one else like him, who takes a genuine interest in your welfare. 21For everyone looks out for his own interests, not those of Jesus Christ. 22But you know that Timothy has proved himself, because as a son with his father he has served with me in the work of the gospel. 23I hope, therefore, to send him as soon as I see how things go with me. 24And I am confident in the Lord that I myself will come soon.

25But I think it is necessary to send back to you Epaphroditus, my brother, fellow worker and fellow soldier, who is also your messenger, whom you sent to take care of my needs. 26For he longs for all of you and is distressed because you heard he was ill. 27Indeed he was ill, and almost died. But God had mercy on him, and not on him only but also on me, to spare me sorrow upon sorrow. 28Therefore I am all the more eager to send him, so that when you see him again you may be glad and I may have less anxiety. 29Welcome him in the Lord with great joy, and honor men like him, 30because he almost died for the work of Christ, risking his life to make up for the help you could not give me.

No Confidence in the Flesh

3 Finally, my brothers, rejoice in the Lord! It is no trouble for me to write the same things to you again, and it is a safeguard for you.

2Watch out for those dogs, those men who do evil, those mutilators of the flesh. 3For it is we who are the circumcision, we who worship by the Spirit of God, who glory in Christ Jesus, and who put no confidence in the flesh— 4though I myself have reasons for such confidence.

If anyone else thinks he has reasons to put confidence in the flesh, I have more: 5circumcised on the eighth day, of the people of Israel, of the tribe of Benjamin, a Hebrew of Hebrews; in regard to the law, a Pharisee; 6as for zeal, persecuting the church; as for legalistic righteousness, faultless.

7But whatever was to my profit I now consider loss for the sake of Christ. 8What is more, I consider everything a loss compared to the surpassing greatness of knowing Christ Jesus my Lord, for whose sake I have lost all things. I consider them rubbish, that I may gain Christ 9and be found in him, not having a righteousness of my own that comes from the law, but that which is through faith in Christ—the righteousness that comes from God and is by faith. 10I want to know Christ and the power of his resurrection and the fellowship of sharing in his sufferings, becoming like him in his death, 11and so, somehow, to attain to the resurrection from the dead.

Pressing on Toward the Goal

12Not that I have already obtained all this, or have already been made perfect, but I press on to take hold of that for which Christ Jesus took hold of me. 13Brothers, I do not consider myself yet to have taken hold of it. But one thing I do: Forgetting what is behind and straining toward what is ahead, 14I press on toward the goal to win the prize for which God has called me heavenward in Christ Jesus.

15All of us who are mature should take such a view of things.

And if on some point you think differently, that too God will make clear to you. [16]Only let us live up to what we have already attained.

[17]Join with others in following my example, brothers, and take note of those who live according to the pattern we gave you. [18]For, as I have often told you before and now say again even with tears, many live as enemies of the cross of Christ. [19]Their destiny is destruction, their god is their stomach, and their glory is in their shame. Their mind is on earthly things. [20]But our citizenship is in heaven. And we eagerly await a Savior from there, the Lord Jesus Christ, [21]who, by the power that enables him to bring everything under his control, will transform our lowly bodies so that they will be like his glorious body.

4 Therefore, my brothers, you whom I love and long for, my joy and crown, that is how you should stand firm in the Lord, dear friends!

Exhortations

[2]I plead with Euodia and I plead with Syntyche to agree with each other in the Lord. [3]Yes, and I ask you, loyal yokefellow,[a] help these women who have contended at my side in the cause of the gospel, along with Clement and the rest of my fellow workers, whose names are in the book of life.

[4]Rejoice in the Lord always. I will say it again: Rejoice! [5]Let your gentleness be evident to all. The Lord is near. [6]Do not be anxious about anything, but in everything, by prayer and petition, with thanksgiving, present your requests to God. [7]And the peace of God, which transcends all understanding, will guard your hearts and your minds in Christ Jesus.

[8]Finally, brothers, whatever is true, whatever is noble, whatever is right, whatever is pure, whatever is lovely, whatever is admirable—if anything is excellent or praiseworthy—think about such things. [9]Whatever you have learned or received or heard from me, or seen in me—put it into practice. And the God of peace will be with you.

Thanks for Their Gifts

[10]I rejoice greatly in the Lord that at last you have renewed your concern for me. Indeed, you have been concerned, but you had no opportunity to show it. [11]I am not saying this because I am in need, for I have learned to be content whatever the circumstances. [12]I know what it is to be in need, and I know what it is to have plenty. I have learned the secret of being content in any and every situation, whether well fed or hungry, whether living in plenty or in want. [13]I can do everything through him who gives me strength.

[14]Yet it was good of you to share in my troubles. [15]Moreover, as you Philippians know, in the early days of your acquaintance with the gospel, when I set out from Macedonia, not one church shared with me in the matter of giving and receiving, except you only; [16]for even when I was in Thessalonica, you sent me aid again and again when I was in need. [17]Not that I am looking for a gift, but I am looking for what may be credited to your account. [18]I have received full payment and even more; I am amply supplied, now that I have received from Epaphroditus the gifts you sent. They are a fragrant offering, an acceptable sacrifice, pleasing to God. [19]And

---

larly the second half), what do you think is going on in this Christian community? **3.** In contrast, what should characterize the "citizens of heaven"?

1. If you had to compare your life in Christ right now to a track race, where would you be: Sitting on the sidelines? Warming up? At the starting blocks? Giving it your all? **2.** What are you passionate about? Are you more likely to strive for excellence in your secular life or your spiritual life? **3.** How would you finish the sentence in verse 13: "But one thing I do ..."

What is the best thing that happened to you this week?

1. How are these women harming the church? **2.** What is Paul's prescription for stress? Compare it to that of modern psychology and New Age religions. **3.** What is Paul's solution to thought pollution? What would he say to the church today about leisure time, reading matter, R-rated movies and football all weekend long on TV? What would he suggest?

On a scale from 1 to 10, what is the stress level in your life? What is your body saying to you?

What do you look back on as the happiest days of your life? Were they really that good?

1. What is Paul's secret to contentment? Where do you think he learned this: From devotional books? Going to church? Graduating from the school of hard knocks? **2.** What is the closest you have come to experiencing what Paul talks about here: Rebounding from loss of freedom? Loss of some physical skill? Loss of some vocational opportunity? Loss of a partner in your life? Or loss of financial security? **3.** What do you learn from Paul in this passage about both contentment and giving and receiving help from others? **4.** In light of Paul's imprisonment for the sake of his preaching, could

---

a3 Or *loyal Syzygus*

some "tongue in cheek" irony be intended in verse 22? (Hint: Caesar Augustus was emperor of Rome at the time.)

♡ **1.** What *outside* force is most likely to upset your contentment? Since God does not always change negative outside forces, what can he change *in you* so that contentment is possible? How can you and your group help the process (see 4:4–8)? **2.** Take turns having one person sit silently while the others share something they are thankful to have received from that person during these study sessions. **3.** What one thing from Philippians do you especially want to apply in your life? In your church?

my God will meet all your needs according to his glorious riches in Christ Jesus.

²⁰To our God and Father be glory for ever and ever. Amen.

Final Greetings

²¹Greet all the saints in Christ Jesus. The brothers who are with me send greetings. ²²All the saints send you greetings, especially those who belong to Caesar's household.

²³The grace of the Lord Jesus Christ be with your spirit. Amen.[a]

---

[a] 23 Some manuscripts do not have *Amen*.

INTRODUCTION to
COLOSSIANS

Book Study Outline: If you are using Colossians for a study course, here is a 4- or 6-week outline. Use the margin questions for your group agenda:

📖 start meeting / 15 min.

📖 read & discuss Bible / 30 min.

♡ close meeting / 15–45 min.

4-week plan	6-week plan	Group Study Passage
1	1	1:1–14/Eternal Redemption in Christ
	2	1:15–23/All Reconciled in Christ
2	3	1:24–2:5/Full Riches in Christ
	4	2:6–23/Firmly Rooted in Christ
3	5	3:1–4:1/Newly Robed in Christ
4	6	4:2–18/New Relationships in Christ

Refer to the Questions and Answers in front of Bible for more information.

Author: The apostle Paul.

Date: Probably in the early A.D. 60s.

Theme: Fullness and freedom in Christ.

Historical Background: Although Paul never visited Colosse, a town about 100 miles east of Ephesus, the church there was probably established as a result of his extended ministry in Ephesus (Ac 19:8–10). Although it had once been a prosperous commercial center, by Paul's day its prominence had diminished. While in prison (see the Introduction to Ephesians), Paul was visited by Epaphras, a native of Colosse who may have founded the church there. His report of a developing problem in the Colosse church prompted Paul to write. It seems that the church was coming under the influence of certain false teachers. The problem for the church seems to have been that of syncretism, i.e., combining various teachings from different religions to come up with something new. Apparently, Greek philosophy, cultic practices, Christianity and Jewish speculations were blended together to offer a "fuller" type of spiritual experience. Jesus was seen as one of several "deities" through which one approaches the Divine. Rigorous ascetic disciplines were used as a means to experience trance-like "visions." In contrast, Paul presents Jesus as the true Lord of the universe (1:15–18; 2:9–10) and highlights love, thankfulness and forgiveness as the marks of true spirituality (3:12–17).

Characteristics: Jesus Christ is central as Paul demonstrates that "in everything he (has) supremacy" (1:18). Chapters 1–2 outline the cosmic nature of Christ who has reconciled all things to himself through his death on the cross, independently of any effort on our part. Chapters 3–4 give the implications of Christ's lordship in terms of how those in union with him are meant to live.

THE LETTERS OF PAUL			
Book	**Time of Writing (A.D.)**	**Place of Writing**	**Theme**
Galatians	48–50 or 51–53	Syrian Antioch or Corinth	Justification by faith alone (Gal)
1 Thessalonians	51	Corinth	Christian living in an immoral world (1Th)
2 Thessalonians	51	Corinth	Life in the light of the coming Christ (2Th)
1 Corinthians	53–55	Ephesus	Glorifying God through Christian living (1Co)
2 Corinthians	55–56	Macedonia	Finding strength in God's true power (2Co)
Romans	56–57	Corinth	Being right with God through faith in Christ (Ro)
Philemon	60	Rome	Mercy and unlimited forgiveness (Phm)
Colossians	60	Rome	Fullness and freedom in Christ (Col)
Ephesians	60	Rome	God's new social order (Eph)
Philippians	61–63	Rome	Joy in Christ, despite hardships (Php)
Titus	63–65	Macedonia	Devotion to duty and doing good (Tit)
1 Timothy	63–65	Macedonia	Faithful leadership through Christ (1Ti)
2 Timothy	67–68	Rome	Exhortation to carry on the ministry (2Ti)

Colossians

Who were your favorite TV or comic book heroes as a child?

1. Paul hasn't met these believers (2:1), yet he is attracted to them. Why? What types of people are you attracted to when you enter a new church group? **2.** Why are faith and love the products of hope (v. 5)? Why must hope exist first? **3.** When did you first come to know the hope offered through Christ in the Gospel? **4.** What does it mean to tell the whole truth about God's grace (v. 6)? Conversely, how does one betray grace? What truth about grace do you see in verses 12–14? **5.** How does what Paul prays for (vv. 9–11) compare with what he thanks God for (vv. 12–14)?

1. How does your prayer for others compare with Paul's: (a) In intensity? (b) In thankfulness? (c) In clarity? (d) In faithfulness? **2.** How is the fruit of hope, faith and love growing in your life: Developing well? Suffering from drought? Destroyed by the last storm? Budding? How will you help this "crop" develop?

What was your favorite animal at the zoo as a child? Your favorite now?

1. The "firstborn" has the rights of an heir. What rights does Jesus have (vv. 15–18)? What is his relationship to "all things"? Why emphasize this? **2.** What is his relationship to God and the church? What does "fullness" imply (v. 19)? **3.** Why did all things need to be reconciled to God (v. 20)? How was this achieved by Jesus? **4.** How much do you identify with verse 21, even now? Do you still sense "evil" in your mind? How do verses 22–23 make you feel?

At times, what people (or forces) seem to be more powerful than Jesus? Why? How do you respond to the fact that

1 Paul, an apostle of Christ Jesus by the will of God, and Timothy our brother,

[2] To the holy and faithful[a] brothers in Christ at Colosse:

Grace and peace to you from God our Father.[b]

Thanksgiving and Prayer

[3] We always thank God, the Father of our Lord Jesus Christ, when we pray for you, [4] because we have heard of your faith in Christ Jesus and of the love you have for all the saints— [5] the faith and love that spring from the hope that is stored up for you in heaven and that you have already heard about in the word of truth, the gospel [6] that has come to you. All over the world this gospel is bearing fruit and growing, just as it has been doing among you since the day you heard it and understood God's grace in all its truth. [7] You learned it from Epaphras, our dear fellow servant, who is a faithful minister of Christ on our[c] behalf, [8] and who also told us of your love in the Spirit.

[9] For this reason, since the day we heard about you, we have not stopped praying for you and asking God to fill you with the knowledge of his will through all spiritual wisdom and understanding. [10] And we pray this in order that you may live a life worthy of the Lord and may please him in every way: bearing fruit in every good work, growing in the knowledge of God, [11] being strengthened with all power according to his glorious might so that you may have great endurance and patience, and joyfully [12] giving thanks to the Father, who has qualified you[d] to share in the inheritance of the saints in the kingdom of light. [13] For he has rescued us from the dominion of darkness and brought us into the kingdom of the Son he loves, [14] in whom we have redemption,[e] the forgiveness of sins.

The Supremacy of Christ

[15] He is the image of the invisible God, the firstborn over all creation. [16] For by him all things were created: things in heaven and on earth, visible and invisible, whether thrones or powers or rulers or authorities; all things were created by him and for him. [17] He is before all things, and in him all things hold together. [18] And he is the head of the body, the church; he is the beginning and the firstborn from among the dead, so that in everything he might have the supremacy. [19] For God was pleased to have all his fullness dwell in him, [20] and through him to reconcile to himself all things, whether things on earth or things in heaven, by making peace through his blood, shed on the cross.

[21] Once you were alienated from God and were enemies in your minds because of[f] your evil behavior. [22] But now he has reconciled you by Christ's physical body through death to present you holy in his sight, without blemish and free from accusation— [23] if you continue in your faith, established and firm, not moved from

---

[a]2 Or *believing*   [b]2 Some manuscripts *Father and the Lord Jesus Christ*   [c]7 Some manuscripts *your*   [d]12 Some manuscripts *us*   [e]14 A few late manuscripts *redemption through his blood*   [f]21 Or *minds, as shown by*

the hope held out in the gospel. This is the gospel that you heard and that has been proclaimed to every creature under heaven, and of which I, Paul, have become a servant.

Paul's Labor for the Church

24Now I rejoice in what was suffered for you, and I fill up in my flesh what is still lacking in regard to Christ's afflictions, for the sake of his body, which is the church. 25I have become its servant by the commission God gave me to present to you the word of God in its fullness— 26the mystery that has been kept hidden for ages and generations, but is now disclosed to the saints. 27To them God has chosen to make known among the Gentiles the glorious riches of this mystery, which is Christ in you, the hope of glory.

28We proclaim him, admonishing and teaching everyone with all wisdom, so that we may present everyone perfect in Christ. 29To this end I labor, struggling with all his energy, which so powerfully works in me.

2 I want you to know how much I am struggling for you and for those at Laodicea, and for all who have not met me personally. 2My purpose is that they may be encouraged in heart and united in love, so that they may have the full riches of complete understanding, in order that they may know the mystery of God, namely, Christ, 3in whom are hidden all the treasures of wisdom and knowledge. 4I tell you this so that no one may deceive you by fine-sounding arguments. 5For though I am absent from you in body, I am present with you in spirit and delight to see how orderly you are and how firm your faith in Christ is.

Freedom From Human Regulations Through Life With Christ

6So then, just as you received Christ Jesus as Lord, continue to live in him, 7rooted and built up in him, strengthened in the faith as you were taught, and overflowing with thankfulness.

8See to it that no one takes you captive through hollow and deceptive philosophy, which depends on human tradition and the basic principles of this world rather than on Christ.

9For in Christ all the fullness of the Deity lives in bodily form, 10and you have been given fullness in Christ, who is the head over every power and authority. 11In him you were also circumcised, in the putting off of the sinful nature,a not with a circumcision done by the hands of men but with the circumcision done by Christ, 12having been buried with him in baptism and raised with him through your faith in the power of God, who raised him from the dead.

13When you were dead in your sins and in the uncircumcision of your sinful nature,b God made youc alive with Christ. He forgave us all our sins, 14having canceled the written code, with its regulations, that was against us and that stood opposed to us; he took it away, nailing it to the cross. 15And having disarmed the powers and authorities, he made a public spectacle of them, triumphing over them by the cross.d

16Therefore do not let anyone judge you by what you eat or drink, or with regard to a religious festival, a New Moon celebration or a Sabbath day. 17These are a shadow of the things that were to come; the reality, however, is found in Christ. 18Do not let anyone who delights in false humility and the worship of angels disqualify you for the prize. Such a person goes into great detail

---

even these are under Christ's authority?

What memories do you have as a child hunting for "buried treasure" or Easter eggs?

1. In what sense are Paul's sufferings a continuation of Jesus' sufferings? Why would this lead him to rejoice (see 2Co 12:9–10)? 2. In 2:3–4, Paul contrasts clever speech and true wisdom. What does this indicate about false teaching infecting the church?

1. Is Paul's stated purpose (1:28; 2:2) a reality in your life? Or are you still somewhere along the way? 2. What "fine sounding arguments" hinder you in following Jesus? How does Paul speak to your concerns? 3. How has finding Christ been like uncovering long-lost buried treasure?

1. As a child, what did you think a "religious" person was like? How did you feel about that person? 2. Did you consider your parents "permissive" or "strict"? Why? (Did they have a lot of rules for you, or just a few? Which one was the biggie?)

1. What does "living in Christ" (v. 6) involve (see 1:10–12)? What does the phrase "rooted and built up" imply to you? 2. What are "the basic principles of this world" (vv. 8,20) and the "powers and authorities" (vv. 10,15)? How did Christ give the Colossians victory over these? 3. What kind of circumcision is done by Christ (v. 11)? How did he do it (vv. 12–15)? 4. What experiences does the believer share with Christ (vv. 9–13)? What implications are drawn from this (vv. 13,16–17, 20–23)? 5. What is the result of trying to base one's relationship with God on rule keeping or on private visions, as the false teachers were doing?

1. When have you felt as if the "roots" of your faith in Christ were barely below the surface? What helps you to sink those roots deeper? 2. What additions to the faith have you encountered from people who try to encourage you to be "more spiritual"? 3. What

---

a 11 Or the flesh   b 13 Or your flesh   c 13 Some manuscripts us   d 15 Or them in him

convinced you that trying to live up to religious rules couldn't change you on the inside? In what area are you still susceptible to getting caught up in rule keeping?

In buying clothes, are you a name-brand buyer? A bargain hunter? Spouse conscious? Quality conscious? Style conscious? (Or could you care less what others think?—Really?)

1. How are we to grow in our spiritual life (vv. 1–4)? How does that contrast with the things that don't lead to growth (see 2:16–23)? How is setting your mind and heart on Christ related to what he *has already done* for us (v. 1)? To what he *will do* for us (v. 4)? **2.** How much contrast is there between the "clothes" of the earthly nature (vv. 5–11) and those of God's chosen people (vv. 12–17)? How hard would it seem to take off the first and put on the second? How is it possible (see 2:6–7,10)? **3.** What practical difference does this "new clothing" make in the relationship between wives and husbands? Between parents and children? Slaves and masters? **4.** What confirms that all these relationships are to be built around Christ? **5.** Is the person in verses 12–17 calm, cool and in control or self-controlled but also lavish in his or her love for others? Do you seek to resemble the first or the second?

1. We get all too used to "earthly nature" clothing. Which aspect of your old nature feels like a comfortable old T-shirt to you now? Why is it difficult to shed or remove? **2.** With what piece of Christ's wardrobe would you like to replace it? Which aspect of Christ's character do you need to clothe yourself with, in relation to your husband or wife? Your parents or children? Your employer or employees? A changing relationship? **3.** How can your small group help with your clothing selection?

about what he has seen, and his unspiritual mind puffs him up with idle notions. [19]He has lost connection with the Head, from whom the whole body, supported and held together by its ligaments and sinews, grows as God causes it to grow.

[20]Since you died with Christ to the basic principles of this world, why, as though you still belonged to it, do you submit to its rules: [21]"Do not handle! Do not taste! Do not touch!"? [22]These are all destined to perish with use, because they are based on human commands and teachings. [23]Such regulations indeed have an appearance of wisdom, with their self-imposed worship, their false humility and their harsh treatment of the body, but they lack any value in restraining sensual indulgence.

Rules for Holy Living

3 Since, then, you have been raised with Christ, set your hearts on things above, where Christ is seated at the right hand of God. [2]Set your minds on things above, not on earthly things. [3]For you died, and your life is now hidden with Christ in God. [4]When Christ, who is your[a] life, appears, then you also will appear with him in glory.

[5]Put to death, therefore, whatever belongs to your earthly nature: sexual immorality, impurity, lust, evil desires and greed, which is idolatry. [6]Because of these, the wrath of God is coming.[b] [7]You used to walk in these ways, in the life you once lived. [8]But now you must rid yourselves of all such things as these: anger, rage, malice, slander, and filthy language from your lips. [9]Do not lie to each other, since you have taken off your old self with its practices [10]and have put on the new self, which is being renewed in knowledge in the image of its Creator. [11]Here there is no Greek or Jew, circumcised or uncircumcised, barbarian, Scythian, slave or free, but Christ is all, and is in all.

[12]Therefore, as God's chosen people, holy and dearly loved, clothe yourselves with compassion, kindness, humility, gentleness and patience. [13]Bear with each other and forgive whatever grievances you may have against one another. Forgive as the Lord forgave you. [14]And over all these virtues put on love, which binds them all together in perfect unity.

[15]Let the peace of Christ rule in your hearts, since as members of one body you were called to peace. And be thankful. [16]Let the word of Christ dwell in you richly as you teach and admonish one another with all wisdom, and as you sing psalms, hymns and spiritual songs with gratitude in your hearts to God. [17]And whatever you do, whether in word or deed, do it all in the name of the Lord Jesus, giving thanks to God the Father through him.

Rules for Christian Households

[18]Wives, submit to your husbands, as is fitting in the Lord.

[19]Husbands, love your wives and do not be harsh with them.

[20]Children, obey your parents in everything, for this pleases the Lord.

[21]Fathers, do not embitter your children, or they will become discouraged.

[22]Slaves, obey your earthly masters in everything; and do it, not only when their eye is on you and to win their favor, but with sincerity of heart and reverence for the Lord. [23]Whatever you do, work at it with all your heart, as working for the Lord, not for men, [24]since you know that you will receive an inheritance from the

---

a4 Some manuscripts *our*   *b6* Some early manuscripts *coming on those who are disobedient*

Lord as a reward. It is the Lord Christ you are serving. 25Anyone who does wrong will be repaid for his wrong, and there is no favoritism.

4 Masters, provide your slaves with what is right and fair, because you know that you also have a Master in heaven.

Further Instructions

2Devote yourselves to prayer, being watchful and thankful. 3And pray for us, too, that God may open a door for our message, so that we may proclaim the mystery of Christ, for which I am in chains. 4Pray that I may proclaim it clearly, as I should. 5Be wise in the way you act toward outsiders; make the most of every opportunity. 6Let your conversation be always full of grace, seasoned with salt, so that you may know how to answer everyone.

Final Greetings

7Tychicus will tell you all the news about me. He is a dear brother, a faithful minister and fellow servant in the Lord. 8I am sending him to you for the express purpose that you may know about our[a] circumstances and that he may encourage your hearts. 9He is coming with Onesimus, our faithful and dear brother, who is one of you. They will tell you everything that is happening here.

10My fellow prisoner Aristarchus sends you his greetings, as does Mark, the cousin of Barnabas. (You have received instructions about him; if he comes to you, welcome him.) 11Jesus, who is called Justus, also sends greetings. These are the only Jews among my fellow workers for the kingdom of God, and they have proved a comfort to me. 12Epaphras, who is one of you and a servant of Christ Jesus, sends greetings. He is always wrestling in prayer for you, that you may stand firm in all the will of God, mature and fully assured. 13I vouch for him that he is working hard for you and for those at Laodicea and Hierapolis. 14Our dear friend Luke, the doctor, and Demas send greetings. 15Give my greetings to the brothers at Laodicea, and to Nympha and the church in her house.

16After this letter has been read to you, see that it is also read in the church of the Laodiceans and that you in turn read the letter from Laodicea.

17Tell Archippus: "See to it that you complete the work you have received in the Lord."

18I, Paul, write this greeting in my own hand. Remember my chains. Grace be with you.

In high school, who were two of your best friends? What was one quality about them that stands out to you?

1. In advancing the Gospel (vv. 2–6), what role is played by prayer? Watchfulness? Thankfulness? Open doors? Closed doors or chains? Wise actions? Opportunism? Graceful talk? Salty talk? 2. Why is thankfulness such a key ingredient in a Christian's life (see 2:7; 3:15,17)? 3. What type of friend is Tychicus (vv.7–8; see Ac 20:4; Eph 6:21; 2Ti 4:12; Tit 3:12)? 4. Likewise, what do you know about Onesimus (v. 9; see Phm 10–16)? Which of Paul's rules, instructions and greetings would be appropriate in preparing to receive this runaway slave from Colosse? How might the Colossians feel about him? 5. Aristarchus (Ac 19:29; 27:2; Phm 24), John Mark (Ac 12:12; 13:5,13; 15:36–40 and the author of Mark), Luke (the author of Luke and Acts), and Demas (Phm 24; 2Ti 4:10) were all with Paul at various times. Why would he include them in his greetings to the church? 6. In light of the influence of the false teachings, why would Paul's commendation of Epaphras be especially important (1:7; 4:12–13)?

1. What has helped you to grow the most in your prayer life? 2. From verses 5–6, what principles do you want to build into your life as you relate to non-believers? 3. Seeing how Paul operated with a team of fellow Christians, what does that imply for you? For your small group? 4. Of the qualities used to describe these people, which one would you like others to say about you in five years? How do 2:6–7 and 3:1–2 suggest you can get moving in that direction? 5. How has your respect and love for Christ grown through this study of Colossians? What from this book has helped you to develop a more thankful heart?

a8 Some manuscripts *that he may know about your*

INTRODUCTION to
1 THESSALONIANS

Book Study Outline: If you are using 1 Thessalonians for a study course, here is a 3- or 6-week outline. Use the margin questions for your group agenda:

3-week plan	6-week plan	Group Study Passage
1	1	1:1–10/Legendary Model of Faith
	2	2:1–16/Lasting Model of Ministry
2	3	2:17–3:13/Longing to Visit This Church
	4	4:1–12/Living to Please God
3	5	4:13–5:11/Living in Light of His Coming
	6	5:12–28/Living in Peace With Others

☕ start meeting / 15 min.

📖 read & discuss Bible / 30 min.

♡ close meeting / 15–45 min.

Refer to the Questions and Answers in the front of this Bible for more information.

Author: The apostle Paul.

Date: Around A.D. 51; either 1 and 2 Thessalonians or Galatians are the earliest letters of Paul in the New Testament.

Theme: Living in light of the coming of Christ.

Historical Background: Paul visited Thessalonica, an important city in Northern Greece, during his second missionary journey (Ac 17:1–9). After preaching for three weeks, he was forced to leave due to mob violence. Jewish leaders accused him of sedition against Caesar. Paul's enemies then used his departure as evidence that he was only a "fly-by-night" religious charlatan (2:3). Concerned about the welfare of the new converts, Paul sent Timothy to encourage them. What Timothy found was twofold. On the one hand, the converts were standing fast in their faith despite persecution and Paul's hasty departure from the city. On the other hand, they were (not unexpectedly) experiencing some problems. Some of the converts had not fully understood the ethical implications of the Gospel. They showed laxity in sexual matters (4:3–8). Furthermore, it seems that some felt it unnecessary to work (in light of the imminence of the Second Coming?) and had become a burden to the others (4:11–12; 5:14). The main problem was that there was a fundamental misunderstanding about the Second Coming (see Introduction for 2 Thessalonians). Timothy later rejoined Paul in Corinth where 1 and 2 Thessalonians were written.

Characteristics: Paul expresses joy at the progress the new converts are making despite their lack of teaching. He then instructs them about the life of holiness they ought to lead as they await the return of Jesus. We catch a glimpse of Paul's approach to ministry (2:1–12; 2:17–3:10) and beautiful summaries of what Christian living is all about (see 1Th 3:11–13; 2Th 1:11–12; 2:16–17).

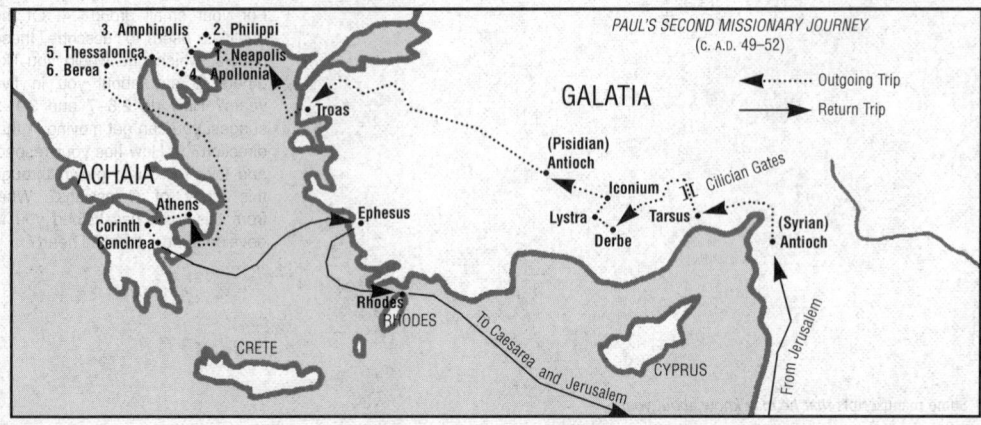

PAUL'S SECOND MISSIONARY JOURNEY (c. A.D. 49–52)

- 3. Amphipolis
- 2. Philippi
- 5. Thessalonica
- 1. Neapolis
- 6. Berea
- 4. Apollonia
- Troas
- GALATIA
- ········> Outgoing Trip
- ───> Return Trip
- (Pisidian) Antioch
- Iconium
- Cilician Gates
- ACHAIA
- Athens
- Ephesus
- Lystra
- Tarsus
- Corinth
- Cenchrea
- Derbe
- (Syrian) Antioch
- Rhodes
- RHODES
- To Caesarea and Jerusalem
- CRETE
- CYPRUS
- From Jerusalem

1 Thessalonians

1 Paul, Silas[a] and Timothy,

To the church of the Thessalonians in God the Father and the Lord Jesus Christ:

Grace and peace to you.[b]

Thanksgiving for the Thessalonians' Faith

[2] We always thank God for all of you, mentioning you in our prayers. [3] We continually remember before our God and Father your work produced by faith, your labor prompted by love, and your endurance inspired by hope in our Lord Jesus Christ.

[4] For we know, brothers loved by God, that he has chosen you, [5] because our gospel came to you not simply with words, but also with power, with the Holy Spirit and with deep conviction. You know how we lived among you for your sake. [6] You became imitators of us and of the Lord; in spite of severe suffering, you welcomed the message with the joy given by the Holy Spirit. [7] And so you became a model to all the believers in Macedonia and Achaia. [8] The Lord's message rang out from you not only in Macedonia and Achaia—your faith in God has become known everywhere. Therefore we do not need to say anything about it, [9] for they themselves report what kind of reception you gave us. They tell how you turned to God from idols to serve the living and true God, [10] and to wait for his Son from heaven, whom he raised from the dead—Jesus, who rescues us from the coming wrath.

Paul's Ministry in Thessalonica

2 You know, brothers, that our visit to you was not a failure. [2] We had previously suffered and been insulted in Philippi, as you know, but with the help of our God we dared to tell you his gospel in spite of strong opposition. [3] For the appeal we make does not spring from error or impure motives, nor are we trying to trick you. [4] On the contrary, we speak as men approved by God to be entrusted with the gospel. We are not trying to please men but God, who tests our hearts. [5] You know we never used flattery, nor did we put on a mask to cover up greed—God is our witness. [6] We were not looking for praise from men, not from you or anyone else.

As apostles of Christ we could have been a burden to you, [7] but we were gentle among you, like a mother caring for her little children. [8] We loved you so much that we were delighted to share with you not only the gospel of God but our lives as well, because you had become so dear to us. [9] Surely you remember, brothers, our toil and hardship; we worked night and day in order not to be a burden to anyone while we preached the gospel of God to you.

[10] You are witnesses, and so is God, of how holy, righteous and blameless we were among you who believed. [11] For you know that we dealt with each of you as a father deals with his own children, [12] encouraging, comforting and urging you to live lives worthy of God, who calls you into his kingdom and glory.

[13] And we also thank God continually because, when you re-

---

a 1 Greek *Silvanus*, a variant of *Silas*   b 1 Some early manuscripts *you from God our Father and the Lord Jesus Christ*

What teams did you belong to (or aspire to) as a child? Of which team were you most proud?

1. What do you know about the Thessalonian church from Paul's experiences in Acts 17:1–9? **2.** What convinced Paul that the Thessalonians were indeed chosen by God? **3.** How did they first become imitators of, and then models for, the faith (vv. 6–10)? What does this tell you about their growth in Christ? **4.** In an age without mass media, how do you suppose their faith became so legendary?

1. What kind of "model" are you in matters of faith: Still on the drawing board? A work in progress? Secured in a private collection? On display at the National Museum? **2.** Which of the qualities in verse 3 do you most wish to see developed in your life now? How can the group help?

What was one of your most memorable failures in junior or senior high school?

1. What rumors about Paul have been spread by his opposition (vv. 1–6)? Does Paul sound reassuring to you? What concerns might linger? **2.** From verses 1–12, what does *ethical* evangelism look like? What would its opposite look like? What do the images of being a mother (v. 7) and father (v. 11) add to this picture? What do these images say about caring for your own children or for "young" believers? **3.** What difficulties were the Thessalonians facing (vv. 14–15)? How would Paul's example of perseverance in the face of persecution encourage them?

1. List the characteristics of a faithful Christian worker given in this passage. Which do you possess? Which do you want to develop? **2.** Who has been a positive influence on you for godly living? How so? How can *you* be a positive influence for someone this week? **3.** What turns you off about the way some people present the Gospel? How are you attempting to avoid these mistakes, and yet maintain a strong witness? **4.** What opposition to your faith are you facing? What encourages you to persevere?

---

1. As a child, when and where did homesickness strike hard? What did you do about it? **2.** What room in your childhood home fills you with warm memories? What happened there?

1. Why do you think Paul called the Thessalonian church his "hope," "joy" and "crown"? **2.** If Paul promised them trials and persecution when he was with them (3:4), why is he writing to them about it now? **3.** What in Timothy's report particularly encourages Paul? What does this tell you about Paul's desires and concerns for the Thessalonians? **4.** What guidelines can you find in Paul's desires, concerns and prayers for those who disciple new Christians today?

1. If someone were to tell you that God promises a trouble-free life to those who are true Christians, how would you respond? What are you struggling with most right now? **2.** In what specific ways have you been encouraged by someone else's faith? Have you told them about it? **3.** Which of Paul's prayer requests would you want someone to pray for you? Do likewise for someone in your small group.

What was the last thing you made from scratch?

1. What three areas of lifestyle, discussed here, most affect a Christian's ministry? How so? **2.** What "behavioral psychology" is Paul using here? What is the guiding principle behind Paul's commands and warnings? What does this passage say to someone

ceived the word of God, which you heard from us, you accepted it not as the word of men, but as it actually is, the word of God, which is at work in you who believe. ¹⁴For you, brothers, became imitators of God's churches in Judea, which are in Christ Jesus: You suffered from your own countrymen the same things those churches suffered from the Jews, ¹⁵who killed the Lord Jesus and the prophets and also drove us out. They displease God and are hostile to all men ¹⁶in their effort to keep us from speaking to the Gentiles so that they may be saved. In this way they always heap up their sins to the limit. The wrath of God has come upon them at last.ᵃ

Paul's Longing to See the Thessalonians

¹⁷But, brothers, when we were torn away from you for a short time (in person, not in thought), out of our intense longing we made every effort to see you. ¹⁸For we wanted to come to you—certainly I, Paul, did, again and again—but Satan stopped us. ¹⁹For what is our hope, our joy, or the crown in which we will glory in the presence of our Lord Jesus when he comes? Is it not you? ²⁰Indeed, you are our glory and joy.

3 So when we could stand it no longer, we thought it best to be left by ourselves in Athens. ²We sent Timothy, who is our brother and God's workerᵇ in spreading the gospel of Christ, to strengthen and encourage you in your faith, ³so that no one would be unsettled by these trials. You know quite well that we were destined for them. ⁴In fact, when we were with you, we kept telling you that we would be persecuted. And it turned out that way, as you well know. ⁵For this reason, when I could stand it no longer, I sent to find out about your faith. I was afraid that in some way the tempter might have tempted you and our efforts might have been useless.

Timothy's Encouraging Report

⁶But Timothy has just now come to us from you and has brought good news about your faith and love. He has told us that you always have pleasant memories of us and that you long to see us, just as we also long to see you. ⁷Therefore, brothers, in all our distress and persecution we were encouraged about you because of your faith. ⁸For now we really live, since you are standing firm in the Lord. ⁹How can we thank God enough for you in return for all the joy we have in the presence of our God because of you? ¹⁰Night and day we pray most earnestly that we may see you again and supply what is lacking in your faith.

¹¹Now may our God and Father himself and our Lord Jesus clear the way for us to come to you. ¹²May the Lord make your love increase and overflow for each other and for everyone else, just as ours does for you. ¹³May he strengthen your hearts so that you will be blameless and holy in the presence of our God and Father when our Lord Jesus comes with all his holy ones.

Living to Please God

4 Finally, brothers, we instructed you how to live in order to please God, as in fact you are living. Now we ask you and urge you in the Lord Jesus to do this more and more. ²For you know what instructions we gave you by the authority of the Lord Jesus.

³It is God's will that you should be sanctified: that you should avoid sexual immorality; ⁴that each of you should learn to control

ᵃ16 Or *them fully*　　ᵇ2 Some manuscripts *brother and fellow worker*; other manuscripts *brother and God's servant* his own body[a] in a way that is holy and honorable, [5]not in passionate lust like the heathen, who do not know God; [6]and that in this matter no one should wrong his brother or take advantage of him. The Lord will punish men for all such sins, as we have already told you and warned you. [7]For God did not call us to be impure, but to live a holy life. [8]Therefore, he who rejects this instruction does not reject man but God, who gives you his Holy Spirit.

[9]Now about brotherly love we do not need to write to you, for you yourselves have been taught by God to love each other. [10]And in fact, you do love all the brothers throughout Macedonia. Yet we urge you, brothers, to do so more and more.

[11]Make it your ambition to lead a quiet life, to mind your own business and to work with your hands, just as we told you, [12]so that your daily life may win the respect of outsiders and so that you will not be dependent on anybody.

The Coming of the Lord

[13]Brothers, we do not want you to be ignorant about those who fall asleep, or to grieve like the rest of men, who have no hope. [14]We believe that Jesus died and rose again and so we believe that God will bring with Jesus those who have fallen asleep in him. [15]According to the Lord's own word, we tell you that we who are still alive, who are left till the coming of the Lord, will certainly not precede those who have fallen asleep. [16]For the Lord himself will come down from heaven, with a loud command, with the voice of the archangel and with the trumpet call of God, and the dead in Christ will rise first. [17]After that, we who are still alive and are left will be caught up together with them in the clouds to meet the Lord in the air. And so we will be with the Lord forever. [18]Therefore encourage each other with these words.

5 Now, brothers, about times and dates we do not need to write to you, [2]for you know very well that the day of the Lord will come like a thief in the night. [3]While people are saying, "Peace and safety," destruction will come on them suddenly, as labor pains on a pregnant woman, and they will not escape.

[4]But you, brothers, are not in darkness so that this day should surprise you like a thief. [5]You are all sons of the light and sons of the day. We do not belong to the night or to the darkness. [6]So then, let us not be like others, who are asleep, but let us be alert and self-controlled. [7]For those who sleep, sleep at night, and those who get drunk, get drunk at night. [8]But since we belong to the day, let us be self-controlled, putting on faith and love as a breastplate, and the hope of salvation as a helmet. [9]For God did not appoint us to suffer wrath but to receive salvation through our Lord Jesus Christ. [10]He died for us so that, whether we are awake or asleep, we may live together with him. [11]Therefore encourage one another and build each other up, just as in fact you are doing.

Final Instructions

[12]Now we ask you, brothers, to respect those who work hard among you, who are over you in the Lord and who admonish you. [13]Hold them in the highest regard in love because of their work. Live in peace with each other. [14]And we urge you, brothers, warn those who are idle, encourage the timid, help the weak, be patient with everyone. [15]Make sure that nobody pays back wrong for wrong, but always try to be kind to each other and to everyone else.

[a]4 Or *learn to live with his own wife*; or *learn to acquire a wife*

who has already made sexual mistakes? **3.** When urged to love "more and more," how do you suppose the Thessalonians felt?

1. How will a lifestyle that bears witness to God affect sexual morality? Work relationships? Time priorities? Small group dynamics? **2.** What do you say to someone who believes you can do anything you want, as long as you mind your own business (v. 11) and no one gets hurt (v. 6)? Would you say anything different to a Christian who believes the same thing about sexual freedom? If so, what?

Who was the first family member you recall dying? Who have you been closest to through their dying days? How did this affect you? What else has shaped your view of death and dying?

1. How would the Thessalonians have felt if they had remained ignorant of the Christian's resurrection and of Christ's return? How would Paul's words have encouraged them? **2.** Do Paul's words about Christ coming as "a thief in the night" (at an unknown time) calm, or stir up fear? How does Paul's analogy of night and day speak to this fear? **3.** How do *faith, love* and *hope* sum up what it means to "belong to the day" (5:8; see 1:3)?

1. Of all the places you live (at home, work, school or church) where do you feel the need for more faith, more hope or more love? How can your group help you? **2.** How can you be better prepared for Christ's return? **3.** How does this passage help you as you consider your own death?

What causes you to "blow a gasket": Traffic jams? Christmas shopping? Bickering children? Burned dinners? Or what?

1. From this passage, what people make up the Christian community? **2.** What attitudes underlie Paul's commands here? What impressions of the Christian life do these commands give you? **3.** How would you summarize the goal and hope of the Christian life

(vv. 23–24) in your own words? **4.** How do the many commands in verses 12–22 relate to the multi-dimensional blessing of verse 23? To the promise of verse 24? To the requests of verses 25–27? To the benediction of verse 28?

♡ **1.** Of the various commands, which are most relevant to your church? Your small group? Your workplace? You? Which do you feel you already are practicing well? Which one will you work on this week? How? **2.** What encouragement, sanctification and grace do you receive from God to fulfill these commands? How has your small group been a help to you in this regard?

¹⁶Be joyful always; ¹⁷pray continually; ¹⁸give thanks in all circumstances, for this is God's will for you in Christ Jesus.

¹⁹Do not put out the Spirit's fire; ²⁰do not treat prophecies with contempt. ²¹Test everything. Hold on to the good. ²²Avoid every kind of evil.

²³May God himself, the God of peace, sanctify you through and through. May your whole spirit, soul and body be kept blameless at the coming of our Lord Jesus Christ. ²⁴The one who calls you is faithful and he will do it.

²⁵Brothers, pray for us. ²⁶Greet all the brothers with a holy kiss. ²⁷I charge you before the Lord to have this letter read to all the brothers.

²⁸The grace of our Lord Jesus Christ be with you.

INTRODUCTION to
2 THESSALONIANS

Book Study Outline: If you are using 2 Thessalonians for a study course, here is a 3-week outline. Use the margin questions for your group agenda:

3-week plan	Group Study Passage
1	1:1–12/Perseverance and God's Judgment
2	2:1–17/Lawlessness and Christ's Coming
3	3:1–18/Idleness and Paul's Authority

☕ start meeting / 15 min.

📖 read & discuss Bible / 30 min.

♡ close meeting / 15–45 min.

Refer to the Questions and Answers in the front of this Bible for more information.

Author: The apostle Paul.

Date: Around A.D. 51; 1 and 2 Thessalonians or Galatians are the earliest letters of Paul in the NT.

Theme: Living in light of the coming of Christ.

Historical Background: First and Second Thessalonians are very much alike (see the Introduction to 1 Thessalonians). The second letter was written within months, if not weeks, of the first. Why was this necessary? The answer may well be that Paul's first letter to these young, untaught Christians produced a serious misunderstanding that necessitated a second, clarifying letter. Specifically, his teaching that "the day of the Lord will come like a thief in the night" (1Th 5:2) may have encouraged people to abandon normal pursuits to prepare for the Second Coming. Thus in 2 Thessalonians 2:1–12 he outlines the events, including the great rebellion, that must take place prior to the return of Christ. The Second Coming is not so imminent that they have to stop everything. Then he goes on to reiterate what he said in his earlier letter: Stand firm and do not be idle. Thus Paul encourages the Thessalonians in responsible Christian living as well as trying to correct some of the misunderstandings they had about the nature and implications of the second coming of Christ.

THE PURPOSE OF 1 AND 2 THESSALONIANS

Paul had left Thessalonica rather abruptly (see Ac 17:5–10) after a brief stay. Recent converts from paganism (1Th 1:9) were thus left with little external support in the midst of persecution. Paul's purpose in writing these letters was:

1. To encourage persecuted believers
(1Th 3:2–5; 2Th 1:3–10)

2. To exhort the Thessalonians to be steadfast, godly and to work for a living
(1Th 4:1–8,11–12; 2Th 2:13–3:15)

3. To correct a misunderstanding and give assurance concerning the Lord's return and the future of believers
(1Th 4:13–15; 2Th 2:1–12)

MACEDONIA

ITALY

Thessalonica

Characteristics: 1 and 2 Thessalonians contain much of the material we have from Paul about the Second Coming. Why did he need to expound on this theme so much at Thessalonica? One suggestion is he may have made use of a popular pagan myth as a point of contact for preaching the Gospel when he was in the city (we have an example of Paul doing something like this when he preached in Athens in Ac 17). Since this myth focused on the hope that one day a hero would return and help the needy, especially those in Thessalonica, Paul would have a ready-made point of entry to tell of the mission of Jesus. His emphasis on the Second Coming in these letters shows that the people may not have fully grasped the differences between Jesus' return and that of their expected hero, especially as it related to their lifestyle.

2 Thessalonians

1 Paul, Silas[a] and Timothy,

To the church of the Thessalonians in God our Father and the Lord Jesus Christ:

²Grace and peace to you from God the Father and the Lord Jesus Christ.

Thanksgiving and Prayer

³We ought always to thank God for you, brothers, and rightly so, because your faith is growing more and more, and the love every one of you has for each other is increasing. ⁴Therefore, among God's churches we boast about your perseverance and faith in all the persecutions and trials you are enduring.

⁵All this is evidence that God's judgment is right, and as a result you will be counted worthy of the kingdom of God, for which you are suffering. ⁶God is just: He will pay back trouble to those who trouble you ⁷and give relief to you who are troubled, and to us as well. This will happen when the Lord Jesus is revealed from heaven in blazing fire with his powerful angels. ⁸He will punish those who do not know God and do not obey the gospel of our Lord Jesus. ⁹They will be punished with everlasting destruction and shut out from the presence of the Lord and from the majesty of his power ¹⁰on the day he comes to be glorified in his holy people and to be marveled at among all those who have believed. This includes you, because you believed our testimony to you.

¹¹With this in mind, we constantly pray for you, that our God may count you worthy of his calling, and that by his power he may fulfill every good purpose of yours and every act prompted by your faith. ¹²We pray this so that the name of our Lord Jesus may be glorified in you, and you in him, according to the grace of our God and the Lord Jesus Christ.[b]

The Man of Lawlessness

2 Concerning the coming of our Lord Jesus Christ and our being gathered to him, we ask you, brothers, ²not to become easily unsettled or alarmed by some prophecy, report or letter supposed to have come from us, saying that the day of the Lord has already come. ³Don't let anyone deceive you in any way, for ⌊that day will not come⌋ until the rebellion occurs and the man of lawlessness[c] is revealed, the man doomed to destruction. ⁴He will oppose and will exalt himself over everything that is called God or is worshiped, so that he sets himself up in God's temple, proclaiming himself to be God.

⁵Don't you remember that when I was with you I used to tell you these things? ⁶And now you know what is holding him back, so that he may be revealed at the proper time. ⁷For the secret power of lawlessness is already at work; but the one who now holds it back will continue to do so till he is taken out of the way.

☕ What did your parents do right in raising you? What rewards and punishments worked best?

📖 **1.** What has happened since Paul wrote 1 Thessalonians (v. 4)? How has persecution affected this church? **2.** What is the evidence that they are "worthy" of God's kingdom (v. 5)? **3.** Who is on trial here? Who is on the witness stand? In the judge's chambers? **4.** Why is God waiting until the Second Coming to punish these persecutors? Who benefits from this delayed justice? How so? **5.** What quality do you think Paul admires most in these Christians? **6.** What do you see as the net effect of Paul's thanksgiving and prayer?

♡ **1.** How will you exercise faith and love this week in a specific way or relationship? **2.** Which of your current struggles are a result of being a Christian? **3.** How do you feel about the punishment mentioned in verses 8–9? How might you feel if you were being severely oppressed? **4.** Pray Paul's prayer (vv. 11–12) in your own words for one another this week.

☕ At what stage in life were you "rebellious"? What memory (painful or humorous) is associated with those times of conflict?

📖 **1.** What must have been happening in Thessalonica to lead Paul to write this (see also Introduction to 2 Thessalonians)? **2.** How much time was Paul able to spend with the Thessalonians (see Ac 17:2)? How would this affect their willingness to believe rumors about Christ's return (v. 2)? **3.** Whom do you think is the restrainer of this lawless one (vv. 6–7)? How do you think this "restraining order" is enforced? **4.** What is God's ultimate purpose in allowing the "man of lawlessness" to deceive people? What signs mark his appearing? **5.**

---

a1 Greek *Silvanus*, a variant of *Silas*   b12 Or *God and Lord, Jesus Christ*
c3 Some manuscripts *sin*

⁸And then the lawless one will be revealed, whom the Lord Jesus will overthrow with the breath of his mouth and destroy by the splendor of his coming. ⁹The coming of the lawless one will be in accordance with the work of Satan displayed in all kinds of counterfeit miracles, signs and wonders, ¹⁰and in every sort of evil that deceives those who are perishing. They perish because they refused to love the truth and so be saved. ¹¹For this reason God sends them a powerful delusion so that they will believe the lie ¹²and so that all will be condemned who have not believed the truth but have delighted in wickedness.

Stand Firm

¹³But we ought always to thank God for you, brothers loved by the Lord, because from the beginning God chose you*a* to be saved through the sanctifying work of the Spirit and through belief in the truth. ¹⁴He called you to this through our gospel, that you might share in the glory of our Lord Jesus Christ. ¹⁵So then, brothers, stand firm and hold to the teachings*b* we passed on to you, whether by word of mouth or by letter.

¹⁶May our Lord Jesus Christ himself and God our Father, who loved us and by his grace gave us eternal encouragement and good hope, ¹⁷encourage your hearts and strengthen you in every good deed and word.

Request for Prayer

3 Finally, brothers, pray for us that the message of the Lord may spread rapidly and be honored, just as it was with you. ²And pray that we may be delivered from wicked and evil men, for not everyone has faith. ³But the Lord is faithful, and he will strengthen and protect you from the evil one. ⁴We have confidence in the Lord that you are doing and will continue to do the things we command. ⁵May the Lord direct your hearts into God's love and Christ's perseverance.

Warning Against Idleness

⁶In the name of the Lord Jesus Christ, we command you, brothers, to keep away from every brother who is idle and does not live according to the teaching*c* you received from us. ⁷For you yourselves know how you ought to follow our example. We were not idle when we were with you, ⁸nor did we eat anyone's food without paying for it. On the contrary, we worked night and day, laboring and toiling so that we would not be a burden to any of you. ⁹We did this, not because we do not have the right to such help, but in order to make ourselves a model for you to follow. ¹⁰For even when we were with you, we gave you this rule: "If a man will not work, he shall not eat."

¹¹We hear that some among you are idle. They are not busy; they are busybodies. ¹²Such people we command and urge in the Lord Jesus Christ to settle down and earn the bread they eat. ¹³And as for you, brothers, never tire of doing what is right.

¹⁴If anyone does not obey our instruction in this letter, take special note of him. Do not associate with him, in order that he may feel ashamed. ¹⁵Yet do not regard him as an enemy, but warn him as a brother.

How will those who refuse Christ respond to this "man"? How does the "powerful delusion" sent by God differ from the deceptive evil of this "man" (vv. 10–12)? How and why will God save his people (vv. 13–14)? In response to God's initiative and Paul's ministry, what are the people to do?

1. How does this passage on Christ's Second Coming, and what will precede it, make you feel? Afraid? Relieved? Rather not think about it? Why? How do you think Paul would have wanted you to feel? **2.** What encouragement do verses 13–14 give you as you face hard times? Where do you need encouragement and strength from God now? **3.** Put this prayer (vv. 16–17) in your own words and pray it for one another this week.

---

1. What is one prayer you were taught to memorize? **2.** What was your first paid job? How long or hard did you work at it? What did you do with your money?

1. Paul has twice prayed for these people (1:11–12; 2:16–17). How does he want them to pray for him and his companions? How would the encouragements in verses 3–5 help them in their trials? **2.** How might a misunderstanding of Paul's earlier teaching (1Th 5:1–3) have led to the problem of idleness? Why would Paul see that as a serious problem *then* (see 1Th 4:11–12) and *now* (see v. 6)? What model does Paul leave for the others to follow (vv. 7–13)? What does this have to do with taking responsibility? **3.** Why does Paul call attention to his handwriting (v. 17)? How else is the close of the letter similar to its beginning? Why do you think Paul emphasizes grace and peace? What does it say about God's will?

1. On a scale from 1 (high anxiety) to 10 (blissfully peaceful), where would you rate your sense of God's peace now? Where in particular do you need group prayer and support? **2.** How

---

a13 Some manuscripts *because God chose you as his firstfruits*   *b15* Or *traditions*
c6 Or *tradition*

are God's love and Christ's perseverance needed in your life now? **3.** What have you found helpful in encouraging you to pray for missionaries? For whom do you regularly pray? What types of pressures may he or she face in that part of the world? **4.** Are you idle, a busybody, a worrywart or a workaholic? What is God's message to you in 2 Thessalonians?

Final Greetings

[16]Now may the Lord of peace himself give you peace at all times and in every way. The Lord be with all of you.

[17]I, Paul, write this greeting in my own hand, which is the distinguishing mark in all my letters. This is how I write.

[18]The grace of our Lord Jesus Christ be with you all.

INTRODUCTION to
1 TIMOTHY

Book Study Outline: If you are using 1 Timothy for a study course, here is a 6- or 8-week outline. Use the margin questions for your agenda:

🍵 start meeting / 15 min.

📖 read & discuss Bible / 30 min.

♡ close meeting / 15–45 min.

6-week plan	8-week plan	Group Study Passage
1	1	1:1–11/False Teachers of the Law
	2	1:12–20/True Mercy for Sinners
2	3	2:1–15/Orderly Worship
3	4	3:1–16/Faithful Leadership
4	5	4:1–16/Redemptive Ministry
5	6	5:1–6:2/Widows, Elders and Slaves
6	7	6:3–10/Love of Money
	8	6:11–21/Fighting the Good Fight

Refer to the Questions and Answers in front of Bible for more information.

Author: The apostle Paul. However, based on considerations of vocabulary and style, the Pauline authorship of the Pastoral Epistles (1 and 2 Timothy, Titus) has been questioned by some scholars.

Date: About A.D. 63–65.

Theme: A faithful ministry.

Historical Background: Timothy, a young man from Lystra, was probably converted during Paul's first missionary journey. When Paul returned to the area a year or two later, Timothy was recommended to him as a faithful disciple of Christ who would make a good traveling companion (Ac 16). From that time on, Timothy is associated with Paul. After Paul was released from his imprisonment in Rome (Ac 28), he, Titus and Timothy went on a preaching tour (see the Introduction to Titus). At Ephesus, Paul discovered that heresy was rotting away the church. It seems that the false teaching involved speculation about obscure matters rather than exposition about Christ and the Christian lifestyle of love. The teachers were characterized as proud, arrogant, contentious and greedy. As a result, Paul excommunicated two of the erring elders (1:19–20) and put Timothy in charge of helping the church recover from its problems (1:3–4). Paul then went on to Macedonia where he wrote this letter to encourage Timothy in his restorative work.

Characteristics: As a result of being called the "Pastoral Epistles," 1 and 2 Timothy and Titus have typically been viewed as manuals for church structure and order. However, 1 Timothy, as well as the other two letters, is a response to a particular crisis in a particular church, not a general commentary on how a church should be run. Its value is not to be found so much in trying to determine church structure (which in the NT appears to be quite fluid), but in determining the character of people who ought to be in leadership. (See the list of qualifications in the Introduction to Titus.)

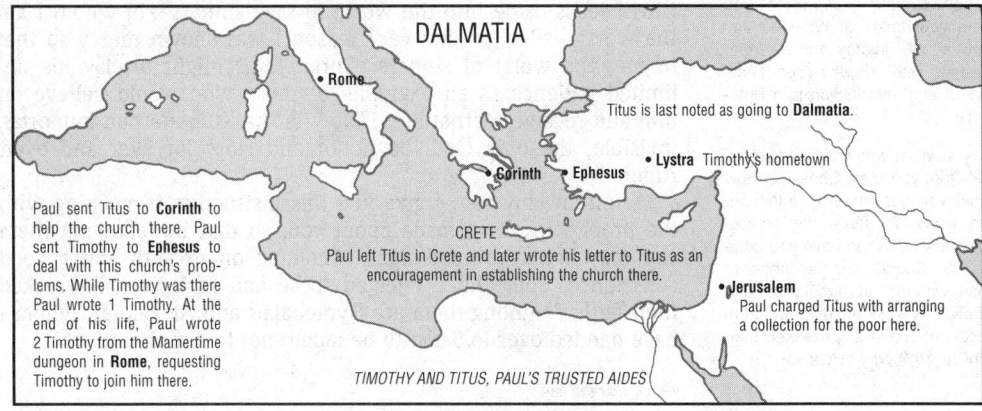

DALMATIA

Rome

Titus is last noted as going to **Dalmatia**.

• **Lystra** Timothy's hometown

Corinth • Ephesus

Paul sent Titus to **Corinth** to help the church there. Paul sent Timothy to **Ephesus** to deal with this church's problems. While Timothy was there Paul wrote 1 Timothy. At the end of his life, Paul wrote 2 Timothy from the Mamertime dungeon in **Rome**, requesting Timothy to join him there.

CRETE
Paul left Titus in Crete and later wrote his letter to Titus as an encouragement in establishing the church there.

• Jerusalem
Paul charged Titus with arranging a collection for the poor here.

TIMOTHY AND TITUS, PAUL'S TRUSTED AIDES

1 Timothy

1. Growing up, what was your father's occupation? Your mother's? **2.** How did they settle sibling fights?

1. What were the problems plaguing the church in Ephesus (vv. 3–4)? How do you think Timothy felt being left in charge of this situation? **2.** What does Paul want Timothy to work toward (v. 5)? How does this differ from the false teachers' work (v. 7)? **3.** For whom is the Law really intended (vv. 9–11)?

1. When did God become your "hope" (v. 1)? In your experience, has God been more of a "lawgiver" or a "lover"? Has your understanding of God changed as you've come to know him? How? **2.** Who in your life would think of you as their "son or daughter in the faith" as Paul addresses Timothy?

Who holds the record in your group for most speeding tickets? Most times "grounded"?

1. What are Paul's credentials—what gives him authority over the false teachers (v. 12)? **2.** Why is someone like Paul such a good witness to unbelievers (v. 16)? How do you feel about talking about your past when you share your faith? **3.** What do you know about Timothy and his relationship with Paul? (See Acts 16:1–5 and Introduction to 1 Timothy.)

1. What was your life like before you knew Christ? **2.** How would you put verse 15 into your own words to share the Gospel with a friend? When have you done this? **3.** Should our response to those who act in "ignorance and unbelief" (v. 13) be different from those who "have shipwrecked their faith" (v. 19)? Why? How so?

1 Paul, an apostle of Christ Jesus by the command of God our Savior and of Christ Jesus our hope,

²To Timothy my true son in the faith:

Grace, mercy and peace from God the Father and Christ Jesus our Lord.

Warning Against False Teachers of the Law

³As I urged you when I went into Macedonia, stay there in Ephesus so that you may command certain men not to teach false doctrines any longer ⁴nor to devote themselves to myths and endless genealogies. These promote controversies rather than God's work—which is by faith. ⁵The goal of this command is love, which comes from a pure heart and a good conscience and a sincere faith. ⁶Some have wandered away from these and turned to meaningless talk. ⁷They want to be teachers of the law, but they do not know what they are talking about or what they so confidently affirm.

⁸We know that the law is good if one uses it properly. ⁹We also know that lawᵃ is made not for the righteous but for lawbreakers and rebels, the ungodly and sinful, the unholy and irreligious; for those who kill their fathers or mothers, for murderers, ¹⁰for adulterers and perverts, for slave traders and liars and perjurers—and for whatever else is contrary to the sound doctrine ¹¹that conforms to the glorious gospel of the blessed God, which he entrusted to me.

The Lord's Grace to Paul

¹²I thank Christ Jesus our Lord, who has given me strength, that he considered me faithful, appointing me to his service. ¹³Even though I was once a blasphemer and a persecutor and a violent man, I was shown mercy because I acted in ignorance and unbelief. ¹⁴The grace of our Lord was poured out on me abundantly, along with the faith and love that are in Christ Jesus.

¹⁵Here is a trustworthy saying that deserves full acceptance: Christ Jesus came into the world to save sinners—of whom I am the worst. ¹⁶But for that very reason I was shown mercy so that in me, the worst of sinners, Christ Jesus might display his unlimited patience as an example for those who would believe on him and receive eternal life. ¹⁷Now to the King eternal, immortal, invisible, the only God, be honor and glory for ever and ever. Amen.

¹⁸Timothy, my son, I give you this instruction in keeping with the prophecies once made about you, so that by following them you may fight the good fight, ¹⁹holding on to faith and a good conscience. Some have rejected these and so have shipwrecked their faith. ²⁰Among them are Hymenaeus and Alexander, whom I have handed over to Satan to be taught not to blaspheme.

ᵃ9 Or *that the law*

Instructions on Worship

2 I urge, then, first of all, that requests, prayers, intercession and thanksgiving be made for everyone— ²for kings and all those in authority, that we may live peaceful and quiet lives in all godliness and holiness. ³This is good, and pleases God our Savior, ⁴who wants all men to be saved and to come to a knowledge of the truth. ⁵For there is one God and one mediator between God and men, the man Christ Jesus, ⁶who gave himself as a ransom for all men— the testimony given in its proper time. ⁷And for this purpose I was appointed a herald and an apostle—I am telling the truth, I am not lying—and a teacher of the true faith to the Gentiles.

⁸I want men everywhere to lift up holy hands in prayer, without anger or disputing.

⁹I also want women to dress modestly, with decency and propriety, not with braided hair or gold or pearls or expensive clothes, ¹⁰but with good deeds, appropriate for women who profess to worship God.

¹¹A woman should learn in quietness and full submission. ¹²I do not permit a woman to teach or to have authority over a man; she must be silent. ¹³For Adam was formed first, then Eve. ¹⁴And Adam was not the one deceived; it was the woman who was deceived and became a sinner. ¹⁵But women*a* will be saved*b* through childbearing—if they continue in faith, love and holiness with propriety.

Overseers and Deacons

3 Here is a trustworthy saying: If anyone sets his heart on being an overseer,*c* he desires a noble task. ²Now the overseer must be above reproach, the husband of but one wife, temperate, self-controlled, respectable, hospitable, able to teach, ³not given to drunkenness, not violent but gentle, not quarrelsome, not a lover of money. ⁴He must manage his own family well and see that his children obey him with proper respect. ⁵(If anyone does not know how to manage his own family, how can he take care of God's church?) ⁶He must not be a recent convert, or he may become conceited and fall under the same judgment as the devil. ⁷He must also have a good reputation with outsiders, so that he will not fall into disgrace and into the devil's trap.

⁸Deacons, likewise, are to be men worthy of respect, sincere, not indulging in much wine, and not pursuing dishonest gain. ⁹They must keep hold of the deep truths of the faith with a clear conscience. ¹⁰They must first be tested; and then if there is nothing against them, let them serve as deacons.

¹¹In the same way, their wives*d* are to be women worthy of respect, not malicious talkers but temperate and trustworthy in everything.

¹²A deacon must be the husband of but one wife and must manage his children and his household well. ¹³Those who have served well gain an excellent standing and great assurance in their faith in Christ Jesus.

¹⁴Although I hope to come to you soon, I am writing you these instructions so that, ¹⁵if I am delayed, you will know how people ought to conduct themselves in God's household, which is the church of the living God, the pillar and foundation of the truth. ¹⁶Beyond all question, the mystery of godliness is great:

Did you go to church as a child? Was worship inspiring?

1. For whom is Paul asking that prayers for salvation be made (vv. 1,4,6–7)? Have you felt certain people were too far gone for salvation? What would Paul say? 2. What seemed to be going on in worship in Ephesus (vv. 8–12)? 3. Are verses 9–15 meant for all times and places, or for a problem at Ephesus (see 1:3–4; 2Ti 3:6–7)? What other principles from Scripture or your experience of God help you decide what women's God-given roles are?

1. What worship attitudes do you want to cultivate? 2. Often the church has not allowed women to use God-given gifts. How does Christ affirm your worth even when others do not?

1. As a child, how did you treat your babysitters? How did they treat you? 2. Do you enjoy babysitting?

1. Why is this list of leadership qualifications focused on the outward as well as the inward? Why is this important considering the Ephesian church's problem with false teachers (v. 5)? 2. How do you interpret "the husband of but one wife" (v. 2)? Does that mean the overseer must not be single? Divorced? Widowed? Remarried? A polygamist? Or does it demand sexual fidelity if married (see also 5:9)? 3. How do you interpret verse 4? What if a godly man who meets the other qualifications has a child who is rebellious and a troublemaker? 4. What central facts about Jesus are summed up in the hymn (v. 16)?

1. Although applied specifically to leaders here, why are these qualities important for all Christians? 2. Of these qualities, what are two or three you have made progress with in this past year? In which area do you want to grow now? How can this group help you? 3. What positions in your church are the equivalent to those of overseers and deacons? Are these basic guidelines followed?

a15 Greek *she*   *b15* Or *restored*   *c1* Traditionally *bishop*; also in verse 2
d11 Or *way, deaconesses*

He*a* appeared in a body, *b*
    was vindicated by the Spirit,
    was seen by angels,
    was preached among the nations,
    was believed on in the world,
    was taken up in glory.

Instructions to Timothy

4 The Spirit clearly says that in later times some will abandon the faith and follow deceiving spirits and things taught by demons. [2]Such teachings come through hypocritical liars, whose consciences have been seared as with a hot iron. [3]They forbid people to marry and order them to abstain from certain foods, which God created to be received with thanksgiving by those who believe and who know the truth. [4]For everything God created is good, and nothing is to be rejected if it is received with thanksgiving, [5]because it is consecrated by the word of God and prayer.

[6]If you point these things out to the brothers, you will be a good minister of Christ Jesus, brought up in the truths of the faith and of the good teaching that you have followed. [7]Have nothing to do with godless myths and old wives' tales; rather, train yourself to be godly. [8]For physical training is of some value, but godliness has value for all things, holding promise for both the present life and the life to come.

[9]This is a trustworthy saying that deserves full acceptance [10](and for this we labor and strive), that we have put our hope in the living God, who is the Savior of all men, and especially of those who believe.

[11]Command and teach these things. [12]Don't let anyone look down on you because you are young, but set an example for the believers in speech, in life, in love, in faith and in purity. [13]Until I come, devote yourself to the public reading of Scripture, to preaching and to teaching. [14]Do not neglect your gift, which was given you through a prophetic message when the body of elders laid their hands on you.

[15]Be diligent in these matters; give yourself wholly to them, so that everyone may see your progress. [16]Watch your life and doctrine closely. Persevere in them, because if you do, you will save both yourself and your hearers.

Advice About Widows, Elders and Slaves

5 Do not rebuke an older man harshly, but exhort him as if he were your father. Treat younger men as brothers, [2]older women as mothers, and younger women as sisters, with absolute purity.

[3]Give proper recognition to those widows who are really in need. [4]But if a widow has children or grandchildren, these should learn first of all to put their religion into practice by caring for their own family and so repaying their parents and grandparents, for this is pleasing to God. [5]The widow who is really in need and left all alone puts her hope in God and continues night and day to pray and to ask God for help. [6]But the widow who lives for pleasure is dead even while she lives. [7]Give the people these instructions, too, so that no one may be open to blame. [8]If anyone does not provide for his relatives, and especially for his immediate family, he has denied the faith and is worse than an unbeliever.

[9]No widow may be put on the list of widows unless she is over

---

What do you do to keep in shape? How physically fit are you?

1. Why is it hypocritical to preach abstinence from marriage and certain foods (see Mk 7:18–19)? What do the teachings in verse 3 imply about these teachers' views of spirituality? 2. What are the limits to the "freedom" principle of verses 4–5? 3. What does Paul mean by "train yourself to be godly" (vv. 7,11–16)?

1. How do you identify hypocrisy versus human imperfection? 2. Do you spend more time and energy on physical training or godliness training? How intense has your godliness training been this year? In the past? With your children? Have you neglected the use of any God-given gifts (v. 14)? 3. What disciplines should be part of a person's spiritual growth program? Which do you want to work on? 4. Some of your coworkers may have been hurt by the church in some way. What in this passage might you practice to influence them toward Christ?

Growing up, what proverb best described the way your family used money: "Waste not, want not"? "Eat, drink and be merry"? "You can't take it with you"? "A penny saved is a penny earned"? "Penny wise, pound foolish"?

1. Reading between the lines, what was the problem with widows in the church? 2. What possible abuses of care for the needy does Paul imply in verses 4–8? Verses 9–10? Verses 11–15? Is a different response to each person in need appropriate in today's church as well? 3. Why are church elders in general to receive "double honor" (v. 17)? Do they receive this honor in your church? Why do some elders deserve pub-

---

a16 Some manuscripts *God*   *b16* Or *in the flesh*

sixty, has been faithful to her husband,[a] [10]and is well known for her good deeds, such as bringing up children, showing hospitality, washing the feet of the saints, helping those in trouble and devoting herself to all kinds of good deeds.

[11]As for younger widows, do not put them on such a list. For when their sensual desires overcome their dedication to Christ, they want to marry. [12]Thus they bring judgment on themselves, because they have broken their first pledge. [13]Besides, they get into the habit of being idle and going about from house to house. And not only do they become idlers, but also gossips and busybodies, saying things they ought not to. [14]So I counsel younger widows to marry, to have children, to manage their homes and to give the enemy no opportunity for slander. [15]Some have in fact already turned away to follow Satan.

[16]If any woman who is a believer has widows in her family, she should help them and not let the church be burdened with them, so that the church can help those widows who are really in need.

[17]The elders who direct the affairs of the church well are worthy of double honor, especially those whose work is preaching and teaching. [18]For the Scripture says, "Do not muzzle the ox while it is treading out the grain,"[b] and "The worker deserves his wages."[c] [19]Do not entertain an accusation against an elder unless it is brought by two or three witnesses. [20]Those who sin are to be rebuked publicly, so that the others may take warning.

[21]I charge you, in the sight of God and Christ Jesus and the elect angels, to keep these instructions without partiality, and to do nothing out of favoritism.

[22]Do not be hasty in the laying on of hands, and do not share in the sins of others. Keep yourself pure.

[23]Stop drinking only water, and use a little wine because of your stomach and your frequent illnesses.

[24]The sins of some men are obvious, reaching the place of judgment ahead of them; the sins of others trail behind them. [25]In the same way, good deeds are obvious, and even those that are not cannot be hidden.

6 All who are under the yoke of slavery should consider their masters worthy of full respect, so that God's name and our teaching may not be slandered. [2]Those who have believing masters are not to show less respect for them because they are brothers. Instead, they are to serve them even better, because those who benefit from their service are believers, and dear to them. These are the things you are to teach and urge on them.

Love of Money

[3]If anyone teaches false doctrines and does not agree to the sound instruction of our Lord Jesus Christ and to godly teaching, [4]he is conceited and understands nothing. He has an unhealthy interest in controversies and quarrels about words that result in envy, strife, malicious talk, evil suspicions [5]and constant friction between men of corrupt mind, who have been robbed of the truth and who think that godliness is a means to financial gain.

[6]But godliness with contentment is great gain. [7]For we brought nothing into the world, and we can take nothing out of it. [8]But if we have food and clothing, we will be content with that. [9]People who want to get rich fall into temptation and a trap and into many foolish and harmful desires that plunge men into ruin and destruc-

lic rebuke? 4. Why doesn't Paul proclaim slavery to be wrong? 5. Why might a Christian slave's lack of respect for his master result in the slander of God's name and Christian teaching (6:1–2)? How does this instruction relate to your work situation?

1. Have you or someone you have known ever suddenly become single? What was that time like? Who in your church needs some help that you or your group can provide? 2. What should be the Christian's/Church's response to the welfare issue?

What was your first job? How much did you get paid?

1. How is the life of one who follows verses 6–8 different from one in verses 9–10? How can you distinguish between them? 2. What is the "great gain" in "godliness with contentment"?

1. When have you struggled most financially? When have you been tempted to be a "lover of money"? 2. Is there a difference between enjoying money and being a lover of money? How fine is the line?

[a]9 Or has had but one husband   [b]18 Deut. 25:4   [c]18 Luke 10:7

1. Growing up, did your parents tend to overprotect you, or push you beyond your limits? 2. With your children, what are you going to do (or have you done) differently when it comes to risk-taking versus playing it safe?

1. What is Timothy told to flee? To pursue (v. 11)? How does a person pursue these qualities? Which one do you particularly want to pursue? 2. How do you think Timothy felt reading the challenge in verses 12–16? How would you respond to this challenge? Why? 3. Why does Paul use battle imagery in verse 12? What does this tell you about what we must expect in the Christian life? 4. Why do you think Paul added more instructions to the wealthy (vv. 17–19)? In your opinion, is it easier for a rich person or a poor person to follow the command in verse 18? Why?

1. What grade would God give you for verse 11? Verses 18–19? 2. What kinds of "godless chatter" and "false knowledge" (v. 20) do Christians need to turn away from today? Which do you need to be especially cautious of? 3. Who in your life may be a "Timothy" for whom God would have you be a "Paul"? 4. What false teachings are you aware of and concerned about today? How can you help your church to be on guard, and to present a strong offense?

tion. ¹⁰For the love of money is a root of all kinds of evil. Some people, eager for money, have wandered from the faith and pierced themselves with many griefs.

Paul's Charge to Timothy

¹¹But you, man of God, flee from all this, and pursue righteousness, godliness, faith, love, endurance and gentleness. ¹²Fight the good fight of the faith. Take hold of the eternal life to which you were called when you made your good confession in the presence of many witnesses. ¹³In the sight of God, who gives life to everything, and of Christ Jesus, who while testifying before Pontius Pilate made the good confession, I charge you ¹⁴to keep this command without spot or blame until the appearing of our Lord Jesus Christ, ¹⁵which God will bring about in his own time—God, the blessed and only Ruler, the King of kings and Lord of lords, ¹⁶who alone is immortal and who lives in unapproachable light, whom no one has seen or can see. To him be honor and might forever. Amen.

¹⁷Command those who are rich in this present world not to be arrogant nor to put their hope in wealth, which is so uncertain, but to put their hope in God, who richly provides us with everything for our enjoyment. ¹⁸Command them to do good, to be rich in good deeds, and to be generous and willing to share. ¹⁹In this way they will lay up treasure for themselves as a firm foundation for the coming age, so that they may take hold of the life that is truly life.

²⁰Timothy, guard what has been entrusted to your care. Turn away from godless chatter and the opposing ideas of what is falsely called knowledge, ²¹which some have professed and in so doing have wandered from the faith.

Grace be with you.

INTRODUCTION to
2 TIMOTHY

Book Study Outline: If you are using 2 Timothy for a study course, here is a 4-week outline. Use the margin questions for your group agenda:

4-week plan	Group Study Passage
1	1:1–2:13/Be Strong in Christ
2	2:14–3:9/Be a Good Workman
3	3:10–4:8/Be Faithful
4	4:9–22/To God Be the Glory

🍵 start meeting / 15 min.

📖 read & discuss Bible / 30 min.

♡ close meeting / 15–45 min.

Refer to the Questions and Answers in front of Bible for more information.

Author: The apostle Paul. However, based on considerations of vocabulary and style, the Pauline authorship of the Pastoral Epistles (1 and 2 Timothy, Titus) has been questioned by some scholars.

Date: Near the end of Paul's life, c. A.D. 67–68.

Theme: Guard the Gospel.

Historical Background: In the spring following the writing of 1 Timothy, Paul was on his way to Ephesus when he was arrested, taken back to Rome, and thrown into prison. It was the time of Nero's insane persecution of Christians, and so he was put in a dungeon "like a criminal" (2:9). He had had a preliminary trial (4:16). His full trial was ahead but Paul did not expect to be released (4:6). In this letter he writes to Timothy encouraging him to hold on to the faith no matter what, and to come to him as soon as he could. Whether he ever saw Timothy again is not known. According to tradition, Paul was beheaded shortly after this letter was written.

Characteristics: Although similar in some ways to 1 Timothy and Titus, 2 Timothy is far more personal in tone. The other two letters were somewhat "business-like" in their discussion of the problems facing the church. This one is the deeply intimate testimony of a man who, having invested his life in the cause of Jesus Christ, wishes to pass on that commitment to a younger man who will carry the torch further. Timothy was the logical choice for this responsibility. He had been a trusted colleague of Paul's for over 15 years and had proved his loyalty to Jesus Christ again and again. This was a critical time for the churches in Europe and Asia. Under Nero's persecution, Rome, which had previously protected the rights of Christians whom they viewed as simply a sect of Jews, had turned against Christianity. Furthermore, there had been widespread apostasy in Asia (1:15). Paul, the missionary who had worked so hard in establishing these churches, was facing death. Now it would be up to Timothy and others to guard the Gospel. Yet, despite the problems, there is a clear note of triumph in this letter. The Gospel cannot be chained (2:9); the church will prevail (4:8); and Paul will be with the Lord (4:18).

THE LAST WORDS OF PAUL

To Timothy

"...fan into flame the gift of God..."
2Ti 1:6

"...do not be ashamed to testify about our Lord..."
2Ti 1:8

"Endure hardship with us like a good soldier of Christ Jesus."
2Ti 2:3

"Do your best to present yourself to God as one approved, a workman who does not need to be ashamed and who correctly handles the word of truth."
2Ti 2:15

"Preach the word; be prepared in season and out of season..."
2Ti 4:2

About Himself

"...I am not ashamed, because I know whom I have believed, and am convinced that he is able to guard what I have entrusted to him for that day."
2Ti 1:12

"I am already being poured out like a drink offering, and the time has come for my departure."
2Ti 4:6

"I have fought the good fight, I have finished the race, I have kept the faith."
2Ti 4:7

"The Lord will rescue me from every evil attack and will bring me safely to his heavenly kingdom."
2Ti 4:18

2 Timothy

☕ **1.** What physical traits have you inherited from your father's side of the family? Your mother's? **2.** Of all your friends from high school, who are still your friends today?

📖 **1.** What do you know or remember about Timothy? (See Introductions to 1 and 2 Timothy; Ac 16:1–3.) **2.** What kind of spiritual heritage did Timothy receive from his family? How does that compare with your spiritual heritage? **3.** Along with being reminded of Timothy's sincere faith, what does Paul remind Timothy to do? **4.** What is one weakness that Timothy has and what does Paul remind him of regarding it (v. 7)? **5.** What pressures might pull at Timothy to be ashamed of the Gospel or of Paul? What kept Paul from being ashamed himself (v. 12)? What keeps you from being ashamed of the Gospel? **6.** How is Timothy to ensure that the message of Christ will live on (2:1–2)? Given Paul's outlook that his days are numbered (see Introduction to 2 Timothy), why was this point particularly crucial to him? **7.** What do the examples of the soldier, athlete and farmer (2:3–7) teach about the Christian life? How would these illustrations encourage Timothy to steadfastly endure his own suffering? **8.** In spite of his suffering, what keeps Paul from giving up (2:8–10)? What has kept you going in times of suffering? **9.** How does the hymn in 2:11–13 pull together the key themes of this passage?

♡ **1.** What were the key factors and events in your life that led to what Paul calls a "sincere faith"? **2.** Have you had a spiritual parent or mentor like Paul? If so, who? **3.** Have you had a spiritual child or trainee like Timothy? If so, who? **4.** When you first decided to follow Jesus, did you assume it would be a bed of roses or a bed of nails? What have you learned about the cost of following Jesus since then? **5.** What role do suffering and endurance play in your life?

1 Paul, an apostle of Christ Jesus by the will of God, according to the promise of life that is in Christ Jesus,

²To Timothy, my dear son:

Grace, mercy and peace from God the Father and Christ Jesus our Lord.

Encouragement to Be Faithful

³I thank God, whom I serve, as my forefathers did, with a clear conscience, as night and day I constantly remember you in my prayers. ⁴Recalling your tears, I long to see you, so that I may be filled with joy. ⁵I have been reminded of your sincere faith, which first lived in your grandmother Lois and in your mother Eunice and, I am persuaded, now lives in you also. ⁶For this reason I remind you to fan into flame the gift of God, which is in you through the laying on of my hands. ⁷For God did not give us a spirit of timidity, but a spirit of power, of love and of self-discipline.

⁸So do not be ashamed to testify about our Lord, or ashamed of me his prisoner. But join with me in suffering for the gospel, by the power of God, ⁹who has saved us and called us to a holy life—not because of anything we have done but because of his own purpose and grace. This grace was given us in Christ Jesus before the beginning of time, ¹⁰but it has now been revealed through the appearing of our Savior, Christ Jesus, who has destroyed death and has brought life and immortality to light through the gospel. ¹¹And of this gospel I was appointed a herald and an apostle and a teacher. ¹²That is why I am suffering as I am. Yet I am not ashamed, because I know whom I have believed, and am convinced that he is able to guard what I have entrusted to him for that day.

¹³What you heard from me, keep as the pattern of sound teaching, with faith and love in Christ Jesus. ¹⁴Guard the good deposit that was entrusted to you—guard it with the help of the Holy Spirit who lives in us.

¹⁵You know that everyone in the province of Asia has deserted me, including Phygelus and Hermogenes.

¹⁶May the Lord show mercy to the household of Onesiphorus, because he often refreshed me and was not ashamed of my chains. ¹⁷On the contrary, when he was in Rome, he searched hard for me until he found me. ¹⁸May the Lord grant that he will find mercy from the Lord on that day! You know very well in how many ways he helped me in Ephesus.

2 You then, my son, be strong in the grace that is in Christ Jesus. ²And the things you have heard me say in the presence of many witnesses entrust to reliable men who will also be qualified to teach others. ³Endure hardship with us like a good soldier of Christ Jesus. ⁴No one serving as a soldier gets involved in civilian affairs—he wants to please his commanding officer. ⁵Similarly, if anyone competes as an athlete, he does not receive the victor's crown unless he competes according to the rules. ⁶The hardworking farmer should be the first to receive a share of the crops. ⁷Reflect on what I am saying, for the Lord will give you insight into all this.

[8]Remember Jesus Christ, raised from the dead, descended from David. This is my gospel, [9]for which I am suffering even to the point of being chained like a criminal. But God's word is not chained. [10]Therefore I endure everything for the sake of the elect, that they too may obtain the salvation that is in Christ Jesus, with eternal glory.

[11]Here is a trustworthy saying:

> If we died with him,
>   we will also live with him;
> [12]if we endure,
>   we will also reign with him.
> If we disown him,
>   he will also disown us;
> [13]if we are faithless,
>   he will remain faithful,
>   for he cannot disown himself.

A Workman Approved by God

[14]Keep reminding them of these things. Warn them before God against quarreling about words; it is of no value, and only ruins those who listen. [15]Do your best to present yourself to God as one approved, a workman who does not need to be ashamed and who correctly handles the word of truth. [16]Avoid godless chatter, because those who indulge in it will become more and more ungodly. [17]Their teaching will spread like gangrene. Among them are Hymenaeus and Philetus, [18]who have wandered away from the truth. They say that the resurrection has already taken place, and they destroy the faith of some. [19]Nevertheless, God's solid foundation stands firm, sealed with this inscription: "The Lord knows those who are his,"[a] and, "Everyone who confesses the name of the Lord must turn away from wickedness."

[20]In a large house there are articles not only of gold and silver, but also of wood and clay; some are for noble purposes and some for ignoble. [21]If a man cleanses himself from the latter, he will be an instrument for noble purposes, made holy, useful to the Master and prepared to do any good work.

[22]Flee the evil desires of youth, and pursue righteousness, faith, love and peace, along with those who call on the Lord out of a pure heart. [23]Don't have anything to do with foolish and stupid arguments, because you know they produce quarrels. [24]And the Lord's servant must not quarrel; instead, he must be kind to everyone, able to teach, not resentful. [25]Those who oppose him he must gently instruct, in the hope that God will grant them repentance leading them to a knowledge of the truth, [26]and that they will come to their senses and escape from the trap of the devil, who has taken them captive to do his will.

Godlessness in the Last Days

3 But mark this: There will be terrible times in the last days. [2]People will be lovers of themselves, lovers of money, boastful, proud, abusive, disobedient to their parents, ungrateful, unholy, [3]without love, unforgiving, slanderous, without self-control, brutal, not lovers of the good, [4]treacherous, rash, conceited, lovers of pleasure rather than lovers of God— [5]having a form of godliness but denying its power. Have nothing to do with them.

a19 Num. 16:5 (see Septuagint)

What did you and your siblings quarrel about as kids?

1. Looking over this passage, what should you pursue (the "Dos"), and flee (the Don'ts)? **2.** What are the effects of false teaching (vv. 17–18)? **3.** What security and challenge do the inscriptions of verse 19 give the church today? **4.** Since repentance means "changing directions," how does repentance (v. 25) relate to fleeing and pursuing (v. 22)?

1. How do you know if you are "quarreling about words" or standing up against false teaching? Which do most Christians spend more time doing? How about you? **2.** Can you be a "noble vessel" (vv. 20–21)? How? **3.** What do you need to flee: Being vulnerable to false teaching and side issues? Arguing about theology? Being a "know-it-all"? Sharing your views unkindly? **4.** What do you need to pursue: Righteousness? Faith? Love? Peace? Other?

1. Contrast the people described here to one who lives by a pure love (see Mt 22:37,39). **2.** According to Jewish tradition, Jannes and Jambres were Egyptian court magicians (see Ex 7:11, 22; 8:7,18). How do "those who oppose the truth" exhibit what Paul means by a "form of godliness"? Why are they dangerous?

1. When have you "looked godly" but lacked a true heart for God? 2. When Paul says, "Have nothing to do with them," (v. 5) is he talking about all evil-doers or only "professing" Christians? Do you reach out to sinners or withdraw into a safe haven?

Have your parents written a will? Have you written one? Why or why not?

1. What areas of Paul's life does he ask Timothy to consider (3:10–13)? 2. What is the crux of what Paul has to say about Timothy's life (3:14–17)? 3. What does Paul state about the origin and purpose of Scripture (3:16)? 4. What nine final orders does Paul solemnly charge Timothy to fulfill (4:1–5)? 5. In the climax of this letter—the last recorded message Paul wrote—how does the apostle sum up his life and ministry.

1. Do you share Paul's hope for the future? How does it motivate you now? 2. How do Paul's words challenge your life? Are you fighting "the good fight" no matter what persecution and suffering you face? 3. How does this Scripture challenge your ministry? What are you doing to build it into your life, and how bold are you to share it faithfully rather than to tell people what they want to hear?

If you "left home without it," what would be the first thing you'd ask someone to send?

1. What do you learn about Paul, the man, in these personal remarks? How do you think he felt—in a cold prison cell, virtually alone because his friends were either busy or had deserted him? 2. What do you remember about the young man Mark, who had accompanied Paul on a missionary trip years earlier (see Ac 13:13; 15:36–41)? What is the lesson here for you? 3. What has the Lord done and what will he do for Paul in the future (vv. 17–18)?

6They are the kind who worm their way into homes and gain control over weak-willed women, who are loaded down with sins and are swayed by all kinds of evil desires, 7always learning but never able to acknowledge the truth. 8Just as Jannes and Jambres opposed Moses, so also these men oppose the truth—men of depraved minds, who, as far as the faith is concerned, are rejected. 9But they will not get very far because, as in the case of those men, their folly will be clear to everyone.

Paul's Charge to Timothy

10You, however, know all about my teaching, my way of life, my purpose, faith, patience, love, endurance, 11persecutions, sufferings—what kinds of things happened to me in Antioch, Iconium and Lystra, the persecutions I endured. Yet the Lord rescued me from all of them. 12In fact, everyone who wants to live a godly life in Christ Jesus will be persecuted, 13while evil men and impostors will go from bad to worse, deceiving and being deceived. 14But as for you, continue in what you have learned and have become convinced of, because you know those from whom you learned it, 15and how from infancy you have known the holy Scriptures, which are able to make you wise for salvation through faith in Christ Jesus. 16All Scripture is God-breathed and is useful for teaching, rebuking, correcting and training in righteousness, 17so that the man of God may be thoroughly equipped for every good work.

4 In the presence of God and of Christ Jesus, who will judge the living and the dead, and in view of his appearing and his kingdom, I give you this charge: 2Preach the Word; be prepared in season and out of season; correct, rebuke and encourage—with great patience and careful instruction. 3For the time will come when men will not put up with sound doctrine. Instead, to suit their own desires, they will gather around them a great number of teachers to say what their itching ears want to hear. 4They will turn their ears away from the truth and turn aside to myths. 5But you, keep your head in all situations, endure hardship, do the work of an evangelist, discharge all the duties of your ministry.

6For I am already being poured out like a drink offering, and the time has come for my departure. 7I have fought the good fight, I have finished the race, I have kept the faith. 8Now there is in store for me the crown of righteousness, which the Lord, the righteous Judge, will award to me on that day—and not only to me, but also to all who have longed for his appearing.

Personal Remarks

9Do your best to come to me quickly, 10for Demas, because he loved this world, has deserted me and has gone to Thessalonica. Crescens has gone to Galatia, and Titus to Dalmatia. 11Only Luke is with me. Get Mark and bring him with you, because he is helpful to me in my ministry. 12I sent Tychicus to Ephesus. 13When you come, bring the cloak that I left with Carpus at Troas, and my scrolls, especially the parchments.

14Alexander the metalworker did me a great deal of harm. The Lord will repay him for what he has done. 15You too should be on your guard against him, because he strongly opposed our message.

16At my first defense, no one came to my support, but everyone deserted me. May it not be held against them. 17But the Lord stood at my side and gave me strength, so that through me the message might be fully proclaimed and all the Gentiles might hear it. And I was delivered from the lion's mouth. [18]The Lord will rescue me from every evil attack and will bring me safely to his heavenly kingdom. To him be glory for ever and ever. Amen.

Final Greetings

[19]Greet Priscilla[a] and Aquila and the household of Onesiphorus. [20]Erastus stayed in Corinth, and I left Trophimus sick in Miletus. [21]Do your best to get here before winter. Eubulus greets you, and so do Pudens, Linus, Claudia and all the brothers. [22]The Lord be with your spirit. Grace be with you.

1. How does Paul's faith and hope, in spite of his suffering, inspire you? **2.** Who are some people who have ministered to you or with you in the past? Why not try to get together again, at least by letter or phone? **3.** What do you most want to apply to your life from 2 Timothy?

---

a 19 Greek *Prisca*, a variant of *Priscilla*

INTRODUCTION to
TITUS

Book Study Outline: If you are using Titus for a study course, here is a 3-week outline. Use the margin questions for your group agenda:

🍵 start meeting / 15 min.

📖 read & discuss Bible / 30 min.

♡ close meeting / 15–45 min.

3-week plan	Group Study Passage
1	1:1–16/Reliable Leaders
2	2:1–15/Sound Doctrine
3	3:1–15/Doing Good

Refer to the Questions and Answers in the front of this Bible for more information.

Author: The apostle Paul. However, based on considerations of vocabulary and style, the Pauline authorship of the Pastoral Epistles (1 and 2 Timothy, Titus) has been questioned by some scholars.

Date: About A.D. 63–65 (at the same time 1 Timothy was written).

Theme: Be devoted to what is good.

Historical Background: Titus was a Gentile who was probably converted through Paul's ministry. He accompanied Paul on his crucial second visit to Jerusalem (Gal 2:1–10). Titus was Paul's trusted friend, sent on difficult assignments. On this trip he was also charged with arranging for a collection for the poor in Jerusalem (2Co 8:16–20). After Paul was released from prison in Rome, Titus and Timothy traveled with him to Crete as part of a preaching tour. Titus was left behind to establish the church they founded there. This letter was written from Macedonia as an encouragement to Titus in that task. Presumably, Titus spent the winter with Paul in Nicopolis after his replacement arrived (see 3:12). In the spring, on their way to Ephesus, Paul was arrested and imprisoned again, probably for the last time. Titus was sent to Dalmatia on yet another mission (2Ti 4:10).

Characteristics: Apart from the greeting and two small sections (2:11–14; 3:3–7, which may be creedal statements), all the material in Titus is parallel to that found in 1 Timothy. Still, differences are notable. Timothy had been left to straighten out an established church that had gone sour because of the false teaching and ungodly lifestyles of its own elders. Titus, on the other hand, had the job of appointing new elders for a new church unstained by such turmoil and controversy. There are no appeals to "keep the faith"; there are few imperatives ("Do this"); there is no mention of the need to endure. Rather, it is primarily a reminder for Christians to live so as to make the teaching about God our Savior attractive to all.

QUALIFICATIONS FOR ELDERS AND DEACONS

Qualification	Office	Reference	Qualification	Office	Reference
Self-controlled	ELDER	1Ti 3:2; Tit 1:8	Husband of one wife	ELDER	1Ti 3:2; Tit 1:6
				DEACON	1Ti 3:12
Hospitable	ELDER	1Ti 3:2; Tit 1:8	Temperate	ELDER	1Ti 3:2; Tit 1:7
Able to teach	ELDER	1Ti 3:2; 5:17; Tit1:9		DEACON	1Ti 3:8
Not violent but gentle	ELDER	1Ti 3:3; Tit 1:7	Respectable	ELDER	1Ti 3:2
Not quarrelsome	ELDER	1Ti 3:3		DEACON	1Ti 3:8
Not a lover of money	ELDER	1Ti 3:3	Not given to	ELDER	1Ti 3:3; Tit 1:7
Not a recent convert	ELDER	1Ti 3:6	drunkenness	DEACON	1Ti 3:8
Has a good reputation with outsiders	ELDER	1Ti 3:7	Manages his own family well	ELDER	1Ti 3:4
				DEACON	1Ti 3:12
Not overbearing	ELDER	Tit 1:7	Sees that his children obey him	ELDER	1Ti 3:4-5; Tit 1:6
Not quick-tempered	ELDER	Tit 1:7		DEACON	1Ti 3:12
Loves what is good	ELDER	Tit 1:8	Does not pursue dishonest gain	ELDER	Tit 1:7
Upright, holy	ELDER	Tit 1:8		DEACON	1Ti 3:8
Disciplined	ELDER	Tit 1:8	Holds to the Truth	ELDER	Tit 1:9
				DEACON	1Ti 3:9
Above reproach	ELDER	1Ti 3:2; Tit 1:6	Sincere	DEACON	1Ti 3:8
(blameless)	DEACON	1Ti 3:9	Tested	DEACON	1Ti 3:10

Titus

1 Paul, a servant of God and an apostle of Jesus Christ for the faith of God's elect and the knowledge of the truth that leads to godliness— ²a faith and knowledge resting on the hope of eternal life, which God, who does not lie, promised before the beginning of time, ³and at his appointed season he brought his word to light through the preaching entrusted to me by the command of God our Savior,

⁴To Titus, my true son in our common faith:

Grace and peace from God the Father and Christ Jesus our Savior.

Titus' Task on Crete

⁵The reason I left you in Crete was that you might straighten out what was left unfinished and appoint*ᵃ* elders in every town, as I directed you. ⁶An elder must be blameless, the husband of but one wife, a man whose children believe and are not open to the charge of being wild and disobedient. ⁷Since an overseer*ᵇ* is entrusted with God's work, he must be blameless—not overbearing, not quick-tempered, not given to drunkenness, not violent, not pursuing dishonest gain. ⁸Rather he must be hospitable, one who loves what is good, who is self-controlled, upright, holy and disciplined. ⁹He must hold firmly to the trustworthy message as it has been taught, so that he can encourage others by sound doctrine and refute those who oppose it.

¹⁰For there are many rebellious people, mere talkers and deceivers, especially those of the circumcision group. ¹¹They must be silenced, because they are ruining whole households by teaching things they ought not to teach—and that for the sake of dishonest gain. ¹²Even one of their own prophets has said, "Cretans are always liars, evil brutes, lazy gluttons." ¹³This testimony is true. Therefore, rebuke them sharply, so that they will be sound in the faith ¹⁴and will pay no attention to Jewish myths or to the commands of those who reject the truth. ¹⁵To the pure, all things are pure, but to those who are corrupted and do not believe, nothing is pure. In fact, both their minds and consciences are corrupted. ¹⁶They claim to know God, but by their actions they deny him. They are detestable, disobedient and unfit for doing anything good.

What Must Be Taught to Various Groups

2 You must teach what is in accord with sound doctrine. ²Teach the older men to be temperate, worthy of respect, self-controlled, and sound in faith, in love and in endurance.

³Likewise, teach the older women to be reverent in the way they live, not to be slanderers or addicted to much wine, but to teach what is good. ⁴Then they can train the younger women to love their husbands and children, ⁵to be self-controlled and pure, to be busy at home, to be kind, and to be subject to their husbands, so that no one will malign the word of God.

⁶Similarly, encourage the young men to be self-controlled. ⁷In everything set them an example by doing what is good. In your

ᵃ5 Or *ordain*   *ᵇ7* Traditionally *bishop*

---

1. While growing up, who always sent you a card or a gift for your birthday? 2. Are you more likely to keep your letters short and to the point, or do you write until you run out of paper?

1. What do you know about the circumstances under which Paul wrote this letter to Titus (see Introduction to Titus). 2. Why is Paul's list of leadership qualifications focused mostly on "being" and not on "doing" (vv. 6–9)? 3. How do you interpret "the husband of but one wife" (v. 6)? Does this exclude bachelors or remarried men? 4. What was going on in Crete that made the appointment of such elders important (vv. 10–16)? Does any of this go on in the church today? In what way?

1. When did you come to a knowledge of the truth of Christ that Paul speaks of in verses 1 and 2? 2. Who in your Christian community have you especially respected for their godly leadership? Which qualities from this passage did you appreciate in them? 3. Which of these qualities do you feel you need to develop in your own life? How can your group help you?

1. As a teenager or college student, how did you decorate your room or living space so that it was really "you"? 2. Who is your favorite elderly person?

1. What is Paul implying about the importance of mentors (trusted guides or models)? 2. What difference does our salvation make in our behavior in this "present age" (v. 12)? What conflicts does this verse imply Christians will face? 3. Why does Paul emphasize "self control" (1:8–10; 2:2,5–6,12; 3:3) and doing "what is

good" (2:3,7,14; 3:1,8)? **4.** How does our new lifestyle relate to Jesus' death (v. 14)? To his glorious appearing (v. 13)?

1. What one quality in each of the groups mentioned do you feel is most important for Christians in our society (look at older men, older women, young women, young men and employees)? **2.** Which group do you fall into? What quality Paul lists for your group catches your attention? Why? **3.** How much have you focused on self-control and doing what is good in your own life? How can you improve?

In what situation do you least exhibit your faith: In a checkout line? In a fender bender? After a tough exam? At the company picnic? In athletics? Other?

1. Why do you think Paul again stresses "doing good" (vv. 1,8,14)? What about human nature makes such reminders necessary (v. 3)? **2.** What do verses 4–7 say about God's character? His work in us? **3.** How does a true understanding of these verses promote humility? Gratitude? A life of service? Have you seen this happen in your life? **4.** What is going on with the people in verses 9–11 (see 2Ti 2:25–26; 3:1–5)? How do Paul's instructions reflect both "tough love" and uncompromising righteousness? What similar situations are occurring in today's church?

1. Does verse 3 paint an accurate picture of you in the past? To what degree? Were these characteristics an obvious part of your life, or more of an underlying reality? **2.** In doing good, what motivates you: (a) Call of duty? (b) Fear of judgment? (c) Hope of Christ's return? (d) Gratitude for what God has done? (e) Desire to make peace in your relationships? (f) Needs of others? **3.** What "good" do you do at home? At church? In your city, state or nation? (Or are you "up to no good"?) **4.** Over the past year, where have you sensed growth in leading a "productive" life for God (see v. 14)?

teaching show integrity, seriousness [8]and soundness of speech that cannot be condemned, so that those who oppose you may be ashamed because they have nothing bad to say about us.

[9]Teach slaves to be subject to their masters in everything, to try to please them, not to talk back to them, [10]and not to steal from them, but to show that they can be fully trusted, so that in every way they will make the teaching about God our Savior attractive.

[11]For the grace of God that brings salvation has appeared to all men. [12]It teaches us to say "No" to ungodliness and worldly passions, and to live self-controlled, upright and godly lives in this present age, [13]while we wait for the blessed hope—the glorious appearing of our great God and Savior, Jesus Christ, [14]who gave himself for us to redeem us from all wickedness and to purify for himself a people that are his very own, eager to do what is good.

[15]These, then, are the things you should teach. Encourage and rebuke with all authority. Do not let anyone despise you.

Doing What Is Good

3 Remind the people to be subject to rulers and authorities, to be obedient, to be ready to do whatever is good, [2]to slander no one, to be peaceable and considerate, and to show true humility toward all men.

[3]At one time we too were foolish, disobedient, deceived and enslaved by all kinds of passions and pleasures. We lived in malice and envy, being hated and hating one another. [4]But when the kindness and love of God our Savior appeared, [5]he saved us, not because of righteous things we had done, but because of his mercy. He saved us through the washing of rebirth and renewal by the Holy Spirit, [6]whom he poured out on us generously through Jesus Christ our Savior, [7]so that, having been justified by his grace, we might become heirs having the hope of eternal life. [8]This is a trustworthy saying. And I want you to stress these things, so that those who have trusted in God may be careful to devote themselves to doing what is good. These things are excellent and profitable for everyone.

[9]But avoid foolish controversies and genealogies and arguments and quarrels about the law, because these are unprofitable and useless. [10]Warn a divisive person once, and then warn him a second time. After that, have nothing to do with him. [11]You may be sure that such a man is warped and sinful; he is self-condemned.

Final Remarks

[12]As soon as I send Artemas or Tychicus to you, do your best to come to me at Nicopolis, because I have decided to winter there. [13]Do everything you can to help Zenas the lawyer and Apollos on their way and see that they have everything they need. [14]Our people must learn to devote themselves to doing what is good, in order that they may provide for daily necessities and not live unproductive lives.

[15]Everyone with me sends you greetings. Greet those who love us in the faith.

Grace be with you all.

INTRODUCTION to
PHILEMON

Book Study Outline: If you are using Philemon for a study course, spend one to two meetings on this short book. Use the questions in the margin for your group agenda:

- start meeting / 15 min.
- read & discuss Bible / 30 min.
- close meeting / 15–45 min.

Refer to the Questions and Answers in the front of this Bible for more information.

Author: The apostle Paul.

Date: Probably in the early A.D. 60s.

Theme: Radical forgiveness.

Historical Background: At this point in history, the 60 million slaves in the Roman Empire made up a critical component of Rome's social and economic structure. Runaways were considered criminals who were punishable by severe measures including death. Philemon, a member of the church at Colosse, was the owner of a slave (Onesimus) who had run away from him. Somehow Onesimus got to Rome, met Paul and became a Christian. We may wonder why Paul did not take this opportunity simply to condemn slavery. The reason is partially clear. For one thing, conditions were not yet right for such a massive social upheaval. The Romans would never have voluntarily freed their slaves. Any revolt would have been savagely crushed. For another thing, unlike the American experience, Roman slavery was not a permanent condition based on race. This meant that slaves could purchase their freedom and enter the mainstream of society. Still, Paul did strike the first note for emancipation by his teaching on how Christians, regardless of race or economic condition, are one "family" in Christ (v. 16; Col. 3:11). This letter is Paul's attempt to persuade Philemon to forgive the crime and receive Onesimus as he would receive Paul himself. Onesimus carried this letter (and possibly Colossians and Ephesians) back to his home (Col. 4:9). The outcome of this story is not recorded in Scripture, but about A.D. 110 Bishop Ignatius of Antioch wrote a letter to the bishop of Ephesus, who was a man named Onesimus. In it, he used the same wordplay on his name as Paul does here in verses 10–11. Since many scholars think that the first collection of Paul's letters was made at Ephesus, Ignatius the bishop may have included this personal note as a vivid demonstration of how Christ can transform and use even a runaway slave.

Characteristics: Philemon is the shortest of Paul's letters, and it is his only private letter preserved in the New Testament. As such, it gives us a valuable glimpse into Paul's personality. He is deeply sympathetic to the plight of Onesimus, so much so that he is willing to deprive himself of Onesimus' help as well as to pay Philemon for any loss Onesimus has caused him (vv. 18–19). This is Christian compassion in action.

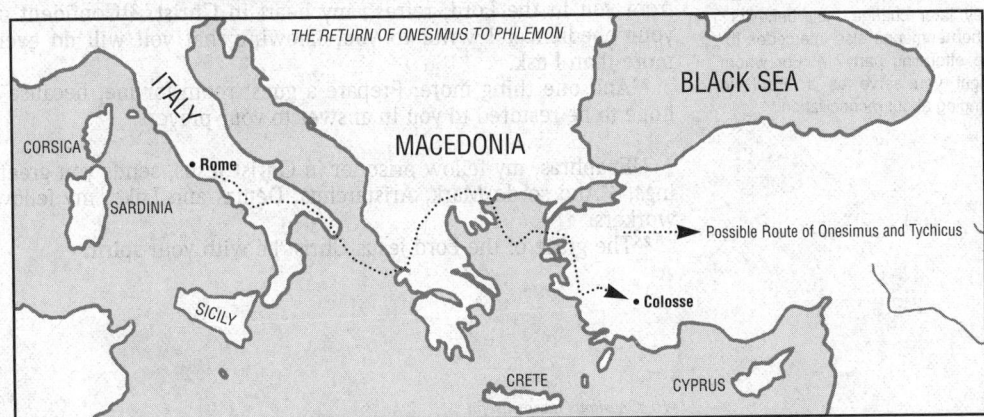

THE RETURN OF ONESIMUS TO PHILEMON

ITALY

CORSICA

Rome

SARDINIA

SICILY

CRETE

BLACK SEA

MACEDONIA

Colosse

CYPRUS

- - - → Possible Route of Onesimus and Tychicus

Philemon

What name were you given at birth? What nicknames have you been given since? What do they mean? How are you living up to their meaning?

1. What qualities in Philemon does Paul commend (vv. 4–7)? How does this prepare the way for Paul's plea in verses 8–10? 2. Given the seriousness of the crime committed by Onesimus (see Introduction to Philemon), what impact will his return have on Philemon's household? On Paul's relationship with Philemon? On Onesimus himself? 3. Does the fact that Onesimus has become a Christian lessen the seriousness of his crime? Why or why not? 4. What is radical about Paul's view of Onesimus (vv. 10–18)? 5. Given Paul's concern and need for Onesimus, why does Paul return Onesimus to Philemon, anyway? Why doesn't Paul exert his apostolic authority, declare Onesimus free, and keep him as a partner in the Gospel? 6. What do you think the chances are that Philemon will do what Paul asks? In what way would Philemon be right to refuse Paul?

1. Which of the qualities in Philemon (vv. 4–7) do you wish to develop for yourself? How could doing so cause you to grow in new areas? 2. Like Onesimus, do you have something you need to return to and make right? Do you have someone else who can help you do that? 3. When do you feel obligated to forgive someone: When they confess their sin? When they later change their behavior? When someone else intercedes for the offending party? 4. For whom might you serve as a "Paul" in bringing about reconciliation?

[1]Paul, a prisoner of Christ Jesus, and Timothy our brother,

To Philemon our dear friend and fellow worker, [2]to Apphia our sister, to Archippus our fellow soldier and to the church that meets in your home:

[3]Grace to you and peace from God our Father and the Lord Jesus Christ.

Thanksgiving and Prayer

[4]I always thank my God as I remember you in my prayers, [5]because I hear about your faith in the Lord Jesus and your love for all the saints. [6]I pray that you may be active in sharing your faith, so that you will have a full understanding of every good thing we have in Christ. [7]Your love has given me great joy and encouragement, because you, brother, have refreshed the hearts of the saints.

Paul's Plea for Onesimus

[8]Therefore, although in Christ I could be bold and order you to do what you ought to do, [9]yet I appeal to you on the basis of love. I then, as Paul—an old man and now also a prisoner of Christ Jesus— [10]I appeal to you for my son Onesimus,[a] who became my son while I was in chains. [11]Formerly he was useless to you, but now he has become useful both to you and to me.

[12]I am sending him—who is my very heart—back to you. [13]I would have liked to keep him with me so that he could take your place in helping me while I am in chains for the gospel. [14]But I did not want to do anything without your consent, so that any favor you do will be spontaneous and not forced. [15]Perhaps the reason he was separated from you for a little while was that you might have him back for good— [16]no longer as a slave, but better than a slave, as a dear brother. He is very dear to me but even dearer to you, both as a man and as a brother in the Lord.

[17]So if you consider me a partner, welcome him as you would welcome me. [18]If he has done you any wrong or owes you anything, charge it to me. [19]I, Paul, am writing this with my own hand. I will pay it back—not to mention that you owe me your very self. [20]I do wish, brother, that I may have some benefit from you in the Lord; refresh my heart in Christ. [21]Confident of your obedience, I write to you, knowing that you will do even more than I ask.

[22]And one thing more: Prepare a guest room for me, because I hope to be restored to you in answer to your prayers.

[23]Epaphras, my fellow prisoner in Christ Jesus, sends you greetings. [24]And so do Mark, Aristarchus, Demas and Luke, my fellow workers.

[25]The grace of the Lord Jesus Christ be with your spirit.

---

a 10 Onesimus means useful.

INTRODUCTION to
HEBREWS

Book Study Outline: If you are using Hebrews for a study course, here is a 7- or 13-week outline. Use the questions in the margin for your group agenda:

☕ start meeting / 15 min.

📖 read & discuss Bible / 30 min.

♡ close meeting / 15–45 min.

Refer to the Questions and Answers in the front of this Bible for more information.

7-week plan	13-week plan	Personal Reading	Group Study Passage
1	1	1:1–14	1:1–14/The Son Reigns
	2	2:1–18	2:5–18/Christ Our Helper
2	3	3:1–19	3:7–19/Don't Turn Back!
	4	4:1–13	4:1–13/The Promised Rest
3	5	4:14–5:10	4:14–5:10/The Great Priest
	6	5:11–6:20	5:11–6:12/Don't Fall Away!
4	7	7:1–28	7:1–28/The New Priest
	8	8:1–13	8:1–13/The New Covenant
5	9	9:1–28	9:11–28/The New Sacrifice
	10	10:1–39	10:19–39/Hold On!
6	11	11:1–40	11:1–40/Examples of Faith
	12	12:1–28	12:1–13/Run the Race!
7	13	13:1–25	13:1–25/A Life of Praise

Author: The author of this letter is nowhere named. Possible authors include Barnabas (Ac 4:36) or Apollos (Ac 18:24).

Date: It is impossible to affix a date to the composition of this letter. However, it seems likely that it was written prior to the destruction of the temple (A.D. 70) since the author consistently refers to it in the present tense.

HEBREWS 11: HEROES OF FAITH

Abel
By faith offered the better sacrifice (v. 4)

Enoch
By faith pleased God and escaped death (v. 5)

Noah
By faith built the ark (v. 7)

Abraham
By faith made his home in a foreign promised land (v. 8)
Abraham and Sarah
By faith became parents when past age (v. 11)
Abraham
By faith offered his son as a sacrifice (vv. 17–19)

Isaac
By faith blessed his sons (v. 20)

Jacob
By faith blessed his grandsons (v. 21)

Joseph
By faith prophesied the Exodus (v. 22)

Moses' Parents
By faith concealed Moses from Pharaoh (v. 23)

Moses
By faith chose mistreatment, left Egypt, and kept the Passover (vv. 24–28)

The Israelites
By faith passed through the Red Sea, and marched around Jericho (vv. 29–30)

Rahab
By faith welcomed the Israelite spies (v. 31)

Theme: The superiority of Jesus.

Historical Background: Hebrews appears to be a written sermon directed to Jewish Christians who were considering whether or not it was worth holding on to Christ any longer. While it is clear that they had suffered great persecution (10:32–34), the nature of their present struggle is less certain. They may have been facing new persecution, rejection by their kin, or the seduction of other teachings that seemed to offer an easier way than the way of Jesus. It appears that they may have been considering a return to Judaism as a way of lessening these tensions. In any case, the temptation to apostasy or reversion was severe enough that the letter to the Hebrews had to be written to encourage these beleaguered Christians to "hold on" (3:6), to "persevere" (10:36), and to "hold unswervingly to the hope we profess" (10:23) lest they compromise Christ and lose the blessings he has won for them.

Characteristics: Hebrews is a marvelous portrait of Jesus Christ seen through the lens of the Old Testament. The author's intent is to show the superiority of Jesus over the prophets, angels, Moses, priests and the whole Old Testament system. Jesus is the new priest with the new sacrifice that establishes a new covenant between people and God.

Hebrews

1. How are you like your mother or father: In artistic talent? Mechanical ability? Athletic ability? Forgetfulness? Distinctive features? **2.** What does your father do? Would you like to take over his business? Why or why not?

1. To what (or whom) is Jesus compared here? **2.** What was the function of the OT prophets (v. 1)? In what ways was Jesus' function similar? How was it different (vv. 2–3)? How is Jesus superior to the prophets? What is the difference between "the past" (v. 1) and "these last days" (v. 2)? **3.** How does Jesus compare with God in terms of activity, authority and relationship (vv. 1–3)? **4.** In verses 5–14, what new facts does the author add to this portrait of Jesus? Which of these OT quotes, first said of the Lord God, is now applied to the Son Jesus? What does that imply? **5.** What do you suppose these readers thought of angels and of prophets that caused the author to write as he does? What counterpoint is the author trying to make about each?

1. When did Jesus become more than just a name to you? **2.** Of all the qualities of Jesus mentioned in verses 2–4, which one are you beginning to appreciate more and more? **3.** Of what help is it for the Christian that God has indeed spoken "at many times and in various ways"? Why not in just one way? Which seems to be God's chosen way of speaking especially to you? **4.** Does this passage imply that Jesus is God's *final* revelation? Most *authoritative* revelation? Most *complete* revelation? Only *self*-revelation? In each instance, tell why you think so.

1 In the past God spoke to our forefathers through the prophets at many times and in various ways, ²but in these last days he has spoken to us by his Son, whom he appointed heir of all things, and through whom he made the universe. ³The Son is the radiance of God's glory and the exact representation of his being, sustaining all things by his powerful word. After he had provided purification for sins, he sat down at the right hand of the Majesty in heaven. ⁴So he became as much superior to the angels as the name he has inherited is superior to theirs.

⁵For to which of the angels did God ever say,

> "You are my Son;
> today I have become your Father*ᵃ"ᵇ*?

Or again,

> "I will be his Father,
> and he will be my Son"*ᶜ*?

⁶And again, when God brings his firstborn into the world, he says,

> "Let all God's angels worship him."*ᵈ*

⁷In speaking of the angels he says,

> "He makes his angels winds,
> his servants flames of fire."*ᵉ*

⁸But about the Son he says,

> "Your throne, O God, will last for ever and ever,
> and righteousness will be the scepter of your kingdom.
> ⁹You have loved righteousness and hated wickedness;
> therefore God, your God, has set you above your companions
> by anointing you with the oil of joy."*ᶠ*

¹⁰He also says,

> "In the beginning, O Lord, you laid the foundations of the earth,
> and the heavens are the work of your hands.
> ¹¹They will perish, but you remain;
> they will all wear out like a garment.
> ¹²You will roll them up like a robe;
> like a garment they will be changed.
> But you remain the same,
> and your years will never end."*ᵍ*

¹³To which of the angels did God ever say,

> "Sit at my right hand

ᵃ5 Or *have begotten you*   *ᵇ5* Psalm 2:7   *ᶜ5* 2 Samuel 7:14; 1 Chron. 17:13
ᵈ6 Deut. 32:43 (see Dead Sea Scrolls and Septuagint)   *ᵉ7* Psalm 104:4
ᶠ9 Psalm 45:6,7   *ᵍ12* Psalm 102:25-27

until I make your enemies
a footstool for your feet"ᵃ?

¹⁴Are not all angels ministering spirits sent to serve those who will inherit salvation?

Warning to Pay Attention

2 We must pay more careful attention, therefore, to what we have heard, so that we do not drift away. ²For if the message spoken by angels was binding, and every violation and disobedience received its just punishment, ³how shall we escape if we ignore such a great salvation? This salvation, which was first announced by the Lord, was confirmed to us by those who heard him. ⁴God also testified to it by signs, wonders and various miracles, and gifts of the Holy Spirit distributed according to his will.

Jesus Made Like His Brothers

⁵It is not to angels that he has subjected the world to come, about which we are speaking. ⁶But there is a place where someone has testified:

"What is man that you are mindful of him,
    the son of man that you care for him?
⁷You made him a littleᵇ lower than the angels;
    you crowned him with glory and honor
⁸   and put everything under his feet."ᶜ

In putting everything under him, God left nothing that is not subject to him. Yet at present we do not see everything subject to him. ⁹But we see Jesus, who was made a little lower than the angels, now crowned with glory and honor because he suffered death, so that by the grace of God he might taste death for everyone.

¹⁰In bringing many sons to glory, it was fitting that God, for whom and through whom everything exists, should make the author of their salvation perfect through suffering. ¹¹Both the one who makes men holy and those who are made holy are of the same family. So Jesus is not ashamed to call them brothers. ¹²He says,

"I will declare your name to my brothers;
    in the presence of the congregation I will sing
        your praises."ᵈ

¹³And again,

"I will put my trust in him."ᵉ

And again he says,

"Here am I, and the children God has given
    me."ᶠ

¹⁴Since the children have flesh and blood, he too shared in their humanity so that by his death he might destroy him who holds the power of death—that is, the devil— ¹⁵and free those who all their lives were held in slavery by their fear of death. ¹⁶For surely it is not angels he helps, but Abraham's descendants. ¹⁷For this reason he had to be made like his brothers in every way, in order that he might become a merciful and faithful high priest in service to God, and that he might make atonement forᵍ the sins of the people.

🔲 **1.** Back in school, what subject matter were you least attentive to? Why? **2.** When your parents went away, who were you "subject to" as a child? How did you look upon this person or the rules imposed on you?

📖 **1.** What danger faces these people? What does it mean to "drift away" (v. 1)? **2.** What is the answer to the rhetorical question in verse 3? **3.** In contrast to the popular expectation of that day (v. 5), to whom does God subject the world (vv. 6–8a)? Why is this rule not yet complete or universal? Who rules instead? **4.** In comparing people and angels (vv. 5–8), how are we both lower and higher? What is the ultimate destiny of humanity? **5.** To what does the phrase "the world to come" refer (v. 5)? How can the kingdom of God exist in both the present (in Jesus, in history) and the future (at the end of time)? **6.** In what respects was Jesus "made lower than the angels" (v. 9)? What elevated him above them? What does Jesus share in common with humanity (vv. 7,9)? In which respect is Jesus unique? **7.** Why did we need someone with flesh and blood like us—not an angel—to die in our place (vv. 14–18)? What did Jesus accomplish by his death as one of us? What is the goal of our salvation (vv. 10–11)? What does it mean that Jesus *authors* salvation? **8.** What is the difference between the way Jesus made atonement (v. 17) and the way the priests mediate atonement?

❤️ **1.** When (if ever) did you drift away from the faith? Why? What evidences for faith helped bring you back? **2.** At what points might you be tempted to lose your faith: After a big loss? When you seem to be making it very well on your own? When things are not going your way? When Christianity is mocked on TV talk shows? **3.** How do the achievements and example of Jesus described here encourage you at such times? **4.** Of Jesus' three titles (brother, v. 11; author of salvation, v. 10; high priest, v. 17) which one means most to you now? Why?

ᵃ13 Psalm 110:1   ᵇ7 Or *him for a little while*; also in verse 9   ᶜ8 Psalm 8:4-6
ᵈ12 Psalm 22:22   ᵉ13 Isaiah 8:17   ᶠ13 Isaiah 8:18   ᵍ17 Or *and that he might turn aside God's wrath, taking away*

¹⁸Because he himself suffered when he was tempted, he is able to help those who are being tempted.

Jesus Greater Than Moses

3 Therefore, holy brothers, who share in the heavenly calling, fix your thoughts on Jesus, the apostle and high priest whom we confess. ²He was faithful to the one who appointed him, just as Moses was faithful in all God's house. ³Jesus has been found worthy of greater honor than Moses, just as the builder of a house has greater honor than the house itself. ⁴For every house is built by someone, but God is the builder of everything. ⁵Moses was faithful as a servant in all God's house, testifying to what would be said in the future. ⁶But Christ is faithful as a son over God's house. And we are his house, if we hold on to our courage and the hope of which we boast.

Warning Against Unbelief

⁷So, as the Holy Spirit says:

> "Today, if you hear his voice,
> ⁸ do not harden your hearts
>   as you did in the rebellion,
>   during the time of testing in the desert,
> ⁹where your fathers tested and tried me
>   and for forty years saw what I did.
> ¹⁰That is why I was angry with that generation,
>   and I said, 'Their hearts are always going astray,
>   and they have not known my ways.'
> ¹¹So I declared on oath in my anger,
>   'They shall never enter my rest.'"ᵃ

¹²See to it, brothers, that none of you has a sinful, unbelieving heart that turns away from the living God. ¹³But encourage one another daily, as long as it is called Today, so that none of you may be hardened by sin's deceitfulness. ¹⁴We have come to share in Christ if we hold firmly till the end the confidence we had at first. ¹⁵As has just been said:

> "Today, if you hear his voice,
>   do not harden your hearts
>   as you did in the rebellion."ᵇ

¹⁶Who were they who heard and rebelled? Were they not all those Moses led out of Egypt? ¹⁷And with whom was he angry for forty years? Was it not with those who sinned, whose bodies fell in the desert? ¹⁸And to whom did God swear that they would never enter his rest if not to those who disobeyedᶜ? ¹⁹So we see that they were not able to enter, because of their unbelief.

A Sabbath-Rest for the People of God

4 Therefore, since the promise of entering his rest still stands, let us be careful that none of you be found to have fallen short of it. ²For we also have had the gospel preached to us, just as they did; but the message they heard was of no value to them, because those who heard did not combine it with faith.ᵈ ³Now we who have believed enter that rest, just as God has said,

*a*11 Psalm 95:7-11   *b*15 Psalm 95:7,8   *c*18 Or *disbelieved*   *d*2 Many
manuscripts *because they did not share in the faith of those who obeyed*

---

1. When lost on a trip, what do you do: Stop and ask directions? Check the map? Wander around until you find the way? 2. Are you usually early or late getting to places, even to your small group? Why?

1. What is the significance of "therefore" (v. 1)? What are the practical implications of what has been written about Jesus in chapters 1 and 2? How is Jesus like an apostle? 2. In what ways are Jesus and Moses similar? In what ways is Jesus greater? Why is that important? 3. What new warning is given (vv. 8,12)? How does this compare with verse 6 and 2:1–4? 4. To what incident does the quotation from Psalms refer (vv. 7–11; see Nu 14)? How did the people of Israel harden their hearts? With what results (vv. 10–11)? What does it mean to turn away from the living God (v. 12)? 5. What role does the Christian community play in keeping each other true to God (v. 13)? What will be the outcome of faithfulness (vv. 14–18)? 6. What does it mean to "enter God's rest" (vv. 11,18–19; see 4:1–11; Mt 11:28–30)?

1. What are some ways your church or small group could put verse 13 into practice? How can that help you? What apprehensions does it cause? 2. What was one of the most rebellious times in your spiritual life? What resulted from it? Who (or what) helped to bring you back? 3. How would you describe your heart now: Soft? Hard? Cold? Warm? Why is that?

What is your favorite way to spend a Sunday afternoon?

1. What is the author warning his readers about from the story of Israel's rebellion? What "message" (v. 2) was given each community (see Ex 3:7; Nu 14:7–9)? With what reception and results? Why is "hearing" not enough? 2. What is this "rest"

"So I declared on oath in my anger,
'They shall never enter my rest.'"[a]

And yet his work has been finished since the creation of the world. [4]For somewhere he has spoken about the seventh day in these words: "And on the seventh day God rested from all his work."[b] [5]And again in the passage above he says, "They shall never enter my rest."

[6]It still remains that some will enter that rest, and those who formerly had the gospel preached to them did not go in, because of their disobedience. [7]Therefore God again set a certain day, calling it Today, when a long time later he spoke through David, as was said before:

"Today, if you hear his voice,
    do not harden your hearts."[c]

[8]For if Joshua had given them rest, God would not have spoken later about another day. [9]There remains, then, a Sabbath-rest for the people of God; [10]for anyone who enters God's rest also rests from his own work, just as God did from his. [11]Let us, therefore, make every effort to enter that rest, so that no one will fall by following their example of disobedience.

[12]For the word of God is living and active. Sharper than any double-edged sword, it penetrates even to dividing soul and spirit, joints and marrow; it judges the thoughts and attitudes of the heart. [13]Nothing in all creation is hidden from God's sight. Everything is uncovered and laid bare before the eyes of him to whom we must give account.

Jesus the Great High Priest

[14]Therefore, since we have a great high priest who has gone through the heavens,[d] Jesus the Son of God, let us hold firmly to the faith we profess. [15]For we do not have a high priest who is unable to sympathize with our weaknesses, but we have one who has been tempted in every way, just as we are—yet was without sin. [16]Let us then approach the throne of grace with confidence, so that we may receive mercy and find grace to help us in our time of need.

5 Every high priest is selected from among men and is appointed to represent them in matters related to God, to offer gifts and sacrifices for sins. [2]He is able to deal gently with those who are ignorant and are going astray, since he himself is subject to weakness. [3]This is why he has to offer sacrifices for his own sins, as well as for the sins of the people.

[4]No one takes this honor upon himself; he must be called by God, just as Aaron was. [5]So Christ also did not take upon himself the glory of becoming a high priest. But God said to him,

"You are my Son;
    today I have become your Father."[e][f]

[6]And he says in another place,

"You are a priest forever,
    in the order of Melchizedek."[g]

[7]During the days of Jesus' life on earth, he offered up prayers and petitions with loud cries and tears to the one who could save him from death, and he was heard because of his reverent submission.

[a]3 Psalm 95:11; also in verse 5   [b]4 Gen. 2:2   [c]7 Psalm 95:7,8   [d]14 Or gone into heaven   [e]5 Or have begotten you   [f]5 Psalm 2:7   [g]6 Psalm 110:4

promised by God: The promised land? Sunday off? Heaven? God's presence? How do verses 3b–10 support your answer? 3. What is the proper response to the warning in verses 1 and 11? What does it mean that God's Word is "living"? Active? That it penetrates? How has the author used the "Word of God" thus far?

1. How would you explain the "promised rest" to someone who is not a Christian? What situations today would make this type of exhortation necessary? 2. What efforts (v. 11) can help you enter into God's rest (see Mt 11:28–30; Jn 6:27–29)? 3. What evidence do you have that the Word of God is living and active in your group study?

1. When you "blew it" as a child, how did you feel about the mistake? About yourself? About others involved? 2. From whom did you then draw comfort: A parent? Sibling? Friend? Your dog?

1. What about Jesus' priesthood is most encouraging (4:14–15; see 2:17; 3:1)? 2. How does the role of the Jewish high priest compare to Jesus' role in terms of: (a) How each is chosen? (5:1) (b) How each relates to sinners? (5:2) (c) How each relates to God? (5:3) 3. What two qualities of Jesus allows the comparison to Melchizedek (5:6,10; see ch. 7; Ge 14:18; Ps 110:4)? 4. What is the significance for our eternal salvation and current situation that Jesus was *fully human*? That Jesus was *without sin*?

1. Why is it hard for many people to trust the love of God? How would you explain the meaning of the priesthood of Jesus to a non-Christian? To someone who doesn't understand the OT sacrificial system? 2. What has made you consider turning away from Christ? At those times, what advantage was it to you to remember Jesus as your high priest?

8Although he was a son, he learned obedience from what he suffered 9and, once made perfect, he became the source of eternal salvation for all who obey him 10and was designated by God to be high priest in the order of Melchizedek.

Warning Against Falling Away

11We have much to say about this, but it is hard to explain because you are slow to learn. 12In fact, though by this time you ought to be teachers, you need someone to teach you the elementary truths of God's word all over again. You need milk, not solid food! 13Anyone who lives on milk, being still an infant, is not acquainted with the teaching about righteousness. 14But solid food is for the mature, who by constant use have trained themselves to distinguish good from evil.

6 Therefore let us leave the elementary teachings about Christ and go on to maturity, not laying again the foundation of repentance from acts that lead to death,*a* and of faith in God, 2instruction about baptisms, the laying on of hands, the resurrection of the dead, and eternal judgment. 3And God permitting, we will do so.

4It is impossible for those who have once been enlightened, who have tasted the heavenly gift, who have shared in the Holy Spirit, 5who have tasted the goodness of the word of God and the powers of the coming age, 6if they fall away, to be brought back to repentance, because*b* to their loss they are crucifying the Son of God all over again and subjecting him to public disgrace.

7Land that drinks in the rain often falling on it and that produces a crop useful to those for whom it is farmed receives the blessing of God. 8But land that produces thorns and thistles is worthless and is in danger of being cursed. In the end it will be burned.

9Even though we speak like this, dear friends, we are confident of better things in your case—things that accompany salvation. 10God is not unjust; he will not forget your work and the love you have shown him as you have helped his people and continue to help them. 11We want each of you to show this same diligence to the very end, in order to make your hope sure. 12We do not want you to become lazy, but to imitate those who through faith and patience inherit what has been promised.

The Certainty of God's Promise

13When God made his promise to Abraham, since there was no one greater for him to swear by, he swore by himself, 14saying, "I will surely bless you and give you many descendants."*c* 15And so after waiting patiently, Abraham received what was promised.

16Men swear by someone greater than themselves, and the oath confirms what is said and puts an end to all argument. 17Because God wanted to make the unchanging nature of his purpose very clear to the heirs of what was promised, he confirmed it with an oath. 18God did this so that, by two unchangeable things in which it is impossible for God to lie, we who have fled to take hold of the hope offered to us may be greatly encouraged. 19We have this hope as an anchor for the soul, firm and secure. It enters the inner sanctuary behind the curtain, 20where Jesus, who went before us, has entered on our behalf. He has become a high priest forever, in the order of Melchizedek.

What do you like hot out of the oven with a glass of cold milk: Chocolate chip cookies? Pound cake? Homemade bread? Apple pie?

1. Why does the author hesitate to give his readers further details? How does solid food help one mature in Christ (5:14)? 2. What's wrong with this prolonged immaturity (6:4–6)? What does each descriptive phrase mean? 3. Is their fate (6:6) reversible? Why (see also Mt 10:33)? What does the agricultural analogy suggest (6:7–8)? 4. Who are these people: (a) True believers gone bad? (b) Those who "hung around" true believers, but ultimately turned away (see 3:16)? (c) Borderline believers who must examine themselves? 5. How and why does the author encourage his readers to do "better" (6:9–12)? What parental logic (positive and negative incentives, praising and prodding) is used here?

1. How would you describe your spiritual appetite now: (a) "I'll just nibble"? (b) "A good meal now and then is nice"? (c) "I'm famished for all I can get"? Why? 2. When have you been spiritually lazy? What motivated you again?

What tries your patience more: Slow elevators? Slow food service? Traffic jams? Christmas sales lines?

1. How does Abraham's example help these people understand God's promise (see 3:12; 6:6)? 2. What effect did God's promise and oath have on Abraham's descendants? How does this affect Christians now?

1. Where in your life does trusting in God come hardest? Easiest? Why? 2. What promises of God are your anchor?

---

a1 Or from useless rituals   b6 Or repentance while   c14 Gen. 22:17

Melchizedek the Priest

7 This Melchizedek was king of Salem and priest of God Most High. He met Abraham returning from the defeat of the kings and blessed him, ²and Abraham gave him a tenth of everything. First, his name means "king of righteousness"; then also, "king of Salem" means "king of peace." ³Without father or mother, without genealogy, without beginning of days or end of life, like the Son of God he remains a priest forever.

⁴Just think how great he was: Even the patriarch Abraham gave him a tenth of the plunder! ⁵Now the law requires the descendants of Levi who become priests to collect a tenth from the people—that is, their brothers—even though their brothers are descended from Abraham. ⁶This man, however, did not trace his descent from Levi, yet he collected a tenth from Abraham and blessed him who had the promises. ⁷And without doubt the lesser person is blessed by the greater. ⁸In the one case, the tenth is collected by men who die; but in the other case, by him who is declared to be living. ⁹One might even say that Levi, who collects the tenth, paid the tenth through Abraham, ¹⁰because when Melchizedek met Abraham, Levi was still in the body of his ancestor.

Jesus Like Melchizedek

¹¹If perfection could have been attained through the Levitical priesthood (for on the basis of it the law was given to the people), why was there still need for another priest to come—one in the order of Melchizedek, not in the order of Aaron? ¹²For when there is a change of the priesthood, there must also be a change of the law. ¹³He of whom these things are said belonged to a different tribe, and no one from that tribe has ever served at the altar. ¹⁴For it is clear that our Lord descended from Judah, and in regard to that tribe Moses said nothing about priests. ¹⁵And what we have said is even more clear if another priest like Melchizedek appears, ¹⁶one who has become a priest not on the basis of a regulation as to his ancestry but on the basis of the power of an indestructible life. ¹⁷For it is declared:

> "You are a priest forever,
>   in the order of Melchizedek." ^a

¹⁸The former regulation is set aside because it was weak and useless ¹⁹(for the law made nothing perfect), and a better hope is introduced, by which we draw near to God.

²⁰And it was not without an oath! Others became priests without any oath, ²¹but he became a priest with an oath when God said to him:

> "The Lord has sworn
>   and will not change his mind:
>   'You are a priest forever.' " ^a

²²Because of this oath, Jesus has become the guarantee of a better covenant.

²³Now there have been many of those priests, since death prevented them from continuing in office; ²⁴but because Jesus lives forever, he has a permanent priesthood. ²⁵Therefore he is able to save completely ^b those who come to God through him, because he always lives to intercede for them.

²⁶Such a high priest meets our need—one who is holy, blameless, pure, set apart from sinners, exalted above the heavens. ²⁷Un-

1. As a child, who was your favorite super-hero? What could he or she do that you wished you could: Fly? Display super-strength? Always win? Talk his way out of anything? 2. If you could live to be 100, but could retain either the *body* or the *mind* of a 30-year-old, which would you choose? Why?

1. Chapter 7 picks up where 5:10 left off. From verses 1–10, what do we know about Melchizedek (see also Ge 14:17–20)? How did Abraham regard him? 2. What is the main point in the comparison between Melchizedek and Abraham? How does Abraham's tithe and the blessing of Melchizedek demonstrate the greatness of Melchizedek? How is his priesthood superior to that which descended from Levi and Aaron (v. 11)? Why is another type of priesthood needed? 3. In what ways is Jesus like the Melchizedek portrayed here (vv. 12–17)? 4. Why was the law set aside (vv. 18–19)? In what sense had it failed? How does the argument in verse 18 parallel that in verse 11? What are the two features of the Jewish religious system that have been superseded? 5. In what ways is Jesus a better priest than those under the Jewish system (vv. 20–28)? What is the relationship between the law and the oath? Why is the oath better?

1. The author was showing Jesus' superiority over the priests to Jews who were tempted to go back to their old ways. What are some of the "old ways" that tempt you to turn from Jesus? How is Jesus superior to those old ways in your life? 2. What difference does Jesus' "once-for-all" sacrifice make to you in terms of your security with God? Your self-image? Your desire to follow Christ?

^a17,21 Psalm 110:4   ^b25 Or *forever*

like the other high priests, he does not need to offer sacrifices day after day, first for his own sins, and then for the sins of the people. He sacrificed for their sins once for all when he offered himself. [28]For the law appoints as high priests men who are weak; but the oath, which came after the law, appointed the Son, who has been made perfect forever.

The High Priest of a New Covenant

8 The point of what we are saying is this: We do have such a high priest, who sat down at the right hand of the throne of the Majesty in heaven, [2]and who serves in the sanctuary, the true tabernacle set up by the Lord, not by man.

[3]Every high priest is appointed to offer both gifts and sacrifices, and so it was necessary for this one also to have something to offer. [4]If he were on earth, he would not be a priest, for there are already men who offer the gifts prescribed by the law. [5]They serve at a sanctuary that is a copy and shadow of what is in heaven. This is why Moses was warned when he was about to build the tabernacle: "See to it that you make everything according to the pattern shown you on the mountain."[a] [6]But the ministry Jesus has received is as superior to theirs as the covenant of which he is mediator is superior to the old one, and it is founded on better promises.

[7]For if there had been nothing wrong with that first covenant, no place would have been sought for another. [8]But God found fault with the people and said[b]:

"The time is coming, declares the Lord,
when I will make a new covenant
with the house of Israel
and with the house of Judah.
[9]It will not be like the covenant
I made with their forefathers
when I took them by the hand
to lead them out of Egypt,
because they did not remain faithful to my
covenant,
and I turned away from them,
declares the Lord.
[10]This is the covenant I will make with the house
of Israel
after that time, declares the Lord.
I will put my laws in their minds
and write them on their hearts.
I will be their God,
and they will be my people.
[11]No longer will a man teach his neighbor,
or a man his brother, saying, 'Know the Lord,'
because they will all know me,
from the least of them to the greatest.
[12]For I will forgive their wickedness
and will remember their sins no more."[c]

[13]By calling this covenant "new," he has made the first one obsolete; and what is obsolete and aging will soon disappear.

---

a5 Exodus 25:40   b8 Some manuscripts may be translated *fault and said to the people.*   c12 Jer. 31:31-34

---

1. What are you best at forgetting: Names? Chores? Birthdays? Scripture references? 2. If your car develops chronic problems, are you the type to keep fixing it up, or to buy a new one? How do you decide it's got to go?

1. What's the point of the previous argument (vv. 1–2)? How would this offer a strong incentive not to turn away from Christianity, as some were considering? 2. Contrast the location, nature and function of the two priesthoods (vv. 1–5; see 5:14–15; 6:19–20; 7:23–28). How does an OT priest prefigure what Jesus would really do? 3. What is a covenant? What is the significance of the fact that God initiates and guarantees it? What is a mediator? Why is one needed? 4. From Exodus 19:5–6, 20:1–17 and 29:35–41, what characterized the old covenant administered by the priests? How does the new covenant mediated by Jesus differ (vv. 10–12)? What four promises does this new covenant involve? 5. Why was a new covenant needed (vv. 7–9,13)?

1. Which aspect of the new covenant brings great joy to you, and why: (a) Having God's law on your heart? (b) Being one of God's people? (c) Knowing God? (d) Having your sins forgiven? 2. Which aspect of the covenant do you wish to experience more? Why? 3. Has your experience of these promises been sudden and dramatic, a gradual awareness, or both? 4. The old covenant ended up focusing on the people's ability (or inability) to measure up to God's demands. How do you still try to come to God on that basis? What happens? What does it mean to you that the new covenant is based on God's actions in Christ, and not on your efforts?

A Call to Persevere

[19] Therefore, brothers, since we have confidence to enter the Most Holy Place by the blood of Jesus, [20] by a new and living way opened for us through the curtain, that is, his body, [21] and since we have a great priest over the house of God, [22] let us draw near to God with a sincere heart in full assurance of faith, having our hearts sprinkled to cleanse us from a guilty conscience and having our bodies washed with pure water. [23] Let us hold unswervingly to the hope we profess, for he who promised is faithful. [24] And let us consider how we may spur one another on toward love and good deeds. [25] Let us not give up meeting together, as some are in the habit of doing, but let us encourage one another—and all the more as you see the Day approaching.

[26] If we deliberately keep on sinning after we have received the knowledge of the truth, no sacrifice for sins is left, [27] but only a fearful expectation of judgment and of raging fire that will consume the enemies of God. [28] Anyone who rejected the law of Moses died without mercy on the testimony of two or three witnesses. [29] How much more severely do you think a man deserves to be punished who has trampled the Son of God under foot, who has treated as an unholy thing the blood of the covenant that sanctified him, and who has insulted the Spirit of grace? [30] For we know him who said, "It is mine to avenge; I will repay," [a] and again, "The Lord will judge his people." [b] [31] It is a dreadful thing to fall into the hands of the living God.

[32] Remember those earlier days after you had received the light, when you stood your ground in a great contest in the face of suffering. [33] Sometimes you were publicly exposed to insult and persecution; at other times you stood side by side with those who were so treated. [34] You sympathized with those in prison and joyfully accepted the confiscation of your property, because you knew that you yourselves had better and lasting possessions.

[35] So do not throw away your confidence; it will be richly rewarded. [36] You need to persevere so that when you have done the will of God, you will receive what he has promised. [37] For in just a very little while,

> "He who is coming will come and will not delay.
> [38] But my righteous one [c] will live by faith.
> And if he shrinks back,
> I will not be pleased with him." [d]

[39] But we are not of those who shrink back and are destroyed, but of those who believe and are saved.

By Faith

11 Now faith is being sure of what we hope for and certain of what we do not see. [2] This is what the ancients were commended for.

[3] By faith we understand that the universe was formed at God's command, so that what is seen was not made out of what was visible.

[4] By faith Abel offered God a better sacrifice than Cain did. By faith he was commended as a righteous man, when God spoke well of his offerings. And by faith he still speaks, even though he is dead.

[5] By faith Enoch was taken from this life, so that he did not

---

How did you meet your spouse or "friend"? What was your first date with him or her?

1. Based on Christ's sacrifice (vv. 19–20; 9:1–10:18) and priesthood (v. 21; 7:1–8:13), what attitudes and actions follow? Note the four "let us" statements in verses 22–25. What does each one mean? What incentives are given? **2.** How do verses 19–25 parallel 4:14–16? Why does the author need to stress this to these readers? **3.** If they habitually reject Christ in favor of sin, what do they forfeit (v. 26; also 3:14; 6:4–6)? What can they expect instead (vv. 27,30–31)? Why is this fate not so unexpected (vv. 28–29; also Dt 17:2–7)? **4.** In rejecting Christ, of what three grievous sins would they be guilty (v. 29)? With what consequence (v. 31)? What false security would make such a warning necessary (see 4:12–13; 6:8)? **5.** After such a dire warning, how does the author appeal to previous testing, present action and future events—all to encourage the Hebrews (vv. 32–39)? Which appeal do you find persuasive?

1. In what specific ways can you spur another Christian on toward love and good deeds? How have you been spurred on by others in your group? Whose exhortation, example or encouragement means the most to you? **2.** How have you seen the difference between someone *assured* of their salvation (vv. 19–25) and someone *presumptuous* about it (vv. 26–31)? How can you develop confidence without presumption? **3.** How does the promise of the Second Coming help you to "keep on keeping on"?

As you consider the people in your small group, what's one positive adjective you would use to describe each person?

1. What are the connections between 10:35–39 and the themes of chapter 11? **2.** In the definition and focus of faith in verses 1 and 6, what verbs describe faith? What is the object of these verbs? Is our faith directed toward the future, toward the present, or toward both? Toward God alone, or people as well? Why do you conclude this? Write your own expanded definition of faith as

---

a30 Deut. 32:35   *b30* Deut. 32:36; Psalm 135:14   *c38* One early manuscript
But the righteous   *d38* Hab. 2:3,4

you try to capture the meaning of verse 1. **3.** How does verse 3 illustrate this understanding of faith? **4.** Why is Abel's sacrifice regarded as better than Cain's (see Ge 4:1–12)? How did Abel's sacrifice prefigure Christ's ultimate sacrifice in a way Cain's did not (recall ch. 9–10)? **5.** What aspect of faith (v. 1) is demonstrated by Enoch (v. 5; Ge 5: 21–24)? By Noah (v. 7; Ge 6:5–22; 7:11–12)? **6.** How is faith demonstrated or explained in each of the three examples from Abraham's life (vv. 8–12,17–19)? What obstacles had to be overcome? What changed for him? For his family? **7.** What group of people does the author use next to illustrate faith (vv. 17–31)? Recall each Old Testament story which is referred to: What do the stories in verses 17–22 have in common? **8.** What do you learn about faith from the example of Moses (vv. 24–28)? **9.** In verses 29–38, what great achievements were accomplished as a result of faith? What price was paid? What came of such faith (vv. 39–40)? How do verses 29–40 encourage you in light of your own suffering and the questions that suffering brings on?

♡ **1.** What are some verbs that describe your present level of faith? Why these? **2.** Of the people mentioned in this section, with whom do you feel you have the most in common? Why? With whom do you have the least in common? Why? Which situation would have been the most difficult for you to face? Why? What does it mean to you that not all these people of faith met with "success"? **3.** How has your life changed as a result of your faith in God? What has your faith cost you? How has your faith affected your neighbors? **4.** Read aloud verses 13–16. What does it mean to *you* to be an alien and a stranger on earth? In what ways do you feel like a stranger in this world? **5.** Who are some contemporary heroes of faith who inspire you today?

experience death; he could not be found, because God had taken him away. For before he was taken, he was commended as one who pleased God. ⁶And without faith it is impossible to please God, because anyone who comes to him must believe that he exists and that he rewards those who earnestly seek him.

⁷By faith Noah, when warned about things not yet seen, in holy fear built an ark to save his family. By his faith he condemned the world and became heir of the righteousness that comes by faith.

⁸By faith Abraham, when called to go to a place he would later receive as his inheritance, obeyed and went, even though he did not know where he was going. ⁹By faith he made his home in the promised land like a stranger in a foreign country; he lived in tents, as did Isaac and Jacob, who were heirs with him of the same promise. ¹⁰For he was looking forward to the city with foundations, whose architect and builder is God.

¹¹By faith Abraham, even though he was past age—and Sarah herself was barren—was enabled to become a father because he*ᵃ* considered him faithful who had made the promise. ¹²And so from this one man, and he as good as dead, came descendants as numerous as the stars in the sky and as countless as the sand on the seashore.

¹³All these people were still living by faith when they died. They did not receive the things promised; they only saw them and welcomed them from a distance. And they admitted that they were aliens and strangers on earth. ¹⁴People who say such things show that they are looking for a country of their own. ¹⁵If they had been thinking of the country they had left, they would have had opportunity to return. ¹⁶Instead, they were longing for a better country—a heavenly one. Therefore God is not ashamed to be called their God, for he has prepared a city for them.

¹⁷By faith Abraham, when God tested him, offered Isaac as a sacrifice. He who had received the promises was about to sacrifice his one and only son, ¹⁸even though God had said to him, "It is through Isaac that your offspring*ᵇ* will be reckoned." *ᶜ* ¹⁹Abraham reasoned that God could raise the dead, and figuratively speaking, he did receive Isaac back from death.

²⁰By faith Isaac blessed Jacob and Esau in regard to their future. ²¹By faith Jacob, when he was dying, blessed each of Joseph's sons, and worshiped as he leaned on the top of his staff. ²²By faith Joseph, when his end was near, spoke about the exodus of the Israelites from Egypt and gave instructions about his bones.

²³By faith Moses' parents hid him for three months after he was born, because they saw he was no ordinary child, and they were not afraid of the king's edict.

²⁴By faith Moses, when he had grown up, refused to be known as the son of Pharaoh's daughter. ²⁵He chose to be mistreated along with the people of God rather than to enjoy the pleasures of sin for a short time. ²⁶He regarded disgrace for the sake of Christ as of greater value than the treasures of Egypt, because he was looking ahead to his reward. ²⁷By faith he left Egypt, not fearing the king's anger; he persevered because he saw him who is invisible. ²⁸By faith he kept the Passover and the sprinkling of blood, so that the destroyer of the firstborn would not touch the firstborn of Israel.

²⁹By faith the people passed through the Red Sea*ᵈ* as on dry land; but when the Egyptians tried to do so, they were drowned.

ᵃ11 Or *By faith even Sarah, who was past age, was enabled to bear children because she*
ᵇ18 Greek *seed*   *ᶜ18* Gen. 21:12   *ᵈ29* That is, Sea of Reeds

³⁰By faith the walls of Jericho fell, after the people had marched around them for seven days.

³¹By faith the prostitute Rahab, because she welcomed the spies, was not killed with those who were disobedient.ᵃ

³²And what more shall I say? I do not have time to tell about Gideon, Barak, Samson, Jephthah, David, Samuel and the prophets, ³³who through faith conquered kingdoms, administered justice, and gained what was promised; who shut the mouths of lions, ³⁴quenched the fury of the flames, and escaped the edge of the sword; whose weakness was turned to strength; and who became powerful in battle and routed foreign armies. ³⁵Women received back their dead, raised to life again. Others were tortured and refused to be released, so that they might gain a better resurrection. ³⁶Some faced jeers and flogging, while still others were chained and put in prison. ³⁷They were stonedᵇ; they were sawed in two; they were put to death by the sword. They went about in sheepskins and goatskins, destitute, persecuted and mistreated— ³⁸the world was not worthy of them. They wandered in deserts and mountains, and in caves and holes in the ground.

³⁹These were all commended for their faith, yet none of them received what had been promised. ⁴⁰God had planned something better for us so that only together with us would they be made perfect.

God Disciplines His Sons

12 Therefore, since we are surrounded by such a great cloud of witnesses, let us throw off everything that hinders and the sin that so easily entangles, and let us run with perseverance the race marked out for us. ²Let us fix our eyes on Jesus, the author and perfecter of our faith, who for the joy set before him endured the cross, scorning its shame, and sat down at the right hand of the throne of God. ³Consider him who endured such opposition from sinful men, so that you will not grow weary and lose heart.

⁴In your struggle against sin, you have not yet resisted to the point of shedding your blood. ⁵And you have forgotten that word of encouragement that addresses you as sons:

> "My son, do not make light of the Lord's
>   discipline,
> and do not lose heart when he rebukes you,
> ⁶because the Lord disciplines those he loves,
> and he punishes everyone he accepts as a
>   son."ᶜ

⁷Endure hardship as discipline; God is treating you as sons. For what son is not disciplined by his father? ⁸If you are not disciplined (and everyone undergoes discipline), then you are illegitimate children and not true sons. ⁹Moreover, we have all had human fathers who disciplined us and we respected them for it. How much more should we submit to the Father of our spirits and live! ¹⁰Our fathers disciplined us for a little while as they thought best; but God disciplines us for our good, that we may share in his holiness. ¹¹No discipline seems pleasant at the time, but painful. Later on, however, it produces a harvest of righteousness and peace for those who have been trained by it.

¹²Therefore, strengthen your feeble arms and weak knees. ¹³"Make level paths for your feet,"ᵈ so that the lame may not be disabled, but rather healed.

1. What discipline did you sometimes resent as a child that you appreciate now: Practicing piano? Having a place for everything and everything in its place? Submitting work on time? Not overspending your allowance? 2. Do you perform better before a crowd or in private? Why is that?

1. How should Christians "run the race"? What does it mean to throw off sin and hindrances? To "run with perseverance"? To "fix our eyes on Jesus"? 2. What does hardship demonstrate about a person's relationship to God? How should a person respond to God when disciplined? How does Christ's discipline differ from human discipline? What benefits does discipline bring?

1. What comfort do you get from knowing that a cloud of witnesses is watching you run the Christian race? 2. What are two obstacles that hinder and entangle you in your race? Why? 3. What have you discovered that helps you keep your eyes fixed on Jesus? 4. How has God disciplined you in the past? How did his discipline lead to peace for you? 5. What's the hardest thing you're going through right now? How is God using this in your life?

ᵃ31 Or *unbelieving*   ᵇ37 Some early manuscripts *stoned; they were put to the test;*   ᶜ6 Prov. 3:11,12   ᵈ13 Prov. 4:26

If you could choose any city to move to with the right job, by what criteria would you choose: Friends or family? Climate? Housing? Cultural or athletic pursuits?

1. How do the instructions and Esau's example (vv. 14–17; see Ge 25:29–34) relate to disciplining your weaker members (vv. 12–13)? 2. What is the point of the comparison between Mt. Sinai (vv. 18–21) and Mt. Zion (vv. 22–24)? 3. What is the "better word" (v. 24) in contrast to "no further word" (v. 19)? What do the words "once more" convey (vv. 26–27)? 4. How does this play on words sum up the author's argument throughout the book? What happens to any who *refuse* to hear God's voice (vv. 18–21,25–29)? To those who *heed* his call?

1. What efforts have you made to "live in peace with all"? 2. In relationships that fail, do you believe it is because one or both parties didn't try hard enough? What can be done to see that people who are torn apart, despite their best efforts, do not also miss the grace of God? 3. What in this passage comforts you? What makes you uneasy? What thrills you most about the city of the living God?

---

1. In one or two words, how would you describe the relationship you had with your brothers and sisters when you were growing up? 2. Who has been as close to you as a brother?

1. In what areas should "brotherly love" define Christians (vv. 1–7)? What consequences are spelled out here for those who do? For those who don't? What help is offered for those who struggle (vv. 6,8)? 2. What does verse 5 say about priorities when making financial decisions? What reason do we have to be worry-free when it comes to money? How are we to regard our leaders (vv. 7,17) and why? How does this reflect our regard for the changeless Christ? What do these verses say about the importance of considering our leaders as Christ's messengers? 3. What "strange teaching" was a particular temptation to Hebrew Christians (vv. 9–10)? What rituals, mores and

Warning Against Refusing God

14Make every effort to live in peace with all men and to be holy; without holiness no one will see the Lord. **15**See to it that no one misses the grace of God and that no bitter root grows up to cause trouble and defile many. **16**See that no one is sexually immoral, or is godless like Esau, who for a single meal sold his inheritance rights as the oldest son. **17**Afterward, as you know, when he wanted to inherit this blessing, he was rejected. He could bring about no change of mind, though he sought the blessing with tears.

18You have not come to a mountain that can be touched and that is burning with fire; to darkness, gloom and storm; **19**to a trumpet blast or to such a voice speaking words that those who heard it begged that no further word be spoken to them, **20**because they could not bear what was commanded: "If even an animal touches the mountain, it must be stoned."[a] **21**The sight was so terrifying that Moses said, "I am trembling with fear."[b]

22But you have come to Mount Zion, to the heavenly Jerusalem, the city of the living God. You have come to thousands upon thousands of angels in joyful assembly, **23**to the church of the firstborn, whose names are written in heaven. You have come to God, the judge of all men, to the spirits of righteous men made perfect, **24**to Jesus the mediator of a new covenant, and to the sprinkled blood that speaks a better word than the blood of Abel.

25See to it that you do not refuse him who speaks. If they did not escape when they refused him who warned them on earth, how much less will we, if we turn away from him who warns us from heaven? **26**At that time his voice shook the earth, but now he has promised, "Once more I will shake not only the earth but also the heavens."[c] **27**The words "once more" indicate the removing of what can be shaken—that is, created things—so that what cannot be shaken may remain.

28Therefore, since we are receiving a kingdom that cannot be shaken, let us be thankful, and so worship God acceptably with reverence and awe, **29**for our "God is a consuming fire."[d]

Concluding Exhortations

13 Keep on loving each other as brothers. **2**Do not forget to entertain strangers, for by so doing some people have entertained angels without knowing it. **3**Remember those in prison as if you were their fellow prisoners, and those who are mistreated as if you yourselves were suffering.

4Marriage should be honored by all, and the marriage bed kept pure, for God will judge the adulterer and all the sexually immoral. **5**Keep your lives free from the love of money and be content with what you have, because God has said,

> "Never will I leave you;
> never will I forsake you."[e]

6So we say with confidence,

> "The Lord is my helper; I will not be afraid.
> What can man do to me?"[f]

7Remember your leaders, who spoke the word of God to you. Consider the outcome of their way of life and imitate their faith. **8**Jesus Christ is the same yesterday and today and forever. **9**Do not be carried away by all kinds of strange teachings. It is

---

a20 Exodus 19:12,13   *b21* Deut. 9:19   *c26* Haggai 2:6   *d29* Deut. 4:24
e5 Deut. 31:6   *f6* Psalm 118:6,7

good for our hearts to be strengthened by grace, not by ceremonial foods, which are of no value to those who eat them. [10]We have an altar from which those who minister at the tabernacle have no right to eat.

[11]The high priest carries the blood of animals into the Most Holy Place as a sin offering, but the bodies are burned outside the camp. [12]And so Jesus also suffered outside the city gate to make the people holy through his own blood. [13]Let us, then, go to him outside the camp, bearing the disgrace he bore. [14]For here we do not have an enduring city, but we are looking for the city that is to come.

[15]Through Jesus, therefore, let us continually offer to God a sacrifice of praise—the fruit of lips that confess his name. [16]And do not forget to do good and to share with others, for with such sacrifices God is pleased.

[17]Obey your leaders and submit to their authority. They keep watch over you as men who must give an account. Obey them so that their work will be a joy, not a burden, for that would be of no advantage to you.

[18]Pray for us. We are sure that we have a clear conscience and desire to live honorably in every way. [19]I particularly urge you to pray so that I may be restored to you soon.

[20]May the God of peace, who through the blood of the eternal covenant brought back from the dead our Lord Jesus, that great Shepherd of the sheep, [21]equip you with everything good for doing his will, and may he work in us what is pleasing to him, through Jesus Christ, to whom be glory for ever and ever. Amen.

[22]Brothers, I urge you to bear with my word of exhortation, for I have written you only a short letter.

[23]I want you to know that our brother Timothy has been released. If he arrives soon, I will come with him to see you.

[24]Greet all your leaders and all God's people. Those from Italy send you their greetings.

[25]Grace be with you all.

other forms of legalism tempt believers of any age? Why? 4. What is the point of the argument in verses 9–14? Based on his argument, what types of "sacrifices" is God concerned with (vv. 15–16)? 5. Why does the author desire their prayers (vv. 18–19)? How would you paraphrase his prayer for them (vv. 20–21)? 6. From verses 1–19, how would you sum up the Christian lifestyle?

1. In which of these six areas have you made the most progress this year: (a) Loving one another as brothers and sisters? (b) Providing hospitality? (c) Caring for those suffering for their faith? (d) Keeping your marriage strong? (e) Staying free from the love of money? (f) Submitting to leaders in authority? Which area do you need the most work on? 2. In which of these six areas is your church the strongest? The weakest? Would you say an obedient congregation prays for its leaders? Or would you say "a praying congregation obeys its leaders"? What's the difference? 3. Considering all you have learned about Jesus in this book, write out a "sacrifice of praise" to him reflecting on all he has done for us. What sacrifice of "doing good and sharing" can you offer this week? 4. What is the most significant thing you've learned from studying Hebrews? How has this affected your life?

INTRODUCTION to
JAMES

Book Study Outline: If you are using James for a study course, here is a 5- or 9-week outline. Use the questions in the margin for your group agenda:

	5-week plan	9-week plan	Group Study Passage
	1	1	1:1–18/Trials and Temptations
		2	1:19–27/Listening and Doing
	2	3	2:1–13/Mercy and Judgment
		4	2:14–26/Faith and Works
	3	5	3:1–12/Taming the Tongue
		6	3:13–18/True and False Wisdom
	4	7	4:1–12/Friendship With God
		8	4:13–5:6/Investing in the Future
	5	9	5:7–20/Suffering and Prayer

🍵 start meeting / 15 min.

📖 read & discuss Bible / 30 min.

♡ close meeting / 15–45 min.

Refer to the Questions and Answers in the front of this Bible for more information.

Author: Traditionally, it has been assumed that the James who wrote this epistle was the brother of Jesus (Mk 6:3), and the leader of the church in Jerusalem (Ac 12:17; Gal 1:19).

Date: Uncertain. Some consider James to be the first New Testament book written (about A.D. 45), while others date it quite late.

Theme: Christianity in action.

THE PROMINENCE OF JAMES IN THE EARLY CHURCH

James was probably the oldest of Christ's several brothers and sisters since he heads the list in Matthew 13:55. At first he did not believe in Jesus and even challenged him and misunderstood his mission (Jn 7:2–5). Later James became a committed disciple. Before his martyrdom c. A.D. 62, James was very prominent in the church:

1. James was one of the select individuals Christ appeared to after his resurrection (1Co 15:7).

2. Paul called him a "pillar" of the church (Gal 2:9).

3. Paul, on his first post-conversion visit to Jerusalem, saw James (Gal 1:19).

4. Paul did the same on his last visit (Ac 21:18).

5. When Peter was rescued from prison, he told his friends to tell James (Ac 12:17).

6. James was a leader in the important council of Jerusalem (Ac 15:13).

7. Jude could identify himself simply as a "brother of James" (Jude 1:1), so well-known was James.

Historical Background: It is not clear to whom James is writing. The inscription in 1:1 ("to the twelve tribes") could refer to Jewish Christians. However, elsewhere in the New Testament this term is used for Gentile believers who, by faith, have become the new Israel. The author's familiarity with the OT and his concern with the Law coupled with his use of Greek literary structure, language and metaphors hint that he may have been writing to God-fearing Gentiles who, having once been attracted to Judaism, were now becoming Christians.

Characteristics: James is closer in style to the book of Proverbs than it is to any New Testament book. James reflects the sermonic style of both Greek philosophers and Jewish rabbis in that it is loosely structured, there is conversation with a hypothetical opponent (2:18ff; 5:13–16), it uses questions to introduce new topics (2:14; 4:1), there are frequent commands (over half of the verses in James are imperatives!), and it proves points by quotes and examples (e.g., 1:11,17). This diversity may be evidence that James is a collection of short sermons on different topics. In terms of content, James has little doctrine; it says surprisingly little about Jesus (it does not mention his atonement or resurrection); nor is the Holy Spirit mentioned. James' focus is not on doctrine, but on how the Christian faith is to be lived on a day-to-day basis. Although Jesus is seldom referred to or quoted, his teaching on the Sermon on the Mount (Mt 5–7) underlies much of this letter.

James

1 James, a servant of God and of the Lord Jesus Christ,

To the twelve tribes scattered among the nations:

Greetings.

Trials and Temptations

²Consider it pure joy, my brothers, whenever you face trials of many kinds, ³because you know that the testing of your faith develops perseverance. ⁴Perseverance must finish its work so that you may be mature and complete, not lacking anything. ⁵If any of you lacks wisdom, he should ask God, who gives generously to all without finding fault, and it will be given to him. ⁶But when he asks, he must believe and not doubt, because he who doubts is like a wave of the sea, blown and tossed by the wind. ⁷That man should not think he will receive anything from the Lord; ⁸he is a double-minded man, unstable in all he does.

⁹The brother in humble circumstances ought to take pride in his high position. ¹⁰But the one who is rich should take pride in his low position, because he will pass away like a wild flower. ¹¹For the sun rises with scorching heat and withers the plant; its blossom falls and its beauty is destroyed. In the same way, the rich man will fade away even while he goes about his business.

¹²Blessed is the man who perseveres under trial, because when he has stood the test, he will receive the crown of life that God has promised to those who love him.

¹³When tempted, no one should say, "God is tempting me." For God cannot be tempted by evil, nor does he tempt anyone; ¹⁴but each one is tempted when, by his own evil desire, he is dragged away and enticed. ¹⁵Then, after desire has conceived, it gives birth to sin; and sin, when it is full-grown, gives birth to death.

¹⁶Don't be deceived, my dear brothers. ¹⁷Every good and perfect gift is from above, coming down from the Father of the heavenly lights, who does not change like shifting shadows. ¹⁸He chose to give us birth through the word of truth, that we might be a kind of firstfruits of all he created.

Listening and Doing

¹⁹My dear brothers, take note of this: Everyone should be quick to listen, slow to speak and slow to become angry, ²⁰for man's anger does not bring about the righteous life that God desires. ²¹Therefore, get rid of all moral filth and the evil that is so prevalent and humbly accept the word planted in you, which can save you.

²²Do not merely listen to the word, and so deceive yourselves. Do what it says. ²³Anyone who listens to the word but does not do what it says is like a man who looks at his face in a mirror ²⁴and, after looking at himself, goes away and immediately forgets what he looks like. ²⁵But the man who looks intently into the perfect law that gives freedom, and continues to do this, not forgetting what he has heard, but doing it—he will be blessed in what he does.

²⁶If anyone considers himself religious and yet does not keep a tight rein on his tongue, he deceives himself and his religion is

---

1. What is the hardest test you remember taking? 2. What do you do to cheer up when you're down? 3. In your family, who does everyone lean on in hard times?

1. What do you know about James? (See Introduction to James.) 2. According to James, what should be a Christian's attitude when facing trials (vv. 2–4)? How realistic is this? 3. How does a person receive wisdom (v. 5)? When asking God for guidance, what must we guard against (v. 6)? 4. How does James turn upside down the assumed status of the rich and poor (vv. 9–10)? 5. What is the promise for one who perseveres under trial (v. 12)? 6. Is there a difference between God "testing our faith" (v. 3) and "tempting" us (v. 13)? Explain.

1. How often is your attitude like James' during trials? How about with any trials you're facing now? How can this group help you in your attitude? 2. When have you prayed for and received God's wisdom? What do you do when you pray but still have doubts? 3. When have you been tempted by something that seemed "good and perfect," but turned out to be disappointing or harmful (vv. 16–17)? What are two good gifts God has given you this year?

Which best describes your temper: Short fuse, big bomb? Long fuse, little fizz? Long fuse, H-bomb?

1. What does James command in verse 19? 2. What is the "righteous life that God desires" (vv. 20,27)? 3. How does the term "Sunday Christian" illustrate James' point in verses 22–24? Conversely, what does the life of someone in verse 25 look like?

1. Does James say anger is wrong? How about "righteous anger" (Mk 11:15–18)? How well do you handle anger? How can we process anger in a healthy way

without breaking God's command here? **2.** How much are you living out verse 27?

---

1. For what event would you buy the "best seats": The World Series? Carnegie Hall? Your child's school play? **2.** What Third World country, or low-income area, have you spent time in?

1. In general, how do people show favoritism (vv. 1–3)? **2.** What two gifts does God give the poor (v. 5)? Why would the poor be rich in faith? **3.** What did James say the rich were doing to the poor? Does this happen today?

1. Who are the "rich" in our churches and communities? Who are the "poor"? **2.** What does this passage say to you about your own conscious or unconscious treatment of others? **3.** How does the love and mercy commanded here relate to God's love and mercy toward you?

Are you more likely to act without thinking or think without acting?

1. In a word or phrase what is the focus of this passage? **2.** What kind of faith is James criticizing? **3.** How do you make sense of this passage in light of Galatians 2:20–21? What is the difference between the Law and deeds?

1. Why is Abraham such a good example of faith in action (see Ge 22)? In Abraham's sandals, would your "faith" have prompted you to do what he did, or to "trust" God to find another way, without climbing the mountain? How do you suppose the audiences of these two passages were different? **2.** When have you been challenged to put your faith to the test in a major way? What happened? **3.** If you were arrested for being a Christian, what evidence would be used to prove the point?

worthless. 27Religion that God our Father accepts as pure and faultless is this: to look after orphans and widows in their distress and to keep oneself from being polluted by the world.

Favoritism Forbidden

2 My brothers, as believers in our glorious Lord Jesus Christ, don't show favoritism. 2Suppose a man comes into your meeting wearing a gold ring and fine clothes, and a poor man in shabby clothes also comes in. 3If you show special attention to the man wearing fine clothes and say, "Here's a good seat for you," but say to the poor man, "You stand there" or "Sit on the floor by my feet," 4have you not discriminated among yourselves and become judges with evil thoughts?

5Listen, my dear brothers: Has not God chosen those who are poor in the eyes of the world to be rich in faith and to inherit the kingdom he promised those who love him? 6But you have insulted the poor. Is it not the rich who are exploiting you? Are they not the ones who are dragging you into court? 7Are they not the ones who are slandering the noble name of him to whom you belong?

8If you really keep the royal law found in Scripture, "Love your neighbor as yourself,"*a* you are doing right. 9But if you show favoritism, you sin and are convicted by the law as lawbreakers. 10For whoever keeps the whole law and yet stumbles at just one point is guilty of breaking all of it. 11For he who said, "Do not commit adultery,"*b* also said, "Do not murder."*c* If you do not commit adultery but do commit murder, you have become a lawbreaker.

12Speak and act as those who are going to be judged by the law that gives freedom, 13because judgment without mercy will be shown to anyone who has not been merciful. Mercy triumphs over judgment!

Faith and Deeds

14What good is it, my brothers, if a man claims to have faith but has no deeds? Can such faith save him? 15Suppose a brother or sister is without clothes and daily food. 16If one of you says to him, "Go, I wish you well; keep warm and well fed," but does nothing about his physical needs, what good is it? 17In the same way, faith by itself, if it is not accompanied by action, is dead.

18But someone will say, "You have faith; I have deeds."

Show me your faith without deeds, and I will show you my faith by what I do. 19You believe that there is one God. Good! Even the demons believe that—and shudder.

20You foolish man, do you want evidence that faith without deeds is useless*d*? 21Was not our ancestor Abraham considered righteous for what he did when he offered his son Isaac on the altar? 22You see that his faith and his actions were working together, and his faith was made complete by what he did. 23And the scripture was fulfilled that says, "Abraham believed God, and it was credited to him as righteousness,"*e* and he was called God's friend. 24You see that a person is justified by what he does and not by faith alone.

25In the same way, was not even Rahab the prostitute considered righteous for what she did when she gave lodging to the spies and sent them off in a different direction? 26As the body without the spirit is dead, so faith without deeds is dead.

a8 Lev. 19:18   *b11* Exodus 20:14; Deut. 5:18   *c11* Exodus 20:13; Deut. 5:17
d20 Some early manuscripts *dead*   *e23* Gen. 15:6

Taming the Tongue

3 Not many of you should presume to be teachers, my brothers, because you know that we who teach will be judged more strictly. ²We all stumble in many ways. If anyone is never at fault in what he says, he is a perfect man, able to keep his whole body in check.

³When we put bits into the mouths of horses to make them obey us, we can turn the whole animal. ⁴Or take ships as an example. Although they are so large and are driven by strong winds, they are steered by a very small rudder wherever the pilot wants to go. ⁵Likewise the tongue is a small part of the body, but it makes great boasts. Consider what a great forest is set on fire by a small spark. ⁶The tongue also is a fire, a world of evil among the parts of the body. It corrupts the whole person, sets the whole course of his life on fire, and is itself set on fire by hell.

⁷All kinds of animals, birds, reptiles and creatures of the sea are being tamed and have been tamed by man, ⁸but no man can tame the tongue. It is a restless evil, full of deadly poison.

⁹With the tongue we praise our Lord and Father, and with it we curse men, who have been made in God's likeness. ¹⁰Out of the same mouth come praise and cursing. My brothers, this should not be. ¹¹Can both fresh water and salt[a] water flow from the same spring? ¹²My brothers, can a fig tree bear olives, or a grapevine bear figs? Neither can a salt spring produce fresh water.

Two Kinds of Wisdom

¹³Who is wise and understanding among you? Let him show it by his good life, by deeds done in the humility that comes from wisdom. ¹⁴But if you harbor bitter envy and selfish ambition in your hearts, do not boast about it or deny the truth. ¹⁵Such "wisdom" does not come down from heaven but is earthly, unspiritual, of the devil. ¹⁶For where you have envy and selfish ambition, there you find disorder and every evil practice.

¹⁷But the wisdom that comes from heaven is first of all pure; then peace-loving, considerate, submissive, full of mercy and good fruit, impartial and sincere. ¹⁸Peacemakers who sow in peace raise a harvest of righteousness.

Submit Yourselves to God

4 What causes fights and quarrels among you? Don't they come from your desires that battle within you? ²You want something but don't get it. You kill and covet, but you cannot have what you want. You quarrel and fight. You do not have, because you do not ask God. ³When you ask, you do not receive, because you ask with wrong motives, that you may spend what you get on your pleasures.

⁴You adulterous people, don't you know that friendship with the world is hatred toward God? Anyone who chooses to be a friend of the world becomes an enemy of God. ⁵Or do you think Scripture says without reason that the spirit he caused to live in us envies intensely?[b] ⁶But he gives us more grace. That is why Scripture says:

> "God opposes the proud
>   but gives grace to the humble."[c]

⁷Submit yourselves, then, to God. Resist the devil, and he will

a11 Greek *bitter* (see also verse 14)   b5 Or *that God jealously longs for the spirit that he made to live in us*; or *that the Spirit he caused to live in us longs jealously*
c6 Prov. 3:34

What radio personality do you appreciate for his or her uplifting words? What radio personality *don't* you appreciate? Why?

1. Why is it such a big responsibility to be a teacher, especially of the Scripture? 2. Why are the illustrations of a bit, a rudder and a fire spark so fitting when talking of the tongue? 3. If verse 8 is true, why should we even try to control our tongues?

1. In your everyday conversation, how seriously do you take verse 9? What does this verse say about the caution and reverence with which we must choose our words? 2. Jesus and the apostles Peter and Paul, were not always very "tame" when it came to the tongue. When is harsh language acceptable? 3. How do verses 2 and 10 make you feel about your tongue? How will they prompt you to pray?

Who deserves the "Wisdom of Solomon Award" in your family?

1. How can you recognize a wise person (v. 13)? 2. What two behaviors indicate a lack of wisdom (v. 16)? 3. What does heavenly wisdom produce?

What is the model here for effective managers, teachers, pastors, parents and coworkers? For friends?

1. Whom did you quarrel with most while growing up? 2. What purchase is highest on your "wish list"?

1. What is at the root of fights and quarrels (vv. 1–2a)? 2. What are the two reasons we don't have what we want (vv. 2b–3)? What if we ask with a good motive and still don't receive? 3. When disagreements arise between people, what needs to happen (vv. 2c,7,11)? 4. What is "the law" in verse 11 (see 1:25; 2:8,12)? What is the difference between slander or judgmentalism and identifying sin in order to stand against it?

1. When you quarrel, do you seek to understand what desire is really motivating you? Do you pray about this desire? Where do you need to improve? 2. How

are you most likely to become a "friend" of the world? Lifestyle? Image? Pleasures of money? How does coming near to God (vv. 7–8) strengthen you? **3.** Can self-assertiveness and humility co-exist? Where does pride come in? **4.** Are Christians supposed to reflect verse 9? When?

---

1. Are you a long-range planner, or do you take one day at a time? **2.** When you were 15, what did you expect to be doing at 25? Were you right?

1. What four areas of life are discussed in 4:13? **2.** What is wrong with this type of planning? Is James putting down long-range planning altogether? Is he against making a profit? **3.** What are the abuses the rich committed (5: 4–6)?

1. Do you approach your career planning in these terms? Your "life planning"? **2.** Take 30 seconds to reflect on how 4:17 is true of you. What situation comes to mind? **3.** How do the abuses of the rich occur today? How should Christians be involved?

---

1. What kind of garden or crop have you planted? How long did it take for the flowers or food crop to appear? **2.** What is the sickest you have been?

1. What does James call Christians to wait for patiently (v. 7)? **2.** As we live out our lives, waiting to be united with Christ, what should we guard against (v. 9)? **3.** What do you recall about the suffering Job experienced? Why does James use the illustration of Job (v. 11)? **4.** What is the point of verse 12? How sincere are you in your commitments?

1. How does the farmer image relate to our waiting? What situation in your life could take a lesson from the farmer? **2.** Have you ever prayed over someone who was sick or had someone pray over you? What was the experience like? **3.** Have you ever confessed your sins to other trusted believers and received prayer? In

flee from you. [8]Come near to God and he will come near to you. Wash your hands, you sinners, and purify your hearts, you double-minded. [9]Grieve, mourn and wail. Change your laughter to mourning and your joy to gloom. [10]Humble yourselves before the Lord, and he will lift you up.

[11]Brothers, do not slander one another. Anyone who speaks against his brother or judges him speaks against the law and judges it. When you judge the law, you are not keeping it, but sitting in judgment on it. [12]There is only one Lawgiver and Judge, the one who is able to save and destroy. But you—who are you to judge your neighbor?

Boasting About Tomorrow

[13]Now listen, you who say, "Today or tomorrow we will go to this or that city, spend a year there, carry on business and make money." [14]Why, you do not even know what will happen tomorrow. What is your life? You are a mist that appears for a little while and then vanishes. [15]Instead, you ought to say, "If it is the Lord's will, we will live and do this or that." [16]As it is, you boast and brag. All such boasting is evil. [17]Anyone, then, who knows the good he ought to do and doesn't do it, sins.

Warning to Rich Oppressors

5 Now listen, you rich people, weep and wail because of the misery that is coming upon you. [2]Your wealth has rotted, and moths have eaten your clothes. [3]Your gold and silver are corroded. Their corrosion will testify against you and eat your flesh like fire. You have hoarded wealth in the last days. [4]Look! The wages you failed to pay the workmen who mowed your fields are crying out against you. The cries of the harvesters have reached the ears of the Lord Almighty. [5]You have lived on earth in luxury and self-indulgence. You have fattened yourselves in the day of slaughter.[a] [6]You have condemned and murdered innocent men, who were not opposing you.

Patience in Suffering

[7]Be patient, then, brothers, until the Lord's coming. See how the farmer waits for the land to yield its valuable crop and how patient he is for the autumn and spring rains. [8]You too, be patient and stand firm, because the Lord's coming is near. [9]Don't grumble against each other, brothers, or you will be judged. The Judge is standing at the door!

[10]Brothers, as an example of patience in the face of suffering, take the prophets who spoke in the name of the Lord. [11]As you know, we consider blessed those who have persevered. You have heard of Job's perseverance and have seen what the Lord finally brought about. The Lord is full of compassion and mercy.

[12]Above all, my brothers, do not swear—not by heaven or by earth or by anything else. Let your "Yes" be yes, and your "No," no, or you will be condemned.

The Prayer of Faith

[13]Is any one of you in trouble? He should pray. Is anyone happy? Let him sing songs of praise. [14]Is any one of you sick? He should call the elders of the church to pray over him and anoint him with oil in the name of the Lord. [15]And the prayer offered in faith will make the sick person well; the Lord will raise him up. If he has

---

[a]5 Or *yourselves as in a day of feasting*

sinned, he will be forgiven. [16]Therefore confess your sins to each other and pray for each other so that you may be healed. The prayer of a righteous man is powerful and effective.

[17]Elijah was a man just like us. He prayed earnestly that it would not rain, and it did not rain on the land for three and a half years. [18]Again he prayed, and the heavens gave rain, and the earth produced its crops.

[19]My brothers, if one of you should wander from the truth and someone should bring him back, [20]remember this: Whoever turns a sinner from the error of his way will save him from death and cover over a multitude of sins.

what way can that experience bring forgiveness, healing and new life? **4.** When you see a fellow Christian stray from God, are you prone to watch in disappointment, keep your distance so that you aren't negatively influenced, or seek ways in which God would have you bring this person back? Why? **5.** When have you come the closest to wandering from the faith? What (or who) helped bring you back? How does that demonstrate the healing body of Christ?

INTRODUCTION to
1 PETER

Book Study Outline: If you are using 1 Peter for a study course, here is a 5- or 9-week outline. Use the margin questions for your group agenda:

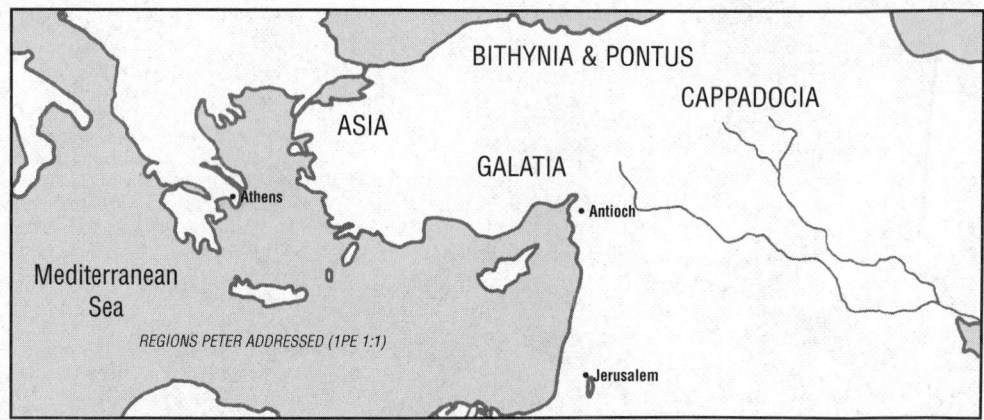

	5-week plan	9-week plan	Group Study Passage
	1	1	1:1–12/Christ Our Hope
		2	1:13–2:3/Christ Our Sacrifice
☕ start meeting / 15 min.	2	3	2:4–12/Christ Our Foundation
		4	2:13–25/Christ Our Example ...
📖 read & discuss Bible / 30 min.	3	5	3:1–7/ ... In Our Relationships
		6	3:8–22/Christ Our Lord
♡ close meeting / 15–45 min.	4	7	4:1–11/Christ Our Strength
		8	4:12–19/Christ Our Joy
	5	9	5:1–14/Christ Our Shepherd

Refer to the Questions and Answers in front of Bible for more information.

Author: Traditionally, the apostle Peter, but some have questioned whether a Galilean fisherman like Peter could have as sophisticated a command of Greek as found in this letter. However in 5:12 he indicates that Silas helped him draft the letter which may explain the excellent style.

Date: Between the great fire in Rome (A.D. 64) and Peter's death (A.D. 68).

Theme: Hope in the midst of suffering.

Historical Background: In the summer of A.D. 64, a great fire destroyed much of Rome. It was widely believed that the Emperor Nero was responsible. Despite his attempts to help the homeless, Nero was unable to allay suspicion. Thus, needing a scapegoat to blame, he selected the Christians for this dubious honor. Up to this point, Christianity had been viewed as simply a sect of Judaism (a legal religion under the Roman system). However, Christianity was now judged to be distinct from Judaism and it was declared a forbidden religion. Waves of oppression and persecution washed over the Empire. During this period Paul was killed by beheading and Peter was crucified upside down. Peter wrote this as a circular letter to the Christians in the Roman provinces of modern-day Turkey (1:1). They were beginning to experience persecution.

Characteristics: The presence of hope in the midst of suffering is the theme throughout this letter. Peter addresses the question of how to live as a Christian in the face of ultimate issues like death, ridicule, persecution and Satanic attack. Throughout the letter, Jesus is held out as their hope (1:3), their Savior (1:18–19), their example (2:21–24), and their Lord (3:15,21b–22). There are numerous Old Testament quotes and allusions, and passages that echo Peter's own sermons as recorded in Acts.

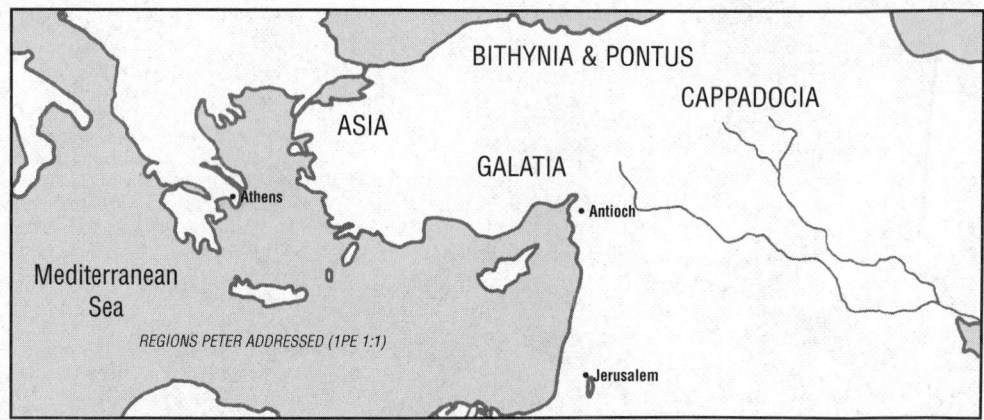

REGIONS PETER ADDRESSED (1PE 1:1)

BITHYNIA & PONTUS

CAPPADOCIA

ASIA

GALATIA

Athens

Antioch

Mediterranean Sea

Jerusalem

1 Peter

1 Peter, an apostle of Jesus Christ,

To God's elect, strangers in the world, scattered throughout Pontus, Galatia, Cappadocia, Asia and Bithynia, ²who have been chosen according to the foreknowledge of God the Father, through the sanctifying work of the Spirit, for obedience to Jesus Christ and sprinkling by his blood:

Grace and peace be yours in abundance.

Praise to God for a Living Hope

³Praise be to the God and Father of our Lord Jesus Christ! In his great mercy he has given us new birth into a living hope through the resurrection of Jesus Christ from the dead, ⁴and into an inheritance that can never perish, spoil or fade—kept in heaven for you, ⁵who through faith are shielded by God's power until the coming of the salvation that is ready to be revealed in the last time. ⁶In this you greatly rejoice, though now for a little while you may have had to suffer grief in all kinds of trials. ⁷These have come so that your faith—of greater worth than gold, which perishes even though refined by fire—may be proved genuine and may result in praise, glory and honor when Jesus Christ is revealed. ⁸Though you have not seen him, you love him; and even though you do not see him now, you believe in him and are filled with an inexpressible and glorious joy, ⁹for you are receiving the goal of your faith, the salvation of your souls.

¹⁰Concerning this salvation, the prophets, who spoke of the grace that was to come to you, searched intently and with the greatest care, ¹¹trying to find out the time and circumstances to which the Spirit of Christ in them was pointing when he predicted the sufferings of Christ and the glories that would follow. ¹²It was revealed to them that they were not serving themselves but you, when they spoke of the things that have now been told you by those who have preached the gospel to you by the Holy Spirit sent from heaven. Even angels long to look into these things.

Be Holy

¹³Therefore, prepare your minds for action; be self-controlled; set your hope fully on the grace to be given you when Jesus Christ is revealed. ¹⁴As obedient children, do not conform to the evil desires you had when you lived in ignorance. ¹⁵But just as he who called you is holy, so be holy in all you do; ¹⁶for it is written: "Be holy, because I am holy." ᵃ

¹⁷Since you call on a Father who judges each man's work impartially, live your lives as strangers here in reverent fear. ¹⁸For you know that it was not with perishable things such as silver or gold that you were redeemed from the empty way of life handed down to you from your forefathers, ¹⁹but with the precious blood of Christ, a lamb without blemish or defect. ²⁰He was chosen before the creation of the world, but was revealed in these last times for your sake. ²¹Through him you believe in God, who raised him from

ᵃ16 Lev. 11:44,45; 19:2; 20:7

---

1. How many times did your family move when you were growing up? Which time was the hardest? 2. How geographically scattered is your family now? How often do you get together?

1. What was the situation in Rome at the writing of this letter (see Introduction to 1 Peter)? 2. What, according to verse 2, is God the Father's role in initiating a Christian's salvation? What part does the Holy Spirit play? 3. What does Peter mean by the "new birth" God, in his mercy, provides (v. 3)? What are God's plans for a Christian's future (vv. 4–5)? 4. What perspective does Peter give suffering in verses 6–7? 5. Despite their suffering, how does Peter describe his audience's spiritual relationship and outlook (vv. 8–9)?

1. When have you felt like a "stranger in the world" (v. 1) because of your faith? What helps you through those times? 2. How has the Spirit stirred a longing for God's forgiveness and holiness within you? 3. How aware are you of God's shielding power that Peter describes? What part do you play (v. 5)? 4. In times of personal crisis, do you tend to lean more on God or blame God? Has suffering made you bitter or "better"?

---

1. How did you get ready for exams in school? Keep up? Cram? Get a good night's sleep? 2. Who was your best coach? How did this person prepare you and help you excel?

1. According to Peter, what does it mean to be holy (1:13–16)? 2. Why would Peter remind Christians who were facing persecution that God is the Judge, and that they should live in fear? Why might they be prone to self-righteousness? 3. What is a good test to see if a Christian has really had a change of heart (1:22)? 4. How is loving deeply and actively possible (1:23–25)?

the dead and glorified him, and so your faith and hope are in God.

²²Now that you have purified yourselves by obeying the truth so that you have sincere love for your brothers, love one another deeply, from the heart.ᵃ ²³For you have been born again, not of perishable seed, but of imperishable, through the living and enduring word of God. ²⁴For,

"All men are like grass,
and all their glory is like the flowers of the field;
the grass withers and the flowers fall,
²⁵   but the word of the Lord stands forever."ᵇ

And this is the word that was preached to you.

2 Therefore, rid yourselves of all malice and all deceit, hypocrisy, envy, and slander of every kind. ²Like newborn babies, crave pure spiritual milk, so that by it you may grow up in your salvation, ³now that you have tasted that the Lord is good.

The Living Stone and a Chosen People

⁴As you come to him, the living Stone—rejected by men but chosen by God and precious to him— ⁵you also, like living stones, are being built into a spiritual house to be a holy priesthood, offering spiritual sacrifices acceptable to God through Jesus Christ. ⁶For in Scripture it says:

"See, I lay a stone in Zion,
a chosen and precious cornerstone,
and the one who trusts in him
will never be put to shame."ᶜ

⁷Now to you who believe, this stone is precious. But to those who do not believe,

"The stone the builders rejected
has become the capstone,ᵈ"ᵉ

⁸and,

"A stone that causes men to stumble
and a rock that makes them fall."ᶠ

They stumble because they disobey the message—which is also what they were destined for.

⁹But you are a chosen people, a royal priesthood, a holy nation, a people belonging to God, that you may declare the praises of him who called you out of darkness into his wonderful light. ¹⁰Once you were not a people, but now you are the people of God; once you had not received mercy, but now you have received mercy.

¹¹Dear friends, I urge you, as aliens and strangers in the world, to abstain from sinful desires, which war against your soul. ¹²Live such good lives among the pagans that, though they accuse you of doing wrong, they may see your good deeds and glorify God on the day he visits us.

Submission to Rulers and Masters

¹³Submit yourselves for the Lord's sake to every authority instituted among men: whether to the king, as the supreme authority, ¹⁴or to governors, who are sent by him to punish those who do wrong and to commend those who do right. ¹⁵For it is God's will that by doing good you should silence the ignorant talk of foolish

---

ᵃ22 Some early manuscripts *from a pure heart*   ᵇ25 Isaiah 40:6-8
ᶜ6 Isaiah 28:16   ᵈ7 Or *cornerstone*   ᵉ7 Psalm 118:22   ᶠ8 Isaiah 8:14

men. [16]Live as free men, but do not use your freedom as a cover-up for evil; live as servants of God. [17]Show proper respect to everyone: Love the brotherhood of believers, fear God, honor the king.

[18]Slaves, submit yourselves to your masters with all respect, not only to those who are good and considerate, but also to those who are harsh. [19]For it is commendable if a man bears up under the pain of unjust suffering because he is conscious of God. [20]But how is it to your credit if you receive a beating for doing wrong and endure it? But if you suffer for doing good and you endure it, this is commendable before God. [21]To this you were called, because Christ suffered for you, leaving you an example, that you should follow in his steps.

> [22]"He committed no sin,
>   and no deceit was found in his mouth." [a]

[23]When they hurled their insults at him, he did not retaliate; when he suffered, he made no threats. Instead, he entrusted himself to him who judges justly. [24]He himself bore our sins in his body on the tree, so that we might die to sins and live for righteousness; by his wounds you have been healed. [25]For you were like sheep going astray, but now you have returned to the Shepherd and Overseer of your souls.

Wives and Husbands

3 Wives, in the same way be submissive to your husbands so that, if any of them do not believe the word, they may be won over without words by the behavior of their wives, [2]when they see the purity and reverence of your lives. [3]Your beauty should not come from outward adornment, such as braided hair and the wearing of gold jewelry and fine clothes. [4]Instead, it should be that of your inner self, the unfading beauty of a gentle and quiet spirit, which is of great worth in God's sight. [5]For this is the way the holy women of the past who put their hope in God used to make themselves beautiful. They were submissive to their own husbands, [6]like Sarah, who obeyed Abraham and called him her master. You are her daughters if you do what is right and do not give way to fear.

[7]Husbands, in the same way be considerate as you live with your wives, and treat them with respect as the weaker partner and as heirs with you of the gracious gift of life, so that nothing will hinder your prayers.

Suffering for Doing Good

[8]Finally, all of you, live in harmony with one another; be sympathetic, love as brothers, be compassionate and humble. [9]Do not repay evil with evil or insult with insult, but with blessing, because to this you were called so that you may inherit a blessing. [10]For,

> "Whoever would love life
>   and see good days
> must keep his tongue from evil
>   and his lips from deceitful speech.
> [11]He must turn from evil and do good;
>   he must seek peace and pursue it.
> [12]For the eyes of the Lord are on the righteous
>   and his ears are attentive to their prayer,
> but the face of the Lord is against those who do
>   evil." [b]

---

tary in nature. How is this different from other interpretations of the word today? **4.** What is Peter's response to one whose master is not a Christian or is just a difficult person (v. 18)? **5.** How does Christ's death result in both an ending and a beginning in our lives (v. 24)?

1. In Peter's day, persecution and slavery made submission to authority difficult. What conditions today make it difficult? **2.** How can Jesus' example help you face hardships you can't change? **3.** What should people do whose legal rights are being violated by authority gone bad? Accept suffering? Insist on justice? Confront the authority? (See also Mk 11:15–16; 15:1–15; Ac 16:35–37).

What have you admired about your grandparents' or other older couples' marriage?

1. See question 3 in the previous "BOOK" questions. In this light, how would you define submission for wives? How are husbands to live "in the same way"? **2.** How can God use the spouse of an unbeliever?

1. When appreciating or striving for beauty, on which do you most often focus (vv. 3–4)? **2.** What does a marriage built on voluntary submission and consideration look like? **3.** Is Peter advocating that spouses stay in cruel situations or that wives never say *no*?

As a child, what can you remember fighting about on family trips?

1. How should we live if we want to "love life and see good days" (v. 10)? How would our society answer this? **2.** How does the quote from Psalm 34 sum up all Peter has said in 2:11–3:9? **3.** How can suffering for what is right be a blessing (v. 14)? **4.** Why is verse 15a the key to following all that Peter says? **5.** What hope does Christ's life and death provide? How does the example of Christ encourage those who suffer?

---

a22 Isaiah 53:9   b12 Psalm 34:12-16

1. How is it really possible to live like verses 8–12? Prayer? Effort? Obedience no matter what? A deepening relationship with Christ? 2. What is the model for evangelism Peter gives in verses 15–16? How closely do you follow this? 3. What fears motivate people today? What fears affect our relationships? How does following Jesus as Lord free you from those fears? 4. How does hope change your behavior and cause people to ask about it? What situation seemed hopeless to you until God brought hope?

How close have you come to dying or being seriously ill?

1. How can suffering change a person's life for the better (vv. 1–2)? 2. Why would a radical change in the lifestyle of Christians be so upsetting to pagan friends or family (v. 4)? 3. How does being clear-minded and self-controlled affect prayer (v. 7)?

1. How have you seen suffering change your own life for the better? 2. How does the reality of judgment (vv. 5–7) and Christ's glory (v. 11) influence your daily behavior? 3. Twice, Peter gives the command to "love each other deeply" (v. 8; 1:22). What comes to mind when you compare your lifestyle of love to this command? 4. Why is using your talents for God important both for yourself and for others?

What kind of pain affects your life the most: physical or emotional?

1. What false assumption does Peter set straight in verse 12? 2. How is rejoicing in suffering different from just enduring suffering? What is meant by "rejoice"? 3. What should be your attitude toward scorn and ridicule of your faith (vv. 16–17)? 4. What is the first and most important course of action amidst suffering (v. 19)?

[13] Who is going to harm you if you are eager to do good? [14] But even if you should suffer for what is right, you are blessed. "Do not fear what they fear[a]; do not be frightened."[b] [15] But in your hearts set apart Christ as Lord. Always be prepared to give an answer to everyone who asks you to give the reason for the hope that you have. But do this with gentleness and respect, [16] keeping a clear conscience, so that those who speak maliciously against your good behavior in Christ may be ashamed of their slander. [17] It is better, if it is God's will, to suffer for doing good than for doing evil. [18] For Christ died for sins once for all, the righteous for the unrighteous, to bring you to God. He was put to death in the body but made alive by the Spirit, [19] through whom[c] also he went and preached to the spirits in prison [20] who disobeyed long ago when God waited patiently in the days of Noah while the ark was being built. In it only a few people, eight in all, were saved through water, [21] and this water symbolizes baptism that now saves you also—not the removal of dirt from the body but the pledge[d] of a good conscience toward God. It saves you by the resurrection of Jesus Christ, [22] who has gone into heaven and is at God's right hand—with angels, authorities and powers in submission to him.

Living for God

4 Therefore, since Christ suffered in his body, arm yourselves also with the same attitude, because he who has suffered in his body is done with sin. [2] As a result, he does not live the rest of his earthly life for evil human desires, but rather for the will of God. [3] For you have spent enough time in the past doing what pagans choose to do—living in debauchery, lust, drunkenness, orgies, carousing and detestable idolatry. [4] They think it strange that you do not plunge with them into the same flood of dissipation, and they heap abuse on you. [5] But they will have to give account to him who is ready to judge the living and the dead. [6] For this is the reason the gospel was preached even to those who are now dead, so that they might be judged according to men in regard to the body, but live according to God in regard to the spirit.

[7] The end of all things is near. Therefore be clear minded and self-controlled so that you can pray. [8] Above all, love each other deeply, because love covers over a multitude of sins. [9] Offer hospitality to one another without grumbling. [10] Each one should use whatever gift he has received to serve others, faithfully administering God's grace in its various forms. [11] If anyone speaks, he should do it as one speaking the very words of God. If anyone serves, he should do it with the strength God provides, so that in all things God may be praised through Jesus Christ. To him be the glory and the power for ever and ever. Amen.

Suffering for Being a Christian

[12] Dear friends, do not be surprised at the painful trial you are suffering, as though something strange were happening to you. [13] But rejoice that you participate in the sufferings of Christ, so that you may be overjoyed when his glory is revealed. [14] If you are insulted because of the name of Christ, you are blessed, for the Spirit of glory and of God rests on you. [15] If you suffer, it should not be as a murderer or thief or any other kind of criminal, or even as a meddler. [16] However, if you suffer as a Christian, do not be ashamed, but praise God that you bear that name. [17] For it is time for judgment to begin with the family of God; and if it begins with

---

a14 Or not fear their threats   b14 Isaiah 8:12   c18,19 Or alive in the spirit, 19through which   d21 Or response

us, what will the outcome be for those who do not obey the gospel of God? [18]And,

> "If it is hard for the righteous to be saved,
>   what will become of the ungodly and the
>   sinner?" [a]

[19]So then, those who suffer according to God's will should commit themselves to their faithful Creator and continue to do good.

To Elders and Young Men

5 To the elders among you, I appeal as a fellow elder, a witness of Christ's sufferings and one who also will share in the glory to be revealed: [2]Be shepherds of God's flock that is under your care, serving as overseers—not because you must, but because you are willing, as God wants you to be; not greedy for money, but eager to serve; [3]not lording it over those entrusted to you, but being examples to the flock. [4]And when the Chief Shepherd appears, you will receive the crown of glory that will never fade away.

[5]Young men, in the same way be submissive to those who are older. All of you, clothe yourselves with humility toward one another, because,

> "God opposes the proud
>   but gives grace to the humble." [b]

[6]Humble yourselves, therefore, under God's mighty hand, that he may lift you up in due time. [7]Cast all your anxiety on him because he cares for you.

[8]Be self-controlled and alert. Your enemy the devil prowls around like a roaring lion looking for someone to devour. [9]Resist him, standing firm in the faith, because you know that your brothers throughout the world are undergoing the same kind of sufferings.

[10]And the God of all grace, who called you to his eternal glory in Christ, after you have suffered a little while, will himself restore you and make you strong, firm and steadfast. [11]To him be the power for ever and ever. Amen.

Final Greetings

[12]With the help of Silas, [c] whom I regard as a faithful brother, I have written to you briefly, encouraging you and testifying that this is the true grace of God. Stand fast in it.

[13]She who is in Babylon, chosen together with you, sends you her greetings, and so does my son Mark. [14]Greet one another with a kiss of love.

Peace to all of you who are in Christ.

♥ **1.** When have you participated in something which was difficult, but eventually became a success (v. 13)? **2.** What form does your suffering for Christ take? How does verse 19 comfort and assure you?

---

1. Were you the youngest, middle or oldest child in your family? How did the family "pecking order" affect your personality? **2.** What is one of the most unruly groups you have had to shepherd: Jr. High kids on a field trip? The church nursery? A small group that wouldn't cooperate? A meeting of competitive professionals?

1. What is Peter warning church leaders about (vv. 2–3)? What are modern-day temptations for leaders? **2.** Who is Peter talking to in verses 5–7? What may be happening in the church? Why might this happen especially during a time of persecution? **3.** How are Christians to deal with stress, tension and hassles (vv. 6–7)? **4.** What theme on suffering in verse 10 summarizes a main theme of 1 Peter? In what way does this promise bring you comfort?

♥ **1.** Who are the "elders" of our day? **2.** What leadership responsibilities do you have? (We all have some!) How do you score on Peter's leadership test? How can you improve your score? **3.** What specific anxiety or concern do you need to cast humbly on the Lord? What gets in your way? **4.** What should Christians be "alert" to? How does this relate to suffering and tensions between people? How does it relate to your own frame of mind? To your belief in the promise in verse 10? **5.** What picture of Christ has Peter drawn in his letter? How does that picture bring peace (5:14) to you?

---

[a]18 Prov. 11:31   [b]5 Prov. 3:34   [c]12 Greek *Silvanus*, a variant of *Silas*

INTRODUCTION to

2 PETER

Book Study Outline: If you are using 2 Peter for a study course, here is a 4-week outline. Use the margin questions for your group agenda:

☕ start meeting / 15 min.

📖 read & discuss Bible / 30 min.

♡ close meeting / 15–45 min.

4-week plan	Group Study Passage
1	1:1–11/Keep On Growing in Christ
2	1:12–21/Authority of True Prophets
3	2:1–22/Destruction of False Prophets
4	3:1–18/Second Coming of Christ

Refer to the Questions and Answers in the front of this Bible for more information.

Author: Traditionally, the apostle Peter, although questions about his authorship have existed since the earliest times because the language and style of this letter differs markedly from 1 Peter. The fact that Peter had different secretaries (Silas, Mark, Glaucias) may explain this difference.

Date: Probably near the time of Peter's death in A.D. 68 (see 1:12–15).

Theme: Be eager and on your guard.

Historical Background: See the Introduction to 1 Peter. Although no specific group is addressed, it appears to have been sent to the same group of Christians who received his first letter (3:1). Persecution from Roman authorities (the major issue in Peter's first letter) was not the only problem facing these people. False teachers had arisen. The fact that Jesus had not yet returned was being interpreted as evidence that the apostles (like Peter and Paul) were not to be trusted. These teachers were apparently insinuating that the Second Coming was sort of a "moral club" invented by the apostles to inhibit the Christian's "freedom." For the false teachers, "freedom" meant the right to indulge in sexual immorality, drunkenness and hedonistic pleasure (2:2,10,13–14,18). Peter fights back in this letter by roaring a "Not so!" He asserts that apostolic teaching was not a matter of spinning their own ideas (1:16,20), but that in reality the false teachers' "authority" stemmed from their own minds (1:21), and their "spiritual freedom" really led to depravity (2:19).

Characteristics: Chapter 1 is an exhortation to grow in the Christian virtues. Chapter 2 is very similar to the epistle of Jude (see the Introduction to Jude). A marked contrast is drawn there between the character and teaching of true apostles (like Peter and Paul) and that of the false teachers whose lives are marked by their denial of Jesus, immorality, rejection of authority, enslavement to sin and misuse of Scripture. Chapter 3 addresses the Second Coming of Christ.

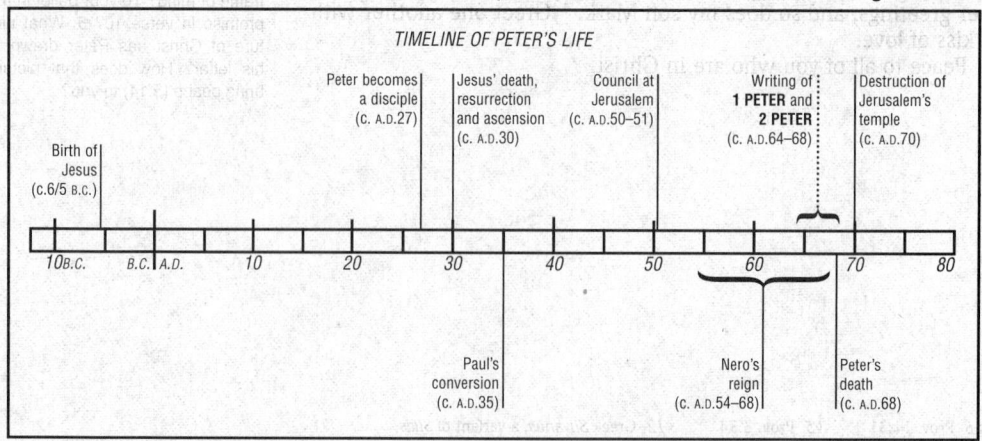

TIMELINE OF PETER'S LIFE

2 Peter

1 Simon Peter, a servant and apostle of Jesus Christ,

To those who through the righteousness of our God and Savior Jesus Christ have received a faith as precious as ours:

²Grace and peace be yours in abundance through the knowledge of God and of Jesus our Lord.

Making One's Calling and Election Sure

³His divine power has given us everything we need for life and godliness through our knowledge of him who called us by his own glory and goodness. ⁴Through these he has given us his very great and precious promises, so that through them you may participate in the divine nature and escape the corruption in the world caused by evil desires.

⁵For this very reason, make every effort to add to your faith goodness; and to goodness, knowledge; ⁶and to knowledge, self-control; and to self-control, perseverance; and to perseverance, godliness; ⁷and to godliness, brotherly kindness; and to brotherly kindness, love. ⁸For if you possess these qualities in increasing measure, they will keep you from being ineffective and unproductive in your knowledge of our Lord Jesus Christ. ⁹But if anyone does not have them, he is nearsighted and blind, and has forgotten that he has been cleansed from his past sins.

¹⁰Therefore, my brothers, be all the more eager to make your calling and election sure. For if you do these things, you will never fall, ¹¹and you will receive a rich welcome into the eternal kingdom of our Lord and Savior Jesus Christ.

Prophecy of Scripture

¹²So I will always remind you of these things, even though you know them and are firmly established in the truth you now have. ¹³I think it is right to refresh your memory as long as I live in the tent of this body, ¹⁴because I know that I will soon put it aside, as our Lord Jesus Christ has made clear to me. ¹⁵And I will make every effort to see that after my departure you will always be able to remember these things.

¹⁶We did not follow cleverly invented stories when we told you about the power and coming of our Lord Jesus Christ, but we were eyewitnesses of his majesty. ¹⁷For he received honor and glory from God the Father when the voice came to him from the Majestic Glory, saying, "This is my Son, whom I love; with him I am well pleased."[a] ¹⁸We ourselves heard this voice that came from heaven when we were with him on the sacred mountain.

¹⁹And we have the word of the prophets made more certain, and you will do well to pay attention to it, as to a light shining in a dark place, until the day dawns and the morning star rises in your hearts. ²⁰Above all, you must understand that no prophecy of Scripture came about by the prophet's own interpretation. ²¹For prophecy never had its origin in the will of man, but men spoke from God as they were carried along by the Holy Spirit.

a17 Matt. 17:5; Mark 9:7; Luke 9:35

1. As a teenager, what did you desire to do most: Career-wise? Sports-wise? Relationship-wise? 2. How have your desires changed since then?

1. From verses 3–4, what is "everything we need for life"? 2. With *everything* given to us, why must we "*add* to our faith"? And with what effort (vv. 5,10)? 3. What seven qualities are we to zealously desire? How does each fit with the one mentioned before it? 4. Why is this moral progress and productive knowledge (v. 8) so desirable for believers (vv. 4,10–11)?

1. In what way are verses 5–10 a prescription for one who is feeling disappointed or unfulfilled? 2. Of the seven qualities in verses 5–7, which two do you possess in the greatest measure? How can you grow in one of the other qualities? How can your group help?

How are you like a tent: Always pulling up stakes, moving on? Resistant to winds of change? Cozy with some, cold to others?

1. What event of Jesus' life does Peter recall (vv. 16–18)? 2. Why (and how) does Peter establish his own authority (v. 16)? Likewise, why does Peter defend the authority and inspiration of the prophets? What problem does this imply his readers may have (vv. 20–21)? 3. If so much prophecy has already been fulfilled in Christ's first coming, how then are we to regard prophecy yet to be fulfilled?

1. If you could have been with Jesus at one event in his life, which would you choose? Why? 2. If a non-Christian asked you to prove the Scriptures are God's Word, on what would you base your answer? 3. How does that answer affect your Bible study habits? Your witness? Your lifestyle?

1. If people have pets that are like them in some way, what does your choice of pet say about you? 2. What "beasts" and other "things which go bump in the night" are you afraid of? Why?

1. Having just commended true prophets (1:12–21), who does Peter now condemn? Why? 2. If it is so plain that judgment awaits these false teachers, why does anyone follow them (vv. 2–3,14,18–19)? If they are so evil, why do you think God allows them to teach in his church? Isn't God's goodness or greatness brought into question by delaying their judgment? 3. In response to that implied question, Peter recites God's track record in dealing with evil: What examples are cited in verses 4–9? 4. If neither angels, the ancient world, nor Sodom and Gomorrah were spared from God's wrath against sin, who does God protect from judgment (v. 9)? Why? How is that a particular comfort to Peter's audience? 5. Who are the gross sinners in verses 13–16? What are they like? On what basis is Peter assured they will be paid back in kind? 6. What other imagery does Peter use to further denounce the false prophets (vv. 17–19)? 7. What "freedom" do they promise: Freedom from sin? From laws? From judgment? From ethical obligations to others and to Christ? All of the above? How is their idea of freedom different from true Christian freedom? 8. What do verses 20–22 imply about a person's salvation? Can one lose it? Or were these people never converted? Why do you think so?

1. How do you know when a preacher is exploiting you with stories they have made up, or feeding you empty promises as "springs without water"? How could the dangers mentioned by Peter affect you now? 2. Do such false teachers upset you as much as Peter? Why or why not? Which preacher do you trust more than others? Why? 3. Amidst all this bad news, what good news is there? Would it be truly good news if there were no judgment? 4. In your experience, does grace ever come through perverse channels (such as the heretics and wicked men depicted here), or only through pure vessels: Always? Sometimes? Never? Why is that?

False Teachers and Their Destruction

2 But there were also false prophets among the people, just as there will be false teachers among you. They will secretly introduce destructive heresies, even denying the sovereign Lord who bought them—bringing swift destruction on themselves. 2Many will follow their shameful ways and will bring the way of truth into disrepute. 3In their greed these teachers will exploit you with stories they have made up. Their condemnation has long been hanging over them, and their destruction has not been sleeping.

4For if God did not spare angels when they sinned, but sent them to hell,[a] putting them into gloomy dungeons[b] to be held for judgment; 5if he did not spare the ancient world when he brought the flood on its ungodly people, but protected Noah, a preacher of righteousness, and seven others; 6if he condemned the cities of Sodom and Gomorrah by burning them to ashes, and made them an example of what is going to happen to the ungodly; 7and if he rescued Lot, a righteous man, who was distressed by the filthy lives of lawless men 8(for that righteous man, living among them day after day, was tormented in his righteous soul by the lawless deeds he saw and heard)— 9if this is so, then the Lord knows how to rescue godly men from trials and to hold the unrighteous for the day of judgment, while continuing their punishment.[c] 10This is especially true of those who follow the corrupt desire of the sinful nature[d] and despise authority.

Bold and arrogant, these men are not afraid to slander celestial beings; 11yet even angels, although they are stronger and more powerful, do not bring slanderous accusations against such beings in the presence of the Lord. 12But these men blaspheme in matters they do not understand. They are like brute beasts, creatures of instinct, born only to be caught and destroyed, and like beasts they too will perish.

13They will be paid back with harm for the harm they have done. Their idea of pleasure is to carouse in broad daylight. They are blots and blemishes, reveling in their pleasures while they feast with you.[e] 14With eyes full of adultery, they never stop sinning; they seduce the unstable; they are experts in greed—an accursed brood! 15They have left the straight way and wandered off to follow the way of Balaam son of Beor, who loved the wages of wickedness. 16But he was rebuked for his wrongdoing by a donkey—a beast without speech—who spoke with a man's voice and restrained the prophet's madness.

17These men are springs without water and mists driven by a storm. Blackest darkness is reserved for them. 18For they mouth empty, boastful words and, by appealing to the lustful desires of sinful human nature, they entice people who are just escaping from those who live in error. 19They promise them freedom, while they themselves are slaves of depravity—for a man is a slave to whatever has mastered him. 20If they have escaped the corruption of the world by knowing our Lord and Savior Jesus Christ and are again entangled in it and overcome, they are worse off at the end than they were at the beginning. 21It would have been better for them not to have known the way of righteousness, than to have known it and then to turn their backs on the sacred command that was passed on to them. 22Of them the proverbs are true: "A dog returns to its vomit,"[f] and, "A sow that is washed goes back to her wallowing in the mud."

a4 Greek Tartarus   b4 Some manuscripts into chains of darkness   c9 Or unrighteous for punishment until the day of judgment   d10 Or the flesh
e13 Some manuscripts in their love feasts   f22 Prov. 26:11

The Day of the Lord

3 Dear friends, this is now my second letter to you. I have written both of them as reminders to stimulate you to wholesome thinking. ²I want you to recall the words spoken in the past by the holy prophets and the command given by our Lord and Savior through your apostles.

³First of all, you must understand that in the last days scoffers will come, scoffing and following their own evil desires. ⁴They will say, "Where is this 'coming' he promised? Ever since our fathers died, everything goes on as it has since the beginning of creation." ⁵But they deliberately forget that long ago by God's word the heavens existed and the earth was formed out of water and by water. ⁶By these waters also the world of that time was deluged and destroyed. ⁷By the same word the present heavens and earth are reserved for fire, being kept for the day of judgment and destruction of ungodly men.

⁸But do not forget this one thing, dear friends: With the Lord a day is like a thousand years, and a thousand years are like a day. ⁹The Lord is not slow in keeping his promise, as some understand slowness. He is patient with you, not wanting anyone to perish, but everyone to come to repentance.

¹⁰But the day of the Lord will come like a thief. The heavens will disappear with a roar; the elements will be destroyed by fire, and the earth and everything in it will be laid bare.ᵃ

¹¹Since everything will be destroyed in this way, what kind of people ought you to be? You ought to live holy and godly lives ¹²as you look forward to the day of God and speed its coming.ᵇ That day will bring about the destruction of the heavens by fire, and the elements will melt in the heat. ¹³But in keeping with his promise we are looking forward to a new heaven and a new earth, the home of righteousness.

¹⁴So then, dear friends, since you are looking forward to this, make every effort to be found spotless, blameless and at peace with him. ¹⁵Bear in mind that our Lord's patience means salvation, just as our dear brother Paul also wrote you with the wisdom that God gave him. ¹⁶He writes the same way in all his letters, speaking in them of these matters. His letters contain some things that are hard to understand, which ignorant and unstable people distort, as they do the other Scriptures, to their own destruction.

¹⁷Therefore, dear friends, since you already know this, be on your guard so that you may not be carried away by the error of lawless men and fall from your secure position. ¹⁸But grow in the grace and knowledge of our Lord and Savior Jesus Christ. To him be glory both now and forever! Amen.

1. When did your dad promise a fishing trip, a ballgame or a graduation present and then fail to deliver? How did that make you feel? 2. When told, "Wait until your birthday," or "Christmas isn't here yet," and "You'd better be good until then," how did that affect your behavior while waiting?

1. Following the digression of chapter 2, to what themes does Peter now return? 2. What "must" the readers first understand (see also 1:20–21)? 3. Why does God's creation of the earth support Peter's contention that he will also destroy the earth (v. 10)? Why is that so difficult for people to believe? What does this tell you about their perception of God? 4. What frustrations does God's patience produce? How is God's patience a benefit (vv. 9,15)? 5. How does God's view of time differ from the readers' view? In this context (vv. 10–16), is Peter addressing the certainty, the timing or the manner of Christ's coming? How is that an effective inducement to godly living now? 6. How does Peter's reference to Paul also encourage his readers in right behavior (v. 15)? 7. What is Peter's final antidote to the false teachers of his day (vv. 17–18)?

1. If you were in charge of the world's clock, would you slow it down or speed it up? Why? 2. If you were in charge of creating, destroying and redeeming the world, which of these would you take more "time" doing? Why? 3. In football strategy "the best defense is a good offense," meaning if the other team never gets the ball they can't score against you. How is Peter's strategy like that in his defense against those who would lead us away from the truth? What can you do to "grow in the grace and knowledge of our Lord"?

ᵃ10 Some manuscripts *be burned up*   ᵇ12 Or *as you wait eagerly for the day of God to come*

INTRODUCTION to
1 JOHN

Book Study Outline: If you are using 1 John for a study course, here is a 4- or 7-week outline. Use the margin questions for your group agenda:

	4-week plan	7-week plan	Group Study Passage
	1	1	1:1–2:14/Walking in the Light
		2	2:15–27/Warning Against Antichrists
	2	3	2:28–3:10/Doing What Is Right
		4	3:11–24/Loving One Another
	3	5	4:1–6/Testing the Spirits
		6	4:7–21/Loving God
	4	7	5:1–21/Believing in Christ

start meeting / 15 min.

read & discuss Bible / 30 min.

close meeting / 15–45 min.

Refer to the Questions and Answers in the front of this Bible for more information.

Author: Traditionally, the apostle John.

Date: Uncertain, but probably in the late A.D. 80s or early 90s when the heresy which is rebuked here (an early form of Gnosticism) began to flourish.

Theme: Walking in the light.

Historical Background: Since in his later years John resided in Ephesus, this letter was probably addressed to the church there. A group had split off from the church (2:19) and began trying to persuade others to espouse their new and "advanced" views (2:26). To help the church discern truth from error, both in doctrine and lifestyle, John wrote this letter. The secessionists did not believe Jesus was the Messiah (2:22), nor that he had come in the flesh (4:2–3). Furthermore, they didn't need Jesus as Savior or mediator, since they claimed to have direct knowledge of and fellowship with God (1:6; 2:4). This spiritual elitism bypassed morality and love as marks of one's spiritual maturity. What was important to them were visions and spiritual revelations.

Characteristics: First John does not have the neat, logical outline found in many New Testament books. Rather, John seems to have written one paragraph and then he would be reminded of a related idea which became the topic of the next paragraph. The structure is more spiral than linear. This epistle is a distillation of all John, now an old man, wants people to remember about the faith. Its essence is that God is light (1:5); God is love (4:16); Jesus is the Messiah (2:22), the Son of God (4:15) who has come in the flesh (4:2) to make us his children (3:1). As such, we have eternal life (2:25) and are called not to sin (2:1), but to love one another (3:11; 4:7–12).

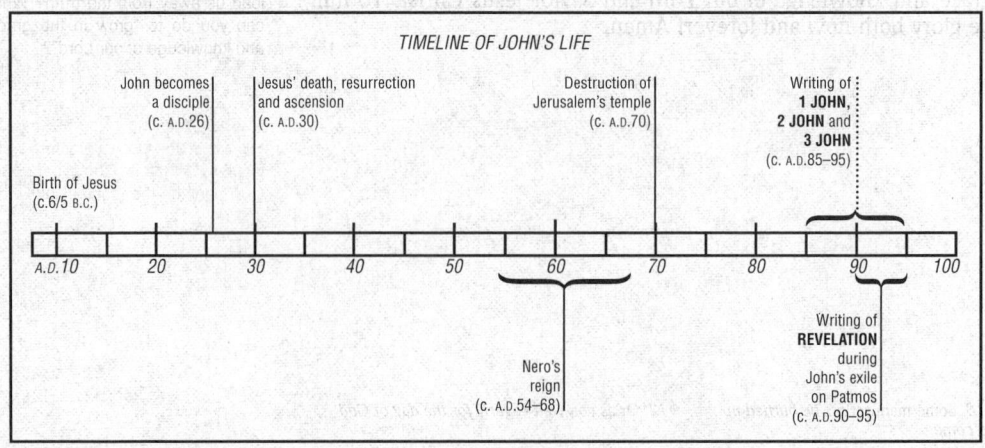

TIMELINE OF JOHN'S LIFE

John becomes a disciple (c. A.D.26)

Jesus' death, resurrection and ascension (c. A.D.30)

Destruction of Jerusalem's temple (c. A.D.70)

Writing of **1 JOHN, 2 JOHN** and **3 JOHN** (c. A.D.85–95)

Birth of Jesus (c.6/5 B.C.)

A.D.10   20   30   40   50   60   70   80   90   100

Nero's reign (c. A.D.54–68)

Writing of **REVELATION** during John's exile on Patmos (c. A.D.90–95)

1 John

The Word of Life

1 That which was from the beginning, which we have heard, which we have seen with our eyes, which we have looked at and our hands have touched—this we proclaim concerning the Word of life. ²The life appeared; we have seen it and testify to it, and we proclaim to you the eternal life, which was with the Father and has appeared to us. ³We proclaim to you what we have seen and heard, so that you also may have fellowship with us. And our fellowship is with the Father and with his Son, Jesus Christ. ⁴We write this to make our[a] joy complete.

Walking in the Light

⁵This is the message we have heard from him and declare to you: God is light; in him there is no darkness at all. ⁶If we claim to have fellowship with him yet walk in the darkness, we lie and do not live by the truth. ⁷But if we walk in the light, as he is in the light, we have fellowship with one another, and the blood of Jesus, his Son, purifies us from all[b] sin.

⁸If we claim to be without sin, we deceive ourselves and the truth is not in us. ⁹If we confess our sins, he is faithful and just and will forgive us our sins and purify us from all unrighteousness. ¹⁰If we claim we have not sinned, we make him out to be a liar and his word has no place in our lives.

2 My dear children, I write this to you so that you will not sin. But if anybody does sin, we have one who speaks to the Father in our defense—Jesus Christ, the Righteous One. ²He is the atoning sacrifice for our sins, and not only for ours but also for[c] the sins of the whole world.

³We know that we have come to know him if we obey his commands. ⁴The man who says, "I know him," but does not do what he commands is a liar, and the truth is not in him. ⁵But if anyone obeys his word, God's love[d] is truly made complete in him. This is how we know we are in him: ⁶Whoever claims to live in him must walk as Jesus did.

⁷Dear friends, I am not writing you a new command but an old one, which you have had since the beginning. This old command is the message you have heard. ⁸Yet I am writing you a new command; its truth is seen in him and you, because the darkness is passing and the true light is already shining.

⁹Anyone who claims to be in the light but hates his brother is still in the darkness. ¹⁰Whoever loves his brother lives in the light, and there is nothing in him[e] to make him stumble. ¹¹But whoever hates his brother is in the darkness and walks around in the darkness; he does not know where he is going, because the darkness has blinded him.

¹²I write to you, dear children,
  because your sins have been forgiven on
    account of his name.

1. What was your house like at age 7? 2. What do you remember about your room? 3. As a child, were you afraid of the dark? What "monsters" were in the dark that scared you?

1. A group in John's church had split off and were teaching that Jesus did not really die. They also believed they were without sin (see Introduction to 1 John). What could not be proclaimed if Jesus hadn't died? 2. What false claims do John's opponents make (1:6,8)? 3. What hope does John give when people fail to live in light of God's love (1:9; 2:1–2)? Explain in your own words what it means that Jesus is the advocate, the righteous one and the atoning sacrifice. 4. How can the command to love God and others (2:7) be new and old at the same time? How is its truth seen in Jesus (think of examples from the Gospels)? 5. What are the two tests given in this passage for determining whether one really knows God (2:3,10)? How are you doing in each of these areas? 6. What three things does John stress again in verses 2:12–14?

1. In what ways have you, like John, "seen," "heard" and "touched" Jesus? 2. Who has been like the apostle John in your life—a person who has cared about your spiritual growth? 3. What characteristics of light reflect who God is? Has God brought light to your life? Or do you more often feel like you're in the dark? 4. How do you feel about the consistency of your own life (1:6,8)? Are you living the truth or a lie? In what area do you especially need improvement? 5. When you know you've sinned, how long do you wait before you confess? What is God's part and your part in the confession process?

---

a4 Some manuscripts your   b7 Or every   c2 Or He is the one who turns aside God's wrath, taking away our sins, and not only ours but also   d5 Or word, love for God   e10 Or it

13I write to you, fathers,
  because you have known him who is from the
    beginning.
I write to you, young men,
  because you have overcome the evil one.
I write to you, dear children,
  because you have known the Father.
14I write to you, fathers,
  because you have known him who is from the
    beginning.
I write to you, young men,
  because you are strong,
  and the word of God lives in you,
  and you have overcome the evil one.

Do Not Love the World

15Do not love the world or anything in the world. If anyone loves the world, the love of the Father is not in him. 16For everything in the world—the cravings of sinful man, the lust of his eyes and the boasting of what he has and does—comes not from the Father but from the world. 17The world and its desires pass away, but the man who does the will of God lives forever.

Warning Against Antichrists

18Dear children, this is the last hour; and as you have heard that the antichrist is coming, even now many antichrists have come. This is how we know it is the last hour. 19They went out from us, but they did not really belong to us. For if they had belonged to us, they would have remained with us; but their going showed that none of them belonged to us.

20But you have an anointing from the Holy One, and all of you know the truth.a 21I do not write to you because you do not know the truth, but because you do know it and because no lie comes from the truth. 22Who is the liar? It is the man who denies that Jesus is the Christ. Such a man is the antichrist—he denies the Father and the Son. 23No one who denies the Son has the Father; whoever acknowledges the Son has the Father also.

24See that what you have heard from the beginning remains in you. If it does, you also will remain in the Son and in the Father. 25And this is what he promised us—even eternal life.

26I am writing these things to you about those who are trying to lead you astray. 27As for you, the anointing you received from him remains in you, and you do not need anyone to teach you. But as his anointing teaches you about all things and as that anointing is real, not counterfeit—just as it has taught you, remain in him.

Children of God

28And now, dear children, continue in him, so that when he appears we may be confident and unashamed before him at his coming.

29If you know that he is righteous, you know that everyone who does what is right has been born of him.

3 How great is the love the Father has lavished on us, that we should be called children of God! And that is what we are! The reason the world does not know us is that it did not know him. 2Dear friends, now we are children of God, and what we will be has not yet been made known. But we know that when he ap-

a20 Some manuscripts *and you know all things*

Are you more likely to err on the side of doing what you shouldn't or not doing what you should?

1. What does John mean by "the world" (vv. 15–17)? Is it wrong to love the outdoors or your pet? Are all human desires contrary to God's will? Why? 2. What is the anointing in verse 20? How does this anointing help a person to know and remain in the truth (vv. 20,24)? 3. In what way are the antichrists in this passage foreshadowing the Antichrist to come? What danger do they pose to the church? 4. Why are there only two options in verse 23?

1. In what areas of your life does love for the world compete with love for God: In your use of money? Time? Priorities? Relationships? Ambitions? 2. What criteria can you use to distinguish between: (a) new insights into Christian truths that the Holy Spirit brings to light, and (b) new teachings that undermine the Christian faith?

Who is the "neat freak" in your family? Are you neat or messy?

1. What tell-tale attitudes and actions characterize a person "born of God" (2:29; 3:1b,3,6–7, 10)? 2. Are Christians sinless (3:6–10)? Does John mean that Christians do not sin: At all? Inadvertently? Deliberately? Habitually? Or is he providing a gauge to evaluate teachers? 3. John says the main source of tension between the world and Christians is sin. De-

pears,[a] we shall be like him, for we shall see him as he is. [3]Everyone who has this hope in him purifies himself, just as he is pure.

[4]Everyone who sins breaks the law; in fact, sin is lawlessness. [5]But you know that he appeared so that he might take away our sins. And in him is no sin. [6]No one who lives in him keeps on sinning. No one who continues to sin has either seen him or known him.

[7]Dear children, do not let anyone lead you astray. He who does what is right is righteous, just as he is righteous. [8]He who does what is sinful is of the devil, because the devil has been sinning from the beginning. The reason the Son of God appeared was to destroy the devil's work. [9]No one who is born of God will continue to sin, because God's seed remains in him; he cannot go on sinning, because he has been born of God. [10]This is how we know who the children of God are and who the children of the devil are: Anyone who does not do what is right is not a child of God; nor is anyone who does not love his brother.

Love One Another

[11]This is the message you heard from the beginning: We should love one another. [12]Do not be like Cain, who belonged to the evil one and murdered his brother. And why did he murder him? Because his own actions were evil and his brother's were righteous. [13]Do not be surprised, my brothers, if the world hates you. [14]We know that we have passed from death to life, because we love our brothers. Anyone who does not love remains in death. [15]Anyone who hates his brother is a murderer, and you know that no murderer has eternal life in him.

[16]This is how we know what love is: Jesus Christ laid down his life for us. And we ought to lay down our lives for our brothers. [17]If anyone has material possessions and sees his brother in need but has no pity on him, how can the love of God be in him? [18]Dear children, let us not love with words or tongue but with actions and in truth. [19]This then is how we know that we belong to the truth, and how we set our hearts at rest in his presence [20]whenever our hearts condemn us. For God is greater than our hearts, and he knows everything.

[21]Dear friends, if our hearts do not condemn us, we have confidence before God [22]and receive from him anything we ask, because we obey his commands and do what pleases him. [23]And this is his command: to believe in the name of his Son, Jesus Christ, and to love one another as he commanded us. [24]Those who obey his commands live in him, and he in them. And this is how we know that he lives in us: We know it by the Spirit he gave us.

Test the Spirits

4 Dear friends, do not believe every spirit, but test the spirits to see whether they are from God, because many false prophets have gone out into the world. [2]This is how you can recognize the Spirit of God: Every spirit that acknowledges that Jesus Christ has come in the flesh is from God, [3]but every spirit that does not acknowledge Jesus is not from God. This is the spirit of the antichrist, which you have heard is coming and even now is already in the world.

[4]You, dear children, are from God and have overcome them, because the one who is in you is greater than the one who is in the

spite this tension, what must go hand-in-hand with obedience for a Christian (3:10)? When is it difficult for you to love?

1. How would you feel if Jesus returned right now? Excited? Relieved? Ashamed? **2.** What do verses 1–3 imply about God? What does this mean for our self-image? How have you experienced God's lavish love this week? **3.** How can a Christian recognize and deal with our society's "whatever is right for you" attitude (moral relativism)?

Who was your first "true love" growing up?

1. What do you think Christians in the first century were encountering from the non-Christian world? From each other? **2.** What is the heart of John's message? **3.** Why does John use the story of Cain and Abel here (see Ge 4:1–8)? Where do you see "Cain-like" attitudes in yourself? **4.** What is John's definition of love (vv. 16–18)? How does this differ from contemporary definitions? **5.** What are we assured of through loving others (vv. 14,19–20,24)?

1. How would you like to consciously practice Jesus-like love this week? With your family? A friend? At church? In politics? In social issues? A difficult person? A person in need? How will doing this affect your own need for love? **2.** How are answered prayers and obedience connected (vv. 18–22)? Will obedience affect what we pray for? How has this been true for you?

How do you stay informed on current events?

1. What does John command in verse 1? What else has he said about false prophets (2:18–29)? **2.** How can a Christian distinguish a true prophet from a false (see also 2:20–23)?

1. What do you believe about Jesus' nature? What difference does it make whether he was

---

[a]2 Or *when it is made known*

truly divine? Truly human? **2.** What "power" equips you to overcome false prophets?

☕ What personality trait or strength did you get from your father? Your mother?

📖 **1.** What is the source of human love? How can God's love be expressed through humans? In our motives? Our actions? Why is it a lie to say you love God but do not show love to your brother (v. 19)? **2.** From verses 8–15, what do you learn about the relationship between the Father, Son and Holy Spirit? About their relationship to us? **3.** How does the message that God's love drives out fear (v. 18) relate to the teaching that God is light (1:5)?

❤ **1.** Is the love discussed here an action or a feeling? What does this tell you about love? **2.** In your life, when has "love" held too much fear? When has God's love cast out fear? **3.** If you want to do a better job of loving others, how should you go about it? What is the only way to improve (see vv. 15–16)? **4.** How do you want to love sacrificially this week? At home? At work? A difficult relationship? In how you plan your time? Your budget?

☕ **1.** In the Aesop's Fable, "The Tortoise and the Hare," are you more like the steady, persistent tortoise, or the fast-starting, easily distracted hare? How so? **2.** Did you say a bedtime prayer as a child? What kind of prayer? Did Mom or Dad join you?

📖 **1.** What kind of love comes along with our new birth (vv. 1–3)? Why are God's commands not a burden? **2.** What is the power source for overcoming the world? How have you seen faith (belief), love and obedience to be interconnected in your life? What lie is John combatting (remember the group who had split off from the church, see Introduction to 1 John)? **3.** What are the three witnesses to Jesus Christ (v. 7)? What do water and blood refer to (see 5:6)? What happened at Jesus' baptism (Mk 1:9–11)? Why is it important to emphasize Jesus' death and resurrection? How does the Spirit testify to

world. **5**They are from the world and therefore speak from the viewpoint of the world, and the world listens to them. **6**We are from God, and whoever knows God listens to us; but whoever is not from God does not listen to us. This is how we recognize the Spirit*a* of truth and the spirit of falsehood.

God's Love and Ours

7Dear friends, let us love one another, for love comes from God. Everyone who loves has been born of God and knows God. **8**Whoever does not love does not know God, because God is love. **9**This is how God showed his love among us: He sent his one and only Son*b* into the world that we might live through him. **10**This is love: not that we loved God, but that he loved us and sent his Son as an atoning sacrifice for*c* our sins. **11**Dear friends, since God so loved us, we also ought to love one another. **12**No one has ever seen God; but if we love one another, God lives in us and his love is made complete in us.

13We know that we live in him and he in us, because he has given us of his Spirit. **14**And we have seen and testify that the Father has sent his Son to be the Savior of the world. **15**If anyone acknowledges that Jesus is the Son of God, God lives in him and he in God. **16**And so we know and rely on the love God has for us.

God is love. Whoever lives in love lives in God, and God in him. **17**In this way, love is made complete among us so that we will have confidence on the day of judgment, because in this world we are like him. **18**There is no fear in love. But perfect love drives out fear, because fear has to do with punishment. The one who fears is not made perfect in love.

19We love because he first loved us. **20**If anyone says, "I love God," yet hates his brother, he is a liar. For anyone who does not love his brother, whom he has seen, cannot love God, whom he has not seen. **21**And he has given us this command: Whoever loves God must also love his brother.

Faith in the Son of God

5 Everyone who believes that Jesus is the Christ is born of God, and everyone who loves the father loves his child as well. **2**This is how we know that we love the children of God: by loving God and carrying out his commands. **3**This is love for God: to obey his commands. And his commands are not burdensome, **4**for everyone born of God overcomes the world. This is the victory that has overcome the world, even our faith. **5**Who is it that overcomes the world? Only he who believes that Jesus is the Son of God.

6This is the one who came by water and blood—Jesus Christ. He did not come by water only, but by water and blood. And it is the Spirit who testifies, because the Spirit is the truth. **7**For there are three that testify: **8**the*d* Spirit, the water and the blood; and the three are in agreement. **9**We accept man's testimony, but God's testimony is greater because it is the testimony of God, which he has given about his Son. **10**Anyone who believes in the Son of God has this testimony in his heart. Anyone who does not believe God has made him out to be a liar, because he has not believed the testimony God has given about his Son. **11**And this is the testimony: God has given us eternal life, and this life is in his Son. **12**He

*a*6 Or *spirit*   *b*9 Or *his only begotten Son*   *c*10 Or *as the one who would turn aside his wrath, taking away*   *d*7,8 Late manuscripts of the Vulgate *testify in heaven: the Father, the Word and the Holy Spirit, and these three are one. 8And there are three that testify on earth: the* (not found in any Greek manuscript before the sixteenth century)

who has the Son has life; he who does not have the Son of God does not have life.

Concluding Remarks

[13]I write these things to you who believe in the name of the Son of God so that you may know that you have eternal life. [14]This is the confidence we have in approaching God: that if we ask anything according to his will, he hears us. [15]And if we know that he hears us—whatever we ask—we know that we have what we asked of him.

[16]If anyone sees his brother commit a sin that does not lead to death, he should pray and God will give him life. I refer to those whose sin does not lead to death. There is a sin that leads to death. I am not saying that he should pray about that. [17]All wrongdoing is sin, and there is sin that does not lead to death.

[18]We know that anyone born of God does not continue to sin; the one who was born of God keeps him safe, and the evil one cannot harm him. [19]We know that we are children of God, and that the whole world is under the control of the evil one. [20]We know also that the Son of God has come and has given us understanding, so that we may know him who is true. And we are in him who is true—even in his Son Jesus Christ. He is the true God and eternal life.

[21]Dear children, keep yourselves from idols.

Jesus? **4.** What is the condition for prayer to be answered (vv. 14–15)? What does it mean to pray in Jesus' name? **5.** How is the assurance of eternal life (v. 13) the key to: (a) Answered prayer (vv. 14–15)? (b) Forgiveness of sin (vv. 16–17)? (c) Deliverance from sin and evil (vv. 18–19)? (d) Avoidance of idols (v. 21)? **6.** What might be the sin that leads to death (see Mk 3:22–30)? Why do the very fears of those who worry about having committed this sin prove that they have not done so?

1. How are you doing at loving God? Using the "love test" from verses 1–3, how are you doing at loving others? How does your obedience to God affect your love for others? **2.** What has convinced you that true life is found in Jesus? What further "proof" do you need? **3.** How often are you prompted to pray for someone you see struggling with sin in their life? Who has prayed for you in the past? What was the result? **4.** If 1 John were dropped from the Bible, what would be missing from the story of God's redemptive work in history?

INTRODUCTION to
2 and 3 JOHN

Book Study Outline: If you are using 2 and 3 John for a study course, spend one meeting on each of these short books. Use the questions in the margin for your group agenda:

start meeting /
15 min.

read & discuss Bible /
30 min.

close meeting /
15–45 min.

Refer to the Questions and Answers in the front of this Bible for more information.

Author: Since the style and content of these two letters is similar to 1 John, it is assumed that the author ("the elder") is John the apostle.

Date: Uncertain, but probably in the late A.D. 80s or early 90s, when the heresy which is rebuked here (an early form of Gnosticism) began to flourish.

Theme: Hospitality for itinerant teachers.

Historical Background: Itinerant missionaries were the means by which Christianity spread throughout the Empire. They looked to local churches to aid in their mission by providing hospitality (Roman inns were notorious for being dirty and flea-infested). The problem was that some of the people seeking room and board were false teachers, expounding erroneous doctrines; others were phonies, pretending to be true prophets in order to get free hospitality. Even the pagan Greek author Lucian noticed this sort of abuse. In his satirical work *Peregrinus,* he wrote about a religious charlatan who lived off the generosity of the church simply as a way to avoid working. The *Didache,* an early church manual, set out guidelines to help the churches discern what types of itinerant teachers should and shouldn't be received. For example, it stated that true prophets were indeed to be entertained—for a day or two. But if a prophet stayed three days, this was a sign that he was false. In the same way, 2 and 3 John were written to help certain local churches sort out the problem. In 2 John, the author warns the church to beware of those who teach false doctrine. "Do not welcome such," he says. In 3 John he addresses the opposite problem: the failure of Christians to provide hospitality for genuine teachers. Here he commends a friend by the name of Gaius who opened his house even to strangers. By so doing, he was entering into their work of spreading the truth.

Characteristics: These are the shortest letters in the New Testament. They are quite similar in style and content and were undoubtedly written by the same person. There is also a close connection between 1 John and these two shorter letters. They reflect John's concern in his first epistle for *truth* (which is mentioned four times in 2 John and seven times in 3 John) and for *love* (which occurs five times in 2 John and two times in 3 John). These two letters provide a glimpse into the life of the early church, and insight into how we should respond to Christian workers.

THE ERRORS OF GNOSTICISM

One of the most dangerous heresies of the first two centuries of the church was Gnosticism. Its central teaching was that salvation is a product of knowledge; that spirit is entirely good and matter is entirely evil. From this unbiblical dualism flowed five important errors:

1. Man's body, which is matter, is therefore evil. It is to be contrasted with God, who is wholly spirit and therefore good.

2. Salvation is escape from the body, achieved not by faith in Christ but by special knowledge (the Greek word for "knowledge" is *gnosis*, hence Gnosticism).

3. Christ's humanity was denied in two ways: (1) Some said that Christ only *seemed* to have a body, a view called Docetism, from the Greek *dokeo* ("to seem"), and (2) others said that the divine Christ joined the man Jesus at baptism and left him before he died, a view called Cerinthianism, after its most prominent spokesman, Cerinthus. This view is the background of much of 1 John (see 1:1; 2:22; 4:2–3).

4. Since the body was considered evil, it was to be treated harshly. This ascetic form of Gnosticism is the background of part of the letter to the Colossians (2:21–23).

5. Paradoxically, this dualism also led to licentiousness. The reason was that, since matter—and not the breaking of God's law (1Jn 3:4)—was considered evil, breaking this law was of no moral consequence.

The Gnosticism addressed in the New Testament was an early form of heresy, not the intricately developed system of the second and third centuries. In addition to that seen in Colossians and in John's letters, acquaintance with early Gnosticism is reflected in 1 and 2 Timothy, Titus, 2 Peter and perhaps 1 Corinthians.

2 John

¹The elder,

To the chosen lady and her children, whom I love in the truth—and not I only, but also all who know the truth— ²because of the truth, which lives in us and will be with us forever:

³Grace, mercy and peace from God the Father and from Jesus Christ, the Father's Son, will be with us in truth and love.

⁴It has given me great joy to find some of your children walking in the truth, just as the Father commanded us. ⁵And now, dear lady, I am not writing you a new command but one we have had from the beginning. I ask that we love one another. ⁶And this is love: that we walk in obedience to his commands. As you have heard from the beginning, his command is that you walk in love.

⁷Many deceivers, who do not acknowledge Jesus Christ as coming in the flesh, have gone out into the world. Any such person is the deceiver and the antichrist. ⁸Watch out that you do not lose what you have worked for, but that you may be rewarded fully. ⁹Anyone who runs ahead and does not continue in the teaching of Christ does not have God; whoever continues in the teaching has both the Father and the Son. ¹⁰If anyone comes to you and does not bring this teaching, do not take him into your house or welcome him. ¹¹Anyone who welcomes him shares in his wicked work.

¹²I have much to write to you, but I do not want to use paper and ink. Instead, I hope to visit you and talk with you face to face, so that our joy may be complete.

¹³The children of your chosen sister send their greetings.

---

1. When you were growing up, where did you gather for family reunions? What was special about those times? Where did the guests stay? 2. Whose home could you drop in on unexpectedly and know that you would be welcome?

1. How are John's twin themes of truth and love interconnected here? 2. If the lady addressed in this letter were to show hospitality to these false teachers who traveled around, would her error be on the side of truth, or on the side of love? What's wrong with welcoming such wandering missionaries? 3. How do John's exhortations to true believers (vv. 4–6) help them resist the deception and wickedness of the religious frauds (vv. 7–11)?

1. Which is easier for you to do—"walk in truth" or "walk in love"? 2. Have you ever been involved in a deep relationship that had to be terminated because of an overriding issue involving your faith? What happened? 3. How do you distinguish between those missionaries you ought not to support and those you should? How can you exercise truth and love in that decision? 4. When was the last time you had someone over who was really hurting, lonely or needing help (no names)? Should you do this more often? What's stopping you?

3 John

1. Did you ever run out of money when you were away from home? What did you do? 2. Who extended loving hospitality to you when you needed it most?

1. What conflicts were going on in the church that prompted John to write this letter (see Introduction to 2 and 3 John)? What personality issues are involved? What type of character sketch would you draw for Gaius? Diotrephes? Demetrius? 2. In what ways does this letter tackle the hospitality issue differently than 2 John? Why is John urging that these teachers be cared for in their travels? Why would this be so important at this time?

1. How can you reflect Gaius' desire to be of help to itinerant Christian workers? 2. Has suspicion about the false motives or messages of some pastors/ teachers soured you against them all? What needs to change so you will not hinder the work of God by failing to encourage his true servants? 3. Do you find opening up your home (or your small group) to new people easy or difficult? Why is that? 4. In picking close friends (like Gaius was to John), what do you look for? How can you be that kind of friend to others?

[1]The elder,

To my dear friend Gaius, whom I love in the truth.

[2]Dear friend, I pray that you may enjoy good health and that all may go well with you, even as your soul is getting along well. [3]It gave me great joy to have some brothers come and tell about your faithfulness to the truth and how you continue to walk in the truth. [4]I have no greater joy than to hear that my children are walking in the truth.

[5]Dear friend, you are faithful in what you are doing for the brothers, even though they are strangers to you. [6]They have told the church about your love. You will do well to send them on their way in a manner worthy of God. [7]It was for the sake of the Name that they went out, receiving no help from the pagans. [8]We ought therefore to show hospitality to such men so that we may work together for the truth.

[9]I wrote to the church, but Diotrephes, who loves to be first, will have nothing to do with us. [10]So if I come, I will call attention to what he is doing, gossiping maliciously about us. Not satisfied with that, he refuses to welcome the brothers. He also stops those who want to do so and puts them out of the church.

[11]Dear friend, do not imitate what is evil but what is good. Anyone who does what is good is from God. Anyone who does what is evil has not seen God. [12]Demetrius is well spoken of by everyone—and even by the truth itself. We also speak well of him, and you know that our testimony is true.

[13]I have much to write you, but I do not want to do so with pen and ink. [14]I hope to see you soon, and we will talk face to face.

Peace to you. The friends here send their greetings. Greet the friends there by name.

INTRODUCTION to
JUDE

Book Study Outline: If you are using Jude for a study course, spend one to two meetings on this short book. Use the questions in the margin for your group agenda:

start meeting /
15 min.

read & discuss Bible /
30 min.

close meeting /
15–45 min.

Refer to the Questions and Answers in the front of this Bible for more information.

Author: Traditionally, Jude, the brother of Jesus (Mt 13:55, Jude is a form of the name "Judas"). After the resurrection, Jesus' brothers came to believe in him and they became missionaries (1Co 9:5).

Date: The date of Jude is hard to ascertain. If 2 Peter made use of it, then it would be dated around A.D. 65; otherwise it could be dated as late as A.D. 80.

Theme: Contend for the faith.

Historical Background: This is a sermon/letter meant to be read to a congregation, warning them against false teachers. Jude's opponents are a band of smooth-talking teachers who go from church to church, receiving hospitality in return for their instruction. In this case, the teachers were *antinomians.* They rejected all moral standards and indulged in immoral behavior; particularly of a sexual kind. The root problem was their misunderstanding of the doctrine of grace. They twisted the truth that people are saved by grace to mean that people could therefore do whatever they pleased. Paul, who was apparently accused of this type of teaching, rejected it in no uncertain terms as a perversion of the Gospel (see Ro 6). These teachers rooted their authority largely in their own ecstatic experiences ("God told me"), and therefore they considered their actions beyond criticism. The book of Jude is a fiery call to defend the faith against these heretics who had wormed their way into the church.

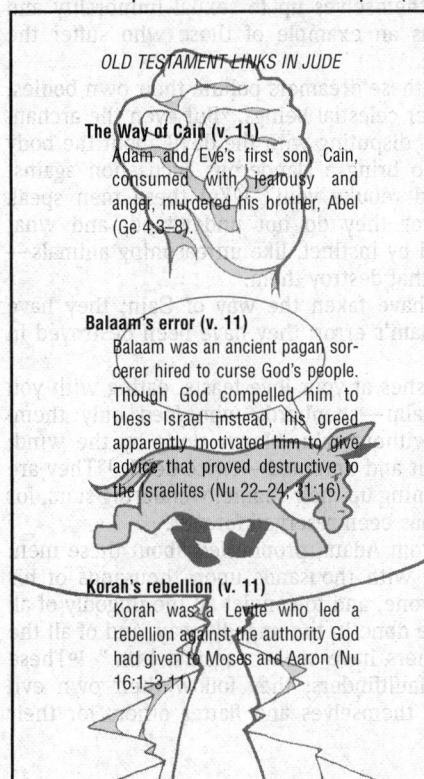

OLD TESTAMENT LINKS IN JUDE

The Way of Cain (v. 11)
Adam and Eve's first son, Cain, consumed with jealousy and anger, murdered his brother, Abel (Ge 4:3–8).

Balaam's error (v. 11)
Balaam was an ancient pagan sorcerer hired to curse God's people. Though God compelled him to bless Israel instead, his greed apparently motivated him to give advice that proved destructive to the Israelites (Nu 22–24; 31:16).

Korah's rebellion (v. 11)
Korah was a Levite who led a rebellion against the authority God had given to Moses and Aaron (Nu 16:1–3,11).

Characteristics: Best known for its doxology (vv. 24–25), Jude is packed with quotes from the Old Testament and the Apocrypha (religious books written by Jews between the time of the Old Testament and New Testament). It uses vivid images and frequent allusions. Jude's themes are summed up in verses 3–4: (a) Christians are to "contend for the faith," and (b) they are to do so against the false teachers who have slipped into their midst. Jude is clearly related to 2 Peter, since 15 of its 25 verses are also found there in whole or in part. However, it is not known which epistle came first, or if they both quoted from a third source. Jude's use of apocryphal literature was of some concern to the early church fathers who concluded (wrongly) that any book that used such literature could not be genuine. However, they failed to recognize that other New Testament writers did the same thing. Paul referred to nonbiblical Jewish writing (2Ti 3:8). He also quoted heathen poets (Ac 17:28; 1Co 15:32–33; Tit 1:12). The author of Hebrews echoes the works of Philo, and James makes reference to nonbiblical sources. The issue is not where the specific words came from but how the New Testament writer used the words to reveal God's truth.

Jude

1. Who was your first boyfriend or girlfriend? Where is that person now? 2. When was the last time someone "read you the riot act"? What had you done wrong? How did it feel to be soundly rebuked? 3. What scary experience with fire have you had?

1. What are your first impressions of Jude, the man and his letter? 2. How does he describe himself and his fellow Christians (vv. 3–5)? From this description, what does it mean to be a Christian? 3. What concerning these "godless men" (v. 4) is so godless? 4. How do each of the examples from history (vv. 5–7,11) relate to problems of unbelief, immorality, violence and rebellion? 5. To someone who questions the certainty, severity or justice of God's judgment, what do these examples teach? How do the vivid images in verses 12–16 further condemn the skeptics? 6. Should Jude's readers have been surprised by this coming judgment (vv. 17–19)? Why or why not? 7. How is the good distinguished from the bad in this divided church (vv. 17–21)? 8. What is our duty to the doubter who is merely flirting with falsehood (v. 22)? To one already singed with evil (v. 23)? How does the rescuer avoid falling into the same danger as those who play with fire? 9. What role does God play in the believer's safety, sacrificial commitment and sense of joy (v. 24)? How do you explain this picture of God with the contrasting one in verses 5–7?

1. What can make a church vulnerable to false teachers today: (a) Boredom? (b) Lust? (c) Attraction to personalities? (d) Apathy? 2. What "spiritual body-building" plan could help to keep you strong in God's love (vv. 20–21)? 3. What goes on daily at your workplace, in your community or even in your church, which would fall within the range of Jude's indicting sermon? 4. Someone has said, "All it takes for evil to prevail is for a few good men to do nothing." What is one thing you could do this week to help keep this truism from becoming a reality where you live and

¹Jude, a servant of Jesus Christ and a brother of James,

To those who have been called, who are loved by God the Father and kept by[a] Jesus Christ:

²Mercy, peace and love be yours in abundance.

The Sin and Doom of Godless Men

³Dear friends, although I was very eager to write to you about the salvation we share, I felt I had to write and urge you to contend for the faith that was once for all entrusted to the saints. ⁴For certain men whose condemnation was written about[b] long ago have secretly slipped in among you. They are godless men, who change the grace of our God into a license for immorality and deny Jesus Christ our only Sovereign and Lord.

⁵Though you already know all this, I want to remind you that the Lord[c] delivered his people out of Egypt, but later destroyed those who did not believe. ⁶And the angels who did not keep their positions of authority but abandoned their own home—these he has kept in darkness, bound with everlasting chains for judgment on the great Day. ⁷In a similar way, Sodom and Gomorrah and the surrounding towns gave themselves up to sexual immorality and perversion. They serve as an example of those who suffer the punishment of eternal fire.

⁸In the very same way, these dreamers pollute their own bodies, reject authority and slander celestial beings. ⁹But even the archangel Michael, when he was disputing with the devil about the body of Moses, did not dare to bring a slanderous accusation against him, but said, "The Lord rebuke you!" ¹⁰Yet these men speak abusively against whatever they do not understand; and what things they do understand by instinct, like unreasoning animals—these are the very things that destroy them.

¹¹Woe to them! They have taken the way of Cain; they have rushed for profit into Balaam's error; they have been destroyed in Korah's rebellion.

¹²These men are blemishes at your love feasts, eating with you without the slightest qualm—shepherds who feed only themselves. They are clouds without rain, blown along by the wind; autumn trees, without fruit and uprooted—twice dead. ¹³They are wild waves of the sea, foaming up their shame; wandering stars, for whom blackest darkness has been reserved forever.

¹⁴Enoch, the seventh from Adam, prophesied about these men: "See, the Lord is coming with thousands upon thousands of his holy ones ¹⁵to judge everyone, and to convict all the ungodly of all the ungodly acts they have done in the ungodly way, and of all the harsh words ungodly sinners have spoken against him." ¹⁶These men are grumblers and faultfinders; they follow their own evil desires; they boast about themselves and flatter others for their own advantage.

---

a1 Or for; or in   b4 Or men who were marked out for condemnation   c5 Some early manuscripts Jesus

Revelation

Prologue

1 The revelation of Jesus Christ, which God gave him to show his servants what must soon take place. He made it known by sending his angel to his servant John, ²who testifies to everything he saw—that is, the word of God and the testimony of Jesus Christ. ³Blessed is the one who reads the words of this prophecy, and blessed are those who hear it and take to heart what is written in it, because the time is near.

Greetings and Doxology

⁴John,

To the seven churches in the province of Asia:

Grace and peace to you from him who is, and who was, and who is to come, and from the seven spirits*a* before his throne, ⁵and from Jesus Christ, who is the faithful witness, the firstborn from the dead, and the ruler of the kings of the earth.

To him who loves us and has freed us from our sins by his blood, ⁶and has made us to be a kingdom and priests to serve his God and Father—to him be glory and power for ever and ever! Amen.

> ⁷Look, he is coming with the clouds,
>   and every eye will see him,
>   even those who pierced him;
>   and all the peoples of the earth will mourn
>   because of him.
>   So shall it be! Amen.

⁸"I am the Alpha and the Omega," says the Lord God, "who is, and who was, and who is to come, the Almighty."

One Like a Son of Man

⁹I, John, your brother and companion in the suffering and kingdom and patient endurance that are ours in Jesus, was on the island of Patmos because of the word of God and the testimony of Jesus. ¹⁰On the Lord's Day I was in the Spirit, and I heard behind me a loud voice like a trumpet, ¹¹which said: "Write on a scroll what you see and send it to the seven churches: to Ephesus, Smyrna, Pergamum, Thyatira, Sardis, Philadelphia and Laodicea."

¹²I turned around to see the voice that was speaking to me. And when I turned I saw seven golden lampstands, ¹³and among the lampstands was someone "like a son of man,"*b* dressed in a robe reaching down to his feet and with a golden sash around his chest. ¹⁴His head and hair were white like wool, as white as snow, and his eyes were like blazing fire. ¹⁵His feet were like bronze glowing in a furnace, and his voice was like the sound of rushing waters. ¹⁶In his right hand he held seven stars, and out of his mouth came a sharp double-edged sword. His face was like the sun shining in all its brilliance.

¹⁷When I saw him, I fell at his feet as though dead. Then he

---

1. What kind of book are you: Mystery? Sports? Technical? Adventure? Poetry? Unreadable? Sealed? Open? Explain. 2. Around the house, are you king, priest or servant? What would your spouse, parent or friend say is your typical role?

1. What is a revelation? In this case, who is revealed? By whom? To whom? For what purpose? 2. Who is John? Who are the recipient churches (vv. 4,11; see Introduction to Revelation)? 3. What is significant about the references to God in verses 4 and 8? 4. What are the meanings of the titles given to Jesus (vv. 5–6)? What three things does Christ do for us? 5. What theme of the book of Revelation is foreshadowed in verse 7? Why is the phrase "every eye will see him" significant?

1. If asked to share three facts about Jesus that are especially significant to you, what would you say? Why are these facts so important to you? 2. How will you personalize and pass along the blessing of verse 3?

---

1. What bizarre dream can you still recall, and why? 2. What religious pictures or statues adorn the walls of your house (or mind)?

1. Why was John on Patmos? What do you know about his assignment there? 2. What is significant about his spiritual condition and the day when he received this vision? 3. Close your eyes and have someone read verses 12–18 slowly, several times if necessary. Meditate on it. What do you see? Feel? What do the images in these verses suggest about Christ (Da 7:9)? 4. What is the meaning of the seven stars? The seven lampstands? What does it mean for a church to be a light?

1. Using the analogy of a lighting fixture to describe the spiritual condition of your church,

---

a4 Or *the sevenfold Spirit*   *b13* Daniel 7:13

what kind fits your situation (a chandelier, a nightlight)? What would help create more illumination? **2.** Are you right now "on Patmos" (suffering) or "in the Spirit" (reigning)? Why? Can both happen at once?

___

What was your "first love" in elementary school like?

1. What do you know about the church at Ephesus (see Ac 19)? **2.** What good things characterize this church? How might its strengths have been the cause of its failure? What do you think their weekly worship was like? **3.** What is repentance? Why is that necessary for the Ephesian church?

1. Of the positive qualities mentioned about this group, which best describes you? Your church? Why? **2.** In what ways have you lost your first love for Christ? What has helped you to keep that love alive?

___

If you were rich, what would you like to do?

1. What problems is this church facing? How can they be both poor and rich? **2.** Why is Jesus known as the First and the Last? **3.** What does this passage teach about suffering?

1. Has it been harder to live out your faith when you've been poor, or when you've had enough money? Why? **2.** In what ways do you feel spiritually rich?

___

As a child, where was the local "haunted house" in your town? Did you ever dare to go in?

1. What pressures are the Christians in Pergamum facing (v. 13)? At what point are they strong? Where are they tempted? Which do you think is easier to endure: Persecution by enemies or seduction by the culture? Why? **2.** Why is the title by which Christ reveals himself so appropriate to these Christians? **3.** What is the significance of the sword (v. 16)? Of the manna and stone (v. 17)?

placed his right hand on me and said: "Do not be afraid. I am the First and the Last. [18]I am the Living One; I was dead, and behold I am alive for ever and ever! And I hold the keys of death and Hades.

[19]"Write, therefore, what you have seen, what is now and what will take place later. [20]The mystery of the seven stars that you saw in my right hand and of the seven golden lampstands is this: The seven stars are the angels[a] of the seven churches, and the seven lampstands are the seven churches.

To the Church in Ephesus

2 "To the angel[b] of the church in Ephesus write:

These are the words of him who holds the seven stars in his right hand and walks among the seven golden lampstands: [2]I know your deeds, your hard work and your perseverance. I know that you cannot tolerate wicked men, that you have tested those who claim to be apostles but are not, and have found them false. [3]You have persevered and have endured hardships for my name, and have not grown weary.

[4]Yet I hold this against you: You have forsaken your first love. [5]Remember the height from which you have fallen! Repent and do the things you did at first. If you do not repent, I will come to you and remove your lampstand from its place. [6]But you have this in your favor: You hate the practices of the Nicolaitans, which I also hate.

[7]He who has an ear, let him hear what the Spirit says to the churches. To him who overcomes, I will give the right to eat from the tree of life, which is in the paradise of God.

To the Church in Smyrna

[8]"To the angel of the church in Smyrna write:

These are the words of him who is the First and the Last, who died and came to life again. [9]I know your afflictions and your poverty—yet you are rich! I know the slander of those who say they are Jews and are not, but are a synagogue of Satan. [10]Do not be afraid of what you are about to suffer. I tell you, the devil will put some of you in prison to test you, and you will suffer persecution for ten days. Be faithful, even to the point of death, and I will give you the crown of life.

[11]He who has an ear, let him hear what the Spirit says to the churches. He who overcomes will not be hurt at all by the second death.

To the Church in Pergamum

[12]"To the angel of the church in Pergamum write:

These are the words of him who has the sharp, double-edged sword. [13]I know where you live—where Satan has his throne. Yet you remain true to my name. You did not renounce your faith in me, even in the days of Antipas, my faithful witness, who was put to death in your city—where Satan lives.

[14]Nevertheless, I have a few things against you: You have people there who hold to the teaching of Balaam, who taught Balak to entice the Israelites to sin by eating food sacrificed to idols and by committing sexual immorality. [15]Likewise you also have those who hold to the teaching of the Nicolaitans.

[a]20 Or messengers   [b]1 Or messenger; also in verses 8, 12 and 18

[16]Repent therefore! Otherwise, I will soon come to you and will fight against them with the sword of my mouth.

[17]He who has an ear, let him hear what the Spirit says to the churches. To him who overcomes, I will give some of the hidden manna. I will also give him a white stone with a new name written on it, known only to him who receives it.

To the Church in Thyatira

[18]"To the angel of the church in Thyatira write:

These are the words of the Son of God, whose eyes are like blazing fire and whose feet are like burnished bronze. [19]I know your deeds, your love and faith, your service and perseverance, and that you are now doing more than you did at first.

[20]Nevertheless, I have this against you: You tolerate that woman Jezebel, who calls herself a prophetess. By her teaching she misleads my servants into sexual immorality and the eating of food sacrificed to idols. [21]I have given her time to repent of her immorality, but she is unwilling. [22]So I will cast her on a bed of suffering, and I will make those who commit adultery with her suffer intensely, unless they repent of her ways. [23]I will strike her children dead. Then all the churches will know that I am he who searches hearts and minds, and I will repay each of you according to your deeds. [24]Now I say to the rest of you in Thyatira, to you who do not hold to her teaching and have not learned Satan's so-called deep secrets (I will not impose any other burden on you): [25]Only hold on to what you have until I come.

[26]To him who overcomes and does my will to the end, I will give authority over the nations—

[27]'He will rule them with an iron scepter;
    he will dash them to pieces like
        pottery'[a]—

just as I have received authority from my Father. [28]I will also give him the morning star. [29]He who has an ear, let him hear what the Spirit says to the churches.

To the Church in Sardis

3 "To the angel[b] of the church in Sardis write:

These are the words of him who holds the seven spirits[c] of God and the seven stars. I know your deeds; you have a reputation of being alive, but you are dead. [2]Wake up! Strengthen what remains and is about to die, for I have not found your deeds complete in the sight of my God. [3]Remember, therefore, what you have received and heard; obey it, and repent. But if you do not wake up, I will come like a thief, and you will not know at what time I will come to you.

[4]Yet you have a few people in Sardis who have not soiled their clothes. They will walk with me, dressed in white, for they are worthy. [5]He who overcomes will, like them, be dressed in white. I will never blot out his name from the book of life, but will acknowledge his name before my Father and his angels. [6]He who has an ear, let him hear what the Spirit says to the churches.

♡ **1.** What cultural influences distract you from your relationship with Christ? How subtle are these influences in your life? How direct? **2.** What weapons has God given you to do battle with? Which has proved very helpful?

☕ As a teenager, what person or group influenced you the most? How?

📖 **1.** What are the strengths of this church? Its weaknesses? **2.** What does the symbolic name "Jezebel" reveal about the woman in this church (1Ki 2:5–25; 2Ki 9:7–37)? **3.** How does Jesus describe himself? How do you interpret this description? What is he saying about himself? Why is this appropriate for the church at Thyatira? **4.** How is the nature and source of the temptation in Thyatira like (and unlike) that in Pergamum? **5.** What do you think Jesus' promise in verses 26–27 means?

♡ **1.** Which of the qualities in verse 19 apply to you this week? Why? **2.** Who or what has played a role similar to Jezebel in your life (names aren't necessary)? How? How did the Lord free you from that influence? **3.** What do you appreciate most about the promise to overcomers in this section?

☕ What team or group of yours had a reputation far better than its performance?

📖 **1.** What is the contrast between reputation and reality in Sardis? What dangers exist for Christians who rely on an image instead of nurturing a genuine spiritual life (v. 2)? **2.** What is the only hope for the survival of the church in Sardis?

♡ **1.** If Jesus addressed this "wake-up call" to you, what would he want you to strengthen? **2.** Right now, would Jesus need a fire alarm to wake you up, or would a quiet call do it? Why?

---

[a]27 Psalm 2:9   [b]1 Or *messenger*; also in verses 7 and 14   [c]1 Or *the sevenfold Spirit*

☕ When have you been "locked out"?

📖 1. What does the "key of David" open (vv. 7–8; 4:1; see Isa 22:22–24; Mt 16:19)? 2. How is this church able to persevere? Describe their enemies. How does their reward (v. 12) fit their faithfulness?

♡ 1. What open doors has Christ placed before you? How have you taken advantage of the pathways he's made available to you? 2. What are some closed doors he's placed in your career? In your social life? In your schooling? How have you responded to each of these closed doors? 3. In what ways are you like the Christians in Philadelphia? Unlike them? Why? 4. What is the Spirit saying to you now?

☕ 1. What is your favorite cold cereal? Hot cereal? Your favorite drink? 2. If you could invite any famous person for dinner, whom would you ask? Why?

📖 1. What does the "faithful and true witness" see when he looks at the Laodicean church (vv. 15–16)? How does the church view itself? Why the contrast? 2. What does Jesus tell them to do in verse 18? Why? What does this say about true wealth? 3. How would you describe Christ, based on what you have read so far in this book? How does this expand the picture of Jesus in the Gospels?

♡ 1. If Jesus took your spiritual temperature today, what would he find? Why? 2. What is Jesus waiting for at the door of your life? Why not let him in?

☕ What is the most memorable storm you have ever been in? What happened?

📖 1. Where does this scene actually take place: In the afterlife? In some perfect order of things after this world has passed away? Or on the level of spiritual reality here and now (as in Eph 2:6), where good and evil are unmasked to be seen for what they really are? 2. Who is the figure on the throne? What is he like? What are the 24

To the Church in Philadelphia

7"To the angel of the church in Philadelphia write:

These are the words of him who is holy and true, who holds the key of David. What he opens no one can shut, and what he shuts no one can open. 8I know your deeds. See, I have placed before you an open door that no one can shut. I know that you have little strength, yet you have kept my word and have not denied my name. 9I will make those who are of the synagogue of Satan, who claim to be Jews though they are not, but are liars—I will make them come and fall down at your feet and acknowledge that I have loved you. 10Since you have kept my command to endure patiently, I will also keep you from the hour of trial that is going to come upon the whole world to test those who live on the earth.

11I am coming soon. Hold on to what you have, so that no one will take your crown. 12Him who overcomes I will make a pillar in the temple of my God. Never again will he leave it. I will write on him the name of my God and the name of the city of my God, the new Jerusalem, which is coming down out of heaven from my God; and I will also write on him my new name. 13He who has an ear, let him hear what the Spirit says to the churches.

To the Church in Laodicea

14"To the angel of the church in Laodicea write:

These are the words of the Amen, the faithful and true witness, the ruler of God's creation. 15I know your deeds, that you are neither cold nor hot. I wish you were either one or the other! 16So, because you are lukewarm—neither hot nor cold—I am about to spit you out of my mouth. 17You say, 'I am rich; I have acquired wealth and do not need a thing.' But you do not realize that you are wretched, pitiful, poor, blind and naked. 18I counsel you to buy from me gold refined in the fire, so you can become rich; and white clothes to wear, so you can cover your shameful nakedness; and salve to put on your eyes, so you can see.

19Those whom I love I rebuke and discipline. So be earnest, and repent. 20Here I am! I stand at the door and knock. If anyone hears my voice and opens the door, I will come in and eat with him, and he with me.

21To him who overcomes, I will give the right to sit with me on my throne, just as I overcame and sat down with my Father on his throne. 22He who has an ear, let him hear what the Spirit says to the churches."

The Throne in Heaven

4 After this I looked, and there before me was a door standing open in heaven. And the voice I had first heard speaking to me like a trumpet said, "Come up here, and I will show you what must take place after this." 2At once I was in the Spirit, and there before me was a throne in heaven with someone sitting on it. 3And the one who sat there had the appearance of jasper and carnelian. A rainbow, resembling an emerald, encircled the throne. 4Surrounding the throne were twenty-four other thrones, and seated on them were twenty-four elders. They were dressed in white and had crowns of gold on their heads. 5From the throne came flashes of lightning, rumblings and peals of thunder. Before the throne, seven

lamps were blazing. These are the seven spirits^a of God. 6Also before the throne there was what looked like a sea of glass, clear as crystal.

In the center, around the throne, were four living creatures, and they were covered with eyes, in front and in back. 7The first living creature was like a lion, the second was like an ox, the third had a face like a man, the fourth was like a flying eagle. 8Each of the four living creatures had six wings and was covered with eyes all around, even under his wings. Day and night they never stop saying:

> "Holy, holy, holy
> is the Lord God Almighty,
> who was, and is, and is to come."

9Whenever the living creatures give glory, honor and thanks to him who sits on the throne and who lives for ever and ever, 10the twenty-four elders fall down before him who sits on the throne, and worship him who lives for ever and ever. They lay their crowns before the throne and say:

> 11"You are worthy, our Lord and God,
> to receive glory and honor and power,
> for you created all things,
> and by your will they were created
> and have their being."

The Scroll and the Lamb

5 Then I saw in the right hand of him who sat on the throne a scroll with writing on both sides and sealed with seven seals. 2And I saw a mighty angel proclaiming in a loud voice, "Who is worthy to break the seals and open the scroll?" 3But no one in heaven or on earth or under the earth could open the scroll or even look inside it. 4I wept and wept because no one was found who was worthy to open the scroll or look inside. 5Then one of the elders said to me, "Do not weep! See, the Lion of the tribe of Judah, the Root of David, has triumphed. He is able to open the scroll and its seven seals."

6Then I saw a Lamb, looking as if it had been slain, standing in the center of the throne, encircled by the four living creatures and the elders. He had seven horns and seven eyes, which are the seven spirits^a of God sent out into all the earth. 7He came and took the scroll from the right hand of him who sat on the throne. 8And when he had taken it, the four living creatures and the twenty-four elders fell down before the Lamb. Each one had a harp and they were holding golden bowls full of incense, which are the prayers of the saints. 9And they sang a new song:

> "You are worthy to take the scroll
> and to open its seals,
> because you were slain,
> and with your blood you purchased men for God
> from every tribe and language and people and nation.
> 10You have made them to be a kingdom and priests
> to serve our God,
> and they will reign on the earth."

a 5,6 Or the sevenfold Spirit

elders like? (Note: 24 seems to represent all of God's people, coming from the 12 tribes before Christ and the 12 apostles after Christ; see 21:12–14.) **3.** What does the scene around the throne include? Note its many OT images (Ge 9:12–17; Ex 19:16–19; 25:31–40; 2Ch 4:2–6; Eze 1). **4.** What about the four living creatures suggests the eternal power of God? What response does the central figure elicit (vv. 7–9)? Why? **5.** What does this say about who God is and how he relates to his creation?

1. Imagine yourself in this scene. What do you see? Hear? Feel? What impresses you about God? **2.** What aspect of creation best demonstrates God's glory and power to you? Why? **3.** How might this vision of God enhance your worship life? Your everyday life?

---

1. What was the best choir or musical group you have ever heard (or participated in)? What was memorable about the group? **2.** Around the house, are you more like a lion or a lamb? Why?

1. What do you think makes the scroll so significant (Jer 36:2–32)? What dilemma does the sealed scroll pose (Isa 29:11)? **2.** Why is Christ the only one worthy enough to open it (vv. 4,9; see Jn 1:29)? What titles are used to describe him? What does it mean that he is both a Lion and a Lamb? Where does he appear? What does this mean for your life? **3.** What is the response when he takes the scroll? Analyze the three songs (vv. 9–10,12–13): How is the Lamb described? Who comprises the first musical group? The second? The third? Who are the true kings and priests on earth? What elements of praise do you sense here?

1. Have different members of your small group try to capture this scene of praise and adoration via a poem, a sketch, a piece of music or a prayer. To do this, put yourself into the scene, seeing and feeling what John saw and felt. Develop a concert of prayer and praise. **2.** What would the visions in chapters 4 and 5 have meant to the persecuted Christians of Asia? What does this vision say to us as we view our out-of-control world? Based on this, what actions will you take this week?

⦿ **1.** What kind of horse are you most like: A Clydesdale? A thoroughbred? An Arabian stallion? Why? **2.** How is your group like a team of four horsemen: Are you each pulling in a different direction, or the same? How so?

📖 **1.** Who (or what) do each of the horsemen represent? Why? **2.** The luxury items (wine and oil) are still available, but the basic foodstuffs are scarce and costly. What does that tell you about their economic situation? **3.** In what sense do the first three horsemen lead to the fourth? How have these forces: conquest (v. 2), strife (v. 3), scarcity (v. 6), and death (v. 8) operated throughout history? How do they prevail today? What does this mean for the interpretation of the vision? **4.** What is revealed by the opening of the fifth seal (v. 9)? How is this related to the suffering of the Christians in John's day? In our day? **5.** What occurs when the sixth seal is broken (vv. 12–13; see Mk 13)? What elements of the Day of Judgment are described? **6.** Who can stand the wrath of God?

♡ **1.** Which seal opening makes the greatest impression on you? Why? **2.** What's the *worst* thing that has happened to you because of your faithfulness to the Word of God? **3.** In what area of your life are you trying to hide from God? What do you need to do to come out of hiding? **4.** How does this passage make you feel about the end times? Why? How will this affect your actions this week?

¹¹Then I looked and heard the voice of many angels, numbering thousands upon thousands, and ten thousand times ten thousand. They encircled the throne and the living creatures and the elders. ¹²In a loud voice they sang:

> "Worthy is the Lamb, who was slain,
>   to receive power and wealth and wisdom and
>   strength
>   and honor and glory and praise!"

¹³Then I heard every creature in heaven and on earth and under the earth and on the sea, and all that is in them, singing:

> "To him who sits on the throne and to the Lamb
>   be praise and honor and glory and power,
>   for ever and ever!"

¹⁴The four living creatures said, "Amen," and the elders fell down and worshiped.

The Seals

6 I watched as the Lamb opened the first of the seven seals. Then I heard one of the four living creatures say in a voice like thunder, "Come!" ²I looked, and there before me was a white horse! Its rider held a bow, and he was given a crown, and he rode out as a conqueror bent on conquest.

³When the Lamb opened the second seal, I heard the second living creature say, "Come!" ⁴Then another horse came out, a fiery red one. Its rider was given power to take peace from the earth and to make men slay each other. To him was given a large sword.

⁵When the Lamb opened the third seal, I heard the third living creature say, "Come!" I looked, and there before me was a black horse! Its rider was holding a pair of scales in his hand. ⁶Then I heard what sounded like a voice among the four living creatures, saying, "A quart*ᵃ* of wheat for a day's wages,*ᵇ* and three quarts of barley for a day's wages,*ᵇ* and do not damage the oil and the wine!"

⁷When the Lamb opened the fourth seal, I heard the voice of the fourth living creature say, "Come!" ⁸I looked, and there before me was a pale horse! Its rider was named Death, and Hades was following close behind him. They were given power over a fourth of the earth to kill by sword, famine and plague, and by the wild beasts of the earth.

⁹When he opened the fifth seal, I saw under the altar the souls of those who had been slain because of the word of God and the testimony they had maintained. ¹⁰They called out in a loud voice, "How long, Sovereign Lord, holy and true, until you judge the inhabitants of the earth and avenge our blood?" ¹¹Then each of them was given a white robe, and they were told to wait a little longer, until the number of their fellow servants and brothers who were to be killed as they had been was completed.

¹²I watched as he opened the sixth seal. There was a great earthquake. The sun turned black like sackcloth made of goat hair, the whole moon turned blood red, ¹³and the stars in the sky fell to earth, as late figs drop from a fig tree when shaken by a strong wind. ¹⁴The sky receded like a scroll, rolling up, and every mountain and island was removed from its place.

¹⁵Then the kings of the earth, the princes, the generals, the rich, the mighty, and every slave and every free man hid in caves and

---

ᵃ6 Greek *a choinix* (probably about a liter)   ᵇ6 Greek *a denarius*

among the rocks of the mountains. [16]They called to the mountains and the rocks, "Fall on us and hide us from the face of him who sits on the throne and from the wrath of the Lamb! [17]For the great day of their wrath has come, and who can stand?"

144,000 Sealed

7 After this I saw four angels standing at the four corners of the earth, holding back the four winds of the earth to prevent any wind from blowing on the land or on the sea or on any tree. [2]Then I saw another angel coming up from the east, having the seal of the living God. He called out in a loud voice to the four angels who had been given power to harm the land and the sea: [3]"Do not harm the land or the sea or the trees until we put a seal on the foreheads of the servants of our God." [4]Then I heard the number of those who were sealed: 144,000 from all the tribes of Israel.

[5]From the tribe of Judah 12,000 were sealed,
from the tribe of Reuben 12,000,
from the tribe of Gad 12,000,
[6]from the tribe of Asher 12,000,
from the tribe of Naphtali 12,000,
from the tribe of Manasseh 12,000,
[7]from the tribe of Simeon 12,000,
from the tribe of Levi 12,000,
from the tribe of Issachar 12,000,
[8]from the tribe of Zebulun 12,000,
from the tribe of Joseph 12,000,
from the tribe of Benjamin 12,000.

The Great Multitude in White Robes

[9]After this I looked and there before me was a great multitude that no one could count, from every nation, tribe, people and language, standing before the throne and in front of the Lamb. They were wearing white robes and were holding palm branches in their hands. [10]And they cried out in a loud voice:

"Salvation belongs to our God,
who sits on the throne,
and to the Lamb."

[11]All the angels were standing around the throne and around the elders and the four living creatures. They fell down on their faces before the throne and worshiped God, [12]saying:

"Amen!
Praise and glory
and wisdom and thanks and honor
and power and strength
be to our God for ever and ever.
Amen!"

[13]Then one of the elders asked me, "These in white robes—who are they, and where did they come from?"

[14]I answered, "Sir, you know."

And he said, "These are they who have come out of the great tribulation; they have washed their robes and made them white in the blood of the Lamb. [15]Therefore,

"they are before the throne of God
and serve him day and night in his temple;
and he who sits on the throne will spread his tent
over them.

What kind of wind (a warm gentle breeze, a cold north wind, a hurricane, etc.) best symbolizes your life? Why?

1. Do you think the work of the four angels is a new woe or a restatement of the events in chapter 6? Why? Likewise, in what sense do the events of chapter 7 come "after" the events in chapter 6: In actual history? Or in John's vision? 2. What is the message of the fifth angel? Who is sealed? When does this occur? What does it mean (see Ge 4:15; Eze 9:4–6; Eph 1:13–14)? 3. Is this "144,000" a symbol or a statistic? Why (see 7:9; 14:1–5)?

1. How have you sensed God's protection in the last six months? Before that? 2. What sort of seal has God placed on your life? How is this seal evident to others?

What piece of clothing (bathrobe, tennis togs, 3-piece suit, jeans, etc.) do you feel expresses your personality best? How do you feel when wearing it?

1. What does John see next? How does he describe the size of the crowd? Is this multitude the same as the 144,000 (v. 4)? Why or why not? What are they doing? Wearing? Carrying? 2. What is the significance of the white robes, the palm branches and the washing? What is the new function of those in white robes? What is their future? How would this encourage the Christians of John's day? Of our day? 3. When the multitude cries out, how do the angels, elders and the four living creatures respond (v. 12)? What does all this say about God's kingdom and Christ's sacrifice? 4. What qualifies this white-robed crowd to stand before God? What is their new role? What is "the great tribulation"—is it a particular event or a general experience? 5. Is the safety, security and service of these Christians a *present* life experience for them, or only a promise to be realized in some vague and distant *future*? Or both?

♡ 1. Have each person meditate on a word ascribed to God (vv. 9–17) and praise him for part of your group prayer time. 2. What is your greatest tribulation or persecution? How difficult does that seem next to the majesty of God pictured here? How will you incorporate this glimpse of heavenly worship into your earthly walk?

☕ When home alone, do you like silence, or do you have to have some noise going on? Why?

📖 1. Amid seals and trumpets, why this silence? Why the golden censer? 2. What do altars and incense teach about prayer (vv. 3–5; see 5:8; 6:9–10; 9:13)?

♡ Does this imagery seem far removed to you? When was the last time you tried silent meditation or cried for justice? What happened?

☕ 1. What is one of the most excruciating pains you've ever experienced? What happened? 2. What color would you use to describe your past week? Why? To describe your past year? Why?

📖 1. What events follow the sounding of each of the first four trumpets (vv. 7–12)? What do the trumpets signify: Triumph or doom? Life or death? Or what? 2. How do these trumpeted events compare with the events inaugurated by the first six seals? 3. Likewise, how do these events compare with the plagues in Exodus 7–10 and Joel 2:1–11? 4. What parallels or repeated patterns do you see between the opening of the seals and sounding of the trumpets, which suggest that these two scenes are in reality two sides of the same coin? (Note how the trumpets focus on what will happen to the unbelieving world, whereas the seals focus on what will happen to the church.) 5. Do these seals and trumpets refer to datable, sequential events or to aspects of the world's condition, which may be true at any point in history? Why? 6. What happens when the fifth trumpet sounds (9:1–11)? Who can the fallen star be (see Lk 10:18; Isa 14:12)? What power do the locusts have? Describe them.

---

[16]Never again will they hunger;
    never again will they thirst.
The sun will not beat upon them,
    nor any scorching heat.
[17]For the Lamb at the center of the throne will be
       their shepherd;
he will lead them to springs of living water.
And God will wipe away every tear from their
       eyes."

The Seventh Seal and the Golden Censer

8 When he opened the seventh seal, there was silence in heaven for about half an hour.

[2]And I saw the seven angels who stand before God, and to them were given seven trumpets.

[3]Another angel, who had a golden censer, came and stood at the altar. He was given much incense to offer, with the prayers of all the saints, on the golden altar before the throne. [4]The smoke of the incense, together with the prayers of the saints, went up before God from the angel's hand. [5]Then the angel took the censer, filled it with fire from the altar, and hurled it on the earth; and there came peals of thunder, rumblings, flashes of lightning and an earthquake.

The Trumpets

[6]Then the seven angels who had the seven trumpets prepared to sound them.

[7]The first angel sounded his trumpet, and there came hail and fire mixed with blood, and it was hurled down upon the earth. A third of the earth was burned up, a third of the trees were burned up, and all the green grass was burned up.

[8]The second angel sounded his trumpet, and something like a huge mountain, all ablaze, was thrown into the sea. A third of the sea turned into blood, [9]a third of the living creatures in the sea died, and a third of the ships were destroyed.

[10]The third angel sounded his trumpet, and a great star, blazing like a torch, fell from the sky on a third of the rivers and on the springs of water— [11]the name of the star is Wormwood.[a] A third of the waters turned bitter, and many people died from the waters that had become bitter.

[12]The fourth angel sounded his trumpet, and a third of the sun was struck, a third of the moon, and a third of the stars, so that a third of them turned dark. A third of the day was without light, and also a third of the night.

[13]As I watched, I heard an eagle that was flying in midair call out in a loud voice: "Woe! Woe! Woe to the inhabitants of the earth, because of the trumpet blasts about to be sounded by the other three angels!"

9 The fifth angel sounded his trumpet, and I saw a star that had fallen from the sky to the earth. The star was given the key to the shaft of the Abyss. [2]When he opened the Abyss, smoke rose from it like the smoke from a gigantic furnace. The sun and sky were darkened by the smoke from the Abyss. [3]And out of the smoke locusts came down upon the earth and were given power like that of scorpions of the earth. [4]They were told not to harm the grass of the earth or any plant or tree, but only those people who did not have the seal of God on their foreheads. [5]They were not

a11 That is, Bitterness

given power to kill them, but only to torture them for five months. And the agony they suffered was like that of the sting of a scorpion when it strikes a man. [6]During those days men will seek death, but will not find it; they will long to die, but death will elude them.

[7]The locusts looked like horses prepared for battle. On their heads they wore something like crowns of gold, and their faces resembled human faces. [8]Their hair was like women's hair, and their teeth were like lions' teeth. [9]They had breastplates like breastplates of iron, and the sound of their wings was like the thundering of many horses and chariots rushing into battle. [10]They had tails and stings like scorpions, and in their tails they had power to torment people for five months. [11]They had as king over them the angel of the Abyss, whose name in Hebrew is Abaddon, and in Greek, Apollyon.[a]

[12]The first woe is past; two other woes are yet to come.

[13]The sixth angel sounded his trumpet, and I heard a voice coming from the horns[b] of the golden altar that is before God. [14]It said to the sixth angel who had the trumpet, "Release the four angels who are bound at the great river Euphrates." [15]And the four angels who had been kept ready for this very hour and day and month and year were released to kill a third of mankind. [16]The number of the mounted troops was two hundred million. I heard their number.

[17]The horses and riders I saw in my vision looked like this: Their breastplates were fiery red, dark blue, and yellow as sulfur. The heads of the horses resembled the heads of lions, and out of their mouths came fire, smoke and sulfur. [18]A third of mankind was killed by the three plagues of fire, smoke and sulfur that came out of their mouths. [19]The power of the horses was in their mouths and in their tails; for their tails were like snakes, having heads with which they inflict injury.

[20]The rest of mankind that were not killed by these plagues still did not repent of the work of their hands; they did not stop worshiping demons, and idols of gold, silver, bronze, stone and wood—idols that cannot see or hear or walk. [21]Nor did they repent of their murders, their magic arts, their sexual immorality or their thefts.

The Angel and the Little Scroll

10 Then I saw another mighty angel coming down from heaven. He was robed in a cloud, with a rainbow above his head; his face was like the sun, and his legs were like fiery pillars. [2]He was holding a little scroll, which lay open in his hand. He planted his right foot on the sea and his left foot on the land, [3]and he gave a loud shout like the roar of a lion. When he shouted, the voices of the seven thunders spoke. [4]And when the seven thunders spoke, I was about to write; but I heard a voice from heaven say, "Seal up what the seven thunders have said and do not write it down."

[5]Then the angel I had seen standing on the sea and on the land raised his right hand to heaven. [6]And he swore by him who lives for ever and ever, who created the heavens and all that is in them, the earth and all that is in it, and the sea and all that is in it, and said, "There will be no more delay! [7]But in the days when the seventh angel is about to sound his trumpet, the mystery of God will be accomplished, just as he announced to his servants the prophets."

7. What events are inaugurated by the sixth trumpet (9:13–16)? What response should this woe elicit from the unbelieving world? Why? Why do you suppose this woe failed to bring the majority to repentance, as intended?

♡ **1.** What do you think of Christians who pray for trouble to strike the unbelieving world? And what do you think of God's answer to such prayers? What modern-day realities does the imagery of these plagues bring to mind for you? How might they have applied equally well in John's day? **2.** How do you feel when you read this account of stranger-than-fiction events? What is the "who" and "why" behind all these events? **3.** How has the star named "Wormwood" or "Bitterness" affected your life? How has your bitterness affected others? What have you discovered as an antidote to bitterness? **4.** What do you have in common with the people mentioned in 9:20–21? What will you do about this today?

Who was one of your fictional heroes when you were a child: Buck Rogers? The Lone Ranger? Superman? Why?

1. Describe the angel who announces the coming of the seventh trumpet? In what ways does this picture contrast with the traditional view of angels? Why would John be forbidden to record the words of the seven thunders (see 2Co 12:3–4)? **2.** What purposes have the disasters of the first six trumpets served? What do you anticipate the seventh trumpet will bring forth? What is the "mystery of God" (v. 7; see Ro 11:25–36; 16:25–27; Eph 1:9–14)? **3.** What happens to the small scroll (v. 9; see also Eze 3:1–3)? How can a revelation from God be both sweet and bitter?

---

[a]11 Abaddon and Apollyon mean Destroyer.   [b]13 That is, projections

♡ 1. When has God led you into a project that you wouldn't have selected for yourself? What happened? 2. What is an experience you once savored for a moment, but that later turned sour? How has God's Word been both sweet and sour to you?

☕ What have been the three greatest years of your life: (a) College? (b) The years without children (or parents) around? (c) The years when the children were _____? (d) The years when you _____? Why do those years stand out?

📖 1. What is John commanded to do? Who will be "measured" (or protected), and why (v. 1)? With the church and the world set in contrast, what do the two indestructible witnesses represent? And their enemies? 2. What happens to these two witnesses (v. 7)? What results from their death and resurrection? 3. If God's witness is faithfully maintained for "1260 days" to offset the "42 months" (which are the times of the Gentiles), then what do the "3 and 1/2 days" mean (vv. 11–12)?

♡ 1. What do you learn in this passage about what it means to be a witness? 2. What has been toughest about living out your faith at work? At school? At home? Why is there such difficulty? 3. How have you felt especially empowered by God in the last six months?

☕ What was the most rewarding job you ever had? What was the best part about it?

📖 1. What does this trumpet herald? How is the Second Coming a "good news/bad news" event? 2. For what is God worshiped? What does this tell you about God's power?

♡ 1. How do you react to God's power over unbelieving people: to *hurt* them (trumpet 5 or 1st woe), to *kill* them (trumpet 6 or 2nd woe), or to *damn* them (trumpet 7

[8]Then the voice that I had heard from heaven spoke to me once more: "Go, take the scroll that lies open in the hand of the angel who is standing on the sea and on the land."

[9]So I went to the angel and asked him to give me the little scroll. He said to me, "Take it and eat it. It will turn your stomach sour, but in your mouth it will be as sweet as honey." [10]I took the little scroll from the angel's hand and ate it. It tasted as sweet as honey in my mouth, but when I had eaten it, my stomach turned sour. [11]Then I was told, "You must prophesy again about many peoples, nations, languages and kings."

The Two Witnesses

11 I was given a reed like a measuring rod and was told, "Go and measure the temple of God and the altar, and count the worshipers there. [2]But exclude the outer court; do not measure it, because it has been given to the Gentiles. They will trample on the holy city for 42 months. [3]And I will give power to my two witnesses, and they will prophesy for 1,260 days, clothed in sackcloth." [4]These are the two olive trees and the two lampstands that stand before the Lord of the earth. [5]If anyone tries to harm them, fire comes from their mouths and devours their enemies. This is how anyone who wants to harm them must die. [6]These men have power to shut up the sky so that it will not rain during the time they are prophesying; and they have power to turn the waters into blood and to strike the earth with every kind of plague as often as they want.

[7]Now when they have finished their testimony, the beast that comes up from the Abyss will attack them, and overpower and kill them. [8]Their bodies will lie in the street of the great city, which is figuratively called Sodom and Egypt, where also their Lord was crucified. [9]For three and a half days men from every people, tribe, language and nation will gaze on their bodies and refuse them burial. [10]The inhabitants of the earth will gloat over them and will celebrate by sending each other gifts, because these two prophets had tormented those who live on the earth.

[11]But after the three and a half days a breath of life from God entered them, and they stood on their feet, and terror struck those who saw them. [12]Then they heard a loud voice from heaven saying to them, "Come up here." And they went up to heaven in a cloud, while their enemies looked on.

[13]At that very hour there was a severe earthquake and a tenth of the city collapsed. Seven thousand people were killed in the earthquake, and the survivors were terrified and gave glory to the God of heaven.

[14]The second woe has passed; the third woe is coming soon.

The Seventh Trumpet

[15]The seventh angel sounded his trumpet, and there were loud voices in heaven, which said:

> "The kingdom of the world has become the
>   kingdom of our Lord and of his Christ,
> and he will reign for ever and ever."

[16]And the twenty-four elders, who were seated on their thrones before God, fell on their faces and worshiped God, [17]saying:

> "We give thanks to you, Lord God Almighty,
>   the One who is and who was,
> because you have taken your great power
>   and have begun to reign.

¹⁸The nations were angry;
    and your wrath has come.
The time has come for judging the dead,
    and for rewarding your servants the prophets
    and your saints and those who reverence your
        name,
    both small and great—
and for destroying those who destroy the earth."

¹⁹Then God's temple in heaven was opened, and within his temple was seen the ark of his covenant. And there came flashes of lightning, rumblings, peals of thunder, an earthquake and a great hailstorm.

The Woman and the Dragon

12 A great and wondrous sign appeared in heaven: a woman clothed with the sun, with the moon under her feet and a crown of twelve stars on her head. ²She was pregnant and cried out in pain as she was about to give birth. ³Then another sign appeared in heaven: an enormous red dragon with seven heads and ten horns and seven crowns on his heads. ⁴His tail swept a third of the stars out of the sky and flung them to the earth. The dragon stood in front of the woman who was about to give birth, so that he might devour her child the moment it was born. ⁵She gave birth to a son, a male child, who will rule all the nations with an iron scepter. And her child was snatched up to God and to his throne. ⁶The woman fled into the desert to a place prepared for her by God, where she might be taken care of for 1,260 days.

⁷And there was war in heaven. Michael and his angels fought against the dragon, and the dragon and his angels fought back. ⁸But he was not strong enough, and they lost their place in heaven. ⁹The great dragon was hurled down—that ancient serpent called the devil, or Satan, who leads the whole world astray. He was hurled to the earth, and his angels with him.

¹⁰Then I heard a loud voice in heaven say:

"Now have come the salvation and the power and
    the kingdom of our God,
    and the authority of his Christ.
For the accuser of our brothers,
    who accuses them before our God day and
        night,
    has been hurled down.
¹¹They overcame him
    by the blood of the Lamb
    and by the word of their testimony;
    they did not love their lives so much
        as to shrink from death.
¹²Therefore rejoice, you heavens
    and you who dwell in them!
But woe to the earth and the sea,
    because the devil has gone down to you!
He is filled with fury,
    because he knows that his time is short."

¹³When the dragon saw that he had been hurled to the earth, he pursued the woman who had given birth to the male child. ¹⁴The woman was given the two wings of a great eagle, so that she might fly to the place prepared for her in the desert, where she would be taken care of for a time, times and half a time, out of the serpent's reach. ¹⁵Then from his mouth the serpent spewed water like a

---

or 3rd woe)? **2.** As God displays this power in response to prayers (8:4), how do you respond to what he has called you to do? What will you pray about? Why?

When you were a child, who was the most important woman in your life besides your mother? Why?

1. Where, in the thematic development of Revelation, does the unveiling of God's heavenly temple and ark of the covenant fit best? (Note: Some or all of the phenomena occurring in 11:19 also occur in 4:5 and 8:5). **2.** Describe the woman, the dragon and the child. Who does the woman represent? The dragon? The child? **3.** Where does the next conflict occur? Who are the protagonists? What is the outcome of this conflict? What is the significance of this outcome for the earth? For Christians? **4.** When do you see this heavenly battle occurring: (a) At some particular time and place in history? (b) Pre-history? (c) Post-history? (d) Any time and any place during the ongoing heavenly battle between the kingdom of God and the kingdom of Satan (that is, in the spiritual realm which is behind *all* of this world's history)? Why do you think so?

1. What do you learn here about conflict between the Christian church and demonic evil? **2.** When has Satan seemed very real to you? Why? How do you overcome Satan (see 12:11)? How could you apply these tactics in your own life? What do you need to do to become stronger for spiritual battle? **3.** How can your Christian friends pray for you in battles you are facing? Likewise, how can you pray for them?

river, to overtake the woman and sweep her away with the torrent.
[16]But the earth helped the woman by opening its mouth and swallowing the river that the dragon had spewed out of his mouth.
[17]Then the dragon was enraged at the woman and went off to make war against the rest of her offspring—those who obey God's com-

13 mandments and hold to the testimony of Jesus. [1]And the dragon[a] stood on the shore of the sea.

The Beast out of the Sea

And I saw a beast coming out of the sea. He had ten horns and seven heads, with ten crowns on his horns, and on each head a blasphemous name. [2]The beast I saw resembled a leopard, but had feet like those of a bear and a mouth like that of a lion. The dragon gave the beast his power and his throne and great authority. [3]One of the heads of the beast seemed to have had a fatal wound, but the fatal wound had been healed. The whole world was astonished and followed the beast. [4]Men worshiped the dragon because he had given authority to the beast, and they also worshiped the beast and asked, "Who is like the beast? Who can make war against him?"

[5]The beast was given a mouth to utter proud words and blasphemies and to exercise his authority for forty-two months. [6]He opened his mouth to blaspheme God, and to slander his name and his dwelling place and those who live in heaven. [7]He was given power to make war against the saints and to conquer them. And he was given authority over every tribe, people, language and nation. [8]All inhabitants of the earth will worship the beast—all whose names have not been written in the book of life belonging to the Lamb that was slain from the creation of the world.[b]

[9]He who has an ear, let him hear.

[10]If anyone is to go into captivity,
    into captivity he will go.
If anyone is to be killed[c] with the sword,
    with the sword he will be killed.

This calls for patient endurance and faithfulness on the part of the saints.

The Beast out of the Earth

[11]Then I saw another beast, coming out of the earth. He had two horns like a lamb, but he spoke like a dragon. [12]He exercised all the authority of the first beast on his behalf, and made the earth and its inhabitants worship the first beast, whose fatal wound had been healed. [13]And he performed great and miraculous signs, even causing fire to come down from heaven to earth in full view of men. [14]Because of the signs he was given power to do on behalf of the first beast, he deceived the inhabitants of the earth. He ordered them to set up an image in honor of the beast who was wounded by the sword and yet lived. [15]He was given power to give breath to the image of the first beast, so that it could speak and cause all who refused to worship the image to be killed. [16]He also forced everyone, small and great, rich and poor, free and slave, to receive a mark on his right hand or on his forehead, [17]so that no one could buy or sell unless he had the mark, which is the name of the beast or the number of his name.

[18]This calls for wisdom. If anyone has insight, let him calculate the number of the beast, for it is man's number. His number is 666.

---

1. Who do you think is one of the most charismatic leaders living today? How has charisma helped him or her to lead? **2.** When you were growing up, who was the most patient person in your family?

1. What is this beast from the sea like (v. 2; Isa 27:1)? What is the source of its power? How does it use its power? What is the extent of its power? What is the relationship between the beast and the dragon? **2.** Who worships the beast? **3.** Who do you think the first-century Christians would have identified as this beast (see Da 7 and Ro 13:1)? **4.** What impact will this beast have on the Christians? How ought they to respond? Why?

1. Who are some of the beasts or idols in your life (people, forces, institutions, etc.) that test your allegiance to Christ? How has talk of patriotism and tradition affected your allegiance to Christ? How is God helping you deal with that? **2.** Is your name written in the Book of Life? How do you know? **3.** What kind of grade would you give yourself on patience and faithfulness? Why?

What costume best hid your identity as a child?

1. What is this beast from the earth like? **2.** If the first beast exercises political power, what authority does this second beast exercise? How are true government and religion connected (and mimicked) by these two beasts? **3.** Since "7" is the number of completeness in Revelation, what might "666" mean? **4.** Compare the view of the Roman Empire here with that in Romans 13:1–7. How had Rome changed since Paul's day?

How can we discern false religion and governments?

---

a 1 Some late manuscripts *And I*   *b 8* Or *written from the creation of the world in the book of life belonging to the Lamb that was slain*   *c 10* Some manuscripts *anyone kills*

The Lamb and the 144,000

14 Then I looked, and there before me was the Lamb, standing on Mount Zion, and with him 144,000 who had his name and his Father's name written on their foreheads. ²And I heard a sound from heaven like the roar of rushing waters and like a loud peal of thunder. The sound I heard was like that of harpists playing their harps. ³And they sang a new song before the throne and before the four living creatures and the elders. No one could learn the song except the 144,000 who had been redeemed from the earth. ⁴These are those who did not defile themselves with women, for they kept themselves pure. They follow the Lamb wherever he goes. They were purchased from among men and offered as firstfruits to God and the Lamb. ⁵No lie was found in their mouths; they are blameless.

The Three Angels

⁶Then I saw another angel flying in midair, and he had the eternal gospel to proclaim to those who live on the earth—to every nation, tribe, language and people. ⁷He said in a loud voice, "Fear God and give him glory, because the hour of his judgment has come. Worship him who made the heavens, the earth, the sea and the springs of water."

⁸A second angel followed and said, "Fallen! Fallen is Babylon the Great, which made all the nations drink the maddening wine of her adulteries."

⁹A third angel followed them and said in a loud voice: "If anyone worships the beast and his image and receives his mark on the forehead or on the hand, ¹⁰he, too, will drink of the wine of God's fury, which has been poured full strength into the cup of his wrath. He will be tormented with burning sulfur in the presence of the holy angels and of the Lamb. ¹¹And the smoke of their torment rises for ever and ever. There is no rest day or night for those who worship the beast and his image, or for anyone who receives the mark of his name." ¹²This calls for patient endurance on the part of the saints who obey God's commandments and remain faithful to Jesus.

¹³Then I heard a voice from heaven say, "Write: Blessed are the dead who die in the Lord from now on."

"Yes," says the Spirit, "they will rest from their labor, for their deeds will follow them."

The Harvest of the Earth

¹⁴I looked, and there before me was a white cloud, and seated on the cloud was one "like a son of man"ᵃ with a crown of gold on his head and a sharp sickle in his hand. ¹⁵Then another angel came out of the temple and called in a loud voice to him who was sitting on the cloud, "Take your sickle and reap, because the time to reap has come, for the harvest of the earth is ripe." ¹⁶So he who was seated on the cloud swung his sickle over the earth, and the earth was harvested.

¹⁷Another angel came out of the temple in heaven, and he too had a sharp sickle. ¹⁸Still another angel, who had charge of the fire, came from the altar and called in a loud voice to him who had the sharp sickle, "Take your sharp sickle and gather the clusters of grapes from the earth's vine, because its grapes are ripe." ¹⁹The angel swung his sickle on the earth, gathered its grapes and threw them into the great winepress of God's wrath. ²⁰They were tram-

ᵃ14 Daniel 7:13

What kind of singer are you: Off-Broadway? Off-key?

1. Given the chaos described in chapters 12–13, what comfort do you find in this passage? What sights? Sounds? Feelings? 2. Who is the Lamb? What has he done? Why are the people following him?

How are you like (and unlike) the 144,000? Why do you follow the Lamb?

Heard any good news lately? Any good news/bad news jokes? Tell one.

1. What is the essence of the "eternal gospel" proclaimed by the angel of grace? Who will hear it? Has this vision yet been fulfilled? What response to the Gospel is called for? 2. By contrast, what message does the angel of doom spread? Who is the fallen Babylon? Who has been infected by the spirit of Babylon? 3. How does Satan's system (13:2–10) differ from God's church (14:1–5)? How does Satan's ideology (13:11–18) differ from God's truth (14:6–13)?

1. What have you done to help proclaim the Gospel to every nation, tribe, language and people? 2. How do you look upon death: As a rest? A reward? A new phase in the journey? 3. What would you like to be doing when God calls you home?

Ever harvest anything? How hard did you work? Did you enjoy it? Why or why not?

1. Identify the four supernatural beings in this fifth vision. What is the role of each? 2. What are the differences between the two parts of the vision (vv. 14–16 and 17–20)? What is the nature of the judgment that will occur (see Mt 13:30,39)? 3. Who might the first figure be (see Da 7:13)?

How ripe do you think the world is now? Do you feel that the end of the world is close at hand? Why or why not? How does this affect your life?

pled in the winepress outside the city, and blood flowed out of the press, rising as high as the horses' bridles for a distance of 1,600 stadia. [a]

Seven Angels With Seven Plagues

15 I saw in heaven another great and marvelous sign: seven angels with the seven last plagues—last, because with them God's wrath is completed. [2]And I saw what looked like a sea of glass mixed with fire and, standing beside the sea, those who had been victorious over the beast and his image and over the number of his name. They held harps given them by God [3]and sang the song of Moses the servant of God and the song of the Lamb:

"Great and marvelous are your deeds,
   Lord God Almighty.
Just and true are your ways,
   King of the ages.
[4]Who will not fear you, O Lord,
   and bring glory to your name?
For you alone are holy.
All nations will come
   and worship before you,
for your righteous acts have been revealed."

[5]After this I looked and in heaven the temple, that is, the tabernacle of the Testimony, was opened. [6]Out of the temple came the seven angels with the seven plagues. They were dressed in clean, shining linen and wore golden sashes around their chests. [7]Then one of the four living creatures gave to the seven angels seven golden bowls filled with the wrath of God, who lives for ever and ever. [8]And the temple was filled with smoke from the glory of God and from his power, and no one could enter the temple until the seven plagues of the seven angels were completed.

The Seven Bowls of God's Wrath

16 Then I heard a loud voice from the temple saying to the seven angels, "Go, pour out the seven bowls of God's wrath on the earth."

[2]The first angel went and poured out his bowl on the land, and ugly and painful sores broke out on the people who had the mark of the beast and worshiped his image.

[3]The second angel poured out his bowl on the sea, and it turned into blood like that of a dead man, and every living thing in the sea died.

[4]The third angel poured out his bowl on the rivers and springs of water, and they became blood. [5]Then I heard the angel in charge of the waters say:

"You are just in these judgments,
   you who are and who were, the Holy One,
   because you have so judged;
[6]for they have shed the blood of your saints and
      prophets,
   and you have given them blood to drink as they
      deserve."

[7]And I heard the altar respond:

"Yes, Lord God Almighty,
   true and just are your judgments."

a20 That is, about 180 miles (about 300 kilometers)

If you could have a bowl full of anything right now, what would you want? Why?

1. How does John describe this new sign? Why does he say these are the last plagues? 2. What picture does he paint in verse 2? Compare Moses' song of deliverance from Egypt (Ex 15:1–18) with the song sung by those delivered from the beast. What praise is given to God? By whom? 3. What does John see next? How does the angels' attire contrast with what they are given to do? 4. What does the temple in heaven mean: A haven of rest and a place to play harps for those who die? Or time to reckon with God's holiness and wrath unveiled in that very temple? Why?

1. How does this passage make you feel? Why? What does it make you want to do? 2. What great and mighty deeds has God done in your life for which you will praise him today? How appropriate is the song in this passage to your experience with God? Why?

1. What firsthand experience have you had with a natural disaster? What happened? What are your most vivid memories about it? 2. What would be the worst plague for you to experience: Sores all over your body? Intense heat without air conditioning? Total darkness? Or great thirst with very little water? Why?

1. What contents are in each bowl of wrath? Why are these plagues worse than those ushered in by the trumpets (contrast, for example, v. 3 with 8:8)? What was the function of the trumpet plagues? What is the function of the plagues in this passage? 2. Why does the angel (speaking on behalf of nature) react to the outpouring of God's wrath, not with pain or sorrow, but with recognition of divine justice? 3. What is described in the interlude (vv. 13–16) between the sixth and seventh bowls? What function did the frogs perform (see Ex 8:2–13)? 4. How will the just purposes of God and the evil purposes of Satan finally and awfully converge at Armaged-

[8]The fourth angel poured out his bowl on the sun, and the sun was given power to scorch people with fire. [9]They were seared by the intense heat and they cursed the name of God, who had control over these plagues, but they refused to repent and glorify him.

[10]The fifth angel poured out his bowl on the throne of the beast, and his kingdom was plunged into darkness. Men gnawed their tongues in agony [11]and cursed the God of heaven because of their pains and their sores, but they refused to repent of what they had done.

[12]The sixth angel poured out his bowl on the great river Euphrates, and its water was dried up to prepare the way for the kings from the East. [13]Then I saw three evil[a] spirits that looked like frogs; they came out of the mouth of the dragon, out of the mouth of the beast and out of the mouth of the false prophet. [14]They are spirits of demons performing miraculous signs, and they go out to the kings of the whole world, to gather them for the battle on the great day of God Almighty.

[15]"Behold, I come like a thief! Blessed is he who stays awake and keeps his clothes with him, so that he may not go naked and be shamefully exposed."

[16]Then they gathered the kings together to the place that in Hebrew is called Armageddon.

[17]The seventh angel poured out his bowl into the air, and out of the temple came a loud voice from the throne, saying, "It is done!" [18]Then there came flashes of lightning, rumblings, peals of thunder and a severe earthquake. No earthquake like it has ever occurred since man has been on earth, so tremendous was the quake. [19]The great city split into three parts, and the cities of the nations collapsed. God remembered Babylon the Great and gave her the cup filled with the wine of the fury of his wrath. [20]Every island fled away and the mountains could not be found. [21]From the sky huge hailstones of about a hundred pounds each fell upon men. And they cursed God on account of the plague of hail, because the plague was so terrible.

The Woman on the Beast

17 One of the seven angels who had the seven bowls came and said to me, "Come, I will show you the punishment of the great prostitute, who sits on many waters. [2]With her the kings of the earth committed adultery and the inhabitants of the earth were intoxicated with the wine of her adulteries."

[3]Then the angel carried me away in the Spirit into a desert. There I saw a woman sitting on a scarlet beast that was covered with blasphemous names and had seven heads and ten horns. [4]The woman was dressed in purple and scarlet, and was glittering with gold, precious stones and pearls. She held a golden cup in her hand, filled with abominable things and the filth of her adulteries. [5]This title was written on her forehead:

MYSTERY
BABYLON THE GREAT
THE MOTHER OF PROSTITUTES
AND OF THE ABOMINATIONS OF THE EARTH.

[6]I saw that the woman was drunk with the blood of the saints, the blood of those who bore testimony to Jesus.

When I saw her, I was greatly astonished. [7]Then the angel said to me: "Why are you astonished? I will explain to you the mystery

don (or "hill of Megiddo," an historic crossroads of the Middle East)? With what result (vv. 17–21)? **5.** Compare the seven seals, seven trumpets and seven bowls to each other and to the 10 plagues of Egypt (Ex 7–10). What examples of contrast (e.g., "not only … but …") can you find in each section? **6.** What is the connection between the three scenes (of seals, trumpets and bowls)? How would these seals, trumpets and bowls comfort John's original readers?

♡ **1.** What has God done in your life to help you repent? How receptive are you to admitting your guilt and repenting when you sin? **2.** If "war is hell," could John be envisioning that "hell is war"? What does this passage tell you about God's judgment? **3.** What are the "frogs" that are battling with you? How is the battle going? **4.** How is the book of Revelation making you feel? Why? What has surprised you about God or about this book? How would you explain the necessity of these plagues to someone who is not a Christian?

☕ **1.** If you could be famous for one hour, for what would you like to be known? Why? **2.** What bumper sticker or sign sums up your life now? Why?

📖 **1.** Who is the central figure in this passage? In what sense is the woman on the Beast influential? Evil? Attractive? Repulsive? Who is she (see also 14:8 and 16:19)? Who appears to be "off-stage"? How is the woman and this beast like the first and second beasts of chapter 13? **2.** What here is the ultimate sin (vv. 5–6)? Why? **3.** What does the angel say about the origin of the beast? Its history? Its future (vv. 8–14)? What response does the beast elicit? Why? **4.** Geographically, historically and spiritually, what do you think the beast's seven heads and 10 horns represent (see also Da 7:15–28)? Why do the kings and the beast join forces? With what result? How can evil turn on itself, Satan (in effect) casting out Satan? How does

---

[a] 13 Greek *unclean*

God's greater purpose triumph in all this? **5.** How are the readers of Revelation comforted by the various "definitions" of the symbols? How do these many symbols draw attention to a single object from different angles?

♥ **1.** In this passage how does Babylon symbolize what is wrong in society today? For example, what institutions have been overthrown by revolution, only to be replaced by new regimes which surrender to the same godless ideology? **2.** Of society's wrongs, which ones have entrapped you from time to time? How has God enabled you to avoid the snares of "the great prostitute"? **3.** Surely by now you are "calling for a mind with wisdom" (v. 9). What wisdom do you want in the next few weeks? What wisdom do you need in understanding the message of Revelation? **4.** If you have not grasped the full meaning of the various beasts, have you at least been frightened by the power of evil? How will you translate that fear into action or hope?

☕ **1.** If you were a piece of merchandise, would you be made of precious stones, fine linens or costly woods? Why? **2.** Remember as a child when you built a tower of dominoes or blocks, only to have it all fall down—what did you like best about it? Least? Why? **3.** If you could be captain of any kind of ship, what kind would you want? Why?

📖 **1.** As compelling as the power of evil is, a more compelling authority shouts an overriding double-edged message: one edge cutting Babylon and her followers, the other exhorting God's people. What are the two voices, the two messages and the two responses from the two audiences? How does God's perspective on Babylon (vv. 2–6) differ from Babylon's self-understanding (v. 7)? **2.** How do the voices from the world greet the fall of Babylon (vv. 9–20)? Contemporarize each of their laments—make them your own. Why do they mourn? Why would you mourn if you were in their situation? **3.** Compare this passage with the following OT prophecies about the fall of the cities of Sodom and Gomorrah (Ge 19), Babylon (Isa 13,47), and Tyre (Eze 27–28). How is each an

of the woman and of the beast she rides, which has the seven heads and ten horns. [8]The beast, which you saw, once was, now is not, and will come up out of the Abyss and go to his destruction. The inhabitants of the earth whose names have not been written in the book of life from the creation of the world will be astonished when they see the beast, because he once was, now is not, and yet will come.

[9]"This calls for a mind with wisdom. The seven heads are seven hills on which the woman sits. [10]They are also seven kings. Five have fallen, one is, the other has not yet come; but when he does come, he must remain for a little while. [11]The beast who once was, and now is not, is an eighth king. He belongs to the seven and is going to his destruction.

[12]"The ten horns you saw are ten kings who have not yet received a kingdom, but who for one hour will receive authority as kings along with the beast. [13]They have one purpose and will give their power and authority to the beast. [14]They will make war against the Lamb, but the Lamb will overcome them because he is Lord of lords and King of kings—and with him will be his called, chosen and faithful followers."

[15]Then the angel said to me, "The waters you saw, where the prostitute sits, are peoples, multitudes, nations and languages. [16]The beast and the ten horns you saw will hate the prostitute. They will bring her to ruin and leave her naked; they will eat her flesh and burn her with fire. [17]For God has put it into their hearts to accomplish his purpose by agreeing to give the beast their power to rule, until God's words are fulfilled. [18]The woman you saw is the great city that rules over the kings of the earth."

The Fall of Babylon

18 After this I saw another angel coming down from heaven. He had great authority, and the earth was illuminated by his splendor. [2]With a mighty voice he shouted:

> "Fallen! Fallen is Babylon the Great!
>> She has become a home for demons
> and a haunt for every evil[a] spirit,
>> a haunt for every unclean and detestable bird.
> [3]For all the nations have drunk
>> the maddening wine of her adulteries.
> The kings of the earth committed adultery with
>> her,
> and the merchants of the earth grew rich from
>> her excessive luxuries."

[4]Then I heard another voice from heaven say:

> "Come out of her, my people,
>> so that you will not share in her sins,
>> so that you will not receive any of her plagues;
> [5]for her sins are piled up to heaven,
>> and God has remembered her crimes.
> [6]Give back to her as she has given;
>> pay her back double for what she has done.
>> Mix her a double portion from her own cup.
> [7]Give her as much torture and grief
>> as the glory and luxury she gave herself.
> In her heart she boasts,
>> 'I sit as queen; I am not a widow,

---

a2 Greek *unclean*

and I will never mourn.'
⁸Therefore in one day her plagues will overtake
    her:
  death, mourning and famine.
  She will be consumed by fire,
    for mighty is the Lord God who judges her.

⁹"When the kings of the earth who committed adultery with her
and shared her luxury see the smoke of her burning, they will
weep and mourn over her. ¹⁰Terrified at her torment, they will
stand far off and cry:

  " 'Woe! Woe, O great city,
    O Babylon, city of power!
  In one hour your doom has come!'

¹¹"The merchants of the earth will weep and mourn over her
because no one buys their cargoes any more— ¹²cargoes of gold,
silver, precious stones and pearls; fine linen, purple, silk and scarlet cloth; every sort of citron wood, and articles of every kind made
of ivory, costly wood, bronze, iron and marble; ¹³cargoes of cinnamon and spice, of incense, myrrh and frankincense, of wine and
olive oil, of fine flour and wheat; cattle and sheep; horses and
carriages; and bodies and souls of men.
¹⁴"They will say, 'The fruit you longed for is gone from you. All
your riches and splendor have vanished, never to be recovered.'
¹⁵The merchants who sold these things and gained their wealth
from her will stand far off, terrified at her torment. They will weep
and mourn ¹⁶and cry out:

  " 'Woe! Woe, O great city,
    dressed in fine linen, purple and scarlet,
    and glittering with gold, precious stones and
      pearls!
  ¹⁷In one hour such great wealth has been brought
    to ruin!'

"Every sea captain, and all who travel by ship, the sailors, and all
who earn their living from the sea, will stand far off. ¹⁸When they
see the smoke of her burning, they will exclaim, 'Was there ever a
city like this great city?' ¹⁹They will throw dust on their heads, and
with weeping and mourning cry out:

  " 'Woe! Woe, O great city,
    where all who had ships on the sea
    became rich through her wealth!
  In one hour she has been brought to ruin!
  ²⁰Rejoice over her, O heaven!
    Rejoice, saints and apostles and prophets!
  God has judged her for the way she treated you.' "

²¹Then a mighty angel picked up a boulder the size of a large
millstone and threw it into the sea, and said:

  "With such violence
    the great city of Babylon will be thrown down,
    never to be found again.
  ²²The music of harpists and musicians, flute players
    and trumpeters,
    will never be heard in you again.
  No workman of any trade
    will ever be found in you again.
  The sound of a millstone

will never be heard in you again.
23The light of a lamp
    will never shine in you again.
The voice of bridegroom and bride
    will never be heard in you again.
Your merchants were the world's great men.
    By your magic spell all the nations were led
        astray.
24In her was found the blood of prophets and of the
        saints,
    and of all who have been killed on the earth."

Hallelujah!

19 After this I heard what sounded like the roar of a great
multitude in heaven shouting:

"Hallelujah!
Salvation and glory and power belong to our God,
2   for true and just are his judgments.
He has condemned the great prostitute
    who corrupted the earth by her adulteries.
He has avenged on her the blood of his servants."

3And again they shouted:

"Hallelujah!
The smoke from her goes up for ever and ever."

4The twenty-four elders and the four living creatures fell down
and worshiped God, who was seated on the throne. And they
cried:

"Amen, Hallelujah!"

5Then a voice came from the throne, saying:

"Praise our God,
    all you his servants,
you who fear him,
    both small and great!"

6Then I heard what sounded like a great multitude, like the roar
of rushing waters and like loud peals of thunder, shouting:

"Hallelujah!
    For our Lord God Almighty reigns.
7Let us rejoice and be glad
    and give him glory!
For the wedding of the Lamb has come,
    and his bride has made herself ready.
8Fine linen, bright and clean,
    was given her to wear."

(Fine linen stands for the righteous acts of the saints.)

9Then the angel said to me, "Write: 'Blessed are those who
are invited to the wedding supper of the Lamb!'" And he added,
"These are the true words of God."

10At this I fell at his feet to worship him. But he said to me, "Do
not do it! I am a fellow servant with you and with your brothers
who hold to the testimony of Jesus. Worship God! For the testimony of Jesus is the spirit of prophecy."

---

1. When was the last time your favorite ball team finally won it all? Tell the group about any ticker tape parades and other local celebrations you may have witnessed. 2. What was the most festive wedding and reception you ever attended? 3. What funeral have you attended where the eulogy was memorable for its praise of God's salvation?

1. In contrast to the silence that comes with the fall of Babylon (18:22), what characterizes the new scene in heaven? Who participates in this praise? 2. Compare and contrast the five songs of praise. What is the most frequent refrain? What do you learn about God's character? 3. Contrast the prostitute of chapters 17 and 18 with the bride of verses 7–8 (see also Eph 5:25–27). What do you find interesting about this contrast? Why? 4. How is John (and how might we be) tempted to worship the angel or messenger of the good news? 5. How is the witness of Jesus related to prophecy?

1. What are four things for which you are extremely grateful to God? How do you usually express your gratitude to him about these things? 2. How has your interest in worshiping God increased or decreased in the last year? Since beginning your study of Revelation? Why? 3. What sounds of worship do you really appreciate? Why? How will you use them this week to worship God? 4. How does the defeat and condemnation of Babylon and the triumph and glory of the Lord God affect your overall view of your problems here and now? What is one problem you hope to manage more confidently and joyfully as a result of your study of Revelation?

The Rider on the White Horse

¹¹I saw heaven standing open and there before me was a white horse, whose rider is called Faithful and True. With justice he judges and makes war. ¹²His eyes are like blazing fire, and on his head are many crowns. He has a name written on him that no one knows but he himself. ¹³He is dressed in a robe dipped in blood, and his name is the Word of God. ¹⁴The armies of heaven were following him, riding on white horses and dressed in fine linen, white and clean. ¹⁵Out of his mouth comes a sharp sword with which to strike down the nations. "He will rule them with an iron scepter."^a He treads the winepress of the fury of the wrath of God Almighty. ¹⁶On his robe and on his thigh he has this name written:

KING OF KINGS AND LORD OF LORDS.

¹⁷And I saw an angel standing in the sun, who cried in a loud voice to all the birds flying in midair, "Come, gather together for the great supper of God, ¹⁸so that you may eat the flesh of kings, generals, and mighty men, of horses and their riders, and the flesh of all people, free and slave, small and great."

¹⁹Then I saw the beast and the kings of the earth and their armies gathered together to make war against the rider on the horse and his army. ²⁰But the beast was captured, and with him the false prophet who had performed the miraculous signs on his behalf. With these signs he had deluded those who had received the mark of the beast and worshiped his image. The two of them were thrown alive into the fiery lake of burning sulfur. ²¹The rest of them were killed with the sword that came out of the mouth of the rider on the horse, and all the birds gorged themselves on their flesh.

The Thousand Years

20 And I saw an angel coming down out of heaven, having the key to the Abyss and holding in his hand a great chain. ²He seized the dragon, that ancient serpent, who is the devil, or Satan, and bound him for a thousand years. ³He threw him into the Abyss, and locked and sealed it over him, to keep him from deceiving the nations anymore until the thousand years were ended. After that, he must be set free for a short time.

⁴I saw thrones on which were seated those who had been given authority to judge. And I saw the souls of those who had been beheaded because of their testimony for Jesus and because of the word of God. They had not worshiped the beast or his image and had not received his mark on their foreheads or their hands. They came to life and reigned with Christ a thousand years. ⁵(The rest of the dead did not come to life until the thousand years were ended.) This is the first resurrection. ⁶Blessed and holy are those who have part in the first resurrection. The second death has no power over them, but they will be priests of God and of Christ and will reign with him for a thousand years.

Satan's Doom

⁷When the thousand years are over, Satan will be released from his prison ⁸and will go out to deceive the nations in the four corners of the earth—Gog and Magog—to gather them for battle. In number they are like the sand on the seashore. ⁹They marched across the breadth of the earth and surrounded the camp of God's people, the city he loves. But fire came down from heaven and

^a*15* Psalm 2:9

When you were young, how much did you want a horse? Why? Who was your favorite fictional or real horse? Why?

1. What regarding the horse, the rider and the setting commands your attention? 2. Who is following Christ: The church *militant* (still on earth)? Or the church *triumphant* (now in heaven)? Why? 3. What weapon does the rider wield (v. 15)? 4. How does this supper (vv. 17–18) compare with the wedding supper (19:9)? 5. Who are the combatants in this war (vv. 19–21)? Who wins? What happens to the enemy leaders? To the army? 6. How does this "last battle" compare to "previous" ones (16:12–16; 17:14–16) and a "later" one (20:7–10)? Do you think these are different accounts of the same battle? Why?

What hopes and fears does this triumphant picture bring out in you? Why? How has Jesus been your deliverer this year?

---

1. When did you last "lose your head"? What happened? 2. Have you read any good books lately? How do you judge a book?

1. Why is Satan bound? By whom? How? 2. Where and when will this 1000-year reign begin: On earth or in heaven? Beginning when Christ first came? Or when he comes again? Why? 3. What will life be like without Satan deceiving the nations, but with the church reigning instead? In what sense is that *already* true? And *not yet* true? 4. What is the first resurrection? The second death (v. 14; see also 20:11–15)? What do these mean to Christians? To the rest of the dead? 5. Why do you think Satan will again try to deceive the nations? Why do you suppose God released him and let him out of the Abyss? 6. Describe this version of the last battle, comparing it to the other versions in Revelation and to Ezekiel 38–39. What is the final fate of the beast and the false prophet? 7. Who is exempted and who is exhumed at the great white throne of judgment? On what basis?

1. What do you find comforting in this chapter? What disturbs you? Why? 2. What is your biggest spiritual battle today? What is the outcome so far? What is the hope in this passage for you? 3. Imagine a book made of your life, with every thought and deed recorded, then read by all. How would you feel? If Jesus edited that book by substituting his works for yours, how would you feel then? How will you then live today?

1. Where is one of the most beautiful places you have ever been? What impressed you about that place? 2. What was one of the most beautiful spots in your hometown when you were growing up? 3. How do you think your city would be different if God were the mayor?

1. Where will the new world be lived out—on earth or in heaven? Why do you think so? 2. Who will be the residents of the New Jerusalem and the "wife" of the Lamb (v. 9)? Whose presence is the vision caught up with? What's missing from this picture? Why? 3. What do you think it will be like living without fear, pain or death and with the continual and direct presence of God? Will this new world to come be recognizable? How so? 4. What is the significance of the names ascribed to God, especially for those who "overcome" and those who do not (vv. 6–8)? 5. What is it about the city that John and his readers are meant to notice in particular? Why? What impresses you the most about the city and its central figure? Why? 6. Compare John's vision of reality here with the related visions in Ezekiel 40–48 and Isaiah 60–66. Accordingly, what was the function of the temple in the old Jerusalem? Why is there no need for a temple in the New Jerusalem? What is more "real": The spiritual things visualized here in the New Jerusalem? Or the physical objects of the old Jerusalem? 7. What features will be found in the New Jerusalem (22:1–6)? Where else do we see these same features (see Ge 1–3; Eze 47:1–2; Joel 3:18; Zec 14:8)? 8. Trace the origin of the riv-

devoured them. [10]And the devil, who deceived them, was thrown into the lake of burning sulfur, where the beast and the false prophet had been thrown. They will be tormented day and night for ever and ever.

The Dead Are Judged

[11]Then I saw a great white throne and him who was seated on it. Earth and sky fled from his presence, and there was no place for them. [12]And I saw the dead, great and small, standing before the throne, and books were opened. Another book was opened, which is the book of life. The dead were judged according to what they had done as recorded in the books. [13]The sea gave up the dead that were in it, and death and Hades gave up the dead that were in them, and each person was judged according to what he had done. [14]Then death and Hades were thrown into the lake of fire. The lake of fire is the second death. [15]If anyone's name was not found written in the book of life, he was thrown into the lake of fire.

The New Jerusalem

21 Then I saw a new heaven and a new earth, for the first heaven and the first earth had passed away, and there was no longer any sea. [2]I saw the Holy City, the new Jerusalem, coming down out of heaven from God, prepared as a bride beautifully dressed for her husband. [3]And I heard a loud voice from the throne saying, "Now the dwelling of God is with men, and he will live with them. They will be his people, and God himself will be with them and be their God. [4]He will wipe every tear from their eyes. There will be no more death or mourning or crying or pain, for the old order of things has passed away."

[5]He who was seated on the throne said, "I am making everything new!" Then he said, "Write this down, for these words are trustworthy and true."

[6]He said to me: "It is done. I am the Alpha and the Omega, the Beginning and the End. To him who is thirsty I will give to drink without cost from the spring of the water of life. [7]He who overcomes will inherit all this, and I will be his God and he will be my son. [8]But the cowardly, the unbelieving, the vile, the murderers, the sexually immoral, those who practice magic arts, the idolaters and all liars—their place will be in the fiery lake of burning sulfur. This is the second death."

[9]One of the seven angels who had the seven bowls full of the seven last plagues came and said to me, "Come, I will show you the bride, the wife of the Lamb." [10]And he carried me away in the Spirit to a mountain great and high, and showed me the Holy City, Jerusalem, coming down out of heaven from God. [11]It shone with the glory of God, and its brilliance was like that of a very precious jewel, like a jasper, clear as crystal. [12]It had a great, high wall with twelve gates, and with twelve angels at the gates. On the gates were written the names of the twelve tribes of Israel. [13]There were three gates on the east, three on the north, three on the south and three on the west. [14]The wall of the city had twelve foundations, and on them were the names of the twelve apostles of the Lamb.

[15]The angel who talked with me had a measuring rod of gold to measure the city, its gates and its walls. [16]The city was laid out like a square, as long as it was wide. He measured the city with the rod and found it to be 12,000 stadia[a] in length, and as wide and high as it is long. [17]He measured its wall and it was 144 cubits[b]

---

[a]16 That is, about 1,400 miles (about 2,200 kilometers)   [b]17 That is, about 200 feet (about 65 meters)

thick,[a] by man's measurement, which the angel was using. [18]The wall was made of jasper, and the city of pure gold, as pure as glass. [19]The foundations of the city walls were decorated with every kind of precious stone. The first foundation was jasper, the second sapphire, the third chalcedony, the fourth emerald, [20]the fifth sardonyx, the sixth carnelian, the seventh chrysolite, the eighth beryl, the ninth topaz, the tenth chrysoprase, the eleventh jacinth, and the twelfth amethyst.[b] [21]The twelve gates were twelve pearls, each gate made of a single pearl. The great street of the city was of pure gold, like transparent glass.

[22]I did not see a temple in the city, because the Lord God Almighty and the Lamb are its temple. [23]The city does not need the sun or the moon to shine on it, for the glory of God gives it light, and the Lamb is its lamp. [24]The nations will walk by its light, and the kings of the earth will bring their splendor into it. [25]On no day will its gates ever be shut, for there will be no night there. [26]The glory and honor of the nations will be brought into it. [27]Nothing impure will ever enter it, nor will anyone who does what is shameful or deceitful, but only those whose names are written in the Lamb's book of life.

The River of Life

22 Then the angel showed me the river of the water of life, as clear as crystal, flowing from the throne of God and of the Lamb [2]down the middle of the great street of the city. On each side of the river stood the tree of life, bearing twelve crops of fruit, yielding its fruit every month. And the leaves of the tree are for the healing of the nations. [3]No longer will there be any curse. The throne of God and of the Lamb will be in the city, and his servants will serve him. [4]They will see his face, and his name will be on their foreheads. [5]There will be no more night. They will not need the light of a lamp or the light of the sun, for the Lord God will give them light. And they will reign for ever and ever.

[6]The angel said to me, "These words are trustworthy and true. The Lord, the God of the spirits of the prophets, sent his angel to show his servants the things that must soon take place."

Jesus Is Coming

[7]"Behold, I am coming soon! Blessed is he who keeps the words of the prophecy in this book."

[8]I, John, am the one who heard and saw these things. And when I had heard and seen them, I fell down to worship at the feet of the angel who had been showing them to me. [9]But he said to me, "Do not do it! I am a fellow servant with you and with your brothers the prophets and of all who keep the words of this book. Worship God!"

[10]Then he told me, "Do not seal up the words of the prophecy of this book, because the time is near. [11]Let him who does wrong continue to do wrong; let him who is vile continue to be vile; let him who does right continue to do right; and let him who is holy continue to be holy."

[12]"Behold, I am coming soon! My reward is with me, and I will give to everyone according to what he has done. [13]I am the Alpha and the Omega, the First and the Last, the Beginning and the End. [14]"Blessed are those who wash their robes, that they may have

---

er and tree of life from its source to its fruit. What does this comparison suggest about the unity of Scripture? The completeness of God's salvation?

1. How must the early Christians have greeted this vision of what was in store for them? How do you feel about knowing that the Holy City will be your hometown? That it will last forever? How do you feel about the fact that this is what Jesus has prepared you for? Does it change your lifestyle? **2.** What has caused you mourning, crying and pain in the past year? What does it mean to you to know that this will pass away? **3.** How has your study of Revelation, and the many parallels to other parts of Scripture enhanced your view of the Bible? Of the completeness of salvation? How has it affected your trust in God? **4.** Now that your study of Revelation is almost over, how do you feel about this book of the Bible? Is this different from how you felt when you began the study? How has God blessed your life through this story? **5.** What do you hope to carry with you from your time spent in the study of Revelation?

If you could give yourself a new name, symbolizing the legacy your family gave you, the God-given potential you have, or some hidden aspiration you have yet to realize, what name would you choose? Why?

1. What words of Christ are repeated three times in this closing (vv. 7,12,20)? How do these words sum up the theme of Revelation? **2.** What significance do you attribute to Jesus' claims and names in verses 12–17? Regarding these claims, how is the final state of humanity determined: By some arbitrary reward system, fixed from eternity? By what we have done in this present life? Or by our response to his *universal* ("whoever thirsts") and *undeserved* ("free gift") invitation to simply "come"? **3.** What then do you make of God's summary of human destiny (vv. 1–6)? Is it ever too late for

---

[a]17 Or *high*   [b]20 The precise identification of some of these precious stones is uncertain.

people to change their ways and come to Christ? Why or why not? **4.** In the contrast between those "inside" the city and those "outside" (vv. 14–15), what is implied about the basis for our salvation and judgment? What does it mean to "wash" one's "robe"? **5.** What is the meaning of God's final curse in verses 18–19? Knowing what you now do about the seven plagues, the tree of life and the Holy City, how seriously do you take this warning?

♡ **1.** How have you prepared yourself for Christ's second coming? In what way has this study of Revelation helped to prepare you? How is your lifestyle in keeping with verse 7? **2.** How have your perceptions of Jesus, Satan, heaven and hell changed? Why? **3.** How will these new perceptions affect your worship? Your lifestyle? **4.** How would you sum up the central truth of this book?

the right to the tree of life and may go through the gates into the city. [15]Outside are the dogs, those who practice magic arts, the sexually immoral, the murderers, the idolaters and everyone who loves and practices falsehood.

[16]"I, Jesus, have sent my angel to give you[a] this testimony for the churches. I am the Root and the Offspring of David, and the bright Morning Star."

[17]The Spirit and the bride say, "Come!" And let him who hears say, "Come!" Whoever is thirsty, let him come; and whoever wishes, let him take the free gift of the water of life.

[18]I warn everyone who hears the words of the prophecy of this book: If anyone adds anything to them, God will add to him the plagues described in this book. [19]And if anyone takes words away from this book of prophecy, God will take away from him his share in the tree of life and in the holy city, which are described in this book.

[20]He who testifies to these things says, "Yes, I am coming soon." Amen. Come, Lord Jesus.

[21]The grace of the Lord Jesus be with God's people. Amen.

a 16 The Greek is plural.

TABLE OF WEIGHTS AND MEASURES

BIBLICAL UNIT		APPROXIMATE AMERICAN EQUIVALENT	APPROXIMATE METRIC EQUIVALENT
WEIGHTS			
talent	(60 minas)	75 pounds	34 kilograms
mina	(50 shekels)	1 1/4 pounds	0.6 kilogram
shekel	(2 bekas)	2/5 ounce	11.5 grams
pim	(2/3 shekel)	1/3 ounce	7.6 grams
beka	(10 gerahs)	1/5 ounce	5.5 grams
gerah		1/50 ounce	0.6 gram
LENGTH			
cubit		18 inches	0.5 meter
span		9 inches	23 centimeters
handbreadth		3 inches	8 centimeters
CAPACITY			
Dry Measure			
cor (homer)	(10 ephahs)	6 bushels	220 liters
lethek	(5 ephahs)	3 bushels	110 liters
ephah	(10 omers)	3/5 bushel	22 liters
seah	(1/3 ephah)	7 quarts	7.3 liters
omer	(1/10 ephah)	2 quarts	2 liters
cab	(1/18 ephah)	1 quart	1 liter
Liquid Measure			
bath	(1 ephah)	6 gallons	22 liters
hin	(1/6 bath)	4 quarts	4 liters
log	(1/72 bath)	1/3 quart	0.3 liter

The figures of the table are calculated on the basis of a shekel equaling 11.5 grams, a cubit equaling 18 inches and an ephah equaling 22 liters. The quart referred to is either a dry quart (slightly larger than a liter) or a liquid quart (slightly smaller than a liter), whichever is applicable. The ton referred to in the footnotes is the American ton of 2,000 pounds.

This table is based upon the best available information, but it is not intended to be mathematically precise; like the measurement equivalents in the footnotes, it merely gives approximate amounts and distances. Weights and measures differed somewhat at various times and places in the ancient world. There is uncertainty particularly about the ephah and the bath; further discoveries may give more light on these units of capacity.

CONTENTS OF BACK MATERIAL

200 Favorite Bible Stories

Courses for Any Group

Lectionary

Index of Maps and Visual Aids

Subject Index

Dictionary Concordance

200 FAVORITE BIBLE STORIES WITH READY-MADE QUESTIONNAIRES

In addition to the 60 courses found on pages 26–45, you can design your own small group course using these 200 questionnaires—such as choosing stories from *Jesus' Last Week and Resurrection Appearances* for a Lenten Series. Or you can use one of the suggested course outlines at the end of this list of the 200 stories.

OLD TESTAMENT

	Scripture Text	Page
Beginnings of God's Creation		
The Beginning	Ge 1:1–2:3	53
Adam and Eve	Ge 2:4–25	54
The Fall	Ge 3:1–24	56
Cain and Abel	Ge 4:1–26	58
The Flood	Ge 6:5–7:12	61
Noah Waits	Ge 8:1–22	62
The Tower of Babel	Ge 11:1–9	66
Founders of Israel		
The Call of Abram	Ge 11:27–12:9	68
Abram and Lot Separate	Ge 13:1–18	69
Hagar and Ishmael	Ge 16:1–16	72
The Three Visitors	Ge 18:1–15	75
Abraham Pleads for Sodom	Ge 18:16–33	76
Isaac's Birth; Hagar's Expulsion	Ge 21:1–21	80
Abraham Tested	Ge 22:1–19	82
Isaac and Rebekah	Ge 24:1–29,50–66	84
Jacob and Esau	Ge 25:19–34	88
Jacob Gets Isaac's Blessing	Ge 27:1–40	91
Jacob Marries Leah and Rachel	Ge 29:1–30	95
Jacob's Children	Ge 29:31–30:24	96
Jacob Flees From Laban	Ge 31:1–21	98
Laban Pursues Jacob	Ge 31:22–55	99
Jacob Prepares to Meet Esau	Ge 32:1–21	101
Jacob Wrestles With God	Ge 32:22–32	103
Jacob Meets Esau	Ge 33:1–20	104
Jacob Returns to Bethel	Ge 35:1–15	106
Joseph's Dreams	Ge 37:1–11	110
Joseph Sold by His Brothers	Ge 37:12–36	111
Israel's Slavery in Egypt		
Joseph and Potiphar's Wife	Ge 39:1–23	114
Joseph Interprets Pharaoh's Dreams	Ge 41:1–40	117
Joseph Makes Himself Known	Ge 45:1–28	123
The Beginning of Moses' Life	Ex 1:22–2:25	135
Moses and the Burning Bush	Ex 3:1–22	136

		Scripture Text	Page
Israel's Slavery in Egypt (continued)	Signs for Moses	Ex 4:1–17	138
	Bricks Without Straw	Ex 5:1–21	140
	God Promises Deliverance	Ex 5:22–6:12	141
	The Plagues Begin	Ex 6:28–7:24	143
Journey to the Promised Land	The Passover	Ex 12:1–30	150
	Crossing the Sea	Ex 14:5–31	153
	Manna From the Lord	Ex 16:1–35	157
	God Uses Moses' Hands	Ex 17:1–16	159
	Jethro Visits Moses	Ex 18:1–27	160
	Receiving the Ten Commandments	Ex 19:10–20:21	162
	The Golden Calf	Ex 32:1–35	178
	The Cloud of Guidance	Nu 9:15–23; 10:11–13,29–36	243
	Quail From the Lord	Nu 11:4–34	245
	Miriam and Aaron Oppose Moses	Nu 12:1–16	247
	Spying on the Promised Land	Nu 13:26–14:10,26–45	249
	Balak, Balaam and His Donkey	Nu 22:1–35	262
	Joshua to Succeed Moses	Nu 27:12–23	271
Life in the Promised Land	Rahab and the Spies	Jos 2:1–24	330
	Crossing the Jordan	Jos 3:14–4:24	332
	The Fall of Jericho	Jos 5:13–6:21	335
	Joshua's Farewell Address	Jos 23:1–16	357
	Joshua Renews the Covenant	Jos 24:1–27	359
	Deborah Leads Israel	Jdg 4:1–24	366
	Gideon's Fear, Faith and Fleece	Jdg 6:1–40	370
	Gideon Defeats the Midianites	Jdg 7:1–25	372
	Samson's Birth	Jdg 13:1–25	381
	Samson's Marriage	Jdg 14:1–20	383
	Samson and Delilah	Jdg 16:1–22	386
	Samson's Death	Jdg 16:23–31	387
	Naomi and Ruth	Ru 1:1–22	396
	Ruth Meets Boaz	Ru 2:1–23	398
	Ruth and Boaz at the Threshing Floor	Ru 3:1–18	400
	Boaz Marries Ruth	Ru 4:1–22	401
Israel's Great Kings	The Birth and Dedication of Samuel	1Sa 1:1–28	405
	Eli's Wicked Sons	1Sa 2:12–26	407
	The Lord Calls Samuel	1Sa 3:1–21	409
	Israel Asks for a King	1Sa 8:1–22	414
	Samuel Anoints Saul	1Sa 9:1–10:8	416
	Samuel Rebukes Saul	1Sa 13:1–15	421
	Samuel Anoints David	1Sa 16:1–13	427
	David in Saul's Service	1Sa 16:14–23	428
	David and Goliath	1Sa 17:12–50	429
	Saul's Jealousy of David	1Sa 18:1–30	432
	David and Jonathan	1Sa 20:1–42	435
	David Spares Saul's Life	1Sa 24:1–22	440
	David Brings the Ark to Jerusalem	2Sa 6:1–23	457
	David and Bathsheba	2Sa 11:1–27	463
	Nathan Rebukes David	2Sa 12:1–14	464
	David Grieves	2Sa 12:15–24	465
	Amnon Rapes Tamar	2Sa 13:1–22	467
	Absalom Kills Amnon	2Sa 13:23–39	468
	Absalom Returns to Jerusalem	2Sa 14:1–33	470
	David's Mighty Men	2Sa 23:8–23	486
	Solomon's Wisdom	1Ki 3:1–28	496
	The Queen of Sheba Visits Solomon	1Ki 10:1–13	508
	Solomon's Splendor; Solomon's Wives	1Ki 10:23–11:13	510

	7-wk plan	13-wk plan			Page
THE LIFE OF CHRIST (continued)	2	3	Jesus Begins Ministry in His Hometown . . .	Lk 4:14–30	1438
		4	Jesus Heals and Prays	Mk 1:29–39	1392
	3	5	Clashes With the Pharisees	Mk 2:23–3:6	1395
		6	The Transfiguration	Mk 9:2–13	1408
	4	7	The Triumphal Entry	Lk 19:28–44	1475
		8	Jesus Clears the Temple	Mk 11:12–19	1414
	5	9	The Last Supper	Lk 22:7–34	1479
		10	Jesus in Gethsemane	Mk 14:32–42	1421
		11	Jesus Before Pilate	Mk 15:1–15	1423
	6	12	The Crucifixion	Jn 19:16–27	1522
	7	13	Resurrection and Great Commission	Mt 28:1–20	1388

	7-wk plan	13-wk plan			
JESUS' MIRACLES	1	1	The Birth of Jesus Foretold	Lk 1:26–38	1429
		2	Jesus Changes Water to Wine	Jn 2:1–11	1490
	2	3	Jesus Heals a Paralytic	Mk 2:1–12	1393
		4	Jesus Walks on Water	Mt 14:22–33	1361
	3	5	Jesus Calms the Storm	Mk 4:35–41	1399
		6	Jesus Heals a Bleeding Woman	Mk 5:24–34	1400
	4	7	Jesus Feeds the 5,000	Mk 6:30–44	1403
		8	The Healing of a Boy With an Evil Spirit . .	Mk 9:14–29	1409
	5	9	Ten Healed of Leprosy	Lk 17:11–19	1469
		10	The Healing at the Pool	Jn 5:1–15	1496
	6	11	Jesus Heals a Man Born Blind	Jn 9:1–34	1505
		12	Jesus Raises Lazarus	Jn 11:1–44	1509
	7	13	Jesus Appears to Thomas	Jn 20:24–31	1525

	7-wk plan	13-wk plan			
JESUS REACHES OUT TO OTHERS		1	Nicodemus	Jn 3:1–21	1492
	1	2	Samaritan Woman	Jn 4:7–30	1494
		3	First Disciples	Lk 5:1–11	1440
	2	4	Levi	Lk 5:27–39	1442
	3	5	Anointed by a Sinful Woman	Lk 7:36–50	1446
		6	The Rich Young Man	Mk 10:17–31	1411
		7	Demon-possessed Man	Lk 8:26–39	1449
	4	8	Woman Caught in Adultery	Jn 7:53–8:11	1502
	5	9	Zacchaeus	Lk 19:1–10	1473
	6	10	Washing the Disciples' Feet	Jn 13:1–17	1513
		11	Mary Magdalene	Jn 20:1–18	1524
		12	Disciples on the Road to Emmaus	Lk 24:13–35	1485
	7	13	Reinstating Peter	Jn 21:1–25	1526

	7-wk plan	13-wk plan			
JESUS' TEACHINGS	1	1	Parable of the Pharisee and Tax Collector .	Lk 18:9–14	1471
		2	Parable of the Prodigal Son	Lk 15:11–32	1465
	2	3	The Beatitudes	Mt 5:1–12	1344
		4	The Wise and Foolish Builders	Mt 7:24–29	1349
	3	5	Parable of the Sower	Mt 13:1–23	1357
		6	Parable of the Unmerciful Servant	Mt 18:21–35	1367
	4	7	Parable of the 10 Virgins	Mt 25:1–13	1379
		8	Parable of the Talents	Mt 25:14–30	1380

	7-wk plan	13-wk plan			Page
JESUS'	5	9	The Sheep and the Goats	Mt 25:31–46	1381
TEACHINGS		10	Parable of the Good Samaritan	Lk 10:25–37	1454
(continued)	6	11	Parable of the Rich Fool...............	Lk 12:13–21	1458
		12	Parable of the Great Banquet..........	Lk 14:15–24	1463
	7	13	Take Up Your Cross	Mt 16:13–28	1364 ...

	7-wk plan			Page
STORIES	1	Called to Follow	Lk 5:1–11	1440
ABOUT PETER	2	Stepping Out of the Boat	Mt 14:22–33	1361
	3	Peter's Confession of Christ...........	Mt 16:13–28	1364
	4	Peter Disowns Jesus	Lk 22:54–62	1481
	5	Peter Reinstated	Jn 21:1–25	1526
	6	Before the Sanhedrin.................	Ac 4:1–31	1535
	7	Peter's Vision	Ac 10:1–23	1548

	7-wk plan	13-wk plan			Page
STORIES		1	An Angel Appears to Joseph	Mt 1:18–25	1339
FROM MATTHEW	1	2	The Baptism and Temptation of Jesus ...	Mt 3:13–4:11	1342
		3	The Beatitudes......................	Mt 5:1–12	1344
	2	4	The Wise and Foolish Builders.........	Mt 7:24–29	1349
	3	5	Parable of the Sower	Mt 13:1–23	1357
	4	6	Jesus Walks on Water	Mt 14:22–33	1361
		7	Christ Must Die	Mt 16:13–28	1364
	5	8	Parable of the Unmerciful Servant	Mt 18:21–35	1367
		9	Parable of the Workers in the Vineyard. ...	Mt 20:1–16	1369
		10	Parable of the 10 Virgins	Mt 25:1–13	1379
		11	Parable of the Talents................	Mt 25:14–30	1380
	6	12	Jesus Is Arrested	Mt 26:47–56	1384
	7	13	Resurrection and Great Commission	Mt 28:1–20	1388

	7-wk plan	13-wk plan			Page
STORIES	1	1	Jesus Heals and Prays	Mk 1:29–39	1392
FROM MARK		2	Jesus Heals a Paralytic	Mk 2:1–12	1393
	2	3	Jesus Faces Criticism	Mk 3:20–35	1396
	3	4	Jesus Calms the Storm	Mk 4:35–41	1399
		5	Jesus Heals a Bleeding Woman	Mk 5:24–34	1400
		6	Jesus Feeds the 5,000	Mk 6:30–44	1403
	4	7	The Transfiguration	Mk 9:2–13	1408
		8	The Healing of a Boy With an Evil Spirit ..	Mk 9:14–29	1409
	5	9	The Rich Young Man..................	Mk 10:17–31	1411
		10	The Request of James and John.......	Mk 10:35–45	1412
	6	11	Jesus Clears the Temple	Mk 11:12–19	1414
		12	Jesus in Gethsemane	Mk 14:32–42	1421
	7	13	Jesus Before Pilate..................	Mk 15:1–15	1423

	7-wk plan	13-wk plan			Page
STORIES FROM LUKE		1	The Birth of Jesus Foretold	Lk 1:26–38	1429
	1	2	The Birth of Jesus	Lk 2:1–20	1432
		3	Jesus Rejected at Nazareth	Lk 4:14–30	1438
	2	4	The Calling of Levi; New Wineskins	Lk 5:27–39	1442
		5	Parable of the Good Samaritan	Lk 10:25–37	1454
	3	6	At the Home of Martha and Mary	Lk 10:38–42	1455
		7	Parable of the Prodigal Son	Lk 15:11–32	1465
	4	8	The Rich Man and Lazarus	Lk 16:19–31	1467
		9	Ten Healed of Leprosy	Lk 17:11–19	1469
	5	10	The Triumphal Entry	Lk 19:28–44	1475
		11	The Last Supper	Lk 22:7–34	1479
	6	12	Jesus' Death	Lk 23:44–49	1484
	7	13	On the Road to Emmaus	Lk 24:13–35	1485

	7-wk plan	12-wk plan			Page
STORIES FROM JOHN	1	1	Jesus Changes Water to Wine	Jn 2:1–11	.1490
	2	2	Jesus Teaches Nicodemus	Jn 3:1–21	1492
	3	3	Jesus Talks With a Samaritan Woman	Jn 4:7–30	1494
		4	The Healing at the Pool	Jn 5:1–15	1496
	4	5	The Woman Caught in Adultery	Jn 7:53–8:11	1502
		6	Jesus Heals a Man Born Blind	Jn 9:1–34	1505
	5	7	Jesus Raises Lazarus	Jn 11:1–44	1509
		8	Jesus Washes the Disciples' Feet	Jn 13:1–17	1513
	6	9	The Crucifixion	Jn 19:16–27	1522
		10	Jesus Appears to Mary Magdalene	Jn 20:1–18	1524
	7	11	Jesus Appears to Thomas	Jn 20:24–31	1525
		12	Jesus Reinstates Peter	Jn 21:1–25	1526

	7-wk plan	13-wk plan			Page
STORIES FROM ACTS	1	1	Jesus Taken Up Into Heaven	Ac 1:1–11	1529
	2	2	The Holy Spirit Comes at Pentecost .	Ac 2:1–24,36–41	1532
		3	The Fellowship of the Believers	Ac 2:42–47	1533
		4	Peter and John Before the Sanhedrin	Ac 4:1–31	1535
	3	5	Ananias and Sapphira	Ac 5:1–11	1538
		6	Philip and the Ethiopian	Ac 8:26–40	1544
	4	7	Saul's Conversion	Ac 9:1–19	1545
	5	8	Peter's Vision	Ac 10:1–23	1548
		9	Peter's Miraculous Escape From Prison . . .	Ac 12:1–19	1551
	6	10	Lydia's Conversion	Ac 16:11–15	1558
		11	Paul and Silas in Prison	Ac 16:16–40	1559
		12	Paul's Vision in Corinth	Ac 18:5–17	1562
	7	13	Paul Before Agrippa	Ac 26:1–32	1574

LECTIONARY YEAR A*

C = Common	R = Roman	L = Lutheran
Absence of letter is same for all		

Alternative Readings and Psalms are not included

	READING 1	READING 2	GOSPEL
ADVENT SEASON			
Advent 1	Isa 2:1–5	Ro 13:11–14	Mt 24:36–44 (C) Mt 24:37–44 (L,R)
Advent 2	Isa 11:1–10	Ro 15:4–13 (C,L) Ro 15:4–9 (R)	Mt 3:1–12
Advent 3	Isa 35:1–10 (C,L) Isa 35:1–6,10 (R)	Jas 5:7–10	Mt 11:2–11
Advent 4	Isa 7:10–16 (C) Isa 7:10–14 (15–17) (L) Isa 7:10–14 (R)	Ro 1:1–7	Mt 1:18–25 (C,L) Mt 1:18–24 (R)
CHRISTMAS DAY	**Nativity of Our Lord** (Primary Service) Isa 9:1–6 (R)[1] Isa 9:2–7 (C,L)	Tit 2:11–14	Lk 2:1–14 (15–20) (C) Lk 2:1–20 (L) Lk 2:1–14 (R)
CHRISTMAS SEASON			
1st Sunday After Christmas Day	Isa 63:7–9 (C,L) Sir 3:2–6,12–14 (R)[9]	Heb 2:10–18 (C) Gal 4:4–7 (L) Col 3:12–21 (R)	Mt 2:13–23 (C) Mt 2:13–15,19–23 (L,R)
2nd Sunday After Christmas Day	Jer 31:7–14 (C) Sir 24:1–4,8–12 (R)[9] Isa 61:10–62:3 (L)	Eph 1:3–14 (C) Eph 1:3–6,15–18 (L,R)	Jn 1:(1–9) 10–18 (C) Jn 1:1–18 (L,R)
EPIPHANY OF OUR LORD	Isa 60:1–6	Eph 3:1–12 (C) Eph 3:2–12 (L) Eph 3:2–3,5–6 (R)	Mt 2:1–12
EPIPHANY SEASON			
Epiphany 1 (Baptism of Our Lord)	Isa 42:1–9 (C) Isa 42:1–7 (L) Isa 42:1–4,6–7 (R)	Ac 10:34–43 (C) Ac 10:34–38 (L,R)	Mt 3:13–17
Epiphany 2	Isa 49:1–7 (C) Isa 49:1–6 (L) Isa 49:3,5–6 (R)	1Co 1:1–9 (C,L) 1Co 1:1–3 (R)	Jn 1:29–42 (C) Jn 1:29–41 (L) Jn 1:29–34 (R)

	READING 1	READING 2	GOSPEL
Epiphany 3	Isa 9:1–4 (C) Isa 9:1b–4 (L) Isa 8:23–9:3 (R)[2]	1Co 1:10–18 (C) 1Co 1:10–17 (L) 1Co 1:10–13,17 (R)	Mt 4:12–23
Epiphany 4	Mic 6:1–8 (C,L) Zep 2:3; 3:12–13 (R)	1Co 1:18–31 (C) 1Co 1:26–31 (L,R)	Mt 5:1–12
Epiphany 5	Isa 58:1–9a (9b–12) (C) Isa 58:5–9a (L) Isa 58:7–10 (R)	1Co 2:1–12 (13–16) (C) 1Co 2:1–5 (R,L)	Mt 5:13–20 (C,L) Mt 5:13–16 (R)
Epiphany 6	Dt 30:15–20 (C,L) Sir 15:15–20 (R)[9]	1Co 3:1–9 (C) 1Co 2:6–13 (L) 1Co 2:6–10 (R)	Mt 5:21–37 (C) Mt 5:20–37 (L) Mt 5:17–37 (R)
Epiphany 7	Lev 19:1–2,9–18 (C) Lev 19:1–2,17–18 (R,L)	1Co 3:10–11,16–23 (C,L) 1Co 3:16–23 (R)	Mt 5:38–48
Epiphany 8	Isa 49:8–16a (C) Isa 49:13–18 (L) Isa 49:14–15 (R)	1Co 4:1–5 (C,R) 1Co 4:1–13 (L)	Mt 6:24–34

(Churches whose calendar requires this Sunday, and do *not* observe the Last Sunday after Epiphany as the Transfiguration)

	READING 1	READING 2	GOSPEL
Epiphany 9	Dt 11:18–21,26–28 (C) Dt 11:18,26–28 (R)	Ro 1:16–17; 3:22b–28 (29–31) (C) Ro 3:21–25,28 (R)	Mt 7:21–29 (C) Mt 7:21–27 (R)
Last Sunday After Epiphany	**Transfiguration of Our Lord** (August 6—R) Ex 24:12–18 (C) Ex 24:12,15–18 (L) Da 7:9–10,13–14 (R)	2Pe 1:16–21 (C) 2Pe 1:16–19 (20–21) (L) 2Pe 1:16–19 (R)	Mt 17:1–9

LENTEN SEASON

	READING 1	READING 2	GOSPEL
Ash Wednesday	Joel 2:1–2,12–17 (C) Joel 2:12–19 (L) Joel 2:12–18 (R)	2Co 5:20b–6:10 (C) 2Co 5:20b–6:2 (L) 2Co 5:20–6:2 (R)	Mt 6:1–6,16–21 (C,L) Mt 6:1–6,16–18 (R)

Lent 1	Ge 2:15–17; 3:1–7 (C)
	Ge 2:7–9,15–17;
	  3:1–7 (L)
	Ge 2:7–9; 3:1–7 (R)
		Ro 5:12–19 (R,C)
		Ro 5:12 (13–16),
		  17–19 (L)
			Mt 4:1–11

Lent 2	Ge 12:1–4 (C,R) Ge 12:1–8 (L)	Ro 4:1–5,13–17 (C,L) 2Ti 1:8–10 (R)	Jn 3:1–17 (C) Jn 4:5–26 (27–30,39–42) (L) Mt 17:1–9 (R)
Lent 3	Ex 17:1–7 (C) Isa 42:14–21 (L) Ex 17:3–7 (R)	Ro 5:1–11 (C) Eph 5:8–14 (L) Ro 5:1–2,5–8 (R)	Jn 4:5–42 (C,R) Jn 9:1–41 (L)
Lent 4	1Sa 16:1–13 (C) Hos 5:15–6:2 (L) 1Sa 16:1,6–7,10–13 (R)	Eph 5:8–14 (C,R) Ro 8:1–10 (L)	Jn 9:1–41 (C,R) Mt 20:17–28 (L)
Lent 5	Eze 37:1–14 (C) Eze 37:1–3 (4–10) 11–14 (L) Eze 37:12–14 (R)	Ro 8:6–11 (C) Ro 8:11–19 (L) Ro 8:8–11 (R)	Jn 11:1–45 (C,R) Jn 11:1–53 (L)

	READING 1	READING 2	GOSPEL
Lent 6 (Passion or Palm Sunday)	Isa 50:4–9a (C,L) Isa 50:4–7 (R)	Php 2:5–11 (C,L) Php 2:6–11 (R)	Mt 26:1–27:66 *or* Mt 27:11–54 (L) Mt 26:14–27:66 *or* Mt 27:11–54 (C,R)
GOOD FRIDAY	Isa 52:13–53:12	Heb 10:16–25 (C) Heb 4:14–16; 5:7–9 (R,L)	Jn 18:1–19:42

EASTER SEASON

	READING 1	READING 2	GOSPEL
Easter Day	The Resurrection of Our Lord		
	Ac 10:34–43 *or* Jer 31:1–6 (C) Ac 10:34–43 (L) Ac 10:34,37–43 (R)	Col 3:1–4	Jn 20:1–18 (C) Jn 20:1–9 (10–18) (L) Jn 20:1–9 (R)
Easter 2	Ac 2:14a,22–32 (C,L) Ac 2:42–47 (R)	1Pe 1:3–9	Jn 20:19–31
Easter 3	Ac 2:14a,36–41 (C) Ac 2:14a,36–47 (L) Ac 2:14,22–28 (R)	1Pe 1:17–23 (C) 1Pe 1:17–21 (L,R)	Lk 24:13–35
Easter 4	Ac 2:42–47 (C) Ac 6:1–9; 7:2a,51–60 (L) Ac 2:14,36–41 (R)	1Pe 2:19–25 (C,L) 1Pe 2:20–25 (R)	Jn 10:1–10
Easter 5	Ac 7:55–60 (C) Ac 17:1–15 (L) Ac 6:1–7 (R)	1Pe 2:2–10 (C) 1Pe 2:4–10 (L) 1Pe 2:4–9 (R)	Jn 14:1–14 (C) Jn 14:1–12 (L,R)
Easter 6	Ac 17:22–31 (C,L) Ac 8:5–8,14–17 (R)	1Pe 3:13–22 (C) 1Pe 3:15–22 (L) 1Pe 3:15–18 (R)	Jn 14:15–21
Ascension of Our Lord	(These readings may be used on Easter 7 in years A, B, C)		
	Ac 1:1–11	Eph 1:15–23 (C) Eph 1:16–23 (L) Eph 1:17–23 (R)	Lk 24:44–53 (C,L) Mt 28:16–20 (R)
Easter 7	Ac 1:6–14 (C) Ac 1:(1–7) 8–14 (L) Ac 1:12–14 (R)	1Pe 4:12–14; 5:6–11 (C) 1Pe 4:12–17; 5:6–11 (L) 1Pe 4:13–16 (R)	Jn 17:1–11

PENTECOST SEASON

	READING 1	READING 2	GOSPEL
Day of Pentecost	Nu 11:24–30 (C) Joel 2:28–29 (L) Ac 2:1–11 (R)	Ac 2:1–21 (C,L) 1Co 12:3–7,12–13 (R)	Jn 20:19–23
First Sunday After Pentecost	Trinity Sunday (Ordinary Time)		
	Ge 1:1–2:4a (C) Ge 1:1–2:3 (L) Ex 34:4–6,8–9 (R)	2Co 13:11–13 (C,R) 2Co 13:11–14 (L)	Mt 28:16–20 (C,L) Jn 3:16–18 (R)

	READING 1	READING 2	GOSPEL
Pentecost 2	Ge 6:9–22; 7:24; 8:14–19 (C) Dt 11:18–21,26–28 (L) Dt 11:18,26–28 (R)	Ro 1:16–17; 3:22b–28 (29–31) (C) Ro 3:21–25a,27–28 (L) Ro 3:21–25,28 (R)	Mt 7:21–29 (C) Mt 7:(15–20) 21–29 (L) Mt 7:21–27 (R)
Pentecost 3	Ge 12:1–9 (C) Hos 5:15–6:6 (L) Hos 6:3–6 (R)	Ro 4:13–25 (C) Ro 4:18–25 (L,R)	Mt 9:9–13,18–26 (C) Mt 9:9–13 (L,R)
Pentecost 4	Ge 18:1–15 (21:1–7) (C) Ex 19:2–8a (L) Ex 19:2–6 (R)	Ro 5:1–8 (C) Ro 5:6–11 (L,R)	Mt 9:35–10:8 (9–23) (C) Mt 9:35–10:8 (L) Mt 9:36–10:8 (R)
Pentecost 5	Ge 21:8–21 (C) Jer 20:7–13 (L) Jer 20:10–13 (R)	Ro 6:1b–11 (C) Ro 5:12–15 (L,R)	Mt 10:24–39 (C) Mt 10:24–33 (L) Mt 10:26–33 (R)
Pentecost 6	Ge 22:1–14 (C) Jer 28:5–9 (L) 2Ki 4:8–11,14–16 (R)	Ro 6:12–23 (C) Ro 6:1b–11 (L) Ro 6:3–4,8–11 (R)	Mt 10:40–42 (C) Mt 10:34–42 (L) Mt 10:37–42 (R)
Pentecost 7	Ge 24:34–38,42–49, 58–67 (C) Zec 9:9–12 (L) Zec 9:9–10 (R)	Ro 7:15–25a (C,L) Ro 8:9,11–13 (R)	Mt 11:16–19,25–30 (C) Mt 11:25–30 (L,R)
Pentecost 8	Ge 25:19–34 (C) Isa 55:10–11 (L,R)	Ro 8:1–11 (C) Ro 8:18–25 (L) Ro 8:18–23 (R)	Mt 13:1–9,18–23 (C,L) Mt 13:1–23 (R)
Pentecost 9	Ge 28:10–19a (C) Isa 44:6–8 (L) Wis 12:13,16–19 (R)[9]	Ro 8:12–25 (C) Ro 8:26–27 (L,R)	Mt 13:24–30 (36–43) (C,L) Mt 13:24–43 (R)
Pentecost 10	Ge 29:15–28 (C) 1Ki 3:5–12 (L) 1Ki 3:5,7–12 (R)	Ro 8:26–39 (C) Ro 8:28–30 (L,R)	Mt 13:31–33,44–52 (C) Mt 13:44–52 (L,R)
Pentecost 11	Ge 32:22–31 (C) Isa 55:1–5 (L) Isa 55:1–3 (R)	Ro 9:1–5 (C) Ro 8:35–39 (L) Ro 8:35,37–39 (R)	Mt 14:13–21
Pentecost 12	Ge 37:1–4,12–28 (C) 1Ki 19:9–18 (L) 1Ki 19:9,11–13 (R)	Ro 10:5–15 (C) Ro 9:1–5 (L,R)	Mt 14:22–33
Pentecost 13	Ge 45:1–15 (C) Isa 56:1,6–8 (L) Isa 56:1,6–7 (R)	Ro 11:1–2a,29–32 (C) Ro 11:13–15, 29–32 (L,R)	Mt 15:(10–20) 21–28 (C) Mt 15:21–28 (L,R)
Pentecost 14	Ex 1:8–2:10 (C) Ex 6:2–8 (L) Isa 22:15,19–23 (R)	Ro 12:1–8 (C) Ro 11:33–36 (L,R)	Mt 16:13–20
Pentecost 15	Ex 3:1–15 (C) Jer 15:15–21 (L) Jer 20:7–9 (R)	Ro 12:9–21 (C) Ro 12:1–8 (L) Ro 12:1–2 (R)	Mt 16:21–28 (C) Mt 16:21–26 (L) Mt 16:21–27 (R)
Pentecost 16	Ex 12:1–14 (C) Eze 33:7–9 (L,R)	Ro 13:8–14 (C) Ro 13:1–10 (L) Ro 13:8–10 (R)	Mt 18:15–20

	READING 1	READING 2	GOSPEL
Pentecost 17	Ex 14:19–31 (C) Ge 50:15–21 (L) Sir 27:30–28:7 (R)[9]	Ro 14:1–12 (C) Ro 14:5–9 (L) Ro 14:7–9 (R)	Mt 18:21–35
Pentecost 18	Ex 16:2–15 (C) Isa 55:6–9 (L,R)	Php 1:21–30 (C) Php 1:1–5 (6–11), 19–27 (L) Php 1:20–24,27 (R)	Mt 20:1–16
Pentecost 19	Ex 17:1–7 (C) Eze 18:1–4,25–32 (L) Eze 18:25–28 (R)	Php 2:1–13 (C) Php 2:1–5 (6–11) (L) Php 2:1–11 (R)	Mt 21:23–32 (C) Mt 21:28–32 (L,R)
Pentecost 20	Ex 20:1–4,7–9, 12–20 (C) Isa 5:1–7 (L,R)	Php 3:4b–14 (C) Php 3:12–21 (L) Php 4:6–9 (R)	Mt 21:33–46 (C) Mt 21:33–43 (L,R)
Pentecost 21	Ex 32:1–14 (C) Isa 25:6–9 (L) Isa 25:6–10 (R)	Php 4:1–9 (C) Php 4:4–13 (L) Php 4:12–14,19–20 (R)	Mt 22:1–14 (C,R) Mt 22:1–10 (11–14) (L)
Pentecost 22	Ex 33:12–23 (C) Isa 45:1–7 (L) Isa 45:1,4–6 (R)	1Th 1:1–10 (C) 1Th 1:1–5a (L) 1Th 1:1–5 (R)	Mt 22:15–22 (C) Mt 22:15–21 (L,R)
Pentecost 23	Dt 34:1–12 (C) Lev 19:1–2,15–18 (L) Ex 22:20–26 (R)	1Th 2:1–8 (C) 1Th 1:5–10 (L,R)	Mt 22:34–46 (C) Mt 22:34–40 (41–46) (L) Mt 22:34–40 (R)

All Saints Day
(November 1)
	Rev 7:9–17 (C)
	Isa 26:1–4,8–9,
	  12–13,19–21 (L)
	Rev 7:2–4,9–14 (R)
		1Jn 3:1–3 (C,R)
		Rev 21:9–11,22–27
		  (22:1–5) (L)
			Mt 5:1–12

Pentecost 24	Jos 3:7–17 (C) Am 5:18–24 (L) Mal 1:14–2:2,8–10 (R)	1Th 2:9–13 (C) 1Th 4:13–14 (15–18) (L) 1Th 2:7–9,13 (R)	Mt 23:1–12 (C,R) Mt 25:1–13 (L)
Pentecost 25	Jos 24:1–3a,14–25 (C) Hos 11:1–4,8–9 (L) Wis 6:12–16 (R)[9]	1Th 4:13–18 (C,R) 1Th 5:1–11 (L)	Mt 25:1–13 (C,R) Mt 25:14–30 (L)
Pentecost 26	Jdg 4:1–7 (C) Mal 2:1–2,4–10 (L) Pr 31:10–13,19–20, 30–31 (R)	1Th 5:1–11 (C) 1Th 2:8–13 (L) 1Th 5:1–6 (R)	Mt 25:14–30 (C,R) Mt 23:1–12 (L)
Pentecost 27 (Lutheran only)	Jer 26:1–6	1Th 3:7–13	Mt 24:1–14
Last Pentecost	**Christ the King Sunday**		
	Eze 34:11–16,20–24 (C) Eze 34:11–16,23–24 (L) Eze 34:11–12, 15–17 (R)	Eph 1:15–23 (C) 1Co 15:20–28 (L) 1Co 15:20–26,28 (R)	Mt 25:31–46

LECTIONARY YEAR B*

C = Common	R = Roman	L = Lutheran
Absence of letter is same for all		

Alternative Readings and Psalms are not included

	READING 1	READING 2	GOSPEL
ADVENT SEASON			
Advent 1	Isa 64:1–9 (C) Isa 63:16b–17; 64:1–8 (L) Isa 63:16–17,19; 64:2–7(R)[3]	1Co 1:3–9	Mk 13:24-37 (C) Mk 13:33–37 (L,R)
Advent 2	Isa 40:1–11 (C,L) Isa 40:1–5,9–11 (R)	2Pe 3:8–15a (C) 2Pe 3:8–14 (L,R)	Mk 1:1–8
Advent 3	Isa 61:1–4,8–11 (C) Isa 61:1–3,10–11 (L) Isa 61:1–2,10–11 (R)	1Th 5:16–24	Jn 1:6–8,19–28
Advent 4	2Sa 7:1–11,16 (C) 2Sa 7:(1–7) 8–11,16 (L) 2Sa 7:1–5,8–11,16 (R)	Ro 16:25–27	Lk 1:26–38
CHRISTMAS DAY	**Nativity of Our Lord** (Primary Service)		
	Isa 9:1–6 (R)[4] Isa 9:2–7 (C,L)	Tit 2:11–14	Lk 2:1–14 (15–20) (C) Lk 2:1–20 (L) Lk 2:1–14 (R)
CHRISTMAS SEASON			
1st Sunday After Christmas Day	Isa 61:10–62:3 (C) Isa 45:22–25 (L) Sir 3:2–6,12–14 (R)[9]	Gal 4:4–7 (C) Col 3:12–17 (L) Col 3:12–21 (R)	Lk 2:22–40 (C,R) Lk 2:25–40 (L)
2nd Sunday After Christmas Day	Jer 31:7–14 (C) Isa 61:10–62:3 (L) Sir 24:1–4,8–12 (R)[9]	Eph 1:3–14 (C) Eph 1:3–6,15–18 (L,R)	Jn 1:(1–9) 10–18 (C) Jn 1:1–18 (L,R)
EPIPHANY OF OUR LORD	Isa 60:1–6	Eph 3:1–12 (C) Eph 3:2–12 (L) Eph 3:2–3,5–6 (R)	Mt 2:1–12

	READING 1	READING 2	GOSPEL
EPIPHANY SEASON			
Epiphany 1 (Baptism of Our Lord)	Ge 1–5 (C) Isa 42:1–7 (L) Isa 42:1–4,6–7 (R)	Ac 19:1–7 (C) Ac 10:34–38 (L,R)	Mk 1:4–11 (C,L) Mk 1:7–11 (R)
Epiphany 2	1Sa 3:1–10(11–20) (C) 1Sa 3:1–10 (L) 1Sa 3:3–10,19 (R)	1Co 6:12–20 (C,L) 1Co 6:13–15, 17–20 (R)	Jn 1:43–51 (C,L) Jn 1:35–42 (R)
Epiphany 3	Jnh 3:1–5,10	1Co 7:29–31	Mk 1:14–20
Epiphany 4	Dt 18:15–20	1Co 8:1–13 (C,L) 1Co 7:32–35 (R)	Mk 1:21–28
Epiphany 5	Isa 40:21–31 (C) Job 7:1–7 (L) Job 7:1–4,6–7 (R)	1Co 9:16–23 (C,L) 1Co 9:16–19, 22–23 (R)	Mk 1:29–39
Epiphany 6	2Ki 5:1–14 (C,L) Lev 13:1–2,44–46 (R)	1Co 9:24–27 (C,L) 1Co 10:31–11:1 (R)	Mk 1:40–45
Epiphany 7	Isa 43:18–25 (C,L) Isa 43:18–19, 21–22,24–25 (R)	2Co 1:18–22	Mk 2:1–12
Epiphany 8	Hos 2:14–20 (C) Hos 2:14–16 (17–18) 19–20 (L) Hos 2:16–17,21–22 (R)[5]	2Co 3:1–6	Mk 2:13–22 (C) Mk 2:18–22 (L,R)
Epiphany 9	(Churches whose calendar requires this Sunday, and do *not* observe the Last Sunday after Epiphany as the Transfiguration)		
	Dt 5:12–15 (C,R)	2Co 4:5–12 (C) 2Co 4:6–11 (R)	Mk 2:23–3:6 (C,R)
Last Sunday After Epiphany	**Transfiguration of Our Lord** (August 6—R)		
	2Ki 2:1–12 (C,L) Da 7:9–10,13–14 (R)	2Co 4:3–6 (C) 2Co 3:12–4:2 (L) 2Pe 1:16–19 (R)	Mk 9:2–9 (C,L) Mk 9:2–10 (R)
LENTEN SEASON			
Ash Wednesday	Joel 2:1–2,12–17 (C) Joel 2: 12–19 (L) Joel 2:12–18 (R)	2Co 5:20b–6:10 (C) 2Co 5:20b–6:2 (L) 2Co 5:20–6:2 (R)	Mt 6:1–6,16–21 (C,L) Mt 6:1–6,16–18 (R)
Lent 1	Ge 9:8–17 (C) Ge 22:1–18 (L) Ge 9:8–15 (R)	1Pe 3:18–22 (C,R) Ro 8:31–39 (L)	Mk 1:9–15 (C) Mk 1:12–15 (L,R)
Lent 2	Ge 17:1–7,15–16 (C) Ge 28:10–17(18–22) (L) Ge 22:1–2,9–13, 15–18 (R)	Ro 4:13–25 (C) Ro 5:1–11 (L) Ro 8:31–34 (R)	Mk 8:31–38 (C,L) Mk 9:2–10 (R)
Lent 3	Ex 20:1–17	1Co 1:18–25 (C) 1Co 1:22–25 (L,R)	Jn 2:13–22 (C,L) Jn 2:13–25 (R)

	READING 1	**READING 2**	**GOSPEL**
Lent 4	Nu 21:4–9 (C,L) 2Ch 36:14–17, 19–23 (R)	Eph 2:1–10 (C) Eph 2:4–10 (L,R)	Jn 3:14–21
Lent 5	Jer 31:31–34	Heb 5:5–10 (C) Heb 5:7–9 (L,R)	Jn 12:20–33
Lent 6 (Passion or Palm Sunday)	Isa 50:4–9a (C) Zec 9:9–10 (L) Isa 50:4–7 (R)	Php 2:5–11 (C,L) Php 2:6–11 (R)	Mk 14:1–15:47
GOOD FRIDAY	Isa 52:13–53:12	Heb 10:16–25 (C) Heb 4:14–15; 5:7–9 (L,R)	Jn 18:1–19:42

**EASTER
SEASON**

Easter Day | **The Resurrection of Our Lord**

	Ac 10:34–43 *or* Isa 25:6–9 (C) Isa 25:6–9 (L) Ac 10:34,37–43 (R)	1Co 15:1–11 (C) 1Co 15:19–28 (L) 1Co 5:6–8 (R)	Mk 16:1–8 (C,L) Jn 20:1–9 (R)
Easter 2	Ac 4:32–35 (C,R) Ac 3:13–15,17–26 (L)	1Jn 1:1–2:2 (C) 1Jn 5:1–6 (L,R)	Jn 20:19–31
Easter 3	Ac 3:12–19 (C) Ac 4:8–12 (L) Ac 3:13–15,17–19 (R)	1Jn 3:1–7 (C) 1Jn 1:1–2:2 (L) 1Jn 2:1–5 (R)	Lk 24:36b–48 (C) Lk 24:36–49 (L) Lk 24:35–48 (R)
Easter 4	Ac 4:5–12 (C) Ac 4:23–33 (L) Ac 4:8–12 (R)	1Jn 3:16–24 (C) 1Jn 3:1–2 (L,R)	Jn 10:11–18
Easter 5	Ac 8:26–40 (C,L) Ac 9:26–31 (R)	1Jn 4:7–21 (C) 1Jn 3:18–24 (L,R)	Jn 15:1–8
Easter 6	Ac 10:44–48 (C) Ac 11:19–30 (L) Ac 10:25–26,34–35, 44–48 (R)	1Jn 5:1–6 (C) 1Jn 4:1–11 (L) 1Jn 4:7–10 (R)	Jn 15:9–17
Ascension of Our Lord	(These readings may be used on Easter 7 in years A, B, C) Ac 1:1–11	Eph 1:15–23 (C) Eph 1:16–23 (L) Eph 1:17–23 (R)	Lk 24:44–53 (C,L) Mk 16:15–20 (R)
Easter 7	Ac 1:15–17,21–26 (C) Ac 1:15–26 (L) Ac 1:15–17,20–26 (R)	1Jn 5:9–13 (C) 1Jn 4:13–21 (L) 1Jn 4:11–16 (R)	Jn 17:6–19 (C) Jn 17:11–19 (L,R)

**PENTECOST
SEASON**

Day of Pentecost	Ac 2:1–21 (C) Eze 37:1–14 (L) Ac 2:1–11 (R)	Ro 8:22–27 (C) Ac 2:1–21 (L) 1Co 12:3–7,12–13 (R)	Jn 15:26–27; 16:4b–15 (C) Jn 7:37–39a (L) Jn 20:19–23 (R)

First Sunday After Pentecost	READING 1	READING 2	GOSPEL
	Trinity Sunday (Ordinary Time)		
	Isa 6:1–8 (C) Dt 6:4–9 (L) Dt 4:32–34,39–40 (R)	Ro 8:12–17 (C) Ro 8:14–17 (L,R)	Jn 3:1–17 (C,L) Mt 28:16–20 (R)
Pentecost 2	1Sa 3:1–10 (11–20) (C) Dt 5:12–15 (L,R)	2Co 4:5–12 (C,L) 2Co 4:6–11 (R)	Mk 2:23–3:6 (C,R) Mk 2:23–28 (L)
Pentecost 3	1Sa 8:4–11 (12–15) 16–20 (11:14–15) (C) Ge 3:9–15 (L,R)	2Co 4:13–5:1 (C,R) 2Co 4:13–18 (L)	Mk 3:20–35
Pentecost 4	1Sa 15:34–16:13 (C) Eze 17:22–24 (L,R)	2Co 5:6–10 (11–13) 14–17 (C) 2Co 5:1–10 (L) 2Co 5:6–10 (R)	Mk 4:26–34
Pentecost 5	1Sa 17:(1a,4–11, 19–23) 32–49 (C) Job 38:1–11 (L) Job 38:1,8–11 (R)	2Co 6:1–13 (C) 2Co 5:14–21 (L) 2Co 5:14–17 (R)	Mk 4:35–41
Pentecost 6	2Sa 1:1,17–27 (C) La 3:22–33 (L) Wis 1:13–15; 2:23–24 (R)[9]	2Co 8:7–15 (C) 2Co 8:1–9,13–14 (L) 2Co 8:7–9,13–15 (R)	Mk 5:21–43 (C,R) Mk 5:21–24a,35–43 (L)
Pentecost 7	2Sa 5:1–5,9–10 (C) Eze 2:1–5 (L) Eze 2:2–5 (R)	2Co 12:2–10 (C) 2Co 12:7–10 (L,R)	Mk 6:1–13 (C) Mk 6:1–6 (L,R)
Pentecost 8	2Sa 6:1–5,12b–19 (C) Am 7:10–15 (L) Am 7:12–15 (R)	Eph 1:3–14	Mk 6:14–29 (C) Mk 6:7–13 (L,R)
Pentecost 9	2Sa 7:1–14a (C) Jer 23:1–6 (L,R)	Eph 2:11–22 (C) Eph 2:13–22 (L) Eph 2:13–18 (R)	Mk 6:30–34,53–56 (C) Mk 6:30–34 (L,R)
Pentecost 10	2Sa 11:1–15 (C) Ex 24:3–11 (L) 2Ki 4:42–44 (R)	Eph 3:14–21 (C) Eph 4:1–7,11–16 (L) Eph 4:1–6 (R)	Jn 6:1–21 (C) Jn 6:1–15 (L,R)
Pentecost 11	2Sa 11:26–12:13a (C) Ex 16:2–15 (L) Ex 16:2–4,12–15 (R)	Eph 4:1–16 (C) Eph 4:17–24 (L) Eph 4:17,20–24 (R)	Jn 6:24–35
Pentecost 12	2Sa 18:5–9,15, 31–33 (C) 1Ki 19:4–8 (L,R)	Eph 4:25–5:2 (C) Eph 4:30–5:2 (L,R)	Jn 6:35,41–51(C) Jn 6:41–52 (L,R)
Pentecost 13	1Ki 2:10–12; 3:3–14 (C) Pr 9:1–6 (L,R)	Eph 5:15–20	Jn 6:51–58
Pentecost 14	1Ki 8:(1,6,10–11) 22–30,41–43 (C) Jos 24:1–2a,14–18 (L) Jos 24:1–2,15–18 (R)	Eph 6:10–20 (C) Eph 5:21–31 (L) Eph 5:21–32 (R)	Jn 6:56–69 (C) Jn 6:60–69 (L,R)
Pentecost 15	SS 2:8–13 (C) Dt 4:1–2,6–8 (L,R)	Jas 1:17–27 (C) Eph 6:10–20 (L) Jas 1:17–18,21–22,27 (R)	Mk 7:1–8,14–15,21–23

	READING 1	READING 2	GOSPEL
Pentecost 3	1Ki 17:8–16 (17–24) (C) 1Ki 17:17–24 (L,R)	Gal 1:11–24 (C,L) Gal 1:11–19 (R)	Lk 7:11–17
Pentecost 4	1Ki 21:1–10 (11–14) 15–21a (C) 2Sa 11:26–12:10, 13–15 (L) 2Sa 12:7–10,13 (R)	Gal 2:15–21 (C) Gal 2:11–21 (L) Gal 2:16,19–21 (R)	Lk 7:36–8:3 (C,R) Lk 7:36–50 (L)
Pentecost 5	1Ki 19:1–4 (5–7) 8–15a (C) Zec 12:7–10 (L) Zec 12:10–11 (R)	Gal 3:23–29 (C,L) Gal 3:26–29 (R)	Lk 8:26–39 (C) Lk 9:18–24 (L,R)
Pentecost 6	2Ki 2:1–2,6–14 (C) 1Ki 19:14–21 (L) 1Ki 19:16,19–21 (R)	Gal 5:1,13–25 (C,L) Gal 5:1,13–18 (R)	Lk 9:51–62
Pentecost 7	2Ki 5:1–14 (C) Isa 66:10–14 (L,R)	Gal 6:(1–6) 7–16 (C) Gal 6:1–10,14–16 (L) Gal 6:14–18 (R)	Lk 10:1–11,16–20 (C) Lk 10:1–12,16 (17–20) (L) Lk 10:1–12,17–20 (R)
Pentecost 8	Am 7:7–17 (C) Dt 30:9–14 (L) Dt 30:10–14 (R)	Col 1:1–14 (C,L) Col 1:15–20 (R)	Lk 10:25–37
Pentecost 9	Am 8:1–12 (C) Ge 18:1–10a (10b–14) (L) Ge 18:1–10 (R)	Col 1:15–28 (C) Col 1:21–28 (L) Col 1:24–28 (R)	Lk 10:38–42
Pentecost 10	Hos 1:2–10 (C) Ge 18:20–32 (L,R)	Col 2:6–15 (16–19) (C) Col 2:6–15 (L) Col 2:12–14 (R)	Lk 11:1–13
Pentecost 11	Hos 11:1–11 (C) Ecc 1:2; 2:18–26 (L) Ecc 1:2; 2:21–23 (R)	Col 3:1–11 (C,L) Col 3:1–5,9–11 (R)	Lk 12:13–21
Pentecost 12	Isa 1:1,10–20 (C) Ge 15:1–6 (L) Wis 18:6–9 (R)[9]	Heb 11:1–3,8–16 (C,L) Heb 11:1–2,8–19 (R)	Lk 12:32–40 (C,L) Lk 12:32–48 (R)
Pentecost 13	Isa 5:1–7 (C) Jer 23:23–29 (L) Jer 38:4–6,8–10 (R)	Heb 11:29–12:2 (C) Heb 12:1–13 (L) Heb 12:1–4 (R)	Lk 12:49–56 (C) Lk 12:49–53 (L,R)
Pentecost 14	Jer 1:4–10 (C) Isa 66:18–23 (L) Isa 66:18–21 (R)	Heb 12:18–29 (C) Heb 12:18–24 (L) Heb 12:5–7,11–13 (R)	Lk 13:10–17 (C) Lk 13:22–30 (L,R)
Pentecost 15	Jer 2:4–13 (C) Pr 25:6–7 (L) Sir 3:17–18,20, 28–29 (R)[9]	Heb 13:1–8,15–16 (C) Heb 13:1–8 (L) Heb 12:18–19,22–24 (R)	Lk 14:1,7–14
Pentecost 16	Jer 18:1–11 (C) Pr 9:8–12 (L) Wis 9:13–18 (R)[9]	Phm 1–21 (C) Phm 1 (2–9), 10–21 (L) Phm 9–10,12–17 (R)	Lk 14:25–33
Pentecost 17	Jer 4:11–12,22–28 (C) Ex 32:7–14 (L) Ex 32:7–11,13–14 (R)	1Ti 1:12–17 Lk 15:1–32 (R)	Lk 15:1–10 (C,L)

	READING 1	READING 2	GOSPEL
Pentecost 18	Jer 8:18–9:1 (C) Am 8:4–7 (L,R)	1Ti 2:1–7 (C) 1Ti 2:1–8 (L,R)	Lk 16:1–13
Pentecost 19	Jer 32:1–3a,6–15 (C) Am 6:1–7 (L) Am 6:1,4–7 (R)	1Ti 6:6–19 (C) 1Ti 6:6–16 (L) 1Ti 6:11–16 (R)	Lk 16:19–31
Pentecost 20	La 1:1–6 (C) Hab 1:1–3; 2:1–4 (L) Hab 1:2–3; 2:2–4 (R)	2Ti 1:1–14 (C) 2Ti 1:3–14 (L) 2Ti 1:6–8,13–14 (R)	Lk 17:5–10 (C,R) Lk 17:1–10 (L)
Pentecost 21	Jer 29:1,4–7 (C) Ru 1:1–19a (L) 2Ki 5:14–17 (R)	2Ti 2:8–15 (C) 2Ti 2:8–13 (L,R)	Lk 17:11–19
Pentecost 22	Jer 31:27–34 (C) Ge 32:22–30 (L) Ex 17:8–13 (R)	2Ti 3:14–4:5 (C,L) 2Ti 3:14–4:2 (R)	Lk 18:1–8
Pentecost 23	Joel 2:23–32 (C) Dt 10:12–22 (L) Sir 35:12–14,16–18 (R)[9]	2Ti 4:6–8,16–18	Lk 18:9–14
All Saints Day (November 1)	Da 7:1–3,15–18 (C) Isa 26:1–4,8–9, 12–13,19–21 (L) Rev 7:2–4,9–14 (R)	Eph 1:11–23 (C) Rev 21:9–11,22–27 (22:1–5) (L) 1Jn 3:1–3 (R)	Lk 6:20–31 (C) Mt 5:1–12 (L,R)
Pentecost 24	Hab 1:1–4; 2:1–4 (C) Ex 34:5–9 (L) Wis 11:22–12:1 (R)[9]	2Th 1:4,11–12 (C) 2Th 1:1–5,11–12 (L) 2Th 1:11–2:2 (R)	Lk 19:1–10
Pentecost 25	Hag 1:15b–2:9 (C) 1Ch 29:10–13 (L) 2Mac 7:1–2,9–14 (R)[9]	2Th 2:1–5,13–17 (C) 2Th 2:13–3:5 (L) 2Th 2:16–3:5 (R)	Lk 20:27–38
Pentecost 26	Isa 65:17–25 (C) Mal 4:1–2a (L) Mal 3:19–20 (R)[8]	2Th 3:6–13 (C,L) 2Th 3:7–12 (R)	Lk 21:5–19
Pentecost 27 (Lutheran only)	Isa 52:1–6	1Co 15:54–58	Lk 19:11–27
Last Pentecost	**Christ the King Sunday**		
	Jer 23:1–6 (C) Jer 23:2–6 (L) 2Sa 5:1–3 (R)	Col 1:11–20 (C) Col 1:13–20 (L) Col 1:12–20 (R)	Lk 23:33–43 (C) Lk 23:35–43 (L,R)

LECTIONARY ENDNOTES

* The Lectionary for Sundays and major festivals is arranged in a three-year cycle of readings from Holy Scripture. Year A is often referred to as the Year of Matthew; Year B, the Year of Mark; and Year C, the Year of Luke.

Year A always begins on the First Sunday of Advent in years evenly divided by three (e.g. Year A, December 3, 1995; November 29, 1998, etc.).

[1] Isa 9:1–6, as found in the New American Bible, has as its equivalent Isa 9:2–7 in the New International Version.

[2] Isa 8:23–9:3, as found in the New American Bible, has as its equivalent Isa 9:1–4 in the New International Version.

[3] Isa 63:16–17,19; 64:2–7, as found in the New American Bible, has as its equivalent Isa 63:16–17,19–64:1; 64:3–8 in the New International Version.

[4] Isa 9:1–6, as found in the New American Bible, has as its equivalent Isa 9:2–7 in the New International Version.

[5] Hos 2:16–17,21–22, as found in the New American Bible, has as its equivalent Hos 2:14–15,19–20 in the New International Version.

[6] Mic 5:1–4, as found in the New American Bible, has as its equivalent Mic 5:2–5 in the New International Version.

[7] Isa 9:1–6, as found in the New American Bible, has as its equivalent Isa 9:2–7 in the New International Version.

[8] Mal 3:19–20, as found in the New American Bible, has as its equivalent Mal 4:1–2 in the New International Version.

[9] The Apocrypha consists of books not included in the Hebrew canon of Holy Scripture, but present in the Greek version of the Old Testament, known as the Septuagint. The Apocryphal, or Deuterocanonical, books are not included in this Bible. The abbreviations for Apocryphal books included in this lectionary are: Bar: Baruch; Mac: Maccabees; Sir: Sirach; Wis: Wisdom.

INDEX OF MAPS AND VISUAL AIDS

BOOK	MAPS	Page
OLD TESTAMENT		
Genesis	Abraham's Journeys	51
Deuteronomy	The Life of Moses and the Exodus	283
Joshua	Land of the 12 Tribes of Israel	328
Judges	The 12 Judges—Located by Home Tribe	361
Ruth	Setting for the Book of Ruth	395
2 Samuel	The Life of David	449
1 Kings	The Life of Elijah	490
2 Kings	Borders of Israel and Judah Under Jeroboam II and Uzziah	533
2 Chronicles	Exile of the Northern and Southern Kingdoms	618
Ezra	The Return From Exile	661
Song of Songs	Setting for the Song of Songs	944
Amos	Judgment on the Nations	1265
Obadiah	Judgment on Edom	1278
Jonah	Jonah's Journey	1281
Micah	Judgment on Israel and Judah	1286
Nahum	Seat of the Assyrian Empire	1297
Habakkuk	Seat of the Babylonian Empire	1302

VISUAL AIDS

Exodus	The Tabernacle	133
Leviticus	Old Testament Sacrifices	191
Numbers	Marching Order of the Tribes	227
1 Samuel	David's Family Tree	403
1 Chronicles	Solomon's Temple	574
Nehemiah	Chronology of Ezra and Nehemiah	676
Esther	Old Testament Feasts and Other Sacred Days	696
Job	Job's Pre-Trial and Post-Trial Possessions	707
Psalms	Types of Psalms	756
Proverbs	Structure of the Old Testament	886
Ecclesiastes	Outline of Ecclesiastes	930
Isaiah	Major and Minor Prophets—Timeline	958
Jeremiah	Pre-Exile Prophets of Israel and Judah—Timeline	1056

BOOK	VISUAL AIDS	Page

OLD TESTAMENT (continued)

Lamentations	Times of Lament in the History of Israel	1144
Ezekiel	Exile and Post-Exile Prophets	1156
Daniel	Identification of the Four Kingdoms From the Vision in Daniel 2	1220
Hosea	Old Testament Prophecies Fulfilled	1242
Joel	Prophecies of Joel	1258
Zephaniah	Zephaniah's Prophecies Against the Nations	1308
Haggai	Timeline for Haggai	1314
Zechariah	Visions of Zechariah	1317
Malachi	From Malachi to Christ—Timeline	1330

BOOK	MAPS	

NEW TESTAMENT

Matthew	Jesus' Early Years	1337
Mark	Jesus in Galilee	1390
John	Jesus in Judea	1487
Acts	Spread of the Gospel	1528
Romans	Paul's Journey to Rome	1579
1 Corinthians	Paul's Third Missionary Journey	1599
Galatians	Paul's First Missionary Journey	1629
1 Thessalonians	Paul's Second Missionary Journey	1654
1 Timothy	Timothy and Titus, Paul's Trusted Aides	1663
Philemon	The Return of Onesimus to Philemon	1677
1 Peter	Regions Peter Addressed	1700
Revelation	The Seven Churches of Revelation	1722

	VISUAL AIDS	

Luke	The Life of Christ—Timeline	1427
2 Corinthians	Structure of the New Testament	1617
Ephesians	The Life of Paul, Part I	1636
Philippians	The Life of Paul, Part II	1643
Colossians	The Letters of Paul	1649
2 Thessalonians	The Purpose of 1 and 2 Thessalonians	1659
2 Timothy	The Last Words of Paul	1669
Titus	Qualifications for Elders and Deacons	1674
Hebrews	Hebrews 11: Heroes of Faith	1679
James	The Prominence of James in the Early Church	1694
2 Peter	Timeline of Peter's Life	1706
1 John	Timeline of John's Life	1710
2 and 3 John	The Errors of Gnosticism	1716
Jude	Old Testament Links in Jude	1719

SUBJECT INDEX

The numbers in heavy type are the page numbers.
The verses containing the reference are given after the page numbers.

A

Aaron
139 Ex 4:14; 139 Ex 5:1;
158 Ex 17:12; 173 Ex 28:29,32;
246 Nu 12; 254 Nu 16:36–50;
255 Nu 17–18; 258 Nu 20;
1541 Ac 7:40; 1683 Heb 5:4;
1685 Heb 7:11; 1687 Heb 9:4

Abel
57 Ge 4:2–9,25; 1376 Mt 23:35;
1457 Lk 11:51; 1689 Heb 11:4;
1692 Heb 12:24

Abraham, Abram
born 67 Ge 11:26
married Sarai 67 Ge 11:29
migrated from Ur to Haran
67 Ge 11:31
called by God 67 Ge 12:1–5
went to Egypt 68 Ge 12:10–20
separated from Lot 69 Ge 13:7–11
rescued Lot 70 Ge 14:13–16
God's covenant with 72 Ge 15:18;
73 Ge 17:1–22
name changed from Abram to
Abraham 73 Ge 17:5
entertained angels 74 Ge 18:1–21
interceded for Sodom
75 Ge 18:22–23
banished Hagar and Ishmael
79 Ge 21:9–21
willing to offer Isaac 81 Ge 22:1–14
buried Sarah 82 Ge 23
married Keturah 86 Ge 25:1
death and burial 86 Ge 25:8–9
see also 1341 Mt 3:9; 1431 Lk 1:73;
1467 Lk 16:22–30;
1503 Jn 8:33–58;
1583 Ro 4:1–22;
1632 Gal 3:6–29;
1690 Heb 11:8–11,17;
1696 Jas 2:21,23

Absalom
453 2Sa 3:3;
468 2Sa 13:21—18:33

Achaia
1561 Ac 18:12,27; 1564 Ac 19:21;
1596 Ro 15:26; 1615 1Co 16:15;
1618 2Co 1:1; 1624 2Co 9:2;
1655 1Th 1:7–8

Adam
57 Ge 3:20–21; 57 Ge 4:1,25;
59 Ge 5:1–5; 1585 Ro 5:12–21;
1614 1Co 15:22,45–49;
1665 1Ti 2:13,14

Adoption, spiritual
1343 Mt 5:9; 1356 Mt 12:50;
1443 Lk 6:35; 1488 Jn 1:12–13;
1510 Jn 11:52; 1584 Ro 4:16–17;
1588 Ro 8:14–29;
1589 Ro 9:4–8,24–26;
1622 2Co 6:16–18;
1632 Gal 3:7,26–29;
1633 Gal 4:1–7; 1637 Eph 1:5;
1638 Eph 2:19; 1645 Php 2:15;
1681 Heb 2:10–13;
1691 Heb 12:5–10;
1712 1Jn 3:1,2,10; 1742 Rev 21:7

Agrippa
1572 Ac 25:13—26:2;
1574 Ac 26:19,27–32

Ahab
520 1Ki 16:28–33;
522 1Ki 18:1—19:1;
526 1Ki 20:2—22:40

Alexandria(n)
1562 Ac 18:24; 1575 Ac 27:6;
1577 Ac 28:11

Almighty
73 Ge 17:1; 127 Ge 48:3;
976 Isa 13:6; 1740 Rev 19:6

Amalek, Amalekite
158 Ex 17:8–16; 369 Jdg 6:3;
373 Jdg 7:12; 424 1Sa 15:2–33;
446 1Sa 30:1–18;
450 2Sa 1:1–13

Amen
791 Ps 41:13; 1599 Ro 16:27;
1612 1Co 14:16; 1617 1Co 16:24;
1636 Gal 6:18; 1649 Php 4:23;
1726 Rev 3:14

Ammon, Ammonite
78 Ge 19:38; 287 Dt 2:37;
378 Jdg 10:7—12:3;
461 2Sa 10:1—11
(603 1Ch 19:1—20:3);
466 2Sa 12:26–31; 646 2Ch 26:8;
647 2Ch 27:5; 1130 Jer 49:1–6;
1180 Eze 21:28–32;
1185 Eze 25:1–7,10

Amorite
249 Nu 13:29; 260 Nu 21:13;
291 Dt 4:47; 341 Jos 10:5–10;
363 Jdg 1:34–35;
379 Jdg 11:19–23

Ananias
1536 Ac 5:1–6; 1545 Ac 9:10–17;
1568 Ac 22:12–16; 1569 Ac 23:2;
1571 Ac 24:1

Andrew
1343 Mt 4:18; 1352 Mt 10:2;
1391 Mk 1:16; 1418 Mk 13:3;
1489 Jn 1:40,44; 1498 Jn 6:8;
1511 Jn 12:22; 1530 Ac 1:13

Angels
messengers and agents of God
76 Ge 19:1,15; 79 Ge 21:17;
93 Ge 28:12; 128 Ge 48:16;
262 Nu 22:22–35;
525 1Ki 19:5–7;
605 1Ch 21:12–30;
845 Ps 103:20; 1339 Mt 1:20–24;
1342 Mt 4:11;
1359 Mt 13:39,41,49;
1364 Mt 16:27; 1377 Mt 24:31;
1380 Mt 25:31; 1388 Mt 28:2–7;
1428 Lk 1:11–19,26–38;
1432 Lk 2:9–21; 1489 Jn 1:51;
1537 Ac 5:19; 1543 Ac 8:26;
1547 Ac 10:3–8;
1550 Ac 12:7–11,15;
1576 Ac 27:23; 1660 2Th 1:7;
1680 Heb 1:4–7; 1723 Rev 1:1;
1743 Rev 22:6,8,16
in heaven 1375 Mt 22:30;
1458 Lk 12:8–9; 1464 Lk 15:10;
1476 Lk 20:36; 1651 Col 2:18;
1665 1Ti 3:16; 1667 1Ti 5:21;
1725 Rev 3:5; 1728 Rev 5:11;
1729 Rev 7:11;
1730 Rev 8:2—11:15;
1735 Rev 14:6–9;
1736 Rev 15:1—16:17;
1737 Rev 17:1; 1738 Rev 18:1,21;
1740 Rev 19:9,17;
1742 Rev 21:9,12
the angel of the Lord
72 Ge 16:7–11; 82 Ge 22:11,16;
136 Ex 3:2; 363 Jdg 2:1–4;
370 Jdg 6:11–22;
381 Jdg 13:3–21
guardian angels 783 Ps 34:7;
784 Ps 35:5–6; 837 Ps 91:11;
1049 Isa 63:9; 1226 Da 3:28;
1232 Da 6:22; 1366 Mt 18:10
guiding angels 83 Ge 24:7;
154 Ex 14:19;
167 Ex 23:20–21,23;
258 Nu 20:16; 363 Jdg 2:1–4
destroying angels
488 2Sa 24:16–17; 565 2Ki 19:35;
605 1Ch 21:12–30;
653 2Ch 32:21; 824 Ps 78:49;
1010 Isa 37:36; 1552 Ac 12:23
devil and his angels 1381 Mt 25:41;
1626 2Co 11:14; 1720 Jude 1:6;
1733 Rev 12:7–9

names:
Apollyon **1731** Rev 9:11
Gabriel **1235** Da 8:16;
　1236 Da 9:21; **1428** Lk 1:11−38
Michael **1237** Da 10:13;
　1240 Da 12:1; **1720** Jude 1:9;
　1733 Rev 12:7−9

Anna
　1433 Lk 2:36

Annas
　1435 Lk 3:2; **1519** Jn 18:13,24;
　1534 Ac 4:6

Anti-Christ/False Christ
　1377 Mt 24:24; **1419** Mk 13:22;
　1712 1Jn 2:18; **1712** 1Jn 2:22;
　1713 1Jn 4:3; **1717** 2Jn 7

Antioch
　1539 Ac 6:5; **1550** Ac 11:19−30;
　1552 Ac 13:1−3;
　1552 Ac 13:14−50;
　1555 Ac 14:19,21;
　1555 Ac 14:26−15:2;
　1557 Ac 15:35; **1631** Gal 2:11;
　1672 2Ti 3:11

Apollos
　1562 Ac 18:24; **1563** Ac 19:1;
　1600 1Co 1:12; **1602** 1Co 3:4—
　6:22; **1603** 1Co 4:6;
　1615 1Co 16:12

Apostle
　1352 Mt 10:2−4;
　1396 Mk 3:14−19; **1403** Mk 6:30;
　1442 Lk 6:13−16;
　1529 Ac 1:2,13,26;
　1721 Jude 1:17; **1742** Rev 21:14

Aquila
　1561 Ac 18:2,18,26; **1597** Ro 16:3;
　1615 1Co 16:19; **1674** 2Ti 4:19

Ararat
　62 Ge 8:4

Areopagus
　1560 Ac 17:19−22

Ark of the Covenant
　169 Ex 25:10−22; **184** Ex 37:1−9;
　297 Dt 10:1−5; **332** Jos 3:13;
　332 Jos 4:5,11; **334** Jos 6:6;
　410 1Sa 4:1−7:1;
　456 2Sa 6:1−17; **503** 1Ki 8:1−9;
　1687 Heb 9:4; **1733** Rev 11:19

Ark, of Noah
　60 Ge 6:14—9:18; **1378** Mt 24:38;
　1690 Heb 11:7; **1704** 1Pe 3:20

Armageddon
　1737 Rev 16:16

Ascension of Christ
　1499 Jn 6:62; **1501** Jn 7:33;
　1515 Jn 14:2,28; **1517** Jn 16:5,7;
　1524 Jn 20:17; **1532** Ac 2:33;
　1588 Ro 8:34; **1637** Eph 1:20−21;
　1639 Eph 4:8−10; **1684** Heb 6:20;
　1687 Heb 9:12,24;
　1688 Heb 10:12; **1704** 1Pe 3:22

Assyria, Assyrian
　65 Ge 10:11; **557** 2Ki 15:19−29;
　559 2Ki 17:3−19:37;
　972 Isa 10:5,24;
　985 Isa 19:23−25;
　1182 Eze 23:5−23;

1248 Hos 5:13; **1253** Hos 10:6;
　1311 Zep 2:13

Athens, Athenian
　1560 Ac 17:15,16,21,22;
　1561 Ac 18:1; **1656** 1Th 3:1

B

Baal
　266 Nu 25:3−5; **364** Jdg 2:11,13;
　371 Jdg 6:25−32; **413** 1Sa 7:4;
　522 1Ki 18:18−40;
　550 2Ki 10:18−28; **1059** Jer 2:23;
　1088 Jer 19:5; **1095** Jer 23:27;
　1244 Hos 2:8,13,17; **1591** Ro 11:4

Babylon
city in Mesopotamia **65** Ge 10:10;
　565 2Ki 20:12−18;
　571 2Ki 24:10−16;
　662 Ezr 2:1−70; **976** Isa 13—14;
　1026 Isa 47:1; **1133** Jer 50−51;
　1228 Da 4:30; **1229** Da 5
figurative name for Rome
　1706 1Pe 5:13; **1735** Rev 14:8;
　1737 Rev 16:19; **1737** Rev 17:5;
　1738 Rev 18:2−24

Balaam
　261 Nu 22:5−24:25;
　275 Nu 31:8,16; **1293** Mic 6:5;
　1708 2Pe 2:15; **1720** Jude 1:11;
　1724 Rev 2:14

Baptism
John the Baptist **1341** Mt 3:1,11−15;
　1391 Mk 1:4−5,8;
　1435 Lk 3:3,7,16;
　1488 Jn 1:25,31−33;
　1492 Jn 3:23; **1529** Ac 1:5;
　1553 Ac 13:24; **1562** Ac 18:25;
　1563 Ac 19:3−4
Jesus **1341** Mt 3:13−17;
　1391 Mk 1:9−11;
　1436 Lk 3:21−22
Christian **1390** Mt 28:19;
　1532 Ac 2:38,41;
　1543 Ac 8:12,13,16,36,38;
　1549 Ac 10:47−48;
　1585 Ro 6:3−4; **1608** 1Co 10:2;
　1610 1Co 12:13; **1633** Gal 3:27;
　1651 Col 2:12; **1704** 1Pe 3:21
with the Spirit **1341** Mt 3:11;
　1391 Mk 1:8; **1436** Lk 3:16;
　1489 Jn 1:33; **1529** Ac 1:5;
　1550 Ac 11:16; **1610** 1Co 12:13;
　1677 Tit 3:5−6

Barabbas
　1386 Mt 27:16−26;
　1424 Mk 15:7−15; **1482** Lk 23:18;
　1521 Jn 18:40

Barnabas
　1536 Ac 4:36;
　1550 Ac 11:22,25,30;
　1552 Ac 12:25; **1552** Ac 13:1—
　15:41; **1607** 1Co 9:6;
　1631 Gal 2:1,9,13; **1654** Col 4:10

Bartholomew
　1352 Mt 10:3; **1396** Mk 3:18;
　1443 Lk 6:14; **1530** Ac 1:13

Bartimaeus
　1413 Mk 10:46

Bathsheba
　462 2Sa 11:3−12:24;
　491 1Ki 1:15−21;
　493 1Ki 2:12−25

Beatitudes
　1343 Mt 5:3−12; **1443** Lk 6:20−23

Beelzebub
　1353 Mt 10:25; **1355** Mt 12:24,27;
　1396 Mk 3:22;
　1456 Lk 11:15,18,19;
see also Devil, Satan

Belshazzar
　1229 Da 5:1−9,30; **1232** Da 7:1;
　1234 Da 8:1

Benjamin—son of Jacob
born **107** Ge 35:16−18
brought to Egypt **120** Ge 43
accused of theft **121** Ge 44
blessed by Jacob **130** Ge 49:27

Bernice
　1572 Ac 25:13,23; **1575** Ac 26:30

Bethany
　1372 Mt 21:17; **1382** Mt 26:6;
　1413 Mk 11:1,11,12;
　1419 Mk 14:3; **1474** Lk 19:29;
　1487 Lk 24:50; **1489** Jn 1:28;
　1508 Jn 11:1,18; **1511** Jn 12:1

Bethel
　68 Ge 12:8; **93** Ge 28:10−19;
　349 Jos 16:2; **363** Jdg 1:22−26;
　392 Jdg 20:18,26; **413** 1Sa 7:16;
　514 1Ki 13:1−32;
　536 2Ki 2:23−24; **1127** Jer 48:13;
　1269 Am 3:14; **1274** Am 7:10−17

Bethlehem
　107 Ge 35:19; **397** Ru 1:19;
　426 1Sa 16:1,4;
　486 2Sa 23:14−16; **1292** Mic 5:2;
　1340 Mt 2:1,5,6,8,16;
　1432 Lk 2:4,15

Bethsaida
　1354 Mt 11:21; **1404** Mk 6:45;
　1406 Mk 8:22; **1450** Lk 9:10;
　1489 Jn 1:44

Bless(es-ed-ing)
　52 Ge 1:22; **67** Ge 12:2,3;
　237 Nu 6:24−26; **757** Ps 1:1;
　781 Ps 32:1; **924** Pr 28:14;
　930 Pr 31:28; **1343** Mt 5:3−11;
　1411 Mk 10:16; **1413** Mk 11:9;
　1430 Lk 1:42; **1525** Jn 20:29;
　1566 Ac 20:35; **1593** Ro 12:14

Blind
　1351 Mt 9:27; **1353** Mt 11:5;
　1355 Mt 12:22; **1362** Mt 15:14;
　1370 Mt 20:30; **1376** Mt 23:16;
　1406 Mk 8:22; **1413** Mk 10:51;
　1444 Lk 6:39; **1445** Lk 7:21;
　1472 Lk 18:35;
　1505 Jn 9:1,20,25,39,41

Blindness
　77 Ge 19:11; **544** 2Ki 6:18

Blood of Christ
　1383 Mt 26:28; **1420** Mk 14:24;
　1479 Lk 22:20; **1499** Jn 6:53−56;
　1523 Jn 19:34; **1608** 1Co 10:16;
　1610 1Co 11:25,27;
　1687 Heb 9:12,14;
　1689 Heb 10:29; **1692** Heb 12:24;

1694 Heb 13:12; **1701** 1Pe 1:2;
1711 1Jn 1:7; **1714** 1Jn 5:6,8;
1729 Rev 7:14; **1733** Rev 12:11;
1741 Rev 19:13

Boaz
397 Ru 2:3–14; **399** Ru 3:6–13;
400 Ru 4:1–22; **1338** Mt 1:5;
1437 Lk 3:32

Bread of Life
1499 Jn 6:32–59

Burial
Jesus **1387** Mt 27:59–60;
1420 Mk 14:8; **1425** Mk 15:46;
1483 Lk 23:53–56; **1511** Jn 12:7;
1523 Jn 19:38–42
others **83** Ge 23:19; **131** Ge 50:13;
328 Dt 34:6; **482** 2Sa 21:14;
1360 Mt 14:12; **1531** Ac 2:29;
1536 Ac 5:6,10; **1542** Ac 8:2
spiritual **1585** Ro 6:4; **1651** Col 2:12

C

Caesar
1374 Mt 22:21;
1416 Mk 12:14–17;
1476 Lk 20:22–25; **1521** Jn 19:15;
1572 Ac 25:10; **1649** Php 4:22

Caesarea
1544 Ac 8:40; **1546** Ac 9:30;
1547 Ac 10:1,24; **1550** Ac 11:11;
1551 Ac 12:19; **1567** Ac 21:8,16;
1570 Ac 23:23,33;
1572 Ac 25:1,4,6,13

Caesarea Philippi
1363 Mt 16:13; **1407** Mk 8:27

Caiaphas
1382 Mt 26:3,57–66; **1435** Lk 3:2;
1510 Jn 11:49;
1519 Jn 18:13,14,24,28;
1534 Ac 4:6

Cain
57 Ge 4:1–24; **1689** Heb 11:4;
1713 1Jn 3:12; **1720** Jude 1:11

Cana
1490 Jn 2:1–11; **1495** Jn 4:46

Canaan
67 Ge 12:5; **126** Ge 47:4;
141 Ex 6:4; **248** Nu 13:2;
324 Dt 32:49; **358** Jos 24:3;
366 Jdg 4:2,23; **847** Ps 105:11;
1170 Eze 16:3

Capernaum
1342 Mt 4:13; **1349** Mt 8:5;
1354 Mt 11:23; **1365** Mt 17:24;
1391 Mk 1:21; **1409** Mk 9:33;
1439 Lk 4:31; **1444** Lk 7:1;
1453 Lk 10:15; **1491** Jn 2:12;
1498 Jn 6:17,24,59

Carmel
522 1Ki 18:17–46; **536** 2Ki 2:25;
539 2Ki 4:25; **1125** Jer 46:18;
1276 Am 9:3

Casting Lots
1386 Mt 27:35; **1424** Mk 15:24;
1483 Lk 23:34; **1522** Jn 19:24;
1530 Ac 1:26

Cephas
1489 Jn 1:42; **1600** 1Co 1:12;
1602 1Co 3:22; **1607** 1Co 9:5;
1613 1Co 15:5; **1631** Gal 2:9

Cherubim
57 Ge 3:24; **169** Ex 25:18–20;
240 Nu 7:89; **410** 1Sa 4:4;
500 1Ki 6:23–28; **503** 1Ki 8:7;
768 Ps 18:10; **1164** Eze 10:1–22;
1210 Eze 41:18; **1687** Heb 9:5

Chief Priest
1340 Mt 2:4; **1372** Mt 21:15;
1385 Mt 27:1,3,6; **1407** Mk 8:31;
1423 Mk 15:1,3,10,11;
1451 Lk 9:22; **1475** Lk 20:1,19;
1501 Jn 7:32; **1521** Jn 19:6,15,21;
1536 Ac 4:23; **1538** Ac 5:24;
1545 Ac 9:14,21; **1572** Ac 25:2,15

Child
912 Pr 20:11; **970** Isa 9:6;
974 Isa 11:6; **1366** Mt 18:2;
1409 Mk 9:36; **1450** Lk 8:54;
1452 Lk 9:47; **1611** 1Co 13:11

Children
930 Pr 31:28; **1348** Mt 7:11;
1368 Mt 19:13,14; **1405** Mk 7:27;
1410 Mk 10:14; **1514** Jn 13:33;
1532 Ac 2:39; **1588** Ro 8:16,17;
1641 Eph 6:1; **1652** Col 3:20;
1712 1Jn 3:1

Christian
1550 Ac 11:26; **1575** Ac 26:28;
1704 1Pe 4:16

Church(es)
1363 Mt 16:18; **1366** Mt 18:17;
1546 Ac 9:31; **1566** Ac 20:28;
1597 Ro 16:1,5,23; **1600** 1Co 1:2;
1611 1Co 12:28;
1611 1Co 14:4–5,12,23–40;
1637 Eph 1:22;
1641 Eph 5:23–32;
1702 1Pe 2:4–10; **1723** Rev 1:11;
1724 Rev 2:1–3:22

Circumcision
73 Ge 17:10–27; **333** Jos 5:2–9;
1431 Lk 1:59; **1433** Lk 2:21;
1540 Ac 7:8; **1555** Ac 15:1,5;
1557 Ac 16:3; **1567** Ac 21:21;
1582 Ro 2:25–29;
1584 Ro 4:9–12;
1605 1Co 7:18–19;
1638 Eph 2:11; **1651** Col 2:11

Coming
Christ's Coming **970** Isa 9;
993 Isa 26:21; **1054** Isa 66:18;
1287 Mic 1:2–5; **1328** Zec 14:5;
1333 Mal 3:1,2
Second Coming **1364** Mt 16:27–28;
1377 Mt 24:3,26–44;
1380 Mt 25:31–46;
1419 Mk 13:24–37;
1459 Lk 12:39–40;
1468 Lk 17:22–30;
1478 Lk 21:25–28;
1515 Jn 14:2–4,18–24;
1530 Ac 1:11; **1647** Php 3:20–21;
1657 1Th 4:15–5:11;
1660 2Th 1:7–10;
1660 2Th 2:1–15;
1688 Heb 9:27–28;

1710 2Pe 3:3–13; **1712** 1Jn 2:28;
1712 1Jn 3:2;
1743 Rev 22:7,12,17,20

Commandments
of Moses **163** Ex 20:2–17;
(**291** Dt 5:6–21); **289** Dt 4–28;
355 Jos 22:5; **1345** Mt 5:21–48;
1368 Mt 19:7,17; **1393** Mk 1:44;
1417 Mk 12:28–34; **1502** Jn 8:5;
1586 Ro 7:7–13;
1594 Ro 13:8–10; **1696** Jas 2:8
Christ's **1345** Mt 5:22,28,32,
1345 Mt 5:34–37,39–42,44–45,4
8; **1513** Jn 12:49–50;
1514 Jn 13:34;
1516 Jn 15:10–14:17;
1711 1Jn 2:7–8;
1713 1Jn 3:21–24; **1717** 2Jn 5,6

Commission—the Great
1390 Mt 28:16–20

Conscience
1569 Ac 23:1; **1571** Ac 24:16;
1581 Ro 2:15; **1589** Ro 9:1;
1594 Ro 13:5; **1606** 1Co 8:7–13;
1608 1Co 10:25–30;
1664 1Ti 1:19; **1670** 2Ti 1:3;
1704 1Pe 3:16,21

Confession
of Christ **1348** Mt 7:21–23;
1353 Mt 10:32–33;
1363 Mt 16:16; **1407** Mk 8:38;
1458 Lk 12:8–9; **1509** Jn 11:27;
1512 Jn 12:42–43; **1561** Ac 18:5;
1590 Ro 10:8–13; **1595** Ro 14:11;
1610 1Co 12:3; **1645** Php 2:11;
1669 1Ti 6:12; **1670** 2Ti 1:18;
1671 2Ti 2:12; **1711** 1Jn 2:4,23;
1713 1Jn 4:2,3,15
of sin **1470** Lk 18:13–14;
1699 Jas 5:16; **1711** 1Jn 1:8–10

Corinth
1561 Ac 18:1–17; **1563** Ac 19:1;
1600 1Co 1:2; **1618** 2Co 1:1

Cornelius
1547 Ac 10:1–48

Cornerstone
996 Isa 28:16; **1638** Eph 2:20;
1702 1Pe 2:6–7

Counselor
970 Isa 9:6; **1515** Jn 14:16;
1517 Jn 15:26; **1517** Jn 16:7

Covenant
with Noah **60** Ge 6:18; **63** Ge 9:9
with Abraham, Isaac, and Jacob
72 Ge 15:18; **73** Ge 17:2;
136 Ex 2:24; **141** Ex 6:4–5
with Phinehas **267** Nu 25:12–13
with David **458** 2Sa 7
with Israel **161** Ex 19:3–8;
168 Ex 24:7,8; **181** Ex 34:10,27;
289 Dt 4:23; **293** Dt 7:9–11;
600 1Ch 16:14–18; **1534** Ac 3:25;
1540 Ac 7:8; **1620** 2Co 3:14;
1632 Gal 3:17; **1638** Eph 2:12;
1687 Heb 9:1,4,15,18,20
new covenant **1107** Jer 31:31–34;
1383 Mt 26:28; **1420** Mk 14:24;
1479 Lk 22:20; **1610** 1Co 11:25;
1619 2Co 3:6; **1685** Heb 7:22;
1686 Heb 8:6–13; **1687** Heb 9:15;

1688 Heb 10:16,29;
1692 Heb 12:24; **1694** Heb 13:20

Create(d)
52 Ge 1:1—2:4; **799** Ps 51:10;
1638 Eph 2:10; **1640** Eph 4:24;
1650 Col 1:16; **1666** 1Ti 4:4

Cross
of Christ **1386** Mt 27:32,40,42;
1600 1Co 1:17—18;
1634 Gal 5:11; **1636** Gal 6:12,14;
1638 Eph 2:16; **1650** Col 1:20;
1651 Col 2:14; **1691** Heb 12:2
of disciples **1363** Mt 10:38;
1364 Mt 16:24; **1407** Mk 8:34;
1451 Lk 9:23; **1463** Lk 14:27

Cyprus
988 Isa 23:1,12; **1188** Eze 27:6;
1536 Ac 4:36; **1550** Ac 11:20;
1552 Ac 13:4—12; **1557** Ac 15:39

Cyrene
1386 Mt 27:32; **1424** Mk 15:21;
1482 Lk 23:26; **1531** Ac 2:10;
1550 Ac 11:20

Cyrus
662 Ezr 1:1—11; **1022** Isa 44:28;
1022 Isa 45:1—14; **1222** Da 1:21;
1232 Da 6:28; **1237** Da 10:1

D

Damascus
70 Ge 14:15; **460** 2Sa 8:5—6;
541 2Ki 5:12; **546** 2Ki 8:7,9;
556 2Ki 14:28; **558** 2Ki 16:5—12;
967 Isa 7:1—8:6;
1544 Ac 9:2—25,27;
1568 Ac 22:5—16;
1573 Ac 26:12—20;
1626 2Co 11:32; **1630** Gal 1:17

Daniel
trained in King's palace
1221 Da 1:1—7
refused King's food **1222** Da 1:8—16
interprets dreams **1222** Da 2:4
interprets handwriting
1229 Da 5:10—29
delivered from lion's den **1230** Da 6
visions and dreams **1232** Da 7;
1234 Da 8:10—12
prays for his people **1235** Da 9

Darius
king of Persia **665** Ezr 4:5;
667 Ezr 5:5—7; **668** Ezr 6:1—15;
692 Ne 12:22; **1315** Hag 1:1;
1318 Zec 1:1
the Mede **1230** Da 5:31;
1230 Da 6:1,6-9,25—28;
1235 Da 9:1

Darkness
literal **52** Ge 1:2; **71** Ge 15:12;
148 Ex 10:21; **877** Ps 139:12;
1387 Mt 27:45; **1424** Mk 15:33;
1692 Heb 12:18
spiritual **966** Isa 5:20; **1343** Mt 4:16;
1480 Lk 22:53; **1488** Jn 1:5;
1492 Jn 3:19; **1512** Jn 12:35,46;
1620 2Co 4:6; **1640** Eph 5:8,11;
1711 1Jn 1:5—6; **1711** 1Jn 2:8—11

David
anointed by Samuel
426 1Sa 16:1—13
played the harp for Saul
427 1Sa 16:14—23
killed Goliath **428** 1Sa 17
won Jonathan's friendship
431 1Sa 18:1—4
Saul's jealousy **431** 1Sa 18:5—9
married Michal **432** 1Sa 18:20—29
fled from Saul **433** 1Sa 19—22
fought against the Philistines
438 1Sa 23
spared Saul at En Gedi **439** 1Sa 24
David and Abigail **441** 1Sa 25
spared Saul at Ziph **443** 1Sa 26
lived among the Philistines
444 1Sa 27:1—28:2; **446** 1Sa 29
destroyed the Amalekites
446 1Sa 30
anointed king over Judah
451 2Sa 2:1—7
becomes king over Israel
455 2Sa 5:1—16
*brought ark of the covenant to
Jerusalem* **456** 2Sa 6
God's promise with **458** 2Sa 7
extended his kingdom **459** 2Sa 8
David and Bathsheba
462 2Sa 11:1—12:25
fled from Absalom **471** 2Sa 15—16
returned to Jerusalem
478 2Sa 19:8—43
David's last words **485** 2Sa 23:2—7
counted Israel and Judah
487 2Sa 24
David's instructions to Solomon
493 1Ki 2:1—9
died **493** 1Ki 2:10—12
see also
593 1Ch 11—29;
1338 Mt 1:1,6,17;
1375 Mt 22:41—45;
1531 Ac 2:25,29,34;
1553 Ac 13:22,34,36; **1580** Ro 1:3;
1583 Ro 4:6; **1727** Rev 5:5;
1744 Rev 22:16

**Day of Judgment (Day of the
Lord)**
976 Isa 13:6,9; **1005** Isa 34:1—15;
1124 Jer 46:10; **1162** Eze 7:7—19;
1193 Eze 30:2—3;
1260 Joel 2:1—2,11,31;
1272 Am 5:18—20;
1309 Zep 1:7—18; **1348** Mt 7:22;
1352 Mt 10:15; **1354** Mt 11:22,24;
1356 Mt 12:36,41,42;
1456 Lk 11:31,32; **1478** Lk 21:34;
1497 Jn 5:24,29; **1512** Jn 12:48;
1581 Ro 2:16; **1657** 1Th 5:2;
1670 2Ti 1:12,18;
1689 Heb 10:25,27;
1708 2Pe 2:4,9;
1710 2Pe 3:3,7,10; **1714** 1Jn 4:17;
1742 Rev 20:11—15

Deacon
1539 Ac 6:1—6; **1665** 1Ti 3:1—13;

Death
physical **55** Ge 2:17; **57** Ge 3:19;
57 Ge 4:8—16; **319** Dt 30:19;
397 Ru 1:17; **711** Job 3:21;

835 Ps 89:48; **859** Ps 116:15;
895 Pr 7:27; **939** Ecc 9:1—6,10;
1508 Jn 11:11—44;
1614 1Co 15:20—28,54—56;
1657 1Th 4:13—16; **1728** Rev 6:8
spiritual **1585** Ro 6:1—11;
1586 Ro 7:4—6,9-13,24;
1695 Jas 1:15; **1700** Jas 5:20;
1713 1Jn 3:14; **1716** 1Jn 5:16,17;
1741 Rev 20:6,14
of Christ **1387** Mt 27:50;
1425 Mk 15:39; **1483** Lk 23:46;
1520 Jn 18:31—32; **1523** Jn 19:30;
1613 1Co 15:3;
1621 2Co 5:14—15; **1645** Php 2:8;
1650 Col 1:22;
1681 Heb 2:9,14—15;
1704 1Pe 3:18

Deborah
366 Jdg 4:4—14; **367** Jdg 5:1—31

Delilah
385 Jdg 16:4—18

Demons
general **1608** 1Co 10:20—21;
1666 1Ti 4:1; **1731** Rev 9:20;
1737 Rev 16:13—14;
1738 Rev 18:2
and Jesus **1343** Mt 4:24;
1349 Mt 8:16,28—34;
1456 Lk 11:14—26;
1504 Jn 8:48—52;
1507 Jn 10:20—21

Derbe
1554 Ac 14:6,20—21;
1557 Ac 16:1

Devil
1342 Mt 4:1—11; **1437** Lk 4:1—13;
1513 Jn 13:2; **1641** Eph 6:11;
1665 1Ti 3:6—7; **1681** Heb 2:14;
1706 1Pe 5:8; **1713** 1Jn 3:8;
1720 Jude 1:9;
1733 Rev 12:9—12;
1741 Rev 20:2,10
see also Beelzebub, Satan

Disciples
1343 Mt 4:18; **1351** Mt 9:9;
1352 Mt 10:1,5; **1439** Lk 5:1—10;
1489 Jn 1:35—50

Divorce
217 Lev 21:7; **274** Nu 30:9;
311 Dt 24:1—4; **1031** Isa 50:1;
1332 Mal 2:16; **1345** Mt 5:31—32;
1368 Mt 19:3—9
1410 Mk 10:2—12; **1467** Lk 16:18;
1605 1Co 7:10—11,12—16

Dorcas
1547 Ac 9:36—41

Dreams
of Joseph **109** Ge 37:5—11
of Jacob **93** Ge 28:10—15
of Pharaoh **116** Ge 41:1—7
of Nebuchadnezzar **1222** Da 2;
1226 Da 4
of Daniel **1232** Da 7; **1234** Da 8;
1237 Da 10
of Peter **1547** Ac 10:9—23
of Paul **1547** Ac 16:6—10
others **71** Ge 15:1; **98** Ge 31:10—14;
115 Ge 40:5—23; **247** Nu 12:6;
373 Jdg 7:13—16;

408 1Sa 3:1–18; **495** 1Ki 3:5;
1203 Eze 37; **1318** Zec 1:7;
1339 Mt 1:20; **1340** Mt 2:13;
1341 Mt 2:19–20; **1386** Mt 27:19;
1731 Rev 9:17

E

Eden
54 Ge 2:8,10,15; **57** Ge 3:23–24;
1190 Eze 28:13;
1195 Eze 31:9,16–18

Egypt(ians)
68 Ge 12:10–14;
111 Ge 37:25–28; **134** Ex 1—15;
245 Nu 11:5; **495** 1Ki 3:1;
659 2Ch 36:3,4; **1058** Jer 2:6;
1121 Jer 42:19; **1182** Eze 23:3;
1196 Eze 32:11–16;
1254 Hos 11:1;
1325 Zec 10:10–11;
1340 Mt 2:13–15,19

Elders, leaders
Israelite **137** Ex 3:16–18;
358 Jos 24:1,31;
400 Ru 4:2,4,9,11; **1361** Mt 15:2;
1372 Mt 21:23;
1382 Mt 26:3,47,57;
1385 Mt 27:1,3,12,20,41;
1534 Ac 4:5,8,23; **1539** Ac 6:12;
1571 Ac 24:1
heavenly **1726** Rev 4:4,10;
1727 Rev 5:5,6,8-11;
1729 Rev 7:11–14;
1732 Rev 11:16; **1740** Rev 19:4

Elect(ion)
1377 Mt 24:22,31;
1419 Mk 13:20,27; **1589** Ro 9:11;
1591 Ro 11:7; **1592** Ro 11:28;
1671 2Ti 2:10; **1707** 2Pe 1:10

Eli
404 1Sa 1:9—4:18; **494** 1Ki 2:27

Elijah
520 1Ki 17:1—2Ki 2:15;
1337 Mal 4:5; **1354** Mt 11:14;
1364 Mt 17:3–13;
1387 Mt 27:47–49; **1428** Lk 1:17;
1438 Lk 4:25–26;
1488 Jn 1:21,25; **1591** Ro 11:2;
1700 Jas 5:17

Elisha
526 1Ki 19:16–21; **535** 2Ki 2:1—
9:3; **554** 2Ki 13:14–21;
1438 Lk 4:27

Elizabeth
1428 Lk 1:5–7,24–25,36,
1430 Lk 1:40–45,57–61

Emmaus
1484 Lk 24:13

Enoch
59 Ge 5:18–24; **1689** Heb 11:5;
1720 Jude 1:14

Epaphras
1650 Col 1:7; **1654** Col 4:12;
1679 Phm 23

Ephesus
1562 Ac 18:19–21,24–26;
1563 Ac 19:1–41;
1565 Ac 20:16–38;
1614 1Co 15:32; **1615** 1Co 16:8;

1637 Eph 1:1; **1664** 1Ti 1:3;
1724 Rev 2:1–7

Epicureans
1560 Ac 17:18

Esau
87 Ge 25:21–26; **90** Ge 27:1–41;
101 Ge 32:3—33:15;
107 Ge 35:29; **286** Dt 2:4–22;
1279 Ob 8,9,19,21;
1331 Mal 1:2–3; **1589** Ro 9:13;
1690 Heb 11:20

Esther
goes to palace **699** Est 2:8–16
made queen **699** Est 2:17–18
Mordecai asks her help **700** Est 4
makes request of the King
701 Est 5:1–7
reveals Haman's plot
703 Est 7:1–10
confirms Purim **707** Est 9:29–32

Ethiopian
1543 Ac 8:26–39

Euphrates
55 Ge 2:14; **72** Ge 15:18;
1731 Rev 9:14; **1737** Rev 16:12

Eutychus
1565 Ac 20:9–12

Eve
57 Ge 3:20; **57** Ge 4:1;
1625 2Co 11:3; **1665** 1Ti 2:13

F

Faith
general **968** Isa 7:9; **992** Isa 26:2;
1304 Hab 2:4; **1350** Mt 9:2;
1365 Mt 17:20;
1372 Mt 21:21–22; **1468** Lk 17:6;
1580 Ro 1:16–17;
1583 Ro 3:27–31; **1584** Ro 5:1;
1621 2Co 5:7; **1632** Gal 3:2,6-
14,22–26; **1689** Heb 11:1;
1695 Jas 1:6; **1696** Jas 2:14–26
in God **823** Ps 78:22;
1415 Mk 11:22–24;
1512 Jn 12:44–45; **1515** Jn 14:1;
1583 Ro 4:1–25;
1689 Heb 11:1–40
in Christ **1349** Mt 8:13;
1351 Mt 9:28–29; **1394** Mk 2:5;
1400 Mk 5:34,36;
1408 Mk 9:23–24;
1488 Jn 1:7,12,50; **1492** Jn 3:16;
1498 Jn 6:29,35,40;
1506 Jn 9:35–38;
1508 Jn 11:15,25–27;
1525 Jn 20:29,31; **1534** Ac 3:16;
1559 Ac 16:31; **1583** Ro 3:22–26;
1590 Ro 10:6–17;
1631 Gal 2:16,20; **1713** 1Jn 3:23;
1714 1Jn 5:1,5,10,13

False gods
559 2Ki 17:15; **790** Ps 40:4;
1075 Jer 10:11; **1082** Jer 14:22

False prophets
300 Dt 13:1–5; **306** Dt 18:20–22;
530 1Ki 22:5–25;
1094 Jer 23:16–32;
1101 Jer 28:15,16;
1168 Eze 13:17,19; **1290** Mic 3:11;

1348 Mt 7:15; **1377** Mt 24:11,24;
1419 Mk 13:22; **1552** Ac 13:6;
1708 2Pe 2:1; **1713** 1Jn 4:1;
1725 Rev 2:20; **1741** Rev 19:20;
1742 Rev 20:10

Famine
68 Ge 12:10; **116** Ge 41:29–30;
396 Ru 1:1; **481** 2Sa 21:1;
522 1Ki 18:2; **544** 2Ki 6:25;
572 2Ki 25:3; **1550** Ac 11:28

Father (title of God)
834 Ps 89:26; **1050** Isa 63:16;
1346 Mt 5:48; **1346** Mt 6:8–9,32;
1348 Mt 7:21; **1354** Mt 11:25–27;
1421 Mk 14:36; **1434** Lk 2:49;
1459 Lk 12:30,32;
1483 Lk 23:34,46; **1488** Jn 1:18;
1496 Jn 5:17–27,36–45;
1507 Jn 10:29–38;
1515 Jn 14:6–11;
1518 Jn 17:1–26; **1588** Ro 8:15;
1633 Gal 4:6; **1691** Heb 12:5–9;
1712 1Jn 3:1–2,9-10

Father in heaven
1344 Mt 5:16,45; **1346** Mt 6:1,9;
1348 Mt 7:11,21; **1356** Mt 12:50;
1363 Mt 16:17;
1366 Mt 18:10,14,19;
1375 Mt 23:9

Feasts
Feast of Unleavened Bread
149 Ex 12:15–20; **152** Ex 13:6–7;
167 Ex 23:15; **627** 2Ch 8:13;
658 2Ch 35:17; **669** Ezr 6:22;
1382 Mt 26:17; **1419** Mk 14:1,12;
1478 Lk 22:1,7; **1550** Ac 12:3;
1565 Ac 20:6
Feast of Harvest or Weeks
167 Ex 23:16; **181** Ex 34:22;
219 Lev 23:15–21;
303 Dt 16:9–12; **627** 2Ch 8:13
Feast of Tabernacles
220 Lev 23:34,42;
303 Dt 16:13–16;
627 2Ch 8:12–13; **665** Ezr 3:4;
1328 Zec 14:16–19;
1500 Jn 7:2,8,10,11,14,37
New Moon **243** Nu 10:10;
627 2Ch 8:13; **434** 1Sa 20:5;
1275 Am 8:5; **1651** Col 2:16
others: Trumpets **273** Nu 29:1
Purim **707** Est 9:21–32
Dedication of Temple **1507** Jn 10:22

Felix
1570 Ac 23:24,26;
1571 Ac 24:2–27

Festus
1572 Ac 24:27; **1572** Ac 25:1—
26:32

Forgiveness
781 Ps 32:1; **871** Ps 130:4;
1004 Isa 33:24;
1295 Mic 7:18–19;
1346 Mt 6:12,14–15;
1350 Mt 9:1–8;
1366 Mt 18:21–35; **1397** Mk 4:12;
1415 Mk 11:25–26; **1435** Lk 3:3;
1446 Lk 7:36–50;
1468 Lk 17:3–4; **1524** Jn 20:23;
1532 Ac 2:38; **1549** Ac 10:43;

1553 Ac 13:38−39;
1574 Ac 26:18; 1619 2Co 2:5−10;
1640 Eph 4:32; 1651 Col 2:13;
1686 Heb 8:12; 1687 Heb 9:22;
1688 Heb 10:17−18;
1711 1Jn 1:9; 1723 Rev 1:5

Friend(s)
908 Pr 16:28; 909 Pr 17:17;
910 Pr 19:4; 916 Pr 22:24;
922 Pr 27:10; 1294 Mic 7:5;
1354 Mt 11:19; 1383 Mt 26:50;
1516 Jn 15:13; 1696 Jas 2:23;
1697 Jas 4:4

G

Gabriel
1235 Da 8:15−26;
1236 Da 9:20−27;
1428 Lk 1:11−20,26

Galatia
1557 Ac 16:6; 1562 Ac 18:23;
1615 1Co 16:1; 1630 Gal 1:2;
1672 2Ti 4:10; 1701 1Pe 1:1

Galilee
557 2Ki 15:29; (587 1Ch 6:76);
970 Isa 9:1; 1343 Mt 4:23;
1368 Mt 19:1; 1388 Mt 28:7,10,16;
1391 Mk 1:9,14,28,39;
1434 Lk 2:39; 1437 Lk 4:14;
1489 Jn 1:43; 1495 Jn 4:43,47;
1500 Jn 7:1,9,41,52;
1546 Ac 9:31; 1549 Ac 10:37;
1553 Ac 13:31

Gamaliel
1539 Ac 5:34; 1568 Ac 22:3

Genealogy
58 Ge 4:17−5:31; 64 Ge 10;
142 Ex 6:14−27; 231 Nu 3;
402 Ru 4:13−22; 575 1Ch 1−9;
674 Ezr 10:9−44;
1338 Mt 1:1−17; 1436 Lk 3:23−38

Gentiles
1352 Mt 10:5,18; 1433 Lk 2:32;
1545 Ac 9:15; 1549 Ac 10:45;
1554 Ac 13:46−48; 1561 Ac 18:6;
1569 Ac 22:21; 1581 Ro 2:12−27;
1583 Ro 3:29;
1595 Ro 15:9−18,27;
1631 Gal 2:2−4; 1632 Gal 3:14;
1638 Eph 3:1−8; 1656 1Th 2:16

Gethsemane
1383 Mt 26:36; 1421 Mk 14:32

Gideon
370 Jdg 6:11−8:27;
1691 Heb 11:32

Gift(s)
910 Pr 18:16; 914 Pr 21:14;
933 Ecc 3:13; 1348 Mt 7:11;
1532 Ac 2:38; 1586 Ro 6:23;
1593 Ro 12:6−8; 1605 1Co 7:7;
1610 1Co 12:4; 1624 2Co 9:15;
1704 1Pe 4:10

Golgotha
1386 Mt 27:33; 1424 Mk 15:22;
1521 Jn 19:17

Goliath
428 1Sa 17:1−58;
437 1Sa 21:9−10; 438 1Sa 22:10

Greece
1235 Da 8:21; 1238 Da 10:20;
1238 Da 11:2; 1324 Zec 9:13;
1405 Mk 7:26; 1501 Jn 7:35;
1511 Jn 12:20; 1521 Jn 19:20;
1550 Ac 11:20; 1565 Ac 20:2,21

Greed
1397 Mk 4:19; 1458 Lk 12:15−21;
1466 Lk 16:13−14;
1536 Ac 5:1−11; 1586 Ro 7:7−8;
1603 1Co 5:9−11;
1604 1Co 6:9−10;
1640 Eph 5:3−5;
1647 Php 3:18−19;
1652 Col 3:1−6; 1665 1Ti 3:3,8;
1667 1Ti 6:5−11; 1671 2Ti 3:2;
1675 Tit 1:7−11; 1692 Heb 13:5;
1697 Jas 4:2; 1706 1Pe 5:2;
1708 2Pe 2:3,14;
1712 1Jn 2:15−17

H

Hagar
72 Ge 16:1−16; 79 Ge 21:9−21;
1633 Gal 4:24−25

Hannah
404 1Sa 1:2−2:11; 407 1Sa 2:21

Heaven
93 Ge 28:12,17; 163 Ex 20:22;
330 Jos 2:11; 504 1Ki 8:27;
845 Ps 103:11; 1053 Isa 66:1;
1341 Mt 3:16; 1344 Mt 5:12;
1346 Mt 6:10,20; 1366 Mt 18:10;
1368 Mt 19:21; 1375 Mt 22:30;
1388 Mt 28:2,18; 1433 Lk 2:15;
1453 Lk 10:18;
1464 Lk 15:7,18,21;
1480 Lk 22:43; 1489 Jn 1:51;
1491 Jn 3:13;
1498 Jn 6:31−33,38,41,42,
1499 Jn 6:50,51,58; 1534 Ac 3:21;
1542 Ac 7:55−56; 1580 Ro 1:18;
1590 Ro 10:6;
1614 1Co 15:47−49;
1626 2Co 12:2; 1641 Eph 6:9;
1647 Php 3:20;
1650 Col 1:5,16,20;
1657 1Th 4:16; 1660 2Th 1:7;
1688 Heb 9:24;
1692 Heb 12:23,25,26;
1700 Jas 5:18; 1701 1Pe 1:4,12;
1704 1Pe 3:22; 1726 Rev 4−5;
1740 Rev 19:1,11−14;
1742 Rev 21:1−2,10

Heaven—Kingdom of God
1341 Mt 3:2; 1343 Mt 4:17;
1343 Mt 5:3,10,19,20;
1348 Mt 7:21; 1349 Mt 8:11;
1352 Mt 10:7; 1354 Mt 11:11,12;
1357 Mt 13:11,24,31,33,
1359 Mt 13:44,45,47,52;
1363 Mt 16:19;
1366 Mt 18:1,3,4,23;
1368 Mt 19:12,14,23;
1369 Mt 20:1; 1374 Mt 22:2;
1375 Mt 23:13; 1378 Mt 25:1

Hell
1345 Mt 5:22,29,30;
1353 Mt 10:28; 1366 Mt 18:9;
1376 Mt 23:15,33;

Herod
1340 Mt 2:1−22;
1359 Mt 14:1−10;
1401 Mk 6:14−27; 1406 Mk 8:15;
1428 Lk 1:5; 1435 Lk 3:1,19;
1450 Lk 9:7,9; 1461 Lk 13:31;
1482 Lk 23:6−12,15;
1536 Ac 4:27; 1552 Ac 13:1

Herodias
1359 Mt 14:3,6;
1401 Mk 6:17,19,22; 1436 Lk 3:19

Hezekiah
561 2Ki 18−20; 648 2Ch 29−32;
1007 Isa 36−39; 1338 Mt 1:9,10

High Priest
Israelite 217 Lev 21:10−15;
281 Nu 35:25,28,32;
567 2Ki 22:4,8; 678 Ne 3:1,20;
1319 Zec 3:1,8;
1382 Mt 26:3,51,57,
1384 Mt 26:58,62,63,65;
1422 Mk 14:47,53,54,
1422 Mk 14:60,61,63,66;
1480 Lk 22:50; 1510 Jn 11:49,51;
1519 Jn 18:13,15,16,19,
1520 Jn 18:22,24,26; 1534 Ac 4:6;
1537 Ac 5:17,21,27; 1540 Ac 7:1;
1571 Ac 24:1; 1686 Heb 8:3;
1687 Heb 9:7,25; 1694 Heb 13:11;
Christ 1681 Heb 2:17;
1682 Heb 3:1; 1683 Heb 4:14,15;
1683 Heb 5:1−6,10;
1684 Heb 6:20;
1685 Heb 7:15−17,21,24,26−28;
1686 Heb 8:1−4

Holy Spirit
1339 Mt 1:18,20; 1341 Mt 3:11,16;
1342 Mt 4:1;
1355 Mt 12:18,28,31,32;
1391 Mk 1:8; 1429 Lk 1:35;
1437 Lk 4:14,18; 1453 Lk 10:21;
1489 Jn 1:33; 1491 Jn 3:5,6,8,34;
1515 Jn 14:17,26; 1517 Jn 15:26;
1517 Jn 16:13; 1524 Jn 20:22;
1529 Ac 1:2,5,8;
1530 Ac 2:1−4,17,18,33,38;
1536 Ac 5:3,9,32;
1543 Ac 8:15−19,29,39;
1545 Ac 9:17,31;
1548 Ac 10:19,38,44−47;
1550 Ac 11:12,15−17,24,28;
1552 Ac 13:2,4,9,52;
1563 Ac 19:1−7; 1587 Ro 8;
1610 1Co 12:1−13; 1634 Gal 5;
1637 Eph 1:13,14,17;
1638 Eph 2:18,22;
1639 Eph 4:3,4,30;
1643 Eph 6:17−18;
1655 1Th 1:5−6; 1657 1Th 4:8;
1659 1Th 5:19; 1677 Tit 3:5−6;
1681 Heb 2:4; 1707 2Pe 1:21;
1713 1Jn 3:24; 1713 1Jn 4:2,13;
1714 1Jn 5:6−8;

Husband
literal 55 Ge 3:6,16; 396 Ru 1:3−12;
697 Est 1:17,20; 901 Pr 12:4;
928 Pr 31:11;

1605 1Co 7:2–4,10–16,34,39;
1641 Eph 5:22–28,33;
1652 Col 3:18–19;
1703 1Pe 3:1,5,7
figurative **1037** Isa 54:5;
1107 Jer 31:31–32;
1244 Hos 2:7,16; **1625** 2Co 11:2;
1634 Gal 4:27; **1742** Rev 21:2

I

Iconium
1554 Ac 13:51–14:6;
1555 Ac 14:19,21; **1557** Ac 16:2;
1672 2Ti 3:11

Idol
214 Lev 19:4; **318** Dt 29:17;
518 1Ki 15:12; **559** 2Ki 17:12,15;
840 Ps 96:5; **857** Ps 115:4–8;
874 Ps 135:15–18;
1013 Isa 40:19; **1015** Isa 41:7;
1021 Isa 44:12–20;
1025 Isa 46:1–7;
1074 Jer 10:3–5; **1202** Eze 36:25;
1247 Hos 4:17; **1541** Ac 7:41;
1560 Ac 17:16;
1606 1Co 8:1,4,7,10;
1622 2Co 6:16; **1655** 1Th 1:9;
1716 1Jn 5:21; **1724** Rev 2:14,20

Immanuel
968 Isa 7:14; **969** Isa 8:8;
1339 Mt 1:23

Isaac
79 Ge 21:1–7; **81** Ge 22:1–19;
83 Ge 24; **87** Ge 25:19–26;
90 Ge 27:1–40; **107** Ge 35:28,29;
1338 Mt 1:2; **1349** Mt 8:11;
1540 Ac 7:8; **1589** Ro 9:7,10;
1634 Gal 4:28;
1690 Heb 11:9,17–18,20;
1696 Jas 2:21

Isaiah
563 2Ki 19–20; **967** Isa 6;
968 Isa 7:3; **1008** Isa 37–39;
1341 Mt 3:3; **1343** Mt 4:14;
1349 Mt 8:17; **1355** Mt 12:17;
1357 Mt 13:14; **1361** Mt 15:7;
1391 Mk 1:2; **1435** Lk 3:4;
1438 Lk 4:17; **1488** Jn 1:23;
1512 Jn 12:38–41;
1543 Ac 8:28,30; **1579** Ac 28:25;
1590 Ro 9:27–29;
1591 Ro 10:16,20–21;
1596 Ro 15:12

Ishmael
73 Ge 16:15; **74** Ge 17:25–26;
79 Ge 21:3–21;
86 Ge 25:9,12–17; **92** Ge 28:9

Israel
102 Ge 32:22–32; **104** Ge 34:7;
177 Ex 32:4; **289** Dt 4:1;
418 1Sa 11:8; **431** 1Sa 17:52;
512 1Ki 11:42; **672** Ezr 9:1;
687 Ne 9:2; **1352** Mt 10:6;
1362 Mt 15:24; **1431** Lk 1:68,80;
1433 Lk 2:25,32,34;
1485 Lk 24:21; **1529** Ac 1:6;
1538 Ac 5:31,35;
1553 Ac 13:16,17,23,24;
1589 Ro 9:6,27,31;
1591 Ro 10:19,21;

1591 Ro 11:2,7,11,25–26;
1686 Heb 8:8–10; **1729** Rev 7:4;
1742 Rev 21:12

Italy
1547 Ac 10:1; **1561** Ac 18:2;
1575 Ac 27:1,6; **1694** Heb 13:24

J

Jacob
87 Ge 25:19–35:29;
124 Ge 46–50; **1338** Mt 1:2;
1349 Mt 8:11; **1429** Lk 1:33;
1493 Jn 4:5,6,12;
1540 Ac 7:8,12,14,15,46;
1589 Ro 9:13;
1690 Heb 11:9,20,21

Jairus
1399 Mk 5:22; **1449** Lk 8:41

James
son of Zebedee **1343** Mt 4:21;
1364 Mt 17:1; **1391** Mk 1:19,29;
1401 Mk 5:37; **1407** Mk 9:2;
1412 Mk 10:35,41; **1418** Mk 13:3;
1421 Mk 14:33; **1440** Lk 5:10;
1452 Lk 9:54; **1530** Ac 1:13;
1550 Ac 12:2
son of Alphaeus **1352** Mt 10:3;
1396 Mk 3:18; **1443** Lk 6:15;
1530 Ac 1:13
son of Mary **1387** Mt 27:56;
1425 Mk 15:40; **1425** Mk 16:1;
1484 Lk 24:10
brother of Jesus **1359** Mt 13:55;
1401 Mk 6:3; **1551** Ac 12:17;
1556 Ac 15:13; **1567** Ac 21:18;
1630 Gal 1:19; **1631** Gal 2:9,12
other **1443** Lk 6:16; **1530** Ac 1:13;
1695 Jas 1:1; **1720** Jude 1:1

Jehoshaphat
518 1Ki 15:24; **530** 1Ki 22:2–50;
635 2Ch 17–20

Jehu
547 2Ki 9–10

Jeremiah
659 2Ch 36:12,21,22;
1057 Jer 1:1; **1235** Da 9:2;
1340 Mt 2:17; **1363** Mt 16:14;
1385 Mt 27:9

Jericho
261 Nu 22:1; **329** Jos 2:1–24;
334 Jos 5:13–6:26;
349 Jos 6:1,7; **520** 1Ki 16:34;
535 2Ki 2:4,5,15,18;
1370 Mt 20:29; **1413** Mk 10:46;
1453 Lk 10:30; **1472** Lk 18:35;
1472 Lk 19:1; **1691** Heb 11:30

Jeroboam
511 1Ki 11:26–14:20;
(**629** 2Ch 10:2–13:20)

Jerusalem
340 Jos 10:1; **349** Jos 15:63;
362 Jdg 1:8; **455** 2Sa 5:6;
555 2Ki 14:13; **571** 2Ki 24:10,14;
572 2Ki 25:10; **662** Ezr 1:2–11;
693 Ne 12:27; **800** Ps 51:18;
868 Ps 122:6; **1022** Isa 44:26;
1073 Jer 9:11; **1265** Joel 3:17;
1326 Zec 12:2–12; **1340** Mt 2:1,3;
1370 Mt 20:17–18;

1371 Mt 21:1,10; **1376** Mt 23:37;
1412 Mk 10:32;
1413 Mk 11:1,11,15;
1433 Lk 2:22,25,38,41,43,45;
1461 Lk 13:33–35; **1474** Lk 19:28;
1477 Lk 21:20,24; **1491** Jn 2:13;
1493 Jn 4:20; **1495** Jn 5:1;
1511 Jn 12:12; **1529** Ac 1:4,8,12;
1555 Ac 15:2; **1557** Ac 16:4;
1633 Gal 4:26; **1692** Heb 12:22;
1726 Rev 3:12; **1742** Rev 21:2,10

Jesse
403 Ru 4:18–22;
426 1Sa 16:1–22;
428 1Sa 17:12–14,17;
974 Isa 11:1,10; **1338** Mt 1:5–6;
1553 Ac 13:22; **1596** Ro 15:12

Jesus Christ
name **1339** Mt 1:21,25;
1429 Lk 1:31; **1433** Lk 2:21
genealogy **1338** Mt 1:1–17;
1436 Lk 3:23–38
birth and infancy **1339** Mt 1:18–
2:23; **1429** Lk 1:26–38;
1432 Lk 2:1–40
twelve years **1434** Lk 2:41–52
baptism and temptation
1341 Mt 3:13–4:11;
1391 Mk 1:9–13;
1436 Lk 3:21–22; **1437** Lk 4:1–13
ministry in Galilee **1342** Mt 4:12–
18:35; **1391** Mk 1:14–9:50;
1437 Lk 4:14–9:50
Sermon on the Mount
1343 Mt 5:1–7:29;
1443 Lk 6:17–49
confession at Caesarea Philippi
1363 Mt 16:13–28;
1407 Mk 8:27–9:1;
1450 Lk 9:18–27
transfiguration **1364** Mt 17:1–13;
1407 Mk 9:2–13;
1451 Lk 9:28–36
last days in Jerusalem
1371 Mt 21:1–27:66;
1413 Mk 11:1–15:47;
1474 Lk 19:28–23:56;
1511 Jn 12:1–19:42
triumphal entry **1371** Mt 21:1–11;
1413 Mk 11:1–11;
1474 Lk 19:29–44;
1511 Jn 12:12–19
in the Temple **1372** Mt 21:12–17;
1414 Mk 11:15–19;
1474 Lk 19:45–48
discourse on last things
1377 Mt 24:1–25:46;
1418 Mk 13:1–37;
1477 Lk 21:5–36
Last Supper **1382** Mt 26:17–35;
1420 Mk 14:12–31;
1478 Lk 22:7–38; **1513** Jn 13:1–
17:26; **1609** 1Co 11:23–26
Gethsemane **1382** Mt 26:36–46;
1421 Mk 14:32–42;
1480 Lk 22:39–46
*arrest, trial, crucifixion, death, and
burial* **1383** Mt 26:47–27:66;
1422 Mk 14:43–15:47;
1480 Lk 22:47–23:56;
1519 Jn 18:1–19:42

resurrection, appearances,
ascension 1388 Mt 28:1–20;
1425 Mk 16:1–20;
1484 Lk 24:1–53; **1523** Jn 20:1—
21:25; **1529** Ac 1:1–11;
1613 1Co 15:4–8

Jezebel
520 1Ki 16:31; **524** 1Ki 19:1–2;
528 1Ki 21:1–25;
548 2Ki 9:7–10,30–37;
1725 Rev 2:20–23

Joab
452 2Sa 2:12–32;
454 2Sa 3:22–30;
462 2Sa 11:6–21;
471 2Sa 14:28–33;
476 2Sa 18:9–17;
480 2Sa 20:4–23;
494 1Ki 2:28–34

Joash
641 2Ch 22:10; **642** 2Ch 24

John
son of Zebedee **1343** Mt 4:21;
1352 Mt 10:2; **1383** Mt 26:37;
1391 Mk 1:19,29; **1401** Mk 5:37;
1407 Mk 9:2,38;
1412 Mk 10:35,41; **1418** Mk 13:3;
1450 Lk 8:51; **1451** Lk 9:28,49,54;
1478 Lk 22:8; **1520** Jn 18:15–16;
1522 Jn 19:26–27;
1525 Jn 21:2,7,20;
1533 Ac 3:1–11; **1534** Ac 4:1–23;
1543 Ac 8:14–17; **1631** Gal 2:9
author of Revelation
1723 Rev 1:1,4,9; **1743** Rev 22:8
father of Simon Peter
1363 Mt 16:17; **1489** Jn 1:42;
1527 Jn 21:15–17
of family of high priest Annas
1534 Ac 4:6

John the Baptist
1341 Mt 3:1–15;
1353 Mt 11:2–19;
1359 Mt 14:2–12;
1372 Mt 21:25–32;
1391 Mk 1:4–11;
1401 Mk 6:14–29;
1415 Mk 11:29–33;
1428 Lk 1:13–25,57–80;
1435 Lk 3:2–20;
1445 Lk 7:18–33; **1454** Lk 11:1;
1488 Jn 1:6–36;
1492 Jn 3:23–30;
1553 Ac 13:24–25

John Mark
1551 Ac 12:12,25;
1552 Ac 13:5,13;
1557 Ac 15:37,39; **1654** Col 4:10;
1672 2Ti 4.11; **1679** Phm 24;
1706 1Pe 5:13

Jonah
556 2Ki 14:25; **1282** Jnh 1:1;
1356 Mt 12:39–41; **1363** Mt 16:4;
1456 Lk 11:29–32

Jonathan
420 1Sa 13:2–4;
422 1Sa 14:1–15,24–48;
431 1Sa 18:1–5; **434** 1Sa 20;
449 1Sa 31:2; **450** 2Sa 1:17–27

Joppa
353 Jos 19:46; **620** 2Ch 2:16;
665 Ezr 3:7; **1282** Jnh 1:3;
1547 Ac 9:36–43;
1547 Ac 10:5–8,23,32;
1549 Ac 11:5,13

Jordan
69 Ge 13:10–11; **101** Ge 32:10;
289 Dt 4:22; **329** Jos 1:2;
332 Jos 3:17; **478** 2Sa 19:15;
535 2Ki 2:7; **541** 2Ki 5:10;
542 2Ki 6:4; **1078** Jer 12:5;
1341 Mt 3:5–6,13; **1391** Mk 1:5,9;
1410 Mk 10:1; **1435** Lk 3:3;
1489 Jn 1:28; **1508** Jn 10:40

Joseph
son of Jacob **96** Ge 30:22–24;
109 Ge 37:5—50:26;
361 Ge 24:32; **848** Ps 105:17–22;
1493 Jn 4:5; **1540** Ac 7:9–14
husband of Mary **1338** Mt 1:16–25;
1340 Mt 2:13–15,19–23;
1429 Lk 1:27; **1432** Lk 2:4,16;
1438 Lk 4:22; **1489** Jn 1:45;
1499 Jn 6:42
of Arimathea **1387** Mt 27:57–60;
1425 Mk 15:42–46;
1483 Lk 23:50–53;
1523 Jn 19:38–42
other **1359** Mt 13:55; **1387** Mt 27:56;
1401 Mk 6:3; **1425** Mk 15:40,47;
1530 Ac 1:23; **1536** Ac 4:36

Joshua
158 Ex 17:8–13; **168** Ex 24:13;
180 Ex 33:11; **248** Nu 13:1–16;
250 Nu 14:6–9;
271 Nu 27:18–23; **321** Dt 31:23;
329 Jos 1—24; **1541** Ac 7:45;
1683 Heb 4:8

Josiah
567 2Ki 21:24—23:30;
(**655** 2Ch 33:25—35:27)

Judea
1340 Mt 2:1,5,22; **1341** Mt 3:1,5;
1368 Mt 19:1; **1377** Mt 24:16;
1431 Lk 1:65; **1492** Jn 3:22;
1500 Jn 7:1,3; **1508** Jn 11:7;
1529 Ac 1:8; **1567** Ac 21:10;
1596 Ro 15:31; **1630** Gal 1:22;
1656 1Th 2:14

Judah
95 Ge 29:35; **111** Ge 37:26–28;
112 Ge 38; **122** Ge 44:14–34;
129 Ge 49:8–12; **324** Dt 33:7;
1685 Heb 7:14

Judas
1359 Mt 13:55; **1401** Mk 6:3;
1515 Jn 14:22; **1539** Ac 5:37;
1545 Ac 9:11;
1556 Ac 15:22,27,32

Judas Iscariot
1352 Mt 10:4;
1382 Mt 26:14,25,47;
1385 Mt 27:3; **1396** Mk 3:19;
1420 Mk 14:10,43;
1478 Lk 22:3,47–48;
1500 Jn 6:71; **1511** Jn 12:4;
1513 Jn 13:2,26,29;
1519 Jn 18:2–3,5;
1530 Ac 1:16,25

Judge/Judgment
of God **71** Ge 15:14; **75** Ge 18:25;
142 Ex 6:6; **379** Jdg 11:27;
504 1Ki 8:32; (**624** 2Ch 6:23);
760 Ps 7:6,8,11;
840 Ps 96:10,12,13;
944 Ecc 12:14; **1162** Eze 7:3,8;
1345 Mt 5:22; **1347** Mt 7:1–2;
1352 Mt 10:15; **1354** Mt 11:22–24;
1356 Mt 12:36,37,41,42;
1444 Lk 6:37; **1452** Lk 10:10–15;
1456 Lk 11:31–32; **1561** Ac 17:31;
1581 Ro 2:2–3,5,16;
1594 Ro 14:10;
1602 1Co 3:12–15; **1602** 1Co 4:5;
1636 Gal 6:7–9; **1684** Heb 6:2–8;
1688 Heb 9:27;
1689 Heb 10:26–31;
1692 Heb 12:23; **1692** Heb 13:4;
1696 Jas 2:12–13; **1697** Jas 3:1;
1698 Jas 4:12; **1735** Rev 14:7;
1742 Rev 20:12–13
of Christ **1341** Mt 3:12;
1348 Mt 7:21–23;
1358 Mt 13:30,40–43,49,50;
1364 Mt 16:27; **1374** Mt 22:13;
1380 Mt 25:31–46; **1407** Mk 8:38;
1436 Lk 3:17;
1457 Lk 12:2–5,47,48;
1460 Lk 13:6–9,24–30;
1473 Lk 19:12–27;
1497 Jn 5:22,27,30;
1503 Jn 8:15–16,26;
1506 Jn 9:39; **1512** Jn 12:47–48;
1549 Ac 10:42; **1621** 2Co 5:10;
1660 2Th 1:7–8; **1672** 2Ti 4:1,8;
1741 Rev 19:11

K

Kadesh, Kadesh Barnea
73 Ge 16:14; **248** Nu 13:26;
258 Nu 20:1–22; **277** Nu 32:8;
284 Dt 1:2; **342** Jos 10:41

King
God **413** 1Sa 8:7; **763** Ps 10:16;
774 Ps 24:7–10; **778** Ps 29:10;
838 Ps 93:1; **839** Ps 95:3;
840 Ps 96:10; **841** Ps 98:6;
841 Ps 99:1; **967** Isa 6:5;
1004 Isa 33:22; **1075** Jer 10:10;
1328 Zec 14:9,16; **1664** 1Ti 1:17;
1736 Rev 15:3
Christ **1381** Mt 25:34,40;
1474 Lk 19:38; **1498** Jn 6:15;
1511 Jn 12:15; **1521** Jn 18:37;
1560 Ac 17:7; **1738** Rev 17:14;
1741 Rev 19:16

King of the Jews
1340 Mt 2:2; **1385** Mt 27:11,29,37;
1423 Mk 15:2,9,12,18,26;
1482 Lk 23:3,37,38;
1520 Jn 18:33,39;
1521 Jn 19:3,14–15,19,21

King of Israel
1387 Mt 27:42; **1424** Mk 15:32;
1489 Jn 1:49; **1511** Jn 12:13

Kingdom of heaven
characteristics of **1349** Mt 8:11–12;
1354 Mt 11:11–12; **1445** Lk 7:28;
1461 Lk 13:28–30;

1468 Lk 17:20−21;
1479 Lk 22:29−30; **1521** Jn 18:36;
1539 Ac 6−7; **1595** Ro 14:17;
1603 1Co 4:20; **1614** 1Co 15:50;
1692 Heb 12:28; **1696** Jas 2:5;
1732 Rev 11:15
entrance into **1343** Mt 5:3,10,19,20;
1347 Mt 6:33; **1348** Mt 7:21;
1366 Mt 18:1−4; **1368** Mt 19:24;
1373 Mt 21:31,43; **1375** Mt 23:13;
1410 Mk 9:47;
1410 Mk 10:14,15,23−25;
1417 Mk 12:34; **1443** Lk 6:20;
1459 Lk 12:31−32; **1466** Lk 16:16;
1471 Lk 18:16,17,24−30;
1483 Lk 23:42; **1491** Jn 3:3−5;
1555 Ac 14:22; **1604** 1Co 6:9−10;
1634 Gal 5:21; **1640** Eph 5:5;
1650 Col 1:13
imminence of **1341** Mt 3:2;
1343 Mt 4:17; **1352** Mt 10:7;
1355 Mt 12:28; **1391** Mk 1:15;
1407 Mk 9:1; **1451** Lk 9:27;
1452 Lk 10:9−11; **1456** Lk 11:20;
1478 Lk 21:31
parables of **1356** Mt 13:1−52;
1367 Mt 18:23−35;
1369 Mt 20:1−16;
1374 Mt 22:2−14;
1378 Mt 25:1−30;
1398 Mk 4:26−32;
1461 Lk 13:18−21;
1462 Lk 14:15−24;
1473 Lk 19:11−17

Knowledge
54 Ge 2:9; **266** Nu 24:16;
876 Ps 139:6; **897** Pr 9:10;
903 Pr 14:6; **905** Pr 15:2;
1240 Da 12:4; **1431** Lk 1:77;
1457 Lk 11:52; **1600** 1Co 1:5;
1606 1Co 8:1,11; **1665** 1Ti 2:4

L

Lamb
81 Ge 22:7−8; **149** Ex 12:3,5;
200 Lev 9:3; **219** Lev 23:19;
658 2Ch 35:11; **1036** Isa 53:7;
1077 Jer 11:19 **1420** Mk 14:12;
1478 Lk 22:7;
figure or title of Christ
1489 Jn 1:29,36; **1603** 1Co 5:7;
1701 1Pe 1:19;
1727 Rev 5:6,8,12,13;
1729 Rev 7:9,10,14,17;
1733 Rev 12:11; **1738** Rev 17:14;
1740 Rev 19:7,9;
1742 Rev 21:9,14,22,23,27;
1743 Rev 22:1,3

Laodicea
1651 Col 2:1; **1654** Col 4:13−16;
1723 Rev 1:11; **1726** Rev 3:14−22

Lazarus
1467 Lk 16:20;
1508 Jn 11:1−16,38−44;
1511 Jn 12:1,10,17

Leper, Leprosy
247 Nu 12:9−15;
540 2Ki 5:1,11,27; **545** 2Ki 7:3,8;
646 2Ch 26:21,23; **1348** Mt 8:1−4;
1382 Mt 26:6; **1393** Mk 1:40;

1419 Mk 14:3; **1438** Lk 4:27;
1440 Lk 5:12−16; **1468** Lk 17:12

Levite
142 Ex 6:16−25;
179 Ex 32:26−29;
229 Nu 1:47−53; **231** Nu 3:5−51;
241 Nu 8:5−26; **281** Nu 35:2−8;
299 Dt 12:12,19; **304** Dt 17:9,18;
305 Dt 18:1−8; **313** Dt 26:11−13;
339 Jos 8:33; **388** Jdg 17:7—
18:20; **390** Jdg 19:1;
630 2Ch 11:14; **669** Ezr 6:18;
671 Ezr 8:15−20;
1111 Jer 33:18,21−22;
1453 Lk 10:32; **1488** Jn 1:19;
1536 Ac 4:36

Lord's Prayer
1346 Mt 6:9−13; **1454** Lk 11:2−4

Lord's Supper
1382 Mt 26:26−30;
1420 Mk 14:22−26;
1478 Lk 22:15−20;
1609 1Co 11:23−25

Lot
went to Canaan **67** Ge 11:31;
67 Ge 12:5
settled in Sodom **69** Ge 13
rescued by Abram **70** Ge 14:1−16
sheltered angels **76** Ge 19:1−11
fled to Zoar **77** Ge 19:15−23
Lot and his daughters
78 Ge 19:30−38

Love
God **163** Ex 20:6; **180** Ex 34:6;
291 Dt 5:10; **293** Dt 7:7;
775 Ps 25:6−7,10; **845** Ps 103:17;
1037 Isa 54:8,10;
1254 Hos 11:1−4,8,9;
1492 Jn 3:16; **1515** Jn 14:23;
1518 Jn 16:27; **1584** Ro 5:5,8;
1589 Ro 8:39; **1637** Eph 1:5;
1638 Eph 2:4; **1712** 1Jn 3:1;
1714 1Jn 4:7−12
Christ **1508** Jn 11:3,5;
1513 Jn 13:1,34; **1516** Jn 14:31;
1516 Jn 15:9−10,12;
1588 Ro 8:35,37; **1621** 2Co 5:14;
1631 Gal 2:20; **1639** Eph 3:19;
1640 Eph 5:2; **1723** Rev 1:5
other **898** Pr 10:12;
1346 Mt 5:43−48; **1368** Mt 19:19;
1443 Lk 6:27−36; **1516** Jn 15:13;
1611 1Co 13; **1634** Gal 5:6,13,14;
1641 Eph 5:22−33;
1712 1Jn 2:15; **1714** 1Jn 4:19−21

Luke
1654 Col 4:14; **1672** 2Ti 4:11;
1679 Phm 24

Lydia
1557 Ac 16:14,40

Lystra
1554 Ac 14:6,8,21;
1557 Ac 16:1−2; **1672** 2Ti 3:11

M

Macedonia
1557 Ac 16:9−10,12;
1564 Ac 19:21−22;
1565 Ac 20:1,3; **1596** Ro 15:26;

1619 2Co 2:13; **1622** 2Co 7:5;
1623 2Co 8:1; **1647** Php 4:15;
1655 1Th 1:7−8; **1664** 1Ti 1:3

Malchus
1383 Mt 26:51; **1422** Mk 14:47;
1480 Lk 22:50−51; **1519** Jn 18:10

Manna
157 Ex 16:22−35; **245** Nu 11:7−9;
334 Jos 5:10−12; **688** Ne 9:20;
1498 Jn 6:31,49; **1687** Heb 9:4;
1725 Rev 2:17

Marriage
94 Ge 29:15−30;
401 Ru 4:10−16; **1345** Mt 5:32;
1490 Jn 2:1−10; **1586** Ro 7;
1641 Eph 5:22−23
1605 1Co 7:1−16,25−40;
1665 1Ti 3:2,12; **1692** Heb 13:4

Martha
1454 Lk 10:38−41;
1508 Jn 11:1−40; **1511** Jn 12:2

Mary
mother of Jesus
1338 Mt 1:16,18,20; **1340** Mt 2:11;
1359 Mt 13:55; **1401** Mk 6:3;
1429 Lk 1:27,30,34,38,39,
1430 Lk 1:41,46,56;
1432 Lk 2:5,16,19,34;
1490 Jn 2:1−5,12;
1522 Jn 19:25−27; **1530** Ac 1:14
Magdalene **1387** Mt 27:56,61;
1388 Mt 28:1; **1425** Mk 15:40,47;
1425 Mk 16:1,9; **1447** Lk 8:2;
1484 Lk 24:10; **1522** Jn 19:25;
1523 Jn 20:1−18
other **1387** Mt 27:56,61;
1388 Mt 28:1; **1425** Mk 15:40,47;
1425 Mk 16:1; **1454** Lk 10:39,42;
1484 Lk 24:10; **1522** Jn 19:25;
1508 Jn 11:1−2,19,20,28,
1509 Jn 11:31−32,45;
1511 Jn 12:3; **1551** Ac 12:12

Matthew
1351 Mt 9:9; **1352** Mt 10:3;
1396 Mk 3:18; **1441** Lk 5:27−29;
1443 Lk 6:15; **1530** Ac 1:13

Matthias
1530 Ac 1:23,26

Melchizedek
70 Ge 14:18−20; **855** Ps 110:4;
1683 Heb 5:6,10; **1684** Heb 6:20;
1685 Heb 7:1−11,15−17

Mercy, pity
180 Ex 33:19; **180** Ex 34:6−7;
290 Dt 4:31; **775** Ps 25:16;
845 Ps 103:8; **1236** Da 9:9;
1286 Jnh 4:2; **1351** Mt 9:27;
1362 Mt 15:22; **1365** Mt 17:15;
1370 Mt 20:30−31;
1430 Lk 1:50,54,58,72,78;
1443 Lk 6:36;
1589 Ro 9:15−16,18,23;
1592 Ro 11:30−32; **1638** Eph 2:4;
1664 1Ti 1:2,13,16; **1677** Tit 3:5;
1681 Heb 2:17; **1701** 1Pe 1:3;
1702 1Pe 2:10; **1722** Jude 1:21

Michael
1237 Da 10:13,21; **1240** Da 12:1;
1720 Jude 1:9; **1733** Rev 12:7

Midian(ites)
86 Ge 25:4; 109 Ge 36:35;
111 Ge 37:28,36; 136 Ex 3:1;
261 Nu 22:4,7; 266 Nu 25;
275 Nu 31; 369 Jdg 6—8;
970 Isa 9:4; 1045 Isa 60:6;
1541 Ac 7:29

Miracles of Jesus
general 1343 Mt 4:23—24;
1349 Mt 8:16; 1352 Mt 9:35;
1355 Mt 12:15;
1360 Mt 14:14,35—36;
1362 Mt 15:30—31; 1368 Mt 19:2;
1372 Mt 21:14;
1392 Mk 1:32—34,39;
1395 Mk 3:9—12;
1401 Mk 6:5,53—56;
1439 Lk 4:40—41; 1440 Lk 5:15;
1443 Lk 6:18—19; 1445 Lk 7:21;
1450 Lk 9:11; 1491 Jn 2:23;
1491 Jn 3:2; 1497 Jn 6:2;
1512 Jn 12:37; 1525 Jn 20:30;
1549 Ac 10:38
driving out demons: blind and dumb
1355 Mt 12:22
daughter of woman of Tyre
1362 Mt 15:21—28;
1405 Mk 7:24—30
dumb man 1352 Mt 9:32—33;
1456 Lk 11:14
epileptic boy 1365 Mt 17:14—20;
1408 Mk 9:14—21;
1451 Lk 9:37—43
Gerasene man 1398 Mk 5:1—20;
1448 Lk 8:26—39
man in Capernaum
1391 Mk 1:23—28;
1439 Lk 4:33—37
Mary Magdalene 1425 Mk 16:9;
1447 Lk 8:2
men of Gadara 1350 Mt 8:28—34
woman in synagogue
1460 Lk 13:10—17
other cures
blind Bartimaeus
1370 Mt 20:29—34;
1413 Mk 10:46—52;
1472 Lk 18:35—43
blind man at Bethsaida
1406 Mk 8:22—26
man born blind 1505 Jn 9:1—7
two blind men 1351 Mt 9:27—31
deaf-mute 1405 Mk 7:31—37
man with leprosy 1348 Mt 8:1—4;
1393 Mk 1:40—45;
1440 Lk 5:12—16
man with shriveled hand
1355 Mt 12:9—14; 1395 Mk 3:1—6;
1442 Lk 6:6—11
man with dropsy 1462 Lk 14:1—6
centurion's servant 1349 Mt 8:5—13;
1444 Lk 7:1—10
paralyzed man in Capernaum
1350 Mt 9:1—8; 1393 Mk 2:1—12;
1441 Lk 5:17—26
paralyzed man in Jerusalem
1495 Jn 5:1—9
Peter's mother-in-law
1349 Mt 8:14—15;
1392 Mk 1:29—31;
1439 Lk 4:38—39

Servant of high priest
1480 Lk 22:50—51
son of official 1495 Jn 4:46—54
ten men with leprosy
1468 Lk 17:11—19
woman with severe bleeding
1351 Mt 9:20—22;
1400 Mk 5:23—34;
1449 Lk 8:43—48
raising of dead:
daughter of Jairus
1351 Mt 9:18—26;
1399 Mk 5:21—43;
1449 Lk 8:40—56
son of widow of Nain
1445 Lk 7:11—17
Lazarus 1508 Jn 11:1—44
other miracles:
coin in the fish's mouth
1365 Mt 17:24—27
cursing the fig tree 1372 Mt 21:19;
1414 Mk 11:14,20
feeding the five thousand
1360 Mt 14:13—21;
1403 Mk 6:30—44;
1450 Lk 9:10—17; 1497 Jn 6:1—14
feeding the four thousand
1362 Mt 15:32—39;
1406 Mk 8:1—10
great catch of fish 1439 Lk 5:4—10
another catch of fish
1526 Jn 21:6—11
calming the storm 1350 Mt 8:23—27;
1398 Mk 4:35—41;
1448 Lk 8:22—25
walking on the water
1360 Mt 14:22—33;
1404 Mk 6:45—52;
1498 Jn 6:16—21
water changed to wine
1490 Jn 2:1—11

Miracles of others
of Moses 138 Ex 4:3—7;
143 Ex 7:10—10:28;
154 Ex 14:21—28; 156 Ex 15:25;
158 Ex 17:6; 254 Nu 16:28—34;
258 Nu 20:11; 259 Nu 21:8—9
of Joshua 331 Jos 3; 334 Jos 6;
341 Jos 10:12—14
of Samuel 419 1Sa 12:18
of Elijah 520 1Ki 17:1,14,22;
524 1Ki 18:38,41—45;
534 2Ki 1:10; 535 2Ki 2:8
of Elisha 535 2Ki 2:14,21,24;
537 2Ki 3:16—20;
537 2Ki 4:4—7,35,41,43—44;
541 2Ki 5:10,14,27;
542 2Ki 6:6,18; 554 2Ki 13:21
of Isaiah 565 2Ki 20:7,11
of Daniel 1232 Da 6:22
of apostles 1352 Mt 10:1,8;
1401 Mk 6:7,13; 1450 Lk 9:2,6;
1537 Ac 5:12,16
of the seventy-two 1452 Lk 10:9,17
of Philip 1542 Ac 8:6,7,13
of Peter 1533 Ac 3:6—8;
1547 Ac 9:34,40—41
of Paul 1552 Ac 13:11;
1554 Ac 14:9,10; 1558 Ac 16:18;
1564 Ac 19:11—12;
1627 2Co 12:12

Moab(ite)
78 Ge 19:37; 155 Ex 15:15;
259 Nu 21:11—15,26—30;
261 Nu 22:1—36; 266 Nu 25:1;
284 Dt 1:5; 326 Dt 34:1—8;
365 Jdg 3:12—30;
396 Ru 1:1—6:22; 536 2Ki 3:4—26;
980 Isa 15:1—9; 980 Isa 16:2—14;
1126 Jer 48:1—47

Moses
born 134 Ex 2:1—4
adopted by Pharaoh's daughter
134 Ex 2:5—10
killed Egyptian 135 Ex 2:11—12
fled to Midian 135 Ex 2:15—20
married Zipporah 136 Ex 2:21—22
called by God 136 Ex 3:1—4:17
returned to Egypt 139 Ex 4:18—31
interceded with Pharaoh
139 Ex 5—11
crossed the Red Sea 152 Ex 14
song of victory 154 Ex 15:1—18
appointed judges 160 Ex 18:13—26
met with God on Sinai
161 Ex 19:3—13; 168 Ex 24—31
enraged by Israel's idolatry
177 Ex 32
talked with the Lord 179 Ex 33—34
built Tabernacle 182 Ex 35—40
counted the people 228 Nu 1
defended before Aaron and Miriam
246 Nu 12
sent twelve spies to Canaan
248 Nu 13:1—20
consecrated Joshua as his
successor 271 Nu 27:18—23;
321 Dt 31:23
described Israel's history
284 Dt 1—3
urged Israel to be obedient
289 Dt 4:1—40
song of Moses 321 Dt 32:1—43
looked at Canaan 288 Dt 3:23—27;
324 Dt 32:48—52; 326 Dt 34:1—4
blessed the tribes 324 Dt 33
death and burial in Moab
327 Dt 34:5—7
see also 329 Jos 1:5; 822 Ps 77:20;
845 Ps 103:7; 1293 Mic 6:4;
1348 Mt 8:4; 1364 Mt 17:3—4;
1368 Mt 19:7—8;
1468 Lk 16:29,31; 1476 Lk 20:37;
1491 Jn 3:14; 1497 Jn 5:45—46;
1506 Jn 9:28—29; 1534 Ac 3:22;
1539 Ac 6:11,14;
1540 Ac 7:20—44;
1555 Ac 15:1,21; 1589 Ro 9:15;
1590 Ro 10:5,19;
1619 2Co 3:7,13;
1682 Heb 3:2—5,16;
1690 Heb 11:23—24;
1720 Jude 1:9; 1736 Rev 15:3
Law of, 339 Jos 8:31—32;
358 Jos 23:6; 493 1Ki 2:3;
570 2Ki 23:25; 664 Ezr 3:2;
685 Ne 8:1; 1417 Mk 12:26;
1433 Lk 2:22; 1487 Lk 24:44;
1488 Jn 1:17,45; 1553 Ac 13:39;
1555 Ac 15:5; 1577 Ac 28:23;
1620 2Co 3:15

Mount of Olives
473 2Sa 15:30; **1328** Zec 14:4;
1371 Mt 21:1; **1377** Mt 24:3;
1383 Mt 26:30; **1413** Mk 11:1;
1418 Mk 13:3; **1420** Mk 14:26;
1474 Lk 19:29,37; **1478** Lk 21:37;
1480 Lk 22:39; **1502** Jn 8:1;
1530 Ac 1:12

N

Naaman
540 2Ki 5:1–27; **1438** Lk 4:27
Nain
1445 Lk 7:11
Naomi
396 Ru 1:2—4:17
Nathan
458 2Sa 7:2–17;
(**601** 1Ch 17:1–15);
464 2Sa 12:1–23; **491** 1Ki 1:8–45
Nathanael
1489 Jn 1:45–49; **1525** Jn 21:2
Nazareth
1341 Mt 2:23; **1372** Mt 21:11;
1391 Mk 1:9; **1392** Mk 1:24;
1429 Lk 1:26; **1437** Lk 4:16;
1489 Jn 1:45–46
Nazirite
236 Nu 6:2–21; **381** Jdg 13:5–7;
386 Jdg 16:17; **1268** Am 2:11–12
Nebuchadnezzar
571 2Ki 24—25; **659** 2Ch 36;
1090 Jer 21:2,7; **1117** Jer 39:1,5;
1123 Jer 46:2,13,26;
1142 Jer 52:4,12,28–30;
1187 Eze 26:7;
1192 Eze 29:18–19;
1222 Da 2—4
Nicodemus
1491 Jn 3:1–10; **1501** Jn 7:50;
1523 Jn 19:39
Nile
116 Ge 41:1–3,17,18;
134 Ex 1:22; **144** Ex 7:17–25;
984 Isa 19:5–8; **1275** Am 8:8
Nineveh
65 Ge 10:11–12; **565** 2Ki 19:36;
1282 Jnh 1:2; **1284** Jnh 3:2–7;
1286 Jnh 4:11; **1298** Na 1:1;
1299 Na 2:8; **1300** Na 3:7;
1356 Mt 12:41; **1456** Lk 11:30,32
Noah
59 Ge 5:29—9:29; **1037** Isa 54:9;
1169 Eze 14:14;
1378 Mt 24:37–38;
1469 Lk 17:26–27;
1690 Heb 11:7; **1704** 1Pe 3:20;
1708 2Pe 2:5

O

Obedience
to God or Christ **161** Ex 19:5;
290 Dt 4:30; **319** Dt 30:2,8,10,16;
361 Jos 24:24; **425** 1Sa 15:22;
1070 Jer 7:23; **1392** Mk 1:27;
1398 Mk 4:41; **1493** Jn 3:36;
1538 Ac 5:29,32; **1684** Heb 5:8–9;
1714 1Jn 5:2

to demands of the gospel
1586 Ro 6:16–17; **1619** 2Co 2:9;
1623 2Co 7:15; **1645** Php 2:12;
1660 2Th 1:8; **1661** 2Th 3:14;
to human beings **92** Ge 28:7;
129 Ge 49:10; **329** Jos 1:17;
699 Est 2:20; **1112** Jer 35:8;
1538 Ac 5:28–29; **1594** Ro 13:1,5;
1641 Eph 6:1,5; **1677** Tit 3:1;
1702 1Pe 2:13–17; **1703** 1Pe 3:6
Onesimus
1654 Col 4:9; **1679** Phm 10

P

Pamphylia
1531 Ac 2:10; **1552** Ac 13:13;
1555 Ac 14:24; **1557** Ac 15:38;
1575 Ac 27:5
Parables of Jesus
reason and use
1356 Mt 13:1–17,34–35;
1397 Mk 4:10–12;
1447 Lk 8:9–10,16–18
told by Jesus:
children playing **1354** Mt 11:16–19;
1445 Lk 7:31–35
faithful servant **1378** Mt 24:45–51;
1459 Lk 12:42–46
fig tree **1378** Mt 24:32–33;
1419 Mk 13:28–29;
1478 Lk 21:29–31
friend at midnight **1455** Lk 11:5–8
Good Samaritan **1453** Lk 10:29–37
great banquet **1462** Lk 14:15–24
hidden treasure **1359** Mt 13:44
house owner **1359** Mt 13:51–52
king going to war **1463** Lk 14:31–32
lamp under a bowl **1344** Mt 5:15;
1397 Mk 4:21; **1447** Lk 8:16;
1456 Lk 11:33
lost coin **1464** Lk 15:8–10
lost sheep **1366** Mt 18:10–14;
1463 Lk 15:3–7
lost son **1464** Lk 15:11–32
mustard seed **1358** Mt 13:31–32;
1398 Mk 4:30–32;
1461 Lk 13:18–19
net **1359** Mt 13:47–50
new patch **1351** Mt 9:16;
1394 Mk 2:21; **1441** Lk 5:36
pearl **1359** Mt 13:45–46
Pharisee and tax collector
1470 Lk 18:9–14
places at wedding banquet
1462 Lk 14:7–11
rich fool **1458** Lk 12:16–21
rich man and Lazarus
1467 Lk 16:19–31
seed growing **1398** Mk 4:26–29
servant **1468** Lk 17:7–10
shrewd manager **1465** Lk 16:1–9
sower **1356** Mt 13:3–9,18–23;
1397 Mk 4:2–9,13–20;
1447 Lk 8:5–8,11–15
ten minas **1473** Lk 19:11–27
ten virgins **1378** Mt 25:1–13
tenants in vineyard
1373 Mt 21:33–46;
1415 Mk 12:1–12;
1475 Lk 20:9–18
talents **1379** Mt 25:14–30

tower builder **1463** Lk 14:28–30
two debtors **1446** Lk 7:40–43
wise and foolish builders
1348 Mt 7:24–27;
1444 Lk 6:47–49
two sons **1373** Mt 21:28–32
unmerciful servant
1367 Mt 18:23–35
unfruitful fig tree **1460** Lk 13:6–9
watchful house owner
1378 Mt 24:42–44;
1459 Lk 12:39–40
watchful servants
1419 Mk 13:33–37;
1459 Lk 12:35–38
wedding banquet **1374** Mt 22:1–14
wedding guests **1351** Mt 9:15;
1394 Mk 2:19–20;
1441 Lk 5:34–35
weeds **1358** Mt 13:24–30,36–43
persistent widow **1470** Lk 18:1–8
wine and wineskins **1351** Mt 9:17;
1394 Mk 2:22; **1441** Lk 5:37–38
workers in vineyard
1369 Mt 20:1–16
yeast **1358** Mt 13:33;
1461 Lk 13:20–21
Paradise
1483 Lk 23:43; **1626** 2Co 12:3–4
Passover
149 Ex 12:18,19,27,43–48;
151 Ex 13:3–10; **303** Dt 16:1–8;
334 Jos 5:10; **570** 2Ki 23:21–23;
(**657** 2Ch 35:1–19);
669 Ezr 6:19–20;
1382 Mt 26:2,5,17–19;
1386 Mt 27:15;
1419 Mk 14:1,2,12,14,16;
1424 Mk 15:6; **1434** Lk 2:41–43;
1478 Lk 22:1,8,13;
1491 Jn 2:13,23; **1497** Jn 6:4;
1510 Jn 11:55–56;
1511 Jn 12:1,12,20;
1513 Jn 13:1,29; **1521** Jn 19:14;
1550 Ac 12:4; **1603** 1Co 5:7;
1690 Heb 11:28
Patmos
1723 Rev 1:9
Paul
early life:
born in Tarsus **1568** Ac 22:3
sister **1570** Ac 23:16
educated in Jerusalem under
Gamaliel **1568** Ac 22:3
tent maker by trade **1561** Ac 18:3
approved of Stephen's death
1542 Ac 7:58; **1542** Ac 8:1
persecuted Christians **1542** Ac 8:3;
1568 Ac 22:4–5;
1573 Ac 26:10–11
see also **1613** 1Co 15:9;
1630 Gal 1:13; **1646** Php 3:6;
1664 1Ti 1:13
conversion **1544** Ac 9:3–19;
1568 Ac 22:6–16;
1573 Ac 26:12–18
early ministry
Arabia **1630** Gal 1:17
Damascus **1545** Ac 9:19b–25;
1574 Ac 26:20;

1626 2Co 11:32–33;
1630 Gal 1:17
Jerusalem **1546** Ac 9:26–29;
  1574 Ac 26:20; **1630** Gal 1:18–19
Tarsus **1546** Ac 9:30
Antioch **1550** Ac 11:25–30;
missionary work
first journey **1552** Ac 13:1—14:28
Jerusalem council
  1555 Ac 15:1–29;
  1631 Gal 2:1–10
second journey **1557** Ac 15:36—
  18:23
third journey **1562** Ac 18:23b—
  20:38
return to be a disciple
  1566 Ac 21:1–26
arrest and imprisonment:
arrest in Jerusalem
  1567 Ac 21:27—23:22
imprisonment and trial in
Caesarea **1570** Ac 23:23—26:32
voyage to Rome
  1575 Ac 27:1—28:16
ministry in Rome **1577** Ac 28:17–31

Peace
  371 Jdg 6:23–24;
  632 2Ch 14:6–7; **778** Ps 29:11;
  970 Isa 9:6; **1037** Isa 54:10;
  1433 Lk 2:14,29; **1516** Jn 14:27;
  1518 Jn 16:33; **1584** Ro 5:1;
  1596 Ro 15:13,33;
  1629 2Co 13:11;
  1638 Eph 2:14–18; **1644** Php 1:2;
  1647 Php 4:7,9; **1650** Col 1:2,20;
  1652 Col 3:15; **1662** 2Th 3:16

Pentecost
  1530 Ac 2:1; **1565** Ac 20:16;
  1615 1Co 16:8

Persia
  661 2Ch 36:20–23;
  662 Ezr 1:1–2,8; **665** Ezr 3:7;
  665 Ezr 4:3–5,24;
  697 Est 1:3,14,18,19;
  1230 Da 5:28; **1231** Da 6:8,12,15;
  1235 Da 8:20

Peter
call to be a disciple
  1343 Mt 4:18–19;
  1391 Mk 1:16–18;
  1439 Lk 5:1–11; **1489** Jn 1:41–42
declaration about Jesus
  1363 Mt 16:13–20;
  1407 Mk 8:27–30;
  1450 Lk 9:18–21;
  1500 Jn 6:68–69
on Mount of Transfiguration
  1364 Mt 17:1–13;
  1407 Mk 9:2–13;
  1451 Lk 9:28–36;
  1707 2Pe 1:16–18
in the Garden of Gethsemane
  1383 Mt 26:36–46;
  1421 Mk 14:32–42;
  1480 Lk 22:39–46
denies Jesus **1385** Mt 26:69–74;
  1422 Mk 14:66–72;
  1480 Lk 22:56–62;
  1520 Jn 18:15–18,25–27
sees risen Lord **1487** Lk 24:36–49;
  1525 Jn 21:1–23; **1613** 1Co 15:5

sermon at Pentecost
  1531 Ac 2:14–41
activity in Jerusalem, Judea, and
  Samaria **1533** Ac 3:1—5:41;
  1543 Ac 8:14–25; **1546** Ac 9:32—
  12:19; **1555** Ac 15:6–11
rebuked by Paul at Antioch
  1631 Gal 2:11–14
prediction of his death
  1528 Jn 21:18–19
letters **1701** 1Pe 1:1; **1707** 2Pe 1:1

Pharaoh
and Abraham **68** Ge 12:15–20
and Joseph **116** Ge 41:1–55;
  126 Ge 47:1–26;
  1540 Ac 7:10,13,21
in bondage **134** Ex 1:8–11,15–22;
  135 Ex 2:15,23
the Exodus **137** Ex 3:11;
  139 Ex 4:21–23; **139** Ex 5:1–23;
  141 Ex 6—14; **155** Ex 15:19;
  1589 Ro 9:17
and Solomon **495** 1Ki 3:1;
  507 1Ki 9:16; **510** 1Ki 11:1
and Hadad of Edom
  511 1Ki 11:18–22
Pharaoh Neco **570** 2Ki 23:29–35
Pharaoh Hophra **1123** Jer 44:30

Pharisees
  1341 Mt 3:7; **1351** Mt 9:11,14,34;
  1354 Mt 12:2,14,24,38;
  1361 Mt 15:1,12;
  1363 Mt 16:1,6,11–12;
  1368 Mt 19:3; **1374** Mt 22:15;
  1375 Mt 23:2,13–15,23,25–29;
  1387 Mt 27:62; **1446** Lk 7:36–50;
  1466 Lk 16:14; **1470** Lk 18:10–11;
  1488 Jn 1:24; **1491** Jn 3:1;
  1501 Jn 7:32,45–48;
  1555 Ac 15:5; **1569** Ac 23:6–9;
  1573 Ac 26:5

Philadelphia
  1726 Rev 3:7

Philemon
  1678 Phm 1

Philip
  1401 Mk 6:17; **1435** Lk 3:1;
  1352 Mt 10:3; **1359** Mt 14:3;
  1489 Jn 1:43–48; **1497** Jn 6:5–7;
  1511 Jn 12:21–22;
  1515 Jn 14:8–9; **1539** Ac 6:5;
  1542 Ac 8:5–40; **1567** Ac 21:8

Philippi
  1557 Ac 16:12; **1565** Ac 20:6;
  1644 Php 1:1; **1655** 1Th 2:2

Philippian jailer
  1559 Ac 16:27–34

Philistines
  65 Ge 10:14; **80** Ge 21:32,34;
  364 Jdg 3:3,31; **378** Jdg 10:6,7,11;
  381 Jdg 13:1,5; **382** Jdg 14:1–4;
  384 Jdg 15—16; **410** 1Sa 4—6;
  420 1Sa 13:1—14:31;
  429 1Sa 17:19–51;
  1126 Jer 47:1–7;
  1186 Eze 25:15–17

Pilate
  1385 Mt 27; **1423** Mk 15;
  1435 Lk 3:1; **1460** Lk 13:1;
  1482 Lk 23; **1519** Jn 18—19;

1534 Ac 3:13; **1536** Ac 4:27;
1553 Ac 13:28; **1669** 1Ti 6:13

Plagues
  143 Ex 7:10–11; **246** Nu 11:33;
  251 Nu 14:37; **254** Nu 16:47;
  267 Nu 25:9; **606** 1Ch 21:22;
  1328 Zec 14:12

Prayers
in OT **87** Ge 25:21;
  404 1Sa 1:10–17,26–27;
  406 1Sa 2:1–10;
  459 2Sa 7:18–27;
  504 1Ki 8:22–54;
  524 1Ki 18:36–37;
  563 2Ki 19:14–19;
  602 1Ch 17:16–27;
  616 1Ch 29:10–19;
  624 2Ch 6:13—7:1;
  677 Ne 1:5–11; **687** Ne 9:5–37;
  758 Ps 4:1; **905** Pr 15:8,29;
  1010 Isa 38:5; **1076** Lk 10:23–25;
  1235 Da 9:3–23; **1283** Jnh 2
teaching of Jesus **1346** Mt 5:44;
  1346 Mt 6:5–15;
  1454 Lk 11:1–13; **1470** Lk 18:1–8
in life of Jesus **1360** Mt 14:19,23;
  1383 Mt 26:36–44; **1392** Mk 1:35;
  1421 Mk 14:32–39; **1436** Lk 3:21;
  1441 Lk 5:16; **1442** Lk 6:12;
  1454 Lk 11:1; **1480** Lk 22:41–45;
  1518 Jn 17:1–26; **1683** Heb 5:7
teaching in the letters **1588** Ro 8:26;
  1612 1Co 14:13–15;
  1643 Eph 6:18; **1647** Php 4:6;
  1659 1Th 5:17; **1665** 1Ti 2:1,8;
  1698 Jas 5:13–18;
  1722 Jude 1:20

Preach
  1343 Mt 4:17,23; **1352** Mt 10:7;
  1353 Mt 11:5; **1377** Mt 24:14;
  1396 Mk 3:14; **1418** Mk 13:10;
  1427 Mk 16:15;
  1438 Lk 4:18–21,43,44;
  1531 Ac 2:14–40;
  1534 Ac 4:8–12;
  1542 Ac 8:4,25,40;
  1549 Ac 10:34–43;
  1553 Ac 13:16–41;
  1565 Ac 20:7–9,18–35;
  1666 1Ti 4:13; **1672** 2Ti 4:2;
  1704 1Pe 3:19; **1704** 1Pe 4:6

Predestined
  1588 Ro 8:30

Priscilla
  1561 Ac 18:2,18,26; **1597** Ro 16:3;
  1615 1Co 16:19; **1674** 2Ti 4:19

Prophets
of OT **78** Ge 20:7; **246** Nu 11:29;
  247 Nu 12:6; **300** Dt 13:1–3,5;
  305 Dt 18:15,18–22;
  328 Dt 34:10–12; **415** 1Sa 9:9;
  417 1Sa 10:5–6,10–13;
  445 1Sa 28:6,15; **1057** Jer 1:5;
  1081 Jer 14:14–16;
  1093 Jer 23:9,11–31;
  1100 Jer 27:9–10,14–18;
  1167 Eze 13.2–10,16;
  1322 Zec 7:3; **1327** Zec 13:3–6;
  1339 Mt 1:22;
  1340 Mt 2:5,15,17,23;

1343 Mt 4:14; **1354** Mt 11:13;
1376 Mt 23:29–31,37;
1461 Lk 13:34; **1531** Ac 2:16,30;
1534 Ac 3:18,21,24,25;
1543 Ac 8:28,30,34; **1580** Ro 1:2;
1680 Heb 1:1; **1701** 1Pe 1:10
of NT
Anna **1433** Lk 2:36
John the Baptist **1353** Mt 11:9;
1359 Mt 14:5; **1372** Mt 21:26;
1415 Mk 11:32; **1431** Lk 1:76;
1445 Lk 7:26; **1475** Lk 20:6
Jesus **1359** Mt 13:57;
1372 Mt 21:11,46; **1401** Mk 6:15;
1445 Lk 7:16,39; **1461** Lk 13:33;
1485 Lk 24:19; **1493** Jn 4:19,44;
1506 Jn 9:17
"the Prophet" **1488** Jn 1:21,25;
1498 Jn 6:14; **1501** Jn 7:40;
1534 Ac 3:22–23
Christian **1550** Ac 11:27–28;
1552 Ac 13:1; **1557** Ac 15:32;
1611 1Co 12:28–29;
1639 Eph 4:11;
1739 Rev 18:20,24;
1743 Rev 22:9
the two witnesses
1732 Rev 11:3–12

Q

Quail
156 Ex 16:13; **246** Nu 11:31,32;
848 Ps 105:40

Quarrel(ing)
908 Pr 17:14; **911** Pr 19:13;
1600 1Co 1:11–17;
1627 2Co 12:20

Quirinius
1432 Lk 2:2

R

Rachel
93 Ge 29:6–31; **95** Ge 30:1–8;
98 Ge 31:4–5,14–16,19,32–35;
102 Ge 33; **107** Ge 35:16–20;
1105 Jer 31:15; **1340** Mt 2:18

Rahab
329 Jos 2:1–21;
336 Jos 6:22–25; **1338** Mt 1:5;
1691 Heb 11:31; **1696** Jas 2:25

Rebecca
82 Ge 22:23; **84** Ge 24:15–67;
87 Ge 25:21–28;
90 Ge 27:1–28:5; **1589** Ro 9:10

Redeemer
728 Job 19:25; **771** Ps 19:14;
824 Ps 78:35; **1015** Isa 41:14;
1020 Isa 44:6; **1026** Isa 47:4;
1037 Isa 54:8; **1044** Isa 59:20;
1136 Jer 50:34

Red Sea
152 Ex 13:18; **152** Ex 14:1–29;
154 Ex 15:1–22;
849 Ps 106:7–9,21–22;
1541 Ac 7:36; **1608** 1Co 10:1–2;
1690 Heb 11:29

Repent
754 Job 42:6; **1318** Zec 1:6;
1341 Mt 3:2,8,11; **1343** Mt 4:17;

1441 Lk 5:32; **1464** Lk 15:7,10;
1487 Lk 24:47; **1532** Ac 2:38;
1550 Ac 11:18; **1561** Ac 17:30;
1566 Ac 20:21

Resurrection
see also Jesus Christ
in OT **522** 1Ki 17:22; **540** 2Ki 4:35;
554 2Ki 13:21
in NT
daughter of Jairus
1351 Mt 9:18–26;
1399 Mk 5:21–43;
1449 Lk 8:40–56
son of widow of Nain
1445 Lk 7:11–17
Lazarus **1508** Jn 11:1–44
Dorcas **1547** Ac 9:36–42

Resurrection of all the dead
taught by Jesus **1370** Mt 20:30–32;
1377 Mt 24:31–32;
1417 Mk 12:25–27;
1462 Lk 14:14; **1476** Lk 20:35–38;
1497 Jn 5:21,24–29;
1499 Jn 6:39,40,44;
1509 Jn 11:23–26
taught by others **1534** Ac 4:2;
1569 Ac 23:6; **1571** Ac 24:15;
1573 Ac 26:8; **1587** Ro 8:11,23;
1604 1Co 6:14;
1613 1Co 15:12–57;
1620 2Co 4:14; **1621** 2Co 5:1–5;
1646 Php 3:11,21;
1657 1Th 4:14–16; **1684** Heb 6:2;
1741 Rev 20:4–6,13

Resurrection of Jesus
foretold **1363** Mt 16:21;
1365 Mt 17:9,23; **1370** Mt 20:19;
1407 Mk 8:31; **1407** Mk 9:9,31;
1412 Mk 10:34; **1451** Lk 9:22,
1472 Lk 18:33; **1484** Lk 24:7,46;
1491 Jn 2:19–22;
1507 Jn 10:17–18; **1515** Jn 14:19
taught by others **1531** Ac 2:24,32;
1534 Ac 3:15,26; **1534** Ac 4:10,33;
1538 Ac 5:30; **1549** Ac 10:40;
1553 Ac 13:30,34–37;
1560 Ac 17:3,18,31;
1584 Ro 4:24–25; **1585** Ro 6:4;
1587 Ro 8:11; **1590** Ro 10:9;
1604 1Co 6:14;
1613 1Co 15:4–8,12–23

Rome
1561 Ac 18:2; **1564** Ac 19:21;
1570 Ac 23:11; **1577** Ac 28:14–16;
1580 Ro 1:7,15; **1670** 2Ti 1:17

Ruth
396 Ru 1:4; **397** Ru 2:2;
399 Ru 3:9; **402** Ru 4:13;
1338 Mt 1:5

S

Sabbath
157 Ex 16:23–29;
177 Ex 31:14–17; **219** Lev 23:3;
291 Dt 5:12–15;
694 Ne 13:15–22;
1039 Isa 56:2–7;
1043 Isa 58:13,14;
1086 Jer 17:21–27;
1354 Mt 12:1–14; **1395** Mk 3:1–4;

1401 Mk 6:2; **1496** Jn 5:9–18;
1506 Jn 9:13–16;
1552 Ac 13:14,42,44;
1557 Ac 16:13; **1651** Col 2:16

Sadducees
1341 Mt 3:7;
1363 Mt 16:1,6,11–12;
1374 Mt 22:23,34; **1416** Mk 12:18;
1476 Lk 20:27; **1534** Ac 4:1;
1537 Ac 5:17; **1569** Ac 23:6–8

Samaria
520 1Ki 16:24; **526** 1Ki 20:1;
544 2Ki 6:19–25; **559** 2Ki 17:5–6;
1256 Hos 13:16; **1287** Mic 1:1–7;
1468 Lk 17:11; **1493** Jn 4:4–43;
1529 Ac 1:8; **1542** Ac 8:1,5–24;
1555 Ac 15:3

Samaritans
560 2Ki 17:29; **1452** Lk 9:52;
1453 Lk 10:33; **1468** Lk 17:16;
1493 Jn 4:9,39–40

Samson
381 Jdg 13:2—16:31;
1691 Heb 11:32

Samuel
404 1Sa 1:19—4:1; **412** 1Sa 7—
12; **424** 1Sa 15—16;
441 1Sa 25:1; **842** Ps 99:6;
1082 Jer 15:1; **1534** Ac 3:24;
1553 Ac 13:20; **1691** Heb 11:32

Sanhedrin
1345 Mt 5:22; **1384** Mt 26:59;
1422 Mk 14:55; **1538** Ac 5:21–41;
1569 Ac 22:30; **1569** Ac 23:1–10;
1573 Ac 26:12

Sapphira
1536 Ac 5:1

Sarah (Sarai)
67 Ge 11:29–30;
68 Ge 12:10–20; **72** Ge 16:1–8;
73 Ge 17:15; **74** Ge 18:9–15;
79 Ge 21:1–11; **82** Ge 23:2,19;
1584 Ro 4:19; **1589** Ro 9:9;
1690 Heb 11:11; **1703** 1Pe 3:6

Sardis
1725 Rev 3:1,4

Satan
see also Beelzebub, Devil
605 1Ch 21:1–8; **708** Job 1:6–12;
709 Job 2:1–7; **1319** Zec 3:1–2;
1342 Mt 4:10; **1355** Mt 12:26;
1364 Mt 16:23; **1391** Mk 1:13;
1396 Mk 3:23,26; **1397** Mk 4:15;
1407 Mk 8:33; **1453** Lk 10:18;
1456 Lk 11:18; **1461** Lk 13:16;
1478 Lk 22:3,31; **1514** Jn 13:27;
1536 Ac 5:3; **1597** Ro 16:20;
1603 1Co 5:5; **1605** 1Co 7:5;
1661 2Th 2:9; **1664** 1Ti 1:20;
1724 Rev 2:9,13,24;
1733 Rev 12:9; **1741** Rev 20:7

Saul
king of Israel **415** 1Sa 9—11;
420 1Sa 13—28; **449** 1Sa 31;
450 2Sa 1; **1553** Ac 13:21
of Tarsus see Paul

Savior
in OT **482** 2Sa 22:2–3;
984 Isa 19:19–20;
1018 Isa 43:3,11; **1256** Hos 13:4
in NT
God **1430** Lk 1:47; **1664** 1Ti 1:1;
1665 1Ti 2:3; **1666** 1Ti 4:10;
1677 Tit 2:10; **1677** Tit 3:4;
1722 Jude 1:25
in NT
Christ **1433** Lk 2:11; **1495** Jn 4:42;
1538 Ac 5:31; **1553** Ac 13:23;
1641 Eph 5:23; **1647** Php 3:20;
1670 2Ti 1:10; **1675** Tit 1:4;
1707 2Pe 1:1,11; **1708** 2Pe 2:20;
1710 2Pe 3:2,18; **1714** 1Jn 4:14

Sea of Galilee
1343 Mt 4:18;
1350 Mt 8:24,26,27,32;
1356 Mt 13:1; **1360** Mt 14:25–26;
1362 Mt 15:29; **1391** Mk 1:16;
1394 Mk 2:13; **1395** Mk 3:7;
1397 Mk 4:1,35; **1398** Mk 5:1;
1404 Mk 6:45,53 (called Sea of
Tiberias)
1497 Jn 6:1; **1525** Jn 21:1 (called
Lake of Gennesaret)
1439 Lk 5:1

Sennacherib
561 2Ki 18:13—19:36;
(**653** 2Ch 32:1–22;
1007 Isa 36:1—37:37)

Sermon on the Mount
1343 Mt 5—7; **1443** Lk 6:20–49

Silas
1556 Ac 15:22,27,32,40;
1558 Ac 16:19,25,29;
1560 Ac 17:4,10,14–15;
1561 Ac 18:5; **1618** 2Co 1:19;
1655 1Th 1:1; **1660** 2Th 1:1;
1706 1Pe 5:12

Siloam
1460 Lk 13:4; **1505** Jn 9:7,11

Simeon
119 Ge 42:24; **1433** Lk 2:25,34

Simon
1359 Mt 13:55; **1382** Mt 26:6;
1386 Mt 27:32; **1401** Mk 6:3;
1419 Mk 14:3; **1424** Mk 15:21;
1446 Lk 7:36–50; **1482** Lk 23:26;
1500 Jn 6:71; **1513** Jn 13:2,26;
1542 Ac 8:9–24; **1547** Ac 9:43;
1547 Ac 10:6,17,32

Simon Peter
see Peter

Simon the Zealot
1352 Mt 10:4; **1396** Mk 3:18;
1443 Lk 6:15; **1530** Ac 1:13

Sinai
161 Ex 19; **168** Ex 24:12–18;
177 Ex 31:18;
180 Ex 34:2–4,29–32;
687 Ne 9:13; **1541** Ac 7:30,38;
1633 Gal 4:24–25

Snake
55 Ge 3:1; **138** Ex 4:3;
143 Ex 7:10; **259** Nu 21:8;
917 Pr 23:32; **1376** Mt 23:33;

1427 Mk 16:18; **1453** Lk 10:19;
1491 Jn 3:14; **1577** Ac 28:4–5;
1625 2Co 11:3

Sodom and Gomorrah
69 Ge 13:1–13;
70 Ge 14:8–12,17–23;
76 Ge 19:1–28; **318** Dt 29:23;
1172 Eze 16:46–56;
1352 Mt 10:15; **1354** Mt 11:23–24;
1453 Lk 10:12; **1469** Lk 17:29;
1590 Ro 9:29; **1708** 2Pe 2:6;
1720 Jude 1:7; **1732** Rev 11:8

Solomon
493 1Ki 2:12—11:43;
693 Ne 12:45; **696** Ne 13:26;
887 Pr 1:1; **945** SS 1:1;
1338 Mt 1:6–7; **1347** Mt 6:29;
1356 Mt 12:42; **1456** Lk 11:31;
1459 Lk 12:27; **1542** Ac 7:47

Son of David
1338 Mt 1:1; **1351** Mt 9:27;
1355 Mt 12:23; **1362** Mt 15:22;
1370 Mt 20:30–31;
1371 Mt 21:9,15;
1375 Mt 22:42,45

Son of God
1341 Mt 3:17; **1342** Mt 4:3,6;
1361 Mt 14:33; **1363** Mt 16:16;
1364 Mt 17:5; **1384** Mt 26:63;
1386 Mt 27:40,43; **1391** Mk 1:1;
1425 Mk 15:39; **1429** Lk 1:32;
1489 Jn 1:34,49;
1496 Jn 5:19–26; **1508** Jn 10:36;
1508 Jn 11:4,27; **1545** Ac 9:20;
1553 Ac 13:33; **1580** Ro 1:3,4,9;
1585 Ro 5:10; **1587** Ro 8:3;
1600 1Co 1:9; **1631** Gal 2:20;
1633 Gal 4:4,6; **1639** Eph 4:13;
1655 1Th 1:10; **1680** Heb 1:2,5,8;
1683 Heb 4:14; **1683** Heb 5:5;
1689 Heb 10:29;
1712 1Jn 2:22–24; **1713** 1Jn 3:8;
1714 1Jn 4:9,10,14,15;
1714 1Jn 5:9–13

Son of Man
1350 Mt 8:20; **1350** Mt 9:6;
1352 Mt 10:23; **1354** Mt 11:19;
1355 Mt 12:8,32,40;
1359 Mt 13:37,41;
1363 Mt 16:13,27,28;
1365 Mt 17:9,12,22;
1369 Mt 19:28; **1370** Mt 20:18,28;
1377 Mt 24:27,30,37,39,44;
1380 Mt 25:31;
1382 Mt 26:2,24,45,64;
1470 Lk 18:8; **1489** Jn 1:51;
1491 Jn 3:13–14; **1497** Jn 5:27;
1498 Jn 6:27,53,62; **1503** Jn 8:28;
1506 Jn 9:35; **1511** Jn 12:23,34;
1514 Jn 13:31; **1542** Ac 7:56

Song of Mary
1430 Lk 1:46–55

Song of Zechariah
1431 Lk 1:68–79

Spirit of God, of the Lord
52 Ge 1:2; **117** Ge 41:38;
177 Ex 31:2–3; **265** Nu 24:2;
365 Jdg 3:10; **379** Jdg 11:29;
417 1Sa 10:6,10; **535** 2Ki 2:16;

799 Ps 51:11; **974** Isa 11:2;
1046 Isa 61:1; **1202** Eze 36:27;
1263 Joel 2:28–29; **1290** Mic 3:8;
1320 Zec 4:6

Spirit—unclean, evil
427 1Sa 16:14–23;
1391 Mk 1:23,26,27;
1395 Mk 3:11,30;
1398 Mk 5:2,8,13;
1408 Mk 9:17,20,25;
1737 Rev 16:13; **1738** Rev 18:2

Stephen
1539 Ac 6:5; **1539** Ac 6:8—8:2;
1569 Ac 22:20

Synagogue
1352 Mt 9:35; **1391** Mk 1:21–27;
1449 Lk 8:41; **1460** Lk 13:10,14;
1506 Jn 9:22; **1545** Ac 9:20;
1552 Ac 13:14; **1560** Ac 17:1,2;
1561 Ac 18:4; **1564** Ac 19:8

T

Tabernacle
169 Ex 25:8–9; **170** Ex 26—27;
174 Ex 29:4,10–11;
177 Ex 31:6–7; **180** Ex 33:7–11;
182 Ex 35:21—36,38; **188** Ex 40;
194 Lev 4:4–7; **229** Nu 1:50–53;
243 Nu 10:11–21; **356** Jos 22:29;
407 1Sa 2:22; **458** 2Sa 7:2;
585 1Ch 6:32,48;
606 1Ch 21:28–30; **1541** Ac 7:44;
1687 Heb 9:1—8,21

Tabitha
1547 Ac 9:36,40

Tarsus
1546 Ac 9:30; **1550** Ac 11:25;
1568 Ac 21:39; **1568** Ac 22:3

Tax
1365 Mt 17:24; **1374** Mt 22:17,19;
1416 Mk 12:14; **1594** Ro 13:6–7

Tax Collector
1351 Mt 9:10–11; **1354** Mt 11:19;
1373 Mt 21:31–32;
1394 Mk 2:15–16; **1436** Lk 3:12;
1441 Lk 5:27,29–30;
1445 Lk 7:29,34; **1463** Lk 15:1;
1470 Lk 18:10–14;
1472 Lk 19:2–10

Temple
Solomon's **498** 1Ki 5:2–18;
499 1Ki 6—8; **561** 2Ki 18:15–16;
571 2Ki 24:12–13;
572 2Ki 25:13–17; **615** 1Ch 28:10;
619 2Ch 2—7:2
Rebuilding of **665** Ezr 3:6–11;
667 Ezr 5:11–17; **668** Ezr 6:5–22;
1315 Hag 1:14; **1320** Zec 4:7,9
Herod's **1342** Mt 4:5;
1372 Mt 21:12–17,23;
1377 Mt 24:1; **1384** Mt 26:55,61;
1385 Mt 27:5,40,51;
1414 Mk 11:15,27; **1418** Mk 13:1;
1425 Mk 15:38;
1428 Lk 1:9,21–22;
1433 Lk 2:27,46;
1474 Lk 19:45,47; **1475** Lk 20:1;
1477 Lk 21:1,5; **1487** Lk 24:53;

1491 Jn 2:14–17;
1500 Jn 7:14,28; **1503** Jn 8:20;
1507 Jn 10.23; **1533** Ac 2:46;
1533 Ac 3:1–3,8,10;
1538 Ac 5:20,21,25;
1567 Ac 21:26–30
figurative **1491** Jn 2:18–22;
1602 1Co 3:16–17;
1622 2Co 6:16; **1638** Eph 2:21

Ten Commandments
163 Ex 20:1–17; **291** Dt 5:1–21

Thaddaeus
1352 Mt 10:3; **1396** Mk 3:18

Thanks
625 2Ch 7:3; **761** Ps 7:17;
779 Ps 30:12; **820** Ps 75:1;
842 Ps 100:4; **851** Ps 107:1;
1223 Da 2:23; **1587** Ro 7:25;
1615 1Co 15:57; **1637** Eph 1:16;
5:20; **1652** Col 3:17;
1659 1Th 5:18

Thessalonica
1560 Ac 17:1,11,13;
1647 Php 4:16; **1655** 1Th 1:1;
1660 2Th 1:1

Thomas
1352 Mt 10:3; **1396** Mk 3:18;
1443 Lk 6:15; **1508** Jn 11:16;
1515 Jn 14:5; **1525** Jn 20:24–28;
1525 Jn 21:2; **1530** Ac 1:13

Tiglath Pileser
557 2Ki 15:29; **558** 2Ki 16:7–10;
583 1Ch 5:6,26;
648 2Ch 28:16–21

Timothy
1557 Ac 16:1,3; **1560** Ac 17:14,15;
1561 Ac 18:5; **1564** Ac 19:22;
1565 Ac 20:4; **1597** Ro 16:21;
1603 1Co 4:17; **1615** 1Co 16:10;
1618 2Co 1:1,19; **1644** Php 1:1;
1646 Php 2:19,22; **1650** Col 1:1;
1655 1Th 1:1; **1656** 1Th 3:2,6;
1660 2Th 1:1; **1664** 1Ti 1:2;
1669 1Ti 6:20; **1670** 2Ti 1:2;
1678 Phm 1; **1694** Heb 13:23

Titus
1619 2Co 2:13;
1622 2Co 7:6,13,14;
1623 2Co 8:6,16,23;
1627 2Co 12:18; **1631** Gal 2:1,3;
1672 2Ti 4:10; **1675** Tit 1:4

Tongues—speaking in
1427 Mk 16:17; **1530** Ac 2:3,4,11;
1549 Ac 10:46; **1563** Ac 19:6;
1610 1Co 12:10,28,30;
1611 1Co 13:1,8;
1611 1Co 14:2–40

Tyre
456 2Sa 5:11; **498** 1Ki 5:1;
501 1Ki 7:13–14;
988 Isa 23:1–18;
1186 Eze 26:1—28:19;
1266 Am 1:9–10;
1354 Mt 11:21–22; **1362** Mt 15:21;
1405 Mk 7:24,31; **1443** Lk 6:17;

1453 Lk 10:13–14; **1552** Ac 12:20;
1566 Ac 21:3,7

U

Understand(ing)
66 Ge 11:7; **735** Job 26:14;
864 Ps 119:100; **874** Ps 136:5;
883 Ps 147:5; **909** Pr 18:2;
923 Pr 28:5; **1035** Isa 52:15;
1357 Mt 13:14; **1417** Mk 12:33;
1434 Lk 2:47; **1543** Ac 8:30;
1579 Ac 28:27

Ur
67 Ge 11:28,31; **71** Ge 15:7;
594 1Ch 11:35; **687** Ne 9:7

Urim and Thummim
173 Ex 28:30; **199** Lev 8:8;
271 Nu 27:21; **325** Dt 33:8–10;
445 1Sa 28:6; **664** Ezr 2:63;
685 Ne 7:65

V

Vine
115 Ge 40:9–10; **375** Jdg 9:8–13;
498 1Ki 4:25; **827** Ps 80:8–9;
1173 Eze 17:6–10;
1176 Eze 19:10–14;
1516 Jn 15:1,4,5; **1735** Rev 14:18

Vineyard
64 Ge 9:20; **528** 1Ki 21:2–16;
964 Isa 5:1–7; **1278** Am 9:14;
1369 Mt 20:1–16;
1373 Mt 21:28–32,33–43;
1415 Mk 12:1–12;
1475 Lk 20:9–18

Virgin
166 Ex 22:16–17;
380 Jdg 11:37–38;
698 Est 2:2–4,16–17;
1271 Am 5:2; **1339** Mt 1:23;
1429 Lk 1:34; **1606** 1Co 7:34;
1625 2Co 11:2

Visions
see Dreams

W

Widow
166 Ex 22:22–24; **297** Dt 10:18;
396 Ru 1:3,5; **521** 1Ki 17:9,10,20;
1145 La 1:1;
1417 Mk 12:40,42–44;
1445 Lk 7:12; **1470** Lk 18:3–5;
1477 Lk 21:2–3; **1539** Ac 6:1;
1547 Ac 9:39,41; **1605** 1Co 7:8;
1666 1Ti 5:3–16

Wife
55 Ge 2:24; **163** Ex 20:17;
(**291** Dt 5:21); **309** Dt 22:13–22;
673 Ezr 10:2–4; **894** Pr 6:27–29;
910 Pr 18:22; **911** Pr 19:14;
1332 Mal 2:13–16;
1605 1Co 7:2–4,10–12,14,
1605 1Co 7:16,27,33,39;
1641 Eph 5:22–33;
1652 Col 3:18–19;
1703 1Pe 3:1–7

Wine
literal **64** Ge 9:21–24;
236 Nu 6:2–4; **375** Jdg 9:13;
381 Jdg 13:2–4,7,13–14;
404 1Sa 1:14–15;
846 Ps 104:14–15; **912** Pr 20:1;
917 Pr 23:29–35; **928** Pr 31:4–7;
1112 Jer 35:2–8; **1222** Da 1:8;
1351 Mt 9:17; **1394** Mk 2:22;
1424 Mk 15:23; **1428** Lk 1:15;
1441 Lk 5:37–39;
1490 Jn 2:3–10; **1595** Ro 14:21;
1641 Eph 5:18; **1665** 1Ti 3:8;
1667 1Ti 5:23
figurative **1038** Isa 55:1;
1097 Jer 25:15–29;
1735 Rev 14:8,10; **1737** Rev 17:2;
1738 Rev 18:3

Wisdom
498 1Ki 4:29; **508** 1Ki 10:4,23;
619 2Ch 1:10; **737** Job 28:12;
750 Job 38:36; **787** Ps 37:30;
856 Ps 111:10; **888** Pr 2:10;
895 Pr 8:9; **907** Pr 16:16;
914 Pr 21:30; **930** Pr 31:26;
932 Ecc 2:12; **937** Ecc 7–8:1;
940 Ecc 9:13; **1359** Mt 13:54;
1435 Lk 2:52; **1477** Lk 21:15;
1592 Ro 11:33;
1600 1Co 1:17,24,25,31;
1601 1Co 2:6,7; **1602** 1Co 3:19;
1610 1Co 12:8; **1637** Eph 1:17;
1695 Jas 1:5

Wrath
178 Ex 32:11–14;
254 Nu 16:43–46;
267 Nu 25:10–11;
568 2Ki 22:11–17;
1310 Zep 1:15,18; **1341** Mt 3:7;
1436 Lk 3:7; **1477** Lk 21:23;
1493 Jn 3:36; **1580** Ro 1:18;
1581 Ro 2:5,8; **1585** Ro 5:9;
1589 Ro 9:22; **1594** Ro 13:4–5;
1638 Eph 2:3; **1640** Eph 5:6;
1652 Col 3:6; **1656** 1Th 2:16;
1729 Rev 6:17;
1735 Rev 14:10,19;
1736 Rev 15:1,7

X

Xerxes
666 Ezr 4:6;
697 Est 1:1—10:3

Y

Yoke
1099 Jer 27:1,2;
1100 Jer 28:2,10–14;
1354 Mt 11:29–30

Youth
430 1Sa 17:33; **775** Ps 25:7;
844 Ps 103:5; **942** Ecc 12:1;
1092 Jer 22:21

Z

Zacchaeus
1472 Lk 19:1–10

Zebedee
1343 Mt 4:21;
1370 Mt 20:20;
1387 Mt 27:56;
1391 Mk 1:19–20;
1412 Mk 10:35;
1440 Lk 5:10; 1525 Jn 21:2

Zechariah
prophet 667 Ezr 5:1; 669 Ezr 6:14;

1318 Zec 1:1;
1322 Zec 7:1
priest, father of John the Baptist
1428 Lk 1:5–67

Zerubbabel
662 Ezr 2:2;
664 Ezr 3:2–8; 667 Ezr 5:2;
1315 Hag 1:1—2:23;
1320 Zec 4:1–10

Zion
455 2Sa 5:7;
593 1Ch 11:5; 796 Ps 48;
841 Ps 97:8;
970 Isa 8:18; 1265 Joel 3:17;
1371 Mt 21:5; 1511 Jn 12:15;
1590 Ro 9:33;
1592 Ro 11:26;
1692 Heb 12:22; 1735 Rev 14:1

Dictionary-Concordance

A

Aaron—the brother of Moses; he served as Moses' spokesman before Pharaoh (Ex 4:14-16,27-31; 7:1-2); he was Israel's first high priest (Ex 28:1; Nu 17; Heb 5:1-4).

Abel—the second son of Adam (Ge 4:2); he offered the proper sacrifice to God (Ge 4:4; Heb 11:4), but was murdered by his brother Cain (Ge 4:8; Mt 23:35; 1Jn 3:12).

abhor—to hate or to turn away from.

abound—to be more than enough; to overflow.
Ex 34:6 slow to anger, *a* in love
Php 1:9 that your love may *a* more

Abraham—the father of the Jewish nation and of all believers. God promised that he would make a mighty nation of Abraham's children and would give them the land of Canaan (Ge 15; 17; 22; Ro 4; Heb 6:13-15). As a test, God told him to offer his son Isaac as a sacrifice (Ge 22; Heb 11:17-19) but withdrew this command when Abraham showed that he would trust the Lord even in this matter.

abstain—to keep from doing something.

abundance, abundant—having plenty, more than enough.
Jude 2 Mercy, peace and love be yours in *a.*

acknowledge—to know and to say that something is true; to recognize.
Mt 10:32 *a* him before my Father in heaven
2Ti 3:7 but never able to *a* the truth.

Adam—the first man God created (Ge 1:26–2:25); he sinned by disobeying God (Ge 3) thereby bringing all people under the curse of sin (Ro 5:12-21).

adultery—having sexual relations with someone other than one's husband or wife. Spiritual adultery means being unfaithful to God (Jer 3).
Ex 20:14 You shall not commit *a.*
Mt 5:28 lustfully has already committed *a*

advice—an opinion given regarding a decision to be made.
1Ki 12:14 he followed the *a* of the young men
Pr 20:18 Make plans by seeking *a;*

affliction—trouble or pain that lasts a long time.
Ro 12:12 patient in *a,* faithful in prayer.

Ahab—a wicked king of Israel; the husband of Jezebel (1Ki 16:31). He caused Israel to worship Baal rather than God (1Ki 16:31-33) and was opposed by God's prophet Elijah (1Ki 17:1; 18; 21).

alien—a foreigner or stranger.
Ex 22:21 "Do not mistreat an *a*
Eph 2:19 no longer foreigners and *a,* but fellow citizens
1Pe 2:11 as *a* and strangers in the world,

allot—to divide and give away in parts. In Old Testament times the land of Canaan was allotted to the twelve tribes of Israel.

Almighty—a name used to show how strong and powerful God is.
Ge 17:1 "I am God *A;* walk before me
Isa 6:3 "Holy, holy, holy is the LORD *A;*

altar—a raised platform, made of stones, metal, dirt or wood, on which sacrifices were made.

Amen—Hebrew word that means "so be it" or "let it become true."

ancient—very old; in existence for many years.

Andrew—one of the twelve apostles; the brother of Peter (Mt 4:18; 10:2; Ac 1:13).

angel—a heavenly being.
Ps 34:7 The *a* of the LORD encamps
Heb 1:14 Are not all *a* ministering spirits
Heb 2:7 made him a little lower than the *a;*
1Pe 1:12 Even *a* long to look

anger—a strong feeling of displeasure; rage; fury.
Ps 103:8 slow to anger, *a,* abounding in love.
Jas 1:20 for a man's *a* does not bring

anguish—extreme pain or distress of mind or body.
Jer 49:24 *a* and pain have seized her,

anoint—to pour oil on a person's head, either for a physical benefit (Jas 5:14) or in order to set apart someone for service to God (Ex 28:41).

antichrist—a person who is against Christ.
1Jn 2:18 have heard that the *a* is coming,
1Jn 2:22 a man is the *a*—he denies

apostle—1. any of the twelve men Jesus chose to work with him during his earthly ministry; after being equipped by the Holy Spirit, they were sent out to preach about Jesus; 2. later, someone who had been with Jesus, had seen his miracles and then taught others about him.
Mk 3:14 twelve—designating them *a*—
1Co 12:28 God has appointed first of all *a,*
1Co 15:9 For I am the least of the *a*

appalled—overcome with shock or dismay.

appeal—to make an earnest request.
Phm 9 I *a* to you on the basis of love.

ark of the Testimony—also called the ark of the covenant; a large gold-covered box, which contained the Ten Commandments (Tablets of Testimony), a jar of manna and Aaron's staff, and was kept inside the Most Holy Place in the tabernacle (Tent of Meeting). It was a reminder to the Israelites of God's presence with them.

arrest—to officially or lawfully make a prisoner of someone.

arrogant—proud; conceited.

assemble—to bring a group of people together; to meet together.

Assyria—one of the powerful nations of Biblical times; it often attacked the Israelites; its capital was Nineveh.

astray—mistaken; not on the right path; lost.
Isa 53:6 We all, like sheep, have gone *a,*

atone—to make right, by paying the penalty, the relationship between God and humans that was broken through sin. In the Old Testament people atoned symbolically for their sins by offering sacrifices to God. In the New Testament Jesus corrected the relationship between God and people once and for all by dying to take away sins.

atonement—the payment that corrects the relationship between God and humans that was broken through sin.
Lev 17:11 it is the blood that makes *a*
Lev 23:27 this seventh month is the Day of *A.*
Ro 3:25 presented him as a sacrifice of *a,*
Heb 2:17 that he might make *a* for the sins

authority—the right and power to give orders.
Mt 9:6 the Son of Man has *a* on earth
Mt 28:18 "All *a* in heaven and on earth has
Ro 13:1 for there is no *a* except that which
Heb 13:17 your leaders and submit to their *a.*

avenge—to get back at or punish someone who has done wrong.
Dt 32:35 It is mine to *a;* I will repay.

awe—respect and wonder; a holy fear of God because of his great power.
Ecc 5:7 Therefore stand in *a* of God.

B

Baal—the name of many false gods in Canaan.
1Ki 18:25 Elijah said to the prophets of *B,*

Babylon—the beautiful capital of Babylonia; it was a powerful and influential city in the Near East from the eighteenth to the sixth centuries B.C. In the New Testament, Babylon represents the godless city.
Ps 137:1 By the rivers of *B* we sat and wept
Rev 14:8 Fallen is *B* the Great,

banish—to force a person away from a place.

baptize—a religious ceremony in which water is used as a symbol of cleansing from sin. Churches today baptize by sprinkling or pouring or immersing in water. Baptism is a sign that sin is washed away.
Mk 1:9 and was *b* by John in the Jordan.
Mk 16:16 believes and is *b* will be saved,
Ac 1:5 but in a few days you will be *b*
Ac 2:38 "Repent and be *b,* every one of you,

barren—1. unable to have children; 2. unable to produce crops.

Beelzebub—the prince of demons; Satan.
Lk 11:15 "By *B,* the prince of demons,

believe—to accept as true; to trust; to have faith.
Mk 1:15 Repent and *b* the good news!"
Mk 9:24 "I do *b;* help me overcome my
Jn 1:7 that through him all men might *b.*
Jn 3:18 does not *b* stands condemned
Jn 20:27 Stop doubting and *b.*"
Ac 16:31 They replied, "*B* in the Lord Jesus,
Ro 3:22 faith in Jesus Christ to all who *b.*
1Th 4:14 We *b* that Jesus died and rose again

besiege—to surround a city or town completely with an army, so that nothing can go in or out.

Bethlehem—the city in Judea where Jesus was born (Mt 2:1).

betray—to turn a friend over to his or her enemies; to be unfaithful to.
Mt 27:3 When Judas, who had *b* him,
1Co 11:23 on the night he was *b,* took bread,

bitter—having harsh or hateful feelings.
Eph 4:31 Get rid of all *b,* rage
Heb 12:15 and that no *b* root grows up

blameless—without fault.
Ge 17:1 walk before me and be *b.*
1Co 1:8 so that you will be *b* on the day

blaspheme—to speak carelessly, falsely or insultingly about God or holy things.
Mk 3:29 whoever *b* against the Holy Spirit

bless—1. to make holy; 2. to show favor to; 3. to ask God to show favor to.

Ge 2:3 And God *b* the seventh day
Ge 12:3 I will *b* those who *b* you,
Mt 5:3 "*B* are the poor in spirit
Ro 12:14 *b* those who persecute you; *b*

blind—unable to see. Spiritual blindness is an inability to understand the things of God.
Mt 11:5 The *b* receive sight, the lame walk,
Jn 9:25 I was *b* but now I see!"

blood—as the life-giving fluid in the body, it represents life itself. In the Old Testament the blood of sacrifices symbolized the giving of life for life. Through the blood of Jesus on the cross, believers are saved from death for their sins.
Ex 12:13 and when I see the *b,* I will pass
Lev 17:11 For the life of a creature is in the *b,*
Mt 26:28 This is my *b* of the covenant,
Eph 1:7 we have redemption through his *b,*
Heb 9:12 once for all by his own *b,*

boast—to brag; to call attention to.
Ps 34:2 My soul will *b* in the LORD;
Gal 6:14 May I never *b* except in the cross

Boaz—a wealthy man who lived in Bethlehem in the days of the judges; he married Ruth (Ru 2; 4).

body—1. physical part of a person; 2. a group working as a unit.
Ro 6:13 Do not offer the parts of your *b*
Ro 12:1 to offer your *b* as living sacrifices,
1Co 6:19 not know that your *b* is a temple
Eph 5:30 for we are members of his *b.*

born again—refers to the experience of salvation; entering God's family through faith in Christ.
Jn 3:3 no one can see the kingdom of God unless he is *b*
1Pe 1:23 For you have been *b*

bribe—money or favor given to influence judgment or conduct.
Ex 23:8 "Do not accept a *b,*

bride—a woman who is about to get married. The church is called Jesus' bride.

bridegroom—a man who is about to get married. Christ is called the church's bridegroom.

burden—a heavy load.
Mt 11:30 my yoke is easy and my *b* is light.
Gal 6:2 Carry each other's *b,*

burnt offering—in the Old Testament a sacrifice to the Lord that expressed devotion and complete surrender (Ge 8:20; Ex 29:18).

C

Caesar—the title of many Roman emperors.
Lk 2:1 In those days *C* Augustus
Mt 22:21 "Give to *C* what is *C*

Cain—Adam and Eve's firstborn son; he murdered his brother Abel (Ge 4:1-16).

camel—a large animal, able to travel long distances and used for transportation of people and goods.

Canaan—1. the land God promised to the nation of Israel; 2. the promised land.

centurion—a Roman army officer in charge of one hundred soldiers.

chariot—a two-wheeled vehicle pulled by horses.
2Ki 6:17 and *c* of fire all around Elisha.

cherub (pl. **cherubim**)—an angel, with an appearance something like a human being.

Christ—the official title of Jesus, meaning "the Anointed One." It is a Greek word, and it means the same as the Hebrew word *Messiah.*
Mt 1:16 was born Jesus, who is called *C.*

Jn 20:31 you may believe that Jesus is the *C,*
Ro 5:8 While we were still sinners, *C* died
Eph 5:23 as *C* is the head of the church,
Php 1:21 to live is *C* and to die is gain.

Christian—a believer in or follower of Christ.
Ac 11:26 The disciples were called *C* first
1Pe 4:16 as a *C,* do not be ashamed,

church—the entire group of people who believe in Christ.
Mt 16:18 and on this rock I will build my *c,*
Eph 5:23 as Christ is the head of the *c,*
Col 1:24 the sake of his body, which is the *c.*

circumcision—the cutting off of the loose fold of skin at the end of the penis; it symbolized the agreement God made with the Israelites, and they came to be known as "the circumcision" (Eph 2:11).
Ge 17:10 Every male among you shall be *c.*

clan—a group of people belonging to the same extended family.
Ge 24:38 to my father's family and to my own *c,*
Zec 12:12 The land will mourn, each *c* by itself,

clean animals—animals God allowed the Israelites to sacrifice and eat.

cleanse—to make clean; to wash.

cloak—a loose-fitting coat without sleeves.

commandment—an order given by God. God gave the Ten Commandments to the Israelites while they were encamped in the area of Mount Sinai.
Ex 20:6 who love me and keep my *c.*
Mt 22:38 This is the first and greatest *c.*
Jn 13:34 "A new *c* I give you: Love one

companion—one who is a friend or associate or helper.

compassion (compassionate)—sympathy; pity.
Ne 9:17 gracious and *c,* slow to anger
Ps 103:4 and crowns you with love and *c,*
Mt 9:36 When he saw the crowds, he had *c*
Ro 9:15 and I will have *c* on whom I have *c.*"
Col 3:12 clothe yourselves with *c,* kindness,

conceive—1. to become pregnant; 2. to think up or imagine.
Mt 1:20 what is *c* in her is from the Holy
1Co 2:9 no mind has *c*

concubine—in Bible times, a woman who belonged to a man but did not have the rights of a wife. She was often one of the spoils of war, and her primary purpose was to bear children for the man.

condemn (condemnation)—to give out punishment to; to pronounce guilty.
Jn 3:17 Son into the world to *c* the world,
Ro 8:1 there is now no *c* for those who are

confess—1. to say what you believe; 2. to tell your sins to someone.
Ro 10:9 That if you *c* with your mouth,
Php 2:11 every tongue *c* that Jesus Christ is
1Jn 1:9 If we *c* our sins, he is faithful

conscience—the sense of knowing if something is good or bad; a sense of right and wrong.
Ro 2:15 their *c* also bearing witness,
Tit 1:15 their minds and *c* are corrupted.
Heb 9:14 cleanse our *c* from acts that lead

consecrate—to set aside or dedicate for God's use.
Ex 13:2 "*C* to me every firstborn male.
Lev 20:7 "*C* yourselves and be holy,

conspire—to plan together to do evil.

consume—1. to use up or eat up; 2. to destroy completely.
Jn 2:17 "Zeal for your house will *c* me."
Heb 12:29 for our "God is a *c* fire."

contempt—lack of respect; looking down on someone or something as being worthless.
Pr 14:31 He who oppresses the poor shows *c*
1Th 5:20 do not treat prophecies with *c*

corrupt—1. (*v.*) to change from good to bad; 2. (*adj.*) wicked.
Ge 6:11 Now the earth was *c* in God's sight
1Co 15:33 "Bad company *c* good character."

counsel—to give advice to.
Pr 15:22 Plans fail for lack of *c,*

Counselor—another name for the Holy Spirit.
Jn 14:26 But the *C,* the Holy Spirit,
Jn 15:26 "When the *C* comes, whom I will

covenant—1. an agreement between two people or two groups of people, in which both usually make specific promises; 2. the promises of God for salvation.
Ge 9:9 "I now establish my *c* with you
Ex 19:5 if you obey me fully and keep my *c,*
Jer 31:31 "when I will make a new *c*
1Co 11:25 "This cup is the new *c* in my blood;
Heb 9:15 Christ is the mediator of a new *c,*

covet—to want for oneself something that belongs to another person.
Ex 20:17 "You shall not *c* your neighbor's

create—to make; to bring into being.
Ge 1:1 In the beginning God *c* the heavens
Ps 51:10 *C* in me a pure heart, O God,
Col 1:16 For by him all things were *c:*
Rev 10:6 who *c* the heavens and all that is

cross—a tall beam with a crossbar on which a criminal was hung or tied to die.
Mt 10:38 and anyone who does not take his *c*
Gal 6:14 in the *c* of our Lord Jesus Christ,
Php 2:8 even death on a *c!*
Col 2:14 he took it away, nailing it to the *c.*
Heb 12:2 set before him endured the *c,*

crown—a headpiece worn to symbolize glory, honor and victory.
1Co 9:25 it to get a *c* that will last forever.
2Ti 4:8 store for me the *c* of righteousness,
Rev 2:10 and I will give you the *c* of life.

crucify—to put to death by nailing or tying a person's body to a cross.
Mt 27:22 They all answered, "*C* him!"
1Co 1:23 but we preach Christ *c:* a stumbling
Gal 2:20 I have been *c* with Christ

curse—1. (*v.*) to ask God to bring evil or injury to; 2. (*n.*) a prayer or desire that evil or injury come upon someone.
Lev 20:9 "If anyone *c* his father or mother,
Lk 6:28 bless those who *c* you, pray
Gal 3:13 "*C* is everyone who is hung on a tree."

D

Daniel—a young Jewish exile; he lived in Babylon during the reign of several kings, including Nebuchadnezzar. He prayed to God rather than obey an order to pray only to the king and was thrown into a lion's den (Da 1-6).

David—the son of Jesse; anointed by Samuel to become king of Israel (1Sa 16:1-13); killed the giant Goliath (1Sa 17); during his reign Israel's place in the land of Canaan was made secure.

day—1. the period of time between dawn and darkness; 2. a specified time.
Ge 1:5 God called the light "*d,*"
Ps 118:24 This is the *d* the Lord has made;
Ecc 12:1 Creator in the *d* of your youth,
Joel 2:31 and dreadful *d* of the Lord.

Mic 4:1 In the last *d*
Lk 11:3 Give us each *d* our daily bread.
Heb 1:2 in these last *d* he has spoken to us
2Pe 3:8 With the Lord a *d* is like

death—the end of physical life; also the penalty for sin (Ro 6:23).
Ps 23:4 the valley of the shadow of *d*,
Ecc 7:2 for *d* is the destiny of every man;
Isa 25:8 he will swallow up *d* forever.
1Co 15:21 For since *d* came through a man,
1Co 15:55 "Where, O *d*, is your sting?"
Rev 21:4 There will be no more *d*

debt—something that one person owes another.
Mt 6:12 Forgive us our *d*,

deceive—(*v.*) to fool or trick; to lie.
Ge 3:13 "The serpent *d* me, and I ate."
Gal 6:7 Do not be *d*: God cannot be
1Jn 1:8 we *d* ourselves and the truth is not

declare—to make known formally; to state forcefully.
Ps 19:1 The heavens *d* the glory of God;
Eph 6:20 Pray that I may *d* it fearlessly,

decree—1. (*v.*) to order or command; 2. (*n.*) an order or law given by someone with power and authority.

dedicate—to set apart for a special purpose, often for God's use.

defile—to make something that is good and pure into something impure or unclean.

demon—evil spirit. A demon-possessed person is one who is controlled by evil spirits.
Mk 5:15 possessed by the legion of *d*,
Jas 2:19 Good! Even the *d* believe that

depraved (depravity)—evil or sinful.
Php 2:15 fault in a crooked and *d* generation,
2Pe 2:19 they themselves are slaves of *d*

descendant—a member of a particular family line.

desecrate—to treat without respect or reverence.

desolate—not lived in; lonely; deserted.

despise—to look down on with contempt.
Pr 1:7 but fools *d* wisdom
Tit 2:15 Do not let anyone *d* you.

destroy—to ruin completely.

detest—to hate.

devil—the great enemy of God and tempter of people.
Lk 4:2 forty days he was tempted by the *d*.
Eph 6:11 stand against the *d* schemes.
2Ti 2:26 and escape from the trap of the *d*,
Jas 4:7 Resist the *d*, and he will flee
1Pe 5:8 Your enemy the *d* prowls

devour—1. to eat up greedily; 2. to destroy.
1Pe 5:8 looking for someone to *d*.

devout—religious; giving much time to prayer and worship.

die—1. to become lifeless; 2. to become insensitive to, as to die to, the law (Gal 2:19).
Ge 2:17 when you eat of it you will surely *d*."
Ecc 3:2 a time to be born and a time to *d*.
Eze 18:4 soul who sins is the one who will *d*.
Jn 11:26 and believes in me will never *d*.
1Co 15:22 in Adam all *d*, so in Christ all will
Php 1:21 to live is Christ and to *d* is gain.

discern—to understand; to come to know the difference between two or more things.
Php 1:10 you may be able to *d* what is best

disciple—a follower or student, especially one who believes what the leader teaches. Anyone who believes in Jesus is his disciple.
Lk 14:27 and follow me cannot be my *d*.
Jn 13:35 men will know that you are my *d*,

discipline—1. (*v.*) to correct; to teach what is right; 2. (*n.*) training that corrects, molds or perfects moral character.
Pr 29:17 *D* your son, and he will give you
Heb 12:6 the Lord *d* those he loves,
Rev 3:19 Those whom I love I rebuke and *d*.

disgrace—to bring shame to.

disown—to reject someone or something so completely that it no longer belongs to you.
Mt 26:34 you will *d* me three times."
2Ti 2:12 If we *d* him,

distress— suffering, misery, agony.
Ps 57:6 I was bowed down in *d*.
Ro 2:9 There will be trouble and *d*

divination—seeing into the future by magic.
Lev 19:26 "Do not practice *d* or sorcery.

divine—given by God; belonging to God.
Ro 1:20 his eternal power and *d* nature

divorce—to legally dissolve a marriage.
Mal 2:16 "I hate *d*," says the LORD God
Mt 19:3 for a man to *d* his wife for any
1Co 7:11 And a husband must not *d* his wife.

dominion—power; rule.
Ps 22:28 for *d* belongs to the LORD
Eph 1:21 far above all rule and authority, power and *d*,

doubt—uncertainty.
Mt 21:21 if you have faith and do not *d*,
Mk 11:23 and does not *d* in his heart
Jas 1:6 he must believe and not *d*,

dread—great fear.

dream—thoughts, images or emotion occurring during sleep; God sometimes spoke to his people through dreams.
Da 2:4 Tell your servants the *d*,

dwelling—place in which people live; house; in Scripture usually refers to the place where God lives.
1Ki 8:30 Hear from heaven, your *d* place,
Ps 84:1 How lovely is your *d* place,

E

earth—the place that God created for human beings to live.
Ge 1:1 God created the heavens and the *e*.
Ps 24:1 *e* is the LORD's and everything
Mt 6:10 done on *e* as it is in heaven.
Mt 24:35 Heaven and *e* will pass away,
Lk 2:14 on *e* peace to men
Php 2:10 in heaven and on *e* and under the *e*,
2Pe 3:13 to a new heaven and a new *e*,

Egypt—one of the most powerful nations of ancient times, located in the northeast corner of Africa; the Israelites were captives in Egypt at the beginning of the book of Exodus.

elders—1. the older men of a town or nation; they were the leaders of their community and made all the important decisions; 2. the leaders of the church.
1Ti 5:17 The *e* who direct the affairs
Tit 1:5 and appoint *e* in every town,

election—the choosing of Christians by God, as people who belong to him. Christians are called "the elect" (2Ti 2:10).
Ro 9:11 God's purpose in *e* might stand:
2Pe 1:10 to make your calling and *e* sure.

Elijah—a prophet of the Lord who predicted a famine in Israel (1Ki 17:1) and defeated the prophets of Baal in the test of whose God would set fire to the altar (1Ki 18:16-46).

Elisha—the prophet who succeeded Elijah. He was present when God took Elijah to heaven, and he took his place as prophet to Israel (2Ki 2:1-18).

encourage—to inspire with courage or hope.
Ps 19:7 Now go out and *e* your men.
1Th 4:18 Therefore *e* each other with these words.

endure—to continue; to keep on going; to bear something that is difficult or painful.
Ps 136:1 His love *e* forever.
Mal 3:2 who can *e* the day of his coming?
2Ti 2:3 *E* hardship with us like a good

envy—to want for oneself something that belongs to another person.
1Co 13:4 It does not *e*, it does not boast,

ephod—a linen apron worn by a priest over his robe. It was decorated with gold, blue, purple and scarlet yarns.

Esau—the firstborn son of Isaac and twin of Jacob (Ge 25:21-26). He sold his birthright to Jacob for a pot of stew (Ge 25:29-34) and was tricked out of his blessing by this same brother (Ge 27).

Esther—a Jewish woman who lived in Persia (Est 2:7) and became queen (Est 2:8-18). Upon being told of a plot to kill the Jews, she went to the king and pleaded for the Jewish people and thus saved them (Est 3–4; 7–9).

eternal—without beginning or end; forever; timeless.
Dt 33:27 The *e* God is your refuge,
Jn 3:16 him shall not perish but have *e* life.
Ro 6:23 but the gift of God is *e* life
1Jn 5:13 you may know that you have *e* life.

eunuch—a man whose sex organs have been removed so that he cannot produce children. Often in Bible times these men were important officials in royal palaces.

Eve—the first woman God created (Ge 2:20-24). Her name means "mother of all the living" (Ge 3:20).

everlasting—forever; without end.
Ps 90:2 from *e* to *e* you are God.
Isa 9:6 *E* Father, Prince of Peace.
Isa 55:3 I will make an *e* covenant with you,
Jn 6:47 the truth, he who believes has *e* life.

evil—wicked; doing things against God's will.
Ge 2:9 of the knowledge of good and *e*.
Ps 23:4 I will fear no *e*.
Mt 6:13 but deliver us from the *e* one."
Ro 12:9 Hate what is *e*; cling
Ro 12:17 Do not repay anyone *e* for *e*.
Eph 6:16 all the flaming arrows of the *e* one.

exalt—to praise; to raise to an important position.
Ps 118:28 you are my God, and I will *e* you.
Ps 148:13 for his name alone is *e*;
Pr 14:34 Righteousness *e* a nation,
Mt 23:12 For whoever *e* himself will be

exile—1. (*v.*) to force someone to leave his or her country or home; 2. (*n.*) forced removal from one's country or home.

Ezekiel—a priest who was called to be a prophet to the Jewish people when they were in exile in Babylon (Eze 1–3). He had many visions from the Lord (Eze 37; 40).

Ezra—a priest and teacher of the Law; he led a group of Jewish exiles back to Israel and helped them reestablish the temple of God and restore proper worship (Ezr 7–8).

F

faith—belief and trust in God; knowing that God is real, even though one can't see him.
Hab 2:4 but the righteous will live by his *f*
Mt 17:20 if you have *f* as small as a mustard
Lk 7:9 I have not found such great *f*

Ro 1:17 "The righteous will live by *f*."
Ro 3:22 comes through *f* in Jesus Christ
1Co 13:2 and if I have a *f* that can move
2Co 5:7 We live by *f*, not by sight.
Eph 6:16 to all this, take up the shield of *f*,
1Ti 6:12 Fight the good fight of the *f*.
Heb 11:1 *f* is being sure of what we hope for
Heb 11:8 By *f* Abraham, when called to go
Heb 12:2 the author and perfecter of our *f*
Jas 2:26 so *f* without deeds is dead.

faithful (faithfulness)—trustworthy; loyal.
Ps 145:13 The LORD is *f* to all his promises
La 3:23 great is your *f*.
Mt 25:21 "Well done, good and *f* servant!
Ro 12:12 patient in affliction, *f* in prayer.
1Co 10:13 And God is *f*; he will not let you
1Jn 1:9 he is *f* and just and will forgive us
Rev 1:5 who is the *f* witness, the firstborn

false (falsehood)—a lie.
Ex 20:16 "You shall not give *f* testimony

family—a group of people who are related to each other.
Ps 68:6 God sets the lonely in *f*,
Lk 9:61 go back and say good-by to my *f*."
1Ti 3:4 He must manage his own *f* well

famine—1. a time when there is not enough food; 2. any severe shortage.
Am 8:11 but a *f* of hearing the words
Mt 24:7 There will be *f* and earthquakes

fast—1. (*adj.*) firmly fixed; not movable; 2. (*v.*) to go without food for a period of time.
Ps 139:10 your right hand will hold me *f*.
Mt 6:16 "When you *f*, do not look somber

father—a male parent; God is also known as one's father.
Ge 2:24 this reason a man will leave his *f*
Ge 17:4 You will be the *f* of many nations.
Ex 20:12 "Honor your *f* and your mother,
Mt 6:9 "Our *F* in heaven,
Lk 11:11 "Which of you *f*, if your son asks
Jn 10:30 I and the *F* are one."
Jn 14:6 No one comes to the *F*

favor—goodwill; a positive attitude toward another person.
1Sa 20:3 I have found *f* in your eyes,

fear—(*v.*) 1. to respect highly; to feel reverence and awe for; 2. to be afraid of; (*n.*) 1. profound reverence toward God; 2. anticipation or awareness of danger.
Dt 6:13 *F* the LORD your God, serve him
Ps 91:5 You will not *f* the terror of night
Ps 111:10 *f* of the LORD is the beginning
Isa 41:10 So do not *f*, for I am with you
Php 2:12 to work out your salvation with *f*

fellowship—companionship or friendship.
1Jn 1:6 claim to have *f* with him yet walk
1Jn 1:7 we have *f* with one another,

fig—1. a brownish pear-shaped fruit that grows in countries near the Mediterranean Sea; 2. the tree that grows this fruit.

firstborn—a family's first child. The firstborn son in an Israelite family became the head of the family when his father died, and he received twice as much money and property as each of his brothers.
Ex 11:5 Every *f* son in Egypt will die,

firstfruits—the first vegetables, fruits and grains harvested from the field.
Ex 23:19 "Bring the best of the *f* of your soil

flesh—1. the soft parts of the bodies of humans and animals; 2. the believer's sinful nature.

Job 6:12 Is my *f* bronze?
Php 3:3 put no confidence in the *f*

fool—a person who is not wise.
Ps 14:1 The *f* says in his heart,
Lk 12:20 "But God said to him, 'You *f*!

forever—for a limitless time.
Dt 32:40 As surely as I live *f*,
Ps 136:1 His love endures *f*.

forgive—to pardon or excuse; to no longer blame or be angry with someone who has done you wrong.
Mt 6:14 For if you *f* men when they sin
Lk 23:34 Jesus said, "Father, *f* them,
Col 3:13 *F* as the Lord forgave you.
1Jn 1:9 and just and will *f* us our sins

forsake—to leave another completely alone, with no hope that you will ever return.
Jos 1:5 I will never leave you nor *f* you.
Isa 55:7 Let the wicked *f* his way
Mt 27:46 my God, why have you *f* me?"

free (freedom)—not bound; liberated.
Jn 8:32 and the truth will set you *f*."
Ro 6:18 You have been set *f* from sin
2Co 3:17 the Spirit of the Lord is, there is *f*.

friend—a person who loves and respects another person.
Pr 18:24 there is a *f* who sticks closer
Jn 15:13 that he lay down his life for his *f*.
Jas 4:4 Anyone who chooses to be a *f*

fruitful—productive; yielding much fruit.
Ge 1:22 "Be *f* and increase in number
Jn 15:2 cleans so that it will be even more *f*.

fulfill (fulfillment)—to complete a promise or project.
Ps 116:14 I will *f* my vows to the LORD
Mk 14:49 But the Scriptures must be *f*."
Ro 13:10 Therefore love is the *f* of the law.

G

generation—the entire number of people born and living at about the same time. Grandparents, parents and children are three different generations.
Ps 102:12 your renown endures through all *g*.
Lk 1:48 now on all *g* will call me blessed,

Gentile—anyone who is not a Jew.
Ro 3:9 and *G* alike are all under sin.
Ro 11:13 as I am the apostle to the *G*,

Gideon—a judge who freed Israel from the rule and terror of the Midianites (Jdg 6–8). He asked for a sign from God, and God showed him his will by means of dew and a fleece (Jdg 6:36-40).

gift—1. a present; 2. a talent or ability.
Ro 6:23 but the *g* of God is eternal life
1Co 12:4 There are different kinds of *g*,
2Co 9:15 be to God for his indescribable *g*!

glorify—to praise and honor in worship.
Ps 34:3 *G* the LORD with me;
Jn 17:1 *G* your Son, that your Son may

glory—1. honor; praise; 2. a source of pride or worthiness.
Ps 8:5 and crowned him with *g* and honor.
Ps 19:1 The heavens declare the *g* of God;
Lk 2:14 "*G* to God in the highest,
Jn 1:14 We have seen his *g*, the *g* of the One
1Co 10:31 whatever you do, do it all for the *g*
Rev 4:11 to receive *g* and honor and power

God—the supreme creator and the powerful force of the universe; the one who is to be worshiped.
Ge 1:1 In the beginning *G* created
Ex 20:5 the LORD your *G*, am a jealous *G*,

Nu 23:19 *G* is not a man, that he should lie,
Dt 6:4 LORD our *G*, the LORD is one.
Dt 6:5 Love the LORD your *G*
Ps 46:1 *G* is our refuge and strength,
Jn 1:18 ever seen *G*, but *G* the One
Jn 3:16 "For *G* so loved the world that he
Jn 4:24 *G* is spirit, and his worshipers must
1Jn 4:16 *G* is love.
Rev 4:8 holy is the Lord *G* Almighty,

godly—to be devoted and loving toward God, wanting to do his will.
1Ti 4:7 train yourself to be *g*.
2Pe 3:11 live holy and *g* lives

Goliath—the Philistine giant who was killed by David (1Sa 17; 21:9).

gospel—1. the good news that Jesus died for sins and rose again; 2. any of the first four books of the New Testament.
Ro 1:16 I am not ashamed of the *g*,
1Co 9:16 Woe to me if I do not preach the *g*!
1Co 15:2 By this *g* you are saved,

grace—an undeserved favor or gift; the undeserved forgiveness, kindness and mercy that God gives us.
Ro 3:24 and are justified freely by his *g*
Ro 5:20 where sin increased, *g* increased all
2Co 12:9 "My *g* is sufficient for you,
Eph 2:5 it is by *g* you have been saved.
Tit 3:7 having been justified by his *g*,

guilty—deserving punishment for having broken a law or commandment.
Ex 34:7 does not leave the *g* unpunished;
Heb 10:22 to cleanse us from a *g* conscience
Jas 2:10 at just one point is *g* of breaking all

H

harvest—the season for gathering in crops.
Ge 8:22 "As long as the earth endures, seedtime and *h*,

hate—to detest, to have extreme dislike for.
Ps 5:5 you *h* all who do wrong.
Mk 13:13 All men will *h* you because of me,

heal—to make well again.
Lk 8:43 but no one could *h* her.
Ac 28:27 I would *h* them.'

heart—the center of a person's life, including the mind, the will and the emotions.
Dt 6:5 LORD your God with all your *h*
1Sa 16:7 but the LORD looks at the *h*."
Ps 51:10 Create in me a pure *h*, O God,
Ps 119:11 I have hidden your word in my *h*
Ps 139:23 Search me, O God, and know my *h*;
Eze 36:26 I will give you a new *h*
Mt 5:8 Blessed are the pure in *h*,

heaven—1. the place where God lives; 2. the sky.
Ge 14:19 Creator of *h* and earth.
Mt 19:23 man to enter the kingdom of *h*.
Mk 16:19 he was taken up into *h*
Php 3:20 But our citizenship is in *h*.
Rev 21:1 I saw a new *h* and a new earth,

Hebrew—1. another name for an Israelite; a descendant of Abraham; 2. the language spoken by the Jews. The Old Testament was written in Hebrew.

heir—someone who receives the property or blessings of a person who has died.
Ro 8:17 then we are *h*—*h* of God
Eph 3:6 gospel the Gentiles are *h* together

Hezekiah—a king of Judah; he restored the temple, reinstituted proper worship and sought the Lord's help against the Assyrians.

high priest—the chief religious official in the Jewish religion. In the Old Testament he offered the most important sacrifices to God in behalf of the people.
> Heb 4:14 have a great *h* who has gone
> Heb 7:26 Such a *h* meets our need

holy—set apart for God; belonging to God; pure; godly.
> Ex 20:8 the Sabbath day by keeping it *h.*
> Lev 11:44 and be *h,* because I am *h.*
> Isa 6:3 "*H, h, h* is the LORD Almighty,
> Ro 12:1 as living sacrifices, *h* and pleasing
> Rev 4:8 "*H, h, h* is the Lord God Almighty,

Holy Spirit—the third person of the Trinity; he lives and works in the hearts and minds of believers; he came at Pentecost in a powerful way (Ac 2). Other names are: the Spirit, Counselor and Comforter.
> Ps 51:11 or take your *H* from me.
> Jn 14:26 But the Counselor, the *H*
> Jn 20:22 and said, "Receive the *H*
> Ac 2:4 of them were filled with the *H*
> Gal 5:22 But the fruit of the *H* is love, joy,

honor—to show respect to; to give credit to.
> Ex 20:12 "*H* your father and your mother,
> Ps 8:5 and crowned him with glory and *h.*

hope—the anticipation of something good.
> Ps 42:5 Put your *h* in God,
> Isa 40:31 but those who *h* in the LORD
> Ro 8:24 But *h* that is seen is no *h* at all.
> 1Co 15:19 for this life we have *h* in Christ,
> Heb 11:1 faith is being sure of what we *h* for

human—like people rather than animals, in actions or thoughts or appearance.

humble—1. (*v.*) to make lower; 2. (*adj.*) not proud; not pretending to be important.
> Ps 147:6 The LORD sustains the *h*
> Mt 23:12 whoever exalts himself will be *h,*
> Jas 4:10 *H* yourselves before the Lord,

humility—the absence of pride.
> Php 2:3 but in *h* consider others better
> 1Pe 5:5 clothe yourselves with *h*

hypocrite—a person who pretends to be better than he or she is.
> Mt 6:5 when you pray, do not be like the *h,*
> Mt 7:5 You *h,* first take the plank out

I

idol—a statue made by people and worshiped as if it had the power of a god; anything that takes the place of God in a person's life. Worshiping idols is called idolatry.
> 1Co 8:4 We know that an *i* is nothing at all
> Col 3:5 evil desires and greed, which is *i.*

image—likeness.
> Ge 1:27 So God created man in his own *i,*
> Da 3:12 nor worship the *i* of gold you have set up."

immoral (immorality)—wicked; not living by right standards.
> 1Co 6:18 Flee from sexual *i.*
> Eph 5:5 No *i,* impure or greedy person

immortal (immortality)—free from death; not able to die.
> 1Co 15:53 and the mortal with *i.*
> 1Ti 1:17 Now to the King eternal, *i,*

imperishable—not able to die or to be destroyed.
> 1Pe 1:23 not of perishable seed, but of *i,*

impure—not pure; not clean.
> Ac 10:15 not call anything *i* that God has
> 1Th 4:7 For God did not call us to be *i,*

incense—1. spices burned to make a sweet-smelling smoke, as a way of worshiping God; 2. the sweet smell or the smoke of burning spices.
> Ps 141:2 my prayer be set before you like *i;*
> Mt 2:11 him with gifts of gold and of *i*

inhabitant—one who lives in a particular place.
> Rev 6:10 the *i* of the earth and avenge

inheritance—money, property or keepsakes received from a person after his or her death.
> Dt 4:20 to be the people of his *i,*
> 1Pe 1:4 and into an *i* that can never perish,

iniquity—sin; wickedness.
> Ps 51:2 Wash away all my *i*
> Ps 103:10 or repay us according to our *i.*
> Isa 53:6 the *i* of us all.

instruction—the action of a teacher; a lesson.
> Ac 1:2 after giving *i* through the Holy Spirit
> 2Ti 4:2 with great patience and careful *i*

interpret—to explain the meaning of.
> Mt 16:3 you cannot *i* the signs of the times.
> 1Co 12:30 Do all *i* ? But eagerly desire

Isaac—the promised son of Abraham and Sarah (Ge 17:19; 21:1-7); offered as a sacrifice by Abraham (Ge 22); married Rebekah (Ge 24) and was the father of Esau and Jacob (Ge 25).

Isaiah—prophet called by God (Isa 6) to prophesy to Judah (Isa 1:1). Some of his prophecies are about the coming Messiah (Isa 53).

Israel—1. the new name God gave to Jacob (Ge 32:28); 2. the nation made up of descendants of the twelve sons of Jacob; 3. the northern ten tribes after they separated from Judah and Benjamin.
> Dt 6:4 Hear, O *I:* The LORD our God,
> Lk 22:30 judging the twelve tribes of *I.*
> Eph 3:6 Gentiles are heirs together with *I,*

J

Jacob—the son of Isaac and Rebekah; he was the twin brother of Esau (Ge 25:21-26); he bought Esau's birthright for a pot of stew (Ge 25:29-34); he wrestled with God, and his name was changed to Israel (Ge 32:22-32); the descendants of his twelve sons became the nation of Israel.

James—1. one of the twelve apostles; the brother of John (Mt 4:21-22); 2. one of the twelve apostles; the son of Alphaeus (Mt 10:3); 3. the brother of Jesus (Mk 6:30); the author of the letter of James (Jas 1:1).

jealous (jealousy)—1. afraid of losing someone's love or affection; 2. angry or unhappy because of what someone else has; 3. careful to guard or keep what one has.
> Joel 2:18 will be *j* for his land
> 2Co 11:2 I am *j* for you with a godly *j.*
> Gal 5:20 hatred, discord, *j,* fits of rage,

Jeremiah—a prophet called by God to prophesy to Judah (Jer 1:1-3). He is often referred to as the prophet of gloom, because he prophesied about the destruction of Judah.

Jerusalem—the political and religious center of the Jews; it was the site of many important events in the Biblical accounts; also called "Zion" and "the City of David."
> 2Ki 23:27 and I will reject *J,* the city I chose,
> Ne 2:17 Come, let us rebuild the wall of *J,*
> Ps 137:5 If I forget you, O *J,*
> Jn 4:20 where we must worship is in *J."*
> Rev 21:2 I saw the Holy City, the new *J,*

Jesus—The Son of God; the Savior of the world; the Messiah, through whom people can be saved.

Mt 1:21 you are to give him the name *J,*
Php 2:10 name of *J* every knee should bow,

Jew—an Israelite; one of the chosen people of God; a descendant of Abraham through Jacob.
Mt 2:2 who has been born king of the *J?*
Ro 3:29 Is God the God of *J* only?
Gal 3:28 There is neither *J* nor Greek,

Job—a wealthy man from the land of Uz who feared God (Job 1:1-5). His righteousness was tested by disaster (Job 1:6-22) and personal affliction (Job 2), but in the end God restored wealth and honor to him (Job 42).

John—1. the Baptist (Mk 1:2-8); the son of Zechariah and Elizabeth (Lk 1). He preached in the desert, preparing the people for Jesus (Mt 3:11-12); baptized Jesus in the Jordan River (Mt 3:13-17); executed by Herod (Mk 6:14-29); 2. one of the twelve apostles; brother of the apostle James (Lk 5:1-10); wrote the Gospel of John, the letters of John (2Jn 1; 3Jn 1) and the book of Revelation (Rev 1:1; 22:8).

John Mark—See Mark, John.

Jonah—a prophet who was called to preach to Nineveh but instead fled to Tarshish (Jnh 1:1-3). While at sea a great storm arose because of his disobedience; he was thrown into the sea and was swallowed by a large fish (Jnh 1:4-17). He then repented and went to Nineveh and preached, telling the people to repent (Jnh 3).

Jordan—a river in Palestine that flows between the Sea of Galilee and the Dead Sea.
Jos 4:22 "Israel crossed the *J* on dry ground."
Mt 3:6 baptized by him in the *J* River.

Joseph—1. the son of Jacob and Rachel (Ge 30:24), who was favored by his father but hated by his brothers (Ge 37:3-4). He was sold into slavery (Ge 37:12-36), taken to Egypt and eventually given a high position under Pharaoh (Ge 41:41-57); 2. the husband of Mary and childhood father of Jesus (Mt 1:16-24; 2:13-19); 3. a disciple of Jesus from Arimathea; he gave his tomb for Jesus' burial (Mt 27:57-61); 4. the original name of Barnabas (Ac 4:36).

Joshua—1. the son of Nun (Nu 13:8); Moses' aide and later his successor (Dt 31:1-18); he led the Israelites across the Jordan River into Canaan (Jos 3-4); was the commander in the conquest of Jericho (Jos 6), Ai (Jos 7-8), and a large part of Canaan (Jos 10-12); oversaw the dividing up of the promised land among the twelve tribes of Israel (Jos 13-22); 2. the high priest in Israel during the rebuilding of both the temple (Hag 1-2) and the altar (Ezr 3:2,8); also called Jeshua.

Judas—1. one of the twelve apostles (Lk 6:16; Ac 1:13); was probably also called Thaddaeus (Mt 10:3); 2. one of the brothers of Jesus (Mt 13:55); author of the last letter in the New Testament (Jude 1); 3. one of the twelve apostles, also called Iscariot; he betrayed Jesus (Mk 3:19; 14:10-50) and then hung himself (Mt 27:3-5).

judge—to decide if something is good or bad; to condemn.
Ps 9:8 He will *j* the world in righteousness;
Mt 7:1 "Do not *j,* or you too will be judged.
2Ti 4:1 who will *j* the living and the dead,

judgment—1. a decision or opinion; 2. a decision of guilt or innocence made by a judge in a court of law; punishment decided on by a court; 3. a decision from God, especially the final judgment when God will reward those who believe in him and condemn all others to hell.
Dt 1:17 of any man, for *j* belongs to God.
Ps 119:66 Teach me knowledge and good *j,*
Isa 66:16 the LORD will execute *j*
Mt 5:21 who murders will be subject to *j.'*
Mt 12:36 have to give account on the day of *j*
Jn 5:22 but has entrusted all *j* to the Son,

Ro 14:10 stand before God's *j* seat.
2Co 5:10 appear before the *j* seat of Christ,

just—righteous, legally correct.
Ps 111:7 The works of his hands are faithful and *j;*
Rev 16:7 true and *j* are your judgments."

justice—fairness.
Isa 30:18 For the LORD is a God of *j.*
Isa 61:8 "For I, the LORD, love *j;*
Zec 7:9 'Administer true *j;* show mercy
Lk 11:42 you neglect *j* and the love of God.

justify (justification)—to erase someone's sins; to declare righteous.
Ac 13:39 him everyone who believes is *j*
Ro 3:24 and are *j* freely by his grace
Ro 4:25 and was raised to life for our *j.*
Ro 5:1 since we have been *j* through faith,
Gal 3:24 to Christ that we might be *j* by faith.

KL

kingdom—an area or group of people headed by a king; God's kingdom, or the kingdom of heaven, is made up of all believers.
Ex 19:6 you will be for me a *k* of priests
Mt 3:2 "Repent, for the *k* of heaven is near."
Mt 5:3 for theirs is the *k* of heaven.
Mt 6:33 But seek first his *k* and his
Mt 16:19 the keys of the *k* of heaven;
Jn 18:36 "My *k* is not of this world.
1Co 15:24 hands over the *k* to God the Father
Rev 11:15 of the world has become the *k*

labor—1. (*v.*) to work; 2. (*n.*) a task; 3. (*n.*) the time just before giving birth.
Ge 5:29 the *l* and painful toil of our hands
Ex 20:9 Six days you shall *l* and do all your work,
Jer 13:21 like that of a woman in *l?*

lack—1. (*v.*) to stand in need of; 2. (*n.*) the state of being in need of something.

lamb—a principal sacrificial animal in the Old Testament; since Jesus is the supreme sacrifice of God, he is called the "Lamb of God."
Isa 53:7 he was led like a *l* to the slaughter,
Jn 1:29 *L* of God, who takes away the sin
1Co 5:7 our Passover *l,* has been sacrificed.
Rev 5:6 Then I saw a *L,* looking

lament, lamentation—a cry of grief.

law—1. God's rules, which help his people know what is right and wrong (the Ten Commandments are part of God's law); 2. (cap.) the first five books of the Bible, written by Moses.
Ps 1:2 and on his *l* he meditates day
Ps 19:7 The *l* of the LORD is perfect,
Ps 119:97 Oh, how I love your *l!*
Mt 22:40 All the *L* and the Prophets hang
Ro 8:3 For what the *l* was powerless to do
Ro 13:10 love is the fulfillment of the *l.*
Gal 3:24 So the *l* was put in charge to lead us

Lazarus—1. the poor man in one of Jesus' parables (Lk 16:19-31); 2. the brother of Mary and Martha; Jesus raised him from the dead (Jn 11:1-12:19).

leprosy—a word used in the Bible for many different skin diseases and infections.

Levite—a member of the tribe of Levi. The Levites took care of the temple. Only Levites could become priests, but not all Levites were priests.

life—the total substance of a person's existence; can refer to both physical and spiritual existence.
Ge 2:7 into his nostrils the breath of *l,*
Jn 3:16 shall not perish but have eternal *l.*
Jn 11:25 "I am the resurrection and the *l.*

Jn 14:6 am the way and the truth and the *l.*
Ro 6:23 but the gift of God is eternal *l*

light—the form of energy that allows a person to see; in the Old Testament it symbolized life and blessing.
Ge 1:3 "Let there be *l,*" and there was *l.*
Ps 27:1 LORD is my *l* and my salvation
Ps 119:105 and a *l* for my path.
Isa 9:2 have seen a great *l;*
Mt 5:16 let your *l* shine before men,
Jn 8:12 he said, "I am the *l* of the world.
1Jn 1:5 God is *l;* in him there is no

Lord—refers to God as the master. (See also LORD.)
Mt 3:3 'Prepare the way for the *L,*
Lk 2:9 glory of the *L* shone around them,
Ac 16:31 replied, "Believe in the *L* Jesus,
Ro 10:13 on the name of the *L* will be saved."
Php 2:11 confess that Jesus Christ is *L,*
2Pe 1:16 and coming of our *L* Jesus Christ,
Rev 17:14 he is *L* of lords and King of kings
Rev 22:20 Come, *L* Jesus.

LORD (Yahweh)—the intimate and personal name of God; it emphasizes his role as Israel's Redeemer and covenant Lord. (See also Lord.)
Ge 2:4 When the *L* God made the earth
Ex 20:2 "I am the *L* your God, who
Ps 23:1 The *L* is my shepherd, I shall not
Ps 103:1 Praise the *L,* O my soul
Pr 1:7 The fear of the *L* is the beginning
Isa 6:3 "Holy, holy, holy is the *L* Almighty;
Isa 55:6 Seek the *L* while he may be found;

lot—one of the ways used in Bible times to find out God's will about a matter. It is something like drawing straws.
Mt 27:35 divided up his clothes by casting *l.*
Ac 1:26 Then they cast *l,* and the *l* fell

love—wanting good to come to another person; being concerned and willing to work for another person's benefit.
Ex 20:6 showing *l* to thousands of those who *l* me
Ps 23:6 Surely goodness and *l* will follow
Ps 136:1-26 His *l* endures forever.
Mt 3:17 "This is my Son, whom I *l;*
Mt 5:44 *L* your enemies and pray
Mt 19:19 and " '*L* your neighbor as yourself.' "
Jn 13:34 I give you: *L* one another.
Jn 15:13 Greater *l* has no one than this,
Ro 13:10 Therefore *l* is the fulfillment
Gal 5:22 But the fruit of the Spirit is *l,* joy,
Eph 1:4 In *l* he predestined us
1Jn 3:10 anyone who does not *l* his brother.
1Jn 3:16 This is how we know what *l* is:
1Jn 4:7 for *l* comes from God.
1Jn 4:10 This is *l:* not that we loved God,
1Jn 4:16 God is *l.*

Luke—a co-worker with Paul; he wrote the books of Luke and Acts (Col 4:14).

lust—a strong desire for something wrong.
Pr 6:25 Do not *l* in your heart
Ro 1:26 God gave them over to shameful *l.*

M

majestic (majesty)—great and powerful.
Ex 15:6 was *m* in power.
Ps 8:1 how *m* is your name in all the earth!
Ps 111:3 Glorious and *m* are his deeds,

manna—the special food God gave daily to the Israelites until they reached the promised land.
Ex 16:31 people of Israel called the bread *m.*
Jn 6:49 Your forefathers ate the *m*

Mark, John—the cousin of Barnabas (Col 4:10); a helper to Paul and Barnabas (Ac 13:5); later a co-worker with Barnabas (Ac 15:39) and then Paul (Phm 24); author of the second Gospel, according to early church tradition.

marriage—the joining together before God and other people of a man and a woman to form a new family.
Mt 22:30 neither marry nor be given in *m;*
Ro 7:2 she is released from the law of *m.*
Heb 13:4 by all, and the *m* bed kept pure,

marvelous—something that surprises, that fills one with wonder.
Ps 118:23 and it is *m* in our eyes.
Lk 2:33 mother *m* at what was said

Mary—1. the mother of Jesus (Mt 1:16-25); 2. Mary Magdalene—a woman whom Jesus freed from demons (Lk 8:2), who was present at the cross (Mk 15:40) and who came on Easter morning to the tomb (Mt 27:61); 3. the sister of Martha and Lazarus; she washed Jesus' feet with expensive perfume (Jn 12:1-8).

Matthew—a tax collector who became one of the twelve apostles (Mt 9:9-13); also called Levi (Mk 2:14-17).

meditate—to think seriously and carefully.
Ps 1:2 and on his law he *m* day and night.
Ps 119:15 I *m* on your precepts

mercy—kindness and forgiveness, especially when given to a person who doesn't deserve it.
Mic 6:8 To act justly and to love *m*
Ro 9:15 "I will have *m* on whom I have *m,*
1Pe 1:3 In his great *m* he has given us new

Messiah—the "Anointed One"; Christ; the one the Jews expected to come and be their king.
Jn 1:41 "We have found the *M*"

minister—1. (*v.*) to serve; to give care or attention to; 2. (*n.*) one who serves others as God directs.
2Co 3:6 as *m* of a new covenant
1Ti 4:6 you will be a good *m*

miracle—an unusual happening, one that goes against the normal laws of nature. Miracles are done by the power of God.
Ps 77:14 You are the God who performs *m;*
Jn 14:11 the evidence of the *m* themselves.
Ac 2:22 accredited by God to you by *m,*
Heb 2:4 it by signs, wonders and various *m,*

mortal—human; able to die.
1Co 15:53 and the *m* with immortality,

Moses—the leader of Israel in the exodus out of Egypt, culminating in their passing through the Red Sea (Ex 12–14). He received the law of God at Sinai (Ex 19–23) and gave it to the people of Israel. Moses was allowed to view the land of Canaan from the top of Mount Nebo, but died without entering it (Nu 20:1-13; Dt 34:5-12).

mourn—to feel deep sorrow; to grieve.
Mt 5:4 Blessed are those who *m,*

murder—to kill someone illegally.
Ex 20:13 "You shall not *m.*

myrrh—the sweet-smelling sap of the myrrh bush. It was used to make the sacred anointing oil.
Mt 2:11 of gold and of incense and of *m.*

N

Naomi—the mother-in-law of Ruth (Ru 1); she advised Ruth to seek marriage with Boaz (Ru 2-4).

Nehemiah—the Jewish "cupbearer" of King Artaxerxes of Persia (Ne 2:1); while in Jerusalem rebuilt the walls of the city (Ne 2–6) and with Ezra reestablished the worship of God there after the Babylonian exile (Ne 8).

neighbor—1. someone who lives nearby; 2. any fellow human being.

Lev 19:18 but love your *n* as yourself.
Lk 10:36 of these three do you think was a *n*

Nile—the primary river in Egypt.

Nineveh—the city to which Jonah was sent to preach (Jnh 1:2); the ancient capital of Assyria.

Noah—"a righteous man" in early Bible times; he built an ark, as God commanded him (Ge 6–8). God made a covenant with him never again to cover the entire earth with a flood (Ge 9).

O

oath—a promise in which one asks God to witness that something is true.

obey (obedience)—to do as asked; to yield to someone's commands or wishes.

Dt 6:3 careful to *o* so that it may go well
1Sa 15:22 To *o* is better than sacrifice,
Jn 14:23 loves me, he will *o* my teaching.
Ac 5:29 "We must *o* God rather than men!
Eph 6:1 *o* your parents in the Lord,

offense—an act that makes someone angry by what was done.

offering—1. something given to God as an act of worship; 2. the sacrifice of an animal to make the relationship between God and man right again. In the Old Testament, animals and grains were regularly used as offerings in an attempt to bring the people closer to God.

Ge 22:8 provide the lamb for the burnt *o*,
Isa 53:10 the LORD makes his life a guilt *o*,
Mk 12:33 is more important than all burnt *o*
Eph 5:2 as a fragrant *o* and sacrifice to God.

offspring—children.

Ge 3:15 and between your *o* and hers;
Ge 12:7 "To your *o* I will give this land."

oil—almost always refers to olive oil; used to anoint someone for a physical benefit or to set someone apart for service.

2Ki 9:6 the prophet poured *o* on Jehu's head
Lk 7:46 You did not pour *o* on my head

oppress—to control people unfairly and cruelly by the use of one's power.

Isa 53:7 He was *o* and afflicted,
Zec 7:10 Do not *o* the widow

overseer—one of the terms used for leaders in the early church.

Ac 20:28 the Holy Spirit has made you *o*.
1Ti 3:2 Now the *o* must be above reproach,

P

pagan—a person who does not worship God, especially someone who worships idols.

1Pe 2:12 such good lives among the *p* that,

parable—a story that tells a special lesson or truth. Jesus told many parables.

Passover—an annual Jewish holiday that yet today reminds the Jewish people of how God freed them from slavery in Egypt. The Lord "passed over" the homes marked with the blood of a lamb on their doorframes, but he killed all the other firstborn in Egypt.

Ex 12:11 Eat it in haste; it is the LORD's *P*.

Passover lamb—the lamb killed on the Passover as a sacrifice. Jesus is our Passover lamb, because he was sacrificed for our deliverance from sin, in the same way a lamb was sacrificed when the Israelites were delivered from Egypt.

1Co 5:7 our *P* lamb, has been sacrificed.

patient (patience)—able to put up with problems or pain without complaining or becoming angry.

Ro 12:12 Be joyful in hope, *p* in affliction,
1Co 13:4 Love is *p*, love is kind.
Gal 5:22 joy, peace, *p*, kindness, goodness

Paul—a Pharisee from Tarsus (Ac 9:11); named Saul at birth (Ac 13:9). Jesus appeared to him on the road to Damascus (Ac 9:4-9), and he became a powerful apostle (Gal 1). His writings make up a significant portion of the New Testament, ranging from intricate theology to passionate letters to struggling churches.

peace—freedom from disturbance; calm.

Isa 9:6 Everlasting Father, Prince of *P*.
Lk 2:14 on earth *p* to men on whom his
Jn 14:27 *P* I leave with you; my *p*
Ro 5:1 we have *p* with God
Gal 5:22 joy, *p*, patience, kindness,

Pentecost—a Jewish feast celebrated fifty days after the Passover. Today the Christian church celebrates Pentecost because it was the day the Holy Spirit came to dwell with Christ's followers (Ac 2:1-4).

people—a collective group.

2Ch 7:14 if my *p*, who are called by my name,
1Pe 2:9 you are a chosen *p*,

persecute (persecution)—to continually treat someone cruelly and unfairly, even though that person has done nothing wrong. The early Christians were persecuted for believing in Jesus as the Son of God.

Jn 15:20 they *p* me, they will *p* you
Ac 26:14 'Saul, Saul, why do you *p* me?
Ro 12:14 Bless those who *p* you; bless

persevere (perseverance)—to refuse to give up; to keep on trying; to continue in one's actions or beliefs in spite of problems.

Ro 5:3 we know that suffering produces *p*;
Heb 10:36 You need to *p* so that

Peter—one of the twelve apostles; the brother of Andrew; also called Simon (Lk 6:14) and Cephas (Jn 1:42); he denied Jesus three times (Mk 14:66-72) but became a bold evangelist. He wrote the books of 1 and 2 Peter.

pharaoh—the title given to the ruler of Egypt.

Pharisees—a group of Jews who obeyed very strictly both God's laws and all their own rules about God's laws.

Mt 5:20 surpasses that of the *P*

Pilate—the governor of Judea who questioned Jesus (Lk 22:66–23:25) and then sent him to Herod (Lk 23:6-12). Pilate finally consented to Jesus' crucifixion when the crowds chose Barabbas rather than Jesus to be released (Lk 23:13-25).

pity—a sympathy or sorrow for the suffering of another.

Mk 9:22 take *p* on us and help us."

plague—1. a disease that kills many people, such as the plague of boils; 2. an event that causes much suffering or loss, especially a trouble in which there is a great number of offending agents, such as the plague of locusts.

plunder—1. (*v.*) to loot or rob during a war; 2. (*n.*) property taken by plundering.

poor—those who have little money.

Dt 15:4 there should be no *p* among you,
Isa 61:1 me to preach good news to the *p*.
Mt 26:11 The *p* you will always have
1Co 13:3 If I give all I possess to the *p*
2Co 8:9 yet for your sakes he became

praise—1. (*v.*) to glorify; to say g[ ]
someone or something; 2. (*n.*) [ ]
Ex 15:2 He is my God, [ ]

Ps 119:175 Let me live that I may *p* you,
Eph 1:12 might be for the *p* of his glory.

pray—to talk with God.
2Ch 7:14 will humble themselves and *p*
Mt 6:5 "And when you *p*, do not be like
Ro 8:26 do not know what we ought to *p*
1Th 5:16-17 Be joyful always; *p* continually;

preach—to tell the message of the gospel in public; to deliver a sermon.
Isa 61:1 me to *p* good news to the poor.
Ro 10:15 how can they *p* unless they are sent?

precious—valuable; of great worth.
Ps 139:17 How *p* to me are your thoughts,

predestine—to decide or decree ahead of time.
Ro 8:30 And those he *p*, he also called;
Eph 1:5 he *p* us to be adopted

pride—1. (negative) the attitude that one is better than others; 2. (positive) a healthy self-respect or sense of satisfaction.
Pr 16:18 *P* goes before destruction,
Gal 6:4 Then he can take *p* in himself,

priest (priesthood)—a Levite who offered sacrifices and prayers to God for the people.
1Pe 2:9 you are a chosen people, a royal *p*,

proclaim—to announce or declare.
1Ch 16:23 *p* his salvation day after day.
Ps 19:1 the skies *p* the work of his hands.
1Co 11:26 you *p* the Lord's death

profane—to make a holy thing impure by treating it with disrespect or irreverence.
Lev 22:32 Do not *p* my holy name.

prophecy—a message from God that a prophet brings to the people.
1Co 13:8 where there are *p*, they will cease;
2Pe 1:20 you must understand that no *p*

prophesy—to give the message of God to the people.
Joel 2:28 Your sons and daughters will *p*,
1Co 14:39 my brothers, be eager to *p*,

prophet—a person who receives messages from God to tell to his people. A prophet is called by God to speak for him.
Dt 18:18 up for them a *p* like you
Lk 24:25 believe all that the *p* have spoken!
Ac 10:43 All the *p* testify about him that
2Pe 1:19 word of the *p* made more certain,

prostitute—a person who lets someone use his or her body for sexual relations in exchange for money.
1Co 6:9 male *p* nor homosexual offenders

proverbs—1. wise sayings; 2. (cap.) a book of the Bible that contains many wise sayings.

psalms—1. poetry written to praise God; 2. (cap.) a book of the Bible contains many psalms.
Eph 5:19 S̲ ̲ ̲e another with *p*,

punish ̲ ̲ ̲ ̲to cause someone to suffer for doi ̲ ̲ ̲

̲ ̲ ̲ I can bear.
̲ ̲ ̲hildren for the sin
̲ ̲ ̲r blemish.
̲ ̲ ̲t, O God,
̲ ̲ ̲n all sin.
̲ ̲ ̲sness.
̲ ̲ ̲e; to chase; 2. to

R

rage—a fit of anger.
Eph 4:31 Get rid of all bitterness, *r*

ransom—the price paid to get back a person who is held as a slave. Because people are slaves of sin, a ransom has to be paid, which is the death of the sinless one, Jesus.
Mt 20:28 and to give his life as a *r* for many."
Heb 9:15 as a *r* to set them free

reap—1. to cut down grain at harvest time; to gather a crop together; 2. to get as a result or reward.
Gal 6:7 A man *r* what he sows.

rebel—1. (*v.*) to disobey and turn against those in authority; 2. (*n.*) a person who disobeys and flaunts authority.

rebuke—to scold sharply.
2Ti 4:2 correct, *r* and encourage
Rev 3:19 Those whom I love I *r*

reconcile (reconciliation)—to return to friendship after a quarrel; human beings are 'reconciled' to God through Christ.
Mt 5:24 First go and be *r* to your brother;
Ro 5:10 we were *r* to him through the death
2Co 5:18 and gave us the ministry of *r*:

redeem (redemption)—1. to free from evil by paying a price (Gal 3:13); 2. to buy back.
Gal 3:13 Christ *r* us from the curse
Eph 1:7 In him we have *r* through his blood,
Col 1:14 in whom we have *r*, the forgiveness

Red Sea—the body of water the Israelites crossed in a miraculous way when they were running from slavery in Egypt.

refuge—a place of shelter and safety.
Ps 46:1 God is our *r* and strength,

regulations—rules dealing with procedure or ceremony.

rejoice—to express joy or gladness.
Ps 118:24 let us *r* and be glad in it.
Lk 1:47 and my spirit *r* in God my Savior,
Php 4:4 *R* in the Lord always.

remnant—a small part remaining; a small surviving group.

repent (repentance)—to turn away from sin; to be sorry for what one has done and to promise not to do it again.
Mt 4:17 "*R*, for the kingdom of heaven is
Lk 3:8 Produce fruit in keeping with *r*.
Ac 2:38 Peter replied, "*R* and be baptized,

restore—to bring back; to return something to its former condition.
Ps 23:3 he *r* my soul.
Ps 51:12 *R* to me the joy of your salvation

resurrection—the act of coming back to life after being dead.
Jn 11:25 Jesus said to her, "I am the *r*
Ro 1:4 Son of God by his *r* from the dead:
1Co 15:12 some of you say that there is no *r*

revelation—the act of making known or telling about.
Gal 1:12 I received it by *r* from Jesus Christ.
Rev 1:1 *r* of Jesus Christ, which God gave

revenge—to hurt or punish a person who has wronged you; to get back at someone who has hurt you.
Lev 19:18 " 'Do not seek *r* or bear a grudge
Ro 12:19 Do not take *r*, my friends,

reverence (revere)—a deep respect, honor and awe.
Ps 5:7 in *r* will I bow down
Col 3:22 of heart and *r* for the Lord.

reward—1. (*v.*) to repay with good for something someone has done; 2. (*n.*) the gift one receives for good behavior or character.
>Ps 127:3 children a *r* from him.
>Jer 17:10 to *r* a man according to his conduct,
>Mt 5:12 because great is your *r* in heaven,
>Mt 6:5 they have received their *r* in full.

righteous (righteousness)—being "in the right" in relation to God; "not guilty" before God.
>Isa 64:6 and all our *r* acts are like filthy rags;
>Ro 3:10 "There is no one *r*, not even one;

Ruth—a Moabite widow who went with her mother-in-law Naomi to Bethlehem (Ru 1). There she gathered the gleanings from the field of Boaz (Ru 2), whom she later married (Ru 3–4:12). She was an ancestor of David (Ru 4:13-22) and of Jesus (Mt 1:5).

S

Sabbath—the seventh day of the week; the Jewish day of rest and worship. It extended from Friday sunset until Saturday sunset.
>Ex 20:8 "Remember the *S* day

sackcloth—a rough cloth, usually woven from goats' hair. Clothing made of sackcloth was worn as a sign of mourning for the dead or as a sign that a person was sorry for his or her sins.

sacred—holy; set apart for God in a special way.

sacrifice—1. (*v.*) to offer something as a gift to God; 2. (*n.*) an offering given to God. In the Old Testament God commanded the people to pay for their sins by sacrificing the blood of cattle, lambs, goats, doves or pigeons. These sacrifices were pictures of Jesus' coming as a once-for-all sacrifice for sinners.
>Ex 12:27 'It is the Passover *s* to the LORD,
>1Sa 15:22 To obey is better than *s*,
>Ro 12:1 to offer your bodies as living *s*,
>Heb 9:28 so Christ was *s* once
>1Jn 2:2 He is the atoning *s* for our sins,

saints—Christians; people whom God has made holy. A saint can be either a Christian who is alive on earth or one who is already in heaven.
>Ro 8:27 intercedes for the *s* in accordance
>Eph 1:1 To the *s* in Ephesus,

salvation—deliverance from the guilt and power of sin. By his death and resurrection, Jesus brings salvation to people who believe in him.
>Ps 27:1 The LORD is my light and my *s*
>Lk 2:30 For my eyes have seen your *s*,
>Ac 4:12 *S* is found in no one else,
>2Co 7:10 brings repentance that leads to *s*
>Php 2:12 to work out your *s* with fear
>Heb 2:3 escape if we ignore such a great *s*?

Samson—an Israelite judge who was known for his great strength. He was betrayed by Delilah but in the end was used by God to punish the Philistines (Jdg 16).

Samuel—often called the last of Israel's judges and the first of her prophets (see also Heb 11:32). His birth was earnestly prayed for by his mother Hannah (1Sa 1:10-18), and when he was old enough she brought him to the temple and he was dedicated to the Lord (1Sa 1:21-28). There he was raised by Eli (1Sa 2:11; 18–26) and was called to be a prophet (1Sa 3).

sanctify (sanctification)—to make holy; sanctification is the ongoing work of the Holy Spirit in the hearts of believers.
>Ro 15:16 to God, *s* by the Holy Spirit.
>1Th 5:23 *s* you through and through.
>2Th 2:13 through the *s* work of the Spirit

sanctuary—a place where God is worshiped; a holy place.

Sarah—the wife of Abraham and mother of Isaac; first called Sarai (Ge 11:29-31). God promised her that, though she had been barren throughout her life, she would give birth to a son in her old age (Ge 17:15-21; 18:10-15).

Satan—the devil; the leader of the fallen spirits; the most powerful enemy of God and humans.
>Mk 4:15 *S* comes and takes away the word
>2Co 11:14 for *S* himself masquerades
>Rev 12:9 serpent called the devil, or *S*,

satisfy—1. to please, to make happy; 2. to fulfill a condition.
>Ps 103:5 who *s* your desires with good things

Saul—1. the first king of Israel (1Sa 9–10). He was anointed by Samuel but was later rejected by God because of disobedience; David was chosen to be his successor; 2. see Paul.

saved—1. (*v.*) rescued from danger; 2. (*n.*) people who acknowledge that by Jesus' death they have been rescued from the punishment of death that their sins deserve.
>Ro 10:13 on the name of the Lord will be *s*."
>Eph 2:8 For it is by grace you have been *s*,

Savior—a name for Jesus that means he saves his people from sin.
>Lk 1:47 and my spirit rejoices in God my *S*,
>1Ti 4:10 who is the *S* of all men,
>1Jn 4:14 Son to be the *S* of the world.

scepter—a rod or stick held by a king or queen as a sign of royal power and authority.
>Ge 49:10 The *s* will not depart from Judah,

scorn—to despise, to reject with anger or contempt.

scribe—a person with the important task of copying letters, books and legal papers.

Scripture—all or part of the Bible. When the Bible uses this word it means the Old Testament, since the New Testament had not yet been written. Today we call the Old and New Testaments the Bible or Scripture.
>Jn 10:35 and the *S* cannot be broken
>2Ti 3:16 All *S* is God-breathed
>2Pe 1:20 that no prophecy of *S* came about

scroll—a book made of a long piece of leather or paper that was rolled around a stick at both ends.
>Eze 3:1 eat what is before you, eat this *s*;

seal—1. a tool with a design raised on it or cut into it; 2. the mark made by pressing this tool onto wax, paper or other soft material. A seal was used to close a letter or legal paper or to prove the authority of the paper.
>2Co 1:22 set his *s* of ownership on us,
>Rev 5:2 "Who is worthy to break the *s*

seer—a prophet; a person who, with God's help, can see what will happen in the future.

self-control—the ability to control one's own actions and feelings.
>Gal 5:23 gentleness and *s*.
>2Pe 1:6 and to knowledge, *s*; and to *s*,

selfish—centered on oneself; not interested in others.
>Php 2:3 Do nothing out of *s* ambition

sexual immorality—using sex in ways God says are wrong.
>1Co 6:13 body is not meant for *s*
>1Th 4:3 that you should avoid *s*

shame—a painful emotion caused guilt or shortcoming.
>Pr 19:26 a son who brings
>1Co 15:34 I say this t

shepherd—someone who takes care of a flock of sheep. It is often used in the Bible as a figure of speech for anyone who cares for a group of people.
> Ps 23:1 LORD is my *s*, I shall not be in want.
> Jer 31:10 will watch over his flock like a *s*.'
> Jn 10:11 The good *s* lays down his life
> Ac 20:28 Be *s* of the church of God,

shield—a defensive weapon, usually carried on the arm; often a figure of speech in the Bible used to describe God's protection of his people.
> Ps 7:10 My *s* is God Most High,

siege—See besiege.

sin—1. (*v.*) to break the law of God; 2. (*n.*) the act of not doing what God wants.
> Nu 32:23 be sure that your *s* will find you
> Ps 51:2 and cleanse me from my *s*.
> Ps 119:11 that I might not *s* against you.
> Isa 1:18 "Though your *s* are like scarlet,
> Mt 1:21 he will save his people from their *s*."
> Lk 11:4 Forgive us our *s*,
> Jn 1:29 who takes away the *s* of the world!
> Ro 3:23 for all have *s* and fall short
> Ro 6:23 For the wages of *s* is death,
> 2Co 5:21 God made him who had no *s* to be *s*
> 1Jn 1:9 If we confess our *s*, he is faithful

Sinai, Mount—the mountain where Moses received the Ten Commandments (Ex 19–20).

sinner—a person who breaks the law of God.
> Ps 1:1 or stand in the way of *s*
> Mt 9:13 come to call the righteous, but *s*."
> Lk 15:7 in heaven over one *s* who repents
> Lk 18:13 'God, have mercy on me, a *s*.'
> Ro 5:8 While we were still *s*, Christ died

slander—1. (*v.*) saying untrue things about another person in order to hurt him or her; 2. (*n.*) false charges or misrepresentations about another person.
> Lev 19:16 " 'Do not go about spreading *s*
> Tit 3:2 to *s* no one, to be peaceable

slaughter—1. the butchering of livestock for food; 2. the killing of great numbers of human beings, as in a battle.

slave—1. a person who is owned by another; 2. a person who is dominated or controlled by an outside force.
> Ro 7:14 I am unspiritual, sold as a *s* to sin.
> Gal 3:28 *s* nor free, male nor female,

slay, slain—to kill violently or in great numbers.

snare—a trap; something risky that tempts or endangers a person.

Solomon—the son of David and Bathsheba (2Sa 12:24). He became king of Israel after David died (1Ki 1). He asked God for wisdom and was given it (1Ki 3), and he built the temple (1Ki 5–7). His many foreign wives turned his heart away from God (1Ki 11:1-13).

Son of Man—a title Jesus used for himself to show his humanity as di[stinct fr]om his divinity. It was also a reference to the [one pro]phesied about in Daniel 7:13.
> Mt 2[6 . . .] be betrayed
> M[. . .] *S* sitting
> [. . .] seek
> [. . . rais]ed up,
> [. . . per]son; the part of a person
> [. . .] your
> [. . .] the *s*.
> [. . . ou]r *s*.
> [. . .] were sown

spirit—1. the part of a person that is not the body; the soul; 2. a being who does not have a body; 3. (cap.) see Holy Spirit.
> Ps 31:5 Into your hands I commit my *s*;
> Eze 36:26 you a new heart and put a new *s*
> Mt 5:3 "Blessed are the poor in *s*,
> Mt 26:41 *s* is willing, but the body is weak."
> 1Jn 4:1 Dear friends, do not believe every *s*,

splendor—something magnificent or splendid.

springs—a source of water coming up from the ground.
> Dt 8:7 with *s* flowing in the valleys
> Rev 7:17 lead them to *s* of living water.

staff—a stick used to lean on; a rod used by a shepherd.
> Ps 23:4 your rod and your *s*,

statutes—established rules or laws.
> Ps 19:7 *s* of the LORD are trustworthy,

stiff-necked—stubborn.

strength—power; forcefulness.
> Ex 15:2 The LORD is my *s* and my song;
> Dt 6:5 all your soul and with all your *s*.
> Ps 46:1 God is our refuge and *s*,
> Isa 40:31 will renew their *s*.
> Php 4:13 through him who gives me *s*.

suffer—to bear or endure something painful.
> Mk 8:31 the Son of Man must *s* many things
> Lk 24:26 the Christ have to *s* these things
> 1Co 12:26 If one part *s*, every part *s* with it;

suffering—the experience of enduring pain.
> Isa 53:3 of sorrows, and familiar with *s*.
> Ac 5:41 worthy of *s* disgrace for the Name.
> Ro 8:17 share in his *s* in order that we may
> 2Ti 1:8 But join with me in *s* for the gospel,

summon—to issue a call to come together; to send for.
> Isa 43:1 I have *s* you by name; you are mine.

swear—to promise forcefully or earnestly.
> 1Sa 30:15 "*S* to me before God that you will

synagogue—the Jewish place of worship and religious teaching.
> Lk 4:16 the Sabbath day he went into the *s*,
> Ac 17:2 custom was, Paul went into the *s*,

T

tabernacle—the tent used by the Israelites for meeting with God; the place where God chose to show his presence. The tabernacle was made by God's command and according to his plans. It is described in detail in Exodus 26. Also called the Tent of Meeting.
> Ex 40:34 the glory of the LORD filled the *t*.

talent—a large amount of silver or gold, worth very much money.
> Mt 25:15 to another one *t*, each according

teach—to instruct; to help someone learn.
> Ex 33:13 *t* me your ways so I may know you
> Ps 90:12 *T* us to number our days aright,
> Lk 11:1 said to him, "Lord, *t* us to pray,
> Jn 14:26 will *t* you all things and will remind

temple—1. the place where the Jewish people worshiped and sacrificed in Jerusalem; the first temple was built by King Solomon as a house for God; 2. any place of worship. In this sense, the human body is referred to as a temple (1Co 6:19).
> 1Ki 8:27 How much less this *t* I have built!
> Ac 17:24 does not live in *t* built by hands.
> 2Co 6:16 For we are the *t* of the living God.

Job 4:8 and those who *s* trouble reap it.
Mk 4:3 A farmer went out to *s* his seed.
Gal 6:7 A man reaps what he *s*.

temptation—trying to get someone to do wrong.
  Mt 4:1 into the desert to be *t* by the devil.
  1Co 10:13 No *t* has seized you except what

Tent of Meeting—See tabernacle.

testimony—a statement made by a witness to prove that something is true.
  Lk 18:20 not give false *t*, honor your father

thanks—the expression of gratitude.
  1Ch 16:8 Give *t* to the LORD, call
  Ps 100:4 give *t* to him and praise his name.
  1Co 15:57 *t* be to God! He gives us the victory
  2Co 9:15 *T* be to God for his indescribable
  1Th 5:18 give *t* in all circumstances,

thanksgiving—recognizing and thanking the one who has provided a gift.
  Ps 100:4 Enter his gates with *t*
  Php 4:6 by prayer and petition, with *t*,

threshing floor—the place where grain was trampled by oxen or beaten with a stick to separate it from the stalk.

Timothy—fellow-traveler and official representative of the apostle Paul. He joined Paul on his second missionary journey (Ac 16–20), and at one point in this journey Paul sent him to minister to the church at Corinth (1Co 4:17; 16:10). He was the leader of the church at Ephesus (1Ti 1:3) and a co-writer with Paul (1Th 1:1; 2Th 1:1; Phm 1).

tithe—the giving to God of one-tenth of what one earns.
  Lev 27:30 " 'A *t* of everything from the land,
  Mal 3:10 the whole *t* into the storehouse,

Titus—a Gentile co-worker with Paul (Gal 2:1-3; 2Ti 4:10). Paul sent him to Corinth to aid in solving some of the problems there (2Co 2:13; 7–8; 12:18).

tomb—a burial place. In Bible times, a tomb was often either a cave or a cavity dug into a stone cliff, with a large stone rolled in front to close it.
  Mt 27:65 make the *t* as secure as you know
  Lk 24:2 the stone rolled away from the *t*,

tongue—1. the organ of speech in the mouth; 2. a language.
  Ps 39:1 and keep my *t* from sin;
  Ac 2:4 and began to speak in other *t*
  Php 2:11 every *t* confess that Jesus Christ
  Jas 1:26 does not keep a tight rein on his *t*,

trample—to walk heavily causing injury or damage.
  Ps 60:12 he will *t* down our enemies.

transgression—sin; disobeying the law of God.
  Ps 32:1 whose *t* are forgiven,
  Isa 53:5 But he was pierced for our *t*,
  Eph 2:1 you were dead in your *t* and sins,

treasure—1. (*n.*) wealth that is stored up or hidden away; 2. (*v.*) to hold or keep something precious, something of value; to cherish.
  Mt 6:21 your *t* is, there your heart will be also.

treaty—an agreement between two people or groups or nations.

trespass—sin; wrongdoing.
  Ro 5:17 For if, by the *t* of the one man,

true—certain; exactly right.
  Ps 119:160 All your words are *t*,
  Jn 17:3 the only *t* God, and Jesus Christ,
  Ro 3:4 Let God be *t*, and every man a liar.
  Php 4:8 whatever is *t*, whatever is noble,

trust—firm belief or faith in another.
  Ps 37:3 *T* in the LORD and do good;
  Pr 3:5 *T* in the LORD with all your heart
  Isa 30:15 in quietness and *t* is your strength,

  Jn 14:1 *T* in God; *t* also in me.
  1Co 4:2 been given a *t* must prove faithful.

trustworthy—deserving of trust; reliable.
  Ps 19:7 The statutes of the LORD are *t*,
  1Ti 1:15 Here is a *t* saying that deserves full

truth—that which conforms to the facts.
  Ps 51:6 Surely you desire *t*
  Zec 8:16 are to do: Speak the *t* to each other,
  Jn 8:32 know the *t* and the *t*
  Jn 14:6 I am the way and the *t* and the life.
  Ro 1:25 They exchanged the *t* of God
  1Co 13:6 in evil but rejoices with the *t*.
  Eph 4:15 Instead, speaking the *t* in love,
  Heb 10:26 received the knowledge of the *t*,
  1Jn 1:6 we lie and do not live by the *t*.
  1Jn 1:8 deceive ourselves and the *t* is not

UV

unbelief—doubt.
  Mk 9:24 help me overcome my *u*!"

unbeliever—one who does not believe in Jesus.
  2Co 6:14 Do not be yoked together with *u*.

unclean—morally or spiritually impure; unclean animals were those which the Israelites were not allowed to sacrifice or to eat.

upright—honest; doing what is right and good.

vain—worthless; unsuccessful; foolish. "In vain" means without success or result.

vengeance—hurt or punishment done to another person who has done something wrong against another.
  Isa 34:8 For the LORD has a day of *v*,

virgin—a woman or girl who has never had sexual intercourse.
  Isa 7:14 The *v* will be with child
  Mt 1:23 "The *v* will be with child

vision—a dream from God.
  Nu 12:6 I reveal myself to him in *v*,
  Joel 2:28 your young men will see *v*.
  Ac 26:19 disobedient to the *v* from heaven.

vow—a solemn promise made before God or to God.
  Jdg 11:30 Jephthah made a *v* to the LORD:
  Ps 116:14 I will fulfill my *v* to the LORD

W

wages—payment received for work completed.

wail—to cry loudly.

walk—to follow a certain course.
  Ps 1:1 who does not *w* in the counsel
  Isa 2:5 let us *w* in the light of the LORD.
  Mic 6:8 and to *w* humbly with your God.
  2Jn 6 his command is that you *w* in love.

wander—to move about without a fixed course.
  Nu 32:13 he made them *w* in the desert forty years,
  Jas 5:19 if one of you should *w* from the truth

warn—to give notice beforehand of danger or evil.

wash—to clean.
  Ps 51:7 *w* me, and I will be whiter
  Ac 22:16 be baptized and *w* your sins away,

watch—to be on the lookout for someone or something
  Jer 31:10 will *w* over his flock like a shepherd.'
  Mt 26:41 "*W* and pray so that you will not fall

way—the means of getting somewhere; th
  2Sa 22:31 "As for God, his *w* is perf
  Ps 1:1 or stand in the *w* of sinn
  Ps 37:5 Commit your *w* to t
  Isa 53:6 each of us ha

Jn 14:6 "I am the *w* and the truth
1Co 12:31 will show you the most excellent *w*.

welcome—1. to greet a person pleasantly; 2. to make a person feel at home.
Jdg 19:20 "You are *w* at my house,"

wicked—sinful.
Ps 1:1 walk in the counsel of the *w*
Isa 55:7 Let the *w* forsake his way

will—desire; seeking God's will means looking for what God wants to be done.
Ps 143:10 Teach me to do your *w*,
Isa 53:10 Yet it was the LORD's *w*
Mt 6:10 your *w* be done
Mt 26:39 Yet not as I *w*, but as you *w*."
Ro 12:2 and approve what God's *w* is
Eph 5:17 understand what the Lord's *w* is.
1Jn 5:14 we ask anything according to his *w*,
Rev 4:11 and by your *w* they were created

wisdom—the understanding that comes from God.
Lk 2:52 And Jesus grew in *w* and stature,
Jas 1:5 of you lacks *w*, he should ask God,

witness—one who personally sees an event take place.
Ac 22:15 You will be his *w* to all men

womb—the organ within a woman's body where a child grows before birth.

word—1. the means of expressing oneself through language; 2. the Bible, as God's written message to people; 3. (cap.) Jesus is the Word sent from God because his life on earth told the message of God.
Jn 1:14 The *W* became flesh and made his
Heb 4:12 For the *w* of God is living

work—1. (n.) employment; duty; 2. (v.) to bring about; to try to achieve a goal.
Ex 23:12 "Six days do your *w*,
Jn 9:4 we must do the *w* of him who sent
Php 2:12 continue to *w* out your salvation
2Ti 3:17 equipped for every good *w*.

world—1. the earth and those who live in it; 2. the secular, as opposed to the spiritual or religious.
Mt 5:14 "You are the light of the *w*.
Mk 16:15 into all the *w* and preach the good
Jn 1:29 who takes away the sin of the *w!*

Jn 3:16 so loved the *w* that he gave his one
Jn 8:12 he said, "I am the light of the *w*.
1Jn 2:15 not love the *w* or anything in the *w*.

worldly—loving the things of the world more than the things of God.
Tit 2:12 to ungodliness and *w* passions,

worship—1. (v.) to give praise, honor and respect to God; 2. (n.) reverence given to God.
Ps 95:6 Come, let us bow down in *w*,
Jn 4:24 and his worshipers must *w* in spirit

worthy—having value; honorable; deserving.
1Ch 16:25 For great is the LORD and most *w*
Eph 4:1 to live a life *w* of the calling you
Rev 5:2 "Who is *w* to break the seals

wrath—great anger; the strong anger of God.
Pr 15:1 A gentle answer turns away *w*,
Ro 5:9 saved from God's *w* through him!

YZ

yeast—the ingredient that makes dough rise; sometimes a figure of speech for the influence someone has over others.
Mt 16:6 guard against the *y* of the Pharisees
Gal 5:9 little *y* works through the whole

yield—1. to submit; 2. to grow or produce fruit.
Ps 67:6 Then the land will *y* its harvest,
Isa 48:11 I will not *y* my glory to another.

yoke—1. (v.) to join together; 2. (n.) a wooden bar that goes over the necks of two animals, usually oxen. The yoke holds the animals together as they pull an object, such as a plow or a cart.
Mt 11:29 Take my *y* upon you and learn
2Co 6:14 Do not be *y* together

youth—the time when a person is young.
Ecc 12:1 Creator in the days of your *y*,

zeal—eagerness; strong desire.
Ro 12:11 Never be lacking in *z*,

Zion—1. the hill on which the city of Jerusalem first stood; David's royal palace and the temple were both built on Mount Zion; 2. the entire city of Jerusalem.
Jer 50:5 They will ask the way to *Z*
Ro 11:26 "The deliverer will come from *Z*;